D0846351

THE FAMINE IMMIGRANTS

Lists of Irish Immigrants
Arriving at the Port of New York,
1846-1851

Illustrated London News

The Departure from Waterloo Docks, Liverpool

The Famine Immigrants

Lists of Irish Immigrants Arriving at the Port of New York, 1846-1851

Ira A. Glazier
Editor
Michael Tepper
Associate Editor

Volume II
July 1847- June 1848

Baltimore
Genealogical Publishing Co., Inc.
1983

Library of Congress Catalogue Card Number 83-80078
International Standard Book Number 0-8063-1045-6
Made in the United States of America

FOREWORD

Irish immigration through the port of New York in 1846 reached a peak on the first day of June with the arrival of ten ships carrying some 2,500 passengers. Throughout the rest of the month immigration levels remained relatively high, and in the end June proved the busiest month of the year, with as many as 10,000 Irish immigrants disembarking at the Battery in Manhattan or at the quarantine station on Staten Island. During the remaining six months of 1846 the number of immigrant arrivals declined, and as winter wore on into the early months of 1847 the decline became even more pronounced. Between April and June of 1847, however, there was a significant increase in the volume of immigration, the number of Irish arrivals in this quarter alone equalling the totals for the other three quarters of the year combined.

From July of 1847, and throughout the remainder of the year, immigration fell off rather sharply, although with a better-than-expected harvest and the temporary abatement of the potato blight, as well as the customary suspension of ocean traffic during the winter months, it would have been surprising if immigration had not declined. However, the Whig Government's decision in the summer of 1847 to transfer responsibility for emergency relief to the already destitute Irish Poor Law Unions provoked fresh misery, and by the spring of 1848, with remittances continuing to arrive from family members who went beforehand to America, immigration picked up in earnest. In May alone some 17,000 Irish refugees arrived at New York, more than in any month during the preceding two-and-a-half years of the Famine.

This second volume of *The Famine Immigrants* commences with the downturn in immigration in July of 1847 and continues through the first half of 1848, terminating with the fair-weather months of the spring and early summer which were the traditional "season" in the passenger trade. As in the first volume, which covered the period from January 1846 through June 1847, the overwhelming majority of emigrants are shown taking ship at Liverpool, which was only a few hours' journey across the Channel from Dublin and by steamer little more than a day's journey from Cork. During the period covered by this volume, however, emigrants are seen with increasing frequency embarking direct from ports at Waterford, Cork, Limerick, Galway, and Sligo in the south and west, and from Londonderry, Belfast, Newry, and Dublin in the north and east. In the twelve months between July 1847 and June 1848, for instance, 109 emigrant vessels reached New York direct from Irish ports as compared with 66 in the equivalent period of 1846/47.

Nevertheless, Liverpool continued to dominate the Atlantic passenger trade, and as in the previous eighteen months the ships transporting the largest number of outward-bound passengers were the wide-hulled American packets on the Liverpool-New York run, many now carrying between 300 and 400 passengers. As a means of comparison, however preliminary at this stage, it is worth noting that in the first half of 1848 141 vessels arrived in New York from Liverpool carrying approximately 31,300 passengers, while in the same period 11,400 passengers on 73 ships reached New York direct from Irish ports, an average of 222 per ship from Liverpool as against 156 per ship from Ireland.* These are mere averages, of course, and in the way of such things conceal the fact that at least a score of ships in the Liverpool trade at this time carried more than 300 passengers. And ships like the *Henry Clay,* the *Columbia,* the *Montezuma,* and the *Princess Royal,* with complements of nearly 400 passengers each, were by no means unusual, or we should otherwise cite as examples such leviathans as the *America,* the *Caleb Grimshaw,* and the *Columbus,* each of which embarked for New York with more than 400 passengers between decks, or the *Constitution,* which carried more than 500. During the same time period not a single vessel left direct from Ireland carrying anything like this number of passengers, and only two, the *Ambassadress* and the *Lord Ashburton,* sailed with as many as 300.

To the Irish emigrant Liverpool offered numerous attractions. The voyage to New York usually took from four to six weeks — longer perhaps in the winter months — and at £3 to £4 for steerage accommodations it was no more expensive to sail from Liverpool than from smaller Irish ports, and in most cases it was just as fast or even faster. (In November 1846, for example, the *Yorkshire* made the crossing from Liverpool to New York in just sixteen days, supposedly the fastest time ever achieved by a packet.) Passage across the Irish Channel to Liverpool could be booked cheaply, or for nothing at all if the passengers were taken on as ballast, and for many emigrants it was simply more expedient to cross the Channel than to travel overland to the nearest seaport

*Figures given are exclusive of merchant-class vessels with complements of less than twenty passengers.

at home where departures were less frequent and accommodations uncertain. At the same time there was a widely-held belief that passengers would be better provided for in the larger vessels departing from Liverpool, and although this was not entirely accurate, particularly since the Passenger Act of 1842 had diluted health and safety requirements, it was certainly true that such vessels were superior to the decrepit "coffin ships" putting out from the coastal ports of Ireland. Liverpool was in any case a flourishing seaport, the heart of Britain's trans-Atlantic trading empire, and in both ships and services it offered the emigrant a greater range of choice than any other port. Equally important, the great thousand-ton packets putting out of Waterloo Docks were sufficiently seaworthy to transport their human cargo in both fair weather and foul, in-season or out, and so offered a distinct advantage to emigrants forced to take flight at unseasonable times of the year. Whether this advantage was maintained throughout the entire period of the Famine, and whether it had any bearing on the character and extent of the Famine emigration itself, will be seen in later volumes.

M.H.T.

KEY

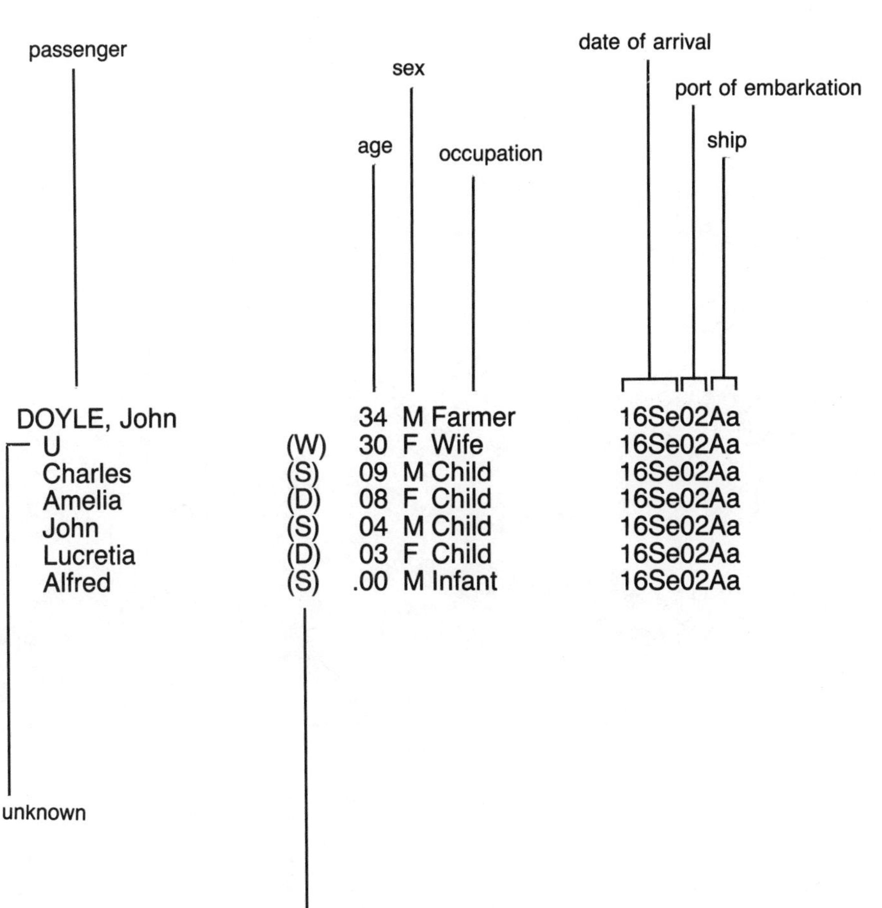

family relationship (wife, son, daughter)

Also *A* aunt; *B* brother; *C* cousin; *F* stepdaughter; *G* stepson; *H* husband; *L* in-law; *M* mother; *N* niece/nephew; *O* widow/widower; *P* father; *R* relative; *T* sister; *Y* grandparent; *Z* grandchild.

List of Ships
With Code Letters

AA GARRICK
AB NIAGARA
AC JOHN-R.SKIDDY
AD SERAPHINE
AE THETIS
AF HUDSON
AG CHAS. MCLAUCHLIN
AH SOUTH ESH
AI EMPIRE
AJ OXFORD
AK JENNY-LIND
AL SWITZERLAND
AM CORNELIA
AO MONTEZUMA
AP VIRGINIA
AQ NEW-ZEALAND
AR COLUMBUS
AS WATERLOO
AT INDIA
AU QUEBEC
AV ST.GEORGE
AW ADAM-CARR
AX FIDELIA
AY VICTORIA
AZ HENRY-HARBECK
BA TORONTO
BB MASSACHUSETTS
BC HOTTINGUER
BD ASHBURTON
BE HUGUENOT
BF ROSCIUS
BG SEA
BH HENDRIK-HUDSON
BI EUROPE
BJ LUCY ANN
BK NEW-YORK
BL WELLINGTON
BM OHIO
BN PRINCE-ALBERT
BO LIVERPOOL
BP IVANHOE
BQ PRINCESS-ROYAL
BR WESTMINSTER
BS SAMUEL-HICKS
BT KALAMAZOO
BU FINGAL
BW ST.PATRICK
BX SIDDONS
BZ YORKSHIRE
CA ERRONDURGA
CB NAOMI
CC LEAR
CD WOLFSVILLE
CE METEOR
CF ISABELLA-STEWART
CG NORTHUMBERLAND
CH ED.AUGUSTA
CI NAPANNA
CJ NELSON-VILLAGE
CK PETER-HATTRICK
CL MARCHIONESS-OF-CLYDESDALE
CM ADIRONDACK
CN QUEEN-OF-THE-WEST
CO HENRY-CLAY
CP BARBARA
CQ SARDINIA
CR BROTHERS
CS EMERALD
CT TUSCAN
CU SIR-HENRY-SMITH
CV CHILDE-HAROLD
CW PATRICK-HENRY
CX JUDAH-FUORO
CY FORFARSHIRE
CZ PHEASANT
DA GEO.A.HOPLEY
DB ANN-HARLEY
DC SARAH-MILLEDGE
DE HOPE
DF MOUNT-VERNON
DG GLADIATOR
DH WARRIOR
DI VENICE
DJ ORPHAN
DK TITCOMB
DL CLARENCE
DM RAPPAHANNOCK
DN JONA
DO SHERIDAN
DP CAITHNESSHIRE
DQ RELIEF
DR PETERSBURG
DS THAETUS
DT MEDIATOR
DU ISABELLA-HELEN
DV JANE
DW RELIANCE
DX SARAH
DY SOUTHERNER
DZ NEBRASKA
EA CAMBRIDGE
EB JANE-GLASSIN
EC ATLAS
ED M.A.FLEMING
EE ANTELEON
EF CREOLE
EG GONDOLA
EH SPEEDWELL
EI A.Z.
EJ BELLE-ISLES
EK ABERDEEN
EL JOHN-R.GARDNER
EM MARGARET-ELIZABETH
EN ERATA
EO GALVESTON
EP DIGBY
EQ GERTRUDE
ER BURGUNDY
ES CAMBRIA
ET GEORGE-MARSDEN
EU MECCA
EV LOUISA
EW COLUMBINE
EX BROOKSBY
EY AUGUSTA
EZ MADAWASKA
FA EFFINGHAM
FB SUPERIOR
FC ELIJAH-SWIFT
FD SOUTH-CAROLINA
FE MARGARET
FF METOKA
FG BROOKLYN
FH MARY-HARRINGTON
FI ROSA-LINDA
FJ INFANTA
FK WOODSIDE
FL INDEPENDENCE
FM MARY-ELIZABETH
FN WASHINGTON
FO EVANDER
FP JOHN-S.DEWOLF
FQ LONDON
FR AURORA
FS GEORGIA
FT STANDARD
FU ARLINGTON
FV UNICORN
FW LIBERTY
FX TAROLINTA
FY HORTENSIA
FZ HAVRE
GA COSMO
GB JANE-H.GLIDEN
GC ORBIT
GD MEMNON
GE CHRISTOPHER-COLUMBUS
GF JAMESTOWN
GG CHAOS
GH VIBILIA
GI PLANT
GJ MANTEO
GK THAMES
GL CHANCELLOR
GM FORREST-KING
GN ZURICH
GO HARRIET-AUGUSTA
GP J.Q.ADAMS
GQ SILVIE-DE-GRASSE
GR CATHERINE
GS RICHARD-ALSOP
GT MISSISSIPPI
GU MARY-PARKINS
GV ADARIO
GW MOSLEM
GX ORPHEUS
GY CONDOR
GZ TROUBADOUR
HA ALCANO
HB STAR-REPUBLIC
HC MARMION
HD JOSEPH-HAM
HE NEW-ORLEANS
HF AMERICA
HG MEMPHIS
HH ENTERPRISE
HI CONSTITUTION
HJ WANDERER
HK CAPT.JOHN
HL NEW-YORK-PACKET
HM HERSILIA
HN INDUSTRY
HO KATE
HP ROSCIOUS
HQ ITALY
HR CHESTER
HS DEFENCE
HT MESSENGER
HU MANCHESTER
HV COSMOS
HW CUSHLAMACHREE
HX COLUMBIA
HY RIO-GRANDE
HZ HAMPDEN
IA COLLOONEY
IB ARETHUSA
IC COMMERCE
ID BLAKE
IE HOME
IF ELIZA-KEITH

IG ABRASIA
IH INTRINSIC
II WAKEFIELD
IJ ELIZABETH
IK ST.JOHN
IL ANDREW-FOSTER
IM WITCH
IN EMPRESS
IO CALEDONIA
IP MARGARET-EVANS
IQ NICHOLAS-BIDDLE
IR ROMANCE
IS SEA-OF-NEW-YORK
IT MARQUIS-OF-CHANDOS
IU FORAGER
IV CAROLINA
IW ANN-D.RICHARDSON
IX SWAN
IY BRILLIANT
IZ NEWCASTLE
JA BURLINGTON
JB HARRIET-NEWELL
JC SARAH-JACKSON
JD HELENA
JE JULINDER
JF LORD-ASHBURTON
JG FANNY
JH LORD-SANDOW
JI CREMONA
JK CALEB-GRIMSHAW
JL EUXINE
JM ELLEN-FORRESTAL
JN ELIZABETH-DENISON
JO CHRISTIANA
JP PLENTY
JQ MILLICETE
JR THOMAS-BENNETT
JS DEBORAH
JT HECLA
JU INA
JV JAMES-FAGAN
JX OCEAN
JZ YORKTOWN
KA AFFGHAN
KB CHARLES
KC ARABIAN
KD MOUNTAINEER
KE ELSINORE
KF BRIDGET
KG ROGER-SHERMAN
KH HEATHER-BELL
KK AMBASSADRESS
KL HYNDERFORD
KM GLENMORE
KN ELIZA-CAROLINE
KO MARTHA-WASHINGTON
KP SARAH-SANDS
KQ KATHLEEN
KR WRENHAM
KS HOWARD
KT SULTANA
KU NEW-WORLD
KV CLUTHA
KW ADONIS
KX ARGYLE
KY GARLAND-GROVE
KZ NANCY
LA ABBY-PRATT
LB GLENLYON
LC MARY-T.RUNDLETT
LD TONQUIN
LE VOLUSIA
LF WIDGEON
LG ANN-SMITH
LH CYNOSURE
LI JAMES-HALL
LJ ADELINE-AND-ELIZA
LK ELIZA
LL CLARISSA
LM MARCELLUS
LN ANCONA
LO PAUL-JONES
LP FALCON
LQ MELAZZO
LR ROWLAND
LS ELEANOR-NEWBOLD
LT BRAZILEINO
LU JUDSON
LV J.W.ANDREWS
LW FANNY-GRAY
LX AGNES
LY ORION
LZ MONTREAL
MO WAVE
MT MONTEREY
MU SIR-ROBERT-PEEL
MY ATLANTIC
NI PRINCE-DE-JOINVILLE
NQ LOUISIANA
NV REPUBLIC
NY ASHLAND
NZ DIANA
OA ELLERSLIE
OE HIGHLAND-MARY
OL MARY-MORRIS
OR JOHN-RAVENEL
OV ALBION
OW ZANONI
PB HIBERNIA
PD SPEED
PN DOWNES
PQ EMBLEM
PU EMIGRANT
QA CHINA
QB JOHN-FIELDING
QC ALICE-WILSON
QD COURIER
QE ENGLAND
QF CHANNING
QG HELEN-MARIA
QH CALIFORNIA
QI M.LIVINGSTON
QJ COLUMBIANA
QK ISAAC-WRIGHT
QL KATE-HUNTER
QM ARGO
QN JOSEPH-HOWE
QO COURIER
QP FLAVIUS
QQ NEUVITAS
QR WARREN
QS JUNIOR
QT MARTHA
QU COLDSTREAM
QV NON-PAREIL
QW EXPRESS
QX QUEEN
QY LISBON
QZ SCHROADIAC
RA SOLDAN
RB AMERICAN-EAGLE
RC TUSKAR
RD DEWDROP
RE GEM
RF PRINCE-RADALI
RG AMBASSADOR
RH ANTWERP
RI SARAH-BROWN
RJ ALBERS
RK WIDOW
RL NATHANIEL-HOOPER
RM CHARLESTOWN
RN EAGLE
RO PHILIP-HONE
RP ROYAL-WILLIAM
RQ EDGAR
RR HARP
RS LANCASHIRE
RT BACHE-MCEVERS
RU ADMIRAL
RV WM.T.DUGGAN
RW PRINCESS-ALICE
RX CHAS.CHALONER
RY GEO.WASHINGTON
RZ ELLEN-BROOKS
SA J.A.MUNN
SB HANNAH-THORTON
SC HARGRAVE
SD EMMA-PRESCOTT
SE ADELBARAN
SF TALBOTT
SG WEST-POINT
SH ARTHUR
SI J.A.JENNER
SJ ELIZA-PERROE
SK JOHN-G.COSTER
SL WAVERLY
SM HARMONIA
SN BACHELOR
SO GUADELQUIVER
SP RICHARD-COBDEN
SQ SENATOR
SR MARY-PHILLIPS
SS PEDRAZA
ST LOTA
SU ADVENTURE
SV NIANTIC
SW BRAZILIAN
SX BREAM
SY JAMES-MARSHALL
SZ TECUMSEH
TA MATILDA
TB EMMA-WATTS
TC PALMETTO
TD JANE-MORISON
TE COLOSSUS
TF ALMEDA
TG MARGARET-SULLIVAN
TH ANN
TI SARDINIA-OF-NEW-YORK
TJ COUNTESS OF DURHAM
TK SARAH-HAND
TL ISAAC-WALTON
TM FANCHION
TN MERCY
TO HECTOR
TP LAURA
TQ LORD-BYRON
TR CHENAGO
TS CHUSAN
TT SAMOSET
TU ACADIA
TV HELENE-CATHERINE
TW CHARTER-OAK
TX OSCAR
TY SIR-JAMES-MCDONALD
TZ MEDEMSEH
UA ANTOLEON
UB GONDAR
UC CHARLES-LOTTIE
UD CHARLES-HAMMOND
UE COHANSEY
UF DORCAS
UG BATAVIA
UH HENRY-ATTKINS
UI GOV. HINCKLEY
UJ GREAT-WESTERN
UK ROSE-STANDISH
UL GERMANIA
UM NOBLE
UN PHILENA

UO TRUE-BLUE
UP GRAMPION
UQ MILAN
UR RAPIDE
US CHRISTINE
UT UNION
UU HEROS
UV OSPRAY
UW LUCONIA
UX OREGON
UY PROGRESS
UZ SEVERN
VA BRITTANIA-OF-GLASGOW
VB CHESHIRE
VC TRITON
VD RADIUS
VE CUGNET
VF LUCINDA-MARIA
VG VINE
VH MADONNAS
VI MARTHA-SANGER
VJ LEONIDAS
VK VANDALIA
VL KATE-HOWE
VM TARQUIN
VN CHARLES-ELLIOT
VO IWANONNER
VP KING PHILIP
VQ SULTAN
VR W.M.VAIL
VS SOPHIA
VT E.Z.
VU HERSCHEL
VV ABEONA
VW BRITISH-QUEEN
VX LYRA
VZ EBENEZEER
WA LADY-OF-THE-LAKE
WB OLAF-KYRRE
WC MADAWASA
WD UNITED-STATES
WE KENT
WF CHIEFTAIN
WG ELIZABETH-DENTLEY
WH ANN-MCLESTER
WI ALPINE
WJ DEVON
WK MARIA
WL ROSETTA

PORTS OF EMBARKATION
With Code Numbers

00 UNKNOWN
01 LONDONDERRY
02 LIVERPOOL
03 QUEENSTOWN
04 GLASGOW
05 HAVRE
06 HAVANA
07 BELFAST
08 MOVILLE
09 SOUTHAMPTON
10 NUEVITAS
11 GALWAY
12 LAGUNA
13 RIO-DE-JANIERO
14 CORK
15 DEMERARA
16 WATERFORD
17 TRINIDAD
18 BRISTOL
19 NEWRY
20 DUBLIN
21 LONDON
22 HALIFAX
23 KINGSTON
24 TURKS-ISLAND
25 LIVERPOOL,QUEENSTOWN
26 GLASGOW,LARNE
27 GLASGOW,MOVILLE
28 SLIGO
29 BARROW,DUBLIN
30 HAITI
31 LIVERPOOL, LONDONDERRY
32 DROGHEDA
33 LIMERICK
34 SYDNEY,CAPE-BRETON
35 BLACK-RIVER
36 PUERTO-CABELLO
37 HULL
38 VERA-CRUZ
39 GUAYAMA,P.R.
40 ST.VINCENT
41 ELEUTHERA
42 FALMOUTH
43 PICTOU,N.S.
44 NEWPORT,WALES
45 GLASGOW,FAYAL
46 FAYAL
47 TORQUAY
48 COLON,R.C.
49 VALPARAISO,CHILE
50 BELIZE
51 PRINCE-EDWARD-ISLAND
52 NASSAU,ELEUTHERA
53 TRALEE
54 MADEIRA
55 LISBON
56 MATANZAS
57 YARMOUTH,N.S.
58 SAGUA-LA-GRANDE
59 DUNDEE
60 KILRUSH
61 NEW-RUSH
62 SAVANILLA
63 MANILA
64 ST.MICHAELS
65 MARANHAM
66 NEWCASTLE
67 RIO-HACHA
68 GREENOCK
69 CAMPECHE
70 SAVANNA-LA-MAR, JAMAICA
71 YOUGHAL
72 CARBONEAR-NF.
73 ST.CROIX
74 TRINIDAD DE CUBA
75 BERMUDA
76 TAMPICO
77 ST.JOHN,CAPE NF.
78 MARSEILLES
79 ST.JOHNS,N.B.
80 CADIZ
81 PUERTO-CABELLO
82 DONEGAL
83 ST.CROIX-VIA-TURKS-IS.
84 SANTO-DOMINGO
85 ST.ANNS-BAY-JAMAICA
86 ST.JOHNS-NF.
87 MALAGA-AND-GIBRALTER
88 PENZANCE
89 CALAIS
90 BREMEN-AND-SOUTHAMPTON
91 MONTEVIDEO
92 WINDSOR
93 NASSAU
94 GLASGOW AND GREENOCK
95 MAYAQUEZ, P.R.
96 OPORTO
97 LIVERPOOL-AND-HALIFAX
98 BREMEN
99 LIVERPOOL, CORK
A1 SANTIAGO DE CUBA
A2 CURACAO
A3 CHARGES, SAN JUAN, HAVANA

LIST OF OCCUPATIONS
With Code Letters

AGRT-MLR	FARMER-MILLER
APTCAST	APOTHECARY'S ASSISTANT
AY-OFF	ARMY OFFICER
BLKP	BLOCK PRINTER
BLR	BOILER MAKER
BLWMKR	BELLOWS MAKER
BRF	BRASS FOUNDER
CBTMKR	CABINET MAKER
CCHBLDR	COACH BUILDER
CFRT	COFFEE ROASTER
CHMD	CHILD MAID
CHPTR	COACH PAINTER
CLCP	CALICO PRINTER
CLD	CLOTH DRAWER
CLDRS	CLOTH DRESSER
CLFN	CLOTH FINISHER
CLSM	CLOTHES SALESMAN
CMCL	COMMERCIAL CLERK
CNDL	CANDLE MAKER
CNF	CONFECTIONER
CRMCHT	CORN MERCHANT
CRPM	CARPET MAKER
CRPW	CARPET WEAVER
CST	CORSET-STAY MAKER
CTLDLR	CATTLE DEALER
CTNDR	COTTON DRESSER
CTNSP	COTTON SPINNER
CVER	CIVIL ENGINEER
EMKR	ENGINE KEEPER
ENGD	ENGINE DRIVER
ENMKR	ENGINE MAKER
FEFNDR	IRON FOUNDER
FLABR	FARM LABORER
FLAXDR	FLAX DRESSER
FMSTWD	FARM STEWARD
FNWK	FURNACE WORKER
FRTDR	FRAME TENDER
FSCTR	FUSTIAN CUTTER
FWK	FRAMEWORK KNITTER
GDNR	GARDENER/GROWER
GLSCTR	GLASS CUTTER
GPEMKR	GOLD PEN MAKER
HJNR	HOUSE JOINER
HOSPINS	HOSPITAL INSPECTOR
HRSDLR	HORSE DEALER
HRSM	HARNESS MAKER
HTLKPR	HOTEL KEEPER
IMKR	INSTRUMENT MAKER
IRNMLDR	IRON MOULDER
JDG-SPCT	JUDGE OF SUPERIOR COURT
JNR-BLDR	JOINER/BUILDER
LAD	LAUNDRY WORKER
LDPR	LINEN DRAPER
LGWVR	LINING WEAVER
LITGR	LITHOGRAPHER
LMNFTR	LEATHER MANUFACTURER
LRCTR	LEATHER CUTTER
LRDR	LARD RENDERER
LRFH	LEATHER FINISHER
MACHMKR	MACHINE MAKER
MLOV	MILL OVERSEER
MMSN	MARBLE MASON
MNFTR	MANUFACTURER
MPOL	MARBLE POLISHER
MRMKR	MIRROR MAKER
MSTA	MASTER OF ARTS
MTMKR	MANTEAU MAKER
MUSTCHR	MUSIC TEACHER
NVYCPT	NAVY CAPTAIN
PASM	PASTRY MAKER
PCLMKR	PENCIL MAKER
PFNL	PROFESSIONAL
PMS	POST MISTRESS
POSTSVYR	POST OFFICE SURVEYOR
PPHGR	PAPER HANGER
PPSTR	PAPER STAINER
PTDSGR	PATTERN DESIGNER
PTMKR	PATTERN MAKER
PVCR	PROVISION CURER
PVMT	PROVISION MERCHANT
PWLWVR	POWER LOOM WEAVER
RCENGR	ROYAL CORPS OF ENGINEERS
REXCV	RAILWAY EXCAVATOR
RLST	RAIL STRAIGHTENER
RRNG	RAILROAD ENGINEER
SCHM	SCHOOL MASTER
SHCHND	SHIP CHANDLER
SHPC	SHIP'S CARPENTER
SLPL	SILVER PLATER
SLT-PLSTR	SLATER-PLASTERER
SP-GVNS	SPINSTER/GOVERNESS
SPDLR	SPIRIT DEALER
SPNRY	YARN SPINNER
SSPNR	SILK SPINNER
STCTR	STONE CUTTER
STDR	STAGE DRIVER
STGKPR	STAGE KEEPER
STKW	STOCKING WEAVER
STWVR	STEAM WEAVER
SWHTR	STRAW BONNET MANUFACTURER
TALCH	TALLOW CHANDLER
TBCMCHT	TOBACCO MERCHANT
TCHRCL	TEACHER OF CLASSICS
TMKR	THREAD MAKER
TNM-BRZ	TINMAN-BRAZIER
TPF	TYPE FOUNDER
W-FMR	WIFE OF FARMER
WDMCHT	WOOD MERCHANT
WI	WIDOW/WIDOWER
WI-FMR	WIDOW/WIDOWER-FARMER
WI-SVNT	WIDOW-SERVANT
WLMCHT	WOOL MERCHANT
WLS	WOOL SPINNER
WMNFTR	WOOL MANUFACTURER
WRHSMN	WAREHOUSE MAN

THE FAMINE IMMIGRANTS

Lists of Irish Immigrants
Arriving at the Port of New York,
1846 - 1851

SOUTH-CAROLINA 02 JULY 1847

From Dublin

NAMES OF PASSENGERS	AGE	SEX	OCCUPATIONS	DATE PORT SHIP
MEDLECOTT, G.	47	M	None	02J120Fd
Hester	32	F	None	02J120Fd
Jane	10	F	None	02J120Fd
Henrietta	08	F	None	02J120Fd
Kate	07	F	None	02J120Fd
Johana	05	F	None	02J120Fd
Martha	04	F	None	02J120Fd
Lucy	02	F	None	02J120Fd
BROWNLOW, Mrt.	22	F	None	02J120Fd
Isbell.	20	F	None	02J120Fd
COSTELLO, D.	40	M	Physician	02J120Fd
U	26	F	Wife	02J120Fd
OKEEFE, J.	22	M	None	02J120Fd
RICHARDSON, W.	42	M	Merchant	02J120Fd
DELANY, P.	23	M	None	02J120Fd
CUMMING, M.	19	M	None	02J120Fd
DONALD, J.M.	20	M	None	02J120Fd
GOUGH, P.	19	M	None	02J120Fd
MONKS, M.	26	M	Laborer	02J120Fd
My.	26	F	None	02J120Fd
Michl.	03	M	Child	02J120Fd
GREEN, T.	26	M	Unknown	02J120Fd
CULLEN, Ellen	24	F	None	02J120Fd
WALSH, Ann	28	F	None	02J120Fd
LARAH, W.	40	M	Unknown	02J120Fd
REILLY, W.	28	M	Unknown	02J120Fd
KELLY, M.	40	M	Unknown	02J120Fd
FEGAN, L.	23	M	Unknown	02J120Fd
My.	24	F	None	02J120Fd
Wm.	20	M	Unknown	02J120Fd
Biddy	40	F	None	02J120Fd
My.	16	F	None	02J120Fd
HARAN, F.	18	M	Unknown	02J120Fd
BRYAN, Ellen	06	F	Child	02J120Fd
MCKEAN, My.	20	F	None	02J120Fd
RICHARDSON, W.	20	M	Unknown	02J120Fd
NUGENT, P.	24	M	Unknown	02J120Fd
LEEDS, A.	18	M	Unknown	02J120Fd
MCCARTY, D.	20	M	Unknown	02J120Fd
LEWIS, Sarah	60	F	None	02J120Fd
MCCARTY, D.	48	M	Unknown	02J120Fd
BRYAN, T.	22	M	Laborer	02J120Fd
MURRY, M.	55	F	None	02J120Fd
MAHONY, Anna	21	F	None	02J120Fd
CONNALLY, Bgt.	22	F	None	02J120Fd
MCKENAN, Anne	33	F	None	02J120Fd
WILLIAMS, Ma.	40	F	None	02J120Fd
POWEL, E.	36	M	Unknown	02J120Fd
NICLESON, U	17	F	None	02J120Fd
RUSSELL, W.	36	M	Unknown	02J120Fd
Elzbt.	32	F	None	02J120Fd
CLOSEN, Cht.	24	F	None	02J120Fd
SALMON, Cath.	35	F	None	02J120Fd
John	19	M	Unknown	02J120Fd
Thos.	12	M	None	02J120Fd
Mary	09	F	Child	02J120Fd
Chas.	07	M	Child	02J120Fd
James	03	M	Child	02J120Fd
LEWIS, My.	25	F	None	02J120Fd
JONSTON, Let.	16	F	None	02J120Fd
KIRWAN, P.	19	M	Unknown	02J120Fd
COYLE, My.	31	F	None	02J120Fd
COOKE, G.	24	M	Unknown	02J120Fd
GALE, T.	26	M	Unknown	02J120Fd
My.	21	F	None	02J120Fd
DULAP, W.	32	M	Unknown	02J120Fd
Ann	32	F	None	02J120Fd
MCANDREW, D.	32	M	Unknown	02J120Fd
Cath.	32	F	None	02J120Fd
DELANEY, J.	25	M	Unknown	02J120Fd
YOUNG, M.	40	M	Unknown	02J120Fd
WILLIS, Jane	23	F	None	02J120Fd
GODFREY, Jane	19	F	None	02J120Fd
MCGOUGH, Mrgt.	21	F	None	02J120Fd
Flann	29	M	Farmer	02J120Fd
COMEFORD, P.	40	M	Mechanic	02J120Fd
BRYAN, T.	13	M	Unknown	02J120Fd
Thos.	21	M	Unknown	02J120Fd
COMEFORD, Cath.	18	F	None	02J120Fd
DENLY, My.	30	F	None	02J120Fd
BYRNE, My.	09	F	Child	02J120Fd
MCGRATH, J.	20	M	Unknown	02J120Fd
Petch.	18	M	Unknown	02J120Fd
Bgt.	17	F	None	02J120Fd
MCCORRISH, C.	27	M	Unknown	02J120Fd
HICKY, J.	37	M	Unknown	02J120Fd
MALLOY, L.	32	M	Unknown	02J120Fd
Cath.	25	F	None	02J120Fd
MCCABE, J.	48	M	Unknown	02J120Fd
GREADY, T.	40	M	Unknown	02J120Fd
MURPHY, J.	35	M	Unknown	02J120Fd
MANGAN, Bgt.	42	F	None	02J120Fd
DARBEY, Anne	22	F	None	02J120Fd
LAWLAR, Ma.	21	F	None	02J120Fd
Biddy	20	F	None	02J120Fd
KEARNY, T.	30	M	Unknown	02J120Fd
Biddy	22	F	None	02J120Fd
Eliza	25	F	None	02J120Fd
Cath.	21	F	None	02J120Fd
Jane	10	F	None	02J120Fd
DURAN, P.	20	M	Laborer	02J120Fd
DALY, J.	30	M	Unknown	02J120Fd
Cath.	25	F	None	02J120Fd
NORTON, M.	19	M	Unknown	02J120Fd
KENNEDY, J.	70	M	Unknown	02J120Fd
Timothy	27	M	Unknown	02J120Fd
Cath.	69	F	None	02J120Fd
Julia	24	F	None	02J120Fd
Kevin	09	M	Child	02J120Fd
ODEALY, M.	38	M	Unknown	02J120Fd
My.	47	F	None	02J120Fd
CORMICK, J.	30	M	Unknown	02J120Fd
Thos.	25	M	Unknown	02J120Fd
CULLEN, P.	25	M	Unknown	02J120Fd
Hannah	26	F	None	02J120Fd
GUESS, T.	30	M	Unknown	02J120Fd
LYNCH, Ann	50	F	None	02J120Fd
Joanne	20	F	None	02J120Fd
Cath.	17	F	None	02J120Fd
Nora	22	F	None	02J120Fd
Ellen	18	F	None	02J120Fd
Patk.	21	M	Unknown	02J120Fd
Michl.	19	M	Unknown	02J120Fd
Chas.	09	M	Child	02J120Fd
STERLING, Bgt.	22	F	None	02J120Fd
BOLAND, P.	28	M	Unknown	02J120Fd
Ann	22	F	None	02J120Fd
Ann	02	F	Child	02J120Fd
RUSSELL, T.	30	M	Unknown	02J120Fd
DILLON, F.	28	M	Unknown	02J120Fd
QUINN, G.	18	M	Unknown	02J120Fd
FALLON, T.	25	M	Unknown	02J120Fd
HURST, A.	50	M	Unknown	02J120Fd
Ann	50	F	None	02J120Fd
Ann	22	F	None	02J120Fd
Chat.	13	F	None	02J120Fd
Wm.	09	M	Child	02J120Fd
DAVIS, M.	25	M	Unknown	02J120Fd
CONROY, M.	24	M	Unknown	02J120Fd
LAWLER, Mt.	32	F	None	02J120Fd

NAMES OF PASSENGERS	A G E	S E X	OCCUPATIONS	DATE PORT SHIP
JACKSON, J.	18	M	Unknown	02JI20Fd
Susan	37	F	None	02JI20Fd
Ann	23	F	None	02JI20Fd
Susan	06	F	Child	02JI20Fd
Mary	16	F	None	02JI20Fd
DORAN, M.	15	M	None	02JI20Fd
Michl.	30	M	Laborer	02JI20Fd
Ann	19	F	None	02JI20Fd
Ellen	15	F	None	02JI20Fd
MURRAY, J.	21	M	Unknown	02JI20Fd
Maria	19	F	None	02JI20Fd
Eliza	18	F	None	02JI20Fd
SHERIDAN, J.	23	M	Unknown	02JI20Fd
MCDAVETT, G.	23	M	Unknown	02JI20Fd
BROWN, Mgrt.	22	F	None	02JI20Fd
BASSETT, T.	24	M	Unknown	02JI20Fd
Jane	23	F	None	02JI20Fd
DONOHUE, M.	31	M	Unknown	02JI20Fd
REGAN, M.	17	M	Unknown	02JI20Fd
RINGWOOD, W.	22	M	Unknown	02JI20Fd
Cath.	20	F	None	02JI20Fd
LUNNERAN, Ma.	18	F	None	02JI20Fd
Sarah	17	F	None	02JI20Fd
Anne	40	F	None	02JI20Fd
DARLING, Mt.	16	F	None	02JI20Fd
Mild.	17	F	None	02JI20Fd
MAGAN, My.	17	F	None	02JI20Fd
MANN, My.	20	F	None	02JI20Fd
BACK, My.A.	17	F	None	02JI20Fd
DOYLE, L.	26	M	Unknown	02JI20Fd
Elza.	23	F	None	02JI20Fd
George	02	M	Child	02JI20Fd
John	01	M	Child	02JI20Fd
Steph.	22	M	Unknown	02JI20Fd
Feny	20	F	None	02JI20Fd
MEREDITH, Ma.	20	F	None	02JI20Fd
MARTIN, R.	30	M	Unknown	02JI20Fd
Phip.	26	M	Unknown	02JI20Fd
My.	20	F	None	02JI20Fd
My.	32	F	None	02JI20Fd
Cath.	20	F	None	02JI20Fd
REILY, G.	17	M	Unknown	02JI20Fd
Ann	18	F	None	02JI20Fd
BURKE, J.	21	M	Unknown	02JI20Fd
MCEVOEY, E.	30	M	Laborer	02JI20Fd
HACKET, P.	25	M	Unknown	02JI20Fd
NOLAN, J.	22	M	Unknown	02JI20Fd
Mgt.	20	F	None	02JI20Fd
NOBB, J.	20	M	Unknown	02JI20Fd
My.	24	F	None	02JI20Fd
CONNELLY, J.	25	M	Unknown	02JI20Fd
Ellen	24	F	None	02JI20Fd
My.	17	F	None	02JI20Fd
Henry	13	M	None	02JI20Fd
LUMSDEN, J.	23	M	Unknown	02JI20Fd
HALAM, M.	20	M	Unknown	02JI20Fd
MOONEY, J.	24	M	Unknown	02JI20Fd
DOWNS, P.	26	M	Unknown	02JI20Fd
DOWNEY, W.	20	M	Unknown	02JI20Fd
John	25	M	Unknown	02JI20Fd
FLYNN, D.	20	M	Unknown	02JI20Fd
Cath.	18	F	None	02JI20Fd
LAWLAR, L.	28	M	Unknown	02JI20Fd
My.	26	F	None	02JI20Fd
BOYLE, J.	22	M	Unknown	02JI20Fd
MURPHY, A.	19	M	Unknown	02JI20Fd
COYNE, J.	33	M	Unknown	02JI20Fd
DOYLE, D.	28	M	Unknown	02JI20Fd
ROURKE, W.	18	M	Unknown	02JI20Fd
CROLEY, Mrgt.	29	F	None	02JI20Fd
DEALY, J.	24	M	Unknown	02JI20Fd
Wm.	20	M	Unknown	02JI20Fd
CARROLE, Ellen	50	F	None	02JI20Fd
PLUNKEET, P.	36	M	Unknown	02JI20Fd
Ann	38	F	None	02JI20Fd

NAMES OF PASSENGERS	A G E	S E X	OCCUPATIONS	DATE PORT SHIP
PLUNKEET, Ann	12	F	None	02JI20Fd
Betty	11	F	None	02JI20Fd
My.	05	F	Child	02JI20Fd
DUFF, P.	21	M	Unknown	02JI20Fd
DELANY, J.	26	M	Unknown	02JI20Fd
FAY, J.	25	M	Unknown	02JI20Fd
BREADY, T.	23	M	Unknown	02JI20Fd
CONER, T.	36	M	Unknown	02JI20Fd
Ellen	28	F	None	02JI20Fd
KENNY, G.	30	M	Unknown	02JI20Fd
COURTNEY, P.	26	M	Unknown	02JI20Fd

WARREN 02 JULY 1847

From Dublin

NAMES OF PASSENGERS	A G E	S E X	OCCUPATIONS	DATE PORT SHIP
MCCAMMAN, P.	20	M	Laborer	02JI20Qr
SHERIDAN, Mich.	09	M	Child	02JI20Qr
SWASEY, Bernard	19	M	Laborer	02JI20Qr
MAGEE, P.	50	M	Laborer	02JI20Qr
Jno.	18	M	Laborer	02JI20Qr
Bernard	18	M	Laborer	02JI20Qr
Charles	24	M	Laborer	02JI20Qr
SHIELD, Richd.	65	M	Mechanic	02JI20Qr
Patt	18	M	Mechanic	02JI20Qr
CARTER, Jas.	20	M	Laborer	02JI20Qr
Bernd.	18	M	Laborer	02JI20Qr
BATES, Richd.	24	M	Laborer	02JI20Qr
MOSSEY, Danl.	19	M	Laborer	02JI20Qr
MORGAN, James	20	M	Laborer	02JI20Qr
RILEY, Peter	25	M	Laborer	02JI20Qr
BERNEY, Jno.	30	M	Laborer	02JI20Qr
NOOLAN, P.	30	M	Laborer	02JI20Qr
BERNEY, Elizth.	15	F	None	02JI20Qr
CARRIGAN, Jas.	18	M	Laborer	02JI20Qr
HETHERTON, P.	20	M	Laborer	02JI20Qr
BUCKLEY, Jno.	60	M	Laborer	02JI20Qr
Richd.	13	M	None	02JI20Qr
CREELY, Mary	35	F	None	02JI20Qr
LOOTZ, Mich.	20	M	Laborer	02JI20Qr
ODONNELL, Jas.	38	M	Laborer	02JI20Qr
Mary	26	F	None	02JI20Qr
RILEY, Jas.	25	M	Laborer	02JI20Qr
MCGAWNCEY, Richd.	20	M	Laborer	02JI20Qr
CALAGHAN, Jno.	20	M	Laborer	02JI20Qr
SHERIDAN, Jas.	30	M	Laborer	02JI20Qr
Peter	38	M	Laborer	02JI20Qr
Chas.	16	M	Laborer	02JI20Qr
LEYNAN, Roger	55	M	Laborer	02JI20Qr
Jno.	18	M	Laborer	02JI20Qr
Hana.	16	F	None	02JI20Qr
BRADDOCK, Jno.	40	M	Laborer	02JI20Qr
Teresa	40	F	None	02JI20Qr
Cath.	19	F	None	02JI20Qr
Johnson	17	M	Laborer	02JI20Qr
Ellen	13	F	None	02JI20Qr
Teresa	08	F	Child	02JI20Qr
SHEHAN, Mary	20	F	None	02JI20Qr
CORREGAN, Alice	16	F	None	02JI20Qr
CARROLL, Winifrid	19	F	None	02JI20Qr
Ellen	25	F	None	02JI20Qr
MALONE, Margt.	18	F	None	02JI20Qr
Elizth.	21	F	None	02JI20Qr
RILEY, Honora	30	F	None	02JI20Qr
Cath.	09	F	Child	02JI20Qr
NAILERS, Sally	21	F	None	02JI20Qr
MARLY, Mary	16	F	None	02JI20Qr
MCCAHERY, Ellen	26	F	None	02JI20Qr
HALL, Jno.	40	M	Mechanic	02JI20Qr

NAMES OF PASSENGERS	AGE	SEX	OCCUPATIONS	DATE PORT SHIP
HALL, Martha	36	F	None	02J120Qr
Mary-Jane	12	F	None	02J120Qr
Robt.	08	M	Child	02J120Qr
Mary-Eliza	.09	F	Infant	02J120Qr
SHERIDAN, Mary	18	F	None	02J120Qr
FLOOD, Cath.	18	F	None	02J120Qr
BOHAM, Jas.	30	M	Farmer	02J120Qr
BOOZ, Jane	19	F	None	02J120Qr
Mary	.00	F	Infant	02J120Qr
CAMPBELL, Elizth.	08	F	Child	02J120Qr
KENNEDY, Mich.	30	M	Farmer	02J120Qr
MCCUNNON, Ann	20	F	None	02J120Qr
SHERIDAN, Rose	28	F	None	02J120Qr
Mary	14	F	None	02J120Qr
Marsella	08	F	Child	02J120Qr
Cath.	06	F	Child	02J120Qr
Elizth.	52	F	None	02J120Qr
MCGEE, Ann	50	F	None	02J120Qr
Cath.	24	F	None	02J120Qr
Honna	22	F	None	02J120Qr
FAGAN, Mary	15	F	None	02J120Qr
Judith	12	F	None	02J120Qr
OCONNER, Johanna	55	F	None	02J120Qr
MCKEON, Elizth.	45	F	None	02J120Qr
Mary	12	F	None	02J120Qr
BLAIE, Margt.	25	F	None	02J120Qr
FINLEY, Martha	22	F	None	02J120Qr
Rebecca	20	F	None	02J120Qr
Eliza	12	F	None	02J120Qr
Jane	13	F	None	02J120Qr
NEVAN, Danl.	30	M	Laborer	02J120Qr
Cath.	10	F	None	02J120Qr
Pat	08	M	Child	02J120Qr
Bridget	06	F	Child	02J120Qr
HOGAN, Mich.	40	M	Laborer	02J120Qr
Bridget	35	F	None	02J120Qr
HOLOHAN, Pat	12	M	None	02J120Qr
Jno.	11	M	None	02J120Qr
KELLY, Mick	08	M	Child	02J120Qr
HAYAN, Jas.	04	M	Child	02J120Qr
DOOLY, Wm.	40	M	Mechanic	02J120Qr
Johana	60	F	None	02J120Qr
Mich.	16	M	None	02J120Qr
Jas.	10	M	None	02J120Qr
Danl.	07	M	Child	02J120Qr
Wm.	05	M	Child	02J120Qr
Jno.	.11	M	Infant	02J120Qr
WALLACE, U	13	F	None	02J120Qr

NEUVITAS 02 JULY 1847

From Londonderry

NAMES OF PASSENGERS	AGE	SEX	OCCUPATIONS	DATE PORT SHIP
RODGERS, Nancy	30	F	None	02J101Qq
Thos.	76	M	Mechanic	02J101Qq
Ann	55	F	None	02J101Qq
Math.	35	F	None	02J101Qq
ROGERS, Jonathan	24	M	Farmer	02J101Qq
ELLIS, James	38	M	Farmer	02J101Qq
Robt.	15	M	None	02J101Qq
Jon.	12	M	None	02J101Qq
Ann	09	F	Child	02J101Qq
Margt.	04	F	Child	02J101Qq
Thos.	01	M	Child	02J101Qq
Matty	38	F	None	02J101Qq
MCCAFFERTY, Jon	20	M	Mechanic	02J101Qq
Hugh	18	M	Mechanic	02J101Qq
Mary	14	F	None	02J101Qq
Margt.	12	F	None	02J101Qq
MCCAFFERTY, Anthony	05	M	Child	02J101Qq
Biddy	40	F	None	02J101Qq
ODONNELL, Phil	30	M	Laborer	02J101Qq
Biddy	40	F	None	02J101Qq
Nancy	19	F	None	02J101Qq
Wm.	17	M	Laborer	02J101Qq
Pat	14	M	None	02J101Qq
Rose	21	F	None	02J101Qq
Mary	07	F	Child	02J101Qq
RODEN, Biddy	17	F	None	02J101Qq
DOHERTY, Edwd.	23	M	Farmer	02J101Qq
Neil	18	M	Farmer	02J101Qq
QUICLEY, Chas.	35	M	Farmer	02J101Qq
Magey	30	F	None	02J101Qq
Bridget	18	F	None	02J101Qq
Rasey	16	F	None	02J101Qq
DURNY, Margt.	39	F	None	02J101Qq
CURREN, Jno.	19	M	Farmer	02J101Qq
U	58	F	WI	02J101Qq
PORTER, Eliza	18	F	None	02J101Qq
SHEARER, Eliza	18	F	None	02J101Qq
CROGHAN, Bernard	60	M	Farmer	02J101Qq
Mary	50	F	None	02J101Qq
COYLE, Margt.	17	F	None	02J101Qq
MOONEY, Hugh	20	M	Farmer	02J101Qq
CALLAHAN, Ann	20	F	None	02J101Qq
DUNCAN, Jno.	19	M	Laborer	02J101Qq
CHRISOM, Wm.J.	17	M	Laborer	02J101Qq
LITTLE, Mary-J.	19	F	None	02J101Qq
MCATHER, Cath.	24	F	None	02J101Qq
Biddy	18	F	None	02J101Qq
TURNER, Jno.	30	M	Laborer	02J101Qq
KERR, Ann	25	F	None	02J101Qq
GILL, Hugh	52	M	Laborer	02J101Qq
Ellen	48	F	None	02J101Qq
Ann	14	F	None	02J101Qq
Susan	12	F	None	02J101Qq
Jane	10	F	None	02J101Qq
KELLY, Philip	29	M	Laborer	02J101Qq
GILL, Bridget	18	F	None	02J101Qq
MOORE, James	18	M	Laborer	02J101Qq
MCKEA, Biddy	16	F	None	02J101Qq
SHANKLIN, M.	21	M	Laborer	02J101Qq
MARSHALL, Wm.	22	M	Farmer	02J101Qq
FLAGGERTY, Francis	20	M	Farmer	02J101Qq
BALLANTINE, Mary-A.	17	F	None	02J101Qq
DEVIN, Mary-A.	17	F	None	02J101Qq
Mary-A.	26	F	None	02J101Qq
WILLIAMSON, Sarah	42	F	None	02J101Qq
MCLAUGHLIN, Ann	22	F	None	02J101Qq
DEALIN, Biddy	16	F	None	02J101Qq
DRACEE, Biddy	17	F	None	02J101Qq
GIBBIN, Peggy	50	F	None	02J101Qq
KERR, James	50	M	Farmer	02J101Qq
Nancy	35	F	None	02J101Qq
Mark	28	M	Farmer	02J101Qq
Jona	18	M	Farmer	02J101Qq
Sally	16	F	None	02J101Qq
Eliza	13	F	None	02J101Qq
Mary	25	F	None	02J101Qq
Robt.	.06	M	Infant	02J101Qq
MCCALGAN, Mary	23	F	None	02J101Qq
AUTHLY, Meth.	20	M	Laborer	02J101Qq
GRAMATTAN, Jas.	34	M	Laborer	02J101Qq
Pat	20	M	Laborer	02J101Qq
KANE, Anthony	24	M	Laborer	02J101Qq
MURRAY, Cath.	16	F	None	02J101Qq

JUNIOR 03 JULY 1847

From Waterford

NAMES OF PASSENGERS	AGE	SEX	OCCUPATIONS	DATE PORT SHIP
SCRUAN, Jos.	38	M	Merchant	03JI16Qs
Henry	28	M	Merchant	03JI16Qs
POWER, B.	72	F	None	03JI16Qs
Pierce	19	M	Laborer	03JI16Qs
Charles	17	M	Laborer	03JI16Qs
PURCELL, Ed.	41	M	Laborer	03JI16Qs
Bridget	28	F	None	03JI16Qs
Ellen	25	F	None	03JI16Qs
Cath.	30	F	None	03JI16Qs
Richd.	13	M	None	03JI16Qs
Julia	07	F	Child	03JI16Qs
William	05	M	Child	03JI16Qs
Ellen	03	F	Child	03JI16Qs
COLEMAN, Mich.	34	M	Farmer	03JI16Qs
Richd.	38	M	Farmer	03JI16Qs
Cath.	28	F	None	03JI16Qs
Jno.	19	M	Farmer	03JI16Qs
Anty	09	F	Child	03JI16Qs
David	07	M	Child	03JI16Qs
Mary	05	F	Child	03JI16Qs
David	03	M	Child	03JI16Qs
Cath.	01	F	Child	03JI16Qs
Edmd.	32	M	Laborer	03JI16Qs
CUTHEY, Richd.	25	M	Laborer	03JI16Qs
GRADY, Pat	22	M	Laborer	03JI16Qs
Thos.	29	M	Laborer	03JI16Qs
KARNEY, Thos.	22	M	Laborer	03JI16Qs
HASTY, Jas.	22	M	Laborer	03JI16Qs
KEMENLY, Mary	00	F	None	03JI16Qs
SHEA, Pat	35	M	Laborer	03JI16Qs
Edwd.	26	M	Mechanic	03JI16Qs
Bridget	26	F	None	03JI16Qs
Anne	29	F	None	03JI16Qs
HOLOHAN, Mat.	27	M	Laborer	03JI16Qs
QUANN, Pat	28	M	Laborer	03JI16Qs
Mary	25	F	None	03JI16Qs
Judy	21	F	None	03JI16Qs
DAMNEY, Judy	24	F	None	03JI16Qs
MCDANIEL, Jno.	24	M	Laborer	03JI16Qs
DOOLAN, Pat	24	M	Laborer	03JI16Qs
BUTLER, Betsey	19	F	None	03JI16Qs
KEAN, William	21	M	Laborer	03JI16Qs
FURLONG, Cath.	31	F	None	03JI16Qs
MURPHY, Jas.	22	M	Laborer	03JI16Qs
BRENNAN, Thos.	25	M	Laborer	03JI16Qs
STAPLETON, Cath.	21	F	None	03JI16Qs
DUGGAN, Mich.	28	M	Laborer	03JI16Qs
Pat.	26	M	Laborer	03JI16Qs
HANAGAN, Man.	40	M	Laborer	03JI16Qs
POWER, Pat	23	M	Laborer	03JI16Qs
RAHER, Thos.	25	M	Laborer	03JI16Qs
Julia	22	F	None	03JI16Qs
QUINGLEY, Thos.	32	M	Laborer	03JI16Qs
SHEA, Bridget	27	F	None	03JI16Qs
AYLEMAND, Anty.	27	M	Laborer	03JI16Qs
BRODRICK, Dennis	22	M	Laborer	03JI16Qs
HENESEY, Pat	20	M	Laborer	03JI16Qs
HENRY, Mat.	19	M	Laborer	03JI16Qs
POWER, Jno.	32	M	Laborer	03JI16Qs
Mich.	27	M	Laborer	03JI16Qs
Cath.	27	F	None	03JI16Qs
Margt.	28	F	None	03JI16Qs
CARROL, May	21	F	None	03JI16Qs
LEAGER, Henry	20	M	Laborer	03JI16Qs
CLADY, Alice	28	F	None	03JI16Qs
CLADY, Edwd.	30	M	Laborer	03JI16Qs
Wm.	05	M	Child	03JI16Qs
Pierce	03	M	Child	03JI16Qs
Jos.	.00	M	Infant	03JI16Qs
DALY, Wm.	24	M	Mechanic	03JI16Qs
SHEA, Andrew	29	M	Laborer	03JI16Qs
Fanny	30	F	None	03JI16Qs
Mary	05	F	Child	03JI16Qs
Joana	03	F	Child	03JI16Qs
Robt.	02	M	Child	03JI16Qs
Wm.	01	M	Child	03JI16Qs
KENEY, Wm.	27	M	Mechanic	03JI16Qs
BOULEE, Alice	20	F	None	03JI16Qs
BAND, Mary	22	F	None	03JI16Qs
REDDY, Pat	30	M	Mechanic	03JI16Qs
QUINN, Jas.	25	M	Mechanic	03JI16Qs
TIELAN, Maria	26	F	None	03JI16Qs
WALSH, Jno.	26	M	Mechanic	03JI16Qs
RODERICK, Mary	22	F	None	03JI16Qs
POWER, Jno.	34	M	Laborer	03JI16Qs
DOLAN, Mich.	24	M	Laborer	03JI16Qs
ODONNELL, Ed.	54	M	Laborer	03JI16Qs
Margt.	62	F	None	03JI16Qs
NOLAN, Ann	22	F	None	03JI16Qs
TEVERTON, Jno.	24	M	Laborer	03JI16Qs
COGLAN, Dennis	30	M	Laborer	03JI16Qs
PURCELL, Mich.	25	M	Laborer	03JI16Qs
Mary	40	F	None	03JI16Qs
Edwd.	28	M	Laborer	03JI16Qs
DRIMING, Jno.	22	M	Laborer	03JI16Qs
Maria	40	F	None	03JI16Qs
Nancy	27	F	None	03JI16Qs
CARROLL, Cath.	30	F	None	03JI16Qs
DRENING, Ann	29	F	None	03JI16Qs
KELLY, Mary	18	F	None	03JI16Qs
FOLEY, Mary	21	F	None	03JI16Qs
KELLY, Mary	22	F	None	03JI16Qs
Edwd.	14	M	None	03JI16Qs
FOLEY, Wm.	20	M	Laborer	03JI16Qs
HEAIRNE, Thos.	28	M	Laborer	03JI16Qs
ROUKE, James	20	M	Laborer	03JI16Qs
MAHER, Jno.	30	M	Laborer	03JI16Qs
Wm.	21	M	Mechanic	03JI16Qs
Ellen	30	F	None	03JI16Qs
RYAN, Thos.	20	M	Mechanic	03JI16Qs
SMITH, Jno.	22	M	Mechanic	03JI16Qs
FLANERTY, Cath.	24	F	None	03JI16Qs
NEAGLE, Edwd.	24	M	Mechanic	03JI16Qs
CONNOR, Margt.	34	F	None	03JI16Qs
Richd.	11	M	None	03JI16Qs
Wm.	09	M	Child	03JI16Qs
Cath.	05	F	Child	03JI16Qs
MCCARTHY, Mary	18	F	Child	03JI16Qs
LUCKEN, Jas.	18	M	Laborer	03JI16Qs
IRELAND, Martin	17	M	Laborer	03JI16Qs
WICKHAM, Jas.	23	M	Laborer	03JI16Qs
WRIGHT, Richd.	30	M	Laborer	03JI16Qs
KELLETT, Ann	23	F	None	03JI16Qs
MCGOUGH, Alice	20	F	None	03JI16Qs
MAHIER, Cath.	20	F	None	03JI16Qs
Ellen	22	F	None	03JI16Qs
STOKES, Pat	45	M	Laborer	03JI16Qs
CONDY, Richd.	16	M	Laborer	03JI16Qs
BODY, Cath.	26	F	None	03JI16Qs
POWER, Thos.	38	M	Laborer	03JI16Qs
HENNEBE, Maria	23	F	None	03JI16Qs
TOUNERING, Ellen	23	F	None	03JI16Qs
RICHARDS, Mariann	00	F	None	03JI16Qs
COUGHLAND, Ellen	00	F	None	03JI16Qs

MARTHA 03 JULY 1847

From Cork

NAMES OF PASSENGERS	AGE	SEX	OCCUPATIONS	DATE PORT SHIP
CALAHAN, Jno.	27	M	Farmer	03J114Qt
MCARTHY, Jno.	30	M	Farmer	03J114Qt
REGAN, Jelly	30	M	Farmer	03J114Qt
Nolly	27	F	None	03J114Qt
DUGGIN, Jelly	27	M	Farmer	03J114Qt
SWEENY, Miles	27	M	Farmer	03J114Qt
Ellen	20	F	None	03J114Qt
DRISCAL, Pat	23	M	Farmer	03J114Qt
LYNCH, Danl.	24	M	Farmer	03J114Qt
HENELLY, Mich.	19	M	Farmer	03J114Qt
SULLIVAN, Mich.	27	M	Farmer	03J114Qt
Joha.	25	F	None	03J114Qt
Pat	23	M	Farmer	03J114Qt
HENNESSY, Ellen	23	F	None	03J114Qt
COHAN, Hain	23	M	Mechanic	03J114Qt
JORDAN, Hern.	20	M	Mechanic	03J114Qt
WALSH, Mich.	27	M	Mechanic	03J114Qt
John.	27	F	None	03J114Qt
Jas.	04	M	Child	03J114Qt
James	01	M	Child	03J114Qt
MULLAWNEY, J.J.	24	M	Mechanic	03J114Qt
CEART, Jno.	54	M	Mechanic	03J114Qt
DALEY, Wm.	21	M	Mechanic	03J114Qt
YOUNG, Wm.	30	M	Mechanic	03J114Qt
MULLONEY, Danl.	32	M	Mechanic	03J114Qt
Ellen	25	F	None	03J114Qt
MURPHY, Jno.	21	M	Mechanic	03J114Qt
TURNBULL, Martin	20	M	Mechanic	03J114Qt
ERWIN, Thos.	42	M	Mechanic	03J114Qt
Ellen	34	F	None	03J114Qt
Margt.	11	F	None	03J114Qt
Honora	08	F	Child	03J114Qt
Bridget	05	F	Child	03J114Qt
Thomas	03	M	Child	03J114Qt
Jno.	02	M	Child	03J114Qt
OSULLIVAN, Briget	19	F	None	03J114Qt
HOGAN, Maget	22	F	None	03J114Qt
MULLANE, David	30	M	Mechanic	03J114Qt
Cath.	26	F	None	03J114Qt
HEALY, David	30	M	Mechanic	03J114Qt
JEWELL, Wm.	22	M	Mechanic	03J114Qt
HENNESSY, Wm.	30	M	Mechanic	03J114Qt
BATEMAN, Jno.	35	M	Mechanic	03J114Qt
AHERAN, Jas.	40	M	Mechanic	03J114Qt
MCARTHEY, Jas.	20	M	Mechanic	03J114Qt
SULLIVAN, Danl.	24	M	Mechanic	03J114Qt
Molly	27	F	None	03J114Qt
Jerry	01	M	Child	03J114Qt
CROE, Dennis	17	M	Mechanic	03J114Qt
COHANE, Richd.	26	M	Mechanic	03J114Qt
Jno.	25	M	Mechanic	03J114Qt
Cate	18	F	None	03J114Qt
BUCKLEY, Jas.	40	M	Mechanic	03J114Qt
Mary	27	F	None	03J114Qt
Peggy	07	F	Child	03J114Qt
Cate	01	F	Child	03J114Qt
Moly	04	F	Child	03J114Qt
Johan	03	M	Child	03J114Qt
WHITE, Maurice	20	M	Mechanic	03J114Qt
SPILLANE, Tim	20	M	Mechanic	03J114Qt
LONG, Mal.	24	M	Mechanic	03J114Qt
Thos.	26	M	Mechanic	03J114Qt
FITZPATRICK, Jno.	25	M	Mechanic	03J114Qt
BAILEY, Madia	30	F	None	03J114Qt
Cate	30	F	None	03J114Qt
BAILEY, Joha	22	F	None	03J114Qt
Mary	.03	F	Infant	03J114Qt
MCSWEENY, Ellen	25	F	None	03J114Qt
Edwd.	20	M	Mechanic	03J114Qt
Bryan	18	M	Mechanic	03J114Qt
MCEVOY, Jno.	24	M	Mechanic	03J114Qt
Margt.	25	F	None	03J114Qt
CALAHANE, Danl.	30	M	Mechanic	03J114Qt
Mary	25	F	None	03J114Qt
BLOW, Jno.	33	M	Mechanic	03J114Qt
LEURY, Bessy	22	F	None	03J114Qt
Mich	03	M	Child	03J114Qt
Danl.	02	M	Child	03J114Qt
ALLEN, Mary	18	F	None	03J114Qt
LEAHRY, Danl.	28	M	Laborer	03J114Qt
CEARY, Tim	20	M	Laborer	03J114Qt
COFFEY, Pat	25	M	Laborer	03J114Qt
MULLANE, Jno.	27	M	Laborer	03J114Qt
MAHONEY, Jas.	23	M	Laborer	03J114Qt
Timm	19	M	Laborer	03J114Qt
REGAN, Jno.	26	M	Laborer	03J114Qt
ROGERS, Mich.	20	M	Laborer	03J114Qt
HARNETT, Jas.	30	M	Laborer	03J114Qt
MULROY, Pat	20	M	Laborer	03J114Qt
RINT, Mary	30	F	None	03J114Qt
MULRAY, Mich.	22	M	Laborer	03J114Qt
COCHRANE, Dennis	24	M	Laborer	03J114Qt
Mich.	28	M	Laborer	03J114Qt
WETTEN, Joh.	24	M	Laborer	03J114Qt
HALKERS, Cate	22	F	None	03J114Qt
COLLINS, Tim	28	M	Laborer	03J114Qt
HOGET, Mary	20	F	None	03J114Qt
FITZPATRICK, Danl.	24	M	Laborer	03J114Qt
SULLIVAN, Timothy	28	M	Laborer	03J114Qt
LYNCH, Jerry	23	M	Laborer	03J114Qt

HUGUENOT 06 JULY 1847

From Liverpool

NAMES OF PASSENGERS	AGE	SEX	OCCUPATIONS	DATE PORT SHIP
THOMAS, Edward	37	M	Mechanic	06J102Be
EVANS, Thomas	33	M	Mechanic	06J102Be
Elizth.	32	F	None	06J102Be
Thomas-Jr.	09	M	Child	06J102Be
JONES, Saml.	40	M	Mechanic	06J102Be
Wm.	20	M	Mechanic	06J102Be
Margt.	39	F	None	06J102Be
WRANGLE, Hugh	46	M	Mechanic	06J102Be
Margt.	46	F	None	06J102Be
HUNG, Geo.	32	M	Farmer	06J102Be
Margt.	36	F	None	06J102Be
Ellen	03	F	Child	06J102Be
WOOD, Peter	18	M	Farmer	06J102Be
CASSERLY, Jas.	35	M	Farmer	06J102Be
DILLON, Bridget	10	F	None	06J102Be
Edwd.	17	M	Laborer	06J102Be
Bridget	20	F	None	06J102Be
HAGAN, Mary	18	F	None	06J102Be
FOX, John	40	M	Laborer	06J102Be
Margt.	35	F	None	06J102Be
Jno.	.00	M	Infant	06J102Be
CHACK, Mich.	60	M	Laborer	06J102Be
Anne	18	F	None	06J102Be
NEIL, James	26	M	Laborer	06J102Be
Thomas	20	M	Laborer	06J102Be
SPENCE, John	47	M	Mechanic	06J102Be
Euph.	46	F	None	06J102Be
Jno.Jr.	14	M	None	06J102Be
Charles	11	M	None	06J102Be

NAMES OF PASSENGERS	AGE	SEX	OCCUPATIONS	DATE PORT SHIP	NAMES OF PASSENGERS	AGE	SEX	OCCUPATIONS	DATE PORT SHIP
SPENCE, Euph.	07	F	Child	06JI02Be	FARREL, Chas.	30	M	Farmer	06JI02Be
CALDER, Jas.	30	M	Mechanic	06JI02Be	Jas.	30	M	Farmer	06JI02Be
GARRETT, Wm.	32	M	Mechanic	06JI02Be	Ann	30	F	None	06JI02Be
Isabel	30	F	None	06JI02Be	GAYNON, John	34	M	Farmer	06JI02Be
DUNN, Jas.	21	M	Mechanic	06JI02Be	Ann	30	F	None	06JI02Be
CULLEN, Jas.	21	M	Mechanic	06JI02Be	POULTON, Solomon	45	M	Farmer	06JI02Be
BYNNE, Jno.	21	M	Mechanic	06JI02Be	SIMMONS, Geo.	25	M	Farmer	06JI02Be
HOCK, Henry	37	M	Farmer	06JI02Be	BAER, Thos.	26	M	Farmer	06JI02Be
Sarah-A.	39	F	None	06JI02Be	MARTIN, John	24	M	Farmer	06JI02Be
BIRMINGHAM, Edwd.	54	M	Farmer	06JI02Be	LUIELL, Jno.	20	M	Farmer	06JI02Be
Martin	25	M	Farmer	06JI02Be	ROBERTS, Jno.	40	M	Farmer	06JI02Be
Mary	18	F	None	06JI02Be	DAVIES, Thos.	20	M	Mechanic	06JI02Be
BENNETT, Ellen	22	F	None	06JI02Be	Jno.	17	M	Mechanic	06JI02Be
HERAN, Ann	22	F	None	06JI02Be	SEAWRIGHT, And.	34	M	Farmer	06JI02Be
KENNEY, John	40	M	Laborer	06JI02Be	Mary	33	F	None	06JI02Be
Thomas	30	M	Laborer	06JI02Be	Jno.	08	M	Child	06JI02Be
FITZSIMMONS, Philip	35	M	Laborer	06JI02Be	Martha	04	F	Child	06JI02Be
Mich.	40	M	Laborer	06JI02Be	Margt.	06	F	Child	06JI02Be
Bridget	60	F	None	06JI02Be	A.J.	03	F	Child	06JI02Be
Ellen	20	F	None	06JI02Be	Geo.	.00	M	Infant	06JI02Be
SMITH, Danl.	15	M	Laborer	06JI02Be	BATES, Susan	20	F	None	06JI02Be
MCCABE, Hugh	20	M	Laborer	06JI02Be	PEPPER, Saml.	40	M	Farmer	06JI02Be
GAFFNEY, Mary	21	F	None	06JI02Be	DUNN, Jno.	40	M	Farmer	06JI02Be
TUCKER, James	40	M	Laborer	06JI02Be	CARRICK, Abraham	17	M	Farmer	06JI02Be
BREWERER, Louis	28	M	Laborer	06JI02Be	GARRETT, Thos.	23	M	Mechanic	06JI02Be
CONNER, Thos.	20	M	Laborer	06JI02Be	FLANNERY, Honor	20	F	None	06JI02Be
Ellen	19	F	None	06JI02Be	SANFORD, Thos.	40	M	Farmer	06JI02Be
MERRITT, Geo.	64	M	Mechanic	06JI02Be	Martha	22	F	None	06JI02Be
Elizth.	54	F	None	06JI02Be	CROCKES, Jno.	28	M	Farmer	06JI02Be
TAGAN, Mich.	24	M	Mechanic	06JI02Be	Alice	30	F	None	06JI02Be
Bridget	20	F	Mechanic	06JI02Be	QUICK, Josh	21	M	Farmer	06JI02Be
RICHARDSON, Jas.	24	M	Farmer	06JI02Be	MCLAUGHLIN, Jno.	19	M	None	06JI02Be
Margt.	24	F	None	06JI02Be	CARBY, Bridg.	17	F	None	06JI02Be
CUMISKEY, Mary	35	F	None	06JI02Be	Ann	16	F	None	06JI02Be
John	14	M	Farmer	06JI02Be	BUCKLEY, Judy	28	F	None	06JI02Be
CONNIGAN, Thomas	40	M	Farmer	06JI02Be	LEWIS, Julius	25	M	Mechanic	06JI02Be
Thomas	17	M	Farmer	06JI02Be	SYLVESTER, Julius	22	M	Mechanic	06JI02Be
GRADY, Mich.	36	M	Laborer	06JI02Be	CARRINGAN, Wm.	25	M	Farmer	06JI02Be
BRADY, Corns.	24	M	Laborer	06JI02Be	Josh	22	M	Farmer	06JI02Be
Mary	22	F	None	06JI02Be	HAYES, Wm.	25	M	Farmer	06JI02Be
CONNER, Jas.	32	M	Laborer	06JI02Be	MCCARTHY, Pat	23	M	Farmer	06JI02Be
KELLEY, Jas.	30	M	Laborer	06JI02Be	BROWN, Chris	26	M	Farmer	06JI02Be
Ellen	28	F	None	06JI02Be	Terence	26	M	Farmer	06JI02Be
GILLEN, Jas.	31	M	Laborer	06JI02Be	MULLIGAN, Pat	30	M	Laborer	06JI02Be
Mary	06	F	Child	06JI02Be	MONOGHAN, Mich.	20	M	Laborer	06JI02Be
Jas.Jr.	03	M	Child	06JI02Be	HENDERSON, Cath.	20	F	None	06JI02Be
WALSH, Martin	32	M	Laborer	06JI02Be	MCCABE, Jno.	22	M	Laborer	06JI02Be
GIBNEY, Thos.	40	M	Laborer	06JI02Be	MCLEAN, Sarah	16	F	None	06JI02Be
Ann	39	F	None	06JI02Be	FANNING, Mary	70	F	None	06JI02Be
STERRETT, Jas.	40	M	Laborer	06JI02Be	HARKER, H.	19	M	Laborer	06JI02Be
Ann	30	F	None	06JI02Be	GORMLY, Thos.	18	M	Laborer	06JI02Be
Chas.	06	M	Child	06JI02Be	MCBRIDE, Mat.	20	M	Laborer	06JI02Be
MOONEY, James	40	M	Laborer	06JI02Be	KELLEY, Pat	25	M	Laborer	06JI02Be
BAINE, Thos.	50	M	Laborer	06JI02Be	DUNAN, Pat	27	M	Mechanic	06JI02Be
Maria	50	F	None	06JI02Be	OBRIEN, Francis	20	M	Laborer	06JI02Be
Pat	22	M	Laborer	06JI02Be	RAE, Margt.	41	F	None	06JI02Be
Thos.Jr.	12	M	None	06JI02Be	HIGGINS, Pat	20	M	Laborer	06JI02Be
Alicia	11	F	None	06JI02Be	CAHILL, Pat	12	M	Laborer	06JI02Be
Maria	20	F	None	06JI02Be	FARLEY, Ellen	17	F	None	06JI02Be
KINSELLA, Pat	40	M	Laborer	06JI02Be	FARRELL, Cath.	24	F	None	06JI02Be
Lucy	38	F	None	06JI02Be	PALMER, Wm.	32	M	Laborer	06JI02Be
Ann	06	F	Child	06JI02Be	HANNON, Ellen	16	F	None	06JI02Be
Mich.	08	M	Child	06JI02Be	DONLY, Alice	14	F	None	06JI02Be
Alicia	05	F	Child	06JI02Be	MCCAUGHY, Sarah	17	F	None	06JI02Be
Mary	03	F	Child	06JI02Be	HOOD, Thos.	22	M	Laborer	06JI02Be
STEWART, Saml.	47	M	Mechanic	06JI02Be	CONNER, Margt.	22	F	None	06JI02Be
Robt.	20	M	Mechanic	06JI02Be	LYNCH, Neil	18	M	Laborer	06JI02Be
MEGRAN, Mich.	20	M	Mechanic	06JI02Be	LEBENNING, Louis	39	M	Laborer	06JI02Be
M.A.	25	F	None	06JI02Be	KENNEY, Patrick	35	M	Laborer	06JI02Be
ROHAN, Timothy	39	M	Mechanic	06JI02Be	YOUNG, Jno.	18	M	Mechanic	06JI02Be
Mary	38	F	None	06JI02Be	Martha	19	F	None	06JI02Be
MCSUIGGAN, Pat	18	M	Laborer	06JI02Be	LEWLER, Peggy	30	F	None	06JI02Be
Bridget	20	F	None	06JI02Be	MARTIN, Jas.	27	M	Mechanic	06JI02Be
KETCHER, Pat	17	M	Laborer	06JI02Be	BIGNALL, Jno.	23	M	Laborer	06JI02Be
SMITH, John	18	M	Laborer	06JI02Be	FURGUSON, Ellen	18	F	None	06JI02Be

NAMES OF PASSENGERS	AGE	SEX	OCCUPATIONS	DATE PORT SHIP
NOULAN, Julia	21	F	None	06JI02Be
MCADOE, Mary	19	F	None	06JI02Be
OHOUGHTON, James	25	M	Laborer	06JI02Be
LAWRENCE, Wm.	30	M	Farmer	06JI02Be
MCLAUGHLIN, Mich.	39	M	Farmer	06JI02Be
MCCALL, Jas.	21	M	Farmer	06JI02Be
REYNOLDS, Mary	17	F	None	06JI02Be
GAFFERY, Thos.	16	M	Farmer	06JI02Be
SMITH, Margt.	20	F	None	06JI02Be
HENDERSON, Wm.	36	M	Farmer	06JI02Be
BAGNILL, Pat	23	M	Laborer	06JI02Be
BROWN, Geo.	22	M	Laborer	06JI02Be
MURPHY, Mary	24	F	None	06JI02Be
KENAN, Bridget	17	F	None	06JI02Be
CAINE, Ann	18	F	None	06JI02Be
MCKENNA, Jane	17	F	None	06JI02Be
CONNELLY, Jas.	25	M	Laborer	06JI02Be
MCTEAGUE, Pat	16	M	Laborer	06JI02Be
MCCUSKER, Rosana.	18	F	None	06JI02Be
FERRIS, Robt.	28	M	Laborer	06JI02Be
RAE, Eliza	40	F	None	06JI02Be
MCCARTY, Callagan	25	M	Laborer	06JI02Be
MCCABE, Bernard	18	M	Laborer	06JI02Be
RINASON, Cath.	17	F	None	06JI02Be
OBRIEN, Jane	28	F	None	06JI02Be
MURPHY, Wm.	21	M	Laborer	06JI02Be

COLDSTREAM 06 JULY 1847

From Liverpool

NAMES OF PASSENGERS	AGE	SEX	OCCUPATIONS	DATE PORT SHIP
MURRY, John	25	M	Laborer	06JI02Qu
Thos.	19	M	Laborer	06JI02Qu
BOYLE, Bartley	26	M	Laborer	06JI02Qu
MURPHY, Biddy	26	F	None	06JI02Qu
GILL, Mich	25	M	Farmer	06JI02Qu
FATRY, Thos.	20	M	Farmer	06JI02Qu
Mary	18	F	None	06JI02Qu
Bridget	16	F	None	06JI02Qu
KELCHAN, Martin	20	M	Farmer	06JI02Qu
WARD, Ellen	19	F	None	06JI02Qu
GLYNN, Jno.	30	M	Laborer	06JI02Qu
CONNELLY, Mary	30	F	None	06JI02Qu
BRODERICK, Ellis	35	M	Laborer	06JI02Qu
SHANENG, Martin	32	M	Laborer	06JI02Qu
NAUGHTON, Jno.	11	M	None	06JI02Qu
Peter	13	M	None	06JI02Qu
Jno.	40	M	Laborer	06JI02Qu
DOUDE, Mich.	17	M	Laborer	06JI02Qu
CONOUGHTON, Pat	19	M	Laborer	06JI02Qu
Brien	40	M	Laborer	06JI02Qu
FUNERAL, Theady	25	M	Laborer	06JI02Qu
CAHILL, Jas.	27	M	Laborer	06JI02Qu
Mary	25	F	None	06JI02Qu
GILL, Thos.	35	M	Mechanic	06JI02Qu
Bridget	32	F	None	06JI02Qu
Mich.	15	M	None	06JI02Qu
Maria	13	F	None	06JI02Qu
Bridget	11	F	None	06JI02Qu
Margt.	08	F	Child	06JI02Qu
POWER, Pat	48	M	Laborer	06JI02Qu
Margt.	40	F	None	06JI02Qu
Mary	18	F	None	06JI02Qu
Mich.	16	M	Laborer	06JI02Qu
Thos.	14	M	Laborer	06JI02Qu
Stephen	12	M	Laborer	06JI02Qu
Bridget	09	F	Child	06JI02Qu
Margt.	05	F	Child	06JI02Qu
Patk.	02	M	Child	06JI02Qu
MCDONALD, Pat	28	M	Laborer	06JI02Qu
Ann	24	F	None	06JI02Qu
Mich.	20	M	Laborer	06JI02Qu
Jas.	18	M	Laborer	06JI02Qu
Cath.	14	F	None	06JI02Qu
Mary	12	F	None	06JI02Qu
Mich.	02	M	Child	06JI02Qu
FLAHERTY, Timothy	30	M	Laborer	06JI02Qu
Bridget	24	F	None	06JI02Qu
CONNOR, Mich.	24	M	Laborer	06JI02Qu
FALEY, Malachi	28	M	Laborer	06JI02Qu
ASSHER, Pat	30	M	Laborer	06JI02Qu
COY, Ann	18	F	None	06JI02Qu
CONNOUGHTON, Edwd.	15	M	None	06JI02Qu
MAY, Jno.	25	M	Laborer	06JI02Qu
BURKE, Thos.	20	M	Laborer	06JI02Qu
FURY, Jno.	24	M	Laborer	06JI02Qu
Patk.	26	M	Laborer	06JI02Qu
MCGUIRE, Peter	23	M	Laborer	06JI02Qu
Cath.	23	F	None	06JI02Qu
HAONLY, Jas.	30	M	Laborer	06JI02Qu
KING, Martha	26	F	None	06JI02Qu
HEALY, Bernard	26	M	Laborer	06JI02Qu
CLARE, Harry	30	M	Laborer	06JI02Qu
CROILY, Jas.	46	M	Laborer	06JI02Qu
Peter	14	M	None	06JI02Qu
JOYCE, Mich.	12	M	None	06JI02Qu
HYNES, Mich.	28	M	Laborer	06JI02Qu
EDWARDS, Mich.	29	M	Laborer	06JI02Qu
Mary	22	F	None	06JI02Qu
CONNELLY, Mich	32	M	Laborer	06JI02Qu
LEECH, Thos.	36	M	Laborer	06JI02Qu
WALSH, Meny.	21	M	Laborer	06JI02Qu
CARLY, Pat	20	M	Laborer	06JI02Qu
Sally	22	F	None	06JI02Qu
HYNES, Mich.	40	M	Laborer	06JI02Qu
Cath.	40	F	None	06JI02Qu
Jno.	05	M	Child	06JI02Qu
Mary-A.	03	F	Child	06JI02Qu
Mich.	07	M	None	06JI02Qu
HUSEY, Cath.	24	F	None	06JI02Qu
Honor	47	F	None	06JI02Qu
MALONEY, Jno.	30	M	Laborer	06JI02Qu
DUFFEY, Cath.	25	F	None	06JI02Qu
Biddy	20	F	None	06JI02Qu
BLAIR, Mary	35	F	None	06JI02Qu
U	20	F	None	06JI02Qu
MALONEY, Mary	28	F	None	06JI02Qu
FEGAN, Bridget	30	F	None	06JI02Qu

NON-PAREIL 06 JULY 1847

From Halifax

NAMES OF PASSENGERS	AGE	SEX	OCCUPATIONS	DATE PORT SHIP
SUTHERLAND, William	25	M	Missionary	06JI22Qv
U	20	F	Wife	06JI22Qv
THERDON, J.	26	M	Merchant	06JI22Qv
TAYLOR, Jas.	24	M	Farmer	06JI22Qv
BRODERICK, Jno.	28	M	Laborer	06JI22Qv

EXPRESS 06 JULY 1847

From Dublin

NAMES OF PASSENGERS	AGE	SEX	OCCUPATIONS	DATE PORT SHIP
REDDINGTON, T.	30	M	Mechanic	06J120Qw
Wm.	34	M	Mechanic	06J120Qw
Thos.	07	M	Child	06J120Qw
Mrgt.	35	F	None	06J120Qw
Mary	30	F	None	06J120Qw
SOULTY, J.	22	M	Mechanic	06J120Qw
FREGULLS, S.	17	M	Mechanic	06J120Qw
DAVEY, J.	24	M	Mechanic	06J120Qw
ORCHARD, W.H.	21	M	Mechanic	06J120Qw
WILLSON, W.	15	M	Mechanic	06J120Qw
TIRENING, W.	27	M	Mechanic	06J120Qw
PIERCE, J.	17	M	Mechanic	06J120Qw
NEWMAN, M.	30	M	Mechanic	06J120Qw
Ann	42	F	None	06J120Qw
KEOHEN, J.	20	M	Mechanic	06J120Qw
Mrgt.	25	F	None	06J120Qw
SMYTH, J.	43	M	Mechanic	06J120Qw
John	18	M	Mechanic	06J120Qw
Wm.	15	M	Mechanic	06J120Qw
ATCHINSON, T.	25	M	Mechanic	06J120Qw
Chas.	30	M	Mechanic	06J120Qw
Mich.	27	M	Mechanic	06J120Qw
Matty	23	M	Mechanic	06J120Qw
Mrgt.	21	F	None	06J120Qw
ROBINSON, J.	30	M	Mechanic	06J120Qw
Jane	30	F	None	06J120Qw
NICHOLSON, Mrgt.	22	F	None	06J120Qw
KELLETT, Elzt.	07	F	Child	06J120Qw
MAHON, P.	26	M	Mechanic	06J120Qw
Mary	40	F	None	06J120Qw
HENRY, J.	21	M	Mechanic	06J120Qw
NORGART, J.	15	M	Mechanic	06J120Qw
KENERING, Sarah	25	F	None	06J120Qw
MACKEN, Mrgt.	21	F	None	06J120Qw
Abme.	20	M	Mechanic	06J120Qw
HARRISON, G.	30	M	Mechanic	06J120Qw
SHEALTON, D.	40	M	Mechanic	06J120Qw
MASON, T.	28	M	Mechanic	06J120Qw
MCREADY, M.	21	M	Mechanic	06J120Qw
CULLEN, T.	23	M	Mechanic	06J120Qw
HUGHES, J.	50	M	Mechanic	06J120Qw
HALY, Mrgt.	24	F	None	06J120Qw
Matilda	22	F	None	06J120Qw

QUEEN 06 JULY 1847

From Liverpool

NAMES OF PASSENGERS	AGE	SEX	OCCUPATIONS	DATE PORT SHIP
MCFARLAN, J.	30	M	Farmer	06J102Qx
Mary	33	F	None	06J102Qx
Cath.	07	F	Child	06J102Qx
DOHERTY, J.	21	M	Farmer	06J102Qx
COLL, F.	40	M	Farmer	06J102Qx
Maggy	13	F	None	06J102Qx
Cath.	35	F	None	06J102Qx
HARKIN, P.	36	M	Farmer	06J102Qx
GALLESTON, A.	16	M	Farmer	06J102Qx
FISHER, J.	35	M	Farmer	06J102Qx
Ann-J.	32	F	None	06J102Qx
FISHER, Bertha	23	F	None	06J102Qx
Lepcon	03	M	Child	06J102Qx
Adellaid	01	F	Child	06J102Qx
Chast.	01	F	Child	06J102Qx
CALSKY, T.	20	M	Farmer	06J102Qx
Pauline	23	F	None	06J102Qx
Yelet	07	M	Child	06J102Qx
Adral	05	F	Child	06J102Qx
HENRY, J.	40	M	Farmer	06J102Qx
Cath.	33	F	None	06J102Qx
Mrgt.	01	F	Child	06J102Qx
FEENY, Alice	23	F	None	06J102Qx
HARLY, J.	12	M	None	06J102Qx
MCGURK, P.	36	M	Farmer	06J102Qx
MCGUINN, E.	25	M	None	06J102Qx
Cath.	30	F	None	06J102Qx
Peter	01	M	Child	06J102Qx
FENNESSON, Mary	01	F	Child	06J102Qx
MCCORMICK, M.	30	M	Farmer	06J102Qx
Bgt.	28	F	None	06J102Qx
James	01	M	Child	06J102Qx
MOSS, M.	40	M	Farmer	06J102Qx
SMITH, J.	35	M	Farmer	06J102Qx
BROWN, W.	35	M	Farmer	06J102Qx
Elzt.	30	F	None	06J102Qx
Mrgt.	04	F	Child	06J102Qx
GREEN, M.A.	20	M	Farmer	06J102Qx
John	07	M	Child	06J102Qx
Charles	04	M	Child	06J102Qx
YOUNG, D.	20	M	Farmer	06J102Qx
MULLEN, Ann	16	F	None	06J102Qx
MILLAN, W.	25	M	Farmer	06J102Qx
WALKER, R.	21	M	Farmer	06J102Qx
MORAN, A.	27	M	Farmer	06J102Qx
TROCON, A.	20	M	Farmer	06J102Qx
ELLIOTT, W.	30	M	Farmer	06J102Qx
MURCHLEDGE, A.	45	M	Farmer	06J102Qx
LODGE, T.	16	M	Farmer	06J102Qx
John	13	M	Farmer	06J102Qx
Mrg.	11	F	None	06J102Qx
Chas.	08	M	Child	06J102Qx
Sarah	06	F	Child	06J102Qx
Richard	01	M	Child	06J102Qx
MALLOHAN, E.C.	46	M	Farmer	06J102Qx
MONTGOMERY, W.	40	M	Farmer	06J102Qx
STEWART, W.	17	M	Farmer	06J102Qx
LODGE, Chast.	42	F	None	06J102Qx
Cath.	21	F	None	06J102Qx
REILLY, Cath.	22	F	None	06J102Qx
GAFNEY, Cath.	20	F	None	06J102Qx
MCINTIRE, Mary	20	F	None	06J102Qx
CAMPBELL, M.	18	M	Farmer	06J102Qx
MCCOURT, P.	30	M	Farmer	06J102Qx
MULLEN, Elzt.	45	F	None	06J102Qx
Cath.	09	F	Child	06J102Qx
SULLIVAN, Betty	26	F	None	06J102Qx
Mary	28	F	None	06J102Qx
MCNALLY, A.	55	M	Farmer	06J102Qx
John	09	M	Child	06J102Qx
Anna	08	F	Child	06J102Qx
OBRIEN, J.	30	M	Farmer	06J102Qx
Francis	18	M	Farmer	06J102Qx
DOLAN, J.	36	M	Farmer	06J102Qx
Edward	20	M	Farmer	06J102Qx
NOLAND, P.	42	M	Farmer	06J102Qx
GRADY, J.	30	M	Farmer	06J102Qx
Cath.	23	F	None	06J102Qx
Mrgt.	17	F	None	06J102Qx
OHARA, P.	50	M	Farmer	06J102Qx
Mrgt.	46	F	None	06J102Qx
Mary	22	F	None	06J102Qx
Cath.	18	F	None	06J102Qx
Francis	16	M	Farmer	06J102Qx
MCGUIRE, Ann	40	F	None	06J102Qx
Mary	18	F	None	06J102Qx

NAMES OF PASSENGERS	A G E	S E X	OCCUPATIONS	DATE PORT SHIP
HENEY, T.	32	M	Farmer	06J102Qx
Pat	20	M	Farmer	06J102Qx
Isaac	18	M	Farmer	06J102Qx
GAFFNEY, P.	47	M	Farmer	06J102Qx
Thomas	30	M	Farmer	06J102Qx
MCGURRY, T.	24	M	Farmer	06J102Qx
Mary	22	F	None	06J102Qx
GARLAN, R.	23	M	Farmer	06J102Qx
MATTHEW, F.	22	M	Farmer	06J102Qx
IVENY, E.	22	M	Farmer	06J102Qx
HAGGANS, R.	22	M	Farmer	06J102Qx
Mrgt.	34	F	None	06J102Qx
Mrgt.A.	33	F	None	06J102Qx
Sarah	20	F	None	06J102Qx
Wm.	07	M	Child	06J102Qx
HIGGINS, W.	01	M	Child	06J102Qx
Sarah	06	F	Child	06J102Qx
MONY, Mary	17	F	None	06J102Qx
SHEO, T.	40	M	Farmer	06J102Qx
Julia	30	F	None	06J102Qx
MURPHY, T.	36	M	Farmer	06J102Qx
Mrgt.	33	F	None	06J102Qx
BRENNER, Jane	19	F	None	06J102Qx
MURPHY, W.	18	M	Farmer	06J102Qx
BOURKE, J.	25	M	Farmer	06J102Qx
CONROY, J.	24	M	Farmer	06J102Qx
SHOCKNESSY, P.	22	M	Farmer	06J102Qx
Mary	18	F	None	06J102Qx
BROWER, P.	24	M	Farmer	06J102Qx
Bgt.	22	F	None	06J102Qx
Eleanor	05	F	Child	06J102Qx
James	01	M	Child	06J102Qx
LAUDER, U	20	F	None	06J102Qx
BENNETT, W.	26	M	Farmer	06J102Qx
Emma	25	F	None	06J102Qx
John	01	M	Child	06J102Qx
Victoria	01	F	Child	06J102Qx
DOLAN, T.	24	M	Farmer	06J102Qx
WEBB, W.	23	M	Farmer	06J102Qx
LIPHELDA, W.	30	M	Farmer	06J102Qx
ROY, J.	30	M	Farmer	06J102Qx
CURTAIN, J.	30	M	Farmer	06J102Qx
PETER, W.	29	M	Farmer	06J102Qx
Cath.	20	F	None	06J102Qx
TENNER, T.	22	M	Farmer	06J102Qx
George	11	M	None	06J102Qx
Joseph	09	M	Child	06J102Qx
MCGUIRE, F.	33	M	Farmer	06J102Qx
GAMBLE, J.	30	M	Farmer	06J102Qx
GURWOOD, W.	20	M	Farmer	06J102Qx
BRENNER, J.	19	M	Farmer	06J102Qx
Bgt.	18	F	None	06J102Qx
CAVENNAH, J.	20	M	Farmer	06J102Qx
May	20	F	None	06J102Qx
MCGWIG, R.	20	M	Farmer	06J102Qx
BUCRUM, T.	20	M	Farmer	06J102Qx
MULLER, J.	20	M	Farmer	06J102Qx

PRINCE-ALBERT 06 JULY 1847

From Liverpool

NAMES OF PASSENGERS	A G E	S E X	OCCUPATIONS	DATE PORT SHIP
CONNELL, Mary	20	F	None	06J102Bn
MCGUGGAN, Mgt.	20	F	None	06J102Bn
GREENWOOD, T.	39	M	Mechanic	06J102Bn
Ann	32	F	None	06J102Bn
FORER, V.	24	M	Mechanic	06J102Bn
JOHNSTON, Soph.	40	F	None	06J102Bn
Mathilda	22	F	None	06J102Bn
JOHNSTON, Sarah	05	F	Child	06J102Bn
George	03	M	Child	06J102Bn
Thos.	02	M	Child	06J102Bn
Thos.	45	M	Farmer	06J102Bn
Mary	60	F	None	06J102Bn
Robt.	20	M	Farmer	06J102Bn
John	18	M	Farmer	06J102Bn
Wm.	13	M	None	06J102Bn
Joseph	12	M	None	06J102Bn
Edward	07	M	Child	06J102Bn
LAURENCE, C.	26	M	Mechanic	06J102Bn
Henry	25	M	Mechanic	06J102Bn
SMITH, Eliza	24	F	None	06J102Bn
TOMAN, H.	24	M	Mechanic	06J102Bn
LAWTON, J.	23	M	Mechanic	06J102Bn
HARLY, W.	22	M	Mechanic	06J102Bn
MURPHY, C.	50	M	Mechanic	06J102Bn
Mary	46	F	None	06J102Bn
Soph.	20	F	None	06J102Bn
Wm.	17	M	None	06J102Bn
Ann	14	F	None	06J102Bn
Fdck.	12	M	None	06J102Bn
John	06	M	Child	06J102Bn
Patck.	04	M	Child	06J102Bn
Joseph	01	M	Child	06J102Bn
BOWE, P.	20	M	Mechanic	06J102Bn
HAGAN, Mary	21	F	None	06J102Bn
Ellen	22	F	None	06J102Bn
THOMPSON, J.	38	F	Farmer	06J102Bn
Cath.	16	F	None	06J102Bn
MCGUINESS, M.	50	M	Farmer	06J102Bn
ROONEY, J.	25	M	Laborer	06J102Bn
NULTY, J.	25	M	Laborer	06J102Bn
DONNELLY, T.	25	M	Laborer	06J102Bn
CUDDEN, J.	27	M	Laborer	06J102Bn
KANE, Judith	20	F	None	06J102Bn
CRIMON, P.	26	M	Laborer	06J102Bn
Bgt.	26	F	None	06J102Bn
Mary	16	F	None	06J102Bn
BROWN, A.	22	M	Laborer	06J102Bn
FANNING, M.	40	M	Laborer	06J102Bn
PARKINSON, R.	19	M	Laborer	06J102Bn
DROGERTY, A.	30	M	Laborer	06J102Bn
Mary	23	F	None	06J102Bn
Danl.	01	M	Child	06J102Bn
WARD, J.	25	M	Laborer	06J102Bn
TONER, J.	19	F	None	06J102Bn
DOWLING, Ellen	24	F	None	06J102Bn
Mary-A.	09	F	Child	06J102Bn
Jane	06	F	Child	06J102Bn
Ellen	04	F	Child	06J102Bn
Richd.	01	M	Child	06J102Bn
KERGAN, W.	18	M	Laborer	06J102Bn
EVANS, Evan	24	M	Laborer	06J102Bn
BULKLY, J.	24	M	Laborer	06J102Bn
CREIGHTON, C.	28	M	Laborer	06J102Bn
Bgt.	25	F	None	06J102Bn
Ann	01	F	Child	06J102Bn
GAFFNEY, Ann	28	F	None	06J102Bn
GIBNEY, Biddy	20	F	None	06J102Bn
CONNELL, R.	28	M	Laborer	06J102Bn
Sarah	20	F	None	06J102Bn
GOGGINS, P.	24	M	Laborer	06J102Bn
LAING, R.	24	M	Laborer	06J102Bn
MARTHER, J.	45	M	Laborer	06J102Bn
Ann	40	F	None	06J102Bn
MCCARTHY, T.	30	M	Laborer	06J102Bn
Ellen	22	F	None	06J102Bn
Ellen	20	F	None	06J102Bn
LEO, Mgt.	20	F	None	06J102Bn
PAWDERLY, J.	23	M	Laborer	06J102Bn
MCCULLO, J.	28	M	Laborer	06J102Bn
SHIPLY, C.	24	M	Laborer	06J102Bn
BRADY, J.	25	M	Laborer	06J102Bn
CROSKY, J.	23	M	Laborer	06J102Bn

NAMES OF PASSENGERS	AGE	SEX	OCCUPATIONS	DATE PORT SHIP
SMITH, H.	21	M	Laborer	06Jl02Bn
LINCH, P.	21	M	Laborer	06Jl02Bn
COOK, O.	18	M	Laborer	06Jl02Bn
CLARK, O.	18	M	Laborer	06Jl02Bn
SMITH, Cath.	17	F	None	06Jl02Bn
CLARK, Ann	17	F	None	06Jl02Bn
COONY, Mary	17	F	None	06Jl02Bn
COOK, Mary	17	F	None	06Jl02Bn
WALKER, J.	25	F	Laborer	06Jl02Bn
CLARK, J.	22	F	Laborer	06Jl02Bn
TULLY, P.	22	F	Laborer	06Jl02Bn
RIELY, T.	23	F	Laborer	06Jl02Bn
HEARNY, Mary	24	F	None	06Jl02Bn
COUGHLIN, J.	24	M	Laborer	06Jl02Bn
FITZSIMMONS, M.	26	M	Laborer	06Jl02Bn
Peter	24	M	Laborer	06Jl02Bn
CLAYTON, T.	26	M	Laborer	06Jl02Bn
LINCH, P.	34	M	Laborer	06Jl02Bn
Patt	30	M	Laborer	06Jl02Bn
Ann	20	F	None	06Jl02Bn
MCDONNELL, P.	21	M	Laborer	06Jl02Bn
GOLLIGHER, Bgt.	22	F	None	06Jl02Bn
MCMANUS, E.	23	M	Laborer	06Jl02Bn
Mrgt.	22	F	None	06Jl02Bn
SULLIVAN, T.	22	M	Laborer	06Jl02Bn
WALSH, M.	22	M	Laborer	06Jl02Bn
MCDERMOTT, Ellen	20	F	None	06Jl02Bn
KANE, Mary	21	F	None	06Jl02Bn
DAVIS, E.	55	M	Laborer	06Jl02Bn
John	26	M	Laborer	06Jl02Bn

VICTORIA 06 JULY 1847

From Galway

NAMES OF PASSENGERS	AGE	SEX	OCCUPATIONS	DATE PORT SHIP
DILLON, J.	30	M	Mechanic	06Jl11Ay
NOLAN, G.	25	M	Mechanic	06Jl11Ay
A.	23	F	None	06Jl11Ay
CUNNINGHAM, M.	28	M	Laborer	06Jl11Ay
CONNORS, J.	32	M	Laborer	06Jl11Ay
P.	28	M	Laborer	06Jl11Ay
E.	26	F	None	06Jl11Ay
P.	25	F	None	06Jl11Ay
P.	.00	M	Infant	06Jl11Ay
P.	.00	M	Infant	06Jl11Ay
N.	.00	M	Infant	06Jl11Ay
J.	.00	M	Infant	06Jl11Ay
JOYCE, R.	23	M	Laborer	06Jl11Ay
LEE, P.	24	M	Laborer	06Jl11Ay
MCMAHON, M.	20	M	Laborer	06Jl11Ay
WALKER, B.	19	F	None	06Jl11Ay
WALSH, A.	18	F	None	06Jl11Ay
M.	17	F	None	06Jl11Ay
HIGGINS, T.	24	M	Laborer	06Jl11Ay
J.	26	M	Laborer	06Jl11Ay
CONNORS, D.	30	M	Laborer	06Jl11Ay
J.	28	M	Laborer	06Jl11Ay
SULLIVAN, J.	30	M	Laborer	06Jl11Ay
MCDERMOTT, J.	19	M	Laborer	06Jl11Ay
M.	18	M	Laborer	06Jl11Ay
HIGGINS, J.	24	F	None	06Jl11Ay
B.	26	F	None	06Jl11Ay
FORAN, Jno.	28	M	Laborer	06Jl11Ay
H.	26	F	None	06Jl11Ay
BRIEN, D.	30	M	Laborer	06Jl11Ay
MCTEREMY, M.	32	M	Laborer	06Jl11Ay
COGHLAR, J.	28	M	Laborer	06Jl11Ay
OCONNER, M.	18	M	Laborer	06Jl11Ay
J.	.00	M	Infant	06Jl11Ay
OCONNER, W.	.00	M	Infant	06Jl11Ay
MCMAHON, J.	32	M	Laborer	06Jl11Ay
J.	30	F	None	06Jl11Ay
HAULD, M.	38	M	Laborer	06Jl11Ay
E.	30	F	None	06Jl11Ay
BURNS, J.	28	M	Laborer	06Jl11Ay
MCDONNELL, A.	30	M	Laborer	06Jl11Ay
OBRIEN, J.	30	M	Laborer	06Jl11Ay
QUIN, J.	26	M	Laborer	06Jl11Ay
MCMAHON, P.	42	M	Laborer	06Jl11Ay
M.	40	F	None	06Jl11Ay
M.	.00	F	Infant	06Jl11Ay
M.	.00	M	Infant	06Jl11Ay
E.	.00	F	Infant	06Jl11Ay
HOULAHAN, M.	29	M	Laborer	06Jl11Ay
GILL, T.	28	M	Laborer	06Jl11Ay
HALLORAN, M.	24	F	None	06Jl11Ay
BROWN, T.	20	M	Laborer	06Jl11Ay
M.	29	F	None	06Jl11Ay
OCONNELL, C.	24	F	None	06Jl11Ay
BROWN, B.	.00	F	Infant	06Jl11Ay
ODONNELL, M.	33	M	Laborer	06Jl11Ay
CLANCY, M.	22	M	Laborer	06Jl11Ay
H.	19	F	None	06Jl11Ay
B.	18	F	None	06Jl11Ay
SACKWELL, A.	18	F	None	06Jl11Ay
FOGARTY, A.	35	M	Laborer	06Jl11Ay
CLANCY, T.	.00	M	Infant	06Jl11Ay
HAYES, N.	23	F	None	06Jl11Ay
MCMAHON, P.	46	M	Laborer	06Jl11Ay
C.	43	F	None	06Jl11Ay
M.	34	M	Laborer	06Jl11Ay
T.	.00	M	Infant	06Jl11Ay
J.	.00	M	Infant	06Jl11Ay
M.	.00	F	Infant	06Jl11Ay
Died-At-Sea				
M.	.00	F	Infant	06Jl11Ay
M.	.00	M	Infant	06Jl11Ay
Died-At-Sea				
DOWNS, W.	39	M	Laborer	06Jl11Ay
FORNENTY, M.	26	M	Laborer	06Jl11Ay
COONIN, P.	26	M	Laborer	06Jl11Ay
WALKER, M.	30	M	Laborer	06Jl11Ay
ODONNELL, S.	.00	M	Infant	06Jl11Ay
BEHAN, J.	36	M	Laborer	06Jl11Ay
DOYLE, M.	43	M	Farmer	06Jl11Ay
C.	38	F	None	06Jl11Ay
P.	.00	M	Infant	06Jl11Ay
D.	.00	M	Infant	06Jl11Ay
BEHAN, M.	20	M	Laborer	06Jl11Ay
CASEY, H.	29	F	None	06Jl11Ay
MCMAHON, S.	.00	F	Infant	06Jl11Ay
DURAN, M.	22	M	Laborer	06Jl11Ay
MCMURRY, B.	.00	F	Infant	06Jl11Ay

LISBON 07 JULY 1847

From Liverpool

NAMES OF PASSENGERS	AGE	SEX	OCCUPATIONS	DATE PORT SHIP
LEHEY, Jane	43	F	None	07Jl02Qy
Mich.	10	M	None	07Jl02Qy
Honora	12	F	None	07Jl02Qy
DEVELIN, Grace	12	F	None	07Jl02Qy
KENELLY, D.	20	M	Laborer	07Jl02Qy
Biddy	28	F	None	07Jl02Qy
LAWLESS, Mary	24	F	None	07Jl02Qy
REILLY, J.	25	M	Laborer	07Jl02Qy
Alice	30	F	None	07Jl02Qy
Mary	09	F	Child	07Jl02Qy

NAMES OF PASSENGERS	AGE	SEX	OCCUPATIONS	DATE PORT SHIP
REILLY, John	09	M	Child	07J102Qy
John	01	M	Child	07J102Qy
GANRY, W.	17	F	None	07J102Qy
MOLENY, Mary	14	F	None	07J102Qy
DUNN, E.	25	M	Laborer	07J102Qy
Johanna	30	F	None	07J102Qy
GALLAGHER, J.	17	M	Laborer	07J102Qy
DALY, L.	27	M	Laborer	07J102Qy
CUSHEN, Mary	19	F	None	07J102Qy
MCGINN, W.	28	M	Laborer	07J102Qy
Danl.	35	M	Laborer	07J102Qy
WELSH, P.	70	M	Unknown	07J102Qy
U	60	F	None	07J102Qy
Edward	05	M	Child	07J102Qy
Pat	06	M	Child	07J102Qy
WELCH, M.	30	F	None	07J102Qy
M.	01	F	Child	07J102Qy
MCGINN, A.	24	M	Laborer	07J102Qy
CORMICK, J.	20	M	Laborer	07J102Qy
Mich.	09	M	Child	07J102Qy
Mich.	19	M	Laborer	07J102Qy
Ned	49	M	Laborer	07J102Qy
Martin	20	M	Laborer	07J102Qy
Biddy	14	F	None	07J102Qy
W.	13	M	None	07J102Qy
Ed.	08	M	Child	07J102Qy
FOLEY, R.	14	M	None	07J102Qy
MURPHY, Mary	20	F	None	07J102Qy
FOLY, Ellen	30	F	None	07J102Qy
SMITH, Bdgt.	35	F	None	07J102Qy
COMERFORD, Mary	20	F	None	07J102Qy
LUNDEGGAN, Betty	20	F	None	07J102Qy
CUMERSFORD, Joe	28	M	Laborer	07J102Qy
MAHON, J.	25	M	Laborer	07J102Qy
Mary	30	F	None	07J102Qy
MAHER, M.	20	M	Laborer	07J102Qy
GOORMAN, J.	22	M	Laborer	07J102Qy
CAHILL, P.	30	M	Laborer	07J102Qy
HAYS, T.	25	M	Laborer	07J102Qy
FITZPATRICK, Mary	22	F	None	07J102Qy
Ann	14	F	None	07J102Qy
ODONELL, Sally	18	F	None	07J102Qy
SLATER, P.	35	M	Laborer	07J102Qy
MCNULTY, M.A.	18	M	Laborer	07J102Qy
Elzt.	24	F	None	07J102Qy
THOMPSON, Mgt.	17	F	None	07J102Qy
HANLY, Cath.	25	F	None	07J102Qy
MURRY, M.	20	M	Laborer	07J102Qy
Wm.	23	M	Laborer	07J102Qy
BYRNES, Mary	20	F	None	07J102Qy
John	20	M	Laborer	07J102Qy
MCCLANE, D.	40	M	Laborer	07J102Qy
MURPHY, U-Mrs.	40	F	None	07J102Qy
John	08	M	Child	07J102Qy
Mrgt.	13	F	None	07J102Qy
Mrgt.	06	F	Child	07J102Qy
Jos.	30	M	Laborer	07J102Qy
Pat	12	M	None	07J102Qy
James	11	M	None	07J102Qy
Bdgt.	12	F	None	07J102Qy
MILES, Bgt.	14	F	None	07J102Qy
HASSELL, J.	24	M	Laborer	07J102Qy
Hannah	14	F	None	07J102Qy
Ellen	24	F	None	07J102Qy
FULLEN, Cath.	30	F	None	07J102Qy
Ellen	05	F	Child	07J102Qy
CONNER, J.	21	M	Laborer	07J102Qy
POWELL, J.	20	M	Laborer	07J102Qy
GLEN, W.	24	M	Laborer	07J102Qy
MCGRATH, J.	28	M	Laborer	07J102Qy
COLLINEN, P.	23	M	Laborer	07J102Qy
RYAN, M.	18	M	Laborer	07J102Qy
GAFFY, Mary	20	F	None	07J102Qy
DUGGAN, Mary	19	F	None	07J102Qy
KELLICH, J.	27	M	Laborer	07J102Qy

NAMES OF PASSENGERS	AGE	SEX	OCCUPATIONS	DATE PORT SHIP
TRENSIN, P.	55	M	Laborer	07J102Qy
James	30	M	Laborer	07J102Qy
BURKE, N.	14	M	Laborer	07J102Qy
HUGHES, P.	30	M	Laborer	07J102Qy
CONN, J.	24	M	Laborer	07J102Qy
Pat	22	M	Laborer	07J102Qy
MCKEOWN, P.	23	M	Laborer	07J102Qy
CORRIE, P.	27	M	Laborer	07J102Qy
BUTLER, P.	20	M	Laborer	07J102Qy
BRIEN, T.	24	M	Laborer	07J102Qy
MCCLEAN, J.	30	M	Laborer	07J102Qy
KILCULLEN, P.	21	M	Laborer	07J102Qy
FAY, Mary	18	F	None	07J102Qy
WHITE, Bgt.	19	F	None	07J102Qy
MADDEN, Mary	19	F	None	07J102Qy
REANY, Betty	13	F	None	07J102Qy
MILAY, Ann	20	F	None	07J102Qy
CANNAGH, Mary	49	F	None	07J102Qy
SCOTT, Ed.	47	M	Laborer	07J102Qy
TOHEDY, Sarah	22	F	None	07J102Qy
DELEY, J.	14	M	Laborer	07J102Qy
MCGINN, J.	21	M	Laborer	07J102Qy
REYNOLDS, P.	23	M	Laborer	07J102Qy
SLATTY, Mary	35	F	None	07J102Qy
SMITH, J.W.	32	M	Laborer	07J102Qy
HOWARD, Betsy	36	F	None	07J102Qy
LAWS, Sarah	18	F	None	07J102Qy

SCHROADIAC 09 JULY 1847

From Liverpool

NAMES OF PASSENGERS	AGE	SEX	OCCUPATIONS	DATE PORT SHIP
KENNAN, S.	45	M	Farmer	09J102Qz
Edw.	11	M	Farmer	09J102Qz
James	10	M	Farmer	09J102Qz
BURNELL, T.	42	M	Farmer	09J102Qz
GRENHEN, Mary	22	F	None	09J102Qz
OZIEN, A.	23	F	None	09J102Qz
GANNON, J.	34	M	Farmer	09J102Qz
U	34	F	Wife	09J102Qz
Julia	11	F	None	09J102Qz
John	06	M	Child	09J102Qz
Ward.	03	M	Child	09J102Qz
Mary	01	F	Child	09J102Qz
FOHOAN, J.	46	M	Farmer	09J102Qz
U	40	F	None	09J102Qz
Jno.	16	M	None	09J102Qz
Mary	15	F	None	09J102Qz
Ridw.	13	M	Farmer	09J102Qz
Mathew	12	M	Farmer	09J102Qz
Mgt.	10	F	None	09J102Qz
Peter	08	M	Child	09J102Qz
Aneler	07	M	Child	09J102Qz
Nicholas	05	M	Child	09J102Qz
Lynn	03	F	Child	09J102Qz
Anelade	01	F	Child	09J102Qz
FERGUS, T.	30	M	Farmer	09J102Qz
U	26	F	None	09J102Qz
MCENY, P.	21	M	Farmer	09J102Qz
FLERGAN, B.	24	M	Farmer	09J102Qz
KENNA, J.	22	M	Farmer	09J102Qz
KELLY, Mary	18	F	None	09J102Qz
CAREGAN, Cath.	22	F	None	09J102Qz
SLATERY, Ellen	25	F	None	09J102Qz
Thos.	25	M	Farmer	09J102Qz
An.	04	M	Child	09J102Qz
NEVES, J.	29	M	Farmer	09J102Qz
U	27	F	None	09J102Qz
Andrew	12	M	Farmer	09J102Qz

NAMES OF PASSENGERS	AGE	SEX	OCCUPATIONS	DATE PORT SHIP	NAMES OF PASSENGERS	AGE	SEX	OCCUPATIONS	DATE PORT SHIP
CORY, H.	30	M	Farmer	09J102Qz	SMITH, Mgt.	13	F	None	09J102Qz
U	23	F	Wife	09J102Qz	CARNAN, L.	27	M	Farmer	09J102Qz
MCANLAN, An.	19	M	Farmer	09J102Qz	KENNAN, P.	26	M	Farmer	09J102Qz
CROGHAN, Jas.	18	M	Farmer	09J102Qz	Cath.	25	F	None	09J102Qz
CUNNINGHAM, M.	18	M	Farmer	09J102Qz	James	22	M	Farmer	09J102Qz
Bdgt.	20	F	None	09J102Qz	QUINN, P.	20	M	Farmer	09J102Qz
HAYES, H.	18	M	Farmer	09J102Qz	MCDERMOTT, J.	18	M	Farmer	09J102Qz
Mary	20	F	None	09J102Qz	Mrgt.	18	F	None	09J102Qz
MCCANN, H.	22	M	Farmer	09J102Qz	BRADSHAW, R.	30	M	Farmer	09J102Qz
MORAN, J.	24	M	Farmer	09J102Qz	Eliza	20	F	None	09J102Qz
DOWD, M.	24	M	Farmer	09J102Qz	Eliza	03	F	Child	09J102Qz
CASEY, Mary	66	F	None	09J102Qz	FOX, J.	20	M	Farmer	09J102Qz
KELLY, Cath.	29	F	None	09J102Qz	LIVINGSTON, Mary	40	F	None	09J102Qz
QUINN, Betty	22	F	None	09J102Qz	STONE, Susana	16	F	None	09J102Qz
WARD, M.	20	M	Farmer	09J102Qz	BURNS, Cath.	26	F	None	09J102Qz
SMITH, A.	25	M	Farmer	09J102Qz	DUFFY, P.	47	M	Farmer	09J102Qz
COATES, H.	35	M	Farmer	09J102Qz	Biddy	44	F	None	09J102Qz
MCQURK, P.	20	M	Farmer	09J102Qz	James	18	M	None	09J102Qz
FLANAGAN, M.	24	M	Farmer	09J102Qz	Pat	16	M	None	09J102Qz
MORAN, P.	25	M	Farmer	09J102Qz	Mrgt.	13	F	None	09J102Qz
MCAVERY, P.	18	M	Farmer	09J102Qz	Jno.	11	M	None	09J102Qz
KELLY, J.	20	M	Farmer	09J102Qz	Bgt.	09	F	Child	09J102Qz
CARTER, Mgt.	20	F	None	09J102Qz	Chsty.	07	F	Child	09J102Qz
FAY, Ann	20	F	None	09J102Qz	Ann	05	F	Child	09J102Qz
REILY, P.	35	M	Farmer	09J102Qz	J.	50	M	Farmer	09J102Qz
MATTHEWS, W.	28	M	Farmer	09J102Qz	Ann	45	F	None	09J102Qz
Hannah	26	F	None	09J102Qz	Ann	20	F	None	09J102Qz
CLERKIN, F.	25	M	Farmer	09J102Qz	Mgt.	18	F	None	09J102Qz
MCCABE, C.	30	M	Farmer	09J102Qz	Jno.	10	M	None	09J102Qz
MCDERMOTT, C.	25	M	Farmer	09J102Qz	KING, J.	27	M	Farmer	09J102Qz
COLEMAN, E.	27	M	Farmer	09J102Qz	Mgt.	25	F	None	09J102Qz
QUINN, J.	25	M	Farmer	09J102Qz	Ann	16	F	None	09J102Qz
SHAKASON, M.	23	M	Farmer	09J102Qz	BRADY, R.	21	M	Farmer	09J102Qz
HOGAN, J.	25	M	Farmer	09J102Qz	Cath.	23	F	None	09J102Qz
James	23	M	Farmer	09J102Qz	Rose	19	F	None	09J102Qz
WHELAN, A.	22	M	Farmer	09J102Qz	CLAIRBEN, J.	21	M	Farmer	09J102Qz
Mary	20	F	None	09J102Qz	DULAP, J.	35	M	Farmer	09J102Qz
CUMMINS, J.	22	M	Farmer	09J102Qz	Mal.	35	M	Farmer	09J102Qz
MCGRATH, J.	23	M	Farmer	09J102Qz	Wm.	09	M	Child	09J102Qz
Patrick	19	M	Farmer	09J102Qz	Robt.	07	M	Child	09J102Qz
HYNES, A.	25	M	Farmer	09J102Qz	Henry	05	M	Child	09J102Qz
U	24	F	Wife	09J102Qz	Jane	03	F	Child	09J102Qz
HEADEN, P.	45	M	Farmer	09J102Qz	Jno.	01	M	Child	09J102Qz
James	16	M	Farmer	09J102Qz	Wm.	23	M	Farmer	09J102Qz
Wm.	14	M	Farmer	09J102Qz	RALEIG, Mary	18	F	None	09J102Qz
Mgt.	12	F	None	09J102Qz	HUGHES, Ann	45	F	None	09J102Qz
Anna	08	F	Child	09J102Qz	Cath.	16	F	None	09J102Qz
Julia	06	F	Child	09J102Qz	Sally	14	F	None	09J102Qz
MORAN, M.	22	M	Farmer	09J102Qz	Dennis	12	M	Farmer	09J102Qz
TAINOR, O.	25	M	Farmer	09J102Qz	Ann	10	F	None	09J102Qz
U	20	F	Wife	09J102Qz	Mrgt.	08	F	None	09J102Qz
Edwd.	01	M	Child	09J102Qz	Jane	03	F	None	09J102Qz
STAMELL, J.	29	M	Farmer	09J102Qz	SHERIDAN, T.	18	M	Farmer	09J102Qz
U	30	F	Wife	09J102Qz	MCCASKER, Sarah	42	F	None	09J102Qz
Gerard	19	M	Farmer	09J102Qz	Saml.	21	M	None	09J102Qz
NELSON, J.	40	M	Farmer	09J102Qz	FREETE, Isb.	12	F	None	09J102Qz
HOIN, W.	40	M	Farmer	09J102Qz	Abraham	09	M	Child	09J102Qz
SANDERS, J.	34	M	Farmer	09J102Qz	STEARN, P.	50	M	Laborer	09J102Qz
Cath.	05	F	Child	09J102Qz	Jacob	24	M	Laborer	09J102Qz
HERLES, J.	24	M	Farmer	09J102Qz	Peter	21	M	Laborer	09J102Qz
MCCANN, Mary	28	F	None	09J102Qz	Julia	11	F	None	09J102Qz
SMITH, Ann	34	F	None	09J102Qz	Chart.	06	F	Child	09J102Qz
Jno.	08	M	Child	09J102Qz	Cath.	49	F	None	09J102Qz
Mgt.	05	F	Child	09J102Qz	CORRIGAN, J.	22	M	Laborer	09J102Qz
Eliza	01	F	Child	09J102Qz	Metus	20	M	Laborer	09J102Qz
CUNNINGHAM, J.	24	M	Farmer	09J102Qz	LAWLESS, C.	22	M	Laborer	09J102Qz
DONOHOE, P.	24	M	Farmer	09J102Qz	TEAG, J.	60	M	Laborer	09J102Qz
Rose	23	F	None	09J102Qz	Winfd.	55	F	None	09J102Qz
Patck.	01	M	Child	09J102Qz	James	25	M	Laborer	09J102Qz
MCGUIRE, T.	35	M	Farmer	09J102Qz	Winnfd.	18	F	None	09J102Qz
Mich.	17	M	Farmer	09J102Qz	Cath.	16	F	None	09J102Qz
Jno.	08	M	Child	09J102Qz	Jno.	10	M	None	09J102Qz
SMITH, Bgt.	35	F	None	09J102Qz	LANGAN, J.	25	M	Laborer	09J102Qz
Cath.	60	F	None	09J102Qz	Cath.	23	F	None	09J102Qz
Cath.	25	F	None	09J102Qz	Ellen	21	F	None	09J102Qz

NAMES OF PASSENGERS	AGE	SEX	OCCUPATIONS	DATE PORT SHIP
LANGAN, Bgt.	19	F	None	09J102Qz
MCLAUGHLAN, P.	30	M	Laborer	09J102Qz
CHARMAN, P.	30	M	Laborer	09J102Qz
LABRIS, D.	20	M	Laborer	09J102Qz
ROGERS, Bgt.	22	F	None	09J102Qz
DOOGAN, L.	40	M	Laborer	09J102Qz
Sally	30	F	None	09J102Qz
Mich.	19	M	Laborer	09J102Qz
Frantz	13	M	None	09J102Qz
Patt	06	M	Child	09J102Qz
Mary	07	F	Child	09J102Qz
BRANGAN, W.	17	M	Laborer	09J102Qz
Mgt.	19	F	None	09J102Qz
HARRISON, H.	24	M	Laborer	09J102Qz
FOX, P.	50	M	Laborer	09J102Qz
FITZSIMMONS, J.	17	M	Laborer	09J102Qz
COLLINS, E.	20	M	Laborer	09J102Qz
SKIFINGTON, C.	22	M	Laborer	09J102Qz
BYRNES, Mary	20	F	None	09J102Qz
DAILY, P.	16	M	Laborer	09J102Qz
REILLY, P.	26	M	Laborer	09J102Qz
FLANAGAN, Cath.	27	F	None	09J102Qz
DOUGHTY, Ann	15	F	None	09J102Qz
MCCORMACK, Ann	40	F	None	09J102Qz
James	17	M	Laborer	09J102Qz
Cath.	50	F	None	09J102Qz
NUGENT, J.	40	M	Laborer	09J102Qz
NOLAN, Mrg.	18	F	None	09J102Qz
Cath.	16	F	None	09J102Qz
Joseph	20	M	None	09J102Qz
LISTANGE, Judy	20	F	None	09J102Qz
CORRIGAN, T.	60	M	Laborer	09J102Qz
Biddy	60	F	None	09J102Qz
Thos.	32	M	Laborer	09J102Qz
Rose	20	F	None	09J102Qz
Peggy	17	F	None	09J102Qz
Mgt.	15	F	None	09J102Qz
Phil	40	M	Laborer	09J102Qz
Matthew	15	M	None	09J102Qz
Cath.	13	F	None	09J102Qz
RULLY, P.	40	M	Laborer	09J102Qz
Mary	30	F	None	09J102Qz
Cath.	04	F	Child	09J102Qz
DUNN, P.	26	M	Laborer	09J102Qz
Anne	30	F	None	09J102Qz
MALONEY, D.	30	M	Laborer	09J102Qz
SARAH, P.	30	M	Laborer	09J102Qz
CONNOR, Mgt.	35	F	None	09J102Qz
MCCOLLY, Mgt.	21	F	None	09J102Qz
Martha	18	F	None	09J102Qz
MCPHILLIP, Cath.	17	F	None	09J102Qz
HEFERN, J.	18	M	Laborer	09J102Qz
NUGENT, M.	30	M	Laborer	09J102Qz
Pat	25	M	Laborer	09J102Qz
Mgt.	27	F	None	09J102Qz
OWENS, J.	27	M	Laborer	09J102Qz
FARRELL, P.	25	M	Laborer	09J102Qz
OWENS, J.	25	M	Laborer	09J102Qz
Cath.	22	F	None	09J102Qz
BROOKS, B.	25	M	Laborer	09J102Qz
FARRELLY, J.	26	M	Laborer	09J102Qz
Peggy	48	F	None	09J102Qz
Wm.	17	M	Laborer	09J102Qz
Mary	19	F	None	09J102Qz
M.	13	M	None	09J102Qz
Pat	11	M	None	09J102Qz
Jno.	09	M	Child	09J102Qz
Thos.	09	M	Child	09J102Qz
Mgt.	02	F	Child	09J102Qz
FLYNN, P.	50	M	Laborer	09J102Qz
Betty	50	F	None	09J102Qz
James	20	M	Laborer	09J102Qz
Jno.	18	M	Laborer	09J102Qz
Mary	16	F	None	09J102Qz
Richd.	13	M	None	09J102Qz
FLYNN, Patck.	11	M	None	09J102Qz
Ellen	09	F	Child	09J102Qz
Mich.	02	M	Child	09J102Qz
CLANCY, P.	34	M	Laborer	09J102Qz
Mary	30	F	None	09J102Qz
COOPIN, Betty	06	F	Child	09J102Qz
CUMBERLAND, J.	30	M	Laborer	09J102Qz
Elzbt.	25	F	None	09J102Qz
MCGREGOR, Mgrt.	18	F	None	09J102Qz
PUGOTT, D.	22	M	Laborer	09J102Qz
LACY, J.	21	M	Laborer	09J102Qz
JONES, R.	28	M	Laborer	09J102Qz
Jno.	23	M	Laborer	09J102Qz
Mary	20	F	None	09J102Qz
CLERK, A.	29	M	Laborer	09J102Qz
STEWART, J.	20	M	Laborer	09J102Qz
Robt.	20	M	Laborer	09J102Qz
Susan	19	F	None	09J102Qz
Rebecca	16	F	None	09J102Qz
Nancy	07	F	Child	09J102Qz
DELANY, W.	34	M	Laborer	09J102Qz
Judith	34	F	None	09J102Qz
Mary	25	F	None	09J102Qz
Mgt.	12	F	None	09J102Qz
James	05	M	Child	09J102Qz

SOLDAN 12 JULY 1847

From Liverpool

NAMES OF PASSENGERS	AGE	SEX	OCCUPATIONS	DATE PORT SHIP
BEBB, Wm.	59	M	Farmer	12J102Ra
M.	44	F	None	12J102Ra
L.	16	F	None	12J102Ra
Wm.	15	M	None	12J102Ra
M.	10	F	None	12J102Ra
M.	08	F	Child	12J102Ra
D.	12	M	Farmer	12J102Ra
F.	05	F	Child	12J102Ra
JONES, L.	23	M	Laborer	12J102Ra
R.	21	F	None	12J102Ra
J.	27	M	Laborer	12J102Ra
R.	19	M	Laborer	12J102Ra
ROBERTS, M.	32	F	None	12J102Ra
OWEN, P.	21	F	None	12J102Ra
JONES, A.	28	M	Laborer	12J102Ra
M.	25	F	None	12J102Ra
W.	.00	F	Infant	12J102Ra
HOWELL, R.	19	M	Laborer	12J102Ra
S.	17	F	None	12J102Ra
WILLIAMS, T.	38	M	Laborer	12J102Ra
C.	33	F	None	12J102Ra
A.	13	F	None	12J102Ra
M.	09	F	Child	12J102Ra
T.	.00	M	Infant	12J102Ra
ROBERTS, G.	31	M	Mechanic	12J102Ra
E.	26	F	None	12J102Ra
J.	07	M	Child	12J102Ra
R.	05	M	Child	12J102Ra
M.	03	F	Child	12J102Ra
C.	.00	F	Infant	12J102Ra
WHITTINGTON, R.	32	M	Mechanic	12J102Ra
M.	23	F	None	12J102Ra
J.	.00	F	Infant	12J102Ra
JERVIS, R.	24	M	Mechanic	12J102Ra
M.	28	F	None	12J102Ra
R.	.00	M	Infant	12J102Ra
BRESS, D.	24	M	Farmer	12J102Ra
HOWELL, D.	38	M	Farmer	12J102Ra
DAVIS, A.	55	F	None	12J102Ra

NAMES OF PASSENGERS	AGE	SEX	OCCUPATIONS	DATE PORT SHIP
DAVIS, M.	27	F	None	12J102Ra
D.	25	M	Farmer	12J102Ra
Jane	19	F	None	12J102Ra
J.	14	M	None	12J102Ra
C.	11	F	None	12J102Ra
MORRIS, M.	65	F	None	12J102Ra
J.	25	F	None	12J102Ra
M.	03	F	Child	12J102Ra
T.	38	M	Farmer	12J102Ra
E.	27	F	None	12J102Ra
E.W.	06	M	Child	12J102Ra
E.	03	F	Child	12J102Ra
R.	.00	F	Infant	12J102Ra
OWEN, C.	21	F	None	12J102Ra
H.	45	M	Farmer	12J102Ra
E.	32	F	None	12J102Ra
R.	17	M	Farmer	12J102Ra
E.	08	F	Child	12J102Ra
E.	06	M	Child	12J102Ra
M.	05	F	Child	12J102Ra
A.	03	F	Child	12J102Ra
CROUGLEY, M.	50	F	None	12J102Ra
T.	28	M	Farmer	12J102Ra
P.	16	M	Farmer	12J102Ra
C.	18	F	None	12J102Ra
B.	16	F	None	12J102Ra
J.	15	F	None	12J102Ra
C.	18	F	None	12J102Ra
MCALLISTER, R.	30	F	None	12J102Ra
B.	03	F	Child	12J102Ra
COONY, M.	20	F	None	12J102Ra
MCDONNELL, A.	20	F	None	12J102Ra
MURPHY, C.	26	F	None	12J102Ra
CLARK, M.	18	F	None	12J102Ra
LUGE, M.	20	F	None	12J102Ra
CARN, N.	55	F	None	12J102Ra
M.	20	M	Farmer	12J102Ra
P.	13	M	Farmer	12J102Ra
EVERET, P.	38	M	Farmer	12J102Ra
C.	26	F	None	12J102Ra
A.	03	F	Child	12J102Ra
RYLEY, R.	45	F	None	12J102Ra
T.	30	M	Farmer	12J102Ra
J.	25	M	Farmer	12J102Ra
M.	23	M	Farmer	12J102Ra
R.	20	F	None	12J102Ra
TULLY, R.	24	F	None	12J102Ra
THOMPSON, M.	21	F	None	12J102Ra
J.	19	F	None	12J102Ra
LYNCH, B.	30	F	None	12J102Ra
KIERIN, P.	24	M	Farmer	12J102Ra
ROBERTS, M.	26	F	None	12J102Ra
RYLEY, C.	21	M	Farmer	12J102Ra
B.	22	F	None	12J102Ra
READEN, W.	30	M	Farmer	12J102Ra
FITZGERALD, M.	30	M	Farmer	12J102Ra
FITZGIVON, T.	26	M	Farmer	12J102Ra
J.	19	M	Farmer	12J102Ra
M.	20	F	None	12J102Ra
C.	50	F	None	12J102Ra
ALLYN, T.	22	M	Farmer	12J102Ra
RIGEN, B.	22	M	Farmer	12J102Ra
LINIHAN, H.	22	F	None	12J102Ra
LINEN, M.A.	21	F	None	12J102Ra
STANTON, W.	36	M	Farmer	12J102Ra
M.	36	F	None	12J102Ra
J.	16	M	Farmer	12J102Ra
E.	09	M	Child	12J102Ra
M.	07	F	Child	12J102Ra
B.	03	F	Child	12J102Ra
MCDONNELL, J.	21	M	Farmer	12J102Ra
QUINN, J.	28	M	Farmer	12J102Ra
POWERS, A.	42	M	Farmer	12J102Ra
J.	30	M	Farmer	12J102Ra
J.	08	M	Child	12J102Ra
POWERS, M.	06	F	Child	12J102Ra
W.	03	M	Child	12J102Ra
GRIFFIN, M.	26	M	Farmer	12J102Ra
HANNEGAN, M.	03	F	Child	12J102Ra
GROCEREY, M.	18	F	None	12J102Ra
BOWNS, M.	25	M	Farmer	12J102Ra
B.	27	F	None	12J102Ra
SHAY, B.	21	F	None	12J102Ra
A.	23	F	None	12J102Ra
ROBERTS, M.	42	M	Farmer	12J102Ra
J.	18	M	Farmer	12J102Ra
FURGUSON, M.	25	F	None	12J102Ra
MARSHALL, E.	22	F	None	12J102Ra
HOWELL, M.	18	F	None	12J102Ra
TUCKER, R.	24	M	Farmer	12J102Ra
E.	30	F	None	12J102Ra
HERTZ, C.	18	F	None	12J102Ra
WALLACE, E.	27	F	None	12J102Ra
CONNERS, A.	27	F	None	12J102Ra
FENTON, B.	18	F	None	12J102Ra
GILBERT, J.	21	M	Farmer	12J102Ra
GILL, D.	30	M	Farmer	12J102Ra
C.	25	F	None	12J102Ra
MCINTIRE, M.	27	M	Farmer	12J102Ra
A.	23	F	None	12J102Ra
M.	21	M	Farmer	12J102Ra
A.	15	F	None	12J102Ra
L.	.00	M	Infant	12J102Ra
RYLEY, E.	26	M	Farmer	12J102Ra
FALLEN, J.	53	M	Farmer	12J102Ra
OWEN, M.	25	M	Farmer	12J102Ra
FARRALLY, P.	28	M	Farmer	12J102Ra
P.	19	M	Farmer	12J102Ra
MURPHY, M.	28	M	Farmer	12J102Ra
M.	25	F	None	12J102Ra
M.	03	F	Child	12J102Ra
H.	.00	F	Infant	12J102Ra
HUSSEY, E.	25	M	Farmer	12J102Ra
CHRISTOPHER, L.	60	M	Farmer	12J102Ra
T.	21	M	Farmer	12J102Ra
M.	19	M	Farmer	12J102Ra
H.	16	M	Farmer	12J102Ra
M.	13	F	None	12J102Ra
M.	06	F	Child	12J102Ra
CARROLL, C.	30	F	None	12J102Ra
CAGINS, E.	19	F	None	12J102Ra
REA, G.	30	M	Farmer	12J102Ra
LANDER, F.	26	F	None	12J102Ra

AMERICAN-EAGLE 12 JULY 1847

From London

NAMES OF PASSENGERS	AGE	SEX	OCCUPATIONS	DATE PORT SHIP
GOODBOURN, D.	35	M	Farmer	12J121Rb
Sarah	29	F	None	12J121Rb
DANSTALE, Eliza	29	F	None	12J121Rb
Frances	20	F	None	12J121Rb
BROWN, Mgrt.	02	F	Child	12J121Rb
MACKS, Morna	21	F	None	12J121Rb
ISAACS, M.	21	M	Farmer	12J121Rb
REDFERN, A.	22	M	Farmer	12J121Rb
Mgrt.	26	F	None	12J121Rb
ALLEN, J.	26	M	Farmer	12J121Rb
Mgt.	34	F	None	12J121Rb
KELH, M.	34	F	None	12J121Rb
SHARP, E.	28	M	Farmer	12J121Rb
MASON, J.	30	M	Farmer	12J121Rb
BARNES, S.	18	M	Farmer	12J121Rb
Richard	39	M	Farmer	12J121Rb

NAMES OF PASSENGERS	AGE	SEX	OCCUPATIONS	DATE PORT SHIP
HARRISS, W.	70	M	Farmer	12J121Rb
RUTT, W.	15	M	Farmer	12J121Rb
Sarah	25	F	None	12J121Rb
CLAYTON, J.	50	M	Farmer	12J121Rb
Sarah	56	F	None	12J121Rb
BRANDON, Ann	22	F	None	12J121Rb
Dann	02	M	Child	12J121Rb
HARRIS, D.	11	M	None	12J121Rb
CLAYTON, J.	18	M	Farmer	12J121Rb
Pan---, W.	30	M	Farmer	12J121Rb
MARSDEN, N.	30	M	Farmer	12J121Rb
ELLIS, G.	22	M	Farmer	12J121Rb
JONES, J.	30	M	Farmer	12J121Rb
DOYLE, Bgt.	22	F	None	12J121Rb
JONES, W.H.	28	M	Farmer	12J121Rb
WALKER, G.	22	M	Farmer	12J121Rb
JONES, J.	27	M	Farmer	12J121Rb
Carolin	25	F	None	12J121Rb
Alfred	04	M	Child	12J121Rb
George	02	M	Child	12J121Rb
Timothy	01	M	Child	12J121Rb
ESSENGER, J.	27	M	Farmer	12J121Rb
HUMPHRY, J.	27	M	Farmer	12J121Rb
TRACY, M.	18	M	Farmer	12J121Rb
GROSSENBACH, W.	24	M	Laborer	12J121Rb
HARSBEY, Ct.	19	F	None	12J121Rb
PLACE, C.	24	M	Laborer	12J121Rb
Carl	21	M	Laborer	12J121Rb
COLLINS, J.	30	M	Laborer	12J121Rb
Amellia	20	F	Spinster	12J121Rb
ELLIOT, T.	45	M	Laborer	12J121Rb
Elzbt.	43	F	None	12J121Rb
Edward	12	M	None	12J121Rb
WHITNEY, J.	26	M	None	12J121Rb
Mgrt.	26	F	None	12J121Rb
Selina	02	F	Child	12J121Rb
BOYD, T.	30	M	Laborer	12J121Rb
KELLING, J.	27	M	Laborer	12J121Rb
BRICK, H.	22	M	Laborer	12J121Rb
REGAN, C.	24	M	Laborer	12J121Rb
FOLY, Mgt.	29	F	None	12J121Rb
COX, W.	21	M	Laborer	12J121Rb
DYANN, W.	36	M	Laborer	12J121Rb
POOR, J.	44	M	Laborer	12J121Rb
Fakan	45	F	None	12J121Rb
Cath.	18	F	None	12J121Rb
Johanes	10	M	None	12J121Rb
Eva	08	F	Child	12J121Rb
Adam	06	M	Child	12J121Rb
Elzbt.	03	F	Child	12J121Rb
MENOCH, H.	38	M	Laborer	12J121Rb
HASTON, Ann-M.	52	F	None	12J121Rb
Phillipa	25	F	None	12J121Rb
Cath.	25	F	None	12J121Rb
Jacob	19	M	None	12J121Rb
Anna-M.	16	F	None	12J121Rb
Henrietta	11	F	None	12J121Rb
Cath.	06	F	Child	12J121Rb
GERHARD, M.	45	M	Laborer	12J121Rb
Dorothea	29	F	None	12J121Rb
Elzbt.	11	F	None	12J121Rb
BRAND, L.	73	M	Laborer	12J121Rb
Elzbt.	60	F	None	12J121Rb
Elzbt.	36	F	None	12J121Rb
Phillipa	01	F	Child	12J121Rb
ESSENGER, P.	26	F	None	12J121Rb
WADE, Janet	67	F	None	12J121Rb
E.W.	27	M	Mechanic	12J121Rb
Janet	27	F	None	12J121Rb
LUBALT, J.R.	62	M	Mechanic	12J121Rb
MASTOLE, F.N.	23	M	Mechanic	12J121Rb
TOAL, Regn.	29	F	None	12J121Rb
DEETY, W.	26	M	Mechanic	12J121Rb
MCRAE, Elza.	27	F	None	12J121Rb
SYDNEY, S.	26	M	Mechanic	12J121Rb

NAMES OF PASSENGERS	AGE	SEX	OCCUPATIONS	DATE PORT SHIP
NEVES, Jas.	32	M	Mechanic	12J121Rb
Cath.	04	F	Child	12J121Rb
KENNY, Elzt.	25	F	None	12J121Rb
TALBOT, M.	25	M	Mechanic	12J121Rb
POOL, W.	21	M	Mechanic	12J121Rb
ADAM, M.	21	M	Mechanic	12J121Rb
MURPHY, W.	32	M	Mechanic	12J121Rb

TUSKAR 13 JULY 1847

From Liverpool

NAMES OF PASSENGERS	AGE	SEX	OCCUPATIONS	DATE PORT SHIP
SCOTT, Jane	20	F	None	13J102Rc
ARMSTRONG, W.	31	M	Farmer	13J102Rc
DUFFERN, W.	30	M	Unknown	13J102Rc
DERBYSHIRE, J.	31	M	Unknown	13J102Rc
HOLDING, H.	33	M	Unknown	13J102Rc
SMITH, S.	48	M	Unknown	13J102Rc
Leah	31	F	None	13J102Rc
NESBITT, J.	60	M	Unknown	13J102Rc
Peggy	55	F	None	13J102Rc
Saml.	17	M	Unknown	13J102Rc
Allen	14	M	None	13J102Rc
Lydia	11	F	None	13J102Rc
KENNEDY, Ellen	54	F	None	13J102Rc
BURKE, D.	30	M	Unknown	13J102Rc
KERWIN, M.	15	M	Laborer	13J102Rc
Rosana	14	F	None	13J102Rc
NESBIT, J.	01	M	Child	13J102Rc
MALONE, Bgt.	24	F	None	13J102Rc
MCKENON, Mgt.	60	F	None	13J102Rc
Francis	14	M	None	13J102Rc
BAGLY, M.	36	M	Unknown	13J102Rc
Jane	36	F	None	13J102Rc
My.	09	F	Child	13J102Rc
Chas.	03	M	Child	13J102Rc
MCINTYRE, D.	26	M	Unknown	13J102Rc
Jno.	21	M	Unknown	13J102Rc
BRANZIE, J.	25	M	Unknown	13J102Rc
MCCORMICK, Elza.	20	F	None	13J102Rc
My.	16	F	None	13J102Rc
CONLIN, Bgt.	19	F	None	13J102Rc
HANLY, Cath.	19	F	None	13J102Rc
NORTON, J.	18	M	None	13J102Rc
MULHOLLAND, T.	40	M	Unknown	13J102Rc
Mgrt.	35	F	None	13J102Rc
Anne	09	F	Child	13J102Rc
Peggy-I.	02	F	Child	13J102Rc
CAUGHY, R.	18	M	Unknown	13J102Rc
MCCARTNEY, Mta.	24	F	None	13J102Rc
BEN, R.	28	M	Unknown	13J102Rc
Agnes	24	F	None	13J102Rc
Elzbt.	24	F	None	13J102Rc
RYAN, M.	23	M	Laborer	13J102Rc
Nancy	19	F	None	13J102Rc
HEFFERNAN, M.	25	M	Unknown	13J102Rc
HENEGAN, W.	25	M	Unknown	13J102Rc
Joseph	24	M	Unknown	13J102Rc
BROWN, C.	26	M	Unknown	13J102Rc
Terence	26	M	Unknown	13J102Rc
DUNN, D.	36	M	Unknown	13J102Rc
Judith	40	F	None	13J102Rc
HACKETT, Ellen	12	F	None	13J102Rc
Thos.	12	M	None	13J102Rc
DUNN, J.	11	M	None	13J102Rc
FITZPATRICK, P.	50	M	Unknown	13J102Rc
Bdgt.	23	F	None	13J102Rc
BELL, J.	02	M	Child	13J102Rc
KENNEDY, J.	24	M	Mechanic	13J102Rc

NAMES OF PASSENGERS	AGE	SEX	OCCUPATIONS	DATE PORT SHIP
SPENCER, G.	27	M	Unknown	13J102Rc
CONSTANTIN, T.	23	M	Unknown	13J102Rc
CLOUGH, G.	24	M	Unknown	13J102Rc
Jno.	21	M	Unknown	13J102Rc
MCNAULTY, Sarah	22	F	None	13J102Rc
DONNELL, T.	30	M	Unknown	13J102Rc
CARDEN, J.	20	M	Unknown	13J102Rc
SMITH, Bgt.	20	F	None	13J102Rc
MONAGHAN, P.	21	M	Unknown	13J102Rc
RIELLY, Rosana	18	F	None	13J102Rc
BRIDE, P.	21	M	Unknown	13J102Rc
CONNERTY, J.	12	M	None	13J102Rc
WHITTEN, J.	59	M	Unknown	13J102Rc
LARKEN, My.	19	F	None	13J102Rc
Sarah	30	F	None	13J102Rc
GOLDING, J.	24	M	Unknown	13J102Rc
LAHY, T.	21	M	Unknown	13J102Rc
MARNIN, A.	24	M	Unknown	13J102Rc
DONLY, T.	20	M	Unknown	13J102Rc
WILLIAMS, T.	40	M	Unknown	13J102Rc
U (W)	40	F	Wife	13J102Rc
BENDESON, J.	19	M	Unknown	13J102Rc
WILLIAMS, J.	16	M	Unknown	13J102Rc
Mgt.	14	F	None	13J102Rc
Martha	12	F	None	13J102Rc
Hannah	09	F	Child	13J102Rc
Sarah	07	F	Child	13J102Rc
Ann	05	F	Child	13J102Rc
Thos.	01	M	Child	13J102Rc
REES, S.	45	M	Unknown	13J102Rc
Eleanor	45	F	None	13J102Rc
Eleanor	15	F	None	13J102Rc
My.	13	F	None	13J102Rc
James	11	M	None	13J102Rc
DAVIS, Hanah	10	F	None	13J102Rc
Elizbt.	04	F	Child	13J102Rc
BEBB, D.	35	F	Unknown	13J102Rc
VAUGHAN, Eleanor	20	F	None	13J102Rc
FANES, T.	25	M	Unknown	13J102Rc
BENNETT, T.	22	F	None	13J102Rc
MCALISTER, Mgt.	22	F	None	13J102Rc
MCHENRY, Elza.	19	F	None	13J102Rc
ORR, Mgt.	24	F	None	13J102Rc
Rebecca	40	F	None	13J102Rc
Sarah	10	F	None	13J102Rc
Rachel	08	F	Child	13J102Rc
Eliza	05	F	Child	13J102Rc
MCGUIN, Jane	34	F	None	13J102Rc
CUNNINGHAM, J.	50	M	Mechanic	13J102Rc
MCHENRY, Wh.	59	M	Unknown	13J102Rc
ORR, T.	26	M	Unknown	13J102Rc
FARRELL, T.	20	M	Unknown	13J102Rc
MAGUIRE, Rosa	18	F	None	13J102Rc
KELLAGHER, P.	19	M	Unknown	13J102Rc
SMITH, J.	18	M	Unknown	13J102Rc
BLAKE, J.	63	M	Laborer	13J102Rc
Elza.	54	F	None	13J102Rc
Wm.	34	M	None	13J102Rc
Jane	14	F	None	13J102Rc
Mar.	12	F	None	13J102Rc
MCBRIDE, P.	24	M	Unknown	13J102Rc
MARTIN, B.	22	M	Unknown	13J102Rc
Cath.	17	F	None	13J102Rc
Ann	16	F	None	13J102Rc
MCMANN, Ann	20	F	None	13J102Rc
Sarah	18	F	None	13J102Rc
Biddy	16	F	None	13J102Rc
HOLT, Ma.	15	F	None	13J102Rc
CLOSE, Cath.	21	F	None	13J102Rc
KINCAID, Jane	42	F	None	13J102Rc
My.	18	F	None	13J102Rc
Jas.	15	M	None	13J102Rc
Saml.	12	M	None	13J102Rc
Jno.	10	M	None	13J102Rc
Eliza.	08	F	Child	13J102Rc
KINCAID, Martha	06	F	Child	13J102Rc
Rosann	04	F	Child	13J102Rc
Wm.	02	M	Child	13J102Rc
COSTIGAN, J.	25	M	Unknown	13J102Rc
LAWLER, J.	55	M	Unknown	13J102Rc
SHEEHAN, D.	22	M	Unknown	13J102Rc
Julia	20	F	None	13J102Rc
CASHMAN, Ellen	24	F	None	13J102Rc
GUNNING, P.	20	M	Laborer	13J102Rc
My.	18	F	None	13J102Rc
Johanna	17	F	None	13J102Rc
Bgt.	16	F	None	13J102Rc
Jno.	12	M	None	13J102Rc
Ellen	08	F	Child	13J102Rc
Cath.	17	F	None	13J102Rc
DENNISON, Cath.	20	F	None	13J102Rc
MCKNIGHT, W.	18	M	Unknown	13J102Rc
Mgt.	12	F	None	13J102Rc
CALLAGHAN, Bgt.	22	F	None	13J102Rc
CLINTON, J.	20	M	Unknown	13J102Rc
My.	18	F	None	13J102Rc
Ann	16	F	None	13J102Rc
BARRETT, J.	21	M	Unknown	13J102Rc
DUNDAN, P.	24	M	Unknown	13J102Rc
Ellen	24	F	None	13J102Rc
CONNERY, D.	28	M	Unknown	13J102Rc
MULLEN, J.	24	M	Unknown	13J102Rc
WALSH, J.	30	M	Unknown	13J102Rc
Mich.	24	M	Unknown	13J102Rc
COLEMAN, R.	40	M	Unknown	13J102Rc
MCQULLAN, B.	30	M	Unknown	13J102Rc
Cath.	20	F	None	13J102Rc
My.	08	F	Child	13J102Rc
Ann	06	F	Child	13J102Rc
Jane	04	F	Child	13J102Rc
MCCANN, Jane	15	F	None	13J102Rc
MCMULLEN, J.	36	M	Unknown	13J102Rc
Harriet	28	F	None	13J102Rc
Nancy	30	F	None	13J102Rc
Alexn.	13	M	None	13J102Rc
STEELE, W.	20	M	Unknown	13J102Rc
MCMULLAN, W.	01	F	Child	13J102Rc
MCQULLAN, J.	53	M	Unknown	13J102Rc
My.	53	F	None	13J102Rc
Wm.	20	M	Unknown	13J102Rc
Rowly	16	M	Unknown	13J102Rc
Hy.	18	M	Unknown	13J102Rc
Bgt.	03	F	Child	13J102Rc
ARMSTRONG, J.	40	M	Unknown	13J102Rc
Jane	38	F	None	13J102Rc
MILLIKEN, Ma.	24	F	None	13J102Rc
My.	16	F	None	13J102Rc
Sarah	14	F	None	13J102Rc
Elzt.	10	F	None	13J102Rc
Wm.	06	M	Child	13J102Rc
Jno.	04	M	Child	13J102Rc
My.	01	F	Child	13J102Rc
MURPHY, W.	20	M	Laborer	13J102Rc
RYAN, T.	24	M	Unknown	13J102Rc
MOORHEAD, My.	61	F	None	13J102Rc
Mgt.	18	F	None	13J102Rc
Ann	20	F	None	13J102Rc
DONNELLY, O.	14	M	Unknown	13J102Rc
Rosey	10	F	None	13J102Rc
REILY, Bidy	20	F	None	13J102Rc
GIBBONS, M.	20	F	None	13J102Rc
DURMODY, D.	20	M	Unknown	13J102Rc
My.	20	F	None	13J102Rc
Mich.	12	M	None	13J102Rc
LEE, Mgt.	50	F	None	13J102Rc
Jane	20	F	None	13J102Rc
Susan	16	F	None	13J102Rc
MURRY, P.	20	M	Unknown	13J102Rc
MCAFEY, Ann	15	F	None	13J102Rc
MORAN, T.	45	M	Unknown	13J102Rc

NAMES OF PASSENGERS	AGE	SEX	OCCUPATIONS	DATE PORT SHIP
MORAN, U (W)	45	F	None	13JI02Rc
Pat	15	M	None	13JI02Rc
Wm.	13	M	None	13JI02Rc
My.	11	F	None	13JI02Rc
Thos.	07	M	Child	13JI02Rc
Kitty	04	F	Child	13JI02Rc
Michl.	02	M	Child	13JI02Rc
CONNOR, Ma.	20	F	None	13JI02Rc
MCMORRAN, C.	20	M	Unknown	13JI02Rc
DRUMMOND, J.	17	M	Unknown	13JI02Rc
OBRIEN, P.	20	M	Unknown	13JI02Rc
Biddy	15	F	None	13JI02Rc
MCCARTHY, T.	12	M	None	13JI02Rc
DOHANNER, J.	30	M	Laborer	13JI02Rc
My.	30	F	None	13JI02Rc
Mgt.	20	F	None	13JI02Rc
Mich	18	M	Unknown	13JI02Rc
Pat	11	M	None	13JI02Rc
Jas.	08	M	Child	13JI02Rc
HALPIN, Ellen	03	F	Child	13JI02Rc
Cath.	01	F	Child	13JI02Rc
ARMSTRONG, My.	50	F	None	13JI02Rc
Jane	12	F	None	13JI02Rc
Bgt.	10	F	None	13JI02Rc
Wm.	08	M	Child	13JI02Rc
Cath.	06	M	Child	13JI02Rc
Jno.	03	M	Child	13JI02Rc
HUGHS, A.	25	M	Unknown	13JI02Rc
MCCARTHY, P.	30	M	Unknown	13JI02Rc
MCGRATH, Mrgt.	30	F	None	13JI02Rc
HANEKIS, J.	26	M	Unknown	13JI02Rc
Mgt.	21	F	None	13JI02Rc
DONNELLY, F.	18	M	Unknown	13JI02Rc
ARNSTY, W.	20	M	Unknown	13JI02Rc
Thos.	13	M	None	13JI02Rc
RYAN, J.	22	M	Unknown	13JI02Rc
Peter	25	M	Unknown	13JI02Rc
Ellen	25	F	None	13JI02Rc
Bgt.	21	F	None	13JI02Rc
DELANY, W.	34	M	Unknown	13JI02Rc
Judith	34	F	None	13JI02Rc
My.	25	F	None	13JI02Rc
Mgt.	12	F	None	13JI02Rc
Jas.	05	M	Child	13JI02Rc
SHELD, M.	21	M	Unknown	13JI02Rc
GREEN, J.	21	M	Unknown	13JI02Rc
SMITH, P.	24	M	Unknown	13JI02Rc
PALMER, Mgt.	20	F	None	13JI02Rc
SMITH, P.	47	M	Unknown	13JI02Rc
KEENAN, T.	24	M	Unknown	13JI02Rc
Ellen	22	F	None	13JI02Rc
CUMINGS, Elzt.	26	F	None	13JI02Rc
WALSH, P.	22	M	Unknown	13JI02Rc
MCONOHY, J.	40	M	Unknown	13JI02Rc
GUNSTON, Wm.	25	M	Unknown	13JI02Rc

NIAGARA 13 JULY 1847

From Liverpool

NAMES OF PASSENGERS	AGE	SEX	OCCUPATIONS	DATE PORT SHIP
AGIN, Cath.	20	F	None	13JI02Ab
Mary	18	F	None	13JI02Ab
Ellen	14	F	None	13JI02Ab
HICKY, Ann	20	F	None	13JI02Ab
SHEEDY, M.	38	M	Laborer	13JI02Ab
Winey	33	F	None	13JI02Ab
Phillip	08	M	Child	13JI02Ab
Cath.	06	F	Child	13JI02Ab
My.	01	F	Child	13JI02Ab
AGIN, M.	63	M	Unknown	13JI02Ab
Mch.Jr.	22	M	Unknown	13JI02Ab
CONALLY, P.	21	M	Unknown	13JI02Ab
TOOLE, J.	20	M	Unknown	13JI02Ab
SHEEDY, J.	35	M	Unknown	13JI02Ab
Ann	25	F	None	13JI02Ab
Mgt.	02	F	Child	13JI02Ab
Phillip	01	M	Child	13JI02Ab
.TINFOUL, My.	28	F	None	13JI02Ab
DUGGAN, My.	20	F	None	13JI02Ab
SMITH, My.	20	F	None	13JI02Ab
FRYER, Ellen	20	F	None	13JI02Ab
GRIFFIN, Mgt.	45	F	None	13JI02Ab
JESSOP, M.	32	M	Unknown	13JI02Ab
Betty	32	F	None	13JI02Ab
Cath.	07	F	Child	13JI02Ab
James	05	M	Child	13JI02Ab
Peter	03	M	Child	13JI02Ab
KALAHAN, C.	25	M	Unknown	13JI02Ab
TOOLAN, W.	18	M	Unknown	13JI02Ab
CASEY, J.	27	M	Unknown	13JI02Ab
FALLON, P.	32	M	Unknown	13JI02Ab
JOHNSON, A.	40	M	Unknown	13JI02Ab
JOHNSTON, Jane	36	F	None	13JI02Ab
SWAN, T.B.	22	M	Unknown	13JI02Ab
My.A.B.	21	F	None	13JI02Ab
RAISTON, Abby	20	F	None	13JI02Ab
LYNCH, Ann	30	F	None	13JI02Ab
SULLIVAN, Cath.	23	F	None	13JI02Ab
DUNAVAN, J.	20	M	Unknown	13JI02Ab
ALTON, My.	48	F	None	13JI02Ab
GRADY, Bgt.	60	F	None	13JI02Ab
Bgt.Jr	18	F	None	13JI02Ab
GORMAN, My.	25	F	None	13JI02Ab
LACEY, J.	18	M	Laborer	13JI02Ab
LYNCH, J.	20	M	Unknown	13JI02Ab
MELON, P.	26	M	Unknown	13JI02Ab
FEGALLY, B.	16	M	Unknown	13JI02Ab
KELLY, J.	21	M	Unknown	13JI02Ab
Biddy	20	F	None	13JI02Ab
James	16	M	Unknown	13JI02Ab
Bgt.	13	F	None	13JI02Ab
FORD, M.	40	M	Unknown	13JI02Ab
REGAN, P.	45	M	Unknown	13JI02Ab
MANEGAN, R.	24	M	Unknown	13JI02Ab
DEVARD, M.	28	M	Unknown	13JI02Ab
QUNLAN, D.	28	M	Unknown	13JI02Ab
Judy	29	F	None	13JI02Ab
Honora	22	F	None	13JI02Ab
CREAM, C.	22	M	Unknown	13JI02Ab
MORAN, E.	23	M	Unknown	13JI02Ab
John	06	M	Child	13JI02Ab
DAVID, J.	40	M	Unknown	13JI02Ab
FRANK, W.	22	M	Unknown	13JI02Ab
Carolin	29	F	None	13JI02Ab
FRYERS, W.	22	M	Unknown	13JI02Ab
SLINY, A.	24	M	Unknown	13JI02Ab
Carolin	40	F	None	13JI02Ab
Christoph	39	M	Unknown	13JI02Ab
Rachael	12	F	None	13JI02Ab
Christiana	01	F	Child	13JI02Ab
CONNOR, My.	09	F	Child	13JI02Ab
Dennis	50	M	Unknown	13JI02Ab
Thos.	16	M	Unknown	13JI02Ab
My.	12	F	None	13JI02Ab
KILGORE, Ellen	14	F	None	13JI02Ab
My.	30	F	None	13JI02Ab
Mgt.	14	F	None	13JI02Ab
Bgt.	11	F	None	13JI02Ab
Kiaron	09	M	Child	13JI02Ab
Hannah	07	F	Child	13JI02Ab
Elzbt.	06	F	Child	13JI02Ab
Cath.	01	F	Child	13JI02Ab
BLAIR, A.	27	M	Unknown	13JI02Ab
ONEILL, J.	25	M	Laborer	13JI02Ab

NAMES OF PASSENGERS	AGE	SEX	OCCUPATIONS	DATE PORT SHIP
RICHARDS, G.	21	M	Unknown	13J102Ab
JACKSON, J.	21	M	Unknown	13J102Ab
PALZAR, Chat.	35	F	None	13J102Ab
RICHARDS, S.	10	M	None	13J102Ab
PALZAR, Jane	01	F	Child	13J102Ab
POTTS, Cath.	21	F	None	13J102Ab
MCCORNISH, T.	24	M	Unknown	13J102Ab
MAGNER, J.	23	M	Unknown	13J102Ab
FITZSIMMONS, T.	30	M	Unknown	13J102Ab
BERM, J.	30	M	Unknown	13J102Ab
HEALT, P.	26	M	Unknown	13J102Ab
Martha	22	F	None	13J102Ab
J.	03	M	Child	13J102Ab
HEECH, P.	01	M	Child	13J102Ab
CLARK, P.	30	M	Unknown	13J102Ab
BRADY, T.	20	M	Unknown	13J102Ab
TULLY, P.	30	M	Unknown	13J102Ab
CLARK, J.	30	M	Unknown	13J102Ab
FARNAN, Bgt.	25	F	None	13J102Ab
CARLAN, Cath.	30	F	None	13J102Ab
CURRAN, My.	20	F	None	13J102Ab
COOLY, Peggy	21	F	None	13J102Ab
ONEIL, J.	44	M	Unknown	13J102Ab
MAGNER, P.	24	M	Unknown	13J102Ab
BROWN, J.	26	M	Unknown	13J102Ab
POWER, J.	35	M	Unknown	13J102Ab
WEENER, D.	38	M	Unknown	13J102Ab
RYAN, W.	34	M	Unknown	13J102Ab
NUNAN, P.	34	F	None	13J102Ab
Mgt.	05	F	Child	13J102Ab
CASEY, T.	29	M	Unknown	13J102Ab
SULLIVAN, D.	27	M	Unknown	13J102Ab
Bgt.	20	F	None	13J102Ab
Michl.	01	M	Child	13J102Ab
BOHLAN, My.	23	F	None	13J102Ab
CLIFFERD, Judy	23	F	None	13J102Ab
BURNES, Math.	21	F	None	13J102Ab
John	20	M	Unknown	13J102Ab
MAHONY, J.	21	M	Unknown	13J102Ab
FINTAN, M.	25	M	Unknown	13J102Ab
BELL, W.	24	M	Unknown	13J102Ab
CASS, P.	24	M	Laborer	13J102Ab
JONES, E.	42	M	Unknown	13J102Ab
DOFF, P.	23	M	Unknown	13J102Ab
CONNAL, My.	26	F	None	13J102Ab
My.	23	F	None	13J102Ab
BERNE, Judy	14	F	None	13J102Ab
ROLFE, E.	36	M	Unknown	13J102Ab
Bgt.	30	F	None	13J102Ab
MCANALLY, T.	55	M	Unknown	13J102Ab
Libby	25	F	None	13J102Ab
CONNER, A.	33	M	Unknown	13J102Ab
MACTEAR, T.	34	M	Unknown	13J102Ab
MALONE, J.	35	M	Unknown	13J102Ab
My.	30	F	None	13J102Ab
My.	10	F	None	13J102Ab
Eliza.	07	F	Child	13J102Ab
Ann	04	F	Child	13J102Ab
DONLY, Ann	17	F	None	13J102Ab
LYNCH, Olive	27	F	None	13J102Ab
REESE, R.	25	M	Unknown	13J102Ab
My.	20	F	None	13J102Ab
GIBBONS, J.	28	M	Unknown	13J102Ab
Peter	24	M	Unknown	13J102Ab
Cath.	25	F	None	13J102Ab
John	04	M	Child	13J102Ab
Cath.	02	F	Child	13J102Ab
KILMARTIN, T.	45	M	Unknown	13J102Ab
My.	40	F	None	13J102Ab
John	22	M	Unknown	13J102Ab
Thos.	08	M	Child	13J102Ab
Ann	13	F	None	13J102Ab
Bgt.	10	F	None	13J102Ab
QUIMLIN, Cath.	17	F	None	13J102Ab
FRANCIS, J.	30	M	Unknown	13J102Ab
FRANCIS, Cath.	27	F	None	13J102Ab
David	01	M	Child	13J102Ab
JONES, J.	24	M	Unknown	13J102Ab
HUMPHRIES, E.	29	M	Unknown	13J102Ab
PUGH, D.	28	M	Unknown	13J102Ab
EVANS, Evan	35	M	Unknown	13J102Ab
ROWLAND, R.	25	M	Unknown	13J102Ab
THOMAS, W.	26	M	Unknown	13J102Ab
JONES, J.	21	M	Farmer	13J102Ab
EVANS, W.	32	M	Unknown	13J102Ab
JOSEPH, H.	23	M	Unknown	13J102Ab
JONES, D.	20	M	Unknown	13J102Ab
PUGH, Ann	22	F	None	13J102Ab
Jane	25	F	None	13J102Ab
OWENS, Eliza.	22	F	None	13J102Ab
EVANS, My.	27	F	None	13J102Ab
ROBERTS, Cath.	22	F	None	13J102Ab
THOMAS, Cath.	21	F	None	13J102Ab
WILLIAMS, Cath.	33	F	None	13J102Ab
COLBY, J.	14	M	Unknown	13J102Ab
Peter	12	M	None	13J102Ab
Patch	09	M	Child	13J102Ab
HONES, T.	23	M	Unknown	13J102Ab
GORMAN, My.	14	F	None	13J102Ab
Owen	35	M	Unknown	13J102Ab
Elizabeth	50	F	None	13J102Ab
FITZPATCK, J.	70	M	Unknown	13J102Ab
James	10	M	None	13J102Ab
Patch	08	M	Child	13J102Ab
Laurence	35	M	Unknown	13J102Ab
Ann	30	F	None	13J102Ab
Maria	06	F	Child	13J102Ab
John	04	M	Child	13J102Ab
FRENCH, C.	33	M	Unknown	13J102Ab
NAVEN, P.	53	M	Unknown	13J102Ab
James	20	M	Unknown	13J102Ab
HEADRY, D.	20	M	Unknown	13J102Ab
SHERIDAN, J.	19	M	Unknown	13J102Ab
CANN, Ann	23	F	None	13J102Ab
My.	25	F	None	13J102Ab
FRANCES, Elza.	22	F	None	13J102Ab
MURRY, Susan	25	F	None	13J102Ab
OBRIEN, D.	23	M	Unknown	13J102Ab
GANNON, L.	27	M	Unknown	13J102Ab
SULLIVAN, My.	40	F	None	13J102Ab
James (H)	50	M	Unknown	13J102Ab
Richd.	16	M	Unknown	13J102Ab
Bat.	10	F	None	13J102Ab
CORMACK, P.	30	M	Unknown	13J102Ab
DILLON, G.	21	M	Unknown	13J102Ab
WELSH, P.	24	M	Laborer	13J102Ab
OHARRA, J.	20	M	Unknown	13J102Ab
CALOHOE, Bgt.	15	F	None	13J102Ab
HUSTON, Cath.	20	F	None	13J102Ab
MCMURRAGH, Susan	20	F	None	13J102Ab
RYE, Mgt.	36	F	None	13J102Ab
MCNULTY, E.	20	M	Unknown	13J102Ab
DOHERTY, H.	20	M	Unknown	13J102Ab
FARRELL, M.	60	M	Unknown	13J102Ab
Barnet	16	M	Unknown	13J102Ab
WYNN, D.	25	M	Unknown	13J102Ab
SYRSON, M.	24	M	Unknown	13J102Ab
EVANS, Elenor	66	F	None	13J102Ab
WILLIAMS, My.	37	F	None	13J102Ab
Eleanor	12	F	None	13J102Ab
Lewis	10	M	None	13J102Ab
My.	08	F	Child	13J102Ab
Evan	06	M	Child	13J102Ab
CONNELL, J.	21	M	Unknown	13J102Ab
STAFFORD, N.	22	M	Unknown	13J102Ab
COCHRAN, J.	27	M	Unknown	13J102Ab
BARRY, J.	27	M	Unknown	13J102Ab
SHOHNALEY, Jn.	41	F	None	13J102Ab
CASEY, My.	18	F	None	13J102Ab
SHALLY, J.	41	M	Unknown	13J102Ab

NAMES OF PASSENGERS	AGE	SEX	OCCUPATIONS	DATE PORT SHIP
SHALLY, Wm.	18	M	Unknown	13J102Ab
Johanna	14	F	None	13J102Ab
SHARP, W.	42	M	Unknown	13J102Ab
Hy.	45	M	Unknown	13J102Ab
Letitia	40	F	None	13J102Ab
Elizbt.	14	F	None	13J102Ab
Eleanor	12	F	None	13J102Ab
Cath.	10	F	None	13J102Ab
Thos.	08	M	Child	13J102Ab
Letitia	05	F	Child	13J102Ab
Wm.	03	M	Child	13J102Ab
MCCARTY, W.	22	M	None	13J102Ab
MULCHAE, M.	21	M	None	13J102Ab
SULLIVAN, J.	23	M	None	13J102Ab
Jeremiah	22	M	None	13J102Ab
MULVEHILL, M.	38	M	None	13J102Ab
Ony	26	F	None	13J102Ab
J.	13	M	None	13J102Ab
James	05	M	Child	13J102Ab
Dominic	02	M	Child	13J102Ab
LYNCH, J.	25	M	Laborer	13J102Ab
FAHEY, T.	23	M	Unknown	13J102Ab
MULVEHILL, P.	27	M	Unknown	13J102Ab
HAGAN, T.	25	M	Unknown	13J102Ab
MULVEHILL, Ann	20	F	None	13J102Ab
CASEY, My.	20	F	None	13J102Ab
HOLLAND, Bgt.	18	F	None	13J102Ab
MULVEHILL, Ann	06	F	Child	13J102Ab
My.	03	F	Child	13J102Ab
NUTALL, T.	41	M	Unknown	13J102Ab
William	21	M	Unknown	13J102Ab
Thos.	15	M	None	13J102Ab
SWEENY, A.	21	M	Unknown	13J102Ab
Bgt.	18	F	None	13J102Ab
THORP, J.	21	M	Unknown	13J102Ab
Eliza	21	F	Unknown	13J102Ab
LARGE, S.	28	M	Unknown	13J102Ab
Susan	24	F	None	13J102Ab
WOODWAND, W.	29	M	Unknown	13J102Ab
Cath.	25	F	None	13J102Ab
WILSON, J.	24	M	Unknown	13J102Ab
GROCK, T.	18	M	Unknown	13J102Ab
WILSON, R.	20	M	Unknown	13J102Ab
Ann	25	F	None	13J102Ab
DORLING, W.	33	M	Unknown	13J102Ab
Cath.	26	F	None	13J102Ab
Janette	13	F	None	13J102Ab
George	17	M	Unknown	13J102Ab
WILSON, M.	67	M	Unknown	13J102Ab
Mgt.	38	F	None	13J102Ab
BELL, G.	22	M	Unknown	13J102Ab
HINDMAN, R.	25	M	Unknown	13J102Ab

DIANA 13 JULY 1847

From London

NAMES OF PASSENGERS	AGE	SEX	OCCUPATIONS	DATE PORT SHIP
GWYN, E.	31	M	Mechanic	13J121Nz
J.	23	M	Mechanic	13J121Nz
PARSONS, W.	33	M	Mechanic	13J121Nz
Mary	30	F	None	13J121Nz
TYRELL, Thos.	21	M	Mechanic	13J121Nz
BISHOP, D.	32	M	Mechanic	13J121Nz
SMITH, C.	26	M	Mechanic	13J121Nz
MORNEY, J.	34	M	Mechanic	13J121Nz
OSULLIVAN, D.	20	M	Mechanic	13J121Nz
DELOES, C.	18	M	Mechanic	13J121Nz
GUNTEN, A.	20	M	Mechanic	13J121Nz
SCHLART, J.	33	M	Mechanic	13J121Nz
ROTENBACH, P.	36	M	Mechanic	13J121Nz
SORTON, J.	25	M	Mechanic	13J121Nz
Me.	25	F	None	13J121Nz
L.	01	F	Child	13J121Nz
U.	.06	M	Infant	13J121Nz
CHITTON, E.	25	M	Farmer	13J121Nz
NELSON, S.	40	M	Farmer	13J121Nz
PITHER, T.	30	M	Mechanic	13J121Nz
GODDARD, W.	33	M	Mechanic	13J121Nz
LONG, A.	43	M	Mechanic	13J121Nz
C.	38	F	None	13J121Nz
A.	18	M	Mechanic	13J121Nz
Phoebe	06	F	Child	13J121Nz
E.	05	F	Child	13J121Nz
ROUAN, J.	30	M	Mechanic	13J121Nz
M.	22	F	None	13J121Nz
MCKAY, H.	33	M	Merchant	13J121Nz
HORNIMAN, H.	20	M	Merchant	13J121Nz
GREGONY, C.H.	28	M	Merchant	13J121Nz
COTES, T.	60	M	Mechanic	13J121Nz
C.	25	F	None	13J121Nz
R.	17	M	Mechanic	13J121Nz
SIMS, W.	40	M	Farmer	13J121Nz
H.	20	M	Farmer	13J121Nz
J.	07	M	Child	13J121Nz
M.J.	16	M	Farmer	13J121Nz
M.T.	11	M	Farmer	13J121Nz
HAVEL, E.S.	25	F	None	13J121Nz

DEWDROP 13 JULY 1847

From Sligo

NAMES OF PASSENGERS	AGE	SEX	OCCUPATIONS	DATE PORT SHIP
MCGOWAN, Pat	20	M	Laborer	13J128Rd
ROONEY, Ann	20	F	None	13J128Rd
BYRNE, Jno.	34	M	Laborer	13J128Rd
ROONEY, Thos.	24	M	Laborer	13J128Rd
Mich.	21	M	Laborer	13J128Rd
JOY, Jno.	17	M	Laborer	13J128Rd
CALLERGAN, Cath.	16	F	None	13J128Rd
EGAN, Thos.	28	M	Laborer	13J128Rd
Bridget	20	F	None	13J128Rd
FOLEY, Chas.	17	M	Laborer	13J128Rd
Mary	19	F	None	13J128Rd
FLANNIGAN, Mary	13	F	None	13J128Rd
DACY, Jno.	38	M	Laborer	13J128Rd
Mary	17	F	None	13J128Rd
Jno.	13	M	Laborer	13J128Rd
BOYLE, Wm.	21	M	Laborer	13J128Rd
CARTY, Patt	30	M	Laborer	13J128Rd
Bridget	32	F	None	13J128Rd
QUINN, Dennis	23	M	Laborer	13J128Rd
Eleanor	19	F	None	13J128Rd
CONNELLY, Patt	19	M	Laborer	13J128Rd
MORAN, Jno.	21	M	Laborer	13J128Rd
Thos.	18	M	Laborer	13J128Rd
GALLAGHER, Cath.	18	F	None	13J128Rd
Margt.	15	F	None	13J128Rd
Bridget	18	F	None	13J128Rd
ROCK, Timothey	30	M	Laborer	13J128Rd
NELSON, Jno.	18	M	Laborer	13J128Rd
Hon.	18	F	None	13J128Rd
MUNN, Bridget	23	F	None	13J128Rd
ROONEY, Mich.	25	M	Laborer	13J128Rd
FINON, Chas.	28	M	Laborer	13J128Rd
FINEGAN, Luke	30	M	Laborer	13J128Rd
Wm.	14	M	Laborer	13J128Rd
MULLEN, Anthony	18	M	Laborer	13J128Rd
Eleanor	35	F	None	13J128Rd

NAMES OF PASSENGERS	AGE	SEX	OCCUPATIONS	DATE PORT SHIP
TIMON, Mary	13	F	None	13JI28Rd
MULLEN, Dord.	16	F	None	13JI28Rd
BOLAND, Pat	10	M	None	13JI28Rd
Mich.	07	M	Child	13JI28Rd
MURRAY, Thady	23	M	Laborer	13JI28Rd
HIGGINS, James	60	M	Laborer	13JI28Rd
Nancey	17	F	None	13JI28Rd
Nancey	50	F	None	13JI28Rd
Peter	20	M	Laborer	13JI28Rd
JORDAN, Jas.	20	M	Laborer	13JI28Rd
GILGAN, Dennis	23	M	Laborer	13JI28Rd
MORROW, Peter	25	M	Laborer	13JI28Rd
Mich.	20	M	Laborer	13JI28Rd
Jno.	27	M	Laborer	13JI28Rd
Darby	17	M	Laborer	13JI28Rd
Ann	19	F	None	13JI28Rd
LACKEN, Ellen	16	F	None	13JI28Rd
HART, Ann	21	F	None	13JI28Rd
SLATTY, Jno.	25	M	Laborer	13JI28Rd
THOMAS, Bridget	23	F	None	13JI28Rd
DUNN, Andrew	26	M	Laborer	13JI28Rd
WALSH, Mich.	26	M	Laborer	13JI28Rd
Ann	20	F	None	13JI28Rd
MCGOWAN, Mary	19	F	None	13JI28Rd
KING, Darby	26	M	Laborer	13JI28Rd
MCGRATH, James	20	M	Laborer	13JI28Rd
MCEWAN, Mich.	16	M	Laborer	13JI28Rd
Biddy	18	F	None	13JI28Rd
FEENY, John	45	M	Laborer	13JI28Rd
Jas.	15	M	Laborer	13JI28Rd
Mary	10	F	None	13JI28Rd
KERR, Bridget	18	F	None	13JI28Rd
HART, Peter	20	M	Laborer	13JI28Rd
REILLY, Edwd.	18	M	Laborer	13JI28Rd
David	20	M	Laborer	13JI28Rd
MULVEY, Jno.	22	M	Laborer	13JI28Rd
Benj.	20	M	Laborer	13JI28Rd
Ann	18	F	None	13JI28Rd
FLANAGAN, Cath.	16	F	None	13JI28Rd
MCGOWAN, Dom.	23	M	Laborer	13JI28Rd
DUNN, Luke	22	M	Laborer	13JI28Rd
RUSH, Patt	22	M	Laborer	13JI28Rd
ROGERS, Jas.	25	M	Laborer	13JI28Rd
GILPATRICK, Lmary	24	F	None	13JI28Rd
CUNNINGHAM, Cath.	20	F	None	13JI28Rd
FLYNN, Patt	23	M	Laborer	13JI28Rd
Mary	19	F	None	13JI28Rd
Margt.	17	F	None	13JI28Rd
DURKEN, Mich.	18	M	Laborer	13JI28Rd
SWEENY, Thos.	22	M	Laborer	13JI28Rd
Edwd.	24	M	Laborer	13JI28Rd
ODONNELL, Mich.	22	M	Laborer	13JI28Rd
CARTY, Cath.	16	F	None	13JI28Rd
MATTINS, Patt	24	M	Laborer	13JI28Rd
Eleanor	20	F	None	13JI28Rd
DUNNE, Jno.	26	M	Laborer	13JI28Rd

MONTEREY 17 JULY 1847

From Dublin

NAMES OF PASSENGERS	AGE	SEX	OCCUPATIONS	DATE PORT SHIP
WRIGHT, R.	25	M	Merchant	17JI20Mt
MCDONNELL, P.	40	M	Merchant	17JI20Mt
FENNELAN, Wm.	40	M	Merchant	17JI20Mt
WILSON, W.	60	M	Farmer	17JI20Mt
My.	49	F	None	17JI20Mt
Robt.	18	M	None	17JI20Mt
George	10	M	None	17JI20Mt
Susan	14	F	None	17JI20Mt
WILSON, My.	12	F	None	17JI20Mt
Ann-J.	08	F	Child	17JI20Mt
ROURKE, T.	45	M	Unknown	17JI20Mt
Cath.	40	F	None	17JI20Mt
John	19	M	Unknown	17JI20Mt
Mary	18	F	None	17JI20Mt
Patch	12	M	None	17JI20Mt
HARLOW, W.	50	M	Unknown	17JI20Mt
Robert	13	M	None	17JI20Mt
M.	12	M	None	17JI20Mt
Cath.	10	F	None	17JI20Mt
RUSSELL, Ann	63	F	None	17JI20Mt
Eltz.	19	F	None	17JI20Mt
My.	15	F	None	17JI20Mt
William	17	M	Unknown	17JI20Mt
Thos.	16	M	Unknown	17JI20Mt
GATELY, T.	17	M	Merchant	17JI20Mt
My.	23	F	None	17JI20Mt
FRAZER, P.	24	M	Mechanic	17JI20Mt
QUINN, Cath.	19	F	None	17JI20Mt
FOGARTY, Bgt.	38	F	None	17JI20Mt
HARTY, R.	18	M	Unknown	17JI20Mt
LYDE, Cath.	22	F	None	17JI20Mt
Rose	01	F	Child	17JI20Mt
LACKEN, My.	18	F	None	17JI20Mt
BREKEN, Cat.	17	F	None	17JI20Mt
MCMAHON, E.	31	M	Unknown	17JI20Mt

SARAH-SANDS 19 JULY 1847

From Liverpool

NAMES OF PASSENGERS	AGE	SEX	OCCUPATIONS	DATE PORT SHIP
WEST, Kath.	26	F	None	19JI02Kp
WILKENS, W.	42	M	Mechanic	19JI02Kp
HICKS, T.	27	M	Unknown	19JI02Kp
Ann	27	F	None	19JI02Kp
Carolin	03	F	Child	19JI02Kp
TRAPWELL, My.A.	31	F	None	19JI02Kp
Joseph	11	M	None	19JI02Kp
John=.	09	M	Child	19JI02Kp
KHOE, My.	24	F	None	19JI02Kp
My.	04	F	Child	19JI02Kp
John	02	M	Child	19JI02Kp
Michl.	01	M	Child	19JI02Kp
BREWER, Ann	27	F	None	19JI02Kp
MAHONY, D.	20	M	Laborer	19JI02Kp
GAIN, J.	40	M	Laborer	19JI02Kp
Cath.	32	F	None	19JI02Kp
My.	11	F	None	19JI02Kp
WILLIAMS, E.	28	M	Unknown	19JI02Kp
POWERS, J.	25	M	Unknown	19JI02Kp
MURPHY, M.	42	M	Unknown	19JI02Kp
Paul	07	M	Child	19JI02Kp
Patch	05	M	Child	19JI02Kp
John	02	M	Child	19JI02Kp
Hugh	09	M	Child	19JI02Kp
HEGAN, Helen	55	F	None	19JI02Kp
WEST, Eliza	30	F	None	19JI02Kp
SHIELDS, D.	30	M	Unknown	19JI02Kp
DIETY, H.	35	M	Unknown	19JI02Kp
Elza.J.	29	F	None	19JI02Kp
Ann-J.	06	F	Child	19JI02Kp
Robt.	04	M	Child	19JI02Kp
Hugh	02	M	Child	19JI02Kp
Wm.J.	01	M	Child	19JI02Kp
William	13	M	None	19JI02Kp
PATTERSON, Elzt.	25	F	None	19JI02Kp
MURPHY, P.	35	M	Unknown	19JI02Kp
Mgt.	26	F	None	19JI02Kp

NAMES OF PASSENGERS	AGE	SEX	OCCUPATIONS	DATE PORT SHIP
MURPHY, Thos.	06	M	Child	19Jl02Kp
Danil	25	M	Unknown	19Jl02Kp
Hanah-A.	04	F	Child	19Jl02Kp
Jeremiah	03	M	Child	19Jl02Kp
WALLACE, Nora	55	F	None	19Jl02Kp
DREWNY, Eliza	23	F	None	19Jl02Kp
BARRY, My.	17	F	None	19Jl02Kp
SQUIRE, G.	40	M	Farmer	19Jl02Kp
BANNON, T.	28	M	Unknown	19Jl02Kp
NOXON, J.	38	M	Unknown	19Jl02Kp
GLINN, J.	20	M	Unknown	19Jl02Kp
ROBSON, D.	20	M	Unknown	19Jl02Kp
BOWEN, T.	32	M	Unknown	19Jl02Kp
DAWS, D.	35	M	Unknown	19Jl02Kp
Mgt.	24	F	None	19Jl02Kp
My.E.	01	M	Child	19Jl02Kp
HOBBS, C.	20	M	Unknown	19Jl02Kp
MICHAEL, D.	26	M	Unknown	19Jl02Kp
COXON, W.	48	M	Unknown	19Jl02Kp
DARCY, P.	30	M	Unknown	19Jl02Kp
Bgt.	28	F	None	19Jl02Kp
MARTIN, D.	28	M	Unknown	19Jl02Kp
CLARK, J.	21	M	Unknown	19Jl02Kp
SMITH, Hanh.N.	58	F	None	19Jl02Kp
Hannah-M.	22	F	None	19Jl02Kp
Robt.F.	15	M	Unknown	19Jl02Kp
HARRIS, D.	40	M	Unknown	19Jl02Kp
CANNING, W.	65	M	Unknown	19Jl02Kp
FOSKES, G.H.	24	M	Unknown	19Jl02Kp
HARRISON, J.	24	M	Unknown	19Jl02Kp
RICHMOND, J.	35	M	Unknown	19Jl02Kp
HDCROFT, G.	24	M	Unknown	19Jl02Kp
FREDLAND, B.	35	M	Unknown	19Jl02Kp
SMITH, J.	35	M	Unknown	19Jl02Kp
MCBRIDE, J.	29	M	Unknown	19Jl02Kp
MULLIGAN, J.	40	M	Unknown	19Jl02Kp

LIVERPOOL 20 JULY 1847

From Liverpool

NAMES OF PASSENGERS	AGE	SEX	OCCUPATIONS	DATE PORT SHIP
PARKER, G.	38	M	Merchant	20Jl02Bo
Mrt.	30	F	None	20Jl02Bo
Sra.	08	F	Child	20Jl02Bo
MCNULTY, Elza.	26	F	None	20Jl02Bo
Pamel.	24	F	None	20Jl02Bo
DAGENS, Elza.	19	F	None	20Jl02Bo
BRUGHES, M.W.	40	F	None	20Jl02Bo
Victoria	04	F	Child	20Jl02Bo
GREGG, D.	34	M	Unknown	20Jl02Bo
My.	29	F	None	20Jl02Bo
MCCARTY, My.	15	F	None	20Jl02Bo
RAFFERTY, Sarah	20	F	None	20Jl02Bo
GORDON, A.	70	M	Unknown	20Jl02Bo
PLEHORN, C.	50	M	Unknown	20Jl02Bo
DORIG, T.	26	M	Unknown	20Jl02Bo
YORK, W.	31	M	Unknown	20Jl02Bo
EWING, R.	20	M	Laborer	20Jl02Bo
BOYLAN, J.	20	M	Unknown	20Jl02Bo
READY, C.	20	M	Unknown	20Jl02Bo
John	34	M	Unknown	20Jl02Bo
BUXTON, J.	20	M	Unknown	20Jl02Bo
Benjn.	22	M	Unknown	20Jl02Bo
PHILLIPS, T.	42	M	Unknown	20Jl02Bo
ROEBUCK, J.	25	M	Unknown	20Jl02Bo
BRYDON, R.	30	M	Unknown	20Jl02Bo
David	37	M	Unknown	20Jl02Bo
My.	37	F	None	20Jl02Bo
My.	05	F	Child	20Jl02Bo
BRYDON, Mgt.	04	F	Child	20Jl02Bo
Arch.	01	M	Child	20Jl02Bo
Jeannette	01	F	Child	20Jl02Bo
WALSH, P.	20	M	Unknown	20Jl02Bo
WARREN, W.	45	M	Unknown	20Jl02Bo
John	17	M	Unknown	20Jl02Bo
GRACE, J.	40	M	Unknown	20Jl02Bo
U	36	F	None	20Jl02Bo
Richd.	22	M	Unknown	20Jl02Bo
James	20	M	Unknown	20Jl02Bo
DALY, Julia	55	F	None	20Jl02Bo
Mich.	12	M	None	20Jl02Bo
WHALLY, Nora	29	F	None	20Jl02Bo
Ellen	12	F	None	20Jl02Bo
FULLEN, B.	26	M	Unknown	20Jl02Bo
KILLAN, Bdgt.	30	F	None	20Jl02Bo
CREAHAN, My.	25	F	None	20Jl02Bo
COLGAN, My.	25	F	None	20Jl02Bo
DANSEY, Bgt.	24	F	None	20Jl02Bo
CREAKEN, Cath.	19	F	None	20Jl02Bo
GREEN, Mich.	30	F	None	20Jl02Bo
DARWIN, Mgt.	20	F	None	20Jl02Bo
MOLLOY, J.	36	M	Unknown	20Jl02Bo
WELLS, Jane	30	F	None	20Jl02Bo
MULHOLLAND, P.	17	M	Unknown	20Jl02Bo
WALLS, B.	20	M	Unknown	20Jl02Bo
Jane	01	F	Child	20Jl02Bo
GOVERN, Cht.	19	F	None	20Jl02Bo
MULHOLLAND, My.J.	18	F	None	20Jl02Bo
LAHON, J.	26	M	Unknown	20Jl02Bo
Mich.	24	M	Unknown	20Jl02Bo
My.	22	F	None	20Jl02Bo
DUNNE, M.	20	M	Unknown	20Jl02Bo
CREAKEN, M.	20	M	Unknown	20Jl02Bo
My.	17	F	None	20Jl02Bo
Hanah	15	F	None	20Jl02Bo
CORBITT, R.	34	M	Unknown	20Jl02Bo
LITTLE, T.	21	M	Unknown	20Jl02Bo
ROWLY, My.	24	F	None	20Jl02Bo
Pat	29	M	Unknown	20Jl02Bo
MALY, Biddy	24	F	None	20Jl02Bo
LYONS, Cath.	20	F	None	20Jl02Bo
HENESY, Cath.	20	F	None	20Jl02Bo
KRENAN, Mgt.	30	F	None	20Jl02Bo
HEEKY, Ann	25	F	None	20Jl02Bo
DAMON, Elza.	25	F	None	20Jl02Bo
HEARNAN, B.	11	M	None	20Jl02Bo
My.	07	F	Child	20Jl02Bo
Thos.	08	M	Child	20Jl02Bo
SCALLON, A.	35	M	Unknown	20Jl02Bo
Moses	26	M	Unknown	20Jl02Bo
M.	24	M	Unknown	20Jl02Bo
Elza.	22	F	None	20Jl02Bo
SULLIVAN, Mgt.	30	F	None	20Jl02Bo
ROURKE, Betsy	20	F	None	20Jl02Bo
John	18	M	Laborer	20Jl02Bo
Peter	17	M	Unknown	20Jl02Bo
MORAN, J.	36	M	Unknown	20Jl02Bo
Wm.	26	M	Unknown	20Jl02Bo
Cath.	30	F	None	20Jl02Bo
Mgt.	10	F	None	20Jl02Bo
Ellen	08	F	Child	20Jl02Bo
John	04	M	Child	20Jl02Bo
Cath.	01	F	Child	20Jl02Bo
Ann	01	F	Child	20Jl02Bo
OBRIEN, M.	25	M	Unknown	20Jl02Bo
RILY, Ann	20	F	None	20Jl02Bo
MCANERY, My.	25	F	None	20Jl02Bo
MCCRUMM, Biddy	13	F	None	20Jl02Bo
RYAN, Bgt.	25	F	None	20Jl02Bo
GREVY, D.	35	M	Unknown	20Jl02Bo
BURNS, A.	20	M	Unknown	20Jl02Bo
CALLEGROHAN, D.	20	M	Unknown	20Jl02Bo
CORMACK, Cath.	24	F	None	20Jl02Bo
WILLS, Bezy.	24	F	None	20Jl02Bo

NAMES OF PASSENGERS	AGE	SEX	OCCUPATIONS	DATE PORT SHIP
WILLS, Ann	14	F	None	20J102Bo
NEELY, J.	70	M	Unknown	20J102Bo
FARRELLY, Cath.	21	F	None	20J102Bo
HOLWELL, A.	35	M	Unknown	20J102Bo
Jane	30	F	None	20J102Bo
LYONS, My.	26	F	None	20J102Bo
HOLWELL, J.	07	M	Child	20J102Bo
Mary	04	F	Child	20J102Bo
Francis	01	F	Child	20J102Bo
LALLY, Cath.	20	F	None	20J102Bo
WILLIS, J.R.	30	M	Unknown	20J102Bo
CONNELL, J.	25	M	Unknown	20J102Bo
HENEAY, T.	30	M	Unknown	20J102Bo
Wm.	20	M	Unknown	20J102Bo
Mich.	16	M	Unknown	20J102Bo
Richd.	56	M	Unknown	20J102Bo
My.	56	F	None	20J102Bo
My.	18	F	None	20J102Bo
Judy	25	F	None	20J102Bo
MCGANN, W.	25	M	Unknown	20J102Bo
BYRNES, L.	21	M	Laborer	20J102Bo
LEES, G.	40	M	Unknown	20J102Bo
Jane	38	F	None	20J102Bo
Joseph	10	M	None	20J102Bo
Elzbt.Jane	08	F	Child	20J102Bo
RILY, Ahe.	18	F	None	20J102Bo
HERN, M.	20	M	Unknown	20J102Bo
CORCORAN, Sarah	20	F	None	20J102Bo
FORNAY, J.	21	M	Unknown	20J102Bo
VERDAN, Cath.	30	F	None	20J102Bo
Ann	05	F	Child	20J102Bo
Mary	01	F	Child	20J102Bo
Cath.	02	F	Child	20J102Bo
DOLAN, My.	35	F	None	20J102Bo
John	10	M	None	20J102Bo
PHILLIPS, M.M.	40	M	Mechanic	20J102Bo
Mary	40	F	None	20J102Bo
Pat	13	M	None	20J102Bo
KENAGH, M.	25	M	None	20J102Bo
NAUGHTON, W.	25	M	None	20J102Bo
Honora	20	F	None	20J102Bo
KENSHALLEN, P.	28	M	Unknown	20J102Bo
DUNN, P.	20	M	Unknown	20J102Bo
GANNON, D.	25	M	Unknown	20J102Bo
CUSAK, T.	20	M	Unknown	20J102Bo
ATKINSON, J.	20	M	Unknown	20J102Bo
GRATTON, J.	25	M	Unknown	20J102Bo
WATE, F.	27	M	Unknown	20J102Bo
My.	22	F	None	20J102Bo
COSTELLO, P.	40	M	Unknown	20J102Bo
My.	40	F	None	20J102Bo
Matilda	01	F	Child	20J102Bo
Bdgt.	04	F	Child	20J102Bo
Wm.	04	M	Child	20J102Bo
LYNCH, N.	24	M	Unknown	20J102Bo
Mgt.	26	F	None	20J102Bo
BYRNES, M.	24	M	Unknown	20J102Bo
RILY, My.	20	F	None	20J102Bo
CAIN, Sally	18	F	None	20J102Bo
STEWART, Mgt.	40	F	None	20J102Bo
Mgt.	21	F	None	20J102Bo
Thos.	24	M	Unknown	20J102Bo
MCANALLY, F.	24	M	Mechanic	20J102Bo
TRAYNOR, T.	20	M	Unknown	20J102Bo
GILLAM, P.	30	M	Unknown	20J102Bo
CUNNINGHAM, My.	20	F	None	20J102Bo
HUGHES, M.	30	M	Unknown	20J102Bo
SCOTT, R.	40	M	Unknown	20J102Bo
Henry	40	M	Unknown	20J102Bo
Ellen	40	F	None	20J102Bo
Jannett	16	F	None	20J102Bo
Henry	14	M	None	20J102Bo
William	09	M	Child	20J102Bo
Thos.	05	M	Child	20J102Bo
COLLINS, Ann	56	F	None	20J102Bo
COLLINS, Martin	30	M	Mechanic	20J102Bo
James	34	M	Unknown	20J102Bo
Edward	20	M	Unknown	20J102Bo
Cath.	18	F	None	20J102Bo
Ann	15	F	None	20J102Bo
CUSACK, J.	16	M	Unknown	20J102Bo
RYAN, T.	25	M	Unknown	20J102Bo
Jas.	20	M	Unknown	20J102Bo
MILLS, J.	20	M	Unknown	20J102Bo
GRAHAM, J.	25	M	Unknown	20J102Bo
WALTERS, M.	28	M	Unknown	20J102Bo
Nelly	28	F	None	20J102Bo
My.	01	F	Child	20J102Bo
WALSH, M.	40	M	Unknown	20J102Bo
MULHALL, J.	26	M	Unknown	20J102Bo
Cath.	21	F	None	20J102Bo
CORLESS, J.	23	M	Unknown	20J102Bo
U	20	F	Wife	20J102Bo
OWENS, Mgt.	16	F	None	20J102Bo
CONELLY, J.	22	M	Unknown	20J102Bo
Bgt.	20	F	None	20J102Bo
MCDONNELL, My.	25	F	None	20J102Bo
KELLY, Bgt.	25	F	None	20J102Bo
TUNNY, B.	20	M	Unknown	20J102Bo
THOMPSON, W.	35	M	Unknown	20J102Bo
Elza.	35	F	None	20J102Bo
George	18	M	Unknown	20J102Bo
Joseph	13	M	None	20J102Bo
HANCOCK, T.	20	M	Unknown	20J102Bo
Augusta	13	F	None	20J102Bo
DUFFY, G.	21	M	Mechanic	20J102Bo
GARRAY, E.	18	M	Unknown	20J102Bo
MCDONAGH, J.	21	M	Unknown	20J102Bo
HARNLY, P.M.	24	M	Unknown	20J102Bo
LONGWOOD, W.	20	M	Unknown	20J102Bo
MCKENNA, E.	25	M	Unknown	20J102Bo
BOLBEN, J.	24	M	Unknown	20J102Bo
Wm.	13	M	None	20J102Bo
BROWN, S.	30	M	Unknown	20J102Bo
LITTLE, J.	35	M	Unknown	20J102Bo
U	30	F	Wife	20J102Bo
W.	15	M	None	20J102Bo
My.	14	F	None	20J102Bo
Isaac	11	M	None	20J102Bo
John	09	M	Child	20J102Bo
Joseph	05	M	Child	20J102Bo
WHEELEN, J.	25	M	Mechanic	20J102Bo
SMALL, J.	30	M	Unknown	20J102Bo
HAYDEN, P.	35	M	Unknown	20J102Bo
ONEILL, J.	22	M	Unknown	20J102Bo
Francis	26	M	Unknown	20J102Bo
Arthur	18	M	Unknown	20J102Bo
Michl.	16	M	Unknown	20J102Bo
Jane	14	F	None	20J102Bo
MCCLOSKY, J.	18	M	Unknown	20J102Bo
SHEPARD, W.	23	M	Unknown	20J102Bo
OBRIEN, P.	28	M	Unknown	20J102Bo
WATSON, J.	30	M	Unknown	20J102Bo
BUTLER, Benjamin	32	M	Unknown	20J102Bo
CROWTHER, R.	30	M	Unknown	20J102Bo
QUAIL, J.	25	M	Unknown	20J102Bo
LOGAN, My.	18	F	None	20J102Bo
SPAUM, T.	70	M	Unknown	20J102Bo
Ann	70	F	None	20J102Bo
Robt.	20	M	Unknown	20J102Bo
RYDER, J.	25	M	Unknown	20J102Bo
Teresa	22	F	None	20J102Bo
LETHAM, J.	20	M	Unknown	20J102Bo
BREADAN, M.	30	M	Unknown	20J102Bo
RYLE, P.	25	M	Unknown	20J102Bo
DIXON, T.	25	M	Unknown	20J102Bo
LOWTHERAND, E.	24	M	Mechanic	20J102Bo
BRESLIN, Ann	18	F	None	20J102Bo
MALONY, Ma.	30	F	None	20J102Bo
QUIGLY, E.	28	M	Unknown	20J102Bo

NAMES OF PASSENGERS	A G E	S E X	OCCUPATIONS	DATE PORT SHIP
BURNEL, T.	20	M	Unknown	20J102Bo
HARPER, T.	30	M	Unknown	20J102Bo
Cath.	40	F	None	20J102Bo
Rose	01	F	Child	20J102Bo
MURRY, J.	41	M	Unknown	20J102Bo
Pat	12	M	None	20J102Bo
LARKIN, P.	25	M	Unknown	20J102Bo
Mich.	16	M	Unknown	20J102Bo
GRAHAM, J.	21	M	Unknown	20J102Bo
CHILD, E.	21	M	Unknown	20J102Bo
KEEFE, B.	50	M	Unknown	20J102Bo
Betty	50	F	None	20J102Bo
John	20	M	Unknown	20J102Bo
Bryan	18	M	Unknown	20J102Bo
Betty	22	F	None	20J102Bo
Mella	20	F	Unknown	20J102Bo
DEAN, J.M.	25	F	Unknown	20J102Bo
RUTLEDGE, Cath.	17	F	None	20J102Bo
HART, M.	20	M	Farmer	20J102Bo
Hannah	20	F	None	20J102Bo
CURRAN, J.	32	M	Unknown	20J102Bo
Hann.	28	F	None	20J102Bo
ALLEN, My.	16	F	None	20J102Bo
CUNELY, D.	22	M	Unknown	20J102Bo
MONKS, M.	24	M	Unknown	20J102Bo
Mgt.	22	F	None	20J102Bo
GUNNELL, W.	40	M	Unknown	20J102Bo
My.	40	F	None	20J102Bo
John	23	M	Unknown	20J102Bo
Jane	13	F	None	20J102Bo
David	08	M	Child	20J102Bo
Wm.	05	M	Child	20J102Bo
HAZEN, W.	26	M	Unknown	20J102Bo
HAMILL, Jane	40	F	None	20J102Bo
Elza.	20	F	None	20J102Bo
Ellen	19	F	None	20J102Bo
CROTHERS, J.	29	M	Unknown	20J102Bo
MCDONNELL, C.	15	M	None	20J102Bo
ADAMS, W.	29	M	Laborer	20J102Bo
Thos.	15	M	Unknown	20J102Bo
THOMAS, J.	30	M	Unknown	20J102Bo
EALERY, Mgt.	10	F	None	20J102Bo
ROCHE, J.	42	M	Unknown	20J102Bo
Betty	36	F	None	20J102Bo
My.	14	F	None	20J102Bo
John	12	M	None	20J102Bo
Elza.	10	F	None	20J102Bo
James	08	M	Child	20J102Bo
Thos.	06	M	Child	20J102Bo
Rosann	02	F	Child	20J102Bo
FEGAN, Rose	40	F	None	20J102Bo
KEY, P.	20	M	Unknown	20J102Bo
MCLOUNFREN, Utt.	20	F	None	20J102Bo
MCGARGEHN, N.	18	M	Unknown	20J102Bo
DALY, P.	26	M	Unknown	20J102Bo
OHARA, Jane	20	F	None	20J102Bo
MULLAN, Bgt.	40	F	None	20J102Bo
Pat	11	M	None	20J102Bo
John	06	M	Child	20J102Bo
Mgt.	06	F	Child	20J102Bo
Cath.	02	F	Child	20J102Bo
HILLON, My.	20	F	None	20J102Bo
FLEMING, J.	40	M	Unknown	20J102Bo
Jane	30	F	None	20J102Bo
WARNOCH, My.	20	F	None	20J102Bo
SMITH, R.	25	M	Unknown	20J102Bo
ROURKE, A.	21	M	Unknown	20J102Bo
HOPE, Mgt.	28	F	None	20J102Bo
Bgt.	20	F	None	20J102Bo
Ellen	18	F	None	20J102Bo
MCGUNN, R.	40	M	Unknown	20J102Bo
Jane	40	F	None	20J102Bo
Robt.	20	M	Unknown	20J102Bo
John	13	M	None	20J102Bo
Jane	20	F	None	20J102Bo
MCGUNN, My.	21	F	None	20J102Bo
DEALIN, P.	28	M	Unknown	20J102Bo
FARLY, P.	20	M	Unknown	20J102Bo
CALLGLIN, My.	20	F	None	20J102Bo
SHENFAHN, My.	15	F	None	20J102Bo
BOGLAN, Elza.	20	F	None	20J102Bo
MCDONNELL, T.	30	M	Laborer	20J102Bo
Jas.	20	M	Unknown	20J102Bo
KENY, My.	40	F	None	20J102Bo
DOOLAN, Bgt.	40	F	None	20J102Bo
Henry	20	M	Unknown	20J102Bo
KENEDY, Hester	11	F	None	20J102Bo
DIMOND, Ann	20	F	None	20J102Bo
CAULFD, J.M.	20	M	Unknown	20J102Bo
BURNS, My.	20	F	None	20J102Bo
MONAGHAN, My.	40	F	None	20J102Bo
Bgt.	28	F	None	20J102Bo
John	08	M	Child	20J102Bo
JAMSEN, W.	20	M	Unknown	20J102Bo
BARDEN, P.	20	M	Unknown	20J102Bo
GEERY, A.	24	M	Unknown	20J102Bo
WILLERS, J.	75	M	Unknown	20J102Bo

SWAN 20 JULY 1847

From Cork

NAMES OF PASSENGERS	A G E	S E X	OCCUPATIONS	DATE PORT SHIP
COSTELLO, Mary	40	F	None	20J114Ix
Tim (H)	40	M	Farmer	20J114Ix
Robt.	13	M	None	20J114Ix
Danl.	04	M	Child	20J114Ix
RUCH, Mike	26	M	Farmer	20J114Ix
COCHRANE, Ellen	20	F	None	20J114Ix
Judy	20	F	None	20J114Ix
HALEY, Mary	20	F	None	20J114Ix
HILL, Mary	20	F	None	20J114Ix
SEALY, Wm.	20	M	Farmer	20J114Ix
REGAN, Jno.	23	M	Farmer	20J114Ix
DONOVAN, Pat	48	M	Farmer	20J114Ix
Mike	18	M	Farmer	20J114Ix
MARLEY, David	30	M	Farmer	20J114Ix
Abby	18	F	None	20J114Ix
KEITH, David	25	M	Farmer	20J114Ix
HENNESSEY, Thomas	28	M	Farmer	20J114Ix
Ellen	28	F	None	20J114Ix
CANLY, Morris	28	M	Farmer	20J114Ix
HENNESSY, Danl.	04	M	Child	20J114Ix
DONALD, Tim	50	M	Farmer	20J114Ix
MCCARTHY, Denis	40	M	Farmer	20J114Ix
Kate	35	F	None	20J114Ix
Sarah	50	F	None	20J114Ix
FEHN, Magt.	20	F	None	20J114Ix
DRADY, Denis	24	M	Farmer	20J114Ix
John	09	M	Child	20J114Ix
Abby	40	F	None	20J114Ix
REY, John	21	M	Farmer	20J114Ix
Mike	17	M	Farmer	20J114Ix
MURPHY, Danl.	35	M	Farmer	20J114Ix
Julia	30	F	None	20J114Ix
Mary	08	F	Child	20J114Ix
Jno.	05	M	Child	20J114Ix
Danl.	06	M	Child	20J114Ix
Tim	.04	M	Infant	20J114Ix
CALLAHAN, Ellen	40	F	None	20J114Ix
Jas.	19	M	Farmer	20J114Ix
Johanna	22	F	None	20J114Ix
SHEEHAN, Edwd.	40	M	Farmer	20J114Ix
LYNCH, Mary	40	F	None	20J114Ix
Mike	26	M	Farmer	20J114Ix

NAMES OF PASSENGERS	AGE	SEX	OCCUPATIONS	DATE PORT SHIP
DRINNERY, Mary	26	F	None	20J114Ix
Abby	20	F	None	20J114Ix
OCALLAHAN, Chas.	28	M	Farmer	20J114Ix
LADLEY, Tim	32	M	Farmer	20J114Ix
CURDEN, Nancy	20	F	None	20J114Ix
LYONS, Jno.	15	M	Farmer	20J114Ix
Kate	22	F	None	20J114Ix
PARKER, Owen	15	M	Farmer	20J114Ix
REORDEN, Joha.	23	F	None	20J114Ix
HENDLIN, Joha.	20	F	None	20J114Ix
DOOLAN, Tim	20	M	Farmer	20J114Ix
David	46	M	Farmer	20J114Ix
HAYS, Mike	18	M	Farmer	20J114Ix
LIMERHAN, Kate	26	F	None	20J114Ix
CONOR, Ellen	24	F	None	20J114Ix
SHEEHAN, Pat	18	M	Farmer	20J114Ix
CARROLL, Roger	29	M	Farmer	20J114Ix
Kate	53	F	None	20J114Ix
Kate	53	F	None	20J114Ix
Patk.	22	M	Farmer	20J114Ix
Ann	20	F	None	20J114Ix
Roger	18	M	Farmer	20J114Ix
Biddy	16	F	None	20J114Ix
FERNEY, Maurice	29	M	Farmer	20J114Ix
GLEESON, Thos.	25	M	Farmer	20J114Ix
BYNEES, Kate	23	F	None	20J114Ix
FITZGERALD, Jno.	40	M	Farmer	20J114Ix
Mary	35	F	None	20J114Ix
Edwd.	10	M	Farmer	20J114Ix
Chas.	10	M	Farmer	20J114Ix
NEEVILL, Joha.	33	F	None	20J114Ix
U	.00	F	Infant	20J114Ix
MCCARTHY, Edwd.	35	M	Farmer	20J114Ix
Ellen	30	F	None	20J114Ix
DWYER, Jno.	06	M	Child	20J114Ix
RYAN, Jas.	30	M	Farmer	20J114Ix
Kate	22	F	None	20J114Ix
HUDDLE, Honora	19	F	None	20J114Ix
Biddy	18	F	None	20J114Ix
EGAN, Wm.	24	M	Farmer	20J114Ix
CONNER, Mary	21	F	None	20J114Ix
CONNELL, Jerry	20	M	Farmer	20J114Ix
HENNESSY, Jno.F.	37	M	Farmer	20J114Ix
Hannah	30	F	None	20J114Ix
Jno.J.	09	M	Child	20J114Ix
Wm.	07	M	Child	20J114Ix
Frances	05	F	Child	20J114Ix
David	04	M	Child	20J114Ix
RUSSELL, Thos.J.	25	M	Farmer	20J114Ix

GEM 20 JULY 1847

From Waterford

NAMES OF PASSENGERS	AGE	SEX	OCCUPATIONS	DATE PORT SHIP
MCGREAN, Magt.	24	F	None	20J116Re
Jno.	15	M	None	20J116Re
Wm.	13	M	None	20J116Re
DOWLING, Wm.	25	M	Mechanic	20J116Re
WALSH, Martin	27	M	Mechanic	20J116Re
MORRISON, Frances	20	F	None	20J116Re
DWYER, Margt.	20	F	None	20J116Re
BERNE, Mich.	25	M	Mechanic	20J116Re
CULLINE, Wm.	22	M	Mechanic	20J116Re
CUMMINS, Jno.	23	M	Mechanic	20J116Re
Mary	25	F	None	20J116Re
MCARTY, Timothy	50	M	Farmer	20J116Re
Chas.	14	M	None	20J116Re
Jas.	16	M	None	20J116Re
Magt.	19	F	None	20J116Re
KEARNY, Mary	15	F	None	20J116Re
CAHILL, Mich.	35	M	Farmer	20J116Re
Pat	23	M	Farmer	20J116Re
CARTY, Denis	19	M	Farmer	20J116Re
Bridget	17	F	None	20J116Re
MORFRENCY, Bridget	30	F	None	20J116Re
REATELY, Thos.	21	M	Laborer	20J116Re
Thos.	25	M	Laborer	20J116Re
WALSH, Jno.	20	M	Laborer	20J116Re
FLINN, Jno.	26	M	Laborer	20J116Re
Margt.	18	F	None	20J116Re
CASY, Thos.	25	M	Laborer	20J116Re
BRUCE, Wm.	23	M	Soldier	20J116Re
CARNAN, Wm.	24	M	Soldier	20J116Re
COPELAND, Robt.	22	M	Soldier	20J116Re
EGNON, Phil	23	M	Soldier	20J116Re
FRAON, Geo.	23	M	Soldier	20J116Re

SIDDONS 24 JULY 1847

From Liverpool

NAMES OF PASSENGERS	AGE	SEX	OCCUPATIONS	DATE PORT SHIP
GRAY, Wilson	34	M	None	24J102Bx
LOGAN, Geo.J.	20	M	None	24J102Bx
GRAY, Alex	20	M	None	24J102Bx
Jos.B.	28	M	None	24J102Bx
RESK, Jno.	26	M	Clerk	24J102Bx
SAUNDERSON, Wm.	25	M	Farmer	24J102Bx
Mary	25	F	None	24J102Bx
MORTHAGH, Mich.	28	M	Farmer	24J102Bx
Mary	22	F	None	24J102Bx
Jno.	01	M	Child	24J102Bx
CONNELLEY, Bess	22	F	None	24J102Bx
KELLEY, R.V.	24	M	Farmer	24J102Bx
OSULLIVAN, Jas.	25	M	Farmer	24J102Bx
OBRIEN, Danl.	25	M	Farmer	24J102Bx
Hona.	21	F	None	24J102Bx
OSULLIVAN, U-Mrs.	18	F	None	24J102Bx
CAMPBELL, Terence	38	M	Farmer	24J102Bx
Cath.	38	F	None	24J102Bx
Anne	17	F	None	24J102Bx
Mary	10	F	None	24J102Bx
Patk.	01	M	Child	24J102Bx
CALDWELL, Jno.	30	M	Laborer	24J102Bx
WALSH, Wm.	65	M	Laborer	24J102Bx
ADELAIDE, Jno.	24	M	Laborer	24J102Bx
Eliz.	24	F	None	24J102Bx
LARNENIAN, Jane	26	F	None	24J102Bx
WRIGHT, Jno.	28	M	Laborer	24J102Bx
FEENEY, Jno.	26	M	Mechanic	24J102Bx
Win.	24	M	Mechanic	24J102Bx
HAIR, Jas.	24	M	Mechanic	24J102Bx
Peter	22	M	Mechanic	24J102Bx
MULVEY, Berd.	30	M	Mechanic	24J102Bx
MCGUIFFE, Jno.	23	M	Mechanic	24J102Bx
WINE, Alex	30	M	Mechanic	24J102Bx
Mary	26	F	None	24J102Bx
HAYRAN, Win.	40	F	None	24J102Bx
KELLY, Anne	25	F	None	24J102Bx
HOBAN, Jno.	50	M	Mechanic	24J102Bx
Bridg.	45	F	None	24J102Bx
Jno.	21	M	Laborer	24J102Bx
Thos.	15	M	Laborer	24J102Bx
Bridg.	24	F	None	24J102Bx
Patk.	14	M	None	24J102Bx
M.	13	M	None	24J102Bx
Wm.	10	M	None	24J102Bx
Danl.	10	M	None	24J102Bx
Jno.	01	M	Child	24J102Bx

NAMES OF PASSENGERS	AGE	SEX	OCCUPATIONS	DATE PORT SHIP	NAMES OF PASSENGERS	AGE	SEX	OCCUPATIONS	DATE PORT SHIP
LUCAS, Geo.	25	M	Laborer	24J102Bx	JACKSON, Jane	18	F	None	24J102Bx
Hana.	21	F	None	24J102Bx	Jas.	16	M	Laborer	24J102Bx
Frans.	04	F	Child	24J102Bx	Jos.	13	M	Laborer	24J102Bx
Frans.	.06	F	Infant	24J102Bx	Jane	22	F	None	24J102Bx
GLANCEY, Peter	22	M	Laborer	24J102Bx	JEFFRY, Fran.	32	M	Laborer	24J102Bx
KEEAN, Owen	40	M	Laborer	24J102Bx	THOMAS, Thos.	27	M	Mechanic	24J102Bx
Biddy	30	F	None	24J102Bx	Nich.	22	M	Mechanic	24J102Bx
Idine	12	F	None	24J102Bx	Catharine	21	F	None	24J102Bx
Mary	08	F	Child	24J102Bx	DORAN, Jno.	24	M	Mechanic	24J102Bx
Jas.	06	M	Child	24J102Bx	BYRNE, Julia	21	F	None	24J102Bx
Jno.	04	M	Child	24J102Bx	Mary	19	F	None	24J102Bx
Sus.	.06	F	Infant	24J102Bx	STANHOUSE, Jas.	25	M	Farmer	24J102Bx
CLARK, Jno.	50	M	Laborer	24J102Bx	THONORD, Jno.	16	M	Farmer	24J102Bx
Maria	45	F	None	24J102Bx	MURPHY, Jas.	30	M	Farmer	24J102Bx
Jno.	30	M	Laborer	24J102Bx	HART, Cath.	22	F	None	24J102Bx
Rachl.	22	F	None	24J102Bx	SAVAN, Patt	36	M	Farmer	24J102Bx
STEINSON, Anne	26	F	None	24J102Bx	GAVAN, Bridy	08	F	Child	24J102Bx
Jas.	20	M	Laborer	24J102Bx	GROWNEY, Owen	50	M	Laborer	24J102Bx
CLARK, Wm.	25	M	Laborer	24J102Bx	Jno.	20	M	Laborer	24J102Bx
ADAMS, Isabela.	18	F	None	24J102Bx	Mary	24	F	None	24J102Bx
KEERS, Mary	17	F	None	24J102Bx	COOKE, Ann	23	F	None	24J102Bx
PRICE, Danl.	15	M	None	24J102Bx	Cath.	07	F	Child	24J102Bx
DONNAGH, Jno.	35	M	Farmer	24J102Bx	DERMOODY, Owen	22	M	Laborer	24J102Bx
Frances	24	F	None	24J102Bx	SMITH, May	24	F	None	24J102Bx
Jas.	24	M	Farmer	24J102Bx	Cath.	22	F	None	24J102Bx
MCLOUGHLIN, Jas.	21	M	Farmer	24J102Bx	LEARY, Danl.	21	M	Laborer	24J102Bx
HIGGINS, Geo.	25	M	Farmer	24J102Bx	DONOVAN, Jno.	18	M	Laborer	24J102Bx
BRIGAN, Bern.	25	M	Farmer	24J102Bx	MCGARRY, Wm.	23	M	Farmer	24J102Bx
MCKEOUGH, Mich.	25	M	Laborer	24J102Bx	CRARIN, Wm.	21	M	Farmer	24J102Bx
DURKAN, Saml.	21	M	Laborer	24J102Bx	JONSON, Geo.	22	M	Farmer	24J102Bx
Agnes	17	F	None	24J102Bx	Esther	20	F	None	24J102Bx
SCOTT, Wm.	25	M	Laborer	24J102Bx	MULLIAN, Wm.	24	M	Farmer	24J102Bx
FIN, Jane	20	F	None	24J102Bx	MOFFIT, Jas.	25	M	Farmer	24J102Bx
CARSON, Agnes	20	F	None	24J102Bx	DAVIS, Wm.	36	M	Laborer	24J102Bx
BARRON, Bern.	25	M	Laborer	24J102Bx	Anne	44	F	None	24J102Bx
Thos.	11	M	Unknown	24J102Bx	David	16	M	Laborer	24J102Bx
FRAONE, Anth.	16	M	Laborer	24J102Bx	ROBERTS, Robt.	30	M	Laborer	24J102Bx
WILLIAMS, Patk.	24	M	Laborer	24J102Bx	HART, Ellen	36	F	None	24J102Bx
CONNIS, Jeffry	38	M	Laborer	24J102Bx	DINER, Patt	25	M	Farmer	24J102Bx
Mary	30	F	None	24J102Bx	LYNCH, Jas.C.	21	M	Farmer	24J102Bx
Mary	11	F	None	24J102Bx	CONWAY, Eugene	28	M	Farmer	24J102Bx
Walter	09	M	Child	24J102Bx	MALONEY, Patk.	27	M	Farmer	24J102Bx
Margt.	07	F	Child	24J102Bx	JERVIS, Thos.	21	M	Farmer	24J102Bx
Bridg.	05	F	Child	24J102Bx	ROBERTS, Ed.	26	M	Laborer	24J102Bx
Jno.	03	M	Child	24J102Bx	Eliza	26	F	None	24J102Bx
Robt.	.00	M	Infant	24J102Bx	BEHAN, Peter	60	M	Laborer	24J102Bx
NOON, Jas.	32	M	Farmer	24J102Bx	ERNSLEY, Jno.	21	M	Laborer	24J102Bx
MURPHY, Jas.	56	M	Farmer	24J102Bx	Ruben	23	M	Laborer	24J102Bx
Cath.	40	F	None	24J102Bx	BOCKELL, Jne.	22	M	Laborer	24J102Bx
Cath.	24	F	None	24J102Bx	DILLON, Cath.	21	F	None	24J102Bx
Sarah-A.	18	F	None	24J102Bx	REED, Biddy	20	F	None	24J102Bx
Mary	13	F	None	24J102Bx	CARSTIN, Mary	21	F	None	24J102Bx
Jas.	11	M	None	24J102Bx	REYNOLDS, Mich.	26	M	Laborer	24J102Bx
LEE, Wm.	25	M	Farmer	24J102Bx	PUGH, Jno.	24	M	Laborer	24J102Bx
Rose	23	F	None	24J102Bx	CARTER, Henry	30	M	Laborer	24J102Bx
Mary	.00	F	Infant	24J102Bx	GREEN, U-Mrs.	60	F	None	24J102Bx
WOODS, Patk.	20	M	Laborer	24J102Bx	Abm.	30	M	Laborer	24J102Bx
MURPHY, Jno.	18	M	Laborer	24J102Bx	PIM, Jno.	24	M	Laborer	24J102Bx
BANON, Anne	20	F	None	24J102Bx	Ellen	22	F	None	24J102Bx
DONIGAN, Jno.	23	M	Laborer	24J102Bx	OHANLON, Ann	24	F	None	24J102Bx
MURPHY, Mich.	35	M	Laborer	24J102Bx	Cath.	06	F	Child	24J102Bx
ARMSTRONG, Jno.	26	M	Laborer	24J102Bx	MCMAHON, Anne	22	F	None	24J102Bx
Jane	20	F	None	24J102Bx	TOWNSEND, Richd.	44	M	Laborer	24J102Bx
Eliza	18	F	None	24J102Bx	LOMITTY, Ellen	21	F	None	24J102Bx
RAHIAL, Jno.	34	M	Farmer	24J102Bx	Maria	20	F	None	24J102Bx
Ann	24	F	None	24J102Bx	REILY, Marten	26	M	Laborer	24J102Bx
TIERNEY, Owen	20	M	Mechanic	24J102Bx	MULLIRN, Wm.	22	M	Laborer	24J102Bx
MOLLONY, Patt.	20	M	Mechanic	24J102Bx	LARDNER, Wm.	21	M	Laborer	24J102Bx
Jno.	20	M	Mechanic	24J102Bx	Jno.	20	M	Laborer	24J102Bx
FEE, Mich.	50	M	Mechanic	24J102Bx	MATTHEWSON, Jno.	30	M	Farmer	24J102Bx
Ellin	40	F	None	24J102Bx	MATHEWS, Albert	30	M	Farmer	24J102Bx
RYAN, Joha.	24	F	None	24J102Bx	Agnes	28	F	None	24J102Bx
GAVAN, Thos.	15	M	Laborer	24J102Bx	Alfred	07	M	Child	24J102Bx
Jno.	32	M	Laborer	24J102Bx	Francis	.00	M	Infant	24J102Bx
JACKSON, Edwd.	23	M	Laborer	24J102Bx	Edwd.	.00	M	Infant	24J102Bx

NAMES OF PASSENGERS	AGE	SEX	OCCUPATIONS	DATE PORT SHIP
MOORE, Jno.	28	M	Farmer	24J102Bx
Julia	17	F	None	24J102Bx
Mary	03	F	Child	24J102Bx
Felix	02	M	Child	24J102Bx
SOMMERS, Maurice	21	M	Farmer	24J102Bx
Ann	20	F	None	24J102Bx
BARRY, Mary	20	F	None	24J102Bx
FORDE, Jno.	25	M	Farmer	24J102Bx
GRIFFIN, Chr.	22	M	Farmer	24J102Bx
CULLIN, Jas.	20	M	Farmer	24J102Bx
DORAN, Mich.	28	M	Laborer	24J102Bx
QUINN, Peter	25	M	Laborer	24J102Bx
Magt.	23	F	None	24J102Bx
MORGAN, Abm.	35	M	Laborer	24J102Bx
Eliza	29	F	None	24J102Bx
Jno.	26	M	Laborer	24J102Bx
RICE, Jos.	16	M	Laborer	24J102Bx
ROBERTS, Jno.	50	M	Farmer	24J102Bx
Ellen	48	F	None	24J102Bx
Henry	28	M	Farmer	24J102Bx
Mary	18	F	None	24J102Bx
Ellen	15	F	None	24J102Bx
Cath.	13	F	None	24J102Bx
Griffith	11	M	None	24J102Bx
Mat.	09	M	Child	24J102Bx
Hanh.	06	F	Child	24J102Bx
Jno.	04	M	Child	24J102Bx
PARRY, Henry	52	M	Farmer	24J102Bx
Mary	13	F	None	24J102Bx
CLARK, Jas.	24	M	Laborer	24J102Bx
STEPHEN, C.E.	20	M	Laborer	24J102Bx
TANBURAN, Wm.	20	M	Laborer	24J102Bx
Jno.	28	M	Laborer	24J102Bx
COFF, Alexs.	28	M	Laborer	24J102Bx
BRANNAN, Patt	22	M	Laborer	24J102Bx
GARLAND, Ed.	21	M	Laborer	24J102Bx
MCGACKAND, Phil.	22	M	Laborer	24J102Bx
COLLINS, Mag.	20	F	None	24J102Bx
NEED, Richd.	20	M	Laborer	24J102Bx
HICKS, Jno.	24	M	Laborer	24J102Bx
MILLER, Mich.	18	M	Laborer	24J102Bx
Thos.	16	M	Laborer	24J102Bx
CONEGAN, Peter	18	M	Laborer	24J102Bx
DUFFY, Ellen	21	F	None	24J102Bx
FERGUSON, Ellen	21	F	None	24J102Bx
BRODRICK, Anne	19	F	None	24J102Bx
FERGUSON, Anne	17	F	None	24J102Bx
TINGLEY, Danl.	21	M	Laborer	24J102Bx
REDDEN, Jno.	22	M	Farmer	24J102Bx
VEY, Patk.	25	M	Farmer	24J102Bx
Keran	24	M	Farmer	24J102Bx
Rose	50	F	None	24J102Bx
MEANY, Mary	20	F	None	24J102Bx
Jas.	21	M	Laborer	24J102Bx
GRIFFIN, Mich.	22	M	Laborer	24J102Bx
FITZGERALD, Mary	22	F	None	24J102Bx
PHEALY, Denis	30	M	Laborer	24J102Bx
COTTER, Jas.	27	M	Farmer	24J102Bx
Cath.	20	F	None	24J102Bx
Cath.	20	F	None	24J102Bx
CAVANAGH, Geo.	21	M	Farmer	24J102Bx
GOUGHLAN, Geo.A.	21	M	Farmer	24J102Bx
SIDNEY, Jno.	18	M	Farmer	24J102Bx
THORT, Mich.	28	M	Mechanic	24J102Bx
Elizth.	19	F	None	24J102Bx
KERMAHON, Susan	22	F	None	24J102Bx
KENNAN, Peter	22	M	Mechanic	24J102Bx
Wm.	05	M	Child	24J102Bx
KERNAN, Peter	28	M	Mechanic	24J102Bx
SWINBORNE, John	23	M	Mechanic	24J102Bx
Jane	20	F	None	24J102Bx
MANNING, Eliza	22	F	None	24J102Bx
CHAUNCY, Jos.	22	M	Mechanic	24J102Bx
SEASDUFF, Jno.	21	M	Mechanic	24J102Bx
LEANY, Jno.	22	M	Mechanic	24J102Bx
LEANY, Cath.	20	F	None	24J102Bx
HITTON, Jno.	28	M	Laborer	24J102Bx
Robt.	30	M	Laborer	24J102Bx
BRADY, Patt	21	M	Laborer	24J102Bx
Mary	21	F	None	24J102Bx
MCDANIEL, Jas.	36	M	Laborer	24J102Bx
MORAN, Bryan	34	M	Laborer	24J102Bx
Anne	25	F	None	24J102Bx
TIGHE, Peter	20	M	Laborer	24J102Bx
DALY, Jno.	40	M	Farmer	24J102Bx
FURNALL, Jno.	40	M	Farmer	24J102Bx
ONEAL, Richd.	44	M	Farmer	24J102Bx
REARDAN, Jas.	19	M	Farmer	24J102Bx
WALSH, Jno.	55	M	Farmer	24J102Bx
Elizth.	50	F	None	24J102Bx
Jno.	25	M	Farmer	24J102Bx
Anastan	25	M	Farmer	24J102Bx
Patk.	24	M	Farmer	24J102Bx
Wm.	22	M	Farmer	24J102Bx
Edwd.	20	M	Farmer	24J102Bx
Thos.	18	M	Farmer	24J102Bx
Mat.	25	M	Farmer	24J102Bx
Mary	20	F	None	24J102Bx
POINEER, Jno.	25	M	Laborer	24J102Bx
Brdgt.	20	F	None	24J102Bx
MCEVOY, Edwd.	25	M	Laborer	24J102Bx
DALEHURST, Anne	25	F	None	24J102Bx
Jno.	22	M	Laborer	24J102Bx
Thos.	20	M	Laborer	24J102Bx
Patt	18	M	Laborer	24J102Bx
DONEVAN, Danl.	25	M	Laborer	24J102Bx
MORRISEY, Mary	17	F	None	24J102Bx
ROYAN, Denis	50	M	Laborer	24J102Bx
GREEN, Matt	56	M	Laborer	24J102Bx
Jane	48	F	None	24J102Bx
Matt	25	M	Laborer	24J102Bx
Thos.	19	M	Laborer	24J102Bx
Nancy	16	F	None	24J102Bx
Elizth.	13	F	None	24J102Bx
Jno.	08	M	Child	24J102Bx
Ellen	03	F	Child	24J102Bx
MCMAHON, Bridy	45	F	None	24J102Bx
Agnes	22	F	None	24J102Bx
Mary	18	F	None	24J102Bx
Peter	20	M	Farmer	24J102Bx
Jas.	11	M	Unknown	24J102Bx
MIDDLETON, Wm.	28	M	Farmer	24J102Bx
MCMAHON, Bridg.	13	F	None	24J102Bx
MURTHA, Rose	13	F	None	24J102Bx
GALLAGER, Jas.	30	M	Laborer	24J102Bx
MORAN, Jas.	60	M	Farmer	24J102Bx
HURLEY, Danl.	40	M	Farmer	24J102Bx
VENTEE, Jno.	25	M	Farmer	24J102Bx
Sarah	22	F	None	24J102Bx
TAYLOR, Geo.	22	M	Farmer	24J102Bx
REILY, Peter	25	M	Farmer	24J102Bx
MARA, Patt	24	M	Farmer	24J102Bx
FEENY, Henry	20	M	Farmer	24J102Bx
DONOUGH, Phil	20	M	Farmer	24J102Bx
ENGLISH, Patk.	28	M	Farmer	24J102Bx
THOMPSON, Jas.	28	M	Merchant	24J102Bx
Mich.	09	M	Child	24J102Bx
COBY, Peter	45	M	Farmer	24J102Bx
Louis	11	M	Farmer	24J102Bx
RAY, Wm.	29	M	Farmer	24J102Bx
Edwd.	20	M	Farmer	24J102Bx
TRACY, Patt	20	M	Farmer	24J102Bx
MCRAY, Mary	17	F	None	24J102Bx
QUILLEN, Jane-M.	21	F	None	24J102Bx
DOLAN, Anne	20	F	None	24J102Bx
MORAN, Cath.	50	F	None	24J102Bx
Cath.	20	F	None	24J102Bx
EGAN, Charlotte	00	F	None	24J102Bx
MANSFIELD, Ellen	21	F	None	24J102Bx
BRADLEY, Bridg.	20	F	None	24J102Bx

NAMES OF PASSENGERS	AGE	SEX	OCCUPATIONS	DATE PORT SHIP
LYONS, Bryan	19	M	Laborer	24JI02Bx
TIGHE, Betty	00	F	None	24JI02Bx
SLATER, Henry	40	M	Laborer	24JI02Bx
GEVIR, Elizth.	40	F	None	24JI02Bx
JACKSON, Wm.	52	M	Laborer	24JI02Bx
Jno.	26	M	Laborer	24JI02Bx
STEENHOUSE, Geo.	20	M	Laborer	24JI02Bx
SHOLENCE, Mary	16	F	None	24JI02Bx
MULLER, Mary	20	F	None	24JI02Bx

PRINCE-RADALI 24 JULY 1847

From Cork

NAMES OF PASSENGERS	AGE	SEX	OCCUPATIONS	DATE PORT SHIP
DORGAN, W.	20	M	Laborer	24JI14Rf
DONNOGHUE, D.	40	U	Unknown	24JI14Rf
Cath.	25	F	Unknown	24JI14Rf
Johanna	20	F	Unknown	24JI14Rf
PERRY, E.	40	M	Unknown	24JI14Rf
CONNELL, T.	40	U	Unknown	24JI14Rf
HADDOGAN, J.	20	U	Unknown	24JI14Rf
DILLON, Ellen	29	F	Unknown	24JI14Rf
TWIGS, Cath.	10	F	Unknown	24JI14Rf
SULLIVAN, Jane	30	F	Unknown	24JI14Rf
EGAN, Bgt.	40	F	Unknown	24JI14Rf
Thomas	30	M	Unknown	24JI14Rf
Edward	25	M	Unknown	24JI14Rf
Johanna	20	F	Unknown	24JI14Rf
ROCHE, J.	40	U	Unknown	24JI14Rf
SULLIVAN, J.	41	U	Unknown	24JI14Rf
HEYERYD, H.	35	U	Unknown	24JI14Rf
Kate	23	F	Unknown	24JI14Rf
SHREHAN, H.	30	F	Unknown	24JI14Rf
CASTY, J.	35	U	Unknown	24JI14Rf
MONIHAN, P.	30	U	Unknown	24JI14Rf
MAHIGAN, My.	30	F	Unknown	24JI14Rf
MURPHY, J.	35	U	Unknown	24JI14Rf
My.	30	F	Unknown	24JI14Rf
DAVIDSON, J.B.	20	U	Unknown	24JI14Rf
HERLY, M.	40	U	Unknown	24JI14Rf
Denis	30	M	Unknown	24JI14Rf
FLYNN, M.	38	U	Unknown	24JI14Rf
MANCALY, Jo.	25	U	Unknown	24JI14Rf
DRISCOLL, D.	40	U	Unknown	24JI14Rf
SULLIVAN, T.	30	U	Unknown	24JI14Rf
Denis	25	M	Unknown	24JI14Rf
David	22	M	Unknown	24JI14Rf
Peggy	20	F	Unknown	24JI14Rf
My.	20	F	Unknown	24JI14Rf
Julia	22	F	Unknown	24JI14Rf
DRISCOLL, J.	20	U	Unknown	24JI14Rf
Kate	01	F	Child	24JI14Rf
CROSBIE, M.	25	F	Unknown	24JI14Rf
MORAN, M.	30	F	Unknown	24JI14Rf
HANLY, M.	30	F	Unknown	24JI14Rf
DRISCOLL, J.	01	M	Child	24JI14Rf
SULLIVAN, C.	40	M	Laborer	24JI14Rf
Margt.	40	F	None	24JI14Rf
William	12	M	None	24JI14Rf
Jeremiah	10	M	None	24JI14Rf
My.	08	F	Child	24JI14Rf
BROWN, D.	27	M	Unknown	24JI14Rf
MOYLAN, J.	30	M	Unknown	24JI14Rf
TOBIN, Ellen	30	F	None	24JI14Rf
MCCARTY, D.	30	M	Unknown	24JI14Rf
KENNEDY, J.	30	M	Unknown	24JI14Rf
KEAN, J.	25	M	Unknown	24JI14Rf
REFFEN, E.	35	M	Unknown	24JI14Rf
Kate	45	F	None	24JI14Rf
FLYNN, Ellen	40	F	None	24JI14Rf
KEARNY, P.	20	M	Unknown	24JI14Rf
James	30	M	Unknown	24JI14Rf
MAHON, M.	30	M	Unknown	24JI14Rf
QUAID, P.	30	M	Unknown	24JI14Rf
DELLON, J.	30	M	Unknown	24JI14Rf
MCCARTY, T.	35	M	Unknown	24JI14Rf
Kate	30	F	None	24JI14Rf
Ellen	20	F	None	24JI14Rf
MCEVOY, P.	28	M	Unknown	24JI14Rf
LOOKEN, D.	25	M	Unknown	24JI14Rf
HERTNY, T.	20	M	Unknown	24JI14Rf
KEENE, P.	25	M	Unknown	24JI14Rf
GRADY, P.	29	M	Unknown	24JI14Rf
COSTELLO, M.	29	M	Unknown	24JI14Rf
EVANS, J.	40	M	Unknown	24JI14Rf
MURRY, J.	40	M	Unknown	24JI14Rf
HACKNY, J.	20	M	Unknown	24JI14Rf
GREGORY, J.	30	M	Unknown	24JI14Rf
LANE, J.	23	M	Unknown	24JI14Rf
MAHONY, P.	25	M	Unknown	24JI14Rf
CLANCY, My.	20	F	Unknown	24JI14Rf
KEELY, J.	25	M	Unknown	24JI14Rf
SHEA, J.	30	M	Unknown	24JI14Rf
BROWN, P.	35	M	Unknown	24JI14Rf
DYSON, J.	30	M	Unknown	24JI14Rf
BOGLY, J.	30	M	Unknown	24JI14Rf
MALONE, M.	40	M	Unknown	24JI14Rf

ANTWERP 24 JULY 1847

From Belfast

NAMES OF PASSENGERS	AGE	SEX	OCCUPATIONS	DATE PORT SHIP
BRYAN, T.	19	M	Laborer	24JI07Rh
J.	17	M	Laborer	24JI07Rh
D.	12	M	None	24JI07Rh
BROWN, W.	19	M	Mechanic	24JI07Rh
BARCKLEY, J.	21	M	Mechanic	24JI07Rh
J.	17	M	Mechanic	24JI07Rh
H.	14	M	Mechanic	24JI07Rh
A.	15	F	Unknown	24JI07Rh
MCCARTHY, J.	26	M	Mechanic	24JI07Rh
THOMPSON, J.	25	M	Mechanic	24JI07Rh
FERGUSON, J.	20	M	Mechanic	24JI07Rh
HAMIL, M.	27	M	Mechanic	24JI07Rh
WHITE, J.	22	M	Laborer	24JI07Rh
GILLON, J.	21	F	Unknown	24JI07Rh
DEURCAN, M.	22	F	Unknown	24JI07Rh
J.	20	F	Unknown	24JI07Rh
M.	18	F	Unknown	24JI07Rh
CORRAN, E.	17	M	Laborer	24JI07Rh
MCFARON, J.	57	M	Farmer	24JI07Rh
E.	50	F	Unknown	24JI07Rh
E.	16	M	Farmer	24JI07Rh
A.	14	M	Farmer	24JI07Rh
S.	11	F	Unknown	24JI07Rh
E.	05	F	Child	24JI07Rh
E.	08	F	Child	24JI07Rh
S.	06	F	Child	24JI07Rh
AYRE, J.	51	M	Farmer	24JI07Rh
S.	40	F	Unknown	24JI07Rh
M.	18	F	Unknown	24JI07Rh
E.	10	F	Unknown	24JI07Rh
J.	07	M	Child	24JI07Rh
QUIN, J.	40	M	Laborer	24JI07Rh
B.	30	F	Unknown	24JI07Rh
M.	05	M	Child	24JI07Rh
S.	02	M	Child	24JI07Rh
THOMPSON, J.	16	M	Laborer	24JI07Rh

NAMES OF PASSENGERS		AGE	SEX	OCCUPATIONS	DATE PORT SHIP
MCGILL, J.		18	F	Unknown	24J107Rh
DOGHERTY, M.		22	F	Unknown	24J107Rh
GALLOWAY, A.		20	F	Unknown	24J107Rh
B.		18	F	Unknown	24J107Rh
GREAVY, P.M.		24	M	Laborer	24J107Rh
ONEIL, C.		19	M	Mechanic	24J107Rh
TEEGLN, W.		17	M	Mechanic	24J107Rh
MCCLUSKEY, A.		57	M	Mechanic	24J107Rh
S.	(W)	54	F	Unknown	24J107Rh
M.J.	(D)	19	F	Unknown	24J107Rh
E.	(D)	17	F	Unknown	24J107Rh
HUMPHRYS, J.		44	M	Farmer	24J107Rh
A.		36	F	Unknown	24J107Rh
A.		66	F	Unknown	24J107Rh
HAMILL, C.		32	F	Unknown	24J107Rh
J.		02	F	Child	24J107Rh
MCNALLY, J.		28	M	Mechanic	24J107Rh
E.		26	F	Unknown	24J107Rh
HEPBOURN, H.		21	M	Mechanic	24J107Rh
HUNTER, A.		20	F	Unknown	24J107Rh
DAYTON, S.		19	M	Mechanic	24J107Rh
CARSON, E.		40	F	Unknown	24J107Rh
T.	(S)	17	M	Mechanic	24J107Rh
W.	(S)	13	M	Mechanic	24J107Rh
R.	(S)	11	M	Mechanic	24J107Rh
TRIMTLE, E.		19	F	Unknown	24J107Rh
MCCULLOUGH, P.		22	M	Mechanic	24J107Rh
MCGARTH, J.		20	M	Mechanic	24J107Rh
TAYLOR, M.		22	F	Unknown	24J107Rh
CULLERN, A.		33	F	Unknown	24J107Rh
A.		14	F	Unknown	24J107Rh
SIMPSON, E.		83	F	Unknown	24J107Rh
THOMPSON, E.		28	M	Mechanic	24J107Rh
MULLEN, P.		18	M	Mechanic	24J107Rh
LAUGHAN, H.		23	F	Unknown	24J107Rh
B.		20	F	Unknown	24J107Rh
CONALLY, J.		20	M	Mechanic	24J107Rh
B.		19	F	Unknown	24J107Rh
SLYMAN, J.		48	M	Mechanic	24J107Rh
C.	(D)	16	F	Unknown	24J107Rh
O.	(D)	14	F	Unknown	24J107Rh
M.	(D)	12	F	Unknown	24J107Rh
WALDEN, J.		20	M	Mechanic	24J107Rh
ELLIFF, P.		20	M	Mechanic	24J107Rh
MCCANN, M.		45	F	Unknown	24J107Rh
TURNER, M.		44	F	Unknown	24J107Rh
A.	(D)	18	F	Unknown	24J107Rh
J.	(S)	11	M	None	24J107Rh
ELLIS, J.		35	M	Laborer	24J107Rh
BOYLE, C.		23	M	Laborer	24J107Rh
MCVEIGH, R.		20	M	Laborer	24J107Rh
J.		21	F	Unknown	24J107Rh
JOHNSON, M.		50	F	Unknown	24J107Rh
M.	(D)	20	F	Unknown	24J107Rh
J.	(D)	18	F	Unknown	24J107Rh
LITTLE, M.		60	F	Unknown	24J107Rh
BOYD, J.		40	M	Laborer	24J107Rh
ADAMS, R.		25	M	Laborer	24J107Rh
R.		22	F	Unknown	24J107Rh
TRUMBLE, M.		20	F	Unknown	24J107Rh
CUNNINGHAM, R.		30	F	Unknown	24J107Rh
E.	(D)	02	F	Child	24J107Rh
MCCANN, O.		50	M	Laborer	24J107Rh
ADAMS, R.		50	M	Farmer	24J107Rh
R.	(S)	30	M	Farmer	24J107Rh
A.	(W)	50	F	Unknown	24J107Rh
M.	(D)	27	F	Unknown	24J107Rh
M.	(D)	24	F	Unknown	24J107Rh
B.	(D)	17	F	Unknown	24J107Rh
T.	(D)	23	F	Unknown	24J107Rh
KELLY, P.		30	M	Mechanic	24J107Rh
A.	(W)	27	F	Unknown	24J107Rh
J.	(S)	01	M	Child	24J107Rh
HARVEY, P.		26	M	Mechanic	24J107Rh
M.		35	F	Unknown	24J107Rh
KEANON, E.		48	F	Unknown	24J107Rh
S.	(D)	08	F	Child	24J107Rh
TAYLOR, M.		15	F	Unknown	24J107Rh
CHAPMAN, N.		33	F	Unknown	24J107Rh
R.	(S)	07	M	Child	24J107Rh
DAVIDSON, A.		24	M	Mechanic	24J107Rh

SARAH-BROWN 26 JULY 1847

From Sligo

NAMES OF PASSENGERS		AGE	SEX	OCCUPATIONS	DATE PORT SHIP
DWYER, M.		50	F	Unknown	26J128Ri
M.		20	F	Unknown	26J128Ri
CAMPBELL, A.		18	F	Unknown	26J128Ri
A.		16	F	Unknown	26J128Ri
FALCON, A.		23	F	Unknown	26J128Ri
CAMBRY, M.		20	F	Unknown	26J128Ri
MALONEY, J.		25	M	Merchant	26J128Ri
M.		20	F	Unknown	26J128Ri
FALCON, P.		45	M	None	26J128Ri
BOLTON, B.		21	M	None	26J128Ri
BUSHE, E.		16	F	Unknown	26J128Ri
BOURKE, C.		22	F	Unknown	26J128Ri
WALDRON, W.J.		28	M	Farmer	26J128Ri
E.	(W)	20	F	Unknown	26J128Ri
M.	(D)	.03	F	Infant	26J128Ri
DAVIS, E.		20	F	Unknown	26J128Ri
GROGAN, L.		39	M	Farmer	26J128Ri
B.		30	F	Unknown	26J128Ri
CRIBBON, M.		18	F	Unknown	26J128Ri
FOLLAND, W.		35	M	Farmer	26J128Ri
B.		20	F	Unknown	26J128Ri
C.		18	F	Unknown	26J128Ri
ELLISS, H.		18	F	Unknown	26J128Ri
HENRY, B.		22	F	Unknown	26J128Ri
DYER, C.		20	F	Unknown	26J128Ri
COLLINS, M.		20	F	Unknown	26J128Ri

SIR-ROBERT-PEEL 26 JULY 1847

From Liverpool

NAMES OF PASSENGERS		AGE	SEX	OCCUPATIONS	DATE PORT SHIP
BUCK, J.		24	M	Physician	26J102Mu
U	(W)	20	F	Wife	26J102Mu
COOPER, My.		30	F	Unknown	26J102Mu
EDWARDS, W.		63	M	Merchant	26J102Mu
My.	(W)	58	F	Unknown	26J102Mu
Fdck.	(S)	21	M	Unknown	26J102Mu
Henry	(S)	15	M	Unknown	26J102Mu
Ellen	(D)	19	F	Unknown	26J102Mu
My.	(D)	19	F	Unknown	26J102Mu
BARRETT, J.		46	M	Mechanic	26J102Mu
Saml.		35	M	Unknown	26J102Mu
THOMPSON, J.		25	M	Unknown	26J102Mu
STOWELL, J.		26	M	Unknown	26J102Mu
NORTHLY, R.		32	M	Unknown	26J102Mu
ROBERTS, J.		20	M	Unknown	26J102Mu
TENBECAST, U		23	M	Unknown	26J102Mu
WILLIAMS, Thy.		27	F	Unknown	26J102Mu
WEBSTER, T.		27	M	Unknown	26J102Mu
Myrt.	(W)	27	F	Unknown	26J102Mu
Thomas	(S)	01	M	Child	26J102Mu
Sally		27	F	Unknown	26J102Mu

NAMES OF PASSENGERS		AGE	SEX	OCCUPATIONS	DATE PORT SHIP
PIERCE, Ann		25	F	Unknown	26J102Mu
SMITH, F.		25	M	Unknown	26J102Mu
Francis		29	M	Unknown	26J102Mu
TRAYLAND, Mgt.		27	F	Unknown	26J102Mu
Mgt.	(D)	01	F	Child	26J102Mu
KELLY, J.		24	M	Unknown	26J102Mu
Mara		18	F	Unknown	26J102Mu
BYRNE, C.		24	M	Laborer	26J102Mu
MCARDLE, O.		45	M	Unknown	26J102Mu
DEVINE, P.		24	M	Unknown	26J102Mu
GLEESON, M.		35	M	Unknown	26J102Mu
KELLY, J.		34	M	Unknown	26J102Mu
DONOHUE, M.		30	M	Unknown	26J102Mu
GRADY, T.		20	M	Unknown	26J102Mu
HESTON, J.		24	M	Unknown	26J102Mu
MULLEN, Bgt.A.		20	F	Unknown	26J102Mu
KELLY, Ann		20	F	Unknown	26J102Mu
GLYNN, J.		30	M	Unknown	26J102Mu
BRADLY, My.		60	F	Unknown	26J102Mu
GLYNN, Sally		22	F	Unknown	26J102Mu
Bgt.		07	F	Child	26J102Mu
MULLEN, Bgt.A.		19	F	Unknown	26J102Mu
GLYNN, J.		35	M	Unknown	26J102Mu
Ann	(W)	28	F	Unknown	26J102Mu
Mgt.	(D)	06	F	Child	26J102Mu
Bgt.	(D)	04	F	Child	26J102Mu
Ann	(D)	01	F	Child	26J102Mu
HEARN, P.		30	M	Laborer	26J102Mu
FAUBMAN, T.		24	M	Unknown	26J102Mu
REILLY, P.		24	M	Unknown	26J102Mu
KIRWEN, P.		26	M	Unknown	26J102Mu
FITZSIMMONS, J.		22	M	Unknown	26J102Mu
KENNY, F.		17	M	Unknown	26J102Mu
LEES, A.		23	M	Unknown	26J102Mu
HANLY, Elza.		55	F	Unknown	26J102Mu
Elza.		25	F	Unknown	26J102Mu
KELLY, J.		24	M	Unknown	26J102Mu
MOON, My.A.		22	F	Unknown	26J102Mu
Isabella		20	F	Unknown	26J102Mu
SMITH, Isb.		19	F	Unknown	26J102Mu
MCGRATH, M.		19	M	Unknown	26J102Mu
REIF, N.		30	M	Unknown	26J102Mu
Ellen		30	F	Unknown	26J102Mu
BOLAND, J.		30	M	Unknown	26J102Mu
WHELAN, W.		15	M	Unknown	26J102Mu
My.		24	F	Unknown	26J102Mu
Ellen		20	F	Unknown	26J102Mu
MCLEAN, C.		25	M	Unknown	26J102Mu
FITZSIMMONS, Ann		20	F	Unknown	26J102Mu
MORRISON, J.		22	M	Unknown	26J102Mu
Martin		20	M	Unknown	26J102Mu
DONNELLY, E.		30	M	Unknown	26J102Mu
SALMONS, P.		22	M	Unknown	26J102Mu
GRIFFETH, Cath.		18	F	Unknown	26J102Mu
KELLY, T.		26	M	Unknown	26J102Mu
MURY, O.		40	M	Unknown	26J102Mu
Bgt.	(D)	18	F	Unknown	26J102Mu
Mgt.	(D)	19	F	Unknown	26J102Mu
Owen	(S)	21	M	Unknown	26J102Mu
Michl.	(S)	18	M	Unknown	26J102Mu
CARROLE, Bgt.		17	F	Unknown	26J102Mu
Elzbt.		16	F	Unknown	26J102Mu
Thos.		15	M	Unknown	26J102Mu
BARNS, C.		21	M	Unknown	26J102Mu
PYE, My.		45	M	Unknown	26J102Mu
FURLONG, J.		19	M	Unknown	26J102Mu
MATTHEWS, A.		16	M	Unknown	26J102Mu
GARGON, C.		10	M	Unknown	26J102Mu

OHIO 27 JULY 1847

From Liverpool

NAMES OF PASSENGERS		AGE	SEX	OCCUPATIONS	DATE PORT SHIP
HUDSON, Thos.		25	M	Mechanic	27J102Bm
Jane		24	F	Unknown	27J102Bm
HANA, Wm.		27	M	Mechanic	27J102Bm
Edna		26	F	Unknown	27J102Bm
RIDDETT, Geo.		29	M	Mechanic	27J102Bm
Ann	(W)	30	F	Unknown	27J102Bm
Geo.	(S)	.00	M	Infant	27J102Bm
ROBINSON, Geo.		30	M	Mechanic	27J102Bm
Jno.		36	M	Mechanic	27J102Bm
Jno.	(P)	69	M	Mechanic	27J102Bm
Rebecca		76	F	Unknown	27J102Bm
STACY, Wm.		28	M	Mechanic	27J102Bm
Hannah		26	F	Unknown	27J102Bm
COULSON, Jno.		38	M	Mechanic	27J102Bm
Elizth.	(W)	34	F	Unknown	27J102Bm
Rebecca	(D)	10	F	Unknown	27J102Bm
Jno.	(S)	07	M	Child	27J102Bm
Hannah	(D)	05	F	Child	27J102Bm
Geo.	(S)	02	M	Child	27J102Bm
GREENWOOD, Jno.		60	M	Farmer	27J102Bm
Adam	(S)	12	M	None	27J102Bm
Geo.	(S)	10	M	None	27J102Bm
PITTERD, Job		32	M	Farmer	27J102Bm
Mary	(W)	30	F	Unknown	27J102Bm
Edith	(D)	04	F	Child	27J102Bm
Geo.	(S)	02	M	Child	27J102Bm
DAVIS, Wm.		22	M	Clerk	27J102Bm
BROWN, Jno.		23	M	Mechanic	27J102Bm
Sarah		20	F	Unknown	27J102Bm
Isaac		20	M	Mechanic	27J102Bm
MILLINGTON, Wm.		22	M	Farmer	27J102Bm
Ann		16	F	Unknown	27J102Bm
MANSON, Henry		21	M	Farmer	27J102Bm
INGRAHAM, Agnes		24	F	Unknown	27J102Bm
PRICE, Elizth.		30	F	Unknown	27J102Bm
WAIT, Jno.		46	M	Farmer	27J102Bm
PERKINS, Thos.		37	M	Farmer	27J102Bm
WARD, Jas.		37	M	Farmer	27J102Bm
Marg.		30	F	Unknown	27J102Bm
Isabella	(D)	10	F	Unknown	27J102Bm
Robt.	(S)	08	M	Child	27J102Bm
Jno.	(S)	06	M	Child	27J102Bm
May.A.	(D)	04	F	Child	27J102Bm
THOMPSON, Jno.		72	M	Farmer	27J102Bm
Alice	(W)	56	F	Unknown	27J102Bm
Magt.	(D)	19	F	Unknown	27J102Bm
Jane	(D)	16	F	Unknown	27J102Bm
PHILIPS, Chas.		40	M	Mechanic	27J102Bm
DRAETTER, Thos.		48	M	Mechanic	27J102Bm
EDYE, Edwd.		45	M	Mechanic	27J102Bm
Mary	(W)	40	F	Unknown	27J102Bm
Elizth.	(D)	11	F	Unknown	27J102Bm
Richd.	(S)	06	M	Child	27J102Bm
ROGERS, Caroline		18	F	Unknown	27J102Bm
PURSEL, Jno.		45	M	Farmer	27J102Bm
JACKSON, Jas.		31	M	Farmer	27J102Bm
Sarah		27	F	Unknown	27J102Bm
SMITH, Wm.		40	M	Farmer	27J102Bm
Ann	(W)	45	F	Unknown	27J102Bm
Jas.	(S)	04	M	Child	27J102Bm
Wm.	(S)	01	M	Child	27J102Bm
TRIGEAR, Henry		48	M	Mechanic	27J102Bm
BROWN, Wm.		22	M	Mechanic	27J102Bm
FERGUSON, Alex		54	M	Farmer	27J102Bm
Jane	(W)	54	F	Unknown	27J102Bm

NAMES OF PASSENGERS		AGE	SEX	OCCUPATIONS	DATE PORT SHIP
FERGUSON, Magt.	(D)	26	F	Unknown	27J102Bm
Mary	(D)	24	F	Unknown	27J102Bm
John	(S)	22	M	Farmer	27J102Bm
Jane	(D)	19	F	Unknown	27J102Bm
Jeanett	(D)	17	F	Unknown	27J102Bm
COURTNEY, Sarah		40	F	Unknown	27J102Bm
Ann		30	F	Unknown	27J102Bm
HILL, Mary		20	F	Unknown	27J102Bm
CAMPBELL, Jas.		69	M	Farmer	27J102Bm
Jane	(W)	72	F	Unknown	27J102Bm
Robt.	(S)	33	M	Farmer	27J102Bm
COULTON, Wm.		21	M	Farmer	27J102Bm
FORELDS, Ellen		21	F	Unknown	27J102Bm
MCGILL, Marion		23	F	Unknown	27J102Bm
REDISON, David		23	M	Farmer	27J102Bm
COUSEN, Jno.		24	M	Farmer	27J102Bm
GLENDENNING, Mary		34	F	Unknown	27J102Bm
MCLAREN, Jeanet		25	F	Unknown	27J102Bm
RICHARDS, Jas.		20	M	Farmer	27J102Bm
VARLIN, Pat		41	M	Farmer	27J102Bm
Phil	(S)	24	M	Farmer	27J102Bm
Pat	(S)	12	M	None	27J102Bm
Alice	(D)	18	F	Unknown	27J102Bm
BRANNIGEN, Felix		50	M	Farmer	27J102Bm
MULLIN, Mich.		22	M	Laborer	27J102Bm
GORMLY, Pat		24	M	Laborer	27J102Bm
CUNNINGHAM, Pat		19	M	Laborer	27J102Bm
NOONAN, Pat		64	M	Laborer	27J102Bm
KIRBY, Jno.		31	M	Laborer	27J102Bm
KENEDY, Mick		17	M	Laborer	27J102Bm
CORR, Thos.		30	M	Laborer	27J102Bm
MADDEN, Jno.		22	M	Laborer	27J102Bm
MCILVIE, Jas.		19	M	Laborer	27J102Bm
Jane		52	F	Unknown	27J102Bm
Sarah		05	F	Child	27J102Bm
BLOOMER, Jno.		16	M	Laborer	27J102Bm
CUNNINGHAM, Jno.		11	M	None	27J102Bm
HACKIN, Cath.		20	F	Unknown	27J102Bm
ELLIOTT, Lucy		22	F	Unknown	27J102Bm
MCGOVERN, Jno.		10	M	None	27J102Bm
DALTON, Mary		24	F	Unknown	27J102Bm
Ohio	(S)	.00	M	Infant	27J102Bm
Died-At-Sea					
LOCKNAN, Ed.		26	M	Laborer	27J102Bm
HARNETT, Jas.		20	M	Laborer	27J102Bm
KENNEDY, Andrew		20	M	Laborer	27J102Bm
MCKEEN, Cath.		50	F	Unknown	27J102Bm
Bridget	(D)	13	F	Unknown	27J102Bm
GARTLAND, Mary		40	F	Unknown	27J102Bm
HUGHES, Jno.		20	M	Laborer	27J102Bm
MCGUIRE, Mary		44	F	Unknown	27J102Bm
ABORN, Mary		15	F	Unknown	27J102Bm
TURNEY, Jas.		20	M	Laborer	27J102Bm
MCNAMEE, Susan		19	F	Unknown	27J102Bm
FERRIS, Jno.		40	M	Laborer	27J102Bm
MITCHELL, Martha		20	F	Unknown	27J102Bm
MENAREIGFEE, Magt.		18	F	Unknown	27J102Bm
ABERDEEN, Cath.		17	F	Unknown	27J102Bm
RILEY, Jas.		28	M	Laborer	27J102Bm
Margt.		30	F	Unknown	27J102Bm
CROWNAN, Jno.		18	M	Laborer	27J102Bm
FAHEE, Jas.		23	M	Mechanic	27J102Bm
Mick		21	M	Mechanic	27J102Bm
TRACEY, Ann		19	F	Unknown	27J102Bm
MADDEN, Bridget		18	F	Unknown	27J102Bm
MAXWELL, Cath.		19	F	Unknown	27J102Bm
MCNEAL, Sarah		21	F	Unknown	27J102Bm
HIGGINS, Thos.		20	M	Laborer	27J102Bm
LANGEN, Thos.		20	M	Laborer	27J102Bm
BRADY, Mary		40	F	Unknown	27J102Bm
Cath.	(D)	13	F	Unknown	27J102Bm
Judy	(D)	10	F	Unknown	27J102Bm
Mary	(D)	08	F	Child	27J102Bm
Rosey	(D)	08	F	Child	27J102Bm
WATERS, M.J.		45	M	Gentleman	27J102Bm

NAMES OF PASSENGERS		AGE	SEX	OCCUPATIONS	DATE PORT SHIP
DRURY, B.H.M.		23	M	Gentleman	27J102Bm
HOOPER, Jno.		25	M	Gentleman	27J102Bm
PERRY, Jas.		35	M	Gentleman	27J102Bm
June		34	F	Unknown	27J102Bm
COLMAN, E.A.		21	F	Unknown	27J102Bm

PATRICK-HENRY 27 JULY 1847

From Liverpool

NAMES OF PASSENGERS		AGE	SEX	OCCUPATIONS	DATE PORT SHIP
TUCKETT, H.		40	M	Merchant	27J102Cw
U	(W)	25	F	Wife	27J102Cw
WARD, U		25	M	Unknown	27J102Cw
BAKER, U		30	M	Unknown	27J102Cw
ELLISON, U		25	M	Unknown	27J102Cw
ALERDICE, U		23	M	Unknown	27J102Cw
JARDINI, U		20	F	Unknown	27J102Cw
FOWLER, U		35	M	Unknown	27J102Cw
MORGAN, U		25	M	Unknown	27J102Cw
COLLESTON, U		25	M	Unknown	27J102Cw
MCCLASHAN, U		40	M	Unknown	27J102Cw
ASHTON, U		40	M	Unknown	27J102Cw
CONNELL, U		28	M	Unknown	27J102Cw
HAYS, U		21	F	Unknown	27J102Cw
LALOR, U		19	F	Unknown	27J102Cw
WARD, U		10	M	None	27J102Cw
ATKINSON, U		22	M	Unknown	27J102Cw
ABRAHAM, U		22	M	Unknown	27J102Cw
IRVIN, J.		28	M	Farmer	27J102Cw
Anne		18	F	Unknown	27J102Cw
Jane		20	F	Unknown	27J102Cw
Elzbt.		21	F	Unknown	27J102Cw
HARPER, R.		90	M	Unknown	27J102Cw
CORR, P.		55	M	Unknown	27J102Cw
Sarah		35	F	Unknown	27J102Cw
Michl.		06	M	Child	27J102Cw
Cath.		04	F	Child	27J102Cw
John		30	M	Unknown	27J102Cw
BURNS, Jane		18	F	Unknown	27J102Cw
DALY, J.		45	M	Unknown	27J102Cw
MCGUIGAN, Eleanor		24	F	Unknown	27J102Cw
MURRY, C.		17	M	Unknown	27J102Cw
DONAGHY, Biddy		15	F	Unknown	27J102Cw
CLANCY, T.		20	M	Unknown	27J102Cw
MURRY, H.		40	M	Unknown	27J102Cw
PARKER, F.		22	M	Unknown	27J102Cw
COLEMAN, P.		22	M	Unknown	27J102Cw
My.		20	F	Unknown	27J102Cw
Biddy		18	F	Unknown	27J102Cw
PALY, W.		40	M	Unknown	27J102Cw
DAVIS, T.		50	M	Unknown	27J102Cw
J.		22	M	Mechanic	27J102Cw
FINEGAN, J.		26	M	Unknown	27J102Cw
Patt		22	M	Unknown	27J102Cw
Bdgt.		20	F	Unknown	27J102Cw
MATHEWS, W.		23	M	Unknown	27J102Cw
REILY, J.		23	M	Unknown	27J102Cw
Mary		20	F	Unknown	27J102Cw
SHEA, G.		20	M	Laborer	27J102Cw
MAHER, J.		24	M	Unknown	27J102Cw
BURKE, E.		28	M	Unknown	27J102Cw
My.	(W)	26	F	Unknown	27J102Cw
Ellen	(D)	04	F	Child	27J102Cw
John	(S)	08	M	Child	27J102Cw
HYLAND, J.		25	M	Unknown	27J102Cw
Edward		20	M	Unknown	27J102Cw
Martha		17	F	Unknown	27J102Cw
MCDONELL, J.		24	M	Unknown	27J102Cw
KEELY, J.		26	M	Unknown	27J102Cw

NAMES OF PASSENGERS		AGE	SEX	OCCUPATIONS	DATE PORT SHIP
BYRNES, Mgt.		18	F	Unknown	27J102Cw
OCONNOR, P.		30	M	Unknown	27J102Cw
DAILY, F.		26	M	Unknown	27J102Cw
Elzbt.		24	F	Unknown	27J102Cw
BARRITT, Cath.		20	F	Unknown	27J102Cw
DILLON, M.		26	M	Unknown	27J102Cw
SHEA, B.		46	M	Unknown	27J102Cw
WAYNE, R.		31	M	Unknown	27J102Cw
My.		32	F	Unknown	27J102Cw
KENNEDY, My.		24	F	Unknown	27J102Cw
PENMAR, My.		51	F	Unknown	27J102Cw
Robt.		19	M	Unknown	27J102Cw
GREENWOOD, B.		24	M	Unknown	27J102Cw
Elizbt.	(W)	26	F	Unknown	27J102Cw
Richd.	(S)	08	M	Child	27J102Cw
Wm.	(S)	01	M	Child	27J102Cw
PENMAR, G.		21	M	Unknown	27J102Cw
Sarah		21	F	Unknown	27J102Cw
SIDES, J.		21	M	Unknown	27J102Cw
LADY, T.		20	M	Unknown	27J102Cw
Elzbt.		21	F	Unknown	27J102Cw
DURNIN, Mgt.		20	F	Unknown	27J102Cw
Anne		18	F	Unknown	27J102Cw
SWEENEY, My.		59	F	Unknown	27J102Cw
TIMMINS, J.		19	M	Laborer	27J102Cw
Thomas		18	M	Laborer	27J102Cw
Anne		16	F	Unknown	27J102Cw
Michl.		24	M	Unknown	27J102Cw
CAMPBELL, J.		30	M	Unknown	27J102Cw
Laurence		19	M	Unknown	27J102Cw
MCEVOY, P.		26	M	Unknown	27J102Cw
MARKEY, My.		18	F	Unknown	27J102Cw
LESTRANG, J.		22	M	Unknown	27J102Cw
STEPHENSON, J.		27	M	Unknown	27J102Cw
Ellen	(W)	26	F	Unknown	27J102Cw
Harriett	(D)	05	F	Child	27J102Cw
Emma	(D)	02	F	Child	27J102Cw
MEREDITH, J.		26	M	Unknown	27J102Cw
My.	(W)	24	F	Unknown	27J102Cw
James	(S)	02	M	Child	27J102Cw
ELLIOTT, J.		30	M	Unknown	27J102Cw
James		10	M	None	27J102Cw
Cath.		34	F	Unknown	27J102Cw
Cath.		19	F	Unknown	27J102Cw
Thomas		13	M	None	27J102Cw
Julia		12	F	Unknown	27J102Cw
Bdgt.		10	F	Unknown	27J102Cw
Jane		08	F	Child	27J102Cw
My.		06	F	Child	27J102Cw
Edwd.		05	M	Child	27J102Cw
Timoty		02	M	Child	27J102Cw
John		04	M	Child	27J102Cw
KANE, J.S.		20	M	Unknown	27J102Cw
SMITH, P.		21	M	Unknown	27J102Cw
Bdgt.		16	F	Unknown	27J102Cw
HANLAN, J.		28	M	Unknown	27J102Cw
RITCHIE, J.		28	M	Unknown	27J102Cw
CROTTY, T.		40	M	Unknown	27J102Cw
My.	(W)	40	F	Unknown	27J102Cw
John	(S)	20	M	Unknown	27J102Cw
Hana	(D)	16	F	Unknown	27J102Cw
Thos.	(S)	14	M	Unknown	27J102Cw
Mgt.	(D)	11	F	Unknown	27J102Cw
My.	(D)	09	F	Child	27J102Cw
Mich.	(S)	05	M	Child	27J102Cw
MCNEAL, M.		29	M	Unknown	27J102Cw
DANIEL, M.		20	M	Farmer	27J102Cw
MARION, M.		22	M	Farmer	27J102Cw
MCQUADE, Naly.		34	F	Unknown	27J102Cw
Sarah		17	F	Unknown	27J102Cw
BROWNE, J.		21	M	Unknown	27J102Cw
WALSH, D.		24	M	Unknown	27J102Cw
Johanna		20	F	Unknown	27J102Cw
REID, Jane		18	F	Unknown	27J102Cw
Andrew		28	M	Unknown	27J102Cw
CONNERS, M.		30	M	Unknown	27J102Cw
Michl.		50	M	Unknown	27J102Cw
Ann	(W)	40	F	Unknown	27J102Cw
Thos.	(S)	12	M	None	27J102Cw
BYRNE, M.		24	M	Unknown	27J102Cw
COONAN, T.		25	M	Unknown	27J102Cw
LYNCH, M.		38	M	Unknown	27J102Cw
My.	(W)	28	F	Unknown	27J102Cw
Anthy.	(S)	12	M	None	27J102Cw
Finela	(D)	10	F	Unknown	27J102Cw
Michl.	(S)	08	M	Child	27J102Cw
Thos.	(S)	06	M	Child	27J102Cw
James	(S)	04	M	Child	27J102Cw
John	(S)	02	M	Child	27J102Cw
NEALAN, W.		28	M	Unknown	27J102Cw
KEEGAN, J.		26	M	Unknown	27J102Cw
My.		24	F	Unknown	27J102Cw
Wm.		23	M	Unknown	27J102Cw
Bdgt.	(D)	01	F	Child	27J102Cw
TAMBLYN, S.		30	M	Unknown	27J102Cw
My.		25	F	Unknown	27J102Cw
NEILL, P.		30	M	Laborer	27J102Cw
My.	(W)	30	F	Unknown	27J102Cw
Elisha	(S)	11	M	None	27J102Cw
DEVAY, P.		26	M	Unknown	27J102Cw
MURPHY, M.		28	M	Unknown	27J102Cw
Cath.		22	F	Unknown	27J102Cw
Brady		20	F	Unknown	27J102Cw
FINLANN, T.		25	M	Unknown	27J102Cw
KEALY, My.		21	F	Unknown	27J102Cw
HALL, J.		30	M	Unknown	27J102Cw
HORGYN, J.		28	M	Unknown	27J102Cw
BLUE, J.		40	M	Laborer	27J102Cw
HINDEN, J.		20	M	Unknown	27J102Cw
Elizbt.		20	F	Unknown	27J102Cw
MULLIGAN, L.		26	M	Unknown	27J102Cw
WALSH, W.		30	M	Unknown	27J102Cw
DOWD, P.		16	M	Unknown	27J102Cw
DUNN, Bgt.		40	F	Unknown	27J102Cw
WRIGHT, E.		22	M	Unknown	27J102Cw
MASON, E.		20	M	Unknown	27J102Cw
Sarah		19	F	Unknown	27J102Cw
BIRCHELL, T.		26	M	Unknown	27J102Cw
MCGEE, D.		20	M	Unknown	27J102Cw
DOONAN, Ellen		20	F	Unknown	27J102Cw
BURBAY, W.		24	M	Unknown	27J102Cw
COSTELLO, My.		60	F	Unknown	27J102Cw
My.		20	F	Unknown	27J102Cw
PYMS, Cath.		24	F	Unknown	27J102Cw
CORBERRY, J.		23	M	Unknown	27J102Cw
DEWS, W.		21	M	Unknown	27J102Cw
HERADIN, My.		26	F	Unknown	27J102Cw
Peter	(S)	04	M	Child	27J102Cw
ARMES, My.		02	F	Child	27J102Cw
CURLY, Lucy		30	F	Unknown	27J102Cw
P.	(S)	09	M	Child	27J102Cw
Wm.	(S)	06	M	Child	27J102Cw
My.A.	(D)	05	F	Child	27J102Cw
My.	(D)	12	F	Unknown	27J102Cw
Lucy	(D)	03	F	Child	27J102Cw
John	(S)	02	M	Child	27J102Cw
Ellen	(D)	01	F	Child	27J102Cw
CARROLL, J.		30	M	Unknown	27J102Cw
MCARDLE, Bgt.		16	F	Unknown	27J102Cw
Rose		15	F	Unknown	27J102Cw
BREEN, O.		25	M	Unknown	27J102Cw
LOUGHRAN, J.		22	M	Unknown	27J102Cw
JACKSON, J.		26	M	Unknown	27J102Cw
HANY, Mgt.		20	F	Unknown	27J102Cw
WHITE, Elza.J.		19	F	Unknown	27J102Cw
CONNERY, J.		21	M	Unknown	27J102Cw
DENNISON, T.		20	M	Unknown	27J102Cw
CAYTON, D.		24	M	Unknown	27J102Cw
PILKINTON, R.		20	M	Laborer	27J102Cw
FITZGIBBONS, Ja.		22	F	Unknown	27J102Cw

NAMES OF PASSENGERS	AGE	SEX	OCCUPATIONS	DATE PORT SHIP
FITZGIBBONS, Ellen	20	F	Unknown	27J102Cw
Cath.	18	F	Unknown	27J102Cw
LEAHY, Mgt.	18	F	Unknown	27J102Cw
Johana	16	F	Unknown	27J102Cw
CRONEN, Mgt.	18	F	Unknown	27J102Cw
LOUGH, L.	30	F	Unknown	27J102Cw
CAMPBELL, E.	21	F	Unknown	27J102Cw
WARD, Ann	19	F	Unknown	27J102Cw
REESY, Ann	06	F	Child	27J102Cw
BARNS, Elza.	21	F	Unknown	27J102Cw
Thos.	19	M	Unknown	27J102Cw
WOODS, W.	23	M	Unknown	27J102Cw
LONDON, My.	24	F	Unknown	27J102Cw
MCGRATH, My.	24	F	Unknown	27J102Cw
MCCARTEY, J.	28	M	Unknown	27J102Cw
HOGAN, Betty	40	F	Unknown	27J102Cw
DONAHUE, C.	25	M	Unknown	27J102Cw
GHELION, J.	26	M	Unknown	27J102Cw
DONAHUE, Anne	21	F	Unknown	27J102Cw
WHITE, W.	20	M	Unknown	27J102Cw
Robt.	20	M	Unknown	27J102Cw
THORNTON, J.	30	M	Unknown	27J102Cw
George	25	M	Unknown	27J102Cw
James	50	M	Unknown	27J102Cw
F.	21	M	Unknown	27J102Cw
Jane-E.	19	F	Unknown	27J102Cw
Hannah	18	F	Unknown	27J102Cw
KING, W.	20	M	Unknown	27J102Cw
CAROLAN, T.	40	M	Unknown	27J102Cw
Bessy	30	F	Unknown	27J102Cw
Bessy	13	F	Unknown	27J102Cw
Cath.	04	F	Child	27J102Cw
Mich.	02	M	Child	27J102Cw
Anne	01	F	Child	27J102Cw
MOLLOY, P.	28	M	Unknown	27J102Cw
Bgt.	25	F	Unknown	27J102Cw
MCGORREY, P.	22	M	Unknown	27J102Cw
DONALY, Betty	09	F	Child	27J102Cw
LIGHTBODY, T.	22	M	Unknown	27J102Cw
ABRAY, G.	32	M	Mechanic	27J102Cw
WALKER, Anne	22	F	Unknown	27J102Cw
WOOGAN, P.	20	M	Unknown	27J102Cw
HUGHES, Bgt.	18	F	Unknown	27J102Cw
CONNAHY, T.	26	M	Laborer	27J102Cw
LARKIN, T.	26	M	Unknown	27J102Cw
SPENCE, W.	18	M	Unknown	27J102Cw
LANNION, J.	23	M	Unknown	27J102Cw
My.	20	F	Unknown	27J102Cw
WOONAN, J.	20	M	Unknown	27J102Cw
Honora	25	F	Unknown	27J102Cw
Cath.	26	F	Unknown	27J102Cw
DUFFY, J.	24	M	Unknown	27J102Cw
Elisbt.	50	F	Unknown	27J102Cw
My.	22	F	Unknown	27J102Cw
Mgt.	20	F	Unknown	27J102Cw
Ann	18	F	None	27J102Cw
COFFEY, D.	25	M	Unknown	27J102Cw
RABBAGH, Ellen	24	F	Unknown	27J102Cw
MITCHELL, My.	16	F	Unknown	27J102Cw
HART, L.	22	M	Unknown	27J102Cw
MURRY, My.	30	F	Unknown	27J102Cw
Bgt.	20	F	Unknown	27J102Cw
Richd.	04	M	Child	27J102Cw
MAHER, My.	18	F	Unknown	27J102Cw
Edward	11	M	None	27J102Cw
REIS, J.	25	M	Unknown	27J102Cw
Anne	19	F	Unknown	27J102Cw
MAHONY, M.	15	M	Unknown	27J102Cw
MCCRENN, P.	22	M	Unknown	27J102Cw
SULLIVAN, Eliza.	20	F	Unknown	27J102Cw
PENDERGAST, My.	12	F	Unknown	27J102Cw
MUNRO, Bgt.	20	F	Unknown	27J102Cw
Chistian	18	M	Unknown	27J102Cw
Luke	19	M	Unknown	27J102Cw
MEALY, Cath.	15	F	Unknown	27J102Cw
MEALY, Carolin	13	F	Unknown	27J102Cw
FARRELL, P.	19	M	Unknown	27J102Cw
Anne	17	F	Unknown	27J102Cw
LOCHAN, P.	16	M	Unknown	27J102Cw
PORTER, A.	16	M	Unknown	27J102Cw
MULLIGAN, Anne	30	F	Unknown	27J102Cw
FITZPATRICK, Bgt.	17	F	None	27J102Cw
LANDRIKER, Judy	20	F	None	27J102Cw
BRENNAN, My.	40	F	None	27J102Cw
WHALEN, Mgt.	20	F	None	27J102Cw
DOWD, Bgt.	55	F	None	27J102Cw
My.	15	F	None	27J102Cw
Stephen	12	M	None	27J102Cw
Patch	10	M	None	27J102Cw
Mgt.	09	F	Child	27J102Cw
REYNOLDS, My.	22	F	Unknown	27J102Cw
MCNALLY, Bgt.	35	F	Unknown	27J102Cw
Cath.	08	F	Child	27J102Cw
Rosanna	09	F	Child	27J102Cw
My.	05	F	Child	27J102Cw
Winfred	03	F	Child	27J102Cw
Anne	01	F	Child	27J102Cw
BARRITT, My.	12	F	Unknown	27J102Cw
BARNS, Cath.	15	F	Unknown	27J102Cw
WARD, My.	20	F	Unknown	27J102Cw
SMITH, Ann	22	F	Unknown	27J102Cw
CONWAY, J.	25	M	Unknown	27J102Cw
CULLIGAN, Bgt.	20	F	Unknown	27J102Cw
Felix	19	M	Unknown	27J102Cw
SHERIDAN, Ann	20	F	Unknown	27J102Cw
Mgt.	22	F	Unknown	27J102Cw
DOLAN, J.	32	M	Unknown	27J102Cw
JORTAN, T.	20	M	Unknown	27J102Cw
RILY, Alice	42	F	Unknown	27J102Cw

WESTMINSTER 27 JULY 1847

From London

NAMES OF PASSENGERS	AGE	SEX	OCCUPATIONS	DATE PORT SHIP
WALLIS, M.	29	M	Mechanic	27J121Br
May	24	F	Unknown	27J121Br
Mark	04	M	Child	27J121Br
James	02	M	Child	27J121Br
Selina	01	F	Child	27J121Br
HILL, Hanah	19	F	Unknown	27J121Br
BROWN, W.	43	M	Unknown	27J121Br
Eleanor	37	F	Unknown	27J121Br
William	11	M	None	27J121Br
George	09	M	Child	27J121Br
Eleanor	07	F	Child	27J121Br
Eliza	03	F	Child	27J121Br
Oliver	04	M	Child	27J121Br
Johan	01	M	Child	27J121Br
PRIOR, J.	45	M	Unknown	27J121Br
Eliza	44	F	Unknown	27J121Br
Amelia	27	F	Unknown	27J121Br
James	23	M	Unknown	27J121Br
Eliza	14	F	Unknown	27J121Br
Rhoda	11	F	Unknown	27J121Br
Laura	02	F	Child	27J121Br
VINCENT, F.A.	19	M	Unknown	27J121Br
WINSLOW, J.	39	M	Unknown	27J121Br
Charlotte	39	F	Unknown	27J121Br
David	10	M	None	27J121Br
Mary	07	F	Child	27J121Br
Rhoda	04	F	Child	27J121Br
Gideon	01	M	Child	27J121Br
BURFORD, W.O.	28	M	Mechanic	27J121Br
WRISCHNER, F.	26	M	Mechanic	27J121Br

NAMES OF PASSENGERS		AGE	SEX	OCCUPATIONS	DATE PORT SHIP
MEGER, G.		30	M	Mechanic	27J121Br
KENNER, J.		23	M	Mechanic	27J121Br
SCHENCK, D.		25	M	Mechanic	27J121Br
PEASE, W.		19	M	Farmer	27J121Br
ACKERMAN, A.		42	M	Unknown	27J121Br
Sophia	(W)	40	F	Unknown	27J121Br
Mry.A.	(D)	16	F	Unknown	27J121Br
Jacob	(S)	12	M	None	27J121Br
Elibt.	(D)	10	F	Unknown	27J121Br
Henry	(S)	08	M	Child	27J121Br
Sarah	(D)	14	F	Unknown	27J121Br
ACKERMANN, Ca.		01	F	Child	27J121Br
STETLER, J.B.		29	M	Mechanic	27J121Br
Victoria		18	F	Unknown	27J121Br
AMBESSTER, Dusan		55	F	Unknown	27J121Br
BLANCK, T.		24	M	Unknown	27J121Br
ZYDA, E.		26	M	Unknown	27J121Br
MEGER, Mry.A.		23	F	Unknown	27J121Br
HENELY, C.		29	M	Unknown	27J121Br
BENSEL, W.		20	M	Unknown	27J121Br
HENNELLY, C.		03	M	Child	27J121Br
GIBBON, J.		25	M	Unknown	27J121Br
Elzbt.		28	F	Unknown	27J121Br
FORBES, W.		13	M	Unknown	27J121Br
SULLIVAN, T.		37	M	Unknown	27J121Br
MILLER, J.		24	M	Unknown	27J121Br
SHECKENDAY, J.		22	M	Unknown	27J121Br
BUCK, N.		22	M	Unknown	27J121Br
HENNINGS, J.		27	M	Unknown	27J121Br
HARPOH, W.		23	M	Unknown	27J121Br
KNIGHT, W.		21	M	Unknown	27J121Br
DETTNAR, D.		25	M	Unknown	27J121Br
BOLTMAN, H.		24	M	Unknown	27J121Br
BERTHAN, Chat.		38	F	Unknown	27J121Br
Eliza	(D)	07	F	Child	27J121Br
Elzbt.	(D)	02	F	Child	27J121Br
JOHNSON, Bgt.		22	F	Unknown	27J121Br
John		26	M	Unknown	27J121Br
MANER, R.		42	M	Unknown	27J121Br
OTTAWA, E.		42	M	Unknown	27J121Br
Mrt.A.		33	F	Unknown	27J121Br
Alfred		09	M	Child	27J121Br
Eliza		07	F	Child	27J121Br
RICHARD, Mry.		60	F	Unknown	27J121Br
Joseph		16	M	Laborer	27J121Br
CUSICK, J.		47	M	Unknown	27J121Br
Ellen	(W)	47	F	Unknown	27J121Br
James	(S)	22	M	Unknown	27J121Br
Ellen	(D)	18	F	Unknown	27J121Br
Wm.	(S)	16	M	Unknown	27J121Br
Thos.	(S)	13	M	None	27J121Br
Sarah	(D)	10	F	Unknown	27J121Br
MOWBERRY, J.		29	M	Unknown	27J121Br
WHEELAN, F.		23	M	Mechanic	27J121Br
CUSICK, R.		29	M	Unknown	27J121Br
PARTON, J.F.		28	M	Unknown	27J121Br
Jane		39	F	Unknown	27J121Br
Francis		02	M	Child	27J121Br
WALLIS, T.		40	M	Unknown	27J121Br
John	(S)	09	M	Child	27J121Br
Emma	(D)	11	F	Unknown	27J121Br
GEER, J.		30	M	Unknown	27J121Br
Wm.		26	M	Unknown	27J121Br
Ann	(W)	23	F	Unknown	27J121Br
David	(S)	04	M	Child	27J121Br
Martha	(D)	03	F	Child	27J121Br
Alfred	(S)	01	M	Child	27J121Br
SETCHFORD, Clara		17	F	Unknown	27J121Br
Silas		11	M	None	27J121Br
KEMP, May		22	F	Unknown	27J121Br
MCGINN, J.		27	M	Unknown	27J121Br

QUEEN 27 JULY 1847

From Liverpool

NAMES OF PASSENGERS		AGE	SEX	OCCUPATIONS	DATE PORT SHIP
HAMPSON, M.		58	M	Laborer	27J102Qx
JONES, F.		25	M	Unknown	27J102Qx
SULLIVAN, T.		30	M	Unknown	27J102Qx
CARTON, H.		40	M	Unknown	27J102Qx
CARTY, Betsy		35	F	Unknown	27J102Qx
My.	(D)	12	F	Unknown	27J102Qx
Wm.	(S)	10	M	None	27J102Qx
Cath.	(D)	07	F	Child	27J102Qx
Mich.	(S)	05	M	Child	27J102Qx
Bgt.	(D)	02	F	Child	27J102Qx
BRANNY, J.		35	M	Unknown	27J102Qx
Cath.	(W)	30	F	Unknown	27J102Qx
Patch	(S)	08	M	Child	27J102Qx
Bdgt.	(D)	06	F	Child	27J102Qx
My.	(D)	04	F	Child	27J102Qx
CALLEN, P.		30	M	Unknown	27J102Qx
STEVENSON, J.		33	M	Unknown	27J102Qx
MOORE, C.		27	M	Unknown	27J102Qx
BURNS, J.		25	M	Unknown	27J102Qx
KAMPETROW, J.		14	M	Unknown	27J102Qx
CROK, S.		56	M	Unknown	27J102Qx
Martha	(W)	56	F	Unknown	27J102Qx
Johnson	(S)	26	M	Unknown	27J102Qx
George	(S)	21	M	Unknown	27J102Qx
Wm.	(S)	18	M	Unknown	27J102Qx
REILLY, N.		25	M	Unknown	27J102Qx
DUNN, L.		23	M	Unknown	27J102Qx
My.		26	F	Unknown	27J102Qx
John	(S)	02	M	Child	27J102Qx
PROBERT, J.		34	M	Unknown	27J102Qx
WATSON, L.		23	M	Unknown	27J102Qx
Patch		18	M	Unknown	27J102Qx
Hy.		16	M	Unknown	27J102Qx
MASKELL, Wm.		28	M	Unknown	27J102Qx
JILES, W.		28	M	Unknown	27J102Qx
TAYLOR, M.		27	M	Unknown	27J102Qx
GANNON, J.		38	M	Unknown	27J102Qx
GALLAGHER, My.		10	F	Unknown	27J102Qx
HUDSON, J.		15	M	Unknown	27J102Qx
FITZPATRICK, J.		21	M	Unknown	27J102Qx
Michael		21	M	Unknown	27J102Qx
MONKS, Silvia		24	F	Unknown	27J102Qx
ONEAL, M.		38	M	Laborer	27J102Qx
Ellen		32	F	Unknown	27J102Qx
MCEVOY, Ann		19	F	Unknown	27J102Qx
MCCEW, C.		25	M	Unknown	27J102Qx
LEMON, Bgt.		17	F	Unknown	27J102Qx
BARK, Ann		20	F	Unknown	27J102Qx
HOURY, W.		24	M	Unknown	27J102Qx
GARDNER, A.		27	M	Unknown	27J102Qx
MURPHY, P.		27	M	Unknown	27J102Qx
GLYNN, P.		65	M	Unknown	27J102Qx
BASSAR, G.		19	M	Unknown	27J102Qx
HOWELL, H.		13	M	Unknown	27J102Qx
FRENCH, Elza.		29	F	Unknown	27J102Qx
KERMAN, J.		20	M	Unknown	27J102Qx
BRADY, B.		23	M	Unknown	27J102Qx
SHAY, P.		35	M	Unknown	27J102Qx
PASCOON, J.		28	M	Unknown	27J102Qx
SMITH, J.		26	M	Unknown	27J102Qx
TUNSTALER, W.		19	M	Unknown	27J102Qx
GEORGE, S.		19	M	Unknown	27J102Qx
TARGUN, T.		16	M	Unknown	27J102Qx
MCGANN, J.		25	M	Unknown	27J102Qx
Sarah		25	F	Unknown	27J102Qx

NAMES OF PASSENGERS		AGE	SEX	OCCUPATIONS	DATE PORT SHIP
HOGAN, T.		35	M	Unknown	27J102Qx
Ellen	(W)	30	F	Unknown	27J102Qx
John	(S)	09	M	Child	27J102Qx
Patch	(S)	07	M	Child	27J102Qx
Ann	(D)	01	F	Child	27J102Qx
CLOSE, Bgt.		21	F	Unknown	27J102Qx
CANNERNAN, B.		24	M	Unknown	27J102Qx
HALLERAN, P.		25	M	Unknown	27J102Qx
MCMAHON, E.		20	M	Unknown	27J102Qx
Denis		28	M	Unknown	27J102Qx
Thos.		22	M	Unknown	27J102Qx
CANN, P.		28	M	Unknown	27J102Qx
BRADY, J.		24	M	Unknown	27J102Qx
HUSSEY, Bgt.		23	F	Unknown	27J102Qx
CARNY, M.		25	M	Unknown	27J102Qx
CARROLE, Bgt.		20	F	Unknown	27J102Qx
COHN, Cath.		23	F	Unknown	27J102Qx
My.		20	F	Unknown	27J102Qx
MARTIN, T.		40	M	Farmer	27J102Qx
ROWELL, J.		25	M	Unknown	27J102Qx
HARTINGTON, Ma.		26	F	Unknown	27J102Qx
FISHER, J.		40	M	None	27J102Qx
ROBERTSON, Elzt.		30	F	Unknown	27J102Qx
MARTIN, My.		15	F	Unknown	27J102Qx
Thos.		30	M	Unknown	27J102Qx
MURSTGAN, P.		25	M	Unknown	27J102Qx
COX, P.		35	M	Unknown	27J102Qx
DUNN, J.		35	M	Unknown	27J102Qx
SINGER, J.		24	M	Unknown	27J102Qx
BIGLY, My.		20	F	Unknown	27J102Qx
SMITH, J.		60	M	Unknown	27J102Qx
Owen	(S)	28	M	Unknown	27J102Qx
Michl.	(S)	26	M	Unknown	27J102Qx
James	(S)	20	M	Unknown	27J102Qx
Michl.	(S)	13	M	None	27J102Qx
Bryan	(S)	11	M	None	27J102Qx
Betty	(D)	11	F	Unknown	27J102Qx
My.	(D)	09	F	Child	27J102Qx
Judy	(D)	07	F	Child	27J102Qx
Beth	(W)	52	F	Unknown	27J102Qx
CADDEN, B.		24	M	Unknown	27J102Qx
CALLY, Cath.		18	F	Unknown	27J102Qx
LAHAHON, D.		25	M	Unknown	27J102Qx
Frans.		18	M	Unknown	27J102Qx
Mgt.		50	F	Unknown	27J102Qx
Mgt.		23	F	Unknown	27J102Qx
FLANGAN, W.		24	M	Unknown	27J102Qx
CARTAN, J.		24	M	Unknown	27J102Qx
CORNER, M.		24	M	Unknown	27J102Qx
FLYNN, Ha.		24	F	Unknown	27J102Qx
KILLEHER, Ha.		24	F	Unknown	27J102Qx
Elzbt.		20	F	Unknown	27J102Qx
KELLY, Cath.		50	F	Unknown	27J102Qx
Mich.	(S)	23	M	Unknown	27J102Qx
Tery.	(S)	14	M	Unknown	27J102Qx
Beng.	(S)	12	M	None	27J102Qx
Peggy	(D)	10	F	Unknown	27J102Qx
Thos.	(S)	08	M	Child	27J102Qx
Bgt.	(D)	20	F	Unknown	27J102Qx
Mgt.	(D)	08	F	Child	27J102Qx
CONNER, D.		25	M	Farmer	27J102Qx
Ellen		18	F	Unknown	27J102Qx
MARTIN, P.		24	M	Unknown	27J102Qx
My.		50	F	Unknown	27J102Qx
HENNESSY, J.		30	M	Unknown	27J102Qx
My.	(W)	28	F	Unknown	27J102Qx
Ellen	(D)	04	F	Child	27J102Qx
My.	(D)	02	F	Child	27J102Qx
John	(S)	01	M	Child	27J102Qx
BARKER, Mgt.		11	F	Unknown	27J102Qx
COSKERRY, J.		31	M	Unknown	27J102Qx
RONAHAN, Sarah		14	F	Unknown	27J102Qx
Ann		10	F	Unknown	27J102Qx
FOLY, B.		20	M	Unknown	27J102Qx
Hannah		30	F	Unknown	27J102Qx

NAMES OF PASSENGERS		AGE	SEX	OCCUPATIONS	DATE PORT SHIP
HIGGINS, My.		06	F	Child	27J102Qx
Nancy		05	F	Child	27J102Qx
THERSTON, R.		30	M	Unknown	27J102Qx
My.		28	F	Unknown	27J102Qx
WARD, S.		30	M	Unknown	27J102Qx
MANAHAN, Cath.		16	F	Unknown	27J102Qx
PACER, W.		28	M	Unknown	27J102Qx
GREEN, G.		30	M	Unknown	27J102Qx
HIGGINS, J.		28	M	Unknown	27J102Qx
MURPHY, P.		40	M	Unknown	27J102Qx
Betsy	(W)	21	F	Unknown	27J102Qx
My.	(D)	01	F	Child	27J102Qx
FANNY, J.		18	M	Unknown	27J102Qx
ADAMS, W.		27	M	Unknown	27J102Qx
SPOELAN, R.		18	M	Unknown	27J102Qx
LOWE, J.		19	M	Unknown	27J102Qx
JONES, J.		38	M	Unknown	27J102Qx
JENKINS, J.		32	M	Unknown	27J102Qx
Elzbt.		24	F	Unknown	27J102Qx
James		11	M	None	27J102Qx
Hannah		16	F	Unknown	27J102Qx
Hannah		50	F	Unknown	27J102Qx
James		15	M	None	27J102Qx
Hestr.		13	F	Unknown	27J102Qx
Berz.		09	F	Child	27J102Qx
Eleanor		09	F	Child	27J102Qx
JONES, D.		39	M	Unknown	27J102Qx
Sarah	(W)	40	F	Unknown	27J102Qx
Denis	(S)	03	M	Child	27J102Qx
FOLEY, U-Mrs.		20	F	Unknown	27J102Qx
HOGAN, F.		24	M	Laborer	27J102Qx
DOWD, P.		32	M	Unknown	27J102Qx
Pat		53	M	Unknown	27J102Qx
TURNEY, Theresa		19	F	Unknown	27J102Qx
MCRULRICH, M.		40	M	Unknown	27J102Qx
BAGLAN, Cath.		21	F	Unknown	27J102Qx
Mich.	(S)	04	M	Child	27J102Qx
Cath.	(D)	02	F	Child	27J102Qx
FITZGERALD, J.		64	M	Unknown	27J102Qx
My.	(D)	22	F	Unknown	27J102Qx
James	(S)	18	M	Unknown	27J102Qx
Cath.	(D)	20	F	Unknown	27J102Qx
HARELTON, My.		20	F	Unknown	27J102Qx
CLARK, Ann		19	F	Unknown	27J102Qx
ONEILL, C.		16	M	Unknown	27J102Qx
MCMANUS, My.		60	F	Unknown	27J102Qx
Rose	(D)	18	F	Unknown	27J102Qx
Chas.	(S)	22	M	Unknown	27J102Qx
ROONEY, My.		57	F	None	27J102Qx
GALLAGHER, M.		65	M	Unknown	27J102Qx
Eleanor	(W)	65	F	Unknown	27J102Qx
John	(S)	22	M	Unknown	27J102Qx
James	(S)	10	M	None	27J102Qx
OLWELL, Ann		17	F	Unknown	27J102Qx
REMPLE, T.		18	M	Unknown	27J102Qx
SHERIDAN, J.		23	M	Unknown	27J102Qx
CAMPBELL, Ellen		21	F	Unknown	27J102Qx
LYON, M.		16	M	Unknown	27J102Qx
HOPE, J.		23	M	Unknown	27J102Qx
Ann		21	F	Unknown	27J102Qx
MASTERSON, T.		20	M	Unknown	27J102Qx
MANIX, Hanah		20	F	Unknown	27J102Qx
MCCULLICH, R.		20	M	Unknown	27J102Qx
CHUTE, J.		16	M	Unknown	27J102Qx
MCBRIDE, Ellen		02	F	Child	27J102Qx
TIMON, J.		21	M	Unknown	27J102Qx
MOORE, P.		33	M	Unknown	27J102Qx
DALY, T.		16	M	Unknown	27J102Qx
COLLINS, D.		25	M	Unknown	27J102Qx
CONLY, Cath.		22	F	Unknown	27J102Qx
BAPFERD, Ellen		30	F	Unknown	27J102Qx
HEWITT, R.		20	M	Laborer	27J102Qx
Thos.	(P)	40	M	Unknown	27J102Qx
Henry		28	M	Unknown	27J102Qx
Robt.		21	M	Unknown	27J102Qx

NAMES OF PASSENGERS		AGE	SEX	OCCUPATIONS	DATE PORT SHIP
SHERIDAN, T.		20	M	Unknown	27JI02Qx
DUFFY, M.		21	M	Unknown	27JI02Qx
MCCANN, M.		19	M	Unknown	27JI02Qx
GUINNESS, P.M.		26	M	Unknown	27JI02Qx
MORSE, J.		40	M	Unknown	27JI02Qx
BRADY, M.		24	M	Unknown	27JI02Qx
RUSSELL, T.		22	M	Unknown	27JI02Qx
GREEN, M.		23	M	Unknown	27JI02Qx
FERRISS, J.		21	M	Unknown	27JI02Qx
HIMPSTER, G.		25	M	Unknown	27JI02Qx
Elzbt.	(W)	23	F	Unknown	27JI02Qx
Phillip	(S)	01	M	Child	27JI02Qx
HOFFMAN, G.		27	M	Unknown	27JI02Qx
My.A.		50	F	Unknown	27JI02Qx
WALSH, M.		62	M	Unknown	27JI02Qx
Patt	(S)	26	M	Unknown	27JI02Qx
Elza.	(D)	22	F	Unknown	27JI02Qx
Kate	(D)	19	F	Unknown	27JI02Qx
GREEVY, G.		19	M	Unknown	27JI02Qx
CLARKE, Bgt.		20	F	None	27JI02Qx
MCCEW, D.		24	M	Unknown	27JI02Qx
Bgt.		25	F	Unknown	27JI02Qx
COONY, E.		24	M	Unknown	27JI02Qx
Peggy		18	F	Unknown	27JI02Qx
QUINLAN, J.		25	M	Unknown	27JI02Qx
Ellen		30	F	Unknown	27JI02Qx
MCGOVERN, J.		28	M	Unknown	27JI02Qx
JACOBS, J.		21	M	Unknown	27JI02Qx
GRAY, M.		21	M	Unknown	27JI02Qx
Marie		21	F	Unknown	27JI02Qx
HESBERT, J.		23	M	Unknown	27JI02Qx
Dolly		60	F	None	27JI02Qx
Cath.		62	F	None	27JI02Qx
BUCK, T.		27	M	Unknown	27JI02Qx
James		19	M	Unknown	27JI02Qx
HALY, W.		20	M	Unknown	27JI02Qx
BAMBERG, E.		27	M	Laborer	27JI02Qx
MADDEN, J.		25	M	Unknown	27JI02Qx
FARLY, Judy		25	F	Unknown	27JI02Qx
OBRIEN, J.		40	M	Unknown	27JI02Qx
OATS, P.		33	M	Unknown	27JI02Qx
LOYD, J.		29	M	Unknown	27JI02Qx
OHARA, T.		34	M	Unknown	27JI02Qx
THOMAS, M.		30	M	Unknown	27JI02Qx
DENNS, J.		21	M	Unknown	27JI02Qx
MULLHERN, J.		22	M	Unknown	27JI02Qx
MULLOY, J.		24	M	Unknown	27JI02Qx
HADLY, J.		51	M	Unknown	27JI02Qx
LITTLE, Judy		28	F	Unknown	27JI02Qx
SMITH, R.		29	M	Unknown	27JI02Qx
Sarah		24	F	Unknown	27JI02Qx
BRAMMER, J.		16	M	Unknown	27JI02Qx
DORAN, W.		30	M	Unknown	27JI02Qx
Francis		20	M	Unknown	27JI02Qx
Fre--KLETON, D.		20	M	Unknown	27JI02Qx
ARMITAGE, J.		18	M	Unknown	27JI02Qx
STOCKDALE, W.		30	M	Unknown	27JI02Qx
MCGUINNESS, E.		50	M	Unknown	27JI02Qx
Pat		30	M	Unknown	27JI02Qx
Edwd.		18	M	Unknown	27JI02Qx
Cath.		14	F	Unknown	27JI02Qx
CARROLL, J.		32	M	Unknown	27JI02Qx
Rose	(W)	30	F	Unknown	27JI02Qx
Mich.	(S)	10	M	None	27JI02Qx
John	(S)	07	M	Child	27JI02Qx
Patt		43	M	Unknown	27JI02Qx
My.	(W)	40	F	Unknown	27JI02Qx
Owen	(S)	17	M	Unknown	27JI02Qx
Isabella	(D)	13	F	Unknown	27JI02Qx
Bernard	(S)	10	M	None	27JI02Qx
James	(S)	07	M	Child	27JI02Qx
Ann	(D)	09	F	Child	27JI02Qx
DORIS, O.		40	M	Unknown	27JI02Qx
Sarah	(W)	38	F	Unknown	27JI02Qx
John	(S)	13	M	None	27JI02Qx
DORIS, Arthur	(S)	13	M	None	27JI02Qx
My.	(D)	08	F	Child	27JI02Qx
James	(S)	06	M	Child	27JI02Qx
H.	(S)	03	M	Child	27JI02Qx
Danl.	(S)	01	M	Child	27JI02Qx
LOGAN, My.		17	F	Unknown	27JI02Qx
Luke		12	M	Unknown	27JI02Qx
Bgt.		09	F	Child	27JI02Qx
BARNES, Cath.		13	F	Unknown	27JI02Qx
DAVIS, J.		23	M	Laborer	27JI02Qx
Mara		33	F	Unknown	27JI02Qx
BYRON, J.		20	M	Unknown	27JI02Qx
KELLY, Rose		25	F	Unknown	27JI02Qx
SHERIDAN, H.		54	M	Unknown	27JI02Qx
Bgt.	(W)	40	F	Unknown	27JI02Qx
James	(S)	20	M	Unknown	27JI02Qx
Bessy	(D)	16	F	Unknown	27JI02Qx
Cath.	(D)	11	F	Unknown	27JI02Qx
Mgt.	(D)	09	F	Child	27JI02Qx
RUNNELS, P.		18	M	Unknown	27JI02Qx
PALLAHAN, My.		24	F	Unknown	27JI02Qx
H----Y, S.		37	M	Unknown	27JI02Qx
Cath.	(W)	38	F	Unknown	27JI02Qx
James	(S)	03	M	Child	27JI02Qx
Mich.	(S)	03	M	Child	27JI02Qx
CANE, Bgt.		21	F	Unknown	27JI02Qx
NEAL, J.M.		20	M	Unknown	27JI02Qx
FOSTER, W.		20	M	Unknown	27JI02Qx
My.		21	F	Unknown	27JI02Qx
CASEY, M.		35	M	Unknown	27JI02Qx
Dennis		22	M	Unknown	27JI02Qx
DONNELLY, J.		24	M	Unknown	27JI02Qx
CARROLL, T.		05	M	Child	27JI02Qx
QUIN, A.		16	M	Unknown	27JI02Qx
KAIN, J.		19	M	Unknown	27JI02Qx
CALWELL, U-Mrs.		30	F	Unknown	27JI02Qx
MCGUINNESS, Ellen		18	F	Unknown	27JI02Qx
SHERIDAN, M.		18	M	Unknown	27JI02Qx

LIBERTY 28 JULY 1847

From Liverpool

NAMES OF PASSENGERS		AGE	SEX	OCCUPATIONS	DATE PORT SHIP
DAVIES, Harry		36	M	Farmer	28JI02Fw
KENNY, Arthur-M.		51	M	Farmer	28JI02Fw
Ann		50	F	Unknown	28JI02Fw
CUMMINS, Jno.		28	M	Laborer	28JI02Fw
Mary		28	F	Unknown	28JI02Fw
KANE, Biddy		26	F	Unknown	28JI02Fw
SHANAGHSY, Biddy		18	F	Unknown	28JI02Fw
WELDON, Mary		03	F	Child	28JI02Fw
COLGAN, Thomas		40	M	Farmer	28JI02Fw
Bently		40	M	Farmer	28JI02Fw
Mary		14	F	Unknown	28JI02Fw
Thos.		18	M	Farmer	28JI02Fw
Mich.		04	M	Child	28JI02Fw
Hanna		02	F	Child	28JI02Fw
MURPHY, Mich.		20	M	Laborer	28JI02Fw
MCCAY, Jas.		20	M	Farmer	28JI02Fw
DEVINE, Anthony		20	M	Farmer	28JI02Fw
ANDERSON, Margt.		54	F	Unknown	28JI02Fw
Joseph	(S)	25	M	Farmer	28JI02Fw
Danl.	(S)	20	M	Farmer	28JI02Fw
BRIDGES, Jno.		30	M	Farmer	28JI02Fw
FINN, Jno.		35	M	Farmer	28JI02Fw
LISKAY, Ann		22	F	Unknown	28JI02Fw
THILLY, Robt.		40	M	Farmer	28JI02Fw
Cath.	(W)	45	F	Unknown	28JI02Fw
Cath.		30	F	Unknown	28JI02Fw

NAMES OF PASSENGERS	AGE	SEX	OCCUPATIONS	DATE PORT SHIP
THILLY, Bridget	23	F	Unknown	28JI02Fw
Biddy	20	F	Unknown	28JI02Fw
Thos.	.00	M	Infant	28JI02Fw
WARD, Saml.	22	M	Mechanic	28JI02Fw
ARMSTRONG, Jas.	40	M	Mechanic	28JI02Fw
BROOKMIER, David	41	M	Mechanic	28JI02Fw
MCKENNY, Mary	28	F	Unknown	28JI02Fw
LANDERS, William	41	M	Mechanic	28JI02Fw
Sarah	34	F	Unknown	28JI02Fw
Wm.	.00	M	Infant	28JI02Fw
MORGAN, Hugh	21	M	Farmer	28JI02Fw
ANDERSON, Margt.	30	F	Unknown	28JI02Fw
Robt.	01	M	Child	28JI02Fw
DOLPHIN, Isaac	18	M	Mechanic	28JI02Fw
Sarah	42	F	Unknown	28JI02Fw
Sarah	06	F	Child	28JI02Fw
Ann	15	F	Unknown	28JI02Fw
GUINE, Jno.	35	M	Mechanic	28JI02Fw
EDWARDS, Jno.	23	M	Mechanic	28JI02Fw
Mary	20	F	Unknown	28JI02Fw
MCSHANE, Joseph	49	M	Mechanic	28JI02Fw
LOWE, Jos.	38	M	Mechanic	28JI02Fw
Sarah	37	F	Unknown	28JI02Fw
Jos.	07	M	Child	28JI02Fw
Mary	07	F	Child	28JI02Fw
Maria	02	F	Child	28JI02Fw
THOMPSON, Laurence	22	M	Mechanic	28JI02Fw
Cath.	20	F	Unknown	28JI02Fw
GLEESON, Jno.D.	26	M	Mechanic	28JI02Fw
RIELY, Mat.	23	M	Farmer	28JI02Fw
KENNEDY, Jas.	21	M	Farmer	28JI02Fw
LALLY, Thos.	24	M	Farmer	28JI02Fw
MOORE, Jas.	34	M	Mechanic	28JI02Fw
DONOHUE, Jas.	21	M	Mechanic	28JI02Fw
MCDONOUGH, Martin	20	M	Mechanic	28JI02Fw
HUTCHINSON, Jos.	21	M	Mechanic	28JI02Fw
COLKINGHAM, Wm.	24	M	Mechanic	28JI02Fw
KNOTTWELL, Hy.R.	22	M	Mechanic	28JI02Fw
CORKING, Wm.	20	M	Mechanic	28JI02Fw
Ezra	16	M	Mechanic	28JI02Fw
ASHBURN, John	30	M	Mechanic	28JI02Fw
POLLARD, Jas.	31	M	Mechanic	28JI02Fw
Sarah	31	F	Unknown	28JI02Fw
Wm.	10	M	None	28JI02Fw
Batt.	05	M	Child	28JI02Fw
Heziah	12	M	None	28JI02Fw
STEACE, Joseph	41	M	Mechanic	28JI02Fw
HOFTUS, Chris.	20	M	Mechanic	28JI02Fw
WALTON, Wm.	30	M	Mechanic	28JI02Fw
HUGHES, Mary	20	F	Unknown	28JI02Fw
LEMAN, Mary	20	F	Unknown	28JI02Fw
HUGHES, Peter	11	M	None	28JI02Fw
MOORE, Cath.	22	F	None	28JI02Fw
Ann	11	F	None	28JI02Fw
SWEENY, Jas.	28	M	Mechanic	28JI02Fw
WARD, Mich.	40	M	Farmer	28JI02Fw
Mary	38	F	Unknown	28JI02Fw
Mary	21	F	Unknown	28JI02Fw
LINSKEY, Mich.	20	M	Laborer	28JI02Fw
BINNS, Bridget	00	F	Unknown	28JI02Fw
JONES, Jno.	24	M	Farmer	28JI02Fw
OWENS, Jno.	21	M	Farmer	28JI02Fw
MOUNTJOY, Thos.	48	M	Mechanic	28JI02Fw
Barbara	48	F	Unknown	28JI02Fw
Maria	21	F	Unknown	28JI02Fw
Jno.	15	M	Mechanic	28JI02Fw
Ann	09	F	Child	28JI02Fw
CLIBBORN, Jos.	20	M	Mechanic	28JI02Fw
CROWLEY, Maria	16	F	Unknown	28JI02Fw
Ann	18	F	Unknown	28JI02Fw
DAVIES, Simeon	24	M	Mechanic	28JI02Fw
MCNIFF, Bryan	38	M	Mechanic	28JI02Fw
Ann	30	F	Unknown	28JI02Fw
Thos.	05	M	Child	28JI02Fw
Biddy	04	F	Child	28JI02Fw
MCNIFF, Cath.	.00	F	Infant	28JI02Fw
LARKINS, Pat	50	M	Laborer	28JI02Fw
Mary	50	F	Unknown	28JI02Fw
Maria	10	F	Unknown	28JI02Fw
Bridget	08	F	Child	28JI02Fw
Mary	06	F	Child	28JI02Fw
Pat	05	M	Child	28JI02Fw
HART, Ellen	18	F	Unknown	28JI02Fw
LARKENS, Mich.	14	M	Laborer	28JI02Fw
DOOLIN, Mich.	58	M	Laborer	28JI02Fw
Cath.	25	F	Unknown	28JI02Fw
REYNOLDS, Mary	61	F	Unknown	28JI02Fw
Mich.	19	M	Laborer	28JI02Fw
MULAY, Ellen	09	F	Child	28JI02Fw
MCGAVOY, Susan	20	F	Unknown	28JI02Fw
DONLY, Dom.	20	M	Laborer	28JI02Fw
KENNEDY, Jos.	20	M	Laborer	28JI02Fw
Mary	16	F	Unknown	28JI02Fw
URHER, Cath.	14	F	Unknown	28JI02Fw
BARRETT, Jno.	09	M	Child	28JI02Fw
Mich.	08	M	Child	28JI02Fw
Martin	06	M	Child	28JI02Fw
MCMULLEN, Mary	19	F	Unknown	28JI02Fw
WELDON, Mat.	64	M	Mechanic	28JI02Fw
Bridget	40	F	Unknown	28JI02Fw
James	18	M	Mechanic	28JI02Fw
Peter	18	M	Mechanic	28JI02Fw
Chris	15	M	None	28JI02Fw
Richd.	12	M	None	28JI02Fw
Bridget	05	F	Child	28JI02Fw
KING, Philip	23	M	Farmer	28JI02Fw
REILY, Ann	20	F	Unknown	28JI02Fw
ANDERSON, Robt.	20	M	Farmer	28JI02Fw
MCCLURE, Ame	60	M	Farmer	28JI02Fw
Mich.	28	M	Farmer	28JI02Fw
CARLIN, Jno.	20	M	Farmer	28JI02Fw
CLARE, Cath.	30	F	Unknown	28JI02Fw
MANNING, Pat	20	M	Farmer	28JI02Fw
DOLING, Jno.	25	M	Farmer	28JI02Fw
Mary	22	F	Unknown	28JI02Fw
Pat	18	M	Farmer	28JI02Fw
Bridget	17	F	Unknown	28JI02Fw
HOLLORAN, Ellen	18	F	Unknown	28JI02Fw
LARKEY, Cath.	25	F	Unknown	28JI02Fw
KELLY, Mary	22	F	Unknown	28JI02Fw
MATHER, Mary	18	F	Unknown	28JI02Fw
DRAKE, Cath.	15	F	Unknown	28JI02Fw
Walter	18	M	Farmer	28JI02Fw
REGAN, Jno.	40	M	Farmer	28JI02Fw
Jas.	16	M	Farmer	28JI02Fw
ESTLAN, Margt.	21	F	Unknown	28JI02Fw
CASSIDY, David	21	M	Laborer	28JI02Fw
KELLY, Peter	24	M	Laborer	28JI02Fw
MCCAIN, Jas.	22	M	Laborer	28JI02Fw
Ellen	16	F	Unknown	28JI02Fw
BOSTWICK, Elizth.	61	F	Unknown	28JI02Fw
STORER, Harriet	23	F	Unknown	28JI02Fw
HARVEY, Geo.	31	M	Laborer	28JI02Fw
Elizth.	30	F	Unknown	28JI02Fw
Mary-A.	10	F	Unknown	28JI02Fw
Geo.	08	M	Child	28JI02Fw
Elizth.	06	F	Child	28JI02Fw
Elizth.	.00	F	Infant	28JI02Fw
BROGAN, Mary	18	F	Unknown	28JI02Fw
MCGARRY, Margt.	24	F	Unknown	28JI02Fw
MONOHAN, Phil	19	M	Mechanic	28JI02Fw
WARMBY, Ann	40	F	Unknown	28JI02Fw
Jane	18	F	Unknown	28JI02Fw
Ann	16	F	Unknown	28JI02Fw
Jno.	14	M	Unknown	28JI02Fw
Harriet	06	F	Child	28JI02Fw
Thos.	02	M	Child	28JI02Fw
REILY, Jno.	21	M	Mechanic	28JI02Fw
MURPHY, Julia	20	F	Unknown	28JI02Fw
Phil.	50	M	Mechanic	28JI02Fw

NAMES OF PASSENGERS	AGE	SEX	OCCUPATIONS	DATE PORT SHIP
MURPHY, Bridget	40	F	Unknown	28JI02Fw
HERLIN, Ann	10	F	Unknown	28JI02Fw
BRADLEY, Martha	28	F	Unknown	28JI02Fw
Alice	11	F	Unknown	28JI02Fw
Jacob	09	M	Child	28JI02Fw
Margt.	05	F	Child	28JI02Fw
Mary-A.	.00	F	Infant	28JI02Fw
HAGAN, Henry	20	M	Laborer	28JI02Fw
MEASONELE, Elizth.	34	F	Unknown	28JI02Fw
M.Jane	06	F	Child	28JI02Fw
Elizth.	02	F	Child	28JI02Fw
Jemima	02	F	Child	28JI02Fw
ISLAND, Ann	22	F	Unknown	28JI02Fw
DUNN, Jno.	26	M	Laborer	28JI02Fw
Jas.	28	M	Laborer	28JI02Fw
Dennis	22	M	Laborer	28JI02Fw
Margt.	25	F	Unknown	28JI02Fw
MACEM, Pat	24	M	Laborer	28JI02Fw
Margt.	26	F	Unknown	28JI02Fw
RICKELL, Jno.	21	M	Laborer	28JI02Fw
CONROY, Mary	19	F	Unknown	28JI02Fw
LOCKLIN, Mich.	20	M	Laborer	28JI02Fw
QUADE, Sarah	40	F	Unknown	28JI02Fw
Barny	25	M	Laborer	28JI02Fw
Peter	28	M	Laborer	28JI02Fw
Margt.	30	F	Unknown	28JI02Fw
SUTTON, Saml.	56	M	Farmer	28JI02Fw
Eliza	52	F	Unknown	28JI02Fw
Richd.	22	M	Laborer	28JI02Fw
George	18	M	Laborer	28JI02Fw
Saml.	14	M	None	28JI02Fw
Hannah	18	F	Unknown	28JI02Fw
Mary	10	F	Unknown	28JI02Fw
Isabella	07	F	Child	28JI02Fw
Eliza	06	F	Child	28JI02Fw
PORTER, Alfred	23	M	Mechanic	28JI02Fw

NATHANIEL-HOOPER 28 JULY 1847

From Sligo

NAMES OF PASSENGERS	AGE	SEX	OCCUPATIONS	DATE PORT SHIP
REDDY, Jno.	20	M	Farmer	28JI28RI
Jerry	18	M	Farmer	28JI28RI
Sarah	55	F	Unknown	28JI28RI
LAGHLIN, Jno.	20	M	Farmer	28JI28RI
ROWAN, Jno.	21	M	Farmer	28JI28RI
ROONEY, Martin	19	M	Farmer	28JI28RI
Anna	17	F	Unknown	28JI28RI
MCKENNA, Honoria	16	F	Unknown	28JI28RI
CULLEN, Peggy	15	F	Unknown	28JI28RI
CAMPBELL, Bridget	20	F	Unknown	28JI28RI
MCGAWAN, Pat	26	M	Farmer	28JI28RI
MULLANY, Wm.	17	M	Farmer	28JI28RI
BRADY, Honora	16	F	Unknown	28JI28RI
MULDOWNEY, Jno.	21	M	Farmer	28JI28RI
BOYD, Margt.	20	F	Unknown	28JI28RI
MURRAY, Mich.	21	M	Farmer	28JI28RI
Eliza	17	F	Unknown	28JI28RI
Maria	14	F	Unknown	28JI28RI
James	16	M	Farmer	28JI28RI
MULDOWNEY, Tim	31	M	Farmer	28JI28RI
MCDOUGHE, Pat	31	M	Farmer	28JI28RI
ROGAN, Mich.	21	M	Farmer	28JI28RI
HORAN, Thos.	22	M	Farmer	28JI28RI
HOPKINS, Jas.	31	M	Farmer	28JI28RI
Anna	20	F	Unknown	28JI28RI
MULVOYE, Jas.	28	M	Farmer	28JI28RI
LAVIN, Mich.	30	M	Farmer	28JI28RI
MCGUIRE, Bridget	19	F	Unknown	28JI28RI
MCDONOUGH, Jno.	21	M	Farmer	28JI28RI
GILGAN, Mary	20	F	Unknown	28JI28RI
CLARKE, Owen	21	M	Farmer	28JI28RI
OCONNER, Mary	20	F	Unknown	28JI28RI
MCGEE, Winfred	21	F	Unknown	28JI28RI
CRAEL, Rose	14	F	Unknown	28JI28RI
Mary	16	F	Unknown	28JI28RI
DRYER, Jno.	41	M	Farmer	28JI28RI
FLANAGAN, Ann	21	F	Unknown	28JI28RI
ANDERSON, Mary	32	F	Unknown	28JI28RI
FOHEY, Ellen	16	F	Unknown	28JI28RI
GILGAN, Mich.	21	M	Farmer	28JI28RI
GILKENTLY, Sarah	22	F	Unknown	28JI28RI
KILGULLAN, Bessy	17	F	Unknown	28JI28RI
LINAN, Brian	21	M	Farmer	28JI28RI
MARTIN, Ann	16	F	Unknown	28JI28RI
CUNNINGHAM, Margt.	20	F	Unknown	28JI28RI
GILMARTIN, James	21	M	Farmer	28JI28RI
TANEY, And.	31	M	Farmer	28JI28RI
TAYLOR, Geo.	31	M	Farmer	28JI28RI
BROWN, Mary	22	F	Unknown	28JI28RI
CAVANAGH, Pat	21	M	Farmer	28JI28RI
GILLEN, Peter	31	M	Farmer	28JI28RI
COSTELLO, Martin	31	M	Farmer	28JI28RI
MCGARVEY, Pat	26	M	Farmer	28JI28RI
MCGARRICK, Bryan	21	M	Farmer	28JI28RI
COOPER, Peter	31	M	Farmer	28JI28RI
Alice	30	F	Unknown	28JI28RI
Pat	04	M	Child	28JI28RI
RAUREN, Luke	52	M	Farmer	28JI28RI
ROPE, James	21	M	Farmer	28JI28RI
LEE, Pat	31	M	Farmer	28JI28RI
MCCARTEY, Mary	40	F	Unknown	28JI28RI
GUNLEY, Mich.	17	M	Farmer	28JI28RI
Nabby	21	F	Unknown	28JI28RI
HARDADON, Chas.	31	M	Farmer	28JI28RI
GALBRAITH, Robt.	31	M	Farmer	28JI28RI
WHITE, Jno.	39	M	None	28JI28RI
Eliza	38	F	None	28JI28RI
Sarah-A.	16	F	None	28JI28RI
Hannah	15	F	None	28JI28RI
Margt.	12	F	None	28JI28RI
Sophia	10	F	None	28JI28RI
Eliza	08	F	Child	28JI28RI
John-J.	07	M	Child	28JI28RI
Olivia	05	F	Child	28JI28RI
KENNY, Mary-Ann	20	F	None	28JI28RI
GRIFFITHS, Geo.	50	M	None	28JI28RI
Jane	30	F	None	28JI28RI
GALBRAITH, Martha	00	F	None	28JI28RI

CHARLESTOWN 28 JULY 1847

From Unknown

NAMES OF PASSENGERS	AGE	SEX	OCCUPATIONS	DATE PORT SHIP
MCGINN, Ellen	30	F	None	28JI00Rm
Thos.	02	M	Child	28JI00Rm
DOLLARD, R.	25	M	Mechanic	28JI00Rm
ROACH, Bgt.	40	F	None	28JI00Rm
WHALEN, Judy	18	F	None	28JI00Rm
QUINN, My.	22	F	None	28JI00Rm
HANDERHON, Ellen	26	F	None	28JI00Rm
MALONE, Cath.	22	F	None	28JI00Rm
RYAN, Ann	23	F	None	28JI00Rm
WELCH, Ann	22	F	None	28JI00Rm
CASSEDY, J.	18	M	Unknown	28JI00Rm
CROAK, M.	33	M	Unknown	28JI00Rm
My.	21	F	None	28JI00Rm
HOGAN, Bgt.	21	F	None	28JI00Rm

NAMES OF PASSENGERS	AGE	SEX	OCCUPATIONS	DATE PORT SHIP
LANNAGAN, J.	15	M	None	28J100Rm
HILAND, W.	16	M	None	28J100Rm
REED, W.	17	M	Farmer	28J100Rm
Ellen	26	F	None	28J100Rm
Judy	28	F	None	28J100Rm
GARAHAN, O.	24	M	Unknown	28J100Rm
Michl.	28	M	Unknown	28J100Rm
Winnfd.	22	F	None	28J100Rm
Sarah	21	F	None	28J100Rm
Reny	20	M	Unknown	28J100Rm
PEYTON, Bgt.	18	F	None	28J100Rm
SHERLOCK, Cath.	23	F	None	28J100Rm
MURPHY, R.	22	M	Unknown	28J100Rm
John	20	M	Unknown	28J100Rm
HUGHES, J.	45	M	Unknown	28J100Rm
GRIFFITH, J.	31	M	Unknown	28J100Rm
CALY, T.	50	M	Unknown	28J100Rm
Ellen-H.	60	F	None	28J100Rm
James	24	M	Unknown	28J100Rm
GLASHAN, W.	23	M	Unknown	28J100Rm
COLLEYIS, My.	28	F	None	28J100Rm
GLASHAN, Ellen	18	F	None	28J100Rm
Thos.	01	M	Child	28J100Rm
John	30	M	Unknown	28J100Rm
Bgt.	09	F	Child	28J100Rm
FINN, W.	23	M	Unknown	28J100Rm
RYAN, R.	21	M	Unknown	28J100Rm
T.	21	M	Laborer	28J100Rm
MORRISLY, J.	30	M	Unknown	28J100Rm
CASSEDY, Betsy	60	F	None	28J100Rm
OCONNOR, B.	20	M	Unknown	28J100Rm
BURKE, M.	33	M	Unknown	28J100Rm
Mgt.	30	F	None	28J100Rm
Mgt.	08	F	Child	28J100Rm
Maria	01	F	Child	28J100Rm
Patch	06	M	Child	28J100Rm
Jeremiah	01	M	Child	28J100Rm
Bgt.	25	F	None	28J100Rm
WHITE, J.	35	M	Unknown	28J100Rm
MANALA, F.	18	M	Unknown	28J100Rm
HAGARTY, M.	16	M	Unknown	28J100Rm
RODERICK, L.	41	M	Unknown	28J100Rm
James	50	M	Unknown	28J100Rm
MCGRATH, M.	35	M	Unknown	28J100Rm
Edwd.	28	M	Unknown	28J100Rm
MYERS, J.	30	M	Unknown	28J100Rm
MCGRATH, Mgt.	26	F	None	28J100Rm
MURPHY, P.	29	M	Unknown	28J100Rm
REYNOLDS, P.	20	M	Unknown	28J100Rm
LEWIS, A.	32	M	Unknown	28J100Rm
MOORE, R.	23	M	Unknown	28J100Rm
COLLINGS, J.	24	M	Unknown	28J100Rm
Martin	17	M	Unknown	28J100Rm
Michl.	13	M	None	28J100Rm
My.	18	F	None	28J100Rm
Peggy	18	F	None	28J100Rm
WHALEY, Joseph	45	M	None	28J100Rm
Rebecca	45	F	None	28J100Rm
SOUTHWELL, Sa.	21	F	None	28J100Rm
Thos.	23	M	Unknown	28J100Rm
WHALEY, Reba.	04	F	Child	28J100Rm
Celia	02	F	Child	28J100Rm
Joshua	16	M	Unknown	28J100Rm
John	13	M	Unknown	28J100Rm
Ebenezer	09	M	Child	28J100Rm
Hanah	12	F	None	28J100Rm
CARR, Bgt.	16	F	None	28J100Rm
MULLEN, D.	65	M	Unknown	28J100Rm
James	20	M	Unknown	28J100Rm
Mgt.	22	F	None	28J100Rm
BURR, M.	25	M	Laborer	28J100Rm
RUSLY, J.	23	M	Laborer	28J100Rm
OGARRA, P.	22	M	Laborer	28J100Rm
LYNCH, M.	25	M	Laborer	28J100Rm
FRAZER, W.	27	M	Laborer	28J100Rm
DELANY, D.	48	M	Laborer	28J100Rm
Elza.	29	F	None	28J100Rm
Sylvester	14	M	None	28J100Rm
DWYER, Ellen	21	F	None	28J100Rm
HEALY, Cath.	20	F	None	28J100Rm
COUGHLAN, P.	20	M	Unknown	28J100Rm
MCMANUS, J.	27	M	Unknown	28J100Rm
DAVIS, J.	26	M	Unknown	28J100Rm
FITZSIMMONS, B.	31	M	Unknown	28J100Rm
My.	24	F	None	28J100Rm
Chast.	22	M	Unknown	28J100Rm
SCANTLAN, F.	22	M	Unknown	28J100Rm
CARVER, J.	17	M	Unknown	28J100Rm
CONNELL, P.	21	M	Unknown	28J100Rm
FENNEGAN, D.	27	M	Unknown	28J100Rm
Cath.	25	F	None	28J100Rm
Patch	03	M	Child	28J100Rm
My.	01	F	Child	28J100Rm
Phillip	29	M	Unknown	28J100Rm
GOVERN, Ann	20	F	None	28J100Rm
CUNNINGHAM, P.	20	M	Unknown	28J100Rm
Ann	18	F	None	28J100Rm
MURRY, Ma.	20	F	None	28J100Rm
HAWLY, A.	23	M	Unknown	28J100Rm
DURKAN, P.	23	M	Unknown	28J100Rm
JORDAN, J.	24	M	Unknown	28J100Rm
SAVAGE, J.	31	M	Unknown	28J100Rm
SULLIVAN, Rose	23	F	None	28J100Rm
GULLESPIE, Ellen	19	F	None	28J100Rm
DONLAN, Bgt.	19	F	None	28J100Rm
GRENAN, M.	37	M	Unknown	28J100Rm
GASNAR, A.	27	M	Unknown	28J100Rm
BALLGAN, L.	25	M	Unknown	28J100Rm
FRANNY, J.	35	M	Unknown	28J100Rm
LEDWITH, P.	32	M	Unknown	28J100Rm
Elzbt.	58	F	None	28J100Rm
MARTIN, Ellen	24	F	None	28J100Rm
DALY, P.	30	M	Laborer	28J100Rm
ODWYER, M.	32	M	Unknown	28J100Rm
Mat.	27	M	Unknown	28J100Rm
Johanah	28	F	None	28J100Rm
DOLAN, J.	19	M	Unknown	28J100Rm
Frances	18	M	Unknown	28J100Rm
WILLEN, Ann	18	F	None	28J100Rm
KING, My.	19	F	None	28J100Rm
CREMIN, W.	47	M	Unknown	28J100Rm
Richd.	14	M	Unknown	28J100Rm
Wm.	10	M	None	28J100Rm
Cath.	08	F	Child	28J100Rm
GERAGHTY, P.	20	M	Unknown	28J100Rm
OCONNER, Ma.	16	F	None	28J100Rm
MCCONNELL, J.	28	M	Unknown	28J100Rm
HUGHES, M.	20	M	Unknown	28J100Rm
GALESHY, Cath.	21	F	None	28J100Rm

EAGLE 28 JULY 1847

From Limerick

NAMES OF PASSENGERS	AGE	SEX	OCCUPATIONS	DATE PORT SHIP
HOWARD, Patt	28	M	Laborer	28J133Rn
Ellen	28	F	None	28J133Rn
Jno.	03	M	Child	28J133Rn
Margt.	48	F	None	28J133Rn
Bridget	25	F	None	28J133Rn
Cath.	18	F	None	28J133Rn
OBRIEN, Jno.	30	M	Mechanic	28J133Rn
Joha.	30	F	None	28J133Rn
Margt.	01	F	Child	28J133Rn
ODONNELL, Chas.	52	M	Mechanic	28J133Rn

NAMES OF PASSENGERS	AGE	SEX	OCCUPATIONS	DATE PORT SHIP
ODONNELL, Cath.	52	F	None	28J133Rn
Jas.	13	M	None	28J133Rn
Thos.	08	M	Child	28J133Rn
OBRIEN, Jonora	21	F	None	28J133Rn
TAFFAN, Mich.	20	M	Mechanic	28J133Rn
Mary	21	F	None	28J133Rn
Cath.	19	F	None	28J133Rn
LYONS, Mary	24	F	None	28J133Rn
SPINY, Walter	36	M	Mechanic	28J133Rn
Anne	30	F	None	28J133Rn
OBRIEN, Bridget	20	F	None	28J133Rn
SHEAHAN, Nelly	25	F	None	28J133Rn
Mary	29	F	None	28J133Rn
CARIG, Patt	28	M	Mechanic	28J133Rn
GRIFFITHS, Jno.	23	M	Merchant	28J133Rn
SHEAHAN, Joseph	24	M	Laborer	28J133Rn
Ellen	17	F	None	28J133Rn
BLAKE, Richd.	21	M	Farmer	28J133Rn
HAYES, Denis	25	M	Farmer	28J133Rn
SEXTON, Maria	20	F	None	28J133Rn
MCNAMARA, Wm.	30	M	None	28J133Rn
DALY, Harriet	35	F	None	28J133Rn
MCNAMARA, Mich.	28	M	Farmer	28J133Rn
Hanna	22	F	None	28J133Rn
CALAHAN, Mich.	27	M	Farmer	28J133Rn
SULLIVAN, Francis	20	M	Farmer	28J133Rn
MEALLY, Edward	11	M	None	28J133Rn
Pat	10	M	None	28J133Rn
SULLIVAN, Cath.	40	F	None	28J133Rn
TOOMEY, Thos.	50	M	Farmer	28J133Rn
Ann	50	F	None	28J133Rn
Thos.	26	M	Farmer	28J133Rn
Bridget	24	F	None	28J133Rn
Cath.	22	F	None	28J133Rn
Honora	20	F	None	28J133Rn
James	12	M	None	28J133Rn
Margt.	10	F	None	28J133Rn
ARTHUR, Francis	25	M	Mechanic	28J133Rn
HOGAN, Law.	20	M	Mechanic	28J133Rn
TUSHY, Cath.	20	F	None	28J133Rn
FOLEY, Tim	48	M	Mechanic	28J133Rn
Bridget	48	F	None	28J133Rn
Patt	22	M	Farmer	28J133Rn
Thos.	16	M	Farmer	28J133Rn
GLYNN, Patt	17	M	Farmer	28J133Rn
FARMAN, Mich.	45	M	Farmer	28J133Rn
Ellen	40	F	None	28J133Rn
Patt	18	M	Farmer	28J133Rn
Mich.	16	M	Farmer	28J133Rn
Jno.	10	M	None	28J133Rn
Bridget	07	F	Child	28J133Rn
BRIEN, Jno.	50	M	Laborer	28J133Rn
GALVIN, Patt	50	M	Laborer	28J133Rn
Johana	48	F	None	28J133Rn
MENTON, Dennis	21	M	Laborer	28J133Rn
MCDONNELL, Dennis	42	M	Farmer	28J133Rn
Mary	35	F	None	28J133Rn
Dennis	16	M	Farmer	28J133Rn
Hanna	14	F	None	28J133Rn
Jno.	12	M	None	28J133Rn
Thos.	11	M	None	28J133Rn
Jas.	09	M	Child	28J133Rn
Mary	07	F	Child	28J133Rn
Bridget	05	F	Child	28J133Rn
Jno.	02	M	Child	28J133Rn
SHEAHAND, Johanna	40	F	None	28J133Rn
Jas.	13	M	None	28J133Rn
Patt	11	M	None	28J133Rn
Honora	06	F	Child	28J133Rn
CONDON, Alicia	25	F	None	28J133Rn
FARNUM, Mary	03	F	Child	28J133Rn
DEWITT, Edwd.	25	M	Laborer	28J133Rn
FITZGERALD, Jas.	24	M	Laborer	28J133Rn
Patt	25	M	Laborer	28J133Rn
Mary	27	F	None	28J133Rn

NAMES OF PASSENGERS	AGE	SEX	OCCUPATIONS	DATE PORT SHIP
FITZGERALD, Honora	29	F	None	28J133Rn
RYAN, Mich.	17	M	Laborer	28J133Rn
GLEESON, Rosana	20	F	None	28J133Rn
SHAUNESSEY, Mich.	32	M	Farmer	28J133Rn
Anne	06	F	None	28J133Rn
DILLON, Nora	20	F	None	28J133Rn
SHAUNESSEY, Jno.	.09	M	Infant	28J133Rn
Mary	04	F	Child	28J133Rn
BLAKE, Bridget	20	F	None	28J133Rn
FLAHERTY, Margt.	18	F	None	28J133Rn
RYAN, Mary	22	F	None	28J133Rn
Ann	20	F	None	28J133Rn

PHILIP-HONE 28 JULY 1847

From Londonderry

NAMES OF PASSENGERS	AGE	SEX	OCCUPATIONS	DATE PORT SHIP
MITCHELL, David	45	M	Farmer	28J101Ro
Eliza	45	F	None	28J101Ro
Ann	16	F	None	28J101Ro
Jane	14	F	None	28J101Ro
Jno.	11	M	None	28J101Ro
Helen	09	F	Child	28J101Ro
Wm.	07	M	Child	28J101Ro
David	05	M	Child	28J101Ro
FRIZ, Latham	29	M	Mechanic	28J101Ro
GOLLA, Wm.	45	M	Farmer	28J101Ro
Sally	38	F	None	28J101Ro
Jno.	16	M	Farmer	28J101Ro
Hugh	14	M	None	28J101Ro
Jack	12	M	None	28J101Ro
Edwd.	09	M	Child	28J101Ro
Jas.	06	M	Child	28J101Ro
Mary	04	F	Child	28J101Ro
TENNEY, Hugh	26	M	Farmer	28J101Ro
SWEENY, Wm.	19	M	Farmer	28J101Ro
DOWNELL, Helen	20	M	Farmer	28J101Ro
HAMILTON, Robt.	25	M	Farmer	28J101Ro
MCODRICK, Ann	21	F	None	28J101Ro
CARNEY, Jno.	17	M	Farmer	28J101Ro
NOXON, Isabella	27	F	None	28J101Ro
DRUAN, Pat	39	M	Farmer	28J101Ro
FULLER, Elizth.	47	F	None	28J101Ro
HARVEY, Eliza	17	F	None	28J101Ro
Chas.	15	M	None	28J101Ro
CASSIDY, Jno.	25	M	Farmer	28J101Ro
MCCOLLUM, Wm.	36	M	Farmer	28J101Ro
Nancy	35	F	None	28J101Ro
Jno.	02	M	Child	28J101Ro
TENSAY, Jno.	19	M	Farmer	28J101Ro
WATTS, Mary-J.	30	F	None	28J101Ro
CASDY, Rose-H.	30	F	None	28J101Ro
WOODWARD, Helen	18	F	None	28J101Ro
MCCOIN, Nancy	21	F	None	28J101Ro
COIL, Hannah	31	F	None	28J101Ro
Jno.	16	M	None	28J101Ro
Ann	08	F	Child	28J101Ro
MCBRIDE, Helena	20	F	None	28J101Ro
MCMICOLL, Sarah	17	F	None	28J101Ro
MCDADE, Danl.	20	M	Mechanic	28J101Ro
FARMER, Jane	21	F	None	28J101Ro
WANELLY, Sidney	50	M	Mechanic	28J101Ro
Thos.	18	M	Mechanic	28J101Ro
PERRY, James	20	M	Mechanic	28J101Ro
BROWNING, Ann	25	F	None	28J101Ro
MCSHANE, Jane	20	F	None	28J101Ro
Betsey-A.	16	F	None	28J101Ro
BLANE, Richd.	50	M	Mechanic	28J101Ro
BLAIR, Eliza	50	F	None	28J101Ro

NAMES OF PASSENGERS	AGE	SEX	OCCUPATIONS	DATE PORT SHIP
BLAIR, Jos.	12	M	None	28J101Ro
Robt.	08	M	Child	28J101Ro
HILLARD, Mary	20	F	None	28J101Ro
Margt.	17	F	None	28J101Ro
DOUGHERTY, Hannah	22	F	None	28J101Ro
Cath.	20	F	None	28J101Ro
MCCALPHY, Jas.	31	M	Mechanic	28J101Ro
CANNON, Pat	12	M	None	28J101Ro
MENELY, Francis	19	M	Mechanic	28J101Ro
LOCHEN, Wm.	50	M	Mechanic	28J101Ro
SCOTT, Rob.	45	M	Mechanic	28J101Ro
Jane	45	F	None	28J101Ro
Margt.	21	F	None	28J101Ro
Jno.S.	16	M	Mechanic	28J101Ro
Jas.	11	M	None	28J101Ro
Barlow	07	M	Child	28J101Ro
MCGILING, Mich.	30	M	Farmer	28J101Ro
Betsey	24	F	None	28J101Ro
Binny	02	M	Child	28J101Ro
Jno.	35	M	Farmer	28J101Ro
SWEENING, Elizth.	17	F	None	28J101Ro
MCMILLEN, Saml.	27	M	Farmer	28J101Ro
Eliza	24	F	None	28J101Ro
Eliza	06	F	Child	28J101Ro
MCCLURE, Jas.	50	M	Farmer	28J101Ro
Ann	50	F	None	28J101Ro
Christ.	20	M	Farmer	28J101Ro
DONNELLY, Sally	29	F	None	28J101Ro
LOGAN, Martha	35	F	None	28J101Ro
MCMICOLL, Jane	18	F	None	28J101Ro

ROYAL-WILLIAM 28 JULY 1847

From Belfast

NAMES OF PASSENGERS	AGE	SEX	OCCUPATIONS	DATE PORT SHIP
MCANALLY, Mich.	17	M	Laborer	28J107Rp
TOOLE, Jno.	20	M	Laborer	28J107Rp
BARKER, Thos.	45	M	Laborer	28J107Rp
Mary	45	F	None	28J107Rp
BURNE, Jas.	30	M	Laborer	28J107Rp
Eliza	20	F	None	28J107Rp
KILESPIE, Mich.	30	M	Laborer	28J107Rp
TOLAN, Pat	24	M	Laborer	28J107Rp
HESTER, Martin	28	M	Laborer	28J107Rp
MAURY, Pat	46	M	Laborer	28J107Rp
Bridget	46	F	None	28J107Rp
KILVERY, Kath.	20	F	None	28J107Rp
MORAN, Mary	18	F	None	28J107Rp
KILNEY, Pat	23	M	Laborer	28J107Rp
HIGGINS, Chas.	24	M	Laborer	28J107Rp
Eliza	20	F	None	28J107Rp
Mary	46	F	None	28J107Rp
FLEMING, Mich.	22	M	Laborer	28J107Rp
MORGAN, Thos.	28	M	Laborer	28J107Rp
Cath.	23	F	None	28J107Rp
MONY, Pat	13	M	Laborer	28J107Rp
MCDONALD, Martin	35	M	Laborer	28J107Rp
MCANALLY, Mich.	30	M	Laborer	28J107Rp
MULLIN, Hester	26	F	None	28J107Rp
READY, Mary	22	F	None	28J107Rp
HIGGIN, Anthony	25	M	Laborer	28J107Rp
MALONE, B.	18	M	Laborer	28J107Rp
CARNAN, Pat	26	M	Laborer	28J107Rp
MCANALLY, Ann	13	F	None	28J107Rp
FREELY, Geo.	26	M	Gentleman	28J107Rp

BROOKSBY 29 JULY 1847

From Glasgow

NAMES OF PASSENGERS	AGE	SEX	OCCUPATIONS	DATE PORT SHIP
GOW, John	40	M	Farmer	29J104Ex
Janet	28	F	None	29J104Ex
GIBSON, Geo.	15	M	Farmer	29J104Ex
WHITEHILL, Robt.	53	M	Mechanic	29J104Ex
Margt.	53	F	None	29J104Ex
Margt.	30	F	None	29J104Ex
Janet	22	F	None	29J104Ex
James	18	M	Mechanic	29J104Ex
Mary	13	F	None	29J104Ex
Robt.	10	M	None	29J104Ex
Hugh	26	M	None	29J104Ex
Jessie	24	F	None	29J104Ex
Robt.	01	M	Child	29J104Ex
FELLOWS, R.	40	M	Farmer	29J104Ex
Mary	36	F	None	29J104Ex
Eliza	13	F	None	29J104Ex
Robt.	12	M	None	29J104Ex
Mary	10	F	None	29J104Ex
Ann	03	F	Child	29J104Ex
Jno.	.08	M	Infant	29J104Ex
ROURK, Peter	40	M	Farmer	29J104Ex
Joana	13	F	None	29J104Ex
Hugh	11	M	None	29J104Ex
Thos.	04	M	Child	29J104Ex
Mary	02	F	Child	29J104Ex
STEVENS, Eliza	32	F	None	29J104Ex
Wm.	02	M	Child	29J104Ex
HARKINS, Ed.	26	M	Mechanic	29J104Ex
MCGILL, Wm.	13	M	Mechanic	29J104Ex
HERON, Margt.	17	F	None	29J104Ex
LATTIMER, Alexs.	20	M	Laborer	29J104Ex
MCMULLEN, Jno.	50	M	Laborer	29J104Ex
Mary	47	F	None	29J104Ex
Jno.	22	M	Laborer	29J104Ex
Jean	15	F	None	29J104Ex
Wm.	13	M	Laborer	29J104Ex
MCMILLAN, D.	17	M	Laborer	29J104Ex
MCDEED, Neil	22	M	Laborer	29J104Ex
CARNY, Ellen	25	F	None	29J104Ex
Mary	16	F	None	29J104Ex
CALLIGAN, Ann	20	F	None	29J104Ex
MOONEY, M.	18	F	None	29J104Ex
CALLIGAN, Neil	29	M	Laborer	29J104Ex
Patrick	20	M	Laborer	29J104Ex
John	18	M	Laborer	29J104Ex
Jean	15	F	None	29J104Ex
HORL, Daniel	22	M	Laborer	29J104Ex
Margt.	20	F	None	29J104Ex
STREET, Mary	21	F	None	29J104Ex
BANKS, Thos.	20	M	Laborer	29J104Ex
CHRISTIG, Mary	20	F	None	29J104Ex
FORD, Bridget	16	F	None	29J104Ex
GROGAN, Edwd.	16	M	Laborer	29J104Ex
THOMPSON, Margt.	18	F	None	29J104Ex
WILSON, Margt.	65	F	None	29J104Ex
Martha	18	F	None	29J104Ex
STEWART, Rachl.	50	F	None	29J104Ex
Isabella	51	F	None	29J104Ex
Jane	18	F	None	29J104Ex
Wm.	17	M	Farmer	29J104Ex
John	16	M	Farmer	29J104Ex
Saml.	15	M	None	29J104Ex
Thos.	13	M	None	29J104Ex
Elizth.	11	F	None	29J104Ex
Susan	09	F	Child	29J104Ex

NAMES OF PASSENGERS	AGE	SEX	OCCUPATIONS	DATE PORT SHIP
STEWART, R.Ann	06	F	Child	29Jl04Ex
Mary	03	F	Child	29Jl04Ex
MCKAY, Elizth.	30	F	None	29Jl04Ex
FORBES, Donald	25	M	Mechanic	29Jl04Ex
Chris.	19	F	None	29Jl04Ex
MCLAUCKLIN, Pat	24	M	Laborer	29Jl04Ex
MCCOMB, Robt.	33	M	Laborer	29Jl04Ex
MALONE, Margt.	19	F	None	29Jl04Ex
Susan	18	F	None	29Jl04Ex
Elizth.	17	F	None	29Jl04Ex
LONGRIN, Margt.	30	F	None	29Jl04Ex
MCMANNING, Robt.	32	M	Laborer	29Jl04Ex
Jas.	05	M	Child	29Jl04Ex
ANDERSON, Janet	45	F	None	29Jl04Ex
John	20	M	Laborer	29Jl04Ex
Archd.	19	M	Laborer	29Jl04Ex
Robt.	12	M	None	29Jl04Ex
Jane	10	F	None	29Jl04Ex
Margaret	08	F	Child	29Jl04Ex
HANSON, Henry	20	M	Laborer	29Jl04Ex
MOORE, Matilda	18	F	None	29Jl04Ex
CLELLAND, John	35	M	Laborer	29Jl04Ex
Mary	34	F	None	29Jl04Ex
Christine	12	F	None	29Jl04Ex
John	10	M	None	29Jl04Ex
Geron.	08	M	Child	29Jl04Ex
ARCHIBALD, Ruth	45	F	None	29Jl04Ex
Ann	32	F	None	29Jl04Ex
MITCHELL, Jane	18	F	None	29Jl04Ex
BEVIS, Jane	16	F	None	29Jl04Ex
MOORE, John	38	M	Laborer	29Jl04Ex
MCCALLUM, Alexs.	30	M	Laborer	29Jl04Ex
SCHOLEY, Ann	54	F	None	29Jl04Ex
ROURKE, Danl.	45	M	Laborer	29Jl04Ex
STEVENSON, James	26	M	Mechanic	29Jl04Ex
WESTON, Gerl.	24	M	Mechanic	29Jl04Ex
LAUCHLEN, Wm.	34	M	Mechanic	29Jl04Ex
CRUIKSHANKS, John	63	M	Farmer	29Jl04Ex
MILLER, Alexs.	32	M	Farmer	29Jl04Ex
CEASY, Robt.	52	M	Farmer	29Jl04Ex
Elizth.	50	F	None	29Jl04Ex
Elizth.	28	F	None	29Jl04Ex
James	26	M	Farmer	29Jl04Ex
John	24	M	Farmer	29Jl04Ex
Margt.	22	F	None	29Jl04Ex
Christa.	20	F	None	29Jl04Ex
Jeffrey	18	M	Farmer	29Jl04Ex
Robt.	16	M	Farmer	29Jl04Ex
GRAY, David	26	M	Farmer	29Jl04Ex
PATRICK, Peter	24	M	Farmer	29Jl04Ex
ODONNEL, Susan	22	F	None	29Jl04Ex
MCLAUCHLIN, Mary	21	F	None	29Jl04Ex
MCCONOWAY, Cath.	20	F	None	29Jl04Ex
STUART, Jno.	28	M	Laborer	29Jl04Ex
DIVIER, Mary	26	F	None	29Jl04Ex
MCGENGLE, Hannah	24	F	None	29Jl04Ex
PARKS, Jos.	22	M	Laborer	29Jl04Ex
MORRISON, Wm.	45	M	Laborer	29Jl04Ex
Ann	45	F	None	29Jl04Ex
Ann	18	F	None	29Jl04Ex
Robt.	16	M	Laborer	29Jl04Ex
Margt.	12	F	None	29Jl04Ex
MCCARREN, Cath.	24	F	None	29Jl04Ex
Margt.	22	F	None	29Jl04Ex
SCANLAN, Eliza	22	F	None	29Jl04Ex
MCEWAN, U-Mrs.	38	F	None	29Jl04Ex
Margt.	24	F	None	29Jl04Ex
Janet	22	F	None	29Jl04Ex
Robt.	20	M	Farmer	29Jl04Ex
Elizth.	18	F	None	29Jl04Ex
Isabella	16	F	None	29Jl04Ex
Mary	14	F	None	29Jl04Ex
BARDON, Eliza	18	F	None	29Jl04Ex
MURDOCK, David	08	M	Child	29Jl04Ex
FINSTDALE, U	20	F	None	29Jl04Ex

VENICE 29 JULY 1847

From Belfast

NAMES OF PASSENGERS	AGE	SEX	OCCUPATIONS	DATE PORT SHIP
HUNTER, Elisabeth	20	F	Spinster	29Jl07Di
THOMSON, Hugh	50	M	Farmer	29Jl07Di
Mary (W)	49	F	Farmer	29Jl07Di
John	21	M	Unknown	29Jl07Di
Hans	21	M	Unknown	29Jl07Di
Eleanor	19	F	Unknown	29Jl07Di
Jane	17	F	Unknown	29Jl07Di
Mary	13	F	Unknown	29Jl07Di
Samuel	11	M	Unknown	29Jl07Di
Hugh	07	M	Child	29Jl07Di
CULISTE, John-C.	21	M	Farmer	29Jl07Di
Hugh	20	M	Unknown	29Jl07Di
Ann	18	F	Unknown	29Jl07Di
HASLETT, William	27	M	Farmer	29Jl07Di
Eliza	18	F	Unknown	29Jl07Di
ANDERSON, Margret	30	F	Unknown	29Jl07Di
STEWART, Robert	13	M	Farmer	29Jl07Di
BUDGET, Samuel	29	M	Farmer	29Jl07Di
William	20	M	Unknown	29Jl07Di
Elizabeth	36	M	Unknown	29Jl07Di
Sarah	12	M	Unknown	29Jl07Di
FORNDEY, Henry	22	M	Unknown	29Jl07Di
MONRO, Ann	18	F	Unknown	29Jl07Di
HILL, Catharine	18	F	Unknown	29Jl07Di
SARJENT, Isabella	25	F	Unknown	29Jl07Di
COULTON, William	30	M	Unknown	29Jl07Di
Mary	18	F	Unknown	29Jl07Di
MCGRATH, Michall	21	M	Machinist	29Jl07Di
MCCUSH, Jane	30	F	Unknown	29Jl07Di
Agnes	21	F	Unknown	29Jl07Di
STEWART, William	24	M	Unknown	29Jl07Di
Robert	23	M	Unknown	29Jl07Di
Ellen	22	F	Unknown	29Jl07Di
COOPER, Achiballd	35	M	Farmer	29Jl07Di
ALAXANDER, Hugh	25	M	Farmer	29Jl07Di
Jane	25	F	Unknown	29Jl07Di
HEWETT, Jam.	27	M	Farmer	29Jl07Di
DOWNY, Robert	22	M	Farmer	29Jl07Di
SANDARSON, Sarah	18	F	Unknown	29Jl07Di
BROWN, Samuel	19	M	Farmer	29Jl07Di
ELDAN, Joseph	28	M	Farmer	29Jl07Di
John	26	M	Farmer	29Jl07Di
Dorrity	55	F	Unknown	29Jl07Di
Elisabeth	34	F	Unknown	29Jl07Di
Dolly	31	F	Unknown	29Jl07Di
Sarah	29	F	Unknown	29Jl07Di
JOYCE, Mary-Jane	36	F	Unknown	29Jl07Di
Thomas	21	M	Farmer	29Jl07Di
Mary-Ann	19	F	Unknown	29Jl07Di
MCMANN, Margret-A.	69	F	Unknown	29Jl07Di
DIXON, Patrick	47	M	Farmer	29Jl07Di
William	10	M	Unknown	29Jl07Di
Hannah	22	F	Unknown	29Jl07Di
Hester	13	F	Unknown	29Jl07Di
OLDA, Robert	25	M	Farmer	29Jl07Di
PATTERSON, James	26	M	Farmer	29Jl07Di
SMITH, Samuel	26	M	Farmer	29Jl07Di
MCCRUCH, Richard	22	M	Farmer	29Jl07Di
WILSON, James	44	M	Farmer	29Jl07Di
WALDRON, Barnard	25	M	Farmer	29Jl07Di
Christaan	24	M	Farmer	29Jl07Di
U	.00	U	Infant	29Jl07Di
William	02	M	Child	29Jl07Di
MCCARTEN, Susan	19	F	Unknown	29Jl07Di
Biddy	22	F	Unknown	29Jl07Di

NAMES OF PASSENGERS		AGE	SEX	OCCUPATIONS	DATE PORT SHIP
HETHERINGTON, Jane		20	F	Unknown	26JI07Di
Sarah		18	F	Unknown	26JI07Di
COCHMAN, Isabella		22	F	Unknown	26JI07Di
Ann-Jane		20	F	Unknown	26JI07Di
James		19	M	Farmer	26JI07Di
Jemima		20	F	Unknown	26JI07Di
HOUSTON, Hellen		21	F	Unknown	26JI07Di
Martha		45	F	Unknown	26JI07Di
Thomas		02	M	Child	26JI07Di
GUBBIN, Mary		22	F	Unknown	26JI07Di
MUGGINS, Alex		20	M	Unknown	26JI07Di
ROSS, James		60	M	Farmer	26JI07Di
Stewart		20	M	Unknown	26JI07Di
Eliza		17	F	Unknown	26JI07Di
Sarah-Ann		13	F	Unknown	26JI07Di
Ruth		12	F	Unknown	26JI07Di
David		10	M	Unknown	26JI07Di
Robert		08	M	Child	26JI07Di
MARSHALL, Eliza		15	F	Unknown	26JI07Di
Sarah-Jane		16	F	Unknown	26JI07Di
Elisabith		13	F	Unknown	26JI07Di
Susan		11	F	Unknown	26JI07Di
Robert		10	M	Unknown	26JI07Di
James		08	M	Child	26JI07Di
WIGTON, James		28	M	Farmer	26JI07Di
Mary	(W)	27	F	Unknown	26JI07Di
U		.00	U	Infant	26JI07Di
James		09	M	Child	26JI07Di
John		07	M	Child	26JI07Di
Thomas		05	M	Child	26JI07Di
Ann		03	F	Child	26JI07Di
NEWELL, Eliza		30	F	Unknown	26JI07Di
MCCULLOCK, Eliza		26	F	Unknown	26JI07Di
GRADIAM, James		31	M	Farmer	26JI07Di
PURDY, James		20	M	Unknown	26JI07Di
Jane		19	F	Unknown	26JI07Di
Ann		17	F	Unknown	26JI07Di
MALROY, James		30	M	Farmer	26JI07Di
Margret		30	F	Unknown	26JI07Di
BIGLAMBE, Sarah		18	F	Unknown	26JI07Di
MCHAUG, Sarah		19	F	Unknown	26JI07Di
MCGUARY, Patrick		20	M	Unknown	26JI07Di
MCCLEARY, Ann		50	F	Unknown	26JI07Di
Bess		25	F	Unknown	26JI07Di
Bridget		20	F	Unknown	26JI07Di
MCREYNOLDS, Boland		44	M	Farmer	26JI07Di
Mary	(W)	35	F	Unknown	26JI07Di
William		17	M	Unknown	26JI07Di
Eliza-Jane		13	F	Unknown	26JI07Di
Agnes		11	F	Unknown	26JI07Di
Mary		09	F	Child	26JI07Di
John		02	M	Child	26JI07Di
HARPER, Isaac		23	M	Machmkr	26JI07Di
Eliza		22	F	Unknown	26JI07Di
COLVITY, William		17	M	Clerk	26JI07Di
MANNING, Mary-A.		27	F	Unknown	26JI07Di
RANAGHAM, Patrick		32	M	Farmer	26JI07Di
Rose	(W)	26	F	Unknown	26JI07Di
U		.00	U	Infant	26JI07Di
U		.00	U	Infant	26JI07Di
Mary		05	F	Child	26JI07Di
Nancy		03	F	Child	26JI07Di
Ann		36	F	Unknown	26JI07Di
BENNETT, George		30	M	Farmer	26JI07Di
Mary	(W)	30	F	Unknown	26JI07Di
Margret		20	F	Unknown	26JI07Di
Jane		10	F	Unknown	26JI07Di
James		05	M	Child	26JI07Di
Mary		02	F	Child	26JI07Di
MCALRICE, David		25	M	Farmer	26JI07Di
CUSANS, James		18	M	Farmer	26JI07Di
WHITE, John		55	M	Farmer	26JI07Di
Sarah	(W)	55	F	Unknown	26JI07Di
Eliza		22	F	Unknown	26JI07Di
Mary		20	F	Unknown	26JI07Di

NAMES OF PASSENGERS		AGE	SEX	OCCUPATIONS	DATE PORT SHIP
WHITE, Susan		13	F	Unknown	26JI07Di
Rebecca		12	F	Unknown	26JI07Di
MILLS, Mary		46	F	Unknown	26JI07Di
Jane		20	F	Unknown	26JI07Di
Samuel		18	M	Unknown	26JI07Di
Andrew		08	M	Child	26JI07Di
Ejiah		05	M	Child	26JI07Di
Susannah		03	F	Child	26JI07Di
QUA, David		30	M	Farmer	26JI07Di
Jane		22	F	Unknown	26JI07Di
SMITH, Andrew		13	M	Farmer	26JI07Di
DUNCAN, Alex		39	M	Farmer	26JI07Di
Robert		13	M	Unknown	26JI07Di
Thomas		12	M	Unknown	26JI07Di
MURPHY, James		25	M	Farmer	26JI07Di
Margret	(W)	35	F	Unknown	26JI07Di
Richard		02	M	Child	26JI07Di
MCMALL, John		20	M	Farmer	26JI07Di
Margret		18	M	Farmer	26JI07Di
CONLY, John		46	M	Farmer	26JI07Di
MCFADANT, Ellen		13	F	Unknown	26JI07Di
CHAMBERS, Alex		86	M	Farmer	26JI07Di
Eliza		47	F	Unknown	26JI07Di
Matilda		18	F	Unknown	26JI07Di
Hugh		13	M	Unknown	26JI07Di
James		12	M	Unknown	26JI07Di
John		11	M	Unknown	26JI07Di
Jane		06	F	Child	26JI07Di
Adam		01	M	Child	26JI07Di
FOSTER, Ann		18	F	Unknown	26JI07Di
JOHNSON, Nancy		25	F	Unknown	26JI07Di
Isabella		05	F	Child	26JI07Di
MCCOW, George		21	M	Unknown	26JI07Di
PORTER, James		21	M	Farmer	26JI07Di
MCSHANNON, William		31	M	Farmer	26JI07Di
Catharine	(W)	30	F	Unknown	26JI07Di
Jane		05	F	Child	26JI07Di
REA, Andrew		25	M	Unknown	26JI07Di
MCGAAY, Catharine		20	F	Unknown	26JI07Di
SMITH, Samuel		20	M	Unknown	26JI07Di
MCDONALL, Ann		21	F	Unknown	26JI07Di
CRAWFORD, Margret		26	F	Unknown	26JI07Di
PUDY, Sarah		60	F	Unknown	26JI07Di
BLACK, William		22	M	Farmer	26JI07Di
CLAPMAN, Thomas		32	M	Farmer	26JI07Di
SCOTT, Robert		32	M	Farmer	26JI07Di
Ellen	(W)	35	F	Unknown	26JI07Di
Margret		04	F	Child	26JI07Di
Mary-Jane		04	F	Child	26JI07Di
William		01	F	Child	26JI07Di
BEATH, Joseph		00	M	Unknown	26JI07Di
WHITE, Fred		00	M	Unknown	26JI07Di
DELZELL, Hugh		00	M	Unknown	26JI07Di
BLAIR, Jane		00	F	Unknown	26JI07Di
Isabella		00	F	Unknown	26JI07Di

WM.T.DUGGAN 30 JULY 1847

From Cork

NAMES OF PASSENGERS	AGE	SEX	OCCUPATIONS	DATE PORT SHIP
MCCARTHY, Chas.	35	M	Laborer	30JI14Rv
Annthy.	27	M	Laborer	30JI14Rv
CADDIGAN, Cornelius	26	F	None	30JI14Rv
Cath.	24	F	None	30JI14Rv
Henry	24	M	Laborer	30JI14Rv
REGAN, Denis	24	M	Laborer	30JI14Rv
LEARY, Tim	22	M	Laborer	30JI14Rv
Margt.	60	F	None	30JI14Rv
BRADSHAW, Wm.	60	M	Laborer	30JI14Rv

NAMES OF PASSENGERS		AGE	SEX	OCCUPATIONS	DATE PORT SHIP
RICHE, David		22	M	Laborer	30JI14Rv
MCCARTHY, Edwd.		22	M	Laborer	30JI14Rv
Joana.		34	F	None	30JI14Rv
SWANTON, Benj.		46	M	Laborer	30JI14Rv
MCGRATH, Timothy		32	M	Laborer	30JI14Rv
James		34	M	Laborer	30JI14Rv
Mich.		26	M	Laborer	30JI14Rv
Martin		25	M	Laborer	30JI14Rv
Mary		60	F	None	30JI14Rv
Ellen		30	F	None	30JI14Rv
Joanna		08	F	Child	30JI14Rv
Margt.		05	F	Child	30JI14Rv
Wm.		.02	M	Infant	30JI14Rv
QUINN, Jas.		58	M	Laborer	30JI14Rv
Jno.		22	M	Laborer	30JI14Rv
Barth.		20	M	Laborer	30JI14Rv
Jas.		17	M	Laborer	30JI14Rv
Mary		23	F	None	30JI14Rv
Mary	(W)	50	F	None	30JI14Rv
Cath.		20	F	None	30JI14Rv
Bridget		22	F	None	30JI14Rv
Joanna		19	F	None	30JI14Rv
Anna		12	F	None	30JI14Rv
OBRIEN, Cath.		30	F	None	30JI14Rv
DALY, Jno.		26	M	Mechanic	30JI14Rv
MAGHEE, Cath.		20	F	None	30JI14Rv
GRIFFIN, Mich.		36	M	Mechanic	30JI14Rv
AHERN, Wm.		40	M	Mechanic	30JI14Rv
Cath.	(W)	32	F	None	30JI14Rv
Wm.		13	M	None	30JI14Rv
Mary		11	F	None	30JI14Rv
Margt.		10	F	None	30JI14Rv
Pat		08	M	Child	30JI14Rv
Jeremiah		06	M	Child	30JI14Rv
Jno.		04	M	Child	30JI14Rv
Ellen		.04	F	Infant	30JI14Rv
WALSH, Edwd.		40	M	Laborer	30JI14Rv
Cath.		06	F	Child	30JI14Rv
Margt.		09	F	Child	30JI14Rv
GIBBS, Smith		50	M	Farmer	30JI14Rv
Mary	(W)	50	F	None	30JI14Rv
Anna		14	F	None	30JI14Rv
Adeline		09	F	Child	30JI14Rv
Jane		92	F	None	30JI14Rv
MARA, Maurice		40	M	Farmer	30JI14Rv
Eliza	(W)	46	F	None	30JI14Rv
Maurice		12	M	None	30JI14Rv
FLYNN, John		26	M	Farmer	30JI14Rv

PRINCESS-ALICE 30 JULY 1847

From Dublin

NAMES OF PASSENGERS		AGE	SEX	OCCUPATIONS	DATE PORT SHIP
FEGAN, J.		57	M	Farmer	30JI20Rw
Rose	(W)	54	F	None	30JI20Rw
Judith		23	F	None	30JI20Rw
Jane		21	F	None	30JI20Rw
Michael		18	M	Unknown	30JI20Rw
Biddy		11	F	None	30JI20Rw
John		09	M	Child	30JI20Rw
Peter		03	M	Child	30JI20Rw
GILSHANAN, Cath.		50	F	None	30JI20Rw
My.		24	F	None	30JI20Rw
Mgt.		22	F	None	30JI20Rw
CONLON, T.		60	M	Unknown	30JI20Rw
U-Mrs.		80	F	None	30JI20Rw
Patch		25	M	Unknown	30JI20Rw
Richd.		18	M	Unknown	30JI20Rw
Mgt.		16	F	None	30JI20Rw
CONLON, Cath.		15	F	None	30JI20Rw
James		08	M	Child	30JI20Rw
Thos.		02	M	Child	30JI20Rw
Christy.		01	M	Child	30JI20Rw
KANE, J.		40	M	Unknown	30JI20Rw
Betty	(W)	45	F	None	30JI20Rw
Thos.		18	M	Unknown	30JI20Rw
Wm.		16	M	Unknown	30JI20Rw
Biddy		12	F	None	30JI20Rw
John		09	M	Child	30JI20Rw
LUDLOW, My.		61	F	None	30JI20Rw
Cath.		28	F	None	30JI20Rw
Patch		36	M	Unknown	30JI20Rw
Biddy		30	F	None	30JI20Rw
CAMPHION, Fanny		26	F	None	30JI20Rw
Cath.		07	F	Child	30JI20Rw
Rose		05	F	Child	30JI20Rw
Edward	(H)	24	M	Unknown	30JI20Rw
LUDLOW, N.		36	M	Unknown	30JI20Rw
Mgt.	(W)	40	F	None	30JI20Rw
James		12	M	None	30JI20Rw
Patch		10	M	None	30JI20Rw
My.		08	F	Child	30JI20Rw
Cath.		06	F	Child	30JI20Rw
Michl.		04	M	Child	30JI20Rw
Mgt.		02	F	Child	30JI20Rw
HARTE, J.		38	M	Farmer	30JI20Rw
Mary	(W)	38	F	None	30JI20Rw
Biddy		11	F	None	30JI20Rw
Cath.		07	F	Child	30JI20Rw
Mary		04	F	Child	30JI20Rw
Bryan		03	M	Child	30JI20Rw
ROURKE, M.		40	M	Unknown	30JI20Rw
MCCORMACK, J.		35	M	Unknown	30JI20Rw
ROURKE, Mgt.		31	F	None	30JI20Rw
Andrew		16	M	Unknown	30JI20Rw
CORMACK, Anne		42	M	Unknown	30JI20Rw
Wm.		20	M	Unknown	30JI20Rw
James		18	M	Unknown	30JI20Rw
Mary		15	F	None	30JI20Rw
Mgt.		13	F	None	30JI20Rw
Cath.		11	F	None	30JI20Rw
WARD, Betty		40	F	None	30JI20Rw
MANTEAGH, J.		35	M	Unknown	30JI20Rw
Ann		31	F	None	30JI20Rw
Patch		26	M	Unknown	30JI20Rw
CAMPION, Tsa.		42	F	None	30JI20Rw
James		20	M	Unknown	30JI20Rw
Mgt.		18	F	None	30JI20Rw
John		01	M	Child	30JI20Rw
MCGRATH, L.		27	M	Unknown	30JI20Rw
Mary	(W)	25	F	None	30JI20Rw
Michl.		02	M	Child	30JI20Rw
Mgt.		01	F	Child	30JI20Rw
EVANS, J.		43	M	Unknown	30JI20Rw
Sally	(W)	40	F	None	30JI20Rw
Michl.		13	M	None	30JI20Rw
Thos.		12	M	None	30JI20Rw
John		10	M	None	30JI20Rw
James		08	M	Child	30JI20Rw
Peter		05	M	Child	30JI20Rw
Mary		01	F	Child	30JI20Rw
DALY, A.		20	M	Unknown	30JI20Rw
Martha		40	F	None	30JI20Rw
Mary		36	F	None	30JI20Rw
Pat		16	M	Unknown	30JI20Rw
Eliza		14	F	None	30JI20Rw
LUNSDEN, J.		21	M	Farmer	30JI20Rw
CONNER, J.		25	M	Unknown	30JI20Rw
Edward		23	M	Unknown	30JI20Rw
Mary		18	F	None	30JI20Rw
Henry		13	M	None	30JI20Rw
MOONY, J.		50	M	Unknown	30JI20Rw
FOGARTY, Biddy		40	F	None	30JI20Rw
MURRAY, J.		24	M	Unknown	30JI20Rw

NAMES OF PASSENGERS		AGE	SEX	OCCUPATIONS	DATE PORT SHIP
MURRAY, Maria		20	F	None	30J120Rw
Eliza		18	F	None	30J120Rw
BROWN, My.A.		22	F	None	30J120Rw
BALANAN, P.		28	M	Unknown	30J120Rw
Anne	(W)	22	F	None	30J120Rw
Anne		02	F	Child	30J120Rw
RUSSELL, T.		30	M	Unknown	30J120Rw
FRASER, P.		20	M	Unknown	30J120Rw
LEARY, U-Mrs.		30	F	None	30J120Rw
My.		01	F	Child	30J120Rw
YOUNG, Pha.		17	F	None	30J120Rw
RYDER, P.		40	M	Unknown	30J120Rw
My.		36	F	None	30J120Rw
CARROLL, W.		38	M	Unknown	30J120Rw
MAHOONY, J.		36	M	Unknown	30J120Rw
Kate		12	F	None	30J120Rw
Eliza		10	F	None	30J120Rw
My.		09	F	Child	30J120Rw
Pat		05	M	Child	30J120Rw
Mara		01	F	Child	30J120Rw
FRAZER, N.		30	M	Unknown	30J120Rw
Bgt.	(W)	25	F	None	30J120Rw
Marcella		05	F	Child	30J120Rw
Pat		04	M	Child	30J120Rw
MARLE, R.		36	M	Unknown	30J120Rw
Phillip		26	M	Unknown	30J120Rw
Morgan		40	M	Unknown	30J120Rw
Nancy		25	F	Unknown	30J120Rw
Cath.		21	F	Unknown	30J120Rw
KILLEN, G.		18	M	Unknown	30J120Rw
Ann		19	F	None	30J120Rw
DOYLE, L.		25	M	Unknown	30J120Rw
TOOLE, Elza.		24	F	None	30J120Rw
George		04	M	Child	30J120Rw
J.		02	M	Child	30J120Rw
CULLEN, Ellen		50	F	None	30J120Rw
CONNELL, J.		28	M	Farmer	30J120Rw
Anne		23	F	None	30J120Rw
Rose		18	F	None	30J120Rw
My.		16	F	None	30J120Rw
Cath.		13	F	None	30J120Rw
Mgt.		11	F	None	30J120Rw
MCCORMICK, Rose		50	F	None	30J120Rw
CALLANAN, P.		20	M	Unknown	30J120Rw
Mary	(W)	22	F	None	30J120Rw
Patch		01	M	Child	30J120Rw
KEAN, J.		35	M	Unknown	30J120Rw
SMITH, T.		30	M	Unknown	30J120Rw
Biddy		04	F	Child	30J120Rw
HARTLAND, P.		42	M	Unknown	30J120Rw
U	(W)	39	F	None	30J120Rw
Christy		16	M	Unknown	30J120Rw
My.		18	F	None	30J120Rw
John		20	M	Unknown	30J120Rw
Michl.		13	M	None	30J120Rw
Anne		10	F	None	30J120Rw
Pat		05	M	Child	30J120Rw
ELDER, J.		30	M	Unknown	30J120Rw
Anne	(W)	26	F	None	30J120Rw
Joseph		07	M	Child	30J120Rw
Anthony		07	M	Child	30J120Rw
John		04	M	Child	30J120Rw
GIFF, Ellen		30	F	None	30J120Rw
IGO, E.		25	M	Unknown	30J120Rw
MELINN, M.		28	M	Unknown	30J120Rw
CORRY, Anne		30	F	None	30J120Rw
Mry.		07	F	Child	30J120Rw
CARTY, My.		22	F	None	30J120Rw
MURRY, Pat		09	M	Child	30J120Rw
Biddy		32	F	None	30J120Rw
GALLAGHER, Biddy		45	F	None	30J120Rw
John		22	M	Unknown	30J120Rw
Sally		18	M	Unknown	30J120Rw
Pat		16	M	Unknown	30J120Rw
Joseph		13	M	None	30J120Rw

NAMES OF PASSENGERS		AGE	SEX	OCCUPATIONS	DATE PORT SHIP
GALLAGHER, My.		09	F	Child	30J120Rw
HOZY, P.		22	M	Farmer	30J120Rw
PETON, Biddy		22	F	None	30J120Rw
CURY, Mgt.		22	F	None	30J120Rw
LLELAN, Ma.		24	F	None	30J120Rw
Biddy		20	F	None	30J120Rw
FOX, J.		30	M	Unknown	30J120Rw
James		07	M	Child	30J120Rw
DARLING, J.		24	M	Unknown	30J120Rw
NUGGING, My.		20	F	None	30J120Rw
DORLING, My.		18	F	None	30J120Rw
WILLIS, Jane		22	F	None	30J120Rw
COOKE, G.		28	M	Unknown	30J120Rw
CORMACK, J.		30	M	Unknown	30J120Rw
Thos.		27	M	Unknown	30J120Rw
Christopher		04	M	Child	30J120Rw
MCGRATH, J.		28	M	Unknown	30J120Rw
Pat		18	M	Unknown	30J120Rw
Biddy		26	F	None	30J120Rw
My.		03	F	Child	30J120Rw
Cath.		01	F	Child	30J120Rw
SALMON, Biddy		20	F	None	30J120Rw
PALMER, J.		22	M	Unknown	30J120Rw
DILLON, N.		24	M	Unknown	30J120Rw
LALOR, T.		40	M	Unknown	30J120Rw
Eliza	(W)	38	F	None	30J120Rw
Biddy		16	F	None	30J120Rw
Cath.		11	F	None	30J120Rw
James		09	M	Child	30J120Rw
JOHNNES, Eliza		20	F	None	30J120Rw
MAHAN, Ellen		20	F	None	30J120Rw
ROBINSON, J.		28	M	Unknown	30J120Rw
CLEARY, Mat.		24	M	Unknown	30J120Rw
John		30	M	Unknown	30J120Rw
Michl.		22	M	Unknown	30J120Rw
FAGAN, J.		40	M	Unknown	30J120Rw
Thos.		07	M	Child	30J120Rw
Jno.		03	M	Child	30J120Rw
MOLLOY, M.		45	M	Unknown	30J120Rw
U	(W)	42	F	Wife	30J120Rw
Pat		13	M	None	30J120Rw
Jas.		10	M	None	30J120Rw
CRAWFORD, N.		26	M	Unknown	30J120Rw
U	(W)	22	F	Wife	30J120Rw
JAMESON, J.		37	M	Farmer	30J120Rw
Ellen		35	F	None	30J120Rw
Pat		15	M	None	30J120Rw
MULLAN, M.		28	M	Unknown	30J120Rw
DYERS, Ann		40	F	None	30J120Rw
BORAN, Ann		01	F	Child	30J120Rw
CARRAN, Libby		60	F	None	30J120Rw

LIVERPOOL 31 JULY 1847

From Liverpool

NAMES OF PASSENGERS		AGE	SEX	OCCUPATIONS	DATE PORT SHIP
SCOTT, Robt.		30	M	Mechanic	31J102Bo
Ellen		30	F	None	31J102Bo
Adam		04	M	Child	31J102Bo
Ellen		01	F	Child	31J102Bo
JACKSON, Ellen		30	F	None	31J102Bo
Molly		37	F	None	31J102Bo
FOSTER, Robt.		23	M	Farmer	31J102Bo
James		20	M	Farmer	31J102Bo
Betsey		13	F	None	31J102Bo
Judy		15	F	None	31J102Bo
Adam		07	M	Child	31J102Bo
John		01	M	Child	31J102Bo
BEATTY, Adam		57	M	Farmer	31J102Bo

NAMES OF PASSENGERS	AGE	SEX	OCCUPATIONS	DATE PORT SHIP
BEATTY, Mary	43	F	None	31J102Bo
Andrew	13	M	Farmer	31J102Bo
Charlotte	28	F	None	31J102Bo
Margt.	18	F	None	31J102Bo
Elizth.	11	F	None	31J102Bo
James	06	M	Child	31J102Bo
LUND, Wm.	30	M	Laborer	31J102Bo
ATKINSON, Geo.	26	M	Laborer	31J102Bo
PYE, Elizth.	30	F	None	31J102Bo
Johanna	05	F	Child	31J102Bo
Thos.	02	M	Child	31J102Bo
TOOLE, Kenny	18	M	Mechanic	31J102Bo
REDFERN, Cath.	22	F	None	31J102Bo
Ann	20	F	None	31J102Bo
MALBURN, Cath.	26	F	None	31J102Bo
Mary	24	F	None	31J102Bo
CASEY, Peter	20	M	Mechanic	31J102Bo
CONNER, Saml.	40	M	Farmer	31J102Bo
Pat	17	M	Farmer	31J102Bo
Jno.	15	M	Farmer	31J102Bo
Mary	13	F	None	31J102Bo
Ann	05	F	Child	31J102Bo
HESLIP, Jno.	34	M	Farmer	31J102Bo
Robt.	26	M	Farmer	31J102Bo
ARMSTRONG, Adam	24	M	Farmer	31J102Bo
Elizth.	24	F	None	31J102Bo
Margt.	03	F	Child	31J102Bo
Jane	01	F	Child	31J102Bo
HESLIP, James	50	M	Farmer	31J102Bo
Jno.	21	M	Farmer	31J102Bo
Geo.	19	M	Farmer	31J102Bo
Isabella	15	F	None	31J102Bo
Elizth.	10	F	None	31J102Bo
James	07	M	Child	31J102Bo
HUMPHREYS, Jno.	20	M	Farmer	31J102Bo
Fanny	13	F	None	31J102Bo
MARTIN, Bridget	20	F	None	31J102Bo
CONNERTON, Henry	20	M	Laborer	31J102Bo
Benj.	24	M	Laborer	31J102Bo
Bernard	18	M	Laborer	31J102Bo
BROPHEY, Mich.	20	M	Farmer	31J102Bo
Jos.	24	M	Farmer	31J102Bo
Jno.	30	M	Farmer	31J102Bo
FARRELL, Patt	21	M	Farmer	31J102Bo
BRAMAN, Jas.	20	M	Farmer	31J102Bo
KAVANAH, Sarah	24	F	None	31J102Bo
Mary-Ann	16	F	None	31J102Bo
MCGUIRE, Thos.	26	M	Farmer	31J102Bo
MCHUGH, Terance	40	M	Farmer	31J102Bo
Honor	40	F	None	31J102Bo
Martin	04	M	Child	31J102Bo
EGAN, Patt	13	M	Farmer	31J102Bo
Ellen	12	F	None	31J102Bo
MCCABE, Ann	20	F	None	31J102Bo
Margt.	18	F	None	31J102Bo
MCHUGH, Rose	21	F	None	31J102Bo
FALLON, Cath.	13	F	None	31J102Bo
Ally	10	F	None	31J102Bo
MCPHILLIPS, Barney	21	M	Farmer	31J102Bo
MEREDITH, Richd.	50	M	None	31J102Bo
Ann	50	F	None	31J102Bo
Mary-Ann	21	F	None	31J102Bo
Elizth.	18	F	None	31J102Bo
John	16	M	None	31J102Bo
Frid.	12	M	None	31J102Bo
Robt.	10	M	None	31J102Bo
MONEGAN, Jno.	26	M	Laborer	31J102Bo
DORLY, Thos.	40	M	Laborer	31J102Bo
Thos.	30	M	Laborer	31J102Bo
LACKIN, Jno.	21	M	Laborer	31J102Bo
MOLD, Mich.	20	M	Laborer	31J102Bo
BERGIN, Fanney	20	F	None	31J102Bo
ONEIL, Patt	21	M	Laborer	31J102Bo
WALSH, James	12	M	Laborer	31J102Bo
GARRIGAN, Jno.	21	M	Laborer	31J102Bo
FAY, Ann	20	F	None	31J102Bo
USHER, Ann	20	F	None	31J102Bo
PIERCE, Jno.	29	M	Laborer	31J102Bo
ROY, Jno.	26	M	Farmer	31J102Bo
AIKAN, Fanny	26	F	None	31J102Bo
CASHAN, J.	.08	M	Infant	31J102Bo
BOYLE, J.	16	M	Farmer	31J102Bo
P.	12	M	None	31J102Bo
MURRAY, A.	26	F	None	31J102Bo
Jerry	10	M	None	31J102Bo
Thos.	08	M	Child	31J102Bo
WARRINGTON, A.	31	M	Laborer	31J102Bo
C.	25	F	None	31J102Bo
C.	03	F	Child	31J102Bo
E.J.	01	F	Child	31J102Bo
E.	35	M	Laborer	31J102Bo
B.	32	M	Laborer	31J102Bo
TAYLER, P.	29	M	Mechanic	31J102Bo
A.	33	F	None	31J102Bo
Wm.	08	M	Child	31J102Bo
G.	05	M	Child	31J102Bo
E.	.04	F	Infant	31J102Bo
LITTLE, J.	32	M	Laborer	31J102Bo
A.	23	F	None	31J102Bo
M.	01	F	Child	31J102Bo
MILLS, J.	50	M	Mechanic	31J102Bo
M.	48	F	None	31J102Bo
T.	20	M	Mechanic	31J102Bo
S.	24	M	Mechanic	31J102Bo
J.	15	M	Mechanic	31J102Bo
S.	18	F	Mechanic	31J102Bo
A.	22	F	Mechanic	31J102Bo
M.	12	F	Mechanic	31J102Bo
FERGUSON, J.	40	M	Farmer	31J102Bo
MCKEON, H.	31	M	Farmer	31J102Bo
NOULAN, Morris	30	M	Farmer	31J102Bo
C.	24	F	None	31J102Bo
MURPHY, J.	21	M	Farmer	31J102Bo
ROURKE, J.	24	M	Farmer	31J102Bo
MENOGAN, T.	15	M	Farmer	31J102Bo
M.	14	M	Farmer	31J102Bo
PRICE, E.	26	M	Farmer	31J102Bo
Jno.	21	F	None	31J102Bo
FLYNN, P.	21	M	Farmer	31J102Bo
HAY, J.	57	M	Farmer	31J102Bo
E.	30	F	None	31J102Bo
C.	20	F	None	31J102Bo
J.	19	M	None	31J102Bo
CARROL, H.	56	F	None	31J102Bo
M.	36	F	None	31J102Bo
C.	18	F	None	31J102Bo
J.	15	F	None	31J102Bo
M.	13	F	None	31J102Bo
E.	11	F	None	31J102Bo
J.	07	M	Child	31J102Bo
PARKER, T.	24	M	Mechanic	31J102Bo
MCHAMLEY, J.	23	M	Mechanic	31J102Bo
CAIN, P.	23	M	Laborer	31J102Bo
ROURKE, T.	24	M	Laborer	31J102Bo
TERNAN, M.	25	M	Laborer	31J102Bo
FLYNN, P.	34	M	Laborer	31J102Bo
FLANNIGAN, T.	23	M	Laborer	31J102Bo
ROWAN, C.	22	F	None	31J102Bo
CAIN, B.	17	F	None	31J102Bo
CONNELLY, M.	40	M	Laborer	31J102Bo
HICKEY, P.	29	M	Laborer	31J102Bo
NULTY, J.	30	M	Laborer	31J102Bo
MARVIN, M.	30	F	None	31J102Bo
P.	27	F	None	31J102Bo
AIGNAN, B.	20	F	None	31J102Bo
CONNELY, M.	25	F	None	31J102Bo
CAULEY, J.	20	M	Laborer	31J102Bo
MCDONALD, P.	20	M	Laborer	31J102Bo
J.	13	F	None	31J102Bo
E.	10	F	None	31J102Bo

NAMES OF PASSENGERS		AGE	SEX	OCCUPATIONS	DATE PORT SHIP
SHEA, J.		20	M	Laborer	31JI02Bo
FARRELL, E.		20	M	Laborer	31JI02Bo
U	(W)	18	F	Wife	31JI02Bo
CASTELLE, W.		21	M	Laborer	31JI02Bo
REYNOLDS, T.		20	M	Laborer	31JI02Bo
MURPHY, B.		20	M	Laborer	31JI02Bo
BRASMAN, M.		20	F	None	31JI02Bo
T.		18	M	Laborer	31JI02Bo
M.		22	F	None	31JI02Bo
RUTHERFORD, J.		48	M	Laborer	31JI02Bo
J.	(W)	36	F	None	31JI02Bo
W.		05	M	Child	31JI02Bo
M.		.08	M	Infant	31JI02Bo
SCOTT, W.		19	M	Laborer	31JI02Bo
HEALY, M.		40	F	None	31JI02Bo
MCGIGINS, J.		23	M	Laborer	31JI02Bo
J.		25	M	Laborer	31JI02Bo
LYNCH, T.		22	M	Laborer	31JI02Bo
B.		20	F	None	31JI02Bo
WALKER, T.		23	M	Mechanic	31JI02Bo
G.	(W)	22	F	None	31JI02Bo
M.		01	F	Child	31JI02Bo
MCGOWAN, P.		20	M	Mechanic	31JI02Bo
MULHONE, C.		26	F	None	31JI02Bo
CANAVAN, J.		20	M	Mechanic	31JI02Bo
MCGUINTY, A.		16	F	None	31JI02Bo
MCGERITY, P.		20	M	Mechanic	31JI02Bo
M.		18	F	None	31JI02Bo
GILLOLY, C.		20	F	None	31JI02Bo
MCGLYNN, M.		14	M	Mechanic	31JI02Bo
HART, C.		20	F	None	31JI02Bo
HAGAN, C.		20	F	None	31JI02Bo
QUINN, P.		24	M	Mechanic	31JI02Bo
CRAWNY, J.		24	M	Laborer	31JI02Bo

SOUTHERNER 31 JULY 1847

From Liverpool

NAMES OF PASSENGERS		AGE	SEX	OCCUPATIONS	DATE PORT SHIP
MONTGOMERY, T.		30	M	Merchant	31JI02Dy
RODERICKSON, R.		00	M	Merchant	31JI02Dy
SMITH, Elza.		00	F	None	31JI02Dy
My.		00	F	None	31JI02Dy
DODGE, J.W.		22	M	Laborer	31JI02Dy
Wm.		19	M	Unknown	31JI02Dy
REGSON, J.		24	M	Unknown	31JI02Dy
LYNCH, A.		27	M	Unknown	31JI02Dy
BENBO, B.		26	M	Unknown	31JI02Dy
My.		03	F	Child	31JI02Dy
JONES, My.		25	F	None	31JI02Dy
PALMER, T.E.		27	M	Unknown	31JI02Dy
WILSON, T.P.		23	M	Unknown	31JI02Dy
GRIGG, E.		21	M	Unknown	31JI02Dy
HILLDARD, J.		16	M	Unknown	31JI02Dy
HUGHES, My.		25	F	None	31JI02Dy
LEWIS, Anna		01	F	Child	31JI02Dy
T.		20	M	Unknown	31JI02Dy
JOSEPH, J.		20	M	Unknown	31JI02Dy
HOOPER, W.		25	M	Unknown	31JI02Dy
CONNOR, J.		14	M	Unknown	31JI02Dy
DOCKERY, P.		24	M	Unknown	31JI02Dy
HAGAN, T.		16	M	Unknown	31JI02Dy
COYLE, T.		26	M	Unknown	31JI02Dy
WEBB, T.		40	M	Unknown	31JI02Dy
HOGG, J.		30	M	Unknown	31JI02Dy
Ellen		03	F	Child	31JI02Dy
OLIVERS, J.		18	M	Unknown	31JI02Dy
CHADWENTY, W.		20	M	Unknown	31JI02Dy
STUART, J.		21	M	Unknown	31JI02Dy
STUART, James		21	M	Unknown	31JI02Dy
ACTON, J.		26	M	Unknown	31JI02Dy
DELON, Hanah		22	F	None	31JI02Dy
HIGGINS, T.		18	M	Unknown	31JI02Dy
SCALLY, W.		23	M	Unknown	31JI02Dy
CONROY, H.		44	M	Unknown	31JI02Dy
CAVANAGH, Rose-E.		18	F	None	31JI02Dy
EICHMANN, J.		29	M	Unknown	31JI02Dy
ROSENBERY, L.		27	M	Unknown	31JI02Dy
DONALD, M.		22	M	Unknown	31JI02Dy
WALLERSON, N.		25	M	Unknown	31JI02Dy
JOLEY, P.		58	M	Laborer	31JI02Dy
THOMAS, J.		52	M	Unknown	31JI02Dy
JONKEN, Anna		21	F	None	31JI02Dy
Edwd.		15	M	None	31JI02Dy
GALLINS, Cath.		26	F	None	31JI02Dy
MURPHY, P.		30	M	Unknown	31JI02Dy
HANNESSY, My.		15	F	None	31JI02Dy
DOWLING, My.		19	F	None	31JI02Dy
FLEESON, Mgt.		40	F	None	31JI02Dy
Mgt.		18	F	None	31JI02Dy
Joel		15	M	Unknown	31JI02Dy
WELSH, D.		12	M	None	31JI02Dy
HAGAN, W.		21	M	Unknown	31JI02Dy
DANIEL, J.M.		20	M	Unknown	31JI02Dy
HENNESY, M.		20	M	Unknown	31JI02Dy
DEEGAN, D.		35	M	Unknown	31JI02Dy
My.	(W)	35	F	None	31JI02Dy
My.		10	F	None	31JI02Dy
Mich.		07	M	Child	31JI02Dy
Patch		05	M	Child	31JI02Dy
Ellen		02	F	Child	31JI02Dy
BERTER, Elst.		27	F	None	31JI02Dy
Wm.		06	M	Child	31JI02Dy
ANAILL, Bgt.		30	F	None	31JI02Dy
CLEG, M.		35	M	Unknown	31JI02Dy
HALY, J.		30	M	Unknown	31JI02Dy
SULLIVAN, M.		29	M	Unknown	31JI02Dy
CORRY, My.		13	F	None	31JI02Dy
MELFEN, D.		28	M	Unknown	31JI02Dy
GRANN, D.		35	M	Unknown	31JI02Dy
CANNEGAN, Biddy		20	F	None	31JI02Dy
BROUGHTON, W.		40	M	Unknown	31JI02Dy
HUGHES, W.		24	M	Unknown	31JI02Dy
SLAY, S.M.		25	M	Unknown	31JI02Dy
CASSIDY, M.		70	M	Unknown	31JI02Dy
Joseph		30	M	Unknown	31JI02Dy
Cath.		24	F	None	31JI02Dy
HOUGH, W.		24	M	Unknown	31JI02Dy
SLAY, J.M.		40	M	Unknown	31JI02Dy
STEVENSON, R.		24	M	Unknown	31JI02Dy
DORMOTT, J.		24	M	Unknown	31JI02Dy
CONALLY, J.		35	M	Unknown	31JI02Dy
ILLENY, Jane		30	F	None	31JI02Dy
HUGHES, My.		28	F	None	31JI02Dy
CORCORAN, J.		18	M	Laborer	31JI02Dy
Bdgt.		21	F	None	31JI02Dy
My.		25	F	None	31JI02Dy
BEGLAN, J.		20	M	Unknown	31JI02Dy
My.		26	F	None	31JI02Dy
CANN, My.		30	F	None	31JI02Dy
MCDONNELL, W.		15	M	None	31JI02Dy
REDDINGTON, Mgt.		20	F	None	31JI02Dy
SULLIVAN, J.		20	M	Unknown	31JI02Dy
JONES, D.		39	M	Unknown	31JI02Dy
David		11	M	None	31JI02Dy
John		08	M	Child	31JI02Dy
Evan		09	M	Child	31JI02Dy
Mgt.		04	F	Child	31JI02Dy
Howell		02	M	Child	31JI02Dy
My.		01	F	Child	31JI02Dy
BEST, Sarah		30	F	None	31JI02Dy
Wm.R.		12	M	None	31JI02Dy
John		09	M	Child	31JI02Dy
Robt.		07	M	Child	31JI02Dy

NAMES OF PASSENGERS	AGE	SEX	OCCUPATIONS	DATE PORT SHIP
BEST, Sarah-A.	03	F	Child	31Jl02Dy
BARCOS, Ann	23	F	None	31Jl02Dy
WHALEN, My.	29	F	None	31Jl02Dy
Fanny	03	F	Child	31Jl02Dy
EAGAN, S.	19	M	Unknown	31Jl02Dy
GADDIS, S.	50	F	None	31Jl02Dy
CAMPBELL, J.	21	M	Unknown	31Jl02Dy
MCKEAN, Rose	22	F	None	31Jl02Dy
CONNOR, Bgt.	32	F	None	31Jl02Dy
Honor	16	F	None	31Jl02Dy
KELLY, Ally	27	F	None	31Jl02Dy
WILSON, Ann	21	F	None	31Jl02Dy
GRAY, Cath.	24	F	None	31Jl02Dy
Abby	20	F	None	31Jl02Dy
GATLEY, T.	14	M	Unknown	31Jl02Dy
DELLY, My.	11	F	Unknown	31Jl02Dy
DUNNIGAN, Ann	16	F	Unknown	31Jl02Dy
RILY, Ann	45	F	Unknown	31Jl02Dy
DELI, Job	15	M	Unknown	31Jl02Dy
Cath.	10	F	None	31Jl02Dy
WILLIAMS, Jane	40	F	None	31Jl02Dy
John	18	M	Laborer	31Jl02Dy
Jeremiah	16	M	Laborer	31Jl02Dy
Chas.	14	M	Laborer	31Jl02Dy
Ann-J.	10	F	None	31Jl02Dy
Wm.	08	M	Child	31Jl02Dy
Robt.	06	M	Child	31Jl02Dy
RILY, Alice	15	F	None	31Jl02Dy
GINLY, J.M.	24	M	Unknown	31Jl02Dy
KEENAN, O.	58	M	Unknown	31Jl02Dy
MCCRADDEN, T.	20	M	Unknown	31Jl02Dy
DOUGHERTY, My.	16	F	None	31Jl02Dy
POWERS, L.	33	M	Unknown	31Jl02Dy
SMITH, W.	19	M	Unknown	31Jl02Dy
MARTIN, N.	24	M	Unknown	31Jl02Dy
GODWIN, T.	20	M	Unknown	31Jl02Dy
SMITH, Ma.	20	F	None	31Jl02Dy
MURRY, P.	23	M	Unknown	31Jl02Dy
Bgt.	19	F	None	31Jl02Dy
CONN, R.	28	M	Unknown	31Jl02Dy
CLIFFORD, P.	11	M	None	31Jl02Dy
MCGOVERN, P.	08	M	Child	31Jl02Dy
DAVENLY, T.	21	M	Unknown	31Jl02Dy
MCGOVERN, Ann	12	F	None	31Jl02Dy
MCGLOIN, T.	22	M	Unknown	31Jl02Dy
May	60	F	None	31Jl02Dy
HENY, J.	22	M	Unknown	31Jl02Dy
ELLERY, M.	40	M	Unknown	31Jl02Dy
Eleanor	10	F	None	31Jl02Dy
James	06	M	Child	31Jl02Dy
John	04	M	Child	31Jl02Dy
PADEN, Sarah	17	F	None	31Jl02Dy
Michl.	01	M	Child	31Jl02Dy
GALLAGHER, J.	30	M	Unknown	31Jl02Dy
CONWAY, My.	36	F	None	31Jl02Dy
Anne-C.	04	F	Child	31Jl02Dy
Sarah	02	F	Child	31Jl02Dy
James	01	M	Child	31Jl02Dy
MCARDLE, Betty	14	F	None	31Jl02Dy
CONNING, W.	30	M	Unknown	31Jl02Dy
KERRIGAN, P.	21	M	Unknown	31Jl02Dy
Anne	19	M	Unknown	31Jl02Dy
Anne	18	M	Unknown	31Jl02Dy
MONAGHAN, P.	24	M	Unknown	31Jl02Dy
ARMSTERY, Elzt.	22	F	None	31Jl02Dy
Fanny	20	F	None	31Jl02Dy

CHAS.CHALONER 31 JULY 1847

From Liverpool

NAMES OF PASSENGERS	AGE	SEX	OCCUPATIONS	DATE PORT SHIP
MCNARY, P.	26	M	Laborer	31Jl02Rx
DENNIS, D.	33	M	Laborer	31Jl02Rx
Sarah (W)	31	F	None	31Jl02Rx
Evan	11	M	None	31Jl02Rx
Jno.	08	M	Child	31Jl02Rx
Ann	06	F	Child	31Jl02Rx
Wm.	04	M	Child	31Jl02Rx
Jane	01	F	Child	31Jl02Rx
JONES, Ann	24	F	None	31Jl02Rx
DAVIS, D.	23	M	Laborer	31Jl02Rx
Eliza	21	F	None	31Jl02Rx
JONES, My.	56	F	None	31Jl02Rx
David	23	M	Laborer	31Jl02Rx
John	22	M	Laborer	31Jl02Rx
EVANS, My.	59	F	None	31Jl02Rx
Wm.	21	M	Laborer	31Jl02Rx
LLOYD, E.	23	M	Laborer	31Jl02Rx
Mgt.	03	F	Child	31Jl02Rx
My.	06	F	Child	31Jl02Rx
David	09	M	Child	31Jl02Rx
BROMLY, J.	33	M	Laborer	31Jl02Rx
DIXON, C.	24	M	Laborer	31Jl02Rx
Ann	04	F	Child	31Jl02Rx
Ann	02	F	Child	31Jl02Rx
Charlotte (W)	24	F	None	31Jl02Rx
SARAHON, Judy	29	F	None	31Jl02Rx
GRIFFIN, Ellen	35	F	None	31Jl02Rx
My.	24	F	None	31Jl02Rx
SHEEHAN, C.	28	M	Laborer	31Jl02Rx
MEERS, Elza.	30	F	None	31Jl02Rx
DUANE, D.	24	M	Laborer	31Jl02Rx
FAZER, G.	30	M	Laborer	31Jl02Rx
BYRNES, J.	26	M	Laborer	31Jl02Rx
Sarah	30	F	None	31Jl02Rx
KEARNS, W.	28	M	Laborer	31Jl02Rx
My.	11	F	None	31Jl02Rx
Wm.	09	M	None	31Jl02Rx
Heny.	07	M	None	31Jl02Rx
Mara	06	F	None	31Jl02Rx
Isaac	05	M	None	31Jl02Rx
Robt.	04	M	None	31Jl02Rx
Isb.	04	F	None	31Jl02Rx
Hanna	02	F	None	31Jl02Rx
MCKENNA, D.	26	M	Laborer	31Jl02Rx
Thos.	24	M	Unknown	31Jl02Rx
Mgt.	18	F	None	31Jl02Rx
WARTON, J.	26	M	Laborer	31Jl02Rx
WHELAN, Mos.	30	F	None	31Jl02Rx
Bgt.	28	F	None	31Jl02Rx
BEMON, J.	24	M	Laborer	31Jl02Rx
REGAN, J.	48	M	Laborer	31Jl02Rx
COOKE, Honor	18	F	None	31Jl02Rx
SARP, Bgt.	16	F	None	31Jl02Rx
REGAN, H.	34	M	Laborer	31Jl02Rx
U (W)	34	F	Wife	31Jl02Rx
LYONS, J.	26	M	Laborer	31Jl02Rx
MCDONOUGH, J.	22	M	Laborer	31Jl02Rx
DEMPSY, P.	27	M	Laborer	31Jl02Rx
Anne	26	F	None	31Jl02Rx
Elzt.	01	F	Child	31Jl02Rx
MCCORMICK, F.	26	M	Laborer	31Jl02Rx
My.	21	F	None	31Jl02Rx
My.	11	F	None	31Jl02Rx
DOWLING, M.	40	M	Laborer	31Jl02Rx
Edwd.	12	M	None	31Jl02Rx

NAMES OF PASSENGERS	AGE	SEX	OCCUPATIONS	DATE PORT SHIP
DOWLING, Elzt.	32	F	None	31J102Rx
DELANY, Cath.	24	F	None	31J102Rx
GLINS, N.	24	M	Laborer	31J102Rx
Honora	24	F	None	31J102Rx
KELLY, J.	20	M	Laborer	31J102Rx
MARSLY, M.	20	M	Laborer	31J102Rx
BARRETT, A.	20	M	Laborer	31J102Rx
FRAHAN, M.	20	M	Laborer	31J102Rx
GARVIN, R.	21	M	Laborer	31J102Rx
Patch	20	M	Laborer	31J102Rx
ALINS, Leila	30	F	None	31J102Rx
Leila	02	F	Child	31J102Rx
RYAN, J.	34	M	Laborer	31J102Rx
Judy	34	F	None	31J102Rx
BENSON, J.	34	M	Laborer	31J102Rx
TROY, Wfd.	25	F	None	31J102Rx
MORNY, P.	25	M	Laborer	31J102Rx
Denis	20	M	Laborer	31J102Rx
MCLOUGHLIN, Bgt.	18	F	None	31J102Rx
SIDDON, My.	22	F	None	31J102Rx
QUIGLY, R.	36	M	Laborer	31J102Rx
Jas.	10	M	None	31J102Rx
COUGHLIN, P.	00	M	Laborer	31J102Rx
SHAW, E.	00	M	Laborer	31J102Rx
FOLY, J.	00	M	Laborer	31J102Rx
HUNT, Honora	00	F	None	31J102Rx
Bgt.	00	F	None	31J102Rx
MULDEY, P.	00	M	None	31J102Rx
CONIGHER, J.	00	M	None	31J102Rx
Jno.	00	M	None	31J102Rx
TRAYNOR, E.	00	M	None	31J102Rx
MCRENAN, P.	00	M	None	31J102Rx
FLEMING, R.	00	M	None	31J102Rx
RYAN, J.	00	M	None	31J102Rx
ONEILL, D.	00	M	None	31J102Rx
OBRIEN, Morgan	00	F	None	31J102Rx
Maga.	00	F	None	31J102Rx
JONES, J.	30	M	Laborer	31J102Rx
Anne	29	F	None	31J102Rx
Anne	08	F	Child	31J102Rx
Evan	05	M	Child	31J102Rx
David	03	M	Child	31J102Rx
Ursula	01	F	None	31J102Rx
JOHNSON, My.	24	F	None	31J102Rx
Mathr.	16	F	None	31J102Rx
CHARLTON, W.	45	M	Laborer	31J102Rx
Ann	45	F	None	31J102Rx
Edwd.	12	M	Laborer	31J102Rx
Jane	10	F	None	31J102Rx
John	06	M	Child	31J102Rx
HARLAN, J.	40	M	Laborer	31J102Rx
My.	10	F	None	31J102Rx
John	08	M	Child	31J102Rx
James	06	M	Child	31J102Rx
QUINN, M.	60	M	Laborer	31J102Rx
Frs.	20	F	None	31J102Rx
Mgt.	22	F	None	31J102Rx
GARETY, M.	13	M	None	31J102Rx
Michl.	03	M	Child	31J102Rx
MURRY, F.	17	M	Laborer	31J102Rx
KELLY, O.	22	M	Laborer	31J102Rx
CONROY, J.	21	M	Laborer	31J102Rx
RYAN, J.	26	M	Laborer	31J102Rx
MARK, R.	00	M	Laborer	31J102Rx
Berdy.	00	F	None	31J102Rx
LANG, J.	40	M	Laborer	31J102Rx
Allen	00	M	Laborer	31J102Rx
ROWLAND, T.	50	M	Laborer	31J102Rx
My.	40	F	None	31J102Rx
Hannah	11	F	None	31J102Rx
THOMAS, D.	31	M	Laborer	31J102Rx
Anne	30	F	None	31J102Rx
ROWLAND, D.	20	M	Laborer	31J102Rx
Elzbt.	24	F	None	31J102Rx
Cath.	20	F	None	31J102Rx

NAMES OF PASSENGERS	AGE	SEX	OCCUPATIONS	DATE PORT SHIP
JONES, E.	24	M	Laborer	31J102Rx
MOREY, R.	25	M	Laborer	31J102Rx
ROWLAND, R.	21	M	Laborer	31J102Rx
RICHARDS, T.	27	M	Laborer	31J102Rx
JONES, T.	30	M	Laborer	31J102Rx
Jane	25	F	None	31J102Rx
CONLAN, Ann	21	F	None	31J102Rx
RISLEY, J.	27	M	Laborer	31J102Rx
Michl.	23	M	Laborer	31J102Rx
CARROLL, G.	22	M	Laborer	31J102Rx
EAMES, J.M.	21	M	Laborer	31J102Rx
MCMANUS, Honor	22	F	None	31J102Rx
CALLAN, Cath.	22	F	None	31J102Rx
MALLAN, E.	40	M	Laborer	31J102Rx
My.	40	F	None	31J102Rx
Martha	11	F	None	31J102Rx
Thos.	07	M	Child	31J102Rx
LAWLER, S.	40	M	Laborer	31J102Rx
Bgt.	40	F	None	31J102Rx
Honor	06	F	Child	31J102Rx
Edwd.	04	M	Child	31J102Rx
Joseph	02	M	Child	31J102Rx
SMITH, A.	30	M	Laborer	31J102Rx
COLLINS, T.	32	M	Laborer	31J102Rx
ROGERS, J.	40	M	Laborer	31J102Rx
Ann	30	F	None	31J102Rx
W.	20	M	Laborer	31J102Rx
My.	08	F	Child	31J102Rx
Bgt.	03	F	Child	31J102Rx
Ann	02	F	Child	31J102Rx
SMITH, W.	40	M	Laborer	31J102Rx
Andrew	30	M	Laborer	31J102Rx
MULLIN, F.	09	M	Child	31J102Rx
NALLY, Honor	38	F	None	31J102Rx
WHITE, P.	44	M	Laborer	31J102Rx
Jas.	11	M	None	31J102Rx
Jane	30	F	None	31J102Rx
Wm.	09	M	Child	31J102Rx
Thos.	08	M	Child	31J102Rx
Ann	06	F	Child	31J102Rx
Kitty	04	F	Child	31J102Rx
DAVIS, J.	36	M	Laborer	31J102Rx
My.	30	F	None	31J102Rx
Eva	08	F	Child	31J102Rx
Ann	05	F	Child	31J102Rx
HEATON, Sarah	18	F	None	31J102Rx
OBRIEN, Bgt.	50	F	None	31J102Rx
Hugh	32	M	None	31J102Rx
Joseph	18	M	None	31J102Rx
Laurence	12	M	None	31J102Rx
LEHAN, J.	56	M	Laborer	31J102Rx
MURRY, W.	00	M	Laborer	31J102Rx
Cath.	01	F	Child	31J102Rx

GEO.WASHINGTON 31 JULY 1847

From BREMEN,Southampton

NAMES OF PASSENGERS	AGE	SEX	OCCUPATIONS	DATE PORT SHIP
CRAWFORD, C.	37	M	Unknown	31J190Ry
BALHON, K.	24	M	Unknown	31J190Ry
CANYERS, M.	22	M	Unknown	31J190Ry
HUNCHTEFORD, N.	37	M	Unknown	31J190Ry
U (W)	28	F	Wife	31J190Ry
BARNS, L-Mrs.	33	F	Wife	31J190Ry
MAWSON, L.	32	M	Unknown	31J190Ry
AUSTIN, U-Mrs.	23	F	None	31J190Ry
U	07	F	Child	31J190Ry
SLOPEN, E.	27	F	Unknown	31J190Ry
BARKER, S.	29	F	Unknown	31J190Ry

NAMES OF PASSENGERS	AGE	SEX	OCCUPATIONS	DATE PORT SHIP
JACKSON, E.	40	M	Mechanic	31Jl90Ry
MULLEN, T.	32	M	Mechanic	31Jl90Ry
CALLAN, J.	30	M	Mechanic	31Jl90Ry
NORTON, J.K.	32	M	Mechanic	31Jl90Ry
BLANE, J.	35	M	Mechanic	31Jl90Ry
SMITH, J.P.	49	M	Mechanic	31Jl90Ry
MILIUS, E.Jr.	18	M	Mechanic	31Jl90Ry
STOMBERG, H.	26	M	Mechanic	31Jl90Ry
SLADE, W.	34	M	Mechanic	31Jl90Ry
KENDALL, J.E.	38	M	None	31Jl90Ry
DEVEREAUX, S.C.	25	M	Unknown	31Jl90Ry
WILLETT, L.	26	M	Unknown	31Jl90Ry
WARNER, A.	24	M	Unknown	31Jl90Ry
LAGRECE, S.	30	M	Unknown	31Jl90Ry
SMITH, J.D.	20	M	Unknown	31Jl90Ry
GRAHAM, G.	38	M	Unknown	31Jl90Ry
ZOYBAUM, J.A.	24	M	Unknown	31Jl90Ry
SOUTHGATE, J.	31	M	Unknown	31Jl90Ry
JACOBS, J.	33	M	Unknown	31Jl90Ry
RENDALL, B.P.	40	M	Unknown	31Jl90Ry
KENDALL, Lit.	35	M	Unknown	31Jl90Ry
COOKE, J.	32	M	Unknown	31Jl90Ry
LANDEN, E.	24	M	Unknown	31Jl90Ry
SMITH, T.	56	M	Unknown	31Jl90Ry
E.	22	F	None	31Jl90Ry
VINCENT, W.	35	F	None	31Jl90Ry
FINCH, U-Mrs.	32	F	None	31Jl90Ry
SWANSON, U	18	F	None	31Jl90Ry
SENNLE, N.	20	F	None	31Jl90Ry
SALCEDO, D.	24	M	Merchant	31Jl90Ry
Anto.	22	M	Merchant	31Jl90Ry
BLACK, T.	23	M	Merchant	31Jl90Ry
C.	32	M	Merchant	31Jl90Ry
HANLOCK, G.	45	M	Merchant	31Jl90Ry
HAWLY, Q.A.	50	M	Merchant	31Jl90Ry

COLUMBIA 02 AUGUST 1847

From Liverpool

NAMES OF PASSENGERS	AGE	SEX	OCCUPATIONS	DATE PORT SHIP
HOPE, Edmd.	32	M	None	02Au02Hx
Mary	30	F	None	02Au02Hx
MCKENSIE, Eliza	40	F	None	02Au02Hx
Frances-N.	13	F	None	02Au02Hx
James-A.	10	M	None	02Au02Hx
PURCELL, Johanna	45	F	None	02Au02Hx
Margt.	45	F	None	02Au02Hx
Kate	40	F	None	02Au02Hx
WILLIAMS, Wm.A.	41	M	None	02Au02Hx
JONES, B.	18	M	None	02Au02Hx
R.	25	M	None	02Au02Hx
LUNT, L.W.	23	M	None	02Au02Hx
LOVE, R.	35	M	None	02Au02Hx
REGAN, Mich.	27	M	Laborer	02Au02Hx
U	22	F	None	02Au02Hx
Cath.	17	F	None	02Au02Hx
Mich.	.00	M	Infant	02Au02Hx
GRATTAN, Bryan	20	M	Laborer	02Au02Hx
SHERLOCK, John	20	M	Laborer	02Au02Hx
CORIGAN, John	24	M	Laborer	02Au02Hx
U	20	F	None	02Au02Hx
U	.00	U	Infant	02Au02Hx
OLINFREL, H.	18	M	Laborer	02Au02Hx
HANLON, Peggy	20	F	None	02Au02Hx
CARNEY, John	40	M	Laborer	02Au02Hx
Died-At-Sea				
U	30	F	None	02Au02Hx
Joanna	60	F	None	02Au02Hx
Cath.	04	F	Child	02Au02Hx
CARNEY, Mary	03	F	Child	02Au02Hx
Johana	.00	F	Infant	02Au02Hx
SHEELY, Mich.	18	M	Laborer	02Au02Hx
Mary	20	F	None	02Au02Hx
Pat	20	M	Laborer	02Au02Hx
CALE, Thos.	29	M	Laborer	02Au02Hx
Corns.	27	M	Laborer	02Au02Hx
Cath.	21	F	None	02Au02Hx
GREENWOOD, Paul	24	M	Laborer	02Au02Hx
BANON, Abraham	24	M	Laborer	02Au02Hx
REMCORN, Rich.H.	00	M	Unknown	02Au02Hx
WALSH, Thos.	23	M	Laborer	02Au02Hx
MCAVOY, Martin	38	M	Laborer	02Au02Hx
BROPHY, Jno.	23	M	Unknown	02Au02Hx
TOBIN, Jno.	35	M	Unknown	02Au02Hx
CONWAY, Christy	33	M	Unknown	02Au02Hx
KENEDY, A.	00	U	Unknown	02Au02Hx
MOONEY, Bernard	32	M	Laborer	02Au02Hx
DASEY, Wm.	24	M	Laborer	02Au02Hx
HENSON, Mich.	25	M	Laborer	02Au02Hx
HOWE, Rebecca	20	F	None	02Au02Hx
Rebecca	.00	F	Infant	02Au02Hx
MOORE, Stewart	13	M	None	02Au02Hx
MCGUIRE, Mary	20	F	None	02Au02Hx
HUGHES, Wm.	28	M	Laborer	02Au02Hx
SCALLY, Pat	20	M	Laborer	02Au02Hx
QUINN, Mich.	36	M	Laborer	02Au02Hx
U	40	F	None	02Au02Hx
ROBINS, Isaac	30	M	Laborer	02Au02Hx
GALAGHER, Mary	19	F	None	02Au02Hx
WHITTELY, Benj.	60	M	Laborer	02Au02Hx
ENTWHISTLE, Ralph	50	M	Laborer	02Au02Hx
NORRIS, Thos.	34	M	Laborer	02Au02Hx
Wm.	23	M	Laborer	02Au02Hx
MANLEY, John	20	M	Laborer	02Au02Hx
LYNCH, Judith	20	F	None	02Au02Hx
U	.00	U	Infant	02Au02Hx
JACKSON, John	36	M	Laborer	02Au02Hx
FAY, James	30	M	Laborer	02Au02Hx
HOOK, David	30	M	Laborer	02Au02Hx
LURIE, David	28	M	Laborer	02Au02Hx
SHIELDS, Owen	40	M	Laborer	02Au02Hx
Mary	30	F	None	02Au02Hx
Biddy	14	F	None	02Au02Hx
MANNERING, Jas.	22	M	Laborer	02Au02Hx
DONNELLY, Jno.	29	M	Laborer	02Au02Hx
MORAN, Thos.	21	M	Laborer	02Au02Hx
Jno.	20	M	Laborer	02Au02Hx
U	60	F	None	02Au02Hx
SHANLY, Frances	21	F	None	02Au02Hx
Anne	20	F	None	02Au02Hx
CAHILL, Robt.	20	M	Laborer	02Au02Hx
Jno.	20	M	Laborer	02Au02Hx
Dennis	19	M	Laborer	02Au02Hx
FRILL, Margt.	40	F	None	02Au02Hx
Wm.	14	M	None	02Au02Hx
James	15	M	None	02Au02Hx
Cath.	18	F	None	02Au02Hx
MULHERAN, Wm.	20	M	Laborer	02Au02Hx
KERIGAN, Francis	40	M	Laborer	02Au02Hx
U	20	F	None	02Au02Hx
Peter	16	M	Laborer	02Au02Hx
BYRNE, Mich.	20	M	Laborer	02Au02Hx
KELLY, Mary	17	F	None	02Au02Hx
CALLAGHAN, Timothy	30	M	Laborer	02Au02Hx
RICE, U-Mrs.	21	F	None	02Au02Hx
Edwd.	27	M	Laborer	02Au02Hx
Bridget	21	F	None	02Au02Hx
Chas.	.00	M	Infant	02Au02Hx
WHITE, Bridget	21	F	None	02Au02Hx
MURRAY, Cath.	20	F	None	02Au02Hx
Sarah	30	F	None	02Au02Hx
FORD, John	32	M	Laborer	02Au02Hx
Cath.	30	F	None	02Au02Hx
U	.00	U	Infant	02Au02Hx

NAMES OF PASSENGERS	AGE	SEX	OCCUPATIONS	DATE PORT SHIP
MCDERMOTT, Patt	36	M	Laborer	02Au02Hx
Mary	32	F	None	02Au02Hx
Margt.	09	F	Child	02Au02Hx
Maria	06	F	Child	02Au02Hx
Pat	04	M	Child	02Au02Hx
REDFORTH, Ellen	40	F	None	02Au02Hx
MCDONNELL, Chas	30	M	Laborer	02Au02Hx
OBRIEN, Maurice	25	M	Laborer	02Au02Hx
SMITH, Jas.	26	F	None	02Au02Hx
BURNETT, Ann	21	F	None	02Au02Hx
LOWRY, Thos.	22	M	Laborer	02Au02Hx
HARTLEY, Saml.	14	M	Laborer	02Au02Hx
SMITH, John	21	M	Laborer	02Au02Hx
CANTIN, Abby	25	F	None	02Au02Hx
COGLE, Edwd.	50	M	Laborer	02Au02Hx
Cath.	50	F	None	02Au02Hx
Judy	24	F	None	02Au02Hx
Ann	18	F	None	02Au02Hx
Biddy	16	F	None	02Au02Hx
DRURY, Pat	30	M	Laborer	02Au02Hx
Rose	12	F	None	02Au02Hx
Mich.	08	M	Child	02Au02Hx
GATLEY, Mich.	20	M	Laborer	02Au02Hx
Edwd.	18	M	Laborer	02Au02Hx
KEGAN, Jno.	08	M	Child	02Au02Hx
CLARK, Jas.	30	M	Laborer	02Au02Hx
OBRIEN, Owen	17	M	Laborer	02Au02Hx
NEVIN, Pat	20	M	Laborer	02Au02Hx
Martin	18	M	Laborer	02Au02Hx
SMITH, Alice	32	F	None	02Au02Hx
Mary	30	F	None	02Au02Hx
LEESON, Betsey	24	F	None	02Au02Hx
BULMAN, Elizth.	27	F	None	02Au02Hx
OLDEN, Jno.	32	M	Laborer	02Au02Hx
MALIN, Jas.	28	M	Laborer	02Au02Hx
REMCORN, Alice	20	F	None	02Au02Hx
Hannah	.00	F	Infant	02Au02Hx
CODY, Wm.	26	M	Laborer	02Au02Hx
U	24	F	None	02Au02Hx
LEPIN, Jas.	13	M	None	02Au02Hx
Mary	09	F	Child	02Au02Hx
HALL, Mary	21	F	None	02Au02Hx
BEARD, Sarah	20	F	None	02Au02Hx
FAGAN, Jas.	25	M	Laborer	02Au02Hx
HUGHES, Ellen	12	F	None	02Au02Hx
Elizth.	30	F	None	02Au02Hx
BURTON, Richd.	40	M	Laborer	02Au02Hx
Ellen	17	F	None	02Au02Hx
Thos.	13	M	None	02Au02Hx
Maria	12	F	None	02Au02Hx
Prudence	10	F	None	02Au02Hx
Timothy	06	M	Child	02Au02Hx
Louisa	03	F	Child	02Au02Hx
Bridget	08	F	Child	02Au02Hx
NOONAN, Pat	26	M	Laborer	02Au02Hx
OKEEFFE, James	26	M	Laborer	02Au02Hx
HALLAHON, Pat	36	M	Laborer	02Au02Hx
Joanna	18	F	None	02Au02Hx
FLYNN, Corns.	00	M	Laborer	02Au02Hx
Eliza	00	F	None	02Au02Hx
STOKES, Cath.	00	F	None	02Au02Hx
LOWLER, Jno.	28	M	Laborer	02Au02Hx
BOW, Margt.	20	F	None	02Au02Hx
GILVEY, Thos.	30	M	Laborer	02Au02Hx
DUFFY, Felix	25	M	Laborer	02Au02Hx
BALDERSON, Kent	40	M	Laborer	02Au02Hx
U	40	F	None	02Au02Hx
U	.00	U	Infant	02Au02Hx
Joseph	07	M	Child	02Au02Hx
Eliza	05	F	Child	02Au02Hx
John	03	M	Child	02Au02Hx
William	09	M	Child	02Au02Hx
Henry	13	M	None	02Au02Hx
FOWLER, Wm.	00	M	Laborer	02Au02Hx
BYRNE, Beny.	00	M	Laborer	02Au02Hx
REILLY, Pat	40	M	Laborer	02Au02Hx
VERNON, Thos.	35	M	Laborer	02Au02Hx
SELLER, Wm.	28	M	Laborer	02Au02Hx
HOGG, John	41	M	Laborer	02Au02Hx
FELLOWS, Caroline	29	F	None	02Au02Hx
Caroline	.00	F	Infant	02Au02Hx
BORTELLA, J.	26	M	Laborer	02Au02Hx
DOLLARD, Sarah	50	F	None	02Au02Hx
FITZGERALD, Thos.	23	M	Laborer	02Au02Hx
BYRNE, Mary	24	F	None	02Au02Hx
WOODS, Eliza	36	F	None	02Au02Hx
Sally	16	F	None	02Au02Hx
Cath.	14	F	None	02Au02Hx
Mary	06	F	Child	02Au02Hx
Eliz.	04	F	Child	02Au02Hx
Charlotte	02	F	Child	02Au02Hx
BROWN, Thos.	24	M	Laborer	02Au02Hx
ROBINSON, Hugh	22	M	Laborer	02Au02Hx
MCGUIRE, Jas.	24	M	Laborer	02Au02Hx
BRENAN, Pat	26	M	Laborer	02Au02Hx
Mary	22	F	None	02Au02Hx
CORRIGAN, Pat	18	M	Laborer	02Au02Hx
BRENAN, Mary	23	F	None	02Au02Hx
U	.00	U	Infant	02Au02Hx
WOOD, Wm.	25	M	Laborer	02Au02Hx
ABBOTT, Joseph	27	M	Laborer	02Au02Hx
DUNN, Margt.	00	F	None	02Au02Hx
CAIN, Thos.	25	M	Laborer	02Au02Hx
John	18	M	Laborer	02Au02Hx
Pat	10	M	Laborer	02Au02Hx
EVANS, Mary	00	F	None	02Au02Hx
Griffith	10	M	None	02Au02Hx
Gevine	08	F	Child	02Au02Hx
Jemima	06	F	Child	02Au02Hx
Robert	03	F	Child	02Au02Hx
LLOYD, Gaylen	11	M	None	02Au02Hx
ONEAL, Daniel	18	M	Laborer	02Au02Hx
Ellen	16	F	None	02Au02Hx
WELCH, Jas.	25	M	Laborer	02Au02Hx
ONEAL, Jane	16	F	None	02Au02Hx
BEARD, James	19	M	Laborer	02Au02Hx
FALLON, Mary	20	F	None	02Au02Hx
GRELOUSE, John	33	M	Laborer	02Au02Hx
U	33	F	None	02Au02Hx
Wm.	09	M	Child	02Au02Hx
Henry	07	M	Child	02Au02Hx
Frank	02	M	Child	02Au02Hx
RYAN, Bridget	20	F	None	02Au02Hx
BRIEN, Nancy	20	F	None	02Au02Hx
John	13	M	Laborer	02Au02Hx
Mary	34	F	None	02Au02Hx
MCGRATH, Mary	20	F	None	02Au02Hx
MCCAFFREY, Peter	20	M	Laborer	02Au02Hx
LYNCH, Ann	18	F	None	02Au02Hx
CAREY, Jas.	20	M	Laborer	02Au02Hx
John	18	M	Laborer	02Au02Hx
HUNTER, Thos.	20	M	Laborer	02Au02Hx
CASSIDY, Susan	18	F	None	02Au02Hx
SLACK, Susan	18	F	None	02Au02Hx
MCGAVIN, Edwd.	24	M	Laborer	02Au02Hx
SHIPLEY, Mary	16	F	None	02Au02Hx
TAAFFE, John	22	M	Laborer	02Au02Hx
CARLE, Cath	50	F	None	02Au02Hx
Peter	20	M	Laborer	02Au02Hx
Mich.	17	M	Laborer	02Au02Hx
Pat	14	M	Laborer	02Au02Hx
HARKIN, Fran	31	M	Laborer	02Au02Hx
QUINN, Mary	30	F	None	02Au02Hx
SWEENEY, Irvin	30	M	Laborer	02Au02Hx
MAHONEY, Mich.	45	M	Laborer	02Au02Hx
KEGANN, Honora	18	F	None	02Au02Hx
GANEN, Barney	20	M	Laborer	02Au02Hx
Mary	16	F	None	02Au02Hx
CARNEY, Jane	00	F	None	2Au02Hx
JAMES, Wm.	15	M	None	02Au02Hx

NAMES OF PASSENGERS	AGE	SEX	OCCUPATIONS	DATE PORT SHIP
JAMES, Thomas	11	M	None	02Au02Hx
Jane	14	F	None	02Au02Hx
MORAN, Pat	12	M	None	02Au02Hx
SHERIDAN, Jane	20	F	None	02Au02Hx
Mary	45	F	None	02Au02Hx
FROLAND, Saml.	28	M	Laborer	02Au02Hx
Ann	22	F	None	02Au02Hx
Mary	20	F	None	02Au02Hx
Wm.	.00	M	Infant	02Au02Hx
WALSH, Joseph	60	M	Laborer	02Au02Hx
Helen	18	F	None	02Au02Hx
KANE, Pat	26	M	Laborer	02Au02Hx
Margt.	20	F	None	02Au02Hx
BYRNE, Wm.	09	M	Child	02Au02Hx
CAMPBELL, James	20	M	Laborer	02Au02Hx
FOX, Anthony	12	M	None	02Au02Hx
HUGHTY, Thos.	44	M	Laborer	02Au02Hx
LASELL, Rose	18	F	None	02Au02Hx
QUILLAN, Philip	30	M	Laborer	02Au02Hx
DALLY, Bridget	45	F	None	02Au02Hx
MORAN, Bridget	11	F	None	02Au02Hx
Mary	09	F	Child	02Au02Hx
CALLAHAN, Jno.	17	M	Laborer	02Au02Hx
MCDONNELL, Hugh	30	M	Laborer	02Au02Hx
U	20	F	None	02Au02Hx
CULLEN, Bridget	00	F	Unknown	02Au02Hx
Cath.	00	F	Unknown	02Au02Hx
WICKINS, Martin	21	M	Laborer	02Au02Hx
DEVINE, Cath.	25	F	None	02Au02Hx
PRIOR, Mary	18	F	None	02Au02Hx
MARNEN, Ellen	19	F	None	02Au02Hx
Anne	17	F	None	02Au02Hx
FAY, Henry	22	M	Laborer	02Au02Hx
SMITH, Eugene	20	M	Laborer	02Au02Hx
VERLY, Ellen	20	F	None	02Au02Hx
BYRNES, Cath.	18	F	None	02Au02Hx
SHIELDS, Mary	14	F	None	02Au02Hx
LYNCH, Mary	18	F	None	02Au02Hx
HUNTER, Rosana	30	F	None	02Au02Hx
FITZPATRICK, Bridget	20	F	None	02Au02Hx
SHERIDAN, Thos.	21	M	Laborer	02Au02Hx
Bridget	40	F	None	02Au02Hx
Rose	30	F	None	02Au02Hx
JOHNSON, Mary	20	F	None	02Au02Hx
MULLIGAN, Jas.	45	M	Laborer	02Au02Hx
Mary	40	F	None	02Au02Hx
Usan (S)	13	F	None	02Au02Hx
SMITH, Mary	21	F	None	02Au02Hx
DEVLIN, Jas.	21	M	Laborer	02Au02Hx
SULLIVAN, Bernard	50	M	Laborer	02Au02Hx
U	50	F	None	02Au02Hx
Thos.	18	M	Laborer	02Au02Hx
BRAMSON, Bridget	50	F	None	02Au02Hx
FIERNEY, Thos.	50	M	Laborer	02Au02Hx
Hugh	20	M	Laborer	02Au02Hx
Ellen	24	F	None	02Au02Hx
GILMORE, Jas.	20	M	Laborer	02Au02Hx
OBRIEN, Rosana	28	F	None	02Au02Hx
FITZPATRICK, Pat	18	M	Laborer	02Au02Hx
CROMWELL, Eliza	00	F	None	02Au02Hx
Magt.	00	F	None	02Au02Hx
Eliza	00	F	None	02Au02Hx
SULLIVAN, Joanna	20	F	None	02Au02Hx
KELLY, Mary	30	F	None	02Au02Hx
Geo.	11	M	None	02Au02Hx
Anne	09	F	Child	02Au02Hx
Robert	07	M	Child	02Au02Hx
MCARDLE, John	25	M	Laborer	02Au02Hx
Mich.	20	M	Laborer	02Au02Hx
CONNELLY, Rose	16	F	None	02Au02Hx
FULLER, Ann	20	F	None	02Au02Hx
COX, Bridget	13	F	None	02Au02Hx
MCDERMOTT, Ann	20	F	None	02Au02Hx
BURNS, John	50	M	Laborer	02Au02Hx
MOORE, John	11	M	None	02Au02Hx

NAMES OF PASSENGERS	AGE	SEX	OCCUPATIONS	DATE PORT SHIP
MOORE, Mary	09	F	Child	02Au02Hx
GALLAMORE, Mary	36	F	None	02Au02Hx
MUTTINGTON, Jonathan	23	M	Laborer	02Au02Hx
HOWAN, Jerry	13	M	Laborer	02Au02Hx
Ellen	18	F	None	02Au02Hx
SCANLAN, Dan	14	M	Laborer	02Au02Hx
SULLIVAN, David	15	M	Laborer	02Au02Hx
ROCHE, Rosanna	30	F	None	02Au02Hx
TITIAN, Joana	60	F	None	02Au02Hx
James	30	M	Laborer	02Au02Hx
Patrick	32	M	Laborer	02Au02Hx
BYRNE, Thos.	17	M	Laborer	02Au02Hx
CANFIELD, Margt.	20	F	None	02Au02Hx
WHITELAN, Wm.	40	M	Laborer	02Au02Hx
U	35	F	None	02Au02Hx
Chas	05	M	Child	02Au02Hx
Geo.	03	M	Child	02Au02Hx
HAIL, Jno.	20	M	Laborer	02Au02Hx
Bridget	19	F	None	02Au02Hx
CAHILL, Cath.	22	F	None	02Au02Hx
MOORE, Bridget	27	F	None	02Au02Hx
ANERNY, Mary	18	F	None	02Au02Hx
MCHUGH, Peter	22	M	Laborer	02Au02Hx
BANEN, Margt.	00	F	None	02Au02Hx
WIPPLE, Mary	38	F	None	02Au02Hx
BROWN, John	20	M	Laborer	02Au02Hx
AHERN, Sarah	22	F	None	02Au02Hx
CALLAGHAN, Jno.	22	M	Laborer	02Au02Hx
LEONARD, Jno.	27	M	Laborer	02Au02Hx
FLYNN, Mich.	26	M	Laborer	02Au02Hx
ONEIL, Pat	00	M	Laborer	02Au02Hx
DUFFIELD, Julia	35	F	None	02Au02Hx
FLYNN, Jno.	38	M	Laborer	02Au02Hx
U	38	F	None	02Au02Hx
Mary-J.	05	F	Child	02Au02Hx
Chas-Wm.	.00	M	Infant	02Au02Hx
WATERLY, Mich.	15	M	Laborer	02Au02Hx
BERMINGHAM, Wm.	24	M	Laborer	02Au02Hx
U	37	F	None	02Au02Hx
CARROLL, Martin	19	M	Laborer	02Au02Hx
WARD, Bridget	40	F	None	02Au02Hx
HURITH, Cath.	16	F	None	02Au02Hx
Sarah	18	F	None	02Au02Hx
CHENY, Isabella	24	F	None	02Au02Hx
RICHE, Wm.	16	M	Laborer	02Au02Hx
MCDONALD, Frances	07	F	Child	02Au02Hx
HICKY, Mary	30	F	None	02Au02Hx
SPENLY, Pat	20	M	Laborer	02Au02Hx
Mary	17	F	None	02Au02Hx
REYNOLDS, Margt.	50	F	None	02Au02Hx
Ann	18	F	None	02Au02Hx
DUNLARN, Pat	20	M	Laborer	02Au02Hx
DAVIS, Arthur	24	M	Laborer	02Au02Hx
Terence	18	M	Laborer	02Au02Hx
KENEY, Ann	20	F	None	02Au02Hx
MURPHY, Mich.	10	M	None	02Au02Hx
DACEES, Eliz.	20	F	None	02Au02Hx
REYNOLDS, Ed.	20	M	Laborer	02Au02Hx
NOONAN, Cath.	18	F	None	02Au02Hx
HARNY, Nancy	20	F	None	02Au02Hx
SHARKY, Ann	20	F	None	02Au02Hx
CHESTEE, Pat	20	M	Laborer	02Au02Hx
Ann	16	F	None	02Au02Hx
BURNS, Jno.	25	M	Laborer	02Au02Hx
DAVIS, Ellen	20	F	None	02Au02Hx
DOYLE, Mary	18	F	None	02Au02Hx

NEW-YORK 03 AUGUST 1847

From Liverpool

NAMES OF PASSENGERS	AGE	SEX	OCCUPATIONS	DATE PORT SHIP
COCHRAN, Jno.	30	M	Laborer	03Au02Bk
LYNCH, Thos.	30	M	Laborer	03Au02Bk
BUTLER, Pat	27	M	Laborer	03Au02Bk
MCPHILLIPS, Betty	35	F	None	03Au02Bk
Ann	30	F	None	03Au02Bk
Pat	11	M	None	03Au02Bk
BELL, Jas.	36	M	Laborer	03Au02Bk
CAHILL, Sarah	25	F	None	03Au02Bk
SULLIVAN, Dan	34	M	Laborer	03Au02Bk
COLLINS, Con	30	M	Laborer	03Au02Bk
HOWELL, Adam	50	M	Laborer	03Au02Bk
Cath.	50	F	None	03Au02Bk
Mary	16	F	None	03Au02Bk
Eliz.	15	F	None	03Au02Bk
Wm.	30	M	Laborer	03Au02Bk
Rebecca	22	F	None	03Au02Bk
Charlotte	02	F	Child	03Au02Bk
Wm.	.00	M	Infant	03Au02Bk
HARPER, Cath.	04	F	Child	03Au02Bk
MCCARTHY, Pat	22	M	Laborer	03Au02Bk
CARTER, Nat	22	M	Laborer	03Au02Bk
CASEY, Jerry	30	M	Laborer	03Au02Bk
U	30	F	Wife	03Au02Bk
HUGHES, Pat	25	M	Laborer	03Au02Bk
FITZGERALD, Mich.	30	M	Laborer	03Au02Bk
DONEY, Mary	24	F	None	03Au02Bk
SHIELDS, Jas.	30	M	Farmer	03Au02Bk
BARRY, Mary	20	F	None	03Au02Bk
BREMEN, Sarah	20	F	None	03Au02Bk
HAY, Margt.	20	F	None	03Au02Bk
LIBERTALLE, Wm.	32	M	Mechanic	03Au02Bk
A.	25	M	Mechanic	03Au02Bk
B.	30	M	Mechanic	03Au02Bk
T.	23	M	Mechanic	03Au02Bk
MCMANUS, Biddy	50	F	None	03Au02Bk
Mary	20	F	None	03Au02Bk
Ann	17	F	None	03Au02Bk
BRADY, Peter	20	M	Mechanic	03Au02Bk
MCGARMEL, Ellen	20	F	None	03Au02Bk
Biddy	18	F	None	03Au02Bk
POLLARD, Margt.	20	F	None	03Au02Bk
Mary	18	F	None	03Au02Bk
WATSON, Bartly	28	M	Laborer	03Au02Bk
WALSH, Edwd.	30	M	Laborer	03Au02Bk
LENDERMN, C.T.	40	M	Laborer	03Au02Bk
Levy	25	M	Laborer	03Au02Bk
U-Mrs.	20	F	None	03Au02Bk
MCCLARY, Margt.A.	25	F	None	03Au02Bk
BOLE, Rob.J.	15	M	Mechanic	03Au02Bk
SHEHON, Pat	24	M	Mechanic	03Au02Bk
BARRETT, Maria	24	F	None	03Au02Bk
WEST, Thos.	30	M	Farmer	03Au02Bk
U	30	F	None	03Au02Bk
Thos.	.00	M	Infant	03Au02Bk
COOPER, U-Mrs.	60	F	None	03Au02Bk
Elsie	22	F	None	03Au02Bk
DENISON, Jno.	20	M	Laborer	03Au02Bk
Mary	23	F	None	03Au02Bk
MULVANY, Jno.	24	M	Laborer	03Au02Bk
DUNN, Mich.	20	M	Laborer	03Au02Bk
BROOKE, Enor.	20	F	None	03Au02Bk
ENGLAND, Geo.	48	M	Farmer	03Au02Bk
MURRAY, Peter	22	M	Farmer	03Au02Bk
MCGARRY, Mary	20	F	None	03Au02Bk
CONNOR, Della	20	F	None	03Au02Bk
CARROLL, Richd.	25	M	Farmer	03Au02Bk
Bridget	25	F	None	03Au02Bk
BARBER, Mary	25	F	None	03Au02Bk
Eliza	10	F	None	03Au02Bk
Leanet	08	F	Child	03Au02Bk
Rob.	06	M	Child	03Au02Bk
BUCKLEY, Mich.	28	M	Laborer	03Au02Bk
CLANCY, David	28	M	Laborer	03Au02Bk
CONNOR, Margt.	20	F	None	03Au02Bk
Joha.	20	F	None	03Au02Bk
PHILLIPS, Phil	25	M	Laborer	03Au02Bk
DWYER, Jas.	30	M	Laborer	03Au02Bk
U	25	F	None	03Au02Bk
Kate	08	F	Child	03Au02Bk
GARRY, Nath.	20	M	Laborer	03Au02Bk
NUGENT, Cath.	20	F	None	03Au02Bk
MCGINES, Pat	30	M	Laborer	03Au02Bk
Jedian	21	F	None	03Au02Bk
WHITAKER, Thos.	30	M	Laborer	03Au02Bk
MULLEN, Ann	23	F	None	03Au02Bk
ARMSTRONG, Jas.	30	M	Laborer	03Au02Bk
FITZPATRICK, Pat	28	M	Laborer	03Au02Bk
FAGAN, Thos.	25	M	Laborer	03Au02Bk
U	23	F	None	03Au02Bk
M.G.	25	M	Laborer	03Au02Bk
U	23	F	None	03Au02Bk
LAMBRET, Margt.	18	F	None	03Au02Bk
MACKLIN, Thos.	36	M	Laborer	03Au02Bk
BERNE, Peter	40	M	Laborer	03Au02Bk
U	28	F	None	03Au02Bk
Thos.	.00	M	Infant	03Au02Bk
BARRY, Wm.	30	M	Laborer	03Au02Bk
Alexn.	26	M	Laborer	03Au02Bk
Joha.	27	F	None	03Au02Bk
WIGGINS, Ann	64	F	None	03Au02Bk
MCDORMNTE, Bend.	30	M	Laborer	03Au02Bk
Mary	50	F	None	03Au02Bk
Thos.	.00	M	Infant	03Au02Bk
Bridget	03	F	Child	03Au02Bk
Peter	25	M	Laborer	03Au02Bk
CUNNINGHAM, Peggy	25	F	None	03Au02Bk
ROCHE, Jno.	20	M	Laborer	03Au02Bk
Jas.	25	M	Laborer	03Au02Bk
BASS, Betty	35	F	None	03Au02Bk
SHANLY, Jno.	20	M	Laborer	03Au02Bk
RIERSON, W.	20	M	Laborer	03Au02Bk
GORMLY, Cath.	18	F	None	03Au02Bk
FLEMING, Esther	40	F	None	03Au02Bk
CARY, And.	30	M	Laborer	03Au02Bk
U	26	F	None	03Au02Bk
Thos.	.00	M	Infant	03Au02Bk
Jane	50	F	None	03Au02Bk
Rob.	18	M	Laborer	03Au02Bk
Mich.	07	M	Child	03Au02Bk
Thos.	06	M	Child	03Au02Bk
And.	04	M	Child	03Au02Bk
Cath.	02	F	Child	03Au02Bk
HEALEY, Pat	20	M	Laborer	03Au02Bk
Margt.	20	F	None	03Au02Bk
Cath.	02	F	Child	03Au02Bk
Ellen	30	F	None	03Au02Bk
Thos.	.00	M	Infant	03Au02Bk
LEARY, Jas.	20	M	Laborer	03Au02Bk
Mary	50	F	None	03Au02Bk
HICKEY, Margt.	15	F	None	03Au02Bk
BRADY, Pat	30	M	None	03Au02Bk
CRANE, U	30	M	None	03Au02Bk
LYNCH, Phil	22	M	None	03Au02Bk
TRESMAN, Louis	20	M	None	03Au02Bk
DEIGNAN, Bridget	20	F	None	03Au02Bk
TIRNEY, Jas.	19	M	Laborer	03Au02Bk
CAREY, Jno.	21	M	Laborer	03Au02Bk
GORMILY, Thos.W.	26	M	Laborer	03Au02Bk
BRADLEY, Jas.	29	M	Laborer	03Au02Bk
Jno.	26	M	Laborer	03Au02Bk

NAMES OF PASSENGERS	AGE	SEX	OCCUPATIONS	DATE PORT SHIP
WITCHUCKER, U-Mrs.	22	F	None	03Au02Bk
BRADSHAW, Fras.	20	M	Laborer	03Au02Bk
DUNN, Thos.	14	M	Laborer	03Au02Bk
FILAN, Fanny	20	F	None	03Au02Bk
MURPHY, Jno.	50	M	Laborer	03Au02Bk
David	22	M	Laborer	03Au02Bk
DUANE, Magt.	60	F	None	03Au02Bk
Wm.	28	M	Laborer	03Au02Bk
Magt.	25	F	None	03Au02Bk
CARROL, Jno.	12	M	None	03Au02Bk
DALEY, Jno.	18	M	Laborer	03Au02Bk
DILLON, Mary-Mrs.	20	F	None	03Au02Bk
MCCLUSKER, Mich.	30	M	Laborer	03Au02Bk
Ann	18	F	None	03Au02Bk
LONG, Ellen	18	F	None	03Au02Bk
GRIFFEN, Jno.	24	M	Laborer	03Au02Bk
SHEELS, Mich.	00	M	Unknown	03Au02Bk
GLYNN, Julia	21	F	None	03Au02Bk
KING, Eliza	.00	F	Infant	03Au02Bk
DURE, Mary-A.	21	F	None	03Au02Bk
KENEDY, Jas.	15	M	Laborer	03Au02Bk
FOLEY, Cath.	21	F	None	03Au02Bk
EGAN, Thos.	21	M	Laborer	03Au02Bk
KENNY, Pat	21	M	Laborer	03Au02Bk
FOLEY, Mary	21	F	None	03Au02Bk
Mich.	21	M	Laborer	03Au02Bk
SHATFORD, Geo.	21	M	Laborer	03Au02Bk
NAUGHTON, Jno.	21	M	Laborer	03Au02Bk
WYNNE, Pat	60	M	Laborer	03Au02Bk
U	40	F	Wife	03Au02Bk
Mary	20	F	None	03Au02Bk
Pat	11	M	None	03Au02Bk
Martin	08	M	Child	03Au02Bk
Thos.	06	M	Child	03Au02Bk
Dan	04	M	Child	03Au02Bk
MULLEN, Cath.	22	F	None	03Au02Bk
MELROY, Chas.	21	M	Laborer	03Au02Bk
GAESY, Henry	21	M	Laborer	03Au02Bk
IRVIN, Jas.	21	M	Laborer	03Au02Bk
MCKEON, And.	21	M	Laborer	03Au02Bk
HORAN, Thos.	21	M	Laborer	03Au02Bk
MCBRACKLY, Mich.	21	M	Laborer	03Au02Bk
MCINTYRE, U-Mrs.	24	F	None	03Au02Bk
DALEY, Cath.	19	F	None	03Au02Bk
Sally	48	F	None	03Au02Bk
WALKER, Ann	21	F	None	03Au02Bk
MANSIN, Jno.	32	M	Laborer	03Au02Bk
Mary	30	F	None	03Au02Bk
Johna.	.00	F	Infant	03Au02Bk
HAGARTY, Ann	42	F	None	03Au02Bk
Mich.	12	M	Laborer	03Au02Bk
MURPHY, Thos.	21	M	Laborer	03Au02Bk
OKEEFE, Wm.	27	M	Laborer	03Au02Bk
BRADIGAN, Mary	19	F	None	03Au02Bk
FLANAGAN, Ann	28	F	None	03Au02Bk
REILY, U	60	F	None	03Au02Bk
BARRY, Cath.	18	F	None	03Au02Bk
Joha.	16	F	None	03Au02Bk
BYRNE, Julia	23	F	None	03Au02Bk
KELLY, Pat	21	M	Laborer	03Au02Bk
ONEIL, Margt.	21	F	None	03Au02Bk
OBRIDE, G.	19	M	Laborer	03Au02Bk
EARLY, M.	31	M	Laborer	03Au02Bk
GALLGER, B.	19	M	Laborer	03Au02Bk
OLROOGE, Mary	35	F	None	03Au02Bk
ELLIOTT, M.E.	20	F	None	03Au02Bk
REED, Wm.	50	M	Farmer	03Au02Bk
Sarah	17	F	None	03Au02Bk
CAMPFIELD, Jno.	21	M	Farmer	03Au02Bk
MCGOWEN, Jas.	55	M	Farmer	03Au02Bk
Mary	50	F	None	03Au02Bk
Jno.	16	M	Farmer	03Au02Bk
Cath.	14	F	None	03Au02Bk
Jane	12	F	None	03Au02Bk
Peter	11	M	None	03Au02Bk

NAMES OF PASSENGERS	AGE	SEX	OCCUPATIONS	DATE PORT SHIP
MCGOWEN, Magt.	10	F	None	03Au02Bk
Ann	08	F	Child	03Au02Bk
RILLY, Rob.	28	M	Farmer	03Au02Bk
NARY, Nancy	22	F	None	03Au02Bk
GERRARD, Jane	23	F	None	03Au02Bk
DONOHUE, Jas.	38	M	Farmer	03Au02Bk
Mary	05	F	Child	03Au02Bk
Thos.	03	M	Child	03Au02Bk
Jas.	02	M	Child	03Au02Bk
BARBER, Alexr.	30	M	Laborer	03Au02Bk
REMAN, Mary	21	F	None	03Au02Bk
GILROY, Jno.	21	M	Laborer	03Au02Bk
MCGARRY, And.	25	M	Laborer	03Au02Bk
SHEEHAN, Geo.	26	M	Laborer	03Au02Bk
U	26	F	None	03Au02Bk
Jas.	04	M	Child	03Au02Bk
Thos.	03	M	Child	03Au02Bk
Ann	06	F	Child	03Au02Bk
DALTON, Jas.	30	M	Laborer	03Au02Bk
WINNE, Ellen	14	F	None	03Au02Bk
Mary	24	F	None	03Au02Bk
HUGHES, Terry	25	M	Laborer	03Au02Bk
Ann	45	F	None	03Au02Bk
HUNTER, Mary	20	F	None	03Au02Bk
Susan	22	F	None	03Au02Bk
NELLIS, Nancy	20	F	None	03Au02Bk
GORMAN, Mary	20	F	None	03Au02Bk
WALSH, Bridget	35	F	None	03Au02Bk
BUCKLEY, Jno.	28	M	Laborer	03Au02Bk
CHESTER, Pat	22	M	Laborer	03Au02Bk
LENON, Peter	12	M	Laborer	03Au02Bk
CONCAN, Magt.	26	F	None	03Au02Bk
Ann	20	F	None	03Au02Bk
MCMULLEN, Mary	20	F	None	03Au02Bk
GAFFNEY, Mary	20	F	None	03Au02Bk
DOD, Ellen	16	F	None	03Au02Bk
Julia	10	F	None	03Au02Bk
BRAY, Jno.	26	M	Farmer	03Au02Bk
NULTY, Phil.	26	M	Farmer	03Au02Bk
RAVENSCROFT, Jno.	26	M	Farmer	03Au02Bk
JOHNSON, And.	30	M	Farmer	03Au02Bk
Jane	32	F	None	03Au02Bk
Jas.	16	M	Farmer	03Au02Bk
Will.	18	M	Farmer	03Au02Bk
Isabella	20	F	None	03Au02Bk
HUTCHINSON, Robt.	26	M	Farmer	03Au02Bk
ELLIOTT, Alexr.	32	M	Farmer	03Au02Bk
Isabella	30	F	None	03Au02Bk
Jane	.00	F	Infant	03Au02Bk
Sarah	.00	F	Infant	03Au02Bk
SMITH, U-Mrs.	25	F	None	03Au02Bk
Jane	02	F	Child	03Au02Bk
DAVIDSON, U	25	F	None	03Au02Bk
GRIFFITH, U	24	F	None	03Au02Bk
OGORMAN, T.	34	M	Physician	03Au02Bk
DOWLING, Robt.	28	M	Merchant	03Au02Bk
IBBOTSON, Laud.	25	M	Merchant	03Au02Bk

REPUBLIC 04 AUGUST 1847

From London

NAMES OF PASSENGERS	AGE	SEX	OCCUPATIONS	DATE PORT SHIP
SNICK, William	42	M	Farmer	04Au21Nv
Cath.	42	F	None	04Au21Nv
Adam	12	M	None	04Au21Nv
Barbara	22	F	None	04Au21Nv
Cath.	14	F	None	04Au21Nv
Nich.	12	M	None	04Au21Nv
Adam	10	M	None	04Au21Nv

NAMES OF PASSENGERS	AGE	SEX	OCCUPATIONS	DATE PORT SHIP
SNICK, Eve	08	F	Child	04Au21Nv
John	05	M	Child	04Au21Nv
Valentine	03	M	Child	04Au21Nv
Michl.	01	M	Child	04Au21Nv
ROSTEL, Martin	24	M	Farmer	04Au21Nv
DESSANER, Jacob	30	M	Farmer	04Au21Nv
KOLL, Cath.	17	F	None	04Au21Nv
BRESTLE, Maria	24	F	None	04Au21Nv
Susa.	17	F	None	04Au21Nv
SORENT, Adam	36	M	Farmer	04Au21Nv
Rosimer	24	F	None	04Au21Nv
BRITZEL, Martin	28	M	Farmer	04Au21Nv
Margt.	22	F	None	04Au21Nv
Elizth.	.00	F	Infant	04Au21Nv
GRAFF, Frank	33	M	Farmer	04Au21Nv
DAVEY, Jacob	27	M	Farmer	04Au21Nv
LAIRD, Peter-H.	31	M	Farmer	04Au21Nv
SHOCK, Jacob	44	M	Farmer	04Au21Nv
Frederica	40	F	None	04Au21Nv
Frederica	11	F	None	04Au21Nv
Goodless	07	M	Child	04Au21Nv
Henry	06	M	Child	04Au21Nv
Cath.	02	F	Child	04Au21Nv
SHOCKH, Andrew	47	M	Farmer	04Au21Nv
Rosina	34	F	None	04Au21Nv
John	04	M	Child	04Au21Nv
Johanna	02	F	Child	04Au21Nv
Frederica	.00	F	Infant	04Au21Nv
Died-At-Sea				
Rosanna	67	F	None	04Au21Nv
Christian	44	M	Farmer	04Au21Nv
ETTMAN, John	29	M	Farmer	04Au21Nv
STOCHT, Jacob	28	M	Farmer	04Au21Nv
MANN, Geo.	34	M	Farmer	04Au21Nv
Magt.	32	F	None	04Au21Nv
Eliza	03	F	Child	04Au21Nv
GRABBEIR, Jacob	29	M	Farmer	04Au21Nv
Fredk.	24	M	Farmer	04Au21Nv
LOERMAN, Peter	40	M	Farmer	04Au21Nv
Magt.	40	F	None	04Au21Nv
Elizth.	15	F	None	04Au21Nv
Louise	11	F	None	04Au21Nv
Eleanor	09	F	Child	04Au21Nv
Magt.	06	F	Child	04Au21Nv
VAHNDERMIRE, Casper	28	M	Farmer	04Au21Nv
Cath.	27	F	None	04Au21Nv
Elizth.	07	F	Child	04Au21Nv
John	04	M	Child	04Au21Nv
ETTMAN, George	44	M	Farmer	04Au21Nv
Margt.	40	F	None	04Au21Nv
Elizth.	14	F	None	04Au21Nv
Hufer	12	M	None	04Au21Nv
George	10	M	None	04Au21Nv
Rosina	05	F	Child	04Au21Nv
Nich.	.00	M	Infant	04Au21Nv
HOOKER, Mich.	43	M	Farmer	04Au21Nv
Margt.	25	F	None	04Au21Nv
Cath.	16	F	None	04Au21Nv
Nich.	11	M	None	04Au21Nv
Susan	19	F	None	04Au21Nv
Eve	07	F	Child	04Au21Nv
Barbara	01	F	Child	04Au21Nv
STOER, Peter	32	M	Farmer	04Au21Nv
Ann-M.	24	F	None	04Au21Nv
Adam	02	M	Child	04Au21Nv
Conrad	01	M	Child	04Au21Nv
MICKLE, Conrad	23	M	Farmer	04Au21Nv
KEONER, Carle	52	M	Farmer	04Au21Nv
Barbara	52	F	None	04Au21Nv
Eliza	22	F	None	04Au21Nv
Jacob	16	M	Farmer	04Au21Nv
ENIGE, Adam	48	M	Farmer	04Au21Nv
Cath.	36	F	None	04Au21Nv
Margt.	15	F	None	04Au21Nv
Munay	11	M	None	04Au21Nv
ENIGE, Martin	08	M	Child	04Au21Nv
Cath.	06	F	Child	04Au21Nv
REINHARDT, Geo.	50	M	Farmer	04Au21Nv
Cath.	50	F	None	04Au21Nv
Jacob	19	M	Farmer	04Au21Nv
BAUGMANN, John	43	M	Farmer	04Au21Nv
Ann	40	F	None	04Au21Nv
John	60	M	Farmer	04Au21Nv
Peter	11	M	None	04Au21Nv
Philip	08	M	Child	04Au21Nv
Fred.	07	M	Child	04Au21Nv
Susan	05	F	Child	04Au21Nv
Adam	01	M	Child	04Au21Nv
SCHILLING, Geo.	40	M	None	04Au21Nv
Mary	40	F	None	04Au21Nv
John	24	M	None	04Au21Nv
Mary	04	F	Child	04Au21Nv
Cath.	02	F	Child	04Au21Nv
KNELL, Henry	39	M	Farmer	04Au21Nv
Margt.	41	F	None	04Au21Nv
Chris.	15	M	None	04Au21Nv
John	09	M	Child	04Au21Nv
Rosina	07	F	Child	04Au21Nv
Tobias	04	M	Child	04Au21Nv
George	15	M	None	04Au21Nv
Eliza	.00	F	Infant	04Au21Nv
VOTTZ, Jacob	43	M	Farmer	04Au21Nv
Eliza	36	F	None	04Au21Nv
Eliza	09	F	Child	04Au21Nv
Jacob	10	M	None	04Au21Nv
Henry	02	M	Child	04Au21Nv
Lovd.	.00	M	Infant	04Au21Nv
WEDENBERG, John	28	M	Farmer	04Au21Nv
KNUCK, John	18	M	Farmer	04Au21Nv
GOURNING, Chris.	35	M	Farmer	04Au21Nv
SENTIMER, Eliza	20	F	None	04Au21Nv
HESTER, John	24	M	Farmer	04Au21Nv
Caroline	44	F	None	04Au21Nv
Johanna	25	F	None	04Au21Nv
Arnold	34	M	Farmer	04Au21Nv
Ellen	10	F	None	04Au21Nv
Dina	50	F	None	04Au21Nv
WARNHOUSE, John	26	M	Farmer	04Au21Nv
Wilhela.	26	F	None	04Au21Nv
DRINKENHOUSE, Denis	39	M	Farmer	04Au21Nv
Margt.	06	F	Child	04Au21Nv
Dora	32	F	None	04Au21Nv
REGINK, Gilbert	22	M	Farmer	04Au21Nv
Wilha.	23	F	None	04Au21Nv
HENDRICKS, Gilbert	45	M	Farmer	04Au21Nv
WILLENS, Hendrik	50	M	Farmer	04Au21Nv
Cath.	47	F	None	04Au21Nv
George	19	M	Farmer	04Au21Nv
Cath.	14	F	None	04Au21Nv
Barbara	10	F	None	04Au21Nv
Susan	07	F	Child	04Au21Nv
Philip	06	M	Child	04Au21Nv
ENZER, Sebastian	47	M	Farmer	04Au21Nv
George	19	M	Farmer	04Au21Nv
HERMAN, Benj.	24	M	Farmer	04Au21Nv
LOOK, John	22	M	Farmer	04Au21Nv
EBBLING, Geo.	31	M	Farmer	04Au21Nv
KNAPP, Jno.	28	M	Farmer	04Au21Nv
LOESS, Cath.	25	F	None	04Au21Nv
DEMPSTON, Wm.	21	M	Farmer	04Au21Nv
WEAVER, Nichs.	28	M	Farmer	04Au21Nv
FISHER, Anton	26	M	Farmer	04Au21Nv
PORUS, Philip	35	M	Farmer	04Au21Nv
CLEAR, Chas.	26	M	Farmer	04Au21Nv
RHEMBCOCK, Chas.	17	M	Farmer	04Au21Nv
CONEN, John	28	M	Farmer	04Au21Nv
OBRIEN, Mich.	27	M	Farmer	04Au21Nv
LEDDES, Phoebe	54	F	None	04Au21Nv
Phoebe	21	F	None	04Au21Nv
Julien	15	M	None	04Au21Nv

NAMES OF PASSENGERS	AGE	SEX	OCCUPATIONS	DATE PORT SHIP
LEDDES, James	23	M	Farmer	04Au21Nv
LENDHAM, Ludwig	28	M	Farmer	04Au21Nv
John	07	M	Child	04Au21Nv
KARLMAN, James	40	M	Farmer	04Au21Nv
COHEN, Abraham	25	M	Farmer	04Au21Nv
BALDWIN, Henry	31	M	Farmer	04Au21Nv
Henry	11	M	None	04Au21Nv
John	09	M	Child	04Au21Nv
GILL, Chas.J.	22	M	Farmer	04Au21Nv
Frances	24	F	None	04Au21Nv
John	.00	M	Infant	04Au21Nv
DOORTY, Julia	17	F	None	04Au21Nv
STENEDECKER, Banl.	38	M	Farmer	04Au21Nv
HEIMMICKE, Jos.	28	M	Farmer	04Au21Nv
Cath.	26	F	None	04Au21Nv
HELLERLY, Wm.	27	M	Farmer	04Au21Nv
David	24	M	Farmer	04Au21Nv
James	22	M	Farmer	04Au21Nv
Ann	20	F	None	04Au21Nv
John	.00	M	Infant	04Au21Nv
MICHAEL, Isaac	24	M	Farmer	04Au21Nv
BARRETT, Isaac	22	M	Farmer	04Au21Nv
ANSPACH, Wolf	22	M	Farmer	04Au21Nv
ALEMANDER, Michael	22	M	Farmer	04Au21Nv
RESSENBERG, Phillip	36	M	Farmer	04Au21Nv
Cath.	18	F	None	04Au21Nv
Garrich	16	M	Farmer	04Au21Nv
Adam	14	M	None	04Au21Nv
Sophia	06	F	Child	04Au21Nv
Maria	05	F	Child	04Au21Nv
Philip	03	M	Child	04Au21Nv
KUTER, Cath.	48	F	None	04Au21Nv
Hendrick	18	M	Farmer	04Au21Nv
Adam	16	M	Farmer	04Au21Nv
John	14	M	None	04Au21Nv
Phillip	12	M	None	04Au21Nv
HOOTER, Jacob	22	M	Farmer	04Au21Nv
LANEBACKER, Andrew	25	M	Farmer	04Au21Nv
NICARD, John	32	M	Farmer	04Au21Nv
HOOTER, Melchor	28	M	Farmer	04Au21Nv
HAMMER, Herns	25	M	Farmer	04Au21Nv
Dedrick	24	M	Farmer	04Au21Nv
KULL, John	46	M	Farmer	04Au21Nv
WEYNK, Phillip	35	M	Farmer	04Au21Nv
Charlotte	36	F	None	04Au21Nv
Martin	03	M	Child	04Au21Nv
HANOW, Phillip	24	M	Farmer	04Au21Nv
Florentine	35	F	None	04Au21Nv
Charlotte	36	F	None	04Au21Nv
Martin	03	M	Child	04Au21Nv
HAVENS, Philip	24	M	Farmer	04Au21Nv
Florentine	35	F	None	04Au21Nv
HAFF, John	35	M	Farmer	04Au21Nv
FELYAR, Kalk.	32	M	Farmer	04Au21Nv
WILKIN, Glvy.	50	M	Farmer	04Au21Nv
WALLER, Fred	31	M	Merchant	04Au21Nv
Elizth.	26	F	None	04Au21Nv
Fred	02	M	Child	04Au21Nv
James	01	M	Child	04Au21Nv
George	.00	M	Infant	04Au21Nv
ULERHAM, Mary	27	F	None	04Au21Nv
GOLSHBEN, Martin	25	M	Merchant	04Au21Nv
VITTAR, Fred	30	M	Merchant	04Au21Nv

JANE 05 AUGUST 1847

From Liverpool

NAMES OF PASSENGERS	AGE	SEX	OCCUPATIONS	DATE PORT SHIP
FAY, Cath.	30	F	None	05Au02Dv
Bridget	42	F	None	05Au02Dv
Margt.	.00	F	Infant	05Au02Dv
Bernard	10	M	None	05Au02Dv
MAHON, Jas.	26	M	Laborer	05Au02Dv
CORGAN, Thos.	21	M	Laborer	05Au02Dv
BUTLER, Mary	21	F	None	05Au02Dv
BRIEN, Judy	21	F	None	05Au02Dv
KILCADDY, Jno.	21	M	Laborer	05Au02Dv
CYRNE, Patt	26	M	Laborer	05Au02Dv
Mary	20	F	None	05Au02Dv
WATERS, Mary	21	F	None	05Au02Dv
MCCAFFRY, Susan	21	F	None	05Au02Dv
ROONEY, Jno.	30	M	Laborer	05Au02Dv
KENNY, Bridget	30	F	None	05Au02Dv
KEEFFY, Cath.	07	F	Child	05Au02Dv
Maria	05	F	Child	05Au02Dv
KENNY, Thos.	21	M	Laborer	05Au02Dv
Mich.	21	M	Laborer	05Au02Dv
GAGHAN, Cath.	17	F	None	05Au02Dv
KENIGAN, Jno.	17	M	Laborer	05Au02Dv
Patk.	18	M	Laborer	05Au02Dv
DUNN, Mich.	23	M	Laborer	05Au02Dv
DONELLY, Ellen	30	F	None	05Au02Dv
IRVIN, Jno.	24	M	Laborer	05Au02Dv
U	20	F	None	05Au02Dv
LOUGHAN, Jane	25	F	None	05Au02Dv
Richd.	29	M	Laborer	05Au02Dv
DILLON, Jas.	50	M	Laborer	05Au02Dv
Mary	50	F	None	05Au02Dv
REILLY, Mich.	29	M	Laborer	05Au02Dv
GALLAGAN, Jas.	24	M	Laborer	05Au02Dv
BARTLEY, Brien	24	M	Laborer	05Au02Dv
MCDONALD, Dudley	27	M	Laborer	05Au02Dv
MCVICARS, Jas.	21	M	Laborer	05Au02Dv
Sarah	21	F	None	05Au02Dv
Margt.	.00	F	Infant	05Au02Dv
THOMPSON, Mary	27	F	None	05Au02Dv
U	25	M	Laborer	05Au02Dv
JENKINS, U	55	M	Farmer	05Au02Dv
Ann	50	F	None	05Au02Dv
Phoebe	25	F	None	05Au02Dv
Margt.	19	F	None	05Au02Dv
Mary	17	F	None	05Au02Dv
Elizth.	13	F	None	05Au02Dv
REESE, Jno.	39	M	Farmer	05Au02Dv
Danl.	20	M	Farmer	05Au02Dv
HUGHES, Hugh	18	M	Farmer	05Au02Dv
STRANGE, Mary	24	F	None	05Au02Dv
Agnes	34	F	None	05Au02Dv
GRADY, John	21	M	Farmer	05Au02Dv
FARROL, Margt.	21	F	None	05Au02Dv
GORMETTE, Ann	24	F	None	05Au02Dv
COYLE, Jno.	16	M	Farmer	05Au02Dv
MCABE, Anna	44	F	None	05Au02Dv
Jas.	18	M	Farmer	05Au02Dv
COFFE, Saml.	26	M	Farmer	05Au02Dv
U	26	F	None	05Au02Dv
JEROFE, Patr.	50	M	Farmer	05Au02Dv
Mary-A.	20	F	None	05Au02Dv
CALAGHAN, Eliza	30	F	None	05Au02Dv
LILLY, Arthur	21	M	Farmer	05Au02Dv
Cath.	21	F	None	05Au02Dv
BOWEN, Farrel	30	M	Farmer	05Au02Dv
Ann	20	F	None	05Au02Dv

NAMES OF PASSENGERS	AGE	SEX	OCCUPATIONS	DATE PORT SHIP
MULHERN, Rose	20	F	None	05Au02Dv
BOWEN, Margt.	20	F	None	05Au02Dv
PURNAUM, Jas.	29	M	Laborer	05Au02Dv
MERIGAN, Ann	20	F	None	05Au02Dv
GUNING, Ann	20	F	None	05Au02Dv
CASEY, Jno.	30	M	Laborer	05Au02Dv
SAGE, Pat	30	M	Laborer	05Au02Dv
REGNEY, Mary	21	F	None	05Au02Dv
Ellen	26	F	None	05Au02Dv
MARTIN, John	21	M	Laborer	05Au02Dv
CARLIN, Cath.	21	F	None	05Au02Dv
KERNAN, Mary	21	F	None	05Au02Dv
MCCAFFRY, Jas.	21	M	Laborer	05Au02Dv
DOBBING, Rob.	26	M	Laborer	05Au02Dv
Jane	20	F	None	05Au02Dv
BECK, Agnes	24	F	None	05Au02Dv
GARNER, William	36	M	Mechanic	05Au02Dv
BRODERICK, Jno.	26	M	Mechanic	05Au02Dv
Cath.	20	F	None	05Au02Dv
TENANT, Mich.	27	M	Mechanic	05Au02Dv
U	27	F	None	05Au02Dv
Maria	07	F	Child	05Au02Dv
Ellen	04	F	Child	05Au02Dv
Mich.	03	M	Child	05Au02Dv
LAWLESS, Nath.	18	M	Laborer	05Au02Dv
KEMP, Elias	30	M	Laborer	05Au02Dv
Catrina	30	F	None	05Au02Dv
Polly	10	F	None	05Au02Dv
ABRAM, Jacob	40	M	Laborer	05Au02Dv
Samuel	22	M	Laborer	05Au02Dv
REYNOLDS, Pat	30	M	Laborer	05Au02Dv
CONLON, Pat	28	M	Laborer	05Au02Dv
Pat	27	M	Laborer	05Au02Dv
Dan	26	M	Laborer	05Au02Dv
RICE, Jno.	36	M	Farmer	05Au02Dv
GANON, Mark	40	M	Farmer	05Au02Dv
U	40	F	None	05Au02Dv
DEMPSEY, Law.	36	M	Farmer	05Au02Dv
U	36	F	None	05Au02Dv
Wm.	25	M	Farmer	05Au02Dv
BAULES, Philip	20	M	Farmer	05Au02Dv
SMITH, Patt	20	M	Farmer	05Au02Dv
Bridget	15	F	None	05Au02Dv
BRODER, Paul	50	M	Farmer	05Au02Dv
Paul	11	M	None	05Au02Dv
James	20	M	Mechanic	05Au02Dv
Mary	21	F	None	05Au02Dv
Bridget	18	F	None	05Au02Dv
Alice	50	F	None	05Au02Dv
DOYLE, Mich.	36	M	Mechanic	05Au02Dv
Mary	28	F	None	05Au02Dv
John	02	M	Child	05Au02Dv
DEVANTY, Mich.	30	M	Mechanic	05Au02Dv
Bridget	12	F	None	05Au02Dv
Winnfred	06	F	Child	05Au02Dv
Pas.	03	F	Child	05Au02Dv
Cath.	04	F	Child	05Au02Dv
SMITH, Phil	30	M	Farmer	05Au02Dv
Ellen	28	F	None	05Au02Dv
Bridget	09	F	Child	05Au02Dv
Jno.	07	M	Child	05Au02Dv
Edwd.	05	M	Child	05Au02Dv
Rose	02	F	Child	05Au02Dv
CASSIDY, Thos.	25	M	Mechanic	05Au02Dv
Bridget	30	F	None	05Au02Dv
WILLIAMS, Sarah	18	F	None	05Au02Dv
GLYNN, Cath.	18	F	None	05Au02Dv
CORROLE, Margt.	17	F	None	05Au02Dv
LERBY, John	23	M	Mechanic	05Au02Dv
MCMULLAN, Alex.	18	M	Mechanic	05Au02Dv
Alick	17	M	Mechanic	05Au02Dv
STEWARD, Margt.	48	F	None	05Au02Dv
Elizth.	17	F	None	05Au02Dv
Olivia	03	F	Child	05Au02Dv
WALSH, Mich.	43	M	Farmer	05Au02Dv
WALSH, Mark	18	M	Farmer	05Au02Dv
Tim	15	M	None	05Au02Dv
Mich.	10	M	None	05Au02Dv
John	09	M	Child	05Au02Dv
Patt	04	M	Child	05Au02Dv
CARROL, Joseph	40	M	Farmer	05Au02Dv
Eliza	40	F	None	05Au02Dv
Eliza	20	F	None	05Au02Dv
HUGHES, Barnerd	22	M	Mechanic	05Au02Dv
HANIGHAN, Martin	18	M	Laborer	05Au02Dv
BARKENFIELD, Andrew	24	M	Laborer	05Au02Dv
U	20	F	None	05Au02Dv
Cath.	23	F	None	05Au02Dv
LYONS, Dennis	25	M	Laborer	05Au02Dv
WILSON, David	49	M	Laborer	05Au02Dv
U	55	F	None	05Au02Dv
Susan	20	F	None	05Au02Dv
James	17	M	Laborer	05Au02Dv
Edwd.	11	M	None	05Au02Dv
LENN, Elizth.	30	F	None	05Au02Dv
Mary	05	F	Child	05Au02Dv
Thos.	03	M	Child	05Au02Dv
Ann	.00	F	Infant	05Au02Dv
Henry	.00	M	Infant	05Au02Dv
FIELE, Mary	60	F	None	05Au02Dv
WAGSTAFF, John	40	M	Mechanic	05Au02Dv
SCOTT, Janet	50	F	None	05Au02Dv
Ellen	25	F	None	05Au02Dv
Jane	20	F	None	05Au02Dv
James	11	M	None	05Au02Dv
HARMON, Patt	24	M	Laborer	05Au02Dv
MCCOY, Thos.	27	M	Laborer	05Au02Dv
DWYRE, Jno.	40	M	Laborer	05Au02Dv
Julia	36	F	None	05Au02Dv
Mary	10	F	None	05Au02Dv
Tim	08	M	Child	05Au02Dv
Pat	06	M	Child	05Au02Dv
Dennis	03	M	Child	05Au02Dv
SHARDY, John	24	M	Laborer	05Au02Dv
RYAN, Dennis	30	M	Laborer	05Au02Dv
Peggy	26	F	None	05Au02Dv
DROGER, Ellen	26	F	None	05Au02Dv
Ellen	12	F	None	05Au02Dv
Fanny	10	F	None	05Au02Dv
James	08	M	Child	05Au02Dv
DWYRE, Pat	27	M	Mechanic	05Au02Dv
RYAN, Law.	20	M	Mechanic	05Au02Dv
VICKERS, Thomas	24	M	Mechanic	05Au02Dv
Mary	20	F	None	05Au02Dv
BROWNE, Jno.	24	M	Laborer	05Au02Dv
DRUNY, Cath.	20	F	None	05Au02Dv
CARDLE, James	21	M	Laborer	05Au02Dv
Mary	22	F	None	05Au02Dv
MAHAR, Mary	20	F	None	05Au02Dv
CANTILL, Patt	26	M	Laborer	05Au02Dv
COSTIGAN, Danl.	26	M	Laborer	05Au02Dv
CAMPBELL, Patt	50	M	Laborer	05Au02Dv
Mary	30	F	None	05Au02Dv
Mary	12	F	None	05Au02Dv
Cecilia	18	F	None	05Au02Dv
ALLEN, George	40	M	Laborer	05Au02Dv
U	40	F	None	05Au02Dv
Isaac	12	M	None	05Au02Dv
PENTNAN, John	24	M	Laborer	05Au02Dv
MAHER, Dennis	20	M	Laborer	05Au02Dv
GRIFFEN, Mich.	18	M	Laborer	05Au02Dv
LENISON, U	40	F	None	05Au02Dv
Thos.	20	M	Farmer	05Au02Dv
COCHRAN, Wm.	20	M	Farmer	05Au02Dv
LYNCH, Jno.	13	M	None	05Au02Dv
MEHAN, Pat	27	M	Farmer	05Au02Dv
MCMAHON, Jas.	18	M	Farmer	05Au02Dv
MCCARTY, Martha	20	F	None	05Au02Dv
HOWARD, Ellen	21	F	None	05Au02Dv
EGAN, Cecelia	20	F	None	05Au02Dv

NAMES OF PASSENGERS	AGE	SEX	OCCUPATIONS	DATE PORT SHIP
HUGHES, Wm.	24	M	Farmer	05Au02Dv
GLEASON, Elen	20	F	None	05Au02Dv
Wm.	15	M	None	05Au02Dv
OBRIEN, Jno.	20	M	Mechanic	05Au02Dv
Bridget	20	F	None	05Au02Dv
Joseph	.00	F	Infant	05Au02Dv
HALLIGAN, Joseph	60	M	Laborer	05Au02Dv
CONROY, Cath.	36	F	None	05Au02Dv
Jno.	18	M	Laborer	05Au02Dv
Mary	24	F	None	05Au02Dv
Margt.	17	F	None	05Au02Dv
ROCHE, Margt.	17	F	None	05Au02Dv
RENDALE, Wm.	20	M	Laborer	05Au02Dv
GARIGAN, James	24	M	Laborer	05Au02Dv
BORDEN, Joseph	30	M	Laborer	05Au02Dv
DEVIS, Jno.	20	M	Farmer	05Au02Dv
WALTON, Jno.	00	M	Farmer	05Au02Dv
MAHON, Pat	30	M	Farmer	05Au02Dv
JASPY, Tom	35	M	Farmer	05Au02Dv
MULROONEY, Thos.	24	M	Laborer	05Au02Dv
MCGARGLE, Cath.	00	F	None	05Au02Dv
MCDEVIRE, Mich.	00	M	Laborer	05Au02Dv
WALTON, U	00	F	None	05Au02Dv
DAVIS, Jno.	00	M	Laborer	05Au02Dv

LOUISIANA 05 AUGUST 1847

From Liverpool

NAMES OF PASSENGERS	AGE	SEX	OCCUPATIONS	DATE PORT SHIP
CURTIS, Bgt.	45	F	None	05Au02Nq
Wm.	22	M	Farmer	05Au02Nq
Mary	13	F	None	05Au02Nq
Ann	11	F	None	05Au02Nq
James	09	M	Child	05Au02Nq
Patck.	04	M	Child	05Au02Nq
DALLY, J.	30	M	Unknown	05Au02Nq
Margt.	24	F	None	05Au02Nq
John-H.	16	M	Mechanic	05Au02Nq
BRESLAND, H.	32	M	Unknown	05Au02Nq
Patch	30	M	Unknown	05Au02Nq
ISAAC, M.	24	M	Unknown	05Au02Nq
Husene	21	M	Unknown	05Au02Nq
Rosly	28	F	Unknown	05Au02Nq
KEHON, J.	24	F	Unknown	05Au02Nq
Mgt.	20	F	None	05Au02Nq
JORDAN, Mgt.	20	F	None	05Au02Nq
SOWOOD, Eliza	20	F	None	05Au02Nq
MELHOLIN, Ann	30	F	None	05Au02Nq
DALE, Eliza	30	F	None	05Au02Nq
DIGHAN, T.	30	M	Unknown	05Au02Nq
DIGNAN, F.	28	M	Unknown	05Au02Nq
BEHAGG, C.	22	F	None	05Au02Nq
Sarah	28	F	Unknown	05Au02Nq
DUFFEY, J.	31	F	Unknown	05Au02Nq
NELSON, My.J.	20	F	None	05Au02Nq
HEATLY, My.A.	18	F	None	05Au02Nq
QUINN, Biddy	28	F	None	05Au02Nq
ROBEY, M.	26	M	Unknown	05Au02Nq
CONNINGHAM, P.	28	M	Unknown	05Au02Nq
MURPHY, P.	18	M	Unknown	05Au02Nq
Michael	16	M	Unknown	05Au02Nq
FOSTER, J.	24	M	Unknown	05Au02Nq
Bgt.	20	F	None	05Au02Nq
READ, J.	24	M	Unknown	05Au02Nq
Kath.	22	F	None	05Au02Nq
HANDY, C.	22	M	Unknown	05Au02Nq
WHITE, J.	27	M	Unknown	05Au02Nq
TUPELL, J.	36	M	Unknown	05Au02Nq
Hannah	28	F	None	05Au02Nq
TUPELL, John	09	M	Child	05Au02Nq
G.	07	M	Child	05Au02Nq
Mary	04	F	Child	05Au02Nq
Ruth	01	F	Child	05Au02Nq
MUMFORD, B.	45	M	Mechanic	05Au02Nq
Elizt.	40	F	None	05Au02Nq
George	20	M	Unknown	05Au02Nq
Mary	16	F	None	05Au02Nq
Edwin	13	M	None	05Au02Nq
Samuel	07	M	Child	05Au02Nq
PARSONS, E.	30	M	Unknown	05Au02Nq
GALLOWAY, P.	35	M	Unknown	05Au02Nq
Mgt.	35	F	None	05Au02Nq
Mary	17	F	None	05Au02Nq
Patrk.	16	M	Unknown	05Au02Nq
John	11	M	None	05Au02Nq
Peter	09	M	Child	05Au02Nq
MCDERMOTT, Ellen	17	F	None	05Au02Nq
HANDY, My.	17	F	None	05Au02Nq
HANLY, Mgt.	18	F	None	05Au02Nq
FARRELL, Mgt.	24	F	None	05Au02Nq
Ann	07	F	Child	05Au02Nq
Patrk.	06	M	Child	05Au02Nq
COLWELL, A.	25	M	Unknown	05Au02Nq
Mry.	20	F	None	05Au02Nq
CLONAN, P.	38	M	Unknown	05Au02Nq
John	18	M	Unknown	05Au02Nq
Mara	17	F	None	05Au02Nq
Ann	17	F	None	05Au02Nq
Danl.	10	M	None	05Au02Nq
Eliza	05	F	Child	05Au02Nq
QUINN, M.	32	M	Unknown	05Au02Nq
DALEHUNT, J.	25	M	Unknown	05Au02Nq
RYAN, P.	25	M	Unknown	05Au02Nq
ETAR, T.M.	26	M	Unknown	05Au02Nq
BROSSIN, J.	27	M	Unknown	05Au02Nq
MCNAMARA, T.	40	M	Unknown	05Au02Nq
Elizt.	35	F	None	05Au02Nq
Bryan	15	M	None	05Au02Nq
Bgt.	12	F	None	05Au02Nq
Thos.	07	M	Child	05Au02Nq
Saml.	04	M	Child	05Au02Nq
Chas.	01	M	Child	05Au02Nq
TERRELL, P.	23	M	Laborer	05Au02Nq
John	21	M	Unknown	05Au02Nq
COLGAN, J.	42	M	Unknown	05Au02Nq
BOGHAN, P.	22	M	Unknown	05Au02Nq
BRIKE, My.	22	F	None	05Au02Nq
FOLEY, F.	24	M	Unknown	05Au02Nq
TRYING, J.	21	M	Unknown	05Au02Nq
GOLDING, J.	26	M	Unknown	05Au02Nq
DICKSON, R.	25	M	Unknown	05Au02Nq
RYON, J.	26	M	Unknown	05Au02Nq
Hugh	23	M	Unknown	05Au02Nq
My.	20	F	None	05Au02Nq
My.	05	F	Child	05Au02Nq
CLINCEY, D.	26	M	Unknown	05Au02Nq
FARMER, Fanny	30	F	None	05Au02Nq
MCNAMARA, My.	20	F	None	05Au02Nq
SKELLY, Jane	20	F	None	05Au02Nq
SMITH, M.	40	M	Unknown	05Au02Nq
WALKER, Cath.	30	F	None	05Au02Nq
QUINN, My.	20	F	None	05Au02Nq
Ann	18	F	None	05Au02Nq
ORINN, C.	24	M	Unknown	05Au02Nq
MCCALISTER, F.	26	M	Unknown	05Au02Nq
WALKER, J.	17	M	Unknown	05Au02Nq
Mgt.	11	F	None	05Au02Nq
Sarah	09	F	Child	05Au02Nq
JOHNSON, J.	38	M	Unknown	05Au02Nq
HARTHILL, W.	30	M	Unknown	05Au02Nq
GARRY, T.	27	M	Unknown	05Au02Nq
SCARCY, J.	20	M	Unknown	05Au02Nq
CONWAY, Cath.	22	F	None	05Au02Nq
MCCARDEN, J.	21	M	Unknown	05Au02Nq

NAMES OF PASSENGERS	AGE	SEX	OCCUPATIONS	DATE PORT SHIP
MCCARDEN, Mary-A.	45	F	None	05Au02Nq
Mary-A.	16	F	None	05Au02Nq
DUNN, J.	60	M	Unknown	05Au02Nq
Rd.	25	M	Unknown	05Au02Nq
John	23	M	Unknown	05Au02Nq
Martin	13	M	None	05Au02Nq
Edwd.	13	M	None	05Au02Nq
Eliza	12	F	None	05Au02Nq
Julia	08	F	Child	05Au02Nq
Wm.	22	M	Unknown	05Au02Nq
MCGRAH, T.	30	M	Laborer	05Au02Nq
Patrk.	26	M	Laborer	05Au02Nq
Bdgt.	05	F	Child	05Au02Nq
Julia	01	F	Child	05Au02Nq
SCULLON, A.	22	M	Unknown	05Au02Nq
HARLY, H.	21	M	Unknown	05Au02Nq
SCHEUL, L.	24	M	Unknown	05Au02Nq
RILY, My.	20	F	None	05Au02Nq
PARKIN, J.	40	M	Unknown	05Au02Nq
Jane	36	F	None	05Au02Nq
Cath.	11	F	None	05Au02Nq
SPERARDEN, Bill	20	M	Unknown	05Au02Nq
CONATY, Ann	20	F	None	05Au02Nq
MCSHEEY, M.	21	M	Unknown	05Au02Nq
Betty	16	F	None	05Au02Nq
GOULD, A.	26	M	Unknown	05Au02Nq
COGAN, J.	24	M	Unknown	05Au02Nq
CAVAN, J.	21	M	Unknown	05Au02Nq
ORONHEALEN, J.	40	M	Unknown	05Au02Nq
Cath.	25	F	None	05Au02Nq
Patrk.	08	M	Child	05Au02Nq
MCHUE, My.	20	F	None	05Au02Nq
RINN, M.	40	M	Unknown	05Au02Nq
Mat.	26	M	Unknown	05Au02Nq
Martha	26	F	None	05Au02Nq
Martin	01	M	Child	05Au02Nq
GALLIGAN, T.	21	M	Unknown	05Au02Nq
Wm.	18	M	Unknown	05Au02Nq
HINLAN, J.	30	M	Unknown	05Au02Nq
Mgt.	20	F	None	05Au02Nq
REYNOLDS, C.	35	M	Unknown	05Au02Nq
DEIGNAN, My.	20	F	None	05Au02Nq
Ann	60	F	None	05Au02Nq
Mgt.	20	F	None	05Au02Nq
Bgt.	20	F	None	05Au02Nq
Hugh	12	M	None	05Au02Nq
MERNAN, Jane	20	F	None	05Au02Nq

ST.PATRICK 09 AUGUST 1847

From Liverpool

NAMES OF PASSENGERS	AGE	SEX	OCCUPATIONS	DATE PORT SHIP
BOLTON, Maria	35	F	None	09Au02Bw
Maria	13	F	None	09Au02Bw
Fanny	09	F	Child	09Au02Bw
Bessy	04	F	Child	09Au02Bw
Richd.	11	M	None	09Au02Bw
HASKETT, Wm.	23	M	Gentleman	09Au02Bw
RIPLEY, Geo.	21	M	Gentleman	09Au02Bw
OWEN, Wm.	60	M	Farmer	09Au02Bw
Mary	71	F	None	09Au02Bw
LAURENCE, Elizth.	33	F	None	09Au02Bw
Mary-L.	13	F	None	09Au02Bw
Jane-T.	04	F	Child	09Au02Bw
Horatio	01	M	Child	09Au02Bw
MILLS, Thos.	63	M	Farmer	09Au02Bw
ATHERTON, Ambrose	29	M	Farmer	09Au02Bw
Matilda	25	F	None	09Au02Bw
Wm.	04	M	Child	09Au02Bw
ATHERTON, John	03	M	Child	09Au02Bw
Elizth.	02	F	Child	09Au02Bw
Thos.	.00	M	Infant	09Au02Bw
BOYD, Eliza	25	F	None	09Au02Bw
ALLISON, Emily	20	F	None	09Au02Bw
MULLANEY, Cath.	20	F	None	09Au02Bw
GALAGHAN, Wm.	11	F	None	09Au02Bw
MILLER, Maria	18	F	None	09Au02Bw
FURLOUGH, Margt.	20	F	None	09Au02Bw
DRAFFIN, Mary	20	F	None	09Au02Bw
Nancy-A.	18	F	None	09Au02Bw
GILLESPIE, Wm.	00	M	Unknown	09Au02Bw
ROWAN, Jno.	32	M	Mechanic	09Au02Bw
Mary	25	F	None	09Au02Bw
Belinda	09	F	Child	09Au02Bw
Thos.	05	M	Child	09Au02Bw
Maria	03	F	Child	09Au02Bw
John	.00	M	Infant	09Au02Bw
COOLAGHAN, Pat	17	M	Mechanic	09Au02Bw
SKIDMORE, Ann	25	F	None	09Au02Bw
Elizth.	06	F	Child	09Au02Bw
SMITHSON, Sarah	18	F	None	09Au02Bw
OBRIEN, Timothy	36	M	Farmer	09Au02Bw
Margt.	30	F	None	09Au02Bw
Mary	18	F	None	09Au02Bw
Jno.	12	M	None	09Au02Bw
Wm.	10	M	None	09Au02Bw
OHARE, Mich.	11	M	None	09Au02Bw
OBRIEN, Tim	.00	M	Infant	09Au02Bw
CRONAN, Wm.	40	M	Laborer	09Au02Bw
Mary	40	F	None	09Au02Bw
RYAN, Jno.	20	M	Laborer	09Au02Bw
Mich.	10	M	None	09Au02Bw
Pat	12	M	None	09Au02Bw
Tim	08	M	Child	09Au02Bw
ONEIL, Thos.	30	M	Laborer	09Au02Bw
John	50	M	None	09Au02Bw
Jno.	20	M	Laborer	09Au02Bw
Harriet	18	F	None	09Au02Bw
Joha.	12	F	None	09Au02Bw
Bridget	09	F	Child	09Au02Bw
BRICKNY, Rody.	25	M	Laborer	09Au02Bw
HAYS, Mich.	40	M	Farmer	09Au02Bw
Jane	40	F	None	09Au02Bw
Jno.	25	M	Farmer	09Au02Bw
Thos.	24	M	Farmer	09Au02Bw
David	20	M	Farmer	09Au02Bw
Jeremiah	18	M	Farmer	09Au02Bw
Jane	12	F	None	09Au02Bw
Jas.	10	M	None	09Au02Bw
ONEIL, Mary	28	F	None	09Au02Bw
RYAN, Mat.	25	M	Farmer	09Au02Bw
RIAL, Thos.	28	M	Farmer	09Au02Bw
OBRIEN, Mich.	30	M	Farmer	09Au02Bw
Ellen	28	F	None	09Au02Bw
Mary	05	F	Child	09Au02Bw
Ellen	03	F	Child	09Au02Bw
Mich.	01	M	Child	09Au02Bw
CORBETT, Roddy	40	M	Laborer	09Au02Bw
Jane	40	F	None	09Au02Bw
Mary	05	F	Child	09Au02Bw
Judy	03	F	Child	09Au02Bw
Biddy	.00	F	Infant	09Au02Bw
KENNY, Mary	20	F	None	09Au02Bw
RYAN, Dennis	25	M	Laborer	09Au02Bw
CRAWFORD, Jas.	25	M	Laborer	09Au02Bw
Eliza	19	F	None	09Au02Bw
MCFARLANE, Ann	36	F	None	09Au02Bw
GILBERT, Edmond	36	M	Laborer	09Au02Bw
Ellen	27	F	None	09Au02Bw
Mary	10	F	None	09Au02Bw
Henry	08	M	Child	09Au02Bw
Robt.	06	M	Child	09Au02Bw
Edmd.	03	M	Child	09Au02Bw
Maurice	28	M	Laborer	09Au02Bw

NAMES OF PASSENGERS	AGE	SEX	OCCUPATIONS	DATE PORT SHIP
GILBERT, Cath.	23	F	None	09Au02Bw
Mary	26	F	None	09Au02Bw
Mary	05	F	Child	09Au02Bw
Henry	02	M	Child	09Au02Bw
MALONEY, Jno.	33	M	Laborer	09Au02Bw
Cath.	33	F	None	09Au02Bw
Margt.	04	F	Child	09Au02Bw
Dennis	03	M	Child	09Au02Bw
Dennis	60	M	Laborer	09Au02Bw
COUNELLY, Cornelius	25	M	Farmer	09Au02Bw
CONNELL, Peter	18	M	Farmer	09Au02Bw
Mary	16	F	None	09Au02Bw
Johanna	14	F	None	09Au02Bw
MCARTHUR, Eliza	20	F	None	09Au02Bw
ENRIGHT, Cath.	20	F	None	09Au02Bw
WAIN, John	25	M	Farmer	09Au02Bw
GILLON, Pat	25	M	Farmer	09Au02Bw
KING, Laurence	33	M	Laborer	09Au02Bw
OBRIEN, Mat.	25	M	Laborer	09Au02Bw
OGNEY, Thos.	23	M	Laborer	09Au02Bw
MAHIN, Thos.	23	M	Laborer	09Au02Bw
OKEEFE, Mary	28	F	None	09Au02Bw
Jno.	04	M	Child	09Au02Bw
DORCEY, Pat	38	M	Laborer	09Au02Bw
FLYNN, Jas.	20	M	Laborer	09Au02Bw
PRINKARD, Saml.	22	M	Laborer	09Au02Bw
GLAY, Jas.	28	M	Laborer	09Au02Bw
DUNN, David	21	M	Laborer	09Au02Bw
GAFFNEY, Mary	20	F	None	09Au02Bw
Luke	50	M	Laborer	09Au02Bw
NEWELL, Jno.	30	M	Laborer	09Au02Bw
Eliza	30	F	None	09Au02Bw
Eliza	.00	F	Infant	09Au02Bw
WALKER, Jno.	32	M	Laborer	09Au02Bw
Margt.	25	F	None	09Au02Bw
Jno.	02	M	Child	09Au02Bw
Geo.	.00	M	Infant	09Au02Bw
OBRYAN, Mich.	52	M	Farmer	09Au02Bw
Betty	45	F	None	09Au02Bw
Nellis	15	M	None	09Au02Bw
Teresa	30	F	None	09Au02Bw
Mich.	13	M	None	09Au02Bw
James	11	M	None	09Au02Bw
Cath.	08	F	Child	09Au02Bw
Henry	03	M	Child	09Au02Bw
FINLY, Jas.	38	M	Laborer	09Au02Bw
Betty	32	F	None	09Au02Bw
WHEELAN, Mary	60	F	None	09Au02Bw
FINLY, Mich.	10	M	None	09Au02Bw
Dennis	08	M	Child	09Au02Bw
Jno.	06	M	Child	09Au02Bw
Pat	04	M	Child	09Au02Bw
Jas.	02	M	Child	09Au02Bw
MARSHALL, Wm.	35	M	None	09Au02Bw
CASSIDY, E.	20	M	Laborer	09Au02Bw
DONOHOO, Wm.	25	M	Laborer	09Au02Bw
HARPER, Wm.	25	M	Laborer	09Au02Bw
DONOHOO, Jas.	20	M	Laborer	09Au02Bw
Mary	18	F	None	09Au02Bw
SHEHAN, Jerry	30	M	Laborer	09Au02Bw
Nelly	30	F	None	09Au02Bw
MCKUNE, Barnard	40	M	Laborer	09Au02Bw
BARNES, Edwd.	30	M	Laborer	09Au02Bw
TRAINER, Cath.	40	F	None	09Au02Bw
Jno.	02	M	Child	09Au02Bw
BYRNE, Bridget	20	F	None	09Au02Bw
DROGAN, Mich.	48	M	Laborer	09Au02Bw
Mary-A.	40	F	None	09Au02Bw
Cath.	18	F	None	09Au02Bw
Rose	14	F	None	09Au02Bw
Matt	12	M	None	09Au02Bw
Bridget	10	F	None	09Au02Bw
Jas.	09	M	Child	09Au02Bw
Pat	07	M	Child	09Au02Bw
Margt.	06	F	Child	09Au02Bw
DROGAN, Nancy	04	F	Child	09Au02Bw
Cath.	02	F	Child	09Au02Bw
FINEGAN, Jno.	60	M	Farmer	09Au02Bw
Cath.	62	F	None	09Au02Bw
Ann	19	F	None	09Au02Bw
Jas.	18	M	Farmer	09Au02Bw
Bridget	16	F	None	09Au02Bw
Mary	14	F	None	09Au02Bw
Jno.	12	M	None	09Au02Bw
Pat	08	M	Child	09Au02Bw
Cath.	05	F	Child	09Au02Bw
Francis	02	M	Child	09Au02Bw
NEAL, Jas.	26	M	Laborer	09Au02Bw
KELLY, Nich.	24	M	Laborer	09Au02Bw
OBRIEN, Mich.	24	M	Laborer	09Au02Bw
Pat	23	M	Laborer	09Au02Bw
CLARK, Peter	30	M	Laborer	09Au02Bw
Margt.	40	F	None	09Au02Bw
SMITH, Jas.	24	M	Farmer	09Au02Bw
Peter	18	M	Farmer	09Au02Bw
Mary	20	F	None	09Au02Bw
Pat	18	M	Farmer	09Au02Bw
Margt.	12	F	None	09Au02Bw
Bridget	06	F	Child	09Au02Bw
ROGERS, Thos.	35	M	Farmer	09Au02Bw
Ann	34	F	None	09Au02Bw
Ann	07	F	Child	09Au02Bw
Thos.	04	M	Child	09Au02Bw
Mary	.00	F	Infant	09Au02Bw
SMITH, Pat	30	M	Mechanic	09Au02Bw
Mary	23	F	None	09Au02Bw
Mary	14	F	None	09Au02Bw
MAURY, Mary	21	F	None	09Au02Bw
COFFRAY, Jno.	20	M	Laborer	09Au02Bw
PATTISON, Jas.	20	M	Laborer	09Au02Bw
CLARK, Mat.	20	M	Laborer	09Au02Bw
MILLER, Saml.	45	M	Farmer	09Au02Bw
MCCLURE, James	10	M	None	09Au02Bw
GILLIAN, Wm.	26	M	Farmer	09Au02Bw
Ann	24	F	None	09Au02Bw
Tim	06	M	Child	09Au02Bw
Elizth.	04	F	Child	09Au02Bw
Edwd.	04	M	Child	09Au02Bw
HEALY, Jno.	30	M	Farmer	09Au02Bw
WALKER, Wm.	50	M	Mechanic	09Au02Bw
TAYLOR, Steph.	24	M	Laborer	09Au02Bw
WARD, Edwd.	20	M	Laborer	09Au02Bw
Joseph	19	M	Laborer	09Au02Bw
Elizth.	60	F	None	09Au02Bw
GARGAN, Jno.	34	M	Laborer	09Au02Bw
TIERNAN, Peter	26	M	Laborer	09Au02Bw
Alice	25	F	None	09Au02Bw
Cath.	12	F	None	09Au02Bw
Peter	10	M	None	09Au02Bw
Mich.	08	M	Child	09Au02Bw
Eliza	04	F	Child	09Au02Bw
DUNN, Wm.	30	M	Farmer	09Au02Bw
Margt.	26	F	None	09Au02Bw
Mary	06	F	Child	09Au02Bw
George	04	M	Child	09Au02Bw
Sarah	02	F	Child	09Au02Bw
David	.00	M	Infant	09Au02Bw
CAVANAGH, Jas.	25	M	Laborer	09Au02Bw
WILEY, Wm.	22	M	Laborer	09Au02Bw
CORINANUN, Ann	21	F	None	09Au02Bw
Hugh	19	M	Laborer	09Au02Bw
ONEIL, Francis	22	M	Laborer	09Au02Bw
MCGUIN, Hugh	17	M	Laborer	09Au02Bw
PERKENS, Wm.	21	M	Laborer	09Au02Bw
EATON, Jas.	30	M	Laborer	09Au02Bw
CHRISTOPHER, Mich.	70	M	Laborer	09Au02Bw
Bridget	60	F	None	09Au02Bw
Mary	20	F	None	09Au02Bw
MOLLETT, Cath.	24	F	None	09Au02Bw
HIGGINS, Biddy	21	F	None	09Au02Bw

NAMES OF PASSENGERS	AGE	SEX	OCCUPATIONS	DATE PORT SHIP
CUANNEIN, Jno.	20	M	Laborer	09Au02Bw
DELANY, Dennis	35	M	Laborer	09Au02Bw
CUNAHAN, Cath.	00	F	None	09Au02Bw
REILY, Phil.	24	M	Farmer	09Au02Bw
Ann	20	F	None	09Au02Bw
HIGGINS, Tereza	13	F	None	09Au02Bw
Jno.	13	M	None	09Au02Bw
Cath.	24	F	None	09Au02Bw
DUNCAN, Mary	00	F	None	09Au02Bw
NOON, Thos.	60	M	Laborer	09Au02Bw
Thos.	16	M	None	09Au02Bw
Mich.	12	M	None	09Au02Bw
Jas.	10	M	None	09Au02Bw
CLANCY, Pat	00	M	Unknown	09Au02Bw
RYAN, Mary	00	F	None	09Au02Bw
SARSEN, Jno.	23	M	Farmer	09Au02Bw
Elizth.	23	F	None	09Au02Bw
U	.00	F	Infant	09Au02Bw
MCKANA, Thos.	25	M	Farmer	09Au02Bw
MCGARVEY, Jas.	30	M	Farmer	09Au02Bw
KOA, Danl.	28	M	Farmer	09Au02Bw
MCMANUS, Cath.	20	F	None	09Au02Bw
LAROOM, Ann	25	F	None	09Au02Bw
ROAN, Biddy	20	F	None	09Au02Bw
BARTET, Bridget	17	F	None	09Au02Bw
MOORE, Rose	35	F	None	09Au02Bw
RIELY, Margt.	37	F	None	09Au02Bw
Susan	19	F	None	09Au02Bw
MOORE, Thos.	09	M	Child	09Au02Bw
Wm.	.00	M	Infant	09Au02Bw
DUFFEE, Susan	39	F	None	09Au02Bw
CRAFTON, Geo.	25	M	Laborer	09Au02Bw
Richd.	23	M	Laborer	09Au02Bw
ADAMS, Thos.	00	M	Unknown	09Au02Bw
OWENS, Thos.	35	M	Laborer	09Au02Bw
Mary-A.	17	F	None	09Au02Bw
CHIVA, Wm.	35	M	Laborer	09Au02Bw
TEVLIN, Wm.	00	M	Laborer	09Au02Bw
DUNN, Danl.	00	M	Laborer	09Au02Bw
MALONE, Jane	00	F	None	09Au02Bw
GILLESPIE, David	00	M	Laborer	09Au02Bw
KELLY, Thos.	20	M	Laborer	09Au02Bw
LENAN, Ann	22	F	None	09Au02Bw
CONNELLY, Mary	20	F	None	09Au02Bw
Eliza	17	F	None	09Au02Bw
DUFFER, Jas.	00	M	Laborer	09Au02Bw
WHORBLE, Wm.	00	M	Laborer	09Au02Bw
POUVIS, Jos.	76	M	Laborer	09Au02Bw
Molly	76	F	None	09Au02Bw
MCKENZIE, Jno.	56	M	Laborer	09Au02Bw
Mercy	26	F	None	09Au02Bw
TOOLE, Francis	40	M	Laborer	09Au02Bw
Patrick	13	M	None	09Au02Bw
Chris	12	M	None	09Au02Bw
Jas.	08	M	Child	09Au02Bw
Sarah	10	F	None	09Au02Bw
Cath.	09	F	Child	09Au02Bw
COROGAN, Thos.	26	M	Laborer	09Au02Bw
BEATY, Bobb	48	M	Laborer	09Au02Bw
Fanny	24	F	None	09Au02Bw
Cath.	22	F	None	09Au02Bw
SHERMAN, Joseph	18	M	Laborer	09Au02Bw
WHELAN, Ann	30	F	None	09Au02Bw
Allen	11	F	None	09Au02Bw
Ann	09	F	Child	09Au02Bw
HOGAN, Ann	20	F	None	09Au02Bw
Sarah	18	F	None	09Au02Bw
SMITH, Wm.	28	M	Laborer	09Au02Bw
Ann	26	F	None	09Au02Bw
MAYLER, Pat	18	M	Laborer	09Au02Bw
CANE, Biddy	16	F	None	09Au02Bw
DILLON, Biddy	50	F	None	09Au02Bw
Martin	25	M	Laborer	09Au02Bw
James	23	M	Laborer	09Au02Bw
Mercy	21	F	None	09Au02Bw
DILLON, Cath.	19	F	None	09Au02Bw
Margt.	18	F	None	09Au02Bw
Biddy	16	F	None	09Au02Bw
Jno.	04	M	Child	09Au02Bw
DAY, Mary	55	F	None	09Au02Bw
Anthony	28	M	Laborer	09Au02Bw
Ellen	26	F	None	09Au02Bw
John	24	M	Laborer	09Au02Bw
DOYLE, Wm.	21	M	Laborer	09Au02Bw
Mich.	19	M	Laborer	09Au02Bw

ANN-HARLEY 10 AUGUST 1847

From Glasgow

NAMES OF PASSENGERS	AGE	SEX	OCCUPATIONS	DATE PORT SHIP
BLACKALAND, Margt.	40	F	None	10Au04Db
Jane	09	F	Child	10Au04Db
Christina	06	F	Child	10Au04Db
James	02	M	Child	10Au04Db
HUTCHINSON, Jane	18	F	None	10Au04Db
STRUTHERS, Agnes	40	F	None	10Au04Db
Wm.	09	M	Child	10Au04Db
Robt.	07	M	Child	10Au04Db
Agnes	05	F	Child	10Au04Db
HOYLE, U	37	F	None	10Au04Db
Margt.	03	F	Child	10Au04Db
STRUTHERS, Jno.	19	M	Laborer	10Au04Db
MOORE, Gavin	33	M	Laborer	10Au04Db
Nancy	25	F	None	10Au04Db
GOLOCHER, Mary	21	F	None	10Au04Db
YOUNG, Jane	40	F	None	10Au04Db
David	10	M	None	10Au04Db
Walter	08	M	Child	10Au04Db
MILL, Jonathan	19	M	Laborer	10Au04Db
FRASER, U	33	F	None	10Au04Db
Smith	10	M	None	10Au04Db
Jonathan	06	M	Child	10Au04Db
FERGUSON, Charlotte	25	F	None	10Au04Db
CRIGHTON, Robt.	25	M	Laborer	10Au04Db
CAMPBELL, Susan	20	F	None	10Au04Db
ROBERTSON, Hannah	60	F	None	10Au04Db
SCOULER, Mary	25	F	None	10Au04Db
Mary	07	F	Child	10Au04Db
Peter	03	M	Child	10Au04Db
Jas.	.10	M	Infant	10Au04Db
HENRY, William	35	M	Farmer	10Au04Db
Mary	35	F	None	10Au04Db
Margt.	10	F	None	10Au04Db
Elizth.	07	F	Child	10Au04Db
Mary-J.	05	F	Child	10Au04Db
Joseph	03	M	Child	10Au04Db
Cath.	.10	F	Infant	10Au04Db
HENDERSON, Biddy	25	F	None	10Au04Db
U	.04	M	Infant	10Au04Db
CUNNINGHAM, U	27	M	Laborer	10Au04Db
Mary	25	F	None	10Au04Db
Jas.	01	M	Child	10Au04Db
MCFARLANE, John	28	M	Farmer	10Au04Db
Jean	24	F	None	10Au04Db
Jno.	02	M	Child	10Au04Db
Wm.	.10	M	Infant	10Au04Db
MILLER, Jas.	54	M	Farmer	10Au04Db
Elizth.	54	F	None	10Au04Db
Wm.	20	M	Farmer	10Au04Db
Jno.	13	M	Farmer	10Au04Db
Jas.	11	M	Farmer	10Au04Db
Jean	09	F	Child	10Au04Db
Grace	05	F	Child	10Au04Db
WITHERSPOON, Jno.	44	M	Farmer	10Au04Db

NAMES OF PASSENGERS	AGE	SEX	OCCUPATIONS	DATE PORT SHIP
WITHERSPOON, Mary-A.	42	F	None	10Au04Db
Robt.	20	M	Farmer	10Au04Db
Jno.	18	M	Farmer	10Au04Db
Thos.	13	M	None	10Au04Db
Wm.	10	M	None	10Au04Db
Elizth.	07	F	Child	10Au04Db
Jas.H.	03	M	Child	10Au04Db
MCGUNES, Malcom	62	M	Farmer	10Au04Db
Charles	23	M	Farmer	10Au04Db
Jno.	21	M	Farmer	10Au04Db
Cath.	28	F	None	10Au04Db
Marion	26	F	None	10Au04Db
WANLESS, Alex.	23	M	Laborer	10Au04Db
Eliza	23	F	None	10Au04Db
SMELLIA, Jean	21	F	None	10Au04Db
REID, Thos.	27	M	Laborer	10Au04Db
ELLIS, Robt.	40	M	Laborer	10Au04Db
Jane	35	F	None	10Au04Db
Elizth.	10	F	None	10Au04Db
George	08	M	Child	10Au04Db
CAMPBELL, Jno.	27	M	Laborer	10Au04Db
LOCKHEAD, Wm.	69	M	Laborer	10Au04Db
Margt.	72	F	None	10Au04Db
MILN, Jean	27	F	None	10Au04Db
Elizth.	22	F	None	10Au04Db
PEARSON, Jno.	19	M	Laborer	10Au04Db
MORRIS, Jno.	28	M	Laborer	10Au04Db
MCQUITTIN, Archd.	21	M	Laborer	10Au04Db
ROSS, Thos.	21	M	Laborer	10Au04Db
HAGERTY, Cannel	21	M	Laborer	10Au04Db
MONWELL, Geo.	35	M	Laborer	10Au04Db
Elizth.	35	F	None	10Au04Db
Geo.	12	M	None	10Au04Db
Adam	07	M	Child	10Au04Db
James	05	M	Child	10Au04Db
WANDWARD, Jno.	21	M	Laborer	10Au04Db
BURNS, Margt.	18	F	None	10Au04Db
ANDERSON, Judy	20	F	None	10Au04Db
TARBET, Mary	25	F	None	10Au04Db
WALKER, Isabilla	28	F	None	10Au04Db
Ruthanne	22	F	None	10Au04Db
BROWN, Helen	22	F	None	10Au04Db
T.	22	M	Laborer	10Au04Db
STEWART, Thos.	19	M	Laborer	10Au04Db
SMITH, James	22	M	Laborer	10Au04Db
MCKENZIE, Jane	18	F	None	10Au04Db
Margt.	16	F	None	10Au04Db
LESLIE, Mary	40	F	None	10Au04Db
Barbara	18	F	None	10Au04Db
Cath.	16	F	None	10Au04Db
Wm.	14	M	None	10Au04Db
Leo	10	M	None	10Au04Db
NINOMS, Thos.	23	M	Gentleman	10Au04Db
ALLISON, Wm.	16	M	Gentleman	10Au04Db
RICKY, And.	19	M	Gentleman	10Au04Db
FAIRFIELD, Jean	21	F	None	10Au04Db
SMITH, Geo.	28	M	Gentleman	10Au04Db
Helen	18	F	None	10Au04Db

EMMA-PRESCOTT 10 AUGUST 1847

From Galway

NAMES OF PASSENGERS	AGE	SEX	OCCUPATIONS	DATE PORT SHIP
BURKE, Mich.	40	M	Mechanic	10Au11Sd
Eliza-M.	30	F	None	10Au11Sd
Cath.	03	F	Child	10Au11Sd
GRADY, Pat	23	M	Mechanic	10Au11Sd
Mary	23	F	None	10Au11Sd
Mich.	02	M	Child	10Au11Sd
TIERNY, Susan	25	F	None	10Au11Sd
TIERNAN, Thos.	25	M	Mechanic	10Au11Sd
Pat	23	M	Mechanic	10Au11Sd
JOYCE, Pat	27	M	Mechanic	10Au11Sd
Ellen	23	F	None	10Au11Sd
LYONS, Mary	23	F	None	10Au11Sd
ROONEY, Peter	26	M	Mechanic	10Au11Sd
Mary	24	F	None	10Au11Sd
CONNOLE, Pat	25	M	Mechanic	10Au11Sd
Peter	18	M	Mechanic	10Au11Sd
HONON, Mich.	23	M	Mechanic	10Au11Sd
HEGARTY, Pat	22	M	Laborer	10Au11Sd
CANNON, Pat	40	M	Laborer	10Au11Sd
CARRIGG, Austin	23	M	Laborer	10Au11Sd
Biddy	23	F	None	10Au11Sd
LEYDEN, Mary	17	F	None	10Au11Sd
AHERN, Bridget	28	F	None	10Au11Sd
Jno.	15	M	None	10Au11Sd
MCDONAGH, Mary	30	F	None	10Au11Sd
Mich	02	M	Child	10Au11Sd
MCDONNELL, Ellen	60	F	None	10Au11Sd
James	04	M	Child	10Au11Sd
OLOUGHLIN, Mary	25	F	None	10Au11Sd
Ellen	17	F	None	10Au11Sd
ONEIL, James	54	M	Laborer	10Au11Sd
Margt.	18	F	None	10Au11Sd
Joseph	12	M	None	10Au11Sd
CONROY, Thos.	38	M	Laborer	10Au11Sd
Bridget	26	F	None	10Au11Sd
Pat	06	M	Child	10Au11Sd
BURKE, Pat	34	M	Laborer	10Au11Sd
Mary	34	F	None	10Au11Sd
COSGRIFFE, Martin	18	M	Laborer	10Au11Sd
CROW, Pat	27	M	Laborer	10Au11Sd
Mary	30	F	None	10Au11Sd
Cath.	19	F	None	10Au11Sd
KELLY, Bridget	40	F	None	10Au11Sd
OBRIEN, Mary	30	F	None	10Au11Sd
Honora	16	F	None	10Au11Sd
FOLAN, Edwd.	25	M	Clerk	10Au11Sd
Mary	57	F	None	10Au11Sd
Cath.	17	F	None	10Au11Sd
READY, Mary	30	F	None	10Au11Sd
SPELMAN, Dom	11	M	Laborer	10Au11Sd
EDWARDS, Anne	18	F	None	10Au11Sd
LYONS, Maria	15	F	None	10Au11Sd
CONNOLE, James	23	M	Laborer	10Au11Sd

ADELBARAN 10 AUGUST 1847

From Cork

NAMES OF PASSENGERS	AGE	SEX	OCCUPATIONS	DATE PORT SHIP
HALEY, Hannah	30	F	None	10Au14Se
Mary-A.	01	F	Child	10Au14Se
SWEENY, Mary	20	F	None	10Au14Se
KENEDY, Peter	28	M	Farmer	10Au14Se
CORBITT, John	50	M	Farmer	10Au14Se
Daniel	20	M	Farmer	10Au14Se
Ellen	50	F	None	10Au14Se
Mary	13	F	None	10Au14Se
Johannah	12	F	None	10Au14Se
Men.	09	F	Child	10Au14Se
BRYON, Mich.	28	M	Farmer	10Au14Se
KIRBY, Phil.	42	M	Farmer	10Au14Se
Cath.	30	F	None	10Au14Se
Mary	10	F	None	10Au14Se
Richd.	08	M	Child	10Au14Se
Cath.	06	F	Child	10Au14Se
Mary	02	F	Child	10Au14Se

NAMES OF PASSENGERS	AGE	SEX	OCCUPATIONS	DATE PORT SHIP
KIRBY, U	.00	U	Infant	10Au14Se
LYONS, Anna	20	F	None	10Au14Se
CURRAN, Patk.	30	M	Mechanic	10Au14Se
Joha.	32	F	None	10Au14Se
BRYAN, Maurice	26	M	Mechanic	10Au14Se
DONOHUE, Pat	32	M	Laborer	10Au14Se
Mary	40	F	None	10Au14Se
MALONEY, Margt.	40	F	None	10Au14Se
Bessy (D)	11	F	None	10Au14Se
Mary (D)	09	F	Child	10Au14Se
CORCORAN, Jno.	40	M	Laborer	10Au14Se
Juda	28	F	None	10Au14Se
Merit	30	M	Laborer	10Au14Se
Ed.	02	M	Child	10Au14Se
U	.00	U	Infant	10Au14Se
COTTER, Pat	40	M	Laborer	10Au14Se
Mary	25	F	None	10Au14Se
FAGHN, James	25	M	Farmer	10Au14Se
Mary	22	F	None	10Au14Se
EGAN, Owen	60	M	Farmer	10Au14Se
Cath.	65	F	None	10Au14Se
Jno.	22	M	Farmer	10Au14Se
Mary	18	F	None	10Au14Se
Elsey	16	F	None	10Au14Se
Ellen	13	F	None	10Au14Se
Owen	11	M	None	10Au14Se
Cath.	09	F	Child	10Au14Se
Jude	07	F	Child	10Au14Se
Nancy	05	F	Child	10Au14Se
Johanna	02	F	Child	10Au14Se
John	21	M	Laborer	10Au14Se
MALONEY, Mary	24	F	None	10Au14Se
HARINGTON, Honora	50	F	None	10Au14Se
MALONY, Mich.	03	M	Child	10Au14Se
U	.00	U	Infant	10Au14Se
RARDEN, Denis	40	M	Mechanic	10Au14Se
Nelly	30	F	None	10Au14Se
Reed	60	M	Mechanic	10Au14Se
U	04	M	Child	10Au14Se
Jasn.	03	M	Child	10Au14Se
DONOVAN, Martin	22	M	Laborer	10Au14Se

AFGHAN 10 AUGUST 1847

From Glasgow

NAMES OF PASSENGERS	AGE	SEX	OCCUPATIONS	DATE PORT SHIP
DEVINE, James	35	M	Mechanic	10Au04Ka
BLACK, Wm.	45	M	Mechanic	10Au04Ka
Bell	47	F	None	10Au04Ka
Mary	19	F	None	10Au04Ka
Thomas	18	M	Mechanic	10Au04Ka
Ann	16	F	None	10Au04Ka
Janet	13	F	None	10Au04Ka
Francis	10	F	None	10Au04Ka
Jane	06	F	None	10Au04Ka
Bell	.10	F	Infant	10Au04Ka
MCLAUGHLIN, Wm.	50	M	Farmer	10Au04Ka
Margt.	47	F	None	10Au04Ka
Margt.	07	F	Child	10Au04Ka
John	05	M	Child	10Au04Ka
PAUL, Andrew	33	M	Mechanic	10Au04Ka
Christine	10	F	None	10Au04Ka
LILING, Agnes	23	F	None	10Au04Ka
David	21	M	Clerk	10Au04Ka
Christine	19	F	None	10Au04Ka
Elizth.	17	F	None	10Au04Ka
Sarah	15	F	None	10Au04Ka
Johanna	13	F	None	10Au04Ka
Andrew	11	M	None	10Au04Ka
LILING, Jemima	09	F	Child	10Au04Ka
Robina	07	F	Child	10Au04Ka
MCKELLAN, Cath.	23	F	None	10Au04Ka
MCLEAN, Elizth.	60	F	None	10Au04Ka
DUNCAN, John	54	M	Mechanic	10Au04Ka
Andrew	21	M	Mechanic	10Au04Ka
Dods.	18	M	Mechanic	10Au04Ka
WIER, Wm.	26	M	Mechanic	10Au04Ka
WOOD, Wm.	28	M	Mechanic	10Au04Ka
WYLIE, Alexd.	26	M	Mechanic	10Au04Ka
Magt.	24	F	None	10Au04Ka
Wm.	06	M	Child	10Au04Ka
Mary	03	F	Child	10Au04Ka
Agnes	.10	F	Infant	10Au04Ka
BROWN, Andrew	22	M	Engineer	10Au04Ka
MCNIEL, Andrew	24	M	Engineer	10Au04Ka
MCLAUGHLAN, Wm.	51	M	Farmer	10Au04Ka
Sarah	51	F	None	10Au04Ka
Cath.	12	F	None	10Au04Ka
John	10	M	None	10Au04Ka
DUNSMORE, Maria	21	F	None	10Au04Ka
Betsey	19	F	None	10Au04Ka
DICKIE, John	25	M	Mechanic	10Au04Ka
Jean	25	F	None	10Au04Ka
MCNEIL, Gordon	22	M	Mechanic	10Au04Ka
John	25	M	Mechanic	10Au04Ka
MIDDLETOWN, Jno.	30	M	Mechanic	10Au04Ka
DODDS, James	55	M	Farmer	10Au04Ka
Mary	55	F	None	10Au04Ka
Jane	15	F	None	10Au04Ka
MULLOY, Mary-A.	19	F	None	10Au04Ka
Elizth.	15	F	None	10Au04Ka
ALLAN, Joseph	20	M	Farmer	10Au04Ka
Richd.	18	M	Farmer	10Au04Ka
Margt.	15	F	None	10Au04Ka
BRIDGES, Jno.	26	M	Farmer	10Au04Ka
Margt.	24	F	None	10Au04Ka
Chas.	17	M	Farmer	10Au04Ka
MCPHAIN, Archibald	22	M	Farmer	10Au04Ka
RATSTON, Agnes	26	F	None	10Au04Ka
GOODWIN, James	27	M	Mechanic	10Au04Ka
Mary	26	F	None	10Au04Ka
Sarah	03	F	Child	10Au04Ka
James	06	M	Child	10Au04Ka
PATERSON, Arn.	28	M	Mechanic	10Au04Ka
DOUGAL, Walter	21	M	Mechanic	10Au04Ka
EWART, Arn.	36	M	Mechanic	10Au04Ka
Agnes	40	F	None	10Au04Ka
Sarah	09	F	Child	10Au04Ka
ORR, Elizth.	35	F	None	10Au04Ka
ODONNELL, Wm.	22	M	Mechanic	10Au04Ka
LONG, Danl.	32	M	Mechanic	10Au04Ka
Mary	25	F	None	10Au04Ka
Ann	06	F	Child	10Au04Ka
CAMPBELL, Hugh	58	M	Mechanic	10Au04Ka
Margt.	49	F	None	10Au04Ka
CUNNINGHAM, Mat.	19	M	Mechanic	10Au04Ka
BREMNER, Donald	23	M	Laborer	10Au04Ka
CARTION, Jas.	27	M	Laborer	10Au04Ka
Thos.	27	M	Laborer	10Au04Ka
MCDUGAL, Dugal	30	M	Farmer	10Au04Ka
GRANT, Rob.	30	M	Farmer	10Au04Ka
MCDOUGAL, Donald	28	M	Farmer	10Au04Ka
Donald	28	M	Farmer	10Au04Ka
Elizth.	36	F	None	10Au04Ka
Alexr.	38	M	Farmer	10Au04Ka
Magt.	24	F	None	10Au04Ka
SCOTT, Donald	23	M	Mechanic	10Au04Ka
Elizth.	20	F	None	10Au04Ka
MCDOUGALL, Elizth.	40	F	None	10Au04Ka
Archibald	18	M	Mechanic	10Au04Ka
STEWART, Jno.	40	M	Mechanic	10Au04Ka
MCKEAN, Wm.	21	M	Mechanic	10Au04Ka
MCKENZIE, Geo.	21	M	Mechanic	10Au04Ka
BAIN, Jno.	33	M	Farmer	10Au04Ka

NAMES OF PASSENGERS	AGE	SEX	OCCUPATIONS	DATE PORT SHIP
JOHNSTON, Wm.	18	M	Farmer	10Au04Ka
TATLOCK, Mary	21	F	None	10Au04Ka
LODGE, Emma	20	F	None	10Au04Ka
EASON, Allen	28	M	Mechanic	10Au04Ka
Betty	29	F	None	10Au04Ka
MCINTOSH, Christina	60	F	Unknown	10Au04Ka
Jane	26	F	None	10Au04Ka
EASON, Betsey	18	F	None	10Au04Ka
ROBERTSON, Jno.	30	M	Farmer	10Au04Ka
Jno.	14	M	Farmer	10Au04Ka
CAMERON, Cath.	20	F	None	10Au04Ka
CAMPBELL, Alex.	60	M	Mechanic	10Au04Ka
Agnes	57	F	None	10Au04Ka
MCALLISTER, Jno.	22	M	Mechanic	10Au04Ka
MITCHELL, Arch.	24	M	Mechanic	10Au04Ka
MCGREARY, Andrew	60	M	Mechanic	10Au04Ka
Nancy	60	F	None	10Au04Ka
Andrew	20	M	Mechanic	10Au04Ka
Hannah	22	F	None	10Au04Ka
Richd.	14	M	Mechanic	10Au04Ka
MCBRIDE, Rachael	16	F	None	10Au04Ka
Sarah	18	F	None	10Au04Ka
HANNAH, Cath.	24	F	None	10Au04Ka
MCMILLAN, Jno.	30	M	Mechanic	10Au04Ka
WUNSCH, Alfred	22	M	Mechanic	10Au04Ka
ROSS, John	32	M	Laborer	10Au04Ka
James	25	M	Laborer	10Au04Ka
ALLARDYCE, Jno.	32	M	Laborer	10Au04Ka
MCHANERY, Wm.	44	M	Laborer	10Au04Ka
Elizth.	40	F	None	10Au04Ka
James	07	M	Child	10Au04Ka
MCKANERY, Archibald	05	M	Child	10Au04Ka
Josh.	05	M	Child	10Au04Ka
Jane	03	F	Child	10Au04Ka
Matilda	.11	F	Infant	10Au04Ka
Mary	13	F	None	10Au04Ka
LORIMER, Jas.	23	M	Mechanic	10Au04Ka
WYSE, Robt.	27	M	Mechanic	10Au04Ka
MCGREGOR, Alex.	32	M	Mechanic	10Au04Ka
MESSER, Alexd.	22	M	Mechanic	10Au04Ka
SCOTT, Jas.	48	M	Mechanic	10Au04Ka
CAMERA, Jno.	28	M	Laborer	10Au04Ka
WILSON, Jno.	32	M	Laborer	10Au04Ka

EMPIRE 10 AUGUST 1847

From Liverpool

NAMES OF PASSENGERS	AGE	SEX	OCCUPATIONS	DATE PORT SHIP
ATKINSON, Lewis-P.	22	M	Merchant	10Au02Al
THORNTON, Benj.	25	M	Merchant	10Au02Al
DAVIDSON, Jno.	16	M	Merchant	10Au02Al
STEAD, Mary	43	F	None	10Au02Al
Bessy	16	F	None	10Au02Al
WILSON, Jno.	22	M	Merchant	10Au02Al
Harry	17	M	Merchant	10Au02Al
WHITTAKER, Caroline-M.	21	F	None	10Au02Al
PEACOCK, Francis-W.	22	M	Merchant	10Au02Al
Annie	25	F	None	10Au02Al
Saml.F.	02	M	Child	10Au02Al
Jno.H.	.03	M	Infant	10Au02Al
MORTON, Elizth.	29	F	None	10Au02Al
Mary-A.	01	F	Child	10Au02Al
H.E.	.02	F	Infant	10Au02Al
BERWICK, Wm.	21	M	Mechanic	10Au02Al
ROBBINS, Geo.	27	M	Mechanic	10Au02Al
COOK, Jno.	29	M	Mechanic	10Au02Al
CRUMP, Henry	49	M	Mechanic	10Au02Al
GRENUP, Rebeca	43	F	None	10Au02Al
Henry	01	M	Child	10Au02Al
FRANKLIN, Elizth.	46	F	None	10Au02Al
BATCHELOR, Jessie	49	M	Merchant	10Au02Al
NEUSON, Edmd.	18	M	Merchant	10Au02Al
BATCHELOR, Wm.	14	M	Merchant	10Au02Al
CROSSLAND, Sarah	32	F	None	10Au02Al
WHALEY, Emma	24	F	None	10Au02Al
TURNER, Elizabeth	21	F	None	10Au02Al
SHELDON, Hannah	28	F	None	10Au02Al
PATTERSON, Mary-A.	21	F	None	10Au02Al
DUNN, Selina	25	F	None	10Au02Al
DRINKEL, Ann	16	F	None	10Au02Al
HOBSON, Betsey	16	F	None	10Au02Al
MORTIMER, Jno.	30	M	None	10Au02Al
PHILLIPS, Wm.	28	M	None	10Au02Al
Fanny	26	F	None	10Au02Al
REECE, Richd.	35	M	Merchant	10Au02Al
HARRISON, James	24	M	Merchant	10Au02Al
Pancha	23	F	None	10Au02Al
GAMBLE, Alfred	15	M	Merchant	10Au02Al
BISHOP, Mary	15	F	None	10Au02Al
JONES, Thos.	34	M	Merchant	10Au02Al
Jane	30	F	None	10Au02Al
Richd.	09	M	Child	10Au02Al
Jno.	06	M	Child	10Au02Al
Chas.	03	M	Child	10Au02Al
BIRTWITH, Jno.	26	M	Mechanic	10Au02Al
Margt.	24	F	None	10Au02Al
DUCKWITH, Sarah	24	F	None	10Au02Al
FURERER, Francis	50	M	None	10Au02Al
THOMAS, Thos.	30	M	Merchant	10Au02Al
POWELL, Llewellyn	35	M	Merchant	10Au02Al
Rebecca	32	F	None	10Au02Al
Frank-O.	04	M	Child	10Au02Al
Sarah-A.	02	F	Child	10Au02Al
ROWLAND, Ann	55	F	None	10Au02Al
ASHTON, Jno.	26	M	Mechanic	10Au02Al
THORNTON, Richd.	25	M	Mechanic	10Au02Al
COYSWELL, Wm.	36	M	Mechanic	10Au02Al
Hannah	17	F	None	10Au02Al
DOUGHERTY, Neal	30	M	Mechanic	10Au02Al
DONELLY, Pat	35	M	Mechanic	10Au02Al
Alice	35	F	None	10Au02Al
Jno.	12	M	None	10Au02Al
Edwd.	10	M	None	10Au02Al
Barnard	08	M	Child	10Au02Al
HUMPHRYS, Richd.	27	M	Mechanic	10Au02Al
Thos.	20	M	Mechanic	10Au02Al
HOWKEY, Elizth.	30	F	None	10Au02Al
MURPHY, Pat	50	M	Mechanic	10Au02Al
Ellen	48	F	None	10Au02Al
MCLOUGHLIN, Pat	28	M	Mechanic	10Au02Al
MCDANIEL, Bridget	40	F	None	10Au02Al
MURPHY, Jas.	12	M	Mechanic	10Au02Al
Bridget	12	F	None	10Au02Al
MAYERS, Jno.	60	M	Mechanic	10Au02Al
Margt.	58	F	None	10Au02Al
MULLEN, Thos.	55	M	Mechanic	10Au02Al
GEORGE, Jno.	10	M	Mechanic	10Au02Al
Sarah	19	F	None	10Au02Al
JOHNSON, Agnes	19	F	None	10Au02Al
HUMPHRIES, Jno.	37	M	Mechanic	10Au02Al
HALL, Henry	19	M	Mechanic	10Au02Al
OWENS, Magt.	20	F	None	10Au02Al
WRIGHT, Haerris	29	M	Laborer	10Au02Al
LLOYD, Pat	24	M	Laborer	10Au02Al
Pat	16	M	Laborer	10Au02Al
Bridget	12	F	None	10Au02Al
Ann	10	F	None	10Au02Al
MENTIN, Francis	25	M	Laborer	10Au02Al
Bernard	19	M	Laborer	10Au02Al
SEELY, Thos.	16	M	Laborer	10Au02Al
CAFLEY, Thos.	18	M	Laborer	10Au02Al
SKEEN, Ros.	50	F	None	10Au02Al
WILSON, Ellen	16	F	None	10Au02Al
Jno.	12	M	None	10Au02Al

NAMES OF PASSENGERS	AGE	SEX	OCCUPATIONS	DATE PORT SHIP
WILSON, Wm.	10	M	None	10Au02AI
BRADY, Thos.	26	M	Laborer	10Au02AI
MURPHY, Mary	19	F	None	10Au02AI
Ellen	16	F	None	10Au02AI
LYNCH, Ann-J.	19	F	None	10Au02AI
CRONIN, Danl.	23	M	Laborer	10Au02AI
CONNELLY, Elizth.	29	F	None	10Au02AI
CUNNINGHAM, Pat	30	M	Laborer	10Au02AI
MCGUIRE, Susan	20	F	None	10Au02AI
James	22	M	Laborer	10Au02AI
TRACEY, Bridget	30	F	None	10Au02AI
CARROL, Eleanor	30	F	None	10Au02AI
Peter	09	M	Child	10Au02AI
Judith	07	F	Child	10Au02AI
Phil	05	M	Child	10Au02AI
Mary	01	F	Child	10Au02AI
FLOOD, Thos.	60	M	Mechanic	10Au02AI
Elizth.	15	F	None	10Au02AI
Mary	50	F	None	10Au02AI
BURNS, Bridget	16	F	None	10Au02AI
Ann-G.	04	F	Child	10Au02AI
KENNEDY, Sarah	55	F	None	10Au02AI
CARR, Wm.	50	M	Laborer	10Au02AI
Margt.	20	F	None	10Au02AI
Thos.	12	M	None	10Au02AI
MAYERS, Jno.	19	M	Laborer	10Au02AI
Steph.	15	M	None	10Au02AI
Biddy	08	F	Child	10Au02AI
REILLY, Pat	50	M	Laborer	10Au02AI
POWELL, Chas.	35	M	Laborer	10Au02AI
Ann	32	F	None	10Au02AI
MALI, Sarah	28	F	None	10Au02AI
POWELL, Joshua	02	M	Child	10Au02AI
Ed.F.	.04	M	Infant	10Au02AI
WILKINS, Jno.	30	M	Mechanic	10Au02AI
ROBINSON, Jonathon	30	M	Mechanic	10Au02AI
Mary	30	F	None	10Au02AI
Wm.	05	M	Child	10Au02AI
Harriet	03	F	Child	10Au02AI
HARRIS, James	23	M	Mechanic	10Au02AI
GILLELY, Brian	30	M	Laborer	10Au02AI
MARTIN, Robert	21	M	Laborer	10Au02AI
Bridget	18	F	None	10Au02AI
KENEDY, Margt.	18	F	None	10Au02AI
DUINN, Jno.	23	M	Laborer	10Au02AI
BURNS, Mary	54	F	None	10Au02AI
DASY, Peter	25	M	Laborer	10Au02AI
Robt.	19	M	Laborer	10Au02AI
Patt	17	M	Laborer	10Au02AI
MORRISON, Wm.	18	M	Mechanic	10Au02AI
STEELE, Thos.	18	M	Mechanic	10Au02AI
Geo.	18	M	Mechanic	10Au02AI
DAVY, Jno.	17	M	Mechanic	10Au02AI
MULLIGAN, Pat	17	M	Laborer	10Au02AI
Thos.	17	M	Laborer	10Au02AI
HARRINGTON, David	76	M	Laborer	10Au02AI
Jno.	30	M	Laborer	10Au02AI
BUCKLEY, Johanna	26	F	None	10Au02AI
Jno.	25	M	Laborer	10Au02AI
REGAN, Simon	32	M	Laborer	10Au02AI
HANLEY, Mich.	28	M	Laborer	10Au02AI
BUTLER, Julia	23	F	None	10Au02AI
DENWOODE, Francis	50	M	Laborer	10Au02AI
CARROL, Cath.	17	F	None	10Au02AI
NORTON, Pat	50	M	Farmer	10Au02AI
Honora	45	F	None	10Au02AI
Mich.	25	M	Farmer	10Au02AI
Math.	14	M	Farmer	10Au02AI
Bridget	22	F	None	10Au02AI
Cath.	20	F	None	10Au02AI
CONNER, Mary	24	F	None	10Au02AI
CUSACK, Mary	23	F	None	10Au02AI
COX, Mich.	25	M	Farmer	10Au02AI
Bridget	25	F	None	10Au02AI
KELLY, Thos.	17	M	Laborer	10Au02AI

NAMES OF PASSENGERS	AGE	SEX	OCCUPATIONS	DATE PORT SHIP
KINNEY, Jas.	21	M	Laborer	10Au02AI
Jane	18	F	None	10Au02AI
Edwd.	14	M	Laborer	10Au02AI
DONENY, Chas.	20	M	Laborer	10Au02AI
COLGAN, Jno.	30	M	Laborer	10Au02AI
Maria	18	F	None	10Au02AI
DONNELLY, Jas.	23	M	Laborer	10Au02AI
SHUMACKER, Jno.	22	M	Laborer	10Au02AI
GROGAN, Jno.	44	M	Laborer	10Au02AI
LENON, Fred.R.	17	M	Laborer	10Au02AI
HEANY, Jno.	26	M	Laborer	10Au02AI
KAY, Judith	14	F	None	10Au02AI
MCGUIRE, Jno.	27	M	Laborer	10Au02AI
BRODIE, Thos.	28	M	Laborer	10Au02AI
REILY, Philip	22	M	Laborer	10Au02AI
Owen	24	M	Laborer	10Au02AI
Jus.	18	M	Laborer	10Au02AI
Cath.	26	F	None	10Au02AI
Eliza	28	F	None	10Au02AI
Mary	11	F	None	10Au02AI
CALLAGHAN, Rose	29	F	None	10Au02AI
CARR, Jas.	07	M	Child	10Au02AI
CALLAGHAN, Julia	13	F	None	10Au02AI
Jno.	12	M	Laborer	10Au02AI
HANLEY, Margt.	20	F	None	10Au02AI
Cath.	14	F	None	10Au02AI
AGNEW, Cath.	15	F	None	10Au02AI
Ellen	15	F	None	10Au02AI
BURNS, James	58	M	Laborer	10Au02AI
NOLAN, Ann	24	F	None	10Au02AI
MORRISON, Sarah	61	F	None	10Au02AI
SHEEHEEN, Jeremiah	27	M	Mechanic	10Au02AI
COYNE, Jno.	37	M	Mechanic	10Au02AI
Wm.	10	M	None	10Au02AI
CAMPBELL, Geo.C.	18	M	Mechanic	10Au02AI
REGAN, Wm.	21	M	Mechanic	10Au02AI
COSS, Edwd.	40	M	Mechanic	10Au02AI
Mary	35	F	None	10Au02AI
THORNTON, Thos.	30	M	Mechanic	10Au02AI
Ann	28	F	None	10Au02AI
Hannah	11	F	None	10Au02AI
Elizth.	09	F	Child	10Au02AI
Wm.	07	M	Child	10Au02AI
Jno.	03	M	Child	10Au02AI
Josh.	01	M	Child	10Au02AI
LYNCH, Josh.	21	M	Laborer	10Au02AI
KNOX, Richd.	47	M	Laborer	10Au02AI
HUGHES, David	40	M	Laborer	10Au02AI
CHURCHILL, Cath.	38	F	None	10Au02AI
BURNS, Mich.	23	M	Laborer	10Au02AI
MORRISON, Sarah	22	F	None	10Au02AI
RICHARDS, Thos.	35	M	Laborer	10Au02AI
TURNER, Saml.	23	M	Laborer	10Au02AI
RIED, Cath.	21	F	None	10Au02AI
Bridget	18	F	None	10Au02AI
BRIGGS, Timothy	22	M	Laborer	10Au02AI
GRANT, Jno.	36	M	Laborer	10Au02AI
Mary	37	F	None	10Au02AI
Cath.	24	F	None	10Au02AI
HURLEY, Law.	32	M	Laborer	10Au02AI
Ellen	30	F	None	10Au02AI
Ellen	02	F	Child	10Au02AI
WADDOCK, Jno.	25	M	Laborer	10Au02AI
MARSHALL, Sarah	60	F	None	10Au02AI
Margt.	32	F	None	10Au02AI
Jas.	29	M	Laborer	10Au02AI
Wm.	19	M	Laborer	10Au02AI
Silas	19	M	Laborer	10Au02AI
Mary-A.	02	F	Child	10Au02AI
OWENS, Hanah	65	F	None	10Au02AI
Richd.	34	M	Laborer	10Au02AI
John	22	M	Laborer	10Au02AI
David	23	M	Mechanic	10Au02AI
Ann	53	F	None	10Au02AI
Joseph	10	M	None	10Au02AI

NAMES OF PASSENGERS	AGE	SEX	OCCUPATIONS	DATE PORT SHIP
OWENS, Ann	08	F	Child	10Au02Al
Hannah	.09	F	Infant	10Au02Al
Benj.	06	M	Child	10Au02Al
Wm.	03	M	Child	10Au02Al
ASHTON, Elizth.	29	F	None	10Au02Al
THICKENS, Sarah	16	F	None	10Au02Al
Martha	14	F	None	10Au02Al
Eleanor	11	F	None	10Au02Al
OWENS, Richd.	35	M	Mechanic	10Au02Al
Jane	35	F	None	10Au02Al
Elizth.	17	F	None	10Au02Al
Richd.	18	M	Mechanic	10Au02Al
Jane	06	F	Child	10Au02Al
J.W.	01	M	Child	10Au02Al
HANLON, Pat	19	M	Laborer	10Au02Al
Wm.	19	M	Laborer	10Au02Al
MCCABE, Pat	45	M	Laborer	10Au02Al
Eliza	19	F	None	10Au02Al
NICHOLAS, Magt.	27	F	None	10Au02Al
Alice	16	F	None	10Au02Al
BROWN, Cath.	09	F	Child	10Au02Al
NOONAN, Wm.	36	M	Laborer	10Au02Al
DEEGAN, Jos.	20	M	Laborer	10Au02Al
Judy	20	F	None	10Au02Al
ROGERS, Hugh	67	M	Laborer	10Au02Al
Hugh	24	M	Laborer	10Au02Al
Mary	22	F	None	10Au02Al
Felix	21	M	Laborer	10Au02Al
Bernard	13	M	Laborer	10Au02Al
GINESS, Edwd.	24	M	Laborer	10Au02Al
MCCABE, Pat	13	M	Laborer	10Au02Al
HENESY, H.	24	M	Laborer	10Au02Al
CARROLL, Jerry	24	M	Laborer	10Au02Al
LEARY, Dan	22	M	Laborer	10Au02Al
MILLER, Andrew	30	M	Laborer	10Au02Al
RYAN, Jno.	30	M	Laborer	10Au02Al
COUNAN, Jerry	40	M	Farmer	10Au02Al
Julia	35	F	None	10Au02Al
Mich.	08	M	Child	10Au02Al
Honora	06	F	Child	10Au02Al
HIGGINS, D.	30	M	Farmer	10Au02Al
SAVAGE, Mich.	54	M	Farmer	10Au02Al
Margt.	56	F	None	10Au02Al
Mary	17	F	None	10Au02Al
Pat	16	M	Farmer	10Au02Al
Danl.	15	M	None	10Au02Al
Jerry	13	M	None	10Au02Al
Margt.	11	F	None	10Au02Al
Eliza	09	F	Child	10Au02Al
Kate	07	F	Child	10Au02Al
OLIVER, Ann	24	F	None	10Au02Al
Sarah	25	F	None	10Au02Al
Mary	28	F	None	10Au02Al
MORGAN, Pat	40	M	Laborer	10Au02Al
BURNETT, Mary	24	F	None	10Au02Al
Margt.	19	F	None	10Au02Al
SCULLY, Mich.	13	M	None	10Au02Al
CARR, Patt	34	M	Laborer	10Au02Al
HIGGINS, Jno.	19	M	Merchant	10Au02Al
KENNEDY, Mich.	35	M	Laborer	10Au02Al
FRAZER, Kenneth	19	M	Laborer	10Au02Al
MARSHALL, Robt.	60	M	Laborer	10Au02Al
ROGERS, Alice	18	F	None	10Au02Al
PARKER, Ann	33	F	None	10Au02Al
Mary	06	F	Child	10Au02Al
Jno.	04	M	Child	10Au02Al
FLYNN, Ellen	20	F	None	10Au02Al
WELSH, Law.	18	M	Laborer	10Au02Al
MCGOVERN, Jno.	18	M	Laborer	10Au02Al
WOODS, Ann	20	F	None	10Au02Al
MCCUE, Mary	16	F	None	10Au02Al
STOCKS, Jno.	30	M	Laborer	10Au02Al
COSER, Pat	25	M	Laborer	10Au02Al
HURLEY, Mary	01	F	Child	10Au02Al
MOORE, Mary	28	F	None	10Au02Al
MOORE, Elizth.	07	F	Child	10Au02Al
Cath.	02	F	Child	10Au02Al

GEORGIA 11 AUGUST 1847

From Glasgow

NAMES OF PASSENGERS	AGE	SEX	OCCUPATIONS	DATE PORT SHIP
CURRIE, Elizth.	45	F	None	11Au04Fs
Lewis	14	M	None	11Au04Fs
Jno.	13	M	None	11Au04Fs
HOUSTON, Jas.	27	M	Farmer	11Au04Fs
ALLAN, Margt.	21	F	None	11Au04Fs
FLEMING, Allen	26	M	Farmer	11Au04Fs
COWIE, Jane	30	F	None	11Au04Fs
Anne	09	F	Child	11Au04Fs
Jane	.07	F	Infant	11Au04Fs
HUNTER, Geo.	24	M	Farmer	11Au04Fs
Wm.	22	M	Physician	11Au04Fs
Susan	24	F	None	11Au04Fs
DORG, Jannet	46	F	None	11Au04Fs
MUTERER, Alexs.	30	M	Mechanic	11Au04Fs
HAMILTON, Thos.	25	M	Farmer	11Au04Fs
Ellen	21	F	None	11Au04Fs
SCOTT, Pat	30	M	Farmer	11Au04Fs
PLUNKETT, Ed.	37	M	Mechanic	11Au04Fs
MCCANNA, Phil	24	M	Mechanic	11Au04Fs
WILSON, Ann	50	F	None	11Au04Fs
Wm.	28	M	Mechanic	11Au04Fs
DUFF, Ann	34	F	None	11Au04Fs
FARRALL, Margt.	07	F	Child	11Au04Fs
Isabella	06	F	Child	11Au04Fs
WATSON, Hugh	30	M	Farmer	11Au04Fs
WILLS, Cath.	24	F	None	11Au04Fs
Mary-A.	03	F	Child	11Au04Fs
Wm.	.06	M	Infant	11Au04Fs

GONDOLA 11 AUGUST 1847

From Dublin

NAMES OF PASSENGERS	AGE	SEX	OCCUPATIONS	DATE PORT SHIP
BURGESS, Julia	18	F	None	11Au20Eg
BEGAN, U-Mrs.	36	F	None	11Au20Eg
BEEGAN, Eliza	30	F	None	11Au20Eg
Sophia	09	F	Child	11Au20Eg
Louisa	06	F	Child	11Au20Eg
Jno.	04	M	Child	11Au20Eg
Mary-F.	02	F	Child	11Au20Eg
Ann-M.	.04	F	Infant	11Au20Eg
KELLY, James	24	M	Laborer	11Au20Eg
MILEY, U-Mrs.	33	F	None	11Au20Eg
Eliza	05	F	Child	11Au20Eg
Jas.	03	M	Child	11Au20Eg
MONK, Jas.	28	M	Mechanic	11Au20Eg
MELVILLE, Andrew	35	M	Mechanic	11Au20Eg
U (W)	30	F	Wife	11Au20Eg
JORDAN, Pat	28	M	Mechanic	11Au20Eg
U (W)	28	F	Wife	11Au20Eg
OCONNER, Maria	20	F	None	11Au20Eg
GLEESON, Thomas	35	M	Mechanic	11Au20Eg
PURCELL, Sarah	19	F	None	11Au20Eg
COLE, Wm.	26	M	Mechanic	11Au20Eg
U (W)	25	F	Wife	11Au20Eg
CAFFREY, Mich.	40	M	Farmer	11Au20Eg

NAMES OF PASSENGERS		AGE	SEX	OCCUPATIONS	DATE PORT SHIP
CAFFREY, Jno.		15	M	Farmer	11Au20Eg
SULLIVAN, Pat		60	M	Farmer	11Au20Eg
KEARNEY, Pat		35	M	Farmer	11Au20Eg
HYDE, Isaac		36	M	Farmer	11Au20Eg
U	(W)	36	F	Wife	11Au20Eg
GAHAN, U-Mrs.		44	F	None	11Au20Eg
Edwd.		15	M	None	11Au20Eg
Winnifred		08	F	Child	11Au20Eg
Milss.		03	M	Child	11Au20Eg
ROACH, Jno.		29	M	Mechanic	11Au20Eg
Phil		27	M	Mechanic	11Au20Eg
HUGHES, Mary		25	F	None	11Au20Eg
Andrew		21	M	Mechanic	11Au20Eg
Thomas		14	M	None	11Au20Eg
WESTERN, Ann		40	F	None	11Au20Eg
Sophia		18	F	None	11Au20Eg
MCDONALD, James		30	M	Farmer	11Au20Eg
U	(W)	29	F	None	11Au20Eg
Pat		08	M	Child	11Au20Eg
Jas.		04	M	Child	11Au20Eg
John		02	M	Child	11Au20Eg
DEVILIN, Ellen		17	F	None	11Au20Eg
SMITH, Chas.		20	M	Farmer	11Au20Eg
Margt.		23	F	None	11Au20Eg
FARWELL, Wm.		35	M	Farmer	11Au20Eg
CULLEN, Jas.		20	M	Clerk	11Au20Eg
FARRELL, Alice		22	F	None	11Au20Eg
WARD, Eliza		24	F	None	11Au20Eg
MYERS, Ellen		28	F	None	11Au20Eg
KIERNAN, Mary		19	F	None	11Au20Eg
MCDONALD, John		24	M	Mechanic	11Au20Eg
MOORE, Martin		32	M	Mechanic	11Au20Eg
GEGARTY, Jas.		22	M	Mechanic	11Au20Eg
BAKER, John		19	M	Mechanic	11Au20Eg
LEE, James		24	M	Mechanic	11Au20Eg
DONOGAN, Jno.		19	M	Mechanic	11Au20Eg
QUIGLEY, Wm.		27	M	Mechanic	11Au20Eg
U	(W)	25	F	Wife	11Au20Eg
HANLON, Jno.		20	M	Mechanic	11Au20Eg
WALTON, Alicia		28	F	None	11Au20Eg
Margt.		22	F	None	11Au20Eg
DELAHANTY, Ann		21	F	None	11Au20Eg
Mary		01	F	Child	11Au20Eg
Ellen		.00	F	Infant	11Au20Eg
SEXTON, Cath.		16	F	None	11Au20Eg
PIERCE, Ann		24	F	None	11Au20Eg
STRANGEWAYS, Cath.		18	F	None	11Au20Eg
FARNELL, Pat		31	M	Mechanic	11Au20Eg
U	(W)	25	F	Wife	11Au20Eg
Cath.		.00	F	Infant	11Au20Eg
CARTHY, Inez		26	F	None	11Au20Eg
MCNALLY, Pat		25	M	Laborer	11Au20Eg
KEEGAN, Law.		26	M	Laborer	11Au20Eg
Mary		22	F	None	11Au20Eg
Ann		03	F	Child	11Au20Eg
BRENAN, Terence		13	M	None	11Au20Eg
Mich.		18	M	Mechanic	11Au20Eg
Jane		20	F	None	11Au20Eg
GRADY, Richd.		30	M	Mechanic	11Au20Eg
U	(W)	24	F	Wife	11Au20Eg
MCKENNA, Phil		18	M	Mechanic	11Au20Eg
DUFFY, Edwd.		22	M	Mechanic	11Au20Eg
U	(W)	27	F	Wife	11Au20Eg
FOLEY, Barth.		22	M	Mechanic	11Au20Eg
CARTHY, Jno.		22	M	Mechanic	11Au20Eg
MURPHY, Jas.		21	M	Mechanic	11Au20Eg
RICE, Law.		19	M	Mechanic	11Au20Eg
PAGE, Jas.		24	M	Mechanic	11Au20Eg
Eliza		21	F	None	11Au20Eg
MALONE, Bernard		24	M	Mechanic	11Au20Eg
KEATING, Jno.		20	M	Mechanic	11Au20Eg
TOOLE, Jer.		25	M	Farmer	11Au20Eg
Cath.		35	F	None	11Au20Eg
James		16	M	Farmer	11Au20Eg
Daniel		14	M	None	11Au20Eg
TOOLE, Richd.		10	M	None	11Au20Eg
Kerr		08	M	Child	11Au20Eg
Jerem.		05	M	Child	11Au20Eg
Pat		01	M	Child	11Au20Eg
DUNNE, Law.		21	M	Farmer	11Au20Eg
MCDONNELL, Jno.		24	M	Farmer	11Au20Eg
BRENNAN, Mich.		20	M	Farmer	11Au20Eg
DULARD, Ellen		30	F	None	11Au20Eg
TOONEY, Wm.		36	M	Farmer	11Au20Eg
HERAN, Jno.		25	M	Farmer	11Au20Eg
DUNN, Mary		25	F	None	11Au20Eg
RIDLY, Margt.		15	F	None	11Au20Eg
GALWAY, Richd.		24	M	Farmer	11Au20Eg
HARDING, James		25	M	Farmer	11Au20Eg
MARTIN, Malachi		21	M	Farmer	11Au20Eg

EMMA-PRESCOTT 11 AUGUST 1847

From Windsor

NAMES OF PASSENGERS	AGE	SEX	OCCUPATIONS	DATE PORT SHIP
CURRY, Jas.E.	21	M	Artist	11Au91Sd

ARTHUR 16 AUGUST 1847

From Kingston

NAMES OF PASSENGERS	AGE	SEX	OCCUPATIONS	DATE PORT SHIP
BADLEY, Chas.	38	M	Laborer	16Au23Sh
Eliz.	40	F	None	16Au23Sh
BONLEY, Jas.	36	M	Laborer	16Au23Sh
Elizth.	30	F	None	16Au23Sh
HIGGONBOTTOM, J.	34	M	Mechanic	16Au23Sh
LENISTALL, W.	29	M	Engineer	16Au23Sh

CATHERINE 17 AUGUST 1847

From Waterford

NAMES OF PASSENGERS	AGE	SEX	OCCUPATIONS	DATE PORT SHIP
PARL, James	45	M	Farmer	17Au16Gr
Mary	36	F	None	17Au16Gr
Edwd.	12	M	None	17Au16Gr
James	08	M	Child	17Au16Gr
Stephen	19	M	Farmer	17Au16Gr
Pat	28	M	Farmer	17Au16Gr
Ellen	36	F	None	17Au16Gr
Thos.	06	M	Child	17Au16Gr
MOORE, Jas.	27	M	Farmer	17Au16Gr
Mary	30	F	None	17Au16Gr
DEVEREUX, Peter	40	M	Farmer	17Au16Gr
KAVANAGH, Thos.	27	M	Farmer	17Au16Gr
TILL, Mich.	48	M	Farmer	17Au16Gr
LAMY, Mich.	28	M	Farmer	17Au16Gr
GLIN, Pat	27	M	Farmer	17Au16Gr
PHALON, Francis	30	M	Farmer	17Au16Gr
SULLIVAN, Joseph	22	M	Farmer	17Au16Gr
MEYERS, Jno.	35	M	Farmer	17Au16Gr
DRUMMOND, Mary	20	F	None	17Au16Gr
POINTY, Magt.	24	F	None	17Au16Gr

NAMES OF PASSENGERS	AGE	SEX	OCCUPATIONS	DATE PORT SHIP
POINTY, Susan	03	F	Child	17Au16Gr
Mich.	09	M	Child	17Au16Gr

SHERIDAN 18 AUGUST 1847

From Liverpool

NAMES OF PASSENGERS	AGE	SEX	OCCUPATIONS	DATE PORT SHIP
HARTLEY, Sarah	26	F	None	18Au02Do
R.A.	03	F	Child	18Au02Do
M.V.	01	F	Child	18Au02Do
CYLE, Jane-A.	40	F	None	18Au02Do
RICHARDS, Wm.	40	M	Merchant	18Au02Do
GUINESS, Wm.	35	M	Laborer	18Au02Do
Eliza	35	F	None	18Au02Do
Adelia	16	F	None	18Au02Do
Emily	13	F	None	18Au02Do
Arthur	12	M	None	18Au02Do
PATTERSON, Wm.	28	M	Printer	18Au02Do
Jannett	24	F	None	18Au02Do
HILL, Susan	35	F	None	18Au02Do
Sophia	09	F	Child	18Au02Do
Theresa	03	F	Child	18Au02Do
Jno.	01	M	Child	18Au02Do
ROSINGTON, Robt.	25	M	Laborer	18Au02Do
Wm.	30	M	Laborer	18Au02Do
U-Mrs.	25	F	None	18Au02Do
BROWNE, Jas.	30	M	Laborer	18Au02Do
CARRINGTON, Robt.	23	M	Laborer	18Au02Do
Eleanor	21	F	None	18Au02Do
MAHON, M.M.	22	M	Clerk	18Au02Do
Sarah	20	F	None	18Au02Do
MCKENNA, Jno.	20	M	Mechanic	18Au02Do
LYNCH, Mich.	23	M	Mechanic	18Au02Do
Margt.	20	F	None	18Au02Do
GRAHAM, John	24	M	Mechanic	18Au02Do
SHAW, David	30	M	Mechanic	18Au02Do
MELHERST, Mathew	45	M	Farmer	18Au02Do
WARBINGTON, Jas.	36	M	Farmer	18Au02Do
IKIN, Benj.	36	M	Farmer	18Au02Do
Eleanor	34	F	None	18Au02Do
Sarah	09	F	Child	18Au02Do
Mary	06	F	Child	18Au02Do
Margt.	04	F	Child	18Au02Do
WILSON, Robt.	60	M	Farmer	18Au02Do
Ann	50	F	None	18Au02Do
Thos.	17	M	Farmer	18Au02Do
SULLIVAN, Mary	25	F	None	18Au02Do
Honora	03	F	Child	18Au02Do
Jno.	.00	M	Infant	18Au02Do
MCCARTY, Nancy	18	F	None	18Au02Do
RULE, James	36	M	Laborer	18Au02Do
BARRETT, John	50	M	Laborer	18Au02Do
Mary	36	F	None	18Au02Do
Timothy	18	M	Laborer	18Au02Do
Jno.	12	M	None	18Au02Do
Wm.	10	M	None	18Au02Do
Edwd.	03	M	Child	18Au02Do
ROACH, Mich.	25	M	Laborer	18Au02Do
Margt.	19	F	None	18Au02Do
BOYLE, Jas.	30	M	Laborer	18Au02Do
CANE, Bryan	23	M	Laborer	18Au02Do
DELANEY, Mathew	24	M	Mechanic	18Au02Do
KONAN, Mich.	32	M	Mechanic	18Au02Do
LOTHERINGTON, Wm.	21	M	Mechanic	18Au02Do
PACK, M.	38	M	Mechanic	18Au02Do
BARBER, Mathew	35	M	Mechanic	18Au02Do
SPEELL, David	40	M	Mechanic	18Au02Do
DUNMORE, Robt.	28	M	Mechanic	18Au02Do
Margt.	27	F	None	18Au02Do
MCGREGOR, Gregor	19	M	Farmer	18Au02Do
JONES, Cath.	27	F	None	18Au02Do
MCGOW, Jno.	19	M	Farmer	18Au02Do
Eliza	17	F	None	18Au02Do
MCSHERRY, Thos.	24	M	Laborer	18Au02Do
TAFFEY, Jno.	36	M	Laborer	18Au02Do
LEDDY, Margt.	18	F	None	18Au02Do
Ann	15	F	None	18Au02Do
MAHON, Law.	26	M	Laborer	18Au02Do
DOUGLAS, Jno.	24	M	Laborer	18Au02Do
THOMPSON, Am.	22	M	Laborer	18Au02Do
GILPIN, Mary-J.	22	F	None	18Au02Do
HUGHES, Jane	19	F	None	18Au02Do
MCLOUGHLIN, Owen	40	M	Laborer	18Au02Do
EVERARD, Julia	45	F	None	18Au02Do
Chris.	21	M	Laborer	18Au02Do
James	15	M	Laborer	18Au02Do
Jane	12	F	None	18Au02Do
William	10	M	None	18Au02Do
Joseph	09	M	Child	18Au02Do
CONNELLY, Jno.	30	M	Laborer	18Au02Do
Ann	26	F	None	18Au02Do
Pat	05	M	Child	18Au02Do
Mary-A.	03	F	Child	18Au02Do
Eliza	.00	F	Infant	18Au02Do
RYAN, Mich.	50	M	Mechanic	18Au02Do
MCELVINEY, John	21	M	Mechanic	18Au02Do
TAYLOR, Jas.	25	M	Mechanic	18Au02Do
MCKEOWN, Felix	21	M	Laborer	18Au02Do
DEVINE, Jas.	50	M	Laborer	18Au02Do
Bridget	16	F	None	18Au02Do
KELLY, Andrew	18	M	Laborer	18Au02Do
LARKINS, Jno.	24	M	Laborer	18Au02Do
DESMOND, Magt.	22	F	None	18Au02Do
GOLLIGHER, Jno.	21	M	Laborer	18Au02Do
Jno.	22	M	Laborer	18Au02Do
Mary	20	F	None	18Au02Do
WALTMAN, Simeon	19	M	Mechanic	18Au02Do
GRANT, M.	35	M	Mechanic	18Au02Do
JONES, Anne	23	F	None	18Au02Do
MOORE, Jos.	28	M	Merchant	18Au02Do
Susan	26	F	None	18Au02Do
Jno.	36	M	Merchant	18Au02Do
Ann	08	F	Child	18Au02Do
LANGTRY, Margt.	14	F	Unknown	18Au02Do
REDDING, Ann	60	F	Unknown	18Au02Do
ROACH, Mary	50	F	Unknown	18Au02Do
Mary	30	F	Unknown	18Au02Do
WALSH, Danl.	23	M	Laborer	18Au02Do
ROACH, Ed.	30	M	Laborer	18Au02Do
ODEA, Jer.	32	M	Laborer	18Au02Do
ROACH, Pat	31	M	Laborer	18Au02Do
Jno.	20	M	Laborer	18Au02Do
Hannah	07	F	Child	18Au02Do
Mary-A.	04	F	Child	18Au02Do
WARMBY, Elisha	24	M	Farmer	18Au02Do
SHAW, J.B.	25	M	Farmer	18Au02Do
MILLCHAM, Joha.	26	F	None	18Au02Do
LONG, Wm.	22	M	Laborer	18Au02Do
CROWLEY, Wm.	38	M	Laborer	18Au02Do
HICKEY, Mich.	20	M	Laborer	18Au02Do
SMITH, Wm.	21	M	Mechanic	18Au02Do
HEANY, Pat	40	M	Mechanic	18Au02Do
BAKER, Jno.	26	M	Mechanic	18Au02Do
Eliza	20	F	None	18Au02Do
MCMULLEN, Robt.	24	M	Mechanic	18Au02Do
DRESCOLL, Mary	25	F	None	18Au02Do
Ellen	09	F	Child	18Au02Do
Eliza	08	F	Child	18Au02Do
Margt.	20	F	None	18Au02Do
MCCARTY, Cath.	19	F	None	18Au02Do
DRESCOLL, Daniel	24	M	Laborer	18Au02Do
BURKE, Ann	17	F	None	18Au02Do
PHEBBS, Jno.	26	M	Laborer	18Au02Do
CLARK, Pat	30	M	Laborer	18Au02Do

NAMES OF PASSENGERS	AGE	SEX	OCCUPATIONS	DATE PORT SHIP
CARROLL, Pat	24	M	Laborer	18Au02Do
Margt.	22	F	None	18Au02Do
Patk.	.00	M	Infant	18Au02Do
COLMAN, Mary	38	F	None	18Au02Do
CAUGHLIN, Mary	04	F	Child	18Au02Do
MURPHY, Mary	20	F	None	18Au02Do
KING, Chas.T.	24	M	Mechanic	18Au02Do
TULLY, Pat	24	M	Mechanic	18Au02Do
CULLEN, Jos.	20	M	Mechanic	18Au02Do
MCDONALD, Wm.	40	M	Mechanic	18Au02Do
HORAN, Jno.	29	M	Mechanic	18Au02Do
Cath.	28	F	None	18Au02Do
Jas.	.00	M	Infant	18Au02Do
SWEENEY, Ed	32	M	Mechanic	18Au02Do
Mary	28	F	None	18Au02Do
Jos.	07	M	Child	18Au02Do
Maria	03	F	Child	18Au02Do
OBRIEN, Morgan	46	M	Laborer	18Au02Do
Thos.	19	M	Laborer	18Au02Do
MEENIS, Benj.	21	M	Laborer	18Au02Do
HASTON, Henry	60	M	Laborer	18Au02Do
Jno.	36	M	Laborer	18Au02Do
Maria	15	F	None	18Au02Do
CROCKETT, Sarah	28	F	None	18Au02Do
EARL, Jno.	25	M	Laborer	18Au02Do
WILSON, Jacob	27	M	Laborer	18Au02Do
LITTLE, Jno.	24	M	Laborer	18Au02Do
GRAHAM, Wm.	28	M	Laborer	18Au02Do
Jane	21	F	None	18Au02Do
Sarah	48	F	None	18Au02Do
Maria	28	F	None	18Au02Do
Ester	26	F	None	18Au02Do
Jno.	21	M	Laborer	18Au02Do
Jackson	14	M	Laborer	18Au02Do
Cath.	12	F	None	18Au02Do
CONLAN, Mary	18	F	None	18Au02Do
Agnes	16	F	None	18Au02Do
MCCAUL, Henry	21	M	Mechanic	18Au02Do
Magt.	23	F	None	18Au02Do
BANNER, Eliza	36	F	None	18Au02Do
Mat.	07	M	Child	18Au02Do
Jno.	04	M	Child	18Au02Do
Thos.	02	M	Child	18Au02Do
Eliza	.00	F	Infant	18Au02Do
CARLIN, Anthony	20	M	Laborer	18Au02Do
Nancy	24	F	None	18Au02Do
MCLAUGHLIN, Rosa.	22	F	None	18Au02Do
SIMMONS, Sophia	28	F	None	18Au02Do
Henry	05	M	Child	18Au02Do
Mary	04	F	Child	18Au02Do
Grace	02	F	Child	18Au02Do
Wm.	.00	M	Infant	18Au02Do
GREEN, Ann	28	F	None	18Au02Do
GLENNAIS, Jno.	32	M	Laborer	18Au02Do
KANE, Jas.	20	M	Laborer	18Au02Do
Cath.	18	F	None	18Au02Do
LEO, Wm.	30	M	Mechanic	18Au02Do
Eliza	25	F	None	18Au02Do
KEEGLEY, Jno.	20	M	Mechanic	18Au02Do
KANE, Mary	18	F	None	18Au02Do
NORRIS, Mich.	20	M	Mechanic	18Au02Do
ROBINSON, Jno.	20	M	Laborer	18Au02Do
Mich.	18	M	Laborer	18Au02Do
BURKE, Bridget	20	F	None	18Au02Do
FAMEN, Francis	30	M	Laborer	18Au02Do
MURPHY, Wm.	28	M	Laborer	18Au02Do
Cath.	50	F	None	18Au02Do
Cath.	28	F	None	18Au02Do
Susan	16	F	None	18Au02Do
Biddy	14	F	None	18Au02Do
Jno.	13	M	Laborer	18Au02Do
Rose	10	F	None	18Au02Do
CROWLEY, Jas.	24	M	Laborer	18Au02Do
Pat	23	M	Laborer	18Au02Do
COUGHLEN, And.	35	M	Laborer	18Au02Do

NAMES OF PASSENGERS	AGE	SEX	OCCUPATIONS	DATE PORT SHIP
HOWELL, Mary	21	F	None	18Au02Do
CONNER, Joha.	46	F	None	18Au02Do
Thos.	20	M	Laborer	18Au02Do
Pat	20	M	Laborer	18Au02Do
SULLIVAN, Jno.	24	M	Farmer	18Au02Do
ENTWHISTLE, U-Mrs.	30	F	None	18Au02Do
U	05	F	Child	18Au02Do
U	02	M	Child	18Au02Do
LUZERNE, Dennis	25	M	Laborer	18Au02Do
SHEEHAN, Dennis	25	M	Laborer	18Au02Do
LUZER, James	25	M	Laborer	18Au02Do
OREILY, Jas.	27	M	Mechanic	18Au02Do
MCDERMOTT, Jas.	17	M	Mechanic	18Au02Do
Lucy	18	F	None	18Au02Do
FAGAN, Betty	20	F	None	18Au02Do
PORTER, Wm.	15	M	Mechanic	18Au02Do
Ann	07	F	Child	18Au02Do
EDGE, Saml.	35	M	Mechanic	18Au02Do
MAGEE, Mich.	30	M	Mechanic	18Au02Do

ELLERSLIE 18 AUGUST 1847

From Liverpool

NAMES OF PASSENGERS	AGE	SEX	OCCUPATIONS	DATE PORT SHIP
MURPHY, Edwd.	30	M	Farmer	18Au020a
CATON, Nat.	28	M	Farmer	18Au020a
Margt.	24	F	None	18Au020a
FOSTER, Jas.	31	M	Farmer	18Au020a
FLETCHER, Jno.	50	M	Farmer	18Au020a
Isabella	20	F	None	18Au020a
KEUGH, Richd.	45	M	Farmer	18Au020a
Roger	20	M	Farmer	18Au020a
James	.00	M	Infant	18Au020a
Mary	18	F	None	18Au020a
Ann	02	F	Child	18Au020a
Walter	05	M	Child	18Au020a
James	17	M	Farmer	18Au020a
HAUKS, Jos.	30	M	Farmer	18Au020a
HANLEY, Jas.	28	M	Farmer	18Au020a
FLETCHER, Isabella	40	F	None	18Au020a
LYON, Lawrence	20	M	Farmer	18Au020a
Ellen	18	F	None	18Au020a
Jas.	04	M	Child	18Au020a
Mary	02	F	Child	18Au020a
Ellen	.00	F	Infant	18Au020a
GARNEY, Jas.	40	M	Farmer	18Au020a
DERBY, Richd.	30	M	Farmer	18Au020a
ONEILL, Eugene	20	M	Farmer	18Au020a
FITZGERALD, Simon	25	M	Farmer	18Au020a
MAHONY, John	49	M	Farmer	18Au020a
U (W)	36	F	Wife	18Au020a
Jno.	27	M	Farmer	18Au020a
Jas.	26	M	Farmer	18Au020a
HEANY, Jno.	30	M	Farmer	18Au020a
SHEA, Jas.	20	M	Farmer	18Au020a
CONNELLY, Patt	26	M	Farmer	18Au020a
SULLIVAN, Patt	21	M	Farmer	18Au020a
CONNOLLY, Rose	70	F	None	18Au020a
SHEHAN, Roger	54	M	Farmer	18Au020a
Roger	30	M	Farmer	18Au020a
Nancy	24	F	None	18Au020a
Mary	20	F	None	18Au020a
Thos.	18	M	Farmer	18Au020a
Cornelius	19	M	Farmer	18Au020a
CONNER, Jas.	28	M	Farmer	18Au020a
HALES, Saml.	36	M	Farmer	18Au020a
REARDEN, Jas.	33	M	Farmer	18Au020a
Mary	29	F	None	18Au020a
LEAL, Edwd.	54	M	Farmer	18Au020a

NAMES OF PASSENGERS	AGE	SEX	OCCUPATIONS	DATE PORT SHIP
LEAL, Susan	50	F	None	18Au020a
Edwd.	05	M	Child	18Au020a
WHITE, James	30	M	Farmer	18Au020a
FARRELL, Bridget	17	F	None	18Au020a
HEALY, Bridget	60	F	None	18Au020a
Mary-A.	20	F	None	18Au020a
GORMAN, Mary	47	F	None	18Au020a
Eliza	12	F	None	18Au020a
BUTTREY, Thos.	26	M	Farmer	18Au020a
Manx.	28	M	Farmer	18Au020a
Walter	04	M	Child	18Au020a
Lucy	.00	F	Infant	18Au020a
Margt.	30	F	None	18Au020a
Rachel	20	F	None	18Au020a
Mary-A.	02	F	Child	18Au020a
GLEASON, Jno.	40	M	Farmer	18Au020a
Edwin	28	M	Farmer	18Au020a
Norah	26	F	None	18Au020a
Jane	22	F	None	18Au020a
Eliza	20	F	None	18Au020a
Sarah	12	F	None	18Au020a
BRADY, Jno.	23	M	Farmer	18Au020a
SHANLY, Thos.	26	M	Farmer	18Au020a
DORAN, Jno.	20	M	Farmer	18Au020a
LAWLESS, Mich.	28	M	Farmer	18Au020a
GARRETTY, Mich.	40	M	Farmer	18Au020a
CADDY, Saml.	28	M	Farmer	18Au020a
CURLEY, Jno.	23	M	Farmer	18Au020a
MCGUIRE, Mary-A.	24	F	None	18Au020a
SULLIVAN, Florence	27	F	None	18Au020a
Dennis	25	M	Farmer	18Au020a
CUNNINGHAM, Jas.	30	M	Farmer	18Au020a
Cath.	24	F	None	18Au020a
MILLS, Richd.	20	M	Farmer	18Au020a
Ann	18	F	None	18Au020a
LYONS, Patt	28	M	Farmer	18Au020a
Cath.	24	F	None	18Au020a
Mary	.00	F	Infant	18Au020a
Jno.	02	M	Child	18Au020a
MCANTA, Pat	25	M	Farmer	18Au020a
Bridget	23	F	None	18Au020a
MCSHEAR, Bridget	20	F	None	18Au020a
GRADY, Mary	20	F	None	18Au020a
CAFREY, Mary	20	F	None	18Au020a
HISLOP, Geo.	40	M	Farmer	18Au020a
MCGEE, Alex.	28	M	Farmer	18Au020a
DONNELLY, Pat	24	M	Farmer	18Au020a
FOLEY, Nich.	24	M	Farmer	18Au020a
SMITH, Thos.	22	M	Farmer	18Au020a
MCCLURE, Jno.	40	M	Farmer	18Au020a
Esther	30	F	None	18Au020a
Sarah	13	F	None	18Au020a
Jane	10	F	None	18Au020a
Maria	07	F	Child	18Au020a
Esther	04	F	Child	18Au020a
Mary-A.	.00	F	Infant	18Au020a
FUERY, Mich.	40	M	Farmer	18Au020a
RONAN, Jas.	30	M	Farmer	18Au020a
LOVATT, Pat	40	M	Farmer	18Au020a
DELANTY, Tim	50	M	Farmer	18Au020a
THORNTON, Robt.	28	M	Farmer	18Au020a
TURNER, Nabby	20	F	None	18Au020a
MCLOUGHLIN, Bridget	37	F	None	18Au020a
FLEMING, Bridget	36	F	None	18Au020a
QUINN, Jno.	40	M	Farmer	18Au020a
MULLIN, Betsey	28	F	None	18Au020a
DURKIN, Bridget	26	F	None	18Au020a
DOWD, Jno.	21	M	Farmer	18Au020a
BURKE, Margt.	18	F	None	18Au020a
HARDES, Thos.	22	M	Farmer	18Au020a
EVERS, Mary	19	F	None	18Au020a
REILLY, Chas.	18	M	Farmer	18Au020a
SHERIDAN, Bridget	18	F	None	18Au020a
COSGROVE, Jas.	30	M	Farmer	18Au020a
Rose	30	F	None	18Au020a
COSGROVE, Rose	30	F	None	18Au020a
MCCORMACK, Susan	31	F	None	18Au020a
COOK, Thos.	23	M	Farmer	18Au020a
Ann	21	F	None	18Au020a
MULLIGAN, Eliza	30	F	None	18Au020a
LAFFEN, Mary	26	F	None	18Au020a
John	26	M	Farmer	18Au020a
Jas.	15	M	Farmer	18Au020a
OBRIEN, Bridget	25	F	None	18Au020a
Francis	28	M	Farmer	18Au020a
Ann	18	F	None	18Au020a
SHARCOE, Bridget	20	F	None	18Au020a
BURKE, Patt	30	M	Farmer	18Au020a
MCDONALD, Jerry	40	M	Farmer	18Au020a
Nancy	37	F	None	18Au020a
KELLY, Jno.	40	M	Farmer	18Au020a
Ellen	08	F	Child	18Au020a
Mary	05	F	Child	18Au020a
Bridget	.00	F	Infant	18Au020a
CURRY, Nancy	40	F	None	18Au020a
Jno.	10	M	None	18Au020a
Bernard	08	M	Child	18Au020a
MAHON, Roger	40	M	Farmer	18Au020a
WALSH, Timothy	30	M	Farmer	18Au020a
SULLIVAN, Mich.	30	M	Farmer	18Au020a
LAPPEN, Robt.	18	M	Farmer	18Au020a
COURTNEY, Eliza	26	F	None	18Au020a
Sarah	24	F	None	18Au020a
KELLY, Daniel	34	M	Farmer	18Au020a
Ellen	30	F	None	18Au020a
CORRIGAN, Ann	30	F	None	18Au020a
ORMOND, Pat	36	M	Farmer	18Au020a
Mary	.00	F	Infant	18Au020a
STANLEY, Jas.	26	M	Farmer	18Au020a
LAVRY, Thos.	30	M	Farmer	18Au020a
CURTIN, Pat	26	M	Farmer	18Au020a
Jeremiah	28	M	Farmer	18Au020a
Jeremiah	.00	M	Infant	18Au020a
Ellen	.00	F	Infant	18Au020a
FARRELY, Thos.	20	M	Farmer	18Au020a
NEWTON, Thos.	50	M	Farmer	18Au020a
NOWLAN, Jno.	21	M	Farmer	18Au020a
CASSIDY, Hugh	18	M	Farmer	18Au020a
WHEATY, Jas.	40	M	Farmer	18Au020a
Ann	38	F	None	18Au020a
Ann	20	F	None	18Au020a
Patt	06	M	Child	18Au020a
Jno.	04	M	Child	18Au020a
Ann	03	F	Child	18Au020a
FLATTERY, Mich.	45	M	Farmer	18Au020a
Peggy	40	F	None	18Au020a
Jno.	20	M	Farmer	18Au020a
Biddy	14	F	None	18Au020a
Mich.	.00	M	Infant	18Au020a
DREW, Jno.	41	M	Farmer	18Au020a
WALL, Wm.	52	M	Farmer	18Au020a
NEILL, Ellen	21	F	None	18Au020a
WARD, Peter	49	M	Farmer	18Au020a
Larry	18	M	Farmer	18Au020a
HAMILTON, Jno.	50	M	Farmer	18Au020a
U (W)	30	F	Wife	18Au020a
Fred	10	M	Farmer	18Au020a
Mary-A.	20	F	None	18Au020a
Fanny	22	F	None	18Au020a
DOLOHAN, Ann	39	F	None	18Au020a
EVANS, David	30	M	Farmer	18Au020a
HARRIS, Jno.	25	M	Farmer	18Au020a
CANNELL, Danl.	28	M	Farmer	18Au020a
CHRISTAIN, Jno.	41	M	Farmer	18Au020a
NORTON, Jno.	49	M	Farmer	18Au020a
Mary	46	F	None	18Au020a
William	30	M	Farmer	18Au020a
John	28	M	Farmer	18Au020a
Michael	26	M	Farmer	18Au020a
Rose	14	F	None	18Au020a

NAMES OF PASSENGERS	AGE	SEX	OCCUPATIONS	DATE PORT SHIP
NORTON, Cath.	12	F	None	18Au020a
CUNNINGHAM, Thos.	33	M	Farmer	18Au020a
REILLY, Owen	18	M	Farmer	18Au020a
NOLLY, Jas.	18	M	Farmer	18Au020a
REILLY, Mary	18	F	None	18Au020a
Margt.	40	F	None	18Au020a
Ann	30	F	None	18Au020a
GANNEA, Hugh	22	M	Farmer	18Au020a
MARTIN, Thos.	20	M	Farmer	18Au020a
MCQUINN, Peter	40	M	Farmer	18Au020a
Dorotey	36	F	None	18Au020a
DONNEGAL, Cath.	36	F	None	18Au020a
MCCABE, Andrew	30	M	Farmer	18Au020a
SAVAGE, Pat	47	M	Farmer	18Au020a
CALLAN, Jno.	25	M	Farmer	18Au020a
NALLY, Pat	41	M	Farmer	18Au020a
Rose	40	F	None	18Au020a
Jas.	09	M	Child	18Au020a
Mary	04	F	Child	18Au020a
Martha	07	F	Child	18Au020a
GREENHAM, Fred.	23	M	Farmer	18Au020a
Chas.	20	M	Farmer	18Au020a
ROACH, Julia	36	F	None	18Au020a
Mary	.00	F	Infant	18Au020a
MANNIGAN, Hugh	20	M	Farmer	18Au020a
MCDONNELL, Ellen	26	F	None	18Au020a
DORAN, Cath.	36	F	None	18Au020a
MCGEE, Jno.	30	M	Farmer	18Au020a
KETTER, Barnet	24	M	Farmer	18Au020a
Mary-A.	25	F	None	18Au020a
Sally	22	F	None	18Au020a
CONNELLY, Henry	14	M	Farmer	18Au020a
Jenny	20	F	None	18Au020a
Mary	26	F	None	18Au020a
HARRISON, Jno.	23	M	Farmer	18Au020a
GANLEY, Jno.	30	M	Farmer	18Au020a
MCNAMARA, Mich.	34	M	Farmer	18Au020a

CORNELIA 23 AUGUST 1847

From Liverpool

NAMES OF PASSENGERS	AGE	SEX	OCCUPATIONS	DATE PORT SHIP
MILLS, Eli.	34	M	Gentleman	23Au02Am
FRANSE, A.St.George-E.	20	M	Gentleman	23Au02Am
FOAME, Wm.	28	M	Laborer	23Au02Am
LALIMORE, Wm.	35	M	Laborer	23Au02Am
U-Miss.	30	F	None	23Au02Am
Margt.	08	F	Child	23Au02Am
Mary	02	F	Child	23Au02Am
ADFIELD, Jos.	30	M	Laborer	23Au02Am
CONLAN, Jno.	34	M	Laborer	23Au02Am
Winifried	28	F	None	23Au02Am
Ann	05	F	Child	23Au02Am
DANIELS, Wm.	29	M	Farmer	23Au02Am
Margt.	26	F	None	23Au02Am
PRITCHARD, Geo.Jas.	28	M	Farmer	23Au02Am
Margt.	26	F	None	23Au02Am
CAVANAGH, Jno.	28	M	Mechanic	23Au02Am
Isabella	30	F	None	23Au02Am
Amy	04	F	Child	23Au02Am
REESE, Mary	30	F	None	23Au02Am
Thos.	12	M	None	23Au02Am
Wm.	10	M	None	23Au02Am
Isaac	05	M	Child	23Au02Am
George	03	M	Child	23Au02Am
Abraham	.06	M	Infant	23Au02Am
HUGHES, Joseph	24	M	Farmer	23Au02Am
Elizth.	22	F	None	23Au02Am
David	.04	M	Infant	23Au02Am
BROWN, Alfred	30	M	Farmer	23Au02Am
Harriet	31	F	None	23Au02Am
James	07	M	Child	23Au02Am
Alfred	05	M	Child	23Au02Am
Fred	03	M	Child	23Au02Am
Richd.	04	M	Child	23Au02Am
MAY, Thos.	30	M	Laborer	23Au02Am
LARKIN, Bridget	18	F	None	23Au02Am
OWENS, Pat	30	M	Laborer	23Au02Am
HEAFORD, Vincent-F.	38	M	Mechanic	23Au02Am
Elizth.	32	F	None	23Au02Am
Mary	13	F	None	23Au02Am
Ann	11	F	None	23Au02Am
Wm.	09	M	Child	23Au02Am
Sarah	07	F	Child	23Au02Am
Eliz.	05	F	Child	23Au02Am
MOORE, Thos.	30	M	Mechanic	23Au02Am
MULLHOLLAND, And.	20	M	Mechanic	23Au02Am
MCAIRLANE, Pat	30	M	Mechanic	23Au02Am
MCPAICK, Mary	19	F	None	23Au02Am
OWEN, Rob.	25	M	Mechanic	23Au02Am
HARROD, Jno.	49	M	Mechanic	23Au02Am
CARR, Jno.	20	M	Laborer	23Au02Am
MURRAY, Pat	20	M	Laborer	23Au02Am
Mary	20	F	None	23Au02Am
GILLIN, Thos.	30	M	Laborer	23Au02Am
NEEGLE, Janette	30	F	None	23Au02Am
KEIFE, Jno.	21	M	Laborer	23Au02Am
THOMAS, Rebecca	28	F	None	23Au02Am
Thos.	02	M	Child	23Au02Am
Emma	01	F	Child	23Au02Am
MARYON, Thos.	24	M	Laborer	23Au02Am
NAYLOR, Eph.	40	M	Mechanic	23Au02Am
Thos.	42	M	Mechanic	23Au02Am
LEROY, Henry	32	M	Mechanic	23Au02Am
Mary-A.	26	F	None	23Au02Am
Esther	01	F	Child	23Au02Am
David	.04	M	Infant	23Au02Am
DOOLIN, Jno.	50	M	Laborer	23Au02Am
Magt.	45	F	None	23Au02Am
Bridget	12	F	None	23Au02Am
Jno.	11	M	None	23Au02Am
Ellen	03	F	Child	23Au02Am
COSS, Mary	24	F	None	23Au02Am
CORMACK, Pat	50	M	Farmer	23Au02Am
Ann	50	F	None	23Au02Am
Joseph	13	M	None	23Au02Am
GILLIN, Mary	32	F	None	23Au02Am
HAUGHTON, Wm.	50	M	Mechanic	23Au02Am
Fred	13	M	Mechanic	23Au02Am
DAVIES, Wm.	60	M	Mechanic	23Au02Am
JONES, Mary	13	F	None	23Au02Am
COUGHLIN, Laurence	22	M	Laborer	23Au02Am
DOOLIG, Jno.	26	M	Laborer	23Au02Am
GALAGAN, Magt.	26	F	None	23Au02Am
GARRITY, Bernard	21	M	Laborer	23Au02Am
KEVEL, Henry	20	M	Laborer	23Au02Am
POLLARD, Jn.	21	M	Laborer	23Au02Am
MCAULIFFE, Mary	22	F	None	23Au02Am
SHEHAN, Elizth.	24	F	None	23Au02Am
FARMER, Jno.	40	M	Laborer	23Au02Am
HARKIN, Jas.	46	M	Laborer	23Au02Am
SHAUGNESSY, Jno.	29	M	Laborer	23Au02Am
MURPHY, Nancy	21	F	None	23Au02Am
CAYNE, Maria	21	F	None	23Au02Am
NEVIN, Maria	21	F	None	23Au02Am
MURDOCK, Elvira	38	F	None	23Au02Am
Margt.	07	F	Child	23Au02Am
MCGLOCKLIN, Margt.	60	F	None	23Au02Am
Rose	05	F	Child	23Au02Am
KENNEDY, Timothy	30	M	Mechanic	23Au02Am
HEAVY, Jas.	26	M	Mechanic	23Au02Am
GILLESPIE, Jane	33	F	None	23Au02Am
JOHNSTON, Margt.	30	F	None	23Au02Am
Ann	23	F	None	23Au02Am

NAMES OF PASSENGERS	AGE	SEX	OCCUPATIONS	DATE PORT SHIP
TAAFE, Peter	35	M	Laborer	23Au02Am
SAMPSON, Margt.	34	F	None	23Au02Am
Elizth.	13	F	None	23Au02Am
LAWDON, Joha.	20	F	None	23Au02Am
Hannah	18	F	None	23Au02Am
COLLINS, Cornelius	25	M	Mechanic	23Au02Am
Ellen	24	F	None	23Au02Am
RIELY, Pat	20	M	Mechanic	23Au02Am
Bridget	19	F	None	23Au02Am
Jas.	18	M	Mechanic	23Au02Am
MCCOOLY, Mich.	21	M	Mechanic	23Au02Am
Mary-A.	04	F	Child	23Au02Am
MCCULLUM, Wm.	36	M	Mechanic	23Au02Am
ALAFFE, Thos.	15	M	Laborer	23Au02Am
MCGOWAN, Simon	16	M	Laborer	23Au02Am
GALVIN, Wm.	21	M	Laborer	23Au02Am
CASE, Mary	20	F	None	23Au02Am
CAZEY, Susan	30	F	None	23Au02Am
Jno.	12	M	None	23Au02Am
Thos.	09	M	Child	23Au02Am
Wm.	07	M	Child	23Au02Am
GARDINER, Jane	50	F	None	23Au02Am
Saml.	32	M	Mechanic	23Au02Am
Jane	12	F	Unknown	23Au02Am
HESLIM, Frank	20	M	Mechanic	23Au02Am
Margt.	17	F	None	23Au02Am
MCGLAUKLIN, Eliza	16	F	None	23Au02Am
Cath.	14	F	None	23Au02Am
MATTESON, Cath.	16	F	None	23Au02Am
Mary	12	F	None	23Au02Am
Jno.	12	M	None	23Au02Am
MURRAY, Jno.	26	M	Laborer	23Au02Am
Pat	09	M	Child	23Au02Am
CANLAN, Ewd.	25	M	Mechanic	23Au02Am
MCGEE, Mary	17	F	None	23Au02Am
Ellen	15	F	None	23Au02Am
Charles	50	M	Laborer	23Au02Am
James	12	M	None	23Au02Am
MCDONALD, Ellen	20	F	None	23Au02Am
DOYLE, Ellen	21	F	None	23Au02Am
CLARKSON, Matt	35	M	Mechanic	23Au02Am
MCCLUSKY, Rose	40	F	None	23Au02Am
Kitty	13	F	None	23Au02Am
Rose	11	F	None	23Au02Am
Mary	05	F	Child	23Au02Am
MCGARITY, Cath.	19	F	None	23Au02Am
RYAN, Mich.	26	M	Mechanic	23Au02Am
ROACH, Wm.	26	M	Mechanic	23Au02Am
Margt.	05	F	Child	23Au02Am
HARE, Ann	30	F	None	23Au02Am
Jno.	09	M	Child	23Au02Am
Wm.	06	M	Child	23Au02Am
Margt.	03	F	Child	23Au02Am
CAUGHLIN, Julia	20	F	None	23Au02Am
MCNAMARA, Pat	25	M	Laborer	23Au02Am
ROBINSON, Jno.	34	M	Laborer	23Au02Am
GORMLEY, Bridget	35	F	None	23Au02Am
Mary	12	F	None	23Au02Am
Jno.	10	M	None	23Au02Am
Jas.	08	M	Child	23Au02Am
CUNNINGHAM, Cath.	09	F	Child	23Au02Am
CARNEY, Jas.	30	M	Laborer	23Au02Am
SHANLE, Nancy	20	F	None	23Au02Am
DONLEY, Pat	20	M	Laborer	23Au02Am
MCLEAN, Jno.	26	M	Laborer	23Au02Am
FAIR, Allen	29	M	Laborer	23Au02Am
KENNEDY, Jno.	28	M	Mechanic	23Au02Am
MONIGAN, Matt	24	M	Laborer	23Au02Am
REILY, Jno.	36	M	Laborer	23Au02Am
REDSHAW, Wm.	22	M	Laborer	23Au02Am
Hannah	30	F	None	23Au02Am
Thos.	11	M	None	23Au02Am
Emma	09	F	Child	23Au02Am
PEACH, Wm.	30	M	Laborer	23Au02Am
BRENNAN, Ewd.	40	M	Laborer	23Au02Am
BRENNAN, U (W)	40	F	Wife	23Au02Am
Ann	13	F	None	23Au02Am
Margt.	12	F	None	23Au02Am
Patt	09	M	Child	23Au02Am
Mich.	06	M	Child	23Au02Am
Ellen	05	F	Child	23Au02Am
BUTTER, Tobias	28	M	Laborer	23Au02Am
GILLAN, Jas.	14	M	None	23Au02Am
Mary-A.	12	F	None	23Au02Am
KING, Jas.	25	M	Laborer	23Au02Am
BRADY, Wm.	25	M	Laborer	23Au02Am
BYRNE, Nancy	25	F	None	23Au02Am
SHARPE, Mary	28	F	None	23Au02Am
COMAN, Ricd.	44	M	Laborer	23Au02Am
COURETTE, Thos.	30	M	Laborer	23Au02Am
WHEELER, Wm.	32	M	Laborer	23Au02Am
BYRNE, Thos.	34	M	Laborer	23Au02Am
KELLY, Edwd.	26	M	Mechanic	23Au02Am
LANGWORTH, Robt.	28	M	Mechanic	23Au02Am
Jas.	30	M	Mechanic	23Au02Am
BYRNE, Pat	21	M	Mechanic	23Au02Am
MURRAY, Jno.	24	M	Mechanic	23Au02Am
BROSIN, Thos.	22	M	Mechanic	23Au02Am
U (W)	26	F	Wife	23Au02Am
Ellen	.06	F	Infant	23Au02Am
LITTEN, Jno.	30	M	Mechanic	23Au02Am
ROACH, David	30	M	Mechanic	23Au02Am
FOGARTY, Tim	44	M	Farmer	23Au02Am
Jno.	21	M	Farmer	23Au02Am
NEAL, Dennis	32	M	Laborer	23Au02Am
Ellen	32	F	None	23Au02Am
Mary	01	F	Child	23Au02Am
HALEY, Hannah	21	F	None	23Au02Am
LANE, Mary	30	F	None	23Au02Am
WOLFE, Maurice	44	M	Farmer	23Au02Am
Ellen	35	F	None	23Au02Am
Jas.	16	M	Farmer	23Au02Am
Ellen	14	F	None	23Au02Am
Maurice	12	M	None	23Au02Am
Mary	08	F	Child	23Au02Am
Joha.	02	F	Child	23Au02Am
CANTILLEN, Pat	30	M	Laborer	23Au02Am
Ellen	30	F	None	23Au02Am
WOLFE, Jno.	35	M	Laborer	23Au02Am
Honora	30	F	None	23Au02Am
Jas.	35	M	Laborer	23Au02Am
MAHER, Honora	20	F	None	23Au02Am
KENNEDY, Hannah	22	F	None	23Au02Am
BUTLER, Edwd.	25	M	Laborer	23Au02Am
Margt.	20	F	None	23Au02Am
CONNER, Mary	16	F	None	23Au02Am
BURKE, Pat	34	M	Laborer	23Au02Am
U (W)	30	F	Wife	23Au02Am
Jane	.04	F	Infant	23Au02Am
Ann	06	F	Child	23Au02Am
Sarah	04	F	Child	23Au02Am
Wm.	05	M	Child	23Au02Am
JOHNSTON, Pat	60	M	Laborer	23Au02Am
U (W)	50	F	Wife	23Au02Am
Jas.	18	M	Laborer	23Au02Am
Eliza	12	F	None	23Au02Am
RIGDEN, Jas.	20	M	Mechanic	23Au02Am
U (W)	20	F	Wife	23Au02Am
Ellen	.04	F	Infant	23Au02Am
SULLIVAN, Danl.	19	M	Mechanic	23Au02Am
Mary	36	F	None	23Au02Am
Ann	.06	F	Infant	23Au02Am
Margt.	16	F	None	23Au02Am
Jno.	13	M	None	23Au02Am
Ellen	10	F	None	23Au02Am
Mary	08	F	Child	23Au02Am
Joha.	05	M	Child	23Au02Am
Honor	02	F	Child	23Au02Am
DALIER, Chas.	48	M	Laborer	23Au02Am
CRENADON, Con.	36	M	Laborer	23Au02Am

NAMES OF PASSENGERS		AGE	SEX	OCCUPATIONS	DATE PORT SHIP
MCCAULY, Jerry		25	M	Mechanic	23Au02Am
ONEIL, Jno.		35	M	Mechanic	23Au02Am
Mary		35	F	None	23Au02Am
Mary		07	F	Child	23Au02Am
Jas.		.06	F	Infant	23Au02Am
Jno.		05	M	Child	23Au02Am
Robt.		03	M	Child	23Au02Am
SHALLON, Henry		40	M	Mechanic	23Au02Am
COLLINS, Pat		35	M	Mechanic	23Au02Am
Sarah		32	F	None	23Au02Am
MCELLIOT, Pat		30	M	Laborer	23Au02Am
Magt.		28	F	None	23Au02Am
Bridget		03	F	Child	23Au02Am
Mary		.06	F	Infant	23Au02Am
MOORE, Mich.		22	M	Laborer	23Au02Am
LENAN, Thos.		22	M	Laborer	23Au02Am
RYAN, Pat		24	M	Laborer	23Au02Am
U	(W)	22	F	Wife	23Au02Am
GRADY, Mary		22	F	Unknown	23Au02Am
DEGAN, Pat		23	M	Laborer	23Au02Am
MCKIERNAN, Mary		23	F	None	23Au02Am
STANTON, Wm.		30	M	Laborer	23Au02Am
BROPHY, Joseph		30	M	Laborer	23Au02Am
KIERNAVAN, M.		28	M	Laborer	23Au02Am
GARRATY, Mary		52	F	None	23Au02Am
Mich.		24	M	Laborer	23Au02Am
Peter		09	M	Child	23Au02Am
DALE, Jno.		26	M	Laborer	23Au02Am
DOLAN, Jno.		30	M	Laborer	23Au02Am
CANNON, James		18	M	Laborer	23Au02Am
OCONNOR, Wm.		27	M	Laborer	23Au02Am
FARRELL, Owen		67	M	Laborer	23Au02Am
U	(W)	60	F	Wife	23Au02Am
Ellen		25	F	None	23Au02Am
Ann		05	F	Child	23Au02Am
Pat		03	M	Child	23Au02Am
HARAN, Pat		37	M	Mechanic	23Au02Am
SWEENEY, Wm.		19	M	Mechanic	23Au02Am
RODGERS, Mich.		24	M	Laborer	23Au02Am
REILY, Thos.		21	M	Laborer	23Au02Am
MURPHY, Ellen		21	F	None	23Au02Am
MCSTRAHEEN, Mary		20	F	None	23Au02Am
SHEELIN, Mary		19	F	None	23Au02Am
DOYLE, Bridget		20	F	None	23Au02Am
DORAN, Jno.		24	M	Mechanic	23Au02Am
KEAN, Cath.		11	F	None	23Au02Am
OSHEIN, Thos.		21	M	Mechanic	23Au02Am
JOHNSTON, Wm.		24	M	Farmer	23Au02Am
Elizth.		20	F	None	23Au02Am
Anne-G.		04	F	Child	23Au02Am
GRAHAM, Geo.		40	M	Farmer	23Au02Am
KELLY, Ann		17	F	None	23Au02Am
MURPHY, Jas.		29	M	Farmer	23Au02Am
DUCHET, Saml.		60	M	Farmer	23Au02Am
Thos.		30	M	Farmer	23Au02Am
Saml.		25	M	Farmer	23Au02Am
Cansly.		18	M	Farmer	23Au02Am
Richd.		15	M	Farmer	23Au02Am
MORGAN, Jno.		24	M	Farmer	23Au02Am
TOPHAM, Henry		26	M	Farmer	23Au02Am
Wm.		24	M	Farmer	23Au02Am
DACHET, Ellen		50	F	None	23Au02Am
Peter		20	M	Farmer	23Au02Am
Ellen		20	F	None	23Au02Am
SULLIVAN, Margt.		25	F	None	23Au02Am
DACHET, Hannah		18	F	None	23Au02Am
Sarah		07	F	Child	23Au02Am
Mary		05	F	Child	23Au02Am
Saml.		.06	M	Infant	23Au02Am
Ellen		05	F	Child	23Au02Am
LYONS, Pat		35	M	Farmer	23Au02Am
MORAN, Pat		31	M	Farmer	23Au02Am
LEWIS, Jno.		40	M	Farmer	23Au02Am
Mary		36	F	None	23Au02Am
Bridget		.04	F	Infant	23Au02Am
LEWIS, Ann		08	F	Child	23Au02Am
Bridget		10	F	None	23Au02Am
Cath.		05	F	Child	23Au02Am
Jno.		03	M	Child	23Au02Am
Mary		13	F	None	23Au02Am
MCGAREG, Pat		30	M	Mechanic	23Au02Am
U	(W)	30	F	Wife	23Au02Am
Mich.		14	M	None	23Au02Am
Jno.		12	M	None	23Au02Am
Pat		06	M	Child	23Au02Am
Jas.		08	M	Child	23Au02Am
HANIGAN, M.		20	F	None	23Au02Am
DOYLE, Bridget		20	F	None	23Au02Am
REILY, Alex		20	M	Laborer	23Au02Am
MCMOONEY, Mary		25	F	None	23Au02Am
MONAGAN, Pat		20	M	Laborer	23Au02Am
BRIEN, Owen		40	M	Laborer	23Au02Am
CLUSKER, Jas.		34	M	Laborer	23Au02Am
Cath.		25	F	None	23Au02Am
Ann		21	F	None	23Au02Am
Thos.		13	M	None	23Au02Am
FRANKLIN, Jno.		28	M	Laborer	23Au02Am
NIELTY, Edwd.		30	M	Laborer	23Au02Am
HOGGINS, M.		19	F	None	23Au02Am
MCFAY, Edwd.		40	M	Laborer	23Au02Am
Pat		20	M	Laborer	23Au02Am
Rose		40	F	Unknown	23Au02Am
Ellen		06	F	Child	23Au02Am
Pat		08	M	Child	23Au02Am
Mary-A.		10	F	None	23Au02Am
Edwd.		06	M	Child	23Au02Am
FRELEY, Harriet		18	F	None	23Au02Am
CORESLEN, Jno.		35	M	Mechanic	23Au02Am
Bridget		50	F	None	23Au02Am
REILY, Jas.		30	M	Mechanic	23Au02Am
JOHNSON, Chas.		20	M	Mechanic	23Au02Am
KELLY, Ann		30	F	None	23Au02Am
HANLY, Mich.		25	M	Mechanic	23Au02Am
HANAGAN, Mary		.06	F	Infant	23Au02Am
MURPHY, Jas.		22	M	Mechanic	23Au02Am

HENRY-CLAY 26 AUGUST 1847

From Liverpool

NAMES OF PASSENGERS		AGE	SEX	OCCUPATIONS	DATE PORT SHIP
CRAWFORD, Dnl.		28	M	Farmer	26Au02Co
Mary-A.		24	F	None	26Au02Co
Frances		03	F	Child	26Au02Co
MINTUM, Mary		39	F	None	26Au02Co
EASTMAN, A.C.		16	M	Farmer	26Au02Co
MONK, G.H.		24	M	Farmer	26Au02Co
Georgiana		24	F	None	26Au02Co
LANLY, Walter		48	M	Mechanic	26Au02Co
Richd.		46	M	Mechanic	26Au02Co
JONES, Jas.A.		42	M	Farmer	26Au02Co
NYE, Marie-J.		12	F	None	26Au02Co
BROLEG, Wm.		26	M	Miner	26Au02Co
Eliza		22	F	None	26Au02Co
MILLS, Joseph		32	M	Mechanic	26Au02Co
Betty		26	F	None	26Au02Co
SHOLES, G.A.		24	M	Mechanic	26Au02Co
BRADY, Jos.		24	M	Mechanic	26Au02Co
LYNNOT, Jas.		28	M	Laborer	26Au02Co
MARSH, Jos.		32	M	Laborer	26Au02Co
Judith		30	F	None	26Au02Co
James		07	M	Child	26Au02Co
Julius		07	M	Child	26Au02Co
FRASER, John		01	M	Child	26Au02Co
Mary		50	F	None	26Au02Co

NAMES OF PASSENGERS	AGE	SEX	OCCUPATIONS	DATE PORT SHIP
FRASER, Etr.	50	F	None	26Au02Co
Mary	20	F	None	26Au02Co
Jane	13	F	None	26Au02Co
Ann	16	F	None	26Au02Co
HARRISS, Jas.	11	M	None	26Au02Co
Susan	25	F	None	26Au02Co
THORN, Ele.	24	M	Laborer	26Au02Co
MORGAN, Robt.	22	M	Laborer	26Au02Co
ARNEY, Jno.	22	M	Laborer	26Au02Co
JOSSON, Jno.	41	M	Mechanic	26Au02Co
Diana	40	F	None	26Au02Co
Ann	16	F	None	26Au02Co
Isabella	05	F	Child	26Au02Co
Sarah	03	F	Child	26Au02Co
Geo.	01	M	Child	26Au02Co
Jno.	76	M	Mechanic	26Au02Co
Jno.	45	M	Mechanic	26Au02Co
WILLIAMSON, Hugh	51	M	Mechanic	26Au02Co
Elizth.	22	F	None	26Au02Co
Jno.	12	M	None	26Au02Co
Elizth.	12	F	None	26Au02Co
Elenor	10	F	None	26Au02Co
Margt.	27	F	None	26Au02Co
HOUSE, Ann	20	F	None	26Au02Co
WILLIAMS, Evan	24	M	Laborer	26Au02Co
GORGAN, Peter	45	M	Laborer	26Au02Co
WYNATT, Matt.	26	F	None	26Au02Co
LLYGES, M.	26	F	None	26Au02Co
Rose	01	F	Child	26Au02Co
MCDOWELL, Ann	30	F	None	26Au02Co
Martha	20	F	None	26Au02Co
Ann	03	F	Child	26Au02Co
Jno.	02	M	Child	26Au02Co
Hamilton	01	M	Child	26Au02Co
ALRENGATE, Josh	35	M	Mechanic	26Au02Co
PARKEY, Chas.	25	M	Mechanic	26Au02Co
ANDREWS, Richd.	34	M	Mechanic	26Au02Co
Eliza	32	F	None	26Au02Co
Edwin	04	M	Child	26Au02Co
Louisa	02	F	Child	26Au02Co
LIQUE, Patt	50	M	Farmer	26Au02Co
RUDDEN, Biddy	20	F	None	26Au02Co
HICKEY, Thos.	23	M	Farmer	26Au02Co
BUNFIELD, H.	28	M	Farmer	26Au02Co
Mary	25	F	None	26Au02Co
PUNTER, Sarah	24	F	None	26Au02Co
M.	10	F	None	26Au02Co
WARD, Jane	21	F	None	26Au02Co
CARRELL, Bynard	21	M	Laborer	26Au02Co
OSLOM, Thos.	26	M	Laborer	26Au02Co
THOMPSON, Joseph	26	M	Laborer	26Au02Co
Mary	24	F	None	26Au02Co
GORDAM, Wm.	25	M	Laborer	26Au02Co
Ann	40	F	None	26Au02Co
Thos.	23	M	Laborer	26Au02Co
Louis	16	M	Laborer	26Au02Co
Cath.	13	F	None	26Au02Co
Mary	30	F	None	26Au02Co
Thos.	04	M	Child	26Au02Co
BERMINGTON, Thos.	40	M	Laborer	26Au02Co
Mary	40	F	None	26Au02Co
Jno.	06	M	Child	26Au02Co
Wm.	04	M	Child	26Au02Co
ASHLEY, Jas.	21	M	Laborer	26Au02Co
DOBBIN, Jane	20	F	None	26Au02Co
REILLY, Pat	26	M	Laborer	26Au02Co
EASTON, Mat.	23	F	None	26Au02Co
DOURNAY, Bessy	21	F	None	26Au02Co
JERMOTT, Magt.	21	F	None	26Au02Co
FROMES, Mary	20	F	None	26Au02Co
SULLIVAN, Jno.	14	M	None	26Au02Co
TOOMES, Mary	02	F	Child	26Au02Co
BUCHANAN, Thos.	22	M	Laborer	26Au02Co
Jane	20	F	None	26Au02Co
OBRIEN, David	35	M	Farmer	26Au02Co
OBRIEN, Elizth.	30	F	None	26Au02Co
Geo.	12	M	None	26Au02Co
Mary	11	F	None	26Au02Co
Thos.	09	M	Child	26Au02Co
MCBIRNIE, Eliza	07	F	Child	26Au02Co
David	06	M	Child	26Au02Co
Wm.	04	M	Child	26Au02Co
Fleming	01	M	Child	26Au02Co
LAURENCE, Geo.	50	M	Laborer	26Au02Co
Jane	51	F	None	26Au02Co
Jane	04	F	Child	26Au02Co
Eliza	02	F	Child	26Au02Co
SHEHAN, Denis	27	M	Laborer	26Au02Co
And.	20	M	Laborer	26Au02Co
Mary	25	F	None	26Au02Co
HARTLEY, Geo.	27	M	Laborer	26Au02Co
Elizth.	24	F	None	26Au02Co
AMY, Ellin	02	F	Child	26Au02Co
PEDDON, Saml.	24	M	Laborer	26Au02Co
PINE, Roll.	39	M	Mechanic	26Au02Co
Abm.	43	M	Mechanic	26Au02Co
BAMWELL, Henry	39	M	Mechanic	26Au02Co
Mary-A.	09	F	Child	26Au02Co
Joseph	07	M	Child	26Au02Co
SMITH, Mary-A.	20	F	None	26Au02Co
MCCLUSKEY, Mich.	20	M	Laborer	26Au02Co
TATER, Wm.	29	M	Laborer	26Au02Co
BRADLY, Pat	21	M	Laborer	26Au02Co
Margt.	20	F	None	26Au02Co
CROWLEY, Jno.	25	M	Laborer	26Au02Co
OWENS, Mary	20	F	None	26Au02Co
Mary-A.	01	F	Child	26Au02Co
COUR, Jno.	41	M	Farmer	26Au02Co
Biddy	40	F	None	26Au02Co
Jan.	30	M	Farmer	26Au02Co
OSTELTEN, Mark	40	M	Farmer	26Au02Co
DAYTON, Mary	28	F	None	26Au02Co
COUR, Hannah	16	F	None	26Au02Co
Mary-A.	13	F	None	26Au02Co
Margt.	12	F	None	26Au02Co
Biddy	11	F	None	26Au02Co
Jno.	07	M	Child	26Au02Co
Thos.	04	M	Child	26Au02Co
Theobald	03	M	Child	26Au02Co
Treesa	08	F	Child	26Au02Co
Margt.	10	F	None	26Au02Co
NOONAN, Jno.	30	M	Mechanic	26Au02Co
CARY, Thos.	40	M	Mechanic	26Au02Co
RENWICK, Geo.	30	M	Mechanic	26Au02Co
Eliza	30	F	None	26Au02Co
Ann	12	F	None	26Au02Co
Emma	08	F	Child	26Au02Co
Mary-A.	07	F	Child	26Au02Co
Wm.	04	M	Child	26Au02Co
Harriet	01	F	Child	26Au02Co
VICKERS, Gerr.	20	M	Mechanic	26Au02Co
LITTLE, Richd.	20	M	Mechanic	26Au02Co
BYRNS, Mary-A.	31	F	None	26Au02Co
EDWARDS, Jas.	04	M	Child	26Au02Co
Hannah	01	F	Child	26Au02Co
BOOTH, Hannah	21	F	None	26Au02Co
CROFT, M.	35	M	Mechanic	26Au02Co
Mary	38	F	None	26Au02Co
Joseph	05	M	Child	26Au02Co
Mary-A.	12	F	None	26Au02Co
DULL, Laurence	01	M	Child	26Au02Co
MORAN, Mary	21	F	None	26Au02Co
TOOL, Cath.	24	F	None	26Au02Co
Jno.	02	M	Child	26Au02Co
LEAVITT, Mich.	29	M	Mechanic	26Au02Co
JAMES, Barn.	34	M	Mechanic	26Au02Co
Louis	39	M	Mechanic	26Au02Co
MORRIS, Morah	17	F	None	26Au02Co
INNES, David	21	M	Mechanic	26Au02Co
SPARKS, Jas.	24	M	Mechanic	26Au02Co

NAMES OF PASSENGERS	AGE	SEX	OCCUPATIONS	DATE PORT SHIP
CLIM, Bridget	21	F	None	26Au02Co
FOOBROOK, Jos.	25	M	Mechanic	26Au02Co
Ann	24	F	None	26Au02Co
William	60	M	Mechanic	26Au02Co
James	01	M	Child	26Au02Co
BALL, Saml.	24	M	Mechanic	26Au02Co
Sarah	18	F	None	26Au02Co
COX, Mary-A.	30	F	None	26Au02Co
DUFFEY, Patt	24	M	Mechanic	26Au02Co
MALONE, Cath.	20	F	None	26Au02Co
KENNALL, Wm.	20	M	Farmer	26Au02Co
ALRIDGE, Al.	23	M	Farmer	26Au02Co
JONES, Jno.	25	M	Farmer	26Au02Co
Jane	22	F	None	26Au02Co
CASWELL, Jno.	40	M	Mechanic	26Au02Co
Elizth.	34	F	None	26Au02Co
Cath.	13	F	None	26Au02Co
Jesmine	06	F	Child	26Au02Co
Mary	01	F	Child	26Au02Co
LYNE, Ann	21	F	None	26Au02Co
HART, Thos.	21	M	Mechanic	26Au02Co
GANSIN, Jno.	24	M	Laborer	26Au02Co
Margt.	15	F	None	26Au02Co
Honoria	12	F	None	26Au02Co
ROWLEY, Geo.	24	M	Laborer	26Au02Co
Julia	22	F	None	26Au02Co
Robt.	01	M	Child	26Au02Co
FLYNN, Jno.	25	M	Mechanic	26Au02Co
Eliza	24	F	None	26Au02Co
BRADY, Chas.	30	M	Mechanic	26Au02Co
SUNDERLAND, Lym	22	M	Farmer	26Au02Co
Ann	21	F	None	26Au02Co
ROBINSON, Eliza	19	F	None	26Au02Co
LOONEY, Ann	22	F	None	26Au02Co
SMITH, John	24	M	Farmer	26Au02Co
SULLIVAN, Dennis	30	M	Farmer	26Au02Co
GALLIGER, Alice	21	F	None	26Au02Co
WALSH, Jno.	21	M	Laborer	26Au02Co
Mary	21	F	None	26Au02Co
GALLIGAN, Ed.	21	M	Laborer	26Au02Co
MCCARTHY, T.	23	M	Laborer	26Au02Co
Maria (W)	24	F	None	26Au02Co
Richd.	07	M	Child	26Au02Co
INHES, Wm.	05	M	Child	26Au02Co
HENDERSON, Robt.	25	M	Farmer	26Au02Co
ILRANN, Josh	22	M	Farmer	26Au02Co
SANDERS, Ben	26	M	Farmer	26Au02Co
ELWITH, Eph.	50	M	Farmer	26Au02Co
Jno.	20	M	Farmer	26Au02Co
DRUMAND, Jas.	30	M	Mechanic	26Au02Co
Francis	25	M	Mechanic	26Au02Co
Bridget	02	F	Child	26Au02Co
Ellen	01	F	Child	26Au02Co
Jno.	16	M	Mechanic	26Au02Co
SWAN, Geo.	21	M	Mechanic	26Au02Co
MCGEE, Ellen	21	F	None	26Au02Co
WALSH, Chris	22	M	Mechanic	26Au02Co
ROUCK, A.	24	M	Mechanic	26Au02Co
Cath.	21	F	None	26Au02Co
CORVILLE, M.	25	M	Farmer	26Au02Co
MILLER, Edw.	18	M	Farmer	26Au02Co
MULLIGAN, Mary	46	F	None	26Au02Co
Diane	17	F	None	26Au02Co
CLINTON, Mich.	30	M	Laborer	26Au02Co
MCMURRY, Pat	30	M	Laborer	26Au02Co
Martha	29	F	None	26Au02Co
VALET, Hen.	22	F	None	26Au02Co
Jno.	35	M	Laborer	26Au02Co
WALTERS, Jno.	35	M	Farmer	26Au02Co
Cath.	09	F	Child	26Au02Co
Jas.	07	M	Child	26Au02Co
Mary	05	F	Child	26Au02Co
Eliza	01	F	Child	26Au02Co
Edwd.	70	M	Farmer	26Au02Co
MCMAHON, Sarah	13	F	None	26Au02Co

NAMES OF PASSENGERS	AGE	SEX	OCCUPATIONS	DATE PORT SHIP
MCMAHON, Elizth.	11	F	None	26Au02Co
James	09	M	Child	26Au02Co
Jno.	30	M	Farmer	26Au02Co
DONALD, Pat	30	M	Farmer	26Au02Co
Mary-A.	31	F	None	26Au02Co
Inna.	10	F	None	26Au02Co
Mich.	07	M	Child	26Au02Co
Wm.	05	M	Child	26Au02Co
Jno.	03	M	Child	26Au02Co
ONEIL, Terence	35	M	Laborer	26Au02Co
Mary	31	F	None	26Au02Co
Rose	09	F	Child	26Au02Co
Pat	06	M	Child	26Au02Co
Ann	03	F	Child	26Au02Co
Cath.	01	F	Child	26Au02Co
CAWLAND, Bridget	15	F	None	26Au02Co
FRYHILL, Pat	23	M	Mechanic	26Au02Co
BROMER, Mary	19	F	None	26Au02Co
LOURY, Jno.	18	M	Mechanic	26Au02Co
MCCAFFERTY, Pat	28	M	Mechanic	26Au02Co
MOONEY, Jno.	20	M	Mechanic	26Au02Co
DOWDALE, Rich.	18	M	Mechanic	26Au02Co
FERGUSON, Josiah	20	M	Mechanic	26Au02Co
Louisa	03	F	Child	26Au02Co
Jno.	01	M	Child	26Au02Co
BROWN, Thos.	20	M	Laborer	26Au02Co
MCIVAN, Chas.	30	M	Laborer	26Au02Co
WATTS, Chas.	22	M	Laborer	26Au02Co
MORY, Elizth.	59	F	None	26Au02Co
KERMAN, Jas.	24	M	Mechanic	26Au02Co
Emily	25	F	None	26Au02Co
ATKINSON, Pat	35	M	Mechanic	26Au02Co
Maria	30	F	None	26Au02Co
Wm.H.	11	M	None	26Au02Co
IRVING, Mary	45	F	None	26Au02Co
Hugh	17	M	Mechanic	26Au02Co
WILKINS, Geo.	37	M	Mechanic	26Au02Co
Elizth.	38	F	None	26Au02Co
LYMINGTON, Robt.	30	M	Mechanic	26Au02Co
DEVIS, Dnl.C.	36	M	Mechanic	26Au02Co
CONVESTON, A.	26	M	Mechanic	26Au02Co
GERHEM, Mary	28	F	None	26Au02Co
LEIGECK, Wm.	23	M	Mechanic	26Au02Co
JAMES, Rob.	22	M	Mechanic	26Au02Co
BURGH, Mary	40	F	None	26Au02Co
Mich.	20	M	Mechanic	26Au02Co
Francis	18	F	None	26Au02Co
Mary	16	F	None	26Au02Co
Margt.	15	F	None	26Au02Co
Jno.	12	M	None	26Au02Co
Geo.	10	M	None	26Au02Co
Cath.	08	F	Child	26Au02Co
LYNCH, Thos.	28	M	Laborer	26Au02Co
CLARK, Eliza	24	F	None	26Au02Co
MCDONALD, Mich.	12	M	None	26Au02Co
HAWTHORN, Chas.	22	M	Mechanic	26Au02Co
MCDALLER, Ellen	35	F	None	26Au02Co
Mary	10	F	None	26Au02Co
Jas.	08	M	Child	26Au02Co
Hugh	06	M	Child	26Au02Co
MCDADE, Jno.	04	M	Child	26Au02Co
Wm.	02	M	Child	26Au02Co
ADAIR, Pat	18	M	Mechanic	26Au02Co
WHITE, Wm.	27	M	Mechanic	26Au02Co
MCCOURMAKEY, Jno.	41	M	Mechanic	26Au02Co
PIGGOT, Thos.	50	M	Mechanic	26Au02Co
Thos.	18	M	Mechanic	26Au02Co
FARNE, Patt	27	M	Mechanic	26Au02Co
MCMULLIN, Cath.	20	F	None	26Au02Co
DOWNEY, Wm.	21	M	Mechanic	26Au02Co
Elizth.	22	F	None	26Au02Co
POLLOCK, James	19	M	Mechanic	26Au02Co
Wm.	22	M	Mechanic	26Au02Co
LOGAN, Jno.	24	M	Mechanic	26Au02Co
Mary	34	F	None	26Au02Co

NAMES OF PASSENGERS	AGE	SEX	OCCUPATIONS	DATE PORT SHIP
LOGAN, Wm.	02	M	Child	26Au02Co
Jas.	01	M	Child	26Au02Co
HAMELTON, Mary-A.	29	F	None	26Au02Co
Alex.	02	M	Child	26Au02Co
DOUGHTY, Jane	20	F	None	26Au02Co
HENRY, Andrew	20	M	Mechanic	26Au02Co
BROOME, Cath.	17	F	None	26Au02Co
ASHLY, Jane	21	F	None	26Au02Co
THOMAS, James	21	M	None	26Au02Co

WAVERLY 28 AUGUST 1847

From Havre

NAMES OF PASSENGERS	AGE	SEX	OCCUPATIONS	DATE PORT SHIP
RICHARDS, Chl.	48	M	None	28Au05Sl
W.D.	08	M	Child	28Au05Sl

HARMONIA 28 AUGUST 1847

From Glasgow

NAMES OF PASSENGERS	AGE	SEX	OCCUPATIONS	DATE PORT SHIP
MCMILLEN, U-Mrs.	46	F	None	28Au04Sm
Jane	30	F	None	28Au04Sm
Jane	23	F	None	28Au04Sm
Benj.	08	M	Child	28Au04Sm
Jno.	02	M	Child	28Au04Sm
U	.00	U	Infant	28Au04Sm
Mary	25	F	None	28Au04Sm
Jane	04	F	Child	28Au04Sm
Rachael	18	F	Child	28Au04Sm
Wm.	16	F	Child	28Au04Sm
James	14	F	Child	28Au04Sm
James	04	M	Child	28Au04Sm
MANON, Wm.	51	M	Mechanic	28Au04Sm
U	51	F	Wife	28Au04Sm
Cath.	14	F	None	28Au04Sm
Matt.	12	M	None	28Au04Sm
GREEN, Jno.	28	M	Clerk	28Au04Sm
GRIEVE, Janet	60	F	None	28Au04Sm
Susan	25	F	None	28Au04Sm
YOUNG, John	29	M	Mechanic	28Au04Sm
KER, Mary	25	F	None	28Au04Sm
STRUTHERS, Cath.	60	F	None	28Au04Sm
Mary-J.	12	F	None	28Au04Sm
Cath.	10	F	None	28Au04Sm
ONEILE, Francis	32	M	Farmer	28Au04Sm
U	32	F	Wife	28Au04Sm
Jas.	12	M	None	28Au04Sm
Cath.	09	F	Child	28Au04Sm
Jno.	04	F	Child	28Au04Sm
Francis	03	F	Child	28Au04Sm
Hanah	.00	F	Infant	28Au04Sm
MCILVEA, Wm.	24	M	Mechanic	28Au04Sm
U	26	F	Wife	28Au04Sm
Math.	04	M	Child	28Au04Sm
U	.00	U	Infant	28Au04Sm
KIRKPATRICK, J.	31	M	Mechanic	28Au04Sm
U	29	F	Wife	28Au04Sm
Agnes	07	F	Child	28Au04Sm
U	.00	U	Infant	28Au04Sm
CONAN, Nancy	35	F	None	28Au04Sm
MCGUILAY, Jno.	30	M	Laborer	28Au04Sm
U	25	F	Wife	28Au04Sm
MCGUILAY, Susan	03	F	Child	28Au04Sm
U	.00	U	Infant	28Au04Sm
MCGINTY, Margt.Mrs.	26	F	None	28Au04Sm
Jno.	04	M	Child	28Au04Sm
Mary	02	F	Child	28Au04Sm
U	.00	U	Infant	28Au04Sm
KENEDY, Daniel	65	M	Farmer	28Au04Sm
Mary-A.	22	F	None	28Au04Sm
Mary	05	F	Child	28Au04Sm
KERR, Agnes	20	F	None	28Au04Sm
MACKINSON, James-A.	24	M	Farmer	28Au04Sm
WALKER, Jas.	25	M	Farmer	28Au04Sm
JONES, Geo.	21	M	Farmer	28Au04Sm
MELL, Mary-A.	24	F	None	28Au04Sm
Joseph	.00	M	Infant	28Au04Sm
SOULTER, Elizth.	36	F	None	28Au04Sm
LEDDELL, Jno.	36	M	Mechanic	28Au04Sm
CARR, Jno.	32	M	Farmer	28Au04Sm
MCGEE, Ellen	28	F	None	28Au04Sm
MCPHIE, Donald	24	M	Farmer	28Au04Sm
Mary	20	F	None	28Au04Sm
FOURNEY, Peter	40	M	Laborer	28Au04Sm
Mary	40	F	None	28Au04Sm
Mary	09	F	Child	28Au04Sm
BLACKWOOD, Peter	38	M	Mechanic	28Au04Sm
Mary	37	F	None	28Au04Sm
Jeanet	13	F	None	28Au04Sm
BAIRD, Robert	13	M	None	28Au04Sm
Isabella	12	F	None	28Au04Sm
Jno.	10	M	None	28Au04Sm
Mary	10	F	None	28Au04Sm
Peter	06	M	Child	28Au04Sm
Jane	03	F	Child	28Au04Sm
U	.00	U	Infant	28Au04Sm
MCGREGOR, Robt.	33	M	Mechanic	28Au04Sm
Ann	30	F	None	28Au04Sm
MORRISON, Jno.	60	M	Mechanic	28Au04Sm
Esph.	60	F	None	28Au04Sm
Esph.	13	F	None	28Au04Sm
SINCLAIR, Archd.	23	M	Farmer	28Au04Sm
BLAKE, Elzth.	26	F	None	28Au04Sm
SMITH, Jas.E.	38	M	Farmer	28Au04Sm
FARNE, Mich.	28	M	Farmer	28Au04Sm
MCBAINE, Wm.	36	M	Farmer	28Au04Sm
Mary	36	F	None	28Au04Sm
Ellen	10	F	None	28Au04Sm
Jas.	08	M	Child	28Au04Sm
Jane	03	F	Child	28Au04Sm
U	.00	U	Infant	28Au04Sm
STUART, Ann	18	F	None	28Au04Sm
MCINTYRE, Geo.	30	M	Mechanic	28Au04Sm
SMITH, Bridget	32	F	None	28Au04Sm
MITCHELL, Jno.	31	M	Mechanic	28Au04Sm
Ann	48	F	None	28Au04Sm
Jean	24	F	None	28Au04Sm
Alex.	23	M	Mechanic	28Au04Sm
Mary	20	F	None	28Au04Sm
Grace	18	F	None	28Au04Sm
Ellen	13	F	None	28Au04Sm
Chris	11	M	Mechanic	28Au04Sm
Jas.	07	M	Child	28Au04Sm
Margt.	05	F	Child	28Au04Sm
Jean	03	F	Child	28Au04Sm
MOORE, Jno.	22	M	Farmer	28Au04Sm
Alex.	20	M	Farmer	28Au04Sm
MCDONALD, Wm.	60	M	Farmer	28Au04Sm
Margt.	55	F	None	28Au04Sm
Jas.	18	M	Farmer	28Au04Sm
Ann	16	F	None	28Au04Sm
Peter	13	M	None	28Au04Sm
Chas.	11	M	None	28Au04Sm
Ellen	06	F	Child	28Au04Sm
REID, Mary	16	F	None	28Au04Sm
ADDISON, Joseph	25	M	Farmer	28Au04Sm
THOMPSON, Geo.	22	M	Farmer	28Au04Sm

NAMES OF PASSENGERS	AGE	SEX	OCCUPATIONS	DATE PORT SHIP
FULLERTON, Pat	19	M	Laborer	28Au04Sm

BACHELOR 30 AUGUST 1847

From Dublin

NAMES OF PASSENGERS	AGE	SEX	OCCUPATIONS	DATE PORT SHIP
OLIVER, Hugh	26	M	Clerk	30Au20Sn
MASON, Jno.	26	M	Clerk	30Au20Sn
JONES, Jno.	30	M	Clerk	30Au20Sn
ARMSTRONG, Jno.	30	M	Farmer	30Au20Sn
BRABSON, Mich.	19	M	Farmer	30Au20Sn
Chas.	13	M	None	30Au20Sn
GRACE, Hebert	13	M	None	30Au20Sn
WOODSIDES, David	14	M	None	30Au20Sn
LEESAM, Jas.	31	M	Laborer	30Au20Sn
PHELAN, Jno.	17	M	Laborer	30Au20Sn
ONEIL, Jno.	50	M	Laborer	30Au20Sn
MARTEN, Jane	40	F	None	30Au20Sn
Jno.	15	M	Laborer	30Au20Sn
ODEA, Thos.	25	M	Laborer	30Au20Sn
Ellen	20	F	None	30Au20Sn
DULLON, Jas.	18	M	Laborer	30Au20Sn
KING, Elizth.	50	F	None	30Au20Sn
Priscilla	19	F	None	30Au20Sn
GAYNOR, Jas.	26	M	Laborer	30Au20Sn
SMITH, Eliza	27	F	None	30Au20Sn
Mary	07	F	Child	30Au20Sn
Wm.	02	M	Child	30Au20Sn
CLARK, Mary	40	F	None	30Au20Sn
MULLEN, Jno.	19	M	Mechanic	30Au20Sn
KELLAN, Thos.	24	M	Mechanic	30Au20Sn
SMITH, Frank	30	M	Mechanic	30Au20Sn
GRACE, Jno.	20	M	Mechanic	30Au20Sn
Margt.	20	F	None	30Au20Sn
LYONS, Cath.	18	F	None	30Au20Sn
Sarah	20	F	None	30Au20Sn
ENESS, Francis	28	M	Mechanic	30Au20Sn
MCCURTEN, Jas.	27	M	Mechanic	30Au20Sn
STOREY, Luke	26	M	Mechanic	30Au20Sn
Magt.	22	F	None	30Au20Sn
U	.00	U	Infant	30Au20Sn
HILL, Jno.	38	M	Farmer	30Au20Sn
Ann	32	F	None	30Au20Sn
Ann	08	F	Child	30Au20Sn
PHILIPS, Ann	44	F	None	30Au20Sn
Ellen	18	F	None	30Au20Sn
Elizth.	11	F	None	30Au20Sn
Henry	21	M	None	30Au20Sn
ROGERS, Robert	25	M	Mechanic	30Au20Sn
SMITH, Magt.	50	F	None	30Au20Sn
Cath.	20	F	None	30Au20Sn
Jas.	22	M	None	30Au20Sn
BALLS, Mary	20	F	None	30Au20Sn
RIELY, Ann	20	F	None	30Au20Sn
LEVIT, Elizth.	50	F	None	30Au20Sn
Cath.	18	F	None	30Au20Sn
Honn.	16	F	None	30Au20Sn
Julia	14	F	None	30Au20Sn
Edmd.	21	M	Mechanic	30Au20Sn
Jas.	12	M	None	30Au20Sn
BEEBY, Caroline	17	F	None	30Au20Sn
DAGNAN, Jno.	27	M	Farmer	30Au20Sn
REDMOND, Magt.	53	F	None	30Au20Sn
Pat	23	M	Farmer	30Au20Sn
John	25	M	Farmer	30Au20Sn
Wm.	22	M	Farmer	30Au20Sn
Jas.	19	M	Farmer	30Au20Sn
Alice	18	F	None	30Au20Sn
HOGLAND, Jno.	19	M	Farmer	30Au20Sn
HODGE, Elizth.	30	F	None	30Au20Sn
Maria	12	F	None	30Au20Sn
Eliza	08	F	Child	30Au20Sn
Bridget	02	F	Child	30Au20Sn
Thos.	11	M	None	30Au20Sn
Jno.	10	M	None	30Au20Sn
Wm.	09	M	Child	30Au20Sn
KARNEY, Cath.	21	F	None	30Au20Sn
FOSTER, Wm.	22	M	Laborer	30Au20Sn
CARY, Cath.	17	F	None	30Au20Sn
SPOLLAN, Bergan	22	M	Laborer	30Au20Sn
Margt.	56	F	None	30Au20Sn
SMITH, Thos.	24	M	Laborer	30Au20Sn
MCDONOUGH, Jas.	25	M	Laborer	30Au20Sn
GREEN, Jas.	20	M	Laborer	30Au20Sn
MARTIN, Pat	35	M	Laborer	30Au20Sn
RYAN, Mary	19	F	None	30Au20Sn
KILRO, Ann	26	F	None	30Au20Sn
BEHAN, Mary	25	F	None	30Au20Sn
NORTON, Magt.	30	F	None	30Au20Sn
RUSH, Ed.	10	M	None	30Au20Sn
GALLIGAN, Julia	32	F	None	30Au20Sn
GALLAGHER, And.	21	M	Clerk	30Au20Sn
CULLEN, Mich.	26	M	Laborer	30Au20Sn
MCMANUS, Jno.	23	M	Laborer	30Au20Sn
FLIN, Ann	52	F	None	30Au20Sn
Mary	20	F	None	30Au20Sn
Margt.	25	F	None	30Au20Sn
ARTENEY, Joseph	35	M	Laborer	30Au20Sn
ANDERSON, Cath.	19	F	None	30Au20Sn
TATE, Ann	21	F	None	30Au20Sn
VINS, Francis	22	F	None	30Au20Sn
DEANAN, Pat	37	M	Laborer	30Au20Sn
HAYDEN, Francis	20	M	Laborer	30Au20Sn
GIVNEY, Mich.	34	M	Laborer	30Au20Sn
Magt.	30	F	None	30Au20Sn
Ann	07	F	Child	30Au20Sn
Edwd.	08	M	Child	30Au20Sn
CADWELL, Jas.	27	M	Laborer	30Au20Sn
Mary	27	F	None	30Au20Sn
Thos.	01	M	Child	30Au20Sn
FITZGERALD, Wm.	65	M	Lawyer	30Au20Sn
Wm.W.	25	M	Gentleman	30Au20Sn
Jas.	21	M	Gentleman	30Au20Sn
Cath.	20	F	None	30Au20Sn
PHIBBS, F.L.E.	28	M	Physician	30Au20Sn

GUADELQUIVER 30 AUGUST 1847

From Liverpool

NAMES OF PASSENGERS	AGE	SEX	OCCUPATIONS	DATE PORT SHIP
CADDY, C.A.	32	M	Physician	30Au02So
DRAPER, W.H.	48	M	Jdg-Spct	30Au02So
HARBOTTLE, John	40	M	Merchant	30Au02So
U	35	F	None	30Au02So
MACKENZIE, Joseph	33	M	Merchant	30Au02So
DECHELL, William-Lt.	25	M	Army	30Au02So
ROBINSON, J.J.	35	M	Nvycpt	30Au02So
SHAW, Charles.T.	32	M	Merchant	30Au02So
SQUIRES, U-Mrs.	40	F	None	30Au02So
Jane	10	F	Child	30Au02So
Mary	09	F	Child	30Au02So
STEWARD, Christina	26	F	Lady'S Maid	30Au02So

ST.GEORGE 01 SEPTEMBER 1847

From Liverpool

NAMES OF PASSENGERS	AGE	SEX	OCCUPATIONS	DATE PORT SHIP
CORCORAN, John	30	M	Laborer	01Se02Av
FINEGAN, Catherine	25	F	Servant	01Se02Av
HICKEY, Michael	42	M	Farmer	01Se02Av
Margaret	34	F	Farmer	01Se02Av
Honora	15	F	None	01Se02Av
Sabina	10	F	None	01Se02Av
Thomas	09	M	Child	01Se02Av
Eduard	07	M	Child	01Se02Av
Michael	05	M	Child	01Se02Av
Eliza	04	F	Child	01Se02Av
Joseph	.00	M	Infant	01Se02Av
MURRAY, James	25	M	Laborer	01Se02Av
Rose	50	F	Laborer	01Se02Av
Mathew	56	M	Farmer	01Se02Av
Maria	40	F	None	01Se02Av
Fanny	10	F	None	01Se02Av
John	09	M	Child	01Se02Av
James	05	M	Child	01Se02Av
Bridget	05	F	Child	01Se02Av
Maria	03	F	Child	01Se02Av
Anna	.00	F	Infant	01Se02Av
Died-At-Sea				
CONDON, Mary	55	F	Unknown	01Se02Av
BOYLAN, Margaret	50	F	None	01Se02Av
CONDON, Mary	22	F	None	01Se02Av
Rose	06	F	Child	01Se02Av
Bridget	.00	F	Infant	01Se02Av
FINEGAN, Matthew	22	M	Laborer	01Se02Av
GALOHER, Peter	37	M	Laborer	01Se02Av
Ellen	20	F	None	01Se02Av
KENNY, William	27	M	Baker	01Se02Av
MCCOY, John	40	M	Thatcher	01Se02Av
MEABE, Patt	25	M	Laborer	01Se02Av
Mary	25	F	None	01Se02Av
CUSACK, John	24	M	Farmer	01Se02Av
Died-At-Sea				
LYNCH, James	20	M	None	01Se02Av
MURPHY, Margaret	45	F	None	01Se02Av
Thomas	20	M	None	01Se02Av
Owen	18	M	None	01Se02Av
John	10	M	None	01Se02Av
Rose	12	F	None	01Se02Av
Ann	11	F	None	01Se02Av
SMITH, Patrick	20	M	None	01Se02Av
GILCHRIST, Anne	20	F	None	01Se02Av
SMITH, Charles	04	M	Child	01Se02Av
Owen	.00	M	Infant	01Se02Av
Catherine	.00	F	Infant	01Se02Av
GRIFFETH, Mary	22	F	None	01Se02Av
Kate	20	F	None	01Se02Av
REILY, Catharine	21	F	None	01Se02Av
MINNIS, Ellen	23	F	None	01Se02Av
MULHOLLAND, John	30	M	None	01Se02Av
COWPER, Charles	20	M	None	01Se02Av
BARNET, Jane	24	F	None	01Se02Av
Eliza	15	F	None	01Se02Av
William	.00	M	Infant	01Se02Av
MCGUIRE, Margaret	13	F	None	01Se02Av
FERRIS, Sarah	18	F	None	01Se02Av
JOHNSON, Catherine	16	F	None	01Se02Av
RAFFERTY, Margaret	16	F	None	01Se02Av
MAGEE, Patt	30	M	Laborer	01Se02Av
MCLEAN, John	23	M	Draper	01Se02Av
BEGAN, Mary	40	F	None	01Se02Av
James	06	M	Child	01Se02Av
BEGAN, Eleanor	12	F	None	01Se02Av
Mary	03	F	Child	01Se02Av
RAFFERTY, Patrick	20	M	Laborer	01Se02Av
CAVENAH, James	20	M	Laborer	01Se02Av
CARBRY, John	25	M	Laborer	01Se02Av
Sally	18	F	Laborer	01Se02Av
Fanny	.00	F	Infant	01Se02Av
Died-At-Sea				
OGARA, Charles	23	M	Laborer	01Se02Av
CARR, Michael	30	M	Laborer	01Se02Av
GALWAY, Robert	50	M	Weaver	01Se02Av
WALPOLE, Thomas	35	M	Laborer	01Se02Av
Mary	27	F	None	01Se02Av
BEGAN, Edward	45	M	Carpenter	01Se02Av
Edward	18	M	None	01Se02Av
Michael	16	M	None	01Se02Av
Robert	09	M	Child	01Se02Av
PATTERSON, Margaret	33	F	None	01Se02Av
John	16	M	None	01Se02Av
Mary	.00	F	Infant	01Se02Av
MCCLUSTY, Margaret	19	F	None	01Se02Av
MITCHELL, George	35	M	Laborer	01Se02Av
Mary	18	F	None	01Se02Av
Jane	16	F	None	01Se02Av
MCLANE, Cristy	15	M	None	01Se02Av
Betty	14	F	None	01Se02Av
Charles	12	M	None	01Se02Av
FITZSIMMONS, Eduard	18	M	Laborer	01Se02Av
SULLIVAN, John	50	M	Laborer	01Se02Av
WALSH, Bartly	25	M	Laborer	01Se02Av
ARMSTRONG, Maria	18	F	None	01Se02Av
LOFTUS, Bridget	16	F	None	01Se02Av
EAGAN, Thomas	26	M	Laborer	01Se02Av
James	30	M	Laborer	01Se02Av
Mary	55	F	None	01Se02Av
Mary	22	F	None	01Se02Av
RYAN, Mick	25	M	Laborer	01Se02Av
Mick	20	M	Laborer	01Se02Av
Biddy	22	F	None	01Se02Av
Michael	.00	M	Infant	01Se02Av
CARSON, John	30	M	Laborer	01Se02Av
MCCORMICK, Jamses	30	M	Laborer	01Se02Av
GRAHAM, John	21	M	Laborer	01Se02Av
BANNAN, John	24	M	Laborer	01Se02Av
RYAN, John	18	M	Laborer	01Se02Av
GALBRETH, Robert	32	M	Laborer	01Se02Av
Sarah	32	F	None	01Se02Av
Robert	07	M	Child	01Se02Av
Sarah-Jane	04	F	Child	01Se02Av
James	02	M	Child	01Se02Av
MCLANE, Matilda	07	F	Child	01Se02Av
FINNEGAN, Hugh	23	M	Grocer	01Se02Av
Elizabeth	20	F	None	01Se02Av
KEOGH, Edward	36	M	Laborer	01Se02Av
Catharine	43	F	None	01Se02Av
Mary	55	F	None	01Se02Av
Patrick	10	M	None	01Se02Av
SHANAHAN, Margaret	20	F	None	01Se02Av
SHEA, Mary	30	F	None	01Se02Av
LENNON, Patrick	28	M	Laborer	01Se02Av
WALSH, Thomas	24	M	Laborer	01Se02Av
OWENS, William	25	M	Laborer	01Se02Av
TRACY, Ellen	50	F	None	01Se02Av
LEE, Mary	17	F	None	01Se02Av
DEALY, Anne	16	F	None	01Se02Av
DARBY, James	50	M	Laborer	01Se02Av
Martin	22	M	Laborer	01Se02Av
Margaret	18	F	None	01Se02Av
WHITE, John	20	M	Laborer	01Se02Av
SNEID, Mary	50	F	None	01Se02Av
Catharine	18	F	None	01Se02Av
SEAVER, Thomas	22	M	Laborer	01Se02Av
SEXTON, John	20	M	Laborer	01Se02Av
NEARY, Josiah	17	M	Laborer	01Se02Av
ELLIS, John	48	M	Laborer	01Se02Av

NAMES OF PASSENGERS	AGE	SEX	OCCUPATIONS	DATE PORT SHIP
HAWKINS, John	25	M	Laborer	01Se02Av
JACKSON, William	23	M	Laborer	01Se02Av
WESTON, John	49	M	Laborer	01Se02Av
DAVID, Thomas	23	M	Laborer	01Se02Av
CAMP, Mary	46	F	None	01Se02Av
William	11	M	Laborer	01Se02Av
David	08	M	Child	01Se02Av
WESTON, Mary	48	F	None	01Se02Av
Herald	10	M	Laborer	01Se02Av
BREWERY, Richard	30	M	Laborer	01Se02Av
ONEIL, David	24	M	Laborer	01Se02Av
Eliza	21	F	None	01Se02Av
LARKIN, Patrick	25	M	Laborer	01Se02Av
MARSHALL, Jane	50	F	None	01Se02Av
FINNEGAN, Owen	50	M	Laborer	01Se02Av
Alfey	15	M	Laborer	01Se02Av
FEE, Mary	24	F	None	01Se02Av
FINNEGAN, Anne	12	F	None	01Se02Av
WATKINS, William	23	M	Collier	01Se02Av
CRAWLENS, John	24	M	Laborer	01Se02Av
FINIS, Robert	25	M	Laborer	01Se02Av
David	23	M	Laborer	01Se02Av
LUDLOW, George	17	M	Laborer	01Se02Av
Anne	16	F	None	01Se02Av
Emily	14	F	None	01Se02Av
Emily	14	F	None	01Se02Av
Lydia	30	F	None	01Se02Av
Richard	08	M	Child	01Se02Av
Richard	08	M	Child	01Se02Av
Charlotte	03	F	Child	01Se02Av
Charlotte	03	F	Child	01Se02Av
GLINN, John	23	M	Laborer	01Se02Av
ELINN, John	23	M	Laborer	01Se02Av
Lucy	28	F	None	01Se02Av
FINNEGAN, John	35	M	Laborer	01Se02Av
Margaret	23	F	None	01Se02Av
Bridget	.00	F	Infant	01Se02Av
SAVAGE, Bridget	50	F	None	01Se02Av
Bessy	16	F	None	01Se02Av
Joseph	13	M	None	01Se02Av
Michael	11	M	None	01Se02Av
MCNAMARA, Bridget	22	F	None	01Se02Av
John	02	M	Child	01Se02Av
Mary-Ann	.00	F	Infant	01Se02Av
CONWAY, Catharine	10	F	None	01Se02Av
Mary	10	F	None	01Se02Av
CALLANAN, Rose	18	F	None	01Se02Av
Catherine	12	F	None	01Se02Av
MURPHY, Mary	20	F	None	01Se02Av
CARABRY, Mary	20	F	None	01Se02Av
HUGHES, Catharine	20	F	None	01Se02Av
CARDELL, Mary-Jane	18	F	None	01Se02Av
GALLIGAN, Joseph	18	M	Laborer	01Se02Av
MOORE, James	29	M	Laborer	01Se02Av
CORBETT, Joseph	29	M	Laborer	01Se02Av
MCCONNELL, Elleck	28	M	Laborer	01Se02Av
Hannah	10	F	None	01Se02Av
Mary	.00	F	Infant	01Se02Av
Elleck	30	M	Laborer	01Se02Av
REILLY, Francis	47	M	Farmer	01Se02Av
Elizabeth	17	F	None	01Se02Av
Jane	15	F	None	01Se02Av
Margaret	09	F	Child	01Se02Av
Thomas	06	M	Child	01Se02Av
Mary-A.	04	F	Child	01Se02Av
Edward	11	M	None	01Se02Av
Charles	02	M	Child	01Se02Av
Died-At-Sea				
BAIRD, James	27	M	Gunsmith	01Se02Av
ERWIN, Anne	14	F	None	01Se02Av
GERENTY, Betty	37	F	None	01Se02Av
MCCABE, Mary	04	F	Child	01Se02Av
BRADY, Catharine	20	F	None	01Se02Av
Jane	26	F	None	01Se02Av
MCLANE, Margaret	51	F	None	01Se02Av
MCLANE, Nancy	16	F	None	01Se02Av
RILEY, Patrick	06	M	Child	01Se02Av
SHAW, William	19	M	Merchant	01Se02Av
BRADBURY, Samuel	18	M	Merchant	01Se02Av
ELLIS, Henry-F.	40	M	Farmer	01Se02Av
U	30	F	Wife	01Se02Av
Ann	60	F	None	01Se02Av
Sarah	23	F	None	01Se02Av
Mary-Ann	21	F	None	01Se02Av
Alexander	35	M	None	01Se02Av
BANNON, Bridget	40	F	Servant	01Se02Av
CAULDFIELD, Abrm.St.Ge	40	M	Clergyman	01Se02Av
U	33	F	Wife	01Se02Av
Hans.	37	M	Physician	01Se02Av

BURLINGTON 02 SEPTEMBER 1847

From Liverpool

NAMES OF PASSENGERS	AGE	SEX	OCCUPATIONS	DATE PORT SHIP
NEALIS, Pat	23	M	Laborer	02Se02Ja
MARDAY, Cath.	18	F	None	02Se02Ja
HARATY, Soph.	30	F	None	02Se02Ja
LYONS, Owen	28	M	Laborer	02Se02Ja
MORRIS, Ellen	40	F	None	02Se02Ja
Anas.	20	F	None	02Se02Ja
CARROL, Ann	45	F	None	02Se02Ja
Biddy	24	F	None	02Se02Ja
Ann	18	F	None	02Se02Ja
Jno.	16	F	None	02Se02Ja
Pat.	11	M	None	02Se02Ja
Thos.	08	M	None	02Se02Ja
HALL, Eliz.	23	F	None	02Se02Ja
HIGGINS, Jno.	32	M	Laborer	02Se02Ja
SHERIDAN, Mich.	26	M	Laborer	02Se02Ja
MULHALL, Jas.	23	M	Laborer	02Se02Ja
BURLIGH, Wm.	30	M	Laborer	02Se02Ja
DUFF, Richd.	60	M	Laborer	02Se02Ja
Jas.	20	M	Laborer	02Se02Ja
Cath.	17	F	None	02Se02Ja
Magt.	22	F	None	02Se02Ja
HERNAN, Ann	07	F	Child	02Se02Ja
DUFF, Ann	00	F	None	02Se02Ja
FALLON, Jno.	24	M	Laborer	02Se02Ja
Maria	20	F	None	02Se02Ja
DOUGHTY, Jno.	26	M	Mechanic	02Se02Ja
MCCORMACK, Ann	34	F	None	02Se02Ja
LEE, Jno.	36	M	Mechanic	02Se02Ja
DUGGAN, Pat	26	M	Mechanic	02Se02Ja
HAYES, Dennis	30	M	Laborer	02Se02Ja
LYNCH, Pat	18	M	Laborer	02Se02Ja
BIDDOCK, Wm.	26	M	Laborer	02Se02Ja
HANELRAN, Bridget	24	F	None	02Se02Ja
HARDEMAN, Winifred	20	M	Laborer	02Se02Ja
Thos.	60	M	Laborer	02Se02Ja
Margt.	50	F	None	02Se02Ja
Jno.	16	M	Laborer	02Se02Ja
Bridget	03	F	Child	02Se02Ja
DUNNING, Honora	22	F	None	02Se02Ja
HINES, Ellen	40	F	None	02Se02Ja
BRENAN, Wm.	21	M	Laborer	02Se02Ja
DEASON, Jno.	18	M	Mechanic	02Se02Ja
JAMESON, Jane	22	F	None	02Se02Ja
HANLEY, Margt.	21	F	None	02Se02Ja
ODONNELL, Rose-A.	18	F	None	02Se02Ja
Eliza	12	F	None	02Se02Ja
MCCLUSKEY, Bessy	21	F	None	02Se02Ja
MORRIS, Pat	38	M	Mechanic	02Se02Ja
Mrgt.	30	F	Wife	02Se02Ja
Thos.	14	M	None	02Se02Ja

NAMES OF PASSENGERS	AGE	SEX	OCCUPATIONS	DATE PORT SHIP
MORRIS, Jno.	10	M	None	02Se02Ja
Richd.	08	M	Child	02Se02Ja
James	05	M	Child	02Se02Ja
Pat	03	M	Child	02Se02Ja
Cath.	00	F	None	02Se02Ja
DAVIS, Edwd.	37	M	Laborer	02Se02Ja
Jno.	21	M	Laborer	02Se02Ja
ELLIOTT, Pat	40	M	Laborer	02Se02Ja
HIGGINS, May	27	F	None	02Se02Ja
Cath	25	F	Wife	02Se02Ja
Bernard	09	M	Child	02Se02Ja
Pat	07	M	Child	02Se02Ja
MCGEE, Wm.	16	M	None	02Se02Ja
MORGAN, Danl.	21	M	Laborer	02Se02Ja
MCCANON, Chas.	36	M	Laborer	02Se02Ja
Ann	36	F	Wife	02Se02Ja
Pat	10	M	None	02Se02Ja
Chas.	08	M	Child	02Se02Ja
Nancy	06	F	Child	02Se02Ja
GORMLEY, Bid.	18	F	None	02Se02Ja
Rosanna	14	F	None	02Se02Ja
MORLAY, Danl.	35	M	Laborer	02Se02Ja
HENERY, Mary	16	F	None	02Se02Ja
NIELL, Mary	24	F	None	02Se02Ja
CUNIFF, Peter	70	M	Laborer	02Se02Ja
Bridget	40	F	None	02Se02Ja
Thos.	08	M	Child	02Se02Ja
MARTIN, Jno.	17	M	Laborer	02Se02Ja
Mary-A.	19	F	None	02Se02Ja
GAFFNEY, Cath.	20	F	None	02Se02Ja
ELROY, Jno.	38	M	Farmer	02Se02Ja
Ann	30	F	Wife	02Se02Ja
Cath.	05	F	Child	02Se02Ja
MILLS, Alice	24	F	None	02Se02Ja
Sarah	15	F	None	02Se02Ja
Julia	06	F	Child	02Se02Ja
James	05	M	Child	02Se02Ja
Thomas	03	M	Child	02Se02Ja
PIERCE, Ann	14	F	None	02Se02Ja
Richd.	04	M	Child	02Se02Ja
Jas.	.00	M	Infant	02Se02Ja
PEALL, Rebecca	40	F	None	02Se02Ja
HANALTY, Cath.	40	F	None	02Se02Ja
Mrgt.	20	F	None	02Se02Ja
BRYAN, Jno.	25	M	Laborer	02Se02Ja
ONEIL, Ann	20	F	None	02Se02Ja
DONIPHAN, M.	24	M	Laborer	02Se02Ja
Cath.	20	F	None	02Se02Ja
DAGG, R.	28	M	Laborer	02Se02Ja
MCELVENE, S.	20	M	Laborer	02Se02Ja
U	25	F	Wife	02Se02Ja
June	05	F	Child	02Se02Ja
U	.00	U	Infant	02Se02Ja
CRONY, J.	33	M	Laborer	02Se02Ja
FETTIGE, E.W.	32	F	None	02Se02Ja
M.	18	F	None	02Se02Ja
S------, A.	36	M	Laborer	02Se02Ja
MCCLASKY, R.	24	M	Laborer	02Se02Ja
DONOVAN, P.	35	M	Laborer	02Se02Ja
M.	16	F	None	02Se02Ja
M.	13	M	None	02Se02Ja
E.	04	F	Child	02Se02Ja
HIGGINS, M.	16	F	None	02Se02Ja
FLOOD, P.	21	M	Laborer	02Se02Ja
A.	20	F	None	02Se02Ja
FARREL, S.	24	F	None	02Se02Ja
MCCABE, A.	20	F	None	02Se02Ja
M.	21	F	None	02Se02Ja
SMITH, P.	23	M	Laborer	02Se02Ja
MURPHY, M.	20	F	None	02Se02Ja
GALLAGHER, F.	20	F	None	02Se02Ja
J.	19	M	Laborer	02Se02Ja
S.	12	M	None	02Se02Ja
BREENAN, A.	20	F	None	02Se02Ja
BURKE, J.	21	M	Laborer	02Se02Ja
BURKE, P.	18	M	Laborer	02Se02Ja
T.	16	M	Laborer	02Se02Ja
JORDAN, T.	20	M	Laborer	02Se02Ja
LACY, M.	20	F	None	02Se02Ja
MAXWELL, A.	19	F	None	02Se02Ja
MCKEE, N.	20	F	None	02Se02Ja
SHAIN, J.	24	M	Laborer	02Se02Ja
KENNEDY, M.	20	M	Laborer	02Se02Ja
E.	20	F	None	02Se02Ja
HANDERS, B.	24	M	Laborer	02Se02Ja
HOGAN, M.	25	M	Laborer	02Se02Ja
LYKE, John	40	M	Laborer	02Se02Ja
T.	29	M	Laborer	02Se02Ja
B.	25	M	Laborer	02Se02Ja
M.	24	M	Laborer	02Se02Ja
FINCH, J.	30	M	Laborer	02Se02Ja
ALLEN, P.	17	M	Laborer	02Se02Ja
DALEY, M.	32	M	Laborer	02Se02Ja
J.	18	M	Laborer	02Se02Ja
M.	18	F	None	02Se02Ja
J.	10	M	None	02Se02Ja
J.	07	M	Child	02Se02Ja
FOSTER, B.	29	M	Laborer	02Se02Ja
HAGHNEY, T.	23	M	Laborer	02Se02Ja
CORNISH, C.	24	M	Laborer	02Se02Ja
WILSON, T.	20	F	None	02Se02Ja
M.	19	M	Laborer	02Se02Ja
REILLY, J.	45	M	Laborer	02Se02Ja
M.	40	F	Wife	02Se02Ja
J.	11	M	None	02Se02Ja
M.	12	F	None	02Se02Ja
B.	07	F	Child	02Se02Ja
J.	.00	M	Infant	02Se02Ja
CARMOIGHT, J.	22	M	Laborer	02Se02Ja
H.	24	M	Laborer	02Se02Ja
CONNERTON, A.	22	M	Laborer	02Se02Ja
ACHESON, S.	00	M	Laborer	02Se02Ja
D.	20	F	None	02Se02Ja
MCGOVERN, A.	18	F	None	02Se02Ja
FAGAN, S.	18	F	None	02Se02Ja
BOYLE, D.	24	M	Laborer	02Se02Ja
L.	20	M	Laborer	02Se02Ja
A.	24	F	None	02Se02Ja
Le-ITY, B.	20	F	None	02Se02Ja
KENNEDY, E.	26	M	Laborer	02Se02Ja
KELLY, J.	26	M	Laborer	02Se02Ja
FLINN, B.	16	M	Laborer	02Se02Ja
M.	13	F	None	02Se02Ja
B.	19	F	None	02Se02Ja
DUNN, E.	18	F	None	02Se02Ja
M.	14	F	None	02Se02Ja
BRYAN, N.	32	M	Laborer	02Se02Ja
B.	30	F	Wife	02Se02Ja
Mat.	14	F	None	02Se02Ja
T.	11	M	None	02Se02Ja
BEHAN, R.	18	M	Laborer	02Se02Ja
REGAN, M.	19	F	None	02Se02Ja
MCILRAE, W.	30	M	Laborer	02Se02Ja
CASEY, D.	20	M	Laborer	02Se02Ja
CONNELLY, J.	29	M	Laborer	02Se02Ja
QUINN, R.	24	F	None	02Se02Ja
BRADY, J.	13	M	Laborer	02Se02Ja
EYRIE, U-Mrs.	40	F	None	02Se02Ja
D.	13	M	None	02Se02Ja
E.	11	F	None	02Se02Ja
E.	09	F	Child	02Se02Ja
M.	05	F	Child	02Se02Ja
D.	07	M	Child	02Se02Ja
L.	00	M	Child	02Se02Ja
WALTON, M.	24	M	Laborer	02Se02Ja
SEAL, M.	50	M	Laborer	02Se02Ja
E.	25	F	None	02Se02Ja
H.	20	F	None	02Se02Ja
M.	16	F	None	02Se02Ja
F.	06	M	Child	02Se02Ja

NAMES OF PASSENGERS	AGE	SEX	OCCUPATIONS	DATE PORT SHIP
CUNNINGHAM, J.	27	M	Laborer	02Se02Ja
DOLAN, M.	20	F	None	02Se02Ja
RYAN, T.	24	M	Laborer	02Se02Ja
B.	20	F	None	02Se02Ja
E.	22	F	None	02Se02Ja
MURPHY, M.	28	F	None	02Se02Ja
OHAGAN, A.	22	F	None	02Se02Ja
MCKENNA, J.	26	M	Laborer	02Se02Ja
CHAPIN, J.	21	M	Farmer	02Se02Ja
BRACKIN, M.P.	17	M	Farmer	02Se02Ja
GRADY, M.	22	F	None	02Se02Ja
C.	22	F	None	02Se02Ja

SENATOR 02 SEPTEMBER 1847

From Liverpool

NAMES OF PASSENGERS	AGE	SEX	OCCUPATIONS	DATE PORT SHIP
KNIGHT, William	32	M	Engineer	02Se02Sq
OCONNELL, John	36	M	Merchant	02Se02Sq
ROBINSON, William	43	M	Tailor	02Se02Sq
Ann	54	F	Unknown	02Se02Sq
Jane	20	F	Spinster	02Se02Sq
Sarah	18	F	Spinster	02Se02Sq
WILLIAMS, William	31	M	Tailor	02Se02Sq
Catherine	32	F	Unknown	02Se02Sq
DAVIES, Samuel	24	M	Tailor	02Se02Sq
PRICE, David	25	M	Laborer	02Se02Sq
CROSS, William	50	M	Servant	02Se02Sq
HURLEY, Margaret	26	F	Spinster	02Se02Sq
KEIN, Ann	60	F	Wi	02Se02Sq
Died-At-Sea				
Ann	20	F	Spinster	02Se02Sq
Ann	08	F	Child	02Se02Sq
John	30	M	Laborer	02Se02Sq
Michael	04	M	Child	02Se02Sq
Mary	25	F	Wife	02Se02Sq
Died-At-Sea				
Henry	02	M	Child	02Se02Sq
Catherine	.06	F	Infant	02Se02Sq
Died-At-Sea				
Cecilia	25	F	Spinster	02Se02Sq
Barnard	13	M	Laborer	02Se02Sq
Jane	17	F	Spinster	02Se02Sq
Michael	06	M	Child	02Se02Sq
Margaret	13	F	Spinster	02Se02Sq
BYRNE, Patrick	22	M	Laborer	02Se02Sq
DARSAY, Frank	30	M	Laborer	02Se02Sq
Margaret	30	F	Wife	02Se02Sq
Mary	17	F	Spinster	02Se02Sq
Mary	13	F	Spinster	02Se02Sq
Bridget	10	F	Spinster	02Se02Sq
Catherine	06	F	Child	02Se02Sq
Jane	08	F	Child	02Se02Sq
KENNY, Honor	30	F	Wi	02Se02Sq
KAIN, Margaret	14	F	Spinster	02Se02Sq
MOONEY, John	54	M	Seaman	02Se02Sq
Catherine	50	F	Wife	02Se02Sq
Catherine	19	F	Spinster	02Se02Sq
WILLIAMS, Catherine	22	F	Spinster	02Se02Sq
Mary-Jane	24	F	Spinster	02Se02Sq
CLARKE, John	.06	M	Infant	02Se02Sq
GALLAGHER, John	44	M	Chandler	02Se02Sq
Bridget	34	F	Wife	02Se02Sq
CUSICK, Anthony	32	M	Laborer	02Se02Sq
GALLAGHER, Ann	13	F	Spinster	02Se02Sq
Pat	10	M	Unknown	02Se02Sq
John	11	M	Unknown	02Se02Sq
Hugh	08	M	Child	02Se02Sq
Bridget	06	F	Child	02Se02Sq

NAMES OF PASSENGERS	AGE	SEX	OCCUPATIONS	DATE PORT SHIP
GALLAGHER, Andrew	04	M	Child	02Se02Sq
Michael	02	M	Child	02Se02Sq
HARDING, Robert	33	M	Farmer	02Se02Sq
Jemima	30	F	Wife	02Se02Sq
Jonathan	09	M	Child	02Se02Sq
OGDEN, Amos	33	M	Mnftr	02Se02Sq
LUDDON, John	26	M	Baker	02Se02Sq
Mary	22	F	Spinster	02Se02Sq
CALLAGHAN, Michael	20	M	Laborer	02Se02Sq
LOVE, James	24	M	Laborer	02Se02Sq
LEACH, Catherine	22	F	Spinster	02Se02Sq
Susan	18	F	Spinster	02Se02Sq
LUGHERY, Thomas	36	M	Farmer	02Se02Sq
Elizabeth	11	F	None	02Se02Sq
Jane	09	F	Child	02Se02Sq
Isabella	07	F	Child	02Se02Sq
Ann	07	F	Child	02Se02Sq
John	04	M	Child	02Se02Sq
Nancy	01	F	Child	02Se02Sq
EWING, Margaret	20	F	Spinster	02Se02Sq
KENNELL, Elizabeth	32	F	Wife	02Se02Sq
Caroline	26	F	Wi	02Se02Sq
SMITH, William	32	M	Tailor	02Se02Sq
KENNELL, Edward	06	M	Child	02Se02Sq
GIBBONS, Lawrence	25	M	Laborer	02Se02Sq
Dominick	20	M	Clergyman	02Se02Sq
HOLDEN, Daniel	49	M	Weaver	02Se02Sq
LYNCH, Thomas	62	M	Farmer	02Se02Sq
Mathew	30	M	Farmer	02Se02Sq
Michael	27	M	Farmer	02Se02Sq
Thomas	21	M	Farmer	02Se02Sq
Eliza	23	F	Spinster	02Se02Sq
CAREY, Jemima	26	F	Spinster	02Se02Sq
MORRIS, William	30	M	Laborer	02Se02Sq
JAMES, William	63	M	Farmer	02Se02Sq
FOX, Charles	22	M	Shoemaker	02Se02Sq
KITCHEN, John	39	M	Jnr-Bldr	02Se02Sq
Mary-Ann	39	F	Wife	02Se02Sq
ASHTON, Josiah	40	M	Car Driver	02Se02Sq
BRIDGE, Charles	21	M	Laborer	02Se02Sq
NIVIN, Luke	35	M	Laborer	02Se02Sq
Nancy	32	F	Wife	02Se02Sq
Nancy	02	F	Child	02Se02Sq
Thomas	.06	M	Infant	02Se02Sq
HILL, Henry	23	M	Japanner	02Se02Sq
Mary	24	F	Wife	02Se02Sq
Rose	01	F	Child	02Se02Sq
ROBINSON, Samuel	52	M	Stkw	02Se02Sq
HANNAH, Martha	26	F	Spinster	02Se02Sq
LARSEN, Bridget	18	F	Spinster	02Se02Sq
SHULTZ, Edward	45	M	Machinist	02Se02Sq
BELGER, Frederick	50	M	Machinist	02Se02Sq
NEWELL, William-B.	23	M	Clerk	02Se02Sq
DANIELS, John	49	M	Engineer	02Se02Sq
Mary-Ann	47	F	Wife	02Se02Sq
Sarah	22	F	Spinster	02Se02Sq
Mary	17	F	Spinster	02Se02Sq
John	12	M	None	02Se02Sq
Ann	10	F	None	02Se02Sq
JAMES, Alexander	25	M	Puddler	02Se02Sq
JONES, Thomas	23	M	Tin Maker	02Se02Sq
MORRIS, John	21	M	Puddler	02Se02Sq
WILSON, John	22	M	Gdnr	02Se02Sq
SAVAGE, John	23	M	Bookbinder	02Se02Sq
WOOD, Thomas	23	M	Tin Maker	02Se02Sq
HOPKINS, Honor	20	F	Spinster	02Se02Sq
FLINN, Sally	36	F	Wife	02Se02Sq
REGAN, Honor	24	F	Wife	02Se02Sq
MCCORMICK, Mary	22	F	Wife	02Se02Sq
RUSSEL, Mary-Ann	23	F	Wife	02Se02Sq
Margaret	21	F	Wife	02Se02Sq
MURRAY, Patrick	47	M	Farmer	02Se02Sq
Margaret	30	F	Wife	02Se02Sq
Ann	10	F	None	02Se02Sq
Margaret	08	F	Child	02Se02Sq

NAMES OF PASSENGERS	AGE	SEX	OCCUPATIONS	DATE PORT SHIP
MURRAY, Elizabeth	04	F	Child	02Se02Sq
Michael	06	M	Child	02Se02Sq
DONOLLY, Grace	20	F	Spinster	02Se02Sq
KELLY, Maurice	27	M	Farmer	02Se02Sq
Margaret	27	F	Wife	02Se02Sq
ROONEY, Ann	25	F	Wife	02Se02Sq
FEATHERSTON, Cecilia	19	F	Spinster	02Se02Sq
CONNOR, Margaret	17	F	Spinster	02Se02Sq
CRAMER, Elizabeth	60	F	Wi	02Se02Sq
James	16	M	Unknown	02Se02Sq
Thomas	07	M	Child	02Se02Sq
DEMPSEY, Mary	18	F	Spinster	02Se02Sq
SHAW, James	55	M	Stoner	02Se02Sq
Ann	56	F	Wife	02Se02Sq
Elizabeth	20	F	Spinster	02Se02Sq
Charles	16	M	Unknown	02Se02Sq
Rachel	12	F	None	02Se02Sq
Margaret	08	F	Child	02Se02Sq
PURCELL, Julia	20	F	Spinster	02Se02Sq
OWENS, Hannah	30	F	Wife	02Se02Sq
Mary	03	F	Child	02Se02Sq
James	01	M	Child	02Se02Sq
GILL, Mary	21	F	Spinster	02Se02Sq
FLINN, Sarah	06	F	Child	02Se02Sq
Patrick	05	M	Child	02Se02Sq
FANNON, John	16	M	Laborer	02Se02Sq
Michael	12	M	Laborer	02Se02Sq
MCGEE, James	60	M	Weaver	02Se02Sq
Mary	60	F	Wife	02Se02Sq
LYNCH, Ann	18	F	Spinster	02Se02Sq
CARR, Ann	36	F	Wife	02Se02Sq
James	13	M	None	02Se02Sq
John	11	M	None	02Se02Sq
Mary-Ann	09	F	Child	02Se02Sq
Charles	07	M	Child	02Se02Sq
Eleanor	03	F	Child	02Se02Sq
BARN, Mark	20	M	Shoemaker	02Se02Sq
GORDON, Mary-Ann	46	F	Wife	02Se02Sq
Margaret	13	F	Spinster	02Se02Sq
SMITH, Mathew	39	M	Potter	02Se02Sq
Eliza	35	F	Wife	02Se02Sq
Tamar	14	F	Spinster	02Se02Sq
William	12	M	Unknown	02Se02Sq
John	08	M	Child	02Se02Sq
Joseph	09	M	Child	02Se02Sq
Mary	06	F	Child	02Se02Sq
Sarah	04	F	Child	02Se02Sq
William	06	M	Child	02Se02Sq
OWENS, Ellen	40	F	Wi	02Se02Sq
BROWN, John	21	M	Laborer	02Se02Sq
THOMPSON, Richard	45	M	Wool Comber	02Se02Sq
CONNELL, James	33	M	Wool Comber	02Se02Sq
DWYER, Michael	25	M	Wool Comber	02Se02Sq
ASHWORTH, Eliza	43	F	Wife	02Se02Sq
William	25	M	Weaver	02Se02Sq
Maria	23	F	Wife	02Se02Sq
James	22	M	Weaver	02Se02Sq
Margaret	20	F	Weaver	02Se02Sq
Ann	17	F	Weaver	02Se02Sq
Esther	15	F	Weaver	02Se02Sq
Thomas	13	M	Weaver	02Se02Sq
John	09	M	Child	02Se02Sq
Charles	05	M	Child	02Se02Sq
Henry	01	M	Child	02Se02Sq
THOMPSON, Charlotte	25	F	Spinster	02Se02Sq
HARDEN, Betty	19	F	Spinster	02Se02Sq
JOHNSON, Samuel	24	M	Clergyman	02Se02Sq
NALL, Ann	48	F	Wife	02Se02Sq
CARGILL, James	27	M	Servant	02Se02Sq
Frances	25	F	Wife	02Se02Sq
HIBBERT, John	41	M	Iron Turner	02Se02Sq
LYONS, William	41	M	Ctndr	02Se02Sq
JACKSON, Abel	23	M	Spinner	02Se02Sq
ASHWORTH, Sarah	18	F	Spinster	02Se02Sq
WILLIAMS, George	28	M	Engineer	02Se02Sq

NAMES OF PASSENGERS	AGE	SEX	OCCUPATIONS	DATE PORT SHIP
LEACH, Mary-Ann	20	F	Spinster	02Se02Sq
MCLAUGHLAN, Mary-Ann	23	F	Spinster	02Se02Sq
COLLINS, Bridget	24	F	Spinster	02Se02Sq
HANDFORD, John	21	M	Laborer	02Se02Sq
CALLAGHAN, Mary	50	F	Wi	02Se02Sq
Jerry	17	M	Unknown	02Se02Sq
Dan	15	M	Unknown	02Se02Sq
Abigail	12	F	Unknown	02Se02Sq
Cornelius	08	M	Child	02Se02Sq
BELL, Ellen	22	F	Spinster	02Se02Sq
Catherine	20	F	Spinster	02Se02Sq
NOLAND, Essy	18	F	Spinster	02Se02Sq
Eliza	14	F	Spinster	02Se02Sq
Julia	12	F	Spinster	02Se02Sq
COMERFORD, Mary	23	F	Spinster	02Se02Sq
FLOOD, Frances	20	M	Tailor	02Se02Sq
STOKES, William	23	M	Farmer	02Se02Sq
Margaret	23	F	Wife	02Se02Sq
RADY, Johannah	18	F	Spinster	02Se02Sq
KENNEDY, John	45	M	Tanner	02Se02Sq
Ann	40	F	Wife	02Se02Sq
Mary	13	F	None	02Se02Sq
USHER, William	45	M	Tanner	02Se02Sq
Jane	35	F	Wife	02Se02Sq
William	21	M	Molder	02Se02Sq
Jane	19	F	Wife	02Se02Sq
Eliza	06	F	Child	02Se02Sq
LEE, Charles	22	M	Stctr	02Se02Sq
FRENY, James	34	M	Laborer	02Se02Sq
CURTIS, Thomas	40	M	Steward	02Se02Sq
Ellen	35	F	Wife	02Se02Sq
John	18	M	Printer	02Se02Sq
Thomas	16	M	Cbtmkr	02Se02Sq
Mary	10	F	None	02Se02Sq
Robert	05	M	Child	02Se02Sq
LESTER, Peter	40	M	Salter	02Se02Sq
WATER, Michael	60	M	Salter	02Se02Sq
MOORE, John	36	M	Salter	02Se02Sq
MURPHY, Pat	55	M	Salter	02Se02Sq
ROACH, Pat	20	M	Salter	02Se02Sq
James	18	M	Salter	02Se02Sq
FITZPATRICK, Thomas	20	M	Laborer	02Se02Sq
HALL, James	30	M	Mechanic	02Se02Sq
CROWTHER, William	27	M	Ctnsp	02Se02Sq
Amelia	25	F	Wife	02Se02Sq
Elizabeth	03	F	Child	02Se02Sq
Mary-Ann	.06	F	Infant	02Se02Sq
MCCARTHY, Susan	26	F	Spinster	02Se02Sq
HOLLAND, Bridget	28	F	Spinster	02Se02Sq
COCHRANE, Hugh	25	M	Laborer	02Se02Sq
Pat	09	M	Child	02Se02Sq
John	07	M	Child	02Se02Sq
ODONNELL, Mary	20	F	Spinster	02Se02Sq
MCPHILIPS, Bridget	32	F	Wi	02Se02Sq
SHEA, Johannah	21	F	Spinster	02Se02Sq
MORIARTY, Michael	22	M	Farmer	02Se02Sq
MIDDELMAN, Judah	40	M	Distiller	02Se02Sq
SULLIVAN, Tim	28	M	Blacksmith	02Se02Sq
Cornelius	32	M	Laborer	02Se02Sq
HUGHES, William	50	M	Laborer	02Se02Sq
Mary	50	F	Wife	02Se02Sq
Margaret	16	F	Spinster	02Se02Sq
William	10	M	None	02Se02Sq
BRADY, Margaret	16	F	Spinster	02Se02Sq
BYRNE, Thomas	20	M	Laborer	02Se02Sq
MCGARRAN, John	47	M	Gdnr	02Se02Sq
MCARVEY, Mary	35	F	Spinster	02Se02Sq
FORD, Bessy	20	F	Spinster	02Se02Sq
FITZGERALD, Martin	23	M	Laborer	02Se02Sq
DRISCOLL, Ellen	20	F	Spinster	02Se02Sq
BIGLEY, Pat	60	M	Weaver	02Se02Sq
James	19	M	Laborer	02Se02Sq
HOUGHTON, Catherine	19	F	Spinster	02Se02Sq
QUIN, James	25	M	Tailor	02Se02Sq
MORAN, James	23	M	Laborer	02Se02Sq

NAMES OF PASSENGERS	AGE	SEX	OCCUPATIONS	DATE PORT SHIP
GUNNING, Laurence	21	M	Laborer	02Se02Sq
Rosey	22	F	Wife	02Se02Sq
LIPSEIN, Himan	29	M	Tailor	02Se02Sq
Charlotte	28	F	Wife	02Se02Sq
LEE, Margaret	21	F	Spinster	02Se02Sq
RYAN, Andw.	27	M	Laborer	02Se02Sq
Mary-Ann	25	F	Spinster	02Se02Sq
MANNING, Michl.	28	M	Laborer	02Se02Sq

TECUMSEH 03 SEPTEMBER 1847

From Glasgow

NAMES OF PASSENGERS	AGE	SEX	OCCUPATIONS	DATE PORT SHIP
MOORE, Gavin	33	M	Miner	03Se04Sz
Ellen	30	F	Wife	03Se04Sz
Thos.	01	M	Unknown	03Se04Sz
REID, David	60	M	Laborer	03Se04Sz
Helen	58	F	Unknown	03Se04Sz
LEWIS, Alex	31	M	Laborer	03Se04Sz
Helen	30	F	Wife	03Se04Sz
Wm.	01	M	Child	03Se04Sz
MCKAIG, Wm.	40	M	Laborer	03Se04Sz
Jane	14	F	Unknown	03Se04Sz
CAMPBELL, Neil	30	M	Laborer	03Se04Sz
U, Robt.	54	M	Miner	03Se04Sz
Catherine	40	F	Wife	03Se04Sz
Jane	23	F	Unknown	03Se04Sz
Margaret	21	F	Unknown	03Se04Sz
William	17	M	Unknown	03Se04Sz
M.Ann	13	F	Unknown	03Se04Sz
Catharine	09	F	Child	03Se04Sz
Thomas	06	M	Child	03Se04Sz
Robt.	04	M	Child	03Se04Sz
Rose	01	F	Child	03Se04Sz
ROGERS, Mary	60	F	Unknown	03Se04Sz
PEARSON, John	20	M	Unknown	03Se04Sz
ELLIS, Jane	57	F	Unknown	03Se04Sz
Elizabeth	23	F	Unknown	03Se04Sz
Robert	18	M	Unknown	03Se04Sz
George	13	M	Unknown	03Se04Sz
HUME, Wm.	46	M	Unknown	03Se04Sz
Elizabeth	46	F	Wife	03Se04Sz
John	19	M	Unknown	03Se04Sz
Alexander	15	M	Unknown	03Se04Sz
Willm.	11	M	Unknown	03Se04Sz
Arthur	10	M	Unknown	03Se04Sz
Colin	03	M	Child	03Se04Sz
Elizabeth	01	F	Child	03Se04Sz
Christina	01	F	Child	03Se04Sz
SHANKE, James	18	M	Unknown	03Se04Sz
John	13	M	Unknown	03Se04Sz
ROBERTSON, Alexander	00	M	Gentleman	03Se04Sz

MATILDA 04 SEPTEMBER 1847

From Liverpool

NAMES OF PASSENGERS	AGE	SEX	OCCUPATIONS	DATE PORT SHIP
TOMAN, Michl.	25	M	Laborer	04Se02Ta
PARKER, Michl.	30	M	Engineer	04Se02Ta
Cathe.	30	F	Wife	04Se02Ta
Sichn.	03	U	Child	04Se02Ta
KIRKHAM, Thomas	30	M	Spinner	04Se02Ta
John	20	M	Spinner	04Se02Ta
KIRKHAM, Eliza	30	F	Spinner	04Se02Ta
Saml.	11	M	Spinner	04Se02Ta
John	09	M	Child	04Se02Ta
Espechan	07	U	Child	04Se02Ta
GREENY, Edmund	28	M	Carpenter	04Se02Ta
OBRIEN, Thos.	45	M	Farmer	04Se02Ta
Dennis	25	M	Farmer	04Se02Ta
Nora	21	F	Farmer	04Se02Ta
FITZGERALD, Mary	24	F	Farmer	04Se02Ta
TROY, Mickl.	20	M	Laborer	04Se02Ta
Cathn.	17	F	Laborer	04Se02Ta
DOYLE, John	22	M	Laborer	04Se02Ta
Mary	22	F	Wife	04Se02Ta
Edward	.06	M	Infant	04Se02Ta
VANCE, Mary	18	F	Seamstress	04Se02Ta
MALLEY, Allice	18	F	Seamstress	04Se02Ta
FLINN, Wm.	23	M	Laborer	04Se02Ta
MCHOLICAN, James	40	M	Laborer	04Se02Ta
WHEIGTON, Richard	40	M	Mason	04Se02Ta
CULVERT, Mary	20	F	Servant	04Se02Ta
MCCOLLIT, Cornelius	30	M	Farmer	04Se02Ta
Abby	25	F	Wife	04Se02Ta
Cathn.	03	F	Child	04Se02Ta
Honor	.00	F	Infant	04Se02Ta
Timothy	30	M	Farmer	04Se02Ta
Mary	28	F	Wife	04Se02Ta
Jeremiah	02	M	Child	04Se02Ta
STOKER, Henry	40	M	Shoemaker	04Se02Ta
John	08	M	Child	04Se02Ta
DUNFORD, John	30	M	Clothier	04Se02Ta
Charlotte	25	F	Clothier	04Se02Ta
LYNCH, Margt.	25	F	Servant	04Se02Ta
Charlot.	.00	F	Infant	04Se02Ta
KING, John	25	M	Laborer	04Se02Ta
DUFFIN, Margh.	20	F	Servant	04Se02Ta
BLUE, John	20	M	Farmer	04Se02Ta
DOGERTY, Rosana	21	F	Servant	04Se02Ta
COSTELLO, Bernd.	20	M	Laborer	04Se02Ta
Thirsa	20	F	Servant	04Se02Ta
WEBSTER, Mary	40	F	Laborer	04Se02Ta
John	30	M	Laborer	04Se02Ta
Margh.	15	F	Servant	04Se02Ta
Rich.	13	M	Laborer	04Se02Ta
SHERDAN, Mary	20	F	Unknown	04Se02Ta
Peter	18	M	Laborer	04Se02Ta
MCNEIL, Mathew	18	M	Laborer	04Se02Ta
KEARNS, Ann	20	F	Unknown	04Se02Ta
BENCANN, Thos.	20	M	Laborer	04Se02Ta
MCLIRIGAN, Pat.	40	M	Shoemaker	04Se02Ta
Mary	40	F	Wife	04Se02Ta
Biddy	20	F	Shoemaker	04Se02Ta
Mary	10	F	Shoemaker	04Se02Ta
Thos.	07	M	Child	04Se02Ta
Fran.	05	U	Child	04Se02Ta
Mathew	.00	M	Infant	04Se02Ta
HAGAN, Pat	08	M	Child	04Se02Ta
LEE, Nancy	20	F	Servant	04Se02Ta
SMITH, Pat	20	M	Laborer	04Se02Ta
CUNNINGHAM, Charles	45	M	Farmer	04Se02Ta
John	.00	M	Infant	04Se02Ta
Ann	45	F	Wife	04Se02Ta
Edwd.	25	M	Farmer	04Se02Ta
Jas.	23	M	Farmer	04Se02Ta
Pat	20	M	Farmer	04Se02Ta
Charles	16	M	Farmer	04Se02Ta
Mary	25	F	Farmer	04Se02Ta
Ann	02	F	Child	04Se02Ta
MARKY, Margh.	50	F	Farmer	04Se02Ta
BURK, Michael	50	M	Farmer	04Se02Ta
Eliza	50	F	Wife	04Se02Ta
Sarah	20	F	Farmer	04Se02Ta
Mary	19	F	Farmer	04Se02Ta
Thos.	17	M	Farmer	04Se02Ta
Henry	15	M	Farmer	04Se02Ta
Michl.	13	M	Farmer	04Se02Ta

NAMES OF PASSENGERS	AGE	SEX	OCCUPATIONS	DATE PORT SHIP	NAMES OF PASSENGERS	AGE	SEX	OCCUPATIONS	DATE PORT SHIP
ROURKE, Francis	20	M	Gdnr	04Se02Ta	CONNELL, Mary	18	F	Servant	04Se02Ta
Mary	18	F	Gdnr	04Se02Ta	LORD, Edward	58	M	Spinner	04Se02Ta
MCMULLAN, James	45	M	Mason	04Se02Ta	Amelia	40	F	Wife	04Se02Ta
Rebecka	40	F	Wife	04Se02Ta	Edwd.	19	M	Spinner	04Se02Ta
Isabella	20	F	Mason	04Se02Ta	Phebe	26	F	Spinner	04Se02Ta
Nancy	18	F	Mason	04Se02Ta	Rebecka	15	F	Spinner	04Se02Ta
Rebecka	17	F	Mason	04Se02Ta	John	13	M	Spinner	04Se02Ta
Mary	16	F	Mason	04Se02Ta	Amelia	13	F	Spinner	04Se02Ta
SHEANE, James	19	M	Laborer	04Se02Ta	Saml.	09	M	Child	04Se02Ta
Owen	20	M	Laborer	04Se02Ta	Allice	04	F	Child	04Se02Ta
MCLOON, Ellen	20	F	Laborer	04Se02Ta	NORTHROP, Wm.	55	M	Spinner	04Se02Ta
MURPHY, Margh.	12	F	Laborer	04Se02Ta	Nancy	54	F	Wife	04Se02Ta
MCLOON, Pat	12	F	Laborer	04Se02Ta	Joseph	24	M	Spinner	04Se02Ta
COPELAND, Josh.	45	M	Weaver	04Se02Ta	Allice	24	F	Spinner	04Se02Ta
Allice	45	F	Wife	04Se02Ta	John	19	M	Spinner	04Se02Ta
Margt.	04	F	Child	04Se02Ta	Wm.	13	M	Spinner	04Se02Ta
MCLOCKLIN, Mary	40	M	Laborer	04Se02Ta	Betty	13	F	Spinner	04Se02Ta
Cath.	30	M	Laborer	04Se02Ta	Ellin	09	F	Child	04Se02Ta
Betsey	18	M	Laborer	04Se02Ta	Hannah	.00	F	Infant	04Se02Ta
MALON, Peter	40	M	Laborer	04Se02Ta	MCMENNAY, James	26	M	Laborer	04Se02Ta
Isabella	40	F	Wife	04Se02Ta	Mary-Ann	24	F	Laborer	04Se02Ta
Rose	20	F	Laborer	04Se02Ta	MCHENY, Danl.	25	F	Laborer	04Se02Ta
Jas.	10	M	Laborer	04Se02Ta	BERRY, John	25	F	Laborer	04Se02Ta
Ann	08	F	Child	04Se02Ta	QUIRK, Martin	25	F	Laborer	04Se02Ta
DUFFY, Ellen	20	F	Servant	04Se02Ta	Ann	14	F	Laborer	04Se02Ta
MULLAN, Charles	22	M	Laborer	04Se02Ta	MORAN, Thos.	40	M	Laborer	04Se02Ta
MCMANUS, Pat.	12	M	Laborer	04Se02Ta	MCGUIRE, Philip	21	M	Laborer	04Se02Ta
MCELLVEEN, Robt.	45	M	Wheelwright	04Se02Ta	DELANY, Robt.	34	M	Farmer	04Se02Ta
John	15	M	Wheelwright	04Se02Ta	DONAHOE, Danl.	48	M	Saddler	04Se02Ta
Margt.	17	F	Wheelwright	04Se02Ta	GIFFEN, John	21	M	Laborer	04Se02Ta
MAHAHAN, Michl.	40	M	Laborer	04Se02Ta	FALLON, Thos.	34	M	Laborer	04Se02Ta
Nancy	40	F	Wife	04Se02Ta	SAUNDERS, David	45	M	Iron Worker	04Se02Ta
Betty	11	F	Laborer	04Se02Ta	Ann	40	F	Wife	04Se02Ta
Ann	09	F	Child	04Se02Ta	Joseph	20	M	Iron Worker	04Se02Ta
Mary	06	F	Child	04Se02Ta	Louisa	25	F	Iron Worker	04Se02Ta
Cathn.	.00	F	Infant	04Se02Ta	GRIFFETHS, John	21	M	Iron Worker	04Se02Ta
Margt.	10	F	Laborer	04Se02Ta	Eliza	24	F	Iron Worker	04Se02Ta
DONALD, Mary	40	F	Laborer	04Se02Ta	SAUNDERS, John	19	M	Iron Worker	04Se02Ta
Margt.	15	F	Laborer	04Se02Ta	PHILIPS, Joseph	28	M	Iron Worker	04Se02Ta
Jas.	12	M	Laborer	04Se02Ta	SAUNDERS, Ger.	11	M	Iron Worker	04Se02Ta
Cath.	10	F	Laborer	04Se02Ta	Ellen	09	F	Child	04Se02Ta
MCENNA, Thos.	20	M	Laborer	04Se02Ta	GRIFFETH, Henry	.00	F	Infant	04Se02Ta
SULIVAN, Cath.	28	M	Laborer	04Se02Ta	SAUNDERS, Jeremiah	.00	F	Infant	04Se02Ta
John	04	M	Child	04Se02Ta	MCLOCKLIN, Thos.	12	M	Sawer	04Se02Ta
Mary	02	F	Child	04Se02Ta	TAYLOR, John	30	M	Laborer	04Se02Ta
IGO, Cathn.	20	F	Servant	04Se02Ta	U	25	F	Wife	04Se02Ta
BRACKEN, Mary	45	F	Laborer	04Se02Ta	Betty	13	F	Laborer	04Se02Ta
Kernan	25	M	Laborer	04Se02Ta	Danl.	12	M	Laborer	04Se02Ta
KEARNEY, Michl.	40	M	Laborer	04Se02Ta	Alex.	09	M	Child	04Se02Ta
Cath.	40	F	Wife	04Se02Ta	SULIVAN, James	20	M	Laborer	04Se02Ta
Pat	10	M	Laborer	04Se02Ta	KENEDY, Philip	25	M	Laborer	04Se02Ta
John	08	M	Child	04Se02Ta	CLARK, John	23	M	Saddler	04Se02Ta
Mary	04	F	Child	04Se02Ta	U	23	F	Wife	04Se02Ta
Mick	02	M	Child	04Se02Ta	U	.00	U	Infant	04Se02Ta
Ellen	.00	F	Infant	04Se02Ta	DUNN, Michl.	30	M	Laborer	04Se02Ta
PATTERSON, Ann	20	F	Servant	04Se02Ta	ELDERTON, Eliza	25	M	Laborer	04Se02Ta
WILLIAMSON, Jas.	40	M	Gdnr	04Se02Ta	Mary	.00	F	Infant	04Se02Ta
Mary	40	F	Wife	04Se02Ta	MANYAN, Bridget	22	F	Servant	04Se02Ta
Charles	14	M	Gdnr	04Se02Ta	DOGERTY, Margt.	20	F	Servant	04Se02Ta
John	13	M	Gdnr	04Se02Ta	FITZGERALD, James	24	M	Carpenter	04Se02Ta
Eloise	11	F	Gdnr	04Se02Ta	MORARTY, Wm.	23	M	Laborer	04Se02Ta
Geo.	09	M	Child	04Se02Ta	NEIL, James	22	M	Laborer	04Se02Ta
Charlotte	07	F	Child	04Se02Ta	MONAHAN, Bridget	22	M	Laborer	04Se02Ta
Robert	04	M	Child	04Se02Ta	U	.00	U	Infant	04Se02Ta
REYNOLDS, Pat	20	M	Laborer	04Se02Ta	BRADY, Pat	22	M	Laborer	04Se02Ta
John	11	M	Laborer	04Se02Ta	MEAN, Thomas	26	M	Laborer	04Se02Ta
BUSBAY, Margh.	20	F	Laborer	04Se02Ta	John	06	M	Child	04Se02Ta
FEGAN, Mary	20	F	Servant	04Se02Ta	KEERNAN, Sarah	20	F	Blacksmith	04Se02Ta
DALEY, Andr.	60	M	Laborer	04Se02Ta	Pat	21	M	Blacksmith	04Se02Ta
Biddy	60	F	Wife	04Se02Ta	MCQUIRE, John	47	M	Laborer	04Se02Ta
CRENAN, Bid.M.	23	F	Laborer	04Se02Ta	Ann	42	F	Laborer	04Se02Ta
KENEDY, Geo.	25	M	Laborer	04Se02Ta	Charles	10	M	Laborer	04Se02Ta
FOSTER, Thos.	47	M	Farmer	04Se02Ta	KELLY, Isabella	20	F	Servant	04Se02Ta
Margt.	46	F	Wife	04Se02Ta	GILLES, Ellen	21	F	Servant	04Se02Ta
Wm.	20	M	Farmer	04Se02Ta	FRAIN, John	40	M	Laborer	04Se02Ta

NAMES OF PASSENGERS	AGE	SEX	OCCUPATIONS	DATE PORT SHIP
FRAIN, Bridget	22	F	Laborer	04Se02Ta
GANNAN, Pat	21	M	Laborer	04Se02Ta
Michl.	20	M	Laborer	04Se02Ta
Judy	21	F	Laborer	04Se02Ta
Anthony	10	M	Laborer	04Se02Ta
SMITH, Cath.	36	F	Laborer	04Se02Ta
John	24	M	Laborer	04Se02Ta
Edward	12	M	Laborer	04Se02Ta
FRYE, Ann	26	F	Laborer	04Se02Ta
Joseph	10	M	Laborer	04Se02Ta
FURLEY, Bridget	18	F	Laborer	04Se02Ta
NOON, Bridget	20	F	Laborer	04Se02Ta
Mary	20	F	Laborer	04Se02Ta
John	40	M	Laborer	04Se02Ta
SHANNON, Mary	08	F	Child	04Se02Ta
MURRY, Jane	50	F	Laborer	04Se02Ta
Pat	28	F	Laborer	04Se02Ta
Mary	27	F	Wife	04Se02Ta
Jane	02	F	Child	04Se02Ta
CASEY, Jeremiah	20	M	Carpenter	04Se02Ta
SMITH, Martha	20	F	Laborer	04Se02Ta
SHERIDAN, Margt.	20	F	Servant	04Se02Ta
GILLESPIE, Isabella	18	F	Servant	04Se02Ta
MATIRSON, Edward	45	M	Laborer	04Se02Ta
Richrd.	13	M	Laborer	04Se02Ta
CARNE, Emanuel	30	M	Tailor	04Se02Ta
RAYLAN, Wm.	35	M	Laborer	04Se02Ta
Elana	35	F	Laborer	04Se02Ta
FITZPATRICK, Bridget	18	F	Servant	04Se02Ta
CURLEY, Margt.	19	F	Servant	04Se02Ta
MCDONALD, James	24	M	Tailor	04Se02Ta
HYMEN, Agness	18	F	Servant	04Se02Ta

BURLINGTON 06 SEPTEMBER 1847

From Liverpool

NAMES OF PASSENGERS	AGE	SEX	OCCUPATIONS	DATE PORT SHIP
NEALIS, Pat	23	M	Laborer	06Se02Ja
MONDAY, Cath.	18	F	Spinster	06Se02Ja
HARATY, Sophia	20	F	Spinster	06Se02Ja
LYONS, Owen	28	M	Laborer	06Se02Ja
MORRIS, Ellen	40	F	Wife	06Se02Ja
Anastasia	20	F	Spinster	06Se02Ja
CARROL, Ann	45	F	Wife	06Se02Ja
Biddy	24	F	Spinster	06Se02Ja
Ann	18	F	Spinster	06Se02Ja
John	16	M	None	06Se02Ja
Patrick	11	M	None	06Se02Ja
Thomas	08	M	Child	06Se02Ja
HALL, Eliz.	23	F	Milliner	06Se02Ja
HIGGINS, John	32	M	Laborer	06Se02Ja
SHERIDAN, Mich.	26	M	Laborer	06Se02Ja
MULHALL, James	23	M	Laborer	06Se02Ja
BURLIGH, Wm.	30	M	Miner	06Se02Ja
DUFF, Richard	60	M	Laborer	06Se02Ja
James	20	M	Shoemaker	06Se02Ja
Cath.	17	F	Spinster	06Se02Ja
Margaret	22	F	Wife	06Se02Ja
HERMAN, Ann	07	F	Child	06Se02Ja
DUFF, Ann	00	F	Child	06Se02Ja
FALLON, John	24	M	Laborer	06Se02Ja
Maria (W)	20	F	Wife	06Se02Ja
MCCORMACK, Ann	34	F	Unknown	06Se02Ja
LEE, John	36	M	Seaman	06Se02Ja
DUGGAN, Pat	26	M	Seaman	06Se02Ja
HAYES, Dennis	30	M	Seaman	06Se02Ja
U, P.	18	M	Clerk	06Se02Ja
HANES, Bridget	00	F	Spinster	06Se02Ja
HARDYMAN, Winifred	20	F	Spinster	06Se02Ja
HARDYMAN, Thomas	60	M	Laborer	06Se02Ja
Margaret	50	F	Wife	06Se02Ja
John	16	M	None	06Se02Ja
Bridget	03	F	Child	06Se02Ja
DUNNING, Honora	22	F	Spinster	06Se02Ja
HINES, Ellen	40	F	Spinster	06Se02Ja
BREENAN, Wm.	21	M	Laborer	06Se02Ja
DEACON, John	18	M	Carpenter	06Se02Ja
PAMISON, Jane	22	F	Dressmaker	06Se02Ja
HANLY, Margaret	21	F	Spinster	06Se02Ja
ODONNEL, Rose-A.	18	F	Spinster	06Se02Ja
Eliza	12	F	None	06Se02Ja
MCCLUSKY, Bessy	21	F	Spinster	06Se02Ja
MORRIS, Pat	38	M	Laborer	06Se02Ja
Margaret (W)	30	F	Wife	06Se02Ja
Thomas	14	M	None	06Se02Ja
John	10	M	None	06Se02Ja
Richard	08	M	Child	06Se02Ja
James	05	M	Child	06Se02Ja
Pat	03	M	Child	06Se02Ja
Cath.	00	F	Child	06Se02Ja
DIVER, Edward	27	M	Laborer	06Se02Ja
John	21	M	Laborer	06Se02Ja
ELLIOT, Pat	40	M	Tailor	06Se02Ja
HIGGINS, Mary	27	F	Wife	06Se02Ja
Catherine	25	F	Spinster	06Se02Ja
Bernard	09	M	Child	06Se02Ja
Pat	07	M	Child	06Se02Ja
MCGEE, Wm.	16	M	Laborer	06Se02Ja
MORGAN, Daniel	21	M	Weaver	06Se02Ja
GORMLEY, Bridget	18	F	Spinster	06Se02Ja
Rosanna	16	F	Spinster	06Se02Ja
MONDAY, Daniel	35	M	Laborer	06Se02Ja
HENERY, Mary	16	F	Spinster	06Se02Ja
NEILL, Mary	24	F	Spinster	06Se02Ja
CUNIFF, Peter	70	M	Laborer	06Se02Ja
Bridget (W)	40	F	Wife	06Se02Ja
Thomas	08	M	Child	06Se02Ja
MARTIN, John	17	M	Laborer	06Se02Ja
Mary-Ann	19	F	Spinster	06Se02Ja
GAFFNEY, Cath.	20	F	Spinster	06Se02Ja
KILROY, John	38	M	Farmer	06Se02Ja
Anne (W)	30	F	Wife	06Se02Ja
Cath.	05	F	Child	06Se02Ja
MILLS, Alice	24	F	Spinster	06Se02Ja
Sarah	15	F	Spinster	06Se02Ja
Julia	06	F	Child	06Se02Ja
James	05	M	Child	06Se02Ja
Thomas	03	M	Child	06Se02Ja
GALLAGHER, Francis	20	M	Laborer	06Se02Ja
Pat.	19	M	Laborer	06Se02Ja
BRENNAN, Ann	20	F	Spinster	06Se02Ja
BURKE, John	21	M	Laborer	06Se02Ja
Pat.	18	M	Laborer	06Se02Ja
Thos.	16	M	Laborer	06Se02Ja
JORDAN, Thomas	20	M	Laborer	06Se02Ja
LONG, Margaret	20	F	Spinster	06Se02Ja
MAXWELL, Ann	19	F	Spinster	06Se02Ja
MCKEE, Nancy	20	F	Spinster	06Se02Ja
SLAVIN, John	24	M	Laborer	06Se02Ja
KENNEDY, Mich.	20	M	Laborer	06Se02Ja
Eleanor	20	F	Spinster	06Se02Ja
SLAVIN, Bernard	24	M	Laborer	06Se02Ja
REEGAN, Matt.	25	M	Laborer	06Se02Ja
MCLIGHE, John	40	M	Laborer	06Se02Ja
Stephen	29	M	Laborer	06Se02Ja
Bryan	25	M	Laborer	06Se02Ja
Martin	24	M	Laborer	06Se02Ja
FINCH, John	30	M	Laborer	06Se02Ja
ALLEN, Peter	19	M	Laborer	06Se02Ja
DALEY, Mich.	32	M	Laborer	06Se02Ja
Jas.	18	M	Gdnr	06Se02Ja
Mary	18	F	Spinster	06Se02Ja
Thos.	12	M	None	06Se02Ja
Joseph	10	M	None	06Se02Ja

NAMES OF PASSENGERS		AGE	SEX	OCCUPATIONS	DATE PORT SHIP
DALEY, Ann		07	F	Child	06Se02Ja
MIVINE, Sarah		20	F	Spinster	06Se02Ja
Mich.		19	M	Laborer	06Se02Ja
REILLY, James		45	M	Laborer	06Se02Ja
Margt.	(W)	40	F	Wife	06Se02Ja
Jerry		11	M	None	06Se02Ja
Mary		12	F	None	06Se02Ja
Bessy		07	F	Child	06Se02Ja
Jas.Jr.		00	M	Child	06Se02Ja
CONNOUGHTON, Jas.		22	M	Laborer	06Se02Ja
Hugh		24	M	Laborer	06Se02Ja
CONNERTON, Aley		22	F	Spinster	06Se02Ja
ACHERSON, Stewart		00	M	Laborer	06Se02Ja
Dorothy		20	F	Spinster	06Se02Ja
MCGOVERN, Ann		18	F	Spinster	06Se02Ja
FAGAN, Susan		18	F	Spinster	06Se02Ja
BOYLE, Dominick		24	M	Laborer	06Se02Ja
Luke		20	M	Laborer	06Se02Ja
Ann		24	F	Spinster	06Se02Ja
FERRITY, Bridget		20	F	Spinster	06Se02Ja
KENNEDY, Edwd.		26	M	Laborer	06Se02Ja
KELLY, John		26	M	Laborer	06Se02Ja
FLINN, Bernard		16	M	Laborer	06Se02Ja
Mary		13	F	None	06Se02Ja
Bridget		19	F	Spinster	06Se02Ja
DUNN, Ellen		18	F	Spinster	06Se02Ja
Mary		14	F	Spinster	06Se02Ja
BRYAN, Neil		32	M	Laborer	06Se02Ja
Bridget	(W)	30	F	Wife	06Se02Ja
Mary-Ann		14	F	None	06Se02Ja
Thomas		11	M	None	06Se02Ja
BEAHAN, Robt.		18	M	Shoemaker	06Se02Ja
RYAN, Martha		19	F	Spinster	06Se02Ja
MCMURA, Wm.		30	M	Laborer	06Se02Ja
CAREY, Daniel		20	M	Laborer	06Se02Ja
CONNOLLY, Pat.		29	M	Laborer	06Se02Ja
QUIN, Rosanna		24	F	Spinster	06Se02Ja
FORNEY, Mich.		26	M	Laborer	06Se02Ja
BRADLEY, John		13	M	None	06Se02Ja
CUNNINGHAM, Pat.		27	M	Laborer	06Se02Ja
DOLAN, Mich.		20	M	Laborer	06Se02Ja
RYAN, Tim		24	M	Laborer	06Se02Ja
Biddy		20	F	Spinster	06Se02Ja
Ellen		22	F	Spinster	06Se02Ja
MURPHY, Margaret		28	F	Spinster	06Se02Ja
OHAGAN, Ann		22	F	Spinster	06Se02Ja
MCKENNA, John		26	M	Laborer	06Se02Ja
CHAPLIN, Samuel		21	M	Physician	06Se02Ja
BRACKIN, J.		19	M	Farmer	06Se02Ja
GRADY, J.Maria		22	F	None	06Se02Ja
Cath.		24	F	None	06Se02Ja

EMMA-WATTS 06 SEPTEMBER 1847

From London

NAMES OF PASSENGERS		AGE	SEX	OCCUPATIONS	DATE PORT SHIP
SMITH, John		38	M	Farmer	06Se21Tb
Ann	(W)	35	F	Wife	06Se21Tb
Mary	(D)	10	F	None	06Se21Tb
Sarah	(D)	08	F	Child	06Se21Tb
Susan	(D)	06	F	Child	06Se21Tb
George	(S)	04	M	Child	06Se21Tb
Charles	(S)	02	M	Child	06Se21Tb
PURVIS, James		46	M	Tailor	06Se21Tb
Mary-Ann	(W)	37	F	Wife	06Se21Tb
John-James	(S)	18	M	Unknown	06Se21Tb
SPENCE, Richard		44	M	Cbtmkr	06Se21Tb
Elizabeth	(W)	43	F	Wife	06Se21Tb
Mary-Ann	(D)	22	F	Unknown	06Se21Tb
SPENCE, Richard	(S)	20	M	Unknown	06Se21Tb
Elizabeth	(D)	18	F	Unknown	06Se21Tb
Charles	(S)	06	M	Child	06Se21Tb
Edward	(S)	04	M	Child	06Se21Tb
Alfred	(S)	03	M	Child	06Se21Tb
Isabella	(D)	.00	F	Infant	06Se21Tb
FORSTER, Kinan		24	M	Cbtmkr	06Se21Tb
SEYMOR, William		24	M	Cbtmkr	06Se21Tb
WOODWARD, Charles		27	M	Cbtmkr	06Se21Tb
SMITH, John		25	M	Cbtmkr	06Se21Tb
SHARP, John-Wilson		22	M	Cbtmkr	06Se21Tb
Ocl--NE, William-H.		28	M	Watchmaker	06Se21Tb
Jane	(W)	21	F	Wife	06Se21Tb
FORD, Owen		30	M	Plasterer	06Se21Tb
Mary	(W)	30	F	Wife	06Se21Tb
Ann	(D)	03	F	Child	06Se21Tb
HUNTER, John		40	M	Unknown	06Se21Tb
GORNER, Patrick		26	M	Unknown	06Se21Tb
HART, Angel		25	M	Tbcmcht	06Se21Tb
Sarah	(W)	25	F	Wife	06Se21Tb
Amelia	(D)	.00	F	Infant	06Se21Tb
WEDD, John		27	M	Farmer	06Se21Tb
Emma	(W)	25	F	Wife	06Se21Tb
Emma	(D)	02	F	Child	06Se21Tb
John	(S)	.00	M	Infant	06Se21Tb
LAZARUS, Joseph		25	M	Farmer	06Se21Tb
HUNTER, Wm.		46	M	Silk Weaver	06Se21Tb
John	(S)	14	M	Silk Weaver	06Se21Tb
David	(S)	13	M	Silk Weaver	06Se21Tb
DAVENPORT, Robert		25	M	Farmer	06Se21Tb
HUSBAND, Charles		27	M	Farmer	06Se21Tb
SHEPARD, John		28	M	Saddler	06Se21Tb
Eliza	(W)	27	F	Wife	06Se21Tb
Benjamin	(S)	.00	M	Infant	06Se21Tb
HENESSY, Robert		20	M	Farmer	06Se21Tb
MCHUGH, Thomas		31	M	Farmer	06Se21Tb
Bridget	(W)	31	F	Wife	06Se21Tb
Mary-Ann	(D)	05	F	Child	06Se21Tb
Thomas	(S)	03	M	Child	06Se21Tb
Annie	(D)	.00	F	Infant	06Se21Tb
SAMUEL, Jacob		23	M	Tailor	06Se21Tb
MYER, Saul		21	M	Tailor	06Se21Tb
LYDEN, B.		19	M	Tailor	06Se21Tb
JACOB, Jacob		22	M	Tailor	06Se21Tb
LAPMAN, Barnard		47	M	Tailor	06Se21Tb
HOUGH, Samuel		47	M	Whitesmith	06Se21Tb
CLARK, John		34	M	Gdnr	06Se21Tb
MYERS, John		39	M	Farmer	06Se21Tb
Margaret	(W)	35	F	Wife	06Se21Tb
Mary	(D)	12	F	Farmer	06Se21Tb
Patrick	(S)	10	M	Farmer	06Se21Tb
Joanna	(D)	08	F	Child	06Se21Tb
Ellen	(D)	04	F	Child	06Se21Tb
Margaret		.00	F	Infant	06Se21Tb
HUSSEY, Charles		25	M	Ppstr	06Se21Tb
Elizabeth		54	F	Unknown	06Se21Tb
Elizabeth	(T)	36	F	Unknown	06Se21Tb
Harriott	(T)	31	F	Unknown	06Se21Tb
Mary-Ann	(T)	22	F	Unknown	06Se21Tb
Isaac		13	M	Unknown	06Se21Tb
PUNTER, Henry		25	M	Ppstr	06Se21Tb

SWITZERLAND 06 SEPTEMBER 1847

From London

NAMES OF PASSENGERS		AGE	SEX	OCCUPATIONS	DATE PORT SHIP
DILLON, Frederick		31	M	Farmer	06Se21Al
Catharine		31	F	Wife	06Se21Al
John	(S)	06	M	Child	06Se21Al

NAMES OF PASSENGERS		AGE	SEX	OCCUPATIONS	DATE PORT SHIP
INESS, U-Mrs.		27	F	None	06Se21AI
U		11	F	None	06Se21AI
YATES, U		30	M	Upholsterer	06Se21AI
WILLOCK, W.		25	M	Clerk	06Se21AI
PONIER, U		21	M	Clerk	06Se21AI

PALMETTO 06 SEPTEMBER 1847

From Rio-De-Janiero

NAMES OF PASSENGERS		AGE	SEX	OCCUPATIONS	DATE PORT SHIP
SAUNDERS, Francis		35	M	Merchant	06Se13Tc

JANE-MORISON 07 SEPTEMBER 1847

From Glasgow

NAMES OF PASSENGERS		AGE	SEX	OCCUPATIONS	DATE PORT SHIP
MCIVER, John		50	M	Farmer	07Se04Td
Jane	(W)	50	F	Wife	07Se04Td
Mary		23	F	Servant	07Se04Td
Daniel		28	M	Farmer	07Se04Td
Alexander		20	M	Farmer	07Se04Td
James		17	M	Farmer	07Se04Td
Elizabeth		13	M	Farmer	07Se04Td
John		11	M	Farmer	07Se04Td
Thomas		09	M	Child	07Se04Td
BROWN, Samuel		33	M	Farmer	07Se04Td
MARTIN, Eliza		15	F	Servant	07Se04Td

CHAOS 08 SEPTEMBER 1847

From Liverpool

NAMES OF PASSENGERS		AGE	SEX	OCCUPATIONS	DATE PORT SHIP
CACHMAN, William		24	M	Wlmcht	08Se02Gg
DONAHOE, Catherine		60	F	None	08Se02Gg
Margaret	(D)	20	F	Servant	08Se02Gg
CRANE, Anthony		20	M	Laborer	08Se02Gg
ADAMS, Isabella		18	F	Servant	08Se02Gg
TRAYNOR, Patt		19	M	Laborer	08Se02Gg
DOWNEY, Isabella		30	F	Servant	08Se02Gg
GRIFFEN, Matthew		26	M	Tailor	08Se02Gg
DERVIN, James		43	M	Laborer	08Se02Gg
Bridgt.		36	F	None	08Se02Gg
Margaret		21	F	None	08Se02Gg
Catherine		19	F	None	08Se02Gg
John		16	M	None	08Se02Gg
Elizabeth		13	F	None	08Se02Gg
Patt		12	M	None	08Se02Gg
Biddy		09	F	Child	08Se02Gg
Thomas		02	M	Child	08Se02Gg
James		23	M	Laborer	08Se02Gg
Mary		23	F	Servant	08Se02Gg
KENNEDY, William		50	M	Laborer	08Se02Gg
KELLY, Ellen		19	F	Servant	08Se02Gg
MCCLOUD, Jackson		20	M	Laborer	08Se02Gg
MURRAY, Bridget		40	F	Servant	08Se02Gg
MOLLOY, John		20	M	Laborer	08Se02Gg
DELANY, William		29	M	Laborer	08Se02Gg
DELANY, Mary		27	F	Servant	08Se02Gg
WALSH, Lucy		30	F	Servant	08Se02Gg
John		04	M	Child	08Se02Gg
MANLY, Patt		18	M	Laborer	08Se02Gg
Nancy		10	F	Servant	08Se02Gg
DORMOTTY, Mary		20	F	Servant	08Se02Gg
LARKIN, Bridget		22	F	Servant	08Se02Gg
Catherine		18	F	Servant	08Se02Gg
MCAVOY, Bridget		16	F	Servant	08Se02Gg
MADDON, Maria		20	F	Servant	08Se02Gg
MURPHY, Mary		20	F	Dressmaker	08Se02Gg
KELLY, Mary		19	F	Servant	08Se02Gg
KENNEDY, Bridget		55	F	Servant	08Se02Gg
Eliza		14	F	Servant	08Se02Gg
DONAHOE, Patt.		30	M	Laborer	08Se02Gg
Catherine		24	F	Servant	08Se02Gg
Catherine		22	F	Servant	08Se02Gg
Ellen		.04	F	Infant	08Se02Gg
ARMSTRONG, Lancelot		30	M	Shoemaker	08Se02Gg
Margaret		30	F	None	08Se02Gg
Ann		09	F	Child	08Se02Gg
Thomas		04	M	Child	08Se02Gg
KELLY, Thomas		21	M	Laborer	08Se02Gg
DOONE, Bernard		45	M	Butcher	08Se02Gg
GOODSON, William		40	M	Laborer	08Se02Gg
Richard		15	M	Laborer	08Se02Gg
GILLAN, Margaret		20	F	Servant	08Se02Gg
CUMMINS, William		32	M	Mason	08Se02Gg
CONLAY, Thomas		36	M	Carpenter	08Se02Gg
QUALE, John		20	M	Boatmaker	08Se02Gg
KEANE, William		17	M	Carpenter	08Se02Gg
MCNALLY, Nancy		27	F	Servant	08Se02Gg
Margaret		20	F	Servant	08Se02Gg
MOONEY, Sarah		37	F	None	08Se02Gg
John		10	M	None	08Se02Gg
Rose		07	F	None	08Se02Gg
William		05	M	None	08Se02Gg
REY, May		13	F	None	08Se02Gg
BANNON, James		30	M	Laborer	08Se02Gg
Ann		30	F	None	08Se02Gg
Thomas		09	M	Child	08Se02Gg
Michael		05	M	Child	08Se02Gg
Timothy		03	M	Child	08Se02Gg
CONNER, Catherine		22	F	Servant	08Se02Gg
Margaret		05	F	Child	08Se02Gg
Mary		04	F	Child	08Se02Gg
MULANY, Anthony		19	M	Laborer	08Se02Gg
KILBRAITH, Elizabeth		32	F	Servant	08Se02Gg
FARRELLY, Mary		22	F	Servant	08Se02Gg
Michael		21	M	Laborer	08Se02Gg
LEE, Hugh		24	M	Laborer	08Se02Gg
Bridget		20	F	Servant	08Se02Gg
BRADY, Honora		30	F	None	08Se02Gg
Mary		00	F	None	08Se02Gg
GAHAGAN, Owen		40	M	Laborer	08Se02Gg
Catherine		30	F	None	08Se02Gg
John		11	M	None	08Se02Gg
Mary		09	F	Child	08Se02Gg
Catherine		05	F	Child	08Se02Gg
Ann		04	F	Child	08Se02Gg
FENY, John		24	M	Laborer	08Se02Gg
Denis		20	M	Laborer	08Se02Gg
Rose		20	F	Servant	08Se02Gg
CONROY, John		20	M	Shoemaker	08Se02Gg
Rose		19	F	Servant	08Se02Gg
Thomas		18	M	Laborer	08Se02Gg
COLLOTON, Sarah		20	F	Servant	08Se02Gg
KILBRIDE, Owen		60	M	None	08Se02Gg
DOLANEY, James		22	M	Laborer	08Se02Gg
Deborah		16	F	None	08Se02Gg
MCGRATH, Hugh		27	M	Carpenter	08Se02Gg
Margaret		20	F	None	08Se02Gg
Jane		13	F	None	08Se02Gg
Jane		04	F	Child	08Se02Gg
Eliza		02	F	Child	08Se02Gg

NAMES OF PASSENGERS		AGE	SEX	OCCUPATIONS	DATE PORT SHIP
MCGRATH, James		.03	M	Infant	08Se02Gg
CUNNINGHAM, John		20	M	Laborer	08Se02Gg
FARRELL, John		29	M	Laborer	08Se02Gg
RICHARDS, Ann		23	F	Servant	08Se02Gg
WINN, Honora		17	F	Servant	08Se02Gg
MCGEE, Ellen		20	F	Servant	08Se02Gg
DOOLEY, Michael		24	M	Laborer	08Se02Gg
KENNEDY, Margaret		19	F	Servant	08Se02Gg
GRAY, Ann		18	F	Servant	08Se02Gg
MOONEY, William		28	M	Laborer	08Se02Gg
KERMODE, Elizabeth		35	F	Cnf	08Se02Gg
BRADY, Rose		28	F	Servant	08Se02Gg
CONNER, U		25	M	Laborer	08Se02Gg
GUGARTY, Thomas		40	M	Laborer	08Se02Gg
Died-At-Sea					
Biddy	(D)	14	F	Servant	08Se02Gg
Catherine	(D)	13	F	Servant	08Se02Gg
COOK, John		28	M	Laborer	08Se02Gg
Mary		40	F	None	08Se02Gg
CARROLL, William		43	M	Coach Maker	08Se02Gg
Joseph	(S)	25	M	Coach Maker	08Se02Gg
Sarah	(W)	46	F	None	08Se02Gg
ENNIS, Daniel		30	M	Blacksmith	08Se02Gg
BOYLE, Henry		21	M	Carpenter	08Se02Gg
FLOOD, James		18	M	Laborer	08Se02Gg
THOMAS, Richard		22	M	Printer	08Se02Gg
CLARK, David		16	M	Printer	08Se02Gg
TRACY, Mary		20	F	Servant	08Se02Gg
Catherine		18	F	Servant	08Se02Gg
GOODWIN, James		39	M	Printer	08Se02Gg
FARRELL, James		20	M	Laborer	08Se02Gg
KELLY, Ann		20	F	Servant	08Se02Gg
THORN, Margaret		43	F	Servant	08Se02Gg
ROURKE, Patt.		20	M	Blacksmith	08Se02Gg
Mary		17	F	Servant	08Se02Gg
FORKEN, James		40	M	Laborer	08Se02Gg
Margaret	(W)	40	F	Wife	08Se02Gg
Esther	(D)	07	F	Child	08Se02Gg
Margaret	(D)	06	F	Child	08Se02Gg
Elizabeth	(D)	04	F	Child	08Se02Gg
Thomas	(S)	02	M	Child	08Se02Gg
Mary	(D)	.03	F	Infant	08Se02Gg
DAVIS, Thomas		19	M	Saddler	08Se02Gg
TULLY, Luke		26	M	Saddler	08Se02Gg
HARRISSON, William		25	M	Engineer	08Se02Gg
Thomas		24	M	Mnftr	08Se02Gg
OCONNER, Michael		21	M	Tailor	08Se02Gg
WHITE, Thomas		39	M	Painter	08Se02Gg
FIELDS, Charles		30	M	Lmnftr	08Se02Gg
Julia	(W)	38	F	Wife	08Se02Gg
John	(S)	07	M	Child	08Se02Gg
ARMSTRONG, Eliza		19	F	None	08Se02Gg
WHITE, Michael		63	M	Mnftr	08Se02Gg
Rose		61	F	None	08Se02Gg
PROTHER, Jane		20	F	None	08Se02Gg
CUNNINGHAM, Patt.		25	M	None	08Se02Gg
MOONEY, Roger		24	M	None	08Se02Gg
HOLIGHENSON, Daniel		30	M	Machinist	08Se02Gg
BANNON, Richard		23	M	Carpenter	08Se02Gg
GARDNER, Thomas		20	M	Shoemaker	08Se02Gg
NUGENT, Michael		20	M	Shoemaker	08Se02Gg
COOPER, Benjamin		23	M	Mnftr	08Se02Gg
WALL, John		25	M	Laborer	08Se02Gg
Margaret		22	F	None	08Se02Gg
Catherine		21	F	Dressmaker	08Se02Gg
CLARK, William		20	M	Laborer	08Se02Gg
WARING, Nancy		19	F	Dressmaker	08Se02Gg
CONNEL, John		21	M	Laborer	08Se02Gg
WELBAT, Christy		70	M	Weaver	08Se02Gg
SULLIVAN, Ann		21	F	Servant	08Se02Gg
DORSEY, Mary		12	F	Servant	08Se02Gg
DWYER, Matthew		40	M	Laborer	08Se02Gg
Margaret	(W)	30	F	Wife	08Se02Gg
Michael	(S)	13	M	None	08Se02Gg
KELLY, Patt.		26	M	Laborer	08Se02Gg
DUNN, Ann		24	F	Servant	08Se02Gg
WRIGLEY, James		24	M	Laborer	08Se02Gg
CHARLEY, John		20	M	Laborer	08Se02Gg
Catherine		18	F	Servant	08Se02Gg
BELLOWS, Allice		20	F	Servant	08Se02Gg
MONOHAN, James		20	M	Laborer	08Se02Gg
HUGHES, Mary		32	F	Laborer	08Se02Gg
John	(S)	13	M	Laborer	08Se02Gg
Michael	(S)	09	M	Child	08Se02Gg
ROGERS, Michael		40	M	Laborer	08Se02Gg
MCNEILL, Ann		25	M	Servant	08Se02Gg
BUNNON, Mary		25	M	Servant	08Se02Gg
HANICHY, Samuel		22	M	Spinner	08Se02Gg
CLENWORTH, Charles		18	M	Dyer	08Se02Gg
CONNER, Edward		22	M	Lrctr	08Se02Gg
OLDFIELD, Joseph		30	M	Spinner	08Se02Gg
DUGGAN, William		31	M	Butcher	08Se02Gg
GAHON, William		30	M	Baker	08Se02Gg
FENY, Elonor		.04	F	Infant	08Se02Gg
MCHENRY, Jane		50	F	None	08Se02Gg
MCKEENY, Elizabeth		18	F	None	08Se02Gg
HANLEY, John		20	M	Laborer	08Se02Gg
COLLINS, James		19	M	Laborer	08Se02Gg
HEENEY, Mary		23	F	None	08Se02Gg
James		10	M	None	08Se02Gg
OBRIEN, James		20	M	Laborer	08Se02Gg
Mary		20	F	Servant	08Se02Gg
DUGGAN, Thomas		25	M	Laborer	08Se02Gg
Catherine		22	F	Servant	08Se02Gg
Daniel		21	M	Laborer	08Se02Gg
SHEEAN, Timothy		25	M	Laborer	08Se02Gg
QUIN, Thomas		27	M	Laborer	08Se02Gg
HENKERSON, William		27	M	Gdnr	08Se02Gg
Ann		23	F	None	08Se02Gg
CALAHAN, Honora		23	M	Servant	08Se02Gg
DONNOLLY, Patt.		23	M	Blacksmith	08Se02Gg
WALKER, Bridget		18	F	Servant	08Se02Gg
MCCARTHY, Florence		14	F	Servant	08Se02Gg
LANE, Honora		10	F	None	08Se02Gg
Nancy		40	F	None	08Se02Gg
Daniel		06	M	Child	08Se02Gg
SULLIVAN, Catherine		20	F	Servant	08Se02Gg
WHITE, Catherine		18	F	Servant	08Se02Gg
MCTEAGUE, Margaret		30	F	Servant	08Se02Gg
LYNCH, Michael		40	M	Laborer	08Se02Gg
GALLAGHER, Thomas		21	M	Carpenter	08Se02Gg
FERGUSON, Thomas		17	M	Carpenter	08Se02Gg
Margaret		46	F	None	08Se02Gg
CONWAY, Rose		48	F	None	08Se02Gg
Rose		18	F	None	08Se02Gg
Catherine		14	F	None	08Se02Gg
COLOGG, Michael		28	M	Laborer	08Se02Gg
FARRELL, Winifred		46	U	Unknown	08Se02Gg
KELLY, Mary		50	F	Servant	08Se02Gg
Ann		20	F	Servant	08Se02Gg
MELLOW, Michael		30	M	Laborer	08Se02Gg
FLYNN, Richard		30	M	Currier	08Se02Gg
LODIN, Margaret		17	F	Servant	08Se02Gg
RILEY, Peter		03	M	Child	08Se02Gg
FLYNN, Martin		19	M	Servant	08Se02Gg
Ann		17	F	Servant	08Se02Gg
MCGLOIN, Michael		26	M	Laborer	08Se02Gg
KELLY, William		27	M	Laborer	08Se02Gg
BAXTER, Elizabeth		17	F	Servant	08Se02Gg
DALY, Cornelius		23	M	Laborer	08Se02Gg
MCCAN, Bernard		14	M	Laborer	08Se02Gg
FREEHILL, Ann		21	F	Laborer	08Se02Gg
CASSIDY, Michael		30	M	Carpenter	08Se02Gg
Mary	(W)	19	F	Wife	08Se02Gg
Mary	(D)	.11	F	Infant	08Se02Gg
Died-At-Sea					
MCLOUGHLAN, Thomas		18	M	Laborer	08Se02Gg
MURPHY, Edward		23	M	Laborer	08Se02Gg
RYAN, Ellen		13	F	None	08Se02Gg
SMITH, Margaret		27	F	Servant	08Se02Gg

NAMES OF PASSENGERS		AGE	SEX	OCCUPATIONS	DATE PORT SHIP
SMITH, Julia		20	F	Servant	08Se02Gg
KILROY, Peter		29	M	Laborer	08Se02Gg
Barbara		22	F	Servant	08Se02Gg
Ann		19	F	Servant	08Se02Gg
Ann		20	F	Servant	08Se02Gg
MOONEY, Ann		20	F	Servant	08Se02Gg
OHARA, Bridget		60	F	Servant	08Se02Gg
FULLERTON, Robert		18	M	Laborer	08Se02Gg
WALLACE, James		52	M	Wheelwright	08Se02Gg
MCBRINE, William		50	M	Blacksmith	08Se02Gg
LYNCH, Ann		18	F	Servant	08Se02Gg
COTTER, William		35	M	Carpenter	08Se02Gg
Isabella	(W)	32	F	Wife	08Se02Gg
Elizabeth	(D)	09	F	Child	08Se02Gg
Mary	(D)	07	F	Child	08Se02Gg
John	(S)	05	M	Child	08Se02Gg
Christy	(S)	00	M	None	08Se02Gg
BRADLEY, Margaret		40	F	None	08Se02Gg
Sarah	(D)	16	F	None	08Se02Gg
Rose	(D)	13	F	None	08Se02Gg
Charles	(S)	09	M	Child	08Se02Gg
Mary	(D)	07	F	Child	08Se02Gg
Margaret	(D)	03	F	Child	08Se02Gg
CARTON, Mary-A.		43	F	None	08Se02Gg
U	(D)	14	F	None	08Se02Gg
Mary	(D)	16	F	None	08Se02Gg
MULVEY, Catherine		21	F	Servant	08Se02Gg
GORMAN, Margaret		18	F	Servant	08Se02Gg
DEMPSEY, Mary-A.		16	F	Servant	08Se02Gg
DONLY, Mary		17	F	Servant	08Se02Gg

ADIRONDACK 08 SEPTEMBER 1847

From Liverpool

NAMES OF PASSENGERS	AGE	SEX	OCCUPATIONS	DATE PORT SHIP
DONOVAN, Jerry	40	M	Laborer	08Se02Cm
SULLIVAN, John	28	M	Laborer	08Se02Cm
MOONEY, James	23	M	Groom	08Se02Cm
Wm.	20	M	Waiter	08Se02Cm
COLLINS, Jas.	34	M	Farmer	08Se02Cm
DORISKAL, Cons.	34	M	Laborer	08Se02Cm
LAREN, Thos.	25	M	Laborer	08Se02Cm
CADRY, Michael	18	M	Laborer	08Se02Cm
DOWLING, Michael	20	M	Drover	08Se02Cm
MADDEN, Cathe.	19	F	Unknown	08Se02Cm
COLLINS, Kitty	19	F	Unknown	08Se02Cm
MCMORRAN, Bridget	19	F	Servant	08Se02Cm
YOUNG, Baptist	51	M	Farmer	08Se02Cm
Martha	42	F	None	08Se02Cm
Robert	19	M	Farmer	08Se02Cm
Price	15	M	Farmer	08Se02Cm
John	04	M	Child	08Se02Cm
Martha	12	F	Unknown	08Se02Cm
Margaret	.00	F	Infant	08Se02Cm
MCQUADE, Mary	20	F	Unknown	08Se02Cm
KEATING, Bernard	49	M	Farmer	08Se02Cm
Mary	42	F	None	08Se02Cm
John	13	M	Unknown	08Se02Cm
Catherine	22	F	Unknown	08Se02Cm
Mary	20	F	Unknown	08Se02Cm
Bridget	17	F	Unknown	08Se02Cm
Elizabeth	11	F	Unknown	08Se02Cm
LYST, John	21	M	Farmer	08Se02Cm
Eliza-Jane	20	F	Unknown	08Se02Cm
GILLASPIE, Mary	18	F	Servant	08Se02Cm
MCGINTY, Michl.	50	M	Merchant	08Se02Cm
CAROLAN, James	16	M	Unknown	08Se02Cm
MCGINNIS, Edwd.	56	M	Dealer	08Se02Cm
MCGLOMAN, Bridget	27	F	Servant	08Se02Cm
FITZGERALD, Joana	27	F	Servant	08Se02Cm
CARRADY, Ellen	24	F	Servant	08Se02Cm
Bridget	23	F	Servant	08Se02Cm
Joana	25	F	Servant	08Se02Cm
FINN, Mary	14	F	Servant	08Se02Cm
SCANLAN, Mary	20	F	Servant	08Se02Cm
RILEY, Edwd.	40	M	Laborer	08Se02Cm
Mary	26	F	None	08Se02Cm
Mary	06	F	Child	08Se02Cm
OCONNOR, Morris	30	M	Shoemaker	08Se02Cm
Mary	28	F	None	08Se02Cm
Ellen	03	F	Child	08Se02Cm
Peter	.00	M	Infant	08Se02Cm
DARGAN, Patc.	24	M	Shoemaker	08Se02Cm
SULLIVAN, Bridget	23	F	Unknown	08Se02Cm
MCGRATHRY, Ellen	58	F	Unknown	08Se02Cm
John	17	M	Unknown	08Se02Cm
MACLOUGH, Arthur	08	M	Child	08Se02Cm
HARLON, Ann	33	F	Unknown	08Se02Cm
Michael	10	M	Unknown	08Se02Cm
Catherine	12	F	Unknown	08Se02Cm
Winifred	07	M	Child	08Se02Cm
Cicily	05	F	Child	08Se02Cm
Maria	02	F	Child	08Se02Cm
Ann	.06	F	Infant	08Se02Cm
COUGHLAN, John	28	M	Tailor	08Se02Cm
Honora	28	F	Unknown	08Se02Cm
DONAVAN, Michael	24	M	Clerk	08Se02Cm
HURLAY, Cathe.	24	F	Servant	08Se02Cm
MCKAY, Cathe.	18	F	Servant	08Se02Cm
SULLIVAN, Nancy	17	F	Hatter	08Se02Cm
PINKERTON, Andrew	20	M	Clerk	08Se02Cm
CARROLL, Pat.W.	29	M	Farmer	08Se02Cm
Margaret	28	F	None	08Se02Cm
Wm.Edward	06	M	Child	08Se02Cm
Kate	03	F	Child	08Se02Cm
CORNELL, Joanna	14	F	Servant	08Se02Cm
MCCARTHY, Dennis	32	M	Draper	08Se02Cm
Ellen	30	F	None	08Se02Cm
John	03	M	Child	08Se02Cm
HANLEN, Danl.	26	M	Carpenter	08Se02Cm
CLAHONE, Michael	23	M	Laborer	08Se02Cm
JOYCE, John	23	M	Tailor	08Se02Cm
WELSH, Thos.	58	M	Farmer	08Se02Cm
Thos.	21	M	Farmer	08Se02Cm
HARRINGTON, Florence	35	F	Laborer	08Se02Cm
KELLY, Danl.	40	M	Laborer	08Se02Cm
Ann	40	F	None	08Se02Cm
William	13	M	Unknown	08Se02Cm
Edward	11	M	Unknown	08Se02Cm
Daniel	09	M	Child	08Se02Cm
Michael	03	M	Child	08Se02Cm
Mary	06	F	Child	08Se02Cm
KERNAYE, Matthew	33	M	Laborer	08Se02Cm
Died-At-Sea				
SHEA, Dennis	40	M	Mason	08Se02Cm
CONDON, Michael	28	M	Upholsterer	08Se02Cm
MCCARTY, John	26	M	Plate Layer	08Se02Cm
Bridget	24	F	None	08Se02Cm
Elizabeth	.08	F	Infant	08Se02Cm
HAGAN, Cathe	19	F	Servant	08Se02Cm
BARRY, Danl.	40	M	Tailor	08Se02Cm
Honora	16	F	Unknown	08Se02Cm
MCGIVAN, Margaret	28	F	Unknown	08Se02Cm
John	09	M	Child	08Se02Cm
MURPHY, Cathe.	48	F	Unknown	08Se02Cm
Ellen	11	F	Unknown	08Se02Cm
CROOK, Walter	28	M	Laborer	08Se02Cm
Mary	28	F	Unknown	08Se02Cm
COLEMAN, Patc.	30	M	Gdnr	08Se02Cm
Ann	30	F	Unknown	08Se02Cm
HAGIN, Thos.	40	M	Laborer	08Se02Cm
James	28	M	Laborer	08Se02Cm
Margaret	30	F	Unknown	08Se02Cm
ODRISCOLL, John	29	M	Clerk	08Se02Cm

NAMES OF PASSENGERS	AGE	SEX	OCCUPATIONS	DATE PORT SHIP
GRIGHTON, Richd.	29	M	Laborer	08Se02Cm
John	18	M	Laborer	08Se02Cm
RAFFERTY, Ann	17	F	Unknown	08Se02Cm
MANAGHAN, James	07	M	Child	08Se02Cm
Maria	04	F	Child	08Se02Cm
DILLON, Ellen	38	F	Unknown	08Se02Cm
Edward	38	M	Laborer	08Se02Cm
Ann	36	F	Unknown	08Se02Cm
Patrick	07	M	Child	08Se02Cm
Mary	05	F	Child	08Se02Cm
Lawrence	03	M	Child	08Se02Cm
Michael	.06	M	Infant	08Se02Cm
DONAVAN, Toms.	23	M	Miner	08Se02Cm
TOBIN, John	28	M	Laborer	08Se02Cm
REGAN, Ann	18	F	Laborer	08Se02Cm
NEAL, Michael	42	M	Laborer	08Se02Cm
MCCARTHY, Andrew	24	M	Laborer	08Se02Cm
DONAVAN, Ellen	21	F	Servant	08Se02Cm
MURPHY, Sarah	33	F	Unknown	08Se02Cm
Patrick	17	M	Laborer	08Se02Cm
Quinlan	12	M	Unknown	08Se02Cm
Mary	10	F	Unknown	08Se02Cm
John	08	M	Child	08Se02Cm
Margaret	04	F	Child	08Se02Cm
CARNEY, Cathe.	40	F	Unknown	08Se02Cm
FINTAN, Patc.	17	M	Saddler	08Se02Cm
MALONE, James	21	M	Laborer	08Se02Cm
Isabella	23	M	Unknown	08Se02Cm
MCWHINNEY, Eugene	23	M	Laborer	08Se02Cm
Julia	20	F	Unknown	08Se02Cm
LANE, John	25	M	Shoemaker	08Se02Cm
LARRY, Ellen	56	F	Unknown	08Se02Cm
Daniel	23	M	Laborer	08Se02Cm
David	09	M	Child	08Se02Cm
Ellen	10	F	Unknown	08Se02Cm
David	06	M	Child	08Se02Cm
Mary	18	F	Unknown	08Se02Cm
FINTAN, Robert	22	M	Laborer	08Se02Cm
Timothy	18	M	Laborer	08Se02Cm
KENNEDAY, Wm.	19	M	Weaver	08Se02Cm
MCGIFFEN, John	68	M	Laborer	08Se02Cm
Ellen	30	F	Unknown	08Se02Cm
LUNEY, Cathe.	60	F	Unknown	08Se02Cm
DORISKAL, Dennis	28	M	Laborer	08Se02Cm
Mary	24	F	None	08Se02Cm
John	03	M	Child	08Se02Cm
Catherine	.07	F	Infant	08Se02Cm
QUIRK, Wm.	52	M	Laborer	08Se02Cm
Catherine	42	F	None	08Se02Cm
Ellen	19	F	Unknown	08Se02Cm
Mary	14	F	Unknown	08Se02Cm
Peter	12	M	Unknown	08Se02Cm
Thomas	10	M	Unknown	08Se02Cm
Catherine	08	F	Child	08Se02Cm
LARRY, Frances	25	F	Servant	08Se02Cm
INNISY, Ellen	25	F	Servant	08Se02Cm
BOWEN, Mary	20	F	Unknown	08Se02Cm
Margaret	19	F	Unknown	08Se02Cm
MERVIN, John	24	M	Laborer	08Se02Cm
BRICK, Ellen	54	F	Unknown	08Se02Cm
Wm.	22	M	Laborer	08Se02Cm
REILLEY, Danl.	20	M	Carpenter	08Se02Cm
MOLANE, John	16	M	Laborer	08Se02Cm
CALLAGHAN, Nancy	34	F	Unknown	08Se02Cm
Michael	.09	M	Infant	08Se02Cm
Mary	20	F	Unknown	08Se02Cm
MCKEAN, Mary	21	F	Servant	08Se02Cm
Ellen	18	F	Servant	08Se02Cm
GILLOGHAR, John	22	M	Laborer	08Se02Cm
KEAN, James	30	M	Carpenter	08Se02Cm
Mary	18	F	Unknown	08Se02Cm
CLARK, James	30	M	Contractor	08Se02Cm
FEENY, Michael	19	M	Laborer	08Se02Cm
DYGNAN, Maria	11	F	Unknown	08Se02Cm
KILLIAN, John	35	M	Laborer	08Se02Cm
HOCKIES, Mary	28	F	Unknown	08Se02Cm
Danl.	03	M	Child	08Se02Cm
BIGG, Ellen	08	F	Child	08Se02Cm
GIBBINS, James	25	M	Laborer	08Se02Cm
GRAY, Wm.	20	M	Laborer	08Se02Cm
NULTY, Peter	22	M	Tailor	08Se02Cm
Mary	20	F	Unknown	08Se02Cm
MCMANUS, Hugh	18	M	Tailor	08Se02Cm
DORAN, Michael	38	M	Farmer	08Se02Cm
Ann	15	F	Unknown	08Se02Cm
Barney	13	M	Unknown	08Se02Cm
MCGINNIS, Sarah	20	F	Servant	08Se02Cm
KENNEDY, Eliza	28	F	Servant	08Se02Cm
Mcma-Y, Kearney	33	M	Laborer	08Se02Cm
Susannah	22	F	Unknown	08Se02Cm
O-AN, Michael	27	M	Laborer	08Se02Cm
COLLINS, Danl.	20	M	Laborer	08Se02Cm
DUFFY, Mary	16	F	Unknown	08Se02Cm
Winifred	21	F	Unknown	08Se02Cm
CANNIGAN, Margaret	20	F	Servant	08Se02Cm
O-AN, Margt.	20	F	Unknown	08Se02Cm
GALLAGHER, Ann	16	F	Unknown	08Se02Cm
Rose	20	F	Unknown	08Se02Cm
CONWAY, Mary	24	F	Unknown	08Se02Cm
KEENAN, Sarah	35	F	Unknown	08Se02Cm
John	03	M	Child	08Se02Cm
Mary	.07	F	Infant	08Se02Cm
BARRY, Thos.	35	M	Butcher	08Se02Cm
BOOTH, Bridget	22	F	Unknown	08Se02Cm
GALLAGHER, Bartle.	34	M	Laborer	08Se02Cm
MCKAY, Bridget	34	F	Unknown	08Se02Cm
Michael	02	M	Child	08Se02Cm
MCCANN, Ann	23	F	Servant	08Se02Cm
Catherine	21	F	Servant	08Se02Cm
Hugh	20	M	Laborer	08Se02Cm
CALLAGHAN, Judy	88	F	Unknown	08Se02Cm
LYNCH, Mary	15	F	Unknown	08Se02Cm
OLEARY, Michael	30	M	Farmer	08Se02Cm
Ann	25	F	None	08Se02Cm
Florence	.06	F	Infant	08Se02Cm
Timothy	21	M	Farmer	08Se02Cm
MCCARTHY, Danl.	21	M	Laborer	08Se02Cm
Susan	23	F	Unknown	08Se02Cm
BATTER, U-Mrs.	56	F	Unknown	08Se02Cm
FARRELL, Elizth.	22	F	Dressmaker	08Se02Cm

MEDIATOR 08 SEPTEMBER 1847

From London

NAMES OF PASSENGERS	AGE	SEX	OCCUPATIONS	DATE PORT SHIP
MCKENNA, J.	35	M	Gentleman	08Se21Dt
U (W)	35	F	Unknown	08Se21Dt
IRVING, M.A.-Mrs.	32	F	Unknown	08Se21Dt
J.R. (D)	.00	F	Infant	08Se21Dt
U, U	00	U	Servant	08Se21Dt
MAXWELL, M.	15	F	Unknown	08Se21Dt
BRYAN, Mary-Ann	01	F	Child	08Se21Dt
ROACH, William	35	M	Gentleman	08Se21Dt
Bridget	08	F	Child	08Se21Dt
CALLAGAN, Dennis	26	M	Laborer	08Se21Dt
BRYAN, Henry	33	M	Laborer	08Se21Dt
Mary	26	F	Unknown	08Se21Dt

NAMES OF PASSENGERS		AGE	SEX	OCCUPATIONS	DATE PORT SHIP

ALMEDA 09 SEPTEMBER 1847

From Liverpool

NAMES OF PASSENGERS		AGE	SEX	OCCUPATIONS	DATE PORT SHIP
TAYLOR, Robert		21	M	Tailor	09Se02Tf
WHRIGHT, Isaac		22	M	Mechanic	09Se02Tf
BATY, Joseph		25	M	Farmer	09Se02Tf
Mary	(W)	26	F	Wife	09Se02Tf
U		.00	U	Infant	09Se02Tf
WHRIGHT, Andrew		18	M	Mechanic	09Se02Tf
BROWN, Charles		42	M	Merchant	09Se02Tf
Fanny		38	F	Lady	09Se02Tf
RUSSELL, Isaac		30	M	Farmer	09Se02Tf
Jane	(W)	28	F	Wife	09Se02Tf
U		.00	U	Infant	09Se02Tf
Sarah		70	F	Lady	09Se02Tf
Sarah	(D)	11	F	Lady	09Se02Tf
John	(S)	10	M	Unknown	09Se02Tf
Andrew	(S)	09	M	Child	09Se02Tf
Wm.	(S)	08	M	Child	09Se02Tf
Isaac	(S)	07	M	Child	09Se02Tf
David	(S)	06	M	Child	09Se02Tf

MARY-MORRIS 09 SEPTEMBER 1847

From Glasgow

NAMES OF PASSENGERS	AGE	SEX	OCCUPATIONS	DATE PORT SHIP
MCVANE, John	32	M	Laborer	09Se040l
TAYLOR, Duncan	20	M	Laborer	09Se040l
FRAZER, Donald	44	M	Laborer	09Se040l
RUSSEL, John	40	M	Shopkeeper	09Se040l
Marion	40	F	None	09Se040l
Marion	11	F	None	09Se040l
Mary	09	F	Child	09Se040l
MCDONNEL, Chas.	29	M	Tailor	09Se040l
Sarah	25	F	None	09Se040l
CRAWFORD, Uney	03	F	Child	09Se040l
MURRAY, Alex	40	M	Laborer	09Se040l
Ann	25	F	None	09Se040l
HINLY, Charles	13	M	Weaver	09Se040l
HIELAN, Bridget	44	F	None	09Se040l
KNOX, John	21	M	Farmer	09Se040l
Mary	60	F	None	09Se040l
Ann	49	F	None	09Se040l
Alex	12	M	None	09Se040l
John	11	M	None	09Se040l
MCDONNEL, John	08	M	Child	09Se040l
ROSENBURG, John	21	M	Tailor	09Se040l
MCGREGOR, George	24	M	Laborer	09Se040l
SMEAL, Thos.	50	M	Weaver	09Se040l
Jean	20	F	Servant	09Se040l
Robert	17	M	Weaver	09Se040l
Thos.	13	M	None	09Se040l
Mary	11	F	None	09Se040l
MCAVOY, Wm.	30	M	Laborer	09Se040l
Marion	26	F	None	09Se040l
KEENAN, Catherine	50	F	None	09Se040l
MCAVOY, Pat	01	M	Child	09Se040l
WEBSTER, David	27	M	Laborer	09Se040l
MCINTOSH, Alex	19	M	Laborer	09Se040l
MCEWEN, James	23	M	Smith	09Se040l
BEYLICE, Thos.	23	M	Painter	09Se040l
AIRD, John	27	M	Smith	09Se040l
MCAULEY, Alex	21	M	Student	09Se040l
Mary	22	F	None	09Se040l
James	.11	M	Infant	09Se040l
BAIRD, John	26	M	Laborer	09Se040l
IRVING, James-O.S.	23	M	Msta	09Se040l
HADDOW, Mathew	50	M	Merchant	09Se040l
BARR, James	27	M	Merchant	09Se040l
GRAHAM, Eliza	19	F	None	09Se040l

CONSTITUTION 09 SEPTEMBER 1847

From Liverpool

NAMES OF PASSENGERS	AGE	SEX	OCCUPATIONS	DATE PORT SHIP
ROTTON, M.A.	29	F	None	09Se02Hi
C.	.08	F	Infant	09Se02Hi
COOK, M.A.	40	F	None	09Se02Hi
MOYLE, G.	30	M	Navy	09Se02Hi
RILEY, Jas.S.	30	M	Gentleman	09Se02Hi
CHARTERS, Jas.R.	25	M	Merchant	09Se02Hi
John	22	M	Merchant	09Se02Hi
JAMESON, J.T.	30	M	Doctor	09Se02Hi
SMITH, Sidney	21	M	Merchant	09Se02Hi
BUCKLEY, Jas.Jr.	21	M	Merchant	09Se02Hi
HATT, Thos.C.	25	M	Gentleman	09Se02Hi
KELETT, J.	26	F	None	09Se02Hi
BRADY, Mary	20	F	Spinster	09Se02Hi
Sally	20	F	Spinster	09Se02Hi
MCGUIRE, Jas.	50	M	Laborer	09Se02Hi
Cathn.	50	F	None	09Se02Hi
Judith	15	F	None	09Se02Hi
James	13	M	None	09Se02Hi
Bridget	09	F	Child	09Se02Hi
Patk.	07	M	Child	09Se02Hi
Magt.	05	F	Child	09Se02Hi
HAYDEN, Wm.	00	M	Unknown	09Se02Hi
Esther	00	F	Unknown	09Se02Hi
DAVIES, Mary	30	F	Spinster	09Se02Hi
REECE, Elizath.	41	F	Spinster	09Se02Hi
Wm.A.	22	M	Mason	09Se02Hi
Lawrence	17	M	None	09Se02Hi
Virginius	13	F	None	09Se02Hi
Rosamond	12	F	None	09Se02Hi
Ruben-Geo.	07	M	Child	09Se02Hi
Fergus-Oconnor	05	M	Child	09Se02Hi
Henry	03	M	Child	09Se02Hi
HAYES, John Died-At-Sea	.00	M	Infant	09Se02Hi
SHEIL, Danl.	27	M	Laborer	09Se02Hi
Cath.	21	F	None	09Se02Hi
LAWLER, Jno.	24	M	Laborer	09Se02Hi
CONNOLLY, Frank	40	M	Laborer	09Se02Hi
Mary	18	F	None	09Se02Hi
Thos.	13	M	None	09Se02Hi
GRIME, Pat	30	M	Laborer	09Se02Hi
GAVANAGH, Jas.	20	M	Laborer	09Se02Hi
ANDREW, John	44	M	Laborer	09Se02Hi
Ann	22	F	Spinster	09Se02Hi
Wm.	14	M	None	09Se02Hi
Mary	13	F	None	09Se02Hi
Eliza	09	F	Child	09Se02Hi
Betty	07	F	Child	09Se02Hi
Alice	03	F	Child	09Se02Hi
HAUGHTON, Ann	30	F	Spinster	09Se02Hi
CAWLIN, Thos.	32	M	Laborer	09Se02Hi
Bridget	26	F	None	09Se02Hi
NASH, John	20	M	Laborer	09Se02Hi
Mary	20	F	Spinster	09Se02Hi
Geo.	20	M	Laborer	09Se02Hi
John	18	M	Laborer	09Se02Hi

NAMES OF PASSENGERS	AGE	SEX	OCCUPATIONS	DATE PORT SHIP
NASH, Barbara	16	F	Laborer	09Se02Hi
Maggy	12	F	None	09Se02Hi
Jane	12	F	None	09Se02Hi
Cath.	09	F	Child	09Se02Hi
LEYDON, Michl.	25	M	Laborer	09Se02Hi
KNOX, Wm.	25	M	Mason	09Se02Hi
KIERNAN, Jane	20	F	Spinster	09Se02Hi
Michl.	20	M	Carpenter	09Se02Hi
BRADY, Michl.	20	M	Laborer	09Se02Hi
CURLEY, Mary	40	F	None	09Se02Hi
Jas.	05	M	Child	09Se02Hi
Michl.	03	M	Child	09Se02Hi
Pat	.00	M	Infant	09Se02Hi
FLEMING, Mary	20	F	Spinster	09Se02Hi
MONEY, Esther	18	F	Spinster	09Se02Hi
ATHREA, Thos.	60	M	Laborer	09Se02Hi
Richd.	20	M	Laborer	09Se02Hi
GERATY, Jno.	30	M	Cobbler	09Se02Hi
Mary	18	F	None	09Se02Hi
JAMES, Erasmus	31	M	Carpenter	09Se02Hi
Eliza	32	F	None	09Se02Hi
Edwd.	06	M	Child	09Se02Hi
Elizath.	04	F	Child	09Se02Hi
Ann	.00	F	Infant	09Se02Hi
HAWKES, John	24	M	Laborer	09Se02Hi
CARNEY, Peter	40	M	Laborer	09Se02Hi
Josh	19	M	Laborer	09Se02Hi
WADDOCK, Frans.	21	M	Laborer	09Se02Hi
TATE, Robt.	50	M	Laborer	09Se02Hi
MCLAUGHLIN, Edwd.	17	M	Laborer	09Se02Hi
FORESTER, Robt.	31	M	Laborer	09Se02Hi
ALKIN, Jas.	35	M	Laborer	09Se02Hi
Thos.	50	M	Laborer	09Se02Hi
Bridget	50	F	None	09Se02Hi
Malachie	32	M	Laborer	09Se02Hi
Jno.	23	M	Laborer	09Se02Hi
DAVENAY, Bridget	20	F	Spinster	09Se02Hi
FORD, Mary	21	F	Spinster	09Se02Hi
FASINTINE, Saml.	30	M	Laborer	09Se02Hi
Thos.	18	M	None	09Se02Hi
Fanny	17	F	None	09Se02Hi
Hugh	13	M	None	09Se02Hi
James	11	M	None	09Se02Hi
Isabella	08	F	Child	09Se02Hi
Robt.	06	M	Child	09Se02Hi
Geo.	04	M	Child	09Se02Hi
John	09	M	Child	09Se02Hi
Wm.	.00	M	Infant	09Se02Hi
AGAR, Maria	40	F	None	09Se02Hi
Richd.	21	M	Mechanic	09Se02Hi
Anna-Maria	17	F	None	09Se02Hi
Joseph	16	M	None	09Se02Hi
Jane	15	F	None	09Se02Hi
Alice	14	F	None	09Se02Hi
Chris.	13	M	None	09Se02Hi
MCCAULEY, Frans.	25	M	Laborer	09Se02Hi
HUTCHINSON, Robt.	22	M	Laborer	09Se02Hi
OCONNOR, Edwd.	36	M	Laborer	09Se02Hi
TULLY, Thos.	30	M	Laborer	09Se02Hi
NOONAN, Cath.	28	F	Spinster	09Se02Hi
CURRAN, Bridget	20	F	Spinster	09Se02Hi
FITZGERALD, Wm.	13	M	None	09Se02Hi
CARNEY, Jno.	25	M	Laborer	09Se02Hi
FITZGERALD, Wm.	40	M	Laborer	09Se02Hi
DOHERTY, Margt.	40	F	None	09Se02Hi
MCBRUTY, Rose	40	F	None	09Se02Hi
DOHERTY, Wm.	18	M	Laborer	09Se02Hi
Pat	14	M	Laborer	09Se02Hi
Mary	12	F	None	09Se02Hi
John	09	M	Child	09Se02Hi
REASTAN, Timy	20	M	Laborer	09Se02Hi
Julia	14	F	Spinster	09Se02Hi
HANLEY, Gerald	30	M	Laborer	09Se02Hi
GRIFFIN, Mary	20	F	Spinster	09Se02Hi
MULCAETRY, John	30	M	Laborer	09Se02Hi
RYAN, Pat	30	M	Laborer	09Se02Hi
GRIFFITH, Wm.	30	M	Laborer	09Se02Hi
KERRICK, Pat	22	M	Laborer	09Se02Hi
LEADSEN, Wm.	50	M	Laborer	09Se02Hi
FOGARTY, Eliza	28	F	Spinster	09Se02Hi
MURRAY, Mary	19	F	Spinster	09Se02Hi
Margt.	22	F	Spinster	09Se02Hi
MASTON, Kitty	19	F	Spinster	09Se02Hi
FOGARTY, Jno.	08	M	Child	09Se02Hi
Danl.	07	M	Child	09Se02Hi
Mary	05	F	Child	09Se02Hi
Thos.	02	M	Child	09Se02Hi
TODD, Geo.	34	M	Laborer	09Se02Hi
MORAN, Jas.	22	M	Laborer	09Se02Hi
MCBRIDE, Ann	20	F	Spinster	09Se02Hi
WALSH, Mary	48	F	Spinster	09Se02Hi
Michl.	18	M	Laborer	09Se02Hi
BRAINS, U-Mrs.	30	F	Spinster	09Se02Hi
John	05	M	Child	09Se02Hi
James	03	M	Child	09Se02Hi
LEVANT, Sally	20	F	Spinster	09Se02Hi
QUINN, Matthew	50	M	Laborer	09Se02Hi
CORSEY, Eliza	17	F	Spinster	09Se02Hi
ROWLAND, Thos.	28	M	Laborer	09Se02Hi
Ann	25	F	None	09Se02Hi
Margt.	06	F	Child	09Se02Hi
BRYANS, Wm.	30	M	Laborer	09Se02Hi
Jolseman	21	F	Spinster	09Se02Hi
MULONEY, Bridget	18	F	Spinster	09Se02Hi
Cath.	17	F	Spinster	09Se02Hi
CHADWICK, Jas.	20	M	Laborer	09Se02Hi
MCKEON, Mary	26	F	Spinster	09Se02Hi
Cath.	22	F	Spinster	09Se02Hi
DAY, Mary	18	F	Spinster	09Se02Hi
CHRISTOPHER, Mary	10	F	Spinster	09Se02Hi
HOPKINS, Mary	18	F	Spinster	09Se02Hi
CHRISTOPHER, Edwd.	12	M	Spinster	09Se02Hi
MITCHELL, Mary	26	F	Spinster	09Se02Hi
Eliza	26	F	Spinster	09Se02Hi
John	.00	M	Infant	09Se02Hi
PUSNELL, Maurice	10	M	None	09Se02Hi
HARRIS, Thos.	40	M	Collier	09Se02Hi
Ann	40	F	None	09Se02Hi
Josh.	20	M	Laborer	09Se02Hi
GREEN, Jas.	26	M	Mason	09Se02Hi
John	36	M	Mason	09Se02Hi
Ann	26	F	Spinster	09Se02Hi
COOK, Mary	20	F	Spinster	09Se02Hi
DEVLIN, Mary	20	F	Spinster	09Se02Hi
KELLY, Bridget	20	F	Spinster	09Se02Hi
ARTHUR, Evan	40	M	Carpenter	09Se02Hi
SWEENEY, Ellen	20	F	Spinster	09Se02Hi
Timy	12	M	None	09Se02Hi
MCDONNELL, Mich.	30	M	Collier	09Se02Hi
Betty	16	F	Spinster	09Se02Hi
FELL, Levi	30	M	Laborer	09Se02Hi
Anna	25	F	Spinster	09Se02Hi
Wm.	25	M	Laborer	09Se02Hi
MAKEY, Thos.	20	M	Carpenter	09Se02Hi
Mary	30	F	Spinster	09Se02Hi
NIXON, Ellen	30	F	Spinster	09Se02Hi
FORREST, Biddy	24	F	Spinster	09Se02Hi
MACKEY, Henry	.00	M	Infant	09Se02Hi
Michl.	.00	M	Infant	09Se02Hi
HAYLIFFE, Chas.	30	M	Miner	09Se02Hi
PASCOE, Ann	25	F	Spinster	09Se02Hi
HARRINGTON, Andw.	30	M	Laborer	09Se02Hi
PENDERGRASS, Cath.	27	F	Spinster	09Se02Hi
Mary	20	F	Spinster	09Se02Hi
SMITH, Abigail	28	F	Spinster	09Se02Hi
QUADE, Thos. Died-At-Sea	30	M	Laborer	09Se02Hi
SULLIVAN, Josh.	30	M	Laborer	09Se02Hi
CORNAN, Corns.	13	M	Laborer	09Se02Hi
WASE, Pat	13	M	Laborer	09Se02Hi

NAMES OF PASSENGERS	AGE	SEX	OCCUPATIONS	DATE PORT SHIP
FAY, John	40	M	Laborer	09Se02HI
CORNAN, Nora	40	F	None	09Se02HI
CAIGHAN, Mary	16	F	None	09Se02HI
FAY, Cath.	24	F	Spinster	09Se02HI
JACKSON, Wm.	30	M	Laborer	09Se02HI
Ann	30	F	None	09Se02HI
PALMER, Alfred	20	M	Laborer	09Se02HI
RAFFERTY, Michl.	28	M	Laborer	09Se02HI
Pat	20	M	Laborer	09Se02HI
Margt.	18	F	Spinster	09Se02HI
Cath.	15	F	Spinster	09Se02HI
Margt.	12	F	Spinster	09Se02HI
KELLY, Thaly	22	M	Carpenter	09Se02HI
LAUGHLIN, Magt.	21	F	Spinster	09Se02HI
MADDEN, Jas.	20	M	Clerk	09Se02HI
FREEL, Bernd.	10	M	Laborer	09Se02HI
CLAFFEY, Rose	20	F	Spinster	09Se02HI
BRETT, Ellen	20	F	Spinster	09Se02HI
HUGHES, Cath.	30	F	Spinster	09Se02HI
DAVIES, Mary	22	F	Spinster	09Se02HI
FITZGERALD, Edmd.	38	M	Farmer	09Se02HI
Ames	30	M	None	09Se02HI
MOTHERNER, Wm.	23	M	Laborer	09Se02HI
Eliza	22	F	None	09Se02HI
KINAFE, Eliza	25	F	Spinster	09Se02HI
BIRD, Wm.	26	M	Laborer	09Se02HI
Margaret	26	F	Spinster	09Se02HI
DAUGHDALE, Esther	24	F	None	09Se02HI
Johanna	16	F	None	09Se02HI
BROWNLAN, Richd.	14	M	None	09Se02HI
WHELDON, Eliza	18	F	Spinster	09Se02HI
BARRY, Mary-Ann	30	F	Spinster	09Se02HI
Edward	20	M	Laborer	09Se02HI
COOPER, Alice	20	F	Spinster	09Se02HI
MOELE, U	29	M	Laborer	09Se02HI
CRUGGER, Robt.	23	M	Laborer	09Se02HI
GRAHAM, Wm.	25	M	Laborer	09Se02HI
Chas.	21	M	Laborer	09Se02HI
POWELL, Josh.	30	M	Laborer	09Se02HI
HAMEL, Owen	18	M	Laborer	09Se02HI
DALEY, Francis	20	M	Laborer	09Se02HI
REECE, Edgar	.00	M	Infant	09Se02HI
MILES, Chas.	30	M	Laborer	09Se02HI
Wm.	11	M	None	09Se02HI
JOHNSTON, Isabella	20	F	Spinster	09Se02HI
FUTT, Arthur	23	M	Laborer	09Se02HI
THORPE, Thos.	23	M	Laborer	09Se02HI
DAVIS, Ann	40	F	Spinster	09Se02HI
Sarah-Ann	16	F	Spinster	09Se02HI
Julia	15	F	Spinster	09Se02HI
Chas.	12	M	None	09Se02HI
Wm.	10	M	None	09Se02HI
Martin	08	M	Child	09Se02HI
Mary	06	F	Child	09Se02HI
Maria	05	F	Child	09Se02HI
Geo.	03	M	Child	09Se02HI
Ann	02	F	Child	09Se02HI
BROWN, U	40	M	Farmer	09Se02HI
MASTERSON, Jno.	34	M	Farmer	09Se02HI
FARUGHTON, Edwd.	26	M	Laborer	09Se02HI
Mary	26	F	None	09Se02HI
Hannah-F.	05	F	Child	09Se02HI
John	03	M	Child	09Se02HI
Lydia	.00	F	Infant	09Se02HI
MCCUSKER, Mary	19	F	Spinster	09Se02HI
MOORE, Mary-A.	19	F	Spinster	09Se02HI
FALKNER, Thos.	30	M	Laborer	09Se02HI
HAWKS, Jas.	21	M	Laborer	09Se02HI
MURPHY, Thos.	35	M	Laborer	09Se02HI
MCLAUGHLIN, Thos.	26	M	Laborer	09Se02HI
WHELAN, Patk.	38	M	Laborer	09Se02HI
OHALERN, Michl.	30	M	Laborer	09Se02HI
Maria	24	F	None	09Se02HI
Michl.	.00	M	Infant	09Se02HI
Geo.	.00	M	Infant	09Se02HI
HANAGHOO, Mary	30	F	Spinster	09Se02HI
MCCOMBRE, Jas.	34	M	Laborer	09Se02HI
Margt.	40	F	None	09Se02HI
Jas.Henry	15	M	None	09Se02HI
Wm.	13	M	None	09Se02HI
Sarah	11	F	None	09Se02HI
Margt.	06	F	Child	09Se02HI
Wm.	04	M	Child	09Se02HI
Hannah	.00	F	Infant	09Se02HI
HAMILTON, Cath.	18	F	Spinster	09Se02HI
DOUGAL, Jane	30	M	Laborer	09Se02HI
MCGUIRE, Wm.	30	M	Laborer	09Se02HI
WELDEN, Hugh	24	M	Laborer	09Se02HI
Abigail	22	F	None	09Se02HI
Ann	02	F	Child	09Se02HI
GORMAN, Danl.	40	M	Laborer	09Se02HI
Eliza	50	F	None	09Se02HI
BRAEN, Betty	55	F	None	09Se02HI
Ann	18	F	None	09Se02HI
Eliza	12	F	None	09Se02HI
MCSHARICK, Hugh	25	M	Laborer	09Se02HI
JEVEL, John	35	M	Laborer	09Se02HI
TODD, Sarah	30	F	Spinster	09Se02HI
LINSEY, Thos.	26	M	Laborer	09Se02HI
GAUGHAN, Robt.	21	M	Carpenter	09Se02HI
MARLIN, Margt.	27	F	Spinster	09Se02HI
DAVISON, Wm.	29	M	Laborer	09Se02HI
Thos.	24	M	Laborer	09Se02HI
Margt.	29	F	Spinster	09Se02HI
COOK, Jno.	14	M	None	09Se02HI
STUBBS, Geo.	60	M	None	09Se02HI
Mary	60	F	None	09Se02HI
CHISFERMY, Wm.	36	M	Laborer	09Se02HI
Marian	38	F	Spinster	09Se02HI
BRAITHWAITH, Jonas	38	M	Laborer	09Se02HI
WHITTY, Jas.	20	M	Laborer	09Se02HI
MORAN, Jno.	20	M	Laborer	09Se02HI
Bernard	27	M	Laborer	09Se02HI
Wm.	17	M	Laborer	09Se02HI
Wm.	23	M	Mason	09Se02HI
MIDDLETON, Thos.	20	M	Laborer	09Se02HI
SHAW, Geo.	20	M	Collier	09Se02HI
TUCK, Barnet	24	M	Collier	09Se02HI
Joseph	27	M	Laborer	09Se02HI
KELLER, A.	22	M	Laborer	09Se02HI
Mark	20	M	Laborer	09Se02HI
HOLLAMAN, Jno.	28	M	Laborer	09Se02HI
Mich.	20	M	Laborer	09Se02HI
MURRY, Rose	40	F	Spinster	09Se02HI
Eliza	20	F	Spinster	09Se02HI
OWENS, Pat	25	M	Laborer	09Se02HI
Thos.	20	M	Laborer	09Se02HI
CLAFEY, Ann	18	F	Spinster	09Se02HI
MILLER, Frans.	25	F	Spinster	09Se02HI
Nancy	20	F	Spinster	09Se02HI
Isab.	18	F	Spinster	09Se02HI
DERBY, Frans.	25	F	Spinster	09Se02HI
MARNNEY, Abm.	25	M	Laborer	09Se02HI
DALEY, Mich.	25	M	Laborer	09Se02HI
Magt.	20	F	Spinster	09Se02HI
MURRAY, Jas.	25	M	Laborer	09Se02HI
ONEILL, Hannah	30	F	Spinster	09Se02HI
John	31	M	Laborer	09Se02HI
SHANLEY, Ellen	20	F	Spinster	09Se02HI
MCCARTNEY, Rose	20	F	Spinster	09Se02HI
Mary	20	F	Spinster	09Se02HI
Cath.	25	F	Spinster	09Se02HI
Sarah	20	F	Spinster	09Se02HI
SHERDEN, Bryan	28	M	Laborer	09Se02HI
DARCEY, Jno.	20	M	Laborer	09Se02HI
COLLENS, Ellen	21	F	Spinster	09Se02HI
REGAN, Danl.	28	M	Mason	09Se02HI
FOLEY, Danl.	25	M	Laborer	09Se02HI
Corns.	25	M	Laborer	09Se02HI
LYNCH, Morris	30	M	Laborer	09Se02HI

NAMES OF PASSENGERS	AGE	SEX	OCCUPATIONS	DATE PORT SHIP
RILEY, Ann	20	F	Spinster	09Se02Hi
WILSON, Mary	20	F	Spinster	09Se02Hi
Margt.	20	F	Spinster	09Se02Hi
COSTELLO, Tim.Y.	25	M	Laborer	09Se02Hi
GREER, Pat	20	M	Laborer	09Se02Hi
MORRISON, Wm.	21	M	Laborer	09Se02Hi
Nancy	18	F	Spinster	09Se02Hi
BRADY, John	20	M	Laborer	09Se02Hi
REGAN, Barba.	20	F	Spinster	09Se02Hi
KILLER, Ed.	45	M	Laborer	09Se02Hi
Died-At-Sea				
John	40	M	Laborer	09Se02Hi
REYNOLDS, Cath.	20	F	Spinster	09Se02Hi
Sarah	18	F	Spinster	09Se02Hi
CRANEN, Biddy	21	F	Spinster	09Se02Hi
THOMPSON, Biddy	21	F	Spinster	09Se02Hi
FALSEY, Jas.	25	M	Laborer	09Se02Hi
Mary	20	F	Spinster	09Se02Hi
MCNALLY, Hannah	21	F	Spinster	09Se02Hi
Jas.	04	M	Child	09Se02Hi
GREY, Eliza	25	F	Spinster	09Se02Hi
Thos.	28	M	Laborer	09Se02Hi
Pat.	21	M	Laborer	09Se02Hi
Died-At-Sea				
Jas.	10	M	None	09Se02Hi
Ann	08	F	Child	09Se02Hi
Robt.	06	M	Child	09Se02Hi
Jno.	03	M	Child	09Se02Hi
Died-At-Sea				
MOLAN, Ann	20	F	Spinster	09Se02Hi
RYAN, Nancy	40	F	Spinster	09Se02Hi
BENNET, Jas.	21	M	Laborer	09Se02Hi
SWEENEY, Jane	20	F	Spinster	09Se02Hi
MALONE, Michl.	30	M	Laborer	09Se02Hi
HAYES, Bridget	30	F	Spinster	09Se02Hi
MCDONNELL, Jas.	20	M	Laborer	09Se02Hi
TOONEY, Johan.	20	F	Spinster	09Se02Hi
RAHELLY, Dennis	25	M	Laborer	09Se02Hi
WELSH, Cath.	21	F	Spinster	09Se02Hi
BYRNES, Margt.	30	F	Spinster	09Se02Hi
FOX, John	25	M	Collier	09Se02Hi
BYRNES, Eliza	12	F	None	09Se02Hi
Ann	18	F	Spinster	09Se02Hi
Thos.	09	M	Child	09Se02Hi
TRAINER, Geo.	25	M	Laborer	09Se02Hi
LAUGHLIN, Thos.	20	M	Laborer	09Se02Hi
MANY, Pat	20	M	Laborer	09Se02Hi
Matilda	06	F	Child	09Se02Hi
Bridget	04	F	Child	09Se02Hi
Ann	03	F	Child	09Se02Hi
HAUGHTON, Sarah	25	F	Spinster	09Se02Hi
Mary	10	F	None	09Se02Hi
Ann	06	F	Child	09Se02Hi
CUNNINGHAM, Peter	20	M	Laborer	09Se02Hi
KIRBY, Mary	20	F	Spinster	09Se02Hi
MCMANUS, Barny	25	M	Laborer	09Se02Hi
MADDEN, Margt.	20	F	Spinster	09Se02Hi
Ann	06	F	Child	09Se02Hi
Died-At-Sea				
Mary	06	F	Child	09Se02Hi
Died-At-Sea				
David	03	M	Child	09Se02Hi
Died-At-Sea				
LEE, Wm.	30	M	Laborer	09Se02Hi
Saml.	25	M	Laborer	09Se02Hi
COSGROVE, Mary	20	F	Spinster	09Se02Hi
WEBB, Mary	30	F	Spinster	09Se02Hi
Ellen	21	F	Spinster	09Se02Hi
John	22	M	Laborer	09Se02Hi
BIRD, Wm.	40	M	Laborer	09Se02Hi
Nancy	30	F	None	09Se02Hi
Robt.	04	M	Child	09Se02Hi
Thos.	.00	M	Infant	09Se02Hi
STAFFORD, Martha	40	F	Spinster	09Se02Hi
Sarah	20	F	Spinster	09Se02Hi

NAMES OF PASSENGERS	AGE	SEX	OCCUPATIONS	DATE PORT SHIP
STAFFORD, Mary	18	F	Spinster	09Se02Hi
Peter	25	M	Laborer	09Se02Hi
FURY, Bridget	20	F	Spinster	09Se02Hi
MAHON, Martha	21	F	Spinster	09Se02Hi
RATIVAN, Thos.	08	M	Child	09Se02Hi
Margt.	10	F	None	09Se02Hi
CROGHEN, Margt.	20	F	Spinster	09Se02Hi
LYNCH, Wm.	28	M	Laborer	09Se02Hi
HICKEY, Jno.	12	M	None	09Se02Hi
Ann	08	F	Child	09Se02Hi
MCINTER, Mary	20	F	Spinster	09Se02Hi
MCCANN, Owen	40	M	Laborer	09Se02Hi
Bridgt.	40	F	None	09Se02Hi
Jas.	10	M	None	09Se02Hi
MCLAUGHLIN, Jas.	30	M	Laborer	09Se02Hi
CONCLIN, Mary	20	F	Spinster	09Se02Hi
SHARKY, Jane	20	F	Spinster	09Se02Hi
BURNS, Ann	20	F	Spinster	09Se02Hi
MCKENNA, Ellen	45	F	Spinster	09Se02Hi
Cath.	21	F	Spinster	09Se02Hi
Ellen	18	F	Spinster	09Se02Hi
FAY, Ellen	28	F	Spinster	09Se02Hi
Chas.	30	M	Laborer	09Se02Hi
Pat	20	M	Laborer	09Se02Hi
Jane	05	F	Child	09Se02Hi
HAMTHON, Mary	15	F	None	09Se02Hi
Robt.	13	M	None	09Se02Hi
REILLY, Francis	30	M	Laborer	09Se02Hi
MASTERSON, Mary	20	F	Spinster	09Se02Hi
Mary	18	F	Spinster	09Se02Hi
John	10	M	None	09Se02Hi
MCGUIRE, Jas.	18	M	Laborer	09Se02Hi
SAVAGE, Jas.	25	M	Laborer	09Se02Hi
COSTELLO, Pat	30	M	Laborer	09Se02Hi
Ann	25	F	Spinster	09Se02Hi
Bridget	12	F	None	09Se02Hi
Eliza	07	F	Child	09Se02Hi
OWEN, Mary	20	F	Spinster	09Se02Hi
OBRIEN, Jas.	20	M	Laborer	09Se02Hi
BIGTON, Alice	20	F	Spinster	09Se02Hi
LAMAN, Martha	25	F	Spinster	09Se02Hi
MASSEY, Mary-Jane	20	F	Spinster	09Se02Hi
LYONS, Martha	21	F	Spinster	09Se02Hi
Mary	18	F	Spinster	09Se02Hi
Edwd.	10	M	None	09Se02Hi
John	08	M	Child	09Se02Hi
HANETT, Mary	20	F	Spinster	09Se02Hi
COX, Mary	40	F	Spinster	09Se02Hi
Thos.	28	M	Laborer	09Se02Hi
Pat	09	M	Child	09Se02Hi
Cath.	07	F	Child	09Se02Hi
Honora	05	F	Child	09Se02Hi
DOONERN, Mary	21	F	Spinster	09Se02Hi
BRAIN, Ann	21	F	Spinster	09Se02Hi
DOHERTY, Harriet	20	F	Spinster	09Se02Hi
CLEWS, Jas.	40	M	Laborer	09Se02Hi
SMITH, Saml.	35	M	Laborer	09Se02Hi
Robt.	09	M	Child	09Se02Hi
John	06	M	Child	09Se02Hi
HASTINGS, John	30	M	Laborer	09Se02Hi
Wm.	28	M	Laborer	09Se02Hi
HUGHES, Nancy	20	F	Spinster	09Se02Hi
MOONEY, Wm.	18	M	Laborer	09Se02Hi
CHUTE, Michl.	25	M	Laborer	09Se02Hi
Mary	20	F	Spinster	09Se02Hi
MCDOWELL, Jas.	20	M	Laborer	09Se02Hi
KENNEDY, Jno.	20	M	Laborer	09Se02Hi
MANY, Danl.	12	M	None	09Se02Hi
HERMAN, John	20	M	Laborer	09Se02Hi
Michl.	13	M	None	09Se02Hi
Cath.	11	F	None	09Se02Hi
THOMPSON, Henry	20	M	Laborer	09Se02Hi
Ann	09	F	Child	09Se02Hi
John	06	M	Child	09Se02Hi
Cath.	04	F	Child	09Se02Hi

MARGARET-SULLIVAN 09 SEPTEMBER 1847

From Newry

NAMES OF PASSENGERS		AGE	SEX	OCCUPATIONS	DATE PORT SHIP
CAREY, Robert		20	M	Clerk	09Se19Tg
LITTLE, James		19	M	Unknown	09Se19Tg
STRINGER, Mary		45	F	Unknown	09Se19Tg
DEVLIN, Bridget		24	F	Unknown	09Se19Tg
SAMSON, Margaret		22	F	Unknown	09Se19Tg
MCBRIDE, Rose		26	F	Unknown	09Se19Tg

COLUMBIA 10 SEPTEMBER 1847

From Liverpool

NAMES OF PASSENGERS		AGE	SEX	OCCUPATIONS	DATE PORT SHIP
BRENNAN, Thos.		26	M	Laborer	10Se02Hx
KEHR, Patrick		40	M	Laborer	10Se02Hx
COMSKY, Mathew		50	M	Farmer	10Se02Hx
Catherine	(W)	40	F	Wife	10Se02Hx
Mathew	(S)	15	M	Unknown	10Se02Hx
Simon	(S)	13	M	Unknown	10Se02Hx
Briget	(D)	11	F	Unknown	10Se02Hx
Catherine	(D)	08	F	Child	10Se02Hx
Patrick	(S)	06	M	Child	10Se02Hx
KERNAN, Biddy		26	F	Unknown	10Se02Hx
Emma		24	F	Unknown	10Se02Hx
SOMERVILLE, John		55	M	Farmer	10Se02Hx
Elizabeth	(W)	48	F	Wife	10Se02Hx
Samuel	(S)	15	M	Unknown	10Se02Hx
Susanna	(D)	17	F	Unknown	10Se02Hx
Ellen-Jane	(D)	10	F	Unknown	10Se02Hx
Jno.	(S)	07	M	Child	10Se02Hx
MCCORMICK, Arthur		30	M	Unknown	10Se02Hx
HARRON, Jas.		09	M	Child	10Se02Hx
WILD, Paul		22	M	Ctnsp	10Se02Hx
BRADLEY, John		27	M	Laborer	10Se02Hx
Rebecca	(W)	24	F	Wife	10Se02Hx
JAMISON, John		27	M	Laborer	10Se02Hx
RODDY, Mary		20	F	Laborer	10Se02Hx
BUCKLEY, Dennis		30	M	Laborer	10Se02Hx
SULIVAN, Henry		20	M	Laborer	10Se02Hx
Julia		20	F	Laborer	10Se02Hx
DELANCEY, Jas.		26	M	Unknown	10Se02Hx
Cath.	(W)	24	F	Wife	10Se02Hx
U		.00	U	Infant	10Se02Hx
MULVEY, Ann		20	F	Unknown	10Se02Hx
MCCARTHY, Timothy		50	M	Unknown	10Se02Hx
Died-At-Sea					
Johanna	(W)	40	F	Wife	10Se02Hx
Ann	(D)	15	F	Unknown	10Se02Hx
Catherine	(D)	14	F	Unknown	10Se02Hx
John	(S)	08	M	Child	10Se02Hx
Timothy	(S)	06	M	Child	10Se02Hx
Jeny	(D)	04	F	Child	10Se02Hx
Mary	(D)	02	F	Child	10Se02Hx
SCANLAN, Briget		16	F	Unknown	10Se02Hx
MCCARTHY, Honora		16	F	Unknown	10Se02Hx
COREY, Margt.		25	F	Unknown	10Se02Hx
CONELL, Patrick		30	M	Trader	10Se02Hx
Cath.	(W)	28	F	Wife	10Se02Hx
U		.00	U	Infant	10Se02Hx
Timothy	(S)	04	M	Child	10Se02Hx
Mary		16	F	Unknown	10Se02Hx
DEVITT, John		24	M	Laborer	10Se02Hx
MCAVELLY, John		14	M	Laborer	10Se02Hx
BARITT, Jas.		40	M	Carpenter	10Se02Hx
Margaret	(D)	16	F	Unknown	10Se02Hx
Mary	(D)	11	F	Unknown	10Se02Hx
BRIEN, Pat		26	M	Teacher	10Se02Hx
MURPHY, J.W.		30	M	Laborer	10Se02Hx
CALLAGHAN, Mary-Mrs.		50	F	Unknown	10Se02Hx
HEALY, Peter		28	M	Laborer	10Se02Hx
SULLIVAN, Fanny		20	F	Unknown	10Se02Hx
U		.00	U	Infant	10Se02Hx
HEALY, Margt.		20	F	Unknown	10Se02Hx
MAHONEY, Kean		40	M	Tailor	10Se02Hx
SULLIVAN, Marty		50	M	Laborer	10Se02Hx
Marty-Jr.	(S)	28	M	Laborer	10Se02Hx
Florence	(D)	14	F	Laborer	10Se02Hx
MOORE, John		40	M	Farmer	10Se02Hx
Mary	(W)	24	F	Wife	10Se02Hx
U		.00	U	Infant	10Se02Hx
Johanna	(D)	02	F	Child	10Se02Hx
Mary		20	F	Unknown	10Se02Hx
MCSWEENEY, Jas.		30	M	Laborer	10Se02Hx
MAHONY, Tim		30	M	Laborer	10Se02Hx
AUGLONE, Thos.		21	M	Laborer	10Se02Hx
MAHONEY, Jas.		28	M	Laborer	10Se02Hx
BUCKLEY, Margt.		27	F	Unknown	10Se02Hx
HOLLAND, Patrick		28	M	Unknown	10Se02Hx
DOLAN, Patrick		50	M	Laborer	10Se02Hx
KUGAN, Richard		30	M	Laborer	10Se02Hx
MCGRATH, Patrick		20	M	Laborer	10Se02Hx
Mary		20	F	Laborer	10Se02Hx
GIBBONS, Barney		30	M	Laborer	10Se02Hx
DURKIN, Betty		19	F	Laborer	10Se02Hx
SHEEHY, Phillip		40	M	Laborer	10Se02Hx
RYAN, Wm.		33	M	Laborer	10Se02Hx
FURY, John		30	M	Laborer	10Se02Hx
Cath.	(W)	28	F	Wife	10Se02Hx
U		.00	U	Infant	10Se02Hx
Michael	(S)	03	M	Child	10Se02Hx
HALLIGAN, John		19	M	Laborer	10Se02Hx
MCNULTY, Pat		19	M	Baker	10Se02Hx
GEAGAN, Edward		50	M	Laborer	10Se02Hx
Julia	(W)	50	F	Wife	10Se02Hx
Jno.	(S)	20	M	Unknown	10Se02Hx
NEILL, Ellen		40	F	Unknown	10Se02Hx
Mary	(D)	14	F	Unknown	10Se02Hx
Eleanor	(D)	11	F	Unknown	10Se02Hx
Eugene	(S)	08	M	Child	10Se02Hx
Ellen	(D)	05	F	Child	10Se02Hx
CONOR, Hannah		57	F	Unknown	10Se02Hx
Peter	(S)	25	M	Blacksmith	10Se02Hx
CAULFIELD, Jno.		18	M	Laborer	10Se02Hx
GRAHAM, John		30	M	Cooper	10Se02Hx
FOX, Anthony		22	M	Laborer	10Se02Hx
Michell		26	M	Laborer	10Se02Hx
Died-At-Sea					
MCDERMOTT, Mary		28	F	Unknown	10Se02Hx
MCGOWAN, Nancy		18	F	Unknown	10Se02Hx
Magt.		28	F	Unknown	10Se02Hx
KELLY, Mary		18	F	Unknown	10Se02Hx
John		09	M	Child	10Se02Hx
KILBANE, Michael		16	M	Laborer	10Se02Hx
Maria		14	F	Unknown	10Se02Hx
CAMPBELL, Letty		56	U	Unknown	10Se02Hx
Wm.	(S)	19	M	Unknown	10Se02Hx
Eliza	(D)	15	F	Unknown	10Se02Hx
MCCANNA, Francis		40	M	Unknown	10Se02Hx
TURNER, Owen		08	M	Child	10Se02Hx
MCCABE, Sarah		20	F	Unknown	10Se02Hx
MURPHY, Michael		30	M	Laborer	10Se02Hx
NOLAN, John		37	M	Mason	10Se02Hx
Ellen	(W)	33	F	Wife	10Se02Hx
U		.00	U	Infant	10Se02Hx
Catharine	(D)	08	F	Child	10Se02Hx
Patrick	(S)	06	M	Child	10Se02Hx

NAMES OF PASSENGERS		AGE	SEX	OCCUPATIONS	DATE PORT SHIP
NOLAN, Mary	(D)	04	F	Child	10Se02Hx
John	(S)	02	M	Child	10Se02Hx
REID, John		50	M	Laborer	10Se02Hx
Died-At-Sea					
Patrick	(S)	22	M	Laborer	10Se02Hx
Maria	(L)	22	F	Wife	10Se02Hx
U		.00	U	Infant	10Se02Hx
MCLOUGHLIN, John		27	M	Unknown	10Se02Hx
Mary	(W)	27	F	Wife	10Se02Hx
DUNCAN, Ellen		17	F	Unknown	10Se02Hx
KELLY, Bridget		27	F	Unknown	10Se02Hx
Betty		40	F	Unknown	10Se02Hx
COSGROVE, Edward		43	M	Flaxdr	10Se02Hx
Ann		23	F	Flaxdr	10Se02Hx
OWENS, Wm.		24	M	Laborer	10Se02Hx
DILLON, Patrick		20	M	Laborer	10Se02Hx
FEENEY, Magt.		24	F	Unknown	10Se02Hx
GRIFFIN, Mary		16	F	Unknown	10Se02Hx
MCCABE, Pete		16	M	Unknown	10Se02Hx
LYNCH, Magt.		29	M	Unknown	10Se02Hx
Mich.	(S)	06	M	Child	10Se02Hx
WARDLE, Tillerton		36	U	Crate Maker	10Se02Hx
Wm.	(S)	13	M	Crate Maker	10Se02Hx
Ann	(D)	12	F	Unknown	10Se02Hx
Sampson	(S)	09	M	Child	10Se02Hx
Lydia	(D)	05	F	Child	10Se02Hx
TURNER, Wm.		59	M	Laborer	10Se02Hx
Elizabeth	(W)	50	F	Wife	10Se02Hx
David	(S)	12	M	Unknown	10Se02Hx
ASKIN, Mary-A.		29	F	Unknown	10Se02Hx
Ann	(D)	09	F	Child	10Se02Hx
SCOTT, James		27	M	Potter	10Se02Hx
BENSON, Catherine		00	F	Unknown	10Se02Hx
Mary		00	F	Unknown	10Se02Hx
CULLEN, Ann		16	F	Unknown	10Se02Hx
Patrick		12	M	Unknown	10Se02Hx
CRAIG, David		20	M	Laborer	10Se02Hx
Jane	(W)	20	F	Wife	10Se02Hx
U		.00	U	Infant	10Se02Hx
RYDER, Bridgt.		24	F	Unknown	10Se02Hx
GREEN, Pat		22	M	Unknown	10Se02Hx
DAVEY, John		00	M	Unknown	10Se02Hx
MCGUIRE, Mathew		00	M	Unknown	10Se02Hx
HUGHES, Mary		00	F	Unknown	10Se02Hx
GARDNER, Wm.		00	M	Unknown	10Se02Hx

ANN 11 SEPTEMBER 1847

From Carbonear-Nf.

NAMES OF PASSENGERS		AGE	SEX	OCCUPATIONS	DATE PORT SHIP
MACCAY, U		34	M	Shoemaker	11Se72Th

SARDINIA-OF-NEW-YORK 11 SEPTEMBER 1847

From Liverpool

NAMES OF PASSENGERS		AGE	SEX	OCCUPATIONS	DATE PORT SHIP
ARTLY, Matilda		30	F	Servant	11Se02Ti
William	(S)	08	M	Child	11Se02Ti
GANTHROP, Dennis		44	M	Laborer	11Se02Ti
Selina	(W)	44	F	Wife	11Se02Ti
Edwin	(S)	20	M	Laborer	11Se02Ti
Joseph	(S)	15	M	Laborer	11Se02Ti
Mary	(D)	12	F	Laborer	11Se02Ti
GANTHROP, Abraham	(S)	10	F	Laborer	11Se02Ti
William	(S)	08	M	Child	11Se02Ti
Robert	(S)	03	M	Child	11Se02Ti
MCKENZIE, John		22	M	Laborer	11Se02Ti
PRIOR, Patrick		30	M	Laborer	11Se02Ti
LOOMEY, Richard		35	M	Laborer	11Se02Ti
PRIOR, Mary		30	F	Laborer	11Se02Ti
DOOLAN, Margrate		40	F	Laborer	11Se02Ti
BURNS, John		30	M	Laborer	11Se02Ti
KENERDY, William		35	M	Laborer	11Se02Ti
MAHANY, Charles		30	M	Laborer	11Se02Ti
MASTON, John		19	M	Laborer	11Se02Ti
Bridget		23	F	Laborer	11Se02Ti
Jane		22	F	Laborer	11Se02Ti
Mary		21	F	Laborer	11Se02Ti
MCCONLLY, Cath.		20	F	Laborer	11Se02Ti
SHAW, John		24	M	Laborer	11Se02Ti
DYKES, Thomas		35	M	Laborer	11Se02Ti
CARR, Patrick		15	M	Laborer	11Se02Ti
BATE, William		29	M	Laborer	11Se02Ti
Elizabeth	(W)	29	F	Wife	11Se02Ti
William	(S)	07	M	Child	11Se02Ti
Edward	(S)	05	M	Child	11Se02Ti
Mary	(D)	03	F	Child	11Se02Ti
Richard	(S)	02	M	Child	11Se02Ti
Elizabeth	(D)	.00	F	Infant	11Se02Ti
EDE, Joseph		29	M	Laborer	11Se02Ti
Blancha	(W)	28	F	Wife	11Se02Ti
John	(S)	05	M	Child	11Se02Ti
BARNAGHER, John		48	M	Laborer	11Se02Ti
Martin	(S)	13	M	Laborer	11Se02Ti
Catherine	(D)	11	F	Laborer	11Se02Ti
DWYER, Daniel		56	M	Laborer	11Se02Ti
Richard	(S)	13	M	Laborer	11Se02Ti
NILON, Bridget		22	F	Farmer	11Se02Ti
Ellen		08	F	Child	11Se02Ti
Mary		06	F	Child	11Se02Ti
Hugh		04	M	Child	11Se02Ti
Patt.		02	M	Child	11Se02Ti
Margrate		.00	F	Infant	11Se02Ti
COYNE, Owin		12	M	Laborer	11Se02Ti
Margrate		10	F	Laborer	11Se02Ti
COLLIS, Patt.		18	M	Laborer	11Se02Ti
CAMMELL, John-S.		41	M	Laborer	11Se02Ti
Ann		41	F	Laborer	11Se02Ti
EDWARDS, Ann-Elizabeth		15	F	Laborer	11Se02Ti
Sarah-Jane		12	F	Laborer	11Se02Ti
Mary		08	F	Child	11Se02Ti
CATO, George		33	M	Laborer	11Se02Ti
Mary-Ann		30	F	None	11Se02Ti
John-Morgan		12	M	Laborer	11Se02Ti
Morgan-John		10	M	Laborer	11Se02Ti
Felix		09	M	Laborer	11Se02Ti
Mary-Ellen		07	F	Laborer	11Se02Ti
Sarah-Jane		06	F	Laborer	11Se02Ti
Henry		05	M	Laborer	11Se02Ti
Elizabeth-Ann		01	F	Laborer	11Se02Ti
Thomas		.00	M	Infant	11Se02Ti
Died-At-Sea					
COLLINS, Samuel		30	M	Laborer	11Se02Ti
Susan	(W)	35	F	Wife	11Se02Ti
Louisa-Ann	(D)	15	F	Laborer	11Se02Ti
John	(S)	12	M	Laborer	11Se02Ti
Samuel	(S)	10	M	Laborer	11Se02Ti
Ellen	(D)	07	F	Laborer	11Se02Ti
George	(S)	03	M	Laborer	11Se02Ti
Jane	(D)	.00	F	Infant	11Se02Ti
BART, Jonas		35	M	Laborer	11Se02Ti
HATCH, Fredrick		30	M	Laborer	11Se02Ti
KERRIGAN, Edward		28	M	Laborer	11Se02Ti
ANDREWS, John		10	M	Laborer	11Se02Ti
MAGHEANAN, Edward		25	M	Laborer	11Se02Ti
Catherine		26	F	Laborer	11Se02Ti
MCLOCKLINE, Bridget		42	F	Laborer	11Se02Ti
John	(S)	13	M	Laborer	11Se02Ti

NAMES OF PASSENGERS		AGE	SEX	OCCUPATIONS	DATE PORT SHIP
MCLOCKLINE, Sarah-A	(D)	10	F	Laborer	11Se02Tl
Daniel	(S)	08	M	Child	11Se02Tl
AGNEW, Richard		26	M	Merchant	11Se02Tl
Mary	(W)	26	F	Wife	11Se02Tl
Mathew-E.R.	(S)	.00	M	Infant	11Se02Tl
HUBBARD, Catharine		18	F	Servant	11Se02Tl
MCKELLOSS, Mary		25	F	Lady	11Se02Tl

SARAH-HAND 13 SEPTEMBER 1847

From Liverpool

NAMES OF PASSENGERS		AGE	SEX	OCCUPATIONS	DATE PORT SHIP
CARRIGAN, John		22	M	Laborer	13Se02Tk
Margt.		20	F	Unknown	13Se02Tk
MCCARTY, Jerry		30	M	Laborer	13Se02Tk
WHITE, Joseph		30	M	Laborer	13Se02Tk
SPANAHAN, Thos.		18	M	Laborer	13Se02Tk
MANAN, Margt.Ann		25	F	Unknown	13Se02Tk
KELLY, R.		28	M	Laborer	13Se02Tk
KURAN, Pat		16	M	Laborer	13Se02Tk
GORDON, Thos.		20	M	Laborer	13Se02Tk
CAFFERTY, Anna		16	F	Unknown	13Se02Tk
CONWAY, Cath.		16	F	Unknown	13Se02Tk
KEVLIN, Eliza		20	F	Unknown	13Se02Tk
BURKE, Edmund		22	M	Laborer	13Se02Tk
HOWARD, Mary		20	F	Unknown	13Se02Tk
Honour		20	F	Unknown	13Se02Tk
MCCARTHY, Edwd.		30	M	Laborer	13Se02Tk
PURCELL, Wm.		33	M	Laborer	13Se02Tk
Anastasia	(W)	30	F	Wife	13Se02Tk
Michel	(S)	06	M	Child	13Se02Tk
Bridget	(D)	03	F	Child	13Se02Tk
Ellen	(D)	.00	F	Infant	13Se02Tk
GRIFFIN, Mich		20	M	Laborer	13Se02Tk
HICKEY, John		25	M	Laborer	13Se02Tk
Cath.		27	F	Unknown	13Se02Tk
MULHALL, William		35	M	Laborer	13Se02Tk
U	(W)	30	F	Wife	13Se02Tk
Nancy	(D)	07	F	Child	13Se02Tk
Cath.	(D)	03	F	Child	13Se02Tk
Mary	(D)	02	F	Child	13Se02Tk
John	(S)	.00	M	Infant	13Se02Tk
MONKS, Thomas		23	M	Laborer	13Se02Tk
WHITE, Wm.		19	M	Laborer	13Se02Tk
DUFFY, Wm.		34	M	Laborer	13Se02Tk
MULLIN, W.		28	M	Laborer	13Se02Tk
U	(W)	24	F	Wife	13Se02Tk
DIXON, Joseph		20	M	Laborer	13Se02Tk
CANBLE, Mary-Jane		28	F	Unknown	13Se02Tk
BRIEN, Pat		26	M	Laborer	13Se02Tk
Mary-Ann		26	F	Unknown	13Se02Tk
John		16	M	Laborer	13Se02Tk
MAULDEN, Mary		45	F	Unknown	13Se02Tk
DELANY, Peter		40	M	Laborer	13Se02Tk
Ellen	(W)	45	F	Wife	13Se02Tk
Mary	(D)	21	F	Laborer	13Se02Tk
Anastasia	(D)	20	F	Laborer	13Se02Tk
Sarah	(D)	20	F	Laborer	13Se02Tk
Cath.	(D)	16	F	Laborer	13Se02Tk
James	(S)	13	M	Laborer	13Se02Tk
Anne	(D)	16	F	Laborer	13Se02Tk
Thomas	(S)	.00	M	Infant	13Se02Tk
COGLIN, Catharine		26	F	Laborer	13Se02Tk
STEWERT, Saml.		25	M	Laborer	13Se02Tk
BIBETS, Usher		25	M	Laborer	13Se02Tk
MURRAY, Andrew		20	M	Laborer	13Se02Tk
GARETY, Martin		18	M	Laborer	13Se02Tk
KERNEN, Pat		18	M	Laborer	13Se02Tk
HARRINGTON, John		23	M	Laborer	13Se02Tk
SHEA, Miles		23	M	Laborer	13Se02Tk
Judith		25	F	Laborer	13Se02Tk
Mary		24	F	Laborer	13Se02Tk
KRUPAN, Abraham		27	M	Laborer	13Se02Tk
U	(W)	27	F	Wife	13Se02Tk
Benjn.	(S)	00	M	Child	13Se02Tk
Mahl.	(S)	02	M	Child	13Se02Tk
BUCK, Hyman-Mrs.		24	F	Laborer	13Se02Tk
SERILH, Myers		08	M	Child	13Se02Tk
BUCK, Marcus		00	M	Unknown	13Se02Tk
MAHONA, Denis		35	M	Laborer	13Se02Tk
SHEA, Pat		26	M	Laborer	13Se02Tk
MCCADDEN, Mich.		20	M	Laborer	13Se02Tk
MCKENNA, Pat		20	M	Laborer	13Se02Tk
SCANNON, Wm.		25	M	Laborer	13Se02Tk
DAVIS, John		28	M	Laborer	13Se02Tk
LITTLE, John		50	M	Laborer	13Se02Tk
JAMES, Benjn.		20	M	Laborer	13Se02Tk
MOORE, U-Mrs.		22	F	Laborer	13Se02Tk
TOBIN, Robt.		27	M	Laborer	13Se02Tk
BRAPSON, Pat		28	M	Laborer	13Se02Tk
Cath.		28	F	Laborer	13Se02Tk
John		21	M	Laborer	13Se02Tk
RANAN, Mich.		21	M	Laborer	13Se02Tk
ROOLEY, Theod.		21	M	Laborer	13Se02Tk
Cath.		23	F	Laborer	13Se02Tk
BURKE, Richard		21	M	Laborer	13Se02Tk
HANAGAN, Pat		40	M	Laborer	13Se02Tk
Mary	(W)	38	F	Wife	13Se02Tk
Judy	(D)	10	F	Laborer	13Se02Tk
Margaret	(D)	05	F	Child	13Se02Tk
MANAY, Lawrence		20	M	Laborer	13Se02Tk
WOODEND, James		25	M	Laborer	13Se02Tk
POLKINTON, Martha		.00	F	Infant	13Se02Tk
ROOLIN, James		35	M	Laborer	13Se02Tk
Bridget		30	F	Laborer	13Se02Tk
CONLIN, Owen		28	M	Laborer	13Se02Tk
Ann	(W)	28	F	Wife	13Se02Tk
Biddy	(D)	03	F	Child	13Se02Tk
Margt.	(D)	.00	F	Infant	13Se02Tk
Pat		20	M	Laborer	13Se02Tk
BROWN, Charles		43	M	Laborer	13Se02Tk
Franny		39	F	Laborer	13Se02Tk
CARROLL, Mich.		32	M	Laborer	13Se02Tk
Mona	(W)	41	F	Wife	13Se02Tk
Ellen	(D)	12	F	Laborer	13Se02Tk
John	(S)	09	M	Child	13Se02Tk
John	(S)	13	M	Laborer	13Se02Tk

SEA-OF-NEW-YORK 13 SEPTEMBER 1847

From Liverpool

NAMES OF PASSENGERS		AGE	SEX	OCCUPATIONS	DATE PORT SHIP
DAVIS, Alexander		30	M	Joiner	13Se02Is
Alice	(W)	30	F	Wife	13Se02Is
Eliza	(D)	09	F	Child	13Se02Is
John	(S)	04	M	Child	13Se02Is
Harriet	(D)	01	F	Child	13Se02Is
CONWAY, Richard		40	M	Laborer	13Se02Is
William	(S)	20	M	Laborer	13Se02Is
Eliza	(D)	21	F	Unknown	13Se02Is
Catherine		13	F	Unknown	13Se02Is
OCONNOR, Daniel		25	M	Gdnr	13Se02Is
TRACEY, Thomas		28	M	Saddler	13Se02Is
BURKE, Peter		36	M	Blacksmith	13Se02Is
SHAW, Christopher		17	M	Clerk	13Se02Is
VILLIERS, Thomas		22	M	Laborer	13Se02Is
Elizabeth		22	F	Unknown	13Se02Is
FULTON, Elizabeth-Jane		22	F	Servant	13Se02Is

NAMES OF PASSENGERS		AGE	SEX	OCCUPATIONS	DATE PORT SHIP
MCMULLEN, Nancy		21	F	Servant	13Se02Is
TAYLOR, Elizabeth		19	F	Servant	13Se02Is
CREIGHTON, Dinah		40	F	Wife	13Se02Is
Mary-Jane	(D)	11	F	Unknown	13Se02Is
Sarah-Ann	(D)	10	F	Unknown	13Se02Is
James	(S)	08	M	Child	13Se02Is
Died-At-Sea					
Fanny	(D)	05	F	Child	13Se02Is
Robert	(S)	02	M	Child	13Se02Is
COUSER, Joseph		18	M	Laborer	13Se02Is
MATTHEWS, Rose		26	F	Unknown	13Se02Is
CONWAY, Ann		18	F	Servant	13Se02Is
WALLACE, Lawrence		27	M	Tailor	13Se02Is
Michael		36	M	Laborer	13Se02Is
Catherine		18	F	Servant	13Se02Is
KILLIAN, Thomas		34	M	Laborer	13Se02Is
KERIGAN, Michael		62	M	Cooper	13Se02Is
LOWE, Bridget		09	F	Child	13Se02Is
CONNELL, Ann		41	F	Unknown	13Se02Is
Marj.	(D)	14	F	Unknown	13Se02Is
Eliza	(D)	06	F	Child	13Se02Is
MCCANN, George		33	M	Dyer	13Se02Is
FERRIGAN, Pat		33	M	Engraver	13Se02Is
GRAHAM, David		37	M	Farmer	13Se02Is
William	(S)	13	M	Farmer	13Se02Is
KELLY, Ann		18	F	Unknown	13Se02Is
MCALEER, Jess		40	M	Laborer	13Se02Is
Mary	(W)	40	F	Wife	13Se02Is
Thomas	(S)	11	M	Laborer	13Se02Is
MCGUINESS, Marj.		40	F	Unknown	13Se02Is
Hugh	(S)	07	M	Child	13Se02Is
John	(S)	05	M	Child	13Se02Is
MCALEER, Jess		13	M	Unknown	13Se02Is
RUTHERFORD, Adam		40	M	Laborer	13Se02Is
Eliza	(W)	30	F	Wife	13Se02Is
Marj.	(D)	17	F	Unknown	13Se02Is
Joseph	(S)	03	M	Child	13Se02Is
Adam	(S)	.11	M	Infant	13Se02Is
IRWIN, Marj.		20	F	Unknown	13Se02Is
MCFADDEN, Gilbert		22	M	Unknown	13Se02Is
SIMPSON, Wm.		60	M	Farmer	13Se02Is
Alice	(W)	44	F	Wife	13Se02Is
John	(S)	18	M	Unknown	13Se02Is
Jane	(D)	17	F	Unknown	13Se02Is
Catherine	(D)	14	F	Unknown	13Se02Is
William	(S)	12	M	Unknown	13Se02Is
Robert	(S)	10	M	Unknown	13Se02Is
Eliza	(D)	08	F	Child	13Se02Is
GRAY, John		18	M	Unknown	13Se02Is
MCALEER, James		43	M	Laborer	13Se02Is
Biddy	(W)	38	F	Wife	13Se02Is
Pat	(S)	11	M	Unknown	13Se02Is
Peter	(S)	10	M	Unknown	13Se02Is
Marj.	(D)	08	F	Child	13Se02Is
Michael	(S)	06	M	Child	13Se02Is
Biddy	(D)	04	F	Child	13Se02Is
Nancy	(D)	.04	F	Infant	13Se02Is
Nancy	(D)	17	F	Unknown	13Se02Is
Ellen	(D)	00	F	Unknown	13Se02Is
MCCUTTOR, John		28	M	Laborer	13Se02Is
LAWLES, Peter		11	M	Unknown	13Se02Is
CURRY, Mary		12	F	Unknown	13Se02Is
BIRMINGHAM, James		28	M	Tailor	13Se02Is
MCKENNA, Sarah		40	F	None	13Se02Is
FITCHILL, Samuel		15	M	None	13Se02Is
Elizabeth		18	F	None	13Se02Is
CALLAHAN, Thos.		27	M	Laborer	13Se02Is
MCCONNELL, Mary		18	F	None	13Se02Is
Pat		28	M	Laborer	13Se02Is
BOYLE, Thomas		50	M	Laborer	13Se02Is
DUNLAVY, Anthony		25	M	Laborer	13Se02Is
CORRIGAN, Ann		45	F	Unknown	13Se02Is
Pat	(S)	11	M	Unknown	13Se02Is
Margaret	(D)	07	F	Child	13Se02Is
James	(S)	02	M	Child	13Se02Is

NAMES OF PASSENGERS		AGE	SEX	OCCUPATIONS	DATE PORT SHIP
MCMANUS, Michae		24	M	Laborer	13Se02Is
BOYLE, James		30	M	Laborer	13Se02Is
KILGART, Margaret		18	F	Laborer	13Se02Is
SORAHAN, Pat.		40	M	Laborer	13Se02Is
CLUKIN, Phil.		20	M	Laborer	13Se02Is
SORAHAN, Bridget		44	F	Wife	13Se02Is
Margaret	(D)	18	F	Servant	13Se02Is
Catherine	(D)	17	F	Servant	13Se02Is
MCENTAGART, Honor		40	F	Fwk	13Se02Is
SMITH, Ann		18	F	Fwk	13Se02Is
LEE, Julia		14	F	Fwk	13Se02Is
JORDAN, Richard		41	M	Laborer	13Se02Is
Catherine	(W)	16	F	Unknown	13Se02Is
DORAN, Catherine		16	F	Unknown	13Se02Is
JORDAN, Mary-Ann		09	F	Child	13Se02Is
Judith		07	F	Child	13Se02Is
Richard	(B)	05	M	Child	13Se02Is
John	(B)	02	M	Child	13Se02Is
FLYNN, Pat		30	M	Groom	13Se02Is
FORD, Ann		22	F	Servant	13Se02Is
Maria		24	F	Unknown	13Se02Is
Barney		48	M	Unknown	13Se02Is
Margaret		08	F	Child	13Se02Is
SCOTT, John		60	M	Laborer	13Se02Is
Thomas	(S)	26	M	Laborer	13Se02Is
Nancy	(W)	60	F	Unknown	13Se02Is
MCGORRUN, Richd.		06	M	Child	13Se02Is
GALLAGHER, Dennis		22	M	Laborer	13Se02Is
LASSLY, Edward		21	M	Laborer	13Se02Is
ODONNELL, Margaret		38	F	Unknown	13Se02Is
MCGLURSKY, John		04	F	Child	13Se02Is
CANNON, Biddy		28	F	Servant	13Se02Is
MONAGHAN, Pat		21	M	Clerk	13Se02Is
Bridget		22	F	Unknown	13Se02Is
PATTERSON, Robert		25	M	Laborer	13Se02Is
QUINN, Wm.		20	M	Nailer	13Se02Is
GIBSON, Jane		21	F	Servant	13Se02Is
FERGUSON, Wm.		40	M	Miller	13Se02Is
Jane		30	F	Unknown	13Se02Is
Mary-Ann		27	F	Unknown	13Se02Is
Robert	(S)	18	M	Unknown	13Se02Is
BRADLEY, Michael		33	M	Laborer	13Se02Is
ONEILL, Bridget		28	F	Dressmaker	13Se02Is
Daniel	(S)	09	M	Child	13Se02Is
MCMICKLE, Rhoda		46	F	None	13Se02Is
PATTERSON, John		29	M	Laborer	13Se02Is
Marg.	(W)	22	F	Unknown	13Se02Is
Isabella	(D)	05	F	Child	13Se02Is
David	(S)	02	M	Child	13Se02Is
TORMEY, James		14	M	None	13Se02Is
CARROLL, Ellen		20	F	Servant	13Se02Is
CARPENTER, Catherine		25	F	Servant	13Se02Is
SMITH, Ann		22	F	Servant	13Se02Is
WILSON, Letitia		26	F	Servant	13Se02Is
LYNCH, Ann		20	F	Servant	13Se02Is
CAHILL, U		26	M	Shoemaker	13Se02Is
COMMONS, Hugh		26	M	Laborer	13Se02Is
Bernard		24	M	Laborer	13Se02Is
KELLY, Mary		16	F	Servant	13Se02Is
DONNELL, Madge		36	F	Unknown	13Se02Is
Sarah	(W)	26	F	Wife	13Se02Is
Ann	(D)	16	F	Unknown	13Se02Is
MCGONIGAL, John		24	M	Laborer	13Se02Is
CANNON, Charles		12	M	Unknown	13Se02Is
MCCROSSON, Michael		29	M	Laborer	13Se02Is
DORAN, Susan		12	F	Unknown	13Se02Is
James		09	M	Child	13Se02Is
MAGUIRE, Patt.		50	M	Farmer	13Se02Is
Rose	(D)	17	F	Unknown	13Se02Is
Margaret	(W)	48	F	Wife	13Se02Is
Patt.	(S)	13	M	Unknown	13Se02Is
Alice	(D)	10	F	Unknown	13Se02Is
Terence	(S)	08	M	Child	13Se02Is
Hugh	(S)	06	M	Child	13Se02Is
MOSS, Stephen		60	M	Unknown	13Se02Is

NAMES OF PASSENGERS		AGE	SEX	OCCUPATIONS	DATE PORT SHIP
SMITH, Mary-Ann		22	F	Servant	13Se02Is

GARRICK 13 SEPTEMBER 1847

From Liverpool

NAMES OF PASSENGERS		AGE	SEX	OCCUPATIONS	DATE PORT SHIP
COURT, James-M.		40	M	Servant	13Se02Aa
WOODS, William		26	M	Laborer	13Se02Aa
Catharen	(W)	00	F	Wife	13Se02Aa
U		00	U	Unknown	13Se02Aa
Catharen	(D)	02	F	Child	13Se02Aa
Alexander	(S)	.00	M	Infant	13Se02Aa
MCWILLIAMS, Bernerd		25	F	Servant	13Se02Aa
Margaret		24	F	Servant	13Se02Aa
Susan		21	F	Servant	13Se02Aa
MURPHEY, Michal		19	M	Laborer	13Se02Aa
Mary		25	F	Servant	13Se02Aa
CAMPBELL, James		30	M	Joiner	13Se02Aa
Ellen	(W)	25	F	Wife	13Se02Aa
Bridget	(D)	05	F	Child	13Se02Aa
Catharin	(D)	05	F	Child	13Se02Aa
James	(S)	04	M	Child	13Se02Aa
Patric		31	M	Laborer	13Se02Aa
Mary		01	F	Child	13Se02Aa
DONIGAN, James		22	M	Blacksmith	13Se02Aa
NOWLAN, James		26	M	Laborer	13Se02Aa
MCDOWAL, Elizabeth		22	F	Servant	13Se02Aa
Sarah		19	F	Dressmaker	13Se02Aa
Mar.Jane		18	F	Dressmaker	13Se02Aa
CAMPBELL, Georg.		00	M	Gdnr	13Se02Aa
ENNIS, Pat		24	M	Coachman	13Se02Aa
Catharin		19	F	Servant	13Se02Aa
LAMB, Agness		50	F	Servant	13Se02Aa
Jane		28	F	Servant	13Se02Aa
James		22	M	Laborer	13Se02Aa
HALLIGAN, Mary		21	F	Servant	13Se02Aa
DENNY, Edd.		23	M	Cooper	13Se02Aa
MORGAN, John		30	M	Laborer	13Se02Aa
KENNEDY, Ann		25	F	Servant	13Se02Aa
BRIDSON, Michal		40	M	Piano Maker	13Se02Aa
Lucy	(W)	40	F	Wife	13Se02Aa
Thomas	(S)	20	M	None	13Se02Aa
Benjamin	(S)	15	M	None	13Se02Aa
Elizabeth	(D)	12	F	None	13Se02Aa
Jordan	(S)	10	M	None	13Se02Aa
Henry	(S)	21	M	None	13Se02Aa
CLOGHER, Michal		14	M	Laborer	13Se02Aa
BRACKEN, Margaret		50	F	Servant	13Se02Aa
Margaret	(D)	18	F	Servant	13Se02Aa
Patric	(S)	07	M	Child	13Se02Aa
BERRY, Joseph		22	M	Farmer	13Se02Aa
MARTIN, Owen		45	M	Laborer	13Se02Aa
Ann		24	F	None	13Se02Aa
Owen		14	M	None	13Se02Aa
Catharin		12	F	None	13Se02Aa
Patric		02	M	Child	13Se02Aa
Mary		.00	F	Infant	13Se02Aa
WALSH, Martin		26	M	Servant	13Se02Aa
Julia		24	F	Servant	13Se02Aa
TOPPIN, Samuel		22	M	Farmer	13Se02Aa
GRAN, Hugh		40	M	Tailor	13Se02Aa
ROONEY, Margaret		50	F	Servant	13Se02Aa
Thomas		20	M	Laborer	13Se02Aa
MCGEE, Mary		30	F	Servant	13Se02Aa
SHARPLES, William		22	M	Saddler	13Se02Aa
CARTER, William		26	M	Glass Maker	13Se02Aa
Ann-Jane	(W)	22	F	Wife	13Se02Aa
Ann	(D)	.00	F	Infant	13Se02Aa
MADOLE, Elizabeth		24	F	Servant	13Se02Aa
MULLINS, Pat		27	M	Laborer	13Se02Aa
Margaret		27	F	None	13Se02Aa
LANDRIDGE, James		17	M	Blacksmith	13Se02Aa
LENAN, William		50	M	Farmer	13Se02Aa
Rose	(W)	40	F	Wife	13Se02Aa
Ellen	(D)	20	F	None	13Se02Aa
Rose	(D)	19	F	None	13Se02Aa
Mary	(D)	17	F	None	13Se02Aa
Patric	(S)	18	M	None	13Se02Aa
Madge	(D)	12	F	None	13Se02Aa
Philip	(S)	09	M	Child	13Se02Aa
Thomas	(S)	07	M	Child	13Se02Aa
LACY, Pat		34	M	Laborer	13Se02Aa
MARTIN, Pat		50	M	Laborer	13Se02Aa
Bridget	(W)	50	F	Wife	13Se02Aa
John	(S)	25	M	Clerk	13Se02Aa
BRYAN, Catherin		40	F	Servant	13Se02Aa
Sarah		03	F	Child	13Se02Aa
SMITH, Rose		40	F	Servant	13Se02Aa
Mary	(D)	23	F	Servant	13Se02Aa
Margaret	(D)	19	F	Servant	13Se02Aa
Rose	(D)	18	F	Servant	13Se02Aa
Catharin	(D)	12	F	Servant	13Se02Aa
John	(S)	18	M	Servant	13Se02Aa
RYAN, Nother		40	M	Laborer	13Se02Aa
CARNEY, Bridget		55	F	None	13Se02Aa
James	(S)	16	M	None	13Se02Aa
Died-At-Sea					
William	(S)	13	M	None	13Se02Aa
DOYLE, Judith		30	F	None	13Se02Aa
Michal		25	M	Laborer	13Se02Aa
NEALE, Dennis		46	M	Laborer	13Se02Aa
MURPHY, Peter		22	M	Laborer	13Se02Aa
CAMPBELL, George		40	M	Weaver	13Se02Aa
Ellin	(W)	38	F	Wife	13Se02Aa
Stafford	(S)	12	M	None	13Se02Aa
Margaret	(D)	10	F	Unknown	13Se02Aa
Maria	(D)	08	F	Child	13Se02Aa
William	(S)	06	M	Child	13Se02Aa
Ellin	(D)	04	F	Child	13Se02Aa
Mary	(D)	02	F	Child	13Se02Aa
FOULKNER, Joseph		18	M	Clerk	13Se02Aa
KING, Eliza		30	F	Dressmaker	13Se02Aa
DANIGAN, Margaret		18	F	Weaver	13Se02Aa
Alice		20	F	Servant	13Se02Aa
BRADEY, Rose		18	F	Milliner	13Se02Aa
Ellin		21	F	Milliner	13Se02Aa
MCANALTY, Mart.		39	F	Milliner	13Se02Aa
Catharin	(D)	07	F	Child	13Se02Aa
Biddy	(D)	05	F	Child	13Se02Aa
Ellin	(D)	02	F	Child	13Se02Aa
DONALY, Hugh		30	M	Laborer	13Se02Aa
Biddy		38	F	None	13Se02Aa
MULLIN, Margat.		08	F	Child	13Se02Aa
FITZGERRALD, Ellin		20	F	Servant	13Se02Aa
CAGNY, Ellin		12	F	Servant	13Se02Aa
Bridgt.		10	F	Servant	13Se02Aa
BRYAN, Ellen		20	F	Servant	13Se02Aa
FENNESSEY, Mart.		30	F	Servant	13Se02Aa
COHREN, James		02	M	Child	13Se02Aa
BRYAN, Hono.		24	F	Servant	13Se02Aa
LAVILL, David		40	M	Weaver	13Se02Aa
Hugh		10	M	None	13Se02Aa
HAMAHAN, Rody		26	M	Farmer	13Se02Aa
WALSH, Charls.		25	M	Laborer	13Se02Aa
MORGAN, James		25	M	Laborer	13Se02Aa
COFFEY, Charles		33	M	Tailor	13Se02Aa
Hannah		30	F	None	13Se02Aa
GAMON, James		30	M	Engineer	13Se02Aa
LAWLIS, Dennis		34	M	Carpenter	13Se02Aa
Mary	(W)	30	F	Wife	13Se02Aa
Jane	(D)	04	F	Child	13Se02Aa
Patric	(S)	02	M	Child	13Se02Aa
Martha	(D)	.00	F	Infant	13Se02Aa
FALLON, Pat		34	M	Carpenter	13Se02Aa

NAMES OF PASSENGERS		AGE	SEX	OCCUPATIONS	DATE PORT SHIP
REID, James		26	M	Carpenter	13Se02Aa
GREEN, Ann		20	F	Servant	13Se02Aa
CLARK, Mary		45	F	Servant	13Se02Aa
MCDERMOTT, Mart.		24	F	Servant	13Se02Aa
CLARK, Lawrence		05	M	Child	13Se02Aa
MASTON, Mart.		35	F	Dressmaker	13Se02Aa
Eliza		18	F	Dressmaker	13Se02Aa
Margaret		17	F	Dressmaker	13Se02Aa
John		13	M	None	13Se02Aa
Richard		11	M	None	13Se02Aa
LEWIS, Richard		45	M	Farmer	13Se02Aa
Margrt.	(W)	38	F	Wife	13Se02Aa
Catharin	(D)	17	F	Unknown	13Se02Aa
Sarah	(S)	16	F	Unknown	13Se02Aa
Charles	(S)	13	F	Unknown	13Se02Aa
George	(S)	07	M	Child	13Se02Aa
Marie	(D)	05	F	Child	13Se02Aa
WEBSTER, George		24	M	Farmer	13Se02Aa
Eliza		22	F	Unknown	13Se02Aa
TURNER, Mary-Ann		19	F	Unknown	13Se02Aa
THOMPSON, Edwd.		19	M	Unknown	13Se02Aa
DAVIS, Thos.		16	M	Unknown	13Se02Aa
FOLEY, Joseph		18	M	Unknown	13Se02Aa
RAFERTY, James-M.		26	M	Mechanic	13Se02Aa
HOWELL, Nichl.		30	M	Merchant	13Se02Aa
Cath.		27	F	Unknown	13Se02Aa
HUTCHINGSON, Ann		25	F	Unknown	13Se02Aa
Mary		20	F	Unknown	13Se02Aa
FLEMMING, Mary		28	F	Unknown	13Se02Aa
DEELIN, Ellyn		19	F	Unknown	13Se02Aa
FELIN, Mary-Ann		20	F	Unknown	13Se02Aa
MCMAHON, Mary		40	F	Servant	13Se02Aa
ROBERTS, Robert-W.		38	M	Laborer	13Se02Aa
Rose	(W)	36	F	Unknown	13Se02Aa
John	(S)	13	M	Unknown	13Se02Aa
Susan	(D)	11	F	Unknown	13Se02Aa
Hugh	(S)	11	M	Unknown	13Se02Aa
Thomas	(S)	06	M	Child	13Se02Aa
James	(S)	03	M	Child	13Se02Aa
David	(S)	.00	M	Infant	13Se02Aa
MCMULLIN, Valentine		26	M	Baker	13Se02Aa
FITZSIMMONS, Robt.		40	F	Servant	13Se02Aa
RYAN, Pat		40	M	Gdnr	13Se02Aa
GRAHAM, James		35	M	Miner	13Se02Aa
Mary	(W)	40	F	Wife	13Se02Aa
Samuel	(S)	13	M	Unknown	13Se02Aa
Michael	(S)	11	M	Unknown	13Se02Aa
Mary	(D)	09	F	Child	13Se02Aa
LONG, Eliza		07	F	Child	13Se02Aa
BROWN, Rose-Ann		20	F	Servant	13Se02Aa
MURTHA, Rose-Ann		16	F	Servant	13Se02Aa
DEVEREUX, Elizabeth		35	F	Servant	13Se02Aa
Mary		10	F	Servant	13Se02Aa
BOOTH, Samuel		26	M	Cbtmkr	13Se02Aa
HIGGINS, Francis		20	M	Cbtmkr	13Se02Aa
BUTLER, Owen		26	M	Laborer	13Se02Aa
ONEIL, Hugh		28	M	Laborer	13Se02Aa
Mary	(W)	26	F	Wife	13Se02Aa
Charles	(S)	03	M	Child	13Se02Aa
John	(S)	.00	M	Infant	13Se02Aa
HELAND, William		18	M	Laborer	13Se02Aa
TAMMEY, Elizabeth		24	F	Unknown	13Se02Aa
DOORAS, Mart.		24	F	Dressmaker	13Se02Aa
Biddy		17	F	Servant	13Se02Aa
BROWN, Eliza		20	F	Servant	13Se02Aa
NOON, John		20	M	Laborer	13Se02Aa
ONEIL, Pat		47	M	Spinner	13Se02Aa
Catherin		50	F	None	13Se02Aa
SHEPHERD, Thomas		36	M	Servant	13Se02Aa
Margaret	(W)	24	F	Wife	13Se02Aa
John	(S)	12	M	None	13Se02Aa
Thomas	(S)	12	M	None	13Se02Aa
William	(S)	10	M	None	13Se02Aa
Edward	(S)	07	M	Child	13Se02Aa
Robinson	(S)	01	M	Child	13Se02Aa

NAMES OF PASSENGERS		AGE	SEX	OCCUPATIONS	DATE PORT SHIP
WILKINS, Margt.		18	F	Servant	13Se02Aa
MONERY, Sarah		21	F	Servant	13Se02Aa
MALLON, Julia		26	F	Servant	13Se02Aa
HAYS, Danl.		47	M	Farmer	13Se02Aa
Catharin	(W)	40	F	Wife	13Se02Aa
William	(S)	20	M	None	13Se02Aa
Michael	(S)	18	M	None	13Se02Aa
John	(S)	18	M	None	13Se02Aa
Edward	(S)	14	M	None	13Se02Aa
Patric	(S)	12	M	None	13Se02Aa
Bryan	(S)	10	M	None	13Se02Aa
Mary	(D)	08	F	Child	13Se02Aa
RYAN, Bridget		18	M	Servant	13Se02Aa
JAMESON, Robert		20	M	Grocer	13Se02Aa
MCNEIL, Thomas		24	M	Bricklayer	13Se02Aa
YOUNG, David		18	M	Draper	13Se02Aa
DOYL, John		24	M	Laborer	13Se02Aa
ACHESON, David		24	M	Butcher	13Se02Aa
LYNAN, James		26	M	Farmer	13Se02Aa
BARRET, Mary		18	F	Dressmaker	13Se02Aa
STERN, George		24	M	Weaver	13Se02Aa
COX, Alex		26	M	Servant	13Se02Aa
Rosanna		21	F	None	13Se02Aa
RAIN, Pat		30	M	Laborer	13Se02Aa
DONAHUE, Edward		20	M	Laborer	13Se02Aa
MASTON, Julia		18	F	Servant	13Se02Aa
Patric		12	F	Servant	13Se02Aa
Ann		09	F	Child	13Se02Aa
HOSTY, Charles		20	M	Clerk	13Se02Aa
HEFFERON, Peter		30	M	Laborer	13Se02Aa
HOWARD, Sarah		18	M	Servant	13Se02Aa
COURTNEY, Owen		42	M	Farmer	13Se02Aa
Catharin	(W)	42	F	Wife	13Se02Aa
Judith	(D)	21	F	None	13Se02Aa
Bridget	(D)	13	F	None	13Se02Aa
Edward	(S)	11	M	None	13Se02Aa
Catharin	(D)	09	F	Child	13Se02Aa
George	(S)	07	M	Child	13Se02Aa
Michael	(S)	04	M	Child	13Se02Aa
KELLY, John		23	M	Paper Maker	13Se02Aa
NESSFIELD, John		21	M	Lrfh	13Se02Aa
BYRN, Edward		24	M	Paper Maker	13Se02Aa
MCGANAY, Mart.		18	F	Servant	13Se02Aa
MARTIN, David		24	M	Joiner	13Se02Aa
LAUNDON, Edward		40	M	Coachman	13Se02Aa
ROONEY, James		23	M	Saddler	13Se02Aa
Mary-Ann		17	F	None	13Se02Aa
MCGEE, Joseph		24	M	Laborer	13Se02Aa
BOWERY, Peter		24	M	Laborer	13Se02Aa
DENNY, Margaret		21	F	None	13Se02Aa
NEIL, Pat		20	M	Laborer	13Se02Aa
STAUNTON, Michal		20	M	Laborer	13Se02Aa
KELLY, Catharin		45	F	Servant	13Se02Aa
DELANY, John		08	M	Child	13Se02Aa
HENNESSEY, Pat		26	M	Laborer	13Se02Aa
Mary		60	F	None	13Se02Aa
Margaret		34	F	Servant	13Se02Aa
Catharin		22	F	Servant	13Se02Aa

ISAAC-WALTON 13 SEPTEMBER 1847

From Liverpool

NAMES OF PASSENGERS		AGE	SEX	OCCUPATIONS	DATE PORT SHIP
SHERIDAN, Bridget		20	F	Spinster	13Se02TI
CAMPBELL, Mary		20	F	Spinster	13Se02TI
BOYLE, Catherine		25	F	Spinster	13Se02TI
MCCABE, Rose		19	F	Spinster	13Se02TI
DRUMGOOLE, Geo.H.		25	M	Solicitor	13Se02TI
Henriette	(W)	24	F	Wife	13Se02TI

NAMES OF PASSENGERS		AGE	SEX	OCCUPATIONS	DATE PORT SHIP
DRUMGOOLE, George	(S)	03	M	Child	13Se02TI
U	(D)	.00	F	Infant	13Se02TI
SULLIVAN, Patrick		24	M	Laborer	13Se02TI
DUFF, Patrick		28	M	Laborer	13Se02TI
FARRELL, Mary		26	F	Spinster	13Se02TI
Margaret		24	F	Spinster	13Se02TI
TWOMEY, Mary		23	F	Spinster	13Se02TI
DALEY, Colney		45	M	Laborer	13Se02TI
Honora		19	F	Spinster	13Se02TI
FERGUSON, James		66	M	Farmer	13Se02TI
KELLY, Peter		27	M	Laborer	13Se02TI
Catherine	(W)	27	F	Wife	13Se02TI
Margaret	(D)	04	F	Child	13Se02TI
Peter	(S)	02	M	Child	13Se02TI
Ann		20	F	Unknown	13Se02TI
POWER, James		46	M	Farmer	13Se02TI
Ann	(W)	42	F	Wife	13Se02TI
Catherine	(D)	14	F	Unknown	13Se02TI
Margaret	(D)	12	F	Unknown	13Se02TI
Mary	(D)	10	F	Unknown	13Se02TI
John	(S)	08	M	Child	13Se02TI
Ellen	(D)	06	F	Child	13Se02TI
James	(S)	04	M	Child	13Se02TI
Ann	(D)	02	F	Child	13Se02TI
JORDAN, Thomas		18	M	Physician	13Se02TI
KELLY, Patrick		19	M	Farmer	13Se02TI
Patrick		12	M	Farmer	13Se02TI
SULLIVAN, Michael		27	M	Laborer	13Se02TI
Mary		09	F	Child	13Se02TI
Ellen		24	F	Unknown	13Se02TI
MCHERR, Peter		26	M	Laborer	13Se02TI
MCLOCHLEN, Mary		25	F	Spinster	13Se02TI
SHEA, Michael		35	M	Laborer	13Se02TI
WARD, Ann		50	F	Wi	13Se02TI
Thomas		30	M	Laborer	13Se02TI
Frank		09	M	Child	13Se02TI
KEEGAN, Mary		12	F	Unknown	13Se02TI
MCCABE, Bessy		09	F	Child	13Se02TI
MCGEE, Owen		26	M	Laborer	13Se02TI
James		24	M	Laborer	13Se02TI
ARMSTRONG, John		50	M	Carpenter	13Se02TI
Judith	(W)	50	F	Wife	13Se02TI
Willm.	(S)	15	M	Unknown	13Se02TI
Pricilla	(D)	12	F	Unknown	13Se02TI
Hugh	(S)	11	M	Unknown	13Se02TI
KELLY, Elizabeth		16	F	Spinster	13Se02TI
RENNITS, James		24	M	Laborer	13Se02TI
SMITH, John		23	M	Shoemaker	13Se02TI
GALLAGHER, Mary		18	F	Spinster	13Se02TI
RAINOLDS, James		18	M	Laborer	13Se02TI
MCQUADE, Margaret		22	F	Wife	13Se02TI
Mary	(D)	03	F	Child	13Se02TI
QUIN, Mary		20	F	Spinster	13Se02TI
Ellen		10	F	Spinster	13Se02TI
KENNEDY, Darby		20	M	Carpenter	13Se02TI
Nathan		06	M	Child	13Se02TI
DRAKE, Ellen		39	F	Wi	13Se02TI
Ellen		23	F	Unknown	13Se02TI
Michael		20	M	Unknown	13Se02TI
Ann		17	F	Unknown	13Se02TI
Mary		10	F	Unknown	13Se02TI
GRAY, Mary		15	F	Spinster	13Se02TI
FARLEY, Bridget		20	F	Spinster	13Se02TI
LEE, Patrick		16	M	Laborer	13Se02TI
COLMAN, Thomas		20	M	Carpenter	13Se02TI
Catharine		21	F	Spinster	13Se02TI
LEARY, John		17	M	Laborer	13Se02TI
Margaret		24	F	Spinster	13Se02TI
MCCORMICK, Michael		24	M	Tailor	13Se02TI
HIGGIN, Michael		17	M	Laborer	13Se02TI
MORRIS, Sarah		18	F	Spinster	13Se02TI
LESLIE, Eliza		30	F	Wi	13Se02TI
Robert	(S)	12	M	Unknown	13Se02TI
MCCOSKER, John		60	M	Butcher	13Se02TI
Nelly	(W)	55	F	Wife	13Se02TI
MCCOSKER, Jane	(D)	13	F	Unknown	13Se02TI
John	(S)	11	M	Unknown	13Se02TI
MCGENNIS, Peter		30	M	Laborer	13Se02TI
GRIFFIN, Michael		32	M	Cbtmkr	13Se02TI
GORDON, Thomas		25	M	Grocer	13Se02TI
CONWAY, Catherine		18	F	Spinster	13Se02TI
CAVERTY, Ann		22	F	Spinster	13Se02TI
DARDIS, Thomas		35	M	Laborer	13Se02TI
Mary	(W)	30	F	Wife	13Se02TI
Patrick	(S)	15	M	Unknown	13Se02TI
Edwin	(S)	10	M	Unknown	13Se02TI
Henry	(S)	10	M	Unknown	13Se02TI
John	(S)	08	M	Child	13Se02TI
Ann	(D)	06	F	Child	13Se02TI
Mary	(D)	02	F	Child	13Se02TI
RATICAN, Mary		16	F	Spinster	13Se02TI
FALLO, Honora		22	F	Spinster	13Se02TI
MCKEEHAN, Martha		20	F	Spinster	13Se02TI
CARTY, Patrick		20	M	Laborer	13Se02TI
MADDEN, Catherine		27	F	Spinster	13Se02TI
DOLAN, Hannah		50	F	Wi	13Se02TI
CAMPBELL, Elizabeth		38	F	Wi	13Se02TI
GRIFFIN, Thomas		24	M	Laborer	13Se02TI
Ellen		20	F	Spinster	13Se02TI
QUIN, Michael		25	M	Grocer	13Se02TI
Catherine	(W)	20	F	Wife	13Se02TI
Martha	(D)	.04	F	Infant	13Se02TI
LEONARD, Jane		14	F	Unknown	13Se02TI
MAHONY, Catherine		30	F	Spinster	13Se02TI
DAWSON, Catherine		19	F	Spinster	13Se02TI
MAHON, Patrick		35	M	Carpenter	13Se02TI
HEALY, Hampton		62	M	Farmer	13Se02TI
DUGAN, Mary		16	F	Spinster	13Se02TI
Eliza		20	F	Spinster	13Se02TI
BEADY, Bridget		14	F	Spinster	13Se02TI
Rose		11	F	Spinster	13Se02TI
NEAVEN, Bridget		24	F	Spinster	13Se02TI
Maria	(D)	.11	F	Infant	13Se02TI

COLLOONEY 13 SEPTEMBER 1847

From London

NAMES OF PASSENGERS		AGE	SEX	OCCUPATIONS	DATE PORT SHIP
TICE, William		30	M	Cbtmkr	13Se21la
FERGUSON, Frederic		27	M	Seaman	13Se21la
Susanna-U.		32	F	None	13Se21la
Susanna-Sophia		03	F	Child	13Se21la
KELLY, John		30	M	Grainer	13Se21la
NEILSON, Thomas-Horati		47	M	Accountant	13Se21la
Robert-Ray		15	M	Accountant	13Se21la
Marion		18	F	None	13Se21la
Annabella		16	F	None	13Se21la
Agnes-Reed		13	F	None	13Se21la
NELSON, Mary-Patterson		13	F	None	13Se21la
GRIFFIN, Patrick		42	M	Farmer	13Se21la
Mary		35	F	None	13Se21la
Patrick		09	M	Child	13Se21la
Margaret		07	F	Child	13Se21la
John		04	M	Child	13Se21la
Maurice		.10	M	Infant	13Se21la
FITZGERALD, William		30	M	Farmer	13Se21la
John		40	M	Farmer	13Se21la

KALAMAZOO 13 SEPTEMBER 1847

From Liverpool

NAMES OF PASSENGERS	AGE	SEX	OCCUPATIONS	DATE PORT SHIP
HACKETT, Pierce	32	M	Laborer	13Se02Bt
Michael	30	M	Laborer	13Se02Bt
Johanna	20	F	Laborer	13Se02Bt
MURPHY, Mary	40	F	Laborer	13Se02Bt
Edward	02	M	Child	13Se02Bt
SMITH, Jane	23	F	Laborer	13Se02Bt
CARMAN, Mary	50	F	Laborer	13Se02Bt
Died-At-Sea				
Elishia	12	F	Laborer	13Se02Bt
DOOGAN, Mary	26	F	Laborer	13Se02Bt
MCFADDEN, Ellen	09	F	Child	13Se02Bt
MCCARTHY, Eugene	30	M	Laborer	13Se02Bt
Catherine	27	F	Wife	13Se02Bt
U	.00	U	Infant	13Se02Bt
MAHONEY, Jane	17	F	None	13Se02Bt
WHALEN, Margt.	26	F	None	13Se02Bt
Martin	02	M	Child	13Se02Bt
ROSS, Honor	25	F	Farmer	13Se02Bt
S-IR, Margt.	14	F	Unknown	13Se02Bt
Mary	12	F	Unknown	13Se02Bt
MCTEAGUE, Bernard	40	M	Laborer	13Se02Bt
JONES, Charles	36	M	Laborer	13Se02Bt
DONLY, Edward	33	M	Laborer	13Se02Bt
Ann	30	F	Wife	13Se02Bt
John	01	M	Child	13Se02Bt
MCCABE, Margret	39	F	None	13Se02Bt
Ann	26	F	Wife	13Se02Bt
Margt.	09	F	Child	13Se02Bt
Micheal	08	M	Child	13Se02Bt
FANEN, William	55	M	Laborer	13Se02Bt
Charlotte	45	F	Wife	13Se02Bt
Elizabeth	19	F	Laborer	13Se02Bt
Maria	16	F	Laborer	13Se02Bt
Isabella	12	F	Laborer	13Se02Bt
William	12	M	Laborer	13Se02Bt
Charlotte	10	F	Laborer	13Se02Bt
Emily	05	F	Child	13Se02Bt
Louisa	03	F	Child	13Se02Bt
MURPHY, Micheal	34	M	Farmer	13Se02Bt
Mary	13	F	Farmer	13Se02Bt
MCKENNA, Teresa	25	M	Spinster	13Se02Bt
Rosanna	01	F	Child	13Se02Bt
NEILL, John	40	M	Laborer	13Se02Bt
Esther	41	F	Spinster	13Se02Bt
Eliza	11	F	Spinster	13Se02Bt
Robert	07	M	Child	13Se02Bt
KENNEDY, Thomas	52	M	Farmer	13Se02Bt
Margaret	19	F	Farmer	13Se02Bt
Anthony	16	M	Farmer	13Se02Bt
Judy	13	F	Farmer	13Se02Bt
Mary	11	F	Farmer	13Se02Bt
William	10	M	Farmer	13Se02Bt
John	09	M	Child	13Se02Bt
JENKINS, Anastatia	24	F	Spinster	13Se02Bt
NOWLAN, Maria	25	F	Spinster	13Se02Bt
HARES, James	32	M	Farmer	13Se02Bt
GILL, William	30	M	Farmer	13Se02Bt
Sarah	20	F	Wife	13Se02Bt
William	01	M	Child	13Se02Bt
MCCONNELL, James	30	M	Laborer	13Se02Bt
Mary	28	F	Wife	13Se02Bt
Mary	09	F	Child	13Se02Bt
Charles	06	M	Child	13Se02Bt
Joseph	04	M	Child	13Se02Bt
MCCABE, Hugh	40	M	Farmer	13Se02Bt
MCCABE, Ellen	34	F	Wife	13Se02Bt
Jane	12	F	Farmer	13Se02Bt
Andrew	10	M	Farmer	13Se02Bt
James	08	M	Child	13Se02Bt
DOYLE, John	40	M	Farmer	13Se02Bt
Mary	30	F	Wife	13Se02Bt
Henry	06	M	Child	13Se02Bt
Mary	.00	F	Infant	13Se02Bt
DAILEY, Hannah	18	F	Spinster	13SeC2Bt
MURPHY, David	23	M	Farmer	13Se02Bt
Michl.	20	M	Farmer	13Se02Bt
Ann	20	F	Farmer	13Se02Bt
Mary	19	F	Farmer	13Se02Bt
MULCAHAY, Patt.	22	M	Laborer	13Se02Bt
Catherine	24	F	Laborer	13Se02Bt
DOYLE, Thomas	34	M	Laborer	13Se02Bt
CONNELL, Simon	27	M	Laborer	13Se02Bt
BURT, Patt.	25	M	Laborer	13Se02Bt
BURKE, Edward	28	M	Farmer	13Se02Bt
FALLEN, Mary	22	F	Farmer	13Se02Bt
Catherine	20	F	Farmer	13Se02Bt
JENKINS, Jane	17	F	Farmer	13Se02Bt
SMITH, William	21	M	Weaver	13Se02Bt
MCCALLY, Bridget	22	F	Spinster	13Se02Bt
STILL, Elizabeth	48	F	Spinster	13Se02Bt
GAMAN, Jane	27	F	Spinster	13Se02Bt
STILL, Mary	24	F	Spinster	13Se02Bt
David	22	M	Farmer	13Se02Bt
John	19	M	Farmer	13Se02Bt
James	13	M	Farmer	13Se02Bt
Eliza	08	F	Child	13Se02Bt
Creighton	06	M	Child	13Se02Bt
Sarah-Jane	06	F	Child	13Se02Bt
FITZGERALD, Edward	26	M	Farmer	13Se02Bt
LINEHAN, John	22	M	Farmer	13Se02Bt
KIRBY, Daniel	12	M	Farmer	13Se02Bt
PRENDERGAST, Patt.	35	M	Laborer	13Se02Bt
Jane	18	F	Laborer	13Se02Bt
Richard	10	M	Laborer	13Se02Bt
GUNN, Patt.	26	M	Laborer	13Se02Bt
KAYE, Joseph	28	M	Laborer	13Se02Bt
Jane	26	F	Laborer	13Se02Bt
WALSH, Eliza	30	F	Spinster	13Se02Bt
MCCORMICK, Mary	19	F	Spinster	13Se02Bt
KELLY, Catherine	30	F	Spinster	13Se02Bt
MCDONALD, Bridget	17	F	Spinster	13Se02Bt
DUGGAN, Michl.	20	M	Laborer	13Se02Bt
JUBB, Mary-Ann	20	F	Spinster	13Se02Bt
PROCTER, Ann	24	F	Spinster	13Se02Bt
Eliza	04	F	Child	13Se02Bt
FOLEY, Denty	40	M	Laborer	13Se02Bt
FALCOLNER, Hugh	40	M	Farmer	13Se02Bt
Catherine	35	F	Farmer	13Se02Bt
MCCULLOCH, Richard	22	M	Farmer	13Se02Bt
Robert	13	M	Farmer	13Se02Bt
Catherine	11	F	Farmer	13Se02Bt
Alexander	08	M	Child	13Se02Bt
James	06	M	Child	13Se02Bt
DAY, Micheal	40	M	Laborer	13Se02Bt
Francis	35	F	Wife	13Se02Bt
James	14	M	Laborer	13Se02Bt
Mary	09	F	Child	13Se02Bt
John	05	M	Child	13Se02Bt
Micheal	03	M	Child	13Se02Bt
KIRWEN, John	24	M	Farmer	13Se02Bt
Jane	22	F	Farmer	13Se02Bt
Catherine	20	F	Farmer	13Se02Bt
Patt.	04	M	Child	13Se02Bt
John	02	M	Child	13Se02Bt
GARDINER, James	60	M	Farmer	13Se02Bt
DECK, Mary	30	F	Spinster	13Se02Bt
FORSYTH, Agnes	25	F	Spinster	13Se02Bt
BUXTON, Mary	22	F	Spinster	13Se02Bt
DONOHOE, Patt.	20	M	Laborer	13Se02Bt
BUXTON, James	15	M	Laborer	13Se02Bt

MARY-PARKINS 14 SEPTEMBER 1847

From PICTOU,N.S.

NAMES OF PASSENGERS	AGE	SEX	OCCUPATIONS	DATE PORT SHIP
MCDONALD, Victor	48	M	Unknown	14Se43Gu

MONTEZUMA 14 SEPTEMBER 1847

From Liverpool

NAMES OF PASSENGERS	AGE	SEX	OCCUPATIONS	DATE PORT SHIP
JACOBS, Joseph	36	M	Merchant	14Se02Ao
HOLLINGSWORTH, Joseph	27	M	Merchant	14Se02Ao
CURTIS, John	23	M	Merchant	14Se02Ao
WILKINSON, Wm.	17	M	Gentleman	14Se02Ao
CARRUTHERS, Archd.	19	M	Gentleman	14Se02Ao
SMITH, William	24	M	Merchant	14Se02Ao
Elizabeth	24	F	Wife	14Se02Ao
Anna	03	F	Child	14Se02Ao
JEFFRYS, Elizabeth-Mrs	60	F	Lady	14Se02Ao
BRISCOE, Mary	26	F	Lady	14Se02Ao
Emma	21	F	Lady	14Se02Ao
COCHRANE, H.	21	M	Merchant	14Se02Ao
CARNEL, Caroline	06	F	Child	14Se02Ao
SCANLAN, Michael	25	M	Clerk	14Se02Ao
DUNCAN, John-Edwd.	30	M	Tailor	14Se02Ao
PURDON, Thomas	30	M	Prntctr	14Se02Ao
Anne	30	F	Unknown	14Se02Ao
Lilly	25	F	Unknown	14Se02Ao
BASTOCK, Geo.	27	M	Farmer	14Se02Ao
LIGGET, James	20	M	Laborer	14Se02Ao
MURPHY, James	23	M	Laborer	14Se02Ao
KINNEAR, Patrick	27	M	Grocer	14Se02Ao
MONAGHAN, James	50	M	Farmer	14Se02Ao
Catherine	15	F	Unknown	14Se02Ao
Mary	40	F	Wife	14Se02Ao
Julia	13	F	Unknown	14Se02Ao
Mary	08	F	Child	14Se02Ao
James	05	M	Child	14Se02Ao
Christopher	17	M	Unknown	14Se02Ao
KELLY, Catherine	40	F	Unknown	14Se02Ao
Anne	12	F	Unknown	14Se02Ao
Patrick	10	M	Unknown	14Se02Ao
BRADLEY, Jane	30	F	Unknown	14Se02Ao
William	12	M	Unknown	14Se02Ao
Bernard	10	M	Unknown	14Se02Ao
Bridget	07	F	Child	14Se02Ao
Margaret	04	F	Child	14Se02Ao
GARDNER, Jno.	27	M	Artist	14Se02Ao
KIELY, Thomas	26	M	Tailor	14Se02Ao
HICKEY, James	28	M	Carpenter	14Se02Ao
CURTIS, John	21	M	Lawyer	14Se02Ao
MACK, James	32	M	Lawyer	14Se02Ao
MURPHY, Rose	16	F	Unknown	14Se02Ao
ROWLEY, Michael	25	M	Unknown	14Se02Ao
KELLY, Mary	21	F	Unknown	14Se02Ao
BRADY, Patrick	20	M	Farmer	14Se02Ao
MORRISON, Catherine	18	F	Unknown	14Se02Ao
HILLIARD, Henry	25	M	Watchmaker	14Se02Ao
Maryanne	21	F	Cnf	14Se02Ao
ERWIN, Hugh	25	M	Tailor	14Se02Ao
Essy	25	F	Wife	14Se02Ao
Rbt.	.00	M	Infant	14Se02Ao
DOWNEY, Thomas	21	M	Laborer	14Se02Ao
PRITCHARD, James	24	M	Unknown	14Se02Ao
LOY, Thomas	20	M	Laborer	14Se02Ao
OCONNOR, Brian	21	M	Clerk	14Se02Ao
GREER, Margaret	24	F	Unknown	14Se02Ao
LOCKART, Jane	52	F	Unknown	14Se02Ao
MORFACE, Patrick	20	M	Laborer	14Se02Ao
Alice	18	F	Unknown	14Se02Ao
RYAN, Robt.	24	M	Laborer	14Se02Ao
Ellen	17	F	Unknown	14Se02Ao
William	27	M	Laborer	14Se02Ao
FARRELL, Thomas	20	M	Laborer	14Se02Ao
CONWAY, Thomas	21	M	Shoemaker	14Se02Ao
KENNEDY, Maryanne	44	F	Unknown	14Se02Ao
James	21	M	Laborer	14Se02Ao
Bridget	20	F	Unknown	14Se02Ao
Patrick	17	M	Unknown	14Se02Ao
Hugh	16	M	Unknown	14Se02Ao
Thomas	13	M	Unknown	14Se02Ao
GILMARTIN, Mary	26	F	Unknown	14Se02Ao
ODONNEL, Bridget	30	F	Unknown	14Se02Ao
FURY, Thomas	20	M	Porter	14Se02Ao
Patrick	18	M	Brush Maker	14Se02Ao
Isabella	18	F	Brush Maker	14Se02Ao
KELLY, Margaret	20	F	Shoemaker	14Se02Ao
SHEEHAN, Jeremiah	22	M	Shoemaker	14Se02Ao
ROTH, Edward	23	M	Teacher	14Se02Ao
DENNY, Geo.	37	M	Weaver	14Se02Ao
Thomas	35	M	Laborer	14Se02Ao
THOMPSON, Lancelot	19	M	Shoemaker	14Se02Ao
CASSIDY, Michael	19	M	Tinsmith	14Se02Ao
Mary	36	F	Unknown	14Se02Ao
Sarah	12	F	Unknown	14Se02Ao
John	07	M	Child	14Se02Ao
Anne	03	F	Child	14Se02Ao
WHITE, Maurice	18	M	Laborer	14Se02Ao
Stephen	19	M	Farmer	14Se02Ao
Margaret	17	F	Unknown	14Se02Ao
Anne	10	F	Unknown	14Se02Ao
MULLEN, Andrew	38	M	Shoemaker	14Se02Ao
REED, Patrick	25	M	Laborer	14Se02Ao
HORAN, John	50	M	Groom	14Se02Ao
RORK, Anne	50	F	Unknown	14Se02Ao
Catherine	12	F	Unknown	14Se02Ao
Maryanne	10	F	Unknown	14Se02Ao
CARRAN, Mary	18	F	Unknown	14Se02Ao
BARRY, Elizabeth	18	F	Unknown	14Se02Ao
MCCAHAN, James	22	M	Laborer	14Se02Ao
KELLY, Patrick	25	M	Laborer	14Se02Ao
Daniel	30	M	Laborer	14Se02Ao
FLINN, Lawrence	60	M	Laborer	14Se02Ao
Margaret	60	F	Unknown	14Se02Ao
FARRELL, Margaret	09	F	Child	14Se02Ao
FLYNN, Anne	25	F	Unknown	14Se02Ao
Lawrence	21	M	Laborer	14Se02Ao
MOORE, Thomas	36	M	Coach Maker	14Se02Ao
JENKINS, John	36	M	Spmk	14Se02Ao
CORRIGAN, Mary	23	F	Unknown	14Se02Ao
CARTY, John	24	M	Tailor	14Se02Ao
HENNING, William	24	M	Peddler	14Se02Ao
Margt.Jane	19	F	Unknown	14Se02Ao
GRIFFITH, Eliza	20	F	Unknown	14Se02Ao
MCLOUGHLAN, Hugh	21	M	Weaver	14Se02Ao
RESLAN, Mary	20	F	Unknown	14Se02Ao
RUSH, Anne	19	F	Unknown	14Se02Ao
SHAFFERY, Michael	40	M	Piper	14Se02Ao
DOHERTY, Catherine	24	M	Unknown	14Se02Ao
PROCTOR, John	20	M	Tinman	14Se02Ao
BURROWES, Charles	21	M	Spdmkr	14Se02Ao
OBRIEN, Mark	19	M	Painter	14Se02Ao
Maurice	25	M	Lace Maker	14Se02Ao
WARD, Hugh	37	M	Painter	14Se02Ao
DUNN, James	16	M	Unknown	14Se02Ao
MANNING, William	37	M	Saddler	14Se02Ao
Ellen	38	F	Dressmaker	14Se02Ao
MCINTYRE, Thomas	20	M	Carpenter	14Se02Ao

NAMES OF PASSENGERS	AGE	SEX	OCCUPATIONS	DATE PORT SHIP
RYAN, Andrew	16	M	Unknown	14Se02Ao
MYERS, John	37	M	Laborer	14Se02Ao
Margaret	37	F	Wife	14Se02Ao
Maryanne	12	F	Unknown	14Se02Ao
Margaret	06	F	Child	14Se02Ao
Robert	03	M	Child	14Se02Ao
Sarah	.00	F	Infant	14Se02Ao
Jane	25	F	Unknown	14Se02Ao
GARREY, Peter	23	M	Laborer	14Se02Ao
Catherine	19	F	Dressmaker	14Se02Ao
FITZPATRICK, Edwd.	21	M	Laborer	14Se02Ao
MCMULLEN, Anne	16	F	Unknown	14Se02Ao
KEEGAN, James	22	M	Heckler	14Se02Ao
MCKANNAH, Catherine	20	F	Unknown	14Se02Ao
REDFORD, John	28	M	Brewer	14Se02Ao
MCCABE, Anne	28	M	Unknown	14Se02Ao
HOWES, Simon	27	M	Shoemaker	14Se02Ao
LYONS, Ellen	23	M	Unknown	14Se02Ao
ECCLESFIELD, Robt.	27	M	Farmer	14Se02Ao
HAVERTY, Bridget	22	M	Unknown	14Se02Ao
Died-At-Sea				
SPRUCE, John	44	M	Weaver	14Se02Ao
FLANNAGAN, John	24	M	Flaxdr	14Se02Ao
CORMICK, Michael	55	M	Laborer	14Se02Ao
Judith	54	F	Unknown	14Se02Ao
SHEEHY, Ellen	22	F	Unknown	14Se02Ao
DONOVAN, Johanna	25	F	Unknown	14Se02Ao
WATERSON, Jane	18	F	Unknown	14Se02Ao
FLANAGAN, Mary	22	F	Unknown	14Se02Ao
MARTIN, Thomas	30	M	Laborer	14Se02Ao
Bridget	30	F	Unknown	14Se02Ao
CALAGHAN, Thomas	27	M	Mmsn	14Se02Ao
MAGRATH, Margaret	16	F	Unknown	14Se02Ao
MACLERATH, John	10	M	Unknown	14Se02Ao
Robt.	16	M	Weaver	14Se02Ao
FINNEGAN, Susan	20	F	Dressmaker	14Se02Ao
LADLEY, Anne	22	F	Dressmaker	14Se02Ao
SLATTERY, William	17	M	Laborer	14Se02Ao
MACKADON, John	22	M	Tailor	14Se02Ao
REILLY, Mary	20	F	Unknown	14Se02Ao
WHITE, Mary	20	F	Unknown	14Se02Ao
MCCABE, Patrick	27	M	Farmer	14Se02Ao
MCAGALA, Eliza	19	F	Unknown	14Se02Ao
MCKEON, Anne-Jane	19	F	Unknown	14Se02Ao
Ellen	17	F	Unknown	14Se02Ao
Sarah-Jane	17	F	Unknown	14Se02Ao
GEOGHAGAN, Daniel	17	M	Laborer	14Se02Ao
WARD, Catherine	39	F	Unknown	14Se02Ao
John	17	M	Plasterer	14Se02Ao
Bernard	07	M	Child	14Se02Ao
Mary	20	F	Unknown	14Se02Ao
Isabella	15	F	Unknown	14Se02Ao
MAGRAME, Margaret	34	F	Dressmaker	14Se02Ao
John	12	M	Unknown	14Se02Ao
MCPEAK, Alicia	17	F	Bookbinder	14Se02Ao
FEILY, Margaret	14	F	Unknown	14Se02Ao
COSTELLO, Mary	02	F	Child	14Se02Ao
CORCORAN, Margaret	22	F	Unknown	14Se02Ao
FLEMING, Michael	26	M	Laborer	14Se02Ao
John	18	M	Laborer	14Se02Ao
Mary	60	F	Unknown	14Se02Ao
REILLY, Matthew	28	M	Laborer	14Se02Ao
BURN, Thomas	15	M	Laborer	14Se02Ao
CONNOR, Mary	20	F	Laborer	14Se02Ao
HICKEY, Fra.	19	U	Laborer	14Se02Ao
Ellen	16	F	Laborer	14Se02Ao
CANON, Charles	21	M	Laborer	14Se02Ao
GILSINNON, Eliza	18	F	Unknown	14Se02Ao
DONOVAN, Margaret	30	F	Unknown	14Se02Ao
SCOTT, John	38	M	Laborer	14Se02Ao
AHERN, Patrick	35	M	Laborer	14Se02Ao
WOODS, Patrick	25	M	Butcher	14Se02Ao
KERNAHAN, Marie	02	F	Child	14Se02Ao
ROSE, Richard	23	M	Clothier	14Se02Ao
MILLIGAN, Margaret	23	F	Unknown	14Se02Ao
TOOLE, Catherine	35	F	Unknown	14Se02Ao
Jeremiah	20	M	Laborer	14Se02Ao
Judith	18	F	Unknown	14Se02Ao
Michael	15	M	Unknown	14Se02Ao
James	10	M	Unknown	14Se02Ao
CANTWELL, John	21	M	Laborer	14Se02Ao
CLANCY, Patrick	35	M	Laborer	14Se02Ao
GUARD, Margaret	63	F	Unknown	14Se02Ao
FORREST, Thomas	20	M	Weaver	14Se02Ao
COLMAN, Alice	50	F	Unknown	14Se02Ao
BROWN, Anne	20	F	Unknown	14Se02Ao
REGAN, Margaret	30	F	Unknown	14Se02Ao
Anne	08	F	Child	14Se02Ao
Catherine	08	F	Child	14Se02Ao
John	06	M	Child	14Se02Ao
Margaret	05	F	Child	14Se02Ao
Daniel	03	M	Child	14Se02Ao
COLMAN, John	14	M	Unknown	14Se02Ao
Alice	10	F	Unknown	14Se02Ao
Catherine	12	F	Unknown	14Se02Ao
REGAN, Mary	03	F	Child	14Se02Ao
GARITY, Winnifred	50	F	Unknown	14Se02Ao
Died-At-Sea				
GILDAY, Peter	19	M	Laborer	14Se02Ao
BARMAN, Catherine	60	F	Unknown	14Se02Ao
DIVANEY, Mary	40	F	Unknown	14Se02Ao
REYNOLDS, Bernard	14	M	Unknown	14Se02Ao
Felix	09	M	Child	14Se02Ao
CARMON, Patrick	29	M	Laborer	14Se02Ao
MCQUADE, Thomas	22	M	Laborer	14Se02Ao
MURPHY, Catherine	23	F	Laborer	14Se02Ao
FARLEY, Peter	20	M	Bootmaker	14Se02Ao
DONOHOE, Anne	23	F	Unknown	14Se02Ao
BRYAN, Mary	25	F	Unknown	14Se02Ao
FOLEY, James	12	F	Unknown	14Se02Ao
Margt.	09	F	Child	14Se02Ao
CABBOT, Mary	25	F	Unknown	14Se02Ao
KENNEDY, John	57	M	Coachman	14Se02Ao
Lawrence	58	M	Laborer	14Se02Ao
Bridget	24	F	Unknown	14Se02Ao
Catherine	22	F	Unknown	14Se02Ao
FOX, Catherine	16	F	Unknown	14Se02Ao
MACRORY, Jane	19	F	Dressmaker	14Se02Ao
Eliza	21	F	Dressmaker	14Se02Ao
BURTON, Elizabeth	16	F	Dressmaker	14Se02Ao
CASSIDY, Catherine	19	F	Unknown	14Se02Ao
OCONNELL, John	58	M	Gdnr	14Se02Ao
MCCALL, Mary	66	F	Unknown	14Se02Ao
Sarah	36	F	Unknown	14Se02Ao
Michael	07	M	Child	14Se02Ao
Mary	05	F	Child	14Se02Ao
Patrick	03	M	Child	14Se02Ao
SCOTT, Thomas	28	M	Laborer	14Se02Ao
Catherine	20	F	Unknown	14Se02Ao
LARKIN, Mary	44	F	Unknown	14Se02Ao
ROONEY, Mary	60	F	Unknown	14Se02Ao
Patrick	10	M	Unknown	14Se02Ao
Terence	36	M	Unknown	14Se02Ao
SHEA, Mary	20	F	Unknown	14Se02Ao
CAFFEY, Mary	50	F	Unknown	14Se02Ao
GAUGHRAN, Patrick	26	M	Stableman	14Se02Ao
DENNERY, Thomas	55	M	Laborer	14Se02Ao
Margaret	17	F	Unknown	14Se02Ao
BYRNE, Brien	27	M	Laborer	14Se02Ao
MCGOVERN, Hugh	40	M	Laborer	14Se02Ao
Anne	40	F	Wife	14Se02Ao
Anne	12	F	Unknown	14Se02Ao
Mary	16	F	Unknown	14Se02Ao
Peter	14	M	Unknown	14Se02Ao
Patrick	05	M	Child	14Se02Ao
Bridget	01	F	Child	14Se02Ao
RIDGATE, Anne	27	F	Dressmaker	14Se02Ao
Josephine	03	F	Child	14Se02Ao
SHORIGHRAN, Jeremiah	32	M	Laborer	14Se02Ao
Bridget	22	F	Unknown	14Se02Ao

NAMES OF PASSENGERS	AGE	SEX	OCCUPATIONS	DATE PORT SHIP
GOFFIN, James	25	M	Blacksmith	14Se02Ao
OCONNELL, Thomas	23	M	Farmer	14Se02Ao
TOWNSEND, John	40	M	Weaver	14Se02Ao
MEARA, Judith	50	F	Unknown	14Se02Ao
Bridget	13	F	Unknown	14Se02Ao
Judith	15	F	Unknown	14Se02Ao
BOWERS, Mary	20	F	Unknown	14Se02Ao
DINEN, John	47	M	Butcher	14Se02Ao
MCCORMICK, John	20	M	Laborer	14Se02Ao
DUGGAN, Michael	18	M	Laborer	14Se02Ao
CUSACK, Margaret	16	M	Laborer	14Se02Ao
BOYLE, Rose	24	M	Laborer	14Se02Ao
MEARA, Martin	19	M	Clerk	14Se02Ao
Patrick	50	M	Weaver	14Se02Ao
Johanna (T)	16	F	Unknown	14Se02Ao
HARTIGAN, Mary	16	F	Dressmaker	14Se02Ao
COOK, Jane	19	F	Unknown	14Se02Ao
BELL, Louisa	22	F	Tirw	14Se02Ao
LEECH, James	21	M	Miner	14Se02Ao
BEAUMONT, Anne Died-At-Sea	75	F	Unknown	14Se02Ao
CASSIDY, Margaret	18	F	Unknown	14Se02Ao
ASHTON, Hariet	26	F	Milliner	14Se02Ao
Eliza	.00	F	Infant	14Se02Ao
William	02	M	Child	14Se02Ao
BARKER, Samuel	28	M	Grocer	14Se02Ao
Sarah	30	F	Wife	14Se02Ao
Samuel	01	M	Child	14Se02Ao
Elizabeth	03	F	Child	14Se02Ao
Richard	05	M	Child	14Se02Ao
William	07	M	Child	14Se02Ao
BARR, William	27	F	Draper	14Se02Ao
Maryanne	26	F	Wife	14Se02Ao
William	04	M	Child	14Se02Ao
Maryanne	01	F	Child	14Se02Ao
FARRELL, Edward	26	M	Laborer	14Se02Ao
Jane	23	F	Unknown	14Se02Ao
CLOUGH, Robt.	47	M	Clothier	14Se02Ao
Sarah	46	F	Wife	14Se02Ao
Sarah-Anne	20	F	Unknown	14Se02Ao
Elizabeth-Anne	15	F	Unknown	14Se02Ao
Hannah	13	F	Unknown	14Se02Ao
Martha	10	F	Unknown	14Se02Ao
PARK, Jonathan	16	M	Cbtmkr	14Se02Ao
MAUD, Wm.H.	40	M	Auctioneer	14Se02Ao
Sarah	30	F	Wife	14Se02Ao
William	14	M	Unknown	14Se02Ao
Valentine	10	M	Unknown	14Se02Ao
DAVIS, Hannah	43	F	Unknown	14Se02Ao
Eliza	22	F	Unknown	14Se02Ao
Eleanor	16	F	Unknown	14Se02Ao
Caroline	13	F	Unknown	14Se02Ao
Francis	10	M	Unknown	14Se02Ao
Edward	06	M	Child	14Se02Ao
Essy	03	F	Child	14Se02Ao
CORBET, Patrick	40	M	Gdnr	14Se02Ao
Catherine	32	F	Unknown	14Se02Ao
HAMILTON, William	33	M	Surgeon	14Se02Ao
Mary	50	F	Unknown	14Se02Ao
MCCUTCHEON, Richard	36	M	Saddler	14Se02Ao
Anne	28	F	Wife	14Se02Ao
Edward	04	M	Child	14Se02Ao
Isabella	03	F	Child	14Se02Ao
Maria	01	F	Child	14Se02Ao
DORLAN, Anne	17	F	Unknown	14Se02Ao
DUFFY, Bernard	22	M	Grocer	14Se02Ao
LEAKE, William	19	M	Tailor	14Se02Ao
Charles	21	M	Hatter	14Se02Ao
Eliza	21	F	Unknown	14Se02Ao
James	11	M	Unknown	14Se02Ao
Elizabeth	08	F	Child	14Se02Ao
WHITE, Stephen Died-At-Sea	.00	M	Infant	14Se02Ao
GEARY, Patrick Died-At-Sea	23	M	Laborer	14Se02Ao
CROGAN, James Died-At-Sea	22	M	Laborer	14Se02Ao
Margaret Died-At-Sea	58	F	Unknown	14Se02Ao
HOGAN, Thomas	21	M	Laborer	14Se02Ao
MCGOVERN, John	23	M	Laborer	14Se02Ao
MANSFIELD, Henry	29	M	Laborer	14Se02Ao
CLANCY, Robert	18	M	Laborer	14Se02Ao
FITZPATRICK, Wm.	21	M	Laborer	14Se02Ao

GLENMORE 15 SEPTEMBER 1847

From Liverpool

NAMES OF PASSENGERS	AGE	SEX	OCCUPATIONS	DATE PORT SHIP
MONTGOMERY, W.H.	22	M	Gentleman	15Se02Km
B.	20	F	Lady	15Se02Km
CONNOR, John	36	M	Gentleman	15Se02Km
KIRLEY, Sarah	20	F	Servant	15Se02Km
TORPY, Pat	26	M	Laborer	15Se02Km
Martin	21	M	Laborer	15Se02Km
Michael	20	M	Laborer	15Se02Km
MCGLONE, Bridget	22	F	Spinster	15Se02Km
DALF, Thomas	24	M	Wheelwright	15Se02Km
TAYLOR, John	20	M	Shoemaker	15Se02Km
MCGUIRE, Pat	22	M	Shoemaker	15Se02Km
Honora	14	F	Spinster	15Se02Km
DORKIN, Winfred	14	F	Spinster	15Se02Km
Sarah	14	F	Spinster	15Se02Km
MCELDERREY, Michael	32	M	Shoemaker	15Se02Km
Rose	32	F	Spinster	15Se02Km
DIAMOND, Sally	18	F	Spinster	15Se02Km
MCGLADE, Sally	21	F	Spinster	15Se02Km
ROSS, John	49	M	Tailor	15Se02Km
George	11	M	Tailor	15Se02Km
DOTTEY, Nicholas	50	M	Tailor	15Se02Km
Nicholas-Jr.	22	M	Tailor	15Se02Km
RYAN, Michael	24	M	Laborer	15Se02Km
DOLAN, Michael	24	M	Unknown	15Se02Km
OBRIEN, Mary	30	F	Spinster	15Se02Km
ONEIL, Wm.	26	M	Laborer	15Se02Km
Pat	20	M	Laborer	15Se02Km
CALLAGER, Ellen	23	F	Spinster	15Se02Km
BRODERICK, Thomas	21	M	Tailor	15Se02Km
BUCKLEY, Edward	23	M	Laborer	15Se02Km
DELANE, Alice	21	F	Spinster	15Se02Km
KENNEDY, Alice	09	F	Child	15Se02Km
SHEA, Timothy	28	M	Laborer	15Se02Km
TOPIN, Hugh	24	M	Tanner	15Se02Km
BEETHAM, Hanah	20	F	Spinster	15Se02Km
Grace	18	F	Spinster	15Se02Km
ROWAN, Essey	18	F	Spinster	15Se02Km
Robt.	22	M	Tanner	15Se02Km
NIBLOCK, Eliza-Jane	19	F	Spinster	15Se02Km
KNOX, John	18	M	Shoemaker	15Se02Km
FINNEGAN, Ann	15	F	Spinster	15Se02Km
POTTS, Mary	19	F	Spinster	15Se02Km
MAXWELL, James	19	M	Weaver	15Se02Km
GARLAND, Patt	26	M	Carver	15Se02Km
Margt.	24	F	Carver	15Se02Km
BROWN, Robt.	36	M	Laborer	15Se02Km
FARRELLY, Patt.	24	M	Laborer	15Se02Km
Bridget	20	F	Spinster	15Se02Km
MCGERRICK, Mary	26	F	Spinster	15Se02Km
Margt.	10	F	Spinster	15Se02Km
BYRNE, Mary	26	F	Spinster	15Se02Km
FITZGERALD, Thos.	48	M	Laborer	15Se02Km
Julia	44	F	Wife	15Se02Km
Abby	16	F	Unknown	15Se02Km
Michael	13	M	Unknown	15Se02Km

NAMES OF PASSENGERS	AGE	SEX	OCCUPATIONS	DATE PORT SHIP
FITZGERALD, Ellen	11	F	Unknown	15Se02Km
Julia	09	F	Child	15Se02Km
Catherine	06	F	Child	15Se02Km
FOX, James	26	M	Blacksmith	15Se02Km
Margaret	26	F	Wife	15Se02Km
Edwd.	13	M	Unknown	15Se02Km
SCULLY, Daniel	60	M	Weaver	15Se02Km
Catherin	60	F	Wife	15Se02Km
Margt.	26	F	Weaver	15Se02Km
HAGERTY, Timothy	30	M	Tailor	15Se02Km
Mary	25	F	Unknown	15Se02Km
Jeremiah	28	M	Laborer	15Se02Km
KELLY, Edward	18	M	Tailor	15Se02Km
COLLINS, Lmary	25	F	Spinster	15Se02Km
Francis	70	M	Farmer	15Se02Km
CALLENDAN, Ann	40	F	Spinster	15Se02Km
HAMMOND, Michael	20	M	Laborer	15Se02Km
KEEFE, Denis	50	M	Laborer	15Se02Km
Julia	40	F	Spinster	15Se02Km
LONG, William	27	M	Laborer	15Se02Km
U	27	F	Spinster	15Se02Km
KANE, William	19	M	Laborer	15Se02Km
MURPHY, Mary	19	F	Spinster	15Se02Km
MACHTADY, Thomas	24	M	Laborer	15Se02Km
LANDRAGAN, Mag.	40	F	Spinster	15Se02Km
Ellen	40	F	Spinster	15Se02Km
Julia	13	F	Spinster	15Se02Km
Thomas	11	M	Spinster	15Se02Km
David	10	M	Spinster	15Se02Km
Bridget	09	F	Child	15Se02Km
FLAHERTY, Margt.	30	F	Unknown	15Se02Km
Thomas	05	M	Child	15Se02Km
CROWLEY, Dennis	25	M	Unknown	15Se02Km
Daniel	04	M	Child	15Se02Km
SHEA, John	22	M	Laborer	15Se02Km
MCGILLCUDDY, B.	13	F	Unknown	15Se02Km
LANE, Edwd.	30	M	Brazier	15Se02Km
MCELROY, James	45	M	Farmer	15Se02Km
Maria	43	F	Spinster	15Se02Km
Margaret	19	F	Spinster	15Se02Km
Mary	19	F	Spinster	15Se02Km
John	15	M	Laborer	15Se02Km
Henry	12	M	Laborer	15Se02Km
Patrick	08	M	Child	15Se02Km
LEHY, Thomas	28	M	Weaver	15Se02Km
GIBONS, Thomas	30	M	Mason	15Se02Km
CAVNAGH, Samuel	18	M	Laborer	15Se02Km
COLLINS, Nancy	25	F	Unknown	15Se02Km
James	17	M	Laborer	15Se02Km
TRAINER, Thomas	40	M	Unknown	15Se02Km
SPAIN, Michael	35	M	Unknown	15Se02Km
DONBURY, Judith	30	F	Spinster	15Se02Km
Maria	17	F	Unknown	15Se02Km
GROGAN, Mary	35	F	Unknown	15Se02Km
Thomas	02	M	Child	15Se02Km
KELLY, Thomas	25	M	Carpenter	15Se02Km
U	25	F	Wife	15Se02Km
Joseph	02	M	Child	15Se02Km
MALONE, Anthony	30	M	Laborer	15Se02Km
MACK, Alexander	25	M	Unknown	15Se02Km
DALTON, Ann	13	F	Unknown	15Se02Km
HARVEY, John	26	M	Laborer	15Se02Km
MULVEY, Ellen	20	F	Unknown	15Se02Km
MOORE, Patt.	40	M	Unknown	15Se02Km
COLLINS, John	25	M	Laborer	15Se02Km
LEAHY, Ellen	30	F	Unknown	15Se02Km
KEHOWN, Ellen	36	F	Unknown	15Se02Km
MCCABE, John	26	M	Unknown	15Se02Km
Ann	08	F	Child	15Se02Km
Judith	06	F	Child	15Se02Km
Catherine	03	F	Child	15Se02Km
Mary	.00	F	Infant	15Se02Km
MURTAGH, James	26	M	Laborer	15Se02Km
Bridget	24	F	Spinster	15Se02Km
Peggy	25	F	Spinster	15Se02Km

NAMES OF PASSENGERS	AGE	SEX	OCCUPATIONS	DATE PORT SHIP
MURTAGH, Mary	28	F	Spinster	15Se02Km
NICHOLS, Ebenezer	22	M	Laborer	15Se02Km
MULLINS, Margt.	22	F	Spinster	15Se02Km
DUGAN, John	45	M	Laborer	15Se02Km
Ellen	22	F	Spinster	15Se02Km
KELLY, John	25	F	Spinster	15Se02Km
IRWIN, James	20	M	Unknown	15Se02Km
DOUGHERTY, Sally	26	F	Spinster	15Se02Km
Mary	21	F	Unknown	15Se02Km
Sarah	27	F	Unknown	15Se02Km

ADARIO 16 SEPTEMBER 1847

From Sligo

NAMES OF PASSENGERS		AGE	SEX	OCCUPATIONS	DATE PORT SHIP
QUINAN, Bryan		20	M	Laborer	16Se28Gv
KAVENY, Mary		22	F	Spinster	16Se28Gv
QUINAN, Eleanor		49	F	Spinster	16Se28Gv
Michael	(S)	18	M	Farmer	16Se28Gv
James	(S)	05	M	Child	16Se28Gv
ORMSBY, Mary		14	F	Spinster	16Se28Gv
MISSETT, Robert		42	M	Carpenter	16Se28Gv
MULLANEY, James		25	M	Tailor	16Se28Gv
PADDEN, Mary		17	F	Spinster	16Se28Gv
MCGLOIN, Patt		23	M	Laborer	16Se28Gv
Eleanor		19	F	Spinster	16Se28Gv
TANSY, John		20	M	Laborer	16Se28Gv
DUFFY, Margt.		17	F	Spinster	16Se28Gv
TANSY, Mary		19	F	Spinster	16Se28Gv
JENNINGS, Honor		21	F	Spinster	16Se28Gv
Malachy		17	M	None	16Se28Gv
MCANDREW, Anne		41	F	Spinster	16Se28Gv
Michael	(S)	19	M	None	16Se28Gv
Bridget	(D)	13	F	None	16Se28Gv
HALE, Barny		20	F	Spinster	16Se28Gv
FURY, Andrew		24	M	Htlkpr	16Se28Gv
DUFFY, Patt.		30	M	Laborer	16Se28Gv
Bridget		30	F	Matron	16Se28Gv
HOGAN, Michael		12	M	None	16Se28Gv
TIERNAN, Besy		24	F	Spinster	16Se28Gv
MCGUIRE, Winefred		20	F	Spinster	16Se28Gv
VENNARD, Esther		47	F	Spinster	16Se28Gv
HERON, Ellen		30	F	Spinster	16Se28Gv
BREADIN, Mary		23	F	Spinster	16Se28Gv
CURRAN, Margt.		28	F	Wi	16Se28Gv
John	(S)	04	M	Child	16Se28Gv
Willliam	(S)	03	M	Child	16Se28Gv
BRENNAN, Anne		18	F	Spinster	16Se28Gv
HEALLY, David		42	M	Merchant	16Se28Gv
Mary	(D)	16	F	Spinster	16Se28Gv
FERGUSON, Bridget		25	F	Spinster	16Se28Gv
FEENY, Michael		17	M	Laborer	16Se28Gv
John		20	M	Laborer	16Se28Gv
MURRAE, Mathew		30	M	Laborer	16Se28Gv
Biddy		20	F	Spinster	16Se28Gv
COSTELLO, Michael		14	M	None	16Se28Gv
COONEY, Michael		30	M	Laborer	16Se28Gv
MOONEY, Anne		19	F	Spinster	16Se28Gv
LANG, Patrick		32	M	Laborer	16Se28Gv
ERDIS, Samuel		22	M	Farmer	16Se28Gv
Jane	(W)	19	F	Wife	16Se28Gv
KILMARTIN, Martin		30	M	Teacher	16Se28Gv
MEANEY, Patt.		29	M	Wheelwright	16Se28Gv
TAYLOR, John		40	M	Tailor	16Se28Gv
SHULTHIESS, Gottfried		23	M	Clock Maker	16Se28Gv
GILLON, James		28	M	Laborer	16Se28Gv
Catherine		31	M	Matron	16Se28Gv
COSTELLO, Maria		12	F	None	16Se28Gv
DEVANY, Mick		30	M	Laborer	16Se28Gv

NAMES OF PASSENGERS		AGE	SEX	OCCUPATIONS	DATE PORT SHIP
MISSETT, John		16	M	None	16Se28Gv
HEAL, Patt.		16	M	None	16Se28Gv
SHAW, Eliza-Jane		20	F	None	16Se28Gv
FEENY, Michael		30	M	Laborer	16Se28Gv
Mary	(W)	30	F	None	16Se28Gv
DEVANEY, Anne		28	F	Spinster	16Se28Gv
GOLDRICK, Owen		17	M	None	16Se28Gv
COWAN, Thomas		25	M	Bootmaker	16Se28Gv

FALCON 17 SEPTEMBER 1847

From Bermuda

NAMES OF PASSENGERS		AGE	SEX	OCCUPATIONS	DATE PORT SHIP
DONOHUE, Patrick		40	M	Laborer	17Se75Lp
Bridget	(W)	30	F	None	17Se75Lp
Michael	(S)	09	M	Child	17Se75Lp
Terence	(S)	07	M	Child	17Se75Lp
Margaret	(D)	05	F	Child	17Se75Lp

CAMBRIDGE 17 SEPTEMBER 1847

From Liverpool

NAMES OF PASSENGERS		AGE	SEX	OCCUPATIONS	DATE PORT SHIP
HURLEY, Ted		27	M	Laborer	17Se02Ea
John		20	M	Laborer	17Se02Ea
DONOVAN, Mary		45	F	Servant	17Se02Ea
Ellen		07	F	Child	17Se02Ea
FINNIGAN, Margt.		18	F	Servant	17Se02Ea
MARON, Cath.		45	F	Servant	17Se02Ea
Ann		10	F	Servant	17Se02Ea
CASE, Eliza		17	F	Servant	17Se02Ea
Died-At-Sea					
EGAN, Mary		21	F	Servant	17Se02Ea
WHEELAN, Thos.		30	M	Laborer	17Se02Ea
Cath.		25	F	Laborer	17Se02Ea
BALL, Jas.		29	M	Smith	17Se02Ea
LARKIN, Peter		30	M	Laborer	17Se02Ea
Rose		26	F	Laborer	17Se02Ea
Patk.		12	M	Laborer	17Se02Ea
Mary		.00	F	Infant	17Se02Ea
Michl.		28	M	Laborer	17Se02Ea
Mary		50	F	Laborer	17Se02Ea
Owen		26	M	Laborer	17Se02Ea
Ann		22	F	Laborer	17Se02Ea
Margt.		20	F	Laborer	17Se02Ea
Pat.		13	M	Laborer	17Se02Ea
James		11	M	Laborer	17Se02Ea
MULLIGAN, Cath.		30	F	Servant	17Se02Ea
HANLON, Margt.		27	F	Servant	17Se02Ea
WHITE, Rose		25	F	Servant	17Se02Ea
HANLON, Mgt.		22	F	Servant	17Se02Ea
FARRELL, Cath.		27	F	Servant	17Se02Ea
MEEGAN, John		02	M	Child	17Se02Ea
Pat		.00	F	Infant	17Se02Ea
POLLOKS, Mary		45	F	Servant	17Se02Ea
Ann		20	F	Servant	17Se02Ea
Barney		18	M	Servant	17Se02Ea
Jas.		12	M	Servant	17Se02Ea
John		09	M	Child	17Se02Ea
Mary		05	F	Child	17Se02Ea
SMITH, Ann		12	F	Servant	17Se02Ea
DERGUE, Francis		20	M	Laborer	17Se02Ea
Cath.		16	F	Servant	17Se02Ea
GILDOY, Winifred		40	F	Servant	17Se02Ea
Michl.		04	M	Child	17Se02Ea
James		.00	M	Infant	17Se02Ea
KENNEDY, Cath.		40	F	Servant	17Se02Ea
Julia		20	F	Servant	17Se02Ea
Bridget		17	F	Servant	17Se02Ea
Ann		14	F	Servant	17Se02Ea
Henry		12	M	Servant	17Se02Ea
Pat		07	M	Child	17Se02Ea
HERNAN, Cath.		30	F	Servant	17Se02Ea
ROUGHAIN, Mary		45	F	Dressmaker	17Se02Ea
Cath.		20	F	Dressmaker	17Se02Ea
MCDERMOTT, Cath.		20	F	Servant	17Se02Ea
Pat		11	M	Laborer	17Se02Ea
REILLEY, Pat		22	M	Laborer	17Se02Ea
SHIELS, Ann		47	F	Servant	17Se02Ea
Rose		12	F	Servant	17Se02Ea
Hugh		10	M	Laborer	17Se02Ea
Mathew		08	M	Child	17Se02Ea
Agnes		04	F	Child	17Se02Ea
James		02	M	Child	17Se02Ea
Luke		.00	M	Infant	17Se02Ea
MCLOUGHLIN, Michl.		48	M	Weaver	17Se02Ea
U		40	F	None	17Se02Ea
DOUGHERTY, Jas.		30	M	Laborer	17Se02Ea
MCLOUGHLIN, Sarah		10	F	Servant	17Se02Ea
Bridget	(T)	08	F	Child	17Se02Ea
Nancy	(T)	06	F	Child	17Se02Ea
Rose	(T)	06	F	Child	17Se02Ea
John	(B)	02	M	Child	17Se02Ea
WISELEY, Mary		50	F	Servant	17Se02Ea
Mary		20	F	Servant	17Se02Ea
John		17	M	Laborer	17Se02Ea
Saml.		15	M	Laborer	17Se02Ea
Isaac		10	M	Laborer	17Se02Ea
CARRON, Jane		16	F	Servant	17Se02Ea
Pat		12	M	Laborer	17Se02Ea
ONEILL, Mary		30	F	Servant	17Se02Ea
BROWN, Maria		04	F	Child	17Se02Ea
MCFETRIDGE, Pat		26	M	Sailor	17Se02Ea
GERAGHTY, Ewd.		40	M	Stone Mason	17Se02Ea
Fras.		17	M	Stone Mason	17Se02Ea
Mary		14	F	Stone Mason	17Se02Ea
CAVANNAH, John		40	M	Laborer	17Se02Ea
MCDONALD, Cath.		10	F	Servant	17Se02Ea
CONNOR, Thos.		50	M	Tailor	17Se02Ea
U		46	F	Tailor	17Se02Ea
WHITE, Jas.		17	M	Laborer	17Se02Ea
MCCANN, John		40	M	Laborer	17Se02Ea
Cath.		36	F	None	17Se02Ea
Michl.		14	M	Laborer	17Se02Ea
Bridget		13	M	Laborer	17Se02Ea
Peter		10	M	Laborer	17Se02Ea
Pat		08	M	Child	17Se02Ea
John		07	M	Child	17Se02Ea
Susan		05	F	Child	17Se02Ea
Wm.		04	M	Child	17Se02Ea
Mary		02	F	Child	17Se02Ea
CONNOR, Abby		20	F	Servant	17Se02Ea
DALY, Ellen		24	F	Servant	17Se02Ea
FARRELL, John		20	M	Laborer	17Se02Ea
WALKER, Eliz.		25	F	Servant	17Se02Ea
DOWNS, John		17	M	Laborer	17Se02Ea
CARSON, Wm.		17	M	Laborer	17Se02Ea
HODDER, John		28	M	Blacksmith	17Se02Ea
HAYDON, Danl.		26	M	Wmcht	17Se02Ea
KELLY, John		26	M	Laborer	17Se02Ea
Eliza		22	F	Servant	17Se02Ea
BRENNAN, Mary		20	F	Servant	17Se02Ea
CAHOON, John		26	M	Laborer	17Se02Ea
Margt.		22	F	None	17Se02Ea
Sarah		.00	F	Infant	17Se02Ea
RAINEY, Wm.		40	M	Farmer	17Se02Ea
Mary		40	F	None	17Se02Ea
Jane		16	F	Farmer	17Se02Ea

NAMES OF PASSENGERS	AGE	SEX	OCCUPATIONS	DATE PORT SHIP
RAINEY, David	14	M	Farmer	17Se02Ea
Eliza	11	F	Farmer	17Se02Ea
Margt.	09	F	Child	17Se02Ea
John	07	M	Child	17Se02Ea
Robt.	.00	M	Infant	17Se02Ea
MULLEN, Bridget	20	F	Servant	17Se02Ea
KELLY, Henry	19	M	Laborer	17Se02Ea
DUFFY, Jas.	17	M	Laborer	17Se02Ea
DIVITT, Jas.	21	M	Draper	17Se02Ea
TWOOY, Bridget	24	F	Servant	17Se02Ea
Mary	.00	F	Infant	17Se02Ea
WELDON, Pat	46	M	Laborer	17Se02Ea
Cath.	40	F	None	17Se02Ea
Died-At-Sea				
Mat.	20	M	Laborer	17Se02Ea
Mary	19	F	Servant	17Se02Ea
SMITH, Mary	20	F	Servant	17Se02Ea
SHAUGHNESSY, Thos.	20	M	Farmer	17Se02Ea
CRONIN, Josh.	18	M	Farmer	17Se02Ea
PEARSON, Ewd.	25	M	Laborer	17Se02Ea
HART, Bridget	30	F	Servant	17Se02Ea
Eliza	12	F	Servant	17Se02Ea
PURCEL, Henry	44	M	Hpntr	17Se02Ea
Jane	46	F	None	17Se02Ea
Jonathan	24	M	Hpntr	17Se02Ea
Thos.	20	M	Hpntr	17Se02Ea
Jas.	18	M	Hpntr	17Se02Ea
Margt.	15	F	Hpntr	17Se02Ea
Eliza	12	F	Hpntr	17Se02Ea
John	09	M	Child	17Se02Ea
Jas.	22	M	Hpntr	17Se02Ea
KEAN, Ewd.	22	M	Laborer	17Se02Ea
Fdk.	20	M	Laborer	17Se02Ea
GANNION, Mary	20	F	Servant	17Se02Ea
Eliza	18	F	Servant	17Se02Ea
DUFFY, Mary	24	F	Servant	17Se02Ea
DILLON, Eliza	18	F	Servant	17Se02Ea
NEAGH, Jas.	20	M	Laborer	17Se02Ea
GORMAN, Margt.	20	F	Servant	17Se02Ea
JORDAN, Cath.	21	F	Servant	17Se02Ea
Johanh.	20	F	Servant	17Se02Ea
LYONS, John	30	M	Laborer	17Se02Ea
U	26	F	None	17Se02Ea
William	03	M	Child	17Se02Ea
Mary	.00	F	Infant	17Se02Ea
DENNEY, Ann	40	F	Milliner	17Se02Ea
Jas.	17	M	Blacksmith	17Se02Ea
Mary	20	F	Servant	17Se02Ea
Kate	12	F	Servant	17Se02Ea
Peter	.00	M	Infant	17Se02Ea
KEARNS, U-Mrs.	45	F	Shopkeeper	17Se02Ea
LYONS, U	20	F	Shopkeeper	17Se02Ea
KEARNS, Pat	17	M	Shopkeeper	17Se02Ea
Thos.	14	M	Shopkeeper	17Se02Ea
John	05	M	Child	17Se02Ea
Margt.	04	F	Child	17Se02Ea
GORMAN, Betty	18	F	Servant	17Se02Ea
Ann	19	F	Servant	17Se02Ea
MCANSONEY, Ann	20	F	Servant	17Se02Ea
CAMPBELL, Thos.	27	M	Laborer	17Se02Ea
KEEFE, Jane	27	F	Servant	17Se02Ea
Wm.	.00	M	Infant	17Se02Ea
Died-At-Sea				
LEARY, Ann	20	F	Servant	17Se02Ea
Jane	20	F	Servant	17Se02Ea
KENIFECK, Wm.	25	M	Seaman	17Se02Ea
MCLOUGHLIN, Thos.	30	M	Farmer	17Se02Ea
DILLON, Ann	17	F	Servant	17Se02Ea
Bridget	16	F	Servant	17Se02Ea
ONEIL, Ewd.	20	M	Laborer	17Se02Ea
MAHER, Ewd.	17	M	Waiter	17Se02Ea
DEMPSEY, Michl.	20	M	Laborer	17Se02Ea
JOHNSON, Ellen	20	F	Servant	17Se02Ea
ONEIL, Hugh	21	M	Accountant	17Se02Ea
HAMILTON, Bridget	30	F	Servant	17Se02Ea
HAMILTON, Bridget	07	F	Child	17Se02Ea
Jas.	04	M	Child	17Se02Ea
Ann	.00	F	Infant	17Se02Ea
BURNS, Eliz.	19	F	Servant	17Se02Ea
CASSON, Jas.	21	M	Painter	17Se02Ea
WINNE, Pat	21	M	Laborer	17Se02Ea
MCANSLEY, Mary	20	F	Servant	17Se02Ea
CARNEY, Honora	20	F	Servant	17Se02Ea
BROWN, Saml.	27	M	Clerk	17Se02Ea
SILVESTER, John	28	M	Accountant	17Se02Ea
DOYLE, Cath.	20	F	Servant	17Se02Ea
DANIEL, Thos.	21	M	Laborer	17Se02Ea
LINDSAY, Teresa	27	F	Servant	17Se02Ea
Josh	05	M	Child	17Se02Ea
John	02	M	Child	17Se02Ea
Mary	04	F	Child	17Se02Ea
FAHEY, Eliza	20	F	Servant	17Se02Ea
Ellen	24	F	Servant	17Se02Ea
OHALLORAN, Jas.	17	M	Printer	17Se02Ea
CROW, Wm.	22	M	Farmer	17Se02Ea
Eliz.	17	F	Servant	17Se02Ea
MONAGHAN, Mary	21	F	Servant	17Se02Ea
OSULLIVAN, Thos.	21	M	Saddler	17Se02Ea
OHARA, Cath.	21	F	Servant	17Se02Ea
OSHAUGHNESSY, Pat	30	M	Sawer	17Se02Ea
Margt.	30	F	None	17Se02Ea
John	02	M	Child	17Se02Ea
Mary	.00	F	Infant	17Se02Ea
BEARY, Johannah	20	F	Servant	17Se02Ea
JONES, Mary	20	F	Servant	17Se02Ea
Thos.	.00	M	Infant	17Se02Ea
MONAGHAN, Jane	45	F	Servant	17Se02Ea
Ann	18	F	Servant	17Se02Ea
Eliza	16	F	Servant	17Se02Ea
Margt.	12	F	Servant	17Se02Ea
Jane	10	F	Servant	17Se02Ea
Marcella	08	F	Child	17Se02Ea
OWENS, Alexr.	17	M	Laborer	17Se02Ea
Wm.	09	M	Child	17Se02Ea
Ann	12	F	Servant	17Se02Ea
Died-At-Sea				
GRANEY, Andrew	17	M	Laborer	17Se02Ea
BRYDE, Thos.	24	M	Laborer	17Se02Ea
MORAN, Mary	20	F	Servant	17Se02Ea
JONES, Ralph	22	M	Weaver	17Se02Ea
MALEY, Barth.	19	M	Laborer	17Se02Ea
CURRY, Pat	20	M	Laborer	17Se02Ea
EGAN, Cath.	20	F	Servant	17Se02Ea
RUDDLES, Ann	35	F	Merchant	17Se02Ea
John	44	M	Merchant	17Se02Ea
John	14	M	Merchant	17Se02Ea
Saml.	12	M	Merchant	17Se02Ea
Geo.	10	M	Merchant	17Se02Ea
Eliza	08	F	Child	17Se02Ea
Jane	06	F	Child	17Se02Ea
Ann	04	F	Child	17Se02Ea
Alice	01	F	Child	17Se02Ea
Died-At-Sea				
CARMICHAEL, Ann	19	F	Servant	17Se02Ea
CONNOR, Mgt.	18	F	Servant	17Se02Ea
Cath.	03	F	Child	17Se02Ea
DONNELLY, Mary	16	F	Servant	17Se02Ea
Thos.	21	M	Laborer	17Se02Ea
LEARY, Margt.	20	F	Servant	17Se02Ea
CASSON, Cath.	20	F	Servant	17Se02Ea
WOODBER, Jas.	24	M	Laborer	17Se02Ea
MCCAULEY, John	20	M	Laborer	17Se02Ea
WELSH, Thos.	28	M	Draper	17Se02Ea
RILEY, Ed.	20	M	Laborer	17Se02Ea
WILSON, John	26	M	Weaver	17Se02Ea
RICKERS, Thos.	30	M	Mason	17Se02Ea
WOODBURN, John	20	M	Laborer	17Se02Ea
ODONNEL, Hugh	26	M	Laborer	17Se02Ea
Henry	17	M	Laborer	17Se02Ea
QUIGLEY, Bartley	40	M	Laborer	17Se02Ea

NAMES OF PASSENGERS		AGE	SEX	OCCUPATIONS	DATE PORT SHIP

VICTORIA 17 SEPTEMBER 1847

From London

NAMES OF PASSENGERS		AGE	SEX	OCCUPATIONS	DATE PORT SHIP
DUGGAN, Joseph		00	M	Musician	17Se21Ay

ORPHEUS 18 SEPTEMBER 1847

From Liverpool

NAMES OF PASSENGERS		AGE	SEX	OCCUPATIONS	DATE PORT SHIP
LEACH, George		38	M	Glazier	18Se02Gx
Mary	(W)	34	F	Wife	18Se02Gx
Briget	(D)	11	F	None	18Se02Gx
John	(S)	09	M	Child	18Se02Gx
Mary	(D)	05	F	Child	18Se02Gx
Cathrine	(D)	.09	F	Infant	18Se02Gx
PHILIPS, Catherine		13	F	None	18Se02Gx
HORNICK, John		28	M	Farmer	18Se02Gx
U-Mrs.	(M)	50	F	None	18Se02Gx
Harriet		30	F	None	18Se02Gx
Sarah		14	F	None	18Se02Gx
MCGORVEN, Magerate		20	F	Tailor	18Se02Gx
GUFFNEY, Brien		30	M	Laborer	18Se02Gx
Margret		28	F	None	18Se02Gx
Jane		18	F	None	18Se02Gx
Marthew		11	M	None	18Se02Gx
Barthy		06	M	Child	18Se02Gx
Ellen		04	F	Child	18Se02Gx
RILEY, Patrick		31	M	Laborer	18Se02Gx
U	(W)	21	F	Wife	18Se02Gx
Patrick-Jr.		14	M	None	18Se02Gx
Mary		09	F	Child	18Se02Gx
CUNNINGHAM, John		26	M	Cooper	18Se02Gx
Mary	(D)	09	F	Child	18Se02Gx

RAPPAHANNOCK 18 SEPTEMBER 1847

From Liverpool

NAMES OF PASSENGERS		AGE	SEX	OCCUPATIONS	DATE PORT SHIP
DAY, Thomas		32	M	Laborer	18Se02Dm
SWEENY, Ann		25	F	None	18Se02Dm
MARTIN, John		25	M	Laborer	18Se02Dm
DELANY, Michael		20	M	Laborer	18Se02Dm
MCKENNA, Cathe.		50	F	None	18Se02Dm
Cathe.		20	F	None	18Se02Dm
INGHAM, John		40	M	Laborer	18Se02Dm
Ellen		42	F	None	18Se02Dm
William		13	M	Laborer	18Se02Dm
James		12	M	Laborer	18Se02Dm
MALLANE, Arthur		26	M	Laborer	18Se02Dm
Sarah		26	F	None	18Se02Dm
Mary		03	F	Child	18Se02Dm
John		.00	M	Infant	18Se02Dm
MAXWELL, Matilda		18	F	None	18Se02Dm
SCOTT, Samuel		40	M	Laborer	18Se02Dm
Mary		40	F	None	18Se02Dm
John		08	M	Child	18Se02Dm
DUFFY, Ellen		34	F	Laborer	18Se02Dm
Joe		20	M	Laborer	18Se02Dm
Francis		12	M	None	18Se02Dm
Laurence		10	M	None	18Se02Dm
Hugh		06	M	Child	18Se02Dm
John		.06	M	Infant	18Se02Dm
MCGLEORON, Bridget		20	F	None	18Se02Dm
MCELIVE, John		30	M	None	18Se02Dm
Eliza		10	F	None	18Se02Dm
Jno.		02	M	Child	18Se02Dm
SWAN, Cathe.		18	F	None	18Se02Dm
GREEN, Dennis		30	M	Laborer	18Se02Dm
Ann		30	F	None	18Se02Dm
Wm. Died-At-Sea	(S)	.06	M	Infant	18Se02Dm
MASTERSON, Patt.		12	M	Laborer	18Se02Dm
GARRICK, Thos.		26	M	Laborer	18Se02Dm
Henry		13	M	None	18Se02Dm
Martha		24	F	Laborer	18Se02Dm
Charles		02	M	Child	18Se02Dm
Lucy		.06	F	Infant	18Se02Dm
OBRIEN, Jno.		30	M	Laborer	18Se02Dm
Charles		30	M	Laborer	18Se02Dm
DALLAS, Elizabeth		35	F	None	18Se02Dm
Elizabeth		25	F	None	18Se02Dm
WHITEHEAD, Wm.		36	M	Laborer	18Se02Dm
Ester		36	F	None	18Se02Dm
Bessy		11	F	None	18Se02Dm
Sarah-Ann		10	F	None	18Se02Dm
Caroline		06	F	Child	18Se02Dm
Lucy		04	F	Child	18Se02Dm
Ellen		.06	F	Infant	18Se02Dm
David		34	M	Laborer	18Se02Dm
WALLACE, Judy		20	F	None	18Se02Dm
MCAVOY, Martin		30	M	None	18Se02Dm
KELLY, Ketty		30	F	None	18Se02Dm
ETCHELL, Jno.		25	M	Laborer	18Se02Dm
FOWLER, Thos.		31	M	Laborer	18Se02Dm
BURTON, George		21	M	Laborer	18Se02Dm
GIMLET, Wm.		20	M	Laborer	18Se02Dm
LEWIS, Sarah		31	F	None	18Se02Dm
MCCARN, Mary		18	F	None	18Se02Dm
Rose		38	F	None	18Se02Dm
MCLAUGHLIN, Hugh		36	M	Laborer	18Se02Dm
Catherine		25	F	None	18Se02Dm
MCGROY, Cath.		21	F	None	18Se02Dm
MCDOUGAL, Margaret		40	F	None	18Se02Dm
Donald		08	M	Child	18Se02Dm
Margaret		04	F	Child	18Se02Dm
HOGAN, Cath.		20	F	None	18Se02Dm
DUFFY, Ann		20	F	None	18Se02Dm
MANIAN, Ann		20	F	None	18Se02Dm
MCCOY, Phil		40	M	Laborer	18Se02Dm
Mary		40	F	Unknown	18Se02Dm
Jane		11	F	None	18Se02Dm
Patt.		09	M	Child	18Se02Dm
Brian		07	M	Child	18Se02Dm
Thos.		05	M	Child	18Se02Dm
TRAINOR, Ed.		20	M	None	18Se02Dm
WHITE, W.		25	M	None	18Se02Dm
OMALLY, Bridget		50	F	None	18Se02Dm
Jno.		13	M	None	18Se02Dm
Martin		12	M	None	18Se02Dm
BURN, Margt.		20	F	None	18Se02Dm
MCDUNAGAN, Mary		18	F	None	18Se02Dm
HANLY, Mary		31	F	None	18Se02Dm
Charles		20	M	Laborer	18Se02Dm
BRANNON, Bridget		40	F	None	18Se02Dm
Thos.		20	M	None	18Se02Dm
James		12	M	None	18Se02Dm
Ann		25	F	None	18Se02Dm
Kate		.06	F	Infant	18Se02Dm
SWITZER, Banlet		40	M	Laborer	18Se02Dm
Margaret		40	F	Unknown	18Se02Dm
Ester		09	F	Child	18Se02Dm

NAMES OF PASSENGERS	AGE	SEX	OCCUPATIONS	DATE PORT SHIP
SWITZER, Margt.	06	F	Child	18Se02Dm
Christopher	05	M	Child	18Se02Dm
Jno.	04	M	Child	18Se02Dm
Hugh	02	M	Child	18Se02Dm
Eliza	.06	F	Infant	18Se02Dm
MANNON, Margt.	20	F	Unknown	18Se02Dm
WATERS, Mgt.	18	F	Unknown	18Se02Dm
TIGHTBURN, H.M.	20	M	Laborer	18Se02Dm
SHARP, Charles	40	M	Laborer	18Se02Dm
Ann	40	F	None	18Se02Dm
Selin	20	F	None	18Se02Dm
Ann	21	F	None	18Se02Dm
Died-At-Sea				
Isabella	18	F	None	18Se02Dm
David	15	M	None	18Se02Dm
Barbara	13	F	None	18Se02Dm
MURRAY, Thos.	30	M	Laborer	18Se02Dm
U (W)	28	F	Wife	18Se02Dm
Wm.	13	M	None	18Se02Dm
Ann	02	F	Child	18Se02Dm
Ellen	.06	F	Infant	18Se02Dm
Died-At-Sea				
SHEPPARD, Henry	25	M	Laborer	18Se02Dm
Mary	20	F	None	18Se02Dm
MCCULLA, Thos.	21	M	None	18Se02Dm
Mary	18	F	None	18Se02Dm
SMITH, Ann	47	F	None	18Se02Dm
SHAW, Jno.	40	M	Laborer	18Se02Dm
Mary	27	F	None	18Se02Dm
Martin	.06	M	Infant	18Se02Dm
DONAVAN, Isabella	23	F	None	18Se02Dm
MCGUIRE, Duncan	27	M	Laborer	18Se02Dm
Donald	20	M	Laborer	18Se02Dm
Arch.	20	M	Laborer	18Se02Dm
MCKENNA, Benjn.	54	M	Laborer	18Se02Dm
DURAGH, Sandy	42	M	Laborer	18Se02Dm
Janet	40	F	None	18Se02Dm
SHAW, Neil	25	M	Laborer	18Se02Dm
DURAGH, Agnes	13	F	None	18Se02Dm
Mary	12	F	None	18Se02Dm
Donald	08	M	Child	18Se02Dm
Janet	05	F	Child	18Se02Dm
Daniel	.06	M	Infant	18Se02Dm
MCLEAN, Malcom	57	M	Laborer	18Se02Dm
Mary	50	F	Unknown	18Se02Dm
Flora	18	F	None	18Se02Dm
James	16	M	None	18Se02Dm
Peter	13	M	None	18Se02Dm
Warren	11	M	None	18Se02Dm
James	06	M	Child	18Se02Dm
BLACK, Alix	31	M	Laborer	18Se02Dm
Margt.	29	F	None	18Se02Dm
Duncan	06	M	Child	18Se02Dm
Neil	04	M	Child	18Se02Dm
Agnes	04	F	Child	18Se02Dm
MCGILBY, Jno.	35	M	Laborer	18Se02Dm
Isabella	28	F	Laborer	18Se02Dm
Duncan	28	M	Laborer	18Se02Dm
Flora	02	F	Child	18Se02Dm
Malcom	.06	M	Infant	18Se02Dm
KENNEDY, Dugald	32	M	Laborer	18Se02Dm
Warren	20	M	Laborer	18Se02Dm
Janet	.06	F	Infant	18Se02Dm
MCCARTHA, Duncan	45	M	Laborer	18Se02Dm
Mary	32	F	Laborer	18Se02Dm
Agnes	06	F	Child	18Se02Dm
Warren	11	M	Laborer	18Se02Dm
Janet	07	F	Child	18Se02Dm
John	05	M	Child	18Se02Dm
Gilbert	11	M	None	18Se02Dm
John	02	M	Child	18Se02Dm
SHAW, Jno.	25	M	Laborer	18Se02Dm
Cath.	25	F	None	18Se02Dm
John	05	M	Child	18Se02Dm
Mary	06	F	Child	18Se02Dm

NAMES OF PASSENGERS	AGE	SEX	OCCUPATIONS	DATE PORT SHIP
SHAW, Rusty	.06	M	Infant	18Se02Dm
WELSH, Joseph	40	M	Laborer	18Se02Dm
U (W)	35	F	None	18Se02Dm
NUGENT, Mary-Ann	20	F	None	18Se02Dm
MCGEE, Mary	25	F	None	18Se02Dm
MCGOWNEL, Mary	20	F	None	18Se02Dm
DROGAN, Martha	20	F	None	18Se02Dm
MCCARRON, Ellen	20	F	None	18Se02Dm
REYNOLDS, Mgt.	17	F	None	18Se02Dm
Anne	22	F	None	18Se02Dm
FLETCHER, J.I.	28	M	Laborer	18Se02Dm
MARTIN, James	25	M	Laborer	18Se02Dm
FARLEY, Patt.	28	M	Laborer	18Se02Dm
Benjn.	23	M	Laborer	18Se02Dm
Ann	04	F	Child	18Se02Dm
Benjn.	.06	M	Infant	18Se02Dm
Died-At-Sea				
ASDEN, Alex.	22	M	Laborer	18Se02Dm
WATSON, Jas.	25	M	Laborer	18Se02Dm
MCGOURLOCK, Bridget	19	F	None	18Se02Dm
LINDEN, Daniel	18	M	None	18Se02Dm
U (M)	40	F	None	18Se02Dm
KEENAN, Rumly	20	M	Laborer	18Se02Dm
KEEF, Tardy	28	M	Laborer	18Se02Dm
KENNEDY, Toby	25	M	Laborer	18Se02Dm
MORAN, Patt.	25	M	Laborer	18Se02Dm
William	22	M	Laborer	18Se02Dm
FILLETT, George	40	M	Laborer	18Se02Dm
Diana	49	F	None	18Se02Dm
Mary	19	F	None	18Se02Dm
David	17	M	None	18Se02Dm
Jonas	13	M	Laborer	18Se02Dm
Toby	11	M	None	18Se02Dm
Caroline	07	F	Child	18Se02Dm
Jnothan	05	M	Child	18Se02Dm
Edwin	.06	M	Infant	18Se02Dm
MURPHY, Hugh	20	M	Laborer	18Se02Dm
Margt.	18	F	None	18Se02Dm
SMITH, Ann	20	F	None	18Se02Dm
MCLANTY, Eliza	20	F	None	18Se02Dm
DOWGAN, Ellen	20	F	None	18Se02Dm
DWYER, Mary	20	F	None	18Se02Dm
GAMMON, Mary	12	F	None	18Se02Dm
MCCAFFERY, Phil	30	M	Laborer	18Se02Dm
Ann	30	F	None	18Se02Dm
LYNCH, Margt.	20	F	None	18Se02Dm
CAFFERY, Patt.	10	M	Laborer	18Se02Dm
Margt.	08	F	Child	18Se02Dm
Laurence	05	M	Child	18Se02Dm
CAVAGHNE, Bridget	20	F	None	18Se02Dm
MCDEVITT, Samuel	50	M	Laborer	18Se02Dm
Mary	50	F	None	18Se02Dm
Sally	20	F	None	18Se02Dm
Jane	25	F	None	18Se02Dm
Nepper	18	F	None	18Se02Dm
Margt.	16	F	None	18Se02Dm
MCSWIGGIN, Michl.	25	M	None	18Se02Dm
MCELWER, Cath.	20	F	None	18Se02Dm
DEVLIN, Jane	20	F	None	18Se02Dm
FOGARTY, Cath.	18	F	None	18Se02Dm
MALEY, Peter	20	M	Laborer	18Se02Dm
MCMACKEN, Patt.	45	M	Laborer	18Se02Dm
Rebecca	45	F	None	18Se02Dm
James	25	M	Laborer	18Se02Dm
Ann	20	F	None	18Se02Dm
Susan	11	F	None	18Se02Dm
Patt.	09	M	Child	18Se02Dm
Michl.	07	M	Child	18Se02Dm
Joseph	.06	M	Infant	18Se02Dm
MCBRIDE, Bridget	28	F	None	18Se02Dm
GARGAN, James	07	M	Child	18Se02Dm
Rosen	03	M	Child	18Se02Dm
Hugh	02	M	Child	18Se02Dm
GOUGH, Wm.	35	M	None	18Se02Dm
KEERY, Thos.	35	M	Laborer	18Se02Dm

NAMES OF PASSENGERS	AGE	SEX	OCCUPATIONS	DATE PORT SHIP
KEERY, John	11	M	None	18Se02Dm
BRAN, Peter	30	M	Laborer	18Se02Dm
Ann	35	F	None	18Se02Dm
John	20	M	None	18Se02Dm
NEUGENT, W.	18	M	None	18Se02Dm
MCGOVERN, Eliza	21	F	None	18Se02Dm
F_IN, Alice	21	F	None	18Se02Dm
SWORDS, Thos.	11	M	Laborer	18Se02Dm
Patt.	07	M	Child	18Se02Dm
John	40	M	Laborer	18Se02Dm
CANNON, Henry	10	M	None	18Se02Dm
Patt.	08	M	Child	18Se02Dm
HUGHS, Ed.	30	M	Laborer	18Se02Dm
MALONY, Cath.	18	F	None	18Se02Dm
MCKEOWN, Ann	18	F	None	18Se02Dm
BRADY, Bidy	35	F	None	18Se02Dm
Bessy	18	F	None	18Se02Dm
EVERET, Margt.	20	F	None	18Se02Dm
RYAN, Michl.	35	M	None	18Se02Dm
DURICK, John	20	M	None	18Se02Dm
ROSS, W.	20	M	None	18Se02Dm
HIGAN, U-Miss.	20	F	None	18Se02Dm
COGHLIN, Mary-A.	20	F	None	18Se02Dm
HAYS, Saly	25	F	None	18Se02Dm
HILL, Jno.	21	M	Laborer	18Se02Dm
GRUSLY, Jno.	41	M	Laborer	18Se02Dm
My.	45	F	Laborer	18Se02Dm
TYLER, Susan	19	F	None	18Se02Dm
GRUSLY, Eliza	12	F	None	18Se02Dm
Sarah-A.	.06	F	Infant	18Se02Dm
KUILLIAN, Patt.	26	M	Laborer	18Se02Dm
BUTLER, Andrew	25	M	Laborer	18Se02Dm
DYHN, John	25	M	Laborer	18Se02Dm
BELL, Sally	25	F	None	18Se02Dm
MCHUGH, Ann	25	F	None	18Se02Dm
Died-At-Sea				
James	20	M	Laborer	18Se02Dm
Died-At-Sea				
Mgt.	18	F	Unknown	18Se02Dm
Biddy	20	F	Unknown	18Se02Dm
KERR, Thomas	25	M	Unknown	18Se02Dm
HANLAN, Mary	18	F	Unknown	18Se02Dm
KURMAN, Ralph	50	M	Laborer	18Se02Dm
Died-At-Sea				
Ralph	19	M	None	18Se02Dm
John	18	M	None	18Se02Dm
Mgt.	15	F	None	18Se02Dm
SHERRY, Margt.	38	F	None	18Se02Dm
HUGHS, Mgt.	30	F	None	18Se02Dm
CRANGHAN, Mary	20	F	None	18Se02Dm
SHERRY, Patt.	38	M	Laborer	18Se02Dm
FARRELL, Thos.	25	M	Laborer	18Se02Dm
SAUL, My.	20	F	None	18Se02Dm
KELLY, Michel	25	M	Laborer	18Se02Dm
John	02	M	Child	18Se02Dm
FARRELL, John	20	M	Laborer	18Se02Dm
MCGILL, Micheal	34	M	Laborer	18Se02Dm
Mary	33	F	None	18Se02Dm
Sandy	08	M	Child	18Se02Dm
Duncan	06	M	Child	18Se02Dm
John	04	M	Child	18Se02Dm
Mary	.06	F	Infant	18Se02Dm
MCELLROY, Wm.	58	M	Laborer	18Se02Dm
My.	50	F	Unknown	18Se02Dm
Stephen	13	M	None	18Se02Dm
Hugh	12	M	Unknown	18Se02Dm
Luke	10	M	None	18Se02Dm
Thos.	04	M	Child	18Se02Dm
Ann	02	F	Child	18Se02Dm
DILLON, Margt.	20	F	None	18Se02Dm
Mary	03	F	Child	18Se02Dm
STONEHORE, Cath.	20	F	None	18Se02Dm
MADE, Johanna	20	F	Laborer	18Se02Dm
HOLLAND, Jer.	25	M	Laborer	18Se02Dm
Patt.	20	M	Laborer	18Se02Dm
BARRY, Honora	50	F	None	18Se02Dm
Thos.	25	M	Laborer	18Se02Dm
David	20	M	Laborer	18Se02Dm
John	08	M	Child	18Se02Dm
Julia	25	F	Laborer	18Se02Dm
James	04	M	Child	18Se02Dm
SULLIVAN, Jer.	45	M	Laborer	18Se02Dm
Ellen	45	F	Unknown	18Se02Dm
Michl.	25	M	Unknown	18Se02Dm
Dennis	20	M	Laborer	18Se02Dm
Mary	11	F	None	18Se02Dm
Illvin	10	M	None	18Se02Dm
BUTLER, Julia	20	F	Laborer	18Se02Dm
BARRY, James	45	M	None	18Se02Dm
James	20	M	None	18Se02Dm
Mgt.	45	F	Unknown	18Se02Dm
My.	15	F	None	18Se02Dm
Johanna	10	F	None	18Se02Dm
Mgt.	06	F	Child	18Se02Dm
Briget	05	F	Child	18Se02Dm
DELANY, Bridget	20	F	None	18Se02Dm
James	10	M	None	18Se02Dm
Patt.	06	M	Child	18Se02Dm
MULLIN, Brid.	20	F	None	18Se02Dm
DUNN, Wm.	25	M	Laborer	18Se02Dm
RILEY, Patt.	25	M	Laborer	18Se02Dm
MCKENNA, Peter	25	M	Laborer	18Se02Dm
HEANY, W.	20	M	Laborer	18Se02Dm
HUES, John	25	M	Laborer	18Se02Dm
FARNEY, Sarah	20	F	None	18Se02Dm
MODS, Alice	20	F	None	18Se02Dm
MCBRIDE, Birnard	25	M	None	18Se02Dm
SULIVAN, Julia	20	F	None	18Se02Dm
COWLEY, Tim	25	M	None	18Se02Dm
BOURK, Daniel	20	M	Laborer	18Se02Dm
COWLEY, Mgt.	20	F	None	18Se02Dm
LOFTUS, Mary	25	F	None	18Se02Dm
Martha	20	F	None	18Se02Dm
KELLGHAN, Ann	20	F	None	18Se02Dm
RUVAN, Sarah	25	F	None	18Se02Dm
Mary	20	F	None	18Se02Dm
MCKENNA, Ann	30	F	None	18Se02Dm
MCGILL, Bridget	32	F	None	18Se02Dm
LOY, Mary	13	F	None	18Se02Dm
MCHUGH, Mary	37	F	None	18Se02Dm
BOOTH, Samuel	30	M	Laborer	18Se02Dm
CROSS, Thos.	34	M	Laborer	18Se02Dm
BRADY, Phil	21	M	Laborer	18Se02Dm
Betsy	21	F	Laborer	18Se02Dm
BUSH, John	18	M	Laborer	18Se02Dm
MARKEY, Catherin	20	F	None	18Se02Dm
GORDON, Bridget	03	F	Child	18Se02Dm
WEAKLEY, Mgt.	20	F	Laborer	18Se02Dm
DERVAS, Mgt.	50	F	None	18Se02Dm
Mgt.	25	F	None	18Se02Dm
James	20	M	None	18Se02Dm
GARRY, Sally	20	F	None	18Se02Dm
SWEENY, Joseph	27	M	Laborer	18Se02Dm
MCGEW, Brid	50	F	None	18Se02Dm
Died-At-Sea				
Mary	30	F	None	18Se02Dm
Mrg.	.06	F	Infant	18Se02Dm
MCKAIN, Hector	35	M	Laborer	18Se02Dm
Mary	25	F	None	18Se02Dm
Letitia	08	F	Child	18Se02Dm
Susan	19	F	None	18Se02Dm
John	03	M	Child	18Se02Dm
James	.06	M	Infant	18Se02Dm
BURN, Wm.	27	M	Laborer	18Se02Dm
Mary	25	F	Laborer	18Se02Dm
DUNN, Micheal	22	M	Laborer	18Se02Dm
BURN, Joseph	22	M	Unknown	18Se02Dm
WHITE, James	27	M	Laborer	18Se02Dm
Isabella	24	F	Unknown	18Se02Dm
Isabella	02	F	Child	18Se02Dm

NAMES OF PASSENGERS	AGE	SEX	OCCUPATIONS	DATE PORT SHIP
WHITE, James Died-At-Sea	.06	M	Infant	18Se02Dm
DUNN, James	50	M	Laborer	18Se02Dm
SHORE, Grace	40	F	None	18Se02Dm
EGAN, Thos.	31	M	Laborer	18Se02Dm
CORRIGAN, James	20	M	Laborer	18Se02Dm
GANNON, Mgt.	30	F	None	18Se02Dm
RICH, Julia	20	F	None	18Se02Dm
LINCH, Micheal	25	M	Laborer	18Se02Dm
MCGILL, Francis	20	M	Laborer	18Se02Dm
LEERY, Ann	19	F	Laborer	18Se02Dm
SHERRY, Mary	45	F	Laborer	18Se02Dm
Patt.	25	M	Laborer	18Se02Dm
John	20	M	Laborer	18Se02Dm
Mary	11	F	None	18Se02Dm
ROPER, Mary	20	F	None	18Se02Dm
James	22	M	None	18Se02Dm
ROCHFORD, Ellen	21	F	None	18Se02Dm
DOYLE, Micheal	30	M	Laborer	18Se02Dm
Mary	20	F	None	18Se02Dm
LEERY, Mary	25	F	None	18Se02Dm
John	08	M	Child	18Se02Dm
Patt.	06	M	Child	18Se02Dm
James	02	M	Child	18Se02Dm
WOODS, Ellen	18	F	Laborer	18Se02Dm
COSEY, Mary	20	F	Laborer	18Se02Dm
SHIEN, Thos.	40	M	Laborer	18Se02Dm
U (W)	30	F	None	18Se02Dm
Patt.	20	M	Laborer	18Se02Dm
James	12	M	Laborer	18Se02Dm
Wm.	10	M	Laborer	18Se02Dm
Catherine	08	F	Child	18Se02Dm
KELLEY, John	30	M	Laborer	18Se02Dm
Margt.	10	F	None	18Se02Dm
Maria	08	F	Child	18Se02Dm
Catherin	06	F	Child	18Se02Dm
LOGAN, Patt.	18	M	Laborer	18Se02Dm
MCGILL, Hugh	31	M	Laborer	18Se02Dm
SMITH, Susan	12	F	None	18Se02Dm
MARKEY, Patt.	25	M	Laborer	18Se02Dm
COSTILLO, Micheal	35	M	Laborer	18Se02Dm
HEANY, Micheal	36	M	Laborer	18Se02Dm
LEADY, Phil	25	M	Laborer	18Se02Dm
Ann	21	F	None	18Se02Dm
GALLAGHER, Thos.	22	M	Laborer	18Se02Dm
WARD, Nora	20	F	Laborer	18Se02Dm
FINGAN, Mary	20	F	Laborer	18Se02Dm
GANNON, Micheal Died-At-Sea	28	M	Laborer	18Se02Dm
FLINN, Patt.	50	M	Laborer	18Se02Dm
DAVINE, James	50	M	Laborer	18Se02Dm
Mary	13	F	None	18Se02Dm
Ellen	12	F	None	18Se02Dm
WHITELAN, Thos.	30	M	Laborer	18Se02Dm
MCANALY, Cath.	17	F	None	18Se02Dm
LYNCH, Patt.	40	M	Laborer	18Se02Dm
Biddy	40	F	Unknown	18Se02Dm
Biddy	20	F	Laborer	18Se02Dm
MURRY, Peter	20	M	Laborer	18Se02Dm
Julia	.06	F	Infant	18Se02Dm
CAMPBELLE, John	35	M	Laborer	18Se02Dm
SMITH, Mary	20	F	None	18Se02Dm
HEALY, Mary	20	F	None	18Se02Dm
NEVAN, Ann	20	F	None	18Se02Dm
Bridget	02	F	Child	18Se02Dm
MULLIN, Jane	25	F	None	18Se02Dm
Thos.	18	M	Laborer	18Se02Dm
BAILY, J.G.	25	M	Laborer	18Se02Dm
TWEDALE, John	25	M	Laborer	18Se02Dm
Mary	20	F	None	18Se02Dm

SEA 18 SEPTEMBER 1847

From Liverpool

NAMES OF PASSENGERS	AGE	SEX	OCCUPATIONS	DATE PORT SHIP
DAVIS, Alx.	30	M	Mechanic	18Se02Bg
Alice	30	F	Unknown	18Se02Bg
Eliza	09	F	Child	18Se02Bg
Jno.	04	M	Child	18Se02Bg
Harriet	01	F	Child	18Se02Bg
JAMES, Geo.	35	M	Mechanic	18Se02Bg
Mary	30	F	Unknown	18Se02Bg
Mary	11	F	None	18Se02Bg
Wm.	02	M	Child	18Se02Bg
Cath.	03	F	Child	18Se02Bg
Geo.	07	M	Child	18Se02Bg
CONWAY, Richd.	40	M	Laborer	18Se02Bg
Wm.	20	M	Laborer	18Se02Bg
Eliza	21	F	None	18Se02Bg
Cath.	13	F	None	18Se02Bg
OCONNER, Danl.	25	M	Laborer	18Se02Bg
TRACEY, Thos.	28	M	Laborer	18Se02Bg
BURKE, Peter	36	M	Laborer	18Se02Bg
SHAW, Chris.	17	M	Laborer	18Se02Bg
VILLIERS, Thos.	22	M	Laborer	18Se02Bg
Elizth.	22	F	None	18Se02Bg
BURDETT, Thos.	28	M	Laborer	18Se02Bg
BEVAN, Elias	46	M	Laborer	18Se02Bg
FULTON, Elizth.	22	F	None	18Se02Bg
MCMULLEN, Nancy	21	F	None	18Se02Bg
TAYLOR, Elizth.	19	F	None	18Se02Bg
EDGAR, Jane	30	M	Laborer	18Se02Bg
Henry	09	M	Child	18Se02Bg
B.J.	07	M	Child	18Se02Bg
Jane	.07	F	Infant	18Se02Bg
CRIGHTON, Dina-L.	40	F	None	18Se02Bg
M.-I.	11	F	None	18Se02Bg
S.A.	10	F	None	18Se02Bg
Jas.	08	M	Child	18Se02Bg
Fanny	06	F	Child	18Se02Bg
Robt.	02	M	Child	18Se02Bg
PRITCHARD, Danl.	23	M	Mechanic	18Se02Bg
AUBREY, Thos.	35	M	Mechanic	18Se02Bg
Magt.	30	F	Unknown	18Se02Bg
Elizth.	10	F	None	18Se02Bg
Magrt.	08	F	Child	18Se02Bg
Wm.	06	M	Child	18Se02Bg
Jane	04	F	Child	18Se02Bg
Mary	.09	F	Infant	18Se02Bg
COWEN, Jos.	18	M	Laborer	18Se02Bg
KUMERMAN, Robt.	43	M	Laborer	18Se02Bg
Magt.	32	F	Unknown	18Se02Bg
Robt.	16	M	Laborer	18Se02Bg
Susan	13	F	None	18Se02Bg
Margt.	12	F	None	18Se02Bg
Jno.	06	M	Child	18Se02Bg
MATHEWS, Rose	26	F	None	18Se02Bg
CONWAY, Ann	18	F	None	18Se02Bg
MARSDEN, Robt.	24	M	Mechanic	18Se02Bg
BRAY, Ann	50	F	None	18Se02Bg
Hannah	15	F	None	18Se02Bg
Mary	09	F	Child	18Se02Bg
Jacob	06	M	Child	18Se02Bg
OLEVIS, Wm.	38	M	Laborer	18Se02Bg
Elizth.	38	F	Unknown	18Se02Bg
Jno.	12	M	None	18Se02Bg
Jno.	12	M	Laborer	18Se02Bg
EVANS, Wm.	25	M	Laborer	18Se02Bg
WALLACE, Law.	27	M	Laborer	18Se02Bg
Mich.	36	M	Laborer	18Se02Bg

NAMES OF PASSENGERS	AGE	SEX	OCCUPATIONS	DATE PORT SHIP
WALLACE, Cath.	18	F	None	18Se02Bg
KILLIAN, Thos.	34	M	Laborer	18Se02Bg
KEEGAN, Mich.	62	M	Laborer	18Se02Bg
LOWE, Bridget	09	F	Child	18Se02Bg
CONNELL, Ann	41	F	None	18Se02Bg
Mary	14	F	None	18Se02Bg
Eliza	06	F	Child	18Se02Bg
FRAITCH, David	28	M	Laborer	18Se02Bg
Deborah	16	F	None	18Se02Bg
MCCAUN, Geo.	31	M	Mechanic	18Se02Bg
FINIGAN, Pat	33	M	Mechanic	18Se02Bg
MANGATE, Hy.	38	M	Mechanic	18Se02Bg
COULTON, Rich.	30	M	Mechanic	18Se02Bg
GRAHAM, David	37	M	Farmer	18Se02Bg
Wm.	13	M	Farmer	18Se02Bg
KELLY, Ann	18	F	None	18Se02Bg
ROBINSON, Cath.	24	F	None	18Se02Bg
Wm.	02	M	Child	18Se02Bg
Euph.	03	F	Child	18Se02Bg
FERGUSON, Robt.	30	M	Laborer	18Se02Bg
MCALIER, Jas.	40	M	Laborer	18Se02Bg
Mary	40	F	Unknown	18Se02Bg
Thos.	11	M	None	18Se02Bg
MCGUINISS, Mary	40	F	None	18Se02Bg
Hugh	07	M	Child	18Se02Bg
Jno.	05	M	Child	18Se02Bg
MCALIER, Jess	13	M	Laborer	18Se02Bg
RUTHERFORD, Adam	40	M	Laborer	18Se02Bg
Eliza	30	F	Unknown	18Se02Bg
Mary	17	F	None	18Se02Bg
Jos.	03	M	Child	18Se02Bg
Adam	.11	M	Infant	18Se02Bg
JERVISS, Mary	20	F	None	18Se02Bg
MCFADDEN, Gilbert	22	M	Farmer	18Se02Bg
SIMPSON, Wm.	60	M	Farmer	18Se02Bg
Alice	44	F	Unknown	18Se02Bg
Jno.	18	M	Farmer	18Se02Bg
Jane	17	F	None	18Se02Bg
Cath.	14	F	None	18Se02Bg
Wm.	12	M	None	18Se02Bg
Robt.	10	M	None	18Se02Bg
Eliza	08	F	Child	18Se02Bg
GRAY, Jno.	18	M	Laborer	18Se02Bg
MCALIER, Jas.	43	M	Laborer	18Se02Bg
Biddy	38	F	Unknown	18Se02Bg
Pat	11	M	None	18Se02Bg
Peter	10	M	None	18Se02Bg
Mary	08	F	Child	18Se02Bg
Mich.	06	M	Child	18Se02Bg
Biddy	04	F	Child	18Se02Bg
James	02	M	Child	18Se02Bg
Nancy	.04	F	Infant	18Se02Bg
Nancy	17	F	None	18Se02Bg
Ellen	42	F	None	18Se02Bg
MCCUTTER, Jno.	28	M	Laborer	18Se02Bg
LAWLESS, Peter	11	M	None	18Se02Bg
CURRY, Mary	12	F	None	18Se02Bg
BIRMINGHAM, Jas.	28	M	Mechanic	18Se02Bg
MCKENNA, Sarah	40	F	None	18Se02Bg
FITSCHILL, Saml.	15	M	None	18Se02Bg
Elizth.	18	F	None	18Se02Bg
CALLAHAN, Thos.	27	M	Laborer	18Se02Bg
MCCONNELL, Mary	18	F	None	18Se02Bg
Pat	28	M	Laborer	18Se02Bg
BOYLE, Thos.	50	M	Laborer	18Se02Bg
DUNLEVY, Anth.	25	M	Laborer	18Se02Bg
COUGAN, Ann	45	F	None	18Se02Bg
Pat	11	M	None	18Se02Bg
Magt.	07	F	Child	18Se02Bg
Jas.	02	M	Child	18Se02Bg
MCMANUS, Mich.	24	M	Laborer	18Se02Bg
MCNAMARA, Jno.	16	M	Laborer	18Se02Bg
BOYLE, Jas.	30	M	Laborer	18Se02Bg
KILGART, Magt.	18	F	None	18Se02Bg
SOIAHAN, Pat	40	M	Laborer	18Se02Bg

NAMES OF PASSENGERS	AGE	SEX	OCCUPATIONS	DATE PORT SHIP
CLERKIN, Phil	20	M	Laborer	18Se02Bg
SOIAHAN, Bridget	44	F	None	18Se02Bg
Mary	18	F	None	18Se02Bg
Cath.	17	F	None	18Se02Bg
COULTIN, Wm.	56	M	Laborer	18Se02Bg
MCENTAGART, Honor	60	F	None	18Se02Bg
SMITH, Ann	18	F	None	18Se02Bg
LEE, Julia	14	F	None	18Se02Bg
MCCUTTY, Joseph	30	M	Laborer	18Se02Bg
WINNIFIELD, Saml.	27	M	Clothier	18Se02Bg
Mary	30	F	Unknown	18Se02Bg
Sarah-J.	05	F	Child	18Se02Bg
Saml.	03	M	Child	18Se02Bg
FRYER, Mary	36	F	None	18Se02Bg
Saml. (S)	02	M	Child	18Se02Bg
SMITH, Mary-A.	19	F	None	18Se02Bg
JORDAN, Richd.	41	M	Laborer	18Se02Bg
Magt.	31	F	None	18Se02Bg
DORAN, Cath.	16	F	None	18Se02Bg
JORDAN, Mary-A.	09	F	Child	18Se02Bg
Judith	07	F	Child	18Se02Bg
Richd.	05	M	Child	18Se02Bg
Jno.	02	M	Child	18Se02Bg
FLYNN, Pat	30	M	Laborer	18Se02Bg
FAREL, Ann	22	F	None	18Se02Bg
Maria	24	F	None	18Se02Bg
Fanny	48	F	None	18Se02Bg
Margt.	08	F	Child	18Se02Bg
SCOTT, Jno.	60	M	Laborer	18Se02Bg
Thos.	26	M	Laborer	18Se02Bg
Nancy	60	F	Unknown	18Se02Bg
MCGARREN, R.	06	M	Child	18Se02Bg
GALLAGER, Dennis	22	M	Laborer	18Se02Bg
LARBY, Edwd.	21	M	Laborer	18Se02Bg
ODONNELL, Magt.	38	F	None	18Se02Bg
MCGLUISKY, Jno.	04	M	Child	18Se02Bg
CANNON, Biddy	28	F	None	18Se02Bg
DANIEL, Saml.	21	M	Clerk	18Se02Bg
CARPENTER, Wm.	24	M	Mechanic	18Se02Bg
JONES, Jos.	22	M	Mechanic	18Se02Bg
MANAHAN, Pat	21	M	Mechanic	18Se02Bg
Bridget	22	F	None	18Se02Bg
PATTERSON, M.	25	M	Laborer	18Se02Bg
HANCOCK, Richd.	30	M	Laborer	18Se02Bg
HAMILTON, Jas.	44	M	Laborer	18Se02Bg
QUINN, Wm.	20	M	Laborer	18Se02Bg
WILLIAMS, Thos.	33	M	Laborer	18Se02Bg
Mary	63	F	None	18Se02Bg
Jane	24	F	None	18Se02Bg
WARE, Jno.	37	M	Mechanic	18Se02Bg
BRACHAN, Ed.	25	M	Mechanic	18Se02Bg
BAILY, Isabella	21	F	None	18Se02Bg
GIBSON, Jane	21	F	None	18Se02Bg
FERGUSON, Wm.	40	M	Mechanic	18Se02Bg
Jane	30	F	None	18Se02Bg
Mary-A.	27	F	None	18Se02Bg
Robt.	18	M	Mechanic	18Se02Bg
BRADLY, Mich.	33	M	Mechanic	18Se02Bg
MCGILVY, Wm.	59	M	Mechanic	18Se02Bg
FRASER, Hugh	33	M	Mechanic	18Se02Bg
MCGILVY, Magt.	55	F	None	18Se02Bg
SHAW, Mgt.	55	F	None	18Se02Bg
MCINTYRE, Alex.	17	M	Mechanic	18Se02Bg
ONEILL, Bridget	28	F	None	18Se02Bg
Saul	09	M	Child	18Se02Bg
MCMICKLE, Rhoda	46	F	None	18Se02Bg
MURDOCK, Danl.	24	M	Laborer	18Se02Bg
MCKAY, Robt.	22	M	Laborer	18Se02Bg
CAMPBELL, Robt.	25	M	Laborer	18Se02Bg
BRICE, Jno.	25	M	Laborer	18Se02Bg
PATTERSON, Jno.	29	M	Laborer	18Se02Bg
Mary	22	F	Unknown	18Se02Bg
Isabella	05	F	Child	18Se02Bg
David	02	M	Child	18Se02Bg
LOCKWOOD, Elizth.	30	F	None	18Se02Bg

NAMES OF PASSENGERS		AGE	SEX	OCCUPATIONS	DATE PORT SHIP
LOCKWOOD, Mich.		18	M	Laborer	18Se02Bg
TOMEY, Jas.		14	M	Laborer	18Se02Bg
CARROLL, Ellen		10	F	None	18Se02Bg
CARPENTER, Cath.		25	F	None	18Se02Bg
SMITH, Ann		22	F	None	18Se02Bg
WILSON, Letitia		26	F	None	18Se02Bg
LYNCH, Ann		20	F	None	18Se02Bg
CASELL, U-Miss.		26	F	None	18Se02Bg
CAMERON, Hugh		26	M	Laborer	18Se02Bg
Bernard		24	M	Laborer	18Se02Bg
KELLY, Mary		16	F	None	18Se02Bg
DONNELL, Mary		36	F	None	18Se02Bg
Sarah		32	F	None	18Se02Bg
Ann		16	F	None	18Se02Bg
MCGONIGAL, Jno.		24	M	Laborer	18Se02Bg
CANNON, Chas.		12	M	None	18Se02Bg
MCCROCKEN, Mich.		20	M	Laborer	18Se02Bg
DORAN, Susan		12	F	None	18Se02Bg
Jas.J.		09	M	Child	18Se02Bg
MAGUIRE, Patt.		50	M	Farmer	18Se02Bg
Rose		17	F	None	18Se02Bg
Mag.		48	F	Unknown	18Se02Bg
Pat		13	M	None	18Se02Bg
Alice		10	F	None	18Se02Bg
Terence		08	M	Child	18Se02Bg
Hugh		06	M	Child	18Se02Bg
MISS, Stephen		60	M	Laborer	18Se02Bg
SMITH, Mary-A.		22	F	None	18Se02Bg

MASSACHUSETTS 20 SEPTEMBER 1847

From Liverpool

NAMES OF PASSENGERS		AGE	SEX	OCCUPATIONS	DATE PORT SHIP
EADY, John		27	M	Bootmaker	20Se02Bb
Eliza	(W)	23	F	Wife	20Se02Bb
John	(S)	.04	M	Infant	20Se02Bb
MARTIN, Phillip		29	M	Miller	20Se02Bb
FENBY, Mary		30	F	Dairymaid	20Se02Bb
LYNCH, Ann		18	F	Dairymaid	20Se02Bb
CLOVIN, William		22	M	Farmer	20Se02Bb
Mary-Jane		21	F	Unknown	20Se02Bb
THOMPSON, Ann		23	F	Unknown	20Se02Bb
STONE, Sarah		20	F	Unknown	20Se02Bb
CHERRY, Sarah		21	F	Unknown	20Se02Bb
DONAHHU, William		40	M	Unknown	20Se02Bb
Mary		36	F	Unknown	20Se02Bb
Margrett		05	F	Child	20Se02Bb
MEARYS, Elizabeth		40	F	Unknown	20Se02Bb
HERN, John		40	M	Farmer	20Se02Bb
Ellen	(W)	35	F	Wife	20Se02Bb
Peter	(S)	13	M	Son	20Se02Bb
Margrett	(D)	11	F	Daughter	20Se02Bb
Abby	(D)	08	F	Child	20Se02Bb
Mary	(D)	06	F	Child	20Se02Bb
Charles	(S)	04	M	Child	20Se02Bb
John	(S)	03	M	Child	20Se02Bb
Ellen	(D)	02	F	Child	20Se02Bb
WOLON, Edward		35	M	Laborer	20Se02Bb
KELLY, Margrett		30	F	Laborer	20Se02Bb
DONEHO, Daniel		28	M	Clerk	20Se02Bb
Ann		30	F	Clerk	20Se02Bb
ENNES, Thomas		36	M	Laborer	20Se02Bb
PRAVIS, Catherine		40	F	Weaver	20Se02Bb
Andrew		18	M	Laborer	20Se02Bb
QUINN, Patrick		25	M	Laborer	20Se02Bb
Sarah		21	F	Laborer	20Se02Bb
CLARS, James		26	M	Farmer	20Se02Bb
Margrett		26	F	Farmer	20Se02Bb
BRIZEN, James		24	M	Weaver	20Se02Bb
BARBER, Mary		12	F	Unknown	20Se02Bb
Ellen		10	F	Unknown	20Se02Bb
MCCAN, Richard		19	M	Watchmaker	20Se02Bb
RANY, Mary		20	F	Unknown	20Se02Bb
BURNS, James		30	M	Currier	20Se02Bb
Michl.		26	M	Currier	20Se02Bb
NORMAN, Theofilus		26	M	Laborer	20Se02Bb
GALIGHER, Patrick		64	M	Farmer	20Se02Bb
Rosa	(W)	60	F	Wife	20Se02Bb
Thomas	(S)	19	M	Son	20Se02Bb
Mary	(D)	13	F	Unknown	20Se02Bb
MCMULLIRY, John		18	M	Farmer	20Se02Bb
SHARP, Robert		12	M	Laborer	20Se02Bb
RAINALS, John		37	M	Mason	20Se02Bb
FATTER, Jame		28	M	Farmer	20Se02Bb
DOUGAN, Daniel		22	M	Laborer	20Se02Bb
BURNS, Dennis		26	M	Laborer	20Se02Bb
LANNAN, Dennis		24	M	Laborer	20Se02Bb
KANNY, Cathrine		30	F	Unknown	20Se02Bb
BURNS, Judid		18	F	Unknown	20Se02Bb
CONEL, An-Elizabeth		25	F	Unknown	20Se02Bb
DOGAN, Bridgett		20	F	Unknown	20Se02Bb
CAMBEL, George		23	M	Tailor	20Se02Bb
Patric		16	M	Laborer	20Se02Bb
COILY, Abby		30	F	Unknown	20Se02Bb
Margrett		15	F	Laborer	20Se02Bb
MURAHA, Patrick		26	M	Laborer	20Se02Bb
COLLINS, Elizabeth		27	F	Laborer	20Se02Bb
John		06	M	Child	20Se02Bb
Michel.		03	M	Child	20Se02Bb
HIGGINS, Ellen		16	F	Laborer	20Se02Bb
CASHIARNE, Julia		20	F	Laborer	20Se02Bb
IGO, Michel.		50	M	Mason	20Se02Bb
Mary		49	F	Unknown	20Se02Bb
Ann		18	F	Unknown	20Se02Bb
John		12	M	Unknown	20Se02Bb
HANLY, Margrett		05	F	Child	20Se02Bb
John		03	M	Child	20Se02Bb
BOID, Robert		28	M	Engineer	20Se02Bb
DUFFEE, Rose		18	F	Unknown	20Se02Bb
MAHARY, Dennis		28	M	Laborer	20Se02Bb
Benjamin		20	M	Laborer	20Se02Bb
THORN, John		21	M	Laborer	20Se02Bb
DRENE, Thomas		26	M	Laborer	20Se02Bb
MARTIN, Mary		20	F	Laborer	20Se02Bb
FITZSIMONS, Judy		46	F	Laborer	20Se02Bb
Betty		12	F	Laborer	20Se02Bb
Edward		10	M	Laborer	20Se02Bb
Catherine		08	F	Child	20Se02Bb
IRVAINY, John		20	M	Laborer	20Se02Bb
DONLAN, John		17	M	Laborer	20Se02Bb
Mathew		50	M	Farmer	20Se02Bb
CAHEL, Patrick		48	M	Weaver	20Se02Bb
Richard		47	M	Unknown	20Se02Bb
Ferril		24	M	Laborer	20Se02Bb
Ann		18	F	Laborer	20Se02Bb
Mary		14	F	Laborer	20Se02Bb

NEW-WORLD 21 SEPTEMBER 1847

From Liverpool

NAMES OF PASSENGERS		AGE	SEX	OCCUPATIONS	DATE PORT SHIP
HARBISON, David		23	M	Farmer	21Se02Ku
MORRISON, Philip-Jas.		20	M	Farmer	21Se02Ku
GRAHAM, Peter		17	M	Laborer	21Se02Ku
LOWE, William		22	M	Tailor	21Se02Ku
Pat		18	M	Laborer	21Se02Ku
MAHER, Edwd.		32	M	Carpenter	21Se02Ku
Mary	(W)	32	F	Wife	21Se02Ku

NAMES OF PASSENGERS		AGE	SEX	OCCUPATIONS	DATE PORT SHIP
MAHER, Ann		20	F	Servant	21Se02Ku
REILLY, James		21	M	Laborer	21Se02Ku
BOLAND, Marg.		21	F	Wife	21Se02Ku
Catha.		20	F	Servant	21Se02Ku
James		28	M	Carpenter	21Se02Ku
MORAN, John		40	M	Coach Maker	21Se02Ku
U	(W)	30	F	Wife	21Se02Ku
James	(S)	09	M	Child	21Se02Ku
Jane	(D)	.00	F	Infant	21Se02Ku
NEDDY, John		25	M	Pvcr	21Se02Ku
CRAIG, John		30	M	Farmer	21Se02Ku
Mary-Jane	(W)	28	F	Wife	21Se02Ku
SOMERVILLE, Matilda		20	F	Dressmaker	21Se02Ku
LEE, James		21	M	Butcher	21Se02Ku
RIARDEN, Pat		22	M	Butcher	21Se02Ku
DOWNEY, Edward		26	M	Pvcr	21Se02Ku
SCANLAN, Peter		25	M	Laborer	21Se02Ku
MURPHY, John		18	M	Tailor	21Se02Ku
COLEMAN, Alice		20	F	Dressmaker	21Se02Ku
BLACK, Archd.		40	M	Merchant	21Se02Ku
U	(W)	35	F	Wife	21Se02Ku
JOHNSTONE, Eliza		17	F	Sister	21Se02Ku
CARLTON, Eliza		17	F	Servant	21Se02Ku
RICHMON, Thos.		20	M	Jeweller	21Se02Ku
DONAHUE, Pat		20	M	Laborer	21Se02Ku
FINLEY, Pat		22	M	Laborer	21Se02Ku
Catha.		15	F	Servant	21Se02Ku
Abby		14	F	Servant	21Se02Ku
KULLAHER, John		20	M	Cooper	21Se02Ku
ASHE, Wm.		20	M	Carver	21Se02Ku
CUSSACK, Mary		20	F	Servant	21Se02Ku
MCDONNELL, Susan		20	F	Servant	21Se02Ku
FLOOD, Rose		23	F	Servant	21Se02Ku
THOMAS, Jam.		21	M	Laborer	21Se02Ku
WARLOW, John		48	M	Laborer	21Se02Ku
Elizabeth	(W)	46	F	Wife	21Se02Ku
Mary	(D)	05	F	Child	21Se02Ku
THOMAS, Richd.		26	M	Miner	21Se02Ku
HOWELL, Eliza		25	F	Wife	21Se02Ku
Catha.-R.		40	F	Daughter	21Se02Ku
WILSON, Archy		25	M	Groom	21Se02Ku
Catha.	(W)	26	F	Wife	21Se02Ku
SWENEY, Hugh		20	M	Laborer	21Se02Ku
MCFADDIN, Margt.		36	F	Servant	21Se02Ku
SMITH, Jane		37	F	Wife	21Se02Ku
Jane	(D)	03	F	Child	21Se02Ku
BEATON, Mary		23	F	Dressmaker	21Se02Ku
MCNULTY, Edwd.		50	M	Shoemaker	21Se02Ku
Alice	(D)	38	F	Unknown	21Se02Ku
Edwd.	(S)	08	M	Child	21Se02Ku
CALTON, John		13	M	Unknown	21Se02Ku
DUFFY, Chas.		22	M	Laborer	21Se02Ku
Margt.	(W)	23	F	Wife	21Se02Ku
MILLER, John		47	M	Farmer	21Se02Ku
Lucy	(W)	40	F	Wife	21Se02Ku
Hannah	(T)	38	F	Unknown	21Se02Ku
MCCALLA, Sarah-Jane		13	F	Daughter	21Se02Ku
MILLER, Ann		11	F	Daughter	21Se02Ku
Mary-Ann	(D)	09	F	Child	21Se02Ku
Hanna	(D)	06	F	Child	21Se02Ku
Margt.	(D)	04	F	Child	21Se02Ku
Elizabeth	(D)	.00	F	Infant	21Se02Ku
WELSH, John		20	M	Clerk	21Se02Ku
ANDERSON, Mary-Jane		.00	F	Infant	21Se02Ku
MOLLOY, Alice		77	F	Wife	21Se02Ku
Thos.		32	M	Farmer	21Se02Ku
Ann-Teresa	(W)	26	F	Wife	21Se02Ku
Thos.	(S)	07	M	Child	21Se02Ku
Maria	(D)	05	F	Child	21Se02Ku
Jessie	(S)	04	M	Child	21Se02Ku
Jos.	(S)	.00	M	Infant	21Se02Ku
ROGERS, Ann		25	F	Servant	21Se02Ku
KEYNON, Catha.		20	F	Servant	21Se02Ku
CARMICHAEL, Ann		25	F	Servant	21Se02Ku
CRAWFORD, Elias		20	M	Laborer	21Se02Ku

NAMES OF PASSENGERS		AGE	SEX	OCCUPATIONS	DATE PORT SHIP
MOORE, Jeremiah		26	M	Tailor	21Se02Ku
MORAN, Martin		25	M	Laborer	21Se02Ku
DEVERAUX, Thos.		40	M	Carpenter	21Se02Ku
Mary	(W)	40	F	Wife	21Se02Ku
Edwd.	(S)	20	M	Son	21Se02Ku
Mary	(D)	18	F	Daughter	21Se02Ku
Margt.	(D)	16	F	Daughter	21Se02Ku
John	(S)	13	M	Son	21Se02Ku
Pat	(S)	11	M	Son	21Se02Ku
James	(S)	09	M	Child	21Se02Ku
CUMMINS, Ann		20	F	Dressmaker	21Se02Ku
Alice		18	F	Dressmaker	21Se02Ku
LYONS, Larry		30	M	Laborer	21Se02Ku
MCCARTHY, Catha.		20	F	Servant	21Se02Ku
Johanna		18	F	Servant	21Se02Ku
CURRON, John		38	M	Laborer	21Se02Ku
Mary	(W)	23	F	Wife	21Se02Ku
SNOW, Elizabeth		30	F	Wife	21Se02Ku
Catha.	(D)	04	F	Child	21Se02Ku
CLANCY, Pat		40	M	Laborer	21Se02Ku
CLARKE, Catha.		12	F	Servant	21Se02Ku
MURPHY, Henry		25	M	Laborer	21Se02Ku
John		23	M	Clerk	21Se02Ku
MCGOVERN, Anthony		20	M	Laborer	21Se02Ku
WELSH, Michl.		26	M	Farmer	21Se02Ku
Thos.		24	M	Farmer	21Se02Ku
U	(W)	22	F	Wife	21Se02Ku
CURRAN, Michl.		23	M	Mason	21Se02Ku
ALLEN, Thos.		24	M	Laborer	21Se02Ku
SOUTHERN, Denis		12	M	Unknown	21Se02Ku
MURPHY, Ellen		30	F	Servant	21Se02Ku
Mary		24	F	Servant	21Se02Ku
REID, U		40	F	Wife	21Se02Ku
Edwd.	(S)	19	M	Son	21Se02Ku
James	(S)	17	M	Son	21Se02Ku
Michl.	(S)	15	M	Son	21Se02Ku
Ellen	(D)	11	F	Daughter	21Se02Ku
MURPHY, Mary		20	F	Servant	21Se02Ku
SOMERVILLE, Alex.		20	M	Farmer	21Se02Ku
TRIG, Mary		40	F	Servant	21Se02Ku
Rosey		18	F	Servant	21Se02Ku
KING, Mary		20	F	Servant	21Se02Ku
MCCALLIN, Ann		18	F	Servant	21Se02Ku
CONNLEY, Catha.		21	F	Servant	21Se02Ku
DOONAN, Nabby		18	F	Servant	21Se02Ku
WARD, Ellen		20	F	Dressmaker	21Se02Ku
FITZPATRICK, Rose		21	F	Dressmaker	21Se02Ku
SWEENY, Ann		20	F	Servant	21Se02Ku
KILLARD, Wm.		25	M	Laborer	21Se02Ku
WHALLEY, Mary		63	F	Servant	21Se02Ku
Ellen		33	F	Servant	21Se02Ku
MCTRAGUE, Pat.		25	M	Laborer	21Se02Ku
Margt.	(W)	18	F	Wife	21Se02Ku
Bridget	(T)	12	F	Unknown	21Se02Ku
James	(B)	11	M	Unknown	21Se02Ku
CANNON, Mary		40	F	Servant	21Se02Ku
Michl.	(S)	10	M	Unknown	21Se02Ku
Judy	(D)	06	F	Child	21Se02Ku
Peter	(S)	.00	M	Infant	21Se02Ku
COONEY, Cornels.		20	M	Laborer	21Se02Ku
ROONEY, John		25	M	Laborer	21Se02Ku
ROWNEY, Ellen		23	F	Servant	21Se02Ku
ANDERSON, Jane		18	F	Servant	21Se02Ku
Sarah	(M)	71	F	Unknown	21Se02Ku
CANN, Michl.		25	M	Laborer	21Se02Ku
Margt.		20	F	Servant	21Se02Ku
BRENNAN, Mary		12	F	Servant	21Se02Ku
Cath.		10	F	Servant	21Se02Ku
MCNALLY, Michl.		40	M	Wheelwright	21Se02Ku
Pat		18	M	Tailor	21Se02Ku
FURY, John		28	M	Clerk	21Se02Ku
Bridget	(W)	28	F	Wife	21Se02Ku
Pat	(B)	10	M	Unknown	21Se02Ku
FINNIGAN, Michl.		20	M	Laborer	21Se02Ku
GALLAGER, Pat		12	M	Laborer	21Se02Ku

NAMES OF PASSENGERS		AGE	SEX	OCCUPATIONS	DATE PORT SHIP
REGAN, Mary		20	F	Servant	21Se02Ku
WHELIHER, Mary		20	F	Servant	21Se02Ku
RAFERTY, Michl.		11	M	Unknown	21Se02Ku
Timothy		09	M	Child	21Se02Ku
BRENNAN, James		40	M	Laborer	21Se02Ku
Alice	(D)	20	F	Unknown	21Se02Ku
Jane	(D)	18	F	Unknown	21Se02Ku
MCCUE, Peter		12	M	Unknown	21Se02Ku
EATON, Mathw.		20	M	Laborer	21Se02Ku
ORMSBY, Ellen		13	F	Servant	21Se02Ku
BRADY, Pat		12	M	Laborer	21Se02Ku
SAMON, Mary		20	F	Servant	21Se02Ku
PLUNKETT, Pat		08	M	Child	21Se02Ku
SILLY, Mathw.		50	M	Laborer	21Se02Ku
MCLAUGHLIN, Winney		13	F	Servant	21Se02Ku
KILOOLY, Sarah		20	F	Servant	21Se02Ku
FLINN, Ellen-Mrs.		40	F	Wife	21Se02Ku
Owen	(S)	12	M	Unknown	21Se02Ku
Thos.	(S)	11	M	Unknown	21Se02Ku
Pat	(S)	08	M	Child	21Se02Ku
Andy	(S)	05	M	Child	21Se02Ku
Margt.	(D)	.00	F	Infant	21Se02Ku
MCGRATH, Johana		20	F	Servant	21Se02Ku
BURKE, Mary-Mrs.		40	F	Wife	21Se02Ku
Thos.	(S)	08	M	Child	21Se02Ku
John	(S)	05	M	Child	21Se02Ku
Edw.	(S)	03	M	Child	21Se02Ku
Bryan	(S)	.00	M	Infant	21Se02Ku
HALL, Margt.		20	F	Servant	21Se02Ku
CUNNINGHAM, Hugh		20	M	Laborer	21Se02Ku
BATELL, John		40	M	Laborer	21Se02Ku
Ellen	(W)	40	F	Wife	21Se02Ku
John	(S)	14	M	Unknown	21Se02Ku
Catha.	(D)	12	F	Unknown	21Se02Ku
James	(S)	10	M	Unknown	21Se02Ku
Luke	(S)	08	M	Child	21Se02Ku
Pat	(S)	.00	M	Infant	21Se02Ku
CARNEY, James		20	M	Laborer	21Se02Ku
MONAGHAN, Catha.		40	F	Servant	21Se02Ku
Barthm.		25	M	Laborer	21Se02Ku
NEAL, Mary		11	F	Servant	21Se02Ku
SWEENEY, Margt.		20	F	Servant	21Se02Ku
BUCK, Esther		18	F	Servant	21Se02Ku
SHARP, Mary-Ann		20	F	Dressmaker	21Se02Ku
MEREDITH, Frances		20	M	Laborer	21Se02Ku
ROONEY, Mathew		40	M	Laborer	21Se02Ku
Ann		40	F	Laborer	21Se02Ku
Pat	(S)	06	M	Child	21Se02Ku
James	(S)	.00	M	Infant	21Se02Ku
BRADY, Ann		20	F	Servant	21Se02Ku
SMITH, Mathw.		28	M	Laborer	21Se02Ku
Pat		25	M	Laborer	21Se02Ku
Bridgt.		20	F	Servant	21Se02Ku
Ealy		12	U	Servant	21Se02Ku
REYNOLDS, Ann		14	F	Servant	21Se02Ku
SER, Rose		20	F	Servant	21Se02Ku
DIXON, Sarah-Mrs.		30	F	Wife	21Se02Ku
Mary	(D)	04	F	Child	21Se02Ku
Alice	(D)	.00	F	Infant	21Se02Ku
CASSIDY, Rose		20	F	Unknown	21Se02Ku
COX, Catha.		40	F	Unknown	21Se02Ku
Bridget		20	F	Unknown	21Se02Ku
MCKINSELL, Robt.		30	M	Weaver	21Se02Ku
Jane	(W)	30	F	Wife	21Se02Ku
James	(S)	11	M	Unknown	21Se02Ku
Samuel	(S)	09	M	Child	21Se02Ku
Robt.	(S)	07	M	Child	21Se02Ku
John	(S)	05	M	Child	21Se02Ku
Sarah	(D)	02	F	Child	21Se02Ku
MILLER, Rachael		20	F	Servant	21Se02Ku
POSTON, Robt.		17	M	Laborer	21Se02Ku
WILSON, Eliza-Mrs.		40	F	Wife	21Se02Ku
William		60	M	Laborer	21Se02Ku
HIGGERTY, John		28	M	Laborer	21Se02Ku
MCGEE, Henry		60	M	Laborer	21Se02Ku
MCGEE, Ann	(W)	60	F	Wife	21Se02Ku
DUNNIGAN, Rose		40	F	Servant	21Se02Ku
Mary		20	F	Servant	21Se02Ku
HERON, Wm.		25	M	Laborer	21Se02Ku
Cath.	(W)	25	F	Wife	21Se02Ku
John	(S)	06	M	Child	21Se02Ku
John	(S)	04	M	Child	21Se02Ku
MCNALLY, James		25	M	Laborer	21Se02Ku
BOYLE, Mary		20	F	Servant	21Se02Ku
ALLISON, Robt.		25	M	Laborer	21Se02Ku
SLOAN, John		20	M	Laborer	21Se02Ku
BRADLEY, Ellen		20	F	Servant	21Se02Ku
John		11	M	Unknown	21Se02Ku
DOUGHERTY, Mary		20	F	Servant	21Se02Ku
MCKANE, Nancy		20	F	Servant	21Se02Ku
FICHRY, John		10	M	Weaver	21Se02Ku
Maria		13	F	Weaver	21Se02Ku
Michael		25	M	Weaver	21Se02Ku
MORRIS, Robert		20	M	Laborer	21Se02Ku
ANDERSON, Robert		35	M	Blacksmith	21Se02Ku
Jane	(W)	28	F	Wife	21Se02Ku
KELLY, Bridget-Mrs.		25	F	Wife	21Se02Ku
Mary		20	F	Servant	21Se02Ku
Maria		02	F	Child	21Se02Ku
William		04	M	Child	21Se02Ku
ANDERSON, Mary		25	F	Servant	21Se02Ku
William		24	M	Laborer	21Se02Ku
James		24	M	Laborer	21Se02Ku
Mary		15	F	Servant	21Se02Ku
MCGOVERN, Catha.		20	F	Servant	21Se02Ku
HAIGHTON, Danl.		25	M	Laborer	21Se02Ku
MURPHY, Jeremiah		12	M	Servant	21Se02Ku
Hanah		10	F	Servant	21Se02Ku
REILLY, Thos.		28	M	Laborer	21Se02Ku
Ellen	(W)	26	F	Wife	21Se02Ku
CREED, Ellen		40	F	Servant	21Se02Ku
Thos.		20	M	Laborer	21Se02Ku
ROURKE, Wm.		25	M	Shoemaker	21Se02Ku
Ellen	(W)	20	F	Unknown	21Se02Ku
FOONEY, Pat		25	M	Laborer	21Se02Ku
Johannah		25	F	Servant	21Se02Ku
KANE, Ellen		18	F	Servant	21Se02Ku
PERRY, Eliza		20	F	Dressmaker	21Se02Ku
MOORE, Mary		20	F	Weaver	21Se02Ku
BRISSELL, John		20	M	Laborer	21Se02Ku
Ellen		20	F	Servant	21Se02Ku
Bridget		09	F	Child	21Se02Ku
SEENEY, Catha.		13	F	Servant	21Se02Ku
KING, John		40	M	Laborer	21Se02Ku
Margt.	(W)	40	F	Wife	21Se02Ku
Margt.	(D)	11	F	Unknown	21Se02Ku
Thos.	(S)	09	M	Child	21Se02Ku
Cath.	(D)	07	F	Child	21Se02Ku
Pat	(S)	03	M	Child	21Se02Ku
Jane	(D)	.00	F	Infant	21Se02Ku
ROACH, Margt.		20	F	Servant	21Se02Ku
DALEY, Wm.		25	M	Laborer	21Se02Ku
MCELROY, Thos.		40	M	Laborer	21Se02Ku
Thos.		20	M	Laborer	21Se02Ku
Rose		18	F	Servant	21Se02Ku
Bridget		20	F	Servant	21Se02Ku
Henry		.00	M	Infant	21Se02Ku
CASSIDY, Ellen		20	F	Servant	21Se02Ku
Eliza		18	F	Servant	21Se02Ku
Mary		20	F	Servant	21Se02Ku
COONEYS, Pat		25	M	Shoemaker	21Se02Ku
OATES, Wm.		20	M	Shoemaker	21Se02Ku
RIARDEN, Johana-Mrs.		25	F	Wife	21Se02Ku
Catha.	(D)	06	F	Child	21Se02Ku
Johan	(S)	04	M	Child	21Se02Ku
MCGOVERN, Chas.		40	M	Laborer	21Se02Ku
Margt.	(D)	08	F	Child	21Se02Ku
Pat	(S)	06	M	Child	21Se02Ku
Edwd.	(S)	04	M	Child	21Se02Ku
MCGUIRE, Bernd.		40	M	Laborer	21Se02Ku

NAMES OF PASSENGERS		AGE	SEX	OCCUPATIONS	DATE PORT SHIP
GRIER, Margt.		50	F	Servant	21Se02Ku
ROACH, Wm.		20	M	Laborer	21Se02Ku
Edwd.		07	M	Child	21Se02Ku
John		05	M	Child	21Se02Ku
HEWITTE, Margt.		20	F	Servant	21Se02Ku
MCKENNA, Catha.Mrs.		40	F	Wife	21Se02Ku
Catha.	(D)	20	F	Unknown	21Se02Ku
Wm.	(S)	18	M	Unknown	21Se02Ku
Ellen	(D)	10	F	Unknown	21Se02Ku
John	(S)	04	M	Child	21Se02Ku
Olinda	(D)	.00	F	Infant	21Se02Ku
ROONEY, Mary		30	F	Servant	21Se02Ku
Wm.Henry	(S)	.00	M	Infant	21Se02Ku
MCKELLUP, Mary		12	F	Servant	21Se02Ku
SCULLY, John		30	M	Carpenter	21Se02Ku
Catha.	(W)	20	F	Wife	21Se02Ku
BRION, Thos.		25	M	Laborer	21Se02Ku
Elisabeth		20	F	Servant	21Se02Ku
CASSIDY, Margt.		20	F	Servant	21Se02Ku
GRIFFITH, Margt.		25	F	Servant	21Se02Ku
WHELAN, Mary		14	F	Servant	21Se02Ku
Cath.		11	F	None	21Se02Ku
John		09	M	Child	21Se02Ku
KEANS, Mary		11	M	None	21Se02Ku
Catha.		09	F	Child	21Se02Ku
DRISCOLL, Denny		25	M	Laborer	21Se02Ku
EVANS, William		30	M	Laborer	21Se02Ku
Eliza	(W)	29	F	Wife	21Se02Ku
BULGER, James		26	M	Druggist	21Se02Ku
KEHOE, Thos.		31	M	Soap Maker	21Se02Ku
KERNY, Michl.		19	M	Laborer	21Se02Ku
MULLONE, Betty		22	F	Servant	21Se02Ku
MOUNTFORD, S.		27	M	Farmer	21Se02Ku
PATTERSON, O.		18	M	Farmer	21Se02Ku
MORTON, James		25	M	Farmer	21Se02Ku
CRIGHTON, Saml.		35	M	Farmer	21Se02Ku
Robt.		18	M	Carpenter	21Se02Ku
MCHUGH, Pat		15	M	Tailor	21Se02Ku
MCCARNEY, Philip		11	M	None	21Se02Ku
JOHNSTON, William		20	M	Farmer	21Se02Ku
U	(W)	25	F	Wife	21Se02Ku
Richd.	(S)	04	M	Child	21Se02Ku
Eliza	(D)	06	F	Child	21Se02Ku
John	(S)	02	M	Child	21Se02Ku
BOURKE, Cathn.		20	F	Servant	21Se02Ku
BRETT, Chas.		25	M	Farmer	21Se02Ku
U	(W)	20	F	Wife	21Se02Ku
HANLY, Amelia		25	F	Servant	21Se02Ku
ROBINSON, Ellen		20	F	Servant	21Se02Ku
Margt.		20	F	Servant	21Se02Ku
DONNELL, Cathn.		20	F	Servant	21Se02Ku
Agnes		18	F	Servant	21Se02Ku
MULDROOM, Andrew		10	M	None	21Se02Ku
MCDERMOTT, Thos.		20	M	Clerk	21Se02Ku
Margt.		18	F	Servant	21Se02Ku
WILSON, Jane-Mrs.		40	F	Wife	21Se02Ku
Wm.		30	M	Tpf	21Se02Ku
Gibbons	(S)	14	M	Unknown	21Se02Ku
Alexander	(S)	12	M	Unknown	21Se02Ku
Eliza-Jane	(D)	10	F	Unknown	21Se02Ku
Mary	(D)	09	F	Child	21Se02Ku
Thos.	(S)	07	M	Child	21Se02Ku
Wm.	(S)	05	M	Child	21Se02Ku
James	(S)	03	M	Child	21Se02Ku
HARKINS, Thos.		22	M	Cooper	21Se02Ku
SIPSETT, James		20	M	Merchant	21Se02Ku
Mary	(M)	40	F	Unknown	21Se02Ku
Rebecca		17	F	Servant	21Se02Ku
DARGAN, Bernd.		20	M	Laborer	21Se02Ku
SHERMAN, Mary		18	F	Servant	21Se02Ku
MONROE, Rose-Mrs.		40	F	Wife	21Se02Ku
Wm.	(S)	17	M	Unknown	21Se02Ku
Sarah	(D)	12	F	Unknown	21Se02Ku
WILSON, William		30	M	Bookbinder	21Se02Ku
John	(S)	08	M	Child	21Se02Ku

NAMES OF PASSENGERS		AGE	SEX	OCCUPATIONS	DATE PORT SHIP
JONES, Michl.		11	M	Bookbinder	21Se02Ku
DALE, Samuel		30	M	Farmer	21Se02Ku
U	(W)	20	F	Wife	21Se02Ku
John	(S)	08	M	Child	21Se02Ku
Samuel	(S)	06	M	Child	21Se02Ku
Stephen	(S)	04	M	Child	21Se02Ku
William	(S)	.00	M	Infant	21Se02Ku
HEANEY, Oliver		20	M	Carpenter	21Se02Ku
WHITE, Jno.		30	M	Merchant	21Se02Ku
LYNCH, John		30	M	Surveyor	21Se02Ku
MARTIN, James		18	M	Laborer	21Se02Ku
Michl.		18	M	Laborer	21Se02Ku
VEASEY, Luke		20	M	Laborer	21Se02Ku
Mary-Mrs.		60	F	Wife	21Se02Ku
CANNON, Opporan		30	M	Peddler	21Se02Ku
Hannah	(W)	19	F	Wife	21Se02Ku
HIGGINS, John		26	M	Merchant	21Se02Ku
Essy	(T)	20	F	Unknown	21Se02Ku
Maria	(T)	10	F	Unknown	21Se02Ku
NAVAN, Ellen		30	F	Servant	21Se02Ku
Margt.		25	F	Servant	21Se02Ku
Catha.		22	F	Servant	21Se02Ku
COUGHLIN, Mary		20	F	Servant	21Se02Ku
BOURKE, J.		20	M	Laborer	21Se02Ku
SEE, Margt.		18	F	Servant	21Se02Ku
GRATTIN, Wm.N.		20	M	Imcht	21Se02Ku
MCGENLEY, Chas.		30	M	Laborer	21Se02Ku
CLARK, Rebecca		18	F	Servant	21Se02Ku
MCBRIDE, Mary		20	F	Servant	21Se02Ku
MALONE, Pat		20	M	Clerk	21Se02Ku
HALLIGAN, Margt.		20	F	Servant	21Se02Ku
KELLY, Timothy		30	M	Miner	21Se02Ku
SHANNON, Francis		20	M	Laborer	21Se02Ku
Margt.	(W)	22	F	Wife	21Se02Ku
CONNOR, Catharine		18	F	Servant	21Se02Ku
Ellen		18	F	Servant	21Se02Ku
CORBETT, Mary		22	F	Servant	21Se02Ku
REILLY, Margt.		18	F	Servant	21Se02Ku
VICTORY, Michl.		20	M	Laborer	21Se02Ku
MCCONNELL, Pat		27	M	Laborer	21Se02Ku
MORRIS, Ann		20	F	Servant	21Se02Ku
CONNOR, Lawrence		24	M	Tailor	21Se02Ku
CURLEY, Pat		20	M	Joiner	21Se02Ku
KEEFE, Chas.		60	M	Farmer	21Se02Ku
FOY, Mary-Mrs.		30	F	Wife	21Se02Ku
Robt.	(S)	.00	M	Infant	21Se02Ku
VICTORY, Ann-Mrs.		30	F	Wife	21Se02Ku
Peter	(S)	.00	M	Infant	21Se02Ku
WILEY, Ellen		17	F	Servant	21Se02Ku
KELLY, Edwd.		00	M	Laborer	21Se02Ku
TOWNS, John		30	M	Laborer	21Se02Ku
Cathn.	(W)	26	F	Wife	21Se02Ku
Maria	(D)	05	F	Child	21Se02Ku
Catherine	(D)	03	F	Child	21Se02Ku
Anne	(D)	01	F	Child	21Se02Ku
MOYLAN, Maria		30	F	Servant	21Se02Ku
WATERMAN, Ann		21	F	Dressmaker	21Se02Ku
Margt.		19	F	Dressmaker	21Se02Ku
Mary		18	F	Dressmaker	21Se02Ku
Bridget		17	F	Servant	21Se02Ku
HARTNELL, Jos.		20	M	Laborer	21Se02Ku
Catha.		18	F	Servant	21Se02Ku
LARRY, Mary		19	F	Servant	21Se02Ku
TOOLEY, Dennis		50	M	Laborer	21Se02Ku
Johana	(W)	40	F	Wife	21Se02Ku
Denis	(S)	14	M	Unknown	21Se02Ku
John	(S)	11	M	Unknown	21Se02Ku
Timothy	(S)	10	M	Unknown	21Se02Ku
Daniel	(S)	07	M	Child	21Se02Ku
Julia	(D)	02	F	Child	21Se02Ku
HIGGINS, Henry		50	M	Laborer	21Se02Ku
SMITHE, Eliza		21	F	Servant	21Se02Ku
Ellen		19	F	Servant	21Se02Ku
MORAN, Helen		20	F	Servant	21Se02Ku
Roseanne		18	F	Servant	21Se02Ku

NAMES OF PASSENGERS		AGE	SEX	OCCUPATIONS	DATE PORT SHIP
GLINN, Peter		35	M	Laborer	21Se02Ku
Thos.		25	M	Laborer	21Se02Ku
CLANCEY, Pat		40	M	Laborer	21Se02Ku
ODONNELL, Wm.		40	M	Farmer	21Se02Ku
Eliza	(W)	33	F	Wife	21Se02Ku
Mary	(T)	33	F	Unknown	21Se02Ku
John	(S)	13	M	Unknown	21Se02Ku
Margt.	(D)	12	F	Unknown	21Se02Ku
Michael	(S)	09	M	Child	21Se02Ku
Edmund	(S)	07	M	Child	21Se02Ku
William	(S)	05	M	Child	21Se02Ku
Thomas	(S)	03	M	Child	21Se02Ku
James	(S)	.00	M	Infant	21Se02Ku
TASSIL, James		23	M	Farmer	21Se02Ku
George		21	M	Farmer	21Se02Ku
Catharine		19	F	Unknown	21Se02Ku
SCOTT, James		25	M	Laborer	21Se02Ku
Wm.		20	M	Shoemaker	21Se02Ku

TROUBADOUR 21 SEPTEMBER 1847

From Liverpool

NAMES OF PASSENGERS		AGE	SEX	OCCUPATIONS	DATE PORT SHIP
SAUL, James		20	M	Gdnr	21Se02Gz
Ann		24	F	Servant	21Se02Gz
ROBINSON, Saml.		32	M	Watchmaker	21Se02Gz
Sarah		33	F	Unknown	21Se02Gz
Ann	(D)	06	F	Child	21Se02Gz
GILMARTIN, Jno.		21	M	Laborer	21Se02Gz
Catherine		20	F	Servant	21Se02Gz
Margt.		17	F	Servant	21Se02Gz
COLEMAN, Mary		32	F	Servant	21Se02Gz
Patrick		12	M	Laborer	21Se02Gz
Thomas		10	M	Laborer	21Se02Gz
Richd.		08	M	Child	21Se02Gz
James		06	M	Child	21Se02Gz
Bridget		03	F	Child	21Se02Gz
MCNALLY, Cate.		22	F	Servant	21Se02Gz
MCGAHON, Bridgt.		21	F	Servant	21Se02Gz
GOODWIN, Mary		20	F	Servant	21Se02Gz
PHILLIPS, Wm.		23	M	Engineer	21Se02Gz
Mary		20	F	Unknown	21Se02Gz
John		.00	M	Infant	21Se02Gz
HEALEY, Abhy.		18	M	Unknown	21Se02Gz
Andw.		16	M	Unknown	21Se02Gz
MCCARTHY, Honora		22	F	Dressmaker	21Se02Gz
Mary		20	F	Dressmaker	21Se02Gz
SULLIVAN, John		20	M	Servant	21Se02Gz
Bridget		26	F	Servant	21Se02Gz
Jno.		05	M	Child	21Se02Gz
COLEMAN, Eliz.		20	F	Servant	21Se02Gz
COTTER, Ellen		60	F	Servant	21Se02Gz
Mary		22	F	Servant	21Se02Gz
Margt.		19	F	Servant	21Se02Gz
MULLEN, Edward		13	M	Servant	21Se02Gz
BURNES, Andw.		25	M	Tailor	21Se02Gz
Mary		25	F	Unknown	21Se02Gz
Mary		00	F	Child	21Se02Gz
Ann		02	F	Child	21Se02Gz
Died-At-Sea					
GOMLAY, David		29	M	Weaver	21Se02Gz
PAUL, Wm.		30	M	Laborer	21Se02Gz
MCELENTOCK, Josh.		20	M	Weaver	21Se02Gz
HAMILTON, Thos.G.		20	M	Joiner	21Se02Gz
SYNTEN, Judy		50	F	Weaver	21Se02Gz
Fanny		21	F	Unknown	21Se02Gz
John		18	M	Laborer	21Se02Gz
MCBRIDE, Francis		21	M	Laborer	21Se02Gz
SCALLIN, Mary		48	F	Laborer	21Se02Gz
SCALLIN, Cate.		18	F	Unknown	21Se02Gz
CALLAHAN, Biddy		21	F	Unknown	21Se02Gz
MCKENOUGH, Jno.		40	M	Nailer	21Se02Gz
James		10	M	Nailer	21Se02Gz
PATTERSON, James		21	M	Nailer	21Se02Gz
STEELE, Mary		50	F	Servant	21Se02Gz
Mary		20	F	Servant	21Se02Gz
HILL, Isabella		20	F	Servant	21Se02Gz
Mary		16	F	Servant	21Se02Gz
MCKEMES, Eliza		21	F	Servant	21Se02Gz
BANESEY, Thomas		19	M	Shoemaker	21Se02Gz
SAMLY, Eliza		26	F	Shoemaker	21Se02Gz
COLLINS, Michael		43	M	Shoemaker	21Se02Gz
Ann		40	F	Unknown	21Se02Gz
Charles		20	M	Laborer	21Se02Gz
Sarah-Ann		.00	F	Infant	21Se02Gz
Thomas		12	M	Unknown	21Se02Gz
ROBINSON, James		20	M	Draper	21Se02Gz
ROBINS, John		20	M	Grocer	21Se02Gz
ARMSTRONG, Edward		22	M	Clerk	21Se02Gz
DELANEY, Micheal		35	M	Shoemaker	21Se02Gz
RYAN, Patrick		12	M	Unknown	21Se02Gz
Edward		11	M	Unknown	21Se02Gz
JOSEPHS, John		22	M	Blacksmith	21Se02Gz
HANLON, Corniels.		19	M	Laborer	21Se02Gz
CONNOR, Bridget		18	F	Laborer	21Se02Gz
MCCUE, Cath.		20	F	Laborer	21Se02Gz
RUDDY, John		32	M	Laborer	21Se02Gz
U-Mrs		20	F	Wife	21Se02Gz
Martin		40	M	Laborer	21Se02Gz
Nancy		32	F	Unknown	21Se02Gz
Bridget		25	F	Unknown	21Se02Gz
CRAWFORD, Aleo.		24	M	Laborer	21Se02Gz
WELSH, Patt.		20	M	Laborer	21Se02Gz
BARRETT, Anthony		30	M	Laborer	21Se02Gz
MCANDIS, Bridget		20	F	Unknown	21Se02Gz
RODDY, John		03	M	Child	21Se02Gz
Sally		05	F	Child	21Se02Gz
Anne		.00	F	Infant	21Se02Gz
BROWN, John		20	M	Laborer	21Se02Gz
MCCARTNEY, Charles		40	M	Farmer	21Se02Gz
Anne		19	F	Unknown	21Se02Gz
Micheal		12	M	Unknown	21Se02Gz
MOORE, John		30	M	Paper Maker	21Se02Gz
Mary-Ann		26	F	Unknown	21Se02Gz
DOODY, John		30	M	Laborer	21Se02Gz
Peil.		07	M	Child	21Se02Gz
MOONEY, Ann		23	F	Weaver	21Se02Gz
CONNELLY, Cath.		19	F	Weaver	21Se02Gz
MOORE, Patrick		25	M	Tailor	21Se02Gz
MCCAFFREY, John		18	M	Laborer	21Se02Gz
Joseph		16	M	Unknown	21Se02Gz
Elya		22	F	Unknown	21Se02Gz
MCSHEFREY, Mary		19	F	Servant	21Se02Gz
Biddy		13	F	Servant	21Se02Gz
MCLUSKEY, Biddy		22	F	Servant	21Se02Gz
Betty		16	F	Servant	21Se02Gz
Margaret		18	F	Servant	21Se02Gz
HIGGINS, Mary		19	F	Servant	21Se02Gz
Nancy		21	F	Servant	21Se02Gz
QUINN, U-Mrs		28	F	Unknown	21Se02Gz
TOONEY, Biddy		30	F	Unknown	21Se02Gz
GARNETT, Patt.		20	M	Laborer	21Se02Gz
CURRAN, Thomas		30	M	Smith	21Se02Gz
U-Mrs.		58	F	Unknown	21Se02Gz
WHITE, Pat.		08	M	Child	21Se02Gz
REID, James		04	M	Child	21Se02Gz
JOHNSTON, Thomas		22	M	Baker	21Se02Gz
CLINTON, Biddy		22	F	Unknown	21Se02Gz
MOORE, Ann		19	F	Unknown	21Se02Gz
CROSS, Ann		24	F	Unknown	21Se02Gz
GRIFFIN, Jerry		25	M	Laborer	21Se02Gz
BRISTLE, Thos.		15	M	Laborer	21Se02Gz
Mary		13	F	Unknown	21Se02Gz
CONDON, Mauric		20	M	Laborer	21Se02Gz

NAMES OF PASSENGERS	AGE	SEX	OCCUPATIONS	DATE PORT SHIP
MCGREVEY, Cor.	17	M	Laborer	21Se02Gz
CONNISER, Rodger	20	M	Laborer	21Se02Gz
CLAREY, Patt.	20	M	Laborer	21Se02Gz
KELLY, Owen	18	M	Laborer	21Se02Gz
TEARNEY, Pat	48	M	Laborer	21Se02Gz
LERVIS, Thos.	27	M	Laborer	21Se02Gz
WESTMAN, James	23	M	Laborer	21Se02Gz
BUCKLEY, Eliza	50	F	Servant	21Se02Gz
Catherine	16	F	Servant	21Se02Gz
BASSETT, Geo.	20	M	Shepherd	21Se02Gz
PRICE, Jno.	25	M	Wool Comber	21Se02Gz
WARREN, William	25	M	Wool Comber	21Se02Gz
BROADHIRST, Thos.	27	M	Silk Weaver	21Se02Gz
GORDON, Harriet	13	F	Sspnr	21Se02Gz
Jane	11	F	Sspnr	21Se02Gz
William	.00	M	Infant	21Se02Gz
BROADHIRST, Harriet	25	F	Unknown	21Se02Gz
CURTIS, Francis	46	M	Wool Comber	21Se02Gz
U-Mrs	44	F	Wife	21Se02Gz
Sarah	10	F	Unknown	21Se02Gz
Jane	08	F	Child	21Se02Gz
Julia	06	F	Child	21Se02Gz
James	03	M	Child	21Se02Gz
HILL, John	22	M	Wool Comber	21Se02Gz
WARREN, Joseph	30	M	Wool Sorter	21Se02Gz
GILLARD, David	43	M	Farmer	21Se02Gz
Ann	40	F	Unknown	21Se02Gz
Almond	12	M	Unknown	21Se02Gz
Anne	11	F	Unknown	21Se02Gz
Jane	08	F	Child	21Se02Gz
TREHEHEY, Saml.	47	M	Farmer	21Se02Gz
ROBERTS, Jno.	28	M	Wool Comber	21Se02Gz
MCNILE, James	25	M	Clerk	21Se02Gz
WARD, Robt.	25	M	Printer	21Se02Gz
GARSIDES, Joseph	34	M	Butcher	21Se02Gz
James	09	M	Laborer	21Se02Gz
John	08	M	Laborer	21Se02Gz
DUNNE, Mary	30	F	Laborer	21Se02Gz
WALSH, William	23	M	Laborer	21Se02Gz
LYNCH, Ellen	03	F	Child	21Se02Gz
Mary	02	F	Child	21Se02Gz
VAUGHN, Thomas	21	M	Laborer	21Se02Gz
GILMORE, Michl.	21	M	Laborer	21Se02Gz
LACKIN, John	28	M	Laborer	21Se02Gz
Rose	32	F	Laborer	21Se02Gz
VAUGHN, Christopher	22	M	Nailer	21Se02Gz
Rose	18	F	Unknown	21Se02Gz
CULLEN, Elizh.	11	F	Unknown	21Se02Gz
James	10	M	Laborer	21Se02Gz
Cath.	07	F	Child	21Se02Gz
OKEEFE, Margt.	21	F	Unknown	21Se02Gz
DUVEROH, Henry	17	M	Tailor	21Se02Gz
MULIGAN, Michael	20	M	Farmer	21Se02Gz
TRACEY, Michael	18	M	Surveyor	21Se02Gz
MAHAR, Margt.	20	F	Unknown	21Se02Gz
MCFARLAND, Matilda	20	F	Unknown	21Se02Gz
GILLISPIE, John	19	M	Blacksmith	21Se02Gz
LAMB, James	19	M	Farmer	21Se02Gz
MURPHY, Jno.	40	M	Pork Cutter	21Se02Gz
GRAHAM, James	45	M	Pork Cutter	21Se02Gz
DONNELLY, Nat	21	M	Pork Cutter	21Se02Gz
CAUGHEY, Jno.	36	M	Ham Curer	21Se02Gz
REYNOLDS, Rob.	29	M	Pork Cutter	21Se02Gz
WATERS, Joseph	26	M	Hairdresser	21Se02Gz
Eliza	28	F	Unknown	21Se02Gz
Ann	50	F	Unknown	21Se02Gz
KEENAN, Jno.	22	M	Laborer	21Se02Gz
SMITH, Jno.	29	M	Laborer	21Se02Gz
HOLT, Richd.	26	M	Shoemaker	21Se02Gz
CARLIN, Bridgt.	31	F	Unknown	21Se02Gz
MULLIGAN, Jno.	30	M	Laborer	21Se02Gz
Kitty	26	F	Unknown	21Se02Gz
Mary	03	F	Child	21Se02Gz
Patrick	02	M	Child	21Se02Gz
Bridget	.00	F	Infant	21Se02Gz
BRADY, Cathn.	50	F	Unknown	21Se02Gz
CRAWFORD, Cate.	25	F	Pwlwvr	21Se02Gz
BURNS, Mary	50	F	Unknown	21Se02Gz
CULLEN, Danl.	40	M	Carpenter	21Se02Gz
Mary	38	F	Unknown	21Se02Gz
FLYNN, Jno.	00	M	Laborer	21Se02Gz
HARKIN, Patt.	00	M	Laborer	21Se02Gz
WALSH, Eliza	00	F	Laborer	21Se02Gz
LEE, Nicholas	00	M	Laborer	21Se02Gz

SARAH-SANDS 23 SEPTEMBER 1847

From Liverpool

NAMES OF PASSENGERS	AGE	SEX	OCCUPATIONS	DATE PORT SHIP
DEER, Mary	54	F	Servant	23Se02Kp
GRIER, John	36	M	Merchant	23Se02Kp
COOK, John	47	M	Teacher	23Se02Kp
LEE, Domenick	37	M	Farmer	23Se02Kp
CORCORAN, Jos.	27	M	Tailor	23Se02Kp
OKEEFE, Jerome	56	M	Teacher	23Se02Kp
RIELLY, John	22	M	Merchant	23Se02Kp
Henry	26	M	Merchant	23Se02Kp
MAGUIRE, John	46	M	Merchant	23Se02Kp

STAR-REPUBLIC 24 SEPTEMBER 1847

From Montevideo

NAMES OF PASSENGERS	AGE	SEX	OCCUPATIONS	DATE PORT SHIP
KENNY, Eliza	20	F	Servant	24Se91Hb

JOHN-R.SKIDDY 24 SEPTEMBER 1847

From Liverpool

NAMES OF PASSENGERS	AGE	SEX	OCCUPATIONS	DATE PORT SHIP
ALLEN, Eliza-J.	46	F	Lady	24Se02Ac
Ann-E.	25	F	Lady	24Se02Ac
Elizth.F.	18	F	Lady	24Se02Ac
Dorothea-E.	15	F	Lady	24Se02Ac
Henry-C.	07	M	Child	24Se02Ac
HORAN, Thos.	45	M	Farmer	24Se02Ac
CASTIGAN, Jno.	25	M	Farmer	24Se02Ac
Mary	22	F	Farmer	24Se02Ac
HORAN, Bridgt.	45	F	Farmer	24Se02Ac
MCGUIRE, U-Mrs.	00	F	Unknown	24Se02Ac
Ellen	10	F	Unknown	24Se02Ac
Jas.	09	M	Child	24Se02Ac
Thos.	03	M	Child	24Se02Ac
CASTIGAN, Bridgt.	.07	F	Infant	24Se02Ac
DELANEY, Kate	22	F	Farmer	24Se02Ac
KELLEY, John	56	M	Publisher	24Se02Ac
Cathn.	45	F	Unknown	24Se02Ac
Michl.	17	M	Unknown	24Se02Ac
Ann	14	F	Unknown	24Se02Ac
Cathn.	11	F	Unknown	24Se02Ac
Margt.	10	F	Unknown	24Se02Ac
John	07	M	Child	24Se02Ac
James	05	M	Child	24Se02Ac

NAMES OF PASSENGERS	AGE	SEX	OCCUPATIONS	DATE PORT SHIP
KELLEY, Eliza	02	F	Child	24Se02Ac
Teresa	.03	F	Infant	24Se02Ac
LAWLER, Elizth.	20	F	Spinster	24Se02Ac
FEEHELY, Ann	25	F	Spinster	24Se02Ac
KILROSE, Mary	20	F	Spinster	24Se02Ac
PATTERSON, Jno.	23	M	Laborer	24Se02Ac
KEAN, Ellen	20	F	Laborer	24Se02Ac
HARRISON, Michael	22	M	Shoemaker	24Se02Ac
Jno.	24	M	Tailor	24Se02Ac
Mary	30	F	Tailor	24Se02Ac
ROURKE, Eliza	20	F	Weaver	24Se02Ac
BAILEY, Honora	19	F	Spinster	24Se02Ac
CASSAN, Biddy	20	F	Spinster	24Se02Ac
MCQUIGAN, Rose	20	F	Spinster	24Se02Ac
MOHAN, Ann	20	F	Spinster	24Se02Ac
DORCEY, Ann	20	F	Spinster	24Se02Ac
CARUTHERS, Margh.	20	F	Currier	24Se02Ac
HUME, Wm.	27	M	Farmer	24Se02Ac
MONGHAN, Alexr.	20	M	Laborer	24Se02Ac
MCQUILLIAN, Jno.	34	M	Blacksmith	24Se02Ac
SAVAGE, Margh.	20	F	Spinster	24Se02Ac
KENNEDY, Cathn.	50	F	Spinster	24Se02Ac
Jno.	40	M	Laborer	24Se02Ac
Pat	29	M	Laborer	24Se02Ac
Cathn.	25	F	Laborer	24Se02Ac
HAYES, James	32	M	Joiner	24Se02Ac
Mary	30	F	Unknown	24Se02Ac
Mary	10	F	Laborer	24Se02Ac
Margh.	07	F	Child	24Se02Ac
Jno.	04	M	Child	24Se02Ac
Michl.	.11	M	Infant	24Se02Ac
HIGNEY, Wm.	25	M	Farmer	24Se02Ac
CONROY, Danl.	25	M	Farmer	24Se02Ac
Mary	11	F	Farmer	24Se02Ac
GALVIN, Pat	22	M	Shoemaker	24Se02Ac
HALWAYS, Ann	19	F	Spinster	24Se02Ac
HAYNS, Ann	21	F	Spinster	24Se02Ac
FITZPATRICK, Ann	22	F	Weaver	24Se02Ac
MCDERMOT, Pat	27	M	Laborer	24Se02Ac
CALLARY, Michl.	30	M	Farmer	24Se02Ac
Elizth.	50	F	Farmer	24Se02Ac
Pat	24	M	Farmer	24Se02Ac
Bridgt.	16	F	Farmer	24Se02Ac
Thos.	12	M	Farmer	24Se02Ac
Mary	10	F	Laborer	24Se02Ac
Bridgt.	09	F	Child	24Se02Ac
MCINTIRE, Mary	24	F	Spinster	24Se02Ac
CARROLL, Martin	14	M	Laborer	24Se02Ac
MOLOY, James	24	M	Laborer	24Se02Ac
Thos.	04	M	Child	24Se02Ac
FITZPATRICK, Philip	20	M	Tailor	24Se02Ac
REILY, Robt.	10	M	Unknown	24Se02Ac
FARLY, Mary	20	F	Spinster	24Se02Ac
SHEA, Cathn.	20	F	Spinster	24Se02Ac
SHARKY, Elizth.	19	F	Dressmaker	24Se02Ac
Mary	16	F	Dressmaker	24Se02Ac
PARKER, Mary	24	F	Spinster	24Se02Ac
JORDAN, Brdgt.	24	F	Spinster	24Se02Ac
EGAN, Keran	24	M	Spinster	24Se02Ac
CONNOR, Jane	24	F	Spinster	24Se02Ac
Henry	.07	M	Infant	24Se02Ac
PURCELL, Fanny	46	F	Spinster	24Se02Ac
TALBOT, Jno.	12	M	Unknown	24Se02Ac
HAGAN, James	36	M	Publisher	24Se02Ac
Elizth.	35	F	Unknown	24Se02Ac
Frs.	10	F	Publisher	24Se02Ac
Ann	09	F	Child	24Se02Ac
James	06	M	Child	24Se02Ac
Jane	.08	F	Infant	24Se02Ac
CONROY, Pat	29	M	Laborer	24Se02Ac
MORRIS, James	21	M	Shoemaker	24Se02Ac
BRANNON, Elizth.	26	F	Spinster	24Se02Ac
Martin	06	M	Child	24Se02Ac
CONLEY, Ann	26	F	Spinster	24Se02Ac
CLARK, Alice	22	F	Spinster	24Se02Ac

NAMES OF PASSENGERS	AGE	SEX	OCCUPATIONS	DATE PORT SHIP
CLARK, Bridgt.	10	F	Spinster	24Se02Ac
QUINN, Cathn.	22	F	Servant	24Se02Ac
LAUGHLIN, Mich.	21	M	Farmer	24Se02Ac
Cathn.	19	F	Farmer	24Se02Ac
FITZGERALD, Thos.	25	M	Farmer	24Se02Ac
GIBBON, Jane	50	F	Farmer	24Se02Ac
PLUNKETT, Mary	19	F	Spinster	24Se02Ac
NEAL, James	40	M	Laborer	24Se02Ac
Margt.	36	F	Unknown	24Se02Ac
Mary	11	F	Laborer	24Se02Ac
NOWLAN, Danl.	60	M	Joiner	24Se02Ac
Mary	21	F	Joiner	24Se02Ac
Bridgt.	15	F	Joiner	24Se02Ac
James	10	M	Joiner	24Se02Ac
Betsey	12	F	Joiner	24Se02Ac
ROGERS, Martin	60	M	Weaver	24Se02Ac
Thos.	27	M	Weaver	24Se02Ac
Bridgt.	30	F	Weaver	24Se02Ac
DELANEY, Mary	25	F	Servant	24Se02Ac
MAXWELL, Cathn.	23	F	Servant	24Se02Ac
CARROLL, Pat	19	M	Laborer	24Se02Ac
GOUGHLIN, Bridgt.	30	F	Servant	24Se02Ac
SHERIDAN, Margt.	25	F	Servant	24Se02Ac
FITZPATRICK, Mary	40	F	Servant	24Se02Ac
Peter	14	M	Servant	24Se02Ac
Margt.	11	F	Servant	24Se02Ac
Wm.	09	M	Child	24Se02Ac
MACENCROW, Cathn.	21	F	Spinster	24Se02Ac
VENABLES, Michl.	20	M	Farmer	24Se02Ac
ROGERS, Honora	20	F	Spinster	24Se02Ac
DOYLE, Lewis	21	M	Laborer	24Se02Ac
Jane	10	F	Laborer	24Se02Ac
James	08	M	Child	24Se02Ac
SMITH, Mary	18	F	Servant	24Se02Ac
Cathn.	16	F	Servant	24Se02Ac
GAFFNEY, Sarah	20	F	Servant	24Se02Ac
OLEARY, Pat	22	M	Laborer	24Se02Ac
Wm.	20	M	Laborer	24Se02Ac
DIXON, Bridgt.	24	F	Servant	24Se02Ac
MCCANN, Mary	.09	F	Infant	24Se02Ac
STEEL, Ann	20	F	Weaver	24Se02Ac
MCCARTY, Thos.	11	M	Weaver	24Se02Ac
BOYLE, Bridgt.	26	F	Weaver	24Se02Ac
CARUTHERS, Mooney	21	F	Weaver	24Se02Ac
DOUGLASS, Martha	16	F	Weaver	24Se02Ac
DELMAR, Mooney	20	M	Servant	24Se02Ac
OBRIEN, Bridgt.	24	F	Child	24Se02Ac
QUADE, Mary	20	F	Child	24Se02Ac
CORCORAN, Tim	22	M	Laborer	24Se02Ac
TROYER, Danl.	20	M	Laborer	24Se02Ac
ARNOLD, Mary	27	F	Laborer	24Se02Ac
PHILLIPS, Jane	30	F	Laborer	24Se02Ac
DIVINE, Jno.	24	M	Laborer	24Se02Ac
MCGAUGHRAN, Ann	20	F	Laborer	24Se02Ac
MCLOMAN, Wm.	25	M	Laborer	24Se02Ac
BRANNAN, Honora	23	F	Laborer	24Se02Ac
MCCANN, Cathn.	39	F	Laborer	24Se02Ac
James	12	M	Laborer	24Se02Ac
Pat	09	M	Child	24Se02Ac
MCKINLEY, Saml.	18	M	Laborer	24Se02Ac
DOUGLASS, Charlotte	18	F	Laborer	24Se02Ac
Jane	15	F	Laborer	24Se02Ac
MCCAHARN, Mary	40	F	Laborer	24Se02Ac
COOKE, Hannah	40	F	Laborer	24Se02Ac
Michl.	16	M	Laborer	24Se02Ac
Thos.	14	M	Laborer	24Se02Ac
Winne	12	F	Laborer	24Se02Ac
Bridgt.	11	F	Laborer	24Se02Ac
Mary	09	F	Child	24Se02Ac
BANKS, Anthony	32	M	Laborer	24Se02Ac
Pat	17	M	Laborer	24Se02Ac
James	15	M	Laborer	24Se02Ac
Ann	14	F	Laborer	24Se02Ac
DEAN, Jno.	19	M	Laborer	24Se02Ac
SWAN, John	30	M	Laborer	24Se02Ac

NAMES OF PASSENGERS	AGE	SEX	OCCUPATIONS	DATE PORT SHIP
TIERNEY, Pat	32	M	Laborer	24Se02Ac
Kerry	16	M	Laborer	24Se02Ac
GANNON, Mary	17	F	Laborer	24Se02Ac
Pat	14	M	Laborer	24Se02Ac
IWELREY, Margt.	22	F	Laborer	24Se02Ac
MCCUNE, Elizth.	36	F	Laborer	24Se02Ac
Jno.	14	M	Laborer	24Se02Ac
Danl.	12	M	Laborer	24Se02Ac
Hugh	09	M	Child	24Se02Ac
MCDERMOT, Bernd.	22	M	Laborer	24Se02Ac
DOHERTY, Wm.	20	M	Laborer	24Se02Ac
ICEMAN, Thos.	26	M	Laborer	24Se02Ac
STARKEL, Jno.	32	M	Laborer	24Se02Ac
Elizabeth	33	F	Unknown	24Se02Ac
Jno.	13	M	Laborer	24Se02Ac
Alice	10	F	Laborer	24Se02Ac
RIGBY, Maria	16	F	Laborer	24Se02Ac
GLYNN, James	31	M	Laborer	24Se02Ac
PIKE, Martin	24	M	Laborer	24Se02Ac
FORD, Saml.	28	M	Laborer	24Se02Ac
BRENNAN, Maria	18	F	Laborer	24Se02Ac
BROWN, Sarah	40	F	Laborer	24Se02Ac
MCELROY, Rose	35	F	Laborer	24Se02Ac
Abala	12	F	Laborer	24Se02Ac
Alexr.	09	M	Child	24Se02Ac
PATTERSON, Thos.	27	M	Laborer	24Se02Ac
RODY, Pat	30	M	Laborer	24Se02Ac

JOSEPH-HAM 28 SEPTEMBER 1847

From Windsor

NAMES OF PASSENGERS	AGE	SEX	OCCUPATIONS	DATE PORT SHIP
ROXBY, Richard	30	M	Farmer	28Se92Hd
Ann	67	F	Farmer	28Se92Hd
Maria	25	F	Farmer	28Se92Hd
Jane	27	F	Farmer	28Se92Hd

AMERICA 28 SEPTEMBER 1847

From Liverpool

NAMES OF PASSENGERS	AGE	SEX	OCCUPATIONS	DATE PORT SHIP
MCGUIRE, Jas.	00	M	Merchant	28Se02Hf
Magth.	00	M	Merchant	28Se02Hf
Kate	00	M	Merchant	28Se02Hf
Peter	07	M	Child	28Se02Hf
SHORTALE, Fanny	30	F	Unknown	28Se02Hf
REID, Ann	20	F	Unknown	28Se02Hf
SHORTALE, Johanna	20	F	Unknown	28Se02Hf
FOWLER, Myles	22	M	Unknown	28Se02Hf
BRENNAN, Pat	40	M	Unknown	28Se02Hf
Mary	35	F	Unknown	28Se02Hf
Margh.	75	F	Unknown	28Se02Hf
BYNE, Lawrence	20	M	Unknown	28Se02Hf
BRENNAN, Anne	13	F	None	28Se02Hf
Margt.	07	F	Child	28Se02Hf
Cathe.	03	F	Child	28Se02Hf
Mary	.00	F	Infant	28Se02Hf
CLARKE, Anne	11	F	Unknown	28Se02Hf
LEWIS, Thos.	30	M	Baker	28Se02Hf
Jane	25	F	Unknown	28Se02Hf
Daniel	.00	M	Infant	28Se02Hf
KERNAN, Maria	16	F	Unknown	28Se02Hf
LYNCH, Thos.	30	M	Coach Maker	28Se02Hf
TAILBET, Henry	23	M	Butcher	28Se02Hf
DOWLEN, Cathe.	25	F	Unknown	28Se02Hf
MULLANY, Cathe.	30	F	Unknown	28Se02Hf
Cathe.	11	F	Unknown	28Se02Hf
Joseph	04	M	Child	28Se02Hf
John	.00	M	Infant	28Se02Hf
DUNAGAN, Ann	14	F	Unknown	28Se02Hf
SYLVESTER, Mark	30	M	Unknown	28Se02Hf
Luke	22	M	Unknown	28Se02Hf
MURPHY, Eliza	19	F	Unknown	28Se02Hf
HART, Ann	25	F	Unknown	28Se02Hf
KYAN, Danl.	29	M	Unknown	28Se02Hf
HODSON, Joseph	24	M	Rope Maker	28Se02Hf
BLAKE, Cath.	25	F	Unknown	28Se02Hf
SKELLY, Jno.	19	M	Unknown	28Se02Hf
DALEY, Pat	46	M	Unknown	28Se02Hf
Mary	46	F	Unknown	28Se02Hf
Rose	24	F	Unknown	28Se02Hf
Pat.	22	M	Unknown	28Se02Hf
Margt.	20	F	Unknown	28Se02Hf
Mary	18	F	Unknown	28Se02Hf
Hester	15	F	Unknown	28Se02Hf
Peter	12	M	Unknown	28Se02Hf
Biddy	10	F	Unknown	28Se02Hf
Martha	08	F	Child	28Se02Hf
CARR, Charlotte	37	F	Unknown	28Se02Hf
Eliza	06	F	Child	28Se02Hf
LOCKMAN, Mary-A.	21	F	Unknown	28Se02Hf
GAFFNEY, Mary	48	F	Unknown	28Se02Hf
MAYNE, Mary	15	F	Unknown	28Se02Hf
MCNULTY, Phillip	28	M	Unknown	28Se02Hf
PENDLEBURRY, John	40	M	Unknown	28Se02Hf
DOWLIN, Wm.	23	M	Unknown	28Se02Hf
BYRNES, John	28	M	Unknown	28Se02Hf
SMYTHE, Pat	26	M	Unknown	28Se02Hf
SKEWELL, Geo.	35	M	Unknown	28Se02Hf
Daniel	11	M	Unknown	28Se02Hf
Mary-A.	05	F	Child	28Se02Hf
Sarah	02	F	Child	28Se02Hf
MCDONAUGH, P.	18	M	Unknown	28Se02Hf
REYNOLDS, George	25	M	Unknown	28Se02Hf
Margaret	07	F	Child	28Se02Hf
Mary	40	F	Unknown	28Se02Hf
Kate	12	F	Unknown	28Se02Hf
Dennis	04	M	Child	28Se02Hf
Wm.	01	M	Child	28Se02Hf
MORAN, Pat	20	M	Unknown	28Se02Hf
LOGAN, Jno.	40	M	Unknown	28Se02Hf
DONNELLY, Jno.	40	M	Unknown	28Se02Hf
POLLOCK, Eliza	38	F	Unknown	28Se02Hf
Mary	12	F	Unknown	28Se02Hf
Robt.	08	M	Child	28Se02Hf
Wm.	04	M	Child	28Se02Hf
Eliza	04	F	Child	28Se02Hf
FALLEN, Jno.	32	M	Farmer	28Se02Hf
Ann	34	F	Unknown	28Se02Hf
Mary	14	F	Unknown	28Se02Hf
James	12	M	Unknown	28Se02Hf
LOWREY, Jno.	40	M	Unknown	28Se02Hf
Rose	30	F	Unknown	28Se02Hf
Thos.	06	M	Child	28Se02Hf
Jno.	04	M	Child	28Se02Hf
Ester	.00	F	Infant	28Se02Hf
STANTON, Miles	40	M	Laborer	28Se02Hf
Ann	35	F	Unknown	28Se02Hf
BRUCE, Dennis	37	M	Unknown	28Se02Hf
BRADY, Biddy	20	F	Unknown	28Se02Hf
DONOHUE, Ann	12	F	Unknown	28Se02Hf
Jno.	10	M	Unknown	28Se02Hf
Biddy	08	F	Child	28Se02Hf
MULLIGAN, Danl.	14	M	Farmer	28Se02Hf
BOBURN, Mary	26	F	Unknown	28Se02Hf
Eliza	30	F	Unknown	28Se02Hf
COIL, Ellen	20	F	Unknown	28Se02Hf
DONNELLY, Michl.	35	M	Unknown	28Se02Hf

NAMES OF PASSENGERS	AGE	SEX	OCCUPATIONS	DATE PORT SHIP
DONNELLY, Biddy	24	F	Unknown	28Se02Hf
James	.00	M	Infant	28Se02Hf
Mary	70	F	Unknown	28Se02Hf
FITZGERALD, Martin	25	M	Mason	28Se02Hf
FITZPATRICK, Mag.	11	F	Unknown	28Se02Hf
CLARK, Jas.	24	M	Blacksmith	28Se02Hf
Eliza	22	F	Unknown	28Se02Hf
Lavinia	.00	F	Infant	28Se02Hf
JARVIS, Mary-Ann	24	F	Unknown	28Se02Hf
COUGHLIN, Paddy	60	M	Farmer	28Se02Hf
Caddy	65	F	Unknown	28Se02Hf
Cath.	22	F	Unknown	28Se02Hf
DEWLY, Jno.	26	M	Shoemaker	28Se02Hf
Briget	26	F	Unknown	28Se02Hf
MULROY, Cath.	58	F	Unknown	28Se02Hf
Mary	03	F	Child	28Se02Hf
Jas.	.00	M	Infant	28Se02Hf
CASSIDY, Michl.	30	M	Laborer	28Se02Hf
SCIVINGTON, Pat	20	M	Tailor	28Se02Hf
BROWN, Henry	20	M	Laborer	28Se02Hf
RILEY, Pat	18	M	Laborer	28Se02Hf
Jno.	20	M	Laborer	28Se02Hf
CLARK, Thos.	21	M	Laborer	28Se02Hf
LALY, Martin	22	M	Laborer	28Se02Hf
EARLY, Pat	40	M	Laborer	28Se02Hf
CONOVAN, Pat	21	M	Unknown	28Se02Hf
BRANSON, Henry	33	M	Carpenter	28Se02Hf
Ann	27	F	Unknown	28Se02Hf
Wm.	11	M	Unknown	28Se02Hf
Ann	.00	F	Infant	28Se02Hf
ELLSLOW, Letetia	23	M	Unknown	28Se02Hf
William	02	M	Child	28Se02Hf
Matilda	04	F	Child	28Se02Hf
Henry	29	M	Laborer	28Se02Hf
QUINN, John	17	M	Shoemaker	28Se02Hf
TUCKER, Martin	16	M	Shoemaker	28Se02Hf
Joseph	12	M	Shoemaker	28Se02Hf
FARLEY, Pat	33	M	Shoemaker	28Se02Hf
Biddy	30	F	Shoemaker	28Se02Hf
LARKIN, Margret	22	F	Shoemaker	28Se02Hf
DONLEN, Cathe.	16	F	Shoemaker	28Se02Hf
PATERSON, Margt.	19	F	Shoemaker	28Se02Hf
CANOVAN, Susan	27	F	Shoemaker	28Se02Hf
MCGRATH, John	50	M	Farmer	28Se02Hf
Mary	50	F	Unknown	28Se02Hf
Mary	21	F	Unknown	28Se02Hf
Biddy	17	F	Unknown	28Se02Hf
Cath.	12	F	Unknown	28Se02Hf
Jno.	10	M	Unknown	28Se02Hf
Frank	08	M	Child	28Se02Hf
Maly	06	M	Child	28Se02Hf
SHERIDAN, Pat	26	M	Bricklayer	28Se02Hf
RILEY, Peter	36	M	Bricklayer	28Se02Hf
CLUNIN, Biddy	20	F	Bricklayer	28Se02Hf
KINGHAY, Mary	28	F	Bricklayer	28Se02Hf
LYMS, Peter	28	M	Laborer	28Se02Hf
WEBB, Thos.	26	M	Blacksmith	28Se02Hf
Mag.	28	F	Unknown	28Se02Hf
TAIS, Mary	18	F	Unknown	28Se02Hf
SCANLIN, Wm.	16	M	Unknown	28Se02Hf
Edward	08	M	Child	28Se02Hf
BOYLAN, Michl.	21	M	Unknown	28Se02Hf
COLEMAN, Thos.	28	M	Tailor	28Se02Hf
Cath.	20	F	Unknown	28Se02Hf
Geo.	20	M	Tailor	28Se02Hf
JOHNSON, Biddy	30	M	Unknown	28Se02Hf
Mary	09	F	Child	28Se02Hf
Jno.	06	M	Child	28Se02Hf
GILLMURY, Cath.	18	F	Unknown	28Se02Hf
JOHNSON, Thos.	27	M	Machinist	28Se02Hf
KEENAN, Jno.	29	M	Baker	28Se02Hf
SHEREDAN, Thos.	28	M	Baker	28Se02Hf
GAUGHLIN, Jno.	35	M	Laborer	28Se02Hf
Ann	30	F	Unknown	28Se02Hf
BRADY, Magt.	20	F	Unknown	28Se02Hf
DUNAVAN, Cath.	18	F	Unknown	28Se02Hf
REILY, Anne	19	F	Unknown	28Se02Hf
CANISTY, James	40	M	Unknown	28Se02Hf
Margt.	35	F	Unknown	28Se02Hf
Bryan	20	M	Unknown	28Se02Hf
Biddy	18	F	Unknown	28Se02Hf
Peter	15	M	Unknown	28Se02Hf
HANEY, Cath.	18	F	Unknown	28Se02Hf
Mary	10	F	Unknown	28Se02Hf
James	15	M	Unknown	28Se02Hf
Lawrence	13	M	Unknown	28Se02Hf
BRADY, Michael	30	M	Unknown	28Se02Hf
Mary	25	F	Unknown	28Se02Hf
Ann	18	F	Unknown	28Se02Hf
John	16	F	Unknown	28Se02Hf
Ellen	04	F	Child	28Se02Hf
Biddy	.00	F	Infant	28Se02Hf
CRAYTON, Thos.	36	M	Unknown	28Se02Hf
CORE, Paddy	24	M	Unknown	28Se02Hf
MCCARTY, Hannah	22	F	Unknown	28Se02Hf
CONNOR, Judy	15	F	Unknown	28Se02Hf
LEONARD, Margt.	25	F	Unknown	28Se02Hf
Alli	02	F	Child	28Se02Hf
TULLY, Biddy	20	F	Unknown	28Se02Hf
FITZSIMMONS, Biddy	19	F	Unknown	28Se02Hf
TULLY, Ann	20	F	Unknown	28Se02Hf
STEWARD, John	20	M	Unknown	28Se02Hf

MEMPHIS 29 SEPTEMBER 1847

From Liverpool

NAMES OF PASSENGERS	AGE	SEX	OCCUPATIONS	DATE PORT SHIP
BRENNAN, Denis	50	M	Laborer	29Se02Hg
Margt.	50	F	Unknown	29Se02Hg
John	25	M	Unknown	29Se02Hg
Philip	23	M	Unknown	29Se02Hg
Edwd.	13	M	Unknown	29Se02Hg
Catherine	11	F	Unknown	29Se02Hg
Ellen	09	F	Child	29Se02Hg
Thomas	07	M	Child	29Se02Hg
SHINE, Denis	25	M	Laborer	29Se02Hg
Catherine	24	F	Unknown	29Se02Hg
OHARA, Hugh	24	M	Laborer	29Se02Hg
HENMER, Bidy	20	F	Unknown	29Se02Hg
TIGHE, Honac	20	U	Unknown	29Se02Hg
MCDONEY, Bridgt.	21	F	Unknown	29Se02Hg
MULDOWNEY, Ann	40	F	Unknown	29Se02Hg
MCCULLON, Mary	13	F	Unknown	29Se02Hg
BROGAN, Thos.	40	M	Unknown	29Se02Hg
Catherin	40	F	Unknown	29Se02Hg
John	13	M	Unknown	29Se02Hg
Richd.	12	M	Unknown	29Se02Hg
Patk.	11	M	Unknown	29Se02Hg
Julia	10	F	Unknown	29Se02Hg
Ann	08	F	Child	29Se02Hg
CULLEN, Julia	20	F	Unknown	29Se02Hg
GOLAHER, And.	22	M	Laborer	29Se02Hg
MUNDY, John	24	M	Laborer	29Se02Hg
James	21	M	Laborer	29Se02Hg
HOGAN, Jane	26	F	Unknown	29Se02Hg
William	02	M	Child	29Se02Hg
DUGAN, Mary	35	F	Unknown	29Se02Hg
John	12	M	Unknown	29Se02Hg
HICKS, John	32	M	Laborer	29Se02Hg
Barbara	29	F	Unknown	29Se02Hg
COGLERAN, Edwd.	20	M	Unknown	29Se02Hg
OKEEFFE, James	22	M	Laborer	29Se02Hg
MCAULIFFE, Malackey	24	M	Laborer	29Se02Hg
QUAIL, Margt.	25	M	Unknown	29Se02Hg

NAMES OF PASSENGERS	AGE	SEX	OCCUPATIONS	DATE PORT SHIP
OWENS, John	40	M	Laborer	29Se02Hg
Died-At-Sea				
Margaret	35	F	Unknown	29Se02Hg
Frances	13	F	Unknown	29Se02Hg
Ann	11	F	Unknown	29Se02Hg
Joseph	09	M	Child	29Se02Hg
Edwd.	07	M	Child	29Se02Hg
John	04	M	Child	29Se02Hg
DUNNE, Wm.	30	M	Laborer	29Se02Hg
Sarah	36	F	Unknown	29Se02Hg
CARDIFFE, John	40	M	Laborer	29Se02Hg
Eliza	25	F	Unknown	29Se02Hg
LEONARD, Mich.	50	M	Laborer	29Se02Hg
Bidy	20	F	Unknown	29Se02Hg
Nelly	13	F	Unknown	29Se02Hg
GRAVEY, Wm.	20	M	Laborer	29Se02Hg
LEONARD, Nancy	07	F	Child	29Se02Hg
WADE, John	25	M	Laborer	29Se02Hg
U (W)	24	F	Wife	29Se02Hg
Wm.	03	M	Child	29Se02Hg
Eliza	.00	F	Infant	29Se02Hg
DUNALEY, Wm.	25	M	Laborer	29Se02Hg
HOUSTON, Margt.	22	F	Unknown	29Se02Hg
MCKINNE, Ann	19	F	Unknown	29Se02Hg
SHEIL, John	22	M	Laborer	29Se02Hg
Matilda	25	F	Unknown	29Se02Hg
GALLAGHER, Jas.	25	M	Laborer	29Se02Hg
MCMANUS, Phil.	30	M	Shoemaker	29Se02Hg
FRIDETAL, Joseph	31	M	Shoemaker	29Se02Hg
SHARAGH, Barnd.	20	M	Unknown	29Se02Hg
MCMANUS, Cath.	19	F	Unknown	29Se02Hg
BRADY, Thos.	29	M	Laborer	29Se02Hg
MCGOWAN, Edward	30	M	Laborer	29Se02Hg
DUNNE, Ann	34	F	Unknown	29Se02Hg
Mary	11	F	Unknown	29Se02Hg
Susan	08	F	Child	29Se02Hg
Ann	02	F	Child	29Se02Hg
Catherine	.00	F	Infant	29Se02Hg
MULHERON, Thos.	27	M	Laborer	29Se02Hg
Mary	20	F	Unknown	29Se02Hg
Bidy	17	F	Unknown	29Se02Hg
Pat	.00	M	Infant	29Se02Hg
MORAN, Owan	36	M	Laborer	29Se02Hg
Catherine	35	F	Unknown	29Se02Hg
Catherine	10	F	Unknown	29Se02Hg
William	07	M	Child	29Se02Hg
John	04	M	Child	29Se02Hg
MURTAGH, Pat	40	M	Laborer	29Se02Hg
Margt.	40	F	Unknown	29Se02Hg
Barney	17	M	Unknown	29Se02Hg
Mary	12	F	Unknown	29Se02Hg
Pat	05	M	Child	29Se02Hg
CONNELL, Jno.	34	M	Unknown	29Se02Hg
Nancy	30	F	Unknown	29Se02Hg
MCCARTY, Nancy	18	F	Unknown	29Se02Hg
Died-At-Sea				
Gaffy	28	M	Unknown	29Se02Hg
LAURENCE, Cornelius	25	M	Laborer	29Se02Hg
SULLIVAN, Thos.	35	M	Laborer	29Se02Hg
LAURENCE, Dinll.	30	M	Enmkr	29Se02Hg
GRIFFIN, Pat	23	M	Unknown	29Se02Hg
MCDADE, Joseph	25	M	Unknown	29Se02Hg
Mary-Jane	13	F	Unknown	29Se02Hg
Mary-Jane	07	F	Child	29Se02Hg
ROONEY, Eliz.	24	F	Unknown	29Se02Hg
SULLIVAN, Danl.	50	M	Unknown	29Se02Hg
MURPHY, Mary	20	F	Unknown	29Se02Hg
GARAGHTY, Thos.	60	M	Laborer	29Se02Hg
Mary	50	F	Unknown	29Se02Hg
Isaac	19	M	Unknown	29Se02Hg
Thomas	10	M	Unknown	29Se02Hg
MYERS, Ann	20	F	Unknown	29Se02Hg
COUGHLIN, Elizbth.	78	F	Unknown	29Se02Hg
Ellen	18	F	Unknown	29Se02Hg
Honora	14	F	Unknown	29Se02Hg
COUGHLIN, Michl.	12	M	Unknown	29Se02Hg

ADAM-CARR 29 SEPTEMBER 1847

From Glasgow

NAMES OF PASSENGERS	AGE	SEX	OCCUPATIONS	DATE PORT SHIP
BRADLEY, Peter	56	M	Laborer	29Se04Aw
HIRLE, Anthony	30	M	Shoemaker	29Se04Aw
Margaret	24	F	Spinster	29Se04Aw
DOHERTY, Patrick	40	M	Laborer	29Se04Aw
Elizabeth	16	F	Spinster	29Se04Aw
William	13	M	None	29Se04Aw

FIDELIA 06 OCTOBER 1847

From Liverpool

NAMES OF PASSENGERS	AGE	SEX	OCCUPATIONS	DATE PORT SHIP
TAIT, Ellen	21	F	None	06Oc02Ax
WILSON, Richard	33	M	None	06Oc02Ax
Mary-Ann	23	F	None	06Oc02Ax
RYAN, George	21	M	None	06Oc02Ax
CAMPBELL, Bridget	22	F	Servant	06Oc02Ax
CUMMINGS, Sarah	25	F	Servant	06Oc02Ax
Sarah-Senr.	62	F	None	06Oc02Ax
MAGUIRE, Winifred	35	F	None	06Oc02Ax
Michael	12	M	None	06Oc02Ax
James	10	M	None	06Oc02Ax
William	07	M	Child	06Oc02Ax
Patrick	04	M	Child	06Oc02Ax
CLARKE, James	22	M	Grocer	06Oc02Ax
KEANY, Patrick	40	M	Laborer	06Oc02Ax
Catherine	38	F	Wife	06Oc02Ax
Mary	18	F	None	06Oc02Ax
Patrick-Junior	13	M	None	06Oc02Ax
John	09	M	Child	06Oc02Ax
Peter	.09	M	Infant	06Oc02Ax
Margaret	04	F	Child	06Oc02Ax
CANNON, Anne	26	F	None	06Oc02Ax
MCCONNELL, Jane	28	F	None	06Oc02Ax
Mary-Jane	04	F	Child	06Oc02Ax
Robert	02	M	Child	06Oc02Ax
GILL, John	23	M	Farmer	06Oc02Ax
COLLINS, Catherine	22	F	None	06Oc02Ax
CURRAN, Patrick	25	M	Farmer	06Oc02Ax
Catherine	28	F	Wife	06Oc02Ax
Thomas	04	M	Child	06Oc02Ax
Michael	03	M	Child	06Oc02Ax
James	.06	M	Infant	06Oc02Ax
TOBIN, Thomas	18	M	Laborer	06Oc02Ax
CORBETT, Mary	45	F	Servant	06Oc02Ax
NAGLE, Richard	23	M	Student	06Oc02Ax
CLANCHY, John	19	M	Accountant	06Oc02Ax
OCONNELL, Delia	17	F	None	06Oc02Ax
OKELLY, Sarah	17	F	None	06Oc02Ax
OSHAUGHNESSY, Catherin	15	F	None	06Oc02Ax
MACKERELL, James	50	M	Laborer	06Oc02Ax
DICKSON, Margaret	16	F	None	06Oc02Ax
LOUGHLIN, Patrick	29	M	Groom	06Oc02Ax
Alicia	20	F	None	06Oc02Ax
DRENNAN, Eliza	36	F	None	06Oc02Ax
PAGE, John	20	M	None	06Oc02Ax
GORMAN, James	15	M	None	06Oc02Ax
MITCHELL, Patrick	20	M	Laborer	06Oc02Ax

NAMES OF PASSENGERS	AGE	SEX	OCCUPATIONS	DATE PORT SHIP
SWEENEY, Peter	25	M	Tailor	060c02Ax
Maria	25	F	Wife	060c02Ax
Michael	02	M	Child	060c02Ax
Patrick	.10	M	Infant	060c02Ax
FARLEY, John	22	M	Surveyor	060c02Ax
LYNCH, Patrick	20	M	Laborer	060c02Ax
DOUGHAN, William	40	M	Laborer	060c02Ax
GLEESON, Oliver	27	M	Laborer	060c02Ax
William	21	M	Shopkeeper	060c02Ax
RILEY, James	25	M	Weaver	060c02Ax
Alicia	27	F	Dressmaker	060c02Ax
MAHAFFY, John	17	M	Laborer	060c02Ax
FOY, James	33	M	Laborer	060c02Ax
WOODS, John	26	M	Victualler	060c02Ax
Mary-Ann	26	F	Unknown	060c02Ax
Mary	06	F	Child	060c02Ax
Eliza	02	F	Child	060c02Ax
Thomas	.04	M	Infant	060c02Ax
GROOGIN, John	35	M	Laborer	060c02Ax
HAPPUR, Harvey	61	M	Farmer	060c02Ax
FAGAN, John	36	M	Stone Mason	060c02Ax
CULLEN, James	45	M	Stone Mason	060c02Ax
DILLON, Mathew	19	M	Laborer	060c02Ax
John	20	M	Laborer	060c02Ax
MADDEN, Anne	22	F	House Maid	060c02Ax
KELLY, Anne	13	F	None	060c02Ax
GERAGHTY, Bridget	20	F	Servant	060c02Ax
HOARE, Martin	15	M	Laborer	060c02Ax
FINN, Bridget	20	F	Servant	060c02Ax
MCDERMOTT, Bridget	20	F	None	060c02Ax
BARRY, Thomas	64	M	Servant	060c02Ax
Margaret	24	F	None	060c02Ax
John	13	M	None	060c02Ax
DALY, Honora	24	F	None	060c02Ax
MULLIGAN, Edward	21	M	None	060c02Ax
WILSON, William	20	M	Farmer	060c02Ax
BYRNE, Connor	18	M	Laborer	060c02Ax
DUNNION, Matthew	18	M	Chandler	060c02Ax
MILLER, John	21	M	Sawer	060c02Ax
MCEVELLY, Patrick	24	M	Accountant	060c02Ax
Louisa	20	F	None	060c02Ax
MCGENNISS, John-James	34	M	Wmcht	060c02Ax
LOCKERY, Oliver-James	25	M	Tailor	060c02Ax
FIFE, James	24	M	Farmer	060c02Ax
CAHILL, Patrick	19	M	Laborer	060c02Ax
KENNY, Edward	15	M	Laborer	060c02Ax
RYAN, John	17	M	None	060c02Ax
MURRAY, John	23	M	None	060c02Ax
SHARKEY, John	25	M	Farmer	060c02Ax
Margaret	20	F	None	060c02Ax
KING, Henry	18	M	Accountant	060c02Ax
KELLY, Patrick	18	M	Accountant	060c02Ax
REYNOLDS, John	22	M	Laborer	060c02Ax
MCKEON, Patrick	22	M	Laborer	060c02Ax
STEELE, Richard-Willia	30	M	Reporter	060c02Ax
KENNELLY, William	27	M	Laborer	060c02Ax
REYNOLDS, Anne	40	F	None	060c02Ax
Mary-Anne	11	F	None	060c02Ax
MCGUINNESS, Mary	23	F	None	060c02Ax
DEVINE, Margaret	20	F	None	060c02Ax
DUFFY, Mary	20	F	Servant	060c02Ax
HODGENS, Margaret	20	F	Servant	060c02Ax
CORMACK, Anne	17	F	None	060c02Ax
MCCORMACK, Maragret	40	F	Servant	060c02Ax
James	17	M	None	060c02Ax
Mary	12	F	None	060c02Ax
Thomas	08	M	Child	060c02Ax
MCDERMOTT, Bridget	20	F	Servant	060c02Ax
BOLAND, Cormack	60	M	Gdnr	060c02Ax
Sarah	60	F	Wife	060c02Ax
Cormack-Junior	18	M	None	060c02Ax
James	07	M	Child	060c02Ax
CARRIGHAN, John	40	M	None	060c02Ax
Timothy	14	M	None	060c02Ax
RYAN, Timothy	40	M	None	060c02Ax
KENRICK, Edward	28	M	Mariner	060c02Ax
CONNOR, Edward	34	M	Laborer	060c02Ax
Johanna	34	F	Wife	060c02Ax
James	01	M	Child	060c02Ax
James	20	M	None	060c02Ax
NELIGAN, Johanna	18	F	None	060c02Ax
SHEA, Catherine	19	F	None	060c02Ax
CAVENAGH, Johanna	20	F	None	060c02Ax
BYRNES, Ellea	25	F	Stgkpr	060c02Ax
Mary	07	F	Child	060c02Ax
MULLINS, Mary	17	F	None	060c02Ax
COWAN, Catherine	18	F	None	060c02Ax
CRAWFORD, Margaret	20	F	Dressmaker	060c02Ax
LINTON, Elizabeth	30	F	Servant	060c02Ax
MORAN, Thomas	26	M	Rexcv	060c02Ax
SHANLY, James	20	R	Rexcv	060c02Ax
MCKENNA, Mary	23	F	None	060c02Ax
PURCELL, Mary	22	F	None	060c02Ax
TIGHE, Ellen	20	F	None	060c02Ax
DIAMOND, Margaret	25	F	None	060c02Ax
Margaret-Jr.	01	F	Child	060c02Ax
Susan	56	F	None	060c02Ax
LYDDY, Anne	40	F	None	060c02Ax
MCCABE, Henry	22	M	None	060c02Ax
LENNON, George-Homan	23	M	None	060c02Ax
Alicia-Maria	23	F	None	060c02Ax
MCCAN, Anne	23	F	None	060c02Ax
Thomas	.03	M	Infant	060c02Ax
GALLAHER, Michael	40	M	Agrt-Mlr	060c02Ax
GIBBONS, Patrick	38	M	Cver	060c02Ax
KEARNEY, James	23	M	Clergyman	060c02Ax
JAAFE, Peter	23	M	Clergyman	060c02Ax
WALSH, John	24	M	Clergyman	060c02Ax
DELANY, Catherine	18	F	Dressmaker	060c02Ax
MANGAN, Bridget	17	F	Servant	060c02Ax
ALEXANDER, James	30	M	Shopkeeper	060c02Ax
Anne	27	F	Wife	060c02Ax
John	.08	M	Infant	060c02Ax
MCDERMOTT, Mary	24	F	None	060c02Ax
SMITH, Winefred	28	F	None	060c02Ax
FITZPATRICK, Anne	26	F	None	060c02Ax
MCLOUGHLIN, Margaret	19	F	Servant	060c02Ax
FARRELL, Honor	19	F	Servant	060c02Ax
MCGUIRE, Owen	20	M	Laborer	060c02Ax
Thomas	55	M	Laborer	060c02Ax
ROBINSON, James-Boyd	26	M	Tchrcl	060c02Ax
MARTIN, Catherine	20	F	None	060c02Ax
Hugh	02	M	Child	060c02Ax
BRENNAN, Catherine	17	F	Servant	060c02Ax
Anstice	16	F	Servant	060c02Ax
HART, Martin	21	M	Baker	060c02Ax
CAULFIELD, Mary	36	F	None	060c02Ax
Mary	.11	F	Infant	060c02Ax
MCGLYNN, Anne	21	F	Servant	060c02Ax
DOLAN, Mary	00	F	None	060c02Ax
HANLY, Michael	20	M	Laborer	060c02Ax
LALLY, Mary	30	F	None	060c02Ax
John	04	M	Child	060c02Ax
MCDERMOTT, Eliza	21	F	Lad	060c02Ax
BRADY, Susan	20	F	None	060c02Ax
TONER, Bridget	25	F	None	060c02Ax
FARRELL, Honor	19	F	None	060c02Ax
BYRNE, Ellen	19	F	Servant	060c02Ax
DARLEY, Thomas	18	M	Servant	060c02Ax

ENTERPRISE 08 OCTOBER 1847

From Liverpool

NAMES OF PASSENGERS	AGE	SEX	OCCUPATIONS	DATE PORT SHIP
BERRY, Catherine	50	F	Unknown	080c02Hh
Caroline	17	F	Unknown	080c02Hh
Jeannette	16	F	Unknown	080c02Hh
Thos.	08	M	Child	080c02Hh
MURPHY, Catherine	18	F	Unknown	080c02Hh
SEARIGHT, Wm.B.	30	M	Unknown	080c02Hh
Mary	27	F	Wife	080c02Hh
James	08	M	Child	080c02Hh
Georgianna	04	F	Child	080c02Hh
Mary	02	F	Child	080c02Hh
WALKER, Geo.H.	32	M	Merchant	080c02Hh

JOSEPH-HOWE 11 OCTOBER 1847

From Halifax

NAMES OF PASSENGERS	AGE	SEX	OCCUPATIONS	DATE PORT SHIP
FRENCH, James	35	M	Tailor	110c22Qn
Thos.	10	M	Child	110c22Qn
Wm.	12	M	Unknown	110c22Qn

ABBY-PRATT 15 OCTOBER 1847

From Liverpool

NAMES OF PASSENGERS	AGE	SEX	OCCUPATIONS	DATE PORT SHIP
WHITE, Patrick	28	M	Builder	150c02La
FITZGERALD, Mary	40	F	Housekeeper	150c02La
Catherine	20	F	Housekeeper	150c02La
Mary	16	F	Housekeeper	150c02La
Murty	10	F	Housekeeper	150c02La
Ann	06	F	Child	150c02La
Andrew	02	M	Child	150c02La
MAHER, Margaret	20	F	Servant	150c02La
RIGNEY, Catherine	40	F	Servant	150c02La
Catherine	18	F	Servant	150c02La
Biddy	14	F	Servant	150c02La
WYLIE, Ann-Mrs.	38	F	Housekeeper	150c02La
Thomas	12	M	Laborer	150c02La
Fanny	08	F	Child	150c02La
Robert	06	M	Child	150c02La
MCCABE, Julia	23	F	Lad	150c02La
HART, Ann	21	F	Housekeeper	150c02La
James	.00	M	Infant	150c02La
MCKENNA, Mary	37	F	Housekeeper	150c02La
Catherine	10	F	Child	150c02La
Dennis	08	M	Child	150c02La
Patrick	05	M	Child	150c02La
Thomas	02	M	Child	150c02La
ECCLETON, Richd.	22	M	Groom	150c02La
RUTLEDGE, Thomas	17	M	Laborer	150c02La
John	15	M	Laborer	150c02La
COMBSKAY, Mary	30	F	Housekeeper	150c02La
SMYTH, Rose	20	F	Housekeeper	150c02La
CONISKY, Patrick	11	M	Housekeeper	150c02La
CONISKY, Cathne.	09	F	Child	150c02La
Terence Died-At-Sea	07	M	Child	150c02La
Rose	05	F	Child	150c02La
Thomas	03	M	Child	150c02La
MORAN, Eliza	20	F	Servant	150c02La
ODONNELL, Eliza	20	F	Servant	150c02La
BURNS, Mary	40	F	Housekeeper	150c02La
MALOY, James	47	M	Laborer	150c02La
CUMMINGS, Patk.	11	M	Laborer	150c02La
Michl.	11	M	Laborer	150c02La
MAGILL, James	24	M	Laborer	150c02La
HEALEY, Dennis	27	M	Blwmkr	150c02La
WELSH, Honora	14	F	Housekeeper	150c02La
Ellen	10	F	Unknown	150c02La
ROACH, Cathne.	20	F	Housekeeper	150c02La
WELSH, Cathne.	18	F	Servant	150c02La
MURPHY, Honora	17	F	Servant	150c02La
KENNERLLY, James	24	M	Smith	150c02La
CONNELL, Peter	67	M	Laborer	150c02La
Cathne.	20	F	Spinster	150c02La
SULLIVAN, Florance	30	F	Laborer	150c02La
BERRY, Patk.	30	M	Laborer	150c02La
MORAN, Wm.	40	M	Laborer	150c02La
Bridget	35	F	Servant	150c02La
Patk.	25	M	Laborer	150c02La
Wm.	30	M	Laborer	150c02La
John	18	M	Laborer	150c02La
Cathne.	12	F	Servant	150c02La
ROY, Robt.	25	M	Laborer	150c02La
Margt.	27	F	Spinster	150c02La
RILEY, Cathne.	10	F	Spinster	150c02La
John	30	M	Laborer	150c02La
BOWES, Joseph	24	M	Cord Winder	150c02La
U (W)	20	F	Spinster	150c02La
SOLDAN, Laurence	23	M	Laborer	150c02La
KELLY, Cathne.	30	F	Dressmaker	150c02La
U, U	.00	F	Infant	150c02La
RILEY, Terence	12	M	Spinner	150c02La
John	09	M	Child	150c02La
Mary	06	F	Child	150c02La
BURK, Patk.	11	M	Laborer	150c02La
John	09	M	Child	150c02La
Mary	07	F	Child	150c02La
RILEY, John	29	M	Laborer	150c02La
KELLY, Martin	23	M	Laborer	150c02La
Michl.	26	M	Laborer	150c02La
Cathne.	14	F	Laborer	150c02La
MCKOEN, Margt.	17	F	Servant	150c02La
GILLIGAN, Honora	11	F	Lad	150c02La
Biddy	17	F	Lad	150c02La
Teressa	47	F	Lad	150c02La
RILEY, Patk.	29	M	Laborer	150c02La
Thomas	.00	M	Infant	150c02La
Honora	26	F	Scourer	150c02La
GORMLEY, Bridget	24	F	Servant	150c02La
WALLACE, Ellen	20	F	Servant	150c02La
BURNS, U	20	M	Smith	150c02La
U (W)	20	F	Servant	150c02La
Joseph	02	M	Child	150c02La
CHIRWIN, John	26	M	Coachman	150c02La
KELLY, Martin	24	M	Laborer	150c02La
QUINN, Patk.	50	M	Laborer	150c02La
BRENNAN, James	24	M	Laborer	150c02La
LEARY, Michael	24	M	Laborer	150c02La
Bridget	20	F	Servant	150c02La
CRIDDEN, Turner	24	M	Laborer	150c02La
MCKEON, Francis	40	M	Gdnr	150c02La
MCKOEN, Eliza	20	F	Servant	150c02La
SOLDEN, Mathew	27	F	Laborer	150c02La
DONAGHO, Thos.	27	F	Builder	150c02La
U (W)	24	F	Servant	150c02La
U	.00	U	Infant	150c02La
REYNOLDS, Ann	18	F	Servant	150c02La
GUMLEY, Mary-Ann	18	F	Servant	150c02La

NAMES OF PASSENGERS	AGE	SEX	OCCUPATIONS	DATE PORT SHIP
GUMLEY, Sarah	20	F	Servant	150c02La
CARROLL, Patk.	27	M	Carpenter	150c02La
WALSH, Mary	20	F	Servant	150c02La
HANNESSY, Thomas	31	M	Farmer	150c02La
GARAN, Thomas	25	M	Laborer	150c02La
MURPHY, Mary	26	F	Spinster	150c02La
HANNEY, Patrick	23	M	Clerk	150c02La
KNIGHT, John	17	M	Clerk	150c02La
DOWLING, Francis	16	M	Laborer	150c02La
Cathne.	26	F	Servant	150c02La
Rose	24	F	Dressmaker	150c02La
MCGARNELL, Thos.	11	M	Laborer	150c02La
MOONEY, Nancy	40	F	Servant	150c02La
LOVE, Hannah	20	F	Dressmaker	150c02La
Cathne.	18	F	Dressmaker	150c02La
GARVEY, Dennis	39	M	Builder	150c02La
Ellen	36	F	Unknown	150c02La
CONNELL, Chas.	25	M	Unknown	150c02La
GARVEYTH, Eliza	20	F	Unknown	150c02La
GARVEYH, Henry	09	M	Child	150c02La
James	07	M	Child	150c02La
GARVETH, Charles	04	M	Child	150c02La
GARVEYH, Richd.	02	M	Child	150c02La
TOOHEY, Thomas	21	M	Clerk	150c02La
BYRNE, John	28	M	Baker	150c02La
Honara	45	F	Unknown	150c02La
Eliza	20	F	Dressmaker	150c02La
MULLOWAY, Bryan	24	M	Laborer	150c02La
STUVIN, Robert	40	M	Butcher	150c02La
U (W)	40	F	Wife	150c02La
U	17	U	Unknown	150c02La
U	15	U	Unknown	150c02La
U	16	U	Unknown	150c02La
MATHEWS, Henry	17	M	Baker	150c02La
CONNELL, Michl.	16	M	Laborer	150c02La
KELLY, Eliza	47	F	Unknown	150c02La
Died-At-Sea				
SMITH, Mary-H.	22	F	Servant	150c02La
Rebecca	13	F	Servant	150c02La
Richd.	02	M	Child	150c02La
Jessie	28	F	None	150c02La
TWINEY, Mary	14	F	None	150c02La
CAMPBELL, Mancy	24	F	Servant	150c02La
SHIELS, Jane	24	F	Servant	150c02La
CARROLL, Mulhart	27	M	Coachman	150c02La
LOUGHLAN, Michael	40	M	Unknown	150c02La
MOONEY, Mancy	49	F	Servant	150c02La
Ann	15	F	Weaver	150c02La
MARTIN, William	27	M	Laborer	150c02La
GREEN, Martin	30	M	Laborer	150c02La
MCEWEN, Peter	21	M	Laborer	150c02La
ROY, Sarah	06	F	Child	150c02La
Wm.	03	M	Child	150c02La
WALSH, Honora	37	F	Housekeeper	150c02La
FOY, John-Hy.	17	M	Accountant	150c02La
DUNDAS, Wm.	21	M	Wlmcht	150c02La
Olivia	21	F	Unknown	150c02La

EUROPE 18 OCTOBER 1847

From Liverpool

NAMES OF PASSENGERS	AGE	SEX	OCCUPATIONS	DATE PORT SHIP
DONAHUE, Henry	28	M	Clerk	180c02Bi
WILLIAMS, Mich.	26	M	Laborer	180c02Bi
DOWNS, Jas.	60	M	Unknown	180c02Bi
Cath.	60	F	None	180c02Bi
Edward	19	M	Unknown	180c02Bi
Ann	16	F	Servant	180c02Bi
FLANAGAN, Michl.	27	M	Laborer	180c02Bi
DOWNS, Mary	13	F	Laborer	180c02Bi
Thos.	48	M	Laborer	180c02Bi
BURNS, Rose	30	F	Servant	180c02Bi
Cath.	16	F	Servant	180c02Bi
KERNEY, Mary	21	F	Servant	180c02Bi
Cath.	06	F	Child	180c02Bi
SHIPMAN, Walter	18	M	Baker	18Cc02Bi
GUNING, Geo.	55	M	Tinman	180c02Bi
DIVINE, Mary	60	F	Servant	180c02Bi
GOSGROVE, Pat	32	M	Laborer	180c02Bi
THOMSON, Adam	53	M	Ctnsp	180c02Bi
Thos.	25	M	Ctnsp	180c02Bi
Jas.	31	M	Ctnsp	180c02Bi
MARUE, Ellen	30	F	Servant	180c02Bi
Francis	06	M	Child	180c02Bi
Died-At-Sea				
Charles	08	M	Child	180c02Bi
Died-At-Sea				
DUFFEE, Michl.	32	M	Servant	180c02Bi
Eliza	32	F	None	180c02Bi
Potter	16	M	Servant	180c02Bi
John	08	M	Child	180c02Bi
Patt	01	M	Child	180c02Bi
Mary	12	F	Servant	180c02Bi
Sarah	04	F	Child	180c02Bi
KALLEY, Mary	50	F	Servant	180c02Bi
John	13	M	Servant	180c02Bi
Cath.	18	F	Servant	180c02Bi
Anne	17	F	Servant	180c02Bi
Mary	15	F	Servant	180c02Bi
Salley	09	F	Child	180c02Bi
Hellen	07	F	Child	180c02Bi
MULANY, Thos.	21	M	Laborer	180c02Bi
KOUGHNAN, Jas.	20	M	Laborer	180c02Bi
MCDONOUGH, Peter	30	M	Laborer	180c02Bi
Margt.	36	F	Servant	180c02Bi
BRANNAN, Jas.	09	M	Child	180c02Bi
Cath.	19	F	Servant	180c02Bi
COBREY, Pat	60	M	Laborer	180c02Bi
Mary	56	F	Servant	180c02Bi
John	23	M	Servant	180c02Bi
James	18	M	Servant	180c02Bi
Cathe.	16	F	Laborer	180c02Bi
Ann	18	F	Servant	180c02Bi
Sarah	12	F	Servant	180c02Bi
COX, Eliza	21	F	Servant	180c02Bi
VAUGAN, Mary	17	F	Servant	180c02Bi
FLANERY, Owen	35	M	Servant	180c02Bi
GANNING, Margt.	40	F	Servant	180c02Bi
BRANNAN, Pat	09	M	Child	180c02Bi
CLARK, Eliza	25	F	Servant	180c02Bi

ELSINORE 21 OCTOBER 1847

From Liverpool

NAMES OF PASSENGERS	AGE	SEX	OCCUPATIONS	DATE PORT SHIP
BAGLEY, James	26	M	Laborer	210c02Ke
Bridget	24	F	Unknown	210c02Ke
OSTEN, Mary	25	F	Unknown	210c02Ke
Mary	02	F	Child	210c02Ke
MCENTIZART, James	20	M	Laborer	210c02Ke
WOOD, James	40	M	Laborer	210c02Ke
Mary	40	F	Unknown	210c02Ke
James	20	M	Laborer	210c02Ke
DEAONLY, Jos.	23	M	Laborer	210c02Ke
Eliza	22	F	Unknown	210c02Ke
Rose	.00	F	Infant	210c02Ke
Sarah	26	F	Unknown	210c02Ke
Ann	05	F	Child	210c02Ke

NAMES OF PASSENGERS	AGE	SEX	OCCUPATIONS	DATE PORT SHIP
HOLMES, David	30	M	Laborer	210c02Ke
MUN, John	45	M	Laborer	210c02Ke
Maria	40	F	Unknown	210c02Ke
Ann	14	F	Unknown	210c02Ke
Joseph	13	M	Unknown	210c02Ke
Emma	06	M	Child	210c02Ke
Jane	05	M	Child	210c02Ke
John	.00	M	Infant	210c02Ke
MARTIN, Geo.	23	M	Laborer	210c02Ke
THORNHILL, Thos.	25	M	Laborer	210c02Ke
Eliza	23	F	Unknown	210c02Ke
ANDERSON, Joseph	35	M	Laborer	210c02Ke
Eliza	30	F	Unknown	210c02Ke
Lorince	10	M	Child	210c02Ke
Sarah	06	F	Child	210c02Ke
Thomas	04	M	Child	210c02Ke
Joseph	.00	M	Infant	210c02Ke
EASTON, James	25	M	Laborer	210c02Ke
Jessey	24	M	Laborer	210c02Ke
Mary	04	F	Child	210c02Ke
Margt.	01	F	Child	210c02Ke
URQUAHART, Arkey	19	F	Unknown	210c02Ke
AUCHANEM, Thos.	21	M	Laborer	210c02Ke
DINEHEN, Thos.	24	M	Laborer	210c02Ke
MCSEN, John	26	M	Laborer	210c02Ke
BELLIN, Richd.	24	M	Laborer	210c02Ke
PRESTON, Mich.	24	M	Laborer	210c02Ke
WATERS, Cathe.	00	F	Unknown	210c02Ke
MORRIS, John	22	M	Laborer	210c02Ke
Mary	21	F	Unknown	210c02Ke
MALONE, Mary	22	F	Unknown	210c02Ke
MATTHEWS, Cathe.	13	F	Unknown	210c02Ke
Margt.	12	F	Unknown	210c02Ke
Jane	08	F	Child	210c02Ke
KEVERLY, Ann	40	F	Unknown	210c02Ke
LIVETON, Benjn.	44	M	Laborer	210c02Ke
Ann	40	F	Unknown	210c02Ke
CHILD, John	24	M	Laborer	210c02Ke
Caroline	27	F	Unknown	210c02Ke
Matthew	09	M	Child	210c02Ke
CONORS, Henry	25	M	Laborer	210c02Ke
Mary	21	F	Unknown	210c02Ke
BRISCOE, Geo.	26	M	Laborer	210c02Ke
Emily	22	F	Unknown	210c02Ke
Ann	03	F	Child	210c02Ke
HINDS, William	24	M	Laborer	210c02Ke
MOORES, Maria	30	F	Unknown	210c02Ke
Henrietta	15	F	Unknown	210c02Ke
BROWN, James	36	M	Laborer	210c02Ke
Thomas	30	M	Laborer	210c02Ke
DALLY, Wm.	45	M	Laborer	210c02Ke
WALLY, John	35	M	Laborer	210c02Ke
SHEPHERD, Henry	21	M	Laborer	210c02Ke
ROWLAND, Thos.	35	M	Laborer	210c02Ke
HOPKINS, Ann	24	F	Unknown	210c02Ke
CONROY, John	25	M	Laborer	210c02Ke
NIELE, Ann	20	F	Unknown	210c02Ke
FITZGERALD, John	67	M	Laborer	210c02Ke
Margt.	47	F	Unknown	210c02Ke
James	17	M	Laborer	210c02Ke
Elisa	11	F	Unknown	210c02Ke
Rose	15	F	Unknown	210c02Ke
Thos.	09	M	Child	210c02Ke
Mary	07	F	Child	210c02Ke
MCCABE, Edwd.	28	M	Laborer	210c02Ke
MURPHY, Pat	28	M	Laborer	210c02Ke
MOLLER, Mary	26	F	Unknown	210c02Ke
GIBNEY, Pat	50	M	Laborer	210c02Ke
Ann	50	F	Unknown	210c02Ke
Rose	17	F	Unknown	210c02Ke
Ann	15	F	Unknown	210c02Ke
Bryan	16	M	Laborer	210c02Ke
Pat	09	M	Child	210c02Ke
OFLARETY, Henry	50	M	Laborer	210c02Ke
DOCHNALL, Edwd.	27	M	Laborer	210c02Ke
SHARP, Bridget	08	F	Child	210c02Ke
MOONEY, Mich.	24	M	Laborer	210c02Ke
CONNELL, Thos.	40	M	Laborer	210c02Ke
RYAN, Pat	21	M	Laborer	210c02Ke
KELLEY, Bernd.	50	M	Laborer	210c02Ke
Thos.	27	M	Laborer	210c02Ke
Mary	26	F	Unknown	210c02Ke
Pat	.00	M	Infant	210c02Ke
FURNEY, James	28	M	Laborer	210c02Ke
COCKAYNE, Jos.	40	M	Laborer	210c02Ke
GASKIN, James	36	M	Laborer	210c02Ke
MCNIEL, James	25	M	Laborer	210c02Ke
DUFFIN, Eliza	26	F	Unknown	210c02Ke
MCGROTTY, Corn.	30	M	Laborer	210c02Ke
HODGE, John	50	M	Laborer	210c02Ke
Jane	40	F	Unknown	210c02Ke
Robert	20	M	Laborer	210c02Ke
Nancy	18	F	Unknown	210c02Ke
Samuel	16	M	Laborer	210c02Ke
John	10	M	Laborer	210c02Ke
James	08	M	Child	210c02Ke
Daniel	06	M	Child	210c02Ke
Jane	04	F	Child	210c02Ke
SHEA, Maurice	20	M	Laborer	210c02Ke
HENISTER, James	30	M	Laborer	210c02Ke
Elisa	18	F	Unknown	210c02Ke
Maurice	.00	M	Infant	210c02Ke
BRIEN, John	24	M	Laborer	210c02Ke
YOUNG, Edwd.	20	M	Laborer	210c02Ke
MCCARTHY, Mary	20	F	Unknown	210c02Ke
OHERELLY, John	19	M	Laborer	210c02Ke
SHEA, Mary	20	F	Unknown	210c02Ke
Johanna	18	F	Unknown	210c02Ke
MURPHY, Dennis	33	M	Laborer	210c02Ke
Elisa	30	F	Unknown	210c02Ke
Michael	04	M	Child	210c02Ke
Elisa	03	F	Child	210c02Ke
Ellen	.00	F	Infant	210c02Ke
FOLLEY, Wm.	30	M	Laborer	210c02Ke
COFFEE, Cathe.	30	F	Unknown	210c02Ke
DALEY, Eolry	20	F	Unknown	210c02Ke
COFFEE, Mary	04	F	Child	210c02Ke
Peggy	02	F	Child	210c02Ke
CURRAN, Mich.	25	M	Laborer	210c02Ke
CROFTEN, Richd.	50	M	Laborer	210c02Ke
Ann	50	F	Unknown	210c02Ke
John	20	M	Laborer	210c02Ke
Cathe.	09	F	Child	210c02Ke
BRADY, Samuel	19	M	Laborer	210c02Ke
Alice	50	F	Unknown	210c02Ke
WELSTRAD, Wm.	56	M	Laborer	210c02Ke
FARR, James	60	M	Laborer	210c02Ke
ONIEL, John	40	M	Laborer	210c02Ke
BROWN, James	24	M	Laborer	210c02Ke
Cathe.	20	F	Unknown	210c02Ke
NORRIS, Thos.	25	M	Laborer	210c02Ke
CAMBLE, Pat	30	M	Laborer	210c02Ke
Jane	20	F	Unknown	210c02Ke
James	22	M	Laborer	210c02Ke
DOLAN, Peter	12	M	Laborer	210c02Ke
WALKER, Wm.	30	M	Laborer	210c02Ke
KNOTT, John	24	M	Laborer	210c02Ke
KERSHAW, Robert	16	M	Laborer	210c02Ke
TAYLOR, Jessey	25	M	Laborer	210c02Ke
HURLEY, Jos.	17	M	Laborer	210c02Ke
COLLINS, Mary	21	F	Unknown	210c02Ke
EUSTACE, Chris	20	M	Laborer	210c02Ke
HAYES, Richd.	18	M	Laborer	210c02Ke
VALLALY, Cathe.	18	F	Unknown	210c02Ke
MCGUIRE, Henry	16	M	Laborer	210c02Ke
BUCKLEY, Jos.	24	M	Laborer	210c02Ke
BELL, Sarah	25	F	Unknown	210c02Ke
BOYLE, Oscar	24	M	Laborer	210c02Ke
Anthony	18	M	Laborer	210c02Ke
DOGHERTY, Anthony	24	M	Laborer	210c02Ke

NAMES OF PASSENGERS	AGE	SEX	OCCUPATIONS	DATE PORT SHIP
KELLY, Letitia	30	F	Unknown	210c02Ke
WOODS, Charles	25	M	Laborer	210c02Ke
NEEL, John	23	M	Laborer	210c02Ke
ATCHENSON, John	25	M	Laborer	210c02Ke
LYNES, Pat	20	M	Laborer	210c02Ke
MARIORITY, Mary	21	F	Unknown	210c02Ke
GARIGHAN, Bridget	27	F	Unknown	210c02Ke
James	17	M	Laborer	210c02Ke
NIGHT, Gabriel	20	M	Laborer	210c02Ke
WARUTHICH, John	50	M	Laborer	210c02Ke
Mary	49	F	Unknown	210c02Ke
James	19	M	Laborer	210c02Ke
Jane	10	F	Child	210c02Ke
Mary	21	F	Unknown	210c02Ke
FIDORK, James	60	M	Laborer	210c02Ke
WELCH, Margt.	20	F	Unknown	210c02Ke
Mary	03	F	Child	210c02Ke
MURRY, Wm.	19	M	Laborer	210c02Ke
Margt.	24	F	Unknown	210c02Ke
ADAMS, Mark	29	M	Laborer	210c02Ke
LURRENS, Fardy	22	M	Laborer	210c02Ke
DOYLE, Aaron	26	M	Laborer	210c02Ke
FITZPATRICK, John	26	M	Laborer	210c02Ke
Mary	02	M	Child	210c02Ke
BRADY, Ann	20	M	Unknown	210c02Ke
STORER, Jane	15	M	Unknown	210c02Ke
Julia	13	M	Unknown	210c02Ke
FITZPATRICK, Margt.	18	M	Unknown	210c02Ke
STEVENS, Stephen	25	M	Laborer	210c02Ke
Mary	24	F	Unknown	210c02Ke
TUCKER, Henry	20	M	Laborer	210c02Ke
SMITH, Richd.	30	M	Laborer	210c02Ke
Mary	26	F	Unknown	210c02Ke
MCGANFLIN, Barnd.	32	M	Laborer	210c02Ke
BOYLE, John	30	M	Laborer	210c02Ke
MOORE, Owen	25	M	Laborer	210c02Ke
KILLDAY, Corn.	20	M	Laborer	210c02Ke
DEVLIN, John	27	M	Laborer	210c02Ke
James	30	M	Laborer	210c02Ke
MORIORITY, Owen	25	M	Laborer	210c02Ke
Ellen	22	F	Unknown	210c02Ke
CROOK, James	40	M	Laborer	210c02Ke
Robert	17	M	Laborer	210c02Ke
MCCRODEN, John	30	M	Laborer	210c02Ke

M.LIVINGSTON 21 OCTOBER 1847

From Liverpool

NAMES OF PASSENGERS	AGE	SEX	OCCUPATIONS	DATE PORT SHIP
ONEILL, H.	27	M	Unknown	210c02Qi
My.	25	F	Unknown	210c02Qi
George	04	M	Child	210c02Qi
ACKERMAN, Bgt.	30	F	Unknown	210c02Qi
DRIVER, My.	65	F	Unknown	210c02Qi
MCCONNER, Rose	45	F	Unknown	210c02Qi
My.	16	F	Unknown	210c02Qi
Rose	12	F	Unknown	210c02Qi
HOLMES, Ellen	20	F	Unknown	210c02Qi
JOHSTON, F.	32	M	Merchant	210c02Qi
Ann	26	F	Unknown	210c02Qi
ARMSTRONG, John	27	M	Mechanic	210c02Qi
My.	24	F	Unknown	210c02Qi
Robt.	04	M	Child	210c02Qi
James	03	M	Child	210c02Qi
Ellen	30	F	Unknown	210c02Qi
Mgt.	22	F	Unknown	210c02Qi
SMITHHEIMER, Ma.	31	F	Unknown	210c02Qi
Sarah	06	F	Child	210c02Qi
PLATT, W.	45	M	Mechanic	210c02Qi

NAMES OF PASSENGERS	AGE	SEX	OCCUPATIONS	DATE PORT SHIP
BATTEMUTT, B.	44	M	Mechanic	210c02Qi
HODGSON, W.	43	M	Mechanic	210c02Qi
BATTENUTT, J.	42	M	Mechanic	210c02Qi
Mgt.	37	F	Unknown	210c02Qi
Joseph	19	M	Unknown	210c02Qi
Ann	17	F	Unknown	210c02Qi
Jane	15	F	Unknown	210c02Qi
Ellen	13	F	Unknown	210c02Qi
Earn.	09	M	Child	210c02Qi
John	07	M	Child	210c02Qi
Saml.	01	M	Child	210c02Qi
SMITH, J.	23	M	Mechanic	210c02Qi
Carl	25	M	Mechanic	210c02Qi
SMELL, Eliza	37	F	Mechanic	210c02Qi
Cath.	11	F	Mechanic	210c02Qi
SNETHER, Eliza	15	F	Mechanic	210c02Qi
Chas.	11	M	None	210c02Qi
HAURS, Eliza	35	F	Unknown	210c02Qi
WATTS, R.	24	M	Unknown	210c02Qi
Jane	63	F	Unknown	210c02Qi
E.	35	M	Unknown	210c02Qi
D.	30	M	Farmer	210c02Qi
Susan	27	F	Unknown	210c02Qi
Mgt.	26	F	Unknown	210c02Qi
My.	26	F	Unknown	210c02Qi
NIELY, R.	13	M	None	210c02Qi
HANNAH, J.	22	M	Farmer	210c02Qi
WALLACE, J.	30	M	Farmer	210c02Qi
Isb.	08	F	Child	210c02Qi
Jas.	05	M	Child	210c02Qi
Ayn	02	F	Child	210c02Qi
EMNETT, W.	38	M	Mechanic	210c02Qi
Ann	42	F	Unknown	210c02Qi
BLENAN, J.	24	M	Mechanic	210c02Qi
Henry	23	M	Mechanic	210c02Qi
ASHWORTH, N.	29	M	Mechanic	210c02Qi
HARGIN, My.	18	F	Unknown	210c02Qi
Cath.	20	F	Unknown	210c02Qi
MCDANIEL, Eliza	17	F	Unknown	210c02Qi
SCOTT, Mgt.	64	F	Unknown	210c02Qi
Walter	15	M	None	210c02Qi
MOORE, P.	32	M	Mechanic	210c02Qi
BURK, P.	26	M	Mechanic	210c02Qi
ADAMS, Eliza	46	F	Unknown	210c02Qi
Thos.	22	M	Mechanic	210c02Qi
Mgt.	19	F	Unknown	210c02Qi
Wm.	11	M	None	210c02Qi
Emma	09	F	Child	210c02Qi
Ellen	07	F	Child	210c02Qi
CREFTON, Mgt.	67	F	Unknown	210c02Qi
Elen	22	F	Unknown	210c02Qi
U	25	F	Unknown	210c02Qi
U	16	F	Unknown	210c02Qi
CLAYTON, U	35	M	Mechanic	210c02Qi
Mt.	08	F	Child	210c02Qi
Emma	02	F	Child	210c02Qi
COFFY, Corns.	22	M	Mechanic	210c02Qi
Timoty	28	M	Mechanic	210c02Qi
Har-----, T.	35	M	Mechanic	210c02Qi
PREASON, Sa.	22	F	Unknown	210c02Qi
HENDERSON, J.	20	M	Mechanic	210c02Qi
GREER, Cath.	40	F	Unknown	210c02Qi
HAMIL, J.	22	M	Mechanic	210c02Qi
J.	23	M	Mechanic	210c02Qi
LAVERTY, J.	23	M	Mechanic	210c02Qi
HAMILL, M.	30	M	Mechanic	210c02Qi
CAIN, My.	10	F	Child	210c02Qi
ROONEY, J.	18	M	Mechanic	210c02Qi
ROBINSON, T.	60	M	Mechanic	210c02Qi
Eliza	45	F	Unknown	210c02Qi
RIGLEY, J.	31	M	Mechanic	210c02Qi
WALLACE, Jane	15	F	Unknown	210c02Qi
GLENNAN, Wfd.	30	F	Unknown	210c02Qi
PENNENTIN, W.	19	M	Mechanic	210c02Qi
MULHOLLAND, Jane	24	F	Unknown	210c02Qi

NAMES OF PASSENGERS	AGE	SEX	OCCUPATIONS	DATE PORT SHIP
REES, Cath.	20	F	Unknown	210c02QI
Eliza	18	F	Unknown	210c02QI
ONSLOW, S.	31	M	Mechanic	210c02QI
GRIFFITH, J.	24	M	Mechanic	210c02QI
ENDOR, T.	35	M	Mechanic	210c02QI
Joseph	27	M	Mechanic	210c02QI
CAIN, B.	30	M	Mechanic	210c02QI
ROURKE, Cath.	30	F	Unknown	210c02QI
COIL, Bgt.	60	F	Unknown	210c02QI
BLACK, Sa.	30	F	Unknown	210c02QI
Mgrt.	43	F	Unknown	210c02QI
Eliza	11	F	Unknown	210c02QI
Chas.	07	M	Child	210c02QI
Jane	11	F	Unknown	210c02QI
My	01	F	Child	210c02QI
WILSON, Cath.	18	F	Unknown	210c02QI
CARNEY, Jas.	16	M	Unknown	210c02QI
John	14	M	None	210c02QI
LINNET, Eliza	79	F	Unknown	210c02QI
Jane	67	F	Unknown	210c02QI
COLLINS, Ann	31	F	Unknown	210c02QI
Wm.	12	M	None	210c02QI
KENDALL, My.	41	M	Unknown	210c02QI
Thos.	41	M	Mechanic	210c02QI
Mem.	13	F	Unknown	210c02QI
Thos.	12	M	None	210c02QI
Eliza	10	F	Unknown	210c02QI
Sa.A.	06	F	Child	210c02QI
LAURIE, Ja.	42	F	Unknown	210c02QI
Ep---	18	F	Unknown	210c02QI
T.	16	M	Laborer	210c02QI
Geg.	13	M	None	210c02QI
Danl.	11	M	None	210c02QI
John	09	M	Child	210c02QI
Mgt.	05	F	Child	210c02QI
Jemima	02	F	Child	210c02QI
TENGE, Mgt.	55	F	Unknown	210c02QI
My.	16	F	Unknown	210c02QI
Patrick	11	M	None	210c02QI
Eliza	09	F	Child	210c02QI
John	06	M	Child	210c02QI
Tmty.	06	M	Child	210c02QI
HINS, My.	50	F	Unknown	210c02QI
Thos.	14	M	None	210c02QI
MOOR, P.	45	M	None	210c02QI
Eliza	45	F	Unknown	210c02QI
Jon	12	M	None	210c02QI
Peter	10	M	None	210c02QI
Mgt.	06	F	Child	210c02QI
BAIN, J.	73	M	Laborer	210c02QI
Jas.	08	M	Child	210c02QI
MALOY, My.	60	F	Unknown	210c02QI
My.	24	F	Unknown	210c02QI
CASEY, Bgt.	60	F	Unknown	210c02QI
Patck.	60	M	Laborer	210c02QI
Thos.	14	M	Laborer	210c02QI
DOWLING, T.	39	M	Laborer	210c02QI
Alice	28	F	Unknown	210c02QI
John	11	M	None	210c02QI
My.	09	F	Child	210c02QI
Cath.	07	F	Child	210c02QI
Patck.	05	M	Child	210c02QI
Johanna	01	F	Child	210c02QI
ROACH, Wfd.	40	F	Unknown	210c02QI
Cath.	11	F	Unknown	210c02QI
Rich.	09	M	Child	210c02QI
Johanna	06	F	Child	210c02QI
John	04	M	Child	210c02QI
SCOLLEN, Mgt.	30	F	Unknown	210c02QI
Patck.	09	M	Child	210c02QI
James	06	M	Child	210c02QI
John	03	M	Child	210c02QI
T.	01	M	Child	210c02QI
BIRCHELL, G.	49	M	Laborer	210c02QI
Ann	50	F	Unknown	210c02QI
BIRCHELL, Geog.	25	M	Laborer	210c02QI
Mt.	22	F	Unknown	210c02QI
John	17	M	Laborer	210c02QI
Thos.	04	M	Child	210c02QI
Jno.	02	M	Child	210c02QI
DOYLE, My.	35	F	Unknown	210c02QI
Luis	30	F	Unknown	210c02QI
Patck.	11	M	None	210c02QI
Jane	07	F	Child	210c02QI
Cath.	04	F	Child	210c02QI
MOUNT, Ann	37	F	Unknown	210c02QI
Mgt.	11	F	Unknown	210c02QI
Mich.	09	M	Child	210c02QI
Pat	05	M	Child	210c02QI
John	03	M	Child	210c02QI
Eliza	01	F	Child	210c02QI
OREILY, J.	28	M	Laborer	210c02QI
Denis	25	M	Laborer	210c02QI
MERATY, Ry.	19	M	Laborer	210c02QI
DOHERTY, J.	45	M	Laborer	210c02QI
GUIRE, A.	35	M	Laborer	210c02QI
Hrty.	35	F	Unknown	210c02QI
John	08	M	Child	210c02QI
Tmty.	07	M	Child	210c02QI
KEEF, J.	34	M	Laborer	210c02QI
CONIF, J.	32	M	Laborer	210c02QI
KEEF, Ann	26	F	Unknown	210c02QI
CLEGUE, Cath.	44	F	Unknown	210c02QI
Jas.	12	M	Unknown	210c02QI
Thos.	10	M	Unknown	210c02QI
MURRY, Jane	40	F	Unknown	210c02QI
Patck.	12	M	None	210c02QI
Cath.	07	F	Child	210c02QI
FLANEGAN, My.	13	F	Unknown	210c02QI
BRENNAN, P.	24	M	Laborer	210c02QI
MCGHEE, Bgt.	20	F	Unknown	210c02QI
Patck.	15	M	Unknown	210c02QI
MCKEAN, Bgt.	22	F	Unknown	210c02QI
RORRY, J.	11	M	None	210c02QI
MCNICOLL, F.	60	M	Laborer	210c02QI
Judith	60	F	Unknown	210c02QI
Susan	15	F	Unknown	210c02QI
CASSEDY, J.	30	M	Laborer	210c02QI
PATTERSON, D.	30	M	Laborer	210c02QI
MCMAHER, Mgt.	22	F	Unknown	210c02QI
HEALY, Brt.	23	F	Unknown	210c02QI
CONWAY, W.	30	M	Laborer	210c02QI
ROCHHE, T.	20	M	Laborer	210c02QI
Tmy.	19	M	Laborer	210c02QI
CLANCY, J.	40	M	Laborer	210c02QI
Ann	35	F	Unknown	210c02QI
My.	05	F	Child	210c02QI
Hh.	03	M	Child	210c02QI
John	01	M	Child	210c02QI
Mth.	25	M	Laborer	210c02QI
R.	40	F	Unknown	210c02QI
Mgt.	27	F	Unknown	210c02QI
MCKEAN, P.	26	M	Laborer	210c02QI
LAMBERT, C.	21	M	Laborer	210c02QI
MOIN, T.	26	M	Laborer	210c02QI
My.	06	F	Child	210c02QI
IVUSH, W.	40	M	Laborer	210c02QI
FREELAN, My.	16	F	Unknown	210c02QI
MCCOY, Rose	50	F	Unknown	210c02QI
HUNTER, F.	21	M	Laborer	210c02QI
BENNETT, Cath.	14	F	Unknown	210c02QI
MCKAY, Ann	15	F	Unknown	210c02QI
MCCABE, J.	26	M	Laborer	210c02QI
Alla	13	F	Unknown	210c02QI
SHAY, Ann	40	F	Unknown	210c02QI
MCCARTY, O.	16	M	Laborer	210c02QI
MCDORN, P.	25	M	Laborer	210c02QI
LYNCH, T.	30	M	Laborer	210c02QI
Pat	03	M	Child	210c02QI
BALEY, Ann	24	F	Unknown	210c02QI

NAMES OF PASSENGERS	A G E	S E X	OCCUPATIONS	DATE PORT SHIP
DEMPSEY, Elen	35	F	Unknown	210c02Qi
MALOY, T.	18	M	Laborer	210c02Qi
GALLAGHER, My.	30	F	Unknown	210c02Qi
MURPHY, T.	25	M	Laborer	210c02Qi
MALY, M.	21	M	Laborer	210c02Qi
DOHERTY, Elen	18	F	Unknown	210c02Qi

OCEAN 22 OCTOBER 1847

From Havre

NAMES OF PASSENGERS	A G E	S E X	OCCUPATIONS	DATE PORT SHIP
MCDONALD, John	30	M	Farmer	220c05Jx
HEYDEN, Thomas	31	M	Farmer	220c05Jx
KEAN, Bill	30	M	Farmer	220c05Jx

COLUMBIANA 22 OCTOBER 1847

From Liverpool

NAMES OF PASSENGERS	A G E	S E X	OCCUPATIONS	DATE PORT SHIP
FIELD, Mary	26	F	Farmer	220c02Qj
Joseph	19	M	Farmer	220c02Qj
Olivia	03	F	Child	220c02Qj
Jane	01	F	Child	220c02Qj
TODD, William	28	M	Farmer	220c02Qj
MCBRIDE, Mary	23	F	Farmer	220c02Qj
GETTRICK, Ann	50	F	Farmer	220c02Qj
HUGHES, Sally	21	F	Farmer	220c02Qj
CONNER, Mary	17	F	Farmer	220c02Qj
MURRY, Mary	21	F	Farmer	220c02Qj
RAFFITY, Dennis	22	M	Farmer	220c02Qj
HUGHES, Sally	25	F	Farmer	220c02Qj
JOHNSTON, Elizabeth	20	F	Farmer	220c02Qj
HILES, Edwd.	32	M	Farmer	220c02Qj
MABEN, Bridget	18	F	Farmer	220c02Qj
CUSSONS, William	34	M	Farmer	220c02Qj
MALAN, James	21	M	Farmer	220c02Qj
WELCH, Wm.	20	M	Farmer	220c02Qj
James	19	M	Farmer	220c02Qj
Simon	16	M	Farmer	220c02Qj
Mary	35	F	Farmer	220c02Qj
KELLEY, Mary	20	F	Farmer	220c02Qj
FLARITY, Margt.	16	F	Farmer	220c02Qj
CRABTREE, Aaron	27	M	Farmer	220c02Qj
U (W)	25	F	Unknown	220c02Qj
Nathaniel	03	M	Child	220c02Qj
WORTH, James	27	M	Farmer	220c02Qj
ROUKE, Honora	13	F	Farmer	220c02Qj
LANDAY, John	43	M	Farmer	220c02Qj
James	29	M	Farmer	220c02Qj
Catherine	63	F	Farmer	220c02Qj
Hannah	09	F	Child	220c02Qj
Catherine	07	F	Child	220c02Qj
COYNE, Brigt.	24	F	Farmer	220c02Qj
ENGLAND, Geo.	30	M	Farmer	220c02Qj
WATT, John	24	M	Farmer	220c02Qj
Mary-Ann	23	F	Unknown	220c02Qj
Sarah	01	F	Child	220c02Qj
MERCHANT, Alfred	32	M	Farmer	220c02Qj
KELLEY, Margret	20	F	Farmer	220c02Qj
JENKINS, Joseph	17	M	Farmer	220c02Qj
HOLLINGS, Wm.	33	M	Farmer	220c02Qj
HUGHES, Wm.	32	M	Farmer	220c02Qj
TYSON, John	30	M	Farmer	220c02Qj
TYSON, Jane	29	F	Unknown	220c02Qj
Elizabeth	06	F	Child	220c02Qj
WALDING, John	23	M	Farmer	220c02Qj
RYAN, Thos.	40	M	Farmer	220c02Qj
Margret	18	F	Farmer	220c02Qj
SUTER, John	24	M	Farmer	220c02Qj
MCGUEIRE, Peggy	22	F	Farmer	220c02Qj
FREBREME, Sholts	24	M	Farmer	220c02Qj
George	24	M	Farmer	220c02Qj
ROSEBOTTOM, Susan	07	F	Child	220c02Qj
OBRIAN, Michl.	60	M	Farmer	220c02Qj
Mary	45	F	Farmer	220c02Qj
Catherine	03	F	Child	220c02Qj
John	01	M	Child	220c02Qj
MCMANIOR, Ann	17	F	Farmer	220c02Qj
DELAHIMLLY, James	16	M	Farmer	220c02Qj
ONEIL, Mary	20	F	Farmer	220c02Qj
REILEY, Yunice	56	F	Farmer	220c02Qj
Ann	10	F	Farmer	220c02Qj
Sylvester	12	M	Farmer	220c02Qj
KELLY, Bridget	30	F	Farmer	220c02Qj
Mary	09	F	Child	220c02Qj
Margret	04	F	Child	220c02Qj
COWLASS, James	30	M	Farmer	220c02Qj
HONORA, Wm.	25	M	Farmer	220c02Qj
STUBBENS, Geo.H.	20	M	Farmer	220c02Qj
TINES, John	28	M	Farmer	220c02Qj
GURTRICK, John	28	M	Farmer	220c02Qj
Margret	29	F	Farmer	220c02Qj
FAHAN, James	28	M	Farmer	220c02Qj
QUINE, Patt	19	M	Farmer	220c02Qj
Ann	25	F	Farmer	220c02Qj
STUART, James	30	M	Farmer	220c02Qj
Susan	28	F	Unknown	220c02Qj
George	08	M	Child	220c02Qj
William	06	M	Child	220c02Qj
David	03	M	Child	220c02Qj
John	.00	M	Infant	220c02Qj
HUGHES, Allace	70	F	Farmer	220c02Qj
CLARK, Mary	35	F	Farmer	220c02Qj
Alexander	11	M	Farmer	220c02Qj
Mary	08	F	Child	220c02Qj
John	04	M	Child	220c02Qj
Thos.	02	M	Child	220c02Qj
GRAY, Sarah	30	F	Farmer	220c02Qj
Edward	01	M	Child	220c02Qj
MAHAN, John-C.	17	M	Farmer	220c02Qj
Mary	11	F	Farmer	220c02Qj
Jeriminah	05	M	Child	220c02Qj
SULIVAN, Hannah	16	F	Farmer	220c02Qj
CARRY, James	27	M	Farmer	220c02Qj
Jane	30	F	Unknown	220c02Qj
Eliza	08	F	Child	220c02Qj
Rebeca	06	F	Child	220c02Qj
HUBLAN, Sophia	17	F	Farmer	220c02Qj
EGAN, Torrell	23	U	Farmer	220c02Qj
STILL, James	27	M	Farmer	220c02Qj
MCMANUS, Mary	29	F	Farmer	220c02Qj
MCQUINNE, Wm.	30	M	Farmer	220c02Qj
Elizebeth	10	F	Child	220c02Qj
Mary	08	F	Child	220c02Qj
John	06	M	Child	220c02Qj
William	04	M	Child	220c02Qj
Sarah	01	F	Child	220c02Qj
HAYNES, Molly	17	F	Farmer	220c02Qj
KELLY, Daniel	40	M	Farmer	220c02Qj
CASSELY, Mary	22	F	Farmer	220c02Qj
HAY, Frances-Ann	17	F	Farmer	220c02Qj
RUTHE, Ellen	50	F	Farmer	220c02Qj
Ann	25	F	Farmer	220c02Qj
OGORMAN, Patt	29	M	Farmer	220c02Qj
DAYAL, Mary	50	F	Farmer	220c02Qj
MCGLADE, Rose	40	F	Farmer	220c02Qj
Mary	37	F	Farmer	220c02Qj
Biddy-Kane	18	F	Farmer	220c02Qj

NAMES OF PASSENGERS	AGE	SEX	OCCUPATIONS	DATE PORT SHIP
HENRY, Ann	20	F	Farmer	220c02Qj
Susan	18	F	Farmer	220c02Qj
WILLIAMS, Catherine	18	F	Farmer	220c02Qj
WRIGHT, Michl.	40	M	Farmer	220c02Qj
Ann	40	F	Unknown	220c02Qj
Jane	13	F	Farmer	220c02Qj
Wm.	11	M	Farmer	220c02Qj
Brigt.	09	F	Child	220c02Qj
John	07	M	Child	220c02Qj
Maria	04	F	Child	220c02Qj
IRTEN, James	25	M	Farmer	220c02Qj
TRACEY, Michel	20	M	Farmer	220c02Qj
IRELAND, John	26	M	Farmer	220c02Qj
KIREVON, Peter	36	M	Farmer	220c02Qj
Mary	34	F	Unknown	220c02Qj
James	10	M	Child	220c02Qj
Patt	08	M	Child	220c02Qj
Bridget	06	F	Child	220c02Qj
MCMANUS, Pill	13	U	Farmer	220c02Qj
Thomas	10	M	Child	220c02Qj
James	08	M	Child	220c02Qj
RAYNOLDS, Sally	18	F	Farmer	220c02Qj
CARR, Catherine	13	F	Farmer	220c02Qj
BURY, Ann	21	F	Farmer	220c02Qj
Margret	03	F	Child	220c02Qj
Elizebeth	23	F	Farmer	220c02Qj
James	.00	M	Infant	220c02Qj
CALLWELL, Patt	24	M	Farmer	220c02Qj
WARD, James	21	M	Farmer	220c02Qj
MERKINS, U	40	M	Farmer	220c02Qj
HONELL, Ann	40	F	Farmer	220c02Qj
Jane	23	F	Farmer	220c02Qj
MCMAHON, Michl.	35	M	Farmer	220c02Qj
Mary	25	F	Unknown	220c02Qj
John	06	M	Child	220c02Qj
CLACKLOW, Ann	25	F	Farmer	220c02Qj
Biddy	26	F	Farmer	220c02Qj
SMITH, John	25	M	Farmer	220c02Qj
Bridget	50	F	Farmer	220c02Qj
ONEAL, Thos.	25	M	Farmer	220c02Qj
GALLCOM, James	30	M	Farmer	220c02Qj
RUSSELL, Wm.	49	M	Farmer	220c02Qj
DORLEY, John	24	M	Farmer	220c02Qj
Thomas	04	M	Child	220c02Qj
MCKENNEY, Sally	50	F	Farmer	220c02Qj
Hugh	17	M	Farmer	220c02Qj
Mary	15	F	Farmer	220c02Qj
Michl.	04	M	Child	220c02Qj
DOLLING, Michl.	08	M	Child	220c02Qj
John	04	M	Child	220c02Qj
Sally	02	F	Child	220c02Qj
ROSE, Martin	24	M	Farmer	220c02Qj
Henor	21	U	Farmer	220c02Qj
DUMGAN, Mary	40	F	Farmer	220c02Qj
Henora	19	F	Farmer	220c02Qj
Margt.	19	F	Farmer	220c02Qj
DUNNAGHAN, Ann	09	F	Child	220c02Qj
Bridget	11	F	Farmer	220c02Qj
Catherine	06	F	Child	220c02Qj
Elizebeth	05	F	Child	220c02Qj
HALEY, Ann	30	F	Farmer	220c02Qj
KENNEY, Bridget	27	F	Farmer	220c02Qj
Bryan	12	M	Farmer	220c02Qj
Mary	10	F	Farmer	220c02Qj
Darly	08	U	Child	220c02Qj
Thomas	06	M	Child	220c02Qj
MULLEN, Thomas	24	M	Farmer	220c02Qj
Mary	20	F	Farmer	220c02Qj
HARREN, Sarah	11	F	Farmer	220c02Qj
MCCARTY, Margret	20	F	Farmer	220c02Qj
Timothy	20	M	Farmer	220c02Qj
OWENS, Ellin	50	F	Farmer	220c02Qj
Cornelius	20	M	Farmer	220c02Qj

THETIS 22 OCTOBER 1847

From Belfast

NAMES OF PASSENGERS		AGE	SEX	OCCUPATIONS	DATE PORT SHIP
BELL, Elizabeth		16	F	Spinster	220c07Ae
MCQUICK, Jane		25	F	Spinster	220c07Ae
Anne	(D)	05	F	Child	220c07Ae
Mary	(D)	03	F	Child	220c07Ae
Alexander	(S)	01	M	Child	220c07Ae
ONEILL, Thomas		48	M	Paper Maker	220c07Ae
Thomasena	(W)	48	F	None	220c07Ae
Margaret	(D)	21	F	Unknown	220c07Ae
Esther	(D)	19	F	Unknown	220c07Ae
Thomasena	(D)	16	F	Unknown	220c07Ae
Eliza	(D)	13	F	Unknown	220c07Ae
Frances	(D)	11	F	Unknown	220c07Ae
Margaret	(D)	09	F	Child	220c07Ae
Isabella	(D)	20	F	Unknown	220c07Ae
Thomasena	(D)	01	F	Child	220c07Ae
Robert	(S)	22	M	Unknown	220c07Ae
MULHOLLAND, Hugh		29	M	Farmer	220c07Ae
John		23	M	Farmer	220c07Ae
BURNSIDE, Rachel		19	F	Spinster	220c07Ae
CRAIG, Nancy		50	F	Spinster	220c07Ae
Mary	(D)	20	F	Spinster	220c07Ae
RAINEY, Hugh		20	M	Farmer	220c07Ae
Eliza		18	F	Spinster	220c07Ae
Martha		15	F	Spinster	220c07Ae
MAWHINNEY, Mary		20	F	Spinster	220c07Ae
LOWNSLEY, Robert		20	M	Farmer	220c07Ae
HEMPHILL, Margeret		09	F	Child	220c07Ae
James		12	M	Unknown	220c07Ae
John		07	M	Child	220c07Ae
EVANS, John		60	M	Farmer	220c07Ae
Andrew	(S)	20	M	Farmer	220c07Ae
Catherine	(W)	50	F	Wife	220c07Ae
Isabella		19	F	Wife	220c07Ae
MCILROY, Ellen		20	F	Spinster	220c07Ae
BLAIR, William		17	M	Clerk	220c07Ae
MCILVENE, John		16	M	Clerk	220c07Ae
DUNCAN, William		21	M	Clerk	220c07Ae
BLACK, Margaret		47	F	Spinster	220c07Ae
MCKEOWN, Samuel		24	M	Farmer	220c07Ae
Margaret	(W)	25	F	None	220c07Ae
KENT, Andrew		46	M	Weaver	220c07Ae
AGNEW, Samuel		50	M	Weaver	220c07Ae
Martha	(W)	48	F	None	220c07Ae
William	(S)	23	M	Weaver	220c07Ae
David	(S)	11	M	Weaver	220c07Ae
Sarah	(D)	17	F	Spinster	220c07Ae
Maria	(D)	13	F	Spinster	220c07Ae
Margaret	(D)	09	F	Child	220c07Ae
NICHOLL, Robert		30	M	Farmer	220c07Ae
William	(S)	05	M	Child	220c07Ae
Ellen	(W)	24	F	None	220c07Ae
Jane	(D)	03	F	Child	220c07Ae
Maria	(D)	01	F	Child	220c07Ae
BAKER, Margaret		18	F	Spinster	220c07Ae
LOUGHRAN, Samuel		00	M	Child	220c07Ae
THOMPSON, William		18	M	Nailer	220c07Ae
Jane		16	F	Spinster	220c07Ae
MOORE, Thomas		56	M	Farmer	220c07Ae
Mary	(W)	50	F	None	220c07Ae
Margaret	(D)	20	F	Spinster	220c07Ae
BEGGS, James		21	M	Spinner	220c07Ae
MCCOLLOUGH, Owen		25	M	Laborer	220c07Ae
MCPEAK, Hugh		21	M	Laborer	220c07Ae
BURNEY, John		22	M	Spinner	220c07Ae
Eliza		20	F	Spinster	220c07Ae

NAMES OF PASSENGERS		AGE	SEX	OCCUPATIONS	DATE PORT SHIP
MAGEE, Mary		28	F	Spinster	220c07Ae
James	(S)	02	M	Child	220c07Ae
Edward	(S)	01	M	Child	220c07Ae
READ, Margaret		20	F	Spinster	220c07Ae
MCCRACKEN, Mary		49	F	Weaver	220c07Ae
Margaret	(D)	22	F	Weaver	220c07Ae
MCQUESTON, Edward		16	M	Painter	220c07Ae
Agnes		20	F	Milliner	220c07Ae
Margaret		18	F	Milliner	220c07Ae
MCGUEGGAN, Eliza		25	F	Spinster	220c07Ae
STEELE, Anne		22	F	Spinster	220c07Ae
HOLMES, William		18	M	Painter	220c07Ae
WILSON, Mary		25	F	Spinster	220c07Ae
MAITLAND, John		19	M	Farmer	220c07Ae
BURNS, James		29	M	Farmer	220c07Ae
TRIMBLE, Eliza		20	F	Spinster	220c07Ae
Jane		19	F	Spinster	220c07Ae
BELL, Robert		30	M	Farmer	220c07Ae
KANE, Rachel		18	F	Spinster	220c07Ae
CORREY, Thomas		41	M	Laborer	220c07Ae
MCQUILLIAMS, Joseph		29	M	Laborer	220c07Ae
CREDY, Thomas		29	M	Laborer	220c07Ae
CONNER, James		20	M	Laborer	220c07Ae
BIRNEY, Sarah		22	F	Spinster	220c07Ae
AGNEW, Elizabeth		20	F	Spinster	220c07Ae
BRANAGH, James		30	M	Farmer	220c07Ae
Henry	(S)	06	M	Child	220c07Ae
James	(S)	04	M	Child	220c07Ae
Catherine	(W)	25	F	None	220c07Ae
Margaret	(D)	02	F	Child	220c07Ae
HYDE, John		35	M	Farmer	220c07Ae
NEVILLE, Elizabeth		28	F	Spinster	220c07Ae
FERGUSON, Agnes		24	F	Spinster	220c07Ae
CAVEN, Bella		30	F	Spinster	220c07Ae
PATTERSON, James		53	M	Farmer	220c07Ae
Jane	(W)	50	F	None	220c07Ae
Richard	(S)	12	M	Unknown	220c07Ae
Abigale	(D)	18	F	Unknown	220c07Ae
Anne	(D)	16	F	Unknown	220c07Ae
Elizabeth	(D)	10	F	Unknown	220c07Ae
Margaret	(D)	06	F	Child	220c07Ae
BROWN, Thomas		42	M	Weaver	220c07Ae
Eliza	(W)	37	F	None	220c07Ae
Robert	(S)	14	M	Unknown	220c07Ae
Thomas	(S)	05	M	Child	220c07Ae
Sarah	(D)	11	F	Unknown	220c07Ae
Mary	(D)	09	F	Child	220c07Ae
Margaret	(D)	07	F	Child	220c07Ae
Anne	(D)	03	F	Child	220c07Ae
MCDOWELL, Eliza		55	F	Wi	220c07Ae
CONNARS, Rose		30	F	Spinster	220c07Ae
Elizabeth		32	F	Spinster	220c07Ae
Mary		26	F	Spinster	220c07Ae
ANDERSON, William		25	M	Farmer	220c07Ae
Mary		27	F	Spinster	220c07Ae
Margaret		20	F	Spinster	220c07Ae
GELLESPIE, William		38	M	Farmer	220c07Ae
Rachel	(W)	38	F	None	220c07Ae
Benjamin	(S)	13	M	Unknown	220c07Ae
Ellen	(D)	09	F	Child	220c07Ae
Margaret	(D)	16	F	Unknown	220c07Ae
JONES, Robert		40	M	Farmer	220c07Ae
Eliza	(W)	40	F	None	220c07Ae
William		13	M	Unknown	220c07Ae
Sarah	(D)	06	F	Child	220c07Ae
Mary	(D)	02	F	Child	220c07Ae
HOUSTON, David		50	M	Farmer	220c07Ae
Jane		50	F	None	220c07Ae
Jane		16	F	Unknown	220c07Ae
Mary		12	F	Unknown	220c07Ae
HILL, Joseph		21	M	Farmer	220c07Ae
BELL, Alex		25	M	Farmer	220c07Ae
RICE, Fanny		25	F	Weaver	220c07Ae
Robert	(S)	07	M	Child	220c07Ae
Fanny	(D)	05	F	Child	220c07Ae
HOLMES, Stewart		00	M	Unknown	220c07Ae

ISAAC-WRIGHT 22 OCTOBER 1847

From Liverpool

NAMES OF PASSENGERS		AGE	SEX	OCCUPATIONS	DATE PORT SHIP
MARSHALL, Mary		20	F	Servant	220c02Qk
Honora		18	F	Servant	220c02Qk
CONDON, Joanna		13	F	Servant	220c02Qk
SMITH, Mary		50	F	Servant	220c02Qk
Anne		08	F	Child	220c02Qk
Michael		21	M	Servant	220c02Qk
Bridget		23	F	Servant	220c02Qk
Betty		22	F	Servant	220c02Qk
Catherine		16	F	Servant	220c02Qk
Mary		15	F	Servant	220c02Qk
MCGOVERN, Christy		27	M	Tailor	220c02Qk
BUTLER, Eliza		24	F	Servant	220c02Qk
FINNIGEN, John		24	M	Servant	220c02Qk
BYRNE, Anne		18	F	Servant	220c02Qk
DUGAN, John		56	M	Spinner	220c02Qk
William		14	M	Servant	220c02Qk
COFFEE, Michael		27	M	Paper Maker	220c02Qk
SULLIVAN, Con.		20	M	Servant	220c02Qk
REYNOLDS, Catherine		20	F	Servant	220c02Qk
DONOVAN, Dennis		21	M	Laborer	220c02Qk
SWEENY, Mathew		13	M	Laborer	220c02Qk
DALEY, Michael		40	M	Laborer	220c02Qk
John		09	M	Child	220c02Qk
CASE, Mary		24	F	Servant	220c02Qk
Ellen		03	F	Child	220c02Qk
REGAN, William		24	M	Laborer	220c02Qk
Mary		24	F	None	220c02Qk
Richard		04	M	Child	220c02Qk
Thomas		02	M	Child	220c02Qk
Bridget		01	F	Child	220c02Qk
Died-At-Sea					
HAYES, Alley		22	F	Servant	220c02Qk
BENSON, Mary		50	F	Servant	220c02Qk
SHEEN, Mary		13	F	Servant	220c02Qk
REILLY, Mary		27	F	Servant	220c02Qk
CUNIFF, Sarah		18	F	Servant	220c02Qk
NOLAN, John		23	M	Shoemaker	220c02Qk
CLIFFORD, Edward		50	M	Miner	220c02Qk
Catherine		40	F	None	220c02Qk
Thomas		20	M	Miner	220c02Qk
Catherine		13	F	Servant	220c02Qk
Joanna		10	F	Servant	220c02Qk
Edward		07	M	Child	220c02Qk
Martin		04	M	Child	220c02Qk
CASEY, Anne		19	F	Servant	220c02Qk
FLYNN, Bridget		20	F	Servant	220c02Qk
GAGEN, Charles		25	M	Surgeon	220c02Qk
Eliza		25	F	None	220c02Qk
Charles		06	M	Child	220c02Qk
William		05	M	Child	220c02Qk
Maria		04	F	Child	220c02Qk
Ellen		.06	F	Infant	220c02Qk
William		30	M	Tailor	220c02Qk
U	(W)	20	F	None	220c02Qk
Jane		.08	F	Infant	220c02Qk
NUGENT, Eliza		50	F	Lady	220c02Qk
FEATHERSTONE, Lucy		50	F	Lady	220c02Qk
MITTY, Charlotte		30	F	Lady	220c02Qk
Jaqueline		30	F	Lady	220c02Qk
HAINE, U		17	M	Molder	220c02Qk
TEENY, Thomas		38	M	Hatter	220c02Qk
COLLOGHEN, Mary		20	F	Servant	220c02Qk
HICKEY, John		22	M	Laborer	220c02Qk

NAMES OF PASSENGERS	AGE	SEX	OCCUPATIONS	DATE PORT SHIP
CREIGHTON, William	24	M	Clerk	220c02Qk
DOUGHERTY, Dan	46	M	Laborer	220c02Qk
BRYAN, James	20	M	Laborer	220c02Qk
BOYLE, Dan	21	M	Laborer	220c02Qk
Jane	18	F	Servant	220c02Qk
LINNEY, Anne	17	F	Servant	220c02Qk
GORMAN, Peter	23	M	Laborer	220c02Qk
OCALLAGHAN, William	40	M	Merchant	220c02Qk
CLARY, Michael	40	M	Laborer	220c02Qk
KILDOY, Dennis	30	M	Laborer	220c02Qk
MULLOY, Pat	20	M	Laborer	220c02Qk
MAHER, Bridget	24	F	Servant	220c02Qk
HAIN, Robert	24	M	Laborer	220c02Qk
Mary	20	F	Servant	220c02Qk
WALSH, Henry	18	M	Laborer	220c02Qk
WALL, Michael	55	M	Finisher	220c02Qk
Pat	20	M	Servant	220c02Qk
John	09	M	Child	220c02Qk
Anne	12	F	Servant	220c02Qk
Mary	05	F	Child	220c02Qk
Catherine	40	F	Servant	220c02Qk
KEENAN, Peter	24	M	Laborer	220c02Qk
Bridget	18	F	Servant	220c02Qk
MCCULEA, James	21	M	Laborer	220c02Qk
MARTIN, Jane	02	F	Child	220c02Qk
ELLIOT, M.B.	27	M	Engineer	220c02Qk
LONGDON, William	30	M	Laborer	220c02Qk
U (W)	30	F	None	220c02Qk
U	.05	F	Infant	220c02Qk
James	35	M	Laborer	220c02Qk
LEE, Rosamend	26	F	Servant	220c02Qk
James	03	M	Child	220c02Qk
Catherine	01	F	Child	220c02Qk
Died-At-Sea				
Barrett	.04	M	Infant	220c02Qk
BURNS, James	22	M	Laborer	220c02Qk
LYNCH, William	36	M	Laborer	220c02Qk
Mary	28	F	Servant	220c02Qk
Pat	04	M	Child	220c02Qk
Mary	.10	F	Infant	220c02Qk
SWAN, Mary	38	F	Servant	220c02Qk
John	22	M	Engineer	220c02Qk
Alexander	20	M	Joiner	220c02Qk
Mary-Jane	17	F	Servant	220c02Qk
James	11	M	Servant	220c02Qk
Margaret	09	F	Child	220c02Qk
MCGINLY, Thomas	44	M	Merchant	220c02Qk
John	16	M	Merchant	220c02Qk
CUMMINGS, Michael	25	M	Blacksmith	220c02Qk
Nancy	20	F	Servant	220c02Qk
KANE, Catherine-L.	20	F	Servant	220c02Qk
HOWLAND, Betty	20	F	Servant	220c02Qk
WINDHAM, Susan	25	F	Servant	220c02Qk
Eliza	30	F	Servant	220c02Qk
CONLEY, Mary	23	F	Servant	220c02Qk
MCCARTLY, Anne	23	F	Servant	220c02Qk
LEO, John	26	M	Laborer	220c02Qk
MCCORMICK, Patrick	21	M	Laborer	220c02Qk
MALONE, Edward	47	M	Laborer	220c02Qk
BROWN, Catherine	22	F	Servant	220c02Qk
BOYLE, Jane	19	F	Servant	220c02Qk
DOUGHERTY, James	25	M	Laborer	220c02Qk
Edward	25	M	Laborer	220c02Qk
John	20	M	Laborer	220c02Qk
Catherine	60	F	Housekeeper	220c02Qk
HAGERTY, James	26	M	Laborer	220c02Qk
VANCE, Bridget	27	F	Servant	220c02Qk
AKEN, Marianne	12	F	Servant	220c02Qk
WOODS, John	18	M	Tailor	220c02Qk
MCGEAGAN, Pat	18	M	Laborer	220c02Qk
LOUGH, John	22	M	Laborer	220c02Qk
DONELLY, Michael	21	M	Laborer	220c02Qk
FARLEY, Thomas	16	M	Laborer	220c02Qk
MIEHAN, Michael	30	M	Laborer	220c02Qk
Joanna	25	F	Servant	220c02Qk

NAMES OF PASSENGERS	AGE	SEX	OCCUPATIONS	DATE PORT SHIP
BOLAN, Ellen	20	F	Servant	220c02Qk
SCOTT, Catherine	20	F	Servant	220c02Qk
TRACY, Sarah	20	F	Servant	220c02Qk
SCULLY, Anne	18	F	Servant	220c02Qk
SHARKY, Ellen	20	F	Servant	220c02Qk
DOWLING, Anne	30	F	Servant	220c02Qk
HALL, Hugh	26	M	Laborer	220c02Qk
Mary	24	F	Servant	220c02Qk
GALLAGHER, Pat	26	M	Laborer	220c02Qk
REID, Edward	14	M	Laborer	220c02Qk
Jane	40	F	Servant	220c02Qk
FANNEGAN, Pat	30	M	Laborer	220c02Qk
Betsy	20	F	Servant	220c02Qk
LHANAHAN, Bridget	44	F	Servant	220c02Qk
CLARK, Anne	30	F	Servant	220c02Qk
BYRON, Thomas	20	M	Laborer	220c02Qk
CLARKE, Stephen	20	M	Laborer	220c02Qk
KEOGH, Thomas	40	M	Laborer	220c02Qk
Catherine	40	F	Housewife	220c02Qk
Ellen	20	F	Servant	220c02Qk
SCANLON, Ellen	30	F	Servant	220c02Qk
John	11	M	Servant	220c02Qk
Ellen	10	F	Servant	220c02Qk
James	08	M	Child	220c02Qk
Edward	06	M	Child	220c02Qk
Rose-Anne	01	F	Child	220c02Qk
LYNCH, Mary	13	F	Servant	220c02Qk
HOWARD, James	37	M	Laborer	220c02Qk
HUGHES, Pat	26	M	Laborer	220c02Qk
MCCAROLL, Anne	30	F	Servant	220c02Qk
COSTELLO, Mathew	20	M	Wool Comber	220c02Qk
FLYNN, John	15	M	Laborer	220c02Qk
MURPHY, Nelly	25	F	Servant	220c02Qk
MAHONY, Thomas	30	M	Wool Comber	220c02Qk
BAKER, James	30	M	Laborer	220c02Qk
MCCARTHY, Mary	30	F	Servant	220c02Qk
Bridget	03	F	Child	220c02Qk
John	.11	M	Infant	220c02Qk
DOUGEAN, Eliza	30	F	Servant	220c02Qk
LYNCH, Mary	18	F	Servant	220c02Qk
GALVIN, Anne	20	F	Servant	220c02Qk
FITZPATRICK, William	24	M	Laborer	220c02Qk
PRESTON, Sarah	18	F	Servant	220c02Qk
MURRAY, John	50	M	Carpenter	220c02Qk
FITZPATRICK, Betty	18	F	Servant	220c02Qk
WOODS, Bridget	20	F	Servant	220c02Qk
FEEHAN, Eliza	20	F	Servant	220c02Qk
Anne	18	F	Servant	220c02Qk
ROACHE, Alice	40	F	Housekeeper	220c02Qk
MCMILLAN, U-Mrs.	25	F	Servant	220c02Qk
Sophia	02	F	Child	220c02Qk
KIRKLAND, Jane	25	F	Servant	220c02Qk
LAW, Anne	20	F	Servant	220c02Qk
Anne	21	F	Servant	220c02Qk
ONEALE, Tim	40	M	Laborer	220c02Qk
MULLIGAN, Anne	17	F	Servant	220c02Qk
MULLER, Catherine	18	F	Servant	220c02Qk
FINNIGAN, Luke	20	M	Servant	220c02Qk
CARNIFF, Mike	25	M	Laborer	220c02Qk
STEELE, Mike	15	M	Laborer	220c02Qk
LEE, Bernard	25	M	Laborer	220c02Qk
DOUGHERTY, Henry	30	M	Laborer	220c02Qk
NOLAN, Catherine	48	F	Servant	220c02Qk
NOLANS, Catherine	13	F	Servant	220c02Qk
WICKHAM, Anne	20	F	Servant	220c02Qk
ELLWOOD, John	25	M	Tailor	220c02Qk
CARR, Margarat	27	F	Servant	220c02Qk
DOUGHEY, Thomas	30	M	Laborer	220c02Qk
Catherine	30	F	Housewife	220c02Qk
CORCORAN, Hugh	27	M	Laborer	220c02Qk
DUNN, Martin	20	M	Laborer	220c02Qk
MOONEY, John	25	M	Laborer	220c02Qk
BARCHARD, Edward	20	M	Laborer	220c02Qk
CULLEY, Catherine	18	F	Servant	220c02Qk
MAHEN, Bridget	18	F	Servant	220c02Qk

NAMES OF PASSENGERS	AGE	SEX	OCCUPATIONS	DATE PORT SHIP
BURNS, Charles	18	M	Servant	220c02Qk
NOLAN, James	15	M	Servant	220c02Qk
SULLIVAN, Biddy	20	F	Servant	220c02Qk
HOY, Catherine	20	F	Servant	220c02Qk

KATE-HUNTER 22 OCTOBER 1847

From Liverpool

NAMES OF PASSENGERS	AGE	SEX	OCCUPATIONS	DATE PORT SHIP
FITZGIBBEN, Patrick	18	M	Shoemaker	220c02Ql
Catherine	16	F	Servant	220c02Ql
John	14	M	Servant	220c02Ql
Mary	12	F	Servant	220c02Ql
James	10	M	Servant	220c02Ql
Ellen	08	F	Child	220c02Ql
Margt.	.02	F	Infant	220c02Ql
Mick	04	M	Child	220c02Ql
MURPHY, Mary	20	F	Seamstress	220c02Ql
DUNN, John	20	M	Carpenter	220c02Ql
Mary	21	F	Tailor	220c02Ql
SHIELDS, Kitty	21	F	Seamstress	220c02Ql
KERNY, Edward	18	M	Tailor	220c02Ql
MORRONY, Michl.	19	M	Tailor	220c02Ql
MCCAME, Peter	30	M	Miller	220c02Ql
HINES, Peter	30	M	Miller	220c02Ql
DALY, Thomas	25	M	Miller	220c02Ql
MONY, Mary	18	F	Vest Maker	220c02Ql
Catherine	20	F	Vest Maker	220c02Ql
FITZSIMONS, Mary	21	F	Servant	220c02Ql
POLAND, Betsey	25	F	Servant	220c02Ql
FARRELL, Thomas	40	M	Servant	220c02Ql
U (W)	30	F	None	220c02Ql
U	.00	U	Infant	220c02Ql
Pat	10	M	Servant	220c02Ql
Herbert	12	M	Servant	220c02Ql
Bridget	07	F	Child	220c02Ql
James	03	M	Child	220c02Ql
KEARNAN, Mary	12	F	Servant	220c02Ql
John	10	M	Servant	220c02Ql
Peter	06	M	Child	220c02Ql
MCCORMICK, Bridget	20	F	Servant	220c02Ql
REDDAN, Maurice	40	M	Miller	220c02Ql
JOHNSON, James	06	M	Child	220c02Ql
Pat	07	M	Child	220c02Ql
BURKE, Pat	27	M	Bootmaker	220c02Ql
DELAHANTY, Michl.	18	M	Servant	220c02Ql
HARDY, Pat	27	M	Servant	220c02Ql
SHERIDAN, Peter	27	M	Servant	220c02Ql
U (W)	30	F	Servant	220c02Ql
NEILL, James	25	M	Servant	220c02Ql
WALSH, Marry	30	F	Seamstress	220c02Ql
BREDMORE, U-Mrs.	30	F	Vest Maker	220c02Ql
Sarah	06	F	Child	220c02Ql
CRERY, Laurence	34	M	Miller	220c02Ql
U (W)	30	F	Servant	220c02Ql
U	.00	U	Infant	220c02Ql
THOMPSON, John	24	M	Tailor	220c02Ql
MCCAMA, Rose	40	F	Lad	220c02Ql
OBRIEN, Julia	44	F	Lad	220c02Ql
SULLIVAN, Johanna	30	F	Lad	220c02Ql
FENNELL, Onny	40	M	Bootmaker	220c02Ql
Marey	36	F	Servant	220c02Ql
Eliza	30	F	Servant	220c02Ql
John	04	M	Child	220c02Ql
Sarah	07	F	Child	220c02Ql
BURKE, James	21	M	Groom	220c02Ql
MURPHY, Shady	22	M	Groom	220c02Ql
IRWIN, William	18	M	Tailor	220c02Ql
John	11	M	Unknown	220c02Ql

NAMES OF PASSENGERS	AGE	SEX	OCCUPATIONS	DATE PORT SHIP
TWOHEY, Thomas	18	M	Servant	220c02Ql
JOURDAN, Michl.	18	M	Servant	220c02Ql
GLEESON, John	30	M	Servant	220c02Ql
LINDSKEY, John	35	M	Servant	220c02Ql
ROCK, Pat	30	M	Servant	220c02Ql
GORRY, James	35	M	Servant	220c02Ql
FARRELLY, James	20	M	Servant	220c02Ql
Pat	14	M	Servant	220c02Ql
LISK, Robert	24	M	Servant	220c02Ql
CRANAGE, John	45	M	Servant	220c02Ql
LOVELL, Thos.	20	M	Servant	220c02Ql
GUTRIDGE, Geo.	20	M	Servant	220c02Ql
PALMER, Bridget	50	F	Servant	220c02Ql
HEALY, Sarah	45	F	Servant	220c02Ql
WALL, Margt.	30	F	Servant	220c02Ql
OLOUGHLIN, Michl.	50	M	Car Driver	220c02Ql
WALLACE, Valentine	24	M	Tailor	220c02Ql
U (W)	20	F	None	220c02Ql
U	.00	U	Infant	220c02Ql
COWAN, Ellen	45	F	Servant	220c02Ql
Mathew	10	M	Servant	020c02Ql
KELMARTIN, Mary	19	F	Servant	220c02Ql
MCGOVERN, Catherine	19	F	Servant	220c02Ql
CAVENY, Mary	25	F	Servant	220c02Ql
CANEMMY, Pat	09	M	Child	220c02Ql
PRIOR, Benard	26	M	Servant	220c02Ql
Mary	24	F	Servant	220c02Ql
John	04	M	Child	220c02Ql
Bridget	40	F	Servant	220c02Ql
WHITE, U-Mrs.	19	F	Milliner	220c02Ql
Mary-Jane	20	F	Milliner	220c02Ql
FLYNN, Mary-Jane	20	F	Tailor	220c02Ql
MATHEWS, Mary	20	F	Tailor	220c02Ql
GAYNOR, Geo.	19	M	Laborer	220c02Ql
CORBETT, Thos.	34	M	Laborer	220c02Ql
MURPHY, John	15	M	Laborer	220c02Ql
HEFFERMAN, Wm.	46	M	Laborer	220c02Ql
U (W)	40	F	None	220c02Ql
CALLAGHAN, Wm.	21	M	Laborer	220c02Ql
Mary	14	F	Laborer	220c02Ql
Eliza	17	F	Laborer	220c02Ql
Margt.	20	F	Laborer	220c02Ql
LARY, James	30	M	Laborer	220c02Ql
Bridget	02	F	Child	220c02Ql
Mary	24	F	Laborer	220c02Ql
Mary	04	F	Child	220c02Ql
Wm.	08	M	Child	220c02Ql
David	10	M	Laborer	220c02Ql
MCDALLEFF, Margt.	10	F	Seamstress	220c02Ql
CUNNINGHAM, Cormick	30	M	Bootmaker	220c02Ql
Fanny	26	F	Lad	220c02Ql
MURRAY, Michl.	12	M	Laborer	220c02Ql
Dan	06	M	Child	220c02Ql
Pat	08	M	Child	220c02Ql
HEFFERMAN, Denis	16	M	Laborer	220c02Ql
John	11	M	Laborer	220c02Ql
Wm.	14	M	Laborer	220c02Ql
Margt.	17	F	Servant	220c02Ql
Johanna	01	F	Child	220c02Ql
Ellen	07	F	Child	220c02Ql
DOOLEY, Thomas	40	M	Laborer	220c02Ql
U (W)	30	F	None	220c02Ql
Emma	.00	F	Infant	220c02Ql
MCGLYNN, John	31	M	Tailor	220c02Ql
U (W)	31	F	None	220c02Ql
U	.00	U	Infant	220c02Ql
Bridget	08	F	Child	220c02Ql
MONE, Bridget	26	F	Servant	220c02Ql
U	.00	U	Infant	220c02Ql
QUEARY, Denis	30	M	Laborer	220c02Ql
WALSH, Wm.	30	M	Laborer	220c02Ql
FLEMMING, Anne	40	F	Servant	220c02Ql
MCCORMICK, John	20	M	Farmer	220c02Ql
DELANY, Pat	22	M	Farmer	220c02Ql
GILMORE, Mary	18	F	Farmer	220c02Ql

NAMES OF PASSENGERS	AGE	SEX	OCCUPATIONS	DATE PORT SHIP
DOOLEY, Mary	19	F	Farmer	220c02QI
HENRY, Owen	35	M	Servant	220c02QI
Thomas	20	M	Servant	220c02QI
Michl.	18	M	Servant	220c02QI
MCGEEN, Thos.	30	M	Servant	220c02QI
GIBLIN, Martin	20	M	Servant	220c02QI
SPELMAN, James	25	M	Laborer	220c02QI
FLEMMING, Johanna	20	F	Servant	220c02QI
Mary	40	F	Servant	220c02QI
Anty	40	F	Servant	220c02QI
QUARY, Ellen	22	F	Servant	220c02QI
GLASS, Mary	20	F	Servant	220c02QI
BYRNE, U-Mrs.	30	F	Servant	220c02QI
U	.00	U	Infant	220c02QI
WALLACE, John	40	M	Laborer	220c02QI
SULLIVAN, Nelly	30	F	Servant	220c02QI
Pat	44	M	Laborer	220c02QI
COFFY, Lucy	20	F	Servant	220c02QI
DUFFY, Margt.	20	F	Servant	220c02QI
MCGARNEY, Anne	20	F	Servant	220c02QI
SPEARS, John	20	M	Laborer	220c02QI
KELLY, Chas.	40	M	Laborer	220c02QI
LEONARD, Mark	26	M	Laborer	220c02QI
HINDS, Pat	20	M	Laborer	220c02QI
BERLIN, Barney	21	M	Laborer	220c02QI
John	20	M	Laborer	220c02QI
FRIMEGAN, James	20	M	Laborer	220c02QI
CONNOR, Dan	30	M	Laborer	220c02QI
GARVEY, Wm.	20	M	Laborer	220c02QI
LENAHAN, James	20	M	Laborer	220c02QI
DUFFY, Pat	40	M	Laborer	220c02QI
PIGHE, Richard	20	M	Laborer	220c02QI
MCFARLAND, James	56	M	Laborer	220c02QI
James	12	M	Laborer	220c02QI
Andrew	13	M	Laborer	220c02QI
THREFALL, Thomas	30	M	Laborer	220c02QI
WHITTOM, Luke	36	M	Laborer	220c02QI
WILLIAMSON, Wm.	30	M	Laborer	220c02QI
RIELY, James	30	M	Farmer	220c02QI
BROWN, Sarah	24	F	Lad	220c02QI
KELLY, John	22	M	Laborer	220c02QI
Charles	18	M	Laborer	220c02QI
BROSNAN, Michl.	25	M	Laborer	220c02QI
FITZGERALD, Pat	30	M	Laborer	220c02QI
DOYLE, Jeremiah	20	M	Laborer	220c02QI
Julia	25	F	Servant	220c02QI
REILY, Mary	18	F	Servant	220c02QI
CONNOR, Ellen	20	F	Servant	220c02QI
PLATT, Mary	20	F	Seamstress	220c02QI
Anna	28	F	Seamstress	220c02QI
WALLA, Betty	27	F	Servant	220c02QI
Sarah	03	F	Child	220c02QI
HITCHMOUGH, Wm.	15	M	Laborer	220c02QI
BOYDE, Wm.	36	M	Laborer	220c02QI
MCCOY, Hugh	15	M	Laborer	220c02QI
Margt.	40	F	Laborer	220c02QI
Thomas	19	M	Laborer	220c02QI
Catherine	28	F	Laborer	220c02QI
Wm.	12	M	Laborer	220c02QI
DUCKETT, Wm.	30	M	Laborer	220c02QI
FEENY, Margt.	22	F	Servant	220c02QI
ELLIS, Ellis	26	M	Laborer	220c02QI
U (W)	27	F	Servant	220c02QI
U	.00	U	Infant	220c02QI
JONES, Griffith	30	M	Servant	220c02QI
U (W)	26	F	Laborer	220c02QI
SCOTT, Winsworth	20	M	Laborer	220c02QI
Margt.	17	F	Laborer	220c02QI
MURRAY, U	40	M	Laborer	220c02QI
Thos.	10	M	Laborer	220c02QI
DUFFY, Michl.	26	M	Laborer	220c02QI
Catherine	30	F	Laborer	220c02QI
HOUSE, Stephen	25	M	Laborer	220c02QI
Henry	19	M	Unknown	220c02QI

ROSCIUS 22 OCTOBER 1847

From Liverpool

NAMES OF PASSENGERS	AGE	SEX	OCCUPATIONS	DATE PORT SHIP
LOUNDS, William	20	M	Farmer	220c02Bf
JAMESON, Thos.	20	M	Laborer	220c02Bf
CHADWICK, James	20	M	Laborer	220c02Bf
MALONE, Henry	25	M	Laborer	220c02Bf
CARTY, Thos.	35	M	Laborer	220c02Bf
Elizabeth	35	F	Laborer	220c02Bf
BOURKS, Pat	20	M	Laborer	220c02Bf
BROWN, James	30	M	Laborer	220c02Bf
MITCHELL, Geo.	56	M	Farmer	220c02Bf
MCCULLY, Hugh	44	M	Farmer	220c02Bf
MCGARIGH, Mary	30	F	Unknown	220c02Bf
MARRIOTT, John	26	M	Laborer	220c02Bf
U (W)	20	F	None	220c02Bf
ASPINALL, Antoy	30	M	Laborer	220c02Bf
DEVERTE, Andw.	13	M	Laborer	220c02Bf
Peter	20	M	Laborer	220c02Bf
BROOKS, Joseph	33	M	Farmer	220c02Bf
Mary	28	F	Farmer	220c02Bf
KELLY, Richard	44	M	Farmer	220c02Bf
COPE, Fredk.	37	M	Farmer	220c02Bf
HILL, John	20	M	Laborer	220c02Bf
MCGOW, Judy	25	F	Laborer	220c02Bf
Ellen	21	F	Laborer	220c02Bf
Cathe.	20	F	Laborer	220c02Bf
Ann	20	F	Laborer	220c02Bf
SMITH, Mary	20	F	Laborer	220c02Bf
HUNTER, Hugh	40	M	Farmer	220c02Bf
Martha	38	F	None	220c02Bf
Hugh	16	M	Farmer	220c02Bf
Joseph	14	M	Farmer	220c02Bf
Martha	12	F	Farmer	220c02Bf
Francis	08	M	Child	220c02Bf
FLINN, Thos.	20	M	Laborer	220c02Bf
Elizth.	14	F	Laborer	220c02Bf
SPENCER, James	24	M	Laborer	220c02Bf
U (W)	21	F	None	220c02Bf
James	04	M	Child	220c02Bf
Francis	02	M	Child	220c02Bf
Micheal	.00	M	Infant	220c02Bf
KERR, Joseph	20	M	Laborer	220c02Bf
MORIARTY, Dennis	26	M	Laborer	220c02Bf
Eugene	20	M	Laborer	220c02Bf
Ellen	23	F	Laborer	220c02Bf
MCCUFFY, Peter	25	M	Laborer	220c02Bf
MADDOCK, Mary	50	F	Laborer	220c02Bf
Mary	28	F	Laborer	220c02Bf
Henry	20	M	Laborer	220c02Bf
Bety	18	F	Laborer	220c02Bf
STEEL, Sarah	30	F	Laborer	220c02Bf
KNIGHT, Elias	50	M	Farmer	220c02Bf
U (W)	48	F	None	220c02Bf
Amelia	30	F	Farmer	220c02Bf
George	20	M	Laborer	220c02Bf
HAMILTON, Mary	27	F	Laborer	220c02Bf
Wm.	07	M	Child	220c02Bf
Eliza	.00	F	Infant	220c02Bf
BURNS, Pat	18	M	Laborer	220c02Bf
Ann	20	F	Laborer	220c02Bf
FINLAY, Henreta	14	F	Laborer	220c02Bf
ODONNELL, Mary-Jane	13	F	Laborer	220c02Bf
FARRAL, James	40	M	Farmer	220c02Bf
Mary	40	F	None	220c02Bf
John	11	M	Farmer	220c02Bf
James	09	M	Child	220c02Bf
Ann	07	F	Child	220c02Bf

NAMES OF PASSENGERS	AGE	SEX	OCCUPATIONS	DATE PORT SHIP
DONNELLY, Mary-Ann	26	F	Farmer	220c02Bf
MCDAID, Domnick	24	M	Farmer	220c02Bf
Sarah	26	F	None	220c02Bf
John	03	M	Child	220c02Bf
FULLERTON, Unity	60	M	Farmer	220c02Bf
FARHAN, Ann	12	F	Farmer	220c02Bf
MCBRIDE, Martha	52	F	Farmer	220c02Bf
MCNIEL, Mary	27	F	Farmer	220c02Bf
Robt.	03	M	Child	220c02Bf
Margret	.00	F	Infant	220c02Bf
FARRALL, John	21	M	Laborer	220c02Bf
BONSON, Sarah	23	F	Laborer	220c02Bf
Lucy	05	F	Child	220c02Bf
Emma	04	F	Child	220c02Bf
Mary-Ann	02	F	Child	220c02Bf
WILLIAMS, Robt.	30	M	Laborer	220c02Bf
Ann	30	F	Laborer	220c02Bf
Ann	07	F	Child	220c02Bf
Emma	05	F	Child	220c02Bf
Jane	03	F	Child	220c02Bf
Margret	.00	F	Infant	220c02Bf
HART, Rowland	28	M	Laborer	220c02Bf
FALLEN, Lawrence	28	M	Laborer	220c02Bf
STEFFEN, Ed.	28	M	Laborer	220c02Bf
CROSS, Hugh	50	M	Farmer	220c02Bf
Cathe.	23	F	Farmer	220c02Bf
BOTTOMLEY, Ed.	28	M	Laborer	220c02Bf
CAREY, Joseph	27	M	Laborer	220c02Bf
Mary	25	F	Laborer	220c02Bf
DONNELLY, Timy.	60	M	Farmer	220c02Bf
BAUKER, Eliza	20	F	Farmer	220c02Bf
MAGUINESS, Wm.	30	M	Laborer	220c02Bf
Mary	20	F	Laborer	220c02Bf
BARKER, Pat	37	M	Laborer	220c02Bf
MCTEAGUE, James	20	M	Laborer	220c02Bf
Mary	25	F	Laborer	220c02Bf
MCKEOWN, Terance	20	M	Laborer	220c02Bf
Pat	.00	M	Infant	220c02Bf
WATLEY, Duke	27	M	Laborer	220c02Bf
Betty	24	F	Laborer	220c02Bf
WARF, Wm.	27	M	Farmer	220c02Bf
Martha	30	F	Farmer	220c02Bf
FLINTON, Mary-Ann	20	F	Farmer	220c02Bf
WILKINSON, Joseph	50	M	Farmer	220c02Bf
Maria	35	F	Farmer	220c02Bf
WALES, Hugh	39	M	Farmer	220c02Bf
Mary	35	F	None	220c02Bf
Sarah	15	F	Farmer	220c02Bf
Julia	13	F	Farmer	220c02Bf
Margret	11	F	Farmer	220c02Bf
Alexander	09	M	Child	220c02Bf
Susan	.00	F	Infant	220c02Bf
Andrew	03	M	Child	220c02Bf
MCASH, Bridget	25	F	Farmer	220c02Bf
RILY, John	30	M	Farmer	220c02Bf
BRADY, Ann	25	F	Farmer	220c02Bf
Joseph	.00	M	Infant	220c02Bf
MAGUINESS, Thos.	45	M	Farmer	220c02Bf
ANDERSON, Robt.	20	M	Farmer	220c02Bf
MAHER, James	12	M	Farmer	220c02Bf
CLARKE, Dennis	20	M	Farmer	220c02Bf
RYAN, Martin	25	M	Farmer	220c02Bf
RIGLY, Edwd.	35	M	Farmer	220c02Bf
COOPER, Wright	36	M	Farmer	220c02Bf
BARRY, Thos.	26	M	Farmer	220c02Bf
Alice	28	F	Farmer	220c02Bf
John	06	M	Child	220c02Bf
Richd.	04	M	Child	220c02Bf
Mary	02	F	Child	220c02Bf
BROFFEN, Ann	20	F	Farmer	220c02Bf
PURCELL, Pat	26	F	Farmer	220c02Bf
Cathe.	25	F	Farmer	220c02Bf
Mary	20	F	Farmer	220c02Bf
Cathe.	12	F	Farmer	220c02Bf
FARRAL, James	24	M	Laborer	220c02Bf
DUNN, Pat	40	M	Laborer	220c02Bf
Ally	36	F	Laborer	220c02Bf
Pat	21	M	Laborer	220c02Bf
Micheal	15	M	Laborer	220c02Bf
James	10	M	Laborer	220c02Bf
Margret	08	F	Child	220c02Bf
FLINN, Edward	30	M	Laborer	220c02Bf
Margret	10	F	Laborer	220c02Bf
HAYES, Edward	20	M	Laborer	220c02Bf
Biddy	13	F	Laborer	220c02Bf
FLAGHETY, Richd.	25	M	Laborer	220c02Bf
MCDERMOTT, Bridget	20	F	Laborer	220c02Bf
FLANIGAN, Maria	20	F	Laborer	220c02Bf
DALY, James	45	M	Laborer	220c02Bf
Wm.	13	M	Laborer	220c02Bf
Anne	11	F	Laborer	220c02Bf
Bridget	09	F	Child	220c02Bf
Mathew	07	M	Child	220c02Bf
Joseph	05	M	Child	220c02Bf
David	02	M	Child	220c02Bf
FARRALL, James	43	M	Laborer	220c02Bf
Mary	28	F	Laborer	220c02Bf
MONAHAN, James	17	M	Laborer	220c02Bf
FARRAL, John	03	M	Child	220c02Bf
Jas.	.00	M	Infant	220c02Bf
JACKS, Jack	35	M	Laborer	220c02Bf
GRAY, Sarah	34	F	Laborer	220c02Bf
Wm.	11	M	Laborer	220c02Bf
Thos.	07	M	Child	220c02Bf
Henry	05	M	Child	220c02Bf
Hamilton	02	M	Child	220c02Bf
Mary-Ann	02	F	Child	220c02Bf
RICHIE, John	50	M	Laborer	220c02Bf
Rachel	35	F	Laborer	220c02Bf
Elizabeth	24	F	Laborer	220c02Bf
James	17	M	Laborer	220c02Bf
George	13	M	Laborer	220c02Bf
Mary-Ann	11	F	Laborer	220c02Bf
Sarah	09	F	Child	220c02Bf
James	06	M	Child	220c02Bf
Wm.	03	M	Child	220c02Bf
James	46	M	Laborer	220c02Bf
Jane	40	F	Laborer	220c02Bf
Eliza	03	F	Child	220c02Bf
Hannah	11	F	Laborer	220c02Bf
George	09	M	Child	220c02Bf
David	07	M	Child	220c02Bf
Mary	04	F	Child	220c02Bf
CRAWFORD, Jessie	19	F	Laborer	220c02Bf
MILLER, Rebecc	34	F	Laborer	220c02Bf
Henry	08	M	Child	220c02Bf
COGHLAN, Jerry	20	M	Laborer	220c02Bf
Bridget	22	F	Laborer	220c02Bf
HARRINGTON, Honora	30	F	Laborer	220c02Bf
GALVINE, Micheal	30	M	Laborer	220c02Bf
FINLY, George	25	M	Laborer	220c02Bf
RYAN, John	40	M	Laborer	220c02Bf
Mary	18	F	Laborer	220c02Bf
Cathe.	09	F	Child	220c02Bf
CARROLL, John	25	M	Laborer	220c02Bf
MURPHY, Jerry	30	M	Laborer	220c02Bf
Wm.	30	M	Laborer	220c02Bf
James	18	M	Laborer	220c02Bf
CONNER, Ellen	18	F	Laborer	220c02Bf
REYNOLDS, James	28	M	Laborer	220c02Bf
Bridget	60	F	Laborer	220c02Bf
Thos.	40	M	Laborer	220c02Bf
John	24	M	Laborer	220c02Bf
Joseph	22	M	Laborer	220c02Bf
Cathe.	02	F	Child	220c02Bf
Bridget	13	F	Laborer	220c02Bf
STEWART, Pat	17	M	Laborer	220c02Bf
Cathe.	25	F	Laborer	220c02Bf
MCDERMOTT, Hu	50	M	Laborer	220c02Bf
Ellen	48	F	Laborer	220c02Bf

NAMES OF PASSENGERS	AGE	SEX	OCCUPATIONS	DATE PORT SHIP
MCDERMOTT, Bernard	28	M	Laborer	220c02Bf
James	26	M	Laborer	220c02Bf
John	24	M	Laborer	220c02Bf
William	18	M	Laborer	220c02Bf
Hugh	12	M	Laborer	220c02Bf
Ann	25	F	Laborer	220c02Bf
Susan	22	F	Laborer	220c02Bf
Bessy	20	F	Laborer	220c02Bf
Rosean	13	F	Laborer	220c02Bf
Ellen	12	F	Laborer	220c02Bf
STEWART, James	63	M	Laborer	220c02Bf
Ellen	60	F	None	220c02Bf
George	20	M	Laborer	220c02Bf
Ellen	18	F	Laborer	220c02Bf
GRAHAM, Pat	28	M	Laborer	220c02Bf
John	24	M	Laborer	220c02Bf
Margret	26	F	Laborer	220c02Bf
CONNOR, Tary	50	M	Laborer	220c02Bf
Mary	35	F	Laborer	220c02Bf
Mary	11	F	Laborer	220c02Bf
Thos.	20	M	Laborer	220c02Bf
COLGAN, Pat	36	M	Laborer	220c02Bf
Mary	40	F	None	220c02Bf
Pat	19	M	Laborer	220c02Bf
Micheal	08	M	Child	220c02Bf
Margret	16	F	Laborer	220c02Bf
Bridget	12	F	Laborer	220c02Bf
Ann	07	F	Child	220c02Bf
MULLEN, Cathe.	20	F	Laborer	220c02Bf
NEARY, Pat	40	M	Laborer	220c02Bf
Mary	28	F	None	220c02Bf
Bridget	.00	F	Infant	220c02Bf
CAROLIN, John	30	M	Laborer	220c02Bf
Honora	40	F	None	220c02Bf
Bridget	13	F	Laborer	220c02Bf
Ellen	09	F	Child	220c02Bf
Mary	07	F	Child	220c02Bf
DONLAN, Martin	32	M	Laborer	220c02Bf
PADEN, Richard	32	M	Laborer	220c02Bf
Mary	30	F	None	220c02Bf
William	12	M	Laborer	220c02Bf
James	09	M	Child	220c02Bf
Bill	10	M	Laborer	220c02Bf
Maria	06	F	Child	220c02Bf
MULROONY, Pat	60	M	Laborer	220c02Bf
U-Mrs.	25	F	None	220c02Bf
Ellen	13	F	Laborer	220c02Bf
Edward	11	M	Laborer	220c02Bf
Pat	09	M	Child	220c02Bf
John	06	M	Child	220c02Bf
Rose-Ann	02	F	Child	220c02Bf
MCBRIAN, Mary	30	F	Laborer	220c02Bf
MAXWILL, John	20	M	Laborer	220c02Bf
TAYLOR, U-Mrs.	40	F	Laborer	220c02Bf
U	23	F	Laborer	220c02Bf
U	20	F	Laborer	220c02Bf
U	18	F	Laborer	220c02Bf
U	12	F	Laborer	220c02Bf
LEE, John	34	M	Laborer	220c02Bf
CONNOR, Bernard	30	M	Laborer	220c02Bf
CANAGHER, Pat	35	M	Laborer	220c02Bf
DONNELLY, Pat	18	M	Laborer	220c02Bf
BOOKES, Wm.	25	M	Laborer	220c02Bf
BLACKMAN, Richd.	30	M	Laborer	220c02Bf
IRWIN, Francis	22	M	Laborer	220c02Bf
HENDERSON, Grace	20	F	Laborer	220c02Bf
OBRIEN, Thos.	50	M	Laborer	220c02Bf
Margret	44	F	None	220c02Bf
Margret	16	F	Laborer	220c02Bf
Anne	18	F	Laborer	220c02Bf
MCCAFFRY, Ann	35	F	Laborer	220c02Bf
COLEMAN, Wm.	35	M	Laborer	220c02Bf
John	08	M	Child	220c02Bf
MCDONALD, U-Mrs.	40	F	Laborer	220c02Bf
Ellen	14	F	Laborer	220c02Bf

NAMES OF PASSENGERS	AGE	SEX	OCCUPATIONS	DATE PORT SHIP
MCDONALD, Kate	12	F	Laborer	220c02Bf
Maria	08	F	Child	220c02Bf
CALLAGHER, Ellen	00	F	Laborer	220c02Bf
BRIDE, John	00	M	Laborer	220c02Bf
Biddy	00	F	Laborer	220c02Bf
DOWNES, Andrew	00	M	Laborer	220c02Bf
MORGAN, John	20	M	Laborer	220c02Bf
HUGHES, Jane	20	F	Laborer	220c02Bf
KNOWLES, Cathne.	25	F	Laborer	220c02Bf
Mary	20	F	Laborer	220c02Bf
HOYSTER, Mary	22	F	Laborer	220c02Bf
DUNN, Mary	02	F	Child	220c02Bf
WILKINSON, John	28	M	Laborer	220c02Bf
ONEILE, Con.	56	M	Laborer	220c02Bf
Biddy	45	F	None	220c02Bf
Sally-Jane	18	F	Unknown	220c02Bf
Henry-Jno.	13	M	Unknown	220c02Bf
James	11	M	Unknown	220c02Bf
Hugh	09	M	Child	220c02Bf
Charles	07	M	Child	220c02Bf
Biddy	05	F	Child	220c02Bf
Elizabeth	02	F	Child	220c02Bf
CUSHLEY, Francis	50	M	Laborer	220c02Bf
Biddy	13	F	Unknown	220c02Bf
KINNEY, Mary-Ann	28	F	Unknown	220c02Bf
Pat	06	M	Child	220c02Bf
Anna	04	F	Child	220c02Bf
HARNEY, Thos.	26	M	Laborer	220c02Bf
REYNOLDS, John	25	M	Laborer	220c02Bf
SELWYN, C.G.Col.	40	M	Rcengr	220c02Bf
U	35	F	None	220c02Bf
U, U	35	U	Servant	220c02Bf
U	35	U	Servant	220c02Bf
STENTON, U-Mrs.	19	F	Unknown	220c02Bf
U	17	F	Unknown	220c02Bf
TAFFE, C.	14	M	Unknown	220c02Bf

HOTTINGUER 22 OCTOBER 1847

From Liverpool

NAMES OF PASSENGERS	AGE	SEX	OCCUPATIONS	DATE PORT SHIP
DARCY, Arthur	21	M	Salesman	220c02Bc
STEPHENSON, Robert	24	M	Surgeon	220c02Bc
CASEY, Cathr.	35	F	None	220c02Bc
Margt.	14	F	Clerk	220c02Bc
SULIVAN, Patrick	40	M	Farmer	220c02Bc
CASEY, Thomas	30	M	Farmer	220c02Bc
William	15	M	Farmer	220c02Bc
SULIVAN, Mary	31	F	Farmer	220c02Bc
Hannah	15	F	Farmer	220c02Bc
Hanorah	09	F	Child	220c02Bc
Ellen	07	F	Child	220c02Bc
John	05	M	Child	220c02Bc
Thomas	02	M	Child	220c02Bc
OBRIAN, Michael	32	M	Seaman	220c02Bc
Matthew	21	M	Seaman	220c02Bc
GOLLAGHER, Mary	29	F	Upholsterer	220c02Bc
Mary	01	F	Child	220c02Bc
GEOGHEGAN, Bridget	59	F	Dealer	220c02Bc
MCGOWAN, Samuel	20	F	Weaver	220c02Bc
MARRY, Brian	21	F	Laborer	220c02Bc
PINTONY, Christopher	35	F	Weaver	220c02Bc
U (W)	29	F	None	220c02Bc
John	08	M	Child	220c02Bc
Patt	06	M	Child	220c02Bc
Christy	03	M	Child	220c02Bc
COUGHLAN, Patt.	56	M	Laborer	220c02Bc
U (W)	50	F	None	220c02Bc
Thomas	19	M	Laborer	220c02Bc

NAMES OF PASSENGERS	AGE	SEX	OCCUPATIONS	DATE PORT SHIP
COUGHLAN, Ellen	17	F	Laborer	200c02Bc
Margaret	13	F	Laborer	200c02Bc
GORDON, Margaret	22	F	Laborer	200c02Bc
FOX, Ellen	14	F	Unknown	200c02Bc
FEGAN, Mary	03	F	Child	200c02Bc
Anne	18	F	Unknown	200c02Bc
Thomas	30	M	Gdnr	200c02Bc
Michael	22	M	Gdnr	200c02Bc
Cathr.	55	F	Gdnr	200c02Bc
Matthew	60	M	Gdnr	200c02Bc
Died-At-Sea				
CAROLIN, Patt.	21	M	Clerk	200c02Bc
GAGAN, Phil.	20	M	Laborer	200c02Bc
CLARK, Patt.	21	M	Shoemaker	200c02Bc
BATH, Agnes	16	F	Servant	200c02Bc
MCGUIRK, Cathr.	16	F	Servant	200c02Bc
MCKENNA, Ellen	14	F	Servant	200c02Bc
Anny	10	F	Servant	200c02Bc
Biddy	06	F	Child	200c02Bc
Francis	30	M	Farmer	200c02Bc
U	36	F	None	200c02Bc
MCKEON, Owen	30	M	Farmer	200c02Bc
U (W)	23	F	None	200c02Bc
Biddy	05	F	Child	200c02Bc
Allice	03	F	Child	200c02Bc
Mary-A.	.06	F	Infant	200c02Bc
HARON, Margt.	18	F	Farmer	200c02Bc
HOLMES, Sarah	18	F	Servant	200c02Bc
FEEGAN, Betsy	25	F	Servant	200c02Bc
MCCANN, John	55	M	Smith	200c02Bc
DORAN, John	11	M	Smith	200c02Bc
MCCANN, Margt.	26	F	Unknown	200c02Bc
John	06	M	Child	200c02Bc
Peter	04	M	Child	200c02Bc
Mary-A.	02	F	Child	200c02Bc
Teresa	.06	F	Infant	200c02Bc
FINEGAN, Miles	21	M	Laborer	200c02Bc
MARRON, Owen	40	M	Laborer	200c02Bc
U (W)	30	F	None	200c02Bc
Peter	01	M	Child	200c02Bc
KELLY, Johanna	20	F	Servant	200c02Bc
MCMAHON, Mary	26	F	Servant	200c02Bc
NULTY, Cathr.	21	F	Servant	200c02Bc
TURNER, John	20	M	Farmer	200c02Bc
MCCARAGHER, Margaret	28	F	Farmer	200c02Bc
Alexr.	.06	M	Infant	200c02Bc
TURNER, James	21	M	Farmer	200c02Bc
HANLON, Anne	17	F	Farmer	200c02Bc
MULTONY, Judy	30	F	Farmer	200c02Bc
GEE, Essy	20	F	Servant	200c02Bc
MCCORD, Jane	33	F	Servant	200c02Bc
Mary-J.	21	F	Weaver	200c02Bc
KELLY, Mary-J.	18	F	Servant	200c02Bc
GRIFFIN, Jane	30	F	Schms	200c02Bc
Martha	04	F	Child	200c02Bc
Joseph	01	M	Child	200c02Bc
John	31	M	Coach Maker	200c02Bc
John	02	M	Child	200c02Bc
MARA, Matthew	38	M	Gdnr	200c02Bc
SHEA, Maria	25	F	Dressmaker	200c02Bc
Matilda	20	F	Dressmaker	200c02Bc
HALL, Anne	25	F	Dressmaker	200c02Bc
DOHERTY, Mary	36	F	Unknown	200c02Bc
HARRISON, Ellen	40	F	Servant	200c02Bc
ROBINSON, John	30	M	Trader	200c02Bc
GILLIGAN, John	27	M	Wegr	200c02Bc
BRADY, F.	25	M	Wegr	200c02Bc
QUINN, John	31	M	Traveller	200c02Bc
MCALENEY, William	36	M	Carpenter	200c02Bc
MURPHY, James	24	M	Farmer	200c02Bc
CUDMER, Nell	57	F	Farmer	200c02Bc
HACID, Peggy	21	F	Servant	200c02Bc
DOUGAN, Rose	14	F	Servant	200c02Bc
KENEDY, Bernard	27	M	Ploughman	200c02Bc
U (W)	28	F	None	200c02Bc

NAMES OF PASSENGERS	AGE	SEX	OCCUPATIONS	DATE PORT SHIP
SEERY, Dan.	21	M	Laborer	200c02Bc
COHOON, George	18	M	Weaver	200c02Bc
GAVIN, Patt.	25	M	Shoemaker	200c02Bc
BRADLY, Patt.	25	M	Laborer	200c02Bc
NUGENT, Tim	19	M	Laborer	200c02Bc
HEAVEY, Michl.	24	M	Clerk	200c02Bc
Sally	18	F	Clerk	200c02Bc
FALLAN, Anne	22	F	Servant	200c02Bc
BRIARTY, Phill	35	M	Farmer	200c02Bc
CULLY, Patt	21	M	Farmer	200c02Bc
FOX, James	26	M	Farmer	200c02Bc
MADDEN, Ellen	22	F	Dressmaker	200c02Bc
COUGHLAN, Ellen	22	F	Dressmaker	200c02Bc
Cathr.	20	F	Dressmaker	200c02Bc
ODONALD, John	28	M	Laborer	200c02Bc
ALLEN, William	19	M	Laborer	200c02Bc
GUNGHEGAN, Bridget	22	F	Servant	200c02Bc
HESHLAN, Biddy	16	F	Servant	200c02Bc
MONAGHAN, James	48	M	Laborer	200c02Bc
James	20	M	Tailor	200c02Bc
Susan	18	F	Servant	200c02Bc
Henry	05	M	Child	200c02Bc
Hugh	14	M	Servant	200c02Bc
Mary	48	F	Servant	200c02Bc
NOLAN, Ellen	19	F	Servant	200c02Bc
Mary	25	F	Servant	200c02Bc
Ellen	40	F	Servant	200c02Bc
CHUOT, George	21	M	Shoemaker	200c02Bc
BOWES, Dennis	26	M	Laborer	200c02Bc
CHUOT, Margt.	25	F	Laborer	200c02Bc
Agnes	17	F	Laborer	200c02Bc
MCGOVERN, Anne	22	F	Servant	200c02Bc
Edward	16	M	Servant	200c02Bc
FARRELL, Bessy	17	F	Servant	200c02Bc
MCGEOWEY, John	50	M	Weaver	200c02Bc
Anne	52	F	None	200c02Bc
HOYE, Jane	40	F	Weaver	200c02Bc
Thomas	19	M	Tailor	200c02Bc
John	17	M	Tailor	200c02Bc
Patt.	15	M	Tailor	200c02Bc
William	14	M	Tailor	200c02Bc
Jane	11	F	Tailor	200c02Bc
James	04	M	Child	200c02Bc
MYRES, John	14	M	Tailor	200c02Bc
DONELLY, Henry	12	M	Tailor	200c02Bc
DONNELLY, Anne	10	F	Tailor	200c02Bc
ONEIL, Rose	29	F	Servant	200c02Bc
HALL, U-Mrs.	22	F	Servant	200c02Bc
Joseph	08	M	Child	200c02Bc
John	05	M	Child	200c02Bc
Thomas	19	M	Weaver	200c02Bc
MCGINITY, Anny	40	F	Weaver	200c02Bc
James	20	M	Laborer	200c02Bc
Patt.	42	M	Laborer	200c02Bc
NEESON, Bridget	18	F	Servant	200c02Bc
MCLOONEY, Patt.	28	M	Farmer	200c02Bc
GEARY, Donald	40	M	Farmer	200c02Bc
David	10	M	Farmer	200c02Bc
DONOHOO, Stephen	30	M	Laborer	200c02Bc
Patt.	12	M	Laborer	200c02Bc
Michl.	09	M	Child	200c02Bc
Anne	07	F	Child	200c02Bc
James	03	M	Child	200c02Bc
PHITZPATRICK, Patt.	27	M	Mason	200c02Bc
Mary-A.	15	F	Dressmaker	200c02Bc
Margaret	13	F	Dressmaker	200c02Bc
CAMPAN, Margaret	20	F	Dressmaker	200c02Bc
DONPHY, Eliza	26	F	Servant	200c02Bc
KENNY, Mary	18	F	Servant	200c02Bc
CAIRY, Cathr.	40	F	Servant	200c02Bc
DUNN, Agnes	33	F	Servant	200c02Bc
Teresa	03	F	Child	200c02Bc
Anne	02	F	Child	200c02Bc
Died-At-Sea				
BROWN, Sally	27	F	Servant	200c02Bc

NAMES OF PASSENGERS	AGE	SEX	OCCUPATIONS	DATE PORT SHIP
BROWN, Cathr. Died-At-Sea	03	F	Child	200c02Bc
MCLOONEY, Cathr. Died-At-Sea	28	F	Servant	200c02Bc
REA, Catharine	30	F	Servant	200c02Bc
Matthew	.06	M	Infant	200c02Bc
LEAN, Margaret	25	F	Servant	200c02Bc
HAMILTON, Elizabeth	30	F	Servant	200c02Bc
Samuel	07	M	Child	200c02Bc
William Died-At-Sea	05	M	Child	200c02Bc
Ellen	03	F	Child	200c02Bc
BERGEN, Patt.	30	M	Laborer	200c02Bc
COSS, John	29	M	Ploughman	200c02Bc
MURPHY, Cathr.	19	F	Servant	200c02Bc
FARRELL, Mary	21	F	Servant	200c02Bc
PIERY, Margaret	17	F	Servant	200c02Bc
MCGLOUGHLAN, Nancy	20	F	Servant	200c02Bc
HEANEY, Anne	60	F	Servant	200c02Bc
Margt.	12	F	Servant	200c02Bc
Francis	07	M	Child	200c02Bc
MCGLOUGHLAN, Mary	20	M	Servant	200c02Bc
FINTON, John	36	M	Laborer	200c02Bc
BRENNON, James	25	M	Laborer	200c02Bc
LYNES, Patt.	27	M	Laborer	200c02Bc
Ellen	40	F	Laborer	200c02Bc
LEHAN, Bridget	18	F	Dressmaker	200c02Bc
CANTY, Eliza	20	F	Servant	200c02Bc
Eliza	02	F	Child	200c02Bc
FEGAN, Patt.	22	M	Dairyman	200c02Bc
Vesty	24	M	Laborer	200c02Bc
PERRY, James	18	M	Servant	200c02Bc
DRAPER, William	18	M	Miner	200c02Bc
LYNCH, Martin	36	M	Musician	200c02Bc
CONNOR, Ellen	14	F	Musician	200c02Bc
WHITE, William	48	M	Whitesmith	200c02Bc
Jane	40	F	None	200c02Bc
Susanna	19	F	Unknown	200c02Bc
Alice	12	F	Unknown	200c02Bc
Eliza	06	F	Child	200c02Bc
Charlotte	05	F	Child	200c02Bc
Frederick-W.	02	M	Child	200c02Bc
BUTLER, Thomas	36	M	Laborer	200c02Bc
FREZAR, William	20	M	Laborer	200c02Bc
Cathr.	18	F	Laborer	200c02Bc
COYNE, Thomas	21	M	Farmer	200c02Bc
GILHOLY, Cathr.	40	F	Farmer	200c02Bc
Mary	13	F	Farmer	200c02Bc
Patt.	10	M	Farmer	200c02Bc
John	08	M	Child	200c02Bc
Cathr.	03	F	Child	200c02Bc
MCKUSKER, Biddy Died-At-Sea	73	F	Farmer	200c02Bc
Nell	36	F	Farmer	200c02Bc
Biddy	29	F	Farmer	200c02Bc
BRADLY, Patt.	11	M	Farmer	200c02Bc
Neil	09	M	Child	200c02Bc
MCNAULTY, Margaret	38	F	Farmer	200c02Bc
John	18	M	Weaver	200c02Bc
Mary-A.	12	F	Weaver	200c02Bc
ROONEY, Mary	49	F	Weaver	200c02Bc
James	20	M	Laborer	200c02Bc
Mary	14	F	Laborer	200c02Bc
HANAN, Mary	05	F	Child	200c02Bc
LOHAN, Biddy	14	F	Servant	200c02Bc
FAVELL, Patt.	29	M	Farmer	200c02Bc
FLAHERTY, Patt.	20	M	Farmer	200c02Bc
LONG, John	25	M	Farmer	200c02Bc
Dan.	17	M	Farmer	200c02Bc
REILANS, John	56	M	Farmer	200c02Bc
Richard	11	M	Farmer	200c02Bc
Cathr.	13	F	Farmer	200c02Bc
FULLAM, Rose	18	F	Farmer	200c02Bc

NICHOLAS-BIDDLE 22 OCTOBER 1847

From Liverpool

NAMES OF PASSENGERS	AGE	SEX	OCCUPATIONS	DATE PORT SHIP
MCCARTNEY, Martin	43	M	Laborer	220c02lq
Elizabeth	38	F	None	220c02lq
Micheal	15	M	Unknown	220c02lq
ROONEY, Bridget	17	F	Servant	220c02lq
MCCARTNEY, Elleneor	09	F	Child	220c02lq
James	06	M	Child	220c02lq
Josh.	03	M	Child	220c02lq
HORN, Wm.	41	M	Laborer	220c02lq
NEAL, Saml.	31	M	Laborer	220c02lq
DOGANE, James	50	M	Laborer	220c02lq
Ellen	50	F	None	220c02lq
Cath.	22	F	Servant	220c02lq
Rosey	20	F	Servant	220c02lq
Grace	18	F	Servant	220c02lq
Mary	14	F	Servant	220c02lq
HOLFORD, Mary	16	F	Servant	220c02lq
TORNY, John	58	M	Farmer	220c02lq
Betty	56	F	None	220c02lq
Christian	16	F	Servant	220c02lq
Biddy	11	F	Unknown	220c02lq
Thomas	12	M	Unknown	220c02lq
SAUL, Rose	20	F	Servant	220c02lq
MONAGAN, Martin	34	M	Servant	220c02lq
SMALL, Ellen	28	F	Servant	220c02lq
BROMILY, Maria	23	F	Servant	220c02lq
MILLICAN, Thomas	58	M	Servant	220c02lq
Jane	54	F	None	220c02lq
Charles	23	M	Farmer	220c02lq
KENNEDY, Mary	22	F	Servant	220c02lq
DUFFY, Mary	30	F	Servant	220c02lq
MADDEN, Mary	50	F	Servant	220c02lq
JACKSON, Ellen	04	F	Child	220c02lq
RILEY, Ann	20	F	Servant	220c02lq
REILLY, Ellen	30	F	Servant	220c02lq
DOWD, Margt.	45	F	Servant	220c02lq
MCMANUS, Jno.	23	M	Servant	220c02lq
MCSHANE, Frank	24	M	Laborer	220c02lq
SMALL, Wm.	12	M	Unknown	220c02lq
GILLEN, Catherine	25	F	Servant	220c02lq
James	03	M	Child	220c02lq
MEEHAN, James	21	M	Servant	220c02lq
MORIS, Henry	37	M	Laborer	220c02lq
Sarah	32	F	None	220c02lq
Janet	09	F	Child	220c02lq
Martha	07	F	Child	220c02lq
Alice	05	F	Child	220c02lq
Henry	03	M	Child	220c02lq
Ann	.00	F	Infant	220c02lq
TEAGUER, James	25	M	Farmer	220c02lq
Ann	04	F	Child	220c02lq
FLOOD, Mary	30	F	Servant	220c02lq
MCENTYRE, Ann	06	F	Child	220c02lq
FOLEY, Thomas	30	M	Farmer	220c02lq
Michl.	20	M	Farmer	220c02lq
James-Jos.	17	M	Farmer	220c02lq
Ellen	22	F	Farmer	220c02lq
Catherine	19	F	Farmer	220c02lq
DORGAN, Sally	25	F	Farmer	220c02lq
SHEEHAN, Nancy	19	F	Servant	220c02lq
MCHARFFNY, Adw.	20	M	Mechanic	220c02lq
MCGUIGAN, John	24	M	Laborer	220c02lq
BARTES, Jane	20	F	Servant	220c02lq
STRINGER, Maria	50	F	Servant	220c02lq
Phebe	30	F	Servant	220c02lq
GILLESPIE, Jane	22	F	Servant	220c02lq

NAMES OF PASSENGERS	AGE	SEX	OCCUPATIONS	DATE PORT SHIP
STRINGER, Mary-Jane	05	F	Child	220c02lq
Eliza	03	F	Child	220c02lq
Betty-Jane	02	F	Child	220c02lq
U	.00	F	Infant	220c02lq
TEAGUE, Ann	24	F	Servant	220c02lq
LEWIS, David	24	M	Servant	220c02lq
RYLEY, Ann	21	F	Servant	220c02lq
UNSWORTH, Thomas	24	M	Laborer	220c02lq
DWYER, Wm.	40	M	Laborer	220c02lq
Margt.	30	F	Unknown	220c02lq
Mary	45	F	Unknown	220c02lq
HOLLAND, Sarah	27	F	Servant	220c02lq
MAHON, Cath.	21	F	Servant	220c02lq
DWIRE, Patrick	25	M	Servant	220c02lq
CURIE, John	40	M	Servant	220c02lq
MCBRIDE, Rose	24	F	Servant	220c02lq
LYTHGOE, James	23	M	Servant	220c02lq
MALLON, Mary	17	F	Servant	220c02lq
BUSSY, James	16	M	Servant	220c02lq
Isabella	10	F	Unknown	220c02lq
SOWTHER, Thomas	16	M	Servant	220c02lq
BRADDEN, Magt.	35	F	Servant	220c02lq
WALTON, Wm.	30	M	Servant	220c02lq
U (W)	26	F	None	220c02lq
John	.00	M	Infant	220c02lq
Mary	15	F	Servant	220c02lq
Albert	28	M	Servant	220c02lq
Sarah	22	F	None	220c02lq
Wm.	.00	M	Infant	220c02lq

ATLANTIC 22 OCTOBER 1847

From Liverpool

NAMES OF PASSENGERS	AGE	SEX	OCCUPATIONS	DATE PORT SHIP
MILLOR, Jane	20	F	Servant	220c02My
GLAKIN, Wm.	50	M	Laborer	220c02My
Margaret	45	F	None	220c02My
Daniel	12	M	Laborer	220c02My
Edward	11	M	Laborer	220c02My
Patrick	11	M	Laborer	220c02My
REWHERN, Rosan	30	F	Laborer	220c02My
TRACY, Ann	25	F	Laborer	220c02My
RUGHAN, Pat	30	M	Farmer	220c02My
MULHERRAN, Danl.	20	M	Laborer	220c02My
John	18	M	Laborer	220c02My
GARRAN, Owen	20	M	Laborer	220c02My
SHERLAN, Margaret	20	M	Servant	220c02My
CONAGHER, Hugh	25	M	Servant	220c02My
COOK, Daniel	23	M	Servant	220c02My
CARLAN, Francis	30	M	Laborer	220c02My
CAMPBELL, John	40	M	Farmer	220c02My
QUINN, Mary	27	F	Servant	220c02My
Margaret	20	F	Servant	220c02My
Francis	03	F	Child	220c02My
Biddy	02	F	Child	220c02My
Hugh	.00	M	Infant	220c02My
MOFFATT, Elizabeth	25	F	Servant	220c02My
KEOWN, Margaret	19	F	Servant	220c02My
FREIL, James	48	M	Mechanic	220c02My
James	22	M	Laborer	220c02My
Maria	19	F	Laborer	220c02My
HARDMAN, Augusta	34	M	Butcher	220c02My
U (W)	23	F	Wife	220c02My
PLINKINTON, James	20	M	Painter	220c02My
LECHIS, Alexr.	20	M	Laborer	220c02My
BLACKING, Henry	25	M	Builder	220c02My
U (W)	21	F	Wife	220c02My
CASSIDAY, James	20	M	Engineer	220c02My
HEMPSON, Francis	25	M	Servant	220c02My
HEMPSON, Charles	.00	M	Infant	220c02My
CARR, Patrick	22	M	Laborer	220c02My
FLAVIN, Robert	50	M	Laborer	220c02My
Mary	48	F	Servant	220c02My
Catharine	26	F	Servant	220c02My
Hannah	24	F	Servant	220c02My
Bridget	20	F	Servant	220c02My
PENDERGRASS, Ellen	23	F	Servant	220c02My
Gr---T, Patrick	17	M	Laborer	220c02My
CROWTHERS, James	30	M	Laborer	220c02My
James	35	M	Laborer	220c02My
Richard	27	M	Laborer	220c02My
James	40	M	Laborer	220c02My
DUFFY, John	40	M	Laborer	220c02My
U (W)	30	F	Servant	220c02My
FARRELL, Patrick	27	M	Servant	220c02My
MURPHY, James	26	M	Servant	220c02My
FILTERS, Mary	12	F	Servant	220c02My
KEHOLEY, Florence	26	F	Servant	220c02My
Thomas	28	M	Servant	220c02My
Martha	21	F	Servant	220c02My
Thomas	.00	M	Infant	220c02My
LEDDY, John	29	M	Laborer	220c02My
TOUCHBONE, James	25	M	Laborer	220c02My
HURST, Robert	46	M	Hrsm	220c02My
Nathaniel	15	M	Hrsm	220c02My
Thomas	11	M	Hrsm	220c02My
CASHEN, Wm.	24	M	Servant	220c02My
RYAN, Ellen	28	F	Servant	220c02My
HOGARTY, Catharine	30	F	Servant	220c02My
Catharine	04	F	Child	220c02My
Isabella	.00	F	Infant	220c02My
DUFFY, Catharine	24	F	Servant	220c02My
CORBETT, Isaac	23	M	Servant	220c02My
HOSLIN, Isaac	25	M	Laborer	220c02My
GORMLY, Henry	20	M	Laborer	220c02My
FITZMORRIS, Thos.	25	M	Laborer	220c02My
U (W)	20	F	Wife	220c02My
William	12	M	Laborer	220c02My
Eliza	09	F	Child	220c02My
Thomas	07	M	Child	220c02My
REIF, Eliza	22	F	Laborer	220c02My
FIELDS, Richard	25	M	Servant	220c02My
ALLISON, Chas.	65	M	Servant	220c02My
William	55	M	Servant	220c02My
Flora	19	F	Servant	220c02My
Phoebe	21	F	Servant	220c02My
Frederick	20	F	Servant	220c02My
Sarah	20	F	Servant	220c02My
BRADY, Michael	30	M	Servant	220c02My
MCKINNA, Thomas	30	M	Laborer	220c02My
SLATE, James	20	M	Laborer	220c02My
HENRY, Daniel	54	M	Laborer	220c02My
Bridget	53	F	Servant	220c02My
Margaret	26	F	Servant	220c02My
Maria	24	F	Servant	220c02My
Michael	18	M	Laborer	220c02My
COCHEREN, Michael	40	M	Laborer	220c02My
Died-At-Sea				
Mary	40	F	Servant	220c02My
BRYAN, Anne	30	F	Servant	220c02My
Thomas	11	M	Servant	220c02My
Patrick	09	M	Child	220c02My
Catharine	03	F	Child	220c02My
Margaret	.00	F	Infant	220c02My
TOOLE, Michael	32	M	Laborer	220c02My
Bridget	30	F	Servant	220c02My
Patrick	10	M	Servant	220c02My
Died-At-Sea				
Anne	07	F	Child	220c02My
Peter	05	M	Child	220c02My
Anne	.00	F	Infant	220c02My
REILLY, Bessy	30	F	Servant	220c02My
Mary	.00	F	Infant	220c02My
HART, Patrick	55	M	Laborer	220c02My

NAMES OF PASSENGERS	AGE	SEX	OCCUPATIONS	DATE PORT SHIP
HART, Michael	09	M	Child	220c02My
TOOLE, Hugh	45	M	Laborer	220c02My
Anne	24	F	Servant	220c02My
Mary	26	F	Servant	220c02My
BYRNE, Betty	20	F	Servant	220c02My
Ethy	18	F	Servant	220c02My
Bridget	16	F	Servant	220c02My
Anne	30	F	Servant	220c02My
Died-At-Sea				
KING, Timothy	26	M	Laborer	220c02My
LINECHAN, Michael	27	M	Laborer	220c02My
DWYER, James	20	M	Laborer	220c02My
MAHONEY, Eliza	40	F	Servant	220c02My
Margaret	16	F	Servant	220c02My
MAHONY, Ellen	14	F	Servant	220c02My
Julia	08	F	Child	220c02My
Bridget	08	F	Child	220c02My
John	04	M	Child	220c02My
John	.00	M	Infant	220c02My
Died-At-Sea				
RONCHE, Bridget	20	F	Servant	220c02My
CONNOR, Cathe.	25	F	Servant	220c02My
SCALLION, Peter	21	M	Farmer	220c02My
MORAN, Luke	22	M	Laborer	220c02My
SHEENAN, Hugh	50	M	Laborer	220c02My
WHELAN, Thomas	20	M	Laborer	220c02My
DERY, John	20	M	Laborer	220c02My
SOMERS, Ann	18	F	Servant	220c02My
MUTTALL, John	20	M	Laborer	220c02My
SHENDAN, Bessy	20	F	Servant	220c02My
Ellen	17	F	Servant	220c02My
STEWART, William	27	M	Servant	220c02My
FALLAN, Danl.	18	M	Laborer	220c02My
OBRIEN, Francis	21	M	Laborer	220c02My
MORAN, Mary	50	F	Laborer	220c02My
Joseph	09	M	Child	220c02My
CANFIELD, Francis	20	M	Laborer	220c02My
Michael	18	M	Laborer	220c02My
Jane	40	F	Laborer	220c02My
John	11	M	Servant	220c02My
Rose	11	F	Servant	220c02My
REILEY, Connor	40	M	Dyer	220c02My
Patrick	23	M	Laborer	220c02My
Mary	11	F	Servant	220c02My
HART, Fanny	22	F	Servant	220c02My
COYLE, Patrick	30	M	Laborer	220c02My
BRADY, Richd.	20	M	Laborer	220c02My
HANLEY, Owen	20	M	Laborer	220c02My
LARY, Thady	20	M	Laborer	220c02My
Stephen	18	M	Laborer	220c02My
SWEENEY, Bryan	20	M	Laborer	220c02My
HOPE, Charles	20	M	Laborer	220c02My
U (W)	20	F	Servant	220c02My
MORRIS, Elizh.	20	F	Servant	220c02My
MCGRANE, Elizh.	20	F	Servant	220c02My
MEATH, Bryan	20	M	Laborer	220c02My
FARLEY, Edwd.	25	M	Laborer	220c02My
Bridget	26	F	Servant	220c02My
CUFF, William	30	M	Laborer	220c02My
Anne	25	F	Servant	220c02My
MCGREAVEY, Ellen	30	F	Servant	220c02My
GREAVY, William	30	M	Laborer	220c02My
Ellen	30	F	Servant	220c02My
QUINTEN, Honora	20	F	Servant	220c02My
John	30	M	Laborer	220c02My
Margaret	20	F	Servant	220c02My
GREAVY, Dennis	04	M	Child	220c02My
Margaret	02	F	Child	220c02My
Thomas	.00	M	Infant	220c02My
GALAGHER, John	15	M	Unknown	220c02My
CAFFREY, Edwd.	28	M	Laborer	220c02My
Wm.Robt.	.00	M	Infant	220c02My
RYAN, Michael	26	M	Laborer	220c02My
CAFFREY, Mary	25	F	Servant	220c02My
MCGRATH, John	21	M	Laborer	220c02My
MCGUIRE, Terrence	53	M	Laborer	220c02My
Mary	23	F	Servant	220c02My
KING, John	44	M	Laborer	220c02My
U (W)	36	F	Servant	220c02My
William	.00	M	Infant	220c02My
Maria	02	F	Child	220c02My
HORY, Bridget	26	F	Servant	220c02My
REYNOLDS, Bridget	26	F	Servant	220c02My
MOORE, Nancy	30	F	Servant	220c02My
Letty	03	F	Child	220c02My
HOWLAND, Martin	20	M	Laborer	220c02My
KEENAN, Patrick	25	M	Laborer	220c02My
DERMY, John	25	M	Laborer	220c02My
DEGNAN, Barnard	21	M	Laborer	220c02My
DERMAN, Edwd.	21	M	Laborer	220c02My
FORBES, John	20	M	Laborer	220c02My
NANY, John	30	M	Laborer	220c02My
BARTHY, Robt.	30	M	Laborer	220c02My
HUGHES, Pat	20	M	Laborer	220c02My
FARRELL, Margaret	14	F	Servant	220c02My
Mary	20	F	Servant	220c02My
COSGRAVE, Cathe.	20	F	Servant	220c02My
MULLAN, Peter	20	M	Laborer	220c02My
BRADY, Maria	20	F	Servant	220c02My
SHANLEY, Wm.	23	M	Laborer	220c02My
WARD, Bryan	36	M	Laborer	220c02My
ROURKE, Margaret	30	F	Servant	220c02My
MCGAHAN, Ann	50	F	Servant	220c02My
RIELLY, Biddy	24	F	Servant	220c02My
FREELY, Patrick	20	M	Laborer	220c02My
CUFF, Bridget	20	F	Servant	220c02My
FALLAN, Patrick	20	M	Laborer	220c02My
DOYLE, Sally	18	F	Servant	220c02My
FITSIMMONS, Margaret	50	F	Servant	220c02My
Rose	21	F	Servant	220c02My
Michael	20	M	Laborer	220c02My
Mary	10	F	Servant	220c02My
MCHUGH, Anthony	20	M	Laborer	220c02My
SHEA, Patrick	40	M	Laborer	220c02My
Sarah	18	F	Servant	220c02My
FITZPATRICK, Thomas	18	M	Laborer	220c02My
HANLEY, Thomas	18	M	Laborer	220c02My
GOLDEN, Sarah	20	F	Servant	220c02My
QUICK, Samuel	30	M	Laborer	220c02My
Ann	30	F	Servant	220c02My
Bridget	04	F	Child	220c02My
Patrick	02	M	Child	220c02My
BANDON, Dennis	40	M	Laborer	220c02My
Mary	40	F	Servant	220c02My
Mary	10	F	Servant	220c02My
CULLEN, Mary	12	F	Servant	220c02My
Bridget	10	F	Servant	220c02My
Francis	08	M	Child	220c02My
DIRINE, Patrick	23	M	Laborer	220c02My
SHEFLIN, Mary	18	F	Servant	220c02My
BARRY, Margt.	50	F	Servant	220c02My
William	30	M	Laborer	220c02My
Died-At-Sea				
Mary	10	F	Servant	220c02My
RAWDON, Ellen	20	F	Servant	220c02My
SEARY, Elizh.	20	F	Servant	220c02My
MAHONEY, Michael	21	M	Laborer	220c02My
CLARKSON, Tilly	21	M	Laborer	220c02My
MCGEE, Daniel	10	M	Laborer	220c02My
Hannah	50	F	Servant	220c02My
KEEGHAN, Thomas	30	M	Laborer	220c02My
MCCARTHY, Bridget	18	F	Servant	220c02My
KELLY, Julia	20	F	Servant	220c02My
GEGHAN, Bridget	20	F	Servant	220c02My
MCGUIN, Ann	20	F	Servant	220c02My
MILLMORE, Thomas	28	M	Laborer	220c02My
BOLAND, Dennis	22	M	Laborer	220c02My
LEE, Patrick	25	M	Laborer	220c02My
James	25	M	Laborer	220c02My
LYNCH, James	23	M	Laborer	220c02My

NAMES OF PASSENGERS	AGE	SEX	OCCUPATIONS	DATE PORT SHIP
DERMOND, Thos.	21	M	Laborer	220c02My
RYAN, Eliza	40	F	Servant	220c02My
FLOX, Michael	16	M	Laborer	220c02My
LYNCH, Thomas	23	M	Laborer	220c02My
Mary	26	F	Servant	220c02My
Patrick	.00	M	Infant	220c02My
LENAHAN, Hugh	40	M	Laborer	220c02My
Ellen	50	F	Servant	220c02My
Ellen	13	F	Servant	220c02My
MCDERMONT, Ann	21	F	Servant	220c02My
HALLY, John	20	M	Laborer	220c02My
DERNE, Pat	20	M	Laborer	220c02My
KERRIGAN, Pat	22	M	Laborer	220c02My
James	11	M	Laborer	220c02My
HOPE, Christopher	20	M	Laborer	220c02My
Catherine	20	F	Servant	220c02My
SMITH, William	28	M	Laborer	220c02My

ASHBURTON 22 OCTOBER 1847

From Liverpool

NAMES OF PASSENGERS	AGE	SEX	OCCUPATIONS	DATE PORT SHIP
NEAL, John	30	M	Farmer	220c02Bd
HARDWAY, Fredk.	44	M	Chandler	220c02Bd
Mary	21	F	Unknown	220c02Bd
Fredk.	21	M	Musician	220c02Bd
MCBRIGHT, Margaret	19	F	Unknown	220c02Bd
WHEELAN, John	32	M	Farmer	220c02Bd
LINDEN, James	28	M	Printer	220c02Bd
Arthur	12	M	Unknown	220c02Bd
HAIN, John	50	M	Shoemaker	220c02Bd
Margaret	44	F	None	220c02Bd
Mary	18	F	Unknown	220c02Bd
Johanna	15	F	Unknown	220c02Bd
Pat	13	M	Unknown	220c02Bd
Richard	02	M	Child	220c02Bd
SHEA, James	20	M	Laborer	220c02Bd
Quintin	18	M	Laborer	220c02Bd
RIVEY, Peter	25	M	Laborer	220c02Bd
SLATTERY, John	28	M	Laborer	220c02Bd
Johanna	26	F	Unknown	220c02Bd
BRADY, Barnard	26	M	Laborer	220c02Bd
Bridget	26	F	Unknown	220c02Bd
HEIRN, John	34	M	Laborer	220c02Bd
Johanna	30	F	None	220c02Bd
Cornelius	06	M	Child	220c02Bd
WALKER, Thomas	22	M	Laborer	220c02Bd
Maria	17	F	Laborer	220c02Bd
HAMMELL, Henry	20	M	Laborer	220c02Bd
HIVIN, Sarah	55	F	Unknown	220c02Bd
Rose	16	F	Unknown	220c02Bd
Hugh	12	M	Unknown	220c02Bd
GRATTIN, John	35	M	Weaver	220c02Bd
HAY, Pat	35	M	Laborer	220c02Bd
Mary	34	F	None	220c02Bd
Margaret	11	F	Unknown	220c02Bd
HARRINGTON, Johanna	22	F	Unknown	220c02Bd
WATTS, James	19	M	Laborer	220c02Bd
HAY, Betty	40	F	Unknown	220c02Bd
Patrick	11	M	Laborer	220c02Bd
James	19	M	Laborer	220c02Bd
HORSON, John	22	M	Laborer	220c02Bd
MCCORMICK, Robt.	36	M	Laborer	220c02Bd
HAGANS, Peter	34	M	Laborer	220c02Bd
HIGGINS, John	20	M	Weaver	220c02Bd
BENNINGTON, Michael	19	M	Tailor	220c02Bd
HIGGIN, Margaret	30	F	Tailor	220c02Bd
ARMSTRONG, John	24	M	Weaver	220c02Bd
DOLAN, John	23	M	Laborer	220c02Bd

NAMES OF PASSENGERS	AGE	SEX	OCCUPATIONS	DATE PORT SHIP
DOLAN, Mary	23	F	Laborer	220c02Bd
GRIFFIN, Cornelius	34	M	Laborer	220c02Bd
DUNN, Martin	54	M	Farmer	220c02Bd
Patrick	25	M	Farmer	220c02Bd
John	16	M	Farmer	220c02Bd
Julia	20	F	Unknown	220c02Bd
JOHNSON, David	40	M	Mason	220c02Bd
Sarah	30	F	None	220c02Bd
Mary-Ann	10	F	Unknown	220c02Bd
Sarah	08	F	Child	220c02Bd
James	06	M	Ch'ld	220c02Bd
David	04	M	Child	220c02Bd
Elizabeth	02	F	Child	220c02Bd
Jane	07	F	Child	220c02Bd
CULLEN, Mary	36	F	Unknown	220c02Bd
Michael	06	M	Child	220c02Bd
CURSEY, Richard	32	M	Laborer	220c02Bd
Ellen	25	F	None	220c02Bd
John	.00	M	Infant	220c02Bd
MCGAFENY, Owen	44	M	Laborer	220c02Bd
STENTON, Lackey	30	M	Laborer	220c02Bd
MCKEY, Andrew	44	M	Mechanic	220c02Bd
KELLEY, Ellen	40	F	Unknown	220c02Bd
William	13	M	Unknown	220c02Bd
John	11	M	Unknown	220c02Bd
Mary-Ann	07	F	Child	220c02Bd
Sally	02	F	Child	220c02Bd
Ellen	.00	F	Infant	220c02Bd
James	05	M	Child	220c02Bd
ROURKE, Michael	42	M	Laborer	220c02Bd
Mary	36	F	None	220c02Bd
Maragret	13	F	Unknown	220c02Bd
John	09	M	Child	220c02Bd
Michael	06	M	Child	220c02Bd
Mary-Ann	03	F	Child	220c02Bd
HARDEN, Ann	20	F	Unknown	220c02Bd
GARVIN, Margaret	54	F	Unknown	220c02Bd
John	14	M	Unknown	220c02Bd
EGAN, Patrick	22	M	Laborer	220c02Bd
SHIDNEN, Joseph	20	M	Laborer	220c02Bd
Mary	18	F	Unknown	220c02Bd
DENIGAN, Patrick	28	M	Laborer	220c02Bd
DOYLE, Honora	20	F	Unknown	220c02Bd
KENNEDY, Bridget	21	F	Unknown	220c02Bd
RAIN, John	30	M	Laborer	220c02Bd
FOREST, Thomas	22	M	Clerk	220c02Bd
RING, David	36	M	Laborer	220c02Bd
CONNELL, Jerry	30	M	Laborer	220c02Bd
RYAN, Ellen	20	F	Laborer	220c02Bd
KIRBY, Redman	30	M	Laborer	220c02Bd
MCCARTY, Callahan	50	M	Laborer	220c02Bd
BRAN, Rebecca	40	F	Unknown	220c02Bd
Vesey	12	M	Unknown	220c02Bd
Jane	10	F	Unknown	220c02Bd
Rebecca	07	F	Child	220c02Bd
John	05	M	Child	220c02Bd
Catherine	02	F	Child	220c02Bd
WHITE, William	54	M	Laborer	220c02Bd
LINER, Mary	40	F	Unknown	220c02Bd
Catherine	14	F	Unknown	220c02Bd
James	05	M	Child	220c02Bd
Margaret	10	F	Unknown	220c02Bd
Barney	12	M	Unknown	220c02Bd
KEENAN, John	13	M	Unknown	220c02Bd
HARRINGTON, Norah	19	F	Unknown	220c02Bd
GOORIN, Ann	19	F	Unknown	220c02Bd
BOYDON, Dan	20	M	Weaver	220c02Bd
DRAUT, Thomas	37	M	Laborer	220c02Bd
William	11	M	Unknown	220c02Bd
Theresa	09	F	Child	220c02Bd
John	07	M	Child	220c02Bd
Sarah	05	F	Child	220c02Bd
MOORE, Daniel	26	M	Laborer	220c02Bd
Patrick	14	M	Laborer	220c02Bd
DUFFY, Ann	18	F	Unknown	220c02Bd

NAMES OF PASSENGERS	AGE	SEX	OCCUPATIONS	DATE PORT SHIP
MORISON, Elizabeth	19	F	Unknown	220c02Bd
FRAZER, Ann	19	F	Unknown	220c02Bd
Elizabeth	16	F	Unknown	220c02Bd
SWINEY, Ellen	20	F	Unknown	220c02Bd
QUEEN, Catharine	20	F	Unknown	220c02Bd
ODONNELL, Bridget	20	F	Unknown	220c02Bd
LIDDY, Ann	40	F	Unknown	220c02Bd
MCCRATE, Esther	16	F	Unknown	220c02Bd
Margaret	19	F	Unknown	220c02Bd
HALEY, Thomas	30	M	Laborer	220c02Bd
DORAN, Patrick	18	M	Laborer	220c02Bd
HYDE, Daniel	20	M	Laborer	220c02Bd
HARGAN, Ann	40	F	Unknown	220c02Bd
Bridget	18	F	Unknown	220c02Bd
Mary	16	F	Unknown	220c02Bd
COLLINS, James	35	M	Laborer	220c02Bd
TAYLOR, James	30	M	Grocer	220c02Bd
MCGUIRE, Catharine	20	F	Unknown	220c02Bd
CLANCY, Winnie	15	F	Unknown	220c02Bd
LANNAN, Margaret	18	F	Unknown	220c02Bd
PIDDET, Bridget	13	F	Unknown	220c02Bd
FLOOD, Michael	22	M	Tailor	220c02Bd
Alice	18	F	Dressmaker	220c02Bd
DIGNAN, Ann	22	F	Unknown	220c02Bd
Peggy	19	F	Unknown	220c02Bd
BOLEN, Mary	40	F	Unknown	220c02Bd
KIAN, Michael	20	M	Shoemaker	220c02Bd
CORDON, Thomas	15	M	Shoemaker	220c02Bd
CORDEN, Charles	12	M	Tailor	220c02Bd
WELSH, Joseph	24	M	Laborer	220c02Bd
HAGAN, Andrew	25	M	Laborer	220c02Bd
DOWLING, James	20	M	Laborer	220c02Bd
BLAINEY, John	35	M	Carpenter	220c02Bd
Ann	37	F	None	220c02Bd
James	12	M	Unknown	220c02Bd
John	10	M	Unknown	220c02Bd
Mary-Ann	.00	F	Infant	220c02Bd
NOONAN, Martin	25	M	Lrdr	220c02Bd
Mary	26	F	None	220c02Bd
James	02	M	Child	220c02Bd
DEARY, Betty	50	F	Unknown	220c02Bd
LANGAN, Ann	18	F	Unknown	220c02Bd
HANBURY, Walter	32	M	Butcher	220c02Bd
Patrick	34	M	Butcher	220c02Bd
FAILANY, William	21	M	Butcher	220c02Bd
MOONEY, William	20	M	Butcher	220c02Bd
MILALLEY, Mary	20	F	Unknown	220c02Bd
Joanna	25	F	Unknown	220c02Bd
KELLEY, Thomas	19	M	Unknown	220c02Bd
GARDNER, Alice	22	F	Unknown	220c02Bd
HARGAN, Peter	12	M	Unknown	220c02Bd
MURPHY, Michael	16	M	Seaman	220c02Bd
HAGAN, Patrick	27	M	Laborer	220c02Bd

ELLEN-BROOKS 25 OCTOBER 1847

From Havre

NAMES OF PASSENGERS	AGE	SEX	OCCUPATIONS	DATE PORT SHIP
MADDEN, P.J.	32	M	Priest	250c05Rz

PRINCE-ALBERT 25 OCTOBER 1847

From London

NAMES OF PASSENGERS	AGE	SEX	OCCUPATIONS	DATE PORT SHIP
CONNOR, Ann-M.	23	F	Servant	250c21Bn

HANNAH-THORTON 25 OCTOBER 1847

From Liverpool

NAMES OF PASSENGERS		AGE	SEX	OCCUPATIONS	DATE PORT SHIP
HERNE, Mary		40	F	Servant	250c02Sb
Bridget	(D)	17	F	Servant	250c02Sb
John	(S)	08	M	Child	250c02Sb
Barney	(S)	05	M	Child	250c02Sb
Mary	(D)	02	F	Child	250c02Sb
EGAN, Barney		40	M	Farmer	250c02Sb
Mary	(W)	36	F	Wife	250c02Sb
Catherine	(D)	12	F	Unknown	250c02Sb
Margret	(D)	10	F	Unknown	250c02Sb
Ann	(D)	08	F	Child	250c02Sb
John	(S)	07	M	Child	250c02Sb
Owen	(S)	02	M	Child	250c02Sb
CALLAGAN, Pat		35	M	Mechanic	250c02Sb
POWER, Phillip		44	M	Mechanic	250c02Sb
Thomas	(S)	14	M	Mechanic	250c02Sb
WELSH, Lawerance		27	M	Mechanic	250c02Sb
SCALLY, Mary		27	F	Servant	250c02Sb
Johanna	(D)	05	F	Child	250c02Sb
Mary	(D)	02	F	Child	250c02Sb
SULLIVAN, Michael		20	M	Mechanic	250c02Sb
BRENON, Catherine		26	F	None	250c02Sb
Margret		03	F	Child	250c02Sb
Johana		28	F	Servant	250c02Sb
Mary		.06	F	Infant	250c02Sb
Died-At-Sea					
Edward		02	M	Child	250c02Sb
BUCKLEY, Mary-E.		30	F	Servant	250c02Sb
MOONY, James		22	M	Mechanic	250c02Sb
Ann	(W)	19	F	Wife	250c02Sb
MCMULLEN, Ann		28	F	Servant	250c02Sb
MILLEN, Michael		30	M	Laborer	250c02Sb
HAMMOND, David		38	M	Mechanic	250c02Sb
Margret	(W)	30	F	Wife	250c02Sb
WALLACE, Robert		25	M	Laborer	250c02Sb
SCHIEL, Bryan		30	M	Mechanic	250c02Sb
DUFFEE, Michael		28	M	Laborer	250c02Sb
Catherine		23	F	Servant	250c02Sb
LEONARD, James		23	M	Mechanic	250c02Sb
HOGAN, Mary		30	F	Servant	250c02Sb
John	(S)	08	M	Child	250c02Sb
Pat	(S)	06	M	Child	250c02Sb
Edward	(S)	04	M	Child	250c02Sb
CONLY, Honnor		20	F	Servant	250c02Sb
KARNIN, Charles		22	M	Laborer	250c02Sb
CASSEY, John		20	M	Laborer	250c02Sb
DONLON, Thomas		47	M	Laborer	250c02Sb
Ellen	(W)	37	F	Wife	250c02Sb
Pat	(S)	17	M	Laborer	250c02Sb
Thomas	(S)	15	M	Laborer	250c02Sb
RAFFERTEY, Pat		46	M	Mechanic	250c02Sb
Ann	(D)	18	F	Servant	250c02Sb
RINKELL, Ann		18	F	Servant	250c02Sb
MORISSEY, Betsy		40	F	Servant	250c02Sb

NAMES OF PASSENGERS		AGE	SEX	OCCUPATIONS	DATE PORT SHIP
WALDRON, Michael		20	M	Mechanic	250c02Sb
GLISSON, Thomas		26	M	Mechanic	250c02Sb
BROWN, Catherine		20	F	Servant	250c02Sb
MCHUGH, Pat		50	M	Mechanic	250c02Sb
Isabella	(W)	48	F	Wife	250c02Sb
GREN, Henry		35	M	Laborer	250c02Sb
FITZPATRICK, Pat		57	M	Laborer	250c02Sb
GREEN, Thomas		31	M	Laborer	250c02Sb
Jane	(W)	31	F	Wife	250c02Sb
Thomas	(S)	12	M	Unknown	250c02Sb
John	(S)	01	M	Child	250c02Sb
RILEY, Barnard		18	F	Laborer	250c02Sb
MCAVENUE, Jane		20	F	Servant	250c02Sb
RILEY, Margret		18	F	Servant	250c02Sb
MCCLEAN, William		56	M	Mechanic	250c02Sb
MCGRATH, Thomas		31	M	Mechanic	250c02Sb
WILDEMAN, John		42	M	Mechanic	250c02Sb
CANISS, James		26	M	Laborer	250c02Sb
TONER, Mary		20	F	Servant	250c02Sb
HUNEWELL, Margret		20	F	Servant	250c02Sb
CARROLL, Pat		28	M	Laborer	250c02Sb
MCCARN, Jane		25	F	Servant	250c02Sb
LAVINE, Bridget		18	F	Servant	250c02Sb
BRENON, Bridget		20	F	Servant	250c02Sb
ROURKE, Mary		26	F	Servant	250c02Sb
SHANLEY, Bridget		20	F	Servant	250c02Sb
DIAMOND, John		28	M	Mechanic	250c02Sb
CONELLY, Mary		50	F	None	250c02Sb
Ellen	(D)	17	F	Unknown	250c02Sb
SHAILLEY, James		18	M	Laborer	250c02Sb
CALFREN, John		22	M	Laborer	250c02Sb
CLASSIN, Martin		24	M	Laborer	250c02Sb
CONAGAN, John		21	M	Laborer	250c02Sb
HUTCHENSON, James		25	M	Laborer	250c02Sb
DALLY, Pat		26	M	Laborer	250c02Sb
COGAN, Pat		28	M	Laborer	250c02Sb
KILROY, Pat		30	M	Laborer	250c02Sb
MCNORTON, Morgan		26	M	Laborer	250c02Sb
SCHIEL, Ellen		24	F	None	250c02Sb
ROWAN, Martin		26	M	Laborer	250c02Sb
HOWARD, Thomas		25	M	Laborer	250c02Sb
Catherine		16	F	Servant	250c02Sb
Mary		14	F	Servant	250c02Sb
Ann		16	F	Servant	250c02Sb
HIGINS, John		50	M	Laborer	250c02Sb
Mary	(W)	45	F	Wife	250c02Sb
Pat	(S)	20	M	Servant	250c02Sb
Ann	(D)	15	F	Servant	250c02Sb
Catherine	(D)	13	F	Servant	250c02Sb
William	(S)	09	M	Child	250c02Sb
Mary	(D)	28	F	Servant	250c02Sb
GORMLEY, Margret	(D)	15	F	Servant	250c02Sb
GARETEY, Pat		30	M	Laborer	250c02Sb
ENART, Brian		25	M	Laborer	250c02Sb
SCHORT, Samuel		46	M	Laborer	250c02Sb
JORDON, Honnor		50	F	Servant	250c02Sb
Ellen	(D)	14	F	Servant	250c02Sb
MCGUIRE, Mary		20	F	Servant	250c02Sb
MULDOON, Elizebeth		14	F	Servant	250c02Sb
Margret		14	F	Servant	250c02Sb
CONLEY, Michel		26	M	Laborer	250c02Sb
Mary	(W)	28	F	Wife	250c02Sb
Michael	(S)	10	M	Unknown	250c02Sb
Mary	(D)	09	F	Child	250c02Sb
LEAREY, Catherine		20	F	Servant	250c02Sb
CURRAN, Margret		26	F	Servant	250c02Sb
Mary	(D)	05	F	Child	250c02Sb
Pat	(S)	01	M	Child	250c02Sb
FLANAGAN, John		47	M	Laborer	250c02Sb
Mary	(W)	47	F	Wife	250c02Sb
Bridget	(D)	22	F	Servant	250c02Sb
Allice	(D)	20	F	Servant	250c02Sb
John	(S)	15	M	Servant	250c02Sb
Joseph	(S)	13	M	Servant	250c02Sb
Peter	(S)	10	M	Servant	250c02Sb
CURREY, Conner		25	M	Laborer	250c02Sb
Joseph		12	M	Unknown	250c02Sb
MCCARDLE, Henry		55	M	Mechanic	250c02Sb
WELSH, Pat		20	M	Mechanic	250c02Sb
ABRAHAM, Mary-Ann		25	F	Servant	250c02Sb
ROONEY, James		26	M	Laborer	250c02Sb
John	(S)	01	M	Child	250c02Sb
Peter	(S)	06	M	Child	250c02Sb
FANNON, Pat		20	M	Mechanic	250c02Sb
MCDONALD, Pat		30	M	Laborer	250c02Sb
ROONEY, Catherine		26	F	None	250c02Sb
MEANEY, John		20	M	Laborer	250c02Sb
--ESSEY, Maria		16	F	Servant	250c02Sb
HEWS, John		14	M	Unknown	250c02Sb
FALEY, Mary		20	F	Servant	250c02Sb
HEWS, Margret		20	F	Laborer	250c02Sb
SPRING, John		25	M	Mechanic	250c02Sb
ONEILE, John		28	M	Laborer	250c02Sb
Died-At-Sea					
DOLAN, Bridget		25	F	Servant	250c02Sb
IRVIN, Catherine		18	F	Unknown	250c02Sb

MANCHESTER 25 OCTOBER 1847

From Liverpool

NAMES OF PASSENGERS		AGE	SEX	OCCUPATIONS	DATE PORT SHIP
DALY, Cathn.		20	F	Milliner	250c02Hu
Mary		15	F	Milliner	250c02Hu
MCCARTY, Mary		40	F	Milliner	250c02Hu
LAFFEY, John		19	M	Farmer	250c02Hu
SMITH, Wiliam		30	M	Laborer	250c02Hu
HOLINDRAKE, Charles		45	M	Laborer	250c02Hu
OLDROLD, David		45	M	Merchant	250c02Hu
TOMLINSON, Isaac		36	M	Farmer	250c02Hu
Susan		14	F	Farmer	250c02Hu
John		12	M	Farmer	250c02Hu
Ann		09	F	Child	250c02Hu
Hugh		07	M	Child	250c02Hu
Mary-Elizabh.		05	F	Child	250c02Hu
NEWTON, Thomas		26	M	Smith	250c02Hu
BURNE, Patk.		23	M	Laborer	250c02Hu
FARRELL, Mary		21	F	Servant	250c02Hu
BURNE, Kitty		21	F	Servant	250c02Hu
MCILHENNY, Rose		20	F	Servant	250c02Hu
Andrew		14	M	Servant	250c02Hu
CARTHY, John		40	M	Farmer	250c02Hu
GIBBS, Mary		24	F	Servant	250c02Hu
SHOOE, Caroline		20	F	Lady	250c02Hu
CONNOR, Mary		19	F	Servant	250c02Hu
BENNETT, Cathn.		13	F	Servant	250c02Hu
BRACKEN, Cathn.		12	F	Servant	250c02Hu
Mary		18	F	Servant	250c02Hu
CERNAN, Eliza		20	F	Servant	250c02Hu
RIELY, Patk.		19	M	Farmer	250c02Hu
BUTLER, Lawrence		40	M	Farmer	250c02Hu
Margaret		20	F	Farmer	250c02Hu
BRENNAN, Eliza		25	F	Servant	250c02Hu
George		.00	M	Infant	250c02Hu
LINNEY, Mary		20	F	Servant	250c02Hu
CONNOR, Edward		27	M	Farmer	250c02Hu
William		30	M	Farmer	250c02Hu
LENARD, Patk.		27	M	Laborer	250c02Hu
LONG, Richard		22	M	Farmer	250c02Hu
Thomas		20	M	Farmer	250c02Hu
QUINN, Margaret		18	F	Servant	250c02Hu
MCCANN, John		21	M	Laborer	250c02Hu
GALBRATH, Edward		35	M	Laborer	250c02Hu
Died-At-Sea					
John		10	M	Laborer	250c02Hu

NAMES OF PASSENGERS		AGE	SEX	OCCUPATIONS	DATE PORT SHIP
GALBRATH, Teresa		07	F	Child	250c02Hu
Edward		05	M	Child	250c02Hu
Ann		02	F	Child	250c02Hu
MCCULLOUGH, Mary-J.		20	F	Servant	250c02Hu
ODONNELL, Mary		25	F	Servant	250c02Hu
BOLAND, Bridget		20	F	Servant	250c02Hu
MOLONEY, Kenon		26	M	Farmer	250c02Hu
LOONEY, Mickl.		25	M	Farmer	250c02Hu
DONOVAN, Cornelious		24	M	Laborer	250c02Hu
John		26	M	Laborer	250c02Hu
Mary		11	F	Laborer	250c02Hu
James		27	M	Laborer	250c02Hu
Michl.		28	M	Farmer	250c02Hu
MCCOLLOUGH, John		25	M	Farmer	250c02Hu
Ellen		20	F	Farmer	250c02Hu
SAMUEL, John		18	M	Mason	250c02Hu
QUIGLY, Mary		20	F	Hatter	250c02Hu
MORAN, Margaret		19	F	Hatter	250c02Hu
MARNON, Mary		20	F	Servant	250c02Hu
MOORE, Timothy		29	M	Stctr	250c02Hu
U	(W)	24	F	Wife	250c02Hu
ANDREWS, Elizth.		40	F	Servant	250c02Hu
DOYLE, James		18	M	Laborer	250c02Hu
Peter		12	M	Laborer	250c02Hu
Eliza		11	F	Laborer	250c02Hu
CURLEY, Michl.		30	M	Laborer	250c02Hu
CUMINS, Thomas		30	M	Tailor	250c02Hu
Julia		26	F	None	250c02Hu
Thomas		07	M	Child	250c02Hu
Julia		05	F	Child	250c02Hu
COLLINS, John		30	M	Tailor	250c02Hu
WILLIAMS, John		27	M	Farmer	250c02Hu
U	(W)	23	F	Wife	250c02Hu
James		25	M	Farmer	250c02Hu
Richd.		21	M	Farmer	250c02Hu
MARTIN, John		24	M	Tailor	250c02Hu
BRANNAN, James		25	M	Farmer	250c02Hu
Thomas		22	M	Farmer	250c02Hu
CORRY, Sarah		17	F	Servant	250c02Hu
DEGGAN, Mary		27	F	Servant	250c02Hu
Bridget		.00	F	Infant	250c02Hu
FELLON, Pat		19	M	Laborer	250c02Hu
FEYGIN, Ann		12	F	Servant	250c02Hu
HANLY, Jno.		39	M	Servant	250c02Hu
BEGAN, Mathew		40	M	Servant	250c02Hu
Dennis		21	M	Servant	250c02Hu
KELLY, Thos.		25	M	Carpenter	250c02Hu
HALY, William		26	M	Mason	250c02Hu
Margaret		28	F	Unknown	250c02Hu
REILEY, Jno.		25	M	Farmer	250c02Hu
GIBSON, Jno.		25	M	Farmer	250c02Hu
BRENNAN, Patk.		25	M	Farmer	250c02Hu
ROWAN, Patk.		21	M	Farmer	250c02Hu
PLAHIRT, Luke		20	M	Farmer	250c02Hu
DAVIS, James		20	M	Farmer	250c02Hu
HACKET, Thomas		40	M	Farmer	250c02Hu
Cathn.		40	F	None	250c02Hu
William		04	M	Child	250c02Hu
James		02	M	Child	250c02Hu
George		.00	M	Infant	250c02Hu
CLAFERTY, Ann		20	F	Servant	250c02Hu
DEADE, Jno.		20	M	Servant	250c02Hu
MCDONOGH, Thomas		21	M	Housekeeper	250c02Hu
KIRWIN, Thomas		30	M	Farmer	250c02Hu
Mcral---, James		24	M	Farmer	250c02Hu
OBRIEN, James		24	M	Smith	250c02Hu
Thomas		29	M	Smith	250c02Hu
FEE, Charles		18	M	Mason	250c02Hu
LENARD, Edmond		22	M	Farmer	250c02Hu
CURRANE, Michl.		10	M	Farmer	250c02Hu
Cathn.		12	F	Farmer	250c02Hu
LENON, Hanna		19	F	Farmer	250c02Hu
RAFFERTY, Patk.		20	M	Farmer	250c02Hu
GINTY, James		20	M	Laborer	250c02Hu
LUMOTT, John		24	M	Laborer	250c02Hu
GINTY, Michl.		21	M	Laborer	250c02Hu
BURNS, Mary		20	F	Servant	250c02Hu
SHEEHAN, James		50	M	Servant	250c02Hu
U	(W)	40	F	Wife	250c02Hu
Cornl.		24	M	Servant	250c02Hu
Dennis		22	M	Servant	250c02Hu
John		19	M	Servant	250c02Hu
Cathn.		13	F	Servant	250c02Hu
William		08	M	Child	250c02Hu
Margaret		06	F	Child	250c02Hu
MCLOUGHLIN, John		32	M	Cooper	250c02Hu
DURNIN, Mary		40	F	Servant	250c02Hu
DEFFAN, Peter		30	M	Servant	250c02Hu
SMITH, Ellen		20	F	Servant	250c02Hu
CONNOLLY, Thomas		18	M	Laborer	250c02Hu
QUINN, Michl.		25	M	Farmer	250c02Hu
Edward		19	M	Farmer	250c02Hu
GONNAN, John		20	M	Farmer	250c02Hu
LYNAN, Mary		18	F	Servant	250c02Hu
HANDRICK, Thomas		50	M	Farmer	250c02Hu
Cathn.		40	F	None	250c02Hu
Patk.		16	M	Farmer	250c02Hu
Ellen		14	F	Farmer	250c02Hu
Thomas		12	M	Farmer	250c02Hu
Christy		10	M	Farmer	250c02Hu
Mary		08	F	Child	250c02Hu
Ellen		06	F	Child	250c02Hu
BRODRICK, Kate		04	F	Child	250c02Hu
Linda		02	F	Child	250c02Hu
BRACKIN, Betty		30	F	Servant	250c02Hu
LENARD, William		35	M	Cooper	250c02Hu

ALBION 25 OCTOBER 1847

From Limerick

NAMES OF PASSENGERS		AGE	SEX	OCCUPATIONS	DATE PORT SHIP
FROST, George		35	M	Farmer	250c330v
Maria		09	F	Child	250c330v
Margaret		07	F	Child	250c330v
Solomon		05	M	Child	250c330v
Eliza		03	F	Child	250c330v
Ann		01	F	Child	250c330v
MARA, Bridget		15	F	Spinster	250c330v
HANNAN, Martin		20	M	Farmer	250c330v
NASH, Johanna		13	F	Unknown	250c330v
LAHEY, James		20	M	Farmer	250c330v
HANNAN, Patrick		26	M	Farmer	250c330v
ODONNELL, John		25	M	Farmer	250c330v
CASEY, Mary		24	F	Spinster	250c330v
WALLACE, Mary		23	F	Spinster	250c330v
Wm.		24	M	Farmer	250c330v
OCONNELL, David		26	M	Farmer	250c330v
LAHY, Deborah		20	F	Spinster	250c330v
DILLON, Catharine		19	F	Spinster	250c330v
HALLINAN, Thomas		00	M	Farmer	250c330v
Ellen	(W)	00	F	Wife	250c330v
Thomas		00	M	Child	250c330v
Margaret		00	F	Child	250c330v
DWYER, Mary		.00	F	Infant	250c330v
BARRETT, Ellen		00	F	Spinster	250c330v
Mary		00	F	Spinster	250c330v
HICKEY, Mary		00	F	Spinster	250c330v
FROST, Mary		00	F	Spinster	250c330v
HIGGINS, Ellen		00	F	Spinster	250c330v
EGAN, Timothy		00	M	Farmer	250c330v
Catharine	(W)	00	F	Wife	250c330v
Honora		00	F	Child	250c330v
MCNAMARA, Johanna		.00	F	Infant	250c330v
COLLINS, Mortimer		00	M	Farmer	250c330v

NAMES OF PASSENGERS		AGE	SEX	OCCUPATIONS	DATE PORT SHIP
COLLINS, Hugh		00	M	None	250c330v
Patt		00	M	Laborer	250c330v
James		12	M	Laborer	250c330v
Bridget		20	F	Spinster	250c330v
Margaret		26	F	Spinster	250c330v
Bridget		50	F	Spinster	250c330v
HEARLEY, Patt		40	M	Farmer	250c330v
Elizabeth	(W)	38	F	Wife	250c330v
Patt		15	M	Laborer	250c330v
MAHER, Simon		25	M	Laborer	250c330v
QUINLINAN, Bridget		20	F	Spinster	250c330v
Mary		15	F	Spinster	250c330v
Margaret		12	F	Spinster	250c330v
MCMAHON, Honor		30	F	Spinster	250c330v
Simon		19	M	Laborer	250c330v
CUSSEN, Michl.		36	M	Laborer	250c330v
MESCALL, Patt		28	M	Laborer	250c330v
Bridget	(W)	24	F	Wife	250c330v
MILLIGAN, Michl.		20	M	Laborer	250c330v
Ellen		12	F	Unknown	250c330v
CASEY, Patt		17	M	Laborer	250c330v
Martin		19	M	Laborer	250c330v
DONOHOE, James		24	M	Laborer	250c330v
CULLINAN, Bridget		18	F	Spinster	250c330v
MARA, John		25	M	Laborer	250c330v
MCMAHON, Simon		33	M	Laborer	250c330v
BUCKLEY, Michael		26	M	Laborer	250c330v
GRADY, Thomas		17	M	Laborer	250c330v
George		20	M	Mason	250c330v
Daniel		25	M	Laborer	250c330v
KANE, John		38	M	Farmer	250c330v
SHEEHAN, Thomas		38	M	Laborer	250c330v
BAKER, Michael		20	M	Laborer	250c330v
MCMAHON, Mary		33	F	Spinster	250c330v
SHEEHY, William		34	M	Laborer	250c330v
SCANLAN, Jane		25	F	Milliner	250c330v
MCMAHON, Michael		37	M	Laborer	250c330v
DALEY, Mary		27	F	Spinster	250c330v
James		07	M	Child	250c330v
Margaret		04	F	Child	250c330v
GRIFFEN, Michael		22	M	Laborer	250c330v
DOWNES, Sarah		25	F	Spinster	250c330v
HALLINAN, Mary		24	F	Spinster	250c330v
FORAN, Michael		45	M	Laborer	250c330v
CAREY, Honor		16	F	Spinster	250c330v
DAVORAN, Thomas		31	M	Laborer	250c330v
GRIFFEN, Ellen		14	F	Spinster	250c330v
OCONNELL, Mary		35	F	Spinster	250c330v
HOWARD, Michael		40	M	Laborer	250c330v
GRIFFEN, John		34	M	Shoemaker	250c330v
BUCKLY, Catharine		40	F	Matron	250c330v
SHEAHAN, Jane		30	F	Wife	250c330v

TALBOTT 25 OCTOBER 1847

From Newcastle

NAMES OF PASSENGERS		AGE	SEX	OCCUPATIONS	DATE PORT SHIP
DENNIS, John		21	M	None	250c66Sf

WEST-POINT 25 OCTOBER 1847

From Liverpool

NAMES OF PASSENGERS		AGE	SEX	OCCUPATIONS	DATE PORT SHIP
LAWRENCE, U-Rev.		30	M	Priest	250c02Sg
COFFEE, Jabey		24	M	Gentleman	250c02Sg
MAXWELL, Eliza		24	F	Unknown	250c02Sg
Thomas		02	M	Child	250c02Sg
Eliza		.00	F	Infant	250c02Sg
DOUGLASS, Jessy		15	F	Servant	250c02Sg
MITCHELL, Thomas		24	M	Laborer	250c02Sg
Isaac		27	M	Laborer	250c02Sg
IGO, Ann		17	F	Servant	250c02Sg
OBRIEN, John		20	M	Laborer	250c02Sg
SCURLETT, James		21	M	Laborer	250c02Sg
KELLY, John		50	M	Laborer	250c02Sg
FAY, Pat		40	M	Laborer	250c02Sg
Bridget		17	F	Servant	250c02Sg
MADDEN, John		24	M	Laborer	250c02Sg
WOODS, Charlott		20	F	Servant	250c02Sg
Matilda		18	F	Servant	250c02Sg
DONLAN, Mary		22	F	Servant	250c02Sg
Ann		18	F	Servant	250c02Sg
Thomas		15	M	Laborer	250c02Sg
FARRELL, Patt		24	M	Laborer	250c02Sg
SHAUGHESSEY, John		24	M	Laborer	250c02Sg
Micheal		20	M	Laborer	250c02Sg
MCCARTY, Myles		24	M	Laborer	250c02Sg
U	(W)	20	F	Wife	250c02Sg
Anthony		.00	M	Infant	250c02Sg
MANGIN, Anne		20	F	Servant	250c02Sg
BARRETT, Richard		40	M	Laborer	250c02Sg
Rosa		16	F	Unknown	250c02Sg
MCGILLICK, Peter		21	M	Laborer	250c02Sg
WALSH, Micheal		24	M	Farmer	250c02Sg
Mathew		18	M	Farmer	250c02Sg
Luke		15	M	Farmer	250c02Sg
Jane		50	F	Unknown	250c02Sg
Jane		17	F	Unknown	250c02Sg
DALEY, Pat		20	M	Laborer	250c02Sg
KEARNS, Pat		20	M	Laborer	250c02Sg
BRADY, Mary		19	F	Servant	250c02Sg
KEELAN, Anne		20	F	Servant	250c02Sg
FREENEY, Mary		18	F	Servant	250c02Sg
MURPHY, John		25	M	Laborer	250c02Sg
MCGATTAN, Bridget		25	F	Servant	250c02Sg
MAHONEY, Ally		22	M	Laborer	250c02Sg
MURPHY, Myles		21	M	Laborer	250c02Sg
GAHAGAN, William		24	M	Laborer	250c02Sg
DOYLE, Pat		24	M	Laborer	250c02Sg
CAVANAH, Sylvester		27	M	Laborer	250c02Sg
BARREN, Richard		21	M	Laborer	250c02Sg
WARREN, Deborah		21	F	Servant	250c02Sg
SAVAGE, Rose		20	F	Servant	250c02Sg
COYLE, Peter		50	M	Farmer	250c02Sg
LAWLESS, Biddy		20	F	Servant	250c02Sg
DELANY, Ony		21	M	Laborer	250c02Sg
Catherine		22	F	Laborer	250c02Sg
GRAHAM, James		36	M	Farmer	250c02Sg
Rose	(W)	35	F	Wife	250c02Sg
James		19	M	Unknown	250c02Sg
Eliza		17	F	Unknown	250c02Sg
Charlott		14	F	Unknown	250c02Sg
LYNCH, Micheal		36	M	Laborer	250c02Sg
U	(W)	30	F	Wife	250c02Sg
Pat		14	M	Unknown	250c02Sg
John		09	M	Child	250c02Sg
James		06	M	Child	250c02Sg
Rosey		.00	F	Infant	250c02Sg

NAMES OF PASSENGERS		AGE	SEX	OCCUPATIONS	DATE PORT SHIP
COYLE, Chas.		24	M	Laborer	250c02Sg
ABBOTT, Nancy		21	F	Servant	250c02Sg
BURNS, Miles		20	M	Laborer	250c02Sg
Leary		32	M	Laborer	250c02Sg
WHITE, Koran		32	M	Laborer	250c02Sg
ODONNELL, Catharine		20	F	Servant	250c02Sg
ROURKE, Mary		20	F	Servant	250c02Sg
WATSON, Lee		32	M	Farmer	250c02Sg
Jas.B.		30	M	Farmer	250c02Sg
LYON, John-T.		25	M	Farmer	250c02Sg
PAINTER, Geo.		45	M	Farmer	250c02Sg
Mary		40	F	None	250c02Sg
GOLD, Eliza		30	F	Unknown	250c02Sg
DOWLING, Geo.		16	M	Engineer	250c02Sg
HATFIELD, Thos.		25	M	Laborer	250c02Sg
Eliza		20	F	None	250c02Sg
HAGGERTY, John		24	M	Laborer	250c02Sg
MONKS, John		26	M	Laborer	250c02Sg
Bridget	(W)	24	F	Wife	250c02Sg
DOHERTY, Sarah		18	F	Servant	250c02Sg
COLLINS, Robert		32	M	Farmer	250c02Sg
U	(W)	27	F	Wife	250c02Sg
U		00	F	Child	250c02Sg
HALEY, M.		24	F	Shopkeeper	250c02Sg
GUNNING, Wm.		20	F	Salesman	250c02Sg
GILLESPIE, Wm.		46	F	Land Agent	250c02Sg
Mary	(W)	46	F	Wife	250c02Sg
Gilbert		20	M	Unknown	250c02Sg
Susan		19	F	Unknown	250c02Sg
Margaret		17	F	Unknown	250c02Sg
William		13	M	Unknown	250c02Sg
Vesay		09	M	Child	250c02Sg
Mary-Anne		06	F	Child	250c02Sg
Oran		11	M	Unknown	250c02Sg
FORTER, Arthur		22	M	Engineer	250c02Sg
BLOOM, Mary		18	F	Servant	250c02Sg
MARROW, Ellen		35	F	Servant	250c02Sg
CLUSKY, Micheal		14	M	Servant	250c02Sg
WILSON, John		07	M	Child	250c02Sg
BYRNE, John		31	M	Laborer	250c02Sg
NIXON, Mary		19	F	Servant	250c02Sg
MARSHALL, Wm.		50	M	Farmer	250c02Sg
U	(W)	55	F	Wife	250c02Sg
Micheal		18	M	Unknown	250c02Sg
Frank		24	M	Unknown	250c02Sg
LONG, Catharine		22	F	Servant	250c02Sg
RAINER, Rose		25	F	Servant	250c02Sg
HISSON, Peggy		24	F	Servant	250c02Sg
SHAIKY, Mary		20	F	Servant	250c02Sg
GINTY, Peter		24	M	Laborer	250c02Sg
KING, Thomas		24	M	Laborer	250c02Sg
Eliza	(W)	20	F	Wife	250c02Sg
DOHERTY, Robert		24	M	Laborer	250c02Sg
Catharine	(W)	20	F	Wife	250c02Sg
CURRAN, Mary		19	F	Servant	250c02Sg
MALLONY, Onny		20	F	Servant	250c02Sg
MCSHANE, Biddy		26	F	Servant	250c02Sg
MCWARD, Catharine		24	F	Unknown	250c02Sg
U		.00	F	Infant	250c02Sg
GALLAHER, Margaret		20	F	Servant	250c02Sg
DUFFEY, Jane		40	F	Unknown	250c02Sg
Died-At-Sea					
Mary		26	F	Unknown	250c02Sg
Fonna		08	F	Child	250c02Sg
Patrick		07	M	Child	250c02Sg
RUDDEN, Catharine		26	F	Servant	250c02Sg
MCMAHON, Mary		11	F	Servant	250c02Sg
Mary		10	F	Servant	250c02Sg
Ellen		06	F	Child	250c02Sg
MCCAFFRUY, Anne		30	F	Servant	250c02Sg
William		11	M	Servant	250c02Sg
Elizabeth		09	F	Child	250c02Sg
Anne		08	F	Child	250c02Sg
OBRIEN, Ellen		20	F	Unknown	250c02Sg
CLARK, Mary		30	F	Unknown	250c02Sg

NAMES OF PASSENGERS		AGE	SEX	OCCUPATIONS	DATE PORT SHIP
CLARK, Micheal		08	M	Child	250c02S
Mary		06	F	Child	250c02S
Anne		04	F	Child	250c02S
MCKEON, Richard		26	M	Laborer	250c02S
Margaret		21	F	None	250c02S
BARNACLE, Ellen		20	F	Servant	250c02S
KELLY, Judy		36	F	Servant	250c02S
Thomas		11	M	Unknown	250c02S
Anne		09	F	Child	250c02S
Sarah		07	F	Child	250c02S
Catharine		06	F	Child	250c02S
Jane		05	F	Child	250c02S
Hugh		03	M	Child	250c02S
MORRISSAY, Hugh		30	M	Laborer	250c02S
COMOAY, Mary		09	F	Child	250c02S
MALLEN, John		12	M	Unknown	250c02S
Henry		10	M	Unknown	250c02S
Anne		08	F	Child	250c02S
FAIRNY, James		24	M	Laborer	250c02S
JONMER, Letitia		30	F	None	250c02S
Alexander		08	M	Child	250c02S
Rose		06	F	Child	250c02S
Thomas		04	M	Child	250c02S
William		.00	M	Infant	250c02S
SPROLE, Mary		17	F	Servant	250c02S
ILHATTEN, Saml.		27	M	Farmer	250c02S
U	(W)	24	F	Wife	250c02S
Racheal		10	F	Unknown	250c02S
Jane		08	F	Child	250c02S
Jas.Alex.		06	M	Child	250c02S
Mary		04	F	Child	250c02S
David		02	M	Child	250c02S
MCKINLY, Saml.		14	M	Unknown	250c02S
MCILHATTEN, Allice		.00	F	Infant	250c02S
MCLOUGHLIN, Hugh		26	M	Farmer	250c02S
KANE, Patrick		20	M	Laborer	250c02S
GILKISSON, Margaret		18	F	Servant	250c02S
COWLEY, Samuel		52	M	Farmer	250c02S
Dorathy		45	F	None	250c02S
Henry		30	M	Unknown	250c02S
Mary		24	F	Unknown	250c02S
Anne		22	F	Unknown	250c02S
Lucy		19	F	Unknown	250c02S
John		13	M	Unknown	250c02S
MORGAN, John		46	M	Laborer	250c02S
ROBINSON, Anne		27	F	Unknown	250c02S
Mary		10	F	Unknown	250c02S
Sarah		08	F	Child	250c02S
GORMAN, Sally		46	F	Unknown	250c02S
James		14	M	Unknown	250c02S
Mary		11	F	Unknown	250c02S
EAGAN, James		24	M	Laborer	250c02S
HART, Jane		20	F	Servant	250c02S
FORD, Margaret		21	F	Servant	250c02S
KILLANY, Sally		21	F	Servant	250c02S
MCCORMACK, Bridget		21	F	Servant	250c02S
CURLEY, Mary		21	F	Servant	250c02S
Thomas		08	M	Child	250c02S
DELANY, William		24	M	Farmer	250c02S
CONNOLLY, Mary		40	F	Unknown	250c02S
MURPHY, Thomas		03	M	Child	250c02S
MULLEN, Mary		20	F	Unknown	250c02S
Mary		04	F	Child	250c02S
COGAN, Rose		20	F	Servant	250c02S
BRYAN, John		22	M	Servant	250c02S
LOOKILL, Daniel		21	M	Laborer	250c02S
QUINN, Honora		35	F	Unknown	250c02S
SHAUGHNESS, Mary		04	F	Child	250c02S
William		.00	M	Infant	250c02S
MASTERSON, Jas.		21	M	Laborer	250c02S
TUITEE, Michl.		24	M	Laborer	250c02S
FOX, Anne		16	F	Servant	250c02S
RADIGAN, Mary		19	F	Servant	250c02S
MCDONALD, Bridget		20	F	Servant	250c02S
LARKIN, Catharine		20	F	Servant	250c02S

NAMES OF PASSENGERS	AGE	SEX	OCCUPATIONS	DATE PORT SHIP
MARSHALL, Francis	24	M	Laborer	250c02Sg
REILLY, Peter	24	M	Laborer	250c02Sg
Mary	05	F	Child	250c02Sg
Catharine	03	F	Child	250c02Sg
BYRNES, James	17	M	Servant	250c02Sg
Cath.	22	F	Servant	250c02Sg
KNOWLAN, John	02	M	Child	250c02Sg
MALLONEY, Mary	25	F	Servant	250c02Sg
ROACH, Patrick	07	M	Child	250c02Sg
WALKER, Chas.	20	M	Laborer	250c02Sg
Catharine	11	F	Unknown	250c02Sg
HALES, Patrick	30	M	Farmer	250c02Sg
WONDERS, William	26	M	Farmer	250c02Sg
U (W)	26	F	Wife	250c02Sg
Joseph	02	M	Child	250c02Sg
Thomas	02	M	Child	250c02Sg
MORRISSAY, Catharine	20	F	Servant	250c02Sg
MULCAHY, James	03	M	Child	250c02Sg
KEELAN, Alice	24	F	Servant	250c02Sg
WILDIN, Anne	46	F	Unknown	250c02Sg
Alex.	12	M	Unknown	250c02Sg
Isabella	10	F	Unknown	250c02Sg
FAWCETT, William	09	M	Child	250c02Sg
Margaret	07	F	Child	250c02Sg
Josephene-Jane	05	F	Child	250c02Sg
TURNAY, James	21	M	Laborer	250c02Sg
CONNER, Anne	20	F	Servant	250c02Sg
SMITH, Bridget	27	F	Unknown	250c02Sg
Anne	12	F	Unknown	250c02Sg
Bridget	09	F	Child	250c02Sg
Mary	07	F	Child	250c02Sg
Elizabeth	05	F	Child	250c02Sg
John	02	M	Child	250c02Sg
DAIN, Margt.	20	F	Servant	250c02Sg
MCCREIGHT, Charlott	11	F	Unknown	250c02Sg
SIMPSON, Eliza	36	F	Unknown	250c02Sg
William	04	M	Child	250c02Sg
GARDNER, Margt.	20	F	Servant	250c02Sg
BUCKLEY, Ellen	16	F	Servant	250c02Sg
Mary	12	F	Servant	250c02Sg
REILLY, Bridget	14	F	Servant	250c02Sg
PUMAS, Mary	12	F	Servant	250c02Sg
Catharine	10	F	Unknown	250c02Sg
MURPHY, Micheal	21	M	Laborer	250c02Sg
OHALLINAN, Micheal	13	M	Laborer	250c02Sg
Sarah	11	F	Unknown	250c02Sg
KELLY, Betsey	26	F	Unknown	250c02Sg
Mary	02	F	Child	250c02Sg
Margaret	04	F	Child	250c02Sg
FLYNN, John	46	M	Farmer	250c02Sg
U (W)	40	F	Wife	250c02Sg
David	24	M	Farmer	250c02Sg
Elizabeth	20	F	Unknown	250c02Sg
LYNCH, William	14	M	Unknown	250c02Sg
Edward	12	M	Unknown	250c02Sg
PRIER, John	16	M	Unknown	250c02Sg
Patrick	08	M	Child	250c02Sg
Francis	06	M	Child	250c02Sg
Anne	10	F	Unknown	250c02Sg
GILLESPIE, Jas.	45	M	Farmer	250c02Sg
BOYLE, Micheal	24	M	Farmer	250c02Sg
Bridget	20	F	Servant	250c02Sg
CURRAN, Margt.	24	F	Servant	250c02Sg
KENNEDY, Patrick	10	M	Unknown	250c02Sg
REILLY, Bridget	46	F	Servant	250c02Sg
GANLY, William	46	M	Farmer	250c02Sg
Catharine	36	F	None	250c02Sg
William	12	M	Unknown	250c02Sg
Anne	10	F	Unknown	250c02Sg
Biddy	08	F	Child	250c02Sg
Michl.	06	M	Child	250c02Sg
Catharine	04	F	Child	250c02Sg
MCAVOY, Francis	27	M	Laborer	250c02Sg
TYRELL, William	50	M	Laborer	250c02Sg
Bridget	50	F	None	250c02Sg

NAMES OF PASSENGERS	AGE	SEX	OCCUPATIONS	DATE PORT SHIP
TYRELL, Patrick	19	M	Unknown	250c02Sg
Pearce	17	M	Unknown	250c02Sg
David	14	M	Unknown	250c02Sg
William	12	M	Unknown	250c02Sg
Eliza	09	F	Child	250c02Sg
LANDERS, Peirce	50	M	Farmer	250c02Sg
OBRIEN, Laurence	25	M	Farmer	250c02Sg
COFFEE, Edmond	25	M	Laborer	250c02Sg
FEELAN, Mary	20	F	Servant	250c02Sg
CORMICK, Ellen	21	F	Servant	250c02Sg
PRESUGEN, Edward	32	M	Farmer	250c02Sg
U (W)	30	F	None	250c02Sg
DAVIDSON, Mary	07	F	Child	250c02Sg
BYRNE, Catharine	30	F	Servant	250c02Sg
HADDEN, Mary	24	F	Servant	250c02Sg
COCKILL, Wm.	21	M	Laborer	250c02Sg
ROONEY, Richd.	24	M	Laborer	250c02Sg
MULHOLLAND, Joseph	44	M	Laborer	250c02Sg
DONAGHEY, Jane	18	F	Servant	250c02Sg
KAVANAGH, Owen	20	M	Laborer	250c02Sg
SIMOND, Peter	20	M	Laborer	250c02Sg
SOMERS, Alley	20	M	Laborer	250c02Sg
SMITH, Thomas	35	M	Laborer	250c02Sg
DYNANE, Bridget	20	F	Servant	250c02Sg
MILES, James	20	M	Laborer	250c02Sg
GRAY, Ann	20	F	Servant	250c02Sg
MCCANNA, Mary	20	F	Servant	250c02Sg
MCGUIRE, Mary	20	F	Servant	250c02Sg
JOHNSTON, Margaret	63	F	Servant	250c02Sg
Jane	26	F	Servant	250c02Sg
Elizabeth	18	F	Servant	250c02Sg
MOONEY, Mary-Ann	20	F	Servant	250c02Sg
ONEIL, Rev.W.	24	M	Priest	250c02Sg
Mary	20	F	Servant	250c02Sg
MORGAN, Mary	17	F	Servant	250c02Sg
DOWLING, Jas.	21	M	Laborer	250c02Sg

ELIZA-PERROE 25 OCTOBER 1847

From Liverpool

NAMES OF PASSENGERS	AGE	SEX	OCCUPATIONS	DATE PORT SHIP
SULLIVAN, Jeremiah	40	M	Laborer	250c02Sj
Cath.	32	F	Spinster	250c02Sj
Mary	12	F	Spinster	250c02Sj
SHIEL, Ann	50	F	Spinster	250c02Sj
LIVERY, Michl. Died-At-Sea	24	M	Laborer	250c02Sj
JONES, Ann	20	F	Spinster	250c02Sj
Honora	18	F	Spinster	250c02Sj
THONE, Mary-A.	24	F	Spinster	250c02Sj
CASEY, John	48	M	Laborer	250c02Sj
Mary	13	F	Unknown	250c02Sj
Pat	11	M	Laborer	250c02Sj
Anna	09	F	Child	250c02Sj
OWENS, Mary	50	F	Unknown	250c02Sj
Mary	20	F	Unknown	250c02Sj
Eliza	10	F	Unknown	250c02Sj
PIERCE, Rebecca	22	F	Unknown	250c02Sj
Wm.	.00	F	Infant	250c02Sj
SHIELS, Jane	20	F	Unknown	250c02Sj
MCDERMOTT, Hugh	26	M	Farmer	250c02Sj
LOUGHRAY, Wm.	40	M	Farmer	250c02Sj
Edwd.	09	M	Child	250c02Sj
MCAVOY, Cath.	20	F	Spinster	250c02Sj
OBRIEN, Ellen	30	F	Spinster	250c02Sj
Mark	11	M	Unknown	250c02Sj
MURRAY, John	12	M	Laborer	250c02Sj
David	10	M	Laborer	250c02Sj
GEDWIN, Pat	20	M	Laborer	250c02Sj

NAMES OF PASSENGERS	AGE	SEX	OCCUPATIONS	DATE PORT SHIP
GEDWIN, Ann	08	F	Child	250c02Sj
BOURKE, Thomas	09	M	Child	250c02Sj
QUINN, Mast.	27	M	Mechanic	250c02Sj
PLUVER, Madgy	20	F	Spinster	250c02Sj
MORAN, Pat	27	M	Laborer	250c02Sj
Celia	24	F	Spinster	250c02Sj
Cath.	.00	F	Infant	250c02Sj
MULHERON, Mary	09	F	Child	250c02Sj
COTTOLAN, Ann	50	F	Spinster	250c02Sj
Sarah	23	F	Spinster	250c02Sj
Ann	21	F	Spinster	250c02Sj
WILSON, Jane	29	F	Spinster	250c02Sj
Elzh.	08	F	Child	250c02Sj
John	06	M	Child	250c02Sj
Wm.	.00	M	Infant	250c02Sj
EAGAN, Mich.	36	M	Laborer	250c02Sj
REILLY, Ellen	15	F	Spinster	250c02Sj
Bridget	12	F	Unknown	250c02Sj
Margt.	11	F	Unknown	250c02Sj
KELLY, Mary	24	F	Spinster	250c02Sj
HANLY, Bridget	22	F	Spinster	250c02Sj
Margt.	28	F	Spinster	250c02Sj
REYNOLDS, Margt.	20	F	Spinster	250c02Sj
Peter	12	M	Laborer	250c02Sj
LEWIS, Wm.	27	M	Laborer	250c02Sj
Margt.	27	F	Spinster	250c02Sj
Geo.Wm.	04	M	Child	250c02Sj
David	.00	M	Infant	250c02Sj
David	.00	M	Infant	250c02Sj
OBRIEN, Edwd.	20	M	Laborer	250c02Sj
CAULFIELD, Nancy	18	F	Spinster	250c02Sj
KELLY, Laned	30	M	Spinner	250c02Sj
MCGUIRE, Luke	32	M	Laborer	250c02Sj
SAVAGE, Jas.	30	M	Laborer	250c02Sj
Alice	26	F	Spinster	250c02Sj
Betty	14	F	Spinster	250c02Sj
Thomas	05	M	Child	250c02Sj
Elizh.	03	F	Child	250c02Sj
Margt.	.00	F	Infant	250c02Sj
HEAP, Elzh. Died-At-Sea	35	F	Unknown	250c02Sj
Hannah	10	F	Unknown	250c02Sj
Elzh.	.00	F	Infant	250c02Sj
Betty	04	F	Child	250c02Sj
HALL, Mary	27	F	Spinster	250c02Sj
Mary	06	F	Child	250c02Sj
Jessey	04	F	Child	250c02Sj
MCCAHILL, Ann	24	F	Spinster	250c02Sj
MURPHY, Margt.	30	F	Spinster	250c02Sj
Michl.	05	M	Child	250c02Sj
Honor	03	F	Child	250c02Sj
CONOVAN, Ellen	19	F	Servant	250c02Sj
Bridget	11	F	Servant	250c02Sj
DANNEGAN, Owen	19	M	Laborer	250c02Sj
U-Mrs.	30	F	Spinster	250c02Sj
Pat	03	M	Child	250c02Sj
Thoms	.00	M	Infant	250c02Sj
GARRETT, Thos.	20	M	Laborer	250c02Sj
TIERNEY, Pat	24	M	Laborer	250c02Sj
Cath.	12	F	Unknown	250c02Sj
LACEY, Mary	24	F	Unknown	250c02Sj
Ann	.00	F	Infant	250c02Sj
Betty	.00	F	Infant	250c02Sj
BURNIE, Jno.	19	M	Laborer	250c02Sj
MCCORMICK, Ann	14	F	Unknown	250c02Sj
DARCEY, Dennis	26	M	Laborer	250c02Sj
BYRON, Dixon	20	M	Laborer	250c02Sj
CASHEN, Jas.	54	M	Laborer	250c02Sj
Cath.	40	F	None	250c02Sj
Ellen	13	F	Unknown	250c02Sj
Margt.	10	F	Unknown	250c02Sj
ELLIOTT, Mary-A.	60	F	Spinster	250c02Sj
FITZPATRICK, James	17	M	Laborer	250c02Sj
SMITH, Ann	20	F	Spinster	250c02Sj
MULLEN, James	20	M	Laborer	250c02Sj
MURPHY, Jas.	32	M	Laborer	250c02Sj
Bridget	26	F	Servant	250c02Sj
Mathew	24	M	Laborer	250c02Sj
Cath.	23	F	Spinster	250c02Sj
FAHEY, Wm.	20	M	Laborer	250c02Sj
MURPHY, Bridget	21	F	Spinster	250c02Sj
PARRY, Richd.	40	M	Laborer	250c02Sj
Francis	11	M	Laborer	250c02Sj
Richd.	06	M	Child	250c02Sj
SAGESON, Elizh.	40	F	Spinster	250c02Sj
Elizabeth	08	F	Child	250c02Sj
Robt.	.00	M	Infant	250c02Sj
MORRIS, T.G.	35	M	Laborer	250c02Sj
RICE, Cath.	21	F	Laborer	250c02Sj
BUTLER, Thomas	16	M	Laborer	250c02Sj
Joseph	12	M	Laborer	250c02Sj
KEARNS, Bridget	17	F	Spinster	250c02Sj
BURNS, Edwd.	23	M	Laborer	250c02Sj
MCMURONY, Wm.	22	M	Laborer	250c02Sj
ROACH, Lawnce.	22	M	Laborer	250c02Sj
BARDIN, Bridget	24	F	Spinster	250c02Sj
HANNAN, Jean	26	F	Spinster	250c02Sj
Ann-Jane	.00	F	Infant	250c02Sj
BULGER, Isabella	26	F	Spinster	250c02Sj
Bridget	04	F	Child	250c02Sj
MOLLY, Elizh.	17	F	Spinster	250c02Sj
Ellen	16	F	Spinster	250c02Sj
MCCAFFRAY, John	26	M	Laborer	250c02Sj
Ann	24	F	None	250c02Sj
Pat	03	M	Child	250c02Sj
James	.00	M	Infant	250c02Sj
Ellen	.00	F	Infant	250c02Sj
BRENNAN, Mary	50	F	Spinster	250c02Sj
Tim.	20	M	Laborer	250c02Sj
MCMANUS, Bridget	34	F	Spinster	250c02Sj
Terence	12	M	Laborer	250c02Sj
John	10	M	Laborer	250c02Sj
Corns.	08	M	Child	250c02Sj
Michl.	06	M	Child	250c02Sj
Mary	04	F	Child	250c02Sj
Margt.	.00	F	Infant	250c02Sj
Ann	12	F	Spinster	250c02Sj
John	18	M	Laborer	250c02Sj
BRENNAN, Michl.	24	M	Laborer	250c02Sj
Winford	20	M	Laborer	250c02Sj
CONORLLE, Jno.	21	M	Laborer	250c02Sj
KELLY, Wm.	45	M	Laborer	250c02Sj
Cath.	18	F	Spinster	250c02Sj
Elizh.	10	F	Unknown	250c02Sj
Pat	09	M	Child	250c02Sj
HIGGINS, Maria	18	F	Spinster	250c02Sj
MURRAY, Martha	16	F	Spinster	250c02Sj
FLEMING, Michl.	36	M	Laborer	250c02Sj
MULLIGAN, Thomas	11	M	Unknown	250c02Sj
Thomas	09	M	Child	250c02Sj
Pat	07	M	Child	250c02Sj
Charles	.00	M	Infant	250c02Sj
DEVINE, John	24	M	Laborer	250c02Sj
Bridget	22	F	Spinster	250c02Sj
Daniel	.00	M	Infant	250c02Sj
RICE, Mary	20	F	Spinster	250c02Sj
KELEHAR, Bridget	22	F	Spinster	250c02Sj
FLAHERTY, Margt.	36	F	Spinster	250c02Sj
ROURKE, Thos.	11	M	Unknown	250c02Sj
Jno.	09	M	Child	250c02Sj
SULLIVAN, Margt.	22	F	Spinster	250c02Sj
Michl.	12	M	Unknown	250c02Sj
DENION, Edwd.	30	M	Laborer	250c02Sj
Mary	70	F	Spinster	250c02Sj
REILLEY, Cath.	06	F	Child	250c02Sj
CARVIN, Mary	16	F	Spinster	250c02Sj
SLATER, Adolph	54	M	Laborer	250c02Sj
KULMAN, Wilhelm	31	M	Laborer	250c02Sj
NEIDHARDT, Jno.	27	M	Laborer	250c02Sj
ROBINSON, Robt.	22	M	Laborer	250c02Sj

NAMES OF PASSENGERS	AGE	SEX	OCCUPATIONS	DATE PORT SHIP
ORMOND, Gerrard	22	M	Laborer	250c02Sj
FINNEGAN, Jno.	27	M	Laborer	250c02Sj
TOBIN, Biddy	22	F	Spinster	250c02Sj
MARKIN, Martin	40	M	Laborer	250c02Sj
DOYLE, Pat	22	M	Laborer	250c02Sj
BRADY, Michl.	23	M	Laborer	250c02Sj
Bridget	20	F	Spinster	250c02Sj
Owen	.00	M	Infant	250c02Sj
SHERIDAN, Jas.	18	M	Laborer	250c02Sj
SAVAGE, Thomas	10	M	Unknown	250c02Sj
U-Mrs.	40	F	Spinster	250c02Sj
MEALY, Maurice	40	M	Laborer	250c02Sj
Ellen	35	F	None	250c02Sj
Cornelius	08	M	Child	250c02Sj
Wm.	03	M	Child	250c02Sj
Maurice	.00	M	Infant	250c02Sj
SPRATT, Jno.	30	M	Laborer	250c02Sj
MCCARTHY, Jane	50	F	Spinster	250c02Sj
Jane	15	F	Spinster	250c02Sj
Hannah	09	F	Child	250c02Sj
Richd.	06	M	Child	250c02Sj
CASSETY, Mary	25	F	Spinster	250c02Sj
RAYSCROFT, Ben	25	M	Laborer	250c02Sj
Margt.	21	F	Spinster	250c02Sj
CONNOR, Mary	50	F	Spinster	250c02Sj
Andrew	18	M	Laborer	250c02Sj
Margt.	12	F	Spinster	250c02Sj
John	48	M	Laborer	250c02Sj
Cath.	46	F	Spinster	250c02Sj
Bridget	21	F	Spinster	250c02Sj
COWAN, Pat	16	M	Laborer	250c02Sj
Ellen	18	F	Spinster	250c02Sj
Chas.	13	M	Unknown	250c02Sj
Wm.	11	M	Unknown	250c02Sj
Ann	09	F	Child	250c02Sj
Cath.	08	F	Child	250c02Sj
Hannah	06	F	Child	250c02Sj
Margt.	04	F	Child	250c02Sj
Jane	02	F	Child	250c02Sj
Jno.	.00	M	Infant	250c02Sj
MUNEGAL, Jno.	35	M	Laborer	250c02Sj
BURNS, Jno.	20	M	Laborer	250c02Sj
GOLDING, Jno.	24	M	Laborer	250c02Sj
Cath.	28	F	Spinster	250c02Sj
Bessey	20	F	Spinster	250c02Sj
SMITH, Eliza	35	F	Spinster	250c02Sj
Mary	09	F	Child	250c02Sj
Robt.	07	M	Child	250c02Sj
Sarah	.00	F	Infant	250c02Sj
HAMELL, Owen	40	M	Laborer	250c02Sj
Jane	25	F	Spinster	250c02Sj
MCMAHON, Michl.	35	M	Laborer	250c02Sj
Mary	25	F	Spinster	250c02Sj
Josh	06	M	Child	250c02Sj
CLOONEY, Pat	20	M	Laborer	250c02Sj
QUINN, Jno.	20	M	Laborer	250c02Sj
LATHER, Henry	40	M	Laborer	250c02Sj
Mary	42	F	Spinster	250c02Sj
Hannah	26	F	Spinster	250c02Sj
Sarah	14	F	Spinster	250c02Sj
Jane	12	F	Spinster	250c02Sj

JOHN-G.COSTER 26 OCTOBER 1847

From Liverpool

NAMES OF PASSENGERS	AGE	SEX	OCCUPATIONS	DATE PORT SHIP
GARRETY, Thos.	32	M	Laborer	260c02Sk
GOGARTY, John	14	M	Laborer	260c02Sk
HAZEE, Thos.	29	M	Mason	260c02Sk
BRISCOE, Jerh.	21	M	Mason	260c02Sk
DILLON, Timothy	20	M	Laborer	260c02Sk
CRONON, James	24	M	Laborer	260c02Sk
FITZGERALD, Mary	36	F	Servant	260c02Sk
WILLIAMS, Elizh.	20	F	Servant	260c02Sk
FOLEY, Mary	16	F	Servant	260c02Sk
CONNER, Cathe.	20	F	Servant	260c02Sk
FITZGERALD, Mary	12	F	Servant	260c02Sk
CULLEY, Mary	19	F	Servant	260c02Sk
HUGHES, Thomas	46	M	Grocer	260c02Sk
Sarah (W)	30	F	Wife	260c02Sk
Cavallah (S)	08	M	Child	260c02Sk
Elizabeth (D)	05	F	Child	260c02Sk
Saml. (S)	.00	M	Infant	260c02Sk
SMITH, James	30	M	Wrhsmn	260c02Sk
DOYLE, Bridget	18	F	Housekeeper	260c02Sk
MONON, Mary	20	F	Housekeeper	260c02Sk
Mary (D)	.00	F	Infant	260c02Sk
MCCONON, Christian	19	F	Housekeeper	260c02Sk
FAGAN, Ann	20	F	Housekeeper	260c02Sk
SKELLY, Judith	21	F	Housekeeper	260c02Sk
MURPHY, Michael	25	M	Laborer	260c02Sk
MORIATY, John	35	M	Laborer	260c02Sk
LYNE, Pat	40	M	Laborer	260c02Sk
SULLIVAN, John	40	M	Laborer	260c02Sk
MCNAMARA, Pat	39	M	Servant	260c02Sk

PRINCE-DE-JOINVILLE 26 OCTOBER 1847

From Liverpool

NAMES OF PASSENGERS	AGE	SEX	OCCUPATIONS	DATE PORT SHIP
BLACK, Jane	19	F	Spinster	260c02Ni
SMITH, John	28	M	Laborer	260c02Ni
SUTTON, James	25	M	Laborer	260c02Ni
DAVIS, John	48	M	Laborer	260c02Ni
FARRELL, John	24	M	Laborer	260c02Ni
Michl.	22	M	Laborer	260c02Ni
HALLON, James	25	M	Laborer	260c02Ni
Ellen (W)	24	F	Spinster	260c02Ni
Charles (S)	09	M	Child	260c02Ni
James (S)	08	M	Child	260c02Ni
Francis (S)	09	M	Child	260c02Ni
Margt. (D)	03	F	Child	260c02Ni
Robert (S)	.00	M	Infant	260c02Ni
HAMILTON, John	17	M	Laborer	260c02Ni
Mary	12	F	Unknown	260c02Ni
Wm.	08	M	Child	260c02Ni
Eliz.	06	F	Child	260c02Ni
JUDGE, Madge	33	M	Laborer	260c02Ni
Mary (D)	11	F	Unknown	260c02Ni
Died-At-Sea				
Saml. (S)	09	M	Child	260c02Ni
Died-At-Sea				
KERNAN, John	49	M	Unknown	260c02Ni
KANE, Jane	20	F	Spinster	260c02Ni
KEHOE, Jane	14	F	Spinster	260c02Ni
MCGARR, Alice	29	F	Spinster	260c02Ni
James	19	M	Laborer	260c02Ni
NICHOLS, W.T.	33	M	Farmer	260c02Ni
Selina (W)	31	F	Wife	260c02Ni
Selina (D)	09	F	Child	260c02Ni
Hephsibah (S)	07	M	Child	260c02Ni
Eliza (D)	04	F	Child	260c02Ni
Thomas (S)	01	M	Child	260c02Ni
Joshua (S)	.00	M	Infant	260c02Ni
LEE, Leonard	24	M	Laborer	260c02Ni
SCHORCK, George	24	M	Laborer	260c02Ni
MCGARRETT, Owen	21	M	Laborer	260c02Ni
WILDE, U	31	M	Laborer	260c02Ni

NAMES OF PASSENGERS		AGE	SEX	OCCUPATIONS	DATE PORT SHIP
WILDE, U	(W)	26	F	Wife	260c02Ni
JACKSON, Saml.		26	M	Laborer	260c02Ni
Thomas		28	M	Laborer	260c02Ni
DRISCOLL, Helen		22	F	Laborer	260c02Ni
LEAHEY, Elizh.		22	F	Laborer	260c02Ni
CRONIN, Murtagh		25	M	Laborer	260c02Ni
Mary		22	F	Laborer	260c02Ni
CASSIDY, Michl.		30	M	Laborer	260c02Ni
Patt		28	M	Laborer	260c02Ni
Cathe.		25	F	Unknown	260c02Ni
CLIFFORD, James		38	M	Unknown	260c02Ni
GORMAN, Mich.		15	M	Unknown	260c02Ni
BRYAN, Morris		09	M	Child	260c02Ni
MCKAY, John		28	M	Unknown	260c02Ni
SHEA, John		21	M	Unknown	260c02Ni
MCCLANE, John		30	M	Unknown	260c02Ni
GORMAN, Johanna		20	F	Unknown	260c02Ni
Danl.		17	M	Unknown	260c02Ni
FORREST, Mary		04	F	Child	260c02Ni
CAMPBELL, Cathe.		45	F	Spinster	260c02Ni
Christianna	(D)	24	F	Spinster	260c02Ni
GORMAN, Cathe.		27	F	Spinster	260c02Ni
Owen	(S)	01	M	Child	260c02Ni
MOYLAN, Jeremiah		45	M	Laborer	260c02Ni
Cathe.	(D)	18	F	Unknown	260c02Ni
SULLIVAN, Patt		21	M	Laborer	260c02Ni
John		19	M	Laborer	260c02Ni
MCGALLIGATT, John		35	M	Laborer	260c02Ni
RILEY, Joseph		26	M	Laborer	260c02Ni
MCELROY, John		26	M	Laborer	260c02Ni
Ann	(D)	06	F	Child	260c02Ni
LEDDY, Nancy		30	F	Spinster	260c02Ni
Mary	(D)	04	F	Child	260c02Ni
REID, Jane		30	F	Unknown	260c02Ni
CRONNIN, Cornelius		22	M	Unknown	260c02Ni
Dennis	(S)	04	M	Child	260c02Ni
MCFARLANE, James		22	M	Unknown	260c02Ni
Margt.		23	F	Spinster	260c02Ni
MCGRECHAN, Henry		25	M	Laborer	260c02Ni
HANTON, John		24	M	Unknown	260c02Ni
FLAHERTY, Bridget		35	F	Unknown	260c02Ni
James	(S)	10	M	Unknown	260c02Ni
Michl.	(S)	08	M	Child	260c02Ni
Matthew	(S)	05	M	Child	260c02Ni
FAGAN, Mary		20	F	Spinster	260c02Ni
BOYD, Edward		50	M	Laborer	260c02Ni
Rachael	(D)	20	F	Laborer	260c02Ni
George	(S)	19	M	Laborer	260c02Ni
Harkness	(S)	12	M	Unknown	260c02Ni
Charlotte	(D)	10	F	Unknown	260c02Ni
MCCONNELL, Wm.H.		23	M	Laborer	260c02Ni
Edward		19	M	Unknown	260c02Ni
HALL, Thomas		22	M	Unknown	260c02Ni
PATTIGAN, Michl.		34	M	Unknown	260c02Ni
George		24	M	Unknown	260c02Ni
Mary		30	F	Unknown	260c02Ni
BYRNE, Mary		31	F	Unknown	260c02Ni
Patrick	(S)	10	M	Unknown	260c02Ni
Ann	(D)	12	F	Unknown	260c02Ni
FLOOD, Ann		20	F	Spinster	260c02Ni
Michl.		10	M	Unknown	260c02Ni
Julia		07	F	Child	260c02Ni
SPIERS, David		20	M	Unknown	260c02Ni
WOODS, Wm.		31	M	Laborer	260c02Ni
OMALEY, Austin		28	M	Laborer	260c02Ni
ODONNELL, Nathl.		20	M	Laborer	260c02Ni
MCGUIRE, Michl.		20	M	Laborer	260c02Ni
MCDERMOTT, John		23	M	Laborer	260c02Ni
Sally		12	F	Unknown	260c02Ni
MCCULLOCK, Ellen		18	F	Spinster	260c02Ni
KELLY, Cath.		32	F	Spinster	260c02Ni
COURRIN, Margt.		30	F	Spinster	260c02Ni
Mary	(D)	06	F	Child	260c02Ni
SHEEHAN, Patk.		30	M	Unknown	260c02Ni
MANNING, Thomas		50	M	Unknown	260c02Ni
MANNING, Eliza		13	F	Unknown	260c02Ni
SANDARS, Eliza		16	F	Unknown	260c02Ni
SHERRY, Barney		30	M	Unknown	260c02Ni
Mary		25	F	Unknown	260c02Ni
ROURK, Danl.		24	M	Unknown	260c02Ni
James		26	M	Unknown	260c02Ni
KEARNES, Mary		24	F	Unknown	260c02Ni
MCGOWAN, Saml.		21	M	Unknown	260c02Ni

YORKSHIRE 27 OCTOBER 1847

From Liverpool

NAMES OF PASSENGERS		AGE	SEX	OCCUPATIONS	DATE PORT SHIP
MCMURRAY, J.Rev.		32	M	Clergyman	270c02Bz
MONTGOMERY, Henry-J.		23	M	Merchant	270c02Bz
LEACH, Stephen-W.		32	M	Musician	270c02Bz
COTES, Christopher		53	M	Unknown	270c02Bz
PALK, William		58	M	Physician	270c02Bz
BECKETT, George-C.		37	M	Bookkeeper	270c02Bz
DAVIS, Fredrick		12	M	Unknown	270c02Bz
LEACH, Harry		05	M	Child	270c02Bz
POULSON, Mary-Ann		14	F	Unknown	270c02Bz
BREMNER, Martha		12	F	Unknown	270c02Bz
IRVING, John		30	M	Unknown	270c02Bz
LEONARD, Ann		20	F	Servant	270c02Bz
SPENCER, Mary		58	F	Servant	270c02Bz
CARROL, Ellen		20	F	Servant	270c02Bz
LEONORD, Ann		18	F	Dressmaker	270c02Bz
Mary	(D)	03	F	Child	270c02Bz
Allice	(D)	02	F	Child	270c02Bz
HILLGROM, Luke		30	M	Mason	270c02Bz
RIODAN, Tim		28	M	Farmer	270c02Bz
SCANLAN, Johannah		18	F	Servant	270c02Bz
Nancy		26	F	Servant	270c02Bz
MCCARTY, Mary		21	F	Servant	270c02Bz
LONGHEAD, William		25	M	Nail Maker	270c02Bz
Robert	(S)	05	M	Child	270c02Bz
FARREL, Francis		25	M	Laborer	270c02Bz
MCHUGH, Peter		27	M	Laborer	270c02Bz
CONASINE, Ann		18	F	Servant	270c02Bz
JARRAN, Biddy		15	F	Servant	270c02Bz
RYAN, Catharine		23	F	House Maid	270c02Bz
DAILEY, Pat		20	M	Servant	270c02Bz
DOCKARTY, Peter		28	M	Laborer	270c02Bz
GILLOOLY, Michael		34	M	Laborer	270c02Bz
BLACK, Mary		22	F	Tailor	270c02Bz
GRIFFIN, Mary		20	F	Servant	270c02Bz
MCTARVY, Francis		12	M	Servant	270c02Bz
RILEY, Barney		26	M	Farmer	270c02Bz
BRADY, Thomas		17	M	Cooper	270c02Bz
FLINN, Bess		19	F	House Maid	270c02Bz
MCGOWEN, Catharine		60	F	Nurse	270c02Bz
MCMAR, Pat		22	M	Weaver	270c02Bz
MCMAHAN, Thomas		19	M	Weaver	270c02Bz
WALL, John		40	M	Gdnr	270c02Bz
FALAN, Bernard		20	M	Laborer	270c02Bz
GRIFFIN, John		38	M	Farmer	270c02Bz
Mary	(W)	36	F	Servant	270c02Bz
Mary	(D)	06	F	Child	270c02Bz
QUIN, Edmond		24	M	Laborer	270c02Bz
CONNOR, Cornel		42	M	Laborer	270c02Bz
BROWN, Joseph		24	M	Farmer	270c02Bz
COILE, Catharine		20	F	Spinster	270c02Bz
RILEY, Michael		09	M	Child	270c02Bz
Mary		05	F	Child	270c02Bz
CUNNINGHAM, Ellen		24	F	Servant	270c02Bz
MCGRATH, Ann		19	F	Servant	270c02Bz
COLEMAN, Catharine		16	F	Servant	270c02Bz
MORRISON, Ann		25	F	Cook	270c02Bz

NAMES OF PASSENGERS		AGE	SEX	OCCUPATIONS	DATE PORT SHIP
MORRISON, Sarah		12	F	Servant	270c02Bz
HEFFORMAN, Mary		22	F	Servant	270c02Bz
MORRIS, Ann		21	F	Servant	270c02Bz
NEGRE, Ellen		19	F	Servant	270c02Bz
BURNS, Michael		22	M	Miner	270c02Bz
WHITE, William		29	M	Tailor	270c02Bz
ODONNELL, William		25	M	Currier	270c02Bz
RICHARDS, Francis		25	M	Shoemaker	270c02Bz
FANSETT, Gewes-S.		29	M	Waiter	270c02Bz
MURREY, Mary		18	F	Housekeeper	270c02Bz
MCGINITY, James		27	M	Cooper	270c02Bz
RUDDAN, Owen		25	M	Hatter	270c02Bz
EARLY, Ann		16	F	Servant	270c02Bz
Biddy		14	F	Servant	270c02Bz
WADE, Michael		18	M	Laborer	270c02Bz
SMITH, Thomas		18	M	Laborer	270c02Bz
DUNN, Margret		20	F	Shoe Binder	270c02Bz
Mary		17	F	Shoe Binder	270c02Bz
MCGEE, Thomas		21	M	Blacksmith	270c02Bz
John		16	M	Farmer	270c02Bz
DONELLY, Ann		21	F	Shoe Binder	270c02Bz
MURPHY, Martha		26	F	Shoe Binder	270c02Bz
Richard	(S)	06	M	Child	270c02Bz
Michael	(S)	04	M	Child	270c02Bz
Mary-Ann	(D)	08	F	Child	270c02Bz
MCMANNERS, Michael		20	M	Laborer	270c02Bz
CAHILL, John		24	M	Bricklayer	270c02Bz
MATERMERS, Catharine		21	F	Child Maid	270c02Bz
KENNEDY, Pat		27	M	Laborer	270c02Bz
HAND, John		18	M	Laborer	270c02Bz
ROCHE, Mary		22	F	Servant	270c02Bz
FARLESS, John		19	M	Laborer	270c02Bz
WILTON, Charles		21	M	Farmer	270c02Bz
BRADLY, Ellen		28	F	Housekeeper	270c02Bz
BRADLEY, Mary		02	F	Child	270c02Bz
Francis		.05	M	Infant	270c02Bz
FARNEY, Mary		23	F	Servant	270c02Bz
BURN, Mary-Ann		24	F	Servant	270c02Bz
Ellen		02	F	Child	270c02Bz
BEAL, Fredrick		20	M	Laborer	270c02Bz
CROTHERS, William		31	M	Unknown	270c02Bz
Sarcham		33	F	Clfn	270c02Bz
Mary		31	F	Unknown	270c02Bz
Sophia		09	F	Child	270c02Bz
Samuel		07	M	Child	270c02Bz
Ruben		23	M	Carder	270c02Bz
Anne		35	F	Unknown	270c02Bz
Abner		45	M	Clfn	270c02Bz
U		.04	M	Infant	270c02Bz
BOOTH, John		70	M	Clfn	270c02Bz
HAYVORE, Bery		33	M	Clfn	270c02Bz
TONA, Lawrance		21	M	Laborer	270c02Bz
MCGLAN, John		19	M	Laborer	270c02Bz
CARNEY, Richard		25	M	Laborer	270c02Bz
MOONEY, Mary		19	F	Servant	270c02Bz
KELLY, Mary		20	F	Servant	270c02Bz
Jane		15	F	Dressmaker	270c02Bz
GALLAGHER, Peter		20	M	Laborer	270c02Bz
Ellen		30	F	Unknown	270c02Bz
Pat		07	M	Child	270c02Bz
HICKNEY, Catharine		27	F	Housekeeper	270c02Bz
Mary	(D)	03	F	Child	270c02Bz
FEENEY, William		30	M	Blacksmith	270c02Bz
DONILY, Catharine		42	F	Servant	270c02Bz
John	(S)	10	M	Unknown	270c02Bz
MCNAMARRAH, Bridget		26	F	Housekeeper	270c02Bz
John	(S)	04	M	Child	270c02Bz
Mary	(D)	02	F	Child	270c02Bz
Anthony	(S)	.04	M	Infant	270c02Bz
WELLS, Catharine		20	F	Servant	270c02Bz
CLARE, Bridget		17	F	Servant	270c02Bz
WELSH, Jerry		27	M	Laborer	270c02Bz
SHERDEN, Ann		65	F	Nurse	270c02Bz
MARGHAR, Mary		15	F	Servant	270c02Bz
HARRINGTON, Catharine		19	F	Servant	270c02Bz

NAMES OF PASSENGERS		AGE	SEX	OCCUPATIONS	DATE PORT SHIP
BALKIN, Pat		18	M	Laborer	270c02Bz
CLAREY, Theodore		23	M	Laborer	270c02Bz
KEELAND, Thomas		55	M	Farmer	270c02Bz
MORRISSY, Lawrance		48	M	Farmer	270c02Bz
KELTER, John		28	M	Laborer	270c02Bz
HUGHES, Barney		20	M	Laborer	270c02Bz
MUCHONE, James		23	M	Laborer	270c02Bz
MCCLARDEN, James		27	M	Laborer	270c02Bz
COPELY, Stephen		18	M	Laborer	270c02Bz
MCGLOSKEY, Biddy		70	F	Nurse	270c02Bz
KELLOLEY, Pat		22	M	Laborer	270c02Bz
ROUKE, James		19	M	Laborer	270c02Bz
MCALARNEY, James		20	M	Laborer	270c02Bz
Honer		12	M	Laborer	270c02Bz
COLWELL, Cornelias		25	M	Laborer	270c02Bz
Mary	(W)	30	F	Wife	270c02Bz
Ann	(D)	04	F	Child	270c02Bz
Michael	(S)	.03	M	Infant	270c02Bz
MCMARNNEY, Owen		45	M	Weaver	270c02Bz
WINSLOW, John		22	M	Farmer	270c02Bz
MERTER, Brian		24	M	Laborer	270c02Bz
MOORE, William		19	M	Cooper	270c02Bz
BRANIGAN, Peter		26	M	Laborer	270c02Bz
FITZSOMERS, James		34	M	Cooper	270c02Bz
Ann	(W)	24	F	Wife	270c02Bz
Elizabeth	(D)	02	F	Child	270c02Bz
CAGHAL, Ann		22	F	Servant	270c02Bz
MCGRAAR, Ann		26	F	Servant	270c02Bz
QUIRK, John		20	M	Laborer	270c02Bz
CAHAN, Abby		30	F	House Maid	270c02Bz
John	(S)	05	M	Child	270c02Bz
Mary-Ann	(D)	02	F	Child	270c02Bz
GERTY, Ann		21	F	Servant	270c02Bz
EDMONSON, Sarah		19	F	Servant	270c02Bz
ADAMSON, Eliza		20	F	Servant	270c02Bz
DOILE, Mary		21	F	Servant	270c02Bz
FLANIGAN, Mary		22	F	Servant	270c02Bz
WALLACE, Francis		18	M	Cooper	270c02Bz
FAGAN, Rosy		24	F	Servant	270c02Bz
Mary	(D)	.05	F	Infant	270c02Bz
MCCLURE, Martha		16	F	Tailor	270c02Bz
Robert		14	M	Tailor	270c02Bz
LYSAGHT, Thomas		19	M	Farmer	270c02Bz
COLLY, William		32	M	Carpenter	270c02Bz
Catharine	(W)	22	F	Wife	270c02Bz
Thomas	(S)	03	M	Child	270c02Bz
Ann	(D)	02	F	Child	270c02Bz
MCGEE, Finton		64	M	Farmer	270c02Bz
Mary		49	F	Unknown	270c02Bz
Judy		23	F	Unknown	270c02Bz
Ellen		17	F	Unknown	270c02Bz
Patrick		28	M	Farmer	270c02Bz
ROUKE, Mathew		58	M	Farmer	270c02Bz
Mary		30	F	Unknown	270c02Bz
Thomas		07	M	Child	270c02Bz
Dennis		05	M	Child	270c02Bz
Fenton		03	M	Child	270c02Bz
Mary		.00	F	Infant	270c02Bz
MCMAHON, Frank		30	M	Weaver	270c02Bz
MCLILOR, Michael		33	M	Farmer	270c02Bz
Catharine	(W)	30	F	Wife	270c02Bz
Maria	(D)	05	F	Child	270c02Bz
WELLEN, Catharine		25	F	House Maid	270c02Bz
Michael	(S)	04	M	Child	270c02Bz
MCLILOR, Patrick		03	M	Child	270c02Bz
CCOCHRAN, Mary		36	F	Dressmaker	270c02Bz
DELANY, Lawrance		38	M	Farmer	270c02Bz
HUCHERSON, James		09	M	Child	270c02Bz
Jane		07	F	Child	270c02Bz
Susan		05	F	Child	270c02Bz
MCGUIRE, Bridget		52	F	Nurse	270c02Bz
WARD, Nancy		23	F	Servant	270c02Bz
MCNEAL, Ann		16	F	Servant	270c02Bz
Mary		12	F	Servant	270c02Bz
TAYLOR, Thomas		30	M	Draper	270c02Bz

NAMES OF PASSENGERS		AGE	SEX	OCCUPATIONS	DATE PORT SHIP
CUMMUSKY, Mathia		30	F	Servant	270c02Bz
MOORE, Francis		38	M	Laborer	270c02Bz
RILEY, Philip		31	M	Laborer	270c02Bz
COILE, Terrance		38	M	Laborer	270c02Bz
Mary		65	F	Nurse	270c02Bz
Ann	(W)	30	F	Servant	270c02Bz
REELLY, Edward		02	M	Child	270c02Bz
KLINE, Bridget		33	F	Housekeeper	270c02Bz
DOWUR, Maria		26	F	Housekeeper	270c02Bz
Mary	(D)	02	F	Child	270c02Bz
BRIAN, William		18	M	Laborer	270c02Bz
QUINN, William		24	M	Laborer	270c02Bz
BANGUS, Thomas		22	M	Locksmith	270c02Bz
RILEY, Sarah		15	F	Servant	270c02Bz
DERKEN, James		20	M	Laborer	270c02Bz
Ann		18	F	Servant	270c02Bz
CARTER, Stephen		22	M	Pit Sawyer	270c02Bz
CARLES, James		22	M	Pit Sawyer	270c02Bz
GRACE, Bridget		20	F	House Maid	270c02Bz
FEE, John		18	M	Farmer	270c02Bz
Henry		13	M	Farmer	270c02Bz
Jane		21	F	House Maid	270c02Bz
RYAN, Mary		34	F	House Maid	270c02Bz
FITZPATRICK, John		15	M	Farmer	270c02Bz
ARNORD, Biddy		50	F	Unknown	270c02Bz
SARNHURST, Mary		20	F	Unknown	270c02Bz
KIEF, Mary		10	F	Unknown	270c02Bz
DONILEY, Peter		22	M	Bootmaker	270c02Bz
CROSBY, Mary		25	F	Servant	270c02Bz
MCNAMARAH, Catharine		24	F	Servant	270c02Bz
DONILEY, Edward		18	M	Laborer	270c02Bz
CASLIN, John		20	M	Laborer	270c02Bz
MCNAMARAH, Ennis		20	M	Laborer	270c02Bz
BARRY, Michael		19	M	Laborer	270c02Bz
DONNELLY, Edward		23	M	Mason	270c02Bz
TOOLIN, Andrew		20	M	Tailor	270c02Bz
KELLY, Simon		22	M	Tailor	270c02Bz
RIELLY, Bridget		14	F	Lad	270c02Bz
CASSIDY, Mary		20	F	Servant	270c02Bz
WORTHINGTON, Michael		40	M	Shoemaker	270c02Bz
DOOLEY, John		18	M	Shoemaker	270c02Bz
KIEF, John		25	M	Laborer	270c02Bz
Timothy		25	M	Laborer	270c02Bz
HORTY, Michael		26	M	Laborer	270c02Bz
GRADY, Catharine		34	F	House Maid	270c02Bz
RYAN, Mary		26	F	Dairymaid	270c02Bz
GRADY, David		13	M	Servant	270c02Bz
Mary		09	F	Child	270c02Bz
Henry		06	M	Child	270c02Bz
RYAN, Dennis		20	M	Shoemaker	270c02Bz
HALEY, Philip		28	M	Laborer	270c02Bz
ODONELD, Jerry		16	M	Laborer	270c02Bz
Catharine		22	F	Servant	270c02Bz
Bridget		17	F	Servant	270c02Bz
COCKLIN, Anora		24	F	Dairymaid	270c02Bz
PARSLEY, Catharine		60	F	Nurse	270c02Bz
LINER, Margret		20	F	Servant	270c02Bz
SHEERER, Elizabeth		19	F	Servant	270c02Bz
George		21	M	Laborer	270c02Bz
MCGAUGHAY, Mary		18	F	Servant	270c02Bz
HUTCHERSON, Catharine		44	F	Servant	270c02Bz
Elizabeth	(D)	11	F	None	270c02Bz
KILLY, James		25	M	Farmer	270c02Bz
LADY, Barned		40	M	Coachman	270c02Bz
John		69	M	Coachman	270c02Bz
Mary		66	F	Unknown	270c02Bz
ANDERSON, Alice		19	F	Servant	270c02Bz
KELLY, Mary		22	F	Servant	270c02Bz
DONAHOE, Ellen		18	F	Servant	270c02Bz
CUNNINGHAM, Thomas		22	M	Laborer	270c02Bz
QUIRLAN, Mary		22	F	Dressmaker	270c02Bz
FARLAN, Bridget		17	F	Servant	270c02Bz
RILEY, Catharine		26	F	Housekeeper	270c02Bz
Peter	(S)	04	M	Child	270c02Bz

REPUBLIC 28 OCTOBER 1847

From Liverpool

NAMES OF PASSENGERS		AGE	SEX	OCCUPATIONS	DATE PORT SHIP
MAGALAIN, Francis		22	M	Farmer	280c02Nv
SMITH, Terrance		27	M	Farmer	280c02Nv
OROURKE, Andrew		25	M	Baker	280c02Nv
WELCH, Batty		34	M	Laborer	280c02Nv
Margaret		30	F	Laborer	280c02Nv
OBRIEN, Mary		27	F	Laborer	280c02Nv
JONES, Mary		38	F	Laborer	280c02Nv
Charles	(S)	13	M	Laborer	280c02Nv
Fredrick	(S)	09	M	Child	280c02Nv
MURPHY, John		26	M	Ppstr	280c02Nv
Jane		24	F	Unknown	280c02Nv
EVANS, Eliza		30	F	Unknown	280c02Nv
Jane		30	F	Unknown	280c02Nv
HANARTY, Michael		31	M	Laborer	280c02Nv
MACANALLY, Mary		35	F	Laborer	280c02Nv
KILROE, Bridget		21	F	Laborer	280c02Nv
KNOWLAND, Ann		19	F	Laborer	280c02Nv
ODONNOLL, John		30	M	Shop Boy	280c02Nv
James		28	M	Shop Boy	280c02Nv
GRIBBIN, James		21	M	Carpenter	280c02Nv
MCMONIGAL, Samuel		38	M	Farmer	280c02Nv
Rebecca	(W)	37	F	Wife	280c02Nv
Mary-Jane	(D)	08	F	Child	280c02Nv
Michael	(S)	06	M	Child	280c02Nv
George	(S)	04	M	Child	280c02Nv
William	(S)	03	M	Child	280c02Nv
Robert	(S)	.00	M	Infant	280c02Nv
Died-At-Sea					
DOLIN, Owen		50	M	Miller	280c02Nv
Catherine	(W)	48	F	Unknown	280c02Nv
Susan	(D)	16	F	Unknown	280c02Nv
Alexander	(S)	17	M	Miller	280c02Nv
John	(S)	25	M	Miller	280c02Nv
Patrick	(S)	19	M	Miller	280c02Nv
KENNAN, Ann		27	F	Unknown	280c02Nv
MAHONEY, Thomas		60	M	Weaver	280c02Nv
CONNELL, Matthew		50	M	Weaver	280c02Nv
MAHONEY, John		24	M	Weaver	280c02Nv
CONLAN, Ann		50	F	Laborer	280c02Nv
Betty	(D)	17	F	Laborer	280c02Nv
Ann	(D)	21	F	Laborer	280c02Nv
DAVIES, Matthew		32	M	Laborer	280c02Nv
MCDONNELL, Mary		50	F	Laborer	280c02Nv
BRADEY, Bridget		50	F	Laborer	280c02Nv
DOLLON, Mary		24	F	Laborer	280c02Nv
FOX, John		23	M	Laborer	280c02Nv
COYLE, Pat		12	M	Laborer	280c02Nv
Rosey		14	F	Unknown	280c02Nv
Catherine		12	F	Unknown	280c02Nv
HARTON, John		22	M	Laborer	280c02Nv
MCQUIRK, John		25	M	Laborer	280c02Nv
DONAHUE, James		25	M	Laborer	280c02Nv
LEAREY, Honora		30	F	Unknown	280c02Nv
NEILL, Ellen		18	F	Unknown	280c02Nv
SULLIVAN, Mary		18	F	Unknown	280c02Nv
MCGUIRE, Mary		42	F	Unknown	280c02Nv
Catherine	(D)	20	F	Unknown	280c02Nv
Francis	(S)	15	M	Unknown	280c02Nv
John	(S)	12	M	Unknown	280c02Nv
Jane	(D)	10	F	Unknown	280c02Nv
Pat	(S)	07	M	Child	280c02Nv
Mary	(D)	05	F	Child	280c02Nv
CONNER, Coney		30	F	Unknown	280c02Nv
Catherine	(W)	25	F	Wife	280c02Nv
Ellen	(D)	.00	F	Infant	280c02Nv

NAMES OF PASSENGERS		AGE	SEX	OCCUPATIONS	DATE PORT SHIP
LYNCH, Owen		30	M	Laborer	280c02Nv
CLARKSON, Andrew		37	M	Laborer	280c02Nv
RILEY, Mat		22	M	Laborer	280c02Nv
KELLY, Thomas		27	M	Laborer	280c02Nv
SMITH, Betsy		25	F	Unknown	280c02Nv
FINNIGAN, James		30	M	Unknown	280c02Nv
RILEY, Catherine		22	F	Unknown	280c02Nv
CASSODY, Ann		30	F	Unknown	280c02Nv
Catherine		20	F	Unknown	280c02Nv
Rose		.00	F	Infant	280c02Nv
STERLING, James		18	M	Painter	280c02Nv
HILL, James		20	M	Unknown	280c02Nv
LONG, Honna		30	F	Unknown	280c02Nv
Mary	(D)	08	F	Child	280c02Nv
LYNCH, Mary		30	F	Unknown	280c02Nv
Catherine		16	F	Unknown	280c02Nv
Honora		08	F	Child	280c02Nv
Julia		06	F	Child	280c02Nv
William		03	M	Child	280c02Nv
Johnnah		.00	F	Infant	280c02Nv
MALLONEY, Pat		25	M	Laborer	280c02Nv
COWEN, William		20	M	Laborer	280c02Nv
Ann		14	F	Unknown	280c02Nv
FLORITEY, William		30	M	Laborer	280c02Nv
WALL, William		56	M	Laborer	280c02Nv
SULLIVAN, Daniel		24	M	Laborer	280c02Nv
Mary	(W)	20	F	Wife	280c02Nv
Dennis	(S)	.00	M	Infant	280c02Nv
HANIGAN, John		20	M	Unknown	280c02Nv
Johannah		16	F	Unknown	280c02Nv
MCGAN, Pat		26	M	Unknown	280c02Nv
CARROL, Daniel		24	M	Laborer	280c02Nv
DOUD, Michael		28	M	Laborer	280c02Nv
Catherine		21	F	Laborer	280c02Nv
Ellen		08	F	Child	280c02Nv
Mary		06	F	Child	280c02Nv
Catherine		03	F	Child	280c02Nv
GRANFIELD, Robert		50	M	Unknown	280c02Nv
Thomas	(S)	22	M	Unknown	280c02Nv
Johannah	(D)	19	F	Unknown	280c02Nv
COLEMAN, James		58	M	Laborer	280c02Nv
Nelly	(W)	50	F	Wife	280c02Nv
Mary	(D)	16	F	Unknown	280c02Nv
James	(S)	13	M	Unknown	280c02Nv
Catherine	(D)	11	F	Unknown	280c02Nv
Ann	(D)	09	F	Child	280c02Nv
John	(S)	09	M	Child	280c02Nv
Bridget	(D)	.00	F	Infant	280c02Nv
CUSHACK, John		24	M	Laborer	280c02Nv
FERGERSON, John		26	M	Laborer	280c02Nv
MCGARAHAN, Mary		19	F	Laborer	280c02Nv
COCHLAN, Catherine		35	F	Unknown	280c02Nv
Daniel		22	M	Laborer	280c02Nv
Margaret		13	F	Unknown	280c02Nv
Bridget		11	F	Unknown	280c02Nv
Ann		06	F	Child	280c02Nv
CEAIN, John		14	M	Laborer	280c02Nv
STANTON, Pat-E.		22	M	Laborer	280c02Nv
KIERNAN, Andrew		20	M	Laborer	280c02Nv
HURSON, Judah		54	M	Laborer	280c02Nv
Henry	(S)	22	M	Laborer	280c02Nv
John	(S)	21	M	Laborer	280c02Nv
Francis	(S)	18	M	Laborer	280c02Nv
James	(S)	11	M	Laborer	280c02Nv
Mary	(D)	09	F	Child	280c02Nv
CONNON, Thomas		24	M	Laborer	280c02Nv
LARKIN, Peter		16	M	Laborer	280c02Nv
HANAHAN, Michael		26	M	Shoemaker	280c02Nv
MAHONEY, Margaret		30	F	Unknown	280c02Nv
Nenny	(D)	03	F	Child	280c02Nv
Dennis	(S)	.00	M	Infant	280c02Nv
RICE, James		34	M	Laborer	280c02Nv
Mary	(W)	33	F	Wife	280c02Nv
Margaret	(D)	13	F	Unknown	280c02Nv
John	(S)	09	M	Child	280c02Nv
RICE, Mary-Ann	(D)	07	F	Child	280c02Nv
Selah	(D)	05	F	Child	280c02Nv
James	(S)	02	M	Child	280c02Nv
GUIGGIN, Lawrence		20	M	Unknown	280c02Nv
ROGAN, John		20	M	Unknown	280c02Nv
HASLAN, Sarah		20	F	Unknown	280c02Nv
GAGHAN, Patrick		23	M	Laborer	280c02Nv
BELL, James		19	M	Laborer	280c02Nv
FOX, William		22	M	Laborer	280c02Nv
Barney		17	M	Laborer	280c02Nv
MCAULEY, P.		35	M	Unknown	280c02Nv

COMMERCE 03 NOVEMBER 1847

From Galway

NAMES OF PASSENGERS		AGE	SEX	OCCUPATIONS	DATE PORT SHIP
FINIGAN, Pat.		40	M	Laborer	03No11c
Margaret		36	F	Spinster	03No11c
Bridget		23	F	Spinster	03No11c
Ann		20	F	Spinster	03No11c
Pat		18	M	Laborer	03No11c
William		15	M	Laborer	03No11c
DEVANE, Mary		19	F	Spinster	03No11c
ODEA, Ellen		19	F	Spinster	03No11c
FINIGAN, Bridget		19	F	Spinster	03No11c
MURRY, Bridget		21	F	Spinster	03No11c
Honor		23	F	Spinster	03No11c
NAUGHTEN, Stephen		24	M	Laborer	03No11c
BRAKERY, Catherine		46	F	Spinster	03No11c
Ann		24	F	Spinster	03No11c
Honor		26	F	Spinster	03No11c
CONNELLY, John		28	M	Laborer	03No11c
WARD, Pat		32	M	Laborer	03No11c
Bridget	(W)	29	F	Spinster	03No11c
Thomas	(S)	14	M	Laborer	03No11c
John	(S)	12	M	Laborer	03No11c
James	(S)	09	M	Child	03No11c
Peter	(S)	07	M	Child	03No11c
Pat	(S)	04	M	Child	03No11c
Julia	(D)	01	F	Child	03No11c
ERWIN, Harry		42	M	Victualler	03No11c
FLAHERTY, Pat		21	M	Victualler	03No11c
BUTLEE, Micheal		28	M	Victualler	03No11c
BURNS, Catherine		21	F	Spinster	03No11c
COLEMAN, Mooney		30	F	Spinster	03No11c
SPELLMAN, Martin		32	M	Laborer	03No11c
DARMODY, Sarah		24	F	Spinster	03No11c
Michael	(S)	02	M	Child	03No11c
MURAN, Catherine		30	F	Spinster	03No11c
Michael	(S)	.00	M	Infant	03No11c
MCDONALD, Mary		24	F	Spinster	03No11c
HANBERRY, Michael		22	M	Servant	03No11c
RIELLEY, William		21	M	Laborer	03No11c
DEVANY, Mary		20	F	Spinster	03No11c
COSTELLO, Michael		22	M	Laborer	03No11c
KERNS, Dennis		29	M	Laborer	03No11c
DARMODY, James		36	M	Laborer	03No11c
HAVERTY, D.		22	M	Victualler	03No11c
GREAVY, John		30	M	Laborer	03No11c
Catherine		30	F	Spinster	03No11c
Bridget		20	F	Spinster	03No11c
CONREY, Winny		35	F	Spinster	03No11c
Thomas		19	M	Laborer	03No11c
Ann		07	F	Child	03No11c
Margaret		18	F	Spinster	03No11c
MACK, Martin		40	M	Laborer	03No11c
PRENDERGRASS, Miles		26	M	Laborer	03No11c
BREADY, Bridget		32	F	Spinster	03No11c
Kate		22	F	Spinster	03No11c

NAMES OF PASSENGERS		AGE	SEX	OCCUPATIONS	DATE PORT SHIP
BREADY, Mary		03	F	Child	03No11Ic
CORLIS, Mary		30	F	Servant	03No11Ic
QUINLAN, Charles		23	M	Laborer	03No11Ic
Emilie		19	F	Spinster	03No11Ic
WALKER, Jane		23	F	Spinster	03No11Ic
RYAN, Mary		25	F	Spinster	03No11Ic
QUIN, Tim		28	M	Laborer	03No11Ic
SOMERLY, John		30	M	Laborer	03No11Ic
Mary	(D)	09	F	Child	03No11Ic
John	(S)	02	M	Child	03No11Ic
BLUNDELL, Ann		26	F	Spinster	03No11Ic
MORAN, Larry		20	M	Laborer	03No11Ic
EDGAR, Jas.		27	M	Gentleman	03No11Ic
SMYTH, Pat		20	M	Gentleman	03No11Ic
GRIFFIN, Wm.		25	M	Laborer	03No11Ic
MURAN, Mary		17	F	Spinster	03No11Ic
BREADY, Pat		01	M	Child	03No11Ic
John		06	M	Child	03No11Ic
RIELLY, Philip		11	M	Unknown	03No11Ic
FLYNN, Ned		30	M	Victualler	03No11Ic
RIDGE, Tim		30	M	Laborer	03No11Ic
HEAVY, John		28	M	Laborer	03No11Ic
Margaret		30	F	Unknown	03No11Ic
Pat		18	M	Laborer	03No11Ic
Nelly		26	F	Spinster	03No11Ic
Mary		17	F	Spinster	03No11Ic
DONOGHOE, Michael		30	M	Servant	03No11Ic
JUDGE, Anna		15	F	Spinster	03No11Ic
MCDONOUGH, Thomas		15	M	Unknown	03No11Ic
Pat		18	M	Laborer	03No11Ic
Michael		12	M	Unknown	03No11Ic
Margaret		35	F	Unknown	03No11Ic
Margaret		15	F	Spinster	03No11Ic
Mary		10	F	Unknown	03No11Ic
GLYNN, Jas.		22	M	Laborer	03No11Ic
QUILAN, Pat		03	M	Child	03No11Ic
MCDONOUGH, Michael		07	M	Child	03No11Ic

MARY-PHILLIPS 04 NOVEMBER 1847

From Dublin

NAMES OF PASSENGERS		AGE	SEX	OCCUPATIONS	DATE PORT SHIP
SCOLLON, Terence-Revd.		28	M	Clergyman	04No20Sr
CROSBY, Eleanor-C.		25	F	Unknown	04No20Sr
BIBBY, Richd.M.		13	M	Unknown	04No20Sr
HAUGHTON, Edwd.W.		20	M	Clerk	04No20Sr
RYAL, Christopher		29	M	Tailor	04No20Sr
Ann		28	F	Unknown	04No20Sr
BOYLEN, Mary		35	F	Unknown	04No20Sr
John	(S)	11	M	Unknown	04No20Sr
Ellen	(D)	02	F	Child	04No20Sr
KERNS, James		24	M	Farmer	04No20Sr
Eliza		24	F	Unknown	04No20Sr
WHELEMAN, Michl.		24	M	Farmer	04No20Sr
VERNON, George		25	M	Wlmcht	04No20Sr
SWEENY, Mary		19	F	Unknown	04No20Sr
SHANLY, Mary		20	F	Unknown	04No20Sr

BROOKSBY 05 NOVEMBER 1847

From Glasgow

NAMES OF PASSENGERS		AGE	SEX	OCCUPATIONS	DATE PORT SHIP
BURK, Saran		26	F	None	05No04Ex
WHITE, Ann		50	F	None	05No04Ex
CUMMING, Mary		23	F	None	05No04Ex
MCGOWN, Ann		17	F	None	05No04Ex
CORCORRAN, Jas.		28	M	Laborer	05No04Ex

ELIZABETH-DENISON 05 NOVEMBER 1847

From Liverpool

NAMES OF PASSENGERS		AGE	SEX	OCCUPATIONS	DATE PORT SHIP
FINLEY, William		35	M	Farmer	05No02Jn
Anne	(W)	35	F	Wife	05No02Jn
Mary-Ann	(D)	11	F	Farmer	05No02Jn
John	(S)	09	M	Child	05No02Jn
Betsey	(D)	07	F	Child	05No02Jn
Sarah	(D)	05	F	Child	05No02Jn
John		44	M	Farmer	05No02Jn
BELL, Anne		27	F	Unknown	05No02Jn
HEYWOOD, Mary		24	F	Laborer	05No02Jn
REILLEY, Thomas		26	M	Laborer	05No02Jn
MCCORMICK, Michael		27	M	Laborer	05No02Jn
GIROM, Thomas		21	M	Laborer	05No02Jn
MULDON, Judy		25	F	Laborer	05No02Jn
Judy	(D)	08	F	Child	05No02Jn
Margarett	(D)	06	F	Child	05No02Jn
Ellen	(D)	02	F	Child	05No02Jn
MCCORMICK, Bridgett		20	F	Laborer	05No02Jn
MURRAY, Anne		20	F	Laborer	05No02Jn
FARRELLY, Anne		16	F	Laborer	05No02Jn
COROLAN, Mary		17	F	Laborer	05No02Jn
BRODY, James		19	M	Laborer	05No02Jn
Mary		17	F	Laborer	05No02Jn
Bridgett		16	F	Laborer	05No02Jn
FARRELLY, James		18	M	Laborer	05No02Jn
MCCANN, Hugh		20	M	Laborer	05No02Jn
SALLERY, Ann		20	F	Laborer	05No02Jn
Died-At-Sea					
MURRY, Rose		24	F	Laborer	05No02Jn
CARNEY, James		24	M	Laborer	05No02Jn
REILLY, Rose		40	F	Laborer	05No02Jn
Rose	(D)	20	F	Laborer	05No02Jn
John	(S)	18	M	Laborer	05No02Jn
Patrick	(S)	16	M	Laborer	05No02Jn
James	(S)	07	M	Child	05No02Jn
MCGUIRE, Susan		40	F	Laborer	05No02Jn
BYRNE, Margarett		21	F	Laborer	05No02Jn
CAROLAN, Owen		20	M	Laborer	05No02Jn
GALVIN, Patrick		36	M	Laborer	05No02Jn
Bridgett	(W)	33	F	Wife	05No02Jn
Maria	(D)	01	F	Child	05No02Jn
BRERLY, Isaac		22	M	Tailor	05No02Jn
MCCRARY, Patrick		24	M	Tailor	05No02Jn
BARRY, Thomas		25	M	Tailor	05No02Jn
FOWLER, Thomas		28	M	Joiner	05No02Jn
Maria		24	F	Unknown	05No02Jn
MOOREHOUSE, Edward		24	M	Laborer	05No02Jn
DORAN, James		35	M	Unknown	05No02Jn
Catharine	(W)	30	F	Wife	05No02Jn
Bridgett	(D)	13	F	Unknown	05No02Jn

NAMES OF PASSENGERS		AGE	SEX	OCCUPATIONS	DATE PORT SHIP
DORAN, Mary	(D)	11	F	Unknown	05No02Jn
Catharine	(D)	09	F	Child	05No02Jn
Ellen	(D)	07	F	Child	05No02Jn
James	(S)	04	M	Child	05No02Jn
MEEHAN, Mary-Ann		20	F	Unknown	05No02Jn
MCCARTHY, Betsey		20	F	Unknown	05No02Jn
HUMPHREY, Patrick		21	M	Unknown	05No02Jn
Anne		40	F	Unknown	05No02Jn
GILLEAS, Mary		22	F	Unknown	05No02Jn
MURPHY, Charles		30	M	Unknown	05No02Jn
CROSSEN, Catharine		40	F	Unknown	05No02Jn
CAREY, Denis		20	M	Unknown	05No02Jn
Patrick		22	M	Unknown	05No02Jn
CARROLL, Joseph		25	M	Tailor	05No02Jn
Ellen	(W)	25	F	Wife	05No02Jn
Mary	(D)	01	F	Child	05No02Jn
James	(S)	.00	M	Infant	05No02Jn
CAREY, Jane		18	F	Unknown	05No02Jn
HOSEY, Bridgett		18	F	Unknown	05No02Jn
MALOY, Eliza		21	F	Unknown	05No02Jn
ONEIL, Johanna		30	F	Unknown	05No02Jn
DONOHUE, Ellen		17	F	Unknown	05No02Jn
BOYLAN, Catharine		60	F	Unknown	05No02Jn
Catharine		20	F	Unknown	05No02Jn
SULLIVAN, Denis		11	M	Laborer	05No02Jn
CREAMER, John		25	M	Tailor	05No02Jn
BRENNON, Margarette		27	F	Unknown	05No02Jn
NOLAN, Peter		21	M	Laborer	05No02Jn
DONIEL, Edward		30	M	Laborer	05No02Jn
GAVIN, Margarette		34	F	Laborer	05No02Jn
Died-At-Sea					
Anne	(D)	05	F	Child	05No02Jn
Catharine	(D)	.00	F	Infant	05No02Jn
Died-At-Sea					
GELSHENON, Christopher		28	M	Tailor	05No02Jn
Mary		18	F	Unknown	05No02Jn
Died-At-Sea					
Judy		16	F	Unknown	05No02Jn
AGAR, Henry		20	M	Blacksmith	05No02Jn
TROEY, Michael		30	M	Laborer	05No02Jn
BOYLON, Edward		40	M	Servant	05No02Jn
PALINER, Hiram		47	M	Gdnr	05No02Jn
Sarah	(W)	48	F	Wife	05No02Jn
John-G.	(S)	13	M	Unknown	05No02Jn
Samuel	(S)	10	M	Unknown	05No02Jn
MILLER, William		36	M	Laborer	05No02Jn
Sarah	(W)	35	F	Wife	05No02Jn
Martha	(D)	.00	F	Infant	05No02Jn
CARROLL, Maria		29	F	Unknown	05No02Jn
Ellen		24	F	Unknown	05No02Jn
Margarette		23	F	Unknown	05No02Jn
Anne		21	F	Unknown	05No02Jn
GROTTON, John		52	M	Laborer	05No02Jn
U	(W)	40	F	Wife	05No02Jn
Peter	(S)	24	M	Laborer	05No02Jn
Lawrence	(S)	22	M	Laborer	05No02Jn
Patrick	(S)	20	M	Laborer	05No02Jn
John	(S)	13	M	Laborer	05No02Jn
Bridgett	(D)	09	F	Child	05No02Jn
Bartholom	(S)	04	M	Child	05No02Jn
CARTE, Eliza		20	F	Laborer	05No02Jn
BLANEY, Jane		25	F	Laborer	05No02Jn
COSTELLO, James		04	M	Child	05No02Jn
DONERLY, Margarett		18	F	Laborer	05No02Jn
GROTTON, Patrick		40	M	Laborer	05No02Jn
Died-At-Sea					
MCGOWAN, Michael		20	M	Laborer	05No02Jn
MCCUE, Frank		21	M	Laborer	05No02Jn
MOLLYHAN, Margarette		41	F	Laborer	05No02Jn
MAYWELL, Brigette		18	F	Laborer	05No02Jn
BYRNE, Margarette		18	F	Laborer	05No02Jn
WINKLEHAM, Sarah		59	F	Laborer	05No02Jn
ROWLEY, George		12	M	Laborer	05No02Jn
Margarett		04	F	Child	05No02Jn
FOX, Margarett		60	F	Laborer	05No02Jn

NAMES OF PASSENGERS		AGE	SEX	OCCUPATIONS	DATE PORT SHIP
FOX, Eliz.		32	F	Laborer	05No02Jn
Patrick		11	M	Laborer	05No02Jn
Margarett		09	F	Child	05No02Jn
John		07	M	Child	05No02Jn
Charles		03	M	Child	05No02Jn
James		.00	M	Infant	05No02Jn
CHENY, Mrs.H.		23	F	Unknown	05No02Jn
Fanny	(D)	.00	F	Infant	05No02Jn
GROLE, James		47	M	Unknown	05No02Jn
Catharine	(W)	36	F	Wife	05No02Jn
Maria	(D)	16	F	Unknown	05No02Jn
Dennis	(S)	02	M	Child	05No02Jn
HINES, Owen		30	M	Unknown	05No02Jn
John		24	M	Unknown	05No02Jn
CHITTICK, James		25	M	Unknown	05No02Jn
Margarett		24	F	Unknown	05No02Jn
Elizabeth		23	F	Unknown	05No02Jn
Margarett		44	F	Unknown	05No02Jn
Christopher		17	M	Unknown	05No02Jn
Christopher		.00	M	Infant	05No02Jn
Catharine		21	F	Unknown	05No02Jn
BRATZ, Francis		36	M	Unknown	05No02Jn
GARRETTY, Bryon		48	M	Unknown	05No02Jn
Catharine	(W)	48	F	Wife	05No02Jn
Michael	(S)	21	M	Unknown	05No02Jn
SCACENEY, James		22	M	Unknown	05No02Jn
LARKIN, Wilson		18	M	Unknown	05No02Jn
MCBRIDE, Patrick		40	M	Unknown	05No02Jn
Margarett	(W)	38	F	Wife	05No02Jn
Andrew	(S)	20	M	Unknown	05No02Jn
MCCARTON, Patrick		19	M	Unknown	05No02Jn
GEE, Anne		18	F	Unknown	05No02Jn
MIMBLE, Margarett		19	F	Unknown	05No02Jn
BAHAN, Rose		20	F	Unknown	05No02Jn
MCGURK, Ellen		18	F	Unknown	05No02Jn
HEARNY, Barthol		18	M	Unknown	05No02Jn
MCCORMICK, James		50	M	Unknown	05No02Jn
James	(S)	19	M	Unknown	05No02Jn
Peter	(S)	17	M	Unknown	05No02Jn
Anne	(D)	16	F	Unknown	05No02Jn
MCGLOCHEN, Henry		40	M	Unknown	05No02Jn
MCHIDLE, Thomas		21	M	Unknown	05No02Jn
MCCONNELL, Patrick		24	M	Unknown	05No02Jn
U	(W)	24	F	Wife	05No02Jn
MATHEWS, Margarett		20	F	Unknown	05No02Jn
SMETHIAN, Mathew		19	M	Unknown	05No02Jn
Died-At-Sea					
WALLACE, Wm.		26	M	Unknown	05No02Jn
CREAMER, Betsey		16	F	Unknown	05No02Jn
FITZGERALD, Judith		20	F	Unknown	05No02Jn
DOBBIN, John		20	M	Unknown	05No02Jn
U	(W)	20	F	Wife	05No02Jn
LYON, James		40	M	Unknown	05No02Jn
U	(W)	30	F	Wife	05No02Jn
James	(S)	12	M	Unknown	05No02Jn
Samuel	(S)	08	M	Child	05No02Jn
Elizabeth	(D)	06	F	Child	05No02Jn
Thomas	(S)	04	M	Child	05No02Jn
LANG, George		19	M	Unknown	05No02Jn
LYONS, Sarah		60	F	Unknown	05No02Jn
Ann	(D)	30	F	Unknown	05No02Jn
PRATT, Charlotte		28	F	Unknown	05No02Jn
Eliza	(D)	08	F	Child	05No02Jn
QUINN, John		22	M	Unknown	05No02Jn
William		20	M	Unknown	05No02Jn
MARSHALL, Scott		25	M	Unknown	05No02Jn
LARKIN, Margarett		22	F	Unknown	05No02Jn
CONREY, Michael		25	M	Unknown	05No02Jn
DOYLE, Margarett		11	F	Unknown	05No02Jn
MOORE, William		25	M	Unknown	05No02Jn
HENEY, Thomas		25	M	Unknown	05No02Jn
Elizabeth		24	F	Unknown	05No02Jn
QUINN, Catherine		20	F	Unknown	05No02Jn
MCCROM, Catherine		20	F	Unknown	05No02Jn
Sarah		18	F	Unknown	05No02Jn

NAMES OF PASSENGERS		AGE	SEX	OCCUPATIONS	DATE PORT SHIP
SULIVAN, Robert		25	M	Unknown	05No02Jn
Jerey		23	M	Unknown	05No02Jn
CASEY, James		37	M	Unknown	05No02Jn
DUCKWORTH, Daniel		13	M	Unknown	05No02Jn
MCGALLEY, Owen		27	M	Unknown	05No02Jn
CALLOHAN, Margarett		19	F	Unknown	05No02Jn
RYAN, John		25	M	Unknown	05No02Jn
BURNS, Joseph		20	M	Unknown	05No02Jn
GALLGER, Margaret		20	F	Unknown	05No02Jn
HEALY, Daniel		22	M	Unknown	05No02Jn
HULY, Mary		18	F	Unknown	05No02Jn
BROWN, Richard		37	M	Unknown	05No02Jn
COLLINS, Christopher		20	M	Unknown	05No02Jn
MALONY, John		20	M	Unknown	05No02Jn
MCFARLAND, Duncan		20	M	Unknown	05No02Jn
STAFFORD, Margarett		25	F	Unknown	05No02Jn

PEDRAZA 09 NOVEMBER 1847

From Nassau

NAMES OF PASSENGERS		AGE	SEX	OCCUPATIONS	DATE PORT SHIP
WEBB, Fredrick		21	M	Merchant	09No93Ss
SYMNETT, Wm.		17	M	Clerk	09No93Ss

WASHINGTON 10 NOVEMBER 1847

From BREMEN,Southampton

NAMES OF PASSENGERS		AGE	SEX	OCCUPATIONS	DATE PORT SHIP
ROBERTS, J.G.		30	M	Gentleman	10No90Fn
U	(W)	18	F	Wife	10No90Fn
NEILL, Hill		20	M	Merchant	10No90Fn
MURPHY, Christian		37	M	Servant	10No90Fn

LOTA 11 NOVEMBER 1847

From Cork

NAMES OF PASSENGERS		AGE	SEX	OCCUPATIONS	DATE PORT SHIP
MCDONNALL, Patrick		35	M	Farmer	11No14St
Jeremiah		29	M	Farmer	11No14St
James		23	M	Farmer	11No14St
SCARNALL, Dennis		63	M	Farmer	11No14St
MCDONNALL, Ellen		19	F	Farmer	11No14St
HANDLAY, Mary		19	F	Farmer	11No14St

LIVERPOOL 12 NOVEMBER 1847

From Liverpool

NAMES OF PASSENGERS		AGE	SEX	OCCUPATIONS	DATE PORT SHIP
BROWN, Joseph		32	M	Gentleman	12No02Bo
STUART, Robert		21	M	Merchant	12No02Bo
FENGAN, Thomas		16	M	Laborer	12No02Bo
FENGAN, Bryan		13	M	Laborer	12No02Bo
KEARNEY, Ellen		20	F	Servant	12No02Bo
SHEEHAN, Mary		14	F	Servant	12No02Bo
Cathe.		12	F	Servant	12No02Bo
HAGAN, Thos.		30	M	Laborer	12No02Bo
CONNER, Pat		40	M	Farmer	12No02Bo
Margt.	(W)	30	F	Wife	12No02Bo
Sarah	(D)	06	F	Child	12No02Bo
Mary	(D)	04	F	Child	12No02Bo
Margt.	(D)	02	F	Child	12No02Bo
Michl.	(S)	.06	M	Infant	12No02Bo
STEWART, Jane		20	F	Servant	12No02Bo
MAHON, Cornelius		20	M	Laborer	12No02Bo
LYNAN, John		25	M	Laborer	12No02Bo
Maria		20	F	Servant	12No02Bo
HEVERNAN, Mary		20	F	Servant	12No02Bo
LIST, George		20	M	Laborer	12No02Bo
Johanna		20	F	Servant	12No02Bo
DEATON, Michl.		54	M	Sawer	12No02Bo
Ellen	(W)	44	F	Wife	12No02Bo
Pat	(S)	11	M	Unknown	12No02Bo
Mary	(D)	09	F	Child	12No02Bo
Betty	(D)	05	F	Child	12No02Bo
Mathew	(S)	07	M	Child	12No02Bo
James Died-At-Sea	(S)	01	M	Child	12No02Bo
GORMAN, John		23	M	Laborer	12No02Bo
WALKER, John		30	M	Carpenter	12No02Bo
Robert		28	M	Carpenter	12No02Bo
GILROY, John		20	M	Farmer	12No02Bo
GILBRIDE, James		21	M	Farmer	12No02Bo
OBOYLE, John		18	M	Farmer	12No02Bo
RILEY, Pat		26	M	Laborer	12No02Bo
Rose	(W)	25	F	Wife	12No02Bo
Nancy	(M)	50	F	Unknown	12No02Bo
John		21	M	Carpenter	12No02Bo
Ann		19	F	Servant	12No02Bo
Bridget		16	F	Servant	12No02Bo
Margt.		12	F	Servant	12No02Bo
Ellen		09	F	Child	12No02Bo
DEATON, Honora		08	F	Child	12No02Bo
RYLEY, William		19	M	Laborer	12No02Bo
Bernard		02	M	Child	12No02Bo
Pat		.04	M	Infant	12No02Bo
CARLAN, Margt.		20	F	Servant	12No02Bo
IAGO, Ann		17	F	Servant	12No02Bo
NOONAN, Dennis		19	M	Farmer	12No02Bo
Eliza	(W)	24	F	Wife	12No02Bo
GLASS, Mary		20	F	Servant	12No02Bo
MCCLUSKEY, Margt.		18	F	Servant	12No02Bo
SAXTON, John		27	M	Laborer	12No02Bo
Margt.	(W)	27	F	Wife	12No02Bo
Francis		20	M	Laborer	12No02Bo
John	(S)	03	M	Child	12No02Bo
GILLDAY, Edward		24	M	Laborer	12No02Bo
SHAW, John-Smith		20	M	Merchant	12No02Bo
BARNES, Edward		27	M	Engineer	12No02Bo
Jane	(W)	26	F	Wife	12No02Bo
Mary	(D)	02	F	Child	12No02Bo
LAW, Thomas		18	M	Laborer	12No02Bo
PURFIAL, Pat		20	M	Butcher	12No02Bo
WILLIAM, Henry-M.		60	M	Storekeeper	12No02Bo
ROUKE, Cathe.		51	F	Servant	12No02Bo
Thomas		14	M	Servant	12No02Bo
CANE, John		22	M	Clerk	12No02Bo
KELLY, Isabella		23	F	Servant	12No02Bo
Ann		23	F	Servant	12No02Bo
FAHY, Eliza		18	F	Servant	12No02Bo
KELLY, Elizebeth		06	F	Child	12No02Bo
Thos.		04	M	Child	12No02Bo
HIGGINBOTTOM, Geo.		23	M	Clerk	12No02Bo
MCCAN, Thos.		31	M	Laborer	12No02Bo
MIKENS, James		34	M	Laborer	12No02Bo
Wm.	(S)	12	M	Laborer	12No02Bo
HUNT, Letitia		40	F	Servant	12No02Bo

NAMES OF PASSENGERS		AGE	SEX	OCCUPATIONS	DATE PORT SHIP
HIGGINS, James		32	M	Laborer	12No02Bo
HENESY, Patrick		25	M	Laborer	12No02Bo
OBRIEN, Johanna		24	M	Servant	12No02Bo
ROCHE, Mary		20	F	Servant	12No02Bo
BURKE, Edward		16	M	Servant	12No02Bo
HILLIRAN, Dennis		23	M	Farmer	12No02Bo
BUCKLEY, Pat		20	M	Laborer	12No02Bo
LILESS, Mary		25	M	Wife	12No02Bo
Cathe.	(D)	05	F	Child	12No02Bo
HORIGAN, Denis		25	M	Laborer	12No02Bo
Cathe.	(W)	18	F	Wife	12No02Bo
GORMAN, John		23	M	Laborer	12No02Bo
DUSEY, James		30	M	Laborer	12No02Bo
ROWLAWAY, James		30	M	Weaver	12No02Bo
WALSH, James		25	M	Laborer	12No02Bo
Mary	(W)	24	F	Wife	12No02Bo
Mary	(D)	04	F	Child	12No02Bo
Saunders	(S)	02	M	Child	12No02Bo
Ann-D.		20	F	Servant	12No02Bo
GROOMLEY, Margt.		23	F	Servant	12No02Bo
MCDONALD, Tim		37	M	Servant	12No02Bo
MURPHY, Pat		22	M	Laborer	12No02Bo
KELLY, Michl.		27	M	Laborer	12No02Bo
SMITH, Cathe.		20	F	Cnf	12No02Bo
Mary		20	F	Dressmaker	12No02Bo
ENNIS, Stephen		20	M	Clerk	12No02Bo
WAGSTAFF, Charlotte		50	F	Servant	12No02Bo
MCGRATH, Owen		50	M	Laborer	12No02Bo
KEARNEY, Honora		30	F	Servant	12No02Bo
WICKHAM, John		30	M	Blacksmith	12No02Bo
MCILHOO, Wm.		55	M	Farmer	12No02Bo
Margt.	(W)	40	F	Wife	12No02Bo
Sarah	(D)	18	F	Unknown	12No02Bo
Benjn.	(S)	23	M	Unknown	12No02Bo
Wm.	(S)	13	M	Unknown	12No02Bo
Hugh	(S)	12	M	Unknown	12No02Bo
Robert	(S)	04	M	Child	12No02Bo
James	(S)	18	M	Unknown	12No02Bo
GALAN, Mary-A.		20	F	Servant	12No02Bo
KANE, Ann		21	F	Servant	12No02Bo
TRACY, Margt.		16	F	Servant	12No02Bo
Ann		16	F	Servant	12No02Bo
MULLIN, Ann		26	F	Servant	12No02Bo
ROBBINS, Margt.		24	F	Teacher	12No02Bo
Jane	(W)	20	F	Wife	12No02Bo
George-J.	(S)	02	M	Child	12No02Bo
Jane-M.	(D)	03	F	Child	12No02Bo
CORBITT, Biddy		20	F	Servant	12No02Bo
SMITH, Cathe.		52	F	Servant	12No02Bo
Mary	(D)	14	F	Unknown	12No02Bo
HAMMON, James		20	M	Laborer	12No02Bo
COYNE, Cecilia		20	F	Servant	12No02Bo
CAHILL, Bridget		27	F	Servant	12No02Bo
MONAGHAN, Ann		20	F	Servant	12No02Bo
QUINN, Mary		18	F	Servant	12No02Bo
CANNON, Bridget		28	F	Servant	12No02Bo
MYLETT, John		28	M	Laborer	12No02Bo
HASTINGS, Timothy		15	M	Laborer	12No02Bo
MCCARTY, John		00	M	Tailor	12No02Bo
Mary		18	F	Servant	12No02Bo
CRAVEN, Mary		06	F	Child	12No02Bo
WARD, John		16	M	Hrsm	12No02Bo
MCCANN, Mary-A.		31	F	Wife	12No02Bo
Margt.	(D)	11	F	Servant	12No02Bo
James	(S)	06	M	Child	12No02Bo
Sarah	(D)	03	F	Child	12No02Bo
Cathe.	(D)	.06	F	Infant	12No02Bo
MCCASKIE, Peter		18	M	Laborer	12No02Bo
ROBINSON, Jane		15	F	Servant	12No02Bo
Margt.		17	F	Servant	12No02Bo
MCGUIRE, Andrew		17	M	Farmer	12No02Bo
Hannah		19	F	Servant	12No02Bo
Joseph		14	M	Servant	12No02Bo
ROUKE, Pat		45	M	Farmer	12No02Bo
BOYLAN, Lawrence		20	M	Laborer	12No02Bo
ONEILL, Tim		25	M	Laborer	12No02Bo
KEENAN, Thos.		24	M	Lawyer	12No02Bo
Margt.	(W)	24	F	Wife	12No02Bo
Mary	(D)	01	F	Child	12No02Bo
DONOVAN, Jerh.		18	M	Laborer	12No02Bo
Ellen		16	F	Servant	12No02Bo
WELSH, Ellen		39	F	Servant	12No02Bo
James		48	M	Farmer	12No02Bo
David	(S)	11	M	Unknown	12No02Bo
James	(S)	09	M	Child	12No02Bo
Edward	(S)	04	M	Child	12No02Bo
Mary	(D)	06	F	Child	12No02Bo
CONARTY, Pat		24	M	Laborer	12No02Bo
KILLAHAN, John		60	M	Laborer	12No02Bo
ROACH, Pat		25	M	Laborer	12No02Bo
MULONEY, Mary		60	F	Wife	12No02Bo
FAHEY, David		26	M	Laborer	12No02Bo
John		22	M	Laborer	12No02Bo
Wm.		20	M	Laborer	12No02Bo
David		26	M	Laborer	12No02Bo
HAFFEY, Honora		18	F	Servant	12No02Bo
MORRISON, Cathe.		18	F	Servant	12No02Bo
CANNON, Sally		16	F	Servant	12No02Bo
FRAIL, Mannas		60	M	Farmer	12No02Bo
Mary	(W)	65	F	Wife	12No02Bo
Grace	(D)	18	F	Servant	12No02Bo
James	(S)	12	M	Unknown	12No02Bo
MCGILL, Daniel		22	M	Laborer	12No02Bo
BARRON, Bernard		09	M	Child	12No02Bo
Mary		06	F	Child	12No02Bo
MORIARTY, Johanna		36	F	Servant	12No02Bo
LYNCH, Ellen		25	F	Servant	12No02Bo
Ann		21	F	Servant	12No02Bo
CONNARTY, Thos.		20	M	Laborer	12No02Bo
DOONEY, Thos.		02	M	Child	12No02Bo
BYRNE, Mary		21	F	Wife	12No02Bo
BRADY, John		19	M	Laborer	12No02Bo
Mary		16	F	Servant	12No02Bo
Eliza		14	F	Servant	12No02Bo
KEEGAN, Cathe.		18	F	Servant	12No02Bo
Eliza		13	F	Servant	12No02Bo
BRANIGAN, Jane		28	F	Wife	12No02Bo
Robert	(S)	04	M	Child	12No02Bo
Thos.	(S)	01	M	Child	12No02Bo
MCCARRILL, Ellen		16	F	Servant	12No02Bo
KANE, Jane		12	F	Servant	12No02Bo
LYNCH, Ellen		25	F	Servant	12No02Bo
BROGAN, Thos.		27	M	Laborer	12No02Bo
CORMICK, Bridget		20	F	Servant	12No02Bo
FINNON, Cathe.		18	F	Servant	12No02Bo
FAGAN, James		15	M	Laborer	12No02Bo
Mary		07	F	Child	12No02Bo
SLATTERY, Bridget		20	F	Servant	12No02Bo
MCMAHON, Frans.		20	M	Laborer	12No02Bo
John		24	M	Laborer	12No02Bo
SMITH, James		27	M	Laborer	12No02Bo
MCGRAUGH, Pat		16	M	Laborer	12No02Bo
CAHILL, John		27	M	Laborer	12No02Bo
KEEFE, Abby		08	F	Child	12No02Bo
Ellen		06	F	Child	12No02Bo
Bessy		04	F	Child	12No02Bo
HOGAN, Margt.		21	F	Milliner	12No02Bo
BUTLER, Michl.		14	M	Hrsm	12No02Bo

TAROLINTA 12 NOVEMBER 1847

From Liverpool

NAMES OF PASSENGERS		AGE	SEX	OCCUPATIONS	DATE PORT SHIP
MCMURRY, Peter		26	M	Laborer	12No02Fx
FLYNN, Owen		23	M	Groom	12No02Fx
TIMONS, James		21	M	Nailer	12No02Fx
MCMULLEN, Thomas		16	M	Farmer	12No02Fx
Wm.		17	M	Farmer	12No02Fx
WALKER, John		23	M	Farmer	12No02Fx
Alice		20	F	Dressmaker	12No02Fx
KEEGAN, John		32	M	Sailor	12No02Fx
CONNERLY, Margaret		18	F	Servant	12No02Fx
MCLOUGHLIN, James		34	M	Rigger	12No02Fx
Mary-Ann	(D)	11	F	Unknown	12No02Fx
Frances	(D)	09	F	Child	12No02Fx
GAYNOR, Nickolus		55	M	Farmer	12No02Fx
Mary		28	F	Farmer	12No02Fx
Sarah		24	F	Farmer	12No02Fx
Margaret		22	F	Farmer	12No02Fx
Bridget		18	F	Farmer	12No02Fx
Michl.		20	M	Farmer	12No02Fx
John		16	M	Farmer	12No02Fx
GREEN, John		35	M	Grocer	12No02Fx
Esther	(W)	30	F	Wife	12No02Fx
NASH, Wm.		28	M	Servant	12No02Fx
Harriet	(W)	23	F	Wife	12No02Fx
COGAN, Pat		35	M	Laborer	12No02Fx
FINAN, Ellen		24	F	Servant	12No02Fx
TORSNEY, Biddy		20	F	Servant	12No02Fx
BOURKE, Pat		52	M	Laborer	12No02Fx
Mary	(W)	40	F	Wife	12No02Fx
Mic.	(S)	20	M	Laborer	12No02Fx
John	(S)	16	M	Laborer	12No02Fx
Mary	(D)	13	F	Unknown	12No02Fx
Richard	(S)	12	M	Unknown	12No02Fx
Kate	(D)	09	F	Child	12No02Fx
Margart.	(D)	06	F	Child	12No02Fx
Pat	(S)	03	M	Child	12No02Fx
KEEN, Wm.		30	M	Laborer	12No02Fx
DOLAN, Wm.		20	M	Miner	12No02Fx
MCMULLEN, Martha		26	F	Dressmaker	12No02Fx
Jane		24	F	Dressmaker	12No02Fx
Nancy		22	F	Seamstress	12No02Fx
CONLEY, Wm.		18	M	Laborer	12No02Fx
HICKS, Eliza		30	F	Spinster	12No02Fx
HANRAHAN, Patk.		26	M	Miner	12No02Fx
Bridget	(W)	24	F	Wife	12No02Fx
Timothey	(S)	.04	M	Infant	12No02Fx
BOYD, John		29	M	Weaver	12No02Fx
Margaret	(W)	28	F	Wife	12No02Fx
Jane	(D)	06	F	Child	12No02Fx
Sarah-Anne	(D)	04	F	Child	12No02Fx
Mary	(D)	.11	F	Infant	12No02Fx
CANNON, Michael		26	M	Laborer	12No02Fx
Catherine		40	F	Wife	12No02Fx
Barnard		30	M	Laborer	12No02Fx
Brigit		22	F	Wife	12No02Fx
Mary		04	F	Child	12No02Fx
Died-At-Sea					
Frances		20	M	Laborer	12No02Fx
FOX, Michael		30	M	Laborer	12No02Fx
Betty	(W)	20	F	Wife	12No02Fx
Kate	(D)	.10	F	Infant	12No02Fx
HACKET, Pat		37	M	Laborer	12No02Fx
MCGUIRE, Biddy		20	F	Servant	12No02Fx
KELLEY, Nancy		20	F	Servant	12No02Fx
FLANAGAN, Pat		20	M	Laborer	12No02Fx
LEE, Ellen		23	F	Servant	12No02Fx
WILLIAMS, Catharine		18	F	Servant	12No02Fx
CLARK, Pat		35	M	Laborer	12No02Fx
COSTELLO, Mary		17	F	Wife	12No02Fx
Michal		65	M	Musician	12No02Fx
Rose		25	F	Servant	12No02Fx
RYAN, Michael		20	M	Laborer	12No02Fx
MCGROVERY, Alice		40	F	Wife	12No02Fx
Frederick		02	M	Child	12No02Fx
Susan		20	F	Servant	12No02Fx
Agnes		18	F	Servant	12No02Fx
Catherine		16	F	Servant	12No02Fx
Rosan		13	F	Servant	12No02Fx
HOUSTON, William		24	M	Farmer	12No02Fx
HARPER, Eliza		23	F	Servant	12No02Fx
BLAKE, Anne		19	F	Milliner	12No02Fx
CONNERLY, Ellen		17	F	Servant	12No02Fx
CROSS, Susan		23	F	Weaver	12No02Fx
GLYNN, John		28	M	Laborer	12No02Fx
Dennis		20	M	Laborer	12No02Fx
MANNING, Christopher		30	M	Weaver	12No02Fx
MURRY, Michal		22	M	Clerk	12No02Fx
CARTER, Stephen		23	M	Laborer	12No02Fx
CURRY, Stephen		21	M	Laborer	12No02Fx
RYAN, William		30	M	Laborer	12No02Fx
DOLAN, Michal		23	M	Clerk	12No02Fx
MCCEW, Phillip		30	M	Laborer	12No02Fx
John		22	M	Laborer	12No02Fx
LYNN, Sam.		28	M	Laborer	12No02Fx
Mathew		23	M	Laborer	12No02Fx
HIGGINS, William		25	M	Laborer	12No02Fx
Bridget	(W)	22	F	Wife	12No02Fx
Mary	(D)	.11	F	Infant	12No02Fx
CARPENTER, Mathew		40	M	Shoemaker	12No02Fx
DYERS, William		50	M	Architect	12No02Fx
Elizabeth	(W)	45	F	Wife	12No02Fx
Anne	(D)	15	F	Unknown	12No02Fx
Jane	(D)	10	F	Unknown	12No02Fx
MCGUIRE, Mary		21	F	Dressmaker	12No02Fx
ACHIBALD, Mary		19	F	Dressmaker	12No02Fx
RILEY, Henry		20	M	Laborer	12No02Fx
MULRANY, Pat		27	M	Coachman	12No02Fx
RILEY, Mary		16	F	Servant	12No02Fx
Ann		15	F	Servant	12No02Fx
MCCANN, Catharine		19	F	Servant	12No02Fx
ROUKE, Michal		20	M	Miller	12No02Fx
GHARRA, John-A.		22	M	Laborer	12No02Fx
CONLEY, Margaret		18	F	Dressmaker	12No02Fx
COGHAN, Cicily		20	F	Servant	12No02Fx
OBRIAN, Rose		26	F	Servant	12No02Fx
MURPHY, Michal		42	M	Laborer	12No02Fx
CAIG, Eliza		16	F	Servant	12No02Fx
GREEN, Martin		22	M	Laborer	12No02Fx
BURNS, Tom		40	M	Laborer	12No02Fx
MCNAMARRA, Teddy		20	M	Laborer	12No02Fx
DUNN, Eliza		32	F	Servant	12No02Fx
DODDS, Susan		18	F	Seamstress	12No02Fx
Mary	(M)	50	F	Seamstress	12No02Fx
WALTER, Wm.		22	M	Laborer	12No02Fx
Kiltura		42	F	Wife	12No02Fx
Luke		08	M	Child	12No02Fx
Ely		06	M	Child	12No02Fx
Richard		04	M	Child	12No02Fx
Frederick		02	M	Child	12No02Fx
Sarah		11	F	Unknown	12No02Fx
GORE, Mary		25	F	Wife	12No02Fx
John	(S)	02	M	Child	12No02Fx
KISAN, William		28	M	Laborer	12No02Fx
Eliza		20	F	Servant	12No02Fx
OCONNER, Michael		45	M	Laborer	12No02Fx
Catherin	(W)	43	F	Wife	12No02Fx
Michael	(S)	20	M	Laborer	12No02Fx
Bridget	(D)	17	F	Servant	12No02Fx
Mathew	(S)	16	M	Laborer	12No02Fx
William	(S)	13	M	Laborer	12No02Fx
Catherine	(D)	10	F	Unknown	12No02Fx

NAMES OF PASSENGERS		AGE	SEX	OCCUPATIONS	DATE PORT SHIP
OCONNER, John	(S)	07	M	Child	12No02Fx
Margaret	(D)	05	F	Child	12No02Fx
Pat	(S)	04	M	Child	12No02Fx
Roger	(S)	01	M	Child	12No02Fx
CONNERAN, William		24	M	Laborer	12No02Fx
TOHEY, Laurence		26	M	Laborer	12No02Fx
TROY, Lawrence		20	M	Laborer	12No02Fx
SALMOND, John		25	M	Laborer	12No02Fx
DUNN, Tom		22	M	Laborer	12No02Fx
FLOOD, Biddy		20	F	Servant	12No02Fx
DOWALL, Wm.		38	M	Laborer	12No02Fx
MCCOY, Pat		30	M	Laborer	12No02Fx
OCONNER, Domenick		50	M	Laborer	12No02Fx
SULIVAN, Dennis		33	M	Laborer	12No02Fx
REVELAN, John		48	M	Laborer	12No02Fx
Jane	(W)	44	F	Wife	12No02Fx
James	(S)	07	M	Child	12No02Fx
ANDREW, Robert		20	M	Laborer	12No02Fx
HALPIN, Mary		17	F	Servant	12No02Fx
BENNET, Winnie		16	F	Servant	12No02Fx
DONLEY, Jane		17	F	Servant	12No02Fx
MCELROY, Pat		19	M	Laborer	12No02Fx
GILROY, James		26	M	Laborer	12No02Fx
KEELAND, Ned		22	M	Cooper	12No02Fx
MALONEY, James		24	M	Blacksmith	12No02Fx
GILBERT, Charles		23	M	Laborer	12No02Fx

JONA 15 NOVEMBER 1847

From Falmouth

NAMES OF PASSENGERS		AGE	SEX	OCCUPATIONS	DATE PORT SHIP
GARDNER, Robert		45	M	Planter	15No42Dn
OGLETON, John		51	M	Planter	15No42Dn

CAITHNESSSHIRE 15 NOVEMBER 1847

From Belfast

NAMES OF PASSENGERS		AGE	SEX	OCCUPATIONS	DATE PORT SHIP
ERVINS, George		40	M	Laborer	15No07Dp
NELSON, William		24	M	Laborer	15No07Dp
MCGONE, Ann		17	F	Spinster	15No07Dp
GARRETTY, John		19	M	Spinner	15No07Dp
ROBINSON, Jno.		28	M	Farmer	15No07Dp
Margaret	(W)	22	F	Wife	15No07Dp
James	(S)	02	M	Child	15No07Dp
Mary	(D)	.00	F	Infant	15No07Dp
FERGUSON, Eliza		15	F	Spinster	15No07Dp
ROBINSON, James		18	M	Laborer	15No07Dp
MOLLVY, Jno.		17	M	Laborer	15No07Dp
LINDSAY, Henry		28	M	Laborer	15No07Dp
MCCLARNON, Mary		30	F	Wife	15No07Dp
Jno.	(S)	04	M	Child	15No07Dp
Patrick	(S)	02	M	Child	15No07Dp
MCCLANE, Jno.		25	M	Laborer	15No07Dp
MCGILL, Andrew		55	M	Laborer	15No07Dp
CANE, Sally		19	F	Spinster	15No07Dp
Nancy		18	F	Spinster	15No07Dp
MCCAKE, Mary		20	F	Spinster	15No07Dp
POTTS, Jno.		15	M	Laborer	15No07Dp
LINDURN, Elizabeth		35	F	Wife	15No07Dp
Mary-Jane	(D)	09	F	Child	15No07Dp
Robt.	(S)	06	M	Child	15No07Dp
HOLMES, Mary		18	F	Spinster	15No07Dp
LOGAN, Jane		21	F	Spinster	15No07Dp
BOYD, Mary		20	F	Spinster	15No07Dp
HASTY, Robt.		20	M	Laborer	15No07Dp
TAYLOR, Ann		16	F	Spinster	15No07Dp
RODGER, James		50	M	Laborer	15No07Dp
Elizabeth		20	F	Spinster	15No07Dp
MELVYN, Thos.		20	M	Laborer	15No07Dp
RAMEY, David		20	M	Laborer	15No07Dp
SAND, Nicholas		20	M	Laborer	15No07Dp
EGAN, Wm.		29	M	Laborer	15No07Dp
PATTERSON, Wm.		20	M	Laborer	15No07Dp
STONE, Wm.		20	M	Laborer	15No07Dp
FERRIS, Jane		35	F	Spinster	15No07Dp
Mary-Anne	(D)	06	F	Child	15No07Dp
HOLMES, Thos.		18	M	Laborer	15No07Dp
LITTLE, Joseph		46	M	Farmer	15No07Dp
Elizth.	(W)	32	F	Wife	15No07Dp
Thos.	(S)	12	M	Unknown	15No07Dp
Margt.	(D)	06	F	Child	15No07Dp
Wm.	(S)	03	M	Child	15No07Dp
Jane		48	F	Spinster	15No07Dp
James		35	M	Laborer	15No07Dp
Mary		30	F	Wife	15No07Dp
Margt.		03	F	Child	15No07Dp
Betty		.00	F	Infant	15No07Dp
Ann		30	F	Spinster	15No07Dp
GRAHAM, James		30	M	Farmer	15No07Dp
Jane	(W)	30	F	Wife	15No07Dp
Isabella	(D)	04	F	Child	15No07Dp
Margt.	(D)	02	F	Child	15No07Dp
Eliza-Ann	(D)	.04	F	Infant	15No07Dp
ABBOTT, Stephen		47	M	Laborer	15No07Dp
Sarah	(W)	40	F	Wife	15No07Dp
Mary-Ann	(D)	05	F	Child	15No07Dp
MCGOURAN, Patrick		17	M	Laborer	15No07Dp
Jno.Cully	(P)	40	M	Farmer	15No07Dp
Mary	(M)	40	F	Wife	15No07Dp
Susan	(T)	13	F	Unknown	15No07Dp
Jno.	(B)	11	M	Unknown	15No07Dp
Rosey	(T)	08	F	Child	15No07Dp
Mary-Ann	(T)	06	F	Child	15No07Dp
Patrick	(B)	03	M	Child	15No07Dp
DARAGH, William		55	M	Farmer	15No07Dp
Allison		25	U	Laborer	15No07Dp
Magt.		29	F	Wife	15No07Dp
Wm.Jno.		02	M	Child	15No07Dp
Mary-Jane		.02	F	Infant	15No07Dp
ARTHUR, James		12	M	Unknown	15No07Dp
REED, Robt.		22	M	Laborer	15No07Dp
LOGAN, Wm.		28	M	Laborer	15No07Dp
BELSHAW, James-B.		27	M	Laborer	15No07Dp
GAHAN, James-B.		26	M	Farmer	15No07Dp
Eliza	(W)	24	F	Wife	15No07Dp
BROWNLER, James		50	M	Laborer	15No07Dp
DONGAN, Henry		55	M	Farmer	15No07Dp
Isabella	(W)	55	F	Wife	15No07Dp
Allan	(S)	09	M	Child	15No07Dp
Henry	(S)	05	M	Child	15No07Dp
Hugh	(S)	02	M	Child	15No07Dp
CLARK, James		56	M	Farmer	15No07Dp
Jane	(W)	56	F	Wife	15No07Dp
James	(S)	20	M	Laborer	15No07Dp
Mary-Jane	(D)	08	F	Child	15No07Dp
Jno.	(S)	26	M	Laborer	15No07Dp
MCDONALD, Ann		30	F	Spinster	15No07Dp
KELLY, William		39	M	Laborer	15No07Dp
Ellen	(W)	30	F	Wife	15No07Dp
MCCAFFERTY, Hugh		22	M	Laborer	15No07Dp
CAVAN, Jno.		58	M	Laborer	15No07Dp
Elizh.	(W)	50	F	Wife	15No07Dp
Jno.	(S)	26	M	Laborer	15No07Dp
Eliza	(D)	23	F	Spinster	15No07Dp
Martha	(D)	19	F	Spinster	15No07Dp
MURPHY, Cathe.		35	F	Wife	15No07Dp
Patrick	(S)	09	M	Child	15No07Dp

NAMES OF PASSENGERS	AGE	SEX	OCCUPATIONS	DATE PORT SHIP
MURPHY, Michl. (S)	05	M	Child	15No07Dp
Rosey (D)	03	F	Child	15No07Dp
CHAMBERS, Eliza	16	F	Spinster	15No07Dp
CAVAN, William	30	M	Laborer	15No07Dp
MURPHY, James	33	M	Laborer	15No07Dp
LAVETT, Thos.	33	M	Laborer	15No07Dp
DYAR, David	22	M	Laborer	15No07Dp
BELL, Abr.	00	M	Laborer	15No07Dp
CORDAKES, Isaac	00	M	Laborer	15No07Dp

ATLAS 15 NOVEMBER 1847

From Liverpool

NAMES OF PASSENGERS	AGE	SEX	OCCUPATIONS	DATE PORT SHIP
MURRAY, John	12	M	Laborer	15No02Ec
LOGAN, Mary-Jane	40	F	Spinster	15No02Ec
Alexander	46	M	Laborer	15No02Ec
Mary-Jane	30	F	Spinster	15No02Ec
Melinda	15	F	Spinster	15No02Ec
Margaret-Ann	18	F	Spinster	15No02Ec
SAGAN, John	30	M	Laborer	15No02Ec
MADGE, Wm.	20	M	Laborer	15No02Ec
Elizabeth	06	F	Child	15No02Ec
Jane	03	F	Child	15No02Ec
James	.00	M	Infant	15No02Ec
MCCUE, Cathe.	18	F	Spinster	15No02Ec
MORGAN, Michael	24	M	Laborer	15No02Ec
Patrick	34	M	Laborer	15No02Ec
BYRNES, Bridget	20	F	Spinster	15No02Ec
MCQUIGAN, Laurence	24	M	Weaver	15No02Ec
SLATER, Wm.	26	M	Machinist	15No02Ec
BARNS, Frances	30	M	Machinist	15No02Ec
WHITE, Patrick	22	M	Laborer	15No02Ec
HENRY, Edward	30	M	Laborer	15No02Ec
Mary	25	F	Spinster	15No02Ec
BURNS, Malachie	30	M	Laborer	15No02Ec
FERGUSON, Cathe.	20	F	Spinster	15No02Ec
CRAGAN, Mathew	15	M	Laborer	15No02Ec
WHITE, Owen	16	M	Laborer	15No02Ec
Winney	21	F	Spinster	15No02Ec
ONEILL, Jno.	21	M	Sawer	15No02Ec
Sarah	22	F	Spinster	15No02Ec
Patrick	.00	M	Infant	15No02Ec
MCGEE, James	20	M	Weaver	15No02Ec
KILMARTIN, Patrick	20	M	Laborer	15No02Ec
CANNON, Daniel	21	M	Laborer	15No02Ec
CREED, Patrick	18	M	Laborer	15No02Ec
Mary	20	F	Spinster	15No02Ec
GANNON, Biddy	20	F	Spinster	15No02Ec
TALMY, Domnick	20	M	Laborer	15No02Ec
CARROLL, Mary	20	F	Spinster	15No02Ec
RAFTAN, Bridget	19	F	Spinster	15No02Ec
KILWOOD, Michael	60	M	Laborer	15No02Ec
Ann	16	F	Spinster	15No02Ec
SHIELDS, John	30	M	Cooper	15No02Ec
VANCE, John	33	M	Piano Maker	15No02Ec
Ann	24	F	Spinster	15No02Ec
HAYDEN, John	26	M	Laborer	15No02Ec
KILBY, John	25	M	Laborer	15No02Ec
WHEELAND, John	30	M	Laborer	15No02Ec
Margaret	27	F	Spinster	15No02Ec
CHRISTEY, Esther	40	F	Spinster	15No02Ec
Margaret	04	F	Child	15No02Ec
Ann	05	F	Child	15No02Ec
Robert	03	M	Child	15No02Ec
DUGGAN, Wm.	36	M	Laborer	15No02Ec
John	12	M	Laborer	15No02Ec
HUNTER, Joseph	30	M	Laborer	15No02Ec
Esther	26	F	Spinster	15No02Ec
HUNTER, John	03	M	Child	15No02Ec
David	01	M	Child	15No02Ec
Wm.	.00	M	Infant	15No02Ec
WELCH, Ellen	25	F	Spinster	15No02Ec
GRANT, Cathrin	04	F	Child	15No02Ec
SMITH, James	50	M	Laborer	15No02Ec
Mary	15	F	Spinster	15No02Ec
Hannah	20	F	Spinster	15No02Ec
Mary	21	F	Spinster	15No02Ec
CLEMENTS, Alexander	26	M	Pfnl	15No02Ec
BALANCE, Joseph	18	M	Carpenter	15No02Ec
Mary	23	F	Spinster	15No02Ec
Wm.	45	M	Laborer	15No02Ec
Rachel	45	F	Spinster	15No02Ec
FOLEY, Peggy	40	F	Spinster	15No02Ec
GEHAN, Mary	12	F	Spinster	15No02Ec
HARE, Julia	25	F	Spinster	15No02Ec
FLEMING, Mary	30	F	Spinster	15No02Ec
REARDON, Ellen	20	F	Spinster	15No02Ec
WELSH, John	35	M	Carpenter	15No02Ec
GRIFFIN, Honor	20	F	Spinster	15No02Ec
RICHARDSON, Jas.	30	M	Cartwright	15No02Ec
YOUNG, Jane	15	F	Spinster	15No02Ec
GEARY, Martin	20	M	Laborer	15No02Ec
Patrick	20	M	Laborer	15No02Ec
MULLAN, Patrick	30	M	Laborer	15No02Ec
MURPHY, Dennis	26	M	Laborer	15No02Ec
COONEY, Daniel	26	M	Laborer	15No02Ec
GANNON, John	23	M	Weaver	15No02Ec
LYONS, Timothy	45	M	Laborer	15No02Ec
Mary	37	F	Spinster	15No02Ec
Cathe.	18	F	Spinster	15No02Ec
John	17	M	Spinner	15No02Ec
Daniel	09	M	Child	15No02Ec
Margaret	05	F	Child	15No02Ec
Ellen	04	F	Child	15No02Ec
John	.00	M	Infant	15No02Ec
MCCOURT, Hugh	56	M	Schm	15No02Ec
U (W)	50	F	Spinster	15No02Ec
Patrick	13	M	Unknown	15No02Ec
Hannah	11	F	None	15No02Ec
Ann	18	F	Spinster	15No02Ec
HICKEY, Wm.	30	M	Laborer	15No02Ec
Norry	30	F	Wife	15No02Ec
John	06	M	Child	15No02Ec
Mary	03	F	Child	15No02Ec
MCGUIRE, Patrick	25	M	Laborer	15No02Ec
Joseph	20	M	Laborer	15No02Ec
REARDON, James	30	M	Smith	15No02Ec
Norry	18	F	Spinster	15No02Ec
James	15	M	None	15No02Ec
Margaret	12	F	None	15No02Ec
Bridget	09	F	Child	15No02Ec
Patrick	06	M	Child	15No02Ec
SHEHANE, Eliza	25	F	Spinster	15No02Ec
DOOLAN, James	50	M	Servant	15No02Ec
KEELY, John	46	M	Laborer	15No02Ec
Mary	20	F	Spinster	15No02Ec
Bridget	18	F	Spinster	15No02Ec
BYRNES, James	30	M	Laborer	15No02Ec
MARTIN, James	18	M	Carpenter	15No02Ec
DEVINE, Patrick	40	M	Laborer	15No02Ec
Wm.	13	M	Laborer	15No02Ec
Mary	11	F	None	15No02Ec
Thomas	09	M	Child	15No02Ec
FITZGERALD, Maurice	17	M	Laborer	15No02Ec
WALSH, Thomas	14	M	Tailor	15No02Ec
FITZGERALD, Wm.	12	M	Laborer	15No02Ec
WALSH, John	09	M	Child	15No02Ec
SULLIVAN, Danl.	40	M	Laborer	15No02Ec
ONEIL, Ellen	18	F	Spinster	15No02Ec
RIELY, Eliza	18	F	Spinster	15No02Ec
MANNING, Thos.	20	M	Laborer	15No02Ec
WALTER, James	28	M	Laborer	15No02Ec
Cathe.	20	F	Spinster	15No02Ec

NAMES OF PASSENGERS	AGE	SEX	OCCUPATIONS	DATE PORT SHIP
WALTER, Eugene	20	M	Laborer	15No02Ec
HELEY, Pattrick	45	M	Laborer	15No02Ec
COHALIN, Elizabeth	30	F	Spinster	15No02Ec
MALONE, Cathe.	10	F	Spinster	15No02Ec
FERRAL, Margaret	30	F	Spinster	15No02Ec
CORNELL, Honor	18	F	Spinster	15No02Ec
SULLIVAN, Jenny	50	F	Laborer	15No02Ec
LYONS, Michael	16	M	Laborer	15No02Ec
MCKENNY, Bridget	25	F	Spinster	15No02Ec
BROWN, Sarah	12	F	None	15No02Ec
CANNING, James	50	M	Fiddler	15No02Ec
Margaret	52	F	None	15No02Ec
MCANN, Ruth	26	F	Spinster	15No02Ec
M.J.	06	F	Child	15No02Ec
Elizabeth-Ann	04	F	Child	15No02Ec
Robert	01	M	Child	15No02Ec
MCBRIDE, Hugh	25	M	Pfnl	15No02Ec
CAR, John-James	22	S	Pfnl	15No02Ec
DOGHERTY, Mary	19	F	Spinster	15No02Ec
MCCARTAN, Sally	24	F	Spinster	15No02Ec
MAGEE, Wm.	50	M	Laborer	15No02Ec
Mary	50	F	Spinster	15No02Ec
Charles	14	M	None	15No02Ec
Cathn.	09	F	Child	15No02Ec
GANNON, John	23	M	Laborer	15No02Ec

THAETUS 18 NOVEMBER 1847

From Londonderry

NAMES OF PASSENGERS	AGE	SEX	OCCUPATIONS	DATE PORT SHIP
RODDEN, Ellen	16	F	Spinster	18No01Ds
RILEY, Anne	20	F	Spinster	18No01Ds
ANDERSON, Robt.	24	M	Laborer	18No01Ds
CONLIN, Anne	40	F	Spinster	18No01Ds
Eliza	18	F	Spinster	18No01Ds
James	07	M	Child	18No01Ds
Bridget	05	F	Child	18No01Ds
DONAGHOE, James	20	M	Laborer	18No01Ds
CONWAY, Peter	28	M	Laborer	18No01Ds
COLLUM, John	18	M	Laborer	18No01Ds
MACMANUS, Susan	30	F	Spinster	18No01Ds
LONG, Edward	10	M	None	18No01Ds
SHERRY, Felix	19	M	Tailor	18No01Ds
COSTELLO, Edward	17	M	Laborer	18No01Ds
WILSON, Eliza	25	F	Spinster	18No01Ds
HUGHES, Cath.	14	F	Spinster	18No01Ds
BLAIR, Jane	30	F	Spinster	18No01Ds
Isabella	10	F	None	18No01Ds
Cath.	06	F	Child	18No01Ds
THOMPSON, Wm.	21	M	Laborer	18No01Ds
LAUGHLIN, Anne	35	F	Spinster	18No01Ds
ONEILL, Margaret	53	F	Spinster	18No01Ds
Mary-J.	12	F	None	18No01Ds
Ha--IL, Cath.	26	F	Spinster	18No01Ds
Mary-J.	03	F	Child	18No01Ds
LAMBERT, Jane	30	F	Chmd	18No01Ds
GUY, Robt.	55	M	Laborer	18No01Ds
Jane	55	F	Spinster	18No01Ds
Jane	21	F	Spinster	18No01Ds
Sarah	19	F	Spinster	18No01Ds
James	17	M	Laborer	18No01Ds
CORRAN, Jane	28	F	Dressmaker	18No01Ds
FULTON, Eliza	50	F	Spinster	18No01Ds
VINEY, Mary-Anne	18	F	Spinster	18No01Ds
CONNOR, Biddy	29	F	Spinster	18No01Ds
MURRY, Cath.	15	F	Spinster	18No01Ds
KANE, Anne	17	F	Spinster	18No01Ds
LITTLE, Jane	19	F	Spinster	18No01Ds
SKIPTON, Edward	49	M	Laborer	18No01Ds

NAMES OF PASSENGERS	AGE	SEX	OCCUPATIONS	DATE PORT SHIP
KERRIGAN, Wm.	25	M	Laborer	18No01Ds
CORRY, Jane	07	F	Child	18No01Ds
Wm.	04	M	Child	18No01Ds
MCCARTEY, James	10	M	Laborer	18No01Ds
CORREY, Susan	30	F	Spinster	18No01Ds
Wm.	25	M	Laborer	18No01Ds
Mary	01	F	Child	18No01Ds
Died-At-Sea				
BIGGES, Margaret	18	F	Weaver	18No01Ds
BARTLEY, John	20	M	Laborer	18No01Ds
Died-At-Sea				
KEMPTON, Andrew	26	M	Laborer	18No01Ds
CONNER, Peter	21	M	Laborer	18No01Ds
Bridget	18	F	Spinster	18No01Ds
MCCULLOCH, Sarah	21	F	Spinster	18No01Ds
SMITH, Cath.	20	F	Spinster	18No01Ds
LITTLE, Sarah	24	F	Dressmaker	18No01Ds
RAFFERTY, Peter	17	M	Laborer	18No01Ds
MACNAMEE, Bell	30	F	Spinster	18No01Ds
Francis	08	M	Child	18No01Ds
Neill	06	M	Child	18No01Ds
Bernard	05	M	Child	18No01Ds
John	04	M	Child	18No01Ds
MCCLINTOCK, Eliza	20	F	Spinster	18No01Ds
LOUGHERY, Andrew	13	M	None	18No01Ds
Cath.	10	F	None	18No01Ds
John	14	M	None	18No01Ds
MCCLEAN, Alexander	17	M	Laborer	18No01Ds
TRAVERS, Hannah	17	F	Spinster	18No01Ds
MITCHELL, John	65	M	Weaver	18No01Ds
MCDIVETT, James	20	M	Weaver	18No01Ds
CORREY, Margt.	19	F	Spinster	18No01Ds
CARR, Daniel	35	M	Laborer	18No01Ds
Biddy	30	F	Spinster	18No01Ds
Eleanor	12	F	None	18No01Ds
Patrick	10	M	None	18No01Ds
Giles	08	M	Child	18No01Ds
Daniel	04	M	Child	18No01Ds
Mary	.04	F	Infant	18No01Ds
DALEY, James	50	M	Bricklayer	18No01Ds
Eliza	40	F	Spinster	18No01Ds
Benisford	20	M	Bricklayer	18No01Ds
Roddy	10	M	None	18No01Ds
James	05	M	Child	18No01Ds
Eliza	02	F	Child	18No01Ds
MCMAKIN, Daniel	30	M	Carpenter	18No01Ds
Patrick	60	M	Laborer	18No01Ds
Cath.	26	F	Spinster	18No01Ds
John	02	M	Child	18No01Ds
HARKEN, Easther	22	F	Spinster	18No01Ds
Wm.	19	M	None	18No01Ds
GILLEN, Ellen	17	F	Spinster	18No01Ds
GORMLEY, Margt.	16	F	Spinster	18No01Ds
HILL, Margt.	50	F	Spinster	18No01Ds
Ellen	18	F	Spinster	18No01Ds
Margery	11	F	None	18No01Ds
MCMENAMIN, Mary	30	F	Spinster	18No01Ds
John	09	M	Child	18No01Ds
Eliza	06	F	Child	18No01Ds
ODONNELL, Margery	34	F	Spinster	18No01Ds
Cath.	10	F	None	18No01Ds
William	07	M	Child	18No01Ds
Margery	05	F	Child	18No01Ds
Margaret	03	F	Child	18No01Ds
MCCRORY, John	36	M	Cooper	18No01Ds
DURNING, Hannah	18	F	Spinster	18No01Ds
Jane	08	F	Child	18No01Ds
Elizabeth	05	F	Child	18No01Ds
John	04	M	Child	18No01Ds
FERGUSON, Hugh	18	M	Laborer	18No01Ds
Patrick	16	M	Laborer	18No01Ds
NELSON, Robt.	16	M	Bookseller	18No01Ds
HEMPHILL, Jane	22	F	Spinster	18No01Ds
DOUGHERTY, John	18	M	Laborer	18No01Ds
KANE, Patrick	30	M	Laborer	18No01Ds

NAMES OF PASSENGERS	AGE	SEX	OCCUPATIONS	DATE PORT SHIP
AIKEN, Robt.	39	M	Laborer	18No01Ds
MCNAMEE, William	28	M	Laborer	18No01Ds

ISABELLA-HELEN 18 NOVEMBER 1847

From St.Johns-Nf.

NAMES OF PASSENGERS	AGE	SEX	OCCUPATIONS	DATE PORT SHIP
FOLEY, Martin	44	M	Laborer	18No86Du
Honor	36	F	Spinster	18No86Du
POWER, Mary	25	F	Spinster	18No86Du
COTTER, Ellen	22	F	Spinster	18No86Du
HEARNE, John	41	M	Laborer	18No86Du
MURPHY, James	40	M	Rope Maker	18No86Du
WALSH, James	26	M	Laborer	18No86Du
WHEALEN, Ferny	26	M	Fisherman	18No86Du
FENTON, Pattk.	35	M	Carpenter	18No86Du

SARAH 19 NOVEMBER 1847

From SYDNEY,Cape-Breton

NAMES OF PASSENGERS	AGE	SEX	OCCUPATIONS	DATE PORT SHIP
MCCOY, William	28	M	Carpenter	19No34Dx

JANE-GLASSIN 20 NOVEMBER 1847

From Liverpool

NAMES OF PASSENGERS	AGE	SEX	OCCUPATIONS	DATE PORT SHIP
MCGRATH, Michel	24	M	Farmer	20No02Eb
BULGER, Wm.	45	M	Farmer	20No02Eb
U (W)	43	F	Unknown	20No02Eb
Isabel	18	F	Farmer	20No02Eb
John	13	M	Farmer	20No02Eb
Wm.	07	M	Farmer	20No02Eb
WALSH, John	36	M	Weaver	20No02Eb
Catherine	27	F	Weaver	20No02Eb
CARMODY, John	30	M	Weaver	20No02Eb
HOGAN, Wm.	18	M	Weaver	20No02Eb
COX, James	20	M	Weaver	20No02Eb
MCGAVIN, Pat	24	M	Weaver	20No02Eb
TURNER, Michel	25	M	Weaver	20No02Eb
GALLAGHER, Owen	30	M	Weaver	20No02Eb
MCCLALKER, Francis	36	M	Weaver	20No02Eb
HEMINGWAY, Elizabeth	09	F	Child	20No02Eb
REILLY, Peter	29	M	Waiter	20No02Eb
HUNT, John	20	M	Waiter	20No02Eb
WHOLLY, Cathrine	20	F	Waiter	20No02Eb
Pat	02	M	Child	20No02Eb
DRISCOLL, Ellen	19	F	Cook-Baker	20No02Eb
John	02	M	Child	20No02Eb
Eleanor	22	F	Cook-Baker	20No02Eb
MCCARTHY, John	20	M	Cook-Baker	20No02Eb
MCKENNA, Cathrine	21	F	Seamstress	20No02Eb
MEES, Mary	42	F	Seamstress	20No02Eb
Phebe	14	F	Seamstress	20No02Eb
Susanna	09	F	Child	20No02Eb
Emma	.00	F	Infant	20No02Eb
Thos.	.00	M	Infant	20No02Eb
MALIA, Ann	02	F	Child	20No02Eb
Martha	07	F	Child	20No02Eb
SMITH, John	16	M	Mechanic	20No02Eb
GEELON, Thos.	44	M	Mechanic	20No02Eb
OBRIEN, Cathrine	23	F	Unknown	20No02Eb
NIXE, Wm.	20	M	Unknown	20No02Eb
DILLON, Thos.	24	M	Unknown	20No02Eb
Mary	22	F	Unknown	20No02Eb
Catharine	20	F	Unknown	20No02Eb
KEVANEY, Michl.	24	M	Unknown	20No02Eb
EDWARDS, Thos.	37	M	Unknown	20No02Eb
Sarah	30	F	Servant	20No02Eb
JACKSON, Joseph-W.	21	M	Servant	20No02Eb
CAMPBELL, Ellen	48	F	Servant	20No02Eb
Rebecca	18	F	Servant	20No02Eb
David	12	M	Milliner	20No02Eb
Wm.	08	M	Child	20No02Eb
MURPHY, John	23	M	Unknown	20No02Eb
CULLY, John	20	M	Unknown	20No02Eb
PRICE, James	22	M	Unknown	20No02Eb
HUTSON, Robt.	47	M	Unknown	20No02Eb
Ann-Mary	46	F	Unknown	20No02Eb
Ann	19	F	Unknown	20No02Eb
Solomon	05	M	Child	20No02Eb
GOODWIN, Mathew	24	M	Watchmaker	20No02Eb
Amelia	22	F	Watchmaker	20No02Eb
Wm.	.00	M	Infant	20No02Eb
BROPHY, Cathrine	28	F	Unknown	20No02Eb
James	23	M	Unknown	20No02Eb
MCCRADDEN, Cathrine	35	F	Unknown	20No02Eb
Mary	18	F	Unknown	20No02Eb
Wm.	09	M	Child	20No02Eb
Elizabeth	11	F	Unknown	20No02Eb
BEGLEY, Thos.	25	M	Unknown	20No02Eb
Mary	28	F	Unknown	20No02Eb
Mary	03	F	Child	20No02Eb
SMITH, Thos.	30	M	Baker	20No02Eb
Mary	06	F	Child	20No02Eb
Sarah-Ann	04	F	Child	20No02Eb
BITY, Mary	40	F	Unknown	20No02Eb
BROPHY, Peter	18	M	Unknown	20No02Eb
MULLIGAN, Matthew	20	M	Unknown	20No02Eb
YOUNG, John	21	M	Unknown	20No02Eb
Mary	20	F	Unknown	20No02Eb
SHANNON, Thos.	22	M	Shoemaker	20No02Eb
Michel	18	M	Shoemaker	20No02Eb
HUNTER, Thos.	17	M	Shoemaker	20No02Eb
DUNN, James	50	M	Shoemaker	20No02Eb
Mary	18	F	Hairdresser	20No02Eb
Ann	30	F	Hairdresser	20No02Eb
John	06	M	Child	20No02Eb
James	.00	M	Infant	20No02Eb
OBRIEN, Ann	20	F	Unknown	20No02Eb
FITZPATRICK, John	50	M	Machinist	20No02Eb
Mary	50	F	Unknown	20No02Eb
Cathrine	20	F	Unknown	20No02Eb
Elizth.	22	F	Unknown	20No02Eb
Judith	15	F	Unknown	20No02Eb
Patrick	14	M	Wig Maker	20No02Eb
Margt.	13	F	Unknown	20No02Eb
Michel	09	M	Child	20No02Eb
Ann	07	F	Child	20No02Eb
JIBB, U	20	F	Unknown	20No02Eb
FOOTE, Mary	24	F	Unknown	20No02Eb
MALREN, James	20	M	Butcher	20No02Eb
SMITH, Jas.	21	M	Butcher	20No02Eb
Mary	19	F	Hat Trimmer	20No02Eb
FOOTE, John-O.	20	M	Butcher	20No02Eb
MCGRATH, Pat	20	M	Butcher	20No02Eb
Mary	22	F	Ctnsp	20No02Eb
James	13	M	Ctnsp	20No02Eb
HOLMES, Adam	20	M	Ctnsp	20No02Eb
WATERS, Mary	15	F	Ctnsp	20No02Eb
DENNIS, Bridget	20	F	Ctnsp	20No02Eb
DEGNAN, Mary	20	F	Ctnsp	20No02Eb

NAMES OF PASSENGERS		AGE	SEX	OCCUPATIONS	DATE PORT SHIP
HINCLLAN, Pate		21	M	Ctnsp	20No02Eb
U	(W)	19	F	Unknown	20No02Eb
U		.00	F	Infant	20No02Eb
HARMON, Bridget		20	F	Ctnsp	20No02Eb
CASSIDY, Rebe.		20	F	Ctnsp	20No02Eb
MURTAGH, Cathrine		15	F	Ctnsp	20No02Eb
Mary		13	F	Ctnsp	20No02Eb
James		11	M	Spnry	20No02Eb
FARRELL, Cathrine		18	F	Spnry	20No02Eb
BAKERMILLER, James		50	M	Spnry	20No02Eb
U	(W)	40	F	Unknown	20No02Eb
Cathr.		10	F	Spnry	20No02Eb
Pat		08	M	Child	20No02Eb
GOLGAN, Pat		21	M	Farmer	20No02Eb
HARMON, Mary		19	F	Farmer	20No02Eb
NAUGHTON, John		22	M	Farmer	20No02Eb
MCCORMICK, John		22	M	Farmer	20No02Eb
CAFFERTY, Michal		21	M	Farmer	20No02Eb
MURRAY, Alice		21	F	Mtmkr	20No02Eb
LAY, Chas.		40	M	Watchmaker	20No02Eb
Thos.		15	M	Watchmaker	20No02Eb
Wm.		12	M	Watchmaker	20No02Eb
CARNEY, John		45	M	Watchmaker	20No02Eb
Cath.		40	F	Pasm	20No02Eb
Wm.		21	M	Pasm	20No02Eb
Catherine		13	F	Pasm	20No02Eb
Margt.		10	F	Pasm	20No02Eb
MURDOCK, Laurence		.00	M	Infant	20No02Eb
BRIDE, Thos.		28	M	Hatter	20No02Eb
Catherine		22	F	Milliner	20No02Eb
Mary		22	F	Milliner	20No02Eb
MURPHY, Bridget		22	F	Milliner	20No02Eb
Owen		38	M	Milliner	20No02Eb
REILLY, Anty.		40	M	Shoemaker	20No02Eb
MURPHY, Dennis		22	M	Shoemaker	20No02Eb
DEVEREAUX, Mary		24	F	Shoemaker	20No02Eb
DUNLOP, Ann		18	F	Seamstress	20No02Eb
KELLY, Nancy		30	F	Seamstress	20No02Eb
Nancy		06	F	Child	20No02Eb
FLATTERY, Catherine		36	F	Seamstress	20No02Eb
Jas.		11	M	Laborer	20No02Eb
Sarah		09	F	Child	20No02Eb
HOGAN, Tim		24	M	Servant	20No02Eb
CONNER, John		30	M	Servant	20No02Eb
Bridget		30	F	Servant	20No02Eb
CAIN, Darby		22	M	Servant	20No02Eb
HAYES, James		23	M	Servant	20No02Eb
CONLEY, Tim		45	M	Servant	20No02Eb
Mary		40	F	Dressmaker	20No02Eb
Daniel		25	M	Unknown	20No02Eb
John		12	M	Unknown	20No02Eb
Pegg		12	F	Unknown	20No02Eb
Honora		02	F	Child	20No02Eb
SULLIVAN, Julia		18	F	Unknown	20No02Eb
DONOVAN, Daniel		50	M	Baker	20No02Eb
Mary		40	F	Unknown	20No02Eb
Patrick		24	M	Unknown	20No02Eb
John		20	M	Unknown	20No02Eb
Catherine		18	F	Unknown	20No02Eb
Thos.		16	M	Unknown	20No02Eb
Margt.		15	F	Milliner	20No02Eb
Mary		13	F	Unknown	20No02Eb
Ellen		12	F	Unknown	20No02Eb
Eliza		10	F	Unknown	20No02Eb
Elizabeth		10	F	Unknown	20No02Eb
Nancy		08	F	Child	20No02Eb
Agnes		04	F	Child	20No02Eb
Julia		.00	F	Infant	20No02Eb
BUCKLEY, Judy		16	F	Weaver	20No02Eb
DUFFEY, Cormack		33	M	Unknown	20No02Eb
Died-At-Sea					
Mary		20	F	Unknown	20No02Eb
MCBENNET, Bety		40	F	Unknown	20No02Eb
BYANTER, Manus		22	M	Unknown	20No02Eb
BYRNE, Mary		19	F	Unknown	20No02Eb

NAMES OF PASSENGERS		AGE	SEX	OCCUPATIONS	DATE PORT SHIP
CARRANY, Pat.		21	M	Unknown	20No02Eb
BULLEN, James		40	M	Unknown	20No02Eb
Jane		08	F	Child	20No02Eb
WALSH, Pat		35	M	Unknown	20No02Eb
BULK, Mary		11	F	Unknown	20No02Eb
Pat		09	M	Child	20No02Eb
Thersa		07	F	Child	20No02Eb
Bridget		05	F	Child	20No02Eb
Margt.		03	F	Child	20No02Eb
CONNER, Ann		20	F	Unknown	20No02Eb
SCHADWELL, Pat		07	M	Child	20No02Eb
MURDOCH, Pat.		60	M	Unknown	20No02Eb
Anne		60	F	Dressmaker	20No02Eb
Mary		15	F	Unknown	20No02Eb
Isabella		25	F	Unknown	20No02Eb
FARMER, Bessy		16	F	Unknown	20No02Eb
GRUNDY, Jas.		22	M	Blacksmith	20No02Eb
Margt.		24	F	Servant	20No02Eb
CURRY, Cornelius		45	M	Servant	20No02Eb
Margt.		21	F	Servant	20No02Eb
HEMINGWAY, Hannah		45	F	Servant	20No02Eb
Margt.		18	F	Servant	20No02Eb
Jane		15	F	Servant	20No02Eb
Eliza		13	F	Servant	20No02Eb
Nancy		11	F	Servant	20No02Eb
BARRY, Ellen		04	F	Child	20No02Eb
GREADY, Mary		30	F	Unknown	20No02Eb
HAMAN, Honora		06	F	Child	20No02Eb
BRENNAN, Bridget		48	F	Unknown	20No02Eb
Mary		07	F	Child	20No02Eb
Bridget		05	F	Child	20No02Eb
John		20	M	Unknown	20No02Eb
James		22	M	Unknown	20No02Eb
John		45	M	Unknown	20No02Eb
KENNEDY, James		40	M	Unknown	20No02Eb
U	(W)	40	F	Cake Baker	20No02Eb
Eliza		08	F	Child	20No02Eb
John		06	M	Child	20No02Eb
Wm.		04	M	Child	20No02Eb
DELEHINTY, Margt.		20	F	Bread Baker	20No02Eb
CONNOLLY, Mary		20	F	Bread Baker	20No02Eb
CARROLL, Joseph		25	M	Bread Baker	20No02Eb
Ellen		25	F	Unknown	20No02Eb
Mary		02	F	Child	20No02Eb
Jane		.00	F	Infant	20No02Eb
CAREY, John		18	M	Pasm	20No02Eb
Patrick		12	M	Pasm	20No02Eb
John		08	M	Child	20No02Eb
MOSEY, Bidy		18	F	Bread Baker	20No02Eb
CAREY, Dennis		20	M	Bread Baker	20No02Eb
Mary		37	F	Bread Baker	20No02Eb
Johanna		20	F	Bread Baker	20No02Eb
FITZGERALD, John		30	M	Philosopher	20No02Eb
U	(W)	35	F	Imkr	20No02Eb
Wm.		08	M	Child	20No02Eb
James		06	M	Child	20No02Eb
Anne		04	F	Child	20No02Eb
Catherine		02	F	Child	20No02Eb
Walter		.00	M	Infant	20No02Eb
John		36	M	Farmer	20No02Eb
Johanna		26	F	Farmer	20No02Eb
Thos.		.00	M	Infant	20No02Eb
Michel		26	M	Farmer	20No02Eb
Mary		20	F	Farmer	20No02Eb
PURTELL, Michel		18	M	Farmer	20No02Eb
Bridget		14	F	Farmer	20No02Eb
WALE, Andrew		26	M	Farmer	20No02Eb
QUINLAN, Pat		50	M	Farmer	20No02Eb
U	(W)	50	F	Unknown	20No02Eb
DEVLEY, Mary		26	F	Farmer	20No02Eb
GARGAN, George		23	M	Farmer	20No02Eb
U	(W)	21	F	Unknown	20No02Eb
John		04	M	Child	20No02Eb
Hannah		02	F	Child	20No02Eb

NAMES OF PASSENGERS	AGE	SEX	OCCUPATIONS	DATE PORT SHIP
MCNAMARA, John	40	M	Unknown	20No02Eb
Died-At-Sea				
KINCLLA, U-Mrs.	19	F	Dressmaker	20No02Eb
U	.00	F	Infant	20No02Eb
CONNER, John	00	M	Unknown	20No02Eb
Died-At-Sea				
DUFFEY, Cormack	33	M	Weaver	20No02Eb
CURRY, Conel	00	M	Unknown	20No02Eb
Died-At-Sea				
Mary	00	F	Unknown	20No02Eb
Died-At-Sea				
SMITH, Patrick	00	M	Unknown	20No02Eb
Died-At-Sea				
HATSON, Elizabeth	00	F	Unknown	20No02Eb
Died-At-Sea				
BEGLEY, Bridget	00	F	Unknown	20No02Eb
Died-At-Sea				
MURTAGH, Mary	00	F	Unknown	20No02Eb
Died-At-Sea				

NEBRASKA 22 NOVEMBER 1847

From Liverpool

NAMES OF PASSENGERS	AGE	SEX	OCCUPATIONS	DATE PORT SHIP
COFFEE, Ellen	30	F	Servant	22No02Dz
GRADY, Michl.	24	M	Unknown	22No02Dz
RYAN, James	26	M	Unknown	22No02Dz
KELLY, Ed.	30	M	Unknown	22No02Dz
CONNOR, Mary	40	F	Unknown	22No02Dz
James	28	M	Unknown	22No02Dz
Richard	12	M	Unknown	22No02Dz
Johanna	10	F	Unknown	22No02Dz
Alice	07	F	Child	22No02Dz
CASHIN, James	13	M	Unknown	22No02Dz
BROWN, Mich.	27	M	Unknown	22No02Dz
BUTLER, John	25	M	Unknown	22No02Dz
SWEENY, Alx	20	M	Unknown	22No02Dz
RANDOLPH, U-Mrs.	18	F	None	22No02Dz
WATSON, Henry	60	M	Farmer	22No02Dz
Ellen	50	F	Farmer	22No02Dz
James	25	M	Farmer	22No02Dz
FLOOD, Cath.	50	F	Servant	22No02Dz
Matt.	30	M	Laborer	22No02Dz
Margt.	20	F	Servant	22No02Dz
COSTELLO, Anne	35	F	Servant	22No02Dz
Cath.	13	F	Servant	22No02Dz
Luke	11	M	Servant	22No02Dz
SMYTH, Mary	20	F	Servant	22No02Dz
MANNING, Michl.	25	M	Farmer	22No02Dz
John	20	M	Farmer	22No02Dz
MCANNA, Mary	22	F	Servant	22No02Dz
CONAGHTON, Mary	22	F	Servant	22No02Dz
MCMULLEN, Mary	20	F	Servant	22No02Dz
CAVANAGH, John	27	M	Servant	22No02Dz
CALLAGHAN, Pat.	26	M	Servant	22No02Dz
Mary	22	F	Servant	22No02Dz
MCART, Jane	20	F	Servant	22No02Dz
MICKELLENNY, Pat	25	M	Farmer	22No02Dz
DANNELLAY, John	50	M	Farmer	22No02Dz
KEELAN, Bridget	18	F	Servant	22No02Dz
MCGOWAN, Wm.	22	M	Farmer	22No02Dz
OBRIEN, Cath.	20	F	Farmer	22No02Dz
CUNNINGHAM, Cath.	18	F	Farmer	22No02Dz
GREENAN, Michl.	16	F	Farmer	22No02Dz
KIRBY, Edward	26	M	Servant	22No02Dz
SIMPSON, Samuel	40	M	Weaver	22No02Dz
SHOESMITH, Ralph	48	M	Unknown	22No02Dz
U (W)	46	F	Unknown	22No02Dz
Jane	04	F	Child	22No02Dz

NAMES OF PASSENGERS	AGE	SEX	OCCUPATIONS	DATE PORT SHIP
FARMINGTON, Thomas	28	M	Unknown	22No02Dz
John	26	M	Unknown	22No02Dz
BOUCHER, Pat	29	M	Unknown	22No02Dz
DIFFLE, John	26	M	Unknown	22No02Dz
DONOHOE, Cath.	24	F	Unknown	22No02Dz
CAHILL, John	17	M	Unknown	22No02Dz
SEAL, Robt.O.	18	M	Unknown	22No02Dz
Anne	16	F	Unknown	22No02Dz
KIRKPATRICK, Kate	19	F	Unknown	22No02Dz
Mary	18	F	Unknown	22No02Dz
MURREY, Gd.	25	M	Unknown	22No02Dz
ELLIOT, Gabriel	26	M	Unknown	22No02Dz
TRAINOR, Felix	35	M	Unknown	22No02Dz
HUGES, John	28	M	Unknown	22No02Dz
BRANDON, Thos.	40	M	Unknown	22No02Dz
TOBIN, John	22	M	Unknown	22No02Dz
LEAHY, James	23	M	Unknown	22No02Dz
MAGUIRE, Rose	22	F	Unknown	22No02Dz
CUNFIELD, Rose	21	F	Unknown	22No02Dz
KILFOIL, Wm.	25	M	Unknown	22No02Dz
YATES, John	50	M	Unknown	22No02Dz
Eliza	45	F	Unknown	22No02Dz
Robt.	23	M	Unknown	22No02Dz
John	20	M	Unknown	22No02Dz
Margt.	16	F	Unknown	22No02Dz
James	13	M	Unknown	22No02Dz
Agnes-Jane	10	F	Unknown	22No02Dz
Saml.	08	M	Child	22No02Dz
David	06	M	Child	22No02Dz
Wm.	04	M	Child	22No02Dz
LANE, Mgt.	40	F	Unknown	22No02Dz
MAGUIRE, James	28	M	Unknown	22No02Dz
James	20	M	Unknown	22No02Dz
John	09	M	Child	22No02Dz
HITCHENS, John	20	M	Unknown	22No02Dz
QUINN, Cath.	18	F	Unknown	22No02Dz
MCCANN, Peter	24	M	Unknown	22No02Dz
HANLEY, Pat	11	M	Unknown	22No02Dz
Bridget	07	F	Child	22No02Dz
DONOHUE, Ellen	16	F	Unknown	22No02Dz
HEETMAN, Henri	33	M	Unknown	22No02Dz
SCHULLER, F.	56	M	Unknown	22No02Dz
SAUSACHER, Carol	43	F	Unknown	22No02Dz
BRODERICK, Wm.	40	M	Collier	22No02Dz
U (W)	36	F	Collier	22No02Dz
Mary	06	F	Child	22No02Dz
Mary	07	F	Child	22No02Dz
John	04	M	Child	22No02Dz
CARBERY, Philip	28	M	Unknown	22No02Dz
OREILY, Robt.	26	M	Unknown	22No02Dz
Fanny	24	F	Unknown	22No02Dz
Died-At-Sea				
Ellen	23	F	Unknown	22No02Dz
FERGUSON, Mary	22	F	Unknown	22No02Dz
GRATH, Jane	20	F	Unknown	22No02Dz
EDWARDS, Margt.	50	F	Unknown	22No02Dz
Mary	18	F	Unknown	22No02Dz
Mgt.	16	F	Unknown	22No02Dz
ROCHE, Cath.	26	F	Unknown	22No02Dz
MURRY, Michl.	49	M	Unknown	22No02Dz
CORBALLE, Patk.	22	M	Unknown	22No02Dz
CARROLL, Sabina	20	F	Unknown	22No02Dz
CAVANAGH, Elizabeth	40	F	Unknown	22No02Dz
Anne	04	F	Child	22No02Dz
Peter	.00	M	Infant	22No02Dz
Died-At-Sea				
OLEERY, Cath.	50	F	Unknown	22No02Dz
BALDWIN, Bridget	36	F	Unknown	22No02Dz
Cath.	06	F	Child	22No02Dz
John	02	M	Child	22No02Dz
Anne	04	F	Child	22No02Dz
BRENNAN, Thos.	18	M	Unknown	22No02Dz
DONNELLY, Mary	45	F	Unknown	22No02Dz
Rose	12	F	Unknown	22No02Dz
Mary	10	F	Unknown	22No02Dz

NAMES OF PASSENGERS	AGE	SEX	OCCUPATIONS	DATE PORT SHIP
DONNELLY, David	06	M	Child	22No02Dz
Harriet	05	F	Child	22No02Dz
DEIGHAN, Hugh	25	M	Unknown	22No02Dz
DEALHEARNE, Margt.	18	F	Unknown	22No02Dz
CARROLL, Mary	19	F	Unknown	22No02Dz
KELLY, James	23	M	Unknown	22No02Dz
MURTAGH, Mgt.	18	F	Unknown	22No02Dz
FOLEY, Patrick	23	M	Unknown	22No02Dz
ENGLAND, Cath.	60	F	Unknown	22No02Dz
FARRELL, Mary	18	F	Unknown	22No02Dz
KAITNEY, Anne	20	F	Unknown	22No02Dz
REYNOLDS, Mary	06	F	Child	22No02Dz
Mgt.	04	F	Child	22No02Dz
OSULLIVAN, John	25	M	Unknown	22No02Dz
FERRAR, Wm.	28	M	Unknown	22No02Dz
Frances	26	F	Unknown	22No02Dz
Henry	04	M	Child	22No02Dz
Benj.	02	M	Child	22No02Dz
James Died-At-Sea	.00	M	Infant	22No02Dz
CASEY, Rich.	22	M	Unknown	22No02Dz
Harriet	26	F	Unknown	22No02Dz
CARTIN, Fanny	22	F	Unknown	22No02Dz
JOHNSON, Hamilton	17	M	Unknown	22No02Dz
HERRITT, Francis	35	M	Unknown	22No02Dz
Mary	30	F	Unknown	22No02Dz
Jas.	11	M	Unknown	22No02Dz
Elley	09	F	Child	22No02Dz
Francis	06	M	Child	22No02Dz
Isabella	05	F	Child	22No02Dz
Wm.	.00	M	Infant	22No02Dz
MCCOY, Rach.	26	F	Unknown	22No02Dz
DICKEY, Dan	25	M	Unknown	22No02Dz
Ann	20	F	Unknown	22No02Dz
DONOGHUE, Thos.	40	M	Unknown	22No02Dz
Mgt.	40	F	Unknown	22No02Dz
Thos.	23	M	Unknown	22No02Dz
Michl.	18	M	Unknown	22No02Dz
DONLOP, Rosanah	28	F	Unknown	22No02Dz
FAGAN, John	30	M	Unknown	22No02Dz
NEWTON, Eliza	30	F	Unknown	22No02Dz
DRAKE, Jas.	33	M	Unknown	22No02Dz
MCALLAY, Pat	45	M	Unknown	22No02Dz
MEEHAN, John	35	M	Unknown	22No02Dz
Mary	30	F	Unknown	22No02Dz
Jane	04	F	Child	22No02Dz
Anne	.00	F	Infant	22No02Dz
GREEN, Lawrence	12	M	Unknown	22No02Dz
Mgt.	10	F	Unknown	22No02Dz
Mary	08	F	Child	22No02Dz
Ellen	06	F	Child	22No02Dz
MCCANNEY, Betsy	18	F	Unknown	22No02Dz
SKELLY, Mary	16	F	Unknown	22No02Dz
PARNELL, Mary	40	F	Unknown	22No02Dz

M.A.FLEMING 22 NOVEMBER 1847

From St.Johns-Nf.

NAMES OF PASSENGERS	AGE	SEX	OCCUPATIONS	DATE PORT SHIP
REILLY, Patrick	17	M	Clerk	22No86Ed
SPENSER, Michael	34	M	Fisherman	22No86Ed
CONDAN, Michael	45	M	Carpenter	22No86Ed
WELSH, Morris	40	M	Fisherman	22No86Ed

ANTELEON 24 NOVEMBER 1847

From SYDNEY,Cape-Breton

NAMES OF PASSENGERS	AGE	SEX	OCCUPATIONS	DATE PORT SHIP
CLIFFORD, M.A.	19	F	Teacher	24No34Ee
Margeret	14	F	Teacher	24No34Ee
HILL, A.	16	F	Lady	24No34Ee

CREOLE 24 NOVEMBER 1847

From Liverpool

NAMES OF PASSENGERS	AGE	SEX	OCCUPATIONS	DATE PORT SHIP
COLLINS, David	36	M	Laborer	24No02Ef
Jane	16	F	Spinster	24No02Ef
Matilda	14	F	Spinster	24No02Ef
Thos.	10	M	Laborer	24No02Ef
HUTCHESON, Geo.	26	M	Laborer	24No02Ef
GORMLY, Edw.	25	M	Laborer	24No02Ef
CONNA, Mary	21	F	Spinster	24No02Ef
HALLINAN, Michl.	25	M	Laborer	24No02Ef
HALLORAN, Mary	22	F	Spinster	24No02Ef
MCGRATH, Thos.	26	M	Laborer	24No02Ef
Mgt.	19	F	Spinster	24No02Ef
MARA, William	26	M	Unknown	24No02Ef
BLAKE, Michl.	24	M	Unknown	24No02Ef
Daniel	25	M	Unknown	24No02Ef
HAYES, Jno.	20	M	Laborer	24No02Ef
CAVIDILLA, Thos.	23	M	Laborer	24No02Ef
DEVILIN, Jno.	14	M	Laborer	24No02Ef
Mich.	16	M	Laborer	24No02Ef
LARKIN, Mich.	20	M	Laborer	24No02Ef
MANSON, Mary	21	F	Spinster	24No02Ef
LARKIN, Pat	15	M	Laborer	24No02Ef
MCGEE, Jno.	56	M	Laborer	24No02Ef
Mary	11	F	Spinster	24No02Ef
Jno.	20	M	Laborer	24No02Ef
MCGUIRE, Mich.	24	M	Laborer	24No02Ef
Cath.	18	F	Spinster	24No02Ef
HALFPENY, Ann	22	F	Spinster	24No02Ef
MCBRIDE, Ann	22	F	Spinster	24No02Ef
COFFREY, Matth.	08	M	Child	24No02Ef
Terence	06	M	Child	24No02Ef
KANE, N.	50	F	Spinster	24No02Ef
CALLAHAN, Ann Died-At-Sea	19	F	Spinster	24No02Ef
Matt.	21	M	Laborer	24No02Ef
Chas. Died-At-Sea	.00	M	Infant	24No02Ef
MCDONAGH, Ann	20	F	Spinster	24No02Ef
MAHON, Thos.	22	M	Laborer	24No02Ef
Mary-Ann	18	F	Spinster	24No02Ef
ROACH, Mary	35	F	Spinster	24No02Ef
John	09	M	Child	24No02Ef
Mich.	06	M	Child	24No02Ef
DONAS, Lewis	27	M	Laborer	24No02Ef
HALLOWAY, Mary	21	F	Spinster	24No02Ef
Ellen	20	F	Spinster	24No02Ef
FRANE, Mary	24	F	Spinster	24No02Ef
MCGARRY, Jas.	20	F	Spinster	24No02Ef
BENZ, Ester	20	F	Spinster	24No02Ef
KANE, Martin	24	M	Laborer	24No02Ef
SHAY, Cath.	24	F	Spinster	24No02Ef
KENY, Mary	24	F	Spinster	24No02Ef

NAMES OF PASSENGERS	AGE	SEX	OCCUPATIONS	DATE PORT SHIP
NAUTON, Mary	21	F	Spinster	24No02Ef
GUINN, David	24	M	Laborer	24No02Ef
BUCKLEY, Mich.	24	M	Laborer	24No02Ef
Timothy	24	M	Laborer	24No02Ef
Magt.	40	F	Spinster	24No02Ef
Magt.	18	F	Spinster	24No02Ef
Biddy	16	F	Spinster	24No02Ef
Ann	10	F	Spinster	24No02Ef
Timothy	09	M	Child	24No02Ef
KANE, James	30	M	Laborer	24No02Ef
PENDERGAST, Jno.	29	M	Laborer	24No02Ef
Mary	29	F	Spinster	24No02Ef
James	08	M	Child	24No02Ef
John	05	M	Child	24No02Ef
Joseph	03	M	Child	24No02Ef
DOUGHERTY, John	20	M	Laborer	24No02Ef
GIBBONS, Wm.	14	M	Laborer	24No02Ef
HANNING, David	22	M	Laborer	24No02Ef
DURNELL, Mich.	26	M	Laborer	24No02Ef
DURNIN, Judith	24	F	Spinster	24No02Ef
KELLY, Ann	20	F	Spinster	24No02Ef
HICKEY, Alice	21	F	Spinster	24No02Ef
WYSE, Magt.	21	F	Spinster	24No02Ef
HARNEY, Wm.	30	M	Laborer	24No02Ef
Isaac	16	M	Laborer	24No02Ef
DEVIN, Jos.	30	M	Laborer	24No02Ef
WILSON, Jas.	35	M	Laborer	24No02Ef
BRADY, Thos.	30	M	Laborer	24No02Ef
Owen	24	M	Laborer	24No02Ef
PERSEYLOVE, Thos.	25	M	Laborer	24No02Ef
Joan	24	F	Spinster	24No02Ef
Robt.	.00	M	Infant	24No02Ef
BEWE, Hugh	14	M	Laborer	24No02Ef
ROONEY, Mich.	20	M	Laborer	24No02Ef
KEENAN, Jas.	24	M	Laborer	24No02Ef
HASKINS, Timothy	80	M	Laborer	24No02Ef
FARRELL, Biddy	25	F	Spinster	24No02Ef
GRAY, Mary	50	F	Spinster	24No02Ef
Thos.	12	M	Laborer	24No02Ef
HENRY, Judy	25	F	Spinster	24No02Ef
MCGANN, Margt.	20	F	Spinster	24No02Ef
ROSS, William	30	M	Laborer	24No02Ef
Elizabeth	22	F	Spinster	24No02Ef
Ellen	55	F	Spinster	24No02Ef
MADLEY, John	37	M	Laborer	24No02Ef
COCKEN, John	35	M	Laborer	24No02Ef
SCHOFIELD, John	47	M	Laborer	24No02Ef
KAYE, James	49	M	Laborer	24No02Ef
DOCKRCY, Pat	45	M	Laborer	24No02Ef
DOGERTY, Ann	45	F	Spinster	24No02Ef
Patrick	16	M	Laborer	24No02Ef
Eliza	18	F	Spinster	24No02Ef
FLANAGAN, Bridget	20	F	Spinster	24No02Ef
DOGERTY, Catherine	40	F	Spinster	24No02Ef
LANAKAN, Patrick	35	M	Laborer	24No02Ef
Catherine	25	F	Spinster	24No02Ef
Bridget	03	F	Child	24No02Ef
Ann	.00	F	Infant	24No02Ef
LENTROLL, William	25	M	Laborer	24No02Ef
RILEY, Mary	48	F	Spinster	24No02Ef
Michael	68	M	Laborer	24No02Ef
Bridget	12	F	Spinster	24No02Ef
Owen	10	M	Laborer	24No02Ef
Rose	08	F	Child	24No02Ef
ROACH, Margt.	30	F	Spinster	24No02Ef
HAGERTY, Mary	18	F	Spinster	24No02Ef
Dennis	06	M	Child	24No02Ef
Catherine	04	F	Child	24No02Ef
BURNS, Biddy	20	F	Spinster	24No02Ef
RUFFLE, Mary	30	F	Spinster	24No02Ef
OBRIEN, Mary-Ann	18	F	Spinster	24No02Ef
MULLIN, Eliza	20	F	Spinster	24No02Ef
FITZGERALD, Michael	24	M	Laborer	24No02Ef
GALLIGAN, Pat	24	M	Laborer	24No02Ef
MURPHY, James	32	M	Laborer	24No02Ef
SULLIVAN, Jno.	30	M	Laborer	24No02Ef
MORRISON, Matthew	22	M	Laborer	24No02Ef
Letty	20	F	Spinster	24No02Ef
CARSON, Ann-J.	20	F	Spinster	24No02Ef
Rachael	17	F	Spinster	24No02Ef
KEEGAN, Pat	30	M	Laborer	24No02Ef
Thos.	35	M	Laborer	24No02Ef
MCDONALD, Catherine	20	F	Spinster	24No02Ef
FITZGERALD, Mary	20	F	Spinster	24No02Ef
GOFFIN, Thomas	30	M	Laborer	24No02Ef
MANCRY, John	30	M	Laborer	24No02Ef
CONNOR, Edwd.	30	M	Laborer	24No02Ef
NORRAN, Michael	20	M	Laborer	24No02Ef
Pat	30	M	Laborer	24No02Ef
BYRNE, Garret	25	M	Laborer	24No02Ef
Cathe.	22	F	Spinster	24No02Ef
GAGHEGAN, James	22	M	Laborer	24No02Ef
CORMICK, Bridget	20	F	Spinster	24No02Ef
MALLANCY, Jimmy	22	M	Laborer	24No02Ef
Edwd.	10	M	Laborer	24No02Ef
FREEMAN, Arthur	25	M	Laborer	24No02Ef
DUFFY, Mary	36	F	Spinster	24No02Ef
James	20	M	Laborer	24No02Ef
CONNOLLY, Bridget	50	F	Spinster	24No02Ef
HIPPET, Thos.	22	M	Laborer	24No02Ef
U	22	F	Spinster	24No02Ef
FLAHERTY, Edwd.	30	M	Laborer	24No02Ef
LARKIN, Jim	26	M	Laborer	24No02Ef
LINN, John	40	M	Laborer	24No02Ef
Mich.	11	M	Laborer	24No02Ef
COGMAN, James	25	M	Laborer	24No02Ef
John	16	M	Laborer	24No02Ef
Cath.	23	F	Spinster	24No02Ef
KIRWIN, Mary	20	F	Spinster	24No02Ef
WILSON, Wm.	25	M	Laborer	24No02Ef
Jane	19	F	Spinster	24No02Ef
SEXTON, Pegg.	25	F	Spinster	24No02Ef
MCDONALD, Pat	22	M	Laborer	24No02Ef
RYON, John	23	M	Laborer	24No02Ef
Cath.	20	F	Spinster	24No02Ef
Johana	02	F	Child	24No02Ef
GRIFFIN, Mary	20	F	Spinster	24No02Ef
FLACK, James	22	M	Laborer	24No02Ef
SHEY, Pat	30	M	Laborer	24No02Ef
Cath.	25	F	Spinster	24No02Ef
HANNAH, John	24	M	Laborer	24No02Ef
OCONNELL, Denis	24	M	Laborer	24No02Ef
Pat	18	M	Laborer	24No02Ef
Cath.	25	F	Spinster	24No02Ef
GEELAN, Sam.	40	M	Laborer	24No02Ef
U	40	M	Laborer	24No02Ef
DONLAN, Biddy	20	F	Spinster	24No02Ef
Mary	08	F	Child	24No02Ef
Pat	05	M	Child	24No02Ef
DONOGHUE, Betsey	25	F	Spinster	24No02Ef
Ann	03	F	Child	24No02Ef
FITZSIMONS, Cath.	20	F	Spinster	24No02Ef
DUFFY, John	20	M	Laborer	24No02Ef
REYNOLDS, James	50	M	Laborer	24No02Ef
Mgr.	19	F	Spinster	24No02Ef
LEVAN, Pat	20	M	Laborer	24No02Ef
REYNOLDS, Wm.	40	M	Laborer	24No02Ef
BRENNAN, Roger	28	M	Laborer	24No02Ef
Wm.	26	M	Laborer	24No02Ef
Danl.	24	M	Laborer	24No02Ef
Gilbert	07	M	Child	24No02Ef
James	18	M	Laborer	24No02Ef
Anne	20	F	Spinster	24No02Ef
FALLEN, Garret	30	M	Laborer	24No02Ef
Eliza	26	F	Spinster	24No02Ef
Thos.	43	M	Laborer	24No02Ef
Mary	18	F	Spinster	24No02Ef
Bridget	20	F	Spinster	24No02Ef
HANLY, Thos.	60	M	Laborer	24No02Ef
Mary	50	F	Spinster	24No02Ef

NAMES OF PASSENGERS	AGE	SEX	OCCUPATIONS	DATE PORT SHIP
HANLY, Pat	24	M	Laborer	24No02Ef
Edw.	18	M	Laborer	24No02Ef
Darby	16	M	Laborer	24No02Ef
Mich.	13	M	Laborer	24No02Ef
Mary	20	F	Spinster	24No02Ef
STEWART, Wm.	47	M	Laborer	24No02Ef
Bridget	43	F	Spinster	24No02Ef
Chas.	14	M	Laborer	24No02Ef
Mal.	12	M	Laborer	24No02Ef
Wm.	08	M	Child	24No02Ef
Eliza	10	F	Spinster	24No02Ef
Pat	60	M	Laborer	24No02Ef
Mary	55	F	Spinster	24No02Ef
Bridget	14	F	Spinster	24No02Ef
MAGHER, John	30	M	Laborer	24No02Ef
Mary	30	F	Spinster	24No02Ef
Pat	05	M	Child	24No02Ef
Mary	03	F	Child	24No02Ef
HANLEY, Jas.	30	M	Laborer	24No02Ef
Susan	30	F	Spinster	24No02Ef
HARRINGTON, John	14	M	Laborer	24No02Ef
HANLEY, John	07	M	Child	24No02Ef
Peter	05	M	Child	24No02Ef
QUINN, Cath.	30	F	Spinster	24No02Ef
Jane	08	F	Child	24No02Ef
Luke	06	M	Child	24No02Ef
John	.00	M	Infant	24No02Ef
Cath.	17	F	Spinster	24No02Ef
DUFFY, James	20	M	Laborer	24No02Ef
Geo.	26	M	Laborer	24No02Ef
Mary	60	F	Spinster	24No02Ef
Died-At-Sea				
MULLEN, James	50	M	Laborer	24No02Ef
Bridget	50	F	Spinster	24No02Ef
Dan.	12	M	Laborer	24No02Ef
Bridget	10	F	Spinster	24No02Ef
M.	07	U	Child	24No02Ef
STEWART, Geo.	40	M	Laborer	24No02Ef
Brig.	32	F	Spinster	24No02Ef
Chas.	06	M	Child	24No02Ef
John	04	M	Child	24No02Ef
Mary	10	F	Spinster	24No02Ef
COSTELLO, Ellen	55	F	Spinster	24No02Ef
John	08	M	Child	24No02Ef
Mary	18	F	Spinster	24No02Ef
Brigh.	16	F	Spinster	24No02Ef
DRUMAN, Pat	65	M	Laborer	24No02Ef
DOULAN, John	36	M	Laborer	24No02Ef
Pat	27	M	Laborer	24No02Ef
Edw.	25	M	Laborer	24No02Ef
Wm.	16	M	Laborer	24No02Ef
Mary	14	F	Spinster	24No02Ef
MCGAN, John	34	M	Laborer	24No02Ef
MCGUIRE, Pat	22	M	Laborer	24No02Ef
Ann	28	F	Spinster	24No02Ef
Ellen	26	F	Spinster	24No02Ef
Cath.	24	F	Spinster	24No02Ef
NEARY, Mary	35	F	Spinster	24No02Ef
John	16	M	Laborer	24No02Ef
Jas.	03	M	Child	24No02Ef
Cathe.	24	F	Spinster	24No02Ef
Bridget	14	F	Spinster	24No02Ef
FALLON, Thos.	33	M	Laborer	24No02Ef
Ann	32	F	Spinster	24No02Ef
Pat	17	M	Laborer	24No02Ef
Martin	05	M	Child	24No02Ef
Ellen	08	F	Child	24No02Ef
Mary	.00	F	Infant	24No02Ef
Bridget	25	F	Spinster	24No02Ef
MULRANEY, Michl.	22	M	Laborer	24No02Ef
Honora	17	F	Spinster	24No02Ef
Sally	16	F	Spinster	24No02Ef
Margt.	22	F	Spinster	24No02Ef
STEWART, John	21	M	Laborer	24No02Ef
Bridgt.	17	F	Spinster	24No02Ef

NAMES OF PASSENGERS	AGE	SEX	OCCUPATIONS	DATE PORT SHIP
STEWART, Cathe.	15	F	Spinster	24No02Ef
DONLAN, Patrick	27	M	Laborer	24No02Ef
Ann	27	F	Spinster	24No02Ef
GREEN, John	25	M	Laborer	24No02Ef
SHELLEY, Cathe.	16	F	Spinster	24No02Ef
LALLY, Mary	19	F	Spinster	24No02Ef
Bridget	09	F	Child	24No02Ef
IRWIN, Ellen	20	F	Spinster	24No02Ef
FALLON, Thos.	30	M	Laborer	24No02Ef

NIAGARA 25 NOVEMBER 1847

From Liverpool

NAMES OF PASSENGERS	AGE	SEX	OCCUPATIONS	DATE PORT SHIP
KENNY, Martin	50	M	Laborer	25No02Ab
Bridget (W)	48	F	Wife	25No02Ab
Michael	04	M	Child	25No02Ab
James	02	M	Child	25No02Ab
Patrick	22	M	Laborer	25No02Ab
Philip	20	M	Laborer	25No02Ab
Martin-Jr.	18	M	Laborer	25No02Ab
Thomas	16	M	Laborer	25No02Ab
Christopher	06	M	Child	25No02Ab
HAYES, Moke	21	M	Laborer	25No02Ab
OATES, Ann	60	F	Wi	25No02Ab
COSTELLO, Ellen	22	F	Domestic	25No02Ab
PRICE, Ann	22	F	Seamstress	25No02Ab
RUARK, Mary	22	F	Seamstress	25No02Ab
KENNY, Catherine	24	F	Seamstress	25No02Ab
Margaret	14	F	Seamstress	25No02Ab
Mary	12	F	Unknown	25No02Ab
Bridget	10	F	Unknown	25No02Ab
CONALLY, Betty	50	F	Domestic	25No02Ab
Died-At-Sea				
BURNES, Edward	45	M	Laborer	25No02Ab
Ann (W)	16	F	Wife	25No02Ab
MATHEWS, Owen	35	M	Laborer	25No02Ab
Patrick	14	M	Laborer	25No02Ab
MURPHY, Nicholas	40	M	Laborer	25No02Ab
Anty. (W)	35	F	Wife	25No02Ab
James	10	M	Unknown	25No02Ab
Patrick	08	M	Child	25No02Ab
John	06	M	Child	25No02Ab
Nicholas-Jr.	04	M	Child	25No02Ab
Walter	.10	M	Infant	25No02Ab
CALLAN, Michael	30	M	Laborer	25No02Ab
OGRADY, Thomas	32	M	Laborer	25No02Ab
KAHALAN, Patrick	30	M	Laborer	25No02Ab
SULLIVAN, William	30	M	Gdnr	25No02Ab
BUTLER, John	16	M	Laborer	25No02Ab
Judy	23	F	Domestic	25No02Ab
James	08	M	Child	25No02Ab
CANNON, Peter	24	M	Laborer	25No02Ab
FORTNER, Michael	25	M	Bootmaker	25No02Ab
CANNON, Patrick	25	M	Shop Boy	25No02Ab
TULLY, Bridget	18	F	Seamstress	25No02Ab
DOYLE, Bridget	20	F	Seamstress	25No02Ab
CARROLL, Margaret	15	F	Seamstress	25No02Ab
SULLIVAN, Eliza	17	F	Seamstress	25No02Ab
OBRIAN, Thomas	30	M	Clerk	25No02Ab
Alice (W)	24	F	Wife	25No02Ab
OATES, Teddy	25	M	Laborer	25No02Ab
KENNY, Thos.Jr.	28	M	Unknown	25No02Ab
Thos.	80	M	Unknown	25No02Ab
Mary	70	F	Wife	25No02Ab
Theresa	18	F	Domestic	25No02Ab
HICKEY, Ann	42	F	Domestic	25No02Ab
RIGNEY, Ann	22	F	Domestic	25No02Ab
SCOTT, James	23	M	Laborer	25No02Ab

NAMES OF PASSENGERS	AGE	SEX	OCCUPATIONS	DATE PORT SHIP
REDEN, Daniel	26	M	Laborer	25No02Ab
TEHAN, Thomas	23	M	Laborer	25No02Ab
KENNEDY, Patrick	23	M	Shepherd	25No02Ab
FEEHAN, Judy	21	F	Shepherd	25No02Ab
COURON, Bridget	24	F	Domestic	25No02Ab
KENNEDY, William	20	M	Laborer	25No02Ab
MELACKY, Edward	21	M	Laborer	25No02Ab
GOSNERS, Hugh	20	M	Laborer	25No02Ab
HANNEGAN, Thos.	25	M	Blacksmith	25No02Ab
TYRELL, Harriet	19	F	Domestic	25No02Ab
HENERY, Ann	28	F	Domestic	25No02Ab
Mary	15	F	Domestic	25No02Ab
CASTLE, Margaret	20	F	Domestic	25No02Ab
CONLEN, Bridget	24	F	Domestic	25No02Ab
CROHAN, Celia	24	F	Domestic	25No02Ab
CAIN, Ellen	20	F	Domestic	25No02Ab
Died-At-Sea				
Norry	22	F	Domestic	25No02Ab
COSGAR, Patrick	21	M	Laborer	25No02Ab
NOCTAN, Dennis	25	M	Laborer	25No02Ab
DONNEGAN, Mary	20	F	Domestic	25No02Ab
Died-At-Sea				
AGAN, Mary	16	F	Domestic	25No02Ab
AILY, Bridget	16	F	Domestic	25No02Ab
QUINLAN, Catherine	19	F	Domestic	25No02Ab
COUGEN, Ann	50	F	Domestic	25No02Ab
John	20	M	Laborer	25No02Ab
Ann-Jr.	10	F	Unknown	25No02Ab
CARROLL, John	30	M	Laborer	25No02Ab
CALLAGAN, Michael	24	M	Laborer	25No02Ab
CAIN, Thomas	28	M	Laborer	25No02Ab
KELLY, Peter	20	M	Laborer	25No02Ab
HART, Mary	55	F	Domestic	25No02Ab
Ellen	14	F	Domestic	25No02Ab
Margaret	12	F	Domestic	25No02Ab
HERSLE, Ellen	20	F	Domestic	25No02Ab
CONARTY, Thomas	22	M	Laborer	25No02Ab
CAIR, John	24	M	Laborer	25No02Ab
DEVAN, Andrew	17	M	Laborer	25No02Ab
MAHON, Michael	19	M	Laborer	25No02Ab
CONARTY, Judy	20	F	Domestic	25No02Ab
MEGAHAN, Mary	18	F	Domestic	25No02Ab
DEVINE, Bridget	14	F	Domestic	25No02Ab
DELANCY, Ann	20	F	Domestic	25No02Ab
DOLAN, Mary	16	F	Domestic	25No02Ab
Ann	17	F	Domestic	25No02Ab
John	09	M	Child	25No02Ab
Rosa	07	F	Child	25No02Ab
FINNEGAN, Catherine	26	F	Domestic	25No02Ab
Edward	02	M	Child	25No02Ab
Died-At-Sea				
MCCANE, Ann	30	F	Domestic	25No02Ab
Peter	12	M	Laborer	25No02Ab
Mathew	09	M	Child	25No02Ab
DONNAHOE, Fanny	35	F	Domestic	25No02Ab
Fanny-Jr.	13	F	Domestic	25No02Ab
Died-At-Sea				
Bartlett	12	M	Laborer	25No02Ab
POWER, Michael	19	M	Weaver	25No02Ab
Margaret	16	F	Weaver	25No02Ab
BURN, Mark	30	M	Weaver	25No02Ab
Mary (W)	30	F	Wife	25No02Ab
John	06	M	Child	25No02Ab
Catherine	03	F	Child	25No02Ab
MCANALLY, Owen	20	M	Laborer	25No02Ab
IRVINE, James-F.	45	M	Surgeon	25No02Ab
James-T.	12	M	Student	25No02Ab

JOHN-R.GARDNER 25 NOVEMBER 1847

From Belize

NAMES OF PASSENGERS	AGE	SEX	OCCUPATIONS	DATE PORT SHIP
MORAN, Dennis	39	M	Carpenter	25No05El

HUGUENOT 26 NOVEMBER 1847

From Liverpool

NAMES OF PASSENGERS	AGE	SEX	OCCUPATIONS	DATE PORT SHIP
HOWE, Cath.	44	F	Servant	26No02Be
John	18	M	Servant	26No02Be
WILTON, Charles-H.	23	M	Clerk	26No02Be
MORROW, Major	60	M	Weaver	26No02Be
BALL, Leonard	26	M	Weaver	26No02Be
JUDGE, Hannah	40	F	Wife	26No02Be
LEAMMALE, Elyone	29	M	Carpenter	26No02Be
HARTEY, James	21	M	Mason	26No02Be
MURAY, Joseph	36	M	Shoemaker	26No02Be
MCGUIRE, William	60	M	Weaver	26No02Be
Sarah	60	F	Unknown	26No02Be
RAMISON, John	35	M	Laborer	26No02Be
Esther	28	F	Wife	26No02Be
Ann	13	F	Unknown	26No02Be
Sally	10	F	Unknown	26No02Be
James	08	M	Child	26No02Be
Eliza-Jane	06	F	Child	26No02Be
William	05	M	Child	26No02Be
Mary	02	F	Child	26No02Be
CONNELL, Luke	28	M	Laborer	26No02Be
MCQUADE, Mary	40	F	Unknown	26No02Be
Ann	19	F	Servant	26No02Be
Ann	30	F	Servant	26No02Be
Mathew	16	M	Unknown	26No02Be
Louisa	08	F	Child	26No02Be
Eugene	06	M	Child	26No02Be
Mary-Ann	04	F	Child	26No02Be
Susan	02	F	Child	26No02Be
Lucinda	.00	F	Infant	26No02Be
TOOMAY, Thomas	30	M	Farmer	26No02Be
SPILLANCE, Daniel	31	M	Laborer	26No02Be
Pat	25	M	Laborer	26No02Be
Peggy	23	F	Laborer	26No02Be
Mary	21	F	Laborer	26No02Be
HIGGINS, James	21	M	Laborer	26No02Be
JOHNSON, James	26	M	Doctor	26No02Be
MILLS, Charles	20	M	Engraver	26No02Be
HYAM, John	20	M	Turner	26No02Be
GALAGER, Thomas	25	M	Laborer	26No02Be
BEAM, Maria	28	F	Housekeeper	26No02Be
Biddy	27	F	Servant	26No02Be
Ellen	26	F	Servant	26No02Be
AIKINS, Bernard	34	M	Tailor	26No02Be
Mary	30	F	Unknown	26No02Be
SMITH, Joseph	21	M	Weaver	26No02Be
MURRAY, Thomas	22	M	Spinster	26No02Be
JOHNSON, William	22	M	Shoemaker	26No02Be
Frances	20	M	Shoemaker	26No02Be
MARRIOT, William	26	M	Spinner	26No02Be
James	25	M	Weaver	26No02Be
ASHWITH, Thomas	28	M	Shoemaker	26No02Be
FLINT, George	20	M	Tailor	26No02Be
CEARDEY, George	24	M	Laborer	26No02Be

NAMES OF PASSENGERS	AGE	SEX	OCCUPATIONS	DATE PORT SHIP
BLODBART, Joseph	21	M	Mechanic	26No02Be
BYRNE, William	22	M	Laborer	26No02Be
LANGAN, James	24	M	Laborer	26No02Be
HAWLES, Pat	26	M	Laborer	26No02Be
WALKER, Pat	25	M	Laborer	26No02Be
PLANT, George	21	M	Laborer	26No02Be
RILEY, Joseph	18	M	Laborer	26No02Be
CATS, Robert	43	M	Weaver	26No02Be
Mary	36	F	Wife	26No02Be
Eliza	15	F	Weaver	26No02Be
William	13	M	Weaver	26No02Be
Mary-Ann	.00	F	Infant	26No02Be
ROGERS, James	21	M	Butcher	26No02Be
Alice	17	F	Unknown	26No02Be
Alice	50	F	Unknown	26No02Be
BOK, Ann	26	F	Unknown	26No02Be
LOVET, Hannah	12	F	Unknown	26No02Be
WAUGONERY, Pat	20	M	Laborer	26No02Be
TRACY, Mary	18	F	Servant	26No02Be
HANLEY, Sally	17	F	Servant	26No02Be
RILEY, James	30	M	Farmer	26No02Be
BRISTOW, Ellen	29	F	Servant	26No02Be
MERRITT, William	36	M	Wood Cutter	26No02Be
RIELLY, Edward	45	M	Laborer	26No02Be
FITZIMANS, Benj.	40	M	Laborer	26No02Be
James	47	M	Laborer	26No02Be
Cath.	46	F	Laborer	26No02Be
Cath.	16	F	Laborer	26No02Be
Malachi	16	M	Laborer	26No02Be
William	13	M	Laborer	26No02Be
Mary	13	F	Laborer	26No02Be
Johanna	11	F	Laborer	26No02Be
MILLCRIK, Morris	40	M	Farmer	26No02Be
Cath.	16	F	Farmer	26No02Be
Johanna	21	F	Farmer	26No02Be
RYAN, Jeremiah	22	M	Laborer	26No02Be
POWELL, Mary	24	F	Housekeeper	26No02Be
Cath.	04	F	Child	26No02Be
William	02	F	Child	26No02Be
VALE, Eliza	25	F	Wife	26No02Be
Stephen	06	M	Child	26No02Be
Died-At-Sea				
Mary-Ann	04	F	Child	26No02Be
John	.00	M	Infant	26No02Be
WILLSON, Ann	30	F	Servant	26No02Be
HEVIKDEFFER, Elijah	53	M	Stone Mason	26No02Be
Hannah (W)	50	F	Wife	26No02Be
Mathias	14	M	Unknown	26No02Be
EVANS, David	56	M	Farmer	26No02Be
Hannah	56	F	Farmer	26No02Be
Mary	24	F	Unknown	26No02Be
Anna	20	F	Unknown	26No02Be
Ann	15	F	Unknown	26No02Be
Thomas	11	M	Unknown	26No02Be
James	09	M	Child	26No02Be
FLANNERY, Bridget	18	F	Servant	26No02Be
Eliza	12	F	Servant	26No02Be
LEECH, Mary	21	F	Servant	26No02Be
DONLY, Mary	20	F	Servant	26No02Be
Mathias	07	M	Child	26No02Be
MCCAUKEREL, Fanny	30	F	Servant	26No02Be
HOOLY, Martha	55	F	Dressmaker	26No02Be
Ann	29	F	Dressmaker	26No02Be
Hannah	27	F	Dressmaker	26No02Be
Lucy	23	F	Dressmaker	26No02Be
TRAINOR, Bridget	56	F	Housekeeper	26No02Be
LYNCH, Richard	30	M	Laborer	26No02Be
Mary	30	F	Laborer	26No02Be
Lynch	.00	M	Infant	26No02Be
PRIOR, Ellen	05	F	Child	26No02Be
CALLSON, Miles	35	M	Laborer	26No02Be
MELEY, Mary	28	F	Unknown	26No02Be
CARR, Pat	14	M	Unknown	26No02Be
RAWOTH, Thomas	37	M	Shoemaker	26No02Be
M.	27	F	Unknown	26No02Be
HALEDAY, Richard	21	M	Unknown	26No02Be
REILLY, Mary	56	F	Unknown	26No02Be
Alfred	18	M	Blacksmith	26No02Be
LINNETE, Joseph	16	M	Laborer	26No02Be
SMEATORS, Mary	21	F	Dressmaker	26No02Be
SMITH, William	27	M	Laborer	26No02Be
COOK, Mary	24	F	Servant	26No02Be
MULLEN, James	20	M	Dyer	26No02Be
FLYNN, Thomas	22	M	Laborer	26No02Be
BAWDEN, James	28	M	Dresser	26No02Be
THOMAS, Thomas	24	M	Carter	26No02Be
MCDANIEL, Lawrence	55	M	Cfrt	26No02Be
Jane	14	F	Unknown	26No02Be
ROWN, Rose	20	F	Servant	26No02Be
DONEVAN, Bridget	18	F	Servant	26No02Be
Mary	17	F	Servant	26No02Be
RAMSDEN, William	17	M	Dyer	26No02Be
MITCHELL, Owen	20	M	Laborer	26No02Be
BROWN, Dennis	30	M	Printer	26No02Be
BRACON, U	25	M	Tailor	26No02Be
WARD, Bart	30	M	Laborer	26No02Be
SMITH, Mich.	22	M	Laborer	26No02Be
Margaret	18	F	Unknown	26No02Be
KIERMAN, Mathew	21	M	Laborer	26No02Be
TIERNEY, Ann	24	F	Servant	26No02Be
SMITH, Ann	16	F	Servant	26No02Be
DANLEAVY, Cath.	22	F	Servant	26No02Be
SEXTON, Cath.	17	F	Servant	26No02Be
BRADY, Honer	30	F	Servant	26No02Be
SMITH, Cath.	16	F	Servant	26No02Be
KELLY, Luke	11	M	Unknown	26No02Be
BRADY, John	09	M	Child	26No02Be
Ann	07	F	Child	26No02Be
Margaret	05	F	Child	26No02Be
Mathew	20	M	Laborer	26No02Be
MATHEW, Lunday	18	M	Laborer	26No02Be
DOYLE, Mary	20	F	Servant	26No02Be
RILLY, Charles	21	M	Laborer	26No02Be
Pete	28	M	Laborer	26No02Be
Margaret	24	F	Unknown	26No02Be
Mich.	01	M	Child	26No02Be
MCGARY, Bridget	25	F	Unknown	26No02Be
Frances	21	M	Laborer	26No02Be
MCINTYRE, Mic.	20	M	Laborer	26No02Be
GRACY, Mary	16	F	Servant	26No02Be
MADDEN, John	20	M	Laborer	26No02Be
Agnes	25	F	Servant	26No02Be
Cath.	23	F	Servant	26No02Be
CURRY, John-J.	38	M	Laborer	26No02Be
Joseph	08	M	Child	26No02Be
RYAN, Joseph	28	M	Butcher	26No02Be
Pat	19	M	Butcher	26No02Be
Bidget	21	F	Servant	26No02Be
SROUGHEY, Pat	50	M	Locksmith	26No02Be
Betty	50	F	Unknown	26No02Be
Cath.	17	F	Unknown	26No02Be
William	17	M	Unknown	26No02Be
DOWNES, John	17	M	Weaver	26No02Be
KAVANAGH, Martin	26	M	Miner	26No02Be
Died-At-Sea				
Cath.	26	F	Unknown	26No02Be
Thos.	10	M	Unknown	26No02Be
Bridget	08	F	Child	26No02Be
John	06	M	Child	26No02Be
Mary	03	F	Child	26No02Be
Mary	25	F	Servant	26No02Be
KEEFE, Bridget	28	F	Unknown	26No02Be
Cath.	13	F	Unknown	26No02Be
John	11	M	Unknown	26No02Be
Mary	09	F	Unknown	26No02Be
Richard	06	M	Unknown	26No02Be
John	.00	M	Infant	26No02Be
HENNEGAN, Thomas	27	M	Laborer	26No02Be
Patt.	25	M	Laborer	26No02Be
GILLESPIE, Martin	20	M	Laborer	26No02Be

NAMES OF PASSENGERS	AGE	SEX	OCCUPATIONS	DATE PORT SHIP
GILLESPIE, Cath.	19	F	Servant	26No02Be
CONWAY, John	21	M	Laborer	26No02Be
MORRISON, Margaret	20	F	Servant	26No02Be
DUROSS, Mich.	11	M	Unknown	26No02Be
Daniel	09	M	Child	26No02Be
James	07	M	Child	26No02Be
FROK, Nath.	20	M	Weaver	26No02Be
BOHAN, Mich.	33	M	Laborer	26No02Be
Bridget	27	F	Unknown	26No02Be
CONNER, Michael	40	M	Laborer	26No02Be
Patt.	40	M	Laborer	26No02Be
LYLE, Thomas	28	M	Laborer	26No02Be
CONNER, Biddy	27	F	Unknown	26No02Be
CLOONAN, James	29	M	Carpenter	26No02Be
CALLANAN, Biddy	22	F	Dressmaker	26No02Be
ARTHUR, William	35	M	Farmer	26No02Be
MANEY, Mary	16	F	Servant	26No02Be
MADDEN, Bessy	17	F	Servant	26No02Be
SUMMERS, Ml.	45	M	Laborer	26No02Be
FARDLES, John	14	M	Laborer	26No02Be
TOWN, Thomas	21	M	Laborer	26No02Be

CONSTITUTION 26 NOVEMBER 1847

From Belfast

NAMES OF PASSENGERS	AGE	SEX	OCCUPATIONS	DATE PORT SHIP
MCCRAW, Charles	30	M	Laborer	26No07Hi
TWEED, Margaret	18	F	Laborer	26No07Hi
Agnes	17	F	Servant	26No07Hi
Barbera	12	F	Servant	26No07Hi
Mary	71	F	Servant	26No07Hi
MCGOREY, Terence	50	M	Laborer	26No07Hi
Mary	40	F	Servant	26No07Hi
Sarah	16	F	Servant	26No07Hi
Terence	13	M	Farmer	26No07Hi
Rosey	13	F	Servant	26No07Hi
HUTCHISON, Christy	40	M	Servant	26No07Hi
Anne	36	F	Servant	26No07Hi
John	06	M	Child	26No07Hi
BURNS, William	40	M	Servant	26No07Hi
Jane	38	F	Servant	26No07Hi
Robert	16	M	Servant	26No07Hi
Mary	14	F	Servant	26No07Hi
Eliza	01	F	Child	26No07Hi
BLOOMER, Annie	20	F	Servant	26No07Hi
MCGARRELL, Dennis	24	M	Servant	26No07Hi
GILROY, Jane	30	F	Servant	26No07Hi
GILSON, Sarah	40	F	Servant	26No07Hi
William	06	M	Child	26No07Hi
Robert	04	M	Child	26No07Hi
Sarah	02	F	Child	26No07Hi
Susan	01	F	Child	26No07Hi
BLACK, Robert	19	M	Servant	26No07Hi
STEWART, Mary	33	F	Farmer	26No07Hi
Martha	16	F	Farmer	26No07Hi
Samuel	12	M	Farmer	26No07Hi
William	09	M	Child	26No07Hi
Thomas	04	M	Child	26No07Hi
Margaret	03	F	Child	26No07Hi
Edward	01	M	Child	26No07Hi
CALIGAN, Jas.	56	M	Farmer	26No07Hi
John	40	M	Farmer	26No07Hi
Hugh	13	M	Farmer	26No07Hi
MCGARTHAND, Bidy	19	F	Farmer	26No07Hi
HARVEY, Bidy	18	F	Farmer	26No07Hi
MULHOLAND, Margaret	45	F	Farmer	26No07Hi
CRAIG, Al.	18	M	Farmer	26No07Hi
Isabella	19	F	Farmer	26No07Hi
Eliza	13	F	Farmer	26No07Hi
CRAIG, Sarah	11	F	Farmer	26No07Hi
MULLIGAN, George	25	M	Farmer	26No07Hi
HILL, William	18	M	Farmer	26No07Hi
SUFFREW, James	21	M	Farmer	26No07Hi
John	19	M	Farmer	26No07Hi
MULHOLLAND, James	46	M	Farmer	26No07Hi
Sarah	40	F	Dressmaker	26No07Hi
Margaret	22	F	Dressmaker	26No07Hi
Eliza	20	F	Dressmaker	26No07Hi
MCCONVILLE, Arthur	23	M	Laborer	26No07Hi
THORSBY, Jane	23	F	Servant	26No07Hi
BLACK, Mary	21	F	Servant	26No07Hi
SERGEANT, James	21	M	Servant	26No07Hi
Agnes	19	F	Servant	26No07Hi
MCGARRELL, Mary	19	F	Servant	26No07Hi
COOPER, Eliza	14	F	Servant	26No07Hi
MCCORMICK, Richard	25	M	Farmer	26No07Hi
Isabella	13	F	Servant	26No07Hi
KILLARDEN, Peter	21	M	Servant	26No07Hi
RANKIN, Robert	24	M	Servant	26No07Hi
MIRES, James-H.	20	M	Servant	26No07Hi
ONEIL, Mary	22	F	Servant	26No07Hi
CHARLETON, Francis	48	M	Servant	26No07Hi
Ellizabeth	40	F	Servant	26No07Hi
Francis	20	M	Servant	26No07Hi
Jane	18	F	Servant	26No07Hi
Elizabeth	13	F	Servant	26No07Hi
Robert	.00	M	Infant	26No07Hi
Sarah	09	F	Child	26No07Hi
William	07	M	Child	26No07Hi
WALLES, Margaret	29	F	Milliner	26No07Hi
AIKINS, William	21	M	Servant	26No07Hi
Eliza	19	F	Servant	26No07Hi
Anna	.00	F	Infant	26No07Hi
Elizabeth	50	F	Servant	26No07Hi
DONAVAN, Bernard	21	M	Servant	26No07Hi
CRAWFORD, Robert	38	M	Servant	26No07Hi
GAMBE, Peter	45	M	Servant	26No07Hi
KELLEY, Sarah	30	F	Servant	26No07Hi
CALLAGHAN, Jane	45	F	Servant	26No07Hi
William	30	M	Servant	26No07Hi
Esther	45	F	Servant	26No07Hi
Thomas	.00	M	Infant	26No07Hi
MARRION, Mathew	22	M	Carpenter	26No07Hi
BIRNES, Mary	20	F	Servant	26No07Hi
ADAMAS, Hugh	16	M	Servant	26No07Hi
FREEBURN, John	32	M	Servant	26No07Hi
Mary	23	F	Servant	26No07Hi
Hanna	07	F	Child	26No07Hi
Margaret	05	F	Child	26No07Hi
William	.00	M	Infant	26No07Hi
Thomas	18	M	Tailor	26No07Hi
GALWAY, Robert	18	M	Servant	26No07Hi
CADOO, James	18	M	Servant	26No07Hi
MCGIVERN, Daniel	18	M	Servant	26No07Hi
Mary	20	F	Servant	26No07Hi
FINLEY, John	22	M	Servant	26No07Hi
MCELVERY, Margaret	40	F	Servant	26No07Hi
Robert	10	M	Servant	26No07Hi
John	08	M	Child	26No07Hi
Samuel	06	M	Child	26No07Hi
MCCRUDDER, Sarah	00	F	Servant	26No07Hi
James	25	M	Farmer	26No07Hi
Sarah	23	F	Servant	26No07Hi
John	20	M	Servant	26No07Hi
Susan	18	F	Servant	26No07Hi
William	14	M	Servant	26No07Hi
GIBBS, Jane	25	F	Servant	26No07Hi
WOODS, Mary	18	F	Servant	26No07Hi
MICHAEL, James	18	M	Servant	26No07Hi
ARMSTRONG, Margaret	19	F	Servant	26No07Hi
FERGUSON, Jane	35	F	Servant	26No07Hi
Ellizabeth	12	F	Servant	26No07Hi
Margaret	10	F	Servant	26No07Hi
Jane	04	F	Child	26No07Hi

NAMES OF PASSENGERS	AGE	SEX	OCCUPATIONS	DATE PORT SHIP
FERGUSON, Robert	.00	M	Infant	26No07Hi
FINLAY, William	21	M	Servant	26No07Hi
NEWELL, John	39	M	Servant	26No07Hi
CARNEY, James	18	M	Servant	26No07Hi
MORROW, Mary	18	F	Servant	26No07Hi
DIAMOND, John	30	M	Carpenter	26No07Hi
James	17	M	Carpenter	26No07Hi
Charles	09	M	Child	26No07Hi
FREEBURN, William	19	M	Tailor	26No07Hi
GRAHAM, Thomas	26	M	Tailor	26No07Hi
Joseph	30	M	Tailor	26No07Hi
Isabella	22	F	Servant	26No07Hi
Jane	.00	F	Infant	26No07Hi
MCCAPPIN, Jane	40	F	Servant	26No07Hi
Catherine	10	F	Servant	26No07Hi
THOMPSON, Isaac	48	M	Servant	26No07Hi
Elizabeth	46	F	Servant	26No07Hi
John	12	M	Servant	26No07Hi
Sarah	09	F	Child	26No07Hi
Eliza	07	F	Child	26No07Hi
Mary	05	F	Child	26No07Hi
James	03	M	Child	26No07Hi
Margaret	.00	F	Infant	26No07Hi
MARKS, Joseph	40	M	Servant	26No07Hi
WRYSTY, Eliza	29	F	Servant	26No07Hi
DYER, Mary	19	F	Servant	26No07Hi
ALL, Mary	27	F	Servant	26No07Hi
BLEAKLY, Margaret	19	F	Servant	26No07Hi
ALL, Robert	.00	M	Infant	26No07Hi
MCDONNELL, Samuel	00	M	Servant	26No07Hi
ENNIS, Henry	19	M	Servant	26No07Hi
SMITH, John	35	M	Farmer	26No07Hi
MCVEIGH, Thomas	21	M	Farmer	26No07Hi
RAFFERTY, John	35	M	Farmer	26No07Hi
MCBRIDE, Mathew	21	M	Farmer	26No07Hi
GRAHAM, William	30	M	Farmer	26No07Hi
WOOD, Mary	29	F	Servant	26No07Hi
Anna	26	F	Servant	26No07Hi
HARPER, Uriah	02	M	Child	26No07Hi
MCMULLEN, Wm.	17	M	Servant	26No07Hi
BELL, Ellen	30	F	Servant	26No07Hi
LAGAN, Mary	18	F	Servant	26No07Hi
GALLAGHER, Mary	13	F	Servant	26No07Hi
MCKNIGHT, John	15	M	Servant	26No07Hi
QUIGLEY, James	25	M	Servant	26No07Hi
John	18	M	Servant	26No07Hi
MOGEY, James	21	M	Servant	26No07Hi
BRADLEY, Sarah	25	F	Dressmaker	26No07Hi
Wm.	30	M	Farmer	26No07Hi
Patrick	22	M	Farmer	26No07Hi
GIBSON, Eliza	15	F	Servant	26No07Hi
WRIGHT, James	13	M	Servant	26No07Hi
Mary	14	F	Servant	26No07Hi
Mary	.00	F	Infant	26No07Hi
GALOGNELY, Anne	20	F	Servant	26No07Hi
BRIGGS, Thomas	32	M	Servant	26No07Hi
CARROLL, John	24	M	Servant	26No07Hi
MCDOWELL, Alex	19	M	Servant	26No07Hi
David	21	M	Servant	26No07Hi
MARLIN, Edward	30	M	Servant	26No07Hi
WOODS, Robert	35	M	Servant	26No07Hi
MCKITTRICK, Eliza	21	F	Servant	26No07Hi
Sarah	18	F	Servant	26No07Hi
Margaret	14	F	Servant	26No07Hi
WILSON, Mary	30	F	Servant	26No07Hi
Cecilia	60	F	Servant	26No07Hi
JOHNSTON, John	26	M	Shoemaker	26No07Hi
MCCARNEY, Sarah	17	F	Shoemaker	26No07Hi
SHEILDS, Sarah	40	F	Shoemaker	26No07Hi
Ann	12	F	Shoemaker	26No07Hi
Jane	10	F	Shoemaker	26No07Hi
JACKSON, Margret	26	F	Dressmaker	26No07Hi
William	.00	M	Infant	26No07Hi
FITZPATRICK, John	26	M	Laborer	26No07Hi
GIBBS, Mdy.	25	F	Servant	26No07Hi

CAROLINA 26 NOVEMBER 1847

From Liverpool

NAMES OF PASSENGERS	AGE	SEX	OCCUPATIONS	DATE PORT SHIP
BYRNE, Lawrence	18	M	Laborer	26No02Lv
DALEY, Michael	40	M	Laborer	26No02Lv
Eliza	30	F	None	26No02Lv
Mary	09	F	Child	26No02Lv
Judy	08	F	Child	26No02Lv
Patrick	02	M	Child	26No02Lv
KEATING, Sally	35	F	Unknown	26No02Lv
Catharine	06	F	Child	26No02Lv
Mary	04	F	Child	26No02Lv
Peggy	01	F	Child	26No02Lv
Thomas	08	M	Child	26No02Lv
KELLEY, James	24	M	Laborer	26No02Lv
FLANNAGAN, John	37	M	Laborer	26No02Lv
Margaret	46	F	Unknown	26No02Lv
GILROY, Catharine	35	F	Unknown	26No02Lv
Ann	20	F	Unknown	26No02Lv
Bernard	17	M	Shoemaker	26No02Lv
MULLIN, Rose	12	F	Unknown	26No02Lv
NIXON, Jane	15	F	Unknown	26No02Lv
MCMURRY, Catharine	22	F	Unknown	26No02Lv
HANNEN, Michael	03	M	Child	26No02Lv
FAHEY, Bridget	20	F	Unknown	26No02Lv
CULLINAN, James	37	M	Miner	26No02Lv
Margaret	36	F	None	26No02Lv
Catharine	13	F	Unknown	26No02Lv
Margaret	08	F	Child	26No02Lv
Bridget	06	F	Child	26No02Lv
Alice	03	F	Child	26No02Lv
Mary	01	F	Child	26No02Lv
Thomas	12	M	Unknown	26No02Lv
Patrick	10	M	Unknown	26No02Lv
POWER, Patrick	45	M	Farmer	26No02Lv
James	13	M	Farmer	26No02Lv
William	11	M	Farmer	26No02Lv
CULLINAN, John	24	M	Laborer	26No02Lv
WALSH, David	25	M	Laborer	26No02Lv
FLINN, Patrick	30	M	Unknown	26No02Lv

LIBERTY 26 NOVEMBER 1847

From Liverpool

NAMES OF PASSENGERS	AGE	SEX	OCCUPATIONS	DATE PORT SHIP
FARMER, John	25	M	None	26No02Fw
FLOOD, James	24	M	Carpenter	26No02Fw
Mary	20	F	None	26No02Fw
DOWD, Margaret	50	F	None	26No02Fw
HARTIN, John	25	M	None	26No02Fw
THOMAS, Mary	18	F	None	26No02Fw
HALLY, Andrew	35	M	None	26No02Fw
Catherine	35	F	None	26No02Fw
Rosanna	02	F	Child	26No02Fw
CLIFFORTY, Owen	30	M	None	26No02Fw
Betty	25	F	None	26No02Fw
QUIGLY, Biddy	20	F	None	26No02Fw
HAND, Alice	30	F	None	26No02Fw
John	08	M	Child	26No02Fw
Margaret	05	F	Child	26No02Fw
Paddy	04	M	Child	26No02Fw
James	04	M	Child	26No02Fw

NAMES OF PASSENGERS	AGE	SEX	OCCUPATIONS	DATE PORT SHIP
SHOULDER, Anne	26	F	Dressmaker	26No02Fw
EBBIT, Rose	24	F	None	26No02Fw
GAYDOR, Judy	26	F	None	26No02Fw
CORMICK, Mary	30	F	None	26No02Fw
Ellen	20	F	None	26No02Fw
Catherine	09	F	Child	26No02Fw
Edmund	07	M	Child	26No02Fw
SCOTT, Catherine	20	F	None	26No02Fw
MOORE, Martin	30	M	None	26No02Fw
DALTON, Thomas	30	M	Butcher	26No02Fw
CONNORTON, Celia	60	F	None	26No02Fw
Celia	18	F	None	26No02Fw
SMITH, Micheal	18	M	None	26No02Fw
Mary	18	F	None	26No02Fw
CALLAGHAN, Thomas	30	M	None	26No02Fw
MCCONCHEY, Thomas	26	M	Gdnr	26No02Fw
William	23	M	None	26No02Fw
Agnes	20	F	Dressmaker	26No02Fw
Elizabeth	17	F	Dressmaker	26No02Fw
Martha	19	F	Dressmaker	26No02Fw
Mary	15	F	Dressmaker	26No02Fw
WARD, John	30	M	None	26No02Fw
William	05	M	Child	26No02Fw
CROAL, Andrew	20	M	Farmer	26No02Fw
MCNULTY, Pat	25	M	None	26No02Fw
LISPITT, James	21	M	None	26No02Fw
LEONARD, Patrick	34	M	None	26No02Fw
BUCKLY, Terence	36	M	Shopkeeper	26No02Fw
BROWN, Ellen	20	F	Dressmaker	26No02Fw
PIERCE, William	36	M	None	26No02Fw
KIRK, Robert	40	M	Grocer	26No02Fw
Faithful	40	F	None	26No02Fw
Robert	12	M	None	26No02Fw
James	10	M	None	26No02Fw
SLARTON, Edward	40	M	None	26No02Fw
Catherine	20	F	None	26No02Fw
HANLIN, Ann	26	F	None	26No02Fw
Mary	25	F	None	26No02Fw
TALBOTT, Richard	26	M	None	26No02Fw
MCENTEE, Philip	49	M	Blacksmith	26No02Fw
Anne	20	F	None	26No02Fw
MONAGHAN, Ann	15	F	None	26No02Fw
MCOLARY, Pat	16	M	None	26No02Fw
CAMPBELL, Francis	25	M	None	26No02Fw
MCCUSKER, Redmund	30	M	None	26No02Fw
BUCHANAN, Mary	40	F	None	26No02Fw
John	13	M	None	26No02Fw
MCMARTIN, Martha	22	F	None	26No02Fw
GLENDINGING, Joseph	30	M	None	26No02Fw
MCQUADE, Rose	22	F	None	26No02Fw
SLADIN, Mary	20	F	None	26No02Fw
COLLINS, John	50	M	None	26No02Fw
YOUNG, Margaret	34	F	None	26No02Fw
James	09	M	Child	26No02Fw
Jane	07	F	Child	26No02Fw
Margaret	03	F	Child	26No02Fw
MITCHELL, Martin	24	M	None	26No02Fw
BUTLER, John	25	M	None	26No02Fw
Margaret	52	F	None	26No02Fw
BRODERIC, Mary	27	F	None	26No02Fw
HEALY, Thomas	40	M	None	26No02Fw
LENAHANE, Thady	30	M	None	26No02Fw
MCCUE, Atty.	21	M	None	26No02Fw
Pat	55	M	None	26No02Fw
HEART, Catherine	60	F	None	26No02Fw
Bartholamew	30	M	None	26No02Fw
ERMINE, Margaret	23	F	None	26No02Fw
BURBITT, Betty	35	F	None	26No02Fw
NEVIN, Fanny	18	F	None	26No02Fw
GALLAGHER, Teddy	19	M	None	26No02Fw
MCDONALD, Luke	24	M	Tailor	26No02Fw
CALHOUN, Mary	24	F	None	26No02Fw
MCGEE, Alice	40	F	None	26No02Fw
Mary	13	F	None	26No02Fw
Sally	09	F	Child	26No02Fw
MCGEE, James	07	M	Child	26No02Fw
Pat	06	M	Child	26No02Fw
Charles	05	M	Child	26No02Fw
Catharine	04	F	Child	26No02Fw
CONOLLY, Eliza	20	F	None	26No02Fw
DOYLE, Edward	40	M	None	26No02Fw
ROWLEY, Bridget	53	F	None	26No02Fw
Luke	08	M	Child	26No02Fw
Thomas	40	M	None	26No02Fw
SLEVIN, Edward	17	M	None	26No02Fw
MCCONLY, James	20	M	None	26No02Fw
Thomas	10	M	None	26No02Fw
CAMPBELL, Fanny	50	F	None	26No02Fw
Isabella	18	F	None	26No02Fw
Barney	15	M	None	26No02Fw
George	12	M	None	26No02Fw
Samuel	08	M	Child	26No02Fw
William	05	M	Child	26No02Fw
Sarah	10	F	Child	26No02Fw
Robert	03	M	Child	26No02Fw
HAWLY, Barbara	20	F	None	26No02Fw
MCKRENLY, Michael	01	M	Child	26No02Fw
BURNS, John	30	M	Tailor	26No02Fw
Ellen	30	F	Tailor	26No02Fw
QUIN, Bridget	60	F	Tailor	26No02Fw
BURNS, John	04	M	Child	26No02Fw
Mary	03	F	Child	26No02Fw
MCNAMAN, Ellen	18	F	None	26No02Fw
SLORO, Pat	31	M	Blacksmith	26No02Fw
Mary	30	F	None	26No02Fw
NAVIN, Amy	20	F	Dressmaker	26No02Fw
MOSTMAN, Alexandre	25	M	None	26No02Fw
FOLEY, Michael	45	M	None	26No02Fw
Thomas	13	M	None	26No02Fw
SMITH, William	60	M	None	26No02Fw
William	35	M	None	26No02Fw
Mary	26	F	Wife	26No02Fw
Sally	06	F	Child	26No02Fw
John	03	M	Child	26No02Fw
James	02	M	Child	26No02Fw
MCALLISTER, John	21	M	None	26No02Fw
THOMPSON, John	22	M	None	26No02Fw
Mary	03	F	Child	26No02Fw
MCNALLE, Thomas	22	M	None	26No02Fw
LANGAN, Ann	22	F	None	26No02Fw
MALOY, Catherine	40	F	None	26No02Fw
GALLOWAY, Robert	17	M	Carpenter	26No02Fw
Catherine	12	F	None	26No02Fw
MCALLAN, John	18	M	None	26No02Fw
Samuel	24	M	None	26No02Fw
James	12	M	None	26No02Fw
SMITH, Catherine	21	F	None	26No02Fw
OBRIAN, William	30	M	None	26No02Fw
Bridget	25	F	None	26No02Fw
FARRALL, Honor	24	F	Dressmaker	26No02Fw
HIGGINS, Margaret	25	F	None	26No02Fw
HANEY, Owen	24	M	None	26No02Fw
Thomas	19	M	None	26No02Fw
KEARNS, Mary	20	F	None	26No02Fw
MADDEN, John	20	M	Blacksmith	26No02Fw
STUART, Thomas	40	M	None	26No02Fw
Ann	40	F	None	26No02Fw
MAHONE, Mary	19	F	None	26No02Fw
MCOLANY, Pat	14	M	None	26No02Fw
CASSIDA, Henry	30	M	None	26No02Fw
Mary	38	F	None	26No02Fw
MCDURMOTT, John	38	F	None	26No02Fw
Jane	21	F	None	26No02Fw
Mary	19	F	None	26No02Fw
CONNELL, Pat	20	M	None	26No02Fw
Bridget (W)	22	F	Wife	26No02Fw
Jane	20	F	None	26No02Fw
Mary	18	F	None	26No02Fw
MATHEWS, Mary	19	F	None	26No02Fw
HYNES, Mary-A.	18	F	None	26No02Fw

NAMES OF PASSENGERS	AGE	SEX	OCCUPATIONS	DATE PORT SHIP
COMMONS, Catherine	18	F	Dressmaker	26No02Fw
COSTELLO, George	28	M	Victualler	26No02Fw
NOONE, Martin	16	M	None	26No02Fw
DURFEY, James	23	M	Tailor	26No02Fw
Pat	21	M	Tailor	26No02Fw
KANE, Luke	35	M	None	26No02Fw
CAMPBELL, Michael	20	M	None	26No02Fw
CLANCY, Catherine	23	F	None	26No02Fw
CONNOR, Ann	20	F	None	26No02Fw
CAMPBELL, Catherine	30	F	None	26No02Fw
KANE, Mary	17	F	None	26No02Fw
MOONEY, William	20	M	Hatter	26No02Fw
RICHARDS, Mary	28	F	None	26No02Fw
Jane	20	F	None	26No02Fw
HART, James	30	M	Carpenter	26No02Fw
John	35	M	None	26No02Fw
DALTON, John	25	M	None	26No02Fw
MADDEN, Pat	25	M	None	26No02Fw
Mary	18	F	None	26No02Fw
Bridget	16	F	None	26No02Fw
FAUGHAN, George	32	M	None	26No02Fw
MCGUIRE, Ann	26	F	None	26No02Fw
LAWLER, Thomas	25	M	None	26No02Fw
DALTON, John	35	M	None	26No02Fw
NISETT, Cathrine	32	F	None	26No02Fw
CARROLL, Dennis	48	M	None	26No02Fw
Dennis	14	M	None	26No02Fw
Judy	20	F	None	26No02Fw
Mary	11	F	None	26No02Fw
Rose	20	F	None	26No02Fw
JEFFRIES, Richard	24	M	Baker	26No02Fw
Mary-Ann	25	F	Baker	26No02Fw
SHERRY, Lucy	21	F	Baker	26No02Fw
LYMAN, Eliza	19	F	Baker	26No02Fw
HALLORAN, Margaret	22	F	Baker	26No02Fw
TORPEY, Mary	24	F	Baker	26No02Fw
RILEY, Henry	33	M	Tailor	26No02Fw
RAFERTY, Pat	25	M	None	26No02Fw
MCCOY, Bridget	34	F	None	26No02Fw
FLYNN, Joseph	20	M	None	26No02Fw
Dennis	18	M	None	26No02Fw
Michael	20	M	None	26No02Fw
HALL, Peter	20	M	None	26No02Fw
GIBBONS, William	20	M	Shoemaker	26No02Fw
BOWMAN, Catherine	18	F	None	26No02Fw
FARLEY, Margaret	27	F	None	26No02Fw
Mary	04	F	Child	26No02Fw
DORNEY, Rose	18	F	None	26No02Fw
DONAHUE, Michael	18	M	None	26No02Fw
BRADY, Pat	24	M	None	26No02Fw
FLANAGAN, Mary	20	F	None	26No02Fw
MILLEGAN, Mary	22	F	None	26No02Fw
Susan	23	F	None	26No02Fw
RILEY, Eliza	18	F	None	26No02Fw
COYLE, Ellen	19	F	None	26No02Fw
Ann	19	F	None	26No02Fw
LEONARD, Alice	20	F	None	26No02Fw
SMITH, James	35	M	None	26No02Fw
Mary	16	F	None	26No02Fw
Pat	12	M	None	26No02Fw
John	08	M	Child	26No02Fw
BURKE, Richard	18	M	None	26No02Fw
CONNELL, Thomas	20	M	None	26No02Fw

WARREN 26 NOVEMBER 1847

From Belfast

NAMES OF PASSENGERS	AGE	SEX	OCCUPATIONS	DATE PORT SHIP
MURPHY, John	18	M	Mechanic	26No07Qr
LEARY, Timothy	20	M	Mechanic	26No07Qr
SMITH, William	27	M	Gentleman	26No07Qr
Martha	20	F	Lady	26No07Qr
FOX, Patrick	48	M	Mechanic	26No07Qr
MCCORMICK, Catharine	22	F	Spinster	26No07Qr
MCADAM, Agnes	30	F	Spinster	26No07Qr
Margaret	11	F	Spinster	26No07Qr
Janet	07	F	Child	26No07Qr
Agnes	05	F	Child	26No07Qr
Alexander	03	F	Child	26No07Qr
U	.06	F	Infant	26No07Qr
HAND, Laurence	22	M	Mechanic	26No07Qr
Elizabeth	22	F	Lady	26No07Qr
John	02	M	Child	26No07Qr
STIRLING, John	28	M	Mechanic	26No07Qr
GREEN, Robert	35	M	Tailor	26No07Qr
John	13	M	None	26No07Qr
LANNAN, Ann	24	F	Spinster	26No07Qr

MARGARET-ELIZABETH 29 NOVEMBER 1847

From PICTOU, N.S.

NAMES OF PASSENGERS	AGE	SEX	OCCUPATIONS	DATE PORT SHIP
FOWLER, Thos.	50	M	Professor	29No43Em

ERATA 29 NOVEMBER 1847

From Malaga-And-Gibralter

NAMES OF PASSENGERS	AGE	SEX	OCCUPATIONS	DATE PORT SHIP
FRASIER, T.W.Capt.	27	M	Army	29No87En

WATERLOO 30 NOVEMBER 1847

From Liverpool

NAMES OF PASSENGERS	AGE	SEX	OCCUPATIONS	DATE PORT SHIP
ROWAN, James	24	M	Mechanic	30No02As
CHAEDEL, Joseph	30	M	Unknown	30No02As
SPRINT, W.G.	50	M	Unknown	30No02As
U (W)	45	F	Wife	30No02As
Isabella	20	F	Unknown	30No02As
JOHNSON, Elizabeth	17	F	Unknown	30No02As
Margaret	15	F	Unknown	30No02As
Charlotte	13	F	Unknown	30No02As
Isabella	09	F	Child	30No02As
MITCHEL, George	26	M	Unknown	30No02As
Catherine	24	F	Unknown	30No02As

NAMES OF PASSENGERS	AGE	SEX	OCCUPATIONS	DATE PORT SHIP
ANDERSON, Richard	27	M	Unknown	30No02As
Mary	22	F	Unknown	30No02As
WALTON, Thomas	37	M	Unknown	30No02As
SUTTON, Thos.	25	M	Unknown	30No02As
TALLAMART, W.	21	M	Unknown	30No02As
HAMPSHIRE, John	22	M	Unknown	30No02As
TROY, Michel	40	M	Unknown	30No02As
MALETON, Bessey	20	F	Unknown	30No02As
FRANKS, James	30	M	Unknown	30No02As
U (W)	30	F	Wife	30No02As
WALSH, William	28	M	Unknown	30No02As
EVANS, Edward	36	M	Unknown	30No02As
JACKSON, M.	26	M	Unknown	30No02As
LAWSON, Joseph	20	M	Unknown	30No02As
Martha	11	F	Unknown	30No02As
Emma	06	F	Child	30No02As
Bada	02	F	Child	30No02As
TILESON, James	26	M	Unknown	30No02As
BANK, W.Win.	27	M	Unknown	30No02As
MANATON, W.	27	M	Unknown	30No02As
COLTES, Thos.	30	M	Unknown	30No02As
Ann	30	F	None	30No02As
Ann	10	F	Unknown	30No02As
Jane	08	F	Child	30No02As
JIMESON, Jacob	21	M	Unknown	30No02As
FITZGERALD, Thos.	21	M	Unknown	30No02As
SCOTT, Samuel	27	M	Unknown	30No02As
SPRATE, Margaret	20	F	Unknown	30No02As
GRAHAM, Eliza	20	F	Unknown	30No02As
MARTIN, Mary-Ann	20	F	Unknown	30No02As
BURK, Michel	20	M	Unknown	30No02As
U-Mrs.	40	F	Unknown	30No02As
James	20	M	Unknown	30No02As
Mary	18	F	Unknown	30No02As
Ellen	16	F	Unknown	30No02As
FURY, Pat	20	M	Unknown	30No02As
COLEMAN, James	20	M	Unknown	30No02As
STOKES, Thos.	28	M	Unknown	30No02As
MILLER, C.	09	M	Child	30No02As
Thos.	07	M	Child	30No02As
ONIONS, Conelus.	56	M	Unknown	30No02As
GRAHAM, Mathew	24	M	Unknown	30No02As
Robert	18	M	Unknown	30No02As
MARTIN, Samuel	20	M	Unknown	30No02As
JOHNSTON, J.	20	M	Unknown	30No02As
ALEXANDER, L.	18	M	Unknown	30No02As
MARTIN, Mary-Ann	18	F	Unknown	30No02As
ARNOTT, Peggy-Jane	18	F	Unknown	30No02As
SAPESLY, George	20	M	Unknown	30No02As
Ann	18	F	Unknown	30No02As
Mary-Jane	.00	F	Infant	30No02As
DONNY, Ebenezer	22	M	Unknown	30No02As
Benjamin	24	M	Unknown	30No02As
ROYLES, John	11	M	Unknown	30No02As
CONNOR, James	45	M	Unknown	30No02As
Eliza	40	F	None	30No02As
Martin	13	M	Unknown	30No02As
Margaret	11	F	Unknown	30No02As
James	09	M	Child	30No02As
Thomas	05	M	Child	30No02As
MCELROY, James	25	M	Unknown	30No02As
Sarah	50	F	Unknown	30No02As
John	17	M	Unknown	30No02As
Martha	16	F	Unknown	30No02As
Esther	12	F	Unknown	30No02As
Sarah	09	F	Child	30No02As
DANILSON, Robt.	20	M	Unknown	30No02As
MARTIN, Mary	17	F	Unknown	30No02As
PATTERSON, John	26	M	Unknown	30No02As
WHITAKER, James	23	M	Unknown	30No02As
BOWLER, John	32	M	Unknown	30No02As
HAGAN, Joseph	25	M	Unknown	30No02As
WOSTENHOLM, Charles	35	M	Unknown	30No02As
BARRETE, Edward	25	M	Unknown	30No02As
TWOMEY, Patrick	25	M	Unknown	30No02As
EWANS, John	30	M	Unknown	30No02As
DUNN, Margart	20	F	Unknown	30No02As
May	23	F	Unknown	30No02As
BOOTH, Joseph	32	M	Unknown	30No02As
HAGEN, Wm.	27	M	Unknown	30No02As
BYRON, Edward	35	M	Unknown	30No02As
James	28	M	Unknown	30No02As
DENNISON, George	25	M	Unknown	30No02As
MARSHALL, Mary	44	F	Unknown	30No02As
Eliz.	13	F	Unknown	30No02As
William	06	M	Child	30No02As
MORSON, James	25	M	Unknown	30No02As
Grace	25	F	None	30No02As
Emma	01	F	Child	30No02As
HIGH, Eliza	40	F	Unknown	30No02As
Ann	18	F	Unknown	30No02As
Eliza	07	F	Child	30No02As
Edwina	05	F	Child	30No02As
PLATT, Thos.	32	M	Unknown	30No02As
HEWITT, Samuel	38	M	Unknown	30No02As
MURREY, U-Mrs.	40	F	Unknown	30No02As
Catherine	06	F	Child	30No02As
James	03	M	Child	30No02As
LYNCH, Mathew	22	M	Laborer	30No02As
LARKIN, John	27	M	Laborer	30No02As
BEATY, James	40	M	Laborer	30No02As
AGNEW, John	20	M	Laborer	30No02As
LOWLEY, Dennis	40	M	Laborer	30No02As
Julia	30	F	None	30No02As
Ann	.00	F	Infant	30No02As
Michel	27	M	Unknown	30No02As
Catherine	27	F	None	30No02As
Johanna	06	F	Child	30No02As
James	04	M	Child	30No02As
John	02	M	Child	30No02As
Susan	.00	F	Infant	30No02As
MOYNE, Dennis	25	M	Laborer	30No02As
Patt.	24	M	Laborer	30No02As
Mary	20	F	Laborer	30No02As
Thomas	26	M	Laborer	30No02As
HASLIN, Richd.	30	M	Laborer	30No02As
BURKE, Michl.	20	M	Laborer	30No02As
MORTON, Mathias	18	M	Laborer	30No02As
RYON, John	40	M	Laborer	30No02As
PIM, James	26	M	Laborer	30No02As
U (W)	24	F	Wife	30No02As
Johanna	04	F	Child	30No02As
John	03	M	Child	30No02As
KEEFE, Michel	26	M	Unknown	30No02As
RYON, Biddy	26	F	Unknown	30No02As
Patt.	.00	M	Infant	30No02As
Mary	20	F	Unknown	30No02As
REILEY, Jake	20	M	Unknown	30No02As
HYLAND, Thomas	20	M	Unknown	30No02As
GAVAN, Thomas	20	M	Unknown	30No02As
NALLEY, Pat	40	M	Unknown	30No02As
MIKOOD, Jane	20	F	Unknown	30No02As
BEGLEY, Mary	20	F	Unknown	30No02As
MARTIN, John	30	M	Unknown	30No02As
YORK, Ellen	40	F	Unknown	30No02As
JURT, Henry	28	M	Unknown	30No02As
MCCAE, John	30	M	Unknown	30No02As
FALLON, Thos.	26	M	Unknown	30No02As
John	24	M	Unknown	30No02As
CONWEY, Sarah	23	F	Unknown	30No02As
ONEAL, James	30	M	Unknown	30No02As
U (W)	25	F	Wife	30No02As
OHEARN, W.	30	U	None	30No02As
John	26	M	None	30No02As
Dennis	20	M	None	30No02As
Mary	55	F	None	30No02As
Mary	11	F	None	30No02As
HIGGINS, Michel	12	M	None	30No02As
LYONS, Pat	30	M	None	30No02As
BRYON, Catherine	25	F	None	30No02As

NAMES OF PASSENGERS	AGE	SEX	OCCUPATIONS	DATE PORT SHIP
BRYON, Winiford	19	U	None	30No02As
FITZSIMMONS, John	20	M	None	30No02As
MCINTIRE, Pat	40	M	Laborer	30No02As
PRINTY, Noody	20	M	Laborer	30No02As
HUGHES, James	40	M	Laborer	30No02As
Mary	40	F	None	30No02As
James	09	M	Child	30No02As
Ellen	14	F	None	30No02As
Jane	12	F	None	30No02As
COOPER, Betey	35	F	None	30No02As
Ann	30	F	None	30No02As
William	16	M	None	30No02As
George	12	M	None	30No02As
Betey	10	F	None	30No02As
Edward	08	M	Child	30No02As
Sarah	06	F	Child	30No02As
Eliza	04	F	Child	30No02As
CLYMES, Daniel	25	M	Unknown	30No02As
LYNCH, James	20	M	Unknown	30No02As
GARDNER, Adam	30	M	Unknown	30No02As
U (W)	30	F	Wife	30No02As
Arch.	10	M	Unknown	30No02As
Catherine	03	F	Child	30No02As
Alexd.	02	M	Child	30No02As
KERNEY, Thomas	21	M	Unknown	30No02As
CANNON, Pat	23	M	Unknown	30No02As
BROUGHTON, Mark-Anthon	25	M	Unknown	30No02As
Martha	53	F	Unknown	30No02As
Grace-Remson	63	F	Unknown	30No02As
Mathias	18	M	Unknown	30No02As
HUGHS, Pat	25	M	Unknown	30No02As
DAVIDSON, Francis	26	M	Unknown	30No02As
MCGURLES, John	26	M	Unknown	30No02As
MCCARLY, Mary	18	F	Unknown	30No02As
TRACY, Hugh	26	M	Unknown	30No02As
GORMLEY, Pat	27	M	Unknown	30No02As
Biddy	20	F	Unknown	30No02As
ROBISON, Tom	20	M	Unknown	30No02As
Pat	20	M	Unknown	30No02As
DEASH, William	30	M	Unknown	30No02As
LEARY, James	20	M	Unknown	30No02As
HACKET, Thomas	20	M	Unknown	30No02As
GORVIN, James	22	M	Unknown	30No02As
CONROY, Ann	20	F	Unknown	30No02As
CORLEY, Bridget	25	F	Unknown	30No02As
LYONS, Ann	20	F	Unknown	30No02As
GRADY, John	17	F	Unknown	30No02As
DUMLIN, Bridget	49	F	Unknown	30No02As
BRYAN, Johannah	49	F	Unknown	30No02As
CALLEHAN, Michl.	21	M	Laborer	30No02As
CLYRE, Margaret	10	F	Laborer	30No02As
ROONEY, Mary	40	F	Laborer	30No02As
Catherine	10	F	Laborer	30No02As
KELLY, John	06	M	Child	30No02As
MALONE, Thos.	35	M	None	30No02As
HEALEY, Wm.	22	M	None	30No02As
FORROTON, Thomas	18	M	None	30No02As
HEALEY, Bridget	23	F	None	30No02As
ABBOTT, Bridget	14	F	None	30No02As
EKESLY, Joseph	18	M	None	30No02As
WEBSTER, William	18	M	None	30No02As
William	18	M	None	30No02As
COOPER, Robert	22	M	None	30No02As
KINNON, John	30	M	None	30No02As
NUGENT, John	20	M	None	30No02As
James	18	M	None	30No02As
Isabella	11	F	None	30No02As
Richard	11	M	None	30No02As
KELLEY, Thomas	20	M	None	30No02As
GRATH, John	20	M	None	30No02As
COOK, Thomas	17	M	None	30No02As
MEEGHAN, Michel	33	M	None	30No02As
RICHARDSON, Pat	24	M	None	30No02As
MCCORMICK, Pat	58	M	None	30No02As
Margaret	58	F	None	30No02As

NAMES OF PASSENGERS	AGE	SEX	OCCUPATIONS	DATE PORT SHIP
MCCORMICK, Thomas	24	M	Laborer	30No02As
Patt	20	M	Laborer	30No02As
Bridget	22	F	Laborer	30No02As
Alice	08	F	Child	30No02As
Michel	03	M	Child	30No02As
CHESTER, John	20	M	Unknown	30No02As
HAY, Mary	30	F	Unknown	30No02As
MCDONALD, John	28	M	Unknown	30No02As
Andrew	26	M	Unknown	30No02As
HART, Pat	21	M	Laborer	30No02As
DONALLY, Mary	20	F	Laborer	30No02As
PENTONY, Cath.	35	F	Laborer	30No02As
John	12	M	Laborer	30No02As
Michael	10	M	Laborer	30No02As
Mary	08	F	Laborer	30No02As
James	06	M	Laborer	30No02As
Pat	04	M	Laborer	30No02As
Cath.	.00	F	Infant	30No02As
GILL, Thomas	20	M	Unknown	30No02As
ERNSLEY, Mary	24	F	Unknown	30No02As
Anna	08	F	Child	30No02As
William	06	M	Child	30No02As
Martha	03	F	Child	30No02As
John	.00	M	Infant	30No02As
MULLEN, Bernard	54	M	Laborer	30No02As
CLARKE, Patt.	30	M	Laborer	30No02As
James	24	M	Laborer	30No02As
DUFFY, James	17	M	Laborer	30No02As
BRADLEY, Thomas	47	M	Laborer	30No02As
Susan	45	F	None	30No02As
Sarah	18	F	Laborer	30No02As
Mary	15	F	Laborer	30No02As
Elizabeth	11	F	Laborer	30No02As
Hannah	08	F	Child	30No02As
Ann	06	F	Child	30No02As
BUCKLEY, John	30	M	Laborer	30No02As
LEACH, Charles	28	M	Laborer	30No02As
DARLEY, John	21	M	Laborer	30No02As
BISHOP, James	47	M	Laborer	30No02As
U (W)	45	F	Wife	30No02As
U	19	M	Laborer	30No02As
U	12	F	Laborer	30No02As
U	10	M	Laborer	30No02As
U, U	00	M	Laborer	30No02As
U	26	M	Laborer	30No02As
U	25	F	Laborer	30No02As
MCGEE, U	26	F	Laborer	30No02As
COCKERN, U	29	M	Laborer	30No02As
Franciss	08	F	Child	30No02As
William	06	M	Child	30No02As
Mary	04	F	Child	30No02As
Harriott	02	F	Child	30No02As
GALLAGHER, Rosey	17	F	Laborer	30No02As
BLAKE, Ann	05	F	Child	30No02As
LARKIN, Ann	30	F	Laborer	30No02As
DONNELLY, Thomas	29	M	Laborer	30No02As
MILLIGAN, John	50	M	Laborer	30No02As
FLINT, John	32	M	Laborer	30No02As
AKIN, Wm.	38	M	Laborer	30No02As
PARRY, Ann	39	F	Laborer	30No02As
MULHERAN, Patt.	22	M	Laborer	30No02As
MURRAY, John	23	M	Laborer	30No02As
WARD, John	27	M	Laborer	30No02As
FITZPATRICK, Laurance	27	M	Laborer	30No02As
NEILL, Henry	20	M	Laborer	30No02As
NESBITT, Mary	22	F	Laborer	30No02As
KENNEY, Edward	36	M	Laborer	30No02As
BOYDE, Michel	20	M	Laborer	30No02As
MCLAUGHLIN, Michel	24	M	Laborer	30No02As
CURRY, Daniel	21	M	Laborer	30No02As
CRONAN, Dennis	20	M	Laborer	30No02As
WALSH, Michel	23	M	Laborer	30No02As
Ann	24	F	Laborer	30No02As
ODLUM, Thomas	27	M	Laborer	30No02As
U (W)	25	F	Wife	30No02As

NAMES OF PASSENGERS	AGE	SEX	OCCUPATIONS	DATE PORT SHIP
OHARA, Wm.	22	M	Laborer	30No02As
ANSLEY, J.	22	M	Laborer	30No02As
BLAKE, Peter	20	M	Laborer	30No02As
Owin	18	M	Laborer	30No02As
LACEY, Pat	26	M	Laborer	30No02As
MARSHALL, Tim	24	M	Laborer	30No02As
SULLIVAN, Paddy	20	M	Laborer	30No02As
FARLY, Mary	18	F	Laborer	30No02As
CONWELL, Mary	16	F	Laborer	30No02As
QAY, Pat	40	M	Laborer	30No02As
U (W)	40	F	Wife	30No02As
May	.00	F	Infant	30No02As
Mary	06	F	Child	30No02As
Bessey	08	F	Child	30No02As
John	04	M	Child	30No02As
CARTY, Sarah	25	F	Unknown	30No02As
MULDOON, Easter	60	F	Unknown	30No02As

PATRICK-HENRY 01 DECEMBER 1847

From Liverpool

NAMES OF PASSENGERS	AGE	SEX	OCCUPATIONS	DATE PORT SHIP
WALMSLEY, Wm.	40	M	Farmer	01De02Cw
CALLIGAN, John	36	M	Farmer	01De02Cw
Eliza	35	F	Farmer	01De02Cw
Mary-Jane	13	F	Farmer	01De02Cw
Wm.George	12	M	Farmer	01De02Cw
James	10	M	Farmer	01De02Cw
Andrew	07	M	Child	01De02Cw
John-Robt.	03	M	Child	01De02Cw
RUSH, Mary	24	F	Draper	01De02Cw
MCGURRY, Owen	30	M	Farmer	01De02Cw
Ann	25	F	Unknown	01De02Cw
Mary	.00	F	Infant	01De02Cw
MCMAHON, Ann	18	F	Unknown	01De02Cw
Mary	19	F	Unknown	01De02Cw
FAYE, Kitty	18	F	Unknown	01De02Cw
SALMON, John	30	M	Farmer	01De02Cw
Ann	25	F	Unknown	01De02Cw
Edwd.	02	M	Child	01De02Cw
ROWLEY, Michael	21	M	Farmer	01De02Cw
Mary	20	F	Unknown	01De02Cw
Patrick	21	M	Farmer	01De02Cw
John	16	M	Farmer	01De02Cw
DOLAN, Edward	40	M	Farmer	01De02Cw
Patrick	30	M	Farmer	01De02Cw
HOARTZ, John	36	M	Farmer	01De02Cw
GANITZ, Michael	32	M	Farmer	01De02Cw
FITZPATRICK, Martin	42	M	Farmer	01De02Cw
MCMAHON, Pat.	35	M	Farmer	01De02Cw
John	30	M	Unknown	01De02Cw
Peter	10	M	Unknown	01De02Cw
GANITZ, Thos.	08	M	Child	01De02Cw
SHAUGHNESSY, Pat.	19	M	Unknown	01De02Cw
MORISON, Barnard	20	M	Laborer	01De02Cw
Bridget	24	F	Unknown	01De02Cw
MALLMAN, Joshua	20	M	Shoemaker	01De02Cw
John	17	M	Shoemaker	01De02Cw
MCMAHON, Mary	30	F	Unknown	01De02Cw
MOORE, Benj.	30	M	Farmer	01De02Cw
Phoebe	30	F	Unknown	01De02Cw
Ann	07	F	Child	01De02Cw
Eliza	03	F	Child	01De02Cw
Jane	.00	F	Infant	01De02Cw
BANKS, Eliz.	20	F	Unknown	01De02Cw
HIGSON, Dennis	29	M	Laborer	01De02Cw
SYKES, Jas.	21	M	Laborer	01De02Cw
LEE, Fanny	28	F	Laborer	01De02Cw
SMITH, Patt.	25	M	Laborer	01De02Cw
MOLYNEUX, John	24	M	Laborer	01De02Cw
DONALD, John	25	M	Carpenter	01De02Cw
HOEY, Robert	30	M	Farmer	01De02Cw
Jane	26	F	Unknown	01De02Cw
John	05	M	Child	01De02Cw
Catherine	02	F	Child	01De02Cw
ANDERSON, Mary	21	F	Unknown	01De02Cw
Eliz.	30	F	Unknown	01De02Cw
FITZPATRICK, Betty	21	F	Unknown	01De02Cw
CUNAN, Michael	26	M	Laborer	01De02Cw
Judith	24	F	Unknown	01De02Cw
MCCABE, Margt.	20	F	Unknown	01De02Cw
HALPIN, Bryan	27	M	Laborer	01De02Cw
WARD, Catherine	25	F	Unknown	01De02Cw
HALPIN, Mary	25	F	Unknown	01De02Cw
Patt.	35	M	Laborer	01De02Cw
KELLY, Dennis	25	M	Laborer	01De02Cw
Bridget	25	F	Unknown	01De02Cw
CULLEN, Jas.	40	M	Unknown	01De02Cw
Eliz.	35	F	Unknown	01De02Cw
Rose	20	F	Unknown	01De02Cw
John	12	M	Unknown	01De02Cw
GAFFNEY, Henry	40	M	Laborer	01De02Cw
Mary	18	F	Unknown	01De02Cw
KINDELLAN, James	25	M	Laborer	01De02Cw
Elizabeth	23	F	Unknown	01De02Cw
Rose	.00	F	Infant	01De02Cw
KELLY, Jas.	21	M	Laborer	01De02Cw
BARDSLEY, Jas.	32	M	Farmer	01De02Cw
Maria	32	F	Unknown	01De02Cw
Mary	10	F	Unknown	01De02Cw
Thomas	.00	M	Infant	01De02Cw
CLEGG, John	22	M	Unknown	01De02Cw
FLINT, Charles	24	M	Laborer	01De02Cw
LAYTON, Thos.	28	M	Laborer	01De02Cw
STINSON, Alfred	22	M	Laborer	01De02Cw
COUSIN, Jas.	30	M	Laborer	01De02Cw
MCWILLIAM, Henry	30	M	Laborer	01De02Cw
MCCUSKY, Arthur	24	M	Laborer	01De02Cw
BLACK, Martha	30	F	Unknown	01De02Cw
Eliza	04	F	Child	01De02Cw
DAILEY, Catherine	20	F	Unknown	01De02Cw
THANLEY, Margt.	20	F	Unknown	01De02Cw
EVANS, Biddy	20	F	Unknown	01De02Cw
MOONEY, Jane	20	F	Unknown	01De02Cw
MAXHAM, John	25	M	Laborer	01De02Cw
Ann	23	F	Unknown	01De02Cw
Catherine	.00	F	Infant	01De02Cw
Henry	01	M	Child	01De02Cw
Mary	20	F	Unknown	01De02Cw
SMITH, Hannah	22	F	Unknown	01De02Cw
Ellen	02	F	Child	01De02Cw
JAMES, Robert	24	M	Farmer	01De02Cw
LEE, Catherine	24	F	Unknown	01De02Cw
BARRETT, Mary	20	F	Unknown	01De02Cw
FINN, Jas.	40	M	Farmer	01De02Cw
Jane	30	F	Unknown	01De02Cw
Bridget	15	F	Unknown	01De02Cw
Peter	14	M	Unknown	01De02Cw
John	12	M	Unknown	01De02Cw
Mary	10	F	Unknown	01De02Cw
Jane	08	F	Child	01De02Cw
Agnes	06	F	Child	01De02Cw
Thos.	02	M	Child	01De02Cw
Eliza	.00	F	Infant	01De02Cw
KELLY, John	45	M	Laborer	01De02Cw
Mary	40	F	Unknown	01De02Cw
Mary	14	F	Unknown	01De02Cw
Ann	04	F	Child	01De02Cw
Thos.	03	M	Child	01De02Cw
Agnes	16	F	Unknown	01De02Cw
BATH, Patt.	23	M	Laborer	01De02Cw
Jas.	21	M	Laborer	01De02Cw
MCCARR, John	17	M	Laborer	01De02Cw
LIDEN, Andrew	35	M	Laborer	01De02Cw

NAMES OF PASSENGERS	AGE	SEX	OCCUPATIONS	DATE PORT SHIP
LEATHAM, Jos.C.	28	M	Farmer	01De02Cw
Charles	00	M	Unknown	01De02Cw
BRADY, Walter	30	M	Unknown	01De02Cw
Susan	20	F	Unknown	01De02Cw
GOLLIGAN, Mary	30	F	Unknown	01De02Cw
FINNEGAN, Bridget	18	F	Unknown	01De02Cw
SHERIDAN, Rose	30	F	Unknown	01De02Cw
DICKASON, Ann	13	F	Unknown	01De02Cw
PHILLIPS, Wm.	26	M	Blacksmith	01De02Cw
RAFFERTY, Patt.	40	M	Laborer	01De02Cw
Bridget	30	F	Unknown	01De02Cw
FANNILLY, Hugh	30	M	Unknown	01De02Cw
Jeremiah	20	M	Unknown	01De02Cw
KINGSTON, Ann	18	F	Unknown	01De02Cw
WOODWARD, U	35	M	Clerk	01De02Cw
U	18	F	Unknown	01De02Cw
MCCABE, Patrick	19	M	Laborer	01De02Cw
COWAN, Mary	60	F	Unknown	01De02Cw
Jas.	23	M	Laborer	01De02Cw
Thos.	20	M	Laborer	01De02Cw
Jane	22	F	Unknown	01De02Cw
Jas.	12	M	Unknown	01De02Cw
STRETTON, Edward	45	M	Gdnr	01De02Cw
MULREYAN, Letitia	20	F	Unknown	01De02Cw
Marcilla	40	F	Unknown	01De02Cw
HARDEN, Mary	30	F	Unknown	01De02Cw
DARCY, Catherine	20	F	Unknown	01De02Cw
OBRIEN, Mary	20	F	Unknown	01De02Cw
HAND, Rose	20	F	Unknown	01De02Cw
CRAWLEY, Mary	25	F	Unknown	01De02Cw
FLYNNE, Dennis	23	M	Laborer	01De02Cw
BROOKS, Wm.	38	M	Laborer	01De02Cw
Ann	34	F	Unknown	01De02Cw
Mary	14	F	Unknown	01De02Cw
BRADLEY, John	30	M	Unknown	01De02Cw
Leppa	21	M	Unknown	01De02Cw
Ellen	24	F	Unknown	01De02Cw
MCGUIRE, Edward	20	M	Farmer	01De02Cw
Jane	21	F	Unknown	01De02Cw
FRANCIS, John	21	M	Farmer	01De02Cw
CONNOLLY, Patt.	30	M	Farmer	01De02Cw
BADDY, Patt.	35	M	Laborer	01De02Cw
Ann	32	F	Unknown	01De02Cw
Jas.	16	M	Unknown	01De02Cw
BRADDY, Peter	35	M	Laborer	01De02Cw
Catherine	13	F	Unknown	01De02Cw
Margt.	11	F	Unknown	01De02Cw
Joseph	07	M	Child	01De02Cw
Ann	.00	F	Infant	01De02Cw
COOK, Hugh	35	M	Unknown	01De02Cw
Matthew	09	M	Child	01De02Cw
Thos.	05	M	Child	01De02Cw
HEALY, Dennis	26	M	Farmer	01De02Cw
Andrew	22	M	Unknown	01De02Cw
Mary	21	F	Unknown	01De02Cw
MCGLEESON, Patt.	30	M	Unknown	01De02Cw
Johanna	28	F	Unknown	01De02Cw
Morris	04	M	Child	01De02Cw
Edmund	.00	M	Infant	01De02Cw
KERRY, Edward	26	M	Carpenter	01De02Cw
MCCURRAN, Arthur	45	M	Farmer	01De02Cw
Margt.	36	F	Unknown	01De02Cw
Isabella	11	F	Unknown	01De02Cw
MCCURKIN, Ellen	08	F	Child	01De02Cw
Peter	06	M	Child	01De02Cw
Margaret	04	F	Child	01De02Cw
Biddy	.00	F	Infant	01De02Cw
DUFFY, Patt.	26	M	Unknown	01De02Cw
DOWNY, John	26	M	Surveyor	01De02Cw
KENWORTHY, Jos.	26	M	Spinner	01De02Cw
Hannah	24	F	Spinner	01De02Cw
ROBINSON, Benj.	25	M	Spinner	01De02Cw
ALATHER, Jas.	30	M	Weaver	01De02Cw
HARVERN, David	22	M	Unknown	01De02Cw
HALFIELD, David	40	M	Grocer	01De02Cw
HALFIELD, Wm.	07	M	Child	01De02Cw
JONES, Thos.	25	M	Unknown	01De02Cw
MCMULTON, Charles	20	M	Farmer	01De02Cw
JONES, S.	55	M	Farmer	01De02Cw
LAMEY, Jas.	28	M	Carpenter	01De02Cw
Henry	20	M	Spinner	01De02Cw
KANE, Charles	50	M	Farmer	01De02Cw
Mary	40	F	Unknown	01De02Cw
Margaret	08	F	Child	01De02Cw
William	05	M	Child	01De02Cw
HUNTER, Patrick	25	M	Carpenter	01De02Cw
LOGAN, Jas.	30	M	Unknown	01De02Cw
CURRINES, Bridget	25	F	Unknown	01De02Cw
MCGRATH, Jas.	24	M	Laborer	01De02Cw
CUNNIF, Brian	20	M	Laborer	01De02Cw
MORGAN, Catherine	20	F	Unknown	01De02Cw
CAMERON, Robt.	18	M	Laborer	01De02Cw
SULLIVAN, Maria	36	F	Servant	01De02Cw
Julia	13	F	Unknown	01De02Cw
Daniel	12	M	Unknown	01De02Cw
Catherine	09	F	Child	01De02Cw
MCCORMICK, James	14	M	Laborer	01De02Cw
William	11	M	Unknown	01De02Cw
Patt	10	M	Unknown	01De02Cw
Mary	07	F	Child	01De02Cw
WALSH, John	30	M	Farmer	01De02Cw
Catherine	20	F	Unknown	01De02Cw
LENNAN, Patt	30	M	Farmer	01De02Cw
RALLEIGH, Thomas	30	M	Farmer	01De02Cw
Johanna	23	F	Unknown	01De02Cw
MCCARTY, Dennis	25	M	Farmer	01De02Cw
GOLDING, Judy	50	F	Unknown	01De02Cw
Timothy	20	M	Farmer	01De02Cw
LUDDIN, Nelly	21	F	Unknown	01De02Cw
MCGUINISS, Bridget	40	F	Unknown	01De02Cw
MURPHY, Margarett	40	F	Unknown	01De02Cw
TULLEY, Rosey	19	F	Unknown	01De02Cw
KENNARD, John	25	M	Laborer	01De02Cw
REILEY, Patt	37	M	Laborer	01De02Cw
MCDONNELL, Ann	40	F	Unknown	01De02Cw
Barnard	09	M	Child	01De02Cw
DERKIN, Thomas	20	M	Laborer	01De02Cw
OBRIEN, Catherine	18	F	Unknown	01De02Cw
MCGUFF, John	21	M	Joiner	01De02Cw
DEVONS, William	20	M	Draper	01De02Cw
WRIGHT, William	19	M	Laborer	01De02Cw
OLAUGHLIN, John	20	M	Laborer	01De02Cw
DERKIN, Patt	20	M	Laborer	01De02Cw
REYNOLDS, Margarett	20	F	Unknown	01De02Cw
WOODS, Charles	30	M	Laborer	01De02Cw
MURRAY, Thomas	16	M	Laborer	01De02Cw
SCANLIN, Martin	21	M	Farmer	01De02Cw
Maria	04	F	Child	01De02Cw
JOHNSTON, Robert	27	M	Carpenter	01De02Cw
MOSS, James	26	M	Gdnr	01De02Cw
AMSON, John	50	M	Carpenter	01De02Cw
BRIGGS, Joseph	26	M	Carpenter	01De02Cw
MORRISS, Patrick	25	M	Farmer	01De02Cw
DAILEY, Philip	24	M	Merchant	01De02Cw
TORMEY, Mary	20	F	Unknown	01De02Cw
MORAN, John-R.	21	M	Laborer	01De02Cw
FITZHARRISS, Mathew	23	M	Unknown	01De02Cw
RICHARDS, William	28	M	Weaver	01De02Cw
BROADHEAD, John	25	M	Weaver	01De02Cw
REILEY, Patrick	20	M	Laborer	01De02Cw
Catherine	16	F	Unknown	01De02Cw
TAYLOR, Henry	40	M	Spinner	01De02Cw
MCCARTNEY, James	26	M	Farmer	01De02Cw
Ellen	24	F	Unknown	01De02Cw
KELLY, Robert	26	M	Farmer	01De02Cw
CLARK, Robert	40	M	Carpenter	01De02Cw
Agnes	38	F	Unknown	01De02Cw
BRAY, Andrew	26	M	Weaver	01De02Cw
BAILEY, Ezra	29	M	Weaver	01De02Cw
ROBERTS, Joseph	21	M	Weaver	01De02Cw

NAMES OF PASSENGERS	AGE	SEX	OCCUPATIONS	DATE PORT SHIP
FITZPATRICK, Francis	20	M	Tailor	01De02Cw
BANE, William	35	M	Baker	01De02Cw
BENNETT, Thomas	13	M	Laborer	01De02Cw
MARTIN, John	20	M	Weaver	01De02Cw
Ann	18	F	Weaver	01De02Cw
LYNCH, Ann	18	F	Weaver	01De02Cw
CLIFFORD, Nichols	18	M	Laborer	01De02Cw
Patt	10	M	Unknown	01De02Cw
THOMPSON, Christian	18	F	Unknown	01De02Cw
MCALLISTER, Margt.	20	F	Unknown	01De02Cw
JOSELY, Richard	24	M	Miner	01De02Cw
RIDDEN, Richd.	20	M	Miner	01De02Cw
CARNEY, Edward	24	M	Unknown	01De02Cw
Margarett	24	F	Unknown	01De02Cw
Ellen	.00	F	Infant	01De02Cw
REILLEY, Mary	30	F	Unknown	01De02Cw
Peter	01	M	Child	01De02Cw

MARMION 01 DECEMBER 1847

From Liverpool

NAMES OF PASSENGERS	AGE	SEX	OCCUPATIONS	DATE PORT SHIP
ELLIOTT, John	22	M	Laborer	01De02Hc
Jane	25	F	Servant	01De02Hc
BOLE, Ambrose	28	M	Farmer	01De02Hc
DOWD, James	26	M	Laborer	01De02Hc
Mary	27	F	Laborer	01De02Hc
KEENAN, Ann	23	F	Laborer	01De02Hc
HICKEY, John	24	M	Laborer	01De02Hc
CORRICAN, Ann	19	F	Servant	01De02Hc
YORK, Kate	16	F	Servant	01De02Hc
DOWD, Winnifred	02	F	Child	01De02Hc
Catherine	.08	F	Infant	01De02Hc
CONNOLLY, Biddy	30	F	Unknown	01De02Hc
Eliza	02	F	Child	01De02Hc
May	.06	F	Infant	01De02Hc
CAMPBELL, Catherine	22	F	Unknown	01De02Hc
MONAGHAN, Mary	10	F	Unknown	01De02Hc
CAMPBELL, Sarah	03	F	Child	01De02Hc
Mary-Ann	.04	F	Infant	01De02Hc
POWER, Richard	18	M	Laborer	01De02Hc
HOPKINS, Martin	25	M	Laborer	01De02Hc
CASEY, Pat	26	M	Laborer	01De02Hc
MCCOY, John	21	M	Laborer	01De02Hc
COFFEY, Mary	40	F	Unknown	01De02Hc
Joseph	22	M	Laborer	01De02Hc
John	20	M	Laborer	01De02Hc
Ellen	15	F	Unknown	01De02Hc
Alice	10	F	Unknown	01De02Hc
Donald	08	M	Child	01De02Hc
Morris	06	M	Child	01De02Hc
MCDONALD, Bryan	21	M	Laborer	01De02Hc
CONROY, Michael	25	M	Laborer	01De02Hc
MCDONALD, Martin	21	M	Laborer	01De02Hc
CONROY, Teresa	25	F	Servant	01De02Hc
MCDONALD, Martha	25	F	Servant	01De02Hc
POTTER, Michael	18	M	Servant	01De02Hc
Mary	19	F	Servant	01De02Hc
CAVANAGH, Wm.	30	M	Carpenter	01De02Hc
BRENNAN, Cathe.	20	F	Servant	01De02Hc
REYNOLDS, Cathe.	50	F	Unknown	01De02Hc
Susan	13	F	Unknown	01De02Hc
Thos.	45	M	Laborer	01De02Hc
GAMBLE, Wm.	20	M	Carpenter	01De02Hc
Thos.	18	M	Laborer	01De02Hc
Johnston	16	M	Laborer	01De02Hc
Jane	45	F	Unknown	01De02Hc
Mary	12	F	Unknown	01De02Hc
MCGEANY, James	17	M	Laborer	01De02Hc
HOLLADY, James	22	M	Tailor	01De02Hc
Eliza-Jane	22	F	None	01De02Hc
James	.06	M	Infant	01De02Hc
DELANY, Dennis	26	M	Laborer	01De02Hc
DUTTON, Wm.	24	M	Laborer	01De02Hc
FLYNN, Peter	32	M	Builder	01De02Hc
Margaret	30	F	None	01De02Hc
John	06	M	Child	01De02Hc
Mary-Ann	04	F	Child	01De02Hc
WAYLAND, James	20	M	Laborer	01De02Hc
HIGGINS, Andrew	25	M	Laborer	01De02Hc
Michael	18	M	Laborer	01De02Hc
MCCABE, Catherine	20	F	Servant	01De02Hc
SMITH, Samuel	24	M	Laborer	01De02Hc
COLLINS, James	21	M	Laborer	01De02Hc
Ellen	20	F	Unknown	01De02Hc
KIRKLAND, Wm.	28	M	Tailor	01De02Hc
MCGOLLICK, John	26	M	Laborer	01De02Hc
MOLLOY, John	24	M	Laborer	01De02Hc
HALL, Mary-Jane	20	F	Servant	01De02Hc
NEWMAN, Phillip	25	M	Blacksmith	01De02Hc
ROURKE, Daniel	25	M	Laborer	01De02Hc
Rose	22	F	Unknown	01De02Hc
DIGNAN, Eleanor	25	F	Unknown	01De02Hc
KIERNAN, Ann	40	F	Unknown	01De02Hc
BYRNE, Thomas	28	M	Laborer	01De02Hc
Alice	24	F	Servant	01De02Hc
Judy	26	F	Servant	01De02Hc
LOUHAN, Mary	20	F	Servant	01De02Hc
BONNY, Margaret	20	F	Servant	01De02Hc
OCONNOR, Edward	20	M	Baker	01De02Hc
FEY, James	20	M	Laborer	01De02Hc
CONNOR, David	40	M	Farmer	01De02Hc
Margaret	40	F	None	01De02Hc
John	21	M	Laborer	01De02Hc
Dennis	19	M	Laborer	01De02Hc
Julia	16	F	Unknown	01De02Hc
DOLAN, Pat	20	M	Laborer	01De02Hc
PATTERSON, Thos.	18	M	Shoemaker	01De02Hc
FLANNAGAN, James	30	M	Blacksmith	01De02Hc
HEALAN, James	30	M	Farmer	01De02Hc
HANNAGAN, Sally	21	F	Servant	01De02Hc
HEALAN, Thomas	10	M	Unknown	01De02Hc
Bridget	08	F	Child	01De02Hc
MCKEENAN, Robt.	16	M	Laborer	01De02Hc
Sarah	17	F	Unknown	01De02Hc
Catherine	12	F	Unknown	01De02Hc
KIMLAHAN, John	40	M	Carpenter	01De02Hc
Julia	40	F	None	01De02Hc
Charlotte	20	F	Unknown	01De02Hc
Thomas	09	M	Child	01De02Hc
Richard	05	M	Child	01De02Hc
John	03	M	Child	01De02Hc
GEDDES, Jane	21	F	Servant	01De02Hc
GRIMES, William	17	M	Carpenter	01De02Hc
ORR, John	20	M	Carpenter	01De02Hc
FEIGHLEY, John	30	M	Laborer	01De02Hc
Bridget	35	F	None	01De02Hc
Pat	02	M	Child	01De02Hc
James	.06	M	Infant	01De02Hc
SCANNON, James	40	M	Laborer	01De02Hc
TIMOTHY, Pat	24	M	Laborer	01De02Hc
CONNOR, Bridget	20	F	Unknown	01De02Hc
GILROY, Ann	18	F	Servant	01De02Hc
FEA, Ann	20	F	Servant	01De02Hc
RYAN, Patrick	06	M	Child	01De02Hc
Michael	02	M	Child	01De02Hc
GOLEY, John	31	M	Laborer	01De02Hc
CONNELL, Elizabeth	25	F	Unknown	01De02Hc
MURRAY, John	54	M	Farmer	01De02Hc
LONG, James	55	M	Laborer	01De02Hc
Alice	60	F	Unknown	01De02Hc
Ellen	19	F	Unknown	01De02Hc
Mary	13	F	Unknown	01De02Hc
JOHNSTONE, Nathaniel	42	M	Weaver	01De02Hc

NAMES OF PASSENGERS		AGE	SEX	OCCUPATIONS	DATE PORT SHIP
MURPHY, Bridget		13	F	Servant	01De02Hc
CULLEN, Patrick		21	M	Laborer	01De02Hc
HARVEY, James		30	M	Laborer	01De02Hc
John		12	M	Laborer	01De02Hc
Cathl.		09	F	Child	01De02Hc
Margaret		18	F	Laborer	01De02Hc
CROSSLEY, Wm.		20	M	Draper	01De02Hc
LILLY, John		60	M	Farmer	01De02Hc
Margaret		50	F	Unknown	01De02Hc
Michael		18	M	Unknown	01De02Hc
Mary		12	F	Unknown	01De02Hc
Edward		10	M	Unknown	01De02Hc
Betsy		06	F	Child	01De02Hc
Rose		07	F	Child	01De02Hc
GUM, John		07	M	Child	01De02Hc
Catherine		05	F	Child	01De02Hc
SHEVLIN, Pat		40	M	Laborer	01De02Hc
Hone		12	U	Laborer	01De02Hc
Pat		10	M	Laborer	01De02Hc
Harry		08	M	Child	01De02Hc
George		05	M	Child	01De02Hc
TOOHY, Malachi		27	M	Laborer	01De02Hc
MILES, Bridget		28	F	Unknown	01De02Hc
RYAN, Wm.		46	M	Tailor	01De02Hc
Betty		40	F	Unknown	01De02Hc
HART, Catherine		20	F	Unknown	01De02Hc
BRYAN, Michael		50	M	Laborer	01De02Hc
MILLER, Mary		40	F	Unknown	01De02Hc
Hugh		01	M	Child	01De02Hc
PLED, Mary		77	F	Unknown	01De02Hc
FREEL, Manessch		16	M	Servant	01De02Hc
MCCELLAN, Jas.		16	M	Laborer	01De02Hc
REILLY, John		20	M	Laborer	01De02Hc
Mary		18	F	Servant	01De02Hc
MCGEOGH, Ann		16	F	Unknown	01De02Hc
Peter		13	M	Unknown	01De02Hc
MCCAUGHEY, Phillip		60	M	Farmer	01De02Hc
BOYLE, Nancy		32	F	Unknown	01De02Hc
Edward		13	M	Unknown	01De02Hc
Mary-Ann		11	F	Unknown	01De02Hc
Hugh		09	M	Child	01De02Hc
Henry		07	M	Child	01De02Hc
Elizabeth		05	F	Child	01De02Hc
William		03	M	Child	01De02Hc
Richard		01	M	Child	01De02Hc
HAGAN, Mary		16	F	Unknown	01De02Hc
Susan		13	F	Unknown	01De02Hc
GOOCH, Thomas		36	M	Shopkeeper	01De02Hc
HENESSY, Bridget		24	F	Unknown	01De02Hc
BURKE, Catherine		25	F	Unknown	01De02Hc
WALSH, Dennis		55	M	Laborer	01De02Hc
St.JOHN, Michael		30	M	Farmer	01De02Hc
Mary		35	F	None	01De02Hc
Mary		09	F	Child	01De02Hc
James		06	M	Child	01De02Hc
Margaret		03	F	Child	01De02Hc
Judith	(D)	.06	F	Infant	01De02Hc
BELL, Eliza		28	F	Unknown	01De02Hc
Catherine		07	F	Child	01De02Hc
GUIRKEN, Peter		20	M	Laborer	01De02Hc
HUTCHINSON, Martha		70	F	Unknown	01De02Hc
James		30	M	Laborer	01De02Hc
FENNELL, Ann		20	F	Servant	01De02Hc
MCALTEE, Pat		20	M	Laborer	01De02Hc
Edward		15	M	Laborer	01De02Hc
CORRIGAN, James		20	M	Laborer	01De02Hc
CLARKE, Mary		40	F	Unknown	01De02Hc
Pat		16	M	Unknown	01De02Hc
James		14	M	Unknown	01De02Hc
Bryan		11	M	Unknown	01De02Hc
CARN, Bridget		60	F	Unknown	01De02Hc
BRATTON, James		16	M	Flaxdr	01De02Hc
Andrew		12	M	Unknown	01De02Hc
Wm.		10	M	Unknown	01De02Hc
MCCROMKEN, Margaret		40	F	Unknown	01De02Hc

NAMES OF PASSENGERS		AGE	SEX	OCCUPATIONS	DATE PORT SHIP
MCCROMKEN, Ann		12	F	Unknown	01De02Hc
Pat		10	M	Unknown	01De02Hc
Terry		08	M	Child	01De02Hc
John		06	M	Child	01De02Hc
Mary		.04	F	Infant	01De02Hc
TIMOTHY, Martin		25	M	Laborer	01De02Hc
CONNOR, Thomas		25	M	Laborer	01De02Hc
DAVIES, John		24	M	Brush Maker	01De02Hc
KENNY, Thomas		20	M	Laborer	01De02Hc
HAND, Rose		45	F	Unknown	01De02Hc
Mary		12	F	Unknown	01De02Hc
Pat		09	M	Child	01De02Hc
James	(S)	05	M	Child	01De02Hc
BURNS, Margaret		45	F	Unknown	01De02Hc
CAROLIN, Bridget		20	F	Unknown	01De02Hc
ELLIS, Thomas		30	M	Farmer	01De02Hc
CONOLLY, Ann		20	F	Servant	01De02Hc
POWER, Patrick		35	M	Laborer	01De02Hc
John		30	M	Farmer	01De02Hc
Catherine		30	F	Unknown	01De02Hc
Mary		13	F	Unknown	01De02Hc
Johanna		09	F	Child	01De02Hc
John		08	M	Child	01De02Hc
Pat		04	M	Child	01De02Hc
James		03	M	Child	01De02Hc
QUIGLEY, Edward		40	M	Dyer	01De02Hc
Mary		13	F	Servant	01De02Hc
MONALLY, Anthony		50	M	Laborer	01De02Hc
Bridget	(W)	48	F	None	01De02Hc
Catherine	(D)	13	F	Unknown	01De02Hc
MURPHY, John		18	M	Unknown	01De02Hc
Maria		14	F	Unknown	01De02Hc
MCKEENAN, Barney		24	M	Farmer	01De02Hc
GREEN, Mary		21	F	Servant	01De02Hc
MCDARROW, Hugh		30	M	Laborer	01De02Hc
Cathe.		25	F	Unknown	01De02Hc
LEE, Bridget		20	F	Servant	01De02Hc
FLOOD, Peter		35	M	Farmer	01De02Hc
Bridget	(W)	29	F	None	01De02Hc
Mary	(D)	09	F	Child	01De02Hc
Francis	(S)	07	M	Child	01De02Hc
John	(S)	03	M	Child	01De02Hc
Charles	(S)	02	M	Child	01De02Hc
MULVEY, Daniel		25	M	Laborer	01De02Hc
KELLY, Bridget		22	F	Servant	01De02Hc
FLEMING, Sarah-Jane		25	F	Unknown	01De02Hc
MORRIS, James		20	M	Laborer	01De02Hc
CONNELL, Patt		40	M	Laborer	01De02Hc
JENNINGS, Thomas		22	M	Laborer	01De02Hc
ELLIOTT, John		33	M	Butcher	01De02Hc
Mary		30	F	Unknown	01De02Hc
BARKER, Patrick		21	F	Striker	01De02Hc
BONNER, Ann		24	F	Servant	01De02Hc
WELSH, William		24	M	Laborer	01De02Hc
CONWAY, Lawrence		22	M	Laborer	01De02Hc
NOWLAN, Bryan		29	M	Laborer	01De02Hc
DUARDEN, Hannah		34	F	Unknown	01De02Hc
Francis		30	M	Unknown	01De02Hc
Isaac		08	M	Child	01De02Hc
KNIPE, Samuel		30	M	Weaver	01De02Hc
BILL, Thomas		26	M	Farmer	01De02Hc
MCCELLAND, Edwd.		24	M	Farmer	01De02Hc
ALLEN, John		28	M	Groom	01De02Hc
Mary		28	F	Unknown	01De02Hc
HAGAN, John		20	M	Laborer	01De02Hc
KELLY, Catharine		18	F	Servant	01De02Hc
MCKENNEY, Thomas		40	M	Laborer	01De02Hc
Ann-Jane		18	F	Unknown	01De02Hc
Martin		11	M	Unknown	01De02Hc
Mary		09	F	Child	01De02Hc
MAXWELL, John		47	M	Mpol	01De02Hc
MCGUIRE, Alice		60	F	Unknown	01De02Hc
John		03	M	Child	01De02Hc
PYM, James		33	M	Wlmcht	01De02Hc
BYRNES, Patt		30	M	Laborer	01De02Hc

NAMES OF PASSENGERS		AGE	SEX	OCCUPATIONS	DATE PORT SHIP
CLUSKY, Patt		25	M	Laborer	01De02Hc
MCCUNE, Pat		28	M	Shoemaker	01De02Hc

AMBASSADOR 01 DECEMBER 1847

From Liverpool

NAMES OF PASSENGERS		AGE	SEX	OCCUPATIONS	DATE PORT SHIP
CLARKE, Catherine		18	F	Unknown	01De02Rg
CARTNEY, Rose		16	F	Unknown	01De02Rg
MCDERMOTT, Michal.		17	M	Laborer	01De02Rg
SMITH, Judy		18	F	Unknown	01De02Rg
MCANNEL, Eliza		20	F	Unknown	01De02Rg
DOONEY, Mary		20	F	Unknown	01De02Rg
LYNCH, Biddy		19	F	Unknown	01De02Rg
MCMAHON, John		30	M	Laborer	01De02Rg
KENNEAR, Wm.		40	M	Laborer	01De02Rg
MALONE, Mary		25	F	Unknown	01De02Rg
MORNEY, Thomas		20	M	Laborer	01De02Rg
Michl.		18	M	Laborer	01De02Rg
GRAHAM, Wm.		21	M	Laborer	01De02Rg
HURLEY, Tim		25	M	Laborer	01De02Rg
Ann		20	F	Unknown	01De02Rg
Mary		18	F	Unknown	01De02Rg
Died-At-Sea					
SULLIVAN, Jerry		45	M	Laborer	01De02Rg
Mary		12	F	Unknown	01De02Rg
Honor		09	F	Child	01De02Rg
Nancy		06	F	Child	01De02Rg
DALEY, Mary		30	F	Unknown	01De02Rg
Died-At-Sea					
SULLIVAN, Mary		20	F	Unknown	01De02Rg
U, Margaret		16	F	Unknown	01De02Rg
John		02	M	Child	01De02Rg
GURLEY, Julia		20	F	Unknown	01De02Rg
LYNCH, John		40	M	Laborer	01De02Rg
Philip		17	M	Laborer	01De02Rg
John		09	M	Child	01De02Rg
MCHEW, Michl.		18	M	Laborer	01De02Rg
MCKEEN, Wm.		11	M	Laborer	01De02Rg
MULLEY, Jane		30	F	Unknown	01De02Rg
MCCONNOR, James		20	M	Laborer	01De02Rg
FITZPATERICK, Wm.		30	M	Laborer	01De02Rg
U	(W)	25	F	None	01De02Rg
U		20	F	Unknown	01De02Rg
BOYLAND, Bridget		21	F	Unknown	01De02Rg
MCGEE, James		50	M	Laborer	01De02Rg
John		19	M	Laborer	01De02Rg
Catherine		20	F	Unknown	01De02Rg
CUNNINGHAM, John		50	M	Laborer	01De02Rg
Thos.		16	M	Laborer	01De02Rg
HANLEY, Berry		34	M	Laborer	01De02Rg
MILLIGAN, Mich.		40	M	Laborer	01De02Rg
Owen		30	M	Laborer	01De02Rg
Mary		18	F	Unknown	01De02Rg
MORAN, Mary		18	F	Unknown	01De02Rg
NANCA, Joseph		24	M	Laborer	01De02Rg
U	(W)	22	F	None	01De02Rg
COYLE, Thos.		40	M	Laborer	01De02Rg
Michael		17	M	Laborer	01De02Rg
Pat		14	M	Laborer	01De02Rg
Richard		11	M	Laborer	01De02Rg
COXON, Joseph		35	M	Laborer	01De02Rg
U	(W)	28	F	None	01De02Rg
Oliver	(S)	03	M	Child	01De02Rg
HINNIFFREY, John		35	M	Laborer	01De02Rg
Edward		34	M	Laborer	01De02Rg
Mary		30	F	Unknown	01De02Rg
Sally		20	F	Unknown	01De02Rg
FOOLEY, Carle		20	M	Laborer	01De02Rg

NAMES OF PASSENGERS		AGE	SEX	OCCUPATIONS	DATE PORT SHIP
KEELY, James		20	M	Laborer	01De02Rg
BRANNAN, Mary		20	F	Unknown	01De02Rg
Catherine		18	F	Unknown	01De02Rg
FOOLEY, Anne		20	F	Unknown	01De02Rg
MCKEAN, U-Mrs.		30	F	Unknown	01De02Rg
Michael	(S)	06	M	Child	01De02Rg
Cissy	(D)	03	F	Child	01De02Rg
Francis	(S)	.11	M	Infant	01De02Rg
FITZPATERICK, Wm.		50	M	Laborer	01De02Rg
TUNOGESTY, Thos.		20	M	Laborer	01De02Rg
Biddy		18	F	Unknown	01De02Rg
Mary		20	F	Unknown	01De02Rg
MCAONEYTH, Thos.		20	M	Laborer	01De02Rg
Michl.		27	M	Laborer	01De02Rg
Anne		40	F	Unknown	01De02Rg
LAFHEAD, John		27	M	Laborer	01De02Rg
MAYORS, Owen		20	M	Laborer	01De02Rg
Thos.		19	M	Laborer	01De02Rg
COONEY, Pat		40	M	Laborer	01De02Rg
Eliza	(W)	40	F	None	01De02Rg
John	(S)	24	M	Laborer	01De02Rg
Margt.	(D)	17	F	Unknown	01De02Rg
Eliza	(D)	15	F	Unknown	01De02Rg
Mary	(D)	12	F	Unknown	01De02Rg
Wm.	(S)	10	M	Unknown	01De02Rg
Anne	(D)	07	F	Child	01De02Rg
Ellen	(D)	04	F	Child	01De02Rg
BURKE, Peter		20	M	Unknown	01De02Rg
Bridget		20	F	Unknown	01De02Rg
MALONE, Ned		30	M	Unknown	01De02Rg
Bridget		30	F	Unknown	01De02Rg
KEENAN, Lawrence		20	M	Laborer	01De02Rg
KILLEN, Sally		20	F	Unknown	01De02Rg
MCGENTY, Peter		26	M	Laborer	01De02Rg
Maria		35	F	Unknown	01De02Rg
CLARK, Biddy		25	F	Unknown	01De02Rg
CURRY, Kitty		39	F	Unknown	01De02Rg
FITZPATRICK, Susan		27	F	Unknown	01De02Rg
MCGENTY, Bernard		.08	M	Infant	01De02Rg
RIGLEY, John		40	M	Laborer	01De02Rg
U	(W)	40	F	None	01De02Rg
Charles	(S)	15	M	Laborer	01De02Rg
Edward	(S)	13	M	Laborer	01De02Rg
Samuel	(S)	19	M	Laborer	01De02Rg
Hannah	(D)	09	F	Child	01De02Rg
Elizabeth	(D)	05	F	Child	01De02Rg
Eliza	(D)	03	F	Child	01De02Rg
Emma	(D)	.08	F	Infant	01De02Rg
HEADSHAW, Thos.		20	M	Laborer	01De02Rg
CROSS, Geo.		24	M	Laborer	01De02Rg
BLUNT, Thos.		40	M	Laborer	01De02Rg
Thos.		11	M	Laborer	01De02Rg
Mary		13	F	Unknown	01De02Rg
Henry		06	M	Child	01De02Rg
BOYLAND, Bryan		20	M	Laborer	01De02Rg
LEACH, John		24	M	Laborer	01De02Rg
FEENEY, Biddy		16	F	Unknown	01De02Rg
Margt.		12	F	Unknown	01De02Rg
RYANS, Anne		30	F	Unknown	01De02Rg
Pat		12	M	Unknown	01De02Rg
Mary		10	F	Unknown	01De02Rg
ANNE, Mary		21	F	Unknown	01De02Rg
HANLEY, Pat		40	M	Laborer	01De02Rg
ARMSTRONG, Thos.		40	M	Laborer	01De02Rg
CUNNINGHAM, Anne		40	F	Unknown	01De02Rg
Died-At-Sea					
DUXBURY, Edward		24	M	Laborer	01De02Rg
Nancy		24	F	Unknown	01De02Rg
MCCAM, James		20	M	Laborer	01De02Rg
LENNAN, Margaret		20	F	Unknown	01De02Rg
LYNCH, Margaret		20	F	Unknown	01De02Rg
MAHONE, Francis		24	M	Laborer	01De02Rg
Anne	(W)	20	F	None	01De02Rg
Mary	(D)	.08	F	Infant	01De02Rg
MCGUIRE, John		25	M	Laborer	01De02Rg

NAMES OF PASSENGERS		AGE	SEX	OCCUPATIONS	DATE PORT SHIP
FLYNN, Thos.		24	M	Laborer	01De02Rg
Anne		04	F	Child	01De02Rg
WOODS, Catherine		18	F	Unknown	01De02Rg
REVILLE, James		24	M	Laborer	01De02Rg
MAILY, Margt.		16	F	Unknown	01De02Rg
REILLY, Elizbth.		22	F	Unknown	01De02Rg
WINN, Andrew		13	M	Laborer	01De02Rg
Mich.		10	M	Laborer	01De02Rg
CONNELL, Paterick		18	M	Laborer	01De02Rg
COYLE, Margaret		20	F	Unknown	01De02Rg
CARRIGAN, Maria		10	F	Unknown	01De02Rg
CARTY, Maurice		20	M	Laborer	01De02Rg
MCCARTY, Jeremiah		30	M	Laborer	01De02Rg
MULLON, James		26	M	Laborer	01De02Rg
HAYES, Roger		22	M	Laborer	01De02Rg
HYAMS, Mary		40	F	Unknown	01De02Rg
Mary		13	F	Unknown	01De02Rg
Anthony		11	M	Laborer	01De02Rg
Libby		09	F	Child	01De02Rg
KEARNEY, Michael		19	M	Laborer	01De02Rg
KILLEN, Mary		20	F	Unknown	01De02Rg
Biddy		12	F	Unknown	01De02Rg
CARROLL, Henry		20	M	Laborer	01De02Rg
HANLEY, Mary		70	F	Unknown	01De02Rg
BRENNAN, James		30	M	Laborer	01De02Rg
U	(W)	25	F	None	01De02Rg
Mary	(D)	04	F	Child	01De02Rg
Wm.	(S)	.10	M	Infant	01De02Rg
Judy	(D)	03	F	Child	01De02Rg
RODERICK, Robert		28	M	Laborer	01De02Rg
U	(W)	23	F	None	01De02Rg
John	(S)	02	M	Child	01De02Rg
FAIR, John		13	M	Laborer	01De02Rg
Eliza		11	F	Unknown	01De02Rg
Mary		09	F	Child	01De02Rg
MOULLON, Eliza		14	F	Unknown	01De02Rg
HERRANE, Wm.		23	M	Laborer	01De02Rg
CONLEY, Mary		19	F	Unknown	01De02Rg

ALBERS 02 DECEMBER 1847

From Liverpool

NAMES OF PASSENGERS		AGE	SEX	OCCUPATIONS	DATE PORT SHIP
STOW, Mary-Ann		28	F	Unknown	02De02RJ
Died-At-Sea					
James		06	M	Child	02De02RJ
BYRNE, Peter		25	M	Laborer	02De02RJ
KELLY, Barney		20	M	Laborer	02De02RJ
BRADY, Jno.		38	M	Laborer	02De02RJ
REILLY, Catherine		30	F	Laborer	02De02RJ
LANGTON, Frank		25	M	Laborer	02De02RJ
GILLESPIE, Margaret		50	F	Unknown	02De02RJ
Ellen		17	F	Unknown	02De02RJ
Michel		04	M	Child	02De02RJ
HOY, Catherine		16	F	Unknown	02De02RJ
MCARDLE, Mary		24	F	Unknown	02De02RJ
CARDEN, Ann		60	F	Unknown	02De02RJ
DWAN, Patrick		50	M	Laborer	02De02RJ
Bridget		30	F	Unknown	02De02RJ
MURRAY, James		12	M	None	02De02RJ
DWAN, Barnard		07	M	Child	02De02RJ
Peter		05	M	Child	02De02RJ
Patrick		03	M	Child	02De02RJ
FOX, Hubert		30	M	Laborer	02De02RJ
Franny		12	M	None	02De02RJ
John		10	M	None	02De02RJ
GOUGH, Christoph.		29	M	Laborer	02De02RJ
BUR, John		30	M	Laborer	02De02RJ
Michl.		28	M	Laborer	02De02RJ
BUR, Mary-Ann		20	F	Unknown	02De02RJ
IHRES, Biddy		23	F	Unknown	02De02RJ
Mary		40	F	Unknown	02De02RJ
Michel		19	M	Laborer	02De02RJ
Mary		12	F	None	02De02RJ
Died-At-Sea					
MCDONNELL, James		24	M	Unknown	02De02RJ
Ann		44	F	Unknown	02De02RJ
Emma		.00	F	Infant	02De02RJ
Ann		13	F	None	02De02RJ
Michel.		1[illegible]	M	None	02De02RJ
James		09	M	Child	02De02RJ
Catherine		04	F	Child	02De02RJ
WELSH, Mary		50	F	Unknown	02De02RJ
HAY, Ann		35	F	Unknown	02De02RJ
MCKENNA, Hugh		40	M	Laborer	02De02RJ
CORNELL, Francis		30	M	Laborer	02De02RJ
LEGGIN, William		22	M	Laborer	02De02RJ
BARRY, Michel.		22	M	Laborer	02De02RJ
FALVEY, Daniel		50	M	Laborer	02De02RJ
HENELLY, Ellen		52	F	Unknown	02De02RJ
Dennis		19	M	Laborer	02De02RJ
LEARY, Howard		50	M	Unknown	02De02RJ
Jno.		21	M	Unknown	02De02RJ
Daniel		17	M	Unknown	02De02RJ
Ellen		13	F	None	02De02RJ
Jane		11	F	None	02De02RJ
Edward		10	M	None	02De02RJ
Patrick		05	M	Child	02De02RJ
MCKENNA, Ellen		11	F	None	02De02RJ
Ann		10	F	None	02De02RJ
DEMODY, Patrick		25	M	Laborer	02De02RJ
Thomas		03	M	Child	02De02RJ
PERSTAGS, Thomas		27	M	Laborer	02De02RJ
Edward		15	M	Unknown	02De02RJ
CAMPRIN, Patrick		19	M	Laborer	02De02RJ
MURPHY, John		31	M	Laborer	02De02RJ
MAHONY, Mary		06	F	Child	02De02RJ
DATULL, Margaret		04	F	Child	02De02RJ
DOWVAN, Charles		05	M	Child	02De02RJ
MURRY, William		12	M	None	02De02RJ
OBURN, Dennis		20	M	Laborer	02De02RJ
DEVINS, Mary		20	F	Unknown	02De02RJ
MURPHY, Jonathan		35	M	Laborer	02De02RJ
CARNY, James		15	M	Unknown	02De02RJ
Catherine		14	F	Unknown	02De02RJ
Julia		12	F	None	02De02RJ
REEGAN, Ellen		20	F	Unknown	02De02RJ
CUNNINGHAM, Jane		30	F	Unknown	02De02RJ
BRADLY, John		45	M	Laborer	02De02RJ
Julia	(W)	35	F	None	02De02RJ
John	(S)	07	M	Child	02De02RJ
MCCARTHY, John		21	M	Laborer	02De02RJ
BOYLE, Thomas		20	M	Laborer	02De02RJ
CONNAN, John		30	M	Laborer	02De02RJ
Patrick		30	M	Laborer	02De02RJ
Edward		28	M	Laborer	02De02RJ
Died-At-Sea					
RATTIGAN, Catherine		22	F	Unknown	02De02RJ
FITZGIBBON, U-Mrs.		47	F	Wi	02De02RJ
CORNELL, Mary		18	F	Unknown	02De02RJ
MURPHY, Honnia		30	M	Laborer	02De02RJ
Edward		.00	M	Infant	02De02RJ
Ellen		10	F	None	02De02RJ
Mary		01	F	Child	02De02RJ
YALHOODY, Catherine		25	F	Unknown	02De02RJ
REYNOLDS, Edw.		30	M	Farmer	02De02RJ
Patrick		20	M	Farmer	02De02RJ
Betty		20	F	Unknown	02De02RJ
JORDAN, John		10	M	None	02De02RJ
GORHAM, Peggy		20	F	Unknown	02De02RJ
Peter		03	M	Child	02De02RJ
FAGAN, Cath.		20	F	Unknown	02De02RJ
FLYNN, Thomas		35	M	Laborer	02De02RJ
Ann		11	F	None	02De02RJ

NAMES OF PASSENGERS		AGE	SEX	OCCUPATIONS	DATE PORT SHIP
FLYNN, James		03	M	Child	02De02Rj
BOOSH, Rose		20	F	None	02De02Rj
OBRIEN, Mary		34	F	Unknown	02De02Rj

GLADIATOR 02 DECEMBER 1847

From London

NAMES OF PASSENGERS		AGE	SEX	OCCUPATIONS	DATE PORT SHIP
ANTHONY, Peter-J.		15	M	Gentleman	02De21Dg
SAMUELS, Elizabeth		30	F	Lady	02De21Dg
HART, Nathan		25	M	Gentleman	02De21Dg
NOYES, Anne		37	F	Unknown	02De21Dg
Mary-A.		05	F	Child	02De21Dg
Eliza		08	F	Child	02De21Dg
NASH, Thomas		40	M	Gentleman	02De21Dg
BRYAN, Dan		50	M	Laborer	02De21Dg
Joseph		15	M	Laborer	02De21Dg
CHANTER, Wm.		35	M	Surgeon	02De21Dg
WITHERS, Gabriel		25	M	Carpenter	02De21Dg
BEENY, Robert		26	M	Baker	02De21Dg
HUMPHREYS, Ann		23	F	Unknown	02De21Dg
Jacob		04	M	Child	02De21Dg
Martha		02	F	Child	02De21Dg
DAWSON, Mary		50	F	Unknown	02De21Dg
JENNY, Mary		33	F	Unknown	02De21Dg
DREW, Matthew-C.		23	M	Surveyor	02De21Dg
BROWN, Abraham		23	M	Butcher	02De21Dg
JEBBETT, Elisha		21	M	Grocer	02De21Dg

ST.PATRICK 04 DECEMBER 1847

From Liverpool

NAMES OF PASSENGERS		AGE	SEX	OCCUPATIONS	DATE PORT SHIP
BARRINGTON, John		60	M	Farmer	04De02Bw
Thomas	(S)	24	M	Carpenter	04De02Bw
Charles	(S)	28	M	Farmer	04De02Bw
James	(S)	26	M	Chandler	04De02Bw
Ann	(W)	56	F	None	04De02Bw
Jno.	(S)	14	M	Unknown	04De02Bw
Jane	(D)	21	F	Spinster	04De02Bw
Mary-Ann	(D)	22	F	Spinster	04De02Bw
TIGHE, Richd.		21	M	Tchrcl	04De02Bw
James		18	M	Tchrcl	04De02Bw
Eliza		16	F	Spinster	04De02Bw
Jane		23	F	Spinster	04De02Bw
CAMPBELL, James		23	M	Soap Maker	04De02Bw
Catherine	(W)	20	F	None	04De02Bw
TRISTRAM, Carey		20	M	Clerk	04De02Bw
WILSON, Ann		20	F	None	04De02Bw
KERWIN, Jno.		36	M	Farmer	04De02Bw
MCMORROUGH, Patk.		28	M	Farmer	04De02Bw
DONALDSON, Mary-Jane		19	F	None	04De02Bw
CRAIG, Elizth.		20	F	Spinster	04De02Bw
Terence		09	M	Child	04De02Bw
Mary		07	F	Child	04De02Bw
DUFFY, Rose		20	F	Servant	04De02Bw
FARRALL, Margt.		26	F	None	04De02Bw
MCCORMICK, Pat		48	M	Farmer	04De02Bw
Died-At-Sea					
Jno.		20	M	Farmer	04De02Bw
QUIN, Bessy		25	F	Servant	04De02Bw
REILLY, Rose		18	F	Servant	04De02Bw
REIRDON, Danl.		32	M	Laborer	04De02Bw
REIRDON, Elizth.		50	F	Wi	04De02Bw
NAUGHTON, Jno.		25	M	Laborer	04De02Bw
REGAN, Jno.		25	M	Laborer	04De02Bw
HYLAND, Mary		30	F	None	04De02Bw
Jno.	(S)	03	M	Child	04De02Bw
Pat	(S)	.11	M	Infant	04De02Bw
LEONARD, Ellen		32	F	None	04De02Bw
Thos.	(S)	07	M	Child	04De02Bw
Margt.	(D)	05	F	Child	04De02Bw
Cathl.	(D)	03	F	Child	04De02Bw
Pat	(S)	.11	M	Infant	04De02Bw
Died-At-Sea					
SHEEHAN, Margt.		27	F	None	04De02Bw
TRILLAIN, Bridget		20	F	Spinster	04De02Bw
GALLIGAN, Michl.		35	M	Grocer	04De02Bw
James		12	M	Grocer	04De02Bw
Edwd.		09	M	Child	04De02Bw
BROGAN, Ann		18	F	Spinster	04De02Bw
Ellen		16	F	Spinster	04De02Bw
TIERNEY, Danl.		35	M	Laborer	04De02Bw
HAYES, Dennis		36	M	Laborer	04De02Bw
CALDWELL, Edwd.		40	M	Laborer	04De02Bw
Cathl.	(W)	32	F	None	04De02Bw
James	(S)	12	M	Unknown	04De02Bw
Mary-Ann	(D)	10	F	Unknown	04De02Bw
Cathl.	(D)	05	F	Child	04De02Bw
FLEMMING, Jno.		35	M	Laborer	04De02Bw
DUNN, Ellen		18	F	Servant	04De02Bw
MURPHY, Thos.		60	M	Carpenter	04De02Bw
Pat	(S)	20	M	Laborer	04De02Bw
Bridget	(W)	50	F	None	04De02Bw
Margt.	(D)	18	F	Spinster	04De02Bw
READ, Mary		25	F	Spinster	04De02Bw
RILEY, Geo.		17	M	Laborer	04De02Bw
LAWLOR, Jas.		24	M	Laborer	04De02Bw
ROUNDTREE, Cathl.		35	F	Wi	04De02Bw
Bridget	(D)	13	F	Unknown	04De02Bw
HEARN, Richd.		27	M	Clerk	04De02Bw
DOOLAN, Fanny		30	F	None	04De02Bw
Dennis	(S)	03	M	Child	04De02Bw
Ann	(D)	02	F	Child	04De02Bw
James		35	M	Laborer	04De02Bw
CAHARTY, Bridget		50	F	Wi	04De02Bw
CONN, Wm.		50	M	Farmer	04De02Bw
Wm.		12	M	Farmer	04De02Bw
Eliza		20	F	Spinster	04De02Bw
Sarah		14	F	Spinster	04De02Bw
QUIN, Cathl.		30	F	Wi	04De02Bw
Ellen	(D)	.10	F	Infant	04De02Bw
FLYNN, Farrall		26	M	Blacksmith	04De02Bw
MOORE, Murtoch		30	M	Laborer	04De02Bw
QUIN, Francis		30	M	Laborer	04De02Bw
Ellen		17	F	Spinster	04De02Bw
Cathl.		09	F	Child	04De02Bw
COSTELLO, Mary-Ann		24	F	None	04De02Bw
MCLOUGHLAN, Cathl.		19	F	Spinster	04De02Bw
ROGERS, Bridget		25	F	Spinster	04De02Bw
CORIGAN, Pat		24	M	Laborer	04De02Bw
DORAN, Andw.		20	M	Flaxdr	04De02Bw
FOLEY, Edwd.		30	M	Laborer	04De02Bw
SMITH, Rose		20	F	Spinster	04De02Bw
MCGAVANNAH, Mary		20	F	Spinster	04De02Bw
FLYNN, Ellen		18	F	Spinster	04De02Bw
MCCORMISH, Jno.		38	M	Butcher	04De02Bw
MALONEY, Wm.		32	M	Laborer	04De02Bw
Cathl.	(W)	24	F	None	04De02Bw
Christopher	(S)	03	M	Child	04De02Bw
Mary-Ann	(D)	.11	F	Infant	04De02Bw
Died-At-Sea					
HAGAN, Peter		24	M	Laborer	04De02Bw
BOYLAN, Jno.		49	M	Laborer	04De02Bw
KELLY, Jno.		11	M	Laborer	04De02Bw
LENIHAN, Jno.		30	M	Laborer	04De02Bw
HENNEBREY, Jas.		40	M	Laborer	04De02Bw
MULLIGAN, Jas.		20	M	Laborer	04De02Bw

NAMES OF PASSENGERS		AGE	SEX	OCCUPATIONS	DATE PORT SHIP
TRAINER, Mary		20	F	Spinster	04De02Bw
LENON, Nancy		19	F	Spinster	04De02Bw
OBRIEN, Chas.		25	M	Farmer	04De02Bw
WELDON, Cathl.		16	F	Spinster	04De02Bw
HOLOHAN, Margt.		20	F	Spinster	04De02Bw
DUFFY, Nancy		19	F	Spinster	04De02Bw
GARVIN, Margt.		19	F	Spinster	04De02Bw
MCCABE, Pat		20	M	Groom	04De02Bw
MCGOWAN, Robt.		26	M	Shoemaker	04De02Bw
REILLY, Mary		20	F	Spinster	04De02Bw
GALWAY, Thos.		26	M	Laborer	04De02Bw
LYNCH, Ann		30	F	None	04De02Bw
SCULLY, Pat		26	M	Laborer	04De02Bw
FARRALL, Pat		20	M	Laborer	04De02Bw
GALLAGHER, Wm.		09	M	Child	04De02Bw
LYONS, Keran		25	M	Laborer	04De02Bw
GALLAGHER, Mary		11	F	Unknown	04De02Bw
LYONS, Mary		50	F	None	04De02Bw
CURRY, Margt.		30	F	None	04De02Bw
Michl.	(S)	06	M	Child	04De02Bw
Jno.	(S)	02	M	Child	04De02Bw
Died-At-Sea					
QUIN, Jno.		20	M	Laborer	04De02Bw
MCCABE, Bernard		25	M	Laborer	04De02Bw
MCKEON, Matthew		17	M	Laborer	04De02Bw
SMITH, Pat		18	M	Laborer	04De02Bw
LYNCH, Cathl.		10	F	Unknown	04De02Bw
MARTIN, Jno.		17	M	Laborer	04De02Bw
CODY, Jno.		17	M	Laborer	04De02Bw
FARMER, Mary		40	F	None	04De02Bw
Pat	(S)	11	M	Unknown	04De02Bw
Sarah	(D)	10	F	Unknown	04De02Bw
Wm.	(S)	09	M	Child	04De02Bw
Mary	(D)	07	F	Child	04De02Bw
Thos.	(S)	03	M	Child	04De02Bw
Ann	(D)	.11	F	Infant	04De02Bw
Bernard	(S)	05	M	Child	04De02Bw
MURPHY, Mary		16	F	Spinster	04De02Bw
QUIN, Rosanna		22	F	Spinster	04De02Bw
Maria		10	F	Spinster	04De02Bw
Ann		08	F	Child	04De02Bw
FINN, Jno.		11	M	Unknown	04De02Bw
WELSH, Cathl.		11	F	Unknown	04De02Bw
LEE, Margt.		11	F	Unknown	04De02Bw
Ellen		09	F	Child	04De02Bw
MAHONEY, Florence		18	M	Laborer	04De02Bw
BROWN, Mary		11	F	Unknown	04De02Bw
MCELROY, Mary		40	F	Wi	04De02Bw
Jno.	(S)	11	M	Unknown	04De02Bw
Cathl.	(D)	09	F	Child	04De02Bw
Wm.	(S)	07	M	Child	04De02Bw
GALLIGAN, Mary-Ann		15	F	Spinster	04De02Bw
HART, Cathl.		30	F	None	04De02Bw
Mary	(D)	10	F	Unknown	04De02Bw
KELLY, Pat		22	M	Laborer	04De02Bw
OLEARY, Margt.		24	F	None	04De02Bw
Dennis	(S)	.11	M	Infant	04De02Bw
REGAN, Jno.		11	M	Unknown	04De02Bw
KELLAGHER, Julia		60	F	Wi	04De02Bw
Murtoch		20	M	Cooper	04De02Bw
BURNS, Thos.		26	M	Laborer	04De02Bw
Jno.		20	M	Laborer	04De02Bw
OHARA, Alice		11	F	Unknown	04De02Bw
DORAN, Jno.		26	M	Laborer	04De02Bw
Mary		23	F	Spinster	04De02Bw
WELDON, Cathl.		40	F	None	04De02Bw
Elizth.	(D)	11	F	Unknown	04De02Bw
CUSACK, Cathl.		26	F	None	04De02Bw
Peter	(S)	09	M	Child	04De02Bw
Pat	(S)	07	M	Child	04De02Bw
BERGEN, Peter		21	M	Laborer	04De02Bw
BURNS, Jane		18	F	Spinster	04De02Bw
ARMSTRONG, Henry		25	M	Carpenter	04De02Bw
JAMESON, Mary		22	F	Spinster	04De02Bw
EWEN, Matthew		19	M	Laborer	04De02Bw
DONLEY, Thos.		11	M	Laborer	04De02Bw
HORAM, Michl.		20	M	Laborer	04De02Bw
BROPHY, Honora		20	F	Spinster	04De02Bw
MAROONEY, Edwd.		19	M	Laborer	04De02Bw
ROONEY, Thos.		26	M	Shoemaker	04De02Bw
Mary-Ann		01	F	Child	04De02Bw
Betsy		11	F	Unknown	04De02Bw
MURPHY, Ellen		11	F	Unknown	04De02Bw
CALLIGAN, Bridget		22	F	Spinster	04De02Bw
GARRAGHAN, Jno.		40	M	Butcher	04De02Bw
Mary	(W)	40	F	None	04De02Bw
CAHILL, Mary		25	F	None	04De02Bw
DOYLE, Jas.		09	M	Child	04De02Bw
CAHILL, Jas.		02	M	Child	04De02Bw
GRIFFIN, Julia		25	F	None	04De02Bw
Winifred	(D)	04	F	Child	04De02Bw
Bridget	(D)	06	F	Child	04De02Bw
SHERIDAN, Pat		20	M	Laborer	04De02Bw
KENNEDY, Mary		15	F	Spinster	04De02Bw
MARA, Peter		46	M	Laborer	04De02Bw
Thom.		11	M	Unknown	04De02Bw
Mary		09	F	Child	04De02Bw
Ellen		08	F	Child	04De02Bw
KELLY, Jno.		21	M	Laborer	04De02Bw
CAHERTY, Jas.		26	M	Laborer	04De02Bw
ROONEY, Mary		28	F	Spinster	04De02Bw
CASEY, Eliza		14	F	Spinster	04De02Bw
KEEGAN, Jno.		09	M	Child	04De02Bw
Chas.		07	M	Child	04De02Bw
Ann		20	F	Spinster	04De02Bw
CARROLL, Jas.		25	M	Laborer	04De02Bw
FERRIS, Pat		46	M	Laborer	04De02Bw
Pat		20	M	Laborer	04De02Bw
Ann		06	F	Child	04De02Bw
FITZPATRICK, Mary		25	F	Spinster	04De02Bw
MCCRORY, Mary		22	F	Spinster	04De02Bw
FARLEY, Ann		20	F	Spinster	04De02Bw
REILLY, Jas.		14	M	Unknown	04De02Bw
Pat		11	M	Unknown	04De02Bw
MCCARROLL, Mary		21	F	Spinster	04De02Bw
HEALLY, Mary		11	F	Unknown	04De02Bw
REILLY, Michl.		40	M	Laborer	04De02Bw
Mary	(W)	40	F	None	04De02Bw
Ann	(D)	16	F	Spinster	04De02Bw
Michl.	(S)	11	M	Unknown	04De02Bw
Felix	(S)	09	M	Child	04De02Bw
Mary	(D)	07	F	Child	04De02Bw
KERAN, Cathl.		20	F	Spinster	04De02Bw
FINNIGAN, David		25	M	Laborer	04De02Bw
Cathl.	(W)	25	F	None	04De02Bw
Mary		16	F	Spinster	04De02Bw
Peter	(S)	05	M	Child	04De02Bw
Thos.	(S)	04	M	Child	04De02Bw
SHEPHERD, Jane		26	F	None	04De02Bw
Jane	(D)	03	F	Child	04De02Bw
MCKINNEY, Elizth.		26	F	None	04De02Bw
Jno.		14	M	Unknown	04De02Bw
Rachel		12	F	Unknown	04De02Bw
Wm.		10	M	Unknown	04De02Bw
Josh.		08	M	Child	04De02Bw
Margt.		06	F	Child	04De02Bw
Eliza		04	F	Child	04De02Bw
James		02	M	Child	04De02Bw
Died-At-Sea					
KELLY, Jas.		25	M	Laborer	04De02Bw
HASLIN, Ann		50	F	Wi	04De02Bw
CULLY, Mary		25	F	Spinster	04De02Bw
Jno.		20	M	Laborer	04De02Bw
OBRIEN, Pat		30	M	Laborer	04De02Bw
GORWIN, Bridget		14	F	Spinster	04De02Bw
SMITH, Cathl.		18	F	Spinster	04De02Bw
Bridget		14	F	Spinster	04De02Bw
Mary		11	F	Unknown	04De02Bw
BONNEY, Winifred		17	F	Unknown	04De02Bw
Barney		04	M	Child	04De02Bw

NAMES OF PASSENGERS		AGE	SEX	OCCUPATIONS	DATE PORT SHIP
BOYLAN, Bridget		24	F	Spinster	04De02Bw
WELSH, Cathl.		10	F	Unknown	04De02Bw
CASEY, Pat		25	M	Carpenter	04De02Bw
CASSERLEY, Ellen		35	F	Wi	04De02Bw
LYNAN, Jas.		20	M	Laborer	04De02Bw
BURNS, Mary		40	F	Wi	04De02Bw
MATTHEWS, Cathl.		14	F	Unknown	04De02Bw
HURLEY, Michl.		40	M	Laborer	04De02Bw
Honora	(W)	40	F	None	04De02Bw
Elizth.	(D)	08	F	Child	04De02Bw
Thos.	(S)	04	M	Child	04De02Bw
Bridget	(D)	.10	F	Infant	04De02Bw
GREY, Edwd.		14	M	Unknown	04De02Bw
Matthew		11	M	Unknown	04De02Bw
FARRALL, Bridget		16	F	Spinster	04De02Bw
TOOLE, Rose		21	F	None	04De02Bw
Bridget	(D)	05	F	Child	04De02Bw
LEDWITH, Maria		14	F	Unknown	04De02Bw
FARLEY, Ann		16	F	Spinster	04De02Bw
HAGERTY, Mary		26	F	Wi	04De02Bw
ROBINSON, Thos.		25	M	Clerk	04De02Bw
Saml.		21	M	Aptcast	04De02Bw
DONLEY, Jno.		40	M	Laborer	04De02Bw
Thos.		19	M	Laborer	04De02Bw
SHUTER, Bridget		19	F	Spinster	04De02Bw
BROWN, Hannah		30	F	None	04De02Bw
CONOLLY, Wm.		15	M	Unknown	04De02Bw
ROWAN, Thos.		35	M	Carpenter	04De02Bw
MCCUNNINGHAM, Jas.		46	M	Laborer	04De02Bw
LYONS, Dennis		25	M	Laborer	04De02Bw
Nancy		25	F	Spinster	04De02Bw
ROWAM, Pat		40	M	Sawer	04De02Bw
LYON, Dolly		20	F	None	04De02Bw
GILLESPIE, Cathl.		20	F	Spinster	04De02Bw
CARR, Hannah		23	F	None	04De02Bw
Jno.	(S)	.03	M	Infant	04De02Bw
SHANDLEY, Bernard		26	M	Laborer	04De02Bw
LEE, Edwd.		23	M	Shoemaker	04De02Bw
CASIDY, Matthew		23	M	Laborer	04De02Bw
BOYLAN, Pat		18	M	Laborer	04De02Bw
Jno.		16	M	Laborer	04De02Bw
Mary		10	F	Unknown	04De02Bw
OSBORN, Thos.		18	M	Laborer	04De02Bw
HENNEBREY, Mary		35	F	None	04De02Bw
Jno.	(S)	07	M	Child	04De02Bw
Thos.	(S)	05	M	Child	04De02Bw
Ellen	(D)	.11	F	Infant	04De02Bw
GALWAY, Margt.		20	F	Spinster	04De02Bw
FARRALL, Thos.		20	M	Laborer	04De02Bw
GALLIGAN, Ellen		11	F	Unknown	04De02Bw
LEE, Thos.		11	M	Unknown	04De02Bw
QUIN, Peter		60	M	Laborer	04De02Bw
Margt.	(W)	55	F	None	04De02Bw
Wm.		23	M	Laborer	04De02Bw
Peter		11	M	Unknown	04De02Bw
Mary		03	F	Child	04De02Bw
GREEN, Thos.		21	M	Laborer	04De02Bw
LEONARD, Jno.		25	M	Laborer	04De02Bw
LYNCH, Susannah		.09	F	Infant	04De02Bw

EDGAR 07 DECEMBER 1847

From Liverpool

NAMES OF PASSENGERS		AGE	SEX	OCCUPATIONS	DATE PORT SHIP
KENOW, Danl.		24	M	Laborer	07De02Rq
John		24	M	Laborer	07De02Rq
BRADY, John		28	M	Laborer	07De02Rq
FLANGAN, Cath.		20	F	Laborer	07De02Rq
Jas.		18	M	Laborer	07De02Rq
CORMICK, Mary		20	F	Laborer	07De02Rq
Beatty		20	F	Laborer	07De02Rq
NIHELSY, Pat		35	M	Laborer	07De02Rq
BRALY, Mary		20	F	Laborer	07De02Rq
GRIRSH, Johann.		16	F	Laborer	07De02Rq
CONNOR, Lawrence		20	M	Laborer	07De02Rq
BAKER, Ellen		30	F	Laborer	07De02Rq
Robert		20	M	Laborer	07De02Rq
COFFEE, Wm.		18	M	Laborer	07De02Rq
CARROLL, Jas.		18	M	Laborer	07De02Rq
GRACE, Ellen		20	F	Laborer	07De02Rq
CAHILL, Cath.		20	F	Laborer	07De02Rq
THOMPSON, Ann		20	F	Laborer	07De02Rq
PRAT, Pat		37	M	Laborer	07De02Rq
Mary		24	F	Laborer	07De02Rq
SCANLAN, Pat		28	M	Laborer	07De02Rq
WHALAN, John		32	M	Laborer	07De02Rq
Mary-W.		32	F	Laborer	07De02Rq
Pat		18	M	Laborer	07De02Rq
DUFFY, Ellen		20	F	Laborer	07De02Rq
MCDERMOT, Hugh		22	M	Laborer	07De02Rq
GURRATY, Beatty		20	F	Laborer	07De02Rq
FALKUOSE, Mary		25	F	Laborer	07De02Rq
IRELAND, Thos.		20	M	Laborer	07De02Rq
BROWN, Mary Died-At-Sea		30	F	Laborer	07De02Rq
MCGARRAN, Bridget		38	F	Laborer	07De02Rq
BRADLEY, John		34	M	Laborer	07De02Rq
Mary		20	F	Laborer	07De02Rq
Nancy		20	F	Laborer	07De02Rq
STACK, Pat		27	M	Laborer	07De02Rq
SHEHAN, Dan		21	M	Laborer	07De02Rq
SALTON, Bridget		20	F	Laborer	07De02Rq
LESLEY, Jas.		24	M	Laborer	07De02Rq
QUIN, Mary		20	F	Laborer	07De02Rq
CAMPBELL, Ann		18	F	Laborer	07De02Rq
MCCOY, Bridget		28	F	Laborer	07De02Rq
MCQUINN, Ann		20	F	Laborer	07De02Rq
ROONEY, Jas.		20	M	Laborer	07De02Rq
LOGAN, L.		27	M	Laborer	07De02Rq
U	(W)	20	F	None	07De02Rq
Jas.	(S)	00	M	Child	07De02Rq
MCDONALD, Owen		40	M	Laborer	07De02Rq
BOOTH, Ann		26	F	Laborer	07De02Rq
MCGURLEY, Philip		30	M	Laborer	07De02Rq
MAXWELL, Jas.		27	M	Laborer	07De02Rq
RYAN, Mich.		24	M	Laborer	07De02Rq
Mary Died-At-Sea		40	F	Laborer	07De02Rq
OBRIEN, Wm.		30	M	Laborer	07De02Rq
MAHON, Mary		20	F	Laborer	07De02Rq
KIRBY, A.		27	F	Laborer	07De02Rq
RAIM, Mary		16	F	Laborer	07De02Rq
SHERIDAN, Pat		27	M	Laborer	07De02Rq
ODELN, Jas.		30	M	Laborer	07De02Rq
HAWLEY, Pat		34	M	Laborer	07De02Rq
MCGUIRE, Mich.		33	M	Laborer	07De02Rq
COTTEN, John		32	M	Laborer	07De02Rq
MOORE, Cath.		15	F	Laborer	07De02Rq
COUGHLAN, Ann		21	F	Laborer	07De02Rq
DUGAN, Cath.-A.		45	F	Laborer	07De02Rq
DYER, Mary		11	F	Laborer	07De02Rq
DRAY, John		55	M	Laborer	07De02Rq
Barnett		26	M	Laborer	07De02Rq
Ellen		24	F	Laborer	07De02Rq
DEASEY, Honora		20	F	Laborer	07De02Rq
HAGERTY, Mich.		25	M	Laborer	07De02Rq
HAYES, Ellen		20	F	Laborer	07De02Rq
HAGERTY, John		23	M	Laborer	07De02Rq
Cath.	(W)	25	F	None	07De02Rq
U	(S)	.00	M	Infant	07De02Rq
BRYAN, Owen		24	M	Laborer	07De02Rq
Wm.		30	M	Laborer	07De02Rq
Joanna	(W)	20	F	None	07De02Rq
Julia	(D)	00	F	Child	07De02Rq

NAMES OF PASSENGERS		A G E	S E X	OCCUPATIONS	DATE PORT SHIP
BRYAN, Patrick		20	M	Laborer	07De02Rq
DOUSHEY, Pat		28	M	Laborer	07De02Rq
DOLAN, Biddy		22	F	Laborer	07De02Rq
MCGUENUSS, F.		24	F	Laborer	07De02Rq
Ann		20	F	Laborer	07De02Rq
MCCAIN, John		27	M	Laborer	07De02Rq
DOYLE, John		40	M	Laborer	07De02Rq
Bernard		20	M	Laborer	07De02Rq
Michael		16	M	Laborer	07De02Rq
MCHUGH, Thos.		19	M	Laborer	07De02Rq
CORNELL, Bridget		20	F	Laborer	07De02Rq
Mich.		01	M	Child	07De02Rq
COROLAN, Mary		18	F	Laborer	07De02Rq
Mich.		14	M	Laborer	07De02Rq
MCCRACKEN, Hugh		51	M	Laborer	07De02Rq
KIRBY, M--.		20	M	Laborer	07De02Rq
BRIEN, Mary		40	F	Laborer	07De02Rq
KELLEY, Mary		14	F	Laborer	07De02Rq
Jno.		25	M	Laborer	07De02Rq
LAHERTY, Wm.		25	M	Laborer	07De02Rq
Philip		22	M	Laborer	07De02Rq
LAWLER, Bridget		22	F	Laborer	07De02Rq
Mich.		12	M	Laborer	07De02Rq
Auty		09	F	Child	07De02Rq
LAHERTY, Mary		26	F	Laborer	07De02Rq
Thos.		16	M	Laborer	07De02Rq
GAFFRAY, Ter.		20	M	Laborer	07De02Rq
BROMY, Thos.		25	M	Laborer	07De02Rq
PHELAN, Mary		20	F	Laborer	07De02Rq
BROPHY, Mary		19	F	Laborer	07De02Rq
CAVANOUGH, Thos.		24	M	Laborer	07De02Rq
BRYAN, Mich.		50	M	Laborer	07De02Rq
Bridget	(W)	40	F	None	07De02Rq
Cath.	(D)	12	F	Unknown	07De02Rq
Pat	(S)	10	M	Unknown	07De02Rq
Ter.	(S)	08	M	Child	07De02Rq
Dan	(S)	06	M	Child	07De02Rq
Maria	(D)	04	F	Child	07De02Rq
Martin	(S)	.00	M	Infant	07De02Rq
DALY, John		20	M	Laborer	07De02Rq
KILLENY, John		20	M	Laborer	07De02Rq
WOODS, Thos.		30	M	Laborer	07De02Rq
GOALY, Mich.		18	M	Laborer	07De02Rq
GALLAGAN, Mich.		24	M	Laborer	07De02Rq
ADAIR, Mary		18	F	Laborer	07De02Rq
Darah		16	F	Laborer	07De02Rq
FLYNN, Peter		20	M	Laborer	07De02Rq
DALOCE, Mary		20	F	Laborer	07De02Rq
BRADY, Ann		20	F	Laborer	07De02Rq
CLUNNSEY, Dan		21	M	Laborer	07De02Rq
CLUMSEY, Mary		20	F	Laborer	07De02Rq
MCCLARY, Mich.		21	M	Laborer	07De02Rq
KELLY, Cath.		10	F	Laborer	07De02Rq
MILES, Mich.		21	M	Laborer	07De02Rq
Mary		20	F	Laborer	07De02Rq
MORAN, Lawrence		22	M	Laborer	07De02Rq
PARDY, Cath.		20	F	Laborer	07De02Rq
MCADLE, Mary		21	F	Laborer	07De02Rq
MCQUITTY, Pat		24	M	Laborer	07De02Rq
KNOX, Mary		20	F	Laborer	07De02Rq
LAWLESS, Jas.		30	M	Laborer	07De02Rq
WELSH, Mary		11	F	Laborer	07De02Rq
SCANLON, James		24	M	Laborer	07De02Rq
FITZPATRICK, Mich.		28	M	Laborer	07De02Rq
JORDAN, Pat		24	M	Laborer	07De02Rq
MAGAGHAN, Ellen		20	F	Laborer	07De02Rq
CURRAN, Ann		60	F	Laborer	07De02Rq
Mich.		20	M	Laborer	07De02Rq
Cath.		18	F	Laborer	07De02Rq
Pat		16	M	Laborer	07De02Rq
Bledgt		07	F	Child	07De02Rq
LENWIN, Cath.		20	F	Laborer	07De02Rq
Thos.		21	M	Laborer	07De02Rq
Winney		18	M	Laborer	07De02Rq
GOLDING, Jas.		09	M	Child	07De02Rq

NAMES OF PASSENGERS		A G E	S E X	OCCUPATIONS	DATE PORT SHIP
BURNS, Ann		18	F	Laborer	07De02Rq
COULSHAW, U		40	F	Wi	07De02Rq
Rose		20	F	Laborer	07De02Rq
OROUKE, Miles		17	M	Laborer	07De02Rq
Bernard		14	M	Laborer	07De02Rq
RYAN, Con.		40	M	Laborer	07De02Rq
GALANS, Nancy		20	F	Laborer	07De02Rq
DONOLLY, Pat		31	M	Laborer	07De02Rq
Jas.		12	M	Laborer	07De02Rq
Mary		12	F	Laborer	07De02Rq
Mary		08	F	Child	07De02Rq
DONNELLY, Mich.		06	M	Child	07De02Rq
DOWERS, Mary		30	F	Laborer	07De02Rq
DAWHURT, Elisa		53	F	Laborer	07De02Rq
Elisa		19	F	Laborer	07De02Rq
BROWN, Wm.		21	M	Laborer	07De02Rq
MCGUIRE, Ellen		30	F	Laborer	07De02Rq
OCONNELLY, Anthony-Dr.		00	M	Surgeon	07De02Rq
CARR, Jane		00	F	Unknown	07De02Rq

HARP 08 DECEMBER 1847

From Maranham

NAMES OF PASSENGERS		A G E	S E X	OCCUPATIONS	DATE PORT SHIP
WALTERS, Wm.-F.		39	M	Juggler	08De65Rr

LANCASHIRE 13 DECEMBER 1847

From Liverpool

NAMES OF PASSENGERS		A G E	S E X	OCCUPATIONS	DATE PORT SHIP
OBRIEN, Wm.		30	M	Farmer	13De02Rs
James		25	M	Laborer	13De02Rs
Elizabeth		30	F	None	13De02Rs
John		09	M	Child	13De02Rs
Thomas		07	M	Child	13De02Rs
Wm.		05	M	Child	13De02Rs
Michael		02	M	Child	13De02Rs
MAHAFFY, Mary		27	F	Doctor	13De02Rs
Anna		06	F	Child	13De02Rs
John		03	M	Child	13De02Rs
MCGARTY, Sally		24	F	Servant	13De02Rs
DOYLE, Mary		18	F	Trader	13De02Rs
WELCH, Michael		24	M	Laborer	13De02Rs
CLAREY, Wm.		26	M	Laborer	13De02Rs
WELCH, Richard		21	M	Laborer	13De02Rs
Mary		20	F	Servant	13De02Rs
PURCELL, John		30	M	Blacksmith	13De02Rs
MOORE, John		30	M	Farmer	13De02Rs
Ellen	(W)	30	F	None	13De02Rs
Mary		16	F	Farmer	13De02Rs
James	(S)	06	M	Child	13De02Rs
Jane	(D)	04	F	Child	13De02Rs
Mary	(D)	02	F	Child	13De02Rs
MCGOUGH, John		21	M	Laborer	13De02Rs
DONNELY, Michael		21	M	Laborer	13De02Rs
DEAREY, Alice		22	F	Servant	13De02Rs
Ann		20	F	Servant	13De02Rs
DARCEY, Dan		26	M	Laborer	13De02Rs

BACHE-MCEVERS 13 DECEMBER 1847

From Cork

NAMES OF PASSENGERS		AGE	SEX	OCCUPATIONS	DATE PORT SHIP
FEHELHY, Margeret		32	F	Laborer	13De14Rt
Mary		04	F	Child	13De14Rt
KNIGHT, Hannah		25	F	Laborer	13De14Rt
GERALD, Edwin		28	M	Laborer	13De14Rt
MOORE, Ellen		23	F	Laborer	13De14Rt
Mary		24	F	Laborer	13De14Rt
FEHELHY, John		01	M	Child	13De14Rt
MCDEALEY, Johana		23	F	Laborer	13De14Rt
John		21	M	Laborer	13De14Rt
GRIFFIN, Mary		25	F	Laborer	13De14Rt
CRONIN, Timothy		28	M	Laborer	13De14Rt
Ellen		37	F	Laborer	13De14Rt
COOKE, Geo.		32	M	Laborer	13De14Rt
DAVIS, Jane		13	F	Laborer	13De14Rt
Mary		10	F	Laborer	13De14Rt
George		27	M	Laborer	13De14Rt
CONNER, Mick		28	M	Laborer	13De14Rt
GALLAHER, Eliza		24	F	Laborer	13De14Rt
LANE, Eliza		28	F	Laborer	13De14Rt
MCGRATH, Thomas		23	M	Laborer	13De14Rt
WALSH, Johana		40	F	Laborer	13De14Rt
Mary	(D)	10	F	Laborer	13De14Rt
Nell	(D)	09	F	Child	13De14Rt
Patt	(S)	03	M	Child	13De14Rt
James		50	M	Laborer	13De14Rt
MORAN, Thomas		32	M	Laborer	13De14Rt
Mary		24	F	Laborer	13De14Rt
WILSON, Ellen		24	F	Laborer	13De14Rt
DONOVAN, Fanny		17	F	Laborer	13De14Rt
DAY, Mary		25	F	Laborer	13De14Rt
WELSH, Thomas		28	M	Laborer	13De14Rt
Mary		22	F	Laborer	13De14Rt
John		28	M	Laborer	13De14Rt
Margeret		23	F	Laborer	13De14Rt
LEARY, Mary		20	F	Laborer	13De14Rt
BROSSENHAM, Thoms.		50	M	Laborer	13De14Rt
Cath.	(W)	40	F	None	13De14Rt
Mary	(D)	18	F	Laborer	13De14Rt
Ellen	(D)	16	F	Laborer	13De14Rt
MAHONY, Julia		41	F	Laborer	13De14Rt
BROSSENHAM, Catherine		13	F	Laborer	13De14Rt
Timothy	(B)	10	M	Laborer	13De14Rt
John	(B)	08	M	Child	13De14Rt
Terrence	(B)	06	M	Child	13De14Rt
Margaret	(T)	02	F	Child	13De14Rt
FOORAN, Timothy		34	M	Laborer	13De14Rt
BURN, Julia		28	F	Laborer	13De14Rt
Honora		25	F	Laborer	13De14Rt
WHEARN, Patt		28	M	Laborer	13De14Rt
LYNCH, Catherine		36	F	Laborer	13De14Rt
NEALE, Michael		40	M	Laborer	13De14Rt
Elizth.		20	F	Laborer	13De14Rt
DILLAN, John		45	M	Laborer	13De14Rt
Mary		40	F	Laborer	13De14Rt
Catherine		32	F	Laborer	13De14Rt
Mary	(D)	12	F	Laborer	13De14Rt
Wm.	(S)	11	M	Laborer	13De14Rt
Patt	(S)	06	M	Child	13De14Rt
Hanh.	(D)	.06	F	Infant	13De14Rt
CORNELL, Cath.		21	F	Laborer	13De14Rt
LOONEY, Ellen		28	F	Laborer	13De14Rt
DOUGHERTY, Mary		21	F	Laborer	13De14Rt
FLYNN, Abbey		25	F	Laborer	13De14Rt
Mathew		21	M	Laborer	13De14Rt
RICE, Richd.		25	M	Laborer	13De14Rt
COLMAN, John		21	M	Laborer	13De14Rt
MCGRATH, Mary		20	F	Laborer	13De14Rt
DONOVAN, John		30	M	Laborer	13De14Rt
Eliza	(W)	25	F	None	13De14Rt
Jacob	(S)	.06	M	Infant	13De14Rt
SULLIVAN, Cors.		69	M	Laborer	13De14Rt
Dennis		25	M	Laborer	13De14Rt
MCCARTHY, Johana		22	F	Laborer	13De14Rt
FLYNN, Kitty		23	F	Laborer	13De14Rt
QUINLAN, Ellen		23	F	Laborer	13De14Rt
RAYNOR, John		40	M	Laborer	13De14Rt
KELLY, Mary		42	F	Laborer	13De14Rt
Anne	(D)	19	F	Laborer	13De14Rt
Bridget		17	F	Laborer	13De14Rt
Kate		13	F	Laborer	13De14Rt
John		11	M	Laborer	13De14Rt
Francis		06	M	Child	13De14Rt
MCCOONEY, Jeremiah		10	M	Laborer	13De14Rt

ADMIRAL 13 DECEMBER 1847

From Liverpool

NAMES OF PASSENGERS		AGE	SEX	OCCUPATIONS	DATE PORT SHIP
LLOYD, William-F.		21	M	Laborer	13De02Ru
MOLLOY, Patrick		40	M	Laborer	13De02Ru
RODDY, Ellen		21	F	None	13De02Ru
MILLIGAN, Michael		40	M	Laborer	13De02Ru
Biddy	(W)	30	F	None	13De02Ru
Ellen	(D)	03	F	Child	13De02Ru
Michael	(S)	.00	M	Infant	13De02Ru
HUNT, John		26	M	Laborer	13De02Ru
HALE, James		24	M	Laborer	13De02Ru
CROTHY, James		24	M	Laborer	13De02Ru
MULEAHY, Patt		24	M	Laborer	13De02Ru
DENNIS, Cath.		20	F	None	13De02Ru
HENESSY, William		25	M	Laborer	13De02Ru
ROCHE, Patt		25	M	Laborer	13De02Ru
OCONNOR, John		32	M	Laborer	13De02Ru
Mary	(W)	28	F	None	13De02Ru
John	(S)	02	M	Child	13De02Ru
Honora		20	F	None	13De02Ru
DONAVAN, Denis		50	M	Laborer	13De02Ru
Ellen	(W)	50	F	None	13De02Ru
John	(S)	20	M	Laborer	13De02Ru
Michael	(S)	13	M	None	13De02Ru
James	(S)	11	M	None	13De02Ru
Ellen	(D)	09	F	Child	13De02Ru
Denis	(S)	07	M	Child	13De02Ru
AHEARN, Daniel		40	M	None	13De02Ru
Margaret		40	F	None	13De02Ru
James		20	M	Laborer	13De02Ru
Catherine		30	F	None	13De02Ru
Eliza		28	F	None	13De02Ru
CONNELL, John		23	M	Laborer	13De02Ru
Jeremiah		.00	M	Infant	13De02Ru
NIX, Anthony		30	M	Laborer	13De02Ru
John		28	M	Laborer	13De02Ru
Catherine		30	F	None	13De02Ru
Anthony		06	M	Child	13De02Ru
Johanna		04	F	Child	13De02Ru
James		.00	M	Infant	13De02Ru
James		28	M	Laborer	13De02Ru
Honora		30	F	None	13De02Ru
HAMRAN, Mary		30	F	None	13De02Ru
BARRETT, John		25	M	Laborer	13De02Ru
NICHOLSON, William		25	M	Laborer	13De02Ru
HOLLAND, William		24	M	Laborer	13De02Ru
KENNEDY, Anne		21	F	None	13De02Ru
HEANY, William		25	M	Laborer	13De02Ru

NAMES OF PASSENGERS		AGE	SEX	OCCUPATIONS	DATE PORT SHIP
HEANY, Mary		24	F	None	13De02Ru
CALLSON, James		20	M	Laborer	13De02Ru
READ, William		37	M	Laborer	13De02Ru
SIMMS, Richd.		39	M	Laborer	13De02Ru
RODGERS, James		23	M	Laborer	13De02Ru
Biddy	(W)	21	F	None	13De02Ru
Thomas	(S)	02	M	Child	13De02Ru
Patrick	(S)	.00	M	Infant	13De02Ru
BRENNAN, Bridget		35	F	None	13De02Ru
Michael		16	M	None	13De02Ru
Ellen		15	F	None	13De02Ru
John		14	M	None	13De02Ru
Bridget		.00	F	Infant	13De02Ru
RODGERS, James		16	M	None	13De02Ru
BOYLE, Mary		20	F	None	13De02Ru
COUNDT, John		38	M	Laborer	13De02Ru
RYDER, Dennis		30	M	Laborer	13De02Ru
STUBBS, Samuel		24	M	Laborer	13De02Ru
BARNES, John		21	M	Laborer	13De02Ru
WYLDE, George		24	M	Laborer	13De02Ru
BYRNE, Rose		50	F	None	13De02Ru
Bridget		20	F	None	13De02Ru
Patrick		18	M	Laborer	13De02Ru
WARD, Mary		19	F	None	13De02Ru
MARTIN, Catherine		20	F	None	13De02Ru
GUNNING, Patt		17	M	None	13De02Ru
CONNOLY, Mary		17	F	None	13De02Ru
KENNEDY, Mary-A.		17	F	None	13De02Ru
Ellen		15	F	None	13De02Ru
RALLY, Bryan		20	M	Laborer	13De02Ru
BROPHY, Thos.		38	M	Laborer	13De02Ru
LEESON, Fanton		36	M	Laborer	13De02Ru
CAMPBELL, Joseph		36	M	Laborer	13De02Ru
Jane		30	F	None	13De02Ru
Martha		20	F	None	13De02Ru
HEYDEN, James		20	M	Laborer	13De02Ru
GALLAGHER, Thos.		25	M	Laborer	13De02Ru
KERLEY, Bridget		20	F	None	13De02Ru
BELL, Edward		21	M	Laborer	13De02Ru
Leela	(W)	20	F	None	13De02Ru
Charles	(S)	.00	M	Infant	13De02Ru
HEATHY, Dorothy		29	F	None	13De02Ru
CAMPBELL, Eliza		19	F	None	13De02Ru
FARRELL, Thos.		50	M	Laborer	13De02Ru
James		21	M	Laborer	13De02Ru
Ellen		19	F	None	13De02Ru
DELANEY, Patt		24	M	Laborer	13De02Ru
DANIEL, William		30	M	Laborer	13De02Ru
Judith	(W)	30	F	None	13De02Ru
Biddy	(D)	04	F	Child	13De02Ru
Ellen	(D)	.00	F	Infant	13De02Ru
HEENAN, Patt		35	M	Laborer	13De02Ru
GANNON, Michl.		14	M	None	13De02Ru
BRANNAN, Dennis		30	M	Laborer	13De02Ru
FOYE, Margt.		21	F	None	13De02Ru
CRAWFORD, Nancy		19	F	None	13De02Ru
DAILY, Peter		17	M	None	13De02Ru
BROWN, Rodger		28	M	Laborer	13De02Ru
KERNEY, Bernard		30	M	Laborer	13De02Ru
KENNY, Margaret		26	F	None	13De02Ru
John		23	M	Laborer	13De02Ru
DOUGHTERY, John		26	M	Laborer	13De02Ru
Mary		23	F	None	13De02Ru
DOWD, James		26	M	Laborer	13De02Ru
Mary		18	F	None	13De02Ru
Bridget		16	F	None	13De02Ru
GARAGAN, Darby		38	M	Laborer	13De02Ru
HENRY, James		13	M	None	13De02Ru
CLYNE, Patt		23	M	Laborer	13De02Ru
FLYNNE, Gilbert		22	M	Laborer	13De02Ru
CORLOS, Anne		30	F	None	13De02Ru
JORDON, Anne		45	F	None	13De02Ru
MAGEE, Michl.		32	M	Laborer	13De02Ru
NEARY, John		32	M	Laborer	13De02Ru
FORMER, Margaret		47	F	None	13De02Ru

NAMES OF PASSENGERS	AGE	SEX	OCCUPATIONS	DATE PORT SHIP
FORMER, Ellen	27	F	None	13De02Ru
Elizabeth	.00	F	Infant	13De02Ru
MASTERTON, Catherine	20	F	None	13De02Ru
Sarah	18	F	None	13De02Ru
OSBOURNE, Michael	21	M	Laborer	13De02Ru
CORCON, Francis	20	M	Laborer	13De02Ru
FLANIGAN, Michael	36	M	Laborer	13De02Ru
MALOWNY, Miles	30	M	Laborer	13De02Ru
HAMMOND, Edward	25	M	Laborer	13De02Ru
SCANLAN, Pat	24	M	Laborer	13De02Ru
SEXTON, Bridget	21	F	None	13De02Ru
NAUGHTON, Margt.	22	F	None	13De02Ru
KEARNEY, Edmund	30	M	Laborer	13De02Ru
FLOOD, John	40	M	Laborer	13De02Ru
TRUSSEL, Jas.	18	M	Laborer	13De02Ru
WALLACE, Thos.	47	M	Laborer	13De02Ru
DOBSON, Sally	38	F	None	13De02Ru
BRADLY, Mary	35	F	None	13De02Ru
COULTER, Mary	30	F	None	13De02Ru
BROWN, Margaret	24	F	None	13De02Ru
DEACON, John	25	M	Laborer	13De02Ru
HARRIGAN, Patk.	23	M	Laborer	13De02Ru
BRENNAN, Wm.	22	M	Laborer	13De02Ru
MAHON, Thos.	63	M	Laborer	13De02Ru
DONOHO, Bernard	26	M	Laborer	13De02Ru
VICTORY, Ann	20	F	None	13De02Ru
TIERNEY, Patt	27	M	Laborer	13De02Ru
MCDONAGH, O.	20	M	Laborer	13De02Ru
MCGLOREN, Martin	20	M	Laborer	13De02Ru
BRANNAN, Patt	20	M	Laborer	13De02Ru
SUE, Mary	20	F	None	13De02Ru
CONNOLY, Patt	21	M	Laborer	13De02Ru
MCDERMOT, Thos.	20	M	Laborer	13De02Ru
MCMAHON, Patt	40	M	Laborer	13De02Ru
BRYAN, Michl.	30	M	Laborer	13De02Ru
DEVLIN, Mary	20	F	None	13De02Ru
KEEF, Joseph	50	M	Laborer	13De02Ru
WEST, Danl.	60	M	Laborer	13De02Ru
SLATTERLY, Dennis	30	M	Laborer	13De02Ru
REYNOLDS, Mary-A.	40	F	None	13De02Ru
MCDONALD, Mary	12	F	None	13De02Ru
James	36	M	Laborer	13De02Ru
FARRELL, Bridget	40	F	None	13De02Ru
KENNY, Eleanor	15	F	None	13De02Ru
LEE, Patt	24	M	Laborer	13De02Ru
BOYLAN, Cathne.	20	F	None	13De02Ru
GINETTY, Patrick	30	M	Laborer	13De02Ru
PETREE, John	24	M	Laborer	13De02Ru
KENNEDY, Anne	30	F	None	13De02Ru
NEWARD, Thos.	27	M	Laborer	13De02Ru
MCCOWEN, Pat	19	M	Laborer	13De02Ru
MCWHEENY, Michl.	40	M	Laborer	13De02Ru
ARMSTRONG, Wm.	13	M	Laborer	13De02Ru
ROBINSON, Eliza	27	F	Laborer	13De02Ru
MCARDLE, Edwd.	20	M	Laborer	13De02Ru
DONELLY, Mary	20	F	Laborer	13De02Ru
KANE, Mary	20	F	Laborer	13De02Ru
BROTHERS, C.	35	M	Laborer	13De02Ru
MURRAY, Joseph	30	M	Laborer	13De02Ru
THOMPSON, Eliza	24	F	Laborer	13De02Ru
KEGLY, Michl.	16	M	Laborer	13De02Ru
QUIGLY, Pat	25	M	Laborer	13De02Ru
NEILL, Patt	32	M	Laborer	13De02Ru
MCCADARN, Patt	18	M	Laborer	13De02Ru
FARRELEY, Edward	28	M	Laborer	13De02Ru
MURPHY, James	16	M	Laborer	13De02Ru
SEXTON, Mary	18	F	None	13De02Ru
MCNAUGHTON, Bridget	20	F	None	13De02Ru
Michael	18	M	Laborer	13De02Ru
KEARNEY, Mary	26	F	None	13De02Ru
Mary	03	F	Child	13De02Ru
WATERS, David	30	M	Laborer	13De02Ru
MCEVANY, Tim	30	M	Laborer	13De02Ru
HOGAN, Patrick	30	M	Laborer	13De02Ru
WALLACE, U-Mrs.	40	F	None	13De02Ru

NAMES OF PASSENGERS		AGE	SEX	OCCUPATIONS	DATE PORT SHIP
WALLACE, Matilda	(D)	07	F	Child	13De02Ru
Robert	(S)	04	M	Child	13De02Ru
Thomas	(S)	.00	M	Infant	13De02Ru
BRADLY, James		10	M	None	13De02Ru
HOLT, Cornelius		19	M	Laborer	13De02Ru
HURRINGTON, Johana		23	F	None	13De02Ru
COULEY, John		22	M	Laborer	13De02Ru
WALSH, Pat		22	M	Laborer	13De02Ru
DONALD, Margaret		26	F	None	13De02Ru
MCDONOUGH, Bridget		45	F	None	13De02Ru
Peter		09	M	Child	13De02Ru
MCGLOVEN, Sarah		26	F	None	13De02Ru
Nelly		14	F	None	13De02Ru
Bridget		60	F	None	13De02Ru
BANIER, Ann		20	F	None	13De02Ru
KILFORNE, Cathr.		03	F	Child	13De02Ru
MCLAUGHLIN, Rodger		19	M	Laborer	13De02Ru
OGLYN, Michael		19	M	Laborer	13De02Ru
MCDENNARD, Mary		19	F	None	13De02Ru
MAHIN, Mary		14	F	None	13De02Ru
Rose		12	F	None	13De02Ru
DEBLIN, Ann		19	F	None	13De02Ru
KEEF, Arthur		30	M	Laborer	13De02Ru
ROACH, James		30	M	Laborer	13De02Ru
David		22	M	Laborer	13De02Ru
SATTERNY, U-Mrs.		24	F	None	13De02Ru
ELLICE, Eliza		20	F	None	13De02Ru
WALTER, Thomas		20	M	Laborer	13De02Ru
REYNOLDS, Mary-A.		40	F	None	13De02Ru
James		13	M	Laborer	13De02Ru
DONALD, Catharine		09	F	Child	13De02Ru
FARREL, Eleanor		13	F	None	13De02Ru
Patt		09	M	Child	13De02Ru
Sarah		07	F	Child	13De02Ru
COSTELLO, Michael		30	M	Laborer	13De02Ru
KENNEY, Laebery		05	M	Child	13De02Ru
LEE, Anne		12	F	None	13De02Ru
MCGUIRE, Alice		30	F	None	13De02Ru
MCCOWAN, Ann		17	F	None	13De02Ru
James		07	M	Child	13De02Ru
Phelise		04	F	Child	13De02Ru
MCSWEENY, Brdget.		39	F	None	13De02Ru
John		13	M	Laborer	13De02Ru
Mary		10	F	None	13De02Ru
Bridget		03	F	Child	13De02Ru
DOYLE, Rose		20	F	None	13De02Ru
GREEN, Mary		20	F	None	13De02Ru
MURRAY, Eliza		35	F	None	13De02Ru
Dennis	(S)	.00	M	Infant	13De02Ru
KEARNEY, J.		27	M	None	13De02Ru
KILLOWEN, Cath.		20	F	None	13De02Ru
MCCOWEN, M.		30	M	Laborer	13De02Ru
MOORE, Archibald		25	M	Laborer	13De02Ru
U	(W)	24	F	None	13De02Ru
Margaret	(D)	.00	F	Infant	13De02Ru
May	(D)	07	F	Child	13De02Ru
U	(D)	.00	F	Infant	13De02Ru
MURRAY, J.		30	M	Laborer	13De02Ru

SWAN 13 DECEMBER 1847

From Cork

NAMES OF PASSENGERS	AGE	SEX	OCCUPATIONS	DATE PORT SHIP
READY, Con	30	U	Laborer	13De14Ix
MCCARTHY, Eugene	25	M	Laborer	13De14Ix
Peter	18	M	Laborer	13De14Ix
Peggy	27	F	Laborer	13De14Ix
Mary	01	F	Child	13De14Ix
CONRY, Eugene	24	M	Laborer	13De14Ix
FOLEY, Jon	32	M	Laborer	13De14Ix
Biddy	21	F	Laborer	13De14Ix
DONOVAN, Mary	28	F	Laborer	13De14Ix
Ellen	25	F	Laborer	13De14Ix
Sally	23	F	Laborer	13De14Ix
PURCELL, Ellen	28	F	Laborer	13De14Ix
LEE, Mary	21	F	Laborer	13De14Ix
COCANE, Patt	24	M	Laborer	13De14Ix
FOLEY, Judy	21	F	Laborer	13De14Ix
KETTEHER, Mary	55	F	Laborer	13De14Ix
BUCKLEY, Bridget	28	F	Laborer	13De14Ix
Tim	13	M	Laborer	13De14Ix
LEAHY, Patt	28	M	Laborer	13De14Ix
SCANNELL, Bridget	25	F	Laborer	13De14Ix
CORNANE, Thomas	34	M	Laborer	13De14Ix
DOOLEY, Wm.	40	M	Laborer	13De14Ix
Jane	13	F	Laborer	13De14Ix
FENNELL, Darby	44	M	Laborer	13De14Ix
Ellen	34	F	None	13De14Ix
Thomas	03	M	Child	13De14Ix
TOWNSEND, Ellen	25	F	Laborer	13De14Ix
MCCARTHY, Mary	21	F	Laborer	13De14Ix
SHEEHAN, Mary	23	F	Laborer	13De14Ix
RONAYNE, Mary	13	F	Laborer	13De14Ix
KINNY, John	25	M	Laborer	13De14Ix
COTTER, Johana	21	F	Laborer	13De14Ix
Honora	23	F	Laborer	13De14Ix
COSTELLO, Margt.	24	F	Laborer	13De14Ix
Tim	00	M	Laborer	13De14Ix
KELLEHAN, Patt	25	M	Laborer	13De14Ix
SHEA, John	23	M	Laborer	13De14Ix
KIDNEY, David	50	M	Laborer	13De14Ix
Johana	45	F	Laborer	13De14Ix
Wm.	21	M	Laborer	13De14Ix
Dennis	18	M	Laborer	13De14Ix
Danl.	17	M	Laborer	13De14Ix
Norry	22	F	Laborer	13De14Ix
AHEARN, Richd.	23	M	Laborer	13De14Ix
LUCY, Dan	25	M	Laborer	13De14Ix
MCCAFFREY, David	40	M	Laborer	13De14Ix
WHOOHILY, Bridget	23	F	Laborer	13De14Ix
WELSH, Robt.	23	M	Laborer	13De14Ix
DRISCOLL, James	21	M	Laborer	13De14Ix
RYAN, Garrett	32	M	Laborer	13De14Ix
MURPHY, Tom	20	M	Laborer	13De14Ix
Michl.	19	M	Laborer	13De14Ix
Margt.	16	F	Laborer	13De14Ix
Mary	15	F	Laborer	13De14Ix
KILTY, Con	25	M	Laborer	13De14Ix
DEADY, Honora	20	F	Laborer	13De14Ix
Bridget	19	F	Laborer	13De14Ix
GAHARAN, John	25	M	Laborer	13De14Ix
HILLANE, John	21	M	Laborer	13De14Ix
BROWN, Ellen	25	F	Laborer	13De14Ix
SULLIVAN, Kitty	50	F	Laborer	13De14Ix
James	24	M	Laborer	13De14Ix
Tim	21	M	Laborer	13De14Ix
Johana	18	F	Laborer	13De14Ix
Mary	30	F	Laborer	13De14Ix
DOHERTY, John	25	M	Laborer	13De14Ix
QUILTY, Dennis	24	M	Laborer	13De14Ix
DEADY, James	35	M	Laborer	13De14Ix
Nelly	23	F	Laborer	13De14Ix
Jeremiah	20	M	Laborer	13De14Ix
Michl.	26	M	Laborer	13De14Ix
John	21	M	Laborer	13De14Ix
SULLIVAN, Norry	50	F	Laborer	13De14Ix
Daniel	21	M	Laborer	13De14Ix
Norry	13	F	Laborer	13De14Ix
Cath.	09	F	Child	13De14Ix
MURPHY, Mary	19	F	Laborer	13De14Ix
BRION, Cather.	25	F	Laborer	13De14Ix
KEEF, Wm.	28	M	Laborer	13De14Ix
Mary	26	F	Laborer	13De14Ix
CUNNINGHAM, Jane	20	F	Laborer	13De14Ix

NAMES OF PASSENGERS	AGE	SEX	OCCUPATIONS	DATE PORT SHIP
HARRAN, Ellen	28	F	Laborer	13De14Ix
Margt.	02	F	Child	13De14Ix
Mary	01	F	Child	13De14Ix
NOONAN, Norry	21	F	Laborer	13De14Ix

NEW-YORK 16 DECEMBER 1847

From Liverpool

NAMES OF PASSENGERS	AGE	SEX	OCCUPATIONS	DATE PORT SHIP
SULLIVAN, John	20	M	Laborer	16De02Bk
GALLAGHER, Owen	14	M	Laborer	16De02Bk
COOPER, Robert	20	M	Laborer	16De02Bk
LAMON, Alex.	22	M	Laborer	16De02Bk
NOONAN, John	27	M	Laborer	16De02Bk
BOYLE, Ann	21	F	Spinster	16De02Bk
MCCAN, Martha	50	F	Wife	16De02Bk
Died-At-Sea				
OBRIEN, Garrett	24	M	Laborer	16De02Bk
Pat	19	M	Laborer	16De02Bk
Alice	25	F	Wife	16De02Bk
Ann	17	F	Wife	16De02Bk
Ellen	20	F	Wife	16De02Bk
CONSTANTINE, Hannah	27	F	Wife	16De02Bk
Francis	03	M	Child	16De02Bk
Alfred	.11	M	Infant	16De02Bk
CUNNINGHAM, David	30	M	Laborer	16De02Bk
MCMAHON, Elizth.	40	F	Wife	16De02Bk
James	20	M	Laborer	16De02Bk
Mattw.	20	M	Laborer	16De02Bk
OHARA, Bridget	20	F	Spinster	16De02Bk
KEENAN, Bridget	27	F	Spinster	16De02Bk
Pat	20	M	Laborer	16De02Bk
WHITE, Winifred	30	F	Wife	16De02Bk
QUIN, James	06	M	Child	16De02Bk
LOUGHLIN, Ellen-W.	30	F	Wife	16De02Bk
Mary	.11	F	Infant	16De02Bk
Died-At-Sea				
GREHERN, Bridget	35	F	Wife	16De02Bk
U	.10	F	Infant	16De02Bk
RUDDEN, Mary	20	F	Spinster	16De02Bk
KIERNAN, Maria	20	F	Spinster	16De02Bk
SMITH, James	20	M	Laborer	16De02Bk
COYLE, Catharine	20	F	Spinster	16De02Bk
CONNOLLY, Mary-Ann	23	F	Spinster	16De02Bk
Ann	03	F	Child	16De02Bk
Ellen	.06	F	Infant	16De02Bk
Died-At-Sea				
HANDY, Ann	16	F	Spinster	16De02Bk
Mary	10	F	Child	16De02Bk
BARKER, John	50	M	Laborer	16De02Bk
Elizth.	17	F	Spinster	16De02Bk
DALEY, John	33	M	Laborer	16De02Bk
ROBINSON, Alfred	29	M	Laborer	16De02Bk
U (W)	23	F	Wife	16De02Bk
Sarah	05	F	Child	16De02Bk
William	.08	M	Infant	16De02Bk
HARTILL, James	28	M	Laborer	16De02Bk
William	07	M	Child	16De02Bk
OCONNOR, Mary	11	F	Child	16De02Bk
Ann	19	F	Spinster	16De02Bk
ODONNNELL, Patr.	28	M	Laborer	16De02Bk
PIERCE, James	21	M	Laborer	16De02Bk
Margt.	18	F	Laborer	16De02Bk
DUNN, Michl.	04	M	Child	16De02Bk
MCMANUS, James	25	M	Laborer	16De02Bk
MCGILLECK, Phillip	26	M	Laborer	16De02Bk
U (W)	28	F	Wife	16De02Bk
NEWMAN, Margt.	30	F	Wife	16De02Bk
Thos.	04	M	Child	16De02Bk
NEWMAN, U	.11	M	Infant	16De02Bk
KEENAN, Dennis	20	M	Laborer	16De02Bk
MULLOWNEY, Richd.	20	M	Laborer	16De02Bk
Owen	18	M	Laborer	16De02Bk
Peter	16	M	Laborer	16De02Bk
Ann	14	F	Spinster	16De02Bk
Cathr.	12	F	Spinster	16De02Bk
WALSH, Peter	30	M	Laborer	16De02Bk
FURY, Cathr.	19	F	Spinster	16De02Bk
CULLEN, Betty	26	F	Wife	16De02Bk
John	02	M	Child	16De02Bk
Mike	.10	M	Infant	16De02Bk
CONNOR, Martin	20	M	Laborer	16De02Bk
KELLY, John	21	M	Laborer	16De02Bk
MURRAY, Nancy	50	F	Wife	16De02Bk
WELDON, Julia	34	F	Wife	16De02Bk
Ann	10	F	Child	16De02Bk
Mary	03	F	Child	16De02Bk
Rosanna	.08	F	Infant	16De02Bk
COUGHLAN, Bridget	25	F	Wife	16De02Bk
Mary-Ann	01	F	Child	16De02Bk
QUIN, Pat	10	M	Child	16De02Bk
Mary	09	F	Child	16De02Bk
OATES, Bridget	30	F	Wife	16De02Bk
Mary	08	F	Child	16De02Bk
LARKIN, Patrick	40	M	Laborer	16De02Bk
Eleanor (W)	57	F	Wife	16De02Bk
Pat	05	M	Child	16De02Bk
WALSH, Ann	21	F	Spinster	16De02Bk
MCGARRESS, John	20	M	Laborer	16De02Bk
ONEILL, Cathr.	20	F	Wife	16De02Bk
MCELROY, James	44	M	Laborer	16De02Bk
U (W)	44	F	Wife	16De02Bk
CAMPBELL, Thos.	10	M	Child	16De02Bk
MCLEER, Mary	07	F	Child	16De02Bk
MCELROY, Eliza	05	F	Child	16De02Bk
BRADLEY, Mathl.	24	M	Laborer	16De02Bk
TIERNAN, Margt.	20	F	Spinster	16De02Bk
Mary	35	F	Spinster	16De02Bk
CAVANAGH, Mary	21	F	Spinster	16De02Bk
LEAHY, Ellen	21	F	Spinster	16De02Bk
ROURKE, Margt.	28	F	Wife	16De02Bk
Mary	08	F	Child	16De02Bk
CONLON, Cathr.	18	F	Spinster	16De02Bk
CURRY, Alice	37	F	Spinster	16De02Bk
Bernard	02	M	Child	16De02Bk
MALLON, Sarah	40	F	Wife	16De02Bk
LEE, Thomas	16	M	Laborer	16De02Bk
MORRIS, Isabella	15	F	Spinster	16De02Bk
KELLY, Mary	35	F	Wife	16De02Bk
Died-At-Sea				
Cathr.	08	F	Child	16De02Bk
Died-At-Sea				
Maria	06	F	Child	16De02Bk
Pat (S)	05	M	Child	16De02Bk
Ann-Mary	03	F	Child	16De02Bk
Died-At-Sea				
MCGUIRE, Mary	20	F	Spinster	16De02Bk
CREMLISK, Mary-A.	18	F	Spinster	16De02Bk
CLARK, Mary	19	F	Spinster	16De02Bk
TRACEY, Ann	22	F	Spinster	16De02Bk
Mary	.10	F	Infant	16De02Bk
MCCULLOCK, Ellen	20	F	Spinster	16De02Bk
NOLAN, Bridget	28	F	Wife	16De02Bk
Nancy	03	F	Child	16De02Bk
TOLAN, James	24	M	Laborer	16De02Bk
MCLOUGHLIN, Thos.	16	M	Laborer	16De02Bk
COUGHLAN, Johana	20	F	Spinster	16De02Bk
BRANNON, Mary	08	F	Child	16De02Bk
Cathr.	06	F	Child	16De02Bk
WHITE, Cathr.	40	F	Wife	16De02Bk
Timy.	20	M	Laborer	16De02Bk
DONOVAN, Norry	06	F	Child	16De02Bk
Timy.	04	M	Child	16De02Bk
John	02	M	Child	16De02Bk

NAMES OF PASSENGERS		AGE	SEX	OCCUPATIONS	DATE PORT SHIP
QUIN, Ann		10	F	Child	16De02
DOWNEY, Rich.		27	M	Laborer	16De02
Thomas		14	M	Laborer	16De02
FLYNN, Bridget		37	F	Wife	16De02
TRAINOR, Hannah		40	F	Wife	16De02
Patk.		54	M	Laborer	16De02
COFFEE, Julia		30	F	Spinster	16De02
GRADY, James		26	M	Laborer	16De02
U		36	M	Laborer	16De02
Pat.		14	M	Laborer	16De02
Nancy		12	F	Child	16De02
Kate		11	F	Child	16De02
Cornl.		09	M	Child	16De02
Eliza		06	F	Child	16De02
CALLAGHAN, Johana		37	F	Unknown	16De02
Pat.		05	M	Child	16De02
Abby		07	F	Child	16De02
KEEFE, Margt.		20	F	Spinster	16De02
NOONAN, Margt.		20	F	Spinster	16De02
Ellen		20	F	Spinster	16De02
Ann		.09	F	Infant	16De02
LEARY, Timy.		21	M	Laborer	16De02
MORRISSEY, Mary		00	F	Wife	16De02
Ellen		24	F	Wife	16De02
John		02	M	Child	16De02
Johanna		.09	F	Infant	16De02
OBRIEN, Michl.		22	M	Laborer	16De02
John		18	M	Laborer	16De02
Rose		50	F	Spinster	16De02
Ally		27	F	Spinster	16De02
FLEMMING, Cathr.		36	F	Spinster	16De02
John		03	M	Child	16De02
Margt.		.10	F	Infant	16De02
DOPSON, Cathr.		30	F	Wife	16De02
May		10	F	Child	16De02
John		07	M	Child	16De02
Ellen		05	F	Child	16De02
Thomas		03	M	Child	16De02
RYAN, Margt.		16	F	Spinster	16De02
FLANNERY, James		08	M	Child	16De02
Mattw.		04	M	Child	16De02
REILLY, Owen		20	M	Laborer	16De02
CONNOR, Patk.		12	M	Child	16De02
LYNCH, Pat.		30	M	Laborer	16De02
Honor	(W)	25	F	Wife	16De02
Ann		03	F	Child	16De02
James		.09	M	Infant	16De02
Mary		.11	F	Infant	16De02
REILLY, Cathr.		25	F	Spinster	16De02
BRADY, Cathr.		20	F	Spinster	16De02
GILKEN, Ann		25	F	Spinster	16De02
GIBBON, Patk.		.11	M	Infant	16De02
John		20	M	Laborer	16De02
KEEFFE, Michl.		40	M	Laborer	16De02
CONNELL, John		20	M	Laborer	16De02
HARRIGAN, Cornl.		26	M	Laborer	16De02
HEFFERNAN, Jerry		27	M	Laborer	16De02
FENTON, James		24	M	Laborer	16De02
Died-At-Sea					
LEARY, John		20	M	Laborer	16De02
Pat		20	M	Laborer	16De02
COFFEE, John		22	M	Laborer	16De02
OCONNOR, William		24	M	Laborer	16De02
WOOD, James		26	M	Laborer	16De02
BANETTEY, James		19	M	Laborer	16De02
MCMALIN, James		18	M	Laborer	16De02
FINLAY, Richd.		18	M	Laborer	16De02
CONNISKEY, James		30	M	Laborer	16De02
U	(W)	30	F	Wife	16De02
Mary		.10	F	Infant	16De02
Died-At-Sea					
GREHARN, James		24	M	Laborer	16De02
POLAGGE, Virgilla		33	M	Laborer	16De02
RAFFERTY, Sally		20	F	Wife	16De02
OBRIEN, Timy.		27	M	Laborer	16De02
CONNELL, William		22	M	Laborer	16De02
Mary	(W)	24	F	Wife	16De02
STAKE, Danl.		16	M	Laborer	16De02
Johana		17	F	Spinster	16De02
BRADY, Cathr.		21	F	Spinster	16De02
SPENCE, Edwin		12	M	Unknown	16De02
TREACY, Michl.		20	M	Unknown	16De02
MCGUIRE, Ann		20	F	Spinster	16De02
TWEED, Joseph		27	M	Laborer	16De02
SMITH, Charles		24	M	Laborer	16De02
SCOFIELD, Isaac		27	M	Laborer	16De02
BYRNE, Patk.		24	M	Laborer	16De02
MCQUADE, James		27	M	Laborer	16De02
MCMAHON, Mary		30	F	Wife	16De02
U		.10	F	Infant	16De02
MCGARRAHAM, Patk.		24	M	Laborer	16De02
SMITH, Judith		18	F	Spinster	16De02
COSTIGAN, Thos.		20	M	Laborer	16De02
QUINLAN, John		30	M	Laborer	16De02
BENSON, William		39	M	Laborer	16De02
CANNON, Dominick		30	M	Laborer	16De02
U	(W)	30	F	Wife	16De02
Margt.		.06	F	Infant	16De02
Cathr.		02	F	Child	16De02
BROWN, John		24	M	Farmer	16De02
Margt.	(W)	22	F	Wife	16De02
Ellen		29	F	Wife	16De02
WOOD, Martha		28	F	Wife	16De02
Emily		.10	F	Infant	16De02
MCDONNELL, Thomas		27	M	Laborer	16De02
LEAHY, Thomas		24	M	Laborer	16De02
GUINNESS, Cathr.		25	F	Spinster	16De02
MCBEAN, Mary		16	F	Spinster	16De02
Rose		09	F	Child	16De02
ODONNELL, Ellen		24	F	Spinster	16De02
BLESSINGTON, Mary		16	F	Spinster	16De02
MILLER, Robert		30	M	Laborer	16De02
HOULAHAN, Ellen		20	F	Spinster	16De02
MANGAN, Bridget		18	F	Spinster	16De02
KEHOUGH, John		32	M	Farmer	16De02
MARA, Pat.		30	M	Farmer	16De02
MADDEN, Honora		40	F	Wife	16De02
PURDON, John		23	M	Laborer	16De02
TRAINOR, Cathr.		20	F	Spinster	16De02
NEWALL, Rich.		21	M	Laborer	16De02
POWELL, Alfred		40	M	Laborer	16De02
MULDOWNEY, Richd.		20	M	Laborer	16De02
FITZPATRICK, Edwd.		27	M	Laborer	16De02
Sally	(W)	20	F	Wife	16De02
MCGOWAN, Jane		30	F	Wife	16De02
Robert		19	M	Laborer	16De02
Mary		30	F	Wife	16De02
James		11	M	Child	16De02
NOONAN, Mary		20	F	Wife	16De02
QUINLAN, Francis		45	M	Laborer	16De02
COURTER, James		30	M	Laborer	16De02
QUINLAN, Joseph		30	M	Laborer	16De02
Sarah		06	F	Child	16De02
MCTIERNEY, Patk.		45	M	Laborer	16De02
DOOLEY, Mary		25	F	Wife	16De02
BRIDE, Mary		16	F	Spinster	16De02
MINALES, Bernd.		32	M	Laborer	16De02
William		26	M	Laborer	16De02
GILLASPEY, Hugh		45	M	Laborer	16De02
BURNAHAND, Dennis		22	M	Laborer	16De02
BAILEY, Kitty		15	F	Spinster	16De02
MOFFATT, James		31	M	Laborer	16De02
Mary	(W)	30	F	Wife	16De02
SWEENY, Mary		30	F	Wife	16De02
KIDNEY, Emily		17	F	Wife	16De02
MCPAROLON, Ann		20	F	Wife	16De02
James		11	M	Child	16De02
MCDONNELL, Patk.		20	M	Laborer	16De02
HYLAND, Dennis		35	M	Laborer	16De02
U	(W)	35	F	Wife	16De02

NAMES OF PASSENGERS		AGE	SEX	OCCUPATIONS	DATE PORT SHIP
HYLAND, Ann		15	F	Spinster	16De02
John		13	M	Child	16De02
Margt.		11	F	Child	16De02
Mary		10	F	Child	16De02
Thomas		09	M	Child	16De02
Dennis		07	M	Child	16De02
Bridget		05	F	Child	16De02
Cathr.		02	F	Child	16De02
BRADY, Bridget		20	F	Spinster	16De02
Ann		21	F	Spinster	16De02
MCGARRY, Ann		40	F	Wife	16De02
Ann		09	F	Child	16De02
Michl.	(S)	05	M	Child	16De02
DEGNAN, Margt.		20	F	Spinster	16De02
Elsie		18	F	Spinster	16De02
WHITE, William-J.		26	M	Merchant	16De02
MCDONALD, U		12	F	Child	16De02
OGORMAN, Thos.Dr.		36	M	Surgeon	16De02

QUEEN-OF-THE-WEST 16 DECEMBER 1847

From Liverpool

NAMES OF PASSENGERS		AGE	SEX	OCCUPATIONS	DATE PORT SHIP
HEANY, Bryan		30	M	Laborer	16De02Cn
U	(W)	21	F	Wife	16De02Cn
Patrick		.00	M	Infant	16De02Cn
Frank		.00	M	Infant	16De02Cn
CARR, Charles		22	M	Shoemaker	16De02Cn
DUFFY, Michael		20	M	Laborer	16De02Cn
Ann		21	F	Unknown	16De02Cn
Charles		12	M	Unknown	16De02Cn
RAFFERTY, Margaret		20	F	Unknown	16De02Cn
PHELAN, Margaret		50	F	Unknown	16De02Cn
Margaret		20	F	Unknown	16De02Cn
MCMANUS, Patrick		30	M	Weaver	16De02Cn
SULLIVAN, Mary		25	F	Unknown	16De02Cn
HUBBARD, Mary-A.		17	F	Unknown	16De02Cn
RYAN, Margaret		16	F	Unknown	16De02Cn
SHEEHAN, Margaret		20	F	Unknown	16De02Cn
WISELY, John		16	M	Unknown	16De02Cn
Margaret		15	F	Unknown	16De02Cn
BULGER, Pat.		24	M	Laborer	16De02Cn
MCWHORTER, Eliza		30	F	Unknown	16De02Cn
LAWLER, Mary		22	F	Unknown	16De02Cn
MCWHORTER, Mary-Ann		03	F	Child	16De02Cn
HORAN, Wm.		20	M	Laborer	16De02Cn
DEMPSEY, Ann		17	F	Unknown	16De02Cn
CAYAL, Susan		36	F	Unknown	16De02Cn
Died-At-Sea					
John		09	M	Child	16De02Cn
Archd.		04	M	Child	16De02Cn
Alexander		.00	M	Infant	16De02Cn
CORRIE, Andrew		20	M	Laborer	16De02Cn
LOUGHMAN, Pat.		20	M	Laborer	16De02Cn
CORRIE, John		09	M	Child	16De02Cn
MCCLURE, Catharine		11	F	Unknown	16De02Cn
RIELLY, Bridget		18	F	Unknown	16De02Cn
MCGARRY, Ellen		20	F	Unknown	16De02Cn
FULLY, Bridget		15	F	Unknown	16De02Cn
CANNON, Bryan		40	M	Laborer	16De02Cn
Biddy	(W)	40	F	Wife	16De02Cn
John		09	M	Child	16De02Cn
CARR, Pat.		30	M	Laborer	16De02Cn
NOBLE, John		27	M	Shoemaker	16De02Cn
SHANNON, Peter		26	M	Shoemaker	16De02Cn
Peter		26	M	Shoemaker	16De02Cn
HAYSETT, Pat.		30	M	Paver	16De02Cn
George		24	M	Plasterer	16De02Cn
ONEAL, Pat.		20	M	Laborer	16De02Cn
CONNOR, Abigail		18	F	Unknown	16De02Cn
KELLY, Jane		26	F	Unknown	16De02Cn
GORMLEY, Barry		25	M	Laborer	16De02Cn
Margt.		12	F	Unknown	16De02Cn
Catharine		12	F	Unknown	16De02Cn
BULMAN, Thos.		30	M	Laborer	16De02Cn
REGAN, Wm.		40	M	Laborer	16De02Cn
HALLERAN, Pat.		26	M	Laborer	16De02Cn
Charles		22	M	Laborer	16De02Cn
Mary		60	F	Unknown	16De02Cn
Abigail		22	F	Unknown	16De02Cn
REGAN, Mary		14	F	Unknown	16De02Cn
HAMILTON, Robert		30	M	Merchant	16De02Cn
COCKLAN, John		36	M	Laborer	16De02Cn
Mary		34	F	Unknown	16De02Cn
W.		.00	U	Infant	16De02Cn
Pat.		34	M	Laborer	16De02Cn
Ellen		50	F	Unknown	16De02Cn
Mary		07	F	Child	16De02Cn
Ellen		05	F	Child	16De02Cn
Maria		04	F	Child	16De02Cn
Pat.		.00	M	Infant	16De02Cn
BUCKLEY, Danl.		40	M	Farmer	16De02Cn
Honora		40	F	None	16De02Cn
Ellen		20	F	Unknown	16De02Cn
Mary		11	F	Unknown	16De02Cn
Larry		08	M	Child	16De02Cn
Timothy		06	M	Child	16De02Cn
Michl.		.00	M	Infant	16De02Cn
Died-At-Sea					
CROFT, Wm.		20	M	Farmer	16De02Cn
HUGHES, Charles		30	M	Flaxdr	16De02Cn
WADE, Peter		23	M	Laborer	16De02Cn
ROURKE, John		28	M	Teacher	16De02Cn
Bridget		25	F	Unknown	16De02Cn
CREGAN, James		20	M	Laborer	16De02Cn
FARRELL, Margt.		20	F	Unknown	16De02Cn
CHESHAN, Eliza		.00	F	Infant	16De02Cn
ROSS, James		20	M	Laborer	16De02Cn
CREGAN, Michl.		20	M	Laborer	16De02Cn
John		25	M	Unknown	16De02Cn
Bessy		20	F	Unknown	16De02Cn
GALLIHER, Mary		22	F	Unknown	16De02Cn
ROBINSON, John		36	M	Carpenter	16De02Cn
NOLAN, Biddy		20	F	Unknown	16De02Cn
DALTON, Daniel		27	M	Carpenter	16De02Cn
RAFFERTY, James		18	M	Laborer	16De02Cn
SHAUGHNESSY, Michl.		30	M	Laborer	16De02Cn
GLEESON, John		30	M	Laborer	16De02Cn
FARRELL, Michl.		24	M	Unknown	16De02Cn
SHAUGHNESSY, Robt.		23	M	Laborer	16De02Cn
KELLY, Ellen		20	F	Unknown	16De02Cn
MCKAHY, Thos.Wm.		24	M	Laborer	16De02Cn
FOX, Biddy		20	F	Unknown	16De02Cn
Hannah		11	F	Unknown	16De02Cn
NAUGHTON, Mary		20	F	Unknown	16De02Cn
BOYLE, Patrick		25	M	Laborer	16De02Cn
CRELLY, James		23	M	Laborer	16De02Cn
ROGAN, Lawrence		25	M	Laborer	16De02Cn
MCCOOBE, Rose		20	F	Unknown	16De02Cn
CAHILL, Mary		20	F	Unknown	16De02Cn
EGAN, Thomas		30	M	Laborer	16De02Cn
HANLEY, Catharine		12	F	Unknown	16De02Cn
DERMODY, Michl.		28	M	Laborer	16De02Cn
John		30	M	Cooper	16De02Cn
Margaret		30	F	Unknown	16De02Cn
Mary		20	F	Unknown	16De02Cn
Catharine		08	F	Child	16De02Cn
LYNCH, Richd.		30	M	Unknown	16De02Cn
MCCARL, Patrick		20	M	Laborer	16De02Cn
MCENTRIE, Rose		20	F	Unknown	16De02Cn
THOMAS, John		40	M	Unknown	16De02Cn
FEELY, Wm.		20	M	Unknown	16De02Cn
ROGAN, Rose		20	F	Unknown	16De02Cn
KELLY, Margt.		35	F	Unknown	16De02Cn

NAMES OF PASSENGERS		AGE	SEX	OCCUPATIONS	DATE PORT SHIP
MCCANN, Patrick		20	M	Blacksmith	16De02Cn
CAHILL, Patrick		60	M	Laborer	16De02Cn
Anne		50	F	Unknown	16De02Cn
James		30	M	Laborer	16De02Cn
MARRION, Pat.		07	M	Child	16De02Cn
CARROLL, John		22	M	Laborer	16De02Cn
MCDONNELL, Ann		20	F	Unknown	16De02Cn
WHITNEY, John		38	M	Laborer	16De02Cn
Anne		15	F	Unknown	16De02Cn
MAHON, Bridget		20	F	Unknown	16De02Cn
QUINN, Ellen		20	F	Unknown	16De02Cn
FLYNN, Mary		18	F	Unknown	16De02Cn
WHITNEY, John		20	M	Laborer	16De02Cn
MOMAILL, Jeremiah		22	M	Laborer	16De02Cn
WARD, Catharine		40	F	Unknown	16De02Cn
John		07	M	Child	16De02Cn
LEDDY, Patrick		30	M	Laborer	16De02Cn
Ellen		14	F	Unknown	16De02Cn
Thomas		20	M	Laborer	16De02Cn
CARROLL, Michael		50	M	Laborer	16De02Cn
Nancy		50	F	Unknown	16De02Cn
Mary		10	F	Unknown	16De02Cn
Patrick		08	M	Child	16De02Cn
Dennis		07	M	Child	16De02Cn
DOOLAN, Judy		20	F	Unknown	16De02Cn
EWINS, Catharine		20	F	Unknown	16De02Cn
BYRNE, Isabella		21	F	Unknown	16De02Cn
DALEY, Mary		16	F	Unknown	16De02Cn
Thomas		13	M	Unknown	16De02Cn
HENRY, Joseph		16	M	Unknown	16De02Cn
Robt.		05	M	Child	16De02Cn
CONNOR, Mary		26	F	Unknown	16De02Cn
Catharine		03	F	Child	16De02Cn
James		.00	M	Infant	16De02Cn
HOLYWOOD, Anne		18	F	Unknown	16De02Cn
Mary		16	F	Unknown	16De02Cn
CAVANAGH, Michael		30	M	Bricklayer	16De02Cn
U	(W)	26	F	Wife	16De02Cn
Margt.		08	F	Child	16De02Cn
Michael		05	M	Child	16De02Cn
Matilda		.00	F	Infant	16De02Cn
MCGOWAN, Francis		16	M	Unknown	16De02Cn
TAYLOR, Benjamin		18	M	Unknown	16De02Cn
FAY, Andrew		60	M	Farmer	16De02Cn
Died-At-Sea					
Margt.		50	F	Unknown	16De02Cn
John		20	M	Farmer	16De02Cn
Catharine		25	F	Unknown	16De02Cn
Catharine		06	F	Child	16De02Cn
Susan		04	F	Child	16De02Cn
Andrew		.00	M	Infant	16De02Cn
Died-At-Sea					
Michael		41	M	Laborer	16De02Cn
Ellen		44	F	Unknown	16De02Cn
Mary		25	F	Unknown	16De02Cn
MARTIN, Mary		20	F	Unknown	16De02Cn
Michael		20	M	Laborer	16De02Cn
MCDOWELL, Grace		52	F	Unknown	16De02Cn
Biddy		20	F	Unknown	16De02Cn
Anne		18	F	Unknown	16De02Cn
Ellen		12	F	Unknown	16De02Cn
John		09	M	Child	16De02Cn
DALY, Patrick		40	M	Laborer	16De02Cn
U	(W)	40	F	Wife	16De02Cn
Biddy		03	F	Child	16De02Cn
Thomas		.00	M	Infant	16De02Cn
Died-At-Sea					
BRACKIN, Mary		20	F	Unknown	16De02Cn
TRACY, Catharine		18	F	Unknown	16De02Cn
GRIFFIN, Ellen		50	F	Unknown	16De02Cn
CROW, Peter		25	M	Laborer	16De02Cn
MCELLEN, Pat.		20	M	Laborer	16De02Cn
KELLY, Thomas		20	M	Laborer	16De02Cn
CONNEAL, John		20	M	Laborer	16De02Cn
TOBY, John		20	M	Laborer	16De02Cn

NAMES OF PASSENGERS		AGE	SEX	OCCUPATIONS	DATE PORT SHIP
FLANNAGAN, Mary		30	F	Unknown	16De02Cn
CANFIELD, Bridget		20	F	Unknown	16De02Cn
COONEY, Pat.		40	M	Laborer	16De02Cn
Jane		18	F	Unknown	16De02Cn
RYLEY, Thos.		35	M	Laborer	16De02Cn
SPORAN, Dan.		28	M	Laborer	16De02Cn
MCMANUS, Lawrence		24	M	Laborer	16De02Cn
MCCABE, Peggy		40	F	Unknown	16De02Cn
NEAL, Catharine		40	F	Unknown	16De02Cn
Bessy		12	F	Unknown	16De02Cn
John		10	M	Unknown	16De02Cn
ALLIWELL, Hugh		29	M	Laborer	16De02Cn
FAY, Catharine		20	F	Unknown	16De02Cn
Anne		20	F	Unknown	16De02Cn
MCCALL, Mary		20	F	Unknown	16De02Cn
Biddy		18	F	Unknown	16De02Cn
WALSH, Robert		30	M	Paper Maker	16De02Cn
FLAVOR, James		20	M	Laborer	16De02Cn
MCCOURT, Michl.		20	M	Laborer	16De02Cn
CAIN, Barthw.		12	M	Unknown	16De02Cn
LEDWAITE, J.W.		40	M	Clerk	16De02Cn
FINNEY, Patrick		20	M	Laborer	16De02Cn
LAUGHLIN, Catharine		30	F	Unknown	16De02Cn

J.A.MUNN 20 DECEMBER 1847

From Halifax

NAMES OF PASSENGERS		AGE	SEX	OCCUPATIONS	DATE PORT SHIP
MURPHY, Patrick		17	M	Laborer	20De22Sa

ASHLAND 20 DECEMBER 1847

From Liverpool

NAMES OF PASSENGERS		AGE	SEX	OCCUPATIONS	DATE PORT SHIP
MCSORLY, John		22	M	Laborer	20De02Ny
CARROLL, Owen		28	M	Laborer	20De02Ny
THOMPSON, Arthur		20	M	Laborer	20De02Ny
Rebecca	(W)	27	F	Wife	20De02Ny
KEOHAN, John		19	M	Laborer	20De02Ny
BRINGLE, Ellen		19	F	Servant	20De02Ny
MCGUIN, Ed.		24	M	Laborer	20De02Ny
Anne	(W)	20	F	Wife	20De02Ny
QUIN, Chas.		20	M	Laborer	20De02Ny
MORRIS, Stephen		50	M	Laborer	20De02Ny
DONNELL, John		37	M	Laborer	20De02Ny
U	(W)	30	F	Wife	20De02Ny
Mary	(D)	.00	F	Infant	20De02Ny
BUCKLEY, Thos.		24	M	Laborer	20De02Ny
RYAN, John		35	M	Mechanic	20De02Ny
U	(W)	30	F	Wife	20De02Ny
Mary	(D)	04	F	Child	20De02Ny
Anne	(D)	02	F	Child	20De02Ny
Jane	(D)	.00	F	Infant	20De02Ny
HAYS, Jas.		30	M	Laborer	20De02Ny
Julia	(W)	30	F	Wife	20De02Ny
Mich.	(S)	13	M	Unknown	20De02Ny
Mary	(D)	04	F	Child	20De02Ny
BRYAN, Lewis		30	M	Mechanic	20De02Ny
Ellen	(W)	30	F	Wife	20De02Ny
Mary	(D)	13	F	Unknown	20De02Ny
Anne	(D)	10	F	Unknown	20De02Ny
Jane	(D)	08	F	Child	20De02Ny
Lewis	(S)	06	M	Child	20De02Ny

NAMES OF PASSENGERS		AGE	SEX	OCCUPATIONS	DATE PORT SHIP
BRYAN, Johann	(D)	03	F	Child	20De02Ny
Ellen	(D)	.00	F	Infant	20De02Ny
CLORATY, Thos.		24	M	Laborer	20De02Ny
GLAVIN, James		15	M	Unknown	20De02Ny
FITZPATRICK, James		16	M	Unknown	20De02Ny
EAGANE, Pat		13	M	Unknown	20De02Ny
TIERNEY, Pat		30	M	Laborer	20De02Ny
Martin		34	M	Laborer	20De02Ny
Cath.	(W)	21	F	Wife	20De02Ny
Mary	(D)	.00	F	Infant	20De02Ny
Sally	(C)	13	F	Unknown	20De02Ny
Honor	(C)	20	F	Unknown	20De02Ny
HUGHTON, Martin		20	M	Laborer	20De02Ny
NEE, Martin		35	M	Laborer	20De02Ny
EAGAN, Michael		40	M	Laborer	20De02Ny
CULLEN, John		30	M	Mechanic	20De02Ny
U	(W)	30	F	Wife	20De02Ny
U	(S)	.00	M	Infant	20De02Ny
REILLY, Jas.		41	M	Laborer	20De02Ny
SPILLAN, Jerry		30	M	Laborer	20De02Ny
KEYS, Pat		60	M	Mechanic	20De02Ny
Pat	(S)	28	M	Unknown	20De02Ny
William	(S)	26	M	Unknown	20De02Ny
James	(S)	24	M	Unknown	20De02Ny
James	(C)	20	M	Unknown	20De02Ny
CARROLL, Cath.Keys		25	F	Unknown	20De02Ny
Dan	(S)	07	M	Child	20De02Ny
Mary-Ann	(D)	.00	F	Infant	20De02Ny
MOFFIT, Jas.		20	M	Mechanic	20De02Ny
MCGRATH, Wm.		30	M	Mechanic	20De02Ny
Sarah	(T)	20	F	Unknown	20De02Ny
MCDONNALD, Cath.		30	F	Unknown	20De02Ny
LAWLER, Pat		20	M	Mechanic	20De02Ny
U	(T)	22	F	Unknown	20De02Ny
FITZPATRICK, Chas.		23	M	Laborer	20De02Ny
WARD, Martin		20	M	Laborer	20De02Ny
QUINN, Owen		20	M	Laborer	20De02Ny
KELLY, Hugh		30	M	Laborer	20De02Ny
DOUD, Jenny		50	F	Laborer	20De02Ny
Mary		13	F	Laborer	20De02Ny
KELLY, Mary		.00	F	Infant	20De02Ny
MCDONELLI, Wm.		36	M	Laborer	20De02Ny
MOORE, Ed.		26	M	Laborer	20De02Ny
U	(W)	22	F	Wife	20De02Ny
Died-At-Sea					
Lewis	(S)	.00	M	Infant	20De02Ny
Mary	(D)	06	F	Child	20De02Ny
MCENTER, Michael		27	M	Laborer	20De02Ny
Jane	(W)	26	F	Wife	20De02Ny
Mary	(N)	20	F	Unknown	20De02Ny
RIELLY, Thos.		28	M	Laborer	20De02Ny
Mary	(T)	25	F	Unknown	20De02Ny
ROLLINSTON, Wm.		25	M	Mechanic	20De02Ny
BRADY, Nicholas		20	M	Laborer	20De02Ny
Rose	(T)	22	F	Unknown	20De02Ny
MCCAUL, Michael		23	M	Laborer	20De02Ny
REILLY, Pat		20	M	Laborer	20De02Ny
FAY, John		25	M	Laborer	20De02Ny
MCCARTHY, Simeon		30	M	Laborer	20De02Ny
U	(W)	30	F	Wife	20De02Ny
Simeon	(S)	06	M	Child	20De02Ny
Daniel	(S)	04	M	Child	20De02Ny
Timothy	(S)	.00	M	Infant	20De02Ny
Died-At-Sea					
Julia	(D)	03	F	Child	20De02Ny
Died-At-Sea					
Daniel		25	M	Laborer	20De02Ny
Mary	(W)	20	F	Wife	20De02Ny
Johanna	(D)	.00	F	Infant	20De02Ny
MAY, Pat		30	M	Mechanic	20De02Ny
Anne	(W)	24	F	Wife	20De02Ny
FLOOD, Michael		23	M	Laborer	20De02Ny
SCULLY, Mary		22	F	Laborer	20De02Ny
COLLINS, Pat		16	M	Laborer	20De02Ny
KEON, Philip		25	M	Laborer	20De02Ny

NAMES OF PASSENGERS		AGE	SEX	OCCUPATIONS	DATE PORT SHIP
GARLAND, Pat		26	M	Laborer	20De02Ny
RUSH, Michael		25	M	Laborer	20De02Ny
Cath.		16	F	Laborer	20De02Ny
CONIGAN, Bridget		17	F	Laborer	20De02Ny
MCMAHON, Anne		18	F	Laborer	20De02Ny
MCGARLIN, Cath.		30	F	Laborer	20De02Ny
Edward	(S)	03	M	Child	20De02Ny
Isabella	(D)	.00	F	Infant	20De02Ny
MURRAY, Charles		22	M	Laborer	20De02Ny
GAHAN, Eliza		26	F	Laborer	20De02Ny
Ellen		.00	F	Infant	20De02Ny
CURLEY, Connor		21	M	Laborer	20De02Ny
BEEGAN, Bridget		28	F	Laborer	20De02Ny
MCGUIRE, Margaret		23	F	Laborer	20De02Ny
EAGAN, Margaret		22	F	Laborer	20De02Ny
MCCARTHY, Mathew		30	M	Laborer	20De02Ny
Margaret	(W)	30	F	Wife	20De02Ny
CAULEY, James		21	M	Laborer	20De02Ny
Danl.		22	M	Laborer	20De02Ny
James		26	M	Laborer	20De02Ny
HALLEHAN, Danl.		50	M	Farmer	20De02Ny
Honor	(W)	40	F	Wife	20De02Ny
Mary	(D)	21	F	Unknown	20De02Ny
Margaret	(D)	16	F	Unknown	20De02Ny
REILLY, Wm.		20	M	Laborer	20De02Ny
COWLEY, Peter		13	M	Unknown	20De02Ny
REAN, Mary		20	F	Unknown	20De02Ny
John		.00	M	Infant	20De02Ny
COWLEY, Anne		18	F	Unknown	20De02Ny
DONOVAN, John		35	M	Laborer	20De02Ny
KEOHAN, Pat		25	M	Laborer	20De02Ny
Mary	(T)	22	F	Unknown	20De02Ny
RABBIT, Ellen		34	F	WI	20De02Ny
Edward	(S)	13	M	Child	20De02Ny
Mary	(D)	07	F	Child	20De02Ny
Patt	(S)	05	M	Child	20De02Ny
Thomas	(S)	.00	M	Infant	20De02Ny
POWELL, John		40	M	Farmer	20De02Ny
U	(W)	40	F	Wife	20De02Ny
Margaret	(D)	22	F	Unknown	20De02Ny
John	(S)	20	M	Unknown	20De02Ny
Michael	(S)	13	M	Unknown	20De02Ny
Robert	(S)	11	M	Unknown	20De02Ny
Henry	(S)	09	M	Child	20De02Ny
DAWSON, Martha		55	F	Unknown	20De02Ny
William	(S)	26	M	Laborer	20De02Ny
MCQUADE, Rose		16	F	Servant	20De02Ny
Cath.	(T)	13	F	Servant	20De02Ny
CROWLEY, John		25	M	Laborer	20De02Ny
FENERAN, John		25	M	Laborer	20De02Ny
MORGAN, Margaret		20	F	Laborer	20De02Ny
NUGENT, Michael		19	M	Laborer	20De02Ny
Maria	(T)	13	F	Unknown	20De02Ny
DOUD, John		21	M	Laborer	20De02Ny
Cath.	(W)	21	F	Wife	20De02Ny
KELLY, Michael		27	M	Laborer	20De02Ny
U	(W)	26	F	Wife	20De02Ny
HOGAN, U-Mrs.		26	F	Wife	20De02Ny
Thos.	(S)	.00	M	Infant	20De02Ny
Died-At-Sea					
REON, Cath.		23	F	Servant	20De02Ny
MCMANUS, U		28	M	Gentleman	20De02Ny
WILLIS, Jeffry		30	M	Laborer	20De02Ny
COLLON, Jerry		20	M	Laborer	20De02Ny
SULLIVAN, Danl.		20	M	Laborer	20De02Ny
CASEY, Ned		26	M	Laborer	20De02Ny
U	(W)	25	F	Wife	20De02Ny
Cath.	(D)	06	F	Child	20De02Ny
Johanna	(D)	.00	F	Infant	20De02Ny
HART, Michael		25	M	Laborer	20De02Ny
Ellen	(M)	50	F	Unknown	20De02Ny
Margaret	(W)	30	F	Wife	20De02Ny
Mathew	(B)	18	M	Laborer	20De02Ny
Daniel	(S)	.00	M	Infant	20De02Ny
Margaret	(T)	20	F	Unknown	20De02Ny

NAMES OF PASSENGERS		AGE	SEX	OCCUPATIONS	DATE PORT SHIP
CONNER, Thos.		20	M	Laborer	20De02Ny
RUSKE, Jas.		20	M	Laborer	20De02Ny
BRIAN, John		26	M	Laborer	20De02Ny
MCBRIDE, Peter		32	M	Laborer	20De02Ny
Mary	(W)	27	F	Wife	20De02Ny
Maria	(D)	05	F	Child	20De02Ny
Anne	(D)	02	F	Child	20De02Ny
Mary	(D)	.00	F	Infant	20De02Ny
ABRAMS, Jos.		26	M	Mechanic	20De02Ny
Ann	(W)	26	F	Wife	20De02Ny
Mary	(D)	.00	F	Infant	20De02Ny
Jane	(D)	03	F	Child	20De02Ny
BELLOWS, Wm.		13	M	Mechanic	20De02Ny
CALLAHAN, Cornelius		25	M	Laborer	20De02Ny
CONWAY, Peter		30	M	Laborer	20De02Ny
DAY, Mary		20	F	Laborer	20De02Ny
RATEGAN, Cath.		28	F	Laborer	20De02Ny
DELLANY, Ellen		20	F	Laborer	20De02Ny
Mary	(T)	20	F	Unknown	20De02Ny
ROONEY, Bridget		30	F	Wi	20De02Ny
Ann	(D)	.00	F	Infant	20De02Ny
GARVIN, Hugh		27	M	Mechanic	20De02Ny
Rose	(W)	24	F	Wife	20De02Ny
Biddy	(D)	.00	F	Infant	20De02Ny
CONNOR, Thos.		27	M	Laborer	20De02Ny
GRAD, Andrew		21	M	Laborer	20De02Ny
SHASKY, John		20	M	Laborer	20De02Ny
TOONY, Teresa		21	F	Laborer	20De02Ny
MULDON, Biddy		20	F	Laborer	20De02Ny
COLLINS, John		21	M	Laborer	20De02Ny
HOGAN, Bridget		21	F	Laborer	20De02Ny
MCDONALD, Mary		06	F	Child	20De02Ny
WADE, Patt		25	M	Laborer	20De02Ny
CARNIFF, Cath.		21	F	Laborer	20De02Ny
MCELROY, Judy		13	F	Laborer	20De02Ny
Owen		30	M	Laborer	20De02Ny
Cath.	(D)	20	F	Unknown	20De02Ny
QUIN, Jas.		29	M	Laborer	20De02Ny
GALLAHAN, John		30	M	Laborer	20De02Ny
WALSH, Ane		13	F	Laborer	20De02Ny
EGAN, Bessy		10	F	Unknown	20De02Ny
Honor	(M)	46	F	Wife	20De02Ny

RELIANCE 21 DECEMBER 1847

From Liverpool

NAMES OF PASSENGERS		AGE	SEX	OCCUPATIONS	DATE PORT SHIP
GOUR, Robert-M.		30	M	Laborer	21De02Dw
HUMPHREYS, Humphrey		36	M	Laborer	21De02Dw
Sarah		34	F	None	21De02Dw
Eliza		32	F	None	21De02Dw
James		07	M	Child	21De02Dw
Thomas		05	M	Child	21De02Dw
Jane		03	F	Child	21De02Dw
Maryann		.00	F	Infant	21De02Dw
NEBLOCH, Robert		45	M	Laborer	21De02Dw
Mary		42	F	None	21De02Dw
Jane		18	F	None	21De02Dw
Isabella		13	F	None	21De02Dw
Matty		11	M	None	21De02Dw
Susan		07	F	Child	21De02Dw
Nancy		05	F	Child	21De02Dw
Mary-A.		.00	F	Infant	21De02Dw
MURRAY, Margaret		25	F	None	21De02Dw
Isabella		10	F	None	21De02Dw
Alexander		05	M	Child	21De02Dw
Henry		02	M	Child	21De02Dw
GRIFFITH, James		26	M	Laborer	21De02Dw
FOX, Ann		40	F	None	21De02Dw
FOX, Peter		40	M	None	21De02Dw
Ann		30	F	None	21De02Dw
Bridget		13	F	None	21De02Dw
Bridget		12	F	None	21De02Dw
Catharine		10	F	None	21De02Dw
Mary		08	F	Child	21De02Dw
Peter		04	M	Child	21De02Dw
Luke		.00	M	Infant	21De02Dw
REID, Bridget		24	F	None	21De02Dw
Ann		22	F	None	21De02Dw
John		20	M	Laborer	21De02Dw
GANTLEY, Mary		40	F	None	21De02Dw
Mary		40	F	None	21De02Dw
Pat		15	M	None	21De02Dw
Daniel		13	M	None	21De02Dw
Dennis		40	M	Laborer	21De02Dw
Ann		09	F	Child	21De02Dw
Michael		07	M	Child	21De02Dw
Ellen		05	F	Child	21De02Dw
Bridget		.00	F	Infant	21De02Dw
RILEY, Mary		35	F	None	21De02Dw
James		12	M	None	21De02Dw
John		10	M	None	21De02Dw
Peter		08	M	Child	21De02Dw
Pat		06	M	Child	21De02Dw
Bernard		04	M	Child	21De02Dw
May		.00	F	Infant	21De02Dw
ROSKIN, Geo.		22	M	Laborer	21De02Dw
CHADUCH, Wm.		22	M	Laborer	21De02Dw
Thomas		16	M	Laborer	21De02Dw
ADAMS, Catharine		40	F	None	21De02Dw
James		20	M	Laborer	21De02Dw
Owen		15	M	None	21De02Dw
Pat		10	M	None	21De02Dw
John		09	M	Child	21De02Dw
KEENAN, Edward		16	M	None	21De02Dw
JOHNSON, Geo.		30	M	Laborer	21De02Dw
Cathan.		31	F	None	21De02Dw
Geo.		07	M	Child	21De02Dw
Eliza		05	F	Child	21De02Dw
John-W.		04	M	Child	21De02Dw
David		.00	M	Infant	21De02Dw
COSTELLO, U		30	F	None	21De02Dw
Margaret		04	F	Child	21De02Dw
Biddy		03	F	Child	21De02Dw
Pat.		02	M	Child	21De02Dw
CASSIDY, Pat.		20	M	Laborer	21De02Dw
WENGES, Pat.		20	M	Laborer	21De02Dw
CARLIN, Ann		37	F	None	21De02Dw
Bridget		02	F	Child	21De02Dw
Mary		.00	F	Infant	21De02Dw
ELHINEY, James-M.		18	M	None	21De02Dw
Eliza		50	F	None	21De02Dw
Alexander		13	M	None	21De02Dw
RIPLEY, Luke		26	M	Laborer	21De02Dw
KENNEDY, Pat		22	M	Laborer	21De02Dw
Hanah		40	F	None	21De02Dw
SULLIVAN, Wm.		35	M	Laborer	21De02Dw
FLAHY, John		45	M	Laborer	21De02Dw
QUINTON, John		30	M	Laborer	21De02Dw
COSEAN, John		29	M	Laborer	21De02Dw
BRIEN, Mary		25	F	None	21De02Dw
ROACHE, John		20	M	Laborer	21De02Dw
WILKINSON, Wm.		25	M	Laborer	21De02Dw
SULLIVAN, Mary		25	F	None	21De02Dw
BARRY, Dennis		28	M	Laborer	21De02Dw
U	(W)	19	F	Wife	21De02Dw
BYRAN, Eliza		17	F	None	21De02Dw
BARNEY, Abiel.		21	M	Laborer	21De02Dw
GREEN, Michael		28	M	Laborer	21De02Dw
Ellen		26	F	None	21De02Dw
David		02	M	Child	21De02Dw
DORAN, Thomas		30	M	Laborer	21De02Dw
MURPHEY, Thomas		21	M	Laborer	21De02Dw
John-N.		18	M	None	21De02Dw

NAMES OF PASSENGERS		AGE	SEX	OCCUPATIONS	DATE PORT SHIP
KANE, James		23	M	Laborer	21De02Dw
NASH, Michael		23	M	Laborer	21De02Dw
HANRAHAN, Wm.		23	M	Laborer	21De02Dw
KAVANAGH, Wm.		21	M	Laborer	21De02Dw
CAIHILL, Biddy		21	F	None	21De02Dw
DAVIDSON, James		21	M	Laborer	21De02Dw
CONNELL, Betty		30	F	None	21De02Dw
YOUNG, Matilda		20	F	None	21De02Dw
BUNN, Bridget		20	F	None	21De02Dw
MCCRACKIN, Ann		16	F	None	21De02Dw
ADAMS, Catharine		40	F	None	21De02Dw
James		20	M	None	21De02Dw
Owen		15	M	None	21De02Dw
Pat		10	M	None	21De02Dw
John		09	M	Child	21De02Dw
HITCHINS, Wm.		28	M	Laborer	21De02Dw
BRONN, Sarah		35	F	None	21De02Dw
Peggy-J.		10	F	None	21De02Dw
CARROLL, Margaret		30	F	None	21De02Dw
Ellen		.00	F	Infant	21De02Dw
KENEDY, Patk.		27	M	Laborer	21De02Dw
CILNER, Catharine		15	F	None	21De02Dw
KERRY, Charles		25	M	Laborer	21De02Dw
JONES, Wm.		25	M	Laborer	21De02Dw
BYRNE, Michael		25	M	Laborer	21De02Dw
SHEANE, Rober.		24	M	Laborer	21De02Dw
CLEAREY, Edwd.		28	M	Laborer	21De02Dw
Eliza		24	F	None	21De02Dw
MCBRIDY, Rober.		24	M	Laborer	21De02Dw
Edwd.		05	M	Child	21De02Dw
BUSHETS, Jane		18	F	None	21De02Dw
FLANIGAN, Martin		41	M	Laborer	21De02Dw
Mary		15	F	None	21De02Dw
James		05	M	Child	21De02Dw
Owen		03	M	Child	21De02Dw
SHENNAN, James		42	M	Laborer	21De02Dw
U	(W)	40	F	Wife	21De02Dw
Thomas		40	M	Laborer	21De02Dw
U-Mrs.		50	F	None	21De02Dw
Sally		22	F	None	21De02Dw
PLUNKETT, Ellen		18	F	None	21De02Dw
SHENNAN, Thomas		19	M	Laborer	21De02Dw
Ann		12	F	None	21De02Dw
Maria		10	F	None	21De02Dw
Edward		08	M	Child	21De02Dw
Ellen		06	F	Child	21De02Dw
Sally		04	F	Child	21De02Dw
Patt		02	M	Child	21De02Dw
U		.00	M	Infant	21De02Dw
MCKEOWN, Sally		24	F	None	21De02Dw
Margaret		22	F	None	21De02Dw
Eliza		.00	F	Infant	21De02Dw
BENNSON, Eliza		18	F	None	21De02Dw
BOYLE, James		24	M	Laborer	21De02Dw
Maria	(W)	21	F	Wife	21De02Dw
Patt	(S)	.00	M	Infant	21De02Dw
Geo.	(S)	.00	M	Infant	21De02Dw
DELANEY, Thomas		30	M	Laborer	21De02Dw
Margaret	(W)	20	F	Wife	21De02Dw
James	(S)	04	M	Child	21De02Dw
DENISON, Ann		24	F	None	21De02Dw
James		13	M	None	21De02Dw
JARDIN, Mary		11	F	None	21De02Dw
LAM, Rebeca		18	F	None	21De02Dw
FARRELL, Mary		50	F	None	21De02Dw
Mathew		30	M	Laborer	21De02Dw
Margaret		28	F	None	21De02Dw
Cath.		20	F	None	21De02Dw
Sarah		16	F	None	21De02Dw
Eliza		14	F	None	21De02Dw
RENAGHAN, John		25	M	Laborer	21De02Dw
EGAN, Thomas		25	M	Laborer	21De02Dw
ROARKE, John		25	M	Laborer	21De02Dw
Bridget		24	F	None	21De02Dw
EGAN, Mary		24	F	None	21De02Dw

NAMES OF PASSENGERS	AGE	SEX	OCCUPATIONS	DATE PORT SHIP
NORKE, Arthur	29	M	None	21De02Dw
Jane	22	F	None	21De02Dw
LUGHRY, Rebecca	24	F	None	21De02Dw
BRADY, Pat	21	M	Laborer	21De02Dw
KENNY, Pat	31	M	Laborer	21De02Dw
CARTER, John	31	M	Laborer	21De02Dw
Mary	28	F	None	21De02Dw
CRANE, Dick	27	M	Laborer	21De02Dw
GILLIGAN, Mick	27	M	None	21De02Dw
CRANE, Edward	30	M	Laborer	21De02Dw
OHARA, Dennis	30	M	Laborer	21De02Dw
MCMAHON, Thomas	31	M	Laborer	21De02Dw
MALCOLM, Michael	40	M	Laborer	21De02Dw
Dennis	20	M	Laborer	21De02Dw
ONEILL, Danl.	25	M	Laborer	21De02Dw
Michl.	20	M	Laborer	21De02Dw
RICE, John	25	M	Laborer	21De02Dw
HOPPENS, Michael	28	M	Laborer	21De02Dw
MORCUM, John	27	M	Laborer	21De02Dw
Mary	24	F	None	21De02Dw
Bridget	.00	F	Infant	21De02Dw
CARROLL, Thos.	17	M	None	21De02Dw
Bridget	16	F	None	21De02Dw
MOLLONY, John	35	M	Laborer	21De02Dw
Mary	30	F	None	21De02Dw
Cathl.	05	F	Child	21De02Dw
Mary	03	F	Child	21De02Dw
Johanna	.00	F	Infant	21De02Dw
ROARKE, James	20	M	Laborer	21De02Dw
BANNERS, Thos.	18	M	None	21De02Dw
NOTTY, U	19	F	None	21De02Dw
CHARLEWORTH, Chas.	24	M	Laborer	21De02Dw
WARLIN, Saml.	27	M	Laborer	21De02Dw
Mary	25	F	None	21De02Dw
John	.00	M	Infant	21De02Dw
COOPER, Geo.	25	M	Laborer	21De02Dw
MIDDLETON, Wm.	30	M	Laborer	21De02Dw
SMITH, Wm.	26	M	Laborer	21De02Dw
GOOSHERY, Joseph	24	M	Laborer	21De02Dw
CARROLL, Dorah	19	F	Laborer	21De02Dw
Charlotte	25	F	Laborer	21De02Dw
Dorah	03	F	Child	21De02Dw
DEVIN, John	20	M	Laborer	21De02Dw
REILLY, Bridget	18	F	None	21De02Dw
Mary	17	F	None	21De02Dw
FARLEY, Margaret	20	F	None	21De02Dw
DELANY, Thomas	20	M	Laborer	21De02Dw
MCCOWAN, Michael	18	M	Laborer	21De02Dw
COURT, Danl.	30	M	Laborer	21De02Dw
Ann	30	F	None	21De02Dw
John	03	M	Child	21De02Dw
Mary	02	F	Child	21De02Dw
MCLAUGHLIN, Cathl.	50	F	None	21De02Dw
Christopher	25	M	Laborer	21De02Dw
Thomas	17	M	Laborer	21De02Dw
COUGHAN, Mary	22	F	None	21De02Dw
MONAHAN, Biddy	24	F	None	21De02Dw
STAFFERY, Mary	19	F	None	21De02Dw
MCCANN, James	21	M	Laborer	21De02Dw
SMITH, Ann	20	F	None	21De02Dw
LEMMON, Patt	20	M	Laborer	21De02Dw
Richd.	21	M	Laborer	21De02Dw
LYNCH, Ann	20	F	None	21De02Dw
CONLAN, Mary	03	F	Child	21De02Dw
Cathr.	21	F	None	21De02Dw
FLANNAGAN, John	20	M	Laborer	21De02Dw
Michl.	04	M	Child	21De02Dw
KEENAN, Mary	18	F	None	21De02Dw
HADDEN, Robt.	28	M	Laborer	21De02Dw
Nancy	23	F	None	21De02Dw
John	.00	M	Infant	21De02Dw
ROARKE, Cath.	16	F	None	21De02Dw
COSGROVE, Michl.	12	M	None	21De02Dw
Esther	09	F	Child	21De02Dw
John	06	M	Child	21De02Dw

NAMES OF PASSENGERS		AGE	SEX	OCCUPATIONS	DATE PORT SHIP
COSGROVE, Charlotte		03	F	Child	21De02Dw
HANLY, Bridget		28	F	None	21De02Dw
Jane		09	F	Child	21De02Dw
CLARK, Cath.		10	F	None	21De02Dw
SMITH, Ann		17	F	None	21De02Dw
DONOHOE, Mary		06	F	Child	21De02Dw
STEWART, Michl.		25	M	Laborer	21De02Dw
Eliza		13	F	None	21De02Dw
BRICHEN, Peter		40	M	Laborer	21De02Dw
U	(W)	35	F	Wife	21De02Dw
William		10	M	Laborer	21De02Dw
Robert		08	M	Child	21De02Dw
Eliza		06	F	Child	21De02Dw
Thomas		05	M	Child	21De02Dw
Richard		03	M	Child	21De02Dw
John		11	M	None	21De02Dw
Geo.		09	M	Child	21De02Dw
Amelia		07	F	Child	21De02Dw
WATT, Nancy		02	F	Child	21De02Dw
MILTON, Geo.		25	M	Laborer	21De02Dw
U	(W)	25	F	Wife	21De02Dw
Thos.		20	M	Laborer	21De02Dw
Ann		05	F	Child	21De02Dw
Eliza		08	F	Child	21De02Dw
Jacob		06	M	Child	21De02Dw
Mary		03	F	Child	21De02Dw
Peter		.00	M	Infant	21De02Dw
GRAVE, Simon		24	M	Laborer	21De02Dw
FARRELL, Martin		24	M	None	21De02Dw
CODIE, Margaret		40	F	None	21De02Dw
Judy		08	F	Child	21De02Dw
Anthony		05	M	Child	21De02Dw
Mary		.00	F	Infant	21De02Dw
DEANE, E.		35	F	None	21De02Dw
C.		27	F	None	21De02Dw
RIPEL, Catharine		18	F	None	21De02Dw
Margaret-K.		20	F	None	21De02Dw
MASON, John		21	M	None	21De02Dw

PETER-HATTRICK 21 DECEMBER 1847

From Liverpool

NAMES OF PASSENGERS		AGE	SEX	OCCUPATIONS	DATE PORT SHIP
DUNN, Charles		31	M	Farmer	21De02Ck
Margaret	(W)	29	F	Wife	21De02Ck
Margaret	(D)	03	F	Child	21De02Ck
KENEDY, John		21	M	Weaver	21De02Ck
Mary		52	F	Nurse	21De02Ck
Nancy		12	F	Child	21De02Ck
MCKAY, James		25	M	Farmer	21De02Ck
Mary	(W)	21	F	Wife	21De02Ck
Henry	(S)	.10	M	Infant	21De02Ck
Patrick		16	M	Farmer	21De02Ck
Catharine		30	F	Servant	21De02Ck
Elizabeth		27	F	Weaver	21De02Ck
Bridget		23	F	Weaver	21De02Ck
Rose		20	F	Servant	21De02Ck
MAHER, Philip		27	M	Farmer	21De02Ck
Joannah	(W)	27	F	Wife	21De02Ck
John	(S)	03	M	Child	21De02Ck
Bridget	(D)	01	F	Child	21De02Ck
FLYNN, Timothy		28	M	Laborer	21De02Ck
Honora	(W)	20	F	Wife	21De02Ck
Mary	(D)	.03	F	Infant	21De02Ck
HOLERAN, Pat		25	M	Laborer	21De02Ck
James		23	M	Laborer	21De02Ck
Mary		28	F	Servant	21De02Ck
MURPHEY, Betsey		22	F	Servant	21De02Ck
Mary		09	F	Child	21De02Ck
CASLIN, Thady		38	M	Laborer	21De02Ck
CUNNINGHAM, Thomas		28	M	Farmer	21De02Ck
BALL, Mary		17	F	Servant	21De02Ck
MCDONALD, Margaret		24	F	Servant	21De02Ck
FITZPATRICK, Michael		50	M	Architect	21De02Ck
Margaret	(W)	42	F	Wife	21De02Ck
Mary		22	F	Unknown	21De02Ck
Albert		09	M	Child	21De02Ck
NOON, Dominick		28	M	Blacksmith	21De02Ck
Mary	(W)	22	F	Wife	21De02Ck
Pat	(S)	03	M	Child	21De02Ck
IRWIN, Jane		15	F	Servant	21De02Ck
MCCRORY, Ann		18	F	Servant	21De02Ck
BURNES, Martin		50	M	Farmer	21De02Ck
Martin		22	M	Farmer	21De02Ck
Mary		20	F	Servant	21De02Ck
Died-At-Sea					
John		13	M	Farmer	21De02Ck
Thomas		08	M	Child	21De02Ck
Bridget		05	M	Child	21De02Ck
DUKE, James		24	M	Farmer	21De02Ck
BURKE, Mary		26	F	Wife	21De02Ck
WARD, Ann		21	F	Servant	21De02Ck
LOUGHLEY, Matt		30	M	Laborer	21De02Ck
BOURKE, Biddy		20	F	Unknown	21De02Ck
LYNCH, Mary		40	F	Unknown	21De02Ck
CONNELY, Sarah		30	F	Wife	21De02Ck
Margaret	(D)	.00	F	Infant	21De02Ck
GARVIN, Catharine		18	F	Servant	21De02Ck
George		50	M	Smith	21De02Ck
SLATER, Margaret		22	F	Servant	21De02Ck
KEIRNARD, Owen		50	M	Laborer	21De02Ck
Ellen	(W)	41	F	Wife	21De02Ck
Michael	(S)	12	M	Child	21De02Ck
Mary	(D)	14	F	Child	21De02Ck
Biddy	(D)	11	F	Child	21De02Ck
MCGALE, James		36	M	Farmer	21De02Ck
Betsey	(W)	40	F	Wife	21De02Ck
John	(S)	11	M	Child	21De02Ck
James	(S)	07	M	Child	21De02Ck
RICE, Mary		45	F	Wife	21De02Ck
Patrick	(S)	18	M	Unknown	21De02Ck
James	(S)	13	M	Unknown	21De02Ck
Charles	(S)	10	M	Unknown	21De02Ck
Michael	(S)	09	M	Child	21De02Ck
MCPEAK, James		21	M	Farmer	21De02Ck
MCANAMIE, Andrew		27	M	Farmer	21De02Ck
MCFILLEN, Pat		20	M	Laborer	21De02Ck
DONOLY, Matilda		18	F	Servant	21De02Ck
DUGGAN, Sally		23	F	Servant	21De02Ck
MORAN, Mary		18	F	Servant	21De02Ck
OBRIEN, Betsey		23	F	Servant	21De02Ck
MILES, Ann		18	F	Servant	21De02Ck
MCBRIDE, Neal		18	M	Clerk	21De02Ck
KELLEY, Margaret		24	F	Servant	21De02Ck
FATTEN, Catharine		21	F	Servant	21De02Ck
CONNER, Honor		36	F	Servant	21De02Ck
NEARY, Edward		40	M	Laborer	21De02Ck
Mary	(W)	30	F	Wife	21De02Ck
Mary		20	F	Servant	21De02Ck
MANYON, Patt		40	M	Laborer	21De02Ck
Michael		10	M	Unknown	21De02Ck
Francis		04	M	Child	21De02Ck
GRADY, Peter		24	M	Farmer	21De02Ck
Margaret		23	F	Servant	21De02Ck
LACEY, Betsey		18	F	Servant	21De02Ck
Catharine		25	F	Servant	21De02Ck
ERVIN, John		40	M	Farmer	21De02Ck
Martha	(W)	40	F	Wife	21De02Ck
James	(S)	20	M	Unknown	21De02Ck
Gabriel	(S)	16	M	Unknown	21De02Ck
Joseph	(S)	13	M	Unknown	21De02Ck
Fanny	(D)	18	F	Unknown	21De02Ck
Martha	(D)	14	F	Unknown	21De02Ck
Rebecca	(D)	15	F	Unknown	21De02Ck

NAMES OF PASSENGERS		AGE	SEX	OCCUPATIONS	DATE PORT SHIP
ERVIN, Jane	(D)	08	F	Child	21De02Ck
Mary	(D)	07	F	Child	21De02Ck
WILKINS, Richard		19	M	Farmer	21De02Ck
DENISON, Wm.		38	M	Farmer	21De02Ck
Margaret	(W)	31	F	Wife	21De02Ck
Mary	(D)	08	F	Child	21De02Ck
Catharine	(D)	.00	F	Infant	21De02Ck
MURRAY, Patrick		24	M	Brush Maker	21De02Ck
MCCULLOUGH, Hannah		20	F	Servant	21De02Ck
GILLESPIE, Wm.		24	M	Weaver	21De02Ck
KIRKPATRICK, John		32	M	Saddler	21De02Ck
MCGRAVY, John		25	M	Tailor	21De02Ck
KILLEN, Wm.		23	M	Tailor	21De02Ck
MOORE, James		23	M	Farrier	21De02Ck
MCCUE, Margaret		21	F	Weaver	21De02Ck
REORDEN, Maurice		22	M	Servant	21De02Ck
Mary		34	F	Servant	21De02Ck
THOMPSON, Jane		27	F	Seamstress	21De02Ck
GEELAN, Mary		16	F	Servant	21De02Ck
BONNAM, John		28	M	Laborer	21De02Ck
DOYLE, Hugh		48	M	Farmer	21De02Ck
CONNEL, James		29	M	Rope Maker	21De02Ck
MAHER, Pat		45	M	Carter	21De02Ck
Ellen	(W)	50	F	Wife	21De02Ck
Mary	(D)	14	F	Unknown	21De02Ck
MCCRORY, Charles		50	M	Farmer	21De02Ck
Susan	(W)	40	F	Wife	21De02Ck
Nancy	(D)	13	F	Unknown	21De02Ck
Mary	(D)	11	F	Twin	21De02Ck
Barney	(S)	11	M	Twin	21De02Ck
Charles	(S)	07	M	Child	21De02Ck
Pat	(S)	05	M	Child	21De02Ck
Henry	(S)	03	M	Child	21De02Ck
QUIN, Daniel		20	M	Farmer	21De02Ck
CUNNINGHAM, Ellen		19	F	Servant	21De02Ck
LARKIN, Michael		30	M	Farmer	21De02Ck
Mary	(W)	30	F	Wife	21De02Ck
Bridget	(D)	16	F	Unknown	21De02Ck
Winney	(D)	00	F	Unknown	21De02Ck
Patrick	(S)	05	M	Child	21De02Ck
MOORE, Mary		22	F	Servant	21De02Ck
ROBERTS, Wm.		12	M	Unknown	21De02Ck
HAUGHNEY, James		28	M	Carpenter	21De02Ck
DONLY, Sarah-Ann		14	F	Servant	21De02Ck
GEELAN, Eliza		19	F	Seamstress	21De02Ck
FARLEY, Sarah		20	F	Servant	21De02Ck
John		16	M	Unknown	21De02Ck
KIERMAN, Elizabeth		03	F	Child	21De02Ck
SPEER, Rachael		20	F	Servant	21De02Ck
Susannah		16	F	Servant	21De02Ck
Eliza		11	F	None	21De02Ck
Morttea		09	F	None	21De02Ck

SHERIDAN 22 DECEMBER 1847

From Liverpool

NAMES OF PASSENGERS	AGE	SEX	OCCUPATIONS	DATE PORT SHIP
SHIELDS, Bernard	30	M	Laborer	22De02Do
HARRAN, Cathn.	24	F	Unknown	22De02Do
KELLY, Sarah	50	F	Servant	22De02Do
MARTIN, Thos.	30	M	Servant	22De02Do
BARRENS, Joseph	45	M	Servant	22De02Do
MURTAGH, Eliza	30	F	Servant	22De02Do
LYNCH, Mary	30	F	Servant	22De02Do
WHITE, Cathn.	50	F	Servant	22De02Do
Cathn.	20	F	Servant	22De02Do
Mary	18	F	Servant	22De02Do
Margret	14	F	Servant	22De02Do
Stephen	16	M	Servant	22De02Do

NAMES OF PASSENGERS	AGE	SEX	OCCUPATIONS	DATE PORT SHIP
WHITE, Michl.	14	M	Servant	22De02Do
DONNELLY, Michl.	32	M	Laborer	22De02Do
WARD, Margt.	50	F	Laborer	22De02Do
Peter	20	M	Laborer	22De02Do
Anne	18	F	Laborer	22De02Do
Cathn.	17	F	Laborer	22De02Do
MCGEE, John	19	M	Laborer	22De02Do
WOODS, Thos.	19	M	Laborer	22De02Do
BREEN, Mathew	24	M	Laborer	22De02Do
WOODS, Thm.	24	U	Laborer	22De02Do
Mary	23	F	Servant	22De02Do
FITZSIMMONS, Anne	16	F	Unknown	22De02Do
CLARK, Patt	24	M	Unknown	22De02Do
CONNOLLY, Ann	40	F	Laborer	22De02Do
Mathew	18	M	Unknown	22De02Do
Ann	17	F	Unknown	22De02Do
Michl.	10	M	Unknown	22De02Do
GLOVER, J.	30	M	Unknown	22De02Do
SANDER, Michel.	22	M	Unknown	22De02Do
MALONE, Fredrick	26	M	Weaver	22De02Do
KELLY, Thos.	21	M	Laborer	22De02Do
FELLON, John	23	M	Unknown	22De02Do
Honora	20	F	Unknown	22De02Do
COLEMAN, Michl.	22	M	Carpenter	22De02Do
CAMPBELL, Robt.	24	M	Shoemaker	22De02Do
DELWORTH, Benjamin	23	M	Carpenter	22De02Do
MCCARTY, Martin	30	M	Unknown	22De02Do
KENNADY, John	26	M	Blacksmith	22De02Do
CONROY, John	26	M	Laborer	22De02Do
LAWLER, Thos.	26	M	Blacksmith	22De02Do
SULLIVAN, John	28	M	Weaver	22De02Do
ONEILL, John	26	M	Dyer	22De02Do
COBBETT, George	30	M	Laborer	22De02Do
CARNEY, John	24	M	Laborer	22De02Do
WHITE, Patt	23	M	Laborer	22De02Do
MCAULEY, Henry	48	M	Laborer	22De02Do
Mary	40	F	Laborer	22De02Do
James	18	M	Laborer	22De02Do
DUNN, Celis	21	F	Servant	22De02Do
PHILLIPS, Julia	17	F	Unknown	22De02Do
RYAN, Bridget	17	F	Unknown	22De02Do
MOORE, James	17	M	Pphgr	22De02Do
SWEENEY, John	27	M	Bookbinder	22De02Do
BRADBURRY, Edwin	24	M	Spinner	22De02Do
Hannah	24	F	Spinner	22De02Do
MCCOCHILL, John	24	M	Laborer	22De02Do
Eliza	23	F	Servant	22De02Do
BURTON, John	26	M	Servant	22De02Do
DONOVAN, Anne	40	F	Servant	22De02Do
Maria	19	F	Servant	22De02Do
DROWLNY, Cathr.	21	F	Servant	22De02Do
LUNCH, Cathr.	22	F	Servant	22De02Do
Michl.	.00	M	Infant	22De02Do
RYAN, Martin	30	M	Laborer	22De02Do
Mary	26	F	Unknown	22De02Do
WYLIE, Wm.	21	M	Shoemaker	22De02Do
CRANFORD, Andrew	21	M	Laborer	22De02Do
FOSSETT, Jane	21	F	Servant	22De02Do
LUBELCOCK, James	19	M	Miner	22De02Do
Nicholas	22	M	Miner	22De02Do
ELLIOTT, Walter	22	M	Laborer	22De02Do
BEAN, Isaac	28	M	Servant	22De02Do
Eliza	26	F	None	22De02Do
Jacob	08	M	Child	22De02Do
ONEILL, Patt	20	M	Laborer	22De02Do
RYAN, Patt	18	M	Laborer	22De02Do
MCCORMICK, James	40	M	Unknown	22De02Do
RYAN, Michl.	40	M	Heckler	22De02Do
Died-At-Sea				
KIRKPATRICK, John	25	M	Unknown	22De02Do
LOFTUS, Thos.	35	M	Unknown	22De02Do
Bridget	32	F	None	22De02Do
John	10	M	Unknown	22De02Do
SHEPPARD, Sarah	24	F	Servant	22De02Do
BLACKLEY, Agnes	22	F	Unknown	22De02Do

NAMES OF PASSENGERS	AGE	SEX	OCCUPATIONS	DATE PORT SHIP
BLACKLEY, Mary	18	F	Unknown	22De02Do
Barbara	10	F	Unknown	22De02Do
MCCOY, Isaac	16	M	Laborer	22De02Do
Died-At-Sea				
Anne	18	F	Servant	22De02Do
BROWN, Abraham	45	M	Weaver	22De02Do
Wm.	24	M	Unknown	22De02Do
Susanna	32	F	Unknown	22De02Do
MURPHY, Maria	20	F	Servant	22De02Do
Alice	25	F	Unknown	22De02Do
MCKENNAN, Mary	20	F	Laborer	22De02Do
HIGGINS, Patk.	13	M	Laborer	22De02Do
KERR, Anne	30	F	Unknown	22De02Do
Biddy	12	F	Unknown	22De02Do
Peter	04	M	Child	22De02Do
U	.00	U	Infant	22De02Do
MORAN, James	50	M	Baker	22De02Do
Mary	40	F	None	22De02Do
Cathn.	06	F	Child	22De02Do
Ellen	03	F	Child	22De02Do
VERDOW, Sarah	30	F	Servant	22De02Do
TALBOTT, James	26	M	Laborer	22De02Do
HENRY, Henry	20	M	Unknown	22De02Do
Isabella	20	F	Unknown	22De02Do
TALBOT, Isabella	26	F	Servant	22De02Do
ROCKFORD, William	20	M	Laborer	22De02Do
MCKEOWN, William	25	M	Laborer	22De02Do
DOLAN, Dennis	38	M	Unknown	22De02Do
MCPOWN, Mary	23	F	Servant	22De02Do
Sarah	01	F	Child	22De02Do
OWENS, Sarah	21	F	Unknown	22De02Do
Eliza	17	F	Unknown	22De02Do
ROBB, James	18	M	Laborer	22De02Do
BEAN, Christopher	17	M	Unknown	22De02Do
RICHARDSON, John	13	M	Unknown	22De02Do
MALONE, Mary	25	F	Servant	22De02Do
Hannah	04	F	Child	22De02Do
Wm.	.00	M	Infant	22De02Do
MCCORMICK, Henry	39	M	Saddler	22De02Do
Charlotte	36	F	None	22De02Do
Ann-Matilda	05	F	Child	22De02Do
Joshua	02	M	Child	22De02Do
Eleanor	.00	F	Infant	22De02Do
LANNILY, Ann	20	F	Servant	22De02Do
HICKEY, John	21	M	Farmer	22De02Do
IVERS, John	22	M	Laborer	22De02Do
U (W)	21	F	Wife	22De02Do
HANNAN, Phillip	28	M	Laborer	22De02Do
MCACAROON, Mary	13	F	Laborer	22De02Do
Cathn.	15	F	Laborer	22De02Do
STEEL, Robert	20	M	Carpenter	22De02Do
KERNAN, Michl.	40	M	Mason	22De02Do
U (W)	40	F	Wife	22De02Do
Margret	17	F	Unknown	22De02Do
Mary	15	F	Unknown	22De02Do
James	12	M	Unknown	22De02Do
Thos.	08	M	Child	22De02Do
Arthr.	05	M	Child	22De02Do
Michl.	.00	M	Infant	22De02Do
SHERIDAN, Thomas	35	M	Laborer	22De02Do
Mary	18	F	Unknown	22De02Do
CAVANNAH, Michl.	25	M	Unknown	22De02Do
Biddy	20	F	Unknown	22De02Do
Patt	08	M	Child	22De02Do
DURNEY, Peggy	46	F	Servant	22De02Do
Mary	25	F	Unknown	22De02Do
GORDON, Mary	18	F	Unknown	22De02Do
FISHER, Charles	24	M	Laborer	22De02Do
CASSON, Wm.F.	30	M	Laborer	22De02Do
CANTY, Michl.	27	M	Laborer	22De02Do
Mary	25	F	Laborer	22De02Do
CLENCY, Ellen	21	F	Laborer	22De02Do
WALSH, David	21	M	Laborer	22De02Do
Patt	28	M	Laborer	22De02Do
PILLOW, Mary	20	F	Servant	22De02Do

NAMES OF PASSENGERS	AGE	SEX	OCCUPATIONS	DATE PORT SHIP
BAILEY, John	30	M	Laborer	22De02Do
Mary	28	F	None	22De02Do
Michl.	02	M	Child	22De02Do
Cathr.	20	F	Servant	22De02Do
Johanna	18	F	Unknown	22De02Do
TAYLOR, William	30	M	Laborer	22De02Do
RODDY, James	24	M	Laborer	22De02Do
William	19	M	Laborer	22De02Do
ROURKE, Wm.	27	M	Laborer	22De02Do
U (W)	25	F	Laborer	22De02Do
CORNEY, Lawrence	35	M	Laborer	22De02Do
John	16	M	Laborer	22De02Do
MARTIN, Joseph	20	M	Laborer	22De02Do
HUGHES, Henry	60	M	Laborer	22De02Do
Died-At-Sea				
Anne	60	F	Laborer	22De02Do
Anne	20	F	Laborer	22De02Do
CUNNINGHAM, Anthony	20	M	Laborer	22De02Do
FEELY, Thos.	20	M	Unknown	22De02Do
Bridget	20	F	Unknown	22De02Do
CUNNINGHAM, Jane	20	F	Servant	22De02Do
PHILLIPS, Phillip	20	M	Laborer	22De02Do
HUGHES, John	25	M	Unknown	22De02Do
CORRIGAN, John	25	M	Mason	22De02Do
Michl.	22	M	Mason	22De02Do
RYAN, Michl.	25	M	Carpenter	22De02Do
ONEILLE, Grace	40	F	Servant	22De02Do
MCSEALE, Dennis	26	M	Laborer	22De02Do
Wm.	24	M	Unknown	22De02Do
MCINNAN, Hannah	20	F	Servant	22De02Do
LYONS, Patt	20	M	Laborer	22De02Do
BURKE, Thos.	30	M	Unknown	22De02Do
TRACY, Hugh	30	M	Unknown	22De02Do
CORBITT, James	40	M	Turner	22De02Do
OBRIAN, Timothy	30	M	Weaver	22De02Do
MURPHY, Stephen	30	M	Unknown	22De02Do
MULLHALE, Fenton	28	M	Unknown	22De02Do
DORAN, Cathn.	24	F	Servant	22De02Do
MONAGHAN, John	24	M	Laborer	22De02Do
DONOHUGH, James	21	M	Unknown	22De02Do
ORR, Peggy	20	F	Servant	22De02Do
WEBHAM, Abby	20	F	Laborer	22De02Do
KEENNAN, Edwd.	20	M	Laborer	22De02Do
CARRIFF, Michl.	40	M	Unknown	22De02Do
SWADES, Mary	30	F	Servant	22De02Do
Thos.Edwin	07	M	Child	22De02Do
Hannah	05	F	Child	22De02Do
Dianna	04	F	Child	22De02Do
HALGATE, John	20	M	Laborer	22De02Do
HARLEY, Sally	20	F	Servant	22De02Do
WILSON, William	02	M	Child	22De02Do
SHERIDAN, Mary	22	F	Unknown	22De02Do
HAUGHLEY, Cathn.	50	F	Unknown	22De02Do
CLEMENTS, Margt.	14	F	Unknown	22De02Do
MURPHY, Alice	25	F	Unknown	22De02Do
SMITH, Saml.	17	M	Blacksmith	22De02Do
ODONNELL, Terrance	34	M	Laborer	22De02Do
John	16	M	Unknown	22De02Do
Mary	12	F	Unknown	22De02Do
LEFTUS, Margt.	10	F	Unknown	22De02Do
Wanney	08	F	Child	22De02Do
MURPHY, Mary	20	F	Servant	22De02Do
ENGLISH, Cathn.	30	F	Unknown	22De02Do
RYAN, Mary	.00	F	Infant	22De02Do
DARCY, Hugh	21	M	Laborer	22De02Do
REYLEY, James	30	M	Laborer	22De02Do
HEARDMAN, Hannah	20	F	Servant	22De02Do
HALLAHAN, Fanny	25	F	Servant	22De02Do
DONNELLEY, Jane	20	F	Unknown	22De02Do
SIMPSON, Patrick	20	M	Laborer	22De02Do
BALL, John	15	M	Unknown	22De02Do
MCGINNISS, Wm.	20	M	Shoemaker	22De02Do
MCGINGER, Alice	47	F	Servant	22De02Do
Rosanna	17	F	Unknown	22De02Do
Francis	16	M	Unknown	22De02Do

NAMES OF PASSENGERS	AGE	SEX	OCCUPATIONS	DATE PORT SHIP
MCGINGER, Cathn.	16	F	Unknown	22De02Do
Maria	12	F	Unknown	22De02Do
Anne	09	F	Child	22De02Do
BLAKE, Lawrence	26	M	Unknown	22De02Do
PURCELL, Mary	25	F	Unknown	22De02Do
GROAN, Fanny	16	F	Unknown	22De02Do
SHELEY, Walter	20	M	Laborer	22De02Do
PRIOR, Margt.	20	F	Servant	22De02Do
GORREGHTY, James	18	M	Laborer	22De02Do
CANTLAN, Peter	26	M	Tailor	22De02Do
FUSLEY, Patt	20	M	Laborer	22De02Do
TRACY, Thomas	18	M	Unknown	22De02Do
BATTLE, Cathn.	08	F	Child	22De02Do
MILLER, Cathn.	23	F	Servant	22De02Do
GRIMES, Eliza	18	F	Unknown	22De02Do
FLOOD, Phillip	25	M	Laborer	22De02Do
MULLIGAN, Mary	20	F	Servant	22De02Do
GAUSSEN, Wm.	21	M	Gentleman	22De02Do

NORTHUMBERLAND 22 DECEMBER 1847

From London

NAMES OF PASSENGERS	AGE	SEX	OCCUPATIONS	DATE PORT SHIP
DONMALL, Chas.	54	M	Professor	22De21Cg
Priscilla	52	F	None	22De21Cg
FARMER, William	36	M	Farmer	22De21Cg
OBRIEN, Bartholomew	30	M	Army	22De21Cg
COLMAN, Wm.T.	45	M	Army	22De21Cg
PRATT, Henry	26	M	Gentleman	22De21Cg
WYATT, Wm.	44	M	Mustchr	22De21Cg
Charlotte	43	F	None	22De21Cg
Charlotte	13	F	None	22De21Cg
Julian	09	M	Child	22De21Cg
MCCLERYN, Frdck.	24	M	Professor	22De21Cg
WALLER, Septor	19	M	Doctor	22De21Cg
PROCTOR, Mary	30	F	None	22De21Cg
Margot	18	F	None	22De21Cg
STONEMAN, Ruth	24	F	None	22De21Cg
Ruth	03	F	Child	22De21Cg
LYONS, Allahan	24	M	Tailor	22De21Cg
Esther	26	F	None	22De21Cg
GREENLAND, Francis	24	M	Miller	22De21Cg
Mini	49	F	None	22De21Cg
Emma	17	F	None	22De21Cg
STEVENS, Harriet	47	F	None	22De21Cg
WILKINSON, Wm.	39	M	Hatter	22De21Cg
Nancy	40	F	None	22De21Cg
Wm.	13	M	None	22De21Cg
Mary-Ann	05	F	Child	22De21Cg
TONE, James	32	M	Hatter	22De21Cg
EYLRS, Elizabeth	37	F	None	22De21Cg
Thos.	13	M	None	22De21Cg
Susan	10	F	None	22De21Cg
U	07	F	Child	22De21Cg
Robt.	05	M	Child	22De21Cg
Ann	03	F	Child	22De21Cg
Richard	01	M	Child	22De21Cg
Elizabeth	01	F	Child	22De21Cg
EDMONDS, Mary	50	F	None	22De21Cg
MARSHALL, Thos.	50	M	Farmer	22De21Cg
HYMEN, A---	28	M	Tailor	22De21Cg
Cath.	25	F	None	22De21Cg
Michael	.08	M	Infant	22De21Cg
LEVY, Saml.	20	M	Cbtmkr	22De21Cg
Judah	19	M	Cbtmkr	22De21Cg
JACOBS, Rebeca	73	F	None	22De21Cg
LAURENCE, Cath.	68	F	None	22De21Cg
MENTER, Will	20	M	Farmer	22De21Cg
RIELEY, Richd.	23	M	Farmer	22De21Cg
GAMBLE, Elizabeth	22	F	None	22De21Cg
HADOVER, John	32	M	Spinner	22De21Cg
WISCOMBE, Will	55	M	Engineer	22De21Cg
Eliza	30	F	None	22De21Cg
FLINDT, Henry	31	M	Tailor	22De21Cg
HART, Eliza	22	F	None	22De21Cg
HARDY, Alixa	25	M	Tailor	22De21Cg
GROSS, Martin	29	M	Farmer	22De21Cg
BURN, James	39	M	Farmer	22De21Cg
EDCOMB, Wm.	52	M	Farmer	22De21Cg
Mary-A.	53	F	None	22De21Cg
Wm.	25	M	Farmer	22De21Cg
WINKLEHOUSE, Grut.	37	M	Laborer	22De21Cg
TONI, M.	40	M	Farmer	22De21Cg
Benjamin	04	M	Child	22De21Cg
SHMIDT, Jacob	23	M	Tailor	22De21Cg
CATTNIG, Robt.	45	M	Farmer	22De21Cg
WATSON, Wm.	32	M	Gdnr	22De21Cg
Charlotte	26	F	None	22De21Cg
Esther	64	F	None	22De21Cg
Saml.	10	M	None	22De21Cg
Wm.	08	M	Child	22De21Cg
George	06	M	Child	22De21Cg
Charlotte	04	F	Child	22De21Cg
Francis	02	M	Child	22De21Cg
Edward	.06	M	Infant	22De21Cg
HILLS, Louisa	17	F	None	22De21Cg
Betsy	15	F	None	22De21Cg
THURSTON, James	48	M	Farmer	22De21Cg
SERN, Wm.	28	M	Clerk	22De21Cg
MONEN, George	31	M	Mason	22De21Cg
TRAPP, Chester	30	M	Tailor	22De21Cg
CASE, Henry-A.	34	M	Farmer	22De21Cg
OPPEINHEIMER, Benjamin	25	M	Furrier	22De21Cg
GRENICAN, G.	27	M	Tailor	22De21Cg
WHITE, Phillip	34	M	Farmer	22De21Cg
Cath.	30	F	None	22De21Cg
Jacob	10	M	None	22De21Cg
Henry	06	M	Child	22De21Cg
Mary	04	F	Child	22De21Cg
WELCH, Wm.	25	M	Clerk	22De21Cg
Ann	23	F	None	22De21Cg
Mary-A.	.09	F	Infant	22De21Cg
BERRY, James	44	M	Tailor	22De21Cg
NEWBACK, Peter	34	M	Tailor	22De21Cg
BONNER, John	24	M	Painter	22De21Cg
Caroline	24	F	None	22De21Cg
MCNOB, John	23	M	Farmer	22De21Cg
CLANCY, Mary	30	F	None	22De21Cg
Wm.	05	M	Child	22De21Cg
Thos.	03	M	Child	22De21Cg
Henry	.06	M	Infant	22De21Cg
BUCKNELL, Chas.	66	M	Wheelwright	22De21Cg
PHILLIPS, Math.	26	M	Porter	22De21Cg
Ann	65	F	None	22De21Cg
ALEXANDER, A.	29	M	Tailor	22De21Cg

ADVENTURE 24 DECEMBER 1847

From PICTOU, N.S.

NAMES OF PASSENGERS	AGE	SEX	OCCUPATIONS	DATE PORT SHIP
MURPHY, Wm.	27	M	Carpenter	24De43Su

HAMPDEN 27 DECEMBER 1847

From Liverpool

NAMES OF PASSENGERS		AGE	SEX	OCCUPATIONS	DATE PORT SHIP
HADFELD, John		24	M	Laborer	27De02Hz
BANCROFT, R.		26	M	Laborer	27De02Hz
THORNLY, Eli		23	M	Laborer	27De02Hz
KILROY, Michael		36	M	Laborer	27De02Hz
Ellen		29	F	None	27De02Hz
CONNER, Henry		24	M	Laborer	27De02Hz
U	(W)	22	F	None	27De02Hz
Prucella	(D)	.00	F	Infant	27De02Hz
KING, John		30	M	Laborer	27De02Hz
CONNER, John		44	M	Laborer	27De02Hz
U	(W)	36	F	None	27De02Hz
Mary	(D)	08	F	Child	27De02Hz
Michael	(S)	06	M	Child	27De02Hz
Bridget	(D)	02	F	Child	27De02Hz
Mark	(S)	.00	M	Infant	27De02Hz
DUFFY, Patk.		30	M	Laborer	27De02Hz
U	(W)	33	F	None	27De02Hz
Mary	(D)	04	F	Child	27De02Hz
Margaret	(D)	.00	F	Infant	27De02Hz
DONAHUE, Thomas		23	M	Laborer	27De02Hz
GILL, Catherine		19	F	None	27De02Hz
DUFFY, Bridget		34	F	None	27De02Hz
Mary		12	F	None	27De02Hz
John		09	M	Child	27De02Hz
Geo.		04	M	Child	27De02Hz
Ellen		.00	F	Infant	27De02Hz
GROWEN, John		30	M	Laborer	27De02Hz
Andy		20	M	Laborer	27De02Hz
Mary		22	F	None	27De02Hz
GILNEY, Ann		17	F	None	27De02Hz
MCELVEY, Hugh		27	M	Laborer	27De02Hz
BARRETT, Mary		40	F	None	27De02Hz
Jane		13	F	None	27De02Hz
John		09	M	Child	27De02Hz
William		07	M	Child	27De02Hz
Bridget		.00	F	Infant	27De02Hz
MCGUIRE, Dan		41	M	Laborer	27De02Hz
U	(W)	36	F	None	27De02Hz
Bridget	(D)	12	F	None	27De02Hz
Hannah	(D)	10	F	None	27De02Hz
REYLEY, Philip		27	M	Laborer	27De02Hz
Margaret		27	F	None	27De02Hz
KING, David		20	M	Laborer	27De02Hz
FITZSIMMONS, Pat		15	M	Laborer	27De02Hz
Edward		13	M	None	27De02Hz
SHANGHNEY, Peter		40	M	Laborer	27De02Hz
MURDOCK, Alexander		23	M	Laborer	27De02Hz
MCKEE, James		20	M	Laborer	27De02Hz
MCMINON, Robert		21	M	Laborer	27De02Hz
BREARD, John		27	M	Laborer	27De02Hz
FAY, Eliza		26	F	None	27De02Hz
SMITH, James		30	M	Laborer	27De02Hz
Jane		30	F	None	27De02Hz
CONOGHY, James		17	M	Laborer	27De02Hz
GRAY, Wm.		20	M	None	27De02Hz
SMITH, Catharine		25	F	None	27De02Hz
ARMSTRONG, Wm.		30	M	Laborer	27De02Hz
U		25	F	None	27De02Hz
LECAS, Daniel		20	M	None	27De02Hz
U	(W)	18	F	None	27De02Hz
James	(S)	.00	M	Infant	27De02Hz
SMYTH, Patk.		20	M	Laborer	27De02Hz
KETTLE, Margaret		18	F	None	27De02Hz
SMITH, Mary		18	F	None	27De02Hz
PENDERS, S.W.		27	M	None	27De02Hz
MCGARR, Allen		41	M	Laborer	27De02Hz
MARTIN, Patk.		26	M	Laborer	27De02Hz
REYNOLDS, Eliza		23	F	None	27De02Hz
SLEVINS, James		22	M	Laborer	27De02Hz
MCMANUS, John		21	M	Laborer	27De02Hz
COLLINS, Michael		37	M	Laborer	27De02Hz
MCAULTY, James		26	M	Laborer	27De02Hz
Ellen		20	F	None	27De02Hz
MCLAUGHLIN, John		20	M	None	27De02Hz
Patrick		15	M	None	27De02Hz
Edward		07	M	None	27De02Hz
BRADEN, Samuel		21	M	Laborer	27De02Hz
GURNGIN, Michael		24	M	Laborer	27De02Hz
HAGUE, Henry		25	M	Laborer	27De02Hz
FLOOD, Owen		24	M	Laborer	27De02Hz
U	(W)	22	F	None	27De02Hz
Margaret		20	F	None	27De02Hz
Mary		20	F	None	27De02Hz
James		22	M	Laborer	27De02Hz
CONNEY, John		22	M	Laborer	27De02Hz
Bridget	(W)	20	F	None	27De02Hz
COSTELLAR, John		20	M	Laborer	27De02Hz
ROWDEN, Andrew		23	M	Laborer	27De02Hz
GRAY, Terrence		40	M	Laborer	27De02Hz
Eliza	(W)	30	F	None	27De02Hz
Catharine		04	F	Child	27De02Hz
MCCROMB, Owen		18	M	None	27De02Hz
BURN, Jos.		31	M	Laborer	27De02Hz
Rachael	(W)	26	F	None	27De02Hz
MCGRATH, Thomas		45	M	Laborer	27De02Hz
Johan		20	M	Laborer	27De02Hz
Margaret		10	F	None	27De02Hz
MEE, Thomas		22	M	Laborer	27De02Hz
DOUD, Wm.		26	M	Laborer	27De02Hz
WHITE, Thomas		20	M	Laborer	27De02Hz
John		16	M	Laborer	27De02Hz
EMEN, Geo.		22	M	Laborer	27De02Hz
COPELAND, Hugh		25	M	Laborer	27De02Hz
POWER, Edward		20	M	Laborer	27De02Hz
FIELDS, Geo.		52	M	Laborer	27De02Hz
CAIN, John		30	M	Laborer	27De02Hz
MILLER, Edward		38	M	Laborer	27De02Hz
U	(W)	38	F	None	27De02Hz
James	(S)	12	M	None	27De02Hz
Thomas	(S)	10	M	None	27De02Hz
Martha	(D)	08	F	Child	27De02Hz
Susan	(D)	06	F	Child	27De02Hz
Eliza	(D)	02	F	Child	27De02Hz
MURPHEY, James		30	M	Laborer	27De02Hz
John		09	M	Child	27De02Hz
James		07	M	Child	27De02Hz
Mary		05	F	Child	27De02Hz
Margaret		04	F	Child	27De02Hz
Edward		02	M	Child	27De02Hz
MORNELL, Rutts		30	M	Laborer	27De02Hz
Sarah-J.		02	F	Child	27De02Hz
DURNE, Catharine		34	F	None	27De02Hz
James		11	M	None	27De02Hz
Ann		09	F	Child	27De02Hz
Jane		07	F	Child	27De02Hz
RIGGS, May-A.		45	F	None	27De02Hz
MUSICA, May-A.		27	F	None	27De02Hz
BRIGGS, James		15	M	Laborer	27De02Hz
MOSSNUN, Charles		18	M	Laborer	27De02Hz
Mary-J.		.00	F	Infant	27De02Hz
MCCUTCHEON, John		30	M	Laborer	27De02Hz
FRANCIS, M.		26	M	Laborer	27De02Hz
James		07	M	Child	27De02Hz
May-A.		05	F	Child	27De02Hz
MCCUTRON, Edward		02	M	Child	27De02Hz
Richard		.00	M	Infant	27De02Hz
RIGGS, Edward		20	M	Laborer	27De02Hz
John		09	M	Child	27De02Hz
May		07	F	Child	27De02Hz
Ellen		05	F	Child	27De02Hz

NAMES OF PASSENGERS		AGE	SEX	OCCUPATIONS	DATE PORT SHIP
RIGGS, Eliza		04	F	Child	27De02Hz
Thomas		02	M	Child	27De02Hz
RENLEY, Mary		36	F	None	27De02Hz
James		15	M	None	27De02Hz
Edward		10	M	None	27De02Hz
Mary		08	F	Child	27De02Hz
Eliza		06	F	Child	27De02Hz
Margaret		04	F	Child	27De02Hz
LEMAN, Martin		25	M	Laborer	27De02Hz
KELLY, John		25	M	Laborer	27De02Hz
MCCORTNEY, Samuel		30	M	Laborer	27De02Hz
FORD, U-Mrs.		32	F	None	27De02Hz
J.A., U		30	F	None	27De02Hz
CLARKIN, Michael		25	M	Laborer	27De02Hz
RAMSBOTTOM, Joshua		24	M	Laborer	27De02Hz
Jane	(W)	23	F	None	27De02Hz
Jane		05	F	Child	27De02Hz
Ann		.00	F	Infant	27De02Hz
CONNELLY, Mary		24	F	None	27De02Hz
FORNEY, Pat.		20	M	Laborer	27De02Hz
Michael		17	M	Laborer	27De02Hz
GOUN, Geo.		20	M	Laborer	27De02Hz
FORNEY, Margaret		20	F	None	27De02Hz
HIGGINS, Ann		20	F	None	27De02Hz
MCGURN, M.		40	M	Laborer	27De02Hz
Bridget		14	F	None	27De02Hz
Eliza		13	F	None	27De02Hz
CANNON, Owen		25	M	Laborer	27De02Hz
U	(W)	24	F	None	27De02Hz
Pat.	(S)	.00	M	Infant	27De02Hz
BREE, Michael		25	M	Laborer	27De02Hz
MENY, Dennis		25	M	Laborer	27De02Hz
HART, Thomas		18	M	Laborer	27De02Hz
Michael		12	M	None	27De02Hz
MCNULTY, Bridget		14	F	None	27De02Hz
COLLINS, Pat		20	M	Laborer	27De02Hz
Richard		19	M	Laborer	27De02Hz
Andrew		18	M	Laborer	27De02Hz
FERGUSON, Francis		26	M	Laborer	27De02Hz
Mary	(W)	24	F	None	27De02Hz
JUDGE, John		30	M	Laborer	27De02Hz
Jane	(W)	26	F	None	27De02Hz
KEANNEY, Elona		26	F	None	27De02Hz
MCGUNNY, Eliza		22	F	None	27De02Hz
THOMAS, John		30	M	Laborer	27De02Hz
U	(W)	30	F	None	27De02Hz
Marie	(D)	12	F	None	27De02Hz
Thomas	(S)	07	M	Child	27De02Hz
James	(S)	05	M	Child	27De02Hz
Henry	(S)	04	M	Child	27De02Hz
CARLIN, John		24	M	Laborer	27De02Hz
WHITETREAD, Andrew		29	M	Laborer	27De02Hz
WATSON, John		24	M	Laborer	27De02Hz
MCCUNLY, Allen		30	M	Laborer	27De02Hz
WALKER, Johana		22	F	None	27De02Hz
MUNCY, Patrick		30	M	Laborer	27De02Hz
SHEA, John-C.		30	M	Laborer	27De02Hz
LYONS, Margaret		16	F	None	27De02Hz
CALLAHAN, John		25	M	Laborer	27De02Hz
SHAUGHNEY, Michael		35	M	Laborer	27De02Hz
Patk.		13	M	None	27De02Hz
MALEY, John		40	M	Laborer	27De02Hz
John		11	M	None	27De02Hz
COSTELLO, John		40	M	Laborer	27De02Hz
Catharine		13	F	None	27De02Hz
Margaret		07	F	Child	27De02Hz
LARKIN, Thomas		25	M	Laborer	27De02Hz
Martin		20	M	Laborer	27De02Hz
CARNEVY, John		35	M	Laborer	27De02Hz
BRODERICK, Patk.		22	M	Laborer	27De02Hz
DOUGLASS, David		25	M	Laborer	27De02Hz
MCQUADE, Francis		26	F	None	27De02Hz
Mary		16	F	None	27De02Hz
Patrick		06	M	Child	27De02Hz
Ann		03	F	Child	27De02Hz
MCQUADE, Francis		.00	F	Infant	27De02Hz
MONGHAN, James		16	M	None	27De02Hz
TRACEY, May		24	F	None	27De02Hz
FITGERALD, Patk.		30	M	Laborer	27De02Hz
WOODS, David		20	M	Laborer	27De02Hz
MCMALAN, Bridget		30	F	None	27De02Hz
HAMILTON, Charles		28	M	Laborer	27De02Hz
KELLEY, Ann		18	F	None	27De02Hz
Surg---, Thomas		17	M	None	27De02Hz
MCMULON, Margaret		40	F	None	27De02Hz
WALSH, Mary		10	F	None	27De02Hz
Michael		08	M	Child	27De02Hz
Wm.		06	M	Child	27De02Hz
Ann		20	F	None	27De02Hz
MCMALON, Catharine		38	F	None	27De02Hz
SWEENEY, Catharine		26	F	None	27De02Hz
CARLIN, Peter		20	M	None	27De02Hz
HENLY, John		08	M	Child	27De02Hz
LEONARD, Ellen		20	F	None	27De02Hz
WALL, Thomas		18	M	Laborer	27De02Hz
Marcy		28	F	None	27De02Hz
HANLY, Honor		03	F	Child	27De02Hz
Martin		27	M	Laborer	27De02Hz
SHUBERRY, M.		25	M	Laborer	27De02Hz
LALE, Wm.		05	M	Child	27De02Hz
SMITH, Andrew		08	M	Child	27De02Hz
CLERKIN, Peter		20	M	Laborer	27De02Hz

NIANTIC 28 DECEMBER 1847

From Liverpool

NAMES OF PASSENGERS		AGE	SEX	OCCUPATIONS	DATE PORT SHIP
MCCORMACK, James		50	M	Farmer	28De02Sv
Kitty	(W)	40	F	None	28De02Sv
Margaret		07	F	Child	28De02Sv
Robert		12	M	None	28De02Sv
Michael		09	M	Child	28De02Sv
CULLEN, Mary		20	F	Servant	28De02Sv
HINLY, John		30	M	Farmer	28De02Sv
VARIS, Thomas		26	M	Laborer	28De02Sv
ENGLAND, Julia		17	F	Servant	28De02Sv
COLLINS, Catherine		30	F	Servant	28De02Sv
QUINN, Bibby		18	F	Servant	28De02Sv
COWLEY, Mary		20	F	Servant	28De02Sv
HOWEY, Hugh		40	M	Servant	28De02Sv
Bibby		16	F	Servant	28De02Sv
LALLY, James		30	M	Farmer	28De02Sv
Mary	(W)	30	F	None	28De02Sv
Mary		16	F	None	28De02Sv
Margaret		03	F	Child	28De02Sv
Michael		13	M	None	28De02Sv
James		10	M	None	28De02Sv
Patrick		07	M	Child	28De02Sv
John		05	M	Child	28De02Sv
MALONE, Peter		18	M	None	28De02Sv
DOLAN, Mary		17	F	None	28De02Sv
KING, Mary		26	F	Servant	28De02Sv
Anne		18	F	Servant	28De02Sv
Bibby		15	F	Servant	28De02Sv
Michael		12	M	Servant	28De02Sv
RYAN, Thomas		21	M	Laborer	28De02Sv
MCCALL, Owen		25	M	Laborer	28De02Sv
CARBENAY, Bibby		34	F	Servant	28De02Sv
BARRY, Ellen		26	F	Servant	28De02Sv
Thomas		12	M	Servant	28De02Sv
CAMERON, Charles		60	M	Servant	28De02Sv

BRAZILIAN 29 DECEMBER 1847

From SYDNEY,Cape-Breton

NAMES OF PASSENGERS		AGE	SEX	OCCUPATIONS	DATE PORT SHIP
RYAN, Wm.		30	M	Laborer	29De34Sw
SKEHAN, John		30	M	Laborer	29De34Sw
MADDOX, John		20	M	Shoemaker	29De34Sw
DOYLE, Dennis		23	M	Laborer	29De34Sw
Patrick		24	M	Laborer	29De34Sw
TOBIN, Pierce		50	M	Laborer	29De34Sw
Patt		20	M	Laborer	29De34Sw
Pierce-Jr.		16	M	Shoemaker	29De34Sw
RYAN, Patrick		45	M	Laborer	29De34Sw

BREAM 29 DECEMBER 1847

From St.JOHNS,N.B.

NAMES OF PASSENGERS		AGE	SEX	OCCUPATIONS	DATE PORT SHIP
MCDERMOTT, James		40	M	Joiner	29De79Sx

SPEEDWELL 03 JANUARY 1848

From St.Anns-Bay-Jamaica

NAMES OF PASSENGERS		AGE	SEX	OCCUPATIONS	DATE PORT SHIP
BARKER, Wm.		23	M	Planter	03Ja85Eh
U		10	M	Planter	03Ja85Eh

TORONTO 05 JANUARY 1848

From London

NAMES OF PASSENGERS		AGE	SEX	OCCUPATIONS	DATE PORT SHIP
LIONS, Pat		30	M	Carpenter	05Ja21Ba
DELANY, John		49	M	Engineer	05Ja21Ba
James		24	M	Mariner	05Ja21Ba

EMBLEM 10 JANUARY 1848

From Londonderry

NAMES OF PASSENGERS		AGE	SEX	OCCUPATIONS	DATE PORT SHIP
NELSON, Elisha		20	M	None	10Ja01Pq
Charlotte		19	F	None	10Ja01Pq
Ellen		15	F	None	10Ja01Pq
Rose		13	F	None	10Ja01Pq
Eliza		11	F	None	10Ja01Pq
John		11	M	None	10Ja01Pq
NELSON, Hugh		06	M	Child	10Ja01Pq
SINCLAIR, Edward		32	M	Farmer	10Ja01Pq
U	(W)	25	F	None	10Ja01Pq
Catherine	(D)	02	F	Child	10Ja01Pq
Marion	(S)	07	M	Child	10Ja01Pq
CORR, Mary		19	F	None	10Ja01Pq
GORMLEY, Michael		28	M	Laborer	10Ja01Pq
Sally	(W)	24	F	None	10Ja01Pq
CRAWLEY, Charles		35	M	Laborer	10Ja01Pq
DEGNUN, Mary		22	F	None	10Ja01Pq
KELLY, Mary		19	F	None	10Ja01Pq
VESEY, Delia		20	F	None	10Ja01Pq
CONNOR, Biddy		19	F	None	10Ja01Pq
SOVATT, Sally		20	F	None	10Ja01Pq
FIGHE, Thomas		21	M	Laborer	10Ja01Pq
LOGAN, Ann		20	F	None	10Ja01Pq
RYLEY, Mary		20	F	None	10Ja01Pq
Ann		18	F	None	10Ja01Pq
Julia		13	F	None	10Ja01Pq
Wm.		11	M	None	10Ja01Pq
CORRIGAN, Edwin		42	M	Farmer	10Ja01Pq
U	(W)	42	F	None	10Ja01Pq
Ann	(D)	19	F	None	10Ja01Pq
KENNEY, Michael		19	M	Laborer	10Ja01Pq
Catherine		23	F	None	10Ja01Pq
CORRIGAN, Catherine		11	F	None	10Ja01Pq
Eliza		09	F	None	10Ja01Pq
Edward		13	M	None	10Ja01Pq
Pat		10	M	None	10Ja01Pq
Biddy		07	F	Child	10Ja01Pq
John		04	M	Child	10Ja01Pq
Jane		11	F	Child	10Ja01Pq
ONEIL, Pat		19	M	Laborer	10Ja01Pq
KELLY, Michael		22	M	Carpenter	10Ja01Pq
MURRY, Edward		24	M	Laborer	10Ja01Pq
KELLY, Mary		20	F	None	10Ja01Pq

ANN-HARLEY 13 JANUARY 1848

From Glasgow

NAMES OF PASSENGERS		AGE	SEX	OCCUPATIONS	DATE PORT SHIP
WILSON, William		45	M	Peddler	13Ja04Db
George		13	M	Peddler	13Ja04Db
DIVAN, James		20	M	Tailor	13Ja04Db
LONG, Ann		28	F	None	13Ja04Db
TURNER, Sarah		18	F	None	13Ja04Db
CASSIDY, Margaret		23	F	Weaver	13Ja04Db
Elisabeth		24	F	Weaver	13Ja04Db
MCDIVIT, James		20	M	Laborer	13Ja04Db

MONTEZUMA 14 JANUARY 1848

From Newcastle

NAMES OF PASSENGERS		AGE	SEX	OCCUPATIONS	DATE PORT SHIP
LENARD, Patrick		46	M	Laborer	14Ja66Ao
Mary		67	F	Laborer	14Ja66Ao
Died-At-Sea					
Simon		32	M	Laborer	14Ja66Ao
Peter		30	M	Laborer	14Ja66Ao
Thomas		15	M	Laborer	14Ja66Ao
Jane		28	F	Laborer	14Ja66Ao
Margaret		19	F	Laborer	14Ja66Ao
MCLAUGHLIN, James		10	M	Laborer	14Ja66Ao

NAMES OF PASSENGERS		AGE	SEX	OCCUPATIONS	DATE PORT SHIP
LENARD, Thomas		08	M	Child	14Ja66Ao
Wynford		04	M	Child	14Ja66Ao
Thomas		.09	M	Infant	14Ja66Ao
James		21	M	Laborer	14Ja66Ao

ABERDEEN 15 JANUARY 1848

From Liverpool

NAMES OF PASSENGERS		AGE	SEX	OCCUPATIONS	DATE PORT SHIP
MCGUIRE, Peter		20	M	Farmer	15Ja02Ek
EDMUNSON, Jane		26	F	None	15Ja02Ek
Margt		26	F	None	15Ja02Ek
CARSON, Isabella		35	F	None	15Ja02Ek
Esther		04	F	Child	15Ja02Ek
ROWAN, Pat		30	M	Farmer	15Ja02Ek
Bridgt.		30	F	None	15Ja02Ek
Martha	(D)	02	F	Child	15Ja02Ek
CRAWFORD, Jane		20	F	None	15Ja02Ek
James		40	M	Farmer	15Ja02Ek
HALLONAN, Pat		30	M	Clerk	15Ja02Ek
James		03	M	Child	15Ja02Ek
Bridgit		30	F	None	15Ja02Ek
Ellen		04	F	Child	15Ja02Ek
TULLY, Mickey		27	M	Farmer	15Ja02Ek
Bridgt.		27	F	None	15Ja02Ek
KELLY, Jane		29	F	None	15Ja02Ek
REILLY, Mick		50	M	Farmer	15Ja02Ek
Margt.		50	F	None	15Ja02Ek
Rose		11	F	None	15Ja02Ek
Ann		09	F	Child	15Ja02Ek
KELLY, John		40	M	Farmer	15Ja02Ek
Thomas		04	M	Child	15Ja02Ek
Margt.		07	F	Child	15Ja02Ek
Bessy		05	F	Child	15Ja02Ek
Ellen		02	F	Child	15Ja02Ek
GIBNAY, Bridgt.		20	F	None	15Ja02Ek
MCCABE, Bridgt.		57	F	None	15Ja02Ek
Mary		20	F	None	15Ja02Ek
Ally		11	F	None	15Ja02Ek
John		51	M	Farmer	15Ja02Ek
COLLINS, Elsoth		28	M	Farmer	15Ja02Ek
CAROLINE, Edward		28	M	Farmer	15Ja02Ek
SANDERSON, Wm.		21	M	Tailor	15Ja02Ek
DUFFIE, Jas.		29	M	Tailor	15Ja02Ek
MCGIRKE, Pat		21	M	Shoemaker	15Ja02Ek
ROONY, Tom		50	M	Shoemaker	15Ja02Ek
U	(W)	50	F	None	15Ja02Ek
MCGUIRE, Jno.		20	M	Farmer	15Ja02Ek
MCGUILLON, Phil		37	M	Farmer	15Ja02Ek
DOOLING, Jas.		39	M	Butcher	15Ja02Ek
RUDDY, Mick		20	M	Farmer	15Ja02Ek
CUNION, Pat		26	M	Laborer	15Ja02Ek
MISULDO, Bessy		12	F	None	15Ja02Ek
LATTIMORE, Geo.		27	M	Teacher	15Ja02Ek
Eliza		31	F	None	15Ja02Ek
Mary		03	F	Child	15Ja02Ek
Ellen		18	F	None	15Ja02Ek
Mary		18	F	None	15Ja02Ek
Jas.		26	M	Farmer	15Ja02Ek
CAULFIELD, John		26	M	Laborer	15Ja02Ek
Wm.		26	M	Laborer	15Ja02Ek
HANNELL, Wm.		26	M	Laborer	15Ja02Ek
Edward		09	M	Child	15Ja02Ek
James		06	M	Child	15Ja02Ek
Arthur		03	M	Child	15Ja02Ek
Robt		02	M	Child	15Ja02Ek
GARGAN, Pat		20	M	Hrsm	15Ja02Ek
MULLIN, Thos.		30	M	Farmer	15Ja02Ek
Micheal		04	M	Child	15Ja02Ek
MULLIN, John		13	M	Farmer	15Ja02Ek
Mick		02	M	Child	15Ja02Ek
U	(W)	30	F	None	15Ja02Ek
WALDRON, Mary		21	F	None	15Ja02Ek
Hanora		20	F	None	15Ja02Ek
FLOYER, U		40	F	None	15Ja02Ek
Thos.		40	M	Laborer	15Ja02Ek
Pat		20	M	Laborer	15Ja02Ek
Mick		12	M	Laborer	15Ja02Ek
Terry		13	M	Laborer	15Ja02Ek
Tom		12	M	Laborer	15Ja02Ek
John		11	M	Laborer	15Ja02Ek
Wm.		06	M	Child	15Ja02Ek
Barny		09	M	Child	15Ja02Ek
James		07	M	Child	15Ja02Ek
HIGGINS, Mary		21	F	None	15Ja02Ek
MCGORMAN, Ellen		20	F	None	15Ja02Ek
PALMER, John		40	M	Organist	15Ja02Ek
DOWEY, John		20	M	Organist	15Ja02Ek
Thos.		13	M	Organist	15Ja02Ek
Barny		11	M	Organist	15Ja02Ek
Levi		09	M	Organist	15Ja02Ek
RIDGE, H.		18	M	Organist	15Ja02Ek
John		13	M	Organist	15Ja02Ek
Geo.		13	M	Organist	15Ja02Ek
MCKEENY, Bryan		40	M	Farmer	15Ja02Ek
Mary	(W)	40	F	None	15Ja02Ek
Bessy	(D)	04	F	Child	15Ja02Ek
Phillis	(D)	02	F	Child	15Ja02Ek
Mary	(D)	01	F	Child	15Ja02Ek
WHALON, U		40	F	None	15Ja02Ek
Andro		40	M	Farmer	15Ja02Ek
COCHLIN, Sam		20	M	Farmer	15Ja02Ek
FEELY, John		21	M	Farmer	15Ja02Ek
WARD, Frank		20	M	Farmer	15Ja02Ek
Owen		21	M	Farmer	15Ja02Ek
Anne		17	F	None	15Ja02Ek
PURCELL, Anty		21	F	None	15Ja02Ek
HARRIS, Mary		20	F	None	15Ja02Ek
Nancy		20	F	None	15Ja02Ek
SHEA, Mary		28	F	None	15Ja02Ek
Michael		32	M	Farmer	15Ja02Ek
Thos.		02	M	Child	15Ja02Ek
TOHEY, Jas.		40	M	Farmer	15Ja02Ek
Jas.		09	M	Child	15Ja02Ek
Anne		08	F	Child	15Ja02Ek
Kate		03	F	Child	15Ja02Ek
Rurson		02	F	Child	15Ja02Ek
WAYNE, John		50	M	Farmer	15Ja02Ek
SCALLY, James		03	M	Child	15Ja02Ek
Mary		29	F	None	15Ja02Ek
Cath.		05	F	Child	15Ja02Ek
Sarah		02	F	Child	15Ja02Ek
LOGAN, Mick		20	M	Blacksmith	15Ja02Ek
John		20	M	Blacksmith	15Ja02Ek
Pat		05	M	Child	15Ja02Ek
Francis		04	M	Child	15Ja02Ek
MCGOVERN, Sally		21	F	None	15Ja02Ek
Bridgt.	(D)	02	F	Child	15Ja02Ek
WANNY, Rose		26	F	None	15Ja02Ek
CONLY, Cecilia		20	F	None	15Ja02Ek
ROBINSON, Caroline		20	F	None	15Ja02Ek
FITZPATRICK, Mary		20	F	None	15Ja02Ek
GARGON, Rose		20	F	None	15Ja02Ek
MONAHAN, Barnd.		20	M	Farmer	15Ja02Ek
MARTIN, Phil		20	M	Farmer	15Ja02Ek
HALFPENNY, Pat		30	M	Farmer	15Ja02Ek
BEGGY, Connor		27	M	Shoemaker	15Ja02Ek
GAYNOR, Pat		20	M	Farmer	15Ja02Ek
MCKERNON, Pat		20	M	Farmer	15Ja02Ek

SEA 17 JANUARY 1848

From Liverpool

NAMES OF PASSENGERS		AGE	SEX	OCCUPATIONS	DATE PORT SHIP
NOLMES, Wm.		20	M	Laborer	17Ja02Bg
HILL, Jesse		28	M	Laborer	17Ja02Bg
HORISH, Widow		40	F	Spinster	17Ja02Bg
ENGLISHBY, Patrick		23	M	Laborer	17Ja02Bg
Cathy		17	F	None	17Ja02Bg
MCGUIRE, John		15	M	Laborer	17Ja02Bg
IRVIR, Namah		16	F	Spinster	17Ja02Bg
Jane		15	F	Spinster	17Ja02Bg
MULKEAMS, John		18	M	Laborer	17Ja02Bg
Bridget		20	F	None	17Ja02Bg
NEAHY, Thos.		40	M	Laborer	17Ja02Bg
FURREY, Mary		16	F	Spinster	17Ja02Bg
MARR, John		32	M	Laborer	17Ja02Bg
DOYLE, Thos.		20	M	Laborer	17Ja02Bg
MCKENNA, Michael		20	M	Laborer	17Ja02Bg
MULOONY, Michael		14	M	Laborer	17Ja02Bg
Pat		11	M	Laborer	17Ja02Bg
MURPHY, Timothy		24	M	Laborer	17Ja02Bg
NELSON, John		19	M	Laborer	17Ja02Bg
Mary		25	F	Spinster	17Ja02Bg
OBRIEN, Cath.		07	F	Child	17Ja02Bg
Mary		04	F	Child	17Ja02Bg
DORGAN, Pat		17	M	Laborer	17Ja02Bg
James		11	M	Laborer	17Ja02Bg
QUINN, Margt		30	F	Spinster	17Ja02Bg
Ann		09	F	Child	17Ja02Bg
Hannah		07	F	Child	17Ja02Bg
Mary		03	F	Child	17Ja02Bg
James		.00	M	Infant	17Ja02Bg
MCDERMAT, Cath.		28	F	None	17Ja02Bg
Peter		03	M	Child	17Ja02Bg
MCGUIRE, Michael		17	M	Laborer	17Ja02Bg
ASH, Cath.		49	F	None	17Ja02Bg
John		16	M	Laborer	17Ja02Bg
Thos.		12	M	Laborer	17Ja02Bg
Bridgit		11	F	None	17Ja02Bg
Mary		09	F	Child	17Ja02Bg
Michael		06	M	Child	17Ja02Bg
Kate		04	F	Child	17Ja02Bg
Jane		02	F	Child	17Ja02Bg
MURRAY, Magt		40	F	None	17Ja02Bg
Phillip		07	M	Child	17Ja02Bg
MULVANEY, Mary		30	F	None	17Ja02Bg
FOYER, Manvah		19	M	Laborer	17Ja02Bg
NUTTER, John		26	M	Laborer	17Ja02Bg
HURRISCH, Wm.		38	M	Laborer	17Ja02Bg
U-Mrs.		36	F	None	17Ja02Bg
Lucy		04	F	Child	17Ja02Bg
Jane		02	F	Child	17Ja02Bg
Ann		.00	F	Infant	17Ja02Bg
COX, Michael		41	M	Laborer	17Ja02Bg
U-Mrs.		38	F	Laborer	17Ja02Bg
DODSON, Danl		48	M	Laborer	17Ja02Bg
U	(W)	46	F	Laborer	17Ja02Bg
Harriet	(D)	20	F	Spinster	17Ja02Bg
Joseph	(S)	18	M	Laborer	17Ja02Bg
Maria	(D)	15	F	Spinster	17Ja02Bg
Sarah	(D)	12	F	Spinster	17Ja02Bg
Elizabeth	(D)	11	F	Spinster	17Ja02Bg
Rich	(S)	08	M	Child	17Ja02Bg
Cath.	(D)	05	F	Child	17Ja02Bg
Hannah	(D)	02	F	Child	17Ja02Bg
TAYLOR, Wm.		25	M	Farmer	17Ja02Bg
U-Mrs.		25	F	None	17Ja02Bg
SUTHERLAND, A.		23	M	Farmer	17Ja02Bg
MCNESPRICK, Hugh		28	M	Farmer	17Ja02Bg
DAILY, Bridgit		20	F	None	17Ja02Bg
KELLY, Edward		40	M	Laborer	17Ja02Bg
Rose		38	F	None	17Ja02Bg
Jane		12	F	None	17Ja02Bg
Thos.		09	M	Child	17Ja02Bg
Mary		07	F	Child	17Ja02Bg
Joseph		05	M	Child	17Ja02Bg
Cath.		02	F	Child	17Ja02Bg
John		.00	M	Infant	17Ja02Bg
CONOLLY, John		18	M	Laborer	17Ja02Bg
MCCOLGAN, Dominick		40	M	Laborer	17Ja02Bg
Elinor		40	F	None	17Ja02Bg
John		17	M	Laborer	17Ja02Bg
Mary		16	F	None	17Ja02Bg
Eliza		13	F	None	17Ja02Bg
Pat		13	M	Laborer	17Ja02Bg
Margt		11	F	None	17Ja02Bg
Susannah		09	F	None	17Ja02Bg
Nancy		07	F	Child	17Ja02Bg
Micheal		04	M	Child	17Ja02Bg
Sarah		02	F	Child	17Ja02Bg
GORMAN, John		22	M	Laborer	17Ja02Bg
SLAVIN, Henry		61	M	Farmer	17Ja02Bg
Hannah		58	F	None	17Ja02Bg
Barney		10	M	None	17Ja02Bg
James		18	M	Farmer	17Ja02Bg
Ann		18	F	None	17Ja02Bg
HAMILTON, Wm.		18	M	Laborer	17Ja02Bg
MELVAN, Ann		25	F	None	17Ja02Bg
BUCKLEY, Edmund		25	M	Laborer	17Ja02Bg
Jas.		28	M	Laborer	17Ja02Bg
BOOTH, James		19	M	Laborer	17Ja02Bg
Sarah		18	F	None	17Ja02Bg
Emily		08	F	Child	17Ja02Bg
BOYLE, Jas.		18	M	Laborer	17Ja02Bg
FAIN, John		50	M	Laborer	17Ja02Bg
NORISH, Pat		35	M	Laborer	17Ja02Bg
CLARK, Teddy		28	M	Laborer	17Ja02Bg
RIELLY, Ellen		18	F	None	17Ja02Bg
NED, John		25	M	Laborer	17Ja02Bg
MCGOVERN, Sarah		40	F	None	17Ja02Bg
Jas.		11	M	None	17Ja02Bg
Cath.		09	F	Child	17Ja02Bg
BARD, Wm.		23	M	Laborer	17Ja02Bg
WILLIAM, John		32	M	Laborer	17Ja02Bg
NEILL, Jas.		30	M	Laborer	17Ja02Bg
U-Mrs.		28	F	None	17Ja02Bg
TOMER, Thos.		56	M	Farmer	17Ja02Bg
HODDELL, Wm.		48	M	Joiner	17Ja02Bg
BENNETT, Edward		21	M	Laborer	17Ja02Bg
NEALE, Wm.		21	M	Laborer	17Ja02Bg
Alphonso		44	M	Laborer	17Ja02Bg
MCLANGLY, John		21	M	Laborer	17Ja02Bg
CLARKSON, Thos.		23	M	Laborer	17Ja02Bg
MCMAHON, Sally		29	F	Spinster	17Ja02Bg
MCCARROLL, Rose		16	F	None	17Ja02Bg
DROSS, George		23	M	Laborer	17Ja02Bg
GILBERT, Eli		32	M	Laborer	17Ja02Bg
GREEN, Jas.		18	M	Laborer	17Ja02Bg
PRICE, Wm.		18	M	Laborer	17Ja02Bg
MCERLAND, Patrick		38	M	Laborer	17Ja02Bg
QUINN, John		41	M	Laborer	17Ja02Bg
DEMPSEY, Bridgit		19	F	Spinster	17Ja02Bg
LARKIN, Ann		28	F	Spinster	17Ja02Bg
Cath.		27	F	Spinster	17Ja02Bg
KANE, Marvin		25	M	Laborer	17Ja02Bg
MCKEOWN, Biddy		30	F	Spinster	17Ja02Bg
PAGE, Wm.		20	M	Laborer	17Ja02Bg
U-Mrs.		20	F	None	17Ja02Bg
GURNSHAW, Solmon		21	M	Laborer	17Ja02Bg
PELLA, Danl.		45	M	Laborer	17Ja02Bg
TUCKER, R.		36	M	Laborer	17Ja02Bg
Ann		28	F	None	17Ja02Bg
MOSS, Elizbth		18	F	None	17Ja02Bg

NAMES OF PASSENGERS	AGE	SEX	OCCUPATIONS	DATE PORT SHIP
MADDON, Winnifred	28	F	None	17Ja02Bg
TERRY, Wm.	22	M	Laborer	17Ja02Bg
CALE, Barney	18	M	Laborer	17Ja02Bg
COBER, Morro	39	M	Laborer	17Ja02Bg
NOTT, Jas.	39	M	Laborer	17Ja02Bg
TAYLOR, Jas.	31	M	Laborer	17Ja02Bg
WEST, Wm.	23	M	Laborer	17Ja02Bg
BERSON, Wm.	22	M	Laborer	17Ja02Bg
HARTLEY, Jas.	28	M	Laborer	17Ja02Bg
MILLTHORPE, Frank	21	M	Laborer	17Ja02Bg
WATERHOUSE, George	56	M	Laborer	17Ja02Bg
John	18	M	Laborer	17Ja02Bg
ROBERTS, Joseph	26	M	Laborer	17Ja02Bg
WEBSTER, Fred	19	M	Laborer	17Ja02Bg
WILSON, Wm.	30	M	None	17Ja02Bg
GREEN, U-Mr.	30	M	None	17Ja02Bg
JONES, U-Mr.	28	M	None	17Ja02Bg

MONTEZUMA 17 JANUARY 1848

From Liverpool

NAMES OF PASSENGERS	AGE	SEX	OCCUPATIONS	DATE PORT SHIP
CREIGHTON, James	24	M	Gentleman	17Ja02Ao
FARLEY, Rod	04	M	Child	17Ja02Ao
Patt	06	M	Child	17Ja02Ao
SMITH, Bridgit	16	F	Laborer	17Ja02Ao
Mary	20	F	Laborer	17Ja02Ao
KEEGAN, Michael	19	M	Laborer	17Ja02Ao
DOUGHTY, Patt	27	M	Laborer	17Ja02Ao
Elizabeth	35	F	Laborer	17Ja02Ao
SACHWELL, Charles	32	M	Carpenter	17Ja02Ao
Mary	38	F	None	17Ja02Ao
Henry	11	M	None	17Ja02Ao
Thomas	08	M	Child	17Ja02Ao
Elizabeth	05	F	Child	17Ja02Ao
Elanore	02	F	Child	17Ja02Ao
LYMAN, Mathew	22	M	Weaver	17Ja02Ao
PASSMORE, William	52	M	Clfn	17Ja02Ao
SWEENY, William	23	M	Carpenter	17Ja02Ao
MCMICHAEEL, Catherine	34	F	Lad	17Ja02Ao
Eliza	12	F	None	17Ja02Ao
Mary-Ann	10	F	None	17Ja02Ao
William	08	M	Child	17Ja02Ao
Margt	06	F	Child	17Ja02Ao
Robert	03	M	Child	17Ja02Ao
KEENAN, Patt	18	M	Farmer	17Ja02Ao
OMALLY, Michael	21	M	Farmer	17Ja02Ao
William	27	M	Farmer	17Ja02Ao
Edward	20	M	Farmer	17Ja02Ao
JONES, Thomas	28	M	Farmer	17Ja02Ao
Mary	18	F	None	17Ja02Ao
PERGMAN, Ann	20	F	Dressmaker	17Ja02Ao
KEENAN, Ann	20	F	Dressmaker	17Ja02Ao
WHALON, Margt.	20	F	Dressmaker	17Ja02Ao
DYAS, Mary	18	F	Dressmaker	17Ja02Ao
Margt.	20	F	Dressmaker	17Ja02Ao
MCDONALD, Maria	18	F	Dressmaker	17Ja02Ao
WHALON, Redmond	24	M	Poulterer	17Ja02Ao
MATHEW, John	35	M	Postillion	17Ja02Ao
THOMPSON, Christy	25	M	Postillion	17Ja02Ao
Mary	45	F	Laborer	17Ja02Ao
GAHORTY, Michael	27	M	Laborer	17Ja02Ao
MCQUICK, William	25	M	Laborer	17Ja02Ao
Mary	24	F	Laborer	17Ja02Ao
KINGSMAN, Elizabeth	33	F	Laborer	17Ja02Ao
Henry	07	M	Child	17Ja02Ao
Luke	06	M	Child	17Ja02Ao
Eliza	05	F	Child	17Ja02Ao
WAPON, David	15	M	Laborer	17Ja02Ao

NAMES OF PASSENGERS	AGE	SEX	OCCUPATIONS	DATE PORT SHIP
WAPON, Isabella	17	F	Laborer	17Ja02Ao
MCKREIG, Patt	22	M	Laborer	17Ja02Ao
KELLY, John	23	M	Laborer	17Ja02Ao
COONEY, Catherine	40	F	Laborer	17Ja02Ao
LOOZ, Hugh	50	M	Laborer	17Ja02Ao
John	15	M	Laborer	17Ja02Ao
CONNELLY, John	20	M	Laborer	17Ja02Ao
SESSON, John	24	M	Laborer	17Ja02Ao
Margt.	18	F	Laborer	17Ja02Ao
KILLORE, Elizabeth	18	F	Laborer	17Ja02Ao
Bridget	13	F	Laborer	17Ja02Ao
BELL, Samuel	22	M	Laborer	17Ja02Ao
MCLELLAND, Robert	23	M	Laborer	17Ja02Ao
KANLY, John	36	M	Laborer	17Ja02Ao
TRACEY, Mary	21	F	Laborer	17Ja02Ao
CARTY, Mary	23	F	Laborer	17Ja02Ao
NAUGHTON, James	35	M	Laborer	17Ja02Ao
LYNCH, Philip	22	M	Laborer	17Ja02Ao
PARLY, Mary	25	F	Laborer	17Ja02Ao
DALY, John	18	M	Laborer	17Ja02Ao
KEENAN, Mary	19	F	Lad	17Ja02Ao
Ann	17	F	Lad	17Ja02Ao
BURKE, Patt	31	M	Wheelwright	17Ja02Ao
Ann	18	F	Dressmaker	17Ja02Ao
Julia	16	F	Dressmaker	17Ja02Ao
MAHONY, James	12	M	Dressmaker	17Ja02Ao
HILL, Charles	24	M	Laborer	17Ja02Ao
DONOGAN, Bartholomew	17	M	Laborer	17Ja02Ao
HARPER, Margt.	19	F	Laborer	17Ja02Ao
MCGOWAN, Eliza	30	F	Laborer	17Ja02Ao
Catherine	08	F	Child	17Ja02Ao
MCCORMAN, Patt	06	M	Child	17Ja02Ao
Bridget	03	F	Child	17Ja02Ao
DURMAN, Julia	30	F	Laborer	17Ja02Ao
Bridget	20	F	Laborer	17Ja02Ao
CAMPBELL, Thomas	25	M	Laborer	17Ja02Ao
LYON, Barnard	25	M	Laborer	17Ja02Ao
LENNON, Ann	17	F	Laborer	17Ja02Ao
Bridget	16	F	Laborer	17Ja02Ao
CONNELY, Mary	24	F	Laborer	17Ja02Ao
BRYAN, Margt.	35	F	Laborer	17Ja02Ao
TOLHER, Margt.	28	F	Laborer	17Ja02Ao
KENNEDY, Margt.	02	F	Child	17Ja02Ao
TOLHER, Johanna	20	F	Laborer	17Ja02Ao
PANAGEN, Ellen	22	F	Laborer	17Ja02Ao
BRENAN, James	21	M	Laborer	17Ja02Ao
HOOLAHAN, Bridget	21	F	Laborer	17Ja02Ao
CLARK, Catherine	35	F	Laborer	17Ja02Ao
SLATTERY, Catherine	19	F	Laborer	17Ja02Ao
Margt.	25	F	Laborer	17Ja02Ao
MCCOLLOUGH, Jane	21	F	Dressmaker	17Ja02Ao
TAHY, Margt.	17	F	Laborer	17Ja02Ao
KELLY, Michael	17	M	Laborer	17Ja02Ao
CALLAGHAN, Abby	22	F	Laborer	17Ja02Ao
BRADY, John	07	M	Child	17Ja02Ao
GRADY, Mary	03	F	Child	17Ja02Ao
OBRIEN, Mary	27	F	Laborer	17Ja02Ao
GILLIDANS, Andrew	20	M	Laborer	17Ja02Ao
KELLY, Johanna	16	F	Laborer	17Ja02Ao
FANELL, Catherine	19	F	Laborer	17Ja02Ao
BURKE, Mary	30	F	Laborer	17Ja02Ao
Mary	03	F	Child	17Ja02Ao
Owen	07	M	Child	17Ja02Ao
ENGLISH, Ellen	17	F	Laborer	17Ja02Ao
MONROE, Bridget	26	F	Laborer	17Ja02Ao
Owen	07	M	Child	17Ja02Ao
Bridget	05	F	Child	17Ja02Ao
Catherine	03	F	Child	17Ja02Ao
QUIN, Margt.	24	F	None	17Ja02Ao
Mary-Ann	02	F	Child	17Ja02Ao
CARNAL, Julia	40	F	None	17Ja02Ao
Catherine	14	F	None	17Ja02Ao
James	12	M	Laborer	17Ja02Ao
LYNCH, Ann	25	F	Laborer	17Ja02Ao
CATON, Peter	27	M	Laborer	17Ja02Ao

NAMES OF PASSENGERS	AGE	SEX	OCCUPATIONS	DATE PORT SHIP
SMITH, John	24	M	Tailor	17Ja02Ao
TAYLOR, Thomas	43	M	Cooper	17Ja02Ao
Ellen	39	F	None	17Ja02Ao
Mary	13	F	None	17Ja02Ao
Jane-Ann	11	F	None	17JaC2Ao
Jason	08	M	Child	17Ja02Ao
Sarah	05	F	Child	17Ja02Ao
Alexander	02	M	Child	17Ja02Ao
ZUBERMAN, Mary	16	F	Laborer	17Ja02Ao
DEVON, Alice	15	F	Laborer	17Ja02Ao
LAVERTY, Ann	20	F	Laborer	17Ja02Ao
BURKE, Margt.	12	F	None	17Ja02Ao
Johanna	40	F	Laborer	17Ja02Ao
WOODS, Patt	21	M	Laborer	17Ja02Ao
MCQUADE, Neil	30	M	Laborer	17Ja02Ao
Onez	30	F	None	17Ja02Ao
Ellen	10	F	None	17Ja02Ao
SHERIDAN, Philip	60	M	Farmer	17Ja02Ao
Mary	56	F	None	17Ja02Ao
Ann	18	F	None	17Ja02Ao
Margt.	17	F	None	17Ja02Ao
Brein	14	U	None	17Ja02Ao
Philip	08	M	Child	17Ja02Ao
William	22	M	Laborer	17Ja02Ao
GIBNEY, Margt.	18	F	None	17Ja02Ao
MCNOBB, Thomas	26	M	Laborer	17Ja02Ao
Mary	24	F	None	17Ja02Ao
REID, Thomas	17	M	Laborer	17Ja02Ao
COOK, Peter	21	M	Laborer	17Ja02Ao
BLACK, Jane	19	F	None	17Ja02Ao
James	25	M	Laborer	17Ja02Ao
LYON, Isaac	35	M	Laborer	17Ja02Ao
COSLEY, Ann	21	F	None	17Ja02Ao
RODNEY, Catherine	30	F	None	17Ja02Ao
ROONEY, John	06	M	Child	17Ja02Ao
Mary	03	F	Child	17Ja02Ao
EDWARDS, Ignatio	17	M	Laborer	17Ja02Ao
NOONAN, Mathew	27	M	Laborer	17Ja02Ao
KERNEY, Peter	18	M	Laborer	17Ja02Ao
CONNAN, James	20	M	Laborer	17Ja02Ao
Michael	56	M	Laborer	17Ja02Ao
CENOUGHLAN, Michael	03	M	Child	17Ja02Ao
REYNOLDS, Ann	24	F	None	17Ja02Ao
GRELSON, Mary	27	F	None	17Ja02Ao
Catherine	21	F	None	17Ja02Ao
KENNY, Mary	26	F	None	17Ja02Ao
Terrance	16	M	Laborer	17Ja02Ao
BROWN, Mary-Ann	20	F	None	17Ja02Ao
JOYCE, Catherine	22	F	None	17Ja02Ao
John	04	M	Child	17Ja02Ao
PHELAN, Ann	45	F	Laborer	17Ja02Ao
Johanna	15	F	Laborer	17Ja02Ao
Maria	12	F	Laborer	17Ja02Ao
James	10	M	Laborer	17Ja02Ao
BROWN, Bridget	18	F	Laborer	17Ja02Ao
SLAVAN, James	17	M	Laborer	17Ja02Ao
Patt	30	M	Laborer	17Ja02Ao
COLGAN, Patt	30	M	Weaver	17Ja02Ao
BLANCH, Patt	19	M	Weaver	17Ja02Ao
CANNON, Joseph	27	M	Mason	17Ja02Ao
Mary	02	F	Child	17Ja02Ao
DILLION, Michael	18	M	Carpenter	17Ja02Ao
Lucy	22	F	None	17Ja02Ao
MURRY, Mary-Ann	04	F	Child	17Ja02Ao
Francis	03	F	Child	17Ja02Ao
Rosanna	14	F	None	17Ja02Ao
LOUGHLY, Thomas	25	M	Laborer	17Ja02Ao
CLOONAN, John	25	M	Laborer	17Ja02Ao
MCGROTH, Mary	50	F	None	17Ja02Ao
Sarah	24	F	None	17Ja02Ao
REYNOLDS, Edward	28	M	Laborer	17Ja02Ao
MULLIGAN, Wm.	21	M	Laborer	17Ja02Ao
VANELL, Bridget	00	F	None	17Ja02Ao
Ellen	30	F	Laborer	17Ja02Ao
Mary	01	F	Child	17Ja02Ao

NAMES OF PASSENGERS	AGE	SEX	OCCUPATIONS	DATE PORT SHIP
ARMSTRONG, Mary	30	F	Laborer	17Ja02Ao
COOK, Mary	20	F	None	17Ja02Ao
REILLY, Mary	20	F	None	17Ja02Ao
KELLY, Ann	13	F	None	17Ja02Ao
John	16	M	Laborer	17Ja02Ao
CARNEY, Patt	20	M	Laborer	17Ja02Ao
Ann	18	F	None	17Ja02Ao
WATSON, Nancy	45	F	None	17Ja02Ao
Samuel	19	M	Laborer	17Ja02Ao
Sarah	17	F	None	17Ja02Ao
Robert	15	M	None	17Ja02Ao
William	13	M	None	17Ja02Ao
Margt.	10	F	None	17Ja02Ao
MCBARN, Margt.	68	F	None	17Ja02Ao
Patt	72	M	Laborer	17Ja02Ao
Conner	20	M	Laborer	17Ja02Ao
Ann	22	F	None	17Ja02Ao
GRIMES, William	60	M	Laborer	17Ja02Ao
William	13	M	Laborer	17Ja02Ao
James	50	M	Laborer	17Ja02Ao
REILLY, John	23	M	Laborer	17Ja02Ao
SINKER, John	30	M	Laborer	17Ja02Ao
Ann	25	F	None	17Ja02Ao
TAYLOR, James	44	M	Laborer	17Ja02Ao
RITCHER, William	30	M	Merchant	17Ja02Ao

HENRY-CLAY 17 JANUARY 1848

From Liverpool

NAMES OF PASSENGERS	AGE	SEX	OCCUPATIONS	DATE PORT SHIP
WEBB, David	27	M	None	17Ja02Co
Hester	30	F	None	17Ja02Co
Job	15	M	None	17Ja02Co
Amellia	.00	F	Infant	17Ja02Co
POLLOCK, Thomas	40	M	None	17Ja02Co
Betty	35	F	None	17Ja02Co
James	20	M	None	17Ja02Co
Thomas	14	M	None	17Ja02Co
CHADWICK, Mw.	40	M	None	17Ja02Co
Elizbth.	12	F	None	17Ja02Co
John	07	M	Child	17Ja02Co
James	05	M	Child	17Ja02Co
FARRWORTH, John	25	M	None	17Ja02Co
Jane	23	F	None	17Ja02Co
Mary	.00	F	Infant	17Ja02Co
CUMMINS, Ruth	26	F	None	17Ja02Co
MURPHY, Darrl.	40	M	None	17Ja02Co
William	22	M	None	17Ja02Co
Ann	18	F	None	17Ja02Co
Bridgt.	.00	F	Infant	17Ja02Co
Math.	20	M	None	17Ja02Co
Christopher	14	M	None	17Ja02Co
REILLY, Mary	12	F	None	17Ja02Co
Bridgt.	15	F	None	17Ja02Co
Michl.	20	M	None	17Ja02Co
Henry	18	M	None	17Ja02Co
Lawrence	16	M	None	17Ja02Co
Ann	15	F	None	17Ja02Co
Catherine	14	F	None	17Ja02Co
Michl.	10	M	None	17Ja02Co
DONNELE, Sarah	21	F	None	17Ja02Co
SMITH, Bryan	40	M	None	17Ja02Co
Patrick	10	M	None	17Ja02Co
REILLY, Frank	20	M	None	17Ja02Co
GILLICK, Ann	20	F	None	17Ja02Co
KERR, Mary	16	F	None	17Ja02Co
CONDY, Mary	18	F	None	17Ja02Co
Madge	12	F	None	17Ja02Co
COOK, Ellen	14	F	None	17Ja02Co

NAMES OF PASSENGERS	AGE	SEX	OCCUPATIONS	DATE PORT SHIP
KERR, Mary	16	F	None	17Ja02Co
MCGUIRE, Patt	13	M	None	17Ja02Co
DALTON, Chr.	22	M	None	17Ja02Co
DOGHERTY, Mary	30	F	None	17Ja02Co
Patrick	10	M	None	17Ja02Co
CASAHIR, Peter	26	M	None	17Ja02Co
Mary	24	F	None	17Ja02Co
Ann	02	F	Child	17Ja02Co
Mary	.00	F	Infant	17Ja02Co
BARRETT, Mary	45	F	None	17Ja02Co
John	20	M	None	17Ja02Co
Rebecca	12	F	None	17Ja02Co
Henry	07	M	Child	17Ja02Co
Margt.	04	F	Child	17Ja02Co
HUER, James	36	M	None	17Ja02Co
MCCABE, Daniel	30	M	None	17Ja02Co
TURNER, John	32	M	None	17Ja02Co
HOFF, John	21	M	None	17Ja02Co
HURRINGHAM, Edwd.	36	M	None	17Ja02Co
ERAUS, Isaac	28	M	None	17Ja02Co
PICKERING, Willm.	26	M	None	17Ja02Co
CARR, Saml.	35	M	None	17Ja02Co
Jane	30	F	None	17Ja02Co
James	02	M	Child	17Ja02Co
Robert	.00	M	Infant	17Ja02Co
BROWN, Wm.	18	M	None	17Ja02Co
DRENAN, Ann	21	F	None	17Ja02Co
YORK, Wm.	16	M	None	17Ja02Co
Died-At-Sea				
GASTLAND, Geo.	11	M	None	17Ja02Co
COHEN, Patk.	24	M	None	17Ja02Co
BOZLAN, Andw.	21	M	None	17Ja02Co
BROADBENT, Jas.	24	M	None	17Ja02Co
Sarah	25	F	None	17Ja02Co
Mary-Alice	08	F	Child	17Ja02Co
Mary	04	F	Child	17Ja02Co
Benjamin	.00	M	Infant	17Ja02Co
SCOON, Chas.	24	M	None	17Ja02Co
LEGERWOOD, Geo.	23	M	None	17Ja02Co
FEDIGAN, Joseph	25	M	None	17Ja02Co
CARTHY, Thos.	30	M	None	17Ja02Co
BERGIN, Margt.	25	F	None	17Ja02Co
John	.00	M	Infant	17Ja02Co
Martin	27	M	None	17Ja02Co
WHITE, Peter	22	M	None	17Ja02Co
KENEDY, Patt	20	M	None	17Ja02Co
MCCABE, James	40	M	None	17Ja02Co
Mary	40	F	None	17Ja02Co
Henry	19	M	None	17Ja02Co
KELLY, Biddy	20	F	None	17Ja02Co
MURPHY, Thos.	26	M	None	17Ja02Co
REGAN, James	22	M	None	17Ja02Co
MURPHY, Thos	28	M	None	17Ja02Co
REGAN, Winney	19	F	None	17Ja02Co
MCDONNELL, Mary	18	F	None	17Ja02Co
BRUER, Elija	12	M	None	17Ja02Co
MURPHY, Saml.	.00	M	Infant	17Ja02Co
HANDCOCK, Elizth.	18	F	None	17Ja02Co
Charles	10	M	None	17Ja02Co
DEVITT, Edw.	26	M	None	17Ja02Co
Elija	22	M	None	17Ja02Co
CASSIDY, James	28	M	None	17Ja02Co
MARA, Martin	25	M	None	17Ja02Co
GLEESON, John	23	M	None	17Ja02Co
Catherine	24	F	None	17Ja02Co
Ann	16	F	None	17Ja02Co
KELLY, Margt.	14	F	None	17Ja02Co
HOWE, Mary	17	F	None	17Ja02Co
MAHER, Bridgt.	24	F	None	17Ja02Co
GLEESON, Wm.	30	M	None	17Ja02Co
RYAN, Margt.	23	F	None	17Ja02Co
QUINN, Mary	24	F	None	17Ja02Co
CAMPBELL, Mary	16	F	None	17Ja02Co
Margt.	25	F	None	17Ja02Co
Daniel	13	M	None	17Ja02Co

NAMES OF PASSENGERS	AGE	SEX	OCCUPATIONS	DATE PORT SHIP
CAMPBELL, Thomas	12	M	None	17Ja02Co
PAUL, William	30	M	None	17Ja02Co
CORNEY, Thos.	26	M	None	17Ja02Co
SMITH, John	35	M	None	17Ja02Co
NEVILL, James	27	M	None	17Ja02Co
Sarah	29	F	None	17Ja02Co
MOCKS, George	32	M	None	17Ja02Co
CLARKE, Ann	27	F	None	17Ja02Co
Mary	24	F	None	17Ja02Co
WALKER, John	30	M	None	17Ja02Co
Mary	26	F	None	17Ja02Co
Henry	24	M	None	17Ja02Co
ROGERS, Patt	21	M	None	17Ja02Co
MONAHAN, Cath.	18	F	None	17Ja02Co
CARPENTER, Margt.	22	F	None	17Ja02Co
FIELDHOUSE, Joseph	25	M	None	17Ja02Co
FERRES, John	24	M	None	17Ja02Co
ROBINSON, John	25	M	None	17Ja02Co
GRADY, John	21	M	None	17Ja02Co
Mary	19	F	None	17Ja02Co
WALSH, Cath.	21	F	None	17Ja02Co
DALEY, William	24	M	None	17Ja02Co
PRICE, John	26	M	None	17Ja02Co
MAHER, Jerimih.	24	M	None	17Ja02Co
Ellen	21	F	None	17Ja02Co
GRAY, Bernd.	22	M	None	17Ja02Co
WALLACE, James	24	M	None	17Ja02Co
MITCHELL, Mathias	30	M	None	17Ja02Co
CARROLL, Michl.	26	M	None	17Ja02Co
Mary-Ann	22	F	None	17Ja02Co
Mary	.00	F	Infant	17Ja02Co
DORAN, Cath.	22	F	None	17Ja02Co
Ellen	21	F	None	17Ja02Co
BULGER, Judy	45	F	None	17Ja02Co
MULHALE, Cath.	08	F	Child	17Ja02Co
MCCONAGHY, Alex.	30	M	None	17Ja02Co
Mary	26	F	None	17Ja02Co
Died-At-Sea				
Charles	07	M	Child	17Ja02Co
Catherine	04	F	Child	17Ja02Co
James	03	M	Child	17Ja02Co
William	01	M	Child	17Ja02Co
WEIS, John	26	M	None	17Ja02Co
MCCONAGHY, Jas.	24	M	None	17Ja02Co
BUTLER, Mary	45	F	None	17Ja02Co
William	10	M	None	17Ja02Co
CONN, Mary	42	F	None	17Ja02Co
Mary	17	F	None	17Ja02Co
Daniel	15	M	None	17Ja02Co
Samuel	11	M	None	17Ja02Co
Letitia	26	F	None	17Ja02Co
PARK, Samul.	24	M	None	17Ja02Co
TURNER, Chas.	23	M	None	17Ja02Co
CODY, Wm.	21	M	None	17Ja02Co
DELANY, Steph.	24	M	None	17Ja02Co
COYNE, Patt	22	M	None	17Ja02Co
Died-At-Sea				
DOYLE, Michl.	20	M	None	17Ja02Co
Mary	20	F	None	17Ja02Co
CORMICK, Mary	19	F	None	17Ja02Co
DELANY, Patr.	28	M	None	17Ja02Co
LESLIE, Geo.	30	M	None	17Ja02Co
WILLSON, Joseph	26	M	None	17Ja02Co
PICKLES, Jessy	21	M	None	17Ja02Co
SHARPE, Mark	26	M	None	17Ja02Co
BULLOUGH, Lucratia	40	F	None	17Ja02Co
Abigal	20	F	None	17Ja02Co
ROBERTS, Wm.	26	M	None	17Ja02Co
CARDIS, Michl.	21	M	None	17Ja02Co
ROBERTS, Betsy	26	F	None	17Ja02Co
WILKINSON, Wm.	30	M	None	17Ja02Co
HENSHAW, Wm.	27	M	None	17Ja02Co
BATTERSBY, Thos.	35	M	None	17Ja02Co
ARNOLD, Joseph	45	M	None	17Ja02Co
MCGEE, Honora	24	F	None	17Ja02Co

NAMES OF PASSENGERS	AGE	SEX	OCCUPATIONS	DATE PORT SHIP
HOWARTH, John	26	M	None	17Ja02Co
Susana	28	F	None	17Ja02Co
POLLARD, Bernd.	26	M	None	17Ja02Co
LONG, James	21	M	None	17Ja02Co
Christn.	22	M	None	17Ja02Co
BARKER, Abram.	24	M	None	17Ja02Co
ROCHE, John	30	M	None	17Ja02Co
DUTTON, Joseph	32	M	None	17Ja02Co
TOWERS, Joseph	28	M	None	17Ja02Co
RIGLEY, John	25	M	None	17Ja02Co
HICKEY, Patk.	24	M	None	17Ja02Co
HAYES, Thomas	22	M	None	17Ja02Co
CONNOLLY, Danl.	21	M	None	17Ja02Co
HAMILTON, Maria	14	F	None	17Ja02Co
CHENERY, Henry	22	M	None	17Ja02Co
MULLEN, Denis	28	M	None	17Ja02Co
Mary	26	F	None	17Ja02Co
MURRAY, Patt	25	M	None	17Ja02Co
STEWART, James	22	M	None	17Ja02Co
RYAN, John	24	M	None	17Ja02Co
HEALY, John	26	M	None	17Ja02Co
SMITH, Henry	17	M	None	17Ja02Co
MAHER, Nichl.	26	M	None	17Ja02Co
NOORAN, Ann	40	F	None	17Ja02Co
FIELD, Mary	23	F	None	17Ja02Co
Margt.	16	F	None	17Ja02Co
Mary-Ann	19	F	None	17Ja02Co
Charles	04	M	Child	17Ja02Co
Mary	02	F	Child	17Ja02Co
Ann-Maria	01	F	Child	17Ja02Co
CAMPBELL, Elizbth.	30	F	None	17Ja02Co
POTTS, Ellen	30	F	None	17Ja02Co
CAMPBELL, Elija	19	M	None	17Ja02Co
Mary	17	F	None	17Ja02Co
Margt.	04	F	Child	17Ja02Co
MITCHELL, Mary-A.	19	F	None	17Ja02Co
KEEGAN, Bathm.	20	M	None	17Ja02Co
Mary	17	F	None	17Ja02Co
COSGROVE, Cath.	30	F	None	17Ja02Co
STANLEY, James	40	M	None	17Ja02Co
Sarah	14	F	None	17Ja02Co
Mary	09	F	Child	17Ja02Co
CONNOR, Ann	20	F	None	17Ja02Co
KELLY, Mary	18	F	None	17Ja02Co
Henry	12	M	None	17Ja02Co
HERMITAGE, Wm.	24	M	None	17Ja02Co
DAVIS, James	32	M	None	17Ja02Co
PARKER, John	25	M	None	17Ja02Co
ROWLAND, Rich.	23	M	None	17Ja02Co
POLLOCK, Rich.	26	M	None	17Ja02Co
FALKNER, Saml.	18	M	None	17Ja02Co
SMITH, Mary	38	F	None	17Ja02Co
Patrick	18	M	None	17Ja02Co
Thomas	15	M	None	17Ja02Co
GLIDDON, Cath.	30	F	None	17Ja02Co
HUGHES, Teresa	40	F	None	17Ja02Co
HILL, Thomas	34	M	None	17Ja02Co
John	09	M	Child	17Ja02Co
Elija	04	M	Child	17Ja02Co
THOMPSON, Mary	44	F	None	17Ja02Co
GEOGAN, John	19	M	None	17Ja02Co
BARRY, Mary	20	F	None	17Ja02Co
Died-At-Sea				
MURPHY, James	19	M	None	17Ja02Co
COSTELLO, Mark	28	M	None	17Ja02Co
Matilda	20	F	None	17Ja02Co
DEVLIN, Michl.	60	M	None	17Ja02Co
Died-At-Sea				
Rose	27	F	None	17Ja02Co
BROOKS, James	20	M	None	17Ja02Co
JAMESON, Biddy	16	F	None	17Ja02Co
DONNELLY, Peter	08	M	Child	17Ja02Co
Peggy	04	F	Child	17Ja02Co
Michael	03	M	Child	17Ja02Co
Mary-Ann	02	F	Child	17Ja02Co
DONNELLY, William	.00	M	Infant	17Ja02Co
WHITTEN, James	19	M	None	17Ja02Co
SMITH, Lawr.	32	M	None	17Ja02Co
CONVILL, Arthur	24	M	None	17Ja02Co
WALLS, Wm.	26	M	None	17Ja02Co
KISSACK, Geo.	25	M	None	17Ja02Co
Ann	22	F	None	17Ja02Co
James	30	M	None	17Ja02Co
William	.00	M	Infant	17Ja02Co
MASTIN, Hugh	50	M	None	17Ja02Co
Ann	45	F	None	17Ja02Co
David	13	M	None	17Ja02Co
William	10	M	None	17Ja02Co
WILKINSON, Robert	18	M	None	17Ja02Co
WILLSON, John	35	M	None	17Ja02Co
MCHIEE, Jon.	25	M	None	17Ja02Co
GRAHAM, Waltr.	30	M	None	17Ja02Co
ASHRETT, Wm.M.	40	M	None	17Ja02Co
Georgiana	17	F	None	17Ja02Co
STANLEY, James	30	M	None	17Ja02Co
Hanna	21	F	None	17Ja02Co
MURPHY, Stephn.	22	M	None	17Ja02Co
Joseph	18	M	None	17Ja02Co
MOLLOY, Biddy	13	F	None	17Ja02Co
Judith	15	F	None	17Ja02Co
SHAUGNESSY, Marg.	17	F	None	17Ja02Co
HIGGINBOTTOM, Rich.	70	M	None	17Ja02Co
Bessy	50	F	None	17Ja02Co
Richard	35	M	None	17Ja02Co
Ann	13	F	None	17Ja02Co
Essy	08	F	Child	17Ja02Co
THOMPSON, Darl.	25	M	None	17Ja02Co
RIDGE, Timt.	40	M	None	17Ja02Co
Ann	30	F	None	17Ja02Co
John	13	M	None	17Ja02Co
Mary	06	F	Child	17Ja02Co
Sarah	01	F	Child	17Ja02Co
ROWLAND, Patk.	40	M	None	17Ja02Co
Bridgt.	30	F	None	17Ja02Co
FITZPATRICK, Rodger	50	M	None	17Ja02Co
Margt.	20	F	None	17Ja02Co
MULLEN, Patt	36	M	None	17Ja02Co
FREGAN, Margt.	12	F	None	17Ja02Co
BYRNE, Wm.	30	M	None	17Ja02Co
OREILLY, Peter	25	M	None	17Ja02Co
CORR, John	20	M	None	17Ja02Co
MOHAHAN, Margt.	20	F	None	17Ja02Co
BARCTER, Saml.	29	M	None	17Ja02Co
BUCK, Robt.	40	M	None	17Ja02Co
CALLAHAN, Winny	19	F	None	17Ja02Co
CAFFNEY, Ann	11	F	None	17Ja02Co
CONNOLLY, Mary	13	F	None	17Ja02Co
MCDONNELL, Ann	20	F	None	17Ja02Co
MARTIN, Eliza	18	F	None	17Ja02Co
MAILLEY, Richard	24	M	None	17Ja02Co
CALLONY, John	24	M	None	17Ja02Co
MEREDITH, Elizth.	15	F	None	17Ja02Co
GRALTON, Cornl.	13	M	None	17Ja02Co
FARRELL, James	25	M	None	17Ja02Co
Eliza	18	F	None	17Ja02Co
HARRINGTON, Michl.	26	M	None	17Ja02Co
STAFFORD, Margt.	22	F	None	17Ja02Co
PASSE, Martha	27	F	None	17Ja02Co
John	20	M	None	17Ja02Co
MULUELL, Michl.	24	M	None	17Ja02Co
Margt.	20	F	None	17Ja02Co
MCDOWELL, Jon.	30	M	None	17Ja02Co
CORNODY, Hanah	22	F	None	17Ja02Co
MCKELGY, Margt.	09	F	Child	17Ja02Co
FITZPATRICK, Ellen	20	F	None	17Ja02Co
MCLOUGHLIN, Ann	12	F	None	17Ja02Co
HENDESON, Margt.	20	F	None	17Ja02Co
SCANLON, John	28	M	None	17Ja02Co
Jeremh.	26	M	None	17Ja02Co
COLLIRES, Richd.	24	M	None	17Ja02Co

NAMES OF PASSENGERS	AGE	SEX	OCCUPATIONS	DATE PORT SHIP
GRAHAM, Margt.	20	F	None	17Ja02Co
COLEMAN, Cath.	22	F	None	17Ja02Co
FAHEY, Joseph	23	M	None	17Ja02Co
CONNOR, Mary	28	F	None	17Ja02Co
TONGUE, Thomas	26	M	None	17Ja02Co
SCHOLFIELD, Joseph	36	M	None	17Ja02Co
HEYDEN, Laur.	40	M	None	17Ja02Co
Andw.	36	M	None	17Ja02Co
John	14	M	None	17Ja02Co
Charles	13	M	None	17Ja02Co
James	09	M	Child	17Ja02Co
William	07	M	Child	17Ja02Co
TURNEY, Edw.	32	M	None	17Ja02Co
MILLER, Joseph	40	M	None	17Ja02Co
W-U	36	F	None	17Ja02Co
A.	.00	U	Infant	17Ja02Co
BOWMERIT, Jas.	26	M	None	17Ja02Co
WRIGLEY, Luse	26	M	None	17Ja02Co
Harriet	24	F	None	17Ja02Co
TOWNLEY, Geo.	24	M	None	17Ja02Co
MORGAN, Thos.	30	M	None	17Ja02Co
MORRIS, Elias	21	M	None	17Ja02Co
WEAVER, Joseph	41	M	None	17Ja02Co
William	17	M	None	17Ja02Co
DUNLEVY, John	30	M	None	17Ja02Co
CAMPBELL, Peter	35	M	None	17Ja02Co
HALSLEY, John	27	M	None	17Ja02Co
MCGUIRE, Cath.	25	F	None	17Ja02Co
CLOUGH, David	23	M	None	17Ja02Co
PAYNE, John	38	M	None	17Ja02Co
ANDERSON, David	25	M	None	17Ja02Co
GREEN, George	38	M	None	17Ja02Co
OCONNOR, David	24	M	None	17Ja02Co
TREES, John	28	M	None	17Ja02Co
Hannah	26	F	None	17Ja02Co
Fredrick	07	M	Child	17Ja02Co
Emily-Margt.	03	F	Child	17Ja02Co
Died-At-Sea				
Thomas	22	M	None	17Ja02Co
POWER, Thomas	27	M	None	17Ja02Co
LURNA, Mary-Ann	35	F	None	17Ja02Co
JONES, John	40	M	None	17Ja02Co
MONOHAN, Sarah	20	F	None	17Ja02Co
GILEHENAN, Michael	21	M	None	17Ja02Co
HATTERY, Richard	24	M	None	17Ja02Co
June	20	F	None	17Ja02Co
DILLON, James	26	M	None	17Ja02Co
Elizabeth	24	F	None	17Ja02Co
GLIDDEN, Caroline	30	F	None	17Ja02Co
Josephine (D)	.00	F	Infant	17Ja02Co
QUIN, Mary-Josephine	00	F	None	17Ja02Co
MCGURCIL, Cath.	00	F	None	17Ja02Co
MONTKITRICK, Rich.	00	M	None	17Ja02Co
WHITEHAM, John	00	M	None	17Ja02Co
SHILLER, John-G.	00	M	None	17Ja02Co
WALES, Jas.G.	00	M	None	17Ja02Co
DING, Jas.D.	00	M	None	17Ja02Co

PRINCESS-ALICE 17 JANUARY 1848

From Liverpool

NAMES OF PASSENGERS	AGE	SEX	OCCUPATIONS	DATE PORT SHIP
HOGAN, Francis	23	M	Laborer	17Ja02Rw
Terence	21	M	Laborer	17Ja02Rw
Mary	25	F	Servant	17Ja02Rw
RAIN, Luke	20	M	Laborer	17Ja02Rw
KAIN, Bridgit	23	F	Servant	17Ja02Rw
REYNOLDS, John	28	M	Laborer	17Ja02Rw
Margaret	18	F	Servant	17Ja02Rw
REYNOLDS, Bridget	26	F	Servant	17Ja02Rw
KAIN, Patrick	20	M	Laborer	17Ja02Rw
WILLIAMS, Bridget	45	F	Servant	17Ja02Rw
HANLON, Marlin	29	M	Laborer	17Ja02Rw
DUNIN, Edward	23	M	Shoemaker	17Ja02Rw
HILAND, John	25	M	Laborer	17Ja02Rw
THOMPSON, John	20	M	Tailor	17Ja02Rw
MOODY, John	27	M	Laborer	17Ja02Rw
LAWLER, Michael	23	M	Laborer	17Ja02Rw
Sarah	30	F	Servant	17Ja02Rw
WINTON, David	29	M	Weaver	17Ja02Rw
BRADY, Bridget	40	F	Servant	17Ja02Rw
Died-At-Sea				
BAILY, Sampson	34	M	Potter	17Ja02Rw
BELL, James	21	M	Cooper	17Ja02Rw
BURKE, Christopher	31	M	Painter	17Ja02Rw
CORRAGAN, John	30	M	Laborer	17Ja02Rw
Margaret	50	F	Servant	17Ja02Rw
Rose	22	F	Servant	17Ja02Rw
KING, Bridget	24	F	Servant	17Ja02Rw
OATES, Hugh	20	M	Laborer	17Ja02Rw
BIRNE, James	30	M	Laborer	17Ja02Rw
Catherine	24	F	Servant	17Ja02Rw
Catherine	02	F	Child	17Ja02Rw
MCDERMID, Bridget	10	F	Servant	17Ja02Rw
GLAFS, John	64	M	Merchant	17Ja02Rw
SERSON, Francis	36	M	Laborer	17Ja02Rw
Elira	17	F	Servant	17Ja02Rw
CHARLTORE, Elira	24	F	Weaver	17Ja02Rw
QUIGLEY, Catherine	23	F	Servant	17Ja02Rw
MACKLE, James	31	M	Weaver	17Ja02Rw
ONEIL, Charles	35	M	Weaver	17Ja02Rw
SMALE, Henry	18	M	Tailor	17Ja02Rw
TONER, Sally	50	F	Servant	17Ja02Rw
Eliza	18	F	Servant	17Ja02Rw
SHAFFREY, Catherine	40	F	Servant	17Ja02Rw
Ellen	06	F	Child	17Ja02Rw
BYRNE, Michael	40	M	Laborer	17Ja02Rw
Mary	12	F	Servant	17Ja02Rw
CASSADY, Patrick	45	M	Laborer	17Ja02Rw
Margaret	20	F	Servant	17Ja02Rw
Judith	18	F	Servant	17Ja02Rw
Edward	16	M	Laborer	17Ja02Rw
MCKENNA, Phelime	28	M	Laborer	17Ja02Rw
Mary	30	F	Servant	17Ja02Rw
CULLAIN, Ann	30	F	Servant	17Ja02Rw
WADE, Mary	20	F	Servant	17Ja02Rw
CULLANE, Michael	08	M	Child	17Ja02Rw
John	05	M	Child	17Ja02Rw
Bridget	03	F	Child	17Ja02Rw
Maria	01	F	Child	17Ja02Rw
Died-At-Sea				
MCKENNA, Maria	04	F	Child	17Ja02Rw
Francis	02	M	Child	17Ja02Rw
BARTON, Robert	34	M	Farmer	17Ja02Rw
Jane	27	F	Servant	17Ja02Rw
Jane	05	F	Child	17Ja02Rw
Charles	04	M	Child	17Ja02Rw
Robert	01	M	Child	17Ja02Rw
DONNIGAN, Hugh	24	M	Cbtmkr	17Ja02Rw
BOYD, William	16	M	Laborer	17Ja02Rw
WALKER, Stewart	45	M	Farmer	17Ja02Rw
Rachel	40	F	Servant	17Ja02Rw
Robert	21	M	Laborer	17Ja02Rw
William	15	M	Laborer	17Ja02Rw
John	13	M	Laborer	17Ja02Rw
Jane	39	F	Servant	17Ja02Rw
Elizabeth	12	F	Servant	17Ja02Rw
GREAVES, William	27	M	Knitter	17Ja02Rw
CHANLIN, Samuel	30	M	Knitter	17Ja02Rw
GRIEVES, Ann	25	F	Servant	17Ja02Rw
Frances	05	M	Child	17Ja02Rw
ARNOLD, Charles	07	M	Child	17Ja02Rw
Oliver	19	M	Knitter	17Ja02Rw
KNOWLES, Robert	22	M	Carder	17Ja02Rw

NAMES OF PASSENGERS	AGE	SEX	OCCUPATIONS	DATE PORT SHIP
GREENALD, John	25	M	Carder	17Ja02Rw
KADIAN, James	35	M	Laborer	17Ja02Rw
LEE, John	35	M	Laborer	17Ja02Rw
BRANUON, Patrick	26	M	Laborer	17Ja02Rw
FAY, Mary	35	F	Servant	17Ja02Rw
Henry	08	M	Child	17Ja02Rw
Thomas	06	M	Child	17Ja02Rw
Daniel	02	M	Child	17Ja02Rw
MAXWELL, Mary	26	F	Servant	17Ja02Rw
COUNIFFE, Ann	16	F	Servant	17Ja02Rw
DELANY, John	30	M	Laborer	17Ja02Rw
Margaret	24	F	Servant	17Ja02Rw
MCDONOUGH, Catherine	19	F	Servant	17Ja02Rw
DALY, Patrick	61	M	Cooper	17Ja02Rw
FOX, William	23	M	Laborer	17Ja02Rw
Mary	20	F	Servant	17Ja02Rw
BARDIN, Simon	34	M	Farmer	17Ja02Rw
BELL, Jane	53	F	Servant	17Ja02Rw
Judith	18	F	Servant	17Ja02Rw
William	19	M	Laborer	17Ja02Rw
Betty	22	F	Servant	17Ja02Rw
William	02	M	Child	17Ja02Rw
MARA, James	50	M	Laborer	17Ja02Rw
Mary	06	F	Child	17Ja02Rw
Julia	18	F	Servant	17Ja02Rw
Elizabeth	16	F	Servant	17Ja02Rw
LEDDY, John	50	M	Laborer	17Ja02Rw
FLAHERTY, Tim	30	M	Laborer	17Ja02Rw
MAGINNIS, John	24	M	Collier	17Ja02Rw
MORAU, Bridget	22	F	Servant	17Ja02Rw
READY, David	28	M	Laborer	17Ja02Rw
Margaret	25	F	Servant	17Ja02Rw
SMITH, William	58	M	Knitter	17Ja02Rw
MALONY, John	50	M	Laborer	17Ja02Rw
John	20	M	Laborer	17Ja02Rw
Honoria	18	F	Servant	17Ja02Rw
James	12	M	Servant	17Ja02Rw
Michael	45	M	Laborer	17Ja02Rw
John	20	M	Laborer	17Ja02Rw
LEARNY, Thomas	22	M	Laborer	17Ja02Rw
HAWKINS, Thomas	22	M	Laborer	17Ja02Rw
ONEIL, Thomas	24	M	Laborer	17Ja02Rw
HAWKINS, John	40	M	Laborer	17Ja02Rw
FAHEY, Bridget	20	F	Servant	17Ja02Rw
OWENS, Hugh	20	M	Laborer	17Ja02Rw
John	26	M	Laborer	17Ja02Rw
MCMANUS, Cornelious	37	M	Weaver	17Ja02Rw
WOLFE, John	26	M	Butcher	17Ja02Rw
Mary	21	F	Servant	17Ja02Rw
James	28	M	Butcher	17Ja02Rw
OBRIAN, William	50	M	Farmer	17Ja02Rw
Catherine	50	F	Servant	17Ja02Rw
Ellen	17	F	Servant	17Ja02Rw
Catherine	19	F	Servant	17Ja02Rw
Bridget	15	F	Servant	17Ja02Rw
Ann	12	F	Servant	17Ja02Rw
WOLFE, Ann	01	F	Child	17Ja02Rw
CASSADY, Hugh	20	M	Shoemaker	17Ja02Rw
BOWMAN, Joseph	26	M	Joiner	17Ja02Rw
RYAN, Mathew	31	M	Laborer	17Ja02Rw
Margaret	25	F	Servant	17Ja02Rw
BERGIN, Dennis	27	M	Baker	17Ja02Rw
Catherine	30	F	Servant	17Ja02Rw
LARKINDS, James	64	M	Farmer	17Ja02Rw
Bridget	16	F	Servant	17Ja02Rw
LARKIN, Daniel	63	M	Farmer	17Ja02Rw
MADDEN, Patrick	29	M	Laborer	17Ja02Rw
BRYAN, Edward	26	M	Laborer	17Ja02Rw
CONSADINE, William	36	M	Draper	17Ja02Rw
RYAN, Mary-Ann	19	F	Servant	17Ja02Rw
LOGUE, Michael	30	M	Laborer	17Ja02Rw
MARSHALL, Elizabeth	34	F	Servant	17Ja02Rw
JOHNSTON, June	21	F	Servant	17Ja02Rw
Mary	26	F	Servant	17Ja02Rw
DOWNEY, Patrick	27	M	Laborer	17Ja02Rw

NAMES OF PASSENGERS	AGE	SEX	OCCUPATIONS	DATE PORT SHIP
DOWNEY, Mary	20	F	Servant	17Ja02Rw
Nicholas	01	M	Child	17Ja02Rw
MCGINNIS, Patrick	21	M	Laborer	17Ja02Rw
Philip	18	M	Laborer	17Ja02Rw
Bridget	50	F	Servant	17Ja02Rw
DALY, John	47	M	Laborer	17Ja02Rw
Mary	16	F	Servant	17Ja02Rw
John	14	M	Laborer	17Ja02Rw
Peter	12	M	Laborer	17Ja02Rw
Owen	09	M	Child	17Ja02Rw
BRIAN, Thomas	26	M	Laborer	17Ja02Rw
John	13	M	Laborer	17Ja02Rw
ODONNELE, William	24	M	Laborer	17Ja02Rw
MCLOUGHLIN, Mary	22	F	Servant	17Ja02Rw
Sarah	19	F	Servant	17Ja02Rw
FINNAGHAN, Henry	40	M	Laborer	17Ja02Rw
RYAN, Bridget	19	F	Servant	17Ja02Rw
BRENNON, James	22	M	Laborer	17Ja02Rw
Jane	23	F	Servant	17Ja02Rw
DOLIN, William	23	M	Carpenter	17Ja02Rw
DORMADY, James	20	M	Laborer	17Ja02Rw
MOORE, Ellen	19	F	Servant	17Ja02Rw
DARCY, John	22	M	Laborer	17Ja02Rw
WINTERBOTTOM, James	25	M	Ctnsp	17Ja02Rw
PEEL, John	27	M	Printer	17Ja02Rw
BLAIR, Eliza	18	F	Servant	17Ja02Rw
Mary	16	F	Servant	17Ja02Rw
MCELHERON, Charles	26	M	Laborer	17Ja02Rw
TAYLOR, Henry	19	M	Bookkeeper	17Ja02Rw
AGG, John	45	M	Gdnr	17Ja02Rw
Rachel	42	F	Servant	17Ja02Rw
Anthony	17	M	Gdnr	17Ja02Rw
Sarah	14	F	None	17Ja02Rw
John	09	M	Child	17Ja02Rw
Henry	05	M	Child	17Ja02Rw
William	02	M	Child	17Ja02Rw
MANTON, George	43	M	Millwright	17Ja02Rw
Sarah	58	F	Servant	17Ja02Rw
SMITH, Hannah	36	F	Stewardess	17Ja02Rw
William (S)	09	M	Child	17Ja02Rw
Thomas (S)	07	M	Child	17Ja02Rw
James (S)	03	M	Child	17Ja02Rw
Joseph (S)	.07	M	Infant	17Ja02Rw
TAYLOR, Richard	24	M	Collier	17Ja02Rw
ANDREWS, Joseph	29	M	Draper	17Ja02Rw
SHEPHERD, James	18	M	Weaver	17Ja02Rw
THOMAS, Benjamin	23	M	Weaver	17Ja02Rw
SMITH, David	28	M	Comb Maker	17Ja02Rw
SWEENY, Charles	40	M	Laborer	17Ja02Rw
CAFFREY, Ellen	42	F	Servant	17Ja02Rw
Eliza	19	F	Servant	17Ja02Rw
Catherine	18	F	Servant	17Ja02Rw
MAQUIRE, Mary	17	F	Servant	17Ja02Rw
CAIN, Patrick	22	M	Laborer	17Ja02Rw
COODY, John	30	M	Blacksmith	17Ja02Rw
HACKETT, Michael	18	M	Laborer	17Ja02Rw
ROBERTS, George	22	M	Blacksmith	17Ja02Rw
ACKROYD, William	59	M	Wool Sorter	17Ja02Rw
DONELLY, James	24	M	Filer	17Ja02Rw
MCKENNY, John	29	M	Laborer	17Ja02Rw
MEAD, John	20	M	Clerk	17Ja02Rw
DUFFY, Michael	50	M	Weaver	17Ja02Rw
Catherine	16	F	Servant	17Ja02Rw
MURRY, Michael	27	M	Cooper	17Ja02Rw
LYNCH, John	24	M	Collier	17Ja02Rw
Margaret	26	F	Servant	17Ja02Rw
MORAN, Edward	42	M	Cooper	17Ja02Rw
MURRY, George	22	M	Weaver	17Ja02Rw
HICKEY, Thomas	22	M	Slater	17Ja02Rw
MCQUANY, Hugh	25	M	Ctnsp	17Ja02Rw
CASTELLO, James	26	M	Laborer	17Ja02Rw
MORAN, Owen	24	M	Laborer	17Ja02Rw
MONTGOMERY, John	12	M	Laborer	17Ja02Rw

JANE-H.GLIDEN 18 JANUARY 1848

From Liverpool

NAMES OF PASSENGERS		AGE	SEX	OCCUPATIONS	DATE PORT SHIP
NEEL, Michael		34	M	Farmer	18Ja02Gb
PARKS, Michael		24	M	Farmer	18Ja02Gb
NOONAN, Jacob		25	M	Farmer	18Ja02Gb
CASHMER, Cornelius		15	M	Farmer	18Ja02Gb
Thomas		17	M	Farmer	18Ja02Gb
WOLF, Richard		20	M	Farmer	18Ja02Gb
HARTWELL, Margaret		22	F	Spinster	18Ja02Gb
Mary		24	F	Spinster	18Ja02Gb
WOOFFE, Peggy		15	F	Spinster	18Ja02Gb
CAPELE, Marie		30	F	Spinster	18Ja02Gb
LUADE, Philip		50	M	Farmer	18Ja02Gb
John		40	M	Farmer	18Ja02Gb
Michael		21	M	Farmer	18Ja02Gb
John		30	M	Farmer	18Ja02Gb
James		19	M	Farmer	18Ja02Gb
Mary		13	F	None	18Ja02Gb
Philip		11	M	None	18Ja02Gb
Betsy		22	F	None	18Ja02Gb
CARFY, Cath.		28	F	None	18Ja02Gb
CALAFHOR, Daniel		30	M	Farmer	18Ja02Gb
Cath.		24	F	Seamstress	18Ja02Gb
Ellen		02	F	Child	18Ja02Gb
Thomas		01	M	Child	18Ja02Gb
MCCIEFY, Margt.		28	F	Seamstress	18Ja02Gb
Constantine		11	M	None	18Ja02Gb
Maryann		08	F	Child	18Ja02Gb
Daniel		06	M	Child	18Ja02Gb
HAIRE, Bridget		35	F	None	18Ja02Gb
Mary		14	F	None	18Ja02Gb
Hale		12	M	None	18Ja02Gb
Ann		10	F	None	18Ja02Gb
Bernerd		08	M	Child	18Ja02Gb
Edwd.		06	M	Child	18Ja02Gb
John		04	M	Child	18Ja02Gb
Patrick		02	M	Child	18Ja02Gb
MCAFREY, John		06	M	Child	18Ja02Gb
MCKINNEY, Ann		14	F	None	18Ja02Gb
ROPERS, Molley		20	F	Seamstress	18Ja02Gb
MUNEY, Sarah		11	F	None	18Ja02Gb
Niel		09	M	Child	18Ja02Gb
MUGIN, Michael		20	M	Servant	18Ja02Gb
LOGAN, James		25	M	Servant	18Ja02Gb
Died-At-Sea					
HUNTER, John		25	M	Servant	18Ja02Gb
ERWIN, Saml.		22	M	Farmer	18Ja02Gb
HUNTER, Marian		25	M	Farmer	18Ja02Gb
HEGINN, Margaret		21	F	Seamstress	18Ja02Gb
QUIN, John		40	M	Farmer	18Ja02Gb
MCJUNKING, Mathew		40	M	Farmer	18Ja02Gb
BARN, Henry		24	M	Farmer	18Ja02Gb
MCKAIN, Elizth.		25	F	Servant	18Ja02Gb
SMITH, Wm.		24	M	Farmer	18Ja02Gb
GRAY, Mathew		40	M	Farmer	18Ja02Gb
U	(W)	30	F	None	18Ja02Gb
Mary	(D)	10	F	None	18Ja02Gb
Patrick	(S)	03	M	Child	18Ja02Gb
Elizth.	(D)	.00	F	Infant	18Ja02Gb
HELEY, Peter		25	M	Farmer	18Ja02Gb
Madame		00	F	None	18Ja02Gb
CAR, Ellen		22	F	Servant	18Ja02Gb
MCMANNERS, Cath.		22	F	Servant	18Ja02Gb
BLAKE, Rose		35	F	Servant	18Ja02Gb
KINNAY, Bridget		20	F	Servant	18Ja02Gb
HAYS, James		25	M	Farmer	18Ja02Gb
HANES, Henry		25	M	Farmer	18Ja02Gb
CAROLL, Patrick		26	M	Farmer	18Ja02Gb
BYRNES, Margaret		22	F	Servant	18Ja02Gb
CORE, Chrish		32	M	Laborer	18Ja02Gb
GALLIGER, Edward		24	M	Laborer	18Ja02Gb
Sally		20	F	Seamstress	18Ja02Gb
ODONNEL, Dennis		26	M	Farmer	18Ja02Gb
GARRIDY, Ann		18	F	Servant	18Ja02Gb
BLAKE, Michael		28	M	Servant	18Ja02Gb
DULAN, Edward		18	M	Farmer	18Ja02Gb
HORINOR, Bettey		20	F	Seamstress	18Ja02Gb
MUNDAY, Pat		30	M	Farmer	18Ja02Gb
Mary		21	F	Seamstress	18Ja02Gb
Daniel		11	M	None	18Ja02Gb
KINNEY, Mary		23	F	Servant	18Ja02Gb
KARNHALL, Elizth.		30	F	Servant	18Ja02Gb
Ann		10	F	None	18Ja02Gb
Rose		08	F	Child	18Ja02Gb
Michael		06	M	Child	18Ja02Gb
Eliza		04	F	Child	18Ja02Gb
Patrick		02	M	Child	18Ja02Gb
MARKEY, Bridget		16	F	Seamstress	18Ja02Gb
DILLEN, Eliza		20	F	Seamstress	18Ja02Gb
MULDON, Bridget		40	F	Seamstress	18Ja02Gb
MUTTAGH, Bridget		22	F	Seamstress	18Ja02Gb
Mary		20	F	Seamstress	18Ja02Gb
DONOGIN, James		20	M	Farmer	18Ja02Gb
KENEDY, Elizth.		50	F	Seamstress	18Ja02Gb
Timothy		03	M	Child	18Ja02Gb
WELSH, Mary		20	F	Seamstress	18Ja02Gb
DURHERN, Judak		20	F	Seamstress	18Ja02Gb
Ann		22	F	Seamstress	18Ja02Gb
MAGUIRE, Wm.		22	M	Farmer	18Ja02Gb
Ann		25	F	Seamstress	18Ja02Gb
Mary		20	F	Seamstress	18Ja02Gb
Thomas		16	M	None	18Ja02Gb
THORPL, Marth.		30	F	Servant	18Ja02Gb
Richard		34	M	Servant	18Ja02Gb
BATES, James		28	M	Farmer	18Ja02Gb
FEGGAN, James		28	M	Farmer	18Ja02Gb
MILLER, Thomas		24	M	Farmer	18Ja02Gb
REGEN, Peter		25	M	Farmer	18Ja02Gb
HAIN, Mary		23	F	Servant	18Ja02Gb
CAROHES, Margaret		25	F	Servant	18Ja02Gb
BOYD, Mary		18	F	Servant	18Ja02Gb
HANDLY, Wm.		24	M	Farmer	18Ja02Gb
WOLFE, John		25	M	Farmer	18Ja02Gb
KINNEY, Dan		30	M	Farmer	18Ja02Gb
Catherine		28	F	Seamstress	18Ja02Gb
Francis		15	F	Seamstress	18Ja02Gb
John		11	M	None	18Ja02Gb
BRADEY, Michael		35	M	Farmer	18Ja02Gb
CALLIGAN, Antoney		20	M	Farmer	18Ja02Gb
CARNEY, James		20	M	Farmer	18Ja02Gb
CALIGON, Daniel		18	M	Farmer	18Ja02Gb
MAHONEY, Henry		21	M	Farmer	18Ja02Gb
SHONEYSEY, John		30	M	Farmer	18Ja02Gb
Frances		28	M	Farmer	18Ja02Gb
James		21	M	Farmer	18Ja02Gb
HALL, Maria		21	F	Teacher	18Ja02Gb
Jane		11	F	None	18Ja02Gb
Maria		16	F	None	18Ja02Gb
Elizth.		17	F	None	18Ja02Gb
WELSH, Jane		20	F	Servant	18Ja02Gb
MURPHEY, Francis		26	M	Farmer	18Ja02Gb
TERRELL, Edwd.		28	M	Farmer	18Ja02Gb
OBRIEN, John		21	M	Farmer	18Ja02Gb
Deboro		26	F	Seamstress	18Ja02Gb
Honore		22	F	Seamstress	18Ja02Gb
SEYMAN, Mary		22	F	Seamstress	18Ja02Gb
Ann		20	F	Seamstress	18Ja02Gb
MCGOVERN, Bridget		21	F	None	18Ja02Gb
SMITH, Honora		20	F	None	18Ja02Gb
HIGON, Bridget		30	F	None	18Ja02Gb
CAR, Margaret		25	F	None	18Ja02Gb
ANDERSON, Susan		45	F	None	18Ja02Gb

NAMES OF PASSENGERS	AGE	SEX	OCCUPATIONS	DATE PORT SHIP
ANDERSON, Mary	26	F	None	18Ja02Gb
Martha	21	F	None	18Ja02Gb
George	01	M	Child	18Ja02Gb
DOOLAN, Rose	28	F	Servant	18Ja02Gb
LEONARD, James	20	M	Servant	18Ja02Gb
LACY, Margaret	24	F	Servant	18Ja02Gb
HUDSON, Edward	19	M	Farmer	18Ja02Gb
ROBINSON, Sarah	27	F	Seamstress	18Ja02Gb
MUNEY, Cath.	18	F	Seamstress	18Ja02Gb
William	12	M	None	18Ja02Gb
DULAN, Mary	19	F	Seamstress	18Ja02Gb
Ann	18	F	Seamstress	18Ja02Gb

CONSTITUTION 18 JANUARY 1848

From Liverpool

NAMES OF PASSENGERS	AGE	SEX	OCCUPATIONS	DATE PORT SHIP
BROWN, A.	40	M	Merchant	18Ja02Hi
A.	24	F	None	18Ja02Hi
MCCREIGHT, Jas.	14	M	None	18Ja02Hi
MIWGER, M.	38	F	None	18Ja02Hi
FENWELL, A.	28	M	None	18Ja02Hi
T.	23	F	None	18Ja02Hi
CARNES, John	24	M	Merchant	18Ja02Hi
DAVIDSON, Jane	22	F	Milliner	18Ja02Hi
Isabella	20	F	Milliner	18Ja02Hi
GREER, Ann	20	F	Milliner	18Ja02Hi
LAFFIN, John	28	M	Laborer	18Ja02Hi
FLECK, John	34	M	Laborer	18Ja02Hi
Cath	24	F	Spinster	18Ja02Hi
Mary-Jane	08	F	Child	18Ja02Hi
Robt.	06	M	Child	18Ja02Hi
Sarah	04	F	Child	18Ja02Hi
James	.00	M	Infant	18Ja02Hi
Died-At-Sea				
Sarah	20	F	Spinster	18Ja02Hi
QUIN, Andw.	16	M	Laborer	18Ja02Hi
BRIDE, Judy	19	F	Spinster	18Ja02Hi
GRAND, Jas.	28	M	Laborer	18Ja02Hi
Mary-Ann	25	F	Spinster	18Ja02Hi
Sarah	06	F	Child	18Ja02Hi
Chas.Fredk.	04	M	Child	18Ja02Hi
Emily	02	F	Child	18Ja02Hi
Maurice-Jas.	.00	M	Infant	18Ja02Hi
CONNOR, Jane	21	F	Spinster	18Ja02Hi
ADAMS, Robt.	24	M	Laborer	18Ja02Hi
M.	21	F	None	18Ja02Hi
LINACRE, Geo.	32	M	Laborer	18Ja02Hi
TAYLOR, Wm.	25	M	Laborer	18Ja02Hi
LETFORD, John	24	M	Laborer	18Ja02Hi
MAXWELL, Matt	22	M	Laborer	18Ja02Hi
BRANNON, Pat	32	M	Laborer	18Ja02Hi
Wm.	04	M	Child	18Ja02Hi
John	02	M	Child	18Ja02Hi
Cath.	06	F	Child	18Ja02Hi
Mary	22	F	Spinster	18Ja02Hi
LARAN, Thos.	21	M	Laborer	18Ja02Hi
FARRELL, Peter	24	M	Laborer	18Ja02Hi
KEOWN, Michl.	24	M	Laborer	18Ja02Hi
John	24	M	Laborer	18Ja02Hi
KENEDY, John	55	M	Laborer	18Ja02Hi
Jane	52	F	Spinster	18Ja02Hi
Maria	23	F	Spinster	18Ja02Hi
Anne	21	F	Spinster	18Ja02Hi
Jane	18	F	Spinster	18Ja02Hi
HYAM, Robt.	40	M	Laborer	18Ja02Hi
CAVANAGH, Pat	20	M	Laborer	18Ja02Hi
QUIN, John	20	M	Laborer	18Ja02Hi
CONNOR, John	20	M	Laborer	18Ja02Hi
CONNOR, Pat	18	M	Laborer	18Ja02Hi
BIRCH, Thos.	24	M	Laborer	18Ja02Hi
HASSELL, Pat	30	M	Laborer	18Ja02Hi
KENWORTHY, Jas.	37	M	Laborer	18Ja02Hi
U (W)	32	F	Spinster	18Ja02Hi
Thos.	19	M	Laborer	18Ja02Hi
Ann	17	F	Spinster	18Ja02Hi
Joseph	15	M	None	18Ja02Hi
LORD, Wm.	14	M	None	18Ja02Hi
KENWORTHY, Caroline	13	F	None	18Ja02Hi
Mary	11	F	None	18Ja02Hi
Sarah-Ann	09	F	Child	18Ja02Hi
Thos.	08	M	Child	18Ja02Hi
John	06	M	Child	18Ja02Hi
BRADY, Berd.	55	M	Laborer	18Ja02Hi
Bridget	39	F	Spinster	18Ja02Hi
Cath.	13	F	Spinster	18Ja02Hi
Biddy	11	F	Spinster	18Ja02Hi
Ann	10	F	Spinster	18Ja02Hi
Berd.	09	M	Child	18Ja02Hi
Jas.	33	M	Laborer	18Ja02Hi
Mary	33	F	Spinster	18Ja02Hi
Wm.	06	M	Child	18Ja02Hi
Ann	05	F	Child	18Ja02Hi
Cath.	02	F	Child	18Ja02Hi
Pat	.00	M	Infant	18Ja02Hi
LEE, Abm.	27	M	Laborer	18Ja02Hi
GALLIGER, Pat	35	M	Laborer	18Ja02Hi
Bridget	30	F	Spinster	18Ja02Hi
Pat	10	M	None	18Ja02Hi
Mary	09	F	Child	18Ja02Hi
Thos.	07	M	Child	18Ja02Hi
SMITH, John	20	M	Laborer	18Ja02Hi
Mary	16	F	Spinster	18Ja02Hi
BRADY, Jas.	20	M	Laborer	18Ja02Hi
BROWN, Alfred	26	M	Laborer	18Ja02Hi
U (W)	26	F	Spinster	18Ja02Hi
Joseph	.00	M	Infant	18Ja02Hi
RADCLIFF, David	30	M	Laborer	18Ja02Hi
Benj.	26	M	Laborer	18Ja02Hi
PARSONS, Wm.	27	M	Laborer	18Ja02Hi
Magt.	24	F	Spinster	18Ja02Hi
Jacob.	17	M	Laborer	18Ja02Hi
JAMES, Jas.	30	M	Laborer	18Ja02Hi
MILLS, Robt.	30	M	Laborer	18Ja02Hi
Wm.	30	M	Laborer	18Ja02Hi
BROWN, John	25	M	Laborer	18Ja02Hi
MURPHY, Owen	36	M	Laborer	18Ja02Hi
CONNOR, Margt.	25	F	Spinster	18Ja02Hi
SULLIVAN, Thos.	30	M	Laborer	18Ja02Hi
FLINN, John	30	M	Laborer	18Ja02Hi
Margt.	20	F	Spinster	18Ja02Hi
Died-At-Sea				
Mary	24	F	Spinster	18Ja02Hi
WALSH, John	40	M	Laborer	18Ja02Hi
BRYSON, Pat	20	M	Laborer	18Ja02Hi
Nancy	18	F	Spinster	18Ja02Hi
HORAN, Julia	24	F	Spinster	18Ja02Hi
BYRNES, Thos.	19	M	Laborer	18Ja02Hi
BLAYNEY, Jas.	26	M	Laborer	18Ja02Hi
DUCK, Lawrence	24	M	Laborer	18Ja02Hi
NAYLOR, John	25	M	Laborer	18Ja02Hi
ECKERSLEY, John	34	M	Laborer	18Ja02Hi
ANDREW, John	43	M	Laborer	18Ja02Hi
COOPER, Taylor	28	M	Laborer	18Ja02Hi
MCQUADE, Henry	35	M	Laborer	18Ja02Hi
Margt.	30	F	Spinster	18Ja02Hi
John	01	M	Child	18Ja02Hi
MILLS, Danl.	35	M	Laborer	18Ja02Hi
DONAVAN, Wm.	40	M	Laborer	18Ja02Hi
WOODS, John	60	M	Laborer	18Ja02Hi
Nancy	60	F	Spinster	18Ja02Hi
Mary-Ann	18	F	Spinster	18Ja02Hi
Jack	20	M	Laborer	18Ja02Hi
Sarah	21	F	Spinster	18Ja02Hi

NAMES OF PASSENGERS	A G E	S E X	OCCUPATIONS	DATE PORT SHIP
FAHEY, Michl.	23	M	Laborer	18Ja02Hi
MCMAHON, Francis	22	M	Laborer	18Ja02Hi
MULCAHEY, Jas.	25	M	Laborer	18Ja02Hi
HANLON, Wm.	29	M	Laborer	18Ja02Hi
Anna	24	F	Spinster	18Ja02Hi
Georgianna	24	F	Spinster	18Ja02Hi
Esther	22	F	Spinster	18Ja02Hi
Anna	.00	F	Infant	18Ja02Hi
Alfred Died-At-Sea	.00	M	Infant	18Ja02Hi
LINDSAY, Alex.	24	M	Laborer	18Ja02Hi
HOUGHTON, Michl.	30	M	Laborer	18Ja02Hi
Mary	24	F	Spinster	18Ja02Hi
KIRKLAND, John	26	M	Laborer	18Ja02Hi
Mary	20	F	Spinster	18Ja02Hi
FARRELL, Pat	24	M	Laborer	18Ja02Hi
RILEY, Thos.	24	M	Laborer	18Ja02Hi
Richd.	24	M	Laborer	18Ja02Hi
FARLEY, Thos.	30	M	Laborer	18Ja02Hi
HOGAN, Pat	22	M	Laborer	18Ja02Hi
SMITH, Mick	24	M	Laborer	18Ja02Hi
SHEA, Patk.	28	M	Laborer	18Ja02Hi
HARRINGTON, John	27	M	Laborer	18Ja02Hi
Mary	30	F	Spinster	18Ja02Hi
KERNEY, Pat	28	M	Laborer	18Ja02Hi
CLARK, Peter	22	M	Laborer	18Ja02Hi
FARRELL, Mary	20	F	Spinster	18Ja02Hi
Eliza	22	F	Spinster	18Ja02Hi
HEALEY, Pat	28	M	Farmer	18Ja02Hi
Cath.	22	F	Spinster	18Ja02Hi
RYAN, Sarah	20	F	Spinster	18Ja02Hi
BOOTHMAN, Joseph	25	M	Laborer	18Ja02Hi
JOHNSTON, John	29	M	Laborer	18Ja02Hi
U	20	F	Spinster	18Ja02Hi
MCNAMARA, Thos.	28	M	Laborer	18Ja02Hi
DUNNE, Margt.	23	F	Spinster	18Ja02Hi
FLOOD, Wm.	42	M	Laborer	18Ja02Hi
James	28	M	Laborer	18Ja02Hi
Rose	32	F	Spinster	18Ja02Hi
Pat	06	M	Child	18Ja02Hi
John	04	M	Child	18Ja02Hi
Mary	03	F	Child	18Ja02Hi
LYNCH, Mary	03	F	Child	18Ja02Hi
Peter	24	M	Laborer	18Ja02Hi
GIBURY, Lawrence	28	M	Laborer	18Ja02Hi
HARGRAVES, Joshua	29	M	Laborer	18Ja02Hi
HARVEY, Benj.	28	M	Laborer	18Ja02Hi
BROPHY, Michl.	27	M	Laborer	18Ja02Hi
FITZSIMMON, Wm.	25	M	Laborer	18Ja02Hi
DUGGAN, Dennis	34	M	Laborer	18Ja02Hi
MCWERNEY, Michl.	30	M	Laborer	18Ja02Hi
PAISLEY, Henry	30	M	Laborer	18Ja02Hi
BARRETT, Geo.	30	M	Farmer	18Ja02Hi
HAMP, Eliza	14	F	Seamstress	18Ja02Hi
BELL, Geo.	25	M	Laborer	18Ja02Hi
ROBINSON, John	27	M	Laborer	18Ja02Hi
MCGEE, Pat	45	M	Laborer	18Ja02Hi
LEES, Geo.	21	M	Laborer	18Ja02Hi
WAKEFIELD, Thos.	32	M	Laborer	18Ja02Hi
EVANS, Thos.	48	M	Laborer	18Ja02Hi
Thos.	18	M	Laborer	18Ja02Hi
CONWAY, Pat	40	M	Laborer	18Ja02Hi
MCMAHON, John	25	M	Laborer	18Ja02Hi
COLLINS, Abm.	40	M	Laborer	18Ja02Hi
MARSHALL, John	29	M	Laborer	18Ja02Hi
MERVILLE, Wm.	30	M	Laborer	18Ja02Hi
DUMPSTER, John	30	M	Laborer	18Ja02Hi
Ann	30	F	None	18Ja02Hi
Thos.	10	M	None	18Ja02Hi
BEAMOUS, Josh.	22	M	Laborer	18Ja02Hi
WILDE, Thos.	30	M	Laborer	18Ja02Hi
Jas.	26	M	Laborer	18Ja02Hi
BUCKLEY, Alfred	31	M	Laborer	18Ja02Hi
WHITTAKER, Jas.	25	M	Laborer	18Ja02Hi
HETHERINGTON, Jas.	40	M	Laborer	18Ja02Hi
SCAMPTON, Joseph	26	M	Laborer	18Ja02Hi
COSGROVE, John	25	M	Laborer	18Ja02Hi
SWEENY, Michl.	20	M	Laborer	18Ja02Hi
HARRIS, Wm.	30	M	Laborer	18Ja02Hi
LEONARD, Pat	24	M	Laborer	18Ja02Hi
LYONS, Michl.	24	M	Laborer	18Ja02Hi
Nelly	19	F	Spinster	18Ja02Hi
Winny	22	F	Spinster	18Ja02Hi
MORAN, Cath.	20	F	Spinster	18Ja02Hi
BROWN, Wm.	27	M	Laborer	18Ja02Hi
Sarah	24	F	Spinster	18Ja02Hi
FRASER, Benj.	23	M	Laborer	18Ja02Hi
WALKER, John	27	M	Laborer	18Ja02Hi
HARDMAN, Wm.	23	M	Laborer	18Ja02Hi
PICKERING, Thos.	45	M	Laborer	18Ja02Hi
HOOLE, Henry	47	M	Laborer	18Ja02Hi
QUIN, Edwd.	20	M	Laborer	18Ja02Hi
KILBY, Jeremiah	24	M	Laborer	18Ja02Hi
SHEEHAN, John	21	M	Laborer	18Ja02Hi
SHEA, Danl.	44	M	Laborer	18Ja02Hi
MOBRAY, Wm.	21	M	Laborer	18Ja02Hi
SIMLIAN, Math.	21	M	Laborer	18Ja02Hi
Mary	50	F	None	18Ja02Hi

CAMBRIA 19 JANUARY 1848

From Halifax

NAMES OF PASSENGERS	AGE	SEX	OCCUPATIONS	DATE PORT SHIP
FITZPATRICK, W.J.	28	M	Gentleman	19Ja22Es
MILLER, Robt.	21	M	Merchant	19Ja22Es
COCHRANE, S.A.	21	M	Merchant	19Ja22Es
WARBURTON, Philip-P.	28	M	Gentleman	19Ja22Es
FLINN, William	49	M	Merchant	19Ja22Es
MURPHY, Alex	43	M	Merchant	19Ja22Es

VICTORIA 19 JANUARY 1848

From London

NAMES OF PASSENGERS	AGE	SEX	OCCUPATIONS	DATE PORT SHIP
ONEAL, Cath.	26	F	Servant	19Ja21Ay
Eliza (W)	24	F	Servant	19Ja21Ay
Charles	22	M	Tailor	19Ja21Ay
MAHONEY, Jerrymiur	24	M	Laborer	19Ja21Ay

MEDIATOR 19 JANUARY 1848

From London

NAMES OF PASSENGERS	AGE	SEX	OCCUPATIONS	DATE PORT SHIP
ROACH, Thos.	34	M	Cooper	19Ja21Dt
CONNER, Mary	27	F	Lady	19Ja21Dt
SEYMOUR, Robt.	33	M	Tailor	19Ja21Dt
Margaret	25	F	None	19Ja21Dt
Robert	04	M	Child	19Ja21Dt

GARRICK 20 JANUARY 1848

From Liverpool

NAMES OF PASSENGERS		AGE	SEX	OCCUPATIONS	DATE PORT SHIP
KERNAN, Thos.		22	M	Laborer	20Ja02Aa
LABB, John		20	M	Carpenter	20Ja02Aa
James		25	M	Laborer	20Ja02Aa
ROBERTS, Thos.		18	M	Laborer	20Ja02Aa
LEAHY, David		30	M	Stone Mason	20Ja02Aa
SEAHY, Mary		28	F	None	20Ja02Aa
John		04	M	Child	20Ja02Aa
David		02	M	Child	20Ja02Aa
Mary		.00	F	Infant	20Ja02Aa
GROOES, Anne		30	F	None	20Ja02Aa
Thos.		03	M	Child	20Ja02Aa
John		05	M	Child	20Ja02Aa
HILCULLEN, Anne		18	F	Servant	20Ja02Aa
PEARD, John		12	M	None	20Ja02Aa
MURPHY, Mary		24	F	None	20Ja02Aa
Mary		.00	F	Infant	20Ja02Aa
Johanna		03	F	Child	20Ja02Aa
DOYLE, Honora		19	F	None	20Ja02Aa
MCCARTHY, Mary		40	F	None	20Ja02Aa
John		09	M	Child	20Ja02Aa
Johanna		07	F	Child	20Ja02Aa
RILEY, Thos.		28	M	Laborer	20Ja02Aa
CALIHAN, Terrence		26	M	Laborer	20Ja02Aa
FLINN, Luke		55	M	Laborer	20Ja02Aa
Sally		52	F	None	20Ja02Aa
Michael		12	M	None	20Ja02Aa
DALY, Bridget		40	F	None	20Ja02Aa
James		30	M	Blacksmith	20Ja02Aa
Daniel		19	M	Clerk	20Ja02Aa
Mary		17	F	None	20Ja02Aa
KEENAN, Anne		18	F	Servant	20Ja02Aa
SHEHAN, Malady		22	M	Laborer	20Ja02Aa
BIRNE, W.A.		36	M	Doctor	20Ja02Aa
U	(W)	26	F	None	20Ja02Aa
W.A.		06	M	Child	20Ja02Aa
Eliza		04	F	Child	20Ja02Aa
Alicia		03	F	Child	20Ja02Aa
John		.00	M	Infant	20Ja02Aa
Died-At-Sea					
MCCARTHY, Ellen		22	F	Servant	20Ja02Aa
Margaret		21	F	Servant	20Ja02Aa
BRIVODY, Mary		30	F	Servant	20Ja02Aa
Bridget		13	F	Servant	20Ja02Aa
John		.00	M	Infant	20Ja02Aa
DOYLE, Patrick		20	M	Laborer	20Ja02Aa
Rose		18	F	None	20Ja02Aa
Mary		.00	F	Infant	20Ja02Aa
MCGROUGH, Julia		20	F	Servant	20Ja02Aa
KING, Mary		42	F	None	20Ja02Aa
Mary		20	F	None	20Ja02Aa
John		18	M	None	20Ja02Aa
James		09	M	Child	20Ja02Aa
Nancy		07	F	Child	20Ja02Aa
Ebenezer		.00	M	Infant	20Ja02Aa
DOYLE, Anne		28	F	Nurse	20Ja02Aa
MCDONALD, Terence		20	M	Laborer	20Ja02Aa
SARKIN, Honora		26	F	Servant	20Ja02Aa
Bridget		20	F	Servant	20Ja02Aa
SALLY, Pat		22	M	Laborer	20Ja02Aa
MANGAN, Pat		20	M	Laborer	20Ja02Aa
MURPHY, Pat		25	M	Laborer	20Ja02Aa
Bridget		20	F	Servant	20Ja02Aa
RIAN, Mary		18	F	Servant	20Ja02Aa
FLANAGEN, Cath.		22	F	Servant	20Ja02Aa
MURPHY, Pat		21	M	Laborer	20Ja02Aa
MURPHY, Anne		20	F	None	20Ja02Aa
MULVEY, Mary		09	F	Child	20Ja02Aa
SHELLY, Michael		13	M	None	20Ja02Aa
NAUGHTEN, Anne		17	F	Servant	20Ja02Aa
DUNN, Mary		16	F	Servant	20Ja02Aa
GORMLY, Teddy		24	M	Laborer	20Ja02Aa
KENALLY, Thos.		25	M	Laborer	20Ja02Aa
U	(W)	25	F	None	20Ja02Aa
Thos.		.00	M	Infant	20Ja02Aa
HOGAN, Thos.		20	M	Laborer	20Ja02Aa
WRIGHT, James		30	M	Laborer	20Ja02Aa
U	(W)	28	F	None	20Ja02Aa
Benj.		02	M	Child	20Ja02Aa
John		.00	M	Infant	20Ja02Aa
LOOHY, Thos.		40	M	Laborer	20Ja02Aa
Thos.		20	M	Laborer	20Ja02Aa
TOSHY, James		22	M	Laborer	20Ja02Aa
BRAMNEY, James		26	M	Laborer	20Ja02Aa
Mary		24	F	None	20Ja02Aa
John		.00	M	Infant	20Ja02Aa
COTELLO, Owen		24	M	Laborer	20Ja02Aa
ROONEY, Onagh		18	F	Servant	20Ja02Aa
SANAHAN, Ellen		17	F	Servant	20Ja02Aa
MCGOVERN, Cath.		22	F	Servant	20Ja02Aa
KERNAN, Pat		20	M	Laborer	20Ja02Aa
KELLY, Michael		30	M	Laborer	20Ja02Aa
Owen		20	M	Laborer	20Ja02Aa
Anne		16	F	None	20Ja02Aa
Mary		08	F	Child	20Ja02Aa
Pat		.00	M	Infant	20Ja02Aa
MAYERS, John		36	M	Laborer	20Ja02Aa
MYERS, Biddy		30	F	None	20Ja02Aa
JOHNSON, John		20	M	Coachman	20Ja02Aa
KIERNAN, Anne		26	F	Servant	20Ja02Aa
Died-At-Sea					
Catherine		05	F	Child	20Ja02Aa
WARD, Cath.		20	F	None	20Ja02Aa
GRANGER, Benj.		23	M	Blacksmith	20Ja02Aa
DARSY, Peter		50	M	Laborer	20Ja02Aa
MCCLUSKY, Henry		20	M	Potter	20Ja02Aa
CONNEL, John		30	M	Carpenter	20Ja02Aa
BOYLE, Brian		24	M	Laborer	20Ja02Aa
BENNET, James		30	M	Laborer	20Ja02Aa
U	(W)	30	F	None	20Ja02Aa
KERNY, Anne		30	F	Servant	20Ja02Aa
Mary		02	F	Child	20Ja02Aa
Bridget		.00	F	Infant	20Ja02Aa
NELSON, Franny		30	F	None	20Ja02Aa
RILEY, Martha		20	F	None	20Ja02Aa
FALLOON, Pat		12	M	None	20Ja02Aa
LECRY, Biddy		20	F	None	20Ja02Aa
BOYLAN, Michael		21	M	Laborer	20Ja02Aa
MURPHY, Mary		18	F	Servant	20Ja02Aa
BOYLAN, Margaret		16	F	Servant	20Ja02Aa
JONES, Wm.		50	M	Farmer	20Ja02Aa
MCGUIRE, Thos.		30	M	Laborer	20Ja02Aa
U	(W)	30	F	None	20Ja02Aa
Mary		.00	F	Infant	20Ja02Aa
REYNOLDS, Pat		30	M	Laborer	20Ja02Aa
U	(W)	30	F	None	20Ja02Aa
Winnefred		09	F	Child	20Ja02Aa
Cath.		08	F	Child	20Ja02Aa
Maria		05	F	Child	20Ja02Aa
Michael		.00	M	Infant	20Ja02Aa
STINSTON, Bridget		20	F	Servant	20Ja02Aa
BURROWS, John		40	M	Farmer	20Ja02Aa
U	(W)	40	F	None	20Ja02Aa
Mary		15	F	None	20Ja02Aa
Margaret		12	F	None	20Ja02Aa
Terence		09	M	Child	20Ja02Aa
Cath.		07	F	Child	20Ja02Aa
Patrick		05	M	Child	20Ja02Aa
John		03	M	Child	20Ja02Aa
James		.00	M	Infant	20Ja02Aa
Michael		20	M	Farmer	20Ja02Aa

NAMES OF PASSENGERS		AGE	SEX	OCCUPATIONS	DATE PORT SHIP
HARVEY, Owen		20	M	Laborer	20Ja02Aa
MORAN, Pat		50	M	Laborer	20Ja02Aa
U	(W)	30	F	None	20Ja02Aa
John		03	M	Child	20Ja02Aa
James		.00	M	Infant	20Ja02Aa
GAROULY, Thos.		30	M	Laborer	20Ja02Aa
Cather.		18	F	None	20Ja02Aa
NALLY, Michael		30	M	Laborer	20Ja02Aa
Cathe.		30	F	None	20Ja02Aa
John		.00	M	Infant	20Ja02Aa
MONTGOMERY, John		20	M	Surveyor	20Ja02Aa
MCMORAN, James		20	M	Laborer	20Ja02Aa
RIAN, John		40	M	Laborer	20Ja02Aa
NALLY, Patt		30	M	Laborer	20Ja02Aa
Biddy		30	F	None	20Ja02Aa
Mary		09	F	Child	20Ja02Aa
Bridget		07	F	Child	20Ja02Aa
John		.00	M	Infant	20Ja02Aa
Died-At-Sea					
CAVANNA, Thos.		20	M	Laborer	20Ja02Aa
MAHONY, Robert		26	M	Weaver	20Ja02Aa
James		08	M	Child	20Ja02Aa
Saml.		10	M	None	20Ja02Aa
DONAHOE, Ellen		20	F	Servant	20Ja02Aa
GANNON, James		25	M	Laborer	20Ja02Aa
MCCABE, James		20	M	Laborer	20Ja02Aa
CORNEL, John		30	M	Laborer	20Ja02Aa
CONNEL, U		30	F	None	20Ja02Aa
GARDNER, Wm.		20	M	Laborer	20Ja02Aa
U	(W)	20	F	None	20Ja02Aa
DALY, Pat		60	M	Farmer	20Ja02Aa
Nelly		50	F	None	20Ja02Aa
John		21	M	None	20Ja02Aa
Dennis		12	M	None	20Ja02Aa
Mary		14	F	None	20Ja02Aa
Michael		19	M	None	20Ja02Aa
BIRNIE, Bridget		18	F	Servant	20Ja02Aa
RAFFERTY, Wm.		22	M	Laborer	20Ja02Aa
FITZPATRICK, Thos.		48	M	Shoemaker	20Ja02Aa
Cath.		46	F	None	20Ja02Aa
Maria		15	F	None	20Ja02Aa
Edward		13	M	None	20Ja02Aa
Thos.		11	M	None	20Ja02Aa
Pat		.00	M	Infant	20Ja02Aa
MCGATH, John		37	M	Carpenter	20Ja02Aa
Isabella		30	F	None	20Ja02Aa
Robert		20	M	Carpenter	20Ja02Aa
Fanny		13	F	None	20Ja02Aa
John-J.		11	M	None	20Ja02Aa
Thos-H.		10	M	None	20Ja02Aa
Isabella		09	F	Child	20Ja02Aa
Issac		06	M	Child	20Ja02Aa
Abraham		04	M	Child	20Ja02Aa
Job		02	M	Child	20Ja02Aa
Ruth		.00	F	Infant	20Ja02Aa
HENDERSON, Wm.		20	M	Weaver	20Ja02Aa
U	(W)	26	F	None	20Ja02Aa
John		07	M	Child	20Ja02Aa
Anne		03	F	Child	20Ja02Aa
Eliza		02	F	Child	20Ja02Aa
DARBY, Thos.		30	M	Laborer	20Ja02Aa
CONNAL, Pat		20	M	Laborer	20Ja02Aa
SMITH, Betsy		20	F	Servant	20Ja02Aa
COONEY, Conner		16	M	Laborer	20Ja02Aa
SHERIDAN, James		30	M	Actor	20Ja02Aa
ONEIL, Cath.		18	F	None	20Ja02Aa
CLEARY, Bridget		20	F	None	20Ja02Aa
FOGARTY, John		26	M	Laborer	20Ja02Aa
SMITH, Cathe.		30	F	Servant	20Ja02Aa
PLACE, John		35	M	Carpenter	20Ja02Aa
Edward		30	M	Laborer	20Ja02Aa
Thos.		26	M	Laborer	20Ja02Aa
ONEIL, Mary		24	F	None	20Ja02Aa
Edward		04	M	Child	20Ja02Aa
John		.00	M	Infant	20Ja02Aa
GILRAY, John		20	M	Stone Mason	20Ja02Aa
DOGHERTY, Frank		26	M	Laborer	20Ja02Aa
MOORE, John		25	M	Laborer	20Ja02Aa
WALSH, Michael		40	M	Farmer	20Ja02Aa
U	(W)	41	F	None	20Ja02Aa
Barbara		20	F	None	20Ja02Aa
Mathew		16	M	None	20Ja02Aa
Frank		12	M	None	20Ja02Aa
CURTIS, Patrick		20	M	Laborer	20Ja02Aa
HOGAN, Tim		25	M	Tailor	20Ja02Aa
DOLAN, Thos.		25	M	Porter	20Ja02Aa
LYONS, George		22	M	Clerk	20Ja02Aa
DOGHERTY, Thos.		18	M	Shoemaker	20Ja02Aa
DONAHOE, Michael		30	M	Blacksmith	20Ja02Aa
Catherine		28	F	None	20Ja02Aa
Mary		16	F	None	20Ja02Aa
HAVERTY, Thos.		30	M	Laborer	20Ja02Aa
NEWMAN, George		36	M	Shopman	20Ja02Aa
Cath.		30	F	None	20Ja02Aa
LUMLEY, Wm.		27	M	Laborer	20Ja02Aa
MUSTAGH, Peter		30	M	Laborer	20Ja02Aa
WELSH, Pat		48	M	Farmer	20Ja02Aa
Winnefred		48	F	None	20Ja02Aa
John		17	M	None	20Ja02Aa
Mary		20	F	None	20Ja02Aa
James		16	M	None	20Ja02Aa
Thos.		15	M	None	20Ja02Aa
Cath.		10	F	None	20Ja02Aa
Mary		08	F	Child	20Ja02Aa
Anne		02	F	Child	20Ja02Aa
Biddy		.00	F	Infant	20Ja02Aa
KELLY, Daniel		34	M	Laborer	20Ja02Aa
MULLEN, Jerry		26	M	Laborer	20Ja02Aa
Cath.		24	F	None	20Ja02Aa
DALY, Charles		18	M	Laborer	20Ja02Aa
FOX, Pat		20	M	Laborer	20Ja02Aa
MCMASTERS, Wm.		21	M	Servant	20Ja02Aa
Thos.		20	M	Waiter	20Ja02Aa
QUIN, Anne		17	F	Servant	20Ja02Aa
SMITH, Cath.		25	F	Cook	20Ja02Aa
Mary		19	F	Servant	20Ja02Aa
RILEY, Anne		19	F	Servant	20Ja02Aa
BROWN, Jane		21	F	Servant	20Ja02Aa
MARTIN, Anne		35	F	Servant	20Ja02Aa
Pat		.00	M	Infant	20Ja02Aa
Mary		10	F	None	20Ja02Aa
Susan		07	F	Child	20Ja02Aa
Jane		04	F	Child	20Ja02Aa
Thos.		24	M	Spinner	20Ja02Aa
MCMANNIS, Eliza		26	F	Servant	20Ja02Aa
Sally		17	F	Servant	20Ja02Aa
DALY, Mary		19	F	Servant	20Ja02Aa
MCCABE, James		14	M	Laborer	20Ja02Aa
Andrew		12	M	Laborer	20Ja02Aa
HANDLY, Martin		19	M	Shoemaker	20Ja02Aa
DOUGHTY, Mathew		21	M	Laborer	20Ja02Aa
MECK, Pat		22	M	Laborer	20Ja02Aa
BRICE, Owen		21	M	Sailor	20Ja02Aa
RYAN, Richard		24	M	Farmer	20Ja02Aa

CAMBRIDGE 20 JANUARY 1848

From Liverpool

NAMES OF PASSENGERS	AGE	SEX	OCCUPATIONS	DATE PORT SHIP
MOFFETT, Edward	25	M	Seaman	20Ja02Ea
Henry	23	M	Seaman	20Ja02Ea
RILEY, Bernard	40	M	Farmer	20Ja02Ea
Ann	45	F	None	20Ja02Ea
James	15	M	None	20Ja02Ea

NAMES OF PASSENGERS	AGE	SEX	OCCUPATIONS	DATE PORT SHIP
CISSIDY, Michiel	19	M	None	20Ja02Ea
Mary	20	F	None	20Ja02Ea
SMITH, Cath.	29	F	None	20Ja02Ea
MAHONY, Pat	25	M	Seaman	20Ja02Ea
BROION, James	23	M	Seaman	20Ja02Ea
CANAY, John	23	M	Seaman	20Ja02Ea
CAREY, Pat	40	M	Seaman	20Ja02Ea
MANNION, Michiel	18	M	Seaman	20Ja02Ea
CAREY, Bridget	34	F	None	20Ja02Ea
Margret	34	F	None	20Ja02Ea
Died-At-Sea				
Thos.	05	M	Child	20Ja02Ea
RILEY, John	37	M	None	20Ja02Ea
HOGIN, Rhody	26	F	None	20Ja02Ea
BRYAN, Pat	22	M	None	20Ja02Ea
CRUNSLEY, Margret	16	F	None	20Ja02Ea
MCCANAHEN, John	24	M	None	20Ja02Ea
HARRISON, David	19	M	None	20Ja02Ea
COOK, Bridget	20	F	None	20Ja02Ea
Mary	18	F	None	20Ja02Ea
RODGERS, Bridget	30	F	None	20Ja02Ea
SCULLEY, Maria	20	F	None	20Ja02Ea
CONLEY, Ellen	20	F	None	20Ja02Ea
GRINNEY, Cornelious	24	M	None	20Ja02Ea
Ellen	20	F	None	20Ja02Ea
MCKEMIE, Pat	26	M	None	20Ja02Ea
OBRIEN, Cate	39	F	None	20Ja02Ea
POWER, John	09	M	Child	20Ja02Ea
SMITH, Pat	40	M	Salesman	20Ja02Ea
Cate	35	F	Salesman	20Ja02Ea
Mary	11	F	Salesman	20Ja02Ea
DOLAN, Bryan	23	M	Salesman	20Ja02Ea
WATERS, Abraham	50	M	Farmer	20Ja02Ea
Ann	50	F	None	20Ja02Ea
GLYNN, James	20	M	None	20Ja02Ea
BUCKLEY, James	27	M	None	20Ja02Ea
MCGINNIS, Michiel	24	M	None	20Ja02Ea
COLSON, Joseph	26	M	None	20Ja02Ea
BARTON, Charles	29	M	None	20Ja02Ea
CAHOON, Daniel	25	M	Laborer	20Ja02Ea
HEART, James	20	M	Laborer	20Ja02Ea
MCCULLCE, Mary	30	F	Laborer	20Ja02Ea
Mary	09	F	Child	20Ja02Ea
HALL, Mary-A.	29	F	None	20Ja02Ea
U	.00	U	Infant	20Ja02Ea
Williams	06	M	Child	20Ja02Ea
Walter	02	M	Child	20Ja02Ea
CLUNNY, James	24	M	Laborer	20Ja02Ea
CANNAL, Wm.	21	M	Laborer	20Ja02Ea
DELANCY, Mary	30	F	None	20Ja02Ea
U	.00	U	Infant	20Ja02Ea
DAILEY, Ellen	04	F	Child	20Ja02Ea
Pat	02	M	Child	20Ja02Ea
HOGEN, Pat	26	M	Laborer	20Ja02Ea
SEARY, Daniel	30	M	Farmer	20Ja02Ea
U (W)	24	F	None	20Ja02Ea
U	.00	F	Infant	20Ja02Ea
Cate	07	F	Child	20Ja02Ea
Ann	05	F	Child	20Ja02Ea
John	03	M	Child	20Ja02Ea
Michiel	02	M	Child	20Ja02Ea
SAMUEL, Mary	18	F	Servant	20Ja02Ea
BUCHFORD, Pat	15	M	Laborer	20Ja02Ea
Bridget	16	F	Servant	20Ja02Ea
BAY, John	16	M	None	20Ja02Ea
BURKE, Toby	34	M	None	20Ja02Ea
U (W)	39	F	None	20Ja02Ea
U	.00	U	Infant	20Ja02Ea
Bridget	16	F	None	20Ja02Ea
Cleary	05	F	None	20Ja02Ea
James	03	M	None	20Ja02Ea
SWEENEY, John	26	M	None	20Ja02Ea
Edward	30	M	None	20Ja02Ea
BOYD, Edward	36	M	None	20Ja02Ea
ODONNEL, Pat	30	M	None	20Ja02Ea
CONNELLE, Cornelious	21	M	Tailor	20Ja02Ea
HUTCHIN, Mary-A.	15	F	Servant	20Ja02Ea
BRENNAN, Andrew	20	M	None	20Ja02Ea
BOWAS, Mary	20	F	None	20Ja02Ea
BROSSEN, Michiel	20	M	Laborer	20Ja02Ea
CONNEL, Michiel	35	M	Laborer	20Ja02Ea
MCCAFFRY, Mary	30	F	None	20Ja02Ea
U	.00	U	Infant	20Ja02Ea
James	09	M	Child	20Ja02Ea
Ann	05	F	Child	20Ja02Ea
BRIDE, Ellen	30	F	None	20Ja02Ea
U	.00	U	Infant	20Ja02Ea
CONNON, James	22	M	Laborer	20Ja02Ea
CART, Mary	25	F	Servant	20Ja02Ea
WARD, Sawnee	24	M	Laborer	20Ja02Ea
Jane	26	F	None	20Ja02Ea
U	.00	U	Infant	20Ja02Ea
Thos.	07	M	Child	20Ja02Ea
James	05	M	Child	20Ja02Ea
James	16	M	None	20Ja02Ea
Pat	13	M	None	20Ja02Ea
Wm.	11	M	None	20Ja02Ea
Thomas	10	M	None	20Ja02Ea
Hannah	24	F	None	20Ja02Ea
U	.00	U	Infant	20Ja02Ea
Anthony	06	M	Child	20Ja02Ea
John	04	M	Child	20Ja02Ea
HIGHLAND, Richard	60	M	None	20Ja02Ea
Bridget	21	F	None	20Ja02Ea
TOONON, Ellen	27	F	Servant	20Ja02Ea
KELLY, Mary	30	F	Servant	20Ja02Ea
Cate	04	F	Child	20Ja02Ea
BIRNKE, Jane	14	F	None	20Ja02Ea
MURPHY, Margret	25	F	None	20Ja02Ea
REARDON, Mary-Ann	56	F	None	20Ja02Ea
SCULLY, Annaleha	17	F	None	20Ja02Ea
SMITH, Pat	18	M	Laborer	20Ja02Ea
PATTERSON, Wm.	22	M	Mason	20Ja02Ea
SHERIDAN, Ann	09	F	Child	20Ja02Ea
HINLY, Mary	30	F	Servant	20Ja02Ea
MULEADY, Pat	50	M	Farmer	20Ja02Ea
LYONS, Pat	30	M	Farmer	20Ja02Ea
RENOLDS, Mary	35	F	Servant	20Ja02Ea
U	.00	U	Infant	20Ja02Ea
James	11	M	None	20Ja02Ea
Cate	09	F	None	20Ja02Ea
Winniah	09	F	None	20Ja02Ea
Ellen	05	F	None	20Ja02Ea
GLENON, John	16	M	Laborer	20Ja02Ea
Martin	14	M	Laborer	20Ja02Ea
Peter	12	M	Laborer	20Ja02Ea
MINTER, William	30	M	Farmer	20Ja02Ea
Mary	28	F	None	20Ja02Ea
SHEA, Timothy	14	M	None	20Ja02Ea
Margret	16	F	None	20Ja02Ea
MILLY, Ellen	20	F	Servant	20Ja02Ea
SHERIDAN, Bridget	14	F	Servant	20Ja02Ea
Philip	16	M	Laborer	20Ja02Ea
FOLARY, Ann	27	F	Servant	20Ja02Ea
GLEARON, Thos.	20	M	Laborer	20Ja02Ea
CLUSKEY, Jane	19	F	Servant	20Ja02Ea
RILEY, Mary	10	F	Servant	20Ja02Ea
Rozanna	08	F	Child	20Ja02Ea
MALOMIN, Wm.	43	M	Laborer	20Ja02Ea
KELLY, Cate	20	F	Servant	20Ja02Ea
MCGRAH, Mary	23	F	Servant	20Ja02Ea
FINIGAN, Cate	21	F	Servant	20Ja02Ea
Owen	11	M	None	20Ja02Ea
CLARY, James	24	M	Laborer	20Ja02Ea
SPELLMAN, Bridget	50	F	Servant	20Ja02Ea
Mary	26	F	Servant	20Ja02Ea
WYNN, Mary	30	F	None	20Ja02Ea
U	.00	U	Infant	20Ja02Ea
Pat	02	M	Child	20Ja02Ea
Nancy	13	F	None	20Ja02Ea

NAMES OF PASSENGERS	AGE	SEX	OCCUPATIONS	DATE PORT SHIP
MILT, Daffy	35	F	None	20Ja02Ea
U	.00	U	Infant	20Ja02Ea
Mary	13	F	None	20Ja02Ea
James	12	M	None	20Ja02Ea
John	07	M	Child	20Ja02Ea
Pegy	09	F	Child	20Ja02Ea
HARRISON, Samuel	21	M	Farmer	20Ja02Ea
DEVINE, Patt	50	M	Farmer	20Ja02Ea
Betsey	50	F	Farmer	20Ja02Ea
Rosanna	07	F	Child	20Ja02Ea
COON, Elizabeth	30	F	Servant	20Ja02Ea
NAHANAY, Mary	36	F	Servant	20Ja02Ea
NAILE, Mary-A.	40	F	Servant	20Ja02Ea
James	20	M	Laborer	20Ja02Ea
Mary	27	F	None	20Ja02Ea
Ann	16	F	None	20Ja02Ea
John	07	M	Child	20Ja02Ea
Stephen	04	M	Child	20Ja02Ea
Mary-A.	05	F	None	20Ja02Ea
DOOLEY, Thos.	27	M	Laborer	20Ja02Ea
MARTIN, Peter	14	M	Laborer	20Ja02Ea
FORD, Nancy	30	F	Servant	20Ja02Ea
MURPHY, William	28	M	Servant	20Ja02Ea
MARTIN, Peter	30	M	Farmer	20Ja02Ea
INESLUNDED, Cate	30	F	None	20Ja02Ea
Pat	05	M	Child	20Ja02Ea
Bridget	02	F	Child	20Ja02Ea
HAYS, Cate	21	F	Servant	20Ja02Ea
LEDWICK, Ellen	50	F	Servant	20Ja02Ea
SCOT, Pat	30	M	Farmer	20Ja02Ea
John	29	M	Farmer	20Ja02Ea
PRIEST, John	31	M	Farmer	20Ja02Ea
TRISTIAN, Thomas	09	M	Child	20Ja02Ea
SULLIVAN, Timothy	55	M	Farmer	20Ja02Ea
Cate	56	F	None	20Ja02Ea
John	30	M	Farmer	20Ja02Ea
Margret	17	F	None	20Ja02Ea
Dennis	12	M	None	20Ja02Ea
DUNNIN, Terrence	19	M	Laborer	20Ja02Ea
GULLUNIN, Francis	20	M	Laborer	20Ja02Ea
TANKARD, Patrick	00	M	None	20Ja02Ea
COXBURY, Peter	00	M	None	20Ja02Ea
SMITH, Peter	00	M	None	20Ja02Ea
MEW, John	00	M	None	20Ja02Ea
DEVAN, John	00	M	None	20Ja02Ea
HALFRIN, P.	00	M	None	20Ja02Ea
SCUFLIN, Mary-A.	00	F	None	20Ja02Ea
BLACKMORY, P.	00	M	None	20Ja02Ea
U (W)	00	F	None	20Ja02Ea
Mary-E.	00	F	None	20Ja02Ea
THOMELL, Hanah	00	F	None	20Ja02Ea
SWEENY, Mary-A.	00	F	None	20Ja02Ea
MOFFET, Fredrick	00	M	None	20Ja02Ea

HENRY-HARBECK 21 JANUARY 1848

From Liverpool

NAMES OF PASSENGERS	AGE	SEX	OCCUPATIONS	DATE PORT SHIP
HEALY, Timothy	36	M	Laborer	21Ja02Az
John	28	M	Laborer	21Ja02Az
DOON, James	60	M	Mechanic	21Ja02Az
Jane	50	F	Baker	21Ja02Az
Laughlin	24	M	Mechanic	21Ja02Az
James	18	M	Mechanic	21Ja02Az
Mary	17	F	Servant	21Ja02Az
John	05	M	Child	21Ja02Az
Terence	14	M	None	21Ja02Az
Betty	11	F	None	21Ja02Az
Bridget	08	F	Child	21Ja02Az
DOON, Hugh	04	M	Child	21Ja02Az
SAVAGE, David	24	M	Mechanic	21Ja02Az
PRITCHARD, Adam	21	M	Mechanic	21Ja02Az
Eliza	20	F	Servant	21Ja02Az
David	14	M	None	21Ja02Az
MOORE, Joseph	27	M	Mechanic	21Ja02Az
SHARP, Cyrus	33	M	Mechanic	21Ja02Az
WITTAM, John	33	M	Mechanic	21Ja02Az
MORE, William	30	M	Mechanic	21Ja02Az
GALLY, John	24	M	Mechanic	21Ja02Az
BROWN, Jane	26	F	Servant	21Ja02Az
Robt.	08	M	Child	21Ja02Az
Margaret	06	F	Child	21Ja02Az
Mary-Ann	04	F	Child	21Ja02Az
Henry	02	M	Child	21Ja02Az
KENNEDY, Margaret	20	F	Servant	21Ja02Az
ORNSBY, John	33	M	Laborer	21Ja02Az
LAUGHLIN, Maria	25	F	Servant	21Ja02Az
Rose	18	F	Servant	21Ja02Az
SCANLLAN, Maria	16	F	Servant	21Ja02Az
HART, Catherine	20	F	Servant	21Ja02Az
BANFORD, William	34	M	Furrier	21Ja02Az
Alexander	11	M	None	21Ja02Az
Matilda	07	F	Child	21Ja02Az
CORBIT, Henry	36	M	Furrier	21Ja02Az
Mary	35	F	Servant	21Ja02Az
Mary-Jane	11	F	None	21Ja02Az
Robert	08	M	Child	21Ja02Az
Hugh	06	M	Child	21Ja02Az
John	03	M	Child	21Ja02Az
MCCAFFIN, Mary	18	F	Servant	21Ja02Az
BRANAGIN, Andrew	46	M	Laborer	21Ja02Az
Margaret	15	F	Servant	21Ja02Az
PAYNAN, Connor	30	M	Laborer	21Ja02Az
Bridget	24	F	Servant	21Ja02Az
MCINTIRE, James	26	M	Laborer	21Ja02Az
William	26	M	Laborer	21Ja02Az
Patt	.00	M	Infant	21Ja02Az
GLYN, Ann	16	F	Servant	21Ja02Az
MADDEN, Margaret	20	F	Servant	21Ja02Az
RYE, Ann	25	F	Servant	21Ja02Az
POLAND, Maria	20	F	Servant	21Ja02Az
WOOD, Henry	34	M	Mechanic	21Ja02Az
WILSON, Issac	30	M	Mechanic	21Ja02Az
HENCHLEY, Wm.	24	M	Mechanic	21Ja02Az
GRIMES, Nicholas	21	M	Mechanic	21Ja02Az
FERGIN, Wm.	21	M	Mechanic	21Ja02Az
TOWER, John	22	M	Mechanic	21Ja02Az
MCBRIEN, Michael	50	M	Mechanic	21Ja02Az
Catherine	40	F	Servant	21Ja02Az
James	18	M	Servant	21Ja02Az
Patt	13	M	Laborer	21Ja02Az
Thomas	12	M	None	21Ja02Az
Alice	10	F	None	21Ja02Az
Thomas	09	M	Child	21Ja02Az
DRUM, John	24	M	Laborer	21Ja02Az
Judy	20	F	Servant	21Ja02Az
GORMBY, Patt	50	M	Laborer	21Ja02Az
Catherine	35	F	Servant	21Ja02Az
Patt	09	M	Child	21Ja02Az
Matthew	07	M	Child	21Ja02Az
Barney	.00	M	Infant	21Ja02Az
Died-At-Sea				
MCGAINERS, Pat	20	M	Laborer	21Ja02Az
TURNER, Mary	25	F	Servant	21Ja02Az
DOUGHERTY, Hugh	25	M	Laborer	21Ja02Az
HORAN, James	30	M	Laborer	21Ja02Az
ORPHAN, Adam	55	M	Laborer	21Ja02Az
COLLINS, Samuel	25	M	Laborer	21Ja02Az
FLANAGAN, Maria	40	F	Servant	21Ja02Az
Maria	08	F	Child	21Ja02Az
Richard	03	M	Child	21Ja02Az
James	.00	M	Infant	21Ja02Az
Died-At-Sea				
FITZSIMMONS, Patt	15	M	None	21Ja02Az

NAMES OF PASSENGERS	AGE	SEX	OCCUPATIONS	DATE PORT SHIP
FITZSIMMONS, Edward	13	M	None	21Ja02Az
TURNER, Pat	20	M	Laborer	21Ja02Az
MARTIN, John	25	M	Laborer	21Ja02Az
MARY, Pat	23	M	Laborer	21Ja02Az
MCGUIRE, John	25	M	Laborer	21Ja02Az
EVANS, Wm.	35	M	Laborer	21Ja02Az
JENKINS, John	70	M	Laborer	21Ja02Az
Elizabeth	28	F	Servant	21Ja02Az
Wm.	08	M	Child	21Ja02Az
Richard	05	M	Child	21Ja02Az
Catherine	02	F	Child	21Ja02Az
THOMAS, Benjamin	36	M	Laborer	21Ja02Az
JONES, Samuel	17	M	Laborer	21Ja02Az
Thomas	16	M	Laborer	21Ja02Az
Jane	28	F	Servant	21Ja02Az
John	01	M	Child	21Ja02Az
STEAD, Richard	30	M	Laborer	21Ja02Az
WHITEHEAD, Wm.	35	M	Laborer	21Ja02Az
RILEY, John	30	M	Laborer	21Ja02Az
Honora	25	F	Servant	21Ja02Az
SHERIDAN, Pat	30	M	Laborer	21Ja02Az
HOLLAND, James	18	M	Laborer	21Ja02Az
CLARK, John	18	M	Laborer	21Ja02Az
KELLY, Pat	20	M	Laborer	21Ja02Az
MARTINSON, Rose	20	F	Servant	21Ja02Az
KERNAN, Ally	20	F	Servant	21Ja02Az
COSTELLO, Mary	19	F	Servant	21Ja02Az
TAGGARD, Jane	40	F	Servant	21Ja02Az
Margaret	14	F	Servant	21Ja02Az
TONER, John	27	M	Laborer	21Ja02Az
FLAMAN, Wm.	55	M	Laborer	21Ja02Az
Wm.	18	M	Laborer	21Ja02Az
Maria	07	F	Child	21Ja02Az
HADDOCK, James	20	M	Laborer	21Ja02Az
PRITCHARD, John	21	M	Laborer	21Ja02Az
WILSON, John	32	M	Laborer	21Ja02Az
HACKETT, Michael	18	M	Laborer	21Ja02Az
MCMULLEN, Eliza	18	F	Servant	21Ja02Az
TONER, Amos	35	M	Laborer	21Ja02Az
PILKINGTON, John	20	M	Laborer	21Ja02Az
James	14	M	None	21Ja02Az
LEARY, Catharine	25	F	Servant	21Ja02Az
SHEEN, Wm.	45	M	Laborer	21Ja02Az
NEAGLE, Frank	21	M	Laborer	21Ja02Az
Johanna	52	F	Servant	21Ja02Az
Margaret	18	F	Servant	21Ja02Az
James	10	M	Child	21Ja02Az
WELSH, Johanna	19	F	Servant	21Ja02Az
RAGAN, John	23	M	Laborer	21Ja02Az
HARGAN, Margaret	20	F	Servant	21Ja02Az
CAMPBELL, Alex.	24	M	Laborer	21Ja02Az
JEWETT, Wm.	21	M	Laborer	21Ja02Az
WILKINSON, Joseph	21	M	Laborer	21Ja02Az
KELLY, Patt	34	M	Laborer	21Ja02Az
FLYNN, Chas.	35	M	Laborer	21Ja02Az
MCGRATH, Eliza	20	F	Servant	21Ja02Az
MCDONNOUGH, Sally	17	F	Servant	21Ja02Az
CLARKE, Pat	60	M	Laborer	21Ja02Az
Margaret	60	F	Servant	21Ja02Az
Ann	19	F	Servant	21Ja02Az
Charles	22	M	Laborer	21Ja02Az
KELLY, Pat	34	M	Laborer	21Ja02Az
FINNIGAN, Ann	18	F	Servant	21Ja02Az
SKEVINGTON, John	19	M	Laborer	21Ja02Az
HAYDON, Mary	17	F	Servant	21Ja02Az
YOUNG, Catharine	24	F	Servant	21Ja02Az
KEARVENY, Stephan	30	M	Laborer	21Ja02Az
MCKEON, James	38	M	Servant	21Ja02Az
Barney	05	M	Child	21Ja02Az
Biddy	03	F	Child	21Ja02Az
Died-At-Sea				
DAY, Deborah	18	F	Servant	21Ja02Az
ODONNELE, Michael	12	M	None	21Ja02Az
Sandy	08	M	Child	21Ja02Az
BROWN, Ann	19	F	Child	21Ja02Az

IVANHOE 21 JANUARY 1848

From Liverpool

NAMES OF PASSENGERS	AGE	SEX	OCCUPATIONS	DATE PORT SHIP
PRENTESS, Edward	24	M	Mechanic	21Ja02Bp
Sarah	22	F	None	21Ja02Bp
EARLES, James	21	M	Laborer	21Ja02Bp
HERBERT, Mary	22	F	Farmer	21Ja02Bp
Eliza	03	F	Child	21Ja02Bp
Alex.	01	M	Child	21Ja02Bp
JORDAN, John	33	M	Laborer	21Ja02Bp
Ann	25	F	None	21Ja02Bp
Mary	07	F	Child	21Ja02Bp
John	06	M	Child	21Ja02Bp
Wm.	03	M	Child	21Ja02Bp
Robert	01	M	Child	21Ja02Bp
CARSON, Isabella	19	F	Servant	21Ja02Bp
MCLIGHO, Bernard	21	M	Scholar	21Ja02Bp
NOLAN, Wm.	21	M	Laborer	21Ja02Bp
STAUNTON, John	37	M	Laborer	21Ja02Bp
FARLEY, John	23	M	Laborer	21Ja02Bp
John	70	M	Laborer	21Ja02Bp
Catherine	40	F	None	21Ja02Bp
Ann	22	F	None	21Ja02Bp
FFONDE, Mary	25	F	None	21Ja02Bp
Patrick	05	M	Child	21Ja02Bp
John	03	M	Child	21Ja02Bp
Mary	02	F	Child	21Ja02Bp
KELLY, Mary	35	F	None	21Ja02Bp
Isabella	09	F	Child	21Ja02Bp
James	01	M	Child	21Ja02Bp
LYNCH, Catherine	28	F	None	21Ja02Bp
BURKE, Peter	21	M	Laborer	21Ja02Bp
REILLY, Daniel	25	M	Laborer	21Ja02Bp
KEYS, George	26	M	Laborer	21Ja02Bp
CANNAY, Edward	18	M	Laborer	21Ja02Bp
DIXON, James	25	M	Laborer	21Ja02Bp
HEGARTY, Richard	35	M	Laborer	21Ja02Bp
HIGNEY, Hugh	20	M	Laborer	21Ja02Bp
Mary	16	F	Servant	21Ja02Bp
MCFARLAND, John	30	M	Laborer	21Ja02Bp
CONNLEY, Terrence	19	M	Laborer	21Ja02Bp
Mary	21	F	None	21Ja02Bp
Margt.	13	F	None	21Ja02Bp
John	10	M	None	21Ja02Bp
RIGLEY, Catherine	35	F	None	21Ja02Bp
John	16	M	None	21Ja02Bp
Mary	09	F	Child	21Ja02Bp
James	06	M	Child	21Ja02Bp
TOGEE, Huston	40	M	Laborer	21Ja02Bp
REGAN, Wm.	28	M	Laborer	21Ja02Bp
COLVIN, Patk.	25	M	Laborer	21Ja02Bp
COLLMAN, Patk.	35	M	Laborer	21Ja02Bp
Anna	30	F	Servant	21Ja02Bp
Patk.	04	M	Child	21Ja02Bp
WILSON, Peter	20	M	Laborer	21Ja02Bp
BRENNAN, Francis	18	F	Tailor	21Ja02Bp
WILLOUGHTY, James	17	F	Tailor	21Ja02Bp
CATON, Mary	50	F	Servant	21Ja02Bp
Bernd.	50	M	Bricklayer	21Ja02Bp
SEYMOUR, Luke	30	M	Laborer	21Ja02Bp
BELL, John	28	M	Laborer	21Ja02Bp
LULLY, Mary	33	F	Servant	21Ja02Bp
Catherine	20	F	Servant	21Ja02Bp
Ann	18	F	Servant	21Ja02Bp
CONNLEY, Francis	21	M	Laborer	21Ja02Bp
LAPPIN, Matilda	18	F	Servant	21Ja02Bp
HOLDEN, Brigt.	45	F	Servant	21Ja02Bp
Catherine	17	F	Servant	21Ja02Bp

NAMES OF PASSENGERS	AGE	SEX	OCCUPATIONS	DATE PORT SHIP
HOLDEN, James	15	M	None	21Ja02Bp
FLOOD, Thomas	35	M	Blacksmith	21Ja02Bp
MCTAGGART, Ann	23	F	Servant	21Ja02Bp
MUNEY, Antony	15	M	Servant	21Ja02Bp
Brigt.	21	F	Servant	21Ja02Bp
MACKIN, James	42	M	Tailor	21Ja02Bp
Mary	44	F	Servant	21Ja02Bp
Mary	15	F	Servant	21Ja02Bp
DOGHERTY, Susan	20	F	Servant	21Ja02Bp
CUSKER, Pat	20	M	Butcher	21Ja02Bp
EGAN, James	20	M	Laborer	21Ja02Bp
Pat	04	M	Child	21Ja02Bp
Martha	24	F	Servant	21Ja02Bp
SHORT, Jane	25	F	Servant	21Ja02Bp
WARD, Tammy	21	F	Servant	21Ja02Bp
GOURLEY, Margt.	15	F	Servant	21Ja02Bp
MCAULEFFE, Brigt.	25	F	Servant	21Ja02Bp
WELSH, Ally	16	F	Servant	21Ja02Bp
HAGGERTY, John	26	M	Laborer	21Ja02Bp
Peter	17	M	Laborer	21Ja02Bp
CUGHAN, John	52	M	Laborer	21Ja02Bp
Sarah	50	F	Servant	21Ja02Bp
Margt.	18	F	Servant	21Ja02Bp
DENOVAN, Lawrence	22	M	Mason	21Ja02Bp
Margt.	17	F	Servant	21Ja02Bp
COKLEY, Ann	19	F	Servant	21Ja02Bp
HAGGERTY, Ellen	17	F	Servant	21Ja02Bp
WALSH, Mick	25	M	Carpenter	21Ja02Bp
MCCARTY, Jeremiah	20	M	Carpenter	21Ja02Bp
MILLER, Ann	27	F	None	21Ja02Bp
Died-At-Sea				
CHRYSTAL, Celia	12	F	None	21Ja02Bp
Ann	07	F	None	21Ja02Bp
DUNN, Mary-C.	16	F	Servant	21Ja02Bp
OLOUGHLAN, Bryan	18	M	Shoemaker	21Ja02Bp
HAGAN, Ann	30	F	Servant	21Ja02Bp
HEFTON, John	25	M	None	21Ja02Bp
AUTHERLY, Thomas	27	M	None	21Ja02Bp

VIRGINIA 22 JANUARY 1848

From Liverpool

NAMES OF PASSENGERS	AGE	SEX	OCCUPATIONS	DATE PORT SHIP
HAGAN, Ellen	20	F	Spinster	22Ja02Ap
HILL, William	35	M	Farmer	22Ja02Ap
Mary	38	F	None	22Ja02Ap
Alfm	15	F	Spinster	22Ja02Ap
WILSON, James	24	M	Laborer	22Ja02Ap
MANSON, Alfred	30	M	Laborer	22Ja02Ap
JONES, Robert	56	M	Laborer	22Ja02Ap
HORRIGAN, Dennis	40	M	Laborer	22Ja02Ap
MURPHY, John	17	M	Laborer	22Ja02Ap
DEMPALSY, Jim	30	M	Laborer	22Ja02Ap
Danl.	23	M	Laborer	22Ja02Ap
HONTERING, Rich	21	M	Laborer	22Ja02Ap
Joseph	20	M	Laborer	22Ja02Ap
MANSON, James	22	M	Laborer	22Ja02Ap
Ellen (W)	19	F	None	22Ja02Ap
CALLAHAN, James	35	M	Farmer	22Ja02Ap
Cath. (W)	32	F	None	22Ja02Ap
Ellen	12	F	None	22Ja02Ap
Michl.	10	M	None	22Ja02Ap
Jon.	07	M	Child	22Ja02Ap
Sarah	04	F	Child	22Ja02Ap
Margt.	02	F	Child	22Ja02Ap
Mary	.00	F	Infant	22Ja02Ap
DAVY, Bridget	20	F	Spinster	22Ja02Ap
Mary	18	F	Spinster	22Ja02Ap
LANGON, Ellen	20	F	Spinster	22Ja02Ap
COCKROME, Honora	18	F	Spinster	22Ja02Ap
John	28	M	Laborer	22Ja02Ap
ROSS, Pat	18	M	Laborer	22Ja02Ap
SMITH, Francis	24	M	Laborer	22Ja02Ap
ODONNELLY, Peter	24	M	Laborer	22Ja02Ap
SMITH, Wm.	25	M	Laborer	22Ja02Ap
James	22	M	Laborer	22Ja02Ap
ASHS, Eliz.	21	F	Spinster	22Ja02Ap
MCCOY, Cath.	20	F	Spinster	22Ja02Ap
DUNN, James	20	M	Farmer	22Ja02Ap
CAMPBELL, Elizth.	20	F	Spinster	22Ja02Ap
WILKINSON, Thos.	32	M	Laborer	22Ja02Ap
John	17	M	Laborer	22Ja02Ap
SHEEHAN, Danl.	23	M	Laborer	22Ja02Ap
LEAVY, Biddy	30	F	None	22Ja02Ap
Danl.	09	M	Child	22Ja02Ap
Cath.	05	F	Child	22Ja02Ap
TRETOS, Alexd.	20	M	Laborer	22Ja02Ap
HINPE, Maria	20	F	Servant	22Ja02Ap
MCCANN, James	20	M	Laborer	22Ja02Ap
WALSH, Pat	18	M	Laborer	22Ja02Ap
MANLY, Barbara	20	F	Spinster	22Ja02Ap
REILLY, Maria	18	F	Spinster	22Ja02Ap
SPRAG, Alexr.	22	M	Farmer	22Ja02Ap
MCGRANE, Ann	24	F	None	22Ja02Ap
CLIFFORD, Margt.	20	F	None	22Ja02Ap
CANNON, Biddy	24	F	None	22Ja02Ap
Biddy	19	F	None	22Ja02Ap
Rose	17	F	None	22Ja02Ap
Michl.	20	M	None	22Ja02Ap
SEXTON, Cornls.	27	M	Laborer	22Ja02Ap
MURPHY, Wm.	21	M	Laborer	22Ja02Ap
DORAN, John	21	M	Laborer	22Ja02Ap
Cath. (W)	20	F	None	22Ja02Ap
WALLIS, Cath.	20	F	None	22Ja02Ap
EARLY, James	30	M	Farmer	22Ja02Ap
Cath. (W)	26	F	None	22Ja02Ap
Rich.	05	M	Child	22Ja02Ap
James	04	M	Child	22Ja02Ap
Robert	02	M	Child	22Ja02Ap
Andw.	.00	M	Infant	22Ja02Ap
DOWNEY, John	21	M	Laborer	22Ja02Ap
SMITH, James	18	M	Laborer	22Ja02Ap
CUSACK, Cath.	21	F	Spinster	22Ja02Ap
CAWLEY, Ellen	21	F	Spinster	22Ja02Ap
LYNCH, Rose	18	F	Spinster	22Ja02Ap
WALLACK, James	39	M	Laborer	22Ja02Ap
Mary (W)	30	F	None	22Ja02Ap
Henry	04	M	Child	22Ja02Ap
FORR, Wm.	23	M	Laborer	22Ja02Ap
NONGHES, Ellen	22	F	Spinster	22Ja02Ap
DONOGHUS, Mary	18	F	Spinster	22Ja02Ap
CLIFFORD, Henry	21	M	Farmer	22Ja02Ap
DAVIES, John	21	M	Farmer	22Ja02Ap
BERGEN, Francis	30	M	Farmer	22Ja02Ap
KERWIN, James	43	M	Farmer	22Ja02Ap
Mary	43	F	None	22Ja02Ap
Cath.	21	F	Spinster	22Ja02Ap
Bridgt.	17	F	Spinster	22Ja02Ap
Ann	13	F	Spinster	22Ja02Ap
Edward	02	M	Child	22Ja02Ap
LUNNA, Wm.	27	M	Laborer	22Ja02Ap
Hugh	24	M	Laborer	22Ja02Ap
GUBBINS, Joseph	20	M	Laborer	22Ja02Ap
MCSTAVOCK, Cath.	23	F	Spinster	22Ja02Ap
RICHARDS, Josh.	43	M	Farmer	22Ja02Ap
COMMANS, Patk.	28	M	Farmer	22Ja02Ap
U (W)	24	F	None	22Ja02Ap
Patk.	.00	M	Infant	22Ja02Ap
BURKE, Francis	30	M	Laborer	22Ja02Ap
COMMONS, Bridgt.	20	F	Servant	22Ja02Ap
WALKER, John	21	M	Laborer	22Ja02Ap
Isabella	24	F	None	22Ja02Ap
SIMPSON, Robt.	22	M	Farmer	22Ja02Ap
JOHNSON, James	56	M	Farmer	22Ja02Ap

NAMES OF PASSENGERS		AGE	SEX	OCCUPATIONS	DATE PORT SHIP
JOHNSON, U	(W)	46	F	None	22Ja02Ap
Mary		29	F	None	22Ja02Ap
John		10	M	None	22Ja02Ap
MCKENNON, Wm.		22	M	Servant	22Ja02Ap
HARWOOD, Geo.		27	M	Servant	22Ja02Ap
Francis		23	F	None	22Ja02Ap
Mary		04	F	Child	22Ja02Ap
Sarah		13	F	None	22Ja02Ap
Geo.		.00	M	Infant	22Ja02Ap
MADDEN, Pat		25	M	Laborer	22Ja02Ap
CARR, John		27	M	Laborer	22Ja02Ap
WILSON, Robt.		27	M	Laborer	22Ja02Ap
MCDORE, Stephen		23	M	Laborer	22Ja02Ap
WARHOOP, Thos.		40	M	Laborer	22Ja02Ap
KENNEDY, Maurich		20	M	Laborer	22Ja02Ap
Margt.	(W)	20	F	None	22Ja02Ap
Thomas		12	M	None	22Ja02Ap
Ellen		20	F	Spinster	22Ja02Ap
GRIFFIN, Johana		30	F	Spinster	22Ja02Ap
MCDERMOTT, Benj.		20	M	Farmer	22Ja02Ap
MULLEN, Mary		20	F	Servant	22Ja02Ap
MCLOUGHLIN, Jane		40	F	None	22Ja02Ap
BRESNAHAN, Pat		20	M	Laborer	22Ja02Ap
KENNEDY, Cath.		20	F	Servant	22Ja02Ap
MINAHAN, Johana		20	F	Servant	22Ja02Ap
MCGINTY, Thos.		35	M	Farmer	22Ja02Ap
THOMSTON, Wm.		25	M	Farmer	22Ja02Ap
Jane	(W)	23	F	None	22Ja02Ap
Margt.		.00	F	Infant	22Ja02Ap
REAY, Wm.		26	M	Laborer	22Ja02Ap
HANNON, Andw.		30	M	Laborer	22Ja02Ap
Margt.		26	F	None	22Ja02Ap
Michl.		07	M	Child	22Ja02Ap
Edwd.		04	M	Child	22Ja02Ap
Wm.		02	M	Child	22Ja02Ap
Margt-Jane		.00	F	Infant	22Ja02Ap
KELLY, Wm.		21	M	Farmer	22Ja02Ap
DAVIES, John		21	M	Farmer	22Ja02Ap
KENNY, Mary		20	F	Spinster	22Ja02Ap
KELLY, Kitty		23	F	Spinster	22Ja02Ap
CONOVAN, Mary		18	F	Spinster	22Ja02Ap
KELLY, Pat		07	M	Child	22Ja02Ap
MCDERMOTT, Jno.		30	M	Servant	22Ja02Ap
Eliza		15	F	Spinster	22Ja02Ap
FLANNELLY, Hugh		20	M	Laborer	22Ja02Ap
Pat		30	M	Laborer	22Ja02Ap
Cath.	(W)	27	F	None	22Ja02Ap
LYNETT, Pat		26	M	Laborer	22Ja02Ap
MCLEAN, Ellen		30	F	None	22Ja02Ap
John		05	M	Child	22Ja02Ap
BEARD, John		22	M	None	22Ja02Ap
KING, Patk.		23	M	None	22Ja02Ap
Margt.	(W)	28	F	None	22Ja02Ap
LAWLESS, Michl.		19	M	Farmer	22Ja02Ap
BRADY, Benj.		60	M	Farmer	22Ja02Ap
John		32	M	Farmer	22Ja02Ap
Mary	(W)	32	F	None	22Ja02Ap
Maria		26	F	None	22Ja02Ap
Barney		18	M	Farmer	22Ja02Ap
Bernard		05	M	Child	22Ja02Ap
Bridgt.		03	F	Child	22Ja02Ap
MULLANEY, Nelly		30	F	None	22Ja02Ap
Mary		06	F	Child	22Ja02Ap
MURRAY, Margt.		45	F	None	22Ja02Ap
Mary		20	F	None	22Ja02Ap
Ellen		18	F	None	22Ja02Ap
Michl.		16	M	Laborer	22Ja02Ap
CONLON, Margt.		16	F	Spinster	22Ja02Ap
DOWD, Hannah		40	F	Spinster	22Ja02Ap
MORIN, Pat		16	M	Laborer	22Ja02Ap
Winnifred		11	F	None	22Ja02Ap
Margt.		40	F	None	22Ja02Ap
James		.00	M	Infant	22Ja02Ap
HEAVAN, Michl.		32	M	Laborer	22Ja02Ap
DEVINE, Mary		45	F	None	22Ja02Ap
DEVINE, Ellen		07	F	Child	22Ja02Ap
CRAIG, Wm.		35	M	None	22Ja02Ap
HILL, Robt.		32	M	Farmer	22Ja02Ap
MCHUGH, John		24	M	Farmer	22Ja02Ap
ANDREW, Margt.		28	F	Farmer	22Ja02Ap
RANKIN, James		26	M	Farmer	22Ja02Ap
LYNCH, Hugh		26	M	Farmer	22Ja02Ap
HAGGERTY, Pat		40	M	Farmer	22Ja02Ap
Mary	(W)	35	F	None	22Ja02Ap
James		05	M	Child	22Ja02Ap
Patk.		03	M	Child	22Ja02Ap
John		.00	M	Infant	22Ja02Ap
ROCHE, Johana		19	F	Spinster	22Ja02Ap
CAMDY, Maria		50	F	None	22Ja02Ap
HAGGERTY, Tim		21	M	Laborer	22Ja02Ap
LEHMAN, Edwd.		20	M	Laborer	22Ja02Ap
MCCARN, Geo.		40	M	Laborer	22Ja02Ap
U	(W)	40	F	None	22Ja02Ap
Geo.		19	M	Farmer	22Ja02Ap
Ann-Jane		17	F	Spinster	22Ja02Ap
Mary		12	F	Spinster	22Ja02Ap
Patt		04	M	Child	22Ja02Ap
HARK, Thomas		30	M	Laborer	22Ja02Ap
THOMPSON, Jane		40	F	None	22Ja02Ap
LYONS, Esther		20	F	None	22Ja02Ap
Margt.		18	F	None	22Ja02Ap
WALKER, Thos.		20	M	Laborer	22Ja02Ap
Margt.	(W)	25	F	None	22Ja02Ap
Isabella		22	F	None	22Ja02Ap
Mary		50	F	None	22Ja02Ap
DINBURY, Wm.		50	M	Farmer	22Ja02Ap
Mary	(W)	24	F	None	22Ja02Ap
James		22	M	Farmer	22Ja02Ap
Richd.		13	M	Farmer	22Ja02Ap
Geo.		11	M	None	22Ja02Ap
Jane		09	F	Child	22Ja02Ap
HARVEY, Henry		25	M	Farmer	22Ja02Ap
GUINNESS, John		41	M	Farmer	22Ja02Ap
Isabella		32	F	None	22Ja02Ap
John		09	M	Child	22Ja02Ap
Charlotte		07	F	Child	22Ja02Ap
Robt.		05	M	Child	22Ja02Ap
Wm-Henry		03	M	Child	22Ja02Ap
Isabella		.00	F	Infant	22Ja02Ap
BRAYURE, Thos.		27	M	Laborer	22Ja02Ap
RAFFERTY, Mary		25	F	None	22Ja02Ap
Elizth.		.00	F	Infant	22Ja02Ap
HEYWOOD, Wm.		36	M	Farmer	22Ja02Ap
PINDER, Issac		23	M	Farmer	22Ja02Ap
SHELDON, Thos.		36	M	Farmer	22Ja02Ap
KELLY, Wm.		34	M	Farmer	22Ja02Ap
MCKEEVES, John		20	M	Farmer	22Ja02Ap
KAY, James		30	M	Laborer	22Ja02Ap
Mary		05	F	Child	22Ja02Ap
Cath.		16	F	Spinster	22Ja02Ap
CLARK, Thos.		24	M	Farmer	22Ja02Ap
U	(W)	24	F	None	22Ja02Ap
Ann		04	F	Child	22Ja02Ap
John		07	M	Child	22Ja02Ap
Michl.		22	M	Laborer	22Ja02Ap
KING, Eliza		24	F	Spinster	22Ja02Ap
REILLY, Margt.		20	F	Spinster	22Ja02Ap
CONLON, Mary		20	F	Spinster	22Ja02Ap
HIGGINS, John		24	M	Farmer	22Ja02Ap
REILLY, Isabella		24	F	Spinster	22Ja02Ap
HIGGINS, Pat		20	M	Laborer	22Ja02Ap
MCDERMOTT, Michl.		32	M	Laborer	22Ja02Ap
FORD, Honora		21	F	Spinster	22Ja02Ap
NOONAN, Ann		17	F	Spinster	22Ja02Ap
Honora		18	F	Spinster	22Ja02Ap
ROGERS, Joseph		46	M	Farmer	22Ja02Ap
BYRNES, Cath.		18	F	Spinster	22Ja02Ap
MCINTSK, Bridgt.		19	F	Spinster	22Ja02Ap
WARDEN, Maria		24	F	Spinster	22Ja02Ap
GERTY, Mary		19	F	Spinster	22Ja02Ap

NAMES OF PASSENGERS	AGE	SEX	OCCUPATIONS	DATE PORT SHIP
GROGAN, Pat	25	M	Laborer	22Ja02Ap
MURPHY, Jno.	30	M	Laborer	22Ja02Ap
SULLIVAN, Dennis	18	M	Laborer	22Ja02Ap
WALL, Jno.	10	M	Laborer	22Ja02Ap
LEAVY, William	.00	M	Infant	22Ja02Ap
Died-At-Sea				
WALLACK, William	06	M	Child	22Ja02Ap
Died-At-Sea				
BRADY, Mary	.00	F	Infant	22Ja02Ap
Died-At-Sea				
FOGGARTY, John	25	M	None	22Ja02Ap
Died-At-Sea				

INDIA 22 JANUARY 1848

From Liverpool

NAMES OF PASSENGERS	AGE	SEX	OCCUPATIONS	DATE PORT SHIP
MCMAHON, Thos.	50	M	Laborer	22Ja02At
Died-At-Sea				
U (W)	50	F	None	22Ja02At
Died-At-Sea				
Maria	27	F	None	22Ja02At
Priscilla	25	F	None	22Ja02At
James	22	M	Laborer	22Ja02At
CASTLE, Mary-Ann	26	F	None	22Ja02At
William	12	M	None	22Ja02At
MCBRIEN, John	20	M	None	22Ja02At
Phillip	11	M	None	22Ja02At
DRISCOLL, Jerry	25	M	None	22Ja02At
Catherine	22	F	None	22Ja02At
HINE, George	24	M	None	22Ja02At
RYAN, Agnes	20	F	None	22Ja02At
BYNNES, James	24	M	None	22Ja02At
MCNUTLY, Sarah	20	F	None	22Ja02At
KENNEDY, Edward	28	M	None	22Ja02At
MARION, John	40	M	None	22Ja02At
LYON, Patrick	18	M	None	22Ja02At
DUFFY, James	18	M	None	22Ja02At
CARNEY, Honora	40	F	None	22Ja02At
Maria	02	F	Child	22Ja02At
James	.00	M	Infant	22Ja02At
FINNEGAN, Patrick	40	M	None	22Ja02At
Catherine	36	F	None	22Ja02At
James	11	M	None	22Ja02At
Catherine	09	F	Child	22Ja02At
Elizabeth	07	F	Child	22Ja02At
Bridget	02	F	Child	22Ja02At
DALEY, John	20	M	None	22Ja02At
Michael	24	M	None	22Ja02At
WILKS, Edward	24	M	None	22Ja02At
BEVIN, Michael	27	M	None	22Ja02At
LEARY, Daniel	14	M	None	22Ja02At
SULLIVAN, Jeffrey	45	M	None	22Ja02At
Died-At-Sea				
DRISCOLL, Julia	25	F	None	22Ja02At
NEAL, Danl.	50	M	None	22Ja02At
Danl.	12	M	None	22Ja02At
Mary	50	F	None	22Ja02At
MCCARTHY, Julia	26	F	None	22Ja02At
Shurly	50	M	None	22Ja02At
MURPHY, Patrick	08	M	Child	22Ja02At
Mary	09	F	Child	22Ja02At
CROWLEY, Darby	25	M	None	22Ja02At
KELLY, Jas.O.	23	M	None	22Ja02At
Mary	23	F	None	22Ja02At
BUCKLEY, Danl.	25	M	None	22Ja02At
WHARTY, Mick	28	M	None	22Ja02At
Elisa	30	F	None	22Ja02At
Richard	03	M	Child	22Ja02At
WHARTY, Mary	.00	F	Infant	22Ja02At
KILMARTIN, Bernard	21	M	None	22Ja02At
Mary	18	F	None	22Ja02At
SWEANY, Roger	30	M	None	22Ja02At
Died-At-Sea				
KENNESSEY, Ann	35	F	None	22Ja02At
QUINN, Mary	20	F	None	22Ja02At
SULLIVAN, Kate	30	F	None	22Ja02At
Mary	06	F	Child	22Ja02At
Michael	04	M	Child	22Ja02At
Died-At-Sea				
John	01	M	Child	22Ja02At
HICKEY, John	23	M	None	22Ja02At
MAELAENN, Francis	20	M	None	22Ja02At
MULLIGAN, Ann	18	F	None	22Ja02At
Mary	08	F	Child	22Ja02At
MARIAN, Hopive	40	M	None	22Ja02At
James	.00	M	Infant	22Ja02At
Mary	14	F	None	22Ja02At
Jane	10	F	None	22Ja02At
John	08	M	Child	22Ja02At
Mark	06	M	Child	22Ja02At
Margaret	05	F	Child	22Ja02At
Mary	02	F	Child	22Ja02At
HENNESY, Hosire	30	M	None	22Ja02At
Patrick	.00	M	Infant	22Ja02At
OHEARN, Mick	23	M	None	22Ja02At
SESSNELL, James	29	M	None	22Ja02At
MURRAY, Peggy	20	F	None	22Ja02At
Kenan	13	M	None	22Ja02At
Patrick	05	M	Child	22Ja02At
BRYAN, Hugh	35	M	None	22Ja02At
AMBROSE, Ann	27	F	None	22Ja02At
Ann	01	F	Child	22Ja02At
ELLIS, Mary	24	F	None	22Ja02At
Mary	06	F	Child	22Ja02At
MORAN, Michl.	23	M	None	22Ja02At
Cath.	17	F	None	22Ja02At
Biddy	14	F	None	22Ja02At
HALL, John	53	M	None	22Ja02At
U (W)	60	F	None	22Ja02At
Emma	.00	F	Infant	22Ja02At
Elizabeth	26	F	None	22Ja02At
Sarah-Ann	19	F	None	22Ja02At
Sarah	16	F	None	22Ja02At
Lucy	13	F	None	22Ja02At
Elizabeth	11	F	None	22Ja02At
Jane	10	F	None	22Ja02At
Charles	09	M	Child	22Ja02At
Died-At-Sea				
Letitia	07	F	Child	22Ja02At
Maria	04	F	Child	22Ja02At
HOLINGSHEAD, Ann	26	F	None	22Ja02At
Thos.	27	M	None	22Ja02At
SMITH, U	27	F	None	22Ja02At
LYONS, Bridget	21	F	None	22Ja02At
Died-At-Sea				
CONNELLY, Michl.	08	M	Child	22Ja02At
BYRNES, Bryan	40	M	None	22Ja02At
Nancy	12	F	None	22Ja02At
Ellen	06	F	Child	22Ja02At
MCKANNA, Ann	33	F	None	22Ja02At
Mary	11	F	None	22Ja02At
Hugh	05	M	Child	22Ja02At
James	02	M	Child	22Ja02At
DEMPSY, Cath.	18	F	None	22Ja02At
REYNOLDS, Edward	20	M	None	22Ja02At
WADE, Felix	24	M	None	22Ja02At
MURPHY, Patrick	35	M	None	22Ja02At
HENNSEEY, Bridget	35	F	None	22Ja02At
DUNN, Cath.	45	F	None	22Ja02At
Mary	18	F	None	22Ja02At
John	10	M	None	22Ja02At
Thomas	07	M	Child	22Ja02At
Martin	06	M	Child	22Ja02At

NAMES OF PASSENGERS		AGE	SEX	OCCUPATIONS	DATE PORT SHIP
DUNN, Catherine		05	F	Child	22Ja02At
Bridget		02	F	Child	22Ja02At
MCDONALD, John		27	M	None	22Ja02At
GAFFNEY, Phillip		20	M	None	22Ja02At
U	(W)	20	F	None	22Ja02At
REILLY, U		30	M	None	22Ja02At
Bridget		30	F	None	22Ja02At
U		.00	U	Infant	22Ja02At
Margaret		18	F	None	22Ja02At
DOLEN, Mary		32	F	None	22Ja02At
HANTON, James		32	M	None	22Ja02At
Died-At-Sea					
CARNEY, Patrick		20	M	None	22Ja02At
MCLEVIN, Dominick		21	M	None	22Ja02At
CAREY, Bryant		30	M	None	22Ja02At
MILLEY, Bridget		30	F	None	22Ja02At
OHARA, Henry		20	M	None	22Ja02At
LENNOX, John		40	M	None	22Ja02At
HENRY, John		24	M	None	22Ja02At
MCCOSKREY, John		24	M	None	22Ja02At
MCGREEN, Sally		20	F	None	22Ja02At
TORYE, Mary-A.		20	F	None	22Ja02At
MADDEN, Margaret		50	F	None	22Ja02At
Mary-Jane		14	F	None	22Ja02At
Susannah		12	F	None	22Ja02At
Catherine		08	F	Child	22Ja02At
Rachel		06	F	Child	22Ja02At
William		04	M	Child	22Ja02At
KANE, Ann		35	F	None	22Ja02At
Died-At-Sea					
TULLY, Michl.		26	M	None	22Ja02At
HANGHAN, Patrick		24	M	None	22Ja02At
MAYLAN, John		38	M	None	22Ja02At
GRAY, Wm.		39	M	None	22Ja02At
GROGIN, John		20	M	None	22Ja02At
Died-At-Sea					
MADDEN, Mary		24	F	None	22Ja02At
NAMVIE, Ellen		23	F	None	22Ja02At
LAWSON, Ann		24	F	None	22Ja02At
BRADLEY, William		22	M	None	22Ja02At
CASEY, James		22	M	None	22Ja02At
Cath.		20	F	None	22Ja02At
John		.00	M	Infant	22Ja02At
Died-At-Sea					
ALLAN, John		00	M	None	22Ja02At
Francis		12	M	None	22Ja02At
Ann		09	F	Child	22Ja02At
HEATH, Bridget		40	F	None	22Ja02At
Ann		12	F	None	22Ja02At
MARK, Ann		10	F	None	22Ja02At
MURRAY, Hugh		24	M	None	22Ja02At
Ellen		23	F	None	22Ja02At
WAPOLE, Thos.		20	M	None	22Ja02At
Died-At-Sea					
Ann		20	F	None	22Ja02At
Petty		18	F	None	22Ja02At
FENEY, Bartley		18	M	None	22Ja02At
MURRAY, Cath.		20	F	None	22Ja02At
MCDUNNOUGH, Rose		17	F	None	22Ja02At
OWENS, Margaret		18	F	None	22Ja02At
LOUGHLIN, Michael		20	M	None	22Ja02At
MURRAY, Martin		20	M	None	22Ja02At
OHARAH, John		40	M	None	22Ja02At
U	(W)	30	F	None	22Ja02At
U		.00	U	Infant	22Ja02At
Died-At-Sea					
Jos.		03	M	Child	22Ja02At
FENEY, Maria		20	F	None	22Ja02At
SNOIN, Geo.		29	M	None	22Ja02At
IRWIN, U		00	F	None	22Ja02At
U		.00	U	Infant	22Ja02At
Thos.		07	M	Child	22Ja02At
James		06	M	Child	22Ja02At
Charles		03	M	Child	22Ja02At
BATES, William		29	M	None	22Ja02At
BATES, Ann		28	F	None	22Ja02At
Emma		.00	F	Infant	22Ja02At
James		17	M	None	22Ja02At
MCGOVEY, Mary		24	F	None	22Ja02At
Cath.		20	F	None	22Ja02At
Died-At-Sea					
James		28	M	None	22Ja02At
KENNEDY, James		40	M	None	22Ja02At
U	(W)	40	F	None	22Ja02At
LYNCH, Patrick		30	M	None	22Ja02At
Michal		20	M	None	22Ja02At
GLYNN, Mary		16	F	None	22Ja02At

NEW-WORLD 22 JANUARY 1848

From Liverpool

NAMES OF PASSENGERS		AGE	SEX	OCCUPATIONS	DATE PORT SHIP
BARROW, Michl.		56	M	Gdnr	22Ja02Ku
DOUGHERTY, Philip		40	M	Mason	22Ja02Ku
RYAN, Michl.		35	M	Farmer	22Ja02Ku
Ellen	(W)	32	F	None	22Ja02Ku
Patrick	(S)	08	M	Child	22Ja02Ku
Mary		06	F	Child	22Ja02Ku
James		05	M	Child	22Ja02Ku
Thomas		04	M	Child	22Ja02Ku
Catherine		03	F	Child	22Ja02Ku
Michl.		.00	M	Infant	22Ja02Ku
Patt		24	M	Laborer	22Ja02Ku
DUNN, Michl.		23	M	Laborer	22Ja02Ku
FARRELL, Edwd.		16	M	None	22Ja02Ku
BRADY, Philip		42	M	Farmer	22Ja02Ku
Bridgt.	(W)	40	F	None	22Ja02Ku
Patt	(S)	21	M	None	22Ja02Ku
Mary	(D)	18	F	None	22Ja02Ku
Catherine	(D)	13	F	None	22Ja02Ku
James	(S)	05	M	Child	22Ja02Ku
NEALAN, John		22	M	Laborer	22Ja02Ku
HANLIN, P.		23	M	Clerk	22Ja02Ku
WIGGINS, Eliza		20	F	Servant	22Ja02Ku
LYNCH, Lauce.		44	M	Blacksmith	22Ja02Ku
BRENNAN, Thos.		24	M	Laborer	22Ja02Ku
MOORE, James		24	M	Laborer	22Ja02Ku
FARMER, James		18	M	Laborer	22Ja02Ku
GAVIN, Michl.		20	M	Laborer	22Ja02Ku
James		12	M	Laborer	22Ja02Ku
CONNOLLY, Bernd.		20	M	Laborer	22Ja02Ku
Patrick		13	M	Laborer	22Ja02Ku
Catherine	(T)	16	F	None	22Ja02Ku
MCGAURAN, Margt.		19	F	Servant	22Ja02Ku
BRENAN, Edward		18	M	Laborer	22Ja02Ku
SHEPHARD, John		12	M	Laborer	22Ja02Ku
CAMPBELL, U		20	F	Servant	22Ja02Ku
BRANAGAN, Thos.		21	M	Laborer	22Ja02Ku
BARRON, James		28	M	Laborer	22Ja02Ku
PLUNKET, Mathw.		20	M	Laborer	22Ja02Ku
KELLY, Edwd.		40	M	Farmer	22Ja02Ku
Eliza	(W)	34	F	None	22Ja02Ku
William	(S)	15	M	None	22Ja02Ku
Edward	(S)	12	M	None	22Ja02Ku
Dyniphria	(D)	08	F	Child	22Ja02Ku
Lance.		06	F	Child	22Ja02Ku
Charles		05	M	Child	22Ja02Ku
Bernard		04	M	Child	22Ja02Ku
Michl.		03	M	Child	22Ja02Ku
Died-At-Sea					
Charles		.00	M	Infant	22Ja02Ku
CADDY, Cath.		30	F	Servant	22Ja02Ku
LUNLEY, Michl.		26	M	Painter	22Ja02Ku
WOODWARD, M.		50	M	Miner	22Ja02Ku

NAMES OF PASSENGERS		AGE	SEX	OCCUPATIONS	DATE PORT SHIP
WOODWARD, William	(S)	16	M	None	22Ja02Ku
Jane	(D)	18	F	None	22Ja02Ku
Mary-Ann	(D)	07	F	Child	22Ja02Ku
Susan	(D)	03	F	Child	22Ja02Ku
MOORHEAD, Willm.		30	M	Laborer	22Ja02Ku
MCNELUS, Patk.		25	M	Laborer	22Ja02Ku
Hannah		17	F	None	22Ja02Ku
DORAIN, John		20	M	Farmer	22Ja02Ku
ONEILL, Michl.		28	M	Carpenter	22Ja02Ku
CAVANAGH, Thos.		20	M	Tailor	22Ja02Ku
SULLIVAN, Michl.		25	M	Farmer	22Ja02Ku
BOLAN, Patk.		25	M	Laborer	22Ja02Ku
MULLEN, Ellen		32	F	None	22Ja02Ku
Hugh		04	M	Child	22Ja02Ku
Susan		02	F	Child	22Ja02Ku
U		.00	U	Infant	22Ja02Ku
HAGGARTY, Margt.		38	F	None	22Ja02Ku
Hugh		06	M	Child	22Ja02Ku
Francis		03	M	Child	22Ja02Ku
TRACEY, Andw.		04	M	Child	22Ja02Ku
BOLAN, Mary		24	F	Servant	22Ja02Ku
HAUGHEY, Patt		20	M	Laborer	22Ja02Ku
ROUGHTON, James		40	M	Laborer	22Ja02Ku
MURRIN, John		18	M	Laborer	22Ja02Ku
MCGRANE, Edwd.		20	M	Servant	22Ja02Ku
MCSHANE, Cath.		36	F	None	22Ja02Ku
Edwd.		10	M	Child	22Ja02Ku
Catherine		06	F	Child	22Ja02Ku
Mary		04	F	Child	22Ja02Ku
Ellen	(L)	20	F	None	22Ja02Ku
REILLY, James		11	M	None	22Ja02Ku
DOYLE, Mary		14	F	None	22Ja02Ku
MALLON, Mary		27	F	None	22Ja02Ku
James		04	M	Child	22Ja02Ku
Michal		02	M	Child	22Ja02Ku
Bridgt.		.00	F	Infant	22Ja02Ku
DOUGHERTY, John		22	M	Laborer	22Ja02Ku
MORAN, Patt		40	M	Laborer	22Ja02Ku
ONEILL, John		29	M	Laborer	22Ja02Ku
Margt.		17	F	None	22Ja02Ku
MCGRATH, John		24	M	Laborer	22Ja02Ku
KELLY, Mary		19	F	Servant	22Ja02Ku
REILLY, Tim		25	M	Carpenter	22Ja02Ku
LAULER, John		32	M	Cbtmkr	22Ja02Ku
LOGUE, Hugh		30	M	Laborer	22Ja02Ku
WILLIAMS, Robt.		40	M	Farmer	22Ja02Ku
STAVOS, William		14	M	Shoemaker	22Ja02Ku
STARS, John		12	M	Servant	22Ja02Ku
DOWLING, John		40	M	Carpenter	22Ja02Ku
MCGUIRE, James		40	M	Farmer	22Ja02Ku
KING, Philip		40	M	Laborer	22Ja02Ku
BAKER, Chas.		35	M	Proprietor	22Ja02Ku
STAFFORD, John		20	M	Spinner	22Ja02Ku
FALLON, Ann		19	F	Servant	22Ja02Ku
KINSLEY, Robert		20	M	Gdnr	22Ja02Ku
FLYNN, Eliz.		13	F	Servant	22Ja02Ku
Hannah	(T)	08	F	Child	22Ja02Ku
BRADY, Mary		18	F	Servant	22Ja02Ku
MCQUILLAN, Cath.		49	F	Servant	22Ja02Ku
Pat		69	M	Servant	22Ja02Ku
MULDONNEY, Cath.		70	F	None	22Ja02Ku
Judith		25	F	None	22Ja02Ku
Cath.		.00	F	Infant	22Ja02Ku
BARRETT, Henry		20	M	Laborer	22Ja02Ku
Mary-Jane	(T)	11	F	None	22Ja02Ku
WIGGINS, Polly		19	F	Dressmaker	22Ja02Ku
GREY, Ann		20	F	Dressmaker	22Ja02Ku
MCCLUSKY, Margt.		07	F	Child	22Ja02Ku
RYLEY, Margt.		30	F	None	22Ja02Ku
Anne		12	F	None	22Ja02Ku
Mary		03	F	Child	22Ja02Ku
Margt.		.00	F	Infant	22Ja02Ku
SMITH, Bridget		28	F	Servant	22Ja02Ku
DEMPSY, James		24	M	Laborer	22Ja02Ku
DRENNAN, Mary		22	F	Servant	22Ja02Ku

NAMES OF PASSENGERS		AGE	SEX	OCCUPATIONS	DATE PORT SHIP
SMALL, Biddy		50	F	None	22Ja02Ku
BARKLEY, Michl.		30	M	Laborer	22Ja02Ku
TORPIE, Maria		23	F	Servant	22Ja02Ku
MCCORMICK, Rich.		30	M	Laborer	22Ja02Ku
U	(W)	28	F	None	22Ja02Ku
Rich.	(S)	10	M	None	22Ja02Ku
James	(S)	04	M	Child	22Ja02Ku
WILSON, Margt.		20	F	None	22Ja02Ku
FITZGERALD, Mary		20	F	None	22Ja02Ku
BOYLE, Dennis		28	M	Blacksmith	22Ja02Ku
BARRETT, Wm.		25	M	Laborer	22Ja02Ku
U	(W)	30	F	None	22Ja02Ku
CONNELL, John		19	M	Butcher	22Ja02Ku
SKEFFINGTON, W.J.		30	M	Clerk	22Ja02Ku
KEMPSTON, Danl.		40	M	Clerk	22Ja02Ku
ARMSTRONG, Thomas		30	M	Laborer	22Ja02Ku
U	(W)	30	F	None	22Ja02Ku
Ellen	(D)	.00	F	Infant	22Ja02Ku
Pat	(S)	09	M	Child	22Ja02Ku
Thos.	(S)	10	M	None	22Ja02Ku
James	(S)	08	M	Child	22Ja02Ku
Mary	(D)	04	F	Child	22Ja02Ku
Luke	(S)	.00	M	Infant	22Ja02Ku
Nancy		18	F	Servant	22Ja02Ku
HAIMS, Margt.		20	F	Servant	22Ja02Ku
FOY, John		20	M	Laborer	22Ja02Ku
SEITH, Robt.		30	M	Farmer	22Ja02Ku
U	(W)	28	F	None	22Ja02Ku
MEIGHAN, Robt.		24	M	Mason	22Ja02Ku
U	(W)	21	F	None	22Ja02Ku
KEENAN, Cath.		13	F	Servant	22Ja02Ku
WALSH, John		30	M	Servant	22Ja02Ku
Dan.		07	M	Child	22Ja02Ku
LEWIS, Richd.		20	M	Laborer	22Ja02Ku
KEHOE, Jno.		44	M	Tanner	22Ja02Ku
U	(W)	21	F	None	22Ja02Ku
CONNER, Peter		20	M	Laborer	22Ja02Ku
BURNS, Franke		20	M	Laborer	22Ja02Ku
LARY, Pate		20	M	Laborer	22Ja02Ku
MCKENNA, Bridg.		30	F	None	22Ja02Ku
Pate		07	M	Child	22Ja02Ku
John		06	M	Child	22Ja02Ku
RIELLY, Fran.		40	M	Laborer	22Ja02Ku
Mary	(T)	35	F	None	22Ja02Ku
DUFFEY, Edwarde		20	M	Laborer	22Ja02Ku
TURNER, Robt.		54	M	None	22Ja02Ku
Robt.		34	M	Farmer	22Ja02Ku
Mary	(W)	30	F	None	22Ja02Ku
Mary-Anne		13	F	None	22Ja02Ku
Jane		11	F	None	22Ja02Ku
Margt.		09	F	Child	22Ja02Ku
Wm.		08	M	Child	22Ja02Ku
Eliz.		06	F	Child	22Ja02Ku
Saml.		03	M	Child	22Ja02Ku
Robt.		.00	M	Infant	22Ja02Ku
TIERNAN, Pat		23	M	Laborer	22Ja02Ku
GILMORE, Thos.		28	M	Weaver	22Ja02Ku
DEVANY, Michl.		20	M	Laborer	22Ja02Ku
U	(W)	20	F	None	22Ja02Ku
Pat		.00	M	Infant	22Ja02Ku
PHELAN, Thos.		37	M	Farmer	22Ja02Ku
Ann	(W)	27	F	None	22Ja02Ku
MCTEAGUE, Jas.		40	M	Laborer	22Ja02Ku
BYRNES, J.		22	M	Doctor	22Ja02Ku
SHAPAR, Richd.		52	M	Merchant	22Ja02Ku

HARMONIA 24 JANUARY 1848

From Glasgow

NAMES OF PASSENGERS		AGE	SEX	OCCUPATIONS	DATE PORT SHIP
DOCHARTY, George		49	M	Carpenter	24Ja04Sm
U	(W)	40	F	None	24Ja04Sm
Cornelius		20	M	None	24Ja04Sm
Nancy		18	F	None	24Ja04Sm
Matty		16	M	None	24Ja04Sm
Biddy		15	F	None	24Ja04Sm
Eliza		13	F	None	24Ja04Sm
James		09	M	Child	24Ja04Sm
George		07	M	Child	24Ja04Sm
Niel		05	M	Child	24Ja04Sm
DONNELLY, Patrick		20	M	Laborer	24Ja04Sm
CANACHAN, C.		59	M	Laborer	24Ja04Sm
Mary		57	F	None	24Ja04Sm
Ann		17	F	None	24Ja04Sm
BRAQUE, Felix-M.		19	M	Laborer	24Ja04Sm
ANDERSON, Robert		15	M	Weaver	24Ja04Sm
Ann		17	F	None	24Ja04Sm
GISTY, Owen		35	M	Laborer	24Ja04Sm
Ann		35	F	None	24Ja04Sm
Catherine		02	F	Child	24Ja04Sm
GOGERTY, Henry		25	M	None	24Ja04Sm
U		.08	U	Infant	24Ja04Sm
CROOKS, Robert		25	M	Miner	24Ja04Sm
RISK, John		52	M	Laborer	24Ja04Sm
Eliza	(W)	48	F	None	24Ja04Sm
Samuel		25	M	Blacksmith	24Ja04Sm
Thos.		22	M	None	24Ja04Sm
John		19	M	None	24Ja04Sm
Eliza		13	F	None	24Ja04Sm
SMITH, Patrick		25	M	Laborer	24Ja04Sm
MCKENNA, James		35	M	Laborer	24Ja04Sm
GRIMASSON, Wm.		30	M	Laborer	24Ja04Sm
Robert		11	M	Laborer	24Ja04Sm
FRASER, John		41	M	Iron Turner	24Ja04Sm
MURDOCK, Hugh		24	M	Iron Turner	24Ja04Sm
MCKENNON, John		24	M	Clcp	24Ja04Sm
HAYES, James		50	M	Clcp	24Ja04Sm
MCDEAMOND, Mary		38	F	None	24Ja04Sm
ANDERSON, David		32	M	Mechanic	24Ja04Sm
U	(W)	36	F	None	24Ja04Sm
Margaret		12	F	None	24Ja04Sm
BAURD, John		26	M	Dyer	24Ja04Sm
ORRMARLEW, James		22	M	Tailor	24Ja04Sm
BURNETT, Alex.		25	M	Baker	24Ja04Sm
MURRAY, Adam		22	M	Servant	24Ja04Sm
TURKIN, John		25	M	Spinner	24Ja04Sm
MENVIRON, Thos.		26	M	Laborer	24Ja04Sm
RONEY, John		31	M	Laborer	24Ja04Sm
WILLSON, John		30	M	Laborer	24Ja04Sm
U	(W)	28	F	None	24Ja04Sm
John		09	M	Child	24Ja04Sm
Mary		06	F	Child	24Ja04Sm
Samuel		04	M	Child	24Ja04Sm
James		01	M	Child	24Ja04Sm
GULIVE, Joseph		16	M	Shoemaker	24Ja04Sm

ERRONDURGA 24 JANUARY 1848

From Glasgow

NAMES OF PASSENGERS	AGE	SEX	OCCUPATIONS	DATE PORT SHIP
TAYLOR, A.B.	45	M	Merchant	24Ja04Ca
RODGERS, James	24	M	Farmer	24Ja04Ca
Maria	22	F	Servant	24Ja04Ca
Hugh	18	M	Farmer	24Ja04Ca
BRUCE, Walter	40	M	Farmer	24Ja04Ca
Mary	35	F	None	24Ja04Ca
Walter	10	M	None	24Ja04Ca
DUNLOP, David	21	M	Blacksmith	24Ja04Ca
DEWAR, Alexander	24	M	Blacksmith	24Ja04Ca
MARTIN, George	30	M	Blacksmith	24Ja04Ca
DOCHERTY, Marjory	30	F	None	24Ja04Ca

NAOMI 24 JANUARY 1848

From Liverpool

NAMES OF PASSENGERS	AGE	SEX	OCCUPATIONS	DATE PORT SHIP
COCHLEN, Bridget	20	F	Servant	24Ja02Cb
Mary	.10	F	Infant	24Ja02Cb
Born-At-Sea				
NICHOLE, Ann	33	F	Servant	24Ja02Cb
James	10	M	None	24Ja02Cb
DUSKIN, William	20	M	Laborer	24Ja02Cb
Bridget	13	F	Servant	24Ja02Cb
MCBRYNE, George	20	M	Laborer	24Ja02Cb
FAY, Patt	20	M	Laborer	24Ja02Cb
Ann	12	F	None	24Ja02Cb
OWEN, Catherine	13	F	None	24Ja02Cb
CONNOR, Sally	20	F	None	24Ja02Cb
COLLEN, Mathew	26	M	Laborer	24Ja02Cb
Margaret	24	F	Servant	24Ja02Cb
Thomas	.11	M	Infant	24Ja02Cb
HAW, Connor	40	M	Laborer	24Ja02Cb
MULLEN, Margaret	13	F	Servant	24Ja02Cb
RYAN, Mary	22	F	Servant	24Ja02Cb
NORTON, Thos.	29	M	Laborer	24Ja02Cb
DOYLE, Catharine	26	F	Servant	24Ja02Cb
Betsy	04	F	Child	24Ja02Cb
Margt.	.11	F	Infant	24Ja02Cb
LONG, John	22	M	Engineer	24Ja02Cb
COSTELLO, John	30	M	Lawyer	24Ja02Cb
RYAN, John	20	M	Lawyer	24Ja02Cb
Mary	07	F	Child	24Ja02Cb
Catharine	06	F	Child	24Ja02Cb
ORMAND, Catharine	20	F	Servant	24Ja02Cb
RYAN, Bridget	25	F	Servant	24Ja02Cb
Samuel	20	M	Laborer	24Ja02Cb
SHANE, Mathew	20	M	Laborer	24Ja02Cb
MCLAUGHLIN, Bridget	20	F	Servant	24Ja02Cb
GANNON, Bridget	40	F	Servant	24Ja02Cb
DALY, Mary	20	F	Servant	24Ja02Cb
Ann	12	F	Servant	24Ja02Cb
MCCARTHY, Morris	30	M	Laborer	24Ja02Cb
FLYNN, Betsey	30	F	Servant	24Ja02Cb
Charles	05	M	Child	24Ja02Cb
John	06	M	Child	24Ja02Cb
BROWN, William	07	M	Child	24Ja02Cb
Edward	30	M	Laborer	24Ja02Cb
Michael	03	M	Child	24Ja02Cb
KILLDAY, Thos.	22	M	Laborer	24Ja02Cb

NAMES OF PASSENGERS	AGE	SEX	OCCUPATIONS	DATE PORT SHIP
WYNNE, Mary	20	F	Servant	24Ja02Cb
CAWLEY, John	20	M	Laborer	24Ja02Cb
DOLAN, Bridget	13	F	Servant	24Ja02Cb
Catharine	18	F	Servant	24Ja02Cb
MULLEN, Honora	11	F	Servant	24Ja02Cb
DOLAN, Eliza	06	F	Child	24Ja02Cb
John	20	M	Servant	24Ja02Cb
MCMANUS, Michael	22	M	Laborer	24Ja02Cb
CONWAY, Martin	20	M	Farmer	24Ja02Cb
Bridget	20	F	None	24Ja02Cb
Nancy	12	F	None	24Ja02Cb
Peggy	20	F	None	24Ja02Cb
NORTON, Lawrence	40	M	Farmer	24Ja02Cb
Margaret	40	F	None	24Ja02Cb
Mary	02	F	Child	24Ja02Cb
Dennis	.08	M	Infant	24Ja02Cb
JORDAN, Thomas	30	M	Farmer	24Ja02Cb
Honora	30	F	None	24Ja02Cb
Patk.	02	M	Child	24Ja02Cb
Mary	.10	F	Infant	24Ja02Cb
LISKEY, Peggy	20	F	Servant	24Ja02Cb
HILL, Patt	21	M	Laborer	24Ja02Cb
CULLEN, Patt	21	M	Laborer	24Ja02Cb
WHITESIDE, Wm.	26	M	Butcher	24Ja02Cb
WYME, Mary	20	F	Servant	24Ja02Cb
MCCABE, Mary	20	F	Servant	24Ja02Cb
KEATING, Isabella	23	F	Servant	24Ja02Cb
DUNN, Margaret	22	F	Servant	24Ja02Cb
MCCORMICK, Daniel	23	M	Carpenter	24Ja02Cb
Charlotte	21	F	None	24Ja02Cb
LYNCH, John	40	M	Farmer	24Ja02Cb
Margaret	30	F	None	24Ja02Cb
Thomas	13	M	Farmer	24Ja02Cb
Michael	12	M	Farmer	24Ja02Cb
SMITH, Peter	20	M	Farmer	24Ja02Cb
CONNELL, Judy	20	F	Farmer	24Ja02Cb
CONROY, Thomas	40	M	Farmer	24Ja02Cb
Mary	40	F	None	24Ja02Cb
Mona	03	F	Child	24Ja02Cb
Patt	.00	M	Infant	24Ja02Cb
STONEY, Ann	25	F	Servant	24Ja02Cb
LAMBS, Martin	20	M	Farmer	24Ja02Cb
Bridget	26	F	None	24Ja02Cb
Martin	10	M	None	24Ja02Cb
Mary	08	F	Child	24Ja02Cb
DUGGAN, Eliza	20	F	Servant	24Ja02Cb
ROACHE, Patt	08	M	Child	24Ja02Cb
KELLY, Michael	31	M	Laborer	24Ja02Cb
CAHEW, John	30	M	Laborer	24Ja02Cb
ROACHE, John	30	M	Laborer	24Ja02Cb
John	12	M	Laborer	24Ja02Cb
Patt	10	M	Laborer	24Ja02Cb
GATELY, John	15	M	Laborer	24Ja02Cb
GARRITY, James	10	M	Laborer	24Ja02Cb
DOYLE, John	21	M	Laborer	24Ja02Cb
Mary	25	F	Servant	24Ja02Cb
MCNAMARA, John	20	M	Laborer	24Ja02Cb
BRADLY, Michael	20	M	Laborer	24Ja02Cb
Bridget	18	F	Servant	24Ja02Cb
FLYNN, John	30	M	Laborer	24Ja02Cb
Peggy	28	F	None	24Ja02Cb
Mary	04	F	Child	24Ja02Cb
Catharine	.10	F	Infant	24Ja02Cb
GARRITY, Richard	40	M	Farmer	24Ja02Cb
LAUGHLIN, Martin	35	M	Farmer	24Ja02Cb
Bridget	30	F	None	24Ja02Cb
Mary	08	F	Child	24Ja02Cb
Bridget	06	F	Child	24Ja02Cb
Margaret	02	F	Child	24Ja02Cb
Patt	.04	M	Infant	24Ja02Cb
Died-At-Sea				
LYNCH, Catharine	21	F	Servant	24Ja02Cb
FITSIMMONS, Pattk.	40	M	Farmer	24Ja02Cb
Mary	40	F	None	24Ja02Cb
Thomas	18	M	Farmer	24Ja02Cb
FITSIMMONS, James	12	M	Farmer	24Ja02Cb
Bridget	10	F	None	24Ja02Cb
Ann	09	F	None	24Ja02Cb
John	07	M	None	24Ja02Cb
Catharine	06	F	Child	24Ja02Cb
Pattk.	04	M	Child	24Ja02Cb
Michael	.08	M	Infant	24Ja02Cb
Died-At-Sea				
KANE, Lawrence	40	M	Farmer	24Ja02Cb
Ann	40	F	None	24Ja02Cb
William	19	M	Farmer	24Ja02Cb
Bridget	17	F	None	24Ja02Cb
Betsy	13	F	None	24Ja02Cb
Francis	11	F	None	24Ja02Cb
James	07	M	Child	24Ja02Cb
Lawrence	06	M	Child	24Ja02Cb
MCLAUGHLIN, Mathew	19	M	Laborer	24Ja02Cb
MCCABE, Denis	24	M	Laborer	24Ja02Cb
Mary	24	F	Servant	24Ja02Cb
Catharine	.06	F	Infant	24Ja02Cb
TOWNSEND, David	30	M	Laborer	24Ja02Cb
CUSHERS, Patt	50	M	Laborer	24Ja02Cb
GARRITY, Sally	40	F	Servant	24Ja02Cb
Died-At-Sea				
Eliza	40	F	Servant	24Ja02Cb
Catharine	07	F	Child	24Ja02Cb
John	05	M	Child	24Ja02Cb
Died-At-Sea				
SULLIVAN, Phillip	40	M	Laborer	24Ja02Cb
SHAUCHUEFEY, Mary	40	F	Servant	24Ja02Cb
GIBB, James	40	M	Laborer	24Ja02Cb
DEVANY, John	40	M	Laborer	24Ja02Cb
KELLY, John	40	M	Farmer	24Ja02Cb
Michael	04	M	Child	24Ja02Cb
Charlotte	40	F	None	24Ja02Cb
Lawrence	.00	M	Infant	24Ja02Cb
GIBBONS, Mary	17	F	Servant	24Ja02Cb
FITZGERALD, Thomas	24	M	Laborer	24Ja02Cb
Honora	50	F	Servant	24Ja02Cb
FANELL, Biddy	20	F	Servant	24Ja02Cb
RYAN, Thos.	33	M	Laborer	24Ja02Cb
HAMDEN, Julia	25	F	Servant	24Ja02Cb
SINCLAIR, James	20	M	Farmer	24Ja02Cb
John	18	M	Farmer	24Ja02Cb
WIGGAN, Catharine	20	F	Servant	24Ja02Cb
GILLISPIE, Thos.	20	M	Laborer	24Ja02Cb
Patt	18	M	Laborer	24Ja02Cb
MCKENNA, James	63	M	Farmer	24Ja02Cb
Died-At-Sea				
Catharine	20	F	None	24Ja02Cb
Catharine	50	F	None	24Ja02Cb
James	19	M	Farmer	24Ja02Cb
MCGRATH, Mary	20	F	Servant	24Ja02Cb
MOONEY, James	40	M	Laborer	24Ja02Cb
Julia	05	F	Child	24Ja02Cb
DORMAN, Patt	20	M	Laborer	24Ja02Cb
MOONEY, Mary	40	F	Servant	24Ja02Cb
MCNAMARA, Denis	40	M	Laborer	24Ja02Cb
MCCABE, James	40	M	Laborer	24Ja02Cb
FINLEY, James	30	M	Farmer	24Ja02Cb
Mary	29	F	None	24Ja02Cb
Catharine	13	F	None	24Ja02Cb
Patt	06	M	Child	24Ja02Cb
Rose	04	F	Child	24Ja02Cb
Terrence	02	M	Child	24Ja02Cb
Ellen	.04	F	Infant	24Ja02Cb
WARE, Mary	20	F	Servant	24Ja02Cb
Betsy	22	F	Servant	24Ja02Cb
FLYNN, Wm.	40	M	Laborer	24Ja02Cb
Bernard	20	M	Laborer	24Ja02Cb
Margaret	13	F	Servant	24Ja02Cb
Catharine	11	F	Servant	24Ja02Cb
John	09	M	Child	24Ja02Cb
EARLES, James	50	M	Laborer	24Ja02Cb
Mary	09	F	Child	24Ja02Cb

NAMES OF PASSENGERS	AGE	SEX	OCCUPATIONS	DATE PORT SHIP
MCMAHON, Dennis	31	M	Laborer	24Ja02Cb
ROGERS, John	23	M	Laborer	24Ja02Cb
Anthony	29	M	Laborer	24Ja02Cb
GILLAN, Michael	21	M	Laborer	24Ja02Cb
GRIFFEN, Wm.	30	M	Farmer	24Ja02Cb
Catharine	30	F	None	24Ja02Cb
Andrew	09	M	Child	24Ja02Cb
John	04	M	Child	24Ja02Cb
Catharine	14	F	None	24Ja02Cb
TWEEDLE, Margaret	40	F	Servant	24Ja02Cb
GARRITY, Margaret	12	F	Servant	24Ja02Cb
MORAN, Michael	40	M	Laborer	24Ja02Cb
LANDRYGAN, Patt	25	M	Laborer	24Ja02Cb
SLYNG, Wm.	25	M	Laborer	24Ja02Cb
MOONEY, Mary	25	F	Servant	24Ja02Cb
ROURKE, Wm.	40	M	Laborer	24Ja02Cb
Ellen	40	F	None	24Ja02Cb
Michael	11	M	Laborer	24Ja02Cb
Johanna	09	F	Child	24Ja02Cb
Mary	.08	F	Infant	24Ja02Cb
BURKE, Michael	35	M	Laborer	24Ja02Cb
FARLEY, Mary	35	F	Servant	24Ja02Cb
BROONEY, Margaret	11	F	Servant	24Ja02Cb
MCKEE, Terry	30	M	Laborer	24Ja02Cb
BAHON, John	24	M	Laborer	24Ja02Cb
TUBIDY, John	35	M	Farmer	24Ja02Cb
Denis	30	M	Farmer	24Ja02Cb
MAHON, Thomas	20	M	Laborer	24Ja02Cb
LANDYGAN, Mary	25	F	Servant	24Ja02Cb
TUBIDY, Mary	26	F	Farmer	24Ja02Cb
Anthony	23	M	Farmer	24Ja02Cb
Patt	22	M	Farmer	24Ja02Cb
William	24	M	Farmer	24Ja02Cb
Edward	19	M	Farmer	24Ja02Cb
Thomas	11	M	Farmer	24Ja02Cb
Margt.	13	F	None	24Ja02Cb
Catharine	60	F	None	24Ja02Cb
WARDE, Wm.	13	M	Laborer	24Ja02Cb
HOLLAND, Ellen	26	F	Servant	24Ja02Cb
WYSE, Mary	27	F	Servant	24Ja02Cb
Died-At-Sea				
GALLAHAN, Catharine	20	F	Servant	24Ja02Cb
LUBBY, Mary	20	F	Servant	24Ja02Cb
Ann	12	F	Servant	24Ja02Cb
MCDERMITT, Patt	29	M	Laborer	24Ja02Cb
GALLAHAN, Peter	.06	M	Infant	24Ja02Cb
KILCANY, Michael	30	M	Farmer	24Ja02Cb
Nelly	30	F	None	24Ja02Cb
John	06	M	Child	24Ja02Cb
Ann	04	F	Child	24Ja02Cb
Michael	02	M	Child	24Ja02Cb
Patt	.08	M	Infant	24Ja02Cb
Died-At-Sea				
DIGNALL, Mary	30	F	Servant	24Ja02Cb
MURRAY, Ann	25	F	Servant	24Ja02Cb
LOVBY, James	26	M	Laborer	24Ja02Cb

SARDINIA 25 JANUARY 1848

From Liverpool

NAMES OF PASSENGERS	AGE	SEX	OCCUPATIONS	DATE PORT SHIP
ROGERSON, Ellen	18	F	Servant	25Ja02Cq
HOFER, Mariah	20	F	Servant	25Ja02Cq
CLIGG, James	28	M	Laborer	25Ja02Cq
Mary	25	F	None	25Ja02Cq
Mary	07	F	Child	25Ja02Cq
Alice	.00	F	Infant	25Ja02Cq
BERRY, Sarah	22	F	None	25Ja02Cq
MCCORMACK, Bryan	32	M	Laborer	25Ja02Cq
MCCORMACK, Owin	22	M	Laborer	25Ja02Cq
DEVLIN, James	33	M	Laborer	25Ja02Cq
HOPKINS, Bridget	25	F	Laborer	25Ja02Cq
CARRIGAN, Edward	45	M	Laborer	25Ja02Cq
Mary	40	F	None	25Ja02Cq
Ann	15	F	None	25Ja02Cq
Johanna	13	F	None	25Ja02Cq
Mary	11	F	None	25Ja02Cq
CANDLY, Bridget	19	F	None	25Ja02Cq
HENY, Bridget	18	F	None	25Ja02Cq
LOUGHAN, John	35	M	Laborer	25Ja02Cq
Mary	13	F	None	25Ja02Cq
MUTTON, John	30	M	None	25Ja02Cq
MALLAY, Peter	24	M	Laborer	25Ja02Cq
GRUHELGH, Abner	29	M	Laborer	25Ja02Cq
WALSH, Mary	18	F	None	25Ja02Cq
James	13	M	None	25Ja02Cq
Patt	12	M	None	25Ja02Cq
CONWAY, Michael	38	M	Laborer	25Ja02Cq
Rose	30	F	None	25Ja02Cq
RIELLY, John	26	M	Laborer	25Ja02Cq
MCMAHAN, Ann	24	F	Laborer	25Ja02Cq
WEINE, John	27	M	Laborer	25Ja02Cq
GROWL, John	32	M	Laborer	25Ja02Cq
Henry	33	M	Laborer	25Ja02Cq
TAYLOR, Elizabeth	35	F	None	25Ja02Cq
Catharine	13	F	None	25Ja02Cq
Elizabeth	11	F	None	25Ja02Cq
Jane	07	F	Child	25Ja02Cq
Victoria	08	F	Child	25Ja02Cq
DUNN, Samuel	20	M	Laborer	25Ja02Cq
MCGEE, Philip	18	M	Laborer	25Ja02Cq
Mary	13	F	None	25Ja02Cq
TUCKEEN, James	13	M	Laborer	25Ja02Cq
Died-At-Sea				
Margrate	15	F	None	25Ja02Cq
FLOOD, Bridget	18	F	None	25Ja02Cq
DARCEY, George	16	M	Laborer	25Ja02Cq
HEANY, Peter	52	M	Laborer	25Ja02Cq
Betsy	48	F	None	25Ja02Cq
Jane	16	F	None	25Ja02Cq
Elizabeth	06	F	Child	25Ja02Cq
William	13	M	Laborer	25Ja02Cq
Peter	11	M	Laborer	25Ja02Cq
John	09	M	Child	25Ja02Cq
James	07	M	Child	25Ja02Cq
CLAFFDA, Margrate	20	F	None	25Ja02Cq
MCKINNAN, Daniel	18	M	Laborer	25Ja02Cq
MCQUIN, Henry	35	M	Laborer	25Ja02Cq
Margrate	36	F	None	25Ja02Cq
Henry	10	M	None	25Ja02Cq
John	08	M	Child	25Ja02Cq
WHILLEY, Mary	36	F	None	25Ja02Cq
Emmas	04	F	Child	25Ja02Cq
DEVLIN, James-P.	18	M	Laborer	25Ja02Cq
MCGUINNESS, Catharine	13	F	None	25Ja02Cq
Barney	12	M	None	25Ja02Cq
MCALLEOY, Catharine	17	F	None	25Ja02Cq
GILSHAM, Ann	50	F	None	25Ja02Cq
Thomas	04	M	Child	25Ja02Cq
Ellen	.00	F	Infant	25Ja02Cq
Brian	17	M	Laborer	25Ja02Cq
CURLIN, Ellen	16	F	None	25Ja02Cq
FLOOD, Ann	21	F	None	25Ja02Cq
HANT, Rosey	16	F	None	25Ja02Cq
BARK, Patrick	22	M	Laborer	25Ja02Cq
BOURK, Bridget	20	F	None	25Ja02Cq
LYON, Eliza-Jane	23	F	None	25Ja02Cq
SULLIVAN, John	48	M	Laborer	25Ja02Cq
Robert	17	M	Laborer	25Ja02Cq
Patrick	14	M	Laborer	25Ja02Cq
MCKENNY, Robert	31	M	Laborer	25Ja02Cq
Agness	31	F	None	25Ja02Cq
William	04	M	Child	25Ja02Cq
CANLEY, James	23	M	Laborer	25Ja02Cq

NAMES OF PASSENGERS		AGE	SEX	OCCUPATIONS	DATE PORT SHIP
COCKLAN, Patt		47	M	Laborer	25Ja02Cq
Rosey		32	F	None	25Ja02Cq
Patt		09	M	Child	25Ja02Cq
Ann		05	F	Child	25Ja02Cq
HAW, William		23	M	Laborer	25Ja02Cq
MYSLIFFE, John		26	M	Laborer	25Ja02Cq
RIGGIN, Ann		40	F	None	25Ja02Cq
Patt		11	M	Laborer	25Ja02Cq
Jane		16	F	None	25Ja02Cq
DEMPSEY, Margrate		30	F	None	25Ja02Cq
Patt		.00	M	Infant	25Ja02Cq
KELLEY, Biddy		40	F	None	25Ja02Cq
James		12	M	Laborer	25Ja02Cq
Honard		06	M	Child	25Ja02Cq
Edward		04	M	Child	25Ja02Cq
DUTTAN, Oliver		28	M	Laborer	25Ja02Cq

EMERALD 25 JANUARY 1848

From Newry

NAMES OF PASSENGERS		AGE	SEX	OCCUPATIONS	DATE PORT SHIP
HEUDY, Francis		23	M	Farmer	25Ja19Cs
HUIDS, Jas.		21	M	Farmer	25Ja19Cs
MACHEW, Jas.		21	M	Farmer	25Ja19Cs
CALLAGHEN, Rose		19	F	Spinster	25Ja19Cs
MACHEW, Mary		19	F	Spinster	25Ja19Cs
RIELLY, Jas.		30	M	Farmer	25Ja19Cs
BRADY, Jas.		24	M	Farmer	25Ja19Cs
FENNER, Dennis		45	M	Farmer	25Ja19Cs
RIELLY, Michl.		30	M	Farmer	25Ja19Cs
KENNAN, Patk.		23	M	Farmer	25Ja19Cs
Thos.		44	M	Farmer	25Ja19Cs
Margt.	(W)	42	F	None	25Ja19Cs
Ann	(D)	17	F	None	25Ja19Cs
KEENAN, Terrence		14	M	Farmer	25Ja19Cs
William		12	M	Farmer	25Ja19Cs
Jas.		10	M	Farmer	25Ja19Cs
Bridget		08	F	Child	25Ja19Cs
Mary		07	F	Child	25Ja19Cs
Cath.		.00	F	Infant	25Ja19Cs
BYRNE, Michl.		50	M	Farmer	25Ja19Cs
Cath.		35	F	None	25Ja19Cs
Charles		08	M	Child	25Ja19Cs
Mary		05	F	Child	25Ja19Cs
Patk.		.00	M	Infant	25Ja19Cs
Died-At-Sea					
Hugh		03	M	Child	25Ja19Cs
Judith		.00	F	Infant	25Ja19Cs
Died-At-Sea					
MADDEN, Rose		27	F	Spinster	25Ja19Cs
JENKINS, Wm.		24	M	Farmer	25Ja19Cs
KENNEDY, Jane		45	F	Spinster	25Ja19Cs
Jane		25	F	Spinster	25Ja19Cs
SMITH, Jas.		40	M	Farmer	25Ja19Cs
GIBSON, Christ.		27	M	Farmer	25Ja19Cs
MAXWELL, Jas.		27	M	Farmer	25Ja19Cs
MCGWEN, Thos.		32	M	Farmer	25Ja19Cs
Elizth.	(W)	27	F	None	25Ja19Cs
Jane	(D)	00	F	Child	25Ja19Cs
OHARA, Patk.		00	M	Farmer	25Ja19Cs
Died-At-Sea					
Bridg.	(T)	35	F	None	25Ja19Cs
MCQUADE, Sicila		30	F	Spinster	25Ja19Cs
SMITH, Mary		40	F	Spinster	25Ja19Cs
KEENAN, Helen		21	F	Spinster	25Ja19Cs
Rose		17	F	Spinster	25Ja19Cs
MAXWELL, Nancy		22	F	Spinster	25Ja19Cs

MARY-MORRIS 25 JANUARY 1848

From Glasgow

NAMES OF PASSENGERS		AGE	SEX	OCCUPATIONS	DATE PORT SHIP
MCKIM, John		22	M	Blacksmith	25Ja04Ol
KELLY, Pat		25	M	Laborer	25Ja04Ol
Mary		25	F	None	25Ja04Ol
Daniel		27	M	Laborer	25Ja04Ol
Elisabeth		27	F	None	25Ja04Ol
Elisabeth		02	F	Child	25Ja04Ol
John		.10	M	Infant	25Ja04Ol
John		26	M	Miner	25Ja04Ol
GLADSTON, Robert		21	M	Unknown	25Ja04Ol
SMITH, Hen.		28	M	Laborer	25Ja04Ol
STEWART, John		21	M	Weaver	25Ja04Ol
GREGARY, Wm.		24	M	Miner	25Ja04Ol
Francis		22	M	Miner	25Ja04Ol
Betsy		14	F	None	25Ja04Ol
Mary		16	F	None	25Ja04Ol
Mary		45	F	None	25Ja04Ol
KERR, Margaret		33	F	None	25Ja04Ol
Marg.		17	F	None	25Ja04Ol
Alex		13	M	None	25Ja04Ol
Jane		13	F	None	25Ja04Ol
David		08	M	Child	25Ja04Ol
DYATT, Wm.		26	M	Laborer	25Ja04Ol
STEWART, Rob		23	M	Laborer	25Ja04Ol
ROBINSON, Wm.		20	M	Laborer	25Ja04Ol
STANLEY, Albert		24	M	Pilot	25Ja04Ol
MCCALL, Wm.		24	M	Laborer	25Ja04Ol
SOUTHALL, Wm.		38	M	Weaver	25Ja04Ol
GALLAGHER, Cor.		20	M	Laborer	25Ja04Ol
MCKENZIE, James		35	M	Printer	25Ja04Ol
MCGEARY, Owen		16	M	Farmer	25Ja04Ol
JOHNSTON, Elis		29	F	Cook	25Ja04Ol
GILLESPIE, Ann		36	F	None	25Ja04Ol
MCQUEEN, And.		30	M	Blacksmith	25Ja04Ol
Johanna		30	F	None	25Ja04Ol
SMITH, Wm.		27	M	Miner	25Ja04Ol
GLENN, Ed		25	M	Laborer	25Ja04Ol
KELLY, And.		29	M	Tailor	25Ja04Ol
STEWARD, Hen.		33	M	Bookbinder	25Ja04Ol
Christiana		35	F	None	25Ja04Ol
HUTCHINSON, Mary		21	F	None	25Ja04Ol
James		53	M	Weaver	25Ja04Ol
Christina		57	F	None	25Ja04Ol
Janet		15	F	None	25Ja04Ol
Barbara		12	F	None	25Ja04Ol
MILLS, James		33	M	Clogger	25Ja04Ol
MANNAGEN, Ann		20	F	None	25Ja04Ol
ROBINSON, Johnston		21	M	Dyer	25Ja04Ol

TUSCAN 26 JANUARY 1848

From Liverpool

NAMES OF PASSENGERS		AGE	SEX	OCCUPATIONS	DATE PORT SHIP
BRATTOW, Pat		21	M	Laborer	26Ja02Ct
Ann		19	F	None	26Ja02Ct
Cath.	(T)	18	F	None	26Ja02Ct
CARSON, Chas.		25	M	Uncle	26Ja02Ct
COFFER, Michl.		25	M	Clerk	26Ja02Ct
BRADWICK, Bridgt.		30	F	Aunt	26Ja02Ct
MINVAIN, S.		40	M	Laborer	26Ja02Ct

NAMES OF PASSENGERS		AGE	SEX	OCCUPATIONS	DATE PORT SHIP
MINVAIN, U	(W)	35	F	None	26Ja02Ct
U	(D)	13	F	None	26Ja02Ct
Cath.	(D)	11	F	None	26Ja02Ct
James	(S)	09	M	Child	26Ja02Ct
Margt.	(D)	07	F	Child	26Ja02Ct
Ellen	(D)	03	F	Child	26Ja02Ct
Jane	(D)	.00	F	Infant	26Ja02Ct
CAHEY, Margt.		06	F	Child	26Ja02Ct
Pat		04	M	Child	26Ja02Ct
Francis		.00	U	Infant	26Ja02Ct
Geh---, Martha		16	F	Servant	26Ja02Ct
Ellen		13	F	Unknown	26Ja02Ct
OBRIEN, Johanna		22	F	Unknown	26Ja02Ct
Jas.		08	M	Child	26Ja02Ct
John		07	M	Child	26Ja02Ct
STEWARD, Anne		20	F	Spinster	26Ja02Ct
COYN, Peter		33	M	Laborer	26Ja02Ct
Cine-AY, Barnam		25	U	Unknown	26Ja02Ct
TIFNEY, Josh.		32	M	Unknown	26Ja02Ct
Michl.		25	M	Unknown	26Ja02Ct
Wm.		19	M	Unknown	26Ja02Ct
Harriet		32	F	Unknown	26Ja02Ct
Elizth.		24	F	Unknown	26Ja02Ct
Ann		10	F	Unknown	26Ja02Ct
Ellen		08	F	Child	26Ja02Ct
Luke		06	M	Child	26Ja02Ct
Alfred		.00	M	Infant	26Ja02Ct
Flan---, Pat		00	M	Unknown	26Ja02Ct
U	(W)	00	F	Unknown	26Ja02Ct
Pat		09	M	Child	26Ja02Ct
KELLY, John		25	M	Fiddler	26Ja02Ct
CAVANAGH, John		40	M	Tailor	26Ja02Ct
DARCY, Michl.		35	M	Laborer	26Ja02Ct
FLYNN, Pat		30	M	Laborer	26Ja02Ct
John		25	M	Laborer	26Ja02Ct
TUNEY, Peter		24	M	Tinker	26Ja02Ct
CAIN, James		30	M	Laborer	26Ja02Ct
Pat		35	M	Laborer	26Ja02Ct
HAYES, Ellen		26	F	Servant	26Ja02Ct
Mary		33	F	Servant	26Ja02Ct
GIBBONS, Mich.		40	M	Mason	26Ja02Ct
DALEY, Thomas		40	M	Weaver	26Ja02Ct
Mary		18	F	None	26Ja02Ct
Thos.		09	M	Child	26Ja02Ct
Edward		12	M	None	26Ja02Ct
MUSA, Michl.		23	M	Painter	26Ja02Ct
Mary		23	F	None	26Ja02Ct
BRYAN, Lenny		24	M	Laborer	26Ja02Ct
Margt.		17	F	None	26Ja02Ct
WATSON, George		25	M	Laborer	26Ja02Ct
Saml.		25	M	Laborer	26Ja02Ct
U	(W)	28	F	None	26Ja02Ct
Sarah		17	F	None	26Ja02Ct
Susan		07	F	Child	26Ja02Ct
PICKET, George		21	M	Peddler	26Ja02Ct
CARRIGAN, Thos.		46	M	Laborer	26Ja02Ct
Rosa		45	F	None	26Ja02Ct
Peter		21	M	None	26Ja02Ct
John		18	M	None	26Ja02Ct
CUNAW, Margt.		50	F	None	26Ja02Ct
Pat		25	U	None	26Ja02Ct
CANIGAN, Thos.		16	M	Laborer	26Ja02Ct
Margt.		15	F	None	26Ja02Ct
Jane		13	F	None	26Ja02Ct
Mich.		11	M	None	26Ja02Ct
GRIFFIN, Esther		22	F	Spinster	26Ja02Ct
SMITH, Pat		13	M	None	26Ja02Ct
Peter		09	M	Child	26Ja02Ct
MACBETH, Jas.		24	M	Artist	26Ja02Ct
STEWARD, E----		37	U	Laborer	26Ja02Ct
MCELSON, Ed		31	M	Laborer	26Ja02Ct
CAHEY, Margt.		35	F	Servant	26Ja02Ct
Biddy		12	F	None	26Ja02Ct
James		10	M	None	26Ja02Ct
William		08	M	Child	26Ja02Ct
U, Peggy		25	F	Servant	26Ja02Ct
Kitty		23	F	Servant	26Ja02Ct
CONNOR, Peter		40	M	Laborer	26Ja02Ct
Margt.		40	F	Servant	26Ja02Ct
SANDS, Eliza		30	F	Servant	26Ja02Ct
Lucy		28	F	Servant	26Ja02Ct
HIATEN, Pat		42	M	Shoemaker	26Ja02Ct
KELLY, Wm.		48	M	Musician	26Ja02Ct
BYRON, Bridget		50	F	Servant	26Ja02Ct
Ellen		14	F	Servant	26Ja02Ct
Pat		21	M	Servant	26Ja02Ct
PINCEL, Cath.		25	F	Servant	26Ja02Ct
Thomas		25	M	Laborer	26Ja02Ct
DOLIN, Pat		32	M	Laborer	26Ja02Ct
PIOYLAND, Thos.		21	M	Laborer	26Ja02Ct
SMITH, Andw.		30	M	Laborer	26Ja02Ct
BURNS, Margt.		30	F	None	26Ja02Ct
FITZSIMMONS, Mary		18	F	None	26Ja02Ct
ALCORN, Thos.		27	M	Peddler	26Ja02Ct
Eliza		25	F	None	26Ja02Ct
EAGAN, John		40	M	Laborer	26Ja02Ct
KELLEY, Louisa		27	F	None	26Ja02Ct
Biddy		17	F	None	26Ja02Ct
DIMSDALE, John		22	M	Laborer	26Ja02Ct
Mary		20	F	None	26Ja02Ct
KRENSHAW, Jas.		26	M	Laborer	26Ja02Ct
ROLLAND, Michl.		40	M	Farmer	26Ja02Ct
U	(W)	35	F	None	26Ja02Ct
Arthur		11	M	None	26Ja02Ct
Mary		08	F	Child	26Ja02Ct
Ellen		09	F	Child	26Ja02Ct
Jas.		05	M	Child	26Ja02Ct
Alley		02	U	Child	26Ja02Ct
CONNELLY, John		40	M	None	26Ja02Ct
GIBBONS, Nancy		50	F	Spinster	26Ja02Ct
James		16	M	None	26Ja02Ct
Bridget		16	M	None	26Ja02Ct
KELLEY, Thomas		40	M	Laborer	26Ja02Ct
GIBBONS, James		30	M	Laborer	26Ja02Ct
MCCLOSKY, Pat		24	M	Laborer	26Ja02Ct
LAUCHANGER, Wm.		28	M	Laborer	26Ja02Ct
MOON, Wm.		28	M	Laborer	26Ja02Ct
WALN, Ellen		45	F	Milliner	26Ja02Ct
Ann		07	F	Child	26Ja02Ct
CARR, Edw.		25	M	Laborer	26Ja02Ct
Ann		24	F	Servant	26Ja02Ct
GILMER, Math.		24	M	Laborer	26Ja02Ct
FAMLER, Richd.		30	M	Laborer	26Ja02Ct
Bridget		18	F	None	26Ja02Ct
DUFFY, Cath.		24	F	None	26Ja02Ct
Laurence		18	M	None	26Ja02Ct
CONNORS, Mary		10	F	None	26Ja02Ct
MULLEN, Cath.		24	F	None	26Ja02Ct
TORLEN, John		23	M	Mason	26Ja02Ct
Bridget		26	F	None	26Ja02Ct
MCBRIDE, Auth.		29	M	Laborer	26Ja02Ct
BYRNE, Bridget		29	F	Servant	26Ja02Ct
DEVOY, Thos.		30	M	None	26Ja02Ct
MCAVOY, Ellen		20	F	None	26Ja02Ct
NEAMAU, Jas.		24	M	Laborer	26Ja02Ct
James		20	M	Laborer	26Ja02Ct
Mary		20	F	None	26Ja02Ct
Andw.		26	M	None	26Ja02Ct
SHANGAU, Pat		24	M	Shoemaker	26Ja02Ct
U	(W)	20	F	None	26Ja02Ct
Jas.		05	M	Child	26Ja02Ct
Bridget		03	F	Child	26Ja02Ct
OBRIEN, Thos.		20	M	Fiddler	26Ja02Ct
GILLARD, Margt.		45	F	Servant	26Ja02Ct
ROGERS, Rose		25	F	Servant	26Ja02Ct
LYNCH, Kab		40	U	None	26Ja02Ct
Mary		20	F	Servant	26Ja02Ct
SMITH, Pat		27	M	Laborer	26Ja02Ct
LYNCH, Thos.		12	M	None	26Ja02Ct
CONNORS, Richd.		25	M	Laborer	26Ja02Ct

NAMES OF PASSENGERS		AGE	SEX	OCCUPATIONS	DATE PORT SHIP
BRADY, Thos.		19	M	Laborer	26Ja02Ct
MULANY, Frank		20	M	Laborer	26Ja02Ct
PINCHIN, Robt.		37	M	Laborer	26Ja02Ct
Ellen		31	F	Servant	26Ja02Ct
STEWARD, Mary		10	F	None	26Ja02Ct
COUGHRAN, Thos.		26	M	Laborer	26Ja02Ct
Alice		24	F	None	26Ja02Ct
John		.00	M	Infant	26Ja02Ct
MCGAM, Pat		30	M	Weaver	26Ja02Ct
BIKAN, Jas.		28	M	Laborer	26Ja02Ct
LARKIN, Richd.		20	M	Laborer	26Ja02Ct
BRYNE, John		30	M	Laborer	26Ja02Ct
HUGHES, Margt.		25	F	Laborer	26Ja02Ct
BRICKLIN, Thos.		32	M	Clerk	26Ja02Ct
LERNED, John		20	M	Laborer	26Ja02Ct
SARGENT, Michl.		21	M	Laborer	26Ja02Ct
CARRY, Michl.		24	M	Laborer	26Ja02Ct
CESSAN, Maria		20	F	None	26Ja02Ct
HUGAN, Pat		35	M	None	26Ja02Ct
MCDERMOT, Pat		36	M	Farmer	26Ja02Ct
Mary		30	F	None	26Ja02Ct
Mary		20	F	None	26Ja02Ct
John		09	M	Child	26Ja02Ct
Mich.		06	M	Child	26Ja02Ct
Pat		04	M	Child	26Ja02Ct
Mary		.00	F	Infant	26Ja02Ct
Susan		.00	F	Infant	26Ja02Ct
BOYLAN, Betty		55	F	Servant	26Ja02Ct
COYLE, Frank		30	M	Laborer	26Ja02Ct
U	(W)	25	F	None	26Ja02Ct
WHELAN, John		25	M	Laborer	26Ja02Ct
U	(W)	25	F	None	26Ja02Ct
BRUNETT, Jas.		27	M	Mason	26Ja02Ct
FOSTER, Martha		28	F	Milliner	26Ja02Ct
Robt.		07	M	Child	26Ja02Ct
Eliza		05	F	Child	26Ja02Ct
John		03	M	Child	26Ja02Ct
Wm.		.00	M	Infant	26Ja02Ct
BLAKELY, John		21	M	Musician	26Ja02Ct
MUSKLY, Chris		24	M	Laborer	26Ja02Ct
Jane		23	F	None	26Ja02Ct
HOLLERAN, Cath.		23	F	Mtmkr	26Ja02Ct
COOK, John		30	M	Peddler	26Ja02Ct
MCKEOWN, Felix		35	M	Cabdriver	26Ja02Ct
BULLY, Thos.		25	M	Pugilist	26Ja02Ct
KRANE, Jas.		30	M	Laborer	26Ja02Ct
DONOGHY, Thos.		32	M	Laborer	26Ja02Ct
BARNES, Joseph		24	M	Laborer	26Ja02Ct
BRADY, Math.		30	M	Laborer	26Ja02Ct
U	(W)	28	F	None	26Ja02Ct
HANAGAN, Wm.		30	M	Shoemaker	26Ja02Ct
James		06	M	Child	26Ja02Ct
HACKETT, Chris		28	M	Laborer	26Ja02Ct
Elizth.		24	F	None	26Ja02Ct
BARKER, Jas-M.		20	M	None	26Ja02Ct
DAVIS, John		21	M	None	26Ja02Ct
MANALO, Barnard		21	M	None	26Ja02Ct
Isabella		18	F	None	26Ja02Ct
CUNNINGHAM, Cath.		18	F	None	26Ja02Ct
GILLARD, Wm.		20	M	None	26Ja02Ct
Pat		19	M	None	26Ja02Ct
COFFER, Eliza		25	F	Servant	26Ja02Ct
CLIFFORD, Mary		20	F	Servant	26Ja02Ct
GLYSON, Wm.		21	M	Servant	26Ja02Ct
CUNIGAN, Thos.		40	M	Laborer	26Ja02Ct
SCOTT, John		25	M	Laborer	26Ja02Ct
MCGOVERN, Biddy		19	F	None	26Ja02Ct
Cath.		20	F	None	26Ja02Ct
Mary		18	F	None	26Ja02Ct
CLARKE, John		45	M	Laborer	26Ja02Ct
Thos.		18	M	Laborer	26Ja02Ct
BLUNETT, Ann		23	F	Servant	26Ja02Ct
MCMANNING, Mary		25	F	Servant	26Ja02Ct
BANNARD, Mary		26	F	Servant	26Ja02Ct
LIDDY, John		20	M	Shoemaker	26Ja02Ct
LIDDY, Cath.		16	F	None	26Ja02Ct
FLETCHER, Jas.		22	M	Laborer	26Ja02Ct
Michl.		13	M	Laborer	26Ja02Ct
Mary		40	F	None	26Ja02Ct
KRIGHAN, Thos.		21	M	Mason	26Ja02Ct
CROLLEY, Cath.		17	F	Servant	26Ja02Ct
GILCHMAN, Jas.		41	M	Laborer	26Ja02Ct
U	(W)	41	F	None	26Ja02Ct
SMITH, Barnd.		24	M	None	26Ja02Ct
Cath.		18	F	None	26Ja02Ct
GILCHMAN, Pat		10	M	None	26Ja02Ct
Chris		08	U	Child	26Ja02Ct
Bridget		.00	F	Infant	26Ja02Ct
MANNING, Jas.		32	M	Laborer	26Ja02Ct
U	(W)	30	F	None	26Ja02Ct
Bridget		12	F	None	26Ja02Ct
Mary		05	F	Child	26Ja02Ct
Thos.		03	M	Child	26Ja02Ct
BOYLAN, Bernard		35	M	Weaver	26Ja02Ct
Owen		60	M	Weaver	26Ja02Ct
MINAR, Mich.		23	M	Tailor	26Ja02Ct
MANAY, Pat		16	M	Laborer	26Ja02Ct
James		08	M	Child	26Ja02Ct
Biddy		22	F	None	26Ja02Ct
Mary		18	F	None	26Ja02Ct
CASEY, Biddy		28	F	Milliner	26Ja02Ct
Winney		25	F	None	26Ja02Ct
James		09	M	Child	26Ja02Ct
Winney		05	F	Child	26Ja02Ct
Pat		03	M	Child	26Ja02Ct
Margt.		.00	F	Infant	26Ja02Ct
MOUSAN, Biddy		25	F	Servant	26Ja02Ct
PAINE, Wm.		30	M	Laborer	26Ja02Ct
Thomas		26	M	Laborer	26Ja02Ct
CONNERS, Satilla		25	M	Soldier	26Ja02Ct
CONAN, Wm.		20	M	Weaver	26Ja02Ct
Richd.		.00	M	Infant	26Ja02Ct
Eliza-Jane		.00	F	Infant	26Ja02Ct
WOOD, Mich.		22	M	Laborer	26Ja02Ct
DALEY, Pat		26	M	Painter	26Ja02Ct
Mary		24	F	None	26Ja02Ct
LOGAN, Thos.		22	M	Musician	26Ja02Ct
FLYNN, John		21	M	Laborer	26Ja02Ct
Margt.		10	F	None	26Ja02Ct
MCGOWAN, Hugh		20	M	Laborer	26Ja02Ct
Pat		12	M	None	26Ja02Ct
Jane		13	F	None	26Ja02Ct
Mary		09	F	Child	26Ja02Ct
INNIS, Wm.		60	M	Schm	26Ja02Ct
MALER, Pat		26	M	Laborer	26Ja02Ct
John		27	M	Laborer	26Ja02Ct
Mary		25	F	None	26Ja02Ct
Biddy		.00	F	Infant	26Ja02Ct
QUINLAHAN, Leo		00	M	Artist	26Ja02Ct
KAUS, Robt.		36	M	Tinker	26Ja02Ct
ASHWORTH, Thos.		27	M	Laborer	26Ja02Ct
KRAU, Jas.		27	M	Laborer	26Ja02Ct
HASD, Grant		39	M	Laborer	26Ja02Ct
DANIEL, Susan		15	F	None	26Ja02Ct
MCLEGHAN, Peter		15	M	None	26Ja02Ct
BOYLE, Wm.		18	M	None	26Ja02Ct
CIMRLE, Thos.		30	M	Tailor	26Ja02Ct
Margt.		28	F	Spinster	26Ja02Ct
LAMB, Jno.		25	M	Butcher	26Ja02Ct
TUMTH, M.		23	U	Actor	26Ja02Ct
DOLAN, Pat		28	M	Laborer	26Ja02Ct
U	(W)	26	F	None	26Ja02Ct
FLUNK, Henry		29	M	Interpreter	26Ja02Ct
LYNDER, Henry		19	M	None	26Ja02Ct
BURNS, Jas.		18	M	None	26Ja02Ct
BRADFORD, Thos.		21	M	None	26Ja02Ct
MCGRATH, Mary		40	F	None	26Ja02Ct
MURPHY, Mary		25	F	None	26Ja02Ct
MCDERMONT, Susan		.00	F	Infant	26Ja02Ct

NAMES OF PASSENGERS	AGE	SEX	OCCUPATIONS	DATE PORT SHIP
MCDURMET, Michl. Died-At-Sea	.00	M	Infant	26Ja02Ct
TIFNEY, Martha Died-At-Sea	53	F	None	26Ja02Ct
MANNING, Cath. Died-At-Sea	.00	F	Infant	26Ja02Ct
MULCAYAN, John Died-At-Sea	40	M	None	26Ja02Ct
FLANNAGAN, Peggy Died-At-Sea	30	F	None	26Ja02Ct
TIFNEY, Elizth. Died-At-Sea	04	F	Child	26Ja02Ct
DAYLON, Tim Died-At-Sea	11	M	None	26Ja02Ct
BOOFIRTE, Michl. Died-At-Sea	12	M	None	26Ja02Ct

MARTHA-WASHINGTON 28 JANUARY 1848

From Liverpool

NAMES OF PASSENGERS	AGE	SEX	OCCUPATIONS	DATE PORT SHIP
WILLSON, Wm.	22	M	Clerk	28Ja02Jw
Anna	21	F	None	28Ja02Jw
FITCH, James	23	M	Painter	28Ja02Jw
GARDNER, Geo.	28	M	Clerk	28Ja02Jw
Elizabeth	23	F	None	28Ja02Jw
Scharlotte	01	F	Child	28Ja02Jw
DOYLE, John	35	M	None	28Ja02Jw

JOHN-FIELDING 29 JANUARY 1848

From Liverpool

NAMES OF PASSENGERS	AGE	SEX	OCCUPATIONS	DATE PORT SHIP
MAHER, John	50	M	Farmer	29Ja02Jy
U (W)	40	F	None	29Ja02Jy
CAMPBELL, Ellen	18	F	Servant	29Ja02Jy
MAHER, Pat	05	M	Child	29Ja02Jy
Dennis	20	M	Laborer	29Ja02Jy
CAMPBELL, Pat	25	M	Laborer	29Ja02Jy
KELLY, Pat	20	M	Laborer	29Ja02Jy
RILEY, Mary	20	F	Servant	29Ja02Jy
CONNOR, Ann	20	F	Servant	29Ja02Jy
FARRALL, James Died-At-Sea	36	M	None	29Ja02Jy
Ann	36	F	Spinner	29Ja02Jy
Maria	07	F	Child	29Ja02Jy
James	.00	M	Infant	29Ja02Jy
FITZSIMONS, Mary	15	F	Housekeeper	29Ja02Jy
MCDONNELL, Owen	06	M	Child	29Ja02Jy
Cath.	03	F	Child	29Ja02Jy
Mary-Ann	.00	F	Infant	29Ja02Jy
FAHY, Mary	25	F	Servant	29Ja02Jy
MARKEY, Cath.	20	F	Servant	29Ja02Jy
Margart	16	F	Servant	29Ja02Jy
JONES, James	43	M	Farmer	29Ja02Jy
CLAY, Dennis	22	M	Farmer	29Ja02Jy
STAVEN, Mathew	18	M	Farmer	29Ja02Jy
Ann	16	F	Spinner	29Ja02Jy
RYAN, Mary	16	F	Dressmaker	29Ja02Jy
Lindy	18	F	Dressmaker	29Ja02Jy
BLAIR, William	28	M	Laborer	29Ja02Jy
ASHTON, John	24	M	Pwlwvr	29Ja02Jy
HAWTH, William	21	M	Weaver	29Ja02Jy
BURKE, John	30	M	Laborer	29Ja02Jy
Ellen	25	F	Servant	29Ja02Jy
Ann	.00	F	Infant	29Ja02Jy
MCDONAGH, John	27	M	Laborer	29Ja02Jy
U (W)	25	F	Servant	29Ja02Jy
Pat	.00	M	Infant	29Ja02Jy
LOUGHLY, John Died-At-Sea	52	M	None	29Ja02Jy
Abby	42	F	Servant	29Ja02Jy
Honor	07	F	Child	29Ja02Jy
Bridget	05	F	Child	29Ja02Jy
Rose	02	F	Child	29Ja02Jy
CAFFREY, John	18	M	Laborer	29Ja02Jy
FOX, Pat	25	M	Wheelwright	29Ja02Jy
Anne	60	F	None	29Ja02Jy
Anne	27	F	Servant	29Ja02Jy
Solomon	11	M	None	29Ja02Jy
BARDEN, Cath.	60	F	None	29Ja02Jy
CARROL, Ellen	30	F	Servant	29Ja02Jy
NAUGHTON, John	40	M	Clerk	29Ja02Jy
U (W)	30	F	None	29Ja02Jy
John	07	M	Child	29Ja02Jy
Mary	04	F	Child	29Ja02Jy
MCALLEN, James	24	M	Laborer	29Ja02Jy
QUINN, Mary	40	F	Servant	29Ja02Jy
Edward	18	M	Laborer	29Ja02Jy
Francis	22	M	Laborer	29Ja02Jy
HENAN, Pat	25	M	Carpenter	29Ja02Jy
Ellen	20	F	Servant	29Ja02Jy
GUFFEY, Ned	25	M	Laborer	29Ja02Jy
MCGRATH, Margt.	50	F	None	29Ja02Jy
Catharine	18	F	None	29Ja02Jy
KANALLY, Alice	50	F	None	29Ja02Jy
Molly	18	F	Servant	29Ja02Jy
GORMLY, Owen Died-At-Sea	40	M	Laborer	29Ja02Jy
HALEY, Thos.	27	M	Laborer	29Ja02Jy
COLLINS, Thos.	30	M	Laborer	29Ja02Jy
GLYNN, Martin	25	M	Laborer	29Ja02Jy
KENIGAN, Mary	29	F	Servant	29Ja02Jy
BURKE, John	20	M	Laborer	29Ja02Jy
MURPHY, John	20	M	Laborer	29Ja02Jy
RABBITS, Thos.	25	M	Laborer	29Ja02Jy
KERRIGAN, Roger	25	M	Laborer	29Ja02Jy
KEARNEY, Michael	25	M	Laborer	29Ja02Jy
KEW, Pat	29	M	Laborer	29Ja02Jy
MISTER, Michael	25	M	Laborer	29Ja02Jy
LISTER, John	23	M	Laborer	29Ja02Jy
FORD, Michael	30	M	Laborer	29Ja02Jy
FARTY, Michael	30	M	Laborer	29Ja02Jy
BEATY, John	25	M	Laborer	29Ja02Jy
DUFFY, Cath.	24	F	Servant	29Ja02Jy
FARTY, Biddy	24	F	Servant	29Ja02Jy
CONLAN, Ellen	30	F	Midwife	29Ja02Jy
Michael	40	M	Carpenter	29Ja02Jy
BLYTHE, Pat	30	M	Laborer	29Ja02Jy
Bridget	25	F	Servant	29Ja02Jy
HALL, John	30	M	Carpenter	29Ja02Jy
Labah	25	F	Servant	29Ja02Jy
LIME, Hannah	40	F	Servant	29Ja02Jy
HALL, James	05	M	Child	29Ja02Jy
Mary	.00	F	Infant	29Ja02Jy
HIGGINS, William	30	M	Farmer	29Ja02Jy
Eliza	25	F	Servant	29Ja02Jy
Anne	25	F	Servant	29Ja02Jy
Maria	05	F	Child	29Ja02Jy
Pat	03	M	Child	29Ja02Jy
Anne	01	F	Child	29Ja02Jy
CROHEM, James	30	M	Farmer	29Ja02Jy
MCCORMACK, James Died-At-Sea	30	M	None	29Ja02Jy
CROHEN, Mary	20	F	Spinner	29Ja02Jy
Maria	50	F	Spinner	29Ja02Jy
DARCEN, Margt-Jane	20	F	Servant	29Ja02Jy
HARDY, Mary-Ann	20	F	Schms	29Ja02Jy

NAMES OF PASSENGERS	AGE	SEX	OCCUPATIONS	DATE PORT SHIP
FAWCETT, James	27	M	Weaver	29Ja02Jy
TAYLOR, James	25	M	Spinner	29Ja02Jy
GRANT, Joseph	25	M	Spinner	29Ja02Jy
SMITH, Sarah	40	F	None	29Ja02Jy
Ann	10	F	None	29Ja02Jy
BAXTER, Bernard	24	M	Profmusc	29Ja02Jy
HALL, Mary-M.	12	F	None	29Ja02Jy
FREENE, William	29	M	Weaver	29Ja02Jy
SMITH, John	27	M	Weaver	29Ja02Jy
ARMSTRONG, Peter	21	M	Laborer	29Ja02Jy
KENZIE, Chas.	25	M	Soap Boiler	29Ja02Jy
GRAY, Levi-D.	30	M	Butcher	29Ja02Jy
COTTER, Andrew	25	M	Carpenter	29Ja02Jy
CONNOR, Thomas	25	M	Laborer	29Ja02Jy
COTTER, Cath.	23	F	Servant	29Ja02Jy
CANNON, Cath.	40	F	None	29Ja02Jy
Maria	20	F	Dressmaker	29Ja02Jy
DONNALLY, Mary	18	F	Servant	29Ja02Jy
COTTER, Maria	02	F	Child	29Ja02Jy
Died-At-Sea				
FARREL, Elizth.	25	F	Servant	29Ja02Jy
GODFREY, George	36	M	Farmer	29Ja02Jy
MCKENNA, John	50	M	Wheelwright	29Ja02Jy
Rose	45	F	None	29Ja02Jy
Robert	14	M	None	29Ja02Jy
James	14	M	None	29Ja02Jy
Elizth.	11	F	None	29Ja02Jy
Mary	03	F	Child	29Ja02Jy
MCKENZIE, Alex.	26	M	Laborer	29Ja02Jy
Mary	24	F	None	29Ja02Jy
MCKENNA, Robert	35	M	Laborer	29Ja02Jy
Mary	34	F	None	29Ja02Jy
Robt-John	09	M	Child	29Ja02Jy
Mary-J.	07	F	Child	29Ja02Jy
James	03	M	Child	29Ja02Jy
Hugh	05	M	Child	29Ja02Jy
MCLAUGHLIN, Mary	19	F	Servant	29Ja02Jy
MCAULIFFE, James	30	M	Farmer	29Ja02Jy
Elizth.	29	F	None	29Ja02Jy
MCCLURE, Hugh	46	M	Laborer	29Ja02Jy
Margt.	09	F	Child	29Ja02Jy
Abby	12	F	None	29Ja02Jy
MINOR, Alley	30	F	Servant	29Ja02Jy
LEYLAND, Bridget	14	F	Weaver	29Ja02Jy
ROGERS, Catharine	21	F	Dressmaker	29Ja02Jy
FLANAGAN, Bridget	47	F	None	29Ja02Jy
HALEY, John	30	M	Laborer	29Ja02Jy
CONNOR, James	30	M	Laborer	29Ja02Jy
Ann	22	F	None	29Ja02Jy
Cath.	.00	F	Infant	29Ja02Jy
MCDONALD, Matthew	31	M	Carpenter	29Ja02Jy
Mary	25	F	None	29Ja02Jy
BOHAN, Owen	20	M	Laborer	29Ja02Jy
Matthew	18	M	Laborer	29Ja02Jy
Elizth.	13	F	Dressmaker	29Ja02Jy
ASPINAL, Bernard	18	M	Groom	29Ja02Jy
CANNON, Pat	20	M	Laborer	29Ja02Jy
Peter	11	M	Laborer	29Ja02Jy
Ann	09	F	Child	29Ja02Jy
LALEY, Ann	20	F	Spinner	29Ja02Jy
GAFFNEY, Mary	24	F	Servant	29Ja02Jy
KANE, Mary	50	F	Servant	29Ja02Jy
Biddy	13	F	Servant	29Ja02Jy
Ann	11	F	Servant	29Ja02Jy
James	09	M	Child	29Ja02Jy
DOLAN, Celia	16	F	Servant	29Ja02Jy
PATTEN, James	60	M	None	29Ja02Jy
Julia	16	F	Servant	29Ja02Jy
FINIRTY, Mary	30	F	Servant	29Ja02Jy
Rose	.00	F	Infant	29Ja02Jy
MCGOWAN, Biddy	26	F	None	29Ja02Jy
FLEMMIE, Winafred	21	F	None	29Ja02Jy
LORAN, Mary	11	F	None	29Ja02Jy
Bridget	10	F	None	29Ja02Jy
John	08	M	Child	29Ja02Jy

NAMES OF PASSENGERS	AGE	SEX	OCCUPATIONS	DATE PORT SHIP
LORAN, Anne	04	F	Child	29Ja02Jy
Died-At-Sea				
CONNOR, Margaret	09	F	Child	29Ja02Jy
STEWART, Francis	20	M	Brf	29Ja02Jy
CLARKE, John	28	M	Mechanic	29Ja02Jy
MAXWELL, Margt.	40	F	Servant	29Ja02Jy
KEEGAN, Rodger	20	M	Laborer	29Ja02Jy
CONNER, Pat	10	M	None	29Ja02Jy
FERAGTY, Cath.	20	F	Servant	29Ja02Jy
BURKE, Bridget	20	F	Housekeeper	29Ja02Jy
Ann	10	F	None	29Ja02Jy
Edward	11	M	None	29Ja02Jy
QUENAN, Winney	20	F	Servant	29Ja02Jy
Ellen	20	F	Servant	29Ja02Jy
LYKES, Jonathan	20	M	Spinner	29Ja02Jy
LUTIFFE, John	40	M	Hatter	29Ja02Jy
CARRINGDALE, James	40	M	Hatter	29Ja02Jy
MAXWELL, Pat	40	M	Laborer	29Ja02Jy
U (W)	40	F	None	29Ja02Jy
Mary	04	F	Child	29Ja02Jy
Michael	25	M	None	29Ja02Jy
Died-At-Sea				
HART, Pat	13	M	Laborer	29Ja02Jy
CLARKE, Thos.	23	M	Laborer	29Ja02Jy
HARDY, Samuel	24	M	Bleacher	29Ja02Jy
TAYLOR, H.	40	M	Laborer	29Ja02Jy
MAXWELL, James	13	M	Laborer	29Ja02Jy
JACKSON, Thomas	40	M	Reed Maker	29Ja02Jy
BRADY, Phil.	30	M	Laborer	29Ja02Jy
Biddy	30	F	Servant	29Ja02Jy
Peter	.00	M	Infant	29Ja02Jy
DUFF, Patt	30	M	Miner	29Ja02Jy
Michael	25	M	Miner	29Ja02Jy
GALLWAY, Martha	29	F	None	29Ja02Jy
James	03	M	Child	29Ja02Jy
Laurence	.00	M	Infant	29Ja02Jy
HAWKINS, Mary	28	F	Servant	29Ja02Jy
MCKEAGHAN, Peter	25	M	Gdnr	29Ja02Jy
BOYLE, William	18	M	Laborer	29Ja02Jy
CARROL, Thomas	30	M	Laborer	29Ja02Jy
Margaret	30	F	None	29Ja02Jy
WALSH, William	40	M	Joiner	29Ja02Jy
EARLY, Peter	50	M	Butcher	29Ja02Jy
Biddy	24	F	Servant	29Ja02Jy
BURKE, Pat	24	M	Laborer	29Ja02Jy
CORMACK, John	25	M	Mason	29Ja02Jy
LOWDIN, John	21	M	Laborer	29Ja02Jy
BRADY, Bridget	25	F	None	29Ja02Jy
Michael	12	M	None	29Ja02Jy
Pat	10	M	None	29Ja02Jy
Margaret	08	F	Child	29Ja02Jy
Terrance	06	M	Child	29Ja02Jy
John	04	M	Child	29Ja02Jy
SHERIDAN, John	18	M	Laborer	29Ja02Jy
CANNON, John	25	M	Farmer	29Ja02Jy
JUNKS, Cath.	21	F	Servant	29Ja02Jy
FEENEY, Patt	40	M	Butcher	29Ja02Jy
SMITH, Pat	20	M	Laborer	29Ja02Jy
FLOOD, Pat	10	M	None	29Ja02Jy
Eliza	18	F	Servant	29Ja02Jy
FARRELL, Thomas	33	M	Laborer	29Ja02Jy
U (W)	24	F	None	29Ja02Jy
Thomas	11	M	None	29Ja02Jy
Ellen	07	F	Child	29Ja02Jy
Maria	.00	F	Infant	29Ja02Jy
Pat	04	M	Child	29Ja02Jy
FITZSIMONS, Mary	16	F	Servant	29Ja02Jy
Margaret	13	F	Servant	29Ja02Jy
QUALAN, Mick	28	M	Laborer	29Ja02Jy
CORRAGIN, Danl.	22	M	Laborer	29Ja02Jy
DALEY, William	32	M	Laborer	29Ja02Jy
CAHAHAN, Pat	30	M	Laborer	29Ja02Jy
CURLEY, William	20	M	Laborer	29Ja02Jy
BEAN, Thos.	26	M	Groom	29Ja02Jy
Mary	18	F	None	29Ja02Jy

NAMES OF PASSENGERS		AGE	SEX	OCCUPATIONS	DATE PORT SHIP
HANLAW, Michael		35	M	Laborer	29Ja02Jy
CANNON, Peter		25	M	Laborer	29Ja02Jy
LITTLE, Dan		30	M	Laborer	29Ja02Jy
Bridget		25	F	None	29Ja02Jy
Pat		08	M	Child	29Ja02Jy
Catherine		06	F	Child	29Ja02Jy
Margaret		05	F	Child	29Ja02Jy
Mary		04	F	Child	29Ja02Jy
Bessy		02	F	Child	29Ja02Jy
Martha		.00	F	Infant	29Ja02Jy
BRENNAN, Anne		30	F	Servant	29Ja02Jy
MOSS, Thos.		29	M	Blacksmith	29Ja02Jy
COLEMAN, Pat		40	M	Farmer	29Ja02Jy
Betty		30	F	None	29Ja02Jy
Michael		05	M	Child	29Ja02Jy
Pat		02	M	Child	29Ja02Jy
Thomas		.00	M	Infant	29Ja02Jy
MONAHAN, Pat		35	M	Fisherman	29Ja02Jy
HURLEY, James		27	M	Hatter	29Ja02Jy
KEAN, Pat		21	M	Laborer	29Ja02Jy
CANNON, Thos.		24	M	Laborer	29Ja02Jy
Mary		25	F	Servant	29Ja02Jy
Michael		.00	M	Infant	29Ja02Jy
Died-At-Sea					
WINTERS, Mary		32	F	None	29Ja02Jy
Thomas		11	M	None	29Ja02Jy
Andrew		03	M	Child	29Ja02Jy
FARMER, William		25	M	Tbcmcht	29Ja02Jy
WATSON, John		30	M	Shoemaker	29Ja02Jy
MCGURNEY, Eliza		18	F	Servant	29Ja02Jy
FURY, Ann		30	F	Servant	29Ja02Jy
SMITH, Thos.		52	M	Laborer	29Ja02Jy
CANNON, Thos.		24	M	Laborer	29Ja02Jy
Mary		25	F	None	29Ja02Jy
Michael		.00	M	Infant	29Ja02Jy
Died-At-Sea					

SWITZERLAND 31 JANUARY 1848

From London

NAMES OF PASSENGERS		AGE	SEX	OCCUPATIONS	DATE PORT SHIP
TOMMY, Thomas		26	M	Farmer	31Ja21Al
Jane		28	F	None	31Ja21Al
DRISCOL, Jeremiah		07	M	None	31Ja21Al
Michael		05	M	None	31Ja21Al
CARTY, James		40	M	Farmer	31Ja21Al
TOMMY, Thomas		26	M	Farmer	31Ja21Al
Jane		28	F	None	31Ja21Al
DRISCOL, Jeremiah		07	M	None	31Ja21Al
Michael		05	M	None	31Ja21Al
CARTY, James		40	M	Farmer	31Ja21Al

MILLICETE 01 FEBRUARY 1848

From Liverpool

NAMES OF PASSENGERS		AGE	SEX	OCCUPATIONS	DATE PORT SHIP
QUIGLEY, Patrick		50	M	Laborer	01Fe02Jq
Ann	(W)	50	F	Wife	01Fe02Jq
Cath.	(D)	21	F	Laborer	01Fe02Jq
Hugh	(S)	20	M	Laborer	01Fe02Jq
Patk.	(S)	18	M	Laborer	01Fe02Jq
Jane	(D)	13	F	Laborer	01Fe02Jq
MULHERON, John		20	M	Laborer	01Fe02Jq
MULHERON, Mary		17	F	Laborer	01Fe02Jq
Brdgt.		16	F	Laborer	01Fe02Jq
Elzth.		46	F	Laborer	01Fe02Jq
MCCARTY, Bridgt.		60	F	Laborer	01Fe02Jq
Danl.	(S)	20	M	Laborer	01Fe02Jq
James	(S)	22	M	Laborer	01Fe02Jq
Mary	(D)	18	F	Laborer	01Fe02Jq
FORREST, Thos.		20	M	Blacksmith	01Fe02Jq
ANDREW, Wm.		20	M	Carpenter	01Fe02Jq
MCNAMARA, James		40	M	Unknown	01Fe02Jq
Betsey		20	F	Servant	01Fe02Jq
ROUTH, Michl.		20	M	Laborer	01Fe02Jq
QUAN, Michl.		26	M	Laborer	01Fe02Jq
Bridgt.		22	F	Laborer	01Fe02Jq
Cath.		20	F	Laborer	01Fe02Jq
HEAGRY, Wm.		20	M	Laborer	01Fe02Jq
DOKERTY, Jane		18	F	Laborer	01Fe02Jq
DEVITT, John		40	M	Laborer	01Fe02Jq
NARY, Mary		20	F	Laborer	01Fe02Jq
HARRISON, John		32	M	Bootmaker	01Fe02Jq
Sarah	(W)	31	F	Wife	01Fe02Jq
U	(S)	.00	M	Infant	01Fe02Jq
CARSEN, Owen		55	M	Laborer	01Fe02Jq
Mary	(W)	55	F	Wife	01Fe02Jq
Lawrence	(S)	14	M	Laborer	01Fe02Jq
James	(S)	12	M	Laborer	01Fe02Jq
Ann	(D)	10	F	Laborer	01Fe02Jq
REGAN, Maria		18	F	Servant	01Fe02Jq
HAMILL, Rose		40	F	Servant	01Fe02Jq
Pat.	(S)	11	M	Servant	01Fe02Jq
Mary	(D)	09	F	Child	01Fe02Jq
Cath.	(D)	04	F	Child	01Fe02Jq
U	(D)	.00	F	Infant	01Fe02Jq
MOSELY, John		24	M	Farmer	01Fe02Jq
Mary	(W)	20	F	Wife	01Fe02Jq
U	(D)	.00	F	Infant	01Fe02Jq
BURKE, Peter		25	M	Baker	01Fe02Jq
DUNN, Bernd.		28	M	Unknown	01Fe02Jq
GANDY, Thos.		40	M	Laborer	01Fe02Jq
Cath.	(W)	35	F	Wife	01Fe02Jq
Mary	(D)	14	F	Laborer	01Fe02Jq
Judith	(D)	11	F	Laborer	01Fe02Jq
U	(D)	.00	F	Infant	01Fe02Jq
DONOHOE, John		38	M	Coppersmith	01Fe02Jq
Charlotte		36	F	Coppersmith	01Fe02Jq
MURRAY, James		23	M	Laborer	01Fe02Jq
Mary		22	F	Laborer	01Fe02Jq
MCGUIRE, Matth.		21	M	Laborer	01Fe02Jq
Margt.		20	F	Laborer	01Fe02Jq
CONNOR, Bridgt.		22	F	Laborer	01Fe02Jq
FELT, Cath.		40	F	House Maid	01Fe02Jq
SLATTERY, Bridgt.		12	F	House Maid	01Fe02Jq
JACKSON, John		45	M	Carpenter	01Fe02Jq
FARRELL, Michl.		40	M	Butcher	01Fe02Jq
Mary	(W)	30	F	Butcher	01Fe02Jq
Michl.	(S)	09	M	Child	01Fe02Jq
Johana	(D)	07	F	Child	01Fe02Jq
U	(D)	.00	F	Infant	01Fe02Jq
MCGILLENON, Jno.		23	M	Laborer	01Fe02Jq
KIERNAN, Francis		43	M	Laborer	01Fe02Jq
HAMLIN, Margt.		20	F	Laborer	01Fe02Jq
Michl.		18	M	Laborer	01Fe02Jq
James		16	M	Laborer	01Fe02Jq
CAMPBELL, Pat		33	M	Clerk	01Fe02Jq
SHORT, Mary		17	F	House Maid	01Fe02Jq
CONNELL, Ellen		21	F	Unknown	01Fe02Jq
DOOLY, Mary		19	F	Unknown	01Fe02Jq
RILEY, Thomas		32	M	Stone Mason	01Fe02Jq
Mary		22	F	Unknown	01Fe02Jq
WARRINGTON, John		40	M	Laborer	01Fe02Jq
Honora		15	F	Unknown	01Fe02Jq
MCCARTY, James		25	M	Unknown	01Fe02Jq
DUFFY, Mary-Ann		18	F	Unknown	01Fe02Jq
COGLIN, Bridgt.		28	F	Tailor	01Fe02Jq
Richard	(S)	05	M	Child	01Fe02Jq

NAMES OF PASSENGERS		AGE	SEX	OCCUPATIONS	DATE PORT SHIP
HEYDEN, Charles		35	M	Tailor	01Fe02Jq
LARKIN, Bridgt.		56	F	Servant	01Fe02Jq
Mary		21	F	Servant	01Fe02Jq
Patk.		20	M	Laborer	01Fe02Jq
Ellen		09	F	Child	01Fe02Jq
BURKE, Ellen		20	F	Laborer	01Fe02Jq
COMERFORD, Cathn.		25	F	Laborer	01Fe02Jq
DUFFY, Michl.		45	M	Laborer	01Fe02Jq
U	(W)	40	F	Wife	01Fe02Jq
Michl.	(S)	19	M	Laborer	01Fe02Jq
Thos.	(S)	17	M	Laborer	01Fe02Jq
Henry	(S)	15	M	Laborer	01Fe02Jq
WALLACE, Mary		18	F	Laborer	01Fe02Jq
PUGH, David		25	M	Weaver	01Fe02Jq
JUREY, Pat		24	M	Laborer	01Fe02Jq
DUNAN, Edwd.		30	M	Laborer	01Fe02Jq
DUNCAN, Christiana		26	F	Laborer	01Fe02Jq
James	(S)	07	M	Child	01Fe02Jq
PEPPER, James		21	M	Tailor	01Fe02Jq
Fanny		19	F	Unknown	01Fe02Jq
Jane		18	F	Unknown	01Fe02Jq
HARRINGTON, Patr.		29	M	Baker	01Fe02Jq
LAUGHTON, Jno.		30	M	Laborer	01Fe02Jq
BRADY, Jno.		27	M	Laborer	01Fe02Jq
HARKIN, Dennis		34	M	Laborer	01Fe02Jq
Bridgt.	(W)	30	F	Wife	01Fe02Jq
Cathn.	(D)	07	F	Child	01Fe02Jq
Bridgt.	(D)	03	F	Child	01Fe02Jq
John		28	M	Laborer	01Fe02Jq
BRANNEN, John		20	M	Laborer	01Fe02Jq
TIMLON, John		26	M	Laborer	01Fe02Jq
Ann		22	F	Laborer	01Fe02Jq
DUFFY, Mary		40	F	Laborer	01Fe02Jq
Mary		26	F	Laborer	01Fe02Jq
MALONEY, James		22	M	Baker	01Fe02Jq
MCCABE, Thos.		32	M	Baker	01Fe02Jq
MURRAY, James		22	M	Baker	01Fe02Jq
SHEAHY, Danl.		21	M	Baker	01Fe02Jq
OBRIAN, Andw.		20	M	Baker	01Fe02Jq
John		12	M	Baker	01Fe02Jq
SMITH, Ann		13	F	Baker	01Fe02Jq
CUNNINGHAM, Francis		20	M	Baker	01Fe02Jq
MAHON, Pat		20	M	Baker	01Fe02Jq
FENESTY, Cath.		40	F	Baker	01Fe02Jq
Thomas		28	M	Baker	01Fe02Jq
Nelly		26	F	Baker	01Fe02Jq
Martin		16	M	Baker	01Fe02Jq
John		13	M	Baker	01Fe02Jq
Cath.		08	F	Child	01Fe02Jq
Patk.		20	M	Laborer	01Fe02Jq
FALLON, Thos.		38	M	Laborer	01Fe02Jq
Cathn.	(W)	38	F	Laborer	01Fe02Jq
Bridgt.	(D)	13	F	Laborer	01Fe02Jq
Jno.	(S)	12	M	Laborer	01Fe02Jq
Martin	(S)	10	M	Laborer	01Fe02Jq
Mary	(D)	08	F	Child	01Fe02Jq
Wm.	(S)	.00	M	Infant	01Fe02Jq
SHAUGHNESSEY, Pat		25	M	Laborer	01Fe02Jq
Edwd.		21	M	Laborer	01Fe02Jq
CONRIFFE, Mary		43	F	Laborer	01Fe02Jq
John	(S)	11	M	Laborer	01Fe02Jq
Peter	(S)	09	M	Child	01Fe02Jq
Patrick	(S)	06	M	Child	01Fe02Jq
James	(S)	04	M	Child	01Fe02Jq
GATELY, John		30	M	Laborer	01Fe02Jq
Peggy	(W)	30	F	Laborer	01Fe02Jq
Mary	(D)	05	F	Child	01Fe02Jq
Thos.	(S)	03	M	Child	01Fe02Jq
Nelly	(D)	.00	F	Infant	01Fe02Jq
Bryan		26	M	Laborer	01Fe02Jq
Peggy		20	F	Laborer	01Fe02Jq
FALLON, Michl.		20	M	Laborer	01Fe02Jq
LIRCKEER, Hinney		30	F	Laborer	01Fe02Jq
FARNIN, John		30	M	Laborer	01Fe02Jq
Mary	(W)	30	F	Laborer	01Fe02Jq
FARNIN, Michl.	(S)	11	M	Laborer	01Fe02Jq
WADE, Bridgt.		28	F	Laborer	01Fe02Jq
Elizth.		26	F	Laborer	01Fe02Jq
FANNON, Wm.		18	M	Laborer	01Fe02Jq
FITZGERALD, Michl.		24	M	Laborer	01Fe02Jq
Richd.		26	M	Laborer	01Fe02Jq
NEELY, Thos.		22	M	Laborer	01Fe02Jq
MORAN, Mary		30	F	Laborer	01Fe02Jq
CORR, Pat		46	M	Laborer	01Fe02Jq
Thos.		16	M	Laborer	01Fe02Jq
Julia		12	F	Laborer	01Fe02Jq
BURKE, Wm.		22	M	Laborer	01Fe02Jq
STEENSON, Wm.		30	M	Laborer	01Fe02Jq
KELLY, Pat		34	M	Laborer	01Fe02Jq
Ellen	(W)	25	F	Laborer	01Fe02Jq
Mary	(D)	03	F	Child	01Fe02Jq
Bridget	(D)	02	F	Child	01Fe02Jq
Died-At-Sea					
Ellen	(D)	.00	F	Infant	01Fe02Jq
DEVINE, Wm.		31	M	Farmer	01Fe02Jq
HAMLIN, Michl.		12	M	Farmer	01Fe02Jq
Michl.		12	M	Farmer	01Fe02Jq
FLANNAGAN, Bernd.		20	M	Laborer	01Fe02Jq
TOOLE, Cath.		17	F	Laborer	01Fe02Jq
WALSH, Martin		28	M	Laborer	01Fe02Jq
Ann	(W)	35	F	Laborer	01Fe02Jq
Cathn.	(D)	.00	F	Infant	01Fe02Jq
Ann	(M)	50	F	Laborer	01Fe02Jq
COX, Paul		24	M	Laborer	01Fe02Jq
KENNY, Mary		50	F	Laborer	01Fe02Jq
LARKIN, Mary		20	F	Laborer	01Fe02Jq
Pat		20	M	Laborer	01Fe02Jq
Lorry	(D)	.00	M	Infant	01Fe02Jq
COCKRANE, Thos.		20	M	Laborer	01Fe02Jq
WALSH, Thos.		30	M	Laborer	01Fe02Jq
KENNIGAN, Thos.		19	M	Laborer	01Fe02Jq
SHERWAN, Edwd.		12	M	Laborer	01Fe02Jq
SMITH, Peter		22	M	Laborer	01Fe02Jq
Bridgt.		22	F	Laborer	01Fe02Jq
RIGNEY, Stephen		21	M	Laborer	01Fe02Jq
SULLIVAN, Thos.		30	M	Laborer	01Fe02Jq
RIGNEY, Michl.		23	M	Laborer	01Fe02Jq
LARKIN, Patk.		22	M	Laborer	01Fe02Jq
Honora		19	F	Laborer	01Fe02Jq
JOHNSON, Henry		21	M	Tailor	01Fe02Jq
CARROLL, Wm.		22	M	Laborer	01Fe02Jq
KEARNEY, Dennis		22	M	Unknown	01Fe02Jq
ALEXANDER, John		23	M	Plasterer	01Fe02Jq
MCGUCKER, Paul		40	M	Weaver	01Fe02Jq
DUNN, Jerh.		40	M	Weaver	01Fe02Jq
DONAN, Margt.		23	F	Weaver	01Fe02Jq
Mary-Ann	(D)	.00	F	Infant	01Fe02Jq
WALSH, John		30	M	Laborer	01Fe02Jq
Bridget		26	F	Laborer	01Fe02Jq
ONEILL, John		18	M	Laborer	01Fe02Jq
KANE, Thos.		40	M	Laborer	01Fe02Jq
LEONARD, Michl.		30	M	Laborer	01Fe02Jq
COURTNEY, Bridgt.		27	F	Laborer	01Fe02Jq
Mary	(D)	03	F	Child	01Fe02Jq
Patk.	(S)	02	M	Child	01Fe02Jq
MEE, Patk.		32	M	Laborer	01Fe02Jq
GRAINGER, Arthur		19	M	Stationer	01Fe02Jq
HANNFORD, Robt.		18	M	Stationer	01Fe02Jq
RYAN, Mathw.		20	M	Bricklayer	01Fe02Jq
SAMPSON, Henry		26	M	Farmer	01Fe02Jq
BURROWS, James		44	M	Farmer	01Fe02Jq
DAVIES, Wm.		28	M	Farmer	01Fe02Jq
Elizth.		25	F	Farmer	01Fe02Jq
QUIN, Bernd.		33	M	Farmer	01Fe02Jq
KELLY, John		20	M	Laborer	01Fe02Jq
Anty.		60	M	Weaver	01Fe02Jq
Anty.		26	M	Weaver	01Fe02Jq
Honora		20	F	Weaver	01Fe02Jq
Sabina		19	F	Weaver	01Fe02Jq
BERNE, James		40	M	Weaver	01Fe02Jq

NAMES OF PASSENGERS		AGE	SEX	OCCUPATIONS	DATE PORT SHIP
BERNE, Bridgt.	(W)	30	F	Weaver	01Fe02Jq
Patk.	(S)	06	M	Child	01Fe02Jq
Honora	(D)	04	F	Child	01Fe02Jq
James	(S)	.00	M	Infant	01Fe02Jq
GAW, Jacob		30	M	Weaver	01Fe02Jq
LIGHT, Andw.		18	M	Weaver	01Fe02Jq
MCHUGH, Margt.		28	F	Weaver	01Fe02Jq
LOFTUS, John		28	M	Weaver	01Fe02Jq
Mary		20	F	Weaver	01Fe02Jq
Kitty		18	F	Weaver	01Fe02Jq
CURLEY, Mary		28	F	Weaver	01Fe02Jq
LOFTUS, Mich.		20	M	Weaver	01Fe02Jq
Mary		18	F	Weaver	01Fe02Jq
Ellen		09	F	Child	01Fe02Jq
Pat		02	M	Child	01Fe02Jq
Wm.		.00	M	Infant	01Fe02Jq
DEVENEY, Mary		20	F	Servant	01Fe02Jq
MCARDLE, Michl.		40	M	Servant	01Fe02Jq
John		05	M	Child	01Fe02Jq
MORAN, Andw.		27	M	Servant	01Fe02Jq
MCMENLEY, Jane		30	F	Servant	01Fe02Jq
Alexr.	(S)	07	M	Child	01Fe02Jq
James	(S)	05	M	Child	01Fe02Jq
Sarah	(D)	03	F	Child	01Fe02Jq
John	(S)	.00	M	Infant	01Fe02Jq
GATELY, John		30	M	Laborer	01Fe02Jq
Peggy	(W)	30	F	Laborer	01Fe02Jq
Mary	(D)	05	F	Child	01Fe02Jq
Thos.	(S)	03	M	Child	01Fe02Jq
Bryan		26	M	Laborer	01Fe02Jq
Peggy		20	F	Laborer	01Fe02Jq
TRACEY, Thos.		30	M	Laborer	01Fe02Jq
CUNNINGHAM, Thos.		20	M	Laborer	01Fe02Jq
WADE, Eliza		28	F	Laborer	01Fe02Jq
FANNON, John		30	M	Laborer	01Fe02Jq
SMITH, Mary		30	F	Laborer	01Fe02Jq
WADE, Elizth.		20	F	Laborer	01Fe02Jq

DIGBY 01 FEBRUARY 1848

From Liverpool

NAMES OF PASSENGERS		AGE	SEX	OCCUPATIONS	DATE PORT SHIP
RILEY, Anthony		25	M	Laborer	01Fe02Ep
DUNN, Bridget		22	F	None	01Fe02Ep
HASTING, James		36	M	Laborer	01Fe02Ep
Eliza	(W)	30	F	None	01Fe02Ep
Geo.	(S)	04	M	Child	01Fe02Ep
DUFFY, John		25	M	Laborer	01Fe02Ep
MURRAY, Catherine		22	F	None	01Fe02Ep
Bridget		17	F	None	01Fe02Ep
Thomas		02	M	Child	01Fe02Ep
GRASSON, Eliza		25	F	None	01Fe02Ep
Eliza	(D)	03	F	Child	01Fe02Ep
John	(S)	02	M	Child	01Fe02Ep
GALLAGHER, Phelim		30	M	Laborer	01Fe02Ep
Libby		22	F	None	01Fe02Ep
Ann		20	F	None	01Fe02Ep
DEAN, Mary		20	F	None	01Fe02Ep
KEAN, Bridget		18	F	None	01Fe02Ep
MURPHY, Catherine		20	F	None	01Fe02Ep
BANNER, James-B.		20	M	Laborer	01Fe02Ep
DIGNEN, Patrick		40	M	Laborer	01Fe02Ep
MALONE, Catherin		25	F	None	01Fe02Ep
Bridget		24	F	None	01Fe02Ep
HURLEY, Mary		21	F	None	01Fe02Ep
Richard		20	M	None	01Fe02Ep
TEAL, Martin		19	M	None	01Fe02Ep
RILEY, Mary		18	F	None	01Fe02Ep
HENNSEY, Ellen		20	F	None	01Fe02Ep

NAMES OF PASSENGERS		AGE	SEX	OCCUPATIONS	DATE PORT SHIP
DALTAN, John		40	M	Laborer	01Fe02Ep
Mary		35	F	None	01Fe02Ep
TRACY, Thoms.		21	M	None	01Fe02Ep
FALLAN, Roger		05	M	Laborer	01Fe02Ep
EARLY, Pat		17	M	Laborer	01Fe02Ep
KEARNY, Michael		25	M	Laborer	01Fe02Ep
Mary		20	F	None	01Fe02Ep
BRADY, Biddy		20	F	None	01Fe02Ep
Eliza		20	F	None	01Fe02Ep
CONNOLY, Patt.		50	M	Laborer	01Fe02Ep
Cath.	(W)	50	F	Wife	01Fe02Ep
Pat	(S)	25	M	Laborer	01Fe02Ep
John	(S)	21	M	Laborer	01Fe02Ep
BARRETT, Pat		21	M	Laborer	01Fe02Ep
CONNOLLY, Nelly		19	F	None	01Fe02Ep
Cathe.		16	F	None	01Fe02Ep
Danl.		11	M	None	01Fe02Ep
Judy		07	F	Child	01Fe02Ep
HARRINGTON, Pat		20	M	Laborer	01Fe02Ep
DOBSON, John		19	M	Laborer	01Fe02Ep
RILEY, Michl.		30	M	Laborer	01Fe02Ep
LOWRY, Bridget		12	F	None	01Fe02Ep
LYNCH, Ann		20	F	None	01Fe02Ep
QUINN, John		40	M	Laborer	01Fe02Ep
TRAINER, Edwd.		19	M	Laborer	01Fe02Ep
Daphney		17	F	Laborer	01Fe02Ep
CLARK, Cathe.		16	F	None	01Fe02Ep
OCONNELL, Christ.		10	M	None	01Fe02Ep
LYNCH, Bridget		17	F	None	01Fe02Ep
FLAHERTY, Honora		29	F	None	01Fe02Ep
SULLIVAN, Michl.		18	M	Laborer	01Fe02Ep
U, Catherine		14	F	None	01Fe02Ep
MCGOVERN, Thos.		17	M	None	01Fe02Ep
John		11	M	None	01Fe02Ep
MURPHY, John		23	M	Laborer	01Fe02Ep
DOYLE, Thos.		36	M	Laborer	01Fe02Ep
ALLEN, Wm.		30	M	Laborer	01Fe02Ep
DAY, Michl.		22	M	Laborer	01Fe02Ep
WALL, John		25	M	Laborer	01Fe02Ep
CARNEY, Ann		40	F	None	01Fe02Ep
MOORE, Mary		12	F	None	01Fe02Ep
Bridget		08	F	Child	01Fe02Ep
Jane		07	F	Child	01Fe02Ep
Rebecca		07	F	Child	01Fe02Ep
MCBRIDE, Elizabeth		25	F	Servant	01Fe02Ep
FINERANE, Thos.		20	M	Laborer	01Fe02Ep
SLAVAN, John		20	M	Laborer	01Fe02Ep
BUCKLEY, Mary		17	F	None	01Fe02Ep
SULLIVAN, Rose		60	M	None	01Fe02Ep
HOOK, Judy		26	F	Servant	01Fe02Ep
WALSH, Margaret		46	F	Servant	01Fe02Ep
Margaret	(D)	.00	F	Infant	01Fe02Ep
BUCKLEY, Bridget		20	F	Servant	01Fe02Ep
KELLY, Peggy		30	F	Servant	01Fe02Ep
DONNELLY, John		23	M	Laborer	01Fe02Ep
FENNERTY, Pat		25	M	Laborer	01Fe02Ep
Cathar.		20	F	None	01Fe02Ep
CUNNINGHAM, Winney		25	F	None	01Fe02Ep
HUGHES, Cathe.		25	F	None	01Fe02Ep
MCMAHON, Bridget		15	F	None	01Fe02Ep
Mary-Ann		16	F	None	01Fe02Ep
ROBINSON, Jas.		40	M	Laborer	01Fe02Ep
Eliza		13	F	None	01Fe02Ep
Jane		09	F	Child	01Fe02Ep
MAGUIRE, Mary		12	F	None	01Fe02Ep
MCINTYRE, Jas.		38	M	Laborer	01Fe02Ep
ASKIN, Pat		23	M	Laborer	01Fe02Ep
HEGARTY, Pat		30	M	Laborer	01Fe02Ep
HANNA, John		32	M	Laborer	01Fe02Ep
GILFILLAN, Wm.		45	M	Laborer	01Fe02Ep
GRIMES, Jas.		40	M	Laborer	01Fe02Ep
U	(W)	40	F	Servant	01Fe02Ep
Michael	(S)	13	M	None	01Fe02Ep
John	(S)	11	M	None	01Fe02Ep
Francis	(S)	09	M	Child	01Fe02Ep

NAMES OF PASSENGERS		AGE	SEX	OCCUPATIONS	DATE PORT SHIP
GRIMES, Wm.	(S)	02	M	Child	01Fe02Ep
Eliza	(D)	18	F	Servant	01Fe02Ep
KENNEY, Thos.		20	M	Laborer	01Fe02Ep
Cath.		11	F	None	01Fe02Ep
MILLIGAN, Pat		30	M	Laborer	01Fe02Ep
GRIMES, Hugh		40	M	Laborer	01Fe02Ep
Mary	(W)	40	F	Servant	01Fe02Ep
Ann	(D)	20	F	Servant	01Fe02Ep
Ellen	(D)	11	F	Servant	01Fe02Ep
John	(S)	12	M	None	01Fe02Ep
Cathe.	(D)	11	F	None	01Fe02Ep
Margaret	(D)	09	F	Child	01Fe02Ep
CUDDY, Thos.		27	M	Laborer	01Fe02Ep
U	(W)	24	F	Wife	01Fe02Ep
CURRY, Peggy		17	F	Servant	01Fe02Ep
CULLEN, Miles		21	M	Laborer	01Fe02Ep
MENEELY, Pat		30	M	Laborer	01Fe02Ep
MOONEY, Peter		26	M	Laborer	01Fe02Ep
SHANDY, Michl.		20	M	Laborer	01Fe02Ep
RAY, David		28	M	Laborer	01Fe02Ep
FAWCETT, Cathe.		33	F	Servant	01Fe02Ep
Ralph	(H)	40	M	Laborer	01Fe02Ep
John	(S)	15	M	None	01Fe02Ep
James	(S)	13	M	None	01Fe02Ep
Isabella	(D)	12	F	None	01Fe02Ep
Ralph	(S)	10	M	None	01Fe02Ep
Wm.	(S)	07	M	Child	01Fe02Ep
Andrew	(S)	05	M	Child	01Fe02Ep
Alex	(S)	03	M	Child	01Fe02Ep
Kate	(D)	.00	F	Infant	01Fe02Ep
CLANCY, John		30	M	Laborer	01Fe02Ep
MULLONY, Michl.		20	M	Laborer	01Fe02Ep
CLANCY, Mary		36	F	Servant	01Fe02Ep
COSTELLO, Thos.		30	M	Laborer	01Fe02Ep
HORAN, Bridget		20	F	Servant	01Fe02Ep
SWEENEY, Pat		22	M	Laborer	01Fe02Ep
MCWHEENY, Michl.		30	M	Laborer	01Fe02Ep
LYMAN, Peter		22	M	Laborer	01Fe02Ep
Honor		45	F	None	01Fe02Ep
Edward		13	M	None	01Fe02Ep
BOLAN, Margaret		45	F	Servant	01Fe02Ep
DARLEY, Lawrence		03	M	Child	01Fe02Ep
NANGLE, Ann		20	F	Servant	01Fe02Ep
BRENNAN, Dennis		21	M	None	01Fe02Ep
Wm.		05	M	Child	01Fe02Ep
WILLIAMS, John		18	M	Laborer	01Fe02Ep
GILLESPIE, Pat		18	M	Laborer	01Fe02Ep
LALLY, Biddy		42	F	Servant	01Fe02Ep
John		40	M	Laborer	01Fe02Ep
Pat		21	M	Laborer	01Fe02Ep
MANLEY, Michl.		25	M	Laborer	01Fe02Ep
OHARA, Richd.		20	M	Laborer	01Fe02Ep
HEARN, Jas.		18	M	Laborer	01Fe02Ep
Thos.		25	M	Laborer	01Fe02Ep
MULLAN, John		50	M	Laborer	01Fe02Ep
Thos.	(S)	26	M	Laborer	01Fe02Ep
Mary	(D)	22	F	Servant	01Fe02Ep
Honora	(D)	17	F	Servant	01Fe02Ep
CONNER, Mary		22	F	Servant	01Fe02Ep
MCDONNELL, Honora		22	F	Servant	01Fe02Ep
NOLAN, Pat		18	M	Laborer	01Fe02Ep
MOONEY, Matthew		20	M	Laborer	01Fe02Ep
WALSH, Wm.		25	M	Laborer	01Fe02Ep
Judith		25	F	Servant	01Fe02Ep
ARTHUR, John		20	M	Laborer	01Fe02Ep
ELLIOTT, Hanna		20	F	Servant	01Fe02Ep
Ann		21	F	Servant	01Fe02Ep
KERR, Betty		60	F	Servant	01Fe02Ep
Margaret	(D)	30	F	Servant	01Fe02Ep
David		03	M	Child	01Fe02Ep
BYRNES, John		35	M	Laborer	01Fe02Ep
Mary	(W)	35	F	Wife	01Fe02Ep
Pat	(S)	08	M	Child	01Fe02Ep
James	(S)	04	M	Child	01Fe02Ep
Mary	(D)	02	F	Child	01Fe02Ep

NAMES OF PASSENGERS		AGE	SEX	OCCUPATIONS	DATE PORT SHIP
BYRNES, Bridget		20	F	Servant	01Fe02Ep
FULLAN, John		21	M	Laborer	01Fe02Ep
Michl.		23	M	Laborer	01Fe02Ep
FOWLER, Wm.		41	M	Laborer	01Fe02Ep
Elizabeth	(W)	39	F	Wife	01Fe02Ep
Elizabeth	(D)	08	F	Child	01Fe02Ep
Wm.	(S)	06	M	Child	01Fe02Ep
Isabella	(D)	03	F	Child	01Fe02Ep
Ellen	(D)	.00	F	Infant	01Fe02Ep
JENKINS, Mary		20	F	Servant	01Fe02Ep
HAPPIKINS, Pat		27	M	Laborer	01Fe02Ep
Mary		21	F	Servant	01Fe02Ep
HUNCH, James		47	M	Laborer	01Fe02Ep
Cathe.		12	F	None	01Fe02Ep
MCANARY, John		20	M	Laborer	01Fe02Ep
BOYLE, Nicholas		21	M	Laborer	01Fe02Ep
SILKE, Thos.		20	M	Laborer	01Fe02Ep
LATHAM, John		40	M	Laborer	01Fe02Ep
EGAN, Mary		20	F	Servant	01Fe02Ep
MAGUIRE, Cathe.		20	F	Servant	01Fe02Ep
MAHON, Peter		40	M	Laborer	01Fe02Ep
MCGORMAN, Pat		24	M	Laborer	01Fe02Ep
MAHON, Ellen		23	F	Servant	01Fe02Ep
Kitty		24	F	Servant	01Fe02Ep
MOORE, Peter		50	M	Laborer	01Fe02Ep
U	(W)	50	F	Wife	01Fe02Ep
James	(S)	17	M	None	01Fe02Ep
Matthew	(S)	15	M	None	01Fe02Ep
Judith	(D)	13	F	None	01Fe02Ep
Bridget	(D)	11	F	None	01Fe02Ep
Chritr.	(S)	06	M	Child	01Fe02Ep
Rose	(D)	06	F	Child	01Fe02Ep
BYRNE, Jas.		24	M	Laborer	01Fe02Ep
MCKNIGHT, Wm.		22	M	Laborer	01Fe02Ep
SMITH, Patk.		24	M	Laborer	01Fe02Ep
DORGAN, Timothy		56	M	Laborer	01Fe02Ep
Abby	(W)	50	F	Laborer	01Fe02Ep
John	(S)	25	M	Laborer	01Fe02Ep
Cas.	(S)	22	M	Laborer	01Fe02Ep
James	(S)	17	M	Laborer	01Fe02Ep
Hannah	(D)	15	F	Servant	01Fe02Ep
Jerry	(S)	11	M	None	01Fe02Ep
Timothy	(S)	09	M	Child	01Fe02Ep
John	(S)	21	M	Laborer	01Fe02Ep
HERRY, Danl.		22	M	Laborer	01Fe02Ep
SMITH, Abby		21	F	Servant	01Fe02Ep
BUTLER, Pat		23	M	Laborer	01Fe02Ep
U	(W)	36	F	Wife	01Fe02Ep
Margaret	(D)	02	F	Child	01Fe02Ep
LYNCH, Pat		20	M	Laborer	01Fe02Ep
MCDONNELL, John		19	M	Laborer	01Fe02Ep
KING, Reuben		30	M	Laborer	01Fe02Ep
WELSH, John		26	M	Laborer	01Fe02Ep
Ann		21	F	Servant	01Fe02Ep
HEART, Michl.		21	M	Laborer	01Fe02Ep
MALCOMSON, Jane		20	F	Servant	01Fe02Ep
CUMSKEY, John		20	M	Laborer	01Fe02Ep
CAMPBELL, Ann		20	F	Servant	01Fe02Ep
LAVERTY, John		20	M	Laborer	01Fe02Ep
HART, Pat		22	M	Laborer	01Fe02Ep
LEE, Kitty		27	F	Servant	01Fe02Ep
MCMANUS, Thos.		25	M	Laborer	01Fe02Ep
Bridget		20	F	Servant	01Fe02Ep
CONNOLY, Pat.		20	M	Laborer	01Fe02Ep
SCOLAN, Bridget		20	F	Servant	01Fe02Ep
Cathe.		14	F	None	01Fe02Ep
TAYLOR, Thos.		00	M	Unknown	01Fe02Ep
COLLART, Jos.		00	M	Unknown	01Fe02Ep
HANLY, Bridget		00	F	Unknown	01Fe02Ep
MULLIGAN, Eliza		00	F	Unknown	01Fe02Ep
HARTLE, Edward		00	M	Unknown	01Fe02Ep
Bridget		00	F	Unknown	01Fe02Ep
BOYLE, Owen		00	M	Unknown	01Fe02Ep
WHITE, Jane		00	F	Unknown	01Fe02Ep
Wm.		00	M	Unknown	01Fe02Ep

NAMES OF PASSENGERS		AGE	SEX	OCCUPATIONS	DATE PORT SHIP
WHITE, John		00	M	Unknown	01Fe02Ep
HUGHES, A.		22	M	Unknown	01Fe02Ep

FIDELIA 03 FEBRUARY 1848

From Liverpool

NAMES OF PASSENGERS		AGE	SEX	OCCUPATIONS	DATE PORT SHIP
SULLIVAN, Michael		26	M	Engineer	03Fe02Ax
COWAN, David		44	M	Farmer	03Fe02Ax
Margaret	(W)	45	F	Wife	03Fe02Ax
Frances	(D)	18	F	Unknown	03Fe02Ax
Esther	(D)	10	F	Unknown	03Fe02Ax
Jane	(D)	08	F	Child	03Fe02Ax
Margt.	(D)	.10	F	Infant	03Fe02Ax
George	(S)	20	M	Unknown	03Fe02Ax
John	(S)	16	M	Unknown	03Fe02Ax
Stafford	(S)	14	M	Unknown	03Fe02Ax
Thomas	(S)	12	M	Unknown	03Fe02Ax
Francis	(S)	06	M	Child	03Fe02Ax
David	(S)	04	M	Child	03Fe02Ax
HANNON, Thomas		30	M	Trader	03Fe02Ax
DALY, Agnes		21	F	Dressmaker	03Fe02Ax
TURNER, Arthur		25	M	Farmer	03Fe02Ax
Anne	(W)	22	F	Wife	03Fe02Ax
George	(S)	.07	M	Infant	03Fe02Ax
Died-At-Sea					
NAUGHTON, Thomas		30	M	Farmer	03Fe02Ax
Catherine	(W)	24	F	Wife	03Fe02Ax
John	(S)	04	M	Child	03Fe02Ax
Anne	(D)	03	F	Child	03Fe02Ax
Catherine	(D)	01	F	Child	03Fe02Ax
U	(S)	.00	M	Infant	03Fe02Ax
Born-At-Sea	Died-At-Sea				
Henry		19	M	Laborer	03Fe02Ax
KERRIENN, Brett		35	M	Laborer	03Fe02Ax
Bridget	(W)	32	F	Wife	03Fe02Ax
Bridget	(D)	12	F	Unknown	03Fe02Ax
John	(S)	10	M	Unknown	03Fe02Ax
Catherine	(D)	06	F	Child	03Fe02Ax
Thomas	(S)	04	M	Child	03Fe02Ax
James	(S)	01	M	Child	03Fe02Ax
MAHER, John		35	M	Weaver	03Fe02Ax
ONEILL, Pat.		18	M	Laborer	03Fe02Ax
KENNY, John		18	M	Laborer	03Fe02Ax
CRAIG, James		26	M	Storekeeper	03Fe02Ax
Sarah	(W)	18	F	Wife	03Fe02Ax
MURPHY, Mary		20	F	Servant	03Fe02Ax
MCFARLANE, John		50	M	Farmer	03Fe02Ax
Armour		17	M	Laborer	03Fe02Ax
WILSON, William		19	M	Laborer	03Fe02Ax
MCDONALD, John		30	M	Laborer	03Fe02Ax
MCGAVIN, Andrew		22	M	Cbtmkr	03Fe02Ax
BRYAN, William		30	M	Laborer	03Fe02Ax
James		20	M	Laborer	03Fe02Ax
KUMISKY, Charles		24	M	Laborer	03Fe02Ax
GALLAGHAN, Peter		21	M	Laborer	03Fe02Ax
CARNEY, John		40	M	Laborer	03Fe02Ax
FARLEY, Michael		39	M	Laborer	03Fe02Ax
MAHERG, John		40	M	Farmer	03Fe02Ax
Margaret	(W)	30	F	Wife	03Fe02Ax
John	(S)	11	M	Unknown	03Fe02Ax
Archd.	(S)	08	M	Child	03Fe02Ax
Robert	(S)	05	M	Child	03Fe02Ax
Margart	(D)	03	F	Child	03Fe02Ax
Mary-Jane	(D)	.04	F	Infant	03Fe02Ax
CARR, Isabella		20	F	Spinster	03Fe02Ax
DILLON, Jared		33	M	Farmer	03Fe02Ax
Mary	(W)	22	F	Wife	03Fe02Ax
James	(S)	01	M	Child	03Fe02Ax

NAMES OF PASSENGERS		AGE	SEX	OCCUPATIONS	DATE PORT SHIP
BRADY, Anne		26	F	Dressmaker	03Fe02Ax
John	(S)	04	M	Child	03Fe02Ax
HILL, Mary		20	F	Servant	03Fe02Ax
CALLUM, Mary		18	F	Servant	03Fe02Ax
MCCUE, Bridget		20	F	Servant	03Fe02Ax
DUFFY, Anne		18	F	Servant	03Fe02Ax
OBRIEN, Catherine		30	F	Brewer	03Fe02Ax
Marianne	(D)	02	F	Child	03Fe02Ax
MCCANN, Cathrine		25	F	Servant	03Fe02Ax
WHITE, Mathew		30	M	Laborer	03Fe02Ax
ARKON, Edwd.		30	M	Laborer	03Fe02Ax
COONEY, Thomas		30	M	Laborer	03Fe02Ax
GARRETY, Pat.		20	M	Laborer	03Fe02Ax
CAIN, Anthony		66	M	Laborer	03Fe02Ax
Anne	(W)	67	F	Wife	03Fe02Ax
Jane	(D)	19	F	Unknown	03Fe02Ax
James	(S)	16	M	Unknown	03Fe02Ax
LEONARD, Patrick		35	M	Unknown	03Fe02Ax
DRAUGHILTY, Mary		31	F	Dressmaker	03Fe02Ax
Michael	(S)	05	M	Child	03Fe02Ax
HARLEY, Pat.		35	M	Laborer	03Fe02Ax
LEARY, Ann		18	F	Dressmaker	03Fe02Ax
Elizabeth		20	F	Dressmaker	03Fe02Ax
FLAHERTY, Margaret		30	F	Dressmaker	03Fe02Ax
FEARNEY, Pat.		27	M	Laborer	03Fe02Ax
Bridget	(W)	30	F	Wife	03Fe02Ax
James		13	M	Laborer	03Fe02Ax
DEVINE, Mary		30	F	Dressmaker	03Fe02Ax
John	(S)	02	M	Child	03Fe02Ax
Francis	(S)	.06	M	Infant	03Fe02Ax
DILLON, Mary		24	F	Servant	03Fe02Ax
SHALLOON, Margaret		19	F	Servant	03Fe02Ax
DOWLING, Agnes		19	F	Servant	03Fe02Ax
COLE, Michael		35	M	Laborer	03Fe02Ax
Mary	(W)	30	F	Wife	03Fe02Ax
Mary	(D)	07	F	Child	03Fe02Ax
James	(S)	04	M	Child	03Fe02Ax
Pat.	(S)	02	M	Child	03Fe02Ax
Died-At-Sea					
WALSH, William		25	M	Laborer	03Fe02Ax
BARRET, Susan		30	F	Servant	03Fe02Ax
SULLIVAN, Dennis		35	M	Laborer	03Fe02Ax
COLE, Mary		40	F	Servant	03Fe02Ax
Pat.	(S)	07	M	Child	03Fe02Ax
William	(S)	04	M	Child	03Fe02Ax
ALLAN, Dennis		25	M	Laborer	03Fe02Ax
Catherin	(M)	60	F	Unknown	03Fe02Ax
LYNCH, Ann		20	F	Servant	03Fe02Ax
GALLAGHER, Mary		22	F	Servant	03Fe02Ax
MCGUINESS, Ann		25	F	Servant	03Fe02Ax
John		13	M	Laborer	03Fe02Ax
NEIL, James		47	M	Farmer	03Fe02Ax
John	(S)	07	M	Child	03Fe02Ax
Joanna	(W)	40	F	Wife	03Fe02Ax
Kate	(D)	10	F	Unknown	03Fe02Ax
Ann	(D)	05	F	Child	03Fe02Ax
Margaret	(D)	03	F	Child	03Fe02Ax
LEAHY, Mary		22	F	Servant	03Fe02Ax
DOWLING, James		29	M	Laborer	03Fe02Ax
FITZPATRICK, Richd.		17	M	Laborer	03Fe02Ax
STOKES, Richd.		14	M	Carpenter	03Fe02Ax
MCCABE, John		20	M	Baker	03Fe02Ax
FALLON, Thomas		30	M	Mason	03Fe02Ax
HEATH, Catherine		26	F	Wife	03Fe02Ax
John	(S)	07	M	Child	03Fe02Ax
Joseph	(S)	05	M	Child	03Fe02Ax
Ann	(D)	03	F	Child	03Fe02Ax
MCNARNEY, James		20	M	Laborer	03Fe02Ax
Helen		22	F	Servant	03Fe02Ax
MADDEN, Bridget		14	F	Servant	03Fe02Ax
Luke		24	M	Laborer	03Fe02Ax
MCCANN, Cathrine		40	F	Wife	03Fe02Ax
Catherine	(D)	01	F	Child	03Fe02Ax
Bridget	(D)	06	F	Child	03Fe02Ax
Charles	(S)	08	M	Child	03Fe02Ax

NAMES OF PASSENGERS		AGE	SEX	OCCUPATIONS	DATE PORT SHIP
WHITE, Rachel		20	F	Dressmaker	03Fe02Ax
BARRY, Mary		22	F	Servant	03Fe02Ax
KEARNAN, James		30	M	Laborer	03Fe02Ax
Elizabeth		24	F	Servant	03Fe02Ax
Mary		20	F	Servant	03Fe02Ax
Ann		18	F	Servant	03Fe02Ax
DUNGAN, Thomas		20	M	Laborer	03Fe02Ax
John		16	M	Laborer	03Fe02Ax
USHER, William		25	M	Laborer	03Fe02Ax
SIMONS, John		19	M	Laborer	03Fe02Ax
KILLIAN, Patrick		30	M	Mason	03Fe02Ax
Dorothy	(W)	30	F	Wife	03Fe02Ax
Mary	(D)	05	F	Child	03Fe02Ax
Anne	(D)	02	F	Child	03Fe02Ax
MCTEAR, William		17	M	Laborer	03Fe02Ax

OXFORD 04 FEBRUARY 1848

From Liverpool

NAMES OF PASSENGERS		AGE	SEX	OCCUPATIONS	DATE PORT SHIP
COCHRANE, T.		24	M	Mechanic	04Fe02Aj
CROFTS, T.		24	M	Mechanic	04Fe02Aj
BARBER, W.		22	M	Mechanic	04Fe02Aj
Elizt.		20	F	None	04Fe02Aj
BEECROFT, F.		21	M	Unknown	04Fe02Aj
Eliza		21	F	None	04Fe02Aj
BOND, R.		28	M	Unknown	04Fe02Aj
My.		27	F	None	04Fe02Aj
BRANT, B.		24	M	Unknown	04Fe02Aj
SMITH, H.		29	M	Unknown	04Fe02Aj
KIMBERLY, J.		26	M	Unknown	04Fe02Aj
HANLON, P.		31	M	Unknown	04Fe02Aj
Rebecca		28	F	None	04Fe02Aj
KINBELLY, Jos.		25	M	Unknown	04Fe02Aj
HANLON, Wm.		12	M	None	04Fe02Aj
Ann-M.		02	F	Child	04Fe02Aj
Fed.		01	M	Child	04Fe02Aj
David		01	M	Child	04Fe02Aj
JOHNSON, Mgt.		22	F	None	04Fe02Aj
PENNINGTON, W.		34	M	Unknown	04Fe02Aj
Richd.		33	M	Unknown	04Fe02Aj
John		26	M	Unknown	04Fe02Aj
Miles		22	M	Unknown	04Fe02Aj
My.		62	F	None	04Fe02Aj
FARLY, P.		38	M	Unknown	04Fe02Aj
My.	(W)	31	F	Wife	04Fe02Aj
Mgt.	(D)	13	F	None	04Fe02Aj
MCCABE, T.		30	M	Unknown	04Fe02Aj
Ellen	(W)	30	F	Wife	04Fe02Aj
My.	(D)	15	F	None	04Fe02Aj
Thos.	(S)	01	M	Child	04Fe02Aj
MAGUIRE, My.		24	F	None	04Fe02Aj
GREIG, Jane		50	F	None	04Fe02Aj
Jane	(D)	30	F	None	04Fe02Aj
Mgt.	(D)	22	F	None	04Fe02Aj
Thos.	(S)	20	M	Unknown	04Fe02Aj
GUFFEY, P.		12	M	None	04Fe02Aj
My.		10	F	None	04Fe02Aj
Mgt.		06	F	Child	04Fe02Aj
LEWIS, H.		24	M	Unknown	04Fe02Aj
DOOLAN, P.		09	F	Child	04Fe02Aj
FARRELL, J.		21	M	Laborer	04Fe02Aj
SMITH, A.		72	M	Laborer	04Fe02Aj
Anthony	(S)	20	M	Laborer	04Fe02Aj
Betty	(W)	60	F	Wife	04Fe02Aj
LYNCH, M.		13	M	None	04Fe02Aj
FEELLY, Ann		17	F	None	04Fe02Aj
CARROLE, Saly		20	F	None	04Fe02Aj
NORTON, Bgt.		32	F	None	04Fe02Aj

NAMES OF PASSENGERS		AGE	SEX	OCCUPATIONS	DATE PORT SHIP
LOFTUS, M.		20	M	Unknown	04Fe02Aj
DONAHUE, Mgt.		30	F	None	04Fe02Aj
MANN, Mgt.		25	F	None	04Fe02Aj
DEVIN, My.		18	F	None	04Fe02Aj
MANSON, Cath.		03	F	Child	04Fe02Aj
CONNELL, Bgt.		18	F	None	04Fe02Aj
BRADY, Mgt.		15	F	None	04Fe02Aj
KENNY, My.		40	F	None	04Fe02Aj
Edwd.	(S)	13	M	None	04Fe02Aj
My.	(D)	12	F	None	04Fe02Aj
COSGROVE, P.		28	M	Unknown	04Fe02Aj
MULLADY, F.		06	M	Child	04Fe02Aj
John		10	M	None	04Fe02Aj
COSGROVE, Ann		01	F	Child	04Fe02Aj
MULLADY, My.		12	F	None	04Fe02Aj
CARR, J.		20	M	Unknown	04Fe02Aj
John		70	M	Unknown	04Fe02Aj
ROONEY, J.		23	M	Unknown	04Fe02Aj
OHARA, J.		22	M	Unknown	04Fe02Aj
FITZPATRICK, J.		16	M	None	04Fe02Aj
MCCANN, Elzt.		23	F	None	04Fe02Aj
Mich.		20	M	Unknown	04Fe02Aj
DONOHUE, F.		30	M	Unknown	04Fe02Aj
DEVIN, Cath.		20	F	None	04Fe02Aj
GREFLLY, Cath.		20	F	None	04Fe02Aj
FAHY, Ann		19	F	None	04Fe02Aj
SWANE, My.		20	F	None	04Fe02Aj
QUIN, An		20	F	None	04Fe02Aj
SMITH, Rose		30	F	None	04Fe02Aj
GRANLY, Mgt.		21	F	None	04Fe02Aj
KIRWAN, Cath.		25	F	None	04Fe02Aj
KIRBY, My.		21	F	None	04Fe02Aj
Pat.		21	M	None	04Fe02Aj
MURPHY, T.		27	M	Laborer	04Fe02Aj
Thos.		30	M	Unknown	04Fe02Aj
DILLON, T.		20	M	Unknown	04Fe02Aj
FLYNN, Mgt.		60	F	None	04Fe02Aj
VAUGHAN, J.		38	M	Unknown	04Fe02Aj
CASEY, Ellen		30	F	None	04Fe02Aj
Mgt.	(D)	06	F	Child	04Fe02Aj
Jas.	(S)	05	M	Child	04Fe02Aj
Jas.	(S)	03	M	Child	04Fe02Aj
John	(S)	01	M	Child	04Fe02Aj
BOYLE, U-Mrs.		21	F	None	04Fe02Aj
ONEILL, Barb.		25	F	None	04Fe02Aj
HAUGHEY, J.		30	M	Unknown	04Fe02Aj
DEEGAN, J.		40	M	Unknown	04Fe02Aj
OONNELL, M.		25	M	Unknown	04Fe02Aj
WALLIS, H.		20	M	Unknown	04Fe02Aj
WALTERS, O.		18	M	Unknown	04Fe02Aj
DEIGAN, T.		30	M	Unknown	04Fe02Aj
Mich.		28	M	Unknown	04Fe02Aj
MAGUIRE, P.		28	M	Unknown	04Fe02Aj
BURN, J.		25	M	Unknown	04Fe02Aj
TWOMY, W.		19	M	Unknown	04Fe02Aj
SMITH, B.		17	M	Unknown	04Fe02Aj
ROSS, Jane		22	F	None	04Fe02Aj
KIRKWAN, T.		11	M	None	04Fe02Aj
Elzt.		18	F	None	04Fe02Aj
MORIARTY, Hanna		20	F	None	04Fe02Aj
MCCALLY, Bgt.		20	F	None	04Fe02Aj
ROARKE, Elzt.		16	F	None	04Fe02Aj
SHORKEY, My.		20	F	None	04Fe02Aj
DENY, My.		30	F	None	04Fe02Aj
WYNN, P.		04	M	Child	04Fe02Aj
Julia	(M)	26	F	None	04Fe02Aj
Bgt.	(T)	05	F	Child	04Fe02Aj
Mathew	(B)	03	M	Child	04Fe02Aj
NOKES, J.		30	M	Unknown	04Fe02Aj
HILTON, R.A.		45	M	Unknown	04Fe02Aj
Elzt.	(W)	46	F	Wife	04Fe02Aj
F.	(S)	19	M	Unknown	04Fe02Aj
Jane	(D)	16	F	Unknown	04Fe02Aj
Mgt.	(D)	17	F	Unknown	04Fe02Aj
Jane	(D)	14	F	Unknown	04Fe02Aj

NAMES OF PASSENGERS		AGE	SEX	OCCUPATIONS	DATE PORT SHIP
HILTON, Robt.	(S)	06	M	Child	04Fe02Aj

JOHN-R.SKIDDY 04 FEBRUARY 1848

From Liverpool

NAMES OF PASSENGERS		AGE	SEX	OCCUPATIONS	DATE PORT SHIP
BUCKLY, Ann		23	F	Seamstress	04Fe02Ac
MURPHY, Martin		20	M	Laborer	04Fe02Ac
MCFALLS, Michl.		19	M	Laborer	04Fe02Ac
BELL, Robert		55	M	Farmer	04Fe02Ac
U	(W)	55	F	Wife	04Fe02Ac
Margt.	(D)	18	F	Farmer	04Fe02Ac
John	(S)	15	M	Farmer	04Fe02Ac
James	(S)	12	M	Farmer	04Fe02Ac
Sarah	(D)	10	F	Farmer	04Fe02Ac
CAMPBILL, Thomas		21	M	Laborer	04Fe02Ac
ERBUCKLE, Andrew		24	M	Farmer	04Fe02Ac
U	(W)	20	F	Wife	04Fe02Ac
BARRY, Michl.		43	M	Mechanic	04Fe02Ac
Patrick		27	M	Mechanic	04Fe02Ac
James		20	M	Mechanic	04Fe02Ac
MCCANN, Francis		24	M	Tailor	04Fe02Ac
ENNIS, Sarah		21	F	Tailor	04Fe02Ac
SLAVIN, William		20	M	Laborer	04Fe02Ac
MCCANN, Owen		18	M	Laborer	04Fe02Ac
HAGAN, Cormack		30	M	Laborer	04Fe02Ac
HAGGERTY, Thomas		36	M	Laborer	04Fe02Ac
John		30	M	Laborer	04Fe02Ac
CHAPMAN, Margt.		50	F	Wi	04Fe02Ac
Ann		28	F	Wi	04Fe02Ac
Thomas	(S)	26	M	Laborer	04Fe02Ac
Mary		24	F	Laborer	04Fe02Ac
John	(S)	22	M	Laborer	04Fe02Ac
James	(S)	17	M	Laborer	04Fe02Ac
William	(S)	13	M	Laborer	04Fe02Ac
Peter	(S)	11	M	Laborer	04Fe02Ac
Cathe.	(D)	09	F	Child	04Fe02Ac
Bridget	(D)	07	F	Child	04Fe02Ac
GILL, Mary		30	F	Laborer	04Fe02Ac
CRONIN, Jeremiah		25	M	Laborer	04Fe02Ac
NOLAN, Stephen		50	M	Laborer	04Fe02Ac
CONNOR, Thomas		24	M	Laborer	04Fe02Ac
DOLAN, Thomas		22	M	Laborer	04Fe02Ac
KELLY, Thomas		27	M	Laborer	04Fe02Ac
RINGFIELD, Mary		20	F	Laborer	04Fe02Ac
MACK, Patrick		26	M	Laborer	04Fe02Ac
TERNAN, James		20	M	Laborer	04Fe02Ac
OGDEN, James		23	M	Laborer	04Fe02Ac
LEES, Abraham		21	M	Laborer	04Fe02Ac
BARNES, John		20	M	Laborer	04Fe02Ac
DOYLE, Thomas		24	M	Laborer	04Fe02Ac
Margt.		20	F	Laborer	04Fe02Ac
James		18	M	Laborer	04Fe02Ac
REYNOLDS, Michl.		41	M	Laborer	04Fe02Ac
GILMORE, Robert		40	M	Farmer	04Fe02Ac
U	(W)	36	F	Farmer	04Fe02Ac
John		32	M	Laborer	04Fe02Ac
George		28	M	Laborer	04Fe02Ac
CONNELLY, James		21	M	Laborer	04Fe02Ac
LEACH, James		20	M	Laborer	04Fe02Ac
HENRY, John		19	M	Laborer	04Fe02Ac
NICHOLLS, George		25	M	Laborer	04Fe02Ac
GALLAGHER, Patt.		30	M	Laborer	04Fe02Ac
U	(W)	26	F	Wife	04Fe02Ac
James	(S)	03	M	Child	04Fe02Ac
U	(S)	.06	M	Infant	04Fe02Ac
BOHEN, Catherine		48	F	None	04Fe02Ac
Michael		33	M	Laborer	04Fe02Ac
BROWN, Edward		20	M	Laborer	04Fe02Ac
MOORE, Thomas-L.		27	M	Laborer	04Fe02Ac
FAWCIT, J.B.		28	M	Laborer	04Fe02Ac
GALLAGHER, John		18	M	Laborer	04Fe02Ac
SESNAN, Mary		16	F	Laborer	04Fe02Ac
Michl.		22	M	Laborer	04Fe02Ac
BRADY, Philip		23	M	Laborer	04Fe02Ac
JOLLY, Philip		23	M	Laborer	04Fe02Ac
Thomas		20	M	Laborer	04Fe02Ac
LANCASTER, Michl.		20	M	Laborer	04Fe02Ac
HENNESSY, Thomas		35	M	Laborer	04Fe02Ac
REILLY, Philip		20	M	Laborer	04Fe02Ac
MCDERMOTT, Michael		48	M	Laborer	04Fe02Ac
Ann	(D)	11	F	None	04Fe02Ac
Maria	(D)	09	F	Child	04Fe02Ac
DUFFY, James		16	M	Laborer	04Fe02Ac
Cathe.	(D)	12	F	Laborer	04Fe02Ac
MULCAHY, John		18	M	Laborer	04Fe02Ac
Ann		17	F	Laborer	04Fe02Ac
James		11	M	Laborer	04Fe02Ac
MCGUIRK, Sarah		20	F	Laborer	04Fe02Ac
MCCANN, Ann		08	F	Child	04Fe02Ac
SHAW, Thomas		38	M	Laborer	04Fe02Ac
Elizabeth	(W)	26	F	Laborer	04Fe02Ac
Joseph	(S)	02	M	Child	04Fe02Ac
Mary	(D)	03	F	Child	04Fe02Ac
MCGLINCHY, Patrick		30	M	Laborer	04Fe02Ac
SULLIVAN, Mary		18	F	Laborer	04Fe02Ac
LYNCH, James		29	M	Laborer	04Fe02Ac
KEENAN, Rosey		20	F	Laborer	04Fe02Ac
FITSIMONS, James		25	M	Laborer	04Fe02Ac
OWEN, T.B.		16	M	Laborer	04Fe02Ac
BRANAGAN, Margaret		24	F	Laborer	04Fe02Ac
BURBLAGE, Catherine		50	F	Laborer	04Fe02Ac
DILLON, John		21	M	Farmer	04Fe02Ac
RUNY, David		21	M	Laborer	04Fe02Ac
TAYLOR, Jas.		40	M	Builder	04Fe02Ac

LIVERPOOL 05 FEBRUARY 1848

From Liverpool

NAMES OF PASSENGERS		AGE	SEX	OCCUPATIONS	DATE PORT SHIP
CULLUMN, Cath.		22	F	Servant	05Fe02Bo
KEARNY, Bridget-Mrs.		22	F	Servant	05Fe02Bo
LANNON, Michl.		35	M	Laborer	05Fe02Bo
MCENTIRE, Terrance		25	M	Laborer	05Fe02Bo
BREIRNE, Michl.		26	M	Laborer	05Fe02Bo
CONROY, Thos.		32	M	Laborer	05Fe02Bo
BRENNAN, James		22	M	Laborer	05Fe02Bo
MURPHY, Margt.		30	F	Wi-Svnt	05Fe02Bo
Bridgt.	(D)	10	F	Servant	05Fe02Bo
John	(S)	08	M	Child	05Fe02Bo
Ann	(D)	06	F	Child	05Fe02Bo
LUCAS, Thos.		24	M	Laborer	05Fe02Bo
TYNON, Michl.		20	M	Laborer	05Fe02Bo
PEPPER, John		21	M	Laborer	05Fe02Bo
MCNAMARA, Michl.		20	M	Laborer	05Fe02Bo
DURAGAN, Bridgt.Mrs.		26	F	Servant	05Fe02Bo
CONROY, Luke		20	M	Laborer	05Fe02Bo
CLARKE, Bryan		22	M	Laborer	05Fe02Bo
BURKE, Alley		18	F	Servant	05Fe02Bo
DIGNAN, John		22	M	Servant	05Fe02Bo
FLYN, Patk.		22	M	Servant	05Fe02Bo
SHERRY, Ann-Mrs.		24	F	Servant	05Fe02Bo
Thos.	(S)	06	M	Child	05Fe02Bo
DOYLE, Cath.Mrs.		24	F	Servant	05Fe02Bo
WALSH, Pierce		31	M	Clerk	05Fe02Bo
MULCHAY, Patk.		20	M	Dyer	05Fe02Bo
CASSERLY, Patk.		35	M	Laborer	05Fe02Bo
Lucy	(W)	30	F	Servant	05Fe02Bo

NAMES OF PASSENGERS		AGE	SEX	OCCUPATIONS	DATE PORT SHIP
FITZPATRICK, Ellen		24	F	Servant	05Fe02Bo
Cath.		18	F	Servant	05Fe02Bo
MURRY, Bridget-Mrs.		22	F	Servant	05Fe02Bo
BEST, James		30	M	Laborer	05Fe02Bo
MARTIN, Thos.		23	M	Laborer	05Fe02Bo
CORRY, Patk.		39	M	Laborer	05Fe02Bo
Bridget		17	F	Servant	05Fe02Bo
LOCHLAN, Peter		19	M	Servant	05Fe02Bo
STOKER, Cathn.Mrs.		36	F	Servant	05Fe02Bo
Ann	(D)	14	F	Servant	05Fe02Bo
Mary	(D)	02	F	Child	05Fe02Bo
HANLEY, Patk.		25	M	Laborer	05Fe02Bo
UNDERWOOD, John		18	M	Gdnr	05Fe02Bo
BYRNES, Wm.		20	M	Laborer	05Fe02Bo
KENSHELA, Patk.		22	M	Lawyer	05Fe02Bo
Margt.	(W)	22	F	Wife	05Fe02Bo
Maria	(D)	01	F	Child	05Fe02Bo
Died-At-Sea					
SLOWEY, Cath.Mrs.		40	F	Wi-Fmr	05Fe02Bo
Margt.	(D)	16	F	Servant	05Fe02Bo
John	(S)	14	M	Servant	05Fe02Bo
Wm.	(S)	13	M	Servant	05Fe02Bo
Michl.	(S)	11	M	Servant	05Fe02Bo
Mary	(D)	08	F	Child	05Fe02Bo
Cath.	(D)	06	F	Child	05Fe02Bo
James	(S)	04	M	Child	05Fe02Bo
DALEY, Patk.		27	M	Laborer	05Fe02Bo
Betsey	(W)	24	F	Servant	05Fe02Bo
Rose	(D)	03	F	Child	05Fe02Bo
Michl.	(S)	01	M	Child	05Fe02Bo
GUY, Betsey		22	F	Servant	05Fe02Bo
WINNE, Bernard		25	M	Servant	05Fe02Bo
Mary		20	F	Servant	05Fe02Bo
CHAMBERS, Hugh		24	M	Farmer	05Fe02Bo
SMITH, Wm.		32	M	Weaver	05Fe02Bo
CANE, Martin		30	M	Laborer	05Fe02Bo
DOLAN, Terrance		25	M	Carpenter	05Fe02Bo
GOLLACHER, Edward		26	M	Laborer	05Fe02Bo
PATON, Wm.		35	M	Laborer	05Fe02Bo
Mary-Jane	(W)	30	F	Wife	05Fe02Bo
John	(S)	11	M	Servant	05Fe02Bo
Ann	(D)	08	F	Child	05Fe02Bo
KENEDY, Patk.		40	M	Laborer	05Fe02Bo
John		18	M	Laborer	05Fe02Bo
NELLY, Michl.		28	M	Laborer	05Fe02Bo
TORMEY, Lawrance		30	M	Laborer	05Fe02Bo
Bridget	(W)	26	F	Wife	05Fe02Bo
OHARA, Michl.		20	M	Laborer	05Fe02Bo
FYG, Domanac		28	M	Laborer	05Fe02Bo
MAGUIRE, Bridgt.		30	F	Servant	05Fe02Bo
WILSON, Alex.		27	M	Engineer	05Fe02Bo
Sarah	(W)	27	F	Wife	05Fe02Bo
Robt.	(S)	10	M	Engineer	05Fe02Bo
ATHY, John		44	M	Wi-Fmr	05Fe02Bo
Andrew	(S)	16	M	Farmer	05Fe02Bo
Maria	(D)	14	F	Farmer	05Fe02Bo
Philip	(S)	12	M	Farmer	05Fe02Bo
Fanny	(D)	10	F	Farmer	05Fe02Bo
Michl.	(S)	06	M	Child	05Fe02Bo
HUGHES, Danl.		25	M	Shopman	05Fe02Bo
MORRISON, David		40	M	Weaver	05Fe02Bo
Mary	(W)	35	F	Wife	05Fe02Bo
Eliza	(D)	16	F	Servant	05Fe02Bo
Mary	(D)	14	F	Servant	05Fe02Bo
John	(S)	12	M	Servant	05Fe02Bo
Eleaner	(D)	06	F	Child	05Fe02Bo
Margt.	(D)	04	F	Child	05Fe02Bo
Sarah-Jane	(D)	01	F	Child	05Fe02Bo
MCCALL, Andrew		37	M	Farmer	05Fe02Bo
Mary		17	F	Servant	05Fe02Bo
Barny		30	M	Servant	05Fe02Bo
Peter		20	M	Servant	05Fe02Bo
RILEY, Michl.		37	M	Laborer	05Fe02Bo
Mary		17	F	Servant	05Fe02Bo
HATTY, John		18	M	Servant	05Fe02Bo

NAMES OF PASSENGERS		AGE	SEX	OCCUPATIONS	DATE PORT SHIP
BELL, Ann-Mrs.		28	F	W-Fmr	05Fe02Bo
Elizabeth	(D)	06	F	Child	05Fe02Bo
SHERMAN, Sarah		18	F	Servant	05Fe02Bo
KERBY, John		55	M	Farmer	05Fe02Bo
Bridgt.		24	F	Dressmaker	05Fe02Bo
Johana		22	F	Servant	05Fe02Bo
Grace		20	F	Servant	05Fe02Bo
Cathn.		18	F	Servant	05Fe02Bo
Dennis		12	M	Servant	05Fe02Bo
MOREARTY, Ellen		26	F	Servant	05Fe02Bo
MCCAN, Wm.		20	M	Servant	05Fe02Bo
MCCLERNAN, Dennis		24	M	Servant	05Fe02Bo
WARD, Peter		22	M	Laborer	05Fe02Bo
WEARE, James		40	M	Laborer	05Fe02Bo
CAR, Sarah-Ann		18	F	Servant	05Fe02Bo
MCCUE, Bridgt.		20	F	Servant	05Fe02Bo
BYRNE, Bridgt.Mrs.		29	F	Servant	05Fe02Bo
Letetia	(D)	02	F	Child	05Fe02Bo
Bridgt.	(D)	02	F	Child	05Fe02Bo
Wm.	(S)	.04	M	Infant	05Fe02Bo
GRIFFIN, Cath.		24	F	Laborer	05Fe02Bo
Mary	(W)	24	F	Wife	05Fe02Bo
Ann	(D)	02	F	Child	05Fe02Bo
Died-At-Sea					
FAIR, John		35	M	Carpenter	05Fe02Bo
BYRNES, Patk.		35	M	Engd	05Fe02Bo
Mary		40	F	Servant	05Fe02Bo
Cath.		12	F	Servant	05Fe02Bo
Jane		05	F	Child	05Fe02Bo
Patk.		01	M	Child	05Fe02Bo
COSE, Nichls.		21	M	Laborer	05Fe02Bo
CAHILL, John		35	M	Laborer	05Fe02Bo
KEHOGH, John		28	M	Laborer	05Fe02Bo
MCAVOY, John		29	M	Cbtmkr	05Fe02Bo
MITCHEL, Timothy		26	M	Laborer	05Fe02Bo
WHALON, John		26	M	Laborer	05Fe02Bo

SARAH-SANDS 10 FEBRUARY 1848

From Liverpool

NAMES OF PASSENGERS		AGE	SEX	OCCUPATIONS	DATE PORT SHIP
MONTGOMERY, Archd.		24	M	Gentleman	10Fe02Kp
PHILPS, T.J.		29	M	Gentleman	10Fe02Kp
GAMBLE, Jas.B.		30	M	Farmer	10Fe02Kp
MCBRIDE, John		30	M	Merchant	10Fe02Kp
ROSS, Jane		27	F	Child	10Fe02Kp
FLANNAGAN, Mary		20	F	Child	10Fe02Kp
THOMPSON, John		32	M	Laborer	10Fe02Kp
QUINN, Henry		25	M	Laborer	10Fe02Kp
Mary-Ann		23	F	Unknown	10Fe02Kp
Jane		21	F	Unknown	10Fe02Kp
CULLOSTON, Wm.H.		22	M	Wlmcht	10Fe02Kp
MYERS, John		45	M	Farmer	10Fe02Kp
MOON, John		40	M	Wrhsmn	10Fe02Kp
GARRY, Edward		25	M	Painter	10Fe02Kp
SMITH, Wm.		32	M	Chemist	10Fe02Kp
WILSON, David		40	M	Hatter	10Fe02Kp
MCALIER, Wm.		28	M	Laborer	10Fe02Kp
RUSSELL, Wm.		35	M	Merchant	10Fe02Kp
MURPHY, Jas.		25	M	Laborer	10Fe02Kp
MALONY, Pat		38	M	Laborer	10Fe02Kp
SMITH, James		25	M	Engineer	10Fe02Kp
Jane	(W)	22	F	Wife	10Fe02Kp
Constantine	(S)	01	M	Child	10Fe02Kp
LARDNER, Martin		36	M	Laborer	10Fe02Kp
MCKONIER, John		30	M	Laborer	10Fe02Kp
MURTY, Bernard		30	M	Laborer	10Fe02Kp
Ann		25	F	Laborer	10Fe02Kp
JOHNSTON, John		25	M	Laborer	10Fe02Kp

NAMES OF PASSENGERS		AGE	SEX	OCCUPATIONS	DATE PORT SHIP
PRENTICE, John		18	M	Laborer	10Fe02Kp
BEAUTY, Mathew		19	M	Laborer	10Fe02Kp
MCKINNEY, Andrew		20	M	Laborer	10Fe02Kp
DAVIES, John		19	M	Laborer	10Fe02Kp
BEAUTY, James		26	M	Baker	10Fe02Kp
William		34	M	Laborer	10Fe02Kp
THOMPSON, John		17	M	Laborer	10Fe02Kp
WILSON, John		60	M	Farmer	10Fe02Kp
RYAN, John		29	M	Farmer	10Fe02Kp
OCONNOR, Owen		33	M	Farmer	10Fe02Kp
John		33	M	Farmer	10Fe02Kp
SMITH, Peter		22	M	Farmer	10Fe02Kp
U	(W)	20	F	Wife	10Fe02Kp

COLLOONEY 10 FEBRUARY 1848

From Glasgow

NAMES OF PASSENGERS		AGE	SEX	OCCUPATIONS	DATE PORT SHIP
FOX, Mary		26	F	Servant	10Fe04Ia

ISAAC-WRIGHT 11 FEBRUARY 1848

From Liverpool

NAMES OF PASSENGERS		AGE	SEX	OCCUPATIONS	DATE PORT SHIP
TEGIT, Martha		36	F	House Maid	11Fe02Qk
Sarah	(D)	14	F	House Maid	11Fe02Qk
Matilda	(D)	15	F	House Maid	11Fe02Qk
Mary	(D)	11	F	House Maid	11Fe02Qk
BOTHWELL, Daniel		20	M	Gdnr	11Fe02Qk
Thomas		18	M	Unknown	11Fe02Qk
BARNES, William		14	M	Unknown	11Fe02Qk
Ellen		18	F	Dressmaker	11Fe02Qk
MCNAMARA, James		17	M	Unknown	11Fe02Qk
Bridget		18	F	Unknown	11Fe02Qk
Catherine		03	F	Child	11Fe02Qk
QUINN, James		12	M	Unknown	11Fe02Qk
Mary		14	F	Unknown	11Fe02Qk
PRIOR, Mary		18	F	Unknown	11Fe02Qk
KINNEY, Patrick		22	M	Farmer	11Fe02Qk
KEENAN, John		20	M	Farmer	11Fe02Qk
DOLTON, John		19	M	Farmer	11Fe02Qk
DOLAN, Brian		20	M	Farmer	11Fe02Qk
MALLEN, Catharine		25	F	Housekeeper	11Fe02Qk
Eliza	(D)	05	F	Child	11Fe02Qk
Mary	(D)	02	F	Child	11Fe02Qk
RILEY, Ann		20	F	Unknown	11Fe02Qk
Michel	(S)	01	M	Child	11Fe02Qk
PRIOR, Tedy		18	M	Farmer	11Fe02Qk
Mary		08	F	Child	11Fe02Qk
HORTON, Pady		41	M	Laborer	11Fe02Qk
John		20	M	Laborer	11Fe02Qk
SWANEY, Peggy		40	F	Unknown	11Fe02Qk
HORTON, Patrick		12	M	Unknown	11Fe02Qk
Nancy		10	F	Unknown	11Fe02Qk
Peggy		06	F	Child	11Fe02Qk
WELDENHEAN, Michel		40	M	Baker	11Fe02Qk
LINCH, Peter		24	M	Laborer	11Fe02Qk
FINAGAN, Peter		24	M	Laborer	11Fe02Qk
Christopher		28	M	Laborer	11Fe02Qk
KERNAN, Rosy		28	F	Servant	11Fe02Qk
BOYLE, Margret		24	F	Servant	11Fe02Qk
MACENROY, Mary		16	F	Servant	11Fe02Qk
FOX, Michel		34	M	Laborer	11Fe02Qk
FOX, Betty	(W)	36	F	Wife	11Fe02Qk
Catharine	(D)	12	F	Unknown	11Fe02Qk
William	(S)	10	M	Unknown	11Fe02Qk
Patt.	(S)	07	M	Child	11Fe02Qk
MCKENSIE, William		20	M	Cooper	11Fe02Qk
MCKINSIE, Catharine		19	F	Unknown	11Fe02Qk
GOULSBERY, Eliza		20	F	Servant	11Fe02Qk
SULIVAN, John		40	M	Overseer	11Fe02Qk
Eliza	(W)	40	F	Wife	11Fe02Qk
Martain	(S)	18	M	Unknown	11Fe02Qk
John	(S)	15	M	Unknown	11Fe02Qk
Mary	(D)	09	F	Child	11Fe02Qk
GRAGI, Mathew		36	M	Farmer	11Fe02Qk
COLLINS, Michel		18	M	Farmer	11Fe02Qk
GASHEEN, Thomas		20	M	Laborer	11Fe02Qk
GILROY, Patt.		21	M	Laborer	11Fe02Qk
LINCH, Connor		32	M	Laborer	11Fe02Qk
Margret	(W)	36	F	Wife	11Fe02Qk
Catherine	(D)	.09	F	Infant	11Fe02Qk
ROAK, Bidy		22	F	Servant	11Fe02Qk
OAKLEY, Ann		20	F	Servant	11Fe02Qk
FEALEY, Ann		20	F	Servant	11Fe02Qk
CONROY, Margret		16	F	Servant	11Fe02Qk
SHAIRE, Bridget		38	F	Servant	11Fe02Qk
Ellen	(D)	13	F	Servant	11Fe02Qk
Maria	(D)	11	F	Servant	11Fe02Qk
Eliza	(D)	09	F	Child	11Fe02Qk
Bridget	(D)	04	F	Child	11Fe02Qk
Patt.	(S)	06	M	Child	11Fe02Qk
MCINIRNEY, Dan		17	M	Unknown	11Fe02Qk
Michl.		14	M	Unknown	11Fe02Qk
Biddy		12	F	Unknown	11Fe02Qk
CRANAN, Ann		40	F	Unknown	11Fe02Qk
Francis	(S)	14	M	Unknown	11Fe02Qk
Catharine	(D)	11	F	Unknown	11Fe02Qk
Mary	(D)	07	F	Child	11Fe02Qk
Thomas	(S)	05	M	Child	11Fe02Qk
Patt.	(S)	.11	M	Infant	11Fe02Qk
MCCAN, Charles		54	M	Weaver	11Fe02Qk
Elizabeth		20	F	Unknown	11Fe02Qk
Felix		21	M	Laborer	11Fe02Qk
Betty		23	F	Unknown	11Fe02Qk
Ellen		17	F	Unknown	11Fe02Qk
Catharine		19	F	Unknown	11Fe02Qk
Charles		14	M	Unknown	11Fe02Qk
MCKAMON, Joseph		09	M	Child	11Fe02Qk
HANALY, Patt.		27	M	Laborer	11Fe02Qk
MAID, James		23	M	Rigger	11Fe02Qk
Margret		22	F	Unknown	11Fe02Qk
MCCANN, Margret		01	F	Child	11Fe02Qk
DONEBRANT, Anthony		52	M	Butcher	11Fe02Qk
DUGAN, Thomas		25	M	Laborer	11Fe02Qk
Margret		27	F	Unknown	11Fe02Qk
NOLAN, John		24	M	Grocer	11Fe02Qk
COFFEE, John		32	M	Laborer	11Fe02Qk
Ann	(W)	30	F	Wife	11Fe02Qk
Juliett	(D)	.10	F	Infant	11Fe02Qk
HINES, Michel		25	M	Laborer	11Fe02Qk
CASSIDY, Michel		32	M	Laborer	11Fe02Qk
MCCANNA, Thomas		26	M	Laborer	11Fe02Qk
John		24	M	Laborer	11Fe02Qk
Mary		20	F	Unknown	11Fe02Qk
LINCH, James		22	M	Laborer	11Fe02Qk
DONOVAN, Margret		20	F	Servant	11Fe02Qk
SULIVAN, Ellen		15	F	Servant	11Fe02Qk
MULCHIN, Johannah		23	F	Servant	11Fe02Qk
FLARTY, Edward		30	M	Brush Maker	11Fe02Qk
CONIGAN, Andrew		25	M	Baker	11Fe02Qk
BOILE, Patt.		17	M	Baker	11Fe02Qk
STROKES, Matt		38	M	Laborer	11Fe02Qk
LUCY, Judy		24	F	Servant	11Fe02Qk
TRIMBLE, Judy		27	F	Servant	11Fe02Qk
Ann		26	F	Servant	11Fe02Qk
BRADY, Patt.		50	M	Laborer	11Fe02Qk
Ellen	(W)	49	F	Wife	11Fe02Qk

NAMES OF PASSENGERS		AGE	SEX	OCCUPATIONS	DATE PORT SHIP
BRADY, John	(S)	26	M	Laborer	11Fe02Qk
MASTERSON, Margret		18	F	Servant	11Fe02Qk
CATE, Ellen		17	F	Servant	11Fe02Qk
MURPHY, Patt.		30	M	Laborer	11Fe02Qk
Mary	(W)	30	F	Wife	11Fe02Qk
Catherine	(D)	07	F	Child	11Fe02Qk
Patt.	(S)	05	M	Child	11Fe02Qk
John	(S)	03	M	Child	11Fe02Qk
Ann	(D)	.03	F	Infant	11Fe02Qk
AGAN, Michel		22	M	Shoemaker	11Fe02Qk
Owen		25	M	Laborer	11Fe02Qk
MICHEL, John		25	M	Laborer	11Fe02Qk
GLINN, Patt.		20	M	Laborer	11Fe02Qk
COLIGAN, Bridget		20	F	Unknown	11Fe02Qk
Barny	(H)	23	M	Laborer	11Fe02Qk
Ann	(D)	.06	F	Infant	11Fe02Qk
KEEAS, Thomas		40	M	Laborer	11Fe02Qk
Christopher		25	M	Laborer	11Fe02Qk
Thomas		20	M	Laborer	11Fe02Qk
William		22	M	Laborer	11Fe02Qk
Charlotte		20	F	Unknown	11Fe02Qk
Jane		22	F	Unknown	11Fe02Qk
FILES, Biddy		22	F	Servant	11Fe02Qk
CUTEY, Biddy		22	F	Servant	11Fe02Qk
FAJOLT, Sarah		22	F	Servant	11Fe02Qk
MULVAYS, Thomas		25	M	Laborer	11Fe02Qk
Thomas		18	M	Laborer	11Fe02Qk
RILEY, John		40	M	Laborer	11Fe02Qk
DIXON, Sparks		25	M	Laborer	11Fe02Qk
FURY, Mary		24	F	Servant	11Fe02Qk
MCCARNNOS, Ellen		22	F	Servant	11Fe02Qk
HOLEHAM, Mary		20	F	Servant	11Fe02Qk
FURY, Catharine		04	F	Child	11Fe02Qk
BRADY, Terance		45	M	Laborer	11Fe02Qk
Michel		50	M	Laborer	11Fe02Qk
BERRENS, John		35	M	Laborer	11Fe02Qk
Bridget	(D)	08	F	Child	11Fe02Qk
MCGUIRE, Ann		20	F	Servant	11Fe02Qk
Peter		18	M	Laborer	11Fe02Qk
MOORE, Patt.		25	M	Laborer	11Fe02Qk
MAHAN, Daniel		21	M	Laborer	11Fe02Qk
KELLY, Michael		18	M	Laborer	11Fe02Qk
MARTIN, Pierceton		25	M	Laborer	11Fe02Qk
DOLAN, Patt.		30	M	Laborer	11Fe02Qk
MACKNAMARAH, Dan		26	M	Laborer	11Fe02Qk
MAYAW, Bethy		21	F	Dressmaker	11Fe02Qk
TONAR, Mary		23	F	Dressmaker	11Fe02Qk
SMITH, John		16	M	Tailor	11Fe02Qk
DUNLOPE, John		26	M	Farmer	11Fe02Qk
Jinny		20	F	Unknown	11Fe02Qk
Grace		18	F	Unknown	11Fe02Qk
John		16	M	Farmer	11Fe02Qk
WILEY, Nancy		20	F	Unknown	11Fe02Qk
CAHILL, Rachal		39	F	Unknown	11Fe02Qk
Samuel	(S)	08	M	Child	11Fe02Qk
ISAACS, Sarah		16	F	Unknown	11Fe02Qk
Pheby		20	F	Unknown	11Fe02Qk
Harriet		18	F	Unknown	11Fe02Qk
CARBARY, Lucinda		20	F	Unknown	11Fe02Qk
WINSLOW, Jane		24	F	Unknown	11Fe02Qk
Elizia		06	F	Child	11Fe02Qk
WHITEHEAD, Julia		20	F	Unknown	11Fe02Qk
NATHAN, George		20	M	Unknown	11Fe02Qk
ROSS, Henry		21	M	Unknown	11Fe02Qk
HOGAN, Martin		18	M	Shoemaker	11Fe02Qk
MALOCHENS, Ann		30	F	Servant	11Fe02Qk
MACKNAMARAH, Mick		24	M	Laborer	11Fe02Qk
JONES, Thomas		26	M	Laborer	11Fe02Qk
RATFORD, Margret		23	F	Servant	11Fe02Qk
JONES, Johannah		01	F	Child	11Fe02Qk
Biddy		04	F	Child	11Fe02Qk
James		02	M	Child	11Fe02Qk
COLLINS, Catharine		16	F	Unknown	11Fe02Qk
Margret		20	F	Servant	11Fe02Qk
DIMPSY, Catharine		21	F	Servant	11Fe02Qk
DIMPSY, Margret		18	F	Servant	11Fe02Qk
Michel		20	M	Farmer	11Fe02Qk
William		19	M	Farmer	11Fe02Qk
FARREL, Michel		30	M	Shoemaker	11Fe02Qk
SMITH, Thomas		32	M	Surveyor	11Fe02Qk
CAHAN, Hue		22	M	Post Boy	11Fe02Qk
MINOKE, Thomas		22	M	Shoemaker	11Fe02Qk
HOGAN, Peter		40	M	Laborer	11Fe02Qk
NOLAN, Edward		35	M	Laborer	11Fe02Qk
THOMAS, Josua		27	M	Talch	11Fe02Qk
CLANCY, Thomas		29	M	Mason	11Fe02Qk

MARGARET-EVANS 14 FEBRUARY 1848

From London

NAMES OF PASSENGERS		AGE	SEX	OCCUPATIONS	DATE PORT SHIP
WHITE, Thomas		34	M	Furrier	14Fe21Ip
PURCELL, John		27	M	Laborer	14Fe21Ip
BAITS, Thomas		48	M	Bricklayer	14Fe21Ip
CONNER, Charles		21	M	Laborer	14Fe21Ip
Owen		39	M	Laborer	14Fe21Ip
FOSTER, Wm.		26	M	Laborer	14Fe21Ip
WHITTAKER, Wm.		35	M	Farmer	14Fe21Ip
Maria		34	F	Unknown	14Fe21Ip
MCMAHON, Henry		16	M	Unknown	14Fe21Ip

HOTTINGUER 15 FEBRUARY 1848

From Liverpool

NAMES OF PASSENGERS		AGE	SEX	OCCUPATIONS	DATE PORT SHIP
OHARA, Catharine		25	F	Unknown	15Fe02Bc
SMYTH, Catharine		20	F	Unknown	15Fe02Bc
Mary		26	F	Unknown	15Fe02Bc
GERDEN, Anthony		30	M	Laborer	15Fe02Bc
SEXTIN, Pat.		27	M	Laborer	15Fe02Bc
Mary		24	F	Laborer	15Fe02Bc
COTTER, John		33	M	Weaver	15Fe02Bc
CAMPBELL, James		20	M	Laborer	15Fe02Bc
PATTERSON, William		19	M	Laborer	15Fe02Bc
DUNLAP, John		70	M	Distiller	15Fe02Bc
Mary-Ann	(W)	65	F	Wife	15Fe02Bc
Jane	(D)	30	F	Unknown	15Fe02Bc
Ellen	(D)	28	F	Unknown	15Fe02Bc
Isabella	(D)	26	F	Unknown	15Fe02Bc
Sarah	(D)	22	F	Unknown	15Fe02Bc
MEEHAN, James		25	M	Shoemaker	15Fe02Bc
KILBRIDE, Mary		20	F	Unknown	15Fe02Bc
RILEY, Ann		20	F	Unknown	15Fe02Bc
KERR, Anthony		30	M	Unknown	15Fe02Bc
MCGUIRE, Pat		20	M	Car Driver	15Fe02Bc
Bridget		20	F	Unknown	15Fe02Bc
John	(S)	.00	M	Infant	15Fe02Bc
CREIGHTON, William		25	M	Clerk	15Fe02Bc
CARLAN, Hugh		20	M	Weaver	15Fe02Bc
CULIAN, Pat.		22	M	Laborer	15Fe02Bc
KIVIL, John		20	M	Laborer	15Fe02Bc
FRAINER, Peter		30	M	Laborer	15Fe02Bc
Margret	(D)	09	F	Child	15Fe02Bc
HAY, James Died-At-Sea		20	M	Laborer	15Fe02Bc
WARD, Pat		26	M	Laborer	15Fe02Bc
NEAL, William		20	M	Laborer	15Fe02Bc
Mary		18	F	Laborer	15Fe02Bc

NAMES OF PASSENGERS		AGE	SEX	OCCUPATIONS	DATE PORT SHIP
KEATING, Jane		20	F	Laborer	15Fe02Bc
RILEY, Thomas		30	M	Laborer	15Fe02Bc
CLUSKEY, Elizabeth-M.		30	F	Unknown	15Fe02Bc
Charles	(S)	12	M	Unknown	15Fe02Bc
Francis	(S)	07	M	Child	15Fe02Bc
Mary	(D)	03	F	Child	15Fe02Bc
David	(S)	01	M	Child	15Fe02Bc
CONVEY, Hugh		25	M	Laborer	15Fe02Bc
Rose		25	F	Unknown	15Fe02Bc
HAWTHORN, Henry		15	M	Unknown	15Fe02Bc
DEAN, William		30	M	Glass Maker	15Fe02Bc
MOORE, William		30	M	Machinist	15Fe02Bc
MCALISTER, Sarah		23	F	Unknown	15Fe02Bc
Biddy		18	F	Unknown	15Fe02Bc
Danial		12	M	Unknown	15Fe02Bc
STANNAGE, Eliza		50	F	Unknown	15Fe02Bc
MILLER, John		30	M	Farmer	15Fe02Bc
Jane		25	F	Unknown	15Fe02Bc
Eliza		30	F	Unknown	15Fe02Bc
CHARLES, Margret		16	F	Unknown	15Fe02Bc
MILLER, Stanage		04	M	Child	15Fe02Bc
John		.06	M	Infant	15Fe02Bc
CAINE, Pat		40	M	Unknown	15Fe02Bc
CORR, Mary		19	F	Unknown	15Fe02Bc
CLELAND, Hans		37	M	Blacksmith	15Fe02Bc
Sarah	(W)	27	F	Wife	15Fe02Bc
Robert	(S)	08	M	Child	15Fe02Bc
Garvin	(S)	04	M	Child	15Fe02Bc
John	(S)	.07	M	Infant	15Fe02Bc
CONNER, John		55	M	Laborer	15Fe02Bc
BARBOUR, James		27	M	Unknown	15Fe02Bc
Joseph		25	M	Laborer	15Fe02Bc
MCGRADE, Francis		30	M	Laborer	15Fe02Bc
COYLE, Pat		23	M	Laborer	15Fe02Bc
HARRISON, James		44	M	Laborer	15Fe02Bc
Jane-A.		44	F	Unknown	15Fe02Bc
WIGGINS, Eliza		17	F	Unknown	15Fe02Bc
John-A.		32	M	Laborer	15Fe02Bc
FLINN, Bartite		30	M	Shepherd	15Fe02Bc
BRADY, John		25	M	Laborer	15Fe02Bc
MATHEWS, John		26	M	Laborer	15Fe02Bc
MCLAUGHLIN, Mary		35	F	Unknown	15Fe02Bc
Mary-Jr.	(D)	14	F	Unknown	15Fe02Bc
John	(S)	11	M	Unknown	15Fe02Bc
Marjery	(D)	10	F	Unknown	15Fe02Bc
Samuel-M.	(S)	08	M	Child	15Fe02Bc
Catharine	(D)	06	F	Child	15Fe02Bc
James	(S)	04	M	Child	15Fe02Bc
Marshall	(S)	02	M	Child	15Fe02Bc
SHEERAN, Thomas		55	M	Laborer	15Fe02Bc
Ann	(W)	48	F	Wife	15Fe02Bc
Bridget	(D)	17	F	Unknown	15Fe02Bc
Ann-Jr.	(D)	15	F	Unknown	15Fe02Bc
John	(S)	12	M	Unknown	15Fe02Bc
Catherine	(D)	10	F	Unknown	15Fe02Bc
Winifred	(D)	08	F	Child	15Fe02Bc
GAWLEY, Jane		30	F	Unknown	15Fe02Bc
John	(S)	08	M	Child	15Fe02Bc
Samuel	(S)	04	M	Child	15Fe02Bc
ODONNELL, Thomas		20	M	Laborer	15Fe02Bc
MCMAHAN, Wm.		24	M	Laborer	15Fe02Bc
James		23	M	Laborer	15Fe02Bc
HUGHES, Margret		27	F	Unknown	15Fe02Bc
THOMPSON, Ann		30	F	Unknown	15Fe02Bc
James	(S)	09	M	Child	15Fe02Bc
Betty	(D)	04	F	Child	15Fe02Bc
William	(S)	.06	M	Infant	15Fe02Bc
Died-At-Sea					
KEENAN, Terance		50	M	Mason	15Fe02Bc
Mary		40	F	Unknown	15Fe02Bc
Catharine		30	F	Unknown	15Fe02Bc
Sally		15	F	Unknown	15Fe02Bc
Hugh		10	M	Unknown	15Fe02Bc
Margret		06	F	Child	15Fe02Bc

HIBERNIA 17 FEBRUARY 1848

From Liverpool

NAMES OF PASSENGERS		AGE	SEX	OCCUPATIONS	DATE PORT SHIP
WALKER, S.A.		29	M	Merchant	17Fe02Pb

MADAWASKA 17 FEBRUARY 1848

From Glasgow

NAMES OF PASSENGERS		AGE	SEX	OCCUPATIONS	DATE PORT SHIP
MCGONEGAL, James		28	M	Miner	17Fe04Ez
U	(W)	24	F	Wife	17Fe04Ez
Mary-Ann	(D)	02	F	Child	17Fe04Ez
Hannah	(D)	.05	F	Infant	17Fe04Ez
MCGUIRE, Unity		38	F	Wi	17Fe04Ez
DUFF, Barnard		18	M	Miner	17Fe04Ez
MCGARIGAL, Martin		22	M	Laborer	17Fe04Ez
MUIRHEAD, Andrew		27	M	Engineer	17Fe04Ez
KINNAY, William		30	M	Engineer	17Fe04Ez
WARD, William		23	M	Laborer	17Fe04Ez
ALLAN, James		32	M	Laborer	17Fe04Ez
SMART, John		21	M	Joiner	17Fe04Ez
U	(W)	20	F	Wife	17Fe04Ez
WHITE, William		31	M	Farmer	17Fe04Ez
CLELAND, James		24	M	Laborer	17Fe04Ez
GALLOWAY, William		26	M	Stctr	17Fe04Ez
PETTIGREW, Thos.		21	M	Engd	17Fe04Ez
GILLIES, Francis		28	M	Miner	17Fe04Ez
LYNCH, John		19	M	Irdr	17Fe04Ez
DUGGAN, Thomas		35	M	Surgeon	17Fe04Ez

ROSCIUS 21 FEBRUARY 1848

From Liverpool

NAMES OF PASSENGERS		AGE	SEX	OCCUPATIONS	DATE PORT SHIP
CRAWLY, Mathew		27	M	Laborer	21Fe02Bf
LAWLOR, Edward		30	M	Laborer	21Fe02Bf
SALMON, Wm.		24	M	Laborer	21Fe02Bf
DOYLE, John		30	M	Tailor	21Fe02Bf
SALMON, Pat.		35	M	Laborer	21Fe02Bf
NOLAN, James		24	M	Laborer	21Fe02Bf
GILBRAITH, Mary		20	F	Servant	21Fe02Bf
FITZPATRICK, Joseph		21	M	Laborer	21Fe02Bf
Mary		20	F	Dressmaker	21Fe02Bf
Ellen		24	F	Servant	21Fe02Bf
MCGIVERN, Philip		27	M	Laborer	21Fe02Bf
Margarett		22	F	Servant	21Fe02Bf
LAURENCE, Robt.		27	M	Packer	21Fe02Bf
LOUGHRY, Pat		16	M	Laborer	21Fe02Bf
GRALY, John		19	M	Laborer	21Fe02Bf
QUINN, Wm.		26	M	Laborer	21Fe02Bf
LOUGHRY, Thos.		26	M	Laborer	21Fe02Bf
Pat		16	M	Laborer	21Fe02Bf
Biddy		18	F	Servant	21Fe02Bf
Rose		11	F	Servant	21Fe02Bf
LENANE, Mary		30	F	Servant	21Fe02Bf
DUNIVAN, Michl.		12	M	Laborer	21Fe02Bf

NAMES OF PASSENGERS	AGE	SEX	OCCUPATIONS	DATE PORT SHIP
DUNIVAN, Cath.	06	F	Child	21Fe02Bf
COWNE, Mary	20	F	Servant	21Fe02Bf
FERLEY, Maria	19	F	Frtdr	21Fe02Bf
MCGUIN, Margarett	21	F	Weaver	21Fe02Bf
HAMILTON, John-Thos.	16	M	Laborer	21Fe02Bf
MCDONALD, Michl.	27	M	Servant	21Fe02Bf
LOONAN, Wm.	23	M	Shoemaker	21Fe02Bf
GOONOTT, John	27	M	Laborer	21Fe02Bf
HANALIN, Lawrence	30	M	Laborer	21Fe02Bf
Ellen	26	F	None	21Fe02Bf
Ann	09	F	Child	21Fe02Bf
John	05	M	Child	21Fe02Bf
Mary	03	F	Child	21Fe02Bf
Pat	01	M	Child	21Fe02Bf
Mary	26	F	None	21Fe02Bf
MCGOVERN, Margarett	10	F	Servant	21Fe02Bf
WHALIN, Kitty	23	F	Dressmaker	21Fe02Bf
WHELEHAN, Luke	20	M	Laborer	21Fe02Bf
Mary	24	F	Servant	21Fe02Bf
James	03	M	Child	21Fe02Bf
Ann	02	F	Child	21Fe02Bf
MURRAY, Francis	13	M	Laborer	21Fe02Bf
Winfred	15	M	Laborer	21Fe02Bf
KENNEDY, John	18	M	Laborer	21Fe02Bf
JENNINGS, James	17	M	Laborer	21Fe02Bf
BROWN, Maria	16	F	Servant	21Fe02Bf
GARVEY, Ann	07	F	Child	21Fe02Bf
Mary	10	F	Servant	21Fe02Bf
Richd.	25	M	Laborer	21Fe02Bf
IGO, John	20	M	Laborer	21Fe02Bf
Pat	15	M	Laborer	21Fe02Bf
CONNOGHTON, Cath.	25	F	Servant	21Fe02Bf
Mary	10	F	Servant	21Fe02Bf
VERDON, Wm.	30	M	Merchant	21Fe02Bf
David	20	M	Merchant	21Fe02Bf
HAY, Susanaha	18	F	Unknown	21Fe02Bf
Wm.	01	M	Child	21Fe02Bf
CHALMERS, Wm.John	40	M	Publican	21Fe02Bf
Harriet	20	M	Publican	21Fe02Bf
DIVIN, John	30	M	Laborer	21Fe02Bf
DALY, Thos.	40	M	Laborer	21Fe02Bf
MAHON, Frank	28	M	Laborer	21Fe02Bf
Ann	26	F	Servant	21Fe02Bf
James	02	M	Child	21Fe02Bf
BRAHANNY, Michl.	35	M	Laborer	21Fe02Bf
HOWE, Bryan	22	M	Laborer	21Fe02Bf
CONNELL, Cecelia	20	F	Servant	21Fe02Bf
ROUIN, Margarett	22	F	Servant	21Fe02Bf
MCGUIRK, Susan	10	F	Servant	21Fe02Bf
MORGAN, Mathew	70	M	Joiner	21Fe02Bf
PARKER, Wm.	36	M	Laborer	21Fe02Bf
QUINN, Mary	13	F	Servant	21Fe02Bf
Norry	12	F	Servant	21Fe02Bf
Biddy	14	F	Servant	21Fe02Bf
DUFFY, Pat.	22	M	Laborer	21Fe02Bf
SWEANEY, Wm.	23	M	Laborer	21Fe02Bf
MCLAUGHLIN, Wm.	22	M	Laborer	21Fe02Bf
MATHEWS, Owen	22	M	Laborer	21Fe02Bf
HEFFERNON, Edwd.	19	M	Laborer	21Fe02Bf
MALONE, Ann	19	F	Servant	21Fe02Bf
SMITH, Mary	22	F	Servant	21Fe02Bf
Catherine	03	F	Child	21Fe02Bf
Thos.	02	M	Child	21Fe02Bf
Peter	32	M	Farmer	21Fe02Bf
Mary	24	F	Servant	21Fe02Bf
Ann	03	F	Child	21Fe02Bf
Juda	02	F	Child	21Fe02Bf
MULLADY, Bryan	26	M	Laborer	21Fe02Bf
KIDNEY, Thos.	36	M	Farmer	21Fe02Bf
MCGILL, Farrel	36	M	Farmer	21Fe02Bf
HARVEY, Rose	22	F	Servant	21Fe02Bf
WALL, Julia	23	F	Servant	21Fe02Bf
MURRAY, Margarett	16	F	Servant	21Fe02Bf
FLINN, Margarett	25	F	Servant	21Fe02Bf
Luke	05	M	Child	21Fe02Bf
FLINN, John	07	M	Child	21Fe02Bf
GORAHAN, Biddy	17	F	Servant	21Fe02Bf
FARLEY, Phillip	40	M	Laborer	21Fe02Bf
Mary	25	F	Servant	21Fe02Bf
Mathew	06	M	Child	21Fe02Bf
Patrick	04	M	Child	21Fe02Bf
Lawrence	01	M	Child	21Fe02Bf
MURPHY, Thos.	20	M	Laborer	21Fe02Bf
Michl.	26	M	Laborer	21Fe02Bf
MCGRAH, Morris	20	M	Laborer	21Fe02Bf
BOYLE, Michl.	27	M	Laborer	21Fe02Bf
CONNIRTON, Margarett	60	F	Servant	21Fe02Bf
DOONEN, Mary	09	F	Child	21Fe02Bf
Margarett	06	F	Child	21Fe02Bf
Ellen	03	F	Child	21Fe02Bf
SHANLY, Cathrine	13	F	Unknown	21Fe02Bf
MULLIN, James	30	M	Laborer	21Fe02Bf
Catharine	20	F	Servant	21Fe02Bf
Alice	12	F	Servant	21Fe02Bf
KELLY, Edwd.	31	M	Laborer	21Fe02Bf
SIMMONS, John	33	M	Bricklayer	21Fe02Bf
GIBBINS, Thos.	25	M	Servant	21Fe02Bf
CONNORY, Thos.	25	M	Carpenter	21Fe02Bf
DILLON, John	23	M	Carpenter	21Fe02Bf
GREEN, John	30	M	Carpenter	21Fe02Bf
MCGEE, James	25	M	Servant	21Fe02Bf
TRACY, John	25	M	Hairdresser	21Fe02Bf
ROBINSON, Thomas	36	M	Baker	21Fe02Bf
MORGAN, Thomas	25	M	Laborer	21Fe02Bf
CAIRNS, Peter	23	M	Laborer	21Fe02Bf
John	10	M	Laborer	21Fe02Bf
RUDDERN, Chas.	64	M	Laborer	21Fe02Bf
Thos.	12	M	Laborer	21Fe02Bf
Winfred	10	M	Laborer	21Fe02Bf
FENLEND, Thos.	60	M	Laborer	21Fe02Bf
MCGEAH, Michael	22	M	Brewer	21Fe02Bf
Dennis	17	M	Laborer	21Fe02Bf
CONNELL, Patrick	23	M	Laborer	21Fe02Bf
MCCARROL, Chas.	35	M	Smith	21Fe02Bf
Mary	35	F	Servant	21Fe02Bf
Ann	17	F	None	21Fe02Bf
ROACHE, David	26	M	Clerk	21Fe02Bf
CLARK, Owen	45	M	Laborer	21Fe02Bf
Mary (D)	10	F	None	21Fe02Bf
Ann (D)	10	F	None	21Fe02Bf
DOROTHY, James	30	M	Laborer	21Fe02Bf
GALLON, Patrick	18	M	Laborer	21Fe02Bf
MCGINGIN, Peter	26	M	Saddler	21Fe02Bf
HALFPENNY, Brine	18	M	Smith	21Fe02Bf
SHARP, Grace-Carr	35	F	Servant	21Fe02Bf
Mary	11	F	Servant	21Fe02Bf
Chas.	08	M	Child	21Fe02Bf
James	06	M	Child	21Fe02Bf
Betty	.11	F	Infant	21Fe02Bf
ONEILL, John	40	M	Laborer	21Fe02Bf
Arthur	18	M	Laborer	21Fe02Bf
Sarah	20	F	Laborer	21Fe02Bf
Rose	16	F	Laborer	21Fe02Bf
SEDLLIN, Betty	17	F	Servant	21Fe02Bf
Mary-Ann	15	F	Servant	21Fe02Bf
ONEIL, John	14	M	Laborer	21Fe02Bf
Stafford	12	M	Laborer	21Fe02Bf
KINSTEN, Dennis	30	M	Laborer	21Fe02Bf
KILFINE, Danl.	30	M	Laborer	21Fe02Bf
JAFFE, Pat.	28	M	Laborer	21Fe02Bf
FEVRON, John	36	M	Laborer	21Fe02Bf
LAWLOR, Cathr.	22	F	Servant	21Fe02Bf
MULLIN, Biddy	20	F	Dressmaker	21Fe02Bf
SULLIVAN, Margarett	22	F	Servant	21Fe02Bf
REALEY, Daniel	18	M	Blacksmith	21Fe02Bf
Catharine	16	F	Servant	21Fe02Bf
Rose-Ann	14	F	Servant	21Fe02Bf
CRAREY, Sally-Sr.	60	F	None	21Fe02Bf
Sally-Jr. (D)	12	F	None	21Fe02Bf
BELL, Anna	10	F	Servant	21Fe02Bf

NAMES OF PASSENGERS		AGE	SEX	OCCUPATIONS	DATE PORT SHIP
CAMPBELL, John		23	M	Laborer	21Fe02Bf
ODONNELL, Dennis		18	M	Laborer	21Fe02Bf
SHARP, James		35	M	Laborer	21Fe02Bf
STANTON, Thos.		16	M	Laborer	21Fe02Bf
SACKROFF, Julia		20	F	Servant	21Fe02Bf
DANIEL, Ann		27	F	Servant	21Fe02Bf
HESLIN, Rose		25	F	Servant	21Fe02Bf
CARROLL, Ann		23	F	Servant	21Fe02Bf

GEO.A.HOPLEY 21 FEBRUARY 1848

From Liverpool

NAMES OF PASSENGERS		AGE	SEX	OCCUPATIONS	DATE PORT SHIP
HUTCHISON, John		28	M	Farmer	21Fe02Da
HARRIS, Geo.		24	M	Farmer	21Fe02Da
HARRISON, Thos.G.		22	M	Plumber	21Fe02Da
HOGAN, Patrick		25	M	Laborer	21Fe02Da
WILLIAMSON, Edw.		26	M	Mariner	21Fe02Da
CROFT, John		40	M	Farmer	21Fe02Da
Eliz.		36	F	None	21Fe02Da
Ann		17	F	None	21Fe02Da
Charlotte		11	F	None	21Fe02Da
Eliza		09	F	Child	21Fe02Da
William		07	M	Child	21Fe02Da
Elizbth.		15	F	Child	21Fe02Da
COATES, James		29	M	Farmer	21Fe02Da
KILLPATRICK, Sam.		30	M	Weaver	21Fe02Da
GILLIGAN, John		25	M	Farmer	21Fe02Da
MAGUINESS, Bridget		46	F	None	21Fe02Da
Bridget		13	F	None	21Fe02Da
Ellen		11	F	None	21Fe02Da
CHAMBERS, Mary		50	F	None	21Fe02Da
Kath.		24	F	None	21Fe02Da
EVANS, Fraas.		31	M	Farmer	21Fe02Da
THOMAS, Philipp		40	M	Miner	21Fe02Da
LOYD, James		40	M	Miner	21Fe02Da
WATERS, Moses		40	M	Forgeman	21Fe02Da
EVANS, William		25	M	Forgeman	21Fe02Da
LAVIS, John		35	M	Forgeman	21Fe02Da
WATERS, Thos.		30	M	Forgeman	21Fe02Da
WILLIAMS, John		29	M	Forgeman	21Fe02Da
REES, D.		31	M	Forgeman	21Fe02Da
HINES, Mary		25	F	None	21Fe02Da
TAMBLE, James		29	M	Laborer	21Fe02Da
SWEENEY, Eliz.		40	F	None	21Fe02Da
Patt.		16	M	None	21Fe02Da
Luke		13	M	None	21Fe02Da
Thomas		10	M	None	21Fe02Da
Margrt.		08	F	Child	21Fe02Da
KENNEDY, Andrew		21	M	Attorney	21Fe02Da
WHITE, Thom.		25	M	Machinist	21Fe02Da
MCDONALD, Edw.		28	M	Shoemaker	21Fe02Da
MCNEA, U-Mrs.		40	F	None	21Fe02Da
Thos.		18	M	None	21Fe02Da
Eliz.		16	F	None	21Fe02Da
John		12	M	None	21Fe02Da
CROZIER, Mary		20	F	None	21Fe02Da
THOMAS, Martin		24	M	Miner	21Fe02Da
RICHARDS, John		25	M	Miner	21Fe02Da
JONES, Robt.		26	M	Miner	21Fe02Da
THOMAS, Fraas.		33	M	Tailor	21Fe02Da
MCMAHON, Owen		36	M	Laborer	21Fe02Da
Jane		27	F	None	21Fe02Da
Mary		.00	F	Infant	21Fe02Da
LALLY, John		22	M	Laborer	21Fe02Da
DEALLY, Mich.		20	M	Laborer	21Fe02Da
GILL, Owen		40	M	Laborer	21Fe02Da
Thomas		20	M	Laborer	21Fe02Da
Ellen		18	F	None	21Fe02Da
MCBATH, William		26	M	Cooper	21Fe02Da
SMITH, John		24	M	Farmer	21Fe02Da
Ann		20	F	None	21Fe02Da
TAMNEY, John		46	M	Farmer	21Fe02Da
MORAN, Thomas		32	M	Tailor	21Fe02Da
U	(W)	34	F	Wife	21Fe02Da
Mary-Ann	(D)	12	F	None	21Fe02Da
Cathar.	(D)	10	F	None	21Fe02Da
Thom.		21	M	Laborer	21Fe02Da
DURK, James		28	M	Laborer	21Fe02Da
Ann		26	F	None	21Fe02Da
U		.00	F	Infant	21Fe02Da
John		06	M	Child	21Fe02Da
Mary		04	F	Child	21Fe02Da
HOPKINSON, Jas.		24	M	Mariner	21Fe02Da
WEAVER, Chas.		45	M	Mariner	21Fe02Da
REID, Wm.		50	M	Tbcmcht	21Fe02Da
Catharine		60	F	None	21Fe02Da
Harriet		07	F	Child	21Fe02Da
MCCABE, Michel.		27	M	Farmer	21Fe02Da
TRAINER, Rose		20	F	None	21Fe02Da
DOWDE, Andrew		30	M	Laborer	21Fe02Da
FALLAN, John		24	M	Carpenter	21Fe02Da
SAMSON, Thos.		24	M	Stkw	21Fe02Da
ADAMS, John		43	M	Miner	21Fe02Da
Eliza		16	F	None	21Fe02Da
Michael		13	M	None	21Fe02Da
Benjamin		11	M	None	21Fe02Da
KELLY, John		30	M	Machinist	21Fe02Da

HYNDERFORD 23 FEBRUARY 1848

From Liverpool

NAMES OF PASSENGERS		AGE	SEX	OCCUPATIONS	DATE PORT SHIP
SWEENY, Daniel		31	M	Laborer	23Fe02Kl
FILLIGAN, Philip		25	M	Laborer	23Fe02Kl
Bridget	(W)	20	F	Wife	23Fe02Kl
Thos.	(S)	.09	M	Infant	23Fe02Kl

EFFINGHAM 25 FEBRUARY 1848

From Cork

NAMES OF PASSENGERS		AGE	SEX	OCCUPATIONS	DATE PORT SHIP
QUIN, Timothy		38	M	Laborer	25Fe14Fa
Ellen		30	F	Laborer	25Fe14Fa
Johanna		13	F	Laborer	25Fe14Fa
Jeremiah		11	M	Laborer	25Fe14Fa
John		.09	M	Infant	25Fe14Fa
DONOVAN, Denis		23	M	Laborer	25Fe14Fa
TELAN, John		44	M	Laborer	25Fe14Fa
Judy		40	F	Laborer	25Fe14Fa
MATHER, John		43	M	Laborer	25Fe14Fa
Mary		40	F	Laborer	25Fe14Fa
John		11	M	Laborer	25Fe14Fa
Mary		10	F	Laborer	25Fe14Fa
Abby		09	F	Child	25Fe14Fa
Tim		08	M	Child	25Fe14Fa
Martin		04	M	Child	25Fe14Fa
Ellen		.03	F	Infant	25Fe14Fa
HORGAN, Edward		23	M	Laborer	25Fe14Fa
Eliz.		23	F	Laborer	25Fe14Fa
CURTISS, Mary		20	F	Laborer	25Fe14Fa
HUDSON, Robt.		30	M	Laborer	25Fe14Fa

NAMES OF PASSENGERS	AGE	SEX	OCCUPATIONS	DATE PORT SHIP
HUDSON, Anne	29	F	Laborer	25Fe14Fa
KEEFE, Ellen	37	F	Laborer	25Fe14Fa
Tom	13	M	Laborer	25Fe14Fa
Ellen	10	F	Laborer	25Fe14Fa
Nelly	09	F	Child	25Fe14Fa
James	08	M	Child	25Fe14Fa
Dennis	07	M	Child	25Fe14Fa
Mary	03	F	Child	25Fe14Fa
KELLEY, John	22	M	Laborer	25Fe14Fa
BYRNE, Margaret	19	F	Laborer	25Fe14Fa
DEASY, Dennis	21	M	Laborer	25Fe14Fa
WALSH, James	40	M	Laborer	25Fe14Fa
Ellen	13	F	Laborer	25Fe14Fa
Richard	10	M	Laborer	25Fe14Fa
James	03	M	Child	25Fe14Fa
ROCHE, Terrence	34	M	Laborer	25Fe14Fa
SUGRU, Danl.	32	M	Laborer	25Fe14Fa
Mary	53	F	Laborer	25Fe14Fa
MULCAHY, Mary	15	F	Laborer	25Fe14Fa
LYONS, John	33	M	Laborer	25Fe14Fa
HARNETT, Danl.	46	M	Laborer	25Fe14Fa
ADAMS, John	25	M	Laborer	25Fe14Fa
John	24	M	Laborer	25Fe14Fa
Wm.	20	M	Laborer	25Fe14Fa
James	70	M	Laborer	25Fe14Fa
HOWLEY, Mary	30	F	Laborer	25Fe14Fa
Kate	07	F	Child	25Fe14Fa
Maurice	05	M	Child	25Fe14Fa
Mary	03	F	Child	25Fe14Fa
Hannah	02	F	Child	25Fe14Fa
U	.00	U	Infant	25Fe14Fa
ELLIGROTT, John	20	M	Laborer	25Fe14Fa
St.JOHN, Phipe.	20	M	Laborer	25Fe14Fa
AHEARNE, David	34	M	Laborer	25Fe14Fa
SHIELS, John	24	M	Laborer	25Fe14Fa
SHEELAN, James	30	M	Laborer	25Fe14Fa
WALSH, Kate	25	F	Laborer	25Fe14Fa
Hannah	21	F	Laborer	25Fe14Fa
James	22	M	Laborer	25Fe14Fa
SULLIVAN, Ellen	50	F	Laborer	25Fe14Fa
Richd.	25	M	Laborer	25Fe14Fa
Matthew	22	M	Laborer	25Fe14Fa
Betty	20	F	Laborer	25Fe14Fa
Johanna	13	F	Laborer	25Fe14Fa
Ellen	10	F	Laborer	25Fe14Fa
DESMOND, Indy	28	U	Laborer	25Fe14Fa
SULLIVAN, Mike	21	M	Laborer	25Fe14Fa
Patk.	21	M	Laborer	25Fe14Fa
CASSEY, Biddy	23	F	Laborer	25Fe14Fa
CONNER, Mike	28	M	Laborer	25Fe14Fa
Johanna	23	F	Laborer	25Fe14Fa
Julia	12	F	Laborer	25Fe14Fa
Norry	28	F	Laborer	25Fe14Fa
PERCALL, Thos.	48	M	Laborer	25Fe14Fa
SHEEHAN, John	26	M	Laborer	25Fe14Fa
RIORDAN, Mike	20	M	Laborer	25Fe14Fa
Ellen	10	F	Laborer	25Fe14Fa
KEEFE, Wm.	23	M	Laborer	25Fe14Fa
COREYRAM, Mary	20	F	Laborer	25Fe14Fa
BUCKLEY, Dennis	21	M	Laborer	25Fe14Fa
LUDDY, Patk.	30	M	Laborer	25Fe14Fa
WALSH, James	28	M	Laborer	25Fe14Fa
MIE, John	21	M	Laborer	25Fe14Fa
DUNN, Terrence	50	M	Laborer	25Fe14Fa
Mike	16	M	Laborer	25Fe14Fa
Andrew	13	M	Laborer	25Fe14Fa
NOLAN, Mike	35	M	Laborer	25Fe14Fa
U	.00	U	Infant	25Fe14Fa
HUGHES, Patk.	50	M	Laborer	25Fe14Fa
Kate	50	F	Laborer	25Fe14Fa
Mike	25	M	Laborer	25Fe14Fa
Ellen	03	F	Child	25Fe14Fa
BROWN, Ellen	00	F	Laborer	25Fe14Fa
MULLIGAN, Kate	19	F	Laborer	25Fe14Fa
MACKIANALE, Mary	20	F	Laborer	25Fe14Fa
MACKIANALE, Margaret	21	F	Laborer	25Fe14Fa
Bridget	19	F	Laborer	25Fe14Fa
CALLAGHAN, Honora	21	F	Laborer	25Fe14Fa
MANGLEE, Luke	19	M	Laborer	25Fe14Fa
SULIVAN, Wm.	10	M	Laborer	25Fe14Fa
Mike	07	M	Child	25Fe14Fa
GARFFAIN, Maurice	28	M	Laborer	25Fe14Fa
U	.00	U	Infant	25Fe14Fa
NOLAN, Jane	40	F	Laborer	25Fe14Fa
BRION, Danl.	30	M	Laborer	25Fe14Fa
John	34	M	Laborer	25Fe14Fa
CASEY, Owen	30	M	Laborer	25Fe14Fa
Kate	28	F	Laborer	25Fe14Fa
CASHEL, Mike	40	M	Laborer	25Fe14Fa
Mary	35	F	Laborer	25Fe14Fa
Patk.	16	M	Laborer	25Fe14Fa
ROWES, Mike	26	M	Laborer	25Fe14Fa
SCANLAN, Mary	28	F	Laborer	25Fe14Fa
TOOMY, John	58	M	Laborer	25Fe14Fa
Mary	12	F	Laborer	25Fe14Fa
Ellen	10	F	Laborer	25Fe14Fa
CULLIMORE, Mary	28	F	Laborer	25Fe14Fa
Patk.	07	M	Child	25Fe14Fa
OCONNELL, James	22	M	Laborer	25Fe14Fa
CONNER, James	25	M	Laborer	25Fe14Fa
WALSH, Mike	28	M	Laborer	25Fe14Fa
GRIFFIN, Thomas	25	M	Laborer	25Fe14Fa
GRIHAN, Wm.	25	M	Laborer	25Fe14Fa
QUAINY, James	27	M	Laborer	25Fe14Fa
CALLIHAN, Danl.	30	M	Laborer	25Fe14Fa
BRION, Maurice	28	M	Laborer	25Fe14Fa
SHEA, Patk.	25	M	Laborer	25Fe14Fa
CALLIHAN, Mary	25	F	Laborer	25Fe14Fa
DESMOND, Mike	16	M	Laborer	25Fe14Fa
Mary	40	F	Laborer	25Fe14Fa
Danl.	20	M	Laborer	25Fe14Fa
KEEFE, Indy	24	U	Laborer	25Fe14Fa
CRANEY, Dennis	25	M	Laborer	25Fe14Fa
MURPHY, Tim	26	M	Laborer	25Fe14Fa
TOBIN, Bartholemew	20	M	Laborer	25Fe14Fa
GRIFFIN, Liman	29	M	Laborer	25Fe14Fa
COLMAN, Margaret	26	F	Laborer	25Fe14Fa
DOOLEY, John	29	M	Laborer	25Fe14Fa
Margaret	29	F	Laborer	25Fe14Fa
Patk.	02	M	Child	25Fe14Fa
KEEFE, Mike	29	M	Laborer	25Fe14Fa
Ann	05	F	Child	25Fe14Fa
John (S)	03	M	Child	25Fe14Fa
DONGAN, John	21	M	Laborer	25Fe14Fa
GANNING, Patk.	22	M	Laborer	25Fe14Fa
Eliza	23	F	Laborer	25Fe14Fa
MADDEN, Edwd.	27	M	Laborer	25Fe14Fa
Edwd.	09	M	Child	25Fe14Fa
REES, James	22	M	Laborer	25Fe14Fa
POUGH, Eliza	20	F	Laborer	25Fe14Fa
COPPET, Joseph	25	M	Laborer	25Fe14Fa
Susan	27	F	Laborer	25Fe14Fa
MORTIMER, Samuel	25	M	Laborer	25Fe14Fa
NOBLE, Thos.	27	M	Laborer	25Fe14Fa
CHARLEY, Patk.	25	M	Laborer	25Fe14Fa
Mary	21	F	Laborer	25Fe14Fa
SALMEO, Julia	20	F	Laborer	25Fe14Fa
CREAMER, John	25	M	Laborer	25Fe14Fa
Kate	18	F	Laborer	25Fe14Fa
MELIA, Patk.	27	M	Laborer	25Fe14Fa
CONNOR, Martin	25	M	Laborer	25Fe14Fa
Owen	22	M	Laborer	25Fe14Fa
HIGGINS, Mike	25	M	Laborer	25Fe14Fa
BAKER, Patk.	27	M	Laborer	25Fe14Fa
Math.	25	M	Laborer	25Fe14Fa
GUNNING, Martin	24	M	Laborer	25Fe14Fa
Kate	23	F	Laborer	25Fe14Fa
MCLOUGHLIN, James	25	M	Laborer	25Fe14Fa
TOULD, Mike	21	M	Laborer	25Fe14Fa
HAWKINS, Patk.	25	M	Laborer	25Fe14Fa

NAMES OF PASSENGERS		AGE	SEX	OCCUPATIONS	DATE PORT SHIP
QUINN, Mary		23	F	Laborer	25Fe14Fa
WARD, John		34	M	Laborer	25Fe14Fa
MORAN, Kate		23	F	Laborer	25Fe14Fa
LEARY, John		23	M	Laborer	25Fe14Fa
DRARVY, Thos.		23	M	Laborer	25Fe14Fa
AHEAN, Simon		40	M	Laborer	25Fe14Fa
Mary		23	F	Laborer	25Fe14Fa
FITZGERALD, Martin		20	F	Laborer	25Fe14Fa
MCAULIFFE, William		24	F	Laborer	25Fe14Fa
LAHER, Patk.		22	F	Laborer	25Fe14Fa
ROHAN, James		23	F	Laborer	25Fe14Fa
OGLE, Chas.		27	F	Laborer	25Fe14Fa
BIGGE, Chas.		25	F	Laborer	25Fe14Fa
BOYD, U		23	U	Laborer	25Fe14Fa
U		15	U	Laborer	25Fe14Fa
BOY, U-Mrs.		43	F	Laborer	25Fe14Fa

BROTHERS 28 FEBRUARY 1848

From Newry

NAMES OF PASSENGERS		AGE	SEX	OCCUPATIONS	DATE PORT SHIP
SHARKEY, Philip		25	M	Clerk	28Fe19Cr
KILLEN, James		45	M	Farmer	28Fe19Cr
Mary	(W)	38	F	Wife	28Fe19Cr
Biddy	(D)	17	F	Unknown	28Fe19Cr
Mary	(D)	15	F	Unknown	28Fe19Cr
Thomas	(S)	13	M	Unknown	28Fe19Cr
Owen	(S)	12	M	Unknown	28Fe19Cr
Peter	(S)	08	M	Child	28Fe19Cr
Anne	(D)	01	F	Child	28Fe19Cr
COYLE, Patrick		35	M	Laborer	28Fe19Cr
Margaret	(W)	30	F	Wife	28Fe19Cr
Catharine	(D)	06	F	Child	28Fe19Cr
Sarah	(D)	04	F	Child	28Fe19Cr
FEARON, Betty		21	F	Spinster	28Fe19Cr
COYLE, Francis		37	M	Laborer	28Fe19Cr
Mary	(W)	35	F	Wife	28Fe19Cr
WARD, Anne		18	F	Spinster	28Fe19Cr
FINNEGAN, James		22	M	Laborer	28Fe19Cr
Elizabeth		24	F	Spinster	28Fe19Cr
CULLEN, Francis		50	M	Laborer	28Fe19Cr
Biddy	(W)	45	F	Wife	28Fe19Cr
John	(S)	20	M	Laborer	28Fe19Cr
Hugh	(S)	18	M	Laborer	28Fe19Cr
James	(S)	16	M	Laborer	28Fe19Cr
Mary	(D)	14	F	Spinster	28Fe19Cr
Catharine	(D)	12	F	Spinster	28Fe19Cr
Francis	(S)	09	M	Child	28Fe19Cr
Ellen	(D)	07	F	Child	28Fe19Cr
OBRIEN, John		23	M	Laborer	28Fe19Cr
SHERIDAN, Patt		25	M	Laborer	28Fe19Cr
DONNELLY, Hugh		22	M	Laborer	28Fe19Cr
BARTON, Margaret		18	F	Spinster	28Fe19Cr
Mary		16	F	Spinster	28Fe19Cr
David		14	M	Laborer	28Fe19Cr
James		13	M	Laborer	28Fe19Cr
RICE, Patt.		25	M	Laborer	28Fe19Cr
MAGENNIS, Felix		24	M	Farmer	28Fe19Cr
Rose	(W)	19	F	Wife	28Fe19Cr
FARRELL, James		18	M	Laborer	28Fe19Cr
RISK, James		35	M	Farmer	28Fe19Cr
Margaret	(W)	30	F	Wife	28Fe19Cr
William	(S)	15	M	Unknown	28Fe19Cr
Margaret	(D)	12	F	Unknown	28Fe19Cr
Thomas	(S)	10	M	Unknown	28Fe19Cr
James	(S)	09	M	Child	28Fe19Cr
STIENSON, Hugh		25	M	Laborer	28Fe19Cr
MCDOOLE, Alice		24	F	Seamstress	28Fe19Cr
MAGONE, John		23	M	Laborer	28Fe19Cr
FINNEGAN, Margaret		20	F	Spinster	28Fe19Cr
MCARDLE, Peter		24	M	Laborer	28Fe19Cr
MARLOW, Robert		35	M	Farmer	28Fe19Cr
Margaret	(W)	28	F	Wife	28Fe19Cr
HUGHES, William		26	M	Farmer	28Fe19Cr
Charles		24	M	Tailor	28Fe19Cr
TREANOR, Mathew		25	M	Laborer	28Fe19Cr
RICE, James		15	M	Farmer	28Fe19Cr
KEENAN, Catharine		50	F	Seamstress	28Fe19Cr
WHITE, Patt.		35	M	Laborer	28Fe19Cr
Margaret	(W)	32	F	Wife	28Fe19Cr
Stephen	(S)	12	M	Unknown	28Fe19Cr
Ann	(D)	10	F	None	28Fe19Cr
MCKEOWN, Joseph		24	M	Laborer	28Fe19Cr
RIELLY, Margaret		19	F	Spinster	28Fe19Cr
LONG, Thomas		35	M	Laborer	28Fe19Cr
MORGAN, John		26	M	Laborer	28Fe19Cr
MCQUADE, John		40	M	Farmer	28Fe19Cr
Ellen	(W)	38	F	Wife	28Fe19Cr
Jane	(D)	15	F	Unknown	28Fe19Cr
Agnes	(D)	14	F	Unknown	28Fe19Cr
Mary-Ann	(D)	12	F	Unknown	28Fe19Cr
Richard	(S)	09	M	Child	28Fe19Cr
HEARTY, Mary		19	F	Spinster	28Fe19Cr
MCCULLEY, Sarah		26	F	Spinster	28Fe19Cr
CAMPBELL, John		28	M	Farmer	28Fe19Cr
Catharine	(W)	26	F	Wife	28Fe19Cr
MCCANN, Hugh		25	M	Tailor	28Fe19Cr
James		23	M	Laborer	28Fe19Cr
MULRAINE, Ellen		18	F	Spinster	28Fe19Cr
Patt.		25	M	Laborer	28Fe19Cr
Michael		23	M	Laborer	28Fe19Cr
Mary		22	F	Spinster	28Fe19Cr
HENDERSON, Robert		25	M	Farmer	28Fe19Cr
CORRY, Terrence		35	M	Laborer	28Fe19Cr
Mary	(W)	32	F	Wife	28Fe19Cr
Phill.	(S)	17	M	Unknown	28Fe19Cr
Daniel	(S)	10	M	Unknown	28Fe19Cr
HOLLAN, Patt.		26	M	Laborer	28Fe19Cr
RICE, Ann		35	F	Spinster	28Fe19Cr
MCMURRIS, James		30	M	Laborer	28Fe19Cr
Rose	(W)	26	F	Wife	28Fe19Cr
Margaret	(D)	02	F	Child	28Fe19Cr
Died-At-Sea					
MCKEEVER, Patt.		34	M	Farmer	28Fe19Cr
Rose	(W)	12	F	Wife	28Fe19Cr
John		18	M	Unknown	28Fe19Cr
Peter	(S)	12	M	Unknown	28Fe19Cr
Margaret	(D)	08	F	Child	28Fe19Cr
MCARDLE, Mary		17	F	Spinster	28Fe19Cr
FEGAN, John		39	M	Laborer	28Fe19Cr
Rose		36	F	Laborer	28Fe19Cr
Eliza		16	F	Spinster	28Fe19Cr
Francis		14	M	Laborer	28Fe19Cr
MCKENNA, Frans.		30	M	Farmer	28Fe19Cr
MCLELLAND, Robert		21	M	Laborer	28Fe19Cr
COYAL, Francis		28	M	Laborer	28Fe19Cr
WHITE, Patt.		12	M	Laborer	28Fe19Cr
MARLOW, U		.00	U	Infant	28Fe19Cr
Born-At-Sea					

UNICORN 29 FEBRUARY 1848

From Liverpool

NAMES OF PASSENGERS		AGE	SEX	OCCUPATIONS	DATE PORT SHIP
JOHNSTON, Charles		21	M	Laborer	29Fe02Fv
GOOLEY, Margaret		50	F	Servant	29Fe02Fv
Patrick		20	M	Laborer	29Fe02Fv
DUNAHO, Thos.		30	M	Laborer	29Fe02Fv

NAMES OF PASSENGERS		AGE	SEX	OCCUPATIONS	DATE PORT SHIP
DUNAHO, Ellen		28	F	Servant	29Fe02Fv
U		.00	U	Infant	29Fe02Fv
Ann		28	F	Spinster	29Fe02Fv
NUGENT, Robert		20	M	Laborer	29Fe02Fv
CORIDAN, Richard		40	M	Laborer	29Fe02Fv
BARTON, Hugh		36	M	Laborer	29Fe02Fv
Margaret		36	F	Servant	29Fe02Fv
Nancy		12	F	Servant	29Fe02Fv
Guy		10	M	None	29Fe02Fv
George		07	M	Child	29Fe02Fv
Catharine		04	F	Child	29Fe02Fv
LOGAN, Con.		25	M	Laborer	29Fe02Fv
CRANLEY, James		25	M	Laborer	29Fe02Fv
MCHUGH, Jas.		24	M	Laborer	29Fe02Fv
BOYLE, Pat.		23	M	Laborer	29Fe02Fv
NEAL, Robert		21	M	Laborer	29Fe02Fv
CABRA, Edward		50	M	Laborer	29Fe02Fv
Mary		18	F	Servant	29Fe02Fv
Daniel		24	M	Laborer	29Fe02Fv
Judy		09	F	Child	29Fe02Fv
Peggy	(W)	40	F	Wife	29Fe02Fv
REYLEY, Rose		19	F	Servant	29Fe02Fv
CARREL, Mary		20	F	Servant	29Fe02Fv
SANFORD, John		22	M	Laborer	29Fe02Fv
COX, John		22	M	Laborer	29Fe02Fv
DUN, Theresa		18	F	Servant	29Fe02Fv
KERRANS, John		21	M	Laborer	29Fe02Fv
Molanfo-, Catharine		19	F	Servant	29Fe02Fv
SHANNON, Ann		17	F	Servant	29Fe02Fv
MCGARITY, James		36	M	Laborer	29Fe02Fv
Mary		20	F	Servant	29Fe02Fv
Bridget		17	F	Servant	29Fe02Fv
MEHAN, Michal		35	M	Laborer	29Fe02Fv
MULLAN, Eliza		24	F	Spinster	29Fe02Fv
OCONNELL, James		40	M	Laborer	29Fe02Fv
HAVENDON, Adam		40	M	Laborer	29Fe02Fv
WILDON, Robert		18	M	Laborer	29Fe02Fv
CARREL, Daniel		40	M	Laborer	29Fe02Fv
GROONEY, Philip		30	M	Laborer	29Fe02Fv
BELOIN, Bridget		29	F	Servant	29Fe02Fv
Ann		07	F	Child	29Fe02Fv
William		06	M	Child	29Fe02Fv
Rose		.00	F	Infant	29Fe02Fv
Catharine		11	F	Unknown	29Fe02Fv
Margaret		20	F	Servant	29Fe02Fv
Mary		22	F	Servant	29Fe02Fv
CONLEN, Hugh		27	M	Laborer	29Fe02Fv
MCDERMOT, Ellen		40	F	Servant	29Fe02Fv
Catharine		20	F	Servant	29Fe02Fv
SCELLEY, Mary		24	F	Servant	29Fe02Fv
William		22	M	Laborer	29Fe02Fv
SMITH, Pat		29	M	Laborer	29Fe02Fv
CASSIDY, Thos.		30	M	Laborer	29Fe02Fv
BELOIN, Terry		07	M	Child	29Fe02Fv
HIGHLAND, John		27	M	Laborer	29Fe02Fv
KESHEN, Charles		36	M	Laborer	29Fe02Fv
Betsey	(W)	35	F	Wife	29Fe02Fv
James	(S)	08	M	Child	29Fe02Fv
Died-At-Sea					
Margaret	(D)	06	F	Child	29Fe02Fv
Michael	(S)	.00	M	Infant	29Fe02Fv
MAHAN, Owen		16	M	Laborer	29Fe02Fv
Mary		15	F	Servant	29Fe02Fv
Judy		11	F	Servant	29Fe02Fv
CONLEY, Owen		48	M	Laborer	29Fe02Fv
Mary	(W)	32	F	Wife	29Fe02Fv
Mary	(D)	10	F	Unknown	29Fe02Fv
Margaret	(D)	08	F	Child	29Fe02Fv
Mary	(D)	06	F	Child	29Fe02Fv
Frances	(D)	04	F	Child	29Fe02Fv
Ellen	(D)	02	F	Child	29Fe02Fv
James	(S)	.00	M	Infant	29Fe02Fv
MCCAUL, Pat		28	M	Laborer	29Fe02Fv
Jane	(W)	24	F	Wife	29Fe02Fv
Ellen		22	F	Servant	29Fe02Fv
MCCAUL, James		13	M	Laborer	29Fe02Fv
MARTIN, John		25	M	Laborer	29Fe02Fv
Mary	(W)	24	F	Wife	29Fe02Fv
Died-At-Sea					
MCINHANAH, Robert		20	M	Laborer	29Fe02Fv
MCCLEAN, James		20	M	Laborer	29Fe02Fv
Mary		30	F	Servant	29Fe02Fv
REID, John		30	M	Laborer	29Fe02Fv
MCCRANON, Charles		18	M	Laborer	29Fe02Fv
FEGAN, Pat.		30	M	Laborer	29Fe02Fv
MULVEY, Owen		22	M	Laborer	29Fe02Fv
LARKIN, Thos.		30	M	Laborer	29Fe02Fv
COOK, David		25	M	Laborer	29Fe02Fv
COATS, John		27	M	Laborer	29Fe02Fv
Mary	(W)	25	F	Wife	29Fe02Fv
Bridget	(D)	.00	F	Infant	29Fe02Fv
Mary		22	F	Servant	29Fe02Fv
Ann		21	F	Servant	29Fe02Fv
Pat		24	M	Laborer	29Fe02Fv
RYAN, James		28	M	Laborer	29Fe02Fv
MACK, Deborah		28	F	Spinster	29Fe02Fv
STANNEY, John		26	M	Laborer	29Fe02Fv
HANORAN, Michal		29	M	Laborer	29Fe02Fv
MELONEY, Thos.		30	M	Laborer	29Fe02Fv
HANORAN, Bridget		24	F	Spinster	29Fe02Fv
MCPEAK, Pat		25	M	Laborer	29Fe02Fv
MCCORDAN, Susan		13	F	Servant	29Fe02Fv
MCWATER, Dias		24	M	Laborer	29Fe02Fv
SCOTT, Peter		28	M	Laborer	29Fe02Fv
LYNCH, James		23	M	Laborer	29Fe02Fv
Died-At-Sea					
John		25	M	Laborer	29Fe02Fv
ADORSLEY, George		28	M	Laborer	29Fe02Fv
BRACKEN, John		29	M	Laborer	29Fe02Fv
MCDERMOTT, Ann		28	F	Spinster	29Fe02Fv
DEVINE, James		30	M	Laborer	29Fe02Fv
WALCH, Margaret		24	F	Spinster	29Fe02Fv
SMITH, Mary-Ann		18	F	Servant	29Fe02Fv
CADIGAN, Pat		24	M	Laborer	29Fe02Fv
COAKLEY, William		32	M	Laborer	29Fe02Fv
VAUGHAN, Nancy		30	F	Servant	29Fe02Fv
Juliana		10	F	Unknown	29Fe02Fv
LYNCH, John		26	M	Laborer	29Fe02Fv
DELANEY, Thos.		29	M	Laborer	29Fe02Fv
Bridget		36	F	Servant	29Fe02Fv
William		06	M	Child	29Fe02Fv
John		07	M	Child	29Fe02Fv
Pat		05	M	Child	29Fe02Fv
Edward		04	M	Child	29Fe02Fv
GOHERTY, Pat		30	M	Laborer	29Fe02Fv
Catharine	(W)	25	F	Wife	29Fe02Fv
Mary	(D)	06	F	Child	29Fe02Fv
Catharine	(D)	05	F	Child	29Fe02Fv
Margaret	(D)	03	F	Child	29Fe02Fv
Pat	(S)	.00	M	Infant	29Fe02Fv
FLYNN, Pat		62	M	Laborer	29Fe02Fv
Pat		29	M	Laborer	29Fe02Fv
Mary-Ann	(W)	27	F	Wife	29Fe02Fv
Jane		25	F	Spinster	29Fe02Fv
GIBSON, Richard		27	M	Laborer	29Fe02Fv
RYAN, James		30	M	Laborer	29Fe02Fv
BRYAN, Pat		26	M	Laborer	29Fe02Fv
STEWARD, William		28	M	Laborer	29Fe02Fv
Eliza	(W)	20	F	Wife	29Fe02Fv
GREEN, Samuel		27	M	Laborer	29Fe02Fv
John		26	M	Laborer	29Fe02Fv
FARREL, Charles		30	M	Laborer	29Fe02Fv
MCDONALD, Michl.		28	M	Laborer	29Fe02Fv
CARNEY, Mary		24	F	Spinster	29Fe02Fv
HICKLEY, Bridget		24	F	Spinster	29Fe02Fv
WIER, Frank		22	M	Laborer	29Fe02Fv
MOCKLEY, Nicholas		20	M	Laborer	29Fe02Fv
HOGAN, Jas.		21	M	Laborer	29Fe02Fv
ARMSTRONG, Charles		20	M	Laborer	29Fe02Fv
MCENNA, Margaret		27	F	Spinster	29Fe02Fv

NAMES OF PASSENGERS		AGE	SEX	OCCUPATIONS	DATE PORT SHIP
DEVLIN, Pat		26	M	Laborer	29Fe02Fv
MCCRANEN, Charles		28	M	Laborer	29Fe02Fv
MCGUIRE, Christy		29	M	Laborer	29Fe02Fv
Bridget	(W)	24	F	Wife	29Fe02Fv
CONLEY, Thos.		29	M	Laborer	29Fe02Fv
EAGAN, James		18	M	Laborer	29Fe02Fv
DAWSON, Jonathan		30	M	Laborer	29Fe02Fv
John		09	M	Child	29Fe02Fv
LYNCH, Michl.		26	M	Laborer	29Fe02Fv
Ann	(W)	26	F	Wife	29Fe02Fv
James	(S)	.00	M	Infant	29Fe02Fv
MOORE, Ann		22	F	Spinster	29Fe02Fv
MCGEE, John		28	M	Laborer	29Fe02Fv
MCHENDRIS, Owen		28	M	Laborer	29Fe02Fv
TEIG, Michl.		17	M	Laborer	29Fe02Fv
MCPETERS, And.		23	M	Laborer	29Fe02Fv
Robert		28	M	Laborer	29Fe02Fv
WALKER, Lawrence		21	M	Laborer	29Fe02Fv
SHARKEY, Nicholas		22	M	Laborer	29Fe02Fv
DAVIS, Jane		40	F	Servant	29Fe02Fv
Catharine		19	F	Servant	29Fe02Fv
Eliza		17	F	Servant	29Fe02Fv
Jane		16	F	Servant	29Fe02Fv
Agnes		12	F	Servant	29Fe02Fv
John		14	M	Servant	29Fe02Fv
GRAHAM, Mary-Ann		21	F	Servant	29Fe02Fv
YOUNG, Thos.		29	M	Laborer	29Fe02Fv
MCAFFERY, Bridget		22	F	Spinster	29Fe02Fv
DEVIT, John		27	M	Laborer	29Fe02Fv
SWENEY, John		26	M	Laborer	29Fe02Fv
ODONEL, John		29	M	Laborer	29Fe02Fv
OHARRAH, John		30	M	Laborer	29Fe02Fv
TAYLOR, Wm.		21	M	Laborer	29Fe02Fv
NASH, J.W.		26	M	Laborer	29Fe02Fv
BRANEN, Michl.		19	M	Laborer	29Fe02Fv
GILLESPIE, Robert		29	M	Laborer	29Fe02Fv
COLLINS, Pat		30	M	Laborer	29Fe02Fv
Peter		25	M	Laborer	29Fe02Fv
Ann		17	F	Servant	29Fe02Fv
MOLIN, Alley		39	M	Laborer	29Fe02Fv
Catharine	(W)	27	F	Wife	29Fe02Fv
Ellen	(D)	06	F	Child	29Fe02Fv
CUNNINGHAM, Margaret		19	F	Servant	29Fe02Fv
BUTLER, James		28	M	Laborer	29Fe02Fv
Judy	(W)	20	F	Wife	29Fe02Fv
Bridget		19	F	Servant	29Fe02Fv
Betsey		10	F	Unknown	29Fe02Fv
Thos.		06	M	Child	29Fe02Fv
Catharine		.00	F	Infant	29Fe02Fv
Johanna		05	F	Child	29Fe02Fv
DEWIRE, Pat		29	M	Laborer	29Fe02Fv
Elizabeth	(W)	27	F	Wife	29Fe02Fv
MAHAN, Thos.		30	M	Laborer	29Fe02Fv
Ann	(W)	29	F	Wife	29Fe02Fv
SMITH, John		27	M	Laborer	29Fe02Fv
MCNALLY, Owen		28	M	Laborer	29Fe02Fv
PARKER, James		29	M	Laborer	29Fe02Fv
George		27	M	Laborer	29Fe02Fv
Matilda		07	F	Child	29Fe02Fv
Margaret		06	F	Child	29Fe02Fv
William		05	M	Child	29Fe02Fv
Thomas		04	M	Child	29Fe02Fv
PERREY, James		28	M	Laborer	29Fe02Fv
HAGERTY, Michl.		45	M	Laborer	29Fe02Fv
Bridget	(W)	42	F	Wife	29Fe02Fv
GOVERIN, John		29	M	Laborer	29Fe02Fv
SMITH, Charles		27	M	Laborer	29Fe02Fv
REYRDEN, Dennis		30	M	Laborer	29Fe02Fv
SHANLEY, John		60	M	Laborer	29Fe02Fv
Died-At-Sea					
John		18	M	Laborer	29Fe02Fv
Thos.		17	M	Laborer	29Fe02Fv
Pat		15	M	Laborer	29Fe02Fv
Andrew		10	M	Laborer	29Fe02Fv
John		.00	M	Infant	29Fe02Fv
SHANLEY, Mary		30	F	Servant	29Fe02Fv
Ann		28	F	Servant	29Fe02Fv
SMITH, Michl.		29	M	Laborer	29Fe02Fv
WALCH, Martin		28	M	Laborer	29Fe02Fv
DONAHU, Margaret		30	F	Spinster	29Fe02Fv
SMITH, Mary		22	F	Spinster	29Fe02Fv
DUNON, Abby		29	M	Laborer	29Fe02Fv
SHERAN, Owen		28	M	Laborer	29Fe02Fv
BUTLER, Michl.		30	M	Laborer	29Fe02Fv
MCLARKEY, John		26	M	Laborer	29Fe02Fv
Frances	(W)	25	F	Wife	29Fe02Fv
TORFEY, James		30	M	Laborer	29Fe02Fv
CONLEN, Ellen		27	F	Spinster	29Fe02Fv
CARR, James		22	M	Laborer	29Fe02Fv
MCGUIKIN, James		30	M	Laborer	29Fe02Fv
John		13	M	Laborer	29Fe02Fv
James		09	M	Child	29Fe02Fv
COONAN, Sarah		24	F	Spinster	29Fe02Fv
MURRAY, Thos.		28	M	Laborer	29Fe02Fv
Catharine	(W)	26	F	Wife	29Fe02Fv
BROWN, John		35	M	Laborer	29Fe02Fv
James		13	M	Laborer	29Fe02Fv
CAMBELL, Thos.		30	M	Laborer	29Fe02Fv
PERREY, James		27	M	Laborer	29Fe02Fv
COX, Patrick		30	M	Laborer	29Fe02Fv
MCCLEAN, John		22	M	Laborer	29Fe02Fv
Michl.		12	M	Laborer	29Fe02Fv
MCQUANEY, Pat		24	M	Laborer	29Fe02Fv
GREENAN, James		22	M	Laborer	29Fe02Fv
FANLEY, Mary		24	F	Servant	29Fe02Fv
Barney		03	M	Child	29Fe02Fv
John		02	M	Child	29Fe02Fv
MCGUIER, Ellen		22	F	Servant	29Fe02Fv
Christy		21	M	Laborer	29Fe02Fv
EAGEN, Lawrence		39	M	Laborer	29Fe02Fv

EMIGRANT 01 MARCH 1848

From Liverpool

NAMES OF PASSENGERS		AGE	SEX	OCCUPATIONS	DATE PORT SHIP
CUNNIFFE, Cathe.		26	F	Servant	01Mr02Pu
COOLIGAN, Cathe.		16	F	Servant	01Mr02Pu
Pat		12	M	None	01Mr02Pu
CONDON, Ann		22	F	Servant	01Mr02Pu
Ellen		20	F	Servant	01Mr02Pu
HUMPHREY, Mary-A.		45	F	Servant	01Mr02Pu
Wm.		18	M	Laborer	01Mr02Pu
George		13	M	None	01Mr02Pu
Thos.		10	M	None	01Mr02Pu
Letitia		08	F	Child	01Mr02Pu
John		07	M	Child	01Mr02Pu
KEEFE, Ellen		29	F	Servant	01Mr02Pu
Dennis		04	M	Child	01Mr02Pu
BURRY, Michael		30	M	Laborer	01Mr02Pu
BRYAN, Pat		11	M	None	01Mr02Pu
Kate		02	F	Child	01Mr02Pu
SHELDON, Jas.		28	M	Laborer	01Mr02Pu
Mary		24	F	Servant	01Mr02Pu
RYAN, Cathe.		20	F	Servant	01Mr02Pu
CASY, Bridget		22	F	Servant	01Mr02Pu
KEARNY, Thos.		26	M	Laborer	01Mr02Pu
REILLY, Philip		22	M	Laborer	01Mr02Pu
GORMLY, Jas.		18	M	Laborer	01Mr02Pu
MCDOWELL, Mary		20	F	Servant	01Mr02Pu
MOORE, Wm.		30	M	Laborer	01Mr02Pu
CONNERS, Felix		25	M	Laborer	01Mr02Pu
MCEVOY, Margt.		30	F	Servant	01Mr02Pu
Thos.		24	M	Laborer	01Mr02Pu
Rose		03	F	Child	01Mr02Pu

NAMES OF PASSENGERS	AGE	SEX	OCCUPATIONS	DATE PORT SHIP
MCEVOY, Bridget	21	F	Servant	01Mr02Pu
DOYLE, Michl.	20	M	Laborer	01Mr02Pu
HIGGANS, Mary	36	F	Servant	01Mr02Pu
Rose	16	F	Servant	01Mr02Pu
Mary	12	F	Servant	01Mr02Pu
Henry	08	M	Child	01Mr02Pu
Ann	03	F	Child	01Mr02Pu
MCKEON, Jas.	26	M	Laborer	01Mr02Pu
Margt.	20	F	None	01Mr02Pu
MCANDREW, Patt.	11	M	None	01Mr02Pu
Jas.	09	M	Child	01Mr02Pu
VELLERY, Mary	24	F	Servant	01Mr02Pu
Thos.	26	M	Laborer	01Mr02Pu
CAIRNES, Margaret	21	F	Servant	01Mr02Pu
MOWBARY, Robt.	03	M	Child	01Mr02Pu
WEBB, Michl.	30	M	Laborer	01Mr02Pu
Dennis	03	M	Child	01Mr02Pu
HUGHES, Ann	40	F	Servant	01Mr02Pu
CHAPMAN, Thos.	06	M	Child	01Mr02Pu
DONOHOE, Bridget	10	F	None	01Mr02Pu
WILSON, Christopher	20	M	Laborer	01Mr02Pu
DONOVAN, Johanna	30	F	Servant	01Mr02Pu
Honora	27	F	Servant	01Mr02Pu
Michael	40	M	Laborer	01Mr02Pu
CATON, Bridget	24	F	Servant	01Mr02Pu
MEHAN, Mary	30	F	Servant	01Mr02Pu
Richd.	04	M	Child	01Mr02Pu
Fanny	10	F	None	01Mr02Pu
FALLON, John	25	M	Laborer	01Mr02Pu
LUNNAN, Ann	23	F	Servant	01Mr02Pu
CALLIGAN, Bridget	23	F	Servant	01Mr02Pu
HIGGINS, Michl.	37	M	Laborer	01Mr02Pu
Mary	30	F	Servant	01Mr02Pu
Patt.	03	M	Child	01Mr02Pu
CONNALE, Peter	02	M	Child	01Mr02Pu
COSGROVE, Jas.	58	M	Laborer	01Mr02Pu
Cathe.	18	F	Servant	01Mr02Pu
BRADY, Jno.	21	M	Laborer	01Mr02Pu
DOHERTY, Bridget	17	F	Servant	01Mr02Pu
POWER, Maurice	40	M	Laborer	01Mr02Pu
LAWLER, Thos.	40	M	Laborer	01Mr02Pu
Bridget	27	F	Servant	01Mr02Pu
MAHER, Judy	15	F	Servant	01Mr02Pu
KERWIN, Jas.	23	M	Laborer	01Mr02Pu
Jno.	25	M	Laborer	01Mr02Pu
Jas.	02	M	Child	01Mr02Pu
Judy	25	F	Servant	01Mr02Pu
Michl.	34	M	Laborer	01Mr02Pu
LANGLEY, Mary	23	F	Servant	01Mr02Pu
CRAWFORD, Mary	18	F	Servant	01Mr02Pu
PATERSON, Mark	29	M	Laborer	01Mr02Pu
DONNELLY, Margt.	16	F	Servant	01Mr02Pu
COWAN, Ann	24	F	Servant	01Mr02Pu
HUGHES, Margaret	45	F	Servant	01Mr02Pu
Jas.	20	M	Laborer	01Mr02Pu
KAVERTY, Ann	18	F	Servant	01Mr02Pu
CORBERRY, Pat	22	M	Laborer	01Mr02Pu
Honora	12	F	None	01Mr02Pu
IRVINE, Jas.	22	M	Laborer	01Mr02Pu
REGAN, Mary	30	F	Servant	01Mr02Pu
BROWN, Thos.	25	M	Laborer	01Mr02Pu
WIDOWS, Wm.	25	M	Laborer	01Mr02Pu
U (W)	22	F	Servant	01Mr02Pu
GRANNEL, John	21	M	Laborer	01Mr02Pu
CULLEN, John	22	M	Laborer	01Mr02Pu
LOWE, Ann	18	F	Servant	01Mr02Pu
MCDONNOUGH, John	40	M	Laborer	01Mr02Pu
U (W)	32	F	Servant	01Mr02Pu
Mary (D)	11	F	None	01Mr02Pu
Agnes (D)	07	F	Child	01Mr02Pu
MCCORMICK, Peter	21	M	Laborer	01Mr02Pu
SHIKAY, Mary	18	F	Servant	01Mr02Pu
FAGAN, Wm.	20	M	Laborer	01Mr02Pu
Margt.	17	F	Servant	01Mr02Pu
BERGAN, Jno.	19	M	Laborer	01Mr02Pu
BOYLE, Jas.	12	M	None	01Mr02Pu
Margt.	10	F	None	01Mr02Pu
Ellen	04	F	Child	01Mr02Pu
MCGINTY, Thos.	20	M	Laborer	01Mr02Pu
ROCHE, Mary	24	F	Servant	01Mr02Pu
MURPHY, Mich.	04	M	Child	01Mr02Pu
Mary	03	F	Child	01Mr02Pu
KIRKPATRICK, Rose	15	F	None	01Mr02Pu
COYNE, Mich.	21	M	Laborer	01Mr02Pu
HAMILTON, Margt.	23	F	Servant	01Mr02Pu
HIGGINS, Phillip	25	M	Laborer	01Mr02Pu
Wm.	12	M	None	01Mr02Pu
Pat	10	M	None	01Mr02Pu
GAHAN, Bernard	40	M	Laborer	01Mr02Pu
Mary	30	F	Servant	01Mr02Pu
James	05	M	Child	01Mr02Pu
Mary	04	F	Child	01Mr02Pu
John	.00	M	Infant	01Mr02Pu
Cathe.	02	F	Child	01Mr02Pu
MCGUIRE, Francis	21	M	Laborer	01Mr02Pu
LYNCH, Cathe.	38	F	Servant	01Mr02Pu
Patk.	17	M	Servant	01Mr02Pu
HAMILTON, Cathe.	20	F	Servant	01Mr02Pu
JOYCE, Eliza	20	F	Servant	01Mr02Pu
FLYNN, Cathe.	40	F	Servant	01Mr02Pu
MONAGHAN, Willm.	50	M	Laborer	01Mr02Pu
DOLLARD, Jas.	30	M	Laborer	01Mr02Pu
MCLEON, Mary	40	F	Servant	01Mr02Pu
George	18	M	Laborer	01Mr02Pu
WALL, Gerald	30	M	Laborer	01Mr02Pu
ROBINSON, Sam	22	M	Laborer	01Mr02Pu
MALONE, Wm.	20	M	Laborer	01Mr02Pu
MCKENNA, John	13	M	None	01Mr02Pu
MONTGOMERY, Alex	25	M	Laborer	01Mr02Pu
CAMPBELL, Pat	20	M	Laborer	01Mr02Pu
CORDON, Robt.	20	M	Laborer	01Mr02Pu
CUNNINGHAM, Robt.	22	M	Laborer	01Mr02Pu
HERDON, Thos.	19	M	Laborer	01Mr02Pu
MCGLESNETT, Thos.	18	M	Laborer	01Mr02Pu
GRANFIELD, Thos.	20	M	Laborer	01Mr02Pu
GIBSON, Jno.	20	M	Laborer	01Mr02Pu
BRADY, Saml.	20	M	Laborer	01Mr02Pu
BURKE, Martin	20	M	Laborer	01Mr02Pu
OWEN, Michl.	20	M	Laborer	01Mr02Pu
CORTY, Bridget	28	F	Servant	01Mr02Pu
Biddy	02	F	Child	01Mr02Pu
AHERN, Jas.	30	M	Laborer	01Mr02Pu
Eliza	28	F	Servant	01Mr02Pu
Mary	23	F	Servant	01Mr02Pu
Jane	05	F	Child	01Mr02Pu
Mary	03	F	Child	01Mr02Pu
James	.00	M	Infant	01Mr02Pu
DESMOND, D.	26	M	Laborer	01Mr02Pu
MCANOCK, Jas.	49	M	Laborer	01Mr02Pu
Rose	47	F	Servant	01Mr02Pu
Jane	15	F	Servant	01Mr02Pu
Jas.	11	M	None	01Mr02Pu
Mary	09	F	Child	01Mr02Pu
Sarah	06	F	Child	01Mr02Pu
Elizabeth	07	F	Child	01Mr02Pu
Arthur	04	M	Child	01Mr02Pu
Harriet	02	F	Child	01Mr02Pu
SLOUGHTON, Pat	28	M	Laborer	01Mr02Pu
MADDEN, Th.	32	M	Laborer	01Mr02Pu
SCALL, Thos.	21	M	Laborer	01Mr02Pu
THOMPSON, Laur.	17	M	Laborer	01Mr02Pu
PEPPER, Thos.	32	M	Laborer	01Mr02Pu
KERWAN, Mich.	27	M	Laborer	01Mr02Pu
DALY, Pat	28	M	Laborer	01Mr02Pu
BOLAN, Geo.	24	M	Laborer	01Mr02Pu
DRISCOLL, Martin	27	M	Laborer	01Mr02Pu
DESMOND, Cathe.	26	F	Servant	01Mr02Pu
GILL, Cathe.	30	F	Servant	01Mr02Pu
Cathe.	04	F	Child	01Mr02Pu
Patt.	08	M	Child	01Mr02Pu

NAMES OF PASSENGERS	AGE	SEX	OCCUPATIONS	DATE PORT SHIP
GILL, Mary	03	F	Child	01Mr02Pu
Edward	07	M	Child	01Mr02Pu
John	25	M	Laborer	01Mr02Pu
Francis	28	M	Laborer	01Mr02Pu
DESMOND, Timothy	25	M	Laborer	01Mr02Pu
HEALY, Bridget	12	F	None	01Mr02Pu
BUCKLEY, Margt.	06	F	Child	01Mr02Pu
Eliza	04	F	Child	01Mr02Pu
SHERIDAN, Danl.	28	M	Laborer	01Mr02Pu
KAINE, Ann	24	F	Servant	01Mr02Pu
MCFADDEN, John	46	M	Laborer	01Mr02Pu
GERITY, Jas.	18	M	Laborer	01Mr02Pu
WILKINSON, Cathe.	30	F	Servant	01Mr02Pu
CONAHAN, Cornelius	22	M	Laborer	01Mr02Pu
CARTY, John	23	M	Laborer	01Mr02Pu
DUNN, Wm.	25	M	Laborer	01Mr02Pu
KEEF, Thomas	00	M	Unknown	01Mr02Pu
Died-At-Sea				
MCEVOY, Thos.	.00	M	Infant	01Mr02Pu
Thos.	.00	M	Infant	01Mr02Pu
SEELEY, Elizabeth	25	F	None	01Mr02Pu
GREENE, David	24	M	Laborer	01Mr02Pu
BROWN, Ann	22	F	None	01Mr02Pu
MCDONOUGH, Edward	19	M	Laborer	01Mr02Pu
Eliza	21	F	None	01Mr02Pu
BOYLE, Mary	42	F	None	01Mr02Pu
BOURKE, Thomas	20	M	Laborer	01Mr02Pu
REARDEN, David	23	M	Laborer	01Mr02Pu
HOLLAND, Robet.	24	M	Laborer	01Mr02Pu
GILL, John	.00	M	Infant	01Mr02Pu
DOYLE, Thoms.	24	M	Laborer	01Mr02Pu
COOPER, Thoms.	35	M	Laborer	01Mr02Pu
GLEASON, Rodger	20	M	Laborer	01Mr02Pu

HORTENSIA 03 MARCH 1848

From Calais

NAMES OF PASSENGERS	AGE	SEX	OCCUPATIONS	DATE PORT SHIP
STARR, Eliza	28	F	None	03Mr89Fy

ZANONI 07 MARCH 1848

From Liverpool

NAMES OF PASSENGERS	AGE	SEX	OCCUPATIONS	DATE PORT SHIP
FITZGERALD, Hannah	44	F	Housekeeper	07Mr02Ow
Susan	08	F	Child	07Mr02Ow
William	06	M	Child	07Mr02Ow
MARSHALL, Alicia	24	F	Housekeeper	07Mr02Ow
MURPHY, James	30	M	Laborer	07Mr02Ow
Patrick	27	M	Laborer	07Mr02Ow
Mary	18	F	Servant	07Mr02Ow
MCANANEY, John	40	M	Laborer	07Mr02Ow
Ann	36	F	Housekeeper	07Mr02Ow
Edward	17	M	Servant	07Mr02Ow
Patrick	15	M	Servant	07Mr02Ow
John	13	M	Servant	07Mr02Ow
Catherine	11	F	Servant	07Mr02Ow
Mathew	09	M	Child	07Mr02Ow
Thomas	07	M	Child	07Mr02Ow
Phillip	05	M	Child	07Mr02Ow
Hugh	.00	M	Infant	07Mr02Ow
MCGUIRE, Bernard	44	M	Laborer	07Mr02Ow
Bridget	40	F	Housekeeper	07Mr02Ow
MCGUIRE, John	12	M	Servant	07Mr02Ow
Mary	11	F	Servant	07Mr02Ow
Peter	09	M	Child	07Mr02Ow
Thomas	06	M	Child	07Mr02Ow
Bernard	04	M	Child	07Mr02Ow
Patrick	02	M	Child	07Mr02Ow
SMITH, John	70	M	Laborer	07Mr02Ow
MCGUIRE, Phillip	40	M	Laborer	07Mr02Ow
MCADAM, Patrick	24	M	Laborer	07Mr02Ow
MONAHON, Patrick	35	M	Laborer	07Mr02Ow
Margaret	40	F	Housekeeper	07Mr02Ow
Mary	16	F	Housekeeper	07Mr02Ow
James	13	M	Servant	07Mr02Ow
Patrick	11	M	Servant	07Mr02Ow
Norah	09	F	Child	07Mr02Ow
Margaret	04	F	Child	07Mr02Ow
FARRELL, Patrick	20	M	Laborer	07Mr02Ow
MCGLEN, Hugh	16	M	Tailor	07Mr02Ow
MCCAFFREY, John	46	M	Laborer	07Mr02Ow
Bernard	16	M	Laborer	07Mr02Ow
Ann	12	F	Servant	07Mr02Ow
MURREY, John	31	M	Laborer	07Mr02Ow
STRONTAGUE, Patrick	29	M	Wheelwright	07Mr02Ow
TIMOTHY, Patrick	25	M	Laborer	07Mr02Ow
MCDONALD, James	20	M	Laborer	07Mr02Ow
Ellen	22	F	Servant	07Mr02Ow
LACY, Edward	23	M	Clerk	07Mr02Ow
NASH, James	38	M	Laborer	07Mr02Ow
Mary	37	F	Servant	07Mr02Ow
Michael	13	M	None	07Mr02Ow
Edward	11	M	None	07Mr02Ow
John	08	M	Child	07Mr02Ow
MULLHOLLAND, Richd.	30	M	Laborer	07Mr02Ow
DEVLIN, James	37	M	Laborer	07Mr02Ow
MCCANN, Bernard	35	M	Laborer	07Mr02Ow
Patrick	40	M	Painter	07Mr02Ow
Margaret	32	F	Servant	07Mr02Ow
MCINTEY, Patrick	20	M	Laborer	07Mr02Ow
Mary	20	F	Housekeeper	07Mr02Ow
Mary	.00	F	Infant	07Mr02Ow
MCNAMARA, James	21	M	Laborer	07Mr02Ow
BURNS, Bridget	13	F	Servant	07Mr02Ow
FENEN, Michael	28	M	Laborer	07Mr02Ow
FLINN, Larry	33	M	Laborer	07Mr02Ow
MULLEGAN, Peter	21	M	Laborer	07Mr02Ow
KEARNON, Patrick	22	M	Laborer	07Mr02Ow
FAGAN, Patrick	28	M	Laborer	07Mr02Ow
Eliza	20	F	Servant	07Mr02Ow
KILROY, Edward	18	M	Laborer	07Mr02Ow
Brian	14	M	Laborer	07Mr02Ow
DUNN, Michael	38	M	Laborer	07Mr02Ow
SACKERTON, Thomas	28	M	Mason	07Mr02Ow
Ann	27	F	Housekeeper	07Mr02Ow
Jane	02	F	Child	07Mr02Ow
Died-At-Sea				
WILLIS, Isabella	18	F	Servant	07Mr02Ow
WELSH, Thomas	26	M	Laborer	07Mr02Ow
BRIAN, Patrick	31	M	Laborer	07Mr02Ow
HALLOWAY, Margaret	30	F	Servant	07Mr02Ow
Mary-Ann	10	F	Servant	07Mr02Ow
GREEN, Caroline	20	F	Servant	07Mr02Ow
CONNER, Patrick	40	M	Laborer	07Mr02Ow
Michael	09	M	Child	07Mr02Ow
Patrick	07	M	Child	07Mr02Ow
John	05	M	Child	07Mr02Ow
SHORTLE, John	30	M	Groom	07Mr02Ow
MCDERMOT, Mary	20	F	Servant	07Mr02Ow
DUNN, Bridget	22	F	Servant	07Mr02Ow
HYLAND, Betsey	21	F	Servant	07Mr02Ow
GROGAN, Fanny	21	F	Servant	07Mr02Ow
BRIAN, William	42	M	Irnmldr	07Mr02Ow
Mary	36	F	Housekeeper	07Mr02Ow
John	10	M	Housekeeper	07Mr02Ow
Edward	07	M	Child	07Mr02Ow
Eliza	06	F	Child	07Mr02Ow

NAMES OF PASSENGERS	AGE	SEX	OCCUPATIONS	DATE PORT SHIP
BRIAN, Margaret	04	F	Child	07Mr020w
Died-At-Sea				
William	01	M	Child	07Mr020w
Died-At-Sea				
LANE, Mary	30	F	Housekeeper	07Mr020w
Mary	12	F	Servant	07Mr020w
Bridget	06	F	Child	07Mr020w
James	.00	M	Infant	07Mr020w
Died-At-Sea				
KAIN, Edward	34	M	Shoemaker	07Mr020w
CAMPEN, William	38	M	Laborer	07Mr020w
MCCOVERN, Peter	32	M	Nail Maker	07Mr020w
Margaret	25	F	Housekeeper	07Mr020w
John	.00	M	Infant	07Mr020w
LOCKERTON, Pat	35	M	Laborer	07Mr020w
LAGAN, Patrick	24	M	Laborer	07Mr020w
MCANALLY, Patrick	21	M	Laborer	07Mr020w
LYNN, Patrick	19	M	Puddler	07Mr020w
MULLBERRY, Letetia	16	F	Servant	07Mr020w
CONNER, Sarah	19	F	Servant	07Mr020w
Ellen	20	F	Servant	07Mr020w
MATHEWS, James	30	M	Laborer	07Mr020w
CAVANAH, John	21	M	Laborer	07Mr020w
QUINN, Peter	26	M	Laborer	07Mr020w
Margaret	19	F	Housekeeper	07Mr020w
MULLIGAN, Catherine	30	F	Housekeeper	07Mr020w
GALLAGAN, Thomas	19	M	Laborer	07Mr020w
RIELLY, Antony	22	M	Laborer	07Mr020w
Ann	13	F	Servant	07Mr020w
GILBERT, Ann	18	F	Servant	07Mr020w
TAGUE, Thomas	55	M	Laborer	07Mr020w
Michael	12	M	Laborer	07Mr020w
Catherine	10	F	Laborer	07Mr020w
KELLY, Thomas	33	M	Laborer	07Mr020w
MCCORMICK, Mary	24	F	Servant	07Mr020w
John	02	M	Child	07Mr020w
MALEY, Michael	28	M	Laborer	07Mr020w
Catherine	23	F	Servant	07Mr020w
HUSSY, Thomas	18	M	Laborer	07Mr020w
STAPLETON, Thomas	25	M	Laborer	07Mr020w
CHALESEA, Michael	25	M	Laborer	07Mr020w
ROGAN, Thomas	23	M	Laborer	07Mr020w
FARLEY, Michael	30	M	Laborer	07Mr020w
FITZPATRICK, Pat	22	M	Laborer	07Mr020w
OCONNER, Peter	18	M	Shepherd	07Mr020w
OLAUCHLEN, Michael	39	M	Laborer	07Mr020w
KELLY, Patrick	20	M	Laborer	07Mr020w
OBRIAN, Daniel	24	M	Laborer	07Mr020w
KEARNEY, Judy	40	F	Housekeeper	07Mr020w
Mary	18	F	Servant	07Mr020w
Bridget	12	F	Servant	07Mr020w
John	20	M	Laborer	07Mr020w
SKULLY, Ann	34	F	Housekeeper	07Mr020w
Peter	17	M	Laborer	07Mr020w
Bridget	14	F	Servant	07Mr020w
Patrick	11	M	Laborer	07Mr020w
Fanny	07	F	Child	07Mr020w
Ann-Jane	05	F	Child	07Mr020w
Thomas	03	M	Child	07Mr020w
William	.00	M	Infant	07Mr020w
MATHEWS, William	23	M	Laborer	07Mr020w
SCANLEN, James	22	M	Carpenter	07Mr020w
CONSIDEN, Thomas	28	M	Laborer	07Mr020w
RIELLY, Bridget	60	F	Housekeeper	07Mr020w
BRANNEN, Bridget	25	F	Servant	07Mr020w
MCMANNIS, Peter	20	M	Laborer	07Mr020w
BRADY, Terrance	26	M	Laborer	07Mr020w
SMITH, Lawrence	17	M	Laborer	07Mr020w
OFARRELL, James	28	M	Laborer	07Mr020w
CORRAGAN, Patrick	40	M	Laborer	07Mr020w
Mary	30	F	Housekeeper	07Mr020w
Bridget	05	F	Child	07Mr020w
Margaret	03	F	Child	07Mr020w
Maria	.00	F	Infant	07Mr020w
Mary	08	F	Child	07Mr020w
CORRAGAN, James	06	M	Child	07Mr020w
William	36	M	Laborer	07Mr020w
BRIAN, Catherine	19	F	Servant	07Mr020w
ROBERTS, William	27	M	Laborer	07Mr020w
Ellen	20	F	Housekeeper	07Mr020w
SMITH, Ann	18	F	Servant	07Mr020w
SALMON, Bridget	19	F	Servant	07Mr020w
Patrick	16	M	Laborer	07Mr020w
DRURY, John	28	M	Shoemaker	07Mr020w
WHALEN, Patrick	28	M	Shoemaker	07Mr020w
ROGUE, Timothy	24	M	Shoemaker	07Mr020w

WEST-POINT 07 MARCH 1848

From Liverpool

NAMES OF PASSENGERS		AGE	SEX	OCCUPATIONS	DATE PORT SHIP
GLESON, John		30	M	Laborer	07Mr02Sg
Mary		30	F	Relative	07Mr02Sg
U		.00	U	Infant	07Mr02Sg
ONEAL, William		20	M	Laborer	07Mr02Sg
KAINE, Mary		36	F	Servant	07Mr02Sg
Margt.		11	F	Relative	07Mr02Sg
U		.00	U	Infant	07Mr02Sg
Owen		09	M	Child	07Mr02Sg
Mary		04	F	Child	07Mr02Sg
DRAPER, John		35	M	Laborer	07Mr02Sg
Frances		35	F	Relative	07Mr02Sg
Margaret		08	F	Child	07Mr02Sg
Willy		06	M	Child	07Mr02Sg
Thomas	(S)	04	M	Child	07Mr02Sg
MALONE, Mary		18	F	Servant	07Mr02Sg
NOON, Matt		23	M	Laborer	07Mr02Sg
Anastatia		16	F	None	07Mr02Sg
HALL, John		23	M	Laborer	07Mr02Sg
DUNN, Peter		20	M	Laborer	07Mr02Sg
HALL, Ann		20	F	Servant	07Mr02Sg
HALORAN, Thos.		30	M	Laborer	07Mr02Sg
BURKE, Pat		25	M	Laborer	07Mr02Sg
MCDONNELL, John		21	M	Laborer	07Mr02Sg
KELLY, Patrick		24	M	Laborer	07Mr02Sg
BYRNE, Richard		35	M	Laborer	07Mr02Sg
MCCAFFERY, Jas.		40	M	Laborer	07Mr02Sg
Pat		17	M	Laborer	07Mr02Sg
CONNELLY, Matt		30	M	Butcher	07Mr02Sg
Mary	(W)	30	F	Wife	07Mr02Sg
MACEUSTACE, James		22	M	Teacher	07Mr02Sg
U-Mrs.		35	F	None	07Mr02Sg
Bridget		20	F	None	07Mr02Sg
Charles		13	M	None	07Mr02Sg
Antony		12	M	None	07Mr02Sg
Honora		10	F	None	07Mr02Sg
Eliza		08	F	Child	07Mr02Sg
Joseph		06	M	Child	07Mr02Sg
Catharine		.00	F	Infant	07Mr02Sg
EGAN, Mary		18	F	Servant	07Mr02Sg
NEALSY, William		20	M	Laborer	07Mr02Sg
U	(W)	20	F	Wife	07Mr02Sg
CARROLE, John		45	M	Laborer	07Mr02Sg
STACK, Mary		91	F	None	07Mr02Sg
MENAGH, John		30	M	Laborer	07Mr02Sg
Margt.	(W)	30	F	Wife	07Mr02Sg
QUINN, Augustas		25	M	Servant	07Mr02Sg
CONALLY, Patrick		35	M	Laborer	07Mr02Sg
LOUD, Eliza		24	F	Servant	07Mr02Sg
BRYAN, Eliza-Mary		31	F	Servant	07Mr02Sg
COOK, Mary		20	F	Servant	07Mr02Sg
Catharn.		20	F	Servant	07Mr02Sg
MONAGHAN, Patrick		18	M	Laborer	07Mr02Sg
ATHENSON, Thos.		30	M	Laborer	07Mr02Sg

NAMES OF PASSENGERS		AGE	SEX	OCCUPATIONS	DATE PORT SHIP
ATHENSON, U	(W)	27	F	Wife	07Mr02Sg
U		.00	U	Infant	07Mr02Sg
Margaret	(D)	04	F	Child	07Mr02Sg
Catharin	(D)	02	F	Child	07Mr02Sg
MORRAN, Alexd.		25	M	Laborer	07Mr02Sg
MCGUIR, Wm.		27	M	Laborer	07Mr02Sg
Stewart		16	M	Laborer	07Mr02Sg
MAXWELL, Edward		22	M	Laborer	07Mr02Sg
OBRIEN, James		45	M	Mariner	07Mr02Sg
U	(W)	30	F	Wife	07Mr02Sg
James	(S)	06	M	Child	07Mr02Sg
CURRAN, Bryan		20	M	Shoemaker	07Mr02Sg
KEEGAN, Thomas		40	M	Laborer	07Mr02Sg
Bo--		16	M	Relative	07Mr02Sg
Margaret	(D)	13	F	Relative	07Mr02Sg
Mary	(D)	15	F	Relative	07Mr02Sg
CONNOR, Eliza		20	F	Servant	07Mr02Sg
KEEGAN, Patt.		36	M	Laborer	07Mr02Sg
Mary		36	F	Relative	07Mr02Sg
U		.00	U	Infant	07Mr02Sg
Rose		34	F	None	07Mr02Sg
James		13	M	None	07Mr02Sg
Laurence		11	M	None	07Mr02Sg
William		09	M	Child	07Mr02Sg
John		07	M	Child	07Mr02Sg
Margaret		05	F	Child	07Mr02Sg
Michael		16	M	None	07Mr02Sg
OAKLEY, H.P.		22	M	Painter	07Mr02Sg
WALSH, Bernard		40	M	Molder	07Mr02Sg
LODGE, William		50	M	Weaver	07Mr02Sg
William		17	M	Relative	07Mr02Sg
Richard	(S)	19	M	Relative	07Mr02Sg
Bridget	(D)	10	F	Relative	07Mr02Sg
BURKE, William		30	M	Weaver	07Mr02Sg
MCLEE, James		34	M	Laborer	07Mr02Sg
U	(W)	35	F	Wife	07Mr02Sg
U		.00	U	Infant	07Mr02Sg
CARROL, John		23	M	Laborer	07Mr02Sg
FITZSIMONS, Micheal		22	M	Laborer	07Mr02Sg
BYRNE, Patt.		22	M	Laborer	07Mr02Sg
GARLAND, Ann		17	F	Servant	07Mr02Sg
KELLY, John		30	M	Laborer	07Mr02Sg
DUNNAYRAN, Chas.		25	M	Laborer	07Mr02Sg
BUNARD, Thos.		34	M	Laborer	07Mr02Sg
U	(W)	28	F	Wife	07Mr02Sg
U		.00	U	Infant	07Mr02Sg
Patrick	(S)	03	M	Child	07Mr02Sg
Micheal		25	M	None	07Mr02Sg
GARREN, Bridget		24	F	Servant	07Mr02Sg
NAUGHTON, Margaret		24	F	Servant	07Mr02Sg
MOONEY, Thos.		23	M	Laborer	07Mr02Sg
NEWMAN, Micheal		22	M	Laborer	07Mr02Sg
GARY, John		23	M	Laborer	07Mr02Sg
DRUMMAN, John		30	M	Laborer	07Mr02Sg
Margaret		27	F	Relative	07Mr02Sg
U		.00	U	Infant	07Mr02Sg
HALLORAN, John		30	M	Baker	07Mr02Sg
FITZPERMICK, William		40	M	Laborer	07Mr02Sg
Judy		14	F	None	07Mr02Sg
Thos.		11	M	None	07Mr02Sg
YORK, Jas.		25	M	Joiner	07Mr02Sg
CATING, Dan		33	M	Stone Mason	07Mr02Sg
Honora	(W)	28	F	Wife	07Mr02Sg
Died-At-Sea					
Tim	(S)	06	M	Child	07Mr02Sg
Dancie	(S)	03	M	Child	07Mr02Sg
Bridget	(D)	02	F	Child	07Mr02Sg
DENNIS, William		28	M	Laborer	07Mr02Sg
Mary	(W)	26	F	Wife	07Mr02Sg
MOONEY, Nichl.		25	M	Laborer	07Mr02Sg
LARKEN, Jas.		21	M	Mason	07Mr02Sg
DOUGHTY, William		23	M	Laborer	07Mr02Sg
CROSSAN, William		36	M	Laborer	07Mr02Sg
Ann	(W)	30	F	Wife	07Mr02Sg
William	(S)	10	M	Relative	07Mr02Sg

NAMES OF PASSENGERS		AGE	SEX	OCCUPATIONS	DATE PORT SHIP
WARD, Mary		18	F	Servant	07Mr02Sg
LYNCH, Cathairn		18	F	Servant	07Mr02Sg
BRYAN, John		26	M	Laborer	07Mr02Sg
Micheal		22	M	Laborer	07Mr02Sg
HARKIN, Dennis		18	M	Laborer	07Mr02Sg
MCCARRON, Nancy		16	F	Servant	07Mr02Sg
SMITH, Bernard		30	M	Shoemaker	07Mr02Sg
Thomas		26	F	Laborer	07Mr02Sg
Mary		20	F	Servant	07Mr02Sg
TRACY, Martin		22	M	Servant	07Mr02Sg
MCGUIRE, John		30	M	Laborer	07Mr02Sg
Bridget	(W)	19	F	Wife	07Mr02Sg
FLOOD, Patrick		45	M	Laborer	07Mr02Sg
FLYNN, Jas.		26	M	Laborer	07Mr02Sg
Biddy	(W)	20	F	Wife	07Mr02Sg
DEVINE, John		19	M	Tailor	07Mr02Sg
WHALON, Margt.		10	F	Servant	07Mr02Sg
Mary		18	F	Servant	07Mr02Sg
ROWLAND, Daniel		28	M	Laborer	07Mr02Sg
James		24	M	Laborer	07Mr02Sg
FAGAN, Pat		35	M	Laborer	07Mr02Sg
BROCK, John		30	M	Laborer	07Mr02Sg
U	(W)	27	F	Wife	07Mr02Sg
KEATING, Kinney		35	F	Relative	07Mr02Sg
Hugh	(S)	07	M	Child	07Mr02Sg
Mary	(D)	05	F	Child	07Mr02Sg
Michael	(S)	.00	M	Infant	07Mr02Sg
SHERIDAN, John		20	M	Laborer	07Mr02Sg
AYTON, James		26	M	Laborer	07Mr02Sg
Marie	(W)	24	F	Wife	07Mr02Sg
DOLAN, Pat		30	M	Laborer	07Mr02Sg
JONES, Henry		26	M	Laborer	07Mr02Sg
U	(W)	22	F	Wife	07Mr02Sg
U		.00	U	Infant	07Mr02Sg
Mary-Jane	(D)	04	F	Child	07Mr02Sg
SCANLIN, James		25	M	Plasterer	07Mr02Sg
U	(W)	18	F	Wife	07Mr02Sg
DOGHERTY, Patrick		21	M	Laborer	07Mr02Sg
Sally	(W)	23	F	Wife	07Mr02Sg
Biddy		18	F	None	07Mr02Sg
KELLY, Hannah		26	F	None	07Mr02Sg
DEEGAN, John		25	M	Laborer	07Mr02Sg
WHEELAN, Patt.		25	M	Laborer	07Mr02Sg
DOOLAN, John		25	M	Blacksmith	07Mr02Sg
Maria	(W)	25	F	Wife	07Mr02Sg
SMITH, Johanna		25	F	Servant	07Mr02Sg
HOGAN, Biddy		25	F	Servant	07Mr02Sg
MULLENS, John		40	M	Gdnr	07Mr02Sg
RABBITT, Bridget		19	F	Servant	07Mr02Sg
SLOAN, Christoph		25	M	Laborer	07Mr02Sg
FITZPATRICK, Micheal		19	M	Laborer	07Mr02Sg
Ann		12	F	None	07Mr02Sg
BRADY, Ann		14	F	None	07Mr02Sg
LIDDEN, Peter		25	M	Laborer	07Mr02Sg
MCNAMARA, Eliza		20	F	Servant	07Mr02Sg
MCCARTY, Daniel		35	M	Mariner	07Mr02Sg
BLESSING, Frances		25	M	Laborer	07Mr02Sg
Peter		18	M	Laborer	07Mr02Sg
FITZPATRICK, Cath.		30	F	Servant	07Mr02Sg
MCGOVERN, James		55	M	Weaver	07Mr02Sg
Catharin		40	F	Relative	07Mr02Sg
Jane		11	F	None	07Mr02Sg
John		09	M	Child	07Mr02Sg
Died-At-Sea					
JENNINGS, Richard		20	M	Laborer	07Mr02Sg
Edward		10	M	Laborer	07Mr02Sg
MCANULTY, Jas.		26	M	Laborer	07Mr02Sg
Ester		20	F	None	07Mr02Sg
KELLY, Judy		20	F	None	07Mr02Sg
MCMAHON, John		19	M	Laborer	07Mr02Sg
CRUDDEN, Frances		24	M	Laborer	07Mr02Sg
MULLIN, Felix		21	M	Laborer	07Mr02Sg
LEVAHAN, Daniel		08	M	Child	07Mr02Sg
MCCARTHY, Jas.		23	M	Laborer	07Mr02Sg
CALLAGHAN, Mary		19	F	Servant	07Mr02Sg

NAMES OF PASSENGERS	AGE	SEX	OCCUPATIONS	DATE PORT SHIP
MURPHY, Bridget	20	F	Servant	07Mr02Sg
GORMLEY, Thomas	26	M	Laborer	07Mr02Sg
LYNCH, Edward	29	M	Laborer	07Mr02Sg
WALSH, Ellen	20	F	Servant	07Mr02Sg
FALVEY, John	26	M	Laborer	07Mr02Sg
MCGUIRE, Hugh	25	M	Laborer	07Mr02Sg
James	21	M	Laborer	07Mr02Sg
HARKNESS, Jas.	50	M	Tailor	07Mr02Sg
U	40	F	Relative	07Mr02Sg
James	20	M	None	07Mr02Sg
George	16	M	None	07Mr02Sg
Charlott	14	F	None	07Mr02Sg
Thomas	09	M	Child	07Mr02Sg
WARD, Ellen	22	F	None	07Mr02Sg
FAGHEY, Mary	26	F	None	07Mr02Sg
KEARNS, Biddy	22	F	None	07Mr02Sg
SWEENEY, Thomas	30	M	Laborer	07Mr02Sg
U (W)	26	F	Wife	07Mr02Sg
ONEAL, Patrick	45	M	Laborer	07Mr02Sg
Winney	22	M	Laborer	07Mr02Sg
MAHER, John	16	M	Laborer	07Mr02Sg
NULTY, Bernard	26	M	Laborer	07Mr02Sg
CLARK, Micheal	22	M	Laborer	07Mr02Sg
SHANLY, Terence	21	M	Laborer	07Mr02Sg
CASEY, John	20	M	Laborer	07Mr02Sg
MCLAUGHLIN, Cath.	16	F	Servant	07Mr02Sg
RYAN, Martin	22	M	Laborer	07Mr02Sg
Patrick	21	M	Laborer	07Mr02Sg
LAW, John	24	M	Laborer	07Mr02Sg
DOYLE, Elicia	20	F	Servant	07Mr02Sg
DEWHOR, Maria	05	F	Child	07Mr02Sg
JOYCE, Micheal	26	M	Laborer	07Mr02Sg
KEATING, Hugh	40	M	Laborer	07Mr02Sg
LEDWORTH, Hiram	20	M	Laborer	07Mr02Sg
STARKEY, William	00	M	Unknown	07Mr02Sg
MCCORMICK, Richard	00	E	Unknown	07Mr02Sg

LOUISIANA 13 MARCH 1848

From Liverpool

NAMES OF PASSENGERS	AGE	SEX	OCCUPATIONS	DATE PORT SHIP
SARAN, Pat	18	M	Laborer	13Mr02Nq
COUNE, Roger	30	M	Laborer	13Mr02Nq
GIBNEY, John	24	M	Laborer	13Mr02Nq
LEDDY, Owen	20	M	Laborer	13Mr02Nq
Mary	10	F	None	13Mr02Nq
Ann	12	F	None	13Mr02Nq
TULLY, Mary	30	F	None	13Mr02Nq
Maria	08	F	Child	13Mr02Nq
NOONE, Thomas	20	M	Laborer	13Mr02Nq
COFFIN, Mary	19	F	Laborer	13Mr02Nq
CARRALL, Thomas	20	M	Laborer	13Mr02Nq
BRADY, Catharin	24	F	Laborer	13Mr02Nq
FLYNN, John	20	M	None	13Mr02Nq
Patrick	13	M	None	13Mr02Nq
James	10	M	None	13Mr02Nq
Bridgett	07	F	Child	13Mr02Nq
DAWSON, William	25	M	None	13Mr02Nq
James	30	M	None	13Mr02Nq
Johanna	36	F	None	13Mr02Nq
Matthew	01	M	Child	13Mr02Nq
REILEY, Owen	26	M	Laborer	13Mr02Nq
FLANAGAN, Thomas	16	M	Laborer	13Mr02Nq
Michael	14	M	Laborer	13Mr02Nq
Bridget	10	F	None	13Mr02Nq
CARTY, Johanna	22	F	None	13Mr02Nq
MILEGAN, John	29	M	None	13Mr02Nq
HICKEY, Sarah	20	F	None	13Mr02Nq
FARRELL, John	26	M	None	13Mr02Nq
HAYES, Charles	21	M	None	13Mr02Nq
GROGAN, Christn.	50	M	Laborer	13Mr02Nq
Ann	50	F	None	13Mr02Nq
Catherin	18	F	None	13Mr02Nq
John	15	M	None	13Mr02Nq
Ann	13	F	None	13Mr02Nq
Mary	10	F	None	13Mr02Nq
HAND, Ann	28	F	None	13Mr02Nq
MARTIN, Biddy	30	F	None	13Mr02Nq
Margrett	03	F	Child	13Mr02Nq
Michael	05	M	Child	13Mr02Nq
Peter	.00	M	Infant	13Mr02Nq
IRVINE, Alexander	25	M	Merchant	13Mr02Nq
CUMMINGS, John	20	M	Merchant	13Mr02Nq
Christina	24	F	None	13Mr02Nq
DUFFY, John	20	M	Laborer	13Mr02Nq
Mary	30	F	None	13Mr02Nq
HARRINGTON, Jerry	28	M	Mechanic	13Mr02Nq
MANIGHAN, Edward	30	M	Mechanic	13Mr02Nq
Mary	30	F	None	13Mr02Nq
Mary	.00	F	Infant	13Mr02Nq
GILL, Hannah	23	F	Servant	13Mr02Nq
CURLY, Edward	27	M	Servant	13Mr02Nq
CROOK, Henry	18	M	Mechanic	13Mr02Nq
MONEGAN, Rose	23	F	Servant	13Mr02Nq
MCGOVERN, Bernard	24	M	Laborer	13Mr02Nq
OHARRA, Patk.	24	M	Laborer	13Mr02Nq
Catharine	20	F	None	13Mr02Nq
KNELSON, Betty	22	F	None	13Mr02Nq
DUNLEVY, Thomas	49	M	Laborer	13Mr02Nq
KOUGH, Edward	24	M	Laborer	13Mr02Nq
REILEY, Judy	40	F	None	13Mr02Nq
DALEY, Ann	07	F	Child	13Mr02Nq
INVELROY, Mary	09	F	Child	13Mr02Nq
OBRIEN, James	26	M	Laborer	13Mr02Nq
SALMON, Daniel	34	M	Laborer	13Mr02Nq
SHAW, Robert	32	M	Laborer	13Mr02Nq
KING, James	16	M	Laborer	13Mr02Nq
JOHNSON, James	32	M	Laborer	13Mr02Nq
Bridget	30	F	None	13Mr02Nq
MULLEN, Julia	30	F	None	13Mr02Nq
JOHNSON, James	04	M	Child	13Mr02Nq
HOPKINS, Hugh	31	M	Mechanic	13Mr02Nq
Sally	19	F	None	13Mr02Nq
FITZSIMONS, Pat.	25	M	Mechanic	13Mr02Nq
MILLAY, Pat.	15	M	None	13Mr02Nq
Thomas	10	M	None	13Mr02Nq
Mary	12	F	None	13Mr02Nq
REDMOND, William	20	M	Laborer	13Mr02Nq
HARRINGTON, Pat	20	M	Laborer	13Mr02Nq
HAGARTY, Thoms.	26	M	Laborer	13Mr02Nq
MATHEWS, Peter	23	M	Laborer	13Mr02Nq
MURRAY, Edward	28	M	Laborer	13Mr02Nq
DEARVAW, Charles	26	M	Laborer	13Mr02Nq
BOURKET, Lawrance	22	M	Mechanic	13Mr02Nq
NELSON, Mathew	19	M	Mechanic	13Mr02Nq
HANLON, Charlotte	20	F	None	13Mr02Nq
DONLON, Pat	19	M	None	13Mr02Nq
John	15	M	None	13Mr02Nq
Mary	12	F	None	13Mr02Nq
James	06	M	Child	13Mr02Nq
MURRAY, Henry	30	M	Mechanic	13Mr02Nq
MCCARTY, J.	40	M	Laborer	13Mr02Nq
Bridget	30	F	None	13Mr02Nq
John	06	M	Child	13Mr02Nq
Michl.	06	M	Child	13Mr02Nq
KELLY, Nancy	30	F	None	13Mr02Nq
HARRIS, Bridget	20	F	None	13Mr02Nq
DURKAN, Mary-Ann	20	F	None	13Mr02Nq
KELLY, Bridget	05	F	Child	13Mr02Nq
John	.00	M	Infant	13Mr02Nq
BARRY, John	25	M	Laborer	13Mr02Nq
MCGOVERN, Michael	30	M	Laborer	13Mr02Nq
KENNY, James	30	M	Laborer	13Mr02Nq
ARMSTRONG, Robt.	37	M	Mechanic	13Mr02Nq

NAMES OF PASSENGERS	AGE	SEX	OCCUPATIONS	DATE PORT SHIP
ARMSTRONG, George	05	M	Child	13Mr02Nq
HOGAN, Pat	22	M	Mechanic	13Mr02Nq
MCGUIRE, Mary	19	F	None	13Mr02Nq
SORLAY, Ellen	18	F	None	13Mr02Nq
CARROLL, James	26	M	Laborer	13Mr02Nq
DURN, Quinlan	30	M	Laborer	13Mr02Nq
MCSHEA, James	30	M	Laborer	13Mr02Nq
CORR, Edward	23	M	Laborer	13Mr02Nq
WALKER, Charles	23	M	Laborer	13Mr02Nq
OSHANNLEY, Margarett	30	F	None	13Mr02Nq
WALKER, Ann	25	F	Unknown	13Mr02Nq
HETHERTON, George	17	M	None	13Mr02Nq
LYNCH, Ann	21	F	None	13Mr02Nq
FLYNN, Catharin	23	F	None	13Mr02Nq
JOHNSON, Robt.	.00	M	Infant	13Mr02Nq
Died-At-Sea				
BARSTON, Nath.	.00	M	Infant	13Mr02Nq
Died-At-Sea				

MEMNON 13 MARCH 1848

From Liverpool

NAMES OF PASSENGERS	AGE	SEX	OCCUPATIONS	DATE PORT SHIP
COMMONS, James	20	M	Laborer	13Mr02Gd
MARSAY, John	28	M	Laborer	13Mr02Gd
JONES, John	13	M	Laborer	13Mr02Gd
TELSON, Henry	24	M	Laborer	13Mr02Gd
MORRIS, David	35	M	Laborer	13Mr02Gd
SMITH, Mary	40	F	Laborer	13Mr02Gd
Rose	05	F	Child	13Mr02Gd
CLARK, John	13	M	Unknown	13Mr02Gd
FLOOD, Ann	16	F	Unknown	13Mr02Gd
CLARK, Pat	18	M	Unknown	13Mr02Gd
COOK, John	26	M	Joiner	13Mr02Gd
WHITE, Edmond	27	M	Shoemaker	13Mr02Gd
HINCLIFF, John	26	M	Tailor	13Mr02Gd
Rebecka	56	F	Unknown	13Mr02Gd
Elen-Emily	15	F	Unknown	13Mr02Gd
GRAY, Anthony	27	M	Weaver	13Mr02Gd
TOOL, Cathrine	31	F	Unknown	13Mr02Gd
PARBIT, Thomas	23	M	Unknown	13Mr02Gd
KEMP, John	17	M	Unknown	13Mr02Gd
MCGEAGH, Partrick	20	M	Unknown	13Mr02Gd
GIBSON, Edward	22	M	Machinist	13Mr02Gd
HANCLIFF, Edward	05	M	Child	13Mr02Gd
SMITH, Wm.	40	M	Spinner	13Mr02Gd
HODSON, John	40	M	Butcher	13Mr02Gd
RYAN, Pat	17	M	Unknown	13Mr02Gd
ONEIL, James	27	M	Mason	13Mr02Gd
RUDDY, Mary	24	F	Unknown	13Mr02Gd
MOONY, John	35	M	Unknown	13Mr02Gd
John	12	M	Unknown	13Mr02Gd
MULIGAN, Ann	13	F	Unknown	13Mr02Gd
PEPPER, Charles	21	M	Bookbinder	13Mr02Gd
FORD, John	38	M	Tailor	13Mr02Gd
BARLOW, Wm.	25	M	Type Cutter	13Mr02Gd
ELLIS, John	29	M	Machinist	13Mr02Gd
BROADBENT, George	24	M	Machinist	13Mr02Gd
ALLAN, Wm.	28	M	Tailor	13Mr02Gd
Teresa	20	F	Unknown	13Mr02Gd
Catherine	04	F	Child	13Mr02Gd
Elen	.10	F	Infant	13Mr02Gd
Teresa	02	F	Child	13Mr02Gd
MOONY, Christopher	20	M	Unknown	13Mr02Gd
Elizabeth	22	F	Unknown	13Mr02Gd
MARTIN, Elizabeth	25	F	Unknown	13Mr02Gd
Hugh	03	M	Child	13Mr02Gd
GERETY, Peter	22	M	Unknown	13Mr02Gd
Mary	21	F	Unknown	13Mr02Gd
FLANAGAN, Cathrine	20	F	Unknown	13Mr02Gd
RYLEY, Phillip	45	M	Butcher	13Mr02Gd
Charles	17	M	Unknown	13Mr02Gd
ROAX, Honor	18	F	Unknown	13Mr02Gd
Mary	16	F	Unknown	13Mr02Gd
BRADLEY, Isaia	22	M	Blacksmith	13Mr02Gd
MONAHAN, Margaret	20	F	Unknown	13Mr02Gd
MCDURMET, Thomas	24	M	Unknown	13Mr02Gd
Margaret	20	F	Unknown	13Mr02Gd
SAVAGE, Bridget	20	F	Unknown	13Mr02Gd
MCDURMOT, Mary	25	F	Unknown	13Mr02Gd
MACKCAY, Micheal	40	M	Tailor	13Mr02Gd
DENAGHY, Mary	18	F	Unknown	13Mr02Gd
FOLY, Mary	12	F	Unknown	13Mr02Gd
SMITH, Henry	30	M	Unknown	13Mr02Gd
NOLAN, Margaret	20	F	Unknown	13Mr02Gd
Pat	19	M	Unknown	13Mr02Gd
COLIHAN, Margaret	10	F	Unknown	13Mr02Gd
BASSIL, John	17	M	Unknown	13Mr02Gd
MCBRIDE, Peter	18	M	Unknown	13Mr02Gd
DOUGHERTY, Elen	12	F	Unknown	13Mr02Gd
TIEF, Cathrine	50	F	Unknown	13Mr02Gd
James	22	M	Unknown	13Mr02Gd
GRIFFITH, Thomas	22	M	Unknown	13Mr02Gd
MCQUADE, Henry	35	M	Unknown	13Mr02Gd
Rose-Ann	25	F	Unknown	13Mr02Gd
Patrick	06	M	Child	13Mr02Gd
Henry	02	M	Child	13Mr02Gd
ONEIL, John	35	M	Tanner	13Mr02Gd
COLLINS, Jeremiah	21	M	Unknown	13Mr02Gd
SMITH, Biddy	14	F	Unknown	13Mr02Gd
HOGAN, Pat	60	M	Butcher	13Mr02Gd
Margaret	60	F	Unknown	13Mr02Gd
Jane	16	F	Unknown	13Mr02Gd
Pat	10	M	Unknown	13Mr02Gd
Elen	04	F	Child	13Mr02Gd
CRAIG, Eliza	34	F	Unknown	13Mr02Gd
Ann	.10	F	Infant	13Mr02Gd
MAGENIS, Honor	40	F	Unknown	13Mr02Gd
JENINGS, Mary	30	F	Unknown	13Mr02Gd
CLARK, Ann	26	F	Milliner	13Mr02Gd
Mary	21	F	Unknown	13Mr02Gd
GORTHY, Robert	27	M	Rope Maker	13Mr02Gd
DRANSFIELD, Wm.	21	M	Unknown	13Mr02Gd
CRIBBIN, James	30	M	Unknown	13Mr02Gd
Died-At-Sea				
Bridget	25	F	Unknown	13Mr02Gd
Thomas	02	M	Child	13Mr02Gd
James	.00	M	Infant	13Mr02Gd
Born-At-Sea				
CLINES, Sally	18	F	Unknown	13Mr02Gd
ROBINSON, Wm.	28	M	Spinner	13Mr02Gd
MARYGRAVE, Richard	27	M	Stctr	13Mr02Gd
MARSHALL, Mathew	22	M	Joiner	13Mr02Gd
CONSTANTINE, Robert	40	M	Wool Comber	13Mr02Gd
Sarah	26	F	Unknown	13Mr02Gd
SEATON, Mark	16	M	Machinist	13Mr02Gd
HOLT, Samuel	25	M	Spinner	13Mr02Gd
GERETY, Thomas	32	M	Unknown	13Mr02Gd
Sibeny	25	F	Unknown	13Mr02Gd
Mary	20	F	Unknown	13Mr02Gd
Margaret	23	F	Unknown	13Mr02Gd
Owen	04	M	Child	13Mr02Gd
Sally	03	F	Child	13Mr02Gd
Thomas	23	M	Unknown	13Mr02Gd
MALONEY, John	30	M	Unknown	13Mr02Gd
MONAHAN, Domnick	25	M	Unknown	13Mr02Gd
Elen	20	F	Unknown	13Mr02Gd
Micheal	26	M	Unknown	13Mr02Gd
HOPKINS, John	27	M	Unknown	13Mr02Gd
Ann	24	F	Unknown	13Mr02Gd
John	04	M	Child	13Mr02Gd
Peter	02	M	Child	13Mr02Gd
U	.00	M	Infant	13Mr02Gd
Born-At-Sea				

NAMES OF PASSENGERS	AGE	SEX	OCCUPATIONS	DATE PORT SHIP
HOPKINS, Christopher	27	M	Unknown	13Mr02Gd
KEPER, David	32	M	Weaver	13Mr02Gd
BROWN, David	24	M	Unknown	13Mr02Gd
Charles	32	M	Unknown	13Mr02Gd
PICK, Thomas	26	M	Unknown	13Mr02Gd
Sarah	26	F	Unknown	13Mr02Gd
BRYNE, Patrick	24	M	Unknown	13Mr02Gd
FANNING, John	20	M	Unknown	13Mr02Gd
Bridget	20	F	Unknown	13Mr02Gd
James	.00	M	Infant	13Mr02Gd
PETERS, Stephen	50	M	Tailor	13Mr02Gd
Joana	20	F	Unknown	13Mr02Gd
Elen	18	F	Unknown	13Mr02Gd
CARROL, Thomas	45	M	Unknown	13Mr02Gd
Margaret	20	F	Unknown	13Mr02Gd
FLETCHER, John	28	M	Unknown	13Mr02Gd
Sarah	22	F	Unknown	13Mr02Gd
James	.11	M	Infant	13Mr02Gd
FANNING, John	20	M	Unknown	13Mr02Gd
DOOLAN, Pat	25	M	Unknown	13Mr02Gd
Juda	20	F	Unknown	13Mr02Gd
FANNING, James	25	M	Unknown	13Mr02Gd
SLATERRY, Bridget	25	F	Unknown	13Mr02Gd
RYAN, Mary	20	F	Unknown	13Mr02Gd
FOGARTY, Wm.	25	M	Unknown	13Mr02Gd
FLETCHER, James	25	M	Unknown	13Mr02Gd
Cathrine	20	F	Unknown	13Mr02Gd
WOODS, Henry	22	M	Unknown	13Mr02Gd
TAYLER, Betsy	50	F	Unknown	13Mr02Gd
Betsy	09	F	Child	13Mr02Gd
BRENAN, Richard	24	M	Unknown	13Mr02Gd
NAUGHTON, Thos.	17	M	Unknown	13Mr02Gd
COLLIGAN, Owen	18	M	Unknown	13Mr02Gd
BAKER, Wm.	17	M	Unknown	13Mr02Gd
CORMICK, Ellen	20	F	Unknown	13Mr02Gd
CHALENGER, Samuel	40	M	Unknown	13Mr02Gd
TAYLOR, Wm.	25	M	Unknown	13Mr02Gd
CHAPMAN, Wm.J.	21	M	Gentleman	13Mr02Gd

CAMBRIA 18 MARCH 1848

From Liverpool

NAMES OF PASSENGERS	AGE	SEX	OCCUPATIONS	DATE PORT SHIP
MARIS, Andrew	34	M	Merchant	18Mr02Es
MCCLEAN, Wm.H.	27	M	Merchant	18Mr02Es
HALLEWELL, Edmund-G.	26	M	Army	18Mr02Es
MAJOR, R.	42	M	Merchant	18Mr02Es
SMITH, Wm.	23	M	Merchant	18Mr02Es
BROADBEAT, Charles	21	M	Merchant	18Mr02Es
ILLINS, Charles	40	M	Merchant	18Mr02Es
PORTER, G.M.	43	M	Merchant	18Mr02Es
GILLON, Robert	22	M	Merchant	18Mr02Es
HEEDSON, Jos.	50	M	Merchant	18Mr02Es
TAYLOR, Wm.	36	M	Merchant	18Mr02Es
RAMSDEN, David	32	M	Merchant	18Mr02Es
Fredk.	56	M	Merchant	18Mr02Es
OSHAUGHESSY, Jno.	29	M	Engineer	18Mr02Es

JAMESTOWN 20 MARCH 1848

From Liverpool

NAMES OF PASSENGERS	AGE	SEX	OCCUPATIONS	DATE PORT SHIP
DOWNAY, Martin	49	M	Laborer	20Mr02Gf
Michael	20	M	Laborer	20Mr02Gf
DOWLING, Mary	40	F	Servant	20Mr02Gf
Margaret	22	F	Servant	20Mr02Gf
Honora	18	F	Servant	20Mr02Gf
Bridget	16	F	Servant	20Mr02Gf
Ann	12	F	Servant	20Mr02Gf
James	11	M	Unknown	20Mr02Gf
BURKE, Catherine	18	F	Servant	20Mr02Gf
Ann	17	F	Servant	20Mr02Gf
MURRAY, James	25	M	Smith	20Mr02Gf
RILEY, John	30	M	Mason	20Mr02Gf
CARROLL, Patrick	25	M	Laborer	20Mr02Gf
Died-At-Sea				
MANION, Patrick	24	M	Laborer	20Mr02Gf
DAILY, William	24	M	Laborer	20Mr02Gf
Allicia	25	F	Servant	20Mr02Gf
Sarah	17	F	Servant	20Mr02Gf
Eliza	16	F	None	20Mr02Gf
Catherine	.00	F	Infant	20Mr02Gf
Thomas	12	M	Unknown	20Mr02Gf
BARRY, John	32	M	Farmer	20Mr02Gf
Mary	30	F	Unknown	20Mr02Gf
BURKE, Ann	20	F	Servant	20Mr02Gf
Died-At-Sea				
BERRY, Robert	05	M	Child	20Mr02Gf
John	04	M	Child	20Mr02Gf
Mary	.00	F	Infant	20Mr02Gf
MADDER, Michael	18	M	Laborer	20Mr02Gf
MANION, John	18	M	Laborer	20Mr02Gf
BILLING, Patrick	40	M	Farmer	20Mr02Gf
Rose	41	F	Unknown	20Mr02Gf
U	.00	U	Infant	20Mr02Gf
Born-At-Sea				
James	20	M	Farmer	20Mr02Gf
John	15	M	Farmer	20Mr02Gf
Mary	12	F	Unknown	20Mr02Gf
Catherine	10	F	Unknown	20Mr02Gf
Clare	02	F	Child	20Mr02Gf
Patrick	04	M	Child	20Mr02Gf
Magaret	07	F	Child	20Mr02Gf
MOORE, Mary	22	F	Servant	20Mr02Gf
BILLING, Francis	18	M	Farmer	20Mr02Gf
MCGERETY, James	35	M	Laborer	20Mr02Gf
Bridget	30	F	Unknown	20Mr02Gf
Patrick	19	M	Laborer	20Mr02Gf
Michael	09	M	Child	20Mr02Gf
Bernard	05	M	Child	20Mr02Gf
James	02	M	Child	20Mr02Gf
John	.00	M	Infant	20Mr02Gf
REILLY, Thomas	50	M	Laborer	20Mr02Gf
Mary	45	F	Unknown	20Mr02Gf
BELLEW, Matthew	21	M	Farmer	20Mr02Gf
MAHONY, Denis	27	M	Carpenter	20Mr02Gf
Ann	23	F	Wife	20Mr02Gf
Bridget	.00	F	Infant	20Mr02Gf
SEARSE, Edward	26	M	Painter	20Mr02Gf
MCDOUGAL, Michael	26	M	Laborer	20Mr02Gf
Margaret	26	F	Cook	20Mr02Gf
Philip	.00	M	Infant	20Mr02Gf
GULSHINA, John	41	M	Laborer	20Mr02Gf
Ann	40	F	Unknown	20Mr02Gf
Patrick	12	M	Unknown	20Mr02Gf
Thomas	10	M	Unknown	20Mr02Gf
Margaret	06	F	Child	20Mr02Gf

NAMES OF PASSENGERS	AGE	SEX	OCCUPATIONS	DATE PORT SHIP
GULSHINA, Ann	.00	F	Infant	20Mr02Gf
BRADY, Mary	20	F	Servant	20Mr02Gf
MAHON, James	32	M	Laborer	20Mr02Gf
Thomas	35	M	Laborer	20Mr02Gf
HEALY, Mary	40	F	Servant	20Mr02Gf
Margaret	20	F	Servant	20Mr02Gf
John	12	M	Unknown	20Mr02Gf
Anthony	09	M	Child	20Mr02Gf
Michael	04	M	Child	20Mr02Gf
DUGGAN, Patrick	21	M	Farmer	20Mr02Gf
John	22	M	Farmer	20Mr02Gf
Mary	20	F	Dressmaker	20Mr02Gf
Ellen	22	F	Servant	20Mr02Gf
BARRY, Mary	20	F	Cook	20Mr02Gf
IRWING, Joseph	24	M	Painter	20Mr02Gf
Mary	21	F	Unknown	20Mr02Gf
MURPHY, John	33	M	Mason	20Mr02Gf
FITZPATRICK, James	30	M	Laborer	20Mr02Gf
William	28	M	Laborer	20Mr02Gf
Peter	20	M	Laborer	20Mr02Gf
Mary	22	F	Cook	20Mr02Gf
CAFFREY, Thomas	17	M	Laborer	20Mr02Gf
FENNEL, Michael	20	M	Laborer	20Mr02Gf
James	19	M	Laborer	20Mr02Gf
Catherine	18	F	Servant	20Mr02Gf
CAIN, Donald	21	M	Laborer	20Mr02Gf
Mary	18	F	Servant	20Mr02Gf
MCNIGHT, Donald	20	M	Laborer	20Mr02Gf
CARTY, William	22	M	Laborer	20Mr02Gf
HUMPHREY, Patrick	30	M	Shoemaker	20Mr02Gf
Patrick	02	M	Child	20Mr02Gf
Ellen	28	F	Unknown	20Mr02Gf
Mary	04	F	Child	20Mr02Gf
CAFFREY, Matthew	47	M	Peddler	20Mr02Gf
CONRONY, Richard	26	M	Smith	20Mr02Gf
MAHON, Sylvan	26	M	Laborer	20Mr02Gf
CORLES, Patrick	45	M	Merchant	20Mr02Gf
Joseph	10	M	Unknown	20Mr02Gf
FITZPATRICK, Patrick	40	M	Laborer	20Mr02Gf
Ann	35	F	Unknown	20Mr02Gf
Ann	27	F	Servant	20Mr02Gf
James	15	M	Unknown	20Mr02Gf
Patrick	12	M	Unknown	20Mr02Gf
QUIN, Francis	32	M	Laborer	20Mr02Gf
COOPER, Charles	20	M	Laborer	20Mr02Gf
LANGIN, Ann	30	F	Servant	20Mr02Gf
Catherine	04	F	Child	20Mr02Gf
Robert	01	M	Child	20Mr02Gf
HOGAN, James	20	M	Laborer	20Mr02Gf
HAMILTON, James	35	M	Fsctr	20Mr02Gf
Jane	30	F	Dressmaker	20Mr02Gf
DIXON, Maria	20	F	Dressmaker	20Mr02Gf
EUSTACE, Patrick	20	M	Laborer	20Mr02Gf
READING, Samuel	44	M	Laborer	20Mr02Gf
John	22	M	Laborer	20Mr02Gf
Thomas	23	M	Laborer	20Mr02Gf
David	21	M	Laborer	20Mr02Gf
NESTON, John	15	M	Laborer	20Mr02Gf
KEEFE, James	30	M	Laborer	20Mr02Gf
Ellen	28	F	Cook	20Mr02Gf
Andrew	01	M	Child	20Mr02Gf
Died-At-Sea				
BURNS, Ann	24	F	Servant	20Mr02Gf
SMITH, John	38	M	Laborer	20Mr02Gf
Bryan	32	M	Laborer	20Mr02Gf
Bridget	08	F	Child	20Mr02Gf
Ellen	30	F	Unknown	20Mr02Gf
Eliza	02	F	Child	20Mr02Gf
GALLIGAN, Patrick	40	M	Laborer	20Mr02Gf
MARTIN, Bridget	20	F	Servant	20Mr02Gf
GIDNEY, Rose	20	F	Servant	20Mr02Gf
MURPHY, Henry	24	M	Laborer	20Mr02Gf
Mary	19	F	Servant	20Mr02Gf
MCSALLY, Peggy	20	F	Servant	20Mr02Gf
Rose	20	F	Servant	20Mr02Gf

NAMES OF PASSENGERS	AGE	SEX	OCCUPATIONS	DATE PORT SHIP
DEARY, Bernard	25	M	Laborer	20Mr02Gf
THORINTON, Judy	20	F	Servant	20Mr02Gf
PAGE, William	35	M	Baker	20Mr02Gf
SMALL, Jane	16	F	Servant	20Mr02Gf
KEEFFE, Jane	17	F	Servant	20Mr02Gf
Andy	40	M	Laborer	20Mr02Gf
William	13	M	Laborer	20Mr02Gf
George	07	M	Child	20Mr02Gf
Winfred	05	M	Child	20Mr02Gf
CUSHALL, James	23	M	Weaver	20Mr02Gf
DUGGAN, Patrick	30	M	Laborer	20Mr02Gf
Catherine	26	F	Servant	20Mr02Gf
Joseph	.00	M	Infant	20Mr02Gf
LAWLER, John	30	M	Laborer	20Mr02Gf
Mary	26	F	Unknown	20Mr02Gf
John	.00	M	Infant	20Mr02Gf
FERRET, Robert	20	M	Laborer	20Mr02Gf
KERR, George	20	M	Farmer	20Mr02Gf
Henry	25	M	Farmer	20Mr02Gf
HAWKES, James	26	M	Farmer	20Mr02Gf
CARROL, Patrick	23	M	Laborer	20Mr02Gf
BELL, William	30	M	Carpenter	20Mr02Gf
Eliza	22	F	Dressmaker	20Mr02Gf
Agnes	15	F	Dressmaker	20Mr02Gf
QUALE, Samuel	40	M	Cbtmkr	20Mr02Gf
MANN, James	30	M	Laborer	20Mr02Gf
Mary	26	F	Dairymaid	20Mr02Gf
MALONE, Eliza	22	F	Dressmaker	20Mr02Gf
SHERIDAN, James	31	M	Farmer	20Mr02Gf
Catherine	18	F	Cook	20Mr02Gf
GLENNIN, Catherine	09	F	Child	20Mr02Gf
MCBRIDE, Thomas	22	M	Farmer	20Mr02Gf
BRIEN, Terence	26	M	Farmer	20Mr02Gf
BOLFE, Edward	35	M	Farmer	20Mr02Gf
FARREL, Rose	35	F	Servant	20Mr02Gf
NEALE, Patrick	33	M	Laborer	20Mr02Gf
RILEY, Oratio	19	M	Clothier	20Mr02Gf
SMITH, Joseph	35	M	Clothier	20Mr02Gf
Cybil	30	F	Unknown	20Mr02Gf
Sarah-Ann	07	F	Child	20Mr02Gf
Ann	03	F	Child	20Mr02Gf
Jabez	05	M	Child	20Mr02Gf
Elijah	01	M	Child	20Mr02Gf
CONNOR, Peter	26	M	Laborer	20Mr02Gf
Eliza	24	F	Servant	20Mr02Gf
ROARKE, Mona	19	F	Servant	20Mr02Gf
Julia	12	F	Servant	20Mr02Gf
Essay	10	F	Servant	20Mr02Gf
WHITE, Mary	19	F	Servant	20Mr02Gf
KNIGHT, Ellen	30	F	Servant	20Mr02Gf
WATERS, James	30	M	Tinsmith	20Mr02Gf
Cath	27	F	Unknown	20Mr02Gf
Mary	.00	F	Infant	20Mr02Gf
CLEMENTS, Rose	07	F	Child	20Mr02Gf
COLMAN, Jane	23	F	Servant	20Mr02Gf
PATHON, Thomas	24	M	Laborer	20Mr02Gf
MCNALTY, Thomas	23	M	Laborer	20Mr02Gf
John	21	M	Laborer	20Mr02Gf
DEMPSEY, Patrick	35	M	Laborer	20Mr02Gf
MCDERMIT, Daniel	24	M	Blacksmith	20Mr02Gf
Catherine	19	F	Unknown	20Mr02Gf
DWYER, James	28	M	Laborer	20Mr02Gf
REYNOLDS, Michaels	19	M	Clerk	20Mr02Gf
DARDIS, Patrick	24	M	Laborer	20Mr02Gf
Thomas	20	M	Laborer	20Mr02Gf
Mary	18	F	Servant	20Mr02Gf
TOOLE, Bridget	30	F	Servant	20Mr02Gf
James	35	M	Laborer	20Mr02Gf
RILEY, Austin	26	M	Laborer	20Mr02Gf
DENISON, Thomas	28	M	Laborer	20Mr02Gf
SHERIDAN, John	21	M	Laborer	20Mr02Gf
RILEY, James	30	M	Laborer	20Mr02Gf
CONNOR, Patrick	30	M	Laborer	20Mr02Gf
COALY, Michael	31	M	Laborer	20Mr02Gf
RITTERICK, Patrick	22	M	Laborer	20Mr02Gf

NAMES OF PASSENGERS	AGE	SEX	OCCUPATIONS	DATE PORT SHIP
FERGUS, John	32	M	Laborer	20Mr02Gf
Bridget	29	F	Servant	20Mr02Gf
FLYNN, Michael	17	M	Butcher	20Mr02Gf
KYLE, Robert	50	M	Farmer	20Mr02Gf
Agnes	55	F	Servant	20Mr02Gf
George	19	M	Farmer	20Mr02Gf
Agnes	12	F	Unknown	20Mr02Gf
Margaret	06	F	Child	20Mr02Gf
Mary	.00	F	Infant	20Mr02Gf
Robert	03	M	Child	20Mr02Gf
RILEY, Catherine	19	F	Servant	20Mr02Gf
HENESSY, Patrick	20	M	Laborer	20Mr02Gf
Andrew	22	M	Laborer	20Mr02Gf
John	25	M	Laborer	20Mr02Gf
CLEMENTS, Mary	40	F	Servant	20Mr02Gf
John	23	M	Laborer	20Mr02Gf
Patrick	17	M	Laborer	20Mr02Gf
Ann	20	F	Servant	20Mr02Gf
CALLIGAN, Mary	44	F	Servant	20Mr02Gf
CLEMENTS, Michael	12	M	Servant	20Mr02Gf
Thomas	09	M	Child	20Mr02Gf
Mary	07	F	Child	20Mr02Gf
Ann	21	F	Servant	20Mr02Gf
RYAN, Denis	18	M	Clerk	20Mr02Gf
Honora	20	F	Cook	20Mr02Gf
TRAYNOR, U-Mrs.	30	F	Dressmaker	20Mr02Gf
MCKEOWN, Pat	30	M	Farmer	20Mr02Gf
Ann	24	F	Unknown	20Mr02Gf
Charles	01	M	Child	20Mr02Gf
BEATTY, Claudius	17	M	Laborer	20Mr02Gf
TURNBULL, John	17	M	Laborer	20Mr02Gf
LEONARD, Antony	20	M	Laborer	20Mr02Gf
MONTGOMERY, Elizabeth	13	F	Servant	20Mr02Gf
COSSY, Ann	14	F	Servant	20Mr02Gf
KENEDY, Alexander	14	M	Unknown	20Mr02Gf
CLURE, Mary	13	F	Servant	20Mr02Gf
KILROY, Patrick	22	M	Laborer	20Mr02Gf
Michael	30	M	Laborer	20Mr02Gf
Mary	18	F	Servant	20Mr02Gf
KILFOYLE, Thomas	28	M	Laborer	20Mr02Gf
GOULDING, Mary	40	F	Unknown	20Mr02Gf
Eliza	08	F	Child	20Mr02Gf
John	35	M	Laborer	20Mr02Gf
James	12	M	Laborer	20Mr02Gf
Frank	06	M	Child	20Mr02Gf
Joseph	04	M	Child	20Mr02Gf
MACKIE, Eliza	12	F	Servant	20Mr02Gf
CONNOLLY, Ann	30	F	Servant	20Mr02Gf
MAHON, Thomas	24	M	Laborer	20Mr02Gf
CLACKIN, Timothy	20	M	Laborer	20Mr02Gf
U, Ellen	20	F	Dressmaker	20Mr02Gf
Jane	18	F	Servant	20Mr02Gf
Mary	22	F	Servant	20Mr02Gf
TURNER, Jane	15	F	Servant	20Mr02Gf
DEVLIN, John	06	M	Child	20Mr02Gf
Mary	07	F	Child	20Mr02Gf
MCKENNA, Patrick	35	M	Laborer	20Mr02Gf
CLINTON, Mary	50	F	Nurse	20Mr02Gf
Patrick	20	M	Mason	20Mr02Gf
Biddy	18	F	Cook	20Mr02Gf
Lawrence	13	M	Mason	20Mr02Gf
Charles	10	M	Mason	20Mr02Gf
Alice	04	F	Child	20Mr02Gf
KENMAN, Michael	22	M	Tinsmith	20Mr02Gf
Honora	19	F	Unknown	20Mr02Gf
HENESSY, James	25	M	Laborer	20Mr02Gf
Catherine	24	F	Unknown	20Mr02Gf
Owen	05	M	Child	20Mr02Gf
RILEY, Andrew	22	M	Laborer	20Mr02Gf
Susan	20	F	Dressmaker	20Mr02Gf
FARRILY, Catherine	17	F	Servant	20Mr02Gf
GOULDING, Henry	21	M	Polisher	20Mr02Gf
EMERS, James	23	M	Laborer	20Mr02Gf
COLLINS, Martin	29	M	Laborer	20Mr02Gf
Michael	20	M	Laborer	20Mr02Gf

NAMES OF PASSENGERS	AGE	SEX	OCCUPATIONS	DATE PORT SHIP
HOGAN, Mary	25	F	Servant	20Mr02Gf
Patrick	.00	M	Infant	20Mr02Gf
MCDONALD, Patrick	30	M	Laborer	20Mr02Gf
Charles	20	M	Laborer	20Mr02Gf

KATE 21 MARCH 1848

From St.JOHNS,N.B.

NAMES OF PASSENGERS	AGE	SEX	OCCUPATIONS	DATE PORT SHIP
FLAHERTY, Michael	45	M	Shpc	21Mr79Ho

PRINCE-ALBERT 22 MARCH 1848

From London

NAMES OF PASSENGERS	AGE	SEX	OCCUPATIONS	DATE PORT SHIP
LOGAN, Patrick	27	M	Laborer	22Mr21Bn
MCALLIGOT, Eugin	31	M	Tailor	22Mr21Bn
David	14	M	None	22Mr21Bn
RIORDEN, Dan	24	M	Tailor	22Mr21Bn
CONNOR, Corn.	23	M	Tailor	22Mr21Bn
Sarah	33	F	Unknown	22Mr21Bn
RIORDAN, Mary	22	F	Unknown	22Mr21Bn
COLEMAN, Wm.	10	M	None	22Mr21Bn
RIORDAN, John	52	M	Tailor	22Mr21Bn
Ann	50	F	Unknown	22Mr21Bn
OKAFF, Patrick	26	M	Laborer	22Mr21Bn
Ann	30	F	None	22Mr21Bn
BOWFIELD, Charlotte	18	F	None	22Mr21Bn
SULLIVAN, Dan	28	M	Tailor	22Mr21Bn
Julia	30	F	Unknown	22Mr21Bn
Jeremiah	02	M	Child	22Mr21Bn
John	.06	M	Infant	22Mr21Bn
KNOWLAND, Julia	36	F	Unknown	22Mr21Bn
SULLIVAN, John	20	M	Laborer	22Mr21Bn
WELSH, Edmond	48	M	Laborer	22Mr21Bn
BIRMINGHAM, Walter	35	M	Laborer	22Mr21Bn
WISS, Levi	25	M	Lace Maker	22Mr21Bn
LYNCH, John	26	M	Laborer	22Mr21Bn
LEARY, James	23	M	Laborer	22Mr21Bn
Jane	28	F	None	22Mr21Bn
Mary	.03	F	Infant	22Mr21Bn
LAVINE, Ellen	24	F	None	22Mr21Bn
BISHOP, Wm.	29	M	Mechanic	22Mr21Bn
Caroline	26	F	Unknown	22Mr21Bn
HULEY, Edm.	26	M	Laborer	22Mr21Bn
PRIARDE, Patr.	37	M	Laborer	22Mr21Bn

SIDDONS 22 MARCH 1848

From Unknown

NAMES OF PASSENGERS	AGE	SEX	OCCUPATIONS	DATE PORT SHIP
MCGOVERN, Chs.	40	M	Laborer	22Mr00Bx
MCHOLLAND, Chs.	48	M	Farmer	22Mr00Bx
Henry	15	M	Farmer	22Mr00Bx
Charles	18	M	Farmer	22Mr00Bx
TURNER, John	26	M	Farmer	22Mr00Bx
HOLDSWORTH, Scholes	26	M	Farmer	22Mr00Bx

NAMES OF PASSENGERS		AGE	SEX	OCCUPATIONS	DATE PORT SHIP
FARRIN, Margt.		24	F	Farmer	22Mr01Bx
PATERS, Patk.		36	M	Mechanic	22Mr01Bx
DOLAN, James		23	M	Mechanic	22Mr01Bx
William		18	M	Mechanic	22Mr01Bx
HUNTER, John		22	M	Mechanic	22Mr01Bx
KELLITT, Eliz.		00	F	Unknown	22Mr01Bx
HEATON, Edward		28	M	Laborer	22Mr01Bx
OVEREND, David		26	M	Laborer	22Mr01Bx
Sarah	(W)	25	F	Laborer	22Mr01Bx
Ann	(D)	03	F	Child	22Mr01Bx
Ruth	(D)	.00	F	Infant	22Mr01Bx
Jonathan		20	M	Laborer	22Mr01Bx
Mary-Ann		22	F	Farmer	22Mr01Bx
BOYS, William		38	M	Farmer	22Mr01Bx
MARRISE, Joseph		30	M	Farmer	22Mr01Bx
BELL, John		20	M	Farmer	22Mr01Bx
LUCAS, Thomas		21	M	Farmer	22Mr01Bx
BEANY, Eliz.		17	F	Farmer	22Mr01Bx
MICHAN, Mich.		21	M	Farmer	22Mr01Bx
CAIN, Denis		35	M	Farmer	22Mr01Bx
BALOY, Joseph		22	M	Farmer	22Mr01Bx
Matilda		24	F	Laborer	22Mr01Bx
STARR, Baxter		24	M	Laborer	22Mr01Bx
Ann		23	F	Laborer	22Mr01Bx
Susana		10	F	Laborer	22Mr01Bx
Amelia		05	F	Child	22Mr01Bx
MALONE, Susan		17	F	Laborer	22Mr01Bx
HYLAND, James		25	M	Laborer	22Mr01Bx
Cath.		24	F	Laborer	22Mr01Bx
SMITH, Eliz.		70	F	Laborer	22Mr01Bx
DELANEY, U-Mrs.		40	F	Laborer	22Mr01Bx
WALSH, John		20	M	Laborer	22Mr01Bx
Wm.		21	M	Laborer	22Mr01Bx
KILLEREDE, Richd.		26	M	Mechanic	22Mr01Bx
MOORE, Joseph		30	M	Mechanic	22Mr01Bx
Martha		30	F	Mechanic	22Mr01Bx
Wm.		05	M	Child	22Mr01Bx
John		04	M	Child	22Mr01Bx
Charlotte		01	F	Child	22Mr01Bx
Wm.		19	M	Mechanic	22Mr01Bx
WILAN, Thos.		24	M	Mechanic	22Mr01Bx
MURRAY, Gilbert		26	M	Mechanic	22Mr01Bx
INGHAM, Nath.		35	M	Mechanic	22Mr01Bx
HARVEY, Terence		35	M	Mechanic	22Mr01Bx
Madge		30	F	Farmer	22Mr01Bx
Mary		20	F	Farmer	22Mr01Bx
Ann		17	F	Farmer	22Mr01Bx
Charlotte		15	F	Farmer	22Mr01Bx
Terence		08	M	Child	22Mr01Bx
James		04	M	Child	22Mr01Bx
Cath.		02	F	Child	22Mr01Bx
CASEY, James		30	M	Farmer	22Mr01Bx
Cath.		22	F	Farmer	22Mr01Bx
Ann		02	F	Child	22Mr01Bx
TRAYNOR, Charles		24	M	Farmer	22Mr01Bx
Mary		20	F	Farmer	22Mr01Bx
James		20	M	Mechanic	22Mr01Bx
Peter		16	M	Mechanic	22Mr01Bx
Cath.		18	F	Mechanic	22Mr01Bx
Brigt.		11	F	Mechanic	22Mr01Bx
Moi--		02	U	Child	22Mr01Bx
DALLEY, James		50	M	Mechanic	22Mr01Bx
Ann		40	F	Mechanic	22Mr01Bx
Ann		12	F	Mechanic	22Mr01Bx
Mary-Ann		10	F	Mechanic	22Mr01Bx
MULLIGAN, Peter		50	M	Mechanic	22Mr01Bx
Maggy		35	F	Mechanic	22Mr01Bx
Ellen		09	F	Child	22Mr01Bx
Chs.		07	M	Child	22Mr01Bx
Maggy		.00	F	Infant	22Mr01Bx
BYRNE, Thomas		16	M	Laborer	22Mr01Bx
Robert		12	M	Laborer	22Mr01Bx
DERMOTT, Jno.M.		25	M	Laborer	22Mr01Bx
GARTY, Cath.		20	F	Laborer	22Mr01Bx
JONES, Robert		23	M	Laborer	22Mr01Bx

NAMES OF PASSENGERS	AGE	SEX	OCCUPATIONS	DATE PORT SHIP
BRYAN, Sarah	24	F	Laborer	22Mr01Bx
ROBINSON, Fred	40	M	Laborer	22Mr01Bx
Charlotte	30	F	Laborer	22Mr01Bx
Fred	11	M	Laborer	22Mr01Bx
SERGEANT, Wm.	30	M	Farmer	22Mr01Bx
JONES, Mary-Ann	30	F	Farmer	22Mr01Bx
DALEY, Brigget	19	F	Farmer	22Mr01Bx
Hugh	16	M	Farmer	22Mr01Bx
FITZGERALD, Mich.	21	M	Farmer	22Mr01Bx
FRACER, Thomas	30	M	Farmer	22Mr01Bx
HANAGIN, Patt	22	M	Farmer	22Mr01Bx
PLENBENERY, James	24	M	Farmer	22Mr01Bx
MONSHAM, John.	28	M	Laborer	22Mr01Bx
Mary	24	F	Laborer	22Mr01Bx
CYRENCE, Thomas	35	M	Laborer	22Mr01Bx
Patt	30	M	Laborer	22Mr01Bx
WARD, Cath.	14	F	Laborer	22Mr01Bx
GREEN, George	07	M	Child	22Mr01Bx
Alice	09	F	Child	22Mr01Bx
BROWN, Joseph	38	M	Laborer	22Mr01Bx
Sarah	25	F	Laborer	22Mr01Bx
CASS, Thomas	18	M	Laborer	22Mr01Bx
NORTH, Abraham	28	U	Laborer	22Mr01Bx
ASQUITH, Danl.	31	M	Laborer	22Mr01Bx
RALLEY, Laurence	21	M	Laborer	22Mr01Bx
FARNY, Patt.	18	M	Laborer	22Mr01Bx
RALLEY, Mich.	28	M	Mechanic	22Mr01Bx
CRAGAN, Francis	17	M	Mechanic	22Mr01Bx
Patt.	30	M	Mechanic	22Mr01Bx
YOUNG, Martin	25	M	Mechanic	22Mr01Bx
Marg.	04	F	Child	22Mr01Bx
John.	16	M	Mechanic	22Mr01Bx
HARNY, Patt.	20	M	Mechanic	22Mr01Bx
SULLIVAN, Mary	20	F	Mechanic	22Mr01Bx
GLANAN, Mary-Ann	32	F	Mechanic	22Mr01Bx
OGLE, Thom.	32	M	Mechanic	22Mr01Bx
BOYLE, Mich.	30	M	Mechanic	22Mr01Bx
Mary	17	F	Mechanic	22Mr01Bx
MCLOUGHLIN, Sarah	32	F	Mechanic	22Mr01Bx
MCCABE, John	32	M	Farmer	22Mr01Bx
Bessy	25	F	Farmer	22Mr01Bx
HOGAN, John	22	M	Farmer	22Mr01Bx
HICKERY, John	30	M	Farmer	22Mr01Bx
NOWLAN, John	32	M	Farmer	22Mr01Bx
STRONG, Thomas	36	M	Farmer	22Mr01Bx
ANDERSON, Thomas-J.	10	M	Farmer	22Mr01Bx
ALLAN, Emanuel	36	M	Farmer	22Mr01Bx
BROMLEY, James	00	M	Farmer	22Mr01Bx
CONROY, Cathne.	30	F	Farmer	22Mr01Bx
Maria	02	F	Child	22Mr01Bx
DOUL, Mickel	20	M	Laborer	22Mr01Bx
THOMAS, James	32	M	Laborer	22Mr01Bx
RICHARDS, Wm.	27	M	Laborer	22Mr01Bx
FARRELL, Thomas	30	M	Laborer	22Mr01Bx
COLLON, Cath.	20	F	Laborer	22Mr01Bx
THOMPSON, Thomas	23	M	Laborer	22Mr01Bx
BIRD, John	24	M	Laborer	22Mr01Bx
NIGHTINGGALE, Patt.	28	M	Laborer	22Mr01Bx
John	02	M	Child	22Mr01Bx
Cath.	28	F	Laborer	22Mr01Bx
Patt.	01	M	Child	22Mr01Bx
BRIEN, Mary	22	F	Laborer	22Mr01Bx
WALLENCE, James	22	M	Laborer	22Mr01Bx
MULVILLE, Charles	27	M	Laborer	22Mr01Bx
COUGHLIN, Patt.	35	M	Laborer	22Mr01Bx
BARKLEY, John	27	M	Laborer	22Mr01Bx
BOWER, Michel	24	M	Laborer	22Mr01Bx
MCLINN, John	22	M	Laborer	22Mr01Bx
WILNER, James	27	M	Laborer	22Mr01Bx
HINKLEY, Eliz.	16	F	Laborer	22Mr01Bx
THOMAS, John-R.	30	M	Mechanic	22Mr01Bx
Charles	26	M	Mechanic	22Mr01Bx
THORNTON, John	22	M	Mechanic	22Mr01Bx
WARD, Wm.	19	M	Mechanic	22Mr01Bx
BRASSWOOD, Eliz.	50	F	Mechanic	22Mr01Bx

NAMES OF PASSENGERS		AGE	SEX	OCCUPATIONS	DATE PORT SHIP
BRASSWOOD, John		12	M	Mechanic	22Mr01Bx
Joseph		09	M	Child	22Mr01Bx
Sarah-Anne		06	F	Child	22Mr01Bx
MIDGLEY, Joseph		22	M	Mechanic	22Mr01Bx
FITZSIMONS, Thomas		38	M	Farmer	22Mr01Bx
Harriet		29	F	Farmer	22Mr01Bx
Harriet		07	F	Child	22Mr01Bx
Margaret		02	F	Child	22Mr01Bx
GLIDDAL, William		80	M	Farmer	22Mr01Bx
MOONEY, Samuel		25	M	Farmer	22Mr01Bx
CROVE, James		21	M	Farmer	22Mr01Bx
YOUNG, James		30	M	Farmer	22Mr01Bx
Jane		19	F	Farmer	22Mr01Bx
DOHERTY, James		19	M	Farmer	22Mr01Bx
MCKEE, James		18	M	Farmer	22Mr01Bx
ATKINSON, John		32	M	Farmer	22Mr01Bx
STANTON, Wm.F.		24	M	Farmer	22Mr01Bx
JONES, John		21	M	Farmer	22Mr01Bx
Abrigel		22	F	Farmer	22Mr01Bx
MASON, John		25	M	Farmer	22Mr01Bx
Hannah		24	F	Farmer	22Mr01Bx
MARTIN, James		35	M	Farmer	22Mr01Bx
Edward		17	M	Farmer	22Mr01Bx
MCELROY, Jane		37	F	Farmer	22Mr01Bx
John		18	M	Farmer	22Mr01Bx
Mary		16	F	Farmer	22Mr01Bx
James		15	M	Mechanic	22Mr01Bx
Alexander		08	M	Child	22Mr01Bx
Jane		05	F	Child	22Mr01Bx
Solomon		03	M	Child	22Mr01Bx
U		.00	U	Infant	22Mr01Bx
SIDWELL, Valentine		24	M	Mechanic	22Mr01Bx
WARD, Wm.		50	M	Mechanic	22Mr01Bx
JOHNSON, Wm.		27	M	Mechanic	22Mr01Bx
PROCTOR, James		21	M	Mechanic	22Mr01Bx
RAYNER, John		21	M	Laborer	22Mr01Bx
VINCENT, Norman		24	M	Laborer	22Mr01Bx
John		20	M	Laborer	22Mr01Bx
GIBSON, John		35	M	Laborer	22Mr01Bx
PARKER, Sam		34	M	Laborer	22Mr01Bx
HANDY, John		24	M	Laborer	22Mr01Bx
DAME, James		22	M	Laborer	22Mr01Bx
LOUGHAN, Thomas		22	M	Laborer	22Mr01Bx
Anne	(W)	20	F	Wife	22Mr01Bx
BRADSHAW, Thomas		24	M	Laborer	22Mr01Bx
STERN, Joseph		20	M	Laborer	22Mr01Bx
FITLEY, Richard		20	M	Laborer	22Mr01Bx
KENEHER, Thomas		24	M	Laborer	22Mr01Bx
Anne		20	F	Laborer	22Mr01Bx
BERRY, Anne		20	F	Laborer	22Mr01Bx
ONEILL, Maria		29	F	Laborer	22Mr01Bx
OAKLEY, George		26	M	Laborer	22Mr01Bx
Mary		25	F	Laborer	22Mr01Bx
George		02	M	Child	22Mr01Bx
Mary		.00	F	Infant	22Mr01Bx
KNOX, Nicholas		28	M	Laborer	22Mr01Bx
U	(W)	24	F	Wife	22Mr01Bx
GARDENER, U		24	M	Laborer	22Mr01Bx
U	(W)	23	F	Wife	22Mr01Bx
STACEPINN, U		20	F	Laborer	22Mr01Bx
YOUNG, Thomas		30	M	Laborer	22Mr01Bx
CONNELL, Francis		21	M	Laborer	22Mr01Bx
FINN, Patk.		30	M	Laborer	22Mr01Bx
CUMINS, Wm.		24	M	Farmer	22Mr01Bx
CAMBELL, James		50	M	Farmer	22Mr01Bx
Mary-Jane		24	F	Farmer	22Mr01Bx
James		21	M	Farmer	22Mr01Bx
Wm.		19	M	Mechanic	22Mr01Bx
Eliz.		16	F	Mechanic	22Mr01Bx
Hugh		13	M	Mechanic	22Mr01Bx
Patk.		09	M	Child	22Mr01Bx
Margaret		07	F	Child	22Mr01Bx
QUIN, John		24	M	Mechanic	22Mr01Bx
BARWILL, Joseph		22	M	Mechanic	22Mr01Bx
QUINLIN, Mich.		28	M	Mechanic	22Mr01Bx
QUINLIN, William		19	M	Mechanic	22Mr01Bx
PARKER, Thomas		30	M	Mechanic	22Mr01Bx
DOWNES, George		26	M	Mechanic	22Mr01Bx
Charles		10	M	Mechanic	22Mr01Bx
WOODS, Robert		24	M	Mechanic	22Mr01Bx
ROLAND, Thomas		25	M	Laborer	22Mr01Bx
JEFFREYS, Jeremia		24	M	Laborer	22Mr01Bx
GELL, Joseph		27	M	Laborer	22Mr01Bx
HAGES, Richard		17	M	Laborer	22Mr01Bx
CALAHAN, Clion		25	U	Laborer	22Mr01Bx
HALL, Thomas		22	M	Laborer	22Mr01Bx
CUNNINGHAM, Thomas		19	M	Laborer	22Mr01Bx
Catherine		20	F	Laborer	22Mr01Bx
HUGES, Sarah		19	F	Laborer	22Mr01Bx
HALL, Sarah		21	F	Laborer	22Mr01Bx
James		28	M	Laborer	22Mr01Bx
CUNNINGHAM, Thos.		30	M	Farmer	22Mr01Bx
HALL, Richard		16	M	Farmer	22Mr01Bx
James		02	M	Child	22Mr01Bx
HOGAN, Mich.		22	M	Laborer	22Mr01Bx
MCNAMARAN, John		50	M	Laborer	22Mr01Bx
Wm.		20	M	Laborer	22Mr01Bx
Johnathan		40	M	Laborer	22Mr01Bx
MCGILMESS, Thos.		36	M	Laborer	22Mr01Bx
BURN, Thomas		30	M	Laborer	22Mr01Bx
DAVENPORT, Joseph		25	M	Laborer	22Mr01Bx
GLENHAN, Kett		25	U	Laborer	22Mr01Bx
GORAN, James		25	M	Laborer	22Mr01Bx
BIRD, Christy		30	M	Laborer	22Mr01Bx
BROWNE, Robert		28	M	Laborer	22Mr01Bx
HARTLEY, Wm.		25	M	Laborer	22Mr01Bx
CUNNINGHAM, John		19	M	Laborer	22Mr01Bx
TIENCEY, Patt		18	M	Laborer	22Mr01Bx
GARDENEER, Wm.		21	M	Laborer	22Mr01Bx
KEEFE, U		23	M	Laborer	22Mr01Bx
BUCKLEY, U		22	M	Laborer	22Mr01Bx
MCSHANE, Solomon		27	M	Laborer	22Mr01Bx
LINAN, James		22	M	Laborer	22Mr01Bx
Wm.		22	M	Farmer	22Mr01Bx
Bridget		21	F	Farmer	22Mr01Bx
SHELL, Mary		23	F	Farmer	22Mr01Bx
FERIN, John		24	M	Farmer	22Mr01Bx
James		22	M	Farmer	22Mr01Bx
Bess		21	F	Farmer	22Mr01Bx
FIRTH, James		24	M	Farmer	22Mr01Bx
SCHOFIELD, Rich.		24	M	Laborer	22Mr01Bx
Sarah		21	F	Laborer	22Mr01Bx
Mary		.00	F	Infant	22Mr01Bx
POWERS, Patk.		20	M	Laborer	22Mr01Bx
Edward		12	M	Laborer	22Mr01Bx
MURRY, U		23	F	Laborer	22Mr01Bx
DAVIS, Wm.		00	M	Laborer	22Mr01Bx
COHAN, Peter		20	M	Laborer	22Mr01Bx
BURNS, Arther		21	M	Laborer	22Mr01Bx
ONEILL, Patt		25	M	Laborer	22Mr01Bx
Bridget		23	F	Laborer	22Mr01Bx
HALL, Cath.		30	F	Laborer	22Mr01Bx
Hannah		16	F	Laborer	22Mr01Bx
Richard		12	M	Laborer	22Mr01Bx
Jane		10	F	Laborer	22Mr01Bx
Charles		06	M	Child	22Mr01Bx
James		40	M	Laborer	22Mr01Bx
Peggy		35	F	Laborer	22Mr01Bx
Dolly		15	F	Laborer	22Mr01Bx
Sophia		12	F	Laborer	22Mr01Bx
John		10	M	Laborer	22Mr01Bx
Mary		08	F	Child	22Mr01Bx
Margt.		06	F	Child	22Mr01Bx
William		04	M	Child	22Mr01Bx
Thomas		40	M	Laborer	22Mr01Bx
ONEILL, Thos.		19	M	Laborer	22Mr01Bx
PREST, Edward		27	M	Laborer	22Mr01Bx
Robert		23	M	Laborer	22Mr01Bx
CANTEN, Mich.		20	M	Laborer	22Mr01Bx
MURPHY, Mich.		20	M	Laborer	22Mr01Bx

NAMES OF PASSENGERS		AGE	SEX	OCCUPATIONS	DATE PORT SHIP
KELLY, Rose		40	F	Laborer	22Mr01Bx
PRICE, James		18	M	Laborer	22Mr01Bx
CANAVAN, Joseph		20	M	Laborer	22Mr01Bx
CARCARAN, Patt		25	M	Farmer	22Mr01Bx
GAHAN, Andrew		22	M	Farmer	22Mr01Bx
LINAN, Mich.		21	M	Farmer	22Mr01Bx
RODGERS, James		20	M	Farmer	22Mr01Bx
CONLAN, Ellen		19	F	Farmer	22Mr01Bx
MURPHY, Christ.		20	M	Mechanic	22Mr01Bx
LANGAN, James		20	M	Mechanic	22Mr01Bx
HORATHY, John		22	M	Mechanic	22Mr01Bx
TAAFFE, Thos.		18	M	Mechanic	22Mr01Bx
STOKES, Mary		17	F	Laborer	22Mr01Bx
CONNOR, Cormick		30	M	Laborer	22Mr01Bx
John		21	M	Laborer	22Mr01Bx
KELLY, Laurence		20	M	Laborer	22Mr01Bx
MORAN, Mary		20	F	Laborer	22Mr01Bx
SHERIDAN, Thomas		37	M	Laborer	22Mr01Bx
BUGERS, Amons		19	M	Laborer	22Mr01Bx
HOLLAND, John		23	M	Laborer	22Mr01Bx
U	(W)	20	F	Wife	22Mr01Bx
DONAHUE, Bernd.		60	M	Laborer	22Mr01Bx
Ellen		21	F	Laborer	22Mr01Bx
LAMAN, Mich.		18	M	Laborer	22Mr01Bx
Thomas		12	M	Laborer	22Mr01Bx
DONALL, Jas.O.		20	M	Mechanic	22Mr01Bx
FRACER, John		30	M	Mechanic	22Mr01Bx
Patt.		18	M	Mechanic	22Mr01Bx
Mary		50	F	Mechanic	22Mr01Bx
BARRON, James		34	M	Mechanic	22Mr01Bx
Cath.		30	F	Mechanic	22Mr01Bx
Mary		07	F	Child	22Mr01Bx
DOOCEY, Garret		20	M	Mechanic	22Mr01Bx
COSTELLO, Ann		11	F	Mechanic	22Mr01Bx
BREAN, Hannach		18	F	Mechanic	22Mr01Bx

HIGHLAND-MARY 23 MARCH 1848

From Liverpool

NAMES OF PASSENGERS		AGE	SEX	OCCUPATIONS	DATE PORT SHIP
SHAFREY, Bryan		30	M	Laborer	23Mr020e
Ellen		30	F	Laborer	23Mr020e
Mary		03	F	Child	23Mr020e
Patrick		02	M	Child	23Mr020e
CALLAGHAN, Mary		20	F	Spinster	23Mr020e
Ann		18	F	Spinster	23Mr020e
GAINER, Bridgt.		18	F	Spinster	23Mr020e
BAGSTER, Rosey		20	F	Spinster	23Mr020e
GILCHRIST, Cath.		20	F	Spinster	23Mr020e
DONOHUE, Bernd.		18	M	Laborer	23Mr020e
Nancy	(W)	20	F	Wife	23Mr020e
Henry		30	M	Servant	23Mr020e
Mary		14	F	Laborer	23Mr020e
WRIGHT, Isabella-Mrs.		25	F	Wife	23Mr020e
Nancy		23	F	Unknown	23Mr020e
GORRY, Michl.		25	M	Laborer	23Mr020e
U-Mrs.		20	F	Wife	23Mr020e
Thomas	(S)	.00	M	Infant	23Mr020e
LINDZAY, William		30	M	Laborer	23Mr020e
MCDONALD, Michl.		28	F	Laborer	23Mr020e
MCANEY, Ann		20	F	Servant	23Mr020e
Mary		18	F	Servant	23Mr020e
CONNOLLY, Patt.		34	M	Laborer	23Mr020e
Bridgt.	(W)	33	F	Wife	23Mr020e
Thomas	(S)	05	M	Child	23Mr020e
Margaret	(D)	03	F	Child	23Mr020e
Bridgt.	(D)	.00	F	Infant	23Mr020e
KELLY, Mary		24	F	Servant	23Mr020e
CORRIGAN, Frances		30	M	Laborer	23Mr020e
MCCORMICK, Michl.		30	M	Laborer	23Mr020e
U	(W)	30	F	Wife	23Mr020e
Biddy	(D)	10	F	None	23Mr020e
Cath.	(D)	08	F	Child	23Mr020e
Mary	(D)	05	F	Child	23Mr020e
Michl.	(S)	.00	M	Infant	23Mr020e
DARCEY, Thomas		30	M	Laborer	23Mr020e
Eliza	(W)	30	F	Wife	23Mr020e
John		19	M	Laborer	23Mr020e
Peter		17	M	Laborer	23Mr020e
Mary		15	F	Spinster	23Mr020e
Richard		12	M	None	23Mr020e
Jane		08	F	Child	23Mr020e
William		01	M	Child	23Mr020e
Thomas		04	M	Child	23Mr020e
Eliza		.00	F	Infant	23Mr020e
LYONS, Mattw.		22	M	Laborer	23Mr020e
KELLY, Michl.		18	M	Laborer	23Mr020e
JORDINE, John		70	M	Laborer	23Mr020e
Matha		20	F	Spinster	23Mr020e
KEVIAN, Cath.		20	F	Spinster	23Mr020e
Mary		07	F	Child	23Mr020e
KENNELLY, Johana		20	F	Spinster	23Mr020e
DORGAN, Pat.		30	M	Laborer	23Mr020e
DOOLANS, Michl.		30	M	Laborer	23Mr020e
Margt.	(W)	25	F	Wife	23Mr020e
DURN, Ellen-Mrs.		25	F	Wife	23Mr020e
Michl.	(S)	.00	M	Infant	23Mr020e
WRIGHT, James		24	M	Unknown	23Mr020e
CUSACKEY, Bessey		19	F	Servant	23Mr020e
Maria		17	F	Spinster	23Mr020e
WOOD, William		20	M	Laborer	23Mr020e
MCLOUGHLIN, Peter		24	M	Laborer	23Mr020e
DOOLIN, Christy		40	M	Laborer	23Mr020e
LAKE, Francis		17	M	Laborer	23Mr020e
MCGRATH, William		30	M	Laborer	23Mr020e
DUNN, Michl.		60	M	Laborer	23Mr020e
Ann		14	F	Spinster	23Mr020e
Michl.		19	M	Laborer	23Mr020e
Francis		09	M	Child	23Mr020e
MCGURTY, John		20	M	Laborer	23Mr020e
BYRNES, Charles		27	M	Laborer	23Mr020e
CONNOR, Mary		30	F	Servant	23Mr020e
John		06	M	Child	23Mr020e
William		04	M	Child	23Mr020e
Ann		.00	F	Infant	23Mr020e
CROTHERS, Wm.		26	M	Servant	23Mr020e
REILLY, John		40	M	Servant	23Mr020e
QUINLAN, Mary-Mrs.		50	F	Wife	23Mr020e
Michl.	(S)	23	M	Laborer	23Mr020e
Bridget	(D)	20	F	Laborer	23Mr020e
PHILIPS, David		40	M	Laborer	23Mr020e
WALTERS, John		22	M	Laborer	23Mr020e
Elizth.	(W)	26	F	Wife	23Mr020e
Joseph	(S)	.00	M	Infant	23Mr020e
GUBBINS, Wm.		26	M	Laborer	23Mr020e
Margt.	(W)	25	F	Wife	23Mr020e
ROURKE, Thos.		26	M	Laborer	23Mr020e
SHEA, Mary-Mrs.		25	F	Wife	23Mr020e
GRACE, Philip		24	M	Laborer	23Mr020e
HUFF, Eliza		16	F	Spinster	23Mr020e
REILLY, Peter		37	M	Laborer	23Mr020e
Mary	(W)	30	F	Wife	23Mr020e
Pat.		45	M	Laborer	23Mr020e
Mary	(W)	45	F	Wife	23Mr020e
Bartly	(S)	18	M	Laborer	23Mr020e
Philip	(S)	17	M	Laborer	23Mr020e
Ann	(D)	16	F	Spinster	23Mr020e
Maria	(D)	14	F	Spinster	23Mr020e
Pat	(S)	09	M	Child	23Mr020e
Rose	(D)	12	F	None	23Mr020e
CLARKE, Bridgt.Mrs.		40	F	Wife	23Mr020e
MCNEILLY, John		25	M	Laborer	23Mr020e
MONTGOMERY, Alexr.		21	M	Laborer	23Mr020e
OBYRNES, Hugh		23	M	Laborer	23Mr020e

NAMES OF PASSENGERS		AGE	SEX	OCCUPATIONS	DATE PORT SHIP
OBYRNES, Nick		25	M	Laborer	23Mr020e
BLYAN, Andw.		28	M	Laborer	23Mr020e
FURY, Mattw.		40	M	Laborer	23Mr020e
WAKEFIELD, Edwd.		32	M	Laborer	23Mr020e
Anna	(W)	23	F	Wife	23Mr020e
WHITELEY, Joseph		36	M	Laborer	23Mr020e
WALKER, Geo.		26	M	Laborer	23Mr020e
MCKENNY, Pat.		18	M	Servant	23Mr020e
MURRAY, Ann		14	F	Spinster	23Mr020e
COOK, Edwd.		22	M	Laborer	23Mr020e
John		20	M	Laborer	23Mr020e
Rose	(W)	21	F	Wife	23Mr020e
LYNCH, Rose		15	F	Spinster	23Mr020e
SMITH, Judith		20	F	Spinster	23Mr020e
COOK, John		07	M	Child	23Mr020e
WRIGHT, Eliza-Mrs.		40	F	Wife	23Mr020e
Nancy		24	F	Spinster	23Mr020e
HARLIN, Andw.		60	M	Laborer	23Mr020e
Cathr.		20	F	Spinster	23Mr020e
LOHANS, John		30	M	Laborer	23Mr020e
HAND, John		30	M	Laborer	23Mr020e
LOHANS, Mary-Mrs.		30	F	Wife	23Mr020e
Honora	(D)	.00	F	Infant	23Mr020e
VILL, John		27	M	Laborer	23Mr020e
LUIS, Dennis		30	M	Laborer	23Mr020e
DOOLAN, Thomas		30	M	Laborer	23Mr020e
Cath.	(W)	24	F	Wife	23Mr020e
HANDLEY, Peter		35	M	Laborer	23Mr020e
U	(W)	21	F	Wife	23Mr020e
Thomas	(S)	.00	M	Infant	23Mr020e
HURLEY, Cathr.		28	F	Servant	23Mr020e
KELLY, Anty.		25	M	Laborer	23Mr020e
FLEMANG, Mary		24	F	Servant	23Mr020e
POWELL, Bartly		46	F	Laborer	23Mr020e
Terance		24	M	Laborer	23Mr020e
Cathr.-Mrs.		23	F	Wife	23Mr020e
Patrick		17	M	Laborer	23Mr020e
Winifred		13	F	Spinster	23Mr020e
Bridgt.		11	F	None	23Mr020e
Bartly		07	M	Child	23Mr020e
MONAGHAN, Mary-Mrs.		21	F	Wife	23Mr020e
NASH, James		40	M	Laborer	23Mr020e
Mary	(W)	30	F	Wife	23Mr020e
Michl.	(S)	10	M	None	23Mr020e
Edmond	(S)	07	M	Child	23Mr020e
John	(S)	06	M	Child	23Mr020e
Ann	(D)	04	F	Child	23Mr020e
Michl.	(S)	02	M	Child	23Mr020e
Mary	(D)	.00	F	Infant	23Mr020e

LIVERPOOL 23 MARCH 1848

From Liverpool

NAMES OF PASSENGERS		AGE	SEX	OCCUPATIONS	DATE PORT SHIP
DIXON, John		26	M	Merchant	23Mr02Bo
U	(W)	19	F	Wife	23Mr02Bo
HONE, Charles		21	M	Physician	23Mr02Bo
SULLIVAN, Daniel		45	M	Laborer	23Mr02Bo
Owen		13	M	Laborer	23Mr02Bo
FISHER, Johanna		21	F	Servant	23Mr02Bo
CALLAGAN, Eliza		18	F	Servant	23Mr02Bo
Hannah		21	F	Servant	23Mr02Bo
CRAMON, Bernard		30	M	Laborer	23Mr02Bo
Ellen		06	F	Child	23Mr02Bo
WELSH, Margret		36	F	Servant	23Mr02Bo
Patrick		12	M	Unknown	23Mr02Bo
John		09	M	Child	23Mr02Bo
Mary		07	F	Child	23Mr02Bo
ONEAL, John		45	M	Laborer	23Mr02Bo
HENRY, George		24	M	Laborer	23Mr02Bo
PINDER, Patrick		30	M	Miner	23Mr02Bo
Edward		28	M	Miner	23Mr02Bo
FARREL, Maria		19	F	Servant	23Mr02Bo
MAJOR, Margret-Mrs.		33	F	Wife	23Mr02Bo
Maria	(D)	11	F	Unknown	23Mr02Bo
Catherine	(D)	09	F	Child	23Mr02Bo
Anne	(D)	04	F	Child	23Mr02Bo
DALTON, John		30	M	Nailer	23Mr02Bo
WHITE, Hannah-Mrs.		27	F	Wife	23Mr02Bo
William	(S)	07	M	Child	23Mr02Bo
MAHER, Alice		22	F	Servant	23Mr02Bo
CULLEN, Antony		19	M	Farmer	23Mr02Bo
GILFOYLE, Patrick		30	M	Laborer	23Mr02Bo
RYLEY, Anne-Mrs.		30	F	Wife	23Mr02Bo
Mary	(D)	09	F	Child	23Mr02Bo
John	(S)	07	M	Child	23Mr02Bo
Anne	(D)	.00	F	Infant	23Mr02Bo
HAND, Geo.		20	M	Laborer	23Mr02Bo
DOW, Catherine		09	F	Child	23Mr02Bo
BURK, Catherine-Mrs.		62	F	Wi	23Mr02Bo
Christopher		29	M	Shoemaker	23Mr02Bo
Jeremiah		16	M	Clerk	23Mr02Bo
William		24	M	Shoemaker	23Mr02Bo
MURTAGH, Bridget		20	F	Servant	23Mr02Bo
BOYD, Hugh		20	M	Laborer	23Mr02Bo
MCGONNEGAL, Thomas		20	M	Laborer	23Mr02Bo
SANDS, William		27	M	Joiner	23Mr02Bo
MCQUEENY, Eliza		21	F	Servant	23Mr02Bo
CASSIDA, Pheobe		20	F	Servant	23Mr02Bo
BURKE, Anne		05	F	Child	23Mr02Bo
FLEENY, Thomas		30	M	Laborer	23Mr02Bo
Margret		18	F	Servant	23Mr02Bo
Mary		20	F	Servant	23Mr02Bo
GREEN, Bridget		21	F	Servant	23Mr02Bo
CONWAY, Nichollas		35	M	Laborer	23Mr02Bo
MANNANY, Rose		18	F	Servant	23Mr02Bo
DONNELL, Edmond		50	M	Laborer	23Mr02Bo
Catherine	(W)	50	F	Wife	23Mr02Bo
Mary	(D)	06	F	Child	23Mr02Bo
MCGARTH, Biddy		24	F	Servant	23Mr02Bo
MYERS, Pat		35	M	Laborer	23Mr02Bo
BIRMINGHAM, Alice		21	F	Servant	23Mr02Bo
MARTIN, Michl.		20	M	Bootmaker	23Mr02Bo
REGAN, Patk.		20	M	Laborer	23Mr02Bo
STAPLETON, John		30	M	Laborer	23Mr02Bo
Mary	(W)	26	F	Wife	23Mr02Bo
DONOHOE, Eliza		20	F	Servant	23Mr02Bo
Rose		22	F	Servant	23Mr02Bo
SMITH, Mary		25	F	Servant	23Mr02Bo
BOLTON, Michael		25	M	Laborer	23Mr02Bo
Pat		20	M	Laborer	23Mr02Bo
BUCKLEY, Danl.		20	M	Laborer	23Mr02Bo
MURRAY, Patrick		22	M	Laborer	23Mr02Bo
GILLON, James		22	M	Mason	23Mr02Bo
DOWNS, Patrick		22	M	Laborer	23Mr02Bo
CLARY, Owen		24	M	Laborer	23Mr02Bo
BOSSELL, Ann		18	F	Servant	23Mr02Bo
CONNERTON, Mary		20	F	Servant	23Mr02Bo
GAMMON, Mary		20	F	Servant	23Mr02Bo
FEENY, Patk.		18	M	Servant	23Mr02Bo
SULLIVAN, Joana		21	F	Servant	23Mr02Bo
MULAGAN, Denis		28	M	Laborer	23Mr02Bo
Betsey-Mrs.		40	F	Laborer	23Mr02Bo
John		12	M	Laborer	23Mr02Bo
Peter		10	M	Laborer	23Mr02Bo
Neal		08	M	Child	23Mr02Bo
Biddy		06	F	Child	23Mr02Bo
James		.00	M	Infant	23Mr02Bo
Biddy Died-At-Sea		65	F	Servant	23Mr02Bo
MCARDLE, Patk.		24	M	Laborer	23Mr02Bo
Mary	(W)	20	F	Wife	23Mr02Bo
Margaret		18	F	Servant	23Mr02Bo
MURRY, Anne		20	F	Servant	23Mr02Bo

NAMES OF PASSENGERS	AGE	SEX	OCCUPATIONS	DATE PORT SHIP
SMITH, Thos.	20	M	Laborer	23Mr02Bo
Mary	18	F	Servant	23Mr02Bc
MURRANNA, Thos.	20	M	Farmer	23Mr02Bo
ODONNELL, Biddy	18	F	Dressmaker	23Mr02Bo
CLINTON, Cath.	18	F	Servant	23Mr02Bo
CARROLL, John	20	M	Ldpr	23Mr02Bo
JOHNSTON, Chas.	25	M	Laborer	23Mr02Bo
MCIVER, Wm.	25	M	Carpenter	23Mr02Bo
HOURIGGAN, Ellen	20	F	Upholsterer	23Mr02Bo
MALLAN, Pat	30	M	Laborer	23Mr02Bo
MCMAHON, Owen	30	M	Laborer	23Mr02Bo
SHARPLEY, Rose	25	F	Servant	23Mr02Bo
CRANTON, Phillip	31	M	Laborer	23Mr02Bo
DRUMSHEY, John	22	M	Bootmaker	23Mr02Bo
LEE, Martha	22	F	Crpm	23Mr02Bo
Cath.	20	F	Servant	23Mr02Bo
NOLAN, Edwd.	20	M	Wrhsmn	23Mr02Bo
FEY, Rose	20	F	Servant	23Mr02Bo
CARLISLE, Samuel	20	M	Joiner	23Mr02Bo
SPROUT, Andrew	30	M	Laborer	23Mr02Bo
Wm.	18	M	Laborer	23Mr02Bo
Margret	40	F	Servant	23Mr02Bo
Esther	20	F	Dressmaker	23Mr02Bo
Deborah	25	F	Milliner	23Mr02Bo
THOMPSN, John	30	M	Shoemaker	23Mr02Bo
CALAGHAN, Wm.	20	M	Laborer	23Mr02Bo
HYNCHY, Pat	25	M	Laborer	23Mr02Bo
MCGRAW, Pat	20	M	Laborer	23Mr02Bo
GIBNEY, Phillip	20	M	Stctr	23Mr02Bo
USHER, James	20	M	Mechanic	23Mr02Bo
COLLON, Wm.	20	M	Mechanic	23Mr02Bo
Mich.	18	M	Mechanic	23Mr02Bo
REYNOLDS, Thos.	20	M	Mechanic	23Mr02Bo
CONNOR, Martin	20	M	Laborer	23Mr02Bo
NEVILLE, Bridget	20	F	Servant	23Mr02Bo
DEMPSEY, Pat	25	M	Laborer	23Mr02Bo
Winnerfred	22	F	Servant	23Mr02Bo
Edward	14	M	Laborer	23Mr02Bo
DELANY, Wm.	22	M	Laborer	23Mr02Bo
FREAMY, Thos.	22	M	Blacksmith	23Mr02Bo
Alice	20	F	Dressmaker	23Mr02Bo
James	06	M	Child	23Mr02Bo
SENIOR, Thos.	28	M	Merchant	23Mr02Bo
Mena	26	F	Dressmaker	23Mr02Bo
BUCKLEY, Wm.	22	M	Gdnr	23Mr02Bo
DUFFY, Thos.	20	M	Shoemaker	23Mr02Bo
CASSIDA, Pat	18	M	Laborer	23Mr02Bo
SMITH, Lenry	24	M	Laborer	23Mr02Bo
LYNCH, Margt.	20	F	Servant	23Mr02Bo
LANGSTAFFE, Wm.	24	M	Shoemaker	23Mr02Bo
DUNN, John	26	M	Shoemaker	23Mr02Bo
MANION, Michl.	21	M	Shoemaker	23Mr02Bo
BYRNE, Robt.	24	M	Merchant	23Mr02Bo
DEVAN, James	20	M	Farmer	23Mr02Bo
QUINN, Rose	30	F	Servant	23Mr02Bo
PHILLIPS, David	25	M	Baker	23Mr02Bo
MALOY, James	20	M	Laborer	23Mr02Bo
CORINGTON, John	24	M	Laborer	23Mr02Bo
CONNELL, Cathe.	28	F	Servant	23Mr02Bo
HORAN, Cath.	19	F	Servant	23Mr02Bo
MAHER, James	20	M	Laborer	23Mr02Bo
FOGARTY, Mary	20	F	Servant	23Mr02Bo
MAHER, Dan	20	M	Servant	23Mr02Bo
BRYAN, Mich.	40	M	Laborer	23Mr02Bo
CAHELL, James	20	M	Laborer	23Mr02Bo
MAHER, Wm.	20	M	Laborer	23Mr02Bo
CAHELL, Billy	20	M	Laborer	23Mr02Bo
DUMPHEY, John	20	M	Laborer	23Mr02Bo
ANDERSON, Wm.	30	M	Laborer	23Mr02Bo
SHARP, Chas.	30	M	Laborer	23Mr02Bo
CLARK, Julia	25	F	Servant	23Mr02Bo
BURNS, Ellen	24	F	Servant	23Mr02Bo
FINNRAN, Bernard	22	M	Laborer	23Mr02Bo
BRYAN, John	22	M	Laborer	23Mr02Bo
MAHER, Michl.	50	M	Laborer	23Mr02Bo

NAMES OF PASSENGERS	AGE	SEX	OCCUPATIONS	DATE PORT SHIP
MAHER, Mary	50	F	Servant	23Mr02Bo
Pat.	20	M	Laborer	23Mr02Bo
Thomas	18	M	Laborer	23Mr02Bo
Ellen	17	F	Servant	23Mr02Bo
FEGAN, Christopher	20	M	Laborer	23Mr02Bo
ROONEY, Cath.	18	F	Servant	23Mr02Bo
FOGARTY, Bridget	17	F	Servant	23Mr02Bo
MCDONALD, James	30	M	Servant	23Mr02Bo
SHARPLEY, Peter	20	M	Servant	23Mr02Bo
LEECH, Martha	46	F	Weaver	23Mr02Bo
John	16	F	Weaver	23Mr02Bo
Robt.	11	M	Servant	23Mr02Bo
Betsy	18	F	Servant	23Mr02Bo
Mary	.00	F	Infant	23Mr02Bo
Jane	04	F	Child	23Mr02Bo
MCKINNERY, Francis	24	M	Tailor	23Mr02Bo
HORAN, Francis	20	M	Carpenter	23Mr02Bo
CONLON, James	20	M	Laborer	23Mr02Bo
IGO, John	18	M	Laborer	23Mr02Bo
SHARP, Chas.	20	M	Laborer	23Mr02Bo
CADDIN, Michl.	40	M	Laborer	23Mr02Bo
Judith	50	F	Unknown	23Mr02Bo
Judith	11	F	Unknown	23Mr02Bo
CONNOLLY, Bridget	20	F	Servant	23Mr02Bo
REYNOLDS, Bridget	20	F	Servant	23Mr02Bo
BAHAM, Michl.	50	M	Farmer	23Mr02Bo
Mich.	30	M	Bricklayer	23Mr02Bo
Thomas	16	M	Laborer	23Mr02Bo
Margret	30	F	Servant	23Mr02Bo
Johannah	26	F	Servant	23Mr02Bo
Bridget	20	F	Servant	23Mr02Bo
Mena	15	F	Servant	23Mr02Bo
HOGAN, Stephen	24	M	Laborer	23Mr02Bo
Margret	24	F	Servant	23Mr02Bo
Michl.	12	M	Servant	23Mr02Bo
Cath.	10	F	Servant	23Mr02Bo
Martin	08	M	Child	23Mr02Bo
FEATHERSTONE, Mary-Ann	18	F	Servant	23Mr02Bo
WALSH, Mark	20	M	Blacksmith	23Mr02Bo
Edw.	22	M	Laborer	23Mr02Bo
SROYTAN, James	25	M	Laborer	23Mr02Bo
RYAN, Catherine	42	F	Servant	23Mr02Bo
Matthew	18	M	Laborer	23Mr02Bo
Patt.	17	M	Laborer	23Mr02Bo
Margret	14	F	Servant	23Mr02Bo
Mary-A.	12	F	Servant	23Mr02Bo
Betty	10	F	Servant	23Mr02Bo
Mary	08	F	Child	23Mr02Bo
James	05	M	Child	23Mr02Bo
Thomas	04	M	Child	23Mr02Bo
Ellen	.00	F	Infant	23Mr02Bo
MACKEY, Mary	18	F	Servant	23Mr02Bo
James	18	M	Laborer	23Mr02Bo
MCGINNES, Edw.	14	M	Laborer	23Mr02Bo
Thos.	11	M	Laborer	23Mr02Bo
DUNN, Hugh	50	M	Weaver	23Mr02Bo
Ellen	46	F	Spinner	23Mr02Bo
Mary	18	F	Spinner	23Mr02Bo
Ann	10	F	Spinner	23Mr02Bo
Sarah	08	F	Child	23Mr02Bo
DORAN, Mary	20	F	Servant	23Mr02Bo
CONWAY, Mary	20	F	Servant	23Mr02Bo
TAYLOR, Sally	17	F	Servant	23Mr02Bo
MATTHEWS, James	20	M	Laborer	23Mr02Bo
Margt.	20	M	Servant	23Mr02Bo
BELLIN, Robt.	20	M	Stctr	23Mr02Bo
Anne	20	F	Dressmaker	23Mr02Bo
Betsey	.00	F	Infant	23Mr02Bo
DORAN, Margt.	20	F	Servant	23Mr02Bo
MAJOR, Margret	06	F	Child	23Mr02Bo
RYLEY, Patt.	05	M	Child	23Mr02Bo
TORPEY, Ellen	18	F	Servant	23Mr02Bo
DEMPSEY, John	22	M	Laborer	23Mr02Bo

NAMES OF PASSENGERS		AGE	SEX	OCCUPATIONS	DATE PORT SHIP

HARRIET-AUGUSTA 24 MARCH 1848

From Liverpool

NAMES OF PASSENGERS		AGE	SEX	OCCUPATIONS	DATE PORT SHIP
MEHAN, Andrew		27	M	Unknown	24Mr02Go
FISHER, Owen		20	M	Unknown	24Mr02Go
COALPIN, Wm.		21	M	Unknown	24Mr02Go
James		11	M	Unknown	24Mr02Go
LONG, Peggy		20	F	Unknown	24Mr02Go
KEANY, Danl.		40	M	Unknown	24Mr02Go
Died-At-Sea					
Thomas		35	M	Unknown	24Mr02Go
GALLAGHER, Teawge		36	M	Unknown	24Mr02Go
Chas.		34	M	Unknown	24Mr02Go
ZEOWLAN, Richd.		35	M	Unknown	24Mr02Go
TORMEY, Mark		20	M	Unknown	24Mr02Go
John		22	M	Unknown	24Mr02Go
DANN, Michael		20	M	Unknown	24Mr02Go
COLLINS, Wm.Wright		23	M	Unknown	24Mr02Go
HOLLINGSWORT, Eligah		32	M	Unknown	24Mr02Go
SPENCER, U-Mrs.		26	F	Unknown	24Mr02Go
CUFF, Pat		20	M	Unknown	24Mr02Go
ROACH, Edwd.		20	M	Unknown	24Mr02Go
Cath.		24	F	Unknown	24Mr02Go
RENNA, Edwd.		18	M	Unknown	24Mr02Go
HOPE, Peter		20	M	Unknown	24Mr02Go
COALMAN, Patr.		20	M	Unknown	24Mr02Go
Biddy		18	F	Unknown	24Mr02Go
COOPER, Anthony		20	M	Unknown	24Mr02Go
Pat.		20	M	Unknown	24Mr02Go
REILLY, Wm.		20	M	Unknown	24Mr02Go
SMITH, Charles		24	M	Unknown	24Mr02Go
HENSHAW, Joseph		23	M	Unknown	24Mr02Go
GANLEY, Margt.		20	F	Unknown	24Mr02Go
CARR, Frances		33	M	Unknown	24Mr02Go
SMITH, Anne		12	F	Unknown	24Mr02Go
BUSH, John		20	M	Unknown	24Mr02Go
MALONY, Oney		50	M	Unknown	24Mr02Go
Owen		12	M	Unknown	24Mr02Go
Margt.		20	F	Unknown	24Mr02Go
BRANNAN, Michl.		20	M	Unknown	24Mr02Go
Thomas		10	M	Unknown	24Mr02Go
ROBBERTS, Robbert		12	M	Unknown	24Mr02Go
Margt.		11	F	Unknown	24Mr02Go
WELSH, Michel		25	M	Unknown	24Mr02Go
Margt.		20	F	Unknown	24Mr02Go
SULLIVAN, Mary		25	F	Unknown	24Mr02Go
BROUGHAN, Pat.		18	M	Unknown	24Mr02Go
COCHAYNE, Thomas		17	M	Unknown	24Mr02Go
HOY, Mary		22	F	Unknown	24Mr02Go
HUNSTON, Alicia		25	F	Unknown	24Mr02Go
HOLDEN, Anne		30	F	Unknown	24Mr02Go
Cath.		50	F	Unknown	24Mr02Go
Andrew		.00	M	Infant	24Mr02Go
ROBINSON, John		26	M	Unknown	24Mr02Go
TOROLAN, Mary		21	F	Unknown	24Mr02Go
CURLEY, Pat		40	M	Unknown	24Mr02Go
Mary		67	F	Unknown	24Mr02Go
EAGAN, Mary		18	F	Unknown	24Mr02Go
COFFEE, Maria		12	F	Unknown	24Mr02Go
BOLAN, James		20	M	Unknown	24Mr02Go
DOLAN, John		22	M	Unknown	24Mr02Go
BLACKWIN, James		22	M	Unknown	24Mr02Go
CANNON, Peter		22	M	Unknown	24Mr02Go
GUFFEY, Pat		22	M	Unknown	24Mr02Go
CROWTHER, Alex		35	M	Unknown	24Mr02Go
CONLAN, Pat		20	M	Unknown	24Mr02Go
Martin		27	M	Unknown	24Mr02Go
DALLON, Anne		28	F	Unknown	24Mr02Go
GROVER, John		56	M	Unknown	24Mr02Go
WHITE, Thomas		21	M	Unknown	24Mr02Go
FAGERY, James		28	M	Unknown	24Mr02Go
Cath		27	F	Unknown	24Mr02Go
BYRNE, Mary		37	F	Unknown	24Mr02Go
FALE, John		18	M	Unknown	24Mr02Go
ODONELL, John		36	M	Unknown	24Mr02Go
GAMELY, Pat		36	M	Unknown	24Mr02Go
U	(W)	28	F	Wife	24Mr02Go
Thos.	(S)	04	M	Child	24Mr02Go
Biddy	(D)	02	F	Child	24Mr02Go
MCKENLA, Anthony		20	M	Unknown	24Mr02Go
MOONEY, Marg.		20	F	Unknown	24Mr02Go
SEREY, James		28	M	Unknown	24Mr02Go
QUIGLEY, Thos.		30	M	Unknown	24Mr02Go
Patk.		10	M	Unknown	24Mr02Go
Cath.		30	F	Unknown	24Mr02Go
Cath.		08	F	Child	24Mr02Go
John		05	M	Child	24Mr02Go
RELLUDE, Judy		18	F	Unknown	24Mr02Go
MCGANELL, Mary		18	F	Unknown	24Mr02Go
DANES, Mary		30	F	Unknown	24Mr02Go
Wm.		09	M	Child	24Mr02Go
John		07	M	Child	24Mr02Go
George		05	M	Child	24Mr02Go
Mary-Anne		.00	F	Infant	24Mr02Go
TUNNEY, Robbert		25	M	Unknown	24Mr02Go
MCGREHIRE, Charles		19	M	Unknown	24Mr02Go
BYRNE, Pat		20	M	Unknown	24Mr02Go
WHITE, Frances		30	M	Unknown	24Mr02Go
TAYLER, Thomas		31	M	Unknown	24Mr02Go
WEIRE, Jame		29	M	Unknown	24Mr02Go
DAVLIN, John		24	M	Unknown	24Mr02Go
HALL, John		35	M	Unknown	24Mr02Go
Eliza		30	F	Unknown	24Mr02Go
William		05	M	Child	24Mr02Go
PORTER, James		25	M	Unknown	24Mr02Go
John		21	M	Unknown	24Mr02Go
FARLEY, Pat		22	M	Unknown	24Mr02Go
GARRITY, Peggy		.00	F	Infant	24Mr02Go
Mary		02	F	Child	24Mr02Go
BOSWELL, James		34	M	Blacksmith	24Mr02Go
COLLINS, William		23	M	Blacksmith	24Mr02Go

YORKSHIRE 24 MARCH 1848

From Liverpool

NAMES OF PASSENGERS		AGE	SEX	OCCUPATIONS	DATE PORT SHIP
GROSLY, Joseph		20	M	Farmer	24Mr02Bz
Jane		20	F	None	24Mr02Bz
U		.00	U	Infant	24Mr02Bz
Elizbh.		02	F	Child	24Mr02Bz
FIELD, Anna		18	F	None	24Mr02Bz
TAYLOR, John		21	M	Farmer	24Mr02Bz
HEYWOOD, Adam		30	M	Farmer	24Mr02Bz
MCCUEN, Elisha		24	M	Farmer	24Mr02Bz
U		.00	U	Infant	24Mr02Bz
KING, Alex.		24	M	Mechanic	24Mr02Bz
U	(W)	20	F	Wife	24Mr02Bz
U		25	U	Unknown	24Mr02Bz
ORMROD, Jas.		50	M	Mechanic	24Mr02Bz
EDWARDS, Jas.		50	M	Mechanic	24Mr02Bz
Jas.		07	M	Child	24Mr02Bz
Charlotte		04	F	Child	24Mr02Bz
RYAN, Patk.		22	M	Laborer	24Mr02Bz
SLATTERY, John		22	M	Laborer	24Mr02Bz
RYAN, Patk.		30	M	Laborer	24Mr02Bz
MCMAHON, Mary		20	F	None	24Mr02Bz
CARRICK, Ellen		24	F	None	24Mr02Bz

NAMES OF PASSENGERS		AGE	SEX	OCCUPATIONS	DATE PORT SHIP
ROOT, Wm.		25	M	Laborer	24Mr02Bz
DENCH, Jonas		25	M	Laborer	24Mr02Bz
MAY, John		30	M	Laborer	24Mr02Bz
NELSON, Wm.		35	M	Laborer	24Mr02Bz
Jane		35	F	Servant	24Mr02Bz
U		.00	U	Infant	24Mr02Bz
John		12	M	None	24Mr02Bz
Jame		10	M	None	24Mr02Bz
Joseph		08	M	Child	24Mr02Bz
Mary		06	F	Child	24Mr02Bz
William		04	M	Child	24Mr02Bz
WORDS, John		20	M	Laborer	24Mr02Bz
CLARK, Alex.		20	M	Laborer	24Mr02Bz
DASSON, Michl.		26	M	Laborer	24Mr02Bz
MCKEON, Patk.		21	M	Farmer	24Mr02Bz
CONAHAN, Jas.		20	M	Farmer	24Mr02Bz
MCGLEE, Mary		25	F	Servant	24Mr02Bz
DONNELL, Susan		20	F	Servant	24Mr02Bz
GRAY, Peter		22	M	Farmer	24Mr02Bz
Mary		20	F	Servant	24Mr02Bz
JONES, Griffy		24	M	Farmer	24Mr02Bz
THOMAS, David		29	M	Farmer	24Mr02Bz
RICHARDS, John		33	M	Farmer	24Mr02Bz
MACY, Peter		25	M	Farmer	24Mr02Bz
KELLY, Michl.		25	M	Farmer	24Mr02Bz
FLYNN, Danl.		25	M	Farmer	24Mr02Bz
CROSBY, Margt.		22	F	Servant	24Mr02Bz
CROKER, Geo.		47	M	Farmer	24Mr02Bz
GIBBS, Saml.		47	M	Farmer	24Mr02Bz
Anna		00	F	None	24Mr02Bz
HOLMES, Ellen		12	F	None	24Mr02Bz
DORKIN, Patk.		30	M	Farmer	24Mr02Bz
HANNON, Mich.		35	M	Farmer	24Mr02Bz
Elizbth.		45	F	None	24Mr02Bz
Alice		12	F	None	24Mr02Bz
Eliz.		10	F	None	24Mr02Bz
Patk.		04	M	Child	24Mr02Bz
COOK, Jas.		29	M	Laborer	24Mr02Bz
Jane		07	F	Child	24Mr02Bz
Elizb.		29	F	Servant	24Mr02Bz
Emma		02	F	Child	24Mr02Bz
PARKIN, Levi		27	M	Laborer	24Mr02Bz
Saml.		29	M	Laborer	24Mr02Bz
Anna		27	F	Servant	24Mr02Bz
COOK, Thos.		15	M	None	24Mr02Bz
Ruth		17	F	Servant	24Mr02Bz
CARTWRIGHT, John		29	M	Laborer	24Mr02Bz
MAHONY, Patk.		21	M	Laborer	24Mr02Bz
NALLY, Thos.		24	M	Laborer	24Mr02Bz
WARBURTON, Jas.		20	M	Laborer	24Mr02Bz
MARRICK, Patk.		27	M	Laborer	24Mr02Bz
Ann		23	F	Servant	24Mr02Bz
Elizabeth		02	F	Child	24Mr02Bz
HOWARD, Alice		26	F	Servant	24Mr02Bz
CLARK, Patk.		22	M	Laborer	24Mr02Bz
AGIN, John		22	M	Laborer	24Mr02Bz
DOWNS, Edwd.		15	M	None	24Mr02Bz
KENNEDY, Ann		24	F	Weaver	24Mr02Bz
NELSON, John		35	M	Weaver	24Mr02Bz
MCCANN, Pat		20	M	Weaver	24Mr02Bz
TULLY, Pat		22	M	Weaver	24Mr02Bz
John		24	M	Weaver	24Mr02Bz
Mary		25	F	Servant	24Mr02Bz
Sarah		25	F	Servant	24Mr02Bz
Peter		20	M	Weaver	24Mr02Bz
DOWNS, Wm.		26	M	Weaver	24Mr02Bz
Cath.		26	F	Servant	24Mr02Bz
RUSHTON, Jas.		30	M	Farmer	24Mr02Bz
Sarah		07	F	Child	24Mr02Bz
Margt.		04	F	Child	24Mr02Bz
PICKLES, Hortly		30	M	Farmer	24Mr02Bz
Jane		03	F	Child	24Mr02Bz
John		02	M	Child	24Mr02Bz
Elizabeth		.00	F	Infant	24Mr02Bz
HARTLEY, Caleb		09	M	Child	24Mr02Bz
HARTLEY, Richd.		13	M	None	24Mr02Bz
PICKLES, Ellen		30	F	Servant	24Mr02Bz
ROSS, Wm.		29	M	Farmer	24Mr02Bz
CLARK, Cath.		22	F	Servant	24Mr02Bz
HAYS, Mary		18	F	Servant	24Mr02Bz
CONNER, Cath.		17	F	Servant	24Mr02Bz
Thos.		23	M	Farmer	24Mr02Bz
Cath.		23	F	Servant	24Mr02Bz
BRYAN, Francis		22	M	Farmer	24Mr02Bz
DARCY, Cath.		16	F	Servant	24Mr02Bz
DONAVAN, Morgan		22	M	Farmer	24Mr02Bz
CASEY, John		32	M	Farmer	24Mr02Bz
Cath.	(W)	30	F	Wife	24Mr02Bz
HARLIGAN, John		31	M	Laborer	24Mr02Bz
CONNER, Thos.		31	M	Laborer	24Mr02Bz
CRONIN, Mary		23	F	Servant	24Mr02Bz
DAILY, Margt.		30	F	Servant	24Mr02Bz
Margt.		04	F	Child	24Mr02Bz
Cath.		06	F	Child	24Mr02Bz
MCGARRY, Henry		20	M	Farmer	24Mr02Bz
Mary	(W)	23	F	Wife	24Mr02Bz
Dominick	(S)	04	M	Child	24Mr02Bz
Wm.	(S)	02	M	Child	24Mr02Bz
DONNELLY, Bridget		26	F	Servant	24Mr02Bz
WORD, Michl.		21	M	Laborer	24Mr02Bz
BAKER, Thos.		28	M	Laborer	24Mr02Bz
Elizbt.		27	F	Servant	24Mr02Bz
Emma		.00	F	Infant	24Mr02Bz
Caroline		02	F	Child	24Mr02Bz
HARWICK, John		40	M	Laborer	24Mr02Bz
Mary		30	F	None	24Mr02Bz
TYLER, Edwd.		45	M	Laborer	24Mr02Bz
Henry		13	M	None	24Mr02Bz
Jane		11	F	None	24Mr02Bz
EVANS, Benj.		25	M	Laborer	24Mr02Bz
HALPIN, Pat		30	M	Laborer	24Mr02Bz
MILLER, John		25	M	Laborer	24Mr02Bz
LYDAN, Bart.		21	M	Laborer	24Mr02Bz
FALLON, Bridget		20	F	Servant	24Mr02Bz
WHELAN, Ann		22	F	Servant	24Mr02Bz
DUFFY, John		30	M	Farmer	24Mr02Bz
FLANAGAN, Henry		19	M	Farmer	24Mr02Bz
MULROY, Patk.		30	M	Farmer	24Mr02Bz
DOOLAN, Phaton		30	M	Farmer	24Mr02Bz
MANGAN, Ann		18	F	Servant	24Mr02Bz
HIGHLAND, Sarah		20	F	Servant	24Mr02Bz
BROWN, Saml.		30	M	Farmer	24Mr02Bz
U	(W)	28	F	Wife	24Mr02Bz
TAYLOR, U		25	M	Farmer	24Mr02Bz
STEPHENS, Wm.		25	M	Farmer	24Mr02Bz
ELLIS, Sarah		20	F	Servant	24Mr02Bz
FURLONG, Francis		49	M	Farmer	24Mr02Bz
U	(W)	49	F	Wife	24Mr02Bz
Cath.	(D)	26	F	Servant	24Mr02Bz
Johanah	(D)	23	F	Servant	24Mr02Bz
Ellen	(D)	20	F	Servant	24Mr02Bz
Jas.	(S)	19	M	Farmer	24Mr02Bz
BENNET, Wm.		26	M	Farmer	24Mr02Bz
DOLEN, John		29	M	Farmer	24Mr02Bz
SHERIDAN, John		20	M	Farmer	24Mr02Bz
Pat		40	M	Farmer	24Mr02Bz
Michl.		15	M	None	24Mr02Bz
Jas.		16	M	None	24Mr02Bz
Ellen		12	F	None	24Mr02Bz
BUCKLEY, Jas.		10	M	None	24Mr02Bz
Ann		45	F	None	24Mr02Bz
Thos.		23	M	Laborer	24Mr02Bz
Matthew		20	M	Laborer	24Mr02Bz
Jas.		18	M	Laborer	24Mr02Bz
John		15	M	None	24Mr02Bz
HOLT, Jas.		40	M	Laborer	24Mr02Bz
DAY, Robt.		20	M	Laborer	24Mr02Bz
U	(W)	20	F	Wife	24Mr02Bz
U		.00	U	Infant	24Mr02Bz
Wm.		01	M	Child	24Mr02Bz

NAMES OF PASSENGERS	AGE	SEX	OCCUPATIONS	DATE PORT SHIP
BENNET, Geo.	20	M	Laborer	24Mr02Bz
U (W)	20	F	Wife	24Mr02Bz
WILLIAMS, Thos.	27	M	Laborer	24Mr02Bz
RAY, John	40	M	Laborer	24Mr02Bz
Robt.	36	M	Laborer	24Mr02Bz
Martha	27	F	None	24Mr02Bz
John	18	M	None	24Mr02Bz
Joseph	20	M	Laborer	24Mr02Bz
Ann	08	F	Child	24Mr02Bz
Thos.	06	M	Child	24Mr02Bz
RILEY, Chas.	20	M	Laborer	24Mr02Bz
GLYN, Margt.	20	F	Servant	24Mr02Bz
ELLIS, Geo.	27	M	Laborer	24Mr02Bz
FERNAN, Thos.	24	M	Laborer	24Mr02Bz
Richd.	26	M	Laborer	24Mr02Bz
Mary	23	F	Servant	24Mr02Bz
WINDLE, Solomon	33	M	Laborer	24Mr02Bz
MADEN, Mary	20	F	Servant	24Mr02Bz
HORAN, Wm.	26	M	Laborer	24Mr02Bz
HICKEY, John	20	M	Laborer	24Mr02Bz
MCGAREY, Bernard	24	M	Laborer	24Mr02Bz
BUTLER, John	30	M	Laborer	24Mr02Bz
BREMNER, Mary	16	F	Servant	24Mr02Bz
HARTY, Mary	30	F	Servant	24Mr02Bz
QUINN, Jas.	24	M	Laborer	24Mr02Bz
KILROY, Thos.	20	M	Laborer	24Mr02Bz
GILL, Patk.	30	M	Laborer	24Mr02Bz
INGRAM, John	23	M	Laborer	24Mr02Bz
DONOHOE, Mary	20	F	Servant	24Mr02Bz
SLATTERY, Julius	20	M	Laborer	24Mr02Bz
KENNEDY, Jeremiah	24	M	Laborer	24Mr02Bz
John	24	M	Laborer	24Mr02Bz
FIENY, Thos.	20	M	Laborer	24Mr02Bz
BALDWIN, Wm.	40	M	Laborer	24Mr02Bz
EMMET, Matthew	30	M	Laborer	24Mr02Bz
U (W)	27	F	Wife	24Mr02Bz
LANGAN, Biddy	27	F	None	24Mr02Bz
CARN, Michl.	25	M	Servant	24Mr02Bz
LOW, John	21	M	Laborer	24Mr02Bz
LEARY, Mich.	21	M	Laborer	24Mr02Bz
BARNES, Jas.	31	M	Laborer	24Mr02Bz
Harriet	26	F	None	24Mr02Bz
DAY, U	.00	F	Infant	24Mr02Bz
BABRIDGE, P.	20	M	Laborer	24Mr02Bz
FARLY, Jas.	20	M	Laborer	24Mr02Bz
MURRAY, Francis	00	M	Laborer	24Mr02Bz
BRAY, Geo.	29	M	Laborer	24Mr02Bz
Ann	24	F	Servant	24Mr02Bz
Hester	07	F	Child	24Mr02Bz
Joseph	02	M	Child	24Mr02Bz
Henry	.00	M	Infant	24Mr02Bz
William	05	M	Child	24Mr02Bz
HENLAY, John	30	M	Laborer	24Mr02Bz
Ellen	34	F	None	24Mr02Bz
CARTY, Pat	18	M	None	24Mr02Bz
DUFFY, Francis	23	M	None	24Mr02Bz
MARTIN, Eleanor	00	F	Unknown	24Mr02Bz
MCCARTY, Jas.	18	M	Laborer	24Mr02Bz
KEAN, Robert	26	M	Laborer	24Mr02Bz
ONEIL, Jas.	18	M	Laborer	24Mr02Bz
John	19	M	Laborer	24Mr02Bz
HAYS, Peter	29	M	Laborer	24Mr02Bz
MONAHAN, Bridget	29	F	Servant	24Mr02Bz
Patk.	20	M	Laborer	24Mr02Bz
MCDONALD, Michl.	02	M	Child	24Mr02Bz
CURRY, Edwrd.	20	M	Laborer	24Mr02Bz
SULLIVAN, John	19	M	Laborer	24Mr02Bz
Fanny	18	F	Servant	24Mr02Bz
FLEMING, Edwd.	20	M	Laborer	24Mr02Bz
SHANTY, Owen	26	M	Laborer	24Mr02Bz
FARRELL, Bridget	26	F	Servant	24Mr02Bz
LANGDON, Mary	21	F	Servant	24Mr02Bz
FARRELL, Thos.	32	M	Laborer	24Mr02Bz
Mary	23	F	Servant	24Mr02Bz
CALLAGHAN, Margt.	27	F	Servant	24Mr02Bz
DOLAN, Patk.	18	M	Laborer	24Mr02Bz
FORD, Ann	25	F	Servant	24Mr02Bz
LANGLEY, Cath.	23	F	Servant	24Mr02Bz
KENNEDY, Mich.	39	M	Laborer	24Mr02Bz
U	.06	M	Infant	24Mr02Bz
KELLY, Bryan	24	M	Laborer	24Mr02Bz
EGAN, Wm.	34	M	Laborer	24Mr02Bz
MADEN, Mary	24	F	Servant	24Mr02Bz
BRISLIN, Michl.	24	M	Laborer	24Mr02Bz
DELANY, Michl.	21	M	Laborer	24Mr02Bz
MURPHY, Mary	23	F	Servant	24Mr02Bz
DORAN, Wm.	18	M	Laborer	24Mr02Bz
OHARE, Mary	18	F	Servant	24Mr02Bz
WILEY, Bridget	05	F	Child	24Mr02Bz
GLOVARD, Margt.	18	F	Servant	24Mr02Bz
MCARDEN, John	20	M	Laborer	24Mr02Bz
SLATTERY, Judy	19	F	Servant	24Mr02Bz
Timothy	10	M	None	24Mr02Bz
Michl.	14	M	None	24Mr02Bz
BIRMINGHAM, Wm.	20	M	Laborer	24Mr02Bz
BINN, Wm.	20	M	Laborer	24Mr02Bz
DELANCY, Julia	30	F	Servant	24Mr02Bz
Cath.	20	F	Servant	24Mr02Bz
John	03	M	Child	24Mr02Bz
Ann	03	F	Child	24Mr02Bz
Maria	.00	F	Infant	24Mr02Bz
SLAYNOR, John	29	M	Laborer	24Mr02Bz
LYNCH, John	19	M	Laborer	24Mr02Bz
CARNESS, Ann	18	F	Servant	24Mr02Bz
MAHON, Martin	21	M	Laborer	24Mr02Bz
NEWMAN, Thos.	30	M	Laborer	24Mr02Bz
MURTOW, Ann	20	F	Servant	24Mr02Bz
REYNOLDS, Margt.	24	F	Servant	24Mr02Bz
Mary	.00	F	Infant	24Mr02Bz
CAMPBELL, Peter	10	M	None	24Mr02Bz
GLENAN, Margt.	50	F	Servant	24Mr02Bz
MCCORMICK, Mary	09	F	Child	24Mr02Bz
MOHAN, Bridget	20	F	Servant	24Mr02Bz
KELLY, Bridget	20	F	Servant	24Mr02Bz
BURNS, Nancy	30	F	Servant	24Mr02Bz
Mary-Ann	07	F	Child	24Mr02Bz
Ellen	05	F	Child	24Mr02Bz
Cath.3	05	F	Child	24Mr02Bz
KELLANY, Bridget	09	F	Child	24Mr02Bz
GRAY, Patk.	20	M	Laborer	24Mr02Bz
Michl.	18	M	Laborer	24Mr02Bz
KENNEDY, Bridget	00	F	Servant	24Mr02Bz
MOONEY, Patk.	39	M	Laborer	24Mr02Bz
Mary	30	F	None	24Mr02Bz
Margt.	.00	F	Infant	24Mr02Bz
REILLY, John-B.	26	M	Laborer	24Mr02Bz
CARTY, John	40	M	Laborer	24Mr02Bz
Martha	07	F	Child	24Mr02Bz
Robt.	13	M	None	24Mr02Bz
Owen	10	M	None	24Mr02Bz
Mary	08	F	None	24Mr02Bz
Bridget	02	F	None	24Mr02Bz
SHORFRY, Ann	30	F	Servant	24Mr02Bz
Ann	06	F	Child	24Mr02Bz
Ann	02	F	Child	24Mr02Bz
BRADY, Mary	03	F	Child	24Mr02Bz
MULLIGAN, Ann	20	F	Servant	24Mr02Bz
OBRIEN, Mich.	22	M	Laborer	24Mr02Bz
NOLIN, Patk.	40	M	None	24Mr02Bz
GAYNOR, Thos.	22	M	Laborer	24Mr02Bz
CONARTY, Cath.	20	F	Servant	24Mr02Bz
LAW, John	21	M	Laborer	24Mr02Bz
Henry	17	M	Laborer	24Mr02Bz
Joseph	14	M	None	24Mr02Bz
Walter	11	M	None	24Mr02Bz
Nancy	06	F	Child	24Mr02Bz
Mary	07	F	Child	24Mr02Bz
COX, Philip	30	M	Laborer	24Mr02Bz
SHEENAN, Thos.	25	M	Laborer	24Mr02Bz
WOODS, Nich.	22	M	Laborer	24Mr02Bz

NAMES OF PASSENGERS	AGE	SEX	OCCUPATIONS	DATE PORT SHIP
LYNCH, Rose	20	F	Servant	24Mr02Bz
BALL, Peter	15	M	None	24Mr02Bz
CORLAN, Patk.	30	M	Laborer	24Mr02Bz
DUFFY, Jas.	29	M	Laborer	24Mr02Bz
CARNY, Julia	20	F	Servant	24Mr02Bz
PLUNKETT, Peter	25	M	Laborer	24Mr02Bz
WATERS, Patk.	27	M	Laborer	24Mr02Bz
MCCORMACK, Thos.	39	M	Laborer	24Mr02Bz
Bridget	00	F	Laborer	24Mr02Bz
MCCALLISTER, Hector	39	M	Laborer	24Mr02Bz
DARBY, Thos.	39	M	Laborer	24Mr02Bz
GORDON, Geo.	24	M	Laborer	24Mr02Bz
PERRY, Jane	14	F	None	24Mr02Bz
ROCH, John	30	M	Laborer	24Mr02Bz
JOHNSON, John	28	M	Laborer	24Mr02Bz
GILLY, Thos.	24	M	Laborer	24Mr02Bz
SMITH, John-M.	32	M	Laborer	24Mr02Bz
BERRY, Saml.	22	M	Laborer	24Mr02Bz
Saml.Geo.	20	M	Laborer	24Mr02Bz
QUINCE, John	23	M	Laborer	24Mr02Bz
Sarah	25	F	Servant	24Mr02Bz
WOOD, Edwd.	25	M	Laborer	24Mr02Bz
FARRELL, Thos.	28	M	Laborer	24Mr02Bz
DAVY, Hugh	21	M	Laborer	24Mr02Bz
BRAY, Jas.	20	M	Laborer	24Mr02Bz
MANY, John	00	M	Unknown	24Mr02Bz
RANCE, George	25	M	Laborer	24Mr02Bz
ROBINSON, Jas.	39	M	Laborer	24Mr02Bz
RICHARDSON, Eliz.	15	F	Servant	24Mr02Bz
WALKER, John	24	M	Laborer	24Mr02Bz
FOX, Jas.	21	M	Laborer	24Mr02Bz
THOMPSON, Chas.	24	M	Laborer	24Mr02Bz
BOOTH, A.P.	25	M	Laborer	24Mr02Bz

MARMION 25 MARCH 1848

From Liverpool

NAMES OF PASSENGERS	AGE	SEX	OCCUPATIONS	DATE PORT SHIP
MCDONNELL, Pat	30	M	Nailer	25Mr02Hc
Mary	23	F	Unknown	25Mr02Hc
ROBERTS, Thomas	30	M	Laborer	25Mr02Hc
Margaret	25	F	Unknown	25Mr02Hc
Mary	25	F	Unknown	25Mr02Hc
Sally	01	F	Child	25Mr02Hc
Jane	.03	F	Infant	25Mr02Hc
TOIPHY, Michael	22	M	Laborer	25Mr02Hc
DAIDY, Thomas	24	M	Dairyman	25Mr02Hc
CRAWFORD, Alexander	21	M	Groom	25Mr02Hc
MULLENS, Thomas	31	M	Laborer	25Mr02Hc
Betty	30	F	Unknown	25Mr02Hc
Mary	00	F	Unknown	25Mr02Hc
Michael	11	M	Unknown	25Mr02Hc
NEALE, Ellen	20	F	Unknown	25Mr02Hc
WALSH, Pat	22	M	Laborer	25Mr02Hc
Mary	12	F	Unknown	25Mr02Hc
JENNINGS, Thomas	22	M	Laborer	25Mr02Hc
QUIRK, William	21	M	Laborer	25Mr02Hc
Thomas	12	M	Laborer	25Mr02Hc
COATES, Patt.	27	M	Laborer	25Mr02Hc
WELSH, Patt.	22	M	Laborer	25Mr02Hc
MURRAN, John	26	M	Laborer	25Mr02Hc
Candy	19	M	Laborer	25Mr02Hc
MCGRATH, Bryan	40	M	Laborer	25Mr02Hc
MCCUSKER, John	52	M	Laborer	25Mr02Hc
FURRELL, Catherine	50	F	Unknown	25Mr02Hc
James	21	M	Laborer	25Mr02Hc
Edward	18	M	Laborer	25Mr02Hc
Mary	16	F	Unknown	25Mr02Hc
HAYES, Catherine	21	F	Servant	25Mr02Hc
HAYES, Johanna	19	F	Servant	25Mr02Hc
BRUNTON, James	26	M	Laborer	25Mr02Hc
Eliza	23	F	Unknown	25Mr02Hc
BRYAN, John	25	M	Laborer	25Mr02Hc
Mary	24	F	Unknown	25Mr02Hc
Thomas	.03	M	Infant	25Mr02Hc
MAHONY, Michael	26	M	Laborer	25Mr02Hc
Judy	24	F	Unknown	25Mr02Hc
Margaret	.05	F	Infant	25Mr02Hc
REEDY, Timothy	24	M	Blacksmith	25Mr02Hc
DONNELL, Nancy	20	F	Servant	25Mr02Hc
BULGER, John	23	M	Laborer	25Mr02Hc
CONNER, Mary	20	F	Servant	25Mr02Hc
Catherine	19	F	Servant	25Mr02Hc
BERGIN, John	23	M	Clerk	25Mr02Hc
HOLOHAN, James	23	M	Laborer	25Mr02Hc
GANNON, James	23	M	Laborer	25Mr02Hc
DUNN, Catherine	23	F	Servant	25Mr02Hc
GANNON, Bridget	20	F	Servant	25Mr02Hc
Bridget	21	F	Servant	25Mr02Hc
DAULTON, Thomas	26	M	Laborer	25Mr02Hc
SWEENEY, John	26	M	Blacksmith	25Mr02Hc
Johanna	22	F	Unknown	25Mr02Hc
QUIRKE, Michael	37	M	Laborer	25Mr02Hc
William	13	M	Unknown	25Mr02Hc
MCGRATH, James	25	M	Unknown	25Mr02Hc
QUINN, Ann	20	F	Servant	25Mr02Hc
WHELAN, Jeremiah	26	M	Laborer	25Mr02Hc
CAUGHLIN, Richard	27	M	Laborer	25Mr02Hc
ROARKE, David	26	M	Laborer	25Mr02Hc
BUTLER, John	24	M	Laborer	25Mr02Hc
TOBIN, Thomas	26	M	Bricklayer	25Mr02Hc
FOLEY, John	44	M	Bricklayer	25Mr02Hc
MORAN, Charles	50	M	Laborer	25Mr02Hc
Ann	45	F	Unknown	25Mr02Hc
PARKBURRY, John	25	M	Hairdresser	25Mr02Hc
Ann	24	F	Unknown	25Mr02Hc
Charles	.00	M	Infant	25Mr02Hc
MURRAY, John	16	M	Carpenter	25Mr02Hc
Catherine	30	F	Unknown	25Mr02Hc
FITZGERALD, Thos.	10	M	Unknown	25Mr02Hc
NYLAND, John	30	M	Laborer	25Mr02Hc
WALSH, John	25	M	Laborer	25Mr02Hc
KILGARIFF, Daniel	21	M	Laborer	25Mr02Hc
CUNIFFE, Thomas	30	M	Laborer	25Mr02Hc
MCSHERRY, John	43	M	Farmer	25Mr02Hc
Mary	11	F	Unknown	25Mr02Hc
REYNOLDS, Celia	28	F	Unknown	25Mr02Hc
John	03	M	Child	25Mr02Hc
DOWLING, James	40	M	Chptr	25Mr02Hc
ROSS, John	26	M	Servant	25Mr02Hc
Alicia	19	F	Servant	25Mr02Hc
CLOONEY, John	28	M	Mason	25Mr02Hc
PHELAN, Patt.	30	M	Weaver	25Mr02Hc
Mary	12	F	Unknown	25Mr02Hc
WHELAN, James	35	M	Laborer	25Mr02Hc
LAWRENCETOWN, John	46	M	Cooper	25Mr02Hc
QUINN, James	29	M	Waiter	25Mr02Hc
Bridget	29	F	Unknown	25Mr02Hc
CORRIGAN, Ann	22	F	Servant	25Mr02Hc
SMITH, Betsey	20	F	Servant	25Mr02Hc
John	50	M	Farmer	25Mr02Hc
Christian	30	M	Farmer	25Mr02Hc
Patt.	25	M	Farmer	25Mr02Hc
John	22	M	Farmer	25Mr02Hc
Thomas	20	M	Farmer	25Mr02Hc
James	18	M	Farmer	25Mr02Hc
Christopher	30	M	Farmer	25Mr02Hc
John	26	M	Farmer	25Mr02Hc
MCNAMEE, Elizabeth	40	F	Unknown	25Mr02Hc
Catherine	03	F	Child	25Mr02Hc
Joseph	35	M	Farmer	25Mr02Hc
Catherine	35	F	Unknown	25Mr02Hc
Catherine	08	F	Child	25Mr02Hc
Richard	06	M	Child	25Mr02Hc

NAMES OF PASSENGERS	A G E	S E X	OCCUPATIONS	DATE PORT SHIP
MURPHY, Thomas	40	M	Farrier	25Mr02Hc
Catherine	38	F	Farrier	25Mr02Hc
Patt.	11	M	Unknown	25Mr02Hc
SLAVIN, Owen	36	M	Laborer	25Mr02Hc
Margt.	50	F	Laborer	25Mr02Hc
MCANEIR, Ann	23	F	Servant	25Mr02Hc
SLAVIN, Marg.	05	F	Child	25Mr02Hc
John	12	M	Unknown	25Mr02Hc
Henry	08	M	Child	25Mr02Hc
Ann	09	F	Child	25Mr02Hc
LAFFERTY, Mary	23	F	Servant	25Mr02Hc
TRAVIS, Patrick	23	M	Laborer	25Mr02Hc
Ellen	20	F	Unknown	25Mr02Hc
Margaret	.00	F	Infant	25Mr02Hc
BYRNE, Catherine	18	F	Servant	25Mr02Hc
KILKENNY, Eliza	20	F	Servant	25Mr02Hc
Ann	18	F	Servant	25Mr02Hc
TONRY, Honora	22	F	Unknown	25Mr02Hc
John	02	M	Child	25Mr02Hc
BURY, Pat	20	M	Laborer	25Mr02Hc
Mary	13	F	Unknown	25Mr02Hc
MORAN, Thomas	12	M	Unknown	25Mr02Hc
HALLAN, Mary	18	F	Unknown	25Mr02Hc
MORAN, Jane	14	F	Unknown	25Mr02Hc
Catherine	10	F	Unknown	25Mr02Hc
CARROLL, Biddy	26	F	Unknown	25Mr02Hc
Charles	02	M	Child	25Mr02Hc
Mary	.00	F	Infant	25Mr02Hc
QUIN, Catherine	30	F	Unknown	25Mr02Hc
Pat	10	M	Unknown	25Mr02Hc
Michael	.00	M	Infant	25Mr02Hc
HACKETT, Julia	20	F	Servant	25Mr02Hc
Kitty	21	F	Servant	25Mr02Hc
CORISH, John	26	M	Nailer	25Mr02Hc
Mary	21	F	Unknown	25Mr02Hc
BRADY, Mary	18	F	Unknown	25Mr02Hc
BURY, Mary	18	F	Dressmaker	25Mr02Hc
BARRATT, John	20	M	Laborer	25Mr02Hc
HAGGARTY, Mary	23	F	Unknown	25Mr02Hc
Wm.	27	M	Laborer	25Mr02Hc
HESHAN, Patrick	32	M	Laborer	25Mr02Hc
CUMMING, Tom	50	M	Laborer	25Mr02Hc
John	22	M	Laborer	25Mr02Hc
MULLEN, Clinton	08	M	Child	25Mr02Hc
Bridget	09	F	Child	25Mr02Hc
Kate	11	F	Unknown	25Mr02Hc
Patrick	40	M	Tailor	25Mr02Hc
John	19	M	Unknown	25Mr02Hc
Mary	36	F	Unknown	25Mr02Hc
MADDEN, John	33	M	Sawer	25Mr02Hc
LEONARD, Roger	10	M	Laborer	25Mr02Hc
HOURY, John	26	M	Laborer	25Mr02Hc
Bridget	26	F	Unknown	25Mr02Hc
Maria	06	F	Child	25Mr02Hc
Bridget	04	F	Child	25Mr02Hc
John	02	M	Child	25Mr02Hc
William	20	M	Laborer	25Mr02Hc
QUIRK, Julia	22	F	Servant	25Mr02Hc
FORD, John	31	M	Laborer	25Mr02Hc
MCTEAGUE, Bridget	31	F	Servant	25Mr02Hc
TIERNEY, Martin	13	M	Unknown	25Mr02Hc
HOARY, Patt.	20	M	Laborer	25Mr02Hc
Mary	13	F	Unknown	25Mr02Hc
MADDEN, John	23	M	Laborer	25Mr02Hc
MCGARL, Margaret	15	F	Servant	25Mr02Hc
HORAY, Essey	10	F	Servant	25Mr02Hc
DOHERTY, Pat	50	M	Tailor	25Mr02Hc
DEAN, John	25	M	Laborer	25Mr02Hc
DOUGHERTY, Dennis	20	M	Laborer	25Mr02Hc
KELLY, John	25	M	Laborer	25Mr02Hc
DEAN, Anthony	22	M	Laborer	25Mr02Hc
Mary	17	F	Servant	25Mr02Hc
ALLAN, John	20	M	Laborer	25Mr02Hc
COSTELLO, Michael	20	M	Servant	25Mr02Hc
OBRIEN, Thos.	12	M	Unknown	25Mr02Hc
HESLIN, Bridget	29	F	Unknown	25Mr02Hc
Mary	06	F	Child	25Mr02Hc
Thomas	04	M	Child	25Mr02Hc
LOVETT, Edward	20	M	Laborer	25Mr02Hc
Michael	16	M	Laborer	25Mr02Hc
DONNELLY, James	20	M	Laborer	25Mr02Hc
MCCLELLAND, Alexr.	20	M	Weaver	25Mr02Hc
MORAN, Patrick	28	M	Laborer	25Mr02Hc
Bernard	25	M	Laborer	25Mr02Hc
FORD, John	28	M	Laborer	25Mr02Hc
Mary	26	F	Unknown	25Mr02Hc
Michael	02	M	Child	25Mr02Hc
FEHELY, Ann	25	F	Servant	25Mr02Hc
MOLLOY, Catherine	28	F	Servant	25Mr02Hc
Margaret	26	F	Servant	25Mr02Hc
BUTLER, Bridget	29	F	Servant	25Mr02Hc
Michael	20	M	Mason	25Mr02Hc
Nicholas	23	M	Mason	25Mr02Hc
TAGGART, Margaret	30	F	Servant	25Mr02Hc
ALLAN, Steward	18	M	Laborer	25Mr02Hc
HUGHES, Margaret	25	F	Servant	25Mr02Hc
KILLAM, Edward	39	M	Mason	25Mr02Hc
HANRATTY, Bryan	35	M	Laborer	25Mr02Hc
Mary	23	F	Unknown	25Mr02Hc
EMMIS, Mary	30	F	Servant	25Mr02Hc
HOWARD, Robert	26	M	Laborer	25Mr02Hc
TAFFE, Patrick	21	M	Coachman	25Mr02Hc
GRIBBIN, Catherine	40	F	Unknown	25Mr02Hc
Mary	15	F	Servant	25Mr02Hc
NOWLAN, Edward	26	M	Laborer	25Mr02Hc
SMITH, Bernard	25	M	Farmer	25Mr02Hc
MEAGHAN, Peter	27	M	Laborer	25Mr02Hc
ANDERSON, Samuel	24	M	Laborer	25Mr02Hc
GORMLEY, Henry	24	M	Laborer	25Mr02Hc
CLARKE, Mary	16	F	Servant	25Mr02Hc
Ann	13	F	Servant	25Mr02Hc
ROURKE, Thomas	20	M	Laborer	25Mr02Hc
KEENAN, John	22	M	Laborer	25Mr02Hc
DEVINE, Thos.	20	M	Laborer	25Mr02Hc
Jane	18	F	Servant	25Mr02Hc
CORRIGAN, Ann	22	F	Servant	25Mr02Hc
GILL, Jane	25	F	Servant	25Mr02Hc
FENEGAN, Patt.	46	M	Laborer	25Mr02Hc
BRADY, Rose	20	F	Servant	25Mr02Hc
Mary	18	F	Servant	25Mr02Hc
Margaret	18	F	Servant	25Mr02Hc
GAFFNEY, Thomas	25	M	Laborer	25Mr02Hc
RILEY, Thomas	28	M	Laborer	25Mr02Hc
Bridget	25	F	Unknown	25Mr02Hc
GREEN, Edward	22	M	Laborer	25Mr02Hc
QUINN, Edward	20	M	Laborer	25Mr02Hc
John	19	M	Laborer	25Mr02Hc
Phillip	12	M	Laborer	25Mr02Hc
KEEGAN, Rose	40	F	Unknown	25Mr02Hc
REILY, Mary	26	F	Servant	25Mr02Hc
Rose	28	F	Servant	25Mr02Hc

COLUMBIA 27 MARCH 1848

From Liverpool

NAMES OF PASSENGERS	A G E	S E X	OCCUPATIONS	DATE PORT SHIP
HALKETT, Charles-Ray	42	M	Gentleman	27Mr02Hx
COCKBURN, Henry-Day	42	M	Gentleman	27Mr02Hx
PERFACT, Francis	42	M	Gentleman	27Mr02Hx
BUCK, James	30	M	Laborer	27Mr02Hx
WOOD, Mary	50	F	Laborer	27Mr02Hx
Betsey	30	F	Laborer	27Mr02Hx
Winney	25	F	Laborer	27Mr02Hx
BAMFORTH, James	30	M	Laborer	27Mr02Hx

NAMES OF PASSENGERS	AGE	SEX	OCCUPATIONS	DATE PORT SHIP
BAMFORTH, Oliver	24	M	Laborer	27Mr02Hx
Harriet	26	F	Laborer	27Mr02Hx
DYSON, Daniel	45	M	Farmer	27Mr02Hx
KELLY, John	25	M	Farmer	27Mr02Hx
Mary	29	F	Farmer	27Mr02Hx
BRADY, Crosly	30	M	Farmer	27Mr02Hx
CULLEN, Patrick	26	M	Laborer	27Mr02Hx
BRANNGAN, Patrick	22	M	Laborer	27Mr02Hx
Eliza	22	F	Laborer	27Mr02Hx
SHIRLY, Richard	22	M	Laborer	27Mr02Hx
CAVNAGH, Peter	22	M	Laborer	27Mr02Hx
HUNT, Thomas	22	M	Laborer	27Mr02Hx
Jane	23	F	Laborer	27Mr02Hx
BUCKLEY, William	22	M	Carpenter	27Mr02Hx
FORBES, Margaret	21	F	Spinster	27Mr02Hx
BOOTHE, Margaret	18	F	Spinster	27Mr02Hx
MILLEN, Anne	42	F	Spinster	27Mr02Hx
BELL, John	20	M	Laborer	27Mr02Hx
FORBES, William	16	M	Laborer	27Mr02Hx
MULLEN, Lewis	22	M	Laborer	27Mr02Hx
GRIFFITHS, Anne	34	F	Laborer	27Mr02Hx
FRANKLIN, John	28	M	Laborer	27Mr02Hx
WRIGHT, George	25	M	Laborer	27Mr02Hx
John	32	M	Laborer	27Mr02Hx
Mary	32	F	Laborer	27Mr02Hx
CLARKE, John	20	M	Laborer	27Mr02Hx
Ellen	20	F	Spinster	27Mr02Hx
COWELL, Thomas	30	M	Farmer	27Mr02Hx
SHERIDAN, Peter	25	M	Farmer	27Mr02Hx
HARTLEY, Wm.	22	M	Farmer	27Mr02Hx
HINDLE, Thomas	24	M	Farmer	27Mr02Hx
SPARKMAN, Ann	50	F	Laborer	27Mr02Hx
HEATH, Alan	22	M	Laborer	27Mr02Hx
GREENE, Richard	40	M	Laborer	27Mr02Hx
COSCLOTH, John	25	M	Laborer	27Mr02Hx
ROBINSON, U	23	M	Laborer	27Mr02Hx
WATLY, Joseph	27	M	Laborer	27Mr02Hx
Ann	25	F	Laborer	27Mr02Hx
Ellen	.11	F	Infant	27Mr02Hx
Joseph	03	M	Child	27Mr02Hx
REYNOLDS, Eliza	26	F	Laborer	27Mr02Hx
Elizabeth	06	F	Child	27Mr02Hx
Mary	04	F	Child	27Mr02Hx
Thomas	.11	M	Infant	27Mr02Hx
MCCORMICK, Edward	20	M	Mechanic	27Mr02Hx
KENNY, William	20	M	Mechanic	27Mr02Hx
SHANDLEY, Jane	20	F	Mechanic	27Mr02Hx
LEES, George	36	M	Mechanic	27Mr02Hx
BRANLEY, Henry	22	M	Mechanic	27Mr02Hx
RYAN, Michel	24	M	Laborer	27Mr02Hx
MCKEE, Robert	30	M	Laborer	27Mr02Hx
William	36	M	Laborer	27Mr02Hx
John	24	M	Laborer	27Mr02Hx
MARSHALL, James	20	M	Laborer	27Mr02Hx
CAHILL, Timothy	35	M	Laborer	27Mr02Hx
MORGAN, Robert	30	M	Laborer	27Mr02Hx
Edwin	12	M	Laborer	27Mr02Hx
WILSON, William	30	M	Laborer	27Mr02Hx
PALMER, Thos.	23	M	Farmer	27Mr02Hx
Ellen	18	F	Spinster	27Mr02Hx
FRAL, Michel	24	M	Mechanic	27Mr02Hx
CLARK, Charles	18	M	Laborer	27Mr02Hx
SMITH, John	15	M	Laborer	27Mr02Hx
MCDURE, James	46	M	Laborer	27Mr02Hx
MCGARRETT, Patrick	26	M	Laborer	27Mr02Hx
Bridget	23	F	Laborer	27Mr02Hx
EGAN, Wm.	24	M	Laborer	27Mr02Hx
DUMPHY, John	22	M	Laborer	27Mr02Hx
CONNELL, Patrick	25	M	Laborer	27Mr02Hx
SMITH, Francis	18	M	Laborer	27Mr02Hx
KIRKPATRICK, James	30	M	Laborer	27Mr02Hx
DWYER, Thomas	30	M	Carpenter	27Mr02Hx
SWEENEY, Nancy	24	F	Spinster	27Mr02Hx
KENNEDY, Catharine	26	F	Spinster	27Mr02Hx
SWEENEY, Catharin	15	F	Spinster	27Mr02Hx

NAMES OF PASSENGERS	AGE	SEX	OCCUPATIONS	DATE PORT SHIP
FOGARTY, Michel	23	M	Laborer	27Mr02Hx
GOODRIDGE, Thomas	17	M	Laborer	27Mr02Hx
EDWARDS, Elizabeth	22	F	Laborer	27Mr02Hx
ONEILE, Cornelius	21	M	Laborer	27Mr02Hx
MCGRATH, James	23	M	Laborer	27Mr02Hx
RYAN, William	23	M	Laborer	27Mr02Hx
SHEA, Michel	21	M	Laborer	27Mr02Hx
SATTINGER, John	20	M	Laborer	27Mr02Hx
Patrick	23	M	Laborer	27Mr02Hx
MULRYAN, John	20	M	Laborer	27Mr02Hx
ANDERSON, John	19	M	Laborer	27Mr02Hx
MCGARHAN, Phillip	20	M	Laborer	27Mr02Hx
GAFFEREY, Ellen	20	F	Laborer	27Mr02Hx
DONNELLY, Ellen	20	F	Laborer	27Mr02Hx
PATTERSON, Robert	22	M	Laborer	27Mr02Hx
GOODTRASS, John	22	M	Laborer	27Mr02Hx
HAMELTON, Isabella	16	F	Laborer	27Mr02Hx
QUINN, Betty	22	F	Laborer	27Mr02Hx
Mary	15	F	Laborer	27Mr02Hx
MURTAGH, Catherin	16	F	Laborer	27Mr02Hx
MCGOWN, Catherin	19	F	Mechanic	27Mr02Hx
MCCURNNY, Edward	20	M	Mechanic	27Mr02Hx
MCENNERY, Edward	22	M	Mechanic	27Mr02Hx
CAFFERY, Margaret	22	F	Mechanic	27Mr02Hx
Biddy	18	F	Mechanic	27Mr02Hx
COOGAN, Mary	23	F	Mechanic	27Mr02Hx
MCDONNELL, Richard	25	M	Mechanic	27Mr02Hx
MAHON, Margaret	23	F	Spinster	27Mr02Hx
MORAN, Ally	24	F	Spinster	27Mr02Hx
GUNN, Mary	25	F	Spinster	27Mr02Hx
Mary	.08	F	Infant	27Mr02Hx
Patrick	07	M	Child	27Mr02Hx
SOMERSHERE, George	29	M	Laborer	27Mr02Hx
Eliza	16	F	Laborer	27Mr02Hx
DONNELLAN, Susan	22	F	Laborer	27Mr02Hx
DALEY, Simon	20	M	Laborer	27Mr02Hx
GRENAN, Patrick	18	M	Laborer	27Mr02Hx
QUINN, Peter	17	M	Laborer	27Mr02Hx
DENT, Mick	30	M	Laborer	27Mr02Hx
KAY, John	40	M	Laborer	27Mr02Hx
HOWARTH, George	41	M	Laborer	27Mr02Hx
BRADLEY, Henrey	26	M	Laborer	27Mr02Hx
U (W)	30	F	Laborer	27Mr02Hx
Jane (D)	.09	F	Infant	27Mr02Hx
ORMOND, Thomas	18	M	Laborer	27Mr02Hx
BRIDGE, Henry	40	M	Laborer	27Mr02Hx
BARROW, Mathew	35	M	Laborer	27Mr02Hx
CASSON, John	45	M	Laborer	27Mr02Hx
PELET, Garret	45	M	Laborer	27Mr02Hx
C. (W)	40	F	Laborer	27Mr02Hx
Catherin (D)	.06	F	Infant	27Mr02Hx
Lawrence (S)	20	M	Laborer	27Mr02Hx
Francis (S)	16	M	Laborer	27Mr02Hx
Mary (D)	12	F	Laborer	27Mr02Hx
Joseph (S)	10	M	Laborer	27Mr02Hx
Bridget (D)	04	F	Child	27Mr02Hx
Catherin (D)	02	F	Child	27Mr02Hx
KILMEANY, Thomas	36	M	Laborer	27Mr02Hx
U (W)	30	F	Wife	27Mr02Hx
Mary (D)	.05	F	Infant	27Mr02Hx
Died-At-Sea				
FOX, James	28	M	Laborer	27Mr02Hx
John	24	M	Laborer	27Mr02Hx
Mary	26	F	Laborer	27Mr02Hx
NOWLAN, Andrew	23	M	Shoemaker	27Mr02Hx
WILSON, John	21	M	Shoemaker	27Mr02Hx
MOLLOY, Ellen	36	F	Spinster	27Mr02Hx
Catherine	15	F	Spinster	27Mr02Hx
James	17	M	Spinster	27Mr02Hx
SHERIDAN, Biddy	13	F	Spinster	27Mr02Hx
HARRINGTON, Ellen	18	F	Spinster	27Mr02Hx
PETET, Barney	34	M	Laborer	27Mr02Hx
SHAUNGHESSY, Jerremah	24	M	Laborer	27Mr02Hx
BRIDGE, Barny	28	M	Laborer	27Mr02Hx
HOLT, William	30	M	Laborer	27Mr02Hx

NAMES OF PASSENGERS	AGE	SEX	OCCUPATIONS	DATE PORT SHIP
TAYLOR, Robt.	44	M	Laborer	27Mr02Hx
RUMNER, James	31	M	Laborer	27Mr02Hx
MULLIGAN, John	46	M	Laborer	27Mr02Hx
CUNDUCK, John	24	M	Laborer	27Mr02Hx
Michel	30	M	Laborer	27Mr02Hx
Ann	25	F	Laborer	27Mr02Hx
MANNAN, Catherin	22	F	Laborer	27Mr02Hx
BURD, James	23	M	Laborer	27Mr02Hx
RHODES, Margaret	34	F	Laborer	27Mr02Hx
Bridget	06	F	Child	27Mr02Hx
Mary-Ann Died-At-Sea	.04	F	Infant	27Mr02Hx
James	04	M	Child	27Mr02Hx
Jane	02	F	Child	27Mr02Hx
HUGHES, William	26	M	Laborer	27Mr02Hx
FOSHER, Samuel	24	M	Laborer	27Mr02Hx
CUNNINGHAM, James	34	M	Laborer	27Mr02Hx
Catherine	30	F	Laborer	27Mr02Hx
Mary	02	F	Child	27Mr02Hx
Catherin	.10	F	Infant	27Mr02Hx
PARKER, John	43	M	Laborer	27Mr02Hx
Joseph	20	M	Laborer	27Mr02Hx
Ann	17	F	Spinster	27Mr02Hx
William	03	M	Child	27Mr02Hx
John	03	M	Child	27Mr02Hx
DOWDELL, Robert	24	M	Laborer	27Mr02Hx
GRATLEY, Timothy	27	M	Laborer	27Mr02Hx
GATELY, Hugh	22	M	Laborer	27Mr02Hx
WORSLEY, Charles	23	M	Laborer	27Mr02Hx
GREGORY, William	36	M	Laborer	27Mr02Hx
DUNGAN, Thomas	20	M	Laborer	27Mr02Hx
Patrick	13	M	Laborer	27Mr02Hx
KELLY, Ann	30	F	Laborer	27Mr02Hx
Ellen	18	F	Laborer	27Mr02Hx
Hannah	16	F	Laborer	27Mr02Hx
BURNEY, James	22	M	Laborer	27Mr02Hx
DOWD, Betty	30	F	Laborer	27Mr02Hx
Mary	11	F	Laborer	27Mr02Hx
James	04	M	Child	27Mr02Hx
Biddy	09	F	Child	27Mr02Hx
JUDGE, Mary	33	F	Laborer	27Mr02Hx
Thomas	.07	M	Infant	27Mr02Hx
Biddy	11	F	Laborer	27Mr02Hx
Ally	09	F	Child	27Mr02Hx
William	03	M	Child	27Mr02Hx
Mary	30	F	Laborer	27Mr02Hx
RUDDEN, Margaret	24	F	Laborer	27Mr02Hx
Mary	.09	F	Infant	27Mr02Hx
MCINNHENY, Catherin	32	F	Laborer	27Mr02Hx
Thomas	14	M	Carpenter	27Mr02Hx
John	32	M	Carpenter	27Mr02Hx
BRUCE, John	20	M	Carpenter	27Mr02Hx
Margaret	15	F	Spinster	27Mr02Hx
HUDDING, Biddy	20	F	Spinster	27Mr02Hx
CARTY, Martin	20	M	Laborer	27Mr02Hx
MCCURTON, Cicily	60	F	Laborer	27Mr02Hx
Mary	18	F	Laborer	27Mr02Hx
BRYAN, Mary	24	F	Laborer	27Mr02Hx
LYON, Charles	30	M	Laborer	27Mr02Hx
William	58	M	Laborer	27Mr02Hx
U-Mrs.	40	F	Spinster	27Mr02Hx
John	26	M	Laborer	27Mr02Hx
Sarah	18	F	Laborer	27Mr02Hx
Thomas	28	M	Laborer	27Mr02Hx
Eliza	24	F	Laborer	27Mr02Hx
BRUD, James	23	M	Laborer	27Mr02Hx
WALTER, John	20	M	Laborer	27Mr02Hx
HANTON, U-Mrs.	20	F	Laborer	27Mr02Hx
Patrick	02	M	Child	27Mr02Hx
Jane	.08	F	Infant	27Mr02Hx
MEGAN, Christy	20	F	Laborer	27Mr02Hx
MAGUIRE, Thomas	17	M	Laborer	27Mr02Hx
FULLAM, Thomas	20	M	Laborer	27Mr02Hx
ROARK, Michel	20	M	Laborer	27Mr02Hx
Bridget	16	F	Laborer	27Mr02Hx

NAMES OF PASSENGERS		AGE	SEX	OCCUPATIONS	DATE PORT SHIP
HANLEY, Liddy		16	F	Laborer	27Mr02Hx
LYNCH, Mychel		21	F	Laborer	27Mr02Hx
FANEY, Rose		18	F	Laborer	27Mr02Hx
CARTY, Julia		20	F	Laborer	27Mr02Hx
MEEHAN, Patrick		20	M	Laborer	27Mr02Hx
LOGAN, Thomas		20	M	Laborer	27Mr02Hx
COLAN, John		40	M	Laborer	27Mr02Hx
CARROLL, Rose		20	F	Laborer	27Mr02Hx
KELLEY, Francis		18	M	Laborer	27Mr02Hx
DUFFY, Patrick		18	M	Laborer	27Mr02Hx
FOX, Owen		34	M	Laborer	27Mr02Hx
Margaret		30	F	Laborer	27Mr02Hx
Patrick		05	M	Child	27Mr02Hx
Peter		03	M	Child	27Mr02Hx
Margaret		.10	F	Infant	27Mr02Hx
TAFFE, Mary		18	F	Laborer	27Mr02Hx
BOW, William		27	M	Mechanic	27Mr02Hx
CAHILL, Patrick		27	M	Mechanic	27Mr02Hx
LENNON, Patrick		25	M	Mechanic	27Mr02Hx
REYNOLDS, James		27	M	Mechanic	27Mr02Hx
HALLAM, Kennon		27	M	Mechanic	27Mr02Hx
LANCASTER, Mathew		17	M	Mechanic	27Mr02Hx
BLAKELEY, Robert		30	M	Mechanic	27Mr02Hx
U	(W)	27	F	Mechanic	27Mr02Hx
Robert	(S)	04	M	Child	27Mr02Hx
Mary	(D)	.11	F	Infant	27Mr02Hx
DICKENS, Eliza		26	F	Mechanic	27Mr02Hx
LOGEN, Edward		21	M	Mechanic	27Mr02Hx
DORLAN, Martin		25	M	Mechanic	27Mr02Hx
HARRINGTON, Eliza		22	F	Spinster	27Mr02Hx
ENTWISTLE, Duncan		28	M	Spinner	27Mr02Hx
DEBB, Joseph		34	M	Laborer	27Mr02Hx
U	(W)	30	F	None	27Mr02Hx
Mary	(D)	.09	F	Infant	27Mr02Hx
WARD, Charles		26	M	Laborer	27Mr02Hx
DEBB, William		02	M	Child	27Mr02Hx
SHANLY, John		20	M	Laborer	27Mr02Hx
Mary		17	F	Laborer	27Mr02Hx
WALLACE, Robert		18	M	Laborer	27Mr02Hx
COX, Catherin		40	F	Laborer	27Mr02Hx
Mary		35	F	Laborer	27Mr02Hx
Peter		35	M	Laborer	27Mr02Hx
John		09	M	Child	27Mr02Hx
Ann		07	F	Child	27Mr02Hx
MARTIN, Mary		45	F	Laborer	27Mr02Hx
Ellen		22	F	Laborer	27Mr02Hx
John		20	M	Laborer	27Mr02Hx
Jane		18	F	Laborer	27Mr02Hx
William		16	M	Laborer	27Mr02Hx
Nancy		10	F	Laborer	27Mr02Hx
Mary		08	F	Child	27Mr02Hx
Peggy		06	F	Child	27Mr02Hx
Robert		02	M	Child	27Mr02Hx
CONLIN, Thomas		20	M	Carpenter	27Mr02Hx
SHEAL, James		20	M	Carpenter	27Mr02Hx
MOONEY, John		40	M	Carpenter	27Mr02Hx
Mary		40	F	Carpenter	27Mr02Hx
Danial		09	M	Child	27Mr02Hx
Sarah		02	F	Child	27Mr02Hx
LEHRE, Thomas		30	M	Spinner	27Mr02Hx
BULLEN, John		29	M	Spinner	27Mr02Hx
U	(W)	30	F	Spinner	27Mr02Hx
MAHER, James		27	M	Spinner	27Mr02Hx
HEALEY, Catherin		50	F	Spinner	27Mr02Hx
Martin		20	M	Spinner	27Mr02Hx
Thomas		18	M	Spinner	27Mr02Hx
REILEY, Rose		30	F	Spinner	27Mr02Hx
BLAND, John		40	M	Spinner	27Mr02Hx
COSGROVE, Philip		20	M	Spinner	27Mr02Hx
Bridget		18	F	Spinner	27Mr02Hx
Mary		08	F	Child	27Mr02Hx
SULLIVAN, Jeremiah		25	M	Spinner	27Mr02Hx
MCGUIRE, John		40	M	Spinner	27Mr02Hx
DICKSON, Eliza		27	F	Spinner	27Mr02Hx
CLARK, Catherin		51	F	Spinster	27Mr02Hx

NAMES OF PASSENGERS	AGE	SEX	OCCUPATIONS	DATE PORT SHIP
CLARK, James	30	M	Laborer	27Mr02Hx
PHILLIPS, Sarah-M.	30	F	Laborer	27Mr02Hx
RIELY, Patrick	40	M	Laborer	27Mr02Hx
BRADY, Ann	11	F	Laborer	27Mr02Hx
EARLY, Ellen	24	F	Laborer	27Mr02Hx
BRADY, Bridget	21	F	Laborer	27Mr02Hx
QUINN, Michel	35	M	Laborer	27Mr02Hx
Michel	11	M	Laborer	27Mr02Hx
Barnard	07	M	Child	27Mr02Hx
Ellen	05	F	Child	27Mr02Hx
CLARK, Rose	18	F	Laborer	27Mr02Hx
GROGHAN, Rose	20	F	Laborer	27Mr02Hx
CORREGAN, Patrick	20	M	Laborer	27Mr02Hx
DOOLAN, James	20	M	Laborer	27Mr02Hx
BAHAN, Ellen	17	F	Laborer	27Mr02Hx
MARTIN, Ellen	20	F	Laborer	27Mr02Hx
REYNOLDS, Margaret	20	F	Laborer	27Mr02Hx
John	20	M	Laborer	27Mr02Hx
LANEY, Hannah	17	F	Laborer	27Mr02Hx
James	24	M	Laborer	27Mr02Hx
HARLY, Bess	30	F	Laborer	27Mr02Hx
Michel	04	M	Child	27Mr02Hx
Mary	02	F	Child	27Mr02Hx
Bridget	.08	F	Infant	27Mr02Hx
REYNOLDS, Alexander-M.	22	M	Laborer	27Mr02Hx
MCKIBBAN, Thomas	21	M	Laborer	27Mr02Hx
BRYAN, Mary	20	F	Laborer	27Mr02Hx
DEEGAN, Michel	20	M	Laborer	27Mr02Hx
WELSH, Martin	20	M	Laborer	27Mr02Hx
LEVINE, Patt.	20	M	Laborer	27Mr02Hx
TULTYTORE, William	24	M	Laborer	27Mr02Hx
Isabella	24	F	Laborer	27Mr02Hx
Isabella	.05	F	Infant	27Mr02Hx
CONNAUGHTON, Pat.	18	M	Laborer	27Mr02Hx
FOX, Pat.	16	M	Laborer	27Mr02Hx
PHILLIPS, David	60	M	Laborer	27Mr02Hx
HADDOCK, Marton	20	M	Laborer	27Mr02Hx
GARNOT, Christy	22	M	Laborer	27Mr02Hx
FOX, Patrick	20	M	Laborer	27Mr02Hx
CONWAY, Thomas	20	M	Laborer	27Mr02Hx
CUMMINS, Sarah	26	F	Laborer	27Mr02Hx
Patrick	28	M	Laborer	27Mr02Hx
Winny	40	F	Spinster	27Mr02Hx
Michel	26	M	Laborer	27Mr02Hx
Bridget	17	F	Laborer	27Mr02Hx
Catherin	14	F	Laborer	27Mr02Hx
Winney	15	F	Laborer	27Mr02Hx
KELLY, Joseph	20	M	Laborer	27Mr02Hx
COGAN, M.	30	F	None	27Mr02Hx
Margaret	03	F	Child	27Mr02Hx
Andrew	10	M	Laborer	27Mr02Hx
BYRNES, Mathew	28	M	Laborer	27Mr02Hx
MCEWIN, James	20	M	Laborer	27Mr02Hx
TYRELL, Patrick	20	M	Laborer	27Mr02Hx
Died-At-Sea				
MURRY, Patrick	20	M	Laborer	27Mr02Hx
Ann	04	F	Child	27Mr02Hx
TYRELL, John	28	M	Laborer	27Mr02Hx
KELHOOLY, Ann	25	F	Laborer	27Mr02Hx
Biddy	04	F	Child	27Mr02Hx
Ann	.09	F	Infant	27Mr02Hx
NOLAN, Ann	25	F	Laborer	27Mr02Hx
BUCKLEY, Danial	20	M	Laborer	27Mr02Hx
LARKIN, Patrick	20	M	Laborer	27Mr02Hx
DELAMVEE, Mary	19	F	Laborer	27Mr02Hx
ROWLEY, Ann	22	F	Laborer	27Mr02Hx
LYNCH, Patrick	15	M	Laborer	27Mr02Hx
Michele	11	M	Laborer	27Mr02Hx
MCGRATH, John	21	M	Laborer	27Mr02Hx
FURLONG, Mary	36	F	Laborer	27Mr02Hx
Johanna	04	F	Child	27Mr02Hx
Mary	.11	F	Infant	27Mr02Hx
FARRELLY, Bridget	30	F	Laborer	27Mr02Hx
CONNOR, Peter	30	M	Laborer	27Mr02Hx
QUINN, Ann	26	F	Laborer	27Mr02Hx

NAMES OF PASSENGERS	AGE	SEX	OCCUPATIONS	DATE PORT SHIP
MULLIGAN, Catherine	20	F	Laborer	27Mr02Hx
FISET, George	20	M	Laborer	27Mr02Hx
TYREL, James	25	M	Laborer	27Mr02Hx
JAMES, Wm.	20	M	Laborer	27Mr02Hx
EARLY, Patrick	23	M	Laborer	27Mr02Hx
DEVINE, Peter	24	M	Laborer	27Mr02Hx
CARRIGAN, James	25	M	Laborer	27Mr02Hx
HALLAHANE, Patrick	14	M	Laborer	27Mr02Hx
SOMAN, Patrick	12	M	Laborer	27Mr02Hx
GORT, Mary	.01	F	Infant	27Mr02Hx

SIR-ROBERT-PEEL 30 MARCH 1848

From Liverpool

NAMES OF PASSENGERS		AGE	SEX	OCCUPATIONS	DATE PORT SHIP
HUGHES, Catherine		28	F	Servant	30Mr02Mu
Mary		23	F	Servant	30Mr02Mu
Ann		21	F	Servant	30Mr02Mu
BRENNAN, Mary-Ann		16	F	Servant	30Mr02Mu
DRISCOLL, Dennis		30	M	Farmer	30Mr02Mu
Jane	(W)	20	F	Wife	30Mr02Mu
Barbara		23	F	Unknown	30Mr02Mu
BRADY, Bernard		40	M	Farmer	30Mr02Mu
John		20	M	Farmer	30Mr02Mu
Ann		16	F	Servant	30Mr02Mu
RECKET, Owen		26	M	Laborer	30Mr02Mu
REILLY, Edward		16	M	Laborer	30Mr02Mu
MCGOWAN, John		20	M	Farmer	30Mr02Mu
Susan	(W)	23	F	Wife	30Mr02Mu
HICKEY, Richard		20	M	Laborer	30Mr02Mu
OKEEFE, David		24	M	Laborer	30Mr02Mu
THOMPSON, John		40	M	Laborer	30Mr02Mu
FLANNERY, John		22	M	Laborer	30Mr02Mu
BROWAN, James		27	M	Unknown	30Mr02Mu
KEARNEY, Patrick		20	M	Carpenter	30Mr02Mu
CAVANAGH, James		16	M	Laborer	30Mr02Mu
DUANE, Michl.		20	M	Laborer	30Mr02Mu
Bridget	(W)	16	F	Wife	30Mr02Mu
QUIN, John		35	M	Laborer	30Mr02Mu
COLLINS, Timothy		25	M	Laborer	30Mr02Mu
MCGUINIS, Hugh		30	M	Laborer	30Mr02Mu
Pat		27	M	Laborer	30Mr02Mu
CONNAUGHTON, Bridget		20	F	Servant	30Mr02Mu
BARRET, James		27	M	Laborer	30Mr02Mu
Ann	(W)	30	F	Wife	30Mr02Mu
Thomas	(S)	09	M	Child	30Mr02Mu
KELLY, Mary		16	F	Servant	30Mr02Mu
KEOGH, Pat		20	M	Laborer	30Mr02Mu
BURKE, Bridget		11	F	Servant	30Mr02Mu
MCGUIRE, Andrew		20	M	Unknown	30Mr02Mu
MCQUADE, James		21	M	Laborer	30Mr02Mu
GARRETT, Philip		22	M	Laborer	30Mr02Mu
BRENNAN, Michl.		28	M	Laborer	30Mr02Mu
MASTERSTON, Michl.		17	M	Laborer	30Mr02Mu
TIRELL, Martin		27	M	Laborer	30Mr02Mu
ROURKE, John		13	M	Laborer	30Mr02Mu
Francis		15	M	Laborer	30Mr02Mu
OATS, Geo.		28	M	Laborer	30Mr02Mu
MULCAHY, Johanna		23	F	Laborer	30Mr02Mu
Nicholas		23	M	Laborer	30Mr02Mu
BRANNAN, Pat		18	M	Laborer	30Mr02Mu
QUIN, Catherine		21	F	Servant	30Mr02Mu
COSTELLO, Miles		50	M	Servant	30Mr02Mu
RYAN, Biddy		48	F	Servant	30Mr02Mu
DORGAN, Michl.		10	M	Unknown	30Mr02Mu
BAILEY, Robert		30	M	Gunsmith	30Mr02Mu
MCSWEENY, Miles		25	M	Laborer	30Mr02Mu
GOULDING, Pat		25	M	Laborer	30Mr02Mu
WISEMAN, Mary		20	F	Servant	30Mr02Mu

NAMES OF PASSENGERS		AGE	SEX	OCCUPATIONS	DATE PORT SHIP
SULLIVAN, Ellen		26	F	Servant	30Mr02Mu
CROWLEY, Philip		27	M	Laborer	30Mr02Mu
Honora		25	F	Servant	30Mr02Mu
Mary		20	F	Servant	30Mr02Mu
BELL, James		23	M	Laborer	30Mr02Mu
DUNN, Pat		21	M	Laborer	30Mr02Mu
DONELLAN, Michl.		27	M	Laborer	30Mr02Mu
MOORE, John		23	M	Butler	30Mr02Mu
Margaret	(W)	23	F	Wife	30Mr02Mu
CRAIG, Ann		20	F	Servant	30Mr02Mu
DEEGAN, Thomas		22	M	Laborer	30Mr02Mu
CARROLL, John		26	M	Laborer	30Mr02Mu
MACKAY, Dennis		24	M	Laborer	30Mr02Mu
EUSTACE, Joseph		28	M	Laborer	30Mr02Mu
TYRRELL, Martin		26	M	Laborer	30Mr02Mu
FERGUSON, Arthur		35	M	Plasterer	30Mr02Mu
JOHNSON, James		28	M	Laborer	30Mr02Mu
VINCENT, John		18	M	Laborer	30Mr02Mu
MIDDLETON, Thos.		20	M	Laborer	30Mr02Mu
MCDONALD, Henry		40	M	Laborer	30Mr02Mu
REID, Patrick		18	M	Shoemaker	30Mr02Mu
DUFFY, Wm.		22	M	Laborer	30Mr02Mu
MCMAHON, Wm.		25	M	Laborer	30Mr02Mu
Mary		21	F	Servant	30Mr02Mu
CORRIGAN, James		24	M	Laborer	30Mr02Mu
Bridget	(W)	21	F	Wife	30Mr02Mu
MCINTYRE, Mary		24	F	Wife	30Mr02Mu
Maria	(D)	11	F	Unknown	30Mr02Mu
TOBIN, Margret		15	F	Servant	30Mr02Mu
BOYLE, Cathrine		20	F	Servant	30Mr02Mu
SHELTON, James		24	M	Laborer	30Mr02Mu
MCNAMARA, John		26	M	Hatter	30Mr02Mu
CAMPBELL, Isabella		20	F	Servant	30Mr02Mu
WOODS, Bessy		22	F	Servant	30Mr02Mu
MURPHY, James		20	M	Laborer	30Mr02Mu
SAWLESS, James		24	M	Laborer	30Mr02Mu
DUANE, Michl.		30	M	Laborer	30Mr02Mu
RYAN, Edwd.		28	M	Laborer	30Mr02Mu
Sally	(W)	28	F	Wife	30Mr02Mu
U		.00	U	Infant	30Mr02Mu
John		20	M	Laborer	30Mr02Mu
Mary		18	F	Servant	30Mr02Mu
Anne		22	F	Servant	30Mr02Mu
RICE, Pat		18	M	Laborer	30Mr02Mu
PHELAN, Thos.		21	M	Laborer	30Mr02Mu
SHERIDAN, John		30	M	Laborer	30Mr02Mu
CORRIGAN, James		25	M	Laborer	30Mr02Mu
WHETTEN, Geo.		28	M	Laborer	30Mr02Mu
PHELAN, John		20	M	Laborer	30Mr02Mu
DWYER, Michl.		24	M	Laborer	30Mr02Mu
CULHAM, Edwd.		18	M	Laborer	30Mr02Mu
Honora		22	F	Servant	30Mr02Mu
Johanna		20	F	Servant	30Mr02Mu
BYRNE, Dennis		22	M	Laborer	30Mr02Mu
MURRAY, David		18	M	Laborer	30Mr02Mu
CARROLL, Martin		30	M	Laborer	30Mr02Mu
MULVANY, Michl.		19	M	Laborer	30Mr02Mu
Ellen	(W)	16	F	Wife	30Mr02Mu
MULDANY, Peter		20	M	Laborer	30Mr02Mu
CARTY, Michl.		40	M	Laborer	30Mr02Mu
MULLIGAN, Anne		20	F	Servant	30Mr02Mu
LAWLESS, Cathrine		22	F	Servant	30Mr02Mu
Jane		.00	F	Infant	30Mr02Mu
RIDDLE, Alex		30	M	Laborer	30Mr02Mu
GRAVES, Mary		30	F	Servant	30Mr02Mu
PRIOR, Thomas-M.		39	M	Saddler	30Mr02Mu
BIRMINGHAM, Edwd.		25	M	Tailor	30Mr02Mu
HALEGAN, Mary		24	F	Servant	30Mr02Mu
Catherine		04	F	Child	30Mr02Mu
BIRMINGHAM, Ellen		20	F	Servant	30Mr02Mu
ROE, Edwd.		24	M	Laborer	30Mr02Mu
MANNING, U		50	F	None	30Mr02Mu
William		28	M	Farmer	30Mr02Mu
Alice		27	F	Wife	30Mr02Mu
James		19	M	Laborer	30Mr02Mu

NAMES OF PASSENGERS		AGE	SEX	OCCUPATIONS	DATE PORT SHIP
CUNNINGHAM, Peter		34	M	Laborer	30Mr02Mu
SWAN, Thomas		18	M	Laborer	30Mr02Mu
Mary	(W)	17	F	Wife	30Mr02Mu
CONNELL, Matthew		30	M	Laborer	30Mr02Mu
Catherine	(W)	25	F	Wife	30Mr02Mu
CUNNINGHAM, Thomas		20	M	Farmer	30Mr02Mu
U	(W)	21	F	Unknown	30Mr02Mu
FARAN, Peter		21	M	Laborer	30Mr02Mu
MURTAGH, Mary		18	F	Spinster	30Mr02Mu
MCHUGH, Anne		21	F	Spinster	30Mr02Mu
CALAHAN, Anne		30	F	Wife	30Mr02Mu
Thos.	(S)	09	M	Child	30Mr02Mu
Patrick	(S)	08	M	Child	30Mr02Mu
FARAN, Biddy		21	F	Wife	30Mr02Mu
Anne	(D)	.00	F	Infant	30Mr02Mu
CARROLL, Patrick		25	M	Laborer	30Mr02Mu
DOWDALE, Richard		25	M	Laborer	30Mr02Mu
MCHUGH, John		30	M	Laborer	30Mr02Mu
Ellen	(W)	28	F	Wife	30Mr02Mu
GREENE, Mary		23	F	Servant	30Mr02Mu
FITZPATRICK, Mary		20	F	Servant	30Mr02Mu
SADDLER, Robt.		23	M	Servant	30Mr02Mu
FRENCH, Ann		20	F	Servant	30Mr02Mu
Susan		16	F	Servant	30Mr02Mu
NOLON, Patrick		22	M	Servant	30Mr02Mu
JAAB, Ann		20	F	Dressmaker	30Mr02Mu
CARROLL, Martin		18	M	Laborer	30Mr02Mu
QUIGLEY, Thos.		19	M	Farmer	30Mr02Mu
KEALLEHER, Michl.		19	M	Laborer	30Mr02Mu
HINDS, Michl.		20	M	Laborer	30Mr02Mu
FLISK, Bridget		19	F	Servant	30Mr02Mu
Mary		17	F	Servant	30Mr02Mu
MALADY, Mary		20	F	Servant	30Mr02Mu
DUNN, Thomas		24	M	Laborer	30Mr02Mu
DAYSY, Tim		22	M	Laborer	30Mr02Mu
HOLTON, Thomas		22	M	Laborer	30Mr02Mu
RUNN, Michal		50	M	Laborer	30Mr02Mu
OREILLY, Charles		20	M	Laborer	30Mr02Mu
BIRMINGHAM, Geo.		29	M	Tailor	30Mr02Mu
ROOKE, Christy		19	M	Laborer	30Mr02Mu
MCELROY, Mary		32	F	Servant	30Mr02Mu
Mick		20	M	Laborer	30Mr02Mu
Julia		20	F	Servant	30Mr02Mu
Catherine		18	F	Servant	30Mr02Mu
James		16	M	Laborer	30Mr02Mu
WELSH, Patrick		24	M	Laborer	30Mr02Mu
MCGOWEN, James		20	M	Laborer	30Mr02Mu
GONNON, Catherine		18	F	Servant	30Mr02Mu
Judy		06	F	Child	30Mr02Mu
MCNABB, John		30	M	Shoemaker	30Mr02Mu
MURTAGH, Thomas		28	M	Farmer	30Mr02Mu
WALL, Christy		27	M	Laborer	30Mr02Mu
BUSBY, Wm.		27	M	Laborer	30Mr02Mu
SULLIVAN, Eliza		23	F	Servant	30Mr02Mu
WISEMAN, Mary		21	F	Servant	30Mr02Mu
CARAHAN, Pat		27	M	Laborer	30Mr02Mu
Alice		25	F	Servant	30Mr02Mu
MONAHAN, Mary		23	F	Servant	30Mr02Mu
Catherine		21	F	Servant	30Mr02Mu
MCKEVER, Mary		19	F	Servant	30Mr02Mu
MURTAGH, Owen		23	M	Laborer	30Mr02Mu
KIRK, Rhoda		21	F	Laborer	30Mr02Mu
DALY, Bridget		19	F	Laborer	30Mr02Mu
KELLY, Wm.		20	M	Laborer	30Mr02Mu
JOHNSON, W.		25	M	Gentleman	30Mr02Mu
HICKEY, Danl.		28	M	Gentleman	30Mr02Mu
CONNELLY, James		28	M	Farmer	30Mr02Mu

AMERICAN-EAGLE 31 MARCH 1848

From London

NAMES OF PASSENGERS		AGE	SEX	OCCUPATIONS	DATE PORT SHIP
DERRYMAN, James		22	M	Carpenter	31Mr21Rb
RILEY, James		20	M	Laborer	31Mr21Rb
Mary		20	F	Servant	31Mr21Rb
FITZGERALD, Catherine		22	F	Servant	31Mr21Rb
SOCKTON, Ellen		30	F	Servant	31Mr21Rb
MCNEAVE, Edward-C.		33	M	Shoemaker	31Mr21Rb
Patrick		24	M	Shoemaker	31Mr21Rb
GARNEER, Michael		23	M	Laborer	31Mr21Rb
Ellen		30	F	Laborer	31Mr21Rb
MUSLEY, James		24	M	Laborer	31Mr21Rb
KNARD, Thomas		18	M	Tailor	31Mr21Rb
HAWLEY, Danl.		30	M	Carpenter	31Mr21Rb
Helen		26	F	Carpenter	31Mr21Rb
Martin		07	M	Child	31Mr21Rb
MCALLEN, Danl.		27	M	Shoemaker	31Mr21Rb
GINNES, Wm.		40	M	Laborer	31Mr21Rb
Margt.		40	F	Laborer	31Mr21Rb
MCCARTY, Danl.		34	M	Laborer	31Mr21Rb
FLINN, Cons.		23	M	Laborer	31Mr21Rb
DUNGOIN, Mary		22	F	Laborer	31Mr21Rb
HATON, Eliz.		40	F	Servant	31Mr21Rb
ODONNELL, Michael		28	M	Farmer	31Mr21Rb
QUINN, Joanna		26	F	Servant	31Mr21Rb
RYAN, John		20	M	Servant	31Mr21Rb
SULLIVAN, Anne		27	F	Servant	31Mr21Rb
WHITSTEAD, Edward		23	M	Unknown	31Mr21Rb
BURK, Thos.		55	M	Laborer	31Mr21Rb
NYRAHER, Dennis		25	M	Unknown	31Mr21Rb
John		21	M	Laborer	31Mr21Rb
Ally		19	F	Laborer	31Mr21Rb
Ellen		28	F	Laborer	31Mr21Rb
BAGGOTT, Catherine		17	F	Servant	31Mr21Rb
DEEDY, Donald		30	M	Farmer	31Mr21Rb
CRAWLEY, James		30	M	Farmer	31Mr21Rb
Mary		32	F	Servant	31Mr21Rb
DECORSEY, Richd.		35	M	Laborer	31Mr21Rb
Ellen		35	F	Laborer	31Mr21Rb

GLENMORE 01 APRIL 1848

From Belfast

NAMES OF PASSENGERS		AGE	SEX	OCCUPATIONS	DATE PORT SHIP
LOAN, James		21	M	Molder	01Ap07Km
MCCARTHY, James		15	M	Molder	01Ap07Km
WARNOCK, William		56	M	Farmer	01Ap07Km
Jane	(W)	54	F	Wife	01Ap07Km
Jane	(D)	24	F	Unknown	01Ap07Km
Eliza	(D)	21	F	Unknown	01Ap07Km
Died-At-Sea					
Anne	(D)	18	F	Unknown	01Ap07Km
James	(S)	11	M	Unknown	01Ap07Km
MCCONNELL, Anne		21	F	Spinster	01Ap07Km
CORDON, John		22	M	Farmer	01Ap07Km
WARREN, John		22	M	Farmer	01Ap07Km
WARWICK, Ellen		18	F	Spinster	01Ap07Km
Sarah		16	F	Spinster	01Ap07Km
THOMPSON, Samuel		29	M	Farmer	01Ap07Km
Anne	(W)	28	F	Wife	01Ap07Km
Eliza	(D)	06	F	Child	01Ap07Km
THOMPSON, Mary	(D)	04	F	Child	01Ap07Km
Anne	(D)	02	F	Child	01Ap07Km
NEILL, Samuel		17	M	Clerk	01Ap07Km
PILSON, Samuel		18	M	Clerk	01Ap07Km
HARBISON, Joseph		35	M	Farmer	01Ap07Km
Hanah	(W)	30	F	Wife	01Ap07Km
William	(S)	15	M	Child	01Ap07Km
Hugh	(S)	13	M	Child	01Ap07Km
Joseph	(S)	11	M	Child	01Ap07Km
Robert	(S)	09	M	Child	01Ap07Km
Lawrence	(S)	07	M	Child	01Ap07Km
John	(S)	05	M	Child	01Ap07Km
Hyndman	(S)	.00	M	Infant	01Ap07Km
MCKEOWN, Jane		19	F	Spinster	01Ap07Km
LONG, William		29	M	Farmer	01Ap07Km
JOHNSTON, William		20	M	Farmer	01Ap07Km
Edward		20	M	Farmer	01Ap07Km
WARWICK, Andrew		30	M	Farmer	01Ap07Km
Mary	(W)	28	F	Wife	01Ap07Km
Robert		19	M	Weaver	01Ap07Km
PIPER, Samuel		21	M	Weaver	01Ap07Km
GRAHAM, Agnes		30	F	Spinster	01Ap07Km
ABERNATHY, Jane		25	F	Spinster	01Ap07Km
TODD, Jane		18	F	Spinster	01Ap07Km
WILIIAMS, John		18	M	Farmer	01Ap07Km
GREIGHTON, Robert		20	M	Farmer	01Ap07Km
TUFTS, John		16	M	Farmer	01Ap07Km
MCMULLEN, Sarah		19	F	Spinster	01Ap07Km
William		18	M	Yeoman	01Ap07Km
SWAN, Mary		17	F	Spinster	01Ap07Km
Anna		16	F	Spinster	01Ap07Km
Daniel		14	M	Laborer	01Ap07Km
MONTGOMERY, John		24	M	Laborer	01Ap07Km
PEOPLES, John		25	M	Laborer	01Ap07Km
Joseph		26	M	Laborer	01Ap07Km
KERNAN, William		25	M	Laborer	01Ap07Km
DONAGHY, James		14	M	Mechanic	01Ap07Km
LILEY, Alexander		20	M	Mechanic	01Ap07Km
HART, John		32	M	Mechanic	01Ap07Km
MULLEN, James		28	M	Mechanic	01Ap07Km
STEWART, Eliza		25	F	Wi	01Ap07Km
Robert	(S)	04	M	Child	01Ap07Km
John	(S)	01	M	Child	01Ap07Km
SHERRARD, James		48	M	Farmer	01Ap07Km
Margaret	(W)	46	F	Wife	01Ap07Km
Thomas	(S)	19	M	Unknown	01Ap07Km
Matilda	(D)	16	F	Unknown	01Ap07Km
Elisabeth	(D)	12	F	Unknown	01Ap07Km
Robert	(S)	10	M	Child	01Ap07Km
Alexander	(S)	08	M	Child	01Ap07Km
HARPIN, Daniel		30	M	Servant	01Ap07Km
LINTON, Thomas		18	M	Servant	01Ap07Km
BARNETT, Francis		20	M	Servant	01Ap07Km
GOWDY, Joseph		23	M	Tailor	01Ap07Km
EARLEY, David		24	M	Tailor	01Ap07Km
HARRISON, Hanna		40	F	Wi	01Ap07Km
BOUCHER, John		24	M	Carpenter	01Ap07Km
William		19	M	Carpenter	01Ap07Km
MCCLEESTER, John		21	M	Carpenter	01Ap07Km
MCCALL, Henry		15	M	Carpenter	01Ap07Km
CREEVY, Thomas		16	M	Carpenter	01Ap07Km
RAINEY, Jane		20	F	Spinster	01Ap07Km
MCGEE, Isaac		29	M	Weaver	01Ap07Km
BROWN, James		21	M	Weaver	01Ap07Km
Jane	(W)	20	F	Wife	01Ap07Km
HULL, George		21	M	Carpenter	01Ap07Km
HUMPHRY, Joseph		21	M	Carpenter	01Ap07Km
SMITH, David		25	M	Carpenter	01Ap07Km
SIMPSON, Robert		21	M	Carpenter	01Ap07Km
BAXTER, Bell		20	F	Spinster	01Ap07Km
Anne		18	F	Spinster	01Ap07Km
MCGUIN, Margaret		20	F	Spinster	01Ap07Km
REDMOND, William		20	M	Weaver	01Ap07Km
MALCOMSON, Robert		25	M	Surgeon	01Ap07Km
ONEILL, Henry		29	M	Farmer	01Ap07Km

NAMES OF PASSENGERS		AGE	SEX	OCCUPATIONS	DATE PORT SHIP
SHEILLS, James		19	M	Farmer	01Ap07Km
LYONS, William		21	M	Farmer	01Ap07Km
FLEMING, Esther		20	F	Spinster	01Ap07Km
MCCORD, Mary		18	F	Spinster	01Ap07Km
AGNEW, Alexander		29	M	Carpenter	01Ap07Km
JORDAN, Thomas		24	M	Carpenter	01Ap07Km
Eliza	(W)	22	F	Wife	01Ap07Km
James	(S)	01	M	Child	01Ap07Km
MURRAY, John		18	M	Carpenter	01Ap07Km
DICKSON, Mary		18	F	Spinster	01Ap07Km
BRIGGS, Alice		22	F	Spinster	01Ap07Km
GOWAN, Thomas		18	M	Carpenter	01Ap07Km
MORRISON, David		20	M	Carpenter	01Ap07Km
MCQUILLAN, James		25	M	Carpenter	01Ap07Km
Catherine	(W)	23	F	Wife	01Ap07Km
MCMASTER, James		20	M	Weaver	01Ap07Km
ESLER, David		26	M	Weaver	01Ap07Km
Isabella	(W)	24	F	Wife	01Ap07Km
Eliza	(D)	.00	F	Infant	01Ap07Km
QUINN, James		22	M	Carpenter	01Ap07Km
CLAMPETT, George		22	M	Carpenter	01Ap07Km
CLELAND, John		18	M	Carpenter	01Ap07Km
STEPHENSON, William		24	M	Tailor	01Ap07Km
Mary	(T)	20	F	Unknown	01Ap07Km
Died-At-Sea					
ROBINSON, Eliza		30	F	Spinster	01Ap07Km
BRIZEL, James		28	M	Carpenter	01Ap07Km
MURDOCK, Eliza		20	F	Spinster	01Ap07Km
KIRKPATRICK, William		29	M	Weaver	01Ap07Km
HAMILTON, Hugh		29	M	Weaver	01Ap07Km
HOLLAND, Eliza		29	F	Wi	01Ap07Km
MEGANE, Isabella		25	F	Wi	01Ap07Km
WOODS, Arthur		19	M	Tailor	01Ap07Km
HALL, John		23	M	Tailor	01Ap07Km
Sarah	(W)	17	F	Wife	01Ap07Km
MARTIN, James		25	M	Weaver	01Ap07Km
MCCRACKEN, Robert		26	M	Weaver	01Ap07Km
DARRATH, John		23	M	Weaver	01Ap07Km
GAMBLE, Henry		25	M	Weaver	01Ap07Km
CONROY, Alexander		51	M	Weaver	01Ap07Km
Died-At-Sea					
HODSMITH, John		18	M	Weaver	01Ap07Km
MORRISON, William		30	M	Weaver	01Ap07Km
FORD, Robert		24	M	Weaver	01Ap07Km
BROWN, James		30	M	Carpenter	01Ap07Km
CAMPBELL, John		20	M	Carpenter	01Ap07Km
Anne	(T)	22	F	Unknown	01Ap07Km
MOOREHEAD, Robert		21	M	Clerk	01Ap07Km
Charlotte	(T)	18	F	Unknown	01Ap07Km
MCCARTNEY, Charles		23	M	Mechanic	01Ap07Km
HACKET, Joseph		29	M	Mechanic	01Ap07Km
MCQUILKAN, John		21	M	Mechanic	01Ap07Km
TURNER, Stewart		18	M	Mechanic	01Ap07Km
POTTS, John		25	M	Mechanic	01Ap07Km
FLEMING, Nathaniel		17	M	Mechanic	01Ap07Km
ANDREW, Robert		29	M	Laborer	01Ap07Km
Thomas		27	M	Laborer	01Ap07Km
MARQUIS, Daniel		35	M	Farmer	01Ap07Km
Mary	(W)	30	F	Wife	01Ap07Km
John	(S)	12	M	Child	01Ap07Km
Jane	(D)	10	F	Child	01Ap07Km
Samuel	(S)	08	M	Child	01Ap07Km
James	(S)	06	M	Child	01Ap07Km
Daniel	(S)	04	M	Child	01Ap07Km
Sarah	(D)	02	F	Child	01Ap07Km
Mary	(D)	.00	F	Infant	01Ap07Km
DUFF, John		50	M	Laborer	01Ap07Km
Ruth	(D)	15	F	Unknown	01Ap07Km
LAFFERTY, Michael		21	M	Laborer	01Ap07Km
MCKEEVER, James		22	M	Laborer	01Ap07Km
JOHNSTON, Patrick		28	M	Laborer	01Ap07Km
HANNY, John		20	M	Weaver	01Ap07Km
CREIGHTON, James		15	M	Laborer	01Ap07Km

JOHN-RAVENEL 01 APRIL 1848

From Liverpool

NAMES OF PASSENGERS		AGE	SEX	OCCUPATIONS	DATE PORT SHIP
GALLAGHER, Owen		30	M	Laborer	01Ap02Or
BRESLIND, John		26	M	Laborer	01Ap02Or
KENNEDY, John		24	M	Laborer	01Ap02Or
MENEALES, Thomas		23	M	Miner	01Ap02Or
FURY, Andrew		25	M	Laborer	01Ap02Or
MCTIGUE, Patrick		26	M	Painter	01Ap02Or
DAVAR, Hugh		24	M	Laborer	01Ap02Or
MENEALES, William		24	M	Laborer	01Ap02Or
HARKIN, Peter		29	M	Laborer	01Ap02Or
WARD, Barney		30	M	Laborer	01Ap02Or
BONNER, James		30	M	Laborer	01Ap02Or
DEVINE, Conner		28	M	Laborer	01Ap02Or
MCCAVARTY, Patrick		28	M	Laborer	01Ap02Or
GALLAGHER, Rose		24	F	Spinster	01Ap02Or
MENEALES, Sarah		21	F	Spinster	01Ap02Or
KILDARE, Mary		21	F	Spinster	01Ap02Or
HARKIN, James		20	M	Laborer	01Ap02Or
FERRITT, Patrick		18	M	Carpenter	01Ap02Or
DONELLY, Bridget		25	F	Spinster	01Ap02Or
Ellen		20	F	Spinster	01Ap02Or
MORRIS, Hugh		36	M	Laborer	01Ap02Or
Rose	(W)	35	F	Wife	01Ap02Or
GAFFNEY, Thomas		40	M	Laborer	01Ap02Or
REILLY, Hugh		40	M	Laborer	01Ap02Or
TULLY, James		47	M	Laborer	01Ap02Or
GALLIGAN, Rose		48	F	Wi	01Ap02Or
FITZSIMMONS, Jane		50	F	Wife	01Ap02Or
SHERIDAN, Catharine		20	F	Spinster	01Ap02Or
GALLIGAN, Ellen		15	F	Spinster	01Ap02Or
Thomas		18	M	Laborer	01Ap02Or
BOYLE, Peter		19	M	Laborer	01Ap02Or
OBRIAN, Martin		30	M	Gdnr	01Ap02Or
REYNOLDS, William		26	M	Butcher	01Ap02Or
REILLY, Peter		30	M	Rrng	01Ap02Or
FARLEY, Bernard		24	M	Laborer	01Ap02Or
CLARKE, Thomas		28	M	Laborer	01Ap02Or
COYLE, Mary		20	F	Servant	01Ap02Or
Catherine		35	F	Wife	01Ap02Or
POORE, Mary		25	F	Spinster	01Ap02Or
HALNON, Mary		25	F	Servant	01Ap02Or
WALSH, Patrick		20	M	Laborer	01Ap02Or
CARNEY, John		24	M	Tailor	01Ap02Or
MCCARTHY, Patrick		24	M	Stone Mason	01Ap02Or
Bridget	(W)	24	F	Wife	01Ap02Or
WARD, James		58	M	Farmer	01Ap02Or
COOGAN, John		30	M	Weaver	01Ap02Or
Bridget	(W)	30	F	Wife	01Ap02Or
Catherine	(D)	.08	F	Infant	01Ap02Or
WARD, Mary		50	F	Wife	01Ap02Or
COOGAN, Mary		07	F	Child	01Ap02Or
Nicholas		05	M	Child	01Ap02Or
CORRIGAN, Judith		09	F	Child	01Ap02Or
SHELBOURNE, Patrick		24	M	Brick Maker	01Ap02Or
BURNE, Margaret		24	F	Wife	01Ap02Or
LENON, Peter		40	M	Laborer	01Ap02Or
MCLOUGHLIN, Patrick		24	M	Tailor	01Ap02Or
BURNE, Stephen		24	M	Coachman	01Ap02Or
Michael		25	M	Farmer	01Ap02Or
BURKE, John		25	M	Laborer	01Ap02Or
WALSH, Bridget		23	F	Milliner	01Ap02Or
REILLY, Owen		33	M	Cbtmkr	01Ap02Or
Sarah	(W)	25	F	Wife	01Ap02Or
Sarah	(D)	.04	F	Infant	01Ap02Or
BYRNES, Peter		24	M	Storekeeper	01Ap02Or
Anne		20	F	Spinster	01Ap02Or

NAMES OF PASSENGERS		AGE	SEX	OCCUPATIONS	DATE PORT SHIP
BRYAN, Patrick		20	M	Laborer	01Ap02Or
SAVAGE, Ellen		18	F	Servant	01Ap02Or
BARNAN, Ann		17	F	Servant	01Ap02Or
HARMAN, Mary		16	F	Servant	01Ap02Or
COUGHLIN, Ellen		17	F	Servant	01Ap02Or
Mary		00	F	Servant	01Ap02Or
CORMICK, Honora		13	F	Servant	01Ap02Or
HALE, Mary		16	F	Spinster	01Ap02Or
DOODY, Etty		20	F	Servant	01Ap02Or
NEALE, Thomas		28	M	Laborer	01Ap02Or
Simon		30	M	Farmer	01Ap02Or
ONEAL, John		25	M	Laborer	01Ap02Or
MARTIN, Patrick		20	M	Laborer	01Ap02Or
Julia		35	F	Wi	01Ap02Or
GRENNON, Mary		30	F	Servant	01Ap02Or
Mary		20	F	Servant	01Ap02Or
POWER, Catherine		25	F	Servant	01Ap02Or
BURNS, Mary		30	F	Wife	01Ap02Or
MEEHAN, Michael		21	M	Laborer	01Ap02Or
GUNNING, Catherine		40	F	Wife	01Ap02Or
Mary	(D)	11	F	Unknown	01Ap02Or
OWENS, James		16	M	Laborer	01Ap02Or
BRAY, Dennis		22	M	Laborer	01Ap02Or
Michael		24	M	Laborer	01Ap02Or
Margaret		24	F	Wife	01Ap02Or
MURPHY, Patrick		24	M	Stctr	01Ap02Or
WOODHEN, Daniel		30	M	Shoemaker	01Ap02Or
CLUSKEY, Rose		20	F	Wife	01Ap02Or
Michael	(H)	25	M	Laborer	01Ap02Or
WEST, Mary		24	F	Wife	01Ap02Or
John		14	M	Unknown	01Ap02Or
ARMSTRONG, Catherine		18	F	Spinster	01Ap02Or
LEDWETH, John		22	M	Laborer	01Ap02Or
Thomas		18	M	Laborer	01Ap02Or
Margaret		20	F	Wife	01Ap02Or
FARRELL, Patrick		20	M	Laborer	01Ap02Or
WALE, Peter		20	M	Laborer	01Ap02Or
Ann		18	F	Servant	01Ap02Or
CASEY, Francis		25	M	Laborer	01Ap02Or
FARRELL, Patrick		25	M	Laborer	01Ap02Or
Mary	(D)	.11	F	Infant	01Ap02Or
GERRARTTY, Andrew		24	M	Farmer	01Ap02Or
MULVEY, Farrell		40	M	Laborer	01Ap02Or
OKEEFE, William		30	M	Laborer	01Ap02Or
Phoebe	(W)	25	F	Wife	01Ap02Or
HART, James		21	M	Printer	01Ap02Or
Catherine	(W)	20	F	Wife	01Ap02Or
KILLAIN, Catherine		20	F	Servant	01Ap02Or
HARFORD, William		34	M	Farmer	01Ap02Or
Mary		12	F	Farmer	01Ap02Or
Rose		10	F	Child	01Ap02Or
Matthew		08	M	Child	01Ap02Or
REED, Christy		20	M	Laborer	01Ap02Or
FOX, John		25	M	Laborer	01Ap02Or
Margaret	(W)	20	F	Wife	01Ap02Or
CUSACK, Mary		20	F	Servant	01Ap02Or
HEALY, Catherine		25	F	Spinster	01Ap02Or
DONOHUE, Mary		24	F	Spinster	01Ap02Or
HORN, William		30	M	Laborer	01Ap02Or
Martin		20	M	Laborer	01Ap02Or
HIGHLAND, Daniel		22	M	Valet	01Ap02Or
DINSMORE, John		20	M	Shst	01Ap02Or
CONNOR, Michael		30	M	Valet	01Ap02Or
Andrew		26	M	Laborer	01Ap02Or
MUNDY, Michael		45	M	Laborer	01Ap02Or
Bridget		16	F	Spinster	01Ap02Or
Mary		12	F	Spinster	01Ap02Or
Anne		10	F	Child	01Ap02Or
MULLIGAN, Phillip		22	M	Laborer	01Ap02Or
KENNY, Fanny		19	F	Servant	01Ap02Or
MCCORMICK, Eliza		16	F	Servant	01Ap02Or
MCHERNARY, Betsy		22	F	Spinster	01Ap02Or
SMITH, Ellen		15	F	Spinster	01Ap02Or
WATSON, George		24	M	Laborer	01Ap02Or
John		20	M	Laborer	01Ap02Or
WATSON, Sarah		22	F	Servant	01Ap02Or
Mary-Ann		24	F	Wife	01Ap02Or
Mary-Ann	(D)	.11	F	Infant	01Ap02Or
MCGARVEY, Michael		20	M	Laborer	01Ap02Or
SMITH, Elizth.		26	F	Spinster	01Ap02Or
Hannah		18	F	Spinster	01Ap02Or
MOORE, Thomas		25	M	Laborer	01Ap02Or
GILL, Patrick		30	M	Valet	01Ap02Or
MOOTY, John		30	M	Laborer	01Ap02Or
BARLOW, Ann		30	F	Wi	01Ap02Or
Richard	(S)	.11	M	Infant	01Ap02Or
DUNN, Susan		29	F	Wife	01Ap02Or
MOORHEAD, Alexander		25	M	Laborer	01Ap02Or
BRENNAN, John		28	M	Fsvnt	01Ap02Or
ODONNELE, John		26	M	Fsvnt	01Ap02Or
MCCUE, Connell		19	M	Fsvnt	01Ap02Or
BRENNAN, Bridget		26	F	Spinster	01Ap02Or
FITZGERALD, Thomas		26	M	Laborer	01Ap02Or
David		23	M	Shoemaker	01Ap02Or
SULLIVAN, Jeremiah		31	M	Laborer	01Ap02Or
Ally	(W)	20	F	Wife	01Ap02Or
OLEARY, Lawrence		18	M	Cmcl	01Ap02Or
DRISCOLE, Timothy		25	M	Laborer	01Ap02Or
CONNOR, John		23	M	Laborer	01Ap02Or
SHEA, Daniel		32	M	Laborer	01Ap02Or
Patrick		24	M	Laborer	01Ap02Or
SULLIVAN, Timothy		28	M	Laborer	01Ap02Or
QUINN, John		42	M	Farmer	01Ap02Or
Ellen	(W)	40	F	Wife	01Ap02Or
Mary	(D)	13	F	Unknown	01Ap02Or
John	(S)	09	M	Child	01Ap02Or
Eliza	(D)	04	F	Child	01Ap02Or
LONG, John		40	M	Laborer	01Ap02Or
CALLAGHAN, John		25	M	Laborer	01Ap02Or
HACKETT, Ellen		20	F	Spinster	01Ap02Or
MCDERMOTT, Mary		25	F	Spinster	01Ap02Or
LYNCH, William		39	M	Carpenter	01Ap02Or
Sarah		16	F	Spinster	01Ap02Or
DRIDMORE, Jane		22	F	Lady'S Maid	01Ap02Or

NEW-YORK 03 APRIL 1848

From Liverpool

NAMES OF PASSENGERS		AGE	SEX	OCCUPATIONS	DATE PORT SHIP
OREILLY, Philip-Rev.		62	M	Gentleman	03Ap02Bk
GRIFFIN, David		26	M	Laborer	03Ap02Bk
Edwin		30	M	Laborer	03Ap02Bk
BREMAN, Edward		20	M	Laborer	03Ap02Bk
Patrick		07	M	Child	03Ap02Bk
HAWIAGHTY, Sarah		35	F	Servant	03Ap02Bk
BARRY, Mary		18	F	Servant	03Ap02Bk
MCNEILLY, Ann		20	F	Servant	03Ap02Bk
K---Y, John		21	M	Servant	03Ap02Bk
GALLAHER, Charles		20	M	Servant	03Ap02Bk
FLANAGEN, Alexander		18	M	Laborer	03Ap02Bk
LYNCH, Hugh		25	M	Laborer	03Ap02Bk
Catherine		22	F	Servant	03Ap02Bk
WARD, John		25	M	Laborer	03Ap02Bk
Mary	(W)	20	F	Wife	03Ap02Bk
Patrick	(S)	03	M	Child	03Ap02Bk
Jane	(D)	02	F	Child	03Ap02Bk
MERSEY, Thomas		14	M	Laborer	03Ap02Bk
Mary		19	F	Servant	03Ap02Bk
Margeret		16	F	Servant	03Ap02Bk
COOK, Owen		18	M	Laborer	03Ap02Bk
Daniel		25	M	Laborer	03Ap02Bk
John		23	M	Laborer	03Ap02Bk
SMITH, Patrick		22	M	Laborer	03Ap02Bk
Bridget		50	F	Servant	03Ap02Bk

NAMES OF PASSENGERS		AGE	SEX	OCCUPATIONS	DATE PORT SHIP
SMITH, Catharine		20	F	Servant	03Ap02Bk
MULLIGAN, Edward		18	M	Laborer	03Ap02Bk
CLARK, Margeret		19	F	Servant	03Ap02Bk
FARRLLY, Patrick		22	M	Laborer	03Ap02Bk
SULLIVAN, Terrence		15	M	Baker	03Ap02Bk
COYLE, Mary		50	F	Servant	03Ap02Bk
Ann		25	F	Servant	03Ap02Bk
COONEY, Ann		25	F	Servant	03Ap02Bk
BRADY, Thomas		20	M	Laborer	03Ap02Bk
GIDSON, Daniel		18	M	Laborer	03Ap02Bk
CARROLAN, Ann		17	F	Servant	03Ap02Bk
ROGERS, Mary		20	F	Servant	03Ap02Bk
FLYNN, John		20	M	Laborer	03Ap02Bk
DUFFY, Charles		20	M	Laborer	03Ap02Bk
COVINGON, Hugh		28	M	Laborer	03Ap02Bk
MCQUIRK, James		24	M	Laborer	03Ap02Bk
DELANY, Patrick		40	M	Laborer	03Ap02Bk
Mary		18	F	Servant	03Ap02Bk
MULLIN, Patrick		28	M	Laborer	03Ap02Bk
Catherine		18	F	Servant	03Ap02Bk
WYNN, John		50	M	Laborer	03Ap02Bk
Bridget	(W)	40	F	Wife	03Ap02Bk
Margeret	(D)	20	F	Servant	03Ap02Bk
Joseph	(S)	18	M	Laborer	03Ap02Bk
James	(S)	16	M	Carpenter	03Ap02Bk
Mary	(D)	15	F	Servant	03Ap02Bk
Betty	(D)	14	F	Servant	03Ap02Bk
CLUSKY, John		61	M	Laborer	03Ap02Bk
Edward		45	M	Laborer	03Ap02Bk
Peter		40	M	Laborer	03Ap02Bk
Patrick		23	M	Gdnr	03Ap02Bk
Batholomew		14	M	Laborer	03Ap02Bk
Jane		20	F	Servant	03Ap02Bk
Ann		18	F	Servant	03Ap02Bk
Rose		14	F	Servant	03Ap02Bk
Mary		16	F	Servant	03Ap02Bk
Bridget		15	F	Servant	03Ap02Bk
BYRNES, Thomas		30	M	Laborer	03Ap02Bk
WEBSTER, Bridget		20	F	Servant	03Ap02Bk
MCCALLIN, John		34	M	Laborer	03Ap02Bk
CORNEY, Mary		18	F	Servant	03Ap02Bk
HANNON, Oliver		20	M	Laborer	03Ap02Bk
Patrick		40	M	Laborer	03Ap02Bk
SORAHAN, Patrick		20	M	Laborer	03Ap02Bk
GOODWIN, Patrick		20	M	Laborer	03Ap02Bk
KILDRA, Hugh		20	M	Sawer	03Ap02Bk
BURK, Margeret		23	F	Servant	03Ap02Bk
REILLY, Margeret		25	F	Servant	03Ap02Bk
MOONEY, Michael		38	M	Farmer	03Ap02Bk
LEDAN, Andrew		19	M	Laborer	03Ap02Bk
DALEY, James		18	M	Baker	03Ap02Bk
MCQUADE, Thomas		20	M	Blacksmith	03Ap02Bk
Eliza		18	F	Servant	03Ap02Bk
MCALIVAN, Mary		16	F	Servant	03Ap02Bk
BIRD, Mary		17	F	Servant	03Ap02Bk
Rose		28	F	Servant	03Ap02Bk
Bernard		05	M	Child	03Ap02Bk
Owen		01	M	Child	03Ap02Bk
NEAL, Bryan		18	M	Laborer	03Ap02Bk
TOONEY, Bridget		30	F	Servant	03Ap02Bk
EARLY, Michael		25	M	Tailor	03Ap02Bk
BYRNES, Henery		25	M	Cooper	03Ap02Bk
HARRISH, James		23	M	Laborer	03Ap02Bk
HUNT, James		20	M	Laborer	03Ap02Bk
TOOMAN, Bridget		19	F	Servant	03Ap02Bk
FITZPATRICK, Mary		23	F	Servant	03Ap02Bk
CASSEY, Patrick		10	M	Laborer	03Ap02Bk
LEMAN, Catharine		22	F	Dressmaker	03Ap02Bk
BYRNE, Mary		20	F	Dressmaker	03Ap02Bk
TOTEN, William		20	M	Laborer	03Ap02Bk
GUNONN, Michael		23	M	Laborer	03Ap02Bk
CLUKEN, Michael		23	M	Laborer	03Ap02Bk
COYLE, John		30	M	Laborer	03Ap02Bk
COGLE, John		25	M	Carpenter	03Ap02Bk
CASSIDY, John		25	M	Carpenter	03Ap02Bk
CASSIDY, Mary-Ann		27	F	Servant	03Ap02Bk
GRAY, U-Mrs.		30	F	Servant	03Ap02Bk
CARNEY, Miles		24	M	Mason	03Ap02Bk
MCGLEGGEN, A.		30	M	Laborer	03Ap02Bk
ROBERTS, William		21	M	Clerk	03Ap02Bk
KELLY, James		30	M	Clerk	03Ap02Bk
SMITH, James		28	M	Laborer	03Ap02Bk
LAWDEN, Sarah		50	F	Housekeeper	03Ap02Bk
MCKEY, Bridget		20	F	Unknown	03Ap02Bk
BURNS, Ellen		60	F	Unknown	03Ap02Bk
Luke		22	M	Laborer	03Ap02Bk
Michael		18	M	Laborer	03Ap02Bk
MEEHAN, Michael		33	M	Laborer	03Ap02Bk
Kitty	(W)	30	F	Servant	03Ap02Bk
Patrick	(S)	04	M	Child	03Ap02Bk
Michell	(S)	.00	M	Infant	03Ap02Bk
HARGRAVES, Janne		22	F	Servant	03Ap02Bk
LEDWIN, Catharine		22	F	Servant	03Ap02Bk
SPELADY, Thomas		27	M	Laborer	03Ap02Bk
MURPHY, Michael		23	M	Laborer	03Ap02Bk
DONOHUE, Patrick		21	M	Laborer	03Ap02Bk
MULLEN, John		22	M	Laborer	03Ap02Bk
MANNION, Thomas		21	M	Tailor	03Ap02Bk
Eliza		03	F	Child	03Ap02Bk
LEARY, Patrick		20	M	Laborer	03Ap02Bk
MCGUIRE, Catharine		50	F	Unknown	03Ap02Bk
CLARK, James		50	M	Shoemaker	03Ap02Bk
Maria	(W)	50	F	Unknown	03Ap02Bk
Michael	(S)	14	M	Laborer	03Ap02Bk
Hugh	(S)	20	M	Shoemaker	03Ap02Bk
Patrick	(S)	05	M	Child	03Ap02Bk
James	(S)	02	M	Child	03Ap02Bk
MURPHY, John		24	M	Laborer	03Ap02Bk
MCGOUGH, Arthur		21	M	Laborer	03Ap02Bk
CANGAN, Michael		19	M	Tailor	03Ap02Bk
RODGERS, Thomas		50	M	Laborer	03Ap02Bk
Catharine	(W)	50	F	Servant	03Ap02Bk
Peter	(S)	20	M	Laborer	03Ap02Bk
Catherina	(D)	19	F	Servant	03Ap02Bk
GAYNOR, Ann		24	F	Servant	03Ap02Bk
MCMANUS, Bridget		40	F	Servant	03Ap02Bk
Patrick	(S)	14	M	Laborer	03Ap02Bk
Mary	(D)	07	F	Servant	03Ap02Bk
Ellen	(D)	11	F	Servant	03Ap02Bk
MCGOWEN, Mary		16	F	Servant	03Ap02Bk
OBRIEN, Felix		17	M	Laborer	03Ap02Bk
GILL, Bryan		21	M	Laborer	03Ap02Bk
BURNS, Mary		15	F	Servant	03Ap02Bk
KEARNS, Bernard		17	M	Laborer	03Ap02Bk
MCCOVEN, Bridget		14	F	Servant	03Ap02Bk
MCCROTHERS, Sarah		18	F	Servant	03Ap02Bk
CARNEY, Daniel		14	M	Laborer	03Ap02Bk
Mary		22	F	Servant	03Ap02Bk
MINTCH, Catharine		20	F	Servant	03Ap02Bk
MINTCHE, Ellen		20	F	Servant	03Ap02Bk
DOOLADY, Patrick		24	M	Hrsm	03Ap02Bk
REYNOLDS, Bernard		26	M	Laborer	03Ap02Bk
TAISLEY, Bridget		17	F	Servant	03Ap02Bk
FAGAN, Bryan		18	M	Laborer	03Ap02Bk
REYNOLDS, Patrick		24	M	Mason	03Ap02Bk
DOLAN, John		23	M	Laborer	03Ap02Bk
Mary		16	F	Servant	03Ap02Bk
LOYD, John		25	M	Laborer	03Ap02Bk
MCDONNELL, John		24	M	Mason	03Ap02Bk
Catharine		20	F	Servant	03Ap02Bk
MOLLOY, Hugh		22	M	Laborer	03Ap02Bk
MORAN, Catharine		20	F	Servant	03Ap02Bk
CARROLL, Mary		33	F	Servant	03Ap02Bk
Ann	(D)	07	F	Child	03Ap02Bk
STANFORD, Susan		35	F	Housekeeper	U3Ap02Bk
Died-At-Sea					
James	(S)	03	M	Child	03Ap02Bk
Mathew	(S)	02	M	Child	03Ap02Bk
Thomas	(S)	.00	M	Infant	03Ap02Bk
TREVAN, Mary		14	F	Servant	03Ap02Bk

NAMES OF PASSENGERS		AGE	SEX	OCCUPATIONS	DATE PORT SHIP
PHELAN, Mary		20	F	Servant	03Ap02Bk
Patrick		22	M	Laborer	03Ap02Bk
CARNEY, Lawrence		27	M	Laborer	03Ap02Bk
REYNOLDS, Patrick		20	M	Laborer	03Ap02Bk
RATTIGAN, Mary		22	F	Servant	03Ap02Bk
HOGAN, Peter		22	M	Laborer	03Ap02Bk
MAHON, Miles		25	M	Laborer	03Ap02Bk
WALSH, Dennis		22	M	Laborer	03Ap02Bk
RODGERSTON, Catharine		21	F	Servant	03Ap02Bk
CROWFORD, Paul		20	M	Laborer	03Ap02Bk
SHERIDAN, Hugh		21	M	Laborer	03Ap02Bk
Ann		20	F	Servant	03Ap02Bk
KEEFE, Mary		18	F	Servant	03Ap02Bk
CONRY, Edward		20	M	Laborer	03Ap02Bk
MURPHY, Thomas		24	M	Laborer	03Ap02Bk
MCSAWYER, John		18	M	Laborer	03Ap02Bk
Alexander		17	M	Laborer	03Ap02Bk
OLIVILL, U-Mrs.		60	F	Housekeeper	03Ap02Bk
Patrick	(S)	23	M	Laborer	03Ap02Bk
Margeret	(D)	22	F	Servant	03Ap02Bk
LEADY, Ann		24	F	Servant	03Ap02Bk
MCKEON, James		24	M	Laborer	03Ap02Bk
CARR, James		20	M	Laborer	03Ap02Bk
REILLY, Mary		14	F	Servant	03Ap02Bk
CAHILL, Mary		20	F	Servant	03Ap02Bk
DALTON, John		20	M	Laborer	03Ap02Bk
MCGEE, Mary		19	F	Servant	03Ap02Bk
John		20	M	Laborer	03Ap02Bk
MCMANUS, Patrick		23	M	Laborer	03Ap02Bk
CUIFFE, Ross		19	M	Laborer	03Ap02Bk
DOHERTY, Peter		20	M	Laborer	03Ap02Bk
MCLEAN, Mary		20	F	Servant	03Ap02Bk
Thomas		19	M	Laborer	03Ap02Bk
Nancey		14	F	Servant	03Ap02Bk
BYRNES, Mary		71	F	Housekeeper	03Ap02Bk
ROVERTY, Daniel		26	M	Laborer	03Ap02Bk
GALLIGER, Grace		16	F	Servant	03Ap02Bk
MONOGHAN, James		26	M	Laborer	03Ap02Bk
SMITH, John		18	M	Clerk	03Ap02Bk
MOONEY, Patrick		20	M	Laborer	03Ap02Bk
BRADY, Henery		17	M	Tailor	03Ap02Bk
LYNCH, Ellen		20	F	Servant	03Ap02Bk
HUGHES, Patrick		25	M	Laborer	03Ap02Bk
Ann		23	F	Servant	03Ap02Bk
LEMON, Margeret		25	F	Servant	03Ap02Bk
MCCLELAND, James		24	M	Laborer	03Ap02Bk
LYONS, Catharine		20	F	Servant	03Ap02Bk
FAGEN, Catharine		19	F	Servant	03Ap02Bk
KELLY, Patrick		20	M	Tailor	03Ap02Bk
CLUSTER, Biddy		24	F	Servant	03Ap02Bk
LUYDEN, Bridget		19	F	Servant	03Ap02Bk
KENNA, Thomas		28	M	Laborer	03Ap02Bk
Ann		20	F	Servant	03Ap02Bk
PHELAN, Michael		20	M	Tailor	03Ap02Bk
Ann		15	F	Servant	03Ap02Bk
MCKINZIE, Roger		56	M	Dish Turner	03Ap02Bk
Nancy	(W)	50	F	Wife	03Ap02Bk
James	(S)	21	M	Dish Turner	03Ap02Bk
William	(S)	20	M	Dish Turner	03Ap02Bk
Margeret	(D)	18	F	Servant	03Ap02Bk
COYLE, Dennis		30	M	Laborer	03Ap02Bk
Catherine		25	F	Servant	03Ap02Bk
KING, James		18	M	Laborer	03Ap02Bk
ALLEN, James		14	M	Laborer	03Ap02Bk
MCNALLY, Charles		21	M	Laborer	03Ap02Bk
PAISLEY, John		50	M	Laborer	03Ap02Bk
KELLY, Mathew		38	M	Turner	03Ap02Bk
BURKE, Ellen		20	F	Servant	03Ap02Bk
DOOLEY, Mary		60	F	Housekeeper	03Ap02Bk
Margeret	(D)	20	F	Servant	03Ap02Bk
Loughlin	(S)	19	M	Laborer	03Ap02Bk
CUNGWILL, Margeret		20	F	Servant	03Ap02Bk
Mary		18	F	Servant	03Ap02Bk
HUKEY, Thomas		22	M	Laborer	03Ap02Bk
Richard		20	M	Laborer	03Ap02Bk

NAMES OF PASSENGERS		AGE	SEX	OCCUPATIONS	DATE PORT SHIP
MULLIGAN, Sarah		18	F	Servant	03Ap02Bk
THOMPSON, Bridget		24	F	Servant	03Ap02Bk
Mary		21	F	Servant	03Ap02Bk
OBRIEN, Timothy		24	M	Laborer	03Ap02Bk
DESMOND, Jeremiah		30	M	Laborer	03Ap02Bk
PURDY, Mary		16	F	Servant	03Ap02Bk
BRENNAN, Ann		18	F	Servant	03Ap02Bk
LEE, Bernard		24	M	Laborer	03Ap02Bk
ONEAL, Ellen		25	F	Servant	03Ap02Bk
HORAN, John		22	M	Laborer	03Ap02Bk
MILLS, James		22	M	Laborer	03Ap02Bk
DAVING, Michael		24	M	Laborer	03Ap02Bk
GRIFFIN, Mary		17	F	Servant	03Ap02Bk
FAGAN, James		22	M	Laborer	03Ap02Bk
SMITH, Margeret		17	F	Servant	03Ap02Bk
SHERIDAN, Patrick		23	M	Laborer	03Ap02Bk
HART, Michael		21	M	Laborer	03Ap02Bk
Catherine		20	F	Servant	03Ap02Bk
CALLERY, John		20	M	Laborer	03Ap02Bk
GUINTY, Bridget		20	F	Servant	03Ap02Bk
MOGAN, Thomas		29	M	Laborer	03Ap02Bk
Died-At-Sea					
MURPHY, Bridget		17	F	Servant	03Ap02Bk
CANAR, John		26	M	Laborer	03Ap02Bk
Mary		26	F	Servant	03Ap02Bk
DAVIS, John		19	M	Laborer	03Ap02Bk
CANAR, Timothy		26	M	Laborer	03Ap02Bk
REILLY, Michael		37	M	Laborer	03Ap02Bk
CARROLL, John		21	M	Laborer	03Ap02Bk
James		30	M	Laborer	03Ap02Bk
MONOGHAM, John		24	M	Blacksmith	03Ap02Bk
MCDONNELL, Mastin		25	M	Laborer	03Ap02Bk
CONWAY, Michael		20	M	Laborer	03Ap02Bk
FANNING, James		20	M	Laborer	03Ap02Bk

SENATOR 03 APRIL 1848

From Liverpool

NAMES OF PASSENGERS		AGE	SEX	OCCUPATIONS	DATE PORT SHIP
COCKSHOTT, James		28	M	Farmer	03Ap02Sq
FANNING, Laurence		30	M	Laborer	03Ap02Sq
DOYLE, Bridget-Mrs.		25	F	Spinster	03Ap02Sq
HALLOREN, John		30	M	Laborer	03Ap02Sq
MURREY, Edward		40	M	Laborer	03Ap02Sq
Bridget	(W)	40	F	Laborer	03Ap02Sq
Edward	(S)	18	M	Laborer	03Ap02Sq
Thomas	(S)	13	M	Laborer	03Ap02Sq
Catherine	(D)	10	F	Spinster	03Ap02Sq
RYLEY, John		21	M	Laborer	03Ap02Sq
SHERIDON, John		23	M	Laborer	03Ap02Sq
BOYLE, Charles		32	M	Tailor	03Ap02Sq
Hugh		25	M	Laborer	03Ap02Sq
ODONALD, John		30	M	Laborer	03Ap02Sq
WARD, Patrick		20	M	Shoemaker	03Ap02Sq
MCCINNON, John		21	M	Laborer	03Ap02Sq
GALLIGHER, Barney		18	M	Laborer	03Ap02Sq
MCCOOK, Connel		20	M	Laborer	03Ap02Sq
Ellen	(W)	18	F	Spinster	03Ap02Sq
ODONALD, Antony		18	M	Laborer	03Ap02Sq
HANLON, Alex		27	M	Laborer	03Ap02Sq
Rebecca	(W)	30	F	Laborer	03Ap02Sq
COLL, James		35	M	Laborer	03Ap02Sq
ODONALD, Daniel		30	M	Laborer	03Ap02Sq
BONNER, Patr.		30	M	Laborer	03Ap02Sq
MCLOY, Neal		27	M	Laborer	03Ap02Sq
MELLEY, James		27	M	Laborer	03Ap02Sq
BONNER, Ann-Mrs.		22	F	Unknown	03Ap02Sq
SWEENEY, Patrick		22	M	Laborer	03Ap02Sq
BOYLE, Bridget		20	F	Spinster	03Ap02Sq

NAMES OF PASSENGERS		AGE	SEX	OCCUPATIONS	DATE PORT SHIP
MCGEEHAN, Daniel		24	M	Blacksmith	03Ap02Sq
SCOTT, Patrick		22	M	Laborer	03Ap02Sq
TREMBLE, John		20	M	Shoemaker	03Ap02Sq
GALLAGHER, Edwd.		25	M	Laborer	03Ap02Sq
MCSHANE, Unity		19	F	Spinster	03Ap02Sq
CONNEL, Margaret-Mrs.		39	F	Unknown	03Ap02Sq
Ed.	(S)	18	M	Laborer	03Ap02Sq
CONNELL, James		16	M	Laborer	03Ap02Sq
Julia		10	F	Spinster	03Ap02Sq
Ann		12	F	Spinster	03Ap02Sq
GERRITY, Patrick		28	M	Laborer	03Ap02Sq
Sylvesta		26	M	Laborer	03Ap02Sq
COONEY, Michael		26	M	Laborer	03Ap02Sq
FAYLE, Nicholas		23	M	Laborer	03Ap02Sq
ROAE, Pat.		19	M	Laborer	03Ap02Sq
OCONNER, Michael		21	M	Painter	03Ap02Sq
KETH, Richd.		54	M	Stone Mason	03Ap02Sq
Ellen		57	F	Unknown	03Ap02Sq
Pat.		23	M	Stone Mason	03Ap02Sq
Catherine		21	F	Spinster	03Ap02Sq
Richd.		02	M	Child	03Ap02Sq
Thomas		01	M	Child	03Ap02Sq
EDWARDS, Henry		23	M	Grocer	03Ap02Sq
Hannah		20	F	Unknown	03Ap02Sq
Henry	(S)	.10	M	Infant	03Ap02Sq
OCONNOR, John		28	M	Tailor	03Ap02Sq
DILLIN, John		26	M	Laborer	03Ap02Sq
BUTLER, Richd.		26	M	Laborer	03Ap02Sq
FARRLLY, James		22	M	Laborer	03Ap02Sq
LISSON, Joseph		19	M	Gdnr	03Ap02Sq
HATHER, Samuel		42	M	Laborer	03Ap02Sq
SMITH, Terrence		30	M	Servant	03Ap02Sq
WATKINS, David		21	M	Miller	03Ap02Sq
QUILT, George		20	M	Sawer	03Ap02Sq
MCGRATH, Thos.		45	M	Grocer	03Ap02Sq
Margt.	(W)	45	F	Unknown	03Ap02Sq
John	(S)	18	M	Grocer	03Ap02Sq
Mary-Ann	(D)	16	F	Spinster	03Ap02Sq
Grace	(D)	12	F	Spinster	03Ap02Sq
HULLIGAN, James		40	M	Laborer	03Ap02Sq
MCAVOY, Paul		25	M	Laborer	03Ap02Sq
WELSH, William		20	M	Laborer	03Ap02Sq
BROPHY, John		21	M	Laborer	03Ap02Sq
Mary		50	F	Laborer	03Ap02Sq
Ann		15	F	Spinster	03Ap02Sq
Keern		22	M	Laborer	03Ap02Sq
Timothy		19	M	Laborer	03Ap02Sq
TRAVERS, Judy		25	F	Spinster	03Ap02Sq
BOYCE, Pat.		25	M	Store Clerk	03Ap02Sq
MORRISSEY, Peter		22	M	Laborer	03Ap02Sq
Maria		20	F	Spinster	03Ap02Sq
WEELING, Judey		20	F	Spinster	03Ap02Sq
HOSEY, Mathew		28	M	Laborer	03Ap02Sq
MCCORT, Joseph		25	M	Weaver	03Ap02Sq
DELAYNEY, Pat.		27	M	Laborer	03Ap02Sq
MATHER, Michael		23	M	Laborer	03Ap02Sq
BROPHEY, Pat.		28	M	Laborer	03Ap02Sq
LOE, Charles		18	M	Laborer	03Ap02Sq
CONINGHAM, Patrick		37	M	Stone Mason	03Ap02Sq
MCLONE, Owen		57	M	Shoemaker	03Ap02Sq
GAVIN, John		30	M	Laborer	03Ap02Sq
Michael		20	M	Laborer	03Ap02Sq
MCLACHLIN, James		30	M	Laborer	03Ap02Sq
Francis		24	M	Laborer	03Ap02Sq
Mary		26	F	Spinster	03Ap02Sq
Margret		18	F	Spinster	03Ap02Sq
Margret		55	F	Unknown	03Ap02Sq
Catherine		14	F	Spinster	03Ap02Sq
HOUGHEY, Owen		30	M	Laborer	03Ap02Sq
LAMB, John		30	M	Laborer	03Ap02Sq
CONINGHAM, Ellen		40	F	Unknown	03Ap02Sq
SMITH, Timothy		28	M	Stay Maker	03Ap02Sq
JAMES, Mary		28	F	Unknown	03Ap02Sq
Mary		08	F	Child	03Ap02Sq
Leo		.11	M	Infant	03Ap02Sq
COSGROVE, Bridget		38	F	Spinster	03Ap02Sq
KEENEAR, John-W.		22	M	Grocer	03Ap02Sq
BOYD, William		21	M	Draper	03Ap02Sq
KNOWLS, Robt.		27	M	Grocer	03Ap02Sq
WOOD, James		40	M	Weaver	03Ap02Sq
HULMA, Joseph		38	M	Farmer	03Ap02Sq
James	(S)	18	M	Farmer	03Ap02Sq
Hannah	(D)	15	F	Spinster	03Ap02Sq
GIRTLAND, Michael		18	M	Laborer	03Ap02Sq
GOLTOGLEY, Thos.		18	M	Laborer	03Ap02Sq
CLUSKEY, Jane		19	F	Spinster	03Ap02Sq
DONLEY, Mary		19	F	Spinster	03Ap02Sq
BURNS, Catherine		16	F	Spinster	03Ap02Sq
CARNEY, Betty		17	F	Spinster	03Ap02Sq
CAVANAH, Bridgett		16	F	Spinster	03Ap02Sq
HALFPENY, Bridgett		17	F	Spinster	03Ap02Sq
HOUSE, Bridgett		19	F	Spinster	03Ap02Sq
DAYLEY, Bridgett		17	F	Spinster	03Ap02Sq
FINAGAN, Pat.		14	M	Laborer	03Ap02Sq
Peter		10	M	Laborer	03Ap02Sq
Thos.		12	M	Laborer	03Ap02Sq
James		42	M	Laborer	03Ap02Sq
Catherine		42	F	Unknown	03Ap02Sq
Mary		16	F	Spinster	03Ap02Sq
Owen		11	M	Unknown	03Ap02Sq
Bridgett		09	F	Spinster	03Ap02Sq
James-J.		.02	M	Infant	03Ap02Sq
MCMAN, Bridget		20	F	Spinster	03Ap02Sq
CONLEY, Margt.		16	F	Spinster	03Ap02Sq
MURPHY, James		27	M	Teacher	03Ap02Sq
John		37	M	Flabr	03Ap02Sq
Mary		36	F	Spinster	03Ap02Sq
Jeohannah		23	F	Wife	03Ap02Sq
Jeohannah	(D)	.05	F	Infant	03Ap02Sq
KING, Mary		17	F	Spinster	03Ap02Sq
MCGLOINE, Michael		15	M	Laborer	03Ap02Sq
MILLER, Edward		26	M	Cbtmkr	03Ap02Sq
GILL, Mary		34	F	Wife	03Ap02Sq
Martin	(S)	04	M	Child	03Ap02Sq
CONERTON, Thos.		25	M	Laborer	03Ap02Sq
ELLIOTT, Mary		30	F	Spinster	03Ap02Sq
CUFF, William		35	M	Laborer	03Ap02Sq
Ann		12	F	Spinster	03Ap02Sq
ROOK, Margret		30	F	Unknown	03Ap02Sq
John	(S)	07	M	Child	03Ap02Sq
LYNCH, Pat.		28	M	Wool Comber	03Ap02Sq
Judy	(W)	30	F	Unknown	03Ap02Sq
Ellen	(D)	.09	F	Infant	03Ap02Sq
BUTTLER, Richd.		40	M	Laborer	03Ap02Sq
SLATERY, James		26	M	Laborer	03Ap02Sq
BUTTLER, Ann		40	F	Unknown	03Ap02Sq
William	(S)	16	M	Laborer	03Ap02Sq
Margrett	(D)	14	F	Unknown	03Ap02Sq
Michell	(S)	12	M	Laborer	03Ap02Sq
James	(S)	07	M	Child	03Ap02Sq
Mary	(D)	04	F	Child	03Ap02Sq
Honey	(D)	.06	F	Infant	03Ap02Sq
ODRISKELL, Joseph		26	M	Chptr	03Ap02Sq
Mary-Ann	(W)	25	F	Unknown	03Ap02Sq
Joseph	(S)	.02	M	Infant	03Ap02Sq
LENORD, Charles		24	M	Gdnr	03Ap02Sq
LAWLESS, Bridget		28	F	Unknown	03Ap02Sq
Ellen	(D)	05	F	Child	03Ap02Sq
Ann	(D)	03	F	Child	03Ap02Sq
Eliza	(D)	.08	F	Infant	03Ap02Sq
Died-At-Sea					
KENEDY, William		20	M	Storekeeper	03Ap02Sq
Grace		20	F	Unknown	03Ap02Sq
GRAY, Mary		45	F	Unknown	03Ap02Sq
GAMBLE, Henry		21	M	Laborer	03Ap02Sq
Mary		18	F	Unknown	03Ap02Sq
GREY, Robt.		10	M	Laborer	03Ap02Sq
HALPENY, Michael		25	M	Gdnr	03Ap02Sq
Peter		27	M	Gdnr	03Ap02Sq
Mary		21	F	Unknown	03Ap02Sq

NAMES OF PASSENGERS		AGE	SEX	OCCUPATIONS	DATE PORT SHIP
HALPENY, Patrick		.09	M	Infant	03Ap02Sq
FLANAGAN, Patrick		27	M	Laborer	03Ap02Sq
COULTER, Alen		18	M	Laborer	03Ap02Sq
KNOX, John		25	M	Laborer	03Ap02Sq
HEANEY, Pat		24	M	Laborer	03Ap02Sq
Bridget		16	F	Spinster	03Ap02Sq
EAGEN, Ellen		16	F	Spinster	03Ap02Sq
HAYSLAP, Peter		27	M	Servant	03Ap02Sq
MCCLAIN, Charles		25	M	Weaver	03Ap02Sq
DRUMOND, Sarah		18	F	Spinster	03Ap02Sq
Susan		17	F	Spinster	03Ap02Sq
CLEARY, James		35	M	Farmer	03Ap02Sq
COLLONS, John		25	M	Tailor	03Ap02Sq
KENEDY, Thos.		30	M	Laborer	03Ap02Sq
Rosey		19	F	Spinster	03Ap02Sq
JOHNSON, James		32	M	Laborer	03Ap02Sq
KELLEY, Hough		22	M	Tailor	03Ap02Sq
IRVIN, Peter		30	M	Laborer	03Ap02Sq
Mary		28	F	Spinster	03Ap02Sq
KELLEY, Catherine		21	F	Spinster	03Ap02Sq
MCDONALD, John		20	M	Laborer	03Ap02Sq
KELLEY, James		26	M	Servant	03Ap02Sq
Michael		22	M	Laborer	03Ap02Sq
CARNEY, Thos.		25	M	Laborer	03Ap02Sq
Honah		21	F	Spinster	03Ap02Sq
FARLEY, John		24	M	Laborer	03Ap02Sq
HOLTON, Margt.		20	F	Spinster	03Ap02Sq
FLIN, Peter		23	M	Farmer	03Ap02Sq
CASEY, Mary		17	F	Spinster	03Ap02Sq
KELLEY, Mary		20	F	Spinster	03Ap02Sq
HOLLIGAN, Catherine		25	F	Spinster	03Ap02Sq
HOWHELL, James		22	M	Flabr	03Ap02Sq
KELLEY, Michael		21	M	Servant	03Ap02Sq
MURPHY, Andrew		27	M	Storekeeper	03Ap02Sq
KEARNON, Barney		21	M	Laborer	03Ap02Sq
DAYLEY, Ann		26	F	Unknown	03Ap02Sq
CAFFRAE, Patrick		22	M	Distiller	03Ap02Sq
Edward		24	M	Distiller	03Ap02Sq
Celia		18	F	Unknown	03Ap02Sq
KENEDY, Peter		36	M	Laborer	03Ap02Sq
SMITH, Patrick		26	M	Laborer	03Ap02Sq
Barnard		28	M	Laborer	03Ap02Sq
MOREHEAD, Hugh		27	M	Laborer	03Ap02Sq
HUGHES, Joseph		23	M	Carpenter	03Ap02Sq
CLASBY, Patrick		21	M	Laborer	03Ap02Sq
ANDREWS, Richd.		33	M	Laborer	03Ap02Sq
Julia	(W)	33	F	Unknown	03Ap02Sq
William	(S)	10	M	Unknown	03Ap02Sq
Michael	(S)	07	M	Child	03Ap02Sq
BUTLER, Richard		35	M	Laborer	03Ap02Sq
JEFFERIES, Patrick		30	M	Laborer	03Ap02Sq
VINCENT, Eliza		19	F	Sp-Gvns	03Ap02Sq
Mary		22	F	Sp-Gvns	03Ap02Sq
MARR, Edward		29	M	Mrmkr	03Ap02Sq
Mary		31	F	Unknown	03Ap02Sq
Christopher		14	M	Mrmkr	03Ap02Sq
PARKES, Stephen		21	M	Laborer	03Ap02Sq
TULLEY, Phillip		23	M	Laborer	03Ap02Sq
Bridget		22	F	Unknown	03Ap02Sq
HOWLDING, James		35	M	Hatter	03Ap02Sq
DOUGHERTY, Hugh-B.		36	M	Boatmaker	03Ap02Sq
FOXLEY, John		27	M	Brick Maker	03Ap02Sq
CARNES, Frederick		33	M	Plasterer	03Ap02Sq
QUARDI, Andrew		26	M	Laborer	03Ap02Sq
KENEDY, Richd.		26	M	Laborer	03Ap02Sq
James		32	M	Laborer	03Ap02Sq
Bridget		38	F	Wife	03Ap02Sq
Judy		31	F	Spinster	03Ap02Sq
Mary		16	F	Spinster	03Ap02Sq
John		29	M	Laborer	03Ap02Sq
RYAN, Michael		32	M	Laborer	03Ap02Sq
DORAN, Marjery		40	F	Unknown	03Ap02Sq
Cath	(D)	20	F	Spinster	03Ap02Sq
Ellen	(D)	18	F	Spinster	03Ap02Sq
Michael	(S)	14	M	Flabr	03Ap02Sq

NAMES OF PASSENGERS		AGE	SEX	OCCUPATIONS	DATE PORT SHIP
DORAN, Mary	(D)	11	F	Spinster	03Ap02Sq
Martha	(D)	07	F	Child	03Ap02Sq
John		22	M	Flabr	03Ap02Sq
MOLAKIN, John		25	M	Carpenter	03Ap02Sq
Mary	(W)	30	F	Wife	03Ap02Sq
MULLIN, John		38	M	Laborer	03Ap02Sq
Mary		30	F	Spinster	03Ap02Sq
MCDONALD, Pat.		20	M	Farmer	03Ap02Sq
DOYLE, Thos.		24	M	Farmer	03Ap02Sq
FLAGHERTY, James		30	M	Cooper	03Ap02Sq
KEELING, William		45	M	Tailor	03Ap02Sq
John		20	M	Tailor	03Ap02Sq
DARMODY, James		18	M	Laborer	03Ap02Sq
BRYAN, Patrick		23	M	Laborer	03Ap02Sq
John		31	M	Laborer	03Ap02Sq
Halley		52	F	Spinster	03Ap02Sq
Halley		21	F	Spinster	03Ap02Sq
Ellen		19	F	Spinster	03Ap02Sq
COINE, James		50	M	Laborer	03Ap02Sq
MCNULTY, John		20	M	Wlmcht	03Ap02Sq
GIVENS, Mary		20	F	Spinster	03Ap02Sq
CONELY, John		36	M	Farmer	03Ap02Sq
ONEAL, Andrew		24	M	Engineer	03Ap02Sq
Eliza	(W)	21	F	Wife	03Ap02Sq
Rachall	(D)	.11	F	Infant	03Ap02Sq
KENEDY, Josiah-W.		16	M	Laborer	03Ap02Sq
CONINGAN, James		26	M	Weaver	03Ap02Sq
LOGAN, Jane		24	F	Spinster	03Ap02Sq
DONELY, Ann		15	F	Spinster	03Ap02Sq
GILLEPSIE, Francis		35	M	Laborer	03Ap02Sq
SMITH, Jane		40	F	Wi	03Ap02Sq
Patrick	(S)	18	M	Laborer	03Ap02Sq
Catherine	(D)	15	F	Spinster	03Ap02Sq
BURNES, James		24	M	Laborer	03Ap02Sq
HARGRAVE, Henry		22	M	Laborer	03Ap02Sq
QUINN, Patrick		27	M	Carpenter	03Ap02Sq
LOWDON, Thos.		30	M	Weaver	03Ap02Sq
BIRCH, Patrick		18	M	Laborer	03Ap02Sq
BONA, Neal		40	M	Laborer	03Ap02Sq
MURPHY, James		40	M	Laborer	03Ap02Sq

PATRICK-HENRY 03 APRIL 1848

From Liverpool

NAMES OF PASSENGERS		AGE	SEX	OCCUPATIONS	DATE PORT SHIP
MILLER, John		26	M	Carpenter	03Ap02Cw
Emma		20	F	Unknown	03Ap02Cw
FURLONG, Thomas		30	M	Laborer	03Ap02Cw
BRAY, James		33	M	Laborer	03Ap02Cw
DICKENSON, John		30	M	Wmnftr	03Ap02Cw
HOLMES, Enor		28	M	Wmnftr	03Ap02Cw
BYRNES, Peter		28	M	Laborer	03Ap02Cw
Mary		28	F	Unknown	03Ap02Cw
Bridget		20	F	Unknown	03Ap02Cw
BREEN, Henry		35	M	Farmer	03Ap02Cw
Margarett	(W)	37	F	Unknown	03Ap02Cw
Sarah	(D)	05	F	Child	03Ap02Cw
FI---, John		22	M	Unknown	03Ap02Cw
RICHARD, Thomas		34	M	Dyer	03Ap02Cw
Elisabeth	(W)	32	F	Unknown	03Ap02Cw
Mary-Ann	(D)	10	F	Child	03Ap02Cw
Rees	(S)	04	M	Child	03Ap02Cw
Philip	(S)	02	M	Child	03Ap02Cw
Ann		60	F	Unknown	03Ap02Cw
Morgan		07	M	Child	03Ap02Cw
FINLAYSON, Kennith		24	M	Laborer	03Ap02Cw
MORGAN, Thos.		22	M	Dyer	03Ap02Cw
HOWELL, John		25	M	Dyer	03Ap02Cw
ELLIS, Evan		25	M	Dyer	03Ap02Cw

NAMES OF PASSENGERS		AGE	SEX	OCCUPATIONS	DATE PORT SHIP
HARRIS, David		20	M	Dyer	03Ap02Cw
GOLESKY, Philip		22	M	Furrier	03Ap02Cw
FELL, Michael		40	M	Laborer	03Ap02Cw
HOWELL, Morgan		23	M	Dyer	03Ap02Cw
MORGAN, Martha		18	F	Unknown	03Ap02Cw
MONAHAN, Dennis		24	M	Farmer	03Ap02Cw
REYNOLDS, John		28	M	Talch	03Ap02Cw
CONNOR, James		24	M	Shoemaker	03Ap02Cw
John		23	M	Shoemaker	03Ap02Cw
BROWN, John		25	M	Laborer	03Ap02Cw
WYNE, William		20	M	Laborer	03Ap02Cw
BOWKETT, Benjamin		32	M	Tailor	03Ap02Cw
DUFFY, Edward		32	M	Tailor	03Ap02Cw
SHEA, Eliza		35	F	Unknown	03Ap02Cw
RABBIT, Mary		16	F	Unknown	03Ap02Cw
Michael		10	M	Unknown	03Ap02Cw
LULLEN, Lawrence		24	M	Farmer	03Ap02Cw
FLYNNE, William		65	M	Laborer	03Ap02Cw
Judith	(W)	60	F	Unknown	03Ap02Cw
Judith	(D)	17	F	Unknown	03Ap02Cw
Catharine	(D)	14	F	Unknown	03Ap02Cw
Bernard	(S)	20	M	Laborer	03Ap02Cw
Peter	(S)	26	M	Laborer	03Ap02Cw
Thomas	(S)	27	M	Laborer	03Ap02Cw
STIVEN, John		30	M	Farmer	03Ap02Cw
MCBRIDE, Jane		58	F	Unknown	03Ap02Cw
Mary		25	F	Unknown	03Ap02Cw
MCFADDEN, James		14	M	Unknown	03Ap02Cw
Patrick		12	M	Unknown	03Ap02Cw
MCNEIL, Rose		45	F	Unknown	03Ap02Cw
Eliza	(D)	18	F	Unknown	03Ap02Cw
Ann	(D)	16	F	Unknown	03Ap02Cw
John	(S)	06	M	Child	03Ap02Cw
FLYNNE, Mary		25	F	Unknown	03Ap02Cw
John	(S)	03	M	Child	03Ap02Cw
Mary	(D)	02	F	Child	03Ap02Cw
REILEY, Catharine		18	F	Unknown	03Ap02Cw
DOWD, Thomas		18	M	Laborer	03Ap02Cw
MCCAVILL, Patt		16	M	Laborer	03Ap02Cw
Joseph		14	M	Laborer	03Ap02Cw
REILLY, Thomas		22	M	Joiner	03Ap02Cw
DOYLE, Edward		22	M	Joiner	03Ap02Cw
TODD, Samuel		15	M	Joiner	03Ap02Cw
KINCELLD, Patt		21	M	Laborer	03Ap02Cw
HAYS, Thomas		27	M	Laborer	03Ap02Cw
POUR, Francis		25	M	Tailor	03Ap02Cw
ROURKE, George		23	M	Tailor	03Ap02Cw
CONNOLY, Michael		30	M	Tailor	03Ap02Cw
DUNNE, Margarett		40	F	Unknown	03Ap02Cw
PLANT, William		24	M	Farmer	03Ap02Cw
Humphrey		26	M	Farmer	03Ap02Cw
Mary		22	F	Unknown	03Ap02Cw
Mary		20	F	Unknown	03Ap02Cw
Wm.		.00	M	Infant	03Ap02Cw
KINCEY, Martha		23	F	Unknown	03Ap02Cw
MCGOWEN, Patt		25	M	Laborer	03Ap02Cw
KELLY, Thomas		45	M	Laborer	03Ap02Cw
MERCER, Henry		20	M	Laborer	03Ap02Cw
QUIGLY, Margarett		30	F	Unknown	03Ap02Cw
FINEGAN, John		10	M	Unknown	03Ap02Cw
EARLY, John		22	M	Laborer	03Ap02Cw
COOKE, Wm.		22	M	Laborer	03Ap02Cw
VOSS, Ann		20	F	Unknown	03Ap02Cw
KELLY, James		25	M	Laborer	03Ap02Cw
HARRINGTON, Patt		26	M	Laborer	03Ap02Cw
Daniel		40	M	Laborer	03Ap02Cw
BIGLY, John		34	M	Farmer	03Ap02Cw
LEERY, Ellen		60	F	Unknown	03Ap02Cw
BROWN, Mary		20	F	Unknown	03Ap02Cw
FARMAN, Michael		20	M	Laborer	03Ap02Cw
James		22	M	Laborer	03Ap02Cw
BRADY, Bernard		22	M	Laborer	03Ap02Cw
WOOD, William		20	M	Laborer	03Ap02Cw
NEWMAN, Daniel		18	M	Laborer	03Ap02Cw
REWIN, Daniel		18	M	Laborer	03Ap02Cw
LANGAN, Mary		18	F	Unknown	03Ap02Cw
FARRELL, Catharine		18	F	Unknown	03Ap02Cw
DAUTTON, William		22	M	Laborer	03Ap02Cw
Catharine		18	F	Unknown	03Ap02Cw
FRAY, Lawrence		18	M	Laborer	03Ap02Cw
MCDERMOTT, Biddy		19	F	Unknown	03Ap02Cw
DUFFY, Peggy		19	F	Unknown	03Ap02Cw
REYNOLDS, Patt		45	M	Laborer	03Ap02Cw
Mary	(W)	40	F	Unknown	03Ap02Cw
SIMONDS, Edward		20	M	Laborer	03Ap02Cw
COFFEY, Patt		20	M	Laborer	03Ap02Cw
SIMONDS, Wm.		20	M	Laborer	03Ap02Cw
CHAPEL, Paul		40	M	Laborer	03Ap02Cw
BURNS, John		23	M	Mechanic	03Ap02Cw
PHILLIPS, James		33	M	Mechanic	03Ap02Cw
IRVINE, Henry		22	M	Reporter	03Ap02Cw
GUTHRIDN, John		24	M	Mechanic	03Ap02Cw
JAMES, Thomas		24	M	Mechanic	03Ap02Cw
ROBERTSON, G.Miss		30	F	Unknown	03Ap02Cw
JACKSON, Thomas		49	M	Turner	03Ap02Cw
Joseph		29	M	Turner	03Ap02Cw
BOOTH, Joseph		24	M	Joiner	03Ap02Cw
JONES, Lewis		24	M	Miner	03Ap02Cw
Elisabeth		23	F	Unknown	03Ap02Cw
EVANS, Evan		40	M	Laborer	03Ap02Cw
Anne		34	F	Unknown	03Ap02Cw
EDWARDS, Maria		19	F	Unknown	03Ap02Cw
JONES, John		26	M	Carpenter	03Ap02Cw
William		24	M	Miner	03Ap02Cw
WATERS, John		36	M	Miner	03Ap02Cw
GRIFFITHS, Thomas		35	M	Farmer	03Ap02Cw
Sarah	(W)	29	F	Unknown	03Ap02Cw
Mary	(D)	11	F	Unknown	03Ap02Cw
CALVEADY, Thomas		22	M	Spinner	03Ap02Cw
William		21	M	Spinner	03Ap02Cw
CULLEN, Michael		25	M	Shoemaker	03Ap02Cw

COLUMBUS 03 APRIL 1848

From Liverpool

NAMES OF PASSENGERS		AGE	SEX	OCCUPATIONS	DATE PORT SHIP
HORSLEY, Howard		42	M	Wrhsmn	03Ap02Ar
Anne	(W)	40	F	Unknown	03Ap02Ar
Sarah	(D)	17	F	Unknown	03Ap02Ar
Ann	(D)	19	F	Unknown	03Ap02Ar
Howard	(S)	06	M	Child	03Ap02Ar
Saml.	(S)	11	M	Unknown	03Ap02Ar
Emma	(D)	04	F	Child	03Ap02Ar
HARRINGTON, Nia.Herber		30	M	Postsvyr	03Ap02Ar
Elizth.	(W)	25	F	Unknown	03Ap02Ar
BAXTER, William		30	M	Merchant	03Ap02Ar
Robt.		25	M	Engineer	03Ap02Ar
Hob---, Henry		28	M	Mariner	03Ap02Ar
PARKER, Jno.F.		33	M	Schm	03Ap02Ar
RAVEN, Jno.		32	M	Gentleman	03Ap02Ar
STEVENS, Saml.		21	M	Chdlr	03Ap02Ar
GALLOWAY, Abraham		23	M	Painter	03Ap02Ar
Esther		23	F	Unknown	03Ap02Ar
BYRON, Honor		30	F	Unknown	03Ap02Ar
WILLIAMS, William		38	M	Grocer	03Ap02Ar
TORKINGTON, Jno.		40	M	Hatter	03Ap02Ar
Adeliza	(W)	40	F	Unknown	03Ap02Ar
ONEIL, Patk.		25	M	Unknown	03Ap02Ar
BUTLER, Fredk.		19	M	Draper	03Ap02Ar
CLARK, Jno.Young		42	M	Weaver	03Ap02Ar
Mary	(W)	40	F	Unknown	03Ap02Ar
CARROLL, Cath.		23	F	Unknown	03Ap02Ar
GALVIN, Mary		22	F	Unknown	03Ap02Ar
FEATHERSTONE, Patk.		25	M	Unknown	03Ap02Ar

NAMES OF PASSENGERS		AGE	SEX	OCCUPATIONS	DATE PORT SHIP
REDDISH, Michael		39	M	Unknown	03Ap02Ar
Thos.		19	M	Laborer	03Ap02Ar
KELLY, Michl.		25	M	Laborer	03Ap02Ar
Bridgt.		20	F	Unknown	03Ap02Ar
Ann		50	F	Unknown	03Ap02Ar
Margt.		06	F	Child	03Ap02Ar
MURPHY, Martin		25	M	Laborer	03Ap02Ar
Francis	(S)	.00	M	Infant	03Ap02Ar
Honor	(W)	23	F	Unknown	03Ap02Ar
FURLEY, Patk.		20	M	Laborer	03Ap02Ar
BOWCOCK, Thos.		22	M	Miner	03Ap02Ar
GRIFFITHS, Jno.		23	M	Miner	03Ap02Ar
ALLEN, Ed.		30	M	Miner	03Ap02Ar
BUXTON, Wm.		20	M	Miner	03Ap02Ar
MURRAY, Danl.		55	M	Bricklayer	03Ap02Ar
Ann	(W)	54	F	Unknown	03Ap02Ar
Ann	(D)	20	F	Unknown	03Ap02Ar
Danl.	(S)	18	M	Bricklayer	03Ap02Ar
Mary	(D)	16	F	Unknown	03Ap02Ar
Winnifd.	(D)	12	F	Unknown	03Ap02Ar
Bridgt.	(D)	24	F	Unknown	03Ap02Ar
Margt.	(D)	10	F	Unknown	03Ap02Ar
FLATLEY, Bryan		36	M	Laborer	03Ap02Ar
Patk.		40	M	Laborer	03Ap02Ar
FINIGAN, Andw.		19	M	Laborer	03Ap02Ar
MURRAY, Michl.		16	M	Laborer	03Ap02Ar
Mary		20	F	Laborer	03Ap02Ar
FLATLEY, Bryan		29	M	Laborer	03Ap02Ar
MCCOY, Patk.		20	M	Laborer	03Ap02Ar
FLATLEY, Hugh		18	M	Laborer	03Ap02Ar
BURKE, Anthy.		18	M	Laborer	03Ap02Ar
SWORDS, Sarah		18	F	Unknown	03Ap02Ar
REILLY, Mary-Ann		17	F	Unknown	03Ap02Ar
FERNY, Luke		15	M	Laborer	03Ap02Ar
Mary		13	F	Unknown	03Ap02Ar
PRIAN, Bridgt.		20	F	Unknown	03Ap02Ar
CALLIGAN, Patk.		27	M	Laborer	03Ap02Ar
BRYAN, Michl.		24	M	Laborer	03Ap02Ar
GREENHALFH, Jas.		44	M	Laborer	03Ap02Ar
LACE, Thos.		35	M	Laborer	03Ap02Ar
CONNELLY, Jno.		33	M	Laborer	03Ap02Ar
MCCARTY, Cath.		30	F	Unknown	03Ap02Ar
DACEY, Bridgt.		19	F	Unknown	03Ap02Ar
Mary		09	F	Child	03Ap02Ar
Jno.		07	M	Child	03Ap02Ar
Bridgt.		.00	F	Infant	03Ap02Ar
JOHNSON, Wm.		25	M	Servant	03Ap02Ar
Mary		28	F	Servant	03Ap02Ar
Mary		.00	F	Infant	03Ap02Ar
MEAGHER, Patk.		30	M	Shoemaker	03Ap02Ar
MCQUAID, Martha		20	F	Unknown	03Ap02Ar
Jno.		12	M	Laborer	03Ap02Ar
LYNCH, Thos.		22	M	Laborer	03Ap02Ar
Michl.		26	M	Laborer	03Ap02Ar
Cath		18	F	Servant	03Ap02Ar
Mary		10	F	Servant	03Ap02Ar
Ellen		08	F	Child	03Ap02Ar
LEE, Christn.		25	M	Laborer	03Ap02Ar
BOYLAN, Owen		18	M	Laborer	03Ap02Ar
MCGEE, Jno.		20	M	Laborer	03Ap02Ar
REILLY, Ann		18	F	Unknown	03Ap02Ar
FAGAN, Jas.		20	M	Laborer	03Ap02Ar
ROONEY, Bryan		24	M	Laborer	03Ap02Ar
BRADY, Peter		25	M	Laborer	03Ap02Ar
RALE, Math.		24	M	Laborer	03Ap02Ar
MCALTER, Elizth.		18	F	Unknown	03Ap02Ar
Ann		24	F	Unknown	03Ap02Ar
FLEMING, Jno.		19	M	Laborer	03Ap02Ar
RYAN, Dennis		23	M	Tailor	03Ap02Ar
MCCREE, Mary		21	F	Unknown	03Ap02Ar
CARROLL, Jno.		26	M	Miner	03Ap02Ar
GANNON, Patk.		14	M	Miner	03Ap02Ar
EDGAR, Saml.		23	M	Miner	03Ap02Ar
DEMPSTER, Edwd.		50	M	Miner	03Ap02Ar
GANNON, Jno.		19	M	Miner	03Ap02Ar

NAMES OF PASSENGERS		AGE	SEX	OCCUPATIONS	DATE PORT SHIP
GANNON, Francis		16	M	Miner	03Ap02Ar
WARD, Philip		20	M	Miner	03Ap02Ar
HAWKINS, Mary		15	F	Unknown	03Ap02Ar
GREEN, Jas.		30	M	Miner	03Ap02Ar
DROUGHERTY, Thos.		25	M	Miner	03Ap02Ar
LYON, Richd.		14	M	Laborer	03Ap02Ar
James		10	M	Laborer	03Ap02Ar
DEVINE, Bridgt.		19	F	Unknown	03Ap02Ar
Ann		18	F	Unknown	03Ap02Ar
DAHILL, Margt.		20	F	Unknown	03Ap02Ar
WALSH, Michl.		16	M	Laborer	03Ap02Ar
GALWAY, Jno.		20	M	Laborer	03Ap02Ar
DIGNAW, Bridgt.		17	F	Unknown	03Ap02Ar
MCCABE, Michl.		14	M	Laborer	03Ap02Ar
Ann		10	F	Unknown	03Ap02Ar
KEEGAN, Michl.		30	M	Laborer	03Ap02Ar
MULVEY, Bridgt.		20	F	Unknown	03Ap02Ar
KIRNAN, Patk.		20	M	Laborer	03Ap02Ar
MCGUINNESS, Jno.		19	M	Laborer	03Ap02Ar
Jane		20	F	Unknown	03Ap02Ar
CONNELL, Mary		20	F	Unknown	03Ap02Ar
HYLAND, Dennis		20	M	Laborer	03Ap02Ar
REILLY, Ann		18	F	Unknown	03Ap02Ar
MCCARTIN, Felix		30	M	Laborer	03Ap02Ar
KEENAN, Bridgt.		20	F	Unknown	03Ap02Ar
QUICKEN, Thos.		24	M	Laborer	03Ap02Ar
ROHALE, Rose		30	F	Unknown	03Ap02Ar
CONNELLY, Mary		16	F	Unknown	03Ap02Ar
CAVIN, Patk.		24	M	Laborer	03Ap02Ar
DALY, Hubert		24	M	Laborer	03Ap02Ar
KEARNY, Keavan		28	M	Laborer	03Ap02Ar
KENNEY, Mary		21	F	Unknown	03Ap02Ar
CURLY, Keaven		14	M	Laborer	03Ap02Ar
MANGAN, Jas.		30	M	Laborer	03Ap02Ar
MCGUINNESS, Mary		20	F	Unknown	03Ap02Ar
HERVISON, Wm.		31	M	Laborer	03Ap02Ar
DUGAN, Peter		20	M	Laborer	03Ap02Ar
KEEGAN, Peter		12	M	Laborer	03Ap02Ar
MCNULLY, Jno.		22	M	Laborer	03Ap02Ar
GALBRAITH, Chs.		20	M	Laborer	03Ap02Ar
MALONE, Thos.		30	M	Laborer	03Ap02Ar
GUFFRY, Mary		21	F	Unknown	03Ap02Ar
KEHOC, Patk.		18	M	Laborer	03Ap02Ar
Mary		27	F	Unknown	03Ap02Ar
CUDDY, Edwd.		23	M	Laborer	03Ap02Ar
Mary		50	F	Unknown	03Ap02Ar
Jno.		30	M	Laborer	03Ap02Ar
Judith		25	F	Unknown	03Ap02Ar
Patk.		18	M	Laborer	03Ap02Ar
Mary		17	F	Unknown	03Ap02Ar
David		12	M	Laborer	03Ap02Ar
Cath.		08	F	Child	03Ap02Ar
FINNERTY, Michl.		36	M	Laborer	03Ap02Ar
Ann		31	F	Unknown	03Ap02Ar
Bridgt.		21	F	Unknown	03Ap02Ar
Bridgt.		.00	F	Infant	03Ap02Ar
CAMPBELL, Mary		30	F	Unknown	03Ap02Ar
Mary	(D)	08	F	Child	03Ap02Ar
Jane	(D)	06	F	Child	03Ap02Ar
Julia	(D)	.00	F	Infant	03Ap02Ar
LEE, Mary-Ann		20	F	Unknown	03Ap02Ar
OLEARY, Jno.		25	M	Laborer	03Ap02Ar
DONEGAN, Thos.		20	M	Laborer	03Ap02Ar
CONNANGHTON, Mary		17	F	Unknown	03Ap02Ar
OWEN, Eleonor		50	F	Unknown	03Ap02Ar
LYNCH, Owen		40	M	Laborer	03Ap02Ar
KEOUGH, Honor		20	F	Servant	03Ap02Ar
Bridgt.		18	F	Servant	03Ap02Ar
OHARE, Ann		20	F	Servant	03Ap02Ar
MCQUINN, Elizth.		40	F	Servant	03Ap02Ar
Peter		25	M	Painter	03Ap02Ar
Susan		20	F	Unknown	03Ap02Ar
BERRYMAN, Jas.		21	M	Farmer	03Ap02Ar
Wm.		18	M	Farmer	03Ap02Ar
Nancy		15	F	Unknown	03Ap02Ar

NAMES OF PASSENGERS		AGE	SEX	OCCUPATIONS	DATE PORT SHIP
MITCHELL, Mary		20	F	Unknown	03Ap02Ar
DELANEY, Ed.		18	M	Laborer	03Ap02Ar
MULLEN, Jno.		20	M	Laborer	03Ap02Ar
Thos.		16	M	Laborer	03Ap02Ar
Ann		11	F	Unknown	03Ap02Ar
MAXWELL, Richd.		20	M	Laborer	03Ap02Ar
GLENNAN, Cath.		18	F	Servant	03Ap02Ar
DOWD, Patk.		20	M	Laborer	03Ap02Ar
GORMLEY, Patk.		40	M	Laborer	03Ap02Ar
Cath.	(W)	40	F	Unknown	03Ap02Ar
Mary	(D)	15	F	Unknown	03Ap02Ar
Nancy	(D)	13	F	Unknown	03Ap02Ar
Margt.	(D)	10	F	Unknown	03Ap02Ar
Jno.	(S)	07	M	Child	03Ap02Ar
Dennis	(S)	05	M	Child	03Ap02Ar
Eliza	(D)	02	F	Child	03Ap02Ar
REDDINGTON, Jas.		20	M	Tailor	03Ap02Ar
MULDAVY, Ellen		18	F	Unknown	03Ap02Ar
DAUGHLAN, Jno.		23	M	Laborer	03Ap02Ar
CLEARY, Thos.		21	M	Laborer	03Ap02Ar
CONNOR, Wm.		34	M	Laborer	03Ap02Ar
Honor		25	F	Unknown	03Ap02Ar
COLLINS, Cath.		24	F	Unknown	03Ap02Ar
CROOK, Thos.		22	M	Laborer	03Ap02Ar
LEARY, Cath.		25	F	Unknown	03Ap02Ar
KEATING, Jane		09	F	Child	03Ap02Ar
DRISCOLL, Jno.		20	M	Laborer	03Ap02Ar
Cornel.		30	M	Laborer	03Ap02Ar
MAHERY, Cornel.		18	M	Laborer	03Ap02Ar
COLLINS, Thady		24	M	Laborer	03Ap02Ar
Danl.		22	M	Laborer	03Ap02Ar
REILLY, Connor		18	M	Laborer	03Ap02Ar
CLOVEN, Thos.		20	M	Laborer	03Ap02Ar
MCADAM, Hugh		20	M	Laborer	03Ap02Ar
HANLEY, Martin		19	M	Laborer	03Ap02Ar
DEVERNEY, Chas.		26	M	Laborer	03Ap02Ar
MCCLEAR, Patk.		30	M	Laborer	03Ap02Ar
MCCORMACK, Patk.		28	M	Laborer	03Ap02Ar
MCKENNA, Jas.		24	M	Laborer	03Ap02Ar
CAMUSKY, Matilda		21	F	Unknown	03Ap02Ar
MCQUINN, Jno.		35	M	Laborer	03Ap02Ar
KENNEDY, Bridgt.		17	F	Unknown	03Ap02Ar
FLANAGAN, Peter		17	M	Laborer	03Ap02Ar
WALKER, Mary		45	F	Unknown	03Ap02Ar
Jsaiah.	(S)	08	M	Child	03Ap02Ar
COYLE, Edwd.		20	M	Laborer	03Ap02Ar
Sarah		20	F	Unknown	03Ap02Ar
KEENAN, Elizth.		17	F	Unknown	03Ap02Ar
GRIFFIN, Patk.		25	M	Laborer	03Ap02Ar
CALLAGAN, Thos.		20	M	Laborer	03Ap02Ar
CONLAN, Rose		09	F	Child	03Ap02Ar
Betsey		28	F	Unknown	03Ap02Ar
BARRY, Norry		55	F	Unknown	03Ap02Ar
Eliza		02	F	Child	03Ap02Ar
REYNOLDS, Jno.		24	M	Laborer	03Ap02Ar
FOX, Elizth.		40	F	Unknown	03Ap02Ar
MCGLYNN, Michl.		20	M	Laborer	03Ap02Ar
Jno.		12	M	Laborer	03Ap02Ar
MCCARTHY, Con.		20	M	Laborer	03Ap02Ar
Dennis		16	M	Laborer	03Ap02Ar
HOGAN, Mary		18	F	Unknown	03Ap02Ar
CONNALL, Michl.		14	M	Laborer	03Ap02Ar
MCLAUGHLIN, Michl.		22	M	Laborer	03Ap02Ar
DUNNIAN, Jas.		17	M	Laborer	03Ap02Ar
CURLY, Thos.		34	M	Laborer	03Ap02Ar
Bridgt.	(D)	06	F	Child	03Ap02Ar
MCCARVIL, Philp.		22	M	Laborer	03Ap02Ar
Cath.		20	F	Unknown	03Ap02Ar
Betsey		22	F	Unknown	03Ap02Ar
MCCABE, Michl.		24	M	Laborer	03Ap02Ar
RATTIGAN, Thos.		30	M	Laborer	03Ap02Ar
CANTY, Jno.		24	M	Laborer	03Ap02Ar
MCGRATH, Martin		30	M	Laborer	03Ap02Ar
MCCARTY, Ellen		20	F	Unknown	03Ap02Ar
WOOD, Felix		40	M	Laborer	03Ap02Ar

NAMES OF PASSENGERS		AGE	SEX	OCCUPATIONS	DATE PORT SHIP
WOOD, Margt.	(W)	40	F	Unknown	03Ap02Ar
Richd.	(S)	20	M	Laborer	03Ap02Ar
Patk.	(S)	13	M	Laborer	03Ap02Ar
Mary	(D)	10	F	Unknown	03Ap02Ar
Francis	(S)	09	M	Child	03Ap02Ar
Letitia	(D)	07	F	Child	03Ap02Ar
STANDEVEN, Joseph		58	M	Laborer	03Ap02Ar
Joseph		30	M	Laborer	03Ap02Ar
CONNOR, Thos.		30	M	Laborer	03Ap02Ar
Mary	(W)	25	F	Unknown	03Ap02Ar
Jas.	(S)	03	M	Child	03Ap02Ar
Jno.	(S)	.00	M	Infant	03Ap02Ar
BAGAN, Berrend		26	M	Blacksmith	03Ap02Ar
Mary		26	F	Unknown	03Ap02Ar
FITZPATRICK, Rose		20	F	Unknown	03Ap02Ar
LEARY, Jas.		21	M	Laborer	03Ap02Ar
QUIGLEY, Michl.		20	M	Laborer	03Ap02Ar
Ann		15	F	Unknown	03Ap02Ar
Susan		13	F	Unknown	03Ap02Ar
MULCAHEY, Ellen		18	F	Unknown	03Ap02Ar
CANTINTTON, Mary		11	F	Unknown	03Ap02Ar
FALLON, Elizth.		20	F	Unknown	03Ap02Ar
MCGOORAN, Jane		29	F	Unknown	03Ap02Ar
LEE, Henry		20	M	Laborer	03Ap02Ar
Elizth.		15	F	Unknown	03Ap02Ar
QUINN, Patk.		20	M	Laborer	03Ap02Ar
Cath.		18	F	Unknown	03Ap02Ar
BOHUN, Cath.		16	F	Unknown	03Ap02Ar
ROGERS, Rose		20	F	Unknown	03Ap02Ar
RATIGAN, Denis		19	M	Laborer	03Ap02Ar
Cawl--, Patk.		21	M	Laborer	03Ap02Ar
EARLY, Jas.		32	M	Laborer	03Ap02Ar
KAVANAGH, Jas.		36	M	Laborer	03Ap02Ar
MCCANIE, Patk.		21	M	Laborer	03Ap02Ar
DOYLE, Timothy		47	M	Laborer	03Ap02Ar
QUIGLEY, Peter		35	M	Laborer	03Ap02Ar
KIERNAN, Edwd.		28	M	Laborer	03Ap02Ar
Cath.		26	F	Unknown	03Ap02Ar
BRENNAN, Bridgt.		29	F	Unknown	03Ap02Ar
KAVANAGH, Michl.		40	M	Laborer	03Ap02Ar
Ann	(W)	40	F	Unknown	03Ap02Ar
Mary	(D)	11	F	Unknown	03Ap02Ar
Ellen	(D)	09	F	Child	03Ap02Ar
Danl.	(S)	06	M	Child	03Ap02Ar
Thos.	(S)	04	M	Child	03Ap02Ar
Elizth.	(D)	02	F	Child	03Ap02Ar
CURRAN, Michl.		29	M	Laborer	03Ap02Ar
HOOKS, Bridgt.		25	F	Unknown	03Ap02Ar
GOULD, Judith		40	F	Unknown	03Ap02Ar
FRANEY, Jno.		05	M	Child	03Ap02Ar
HARDACRE, Saml.		31	M	Laborer	03Ap02Ar
Mary	(W)	28	F	Unknown	03Ap02Ar
Winifred	(D)	02	F	Child	03Ap02Ar
WHITTAKER, Thos.		22	M	Laborer	03Ap02Ar
LYNCH, Jno.		20	M	Miner	03Ap02Ar
CURIVEN, Dennis		26	M	Miner	03Ap02Ar
Ann		20	F	Unknown	03Ap02Ar
MCGOWAN, Peter		25	M	Miner	03Ap02Ar
WHITE, Martha		24	F	Unknown	03Ap02Ar
Patk.		25	M	Miner	03Ap02Ar
Ann		18	F	Unknown	03Ap02Ar
NORTH, Andw.		20	M	Miner	03Ap02Ar
MCGOWAN, Bridgt.		18	F	Unknown	03Ap02Ar
Patk.		24	M	Miner	03Ap02Ar
FINNERTY, Thos.		23	M	Miner	03Ap02Ar
Peter		22	M	Miner	03Ap02Ar
HALEY, Denis		26	M	Miner	03Ap02Ar
BENNETT, Mary		17	F	Unknown	03Ap02Ar
DUNN, Ann		30	F	Unknown	03Ap02Ar
Jno.		14	M	Miner	03Ap02Ar
Margt.		12	F	Unknown	03Ap02Ar
Michl.		09	M	Child	03Ap02Ar
Patk.		07	M	Child	03Ap02Ar
Ann		03	F	Child	03Ap02Ar
DONELEY, Robt.		24	M	Miner	03Ap02Ar

NAMES OF PASSENGERS		AGE	SEX	OCCUPATIONS	DATE PORT SHIP
FINEGAN, Patk.		20	M	Laborer	03Ap02Ar
U		48	F	Wi	03Ap02Ar
David	(S)	16	M	Laborer	03Ap02Ar
Cath.	(D)	13	F	Unknown	03Ap02Ar
Bridgt.	(D)	10	F	Unknown	03Ap02Ar
Honor	(D)	03	F	Child	03Ap02Ar
GALAGHER, Ellen		25	F	Unknown	03Ap02Ar
MCSHARRICK, Jno.		21	M	Laborer	03Ap02Ar
LYNCH, Michl.		26	M	Laborer	03Ap02Ar
PRYALE, Michl.		30	M	Laborer	03Ap02Ar
PEARCE, Jno.		32	M	Laborer	03Ap02Ar
STOKES, Jno.		31	M	Laborer	03Ap02Ar
Wm.		19	M	Laborer	03Ap02Ar
HAWKINS, Joseph		16	M	Laborer	03Ap02Ar
LEDDY, Patk.		30	M	Laborer	03Ap02Ar
Cath.	(W)	26	F	Unknown	03Ap02Ar
Jno.	(S)	06	M	Child	03Ap02Ar
Matw.	(S)	04	M	Child	03Ap02Ar
Patk.	(S)	02	M	Child	03Ap02Ar
Cath.	(D)	.00	F	Infant	03Ap02Ar
FITZPATRICK, Michl.		19	M	Laborer	03Ap02Ar
MULAVEY, Cath.		16	F	Unknown	03Ap02Ar
KELLY, Honor		16	F	Unknown	03Ap02Ar
Mary		20	F	Unknown	03Ap02Ar
MCDONOUGH, Hugh		20	M	Laborer	03Ap02Ar
Jno.		25	M	Laborer	03Ap02Ar
Mary		23	F	Unknown	03Ap02Ar
Ann	(D)	01	F	Child	03Ap02Ar
CARROLE, Patk.		28	M	Laborer	03Ap02Ar
HANAGAN, Mary		22	F	Unknown	03Ap02Ar
MURIN, Bryan		40	M	Laborer	03Ap02Ar
Chas.	(S)	18	M	Laborer	03Ap02Ar
Ellen	(D)	16	F	Unknown	03Ap02Ar
GORMAN, Michl.		40	M	Laborer	03Ap02Ar
Patk.		22	M	Laborer	03Ap02Ar
Jno.		20	M	Laborer	03Ap02Ar
Margt.		17	F	Unknown	03Ap02Ar
FLANAGAN, Mary		20	F	Unknown	03Ap02Ar
Bryan		16	M	Laborer	03Ap02Ar
CANAVERN, Jas.		40	M	Laborer	03Ap02Ar
Margt.		28	F	Unknown	03Ap02Ar
KEARNES, Thos.		22	M	Laborer	03Ap02Ar
DEVERY, Patk.		21	M	Laborer	03Ap02Ar
MCLAUGHLIN, Jas.		24	M	Laborer	03Ap02Ar
MCNAIN, Jas.		18	M	Laborer	03Ap02Ar
FITZPATRICK, Jas.		00	M	Laborer	03Ap02Ar
KELLY, Honor		19	F	Unknown	03Ap02Ar
ROCHFORD, Maria		19	F	Unknown	03Ap02Ar
Ann		20	F	Unknown	03Ap02Ar
MULLEN, Patk.		22	M	Laborer	03Ap02Ar
Bridgt.		20	F	Unknown	03Ap02Ar
MCCUE, Mary		20	F	Unknown	03Ap02Ar
KAVANAGH, Michl.		20	M	Laborer	03Ap02Ar
Ann		19	F	Unknown	03Ap02Ar
ROGERS, Jas.		26	M	Laborer	03Ap02Ar
OHARA, Jas.		22	M	Laborer	03Ap02Ar
Mary		20	F	Unknown	03Ap02Ar
FALLOON, Patk.		19	M	Laborer	03Ap02Ar
NEWELL, Francis		25	M	Laborer	03Ap02Ar
TREBBLE, Jas.		25	M	Laborer	03Ap02Ar
MCCARTNEY, Peter		22	M	Laborer	03Ap02Ar
KERRIGAN, Simeon		27	M	Laborer	03Ap02Ar
OCONNOR, Mat.		26	M	Laborer	03Ap02Ar
WHITE, Jno.		28	M	Laborer	03Ap02Ar
MCDILL, Jno.		25	M	Laborer	03Ap02Ar
Jno.		20	M	Laborer	03Ap02Ar
JOHNSTON, Mary		21	F	Unknown	03Ap02Ar
Cath.		14	F	Unknown	03Ap02Ar
BIRNIE, Thos.		35	M	Laborer	03Ap02Ar
Ellen		20	F	Unknown	03Ap02Ar
LALLY, Anthony		10	M	Laborer	03Ap02Ar
BRADY, Margt.		20	F	Unknown	03Ap02Ar
CONLON, Jno.		22	M	Laborer	03Ap02Ar
Margt.		24	F	Unknown	03Ap02Ar
DUGGAN, Isaih.		20	M	Laborer	03Ap02Ar
CAMPBELL, Hugh		27	M	Laborer	03Ap02Ar
MCGUFFREY, Peter		19	M	Laborer	03Ap02Ar
DRWE, Wm.		20	M	Laborer	03Ap02Ar
NELSON, Jno.		18	M	Laborer	03Ap02Ar
Cath.		20	F	Unknown	03Ap02Ar
MORRISON, Wm.		31	M	Laborer	03Ap02Ar
CLEARY, Ann		24	F	Unknown	03Ap02Ar
QUINLAN, Jas.		37	M	Farmer	03Ap02Ar
TRAVERS, Edwd.		22	M	Farmer	03Ap02Ar
ROURKE, Mary		12	F	Unknown	03Ap02Ar
HYLAND, Jas.		24	M	Farmer	03Ap02Ar
FAHEY, Jas.		21	M	Farmer	03Ap02Ar
CASHEL, Michl.		19	M	Farmer	03Ap02Ar
Maria		25	F	Unknown	03Ap02Ar
BROPHY, Maria		21	F	Unknown	03Ap02Ar
GORMAN, Jas.		30	M	Laborer	03Ap02Ar
Eliza	(W)	28	F	Unknown	03Ap02Ar
Jno.	(S)	08	M	Child	03Ap02Ar
Mary	(D)	02	F	Child	03Ap02Ar
ECKROYD, Eliza		22	F	Unknown	03Ap02Ar
Hargreaves		20	M	Laborer	03Ap02Ar
MCDERMOT, Patk.		22	M	Laborer	03Ap02Ar
SHALE, Elizth.		30	F	Unknown	03Ap02Ar
Thos.	(S)	.00	M	Infant	03Ap02Ar
GALAGHER, Ann		28	F	Unknown	03Ap02Ar
FITZPATRICK, Pat.		28	M	Laborer	03Ap02Ar
FALLON, Margt.		18	F	Unknown	03Ap02Ar
COSTELLO, Margt.		09	F	Child	03Ap02Ar
BROWNE, Cath.		18	F	Unknown	03Ap02Ar
Julia		21	F	Unknown	03Ap02Ar
LEDDY, Margt.		15	F	Unknown	03Ap02Ar
KELLY, Mgt.		20	F	Unknown	03Ap02Ar
Jas.		21	M	Miner	03Ap02Ar
LENNEY, Patk.		27	M	Miner	03Ap02Ar
MCDERMOTT, Jno.		20	M	Miner	03Ap02Ar
Ann		19	F	Unknown	03Ap02Ar
MCSHELLY, Jas.		22	M	Miner	03Ap02Ar
HANLON, Anthy.		37	M	Miner	03Ap02Ar
Mary		19	F	Unknown	03Ap02Ar
MCNULTY, Mary		30	F	Unknown	03Ap02Ar
Bridgt.		25	F	Unknown	03Ap02Ar
MCGUINNESS, Rose		20	F	Unknown	03Ap02Ar
DALTON, Jno.		40	M	Miner	03Ap02Ar
Eliza		20	F	Unknown	03Ap02Ar
KELLY, Cath.		21	F	Unknown	03Ap02Ar
DUFFY, Ann		11	F	Unknown	03Ap02Ar
U, U		00	U	Unknown	03Ap02Ar
Died-At-Sea					

ORPHAN 03 APRIL 1848

From Liverpool

NAMES OF PASSENGERS	AGE	SEX	OCCUPATIONS	DATE PORT SHIP
BARLOW, Richard	40	M	Laborer	03Ap02Dj
FORSIDE, James	30	M	Laborer	03Ap02Dj
GALVIN, William	32	M	Laborer	03Ap02Dj
MADDEN, John	30	M	Laborer	03Ap02Dj
CAHILL, Mary	20	F	Laborer	03Ap02Dj
SWEENY, Catharine	18	F	Laborer	03Ap02Dj
Ellen	15	F	Laborer	03Ap02Dj
Owen	12	M	Laborer	03Ap02Dj
Honorah	10	F	Laborer	03Ap02Dj
MURPHY, Mary	22	F	Laborer	03Ap02Dj
Jeremiah	24	M	Laborer	03Ap02Dj
MCGARTY, Sicily	30	M	Laborer	03Ap02Dj
DOYLE, Owen	22	M	Laborer	03Ap02Dj
Thomas	20	M	Laborer	03Ap02Dj
Ellen	20	F	Laborer	03Ap02Dj
MARIAN, Margret	20	F	Laborer	03Ap02Dj

NAMES OF PASSENGERS	AGE	SEX	OCCUPATIONS	DATE PORT SHIP
MINNS, Ellen	20	F	Laborer	03Ap02Dj
MARIAN, John	60	M	Laborer	03Ap02Dj
MINS, Essy	20	M	Laborer	03Ap02Dj
LAWSON, Michael	20	M	Laborer	03Ap02Dj
Michael	20	M	Laborer	03Ap02Dj
Mary	20	F	Laborer	03Ap02Dj
KELLY, Jane	16	F	Laborer	03Ap02Dj
Biddy	20	F	Laborer	03Ap02Dj
CONLAN, Judy	20	F	Laborer	03Ap02Dj
DOWNEY, David	20	M	Laborer	03Ap02Dj
FAUGHNER, Bryan	20	M	Laborer	03Ap02Dj
CONNELLY, Mathew	40	M	Laborer	03Ap02Dj
Anna	20	F	Laborer	03Ap02Dj
Catharine	18	F	Laborer	03Ap02Dj
Margret	12	F	Laborer	03Ap02Dj
CASSIN, Michael	20	M	Laborer	03Ap02Dj
DONAGHO, James	20	M	Laborer	03Ap02Dj
CARRY, William	40	M	Laborer	03Ap02Dj
BYRNE, Pat	20	M	Laborer	03Ap02Dj
CLARKE, Richard	23	M	Laborer	03Ap02Dj
REDDY, James	20	M	Laborer	03Ap02Dj
MCLAWNEY, Mark	19	M	Laborer	03Ap02Dj
MCQUINN, James	18	M	Laborer	03Ap02Dj
DOVER, Hugh	30	M	Laborer	03Ap02Dj
James	28	M	Laborer	03Ap02Dj
MURPHY, James	20	M	Laborer	03Ap02Dj
CONNER, James	30	M	Laborer	03Ap02Dj
CONREY, Biddy	20	F	Laborer	03Ap02Dj
FARNELL, Rose	20	F	Laborer	03Ap02Dj
KILMARTS, Jane	20	F	Laborer	03Ap02Dj
JONES, William	24	M	Laborer	03Ap02Dj
CROPPER, Samuel	26	M	Laborer	03Ap02Dj
MATHEWS, James	20	M	Laborer	03Ap02Dj
GILLMORE, Patrick	30	M	Laborer	03Ap02Dj
LYNAN, John	18	M	Laborer	03Ap02Dj
Patrick	20	M	Laborer	03Ap02Dj
BRODDAN, Barry	26	M	Laborer	03Ap02Dj
Judy	22	F	Laborer	03Ap02Dj
Pat	.00	M	Infant	03Ap02Dj
CONLAN, Honlan	27	M	Laborer	03Ap02Dj
BOLAND, John	19	M	Laborer	03Ap02Dj
MCSWEENY, William	20	M	Laborer	03Ap02Dj
MASTERSON, Mary	20	F	Laborer	03Ap02Dj
BRANNON, William	40	M	Laborer	03Ap02Dj
CANNON, Anne	22	F	Laborer	03Ap02Dj
BRANNON, Michael	40	M	Laborer	03Ap02Dj
EAGAN, Evan	28	M	Laborer	03Ap02Dj
Mary	24	F	Laborer	03Ap02Dj
James	.00	M	Infant	03Ap02Dj
DUGAN, Thomas	27	M	Laborer	03Ap02Dj
RAGAN, Mary	20	F	Laborer	03Ap02Dj
GARNER, Silas	28	M	Laborer	03Ap02Dj
GASLIN, William	27	M	Laborer	03Ap02Dj
HAWTHORN, Charles	26	M	Laborer	03Ap02Dj
BARKER, William	26	M	Laborer	03Ap02Dj
GREENWOOD, William	25	M	Laborer	03Ap02Dj
SWEENEY, James	28	M	Laborer	03Ap02Dj
WHITEHEAD, Edward	29	M	Laborer	03Ap02Dj
CAIN, Michael	30	M	Laborer	03Ap02Dj
Anna	18	F	Laborer	03Ap02Dj
MCCONDRA, Thomas	20	M	Laborer	03Ap02Dj
BARBER, George	23	M	Laborer	03Ap02Dj
HYLIN, Biddy	20	F	Laborer	03Ap02Dj
SCHOFIELD, Albert	22	M	Laborer	03Ap02Dj
MILLER, John	23	M	Laborer	03Ap02Dj
MCDERMOTT, Michael	30	M	Laborer	03Ap02Dj
GOLDING, Thomas	24	M	Laborer	03Ap02Dj
MCDERMOTT, Anna	20	F	Laborer	03Ap02Dj
DEVINE, Mary	20	F	Laborer	03Ap02Dj
ROONEY, Pat	20	M	Laborer	03Ap02Dj
Mary	40	F	Laborer	03Ap02Dj
SWEENEY, Peter	24	M	Laborer	03Ap02Dj
CLARK, Michael	23	M	Laborer	03Ap02Dj
Martin	30	M	Laborer	03Ap02Dj
MEMLEY, Michael	20	M	Laborer	03Ap02Dj

NAMES OF PASSENGERS	AGE	SEX	OCCUPATIONS	DATE PORT SHIP
CONWAY, James	18	M	Laborer	03Ap02Dj
Rose	22	F	Laborer	03Ap02Dj
DOWD, Michael	22	M	Laborer	03Ap02Dj
COOLEY, Luke	25	M	Laborer	03Ap02Dj
SCULLY, William	18	M	Laborer	03Ap02Dj
RICKEY, Michael	30	M	Laborer	03Ap02Dj
CLARY, Rose	39	F	Laborer	03Ap02Dj
Patrick	.00	M	Infant	03Ap02Dj
MURRAY, Patrick	40	M	Laborer	03Ap02Dj
Mary	40	F	Laborer	03Ap02Dj
WALSH, Michael	50	M	Laborer	03Ap02Dj
SHERIDAN, Michael	24	M	Laborer	03Ap02Dj
MONNEGAN, Hugh	25	M	Laborer	03Ap02Dj
BRANDY, Mary	25	F	Laborer	03Ap02Dj
SIMON, Michael	20	M	Laborer	03Ap02Dj
BENNETT, Bart.	24	M	Laborer	03Ap02Dj
Anne	24	F	Laborer	03Ap02Dj
QUINN, Peter	22	M	Laborer	03Ap02Dj
WALSH, Michael	20	M	Laborer	03Ap02Dj
PORTER, John	20	M	Laborer	03Ap02Dj
CUNIN, Pat.	12	M	Laborer	03Ap02Dj
Mathew	25	M	Laborer	03Ap02Dj
MILLIGAN, Pat.	24	M	Laborer	03Ap02Dj
Thos.	22	M	Laborer	03Ap02Dj
NAUGHTEN, Mary	20	F	Unknown	03Ap02Dj
REDDY, Nell	18	M	Unknown	03Ap02Dj
WHELAN, Bernard	12	M	Unknown	03Ap02Dj
Patrick	11	M	Unknown	03Ap02Dj
Anne	10	F	Unknown	03Ap02Dj
FALLAN, Honora	61	F	Unknown	03Ap02Dj
Mary	05	F	Child	03Ap02Dj
John	.00	M	Infant	03Ap02Dj
MARION, Thomas	23	M	Unknown	03Ap02Dj
MURPHY, Mark	29	M	Unknown	03Ap02Dj
COUGHLAN, Mary	18	F	Unknown	03Ap02Dj
GARVEY, Mary	30	F	Unknown	03Ap02Dj
James	20	M	Unknown	03Ap02Dj
COHAN, Peter	26	M	Laborer	03Ap02Dj
John	26	M	Laborer	03Ap02Dj
Pat.	30	M	Laborer	03Ap02Dj
Catherine	06	F	Child	03Ap02Dj
Mary	.00	F	Infant	03Ap02Dj
Michael	.00	M	Infant	03Ap02Dj
HART, Pat.	21	M	Laborer	03Ap02Dj
MCDONNER, Luke	23	M	Laborer	03Ap02Dj
SUMMER, John	24	M	Laborer	03Ap02Dj
WHITE, Owen	40	M	Laborer	03Ap02Dj
John	14	M	Laborer	03Ap02Dj
Pat.	12	M	Laborer	03Ap02Dj
REGAN, Mary	17	F	Laborer	03Ap02Dj
Anna	11	F	Laborer	03Ap02Dj
Hugh	08	M	Child	03Ap02Dj
MCMANUS, Rose	04	F	Child	03Ap02Dj
Honora	07	F	Child	03Ap02Dj
Peter	03	M	Child	03Ap02Dj
COUGHLAN, John	20	M	Laborer	03Ap02Dj
KILLIHAN, Bart.	18	M	Laborer	03Ap02Dj
SHEEAN, Mary	26	F	Laborer	03Ap02Dj
Johanna	19	F	Laborer	03Ap02Dj
BANKS, John	23	M	Laborer	03Ap02Dj
Catharine	27	F	Laborer	03Ap02Dj
KANAGAN, Edward	40	M	Laborer	03Ap02Dj
WELTH, Briget	40	F	Laborer	03Ap02Dj
Maria	05	F	Child	03Ap02Dj
Michael	09	M	Child	03Ap02Dj
John	07	M	Child	03Ap02Dj
DEGMAN, Roger	30	M	Laborer	03Ap02Dj
Peter	07	M	Child	03Ap02Dj
Michael	09	M	Child	03Ap02Dj
HYLIN, Danall	21	M	Laborer	03Ap02Dj
Julia	22	F	Laborer	03Ap02Dj
SANDS, Benjamin	23	M	Laborer	03Ap02Dj
BRENNON, Catharine	25	F	Laborer	03Ap02Dj
DEVINE, Patrick	28	M	Laborer	03Ap02Dj
MURPHY, Charles	20	M	Laborer	03Ap02Dj

NAMES OF PASSENGERS	AGE	SEX	OCCUPATIONS	DATE PORT SHIP
QUINNIN, Briget	20	F	Laborer	03Ap02Dj
KELLY, John	21	M	Laborer	03Ap02Dj
Anne	20	F	Laborer	03Ap02Dj
MCKEOWN, William	25	M	Laborer	03Ap02Dj
BRIAN, Margeret	22	F	Laborer	03Ap02Dj
HARTNELL, John	20	M	Laborer	03Ap02Dj
RILEY, Catharine	24	F	Laborer	03Ap02Dj
Patrick	20	M	Laborer	03Ap02Dj
EVANS, Enoch	32	M	Laborer	03Ap02Dj
COLE, James	32	M	Laborer	03Ap02Dj
GARRETTE, Charles	27	M	Laborer	03Ap02Dj
REYNOLDS, Mary	20	F	Laborer	03Ap02Dj
Ellen	20	F	Laborer	03Ap02Dj
KEGAN, John	22	M	Laborer	03Ap02Dj
WHITE, Eliza	40	F	Laborer	03Ap02Dj
Dennis	19	M	Laborer	03Ap02Dj
Eliza	11	F	Laborer	03Ap02Dj
Edward	09	M	Child	03Ap02Dj
Ellen	06	F	Child	03Ap02Dj
Michael	.00	M	Infant	03Ap02Dj
CALLIGAN, James	26	M	Farmer	03Ap02Dj
KITTIGHARTY, Rose	22	F	Farmer	03Ap02Dj
KELLY, Anne	21	F	Farmer	03Ap02Dj
BRANNON, Pat	20	M	Farmer	03Ap02Dj
QUINN, Pat	20	M	Farmer	03Ap02Dj
FARRE, Richd.	18	M	Farmer	03Ap02Dj
MEHONE, John	19	M	Farmer	03Ap02Dj
CARTY, Margaret	19	F	Farmer	03Ap02Dj
Pat	.00	M	Infant	03Ap02Dj
FARLY, Christ.	20	M	Farmer	03Ap02Dj
ODONNELL, May	20	F	Farmer	03Ap02Dj
Cath.	28	F	Farmer	03Ap02Dj
RYMOND, Henry	38	M	Farmer	03Ap02Dj
MCGRATY, Niel	12	M	Farmer	03Ap02Dj

ENTERPRISE 04 APRIL 1848

From Liverpool

NAMES OF PASSENGERS	AGE	SEX	OCCUPATIONS	DATE PORT SHIP
OBRIEN, Patt.	50	M	Farmer	04Ap02Hh
Johanna	50	F	Unknown	04Ap02Hh
Patrick (S)	18	M	Unknown	04Ap02Hh
KOWAHAN, Thos.	26	M	Musician	04Ap02Hh
MCGUIRE, Michael	45	M	Carpenter	04Ap02Hh
MCDERMOTT, Thos.	30	M	Painter	04Ap02Hh
GOLLIGER, Lawr.	24	M	Trade Man	04Ap02Hh
HORARE, Lawr.	20	M	Trade Man	04Ap02Hh
REILY, Thomas	17	M	Trade Man	04Ap02Hh
MCCABE, Rose	33	F	Unknown	04Ap02Hh
GOLLIGER, Jane	18	F	Unknown	04Ap02Hh
MCDERMOTT, Bridget	24	F	Unknown	04Ap02Hh
HANNORE, Patt.	30	M	Laborer	04Ap02Hh
ROMAINE, Thomas	50	M	Laborer	04Ap02Hh
Cath.	40	F	Unknown	04Ap02Hh
Francis	21	M	Unknown	04Ap02Hh
Michael	12	M	Unknown	04Ap02Hh
John	09	M	Child	04Ap02Hh
Thomas	06	M	Child	04Ap02Hh
HUERTON, Thomas	25	M	Laborer	04Ap02Hh
LERIARD, Benjamin	22	M	Laborer	04Ap02Hh
BISHOP, John	30	M	Laborer	04Ap02Hh
Mary	30	F	Unknown	04Ap02Hh
Wm.	06	M	Child	04Ap02Hh
QUINLAW, Patt	30	M	Laborer	04Ap02Hh
Bridget	20	F	Unknown	04Ap02Hh
EDWARDS, Cath.	50	F	Mother	04Ap02Hh
QUINLAN, Betty	30	F	Unknown	04Ap02Hh
WHILAN, Michl.	25	M	Laborer	04Ap02Hh
QUINLAN, Wm.	18	M	Tailor	04Ap02Hh

NAMES OF PASSENGERS	AGE	SEX	OCCUPATIONS	DATE PORT SHIP
QUINLAN, Patt.	10	M	Unknown	04Ap02Hh
Mary	07	F	Child	04Ap02Hh
Michl.	01	M	Child	04Ap02Hh
Mary	.00	F	Infant	04Ap02Hh
COADY, Patt.	23	M	Laborer	04Ap02Hh
BULLIKIN, Jno.	24	M	Laborer	04Ap02Hh
SANDFORD, Mary	20	F	Servant	04Ap02Hh
COADY, Mary	20	F	Servant	04Ap02Hh
KINNEDY, Bridget	20	F	Servant	04Ap02Hh
MCKINNA, Mary	55	F	Servant	04Ap02Hh
Ann	40	F	Servant	04Ap02Hh
James	36	M	Carpenter	04Ap02Hh
John	26	M	Bricklayer	04Ap02Hh
Phillix	24	M	Bricklayer	04Ap02Hh
Neale	20	M	Bricklayer	04Ap02Hh
ROGERS, Patt.	22	M	Laborer	04Ap02Hh
MCKINNA, Dennis	20	M	Laborer	04Ap02Hh
GAVIN, Rosey	20	F	Servant	04Ap02Hh
SHANNON, Michl.	47	M	Laborer	04Ap02Hh
ROGERS, John	50	M	Peddler	04Ap02Hh
Wm.	26	M	Peddler	04Ap02Hh
John	20	M	Peddler	04Ap02Hh
Elizabeth	19	F	Peddler	04Ap02Hh
Peter	12	M	Unknown	04Ap02Hh
LEWIS, John	22	M	Puddler	04Ap02Hh
CORBECK, Thos.	24	M	Puddler	04Ap02Hh
TURLEY, Edward	29	M	Puddler	04Ap02Hh
JONES, Thos.	25	M	Puddler	04Ap02Hh
WOODBRIDGE, Danl.	35	M	Puddler	04Ap02Hh
JOHNSTONE, Josiah	26	M	Roller	04Ap02Hh
SWIFTLEY, John	28	M	Puddler	04Ap02Hh
BALL, James	25	M	Puddler	04Ap02Hh
LEECHE, Wm.	50	M	Puddler	04Ap02Hh
Moses	29	M	Puddler	04Ap02Hh
MCCLINNEY, Thos.	21	M	Carpenter	04Ap02Hh
MCCONNELL, Charles	20	M	Laborer	04Ap02Hh
John	20	M	Laborer	04Ap02Hh
Michl.	21	M	Laborer	04Ap02Hh
MCCOWD, Ellen	18	F	Servant	04Ap02Hh
MOSS, Mary	18	F	Servant	04Ap02Hh
MANION, Margt.	17	F	Servant	04Ap02Hh
RIGAN, Michl.	24	M	Clerk	04Ap02Hh
MCLOUGHLIN, Jno.	30	M	Unknown	04Ap02Hh
FITZGERALD, Ellen	30	F	Servant	04Ap02Hh
Patt.	25	M	Laborer	04Ap02Hh
MCQUADE, James	22	M	Laborer	04Ap02Hh
CORRIGAN, Owen	22	M	Laborer	04Ap02Hh
KEATON, Mary	25	F	Unknown	04Ap02Hh
CONNELL, Michl.	20	M	Shoemaker	04Ap02Hh
Ann	20	F	Servant	04Ap02Hh
MCHUGH, Patt	20	M	Laborer	04Ap02Hh
Ellen	21	F	Unknown	04Ap02Hh
GIBSON, Thos.	25	M	Haberdasher	04Ap02Hh
MCCANNA, Cathr.	20	F	Unknown	04Ap02Hh
CUSH, Mary	18	F	Servant	04Ap02Hh
SHARKEY, Mary	30	F	Servant	04Ap02Hh
MCKENNA, Jno.	21	M	Mason	04Ap02Hh
LOROHAN, Margarett	16	F	Unknown	04Ap02Hh
MCGUIRE, Judith	17	F	Servant	04Ap02Hh
Bridget	15	F	Servant	04Ap02Hh
MCANANY, Rosey	16	F	Servant	04Ap02Hh
MCKEOWN, Jno.	60	M	Farmer	04Ap02Hh
Mary	45	F	Unknown	04Ap02Hh
John	22	M	Unknown	04Ap02Hh
Alex	18	M	Unknown	04Ap02Hh
Mary-Ann	16	F	Unknown	04Ap02Hh
Eliza	13	F	Unknown	04Ap02Hh
Margarett	10	F	Unknown	04Ap02Hh
CONLAN, John	25	M	Laborer	04Ap02Hh
NORRY, Maria	08	F	Child	04Ap02Hh
MCARDLE, Patt.	32	M	Laborer	04Ap02Hh
Bridget	25	F	Servant	04Ap02Hh
LANNOR, Cathr.	19	F	Servant	04Ap02Hh
KELLY, Darby	18	M	Laborer	04Ap02Hh
CROSSON, Jno.	25	M	Laborer	04Ap02Hh

NAMES OF PASSENGERS	AGE	SEX	OCCUPATIONS	DATE PORT SHIP
GIBBONS, Isabella	14	F	Servant	04Ap02Hh
James	11	M	Unknown	04Ap02Hh
MCGUIRE, James	17	M	Laborer	04Ap02Hh
SHANNON, Owen	19	M	Laborer	04Ap02Hh
SIRAHAN, Patt.	22	M	Laborer	04Ap02Hh
CORCORAN, Thos.	25	M	Laborer	04Ap02Hh
Mary (W)	23	F	Unknown	04Ap02Hh
Ann (D)	07	F	Child	04Ap02Hh
AGNEW, James	22	M	Farmer	04Ap02Hh
MCKEOWN, James	18	M	Fireman	04Ap02Hh
RYAN, Jno.	40	M	Farmer	04Ap02Hh
Mathew	22	M	Farmer	04Ap02Hh
Judy	40	F	Unknown	04Ap02Hh
Peggy	15	F	Unknown	04Ap02Hh
Judy	12	F	Unknown	04Ap02Hh
Nelly	07	F	Child	04Ap02Hh
Timey	06	F	Child	04Ap02Hh
Johnney	.00	F	Infant	04Ap02Hh
KEARNS, John	25	M	Grocer	04Ap02Hh
Cathr.	20	F	Unknown	04Ap02Hh
TORMOY, Bessy	20	F	Unknown	04Ap02Hh
CRAVEN, Jno.	40	M	Laborer	04Ap02Hh
Ann	38	F	Unknown	04Ap02Hh
Ann	17	F	Unknown	04Ap02Hh
Dennis	18	M	Laborer	04Ap02Hh
DOYLE, Patt.	30	M	Saddler	04Ap02Hh
LYNCH, John	36	M	Laborer	04Ap02Hh
Bridget	30	F	Servant	04Ap02Hh
SMITH, James	19	M	Laborer	04Ap02Hh
Biddy	21	F	Servant	04Ap02Hh
Thomas	18	M	Laborer	04Ap02Hh
Peter	55	M	None	04Ap02Hh
Rose	50	F	None	04Ap02Hh
John	21	M	Laborer	04Ap02Hh
Patt.	18	M	Laborer	04Ap02Hh
Bridget	17	F	Servant	04Ap02Hh
Peter	14	M	Unknown	04Ap02Hh
James	02	M	Child	04Ap02Hh
MCGUIRE, Patt.	14	M	Unknown	04Ap02Hh
KURAN, Margarett	22	F	Servant	04Ap02Hh
REILEY, Ann	17	F	Laborer	04Ap02Hh
SMITH, Rose	17	F	Servant	04Ap02Hh
REILEY, Mary	40	F	Unknown	04Ap02Hh
Richd.	20	M	Laborer	04Ap02Hh
MCLOUGHLIN, Michl.	40	M	Laborer	04Ap02Hh
KNOWLES, Patt.	30	M	Laborer	04Ap02Hh
Mary	30	F	Servant	04Ap02Hh
HORLEY, Lacey	22	F	Servant	04Ap02Hh
PORTER, Wm.	22	M	Laborer	04Ap02Hh
Cathr.	20	F	Servant	04Ap02Hh
CLEAREY, Peter	30	M	Blacksmith	04Ap02Hh
SPAIN, Michl.	25	M	Laborer	04Ap02Hh
MCRDLE, John	00	M	Unknown	04Ap02Hh
WILLIAMS, Wm.	00	M	Unknown	04Ap02Hh
MCKEOWN, Matilda	08	F	Child	04Ap02Hh
Isabella	07	F	Child	04Ap02Hh
KEARY, Jas.	30	M	Laborer	04Ap02Hh
Cath.	25	F	Unknown	04Ap02Hh
U	.00	U	Infant	04Ap02Hh
COWAN, Jno.	27	M	Laborer	04Ap02Hh
MCGUGGAN, Bernd.	25	M	Tailor	04Ap02Hh
QUINN, Patt.	22	M	Carpenter	04Ap02Hh
NEIL, Jno.	20	M	Tinker	04Ap02Hh
MCANALLY, Jno.	25	M	Barber	04Ap02Hh
LYON, Henry	20	M	Clerk	04Ap02Hh
MCHULL, Cyles	01	M	Child	04Ap02Hh
CONLAN, Jane	20	F	Servant	04Ap02Hh
Mary	24	F	Servant	04Ap02Hh
MURRAY, Mary	12	F	Servant	04Ap02Hh
MALONE, Nancy	20	F	Servant	04Ap02Hh
CONLAN, James	.00	M	Infant	04Ap02Hh
HANNON, Mary	21	F	Servant	04Ap02Hh
MILLER, John	25	M	Laborer	04Ap02Hh
HANNON, Patt.	25	M	Farmer	04Ap02Hh
BUTLER, Lawr.	35	M	Laborer	04Ap02Hh
BUTLER, Mary	30	F	Unknown	04Ap02Hh
Thomas	05	M	Child	04Ap02Hh
James	.00	M	Infant	04Ap02Hh
MURRAY, Patt.	25	M	Laborer	04Ap02Hh
Margt.	25	F	Unknown	04Ap02Hh
Ann	25	F	Unknown	04Ap02Hh
CUMMINS, Patt.	30	M	Laborer	04Ap02Hh
RYAN, Matt.	21	M	Laborer	04Ap02Hh
DUNN, James	24	M	Laborer	04Ap02Hh
Cathr.	24	F	Unknown	04Ap02Hh
James	.00	M	Infant	04Ap02Hh
KENNEY, Thos.	18	M	Laborer	04Ap02Hh
CANDELLAN, Honon	16	M	Unknown	04Ap02Hh
Barnes	17	M	Unknown	04Ap02Hh
REILEY, Joseph	18	M	Carpenter	04Ap02Hh
DOWD, Bernd.	19	M	Laborer	04Ap02Hh
MCDERMOTTS, Jno.	39	M	Laborer	04Ap02Hh
REILEY, Danl.	25	M	Blacksmith	04Ap02Hh
SMITH, Cath.	22	F	Servant	04Ap02Hh
Bridgt.	14	F	Servant	04Ap02Hh
Jno.	50	M	Servant	04Ap02Hh
Margt.	25	F	Servant	04Ap02Hh
John	26	M	Servant	04Ap02Hh
Ann	27	F	Servant	04Ap02Hh
DEVINE, Jno.	22	M	Laborer	04Ap02Hh
MCMANUS, Patt.	20	M	Fireman	04Ap02Hh
FITZSIMMONS, Thos.	27	M	Laborer	04Ap02Hh
CROWLEY, Corns.	40	M	Laborer	04Ap02Hh
MURPHY, Mary	30	F	Wife	04Ap02Hh
MCCAFFREY, Hugh	25	M	Laborer	04Ap02Hh
LIDDY, Owen	24	M	Laborer	04Ap02Hh
YOUNG, Bernd.	28	M	Laborer	04Ap02Hh
Martha	16	F	Unknown	04Ap02Hh
Ann	18	F	Unknown	04Ap02Hh

QUEEN-OF-THE-WEST 04 APRIL 1848

From Liverpool

NAMES OF PASSENGERS	AGE	SEX	OCCUPATIONS	DATE PORT SHIP
HENNESSY, Thomas	22	M	Laborer	04Ap02Cn
MCALEY, Hannah	20	F	Unknown	04Ap02Cn
GALLAGHAN, Mary	20	F	Seamstress	04Ap02Cn
GILBERT, Eliza	20	F	Seamstress	04Ap02Cn
OBRIEN, James	53	M	Mason	04Ap02Cn
Thos.	00	M	Mason	04Ap02Cn
KELLY, Cath.	17	F	Unknown	04Ap02Cn
DROGEE, Mich.	20	M	Laborer	04Ap02Cn
Catharine	20	F	Unknown	04Ap02Cn
BURNS, William	20	M	Laborer	04Ap02Cn
Mary	20	F	Unknown	04Ap02Cn
CARLIN, Ellen	20	F	Unknown	04Ap02Cn
CONIGHAM, Anne	20	F	Unknown	04Ap02Cn
MCARDLE, Ann	18	F	Unknown	04Ap02Cn
Jane	12	F	Unknown	04Ap02Cn
PELES, Mary	20	F	Unknown	04Ap02Cn
FEARN, Jno.	21	M	Shoemaker	04Ap02Cn
MCQUILLAN, Thomas	20	M	Laborer	04Ap02Cn
Pat.	23	M	Laborer	04Ap02Cn
Margt.	12	F	Unknown	04Ap02Cn
LORKIN, James	20	M	Laborer	04Ap02Cn
GALLAGHER, Mary	48	F	Unknown	04Ap02Cn
Ellen	18	F	Unknown	04Ap02Cn
James	16	M	Laborer	04Ap02Cn
Thomas	14	M	Laborer	04Ap02Cn
Judy	12	F	Unknown	04Ap02Cn
WOODS, James	21	M	Laborer	04Ap02Cn
REENHOLDS, Michl.	20	M	Laborer	04Ap02Cn
MAKIN, Michl.	12	M	Laborer	04Ap02Cn
MCAULY, Thomas	18	M	Laborer	04Ap02Cn

NAMES OF PASSENGERS	AGE	SEX	OCCUPATIONS	DATE PORT SHIP
GILL, Thomas	27	M	Laborer	04Ap02Cn
SMITH, James	27	M	Unknown	04Ap02Cn
Jane	20	F	Unknown	04Ap02Cn
Pat.	11	M	Unknown	04Ap02Cn
MASTERSON, Pat.	15	M	Unknown	04Ap02Cn
Thomas	20	M	Unknown	04Ap02Cn
FLOOD, Ellen	27	F	Unknown	04Ap02Cn
MCANELLY, Mary	19	F	Unknown	04Ap02Cn
STONES, Lawrence	20	M	Laborer	04Ap02Cn
DELANY, James	50	M	Laborer	04Ap02Cn
Peter	40	M	Laborer	04Ap02Cn
Mary	38	F	Unknown	04Ap02Cn
Peter	.00	M	Infant	04Ap02Cn
BRADY, Mary	24	F	Unknown	04Ap02Cn
RILEY, Margt.	24	F	Unknown	04Ap02Cn
Cath.	23	F	Unknown	04Ap02Cn
FITZGERALD, Eliza	21	F	Unknown	04Ap02Cn
CAMPBELL, Susan	20	F	Unknown	04Ap02Cn
MCEBRATH, Jno.	18	M	Weaver	04Ap02Cn
Jno.	20	M	Unknown	04Ap02Cn
STRACHAN, Jane	17	F	Seamstress	04Ap02Cn
Wm.	12	M	Unknown	04Ap02Cn
RIGNEY, Jno.	60	M	Unknown	04Ap02Cn
Eliza	60	F	Unknown	04Ap02Cn
Pat.	08	M	Child	04Ap02Cn
Jno.	06	M	Child	04Ap02Cn
SIGER, Zachariah	40	M	Unknown	04Ap02Cn
Rebecca	40	F	Unknown	04Ap02Cn
Zachariah	16	M	Farmer	04Ap02Cn
Mary-Jane	06	F	Child	04Ap02Cn
LYNCH, Terence	10	M	Laborer	04Ap02Cn
RIELLY, Mich.	20	M	Unknown	04Ap02Cn
REYNOLDS, Jno.	20	M	Unknown	04Ap02Cn
BRODY, Pat.	12	M	Unknown	04Ap02Cn
Anne	11	F	Unknown	04Ap02Cn
Catharine	00	F	Unknown	04Ap02Cn
Bridget	09	F	Child	04Ap02Cn
MCSALLA, Mary	22	F	Unknown	04Ap02Cn
EIVENS, Thomas	20	M	Farmer	04Ap02Cn
TRACY, Michl.	25	M	Unknown	04Ap02Cn
Margret	20	F	Unknown	04Ap02Cn
RIELLY, Honer	25	F	Unknown	04Ap02Cn
Cath.	04	F	Child	04Ap02Cn
Edward	03	M	Child	04Ap02Cn
DILLONS, Thomas	15	M	Laborer	04Ap02Cn
GREEN, James	18	M	Unknown	04Ap02Cn
MALLOY, Cath.	18	F	Unknown	04Ap02Cn
GALLAGHER, Bridget	26	F	Unknown	04Ap02Cn
POWELL, Eliza	36	F	Unknown	04Ap02Cn
LACEY, Mary	.02	F	Infant	04Ap02Cn
BRANDON, Thomas	20	M	Laborer	04Ap02Cn
MCCABE, Mary	19	F	Unknown	04Ap02Cn
FERGUSON, Jno.	36	M	Lawyer	04Ap02Cn
LOOBY, Thomas	40	M	Unknown	04Ap02Cn
Biddy	38	F	Unknown	04Ap02Cn
Thomas	11	M	Unknown	04Ap02Cn
Richard	07	M	Child	04Ap02Cn
Connor	05	M	Child	04Ap02Cn
MCADAM, Francis	15	M	Shoemaker	04Ap02Cn
MCANELLY, James	16	M	Unknown	04Ap02Cn
GALLAGHER, Luke	19	M	Unknown	04Ap02Cn
GEEGAN, Mary	46	F	Unknown	04Ap02Cn
Pat.	.00	M	Infant	04Ap02Cn
WYNN, Eliza	26	F	Unknown	04Ap02Cn
BROPHY, Dennis	23	M	Laborer	04Ap02Cn
KILMINRY, Cath.	20	F	Unknown	04Ap02Cn
MORRIS, Jno.	24	M	Unknown	04Ap02Cn
Maria	24	F	Unknown	04Ap02Cn
PIERCE, Jno.	23	M	Unknown	04Ap02Cn
STOKES, Jno.	31	M	Unknown	04Ap02Cn
Jno.	07	M	Child	04Ap02Cn
BRYAN, Joseph	25	M	Unknown	04Ap02Cn
CUNIFF, Pat.	20	M	Unknown	04Ap02Cn
GILBERT, Geo.	40	M	Unknown	04Ap02Cn
Alley	40	F	Unknown	04Ap02Cn
GILBERT, Thomas	18	M	Unknown	04Ap02Cn
Mary	30	F	Unknown	04Ap02Cn
TRACEY, Robert	20	M	Laborer	04Ap02Cn
DUGAN, Francis	20	M	Laborer	04Ap02Cn
SWEENEY, James	20	M	Laborer	04Ap02Cn
DUNGHAN, Danl.	26	M	Servant	04Ap02Cn
HURST, Pat	20	M	Laborer	04Ap02Cn
GRIFFITH, Wm.	27	M	Gdnr	04Ap02Cn
Pat	29	M	Gdnr	04Ap02Cn
U-Mrs.	27	F	Unknown	04Ap02Cn
MAOAN, Michael	30	M	Farmer	04Ap02Cn
Mary (W)	29	F	Unknown	04Ap02Cn
Barbara (D)	10	F	Unknown	04Ap02Cn
Bridget	16	F	Unknown	04Ap02Cn
GLASS, Neal	30	M	Farmer	04Ap02Cn
Mary	26	F	Unknown	04Ap02Cn
Jane	18	F	Unknown	04Ap02Cn
MCGUAIG, Mary	18	F	Unknown	04Ap02Cn
MCKURHAN, Jno.	26	M	Laborer	04Ap02Cn
CARIG, Jane	26	F	Unknown	04Ap02Cn
CATHNEY, Samuel	20	M	Laborer	04Ap02Cn
MURPHY, Michael	20	M	Laborer	04Ap02Cn
NOON, Biddy	20	F	Unknown	04Ap02Cn
MAXWELL, Robert	24	M	Bricklayer	04Ap02Cn
CARNALL, Wm.	26	M	Gdnr	04Ap02Cn
MCARNOTT, Thomas	26	M	Laborer	04Ap02Cn
BENT, Wm.	20	M	Laborer	04Ap02Cn
PUGAHAM, Wm.	40	M	Laborer	04Ap02Cn
COFFNEY, Andrew	30	M	Laborer	04Ap02Cn
CAMPBELL, Jno.	25	M	Laborer	04Ap02Cn
DUFF, Thomas	21	M	Laborer	04Ap02Cn
WALKER, Jno.	23	M	Laborer	04Ap02Cn
MCBRIDE, Bernard	24	M	Laborer	04Ap02Cn
Jno.	23	M	Laborer	04Ap02Cn
CONNALLY, Robert	25	M	Laborer	04Ap02Cn
CAMPBELL, Mary-Ann	25	F	Unknown	04Ap02Cn
BRYAN, Michael	20	M	Laborer	04Ap02Cn
BARNETT, Margt.	20	F	Unknown	04Ap02Cn
MAYERS, Cath.	20	F	Unknown	04Ap02Cn
BRENNAN, Michl.	20	M	Laborer	04Ap02Cn
KELLY, Thomas	20	M	Laborer	04Ap02Cn
HOLMES, Mary-Ann	20	F	Laborer	04Ap02Cn
HUNTER, David	27	M	Farmer	04Ap02Cn
STANLEY, Daniel	19	M	Farmer	04Ap02Cn
DANE, William	20	M	Farmer	04Ap02Cn
GAGE, Wm.	28	M	Farmer	04Ap02Cn
U (W)	26	F	Unknown	04Ap02Cn
COCKRAN, Rode	20	M	Farmer	04Ap02Cn
MARSHALL, Jane	30	F	Unknown	04Ap02Cn
DOHERTY, Margt.	29	F	Unknown	04Ap02Cn
Lorna	03	F	Child	04Ap02Cn
MCKARNEY, Pat.	30	M	Laborer	04Ap02Cn
DOHERTY, Fanny	.00	F	Infant	04Ap02Cn
JAMES, Richard	24	M	Gentleman	04Ap02Cn
CONNOLLY, Hugh	20	M	Laborer	04Ap02Cn
BURN, Mick	26	M	Laborer	04Ap02Cn
HAMILTON, Jno.	20	M	Laborer	04Ap02Cn
BURN, Mary	20	F	Unknown	04Ap02Cn
BUTLER, James	20	M	Laborer	04Ap02Cn
DEMPSEY, Rose	20	F	Unknown	04Ap02Cn
LACEY, Hugh	30	M	Hatter	04Ap02Cn
Margt.	28	F	Unknown	04Ap02Cn
Ellen	24	F	Unknown	04Ap02Cn
MALONE, Samuel	22	M	Hatter	04Ap02Cn
MOORE, Bryan	27	M	Hatter	04Ap02Cn
IRVINE, Ally	25	F	Unknown	04Ap02Cn
LINER, Pat.	26	M	Laborer	04Ap02Cn
MCGILL, Samuel	20	M	Currier	04Ap02Cn
U (W)	20	F	Unknown	04Ap02Cn
CRAIG, Wm.	20	M	Currier	04Ap02Cn
DUGAN, Henry	20	M	Currier	04Ap02Cn
BARNEY, Betty-J.	16	F	Unknown	04Ap02Cn
STEWART, Mary	16	F	Unknown	04Ap02Cn
MCAREA, Cath.	20	F	Unknown	04Ap02Cn
STEWART, Betty	16	F	Unknown	04Ap02Cn

NAMES OF PASSENGERS	A G E	S E X	OCCUPATIONS	DATE PORT SHIP
WELSH, Pat.	40	M	Laborer	04Ap02Cn
Margt.	40	F	Unknown	04Ap02Cn
CORRIGAN, Thomas	20	M	Unknown	04Ap02Cn
WELSH, Cath.	20	F	Unknown	04Ap02Cn
CARTY, Bart.	40	M	Piper	04Ap02Cn
COSTELLO, John	20	M	Unknown	04Ap02Cn
CAHILL, Pat.	20	M	Unknown	04Ap02Cn
FITZSIMONS, Jno.	20	M	Unknown	04Ap02Cn
Anne	20	F	Unknown	04Ap02Cn
KELLY, Bart.	26	M	Laborer	04Ap02Cn
Michail	24	M	Laborer	04Ap02Cn
MCCANN, James	18	M	Laborer	04Ap02Cn
FARRELL, Biddy	25	F	Unknown	04Ap02Cn
GRUITTY, Jno.	16	M	Laborer	04Ap02Cn
BRAMAN, Jno.	20	M	Laborer	04Ap02Cn
Anne	20	F	Unknown	04Ap02Cn
MCGOVEN, Michael	28	M	Gdnr	04Ap02Cn
U	25	F	Unknown	04Ap02Cn
Michl.	.00	M	Infant	04Ap02Cn
PISUM, Owen	25	M	Laborer	04Ap02Cn
MURREY, James	26	M	Laborer	04Ap02Cn
CULLIN, Michl.	20	M	Laborer	04Ap02Cn
REID, Margt.	24	F	Unknown	04Ap02Cn
PLUNKET, Anne	20	F	Unknown	04Ap02Cn
Cath.	18	F	Unknown	04Ap02Cn
CULLIGAN, Cath.	24	F	Unknown	04Ap02Cn
OCONNELL, David	26	M	Dyer	04Ap02Cn
MCCARTY, James	25	M	Laborer	04Ap02Cn
Honor	20	F	Unknown	04Ap02Cn
FERRAN, Thomas	24	M	Laborer	04Ap02Cn
MORANS, James	20	M	Laborer	04Ap02Cn
GERREY, Bernard	20	M	Laborer	04Ap02Cn
FEE, Jno.	18	M	Shoemaker	04Ap02Cn
Michl.	24	M	Shoemaker	04Ap02Cn
CREGG, Jane	20	F	Unknown	04Ap02Cn
ROONEY, Mary	26	F	Unknown	04Ap02Cn
TOBAN, Jno.	45	M	Coachman	04Ap02Cn
Wm.	40	M	Unknown	04Ap02Cn
CLARK, Mary	11	M	Unknown	04Ap02Cn
HEWITT, Peter	28	M	Joiner	04Ap02Cn
RILEY, Mary	18	F	Unknown	04Ap02Cn
LEONARD, Jno.	21	M	Shoemaker	04Ap02Cn
MCDONALD, Margt.	20	F	Unknown	04Ap02Cn
FITZPATRICK, Fill	24	M	Farmer	04Ap02Cn
LITTLE, Wm.	21	M	Farmer	04Ap02Cn
MCGLEN, Owen	23	M	Laborer	04Ap02Cn
MCGILLIN, Edward	24	M	Laborer	04Ap02Cn
LOUNING, Pat.	25	M	Laborer	04Ap02Cn
Teague	25	M	Laborer	04Ap02Cn
HALPIN, Rose	26	F	Unknown	04Ap02Cn
MALOY, Bernard	26	M	Laborer	04Ap02Cn
DOUGHERTY, Edward	21	M	Laborer	04Ap02Cn
CLARK, Peter	12	M	Laborer	04Ap02Cn
MALOY, Thomas	20	M	Laborer	04Ap02Cn
MINGG, Anne	20	F	Unknown	04Ap02Cn
DESMOND, Daniel	35	M	Laborer	04Ap02Cn
SULIVAN, Michl.	09	M	Child	04Ap02Cn
Bridget	07	F	Child	04Ap02Cn
FOGARTY, Jno.	21	M	Laborer	04Ap02Cn
Antony	20	M	Laborer	04Ap02Cn
SANGFORD, Thomas	25	M	Laborer	04Ap02Cn
Margt.	19	F	Unknown	04Ap02Cn
CONNALLY, Pat.	20	M	Laborer	04Ap02Cn
Peter	19	M	Laborer	04Ap02Cn
KELLY, Charlotte	24	F	Unknown	04Ap02Cn
Matilda	.00	F	Infant	04Ap02Cn
MCKENNA, Michl.	28	M	Laborer	04Ap02Cn
Luke	18	M	Laborer	04Ap02Cn
FLYNN, Lawrence	23	M	Laborer	04Ap02Cn
RYAN, Cath.	20	F	Unknown	04Ap02Cn
PHILLIPS, Edward	21	M	Laborer	04Ap02Cn
WYNN, Thomas	26	M	Laborer	04Ap02Cn
Farrell	20	M	Laborer	04Ap02Cn
BOYLE, Jno	11	M	Unknown	04Ap02Cn
CASSIDY, Rose	20	F	Unknown	04Ap02Cn

NAMES OF PASSENGERS	A G E	S E X	OCCUPATIONS	DATE PORT SHIP
CASSIDY, Betty	11	F	Unknown	04Ap02Cn
FLYNN, Dennis	25	M	Sailor	04Ap02Cn
BURNS, Tim	24	M	Sailor	04Ap02Cn
FALLOON, James	18	M	Sailor	04Ap02Cn
BRANNAN, Thomas	18	M	Sailor	04Ap02Cn
SHEEHAN, Terence	20	M	Laborer	04Ap02Cn
Ellen	15	F	Unknown	04Ap02Cn
Priscilla	15	F	Unknown	04Ap02Cn
GEHERTY, Mary	25	F	Unknown	04Ap02Cn
Edward	12	M	Unknown	04Ap02Cn
CONAN, Bridget	10	F	Unknown	04Ap02Cn
COYLE, Bridget	20	F	Unknown	04Ap02Cn
GUCKIARE, Thomas	10	M	Unknown	04Ap02Cn
Ellen	12	F	Unknown	04Ap02Cn
SANGFORD, Jno.	20	M	Laborer	04Ap02Cn
BRYAN, Pat.	20	M	Laborer	04Ap02Cn
DESMOND, Mary	20	F	Unknown	04Ap02Cn
BRYAN, Peggy	13	F	Unknown	04Ap02Cn
BATTLE, Jno.	20	M	Laborer	04Ap02Cn
HENNESSY, Mark	28	M	Laborer	04Ap02Cn
KENNY, James	20	M	Laborer	04Ap02Cn
MULLEN, James	20	M	Laborer	04Ap02Cn
MCLOUGHLIN, James	20	M	Laborer	04Ap02Cn
WELLS, Samuel	35	M	Laborer	04Ap02Cn
HOWLEY, Thomas	25	M	Laborer	04Ap02Cn
Biddy	20	F	Unknown	04Ap02Cn
HAHAN, Anne	20	F	Unknown	04Ap02Cn
KELLY, Biddy	20	F	Unknown	04Ap02Cn
DOHERTY, Pat.	20	M	Laborer	04Ap02Cn
WHALAN, Wm.	22	M	Laborer	04Ap02Cn
JOHNSON, Martin	25	M	Laborer	04Ap02Cn
Cath.	20	F	Unknown	04Ap02Cn
FARRELL, Pat.	35	M	Laborer	04Ap02Cn
Anne	32	F	Unknown	04Ap02Cn
FLINN, Mary	26	F	Unknown	04Ap02Cn
GILLAN, Bro.	20	M	Laborer	04Ap02Cn
James	.00	M	Infant	04Ap02Cn
TUMEY, Wm.	18	M	Laborer	04Ap02Cn
BEROLEY, Bridget	20	F	Unknown	04Ap02Cn
WREEN, Anne	20	F	Unknown	04Ap02Cn
CORCORAN, Jno.	20	M	Laborer	04Ap02Cn
LANG, Wm.	35	M	Laborer	04Ap02Cn
KERLAN, Pat.	20	M	Laborer	04Ap02Cn
HUNT, Mag.	30	F	Unknown	04Ap02Cn
Jno.	05	M	Child	04Ap02Cn
FAGAN, Hugh	20	M	Laborer	04Ap02Cn
KELLY, Owen	20	M	Laborer	04Ap02Cn
CAMBELL, Chas.	20	M	Laborer	04Ap02Cn
SUNTALL, Jno.	25	M	Laborer	04Ap02Cn
MCGUM, Jno.	20	M	Laborer	04Ap02Cn
CASEY, Andrew	25	M	Laborer	04Ap02Cn
MORGAN, Hugh	20	M	Joiner	04Ap02Cn
DOUGHERTY, Jno.	20	M	Laborer	04Ap02Cn
MALONY, Jno.	22	M	Laborer	04Ap02Cn
CORRIGAN, Jno.	11	M	Laborer	04Ap02Cn
GARNEY, Maria	22	F	Unknown	04Ap02Cn
DONOHUE, Michael	27	M	Gdnr	04Ap02Cn
FLARIGN, Richard	20	M	Laborer	04Ap02Cn

GLADIATOR 04 APRIL 1848

From London

NAMES OF PASSENGERS	A G E	S E X	OCCUPATIONS	DATE PORT SHIP
LEONARD, Henry	36	M	Blacksmith	04Ap21Dg
Elizabeth	30	F	Blacksmith	04Ap21Dg
Margaret	38	F	Blacksmith	04Ap21Dg
KELLY, John	39	M	Laborer	04Ap21Dg
Ellen	39	F	Laborer	04Ap21Dg
Anna	19	F	Laborer	04Ap21Dg

NAMES OF PASSENGERS	AGE	SEX	OCCUPATIONS	DATE PORT SHIP
KELLY, John	11	M	Laborer	04Ap21Dg
SULLIVAN, James	33	M	Shoemaker	04Ap21Dg
RYAN, Elizabeth	22	F	Unknown	04Ap21Dg
BURKE, John	40	M	Saddler	04Ap21Dg
JONES, Mary	27	F	Unknown	04Ap21Dg
DRISCOLL, Michael	30	M	Laborer	04Ap21Dg
DONOHUE, Elizabeth	28	F	Unknown	04Ap21Dg
OLEARY, John	47	M	Schm	04Ap21Dg
Honorah	45	F	Unknown	04Ap21Dg
Cornelius	20	M	Unknown	04Ap21Dg
Daniel	13	M	Unknown	04Ap21Dg
Michael	04	M	Child	04Ap21Dg
Mary	28	F	Unknown	04Ap21Dg
MAROE, Abbey	29	F	Unknown	04Ap21Dg
CHOWLEY, Patrick	43	M	Laborer	04Ap21Dg
Mary	42	F	Unknown	04Ap21Dg
James	11	M	Unknown	04Ap21Dg
DEMPSEY, Patrick	24	M	Laborer	04Ap21Dg
HORN, William	23	M	Laborer	04Ap21Dg
DEMPSEY, Ann	16	F	Unknown	04Ap21Dg
HORN, Catharine	26	F	Unknown	04Ap21Dg
MAWE, Johanna	21	F	Unknown	04Ap21Dg
MCCARTHY, Charles	40	M	Laborer	04Ap21Dg
GARLAND, Mary	38	F	Unknown	04Ap21Dg
LYON, Julia	27	F	Unknown	04Ap21Dg
LEWIS, Mary	22	F	Unknown	04Ap21Dg

HUDSON 04 APRIL 1848

From Glasgow

NAMES OF PASSENGERS	AGE	SEX	OCCUPATIONS	DATE PORT SHIP
CAMBEL, Neil	23	M	Engineer	04Ap04Af
Janet	30	F	Unknown	04Ap04Af
SCOTT, James	26	M	Weaver	04Ap04Af
MURPHY, James	47	M	Merchant	04Ap04Af
CAMMERON, Samuel	35	M	Clerk	04Ap04Af
Catharine	25	F	None	04Ap04Af
RUSSELL, Wm.	30	M	None	04Ap04Af
RALATION, Jessie	58	F	None	04Ap04Af
James	21	M	Miner	04Ap04Af
WOOD, Janet	13	F	None	04Ap04Af
KIETH, Elexande	35	M	Grocer	04Ap04Af
SLAIN, James	27	M	Agent	04Ap04Af
NIEL, Edward	25	M	Laborer	04Ap04Af
MILES, Thomas	21	M	Miner	04Ap04Af
BUTTER, Thomas	32	M	Miner	04Ap04Af
MCCAMINAGE, John	21	M	Miner	04Ap04Af
PATRICK, James	21	M	Miner	04Ap04Af
KING, Wm.	22	M	Engineer	04Ap04Af
ALLISON, James	20	M	Smith	04Ap04Af
MCGURK, Patrick	35	M	Miner	04Ap04Af
Mary	35	F	None	04Ap04Af
Frances	13	F	Unknown	04Ap04Af
Patrick	09	M	Child	04Ap04Af
Ellen	07	F	Child	04Ap04Af
Betsy	05	F	Child	04Ap04Af
Mary	03	F	Child	04Ap04Af
John	.03	M	Infant	04Ap04Af
MCFADYN, John	31	M	None	04Ap04Af
BOUNDMAN, Robert	33	M	Weaver	04Ap04Af
MCKNIGTT, David	31	M	Shoemaker	04Ap04Af
Jane	27	F	None	04Ap04Af
Ellen	05	F	Child	04Ap04Af
GIBSON, Janet	20	F	None	04Ap04Af
MUREY, Peter	35	M	None	04Ap04Af
Catharine	29	F	Weaver	04Ap04Af
CURREE, John	29	M	Tailor	04Ap04Af
MCALLISTER, John	30	M	Joiner	04Ap04Af
Marion	27	F	Dressmaker	04Ap04Af
MCALLISTER, John	07	M	Child	04Ap04Af
Wm.	01	M	Child	04Ap04Af
STALL, Mathew	21	M	Accountant	04Ap04Af
AUTHER, David	24	M	Farmer	04Ap04Af
LIVINGSTON, David	34	M	Weaver	04Ap04Af
AUTHER, John	21	M	Weaver	04Ap04Af
MCKENLY, Cheny	27	M	None	04Ap04Af
MCCORD, David	45	M	None	04Ap04Af
LANG, David	45	M	Miner	04Ap04Af
Jirlett	46	F	Unknown	04Ap04Af
Jame	20	M	Miner	04Ap04Af
Betsy	25	F	None	04Ap04Af
Thomas	12	M	None	04Ap04Af
Agnes	02	F	Child	04Ap04Af
David	.09	M	Infant	04Ap04Af
MCGURK, Frances	35	M	Unknown	04Ap04Af

HOWARD 04 APRIL 1848

From Liverpool

NAMES OF PASSENGERS	AGE	SEX	OCCUPATIONS	DATE PORT SHIP
DALAY, John	60	M	Stone Mason	04Ap02Kj
Bridget (W)	60	F	Wife	04Ap02Kj
Thomas	20	M	Laborer	04Ap02Kj
Owen	22	M	Laborer	04Ap02Kj
Bridget	12	F	Unknown	04Ap02Kj
Bridget	04	F	Child	04Ap02Kj
MCGRATH, Catharine	35	F	House Maid	04Ap02Kj
LOVELL, Patrick	12	M	Unknown	04Ap02Kj
Bridget	10	F	Unknown	04Ap02Kj
Ann	07	F	Child	04Ap02Kj
MCGRATH, Peter	25	M	Laborer	04Ap02Kj
Mary (W)	26	F	Wife	04Ap02Kj
LINCH, Catharine	30	F	Wife	04Ap02Kj
LUNAN, James	40	M	Laborer	04Ap02Kj
Bridget	12	F	Unknown	04Ap02Kj
MCNALLY, John	24	M	Spinner	04Ap02Kj
Hu----, Eliza	30	F	House Maid	04Ap02Kj
KENNEDY, Jane	08	F	Child	04Ap02Kj
GARVAY, Bridget	40	F	Unknown	04Ap02Kj
Mickeal	20	M	Laborer	04Ap02Kj
Patrick	15	M	Unknown	04Ap02Kj
Barnet	13	M	Unknown	04Ap02Kj
WELSH, Mickeal	30	M	Laborer	04Ap02Kj
BURNES, John	45	M	Laborer	04Ap02Kj
DIGGIN, David	30	M	Carpenter	04Ap02Kj
BURNOCK, Margaret	25	F	House Maid	04Ap02Kj
MCGUIRE, James	22	M	Clerk	04Ap02Kj
Mary (W)	20	F	Wife	04Ap02Kj
WILMAN, Mary	26	F	House Maid	04Ap02Kj
BURNES, Elizabeth	25	F	Wife	04Ap02Kj
MACMAN, Peter	20	M	Laborer	04Ap02Kj
FENIE, Lawrance	30	M	Laborer	04Ap02Kj
GRIFFIN, Mickeal	25	M	Laborer	04Ap02Kj
FENIE, Eliza	21	F	Wife	04Ap02Kj
MCNARLON, Jane	62	F	Unknown	04Ap02Kj
MCARALD, Jane	21	F	House Maid	04Ap02Kj
BURKE, Mary	26	F	House Maid	04Ap02Kj
Died-At-Sea				
NOLAND, Mickeal	29	M	Laborer	04Ap02Kj
Mar--- (W)	25	F	Wife	04Ap02Kj
RYAN, Patrick	40	M	Laborer	04Ap02Kj
Rose (W)	34	F	Wife	04Ap02Kj
Ann	50	F	Unknown	04Ap02Kj
Catharine	19	F	House Maid	04Ap02Kj
Ann	16	F	House Maid	04Ap02Kj
JENKINS, Andrew	28	M	Clerk	04Ap02Kj
DILE, Patrick	25	M	Laborer	04Ap02Kj
Jar---, Bridget	00	F	Unknown	04Ap02Kj

NAMES OF PASSENGERS	AGE	SEX	OCCUPATIONS	DATE PORT SHIP
MCANDREW, Jane	30	F	House Maid	04Ap02KJ
DAVIS, Daniel	45	M	Schm	04Ap02KJ
KELLY, Jeremiah	24	M	Laborer	04Ap02KJ
Eliza	20	F	House Maid	04Ap02KJ
Ann	16	F	House Maid	04Ap02KJ
KALAM, Mary	17	F	House Maid	04Ap02KJ
WARD, James	35	M	Laborer	04Ap02KJ
MCDONALD, John	35	M	Laborer	04Ap02KJ
SHIRDEN, Francis	23	M	Laborer	04Ap02KJ
GULSHANNON, Thomas	24	M	Laborer	04Ap02KJ
CUNNINGHAM, Margaret	20	F	House Maid	04Ap02KJ
MCGUSHAN, Bridget	16	F	House Maid	04Ap02KJ
MOORE, Martin	26	M	Laborer	04Ap02KJ
MANALLY, Mickeal	22	M	Laborer	04Ap02KJ
MULLAGAN, Thomas	25	M	Laborer	04Ap02KJ
Lawrance	23	M	Laborer	04Ap02KJ
Thomas	00	M	Whitesmith	04Ap02KJ
Elizabeth	14	F	Unknown	04Ap02KJ
BURGAN, Patrick	27	M	Mason	04Ap02KJ
GORMER, John	23	M	Laborer	04Ap02KJ
KING, Thomas	45	M	Laborer	04Ap02KJ
KELLY, Catharine	30	F	Wife	04Ap02KJ
BEAR, Ann	18	F	House Maid	04Ap02KJ
FITZPATRICK, Mary	30	F	Wife	04Ap02KJ
RILEY, Peter	20	M	Laborer	04Ap02KJ
KELLY, Peter	22	M	Unknown	04Ap02KJ
DONALLY, James	23	M	Butcher	04Ap02KJ
ENAS, Christie	21	M	Laborer	04Ap02KJ
MCAUSLY, Patrick	24	M	Laborer	04Ap02KJ
NEWMAN, Mary	19	F	House Maid	04Ap02KJ
TURNER, Ann	30	F	House Maid	04Ap02KJ
DOOLEY, Margaret	20	F	House Maid	04Ap02KJ
DONOVAN, Jerry	00	M	Laborer	04Ap02KJ
C-----, Patrick	00	M	Laborer	04Ap02KJ
Ru--, Mary	16	F	House Maid	04Ap02KJ
COYLE, Ann	16	F	House Maid	04Ap02KJ
BRANNON, Catharine	24	F	House Maid	04Ap02KJ
LOADE, Catharine	12	F	Unknown	04Ap02KJ
BOYLN, Mathew	20	M	Laborer	04Ap02KJ
Edward	18	M	Unknown	04Ap02KJ
MCMARN, Barnard	22	M	Unknown	04Ap02KJ
LENCH, Catharine	18	F	House Maid	04Ap02KJ
RYAN, Judy	16	F	Unknown	04Ap02KJ
Kennedy	12	F	Unknown	04Ap02KJ
SULLAVAN, Owen	36	M	Land Agent	04Ap02KJ
Owen	21	M	Laborer	04Ap02KJ
MCKAY, John	25	M	Unknown	04Ap02KJ
MALLAVIN, Ann	35	F	House Maid	04Ap02KJ
BRANNARD, Bridget	21	F	House Maid	04Ap02KJ
U, U	16	F	House Maid	04Ap02KJ
U	18	M	Clerk	04Ap02KJ
Robert	00	M	Laborer	04Ap02KJ
Died-At-Sea				
MENALTY, Andrew	70	M	Laborer	04Ap02KJ
OBRIAN, Ann	50	F	Unknown	04Ap02KJ
Elizabeth	22	F	House Maid	04Ap02KJ
Ann	20	F	House Maid	04Ap02KJ
Rosanna	18	F	House Maid	04Ap02KJ
Margaret	16	F	House Maid	04Ap02KJ
Elesha	44	F	House Maid	04Ap02KJ
Catharine	12	F	House Maid	04Ap02KJ
Teresa	08	F	House Maid	04Ap02KJ
James	10	M	Unknown	04Ap02KJ
NUGENT, Peter	22	M	Laborer	04Ap02KJ
DORTY, James	24	M	Laborer	04Ap02KJ
MCDORMOUT, John	24	M	Laborer	04Ap02KJ
BROWN, Catharine	20	F	House Maid	04Ap02KJ
MCKAN, Margaret	18	F	House Maid	04Ap02KJ
BRANET, Catharine	24	F	House Maid	04Ap02KJ
BURNES, Peter	50	M	Cooper	04Ap02KJ
Margaret (W)	45	F	Wife	04Ap02KJ
James	24	M	Cooper	04Ap02KJ
Peter	22	M	Cooper	04Ap02KJ
John	14	M	Cooper	04Ap02KJ
Francis	12	M	Cooper	04Ap02KJ

NAMES OF PASSENGERS	AGE	SEX	OCCUPATIONS	DATE PORT SHIP
BURNES, William	07	M	Child	04Ap02KJ
Mary	19	F	House Maid	04Ap02KJ
Margaret	10	F	Unknown	04Ap02KJ
FITZGARALD, Mary	23	F	House Maid	04Ap02KJ
RYAN, John	23	M	Laborer	04Ap02KJ
MAHAR, Mickeal	24	M	Laborer	04Ap02KJ
CARCORILL, James	20	M	Laborer	04Ap02KJ
KIRVAN, John	23	M	Laborer	04Ap02KJ
MONOLLY, John	30	M	Laborer	04Ap02KJ
KING, Thomas	22	M	Laborer	04Ap02KJ
Patrick	22	M	Laborer	04Ap02KJ
TOBAR, Patrick	40	M	Laborer	04Ap02KJ
Mary	50	F	Wife	04Ap02KJ
Mary	09	F	Child	04Ap02KJ
Thomas	08	M	Child	04Ap02KJ
Margaret	06	F	Child	04Ap02KJ
Judy	04	F	Child	04Ap02KJ
La------N, John	21	M	Laborer	04Ap02KJ
HAYES, James	16	M	Laborer	04Ap02KJ
GARTLARED, Thomas	28	M	Laborer	04Ap02KJ
LARDRAGAN, Elizabeth	22	F	House Maid	04Ap02KJ
FLYNN, Timothy	29	M	Laborer	04Ap02KJ
BURNES, Rose	19	F	House Maid	04Ap02KJ
BURN, James	22	M	Laborer	04Ap02KJ
FEE, James	19	M	Laborer	04Ap02KJ
Mary	15	F	Unknown	04Ap02KJ
Margaret	12	F	Unknown	04Ap02KJ
QUIGLEY, Mickeal	26	M	Laborer	04Ap02KJ
Ann	21	F	House Maid	04Ap02KJ
Edward	23	M	Laborer	04Ap02KJ
DORTLEY, Dumrick	21	M	Laborer	04Ap02KJ
MOSS, Daniel	25	M	Laborer	04Ap02KJ
CRALLION, Charles	26	M	Laborer	04Ap02KJ
Sarah (W)	21	F	Wife	04Ap02KJ
GULLIVER, Patrick	35	M	Laborer	04Ap02KJ
BROPHELL, Patrick	38	M	Laborer	04Ap02KJ
Mary (W)	40	F	Wife	04Ap02KJ
Mary	17	F	House Maid	04Ap02KJ
John	11	M	Unknown	04Ap02KJ
Mickeal	09	M	Child	04Ap02KJ
William	08	M	Child	04Ap02KJ
Ann	07	F	Child	04Ap02KJ
SKELLY, Patrick	40	M	Pvmt	04Ap02KJ
Eliza (W)	38	F	Wife	04Ap02KJ
Sarah	15	F	Unknown	04Ap02KJ
John	06	M	Child	04Ap02KJ
Patrick	05	M	Child	04Ap02KJ
BREE, Ellen	50	F	Unknown	04Ap02KJ
GALLAVAN, Thomas	36	M	Laborer	04Ap02KJ
Mary (W)	36	F	Wife	04Ap02KJ
Catharine	11	F	Unknown	04Ap02KJ
LEESON, Thomas	30	M	Cooper	04Ap02KJ
RYAN, Anthony	30	M	Laborer	04Ap02KJ
SCULLY, James	20	M	Laborer	04Ap02KJ
MURPHY, Ann	30	F	House Maid	04Ap02KJ
FLYNN, Elesha	17	F	House Maid	04Ap02KJ
MCMAN, Mary	18	F	House Maid	04Ap02KJ
HOR, Joseph	20	M	House Maid	04Ap02KJ
CLOWN, James	25	M	Laborer	04Ap02KJ
MURPHY, John	20	M	Laborer	04Ap02KJ
James	20	M	Laborer	04Ap02KJ
AGAN, Mickeal	18	M	Laborer	04Ap02KJ
MURPHY, Catharine	50	F	Unknown	04Ap02KJ
Catharine	18	F	House Maid	04Ap02KJ
Bridget	16	F	House Maid	04Ap02KJ
BUCKLEY, Alice	18	F	House Maid	04Ap02KJ
MARARTHY, Owen	24	M	Laborer	04Ap02KJ
MACARTHY, John	18	M	Laborer	04Ap02KJ
BRICK, Jeremiah	24	M	Laborer	04Ap02KJ
MARATLY, Patrick	19	M	Laborer	04Ap02KJ
--NALTY, Sarah	65	F	Wife	04Ap02KJ
Died-At-Sea				
M-----, John	30	M	Laborer	04Ap02KJ
M----N, Peter	28	M	Laborer	04Ap02KJ
MCGEE, Conel.	25	M	Laborer	04Ap02KJ

NAMES OF PASSENGERS	AGE	SEX	OCCUPATIONS	DATE PORT SHIP
STEEN, James	18	M	Laborer	04Ap02Kj
BOYLE, John	25	M	Laborer	04Ap02Kj
BONER, James	21	M	Laborer	04Ap02Kj
ODONNELL, James	30	M	Laborer	04Ap02Kj
MCMONOGAL, Sarah	20	F	House Maid	04Ap02Kj
QUIN, Bridget	25	F	House Maid	04Ap02Kj
COLLINS, Mickeal	20	M	Laborer	04Ap02Kj
Died-At-Sea				
MCCABE, Peter	35	M	Laborer	04Ap02Kj
Tuc-NEY, Phonix	44	M	Laborer	04Ap02Kj
WALSH, Richard	21	M	Laborer	04Ap02Kj
NOX, Mary	28	F	House Maid	04Ap02Kj
PENDERGRESS, Catharine	23	F	House Maid	04Ap02Kj
ORAN, Patrick	38	M	Laborer	04Ap02Kj
DRUGAN, James	60	M	Laborer	04Ap02Kj
ROKE, Patrick	28	M	Laborer	04Ap02Kj
MCARNE, Mary	18	F	House Maid	04Ap02Kj
MCGOUGH, Bridget	17	F	House Maid	04Ap02Kj
BARTLEY, Bridget	13	F	House Maid	04Ap02Kj
LENCH, Mickeal	20	M	Laborer	04Ap02Kj
Bridget	20	F	House Maid	04Ap02Kj
MELENEY, Bridget	22	F	Unknown	04Ap02Kj
DUNN, John	25	M	Laborer	04Ap02Kj
HARTON, Hugh	40	M	Laborer	04Ap02Kj
QUIN, John	30	M	Laborer	04Ap02Kj
James	08	M	Laborer	04Ap02Kj
Died-At-Sea				
M-HNE, John	20	M	Laborer	04Ap02Kj
MOORE, Thomas	50	M	Laborer	04Ap02Kj
GRIFFIN, Patrick	25	M	Laborer	04Ap02Kj
COMER, Morris	20	M	Laborer	04Ap02Kj
MCABE, James	02	M	Child	04Ap02Kj
NOX, J.Bridget	03	F	Child	04Ap02Kj
Mary	02	F	Child	04Ap02Kj
ROBINSON, Thomas	03	M	Child	04Ap02Kj
KENNEDY, Thomas	46	M	Laborer	04Ap02Kj
WARD, John	24	M	Laborer	04Ap02Kj
U, U	.00	U	Infant	04Ap02Kj
Died-At-Sea				
U	.00	U	Infant	04Ap02Kj
Died-At-Sea				
U	.00	U	Infant	04Ap02Kj
Died-At-Sea				
U	.00	U	Infant	04Ap02Kj
Died-At-Sea				
U	.00	U	Infant	04Ap02Kj
Died-At-Sea				
PATENT, Edward	46	M	Laborer	04Ap02Kj
HARLEY, Patrick	40	M	Laborer	04Ap02Kj
James	12	M	Laborer	04Ap02Kj
Patrick	08	M	Laborer	04Ap02Kj
Mary (W)	40	F	Wife	04Ap02Kj
Mary	22	F	House Maid	04Ap02Kj
BOYLE, James	54	M	Laborer	04Ap02Kj
HILL, Margaret	26	F	House Maid	04Ap02Kj
Peter	02	M	Child	04Ap02Kj
GRIFFIN, Hannah	19	F	House Maid	04Ap02Kj
GALLAGAN, Thomas	55	M	Laborer	04Ap02Kj
Died-At-Sea				
GALLAVAN, Mary	04	F	Child	04Ap02Kj
SKELLY, Eliza	03	F	Child	04Ap02Kj
Ann	02	F	Child	04Ap02Kj
KELLY, Patrick	20	M	Laborer	04Ap02Kj
BURNES, Emma	02	F	Child	04Ap02Kj
Edward	04	M	Child	04Ap02Kj
TOWLAND, Rose	02	F	Child	04Ap02Kj
LINCH, Mary	02	F	Child	04Ap02Kj
CRALLION, William	02	M	Child	04Ap02Kj
RYAN, John	02	M	Child	04Ap02Kj

WATERLOO 05 APRIL 1848

From Liverpool

NAMES OF PASSENGERS	AGE	SEX	OCCUPATIONS	DATE PORT SHIP
EWING, W.D.	22	M	None	05Ap02As
HEWITSON, Richd.	35	M	None	05Ap02As
John	45	M	None	05Ap02As
NOTE, John	25	M	None	05Ap02As
BYRN, Eliza-Mrs.	45	F	Unknown	05Ap02As
Mary-Ann	14	F	Unknown	05Ap02As
HEART, Henry	42	M	Clothier	05Ap02As
Abram.	23	M	Clothier	05Ap02As
Joseph	20	M	Clothier	05Ap02As
Mary	40	F	Clothier	05Ap02As
Fanny	12	F	Clothier	05Ap02As
Caroline	07	F	Child	05Ap02As
George	09	M	Child	05Ap02As
Sarah	25	F	Clothier	05Ap02As
Edward	.00	M	Infant	05Ap02As
Sarah	.00	F	Infant	05Ap02As
KELSO, Paul	40	M	Printer	05Ap02As
Agnes	39	F	Printer	05Ap02As
Charles	19	M	Printer	05Ap02As
Mary	17	F	Printer	05Ap02As
Patrick	14	M	Printer	05Ap02As
Robert	13	M	Printer	05Ap02As
James	10	M	Printer	05Ap02As
MACKMENDO, James	23	M	Surgeon	05Ap02As
CHARLES, A.	50	M	Clcp	05Ap02As
BANNING, Joshua	31	M	None	05Ap02As
MAHON, Adolphus	29	M	Farmer	05Ap02As
LEE, Thomas	24	M	Clothier	05Ap02As
HENNEFERD, Edward	26	M	Grinder	05Ap02As
ISHERWOOD, Squire	23	M	Spinner	05Ap02As
HACAMAN, James	25	M	Irnmldr	05Ap02As
ROBERTS, Robert	27	M	Ctnsp	05Ap02As
WHITWORTH, William	26	M	Butcher	05Ap02As
BENTLEY, John	25	M	Mechanic	05Ap02As
PILING, Thomas	33	M	Miner	05Ap02As
Margaret	29	F	Miner	05Ap02As
Mary-Jane	07	F	Child	05Ap02As
MILLS, William	27	M	Weaver	05Ap02As
MCGUFFOG, Mary-Ann	22	F	Weaver	05Ap02As
MCDONAL, Daniel	25	M	Farmer	05Ap02As
HERBERT, Withs	27	M	Forgeman	05Ap02As
CALION, James	23	M	Laborer	05Ap02As
Martin	30	M	Laborer	05Ap02As
NICHOLS, Henry	24	M	Joiner	05Ap02As
Ann (W)	24	F	Joiner	05Ap02As
FARRINGTON, Robert	32	M	Miller	05Ap02As
William	26	M	Ctnsp	05Ap02As
COY, Thomas	25	M	Weaver	05Ap02As
KING, Christina	19	F	Weaver	05Ap02As
AMATHUS, Hety	20	F	Weaver	05Ap02As
HAINDEN, Catherine	21	F	Weaver	05Ap02As
KING, James	22	M	Shopman	05Ap02As
HAINDEN, Walter	27	M	Mason	05Ap02As
RIGNEY, Pat	21	M	Laborer	05Ap02As
PINSAL, James	22	M	Laborer	05Ap02As
GRIFFITH, John	25	M	Laborer	05Ap02As
GOOD, George	30	M	Teacher	05Ap02As
Mary	30	F	Teacher	05Ap02As
CALLIHAN, Catherine	18	F	Teacher	05Ap02As
MAGINLEY, Mary	20	F	Teacher	05Ap02As
LITTLE, Sarah	23	F	Teacher	05Ap02As
TROY, Johana	25	F	Teacher	05Ap02As
LITTLE, John	25	M	Teacher	05Ap02As
REYNOLDS, Connak	50	M	Laborer	05Ap02As
Jane	45	F	Laborer	05Ap02As

NAMES OF PASSENGERS	AGE	SEX	OCCUPATIONS	DATE PORT SHIP
REYNOLDS, Rose	12	F	Laborer	05Ap02As
Bridget	10	F	Laborer	05Ap02As
Francis	08	M	Child	05Ap02As
Lawrance	06	M	Child	05Ap02As
Jane	04	F	Child	05Ap02As
Bernard	.00	M	Infant	05Ap02As
BURNES, Robert	40	M	Printer	05Ap02As
William	20	M	Spinner	05Ap02As
GREENWOOD, James	40	M	Blkp	05Ap02As
CLEGG, Abel	19	M	Weaver	05Ap02As
BRITLAFFE, James	43	M	Blkp	05Ap02As
TAYLOR, John	20	M	Weaver	05Ap02As
CANLIFF, Abram.	42	M	Spinner	05Ap02As
WINTERBOTTUM, Robert	22	M	Spinner	05Ap02As
BAGLEY, James	20	M	Spinner	05Ap02As
ASHWORTH, Henry	28	M	Bookkeeper	05Ap02As
Mary	26	F	Unknown	05Ap02As
Maria	05	F	Child	05Ap02As
HORN, Benjamin	23	M	Weaver	05Ap02As
LYTHA, John	19	M	Butcher	05Ap02As
LEE, Thomas	30	M	Laborer	05Ap02As
Ann	30	F	Laborer	05Ap02As
Bernard	.00	M	Infant	05Ap02As
RHATIGAN, Maria	32	F	Laborer	05Ap02As
Patrick	.00	M	Infant	05Ap02As
RAYERDON, Catherine	25	F	Laborer	05Ap02As
LANNEY, Jane	25	F	Laborer	05Ap02As
MCFADDEN, John	22	M	Laborer	05Ap02As
Conn	21	M	Laborer	05Ap02As
CONWILL, Patrick	22	M	Laborer	05Ap02As
ALLEN, Francis	32	M	Farmer	05Ap02As
CASSADY, Owen	26	M	Teacher	05Ap02As
GOLDEN, William	34	M	Mason	05Ap02As
LAINEY, Pat	20	M	Laborer	05Ap02As
RUSHWORTH, William	28	M	Spinner	05Ap02As
CHADWICK, James	30	M	Spinner	05Ap02As
RUSHWORTH, James	26	M	Spinner	05Ap02As
HARGRAVES, John	18	M	Farmer	05Ap02As
GOTT, Joseph	23	M	Molder	05Ap02As
SANDERLAND, William	22	M	Spinner	05Ap02As
Peter	27	M	Spinner	05Ap02As
Ellen	28	F	Spinner	05Ap02As
RUSHWORTH, George	32	M	Spinner	05Ap02As
LEAVER, Charles	26	M	Spinner	05Ap02As
WHITNEY, Ely	33	M	Spinner	05Ap02As
BREAR, Abram	28	M	Farmer	05Ap02As
SANDERSON, James	26	M	Spinner	05Ap02As
PAYTON, Robert	22	M	Laborer	05Ap02As
OHAR, Patrick	23	M	Laborer	05Ap02As
PAYTON, Bess	18	F	Laborer	05Ap02As
MAINY, Ellen	22	F	Laborer	05Ap02As
SHAEE, James	24	M	Laborer	05Ap02As
GUILT, Morris	23	M	Laborer	05Ap02As
DAGIN, Daniel	24	M	Laborer	05Ap02As
KEEF, James	19	M	Laborer	05Ap02As
FOLLEY, Edmond	22	M	Laborer	05Ap02As
BRATT, Rich.	25	M	Laborer	05Ap02As
BINNETT, Morris	23	M	Laborer	05Ap02As
BENNETT, Denniss	24	M	Laborer	05Ap02As
MAHONEY, Denniss	26	M	Laborer	05Ap02As
LINCHAN, Denniss	24	M	Laborer	05Ap02As
DAYLA, Pat	20	M	Laborer	05Ap02As
Barney	18	M	Laborer	05Ap02As
James	16	M	Laborer	05Ap02As
Edward	14	M	Laborer	05Ap02As
Mary	11	F	Laborer	05Ap02As
Ann	40	F	Laborer	05Ap02As
MCABE, Henry	16	M	Laborer	05Ap02As
CRUGAN, Mary	19	F	Laborer	05Ap02As
MCABE, Catherine	20	F	Laborer	05Ap02As
DUFFEY, Mary	20	F	Laborer	05Ap02As
MCCARROL, Mary	16	F	Laborer	05Ap02As
CAINES, Catherine	25	F	Laborer	05Ap02As
TRACEY, Hugh	36	M	Laborer	05Ap02As
Mary	28	F	Laborer	05Ap02As
TRACEY, Joseph	05	M	Child	05Ap02As
Hugh	.00	M	Infant	05Ap02As
RAGAN, Pat	21	M	Laborer	05Ap02As
MCDONNOUGH, Francis	26	M	Laborer	05Ap02As
DUFFEY, John	20	M	Laborer	05Ap02As
Betty	20	F	Laborer	05Ap02As
Mary	12	F	Laborer	05Ap02As
MARTIN, Betty	33	F	Laborer	05Ap02As
SHELLY, Ann	19	F	Laborer	05Ap02As
MULVARNEY, Mary	19	F	Laborer	05Ap02As
MAHON, Jane	17	F	Laborer	05Ap02As
LEE, Peter	22	M	Laborer	05Ap02As
Bridget	55	F	Laborer	05Ap02As
Maria	18	F	Laborer	05Ap02As
MEHAN, Mary	19	F	Laborer	05Ap02As
MORAN, Bridget	30	F	Laborer	05Ap02As
CLARK, Margaret	21	F	Laborer	05Ap02As
BAIN, Catherine	23	F	Laborer	05Ap02As
MITCHEL, Honora	16	F	Laborer	05Ap02As
MCCUIN, Pat	19	M	Laborer	05Ap02As
MCCRAN, Pat	28	M	Laborer	05Ap02As
FINN, Terrance	25	M	Laborer	05Ap02As
CRONOGA, Jane	16	F	Laborer	05Ap02As
BOHIN, James	15	M	Laborer	05Ap02As
BOYLE, Pat	35	M	Laborer	05Ap02As
NIMAN, David	18	M	Laborer	05Ap02As
LEE, Margaret	56	F	Laborer	05Ap02As
Lochtan	10	U	Laborer	05Ap02As
LYNCH, Bridget	18	F	Laborer	05Ap02As
CURIGAN, Bida	10	F	Laborer	05Ap02As
Mary	08	F	Child	05Ap02As
MONAHAN, Thomas	35	M	Laborer	05Ap02As
Ann	30	F	Laborer	05Ap02As
DIXON, Thomas	40	M	Laborer	05Ap02As
COLLINS, Michel	23	M	Baker	05Ap02As
SAVAGE, John	30	M	Tailor	05Ap02As
CUDDY, John	22	M	Clerk	05Ap02As
HADEN, Pat	26	M	Engineer	05Ap02As
KARON, John	35	M	Weaver	05Ap02As
HUGHS, Robert	60	M	Weaver	05Ap02As
MURPHY, Owen	25	M	Laborer	05Ap02As
Bernard	20	M	Laborer	05Ap02As
BOWA, James	29	M	Laborer	05Ap02As
BOLJAR, Edward	28	M	Laborer	05Ap02As
DAVIS, George	34	M	Mnftr	05Ap02As
TIFFNEY, Amos	30	M	Mnftr	05Ap02As
RYAN, Margaret	18	F	Mnftr	05Ap02As
LAWLESS, Mary	25	F	Mnftr	05Ap02As
RYAN, Mary-Ann	25	F	Mnftr	05Ap02As
SMITH, Margaret	25	F	Mnftr	05Ap02As
RYAN, Patrick	24	M	Gdnr	05Ap02As
MCKNIGHT, Robert	22	M	Farmer	05Ap02As
RUSSELLS, Joseph	27	M	Tailor	05Ap02As
MCDERMONT, Mary	45	F	Tailor	05Ap02As
James	11	M	Tailor	05Ap02As
Maria	16	F	Tailor	05Ap02As
Eliza	09	F	Child	05Ap02As
Catherine	06	F	Child	05Ap02As
HANDLEY, John	28	M	Tailor	05Ap02As
HAMILTON, James	40	M	Farmer	05Ap02As
Robert	20	M	Farmer	05Ap02As
RICHMOND, William	23	M	Spinner	05Ap02As
Eliza	26	F	Overseer	05Ap02As
Richd.	20	M	Overseer	05Ap02As
DUFFY, Patrick	19	M	Shopkeeper	05Ap02As
ONIEL, John	24	M	Laborer	05Ap02As
CALLIN, William	18	M	Farmer	05Ap02As
CASTILLO, Patrick	23	M	Laborer	05Ap02As
LOUGHRIN, Martha	25	F	Hrsm	05Ap02As
Catherine	25	F	Hrsm	05Ap02As
Mary	20	F	Hrsm	05Ap02As
Bridget	.00	F	Infant	05Ap02As
CLAFFY, Owin	30	M	Laborer	05Ap02As
HANDEBORD, James	25	M	Laborer	05Ap02As
RYAN, Peter	27	M	Laborer	05Ap02As

NAMES OF PASSENGERS	AGE	SEX	OCCUPATIONS	DATE PORT SHIP
MERNORY, Pat	27	M	Laborer	05Ap02As
Mike	25	M	Laborer	05Ap02As
MCNINEY, Bridget	60	F	Laborer	05Ap02As
Bridget	20	F	Laborer	05Ap02As
Mary	25	F	Laborer	05Ap02As
MURPHY, Eliza	13	F	Laborer	05Ap02As
NERY, Pat	22	M	Stctr	05Ap02As
CRONIN, Pat	25	M	Stctr	05Ap02As
COLOHAN, Johanah	20	F	Unknown	05Ap02As
MCVANE, Catherine	25	F	Unknown	05Ap02As
MAHANEY, Michel	28	M	Laborer	05Ap02As
Catherine	30	F	Laborer	05Ap02As
MCBRUITY, John	40	M	Laborer	05Ap02As
Ann	30	F	Laborer	05Ap02As
John	.00	M	Infant	05Ap02As
DOWNS, Richard	20	M	Laborer	05Ap02As
TILTON, Richard	25	M	Laborer	05Ap02As
CORMICK, Pat	36	M	Laborer	05Ap02As
CARROL, Pat	27	M	Laborer	05Ap02As
DUNN, Dan	23	M	Laborer	05Ap02As
CONNAN, Peter	23	M	Laborer	05Ap02As
HOPKINS, John	23	M	Laborer	05Ap02As
FARRALE, Pat	20	M	Laborer	05Ap02As
DOLAN, Thomas	28	M	Laborer	05Ap02As
LAWLEE, John	35	M	Laborer	05Ap02As
Thomas	36	M	Laborer	05Ap02As
WILTON, Fanny	16	F	Laborer	05Ap02As
CONNOR, Ann	18	F	Laborer	05Ap02As
Catherine	17	F	Laborer	05Ap02As
BUIK, Pat	25	M	Laborer	05Ap02As
BOGANON, Lawrance	35	M	Laborer	05Ap02As
BUIK, Mary	20	F	Laborer	05Ap02As
HALL, Mary	30	F	Laborer	05Ap02As
ROHE, Cornelius	20	M	Laborer	05Ap02As
KING, Benjaman	30	M	Laborer	05Ap02As
DAY, Isaach	23	M	Laborer	05Ap02As
KING, Joseph	27	M	Laborer	05Ap02As
REIGLEY, Bridget	16	F	Laborer	05Ap02As
Rosana	06	F	Child	05Ap02As
QUIN, Nancy	50	F	Laborer	05Ap02As
WRIN, John	37	M	Laborer	05Ap02As
NULDOON, John	40	M	Laborer	05Ap02As
MOLARCHIN, John	17	M	Laborer	05Ap02As
SHERIDAN, Pat	25	M	Laborer	05Ap02As
QUIN, James	18	M	Laborer	05Ap02As
MCNULTY, Hugh	24	M	Laborer	05Ap02As
SMITH, John	20	M	Laborer	05Ap02As
RIGHLEY, Francis	24	M	Laborer	05Ap02As
FOLAN, Pat	40	M	Laborer	05Ap02As
THORNTON, Thomas	30	M	Laborer	05Ap02As
Philip	28	M	Laborer	05Ap02As
Richard	25	M	Laborer	05Ap02As
DONNAL, Patrick	23	M	Laborer	05Ap02As
CUMMANS, Tim	40	M	Laborer	05Ap02As
CLEARY, John	28	M	Laborer	05Ap02As
Thomas	26	M	Laborer	05Ap02As
William	16	M	Laborer	05Ap02As
Judy	29	F	Laborer	05Ap02As
Mary	14	F	Laborer	05Ap02As
BRADY, James	22	M	Laborer	05Ap02As
DIVINE, Thomas	36	M	Laborer	05Ap02As
Ann	17	F	Laborer	05Ap02As
MCDONNEL, Michel	50	M	Laborer	05Ap02As
MURPHY, John	17	M	Laborer	05Ap02As
JOHN, Mccan	25	M	Laborer	05Ap02As
MCCLARIN, Andrew	17	M	Laborer	05Ap02As
MURPHY, Ellen	21	F	Laborer	05Ap02As
Thomas	.00	M	Infant	05Ap02As
John	02	M	Child	05Ap02As
BRADY, Owen	50	M	Laborer	05Ap02As
Pat	19	M	Laborer	05Ap02As
MCGOVARN, Firnl	56	U	Laborer	05Ap02As
Pat	17	M	Laborer	05Ap02As
William	14	M	Laborer	05Ap02As
TYE, Lilliy	13	F	Laborer	05Ap02As
LAWLESS, Andrew	28	M	Laborer	05Ap02As
BARNEY, John	24	M	Laborer	05Ap02As
SHINE, William	36	M	Laborer	05Ap02As
HAGOR, Henry	24	M	Laborer	05Ap02As
MCDERMOT, Ann	20	F	Laborer	05Ap02As
SHINE, Mary	20	F	Laborer	05Ap02As
LAIGAN, Catherine	18	F	Laborer	05Ap02As
CONVENT, Betty	17	F	Laborer	05Ap02As
DAVIS, Thomas	35	M	Collier	05Ap02As
Margaret	22	F	Laborer	05Ap02As
KILTY, Anthony	24	M	Laborer	05Ap02As
Thomas	15	M	Laborer	05Ap02As
Biddy	21	F	Laborer	05Ap02As
SCILY, James	22	M	Laborer	05Ap02As
WELSH, John	22	M	Laborer	05Ap02As
FARRALE, Barney	24	M	Laborer	05Ap02As
DENNISON, Ellen	18	F	Laborer	05Ap02As
BYRNES, Maria	17	F	Laborer	05Ap02As
MAGNEE, John	20	M	Laborer	05Ap02As
GILL, John	21	M	Laborer	05Ap02As
KENNEY, William	19	M	Laborer	05Ap02As
MALONEY, John	29	M	Laborer	05Ap02As
WILTTON, William	20	M	Laborer	05Ap02As
STACK, John	32	M	Laborer	05Ap02As
Julia	26	F	Laborer	05Ap02As
Pat	03	M	Child	05Ap02As
Mary	.00	F	Infant	05Ap02As
KINNAI, Betty	20	F	Laborer	05Ap02As
CORRIGAN, Pat	23	M	Laborer	05Ap02As
CASEY, Thomas	27	M	Laborer	05Ap02As
CUNNINGHAM, Kain	25	M	Laborer	05Ap02As
SWEENEY, Pat	36	M	Laborer	05Ap02As
TEARNEY, Mary-Ann	20	F	Laborer	05Ap02As
HORIN, Bridget	23	F	Laborer	05Ap02As
Mary	35	F	Laborer	05Ap02As
KELLEY, Ann	19	F	Laborer	05Ap02As
SMITH, Rosey	17	F	Laborer	05Ap02As
CUMAHY, John	11	M	Laborer	05Ap02As
CASSADY, Ellin	18	F	Laborer	05Ap02As
Catherine	16	F	Laborer	05Ap02As
MALONE, Margaret	24	F	Laborer	05Ap02As
MCBRIDE, Fanny	15	F	Laborer	05Ap02As
MURN, Mary	25	F	Laborer	05Ap02As
MORIN, Mary	25	F	Laborer	05Ap02As
Unity	.00	F	Infant	05Ap02As
SHEAN, James	20	M	Laborer	05Ap02As
William	50	M	Laborer	05Ap02As
Died-At-Sea				
BOHEAN, Mathew	60	M	Laborer	05Ap02As
Died-At-Sea				
GAFFOY, William	.00	M	Infant	05Ap02As
Died-At-Sea				
BACKWHISTLE, Nathanl.	45	M	Laborer	05Ap02As
Died-At-Sea				

NEW-ORLEANS 05 APRIL 1848

From Bermuda

NAMES OF PASSENGERS	AGE	SEX	OCCUPATIONS	DATE PORT SHIP
GRAY, J.G.	27	M	Doctor	05Ap75He

NAMES OF PASSENGERS	AGE	SEX	OCCUPATIONS	DATE PORT SHIP

BROOKLYN 05 APRIL 1848

From Glasgow

NAMES OF PASSENGERS	AGE	SEX	OCCUPATIONS	DATE PORT SHIP
CRAWFORD, Mary	20	F	Spinster	05Ap04Fg
HIGGINNS, Jno.	30	M	Laborer	05Ap04Fg
SHIELY, Martha	25	F	Spinster	05Ap04Fg
MURPHY, Bernd.	29	M	Laborer	05Ap04Fg
TOIL, Danl.	38	M	Shoemaker	05Ap04Fg
Eliz.	15	F	None	05Ap04Fg
David	12	M	None	05Ap04Fg
WALLACE, Hamilton	26	M	Laborer	05Ap04Fg
Mary	25	F	None	05Ap04Fg
Thos.	12	M	None	05Ap04Fg
John	02	M	Child	05Ap04Fg
Ellen	.07	F	Infant	05Ap04Fg
MARSHALL, Wm.	24	M	Weaver	05Ap04Fg
THOMPSON, John	29	M	Tailor	05Ap04Fg
MCCUSKLE, Henry	48	M	Laborer	05Ap04Fg
Susan	48	F	None	05Ap04Fg
STOCKS, Walter	30	M	Miner	05Ap04Fg
DWAIN, John	26	M	Laborer	05Ap04Fg
Catherine	24	F	None	05Ap04Fg
LAIN, Patrick	29	M	Laborer	05Ap04Fg
DRUMMOND, Thos.	32	M	Laborer	05Ap04Fg
BROWN, Eliza	17	F	Spinster	05Ap04Fg
MCHUFFY, Agness	20	F	Spinster	05Ap04Fg
MCSWEENI, Bernd.	22	M	Laborer	05Ap04Fg

WOODSIDE 05 APRIL 1848

From Liverpool

NAMES OF PASSENGERS	AGE	SEX	OCCUPATIONS	DATE PORT SHIP
WILLIAMS, John	22	M	Farmer	05Ap02Fk
Mary	21	F	Milliner	05Ap02Fk
Henry	.03	M	Infant	05Ap02Fk
NAUGHN, John	24	M	Blacksmith	05Ap02Fk
HAMSON, James	24	M	Carpenter	05Ap02Fk
OHARRA, Oliver	29	M	Farmer	05Ap02Fk
Margaret	28	F	Dressmaker	05Ap02Fk
SMITH, Thomas	40	M	Farmer	05Ap02Fk
Terence	15	M	Weaver	05Ap02Fk
Mathew	13	M	Weaver	05Ap02Fk
TIERNEY, Patt.	20	M	Blacksmith	05Ap02Fk
PHARLEY, Phill	19	M	Farmer	05Ap02Fk
DONOHOE, George	45	M	Miner	05Ap02Fk
Eliza	13	F	Servant	05Ap02Fk
Mary	11	F	Childnurse	05Ap02Fk
Ann	'09	F	Childnurse	05Ap02Fk
Patrick	10	M	Butcher	05Ap02Fk
Catharine	05	F	Child	05Ap02Fk
MURRAY, Patt.	22	M	Miner	05Ap02Fk
Mary	20	F	Milliner	05Ap02Fk
Patt.	02	M	Child	05Ap02Fk
Bryan	.02	M	Infant	05Ap02Fk
OBRIEN, James	19	M	Miner	05Ap02Fk
LEADEN, Patt.	25	M	Miner	05Ap02Fk
CAHILL, Mary	30	M	Cook	05Ap02Fk
Margaret	35	F	Servant	05Ap02Fk
BRADY, Owen	38	M	Farmer	05Ap02Fk

ANN 06 APRIL 1848

From Drogheda

NAMES OF PASSENGERS	AGE	SEX	OCCUPATIONS	DATE PORT SHIP
MAHOLIN, James	32	M	Farmer	06Ap32Th
CLARK, William	49	M	Unknown	06Ap32Th
COOPER, Geo.	21	M	Cooper	06Ap32Th
SAVAGE, Richd.	24	M	Hrsm	06Ap32Th
HARMAN, John	52	M	Butcher	06Ap32Th
HANNAGAN, John	16	M	Farmer	06Ap32Th
PRIOR, Hugh	34	M	Unknown	06Ap32Th
GRAHAM, Richd.	22	M	Carpenter	06Ap32Th
HICKEY, Terrance	20	M	Laborer	06Ap32Th
MCGOVERN, Thomas	40	M	Unknown	06Ap32Th
MINSTER, Pat	19	M	Farmer	06Ap32Th
POULTANEY, Stephen	21	M	Farmer	06Ap32Th
COMMISKEY, Hugh	17	M	Farmer	06Ap32Th
ROGERS, Michl.	17	M	Laborer	06Ap32Th
Miles	18	M	Laborer	06Ap32Th
CLARK, James	18	M	Laborer	06Ap32Th
NULTY, John	19	M	Laborer	06Ap32Th
THOMPSON, Thos.	20	M	Laborer	06Ap32Th
CAIN, Pat	25	M	Laborer	06Ap32Th
MOONEY, John	24	M	Weaver	06Ap32Th
HANNIGAN, John	20	M	Laborer	06Ap32Th
REELY, Pat	19	M	Servant	06Ap32Th
MCAVOY, James	50	M	Weaver	06Ap32Th
James	19	M	Farmer	06Ap32Th
HERDIGAN, Thos.	15	M	Laborer	06Ap32Th
ROMKI, Pat	18	M	Laborer	06Ap32Th
MONAHAM, Thos.	18	M	Painter	06Ap32Th
CASEY, David	21	M	Tailor	06Ap32Th
CAVANAGH, Thos.	20	M	Laborer	06Ap32Th
CASSIDY, Pat	22	M	Laborer	06Ap32Th
CAVANAGH, Pat	25	M	Laborer	06Ap32Th
MCGEE, Pat	20	M	Grocer	06Ap32Th
CRILLY, James	20	M	Servant	06Ap32Th
SIMMONS, James	26	M	Unknown	06Ap32Th
COLLINS, Pat	20	M	Unknown	06Ap32Th
SMITH, Pat	22	M	Farmer	06Ap32Th
MCGEE, Michael	53	M	Unknown	06Ap32Th
HARMAN, Andw.	22	M	Laborer	06Ap32Th
CLARK, Pat	02	M	Child	06Ap32Th
LENNON, John	40	M	Laborer	06Ap32Th
HANNIGAN, Peter	08	M	Child	06Ap32Th
Pat	12	M	None	06Ap32Th
MCGOVERN, Pat	10	M	None	06Ap32Th
DOYLE, Thos.	11	M	None	06Ap32Th
BAGNALL, John	03	M	Child	06Ap32Th
WARD, Loughlin	12	M	None	06Ap32Th
MALHOLM, Matilda	21	F	Wife	06Ap32Th
Ann (D)	.06	F	Infant	06Ap32Th
CASEY, Mary	30	F	Servant	06Ap32Th
CLARK, Mary	18	F	Dairymaid	06Ap32Th
Marg.	15	F	Dairymaid	06Ap32Th
Mary	40	F	Dairymaid	06Ap32Th
LENNON, Mary-Ann	30	F	Dressmaker	06Ap32Th
CRANEN, Theresa	18	F	Milliner	06Ap32Th
MCGUIRE, Ann	25	F	Servant	06Ap32Th
SAVAGE, Mary	56	F	Unknown	06Ap32Th
HARMAN, Bridgt.	17	F	Dressmaker	06Ap32Th
Christina	15	F	Dressmaker	06Ap32Th
MCCOW, Eliza	28	F	Dressmaker	06Ap32Th
HARMAN, Janis	19	F	Dressmaker	06Ap32Th
SAVAGE, Maria	18	F	Dressmaker	06Ap32Th
HANNIGAN, Judith	36	F	Dressmaker	06Ap32Th
MCMANNS, Mary	28	F	Dressmaker	06Ap32Th
THORNTON, Mary	16	F	Servant	06Ap32Th
OWENS, Mary	21	F	Spinster	06Ap32Th

NAMES OF PASSENGERS	AGE	SEX	OCCUPATIONS	DATE PORT SHIP
NELSON, Cathn.	20	F	Servant	06Ap32Th
HAMILTON, Mary	20	F	Servant	06Ap32Th
BARNES, Mary	25	F	Servant	06Ap32Th
REILLY, Cathn.	20	F	Servant	06Ap32Th
DOYLE, Ann	21	F	Servant	06Ap32Th
HENRY, Margt.	20	F	Servant	06Ap32Th
FRITZGREW, Maria	20	F	Servant	06Ap32Th
MURPHY, Mary	23	F	Servant	06Ap32Th
DOYLE, Mary	16	F	Servant	06Ap32Th
HENRY, Mary	20	F	Servant	06Ap32Th
MCCABE, Ann	16	F	Servant	06Ap32Th
ROGERS, Ann	20	F	Servant	06Ap32Th
CARTIN, Alice	28	F	Wife	06Ap32Th
LEECH, Mary	18	F	Servant	06Ap32Th
HAY, Jane	20	F	Servant	06Ap32Th
MAGEE, Margt.	32	F	Servant	06Ap32Th
MCMENNS, Margt.	16	F	Spinster	06Ap32Th
KING, Margt.	20	F	Unknown	06Ap32Th
FETZGAN, Ann	42	F	Wife	06Ap32Th
Margt.	16	F	Spinster	06Ap32Th
MEATH, Rose	16	F	Unknown	06Ap32Th
CASEY, Cathn.	23	F	Wife	06Ap32Th
BOYLE, Mary-Eliza	21	F	Wife	06Ap32Th
CLEARY, Jane	06	F	Child	06Ap32Th
CLARK, Rose	04	F	Child	06Ap32Th
Eliza	08	F	Child	06Ap32Th
Kate	10	F	None	06Ap32Th
Ann	12	F	None	06Ap32Th
LENNON, Ann	06	F	Child	06Ap32Th
ROURKE, Eliza	14	F	Spinster	06Ap32Th
LEWIS, Kate	12	F	None	06Ap32Th
HANNIGAN, Ann	10	F	None	06Ap32Th
MCMANUS, Cathn.	04	F	Child	06Ap32Th
MCGOVERN, Mary	12	F	None	06Ap32Th
MAGEE, Jane	03	F	Child	06Ap32Th
Mary	09	F	Child	06Ap32Th
WARD, Ann	10	F	None	06Ap32Th
ROGERS, Rose	18	F	Spinster	06Ap32Th
DONOHUE, James	22	M	Laborer	06Ap32Th
MAXWELL, William	25	M	Unknown	06Ap32Th
Died-At-Sea				
MCMANUS, Dennis	28	M	Unknown	06Ap32Th
Died-At-Sea				

WARREN 06 APRIL 1848

From Glasgow And Grenock

NAMES OF PASSENGERS	AGE	SEX	OCCUPATIONS	DATE PORT SHIP
BRODIE, James	24	M	Writer	06Ap94Qr
MCCLUSKY, Catherine	17	F	Spinster	06Ap94Qr
MCCREDIE, Helen	17	F	Spinster	06Ap94Qr
WELCH, James	27	M	Slater	06Ap94Qr
MCDOUGALL, John	39	M	Warper	06Ap94Qr
MCKEAN, Ann	22	F	Spinster	06Ap94Qr
Juhann	.09	F	Infant	06Ap94Qr
Mary	24	F	Spinster	06Ap94Qr
MCCAULEY, Ann	20	F	Spinster	06Ap94Qr
James	.08	M	Infant	06Ap94Qr
ROLEH, John	31	M	Farmer	06Ap94Qr
RUSSELL, John	42	M	Laborer	06Ap94Qr
GEMMELL, John	40	M	Farmer	06Ap94Qr
Margaret	40	F	Spinster	06Ap94Qr
Mary-Ann	19	F	Spinster	06Ap94Qr
Catherine	13	F	Spinster	06Ap94Qr
Henry	10	M	None	06Ap94Qr
Charles	08	M	Child	06Ap94Qr
Robert	06	M	Child	06Ap94Qr
Margaret	04	F	Child	06Ap94Qr
Moses	.08	M	Infant	06Ap94Qr
COLLINS, Joseph	20	M	Laborer	06Ap94Qr
PRICE, Elizabeth	20	F	Spinster	06Ap94Qr
FORBES, Samuel	28	M	Farmer	06Ap94Qr
NICOLSON, Walter	25	M	Laborer	06Ap94Qr
WELCH, William	53	M	Laborer	06Ap94Qr

ITALY 06 APRIL 1848

From Liverpool

NAMES OF PASSENGERS	AGE	SEX	OCCUPATIONS	DATE PORT SHIP
QUINN, John	16	M	Laborer	06Ap02Hq
Patrick	12	M	Laborer	06Ap02Hq
CROWLEY, Mathew	28	M	Laborer	06Ap02Hq
Julia (W)	26	F	Laborer	06Ap02Hq
U	.00	U	Infant	06Ap02Hq
William (S)	03	M	Child	06Ap02Hq
JUCE, Elizh.	43	F	Laborer	06Ap02Hq
William	20	M	Laborer	06Ap02Hq
Thomas	18	M	Laborer	06Ap02Hq
Amelia	07	F	Child	06Ap02Hq
WHALIN, Wm.	35	M	Laborer	06Ap02Hq
CARTHUSE, Bernard	25	M	Laborer	06Ap02Hq
MCCORMICK, William	25	M	Laborer	06Ap02Hq
Jane	18	F	Unknown	06Ap02Hq
HOLMES, Mary	19	F	Unknown	06Ap02Hq
HOUSTON, John	24	M	Laborer	06Ap02Hq
MCCAMAY, Mick	19	M	Laborer	06Ap02Hq
Mary	10	F	Unknown	06Ap02Hq
Susan	09	F	Child	06Ap02Hq
Mitchell	17	M	Laborer	06Ap02Hq
DIAMOND, Jane	19	F	Unknown	06Ap02Hq
Catharine	28	F	Unknown	06Ap02Hq
JONES, Wm.	35	M	Laborer	06Ap02Hq
Sarah	32	F	Unknown	06Ap02Hq
Margaret	10	F	Unknown	06Ap02Hq
John	07	M	Child	06Ap02Hq
EDWARDS, Daniel	26	M	Laborer	06Ap02Hq
Catharine	25	F	Unknown	06Ap02Hq
THOMAS, Evan	60	M	Laborer	06Ap02Hq
BOWEN, Thomas	22	M	Laborer	06Ap02Hq
Wm.	25	M	Laborer	06Ap02Hq
MORGAN, John	24	M	Laborer	06Ap02Hq
PRICE, John	24	M	Laborer	06Ap02Hq
WOODS, Jane	25	F	Unknown	06Ap02Hq
LORD, Eliza	23	F	Unknown	06Ap02Hq
CAMEY, Thomas	50	M	Laborer	06Ap02Hq
Joseph	28	M	Laborer	06Ap02Hq
Cath.	28	F	Laborer	06Ap02Hq
Maria	21	F	Laborer	06Ap02Hq
Thomas	18	M	Laborer	06Ap02Hq
ROBINSON, Patrick	55	M	Laborer	06Ap02Hq
FITZPATRICK, Dennis	26	M	Laborer	06Ap02Hq
Eliza	23	F	Unknown	06Ap02Hq
GAFFNEY, Richard	30	M	Laborer	06Ap02Hq
Mary	30	F	Unknown	06Ap02Hq
Mary	10	F	Unknown	06Ap02Hq
CAUGHLAN, John	34	M	Laborer	06Ap02Hq
Mary (W)	26	F	Unknown	06Ap02Hq
U	.00	U	Infant	06Ap02Hq
FAHEY, Mich.	25	M	Laborer	06Ap02Hq
JONES, John	32	M	Laborer	06Ap02Hq
KENNEDY, David	24	M	Laborer	06Ap02Hq
Christiana (W)	22	F	Unknown	06Ap02Hq
U	.00	U	Infant	06Ap02Hq
ARNDT, William	34	M	Laborer	06Ap02Hq
David	23	M	Laborer	06Ap02Hq
LAWLER, Edward	22	M	Laborer	06Ap02Hq
WHALIN, Martin	22	M	Laborer	06Ap02Hq
Eliza (W)	20	F	Unknown	06Ap02Hq

NAMES OF PASSENGERS		AGE	SEX	OCCUPATIONS	DATE PORT SHIP
WHALIN, U		.00	U	Infant	06Ap02Hq
GARRY, Michl.		24	M	Butcher	06Ap02Hq
Catharine		22	F	Unknown	06Ap02Hq
GINDHAM, Wm.		24	M	Laborer	06Ap02Hq
MCCARTHY, Wm.		20	M	Laborer	06Ap02Hq
MCCARNE, B.		30	U	Laborer	06Ap02Hq
HUGHES, Alex		25	M	Laborer	06Ap02Hq
HANLIN, James		35	M	Laborer	06Ap02Hq
Mary		20	F	Unknown	06Ap02Hq
FALLAM, James		20	M	Laborer	06Ap02Hq
MCGEE, Trumen		19	M	Laborer	06Ap02Hq
MORGAN, Barney		35	M	Laborer	06Ap02Hq
DRISWELL, Cornelius		20	M	Laborer	06Ap02Hq
Mary		18	F	Unknown	06Ap02Hq
Michl.		20	M	Laborer	06Ap02Hq
MAHONY, Cornelius		32	M	Unknown	06Ap02Hq
Mary		20	F	Laborer	06Ap02Hq
SULLIVAN, Cornelius		20	M	Laborer	06Ap02Hq
CASY, Thomas		25	M	Laborer	06Ap02Hq
Catharine		22	F	Unknown	06Ap02Hq
MURPHY, John		24	M	Laborer	06Ap02Hq
SULLIVAN, Patrick		40	M	Laborer	06Ap02Hq
Mary		20	F	Unknown	06Ap02Hq
GOVIN, Biddy		16	F	Laborer	06Ap02Hq
WALSH, James		24	M	Laborer	06Ap02Hq
MURPHY, Thomas		22	M	Laborer	06Ap02Hq
SULLIVAN, Michl.		34	M	Laborer	06Ap02Hq
Cornelius		21	M	Laborer	06Ap02Hq
GALLUNDAY, Michael		24	M	Laborer	06Ap02Hq
GARNET, Mary		20	F	Unknown	06Ap02Hq
SHERIDAN, Hugh		26	M	Laborer	06Ap02Hq
U	(W)	24	F	Unknown	06Ap02Hq
SMITH, Michael		40	M	Laborer	06Ap02Hq
Catharine		30	F	Unknown	06Ap02Hq
Bridget		28	F	Unknown	06Ap02Hq
U		.00	U	Infant	06Ap02Hq
Bryan		05	M	Child	06Ap02Hq
TRUNON, Wm.		31	M	Laborer	06Ap02Hq
BOANNAND, Patrick		40	M	Laborer	06Ap02Hq
U	(W)	35	F	Unknown	06Ap02Hq
U		.00	U	Infant	06Ap02Hq
Mary	(D)	10	F	Unknown	06Ap02Hq
Margaret	(D)	11	F	Unknown	06Ap02Hq
Patrick	(S)	09	M	Laborer	06Ap02Hq
BELSON, John		40	M	Laborer	06Ap02Hq
U	(W)	32	F	Unknown	06Ap02Hq
U		.00	U	Infant	06Ap02Hq
MAHER, John		30	M	Laborer	06Ap02Hq
THOMAS, Thomas		35	M	Unknown	06Ap02Hq
Margaret	(W)	35	F	Unknown	06Ap02Hq
U		.00	U	Infant	06Ap02Hq
DAVIS, Famey		27	M	Laborer	06Ap02Hq
GAYNOR, Martin		22	M	Laborer	06Ap02Hq
CLARK, Joseph		20	M	Laborer	06Ap02Hq
LANY, John		23	M	Laborer	06Ap02Hq
MAKINS, Peter		20	M	Laborer	06Ap02Hq
LAWLER, Mary		30	F	Unknown	06Ap02Hq
HAUGHEY, Mich.		22	M	Laborer	06Ap02Hq
EVANS, George		30	M	Laborer	06Ap02Hq
MILLER, Mary		25	F	Unknown	06Ap02Hq
MARTIN, Edward		34	M	Carpenter	06Ap02Hq
Jane	(W)	26	F	Unknown	06Ap02Hq
U		.00	U	Infant	06Ap02Hq
MOORON, Dana		20	U	Unknown	06Ap02Hq
CALLINDER, Robert		19	M	Carpenter	06Ap02Hq
MARTIN, John		30	M	Carpenter	06Ap02Hq
Thomas		29	M	Carpenter	06Ap02Hq
Mary-Ann		21	F	Unknown	06Ap02Hq
SPEAKMAN, William		29	M	Farmer	06Ap02Hq
ROSE, George		23	M	Farmer	06Ap02Hq
John		20	M	Farmer	06Ap02Hq
FLYNN, John		50	M	Farmer	06Ap02Hq
Daniel		22	M	Farmer	06Ap02Hq
Patrick		14	M	Farmer	06Ap02Hq
Margaret		24	F	Unknown	06Ap02Hq
ALLISON, William		19	M	Farmer	06Ap02Hq
DOND, Michael		18	M	Farmer	06Ap02Hq
DOLAN, Ann		18	F	Unknown	06Ap02Hq
BRYAN, Patrick		24	M	Laborer	06Ap02Hq
John		21	M	Laborer	06Ap02Hq
James		20	M	Laborer	06Ap02Hq
DOUGHERTY, Celia		27	F	Unknown	06Ap02Hq
Hugh		07	M	Child	06Ap02Hq
Mary		03	F	Child	06Ap02Hq
LANKLER, John		27	M	Laborer	06Ap02Hq
Ann	(W)	26	F	Unknown	06Ap02Hq
U		.00	U	Infant	06Ap02Hq
John	(S)	07	M	Child	06Ap02Hq
Young	(S)	05	M	Child	06Ap02Hq
SMITH, William		29	M	Laborer	06Ap02Hq
STUSTLER, William		26	M	Laborer	06Ap02Hq
Joseph		23	M	Laborer	06Ap02Hq
Rebecca		17	F	Unknown	06Ap02Hq
Martha		26	F	Unknown	06Ap02Hq
U		.00	U	Infant	06Ap02Hq
HIAMS, James		20	M	Laborer	06Ap02Hq
HARNEY, Daniel		03	M	Child	06Ap02Hq
DALIHANEY, Mary		30	F	Unknown	06Ap02Hq
CLARKE, Cath.		18	F	Unknown	06Ap02Hq
Patrick		30	M	Laborer	06Ap02Hq
DUADE, Joseph		38	M	Laborer	06Ap02Hq
Jane	(W)	36	F	Unknown	06Ap02Hq
U		.00	U	Infant	06Ap02Hq
Hannah	(D)	10	F	Unknown	06Ap02Hq
Mary	(D)	09	F	Child	06Ap02Hq
John	(S)	05	M	Child	06Ap02Hq
Susanah	(D)	03	F	Child	06Ap02Hq
HANLEY, Francis		24	M	Laborer	06Ap02Hq
BYRNE, Mary		22	F	Unknown	06Ap02Hq
MAHER, Tim		20	M	Laborer	06Ap02Hq
Mary		18	F	Unknown	06Ap02Hq
KENNEDY, James		24	M	Laborer	06Ap02Hq
MILES, Ellen		40	F	Unknown	06Ap02Hq
William		18	M	Laborer	06Ap02Hq
Michael		12	M	Laborer	06Ap02Hq
SULLIVAN, John		22	M	Laborer	06Ap02Hq
HARRINGTON, Michael		06	M	Child	06Ap02Hq
BRYAN, Cath.		30	F	Unknown	06Ap02Hq
U		.00	U	Infant	06Ap02Hq
Michael		12	M	Laborer	06Ap02Hq
Ann		10	F	Unknown	06Ap02Hq
BURTIE, Alexander		25	M	Laborer	06Ap02Hq
HORY, Catharine		18	F	Unknown	06Ap02Hq
WARD, William		20	M	Laborer	06Ap02Hq
WATSON, Michl.		16	M	Laborer	06Ap02Hq
Julia		11	F	Unknown	06Ap02Hq
Bridget		17	F	Unknown	06Ap02Hq
BRIMAND, Thomas		20	M	Laborer	06Ap02Hq
MADDEN, Owen		22	M	Laborer	06Ap02Hq
NIX, Margaret		30	F	Unknown	06Ap02Hq
Mary		50	F	Unknown	06Ap02Hq
Martin		07	M	Child	06Ap02Hq
Patrick		05	M	Child	06Ap02Hq
Thomas		03	M	Child	06Ap02Hq
FOX, Bridget		17	F	Unknown	06Ap02Hq
MASTERSON, Patrick		18	M	Laborer	06Ap02Hq
CLYNCH, Martin		20	M	Laborer	06Ap02Hq
FEENEY, Margaret		40	F	Unknown	06Ap02Hq
MCPARTTIN, Owen		12	M	Laborer	06Ap02Hq
BOHAN, Mary		17	F	Unknown	06Ap02Hq
DOLAN, Michl.		18	M	Laborer	06Ap02Hq
MCLOUGHLIN, James		30	M	Laborer	06Ap02Hq
BRANMAN, Peter		20	M	Laborer	06Ap02Hq
BRIEN, Mary		18	F	Unknown	06Ap02Hq
DOONER, John		18	M	Laborer	06Ap02Hq
HARAN, Michl.		20	M	Laborer	06Ap02Hq
DOOLAN, Thomas		20	M	Laborer	06Ap02Hq
GANNON, John		22	M	Laborer	06Ap02Hq
DIVINE, Thomas		20	M	Laborer	06Ap02Hq
Catharine		16	F	Unknown	06Ap02Hq

NAMES OF PASSENGERS		AGE	SEX	OCCUPATIONS	DATE PORT SHIP
DONOHUE, Catharine		26	F	Unknown	06Ap02Hq
Thomas		03	M	Child	06Ap02Hq
CONWAY, Robert		21	M	Laborer	06Ap02Hq
QUICK, Mary		30	F	Unknown	06Ap02Hq
Margaret		25	F	Unknown	06Ap02Hq
STAPLETON, Hannah		08	F	Child	06Ap02Hq
Lawrence		10	M	Laborer	06Ap02Hq
BUTLER, Samuel		40	M	Laborer	06Ap02Hq
CAFFEY, James		36	M	Laborer	06Ap02Hq
CAFFER, Mary		24	F	Unknown	06Ap02Hq
BEGGAN, Bernard		75	M	Laborer	06Ap02Hq
MCGUIRE, John		23	M	Laborer	06Ap02Hq
LIEVIN, John		20	M	Laborer	06Ap02Hq
DEVINE, Daniel		16	M	Laborer	06Ap02Hq
BAITING, Edmud		20	M	Laborer	06Ap02Hq
DALEY, Thomas		25	M	Laborer	06Ap02Hq
ALWILL, Ellen		25	F	Unknown	06Ap02Hq
Mary		24	F	Unknown	06Ap02Hq
Catharine		33	F	Unknown	06Ap02Hq
MCGRATH, Ellen		20	F	Unknown	06Ap02Hq
MURPHY, Lawrence		30	M	Laborer	06Ap02Hq
U	(W)	20	F	Unknown	06Ap02Hq
U		.00	U	Infant	06Ap02Hq
SIMINS, Margaret		15	F	Unknown	06Ap02Hq
Ann		13	F	Unknown	06Ap02Hq
KEENAN, Luke		24	M	Laborer	06Ap02Hq
WALKER, Isabella		18	F	Unknown	06Ap02Hq
BOHAN, Peter		21	M	Laborer	06Ap02Hq
CONLAN, Charles		21	M	Laborer	06Ap02Hq
DOONES, Edward		21	M	Laborer	06Ap02Hq
CONLIN, Ellen		20	F	Unknown	06Ap02Hq
CAVANNAH, C.		23	U	Laborer	06Ap02Hq
DOHERTY, M.		26	U	Laborer	06Ap02Hq
MCGUIRE, Eliza		15	F	Unknown	06Ap02Hq
Patrick		11	M	Laborer	06Ap02Hq
James		09	M	Laborer	06Ap02Hq
HINDS, John		30	M	Laborer	06Ap02Hq
BROPHY, Michael		21	M	Laborer	06Ap02Hq
KILCULLIN, Owen		24	M	Laborer	06Ap02Hq
MCCANN, Mary		45	F	Unknown	06Ap02Hq
Elizabeth		13	F	Unknown	06Ap02Hq
WALSH, John		16	M	Laborer	06Ap02Hq
Mary		14	F	Unknown	06Ap02Hq
DONOHUE, Elizabeth		21	F	Unknown	06Ap02Hq
Rose		18	F	Unknown	06Ap02Hq
U		.00	U	Infant	06Ap02Hq
STANLEY, Thomas		17	M	Laborer	06Ap02Hq
Ann		15	F	Unknown	06Ap02Hq
Martin		12	M	Laborer	06Ap02Hq
DONOHUE, Mary		12	F	Unknown	06Ap02Hq
Margaret		05	F	Child	06Ap02Hq
Michael		03	M	Child	06Ap02Hq
Jane		02	F	Child	06Ap02Hq
GANY, Wm.		17	M	Laborer	06Ap02Hq
TOOKER, Riddis		19	M	Laborer	06Ap02Hq
FALLEN, Daniel		60	M	Laborer	06Ap02Hq
HAENCY, Thomas		23	M	Laborer	06Ap02Hq
Honor		09	F	Child	06Ap02Hq
Owen		04	M	Child	06Ap02Hq
TARBET, Ann		20	F	Unknown	06Ap02Hq
SHANLES, Cath.		21	F	Unknown	06Ap02Hq
MCMANN, Michael		25	M	Laborer	06Ap02Hq
SIDES, William		20	M	Laborer	06Ap02Hq
KILIGHAN, Francis		18	M	Laborer	06Ap02Hq
CONNEL, Daniel		32	M	Laborer	06Ap02Hq
KENNEDY, Michael		25	M	Laborer	06Ap02Hq
FAIEL, Patrick		40	M	Laborer	06Ap02Hq
MCGINNIS, Rose		20	F	Unknown	06Ap02Hq
REYNOLDS, Jane		18	F	Unknown	06Ap02Hq
WYATT, Maria		28	F	Unknown	06Ap02Hq
David		05	M	Child	06Ap02Hq

ARETHUSA 06 APRIL 1848

From Belfast

NAMES OF PASSENGERS		AGE	SEX	OCCUPATIONS	DATE PORT SHIP
LENNON, Michl.		35	M	Weaver	06Ap07Ib
MAGILLL, Wm.		25	M	Farmer	06Ap07Ib
SCULLY, Henry		35	M	Farmer	06Ap07Ib
MAHON, James		21	M	Servant	06Ap07Ib
Hugh		18	M	Servant	06Ap07Ib
STEWART, Hugh		18	M	Servant	06Ap07Ib
HERON, David		25	M	Weaver	06Ap07Ib
Elizth.	(W)	25	F	Wife	06Ap07Ib
LAWDERDALE, Saml.		50	M	Farmer	06Ap07Ib
Martha	(W)	40	F	Wife	06Ap07Ib
Saml.	(S)	03	M	Child	06Ap07Ib
HIGGINS, John		30	M	Servant	06Ap07Ib
Patk.		.10	M	Infant	06Ap07Ib
Magie	(W)	25	F	Wife	06Ap07Ib
Eliza	(D)	02	F	Child	06Ap07Ib
CAMPBELL, John		26	M	Farmer	06Ap07Ib
OKANE, Jas.O.		30	M	Laborer	06Ap07Ib
Mary		26	F	None	06Ap07Ib
KENNEDY, Michl.		70	M	Farmer	06Ap07Ib
Margt.	(W)	66	F	Wife	06Ap07Ib
Hugh	(S)	42	M	Unknown	06Ap07Ib
Grace	(D)	36	F	Unknown	06Ap07Ib
John	(H)	36	M	Unknown	06Ap07Ib
Jane	(T)	28	F	Unknown	06Ap07Ib
John		17	M	None	06Ap07Ib
MCDONNELL, Robt.		19	M	Weaver	06Ap07Ib
MCNAMMIN, Eleanor		26	F	Servant	06Ap07Ib
DIXON, Wm.		32	M	Farmer	06Ap07Ib
Sophia	(W)	28	F	Wife	06Ap07Ib
Wm.	(S)	08	M	Child	06Ap07Ib
Sarah	(D)	04	F	Child	06Ap07Ib
John	(S)	02	M	Child	06Ap07Ib
GORDON, Wm.		24	M	Farmer	06Ap07Ib
Mary	(W)	30	F	Wife	06Ap07Ib
Eliz.		13	F	None	06Ap07Ib
MCMASTER, Thomas		24	M	Laborer	06Ap07Ib
MCGUIRE, Francis		22	M	Laborer	06Ap07Ib
WARD, John		35	M	Carpenter	06Ap07Ib
Nancy	(W)	30	F	Unknown	06Ap07Ib
Chas.		07	M	Child	06Ap07Ib
Agnes		04	F	Child	06Ap07Ib
U		.00	U	Infant	06Ap07Ib
BROWNE, David		30	M	Cooper	06Ap07Ib
DORAN, Alice		28	F	Wi	06Ap07Ib
John		08	M	Child	06Ap07Ib
GORDON, Patk		40	M	Farmer	06Ap07Ib
Nath.		15	M	Unknown	06Ap07Ib
Eliz.		13	F	None	06Ap07Ib
James		11	M	None	06Ap07Ib
Thos.		09	M	Child	06Ap07Ib
Mary .		07	F	Child	06Ap07Ib
NEALE, Patk.		20	M	Laborer	06Ap07Ib
Edwd.		25	M	Laborer	06Ap07Ib
KIDLY, John		25	M	Unknown	06Ap07Ib
Ann		19	F	Ctnsp	06Ap07Ib
DEVELIN, Chas.		47	M	Spinster	06Ap07Ib
MCCRACKIN, Robt.		35	M	Laborer	06Ap07Ib
MCMAHON, Jas.		45	M	Farmer	06Ap07Ib
Mary	(W)	34	F	Unknown	06Ap07Ib
Ann		13	F	None	06Ap07Ib
Cath.		11	F	None	06Ap07Ib
Margt.		09	F	Child	06Ap07Ib
Francis		07	M	Child	06Ap07Ib
John		03	M	Child	06Ap07Ib
Chas.		.00	M	Infant	06Ap07Ib

NAMES OF PASSENGERS	AGE	SEX	OCCUPATIONS	DATE PORT SHIP
COOKE, Sarah	10	F	Spinster	06Ap07Ib
MCGRAGH, Hugh	45	M	Laborer	06Ap07Ib
GRAHAM, Patk.	29	M	Laborer	06Ap07Ib
BURNE, Stephen	30	M	Laborer	06Ap07Ib
Patk.	03	M	Child	06Ap07Ib
MCKEE, Hugh	22	M	Farmer	06Ap07Ib
Margt. (W)	22	F	Unknown	06Ap07Ib
Em.Jane	.00	F	Infant	06Ap07Ib
OWENS, Edwd.	25	M	Butler	06Ap07Ib
MCCULLOUGH, Wm.	25	M	Butler	06Ap07Ib
BIGGER, Henry	26	M	Servant	06Ap07Ib
RITCHIE, Ellen	27	F	Spinster	06Ap07Ib
MULHOLLAND, Jane	25	F	Spinster	06Ap07Ib
NELSON, Wm.	30	M	Mechanic	06Ap07Ib
Mary (W)	30	F	Unknown	06Ap07Ib
Wm.Jno.	08	M	Child	06Ap07Ib
Danl.	.00	M	Infant	06Ap07Ib
MCGUADE, Tobias	21	M	Mechanic	06Ap07Ib
HUNTER, Joseph	19	M	Baker	06Ap07Ib
Isaac	22	M	Baker	06Ap07Ib
Jane (W)	21	F	Wife	06Ap07Ib
Abbey	04	F	Child	06Ap07Ib
Joseph	02	M	Child	06Ap07Ib
FRANCIS, John	30	M	Mechanic	06Ap07Ib
REYNOLDS, Patk.	21	M	Farmer	06Ap07Ib
SMALLAN, Hannah	30	F	Lad	06Ap07Ib
Margt.	08	F	Child	06Ap07Ib
James	06	M	Child	06Ap07Ib
Thos.	02	M	Child	06Ap07Ib
ONEIL, Hessey	46	M	Servant	06Ap07Ib
Hugh	17	M	None	06Ap07Ib
Hessey	15	M	None	06Ap07Ib
Samuel	13	M	None	06Ap07Ib
George	11	M	None	06Ap07Ib
STEELE, John	27	M	Flaxdr	06Ap07Ib
HENRATTY, Patk.	27	M	Flaxdr	06Ap07Ib
FERRIS, Robt.	20	M	Laborer	06Ap07Ib
Mary-Ann (W)	23	F	Unknown	06Ap07Ib
GORMLEY, Margt.	19	F	Spinster	06Ap07Ib
Maria	13	F	Spinster	06Ap07Ib
MARTIN, Jas.	30	M	Farmer	06Ap07Ib
Margt. (W)	24	F	Unknown	06Ap07Ib
Margt.	20	F	Spinster	06Ap07Ib
Robert	04	M	Child	06Ap07Ib
Elizabeth	02	F	Child	06Ap07Ib
Jas.	.00	M	Infant	06Ap07Ib
HENRY, Alex	22	M	Laborer	06Ap07Ib
Jane	20	F	Spinster	06Ap07Ib
MURPHY, Mary	18	F	Spinster	06Ap07Ib
CONN, David	40	M	Laborer	06Ap07Ib
Elizh. (W)	40	F	Unknown	06Ap07Ib
Jane	18	F	None	06Ap07Ib
Eliza	16	F	None	06Ap07Ib
Robt.	13	M	None	06Ap07Ib
Sally-Ann	11	F	None	06Ap07Ib
Margt.	07	F	Child	06Ap07Ib
MCKAY, Patk.	40	M	Laborer	06Ap07Ib
Biddy	16	F	None	06Ap07Ib
Hugh	13	M	None	06Ap07Ib
Jas.	12	M	None	06Ap07Ib
WOODY, Owen	47	M	Weaver	06Ap07Ib
WOODS, John	30	M	Spinner	06Ap07Ib
MCKEARNEY, Mary	40	F	Spinster	06Ap07Ib
Jas.	17	M	Laborer	06Ap07Ib
Eliza	15	F	Spinster	06Ap07Ib
Thos.	13	M	None	06Ap07Ib
OHARPER, Shibby	25	F	Spinster	06Ap07Ib
Cathe	20	F	Spinster	06Ap07Ib
Michl.	18	M	Laborer	06Ap07Ib
MCGUIRKEN, Jno.	40	M	Laborer	06Ap07Ib
Mary (W)	40	F	Unknown	06Ap07Ib
DOE, Chas.	20	M	Clerk	06Ap07Ib
HARGARTY, Margt.	22	F	Spinster	06Ap07Ib
KERR, Thos.	22	M	Laborer	06Ap07Ib
LOWDEN, Ellen	18	F	Spinster	06Ap07Ib
HARDY, Rich.	17	M	Laborer	06Ap07Ib
MARTIN, Jas.	36	M	Laborer	06Ap07Ib
Mary-Ann	12	F	None	06Ap07Ib
GORDON, Thos.	18	M	Laborer	06Ap07Ib
ADAMS, Hugh	49	M	Farmer	06Ap07Ib
Mary (W)	47	F	Unknown	06Ap07Ib
Jas.	19	M	Laborer	06Ap07Ib
Martha	15	F	Spinster	06Ap07Ib
Robert	13	M	None	06Ap07Ib
Jane	08	F	Child	06Ap07Ib
Hugh	05	M	Child	06Ap07Ib
William	03	M	Child	06Ap07Ib
BARRIS, Alex	30	M	Farmer	06Ap07Ib
Jane (W)	30	F	Unknown	06Ap07Ib
John	04	M	Child	06Ap07Ib
Mary-J.	02	F	Child	06Ap07Ib
Sarah	01	F	Child	06Ap07Ib
CONNER, Martha	17	F	Spinster	06Ap07Ib
BROWN, Peter	27	M	Laborer	06Ap07Ib
Elizab. (W)	24	F	Unknown	06Ap07Ib
Alex	06	M	Child	06Ap07Ib
John	04	M	Child	06Ap07Ib
TYFORD, Thos.	20	M	Laborer	06Ap07Ib
TAYLOR, Wm.Jno.	22	M	Laborer	06Ap07Ib
Martha (W)	24	F	Unknown	06Ap07Ib
Joseph	03	M	Child	06Ap07Ib
Eliza	02	F	Child	06Ap07Ib
Martha	.00	F	Infant	06Ap07Ib
MORGAN, John	43	M	Laborer	06Ap07Ib
Margt.	27	F	Spinster	06Ap07Ib
Eliza	20	F	Spinster	06Ap07Ib
MCLAUGHLIN, Peter	48	M	Farmer	06Ap07Ib
Ann (W)	40	F	Unknown	06Ap07Ib
Mary	20	F	None	06Ap07Ib
Jno.	15	M	None	06Ap07Ib
Francis	13	M	None	06Ap07Ib
Elizabeth	11	F	None	06Ap07Ib
Bridget	09	F	Child	06Ap07Ib
Cathe	07	F	Child	06Ap07Ib
Peter	03	M	Child	06Ap07Ib
KILLEN, Ann	10	F	None	06Ap07Ib
Margt.	13	F	None	06Ap07Ib
GOODMAN, Susan	08	F	Child	06Ap07Ib
MCLAUGHLIN, Francis	20	M	Laborer	06Ap07Ib
MCAVOY, Jno.	24	M	Laborer	06Ap07Ib
TOLAN, Arthur	17	M	Laborer	06Ap07Ib
MCCONRIT, John	30	M	Laborer	06Ap07Ib
Bridget (W)	30	F	Unknown	06Ap07Ib
GORMAN, Mary	22	F	Spinster	06Ap07Ib
MCCONVILL, Mary	13	F	None	06Ap07Ib
Barnett	03	M	Child	06Ap07Ib
Biddy	02	F	Child	06Ap07Ib
DOHERTY, Mary	35	F	Seamstress	06Ap07Ib
KING, Rose	20	F	Seamstress	06Ap07Ib
FITZPATRICK, Mary	18	F	Seamstress	06Ap07Ib
Cath.	18	F	Seamstress	06Ap07Ib
DOHERTY, Elizabeth	16	F	Seamstress	06Ap07Ib
Edward	13	M	None	06Ap07Ib
Mary	10	F	None	06Ap07Ib
Cathe.	07	F	Child	06Ap07Ib
Rose	05	F	Child	06Ap07Ib
HOGAN, Peter	21	M	Laborer	06Ap07Ib
IRWIN, Jas.	24	M	Laborer	06Ap07Ib
JOHNSON, Jacob	20	M	Laborer	06Ap07Ib
BUNKER, Margt.	25	F	Spinster	06Ap07Ib
MCCLUNG, Jas.	20	M	Laborer	06Ap07Ib
WALTERS, Jas.	24	M	Seamstress	06Ap07Ib
DOHERTY, Bridget	15	F	Seamstress	06Ap07Ib
QUINN, Danl.	30	M	Laborer	06Ap07Ib
STEWART, Margt.	21	F	Seamstress	06Ap07Ib
Ann	19	F	Seamstress	06Ap07Ib
BORRIS, Jane	22	F	Seamstress	06Ap07Ib
Ann	19	F	Seamstress	06Ap07Ib
DOUGHERTY, Wm.	22	M	Farmer	06Ap07Ib
DICKEY, Margt.	26	F	Seamstress	06Ap07Ib

NAMES OF PASSENGERS		AGE	SEX	OCCUPATIONS	DATE PORT SHIP
DICKEY, Robt.		12	M	None	06Ap07Ib
MCGEE, Eliza		30	F	Servant	06Ap07Ib
GARDNER, John		20	M	Farmer	06Ap07Ib
MCKENNA, Jas.		23	M	Servant	06Ap07Ib
WELF, Mary-A.		23	F	Servant	06Ap07Ib
ANDERSON, Jane		16	F	Servant	06Ap07Ib
STEVENSON, Robt.		17	M	Farmer	06Ap07Ib
MUCKLE, Hugh		20	M	Farmer	06Ap07Ib
EASER, John		45	M	Farmer	06Ap07Ib
Margt.	(W)	45	F	Unknown	06Ap07Ib
Saml.	(S)	15	M	Unknown	06Ap07Ib
John	(S)	13	M	Unknown	06Ap07Ib
Joseph	(S)	11	M	Unknown	06Ap07Ib
Alex	(S)	07	M	Child	06Ap07Ib
Jas.	(S)	04	M	Child	06Ap07Ib
Mary	(D)	02	F	Child	06Ap07Ib
DOUGLASS, Ann		24	F	Servant	06Ap07Ib
GARRETT, Hugh		20	M	Farmer	06Ap07Ib
Mary	(T)	18	F	Unknown	06Ap07Ib
CONNING, Margt.		.06	F	Infant	06Ap07Ib
REILLY, Ann		23	F	Servant	06Ap07Ib
GREEN, John		24	M	Farmer	06Ap07Ib
Robt.		22	M	Farmer	06Ap07Ib
GORMAN, Jas.		20	M	Farmer	06Ap07Ib
MCKEOWN, Jane		33	F	Seamstress	06Ap07Ib
Jas.		13	M	None	06Ap07Ib
Robt.		10	M	None	06Ap07Ib
Alex		08	M	Child	06Ap07Ib
Eliza-J.		04	F	Child	06Ap07Ib
Hugh		.04	M	Infant	06Ap07Ib
MCCULLY, Jas.		20	M	Clerk	06Ap07Ib
ABRAHAM, Wm.		25	M	Gameskeeper	06Ap07Ib
DOHERTY, Mich.		18	M	Laborer	06Ap07Ib
WINCHESTER, Wm.		35	M	Laborer	06Ap07Ib
WARD, Thos.		30	M	Mechanic	06Ap07Ib

WITCH 07 APRIL 1848

From Liverpool

NAMES OF PASSENGERS		AGE	SEX	OCCUPATIONS	DATE PORT SHIP
MANCHEN, Tirone		38	M	Laborer	07Ap02Im
Ann	(W)	32	F	Laborer	07Ap02Im
John	(S)	13	M	Laborer	07Ap02Im
Martin	(S)	11	M	Laborer	07Ap02Im
Michael	(S)	09	M	Laborer	07Ap02Im
Patrick	(S)	06	M	Laborer	07Ap02Im
BANK, Mary		22	F	Laborer	07Ap02Im
PATTIGAN, Mary		17	F	Laborer	07Ap02Im
BYRNE, Charles		25	M	Laborer	07Ap02Im
LOW, John		21	M	Laborer	07Ap02Im
WELCH, John		20	M	Laborer	07Ap02Im
MCCHOLE, John		30	M	Laborer	07Ap02Im
Bridget	(W)	24	F	Laborer	07Ap02Im
Thos.	(S)	04	M	Child	07Ap02Im
Catherine	(D)	01	F	Child	07Ap02Im
ARLEY, Edward		20	M	Laborer	07Ap02Im
NODY, Michael		18	M	Laborer	07Ap02Im
CRONEY, Thos.		24	M	Laborer	07Ap02Im
Bridget		17	F	Laborer	07Ap02Im
QUILLAN, Bryan		20	M	Laborer	07Ap02Im
RYNE, John		20	M	Laborer	07Ap02Im
FINLEY, Ann		20	F	Laborer	07Ap02Im
Mary		18	F	Laborer	07Ap02Im
ROGLEY, Mary		13	F	Laborer	07Ap02Im
LOUGHON, James		23	M	Laborer	07Ap02Im
HANLEY, Mary		20	F	Laborer	07Ap02Im
Catherine		18	F	Laborer	07Ap02Im
Wm.		08	M	Laborer	07Ap02Im
MAHER, Tim		25	M	Laborer	07Ap02Im
DARMODY, Wm.		32	M	Laborer	07Ap02Im
BYRNO, Pat		23	M	Laborer	07Ap02Im
CODY, John		32	M	Laborer	07Ap02Im
GARVIN, James		21	M	Laborer	07Ap02Im
LOUCHNEY, Mich.		21	M	Laborer	07Ap02Im
MCQUAD, Martin		26	M	Laborer	07Ap02Im
Margaret		21	F	Laborer	07Ap02Im
WATER, Mary		20	F	Laborer	07Ap02Im
FLYN, John		21	M	Laborer	07Ap02Im
BREEN, John		26	M	Laborer	07Ap02Im
CASTILL, Wm.		36	M	Laborer	07Ap02Im
Catherine	(W)	24	F	Laborer	07Ap02Im
Ellen	(D)	02	F	Child	07Ap02Im
Philip	(S)	01	M	Child	07Ap02Im
DUGAN, Bridget		18	F	Laborer	07Ap02Im
MAUGHER, John		30	M	Laborer	07Ap02Im
MCCAVE, Bridy		28	F	Laborer	07Ap02Im
HIGGINS, Mary		28	F	Laborer	07Ap02Im
JORDEN, Thomas		22	M	Laborer	07Ap02Im
MALLAY, John		25	M	Laborer	07Ap02Im
HART, Thos.		19	M	Laborer	07Ap02Im
HOULDAN, Pat		40	M	Laborer	07Ap02Im
Margeret		35	F	Laborer	07Ap02Im
Wm.		01	M	Child	07Ap02Im
QUEEN, Richard		26	M	Laborer	07Ap02Im
NANULTON, Thos.		20	M	Laborer	07Ap02Im
BARNES, Mathew		34	M	Laborer	07Ap02Im
SANDS, James		24	M	Laborer	07Ap02Im
Mary		25	F	Laborer	07Ap02Im
CALLAGHER, Michael		26	M	Laborer	07Ap02Im
MOORE, Battle		29	M	Laborer	07Ap02Im
Eliza		23	F	Laborer	07Ap02Im
FILANNOREY, Daniel		35	M	Laborer	07Ap02Im
MARRA, James		28	M	Laborer	07Ap02Im
Alice		33	F	Laborer	07Ap02Im
HARRINGTON, Nicholas		25	M	Laborer	07Ap02Im
Thos.		20	M	Laborer	07Ap02Im
ONEIL, James		25	M	Laborer	07Ap02Im
Betsey		20	F	Laborer	07Ap02Im
MCDONNA, Patrick		50	M	Laborer	07Ap02Im
Owen		20	M	Laborer	07Ap02Im
Pat		17	M	Laborer	07Ap02Im
Thos.		13	M	Laborer	07Ap02Im
Michael		10	M	Laborer	07Ap02Im
WELCH, Peter		25	M	Laborer	07Ap02Im
CAMPBELL, Pat		25	M	Laborer	07Ap02Im
MCSHANE, Peter		25	M	Laborer	07Ap02Im
Wm.		13	M	Laborer	07Ap02Im
Ann		11	F	Laborer	07Ap02Im
ROWANNE, Thos.		28	M	Laborer	07Ap02Im
Michael		25	M	Laborer	07Ap02Im
BRENNAN, James		40	M	Laborer	07Ap02Im
LINNER, Lawrence		30	M	Laborer	07Ap02Im
Thedore		30	M	Laborer	07Ap02Im

JAMES-FAGAN 08 APRIL 1848

From Dublin

NAMES OF PASSENGERS		AGE	SEX	OCCUPATIONS	DATE PORT SHIP
KEARNES, Thos.		23	M	Laborer	08Ap20Jv
Daniel		20	M	Laborer	08Ap20Jv
James		15	M	Laborer	08Ap20Jv
MCARDELL, Peter		30	M	Mason	08Ap20Jv
LOUGHRAN, Jas.		40	M	Tailor	08Ap20Jv
Sarah		40	F	Unknown	08Ap20Jv
Mary		20	F	Unknown	08Ap20Jv
Michael		19	M	Tailor	08Ap20Jv
Sarah		05	F	Child	08Ap20Jv
Joseph		.00	M	Infant	08Ap20Jv

NAMES OF PASSENGERS	AGE	SEX	OCCUPATIONS	DATE PORT SHIP
NUILHALE, Mary	24	F	Spinster	08Ap20Jv
SMITH, Bridget	21	F	Spinster	08Ap20Jv
DOWD, John	21	M	Laborer	08Ap20Jv
Fanny	20	F	Spinster	08Ap20Jv
COSTELLO, Frank	25	M	Laborer	08Ap20Jv
Mary	20	F	Spinster	08Ap20Jv
Mary	20	F	Spinster	08Ap20Jv
DOYLE, Jas.	50	M	Laborer	08Ap20Jv
Jas.	18	M	Laborer	08Ap20Jv
ONEILL, John	36	M	Servant	08Ap20Jv
Richd.	27	M	Servant	08Ap20Jv
Mary	25	F	Servant	08Ap20Jv
Eliza	25	F	Servant	08Ap20Jv
John	.00	M	Infant	08Ap20Jv
SANDERS, John	28	M	Carpenter	08Ap20Jv
Eliza	25	F	Spinster	08Ap20Jv
DUNN, Edwd.	30	M	Laborer	08Ap20Jv
RICHMOND, Francis	20	M	Laborer	08Ap20Jv
Mary	20	F	Spinster	08Ap20Jv
ONEILL, Mary	20	F	Spinster	08Ap20Jv
COSTELLO, Mary	20	F	Spinster	08Ap20Jv
FITZPATRICK, Peter	30	M	Printer	08Ap20Jv
Hannah	25	F	Spinster	08Ap20Jv
Eliza	11	F	Spinster	08Ap20Jv
William	.03	M	Infant	08Ap20Jv
Margt.	04	F	Child	08Ap20Jv
Martha	00	F	Unknown	08Ap20Jv
TRACEY, Patt	30	M	Laborer	08Ap20Jv
FITZPATRICK, Jas.	22	M	Laborer	08Ap20Jv
ROGERSON, Ann	25	F	Laborer	08Ap20Jv
Essey	38	F	Spinster	08Ap20Jv
MASTERSON, Henry	44	M	Carpenter	08Ap20Jv
Eliza	38	F	Spinster	08Ap20Jv
HAMING, Mary-A.	18	F	Unknown	08Ap20Jv
CARTON, Williuam	38	M	Laborer	08Ap20Jv
William	17	M	Laborer	08Ap20Jv
Ann	38	F	Spinster	08Ap20Jv
Margt.A.	11	F	Spinster	08Ap20Jv
BUCKLEY, Harriett	25	F	Spinster	08Ap20Jv
COYLE, Stephen	40	M	Carpenter	08Ap20Jv
Jas.	12	M	Child	08Ap20Jv
BELAN, Michl.	19	M	Carpenter	08Ap20Jv
BULGER, Jas.	20	M	Carpenter	08Ap20Jv
DOYLES, John	20	M	Carpenter	08Ap20Jv
CEORBALLY, Richd.	23	M	Carpenter	08Ap20Jv
MURPHY, John	28	M	Carpenter	08Ap20Jv
Ann	26	F	Spinster	08Ap20Jv
DOWD, Mary	21	F	Spinster	08Ap20Jv
MATHEWS, Patrick	25	M	Laborer	08Ap20Jv
MORGAN, Bridget	30	F	Spinster	08Ap20Jv
MOHER, John	38	M	Carpenter	08Ap20Jv
Edwd.	07	M	Child	08Ap20Jv
COWLEY, Peter	26	M	Carpenter	08Ap20Jv
KEOGH, Patt	28	M	Carpenter	08Ap20Jv
Mary	28	F	Spinster	08Ap20Jv
Bridget	25	F	Spinster	08Ap20Jv
MUNTAGH, Peter	25	M	Laborer	08Ap20Jv
FITZCHARY, Wm.	28	M	Laborer	08Ap20Jv
Ann	28	F	Spinster	08Ap20Jv
GLENNON, Ann	14	F	Spinster	08Ap20Jv
HENREY, Thos.	20	M	Laborer	08Ap20Jv
Ann	15	F	Unknown	08Ap20Jv
Bridget	25	F	Unknown	08Ap20Jv
BUCKLEY, Francis	30	M	Laborer	08Ap20Jv
LAME, Mary	20	F	Spinster	08Ap20Jv
KARGH, John	25	M	Laborer	08Ap20Jv
Fanny	20	F	Spinster	08Ap20Jv
DARCEY, William	31	M	Laborer	08Ap20Jv
KEENAN, Mary	20	F	Spinster	08Ap20Jv
INGOLDSBY, Patt	45	M	Farmer	08Ap20Jv
HIGGINS, Martin	35	M	Farmer	08Ap20Jv
Cathe.	36	F	Spinster	08Ap20Jv
Sophia	22	F	Spinster	08Ap20Jv
Cathe.	20	F	Spinster	08Ap20Jv
Maria	17	F	Spinster	08Ap20Jv
HIGGINS, Margt.	08	F	Child	08Ap20Jv
BRADY, Jas.	28	M	Farmer	08Ap20Jv
HANAGAN, Stephan	28	M	Farmer	08Ap20Jv
SHEIL, Jas.	24	M	Farmer	08Ap20Jv
CONROY, Jas.	32	M	Farmer	08Ap20Jv
GALLAGHER, Cocelia	20	F	Spinster	08Ap20Jv
DOYLE, Patt	22	M	Laborer	08Ap20Jv
Lewis	18	M	Laborer	08Ap20Jv
LONETT, Chas.	25	M	Laborer	08Ap20Jv
Isabella	25	F	Unknown	08Ap20Jv
FORSYTH, Alex	20	M	Laborer	08Ap20Jv
MURPHEY, Thos.	40	M	Laborer	08Ap20Jv
Eliza	28	F	Spinster	08Ap20Jv
Michael	14	M	Servant	08Ap20Jv
Eliza	09	F	Child	08Ap20Jv
DOLAN, Peter	40	M	Unknown	08Ap20Jv
Mary	38	F	Spinster	08Ap20Jv
Michael	12	M	Servant	08Ap20Jv
Peter	08	M	Child	08Ap20Jv
Margt.A.	04	F	Child	08Ap20Jv
BARNETT, Alley	21	F	Spinster	08Ap20Jv
WALSH, John	20	M	Stctr	08Ap20Jv
Margt.	30	F	Unknown	08Ap20Jv
MAHER, Lawrence	30	M	Stctr	08Ap20Jv
CASSIDY, P.	18	M	Painter	08Ap20Jv
REILLY, Daniel	22	M	Painter	08Ap20Jv
Margt.	22	F	Spinster	08Ap20Jv
HERBERT, Eliza	18	F	Spinster	08Ap20Jv
Charlotte	30	F	Spinster	08Ap20Jv
CONNOR, Henry	18	M	Laborer	08Ap20Jv
EVANS, Henry	40	M	Laborer	08Ap20Jv
GLENNON, Pat	22	M	Laborer	08Ap20Jv
ARMSTONG, Thos.	15	M	Laborer	08Ap20Jv
BIRAGE, Jas.	18	M	Laborer	08Ap20Jv
DERMOTT, John	38	M	Laborer	08Ap20Jv
Righd.	19	M	Laborer	08Ap20Jv
MURPHY, Margt.	21	F	Spinster	08Ap20Jv
CLARKE, Patt	18	M	Laborer	08Ap20Jv
Mary	24	F	Spinster	08Ap20Jv
Mary	15	F	Spinster	08Ap20Jv
COYLE, Mary	40	F	Spinster	08Ap20Jv
Fanny	14	F	Spinster	08Ap20Jv
Wm.	04	M	Child	08Ap20Jv
NUGENT, John	30	M	Unknown	08Ap20Jv
Rebecca	26	F	Spinster	08Ap20Jv
DOYLE, John	25	M	Unknown	08Ap20Jv
CONLAN, Thos.	18	M	Unknown	08Ap20Jv
HORNE, Mary	30	F	Spinster	08Ap20Jv
William	15	M	Laborer	08Ap20Jv
BELL, William	24	M	Laborer	08Ap20Jv
Saml.	24	M	Laborer	08Ap20Jv
Jas.	21	M	Laborer	08Ap20Jv
MULHOLLAND, J.	26	M	Bricklayer	08Ap20Jv
LOAGAN, Mary	18	F	Spinster	08Ap20Jv
NEILL, John	20	M	Laborer	08Ap20Jv
Michl.	19	M	Laborer	08Ap20Jv
BRADEY, Denis	26	M	Laborer	08Ap20Jv
MURRAY, Andw.	30	M	Laborer	08Ap20Jv
DUFFY, Chas.	25	M	Laborer	08Ap20Jv
HULHART, Sophia	17	F	Spinster	08Ap20Jv
SMITH, Michl.	25	M	Laborer	08Ap20Jv
Ann	20	F	Laborer	08Ap20Jv
Robt.	.00	M	Infant	08Ap20Jv
MCDONAGH, P.	20	M	Laborer	08Ap20Jv
CORCORAN, John	20	M	Laborer	08Ap20Jv
BYRNES, P.	20	M	Laborer	08Ap20Jv
BRADLEY, John	24	M	Laborer	08Ap20Jv
BYRNE, Anthony	21	M	Laborer	08Ap20Jv
BURKE, John	24	M	Laborer	08Ap20Jv
DONNELLY, M.J.	40	M	Laborer	08Ap20Jv
KAVANAGH, Dora	20	F	Unknown	08Ap20Jv
GALLAGHER, J.O.	20	M	Laborer	08Ap20Jv
Danl.	24	M	Laborer	08Ap20Jv
MCKIN, John	22	M	Laborer	08Ap20Jv
FULERTON, Jas.	30	M	Laborer	08Ap20Jv

NAMES OF PASSENGERS		AGE	SEX	OCCUPATIONS	DATE PORT SHIP
FULERTON, Jas.		16	M	Laborer	08Ap20Jv
CRAVEN, Wm.		40	M	Laborer	08Ap20Jv
Ann		17	F	Spinster	08Ap20Jv
William		16	M	Servant	08Ap20Jv
MCLAUGHLIN, Hainett		10	M	Servant	08Ap20Jv
FLAGAN, Caht.		21	F	Servant	08Ap20Jv
GAFNEY, Mary		26	F	Servant	08Ap20Jv
WALDREN, George		30	M	Servant	08Ap20Jv
WIER, Peter		28	M	Servant	08Ap20Jv
BRADEY, U-Mrs.		40	F	Spinster	08Ap20Jv
Cathn.		23	F	Spinster	08Ap20Jv
Mary		21	F	Spinster	08Ap20Jv
Ann		17	F	Spinster	08Ap20Jv
EGAN, Mary		23	F	Spinster	08Ap20Jv
BYRNE, U-Mrs.		25	F	Spinster	08Ap20Jv
GRANT, Thos.		25	M	Laborer	08Ap20Jv
Margt.		28	F	Spinster	08Ap20Jv
BRIDE, John		25	M	Carpenter	08Ap20Jv
SMITH, John		22	M	Carpenter	08Ap20Jv
SHARKEY, Geo.		25	M	Carpenter	08Ap20Jv
LENNON, Matt		22	M	Carpenter	08Ap20Jv
MONTGOMERY, Mary		20	F	Spinster	08Ap20Jv
MURPHEY, Saml.		20	M	Laborer	08Ap20Jv
DOYLE, Eliza		21	F	Spinster	08Ap20Jv
Mary		18	F	Spinster	08Ap20Jv
CLARKE, Mary		35	F	Spinster	08Ap20Jv
DEVANE, Julia		20	F	Spinster	08Ap20Jv
WYNNE, Thos.		25	M	Carpenter	08Ap20Jv
MCGRATH, Mary		20	F	Spinster	08Ap20Jv
RENTONY, Mary		20	F	Spinster	08Ap20Jv
BURKE, Jas.		26	M	Laborer	08Ap20Jv
LEE, Ellen		20	F	Spinster	08Ap20Jv
STRONG, John		25	M	Carpenter	08Ap20Jv
CONSTANTINE, Ann		16	F	Spinster	08Ap20Jv
LONG, John		50	M	Laborer	08Ap20Jv
John		17	M	Laborer	08Ap20Jv
BROPHY, Geo.		25	M	Laborer	08Ap20Jv
U	(W)	25	F	Spinster	08Ap20Jv
CATLY, Richd.		25	M	Carpenter	08Ap20Jv
U	(W)	25	F	Spinster	08Ap20Jv
SPOLLEN, Eliza		25	F	Spinster	08Ap20Jv
SHEERAN, Eliza		25	F	Spinster	08Ap20Jv
DIMPSEY, Cath.		25	F	Spinster	08Ap20Jv
LOLIN, Joseph		25	M	Unknown	08Ap20Jv

HIBERNIA 10 APRIL 1848

From Liverpool

NAMES OF PASSENGERS	AGE	SEX	OCCUPATIONS	DATE PORT SHIP
EDMONSTON, U	32	M	Merchant	10Ap02Pb
RICHARDSON, John	60	M	Hospins	10Ap02Pb
RAE, U-Dr.	34	M	Surgeon	10Ap02Pb
CLEWS, James	54	M	Gentleman	10Ap02Pb
REID, U	38	M	Merchant	10Ap02Pb
SIMPSON, W.	23	M	Gentleman	10Ap02Pb
HOLLAND, U	54	M	Merchant	10Ap02Pb
EVANS, Jos.	27	M	Merchant	10Ap02Pb
MCKEAND, A.	28	M	Merchant	10Ap02Pb
HADWELL, U	30	M	Gentleman	10Ap02Pb
BONNIN, W.W.	30	M	Merchant	10Ap02Pb
DOHERTY, Jas.	25	M	Merchant	10Ap02Pb
ARMITAGE, Jas.	30	M	Merchant	10Ap02Pb
THOMAS, U	29	M	Merchant	10Ap02Pb
COOPER, U	38	M	Merchant	10Ap02Pb
NORTON, U	25	M	Merchant	10Ap02Pb
FLINN, U	27	M	Merchant	10Ap02Pb

AMBASSADRESS 10 APRIL 1848

From Cork

NAMES OF PASSENGERS	AGE	SEX	OCCUPATIONS	DATE PORT SHIP
CALLAGHAN, Mary	45	F	Spinster	10Ap14Kk
CAHILL, Hannora	25	F	Spinster	10Ap14Kk
MURPHY, Patrick	21	M	Laborer	10Ap14Kk
DONOGHUE, Daniel	18	M	Laborer	10Ap14Kk
Mary	22	F	Spinster	10Ap14Kk
REGAN, Jerry	22	M	Laborer	10Ap14Kk
CARTHY, Owen	15	M	Laborer	10Ap14Kk
KEOHANE, John	31	M	Laborer	10Ap14Kk
Died-At-Sea				
SHEEAN, Daniel	36	M	Laborer	10Ap14Kk
Catharine	30	F	Spinster	10Ap14Kk
CUNNINGHAM, James	38	M	Laborer	10Ap14Kk
Alice	35	F	Spinster	10Ap14Kk
John	00	M	Child	10Ap14Kk
Mary	00	F	Child	10Ap14Kk
Ellen	00	F	Child	10Ap14Kk
William-D.	00	M	Child	10Ap14Kk
Michael	00	M	Child	10Ap14Kk
EARLS, John	35	M	Laborer	10Ap14Kk
Catharine	35	F	Spinster	10Ap14Kk
Catharine	00	F	Child	10Ap14Kk
CAHILL, Edward	22	M	Laborer	10Ap14Kk
KELLY, John	33	M	Laborer	10Ap14Kk
SULLIVAN, Cornelius	22	M	Laborer	10Ap14Kk
OBRIEN, Richard	28	M	Laborer	10Ap14Kk
Ellen	28	F	Spinster	10Ap14Kk
CALLAGHAN, John-C.	40	M	Laborer	10Ap14Kk
Mary	40	F	Spinster	10Ap14Kk
John	00	M	Child	10Ap14Kk
Died-At-Sea				
Cornelius	04	M	Child	10Ap14Kk
EGAN, Andrew	44	M	Laborer	10Ap14Kk
Died-At-Sea				
SHEA, Michael	44	M	Laborer	10Ap14Kk
CULLMANE, John	20	M	Laborer	10Ap14Kk
Margt.	20	F	Spinster	10Ap14Kk
Judy	00	F	Child	10Ap14Kk
SHINNOCK, Thos.	24	M	Laborer	10Ap14Kk
SULLIVAN, Dennis	30	M	Laborer	10Ap14Kk
CONNOR, John	30	M	Laborer	10Ap14Kk
FLYNN, Michl.	30	M	Laborer	10Ap14Kk
DRAKE, Wm.	20	M	Laborer	10Ap14Kk
Richard	19	M	Laborer	10Ap14Kk
DOWLING, John	48	M	Laborer	10Ap14Kk
Mary	00	F	Spinster	10Ap14Kk
Ellen	00	F	Spinster	10Ap14Kk
Philip	17	M	Laborer	10Ap14Kk
Wm.	15	M	Laborer	10Ap14Kk
Thomas	00	M	Child	10Ap14Kk
Patrick	00	M	Child	10Ap14Kk
Mary	00	F	Child	10Ap14Kk
Thomas	00	M	Child	10Ap14Kk
Mary	00	F	Child	10Ap14Kk
John	00	M	Child	10Ap14Kk
RIORDAN, Owen	30	M	Laborer	10Ap14Kk
Catharine	00	F	Spinster	10Ap14Kk
MURPHY, Timothy	23	M	Laborer	10Ap14Kk
WALSH, James	24	M	Laborer	10Ap14Kk
Biddy	00	F	Spinster	10Ap14Kk
BRIEN, Dennis	22	M	Laborer	10Ap14Kk
OBRIEN, James	30	M	Laborer	10Ap14Kk
MURRY, Benjamin	30	M	Laborer	10Ap14Kk
LYONS, Patrick	30	M	Laborer	10Ap14Kk
MULLONE, Judy	00	F	Spinster	10Ap14Kk
SHEA, Catharine	00	F	Spinster	10Ap14Kk

NAMES OF PASSENGERS	AGE	SEX	OCCUPATIONS	DATE PORT SHIP
SHEA, Corneluis	17	M	Laborer	10Ap14Kk
Peggy	00	F	Spinster	10Ap14Kk
Died-At-Sea				
SULLIVAN, Dennis	25	M	Laborer	10Ap14Kk
Catharine	00	F	Spinster	10Ap14Kk
John	00	M	Child	10Ap14Kk
Patrick	00	M	Child	10Ap14Kk
BREHILL, Peter	20	M	Laborer	10Ap14Kk
BRIEN, Mary	00	F	Spinster	10Ap14Kk
Judy	00	F	Child	10Ap14Kk
MCCAN, Wm.	25	M	Engineer	10Ap14Kk
RIORDAN, Mary	00	F	Spinster	10Ap14Kk
SHEA, Patrick	28	M	Laborer	10Ap14Kk
BEVILLE, Joseph	35	M	Laborer	10Ap14Kk
Susanna	00	F	Spinster	10Ap14Kk
Charles	00	M	Child	10Ap14Kk
Melina	00	F	Child	10Ap14Kk
Joseph	00	M	Child	10Ap14Kk
U	.00	M	Infant	10Ap14Kk
WALSH, Johana	00	F	Spinster	10Ap14Kk
HUELEY, James	23	M	Laborer	10Ap14Kk
Mary	00	F	Spinster	10Ap14Kk
DONAVAN, Elizabeth	00	F	Spinster	10Ap14Kk
ROACH, David	21	M	Laborer	10Ap14Kk
CONNOR, Corneluis	21	M	Laborer	10Ap14Kk
GREEHY, Michael	36	M	Laborer	10Ap14Kk
FLYNN, Mary	00	F	Spinster	10Ap14Kk
BUCKLEY, William	36	M	Laborer	10Ap14Kk
Ellen	00	F	Spinster	10Ap14Kk
ROACH, Richard	25	M	Laborer	10Ap14Kk
Mary	00	F	Spinster	10Ap14Kk
Wm.	00	M	Child	10Ap14Kk
LEARY, Dennis	25	M	Laborer	10Ap14Kk
MCCONNEL, Ellen	00	F	Spinster	10Ap14Kk
Mary	00	F	Spinster	10Ap14Kk
Bridget	00	F	Child	10Ap14Kk
Johana	00	F	Child	10Ap14Kk
BUCKLEY, Michl.	00	M	Laborer	10Ap14Kk
WARNER, John	20	M	Laborer	10Ap14Kk
Sarah	00	F	Spinster	10Ap14Kk
CALLAGHAN, Thos.	00	M	Laborer	10Ap14Kk
COLLINS, Ellen	00	F	Spinster	10Ap14Kk
Died-At-Sea				
CALLAGHAN, Johana	00	F	Spinster	10Ap14Kk
HENESEY, Humphrey	30	M	Laborer	10Ap14Kk
LEARY, James	25	M	Laborer	10Ap14Kk
KEIFFE, Patrick	27	M	Laborer	10Ap14Kk
TRACY, Roger	29	M	Laborer	10Ap14Kk
PARKER, Susan	00	F	Spinster	10Ap14Kk
RYAN, Margaret	00	F	Spinster	10Ap14Kk
RIORDAN, Timothy	28	M	Laborer	10Ap14Kk
ROACH, Michael	28	M	Laborer	10Ap14Kk
GALLAVERN, Honora	00	F	Spinster	10Ap14Kk
COLLINS, Eliza	00	F	Spinster	10Ap14Kk
BUCKLEY, Jenny	28	F	Spinster	10Ap14Kk
HAYS, William	35	M	Laborer	10Ap14Kk
Pat	38	M	Laborer	10Ap14Kk
MORAN, James	28	M	Laborer	10Ap14Kk
HUILEY, Daniel	20	M	Laborer	10Ap14Kk
ROBINSON, John	25	M	Laborer	10Ap14Kk
WIILIAMSON, John	23	M	Laborer	10Ap14Kk
FOLEY, Patk.	25	M	Laborer	10Ap14Kk
MAHONY, Judy	25	F	Spinster	10Ap14Kk
SMITH, Bat.	24	M	Laborer	10Ap14Kk
ALLEN, Edward	36	M	Laborer	10Ap14Kk
Catharine	35	F	Spinster	10Ap14Kk
Mary	00	F	Spinster	10Ap14Kk
CUNNINGHAM, William	32	M	Laborer	10Ap14Kk
DROUGHT, Mary	00	F	Spinster	10Ap14Kk
MCNAMARA, Susan	00	F	Spinster	10Ap14Kk
FIX, John	38	M	Laborer	10Ap14Kk
Died-At-Sea				
Maria	00	F	Spinster	10Ap14Kk
HOWARD, George	40	M	Laborer	10Ap14Kk
William	00	M	Laborer	10Ap14Kk

NAMES OF PASSENGERS	AGE	SEX	OCCUPATIONS	DATE PORT SHIP
MULHEIN, Hugh	27	M	Laborer	10Ap14Kk
FINEM, Mat	29	M	Laborer	10Ap14Kk
DRAKE, Patk.	24	M	Laborer	10Ap14Kk
HANNIGAN, Thomas	20	M	Laborer	10Ap14Kk
MEEHAN, Mary	00	F	Spinster	10Ap14Kk
Wm.	00	M	Laborer	10Ap14Kk
LYNCH, Wm.	50	M	Laborer	10Ap14Kk
Died-At-Sea				
Ann	00	F	Spinster	10Ap14Kk
Alice	00	F	Spinster	10Ap14Kk
Betty	00	F	Spinster	10Ap14Kk
Catharine	0u	F	Spinster	10Ap14Kk
KEVI, William	38	M	Laborer	10Ap14Kk
GREGAN, Thomas	32	M	Laborer	10Ap14Kk
Jane	00	F	Spinster	10Ap14Kk
RYAN, Richard	24	M	Laborer	10Ap14Kk
MCGOVERN, Thos.	15	M	Laborer	10Ap14Kk
QUEENY, Biddy	00	F	Spinster	10Ap14Kk
NOWBAN, Patk.	19	M	Laborer	10Ap14Kk
MULLIGAN, Mary	00	F	Spinster	10Ap14Kk
LYONS, Robert	29	M	Laborer	10Ap14Kk
Eliza	00	F	Spinster	10Ap14Kk
John	00	M	Child	10Ap14Kk
Robt.	00	M	Child	10Ap14Kk
Richd.	00	M	Child	10Ap14Kk
GAHERN, Hugh	17	M	Laborer	10Ap14Kk
GONNAN, Patrick	25	M	Laborer	10Ap14Kk
HOPSON, Honey	00	F	Spinster	10Ap14Kk
GERATHY, Bridget	00	F	Spinster	10Ap14Kk
MCFEELY, Hugh	20	M	Laborer	10Ap14Kk
Died-At-Sea				
GERATHY, Eliza	00	F	Spinster	10Ap14Kk
MCFRYLEY, Rose	00	F	Spinster	10Ap14Kk
Ann	00	F	Child	10Ap14Kk
John	00	M	Child	10Ap14Kk
Eliza	00	F	Child	10Ap14Kk
WILSON, Jas.	40	M	Laborer	10Ap14Kk
GRITCHY, Thos.	20	M	Laborer	10Ap14Kk
Margt.	00	F	Spinster	10Ap14Kk
BRADLEY, John	50	M	Laborer	10Ap14Kk
GREEN, Michl.	28	M	Laborer	10Ap14Kk
Ellen	00	F	Spinster	10Ap14Kk
David	00	M	Laborer	10Ap14Kk
DOORAN, Thomas	30	M	Laborer	10Ap14Kk
MURPHY, Thomas	21	M	Laborer	10Ap14Kk
John	21	M	Laborer	10Ap14Kk
KEAN, Jas.	23	M	Laborer	10Ap14Kk
JONES, Jane	00	F	Spinster	10Ap14Kk
RAFTERY, Lary	28	M	Laborer	10Ap14Kk
Sally	00	F	Spinster	10Ap14Kk
POWELL, Pat	32	M	Laborer	10Ap14Kk
WALSH, Johana	00	F	Spinster	10Ap14Kk
Cath.	00	F	Spinster	10Ap14Kk
Michl.	14	M	Laborer	10Ap14Kk
OKEIFFE, Ellen	00	F	Spinster	10Ap14Kk
Daniel	00	M	Laborer	10Ap14Kk
Ann	00	F	Laborer	10Ap14Kk
CONDRON, Bess	10	F	Child	10Ap14Kk
CAMPBELL, Mary	00	F	Child	10Ap14Kk
ARMSTRONG, James	45	M	Laborer	10Ap14Kk
Rose	00	F	Child	10Ap14Kk
Honora	00	F	Child	10Ap14Kk
MEEHAN, Margaret	00	F	Spinster	10Ap14Kk
PRATT, Ellen	00	F	Spinster	10Ap14Kk
Robert	20	M	Laborer	10Ap14Kk
John	16	M	Laborer	10Ap14Kk
SMITH, Ellen	00	F	Spinster	10Ap14Kk
BALDWIN, Mary	00	F	Spinster	10Ap14Kk
DOYLE, Patrick	19	M	Laborer	10Ap14Kk
BRADY, Edward	20	M	Laborer	10Ap14Kk
Ann	00	F	Spinster	10Ap14Kk
RALY, Judy	00	F	Spinster	10Ap14Kk
RILEY, Thos.	18	M	Laborer	10Ap14Kk
Hugh	00	M	Laborer	10Ap14Kk
FOX, Thomas	60	M	Laborer	10Ap14Kk

NAMES OF PASSENGERS	AGE	SEX	OCCUPATIONS	DATE PORT SHIP
RULE, Edward	20	M	Laborer	10Ap14Kk
Catharine	00	F	Spinster	10Ap14Kk
CARTY, Timothy	40	M	Laborer	10Ap14Kk
MOONEY, Margaret	00	F	Spinster	10Ap14Kk
John	00	M	Child	10Ap14Kk
Margt.	00	F	Child	10Ap14Kk
James	00	M	Child	10Ap14Kk
KILEGREN, Richd.	40	M	Laborer	10Ap14Kk
John	00	M	Laborer	10Ap14Kk
LADEN, Susan	00	F	Spinster	10Ap14Kk
Rose	00	F	Child	10Ap14Kk
GRADY, Thos.	33	M	Laborer	10Ap14Kk
Daniel	16	M	Laborer	10Ap14Kk
Eliza	24	F	Spinster	10Ap14Kk
Mary	20	F	Spinster	10Ap14Kk
GORMAN, Honora	22	F	Spinster	10Ap14Kk
MAHER, Johana	25	F	Spinster	10Ap14Kk
CAHILL, Ellen	20	F	Spinster	10Ap14Kk
KEIFFE, Eliza	25	F	Spinster	10Ap14Kk
DEAPRY, Pat	25	M	Laborer	10Ap14Kk
HEALY, Pat	22	M	Laborer	10Ap14Kk
DOOLEY, John	27	M	Laborer	10Ap14Kk
BOURKE, Thomas	21	M	Laborer	10Ap14Kk
MCGAGHAN, Hugh	24	M	Laborer	10Ap14Kk
HUNTER, Francis	24	M	Laborer	10Ap14Kk
HARRY, Jane	20	F	Spinster	10Ap14Kk
IRVINE, Margaret	19	F	Spinster	10Ap14Kk
COONEY, Richard	30	M	Laborer	10Ap14Kk
FEDIGAN, Edward	20	M	Laborer	10Ap14Kk
HEAVY, Darby	42	M	Laborer	10Ap14Kk
Ellen	40	F	Spinster	10Ap14Kk
Patk.	00	M	Laborer	10Ap14Kk
Betsey	00	F	Child	10Ap14Kk
Biddy	00	F	Child	10Ap14Kk
Alice	00	F	Child	10Ap14Kk
MORRISY, Thos	35	M	Laborer	10Ap14Kk
COONY, Mary	16	F	Spinster	10Ap14Kk
GARY, John	30	M	Laborer	10Ap14Kk
MAGRATH, Cath.	25	F	Spinster	10Ap14Kk
BUCKLEY, John	22	M	Laborer	10Ap14Kk
Esther	26	F	Spinster	10Ap14Kk
BYRNE, Mary	20	F	Spinster	10Ap14Kk
WARD, Patk.	00	M	Laborer	10Ap14Kk
Cath.	00	F	Spinster	10Ap14Kk
MEEHAN, Cath.	00	F	Spinster	10Ap14Kk
Nancy	00	F	Child	10Ap14Kk
U, Bernard	19	M	Laborer	10Ap14Kk
FALLON, John	25	M	Laborer	10Ap14Kk
CARRON, Margt.	00	F	Spinster	10Ap14Kk
Margt.	00	F	Child	10Ap14Kk
KELLY, Christopher	38	M	Laborer	10Ap14Kk
Michael	14	M	Laborer	10Ap14Kk
MILLER, Nathan	24	M	Laborer	10Ap14Kk
BYRNES, John	27	M	Laborer	10Ap14Kk
KEAN, Patk.	24	M	Laborer	10Ap14Kk
Eliza	24	F	Spinster	10Ap14Kk
WOLLAGHAN, John	20	M	Laborer	10Ap14Kk
Joseph	20	M	Laborer	10Ap14Kk
Benjamin	21	M	Laborer	10Ap14Kk
Richd.	17	M	Laborer	10Ap14Kk
Maryann	00	F	Child	10Ap14Kk
Charlotte	00	F	Child	10Ap14Kk
Charlotte	00	F	Child	10Ap14Kk
Robert	00	M	Child	10Ap14Kk
Margt.	00	F	Child	10Ap14Kk
DOYLD, Pat	18	M	Laborer	10Ap14Kk
SCANLAN, Ann	00	F	Child	10Ap14Kk
Wrinkle-BURKE, Jas.	00	M	Child	10Ap14Kk
FEENY, Ann	00	F	Child	10Ap14Kk
Bridget	00	F	Child	10Ap14Kk
REGAN, Con.	40	M	Laborer	10Ap14Kk
Cath.	40	F	Spinster	10Ap14Kk
Jas.	00	M	Child	10Ap14Kk
John	00	M	Child	10Ap14Kk
BULGER, Edward	30	M	Laborer	10Ap14Kk
BULGER, Ellen	30	F	Spinster	10Ap14Kk
Jane	12	F	Spinster	10Ap14Kk
FITZPATRICK, Mary	50	F	Spinster	10Ap14Kk
John	08	M	Child	10Ap14Kk
HORAN, Michl.	22	M	Laborer	10Ap14Kk
COLLAGHAN, Maria	21	F	Spinster	10Ap14Kk
KELLY, Cath.	20	F	Spinster	10Ap14Kk
DINEEN, Michl.	20	M	Laborer	10Ap14Kk
Michl.	27	M	Laborer	10Ap14Kk
HOLMES, Thomas	24	M	Laborer	10Ap14Kk
ARMSTRONG, John	27	M	Laborer	10Ap14Kk
WALLACE, Thos.	24	M	Laborer	10Ap14Kk
Honora	28	F	Spinster	10Ap14Kk
MAGENIS, Mary	19	F	Spinster	10Ap14Kk
STAPELTON, Pat	28	M	Laborer	10Ap14Kk
DEVERELL, Sarelton	19	M	Laborer	10Ap14Kk
MAGRUIK, Michl.	27	M	Laborer	10Ap14Kk
Cath.	00	F	Spinster	10Ap14Kk
DONOHOE, Cath.	00	F	Spinster	10Ap14Kk
FERGUSON, Danl.	45	M	Laborer	10Ap14Kk
MEADOWS, John	25	M	Laborer	10Ap14Kk
BLAKELY, Ellen	27	F	Spinster	10Ap14Kk
MCLOUGHLAN, Thos.	28	M	Laborer	10Ap14Kk
Jas.	24	M	Laborer	10Ap14Kk
HACKETT, Martin	24	M	Laborer	10Ap14Kk
Catharine	22	F	Spinster	10Ap14Kk
POUGH, Eliza	22	F	Spinster	10Ap14Kk
KITSON, Bridget	00	F	Child	10Ap14Kk
John	00	M	Child	10Ap14Kk
Margaret	00	F	Child	10Ap14Kk
Thomas	00	M	Child	10Ap14Kk
LELLIS, Thomas	00	M	Child	10Ap14Kk
STAFFORD, Peter	00	M	Child	10Ap14Kk

CHINA 13 APRIL 1848

From Liverpool

NAMES OF PASSENGERS	AGE	SEX	OCCUPATIONS	DATE PORT SHIP
CUMMINS, James	27	M	Laborer	13Ap02Kn
REILY, John	32	M	Laborer	13Ap02Kn
COADY, Thos.	20	M	Laborer	13Ap02Kn
John	24	M	Laborer	13Ap02Kn
Ellen	20	F	Spinster	13Ap02Kn
CONISKY, Patrick	24	M	Laborer	13Ap02Kn
Alice	20	F	Spinster	13Ap02Kn
ROURK, Elen	16	F	Spinster	13Ap02Kn
PHILLIPS, John	28	M	Miner	13Ap02Kn
WATKINS, William	34	M	Miner	13Ap02Kn
LEWIS, David	22	M	Miner	13Ap02Kn
READY, Bridet	25	F	Spinster	13Ap02Kn
GERRILL, Robert	00	M	Wmnftr	13Ap02Kn
ODONNELL, Neil	24	M	Laborer	13Ap02Kn
LOUGHNEY, James	24	M	Laborer	13Ap02Kn
HOWARD, John	20	M	Shoemaker	13Ap02Kn
SPILANE, James	30	M	Shoemaker	13Ap02Kn
REGAN, Susan	23	F	Dressmaker	13Ap02Kn
HUGHES, Peter	40	M	Stone Mason	13Ap02Kn
Jane	30	F	Unknown	13Ap02Kn
U	.00	U	Infant	13Ap02Kn
KELLY, Cath.	40	F	Spinster	13Ap02Kn
Nancy	15	F	Spinster	13Ap02Kn
FREMAN, William	27	M	Miner	13Ap02Kn
DANIEL, Thomas	25	M	Miner	13Ap02Kn
Dina	24	F	Unknown	13Ap02Kn
U	.00	U	Infant	13Ap02Kn
EDWARDS, Daniel	24	M	Miner	13Ap02Kn
ARMSTRONG, James	34	M	Laborer	13Ap02Kn
Ellen	30	F	Unknown	13Ap02Kn
U	.00	U	Infant	13Ap02Kn

NAMES OF PASSENGERS	AGE	SEX	OCCUPATIONS	DATE PORT SHIP
RMSTRONG, Luke	12	M	Child	13Ap02Kn
Francis	25	M	Laborer	13Ap02Kn
ARROLL, Michl.	24	M	Laborer	13Ap02Kn
Margrt.	20	F	Spinster	13Ap02Kn
ARREL, Michl.	24	M	Laborer	13Ap02Kn
Mary	14	F	Spinster	13Ap02Kn
CGINN, Edward	40	M	Joiner	13Ap02Kn
U (W)	34	F	Unknown	13Ap02Kn
U	.00	U	Infant	13Ap02Kn
OONAN, Edwd.	48	M	Joiner	13Ap02Kn
Michl.	24	M	Joiner	13Ap02Kn
Catherine	18	F	Midwife	13Ap02Kn
U	.00	U	Infant	13Ap02Kn
Ellen	16	F	Unknown	13Ap02Kn
Ann	05	F	Child	13Ap02Kn
ARRINGTON, Ellen	16	F	Laborer	13Ap02Kn
REMAN, Owen	40	M	Laborer	13Ap02Kn
U (W)	36	F	Laborer	13Ap02Kn
John	12	M	Spinner	13Ap02Kn
Ann	08	F	Spinster	13Ap02Kn
ORMON, Ann	18	F	Spinster	13Ap02Kn
ALL, Gilbert	24	M	Spinster	13Ap02Kn
EATY, Daniel	24	M	Spinster	13Ap02Kn
OMERS, Thomas	20	M	Spinster	13Ap02Kn
U	.00	U	Infant	13Ap02Kn
ALTON, Marten	40	U	Infant	13Ap02Kn
U (W)	36	F	Unknown	13Ap02Kn
Garrett	20	M	Spinner	13Ap02Kn
James	17	M	Bricklayer	13Ap02Kn
ILSON, Eliza	23	F	Laborer	13Ap02Kn
EMON, Mary	25	F	Spinster	13Ap02Kn
RONIN, Daniel	36	M	Wool Comber	13Ap02Kn
ALLAGHAR, Ellen	18	F	Spinster	13Ap02Kn
Bridget	19	F	Spinster	13Ap02Kn
Honora	17	F	Spinster	13Ap02Kn
ROWE, Peter	24	M	Clerk	13Ap02Kn
CNALLY, Patk.	24	M	Baker	13Ap02Kn
EDREDGE, Mary	35	F	Servant	13Ap02Kn
ONNELE, Patk.	22	M	Laborer	13Ap02Kn
Margt.	23	F	Servant	13Ap02Kn
ONNINGHANSEN, U	23	M	Tailor	13Ap02Kn
MITH, Ann	30	F	Unknown	13Ap02Kn
U	.00	U	Infant	13Ap02Kn
Margt.	03	F	Child	13Ap02Kn
ITZGERALD, Thos.	24	M	Laborer	13Ap02Kn
YNCH, Maurice	23	M	Laborer	13Ap02Kn
USELL, Nicholas	23	M	Laborer	13Ap02Kn
SH, John	20	M	Laborer	13Ap02Kn
OY, James	20	M	Laborer	13Ap02Kn
RAHAM, Timothy	40	M	Laborer	13Ap02Kn
Patrick	13	M	Laborer	13Ap02Kn
ONNOR, Thos.	21	M	Laborer	13Ap02Kn
ONG, Nelly	20	F	Spinster	13Ap02Kn
ONNER, Norry	22	M	Spinner	13Ap02Kn
EVAN, Nancy	21	F	Spinster	13Ap02Kn
ARTIN, John	40	M	Laborer	13Ap02Kn
ARRETT, Thos.	22	M	Painter	13Ap02Kn
Mary	23	F	Painter	13Ap02Kn
ITZPATRICK, James	30	M	Laborer	13Ap02Kn
YRNE, Patrick	20	M	Unknown	13Ap02Kn
Died-At-Sea				
RADY, Alice	22	F	Spinster	13Ap02Kn
CMAHON, Rose	16	F	Spinster	13Ap02Kn
ENEY, Dennis	34	M	Laborer	13Ap02Kn
USSEY, John	30	M	Laborer	13Ap02Kn
Julia	32	F	Laborer	13Ap02Kn
Patrick	01	M	Unknown	13Ap02Kn
SHEEHY, Thomas	22	M	Laborer	13Ap02Kn
BOARDMAN, David	33	M	Tailor	13Ap02Kn
ONKERAN, Thomas	35	M	Laborer	13Ap02Kn
MARTIN, Daniel	26	M	Laborer	13Ap02Kn
SCANLAN, Magaret	20	F	Unknown	13Ap02Kn
Died-At-Sea				
HINLY, Patrick	35	M	Laborer	13Ap02Kn
Catherine	25	F	Spinster	13Ap02Kn

NAMES OF PASSENGERS	AGE	SEX	OCCUPATIONS	DATE PORT SHIP
MULICK, Patrick	13	M	Laborer	13Ap02Kn
Bridget	15	F	Spinster	13Ap02Kn
HYMAN, Thos.	40	M	Laborer	13Ap02Kn
Mary	16	F	Spinster	13Ap02Kn
Margt.	15	F	Spinster	13Ap02Kn
SOMERS, Hugh	27	M	Laborer	13Ap02Kn
Mary	24	F	Laborer	13Ap02Kn
STANTON, David	25	M	Laborer	13Ap02Kn
Rodger	30	M	Laborer	13Ap02Kn
Mary	20	F	Spinster	13Ap02Kn
SMIDDY, David	30	M	Laborer	13Ap02Kn
BURKE, Patrick	00	M	Laborer	13Ap02Kn
Michael	06	M	Child	13Ap02Kn
LOUGHRAN, James	30	M	Coachman	13Ap02Kn
Ann	25	F	Spinster	13Ap02Kn
CAMINS, Mar.	25	F	Spinster	13Ap02Kn
RONANS, Thos.	40	M	Spinner	13Ap02Kn
John	22	M	Laborer	13Ap02Kn
William	14	M	Laborer	13Ap02Kn
Mary	20	F	Spinster	13Ap02Kn
LAUGHRAN, Jane	00	F	Spinster	13Ap02Kn
RONANS, Julia	08	F	Child	13Ap02Kn
David	14	M	Unknown	13Ap02Kn
Thomas	00	M	Unknown	13Ap02Kn
FAY, Michael	20	M	Laborer	13Ap02Kn
CLARKE, Patrick	25	M	Laborer	13Ap02Kn
Julia	30	F	Unknown	13Ap02Kn
U	.00	U	Infant	13Ap02Kn
Michael	02	M	Child	13Ap02Kn
FAVERLY, Bernard	20	M	Laborer	13Ap02Kn
SLAVIN, John	30	M	Laborer	13Ap02Kn
Ann	26	F	Unknown	13Ap02Kn
U	.00	U	Infant	13Ap02Kn
Ann	09	F	Child	13Ap02Kn
James	03	M	Child	13Ap02Kn
Mary	18	F	Spinster	13Ap02Kn
HAWLEY, Michael	30	M	Laborer	13Ap02Kn
Rose	22	F	Unknown	13Ap02Kn
U	.00	U	Infant	13Ap02Kn
Mary	03	F	Child	13Ap02Kn
CORMICK, Catherine	18	F	Spinster	13Ap02Kn
CARRY, Eliza	18	F	Spinster	13Ap02Kn
BROWNING, John	22	M	Laborer	13Ap02Kn
Michael	20	M	Laborer	13Ap02Kn
Ann	15	F	Spinster	13Ap02Kn
GILUAN, James	20	M	Laborer	13Ap02Kn
MATHEW, James	20	M	Laborer	13Ap02Kn
HILL, Wm.	30	M	Tailor	13Ap02Kn
HOPKINS, Thos.	22	M	Baker	13Ap02Kn
U (W)	20	F	Unknown	13Ap02Kn
KAY, Thomas	22	M	Laborer	13Ap02Kn
WRIGHT, Ann	20	F	Spinster	13Ap02Kn
GALAGAN, Julia	21	F	Spinster	13Ap02Kn
ROCHE, Francis	20	M	Plasterer	13Ap02Kn
BECKWITH, William	24	M	Wheelwright	13Ap02Kn
BRADBERRY, Chas.	25	M	Silk Weaver	13Ap02Kn
CLARKE, Patrick	30	M	Laborer	13Ap02Kn
Fanny	21	F	Unknown	13Ap02Kn
U	.00	U	Infant	13Ap02Kn
Owen	40	M	Gdnr	13Ap02Kn
Margaret	09	F	Unknown	13Ap02Kn
Julia	13	F	Unknown	13Ap02Kn
Eliza	02	F	Unknown	13Ap02Kn
DELUCIA, John	33	M	Laborer	13Ap02Kn
U (W)	33	F	Unknown	13Ap02Kn
U	.00	U	Infant	13Ap02Kn
James	02	M	Unknown	13Ap02Kn
Mary	40	F	Spinster	13Ap02Kn
CONNOR, Edward	30	M	Laborer	13Ap02Kn
MARTIN, Thos.	30	M	Laborer	13Ap02Kn
Julia	28	F	Unknown	13Ap02Kn
U	.00	U	Infant	13Ap02Kn
BUTLER, Thos.	25	M	Laborer	13Ap02Kn
TRAVERS, Mary	25	F	Servant	13Ap02Kn
U	.00	U	Infant	13Ap02Kn

NAMES OF PASSENGERS		AGE	SEX	OCCUPATIONS	DATE PORT SHIP
MARTIN, Julia		30	F	Servant	13Ap02Kn
HUGHES, Cath.		00	F	Servant	13Ap02Kn
Daniel		08	M	Unknown	13Ap02Kn
Thomas		06	M	Unknown	13Ap02Kn
FARRELL, Mary		60	F	Servant	13Ap02Kn
Patrick		29	M	Laborer	13Ap02Kn
Edward		11	M	Laborer	13Ap02Kn
Eliza		08	F	Unknown	13Ap02Kn
REANS, John		21	M	Baker	13Ap02Kn
DUGAN, Bridget		20	F	Spinster	13Ap02Kn
SIMMONS, Ja.		21	M	Laborer	13Ap02Kn
Ellen		18	F	Servant	13Ap02Kn
Mary		10	F	Servant	13Ap02Kn
MAHON, Nicholas		21	M	Laborer	13Ap02Kn
HOWARD, Ellen		14	F	Dressmaker	13Ap02Kn
FEULEY, David		22	M	Laborer	13Ap02Kn
FINLY, Mary		24	F	Servant	13Ap02Kn
CREIGH, W.		02	M	Weaver	13Ap02Kn
CONDOR, Bridget		20	F	Servant	13Ap02Kn
DONAVAN, Ellen		23	F	Dressmaker	13Ap02Kn
TRAVERS, Bridget		25	F	Servant	13Ap02Kn
HUSSEY, Bartholomew		02	M	Child	13Ap02Kn
Died-At-Sea					
HUGHES, Ellen		01	F	Child	13Ap02Kn
Died-At-Sea					
ARMSTRONG, John		01	M	Child	13Ap02Kn
Died-At-Sea					

SULTANA 13 APRIL 1848

From Liverpool

NAMES OF PASSENGERS		AGE	SEX	OCCUPATIONS	DATE PORT SHIP
JOHNSTONE, James		45	M	Laborer	13Ap02Kt
Mary		40	F	Unknown	13Ap02Kt
Jane		13	F	Unknown	13Ap02Kt
Ann		02	F	Unknown	13Ap02Kt
CLARK, Bess		20	F	Unknown	13Ap02Kt
DRIVER, Wm.		32	M	Unknown	13Ap02Kt
Hester		32	F	Unknown	13Ap02Kt
Selina		15	F	Unknown	13Ap02Kt
Mary-Ann		11	F	Unknown	13Ap02Kt
Charles		29	M	Unknown	13Ap02Kt
Ann		27	F	Unknown	13Ap02Kt
U		.00	F	Infant	13Ap02Kt
ANDREWS, Fredr.		30	M	Laborer	13Ap02Kt
EDWARDS, John		35	M	Laborer	13Ap02Kt
NALLY, Saml.		27	M	Laborer	13Ap02Kt
Mary		27	F	Laborer	13Ap02Kt
Mary		05	F	Laborer	13Ap02Kt
BROWN, J.		20	F	Laborer	13Ap02Kt
MCGOLICK, Joseph		18	M	Laborer	13Ap02Kt
Sarah		16	M	Laborer	13Ap02Kt
REILLY, Dennis		16	M	Laborer	13Ap02Kt
CONWAY, U-Mrs.		25	F	Laborer	13Ap02Kt
Michael		27	M	Laborer	13Ap02Kt
U	(W)	22	F	Laborer	13Ap02Kt
Danl.		22	M	Laborer	13Ap02Kt
James		15	M	Laborer	13Ap02Kt
James		10	M	Laborer	13Ap02Kt
PEEL, James		29	M	Laborer	13Ap02Kt
KENWORTHY, John		36	M	Laborer	13Ap02Kt
TAYLOR, Wm.		30	M	Laborer	13Ap02Kt
KELES, Thos.		25	M	Laborer	13Ap02Kt
HARKET, Andr.		20	M	Laborer	13Ap02Kt
CONWAY, Mgt.		06	F	Laborer	13Ap02Kt
TOY, Jos.		54	M	Laborer	13Ap02Kt
Wm.		44	M	Laborer	13Ap02Kt
SHEVLIN, Michl.		50	M	Laborer	13Ap02Kt
U	(W)	50	F	Laborer	13Ap02Kt
Died-At-Sea					
Wm.		22	M	Laborer	13Ap02Kt
Biddy		20	F	Laborer	13Ap02Kt
James		12	M	Child	13Ap02Kt
DOWNEY, James		20	M	Laborer	13Ap02Kt
SUNDRAN, Brigt		25	F	Wife	13Ap02Kt
MCBORAN, Margt.		20	F	Unknown	13Ap02Kt
KELLY, Pat		19	M	Laborer	13Ap02Kt
MCGUARE, Bernd.		24	M	Laborer	13Ap02Kt
Died-At-Sea					
HENNAN, Chas.		32	M	Laborer	13Ap02Kt
Elizth.		30	F	Wife	13Ap02Kt
Eliz.		05	F	Child	13Ap02Kt
JOICE, Michl.		40	M	Laborer	13Ap02Kt
Edwd.		50	M	Laborer	13Ap02Kt
Miles		12	M	Laborer	13Ap02Kt
GIBLIN, Cathr.		50	F	Laborer	13Ap02Kt
John		21	M	Laborer	13Ap02Kt
MEALY, Patr.		40	M	Laborer	13Ap02Kt
Michl.		10	M	Laborer	13Ap02Kt
John		08	M	Laborer	13Ap02Kt
MARKHAM, James		25	M	Laborer	13Ap02Kt
OBRIEN, Edwd.		18	M	Laborer	13Ap02Kt
DALY, Dennis		30	M	Laborer	13Ap02Kt
Died-At-Sea					
MCGARRD, Wm.		18	M	Laborer	13Ap02Kt
MCCORMICK, Pat		20	M	Laborer	13Ap02Kt
YORK, Bess		20	F	Laborer	13Ap02Kt
DUCKE, Julia		26	F	Wife	13Ap02Kt
Michl.		06	M	Child	13Ap02Kt
Margt.		03	F	Child	13Ap02Kt
Cath.		.00	F	Infant	13Ap02Kt
Died-At-Sea					
FEENY, Pat		30	M	Laborer	13Ap02Kt
Mary		20	F	None	13Ap02Kt
Ann		18	F	Spinster	13Ap02Kt
John		12	M	None	13Ap02Kt
Bridgt.		10	F	None	13Ap02Kt
DOLAN, Biddy		35	F	None	13Ap02Kt
FALLEN, Michl.		35	M	None	13Ap02Kt
Died-At-Sea					
MCLOUGHLIN, John		25	M	None	13Ap02Kt
NANERY, Thos.		25	M	Laborer	13Ap02Kt
MCKENNAY, Danl.		35	M	Laborer	13Ap02Kt
GALLAGHER, John		27	M	Laborer	13Ap02Kt
ROONEY, John		24	M	Laborer	13Ap02Kt
BURNS, Arthur		30	M	Laborer	13Ap02Kt
BRESLIN, Charles		25	M	Laborer	13Ap02Kt
Cath.	(W)	20	F	None	13Ap02Kt
U		.00	U	Infant	13Ap02Kt
John		17	M	Laborer	13Ap02Kt
Ellen		18	F	None	13Ap02Kt
Sally		16	F	None	13Ap02Kt
GAVIN, John		22	M	Laborer	13Ap02Kt
James		17	M	Laborer	13Ap02Kt
GALLAGHER, Pat		15	M	Laborer	13Ap02Kt
Ann	(W)	20	F	None	13Ap02Kt
MCGURN, Andw.		27	M	Laborer	13Ap02Kt
MCDONNELL, Owen		31	M	Laborer	13Ap02Kt
BOYLE, Thomas		34	M	Laborer	13Ap02Kt
BRESLIN, John		22	M	Laborer	13Ap02Kt
GALLAGHER, Mary		20	F	Laborer	13Ap02Kt
THEVLIN, Danl.		24	M	Laborer	13Ap02Kt
Dennis		22	M	Laborer	13Ap02Kt
MCCURL, Thos.		22	M	Laborer	13Ap02Kt
MCCABE, Bernd.		28	M	Laborer	13Ap02Kt
Ann		26	F	Laborer	13Ap02Kt
U		.00	U	Infant	13Ap02Kt
Owen		16	M	Laborer	13Ap02Kt
Charles		14	M	Laborer	13Ap02Kt
RODGERS, Michl.		30	M	Laborer	13Ap02Kt
DENAN, James		36	M	Laborer	13Ap02Kt
MCNAMARA, Mary		26	F	Laborer	13Ap02Kt
RODGERS, Pat		21	M	Laborer	13Ap02Kt

NAMES OF PASSENGERS	AGE	SEX	OCCUPATIONS	DATE PORT SHIP
SCANLON, John	25	M	Laborer	13Ap02Kt
DEWITT, Francis	15	M	Laborer	13Ap02Kt
Bernd.	18	M	Laborer	13Ap02Kt
DONNELLY, James	25	M	Laborer	13Ap02Kt
BURKE, Walter	36	M	Laborer	13Ap02Kt
Bridgt.	13	F	Spinster	13Ap02Kt
DWYER, Pat	32	M	Laborer	13Ap02Kt
Ann (W)	26	F	Unknown	13Ap02Kt
COLLINS, Michl.	20	M	Laborer	13Ap02Kt
Jim	24	M	Laborer	13Ap02Kt
FITZGERALD, James	28	M	Laborer	13Ap02Kt
MCGUINESS, Owen	28	M	Laborer	13Ap02Kt
BRADY, Mary	20	F	Laborer	13Ap02Kt
SMITH, Mary	21	F	Laborer	13Ap02Kt
REAGON, Thos.	19	M	Laborer	13Ap02Kt
DUFFY, Mary	20	F	Laborer	13Ap02Kt
KELLY, Pat	24	M	Laborer	13Ap02Kt
Celia	28	F	Laborer	13Ap02Kt
MURPHY, Bridgt.	24	F	Laborer	13Ap02Kt
FITZSIMMONS, John	21	M	Laborer	13Ap02Kt
DUFFY, Edwd.	26	M	Laborer	13Ap02Kt
CAREY, Wm.	36	M	Laborer	13Ap02Kt
Peggy	30	F	Laborer	13Ap02Kt
Wm.	06	M	Child	13Ap02Kt
John	03	M	Child	13Ap02Kt
Nicholas	01	M	Child	13Ap02Kt
STANTON, Charles	36	M	Laborer	13Ap02Kt
MURPHY, Michl.	32	M	Laborer	13Ap02Kt
HENDERSON, John	32	M	Laborer	13Ap02Kt
Sarah-Ann	15	F	Spinster	13Ap02Kt
William	13	M	None	13Ap02Kt
Saml.	10	M	Laborer	13Ap02Kt
JUDGE, Geo.	18	M	Laborer	13Ap02Kt
Arthur	20	M	Laborer	13Ap02Kt
FLANNAGAN, Thos.	22	M	Laborer	13Ap02Kt
Christ.	18	M	Laborer	13Ap02Kt
HACKETT, Wm.	25	M	Laborer	13Ap02Kt
DROOK, John	25	M	Laborer	13Ap02Kt
SHERIDAN, Martin	21	M	Laborer	13Ap02Kt
THOMPSON, John	50	M	Laborer	13Ap02Kt
POTTERS, James	35	M	Laborer	13Ap02Kt
VAUGHEN, Peter	23	M	Laborer	13Ap02Kt
MCKEIRNAN, John	32	M	Laborer	13Ap02Kt
CRAVEN, Thos.	32	M	Laborer	13Ap02Kt
WRIGLEY, Abram	32	M	Laborer	13Ap02Kt
JACKSON, John	25	M	Laborer	13Ap02Kt
MILLY, Martin	20	M	Laborer	13Ap02Kt
Jane	18	F	Spinster	13Ap02Kt
BYRNE, John	30	M	None	13Ap02Kt
Betty	30	F	None	13Ap02Kt
Margt.	10	F	None	13Ap02Kt
Mary	08	F	Child	13Ap02Kt
Ann	.00	F	Infant	13Ap02Kt
Pat	38	M	Laborer	13Ap02Kt
Rose (W)	30	F	None	13Ap02Kt
Mary	12	F	None	13Ap02Kt
Margt.	10	F	None	13Ap02Kt
Andrew	06	M	Child	13Ap02Kt
John	04	M	Child	13Ap02Kt
Peter	.00	M	Infant	13Ap02Kt
Bbryan	36	M	None	13Ap02Kt
Ellen (W)	34	F	None	13Ap02Kt
Mary	04	F	Child	13Ap02Kt
Margt.	.00	F	Infant	13Ap02Kt
CALLEN, Mary	40	F	None	13Ap02Kt
Ann	14	F	None	13Ap02Kt
James	12	M	None	13Ap02Kt
John	09	M	Child	13Ap02Kt
COLLINS, James	20	M	Laborer	13Ap02Kt
BRENTON, Frank	25	M	Laborer	13Ap02Kt
Sally	24	F	Laborer	13Ap02Kt
Joel	18	M	Laborer	13Ap02Kt
HINKS, Thos.	30	M	Laborer	13Ap02Kt
HASTINGS, Hugh	17	M	Laborer	13Ap02Kt
Mary (W)	50	F	Wife	13Ap02Kt
HASTINGS, James	21	M	Laborer	13Ap02Kt
Thomas	19	M	Laborer	13Ap02Kt
Jane	18	F	Spinster	13Ap02Kt
Mile	11	M	None	13Ap02Kt
Patk.	08	M	Child	13Ap02Kt
Henry	20	M	None	13Ap02Kt
REID, John	19	M	Laborer	13Ap02Kt
Betsey	16	F	Spinster	13Ap02Kt
BREADON, Margt.	18	F	Spinster	13Ap02Kt
Mary	17	F	Spinster	13Ap02Kt
JOHNSTON, Betsey	40	F	Spinster	13Ap02Kt
NEILLY, Bella	20	F	Spinster	13Ap02Kt
ROONEY, Thomas	18	M	None	13Ap02Kt
KNOWLES, John	30	M	Laborer	13Ap02Kt
Julia	30	F	None	13Ap02Kt
CULLEN, Michl.	35	M	None	13Ap02Kt
Mary	30	F	None	13Ap02Kt
SMITH, Thos.	27	M	Laborer	13Ap02Kt
Bridgt.	25	F	Laborer	13Ap02Kt
James	24	M	Laborer	13Ap02Kt
BERNARD, John	20	M	Laborer	13Ap02Kt
HOGAN, Peter	40	M	Laborer	13Ap02Kt
DOWNY, Thos.	24	M	Laborer	13Ap02Kt
HALBERT, Jos.	24	M	Laborer	13Ap02Kt
NARYLAND, James	27	M	Laborer	13Ap02Kt
FEGAN, James	27	M	Laborer	13Ap02Kt
Matth.	28	M	Laborer	13Ap02Kt
Farrell	20	M	Laborer	13Ap02Kt
Cath.	22	F	Wife	13Ap02Kt
DOOLAN, Bartly	22	M	Laborer	13Ap02Kt
Alice	20	F	Laborer	13Ap02Kt
HANAPHY, Michl.	30	M	Laborer	13Ap02Kt
HAFFORD, John	30	M	Laborer	13Ap02Kt
PIGGOTT, James	26	M	Laborer	13Ap02Kt
MAHER, Mary	20	F	Laborer	13Ap02Kt
ANDERSON, John	40	M	Laborer	13Ap02Kt
Bridgt.	40	M	F	13Ap02Kt
Bridgt.	24	F	Laborer	13Ap02Kt
James	23	M	Laborer	13Ap02Kt
Jane	20	F	Laborer	13Ap02Kt
Thomas	18	M	Laborer	13Ap02Kt
Margt.	16	F	Laborer	13Ap02Kt
Patrick	13	M	Laborer	13Ap02Kt
Michl.	11	M	Laborer	13Ap02Kt
John	08	M	Child	13Ap02Kt
KENNY, John	30	M	Laborer	13Ap02Kt
Cath.	26	F	Laborer	13Ap02Kt
John	10	M	Laborer	13Ap02Kt
Thomas	08	M	Child	13Ap02Kt
PERCIVAL, Ann	36	F	Wife	13Ap02Kt
Margt.	12	F	None	13Ap02Kt
PURCELL, Michl.	21	M	Laborer	13Ap02Kt
MULONEY, Pat	22	M	Laborer	13Ap02Kt
QUEENEY, Michl.	25	M	Laborer	13Ap02Kt
U (W)	20	F	Laborer	13Ap02Kt
Winifred	28	F	Laborer	13Ap02Kt
VANGHAN, Teddy	22	M	Laborer	13Ap02Kt
MCHENRY, Michl.	40	M	Laborer	13Ap02Kt
VANGHAN, Michl.	30	M	Laborer	13Ap02Kt
BURKE, Wm.	24	M	Laborer	13Ap02Kt
MALONEY, Mary	22	F	Laborer	13Ap02Kt
FLEMMING, Mary	15	F	Spinster	13Ap02Kt
John	09	M	Child	13Ap02Kt
HIGGINS, Chas.	28	M	Laborer	13Ap02Kt
WATERS, Wm.	30	M	Laborer	13Ap02Kt
BETHELL, Saml.	26	M	Laborer	13Ap02Kt
KERWIN, Jane	18	F	Laborer	13Ap02Kt
Eliza	16	F	Spinster	13Ap02Kt
MCFARLANE, Mary	40	F	Spinster	13Ap02Kt
Margt.	10	F	Spinster	13Ap02Kt
WHELAN, Danl.	40	M	Laborer	13Ap02Kt
MORRIS, James	27	M	Laborer	13Ap02Kt
PHELAN, Edwd.	21	M	Laborer	13Ap02Kt
CARSON, Wm.	22	M	Laborer	13Ap02Kt
MORRISEY, Ellen	21	F	Wife	13Ap02Kt

NAMES OF PASSENGERS		AGE	SEX	OCCUPATIONS	DATE PORT SHIP
DORAN, John		21	M	Laborer	13Ap02Kt
Judy	(W)	18	F	Laborer	13Ap02Kt
NONLAN, Pat		18	M	Laborer	13Ap02Kt
OLDHAND, Wm.		28	M	Laborer	13Ap02Kt
Betsey		26	F	Laborer	13Ap02Kt
MURPHY, Wm.		28	M	Laborer	13Ap02Kt
FURLONG, John		25	M	Laborer	13Ap02Kt
CONREY, Margt.		25	F	Laborer	13Ap02Kt
James		20	M	Laborer	13Ap02Kt
SMITH, Ann		26	F	Laborer	13Ap02Kt
Mary		.00	F	Infant	13Ap02Kt
BROWN, Ralph		35	M	Laborer	13Ap02Kt
U	(W)	36	F	Laborer	13Ap02Kt
HILTON, John		35	M	Laborer	13Ap02Kt
U	(W)	34	F	Laborer	13Ap02Kt
WALLACK, James		20	M	Laborer	13Ap02Kt
RYAN, Pat		25	M	Laborer	13Ap02Kt
BENSON, John		21	M	Laborer	13Ap02Kt
WHELAN, John		23	M	Laborer	13Ap02Kt
JOHNSTONE, Geo.		36	M	Laborer	13Ap02Kt
Harriett		31	F	Laborer	13Ap02Kt
Harriett		11	F	None	13Ap02Kt
James		09	M	Child	13Ap02Kt
Thomas		05	M	Child	13Ap02Kt
Joseph		.00	M	Infant	13Ap02Kt
MCKENNA, Ellen		18	F	None	13Ap02Kt
MCBRIEN, Ann		48	F	None	13Ap02Kt
REILLY, James		37	M	Laborer	13Ap02Kt
FEE, Chas.		40	M	Laborer	13Ap02Kt
Susan	(W)	32	F	None	13Ap02Kt
HOEY, Ann		26	F	None	13Ap02Kt
MULRANEY, Pat		30	M	Farmer	13Ap02Kt
LORMOUS, Cept.		35	M	Laborer	13Ap02Kt
SMITH, John		38	M	Laborer	13Ap02Kt
REAGAN, Edwd.		42	M	Laborer	13Ap02Kt
DALEY, James		42	M	Laborer	13Ap02Kt
DUGARHTY, John		16	M	Laborer	13Ap02Kt
Judy		14	F	Spinster	13Ap02Kt
Margt.		08	F	Child	13Ap02Kt
RICE, Thomas		34	M	Laborer	13Ap02Kt
MCGUINESS, John		25	M	Laborer	13Ap02Kt
DEVINE, James		41	M	Laborer	13Ap02Kt
DONOHUE, John		29	M	Laborer	13Ap02Kt
JACKBYEND, Thos.		30	M	Laborer	13Ap02Kt
CRONIN, Edwd.		25	M	Laborer	13Ap02Kt
Francis		20	M	Laborer	13Ap02Kt
MCCABE, Owen		20	M	Laborer	13Ap02Kt
MOYNECH, Barnard		21	M	Laborer	13Ap02Kt
MCGORT, Michl.		24	M	Laborer	13Ap02Kt
NUTTY, Hugh		20	M	Laborer	13Ap02Kt
BROWN, Dennis		30	M	Laborer	13Ap02Kt
BYRNES, John		25	M	Laborer	13Ap02Kt
REALY, James		22	M	Laborer	13Ap02Kt
MILLS, Eliza		20	F	Spinster	13Ap02Kt
KILPATRICK, Frank		25	M	Laborer	13Ap02Kt
MCNUTTY, Robt.		21	M	Laborer	13Ap02Kt
MCMANN, Danl.		20	M	Laborer	13Ap02Kt
BURNETT, Jas.		22	M	Laborer	13Ap02Kt
William		28	M	Laborer	13Ap02Kt
QUIN, John		25	M	Laborer	13Ap02Kt
COLSTON, John		28	M	Laborer	13Ap02Kt
ODONNELL, Mary		25	F	Wife	13Ap02Kt
John		02	M	Child	13Ap02Kt
Died-At-Sea					
Peter		.00	M	Infant	13Ap02Kt
QUINNISS, Martha		40	F	None	13Ap02Kt
HOWELL, Eliza		35	F	None	13Ap02Kt
JONES, Joseph		30	M	Laborer	13Ap02Kt
WILLIAMS, Martha		28	F	Wife	13Ap02Kt
Ann		05	F	Child	13Ap02Kt
Martha		04	F	Child	13Ap02Kt
Died-At-Sea					
DERRING, James		20	M	Laborer	13Ap02Kt
Eliza		20	F	Laborer	13Ap02Kt
HENHAN, John		20	M	Laborer	13Ap02Kt

NAMES OF PASSENGERS		AGE	SEX	OCCUPATIONS	DATE PORT SHIP
BREMAN, Michl.		25	M	Laborer	13Ap02Kt
FARRELL, Patk.		40	M	Laborer	13Ap02Kt
Michl.		48	M	Laborer	13Ap02Kt
Gerald		48	M	Laborer	13Ap02Kt
Peter		14	M	Laborer	13Ap02Kt
Mary		13	F	Laborer	13Ap02Kt
Biddy		11	F	Laborer	13Ap02Kt
Thomas		09	M	Child	13Ap02Kt
HALLORAN, Anthony		25	M	Laborer	13Ap02Kt
MALONEY, James		20	M	Laborer	13Ap02Kt
NASTY, Martin		25	M	Laborer	13Ap02Kt
MCNAMARA, Mary		35	F	Laborer	13Ap02Kt
ANDREWS, Thos.		20	M	Laborer	13Ap02Kt
BEGLEY, A.		28	M	Laborer	13Ap02Kt
NASH, Honney		30	F	Spinster	13Ap02Kt
U		.00	U	Infant	13Ap02Kt
GROGAN, Thomas		20	M	Laborer	13Ap02Kt
Died-At-Sea					
MADDEN, Thomas		30	M	Laborer	13Ap02Kt
MULLONEY, James		28	M	Laborer	13Ap02Kt
Dennis		23	M	Laborer	13Ap02Kt
BYRNES, Michl.		24	M	Laborer	13Ap02Kt
Mary		23	F	Laborer	13Ap02Kt
MACKETT, Mary		24	F	Wife	13Ap02Kt
COOGAN, Michl.		26	M	Laborer	13Ap02Kt
JOYCE, Ann		30	F	Wife	13Ap02Kt
U		.00	U	Infant	13Ap02Kt
MCGREING, Biddy		20	F	Laborer	13Ap02Kt
MORRISON, Wm.		40	M	Laborer	13Ap02Kt
Jane		34	F	Laborer	13Ap02Kt
Ann		12	F	Laborer	13Ap02Kt
Mary		10	F	Laborer	13Ap02Kt
John		08	M	Child	13Ap02Kt
Susan		06	F	Child	13Ap02Kt
Samuel		04	M	Child	13Ap02Kt
Grace		02	F	Child	13Ap02Kt
James		.00	M	Infant	13Ap02Kt
KENNEDY, Mary		20	F	Spinster	13Ap02Kt
MCNAMARA, U		.00	U	Infant	13Ap02Kt
Born-At-Sea					
U		.00	U	Infant	13Ap02Kt
Born-At-Sea	Died-At-Sea				

MONTEZUMA 15 APRIL 1848

From Liverpool

NAMES OF PASSENGERS		AGE	SEX	OCCUPATIONS	DATE PORT SHIP
BATES, John		43	M	Clergyman	15Ap02Ao
ONEIL, John		33	M	Merchant	15Ap02Ao
Mary-Ann	(W)	26	F	None	15Ap02Ao
Anthony		07	M	Child	15Ap02Ao
Charles		06	M	Child	15Ap02Ao
Ann		03	F	Child	15Ap02Ao
WILD, William		40	M	Merchant	15Ap02Ao
CALLAN, John		36	M	Clergyman	15Ap02Ao
WILCOX, Ann		23	F	Weaver	15Ap02Ao
CORBITT, Ellen		25	F	Weaver	15Ap02Ao
RUGAN, Edwd.		30	M	Laborer	15Ap02Ao
John		24	M	Laborer	15Ap02Ao
ROBERTS, Mark		30	M	Blacksmith	15Ap02Ao
CORCORAN, Michael		28	M	Laborer	15Ap02Ao
FALIN, John		24	M	Laborer	15Ap02Ao
DORAN, Brien		25	M	Carpenter	15Ap02Ao
BAHERN, Julia		28	F	Carpenter	15Ap02Ao
BUCKLEY, Jesse		40	M	Gdnr	15Ap02Ao
WHITEHEAD, Andrew		36	M	Laborer	15Ap02Ao
BOYDS, Robert		28	M	Laborer	15Ap02Ao
KNOX, James		28	M	Laborer	15Ap02Ao
ONEILL, Martin		28	M	Baker	15Ap02Ao

NAMES OF PASSENGERS	AGE	SEX	OCCUPATIONS	DATE PORT SHIP
ROSS, Catharine	20	F	Servant	15Ap02Ao
POWER, Michael	30	M	Laborer	15Ap02Ao
BRIAN, Mary	27	F	Laborer	15Ap02Ao
WALSH, Mary	01	F	Child	15Ap02Ao
WHITE, Peter	20	M	Laborer	15Ap02Ao
FULLUR, Mary	23	F	Laborer	15Ap02Ao
DORAN, James	22	M	Laborer	15Ap02Ao
RUSH, James	20	M	Laborer	15Ap02Ao
DIVAN, Mary	24	F	Laborer	15Ap02Ao
CONLY, Betty	40	F	Laborer	15Ap02Ao
Ally	18	F	Laborer	15Ap02Ao
Died-At-Sea				
Mary	16	F	Laborer	15Ap02Ao
Died-At-Sea				
Catharine	14	F	Laborer	15Ap02Ao
Biddy	12	F	Laborer	15Ap02Ao
Nancy	10	F	Laborer	15Ap02Ao
LARKIN, Richard	22	M	Laborer	15Ap02Ao
CLINCLE, Judith	20	F	Laborer	15Ap02Ao
HEARY, Lawrence	20	M	Laborer	15Ap02Ao
MURPHY, Dennis	25	M	Laborer	15Ap02Ao
CONNELL, Bridget	02	F	Child	15Ap02Ao
CARNEY, Hannah	25	F	Laborer	15Ap02Ao
DONOVAN, Richard	24	M	Laborer	15Ap02Ao
KELLY, James	24	M	Laborer	15Ap02Ao
DONOVAN, Norry	20	M	Laborer	15Ap02Ao
DALY, Mary	20	F	Laborer	15Ap02Ao
HAGGERTY, Fanny	18	F	Laborer	15Ap02Ao
Peggy	18	F	Laborer	15Ap02Ao
SHEA, Roger	22	M	Laborer	15Ap02Ao
OMEARA, Lawrence	30	M	Laborer	15Ap02Ao
Martin	21	M	Laborer	15Ap02Ao
Honora	29	F	Laborer	15Ap02Ao
BURNS, Mary	17	F	Laborer	15Ap02Ao
HARTIGAN, Thomas	20	M	Laborer	15Ap02Ao
CARSTON, Ann	22	F	Laborer	15Ap02Ao
CARREN, Cecilia	21	F	Laborer	15Ap02Ao
MCMAHON, Bridget	14	F	Laborer	15Ap02Ao
HORTIGAN, Catharine	29	F	Laborer	15Ap02Ao
GILMAN, Bridget	20	F	Laborer	15Ap02Ao
KELCHER, Honor	20	F	Laborer	15Ap02Ao
HANNIN, John	21	M	Laborer	15Ap02Ao
OBRIEN, Catharine	24	F	Laborer	15Ap02Ao
Mary	23	F	Laborer	15Ap02Ao
FITZGIBBONS, Pat	24	M	Laborer	15Ap02Ao
MCCALNEY, David	24	M	Laborer	15Ap02Ao
MCKEOWN, Rosanna	21	F	Laborer	15Ap02Ao
MCENERSIE, Mary	20	F	Laborer	15Ap02Ao
BRENNAN, Peter	30	M	Laborer	15Ap02Ao
REILLY, James	20	M	Laborer	15Ap02Ao
BEYTON, Catharine	25	F	Laborer	15Ap02Ao
LYNCH, Biddy	22	F	Laborer	15Ap02Ao
MOORE, Martin	25	M	Laborer	15Ap02Ao
Martin	24	M	Laborer	15Ap02Ao
SPALLON, Mary	20	F	Laborer	15Ap02Ao
WELSH, Anty	20	F	Laborer	15Ap02Ao
LACEY, Biddy	28	F	Laborer	15Ap02Ao
LAWEN, Bess	25	F	Dressmaker	15Ap02Ao
BUTTER, Mary	20	F	Dressmaker	15Ap02Ao
ROBINSON, John	21	M	Laborer	15Ap02Ao
NORRIS, John	28	M	Laborer	15Ap02Ao
Fa----, Garriett	28	M	Laborer	15Ap02Ao
SMITH, Phillip	30	M	Laborer	15Ap02Ao
BRADY, Luke	20	M	Laborer	15Ap02Ao
MORAN, Betty	22	F	Laborer	15Ap02Ao
BRADY, Mary	20	F	Laborer	15Ap02Ao
BURDEN, Henry	21	M	Dealer	15Ap02Ao
LORK, Henry	20	M	Grocer	15Ap02Ao
CAMPBELL, James	28	M	Tailor	15Ap02Ao
SHEVLIN, Pat	28	M	Cord Winder	15Ap02Ao
ANDERSON, Eliza	00	F	Lady	15Ap02Ao
BROADE, Charles	23	M	Cooper	15Ap02Ao
Martha	21	F	Cooper	15Ap02Ao
THOMBY, U	48	F	Baker	15Ap02Ao
Joshua	18	M	Baker	15Ap02Ao
THOMBY, Harriet	12	F	Baker	15Ap02Ao
Grattan	10	M	Baker	15Ap02Ao
SMITH, George	26	M	Weaver	15Ap02Ao
Hannah	27	F	Weaver	15Ap02Ao
MURRAY, James	20	M	Tailor	15Ap02Ao
GREENWOOD, Wm.	28	M	Cord Winder	15Ap02Ao
WILSON, James	16	M	Packer	15Ap02Ao
BOSTICK, George	28	M	Grocer	15Ap02Ao
John	67	M	Grocer	15Ap02Ao
CARR, John	48	M	Laborer	15Ap02Ao
MCNALLY, John	20	M	Bookmaker	15Ap02Ao
TRAINER, Catharine	24	F	Servant	15Ap02Ao
COUNERY, Mary	23	F	Laborer	15Ap02Ao
HESLIN, Andrew	22	M	Laborer	15Ap02Ao
DALEY, Bridget	22	F	Laborer	15Ap02Ao
ROBINSON, Wm.	22	M	Laborer	15Ap02Ao
GORMAN, Margaret	16	F	Laborer	15Ap02Ao
REILLY, Bridget	18	F	Laborer	15Ap02Ao
GILLERAN, Mary	18	F	Laborer	15Ap02Ao
STINITON, John	17	M	Laborer	15Ap02Ao
MCTAGUE, Rose	17	F	Laborer	15Ap02Ao
WILLIAMS, Margt.	18	F	Laborer	15Ap02Ao
CARTY, John	18	M	Laborer	15Ap02Ao
Margt.	40	F	Laborer	15Ap02Ao
OLWELL, Bridget	18	F	Laborer	15Ap02Ao
Mary	15	F	Laborer	15Ap02Ao
KELLY, Mary	22	F	Laborer	15Ap02Ao
MUBRAY, Winifred	12	F	Laborer	15Ap02Ao
BRYAN, Maria	26	F	Laborer	15Ap02Ao
HAGAN, Bridget	06	F	Child	15Ap02Ao
Catharine	02	F	Child	15Ap02Ao
MCMANUS, James	18	M	Laborer	15Ap02Ao
SMITH, Bridget	20	F	Laborer	15Ap02Ao
WALTERS, Mary	20	F	Laborer	15Ap02Ao
GALLAGHER, Bridget	22	F	Laborer	15Ap02Ao
DONNELLY, Pat	57	M	Laborer	15Ap02Ao
Margaret	22	F	Laborer	15Ap02Ao
Jane	19	F	Laborer	15Ap02Ao
HOWLEY, Ann	17	F	Laborer	15Ap02Ao
MOSSE, James	20	M	Laborer	15Ap02Ao
BROPHEY, James	30	M	Laborer	15Ap02Ao
DONNELLY, Ellen	30	F	Laborer	15Ap02Ao
Felix	05	M	Child	15Ap02Ao
John	03	M	Child	15Ap02Ao
Wm.	.00	M	Infant	15Ap02Ao
LOUGHRY, Wm.	21	M	Laborer	15Ap02Ao
MCCORMICK, James	04	M	Child	15Ap02Ao
WALSH, Stephen	34	M	Laborer	15Ap02Ao
Peggy	30	F	Laborer	15Ap02Ao
WHITE, Catharine	28	F	Laborer	15Ap02Ao
Pat	07	M	Child	15Ap02Ao
John	08	M	Child	15Ap02Ao
Edmund	06	M	Child	15Ap02Ao
Mary	04	F	Child	15Ap02Ao
STEWART, James	20	M	Laborer	15Ap02Ao
RAFFERTY, Mary	17	F	Laborer	15Ap02Ao
Michael	09	M	Child	15Ap02Ao
FULLEN, Thomas	30	M	Laborer	15Ap02Ao
MCWESTERN, Alexr.	26	M	Laborer	15Ap02Ao
GARNEY, Hannah	18	F	Laborer	15Ap02Ao
LYNCH, Lawrence	20	M	Laborer	15Ap02Ao
Matthew	21	M	Laborer	15Ap02Ao
CUNNINGHAM, Catharine	46	F	Laborer	15Ap02Ao
NOLLAN, Ellen	10	F	Laborer	15Ap02Ao
James	07	M	Child	15Ap02Ao
THANE, Maria	10	F	Laborer	15Ap02Ao
BARKER, James	23	M	Laborer	15Ap02Ao
HUGHES, Pat	19	M	Laborer	15Ap02Ao
GREEGAN, Mary	18	F	Laborer	15Ap02Ao
PADDEN, Betsey	18	F	Laborer	15Ap02Ao
WARD, John	25	M	Laborer	15Ap02Ao
MCLAUGHLIN, Grace	30	F	Laborer	15Ap02Ao
WARD, James	10	M	Laborer	15Ap02Ao
John	07	M	Child	15Ap02Ao
Pat	04	M	Child	15Ap02Ao

NAMES OF PASSENGERS	AGE	SEX	OCCUPATIONS	DATE PORT SHIP
WARD, Wm.	.00	M	Infant	15Ap02Ao
MCLEE, Catharine	20	F	Laborer	15Ap02Ao
CROSSIN, Margaret	20	F	Laborer	15Ap02Ao
REILLY, Joseph	18	M	Laborer	15Ap02Ao
Frances	20	M	Laborer	15Ap02Ao
COUGHLY, Pat	18	M	Laborer	15Ap02Ao
Ann	16	F	Laborer	15Ap02Ao
HAYES, Winifred	20	F	Laborer	15Ap02Ao
GALLAGHER, Charles	20	M	Laborer	15Ap02Ao
DONERN, Ellen	50	F	Laborer	15Ap02Ao
CAREY, Ann	20	F	Laborer	15Ap02Ao
DOYLE, John	26	M	Laborer	15Ap02Ao
James	21	M	Laborer	15Ap02Ao
HIGGINS, Eliza	17	F	Laborer	15Ap02Ao
GALLOUGHLY, Susan	22	F	Laborer	15Ap02Ao
CARR, Bridget	18	F	Laborer	15Ap02Ao
KIERNAN, Mary	20	F	Laborer	15Ap02Ao
KENNEDY, John	16	M	Laborer	15Ap02Ao
KEENAN, Bridget	16	F	Laborer	15Ap02Ao
MCPEAK, Margaret	18	F	Laborer	15Ap02Ao
Hugh	17	M	Laborer	15Ap02Ao
STEVENSON, Ann	20	F	Laborer	15Ap02Ao
SPEILMAN, Pat	22	M	Laborer	15Ap02Ao
CAMPBELL, James	21	M	Laborer	15Ap02Ao
QUINN, Bridget	20	F	Laborer	15Ap02Ao
CLARK, Nancy	24	F	Laborer	15Ap02Ao
DOWDS, Ellen	18	F	Laborer	15Ap02Ao
REILLY, Francis	20	M	Laborer	15Ap02Ao
MULLABY, Michael	23	M	Laborer	15Ap02Ao
HALPIN, Michael	20	M	Laborer	15Ap02Ao
ROHALLY, John	15	M	Laborer	15Ap02Ao
MASON, Garritt	24	M	Laborer	15Ap02Ao
WARD, John	22	M	Laborer	15Ap02Ao
MCKARMA, Mary	17	F	Laborer	15Ap02Ao
WARD, Hugh	15	M	Laborer	15Ap02Ao
Mary	20	F	Laborer	15Ap02Ao
CASEY, Domnick	31	M	Laborer	15Ap02Ao
FITZSIMMONS, Mary	20	F	Laborer	15Ap02Ao
MCKEON, Peter	35	M	Laborer	15Ap02Ao
FINNIGAN, Thomas	10	M	Laborer	15Ap02Ao
FITZGERRALD, John	30	M	Laborer	15Ap02Ao
Catharine	16	F	Laborer	15Ap02Ao
MARTIN, Catharine	18	F	Laborer	15Ap02Ao
SCOTT, Ann	19	F	Laborer	15Ap02Ao
MORAN, Thomas	20	M	Laborer	15Ap02Ao
MURRAY, Honor	15	F	Laborer	15Ap02Ao
MCCARTY, Daniel	25	M	Laborer	15Ap02Ao
Died-At-Sea				
REGAN, Thomas	25	M	Laborer	15Ap02Ao
Michael	30	M	Laborer	15Ap02Ao
CAREY, William	26	M	Laborer	15Ap02Ao
QUINNA, Joanna	60	F	Laborer	15Ap02Ao
HARMON, Bridget	22	F	Laborer	15Ap02Ao
CONLON, Michael	23	M	Laborer	15Ap02Ao
Ellen	19	F	Laborer	15Ap02Ao
Rose	15	F	Laborer	15Ap02Ao
Alice	13	F	Laborer	15Ap02Ao
TWISS, Bridget	49	F	Laborer	15Ap02Ao
OCONNOR, Dennis	35	M	Laborer	15Ap02Ao
MOLLY, Pat	32	M	Laborer	15Ap02Ao
CASEY, Pat	20	M	Laborer	15Ap02Ao
REILLY, James	20	M	Laborer	15Ap02Ao
OCONNELL, John	40	M	Laborer	15Ap02Ao
Ellen	32	F	Laborer	15Ap02Ao
SHEAHER, Catharine	16	F	Laborer	15Ap02Ao
DORAN, Ellen	13	F	Laborer	15Ap02Ao
Mary	16	F	Laborer	15Ap02Ao
Pat	40	M	Laborer	15Ap02Ao
MCGAHERTY, Bridget	25	F	Laborer	15Ap02Ao
Catharine	.00	F	Infant	15Ap02Ao
BARRY, Mary	22	F	Laborer	15Ap02Ao
DELOUGHRY, David	24	M	Laborer	15Ap02Ao
ONEILL, Michael	22	M	Laborer	15Ap02Ao
MURPHY, James	20	M	Laborer	15Ap02Ao
John	22	M	Laborer	15Ap02Ao

NAMES OF PASSENGERS	AGE	SEX	OCCUPATIONS	DATE PORT SHIP
FAGAN, Bridget	22	F	Laborer	15Ap02Ao
Pat	.00	M	Infant	15Ap02Ao
CARROLL, James	21	M	Laborer	15Ap02Ao
Catharine	18	F	Laborer	15Ap02Ao
MAHONY, Mary	20	F	Laborer	15Ap02Ao
Margaret	21	F	Laborer	15Ap02Ao
CUNNINGHAM, Daniel	27	M	Laborer	15Ap02Ao
Bridget	24	F	Laborer	15Ap02Ao
CARTEN, Wm.	29	M	Laborer	15Ap02Ao
KELLY, Hugh	30	M	Laborer	15Ap02Ao
MCGRAW, Catharine	26	F	Laborer	15Ap02Ao
Died-At-Sea				
BOYLAN, James	20	M	Laborer	15Ap02Ao
Rose	14	F	Laborer	15Ap02Ao
CORCORAN, Eliza	21	F	Laborer	15Ap02Ao
MOORE, Anna	17	F	Laborer	15Ap02Ao
CAHILL, Cathn.	19	F	Laborer	15Ap02Ao
FITZPATRICK, Thomas	18	M	Laborer	15Ap02Ao
BYRNE, Mary	35	F	Laborer	15Ap02Ao
Mary	06	F	Child	15Ap02Ao
Ann	04	F	Child	15Ap02Ao
Catharine	02	F	Child	15Ap02Ao
MCABOY, Pat	20	M	Laborer	15Ap02Ao
Ann	16	F	Laborer	15Ap02Ao
DONOVAN, Mary	17	F	Laborer	15Ap02Ao
MCCLEUR, Saml.	30	M	Laborer	15Ap02Ao
Jane	30	F	Laborer	15Ap02Ao
Robt.	08	M	Child	15Ap02Ao
David	05	M	Child	15Ap02Ao
Nancy	03	F	Child	15Ap02Ao
FARRELL, Mary	32	F	Laborer	15Ap02Ao
FAGAN, Richard	21	M	Laborer	15Ap02Ao
DEVITT, Peter	20	M	Laborer	15Ap02Ao
SIMPSON, Thomas	20	M	Laborer	15Ap02Ao
COLEMAN, Alice	40	F	Laborer	15Ap02Ao
Matthew	19	M	Laborer	15Ap02Ao
Thomas	11	M	Laborer	15Ap02Ao
CLARK, Margaret	19	F	Laborer	15Ap02Ao
MCKEOWN, John	32	M	Laborer	15Ap02Ao
BRYANS, Saml.	17	M	Laborer	15Ap02Ao
BARRE, Saml.	34	M	Laborer	15Ap02Ao
CONNER, Joseph	19	M	Laborer	15Ap02Ao
WALSH, Ellen	34	F	Laborer	15Ap02Ao
HIGGINS, Bridget	15	F	Laborer	15Ap02Ao
OKEEFE, Johanna	50	F	Laborer	15Ap02Ao
Catharine	17	F	Laborer	15Ap02Ao
Margaret	12	F	Laborer	15Ap02Ao
BROWN, Peter	20	M	Laborer	15Ap02Ao
MURPHY, Julia	26	F	Laborer	15Ap02Ao
CALLAGHAN, Honesty	23	F	Laborer	15Ap02Ao
CARROLL, Catharine	23	F	Laborer	15Ap02Ao
THOMPSON, Ann	16	F	Laborer	15Ap02Ao
ONEILL, Alexr.	32	M	Laborer	15Ap02Ao
DAVIDSON, John	22	M	Laborer	15Ap02Ao
BOYLE, Hughe	20	M	Laborer	15Ap02Ao
FARRELL, Terrance	20	M	Laborer	15Ap02Ao
COSTELLO, U	30	F	Laborer	15Ap02Ao
John	.00	M	Infant	15Ap02Ao
RYAN, Ellen	20	F	Laborer	15Ap02Ao
BLACKWELL, Ann	34	F	Laborer	15Ap02Ao
John	17	M	Laborer	15Ap02Ao
George	16	M	Laborer	15Ap02Ao
Henry	14	M	Laborer	15Ap02Ao
Fanny	04	F	Child	15Ap02Ao
Frank	.00	M	Infant	15Ap02Ao
MULLANY, Thos.	29	M	Laborer	15Ap02Ao
THOMPSON, Rose	50	F	Laborer	15Ap02Ao
Cathn.	17	F	Laborer	15Ap02Ao
Ellen	15	F	Laborer	15Ap02Ao
REILLY, Hugh	20	M	Laborer	15Ap02Ao
MCCABE, James	20	M	Laborer	15Ap02Ao
Ann	35	F	Laborer	15Ap02Ao
REILLY, Pat	25	M	Laborer	15Ap02Ao
MOORE, Margt.	50	F	Laborer	15Ap02Ao
BRIGAN, Mary	20	F	Laborer	15Ap02Ao

NAMES OF PASSENGERS	AGE	SEX	OCCUPATIONS	DATE PORT SHIP
SWEENY, Pat	22	M	Laborer	15Ap02Ao
LANE, Jas.	21	M	Laborer	15Ap02Ao
Bridget	18	F	Laborer	15Ap02Ao
CONLAN, Thos.	30	M	Laborer	15Ap02Ao
CONLAR, Margt.	14	F	Laborer	15Ap02Ao
CONLAN, Thos.	07	M	Child	15Ap02Ao
Michael	05	M	Child	15Ap02Ao
LAKY, James	20	M	Laborer	15Ap02Ao
KENNY, Thos.	18	M	Laborer	15Ap02Ao
KIERNAN, Thos.	20	M	Laborer	15Ap02Ao
Rose	18	F	Laborer	15Ap02Ao
ROBERTS, Ann	22	F	Laborer	15Ap02Ao
MCDONNELL, John	17	M	Laborer	15Ap02Ao
Edward	03	M	Child	15Ap02Ao
MCGOWAN, Cath.	16	F	Laborer	15Ap02Ao
KING, Mary	19	F	Laborer	15Ap02Ao
Catharine	17	F	Laborer	15Ap02Ao
WHITEHEAD, James	34	M	Laborer	15Ap02Ao
Saml.	34	M	Laborer	15Ap02Ao
Robt.	12	M	Laborer	15Ap02Ao
Elizth.	10	F	Laborer	15Ap02Ao
John	04	M	Child	15Ap02Ao
MOFFAT, Ann	20	F	Laborer	15Ap02Ao
LYNCH, Pat	20	M	Laborer	15Ap02Ao
WELDON, Bridget	17	F	Laborer	15Ap02Ao
LOUGHRAN, John	22	M	Laborer	15Ap02Ao
CREATON, Rosey	15	F	Laborer	15Ap02Ao
Hugh	10	M	Laborer	15Ap02Ao
MORAN, James	22	M	Laborer	15Ap02Ao
MCKEON, Catherine	35	F	Laborer	15Ap02Ao
MCIVER, Alice	30	F	Laborer	15Ap02Ao
CANILY, Bernard	19	M	Laborer	15Ap02Ao
MANNING, James	19	M	Laborer	15Ap02Ao
EDWARDS, Edward	15	M	Laborer	15Ap02Ao
WARD, Dennis	18	M	Laborer	15Ap02Ao

SHERIDAN 17 APRIL 1848

From Liverpool

NAMES OF PASSENGERS	AGE	SEX	OCCUPATIONS	DATE PORT SHIP
HALL, Elija	28	M	Laborer	17Ap02Do
MORRIS, Roger	24	M	Carpenter	17Ap02Do
WALLACE, Mary	24	F	Servant	17Ap02Do
CAUFIELD, Anne	14	F	Servant	17Ap02Do
DONNELLY, Patt	23	M	Shoemaker	17Ap02Do
MCGRATH, Patt	21	M	None	17Ap02Do
Died-At-Sea				
BEAMMAR, Richd.	26	M	Laborer	17Ap02Do
JONES, David	28	M	None	17Ap02Do
TORRININ, John	40	M	Laborer	17Ap02Do
John	21	M	Butcher	17Ap02Do
FLYNORE, John	29	M	Tailor	17Ap02Do
CURLEW, Mathew	26	M	Weaver	17Ap02Do
MCDONNELL, Luke	34	M	Baker	17Ap02Do
THEARNEY, James	29	M	Carpenter	17Ap02Do
CASEY, Michl.	29	M	Laborer	17Ap02Do
CAVANAH, Edwd.	29	M	Laborer	17Ap02Do
KEARNEY, Anne	18	F	Weaver	17Ap02Do
FITZGERALD, Bridget	16	F	Tailor	17Ap02Do
KELLEN, James	21	M	Laborer	17Ap02Do
BARDUE, Patk.	21	M	Laborer	17Ap02Do
DONNELL, Thos.O	19	M	Laborer	17Ap02Do
MOONEY, John	24	M	Carpenter	17Ap02Do
DOUGLAS, John	28	M	Doctor	17Ap02Do
MOONEY, Mary	24	F	Servant	17Ap02Do
DALEY, John	36	M	Laborer	17Ap02Do
Cath.	36	F	Servant	17Ap02Do
Anne	.09	F	Infant	17Ap02Do
DUFFEY, Maria	16	F	Servant	17Ap02Do
BUTLER, Betty	24	F	Servant	17Ap02Do
TEIRNEY, James	22	M	Laborer	17Ap02Do
Patk.	21	M	Laborer	17Ap02Do
KIDD, Thos.	24	M	Laborer	17Ap02Do
DOWLING, Edwd.	23	M	Laborer	17Ap02Do
COYLE, Michl.	24	M	Laborer	17Ap02Do
MATHEWS, Michl.	22	M	Laborer	17Ap02Do
Eliza	22	F	Laborer	17Ap02Do
Eliza	.00	F	Infant	17Ap02Do
Born-At-Sea	Died-At-Sea			
CONNILE, Patt	20	M	Laborer	17Ap02Do
DARNING, Wm.	25	M	None	17Ap02Do
SPENCER, Henry	24	M	Laborer	17Ap02Do
FARLEY, Edwd.	27	M	Laborer	17Ap02Do
CARNEY, Michl.	26	M	Laborer	17Ap02Do
ATKINSON, Francis	21	M	Shoemaker	17Ap02Do
NORTON, Peter	21	M	Laborer	17Ap02Do
BURKE, Thos.	24	M	Laborer	17Ap02Do
Cathn.	24	F	Laborer	17Ap02Do
Mary	06	F	Child	17Ap02Do
MALONE, Cathn.	22	F	Servant	17Ap02Do
MATHEWS, Bernard	28	M	Shoemaker	17Ap02Do
HERON, Nicholes	28	M	Shoemaker	17Ap02Do
BENNET, William	29	M	Carpenter	17Ap02Do
HENDRICK, Edwd.	28	M	Laborer	17Ap02Do
GORNSLEY, Julia	40	F	Servant	17Ap02Do
BLAKE, Ellen	22	F	None	17Ap02Do
MURPHY, William	24	M	Miller	17Ap02Do
FISHER, William	25	M	Laborer	17Ap02Do
GIBSON, Thos.	22	M	Tailor	17Ap02Do
WILLIAMS, Richd.	27	M	Laborer	17Ap02Do
Rachel	22	F	None	17Ap02Do
Charles	02	M	Child	17Ap02Do
Sarah	.00	F	Infant	17Ap02Do
PATTEN, Mary	24	F	Servant	17Ap02Do
CAMPBELL, Margt.	18	F	Servant	17Ap02Do
HENLESTON, Letty	20	F	Servant	17Ap02Do
PATTEN, Jane	28	F	Servant	17Ap02Do
Mary-Ann	17	F	Servant	17Ap02Do
Hickey	14	U	Servant	17Ap02Do
Eliza-Jane	11	F	None	17Ap02Do
HAMILL, Saml.	26	M	Carpenter	17Ap02Do
TWEED, John	24	M	Engineer	17Ap02Do
Anne	16	F	None	17Ap02Do
MCAUSTIN, James	24	M	Weaver	17Ap02Do
BALL, Robert	20	M	Rope Maker	17Ap02Do
ANDERSON, James	20	M	Rope Maker	17Ap02Do
William	22	M	Rope Maker	17Ap02Do
Eliza	20	F	Rope Maker	17Ap02Do
Anne	.00	F	Infant	17Ap02Do
MCELHATTEN, Amos	40	M	Laborer	17Ap02Do
Margt.	40	F	Laborer	17Ap02Do
Margt.	18	F	Laborer	17Ap02Do
Alesander	16	M	Laborer	17Ap02Do
Amos	14	M	Laborer	17Ap02Do
Thos.	11	M	Laborer	17Ap02Do
Francis	10	M	Laborer	17Ap02Do
James	08	M	Child	17Ap02Do
MARTIN, William	21	M	Laborer	17Ap02Do
JONES, William	26	M	Laborer	17Ap02Do
Mary	24	F	Laborer	17Ap02Do
Evan	22	M	Laborer	17Ap02Do
Jane	21	F	Laborer	17Ap02Do
WOODS, Cathn.	26	F	Laborer	17Ap02Do
HENIDY, William	30	M	Turner	17Ap02Do
Sarah-Jane	25	F	Turner	17Ap02Do
John-Jane	04	M	Child	17Ap02Do
Eliza-Jane	03	F	Child	17Ap02Do
Wilson-Jane	.00	M	Infant	17Ap02Do
BELL, Henry	23	M	Baker	17Ap02Do
Margt-Jane	20	F	Baker	17Ap02Do
Eliza	23	F	Baker	17Ap02Do
MOSHER, Mary	23	F	Baker	17Ap02Do
QUINN, Mary	23	F	Baker	17Ap02Do
BARRODOUGH, John	24	M	Baker	17Ap02Do

NAMES OF PASSENGERS	AGE	SEX	OCCUPATIONS	DATE PORT SHIP	NAMES OF PASSENGERS	AGE	SEX	OCCUPATIONS	DATE PORT SHIP
JONES, Thos.	45	M	Baker	17Ap02Do	MURPHY, Edwd.	20	M	Laborer	17Ap02Do
William	21	M	Baker	17Ap02Do	WARD, Michl.	19	M	Laborer	17Ap02Do
RABBIT, Thos.	24	M	Laborer	17Ap02Do	MURPHY, Elizabeth	20	F	Servant	17Ap02Do
DORRLEY, Cathn.	22	F	Servant	17Ap02Do	CLARK, Lewis	24	M	Laborer	17Ap02Do
Peggy	20	F	Servant	17Ap02Do	Emily	20	F	None	17Ap02Do
ROBERTS, James	30	M	Carpenter	17Ap02Do	SULLY, John	18	M	Blacksmith	17Ap02Do
Mary	25	F	None	17Ap02Do	PATTEN, Bridget	24	F	Servant	17Ap02Do
GERRARD, Mary-A.	22	F	Servant	17Ap02Do	BOYCE, Frank	40	M	Brewer	17Ap02Do
FARLEY, Mary	20	F	Servant	17Ap02Do	James	21	M	Laborer	17Ap02Do
BRUNDLY, Biddy	18	F	Servant	17Ap02Do	BURKE, Owen	21	M	None	17Ap02Do
SMITH, Anne	18	F	Servant	17Ap02Do	BOYCE, Thos.	06	M	Child	17Ap02Do
CHAILL, Owen	16	M	Laborer	17Ap02Do	WALKER, William	30	M	None	17Ap02Do
REILEY, John	20	M	Laborer	17Ap02Do	ROND, Mark	40	M	None	17Ap02Do
PADLEY, Connor	24	M	Laborer	17Ap02Do	TRANT, Garret	28	M	None	17Ap02Do
DOLAN, Thos.	24	M	Laborer	17Ap02Do	DALEY, Bryan	22	M	None	17Ap02Do
MORAN, Lawrence	24	M	Laborer	17Ap02Do	GORE, Mary	18	F	Servant	17Ap02Do
WHALAN, Thos.	24	M	Laborer	17Ap02Do	CIVOREN, Martin	25	M	Butcher	17Ap02Do
BURKE, John	26	M	Laborer	17Ap02Do	DELANY, John	20	M	Weaver	17Ap02Do
MONAHAN, Mary	24	F	Servant	17Ap02Do	SMITH, William	28	M	None	17Ap02Do
TRACEY, Honora	18	F	Servant	17Ap02Do	HOPKINSON, Joseph	35	M	Cutter	17Ap02Do
HEAD, Mary	18	F	Servant	17Ap02Do	HOWARD, Benjamin	45	M	Laborer	17Ap02Do
BRENNAN, Margt.	18	F	Servant	17Ap02Do	WILKINSON, Henry	44	M	None	17Ap02Do
RYAN, Jane	22	F	Servant	17Ap02Do	LADDEN, James	24	M	None	17Ap02Do
CHAMBERS, Thos.	20	M	Laborer	17Ap02Do	Winifred	22	F	None	17Ap02Do
NOWLAN, James	24	M	Carpenter	17Ap02Do	REORDON, Honora	22	F	None	17Ap02Do
Mary	26	F	None	17Ap02Do	Cathn.	20	F	Servant	17Ap02Do
MCINTYRE, Robert	22	M	Spinner	17Ap02Do	BURKE, Edwd.	30	M	Engineer	17Ap02Do
GEORGE, William	22	M	None	17Ap02Do	KEIRVAN, Patt	12	M	None	17Ap02Do
TIPLER, William	22	M	None	17Ap02Do	---CLE, Kitty	18	U	Servant	17Ap02Do
BRYAN, Geo.	23	M	None	17Ap02Do	BRADLEY, John	16	M	Laborer	17Ap02Do
GRADY, Patk.	32	M	Laborer	17Ap02Do	SULLIVAN, William	22	M	Saddler	17Ap02Do
KELLY, John	40	M	None	17Ap02Do	NORTON, Henry	26	M	Clerk	17Ap02Do
Robert	16	M	Laborer	17Ap02Do	BRASINGTON, Daniel	22	M	Cutler	17Ap02Do
Jane	14	F	Laborer	17Ap02Do	COATTS, Harland	30	M	Merchant	17Ap02Do
Thos.	10	M	Laborer	17Ap02Do	Lena	24	F	None	17Ap02Do
MOORE, Geo.	22	M	Butcher	17Ap02Do	PHILPS, John-W-Jr.	.00	M	Infant	17Ap02Do
Margt.	20	F	None	17Ap02Do	WARD, Jonathan	20	M	Accountant	17Ap02Do
NEAL, David	22	M	Laborer	17Ap02Do	DOUGLAS, John	25	M	Printer	17Ap02Do
RUSSELL, Jane	20	F	Servant	17Ap02Do	GALAHER, Robert	24	M	Tailor	17Ap02Do
TEUNCANS, Mary-A.	25	F	None	17Ap02Do	CARTER, John	21	M	Chemist	17Ap02Do
CLEARY, William	20	M	Tanner	17Ap02Do	GRAHAM, Francis-W.	22	M	Farmer	17Ap02Do
MAHER, Jane	25	F	Servant	17Ap02Do	TOOLE, James	30	M	Coach Maker	17Ap02Do
PETIT, Edwd.	27	M	Shoemaker	17Ap02Do	JONES, M.	28	U	None	17Ap02Do
FAVRELE, Thos.	30	M	Laborer	17Ap02Do	U (W)	24	F	None	17Ap02Do
MCEVOY, James	40	M	Laborer	17Ap02Do	JAMES, John	32	M	None	17Ap02Do
Margt.	36	F	Laborer	17Ap02Do	Thos.	03	M	Child	17Ap02Do
Peter	11	M	Laborer	17Ap02Do	CROSS, John	21	M	Farmer	17Ap02Do
James	07	M	Child	17Ap02Do	ROURKE, Peter	21	M	None	17Ap02Do
Patk.	05	M	Child	17Ap02Do	WALSH, Kate	19	F	Servant	17Ap02Do
MARLEY, Patk.	35	M	Carpenter	17Ap02Do	BRICKWOOD, John	38	M	Farmer	17Ap02Do
Ruth	25	F	None	17Ap02Do	Maria	32	F	Farmer	17Ap02Do
Mary	07	F	Child	17Ap02Do	Celina	07	F	Child	17Ap02Do
James	05	M	Child	17Ap02Do	Adelaide	05	F	Child	17Ap02Do
Thos.	02	M	Child	17Ap02Do	Maria	03	F	Child	17Ap02Do
WALSH, John	28	M	Carpenter	17Ap02Do	Charlotte	.00	F	Infant	17Ap02Do
FARRELLY, Charles	25	M	Spinner	17Ap02Do	BARBAZON, Charlotte	25	F	Servant	17Ap02Do
CAREY, Patk.	22	M	Clerk	17Ap02Do	BRYNE, Peter	27	M	Farmer	17Ap02Do
TWINEY, John	23	M	Laborer	17Ap02Do	Michl.	19	M	Carpenter	17Ap02Do
COREY, Thos.	22	M	Laborer	17Ap02Do	Michl.	21	M	Clerk	17Ap02Do
DWYER, Daniel	24	M	Laborer	17Ap02Do	DOWLING, Julia	16	F	Clerk	17Ap02Do
GORMAN, Mary	21	M	Laborer	17Ap02Do	Mary	18	F	Clerk	17Ap02Do
FALLOW, John	36	M	Laborer	17Ap02Do	John	19	M	Butcher	17Ap02Do
LOUGHLIN, Dennis	24	M	Laborer	17Ap02Do	PATTEN, William	19	M	Carpenter	17Ap02Do
FLYNN, Hannah	22	F	Servant	17Ap02Do	WALKER, Saml.	21	M	Weaver	17Ap02Do
BROGAN, James	30	M	Crpw	17Ap02Do	MULLEN, Owen	25	M	None	17Ap02Do
MULLIN, Mary	18	F	Spinner	17Ap02Do	CANEFORD, Geo.	40	M	Laborer	17Ap02Do
CURREY, Margt.J.	19	F	Servant	17Ap02Do	LABIN, John	28	M	Laborer	17Ap02Do
MCFADDEN, Dennis	22	M	Laborer	17Ap02Do	Margt.	26	F	Laborer	17Ap02Do
MCDONNELL, Michl.	25	M	Laborer	17Ap02Do	Ellen	13	F	Laborer	17Ap02Do
Cathn.	20	F	None	17Ap02Do	MCBRIDE, John	24	M	Farmer	17Ap02Do
HANGBY, Edwd.	30	M	Weaver	17Ap02Do	BERNES, Thos.	23	M	None	17Ap02Do
REILEY, Patk.	17	M	Laborer	17Ap02Do	Barney	19	M	Farmer	17Ap02Do
CONNOR, Cathn.	20	F	Servant	17Ap02Do	GLENNEN, Owen	20	M	Farmer	17Ap02Do
BUTERWORTH, John	45	M	Dyer	17Ap02Do	DOWNES, John	40	M	Farmer	17Ap02Do
FOSTER, William	24	M	Clerk	17Ap02Do	MCLOGHLIN, Cathn.	20	F	Servant	17Ap02Do

NAMES OF PASSENGERS	AGE	SEX	OCCUPATIONS	DATE PORT SHIP
KEATING, Thos.	22	M	Laborer	17Ap02Do
MARKEY, John	20	M	Laborer	17Ap02Do
SMITH, Mary	24	F	Servant	17Ap02Do
MATHEWS, Joseph	20	M	Laborer	17Ap02Do
KING, Mary	22	F	Servant	17Ap02Do
MCANADE, Margt.	20	F	Servant	17Ap02Do
PYLLEN, Margt.	18	F	Servant	17Ap02Do
CARR, Thos.	16	M	Tailor	17Ap02Do
MCCABE, James	27	M	None	17Ap02Do
CHAILL, Rose	20	F	Servant	17Ap02Do
DUFF, Margt.	18	F	Servant	17Ap02Do
STANFORD, Betty	18	F	None	17Ap02Do
FLYNN, Bridget	09	F	Child	17Ap02Do
Ellen	07	F	Child	17Ap02Do
MCGININY, James	20	M	Carpenter	17Ap02Do
WILLIAMS, Herbert	20	M	Miner	17Ap02Do
KUF, Thomas	23	M	Miner	17Ap02Do
THOMAS, Evan	29	M	Miner	17Ap02Do
PHILIPS, David	18	M	None	17Ap02Do
LAWRENCE, Thos.	20	M	Butcher	17Ap02Do
PHELLPS, William	20	M	Tinman	17Ap02Do
KERR, Mathew	24	M	Cord Winder	17Ap02Do
PHILIPS, Mary-A.	19	F	None	17Ap02Do
MURPHY, Bartle	12	M	Laborer	17Ap02Do
Ellen	14	F	Servant	17Ap02Do
CASSIDY, Edwd.	19	M	Laborer	17Ap02Do
BLESSINGTON, Cathn.	36	F	Laborer	17Ap02Do
Bernard	07	M	Child	17Ap02Do
Mary	05	F	Child	17Ap02Do
MALONE, James	26	M	Laborer	17Ap02Do
HADRAGAN, Patt	24	M	Laborer	17Ap02Do
BLAKE, Ally	41	M	Laborer	17Ap02Do
HEPPLE, Thos.	35	M	Laborer	17Ap02Do
Margt.	12	F	Laborer	17Ap02Do
Mary	08	F	Child	17Ap02Do
Martin	06	M	Child	17Ap02Do
HADRAGAN, Margret	20	F	None	17Ap02Do
SMITH, Mary	18	F	None	17Ap02Do
DAVIES, Wm.	22	M	Unknown	17Ap02Do
DORAN, James	25	M	None	17Ap02Do

AMERICA 17 APRIL 1848

From Liverpool

NAMES OF PASSENGERS	AGE	SEX	OCCUPATIONS	DATE PORT SHIP
COCKING, William	25	M	Wool Comber	17Ap02Hf
CHEULEY, Phillip	27	M	Wool Comber	17Ap02Hf
COCKING, George	20	M	Wool Comber	17Ap02Hf
John	22	M	Wool Comber	17Ap02Hf
KELLAGHER, Charles	19	M	Laborer	17Ap02Hf
RILEY, Nehemiah	17	M	Brush Maker	17Ap02Hf
FALLON, Pat	19	M	Laborer	17Ap02Hf
MAGUIRE, Anne	20	F	Spinster	17Ap02Hf
MAGINN, Anne	40	F	Laborer	17Ap02Hf
Pat	16	M	Laborer	17Ap02Hf
Thomas	14	M	None	17Ap02Hf
Daniel	11	M	None	17Ap02Hf
James	09	M	Child	17Ap02Hf
ENGLISH, John	17	M	None	17Ap02Hf
HANLON, Wm.	20	M	Laborer	17Ap02Hf
MACNAMEE, John	20	M	Carpenter	17Ap02Hf
SPROUD, Wm.	20	M	Laborer	17Ap02Hf
MILLARD, Wm.	20	M	Laborer	17Ap02Hf
HANLON, Jane	25	F	None	17Ap02Hf
BOYD, John	35	M	Shoemaker	17Ap02Hf
COLLAGHER, Owen	23	M	Laborer	17Ap02Hf
KINNY, Charles	21	M	Miner	17Ap02Hf
SWEENEY, Michael	18	M	Laborer	17Ap02Hf
GOLLAGHER, Grace	20	F	None	17Ap02Hf
BYRNE, Hugh	20	M	Laborer	17Ap02Hf
Pat	20	M	Laborer	17Ap02Hf
MOONEY, John	18	M	Laborer	17Ap02Hf
MCCAFFERTY, John	13	M	None	17Ap02Hf
GIFFIN, Wm.	12	M	None	17Ap02Hf
FISHER, James	14	M	None	17Ap02Hf
OHARA, Pat	22	M	Laborer	17Ap02Hf
BRENNAN, Mary	20	F	None	17Ap02Hf
MOONEY, Biddy	20	F	None	17Ap02Hf
COMMON, Peggy	18	F	None	17Ap02Hf
FISHER, Margaret	42	F	None	17Ap02Hf
Dennis	18	M	Laborer	17Ap02Hf
CARR, Jane	14	F	None	17Ap02Hf
RILEY, Catherine	20	F	None	17Ap02Hf
HILL, Marlin	27	M	Baker	17Ap02Hf
VANCE, Elizabeth	28	F	None	17Ap02Hf
Mary-Jane	06	F	Child	17Ap02Hf
Catherine	03	F	Child	17Ap02Hf
Samuel	02	M	Child	17Ap02Hf
John	.06	M	Infant	17Ap02Hf
MONAGHON, Francis	21	M	Laborer	17Ap02Hf
BLAKE, Andrew	25	M	Accountant	17Ap02Hf
BRADY, James	20	M	Laborer	17Ap02Hf
MURPHY, John	11	M	None	17Ap02Hf
SMITH, Felix	40	M	Laborer	17Ap02Hf
Mary	20	F	None	17Ap02Hf
REGAN, Jeremiah	20	M	Laborer	17Ap02Hf
MCNUTTY, James	17	M	Laborer	17Ap02Hf
John	19	M	Carter	17Ap02Hf
BOWER, Biddy	20	F	None	17Ap02Hf
Michael	17	M	Laborer	17Ap02Hf
WELSH, Daniel	17	M	Laborer	17Ap02Hf
GORMAN, James	22	M	Laborer	17Ap02Hf
MCCORMICK, Bridget	18	F	None	17Ap02Hf
DONOVAN, Susan	20	F	None	17Ap02Hf
CASHMAN, Pat	24	M	Laborer	17Ap02Hf
HANLON, John	29	M	Slater	17Ap02Hf
BEHREN, John	26	M	Herd	17Ap02Hf
JONES, Elizabeth	22	F	None	17Ap02Hf
WILLIAMS, Martha	30	F	None	17Ap02Hf
CLONREY, Maria	22	F	None	17Ap02Hf
MILESTON, Peter	21	M	Saddler	17Ap02Hf
Mary-Anne	23	F	Dressmaker	17Ap02Hf
MASKILL, Thomas	23	M	Dressmaker	17Ap02Hf
CASE, Michael	19	M	Servant	17Ap02Hf
GAFFAKIN, Mary	30	F	None	17Ap02Hf
Jane	13	F	None	17Ap02Hf
John	06	M	Child	17Ap02Hf
Pat	04	M	Child	17Ap02Hf
Julia	01	F	Child	17Ap02Hf
SELLY, Catherine	22	F	None	17Ap02Hf
MURPHY, Pat	29	M	Laborer	17Ap02Hf
Anne	28	F	None	17Ap02Hf
Mary	03	F	Child	17Ap02Hf
Michael	01	M	Child	17Ap02Hf
Thomas	32	M	Laborer	17Ap02Hf
Judith	60	F	None	17Ap02Hf
Mary	20	F	None	17Ap02Hf
James	17	M	Laborer	17Ap02Hf
William	14	M	None	17Ap02Hf
KAVENAGH, Thomas	29	M	Farmer	17Ap02Hf
KINSALLA, Pat	25	M	Laborer	17Ap02Hf
FOLEY, Edward	20	M	Laborer	17Ap02Hf
NEAL, James	21	M	Laborer	17Ap02Hf
DRULAND, James	28	M	Laborer	17Ap02Hf
MALEY, Sarah	25	F	None	17Ap02Hf
BYRNE, Patrick	38	M	Laborer	17Ap02Hf
BEEHAN, Wm.	40	M	Laborer	17Ap02Hf
DOYLE, Martin	20	M	Laborer	17Ap02Hf
Anne	17	F	None	17Ap02Hf
REDMAN, Mary	21	F	None	17Ap02Hf
MCCONNELL, James	24	M	Laborer	17Ap02Hf
MURPHY, Pat	30	M	Shoemaker	17Ap02Hf
TUCKER, James	30	M	Miner	17Ap02Hf
CARBETT, Benjamin	27	M	Miner	17Ap02Hf

NAMES OF PASSENGERS	AGE	SEX	OCCUPATIONS	DATE PORT SHIP
THOMPSON, John	21	M	Miner	17Ap02Hf
WESTWOOD, Wm.	21	M	Miner	17Ap02Hf
MANSELL, Richard	21	M	Miner	17Ap02Hf
BURNS, Richard	22	M	Carpenter	17Ap02Hf
Michael	21	M	Carpenter	17Ap02Hf
HORAN, Daniel	17	M	Laborer	17Ap02Hf
Margaret	20	F	None	17Ap02Hf
CULLIEN, Catherine	22	F	None	17Ap02Hf
SHEALS, Thomas	25	M	Laborer	17Ap02Hf
Anne	25	F	None	17Ap02Hf
Rose-Anne	.06	F	Infant	17Ap02Hf
Died-At-Sea				
Phill	18	M	Laborer	17Ap02Hf
MURPHY, James	20	M	Laborer	17Ap02Hf
Pat	20	M	Laborer	17Ap02Hf
GAFFNEY, Owen	20	M	Laborer	17Ap02Hf
Margaret	18	F	None	17Ap02Hf
DONOHOR, John	18	M	Laborer	17Ap02Hf
Michael	07	M	Child	17Ap02Hf
MYERS, Rose	20	F	None	17Ap02Hf
SHERIDAN, Sarah	20	F	None	17Ap02Hf
WOODS, Edward	10	M	None	17Ap02Hf
Thomas	07	M	Child	17Ap02Hf
SHERRY, Mary	21	F	None	17Ap02Hf
SMITH, James	20	M	Laborer	17Ap02Hf
SHERRY, Owen	24	M	Laborer	17Ap02Hf
CONOFREY, John	28	M	Laborer	17Ap02Hf
MILLIGAN, Margaret	40	F	None	17Ap02Hf
MASTERSON, Francis	16	M	None	17Ap02Hf
Pat	18	M	None	17Ap02Hf
MCLAUGHLIN, Thomas	21	M	None	17Ap02Hf
JULES, Betty	26	F	Laborer	17Ap02Hf
GROGAN, Mary	20	F	None	17Ap02Hf
DIGNAN, Pat	14	M	None	17Ap02Hf
CONLAN, Mary	16	F	None	17Ap02Hf
GETTY, James-S.	20	M	Tailor	17Ap02Hf
MADDEN, Pat	22	M	Weaver	17Ap02Hf
DOULAN, Francis	19	M	Shoemaker	17Ap02Hf
KEARNS, Pat	30	M	Laborer	17Ap02Hf
Michael	20	M	Laborer	17Ap02Hf
FITZSIMMONS, Mary	20	F	None	17Ap02Hf
HARRIS, Morris	40	M	Merchant	17Ap02Hf
Anne	40	F	None	17Ap02Hf
Lewis	16	M	None	17Ap02Hf
Rosetta	07	F	Child	17Ap02Hf
Rebecca	02	F	Child	17Ap02Hf
Reuben	03	M	Child	17Ap02Hf
Matilda	02	F	Child	17Ap02Hf
Simon	09	M	Child	17Ap02Hf
Rosetta	.06	F	Infant	17Ap02Hf
LEVINSON, J.	25	M	Merchant	17Ap02Hf
Leah	20	F	None	17Ap02Hf
Phillip	19	M	Merchant	17Ap02Hf
LEVI, Moses	17	M	Tailor	17Ap02Hf
RICHMOND, Rachel	22	F	None	17Ap02Hf
SAUFT, Phillip	22	M	Tailor	17Ap02Hf
GETTY, Hester	22	F	None	17Ap02Hf
HARRIS, Sampson	11	M	None	17Ap02Hf
Michael	09	M	Child	17Ap02Hf
Eve	07	F	Child	17Ap02Hf
SAUFT, Eve	28	F	None	17Ap02Hf
HARRIS, Elkin	42	M	Tailor	17Ap02Hf
Amelia	38	F	None	17Ap02Hf
LEVY, Hyman	30	M	Tailor	17Ap02Hf
SAUFT, Lewis	.06	M	Infant	17Ap02Hf
THACKER, Will	40	M	None	17Ap02Hf
ATKINS, Robert	28	M	Shoemaker	17Ap02Hf
COGSWELL, Elizabeth	36	F	None	17Ap02Hf
Simeon	16	M	None	17Ap02Hf
Mary-Anne	14	F	None	17Ap02Hf
Emily	12	F	None	17Ap02Hf
Benjamin	08	M	Child	17Ap02Hf
James	04	M	Child	17Ap02Hf
Samuel	.10	M	Infant	17Ap02Hf
SCEWL, Phillip	36	M	Mnftr	17Ap02Hf

NAMES OF PASSENGERS	AGE	SEX	OCCUPATIONS	DATE PORT SHIP
SCEWL, Anne	36	F	None	17Ap02Hf
MORRIS, Samuel	25	M	Weaver	17Ap02Hf
James	16	M	Weaver	17Ap02Hf
SCEWL, James	14	M	None	17Ap02Hf
Mary-Anne	13	F	None	17Ap02Hf
Nehomi	12	F	None	17Ap02Hf
Ruth	09	F	Child	17Ap02Hf
David	.06	M	Infant	17Ap02Hf
EARL, John	39	M	Draper	17Ap02Hf
REYNOLDS, Samuel	19	M	Carpenter	17Ap02Hf
WILLIAMS, Wm.	30	M	Master	17Ap02Hf
JONES, James	33	M	Founder	17Ap02Hf
FRANCIS, Wm.	30	M	Vender	17Ap02Hf
WILLIAMS, Edward	40	M	Collier	17Ap02Hf
Elizabeth	.06	F	Infant	17Ap02Hf
JONES, Elizabeth	.06	F	Infant	17Ap02Hf
PHILLIPS, Thomas	35	M	Peddler	17Ap02Hf
Wm.	16	M	Peddler	17Ap02Hf
Catherine	40	F	None	17Ap02Hf
JONES, Wm.	40	M	Gdnr	17Ap02Hf
Ellen	40	F	None	17Ap02Hf
DAVIS, John	21	M	Saddler	17Ap02Hf
JONES, Mary	12	F	None	17Ap02Hf
Ellen	13	F	None	17Ap02Hf
Wm.	09	M	Child	17Ap02Hf
Susannah	07	F	Child	17Ap02Hf
GORMAN, James	22	F	Laborer	17Ap02Hf
MCCORMICK, Bridget	18	F	None	17Ap02Hf
THOMPSON, Wm.	20	M	Baker	17Ap02Hf
MCCORMICK, Ellen	30	F	None	17Ap02Hf
COOLDRICK, John	28	M	Laborer	17Ap02Hf
OWENS, Owen	35	M	Laborer	17Ap02Hf
SMITH, Rose	12	F	None	17Ap02Hf
BRADY, Phill	30	M	None	17Ap02Hf
FINEGAN, Dennis	36	M	None	17Ap02Hf
KELLY, Elizabeth	25	F	None	17Ap02Hf
WARNER, Wm.	18	M	None	17Ap02Hf
DONOHOE, Kate	46	F	None	17Ap02Hf
Mary	25	F	None	17Ap02Hf
Biddy	23	F	None	17Ap02Hf
Abby	20	F	None	17Ap02Hf
John	19	M	None	17Ap02Hf
Ellen	11	F	None	17Ap02Hf
Patrick	15	M	None	17Ap02Hf
Florry	12	F	None	17Ap02Hf
Peter	09	M	Child	17Ap02Hf
Norry	10	F	None	17Ap02Hf
Ellen	08	F	Child	17Ap02Hf
Florry	06	M	Child	17Ap02Hf
Died-At-Sea				
Arthur	03	M	Child	17Ap02Hf
SHEVLIN, Michael	22	M	Laborer	17Ap02Hf
GALLAGHER, Daniel	19	M	Laborer	17Ap02Hf
ODONOLD, Con.	40	M	Laborer	17Ap02Hf
BRESLAN, Bryan	25	M	Blacksmith	17Ap02Hf
KEENY, Peggy	07	F	Child	17Ap02Hf
KENNEDY, Nancy	40	F	None	17Ap02Hf
Honor	20	F	None	17Ap02Hf
Pat	12	M	None	17Ap02Hf
Mary	10	F	None	17Ap02Hf
MCNOLIS, Pat	20	M	Laborer	17Ap02Hf
JOHNSON, Isaac	23	M	Farmer	17Ap02Hf
MCCORMICK, Bridget	28	F	None	17Ap02Hf
CARROLL, Mary	20	F	None	17Ap02Hf
KENNY, Margaret	22	F	None	17Ap02Hf
MOONEY, Elizabeth	70	F	None	17Ap02Hf
Patrick	30	M	Laborer	17Ap02Hf
BOA, Bridget	20	F	None	17Ap02Hf
GRACE, Edward	38	M	Waterman	17Ap02Hf
SHAY, Phill	25	M	Laborer	17Ap02Hf
MURRAY, Ann	18	F	None	17Ap02Hf
KENNEDY, Catherine	50	F	None	17Ap02Hf
Pat	18	M	Laborer	17Ap02Hf
Bridget	21	F	None	17Ap02Hf
DICKINSON, Wm.	40	M	Hatter	17Ap02Hf

NAMES OF PASSENGERS	AGE	SEX	OCCUPATIONS	DATE PORT SHIP
DICKINSON, U (W)	25	F	Trimmer	17Ap02Hf
Emma	03	F	Child	17Ap02Hf
MURPHY, Ann	20	F	None	17Ap02Hf
Pat	30	M	Laborer	17Ap02Hf
FEENEY, Pat	24	M	Butcher	17Ap02Hf
MAXWELL, Hubert	20	M	Laborer	17Ap02Hf
MCGORELL, Mary	23	F	None	17Ap02Hf
FISHER, Hugh	38	M	Wool Comber	17Ap02Hf
FRAYNE, Peter	21	M	Wool Comber	17Ap02Hf
GUNCH, Jane	16	F	None	17Ap02Hf
CONLY, Margaret	20	F	None	17Ap02Hf
MOORE, Thomas	18	M	Laborer	17Ap02Hf
DONNELY, Neil	19	M	Laborer	17Ap02Hf
STAFFORD, James	20	M	Laborer	17Ap02Hf
ONEIL, Barney	30	M	Tailor	17Ap02Hf
Mary	25	F	None	17Ap02Hf
Hugh	.06	M	Infant	17Ap02Hf
MAGNUM, Thomas	20	M	Laborer	17Ap02Hf
MULHOLLAND, Agnes	34	F	None	17Ap02Hf
Margaret	13	F	None	17Ap02Hf
Eliza	11	F	None	17Ap02Hf
Charles	08	M	Child	17Ap02Hf
SMITH, Terence	19	M	Laborer	17Ap02Hf
Bridget	38	F	None	17Ap02Hf
GAVIN, Ann	35	F	None	17Ap02Hf
RILEY, Pat	20	M	Laborer	17Ap02Hf
Mary	18	F	None	17Ap02Hf
MULHOLLAND, Thomas	04	M	Child	17Ap02Hf
Samuel	02	M	Child	17Ap02Hf
MAGIE, Peter	24	M	Laborer	17Ap02Hf
WELSH, Mary	01	F	Child	17Ap02Hf
MCNOMEE, Catherine	30	F	None	17Ap02Hf
Pat	08	M	Child	17Ap02Hf
Susan	04	F	Child	17Ap02Hf
Anne	01	F	Child	17Ap02Hf
BRENNAN, Pat	18	M	Laborer	17Ap02Hf
MAGNINER, Catherine	20	F	None	17Ap02Hf
WELSH, Margaret	30	F	None	17Ap02Hf
FITZGERRALD, John	25	M	Laborer	17Ap02Hf
BUCKLEY, Edward	20	M	Laborer	17Ap02Hf
DONEVAN, Jerry	20	M	Joiner	17Ap02Hf
Daniel	20	M	Joiner	17Ap02Hf
COTTER, John	27	M	Laborer	17Ap02Hf
CASHMAN, Mary	13	F	None	17Ap02Hf
Ellen	16	F	None	17Ap02Hf
AGRATH, John	40	M	Laborer	17Ap02Hf
Mary	30	F	None	17Ap02Hf
Mary	10	F	None	17Ap02Hf
Anne	08	F	Child	17Ap02Hf
Sarah	06	F	Child	17Ap02Hf
MORRIS, Michael	20	M	Laborer	17Ap02Hf
James	15	M	Laborer	17Ap02Hf
LINISTER, Wm.	44	M	Draper	17Ap02Hf
Alfred	12	M	None	17Ap02Hf
DAVIES, George	23	M	Spinner	17Ap02Hf
REED, Felix	50	M	Laborer	17Ap02Hf
Susan	40	F	None	17Ap02Hf
Pat	00	M	Laborer	17Ap02Hf
Mary	00	F	None	17Ap02Hf
CORVON, Eliza	00	F	None	17Ap02Hf
MORRAW, Catherine	35	F	None	17Ap02Hf
SULLIVAN, Ellen	25	F	None	17Ap02Hf
OBRIEN, Julia	30	F	None	17Ap02Hf
RIGBY, Johanna	19	F	None	17Ap02Hf
SIMMS, James	20	M	Laborer	17Ap02Hf
Isabella	16	F	None	17Ap02Hf
BRADY, Bartholomew	45	M	Laborer	17Ap02Hf
Elizabeth	07	F	Child	17Ap02Hf
BRENNAN, Richard	24	M	Blacksmith	17Ap02Hf
BURKE, Catherine	20	F	None	17Ap02Hf
HARROLD, Ellen	15	F	None	17Ap02Hf
MAXWELL, Pat	24	M	Laborer	17Ap02Hf
MULVEY, Mary	20	F	None	17Ap02Hf
READDY, Jerry	25	M	Laborer	17Ap02Hf
SMITH, Margaret	24	F	None	17Ap02Hf

NAMES OF PASSENGERS	AGE	SEX	OCCUPATIONS	DATE PORT SHIP
MCKENNA, Wm.	36	M	Laborer	17Ap02Hf
Catherine	36	F	None	17Ap02Hf
DUCKETT, David	24	M	Farmer	17Ap02Hf
RICHARDSON, Wm.	20	M	Unknown	17Ap02Hf
DISTON, Thomas	26	M	Laborer	17Ap02Hf
PEACOCK, Thomas	28	M	Miner	17Ap02Hf
NUNNY, Charles	37	M	Master	17Ap02Hf
BRADLEY, John	19	M	Butcher	17Ap02Hf
WALTERS, James	22	M	Glsbr	17Ap02Hf
HUGHES, Charles	22	M	Ptmkr	17Ap02Hf
LANCASTER, Edward	19	M	Glsbr	17Ap02Hf
BAKER, Y-George	23	M	Engineer	17Ap02Hf
DIRER, Con.	39	M	Saddler	17Ap02Hf
KELLY, Thomas	19	M	None	17Ap02Hf
MULLIGAN, Mary	30	F	None	17Ap02Hf
TANE, Elizabeth	21	F	None	17Ap02Hf
DUFFY, Robert	30	M	Wool Comber	17Ap02Hf
U (W)	24	F	None	17Ap02Hf
ODYER, Phillip	23	M	Surveyor	17Ap02Hf
MOORE, Martin	26	M	Engineer	17Ap02Hf
Martin	29	M	Dyer	17Ap02Hf
LINDER, B.	30	U	None	17Ap02Hf
CAVENAGH, John	28	M	Tailor	17Ap02Hf
BARRETT, Henry	24	M	Shoemaker	17Ap02Hf
WARD, Thomas	20	M	Wool Comber	17Ap02Hf
JENKINS, Wm.	39	M	Mnftr	17Ap02Hf
SEAGROVE, Wm.	30	M	Lace Maker	17Ap02Hf
HUICHCLIFFE, Fredk.	30	M	Tailor	17Ap02Hf
MULLIGAN, John	24	M	Laborer	17Ap02Hf
HIGGINS, Patt	19	M	Laborer	17Ap02Hf
BANNON, James	24	M	Laborer	17Ap02Hf
KING, John	24	M	Laborer	17Ap02Hf
Bridget	22	F	None	17Ap02Hf
DAVY, Honor	21	F	None	17Ap02Hf
TAUSEY, Patt	20	M	Laborer	17Ap02Hf
GOLLAGHER, Mary	20	F	None	17Ap02Hf
Nelly	25	F	None	17Ap02Hf
HANNON, Mary-Anne	08	F	Child	17Ap02Hf
CONLIN, Hugh	35	M	Laborer	17Ap02Hf
BARRETT, James	24	M	Laborer	17Ap02Hf
Mary	22	F	None	17Ap02Hf
PARKS, Arthur	16	M	Laborer	17Ap02Hf
Wm.	14	M	Laborer	17Ap02Hf
WRIGHT, James	12	M	None	17Ap02Hf
Eliza	39	F	None	17Ap02Hf
DOOLY, James	22	M	None	17Ap02Hf
Brothel--, Patt	21	M	Laborer	17Ap02Hf
KILLALA, Michl.	22	M	Bricklayer	17Ap02Hf
RIELLY, Peter	27	M	Laborer	17Ap02Hf
SWIFT, John	25	M	Baker	17Ap02Hf
GILMARTIN, John	20	M	Clerk	17Ap02Hf
MEICKELES, Patt	25	M	None	17Ap02Hf
Margt.	20	F	None	17Ap02Hf
ROLLER, John	28	M	Gdnr	17Ap02Hf
Mary	00	F	None	17Ap02Hf
Mary	39	F	None	17Ap02Hf
Ann	20	F	None	17Ap02Hf
Cathn.	18	F	None	17Ap02Hf
NOWLAN, Patt	13	M	None	17Ap02Hf
Thomas	11	M	None	17Ap02Hf
James	08	M	Child	17Ap02Hf
Mary	08	F	Child	17Ap02Hf
Henry	00	F	Unknown	17Ap02Hf
Edmund	00	F	Unknown	17Ap02Hf
Michl.	04	F	Child	17Ap02Hf
GLEESON, John	26	F	Laborer	17Ap02Hf
PLUNKETT, Elisha	16	F	Laborer	17Ap02Hf
SLEASON, John	07	M	Child	17Ap02Hf
Elizth.	05	F	Child	17Ap02Hf
Teresa	03	F	Child	17Ap02Hf
BARNEY, Nichs.	28	M	Laborer	17Ap02Hf
MCBRIEN, Peter	28	M	Laborer	17Ap02Hf
CAHERN, Cath.	20	F	None	17Ap02Hf
SMALL, John	30	M	Laborer	17Ap02Hf
MCGRATH, Tim	20	M	Laborer	17Ap02Hf

NAMES OF PASSENGERS	AGE	SEX	OCCUPATIONS	DATE PORT SHIP
LARKIN, Mary	20	F	None	17Ap02Hf
TAFFE, Richard	38	M	Laborer	17Ap02Hf
MCDONOUGH, James	18	M	Laborer	17Ap02Hf
KILLOWHOE, Patt	25	M	Groom	17Ap02Hf
MYLER, Patt	25	M	Laborer	17Ap02Hf
MCDONOUGH, Thos.	02	M	Child	17Ap02Hf
CROSBY, James	39	M	Engineer	17Ap02Hf
Sophia	36	F	None	17Ap02Hf
Mary	37	F	None	17Ap02Hf
James	07	M	Child	17Ap02Hf
Wm.	02	M	Child	17Ap02Hf
BROOKS, Joseph	27	M	Unknown	17Ap02Hf
WARING, Peter	31	M	Shoemaker	17Ap02Hf
KAY, Wm.	31	M	Sawer	17Ap02Hf
Alice	38	F	None	17Ap02Hf
John	02	M	Child	17Ap02Hf
WEADON, John	25	M	Weaver	17Ap02Hf
BARLON, Samuel	25	M	Professor	17Ap02Hf
CRAYNER, Thos.	18	M	Laborer	17Ap02Hf
MCCONNLY, Morris	21	M	Laborer	17Ap02Hf
MARRA, Patt	30	M	Laborer	17Ap02Hf
Ann	22	F	None	17Ap02Hf
HAGAN, Thos.	21	M	Laborer	17Ap02Hf
MURRAY, Edward	22	M	Laborer	17Ap02Hf
JONES, Joseph	23	M	Blacksmith	17Ap02Hf
LORD, Joseph	37	M	Engineer	17Ap02Hf
Mary	22	F	None	17Ap02Hf
MORRIS, Mathau	40	M	Miner	17Ap02Hf
ROBERTS, Thos.	40	M	Miner	17Ap02Hf
SAMPSON, Thos.	37	M	Miner	17Ap02Hf
ROBERTS, Rd.	00	M	Unknown	17Ap02Hf
U, G--	36	U	Unknown	17Ap02Hf
CASSIDY, Patt	29	U	Weaver	17Ap02Hf
WILSON, David	25	U	Weaver	17Ap02Hf
GLASS, Patt	22	U	Laborer	17Ap02Hf
LAIDLEY, Maddy	20	F	None	17Ap02Hf
MOONEY, Daniel	19	M	Wheelwright	17Ap02Hf
HODDER, Chris.	25	M	Laborer	17Ap02Hf
Patt	28	M	Laborer	17Ap02Hf
LEWIS, John	22	M	Bricklayer	17Ap02Hf
LAWLER, Christ.	20	M	Laborer	17Ap02Hf
GAFFNEY, Jas.M.	29	M	Blacksmith	17Ap02Hf
CARTER, Samuel	23	M	Butcher	17Ap02Hf
HOLDSMORTH, Enoch	24	M	Dyer	17Ap02Hf
TOPPING, Joseph	26	M	Dyer	17Ap02Hf
BATEMAN, Luke	28	M	Weaver	17Ap02Hf
THOMPSON, John	22	M	Musician	17Ap02Hf
Ann	26	F	None	17Ap02Hf
U, U	00	U	Unknown	17Ap02Hf

HECLA 18 APRIL 1848

From MAYAQUEZ, P.R.

NAMES OF PASSENGERS	AGE	SEX	OCCUPATIONS	DATE PORT SHIP
BEATIE, Joseph	28	M	Physician	18Ap95Jt

FANNY 18 APRIL 1848

From Londonderry

NAMES OF PASSENGERS	AGE	SEX	OCCUPATIONS	DATE PORT SHIP
ARTHUR, James	20	M	Unknown	18Ap01Jg
MCGOLDRICK, Mary	18	F.	Unknown	18Ap01Jg
MOODY, Mickel	16	M	Unknown	18Ap01Jg
SWANSON, Simon	19	M	Unknown	18Ap01Jg
HUGHES, Barney	40	M	Unknown	18Ap01Jg
James	35	M	Unknown	18Ap01Jg
Susan	09	F	Child	18Ap01Jg
Alexander	06	M	Child	18Ap01Jg
Mary	04	F	Child	18Ap01Jg
Mary-Ann	02	F	Child	18Ap01Jg
CROSCADEN, Arthur	19	M	Unknown	18Ap01Jg
Thomas	18	M	Unknown	18Ap01Jg
GALLAGHER, Patrick	25	M	Unknown	18Ap01Jg
Cath.	18	F	None	18Ap01Jg
John	01	M	Child	18Ap01Jg
BARR, Philip	21	M	Unknown	18Ap01Jg
CROMES, John	22	M	Unknown	18Ap01Jg
JOHNSTON, Francis	25	M	Unknown	18Ap01Jg
GARVEY, Sally	40	F	None	18Ap01Jg
Hannah	30	F	None	18Ap01Jg
John	10	M	None	18Ap01Jg
Patrick	08	M	Child	18Ap01Jg
Mary	06	F	Child	18Ap01Jg
Dimer	04	M	Child	18Ap01Jg
LUCAS, Wm.	20	M	Unknown	18Ap01Jg
HUTTON, Mary	22	F	Dressmaker	18Ap01Jg
Sarah	16	F	Dressmaker	18Ap01Jg
MCALICE, Hannah	20	F	Unknown	18Ap01Jg
WALSH, Mary	20	F	Unknown	18Ap01Jg
WARD, William	25	M	Laborer	18Ap01Jg
DONNELLY, Bernard	21	M	Laborer	18Ap01Jg
Elizabeth	23	F	None	18Ap01Jg
CURREN, Patrick	25	M	None	18Ap01Jg
DAVIS, Thomas	28	M	None	18Ap01Jg
MCKINLEY, Matty	23	M	None	18Ap01Jg
Mary	18	F	None	18Ap01Jg
CARLAND, Geo.	20	M	Laborer	18Ap01Jg
MCCRACKEN, William	23	M	Laborer	18Ap01Jg
WILSON, Elisa	50	F	None	18Ap01Jg
Geo.	24	M	Laborer	18Ap01Jg
Mary	22	F	None	18Ap01Jg
James	34	M	Laborer	18Ap01Jg
BURNS, Mary	23	F	None	18Ap01Jg
MCNAUGHT, Johnston	35	M	Laborer	18Ap01Jg
Eliza-Jane	18	F	None	18Ap01Jg
JIMISON, Ann-Jane	22	F	None	18Ap01Jg
RAY, Thos.	56	M	Farmer	18Ap01Jg
Elisabeth	45	F	None	18Ap01Jg
Isabella	20	F	None	18Ap01Jg
James	18	M	Farmer	18Ap01Jg
Elisabeth	15	F	None	18Ap01Jg
John	13	M	Farmer	18Ap01Jg
Jane	12	F	None	18Ap01Jg
Cath.	10	F	None	18Ap01Jg
Thomas	08	M	Child	18Ap01Jg
Barbara	07	F	Child	18Ap01Jg
Mary	05	F	Child	18Ap01Jg
Matthew	03	M	Child	18Ap01Jg
Margaret	.06	F	Infant	18Ap01Jg
HOUSTON, Jane	21	F	None	18Ap01Jg
GREGG, William	55	M	Farmer	18Ap01Jg
Ellen	55	F	None	18Ap01Jg
Essey	30	F	None	18Ap01Jg
William	25	M	Farmer	18Ap01Jg
QUINN, Mary	25	F	None	18Ap01Jg
SPENCER, William	18	M	Farmer	18Ap01Jg
MCCANN, John	40	M	Farmer	18Ap01Jg
WALTERS, James	21	M	Farmer	18Ap01Jg
BRADLEY, Wm.	25	M	Farmer	18Ap01Jg
Andrew	19	M	Farmer	18Ap01Jg
DOHERTY, Mary	24	F	None	18Ap01Jg
LONG, Cath.	22	F	None	18Ap01Jg
MULLHEREN, Ann	19	F	None	18Ap01Jg
CALL, Edward	21	M	Farmer	18Ap01Jg
WALKER, Charles	25	M	Farmer	18Ap01Jg
BURNS, Hugh	32	M	Farmer	18Ap01Jg
Ann	14	F	None	18Ap01Jg
Mary	11	F	None	18Ap01Jg

NAMES OF PASSENGERS	AGE	SEX	OCCUPATIONS	DATE PORT SHIP
BURNS, Cath.	30	F	None	18Ap01Jg
Mary	08	F	Child	18Ap01Jg
REID, Mary	16	F	None	18Ap01Jg
GALLAGHER, Peter	42	M	Farmer	18Ap01Jg
BRADLEY, John	30	M	Farmer	18Ap01Jg
Jane	30	F	None	18Ap01Jg
Mary	04	F	Child	18Ap01Jg
Sarah	28	F	None	18Ap01Jg
MCGURY, Fanny	28	F	None	18Ap01Jg
Mary	26	F	None	18Ap01Jg
DOHERTY, Sarah	20	F	None	18Ap01Jg
GALLAGHER, Ellen	16	F	None	18Ap01Jg
MILLS, Sally	49	F	None	18Ap01Jg
MCELWOOD, John	19	F	None	18Ap01Jg
TAGGART, Sarah	20	F	None	18Ap01Jg
RUSSELL, Isabella	16	F	None	18Ap01Jg
FERGUSON, John	50	M	Farmer	18Ap01Jg
Letitia	45	F	None	18Ap01Jg
Mary	22	F	None	18Ap01Jg
Cath.	16	F	None	18Ap01Jg
Letitia	14	F	None	18Ap01Jg
Rebecca	12	F	None	18Ap01Jg
Jane	06	F	Child	18Ap01Jg
Archbold	04	M	Child	18Ap01Jg
MULLENS, Mary	19	F	None	18Ap01Jg
REID, John	24	M	Farmer	18Ap01Jg
LAIRD, Mary-Jane	18	F	None	18Ap01Jg
HAGGAN, Cath.	18	F	None	18Ap01Jg
DUGGAN, Charles	20	M	Farmer	18Ap01Jg
Hannah	15	F	None	18Ap01Jg
COIL, Patrick	26	M	Farmer	18Ap01Jg
FERRIS, Mannus	21	M	Farmer	18Ap01Jg
MCFADDEN, John	20	M	Farmer	18Ap01Jg
Cath.	22	F	None	18Ap01Jg
SHARKEY, Patrick	25	M	Farmer	18Ap01Jg
OBRIEN, Mary	15	F	None	18Ap01Jg
DUFFEY, Mary	23	F	None	18Ap01Jg
LYNCH, John	25	M	Farmer	18Ap01Jg
POAK, John	40	M	Farmer	18Ap01Jg
Mary-Jane	22	F	None	18Ap01Jg
Margt.	48	F	None	18Ap01Jg
Ann	21	F	None	18Ap01Jg
Mary	19	F	None	18Ap01Jg
John	09	M	Child	18Ap01Jg
Elisabeth	12	F	None	18Ap01Jg
Agnes	04	F	Child	18Ap01Jg
Robert	07	M	Child	18Ap01Jg
Sarah	15	F	None	18Ap01Jg
Martha	.06	F	Infant	18Ap01Jg
MULLAN, Elisabeth	31	F	None	18Ap01Jg
MCCLAY, William	16	M	Farmer	18Ap01Jg
SWEENEY, Edward	35	M	Farmer	18Ap01Jg
BRADLEY, Fredk.	27	M	Farmer	18Ap01Jg
HART, Mary	22	F	None	18Ap01Jg
BRESLAND, John	18	M	Farmer	18Ap01Jg
POLLOCK, Mary	17	F	None	18Ap01Jg
Jane	15	F	None	18Ap01Jg
DONAGHY, Susan	25	F	None	18Ap01Jg
FARREL, James	27	M	Farmer	18Ap01Jg
KINLEY, Mary	22	F	None	18Ap01Jg
John	22	M	Farmer	18Ap01Jg
Thomas	25	M	Farmer	18Ap01Jg
MITCHELL, David	20	M	Farmer	18Ap01Jg
COCHRAN, Wm.	23	M	Farmer	18Ap01Jg
KING, James	63	M	Farmer	18Ap01Jg
Anne	55	F	None	18Ap01Jg
Wm.	32	M	Farmer	18Ap01Jg
Daniel	17	M	Farmer	18Ap01Jg
James	12	M	Farmer	18Ap01Jg
Lucy	12	F	None	18Ap01Jg
ROWE, Daniel	23	M	Farmer	18Ap01Jg
RAMSEY, Susan	21	F	None	18Ap01Jg
GALLAGHER, Sally	60	F	None	18Ap01Jg
MCKEEN, Mary	29	F	None	18Ap01Jg
MCKEVER, James	33	M	Farmer	18Ap01Jg
FLAKENDER, Charles	27	M	Farmer	18Ap01Jg
MCCORRESTON, John	33	M	Farmer	18Ap01Jg
Mary	24	F	None	18Ap01Jg
Patrick	32	M	Farmer	18Ap01Jg
DOHERTY, Mary	19	F	None	18Ap01Jg
CURDEY, Jane	22	F	None	18Ap01Jg
CRAWFORD, Cath.	37	F	None	18Ap01Jg
MCLEAN, Philip	20	M	Farmer	18Ap01Jg
GALLAGHER, Anty.	35	M	Farmer	18Ap01Jg
RUSSEL, Mary-Ann	15	F	None	18Ap01Jg

CHANNING 18 APRIL 1848

From Liverpool

NAMES OF PASSENGERS	AGE	SEX	OCCUPATIONS	DATE PORT SHIP
KELLY, James	45	M	Laborer	18Ap02Qf
Mary	40	F	None	18Ap02Qf
Edward	18	M	Laborer	18Ap02Qf
John	16	M	Laborer	18Ap02Qf
Mary	20	F	Laborer	18Ap02Qf
Ann	12	F	Laborer	18Ap02Qf
Cath.	14	F	Laborer	18Ap02Qf
Elisa	10	F	Laborer	18Ap02Qf
Ellen	07	F	Child	18Ap02Qf
COSTELLO, Thos.	46	M	Laborer	18Ap02Qf
Mary	45	F	None	18Ap02Qf
Pat	17	M	None	18Ap02Qf
Michl.	14	M	None	18Ap02Qf
Martin	12	M	None	18Ap02Qf
Thos.	06	M	Child	18Ap02Qf
Ann	16	F	None	18Ap02Qf
MCGANN, Mary	40	F	None	18Ap02Qf
Jas.	18	M	None	18Ap02Qf
Thos.	08	M	Child	18Ap02Qf
John	05	M	Child	18Ap02Qf
Eliza	14	F	None	18Ap02Qf
Bridget	10	F	None	18Ap02Qf
Ann	.00	F	Infant	18Ap02Qf
John	24	M	Laborer	18Ap02Qf
Luke	20	M	Laborer	18Ap02Qf
Atty	19	F	None	18Ap02Qf
John	.00	M	Infant	18Ap02Qf
Ann	26	F	None	18Ap02Qf
Mary	15	F	None	18Ap02Qf
MCCORMICK, Pat	32	M	Laborer	18Ap02Qf
Cath.	28	F	None	18Ap02Qf
Mary	04	F	Child	18Ap02Qf
Pat	06	M	Child	18Ap02Qf
Ann	02	F	Child	18Ap02Qf
MCMANNIS, Thos.	29	M	Farmer	18Ap02Qf
Jas.	20	M	Farmer	18Ap02Qf
MULLERA, Ann	25	F	None	18Ap02Qf
Pat	24	M	Tailor	18Ap02Qf
WINN, Bridget	30	F	None	18Ap02Qf
MCDONALD, Andrew	18	M	None	18Ap02Qf
Ann	22	F	None	18Ap02Qf
Ellen	16	F	None	18Ap02Qf
CLAINE, Wm.	56	M	Farmer	18Ap02Qf
WINN, Michl.	60	M	Farmer	18Ap02Qf
Wm.	55	M	Farmer	18Ap02Qf
Jas.	16	M	Farmer	18Ap02Qf
Mary	18	F	None	18Ap02Qf
Catherine	03	F	Child	18Ap02Qf
FARRELL, Pat	55	M	Laborer	18Ap02Qf
Mary	50	F	None	18Ap02Qf
Wm.	18	M	Laborer	18Ap02Qf
Margret	16	F	None	18Ap02Qf
Bridget	14	F	None	18Ap02Qf
MADDEN, Mary	46	F	None	18Ap02Qf

NAMES OF PASSENGERS	AGE	SEX	OCCUPATIONS	DATE PORT SHIP
MADDEN, Thos.	13	M	None	18Ap02Qf
Cath.	16	F	None	18Ap02Qf
COLGIN, Margaret	66	F	None	18Ap02Qf
Honora	30	F	None	18Ap02Qf
Mary	28	F	None	18Ap02Qf
GILL, Bernard	30	M	Blacksmith	18Ap02Qf
Catherine	25	F	None	18Ap02Qf
Ann	.00	F	Infant	18Ap02Qf
Pat	02	M	Child	18Ap02Qf
MCDONALD, Michl.	50	M	Farmer	18Ap02Qf
Michl.	21	M	Farmer	18Ap02Qf
Cath.	24	F	None	18Ap02Qf
Mary	18	F	None	18Ap02Qf
FARRELL, Bridget	36	F	None	18Ap02Qf
FOSE, Francis	35	M	Shoemaker	18Ap02Qf
Mary	33	F	None	18Ap02Qf
Thos.	26	M	Shoemaker	18Ap02Qf
Pat	07	M	Child	18Ap02Qf
Francis	14	M	None	18Ap02Qf
Cath.	16	F	None	18Ap02Qf
STEWARD, Bridget	35	F	None	18Ap02Qf
STEWART, James	17	M	None	18Ap02Qf
Michl.	05	M	Child	18Ap02Qf
Bridget	14	F	None	18Ap02Qf
Ann	59	F	None	18Ap02Qf
John	30	M	Tailor	18Ap02Qf
HOARE, Mary	39	F	None	18Ap02Qf
Michl.	36	M	Tailor	18Ap02Qf
John	07	M	Child	18Ap02Qf
Thos.	02	M	Child	18Ap02Qf
Mary	11	F	None	18Ap02Qf
Bridget	08	F	Child	18Ap02Qf
James	05	M	Child	18Ap02Qf
MULLERA, John	35	M	Farmer	18Ap02Qf
Sarah	30	F	None	18Ap02Qf
Pat	25	M	Farmer	18Ap02Qf
Pat	12	M	None	18Ap02Qf
Thos.	10	M	None	18Ap02Qf
John	08	M	Child	18Ap02Qf
Francis	06	M	Child	18Ap02Qf
James	04	M	Child	18Ap02Qf
Died-At-Sea				
NEARY, Bart.	46	M	Tailor	18Ap02Qf
Wm.	36	M	Tailor	18Ap02Qf
Michl.	26	M	Tailor	18Ap02Qf
MARCUS, Thos.	24	M	Tailor	18Ap02Qf
Pat	23	M	Tailor	18Ap02Qf
Andw.	21	M	Tailor	18Ap02Qf
Mary	18	F	None	18Ap02Qf
MULLERA, Thos.	36	M	Farmer	18Ap02Qf
Mary	30	F	None	18Ap02Qf
Bridget	55	F	None	18Ap02Qf
Thos.	06	M	Child	18Ap02Qf
Ann	02	F	Child	18Ap02Qf
BECKETT, James	25	M	Carpenter	18Ap02Qf
Mary	18	F	None	18Ap02Qf
John	15	M	None	18Ap02Qf
REYNOLDS, Michl.	09	M	Child	18Ap02Qf
GALLAGHER, Jane	20	F	None	18Ap02Qf
KELLY, John	70	M	Farmer	18Ap02Qf
BUCKLEY, Tim	40	M	Farmer	18Ap02Qf
Bridget	40	F	None	18Ap02Qf
Pat	22	M	None	18Ap02Qf
Elizth.	13	F	None	18Ap02Qf
Joanna	11	F	None	18Ap02Qf
Mary	09	F	Child	18Ap02Qf
MURPHY, John	40	M	Laborer	18Ap02Qf
MCCARTHY, Francis	21	M	Laborer	18Ap02Qf
FLEAN, John	24	M	Laborer	18Ap02Qf
Mary	20	F	None	18Ap02Qf
Elisa	22	F	None	18Ap02Qf
FARMER, Bridget	22	F	None	18Ap02Qf
KEATING, Martin	18	M	None	18Ap02Qf
DEVIN, Edwin	32	M	Tailor	18Ap02Qf
QUIN, Mary	30	F	None	18Ap02Qf

NAMES OF PASSENGERS	AGE	SEX	OCCUPATIONS	DATE PORT SHIP
QUIN, Francis	05	M	Child	18Ap02Qf
MCKENNA, Peter	20	M	Shoemaker	18Ap02Qf
WALSH, John	25	M	Shoemaker	18Ap02Qf
Nara	25	F	None	18Ap02Qf
MCGAHAN, Ann	20	F	None	18Ap02Qf
SIMS, Thos.	30	M	Miner	18Ap02Qf
Mary	30	F	None	18Ap02Qf
FLAHERTY, Mary	20	F	None	18Ap02Qf
Catherine	04	F	Child	18Ap02Qf
GRIFFIN, Margret	18	F	None	18Ap02Qf
HAYES, John	26	M	Tailor	18Ap02Qf
NEVILLE, Thos.	24	M	Tailor	18Ap02Qf
Henry	23	M	Tailor	18Ap02Qf
HAYES, Bridget	20	F	None	18Ap02Qf
RYAN, Pat	28	M	Laborer	18Ap02Qf
GARRITY, Esther	30	F	None	18Ap02Qf
GOLDING, Martin	22	M	Blacksmith	18Ap02Qf
FEHREWDY, Pat	21	M	Blacksmith	18Ap02Qf
CONNOR, Pat	20	M	Blacksmith	18Ap02Qf
KENNA, Ann	40	F	None	18Ap02Qf
Valentine	11	F	None	18Ap02Qf
Mary	06	F	Child	18Ap02Qf
MOSS, Joseph	25	M	Farmer	18Ap02Qf
Michl.	25	M	Farmer	18Ap02Qf
Jas.	15	M	Farmer	18Ap02Qf
PERKINS, Thos.	29	M	Farmer	18Ap02Qf
BINGLEY, Thos.	28	M	Farmer	18Ap02Qf
GALESMAN, Fredk.	23	M	Farmer	18Ap02Qf
GAUSDEN, Wm.	26	M	Farmer	18Ap02Qf
SCLWRIGHT, John	20	M	Farmer	18Ap02Qf
PETRIE, Wm.	11	M	None	18Ap02Qf
MONTGOMERY, Eliza	20	F	None	18Ap02Qf
BOWLES, James	16	M	None	18Ap02Qf
HOEY, James	16	M	None	18Ap02Qf
SWIFT, Peter	26	M	Laborer	18Ap02Qf
LIDDLE, Wm.	27	M	Farmer	18Ap02Qf
NEALE, John	27	M	Farmer	18Ap02Qf
POWER, Michl.	28	M	Farmer	18Ap02Qf
Mary	28	F	None	18Ap02Qf
PETERS, Wm.	26	M	None	18Ap02Qf
CAMPBELL, Robert	26	M	None	18Ap02Qf
Ann	22	F	None	18Ap02Qf
MELAY, Owen	22	M	Farmer	18Ap02Qf
BONNER, Chas.	22	M	Farmer	18Ap02Qf
KENNAN, John	22	M	Farmer	18Ap02Qf
Owen	22	M	Farmer	18Ap02Qf
GOWNEY, Bridget	50	F	None	18Ap02Qf
Owen	20	M	None	18Ap02Qf
MARCHAND, Pat	20	M	Laborer	18Ap02Qf
MCGEAR, John	21	M	Laborer	18Ap02Qf
MANA, Michl.	23	M	Laborer	18Ap02Qf
MARRA, Pat	20	M	Laborer	18Ap02Qf
MELOY, Bernard	24	M	Laborer	18Ap02Qf
LANGDON, Mary	20	F	None	18Ap02Qf
MCGEE, Cecilia	19	F	None	18Ap02Qf
HICKEY, James	25	M	Joiner	18Ap02Qf
SEALY, Richd.	30	M	Doctor	18Ap02Qf

ST.GEORGE 18 APRIL 1848

From Liverpool

NAMES OF PASSENGERS	AGE	SEX	OCCUPATIONS	DATE PORT SHIP
GARVIN, Dominick	16	M	Laborer	18Ap02Av
BRENNAN, John	22	M	Laborer	18Ap02Av
GARVIN, Martin	12	M	None	18Ap02Av
Thomas	18	M	Laborer	18Ap02Av
FALLON, Peter	24	M	Laborer	18Ap02Av
CORELOHAN, Ann	18	F	Servant	18Ap02Av
Patrick	14	M	Laborer	18Ap02Av

NAMES OF PASSENGERS	AGE	SEX	OCCUPATIONS	DATE PORT SHIP
CUNNINGHAM, Micheal	18	M	Laborer	18Ap02Av
QUAILS, William	20	M	Servant	18Ap02Av
CASSINS, Dennis	14	M	None	18Ap02Av
GARREY, James	21	M	Blacksmith	18Ap02Av
Mary	26	F	Servant	18Ap02Av
BOUCHER, Maria	17	F	None	18Ap02Av
Thomas	30	M	Laborer	18Ap02Av
FARRELL, Winny	36	F	Servant	18Ap02Av
MCDONALD, Luke	22	M	Baker	18Ap02Av
FLANEY, Michael	25	M	Laborer	18Ap02Av
MARITN, Rose	20	F	Servant	18Ap02Av
RIELLY, Betty	24	F	Servant	18Ap02Av
MITCHELL, Hugh	22	M	Plumber	18Ap02Av
MURPHY, Hugh	28	M	Carpenter	18Ap02Av
MCGUIRE, Peter	23	M	Bookkeeper	18Ap02Av
MOORE, John	22	M	Laborer	18Ap02Av
BRANNON, Thomas	21	M	Laborer	18Ap02Av
MCCARTY, Daniel	22	M	Watchmaker	18Ap02Av
CUNNINGHAM, James	23	M	Farmer	18Ap02Av
Bridget	19	F	Dressmaker	18Ap02Av
MCCARTY, Honor	26	F	Servant	18Ap02Av
John	.08	M	Infant	18Ap02Av
SMITH, John	30	M	Carpenter	18Ap02Av
DONAVAN, Danl.	22	M	Laborer	18Ap02Av
MCCORMICK, Nicholas	48	M	Laborer	18Ap02Av
James	16	M	Laborer	18Ap02Av
Pat	18	M	Laborer	18Ap02Av
Mary	45	F	Servant	18Ap02Av
Catherine	19	F	Servant	18Ap02Av
Michael	13	M	None	18Ap02Av
KELLY, John	30	M	Laborer	18Ap02Av
FOY, Francis	30	M	Mason	18Ap02Av
Ruth	24	F	None	18Ap02Av
Mary	.10	F	Infant	18Ap02Av
LANE, Patrick	30	F	Laborer	18Ap02Av
GARY, James	17	F	Laborer	18Ap02Av
CAIN, James	22	F	Shopkeeper	18Ap02Av
Isabella	22	F	None	18Ap02Av
William	.11	M	Infant	18Ap02Av
CAMPBELL, Maria	23	F	None	18Ap02Av
FLANAGAN, John	35	M	Servant	18Ap02Av
Elsey	33	F	Servant	18Ap02Av
Ellizabeth	03	F	Child	18Ap02Av
Mary	50	F	None	18Ap02Av
Joseph	13	M	None	18Ap02Av
CASELBURY, John	32	M	Potter	18Ap02Av
POULSON, Theophilus	22	M	Potter	18Ap02Av
DUNN, James	25	M	Laborer	18Ap02Av
FINLEY, Pat	30	M	Laborer	18Ap02Av
DELANY, Martin	30	M	Laborer	18Ap02Av
DONAGAN, Michael	21	M	Laborer	18Ap02Av
MCGLAUCER, Andrew	20	M	Laborer	18Ap02Av
HARGAN, Pat	25	M	Mason	18Ap02Av
GARVERS, Barnard	20	M	Servant	18Ap02Av
MMCKINNY, Michl.	20	M	Laborer	18Ap02Av
MCDONALD, Mary	19	F	Servant	18Ap02Av
HOLLAND, Julia	25	F	Servant	18Ap02Av
CONWAY, Mary	22	F	Servant	18Ap02Av
MCKINNY, Catherine	21	F	Servant	18Ap02Av
MCCABE, Ann	16	F	Servant	18Ap02Av
NEALE, Catherine	24	F	Dressmaker	18Ap02Av
TAND, Peter	28	M	Engd	18Ap02Av
MCLINA, James	25	M	Laborer	18Ap02Av
PHILLIPS, Richard	48	M	Weaver	18Ap02Av
Matilda	20	F	Seamstress	18Ap02Av
LEWIS, Arthur	23	M	Blacksmith	18Ap02Av
SARP, John	19	M	Laborer	18Ap02Av
KILLIAN, Thos.	19	M	Laborer	18Ap02Av
MCTEAGUE, John	21	M	Laborer	18Ap02Av
Frank	19	M	Laborer	18Ap02Av
Pat	12	M	Laborer	18Ap02Av
Ann	60	F	None	18Ap02Av
Mary	18	F	None	18Ap02Av
Susan	10	F	None	18Ap02Av
Margaret	20	F	None	18Ap02Av
MCTEAGUE, Patrick	.02	M	Infant	18Ap02Av
FITZPATRICK, Pat	21	M	Laborer	18Ap02Av
MCMANNUS, Ann	18	F	Servant	18Ap02Av
FAY, Ann	19	F	Servant	18Ap02Av
GORVAN, Cath.	27	F	Servant	18Ap02Av
MURPHY, Francis	22	M	Laborer	18Ap02Av
BRADY, Thos.	20	M	Laborer	18Ap02Av
Jas.	22	M	Laborer	18Ap02Av
FLANAGAN, Hugh	20	M	Laborer	18Ap02Av
Cath.	17	F	Servant	18Ap02Av
HEAGAN, Mary	14	F	Servant	18Ap02Av
MCCUE, Pat	56	M	Laborer	18Ap02Av
Margaret	25	F	Servant	18Ap02Av
Honor	10	F	Servant	18Ap02Av
James	03	M	Child	18Ap02Av
BURNES, Mary	40	F	Servant	18Ap02Av
Julia	16	F	Servant	18Ap02Av
Margaret	11	F	Servant	18Ap02Av
Mary	08	F	Child	18Ap02Av
Owen	04	M	Child	18Ap02Av
COYLE, Pat	18	M	Carpenter	18Ap02Av
Francis	14	M	Laborer	18Ap02Av
Susan	19	F	Servant	18Ap02Av
SAULAN, Thomas	22	M	Laborer	18Ap02Av
SCANLON, Patrick	20	M	Laborer	18Ap02Av
CHRISTOPHER, Mary	26	F	Dressmaker	18Ap02Av
MCINERY, Francis	40	M	Laborer	18Ap02Av
Bridget	40	F	Laborer	18Ap02Av
Mary	10	F	Laborer	18Ap02Av
Owen	04	M	Child	18Ap02Av
WHELER, Ellen	20	F	Servant	18Ap02Av
QUAILIN, John	24	M	Laborer	18Ap02Av
POWER, Micheal	21	M	Laborer	18Ap02Av
FITZGERALD, Peggy	20	F	Servant	18Ap02Av
CONNER, Catherine	22	F	Servant	18Ap02Av
CAMEYS, Betty	36	F	Servant	18Ap02Av
James	05	M	Child	18Ap02Av
FLANAGAN, Ann	20	F	Servant	18Ap02Av
Catherine	26	F	Servant	18Ap02Av
ROONEY, James	31	M	Laborer	18Ap02Av
Ann	30	F	Servant	18Ap02Av
Margaret	.10	F	Infant	18Ap02Av
Mary	09	F	Child	18Ap02Av
Pat	07	M	Child	18Ap02Av
John	04	M	Child	18Ap02Av
MILLIGAN, Bridget	20	F	Servant	18Ap02Av
LOORY, Catherine	17	F	Servant	18Ap02Av
MULLIGAN, Mary	20	F	Servant	18Ap02Av
SLOANE, Maria	40	F	Servant	18Ap02Av
John	.09	M	Infant	18Ap02Av
Ann	21	F	Servant	18Ap02Av
KELLY, Mary	20	F	Servant	18Ap02Av
MCCOSKY, Betty	26	F	Servant	18Ap02Av
Sarah	24	F	Servant	18Ap02Av
James	60	M	Weaver	18Ap02Av
James	22	M	Weaver	18Ap02Av
HICKEY, Julia	50	F	None	18Ap02Av
Edmund	20	M	Laborer	18Ap02Av
Bridget	22	F	Servant	18Ap02Av
Peter	18	M	Servant	18Ap02Av
ROWAN, William	20	M	Laborer	18Ap02Av
CAFFREY, Eva	32	F	Laborer	18Ap02Av
SUFFY, Owen	23	M	Laborer	18Ap02Av
CARBERRY, Ewd.	23	M	Laborer	18Ap02Av
BURNS, Joseph	23	M	Laborer	18Ap02Av
MCGOUTRY, Owen	21	M	Laborer	18Ap02Av
MCGORVALL, Farrell	24	M	Laborer	18Ap02Av
CLEMMINS, Joseph	19	M	Laborer	18Ap02Av
Mary	61	F	None	18Ap02Av
QUICK, Thomas	20	M	Laborer	18Ap02Av
MARTIN, Martin	46	M	Laborer	18Ap02Av
WILKS, Catherine	22	F	Servant	18Ap02Av
CURTIN, Mary	23	F	Servant	18Ap02Av
CUNNINGHAM, Edwd.	20	M	Shoemaker	18Ap02Av
Mary	20	F	Dressmaker	18Ap02Av

NAMES OF PASSENGERS	A G E	S E X	OCCUPATIONS	DATE PORT SHIP
CUNNINGHAM, Bridget	18	F	Dressmaker	18Ap02Av
SHEA, Thomas	20	M	Laborer	18Ap02Av
DALY, Jeremiah	24	M	Laborer	18Ap02Av
JORAN, John	30	M	Laborer	18Ap02Av
Mary	07	F	Child	18Ap02Av
GILMAN, John	20	M	Boatman	18Ap02Av
Ann	11	F	None	18Ap02Av
CLOFFEY, James	30	M	Laborer	18Ap02Av
BUINN, John	26	M	Laborer	18Ap02Av
BYRNE, Elizabeth	27	F	Servant	18Ap02Av
BACON, Mary	26	F	Servant	18Ap02Av
FAGAN, Mary	21	F	Servant	18Ap02Av
MCGOVVALL, Thomas	24	M	Laborer	18Ap02Av
CADY, Ann	18	F	Servant	18Ap02Av
SHEA, Maria	17	F	Servant	18Ap02Av
CONNORTON, Michl.	28	M	Laborer	18Ap02Av
COLEMAN, John	17	M	Laborer	18Ap02Av
BARNES, Micheal	50	M	Laborer	18Ap02Av
Catherine	51	F	Servant	18Ap02Av
Mary	23	F	Servant	18Ap02Av
John	21	M	Laborer	18Ap02Av
Peter	15	M	Laborer	18Ap02Av
Catherine	18	F	None	18Ap02Av
Micheal	12	M	Laborer	18Ap02Av
Owen	10	M	Laborer	18Ap02Av
RYAN, Dennis	28	M	Laborer	18Ap02Av
Cornelius	26	M	Laborer	18Ap02Av
John	30	M	Bootmaker	18Ap02Av
CONNELLY, Phillip	21	M	Laborer	18Ap02Av
BLAND, Cain	25	M	Laborer	18Ap02Av
REED, John	24	M	Shopkeeper	18Ap02Av
CALLAN, Margaret	36	F	Housekeeper	18Ap02Av
HAYSE, Margaret	30	F	Housekeeper	18Ap02Av
KEENAN, Mary	18	F	Servant	18Ap02Av
CALEROR, Cath.	18	F	Servant	18Ap02Av
DRISCOLL, Mary	08	F	Child	18Ap02Av
MCILLEAR, James	20	M	Engd	18Ap02Av
HYNES, John	20	M	Laborer	18Ap02Av
CAHAL, Mathias	40	M	Laborer	18Ap02Av
MORRAH, John	28	M	Laborer	18Ap02Av
BOLAN, John	29	M	Laborer	18Ap02Av
WELCH, Micheal	35	M	Laborer	18Ap02Av
CRONAN, John	30	M	Laborer	18Ap02Av
REYNOLDS, John	15	M	Servant	18Ap02Av
WALLS, John	26	M	Laborer	18Ap02Av
MULLIN, Catherine	15	F	None	18Ap02Av
BARMON, Catherine	19	F	Servant	18Ap02Av
DEMPSEY, Alexd.	19	M	Laborer	18Ap02Av
MALONY, Fanny	24	F	Milliner	18Ap02Av
Mary	.10	F	Infant	18Ap02Av
CURGAN, Mary	23	F	Seamstress	18Ap02Av
CAMPBELL, Maria	23	F	Dressmaker	18Ap02Av
ENGLISH, Walter-A.	32	M	Engineer	18Ap02Av
George-A.	27	M	Engineer	18Ap02Av
Henry	22	M	Engineer	18Ap02Av
Beveryly	16	M	Engineer	18Ap02Av
Christopher-M.	19	M	Engineer	18Ap02Av
WALKER, Chamberland-R.	24	M	Solicitor	18Ap02Av
ELLIS, Hawkes	20	M	None	18Ap02Av
BYRNE, John	26	M	Servant	18Ap02Av
JORDAN, David	51	M	Lamp Maker	18Ap02Av
NISBIT, William	18	M	Bleacher	18Ap02Av
SLOAN, Thompson	22	M	Clerk	18Ap02Av
Saml.	19	M	Clerk	18Ap02Av
MOFFATT, Thomas	16	M	Clerk	18Ap02Av
LEWERS, William	18	M	Clerk	18Ap02Av

ATLAS 20 APRIL 1848

From Liverpool

NAMES OF PASSENGERS	A G E	S E X	OCCUPATIONS	DATE PORT SHIP
JEFFERS, Jm.	20	M	Laborer	20Ap02Ec
Stephen	22	M	Laborer	20Ap02Ec
Elizabeth	25	F	Laborer	20Ap02Ec
MORAN, Anastasia	23	F	Laborer	20Ap02Ec
Lawrence	21	M	Laborer	20Ap02Ec
Mark	18	M	Tailor	20Ap02Ec
HADEN, Michael	18	M	Laborer	20Ap02Ec
Mary	16	F	None	20Ap02Ec
Ann	22	F	None	20Ap02Ec
CONNOR, Mc.	30	M	Laborer	20Ap02Ec
HAUDS, Jeny	15	F	Laborer	20Ap02Ec
DOYLE, Biddy	20	F	Laborer	20Ap02Ec
DAILY, Mc.	26	M	Laborer	20Ap02Ec
Michael	24	M	Laborer	20Ap02Ec
Matt	22	M	Laborer	20Ap02Ec
Thos.	17	M	Laborer	20Ap02Ec
Anne	20	F	None	20Ap02Ec
Dennis	25	M	Laborer	20Ap02Ec
HAUDY, Cath.	15	F	None	20Ap02Ec
DAILY, Mary-Ann	02	F	Child	20Ap02Ec
MALONE, Biddy	25	F	None	20Ap02Ec
CONLAN, Peter	25	M	None	20Ap02Ec
BLESSARY, Judy	30	F	None	20Ap02Ec
Mary-Ann	14	F	None	20Ap02Ec
Mary	10	F	None	20Ap02Ec
DORIGAN, Mc.	42	M	Laborer	20Ap02Ec
CLARK, Jno.	45	M	Laborer	20Ap02Ec
Judy	45	F	None	20Ap02Ec
Mary	09	F	Child	20Ap02Ec
Biddy	15	F	None	20Ap02Ec
Rosey	45	F	None	20Ap02Ec
SCANLAN, Wm.	28	M	Laborer	20Ap02Ec
SCOTT, Wm.	60	M	Laborer	20Ap02Ec
Wm.Jr.	22	M	Laborer	20Ap02Ec
Michl.	18	M	Laborer	20Ap02Ec
Thomas	16	M	Laborer	20Ap02Ec
Mary	55	F	Laborer	20Ap02Ec
Robert	12	M	Laborer	20Ap02Ec
Sarah	16	F	Laborer	20Ap02Ec
CANAN, Luke	22	M	Laborer	20Ap02Ec
MURRY, Patt	30	M	Laborer	20Ap02Ec
DENLEN, John	30	M	Laborer	20Ap02Ec
DEVLIN, Cath.	30	F	Laborer	20Ap02Ec
Jno.Jr.	12	M	Laborer	20Ap02Ec
Jane	04	F	Child	20Ap02Ec
CORIGAN, Jno.	26	M	Laborer	20Ap02Ec
Margaret	24	F	None	20Ap02Ec
Wm.	05	M	Child	20Ap02Ec
Anne	04	F	Child	20Ap02Ec
SMITH, Wm.	30	M	Clerk	20Ap02Ec
GARNETT, U	28	F	None	20Ap02Ec
SMITH, M.	35	M	Servant	20Ap02Ec
WILSON, Jno.	22	M	Miner	20Ap02Ec
Hugh	27	M	Miner	20Ap02Ec
CLARK, Richd.	30	M	Laborer	20Ap02Ec
George	04	M	Child	20Ap02Ec
Hannah	02	F	Child	20Ap02Ec
Eliza	30	F	None	20Ap02Ec
FITZPATRICK, David	20	M	Laborer	20Ap02Ec
DONOHUE, Jno.	25	M	Laborer	20Ap02Ec
COPP, Will.	20	M	Laborer	20Ap02Ec
Chas.	19	M	Laborer	20Ap02Ec
GARNN, Jno.	20	M	Laborer	20Ap02Ec
BURK, Will.	21	M	Laborer	20Ap02Ec
CLARK, Richd.	27	M	Laborer	20Ap02Ec

NAMES OF PASSENGERS		AGE	SEX	OCCUPATIONS	DATE PORT SHIP
MOTTGAN, Thomas		23	M	Laborer	20Ap02Ec
ONEIL, Dennis		23	M	Laborer	20Ap02Ec
HANDLY, Eglli		25	M	Laborer	20Ap02Ec
MCINTIRE, Jno.		28	M	Laborer	20Ap02Ec
SHORT, Mary		60	F	Laborer	20Ap02Ec
MCINANNA, John		40	F	Laborer	20Ap02Ec
SHARLES, Bryan		19	M	Laborer	20Ap02Ec
MCGUIRE, Pat		18	M	Laborer	20Ap02Ec
GAVIN, Rosey		18	M	Laborer	20Ap02Ec
MCCALL, Mary		18	F	Laborer	20Ap02Ec
CASEY, Rosey		16	F	Laborer	20Ap02Ec
MCCORMICK, Benj.		55	M	Laborer	20Ap02Ec
Jno.		26	M	Laborer	20Ap02Ec
Cath.		12	F	Laborer	20Ap02Ec
MONAHUE, Denis		27	M	Laborer	20Ap02Ec
MCMANUS, Pat		18	M	Laborer	20Ap02Ec
FITZGERALD, Mary		48	F	Laborer	20Ap02Ec
Stephen		16	M	Laborer	20Ap02Ec
Pat		10	M	Laborer	20Ap02Ec
MARTIN, Owen		25	M	Laborer	20Ap02Ec
Margaret		20	F	Laborer	20Ap02Ec
JEFFREY, Mary		15	F	Laborer	20Ap02Ec
CALLAN, Hugh		30	M	Laborer	20Ap02Ec
Jno.		24	M	Laborer	20Ap02Ec
DORLEY, Jno.		44	M	Laborer	20Ap02Ec
Jno.Jr.		25	M	Laborer	20Ap02Ec
Cath.		17	F	Laborer	20Ap02Ec
Mary		15	F	Laborer	20Ap02Ec
CAMBOY, John		18	F	Laborer	20Ap02Ec
HANNEGAN, James		30	M	Laborer	20Ap02Ec
BURK, Jane		24	F	Laborer	20Ap02Ec
MCGREGAN, Corry		60	M	Farmer	20Ap02Ec
Mary		50	F	None	20Ap02Ec
James		25	M	Farmer	20Ap02Ec
MCGUGAN, Biddy		22	F	None	20Ap02Ec
Dennis		18	M	Farmer	20Ap02Ec
Cormick		14	M	Farmer	20Ap02Ec
Honor		16	F	Farmer	20Ap02Ec
Cath.		18	F	Farmer	20Ap02Ec
HAUDY, Pat		21	M	Laborer	20Ap02Ec
FOX, Mary		20	F	Laborer	20Ap02Ec
DONOHAN, Batty		24	M	Laborer	20Ap02Ec
Biddy		20	F	Laborer	20Ap02Ec
Johana		66	F	Laborer	20Ap02Ec
MCKENNA, Corry		60	M	Laborer	20Ap02Ec
Died-At-Sea					
NEWIN, Jno.		27	M	Blacksmith	20Ap02Ec
HORAN, Will.		25	M	Shoemaker	20Ap02Ec
Biddy		11	F	None	20Ap02Ec
Anne		09	F	Child	20Ap02Ec
FIMMONY, Pat		25	M	Laborer	20Ap02Ec
TRAYNON, Ben		40	M	Laborer	20Ap02Ec
BROWN, Mark		46	M	Laborer	20Ap02Ec
Mary		18	F	Laborer	20Ap02Ec
LYNCH, Ganit		28	M	Laborer	20Ap02Ec
CAVANAGH, Pat		22	M	Laborer	20Ap02Ec
MURPHY, Jno.		18	M	Laborer	20Ap02Ec
Bridget		21	F	Laborer	20Ap02Ec
HUGHES, Pat		28	M	Laborer	20Ap02Ec
James		22	M	Laborer	20Ap02Ec
Mary		26	F	Laborer	20Ap02Ec
DOWNS, Margaret		25	F	Laborer	20Ap02Ec
NEAL, Michael		28	M	Laborer	20Ap02Ec
MIEL, Rosey		21	F	Laborer	20Ap02Ec
SHEEL, Edwd.		27	M	Laborer	20Ap02Ec
Anna		28	F	Laborer	20Ap02Ec
MCINRY, Matt		28	M	Laborer	20Ap02Ec
Died-At-Sea					
FLANAGAN, Mary		18	F	None	20Ap02Ec
MOLAN, Cath.		27	F	None	20Ap02Ec
SHIRE, Wm.		23	M	None	20Ap02Ec
NORTH, Wm.		24	M	None	20Ap02Ec
U	(W)	24	F	None	20Ap02Ec
THOMAS, Thomas		33	M	None	20Ap02Ec
Hannah		28	F	None	20Ap02Ec

NAMES OF PASSENGERS	AGE	SEX	OCCUPATIONS	DATE PORT SHIP
THOMAS, Rice	02	F	Child	20Ap02Ec
THORTON, Wm.	26	M	None	20Ap02Ec
MCCORNELL, Alex.	24	M	Carpenter	20Ap02Ec
WEBB, Thos.	30	M	Laborer	20Ap02Ec
HARDY, Wm.	45	M	Laborer	20Ap02Ec
CLARK, Robert	27	M	Laborer	20Ap02Ec
FREER, George	17	M	Laborer	20Ap02Ec
EVANS, Jno.	27	M	Laborer	20Ap02Ec
THOMOSON, Alex.	27	M	Laborer	20Ap02Ec
BYRNE, Mary	18	F	Laborer	20Ap02Ec
MURNEY, Bridget	22	F	Laborer	20Ap02Ec
LYON, Cath.	20	F	Laborer	20Ap02Ec
ACKROY, Joseph	24	M	Laborer	20Ap02Ec
BENTHOW, Robert	26	M	Laborer	20Ap02Ec
SPENCER, Jno.	24	M	Laborer	20Ap02Ec
LANCASTER, Wm.	24	M	Laborer	20Ap02Ec
HARGNAN, Richd.	28	M	Laborer	20Ap02Ec
MONOGAN, Chas.	25	M	Laborer	20Ap02Ec
MUNY, Thos.	21	M	Laborer	20Ap02Ec
Eliza	21	F	Laborer	20Ap02Ec
SMITH, Pat	41	F	Laborer	20Ap02Ec
Ellen	42	F	None	20Ap02Ec
FRAGNON, Jno.	30	M	None	20Ap02Ec
U	25	F	None	20Ap02Ec
James	25	M	Laborer	20Ap02Ec
MULTES, Stephen	17	M	Laborer	20Ap02Ec
FOOT, Robert	36	M	Laborer	20Ap02Ec
DAVIS, Jno.	30	M	Laborer	20Ap02Ec
KILSO, Richd.	20	M	Laborer	20Ap02Ec
DAVISON, Andrew	24	M	Laborer	20Ap02Ec
BUTLER, Richd.	45	M	Laborer	20Ap02Ec
MURPHY, Edwd.	27	M	Laborer	20Ap02Ec
FOGARTES, Martin	40	M	Laborer	20Ap02Ec
TURNER, Robt.	23	M	Laborer	20Ap02Ec
Saml.	15	M	Laborer	20Ap02Ec
Chas.	21	M	Laborer	20Ap02Ec
Cath.	17	F	Laborer	20Ap02Ec
CARTWRIGHT, Joseph	27	M	Laborer	20Ap02Ec
Rebecca	24	F	Laborer	20Ap02Ec
KUTTSELL, Charles	24	M	Laborer	20Ap02Ec
Anne	22	F	Laborer	20Ap02Ec
NOONY, Mary	23	F	Laborer	20Ap02Ec
JENNINGS, Wm.	33	M	Laborer	20Ap02Ec
TRAYNOR, Anne	18	F	Laborer	20Ap02Ec
CONINS, Pat	25	M	Laborer	20Ap02Ec
Mary	23	F	Laborer	20Ap02Ec
COHAN, John	25	M	Laborer	20Ap02Ec
MARTIN, Pat	30	M	Laborer	20Ap02Ec
GOMAN, Eliza	26	F	Laborer	20Ap02Ec
SHEELS, Eliza	25	F	Laborer	20Ap02Ec
SONG, Jno.	17	M	Laborer	20Ap02Ec
MCKEE, Stewart	30	M	Laborer	20Ap02Ec
Ann	30	F	Laborer	20Ap02Ec
Jane	32	F	Laborer	20Ap02Ec
SANCET, Ellis	23	M	Laborer	20Ap02Ec
Robt.	03	M	Child	20Ap02Ec
Wm.	01	M	Child	20Ap02Ec
SAMOUT, Hanty	20	M	None	20Ap02Ec
MCCAMBELL, Jno.	23	M	None	20Ap02Ec
BYNE, Jno.	30	M	None	20Ap02Ec
Cath.	23	F	None	20Ap02Ec
Mary	03	F	Child	20Ap02Ec
LAFFY, Jno.	25	M	None	20Ap02Ec
HIGGINS, Bensy	26	M	None	20Ap02Ec
QUALY, James	22	M	None	20Ap02Ec
KENNEDY, Ann	12	F	None	20Ap02Ec
FATHAN, Chas.	26	M	None	20Ap02Ec
PIFF, Thos.	27	M	None	20Ap02Ec
HEALY, James	26	M	None	20Ap02Ec
MCCANN, Richd.	26	M	None	20Ap02Ec
ROBERTS, Edwd.	60	M	None	20Ap02Ec
ROTHWELL, Beu.	24	M	None	20Ap02Ec
BLAKELY, Jno.	37	M	None	20Ap02Ec
WALSH, Margaret	26	F	None	20Ap02Ec
FITZGERALD, Biddy	20	F	None	20Ap02Ec

NAMES OF PASSENGERS	AGE	SEX	OCCUPATIONS	DATE PORT SHIP
PUSTON, Mary	16	F	None	20Ap02Ec
PRESTON, Biddy	18	F	None	20Ap02Ec
Michl.	40	M	None	20Ap02Ec
MORGAN, Michl.	25	M	None	20Ap02Ec
FRAYES, Michael	20	M	None	20Ap02Ec
ROGERS, Mily	18	M	None	20Ap02Ec
COHALAN, Jas.	21	M	None	20Ap02Ec
CONOL, Terence	47	M	None	20Ap02Ec
Robt.	21	M	None	20Ap02Ec
HAWLY, Wm.	24	M	None	20Ap02Ec
HUTTCHINSON, Stephen	23	M	None	20Ap02Ec
JONES, Thos.	25	M	None	20Ap02Ec
MCPHAIL, Andrew	25	M	None	20Ap02Ec
LACE, Saml.	25	M	None	20Ap02Ec
MCGWEN, Chas.	20	M	None	20Ap02Ec
DOUGAN, Peter	16	M	None	20Ap02Ec
SCULLION, Jane	20	F	None	20Ap02Ec
MURRY, Jno.	41	M	None	20Ap02Ec
Mary	41	F	None	20Ap02Ec
Mary	13	F	None	20Ap02Ec
HUNTER, Margaret	51	F	None	20Ap02Ec
ROY, James	12	M	None	20Ap02Ec
BELL, Francis	32	M	None	20Ap02Ec
FAU, Jane	18	F	None	20Ap02Ec
SWEENY, James	22	M	None	20Ap02Ec
CATHER, Jno.	48	M	None	20Ap02Ec
Susan	48	F	None	20Ap02Ec
LYNDSAY, Jno.	33	M	None	20Ap02Ec
CASE, Andrew	23	M	None	20Ap02Ec
SWEENY, Thos.	19	M	None	20Ap02Ec
BOYLE, Wm.	22	M	None	20Ap02Ec
MCSHAN, Margaret	27	F	None	20Ap02Ec
KELLY, Michl.	19	M	None	20Ap02Ec
GANETT, Alford	20	M	None	20Ap02Ec
DORLY, Margaret	19	F	None	20Ap02Ec
MAHONY, Concelez	18	M	None	20Ap02Ec
MCDOUGAL, George	30	M	None	20Ap02Ec
OWENS, Jane	24	F	None	20Ap02Ec
HURST, Joseph	51	M	None	20Ap02Ec
HUNT, Edwd.	16	M	None	20Ap02Ec
MCNUTLY, James	33	M	None	20Ap02Ec
NEWCOMB, James	25	M	None	20Ap02Ec
MOUAHAN, Wm.	38	M	None	20Ap02Ec
FANCE, Chas.	21	M	None	20Ap02Ec
HAYDEN, Jno.	18	M	None	20Ap02Ec
MCMANUS, Jno.	25	M	None	20Ap02Ec
CEARNS, Jacb.	23	M	None	20Ap02Ec
FANCER, Patt	20	M	None	20Ap02Ec
DOUGEN, James	30	M	None	20Ap02Ec
YANLY, Jarry	20	M	None	20Ap02Ec
CREGGAN, Michl.	20	M	None	20Ap02Ec
SENER, Andrew	26	M	None	20Ap02Ec
CLARKSON, Thos.	33	M	None	20Ap02Ec
Judith	29	F	None	20Ap02Ec
Jno.	14	M	None	20Ap02Ec
Rachel	10	F	None	20Ap02Ec
Martha	06	F	Child	20Ap02Ec
Mary	03	F	Child	20Ap02Ec
CONIGAN, Eliza	.09	F	Infant	20Ap02Ec
SHIEL, Edwd.	.09	M	Infant	20Ap02Ec
MENY, Pat	.10	M	Infant	20Ap02Ec
TRAYNON, Wm.	.10	M	Infant	20Ap02Ec
CARTWRIGHT, Eliza	.10	F	Infant	20Ap02Ec
Thos.	.02	M	Infant	20Ap02Ec
DEVLIN, Pat	.09	M	Infant	20Ap02Ec
CLARK, Alfred	00	M	None	20Ap02Ec
Died-At-Sea				
MCINTERN, Peter	.00	M	Infant	20Ap02Ec
Died-At-Sea				
MCKENNA, Corry	60	M	None	20Ap02Ec
Died-At-Sea				

CLARENCE 21 APRIL 1848

From Galway

NAMES OF PASSENGERS	AGE	SEX	OCCUPATIONS	DATE PORT SHIP
OBRIEN, Martin	23	M	Laborer	21Ap11Dl
ROONEY, Thomas	30	M	Laborer	21Ap11Dl
FAHEY, Michl.	30	M	Laborer	21Ap11Dl
TUOHEY, Winifred	20	F	Spinster	21Ap11Dl
GLYNN, Winifred	20	F	Spinster	21Ap11Dl
LAWLESS, Mary	20	F	Spinster	21Ap11Dl
GOLDING, Mary	20	F	Spinster	21Ap11Dl
GALVIN, Mary	25	F	Spinster	21Ap11Dl
CARTY, John	01	M	Child	21Ap11Dl
SHAUGHNESSY, Peter	28	M	Laborer	21Ap11Dl
Honor	20	F	None	21Ap11Dl
FRIENDS, Patt	25	M	Laborer	21Ap11Dl
CRON, John	30	M	Laborer	21Ap11Dl
LANE, Thos.	25	M	Laborer	21Ap11Dl
MULLANY, John	30	M	Laborer	21Ap11Dl
FOHEY, Michael	32	M	Laborer	21Ap11Dl
LANEY, Michael	32	M	Laborer	21Ap11Dl
FOHEY, Tim	26	M	Laborer	21Ap11Dl
SHAUGHNESSY, John	32	M	Laborer	21Ap11Dl
Mary	30	F	Spinster	21Ap11Dl
Patt	03	M	Child	21Ap11Dl
BRODERICK, Patt	32	M	Laborer	21Ap11Dl
CONNELLY, Montis	20	M	Laborer	21Ap11Dl
MURRAY, Patt	00	M	Laborer	21Ap11Dl
NOON, Michael	00	M	Laborer	21Ap11Dl
PIGOTT, John	18	M	Laborer	21Ap11Dl
Mary	16	F	Spinster	21Ap11Dl
SILK, James	40	M	Laborer	21Ap11Dl
Bridget	17	F	Spinster	21Ap11Dl
SULLY, Michael	22	M	Laborer	21Ap11Dl
DAILY, Martin	30	M	Laborer	21Ap11Dl
KANE, Michael	25	M	Laborer	21Ap11Dl
Winifred	21	M	Laborer	21Ap11Dl
GILL, Bridgett	17	F	Spinster	21Ap11Dl
DEVANY, Winifred	20	M	Laborer	21Ap11Dl
FANNOHER, Michal	26	M	Laborer	21Ap11Dl
OSHEA, James	22	M	Laborer	21Ap11Dl
Lally	22	F	Spinster	21Ap11Dl
Mary	00	F	Spinster	21Ap11Dl
GLEESON, John	20	M	Laborer	21Ap11Dl
DEALY, Francis	20	M	Laborer	21Ap11Dl
KINNAVEY, Martin	20	M	Laborer	21Ap11Dl
Honor	22	F	Spinster	21Ap11Dl
Daniel	43	M	Laborer	21Ap11Dl
MADDENS, Henry	30	M	Laborer	21Ap11Dl
Winifred	22	M	Laborer	21Ap11Dl
MURPHY, John	33	M	Laborer	21Ap11Dl
MONAGHAN, Michael	28	M	Laborer	21Ap11Dl
FAHEY, Michael	25	M	Laborer	21Ap11Dl
Honor	25	M	Laborer	21Ap11Dl
WALSH, James	22	M	Laborer	21Ap11Dl
CONNELLY, Mary	17	F	Spinster	21Ap11Dl
CARTY, Patt	30	M	Laborer	21Ap11Dl
Michael	25	M	Laborer	21Ap11Dl
FORD, Patt	20	M	Laborer	21Ap11Dl
KELLY, Michael	23	M	Laborer	21Ap11Dl
BARRETT, Michael	26	M	Laborer	21Ap11Dl
KENSING, Brigt.	22	F	Spinster	21Ap11Dl
FRANCIS, Richard	30	M	Laborer	21Ap11Dl
REYNOLDS, Joseph	30	M	Laborer	21Ap11Dl
MULLONNEY, Michl.	20	M	Laborer	21Ap11Dl
KEANY, Mary	20	F	Spinster	21Ap11Dl
KEOGH, Patt	40	M	Laborer	21Ap11Dl
DOYLE, Patt	26	M	Laborer	21Ap11Dl
Mary	18	F	Spinster	21Ap11Dl

NAMES OF PASSENGERS	AGE	SEX	OCCUPATIONS	DATE PORT SHIP
OLOUGHLIN, John	32	M	Laborer	21Ap11DI
LOFTESS, Dorly	29	M	Laborer	21Ap11DI
SCAHILL, Tim	29	M	Laborer	21Ap11DI
FINN, Michael	29	M	Laborer	21Ap11DI
FLAHERTY, Michael	19	F	Spinster	21Ap11DI
DONAHOUGH, Mary	18	F	Spinster	21Ap11DI
SHELLY, Miss	16	M	Laborer	21Ap11DI
GANNON, Stephen	30	M	Laborer	21Ap11DI
MCCARTY, Peter	26	M	Laborer	21Ap11DI
Mary	20	F	Spinster	21Ap11DI
LUCAS, Patt	20	M	Laborer	21Ap11DI
MCDERMONT, John	30	M	Laborer	21Ap11DI
Mary	30	F	Spinster	21Ap11DI
CULLIMAN, Andw.	25	M	Laborer	21Ap11DI
Bridget	21	F	Spinster	21Ap11DI
MCGRATH, Kitty	16	F	Spinster	21Ap11DI
SALLY, Pat	16	M	Laborer	21Ap11DI
MULLAN, Margaret	21	F	Spinster	21Ap11DI
MOSTYN, William	33	M	Laborer	21Ap11DI
MORTEN, Mary	26	F	Spinster	21Ap11DI
SHAUGHNESSYY, James	20	M	Laborer	21Ap11DI
HYGINS, Daniel	19	M	Laborer	21Ap11DI
WHEELAN, Michael	19	M	Laborer	21Ap11DI
CASEY, Bridget	24	F	Spinster	21Ap11DI
COHEN, Margt.	24	F	Spinster	21Ap11DI
MURPHEY, Michael	22	M	Laborer	21Ap11DI
HEALY, Ellen	00	F	Spinster	21Ap11DI
HUNNING, John	00	M	Laborer	21Ap11DI
FAHEY, Michael	17	M	Laborer	21Ap11DI
GILL, Misia	17	F	Spinster	21Ap11DI
FOLEY, Peter	24	M	Laborer	21Ap11DI
FOLON, Ellen	20	F	Spinster	21Ap11DI
CAVNEY, Mark	20	M	Laborer	21Ap11DI
KING, John	28	M	Laborer	21Ap11DI
TUFFY, Thos.	28	M	Laborer	21Ap11DI
JENNINGS, Thos.	22	M	Laborer	21Ap11DI
DAMILLAN, Brigt.	18	F	Spinster	21Ap11DI
BYRNE, Martyn	22	M	Laborer	21Ap11DI
HARE, Catheryne	22	F	Spinster	21Ap11DI
Patt	04	M	Child	21Ap11DI
MURPHY, Patt	00	M	None	21Ap11DI
FEELY, Michael	00	M	Merchant	21Ap11DI
MAHON, Edward	00	M	Merchant	21Ap11DI
BOTHELL, Joseph	00	M	Merchant	21Ap11DI

SUPERIOR 21 APRIL 1848

From Belfast

NAMES OF PASSENGERS	AGE	SEX	OCCUPATIONS	DATE PORT SHIP
WINTON, Thomas	18	M	Painter	21Ap07Fb
MURPHY, Margt.	29	F	Servant	21Ap07Fb
FERGUSON, Margt.	20	F	Servant	21Ap07Fb
FORSTER, Susan	40	F	WI	21Ap07Fb
MONTGOMERY, Mary	20	F	Spinster	21Ap07Fb
GRAHAMS, Jane	30	F	Spinster	21Ap07Fb
Rebecca	09	F	Child	21Ap07Fb
Jane	05	F	Child	21Ap07Fb
Hannah	.00	F	Infant	21Ap07Fb
BRADLEY, Biddy	10	F	Unknown	21Ap07Fb
Pat	30	M	Laborer	21Ap07Fb
Felix	25	M	Laborer	21Ap07Fb
JOHNSON, James	20	M	Laborer	21Ap07Fb
MONTGOMERY, John	40	M	Laborer	21Ap07Fb
Jane	39	F	Unknown	21Ap07Fb
Richard	20	M	Unknown	21Ap07Fb
Diana	17	F	Spinster	21Ap07Fb
Robert	14	M	Unknown	21Ap07Fb
William	09	M	Child	21Ap07Fb
Thomas	07	M	Child	21Ap07Fb
Died-At-Sea				
Sarah	05	F	Child	21Ap07Fb
KITCHART, John	20	M	Unknown	21Ap07Fb
CURO, Pat	20	M	Laborer	21Ap07Fb
SHANE, James	29	M	Laborer	21Ap07Fb
MCKEE, James	27	M	Laborer	21Ap07Fb
PLUNKETT, Ann	60	F	Wife	21Ap07Fb
John	23	M	Unknown	21Ap07Fb
James	21	M	Laborer	21Ap07Fb
Alice	18	F	Unknown	21Ap07Fb
ONEILE, Cathr.	28	F	Unknown	21Ap07Fb
Isabella	24	F	Unknown	21Ap07Fb
MCALEEMAN, Roger	29	M	Unknown	21Ap07Fb
Mary	26	F	Unknown	21Ap07Fb
Mary	18	F	Unknown	21Ap07Fb
Mary	17	F	Unknown	21Ap07Fb
Margt.	24	F	Unknown	21Ap07Fb
Catharine	26	F	Unknown	21Ap07Fb
GALLAGHER, Mary	22	F	Unknown	21Ap07Fb
Margt.	20	F	Wife	21Ap07Fb
Mary	.00	F	Infant	21Ap07Fb
MCALLEEMAN, Agnes	24	F	Unknown	21Ap07Fb
HOGG, Robt.	24	M	Laborer	21Ap07Fb
HAGAN, Michl.	22	M	Laborer	21Ap07Fb
CUBITT, John	40	M	Laborer	21Ap07Fb
KERR, Joseph	40	M	Laborer	21Ap07Fb
Jane (W)	42	F	Wife	21Ap07Fb
Margt.	13	F	Unknown	21Ap07Fb
Joseph	09	M	Child	21Ap07Fb
Thomas	03	M	Child	21Ap07Fb
Jane	.00	F	Infant	21Ap07Fb
WATTERSON, Sally	20	F	Unknown	21Ap07Fb
BARRY, Thomas	20	M	Laborer	21Ap07Fb
MOORE, James	20	M	Laborer	21Ap07Fb
ARMSTRONG, James	47	M	Laborer	21Ap07Fb
Eliza	40	F	Wife	21Ap07Fb
Rose	13	F	Child	21Ap07Fb
Eliza	11	F	Child	21Ap07Fb
Jane	09	F	Child	21Ap07Fb
Thomas	08	M	Child	21Ap07Fb
Ellen	07	F	Child	21Ap07Fb
Francis	04	F	Child	21Ap07Fb
Mary-Ann	.00	F	Infant	21Ap07Fb
BROWN, Sarah	30	F	Unknown	21Ap07Fb
Sarah	09	F	Child	21Ap07Fb
Thos.	07	M	Child	21Ap07Fb
Eliza	05	F	Child	21Ap07Fb
John	04	M	Child	21Ap07Fb
Joseph	03	M	Child	21Ap07Fb
Margt.	.00	F	Infant	21Ap07Fb
BOYLE, Patk.	35	M	Laborer	21Ap07Fb
Biddy	35	F	Wife	21Ap07Fb
Thomas	04	M	Child	21Ap07Fb
Mary	20	F	Unknown	21Ap07Fb
Biddy	20	F	Unknown	21Ap07Fb
CUOHS, Pat	13	M	Unknown	21Ap07Fb
MCNABB, Robt.	20	M	Laborer	21Ap07Fb
LENNOCH, Francis	20	M	Laborer	21Ap07Fb
MCLEAN, Saml.	18	M	Laborer	21Ap07Fb
DUNLAP, John	20	M	Laborer	21Ap07Fb
PUTTON, Edwd.	19	M	Laborer	21Ap07Fb
KANT, Joseph	26	M	Laborer	21Ap07Fb
CASON, Robert	20	M	Laborer	21Ap07Fb
Eliza	18	F	Laborer	21Ap07Fb
CUSHIKERIN, Henry	21	M	Laborer	21Ap07Fb
Francis	24	M	Laborer	21Ap07Fb
DICKSON, Thomas	28	M	Laborer	21Ap07Fb
BEATTY, James	21	M	Laborer	21Ap07Fb
LYLES, Jane	22	F	Wife	21Ap07Fb
Sarah	12	F	Child	21Ap07Fb
Margt.	21	F	Unknown	21Ap07Fb
John	09	M	Child	21Ap07Fb
Robert	07	M	Child	21Ap07Fb
Rebecca	03	F	Child	21Ap07Fb

NAMES OF PASSENGERS	AGE	SEX	OCCUPATIONS	DATE PORT SHIP
MCCONNELL, John	23	M	Laborer	21Ap07Fb
Jane	21	F	Wife	21Ap07Fb
KERRY, Mary	20	F	Unknown	21Ap07Fb
GALLAGHER, Pat	20	M	Laborer	21Ap07Fb
RAMSEY, Saml.	21	M	Laborer	21Ap07Fb
Thos.	22	M	Laborer	21Ap07Fb
KYLE, Robert	20	M	Laborer	21Ap07Fb
DICKSON, Mary	22	F	Laborer	21Ap07Fb
HUNTER, John	30	M	Laborer	21Ap07Fb
LINN, Geo.	20	M	Laborer	21Ap07Fb
HONSTON, James	18	M	Laborer	21Ap07Fb
HIBBARD, Thos.	15	M	Laborer	21Ap07Fb
SMITH, Thos.	18	M	Laborer	21Ap07Fb
Andw.	19	M	Laborer	21Ap07Fb
MCCURDY, Archy	21	M	Laborer	21Ap07Fb
DESMOND, Cath.	40	F	Wife	21Ap07Fb
DIAMOND, Wm.	18	M	Laborer	21Ap07Fb
Pat	15	M	Laborer	21Ap07Fb
KELLY, Henry	35	M	Laborer	21Ap07Fb
DEVLIN, Bridgt.	20	F	Unknown	21Ap07Fb
MURPHY, Ann	20	F	Unknown	21Ap07Fb
HARVEY, Mary	17	F	Unknown	21Ap07Fb
GORMIG, Wm.	40	M	Unknown	21Ap07Fb
Jane	38	F	Wife	21Ap07Fb
ROBERTSON, Robt.	32	M	Laborer	21Ap07Fb
MCNIGHT, Mary	40	F	Laborer	21Ap07Fb
NICHOLL, James	25	M	Laborer	21Ap07Fb
STEPHERD, James	20	M	Laborer	21Ap07Fb
LOUGHLIN, Ann	13	F	Unknown	21Ap07Fb
Dominick	11	M	Unknown	21Ap07Fb
GRAHAM, Alex.	30	M	Unknown	21Ap07Fb
REA, Reubin	19	M	Unknown	21Ap07Fb
Eliza	18	F	Unknown	21Ap07Fb
Mary	26	F	Unknown	21Ap07Fb
LIVINGSTON, William	22	M	Unknown	21Ap07Fb
Eliza	40	F	Wife	21Ap07Fb
Sarah-Elizth.	20	F	Unknown	21Ap07Fb
Margt.	24	F	Unknown	21Ap07Fb
DAVISON, John	24	M	Laborer	21Ap07Fb
HASTY, Thos.	16	M	Laborer	21Ap07Fb
LYLE, Robt.	40	M	Laborer	21Ap07Fb
Margt.	01	F	Child	21Ap07Fb
TAYLOR, Mary	16	F	Unknown	21Ap07Fb
Eliza	14	F	Unknown	21Ap07Fb
PRIMROSE, Wm.	22	M	Unknown	21Ap07Fb
BRADLEY, John	18	M	Laborer	21Ap07Fb
LITTLE, Alex.	22	M	Laborer	21Ap07Fb
CRILLY, Danl.	20	M	Laborer	21Ap07Fb
HENRY, Henry	21	M	Laborer	21Ap07Fb
Catharine	31	F	Wife	21Ap07Fb
MCCOTTON, Jane	27	F	Unknown	21Ap07Fb
CAMPBELL, Stewart	26	M	Farmer	21Ap07Fb
KAND, James	23	M	Unknown	21Ap07Fb
HENRY, Mary	.00	F	Infant	21Ap07Fb
ROBINSON, Andrew	20	M	Laborer	21Ap07Fb
CALLAGHEN, Felix	37	M	Laborer	21Ap07Fb
Felina	16	F	Laborer	21Ap07Fb
DONGHERTY, John	30	M	Laborer	21Ap07Fb
MCMURRAY, Danl.	50	M	Laborer	21Ap07Fb
Sarah	45	F	Wife	21Ap07Fb
HONAN, Hugh	30	M	Laborer	21Ap07Fb
Eliza	30	F	Laborer	21Ap07Fb
Sarah	14	F	Unknown	21Ap07Fb
Wm.	03	M	Child	21Ap07Fb
VANCH, James	24	M	Laborer	21Ap07Fb
Richd.	20	M	Laborer	21Ap07Fb
MAY, Ann	22	F	Unknown	21Ap07Fb
WALLS, Thos.	23	M	Unknown	21Ap07Fb
SERTWOOD, Thos.	24	M	Unknown	21Ap07Fb
DICKSON, Wm.	28	M	Unknown	21Ap07Fb
John	20	M	Unknown	21Ap07Fb
KEARNY, James	23	M	Unknown	21Ap07Fb
NUGENT, Terrance	18	M	Unknown	21Ap07Fb
Francis	15	M	Unknown	21Ap07Fb
MCELROY, Robt.	22	M	Unknown	21Ap07Fb
BEAR, John	20	M	Unknown	21Ap07Fb
BELL, Henry	30	M	Unknown	21Ap07Fb
HIGGINS, Mary	21	F	Spinster	21Ap07Fb
HARRIGAN, Ellen	25	F	Spinster	21Ap07Fb
SANDFORD, John	25	M	Laborer	21Ap07Fb
Michl.	22	M	Laborer	21Ap07Fb
MULLIN, Hugh	21	M	Laborer	21Ap07Fb
Cathr.	20	F	Spinster	21Ap07Fb
LAVERTY, Neill	20	M	Laborer	21Ap07Fb
Cathr.	20	F	Spinster	21Ap07Fb
VENEY, Robt.	12	M	Unknown	21Ap07Fb
CUNNINGHAM, Andw.	21	M	Laborer	21Ap07Fb
MCKEE, Robt.	20	M	Laborer	21Ap07Fb
JACKSON, Leslie	30	M	Laborer	21Ap07Fb
MCMIUM, Williams	28	M	Laborer	21Ap07Fb
MEEHAN, Williams	26	M	Laborer	21Ap07Fb
DERRY, John	21	M	Laborer	21Ap07Fb
LINDSAY, David	21	M	Laborer	21Ap07Fb
MCKEAGH, Bernd.	20	M	Laborer	21Ap07Fb
SANDFORD, Thos.	29	M	Laborer	21Ap07Fb
VANCE, Eliza	21	F	Spinster	21Ap07Fb
MCALLAHAN, Geo.	21	M	Laborer	21Ap07Fb
BUCHANAN, Wm.	29	M	Laborer	21Ap07Fb
Sarah	28	F	Wife	21Ap07Fb
DUROSS, Mary	12	F	Child	21Ap07Fb
CONLON, Bernd.	20	M	Farmer	21Ap07Fb
GIBSON, Ann	20	F	Spinster	21Ap07Fb
CROPLEY, John	25	M	Farmer	21Ap07Fb
MCGUIRE, Biddy	40	F	Farmer	21Ap07Fb
SIMPSON, Wm.	30	M	Farmer	21Ap07Fb
Jane	30	F	Wife	21Ap07Fb
James	.00	M	Infant	21Ap07Fb
Died-At-Sea				
WARD, Pat	40	M	Laborer	21Ap07Fb
MARKEY, John	20	M	Laborer	21Ap07Fb
BROWN, U	.00	U	Infant	21Ap07Fb
Born-At-Sea				

ELIJAH-SWIFT 21 APRIL 1848

From Glasgow

NAMES OF PASSENGERS	AGE	SEX	OCCUPATIONS	DATE PORT SHIP
WOODS, Mary	16	F	Weaver	21Ap04Fc
GIBNEY, Patk.	22	M	Blacksmith	21Ap04Fc
FREED, John	34	M	Miner	21Ap04Fc
GIBRAN, Peter	30	M	Shoemaker	21Ap04Fc
Christina	30	F	None	21Ap04Fc
ELLIOTT, Henry	26	M	Mason	21Ap04Fc
Penelighy	21	M	Furrier	21Ap04Fc
MCCABE, John	38	M	Collier	21Ap04Fc
Mary	36	F	None	21Ap04Fc
Patrick	16	M	Collier	21Ap04Fc
John	06	M	Child	21Ap04Fc
CLERKEN, Patk.	21	M	Unknown	21Ap04Fc
BROADY, Frances	17	F	None	21Ap04Fc
MCGARVEY, Michl.	20	M	None	21Ap04Fc
CUNNINGHAM, John	31	M	Miner	21Ap04Fc
KALLAGHAN, Francis	24	M	Laborer	21Ap04Fc
MCCULLOCH, James	28	M	Collier	21Ap04Fc
MOORE, Alexander	27	M	Salesman	21Ap04Fc
Margaret	27	F	None	21Ap04Fc
Samuel	04	M	Child	21Ap04Fc
Elizabeth	.08	F	Infant	21Ap04Fc
BARR, Mary	19	F	None	21Ap04Fc
CALLUM, Geo.M.	16	M	Weaver	21Ap04Fc
DUGHAN, Thomas	26	M	Laborer	21Ap04Fc
BRASLAND, Neil	24	M	Laborer	21Ap04Fc
MUNDY, Jas.	32	M	Laborer	21Ap04Fc
BROWN, Cen	32	M	Laborer	21Ap04Fc

NAMES OF PASSENGERS	AGE	SEX	OCCUPATIONS	DATE PORT SHIP
MUNDY, Sallay	28	F	None	21Ap04Fc
BROWN, Mary	23	F	None	21Ap04Fc
MUNDY, Rosanna	03	F	Child	21Ap04Fc
BROWN, John	04	M	Child	21Ap04Fc
WILLIAMSON, Adam	32	M	Laborer	21Ap04Fc
Ann	09	F	Child	21Ap04Fc
John	08	M	Child	21Ap04Fc
James	49	M	Laborer	21Ap04Fc
BRADEN, Jas.	25	M	Miner	21Ap04Fc
WILLIAMSON, Jas.	20	M	Miner	21Ap04Fc
MCWILLIAMS, Archy	40	M	Mason	21Ap04Fc
Esther	32	F	None	21Ap04Fc
Mary	15	F	None	21Ap04Fc
Jane	13	F	None	21Ap04Fc
Archy	05	M	Child	21Ap04Fc
William	03	M	Child	21Ap04Fc
Esther	01	F	Child	21Ap04Fc
MCAULEY, Jas.	28	M	Mariner	21Ap04Fc
Mary	21	F	None	21Ap04Fc
Mary	07	F	Child	21Ap04Fc
Katy	04	F	Child	21Ap04Fc
John	02	M	Child	21Ap04Fc
James	.03	M	Infant	21Ap04Fc

OHIO 21 APRIL 1848

From Liverpool

NAMES OF PASSENGERS	AGE	SEX	OCCUPATIONS	DATE PORT SHIP
RAGEN, Thos.	30	M	Grocer	21Ap02Bm
Mary	29	F	None	21Ap02Bm
Mickl.	10	M	None	21Ap02Bm
NUGENT, John	20	M	Laborer	21Ap02Bm
DALEY, Thos.	32	M	Farmer	21Ap02Bm
Mary	32	F	None	21Ap02Bm
Terrence	22	M	Farmer	21Ap02Bm
John	20	M	Farmer	21Ap02Bm
John	20	M	Farmer	21Ap02Bm
Mara	20	F	None	21Ap02Bm
Thos.	14	M	None	21Ap02Bm
Jullett	11	F	None	21Ap02Bm
Mare	09	F	None	21Ap02Bm
Ellen	02	F	Child	21Ap02Bm
Ann	.03	F	Infant	21Ap02Bm
GILLON, John	24	M	Servant	21Ap02Bm
RAHALL, Mary	22	F	Servant	21Ap02Bm
KENNEDY, Patt	24	M	Farmer	21Ap02Bm
Marg.	20	F	None	21Ap02Bm
Bridgett	18	F	None	21Ap02Bm
DUGEN, Pat	20	M	Laborer	21Ap02Bm
Ellen	20	F	None	21Ap02Bm
SHOUGHANY, John	30	M	Laborer	21Ap02Bm
BRADY, Mary	19	F	None	21Ap02Bm
CARROLL, Patk.	35	M	Laborer	21Ap02Bm
FEENEY, Mary	17	F	None	21Ap02Bm
CONREY, Cath.	19	F	Milliner	21Ap02Bm
EAGLESTON, Elizebeth	60	F	None	21Ap02Bm
Elizebeth-Ellen	16	F	None	21Ap02Bm
Cath.	09	F	Child	21Ap02Bm
MCCABE, Pat	40	M	Laborer	21Ap02Bm
Elizebeth	30	F	None	21Ap02Bm
MCENNERNEY, Ann	20	F	None	21Ap02Bm
DONNELLY, Jane	55	F	None	21Ap02Bm
HAVEN, Bridgett	26	F	None	21Ap02Bm
Mary	21	F	None	21Ap02Bm
Marg.	16	F	None	21Ap02Bm
Ann	06	F	Child	21Ap02Bm
John	04	M	Child	21Ap02Bm
RILEY, Mary	16	F	None	21Ap02Bm
SMITH, Patk.	35	M	Laborer	21Ap02Bm
SMITH, Marg.	30	F	None	21Ap02Bm
Mary	20	F	None	21Ap02Bm
Cath.	09	F	Child	21Ap02Bm
Rose	05	F	Child	21Ap02Bm
MCCABE, Judy	18	F	None	21Ap02Bm
MCGARRETY, Ellen	20	F	None	21Ap02Bm
Margt.	17	F	None	21Ap02Bm
CURREN, Susan	21	F	None	21Ap02Bm
GORDON, Henr.	40	M	Shoemaker	21Ap02Bm
MCCAFFREY, Bridgett	44	F	None	21Ap02Bm
DAVLIN, Mary	30	F	None	21Ap02Bm
Ann	07	F	Child	21Ap02Bm
Mary	05	F	Child	21Ap02Bm
FOX, Francis	23	M	Laborer	21Ap02Bm
KEENAN, Ann	24	F	None	21Ap02Bm
ROGERS, Mary	40	F	None	21Ap02Bm
James	20	M	Laborer	21Ap02Bm
LAUGHNIN, Ann	19	F	None	21Ap02Bm
Alice	20	F	None	21Ap02Bm
CONWAY, John	21	M	Laborer	21Ap02Bm
MCGUIRE, Thos.	20	M	Baker	21Ap02Bm
RILEY, Andw.	30	M	Laborer	21Ap02Bm
BEST, Mary	25	F	None	21Ap02Bm
Mary-Ann	02	F	None	21Ap02Bm
LEONARD, Patt	30	M	Farmer	21Ap02Bm
LURNEY, John	25	M	Farmer	21Ap02Bm
WALCH, Margt.	26	F	None	21Ap02Bm
FORUM, Pat	18	M	None	21Ap02Bm
MURPHY, Pat	18	M	None	21Ap02Bm
DENOUGH, Jas.	17	M	None	21Ap02Bm
KENNY, Rose	19	F	None	21Ap02Bm
MCGOWEN, Mary	18	F	None	21Ap02Bm
MURPHY, Cath.	16	F	None	21Ap02Bm
BLOYD, Jas.	21	M	None	21Ap02Bm
HESTER, Martin	30	M	Laborer	21Ap02Bm
SACHELL, John	20	M	Laborer	21Ap02Bm
ROACH, John	24	M	Laborer	21Ap02Bm
Francis	18	M	Laborer	21Ap02Bm
MCLAUGLIN, Saml.	25	M	Carpenter	21Ap02Bm
WALDREN, Mickl.	30	M	Laborer	21Ap02Bm
Willm.	20	M	Laborer	21Ap02Bm
BOWEN, John	25	M	Laborer	21Ap02Bm
KOWEN, Owen	28	M	Laborer	21Ap02Bm
WARD, Peter	20	M	Laborer	21Ap02Bm
MULLORE, Mary	28	F	None	21Ap02Bm
LEFFEN, Thos.	32	M	None	21Ap02Bm
DAY, Thos.	22	M	None	21Ap02Bm
DABER, Margt.	60	F	None	21Ap02Bm
Dennis	32	M	None	21Ap02Bm
Johanna	30	F	None	21Ap02Bm
Willm.	06	M	Child	21Ap02Bm
DASER, James	04	M	Child	21Ap02Bm
Pat	02	M	Child	21Ap02Bm
MULLER, Mary	20	F	None	21Ap02Bm
DALLIS, Pat	21	M	Laborer	21Ap02Bm
SWEENER, Danl.	18	M	Laborer	21Ap02Bm
Bridgett	17	F	None	21Ap02Bm
MILLER, John	22	M	None	21Ap02Bm
HOPKINS, Martin	25	M	None	21Ap02Bm
LOGAN, John	20	M	None	21Ap02Bm
Mary	18	F	None	21Ap02Bm
CARROLL, Pat	45	M	Laborer	21Ap02Bm
SHAY, Ellen	25	F	None	21Ap02Bm
Mary	20	F	None	21Ap02Bm
MULLIGEN, Pat	36	M	Laborer	21Ap02Bm
Ann	30	F	None	21Ap02Bm
Cath.	08	F	Child	21Ap02Bm
Ann	04	F	Child	21Ap02Bm
Bridgett	.11	F	Infant	21Ap02Bm
GILLON, Thos.	22	M	Laborer	21Ap02Bm
Margt.	20	F	None	21Ap02Bm
BARRIS, Edmund	25	M	None	21Ap02Bm
ROUSK, Pat	25	M	None	21Ap02Bm
CRINGLE, Willm.	25	M	None	21Ap02Bm
HAINEY, John	30	M	None	21Ap02Bm

NAMES OF PASSENGERS	AGE	SEX	OCCUPATIONS	DATE PORT SHIP
LOGAN, Luke	43	M	None	21Ap02Bm
Cath.	18	F	None	21Ap02Bm
DAVIN, Willm.	20	M	Miller	21Ap02Bm
Hannah	19	F	None	21Ap02Bm
HIFFEREN, James	21	M	Miller	21Ap02Bm
DENNIS, Bridgett	30	F	None	21Ap02Bm
Ann	13	F	None	21Ap02Bm
John	09	M	Child	21Ap02Bm
Richd.	02	M	Child	21Ap02Bm
Margt.	.11	F	Infant	21Ap02Bm
CARROLL, Richd.	20	M	Miller	21Ap02Bm
BIRCH, Mary	17	F	None	21Ap02Bm
DUNN, Bridgett	25	F	None	21Ap02Bm
SAVAGE, Walter	25	M	Laborer	21Ap02Bm
Mary	25	F	None	21Ap02Bm
GRIMES, Richd.	18	M	Laborer	21Ap02Bm
GARTLAND, Ann	32	F	None	21Ap02Bm
MULLONEY, Pat	19	M	Laborer	21Ap02Bm
HEMMETT, Mary	24	F	None	21Ap02Bm
JESSEP, Eliza	19	F	None	21Ap02Bm
GALNIN, Mare	22	F	None	21Ap02Bm
CUMSKY, Cristy	30	M	Laborer	21Ap02Bm
BOYL, Rose	22	F	None	21Ap02Bm
TIGH, Pat	28	M	Farmer	21Ap02Bm
Mick	27	M	Farmer	21Ap02Bm
Bridgett	23	F	None	21Ap02Bm
Ann	20	F	None	21Ap02Bm
Cath.	16	F	None	21Ap02Bm
Bryen	14	M	None	21Ap02Bm
Bridgett	50	F	None	21Ap02Bm
John	24	M	Farmer	21Ap02Bm
Mathew	23	M	Farmer	21Ap02Bm
RUSK, Eliza	30	F	None	21Ap02Bm
MCDONNA, Pat	38	M	Laborer	21Ap02Bm
BRANNEN, Ann	36	F	None	21Ap02Bm
KOWIN, James	11	M	None	21Ap02Bm
Honor	08	F	Child	21Ap02Bm
BRANNOCK, James	40	M	Laborer	21Ap02Bm
RYEN, John	40	M	Bricklayer	21Ap02Bm
CASSIDY, Ellen	21	F	None	21Ap02Bm
MORAN, Eliza	18	F	None	21Ap02Bm
BLEWITT, Ellen	30	F	None	21Ap02Bm
Mary	.11	F	Infant	21Ap02Bm
FLOOD, Rosey	15	F	None	21Ap02Bm
SHAVLER, Mary	23	F	None	21Ap02Bm
MCCANN, Edwd.	25	M	Laborer	21Ap02Bm
John	19	M	Laborer	21Ap02Bm
MANNION, Ellen	28	F	None	21Ap02Bm
Thos.	05	M	Child	21Ap02Bm
Danl.	03	M	Child	21Ap02Bm
Martin	.00	M	Infant	21Ap02Bm
MCKENNA, Sarrah	30	F	None	21Ap02Bm
Sarah	22	F	None	21Ap02Bm
Cath.	17	F	None	21Ap02Bm
John	20	M	Laborer	21Ap02Bm
Mary	18	F	None	21Ap02Bm
Mick.	12	M	None	21Ap02Bm
Rose	10	F	None	21Ap02Bm
Pat	.11	M	Infant	21Ap02Bm
DRUDY, Mary	20	F	None	21Ap02Bm
PHALEY, Ann	24	F	None	21Ap02Bm
DRUDY, John	05	M	Child	21Ap02Bm
MANNION, Cath.	19	F	None	21Ap02Bm
DOYLE, James	33	M	Laborer	21Ap02Bm
Bridgett	33	F	None	21Ap02Bm
Cristy	.04	M	Infant	21Ap02Bm
FARRY, Mary	50	F	None	21Ap02Bm
Margt.	10	F	None	21Ap02Bm
Michl.	06	M	Child	21Ap02Bm
Rose	03	F	Child	21Ap02Bm
KING, Mary	40	F	None	21Ap02Bm
Francis	08	F	Child	21Ap02Bm
Thos.	06	M	Child	21Ap02Bm
BRADY, Rose	30	F	None	21Ap02Bm
Rose	16	F	None	21Ap02Bm
ODONALD, Mick.	18	M	None	21Ap02Bm
MCGATNEY, Ann	22	F	None	21Ap02Bm
LEE, Mary	30	F	None	21Ap02Bm
Bridgett	03	F	Child	21Ap02Bm
CONNELL, Bridgett	20	F	None	21Ap02Bm
MURPHY, Johanna	28	F	None	21Ap02Bm
Chas.	04	M	Child	21Ap02Bm
CHICKLEY, John	25	M	Laborer	21Ap02Bm
Mary	23	F	Laborer	21Ap02Bm
STEWART, Cath.	19	F	Laborer	21Ap02Bm
LEONARD, Ann	30	F	Laborer	21Ap02Bm
RUSSELL, Silvestor	07	M	Child	21Ap02Bm
KOUGHAN, Pat	20	M	Laborer	21Ap02Bm
MURPHY, Mary	30	F	Laborer	21Ap02Bm
Julia	12	F	Laborer	21Ap02Bm
Cin	08	M	Child	21Ap02Bm
MCKENNA, Ann	27	F	None	21Ap02Bm
Cath.	.07	F	Infant	21Ap02Bm
DONNELLY, Rossanna	20	F	None	21Ap02Bm
Ellen	18	F	None	21Ap02Bm
HARNON, John	26	M	Laborer	21Ap02Bm
MCKENNA, Bernard	35	M	Laborer	21Ap02Bm
Margt.	30	F	None	21Ap02Bm
SCHWEB, John	26	M	Laborer	21Ap02Bm
Mary	20	F	None	21Ap02Bm

NORTHUMBERLAND 21 APRIL 1848

From London

NAMES OF PASSENGERS	AGE	SEX	OCCUPATIONS	DATE PORT SHIP
FINIE, Adam	34	M	Merchant	21Ap21Cg
Jane	24	F	None	21Ap21Cg
James	05	M	Child	21Ap21Cg
TAYLOR, Joseph	28	M	Gentleman	21Ap21Cg
FISHER, James	21	M	Gentleman	21Ap21Cg
CAUSLAND, Charly	33	M	Ba	21Ap21Cg
PRATT, Henry-C.	26	M	Farmer	21Ap21Cg
Jane	30	F	Farmer	21Ap21Cg
PLANT, Emma	30	F	Farmer	21Ap21Cg
Emma	08	F	Child	21Ap21Cg
Ceuissidy	06	F	Child	21Ap21Cg
Henry	05	M	Child	21Ap21Cg
Frank	04	M	Child	21Ap21Cg
CHILANEN, Richard	23	M	Farmer	21Ap21Cg
Elizbth.	25	F	Farmer	21Ap21Cg
BERMAN, Wm.	23	M	Miller	21Ap21Cg
Benjamen	19	M	Miller	21Ap21Cg
BROOKS, Wm.T.	22	M	Carpenter	21Ap21Cg
LEAREA, Mark	24	M	Carpenter	21Ap21Cg
LAMBERT, John	34	M	Hatter	21Ap21Cg
CHEAKFIELD, Thos.	33	M	Farmer	21Ap21Cg
WALSCH, John	22	M	Clerk	21Ap21Cg
WILKIE, John	22	M	Farmer	21Ap21Cg
LANG, Francis	26	M	Farmer	21Ap21Cg
SIMMONS, Thos.	49	M	Farmer	21Ap21Cg
GUNTHER, Frank-R.	23	M	Brewer	21Ap21Cg
MEYERS, Christian	22	M	Unknown	21Ap21Cg
WORMACK, William-G.	38	M	Painter	21Ap21Cg
Caroline	29	F	None	21Ap21Cg
WRIGHT, Thomas	40	M	Currier	21Ap21Cg
Emma	36	F	Currier	21Ap21Cg
CARR, John	09	M	Child	21Ap21Cg
GREEN, George	50	M	Gdnr	21Ap21Cg
Mary	50	F	Gdnr	21Ap21Cg
James	22	M	Gdnr	21Ap21Cg
George	21	M	Gdnr	21Ap21Cg
William	11	M	Gdnr	21Ap21Cg
LYONS, Charlotte	45	F	Gdnr	21Ap21Cg
GEAR, William	55	M	Gdnr	21Ap21Cg

NAMES OF PASSENGERS	AGE	SEX	OCCUPATIONS	DATE PORT SHIP
GEAR, Fanny	50	F	None	21Ap21Cg
MCKENSIE, Stephen	20	M	Joiner	21Ap21Cg
MORRIS, Thomas	50	M	Tailor	21Ap21Cg
Ann	46	F	Tailor	21Ap21Cg
FOY, Thomas	30	M	Painter	21Ap21Cg
Sarah	21	F	None	21Ap21Cg
Catherine	.00	F	Infant	21Ap21Cg
Winefred	.00	F	Infant	21Ap21Cg
GRAVES, Andrew	23	M	Wheelwright	21Ap21Cg
Mary	22	F	None	21Ap21Cg
HEATH, William	22	M	Dyer	21Ap21Cg
LAWRENCE, Thomas	32	M	Milkman	21Ap21Cg
HUSLEY, David	16	M	Milkman	21Ap21Cg
BRYAN, Cornelius	50	M	Laborer	21Ap21Cg
Rrichard	20	M	Mason	21Ap21Cg
Cornelius	12	M	Mason	21Ap21Cg
ROURKE, Michael	21	M	Laborer	21Ap21Cg
SHEEN, Michael	29	M	Laborer	21Ap21Cg
Timothy	21	M	Laborer	21Ap21Cg
LEANEY, Morris	37	M	Painter	21Ap21Cg
FOWLER, John	35	M	Draper	21Ap21Cg
Harriet	38	F	Draper	21Ap21Cg
George	13	M	Draper	21Ap21Cg
Thomas	10	M	Draper	21Ap21Cg
William	08	M	Child	21Ap21Cg
Ellen	07	F	Child	21Ap21Cg
Richard	05	M	Child	21Ap21Cg
Oliver	03	M	Child	21Ap21Cg
Elizabeth	.00	F	Infant	21Ap21Cg
VALANTUCE, Isaac	27	M	Tailor	21Ap21Cg
CARTER, Oscar	23	M	Cndl	21Ap21Cg
TAYLOR, William	28	M	Carpenter	21Ap21Cg
TOBIN, Patrick	27	M	Laborer	21Ap21Cg
SULLIVAN, Timothy	24	M	Laborer	21Ap21Cg
LAMING, Frederick	28	M	Paper Maker	21Ap21Cg
Mary	23	F	Paper Maker	21Ap21Cg
Fredrick	03	M	Child	21Ap21Cg
DINMORE, Henry	24	M	Clerk	21Ap21Cg
Maria	26	F	Clerk	21Ap21Cg
Maria	.00	F	Infant	21Ap21Cg
WARNER, Benjamin	56	M	Watchmaker	21Ap21Cg
Sarah	51	F	Watchmaker	21Ap21Cg
Catharine	21	F	Watchmaker	21Ap21Cg
Leonard	13	M	Watchmaker	21Ap21Cg
Elizabeth	11	F	Watchmaker	21Ap21Cg
Margaret	08	F	Child	21Ap21Cg
PACKMAN, Thomas	08	M	Child	21Ap21Cg
Fredrick	07	M	Child	21Ap21Cg
COLMAN, Thomas	30	M	Farmer	21Ap21Cg
Susan	25	F	None	21Ap21Cg
Robert	.00	M	Infant	21Ap21Cg
SALMON, Charles	24	M	Farmer	21Ap21Cg
TURNER, William	15	M	Farmer	21Ap21Cg
DIBBELL, Robert	21	M	Farmer	21Ap21Cg
WEAVER, John	49	M	Gdnr	21Ap21Cg
Elizabeth	47	F	Gdnr	21Ap21Cg
MILLMAN, Hannah	38	F	Gdnr	21Ap21Cg
CROFT, Joseph	24	M	Farmer	21Ap21Cg
DAVIS, William	23	M	Laborer	21Ap21Cg
Thomas	18	M	Laborer	21Ap21Cg
WILSON, Willm-Thos.	37	M	Watchmaker	21Ap21Cg
Matilda	29	F	Watchmaker	21Ap21Cg
TILLEY, Richard	69	M	Shoemaker	21Ap21Cg
Ann	68	F	Shoemaker	21Ap21Cg
SHARP, John	28	M	Butcher	21Ap21Cg
Sarah	31	F	Unknown	21Ap21Cg
GALWIN, James	36	M	Hatter	21Ap21Cg
BRUNCE, Johanna	32	F	Sugar Baker	21Ap21Cg
HUGHES, Frederick	26	M	Cbtmkr	21Ap21Cg
LYNCH, John	26	M	Boatmaker	21Ap21Cg
Sarah	22	F	None	21Ap21Cg
RATCHETT, William	23	M	Sugar Baker	21Ap21Cg
HOPE, Thomas	32	M	Laborer	21Ap21Cg
Phoeby	29	F	Laborer	21Ap21Cg
WINKLEMAN, Johannes	23	M	Laborer	21Ap21Cg

NAMES OF PASSENGERS	AGE	SEX	OCCUPATIONS	DATE PORT SHIP
GREEN, Mary	17	F	Laborer	21Ap21Cg
Sarah	15	F	Laborer	21Ap21Cg
VERLINGER, Phillip	18	M	Laborer	21Ap21Cg
SALMON, William	22	M	Farmer	21Ap21Cg
FROST, Thomas	36	M	Miller	21Ap21Cg
HYAMS, Isaac	21	M	Tailor	21Ap21Cg
HART, David	25	M	Pclmkr	21Ap21Cg
OTTAWAY, Edward	24	M	Farmer	21Ap21Cg
Elizabeth	23	F	None	21Ap21Cg
Anna	.00	F	Infant	21Ap21Cg
Elizabeth	.00	F	Infant	21Ap21Cg
DUNGEY, James	19	M	Farmer	21Ap21Cg
James	50	M	Farmer	21Ap21Cg
Sarah	50	F	Unknown	21Ap21Cg
PARRY, Thomas	24	M	Musician	21Ap21Cg
KOZALOW, Carlton	20	M	Sugar Baker	21Ap21Cg
JOLTER, Herman	21	M	Sugar Baker	21Ap21Cg
SCHMEDED, Albert	22	M	Sugar Baker	21Ap21Cg
BELEMEIN, Welahard	22	M	Sugar Baker	21Ap21Cg
GUDEKAN, Johanns	25	M	Sugar Baker	21Ap21Cg
MCCARTHY, Catharine	20	F	Sugar Baker	21Ap21Cg
GIBBS, James	40	M	Sugar Baker	21Ap21Cg
Celia	34	F	Sugar Baker	21Ap21Cg
Esther	12	F	Sugar Baker	21Ap21Cg
Thomas	10	M	Sugar Baker	21Ap21Cg
Elizabeth	07	F	Child	21Ap21Cg
James	06	M	Child	21Ap21Cg
Aurelia	04	F	Child	21Ap21Cg
William	.00	M	Infant	21Ap21Cg
SCHELLEY, Richard	25	M	Wrhsmn	21Ap21Cg
ROBINS, Phillip	20	M	Tailor	21Ap21Cg
SHOTTEN, George	24	M	Grocer	21Ap21Cg
Henry	19	M	Draper	21Ap21Cg
ROBINSON, Mary	18	F	Draper	21Ap21Cg
Margret	16	F	Draper	21Ap21Cg
ROCKLETH, Thos.	23	M	Sailor	21Ap21Cg
WILLIAM, Chas.	30	M	Sailor	21Ap21Cg
MITCHELL, Chas.	21	M	Steward	21Ap21Cg

INFANTA 21 APRIL 1848

From Belfast

NAMES OF PASSENGERS	AGE	SEX	OCCUPATIONS	DATE PORT SHIP
CRAWFORD, Alexander	18	M	Unknown	21Ap07Fj
JORDAN, Robert	34	M	Surgeon	21Ap07Fj
Eliza	29	F	Unknown	21Ap07Fj
Ann	10	F	Unknown	21Ap07Fj
Thos.A.	08	M	Unknown	21Ap07Fj
Henry	06	M	Unknown	21Ap07Fj
Sarah	03	F	Unknown	21Ap07Fj
Joseph	01	M	Unknown	21Ap07Fj
WILSON, Charlotte	18	F	Servant	21Ap07Fj
ROBINSON, William	15	M	Servant	21Ap07Fj
MONAGHAN, Patrick	40	M	Mason	21Ap07Fj
Mary	38	F	Unknown	21Ap07Fj
Henry	14	M	Unknown	21Ap07Fj
Sarah	11	F	Unknown	21Ap07Fj
John	09	M	Unknown	21Ap07Fj
Mary-Ann	05	F	Unknown	21Ap07Fj
Catherine	04	F	Unknown	21Ap07Fj
WATTS, Robert	21	M	Farmer	21Ap07Fj
BOYER, Henry	20	M	None	21Ap07Fj
MCBRIDE, James	18	M	None	21Ap07Fj
DONALDSON, John	65	M	None	21Ap07Fj
Jane	40	F	None	21Ap07Fj
BURNEY, Hopewell	38	M	None	21Ap07Fj
SHAW, Phillip	50	M	None	21Ap07Fj
Margaret	18	F	None	21Ap07Fj
Wm.	09	M	Child	21Ap07Fj

NAMES OF PASSENGERS	AGE	SEX	OCCUPATIONS	DATE PORT SHIP
PHILLIPS, John	23	M	None	21Ap07Fj
QUIN, Catherine	22	F	None	21Ap07Fj
MCVEIGH, Catherine	21	F	None	21Ap07Fj
KELLY, Ellen	30	F	None	21Ap07Fj
BROWN, Robert	30	M	None	21Ap07Fj
Eliza	22	F	None	21Ap07Fj
William	20	M	None	21Ap07Fj
James	18	M	None	21Ap07Fj
DAVIDSON, Wm.	65	M	None	21Ap07Fj
Died-At-Sea				
Margaret	48	F	None	21Ap07Fj
Mary	66	F	None	21Ap07Fj
Hugh	17	M	None	21Ap07Fj
Mary	14	F	None	21Ap07Fj
William	11	M	None	21Ap07Fj
Eliza	09	F	Child	21Ap07Fj
Margaret	06	F	Child	21Ap07Fj
MCGUINESS, Patk.	21	M	None	21Ap07Fj
MCHOE, Joseph	28	M	None	21Ap07Fj
Mary	21	F	None	21Ap07Fj
CAMPBELL, James	25	M	None	21Ap07Fj
PARKER, Wm.	25	M	None	21Ap07Fj
HENDRICK, Mary	26	F	None	21Ap07Fj
MCADOO, David	28	M	None	21Ap07Fj
Eliza	25	F	None	21Ap07Fj
Samuel	03	M	Child	21Ap07Fj
Ann-Jane	01	F	Child	21Ap07Fj
GRAY, Fanny	35	F	None	21Ap07Fj
John	07	M	Child	21Ap07Fj
BROWN, John	18	M	None	21Ap07Fj
Margaret	19	F	None	21Ap07Fj
Ann	50	F	None	21Ap07Fj
KINNEAR, Robert	17	M	None	21Ap07Fj
SMYTH, James	27	M	None	21Ap07Fj
KINNEAR, James	20	M	None	21Ap07Fj
MAWHINNEY, James	30	M	None	21Ap07Fj
WORTHY, Joseph	35	M	None	21Ap07Fj
Thomas	22	M	None	21Ap07Fj
Ellen	50	F	None	21Ap07Fj
Rachael	25	F	None	21Ap07Fj
Isabella	23	F	None	21Ap07Fj
Mary-Jane	20	F	None	21Ap07Fj
Sally-Ann	18	F	None	21Ap07Fj
James	14	M	None	21Ap07Fj
Joseph	04	M	Child	21Ap07Fj
George	02	M	Child	21Ap07Fj
William	02	M	Child	21Ap07Fj
Rachael	02	F	Child	21Ap07Fj
STARS, Peter	18	M	None	21Ap07Fj
TIERNEY, Catherine	16	F	None	21Ap07Fj
HORNISK, Francis	22	M	None	21Ap07Fj
MULLER, Patrick	30	M	None	21Ap07Fj
Bridget	25	F	None	21Ap07Fj
Thomas	07	M	Child	21Ap07Fj
BURLUGH, Andrew	56	M	None	21Ap07Fj
Eliza	58	F	None	21Ap07Fj
Mary	26	F	None	21Ap07Fj
Henry	24	M	None	21Ap07Fj
TONNELEY, John	20	M	None	21Ap07Fj
Jane	16	F	None	21Ap07Fj
HENRY, Lawrence	25	M	None	21Ap07Fj
THURLEY, Sarah	30	F	None	21Ap07Fj
Joseph	14	M	None	21Ap07Fj
Susan	18	F	None	21Ap07Fj
Francis	06	M	Child	21Ap07Fj
LAMB, Ann	16	F	None	21Ap07Fj
MCGOUGH, Patrick	33	M	None	21Ap07Fj
Eliza	33	F	None	21Ap07Fj
Alice	07	F	Child	21Ap07Fj
Edward	05	M	Child	21Ap07Fj
Bridget	02	F	Child	21Ap07Fj
CULBERT, Thomas	19	M	None	21Ap07Fj
HUGHES, Michael	40	M	None	21Ap07Fj
Bridget	40	F	None	21Ap07Fj
Patrick	13	M	None	21Ap07Fj
HUGHES, Bridget	09	F	Child	21Ap07Fj
Francis	02	M	Child	21Ap07Fj
RYAN, Eliza	17	F	None	21Ap07Fj
DONNAGHY, Patrick	28	M	None	21Ap07Fj
HOLMES, John	24	M	None	21Ap07Fj
MCCLURE, James	30	M	None	21Ap07Fj
Ann	26	F	None	21Ap07Fj
Mary-Ann	03	F	None	21Ap07Fj
WILGER, Samuel	20	M	None	21Ap07Fj
RADCLIFFE, Wallace	35	M	None	21Ap07Fj
Mary	35	F	None	21Ap07Fj
Nancy	15	F	None	21Ap07Fj
Eliza	13	F	None	21Ap07Fj
Ann-Jane	09	F	Child	21Ap07Fj
HENRY, Sarah	20	F	None	21Ap07Fj
Mary	18	F	None	21Ap07Fj
HEGAN, Hannah	18	F	None	21Ap07Fj
GIBNEY, Mary	18	F	None	21Ap07Fj
MCELROY, Betty	60	F	None	21Ap07Fj
HUGHES, Margaret	33	F	None	21Ap07Fj
Rose	20	F	None	21Ap07Fj
Mary	18	F	None	21Ap07Fj
Patrick	12	M	None	21Ap07Fj
Ellen	10	F	None	21Ap07Fj
Matilda	08	F	Child	21Ap07Fj
Mary-Ann	06	F	Child	21Ap07Fj
Margaret	04	F	Child	21Ap07Fj
David	02	M	Child	21Ap07Fj
Mary	25	F	None	21Ap07Fj
Letitia	18	F	None	21Ap07Fj
MCKIBBEN, John	37	M	None	21Ap07Fj
Ellen	36	F	None	21Ap07Fj
Jane	06	F	Child	21Ap07Fj
HERRICK, Mary	26	F	None	21Ap07Fj
HUGHES, George	28	M	None	21Ap07Fj
Thomas	18	M	None	21Ap07Fj
MARTIN, Samuel	22	M	None	21Ap07Fj
Sarah	20	M	None	21Ap07Fj
Eliza	55	F	None	21Ap07Fj
BURDEN, George	20	M	None	21Ap07Fj
DAVIS, James	20	M	None	21Ap07Fj
DUGAN, Hugh	20	M	None	21Ap07Fj
GILLISPIE, Eliza	20	F	None	21Ap07Fj
TRIMBLE, Mary	22	F	None	21Ap07Fj
MILLER, Wm.	27	M	None	21Ap07Fj
John	21	M	None	21Ap07Fj
MCKEAGAN, Thomas	61	M	None	21Ap07Fj
Alice	22	F	None	21Ap07Fj
CLARKE, Mary-Ann	17	F	None	21Ap07Fj
MCGUINISS, Ann	21	F	None	21Ap07Fj
MCELROY, William	24	M	None	21Ap07Fj
Jane	20	F	None	21Ap07Fj
RYAN, Joseph	18	M	None	21Ap07Fj
MAGIE, Terence	26	M	None	21Ap07Fj
Susan	24	F	None	21Ap07Fj
MCCRACKEN, James	20	M	None	21Ap07Fj
MCMANUT, Hugh	25	M	None	21Ap07Fj
WEBSTER, Jane	20	F	None	21Ap07Fj
MURGRAVE, Catherine	21	F	None	21Ap07Fj
Mary	19	F	None	21Ap07Fj
MURPHY, Ann	21	F	None	21Ap07Fj
MCCLURE, Thomas	30	M	None	21Ap07Fj
Elizabeth	25	F	None	21Ap07Fj
Eliza	20	F	None	21Ap07Fj
James	06	M	Child	21Ap07Fj
John	03	M	Child	21Ap07Fj
Eliza	11	F	None	21Ap07Fj
MCGUINISS, Catharine	21	F	None	21Ap07Fj
CANNA, Margaret	24	F	None	21Ap07Fj
ROE, Felix	30	M	None	21Ap07Fj
Ann	32	F	None	21Ap07Fj
GRIMES, Robert	28	M	None	21Ap07Fj
HILL, Ann	21	F	None	21Ap07Fj
HOUSK, Mary	16	F	None	21Ap07Fj
Sarah	22	F	None	21Ap07Fj

NAMES OF PASSENGERS	AGE	SEX	OCCUPATIONS	DATE PORT SHIP
MCDOWELL, Ann	62	F	None	21Ap07Fj
Mary	26	F	None	21Ap07Fj
John	60	M	None	21Ap07Fj
Alexander	26	M	None	21Ap07Fj
Jane	22	F	None	21Ap07Fj
Eliza	20	F	None	21Ap07Fj
Hugh	18	M	None	21Ap07Fj
Isabella	50	F	None	21Ap07Fj
Samuel	17	M	None	21Ap07Fj
Isabella	11	F	None	21Ap07Fj
Eliza	08	F	Child	21Ap07Fj
HUGHS, Mary	60	F	None	21Ap07Fj
John	20	M	None	21Ap07Fj
MUIR, Alexander	26	M	None	21Ap07Fj
MCILVAIN, James	27	M	None	21Ap07Fj
LOY, Andrew	28	M	None	21Ap07Fj
HUNTER, Wm.	27	M	None	21Ap07Fj
KEENAN, Michael	37	M	None	21Ap07Fj
KELLY, Bridget	26	F	None	21Ap07Fj
Patk.	03	M	Child	21Ap07Fj
Isabella	01	F	Child	21Ap07Fj
DALY, Dennis	17	M	None	21Ap07Fj
DENNY, John	22	M	None	21Ap07Fj
MCGEE, Patrick	22	M	None	21Ap07Fj
Owen	18	M	None	21Ap07Fj
MCVEAGH, John	19	M	None	21Ap07Fj
GUCHEAN, Francis	30	M	None	21Ap07Fj
KEEN, Joseph	20	M	None	21Ap07Fj
MCCANN, Sarah	21	F	None	21Ap07Fj
WHITE, James	25	M	None	21Ap07Fj
Maria	21	F	None	21Ap07Fj
Ann	22	F	None	21Ap07Fj
MCILROY, Jane	21	F	None	21Ap07Fj
PARK, Alex.	26	M	None	21Ap07Fj
CAINS, Edward	22	M	None	21Ap07Fj
Michael	29	M	None	21Ap07Fj
MCPHILLIPS, Wm.	55	M	None	21Ap07Fj
Eliza	51	M	None	21Ap07Fj
Mary	16	F	None	21Ap07Fj
Owen	15	M	None	21Ap07Fj
Eliza	10	F	None	21Ap07Fj
Peter	08	M	Child	21Ap07Fj
Sarah	06	F	Child	21Ap07Fj
Mary-A.	21	F	None	21Ap07Fj
Edward	21	M	None	21Ap07Fj
James	01	M	Child	21Ap07Fj
MCCLURE, Holt	26	M	None	21Ap07Fj
TURKINGTON, Saml.	40	M	None	21Ap07Fj
James	14	M	None	21Ap07Fj
MCDOWELL, James	20	M	None	21Ap07Fj
BELL, Alexd.	22	M	None	21Ap07Fj
John	25	M	None	21Ap07Fj
Matthew	26	M	None	21Ap07Fj
WHITE, Charles	25	M	None	21Ap07Fj
CUMNY, James	25	M	None	21Ap07Fj
ARMSTRONG, Mary	19	F	None	21Ap07Fj
CAMPBELL, Catharine	19	F	None	21Ap07Fj
MCGILL, Sarah-A.	20	F	None	21Ap07Fj
BOYLE, Hugh	20	F	None	21Ap07Fj
MCTAGGART, James	20	F	None	21Ap07Fj
DIVEN, Michael	20	F	None	21Ap07Fj
MADDEN, Sarah	18	F	None	21Ap07Fj
MCVEIGH, Ellen	19	F	None	21Ap07Fj
FOX, Jane	23	F	None	21Ap07Fj
Mary-A.	19	F	None	21Ap07Fj
MCVEAGH, Mary	23	F	None	21Ap07Fj
CASEY, John	20	M	None	21Ap07Fj
HUGHES, Catherine	25	F	None	21Ap07Fj
FOX, Michael	22	M	None	21Ap07Fj
MCTAGGART, James	20	M	None	21Ap07Fj
DAVIN, Michael	20	M	None	21Ap07Fj
DUFF, Jas.Michael	18	M	None	21Ap07Fj
STAR, Peter	18	M	None	21Ap07Fj
MCCOOL, Patrick	45	M	None	21Ap07Fj
Catherine	40	F	None	21Ap07Fj
MCCOOL, Dan	18	M	None	21Ap07Fj
Ellen	16	F	None	21Ap07Fj
Thomas	14	M	None	21Ap07Fj
Francis	06	M	Child	21Ap07Fj
Biddy	04	F	Child	21Ap07Fj
MCCANN, Susan	26	F	None	21Ap07Fj
Ann	24	F	None	21Ap07Fj
MCCAY, Ellen	36	F	None	21Ap07Fj
Patrick	12	M	None	21Ap07Fj
James	10	M	None	21Ap07Fj
Ellen	05	F	Child	21Ap07Fj
MCCARTY, Dennis	20	M	None	21Ap07Fj

MARGARET 22 APRIL 1848

From Cork

NAMES OF PASSENGERS		AGE	SEX	OCCUPATIONS	DATE PORT SHIP
SULLIVAN, John		28	M	Farmer	22Ap14Fe
BRUCHELL, Mary		28	F	Servant	22Ap14Fe
DOYLE, Michael		44	M	Farmer	22Ap14Fe
DUGGAN, Edward		27	M	Farmer	22Ap14Fe
Catharine		26	F	Spinster	22Ap14Fe
Ellen		22	F	Spinster	22Ap14Fe
COTTER, John		24	M	Farmer	22Ap14Fe
BROWN, Mary		20	F	Spinster	22Ap14Fe
FARMER, Joseph		20	M	Laborer	22Ap14Fe
SULLIVAN, Cornelius		19	M	Laborer	22Ap14Fe
MURPHY, John		26	M	Laborer	22Ap14Fe
OHERN, Thomas		24	M	Laborer	22Ap14Fe
FLYNN, Ellen		18	F	Servant	22Ap14Fe
BRIEN, Denis		18	M	Laborer	22Ap14Fe
GLEESON, James		34	M	Farmer	22Ap14Fe
Margaret	(W)	26	F	None	22Ap14Fe
SWEENEY, Bridget		22	F	None	22Ap14Fe
GLEESON, Patrick		06	M	Child	22Ap14Fe
Catharine		03	F	Child	22Ap14Fe
NEIL, Margaret		18	F	Spinster	22Ap14Fe
MAHONY, Catharine		48	F	Servant	22Ap14Fe
Margaret		18	F	Spinster	22Ap14Fe
RYAN, Matthew		16	M	Laborer	22Ap14Fe
NOONAN, John		16	M	Laborer	22Ap14Fe
RYAN, Patrick		26	M	Laborer	22Ap14Fe
Mary	(W)	24	F	None	22Ap14Fe
HEFFERMAN, Mary		26	F	Servant	22Ap14Fe
WIGMORE, Margaret		20	F	Servant	22Ap14Fe
KENNEALLY, Margaret		20	F	Servant	22Ap14Fe
Ellen		18	F	Servant	22Ap14Fe
ROCHE, Johanna		32	F	Servant	22Ap14Fe
John		08	M	Child	22Ap14Fe
Margaret		02	F	Child	22Ap14Fe
Ellen		22	F	Spinster	22Ap14Fe
BEZENT, Henry		30	M	Butler	22Ap14Fe
Bridget	(W)	30	F	None	22Ap14Fe
John		20	M	Shoemaker	22Ap14Fe
Catherine		21	F	Spinster	22Ap14Fe
GARDNER, Robert		32	M	Gdnr	22Ap14Fe
Jane	(W)	30	F	None	22Ap14Fe
Catherine		50	F	Servant	22Ap14Fe
MOLLONEY, Ann		50	F	Servant	22Ap14Fe
FITZGERALD, Thomas		30	M	Laborer	22Ap14Fe
HEYNEY, Bridget		30	F	Servant	22Ap14Fe
GARDNER, Joseph		06	M	Child	22Ap14Fe
Charles		04	M	Child	22Ap14Fe
CURTIN, John		28	M	Laborer	22Ap14Fe
HEALY, John		32	M	Laborer	22Ap14Fe
COPPINGER, Patrick		36	M	Farmer	22Ap14Fe
Ellen	(W)	38	F	None	22Ap14Fe
MAHONY, Thomas		38	M	Farmer	22Ap14Fe
FITZPATRICK, Margaret		26	F	Servant	22Ap14Fe

NAMES OF PASSENGERS	AGE	SEX	OCCUPATIONS	DATE PORT SHIP
PINE, Elizabeth	18	F	Servant	22Ap14Fe
SHEEHAN, Eliza	24	F	Servant	22Ap14Fe
Eliza	02	F	Child	22Ap14Fe
MINHANE, Timothy	25	M	Laborer	22Ap14Fe
MCGUIRE, U	30	M	Laborer	22Ap14Fe
FLYNN, Ellen	18	F	Spinster	22Ap14Fe

AURORA 22 APRIL 1848

From Liverpool

NAMES OF PASSENGERS	AGE	SEX	OCCUPATIONS	DATE PORT SHIP
LEESE, Betty	33	F	Servant	22Ap02Fr
Mailtia	12	F	None	22Ap02Fr
John	10	M	None	22Ap02Fr
George	08	M	Child	22Ap02Fr
KIRKLAND, Hannole	24	F	Servant	22Ap02Fr
Albert	.00	M	Infant	22Ap02Fr
QUIN, Maucis	35	M	Mechanic	22Ap02Fr
Betsey	30	F	None	22Ap02Fr
RYAN, John	21	M	Laborer	22Ap02Fr
BOYAN, Catharine	50	F	None	22Ap02Fr
Michael	18	M	Laborer	22Ap02Fr
Maucis	15	M	Laborer	22Ap02Fr
Mary	20	F	Servant	22Ap02Fr
KELLY, Michl.	26	M	Laborer	22Ap02Fr
WARD, Polk	26	M	Laborer	22Ap02Fr
SEYMOUR, John	29	M	Laborer	22Ap02Fr
U (W)	22	F	Servant	22Ap02Fr
HUNY, Thomas	30	M	Mechanic	22Ap02Fr
CORBELLE, Martin	17	M	Laborer	22Ap02Fr
PENDERGAST, Thos.	18	M	Laborer	22Ap02Fr
DUFFY, Francis	50	M	Farmer	22Ap02Fr
Polk	13	M	Farmer	22Ap02Fr
KEARNEY, Thos.	20	M	Farmer	22Ap02Fr
Ann	20	F	Servant	22Ap02Fr
WARDEN, James	21	M	Mechanic	22Ap02Fr
Alice	21	F	Servant	22Ap02Fr
TULLY, Polk	18	M	Laborer	22Ap02Fr
Bardget	21	F	Servant	22Ap02Fr
Winifred	11	F	Servant	22Ap02Fr
RIELLY, Michael	21	M	Laborer	22Ap02Fr
KEEGAN, Danl.	21	M	Laborer	22Ap02Fr
LUSE, Robt.	21	M	Laborer	22Ap02Fr
WALSH, James	21	M	Servant	22Ap02Fr
Bridget	21	F	Servant	22Ap02Fr
DOOLEY, James	21	M	Laborer	22Ap02Fr
MULLOY, Blecher	20	M	Laborer	22Ap02Fr
HUGHES, John	26	M	Laborer	22Ap02Fr
WALSH, Michl.	26	M	Laborer	22Ap02Fr
FARRELL, Polk	25	M	Laborer	22Ap02Fr
KELLY, Bridget	25	F	Servant	22Ap02Fr
DWIGHT, John	50	M	Mechanic	22Ap02Fr
MCCANN, James	50	M	Mechanic	22Ap02Fr
Mary	25	F	None	22Ap02Fr
Owen	03	M	Child	22Ap02Fr
MURPHY, John	21	M	Laborer	22Ap02Fr
TOGASH, Mary	20	F	Servant	22Ap02Fr
MCCOLE, John	26	M	Laborer	22Ap02Fr
MCENNIS, Polk	26	M	Laborer	22Ap02Fr
LANGDAN, Terrence	26	M	Laborer	22Ap02Fr
Caller	26	M	Laborer	22Ap02Fr
SUCHAW, Mary	20	F	Servant	22Ap02Fr
ROURKE, Bridget	28	F	Servant	22Ap02Fr
MURPHY, Edward	24	M	Laborer	22Ap02Fr
WALSH, Nancy	50	F	None	22Ap02Fr
Nancy	20	F	Servant	22Ap02Fr
Bridget	13	F	Servant	22Ap02Fr
Mark	17	M	Laborer	22Ap02Fr
WHITENEY, John	45	M	Mechanic	22Ap02Fr

NAMES OF PASSENGERS	AGE	SEX	OCCUPATIONS	DATE PORT SHIP
FLEMMING, Ellen	20	F	Servant	22Ap02Fr
RYAN, John	20	M	Laborer	22Ap02Fr
LONG, Betsey	25	F	Servant	22Ap02Fr
COWLEY, Polk	20	M	Laborer	22Ap02Fr
John	20	M	Laborer	22Ap02Fr
MCEUPSISS, Polk	17	M	Laborer	22Ap02Fr
DIXON, Ann	20	F	Servant	22Ap02Fr
HEUTLEY, James	34	M	Mechanic	22Ap02Fr
HART, Margt.	24	F	Servant	22Ap02Fr
RIELLY, John	25	M	Laborer	22Ap02Fr
Mary	20	F	Servant	22Ap02Fr
Hugh	25	M	Laborer	22Ap02Fr
SULLIVAN, Johanna	20	F	Laborer	22Ap02Fr
MARA, Collec.	22	F	Servant	22Ap02Fr
COLEMAN, Polk	20	M	Laborer	22Ap02Fr
ONEIL, James	22	M	Laborer	22Ap02Fr
MARA, Mary	19	F	Servant	22Ap02Fr
OBRIEN, Francis	25	M	Mechanic	22Ap02Fr
RAFFERTY, Wm.	18	M	Laborer	22Ap02Fr
MOLEON, Michael	25	M	Laborer	22Ap02Fr
Jerrimiah	20	M	Laborer	22Ap02Fr
HACKET, Polk	20	M	Laborer	22Ap02Fr
MCGERNY, Benjamin	25	M	Laborer	22Ap02Fr
Betty	21	F	None	22Ap02Fr
KERNAN, Andrew	30	M	Mechanic	22Ap02Fr
ODORN, Polk	20	M	Mechanic	22Ap02Fr
LEESE, James	46	M	Mechanic	22Ap02Fr
U (W)	41	F	None	22Ap02Fr
William	30	M	Mechanic	22Ap02Fr
MILENES, James	30	M	Mechanic	22Ap02Fr
Mary	18	F	Servant	22Ap02Fr
George	01	M	Child	22Ap02Fr
John	22	M	None	22Ap02Fr
Edward	22	M	Mechanic	22Ap02Fr
OHARA, Sarah	26	F	Servant	22Ap02Fr
OBOYLE, Mary	21	F	Servant	22Ap02Fr
CONOGAN, Mary	26	F	Servant	22Ap02Fr
MOOLEY, Alice	21	F	Servant	22Ap02Fr
Anne	.00	F	Infant	22Ap02Fr
HACKY, James	40	M	Mechanic	22Ap02Fr
Coleen	38	F	None	22Ap02Fr
Henry	22	M	Mechanic	22Ap02Fr
Margt.	18	F	None	22Ap02Fr
SMITH, Bartley	30	M	Farmer	22Ap02Fr
Anne	25	F	None	22Ap02Fr
Jane	03	F	Child	22Ap02Fr
James	01	M	Child	22Ap02Fr
FITZGERALD, Wm.	31	M	Clerk	22Ap02Fr
BOYLE, Arthur	20	M	Clerk	22Ap02Fr
DOUGHT, Barney	38	M	Mechanic	22Ap02Fr
MCQUINN, Margt.	16	F	Servant	22Ap02Fr
WOODS, James	20	M	Laborer	22Ap02Fr
GALLAGHER, Hugh	36	M	Laborer	22Ap02Fr
SHERIDEN, Michl.	35	M	Laborer	22Ap02Fr
Mary	13	F	Servant	22Ap02Fr
Coleen	10	F	None	22Ap02Fr
CEUSON, Wm.	25	M	Mechanic	22Ap02Fr
WRIGHT, Wm.	28	M	Mechanic	22Ap02Fr
MCCLUIRE, Bridget	20	F	Servant	22Ap02Fr
HERMAN, Edwd.	21	M	Laborer	22Ap02Fr
Polk	32	M	Laborer	22Ap02Fr
Bryan	17	M	Laborer	22Ap02Fr
Maria	50	F	None	22Ap02Fr
Betsey	30	F	None	22Ap02Fr
News	06	M	Child	22Ap02Fr
Mary	08	F	Child	22Ap02Fr
Peter	04	M	Child	22Ap02Fr
QUSKART, Margt.	29	F	Servant	22Ap02Fr
Mary	13	F	Servant	22Ap02Fr
RIELLY, Mary	26	F	Servant	22Ap02Fr
FOX, Mary	22	F	Servant	22Ap02Fr
QUIT, Bridget	35	F	Servant	22Ap02Fr
EVIGAN, Hugh	30	M	Mechanic	22Ap02Fr
MCNUTLY, Colter	12	F	Servant	22Ap02Fr
MCKENNA, Jas.	29	M	Laborer	22Ap02Fr

NAMES OF PASSENGERS	AGE	SEX	OCCUPATIONS	DATE PORT SHIP
MCKENNA, Margt.	29	F	Servant	22Ap02Fr
BRIEN, Edwd.	40	M	Mechanic	22Ap02Fr
Wm.	36	M	Mechanic	22Ap02Fr
KORAN, Wm.	40	M	Mechanic	22Ap02Fr
Ann	18	F	Servant	22Ap02Fr
John	17	M	Laborer	22Ap02Fr
Henry	12	M	None	22Ap02Fr
Wm.	10	M	None	22Ap02Fr
David	11	M	None	22Ap02Fr
KING, Jas. Died-At-Sea	49	M	None	22Ap02Fr
KORAN, Eliza	18	F	Servant	22Ap02Fr
MCNUTLY, Margt.	40	F	Servant	22Ap02Fr
James	24	M	Laborer	22Ap02Fr
Henry	20	M	Laborer	22Ap02Fr
David	19	M	Laborer	22Ap02Fr
James	.00	M	Infant	22Ap02Fr
Nancy	20	F	Servant	22Ap02Fr
Margt.	20	F	Servant	22Ap02Fr
Mary	30	F	Servant	22Ap02Fr
Bridget	20	F	Servant	22Ap02Fr
Bridget	21	F	Servant	22Ap02Fr
Mary	21	F	Servant	22Ap02Fr
CORDWON, Dennis	40	M	Mechanic	22Ap02Fr
CONNOR, Jolius	40	M	Mechanic	22Ap02Fr
LEMPLEY, Dennis	30	M	Mechanic	22Ap02Fr
Bridget	21	F	Servant	22Ap02Fr
Mary	00	F	None	22Ap02Fr
MOLEAU, Ann	24	F	Servant	22Ap02Fr
Margt.	25	F	Servant	22Ap02Fr
BURKE, Polk	21	M	Laborer	22Ap02Fr
Ann	18	F	Servant	22Ap02Fr
HAUS, Mary	12	F	Servant	22Ap02Fr
BYRINE, John	30	M	Farmer	22Ap02Fr
Bridget	12	F	None	22Ap02Fr
EIFFEN, Lucile	20	M	Laborer	22Ap02Fr
MCDONALD, Wm.	29	M	Laborer	22Ap02Fr
MALONY, Michl.	30	M	Laborer	22Ap02Fr
MORAN, John	30	M	Laborer	22Ap02Fr
Quin	13	M	None	22Ap02Fr
Mary	11	F	None	22Ap02Fr
Maria	08	F	Child	22Ap02Fr
Robt.	05	M	Child	22Ap02Fr
John	01	M	Child	22Ap02Fr
LUCLE, Wm.	25	M	Mechanic	22Ap02Fr
TAYLOR, Josh	25	M	Mechanic	22Ap02Fr
THOMPSON, Wm.	30	M	Mechanic	22Ap02Fr
DUKE, Wm.	26	M	Mechanic	22Ap02Fr
MULLIGAN, Thos.	34	M	Mechanic	22Ap02Fr
Coleen	30	F	None	22Ap02Fr
Ellen	06	F	Child	22Ap02Fr
Michl.	04	M	Child	22Ap02Fr
KELLY, Michael	22	M	Laborer	22Ap02Fr
Bridget	.00	F	Infant	22Ap02Fr
WALLACE, James	30	M	Mechanic	22Ap02Fr
FLANNIGAN, Barney	60	M	Mechanic	22Ap02Fr
U (W)	50	F	None	22Ap02Fr
John	50	M	Mechanic	22Ap02Fr
Thomas	21	M	Mechanic	22Ap02Fr
Mary	10	F	None	22Ap02Fr
Michael	12	M	None	22Ap02Fr
Margt.	07	F	Child	22Ap02Fr
George	30	M	Mechanic	22Ap02Fr
MOREY, Austin	38	M	Mechanic	22Ap02Fr
GRADY, Eliza	22	F	Servant	22Ap02Fr
BURKE, Michl.	20	M	Laborer	22Ap02Fr
CONNEL, John	20	M	Laborer	22Ap02Fr
Matthew	20	M	Laborer	22Ap02Fr
BRENAN, Thos.	21	M	Laborer	22Ap02Fr
WEIR, Thos.	21	M	Laborer	22Ap02Fr
TULLY, Wm.	22	M	Laborer	22Ap02Fr
MCMANUS, Jas.	24	M	Laborer	22Ap02Fr
OHARA, Bayan	21	M	Laborer	22Ap02Fr
FITZGERALD, Jas.	27	M	Farmer	22Ap02Fr
SHERWIN, John	26	M	Farmer	22Ap02Fr
HARTWELL, James	30	M	Farmer	22Ap02Fr
LEVY, John	25	M	Farmer	22Ap02Fr
KELLY, Michl.	27	M	Farmer	22Ap02Fr
WALL, Ellen	19	F	Servant	22Ap02Fr
GILLANY, Winny	17	F	Servant	22Ap02Fr
Ellen	14	F	Servant	22Ap02Fr
Mary	16	F	Servant	22Ap02Fr
LYNCH, Owen	40	M	Farmer	22Ap02Fr

SARAH-SANDS 22 APRIL 1848

From Liverpool

NAMES OF PASSENGERS	AGE	SEX	OCCUPATIONS	DATE PORT SHIP
GWYNE, Harriet	25	F	None	22Ap02Kp
ANDERSON, Hobart	35	M	Unknown	22Ap02Kp
Eliza	25	F	None	22Ap02Kp
BISHOP, John	50	M	Merchant	22Ap02Kp
Frank	12	M	Merchant	22Ap02Kp
Ellen	10	F	None	22Ap02Kp
STEPHENS, Wm.	30	M	Merchant	22Ap02Kp
DICKENSON, 53	30	D	Merchant	22Ap02Kp
Grace	33	F	None	22Ap02Kp
BILLIS, Edward	20	M	Draper	22Ap02Kp
Samuel	17	M	Draper	22Ap02Kp
POLLARD, Geo.	13	M	Draper	22Ap02Kp
THRUSH, Rowland	14	M	Farmer	22Ap02Kp
WHEELER, Mary-A.	15	F	None	22Ap02Kp
POWER, John	32	M	Mechanic	22Ap02Kp
Hannah	39	F	None	22Ap02Kp
Jane-Eliza	05	F	Child	22Ap02Kp
GREEN, Chas.	24	M	Spinner	22Ap02Kp
Ann	24	F	None	22Ap02Kp
Mathew	.08	M	Infant	22Ap02Kp
OKEEFE, Pierce	30	M	Miller	22Ap02Kp
Andrew	40	M	Miller	22Ap02Kp
Catherine	26	F	None	22Ap02Kp
Honora	03	F	Child	22Ap02Kp
FOGARTY, Maria	23	F	None	22Ap02Kp
Pat	04	M	Child	22Ap02Kp
BECREESS, Jas.	23	M	Merchant	22Ap02Kp
FORBES, Wm.	29	M	Merchant	22Ap02Kp
HYATT, E.A.C.	26	M	Musician	22Ap02Kp
HUME, John	24	M	Butcher	22Ap02Kp
MCKIBBIN, Jane	21	F	None	22Ap02Kp
ALLAN, Catherine	40	F	None	22Ap02Kp
Mary	20	F	None	22Ap02Kp
Ann	20	F	None	22Ap02Kp
Kate	14	F	None	22Ap02Kp
WEBBER, Mary	17	F	None	22Ap02Kp
DUNLOP, Harry	40	M	Crmcht	22Ap02Kp
Ellen	36	F	None	22Ap02Kp
Wm.	09	M	Child	22Ap02Kp
Frank	07	M	Child	22Ap02Kp
Harry	05	M	Child	22Ap02Kp
Ellen	03	F	Child	22Ap02Kp
WEST, Geo.	25	M	Farmer	22Ap02Kp
Mary	23	F	None	22Ap02Kp
Wm.	24	M	Farmer	22Ap02Kp
Thomas	22	M	Farmer	22Ap02Kp
Robt.	26	M	Farmer	22Ap02Kp
John	23	M	Farmer	22Ap02Kp
Mary-Ann	20	F	None	22Ap02Kp
Abel	19	M	Farmer	22Ap02Kp
Sarah	17	F	Farmer	22Ap02Kp
HOCRECOTT, James	26	M	Merchant	22Ap02Kp
Sarah	24	F	Merchant	22Ap02Kp
KENNEDY, Wm.	22	M	Builder	22Ap02Kp
TALBOT, Jas.	21	M	Merchant	22Ap02Kp
TAYLOR, Harry	22	M	Engineer	22Ap02Kp

NAMES OF PASSENGERS		AGE	SEX	OCCUPATIONS	DATE PORT SHIP
TAITE, Wm.		25	M	Farmer	22Ap02Kp
BRENNAN, Martin		26	M	Draper	22Ap02Kp
ROBB, Alex-R		24	M	Coppersmith	22Ap02Kp
FINDEN, Wm.		21	M	Merchant	22Ap02Kp
THOMPSON, Jas.		21	M	Machinist	22Ap02Kp
LISK, Mary-Ann		24	F	None	22Ap02Kp
BURKE, Ellen		22	F	None	22Ap02Kp
BRACKEN, Laurence		28	M	Laborer	22Ap02Kp
Biddy		26	F	None	22Ap02Kp
Chas.		03	M	Child	22Ap02Kp
SUTHERLAND, Wm.		55	M	Laborer	22Ap02Kp
Hester		49	F	None	22Ap02Kp
Caroline		26	F	None	22Ap02Kp
Fanny		16	F	None	22Ap02Kp
KNOTT, John		22	M	Cook	22Ap02Kp
WARD, John		35	M	Lace Maker	22Ap02Kp
Jane	(W)	29	F	None	22Ap02Kp
Jane-Elizabeth	(D)	09	F	Child	22Ap02Kp
John-Wm.	(S)	.07	M	Infant	22Ap02Kp
James-Edwd.		08	M	Child	22Ap02Kp
JONES, Wm.		20	M	Unknown	22Ap02Kp
BROWN, John		22	M	Mechanic	22Ap02Kp
Jane		49	F	None	22Ap02Kp
POVEY, Chas.		24	M	Mechanic	22Ap02Kp
FITZGIBBON, John		32	M	Laborer	22Ap02Kp
FRANCIS, Michl.		32	M	Laborer	22Ap02Kp
COSTELLO, John		28	M	Laborer	22Ap02Kp
LACES, Wm.		18	M	Joiner	22Ap02Kp
Phillip		16	M	Joiner	22Ap02Kp
FORRESTER, Thos.		23	M	Laborer	22Ap02Kp
Andrew		23	M	Laborer	22Ap02Kp
ASHTON, Jonathan		54	M	Laborer	22Ap02Kp
BAILEY, Thos.		25	M	Laborer	22Ap02Kp
LEES, Thos.		20	M	Miner	22Ap02Kp
BAILEY, Betty		20	F	Miner	22Ap02Kp
Elizabeth		21	F	Miner	22Ap02Kp
Elizabeth		00	F	Miner	22Ap02Kp
Ann		23	F	Miner	22Ap02Kp
ASHTON, Betty		30	F	Miner	22Ap02Kp
MCCUEN, Duncan		32	M	Mechanic	22Ap02Kp
Susan		.00	F	Infant	22Ap02Kp
Janet		.00	F	Infant	22Ap02Kp
OSWALD, James		34	M	Mechanic	22Ap02Kp
CRAWFORD, Saml.		24	M	Farmer	22Ap02Kp
Jane		.00	F	Infant	22Ap02Kp
NONILAS, Michael		25	F	Laborer	22Ap02Kp
KEITH, James		28	F	Laborer	22Ap02Kp
BYRNES, Luke		21	F	Laborer	22Ap02Kp
CARTY, John		35	F	Laborer	22Ap02Kp
HEOLNE, James		31	F	Mechanic	22Ap02Kp
Henry		15	F	Mechanic	22Ap02Kp
William		03	F	Child	22Ap02Kp
THOMPSON, Geo.		21	F	Laborer	22Ap02Kp
WILKINSON, Wm.		24	F	Laborer	22Ap02Kp
Sarah		22	F	None	22Ap02Kp
DENT, Mathew		38	M	Butcher	22Ap02Kp
LUCKING, Joseph		24	M	Hatter	22Ap02Kp
MOORE, Elisha		40	F	Spinner	22Ap02Kp
DAY, Bridget		31	F	Spinner	22Ap02Kp
Patrick		15	M	None	22Ap02Kp
Mary-Ann		.09	F	Infant	22Ap02Kp
SCOTT, Hannillon		30	M	Mechanic	22Ap02Kp
JOHNSTON, James		25	M	Barber	22Ap02Kp
FAZAKERLY, Thomas		17	M	Farmer	22Ap02Kp
ANDERSON, Geo.T.		23	M	Farmer	22Ap02Kp
Mary		22	F	None	22Ap02Kp
George		.06	M	Infant	22Ap02Kp
Ann		04	F	Child	22Ap02Kp
BALINE, Ann		25	F	None	22Ap02Kp
LAMBERT, Thomas		49	M	Spinner	22Ap02Kp
MUSTRIDGE, Richd.		23	M	Farmer	22Ap02Kp
SMITH, Williams		32	M	Farmer	22Ap02Kp
Hannah		31	F	None	22Ap02Kp
Benjamin		07	M	Child	22Ap02Kp
James		04	M	Child	22Ap02Kp

NAMES OF PASSENGERS	AGE	SEX	OCCUPATIONS	DATE PORT SHIP
RAFERTY, Thos.	24	M	Laborer	22Ap02Kp
Margt.	20	F	None	22Ap02Kp
Mary	21	F	None	22Ap02Kp
HEILES, Edwin	27	M	Painter	22Ap02Kp
GLENNAN, Bridget	21	F	None	22Ap02Kp
HALLWELL, Maria	30	F	None	22Ap02Kp
Jonathan	10	M	None	22Ap02Kp
Joseph	09	M	Child	22Ap02Kp
STAFFORD, U	35	M	Spinner	22Ap02Kp
Sarah	28	F	None	22Ap02Kp
Joseph	24	M	None	22Ap02Kp
James	12	M	None	22Ap02Kp
Jane	14	F	None	22Ap02Kp
Edwin	08	M	Child	22Ap02Kp
Elizabeth	04	F	Child	22Ap02Kp
John	.07	M	Infant	22Ap02Kp
RENGON, John	35	M	Mechanic	22Ap02Kp
HOOTAN, Walter	28	M	Clerk	22Ap02Kp
Selina	26	F	None	22Ap02Kp
Samuel	50	M	Clerk	22Ap02Kp
LYON, Elizabeth	40	F	None	22Ap02Kp
RYCROFT, Edward	22	M	Bookbinder	22Ap02Kp
PATTERSON, Thos.	24	M	Laborer	22Ap02Kp
FLOOD, Alice	12	F	None	22Ap02Kp
Rose	11	F	None	22Ap02Kp
BANDLEY, Sidney	45	M	Hatter	22Ap02Kp
Jane	40	F	None	22Ap02Kp
NELSON, Henry	20	M	Blacksmith	22Ap02Kp
GOSLING, Ann	04	F	Child	22Ap02Kp
BLACKSMITH, John	40	M	Blacksmith	22Ap02Kp
BROWN, Jane	30	F	None	22Ap02Kp
GRIBBON, John	30	M	Mechanic	22Ap02Kp
JAMES, Anne	30	F	None	22Ap02Kp
William	.00	M	Infant	22Ap02Kp
MOORE, George	23	M	Mechanic	22Ap02Kp
SHAW, Cathr.	19	F	None	22Ap02Kp
HEARY, Mary	14	F	None	22Ap02Kp
SPENCER, Geo.	36	M	Laborer	22Ap02Kp
Sarah	30	F	None	22Ap02Kp
Elizabeth	06	F	Child	22Ap02Kp
Sarah	04	F	Child	22Ap02Kp
Ann	.00	F	Infant	22Ap02Kp
ANTHONY, Noah	30	M	Laborer	22Ap02Kp
Anne	26	F	None	22Ap02Kp
Herbert	05	M	Child	22Ap02Kp
Susanna	03	F	Child	22Ap02Kp
Arthur	.00	M	Infant	22Ap02Kp
OWENS, Thos.C.	20	M	Blacksmith	22Ap02Kp
BLUNDER, Wm.	26	M	Blacksmith	22Ap02Kp
Honora	25	F	None	22Ap02Kp
SHIELS, Martin	40	M	Mechanic	22Ap02Kp
SMITH, Mathew	40	M	Laborer	22Ap02Kp
MARTIN, John	31	M	Shoemaker	22Ap02Kp
Sarah	30	F	None	22Ap02Kp
Samuel	15	M	None	22Ap02Kp
Ann	11	F	None	22Ap02Kp
Thomas	06	M	Child	22Ap02Kp
Mary	02	F	Child	22Ap02Kp
Jane	.00	F	Infant	22Ap02Kp
MARRYATT, Thos.	20	M	Shoemaker	22Ap02Kp
RAMSAY, Lydia	28	F	None	22Ap02Kp
BISHOP, Jane	21	F	None	22Ap02Kp
RUSSELL, Geo.	40	M	Farmer	22Ap02Kp
Jane	40	F	None	22Ap02Kp
Eliza	19	F	None	22Ap02Kp
GROVES, Eliza	19	F	None	22Ap02Kp
Robert	07	M	Child	22Ap02Kp
LINDSAY, James	25	M	Farmer	22Ap02Kp
MCMAHON, Edward	20	M	Farmer	22Ap02Kp
KAIN, James	26	M	Joiner	22Ap02Kp
John	25	M	Joiner	22Ap02Kp
GEORGE, Mary	45	F	None	22Ap02Kp
Mary	20	F	None	22Ap02Kp
ELLRA, Ann	19	F	None	22Ap02Kp
Margt.	16	F	None	22Ap02Kp

NAMES OF PASSENGERS	AGE	SEX	OCCUPATIONS	DATE PORT SHIP
FERGUSON, Jane	20	F	None	22Ap02Kp
Eleanore	20	F	None	22Ap02Kp
COOK, Elvira	50	F	None	22Ap02Kp
LEADLIE, Elvira	50	F	None	22Ap02Kp
BLADEWOOD, Eliza	15	F	None	22Ap02Kp
GEORGE, Danl.	55	M	Farmer	22Ap02Kp
Mathew	19	M	Farmer	22Ap02Kp
John	08	M	Child	22Ap02Kp
WALLACE, Geo.	21	M	Clerk	22Ap02Kp
FERGUSON, James	30	M	Laborer	22Ap02Kp
Benjamin	20	M	Laborer	22Ap02Kp
LEADLIE, Geo.	55	M	Laborer	22Ap02Kp
DOGHERTY, Jane	16	F	None	22Ap02Kp
BLACKSMITH, Joseph	30	M	Blacksmith	22Ap02Kp
MILLS, John	21	M	Miner	22Ap02Kp
LEES, Charles	25	M	Miner	22Ap02Kp
WARD, Hugh	15	M	Miner	22Ap02Kp
LACKAY, Wm.	20	M	Joiner	22Ap02Kp
CRAWFORD, Wm.	26	M	Mechanic	22Ap02Kp
NORRIS, Michael	21	M	Clerk	22Ap02Kp
RUSK, Margt.	24	F	None	22Ap02Kp
SWIFS, Wm.	30	M	Mechanic	22Ap02Kp
MCCANN, Wm.	29	M	Mechanic	22Ap02Kp
BOWIE, Geo.	27	M	Joiner	22Ap02Kp
Mary	25	F	None	22Ap02Kp
HAWKINS, John	46	M	Farmer	22Ap02Kp
Rachl.	54	F	None	22Ap02Kp
Eliza-Ellen	09	F	Child	22Ap02Kp
Anne-Jane	06	F	Child	22Ap02Kp
SMITH, Wm.	24	M	Shoemaker	22Ap02Kp
Ruth	26	F	None	22Ap02Kp
PARKER, Wm.	23	M	Shoemaker	22Ap02Kp
WHITNELL, Ell.	22	M	Shoemaker	22Ap02Kp
OLIVER, James	39	M	Shoemaker	22Ap02Kp
DUDLEY, John	40	M	Shoemaker	22Ap02Kp
EDWARDS, Richd.	36	M	Shoemaker	22Ap02Kp
MORTON, Thos.	50	M	Shoemaker	22Ap02Kp
Sanders	19	M	Shoemaker	22Ap02Kp
DUDD, Ann	16	F	None	22Ap02Kp
BOLIVENS, John	22	M	None	22Ap02Kp
Edith	21	F	None	22Ap02Kp
Thomas	20	M	None	22Ap02Kp
ALDEMANN, Richd.	24	M	Joiner	22Ap02Kp
John	22	M	Butcher	22Ap02Kp
MCCANN, William	29	M	Joiner	22Ap02Kp
Margt.	25	F	None	22Ap02Kp
LAWLER, John	40	M	Laborer	22Ap02Kp
CARROLL, Phil.	22	M	Laborer	22Ap02Kp
MCHINAY, Mathew	29	M	Laborer	22Ap02Kp
KELLY, John	22	M	Clerk	22Ap02Kp
Bridget	40	F	None	22Ap02Kp
LOGLIN, Catherine	23	F	None	22Ap02Kp
HIGMAN, John	23	M	Hatter	22Ap02Kp
MCCABE, Patt	32	M	Hatter	22Ap02Kp
MAYLARD, Jonathan	34	M	Hatter	22Ap02Kp
ENSIGHT, Michl.	21	M	Laborer	22Ap02Kp
COOK, John	27	M	Laborer	22Ap02Kp
WOOD, Michl.	23	M	Laborer	22Ap02Kp
CLANCEY, Patt	23	M	Laborer	22Ap02Kp
HAYS, Dennis	18	M	Laborer	22Ap02Kp
COSGROVE, Ellen	18	F	None	22Ap02Kp
U	.00	U	Infant	22Ap02Kp
COFFEY, Phillip	22	M	Laborer	22Ap02Kp
WARTON, Joseph	45	M	Baker	22Ap02Kp
Sidney	18	M	Baker	22Ap02Kp
JOHNSTON, Hugh	17	M	Laborer	22Ap02Kp
WARD, Jane	12	F	None	22Ap02Kp
OAKES, Geo.	60	M	Laborer	22Ap02Kp
Mary	58	F	None	22Ap02Kp
Betsy	10	F	None	22Ap02Kp
TREGAN, Ann	59	F	None	22Ap02Kp
Mary-Ann	33	F	None	22Ap02Kp
Rose	03	F	Child	22Ap02Kp
Henry	00	M	Unknown	22Ap02Kp
WHISTLER, Ann	60	F	None	22Ap02Kp
DALLIOT, Pat	59	M	Laborer	22Ap02Kp
Ann	18	F	None	22Ap02Kp

CUSHLAMACHREE 23 APRIL 1848

From Laguna

NAMES OF PASSENGERS	AGE	SEX	OCCUPATIONS	DATE PORT SHIP
MCDONNELL, Michael	30	M	Laborer	23Ap12Hw
Catherine	30	F	Spinster	23Ap12Hw
CUNAN, Stephen	23	M	Laborer	23Ap12Hw
Bidelia	24	F	Spinster	23Ap12Hw
HOCKET, Biddy	30	F	Spinster	23Ap12Hw
MULLIN, William	22	M	Laborer	23Ap12Hw
MCLOUGHLIN, William	30	M	Laborer	23Ap12Hw
Bridget	26	F	Spinster	23Ap12Hw
Patrick	01	M	Child	23Ap12Hw
BURKE, Mary	40	F	Spinster	23Ap12Hw
KANE, Michael	40	M	Laborer	23Ap12Hw
BURKE, George	24	M	Laborer	23Ap12Hw
FRANCIS, Biddy	20	F	Spinster	23Ap12Hw
CLARKE, May	45	F	Spinster	23Ap12Hw
Thomas	13	M	Laborer	23Ap12Hw
FLYNN, Catharine	22	F	Spinster	23Ap12Hw
BODKIN, John	48	M	Laborer	23Ap12Hw
JONES, Elenor	17	F	Spinster	23Ap12Hw
BODKIN, Elenor	44	F	Spinster	23Ap12Hw
Catharin	19	F	Spinster	23Ap12Hw
Elenor	07	F	Child	23Ap12Hw
Billdia	15	F	Spinster	23Ap12Hw
Danl.	13	M	None	23Ap12Hw
Martin	11	M	None	23Ap12Hw
Lawrence	09	M	Child	23Ap12Hw
John-Jr.	07	M	Child	23Ap12Hw
ODONNELL, Patrick	17	M	Laborer	23Ap12Hw
DALY, Kitty	20	F	Spinster	23Ap12Hw
FAHY, Patrick	21	M	Laborer	23Ap12Hw
MORAN, John	28	M	Laborer	23Ap12Hw
HOGAN, John	27	M	Laborer	23Ap12Hw
COMMES, Michael	21	M	Laborer	23Ap12Hw
Mary	21	F	Spinster	23Ap12Hw
MOLLOY, James	23	M	Laborer	23Ap12Hw
MCDONNELL, Timothy	30	M	Laborer	23Ap12Hw
CREAN, Roger	32	M	Laborer	23Ap12Hw
CONNER, Michael	22	M	Laborer	23Ap12Hw
MARTIN, John	26	M	Laborer	23Ap12Hw
Winifred	22	F	Spinster	23Ap12Hw
Magt.	18	F	Spinster	23Ap12Hw
Cecelia	15	F	None	23Ap12Hw
BOLER, Mary-Ann	23	F	Spinster	23Ap12Hw
Bridget	20	F	Spinster	23Ap12Hw
FORD, Fergus	25	M	Laborer	23Ap12Hw
SOUTHWELL, James	23	M	Laborer	23Ap12Hw
TULLY, Catharine	22	F	Spinster	23Ap12Hw
CULLEN, Eliza	40	F	Spinster	23Ap12Hw
HANE, Michael	30	M	Laborer	23Ap12Hw
WILLIAM, John	24	M	Laborer	23Ap12Hw
FAHERTY, Margret	20	F	Spinster	23Ap12Hw
COOK, Bridget	40	F	Spinster	23Ap12Hw
DUFFY, John	18	M	Laborer	23Ap12Hw
ODEA, Michael	28	M	Laborer	23Ap12Hw
Mary	28	F	Spinster	23Ap12Hw
Edward	01	M	Child	23Ap12Hw
Catherine	01	F	Child	23Ap12Hw
HEARY, Michael	22	M	Laborer	23Ap12Hw
BURKE, Patrick	21	M	Laborer	23Ap12Hw
Mary	50	F	Spinster	23Ap12Hw
Mary-Jr.	20	F	Spinster	23Ap12Hw
Francis	18	M	Laborer	23Ap12Hw
MANNION, John	21	M	Laborer	23Ap12Hw

NAMES OF PASSENGERS	AGE	SEX	OCCUPATIONS	DATE PORT SHIP
MANNION, Cathrine	21	F	Spinster	23Ap12Hw
COONEY, Ellen	21	F	Spinster	23Ap12Hw
ODEA, Mary	22	F	Spinster	23Ap12Hw
LOUGHAN, Patrick	27	M	Laborer	23Ap12Hw
MALLOWNEY, Betty	18	F	Spinster	23Ap12Hw
FITZPATRICK, Marie	17	F	Spinster	23Ap12Hw
WARD, Catharine	20	F	Spinster	23Ap12Hw
DEMPSEY, Michael	23	M	Laborer	23Ap12Hw
HEARN, Bridget	30	F	Spinster	23Ap12Hw
EGAN, Bridget	30	F	Spinster	23Ap12Hw
SWIFT, Martin	19	M	Laborer	23Ap12Hw
Bridget	18	F	Spinster	23Ap12Hw
NEILAND, Patrick	35	M	Laborer	23Ap12Hw
Thomas	18	M	Laborer	23Ap12Hw
John	11	M	Laborer	23Ap12Hw
Biddy	09	F	Child	23Ap12Hw
Mary	06	F	Child	23Ap12Hw
MCLOUGHLIN, Michael	22	M	Laborer	23Ap12Hw
CONTELLO, Julia	19	F	Spinster	23Ap12Hw
FAHY, Patrick	22	M	Laborer	23Ap12Hw
SMITH, Martin	16	M	Laborer	23Ap12Hw
ONEAL, Michael	18	M	Laborer	23Ap12Hw
HARBY, Stephen	40	M	Laborer	23Ap12Hw
ROONEY, Michael	34	M	Laborer	23Ap12Hw
DALY, Peter	22	M	Laborer	23Ap12Hw
WALSH, Walter	24	M	Laborer	23Ap12Hw
MORAN, William	27	M	Laborer	23Ap12Hw
Mary	24	F	Spinster	23Ap12Hw
SEAGAN, Thomas	35	M	Laborer	23Ap12Hw
MALLOWNEY, Peter	23	M	Laborer	23Ap12Hw
TRAEY, Martin	23	M	Laborer	23Ap12Hw
COCKLAN, James	27	M	Laborer	23Ap12Hw
Catharine	18	F	Spinster	23Ap12Hw
LYDON, John	20	M	Laborer	23Ap12Hw
FINNEGAN, Patrick	20	M	Laborer	23Ap12Hw
HAIR, Dennis	30	M	Laborer	23Ap12Hw
MARTEN, Patrick	32	M	Laborer	23Ap12Hw
Biddy	24	F	Spinster	23Ap12Hw
John	01	M	Child	23Ap12Hw
CAHILL, Patrick	40	M	Laborer	23Ap12Hw
Margret	38	F	Spinster	23Ap12Hw
Daniel	13	M	Laborer	23Ap12Hw
John	11	M	Laborer	23Ap12Hw
Mary	00	F	None	23Ap12Hw
Bridget	05	F	Child	23Ap12Hw
Margret	01	F	Child	23Ap12Hw
GEANER, John	18	M	Laborer	23Ap12Hw
SHERRIDAN, Thomas	20	M	Laborer	23Ap12Hw
GEANER, Patrick	16	M	Laborer	23Ap12Hw
FAHEY, Patrick	45	M	Laborer	23Ap12Hw
BRODERICK, Bartly	23	M	Laborer	23Ap12Hw
Cathrine	20	F	Spinster	23Ap12Hw
COOLEHAN, Michl.	25	M	Laborer	23Ap12Hw
HOLAN, Thomas	21	M	Laborer	23Ap12Hw
COOLEHAN, Ellen	22	F	Spinster	23Ap12Hw
DONOHUE, James	28	M	Laborer	23Ap12Hw
CAMMEVAN, John	16	M	Laborer	23Ap12Hw
MARTIN, John	20	M	Laborer	23Ap12Hw
HICKEY, John	20	M	Laborer	23Ap12Hw
CONROY, Fergus	20	M	Laborer	23Ap12Hw
HEAVY, Michael	22	M	Laborer	23Ap12Hw
LYNCH, Patrick	13	M	Laborer	23Ap12Hw
NEILAN, Thomas	30	M	Laborer	23Ap12Hw
KELLY, William	50	M	Laborer	23Ap12Hw
MANNION, Patrick	13	M	Laborer	23Ap12Hw
DAY, John	26	M	Laborer	23Ap12Hw
CREHAN, Mary	22	F	Spinster	23Ap12Hw
CLUHERTY, James	00	M	Unknown	23Ap12Hw
BALTON, Thomas	00	M	Unknown	23Ap12Hw

SARAH 24 APRIL 1848

From Dublin

NAMES OF PASSENGERS		AGE	SEX	OCCUPATIONS	DATE PORT SHIP
LEE, David		28	M	Farmer	24Ap20Dx
U	(W)	23	F	None	24Ap20Dx
Margret		17	F	None	24Ap20Dx
Margret-Ann		22	F	None	24Ap20Dx
Charlotte		01	F	Child	24Ap20Dx
Michael		.00	M	Infant	24Ap20Dx
CEULY, James		27	M	Farmer	24Ap20Dx
U	(W)	22	F	None	24Ap20Dx
BOURKE, Michael		20	M	Farmer	24Ap20Dx
SMITH, Philip		24	M	Farmer	24Ap20Dx
U	(W)	22	F	None	24Ap20Dx
BURELL, Edwd.		21	M	Farmer	24Ap20Dx
CANNEY, Stephan		18	M	Farmer	24Ap20Dx
TUNY, Patrick		24	M	Farmer	24Ap20Dx
LOULEV, John		14	M	Farmer	24Ap20Dx
HUNARY, Paul		20	M	Farmer	24Ap20Dx
HOGAN, Eliza		22	F	None	24Ap20Dx
KELLY, Thomas		20	M	Farmer	24Ap20Dx
KENNY, James		20	M	Farmer	24Ap20Dx
TYNELL, Mary-A.		20	F	None	24Ap20Dx
CASSIDY, Owen		45	M	Farmer	24Ap20Dx
Bridget		45	F	None	24Ap20Dx
James		03	M	Child	24Ap20Dx
HENRY, Christopher		32	M	Farmer	24Ap20Dx
Owen		36	M	Farmer	24Ap20Dx
James		03	M	Child	24Ap20Dx
John		.00	M	Infant	24Ap20Dx
GALLIGAN, James		20	M	Farmer	24Ap20Dx
Catherine		17	F	None	24Ap20Dx
SMITH, John		44	M	Farmer	24Ap20Dx
Anne		36	F	Farmer	24Ap20Dx
James		28	M	Farmer	24Ap20Dx
Thomas		28	M	Farmer	24Ap20Dx
Mary		16	F	None	24Ap20Dx
Bernard		14	M	Farmer	24Ap20Dx
Catherine		12	F	None	24Ap20Dx
Rose		10	F	None	24Ap20Dx
David		16	M	Farmer	24Ap20Dx
Nick		11	M	Farmer	24Ap20Dx
MARA, Judy		25	F	None	24Ap20Dx
Mary		24	F	None	24Ap20Dx
CAPRICE, Mary		35	F	None	24Ap20Dx
Anne		14	F	None	24Ap20Dx
John		10	M	None	24Ap20Dx
JOHNSON, Pat		38	M	Farmer	24Ap20Dx
Joseph		28	M	Farmer	24Ap20Dx
James		27	M	Farmer	24Ap20Dx
Tim		24	M	Farmer	24Ap20Dx
Mary		35	F	None	24Ap20Dx
Catherine		23	F	None	24Ap20Dx
TYMAN, Mick		25	M	None	24Ap20Dx
Andy		23	M	None	24Ap20Dx
Mary		20	F	None	24Ap20Dx
Ellen		26	F	None	24Ap20Dx
Peter		.00	M	Infant	24Ap20Dx
BURKE, William		30	M	Farmer	24Ap20Dx
DOYLE, Mary		18	F	None	24Ap20Dx
COYN, Denice		40	M	Farmer	24Ap20Dx
Nelly		27	F	None	24Ap20Dx
COYNE, Margt.		25	F	None	24Ap20Dx
BUFFERTY, Cather.		61	F	None	24Ap20Dx
Bridget		21	F	None	24Ap20Dx
MCANLY, Bridget		30	F	None	24Ap20Dx
MAHN, Mary		34	F	None	24Ap20Dx
Elly		12	F	None	24Ap20Dx

NAMES OF PASSENGERS	AGE	SEX	OCCUPATIONS	DATE PORT SHIP
MAHN, John	05	M	Child	24Ap20Dx
Mary	.00	F	Infant	24Ap20Dx
BONE, Britle	40	M	Farmer	24Ap20Dx
Catherine	35	F	None	24Ap20Dx
James	11	M	Farmer	24Ap20Dx
Michl.	09	M	Child	24Ap20Dx
John	07	M	Child	24Ap20Dx
William	04	M	Child	24Ap20Dx
PHELAN, David	.00	M	Infant	24Ap20Dx
PAULORY, Willm.	22	M	Farmer	24Ap20Dx
SHULUK, Mathew	18	M	Farmer	24Ap20Dx
FETHARDON, Mary	40	F	None	24Ap20Dx
Anne	.00	F	Infant	24Ap20Dx
BURKE, John	21	M	Farmer	24Ap20Dx
DUGGAN, John	20	M	Farmer	24Ap20Dx
BOBULSON, Miss	20	F	None	24Ap20Dx
EVENS, Joseph	40	M	Farmer	24Ap20Dx
U (W)	40	F	None	24Ap20Dx
James	23	M	Farmer	24Ap20Dx
Ellen	20	F	None	24Ap20Dx
Joseph	08	M	Child	24Ap20Dx
John	.00	M	Infant	24Ap20Dx
Pat	.00	M	Infant	24Ap20Dx
ARMSTRONG, Thomas	25	M	Farmer	24Ap20Dx
COYAL, Mick	27	M	Farmer	24Ap20Dx
GULAN, Johan	20	M	Farmer	24Ap20Dx
GRETIUM, Ann	20	F	None	24Ap20Dx
Ellen	20	F	None	24Ap20Dx
TAHLE, Biddy	20	F	None	24Ap20Dx
CONSORY, Michal	24	M	Farmer	24Ap20Dx
DOYLE, Michal	26	M	Farmer	24Ap20Dx
WHELAN, David	26	M	Farmer	24Ap20Dx
COYNEE, Ellen	40	F	None	24Ap20Dx
Thomas	.00	M	Infant	24Ap20Dx
KEAN, Samuel	34	M	Farmer	24Ap20Dx
PENDEN, Mick	21	M	Farmer	24Ap20Dx
Mary	20	F	None	24Ap20Dx
CARNEY, Jayne	20	F	None	24Ap20Dx
FLANAGAN, Thomas	22	M	Farmer	24Ap20Dx
Bridget	19	F	None	24Ap20Dx
Andrew	17	M	Farmer	24Ap20Dx
Mary	14	F	None	24Ap20Dx
RUSS, James	40	M	Farmer	24Ap20Dx
Thomas	19	M	Farmer	24Ap20Dx
Anthony	17	M	Farmer	24Ap20Dx
Patt	17	M	Farmer	24Ap20Dx
Rose	22	F	None	24Ap20Dx
Cathern	20	F	None	24Ap20Dx
Margret	18	F	None	24Ap20Dx
MACHEN, Muff	20	F	None	24Ap20Dx
KENNEDY, Anne	26	F	None	24Ap20Dx
CONNDLY, Mick	50	M	Farmer	24Ap20Dx
Honor	48	F	None	24Ap20Dx
Bess	24	F	None	24Ap20Dx
CAUNALLY, Pat	18	M	Farmer	24Ap20Dx
John	16	M	Farmer	24Ap20Dx
Andy	13	M	Farmer	24Ap20Dx
Cathern	10	F	None	24Ap20Dx
KELLY, James	52	M	Farmer	24Ap20Dx
Mary	54	F	None	24Ap20Dx
Thomas	28	M	Farmer	24Ap20Dx
James	20	M	Farmer	24Ap20Dx
Mary	24	F	None	24Ap20Dx
Margret	22	F	None	24Ap20Dx
MAHN, David	60	M	Farmer	24Ap20Dx
Briddy	56	F	None	24Ap20Dx
Cathern	28	F	None	24Ap20Dx
John	26	M	Farmer	24Ap20Dx
James	24	M	Farmer	24Ap20Dx
Briddy	20	F	None	24Ap20Dx
SMITH, John	28	M	None	24Ap20Dx
Mary	30	F	None	24Ap20Dx
Phillip	06	M	Child	24Ap20Dx
Mary	04	F	Child	24Ap20Dx
Patt	.00	M	Infant	24Ap20Dx

NAMES OF PASSENGERS	AGE	SEX	OCCUPATIONS	DATE PORT SHIP
COYNE, Thomas	40	M	Farmer	24Ap20Dx
Catherine	30	F	None	24Ap20Dx
John	06	M	Child	24Ap20Dx
GATHY, Pat	15	M	Farmer	24Ap20Dx
Cathern	17	F	None	24Ap20Dx
Mary	20	F	None	24Ap20Dx
BYRD, Denis	21	M	Farmer	24Ap20Dx
HEALY, Bridget	60	F	None	24Ap20Dx
KENEDY, Bridget	30	F	None	24Ap20Dx
KENNDY, Maria	10	F	None	24Ap20Dx
Pat	09	M	Child	24Ap20Dx
John	.00	M	Infant	24Ap20Dx
Biddy	07	F	Child	24Ap20Dx
FALLEN, Ellen	19	F	None	24Ap20Dx
QUINNY, Bridget	18	F	None	24Ap20Dx
GILLEN, James	73	M	Farmer	24Ap20Dx
John	19	M	Farmer	24Ap20Dx
U (W)	60	F	None	24Ap20Dx
FANSAN, Edward	40	M	Farmer	24Ap20Dx
Mary	40	F	None	24Ap20Dx
Mary	18	F	None	24Ap20Dx
DALY, Michal	18	M	Farmer	24Ap20Dx
FANN, Thomas	18	M	Farmer	24Ap20Dx
MERIDTH, Jane	20	F	None	24Ap20Dx
MYLY, Francis	17	F	None	24Ap20Dx
RICHARDSON, Wm.	21	M	None	24Ap20Dx
MORGAN, John	20	M	None	24Ap20Dx

RIO-GRANDE 24 APRIL 1848

From Liverpool

NAMES OF PASSENGERS	AGE	SEX	OCCUPATIONS	DATE PORT SHIP
FITZGERALD, Peter	42	M	Laborer	24Ap02Hy
FARRELL, Mary	20	F	Servant	24Ap02Hy
LYONS, Mary	16	F	Servant	24Ap02Hy
TOBEN, Wm.	24	M	Mason	24Ap02Hy
John	30	M	Mason	24Ap02Hy
Katherine	25	F	None	24Ap02Hy
Wm.	.05	M	Infant	24Ap02Hy
OCONNOLL, John	23	M	Farmer	24Ap02Hy
KILDRUFF, Byrum	25	M	Farmer	24Ap02Hy
Bridget	25	F	None	24Ap02Hy
Marsella	.09	F	Infant	24Ap02Hy
HAYES, John	28	M	Farmer	24Ap02Hy
Daniel	23	M	Farmer	24Ap02Hy
MULCARHY, Danl.	35	M	Farmer	24Ap02Hy
JONES, Wm.	23	M	Farmer	24Ap02Hy
LOUGHNAN, Edmond	23	M	Farmer	24Ap02Hy
HAYS, Katherine	20	F	Servant	24Ap02Hy
JONES, Patk.	28	M	Farmer	24Ap02Hy
SULIVAN, Katherine	28	F	Servant	24Ap02Hy
TYNAN, Mary	21	F	Dressmaker	24Ap02Hy
HAYS, Margaret	17	F	Servant	24Ap02Hy
GILLIGAN, Patrick	24	M	Clerk	24Ap02Hy
Mary	20	F	None	24Ap02Hy
GARDNER, Katherine	33	F	None	24Ap02Hy
EAGAN, Bridget	40	F	None	24Ap02Hy
Patrick	10	M	Servant	24Ap02Hy
EAMES, Mary	30	F	Servant	24Ap02Hy
BURKE, Thomas	18	M	Servant	24Ap02Hy
LAMB, Sidney	37	M	Servant	24Ap02Hy
John	11	M	Servant	24Ap02Hy
Patrick	11	M	Servant	24Ap02Hy
JAMES, Ann	19	F	Servant	24Ap02Hy
LAVEY, John	21	M	Laborer	24Ap02Hy
WELSH, James	24	M	Farmer	24Ap02Hy
Michael	27	M	Farmer	24Ap02Hy
David	23	M	Bootmaker	24Ap02Hy
Katherine	25	F	Servant	24Ap02Hy

NAMES OF PASSENGERS	AGE	SEX	OCCUPATIONS	DATE PORT SHIP
BANVEY, Wm.	26	M	Shoemaker	24Ap02Hy
BARRY, Edmond	26	M	Farmer	24Ap02Hy
Mary	14	F	Servant	24Ap02Hy
LAVEY, John	26	M	Tailor	24Ap02Hy
LEAHY, Timothy	27	M	Hrsm	24Ap02Hy
ADRISCAL, Timothy	26	M	Shoemaker	24Ap02Hy
MCAULIFF, Daniel	27	M	Farmer	24Ap02Hy
Betsy	26	F	None	24Ap02Hy
Edmond	18	M	Farmer	24Ap02Hy
Hannah	02	F	Child	24Ap02Hy
MAHONY, Edward	21	M	Laborer	24Ap02Hy
CALLAHAN, Margaret	18	F	Servant	24Ap02Hy
WILLS, John	24	M	Clerk	24Ap02Hy
MILLS, Jane	20	F	Servant	24Ap02Hy
CALLAHAN, Cornelius	15	M	Servant	24Ap02Hy
Thomas	18	M	Servant	24Ap02Hy
MALLAN, Mary	21	F	Servant	24Ap02Hy
HILL, Susan	22	F	Servant	24Ap02Hy
MALONY, Jane	17	F	Servant	24Ap02Hy
OFARRELL, Mathew	26	M	Laborer	24Ap02Hy
Mary	21	F	Servant	24Ap02Hy
Katherine	19	F	Servant	24Ap02Hy
GREEN, Michael	21	M	Laborer	24Ap02Hy
SMITH, Michael	22	M	Laborer	24Ap02Hy
Bridget	26	F	None	24Ap02Hy
James	.11	M	Infant	24Ap02Hy
QUINN, John	25	M	Laborer	24Ap02Hy
HART, Ann	16	F	Servant	24Ap02Hy
CONIGAN, Ann	19	F	Servant	24Ap02Hy
NORTON, Wm.	50	M	Farmer	24Ap02Hy
Jane	50	F	Farmer	24Ap02Hy
Bridget	20	F	Servant	24Ap02Hy
Owen	17	M	Laborer	24Ap02Hy
Katherine	15	F	Servant	24Ap02Hy
James	08	M	Child	24Ap02Hy
Margaret	06	F	Child	24Ap02Hy
Ann	06	F	Child	24Ap02Hy
QUINDON, John	43	M	Farmer	24Ap02Hy
Bridget	23	F	None	24Ap02Hy
Joanna	.06	F	Infant	24Ap02Hy
BURK, Bridget	32	F	Servant	24Ap02Hy
Mary	22	F	None	24Ap02Hy
CATTERY, James	45	M	Farmer	24Ap02Hy
Alice	38	F	None	24Ap02Hy
Ellen	13	F	None	24Ap02Hy
Eliza	11	F	None	24Ap02Hy
Mary	09	F	Child	24Ap02Hy
Timothy	06	M	Child	24Ap02Hy
Alice	03	F	Child	24Ap02Hy
Michael	.10	M	Infant	24Ap02Hy
MACKLIN, Thos.	50	M	Farmer	24Ap02Hy
Norry	43	M	None	24Ap02Hy
Nancy	15	F	None	24Ap02Hy
John	05	M	Child	24Ap02Hy
Ann	03	F	Child	24Ap02Hy
Thomas	.11	M	Infant	24Ap02Hy
CARTY, Patrick	40	M	Laborer	24Ap02Hy
HOGAN, James	28	M	Laborer	24Ap02Hy
GRIFFITH, Ellen	26	F	Servant	24Ap02Hy
HENNSY, Patrick	24	M	Laborer	24Ap02Hy
DUNIVAN, Patrick	26	M	Laborer	24Ap02Hy
Ellen	20	F	Servant	24Ap02Hy
DONSEY, Wm.	23	M	Laborer	24Ap02Hy
BARREY, Bridget	27	F	Servant	24Ap02Hy
HOGAN, Martin	29	M	Laborer	24Ap02Hy
HENNLESSEG, Joanna	28	F	Servant	24Ap02Hy
WARD, George	30	M	Laborer	24Ap02Hy
DIFFLEY, John	20	M	Clerk	24Ap02Hy
NORRY, John	24	M	Laborer	24Ap02Hy
James	19	M	Laborer	24Ap02Hy
Eliza	09	F	Servant	24Ap02Hy
Margaret	11	F	Servant	24Ap02Hy
MAHALY, Eliza	20	F	Servant	24Ap02Hy
MCKEEN, Elizabeth	24	F	Servant	24Ap02Hy
HOGAN, Patrick	30	M	Farmer	24Ap02Hy
HOGAN, May	40	F	None	24Ap02Hy
Biddy	49	F	None	24Ap02Hy
Ellen	17	F	None	24Ap02Hy
Ann	15	F	None	24Ap02Hy
Mary	07	F	Child	24Ap02Hy
Joseph	03	M	Child	24Ap02Hy
John	.11	M	Infant	24Ap02Hy
KENNEDY, Jas.	20	M	Laborer	24Ap02Hy
MCDONALD, Bridget	15	F	Servant	24Ap02Hy
FLEMING, Mary	46	F	Servant	24Ap02Hy
Margaret	20	F	Servant	24Ap02Hy
Mary	18	F	Servant	24Ap02Hy
Patrick	17	M	Laborer	24Ap02Hy
Eliza	15	F	Servant	24Ap02Hy
Joanna	13	F	Servant	24Ap02Hy
Catherine	09	F	Child	24Ap02Hy
Ellen	05	F	Child	24Ap02Hy
Ann	03	F	Child	24Ap02Hy
DOYER, Patrick	19	M	Laborer	24Ap02Hy
BREEN, Julia	25	F	Dressmaker	24Ap02Hy
DAYER, Bridget	17	F	Servant	24Ap02Hy
Mary	07	F	Child	24Ap02Hy
Michael	03	M	Child	24Ap02Hy

HOME 24 APRIL 1848

From Liverpool

NAMES OF PASSENGERS	AGE	SEX	OCCUPATIONS	DATE PORT SHIP
CONLAN, Pat	42	M	Laborer	24Ap02Ie
Mary (W)	16	F	None	24Ap02Ie
Nancy	12	F	Spinster	24Ap02Ie
GRANT, Lance	34	M	None	24Ap02Ie
Nancy	07	F	Child	24Ap02Ie
BAISEL, Pat	17	M	Laborer	24Ap02Ie
DEVENEY, John	20	M	Laborer	24Ap02Ie
MCGINLEY, Pat	30	M	Laborer	24Ap02Ie
MCBRETON, John	31	M	Laborer	24Ap02Ie
WOOLY, John	40	M	Laborer	24Ap02Ie
U (W)	30	F	None	24Ap02Ie
William	17	M	Laborer	24Ap02Ie
John	12	M	Laborer	24Ap02Ie
WALSH, Cath.	28	F	None	24Ap02Ie
MCCOY, Pat	25	M	Laborer	24Ap02Ie
LEARY, Ellen	20	F	None	24Ap02Ie
RICE, James	27	M	Laborer	24Ap02Ie
MCBRIDE, Alexr.	25	M	Laborer	24Ap02Ie
MULLEN, James	25	M	Laborer	24Ap02Ie
MAHON, Robt.	25	M	Laborer	24Ap02Ie
MCGARVEY, James	25	M	Laborer	24Ap02Ie
GALLAGHER, Patk.	25	M	Laborer	24Ap02Ie
MCGROTTY, John	24	M	Laborer	24Ap02Ie
CONORON, Ellen	20	F	None	24Ap02Ie
Thomas	.00	M	Infant	24Ap02Ie
Mary	20	F	None	24Ap02Ie
EAGAN, Martin	35	M	Laborer	24Ap02Ie
Winney	03	F	Child	24Ap02Ie
MORAN, Martin	25	M	Laborer	24Ap02Ie
MCGAVIN, Michl.	22	M	Laborer	24Ap02Ie
NEARY, Mark	18	M	Laborer	24Ap02Ie
Ellen	20	F	Laborer	24Ap02Ie
KELLY, James	14	M	Laborer	24Ap02Ie
DEVENAY, Danl.	19	M	Laborer	24Ap02Ie
Nancy	10	F	Laborer	24Ap02Ie
WARD, Thos.	36	M	Laborer	24Ap02I
FORD, Pat	34	M	Laborer	24Ap02I
FINNEGAN, Nancy	20	F	Laborer	24Ap02I
MURRAY, Biddy	37	F	Wife	24Ap02I
James	13	M	Laborer	24Ap02I
Michl.	11	M	Laborer	24Ap02I

NAMES OF PASSENGERS		AGE	SEX	OCCUPATIONS	DATE PORT SHIP
MURRAY, Thomas		06	M	Child	24Ap02le
George		03	M	Child	24Ap02le
KENNEDY, Mary		20	F	Wife	24Ap02le
Cath.		20	F	Wife	24Ap02le
GRAHAM, Saml.		18	M	Laborer	24Ap02le
DORLY, Mary		19	F	Wife	24Ap02le
GILLESPIE, Robert		40	M	Laborer	24Ap02le
Margt.		25	F	Wife	24Ap02le
DELANEY, Cath.		30	F	Wife	24Ap02le
CAVANAGH, Margt.		25	F	Wife	24Ap02le
Maria		20	F	Wife	24Ap02le
Thomas		.00	M	Infant	24Ap02le
Catharine		03	F	Child	24Ap02le
WARD, Biddy		30	F	None	24Ap02le
CAVANAGH, J.F.		32	M	Laborer	24Ap02le
TOOLE, Patk.		33	M	Unknown	24Ap02le
HALLOGAN, John		33	M	Unknown	24Ap02le
WHOLEHAN, Rose		27	F	Spinster	24Ap02le
ASAIR, John		30	M	Laborer	24Ap02le
MORAN, Alexr.		20	M	Laborer	24Ap02le
FITZGERALD, Patk.		50	M	Laborer	24Ap02le
MCBRIDE, James		22	M	Laborer	24Ap02le
MITCHELL, Robt.		42	M	Laborer	24Ap02le
BREEN, Henry		20	M	Laborer	24Ap02le
U	(W)	18	F	Wife	24Ap02le
CAIN, Anthony		28	M	Laborer	24Ap02le
U	(W)	26	F	Wife	24Ap02le
Biddy		.00	F	Infant	24Ap02le
BERRY, James		21	M	Laborer	24Ap02le
Mary		21	F	Wife	24Ap02le
BOYD, Jane		21	F	None	24Ap02le
MCCARNEY, Bridgt.		19	F	None	24Ap02le
DUFFEY, Mary		19	F	None	24Ap02le
BERRY, Jane		.00	F	Infant	24Ap02le
BOYD, Eliza		.00	F	Infant	24Ap02le
WATSON, Margt.		40	F	None	24Ap02le
Hugh		25	M	Laborer	24Ap02le
WALLACE, Sarah		25	F	Wife	24Ap02le
EDWARDS, Thomas		32	M	Laborer	24Ap02le
PENN, John		23	M	Laborer	24Ap02le
Cath.		24	F	Wife	24Ap02le
James		19	M	Laborer	24Ap02le
EDWARDS, Margt.		03	F	Child	24Ap02le
Thomas		05	M	Child	24Ap02le
EVANS, Geo.		29	M	Laborer	24Ap02le
Ann	(W)	21	F	None	24Ap02le
GREGG, Thos.		29	M	Laborer	24Ap02le
JONES, Wm.		30	M	Laborer	24Ap02le
LOWE, Wm.		06	M	Child	24Ap02le
EDWARDS, James		26	M	Laborer	24Ap02le
WALSH, Rose		20	F	Wife	24Ap02le
Donovan/DORAN, Mike		25	M	Laborer	24Ap02le
U	(W)	25	F	Wife	24Ap02le
Margt.		.00	F	Infant	24Ap02le
Died-At-Sea					
SULLIVAN, Michl.		25	M	Laborer	24Ap02le
COX, Thos.		26	M	Laborer	24Ap02le
MCCORMICK, Mary		17	F	Spinster	24Ap02le
Nancy		22	F	Spinster	24Ap02le
Cath.		19	F	Spinster	24Ap02le
GARLAND, Mary		22	F	Spinster	24Ap02le
WILSON, John		24	M	Laborer	24Ap02le
CORRIGAN, Michl.		30	M	Laborer	24Ap02le
U	(W)	30	F	Wife	24Ap02le
John		30	M	Laborer	24Ap02le
Mathw.		.00	M	Infant	24Ap02le
Died-At-Sea					
SMITH, Patk.		26	M	Laborer	24Ap02le
CALLRON, Michl.		28	M	Laborer	24Ap02le
Mary	(W)	24	F	Wife	24Ap02le
MONKS, Danl.		50	M	Laborer	24Ap02le
DUFFY, Anty.		30	M	Laborer	24Ap02le
U	(W)	30	F	Wife	24Ap02le
James		05	M	Child	24Ap02le
Thomas		02	M	Child	24Ap02le
DUFFY, Anthony		.00	M	Infant	24Ap02le
BOYLE, Ann		20	F	None	24Ap02le
GRIFFIN, John		20	M	Laborer	24Ap02le
Ellen		20	F	Laborer	24Ap02le
DAULTON, Danl.		25	M	Laborer	24Ap02le
REAGAN, Bridgt.		19	F	Laborer	24Ap02le
DORAN, Michl.		20	M	Laborer	24Ap02le
Hannah		18	F	Laborer	24Ap02le
COLLINS, James		20	M	Laborer	24Ap02le
CAMPBELL, Edwd.		20	M	Laborer	24Ap02le
HALCOME, Robt.		22	M	Laborer	24Ap02le
Peggy		20	F	Laborer	24Ap02le
LYONS, John		30	M	Laborer	24Ap02le
Margt.		30	F	Laborer	24Ap02le
KENNEDY, Margt.		19	F	Laborer	24Ap02le
COMFORT, Michl.		25	M	Laborer	24Ap02le
SHIELDS, James		25	M	Laborer	24Ap02le
KING, Pat		20	M	Laborer	24Ap02le
U	(W)	30	F	None	24Ap02le
Ann		12	F	None	24Ap02le
Pat		03	M	Child	24Ap02le
KERNAN, Pat		20	M	Laborer	24Ap02le
OBRIAN, Thos.		20	M	Laborer	24Ap02le
KING, Ann		40	F	None	24Ap02le
MCGETTINGAR, Danl.		20	M	Laborer	24Ap02le
GREEN, Chas.		25	M	Laborer	24Ap02le
FLOOD, John		25	M	Laborer	24Ap02le
SMITH, James		20	M	Laborer	24Ap02le
JONES, Wm.		25	M	Laborer	24Ap02le
NURSE, Saml.		20	M	Laborer	24Ap02le
DORAN, John		20	M	Laborer	24Ap02le
GAVIN, Thos.		20	M	Laborer	24Ap02le
WALKER, Margt.		20	F	None	24Ap02le
MAHER, Thos.		23	M	Laborer	24Ap02le
KEARNS, Eliza		19	F	Spinster	24Ap02le
GREEN, Mary		19	F	Spinster	24Ap02le
MCDONALD, James		22	M	Laborer	24Ap02le
GEESHAM, Thos.		21	M	Laborer	24Ap02le
MURPHY, Thos.		25	M	Laborer	24Ap02le
MCGRATH, Christy		24	M	Laborer	24Ap02le
Elizth.	(W)	24	F	None	24Ap02le
CARNEY, Eliza		21	F	None	24Ap02le
RICHARDS, Edwd.		26	M	Laborer	24Ap02le
DERNWELL, John		30	M	Laborer	24Ap02le
MURPHY, John		20	M	Laborer	24Ap02le
Ann		18	F	None	24Ap02le
DRUM, Ann		25	F	None	24Ap02le
TWEENEY, James		18	M	Laborer	24Ap02le
MCGOGAN, Chas.		22	M	Laborer	24Ap02le
MCDEVITT, Danl.		18	M	Laborer	24Ap02le
RYAN, Michl.		40	M	Laborer	24Ap02le
U	(W)	40	F	None	24Ap02le
Ellen		10	F	None	24Ap02le
Pat		06	M	Child	24Ap02le
John		04	M	Child	24Ap02le
Teddy		.00	M	Infant	24Ap02le
Margt.		08	F	Child	24Ap02le
SMITH, Pat		26	M	Laborer	24Ap02le
CLEARY, John		24	M	Laborer	24Ap02le
Bridgt.		20	F	None	24Ap02le
KEEFFE, Michl.		24	M	Laborer	24Ap02le
Cath.		23	F	None	24Ap02le
Ellen		20	F	None	24Ap02le
MULVEY, James		40	M	Laborer	24Ap02le
Patk.		17	M	Laborer	24Ap02le
WALSH, Pat		22	M	Laborer	24Ap02le
Mary		21	F	Wife	24Ap02le
Norry		20	F	None	24Ap02le
ODONNELL, Wm.		24	M	Laborer	24Ap02le
LYNCH, Mary-A.		21	F	None	24Ap02le
ELLISON, Joseph		40	M	Laborer	24Ap02le
OATES, Sarah		35	F	None	24Ap02le
Eleanor		16	F	None	24Ap02le
Alfred		10	M	None	24Ap02le
CLARKE, Thos.		44	M	Laborer	24Ap02le

NAMES OF PASSENGERS		AGE	SEX	OCCUPATIONS	DATE PORT SHIP
CLARKE, Mary	(W)	44	F	None	24Ap02Ie
MCCARTHY, Michl.		24	M	Laborer	24Ap02Ie
COSGROVE, Ann		21	F	None	24Ap02Ie
HARVEST, Geo.		24	M	Laborer	24Ap02Ie
WALKER, John		22	M	Laborer	24Ap02Ie
LONGDEN, Abram		30	M	Laborer	24Ap02Ie
Sarah		28	F	None	24Ap02Ie
Emily		03	F	Child	24Ap02Ie
CLEARY, Wm.		20	M	Laborer	24Ap02Ie
MAHER, Jane		25	F	None	24Ap02Ie
PETITT, Edwd.		27	M	Laborer	24Ap02Ie
MCNAMARA, John		22	M	Laborer	24Ap02Ie
NEWTON, Robt.O.		24	M	Laborer	24Ap02Ie
HANDS, James-H.		20	M	Laborer	24Ap02Ie
MAWRY, Edwd.		26	M	Laborer	24Ap02Ie
MIILLIGAN, Richd.		23	M	Laborer	24Ap02Ie
GROKER, Joseph		24	M	Laborer	24Ap02Ie
BYRNE, James		30	M	Laborer	24Ap02Ie
MOORE, Mary		28	F	None	24Ap02Ie
LAWLER, Cath.		22	F	None	24Ap02Ie
NIGHTINGALE, Henry		36	M	Laborer	24Ap02Ie
Charlotte		30	F	None	24Ap02Ie
Ann		15	F	None	24Ap02Ie
Wm.		12	M	Laborer	24Ap02Ie
Mary		10	F	None	24Ap02Ie
DELANEY, Mary		30	F	None	24Ap02Ie
HALPIN, Bridgt.		32	F	None	24Ap02Ie
MOONEY, Ann		28	F	None	24Ap02Ie
John		11	M	Laborer	24Ap02Ie
Ellen		09	F	Child	24Ap02Ie
Thomas		05	M	Child	24Ap02Ie
Rose		03	F	Child	24Ap02Ie
Pat		01	M	Child	24Ap02Ie
MAGILL, Danl.		18	M	Laborer	24Ap02Ie
DENNON, John		09	M	Child	24Ap02Ie
Patk.		07	M	Child	24Ap02Ie
SHARPE, Condy		27	M	Laborer	24Ap02Ie
FISHER, Condy		13	M	Laborer	24Ap02Ie
BOYLE, Neill		20	M	Laborer	24Ap02Ie
MULLOWNEY, Edwd.		22	M	Laborer	24Ap02Ie
JOHNSON, John		28	M	Laborer	24Ap02Ie
Neil		21	M	Laborer	24Ap02Ie
FLEMMING, Mary		20	F	Spinster	24Ap02Ie
MCGILLEN, Ann		19	F	Spinster	24Ap02Ie
KENNEDY, Arthur		30	M	Laborer	24Ap02Ie
Ann		25	F	None	24Ap02Ie
Rose		.00	F	Infant	24Ap02Ie
JOHNSON, Saml.		21	M	Laborer	24Ap02Ie
LEE, Arhtur		24	M	Laborer	24Ap02Ie
MCDERMOTT, John		40	M	Laborer	24Ap02Ie
Jane		25	F	None	24Ap02Ie
Pat		.00	M	Infant	24Ap02Ie
FITZPATRICK, Cath.		21	F	None	24Ap02Ie
KENNEDY, Owen		16	M	Laborer	24Ap02Ie
FITZPATRICK, Owen		27	M	Laborer	24Ap02Ie
MCBRINE, Thos.		35	M	Laborer	24Ap02Ie
Margt.		40	F	None	24Ap02Ie
Betsey		15	F	None	24Ap02Ie
Thomas		13	M	Laborer	24Ap02Ie
Rosetta		08	F	Child	24Ap02Ie
Joseph		05	M	Child	24Ap02Ie
Mary-Ann		.00	F	Infant	24Ap02Ie
MCGLAYDEN, John		25	M	Laborer	24Ap02Ie
Isabella	(W)	20	F	None	24Ap02Ie
MURRAY, Thomas		17	M	Laborer	24Ap02Ie
MURPHY, Mary-A.		20	F	None	24Ap02Ie
GOODWYN, James		20	M	Laborer	24Ap02Ie
REYNOLDS, Peter		19	M	Laborer	24Ap02Ie
MCCORMICK, Michl.		20	M	Laborer	24Ap02Ie
THOMPSON, Walter		26	M	Laborer	24Ap02Ie
HARRINGTON, Pat		40	M	Laborer	24Ap02Ie
Jane		30	F	Spinster	24Ap02Ie
Peter		02	M	Child	24Ap02Ie
MONROE, Thos.		24	M	Laborer	24Ap02Ie
MAKER, Margt.		30	F	Laborer	24Ap02Ie
KILMARTIN, Mary		30	F	Laborer	24Ap02Ie
BUCKLEY, Mary		27	F	Laborer	24Ap02Ie
GREEN, Michl.		21	M	Laborer	24Ap02Ie
MCBRIEN, Pat		19	M	Laborer	24Ap02Ie
MCGOVY, Wm.		11	M	Laborer	24Ap02Ie
U	(W)	30	F	Wife	24Ap02Ie
GRAY, Rose		22	F	Wife	24Ap02Ie
BURKE, Ellen		20	F	Spinster	24Ap02Ie
Duffey		.00	M	Infant	24Ap02Ie
Born-At-Sea	Died-At-Sea				
Edwards		.00	M	Infant	24Ap02Ie
Born-At-Sea	Died-At-Sea				

INA 25 APRIL 1848

From Liverpool

NAMES OF PASSENGERS		AGE	SEX	OCCUPATIONS	DATE PORT SHIP
PARKER, Thomas		.00	M	Infant	25Ap02Ju
MCAVEY, Francis		40	M	Laborer	25Ap02Ju
U	(W)	31	F	None	25Ap02Ju
Eliza		08	F	Child	25Ap02Ju
Peter		14	M	None	25Ap02Ju
MCADAM, T.T.		66	M	None	25Ap02Ju
Bridget		22	F	None	25Ap02Ju
Mary		20	F	None	25Ap02Ju
Banded		18	F	None	25Ap02Ju
Cathrine		16	F	None	25Ap02Ju
Arthur		12	M	None	25Ap02Ju
Anne		09	F	Child	25Ap02Ju
Johanna		50	F	None	25Ap02Ju
Patrick		21	M	None	25Ap02Ju
Mich.		13	M	None	25Ap02Ju
Mary		11	F	None	25Ap02Ju
DELANO, William		30	M	None	25Ap02Ju
BUSHMAN, John		25	M	None	25Ap02Ju
MCKENNA, Paul		20	M	None	25Ap02Ju
Sally		40	F	None	25Ap02Ju
Sally		10	F	None	25Ap02Ju
John		05	M	Child	25Ap02Ju
CONWAY, B.		21	M	None	25Ap02Ju
HOGMAN, J.		20	M	None	25Ap02Ju
BLADDY, C.		06	M	Child	25Ap02Ju
MURPHY, T.		20	M	None	25Ap02Ju
SULLIVAN, J.		21	M	None	25Ap02Ju
OLEARY, John		26	M	None	25Ap02Ju
LYND, Daniel		26	M	None	25Ap02Ju
SMITH, Jane		25	F	None	25Ap02Ju
MINTH, Rose		21	F	None	25Ap02Ju
Bridget		20	F	None	25Ap02Ju
Mary		20	F	Laborer	25Ap02Ju
HARRINGTON, Catharine		12	F	Laborer	25Ap02Ju
MCCARTHY, Marthy		35	F	Laborer	25Ap02Ju
Mary		22	F	Laborer	25Ap02Ju
Mary		04	F	Child	25Ap02Ju
Cath.		.00	F	Infant	25Ap02Ju
LEARY, Tim		20	M	None	25Ap02Ju
Darby		23	M	None	25Ap02Ju
Ellen		11	F	None	25Ap02Ju
KELLY, Patrick		17	M	None	25Ap02Ju
Patrick		18	M	None	25Ap02Ju
DEVLIN, John		29	M	None	25Ap02Ju
MCGRANE, Mich.		24	M	None	25Ap02Ju
ONEIL, Mich.		20	M	None	25Ap02Ju
CARLIN, Henry		19	M	None	25Ap02Ju
CARRIFFE, Margret		20	F	None	25Ap02Ju
GRIFFIN, Wm.		24	M	None	25Ap02Ju
Nancy		13	F	None	25Ap02Ju
Peggy		11	F	None	25Ap02Ju
Cath.		20	F	None	25Ap02Ju

NAMES OF PASSENGERS	AGE	SEX	OCCUPATIONS	DATE PORT SHIP
GREEN, Geo.	18	M	None	25Ap02Ju
Cathy.	40	F	None	25Ap02Ju
Cath.	12	F	None	25Ap02Ju
Bartley	09	M	Child	25Ap02Ju
Peter	06	M	Child	25Ap02Ju
Mary	04	F	Child	25Ap02Ju
John	.00	M	Infant	25Ap02Ju
Mary	13	F	None	25Ap02Ju
MCBABE, Peter	36	M	None	25Ap02Ju
CARTY, Tim	36	M	None	25Ap02Ju
RILFOYLE, Mary	40	F	None	25Ap02Ju
BARKLEY, John	27	M	None	25Ap02Ju
FARNELL, Rogard	45	M	None	25Ap02Ju
John	12	M	None	25Ap02Ju
BOLSTON, W.	52	M	Laborer	25Ap02Ju
RYAN, Fras.	30	M	Laborer	25Ap02Ju
THANDEN, Mary	10	F	None	25Ap02Ju
RENNY, John	16	M	None	25Ap02Ju
Cath.	13	F	None	25Ap02Ju
John	11	M	None	25Ap02Ju
Thomas	08	M	Child	25Ap02Ju
RYAN, Honora	30	F	None	25Ap02Ju
Quinn	26	M	None	25Ap02Ju
Edmund	10	M	None	25Ap02Ju
Anna	08	F	Child	25Ap02Ju
MORRIS, Thos.	35	M	None	25Ap02Ju
OLDFIELD, John	16	M	None	25Ap02Ju
CARMONDY, John	09	M	Laborer	25Ap02Ju
Cath.	28	F	None	25Ap02Ju
Margret	24	F	None	25Ap02Ju
COLLINS, Maurice	22	M	None	25Ap02Ju
HANGADHY, Mich.	24	M	None	25Ap02Ju
HARTFORD, John	22	M	None	25Ap02Ju
PIGGART, James	.00	M	Infant	25Ap02Ju
KANNY, John	16	M	None	25Ap02Ju
Cath.	13	F	None	25Ap02Ju
John	19	M	None	25Ap02Ju
Thos.	08	M	Child	25Ap02Ju
QUINN, Dennis	36	M	None	25Ap02Ju
Mary	26	F	None	25Ap02Ju
Ann	11	F	None	25Ap02Ju
Edward	08	M	Child	25Ap02Ju
Celia	52	F	None	25Ap02Ju
John	45	M	None	25Ap02Ju
Maria	17	F	None	25Ap02Ju
Hespy	15	F	None	25Ap02Ju
Matilda	13	F	None	25Ap02Ju
GILLEN, Francis	22	M	None	25Ap02Ju
Mary	20	F	None	25Ap02Ju
DOGERTY, J.	22	M	None	25Ap02Ju
Owen	21	M	None	25Ap02Ju
KELLY, Nancy	20	F	None	25Ap02Ju
LUGERTY, B.	23	M	None	25Ap02Ju
Mary	20	F	None	25Ap02Ju
Sally	24	F	None	25Ap02Ju
MCINTER, L.	30	M	None	25Ap02Ju
CAVANAGH, J.	28	M	None	25Ap02Ju
SMITH, John	21	M	None	25Ap02Ju
Mary	35	F	None	25Ap02Ju
Jane	14	F	None	25Ap02Ju
Anne	12	F	None	25Ap02Ju
COYNE, Stephen	34	M	None	25Ap02Ju
HUGHES, Catharine	40	F	None	25Ap02Ju
James	60	F	None	25Ap02Ju
J.	48	F	None	25Ap02Ju
L.	12	F	None	25Ap02Ju
Cath.	09	F	Child	25Ap02Ju
Brosman	24	M	None	25Ap02Ju
Bridget	20	F	None	25Ap02Ju

SAMUEL-HICKS 26 APRIL 1848

From Liverpool

NAMES OF PASSENGERS	AGE	SEX	OCCUPATIONS	DATE PORT SHIP
CANE, Cath.	30	F	Wife	26Ap02Bs
Mary	10	F	None	26Ap02Bs
Mgt.	08	F	Child	26Ap02Bs
Bridt.	06	F	Child	26Ap02Bs
CASSIDY, Henry	16	M	Laborer	26Ap02Bs
MORGAN, Michl.	19	M	Laborer	26Ap02Bs
John	17	M	Laborer	26Ap02Bs
MURPHY, Edwd.	21	M	Laborer	26Ap02Bs
MCKENAN, Rosana	18	F	Dressmaker	26Ap02Bs
EDWARDS, James	14	M	None	26Ap02Bs
DEMPSY, Rose	21	F	Servant	26Ap02Bs
KELLY, Laune.	17	M	Laborer	26Ap02Bs
MULHOONY, Michl.	25	M	Laborer	26Ap02Bs
DOUNNY, Patk.	20	M	Laborer	26Ap02Bs
CAHILL, Mathw.	25	M	Laborer	26Ap02Bs
KELLY, Michl.	34	M	Laborer	26Ap02Bs
MANNICKS, Patk.	24	M	Laborer	26Ap02Bs
FITZPATRICK, Mary	21	F	Dressmaker	26Ap02Bs
MCNALLY, Cath.	22	F	Spinster	26Ap02Bs
MAHONEY, Biddy	50	F	Wi	26Ap02Bs
John	18	M	Laborer	26Ap02Bs
MUHOONEY, Mary	18	F	Servant	26Ap02Bs
FLANIGAN, Bridt.	24	F	Servant	26Ap02Bs
BYRNE, Patk.	22	M	Laborer	26Ap02Bs
GILLIGAN, Thos.	40	M	Laborer	26Ap02Bs
BACON, Anne	23	F	Servant	26Ap02Bs
OFLAHERTY, Ellen	50	F	Seamstress	26Ap02Bs
Bridt.	34	F	Seamstress	26Ap02Bs
Mary	22	F	Seamstress	26Ap02Bs
FEGAN, Eliza	40	F	Spinster	26Ap02Bs
HOSTER, Jane-M.	20	F	Dressmaker	26Ap02Bs
Isabella	17	F	Dressmaker	26Ap02Bs
MCCUDY, Patk.	28	M	Laborer	26Ap02Bs
John	23	M	Laborer	26Ap02Bs
Robt.	18	M	Laborer	26Ap02Bs
William	10	M	None	26Ap02Bs
James	09	M	Child	26Ap02Bs
BUCHANAN, Deborah	55	F	Wi	26Ap02Bs
Joseph	19	M	Weaver	26Ap02Bs
MILLER, Mgt.	17	F	Dressmaker	26Ap02Bs
FARRELL, Mary	19	F	Servant	26Ap02Bs
WALSH, Thomas	48	M	Laborer	26Ap02Bs
Eliza (W)	48	F	None	26Ap02Bs
Eliza	20	F	Spinster	26Ap02Bs
Cath.	18	F	Spinster	26Ap02Bs
Anne	15	F	Spinster	26Ap02Bs
Martin	12	M	None	26Ap02Bs
Cath.	.00	F	Infant	26Ap02Bs
IGO, Thomas	21	M	Laborer	26Ap02Bs
FARRELL, Francis	20	M	Laborer	26Ap02Bs
LEVY, Cath.	20	F	Spinster	26Ap02Bs
DUNNE, Mary	24	F	Servant	26Ap02Bs
MATHEWS, John	28	M	Laborer	26Ap02Bs
SHEENAN, Judy	35	F	Servant	26Ap02Bs
DUNNE, Launce.	28	M	Laborer	26Ap02Bs
Michl.	24	M	Laborer	26Ap02Bs
NEILL, Peter	24	M	Laborer	26Ap02Bs
WARD, Patk.	15	M	Laborer	26Ap02Bs
MCDERMOTT, John	17	M	Laborer	26Ap02Bs
MORGAN, Betty	26	F	Spinster	26Ap02Bs
HARDMAN, Cath.	17	F	Spinster	26Ap02Bs
KELLY, Bridt.	17	F	Spinster	26Ap02Bs
Hannah	15	F	Servant	26Ap02Bs
Judith	19	F	Servant	26Ap02Bs
BOLTON, Anne	19	F	Servant	26Ap02Bs

NAMES OF PASSENGERS	AGE	SEX	OCCUPATIONS	DATE PORT SHIP
MCKENNA, Thomas	25	M	Laborer	26Ap02Bs
John	28	M	Laborer	26Ap02Bs
GENAGHTY, Thomas	25	M	Butcher	26Ap02Bs
LAMB, John	28	M	Farmer	26Ap02Bs
Isabella	22	F	Spinster	26Ap02Bs
Mgt.	19	F	Spinster	26Ap02Bs
Bridt.	15	F	Spinster	26Ap02Bs
MAHON, John	27	M	Laborer	26Ap02Bs
GUINTY, Michl.	30	M	Laborer	26Ap02Bs
Francis	12	M	None	26Ap02Bs
DONOHOE, Daniel	21	M	Carpenter	26Ap02Bs
WALSH, Mary	20	F	Servant	26Ap02Bs
OHARA, Michl.	30	M	Laborer	26Ap02Bs
NOONAN, Thomas	34	M	Laborer	26Ap02Bs
FARRELL, Wm.	20	M	Laborer	26Ap02Bs
Jno.	18	M	Laborer	26Ap02Bs
DUFFY, Patk.	35	M	Laborer	26Ap02Bs
KEENAN, Patk.	21	M	Carpenter	26Ap02Bs
May	19	F	Spinster	26Ap02Bs
CRAWFORD, Rose	21	F	Servant	26Ap02Bs
MCEVOY, John	17	M	Laborer	26Ap02Bs
FARLEY, Anne	18	F	Spinster	26Ap02Bs
HOLLAND, Dominick	20	M	Laborer	26Ap02Bs
REILLY, Jane	20	F	Spinster	26Ap02Bs
Anne	40	F	Spinster	26Ap02Bs
EAKINS, Mgt.	25	F	Dressmaker	26Ap02Bs
MULLINS, Chas.	24	M	Laborer	26Ap02Bs
Neil	22	M	Blacksmith	26Ap02Bs
James	20	M	Laborer	26Ap02Bs
ROLSTON, Anne	20	F	Servant	26Ap02Bs
GILLESPIE, Chas.	27	M	Carpenter	26Ap02Bs
Mary	20	F	Servant	26Ap02Bs
LYONS, Michl.	22	M	Laborer	26Ap02Bs
CANNON, Mary	20	F	Servant	26Ap02Bs
GILLESPIE, Henry	22	M	Carpenter	26Ap02Bs
CUNAN, Patk.	08	M	Child	26Ap02Bs
Dennis	20	M	Laborer	26Ap02Bs
DUGGAN, John	20	M	Laborer	26Ap02Bs
NICHOLL, Mary	22	F	Spinster	26Ap02Bs
Eliza	20	F	Spinster	26Ap02Bs
COLLINS, Nancy	20	F	Servant	26Ap02Bs
MOLLOY, Patk.	21	M	Laborer	26Ap02Bs
MCAULEY, Susan	18	F	Spinster	26Ap02Bs
ROBINSON, James	24	M	Fisherman	26Ap02Bs
DOUGHERTY, Danl.	23	M	Butcher	26Ap02Bs
Mgt.	27	F	Seamstress	26Ap02Bs
RODNY, Mary	18	F	Wife	26Ap02Bs
LAVAN, Patk.	20	M	Laborer	26Ap02Bs
MARTIN, Cath.	21	F	Servant	26Ap02Bs
CORRIGAN, Francis	25	M	Carpenter	26Ap02Bs
Mary	21	F	Seamstress	26Ap02Bs
GILLANS, Daniel	20	M	Laborer	26Ap02Bs
SMITH, James	12	M	None	26Ap02Bs
Alice	11	F	None	26Ap02Bs
MCGUIRE, Thomas	25	M	Groom	26Ap02Bs
STERLING, John	18	M	Laborer	26Ap02Bs
QUIGLY, John	24	M	Laborer	26Ap02Bs
Jane	24	F	Wife	26Ap02Bs
James	.00	M	Infant	26Ap02Bs
FEEHAN, Mary	17	F	Servant	26Ap02Bs
REILLY, John	28	M	Laborer	26Ap02Bs
Patk.	22	M	Laborer	26Ap02Bs
MCHUGHES, James	26	M	Laborer	26Ap02Bs
MARTIN, Mgt.	26	F	Servant	26Ap02Bs
FARRELL, Mary	27	F	Servant	26Ap02Bs
QUINN, B.	20	F	Servant	26Ap02Bs
YOUNAY, John	18	M	Laborer	26Ap02Bs
MURPHY, John	20	M	Weaver	26Ap02Bs
MOLLOY, Bridt.	07	F	Child	26Ap02Bs
Thomas	40	M	Laborer	26Ap02Bs
KILLEEN, Anne	17	F	Servant	26Ap02Bs
QUINN, Mary	18	F	Servant	26Ap02Bs
EAGAN, John	30	M	Laborer	26Ap02Bs
REILLY, Dennis	20	M	Laborer	26Ap02Bs
BUTLER, James	40	M	Laborer	26Ap02Bs

NAMES OF PASSENGERS	AGE	SEX	OCCUPATIONS	DATE PORT SHIP
MORAN, John	18	M	Laborer	26Ap02Bs
MULLINS, James	17	M	Laborer	26Ap02Bs
Michael	20	M	Laborer	26Ap02Bs
MCKEON, Cath.	16	F	Spinster	26Ap02Bs
REILLY, Anne	30	F	Servant	26Ap02Bs
Bridgt.	28	F	Servant	26Ap02Bs
TOUNEY, Patk.	16	M	None	26Ap02Bs
CONNELL, James	30	M	Laborer	26Ap02Bs
HUGHES, Owen	36	M	Laborer	26Ap02Bs
Francis	30	M	Laborer	26Ap02Bs
Cath.	24	F	Spinster	26Ap02Bs
James	20	M	Laborer	26Ap02Bs
MCDERMOTT, Patk.	20	M	Laborer	26Ap02Bs
DEVINE, Susan	15	F	Dressmaker	26Ap02Bs
BURNES, Rose	24	F	Wife	26Ap02Bs
SHULAN, Michl.	19	M	Blacksmith	26Ap02Bs
FLYNN, John	20	M	Laborer	26Ap02Bs
Thomas	18	M	Laborer	26Ap02Bs
Bridt. (W)	50	F	Wife	26Ap02Bs
Bridt.	20	F	Spinster	26Ap02Bs
REILLY, Mary	21	F	Spinster	26Ap02Bs
MCBRIDE, Bridt.	24	F	Servant	26Ap02Bs
Julia	20	F	Dressmaker	26Ap02Bs
MCDONALD, Mary	20	F	Servant	26Ap02Bs
MCCABE, Bridt.	16	F	Servant	26Ap02Bs
LAWLER, Edwd.	20	M	Laborer	26Ap02Bs
SCULLY, James	20	M	Tailor	26Ap02Bs
MCEVOY, Steven	20	M	Laborer	26Ap02Bs
Patk.	26	M	Laborer	26Ap02Bs
MULVEY, John	20	M	Laborer	26Ap02Bs
MAHER, Francis	21	M	Laborer	26Ap02Bs
Bessy	08	F	Child	26Ap02Bs
RICE, John	20	M	Clerk	26Ap02Bs
NUGENT, Maria	20	F	Spinster	26Ap02Bs
FANELL, John	24	M	Lawyer	26Ap02Bs
MCGOVERN, Michl.	20	M	Laborer	26Ap02Bs
CLINTON, Mary	01	F	Child	26Ap02Bs
CALLAGHAN, Thomas	35	M	Laborer	26Ap02Bs
LEAHY, Ellen	30	F	Servant	26Ap02Bs
FITZGERALD, Cath.	18	F	Servant	26Ap02Bs
BERGAN, Edwd.	18	M	Laborer	26Ap02Bs
FEELAN, Cath.	18	F	Servant	26Ap02Bs
GUY, Thomas	23	M	Farmer	26Ap02Bs
MOONEY, Anne	24	F	Servant	26Ap02Bs
KENNY, Cath.	20	F	Servant	26Ap02Bs
KELLY, Martin	25	M	Laborer	26Ap02Bs
Judy	20	F	Servant	26Ap02Bs
DOOLEY, Bridgt.	20	F	Spinster	26Ap02Bs
FLYNN, Edwd.	55	M	Carpenter	26Ap02Bs
BUCHANON, Mary	15	F	Spinster	26Ap02Bs
Samuel	25	M	Weaver	26Ap02Bs
Joshua	28	M	Weaver	26Ap02Bs
MARTIN, Wm.	07	M	Child	26Ap02Bs
Mary	14	F	None	26Ap02Bs
Eliza	12	F	None	26Ap02Bs
John	10	M	None	26Ap02Bs
Sarah	08	F	Child	26Ap02Bs
Eliza	48	F	Wife	26Ap02Bs
WEIR, Robert	25	M	Carpenter	26Ap02Bs
FOSTER, John	24	M	Laborer	26Ap02Bs
TALFORD, Mary-Jane	20	F	Housekeeper	26Ap02Bs
WHEELAN, Mary	35	F	Dressmaker	26Ap02Bs
HEFFERAN, Bridt.	21	F	Servant	26Ap02Bs
IGO, Patk.	27	M	Laborer	26Ap02Bs
BERGAN, Mgt.	26	F	Servant	26Ap02Bs
CLABBY, Patk.	28	M	Tailor	26Ap02Bs
KERWAN, James	20	M	Laborer	26Ap02Bs
LESLIE, Cath.	25	F	Servant	26Ap02Bs
STANLEY, Thomas	25	M	Laborer	26Ap02Bs
KELLY, Eleanor	15	F	Servant	26Ap02Bs
MADDEN, Mary	16	F	Servant	26Ap02Bs
HORAN, John	01	M	Child	26Ap02Bs
OLLO, Mary	23	F	Dressmaker	26Ap02Bs
KEELAN, James	20	M	Laborer	26Ap02Bs
John	24	M	Laborer	26Ap02Bs

NAMES OF PASSENGERS	AGE	SEX	OCCUPATIONS	DATE PORT SHIP
WILLIAMS, Jane	30	F	Servant	26Ap02Bs
MCGUILCAN, Ellen	18	F	Spinster	26Ap02Bs
ODONNELL, Hugh	23	M	Laborer	26Ap02Bs
HIGGINS, Monty	21	M	Groom	26Ap02Bs
GILLESPIE, Thomas	25	M	Laborer	26Ap02Bs
GALLAGHER, Lanty	20	F	Groom	26Ap02Bs
MARTIN, Daniel	18	M	Laborer	26Ap02Bs
DIXON, Mary	19	F	Servant	26Ap02Bs
MCGINNES, Magt.	70	F	Spinster	26Ap02Bs
LOGHLIN, Martin	32	M	Laborer	26Ap02Bs
LEONARD, Edward	20	M	Laborer	26Ap02Bs
YOUNG, Wm.	30	M	Laborer	26Ap02Bs
U (W)	30	F	None	26Ap02Bs
GRIMES, Michael	70	M	Laborer	26Ap02Bs
Died-At-Sea				
MCDONNELL, Owen	20	M	Laborer	26Ap02Bs
WINN, Thomas	20	M	(Maloser	26Ap02Bs
CONNELY, James	20	M	Laborer	26Ap02Bs
ROE, Joseph	18	M	Shopman	26Ap02Bs
CASEY, James	39	M	Laborer	26Ap02Bs
LAWLER, Edward	25	M	Laborer	26Ap02Bs
MCEVOY, Judith	20	F	Servant	26Ap02Bs
Mary	18	F	Servant	26Ap02Bs
ROE, Ann	20	F	Servant	26Ap02Bs
FLOOD, Cath.	20	F	Servant	26Ap02Bs
FARRELL, Mary	16	F	Spinster	26Ap02Bs
DUGGAN, Maria	20	F	Spinster	26Ap02Bs
HANNAWAY, Cath.	20	F	Spinster	26Ap02Bs
FARRELL, Margt.	16	F	Spinster	26Ap02Bs
KEENAN, Peter	20	M	Laborer	26Ap02Bs
KENNEY, Peter	21	M	Laborer	26Ap02Bs
CONLEY, Bridget	17	F	Servant	26Ap02Bs
WALSH, Richd.	27	M	Slater	26Ap02Bs
MURRY, Michl.	20	M	Laborer	26Ap02Bs
DONLAN, Mary	20	F	Servant	26Ap02Bs
KELLAHER, Cath.	20	F	Servant	26Ap02Bs
COLLINS, Richd.	28	M	Coachman	26Ap02Bs
Ann (W)	19	F	None	26Ap02Bs
KEENAN, Edwd.	20	M	Laborer	26Ap02Bs
Mary	48	F	Wi	26Ap02Bs
ROBIN, James	30	M	Laborer	26Ap02Bs
ROONEY, James	21	M	Laborer	26Ap02Bs
MAHON, Patk.	22	M	Laborer	26Ap02Bs
CAVANAGH, Patk.	26	M	Farmer	26Ap02Bs
BURNES, Thomas	24	M	Laborer	26Ap02Bs
MCDONNALD, Timothy	35	M	Butcher	26Ap02Bs
BAGNELL, Michael	23	M	Farmer	26Ap02Bs
Edwd.	19	M	Farmer	26Ap02Bs
Cath.	20	F	Spinster	26Ap02Bs
BURNES, Eliza	19	F	Spinster	26Ap02Bs
DEVOY, Wm.	24	M	Groom	26Ap02Bs
DOUGHETY, John	30	M	Mason	26Ap02Bs
CHADWICK, Abram.	32	M	Ctnsp	26Ap02Bs
CRAWFORD, Michl.	45	M	Dealer	26Ap02Bs
Rose (W)	40	F	None	26Ap02Bs
James	20	M	Dealer	26Ap02Bs
Patk.	14	M	None	26Ap02Bs
MCBRIETY, Condy	20	M	Laborer	26Ap02Bs
Susan (W)	20	F	None	26Ap02Bs
Condy	.09	M	Infant	26Ap02Bs
GAITLEY, Thomas	20	M	Farmer	26Ap02Bs
WATSON, James	18	M	Laborer	26Ap02Bs
Alex.	16	M	Laborer	26Ap02Bs
DUDGEON, Andrew	30	M	Laborer	26Ap02Bs
SMITH, Harriet	20	F	Servant	26Ap02Bs
MACKEY, John	30	M	Laborer	26Ap02Bs
MCBRIETY, Hannah	20	F	Servant	26Ap02Bs
GILLESPIE, Mary	18	F	Servant	26Ap02Bs
Biddy	17	F	Servant	26Ap02Bs
MULHONEY, Jno.	20	M	Laborer	26Ap02Bs
MCSHANE, Connell	21	M	Laborer	26Ap02Bs
CASHUIRE, Sydney	24	M	Servant	26Ap02Bs
HORAN, James	23	M	Laborer	26Ap02Bs
Wm.	24	M	Laborer	26Ap02Bs
FANDLY, Connor	21	M	Dealer	26Ap02Bs
GAYNOR, Patk.	27	M	Groom	26Ap02Bs
NUGENT, Bridgt.	24	F	Dealer	26Ap02Bs
DUNNE, Patk.	21	M	Laborer	26Ap02Bs
COONY, James	20	M	Laborer	26Ap02Bs
RYAN, Andrew	15	M	Laborer	26Ap02Bs
PHELAN, Cath.	20	F	Dressmaker	26Ap02Bs
CANCLE, Anty.	20	M	Servant	26Ap02Bs
KELLY, Patrick	20	M	Blacksmith	26Ap02Bs

ELIZA-KEITH 29 APRIL 1848

From Liverpool

NAMES OF PASSENGERS	AGE	SEX	OCCUPATIONS	DATE PORT SHIP
RYAN, Richd.	28	M	Laborer	29Ap02If
ROWLEY, Bridget	20	F	Laborer	29Ap02If
MEES, Ann	20	F	Laborer	29Ap02If
GANNON, Jno.	22	M	Laborer	29Ap02If
REACH, Ellen	18	F	Laborer	29Ap02If
FOX, Biddy	20	F	Laborer	29Ap02If
HENAN, Jno.	20	M	Laborer	29Ap02If
COTTER, Mary	18	F	Laborer	29Ap02If
HASSEY, Pat	25	M	Laborer	29Ap02If
LYNCH, Pat	25	M	Laborer	29Ap02If
HASSEY, Bridget	23	F	Laborer	29Ap02If
CAVANAGH, Mary	19	F	Laborer	29Ap02If
FLYNN, Francis	20	F	Laborer	29Ap02If
MCCURRY, Michl.	20	M	Laborer	29Ap02If
POWDERLY, Biddy	20	F	Laborer	29Ap02If
KENNY, Mary	20	F	Laborer	29Ap02If
DELANEY, Mary	20	F	Laborer	29Ap02If
LIVEANY, Cath.	20	F	Laborer	29Ap02If
GRACE, Betsey	20	F	Laborer	29Ap02If
MADDEN, Michl.	20	M	Laborer	29Ap02If
WELSH, Robt.	30	M	Laborer	29Ap02If
FANIL, Pat	25	M	Laborer	29Ap02If
COLLUM, William	20	M	Laborer	29Ap02If
CASMOODY, Thomas	20	M	Laborer	29Ap02If
OBRIEN, Jno.	20	M	Laborer	29Ap02If
POWERS, Mary	20	F	Laborer	29Ap02If
Cath.	20	F	Laborer	29Ap02If
TURRY, James	20	M	Laborer	29Ap02If
CREE, Ellen	20	F	Laborer	29Ap02If
DITTY, Jno.	22	M	Laborer	29Ap02If
TOOLEY, Peggy	20	F	Laborer	29Ap02If
ARISKILL, Perty	20	M	Laborer	29Ap02If
Biddy	20	F	Laborer	29Ap02If
Edward	.00	M	Infant	29Ap02If
CRUE, Kate	20	F	Laborer	29Ap02If
TURNEY, Pat	20	M	Laborer	29Ap02If
MCGRATH, Degan	20	M	Laborer	29Ap02If
TOOLEY, Pat	20	M	Laborer	29Ap02If
Richard	20	M	Laborer	29Ap02If
COWAN, Essy	20	M	Laborer	29Ap02If
CRUK, Johan	20	M	Laborer	29Ap02If
MCCARTHY, William	26	M	Laborer	29Ap02If
Pat	24	M	Laborer	29Ap02If
BRIEN, Pat	20	M	Laborer	29Ap02If
DESMOND, Nory	20	F	Laborer	29Ap02If
BYME, Pegy	13	F	Laborer	29Ap02If
MCCARTHY, Julia	.00	F	Infant	29Ap02If
HUNT, Mary	30	F	Laborer	29Ap02If
Jno.	05	M	Child	29Ap02If
CORTICAN, Jno.	20	M	Laborer	29Ap02If
LANG, Wm.	25	M	Laborer	29Ap02If
KATES, Pat	20	M	Laborer	29Ap02If
MURPHY, Edwd.	20	M	Laborer	29Ap02If
Elizabeth	20	F	Laborer	29Ap02If
HENESY, Jno.	20	M	Laborer	29Ap02If
MCCABE, James	20	M	Laborer	29Ap02If

NAMES OF PASSENGERS	AGE	SEX	OCCUPATIONS	DATE PORT SHIP
BARKER, Wm.	20	M	Laborer	29Ap02If
CONNER, Thomas	18	M	Laborer	29Ap02If
GODDARD, Edwd.	28	M	Laborer	29Ap02If
GRAHAM, Luke	24	M	Laborer	29Ap02If
FEENEY, Pat	20	M	Laborer	29Ap02If
NOONAN, Pat	20	M	Laborer	29Ap02If
KILLINAB, Mary	20	F	Laborer	29Ap02If
Biddy	20	F	Laborer	29Ap02If
FAHEY, Biddy	20	F	Laborer	29Ap02If
BRANLEY, Thomas	21	M	Laborer	29Ap02If
MCKEVIN, Pat	40	M	Laborer	29Ap02If
Mary	50	F	Laborer	29Ap02If
Jno.	14	M	Laborer	29Ap02If
DONOHOE, Michl.	20	M	Laborer	29Ap02If
Ann	18	F	Laborer	29Ap02If
DEVLIN, Conner	20	M	Laborer	29Ap02If
DEENAN, Mary	15	F	Laborer	29Ap02If
MORAN, Cath.	20	F	Laborer	29Ap02If
CLEANY, Jno.	25	M	Laborer	29Ap02If
Wm.	20	M	Laborer	29Ap02If
Ellen	13	F	Laborer	29Ap02If
FAY, Bernard	21	M	Laborer	29Ap02If
Jno.	20	M	Laborer	29Ap02If
MURPHY, Jno.	11	M	Laborer	29Ap02If
MULLOY, Edmund	20	M	Laborer	29Ap02If
Terressa	09	F	Child	29Ap02If
GROGAN, Thomas	20	M	Laborer	29Ap02If
DAY, Ann	30	F	Laborer	29Ap02If
Thos.	.00	M	Infant	29Ap02If
KENNIGAN, Jno.	20	M	Laborer	29Ap02If
BOYHAN, Peter	21	M	Laborer	29Ap02If
DUFFY, James	25	M	Laborer	29Ap02If
Michl.	20	M	Laborer	29Ap02If
MCCLOSKEY, Margt.	30	F	Laborer	29Ap02If
Jno.	04	M	Child	29Ap02If
Bessy	02	F	Child	29Ap02If
CAVAN, Michl.	23	M	Laborer	29Ap02If
GOGGIN, Michl.	55	M	Laborer	29Ap02If
Jno.	33	M	Laborer	29Ap02If
Thomas	56	M	Laborer	29Ap02If
Cath.	56	F	Laborer	29Ap02If
MALOONY, Cath.	12	F	Laborer	29Ap02If
Mary	18	F	Laborer	29Ap02If
DUNLEAVEY, Barben	40	F	Laborer	29Ap02If
MAHON, Bridget	15	F	Laborer	29Ap02If
MURPHY, Thomas	25	M	Laborer	29Ap02If
Cath.	24	F	Laborer	29Ap02If
SHEEHAN, Terence	20	M	Laborer	29Ap02If
Ellen	15	F	Laborer	29Ap02If
Priscella	15	F	Laborer	29Ap02If
KEENAN, Jno.	21	M	Laborer	29Ap02If
Cath.	18	F	Laborer	29Ap02If
Mary	25	F	Laborer	29Ap02If
CASSENLY, Fanell	20	M	Laborer	29Ap02If
KING, Pat	22	M	Laborer	29Ap02If
Cath.	18	F	Laborer	29Ap02If
Bridget	18	F	Laborer	29Ap02If
TIENEY, Jno.	20	M	Laborer	29Ap02If
ASSPEY, James	20	M	Laborer	29Ap02If
GAHAYGEN, Nancy	17	F	Laborer	29Ap02If
Ellen	12	F	Laborer	29Ap02If
CASAN, Anthy.	20	M	Laborer	29Ap02If
READY, William	23	M	Laborer	29Ap02If
KELLY, Eliza	20	M	Laborer	29Ap02If
BESGAN, Mary	30	M	Laborer	29Ap02If
READY, Tim	20	M	Laborer	29Ap02If
Mary	.00	F	Infant	29Ap02If
DONNELLY, John	20	M	Laborer	29Ap02If
HENNESSEY, Mary	27	F	Laborer	29Ap02If
MOLIHAN, Laurence	26	M	Laborer	29Ap02If
Margt.	28	F	Laborer	29Ap02If
MCDERMONTT, Jno.	45	M	Laborer	29Ap02If
LYNCH, Charles	17	M	Laborer	29Ap02If
CELLERY, Ann	20	F	Laborer	29Ap02If
SMYTH, Ellen	20	F	Laborer	29Ap02If
HUGHS, James	21	M	Laborer	29Ap02If
Mary	18	F	Laborer	29Ap02If
WINN, Thomas	21	M	Laborer	29Ap02If
Bridget	12	F	Laborer	29Ap02If
MORAN, Cath.	40	F	Laborer	29Ap02If
Ann	13	F	Laborer	29Ap02If
Jno.	10	M	Laborer	29Ap02If
James	06	M	Child	29Ap02If
Cath.	05	F	Child	29Ap02If
Harriet	04	F	Child	29Ap02If
Jane	02	F	Child	29Ap02If
Maria	.00	F	Infant	29Ap02If
LEACH, Mary	30	F	None	29Ap02If
Nancy	12	F	None	29Ap02If
Julia	08	F	Child	29Ap02If
Johanna	06	F	Child	29Ap02If
Elizabeth	04	F	Child	29Ap02If
Ann	02	F	Child	29Ap02If
Mary	.00	F	Infant	29Ap02If
KYLIE, Thomas	20	M	Laborer	29Ap02If
QUINN, Kelly	20	F	None	29Ap02If
Bridget	20	F	None	29Ap02If
CORCORAN, Johanna	30	F	None	29Ap02If
FREY, Jno.	20	M	None	29Ap02If
POWERS, Jno.	30	M	None	29Ap02If
Mary	30	F	None	29Ap02If
Willm.	16	M	None	29Ap02If
Bridgt.	15	F	None	29Ap02If
Jno.	09	M	Child	29Ap02If
Cath.	07	F	Child	29Ap02If
WERM, Thomas	20	M	None	29Ap02If
Farril	20	M	None	29Ap02If
MUSSEY, Joseph	33	M	None	29Ap02If
Charles	10	M	None	29Ap02If
HALPIN, Rose	18	F	None	29Ap02If
GENARTY, Owen	17	M	None	29Ap02If
Mich.	13	M	None	29Ap02If
CONYLE, Bridget	20	F	None	29Ap02If
GEHARTY, Mary	28	F	None	29Ap02If
Edwd.	12	M	None	29Ap02If
CARTY, Mary	20	F	None	29Ap02If
MCCLARSKEY, Hugh	25	M	None	29Ap02If
Mary	25	F	None	29Ap02If
Cath.	07	F	Child	29Ap02If
William	05	M	Child	29Ap02If
Susan	.00	F	Infant	29Ap02If
HAWKINS, Jno.	18	M	None	29Ap02If
CULLIN, Margt.	04	F	Child	29Ap02If
HURRAN, Bridget	18	F	None	29Ap02If
MCGREW, Margt.	15	F	None	29Ap02If
BRUNT, Timothy	24	M	None	29Ap02If
FLYNN, Dennis	25	M	None	29Ap02If
ROGERS, Mary	16	F	None	29Ap02If
Ellen	17	F	None	29Ap02If
Margt.	16	F	None	29Ap02If
PHILLIPS, Edwd.	21	M	None	29Ap02If
WOODS, Mary	20	F	None	29Ap02If
Andrew	08	M	Child	29Ap02If
FANELL, Thomas	17	M	None	29Ap02If
RILEY, Mary	20	F	None	29Ap02If
COUGHLAN, Jno.	20	M	None	29Ap02If
DONNELLY, Michl.	20	M	None	29Ap02If
Bridget	20	F	None	29Ap02If
OBRIEN, Margt.	11	F	None	29Ap02If
MATHER, Margt.	17	F	None	29Ap02If
MCDONNELL, Cath.	20	F	None	29Ap02If
LANCEY, Ellen	16	F	None	29Ap02If
Pat	12	M	None	29Ap02If
DEMPSEY, Thos.	24	M	None	29Ap02If
Jno.	20	M	None	29Ap02If

NAMES OF PASSENGERS		AGE	SEX	OCCUPATIONS	DATE PORT SHIP

AMERICA 29 APRIL 1848

From Liverpool

NAMES OF PASSENGERS		AGE	SEX	OCCUPATIONS	DATE PORT SHIP
WOODWARD, Sarah-C.		60	F	None	29Ap02Hf
KING, A.		30	M	Minister	29Ap02Hf
REIDY, Thomas.		35	M	Merchant	29Ap02Hf
LYNCH, John		36	M	Merchant	29Ap02Hf

RAPPAHANOCK 01 MAY 1848

From Liverpool

NAMES OF PASSENGERS		AGE	SEX	OCCUPATIONS	DATE PORT SHIP
LAWLER, Richard		30	M	Laborer	01Ma02Dm
THOMSON, Thomas		30	M	Laborer	01Ma02Dm
BETTS, Wm.		19	M	Laborer	01Ma02Dm
Pat		13	M	Laborer	01Ma02Dm
SULLIVAN, Nancy		20	F	Servant	01Ma02Dm
CROFTON, Cath.		20	F	Servant	01Ma02Dm
KELLY, Maria		25	F	Servant	01Ma02Dm
John		25	M	Laborer	01Ma02Dm
KEEF, Mary		15	F	Servant	01Ma02Dm
CRAWLEY, John		25	M	Laborer	01Ma02Dm
Caf---, Pat		20	M	Laborer	01Ma02Dm
CARELIN, James		30	M	Laborer	01Ma02Dm
CARROLL, Cornick		20	M	Laborer	01Ma02Dm
Peter		21	M	Laborer	01Ma02Dm
Ann		18	F	Servant	01Ma02Dm
RYAN, Michael		20	M	Farmer	01Ma02Dm
Mary	(W)	20	F	Wife	01Ma02Dm
COMFEY, John		25	M	Farmer	01Ma02Dm
Jane	(W)	25	F	Wife	01Ma02Dm
NOLAN, Mary		20	F	Servant	01Ma02Dm
CULLEN, Thomas		23	M	Printer	01Ma02Dm
Michael		18	M	Printer	01Ma02Dm
Mary		16	F	Printer	01Ma02Dm
DRUIN, John		36	M	Laborer	01Ma02Dm
CHESTER, Pat		26	M	Laborer	01Ma02Dm
Cathe.		50	F	Wife	01Ma02Dm
HUGHS, Mary		45	F	Unknown	01Ma02Dm
Betty		17	F	Unknown	01Ma02Dm
Margaret		15	F	Unknown	01Ma02Dm
Ann		13	F	Unknown	01Ma02Dm
BASTELLA, Catherine		20	F	Servant	01Ma02Dm
MUNOTT, Bett		20	F	Servant	01Ma02Dm
DWYER, Lawrence		25	M	Farmer	01Ma02Dm
BRENNAN, Pat		18	M	Farmer	01Ma02Dm
MANE, Thomas		25	M	Farmer	01Ma02Dm
HARVEY, Isaac		28	M	Tailor	01Ma02Dm
Mary	(W)	26	F	Wife	01Ma02Dm
Ann-Jane	(D)	.06	F	Infant	01Ma02Dm
WELHAM, Margaret		20	F	Servant	01Ma02Dm
WADDLE, Hamilton		26	M	Baker	01Ma02Dm
Mary	(W)	22	F	Wife	01Ma02Dm
Thoms.		12	M	None	01Ma02Dm
James		05	M	Child	01Ma02Dm
George		07	M	Child	01Ma02Dm
LEE, Robt.		22	M	Farmer	01Ma02Dm
Elicia	(W)	18	F	Wife	01Ma02Dm
POOLE, John		22	M	Farmer	01Ma02Dm
BOLTON, Wm.		40	M	Farmer	01Ma02Dm
FITZGERALD, Wm.		35	M	Farmer	01Ma02Dm
Mary	(W)	35	F	Wife	01Ma02Dm
FITZGERALD, James	(S)	11	M	None	01Ma02Dm
Mary	(D)	09	F	Child	01Ma02Dm
Johanna	(D)	07	F	Child	01Ma02Dm
Susan	(D)	05	F	Child	01Ma02Dm
William	(S)	.08	M	Infant	01Ma02Dm
CAUGLIN, Anld.		21	M	Farmer	01Ma02Dm
MORE, Elisabeth		47	F	Tinker	01Ma02Dm
John		26	M	Tinker	01Ma02Dm
Lindsay		20	M	Tinker	01Ma02Dm
Elizabeth		13	F	None	01Ma02Dm
Margaret		20	F	None	01Ma02Dm
Nancy		11	F	None	01Ma02Dm
Ann-Jane		09	F	Child	01Ma02Dm
Mary		07	F	Child	01Ma02Dm
MCKENNA, Mary		18	F	Servant	01Ma02Dm
CANNEVAN, Cornelius		45	M	Farmer	01Ma02Dm
Catherine	(W)	40	F	Wife	01Ma02Dm
Daniel	(S)	17	M	Unknown	01Ma02Dm
Honorah	(D)	16	F	Unknown	01Ma02Dm
Mary	(D)	12	F	Unknown	01Ma02Dm
James	(S)	13	M	Unknown	01Ma02Dm
Biddy	(D)	08	F	Child	01Ma02Dm
Margaret	(D)	06	F	Child	01Ma02Dm
Ellen	(D)	03	F	Child	01Ma02Dm
Catherine	(D)	.06	F	Infant	01Ma02Dm
Honorah		20	F	Servant	01Ma02Dm
LEDGER, Daniel-S.		06	M	Child	01Ma02Dm
BRYANT, Thomas		24	M	Farmer	01Ma02Dm
COLLINS, James		20	M	Laborer	01Ma02Dm
Patt.		21	M	Laborer	01Ma02Dm
Ann		19	F	Laborer	01Ma02Dm
MULLAN, John		18	M	Laborer	01Ma02Dm
Thomas		18	M	Laborer	01Ma02Dm
COALMAN, Michael		23	M	Farmer	01Ma02Dm
MCMAHR, Stephen		27	M	Farmer	01Ma02Dm
Jane	(W)	25	F	Wife	01Ma02Dm
KIELY, Peter		27	M	Farmer	01Ma02Dm
MCMAHON, John		30	M	Farmer	01Ma02Dm
GREEN, Daniel		30	M	Farmer	01Ma02Dm
PRINDALL, Thomas		28	M	Shoemaker	01Ma02Dm
ROWLAND, John		20	M	Shoemaker	01Ma02Dm
Michael		18	M	Shoemaker	01Ma02Dm
STASHARD, Wm.		26	M	Laborer	01Ma02Dm
CORMIC, J.		22	M	Laborer	01Ma02Dm
HAY, Ellen		23	F	Servant	01Ma02Dm
KIRON, Ann		18	F	Servant	01Ma02Dm
MURPHY, Owen		20	M	Laborer	01Ma02Dm
FREMAY, Edward		20	M	Laborer	01Ma02Dm
MCCRAE, Pat		14	M	None	01Ma02Dm
MCDONEL, Patt.		20	M	Laborer	01Ma02Dm
HARMAN, James		14	M	None	01Ma02Dm
Margt.		14	F	None	01Ma02Dm
HUBBARD, Wm.		26	M	Laborer	01Ma02Dm
MORRISON, Wm.		20	M	Laborer	01Ma02Dm
HALLIGAN, Thomas		28	M	Laborer	01Ma02Dm
MCDAVID, Richard		21	M	Laborer	01Ma02Dm
MANN, Peter		20	M	Laborer	01Ma02Dm
WALL, Catherine		20	F	Servant	01Ma02Dm
CONLAN, Ann		20	F	Servant	01Ma02Dm
John		21	M	Laborer	01Ma02Dm
BLUNT, Patt.		26	M	Laborer	01Ma02Dm
BODEN, Judith		20	F	Servant	01Ma02Dm
CRAWLEY, Thomas		20	M	Laborer	01Ma02Dm
HANLEY, John		26	M	Laborer	01Ma02Dm
SNOWMAN, John		18	M	Laborer	01Ma02Dm
FITZPATRICK, Patt.		40	M	Laborer	01Ma02Dm
Mary	(W)	38	F	Wife	01Ma02Dm
Patt.	(S)	04	M	Child	01Ma02Dm
Michael	(S)	.08	M	Infant	01Ma02Dm
Michael		30	M	Laborer	01Ma02Dm
Rose		60	F	None	01Ma02Dm
MCGLINN, John		20	M	Laborer	01Ma02Dm
CORKEN, Fanny		26	F	Servant	01Ma02Dm
DAILEY, Pat		29	M	Laborer	01Ma02Dm
MCCALL, James		12	M	Laborer	01Ma02Dm

NAMES OF PASSENGERS		AGE	SEX	OCCUPATIONS	DATE PORT SHIP
GAHAGAN, Andrew		30	M	Farmer	01Ma02Dm
Mary	(W)	30	F	Wife	01Ma02Dm
MOONY, Pat		26	M	Laborer	01Ma02Dm
Mathew		11	M	Laborer	01Ma02Dm
DUNN, Bryan		18	M	Farmer	01Ma02Dm
Mary	(W)	20	F	Wife	01Ma02Dm
BRYAN, Benjamin		20	M	Laborer	01Ma02Dm
KELLY, Mary		21	F	Servant	01Ma02Dm
EAGAN, John		21	M	Laborer	01Ma02Dm
FIGHE, Patt.		22	M	Laborer	01Ma02Dm
Hugh		17	M	Laborer	01Ma02Dm
LASLEY, Jeramiah		21	M	Laborer	01Ma02Dm
WELCH, James		20	M	Laborer	01Ma02Dm
Mary	(W)	18	F	Wife	01Ma02Dm
CONLAN, Sarah		20	F	Servant	01Ma02Dm
GORMAN, Rody		18	F	Servant	01Ma02Dm
WELCH, Margaret		18	F	Servant	01Ma02Dm
HOTCHING, James		40	M	Farmer	01Ma02Dm
Sarah	(W)	36	F	Wife	01Ma02Dm
John	(S)	08	M	Child	01Ma02Dm
Rachel	(D)	.06	F	Infant	01Ma02Dm
WILSON, Wm.John		15	M	Laborer	01Ma02Dm
FLANELL, Thomas		22	M	Laborer	01Ma02Dm
ARCHELL, Samuel		20	M	Laborer	01Ma02Dm
SMITH, Elijah		31	M	Laborer	01Ma02Dm
SIMPSON, Wm.		20	M	Laborer	01Ma02Dm
MCNONELL, John		20	M	Laborer	01Ma02Dm
Biddy	(W)	23	F	Wife	01Ma02Dm
CONLIN, John		20	M	Laborer	01Ma02Dm
SHAMLY, John		10	M	Laborer	01Ma02Dm
TAYLOR, Sally		18	F	Servant	01Ma02Dm
MARTIN, John		42	M	Farmer	01Ma02Dm
John		15	M	Farmer	01Ma02Dm
HOLLAND, George		18	M	Farmer	01Ma02Dm
CARPENTER, Pat		20	M	Farmer	01Ma02Dm
BELTON, Peter		19	M	Farmer	01Ma02Dm
KENNY, Maria		10	F	Servant	01Ma02Dm
Mary		07	F	Child	01Ma02Dm
Tint.		20	F	Servant	01Ma02Dm
Mark		22	M	Laborer	01Ma02Dm
Mary-M.		18	F	Servant	01Ma02Dm
HYLAND, Pat		20	M	Laborer	01Ma02Dm
MURPHY, Richard		30	M	Laborer	01Ma02Dm
Ann	(W)	20	F	Wife	01Ma02Dm
MCELLEN, Mary		20	F	Farmer	01Ma02Dm
DALTON, Mareella		25	F	Farmer	01Ma02Dm
Ellis		15	M	Unknown	01Ma02Dm
James		12	M	Unknown	01Ma02Dm
Michael		12	M	Unknown	01Ma02Dm
PERRY, Thomas		20	M	Laborer	01Ma02Dm
Mary	(W)	20	F	Wife	01Ma02Dm
QUIN, Margaret		20	F	Servant	01Ma02Dm
MULHERN, Ann		25	F	Servant	01Ma02Dm
QUIN, Michael		30	M	Laborer	01Ma02Dm
MCGLEEM, John		25	M	Laborer	01Ma02Dm
Ellen	(W)	24	F	Wife	01Ma02Dm
U		.00	U	Infant	01Ma02Dm
MCFELLEGAN, Owen		40	M	Laborer	01Ma02Dm
Ann	(W)	35	F	Wife	01Ma02Dm
CAILE, Owen		20	M	Laborer	01Ma02Dm
MCGLIN, Pat		21	M	Laborer	01Ma02Dm
HANNAGAN, Ann		20	F	Servant	01Ma02Dm
MCGRATH, Catherine		20	F	Servant	01Ma02Dm
HERON, Thomas		16	M	None	01Ma02Dm
MCGLINN, John		22	M	Laborer	01Ma02Dm
GALLAGAN, John		22	M	Laborer	01Ma02Dm
CASADA, Rose		15	F	Servant	01Ma02Dm
BAUGHTON, John		19	M	Laborer	01Ma02Dm
FRELLEPPER, Ann		05	F	Child	01Ma02Dm
QUIGLY, Michael		13	M	Shoemaker	01Ma02Dm
JAWELL, Henry		18	M	Printer	01Ma02Dm
FOX, Peter		16	M	Laborer	01Ma02Dm
MAXWELL, John		18	M	Laborer	01Ma02Dm
WALTON, Thomas		20	M	Laborer	01Ma02Dm
OHARE, John		20	M	Carpenter	01Ma02Dm

NAMES OF PASSENGERS		AGE	SEX	OCCUPATIONS	DATE PORT SHIP
BEALE, Clendine		18	M	Tailor	01Ma02Dm
MCCLAUGHEY, Wm.		17	M	Tailor	01Ma02Dm
Anson		14	M	Tailor	01Ma02Dm
ELLIOT, Mary		40	F	None	01Ma02Dm
CRAIG, Mary		16	F	None	01Ma02Dm
BAGLEY, Patrick		40	M	Laborer	01Ma02Dm
DANSEY, Peter		22	M	Joiner	01Ma02Dm
LAW, Conrad		42	M	Laborer	01Ma02Dm
John	(S)	20	M	Unknown	01Ma02Dm
Mary	(W)	25	F	Wife	01Ma02Dm
Jane		16	F	None	01Ma02Dm
Mary		15	F	None	01Ma02Dm
YOUNG, George		20	M	Laborer	01Ma02Dm
HYSON, Margt.		14	F	None	01Ma02Dm
QUIGLY, Thomas		20	M	Laborer	01Ma02Dm
Pat		07	M	Child	01Ma02Dm
HOWEL, Robert		26	M	Printer	01Ma02Dm
CLARK, Pat		17	M	Laborer	01Ma02Dm
DEWY, Edward		18	M	Laborer	01Ma02Dm
Pat		20	M	Laborer	01Ma02Dm
SHIEL, Thomas		18	M	Carpenter	01Ma02Dm
MCHENRY, Pat		16	M	Shoemaker	01Ma02Dm
CANE, Lawrence		20	M	Carpenter	01Ma02Dm
EUSTACE, Henry		18	M	Laborer	01Ma02Dm
REED, Thomas		14	M	Hrsm	01Ma02Dm
BRANIGAN, Michael		22	M	Hrsm	01Ma02Dm
WARD, John		20	M	Laborer	01Ma02Dm
John		17	M	Laborer	01Ma02Dm
MORE, Thomas		16	M	Laborer	01Ma02Dm
CANAGAN, Mary		25	F	Servant	01Ma02Dm
Judy		18	F	Servant	01Ma02Dm
HARVEY, Ann		18	F	Servant	01Ma02Dm
MULLEN, Margt.		20	F	Servant	01Ma02Dm
MANGEN, Catherine		20	F	Servant	01Ma02Dm
BERRY, Margt.		16	F	Servant	01Ma02Dm
Teresa		15	F	Servant	01Ma02Dm
WHITMORE, Julia-Ann		18	F	Servant	01Ma02Dm
BARRY, Terence		25	M	Laborer	01Ma02Dm
Mary	(W)	25	F	Wife	01Ma02Dm
MURRAY, John		17	M	Carpenter	01Ma02Dm
MCCARTY, Peter		17	M	Carpenter	01Ma02Dm
DERMADY, Anne		16	F	Carpenter	01Ma02Dm
LYONS, Pat		20	M	Laborer	01Ma02Dm
STEPHENSON, Pat		23	M	Laborer	01Ma02Dm
HALES, John		24	M	Laborer	01Ma02Dm
HURLEY, Murnt.		31	M	Laborer	01Ma02Dm
MURPHY, Conney		26	M	Laborer	01Ma02Dm
CALLAPH, Hoyt		24	M	Laborer	01Ma02Dm
BURN, James		18	M	Blacksmith	01Ma02Dm
MAKIN, Thomas		35	M	Blacksmith	01Ma02Dm
DOWNY, John		22	M	Laborer	01Ma02Dm
MADKIN, Mary		19	F	Servant	01Ma02Dm
MCVAY, Sarah		21	F	Servant	01Ma02Dm
MCCARROLL, Margaret		25	F	Servant	01Ma02Dm
QUIN, James		20	M	Laborer	01Ma02Dm
BULLER, Ann		20	F	Servant	01Ma02Dm
HEAVY, Michael		20	M	Laborer	01Ma02Dm
GRIMES, John		19	M	Laborer	01Ma02Dm
Mary		16	F	None	01Ma02Dm
GAFFENY, Francis		30	M	Laborer	01Ma02Dm
TAFEE, Lawrence		20	M	Laborer	01Ma02Dm
MCGOWEN, Thomas		30	M	Laborer	01Ma02Dm
MARTIN, John		30	M	Laborer	01Ma02Dm
MCGOWEN, Cathe.		26	F	None	01Ma02Dm
MARTIN, Ann		20	F	Servant	01Ma02Dm
COLLANNY, James		30	M	Laborer	01Ma02Dm
GALLAGHER, John		30	M	Laborer	01Ma02Dm
BELL, Eliza		25	F	Servant	01Ma02Dm
MALONE, Jane		23	F	Servant	01Ma02Dm
Sarah		13	F	Servant	01Ma02Dm
KELLY, Felix		36	M	Farmer	01Ma02Dm
Mary	(W)	36	F	Wife	01Ma02Dm
Joseph	(S)	13	M	Unknown	01Ma02Dm
Rose	(D)	11	F	Unknown	01Ma02Dm
John	(S)	09	M	Child	01Ma02Dm

NAMES OF PASSENGERS		AGE	SEX	OCCUPATIONS	DATE PORT SHIP
KELLY, Mary	(D)	07	F	Child	01Ma02Dm
Pat	(S)	05	M	Child	01Ma02Dm
Felix	(S)	.05	M	Infant	01Ma02Dm
SHEA, James		30	M	Laborer	01Ma02Dm
ODONNELL, Pat		20	M	Laborer	01Ma02Dm
MEADLY, James		20	M	Laborer	01Ma02Dm
HANDLY, John		20	M	Laborer	01Ma02Dm
FISH, Biddy		18	F	Servant	01Ma02Dm
KENNY, Mary		18	F	Servant	01Ma02Dm
DAVISON, Catherine		20	F	Servant	01Ma02Dm
MCCUE, Martin		20	M	Laborer	01Ma02Dm
BOYLE, Hannah		20	F	Servant	01Ma02Dm
MCGINKEY, Annabella		60	F	Servant	01Ma02Dm
DOWNLY, John		25	M	Mason	01Ma02Dm
Andrew		21	M	Mason	01Ma02Dm
FRIHY, Catherine		60	F	None	01Ma02Dm
Honora		16	F	None	01Ma02Dm
BURNS, Mary		21	F	Servant	01Ma02Dm
BREACH, Robert		40	M	Laborer	01Ma02Dm
PEEL, Joseph		40	M	Laborer	01Ma02Dm
LENNAN, Bartly		30	M	Laborer	01Ma02Dm
PEEL, Ann		28	F	Wife	01Ma02Dm
LENAN, Catherine		28	F	Wife	01Ma02Dm
PENTLAR, Margaret		20	F	None	01Ma02Dm
Marjery		40	F	None	01Ma02Dm
MCCARTY, Teddy		25	M	Laborer	01Ma02Dm
QUIN, Sally		20	F	Servant	01Ma02Dm
MCNAMEE, Susan		16	F	Servant	01Ma02Dm
CARTY, Bryan		22	M	Laborer	01Ma02Dm
GLASSAN, Michael		20	M	Laborer	01Ma02Dm
QUIGLEY, John		20	M	Laborer	01Ma02Dm
CASIDY, Pat		20	M	Laborer	01Ma02Dm
MCGROENTY, Mary		18	F	Servant	01Ma02Dm
GORMAN, Cathe.		20	F	Servant	01Ma02Dm
COMBE, Thomas		45	M	Farmer	01Ma02Dm
LOYD, Charles		24	M	Laborer	01Ma02Dm
Ann	(W)	22	F	Wife	01Ma02Dm
OWEN, Joseph		24	M	Laborer	01Ma02Dm
FOX, John		28	M	Laborer	01Ma02Dm
HOWLAN, Thomas		21	M	Laborer	01Ma02Dm
BEGAM, James		20	M	Laborer	01Ma02Dm
CHERRY, Mary		21	F	Servant	01Ma02Dm
Ann		20	F	Servant	01Ma02Dm
RENSALL, Carl		25	M	Laborer	01Ma02Dm
MORNITT, Mary		25	F	Servant	01Ma02Dm
CAFFIN, Patt.		20	M	Laborer	01Ma02Dm
WILKISON, Margaret		20	F	Servant	01Ma02Dm
QUIN, Patrick		23	M	Farmer	01Ma02Dm
Bridget	(W)	21	F	Wife	01Ma02Dm
Mary	(D)	.08	F	Infant	01Ma02Dm
JONES, James		23	M	Farmer	01Ma02Dm
QUIN, Terence		25	M	Servant	01Ma02Dm
OHARA, Henry		28	M	Laborer	01Ma02Dm
GIBSON, Wm.John		26	M	Laborer	01Ma02Dm
MURPHY, Patt.		21	M	Laborer	01Ma02Dm
Jane		20	F	None	01Ma02Dm
John		13	M	None	01Ma02Dm
MCCONNELL, Michael		20	M	Laborer	01Ma02Dm
JOHNSON, Thomas		35	M	Painter	01Ma02Dm
WILKINS, John		29	M	Draper	01Ma02Dm
George		12	M	Unknown	01Ma02Dm
Lucy		14	F	Unknown	01Ma02Dm
RILEY, Bridget		20	F	Servant	01Ma02Dm
MURPHY, Wm.		18	M	Laborer	01Ma02Dm

RICHARD-ALSOP 01 MAY 1848

From Liverpool

NAMES OF PASSENGERS	AGE	SEX	OCCUPATIONS	DATE PORT SHIP
HEATON, Honora	27	F	Servant	01Ma02Gs
John	.08	M	Infant	01Ma02Gs
MCDONALD, Christopher	22	M	Laborer	01Ma02Gs
SHAWLEY, Winney	19	F	Servant	01Ma02Gs
FAGAN, M.J.	20	M	Laborer	01Ma02Gs
WALSH, Jas.	21	M	Laborer	01Ma02Gs
Maria	20	F	Laborer	01Ma02Gs
HAGARTY, John	21	M	Farmer	01Ma02Gs
LOVILL, Martin	25	M	Laborer	01Ma02Gs
John	21	M	Laborer	01Ma02Gs
MCKEOWAN, Rose	19	F	Servant	01Ma02Gs
DONOHOE, Patk.	10	M	Unknown	01Ma02Gs
MURPHY, Mckl.	16	M	Laborer	01Ma02Gs
MACMAN, Owen	19	M	Laborer	01Ma02Gs
Thos.	16	M	Laborer	01Ma02Gs
ROSS, Mary	50	F	Cloth Maker	01Ma02Gs
Elyza.	19	F	Cloth Maker	01Ma02Gs
John	17	M	Cloth Maker	01Ma02Gs
Walter	15	M	Cloth Maker	01Ma02Gs
Mary	12	F	Cloth Maker	01Ma02Gs
Martha	12	F	Cloth Maker	01Ma02Gs
MOONEY, Thos.	25	M	Laborer	01Ma02Gs
MCGUIRE, Maggey	06	F	Child	01Ma02Gs
FAWLEY, Ann	16	F	Servant	01Ma02Gs
CORRIGAN, Pat	17	M	Laborer	01Ma02Gs
Rd.	15	M	Laborer	01Ma02Gs
RELLY, Abby	20	F	Servant	01Ma02Gs
FITZPATRICK, Cathn.	19	F	Servant	01Ma02Gs
WARD, Mary	17	F	Servant	01Ma02Gs
DAYLY, Patk.	28	M	Laborer	01Ma02Gs
GORDON, Peter	17	M	Laborer	01Ma02Gs
JONES, Benjmn.	30	M	Collier	01Ma02Gs
Geo.	22	M	Collier	01Ma02Gs
HEWSON, Elizth.	16	F	Servant	01Ma02Gs
RIELLY, Thos.	18	M	Laborer	01Ma02Gs
BRENNAN, Cornelius	20	M	Laborer	01Ma02Gs
MACNAMAUGH, Cath.	16	F	Servant	01Ma02Gs
MORAN, John	24	M	Laborer	01Ma02Gs
MCKENNAN, Wm.	21	M	Laborer	01Ma02Gs
COURRY, Ann	30	F	Servant	01Ma02Gs
MCCABE, Francis	21	M	Laborer	01Ma02Gs
REILLY, Ewd.	23	M	Carpenter	01Ma02Gs
SMITH, John	23	M	Laborer	01Ma02Gs
GALLIGHAN, Mary	21	F	Servant	01Ma02Gs
REILLY, Patrick	20	M	Laborer	01Ma02Gs
SHERIDAN, Ellen	25	F	Unknown	01Ma02Gs
Wm.	20	M	Carpenter	01Ma02Gs
Brid.	19	F	Unknown	01Ma02Gs
Mary	18	F	Unknown	01Ma02Gs
Thos.	25	M	Unknown	01Ma02Gs
Ewd.	24	M	Unknown	01Ma02Gs
DONNELLY, Patk.	26	M	Unknown	01Ma02Gs
Mary	24	F	Servant	01Ma02Gs
CAMPION, Thos.	14	M	Laborer	01Ma02Gs
FITZGERALD, Mgt.	18	F	Dressmaker	01Ma02Gs
HAUGHY, Patk.	20	M	Laborer	01Ma02Gs
CUNNINGHAM, Ellen	16	F	Servant	01Ma02Gs
MANDAY, Bridt.	20	F	Servant	01Ma02Gs
HAGERTY, Francis	24	M	Laborer	01Ma02Gs
Pat	15	M	Laborer	01Ma02Gs
MCGUINLEY, Owen	25	M	Laborer	01Ma02Gs
CUNNINGHAM, Mgt.	16	F	Servant	01Ma02Gs
Cathn.	15	F	Servant	01Ma02Gs
ODONNELL, Pat	18	M	Tailor	01Ma02Gs
STANNWELL, Mcl.	18	M	Laborer	01Ma02Gs

NAMES OF PASSENGERS		AGE	SEX	OCCUPATIONS	DATE PORT SHIP
STANNWELL, Ann		16	F	Servant	01Ma02Gs
CALAGHAN, Peter		20	M	Laborer	01Ma02Gs
CUNNINGHAM, James		20	M	Shop Boy	01Ma02Gs
MCALLISTER, Eliza		38	F	Unknown	01Ma02Gs
Nancy		14	F	Unknown	01Ma02Gs
Wm.		11	M	Unknown	01Ma02Gs
John		09	M	Child	01Ma02Gs
Saml.		07	M	Child	01Ma02Gs
R.Ann		05	F	Child	01Ma02Gs
Andw.		03	M	Child	01Ma02Gs
BURNS, Sammy		22	M	Laborer	01Ma02Gs
HOGAN, Peter		33	M	Gdnr	01Ma02Gs
U	(W)	29	F	Wife	01Ma02Gs
Joseph	(S)	03	M	Child	01Ma02Gs
Pat	(S)	.02	M	Infant	01Ma02Gs
ROLANDS, Cornl.		18	M	Laborer	01Ma02Gs
TAYLOR, Elizbt.		35	F	Unknown	01Ma02Gs
Mary		.02	F	Infant	01Ma02Gs
DORLAND, Thos.		22	M	Laborer	01Ma02Gs
HARRINGTON, Henry		25	M	Laborer	01Ma02Gs
Mary		20	F	Unknown	01Ma02Gs
OKRUFTS, Margh.		21	F	Unknown	01Ma02Gs
DERANS, Mary		23	F	Servant	01Ma02Gs
WRENAUS, Bridget		00	F	Servant	01Ma02Gs
DONOHOE, Owen		22	M	Shoemaker	01Ma02Gs
SHEA, Julia		16	F	Servant	01Ma02Gs
Honora		19	F	Servant	01Ma02Gs
Bridt.		25	F	Servant	01Ma02Gs
DONNELLY, Elizth.		21	F	Servant	01Ma02Gs
ROACH, Jas.		20	M	Laborer	01Ma02Gs
MURTAGH, Mary		50	F	Servant	01Ma02Gs
Ann		18	F	Servant	01Ma02Gs
MORRISONS, Owen		35	M	Laborer	01Ma02Gs
MALONE, Rose		18	F	Unknown	01Ma02Gs
DUNLOP, Wm.		20	M	Blacksmith	01Ma02Gs
CORRIGAN, Ann		20	F	None	01Ma02Gs
MCGUIN, Chas.		25	M	Laborer	01Ma02Gs
PATTEN, Martha		18	F	Servant	01Ma02Gs
Jane		16	F	Servant	01Ma02Gs
MCMULLEN, Rosana		20	F	Miller	01Ma02Gs
MCGUIN, Owen		21	M	Laborer	01Ma02Gs
Michl.		21	M	Laborer	01Ma02Gs
MAHANS, John		24	M	Laborer	01Ma02Gs
Rose		17	F	None	01Ma02Gs
Cath.		25	F	None	01Ma02Gs
MCMAHON, Owen		19	M	Laborer	01Ma02Gs
JACKSON, Mary		18	F	Servant	01Ma02Gs
BRAWLY, Ann		18	F	Servant	01Ma02Gs
BRADY, Mcl.		18	M	Laborer	01Ma02Gs
WHITE, Pat		30	M	Laborer	01Ma02Gs
SCOTT, Wm.		20	M	Salesman	01Ma02Gs
CALIGAN, Pat		17	M	Laborer	01Ma02Gs
BOYLAN, Jas.		22	M	Laborer	01Ma02Gs
Rose		18	F	None	01Ma02Gs
BRADY, Ann		17	F	Servant	01Ma02Gs
HOWARD, Thos.		16	M	Unknown	01Ma02Gs
HARDMAN, John		19	M	Laborer	01Ma02Gs
MURRY, Jas.		08	M	Child	01Ma02Gs
SHEA, Ellen		20	F	Servant	01Ma02Gs
Patk.		25	M	Tailor	01Ma02Gs
MCLAUGHLIN, Patk.		18	M	None	01Ma02Gs
James		09	M	Child	01Ma02Gs
Mgt.		07	F	Child	01Ma02Gs
MCGRATH, Jas.		19	M	Laborer	01Ma02Gs
GUIDA, Cathn.		40	F	None	01Ma02Gs
ODONOVAN, Wm.		10	M	None	01Ma02Gs
WHEELAN, Jas.		24	M	Laborer	01Ma02Gs
CARLAN, Jas.		22	M	Laborer	01Ma02Gs
HAYES, Thos.		26	M	Baker	01Ma02Gs
GAFF, Hy.		28	M	Baker	01Ma02Gs
Ewd.		24	M	Baker	01Ma02Gs
Elizth.		20	F	None	01Ma02Gs
SWORDS, Henry		08	M	Child	01Ma02Gs
Fanny		10	F	None	01Ma02Gs
DUFFY, Mary		18	F	Servant	01Ma02Gs
DUNLOP, Jas.		20	M	Farmer	01Ma02Gs
GAYSONS, Edwd.		10	M	None	01Ma02Gs
MOFFITT, Saml.		34	M	Farmer	01Ma02Gs
U	(W)	27	F	Wife	01Ma02Gs
Jane	(D)	07	F	Child	01Ma02Gs
Thos.	(S)	05	M	Child	01Ma02Gs
Rob.	(S)	03	M	Child	01Ma02Gs
Elizth.	(D)	.10	F	Infant	01Ma02Gs
PETERS, James		00	M	Farmer	01Ma02Gs
THOMAS, Thos.		24	M	Plasterer	01Ma02Gs
MULLINS, John		24	M	Plasterer	01Ma02Gs
MCEVOY, Judy		21	F	Servant	01Ma02Gs
LANE, Richd.		28	M	Servant	01Ma02Gs
MALONE, Jas.		22	M	Tchrc	01Ma02Gs
U	(W)	22	F	Unknown	01Ma02Gs
Mck.	(S)	02	M	Child	01Ma02Gs
Mary	(D)	.00	F	Infant	01Ma02Gs
Cornls.		20	M	Unknown	01Ma02Gs
DILLON, Edw.		28	M	Laborer	01Ma02Gs
Mary		26	F	Unknown	01Ma02Gs
U		.00	U	Infant	01Ma02Gs
Ann		24	F	Unknown	01Ma02Gs
REID, John		40	M	Shopkeeper	01Ma02Gs
RAFFERTY, Thos.		20	M	Laborer	01Ma02Gs
CARROLL, Pat		21	M	Laborer	01Ma02Gs
DOLAN, James		23	M	Laborer	01Ma02Gs
MAHON, Thomas		21	M	Laborer	01Ma02Gs
RIELLY, Ellen		18	F	Servant	01Ma02Gs
HARTNETT, David		24	M	Laborer	01Ma02Gs
ODONNELL, Cathrn.		20	F	Servant	01Ma02Gs
MORAN, Patk.		24	M	Laborer	01Ma02Gs
RODGERS, John		23	M	Miller	01Ma02Gs
SWEENY, Neil		30	M	Miller	01Ma02Gs
LYONS, Owen		30	M	Laborer	01Ma02Gs
KENNEDY, James		12	M	Laborer	01Ma02Gs
Mgt.		14	F	Laborer	01Ma02Gs
Susan		16	F	Laborer	01Ma02Gs
HILL, Andy		20	M	Farmer	01Ma02Gs
WALSH, Geo.		30	M	Farmer	01Ma02Gs
John		27	M	Farmer	01Ma02Gs
CALLING, Peter		20	M	Farmer	01Ma02Gs
MCLEAN, Jas.		18	M	Farmer	01Ma02Gs
REILLY, Maria		16	F	Farmer	01Ma02Gs
Jenny		18	F	Farmer	01Ma02Gs
LEES, Mcl.		28	M	Laborer	01Ma02Gs
Mgt.		24	F	Laborer	01Ma02Gs
KENNAN, Bernd.		40	M	Unknown	01Ma02Gs
CALLAGHAN, Mgr.		20	F	Servant	01Ma02Gs
Johana		21	F	Servant	01Ma02Gs
MORRISON, Rebecka		21	F	Servant	01Ma02Gs
EVITT, Eliza		18	F	Unknown	01Ma02Gs
BURNS, John		40	M	Farmer	01Ma02Gs
JAMESON, James		20	M	Laborer	01Ma02Gs
WARNOCK, Robt.		25	M	Laborer	01Ma02Gs
MCNAMEE, Hugh		28	M	Laborer	01Ma02Gs
CASEY, Wm.		36	M	Joiner	01Ma02Gs
U	(W)	30	F	Wife	01Ma02Gs
Cathn.	(D)	04	F	Child	01Ma02Gs
TOOLE, Pat		31	M	Laborer	01Ma02Gs
WALSH, Mcl.		20	M	Laborer	01Ma02Gs
Biddy		21	F	Unknown	01Ma02Gs
John		30	M	Unknown	01Ma02Gs
CORKERRY, John		30	M	Unknown	01Ma02Gs
BARRY, Rd.		38	M	Joiner	01Ma02Gs
ODONNELL, Mgh.		21	F	Unknown	01Ma02Gs
HOGAN, Mary		14	F	Servant	01Ma02Gs
DORAN, Mckl.		21	M	Laborer	01Ma02Gs
Ellen		18	F	Unknown	01Ma02Gs
BRADLEY, Dennis		22	M	Laborer	01Ma02Gs
Mary		18	F	Unknown	01Ma02Gs
BURK, John		25	M	Unknown	01Ma02Gs
RAWLEY, Ellen		25	F	Unknown	01Ma02Gs
RYAN, Mary		20	F	Unknown	01Ma02Gs
DUFFY, Pat		30	M	Laborer	01Ma02Gs
John		24	M	Laborer	01Ma02Gs

NAMES OF PASSENGERS	A G E	S E X	OCCUPATIONS	DATE PORT SHIP
DUFFY, Anthy.	20	M	Laborer	01Ma02Gs
Cathn.	19	F	Unknown	01Ma02Gs
ROGERS, Biddy	17	F	Unknown	01Ma02Gs
MUNNELLY, Mary	12	F	Unknown	01Ma02Gs
BARROW, John	25	M	Currier	01Ma02Gs
John	21	M	Butcher	01Ma02Gs
DOGGETT, Rd.	20	M	Currier	01Ma02Gs
FITZPATRICK, Patk.	20	M	Laborer	01Ma02Gs
MCADDAM, Mcl.	21	M	Laborer	01Ma02Gs
JONES, John	21	M	Laborer	01Ma02Gs
JAMES, Mgt.	50	F	Unknown	01Ma02Gs
Ann	23	F	Unknown	01Ma02Gs
Sarah	12	F	Unknown	01Ma02Gs
JACKSON, Martha	08	F	Child	01Ma02Gs
PLUNKET, Thos.	23	M	Tailor	01Ma02Gs
MARTEAL, Christy	15	F	Tailor	01Ma02Gs
CARROLL, James	50	M	Mason	01Ma02Gs
MCNALLY, John	26	M	Laborer	01Ma02Gs
U (W)	22	F	Unknown	01Ma02Gs
Pat	20	M	Unknown	01Ma02Gs
Mcl.	12	M	Unknown	01Ma02Gs
Mgt.	02	F	Child	01Ma02Gs
Mgt.	.00	F	Infant	01Ma02Gs
ADDAMS, Robt.	56	M	Farmer	01Ma02Gs
Mgt.	56	F	Farmer	01Ma02Gs
Robt.	25	M	Farmer	01Ma02Gs
Pat	20	M	Farmer	01Ma02Gs
Mary	23	F	Farmer	01Ma02Gs
Sarah	22	F	Farmer	01Ma02Gs
Wm.	17	M	Farmer	01Ma02Gs
GORMAN, Pat	50	M	Farmer	01Ma02Gs
FITZGERALD, Thos.	23	M	Farmer	01Ma02Gs
RYAN, Mgt.	23	F	Farmer	01Ma02Gs
MORTON, Lance	30	M	Blacksmith	01Ma02Gs
FINNIGAN, Thos.	30	M	Blacksmith	01Ma02Gs
CLARKEY, Mckl.	25	M	Hrsm	01Ma02Gs
CULLANS, Cathn.	20	F	Hrsm	01Ma02Gs
MEHAN, Bridgt.	19	F	Hrsm	01Ma02Gs
PEMBROKE, Robt.	21	M	Nailer	01Ma02Gs
Bridt.	19	F	Dressmaker	01Ma02Gs
HAYES, Johana	21	F	Dressmaker	01Ma02Gs
LEAHY, David	21	M	Dressmaker	01Ma02Gs
MANN, Geo.	24	M	Carpenter	01Ma02Gs
ELLIS, Wm.	25	M	Farmer	01Ma02Gs
My.Ann	23	F	Farmer	01Ma02Gs
BAKER, Wm.	29	M	Farmer	01Ma02Gs
Mgt.	25	F	Unknown	01Ma02Gs
MCDUNOUGH, John	25	M	Laborer	01Ma02Gs
DOUGHERTY, Jas.	13	M	Laborer	01Ma02Gs
Elizth.	12	F	Laborer	01Ma02Gs
Cathrn.	10	F	Laborer	01Ma02Gs
HARDEN, Pat	45	M	Laborer	01Ma02Gs
Dennys	13	M	Laborer	01Ma02Gs
MAURRY, Math.	20	M	Laborer	01Ma02Gs
MCGOWAN, Bridt.	20	F	Unknown	01Ma02Gs
WALSH, Mgt.	20	F	Unknown	01Ma02Gs
Thos.	03	M	Child	01Ma02Gs
Pat	03	M	Child	01Ma02Gs
U	.00	F	Infant	01Ma02Gs
MENRAW, Patk.	22	M	Laborer	01Ma02Gs

INDEPENDENCE 01 MAY 1848

From London

NAMES OF PASSENGERS	A G E	S E X	OCCUPATIONS	DATE PORT SHIP
KINNA, William-S.	30	M	Farmer	01Ma21Hf
Ann	34	F	Unknown	01Ma21Hf
William	18	M	Unknown	01Ma21Hf
Stephen	13	M	Unknown	01Ma21Hf
KINNA, James	11	M	Unknown	01Ma21Hf
Alfred	09	M	Child	01Ma21Hf
Edward	07	M	Child	01Ma21Hf
John	05	M	Child	01Ma21Hf
Rhoda	03	F	Child	01Ma21Hf
Thomas	42	M	Unknown	01Ma21Hf
Harriett	35	F	Unknown	01Ma21Hf
Louisa	18	F	Unknown	01Ma21Hf
Mary-Ann	15	F	Unknown	01Ma21Hf
Phoebe	13	F	Unknown	01Ma21Hf
William	11	M	Unknown	01Ma21Hf
Edward	09	M	Child	01Ma21Hf
Thomas	07	M	Child	01Ma21Hf
Harriet	05	F	Child	01Ma21Hf
U	00	U	Unknown	01Ma21Hf
FERRY, John	30	M	Laborer	01Ma21Hf
Francis	24	U	Unknown	01Ma21Hf
Francis	06	U	Child	01Ma21Hf
Mary-Ann	04	F	Child	01Ma21Hf
Sarah-Ann	.00	F	Infant	01Ma21Hf
SIMONS, Solomans	40	M	Clothier	01Ma21Hf
Joshua	28	M	Unknown	01Ma21Hf
Sarah	26	F	Unknown	01Ma21Hf
Julia	23	F	Unknown	01Ma21Hf
Rosetta	17	F	Unknown	01Ma21Hf
Elizabeth	14	F	Unknown	01Ma21Hf
ISAACS, George	22	M	Unknown	01Ma21Hf
JACOBS, Gabriel	20	M	Unknown	01Ma21Hf
Henry	24	M	Unknown	01Ma21Hf
HAGON, John	24	M	Jwlplh	01Ma21Hf
Mary	23	F	Unknown	01Ma21Hf
Thomas	.00	M	Infant	01Ma21Hf
DELAY, Dennis	28	M	Laborer	01Ma21Hf
TURNER, William	30	M	Carpenter	01Ma21Hf
Elizabeth	30	F	Unknown	01Ma21Hf
Philip	02	M	Child	01Ma21Hf
James	.00	M	Infant	01Ma21Hf
HAILE, William	29	M	Shoemaker	01Ma21Hf
MORGAN, George	25	M	Laborer	01Ma21Hf
CHURCH, Charles	21	M	Unknown	01Ma21Hf
ELLIOT, Edward	30	M	Unknown	01Ma21Hf
SMITH, William	52	M	Unknown	01Ma21Hf
BRAND, John-E.	31	M	Merchant	01Ma21Hf
Sarah	28	F	Merchant	01Ma21Hf
WILLIAMS, James	40	M	Merchant	01Ma21Hf
Elizabeth	41	F	Merchant	01Ma21Hf
BOULTER, William	24	M	Optician	01Ma21Hf
GILBERT, Susanah-Sarah	45	F	Unknown	01Ma21Hf
Charlotte	18	F	Unknown	01Ma21Hf
Joseph	14	M	Unknown	01Ma21Hf
Sarah-Ann	12	F	Unknown	01Ma21Hf
WASHINGTON, William	06	M	Child	01Ma21Hf
CHATTERTON, Sarah	27	F	Unknown	01Ma21Hf
Mary	34	F	Unknown	01Ma21Hf
Susanah	05	F	Child	01Ma21Hf
Ellen	04	F	Child	01Ma21Hf
John	02	M	Child	01Ma21Hf
Sarah	.00	F	Infant	01Ma21Hf
LEWIS, Henry	34	M	Farmer	01Ma21Hf
FABRIAN, John-Albert	30	M	Unknown	01Ma21Hf
GREAVES, Sophia	30	F	Unknown	01Ma21Hf
Francis	09	M	Child	01Ma21Hf
SOUTHAN, Henry	28	M	Unknown	01Ma21Hf
BAILEY, John	28	M	Unknown	01Ma21Hf
LOVE, Charles	00	M	Laborer	01Ma21Hf
REYNOLDS, Charles	00	M	Actor	01Ma21Hf

DOWNES 01 MAY 1848

From Waterford

NAMES OF PASSENGERS	AGE	SEX	OCCUPATIONS	DATE PORT SHIP
LYNAGH, John	35	M	Tailor	01Ma16Pn
Peter	28	M	Shoemaker	01Ma16Pn
FAGAN, Christo.	40	M	Laborer	01Ma16Pn
STAFFORD, John	26	M	Laborer	01Ma16Pn
HEANE, Richard	28	M	Laborer	01Ma16Pn
BYRNE, Richard	30	M	Laborer	01Ma16Pn
NEILL, Richard	35	M	Laborer	01Ma16Pn
MOORE, Margaret	33	F	Spinster	01Ma16Pn
POWER, Bridgt.	27	F	Spinster	01Ma16Pn
HOLDEN, Cath.	26	F	Spinster	01Ma16Pn
WHITTY, James	24	M	Laborer	01Ma16Pn
MOLLOY, Tho.	23	M	Laborer	01Ma16Pn
FITZGERALD, Tho.	19	M	Laborer	01Ma16Pn
PHELAN, Michl.	18	M	Laborer	01Ma16Pn
FAGAN, Cath.	37	F	Spinster	01Ma16Pn
KENT, Michael	29	M	Laborer	01Ma16Pn
COONEY, Tho.	23	M	Laborer	01Ma16Pn
James	31	M	Laborer	01Ma16Pn
Ellen	29	F	Spinster	01Ma16Pn
BRIEN, Bridget	28	F	Spinster	01Ma16Pn
MAHONEY, Rody.	35	M	Laborer	01Ma16Pn
Ellen (W)	30	F	Wife	01Ma16Pn
U	.06	U	Infant	01Ma16Pn
COGHLAN, Julia	35	F	Spinster	01Ma16Pn
SHEA, Walter	19	M	Laborer	01Ma16Pn
RELLY, Walter	18	M	Laborer	01Ma16Pn
MURPHY, Thos.	33	M	Laborer	01Ma16Pn
RELLY, Cath.	26	F	Spinster	01Ma16Pn
KELLY, Cath.	25	F	Spinster	01Ma16Pn
HOGAN, Patk.	24	M	Laborer	01Ma16Pn
QUINN, Tho.	23	M	Laborer	01Ma16Pn
LARKIN, Ths.	29	M	Laborer	01Ma16Pn
CARROLL, Mary	32	F	Spinster	01Ma16Pn
RYAN, John	28	M	Laborer	01Ma16Pn
MAHONY, John	25	M	Laborer	01Ma16Pn
BUTLER, Ellen	24	F	Spinster	01Ma16Pn
KING, Tho.	19	M	Laborer	01Ma16Pn
VEREKEN, Wm.	21	M	Laborer	01Ma16Pn
KING, James	22	M	Laborer	01Ma16Pn
DOWER, Thos.	25	M	Laborer	01Ma16Pn
WALSH, Patk.	28	M	Laborer	01Ma16Pn
JOHNSON, Ally	26	F	Spinster	01Ma16Pn
CURTIS, Patk.	33	M	Laborer	01Ma16Pn
MURPHY, Jas.	14	M	Laborer	01Ma16Pn
CANTWELL, Michl.	16	M	Laborer	01Ma16Pn
Bridgt.	21	F	Spinster	01Ma16Pn
GUINAN, Joha.	24	F	Spinster	01Ma16Pn
BROWNE, Margt.	29	F	Spinster	01Ma16Pn
LAGAN, Bridgt.	32	F	Spinster	01Ma16Pn
AYBRARD, Joha.	31	F	Spinster	01Ma16Pn
CUMMINS, Michl.	17	M	Spinner	01Ma16Pn
KENNEDY, Patrick	19	M	Spinner	01Ma16Pn
HENNESY, Michl.	33	M	Spinner	01Ma16Pn
MALONY, Andw.	35	M	Spinner	01Ma16Pn
MCGRATH, Michl.	39	M	Spinner	01Ma16Pn
TORPEY, Patk.	28	M	Spinner	01Ma16Pn
Mary	26	F	Spinster	01Ma16Pn
PHELAN, Tho.	25	M	Laborer	01Ma16Pn
Ellen	33	F	Spinster	01Ma16Pn
DROHAN, Joha.	20	F	Spinster	01Ma16Pn
BUTLER, Mary	39	F	Spinster	01Ma16Pn
CONNING, Cath.	35	F	Spinster	01Ma16Pn
SULLIVAN, John	33	M	Laborer	01Ma16Pn
CARROLL, John	27	M	Laborer	01Ma16Pn
MERGAN, Robt.	30	M	Laborer	01Ma16Pn
WALSH, John	22	M	Laborer	01Ma16Pn
LARKIN, Margt.	24	F	Spinster	01Ma16Pn
MURPHY, Ally	25	F	Spinster	01Ma16Pn
FITZGERALD, James	25	M	Laborer	01Ma16Pn
MAHONY, Mary-A.	26	F	Spinster	01Ma16Pn
Francis	19	M	Tailor	01Ma16Pn
MURPHY, James	17	M	Laborer	01Ma16Pn
WALSH, Ths.	15	M	Laborer	01Ma16Pn
Patk.	21	M	Laborer	01Ma16Pn
ONEILL, Con.	26	M	Laborer	01Ma16Pn
MURPHY, Edwd.	28	M	Laborer	01Ma16Pn
CONNORS, Michl.	30	M	Laborer	01Ma16Pn
KELLY, Patk.	33	M	Laborer	01Ma16Pn
CONNELL, Joha.	35	F	Spinster	01Ma16Pn
COMERFORD, Patk.	37	M	Laborer	01Ma16Pn
EGAN, Patk.	28	M	Laborer	01Ma16Pn
John	19	M	Laborer	01Ma16Pn
Edwd.	18	M	Laborer	01Ma16Pn
Mich.	16	M	Laborer	01Ma16Pn
BRIEN, Tho.	21	M	Laborer	01Ma16Pn

WAVE 01 MAY 1848

From Dublin

NAMES OF PASSENGERS	AGE	SEX	OCCUPATIONS	DATE PORT SHIP
BUCKLEY, Arnold	40	M	Farmer	01Ma20Mo
Mary	35	F	Farmer	01Ma20Mo
Robert	20	M	Farmer	01Ma20Mo
Eliza	13	F	Farmer	01Ma20Mo
Jane	12	F	Farmer	01Ma20Mo
Sarah	10	F	Farmer	01Ma20Mo
William	09	M	Child	01Ma20Mo
John	07	M	Child	01Ma20Mo
Mary	06	F	Child	01Ma20Mo
Thomas	.00	M	Infant	01Ma20Mo
Samuel	.00	M	Infant	01Ma20Mo
COSTELLO, James	40	M	Farmer	01Ma20Mo
Mary	12	F	Farmer	01Ma20Mo
KALLY, Frank	28	M	Farmer	01Ma20Mo
U (W)	28	F	Wife	01Ma20Mo
FLANAGAN, Charles	40	M	Farmer	01Ma20Mo
James	20	M	Farmer	01Ma20Mo
PETON, Jane	20	F	Farmer	01Ma20Mo
EMBSON, Catherine	20	F	Farmer	01Ma20Mo
Bessy	18	F	Farmer	01Ma20Mo
BYRNE, John	40	M	Farmer	01Ma20Mo
Cath.	40	F	Farmer	01Ma20Mo
Ann	20	F	Farmer	01Ma20Mo
Mick	18	M	Farmer	01Ma20Mo
Tim	16	M	Farmer	01Ma20Mo
John	12	M	Farmer	01Ma20Mo
BYRNES, Catherine	28	F	Farmer	01Ma20Mo
SMITH, Mary	24	F	Farmer	01Ma20Mo
BLACKBURN, Michl.	17	M	Farmer	01Ma20Mo
OHALLORAN, Wm.	20	M	Farmer	01Ma20Mo
MAYFEAR, Alfred	25	M	Farmer	01Ma20Mo
SPRING, John	21	M	Farmer	01Ma20Mo
TAITE, Patrick	24	M	Farmer	01Ma20Mo
FLINN, Patrick	36	M	Farmer	01Ma20Mo
Anne	33	F	Farmer	01Ma20Mo
Bridget	04	F	Child	01Ma20Mo
Mary	.00	F	Infant	01Ma20Mo
SMITH, Pat	45	M	Farmer	01Ma20Mo
Ann	45	F	Farmer	01Ma20Mo
Bridget	14	F	Farmer	01Ma20Mo
Rose	04	F	Child	01Ma20Mo
Margery	.00	F	Infant	01Ma20Mo
FEGAN, Pat	30	M	Farmer	01Ma20Mo
MORNEY, Francis	26	M	Farmer	01Ma20Mo

NAMES OF PASSENGERS	AGE	SEX	OCCUPATIONS	DATE PORT SHIP
MURRAY, Mary	24	F	Farmer	01Ma20Mo
POWER, John	20	M	Farmer	01Ma20Mo
TIMINS, Ellen	20	F	Farmer	01Ma20Mo
FITZGIBBON, John	50	M	Farmer	01Ma20Mo
John	25	M	Farmer	01Ma20Mo
BENARD, Thomas	50	M	Farmer	01Ma20Mo
Mary	40	F	Farmer	01Ma20Mo
Nora	17	F	Farmer	01Ma20Mo
Catherine	09	F	Child	01Ma20Mo
Michael	.00	M	Infant	01Ma20Mo
AMBROSE, Catherine	54	F	Farmer	01Ma20Mo
William	22	M	Farmer	01Ma20Mo
John	20	M	Farmer	01Ma20Mo
Ellen	18	F	Farmer	01Ma20Mo
Winney	16	F	Farmer	01Ma20Mo
CORCORAN, Edward	40	M	Farmer	01Ma20Mo
Bridget	17	F	Farmer	01Ma20Mo
Margt.	14	F	Farmer	01Ma20Mo
Michael	13	M	Farmer	01Ma20Mo
HENRY, Mary	13	F	Farmer	01Ma20Mo
Dennis	58	M	Farmer	01Ma20Mo
Bridget	21	F	Farmer	01Ma20Mo
MCCABE, Dennis	22	M	Farmer	01Ma20Mo
Honor	00	F	Farmer	01Ma20Mo
John	19	M	Farmer	01Ma20Mo
Mary	18	F	Farmer	01Ma20Mo
Judy	15	F	Farmer	01Ma20Mo
Denis	09	M	Child	01Ma20Mo
COFFE, Patrick	30	M	Farmer	01Ma20Mo
MCCABE, Ann	11	F	Farmer	01Ma20Mo
LYONS, James	30	M	Farmer	01Ma20Mo
U (W)	30	F	Wife	01Ma20Mo
William (S)	06	M	Child	01Ma20Mo
Michael (S)	.00	M	Infant	01Ma20Mo
MCCORMICK, Catherine	50	F	Farmer	01Ma20Mo
SHERIDAN, Mary	20	F	Farmer	01Ma20Mo
TOOLE, Pierce	30	M	Farmer	01Ma20Mo
U (W)	30	F	Wife	01Ma20Mo
BOLAND, Patrick	27	M	Farmer	01Ma20Mo
MCDONELL, John	27	M	Farmer	01Ma20Mo
TOOLE, Bridget	04	F	Child	01Ma20Mo
Anne	.00	F	Infant	01Ma20Mo
Pat	05	M	Child	01Ma20Mo
DELANY, U	20	F	Farmer	01Ma20Mo
KENT, And	24	M	Farmer	01Ma20Mo
U (W)	20	F	Wife	01Ma20Mo
QUIRK, Thomas	24	M	Farmer	01Ma20Mo
MCCANN, Terence	35	M	Farmer	01Ma20Mo
U (W)	30	F	Wife	01Ma20Mo
Robt.	03	M	Child	01Ma20Mo
Maria	.00	F	Infant	01Ma20Mo
HAYDEN, Dennis	36	M	Farmer	01Ma20Mo
Judy	30	F	Farmer	01Ma20Mo
Mary	10	F	Farmer	01Ma20Mo
Margt.	07	F	Child	01Ma20Mo
Michael	08	M	Child	01Ma20Mo
John	05	M	Child	01Ma20Mo
Denis	03	M	Child	01Ma20Mo
Pat	.00	M	Infant	01Ma20Mo
LALOR, John	24	M	Unknown	01Ma20Mo
PHELAN, Dennis	56	M	Unknown	01Ma20Mo
Betty	54	F	Unknown	01Ma20Mo
Martin	28	M	Unknown	01Ma20Mo
Kitty	22	F	Unknown	01Ma20Mo
Margt.	19	F	Unknown	01Ma20Mo
William	13	M	Unknown	01Ma20Mo
Mary	10	F	Unknown	01Ma20Mo
Eliza	.00	F	Infant	01Ma20Mo
LYNCH, Pat	48	M	Farmer	01Ma20Mo
Cath.	36	F	Farmer	01Ma20Mo
John	07	M	Child	01Ma20Mo
James	06	M	Child	01Ma20Mo
Bridget	.00	F	Infant	01Ma20Mo
Mary	.00	F	Infant	01Ma20Mo
DOWD, Terence	33	M	Farmer	01Ma20Mo
DOWD, Cath.	37	F	Farmer	01Ma20Mo
Mary	08	F	Child	01Ma20Mo
Cath.	04	F	Child	01Ma20Mo
James	.00	M	Infant	01Ma20Mo
EDWARDS, Pat	40	M	Farmer	01Ma20Mo
Mary	48	F	Farmer	01Ma20Mo
Christopher	18	M	Farmer	01Ma20Mo
John	15	M	Farmer	01Ma20Mo
Cath.	13	F	Farmer	01Ma20Mo
Pat	09	M	Child	01Ma20Mo
Margt.	16	F	Farmer	01Ma20Mo
KENNEDY, John	52	M	Farmer	01Ma20Mo
Ann	46	F	Farmer	01Ma20Mo
John	22	M	Farmer	01Ma20Mo
Catherine	20	F	Farmer	01Ma20Mo
Mary	15	F	Farmer	01Ma20Mo
James	17	M	Farmer	01Ma20Mo
Margt.	.00	F	Infant	01Ma20Mo
TIERNAN, John	37	M	Farmer	01Ma20Mo
Catherine	38	F	Farmer	01Ma20Mo
Catherine	41	F	Farmer	01Ma20Mo
Anne	39	F	Farmer	01Ma20Mo
Michael	15	M	Farmer	01Ma20Mo
Margt.	11	F	Farmer	01Ma20Mo
Jane	09	F	Child	01Ma20Mo
Owen	07	M	Child	01Ma20Mo
John	.00	M	Infant	01Ma20Mo
Edward	.00	M	Infant	01Ma20Mo
Catherine	03	F	Child	01Ma20Mo
SMITH, Pat	40	M	Farmer	01Ma20Mo
Mary	40	F	Farmer	01Ma20Mo
Mary	18	F	Farmer	01Ma20Mo
Rose	16	F	Farmer	01Ma20Mo
Pat	14	M	Farmer	01Ma20Mo
Catherine	12	F	Farmer	01Ma20Mo
MCGRATH, Thomas	53	M	Farmer	01Ma20Mo
Ann	31	F	Farmer	01Ma20Mo
Mary	28	F	Farmer	01Ma20Mo
Bridget	24	F	Farmer	01Ma20Mo
Margt.	35	F	Farmer	01Ma20Mo
Bridgt.	16	F	Farmer	01Ma20Mo
HEEVEY, Thomas	38	M	Farmer	01Ma20Mo
Eliza	36	F	Farmer	01Ma20Mo
Margt.	16	F	Farmer	01Ma20Mo
Philip	10	M	Farmer	01Ma20Mo
Bernard	08	M	Child	01Ma20Mo
Eliza	.00	F	Infant	01Ma20Mo
Mary	04	F	Child	01Ma20Mo
MORRISS, Connor	26	M	Farmer	01Ma20Mo
James	23	M	Farmer	01Ma20Mo
Nichlas	19	M	Farmer	01Ma20Mo
Mary	26	F	Farmer	01Ma20Mo
Betty	20	F	Farmer	01Ma20Mo
Patrick	33	M	Farmer	01Ma20Mo
Rose	30	F	Farmer	01Ma20Mo
Bridget	03	F	Child	01Ma20Mo
John	.00	M	Infant	01Ma20Mo
SMITH, Mat.	45	M	Farmer	01Ma20Mo
Mary	40	F	Farmer	01Ma20Mo
Patrick	19	M	Farmer	01Ma20Mo
Ann	15	F	Farmer	01Ma20Mo
John	17	M	Farmer	01Ma20Mo
Mary	13	F	Farmer	01Ma20Mo
MURPHY, Mick	30	M	Farmer	01Ma20Mo
Bridget	25	F	Farmer	01Ma20Mo
Judy	.00	F	Infant	01Ma20Mo
Mary	05	F	Child	01Ma20Mo
FITZSIMONS, Michl.	24	M	Farmer	01Ma20Mo
Cath.	28	F	Farmer	01Ma20Mo
Thomas	21	M	Farmer	01Ma20Mo
James	.00	M	Infant	01Ma20Mo
Richard	19	M	Farmer	01Ma20Mo
Bridget	17	F	Farmer	01Ma20Mo
MCLOGHLIN, James	30	M	Farmer	01Ma20Mo
Francis	25	M	Farmer	01Ma20Mo

NAMES OF PASSENGERS	AGE	SEX	OCCUPATIONS	DATE PORT SHIP
MCLOGHLIN, Peter	17	M	Farmer	01Ma20Mo
Joseph	30	M	Farmer	01Ma20Mo
WARD, Mat.	35	M	Farmer	01Ma20Mo
BOHEN, Mat.	51	M	Farmer	01Ma20Mo
Ann	49	F	Farmer	01Ma20Mo
Michael	23	M	Farmer	01Ma20Mo
James	17	M	Farmer	01Ma20Mo
John	16	M	Farmer	01Ma20Mo
Mat.	12	M	Farmer	01Ma20Mo
Margaret	21	F	Farmer	01Ma20Mo
FLOOD, William	57	M	Farmer	01Ma20Mo
Bridget	22	F	Farmer	01Ma20Mo
Patrick	30	M	Farmer	01Ma20Mo
James	23	M	Farmer	01Ma20Mo
Anne	15	F	Farmer	01Ma20Mo
Margt.	17	F	Farmer	01Ma20Mo
DONOHUE, Michael	40	M	Farmer	01Ma20Mo
Rose	40	F	Farmer	01Ma20Mo
Peter	18	M	Farmer	01Ma20Mo
Thomas	16	M	Farmer	01Ma20Mo
James	12	M	Farmer	01Ma20Mo
Julia	05	F	Child	01Ma20Mo
Michael	14	M	Child	01Ma20Mo
Ann	10	F	Child	01Ma20Mo

SWAN 01 MAY 1848

From Cork

NAMES OF PASSENGERS	AGE	SEX	OCCUPATIONS	DATE PORT SHIP
MURPHY, Patrick	28	M	Farmer	01Ma14Ix
Eliza	22	F	Farmer	01Ma14Ix
AHERN, Michel	20	M	Farmer	01Ma14Ix
HART, Martin	24	M	Farmer	01Ma14Ix
CROWLY, Honra.	28	F	Farmer	01Ma14Ix
REARDON, Mary	13	F	Farmer	01Ma14Ix
Cathe.	23	F	Farmer	01Ma14Ix
Jesh.	18	M	Farmer	01Ma14Ix
MCDONNELL, Timy	25	M	Farmer	01Ma14Ix
MURPHY, Michl.	23	M	Farmer	01Ma14Ix
Mary	30	F	Farmer	01Ma14Ix
HECKY, Danl.	20	M	Farmer	01Ma14Ix
William	22	M	Farmer	01Ma14Ix
LACY, Corris	25	M	Farmer	01Ma14Ix
DUNAEVY, Wm.	30	M	Farmer	01Ma14Ix
HOCKSHAW, John	34	M	Farmer	01Ma14Ix
COOMLY, Thos.	18	M	Farmer	01Ma14Ix
HANNAN, Patrick	30	M	Farmer	01Ma14Ix
Mary	22	F	Farmer	01Ma14Ix
Conn.	.02	M	Infant	01Ma14Ix
MAHER, Patrick	30	M	Farmer	01Ma14Ix
Eliza	25	F	Farmer	01Ma14Ix
DONOVAN, Jas.	54	M	Farmer	01Ma14Ix
Jesh.	18	M	Farmer	01Ma14Ix
David	13	M	Farmer	01Ma14Ix
HALY, Thos.	30	M	Farmer	01Ma14Ix
ALISEN, John	20	M	Farmer	01Ma14Ix
Mary-Ann	19	F	Farmer	01Ma14Ix
SHERIDAN, Jas.	23	M	Farmer	01Ma14Ix
CRONIN, Wm.	30	M	Farmer	01Ma14Ix
CORKERY, John	17	M	Farmer	01Ma14Ix
SCANLAND, Michl.	55	M	Farmer	01Ma14Ix
Michl.	16	M	Farmer	01Ma14Ix
Mary	55	F	Farmer	01Ma14Ix
HARRIGAN, Jas.	25	M	Farmer	01Ma14Ix
GUINAN, Angt.	17	F	Farmer	01Ma14Ix
Michl.	28	M	Farmer	01Ma14Ix
SLINEY, Patrick	28	M	Farmer	01Ma14Ix
MCCARTHY, Owen	40	M	Farmer	01Ma14Ix
LONDRIGAN, Thos.	40	M	Farmer	01Ma14Ix
CAREY, Patrick	50	M	Farmer	01Ma14Ix
Johanna	13	F	Farmer	01Ma14Ix
CONNOR, John	20	M	Farmer	01Ma14Ix
ORMOND, Wm.	44	M	Farmer	01Ma14Ix
HUSLY, Ellen	20	F	Farmer	01Ma14Ix
WHELAN, Michl.	22	M	Farmer	01Ma14Ix
CARROLL, Johanna	22	F	Farmer	01Ma14Ix
CAREY, Ellen	22	F	Farmer	01Ma14Ix
DACCLEN, Mary	30	F	Farmer	01Ma14Ix
HOGAN, John	20	M	Farmer	01Ma14Ix
BUCKLY, Patk.	60	M	Farmer	01Ma14Ix
Jesh.	21	M	Farmer	01Ma14Ix
SHEELAN, Maneel	21	M	Farmer	01Ma14Ix
CRONEN, John	20	M	Farmer	01Ma14Ix
SULLIVAN, Cath.	20	F	Farmer	01Ma14Ix
HAYES, Thos.	24	M	Farmer	01Ma14Ix
ODONNELL, Bridget	24	F	Farmer	01Ma14Ix
FARRELL, Ellen	18	F	Farmer	01Ma14Ix
BYRNE, Ellen	18	F	Farmer	01Ma14Ix
CRONEN, Michl.	21	M	Farmer	01Ma14Ix
FITZGERALD, Wm.	38	M	Farmer	01Ma14Ix
Honora	38	F	Farmer	01Ma14Ix
COGHLAN, Mary	18	F	Farmer	01Ma14Ix
FITZGERALD, Mary	09	F	Child	01Ma14Ix
Johanna	07	F	Child	01Ma14Ix
John	06	M	Child	01Ma14Ix
Fany	04	F	Child	01Ma14Ix
James	02	M	Child	01Ma14Ix
KELEY, Michl.	40	M	Farmer	01Ma14Ix
MEEHAN, John	20	M	Farmer	01Ma14Ix
MCCARTHY, Felix	20	M	Farmer	01Ma14Ix
DONOVAN, Patrick	29	M	Farmer	01Ma14Ix
Julia	19	F	Farmer	01Ma14Ix
Bridget	24	F	Farmer	01Ma14Ix
MOLONY, Bridget	24	F	Farmer	01Ma14Ix
DONAVAN, John	17	M	Farmer	01Ma14Ix
Cath.	21	F	Farmer	01Ma14Ix
CONNELL, Daniel	28	M	Farmer	01Ma14Ix
Mary	26	F	Farmer	01Ma14Ix
John	04	M	Child	01Ma14Ix
Thos.	01	M	Child	01Ma14Ix
LINAM, Honora	24	F	Farmer	01Ma14Ix
Johana	.09	F	Infant	01Ma14Ix
DARCY, Bridgt.	25	F	Farmer	01Ma14Ix
SULLIVAN, Roger	20	M	Farmer	01Ma14Ix
MURPHY, Mary	17	F	Farmer	01Ma14Ix
HAMPTON, Peter	19	M	Farmer	01Ma14Ix
MULLINS, Robt.	20	M	Farmer	01Ma14Ix
DREW, Pat	30	M	Farmer	01Ma14Ix
Margt.	25	F	Farmer	01Ma14Ix
JOY, Thos.	28	M	Farmer	01Ma14Ix
KEEFFFE, Ellen	21	F	Farmer	01Ma14Ix
MEEHAN, Andrew	16	M	Farmer	01Ma14Ix

CHAS. MCLAUCHLIN 01 MAY 1848

From Newry

NAMES OF PASSENGERS	AGE	SEX	OCCUPATIONS	DATE PORT SHIP
OHEAR, Mary	18	F	Spinster	01Ma19Ag
HARVEY, Jane	16	F	Spinster	01Ma19Ag
BURNS, Felix	20	M	Farmer	01Ma19Ag
Margaret	18	F	Relative	01Ma19Ag
Felix	16	M	Relative	01Ma19Ag
Mary	22	F	Relative	01Ma19Ag
Rose	12	F	Relative	01Ma19Ag
Patrick	11	M	Relative	01Ma19Ag
WATSON, Wm.	20	M	Laborer	01Ma19Ag
THOMPSON, Mary	40	F	Relative	01Ma19Ag
Elizabeth	16	F	Relative	01Ma19Ag

NAMES OF PASSENGERS		AGE	SEX	OCCUPATIONS	DATE PORT SHIP
THOMPSON, Robert		18	M	Relative	01Ma19Ag
John		13	M	Relative	01Ma19Ag
James		11	M	Relative	01Ma19Ag
Henry		09	M	Relative	01Ma19Ag
Susan		02	F	Relative	01Ma19Ag
KEENAN, Biddy		30	F	Servant	01Ma19Ag
Catherine		28	F	Servant	01Ma19Ag
BURNS, Laughlin		28	M	Laborer	01Ma19Ag
CAMPBELL, Michael		22	M	Laborer	01Ma19Ag
OHEAR, Michael		24	M	Laborer	01Ma19Ag
BURNS, Rose		20	F	Seamstress	01Ma19Ag
MCDONALD, Ann		18	F	Servant	01Ma19Ag
WOODS, Mary		18	F	Servant	01Ma19Ag
James		24	M	Servant	01Ma19Ag
MULLIGAN, Ann		20	F	Servant	01Ma19Ag
HUGHES, Ellen		20	F	Servant	01Ma19Ag
TREANOR, Ann		18	F	Servant	01Ma19Ag
MOAN, Henry		30	M	Farmer	01Ma19Ag
Rose	(W)	19	F	Wife	01Ma19Ag
MAGILL, John		22	M	Laborer	01Ma19Ag
DEVLIN, Nancy		16	F	Servant	01Ma19Ag
BOYLAN, Bridget		26	F	Servant	01Ma19Ag
HANLON, Michael		25	M	Farmer	01Ma19Ag
Mary		18	F	Servant	01Ma19Ag
MCKEVITT, Michael		20	M	Laborer	01Ma19Ag
TREANOR, James		40	M	Laborer	01Ma19Ag
Catharine	(W)	30	F	Wife	01Ma19Ag
John		10	M	Unknown	01Ma19Ag
KERR, Peter		20	M	Farmer	01Ma19Ag
Mary	(W)	22	F	Wife	01Ma19Ag
CAMPBELL, Robert		18	M	Laborer	01Ma19Ag
THOMPSON, Elizabeth		40	F	Servant	01Ma19Ag
Mary-Ann		18	F	Servant	01Ma19Ag
MAGUINNISS, Anne		20	F	Servant	01Ma19Ag
MCALISTER, Jane		30	F	Servant	01Ma19Ag
MCATEE, J.		22	M	Laborer	01Ma19Ag
MALLON, Bridget		18	F	Spinster	01Ma19Ag
BARLOW, Margaret		16	F	Spinster	01Ma19Ag
PORTER, Thomas		28	M	Laborer	01Ma19Ag
LENNON, Cathrine		25	F	Servant	01Ma19Ag
ROGAN, John		20	M	Laborer	01Ma19Ag
Ann		18	F	Servant	01Ma19Ag
Peter		22	M	Unknown	01Ma19Ag
DEEHAN, Mary		20	F	Spinster	01Ma19Ag
MCCOURT, Sally		18	F	Spinster	01Ma19Ag
MCKENA, Catherine		22	F	Spinster	01Ma19Ag
MORROW, Alexander		20	M	Farmer	01Ma19Ag
Wm.		.00	M	Infant	01Ma19Ag
CAMPBELL, James		25	M	Farmer	01Ma19Ag
Mary		20	F	Spinster	01Ma19Ag
Jos.		.00	M	Infant	01Ma19Ag
MONAGHAN, James		32	M	Laborer	01Ma19Ag
RICE, Mary		20	F	Spinster	01Ma19Ag
CRILLY, Mary		18	F	Spinster	01Ma19Ag
Wm.		22	M	Laborer	01Ma19Ag
RICE, Patt.		18	M	Laborer	01Ma19Ag
Ellen		16	F	Spinster	01Ma19Ag
John		20	M	Spinner	01Ma19Ag
DONNELLY, James		25	M	Laborer	01Ma19Ag
MALLEN, Michael		22	M	Laborer	01Ma19Ag
OHARE, Catherine		25	F	Spinster	01Ma19Ag
KELLY, John		25	M	Laborer	01Ma19Ag
Catherine		30	F	Seamstress	01Ma19Ag
FLANAGAN, Thos.		38	M	Blacksmith	01Ma19Ag
LUNDY, Richard		20	M	Shoemaker	01Ma19Ag

CAMBRIDGE 04 MAY 1848

From Liverpool

NAMES OF PASSENGERS	AGE	SEX	OCCUPATIONS	DATE PORT SHIP
CULLEN, Peggy	30	F	Servant	04Ma02Ea
KELLEHER, Dennis	39	M	Laborer	04Ma02Ea
U	30	F	Laborer	04Ma02Ea
John	.00	M	Infant	04Ma02Ea
Margaret	20	F	None	04Ma02Ea
Robt.	15	M	None	04Ma02Ea
John	10	M	None	04Ma02Ea
MCKEARIN, Hannah	18	F	Servant	04Ma02Ea
CARNIN, Patrick	26	M	Laborer	04Ma02Ea
Mary	26	F	Laborer	04Ma02Ea
FINCH, John	32	M	Carpenter	04Ma02Ea
MONAGHAN, Jas.	23	M	Farmer	04Ma02Ea
HILLOUGHLY, Ann	40	F	Farmer	04Ma02Ea
Jas.	14	M	Farmer	04Ma02Ea
BRENNAN, Jas.	27	M	Servant	04Ma02Ea
CONNGAN, Patrick	26	M	Laborer	04Ma02Ea
MCGARINGAN, Chas.	27	M	Laborer	04Ma02Ea
CLANCY, John	25	M	Laborer	04Ma02Ea
MOLLOY, Wm.	22	M	Laborer	04Ma02Ea
RAIL, Patrick	22	M	Laborer	04Ma02Ea
FLEMING, Geo.	18	M	Laborer	04Ma02Ea
HORRIGAN, Wm.	30	M	Laborer	04Ma02Ea
DOLAN, Mary	20	F	Servant	04Ma02Ea
KEANE, John	27	M	Laborer	04Ma02Ea
MURPHY, Peggy	28	F	Laborer	04Ma02Ea
TOWHEY, Thos.	55	M	Laborer	04Ma02Ea
Cornelius	25	M	Laborer	04Ma02Ea
Danl.	23	M	Laborer	04Ma02Ea
Timothy	18	M	Laborer	04Ma02Ea
Richd.	09	M	Child	04Ma02Ea
Johanna	17	F	Laborer	04Ma02Ea
John	50	M	Laborer	04Ma02Ea
Maria	15	F	Laborer	04Ma02Ea
Margaret	12	F	Laborer	04Ma02Ea
Danl.	32	M	Laborer	04Ma02Ea
Catherine	30	F	Laborer	04Ma02Ea
Honora	02	F	Child	04Ma02Ea
CIRNIN, Dennis	24	M	Servant	04Ma02Ea
HANESSY, Eliza	24	F	Servant	04Ma02Ea
SULLIVAN, Julia	24	F	Servant	04Ma02Ea
NOONAN, Thos.	30	M	Laborer	04Ma02Ea
RIGNEY, Michl.	22	M	Laborer	04Ma02Ea
WELSH, Martin	22	M	Laborer	04Ma02Ea
CUSSACK, Rose	18	F	Servant	04Ma02Ea
Margaret	22	F	Servant	04Ma02Ea
Catherine	20	F	Servant	04Ma02Ea
CASSIDY, Peter	30	M	Laborer	04Ma02Ea
MYERS, Pat	26	M	Laborer	04Ma02Ea
SANDERS, Bridget	21	F	Servant	04Ma02Ea
FOGARTY, Jas.	22	M	Gdnr	04Ma02Ea
Wm.	23	M	Gdnr	04Ma02Ea
DELANY, Mary	18	F	Servant	04Ma02Ea
Elizabeth	15	F	Servant	04Ma02Ea
SCULLIN, Patrick	25	M	Porter	04Ma02Ea
MYERS, Catherine	30	F	Servant	04Ma02Ea
OBRIEN, Ann	19	F	Servant	04Ma02Ea
FITZSIMMONS, Thos.	40	M	Farmer	04Ma02Ea
Margaret	37	F	Farmer	04Ma02Ea
Eliza	14	F	Farmer	04Ma02Ea
Jas.	12	M	Farmer	04Ma02Ea
John	09	M	Child	04Ma02Ea
MCANN, Ann	03	F	Child	04Ma02Ea
BURKE, Mary	30	F	Servant	04Ma02Ea
EGAN, Ellen	40	F	Servant	04Ma02Ea
John	16	M	Servant	04Ma02Ea

NAMES OF PASSENGERS	AGE	SEX	OCCUPATIONS	DATE PORT SHIP
EGAN, Jas.	10	M	Servant	04Ma02Ea
Betty	08	F	Child	04Ma02Ea
Ellen	06	F	Child	04Ma02Ea
MCGRATH, Stephen	25	M	Cork Cutter	04Ma02Ea
MURRAY, Mary	35	F	Cork Cutter	04Ma02Ea
U	.00	U	Infant	04Ma02Ea
Mary	03	F	Child	04Ma02Ea
MCDONNELL, Bridget	45	F	Unknown	04Ma02Ea
Chas.	20	M	Unknown	04Ma02Ea
CUNNINGHAM, Patrick	33	M	Carpenter	04Ma02Ea
Michael	27	M	Carpenter	04Ma02Ea
REGAN, Johanna	18	F	Servant	04Ma02Ea
CONAGHAN, Richd.	16	M	Laborer	04Ma02Ea
Susan	14	F	Laborer	04Ma02Ea
KEEGAN, Bridget	20	F	Servant	04Ma02Ea
MCCANN, Bryan	20	M	Tailor	04Ma02Ea
GALLAN, John	29	M	Laborer	04Ma02Ea
FEENRY, Edwd.	30	M	Laborer	04Ma02Ea
MARA, Honora	20	F	Servant	04Ma02Ea
SHEEHAN, Ellen	20	F	Servant	04Ma02Ea
LYNCH, Owen	30	M	Rope Maker	04Ma02Ea
Owen	06	M	Child	04Ma02Ea
REGAN, John	27	M	Laborer	04Ma02Ea
CURTAIN, Thos.	25	M	Laborer	04Ma02Ea
SCANLAN, Timothy	30	M	Laborer	04Ma02Ea
Ellen	25	F	Laborer	04Ma02Ea
MCCANLEY, Michl.	40	M	Boatmaker	04Ma02Ea
John	09	M	Child	04Ma02Ea
Patrick	13	M	Child	04Ma02Ea
Rose	07	F	Child	04Ma02Ea
BARRETT, Edwd.	20	M	Drover	04Ma02Ea
GALLAHER, John	18	M	Laborer	04Ma02Ea
MAHANY, Jas.	20	M	Laborer	04Ma02Ea
Dennis	24	M	Laborer	04Ma02Ea
ARMSTRONG, John	45	M	Laborer	04Ma02Ea
Wm.	20	M	Laborer	04Ma02Ea
MCAVOY, Mary	20	F	Servant	04Ma02Ea
BYRNES, Terence	35	M	Laborer	04Ma02Ea
Bridget	30	F	Laborer	04Ma02Ea
Ann	05	F	Child	04Ma02Ea
SHERIDAN, Mary	25	F	Servant	04Ma02Ea
MAHAN, Robt.	30	M	Laborer	04Ma02Ea
OCONNOR, Michl.	18	M	Laborer	04Ma02Ea
CLANCY, Bridget	30	F	Servant	04Ma02Ea
KILCREAT, Chas.	25	M	Farmer	04Ma02Ea
KELLY, Ellen	22	F	Servant	04Ma02Ea
Esther	22	F	Servant	04Ma02Ea
TOORNEY, Honora	25	F	Servant	04Ma02Ea
Thos.	18	M	Porter	04Ma02Ea
DONOHUE, Mary	21	F	Porter	04Ma02Ea
U	.00	U	Infant	04Ma02Ea
HANLEY, Margaret	20	F	None	04Ma02Ea
ALWELL, Laughlin	30	M	Laborer	04Ma02Ea
CRUDEN, Catherine	20	F	Servant	04Ma02Ea
GONNLEY, Thos.	26	M	Butcher	04Ma02Ea
CONVESS, Wm.	25	M	Carpenter	04Ma02Ea
Ann	17	F	Carpenter	04Ma02Ea
MULLETT, Nabby	13	F	Carpenter	04Ma02Ea
Patrick	10	M	Carpenter	04Ma02Ea
Jas.	09	M	Child	04Ma02Ea
MURPHY, Jas.	23	M	Rope Maker	04Ma02Ea
FESS, Catherine	20	F	None	04Ma02Ea
ENNIS, John	20	M	Laborer	04Ma02Ea
BLANEY, Catherine	46	F	Laborer	04Ma02Ea
Catherine	08	F	Child	04Ma02Ea
MCMANUS, Eliza	19	F	Servant	04Ma02Ea
Margaret	16	F	Servant	04Ma02Ea
MARTIN, Mary-Jane	19	F	Servant	04Ma02Ea
DOYLE, Jas.	30	M	Laborer	04Ma02Ea
LARKIN, John	19	M	Laborer	04Ma02Ea
BRENNAN, Ann	50	F	Servant	04Ma02Ea
Died-At-Sea				
MONOGHAN, Mary	20	F	None	04Ma02Ea
U	.00	U	Infant	04Ma02Ea
Ann-Jane	02	F	Child	04Ma02Ea

NAMES OF PASSENGERS	AGE	SEX	OCCUPATIONS	DATE PORT SHIP
BANOR, Mathew	11	M	Servant	04Ma02Ea
HANLEY, Bridget	30	F	Servant	04Ma02Ea
CONNELLY, Michael	30	M	Laborer	04Ma02Ea
DUGAN, Patrick	30	M	Laborer	04Ma02Ea
MCCARTHY, Ann	18	F	Servant	04Ma02Ea
YOUNG, Betsy	18	F	Servant	04Ma02Ea
KEEGAN, Ellen	35	F	Servant	04Ma02Ea
COYNE, Ann	17	F	Servant	04Ma02Ea
Bridget	14	F	Servant	04Ma02Ea
OBRIEN, John	20	M	Laborer	04Ma02Ea
MCGUIRE, John	20	M	Laborer	04Ma02Ea
MCDERMITT, Jas.	20	M	Laborer	04Ma02Ea
DELAHANTY, Cornelius	20	M	Laborer	04Ma02Ea
Mathew	22	M	Laborer	04Ma02Ea
KELLOUGHLY, Daniel	26	M	Laborer	04Ma02Ea
RAY, Maria	28	F	Servant	04Ma02Ea
Margt.	22	F	Servant	04Ma02Ea
HUGHES, Patrick	24	M	Laborer	04Ma02Ea
MULLIN, Bridget	34	F	Servant	04Ma02Ea
Bridget	18	F	Servant	04Ma02Ea
Ellen	30	F	Servant	04Ma02Ea
MCCOFFREY, Mary	24	F	Servant	04Ma02Ea
MCKAY, Danl.	40	M	Laborer	04Ma02Ea
SHEEHAN, Mary	11	F	Laborer	04Ma02Ea
BALFORD, Wm.	24	M	Farmer	04Ma02Ea
MOORE, Bridget	18	F	Farmer	04Ma02Ea
CLOSEKY, Owen	40	M	Laborer	04Ma02Ea
LAMBERT Jas.	27	M	Laborer	04Ma02Ea
NEAL, Nancy	37	F	Servant	04Ma02Ea
SCULLEN, Margaret	20	F	Nurse	04Ma02Ea
Patrick	25	M	Laborer	04Ma02Ea
KANE, Susan	25	F	Servant	04Ma02Ea
NOTTON, Patrick	30	M	Laborer	04Ma02Ea
MURRAY, Bridget	12	F	Farmer	04Ma02Ea
DOLAN, John	46	M	Carpenter	04Ma02Ea
Ellen	26	F	Carpenter	04Ma02Ea
BRASSEL, Jane	30	F	Servant	04Ma02Ea
Jas.	07	M	Child	04Ma02Ea
Roddy	03	F	Child	04Ma02Ea
BRYAN, Mary	30	F	Servant	04Ma02Ea
Mary	04	F	Child	04Ma02Ea
DOWD, Patrick	19	M	Laborer	04Ma02Ea
Thos.	16	M	Laborer	04Ma02Ea
NOTTON, Catherine	30	F	Servant	04Ma02Ea
DALEY, Bridget	40	F	Servant	04Ma02Ea
Bridget	20	F	Servant	04Ma02Ea
Ann	25	F	Servant	04Ma02Ea
Patrick	21	M	Servant	04Ma02Ea
Thos.	19	M	Servant	04Ma02Ea
BRADY, John	20	M	Laborer	04Ma02Ea
DEMPSEY, Bridget	21	F	Servant	04Ma02Ea
Mary	18	F	Servant	04Ma02Ea
DWYER, John	25	M	Laborer	04Ma02Ea
ARMSTRONG, Ellen	20	F	Servant	04Ma02Ea
FAINLY, Andrew	20	M	Laborer	04Ma02Ea
Mary	20	F	Laborer	04Ma02Ea
Philip	09	M	Child	04Ma02Ea
Maurice	07	M	Child	04Ma02Ea
Owen	05	M	Child	04Ma02Ea
HARTY, Catherine	20	F	Servant	04Ma02Ea
GALLAGHER, Lawrence	30	M	Laborer	04Ma02Ea
REYNOLDS, Chas.	16	M	Laborer	04Ma02Ea
MCGUIRE, Ann	22	F	Servant	04Ma02Ea
PETTS, Nancy	40	F	Housekeeper	04Ma02Ea
U	00	U	Housekeeper	04Ma02Ea
Nancy-Jane	15	F	Housekeeper	04Ma02Ea
Mary	12	F	Housekeeper	04Ma02Ea
Esther	10	F	Housekeeper	04Ma02Ea
Jas.	08	M	Child	04Ma02Ea
Margaret	06	F	Child	04Ma02Ea
John	04	M	Child	04Ma02Ea
MAHANY, Mary	28	F	Servant	04Ma02Ea
COYLE, Catherine	16	F	Servant	04Ma02Ea
KENON, John	12	M	Farmer	04Ma02Ea
Kate	20	F	Servant	04Ma02Ea

NAMES OF PASSENGERS		AGE	SEX	OCCUPATIONS	DATE PORT SHIP
MCNALLEY, Mary		20	F	Seamstress	04Ma02Ea

SOUTH ESH 04 MAY 1848

From Belfast

NAMES OF PASSENGERS		AGE	SEX	OCCUPATIONS	DATE PORT SHIP
CARSON, William		30	M	Laborer	04Ma07Ah
MCMILLEN, Hugh		35	M	Farmer	04Ma07Ah
Jane	(W)	34	F	Wife	04Ma07Ah
William	(S)	17	M	Unknown	04Ma07Ah
Alexander	(S)	09	M	Child	04Ma07Ah
James	(S)	07	M	Child	04Ma07Ah
Eliza	(D)	05	F	Child	04Ma07Ah
Sam	(S)	03	M	Child	04Ma07Ah
MCGEE, James		23	M	Bleacher	04Ma07Ah
Rose	(W)	26	F	Wife	04Ma07Ah
Mary-Jane	(D)	.00	F	Infant	04Ma07Ah
WILLIAMSON, Victor		18	M	Bleacher	04Ma07Ah
SMYLIE, Thomas		28	M	Laborer	04Ma07Ah
Jas.		19	M	Laborer	04Ma07Ah
Jno.		25	M	Laborer	04Ma07Ah
Georgiana		21	F	Laborer	04Ma07Ah
REED, Saml.		23	M	Farmer	04Ma07Ah
Mary	(W)	21	F	Wife	04Ma07Ah
Thomas	(S)	02	M	Child	04Ma07Ah
BEATTY, Ann		23	F	Spinster	04Ma07Ah
ROLSTAN, Jas.		22	M	Farmer	04Ma07Ah
Ann	(W)	21	F	Wife	04Ma07Ah
TURBOT, Jno.		12	M	Unknown	04Ma07Ah
MCCARL, Ann		22	F	Spinster	04Ma07Ah
MCGEE, Edwd.		20	M	Laborer	04Ma07Ah
ELLIOT, Eliza		23	F	Spinster	04Ma07Ah
Margt.		18	F	Spinster	04Ma07Ah
Rose-A.		13	F	Spinster	04Ma07Ah
IRVIN, Hugh		16	M	Laborer	04Ma07Ah
RIELLY, Thos.		35	M	Laborer	04Ma07Ah
MCMICHAEL, Jane		25	F	Spinster	04Ma07Ah
SCOTT, Jas.		20	M	Laborer	04Ma07Ah
MCKEOWN, Hugh		20	M	Farmer	04Ma07Ah
Starke		15	M	Farmer	04Ma07Ah
ANDERSON, Wm.		25	M	Farmer	04Ma07Ah
MCKEE, Wm.		22	M	Farmer	04Ma07Ah
Jno.		20	M	Farmer	04Ma07Ah
TRAINER, Margt.		20	F	Spinster	04Ma07Ah
GORMAN, Francis		20	M	Farmer	04Ma07Ah
MCCORT, Mary		20	F	Spinster	04Ma07Ah
Nancy		18	F	Spinster	04Ma07Ah
FOX, Jas.		18	M	Laborer	04Ma07Ah
MCGINN, Michl.		19	M	Laborer	04Ma07Ah
MCFALL, Patrk.		25	M	Laborer	04Ma07Ah
RAFFERTY, Patrk.		18	M	Laborer	04Ma07Ah
RICKEY, Margt.		30	F	Wi	04Ma07Ah
Francis	(S)	11	M	Unknown	04Ma07Ah
WILLIAMSON, Elizbth.		23	F	Spinster	04Ma07Ah
MAXWELL, Robt.		22	M	Farmer	04Ma07Ah
Eliza	(W)	30	F	Wife	04Ma07Ah
Wm.		12	M	Unknown	04Ma07Ah
John		10	M	Unknown	04Ma07Ah
George		08	M	Child	04Ma07Ah
GUNNING, Hugh		28	M	Farmer	04Ma07Ah
WIER, Cherry		23	F	Spinster	04Ma07Ah
Mary-Jane		21	F	Spinster	04Ma07Ah
Jas.		16	M	Laborer	04Ma07Ah
Emily		10	F	Unknown	04Ma07Ah
GIVIN, Elizth.		45	F	Unknown	04Ma07Ah
Nancy		18	F	Spinster	04Ma07Ah
Betty-Ann		18	F	Spinster	04Ma07Ah
Jane		20	F	Spinster	04Ma07Ah
John		21	M	Laborer	04Ma07Ah
GIVIN, Martha		20	F	Spinster	04Ma07Ah
Mary-Jane		10	F	Unknown	04Ma07Ah
Margaret		06	F	Child	04Ma07Ah
Adam		04	M	Child	04Ma07Ah
David		03	M	Child	04Ma07Ah
Mary-Eliza		.00	F	Infant	04Ma07Ah
AGNEW, Isabella		20	F	Unknown	04Ma07Ah
GORDON, Hugh		29	M	Laborer	04Ma07Ah
KILPATRICK, John		32	M	Laborer	04Ma07Ah
Sarah		32	F	Laborer	04Ma07Ah
Sarah		08	F	Child	04Ma07Ah
Eliza		06	F	Child	04Ma07Ah
Thomas		04	M	Child	04Ma07Ah
John		02	M	Child	04Ma07Ah
MORGAN, Michl.		17	M	Laborer	04Ma07Ah
Sarah		22	F	Spinster	04Ma07Ah
BRANNAN, Nancy		19	F	Spinster	04Ma07Ah
ARMSTRONG, Thomas		35	M	Laborer	04Ma07Ah
Catherine		12	F	Unknown	04Ma07Ah
John		06	M	Child	04Ma07Ah
Sally		07	F	Child	04Ma07Ah

ALBION 04 MAY 1848

From Halifax

NAMES OF PASSENGERS		AGE	SEX	OCCUPATIONS	DATE PORT SHIP
STEWART, Ann		21	F	None	04Ma22Ov
MOONEY, Ellen		20	F	None	04Ma22Ov
WOODS, Mary		25	F	None	04Ma22Ov
MATHEWS, John		22	M	Tailor	04Ma22Ov
VAUGHAN, William		20	M	Butcher	04Ma22Ov
MCNALLEY, Thos.		22	M	Lawyer	04Ma22Ov
NEWMAN, John		25	M	Groom	04Ma22Ov
MCCROONEY, John		20	M	Laborer	04Ma22Ov
HYLAND, Michael		17	M	Laborer	04Ma22Ov
LYNCH, Michael		18	M	Laborer	04Ma22Ov
HYLAND, Patrick		17	M	Laborer	04Ma22Ov
MCCORMICK, Patrick		24	M	Laborer	04Ma22Ov
MURTAGH, Michael		18	M	Laborer	04Ma22Ov

ST.PATRICK 05 MAY 1848

From Liverpool

NAMES OF PASSENGERS		AGE	SEX	OCCUPATIONS	DATE PORT SHIP
MEARN, Bridget		28	F	Spinster	05Ma02Bw
LENNON, Nicks.		30	M	Grocer	05Ma02Bw
Maria	(W)	29	F	Wife	05Ma02Bw
Mary-Ann	(D)	06	F	Child	05Ma02Bw
Michael	(S)	04	M	Child	05Ma02Bw
Hughson	(S)	02	M	Child	05Ma02Bw
Honora	(D)	.00	F	Infant	05Ma02Bw
Mary		20	F	Spinster	05Ma02Bw
BUTLER, Mary		50	F	Mother	05Ma02Bw
LAWLER, Henry		26	M	Laborer	05Ma02Bw
DALY, Margeret-Mrs.		40	F	Unknown	05Ma02Bw
Patrick		13	M	Laborer	05Ma02Bw
THORNTON, Patrick		24	M	Mason	05Ma02Bw
DEMPSY, Peter		26	M	Laborer	05Ma02Bw
Anna	(W)	22	F	Wife	05Ma02Bw
Michal	(S)	.00	M	Infant	05Ma02Bw
DUNN, Mathew		24	M	Laborer	05Ma02Bw
LILLY, Michal		30	M	Grocer	05Ma02Bw
Catherine	(W)	20	F	Wife	05Ma02Bw

NAMES OF PASSENGERS		AGE	SEX	OCCUPATIONS	DATE PORT SHIP
FITZSIMMONS, James		26	M	Laborer	05Ma02Bw
GRENON, Mary		40	F	Unknown	05Ma02Bw
James		20	M	Laborer	05Ma02Bw
Rose		18	F	Spinster	05Ma02Bw
Bridget		15	F	Spinster	05Ma02Bw
Laurice		13	U	Unknown	05Ma02Bw
Mary		12	F	Unknown	05Ma02Bw
John		10	M	Unknown	05Ma02Bw
Catherine		08	F	Child	05Ma02Bw
Patrick		05	M	Child	05Ma02Bw
CLARKEN, Mary		35	F	Wi	05Ma02Bw
U		.00	U	Infant	05Ma02Bw
Born-At-Sea					
MCCABE, Thomas		40	M	Laborer	05Ma02Bw
OWEN, Hugh		20	M	Student	05Ma02Bw
MCMANDHAM, Felix		24	M	Laborer	05Ma02Bw
Patrick		32	M	Butcher	05Ma02Bw
JOYCE, Bridget		21	F	Spinster	05Ma02Bw
GOODWIN, Peter		19	M	Laborer	05Ma02Bw
DOWRING, Samuel		24	M	Draper	05Ma02Bw
Thomas		20	M	Draper	05Ma02Bw
SMITH, U		31	M	Tailor	05Ma02Bw
U	(W)	23	F	Wife	05Ma02Bw
MURRAY, Catherine		22	F	Spinster	05Ma02Bw
WALSH, William		34	M	Laborer	05Ma02Bw
MARSHALL, Samuel		28	M	Shoemaker	05Ma02Bw
Isabella	(W)	27	F	Wife	05Ma02Bw
MCCABE, Rose		20	F	Spinster	05Ma02Bw
MAYON, Pat		45	M	Laborer	05Ma02Bw
CONLON, Bernard		23	M	Laborer	05Ma02Bw
HENNY, Margaret		23	F	Spinster	05Ma02Bw
Allen		20	M	Laborer	05Ma02Bw
HEDDON, Mary-Ann		18	F	Spinster	05Ma02Bw
DUNN, Michal		25	M	Laborer	05Ma02Bw
KELLY, James		23	M	Laborer	05Ma02Bw
FOGARTY, James		20	M	Tailor	05Ma02Bw
DOOLAN, John		23	M	Laborer	05Ma02Bw
HOLOHAM, Bridget		22	F	Spinster	05Ma02Bw
DONALLY, Mary		13	F	Spinster	05Ma02Bw
BRENNAN, John		50	M	Laborer	05Ma02Bw
Ann	(W)	50	F	Wife	05Ma02Bw
Bridget	(D)	16	F	Spinster	05Ma02Bw
John	(S)	14	M	Unknown	05Ma02Bw
Ellen	(D)	12	F	Unknown	05Ma02Bw
DOWNEY, Denis		24	M	Cbtmkr	05Ma02Bw
HUGHES, Ellen		20	F	Spinster	05Ma02Bw
HEALLY, Richard		24	M	Laborer	05Ma02Bw
Julia		22	F	Spinster	05Ma02Bw
MCEVOY, Andrew		55	M	Laborer	05Ma02Bw
Anna	(W)	40	F	Wife	05Ma02Bw
Anna	(D)	19	F	Spinster	05Ma02Bw
Mary	(D)	13	F	Unknown	05Ma02Bw
Andrew	(S)	11	M	Unknown	05Ma02Bw
Jane	(D)	09	F	Child	05Ma02Bw
Henry-George	(S)	.00	M	Infant	05Ma02Bw
CORRORAN, Sarah		40	F	Spinster	05Ma02Bw
MCCORD, Anna		20	F	Spinster	05Ma02Bw
SPROLL, Martha-Jane		21	F	Spinster	05Ma02Bw
CLARKE, Mary		20	F	Spinster	05Ma02Bw
Letteia		45	F	Wi	05Ma02Bw
LOCKART, Hugh		30	M	Farmer	05Ma02Bw
U	(W)	25	F	Wife	05Ma02Bw
BEATTY, Alexander		40	M	Wife	05Ma02Bw
Martha	(W)	36	F	Wife	05Ma02Bw
John	(S)	15	M	Farmer	05Ma02Bw
William	(S)	12	M	Farmer	05Ma02Bw
Robert	(S)	11	M	Farmer	05Ma02Bw
George	(S)	08	M	Child	05Ma02Bw
James-Alexander	(S)	.00	M	Infant	05Ma02Bw
MCNICKOL, Robert		40	M	Carpenter	05Ma02Bw
Alexander		16	M	Laborer	05Ma02Bw
BEATTY, Robert		35	M	Laborer	05Ma02Bw
Martha	(W)	30	F	Wife	05Ma02Bw
Mary-Ann	(D)	16	F	Spinster	05Ma02Bw
Margaret	(D)	16	F	Spinster	05Ma02Bw
BEATTY, Eliza	(D)	14	F	Spinster	05Ma02Bw
Ann	(D)	12	F	Spinster	05Ma02Bw
James	(S)	11	M	Unknown	05Ma02Bw
John	(S)	09	M	Child	05Ma02Bw
Jane	(D)	08	F	Child	05Ma02Bw
Alexander	(S)	06	M	Child	05Ma02Bw
Martha	(D)	04	F	Child	05Ma02Bw
Robert	(S)	.00	M	Infant	05Ma02Bw
GRIFFITH, Pat		23	M	Laborer	05Ma02Bw
ALCOCK, Thomas		61	M	Laborer	05Ma02Bw
U	(W)	61	F	Wife	05Ma02Bw
John		36	M	Laborer	05Ma02Bw
Anna		24	F	Spinster	05Ma02Bw
Peter		18	M	Laborer	05Ma02Bw
Conner		14	M	Laborer	05Ma02Bw
Mary		08	F	Child	05Ma02Bw
GARRION, Margaret		21	F	Spinster	05Ma02Bw
MURROW, Pat		57	M	Laborer	05Ma02Bw
DODD, Thomas		25	M	Laborer	05Ma02Bw
Betty		20	F	Spinster	05Ma02Bw
James		16	M	Laborer	05Ma02Bw
Margaret		12	F	Spinster	05Ma02Bw
Peter		22	M	Laborer	05Ma02Bw
TAYLOR, Luke		23	M	Laborer	05Ma02Bw
KILLDANT, John		30	M	Laborer	05Ma02Bw
MCDONAGH, Peter		30	M	Laborer	05Ma02Bw
DELARAY, Peter		20	M	Laborer	05Ma02Bw
HART, Pat		20	M	Laborer	05Ma02Bw
SMITH, Catherine		24	F	Spinster	05Ma02Bw
FARRELL, Margaret		25	F	Spinster	05Ma02Bw
Anna		14	F	Spinster	05Ma02Bw
CHAMBERLAIN, John		19	M	Farmer	05Ma02Bw
Richard		23	M	Farmer	05Ma02Bw
HENRY, Betty		40	F	Spinster	05Ma02Bw
FITZGERALD, Margaret		30	F	Wi	05Ma02Bw
COWLY, Margaret		16	F	Spinster	05Ma02Bw
FITZGERALD, Michal		09	M	Child	05Ma02Bw
CONNER, Pat		25	M	Laborer	05Ma02Bw
Laurence		35	M	Laborer	05Ma02Bw
U	(W)	35	F	Wife	05Ma02Bw
PURDIM, Biddy		17	F	Spinster	05Ma02Bw
MCCORMICK, John		24	M	Laborer	05Ma02Bw
KENNELLY, John		35	M	Laborer	05Ma02Bw
CAVANAGH, Mary		20	F	Spinster	05Ma02Bw
KENNELLY, Jane		24	F	Spinster	05Ma02Bw
KIRK, John		20	M	Laborer	05Ma02Bw
John		50	M	Laborer	05Ma02Bw
COUGHLIN, William		30	M	Coach Maker	05Ma02Bw
U	(W)	30	F	Wife	05Ma02Bw
BROADRICK, Edward		50	M	Laborer	05Ma02Bw
U	(W)	40	F	Wife	05Ma02Bw
Biddy		25	F	Spinster	05Ma02Bw
Thomas		20	M	Laborer	05Ma02Bw
Edward		11	M	Laborer	05Ma02Bw
Daniel-Ernest		20	M	Laborer	05Ma02Bw
MOONEY, Thomas		25	M	Laborer	05Ma02Bw
RYAN, Pat		25	M	Laborer	05Ma02Bw
Catherine	(M)	50	F	Mother	05Ma02Bw
Anthony		24	F	Spinster	05Ma02Bw
Michal		20	M	Laborer	05Ma02Bw
Peggy		30	F	Spinster	05Ma02Bw
MULLOUGHY, Mary		20	F	Spinster	05Ma02Bw
Thomas		26	M	Laborer	05Ma02Bw
WALSH, Judy		25	F	Spinster	05Ma02Bw
SADLER, Edward		30	M	Smith	05Ma02Bw
WALDON, Michal		15	M	Laborer	05Ma02Bw
CROWN, Thomas		20	M	Laborer	05Ma02Bw
MONAGHAN, John		24	M	Carpenter	05Ma02Bw
Catherine		20	F	Spinster	05Ma02Bw
CAMPBELL, Mary		29	F	Spinster	05Ma02Bw
FERRIS, James		21	M	Clerk	05Ma02Bw
CUNNINGHAM, Martin		17	M	Laborer	05Ma02Bw
CULLIN, Rose		22	F	Spinster	05Ma02Bw
HUGHES, Mary		23	F	Spinster	05Ma02Bw
DUNN, John		27	M	Laborer	05Ma02Bw

NAMES OF PASSENGERS	AGE	SEX	OCCUPATIONS	DATE PORT SHIP
MANSFIELD, Thomas	20	M	Farmer	05Ma02Bw
Mary-Ann	20	F	Spinster	05Ma02Bw
Margaret	18	F	Spinster	05Ma02Bw
TURNER, Alexander	20	M	Laborer	05Ma02Bw
GARNET, James	26	M	Tailor	05Ma02Bw
DERNIAN, Tim	25	M	Laborer	05Ma02Bw
FOGERTY, Jane	22	F	Spinster	05Ma02Bw
DUPLEX, Richard	24	M	Farmer	05Ma02Bw
Sarah	18	F	Spinster	05Ma02Bw
DUFFORD, Thomas	22	M	Laborer	05Ma02Bw
Anna (T)	20	F	Unknown	05Ma02Bw
THORMONEY, Michal	25	M	Farmer	05Ma02Bw
Michel	16	M	Farmer	05Ma02Bw
STORES, Michel	26	M	Laborer	05Ma02Bw
BRIORLY, Thomas	21	M	Laborer	05Ma02Bw
CAMPBELL, James	21	M	Laborer	05Ma02Bw
ENRIGHT, Thomas	35	M	Carpenter	05Ma02Bw
U (W)	25	F	Wife	05Ma02Bw
MALBY, Edward	20	M	Laborer	05Ma02Bw
MODIGAN, John	20	M	Laborer	05Ma02Bw
CONWAY, Martin	50	M	Laborer	05Ma02Bw
Honora (W)	50	F	Wife	05Ma02Bw
John (S)	11	M	Unknown	05Ma02Bw
Martin (S)	09	M	Child	05Ma02Bw
BROWN, Johanna	20	F	Spinster	05Ma02Bw
MOORE, Pat	30	M	Laborer	05Ma02Bw
U (W)	25	F	Wife	05Ma02Bw
CASEY, Jeremiah	26	M	Laborer	05Ma02Bw
John	20	M	Laborer	05Ma02Bw
Owen	24	M	Laborer	05Ma02Bw
ARCHIBALD, Robert	33	M	Farmer	05Ma02Bw
U (W)	33	F	Wife	05Ma02Bw
Ellen (D)	10	F	Unknown	05Ma02Bw
David (S)	08	M	Child	05Ma02Bw
Edward (S)	06	M	Child	05Ma02Bw
Mary-Jane (D)	.00	F	Infant	05Ma02Bw
DUNLOP, Ellen	24	F	Spinster	05Ma02Bw
THORNE, John	60	M	Laborer	05Ma02Bw
Isabella (W)	60	F	Wife	05Ma02Bw
MCCAMBRIDGE, William	21	M	Laborer	05Ma02Bw
MCGARVEY, John	21	M	Laborer	05Ma02Bw
HIGGINS, James	20	M	Laborer	05Ma02Bw
EGAN, William	17	M	Laborer	05Ma02Bw
George	27	M	Laborer	05Ma02Bw
TENNANT, William	24	M	Cbtmkr	05Ma02Bw
MURPHY, Joseph	22	M	Laborer	05Ma02Bw
THORNTON, James	22	M	Laborer	05Ma02Bw
Ellen (T)	20	F	Unknown	05Ma02Bw
DONELLY, John	26	M	Laborer	05Ma02Bw
RYAN, Pat	35	M	Laborer	05Ma02Bw
MCCUSKIN, U-Mrs.	30	F	Unknown	05Ma02Bw
James (S)	08	M	Child	05Ma02Bw
Eliza-Ann (D)	07	F	Child	05Ma02Bw
John (S)	05	M	Child	05Ma02Bw
Felix (S)	04	M	Child	05Ma02Bw
Mary-Ann	34	F	Spinster	05Ma02Bw
GOODWIN, Mary	20	F	Spinster	05Ma02Bw
MURPHY, John	26	M	Baker	05Ma02Bw
PENNANT, Esther	19	F	Spinster	05Ma02Bw
CARRAHER, Patrick	21	M	Clerk	05Ma02Bw
LENNON, Anna	21	F	Spinster	05Ma02Bw
WEALON, John	28	M	Laborer	05Ma02Bw
WAKELY, Maria	16	F	Spinster	05Ma02Bw
DOOLY, James	27	M	Laborer	05Ma02Bw
LAWLER, James	25	M	Laborer	05Ma02Bw
GLEESON, Andrew	25	M	Laborer	05Ma02Bw
SMITH, Sarah	40	F	Spinster	05Ma02Bw
Terence	07	M	Child	05Ma02Bw
HAYDEN, Michal	24	M	Laborer	05Ma02Bw
Patrick	28	M	Laborer	05Ma02Bw
CONRY, Catherine	21	F	Spinster	05Ma02Bw
CURLEY, Anna	24	F	Spinster	05Ma02Bw
Betsy	21	F	Spinster	05Ma02Bw
SHEA, Robt.	40	M	Farmer	05Ma02Bw
Catherine (W)	36	F	Wife	05Ma02Bw
SHEA, Richd.	19	M	Farmer	05Ma02Bw
Wm.	17	M	Farmer	05Ma02Bw
Nicks.	15	M	Farmer	05Ma02Bw
John	12	M	Farmer	05Ma02Bw
Robt.	07	M	Child	05Ma02Bw
Mary-Ann	23	F	Spinster	05Ma02Bw
Johanna	14	F	Spinster	05Ma02Bw
Catherine	09	F	Child	05Ma02Bw
KENEDY, Walter	25	M	Laborer	05Ma02Bw
LENNON, Patrick	32	M	Laborer	05Ma02Bw
PHAIR, Thos.	25	M	Gdnr	05Ma02Bw
OBRIEN, Timothy	30	M	Gdnr	05Ma02Bw
ODUGGAN, Timothy	21	M	Laborer	05Ma02Bw
SPEED, James	21	M	Molder	05Ma02Bw
MAHER, Michael	35	M	Laborer	05Ma02Bw
DERMODY, Thomas	30	M	Laborer	05Ma02Bw

LUCY ANN 05 MAY 1848

From Cork

NAMES OF PASSENGERS	AGE	SEX	OCCUPATIONS	DATE PORT SHIP
WISEMAN, Robert	25	M	Laborer	05Ma14Bj
CARDEN, Robt.	30	M	Laborer	05Ma14Bj
KEARNE, Julia	36	F	Laborer	05Ma14Bj
KEARNEY, Cathe.	12	F	Laborer	05Ma14Bj
COLLINS, Cath.	40	F	Laborer	05Ma14Bj
Timothy	08	M	Child	05Ma14Bj
Ellen	15	F	Laborer	05Ma14Bj
Magt.	04	F	Child	05Ma14Bj
HERLIHY, David	22	M	Laborer	05Ma14Bj
STANNTON, Johanna	22	F	Laborer	05Ma14Bj
HERLIHY, Pat	25	M	Laborer	05Ma14Bj
Ellen	22	F	Laborer	05Ma14Bj
MURPHY, John	20	M	Laborer	05Ma14Bj
John	20	M	Laborer	05Ma14Bj
COLLINS, Jerry	18	M	Laborer	05Ma14Bj
SEYMOUR, Wm.	13	M	Laborer	05Ma14Bj
SHECKARN, Annie	21	F	Laborer	05Ma14Bj
WALSH, Edwd.	25	M	Laborer	05Ma14Bj
CALLAGHAN, Dennis	25	M	Laborer	05Ma14Bj
CADDIGAN, Daniel	22	M	Laborer	05Ma14Bj
Maurice	18	M	Laborer	05Ma14Bj
Edmund	15	M	Laborer	05Ma14Bj
Johanna	20	F	Laborer	05Ma14Bj
Margt.	18	F	Laborer	05Ma14Bj
DUNNE, Margt.	30	F	Laborer	05Ma14Bj
Ellen	20	F	Laborer	05Ma14Bj
Cathe.	18	F	Laborer	05Ma14Bj
MURPHY, John	32	M	Laborer	05Ma14Bj
Robert	50	M	Laborer	05Ma14Bj
DESMOND, Ellen	24	F	Laborer	05Ma14Bj
CRONIN, Philip	25	M	Laborer	05Ma14Bj
Daniel	22	M	Laborer	05Ma14Bj
SHEEHAN, John	45	M	Laborer	05Ma14Bj
HANNON, Margt.	40	F	Laborer	05Ma14Bj
Johanna	13	F	Laborer	05Ma14Bj
John	10	M	Laborer	05Ma14Bj
Pat	.00	M	Infant	05Ma14Bj
FLANNIGAN, John	24	M	Laborer	05Ma14Bj
BARRY, Cathe.	30	F	Laborer	05Ma14Bj
KENNY, Jude	30	F	Laborer	05Ma14Bj
GOGGIN, Magt.	26	F	Laborer	05Ma14Bj
LOONY, Pat	20	M	Laborer	05Ma14Bj
Anne	26	F	Laborer	05Ma14Bj
HEGARTHY, Pat	25	M	Laborer	05Ma14Bj
MURPHY, Michael	20	M	Laborer	05Ma14Bj
Johanna	55	F	Laborer	05Ma14Bj
Judy	22	F	Laborer	05Ma14Bj
Dan	18	M	Laborer	05Ma14Bj

NAMES OF PASSENGERS	AGE	SEX	OCCUPATIONS	DATE PORT SHIP
LINN, Timothy	27	M	Laborer	05Ma14Bj
KENIEFICK, Wm.	25	M	Laborer	05Ma14Bj
Mary	30	F	Laborer	05Ma14Bj
KEEFFE, James	20	M	Laborer	05Ma14Bj
MURPHY, John	18	M	Laborer	05Ma14Bj
DONNOGHUE, Jerry	40	M	Laborer	05Ma14Bj
Johanna	30	F	Laborer	05Ma14Bj
SULLIVAN, Cath.	38	F	Laborer	05Ma14Bj
Mary	13	F	Laborer	05Ma14Bj
Johanna	11	F	Laborer	05Ma14Bj
SPILLANE, Mary	31	F	Laborer	05Ma14Bj
Mary	03	F	Child	05Ma14Bj
CONNOR, Ellen	20	F	Laborer	05Ma14Bj
SPILLANE, Patk.	07	M	Child	05Ma14Bj
Johanna	05	F	Child	05Ma14Bj
HAYES, Mary	30	F	Laborer	05Ma14Bj
GEARY, Thomas	20	M	Laborer	05Ma14Bj
Cathe.	20	F	Laborer	05Ma14Bj
CLAVEEN, Margt.	25	F	Laborer	05Ma14Bj
DONOVAN, Lawrence	30	M	Laborer	05Ma14Bj
Johanna	24	F	Laborer	05Ma14Bj
NEIL, Abby	22	F	Laborer	05Ma14Bj
BIRMINGHAM, John	23	M	Laborer	05Ma14Bj
Michael	20	M	Laborer	05Ma14Bj
BARRY, Wm.	30	M	Laborer	05Ma14Bj
Garrett	21	M	Laborer	05Ma14Bj
Larry	20	M	Laborer	05Ma14Bj
John	20	M	Laborer	05Ma14Bj
HEFFERMAN, Pat	19	M	Laborer	05Ma14Bj
MCDONNELL, Mary	20	F	Laborer	05Ma14Bj
CLIFFORD, Mary	22	F	Laborer	05Ma14Bj
Johanna	20	F	Laborer	05Ma14Bj
PARKER, Ann	25	F	Laborer	05Ma14Bj
KINGSTON, Thomas	50	M	Laborer	05Ma14Bj
Thomas	18	M	Laborer	05Ma14Bj
Paul	14	M	Laborer	05Ma14Bj
Wm.	09	M	Child	05Ma14Bj
Rebecca	50	F	Laborer	05Ma14Bj
Sarah	11	F	Laborer	05Ma14Bj
GIBSON, Joseph	15	M	Laborer	05Ma14Bj
Isabella	17	F	Laborer	05Ma14Bj
Mary	13	F	Laborer	05Ma14Bj
James	03	M	Child	05Ma14Bj
CUSHMAN, Magt.	18	F	Laborer	05Ma14Bj
RINDAW, John	20	M	Laborer	05Ma14Bj
LINEHAN, Cornelius	36	M	Laborer	05Ma14Bj
Ellen	30	F	Laborer	05Ma14Bj
Cornelius	04	M	Child	05Ma14Bj
MURPHY, Mary	38	F	Laborer	05Ma14Bj
Bessy	26	F	Laborer	05Ma14Bj
WILLIS, Ann	20	F	Laborer	05Ma14Bj
MOLONEY, Jeremiah	21	M	Laborer	05Ma14Bj
BRION, David	30	M	Laborer	05Ma14Bj
CASEY, Mary-Ann	18	F	Laborer	05Ma14Bj
CRONIN, Timothy	22	M	Laborer	05Ma14Bj
FORREST, Edwd.	18	M	Laborer	05Ma14Bj
CONNOR, Thomas	47	M	Laborer	05Ma14Bj
Mary	24	F	Laborer	05Ma14Bj
COLLINS, Betty	47	F	Laborer	05Ma14Bj
TOBIN, Michael	30	M	Laborer	05Ma14Bj
MURPHY, Mary	38	F	Laborer	05Ma14Bj
Margt.	.00	F	Infant	05Ma14Bj
James	07	M	Child	05Ma14Bj
Daniel	.00	M	Infant	05Ma14Bj
MALONEY, John	30	M	Laborer	05Ma14Bj
U	.00	M	Infant	05Ma14Bj
STAMMEY, Anne	14	F	Laborer	05Ma14Bj
Emily	18	F	Laborer	05Ma14Bj

MEDIATOR 05 MAY 1848

From London

NAMES OF PASSENGERS	AGE	SEX	OCCUPATIONS	DATE PORT SHIP
BURKE, Edwd.	29	M	Butcher	05Ma21Dt
John	23	M	Engineer	05Ma21Dt
Eliza	20	F	Dressmaker	05Ma21Dt

JENNY-LIND 06 MAY 1848

From Liverpool

NAMES OF PASSENGERS		AGE	SEX	OCCUPATIONS	DATE PORT SHIP
HEFFERNAN, Michl.		35	M	Laborer	06Ma02Ak
DILLON, Martin		45	M	Laborer	06Ma02Ak
Cath.		40	F	Laborer	06Ma02Ak
Pat		07	M	Child	06Ma02Ak
GIBBONS, James		30	M	Laborer	06Ma02Ak
MCGUIRE, Pat		30	M	Laborer	06Ma02Ak
BRENNAN, Edwd.		25	M	Laborer	06Ma02Ak
OBRIEN, Michl.		20	M	Laborer	06Ma02Ak
BRENNAN, Honor		21	F	Laborer	06Ma02Ak
Cathe.		02	F	Child	06Ma02Ak
Eliza		.00	F	Infant	06Ma02Ak
BURKE, Bridgt.		20	F	Laborer	06Ma02Ak
SHERRY, Hugh		45	M	Laborer	06Ma02Ak
Mary		40	F	Laborer	06Ma02Ak
Michl.		18	M	Laborer	06Ma02Ak
Francis		45	F	Laborer	06Ma02Ak
DUFFEY, Peter		48	M	Laborer	06Ma02Ak
Ellen		14	F	Laborer	06Ma02Ak
CRAWFORD, Richd.		40	M	Laborer	06Ma02Ak
U	(W)	35	F	Wife	06Ma02Ak
Letetia	(D)	15	F	Laborer	06Ma02Ak
William	(S)	17	M	Laborer	06Ma02Ak
John	(S)	13	M	Laborer	06Ma02Ak
Isabella	(D)	11	F	Laborer	06Ma02Ak
Francis-Ann	(D)	05	F	Child	06Ma02Ak
Joseph	(S)	02	M	Child	06Ma02Ak
Richd.	(S)	.00	M	Infant	06Ma02Ak
DELANEY, James		26	M	Laborer	06Ma02Ak
Sarah		21	F	Laborer	06Ma02Ak
DUNN, James		28	M	Laborer	06Ma02Ak
CAVANAGH, James		30	M	Laborer	06Ma02Ak
Margt.		23	F	Laborer	06Ma02Ak
SHEALEY, Mary		20	F	Laborer	06Ma02Ak
FIELDING, Ann		20	F	Laborer	06Ma02Ak
CARR, Walter		30	M	Laborer	06Ma02Ak
REILLY, Thomas		24	M	Laborer	06Ma02Ak
MCVEIGH, Henry		22	M	Laborer	06Ma02Ak
OHEARN, Michl.		40	M	Laborer	06Ma02Ak
U	(W)	35	F	Wife	06Ma02Ak
Pat		20	M	Laborer	06Ma02Ak
Lawrence		.00	M	Infant	06Ma02Ak
CULL, Danl.		25	M	Laborer	06Ma02Ak
MCMANUS, Pat		19	M	Laborer	06Ma02Ak
MCAVERY, James		17	M	Laborer	06Ma02Ak
Cathe.		13	F	Laborer	06Ma02Ak
ROGERS, John		18	M	Laborer	06Ma02Ak
Ellen		21	F	Laborer	06Ma02Ak
RICE, James		50	M	Laborer	06Ma02Ak
U	(W)	55	F	Wife	06Ma02Ak
Owen		22	M	Laborer	06Ma02Ak
Ann		21	F	Laborer	06Ma02Ak

NAMES OF PASSENGERS		AGE	SEX	OCCUPATIONS	DATE PORT SHIP
RICE, Alice		13	F	Laborer	06Ma02Ak
B.		11	M	Laborer	06Ma02Ak
Johnny		07	M	Child	06Ma02Ak
Mary		02	F	Child	06Ma02Ak
MCGUIRE, Pat		21	M	Laborer	06Ma02Ak
BELTON, Pat		40	M	Laborer	06Ma02Ak
Mary		19	F	Laborer	06Ma02Ak
Ann		15	F	Laborer	06Ma02Ak
Eliza		13	F	Laborer	06Ma02Ak
Richd.		09	M	Child	06Ma02Ak
KING, Michl.		20	M	Laborer	06Ma02Ak
LOFTIS, Michl.		26	M	Laborer	06Ma02Ak
Mary		22	F	Laborer	06Ma02Ak
KING, Cathr.		18	F	Laborer	06Ma02Ak
MADDEN, Owen		17	M	Laborer	06Ma02Ak
KING, Nancy		09	F	Child	06Ma02Ak
LOFTIS, Maria		.00	F	Infant	06Ma02Ak
CAFFREY, James		22	M	Laborer	06Ma02Ak
Jane		20	F	Laborer	06Ma02Ak
FITZPATRICK, Michl.		50	M	Laborer	06Ma02Ak
FARRELL, John		22	M	Laborer	06Ma02Ak
STEWART, Andw.		39	M	Laborer	06Ma02Ak
OCONNOR, Ann		22	F	Laborer	06Ma02Ak
Margt.		20	F	Laborer	06Ma02Ak
MCGRATH, James		29	M	Laborer	06Ma02Ak
MCCANN, John		30	M	Laborer	06Ma02Ak
ROONEY, Thomas		29	M	Laborer	06Ma02Ak
FINNEGAN, Margt.		20	F	Laborer	06Ma02Ak
DUFFY, Judy		21	F	Laborer	06Ma02Ak
FARRELL, James		09	M	Child	06Ma02Ak
NAUGHTON, Isaac		19	M	Laborer	06Ma02Ak
KENNY, Darby		23	M	Laborer	06Ma02Ak
SHANDEY, John		22	M	Laborer	06Ma02Ak
TROY, Mat.		40	M	Laborer	06Ma02Ak
WOODHOUSE, Geo.		30	M	Laborer	06Ma02Ak
MATHEWMAN, Nathan		26	M	Laborer	06Ma02Ak
ORCORAN, Henry		30	M	Laborer	06Ma02Ak
FITZSIMMONS, Ann		23	F	Laborer	06Ma02Ak
HORAN, Kernan		30	M	Laborer	06Ma02Ak
Pat		24	M	Laborer	06Ma02Ak
ODONNELL, James		20	M	Laborer	06Ma02Ak
WALSH, Thos.		37	M	Laborer	06Ma02Ak
DOWNEY, Martin		13	M	Laborer	06Ma02Ak
SHERRY, Terence		42	M	Laborer	06Ma02Ak
FRAWLEY, Thos.		29	M	Laborer	06Ma02Ak
RUSSELL, Thos.		05	M	Child	06Ma02Ak
SULLIVAN, Michl.		26	M	Laborer	06Ma02Ak
Michl.		40	M	Laborer	06Ma02Ak
MURPHY, Pat		28	M	Laborer	06Ma02Ak
TIERNAN, Mary		20	F	Laborer	06Ma02Ak
MURPHY, Mary		20	F	Laborer	06Ma02Ak
HALLORAN, Bessey		20	F	Laborer	06Ma02Ak
BRIEN, James		20	M	Laborer	06Ma02Ak
TOOHEY, Thomas		23	M	Laborer	06Ma02Ak
BERRIGAN, Martin		24	M	Laborer	06Ma02Ak
POWER, Pat		20	M	Laborer	06Ma02Ak
U	(W)	20	F	Wife	06Ma02Ak
HARE, John		35	M	Gentleman	06Ma02Ak
FRENCH, Patk.		45	M	Gentleman	06Ma02Ak
Cathr.	(W)	40	F	Wife	06Ma02Ak
Cathr.	(D)	06	F	Child	06Ma02Ak
Mary-Ann	(D)	04	F	Child	06Ma02Ak
Peirce	(S)	02	M	Child	06Ma02Ak

FINGAL 06 MAY 1848

From Liverpool

NAMES OF PASSENGERS	AGE	SEX	OCCUPATIONS	DATE PORT SHIP
RANKIN, Samuel-S.	23	M	Merchant	06Ma02Al
THOMPSON, David	30	M	Publican	06Ma02Al
GRANT, James	28	M	Tailor	06Ma02Al
FLAVIN, John	22	M	Farmer	06Ma02Al
RYANS, Charles	24	M	Gentleman	06Ma02Al
MOORE, Joseph	48	M	Doctor	06Ma02Al
John	24	M	Unknown	06Ma02Al
Joseph	13	M	Unknown	06Ma02Al
Ellon	17	F	Unknown	06Ma02Al
Margrt.	16	F	Unknown	06Ma02Al
MAGUIRE, Mary	16	F	Spinster	06Ma02Al
MADDEN, Elizabeth	20	F	Spinster	06Ma02Al
REID, Arthur	41	M	Farmer	06Ma02Al
STEPHEN, Mary-Jane	23	F	Spinster	06Ma02Al
ARMSTRONG, Elizabeth	25	F	Spinster	06Ma02Al
HURRY, William	24	M	Laborer	06Ma02Al
GLEMMENY, James	30	M	Laborer	06Ma02Al
KELLY, Thomas	25	M	Laborer	06Ma02Al
OWENS, Thomas	26	M	Shoemaker	06Ma02Al
OLIVES, Chas.	17	M	Laborer	06Ma02Al
RYON, James	33	M	Unknown	06Ma02Al
OLLIVES, Margret	29	F	Unknown	06Ma02Al
MATHEWS, John	27	M	Unknown	06Ma02Al
Helen	38	F	Unknown	06Ma02Al
MARTIN, Ann	30	F	Unknown	06Ma02Al
Cathn.	.00	F	Infant	06Ma02Al
SULLIVAN, Margret	19	F	Unknown	06Ma02Al
WARD, James	07	M	Child	06Ma02Al
KARNEY, Patrick	20	M	Laborer	06Ma02Al
MARTIN, Patk.	22	M	Laborer	06Ma02Al
SEVELL, Jane	26	F	Spinster	06Ma02Al
MCCARDELL, Patrick	25	M	Clerk	06Ma02Al
Dinnes	25	M	Shoemaker	06Ma02Al
Mary	19	F	Spinster	06Ma02Al
MURPHEY, James	29	M	Joiner	06Ma02Al
MILDOWN, Bryan	21	M	Laborer	06Ma02Al
BENNETT, John	23	M	Smith	06Ma02Al
RATTIGAN, Lewis	32	M	Laborer	06Ma02Al
RAYNOLDS, Edward	27	M	Laborer	06Ma02Al
ODONNAGHY, Hanna	25	F	Spinster	06Ma02Al
DOYEL, Mary	17	F	Spinster	06Ma02Al
WHALING, Margt.	18	F	Spinster	06Ma02Al
ONEILL, Morton	38	M	Laborer	06Ma02Al
Morton	12	M	Unknown	06Ma02Al
WHALING, John	21	M	Joiner	06Ma02Al
KANE, Michael	24	M	Laborer	06Ma02Al
LONERGAN, James	24	M	Farmer	06Ma02Al
CONNELY, John	25	M	Laborer	06Ma02Al
BYWATERS, James	27	M	Laborer	06Ma02Al
HARNEY, Margrett	25	F	Spinster	06Ma02Al
KANE, Margrett	24	F	Spinster	06Ma02Al
DORSEY, Margrett	26	F	Spinster	06Ma02Al
GOODWIN, John	38	M	Tailor	06Ma02Al
MCNOTTY, John	14	M	Tailor	06Ma02Al
FINLAY, James	28	M	Laborer	06Ma02Al
Catherin	20	F	Unknown	06Ma02Al
ONAIL, James	13	M	Unknown	06Ma02Al
CASSIDY, Laurance	25	M	Farmer	06Ma02Al
GORMAN, Michael	29	M	Joiner	06Ma02Al
Catherin	30	F	Spinster	06Ma02Al
SMYTH, Michael	30	M	Laborer	06Ma02Al
COMMINS, Marck	30	M	Carpenter	06Ma02Al
Bridget	28	F	Unknown	06Ma02Al
Mary-Ann	.00	F	Infant	06Ma02Al
Elizabeth	.00	F	Infant	06Ma02Al

NAMES OF PASSENGERS		AGE	SEX	OCCUPATIONS	DATE PORT SHIP
GIERY, Margret		34	F	Spinster	06Ma02AI
CLYENE, James		15	M	Laborer	06Ma02AI
Danial		12	M	Laborer	06Ma02AI
Thos.		07	M	Child	06Ma02AI
Mary		09	F	Child	06Ma02AI
GARREY, Ellen		20	F	Spinster	06Ma02AI
MCKAVER, Michael		21	M	Laborer	06Ma02AI
ROGAN, Hennery		22	M	Laborer	06Ma02AI
SANDS, James		22	M	Laborer	06Ma02AI
TOOL, John		21	M	Laborer	06Ma02AI
U, Ann		20	F	Spinster	06Ma02AI
ROGAN, Ann		20	F	Spinster	06Ma02AI
MCGINN, Mary		34	F	Spinster	06Ma02AI
Ann		05	F	Child	06Ma02AI
Allice		03	F	Child	06Ma02AI
Mary		.00	F	Infant	06Ma02AI
CASSIDAY, Edward		18	M	Laborer	06Ma02AI
James		14	M	Unknown	06Ma02AI
Peter		09	M	Child	06Ma02AI
MILES, Lawrence		19	M	Laborer	06Ma02AI
CASSIDY, Margret		54	F	Spinster	06Ma02AI
Scerah		11	F	Unknown	06Ma02AI
Mary		13	F	Unknown	06Ma02AI
Terressa		29	F	Spinster	06Ma02AI
BURNS, Mary		19	F	Spinster	06Ma02AI
CALLAND, Elizabeth		20	F	Spinster	06Ma02AI
GALLAGHER, John		19	M	Cooper	06Ma02AI
Thos.		15	M	Laborer	06Ma02AI
Janet		21	F	Spinster	06Ma02AI
MEE, Ann		24	F	Spinster	06Ma02AI
Ellon		22	F	Spinster	06Ma02AI
HAMMILL, Mary		22	F	Spinster	06Ma02AI
MAREN, Owen		.00	M	Infant	06Ma02AI
BURGES, Owen		21	M	Laborer	06Ma02AI
James		19	M	Laborer	06Ma02AI
FELEY, James		22	M	Laborer	06Ma02AI
CROTTY, John		15	M	Laborer	06Ma02AI
Thos.		25	M	Laborer	06Ma02AI
Michael		23	M	Laborer	06Ma02AI
Thos.Jnr.		10	M	Laborer	06Ma02AI
Ellen		44	F	Unknown	06Ma02AI
Bridget		15	F	Spinster	06Ma02AI
Margrett		22	F	Spinster	06Ma02AI
Elizabeth		19	F	Spinster	06Ma02AI
Hanna		11	F	Spinster	06Ma02AI
KANE, John		33	M	Laborer	06Ma02AI
Stephon		18	M	Laborer	06Ma02AI
MULLALY, Rorey		23	M	Laborer	06Ma02AI
John		21	M	Laborer	06Ma02AI
DOWD, Martan		22	M	Laborer	06Ma02AI
FOUGHLIN, Tim		21	M	Laborer	06Ma02AI
LAWLER, Michael		28	M	Laborer	06Ma02AI
Seragh		18	F	Spinster	06Ma02AI
Mary		15	F	Spinster	06Ma02AI
CROSSGROVE, John		35	M	Farmer	06Ma02AI
FAGAN, John		18	M	Laborer	06Ma02AI
GAFFNEY, Alexander		25	M	Laborer	06Ma02AI
FEGAN, John		45	M	Farmer	06Ma02AI
Edward	(S)	09	M	Child	06Ma02AI
Margret	(W)	46	F	Wife	06Ma02AI
Bridget		28	F	Spinster	06Ma02AI
Margrett		25	F	Spinster	06Ma02AI
Mary		22	F	Spinster	06Ma02AI
COTT, Maria		17	F	Spinster	06Ma02AI
SLATTERY, Bridgett		16	F	Spinster	06Ma02AI
MADDEN, Roze		20	F	Spinster	06Ma02AI
EGAN, Thos.		22	M	Farmer	06Ma02AI
Laurance		19	M	Farmer	06Ma02AI
Patrick		16	M	Laborer	06Ma02AI
BYRNE, John		21	M	Laborer	06Ma02AI
Mary		22	F	Spinster	06Ma02AI
Elizabeth		15	F	Spinster	06Ma02AI
TRACY, Mary		50	F	Wi	06Ma02AI
Margret		21	F	Spinster	06Ma02AI
FLIN, Patrick		32	M	Farmer	06Ma02AI
BARRETT, John		27	M	Gdnr	06Ma02AI
MULLINE, Owen		22	M	Farmer	06Ma02AI
Catherine		48	F	Unknown	06Ma02AI
CONNER, Mary		19	F	Spinster	06Ma02AI
BARRETT, Margrett		25	F	Spinster	06Ma02AI
FLIN, Hanna		30	F	Cook	06Ma02AI
Julia		28	F	Spinster	06Ma02AI
KEEFFE, Ellan		18	F	Spinster	06Ma02AI
ALLEN, Michael		30	M	Laborer	06Ma02AI
ENGLISH, Michael		22	M	Laborer	06Ma02AI
SYNOTT, Phillip		24	M	Carpenter	06Ma02AI
ALLEN, Scera		26	F	Unknown	06Ma02AI
MULLIGAN, Mary		60	F	Wi	06Ma02AI
Shusan		29	F	Spinster	06Ma02AI
William		17	M	Tailor	06Ma02AI
HELAPEN, William		35	M	Laborer	06Ma02AI
LYANS, James		25	M	Shoemaker	06Ma02AI
HICKEY, Patk.		40	M	Laborer	06Ma02AI
Patk.Jnr.	(S)	05	M	Child	06Ma02AI
Bridgett	(W)	38	F	Wife	06Ma02AI
BURN, Wm.		36	M	Laborer	06Ma02AI
GORE, Mathew		25	M	Laborer	06Ma02AI
NOTTIN, Michael		23	M	Laborer	06Ma02AI
LEDWIG, Thos.		22	M	Laborer	06Ma02AI
Mary		28	F	Spinster	06Ma02AI
MARESY, Patrick		25	M	Laborer	06Ma02AI
BRYON, William		30	M	Laborer	06Ma02AI
MARESY, Catherine		30	F	Wife	06Ma02AI
SHIELD, Patrick		43	M	Laborer	06Ma02AI
MILLER, John		40	M	Cbtmkr	06Ma02AI
HUGHES, Patk.		25	M	Laborer	06Ma02AI
BUCKLEY, Smyth		24	M	Tailor	06Ma02AI
MCLINDAN, Patk.		24	M	Carpenter	06Ma02AI
SHIELD, Ann		16	F	Spinster	06Ma02AI
CORNER, Patrick		26	M	Laborer	06Ma02AI
CONNELLY, Patrick		26	M	Laborer	06Ma02AI
Catherina	(W)	25	F	Wife	06Ma02AI
MORRAN, Patk.		25	M	Laborer	06Ma02AI
BARKLEY, Michael		26	M	Laborer	06Ma02AI
HODSON, James		21	M	Laborer	06Ma02AI
LINDSAY, William		21	M	Tailor	06Ma02AI
HOYE, James		19	M	Spinner	06Ma02AI
HIGGINS, Thos.		19	M	Laborer	06Ma02AI
BURKE, Edwd.		20	M	Gdnr	06Ma02AI
BRYON, Ann		19	F	Spinster	06Ma02AI
DAILEY, Margrett		16	F	Spinster	06Ma02AI
HANDLEY, Ann		18	F	Spinster	06Ma02AI
MAYERS, Lewis		30	M	Farmer	06Ma02AI
Thomas	(S)	04	M	Child	06Ma02AI
John	(S)	.00	M	Infant	06Ma02AI
Margrett	(W)	25	F	Wife	06Ma02AI
MURPHY, Edward		20	M	Laborer	06Ma02AI
MACHAR, Jno.		20	M	Laborer	06Ma02AI
ROYN, Edward		23	M	Laborer	06Ma02AI
LATNEY, Samuel		18	M	Laborer	06Ma02AI
Michael		12	M	Unknown	06Ma02AI
Thos.		10	M	Unknown	06Ma02AI
FAUMELY, Edward		22	M	Carpenter	06Ma02AI
GLEESON, Danial		30	M	Laborer	06Ma02AI
LONG, Jeremia		21	M	Laborer	06Ma02AI
GLEESON, Juda-Mrs.		26	F	Wife	06Ma02AI
Mary		18	F	Spinster	06Ma02AI
Judy		17	F	Spinster	06Ma02AI
MCCALL, Margrett		18	F	Spinster	06Ma02AI
MCNOLAND, Patk.		32	M	Laborer	06Ma02AI
FLAMMIN, James		39	M	Sawer	06Ma02AI
MCCORMICK, Ann-Mrs.		26	F	Wife	06Ma02AI
HOLLARN, Judy		30	F	Wife	06Ma02AI
Judy		10	F	Spinster	06Ma02AI
KATING, Ellon		08	F	Child	06Ma02AI
Richd.		50	M	Farmer	06Ma02AI
Norah		40	F	Wife	06Ma02AI
Martan	(B)	.00	M	Infant	06Ma02AI
Wm.		.00	M	Infant	06Ma02AI
Kathering		14	F	Spinster	06Ma02AI

NAMES OF PASSENGERS		AGE	SEX	OCCUPATIONS	DATE PORT SHIP
KATING, Mary		16	F	Spinster	06Ma02Al
RYAN, Margret		19	F	Spinster	06Ma02Al
DYRS, Thos.		25	M	Laborer	06Ma02Al
MULLY, Jno.		23	M	Laborer	06Ma02Al
BARDON, Allise		19	F	Spinster	06Ma02Al
GREEN, Ellon		20	F	Spinster	06Ma02Al
SMYTH, Bernard		25	M	Shoemaker	06Ma02Al
MCCOLL, Michael		20	M	Shoemaker	06Ma02Al
Thos.		21	M	Laborer	06Ma02Al
MOORE, Robt.		22	M	Gdnr	06Ma02Al
SCOTT, James		26	M	Cldrs	06Ma02Al

NEW-ZEALAND 06 MAY 1848

From Newry

NAMES OF PASSENGERS		AGE	SEX	OCCUPATIONS	DATE PORT SHIP
DEVLIN, Samuel		31	M	Servant	06Ma19Aq
ROSS, Joseph		28	M	Laborer	06Ma19Aq
ONEIL, Francis		33	M	Farmer	06Ma19Aq
KERR, John		18	M	Ploughman	06Ma19Aq
ANDERSON, William		25	M	Laborer	06Ma19Aq
MCSHANE, Catherine		21	F	Seamstress	06Ma19Aq
Susan		18	F	Seamstress	06Ma19Aq
SCOTT, James		38	M	Farmer	06Ma19Aq
Jane	(W)	36	F	Wife	06Ma19Aq
Mary	(D)	14	F	Unknown	06Ma19Aq
Elizabeth	(D)	12	F	Unknown	06Ma19Aq
Ellen	(D)	11	F	Unknown	06Ma19Aq
Jane	(D)	09	F	Child	06Ma19Aq
WHITEMAN, John		45	M	Farmer	06Ma19Aq
Margaret	(W)	40	F	Wife	06Ma19Aq
John	(S)	19	M	Unknown	06Ma19Aq
Mary-Jane	(D)	17	F	Unknown	06Ma19Aq
Betty-Ann	(D)	15	F	Unknown	06Ma19Aq
William	(S)	12	M	Unknown	06Ma19Aq
MCCANN, Thomas		33	M	Laborer	06Ma19Aq
Ann	(W)	30	F	Wife	06Ma19Aq
MCVEIGH, Eliza		06	F	Child	06Ma19Aq
HENRY, Thomas		31	M	Farmer	06Ma19Aq
Rose	(W)	28	F	Wife	06Ma19Aq
Andrew		26	M	None	06Ma19Aq
Rose		62	F	None	06Ma19Aq
Ann		22	F	None	06Ma19Aq
Bernard		18	M	None	06Ma19Aq
Patrick		15	M	None	06Ma19Aq
Lawrence		13	M	None	06Ma19Aq
Peter		.02	M	Infant	06Ma19Aq
Bridget		26	F	Spinster	06Ma19Aq
MCALISTER, Dennis		41	M	Laborer	06Ma19Aq
Jane	(W)	38	F	Wife	06Ma19Aq
Maria	(D)	05	F	Child	06Ma19Aq
John	(S)	.04	M	Infant	06Ma19Aq
MCKEWN, Michael		22	M	Unknown	06Ma19Aq
CONNOR, Patt.		27	M	Laborer	06Ma19Aq
CARROLL, Bernard		28	M	Servant	06Ma19Aq
LEE, Fanny		48	F	Spinster	06Ma19Aq
John	(S)	17	M	Unknown	06Ma19Aq
Margaret	(D)	19	F	Unknown	06Ma19Aq
Jane	(D)	15	F	Unknown	06Ma19Aq
Wm.	(S)	11	M	Unknown	06Ma19Aq
MCPARTLAND, William		30	M	Servant	06Ma19Aq
CARR, Ann		24	F	Seamstress	06Ma19Aq
MURPHY, Mary		23	F	Spinster	06Ma19Aq
BOYLE, Michael		38	M	Farmer	06Ma19Aq
Margaret	(W)	36	F	Wife	06Ma19Aq
Patt.	(S)	12	M	Unknown	06Ma19Aq
Michael	(S)	11	M	Unknown	06Ma19Aq
Mary	(D)	10	F	Unknown	06Ma19Aq
Rose	(D)	09	F	Child	06Ma19Aq
BOYLE, Alicia	(D)	08	F	Child	06Ma19Aq
Betty	(D)	07	F	Child	06Ma19Aq
John	(S)	06	M	Child	06Ma19Aq
Rose	(D)	04	F	Child	06Ma19Aq
CALDWELL, Robert		34	M	Ploughman	06Ma19Aq
MCKEWN, Peter		29	M	Laborer	06Ma19Aq
Bridgit		27	F	Servant	06Ma19Aq
MURPHY, Patrick		55	M	Farmer	06Ma19Aq
Margaret	(W)	48	F	Wife	06Ma19Aq
Edward	(S)	22	M	Unknown	06Ma19Aq
Margaret	(D)	19	F	Unknown	06Ma19Aq
Patrick	(S)	18	M	Unknown	06Ma19Aq
Mary	(D)	13	F	Unknown	06Ma19Aq
John	(S)	12	M	Unknown	06Ma19Aq
James	(S)	10	M	Unknown	06Ma19Aq
Michael	(S)	09	M	Child	06Ma19Aq
Anne	(D)	08	F	Child	06Ma19Aq
HANLON, Redmond		33	M	Farmer	06Ma19Aq
FREEBORN, John		29	M	Servant	06Ma19Aq
PIPER, Adam		25	M	Ploughman	06Ma19Aq
MCKEVER, James		27	M	Farmer	06Ma19Aq
Catherine		26	F	Spinster	06Ma19Aq
Mary		18	F	None	06Ma19Aq
James		16	M	None	06Ma19Aq
ONEIL, Margaret		18	F	Seamstress	06Ma19Aq
COYLE, Owen		35	M	Farmer	06Ma19Aq
Ellen	(W)	32	F	Wife	06Ma19Aq
Bernard	(S)	10	M	Unknown	06Ma19Aq
James	(S)	09	M	Child	06Ma19Aq
Mary	(D)	08	F	Child	06Ma19Aq
Rose	(D)	07	F	Child	06Ma19Aq
Margaret	(D)	06	F	Child	06Ma19Aq
LYNCHEY, Patt.		32	M	Gdnr	06Ma19Aq
MCENALLY, Margaret		20	F	Servant	06Ma19Aq
BOYLAN, Patrick		22	M	Laborer	06Ma19Aq
WALTERS, Mary		19	F	Spinster	06Ma19Aq
MEDOLE, Mary		25	F	Servant	06Ma19Aq
MURPHY, Eleanor		30	F	Seamstress	06Ma19Aq
HAROLD, Eleanor		24	F	Spinster	06Ma19Aq
MCDERMOTT, Peter		57	M	Land Agent	06Ma19Aq
Peggy	(W)	56	F	Wife	06Ma19Aq
Thomas		32	M	Laborer	06Ma19Aq
James		30	M	Laborer	06Ma19Aq
John		23	M	Servant	06Ma19Aq
Anne		21	F	Spinster	06Ma19Aq
Mary		18	F	Spinster	06Ma19Aq
Andrew		13	M	Servant	06Ma19Aq
CALLON, Bernard		29	M	Farmer	06Ma19Aq
Ann	(W)	27	F	Wife	06Ma19Aq
Biddy		20	F	Seamstress	06Ma19Aq
WHITE, Catherine		23	F	Servant	06Ma19Aq
Biddy		14	F	Servant	06Ma19Aq
PATTERSON, Ellen		25	F	Seamstress	06Ma19Aq
SEARIGHT, James		22	M	Shopkeeper	06Ma19Aq
Mary-Ann		21	F	None	06Ma19Aq
Maria		20	F	None	06Ma19Aq
GRIFFEN, Jackson		40	M	Painter	06Ma19Aq
Eliza	(W)	38	F	Wife	06Ma19Aq
Thomas	(S)	17	M	Painter	06Ma19Aq
MDKEWN, Andrew		30	M	Shopkeeper	06Ma19Aq
Mary-Ann		25	F	None	06Ma19Aq
Walter		18	M	None	06Ma19Aq
James		00	M	None	06Ma19Aq
Died-At-Sea					
MCCONVILL, Ellen		20	F	Servant	06Ma19Aq
Ellen		20	F	Servant	06Ma19Aq
MCKEWN, Patt.		30	M	Laborer	06Ma19Aq
WEIR, Henry		22	M	Servant	06Ma19Aq
QUINLEY, Susan		25	F	Spinster	06Ma19Aq
Ellen		.06	F	Infant	06Ma19Aq
Ann		18	F	None	06Ma19Aq
HARVEY, Patrick		27	M	Farmer	06Ma19Aq
Ellen		25	F	Spinster	06Ma19Aq
CAMPBELL, James		23	M	Laborer	06Ma19Aq
DALY, Philip		22	M	Ploughman	06Ma19Aq

NAMES OF PASSENGERS		AGE	SEX	OCCUPATIONS	DATE PORT SHIP
CARROLL, Patt.		28	M	Farmer	06Ma19Aq
MILLS, Elizabeth		24	F	Seamstress	06Ma19Aq
HANLON, Catherine		19	F	Seamstress	06Ma19Aq
DRUMGOOLE, Patt.		19	M	Laborer	06Ma19Aq
FERGUSON, Mary		18	F	Servant	06Ma19Aq
DONNOLLY, David		50	M	Land Agent	06Ma19Aq
LEE, James		35	M	Gdnr	06Ma19Aq
TREANOR, Rose		28	F	Spinster	06Ma19Aq
MURPHY, Margaret		19	F	Servant	06Ma19Aq
BURKE, Richard		33	M	Laborer	06Ma19Aq
Matilda		32	F	Seamstress	06Ma19Aq
Ellen		18	F	None	06Ma19Aq
Margaret		17	F	None	06Ma19Aq
Mary-Ann		16	F	None	06Ma19Aq
Esther		04	F	Child	06Ma19Aq
LACKEN, Mary		25	F	Spinster	06Ma19Aq
MACKEN, Terence		29	M	Laborer	06Ma19Aq
CLARKE, Thomas		34	M	Carpenter	06Ma19Aq
Eliza	(W)	30	F	Wife	06Ma19Aq
William-John	(S)	.03	M	Infant	06Ma19Aq
DONNOLLY, John		26	M	Farmer	06Ma19Aq
CARROLL, John		24	M	Ploughman	06Ma19Aq
WARD, John		40	M	Land Agent	06Ma19Aq
SWAIL, Ann		31	F	Spinster	06Ma19Aq
STEWART, Thomas		25	M	Laborer	06Ma19Aq
DONOHAN, Bridget		20	F	Servant	06Ma19Aq
WOODS, Thomas		18	M	Farmer	06Ma19Aq
TOAL, James		14	M	Servant	06Ma19Aq
SHIELDS, John		30	M	Miller	06Ma19Aq
Nancy		28	F	Unknown	06Ma19Aq
Mary		14	F	Seamstress	06Ma19Aq
KENNEDY, Hannah		29	F	Servant	06Ma19Aq
LAMB, Patrick		25	M	Laborer	06Ma19Aq
STEVENSON, Thomas		40	M	Laborer	06Ma19Aq
Elizabeth	(T)	30	F	Unknown	06Ma19Aq
John		25	M	Servant	06Ma19Aq
Rachel		.00	F	Infant	06Ma19Aq
Mary	(T)	10	F	Unknown	06Ma19Aq
MCCLURE, William		35	M	Wood Ranger	06Ma19Aq
Betty	(W)	36	F	Wife	06Ma19Aq
William		22	M	None	06Ma19Aq
Samuel		18	M	None	06Ma19Aq
Mary-Jane		17	F	None	06Ma19Aq
Eliza		14	F	None	06Ma19Aq
MAGILL, Jane		14	F	Servant	06Ma19Aq
William		01	M	Child	06Ma19Aq
GRANT, Hugh		45	M	Farmer	06Ma19Aq
Ann	(W)	39	F	Wife	06Ma19Aq
Sarah	(T)	24	F	Unknown	06Ma19Aq
MCALINDEN, Catherine		25	F	Spinster	06Ma19Aq
MCFARLAND, Jane		23	F	Spinster	06Ma19Aq
CAVANAGH, Catherine		23	F	Servant	06Ma19Aq
RATRILL, Catherine		20	F	Servant	06Ma19Aq
Ellen		08	F	Child	06Ma19Aq
Andrew		06	M	Child	06Ma19Aq
CONNOLLY, Phill.		22	M	Laborer	06Ma19Aq
DONNEY, Rose		20	F	Milliner	06Ma19Aq
MCSHANE, John		25	M	Farmer	06Ma19Aq
Mary-Ann	(W)	24	F	Wife	06Ma19Aq
DAVIDSON, Mary-Ann		30	F	Servant	06Ma19Aq
Elizabeth	(T)	28	F	Unknown	06Ma19Aq
RICHARDSON, Jane		19	F	Spinster	06Ma19Aq
MURPHY, John		27	M	Fmstwd	06Ma19Aq
DEVINE, Peter		72	M	Pouterer	06Ma19Aq
REILLY, Mary		59	F	Servant	06Ma19Aq
DEVINE, Richard		25	M	Servant	06Ma19Aq
Rose		18	F	None	06Ma19Aq
Patt.		22	M	None	06Ma19Aq
ARMSTRONG, Andrew		26	M	Ploughman	06Ma19Aq
Mary-Ann	(W)	35	F	Wife	06Ma19Aq
MARKS, Margaret		20	F	Servant	06Ma19Aq
Mary-Jane		.06	F	Infant	06Ma19Aq
HANLON, Mary		23	F	Spinster	06Ma19Aq
BOYLE, Mary-Ann		20	F	Seamstress	06Ma19Aq
DORAN, Arthur		50	M	Farmer	06Ma19Aq

NAMES OF PASSENGERS		AGE	SEX	OCCUPATIONS	DATE PORT SHIP
DORAN, Bernard	(S)	20	M	Unknown	06Ma19Aq
MCFARLAND, Rose		30	F	Servant	06Ma19Aq
DORAN, Michael		35	M	Farmer	06Ma19Aq
DEANNY, Nathan		40	M	Land Agent	06Ma19Aq
WHITEMAN, Eliza		40	F	Spinster	06Ma19Aq
MURPHY, Mary		25	F	Seamstress	06Ma19Aq
YOUNG, William		15	M	Servant	06Ma19Aq
HILL, James		40	M	Servant	06Ma19Aq
SMITH, George		35	M	Laborer	06Ma19Aq
Mary	(W)	32	F	Wife	06Ma19Aq
MCGRATH, Charles		30	M	Plough Man	06Ma19Aq
SMALL, Ann		22	F	Spinster	06Ma19Aq
KEARNEY, John		30	M	Servant	06Ma19Aq
BRADLY, Margaret		18	F	Servant	06Ma19Aq
ABBOTT, Edward		23	M	Farmer	06Ma19Aq
MCKEAVITT, Ann		20	F	Spinster	06Ma19Aq
COMESKY, Matthew		25	M	Laborer	06Ma19Aq

PRINCESS-ROYAL 06 MAY 1848

From Liverpool

NAMES OF PASSENGERS		AGE	SEX	OCCUPATIONS	DATE PORT SHIP
CAHILL, Bernard		20	M	Laborer	06Ma02Bs
MORE, Ned		20	M	Laborer	06Ma02Bs
IVERS, Ann		20	F	Laborer	06Ma02Bs
BEECHEN, John		20	M	Laborer	06Ma02Bs
NELSON, Louis		33	M	Laborer	06Ma02Bs
Mary		32	F	Laborer	06Ma02Bs
TUNCLIFFE, Jas.		22	M	Laborer	06Ma02Bs
Isaac		07	M	Child	06Ma02Bs
NELSON, Mary		.00	F	Infant	06Ma02Bs
RANKIN, Jas.		20	M	Laborer	06Ma02Bs
BOYLE, Jas.		20	M	Laborer	06Ma02Bs
MCCABE, Edwd.		20	M	Laborer	06Ma02Bs
MCGRATH, Mary		20	F	Laborer	06Ma02Bs
NEAL, Matthew		20	M	Laborer	06Ma02Bs
MALONEY, Thos.		20	M	Laborer	06Ma02Bs
Mary		20	F	Laborer	06Ma02Bs
IGO, Mary		40	F	Laborer	06Ma02Bs
Mary		24	F	Laborer	06Ma02Bs
BURKE, Mary		22	F	Laborer	06Ma02Bs
Bredget		15	F	Laborer	06Ma02Bs
Julia		16	F	Laborer	06Ma02Bs
Mary		18	F	Laborer	06Ma02Bs
HAREY, Edwd.		20	M	Laborer	06Ma02Bs
BRADY, Mary		20	F	Laborer	06Ma02Bs
GORMAN, Mary		18	F	Laborer	06Ma02Bs
CONNOR, Margt.		18	F	Laborer	06Ma02Bs
BARRETT, Andrew		40	M	Laborer	06Ma02Bs
Ann		38	F	Laborer	06Ma02Bs
Mary		16	F	Laborer	06Ma02Bs
Anna		15	F	Laborer	06Ma02Bs
Jno.		10	M	Laborer	06Ma02Bs
Biddy		08	F	Child	06Ma02Bs
BARNELLY, Andrew		40	M	Laborer	06Ma02Bs
Mary		15	F	Laborer	06Ma02Bs
BELSH, Edwd.		21	M	Laborer	06Ma02Bs
Bredget		13	F	Laborer	06Ma02Bs
DOHERTY, Cathe.		15	F	Laborer	06Ma02Bs
MAXWELL, Thos.		21	M	Laborer	06Ma02Bs
LARKIN, Jas.		20	M	Laborer	06Ma02Bs
Mary		21	F	Laborer	06Ma02Bs
Betty		18	F	Laborer	06Ma02Bs
RAWDEN, Pat		30	M	Laborer	06Ma02Bs
JERMAN, Mary		20	F	Laborer	06Ma02Bs
SMITH, Danl.		20	M	Laborer	06Ma02Bs
HANNEY, Michl.		29	M	Laborer	06Ma02Bs
U	(W)	29	F	Wife	06Ma02Bs
Margt.	(D)	09	F	Child	06Ma02Bs

NAMES OF PASSENGERS		AGE	SEX	OCCUPATIONS	DATE PORT SHIP
HANNEY, Pat	(S)	07	M	Child	06Ma02Bs
Edwd.	(S)	04	M	Child	06Ma02Bs
Jas.	(S)	.00	M	Infant	06Ma02Bs
THOMPSON, Eliza		26	F	Laborer	06Ma02Bs
NORWOOD, Hugh		20	M	Laborer	06Ma02Bs
INNERHAN, Andrew		24	M	Laborer	06Ma02Bs
JOHNSTON, C.D.		20	M	Laborer	06Ma02Bs
RAFFERTY, Richd.		27	M	Laborer	06Ma02Bs
GLENNAN, Pat		29	M	Laborer	06Ma02Bs
Christy		20	M	Laborer	06Ma02Bs
HORY, Bridget		20	F	Laborer	06Ma02Bs
MOONEY, Peter		20	M	Laborer	06Ma02Bs
GAFFNEY, Thos.		20	M	Laborer	06Ma02Bs
DUFFEY, Phil.		25	M	Laborer	06Ma02Bs
COY, Jno.		18	M	Laborer	06Ma02Bs
CAHILL, Mary		18	F	Laborer	06Ma02Bs
STAPLETON, Wm.		56	M	Laborer	06Ma02Bs
SMITH, Owen		30	M	Laborer	06Ma02Bs
Ann		24	F	Laborer	06Ma02Bs
SHEVELL, Rob.		21	M	Laborer	06Ma02Bs
Sarah		.00	F	Infant	06Ma02Bs
THOMAS, Philip		30	M	Laborer	06Ma02Bs
MOONEY, Jas.		30	M	Laborer	06Ma02Bs
Wm.		17	M	Laborer	06Ma02Bs
BRYAN, Margt.		21	F	Laborer	06Ma02Bs
Ellen		24	F	Laborer	06Ma02Bs
CONNOR, Jas.		20	M	Laborer	06Ma02Bs
MCMAHON, Arthur		20	M	Laborer	06Ma02Bs
FARRELL, Ann		35	F	Laborer	06Ma02Bs
QUINN, Biddy		30	F	Laborer	06Ma02Bs
Mary		20	F	Laborer	06Ma02Bs
Margt.		18	F	Laborer	06Ma02Bs
Jane		13	F	Laborer	06Ma02Bs
HURD, Jno.		20	M	Laborer	06Ma02Bs
SULLIVAN, Jerry		26	M	Laborer	06Ma02Bs
Ellen		19	F	Laborer	06Ma02Bs
OCONNOR, Ellen		60	F	Laborer	06Ma02Bs
Jane		23	F	Laborer	06Ma02Bs
MCDONOUGH, Jas.		71	M	Laborer	06Ma02Bs
Ellen		65	F	Laborer	06Ma02Bs
Michl.		45	M	Laborer	06Ma02Bs
Nancy		30	F	Laborer	06Ma02Bs
Chas.		23	M	Laborer	06Ma02Bs
Fanny		20	F	Laborer	06Ma02Bs
SUTTON, Wm.		23	M	Laborer	06Ma02Bs
Alx.		21	M	Laborer	06Ma02Bs
MCGOVERN, Jas.		21	M	Laborer	06Ma02Bs
NEAL, Bessy		24	F	Laborer	06Ma02Bs
MULLEN, Peter		23	M	Laborer	06Ma02Bs
HARK, Bessy		26	F	Laborer	06Ma02Bs
GORMAN, Jas.		50	M	Laborer	06Ma02Bs
Margt.		40	F	Laborer	06Ma02Bs
Patt.		15	M	Laborer	06Ma02Bs
Jno.		15	M	Laborer	06Ma02Bs
Eliza		11	F	Laborer	06Ma02Bs
WALSH, Jas.		21	M	Laborer	06Ma02Bs
EGAN, Margt.		25	F	Laborer	06Ma02Bs
DEVANY, Eliza		23	F	Laborer	06Ma02Bs
GORDAN, Jas.		26	M	Laborer	06Ma02Bs
Cathe.		24	F	Laborer	06Ma02Bs
MORAN, Bridget		21	F	Laborer	06Ma02Bs
ROWLAND, Pat		30	M	Laborer	06Ma02Bs
FARRELL, Francis		25	M	Laborer	06Ma02Bs
SEXTON, Mary		18	F	Laborer	06Ma02Bs
MANGAN, Wm.		20	M	Laborer	06Ma02Bs
RYAN, Danl.		22	M	Laborer	06Ma02Bs
Pat		19	M	Laborer	06Ma02Bs
Cathe.		21	F	Laborer	06Ma02Bs
DARCY, Mary		21	F	Laborer	06Ma02Bs
FRANKLIN, Thos.		18	M	Laborer	06Ma02Bs
BARRET, Pat		15	M	Laborer	06Ma02Bs
MORGAN, Mary		14	F	Laborer	06Ma02Bs
ENGLISH, Mary		14	F	Laborer	06Ma02Bs
Michl.		11	M	Laborer	06Ma02Bs
DUFFY, Alice		20	F	Laborer	06Ma02Bs

NAMES OF PASSENGERS	AGE	SEX	OCCUPATIONS	DATE PORT SHIP
DUFFY, Ann	18	F	Laborer	06Ma02Bs
FLEMING, Bridget	20	F	Laborer	06Ma02Bs
CLARK, Sarah	24	F	Laborer	06Ma02Bs
CAHILL, Cathe.	20	C	Laborer	06Ma02Bs
Mary	20	C	Laborer	06Ma02Bs
KEATING, Jas.	40	M	Laborer	06Ma02Bs
QUIGLEY, Thos.	26	M	Laborer	06Ma02Bs
Mary	20	F	Laborer	06Ma02Bs
Margt.	.00	F	Infant	06Ma02Bs
ROW, Lawce.	20	M	Smith	06Ma02Bs
Matthew	04	M	Child	06Ma02Bs
CASSIDY, Barney	22	M	Laborer	06Ma02Bs
Susan	24	F	Laborer	06Ma02Bs
HENRY, Richd.	20	M	Laborer	06Ma02Bs
Richd.	20	M	Laborer	06Ma02Bs
KELLISHER, Margt.	20	F	Laborer	06Ma02Bs
MCGOVERN, Phillip	19	M	Laborer	06Ma02Bs
CARROLL, Math.	20	M	Laborer	06Ma02Bs
Thos.	18	M	Laborer	06Ma02Bs
BAKER, Ann	30	F	Laborer	06Ma02Bs
Ann	11	F	Laborer	06Ma02Bs
Walter	09	M	Child	06Ma02Bs
Mark	04	M	Child	06Ma02Bs
SURON, Wm.	28	M	Laborer	06Ma02Bs
Mary-Ann	26	F	Laborer	06Ma02Bs
Rebecca	08	F	Child	06Ma02Bs
BRADY, Julia	40	F	Laborer	06Ma02Bs
Hugh	30	M	Laborer	06Ma02Bs
Jno.	20	M	Laborer	06Ma02Bs
Ann	19	F	Laborer	06Ma02Bs
BROGAN, Mary	20	F	Laborer	06Ma02Bs
MULVEY, Pat	21	M	Laborer	06Ma02Bs
BERGES, Jos.	26	M	Laborer	06Ma02Bs
CONNELL, Jno.	30	M	Laborer	06Ma02Bs
HUSKEY, Michl.	35	M	Laborer	06Ma02Bs
Jno.	30	M	Laborer	06Ma02Bs
Jno.	13	M	Laborer	06Ma02Bs
Wm.	10	M	Laborer	06Ma02Bs
Thos.	06	M	Child	06Ma02Bs
Cathe.	04	F	Child	06Ma02Bs
Pat	.00	M	Infant	06Ma02Bs
RYAN, Jas.	30	M	Laborer	06Ma02Bs
MARTIN, Michl.	17	M	Laborer	06Ma02Bs
HICKEY, Biddy	26	F	Laborer	06Ma02Bs
Theresa	10	F	Laborer	06Ma02Bs
Mary	07	F	Child	06Ma02Bs
Cathe.	04	F	Child	06Ma02Bs
MALON, Thos.	22	M	Laborer	06Ma02Bs
KILLFOYLE, Chas.	30	M	Laborer	06Ma02Bs
Julia	28	F	Laborer	06Ma02Bs
Timothy	18	M	Laborer	06Ma02Bs
Stephen	08	M	Child	06Ma02Bs
Jno.	04	M	Child	06Ma02Bs
Hanna	04	F	Child	06Ma02Bs
DOHERTY, Mary	20	F	Laborer	06Ma02Bs
CAMPBELL, Wm.	21	M	Laborer	06Ma02Bs
Ann	09	F	Child	06Ma02Bs
Cathe.	04	F	Child	06Ma02Bs
HADDINGTON, Mary	14	F	Laborer	06Ma02Bs
HOY, Edwd.	21	M	Laborer	06Ma02Bs
HENCHYE, Jas.	27	M	Laborer	06Ma02Bs
BLACKEN, Jno.	24	M	Laborer	06Ma02Bs
ALLISON, Jno.	23	M	Laborer	06Ma02Bs
HARRIGAN, Cathe.	20	F	Laborer	06Ma02Bs
SULLIVAN, Margt.	08	F	Child	06Ma02Bs
DONOVAN, Pat	21	M	Laborer	06Ma02Bs
Neddy	18	M	Laborer	06Ma02Bs
Margt.	13	F	Laborer	06Ma02Bs
Rodger	12	M	Laborer	06Ma02Bs
CASHELL, Jas.	30	M	Laborer	06Ma02Bs
Edwin	12	M	Laborer	06Ma02Bs
Pat	10	M	Laborer	06Ma02Bs
Ann	08	F	Child	06Ma02Bs
MCDONALD, Cathe.	20	F	Laborer	06Ma02Bs
SWEENEY, Martin	35	M	Laborer	06Ma02Bs

NAMES OF PASSENGERS		AGE	SEX	OCCUPATIONS	DATE PORT SHIP
BROWN, Jas.		40	M	Laborer	06Ma02Bs
CLEGG, Jas.		30	M	Laborer	06Ma02Bs
WARD, Jas.		30	M	Laborer	06Ma02Bs
Ellen		27	F	Laborer	06Ma02Bs
MCDONALD, Rose		18	F	Laborer	06Ma02Bs
Hanna		19	F	Laborer	06Ma02Bs
Jno.		18	M	Laborer	06Ma02Bs
Bridget		16	F	Laborer	06Ma02Bs
Michl.		20	M	Laborer	06Ma02Bs
Ellen		19	F	Laborer	06Ma02Bs
Mary		08	F	Child	06Ma02Bs
Hanna		04	F	Child	06Ma02Bs
Judith		02	F	Child	06Ma02Bs
MALLONEY, Jno.		27	M	Laborer	06Ma02Bs
HOWE, Sathe.		22	M	Laborer	06Ma02Bs
KEEFE, Michl.		21	M	Laborer	06Ma02Bs
QUIRK, Pat		25	M	Laborer	06Ma02Bs
COSHIN, Jno.		25	M	Laborer	06Ma02Bs
PAYLAND, Geo.		27	M	Laborer	06Ma02Bs
Alice		25	F	Laborer	06Ma02Bs
MALONEY, Peter		40	M	Laborer	06Ma02Bs
BARRETT, Peter		18	M	Laborer	06Ma02Bs
GALLIGAN, Jno.		35	M	Laborer	06Ma02Bs
FARR, Jas.		46	M	Laborer	06Ma02Bs
FAHY, Jno.		20	M	Laborer	06Ma02Bs
COSGROVE, Bridget		20	F	Laborer	06Ma02Bs
MCCANN, Wm.		30	M	Laborer	06Ma02Bs
Danl.		20	M	Laborer	06Ma02Bs
CARROLL, Mary		20	F	Laborer	06Ma02Bs
JONES, Ras.		27	M	Laborer	06Ma02Bs
Eliza		20	F	Laborer	06Ma02Bs
ANDROES, Wm.		27	M	Laborer	06Ma02Bs
Margt.		21	F	Laborer	06Ma02Bs
OWENS, Jane		21	F	Laborer	06Ma02Bs
RANKIN, Jno.		40	M	Laborer	06Ma02Bs
Jas.		42	M	Laborer	06Ma02Bs
DRUMMOND, Jas.		40	M	Laborer	06Ma02Bs
Mary		20	F	Laborer	06Ma02Bs
Ann		08	F	Child	06Ma02Bs
HOYD, Hugh		30	M	Laborer	06Ma02Bs
CARROLL, Pat		20	M	Laborer	06Ma02Bs
CLARK, Mary		18	F	Laborer	06Ma02Bs
Judy		16	F	Laborer	06Ma02Bs
QUIGLEY, Bridget		15	F	Laborer	06Ma02Bs
Mary		18	F	Laborer	06Ma02Bs
FAY, Margt.		18	F	Laborer	06Ma02Bs
NOON, Bridget		16	F	Laborer	06Ma02Bs
FORD, Jas.		29	M	Laborer	06Ma02Bs
DILLON, Rose		24	F	Laborer	06Ma02Bs
HENEHER, Mary		30	F	Laborer	06Ma02Bs
SHEGRAN, Pat		20	M	Laborer	06Ma02Bs
KIRK, Geo.		45	M	Laborer	06Ma02Bs
MERWIN, Rob.		30	M	Laborer	06Ma02Bs
CALERY, Pat		20	M	Laborer	06Ma02Bs
MORONEY, Jno.		20	M	Laborer	06Ma02Bs
CARROLL, Michl.		20	M	Laborer	06Ma02Bs
MEEHAN, Pat		28	M	Laborer	06Ma02Bs
U	(W)	26	F	Wife	06Ma02Bs
Biddy	(D)	.00	F	Infant	06Ma02Bs
CORCORAN, Jas.		25	M	Laborer	06Ma02Bs
U	(W)	25	F	Wife	06Ma02Bs
Edwd.		30	M	Laborer	06Ma02Bs
Michl.		30	M	Laborer	06Ma02Bs
FELIN, Martin		20	M	Laborer	06Ma02Bs
U	(W)	40	F	Wife	06Ma02Bs
CONNOR, Pat		25	M	Laborer	06Ma02Bs
PHELEN, Jno.		20	M	Laborer	06Ma02Bs
GURMEN, Pat		27	M	Laborer	06Ma02Bs
Mary		20	F	Laborer	06Ma02Bs
QUINN, Jno.		20	M	Laborer	06Ma02Bs
DRUM, Jno.		20	M	Laborer	06Ma02Bs
Mary		20	F	Laborer	06Ma02Bs
CLAREY, Jno.		20	M	Laborer	06Ma02Bs
MCAVERY, Mary		20	F	Laborer	06Ma02Bs
STAMES, Mary		17	F	Laborer	06Ma02Bs

NAMES OF PASSENGERS		AGE	SEX	OCCUPATIONS	DATE PORT SHIP
GRUGEN, Michl.		27	M	Laborer	06Ma02Bs
DOLAN, Ann		20	F	Laborer	06Ma02Bs
BYRNES, Peter		40	M	Laborer	06Ma02Bs
BRANNEN, Edwd.		25	M	Laborer	06Ma02Bs
MATTHEWS, Pat		18	M	Laborer	06Ma02Bs
MCGUIRE, Cathe.		40	F	Laborer	06Ma02Bs
Mary		10	F	Laborer	06Ma02Bs
Cathe.		08	F	Child	06Ma02Bs
Roger		06	M	Child	06Ma02Bs
Mary		04	F	Child	06Ma02Bs
Pat		.00	M	Infant	06Ma02Bs
MADDEN, Andrew		30	M	Laborer	06Ma02Bs
Thos.		06	M	Child	06Ma02Bs
James		05	M	Child	06Ma02Bs
BRENNAN, Biddy		20	F	Child	06Ma02Bs
CANE, Pat		50	M	Unknown	06Ma02Bs
Bridget		48	F	Unknown	06Ma02Bs
Owen		20	M	Unknown	06Ma02Bs
Pat		16	M	Unknown	06Ma02Bs
CLARK, Saml.		26	M	Unknown	06Ma02Bs
Margt.		27	F	Unknown	06Ma02Bs
Wm.		05	M	Child	06Ma02Bs
Saml.		03	M	Child	06Ma02Bs
Rob.		.00	M	Infant	06Ma02Bs
TURNER, Jno.		22	M	Unknown	06Ma02Bs
MITCHELL, Jas.		32	M	Unknown	06Ma02Bs
TURNER, Jane		32	F	Unknown	06Ma02Bs
MITCHELL, U-Mrs.		32	F	Unknown	06Ma02Bs
Louisa	(D)	05	F	Child	06Ma02Bs
Hanna	(D)	02	F	Child	06Ma02Bs
LESTER, Jas.		20	M	Unknown	06Ma02Bs
BROGAN, Andrew		28	M	Unknown	06Ma02Bs
Sarah		28	F	Unknown	06Ma02Bs
Mary		07	F	Child	06Ma02Bs
Jno.		.00	M	Infant	06Ma02Bs
WEEKS, Edwd.		35	M	Unknown	06Ma02Bs
RICH, Chas.		31	M	Unknown	06Ma02Bs
Joseph		36	M	Unknown	06Ma02Bs
SCRINEGER, Wm.		26	M	Unknown	06Ma02Bs
DOLAN, Danl.		20	M	Unknown	06Ma02Bs
DENNING, Thos.		20	M	Unknown	06Ma02Bs
FLAHERTY, Jno.		20	M	Unknown	06Ma02Bs
SOOBY, Jas.		25	M	Unknown	06Ma02Bs
U	(W)	25	F	Wife	06Ma02Bs
Jno.	(S)	.00	M	Infant	06Ma02Bs
Wm.	(S)	02	M	Child	06Ma02Bs
BRADY, Bernard		20	M	Unknown	06Ma02Bs
MCKEOWN, Jno.		20	M	Unknown	06Ma02Bs
SHEAL, Jno.		24	M	Unknown	06Ma02Bs
KELLY, Mary		20	F	Unknown	06Ma02Bs
GREY, Cathe.		20	F	Unknown	06Ma02Bs
KELLY, Mary		20	F	Unknown	06Ma02Bs
Pat		25	M	Unknown	06Ma02Bs
Jane		30	F	Unknown	06Ma02Bs
U		20	F	Unknown	06Ma02Bs
SEMOR, Jno.		30	M	Unknown	06Ma02Bs
MAHER, Margt.		20	F	Unknown	06Ma02Bs
BRADY, Catherine		20	F	Unknown	06Ma02Bs
FARMER, Hugh		21	M	Unknown	06Ma02Bs
Sarah		21	F	Unknown	06Ma02Bs
Mary		.00	F	Infant	06Ma02Bs
WATKINS, Saml.		20	M	Unknown	06Ma02Bs
CONROY, James		26	M	Unknown	06Ma02Bs
U	(W)	24	F	Wife	06Ma02Bs
Mary	(D)	.00	F	Infant	06Ma02Bs
FAHEY, Martin		30	M	Unknown	06Ma02Bs
CAMPBELL, Jas.		30	M	Unknown	06Ma02Bs
PATTERSON, John		21	M	Unknown	06Ma02Bs
QUEAD, Eliza		20	F	Unknown	06Ma02Bs
Michl.		28	M	Unknown	06Ma02Bs
SHANLEY, Thomas		10	M	Unknown	06Ma02Bs
MAGAN, Hannah		20	F	Unknown	06Ma02Bs
Matt.		.00	M	Infant	06Ma02Bs
LUKE, Jas.		31	M	Unknown	06Ma02Bs
KEENAN, Patk.		19	M	Unknown	06Ma02Bs

NAMES OF PASSENGERS	AGE	SEX	OCCUPATIONS	DATE PORT SHIP
TIERNAN, James	19	M	Unknown	06Ma02Bs
KEAN, Ann	26	F	Unknown	06Ma02Bs
OBRIEN, Michl.	20	M	Unknown	06Ma02Bs
Ellen	18	F	Unknown	06Ma02Bs
CONLAN, Margt.	19	F	Unknown	06Ma02Bs
CONNAGHTON, Biddy	20	F	Unknown	06Ma02Bs
Patk.	20	M	Unknown	06Ma02Bs
MCMORAN, Jas.	20	M	Unknown	06Ma02Bs
Eliza	20	F	Unknown	06Ma02Bs
WHITE, Patt.	29	M	Unknown	06Ma02Bs
MCMEEKER, Anthony	23	M	Unknown	06Ma02Bs
CONNELL, Michl.	18	M	Unknown	06Ma02Bs
Margt.	20	F	Unknown	06Ma02Bs
HANNAGAN, John	20	M	Unknown	06Ma02Bs
LEESEESHER, Mary-Ann	08	F	Child	06Ma02Bs
MONTAGUE, Allen	20	M	Unknown	06Ma02Bs
DONNELLY, Pat	20	M	Unknown	06Ma02Bs
PEDAR, Thos.	22	M	Unknown	06Ma02Bs
PRIDE, Jno.	25	M	Unknown	06Ma02Bs
BARRETT, Ann	14	F	Unknown	06Ma02Bs
Peter	18	M	Unknown	06Ma02Bs
Anthony	06	M	Child	06Ma02Bs
STECKEY, Jas.	30	M	Unknown	06Ma02Bs
CAREY, Henry	28	M	Unknown	06Ma02Bs
BARRETT, Hanna	15	F	Unknown	06Ma02Bs
JACKSON, Patk.	20	M	Unknown	06Ma02Bs

SERAPHINE 06 MAY 1848

From London

NAMES OF PASSENGERS	AGE	SEX	OCCUPATIONS	DATE PORT SHIP
QUIN, Thomas	50	M	Painter	06Ma21Ad
Edward	28	M	Painter	06Ma21Ad
WILKERSON, James	24	M	Gpemkr	06Ma21Ad
Sarah	24	F	Gpemkr	06Ma21Ad
Edwin	22	M	Gpemkr	06Ma21Ad
BENNETT, Mary	29	F	Servant	06Ma21Ad
Olive	19	F	Servant	06Ma21Ad
DUDLEY, William	48	M	Wheelwright	06Ma21Ad
JORDAN, Edward	25	M	Laborer	06Ma21Ad
DYER, Matthew	28	M	Laborer	06Ma21Ad
Ellen	28	F	Laborer	06Ma21Ad
TELFER, John	27	M	Chair Maker	06Ma21Ad
Sophia	26	F	Chair Maker	06Ma21Ad
RIGLEY, William	26	M	Weaver	06Ma21Ad
Sarah	28	F	Weaver	06Ma21Ad
William	03	M	Child	06Ma21Ad
BERNIER, William	31	M	Blacksmith	06Ma21Ad
Mary-Ann	31	F	Blacksmith	06Ma21Ad
William	04	M	Child	06Ma21Ad
OBRIEN, John	21	M	Tailor	06Ma21Ad
EVANS, Thomas	27	M	Hrsdlr	06Ma21Ad
Anne	21	F	Hrsdlr	06Ma21Ad
Margaret	02	F	Child	06Ma21Ad
OBRIEN, John	45	M	Tailor	06Ma21Ad
Esther	40	F	Tailor	06Ma21Ad
Eliza	20	F	Tailor	06Ma21Ad
Esther	18	F	Tailor	06Ma21Ad
James	16	M	Tailor	06Ma21Ad
Samuel	15	M	Tailor	06Ma21Ad
Sarah	13	F	Tailor	06Ma21Ad
Catherine	10	F	Tailor	06Ma21Ad
Mary	08	F	Child	06Ma21Ad
Peter	04	M	Child	06Ma21Ad
Anne	06	F	Child	06Ma21Ad
Rose	03	F	Child	06Ma21Ad
Edward	00	M	Child	06Ma21Ad
Amelia	00	F	Child	06Ma21Ad
MEDWINTER, Charles	28	M	Carpenter	06Ma21Ad

NAMES OF PASSENGERS	AGE	SEX	OCCUPATIONS	DATE PORT SHIP
MEDWINTER, Mary-Ann	23	F	Carpenter	06Ma21Ad
Ann	23	F	Carpenter	06Ma21Ad
PACKHAM, Edward	24	M	Farmer	06Ma21Ad
Jane	19	F	Farmer	06Ma21Ad
HARVEY, George	25	M	Saddler	06Ma21Ad
HUNTER, Thomas	30	M	Plasterer	06Ma21Ad
RUDMORE, Thomas	28	M	Clerk	06Ma21Ad
HARVEY, Thomas	32	M	Laborer	06Ma21Ad
Mary	36	F	Laborer	06Ma21Ad
Thomas	00	M	Laborer	06Ma21Ad
Mary	02	F	Child	06Ma21Ad
POTTER, William	28	M	Clerk	06Ma21Ad
SPARROW, Bridget	37	F	Seamstress	06Ma21Ad
Elizabeth	07	F	Child	06Ma21Ad
Bridget	05	F	Child	06Ma21Ad
John	03	M	Child	06Ma21Ad
Maria	00	F	Child	06Ma21Ad
HILL, John	21	M	Laborer	06Ma21Ad
SULLIVAN, Owen	21	M	Laborer	06Ma21Ad
MYERS, Caroline	25	F	Tailor	06Ma21Ad
Rosina	08	F	Child	06Ma21Ad
Jacob	07	M	Child	06Ma21Ad
Henry	03	M	Child	06Ma21Ad
NELSON, Oliver	28	M	Shoemaker	06Ma21Ad
COHEN, Charles	19	M	Pcimkr	06Ma21Ad
STEVENS, Elizabeth	27	F	Tailor	06Ma21Ad
Mary-Ann	06	F	Child	06Ma21Ad
Raechel	03	F	Child	06Ma21Ad
John	00	M	Unknown	06Ma21Ad
U	.00	U	Infant	06Ma21Ad
Died-At-Sea				
FISHER, Edward	23	M	Baker	06Ma21Ad
WENT, Robert	28	M	Sail Maker	06Ma21Ad
Susanna	28	F	Sail Maker	06Ma21Ad
James	02	M	Child	06Ma21Ad
COLE, William	28	M	Weaver	06Ma21Ad
FLANNAGAN, Thomas	31	M	Laborer	06Ma21Ad
DONAHU, Mary	36	F	Servant	06Ma21Ad
FLANNAGAN, Agnes	26	F	Servant	06Ma21Ad
WESTBROOK, Thomas	24	M	Printer	06Ma21Ad
WENT, Benjamin	24	M	Sail Maker	06Ma21Ad
KOCHLEY, John	38	M	Laborer	06Ma21Ad
Margaret	32	F	Laborer	06Ma21Ad
Margaret	00	F	Unknown	06Ma21Ad
WELLS, John	30	M	Laborer	06Ma21Ad
PEDLEY, John	44	M	Carpenter	06Ma21Ad
Caroline	42	F	Carpenter	06Ma21Ad
HUMPHREYS, Julian	31	M	Miner	06Ma21Ad
PHILLIPE, Edith	22	F	Tailor	06Ma21Ad
CONRAD, Jacob	58	M	Clerk	06Ma21Ad
DEGENHART, George	33	M	Mechanic	06Ma21Ad
ALDER, Henry	31	M	Baker	06Ma21Ad
MURPHY, Caroline	26	F	Servant	06Ma21Ad
ALLEN, Joseph	31	M	Baker	06Ma21Ad
Jane	26	F	Baker	06Ma21Ad
Joseph	02	M	Child	06Ma21Ad
BERGER, Antine	35	M	Watchmaker	06Ma21Ad
GRAY, William	54	M	Laborer	06Ma21Ad
EVANS, Samuel	34	M	Carpenter	06Ma21Ad
WHICHELLOW, Charles	25	M	Lrfh	06Ma21Ad
WATERFIELD, Isaacs	50	M	Hatter	06Ma21Ad
Elizabeth	50	F	Hatter	06Ma21Ad
Isaac	04	M	Child	06Ma21Ad
Therese	03	F	Child	06Ma21Ad
CHATTAN, John	47	M	Thatcher	06Ma21Ad
Mary	45	F	Thatcher	06Ma21Ad
Died-At-Sea				
Mary	17	F	Thatcher	06Ma21Ad
Edward	14	M	Thatcher	06Ma21Ad
Sarah	10	F	Thatcher	06Ma21Ad
Ann	07	F	Child	06Ma21Ad
Emma	04	F	Child	06Ma21Ad
Henry	00	M	Unknown	06Ma21Ad
William	00	M	Unknown	06Ma21Ad

NAMES OF PASSENGERS	AGE	SEX	OCCUPATIONS	DATE PORT SHIP
U Died-At-Sea	.00	U	Infant	06Ma21Ad
SULLIVAN, Ugent	20	M	Fiddler	06Ma21Ad
JULIAN, Elizabeth	22	F	Seamstress	06Ma21Ad
MAHONEY, Peter	22	M	Wheelwright	06Ma21Ad
Mary	25	F	Wheelwright	06Ma21Ad
DREW, Thomas	25	M	Laborer	06Ma21Ad
MURRAY, James	25	M	Tailor	06Ma21Ad
Mary	44	F	Tailor	06Ma21Ad
Mary-Ann	25	F	Tailor	06Ma21Ad
Sarah	12	F	Tailor	06Ma21Ad
William	09	M	Child	06Ma21Ad
Maria	07	F	Child	06Ma21Ad
Augustine	04	M	Child	06Ma21Ad
HAY, Alexander	28	M	Clerk	06Ma21Ad
WATKINS, Henry	38	M	Shoemaker	06Ma21Ad
Mary-Ann	40	F	Shoemaker	06Ma21Ad
Eliza	17	F	Shoemaker	06Ma21Ad
Mary-Ann	13	F	Shoemaker	06Ma21Ad
Henry	12	M	Shoemaker	06Ma21Ad
LAVER, Nathan	23	M	Dyer	06Ma21Ad
ADJE, John	46	M	Dresser	06Ma21Ad
WARNER, Charles	23	M	Engineer	06Ma21Ad
Charlotte	23	F	Engineer	06Ma21Ad
BOLTON, John	26	M	Dyer	06Ma21Ad
WENT, George	26	M	Bookbinder	06Ma21Ad
COOPER, Edward	27	M	Painter	06Ma21Ad
MEARTON, Wearnor	30	M	Painter	06Ma21Ad
Margaret	26	F	Painter	06Ma21Ad
CORNEY, William	21	M	Plasterer	06Ma21Ad
MAHONEY, Bridget	24	F	Servant	06Ma21Ad
SMITH, Joseph	26	M	Plasterer	06Ma21Ad
HARRINGTON, John	21	M	Dyer	06Ma21Ad
WEBSTER, Thomas	24	M	Farmer	06Ma21Ad
James	30	M	Farmer	06Ma21Ad
FINCH, Levy	28	M	Farmer	06Ma21Ad
CARTER, Alice	50	F	Servant	06Ma21Ad
FRENCH, Joseph	30	M	Farmer	06Ma21Ad
Sarah-Ann	04	F	Child	06Ma21Ad
Robert	05	M	Child	06Ma21Ad
Mary-Ann	03	F	Child	06Ma21Ad
Ann	00	F	Unknown	06Ma21Ad
COCKERTON, John	22	M	Farmer	06Ma21Ad
Anna	21	F	Farmer	06Ma21Ad
ERITH, Isaac	22	M	Farmer	06Ma21Ad
STANDGATE, James	28	M	Farmer	06Ma21Ad
Sophia	25	F	Farmer	06Ma21Ad
Ellen	06	F	Child	06Ma21Ad
PATE, William	25	M	Laborer	06Ma21Ad
HARDING, William	30	M	Bookbinder	06Ma21Ad
SHEERWOOD, John	30	M	Bookbinder	06Ma21Ad
FALKNER, James	25	M	Bookbinder	06Ma21Ad
LOVE, Henry	23	M	Clerk	06Ma21Ad
LOVELL, Edward	23	M	Clerk	06Ma21Ad
BROADWELL, Thomas	48	M	Farmer	06Ma21Ad
Sarah	45	F	Farmer	06Ma21Ad
Mary	19	F	Farmer	06Ma21Ad
Joel	13	M	Farmer	06Ma21Ad
George	11	M	Farmer	06Ma21Ad
Ann	07	F	Child	06Ma21Ad
Raechel	05	F	Child	06Ma21Ad
BEAL, Susannah	36	F	Seamstress	06Ma21Ad
Frank	12	M	Seamstress	06Ma21Ad
Henry	10	M	Seamstress	06Ma21Ad
Sarah	08	F	Child	06Ma21Ad
COLBURN, Thomas	34	M	Clerk	06Ma21Ad
GRIFFITHS, William	23	M	Laborer	06Ma21Ad
MCDONALD, Joseph	36	M	Sailor	06Ma21Ad
RUTFORD, Eliza	23	F	Servant	06Ma21Ad
FEARBOR, Henry	26	M	Laborer	06Ma21Ad
WOLF, Earl	30	M	Laborer	06Ma21Ad
Frances	24	F	Laborer	06Ma21Ad
EMANUEL, Charles	36	M	Laborer	06Ma21Ad
HENNESSE, Margt.	25	F	Servant	06Ma21Ad
TAGGE, Joseph	17	M	Laborer	06Ma21Ad
REARDEN, Edward	28	M	Carpenter	06Ma21Ad
SHAW, Thomas	20	M	Laborer	06Ma21Ad
ELLREY, Edward	30	M	Painter	06Ma21Ad
Martha	30	F	Painter	06Ma21Ad

ATLANTIC 06 MAY 1848

From Liverpool

NAMES OF PASSENGERS	AGE	SEX	OCCUPATIONS	DATE PORT SHIP
LYNCH, Pat	20	M	Laborer	06Ma02My
NOLAND, Pat	18	M	Laborer	06Ma02My
DOREY, Mary	22	F	None	06Ma02My
Cathe.	18	F	None	06Ma02My
SURNER, Joseph	20	M	Carpenter	06Ma02My
James	18	M	Carpenter	06Ma02My
PRENETY, Caroline	24	F	None	06Ma02My
WHALIN, John	23	M	Laborer	06Ma02My
KING, James	49	M	Farmer	06Ma02My
Winefred	48	F	Farmer	06Ma02My
Pat	18	M	Laborer	06Ma02My
Mary	16	F	None	06Ma02My
John	14	M	None	06Ma02My
Pat	12	M	None	06Ma02My
James	10	M	None	06Ma02My
William	08	M	Child	06Ma02My
Edwd.	07	M	Child	06Ma02My
Thos.	.00	M	Infant	06Ma02My
LAWLER, Wm.	25	M	Farmer	06Ma02My
GRIFFITHS, Benj.	23	M	None	06Ma02My
CARTER, Robert	23	M	None	06Ma02My
HARRISON, Wm.	18	M	None	06Ma02My
ELLERLY, Robt.	24	M	None	06Ma02My
Joseph	22	M	None	06Ma02My
STANSFIELD, James	25	M	Laborer	06Ma02My
HUTLEY, U-Mrs.	28	F	None	06Ma02My
Margt.	26	F	None	06Ma02My
John	.00	M	Infant	06Ma02My
PRICE, John	30	M	Laborer	06Ma02My
NARRY, Edwd.	28	M	Laborer	06Ma02My
Cathr.	22	F	None	06Ma02My
SWEENEY, Pat	23	M	Laborer	06Ma02My
Pat	18	M	Laborer	06Ma02My
DOYLE, Michel	18	M	Laborer	06Ma02My
LYONS, James	24	M	Laborer	06Ma02My
MCNAMARA, Pat	22	M	Laborer	06Ma02My
OHERE, Nancy	21	F	None	06Ma02My
LUHEEN, John	23	M	Laborer	06Ma02My
DYKES, U-Mrs.	20	F	None	06Ma02My
MARTIN, Bridgt.	32	F	None	06Ma02My
DUNNE, Margt.	13	F	None	06Ma02My
MAHONE, Margt.	20	F	None	06Ma02My
John	22	M	Laborer	06Ma02My
James	25	M	Laborer	06Ma02My
GARY, Bessy	24	F	None	06Ma02My
MCGOWAN, Pat	25	M	None	06Ma02My
LAURENCE, John	33	M	Laborer	06Ma02My
BRANNAN, Laurence	25	M	Farmer	06Ma02My
LAURENCE, Mary	28	F	None	06Ma02My
TEMPLETON, John	30	M	Farmer	06Ma02My
Mary	30	F	None	06Ma02My
FORRESTER, John	30	M	Farmer	06Ma02My
James	30	M	Farmer	06Ma02My
LEEK, Christ.	63	M	Farmer	06Ma02My
Mary	48	F	None	06Ma02My
Rebecca	11	F	Child	06Ma02My
Isaac	06	M	Child	06Ma02My
Mary	04	F	Child	06Ma02My
Rachel	03	F	Child	06Ma02My
WOODS, U	50	M	Laborer	06Ma02My

NAMES OF PASSENGERS		AGE	SEX	OCCUPATIONS	DATE PORT SHIP
WOODS, Hannah		50	F	None	06Ma02My
Mary		26	F	None	06Ma02My
Samuel		36	M	None	06Ma02My
U	(W)	36	F	None	06Ma02My
BRACEY, John		25	M	Laborer	06Ma02My
U	(W)	25	F	None	06Ma02My
John	(S)	05	M	Child	06Ma02My
BESCOLEY, John		30	M	Laborer	06Ma02My
SMITH, Thos.		24	M	Laborer	06Ma02My
U	(W)	24	F	None	06Ma02My
Mary	(D)	.00	F	Infant	06Ma02My
PRYER, James		25	M	Laborer	06Ma02My
U	(W)	25	F	None	06Ma02My
James		11	M	None	06Ma02My
Wm.		12	M	None	06Ma02My
John		10	M	None	06Ma02My
Jane		09	F	Child	06Ma02My
COOPER, Francis		25	F	Farmer	06Ma02My
Mary		30	F	None	06Ma02My
DEMPSEY, Ann		18	F	None	06Ma02My
Owen		15	M	None	06Ma02My
MCNAMARA, Michel.		62	M	Laborer	06Ma02My
Hannah		49	F	None	06Ma02My
Michel		18	M	None	06Ma02My
SHORT, John		19	M	Laborer	06Ma02My
GALLAGHER, Mary		28	F	None	06Ma02My
RAFERTY, Mary		18	F	None	06Ma02My
WHITE, Wm.		22	M	None	06Ma02My
BLACK, John		22	M	Laborer	06Ma02My
RESIDE, Brdgt.		45	F	None	06Ma02My
MCAFFEE, Ann		27	F	None	06Ma02My
BEMPESTON, Robert		02	M	Child	06Ma02My
MCRIEN, Dan		22	M	Laborer	06Ma02My
BERNSIDE, Ellen		16	F	None	06Ma02My
MCBRIDE, Sally		27	F	None	06Ma02My
BROWN, Thos.		40	M	Farmer	06Ma02My
Jane		40	F	None	06Ma02My
Wm.		.00	M	Infant	06Ma02My
ROSS, James		45	M	Laborer	06Ma02My
Jane		50	F	None	06Ma02My
Wm.		18	M	None	06Ma02My
James		13	M	None	06Ma02My
Jane		11	F	None	06Ma02My
HENDERSON, Wm.		20	M	Laborer	06Ma02My
DENING, John		35	M	Laborer	06Ma02My
WALKER, Robt.		37	M	Laborer	06Ma02My
SPAID, John		20	M	Laborer	06Ma02My
BLAKE, Ann		20	F	Laborer	06Ma02My
STANFORD, Cathe.		27	M	None	06Ma02My
CALLAN, Hanna		20	F	None	06Ma02My
STANFORD, Brigt.		25	F	None	06Ma02My
HUMPHREYS, Pat		24	M	Laborer	06Ma02My
FLYNN, Phillip		25	M	Laborer	06Ma02My
MATTHEWS, Michl.		40	M	Laborer	06Ma02My
BAXTER, James		25	M	Laborer	06Ma02My
Margt.		27	F	Laborer	06Ma02My
MARTIN, Bernard		24	M	Laborer	06Ma02My
RAY, Thos.		20	M	Laborer	06Ma02My
STEWART, Danil		25	M	Laborer	06Ma02My
PHALIN, Preice		30	M	Laborer	06Ma02My
KATEING, Edwd.		30	M	Laborer	06Ma02My
MULLIN, Thos.		30	M	Laborer	06Ma02My
KELLY, Martin		30	M	Laborer	06Ma02My
U	(W)	25	F	None	06Ma02My
Jas.	(S)	07	M	Child	06Ma02My
Mary	(D)	05	F	Child	06Ma02My
John	(S)	02	M	Child	06Ma02My
KINLAN, Cathr.		16	F	None	06Ma02My
HUDSON, Richd.		39	M	Laborer	06Ma02My
BOYLE, Ben		30	M	Laborer	06Ma02My
MCGRATH, Michl.		25	M	Laborer	06Ma02My
Edwd.		25	M	Laborer	06Ma02My
MCCARRAN, Pat		20	M	Laborer	06Ma02My
CLLARY, Mary		20	F	None	06Ma02My
Mary		35	F	None	06Ma02My

NAMES OF PASSENGERS		AGE	SEX	OCCUPATIONS	DATE PORT SHIP
PRANDY, Thos.		40	M	Farmer	06Ma02My
Sarah		20	F	None	06Ma02My
BRANDY, Pat		12	M	None	06Ma02My
Betty		13	F	None	06Ma02My
Cath.		09	F	Child	06Ma02My
Michl.		07	M	Child	06Ma02My
Thos.		04	M	Child	06Ma02My
CHAMBERS, Wm.		18	M	Laborer	06Ma02My
DALEY, Mary		50	F	None	06Ma02My
Pat		25	M	Laborer	06Ma02My
James		20	M	Laborer	06Ma02My
Biddy		20	F	None	06Ma02My
Ellen		17	F	None	06Ma02My
MARTIN, John		24	M	Laborer	06Ma02My
WELSH, John		21	M	Laborer	06Ma02My
BRIEN, John		23	M	Laborer	06Ma02My
COWAN, Darby		24	M	Laborer	06Ma02My
WALKER, Ann		45	F	None	06Ma02My
James		18	M	None	06Ma02My
Ellen		22	F	None	06Ma02My
Ann		18	F	None	06Ma02My
Joseph		12	M	None	06Ma02My
COIL, Ambroise		23	M	Laborer	06Ma02My
Mary		22	F	None	06Ma02My
Theresa		.00	F	Infant	06Ma02My
HUGHS, Peter		20	M	Farmer	06Ma02My
Mary		18	F	None	06Ma02My
OBRIEN, Jas.		25	M	Laborer	06Ma02My
MONAGHAN, Pat		20	M	Laborer	06Ma02My
MURREY, Richd.		26	M	Laborer	06Ma02My
NAUGHON, Thos.		26	M	Laborer	06Ma02My
U	(W)	23	F	None	06Ma02My
CAMPBELL, Bridgt.		22	F	None	06Ma02My
Mary		16	F	None	06Ma02My
JOSEPH, Daniel		57	M	Laborer	06Ma02My
U	(W)	57	F	None	06Ma02My
Sarah		52	F	None	06Ma02My
Ann		20	F	None	06Ma02My
Morgan		25	M	Laborer	06Ma02My
Eliza		20	F	None	06Ma02My
ISERAL, James		46	M	Laborer	06Ma02My
U	(W)	45	F	None	06Ma02My
Sarah	(D)	24	F	None	06Ma02My
Margret	(D)	13	F	None	06Ma02My
David	(S)	10	M	None	06Ma02My
DENNY, Phillip		25	M	Laborer	06Ma02My
MCFARLANE, Duncan		24	M	Laborer	06Ma02My
HUDSON, Isabella		40	F	None	06Ma02My
SMITHE, John		44	M	Laborer	06Ma02My
MACLACE, Richd.		20	M	Laborer	06Ma02My
WHITKER, Robt.		38	M	Laborer	06Ma02My
RIDDLE, Jams.		38	M	Laborer	06Ma02My
U	(W)	37	F	Wife	06Ma02My
John	(S)	17	M	None	06Ma02My
Martha	(D)	13	F	None	06Ma02My
Ann	(D)	11	F	None	06Ma02My
James	(S)	08	M	Child	06Ma02My
Eliza	(D)	02	F	Child	06Ma02My
PREISON, John		30	M	Farmer	06Ma02My
U	(W)	30	F	None	06Ma02My
Thos.		25	M	Farmer	06Ma02My
Maryann		30	F	None	06Ma02My
MALLON, Eliza		12	F	None	06Ma02My
Wm.		30	M	Laborer	06Ma02My
MYRINCK, Wm.		30	M	Laborer	06Ma02My
Bridgt.		18	F	None	06Ma02My
BROTHERICK, John		25	M	Farmer	06Ma02My
U-Mrs.		38	F	None	06Ma02My
John		10	M	None	06Ma02My
Mary		08	F	Child	06Ma02My
KELLY, James		30	M	Laborer	06Ma02My
Bridgt.		28	F	None	06Ma02My
MARIEN, Mary		20	F	None	06Ma02My
KERINEN, Mary		18	F	None	06Ma02My
MARIEN, Ellen		25	F	None	06Ma02My

NAMES OF PASSENGERS		AGE	SEX	OCCUPATIONS	DATE PORT SHIP
MCCLUGH, Mary		30	F	None	06Ma02My
RIDDIGEN, Michel		23	M	Farmer	06Ma02My
FOLEY, Wm.		22	M	Farmer	06Ma02My
HANNINGTON, Eliza		28	F	None	06Ma02My
Jeremiah		26	M	Laborer	06Ma02My
WHELAN, Daniel		30	M	Laborer	06Ma02My
MCMANUS, Jas.		24	M	Laborer	06Ma02My
DALEY, Jas.		20	M	Laborer	06Ma02My
Matthew		18	M	Laborer	06Ma02My
BURKE, Thos.		35	M	Farmer	06Ma02My
Wm.		24	M	Farmer	06Ma02My
Michl.		.00	M	Infant	06Ma02My
MCGRATH, Mary		28	F	None	06Ma02My
CLOUGH, Thos.		28	M	Laborer	06Ma02My
MURRAY, Thos.		30	M	Laborer	06Ma02My
Ann		26	F	None	06Ma02My
Julia		.00	F	Infant	06Ma02My
DRISCOLL, Betty		25	F	None	06Ma02My
CRAUTHEY, Augt.		23	M	Laborer	06Ma02My
HENRIE, Margt.		24	F	None	06Ma02My
DORAN, Ellen		23	F	None	06Ma02My
BYRNE, Thos.		35	M	Laborer	06Ma02My
Mary		34	F	None	06Ma02My
David		12	M	None	06Ma02My
Mary		10	F	None	06Ma02My
Magt.		08	F	Child	06Ma02My
Mullen		06	M	Child	06Ma02My
Anthony		04	M	Child	06Ma02My
CARTER, Drannon		30	M	Laborer	06Ma02My
CONERYTON, Eliza		25	F	Laborer	06Ma02My
Sarah		23	F	Laborer	06Ma02My
HOLLAND, John		.00	M	Infant	06Ma02My

SERAPHINE 08 MAY 1848

From Newry

NAMES OF PASSENGERS		AGE	SEX	OCCUPATIONS	DATE PORT SHIP
MARDREW, Andrew		40	M	Farmer	08Ma19Ad
Betty-Ann	(W)	28	F	Wife	08Ma19Ad
William		22	M	None	08Ma19Ad
Andrew		18	M	None	08Ma19Ad
KENSEY, Arthur		28	M	Laborer	08Ma19Ad
John		30	M	Laborer	08Ma19Ad
WOODS, Margaret		29	F	Spinster	08Ma19Ad
GREEDEN, James		32	M	Laborer	08Ma19Ad
Elizabeth	(W)	31	F	Wife	08Ma19Ad
David-Wm.		26	M	None	08Ma19Ad
Robert		20	M	None	08Ma19Ad
TATE, John		35	M	Laborer	08Ma19Ad
Solomon		32	M	Laborer	08Ma19Ad
James		29	M	Laborer	08Ma19Ad
RILEY, Philipp		44	M	Laborer	08Ma19Ad
Mary	(W)	40	F	Wife	08Ma19Ad
Thomas		26	M	None	08Ma19Ad
Rose		24	F	None	08Ma19Ad
Bridget		19	F	None	08Ma19Ad
PATTERSON, James		36	M	Laborer	08Ma19Ad
Jane	(W)	33	F	Wife	08Ma19Ad
Wm.George	(S)	12	M	Unknown	08Ma19Ad
James	(S)	11	M	Unknown	08Ma19Ad
Mary-Ann	(D)	.00	F	Infant	08Ma19Ad
ALLEN, William		28	M	Laborer	08Ma19Ad
Mary	(W)	26	F	Wife	08Ma19Ad
Anne		24	F	Spinster	08Ma19Ad
MCCONVILL, Thomas		36	M	Farmer	08Ma19Ad
Mary	(W)	32	F	Wife	08Ma19Ad
WHITE, James		36	M	Laborer	08Ma19Ad
Margaret	(W)	24	F	Wife	08Ma19Ad
MCCANN, Mary		24	F	Spinster	08Ma19Ad
MCCOMB, Rachel		28	F	Spinster	08Ma19Ad
BAXTER, William		35	M	Farmer	08Ma19Ad
Nancy	(W)	32	F	Wife	08Ma19Ad
James		29	M	None	08Ma19Ad
Margaret-Jane		22	F	None	08Ma19Ad
Adam		18	M	None	08Ma19Ad
Joseph		16	M	None	08Ma19Ad
MURPHY, Patt		14	M	Laborer	08Ma19Ad
Owen		22	M	Laborer	08Ma19Ad
PACKSTON, Hugh		22	M	Farmer	08Ma19Ad
Margaret	(W)	28	F	Wife	08Ma19Ad
MCALAIRDEN, James		29	M	Laborer	08Ma19Ad
MCCONVILL, Ed.		36	M	Laborer	08Ma19Ad
KERR, Mary		29	F	Spinster	08Ma19Ad
MCMILLEN, Rose		27	F	Spinster	08Ma19Ad
FEGAN, Mary		37	F	Farmer	08Ma19Ad
Patt.	(H)	34	M	Farmer	08Ma19Ad
Catherine		21	F	None	08Ma19Ad
Ellen		18	F	None	08Ma19Ad
Margaret		16	F	None	08Ma19Ad
Peter		13	M	None	08Ma19Ad
DOYLE, James		42	M	Farmer	08Ma19Ad
Rose	(W)	40	F	Wife	08Ma19Ad
James	(S)	22	M	None	08Ma19Ad
John	(S)	19	M	None	08Ma19Ad
Bridget	(D)	18	F	None	08Ma19Ad
Marta	(D)	17	F	None	08Ma19Ad
Mary	(D)	16	F	None	08Ma19Ad
Arthur	(S)	14	M	None	08Ma19Ad
Felix	(S)	13	M	None	08Ma19Ad
Bernard	(S)	10	M	None	08Ma19Ad
AGNEW, Andrew		48	M	Laborer	08Ma19Ad
Sarah	(W)	46	F	Wife	08Ma19Ad
Mary	(D)	20	F	None	08Ma19Ad
William	(S)	19	M	None	08Ma19Ad
Andrew	(S)	17	M	None	08Ma19Ad
Edward	(S)	14	M	None	08Ma19Ad
Sarah	(D)	12	F	None	08Ma19Ad
DENNON, Thomas		36	M	Farmer	08Ma19Ad
Agnes	(W)	33	F	Wife	08Ma19Ad
Eliza		20	F	None	08Ma19Ad
Catherine		18	F	None	08Ma19Ad
Hugh		17	M	None	08Ma19Ad
Eliza		14	F	None	08Ma19Ad
Margaret		12	F	None	08Ma19Ad
John		09	M	Child	08Ma19Ad
TAYLOR, Samuel		26	M	Laborer	08Ma19Ad
Sarah-Ann	(W)	24	F	Wife	08Ma19Ad
Eliza		22	F	Spinster	08Ma19Ad
KERNIGHAN, James		21	M	Laborer	08Ma19Ad
Margaret-Jane	(W)	19	F	Wife	08Ma19Ad
KILPATRICK, Morris		46	M	Farmer	08Ma19Ad
Alice	(W)	41	F	Wife	08Ma19Ad
Bridget	(D)	20	F	None	08Ma19Ad
Sarah	(D)	19	F	None	08Ma19Ad
Alice	(D)	17	F	None	08Ma19Ad
FEGAN, William		34	M	Farmer	08Ma19Ad
Rose	(W)	28	F	Wife	08Ma19Ad
Margaret		16	F	None	08Ma19Ad
Eliza		13	F	None	08Ma19Ad
BRANGAN, Isabella		33	F	Spinster	08Ma19Ad
FEGAN, Felix		42	M	Farmer	08Ma19Ad
Mick		26	M	None	08Ma19Ad
Sella		24	F	None	08Ma19Ad
Mary		22	F	None	08Ma19Ad
CRUTHERS, Hana		28	F	Laborer	08Ma19Ad
MCCONVILL, Matt		24	M	Laborer	08Ma19Ad
BURNS, Edward		38	M	Farmer	08Ma19Ad
Isabella	(W)	32	F	Wife	08Ma19Ad
John	(S)	16	M	None	08Ma19Ad
Catherine	(D)	17	F	None	08Ma19Ad
Edward	(S)	10	M	None	08Ma19Ad
COOPER, Mary		28	F	Spinster	08Ma19Ad
Betty-Jane		22	F	Spinster	08Ma19Ad
MCCONVILL, Arthur		29	M	Farmer	08Ma19Ad

NAMES OF PASSENGERS	AGE	SEX	OCCUPATIONS	DATE PORT SHIP
MCCONVILL, Margaret (W)	19	F	Wife	08Ma19Ad
Catherine	22	F	Spinster	08Ma19Ad
FOY, Henry	21	M	Laborer	08Ma19Ad
STEVENSON, Hannah	27	F	Spinster	08Ma19Ad
BURNS, James	24	M	Laborer	08Ma19Ad
Hugh	26	M	Laborer	08Ma19Ad
ANDERSON, Alex	32	M	Laborer	08Ma19Ad
MCKEE, John	28	M	Laborer	08Ma19Ad
CHAMBERS, John	27	M	Laborer	08Ma19Ad
FOY, Edward	22	M	Laborer	08Ma19Ad
CONNER, Sarah	31	F	Spinster	08Ma19Ad
MCKENNA, Bernard	32	M	Laborer	08Ma19Ad
Biddy (W)	28	F	Wife	08Ma19Ad
HAMELTON, Margaret	34	F	Spinster	08Ma19Ad
Jane	30	F	Spinster	08Ma19Ad
MCILDOE, James	32	M	Laborer	08Ma19Ad
WHITE, Patt.	24	M	Laborer	08Ma19Ad
MCGINITY, Anne	21	F	Spinster	08Ma19Ad
MCTEER, Mary-Ann	20	F	Spinster	08Ma19Ad
WHITE, Stephen	28	M	Laborer	08Ma19Ad
Catherine	26	F	Spinster	08Ma19Ad
Anne	21	F	Spinster	08Ma19Ad
DOYLE, Daniel	24	M	Laborer	08Ma19Ad
Bridget (W)	22	F	Wife	08Ma19Ad
BEAKE, Sarah	21	F	Spinster	08Ma19Ad
BARK, Wm.	27	M	Laborer	08Ma19Ad
RILEY, Michael	40	M	Joiner	08Ma19Ad
Anne (W)	38	F	Wife	08Ma19Ad
Michael	22	M	None	08Ma19Ad
Francis	20	M	None	08Ma19Ad
James	18	M	None	08Ma19Ad
Anne	16	F	None	08Ma19Ad
Matthew	14	M	None	08Ma19Ad
FEGAN, John	26	M	Laborer	08Ma19Ad
ORAULK, Mary	22	F	Spinster	08Ma19Ad
Mary	22	F	Spinster	08Ma19Ad
DONLY, John	36	M	Farmer	08Ma19Ad
BROWN, Sarah	22	F	Spinster	08Ma19Ad
HANLIN, John	41	M	Laborer	08Ma19Ad
Bridget (W)	41	F	Wife	08Ma19Ad
Margaret	38	F	None	08Ma19Ad
Catherine	26	F	None	08Ma19Ad
Anne	22	F	None	08Ma19Ad
John	14	M	None	08Ma19Ad
Teresa	04	F	Child	08Ma19Ad
MURPHY, Edward	42	M	Farmer	08Ma19Ad
Anne (W)	37	F	Wife	08Ma19Ad
Anne	21	F	None	08Ma19Ad
Michael	19	M	None	08Ma19Ad
Patt.	16	M	None	08Ma19Ad
Ellen	13	F	None	08Ma19Ad
Peter	10	M	None	08Ma19Ad
FITZPATRICK, Michael	28	M	Unknown	08Ma19Ad
Margaret	32	F	None	08Ma19Ad
Hugh	06	M	Child	08Ma19Ad
CALLAGHAN, Thomas	28	M	Farmer	08Ma19Ad
Betty (W)	26	F	Wife	08Ma19Ad
IRVINE, Walter	38	M	Unknown	08Ma19Ad
Mary (W)	36	F	Wife	08Ma19Ad
John (S)	16	M	None	08Ma19Ad
Mary (D)	14	F	None	08Ma19Ad
Nancy (D)	12	F	None	08Ma19Ad
Fanny (D)	10	F	None	08Ma19Ad
William (S)	09	M	Child	08Ma19Ad
Henry (S)	06	M	Child	08Ma19Ad
BLCK, Louis	28	M	Laborer	08Ma19Ad
WYLIE, John	24	M	Laborer	08Ma19Ad
Robert	26	M	Laborer	08Ma19Ad
DONALLY, Margaret	32	F	Wife	08Ma19Ad
Mary	30	F	None	08Ma19Ad
Michael	18	M	None	08Ma19Ad
John	14	M	None	08Ma19Ad
BURKE, Anne-Mrs.	40	F	Wife	08Ma19Ad
Mary-Ann (D)	20	F	None	08Ma19Ad
Dan (S)	18	M	None	08Ma19Ad
Walter (S)	16	M	None	08Ma19Ad
Arthur (S)	12	M	None	08Ma19Ad
KELLY, Thomas	42	M	Farmer	08Ma19Ad
Ally (W)	40	F	Wife	08Ma19Ad
Owen	28	M	None	08Ma19Ad
Patt.	26	M	None	08Ma19Ad
Hugh	18	M	None	08Ma19Ad
Thomas	.00	M	Infant	08Ma19Ad
DOOGAN, Richard	21	M	Laborer	08Ma19Ad
ANDREWS, Isaac	20	M	Laborer	08Ma19Ad
BURNS, William	22	M	Laborer	08Ma19Ad
MCALISTER, Sussanah	20	F	Spinster	08Ma19Ad
MCGOW, Mary	18	F	Spinster	08Ma19Ad
MCGUGAN, Catherine	22	F	Spinster	08Ma19Ad
CALLAGHAN, Bernard	18	M	Laborer	08Ma19Ad
GUFT, Andrew	24	M	Laborer	08Ma19Ad
Mary (W)	22	F	Wife	08Ma19Ad
KERR, Mary	28	F	Spinster	08Ma19Ad
FEARON, Michael	22	M	Laborer	08Ma19Ad
Hannah (W)	18	F	Wife	08Ma19Ad
TREANOR, James	24	M	Laborer	08Ma19Ad
Judith (W)	22	F	Wife	08Ma19Ad
GORDON, Thomas	28	M	Laborer	08Ma19Ad
Sarah (W)	26	F	Wife	08Ma19Ad
Thomas (S)	.00	M	Infant	08Ma19Ad
DONALY, Catherine	24	F	Spinster	08Ma19Ad
BROWN, David	36	M	Laborer	08Ma19Ad
GUIDEE, Phillip	32	M	Laborer	08Ma19Ad
PARKER, William	21	M	Laborer	08Ma19Ad
MURPHY, Catherine	20	F	Spinster	08Ma19Ad
SMITH, Philip	28	M	Laborer	08Ma19Ad
OWENS, Mary	31	F	Spinster	08Ma19Ad
BRANGAN, Arthur	28	M	Laborer	08Ma19Ad
Mccor---, Anne	32	F	Spinster	08Ma19Ad
CUTHBERTSON, George	40	M	Unknown	08Ma19Ad
Fanny	30	F	Unknown	08Ma19Ad
GLASS, David	22	M	Unknown	08Ma19Ad

CONSTITUTION 08 MAY 1848

From Liverpool

NAMES OF PASSENGERS	AGE	SEX	OCCUPATIONS	DATE PORT SHIP
PHELIPS, Chas.	23	M	Unknown	08Ma02Hi
IVESON, Launcelot	22	M	Unknown	08Ma02Hi
JONES, E.M.	23	M	Mnftr	08Ma02Hi
ANDERSON, John	24	M	Merchant	08Ma02Hi
SHERWELL, Richd.	45	M	Merchant	08Ma02Hi
Mary	20	F	Unknown	08Ma02Hi
DARLING, David	22	M	Merchant	08Ma02Hi
BAKER, Andrew	60	M	Farmer	08Ma02Hi
MCLELLAND, Robert	45	M	Mnftr	08Ma02Hi
Rose-Etta	40	F	Unknown	08Ma02Hi
John	01	M	Child	08Ma02Hi
BRENNAN, Jno.	31	M	Mechanic	08Ma02Hi
PAPE, Wm.	22	M	Mechanic	08Ma02Hi
BOARDMAN, Robert	20	M	Farmer	08Ma02Hi
William	18	M	Farmer	08Ma02Hi
Elizabeth	19	F	Unknown	08Ma02Hi
WOODS, Joseph	33	M	Laborer	08Ma02Hi
Mary	29	F	Spinster	08Ma02Hi
William	10	M	Unknown	08Ma02Hi
THOMPSON, Stephen	23	M	Laborer	08Ma02Hi
Alice	22	F	Spinster	08Ma02Hi
Eliza	.00	F	Infant	08Ma02Hi
GOTHERIDGE, Geo.	27	M	Laborer	08Ma02Hi
MARCH, Thos.	29	M	Laborer	08Ma02Hi
SIMPSON, Wm.	29	M	Laborer	08Ma02Hi
HOLMES, Wm.	20	M	Laborer	08Ma02Hi
MURRAY, A.	20	M	Laborer	08Ma02Hi

NAMES OF PASSENGERS	AGE	SEX	OCCUPATIONS	DATE PORT SHIP
WRIGHT, Jas.	20	M	Laborer	08Ma02Hi
ANELEY, Chas.	24	M	Laborer	08Ma02Hi
U (W)	21	F	Spinster	08Ma02Hi
HATTERLY, Wm.	25	M	Laborer	08Ma02Hi
Joseph	25	M	Laborer	08Ma02Hi
MENELL, Edward	24	M	Laborer	08Ma02Hi
MEEKS, John	25	M	Mechanic	08Ma02Hi
COOPER, Edward	32	M	Mechanic	08Ma02Hi
JONES, Wm.	30	M	Laborer	08Ma02Hi
BELL, Thos.	33	M	Laborer	08Ma02Hi
Rachel	30	F	Spinster	08Ma02Hi
Enoch	13	M	Unknown	08Ma02Hi
Anne	10	F	Unknown	08Ma02Hi
AUSTIN, Peter	36	M	Laborer	08Ma02Hi
Ellen	43	F	Spinster	08Ma02Hi
Isaac	13	M	Unknown	08Ma02Hi
Francis	11	M	Unknown	08Ma02Hi
GIBSON, Noah	21	M	Laborer	08Ma02Hi
Sarah	28	F	Spinster	08Ma02Hi
Joseph	04	M	Child	08Ma02Hi
BUTLER, Eliza	16	F	Unknown	08Ma02Hi
STANLEY, Chas.	35	M	Laborer	08Ma02Hi
LIDDY, Pat	24	M	Laborer	08Ma02Hi
BRADY, Pat	24	M	Laborer	08Ma02Hi
BEST, Jno.	24	M	Laborer	08Ma02Hi
BOLTON, Geo.	36	M	Laborer	08Ma02Hi
RICHARDSON, Joseph	20	M	Laborer	08Ma02Hi
PURCELL, Joseph	20	M	Laborer	08Ma02Hi
EDWARDS, Evan	28	M	Laborer	08Ma02Hi
CREEMELL, Pil.	28	M	Laborer	08Ma02Hi
LOWE, Tho.	42	M	Laborer	08Ma02Hi
JONES, John	25	M	Laborer	08Ma02Hi
HUGHES, Thos.	60	M	Laborer	08Ma02Hi
U	20	M	Laborer	08Ma02Hi
U	18	M	Laborer	08Ma02Hi
U	10	M	Laborer	08Ma02Hi
ROBERTS, Thos.	30	M	Laborer	08Ma02Hi
JONES, Jacob	24	M	Laborer	08Ma02Hi
Elias	23	M	Laborer	08Ma02Hi
Joseph	21	M	Laborer	08Ma02Hi
MORRIS, David	20	M	Laborer	08Ma02Hi
WILLEY, Thos.	30	M	Laborer	08Ma02Hi
MALLAHAN, Thos.	23	M	Laborer	08Ma02Hi
Geo.	21	M	Laborer	08Ma02Hi
MCFOLEY, Chas.	25	M	Laborer	08Ma02Hi
HARDY, Wm.	25	M	Laborer	08Ma02Hi
KENNEDY, Pat	35	M	Laborer	08Ma02Hi
DOHARY, Jno.	34	M	Laborer	08Ma02Hi
Mich.	31	M	Laborer	08Ma02Hi
MACKFEE, Wm.	33	M	Laborer	08Ma02Hi
U (W)	26	F	Spinster	08Ma02Hi
PRATT, Edward	22	M	Laborer	08Ma02Hi
Sarah	18	F	Unknown	08Ma02Hi
PATTERSON, Robert	20	M	Unknown	08Ma02Hi
MAZWELL, Elizth.	60	F	Unknown	08Ma02Hi
Mary-Jane	18	F	Unknown	08Ma02Hi
Elizabth.	14	F	Unknown	08Ma02Hi
PORTER, Robert	28	M	Laborer	08Ma02Hi
STEEN, Saml.	26	M	Laborer	08Ma02Hi
NAIL, Pat	50	M	Laborer	08Ma02Hi
John	20	M	Laborer	08Ma02Hi
Mich	20	M	Laborer	08Ma02Hi
CARNEY, Peter	25	M	Laborer	08Ma02Hi
PATER, Andrew	28	M	Laborer	08Ma02Hi
KELLY, Ann	25	F	Spinster	08Ma02Hi
HAYS, Bridget	22	F	Spinster	08Ma02Hi
ONEIL, Jas.	23	M	Laborer	08Ma02Hi
WHITEOBAN, Mary	20	F	Spinster	08Ma02Hi
HAYS, Edward	24	M	Laborer	08Ma02Hi
BURK, Wm.	21	M	Laborer	08Ma02Hi
Jno.	22	M	Laborer	08Ma02Hi
PHINN, Thos.	26	M	Laborer	08Ma02Hi
Ann	21	F	Spinster	08Ma02Hi
PHILLIPS, Maria	16	F	Spinster	08Ma02Hi
FOGARTY, Pat	35	M	Laborer	08Ma02Hi

NAMES OF PASSENGERS	AGE	SEX	OCCUPATIONS	DATE PORT SHIP
ARTHUR, Jane	27	F	Spinster	08Ma02Hi
TOPHAM, James	22	M	Laborer	08Ma02Hi
ARMSTRONG, Jno.	22	M	Laborer	08Ma02Hi
OKEEF, Jno.	21	M	Laborer	08Ma02Hi
HOLLIGAN, Jas.	17	M	Laborer	08Ma02Hi
GEEHAN, Mark	18	M	Laborer	08Ma02Hi
Daniel	13	M	Laborer	08Ma02Hi
Jas.	11	M	Laborer	08Ma02Hi
GALLIGHAR, Saml.	30	M	Mechanic	08Ma02Hi
KELLY, Jas.	20	M	Mechanic	08Ma02Hi
BRAECAN, Bridget	20	F	Spinster	08Ma02Hi
BACON, Thos.	30	M	Laborer	08Ma02Hi
Margt.	30	F	Spinster	08Ma02Hi
MORTIMER, U-Mrs.	40	F	Spinster	08Ma02Hi
Mary	09	F	Child	08Ma02Hi
Jane	07	F	Child	08Ma02Hi
Emma	.00	F	Infant	08Ma02Hi
LOWDEN, Jno.	33	M	Laborer	08Ma02Hi
Eliza	30	F	Spinster	08Ma02Hi
CAHILL, Eliza	20	F	Spinster	08Ma02Hi
COTTIER, John	29	M	Laborer	08Ma02Hi
U	26	F	Spinster	08Ma02Hi
Wm.	08	M	Child	08Ma02Hi
Jno.	04	M	Child	08Ma02Hi
WILLIAMS, Jno.	36	M	Laborer	08Ma02Hi
MORELL, Saml.	25	M	Laborer	08Ma02Hi
MCIVEY, Isaac	36	M	Laborer	08Ma02Hi
Isaac	19	M	Laborer	08Ma02Hi
PLATT, Joseph	18	M	Laborer	08Ma02Hi
JONES, David	35	M	Laborer	08Ma02Hi
Evan	20	M	Laborer	08Ma02Hi
HUGHES, John	18	M	Laborer	08Ma02Hi
QUINN, Jno.	28	M	Laborer	08Ma02Hi
ROCK, Wm.B.	20	M	Laborer	08Ma02Hi
DALEY, Danl.	26	M	Laborer	08Ma02Hi
PREST, Chas.	20	M	Laborer	08Ma02Hi
GANNON, Pat	25	M	Laborer	08Ma02Hi
FORK, Mary	20	F	Spinster	08Ma02Hi
DUNLEA, Cath.	20	F	Spinster	08Ma02Hi
ELY, Elphin	21	M	Laborer	08Ma02Hi
HEGARTY, Wm.	20	M	Laborer	08Ma02Hi
CALLAN, Ann	26	F	Spinster	08Ma02Hi
Cath.	20	F	Spinster	08Ma02Hi
CAREY, Ellen	19	F	Spinster	08Ma02Hi
DUFFAN, Jenny	25	F	Spinster	08Ma02Hi
LYNCH, Pat	25	M	Laborer	08Ma02Hi
HUGHES, Jno.	24	M	Laborer	08Ma02Hi
U (W)	21	F	Spinster	08Ma02Hi
Ann	16	F	Spinster	08Ma02Hi
Margt.	10	F	Spinster	08Ma02Hi
Wm.	18	M	Laborer	08Ma02Hi
John	08	M	Child	08Ma02Hi
FRITCHELY, Wm.	50	M	Laborer	08Ma02Hi
Jane	36	F	Spinster	08Ma02Hi
Joseph	08	M	Child	08Ma02Hi
Lucy	06	F	Child	08Ma02Hi
David	.00	M	Infant	08Ma02Hi
JACKSON, Jno.	29	M	Laborer	08Ma02Hi
Sarah	33	F	Spinster	08Ma02Hi
TAYLOR, Thomas	29	M	Laborer	08Ma02Hi
STORER, Henry	22	M	Laborer	08Ma02Hi
BAKER, Wm.	24	M	Laborer	08Ma02Hi
CARROLL, Johanna	18	F	Spinster	08Ma02Hi
JONES, Robert	20	M	Laborer	08Ma02Hi
ROBERTS, Hugh	20	M	Laborer	08Ma02Hi
GIBSON, Wm.	27	M	Laborer	08Ma02Hi
MARSHALL, Wm.	26	M	Laborer	08Ma02Hi
TAYLOR, Edwin	24	M	Laborer	08Ma02Hi
HICKSON, Jane	20	F	Spinster	08Ma02Hi
JOHNSON, Mary-Ann	21	F	Governess	08Ma02Hi
MCGILL, Thos.	45	M	Shopkeeper	08Ma02Hi
Ann	40	F	Spinster	08Ma02Hi
Mary	19	F	Spinster	08Ma02Hi
Sally	09	F	Child	08Ma02Hi
Thos.	05	M	Child	08Ma02Hi

NAMES OF PASSENGERS	AGE	SEX	OCCUPATIONS	DATE PORT SHIP
MCGILL, Ephin.	03	M	Child	08Ma02Hi
ELDERS, Richard	87	M	Unknown	08Ma02Hi
Died-At-Sea				
MCCARTY, Joseph	24	M	Laborer	08Ma02Hi
MCGILL, Richard	20	M	Laborer	08Ma02Hi
Jas.	15	M	Laborer	08Ma02Hi
KEARNEY, Eliza	46	F	Spinster	08Ma02Hi
GORMAN, Edwd.	24	M	Laborer	08Ma02Hi
Edwd.	21	M	Laborer	08Ma02Hi
HIGGANS, Thos.	20	M	Laborer	08Ma02Hi
REIVINE, Edwd.	19	M	Laborer	08Ma02Hi
Chas.	17	M	Laborer	08Ma02Hi
WILLING, James	21	M	Laborer	08Ma02Hi
YATES, Wm.	19	M	Laborer	08Ma02Hi
WILLING, Ann	20	F	Spinster	08Ma02Hi
YATES, Elizabeth	10	F	Spinster	08Ma02Hi
Mary	20	F	Spinster	08Ma02Hi
CULLINGTON, Michl.	29	M	Laborer	08Ma02Hi
LOOSEBERRY, Jas.	21	M	Laborer	08Ma02Hi
RILEY, Danl.	20	M	Laborer	08Ma02Hi
Jno.	23	M	Laborer	08Ma02Hi
BROWN, Lewis	20	M	Laborer	08Ma02Hi
LOCHER, Thos.	20	M	Laborer	08Ma02Hi
MILLER, John	20	M	Laborer	08Ma02Hi
HERD, Benjh.	20	M	Laborer	08Ma02Hi
STEEL, John	20	M	Laborer	08Ma02Hi
POWELL, John	50	M	Laborer	08Ma02Hi
Susan	19	F	None	08Ma02Hi
Peggy	17	F	None	08Ma02Hi
John	12	M	Laborer	08Ma02Hi
MIGHT, Wm.	22	M	Laborer	08Ma02Hi
JONES, Henry	20	M	Laborer	08Ma02Hi
BEAN, Margt.	30	F	None	08Ma02Hi
MCCULLOUGH, John	40	M	Laborer	08Ma02Hi
MOLLEY, Wm.	35	M	Laborer	08Ma02Hi
WILLIAMS, Thos.	24	M	Laborer	08Ma02Hi
OGRADY, Andrew	29	M	Laborer	08Ma02Hi
KEARNEY, Mary	40	F	None	08Ma02Hi
CLANRRY, Alexn.	20	M	Laborer	08Ma02Hi
CAMPBELL, Mary	20	F	None	08Ma02Hi
MCLEAN, Isabella	21	F	None	08Ma02Hi
MCCARLINE, Mary	40	F	None	08Ma02Hi
PHELAN, Eliza	20	F	None	08Ma02Hi
MCKAY, Thos.	40	M	Laborer	08Ma02Hi
JOHNSTON, Wm.	13	M	Laborer	08Ma02Hi
DEMPSTER, Edward	24	M	Laborer	08Ma02Hi
ALLEN, John	28	M	Laborer	08Ma02Hi
NANESS, Eliza	24	F	None	08Ma02Hi
MULLENS, Mary	21	F	None	08Ma02Hi
COFFEE, Jeremiah	30	M	Laborer	08Ma02Hi
SMITH, Robert	24	M	Laborer	08Ma02Hi
PURCELL, Wm.	21	M	Laborer	08Ma02Hi
CORTLYAND, Jacob	50	M	Merchant	08Ma02Hi
Edwin	22	M	Merchant	08Ma02Hi
Mary	50	F	None	08Ma02Hi
Ann	17	F	None	08Ma02Hi
WARNOW, Hannah	32	F	None	08Ma02Hi
HOEY, James	17	M	Laborer	08Ma02Hi
TAYLOR, Robert	35	M	Laborer	08Ma02Hi
GEE, Benjn.	32	M	Laborer	08Ma02Hi
Mary	35	F	None	08Ma02Hi
FINNEY, Honora	50	F	None	08Ma02Hi
Bridget	25	F	None	08Ma02Hi
John	20	M	Laborer	08Ma02Hi
REILLY, Ellen	20	F	None	08Ma02Hi
HICKEY, Cathe.	20	F	None	08Ma02Hi
HOUGHEY, Pat	20	M	Laborer	08Ma02Hi
MALONE, Judith	50	F	None	08Ma02Hi
Wm.	23	M	Laborer	08Ma02Hi
PRENDERGAST, Garret	14	M	Laborer	08Ma02Hi
Mary	17	F	None	08Ma02Hi
KENNEDY, Edmond	24	M	Laborer	08Ma02Hi
DALEY, Henry	14	M	Laborer	08Ma02Hi
BYRNE, Danl.	12	M	Laborer	08Ma02Hi
Margt.	14	F	None	08Ma02Hi

NAMES OF PASSENGERS	AGE	SEX	OCCUPATIONS	DATE PORT SHIP
MALONEY, Mary	15	F	None	08Ma02Hi
SEXTON, Ellen	25	F	None	08Ma02Hi
Kitty	20	F	None	08Ma02Hi
BIRCH, Thos.	50	M	Laborer	08Ma02Hi
Marcella	45	F	None	08Ma02Hi
HALBACK, Daniel	45	M	Laborer	08Ma02Hi
Mary	50	F	None	08Ma02Hi
GREEN, Sarah	25	F	None	08Ma02Hi
GREENHAIGH, Robert	24	M	Laborer	08Ma02Hi
Alex.	27	M	Laborer	08Ma02Hi
WARD, James	27	M	Laborer	08Ma02Hi
HALLIGAN, Pat	20	M	Laborer	08Ma02Hi
Ellen	16	F	None	08Ma02Hi
DOOLEY, Rose	45	F	None	08Ma02Hi
MILLWARD, Joseph	40	M	Laborer	08Ma02Hi
U (W)	37	F	Wife	08Ma02Hi
James	19	M	Laborer	08Ma02Hi
Jane	18	F	None	08Ma02Hi
Ann	17	F	None	08Ma02Hi
Wm.	12	M	Laborer	08Ma02Hi
John	11	M	Laborer	08Ma02Hi
Thos.	05	M	Child	08Ma02Hi
George	03	M	Child	08Ma02Hi
GILBERT, Joseph	30	M	Laborer	08Ma02Hi
U (W)	30	F	Wife	08Ma02Hi
Wm.	09	M	Child	08Ma02Hi
Herbert	07	M	Child	08Ma02Hi
U	.00	M	Infant	08Ma02Hi
ROBERTS, Edward	30	M	Mechanic	08Ma02Hi
Jane	27	F	None	08Ma02Hi
Betsey	17	F	None	08Ma02Hi
U	.00	F	Infant	08Ma02Hi
COOPER, Joseph	25	M	Laborer	08Ma02Hi
GAIST, John	30	M	Laborer	08Ma02Hi
U (W)	20	F	None	08Ma02Hi
CHATWIN, Thos.	28	M	Laborer	08Ma02Hi
U (W)	28	F	None	08Ma02Hi
Amelia	22	F	None	08Ma02Hi
GAIST, Betsey	.00	F	Infant	08Ma02Hi
Frederick	13	M	Laborer	08Ma02Hi
RIGLEY, Wm.	50	M	Laborer	08Ma02Hi
MCHODSON, Donald	22	M	Laborer	08Ma02Hi
SHACKELTON, John	24	M	Laborer	08Ma02Hi
Benjn.	21	M	Laborer	08Ma02Hi
JENKINS, John	24	M	Laborer	08Ma02Hi
HOPKINS, Hugh	27	M	Laborer	08Ma02Hi
CARR, John	25	M	Laborer	08Ma02Hi
WOOLMAN, Wm.	35	M	Laborer	08Ma02Hi
U (W)	40	F	Wife	08Ma02Hi
Thos.	25	M	Laborer	08Ma02Hi
Ann	23	F	None	08Ma02Hi
Eliza	17	F	None	08Ma02Hi
SMITH, John-Jnr.	30	M	Laborer	08Ma02Hi
John-Senr.	65	M	Laborer	08Ma02Hi
John	30	M	Laborer	08Ma02Hi
LIBEY, Thos.	28	M	Laborer	08Ma02Hi
U (W)	35	F	None	08Ma02Hi
U	.00	F	Infant	08Ma02Hi
SMITH, Ann	30	F	None	08Ma02Hi
EVANS, John	25	M	Laborer	08Ma02Hi
COOKE, Thos.	40	M	Laborer	08Ma02Hi
Thos.	23	M	Laborer	08Ma02Hi
BALDERSIN, Benjh.	19	M	Laborer	08Ma02Hi
BENDETT, Wm.	25	M	Laborer	08Ma02Hi
Saml.	12	M	Laborer	08Ma02Hi
Clara	19	F	None	08Ma02Hi
Saml.	21	M	Laborer	08Ma02Hi
RYAN, Pat	25	M	Laborer	08Ma02Hi
OLWELL, Ann	20	F	None	08Ma02Hi
Cathe.	18	F	None	08Ma02Hi
Jane	21	F	None	08Ma02Hi
BYRNE, Michl.	30	M	Laborer	08Ma02Hi
MATHEW, John	33	M	Laborer	08Ma02Hi
CASHELL, Pat	30	M	Laborer	08Ma02Hi
SMITH, John	30	M	Laborer	08Ma02Hi

NAMES OF PASSENGERS	AGE	SEX	OCCUPATIONS	DATE PORT SHIP	NAMES OF PASSENGERS	AGE	SEX	OCCUPATIONS	DATE PORT SHIP
MCWARREN, John	36	M	Laborer	08Ma02Hi	MULLALLEY, Bryan	28	M	Laborer	08Ma02Hi
ROBINSON, Mary	34	F	None	08Ma02Hi	WESTON, James	26	M	Laborer	08Ma02Hi
CREATON, James	36	M	Laborer	08Ma02Hi	PEARSON, Joseph	24	M	Laborer	08Ma02Hi
LADELER, James	21	M	Laborer	08Ma02Hi	BIRMINGHAM, John	25	M	Laborer	08Ma02Hi
BRADLEY, Thos.	24	M	Laborer	08Ma02Hi	RUSSEL, Ann	20	F	None	08Ma02Hi
ROCHFORD, Margt.	24	F	None	08Ma02Hi	Bridget	22	F	None	08Ma02Hi
GIBSDEY, Benjn.	21	M	Laborer	08Ma02Hi	COSGROVE, Martin	25	M	Laborer	08Ma02Hi
ARTHUR, Richd.	24	M	Laborer	08Ma02Hi	GRANT, Martin	26	M	Laborer	08Ma02Hi
Nicholas	12	M	Laborer	08Ma02Hi	BUTLER, Ann	30	F	None	08Ma02Hi
Susan	23	F	None	08Ma02Hi	GOLDRICH, James	30	M	Laborer	08Ma02Hi
Elizabeth	.00	F	Infant	08Ma02Hi	Bridget	20	F	None	08Ma02Hi
MURRITT, Peter	23	M	Laborer	08Ma02Hi	MCCARTIN, Pat	18	M	Laborer	08Ma02Hi
GLOVER, James	23	M	Laborer	08Ma02Hi	QUINN, Sally	19	F	None	08Ma02Hi
U (W)	20	F	None	08Ma02Hi	LIGHTBURNE, James	40	M	Laborer	08Ma02Hi
TYGHE, Michl.	45	M	Mechanic	08Ma02Hi	Ann	40	F	None	08Ma02Hi
Mary	45	F	None	08Ma02Hi	Wm.	02	M	Child	08Ma02Hi
Ann	16	F	None	08Ma02Hi	WESTON, Edwd.	24	M	Laborer	08Ma02Hi
Peter	14	M	Mechanic	08Ma02Hi	Edward	14	M	Laborer	08Ma02Hi
LONGBOTTOM, Ralph	25	M	Laborer	08Ma02Hi	FITZSIMMONS, Michl.	20	M	Laborer	08Ma02Hi
DINERSLY, Ralph	25	M	Laborer	08Ma02Hi	REILLY, John	26	M	Laborer	08Ma02Hi
Betty	24	F	None	08Ma02Hi	BYRNE, Michl.	30	M	Laborer	08Ma02Hi
Ruth	20	F	None	08Ma02Hi	U (W)	28	F	None	08Ma02Hi
Saml.	16	M	Laborer	08Ma02Hi	John	04	M	Child	08Ma02Hi
FITZSIMMONS, Bridget	30	F	None	08Ma02Hi	James	01	M	Child	08Ma02Hi
Thos.	20	M	Laborer	08Ma02Hi	Mary	06	F	Child	08Ma02Hi
Edward	08	M	Child	08Ma02Hi	MCGINNESS, Edward	23	M	Laborer	08Ma02Hi
MCGUIRE, John	20	M	Laborer	08Ma02Hi	Ann	20	F	None	08Ma02Hi
WHITTAKER, Robert	21	M	Laborer	08Ma02Hi	MCKEON, Thos.	20	M	Laborer	08Ma02Hi
FROARY, Jonathan	23	M	Laborer	08Ma02Hi	DURNAN, James	35	M	Laborer	08Ma02Hi
HARRIS, Wm.	22	M	Laborer	08Ma02Hi	Ann	35	F	None	08Ma02Hi
CAMPIN, Margt.	20	F	None	08Ma02Hi	CARROLL, Peter	16	M	None	08Ma02Hi
DELANEY, Margt.	21	F	None	08Ma02Hi	CARR, Margt.	17	F	None	08Ma02Hi
KERRINS, Terrence	28	M	Laborer	08Ma02Hi	DUFFY, Bridget	17	F	None	08Ma02Hi
ADAMS, Richard	27	M	Laborer	08Ma02Hi	HARNELL, Cathe.	17	F	None	08Ma02Hi
BOWNE, Anne	25	F	None	08Ma02Hi	CURTIS, Nichls.	28	M	Laborer	08Ma02Hi
SWEENEY, Danl.	45	M	Laborer	08Ma02Hi	Bridgt.	23	F	None	08Ma02Hi
Eliza	35	F	None	08Ma02Hi	Margt.	20	F	None	08Ma02Hi
Ann	10	F	None	08Ma02Hi	RICHARDS, James	26	M	Laborer	08Ma02Hi
Mary	08	F	Child	08Ma02Hi	NOONDER, Michl.	24	M	Laborer	08Ma02Hi
John	02	M	Child	08Ma02Hi	HONRIGAN, James	25	M	Laborer	08Ma02Hi
Agnes	.00	F	Infant	08Ma02Hi	MURPHY, Wm.	31	M	Laborer	08Ma02Hi
EDWARD, Thos.	28	M	Laborer	08Ma02Hi	Winfrd.	26	M	Laborer	08Ma02Hi
KING, Wm.	30	M	Laborer	08Ma02Hi	MCDONALD, Ned	35	M	Laborer	08Ma02Hi
Sarah	25	F	None	08Ma02Hi	FLOOD, Edwd.	20	M	Laborer	08Ma02Hi
REYNOLDS, Mary	20	F	None	08Ma02Hi	Pat	30	M	Laborer	08Ma02Hi
WHITEHEAD, Wm.	20	M	Laborer	08Ma02Hi	Ellen	10	F	None	08Ma02Hi
SMITH, Mary	20	F	None	08Ma02Hi	Mary	.00	F	Infant	08Ma02Hi
LARKIN, Pat	21	M	Laborer	08Ma02Hi	KING, Edward	32	M	Laborer	08Ma02Hi
Hanora	20	F	None	08Ma02Hi	MCDONALD, John	25	M	Laborer	08Ma02Hi
MCGUINNESS, Bridget	24	F	None	08Ma02Hi	WEBSTER, Geo.	23	M	Laborer	08Ma02Hi
SMITH, Pat	24	M	Laborer	08Ma02Hi	BURNEY, Judy	28	F	None	08Ma02Hi
REILLY, James	24	M	Laborer	08Ma02Hi	MULCHANEY, Mary	04	F	Child	08Ma02Hi
Pat	23	M	Laborer	08Ma02Hi	DEVANE, Danl.	26	M	Laborer	08Ma02Hi
HARKEY, Pat	25	M	Laborer	08Ma02Hi	CAREY, Wm.	26	M	Laborer	08Ma02Hi
FLEMMIN, Peter	30	M	Laborer	08Ma02Hi	BOWHINE, Bridget	23	F	None	08Ma02Hi
Richd.	24	M	Laborer	08Ma02Hi	DARCEY, Ellen	30	F	None	08Ma02Hi
FITZSIMMONS, Pat	24	M	Laborer	08Ma02Hi	JONES, Mary	44	F	None	08Ma02Hi
HUGHES, Pat	30	M	Laborer	08Ma02Hi	Eliza	15	F	None	08Ma02Hi
Judy	30	F	None	08Ma02Hi	John	10	M	Laborer	08Ma02Hi
FLEMING, Mary	24	F	None	08Ma02Hi	SLEVIN, Thos.	21	M	Laborer	08Ma02Hi
JOHNSON, Mary	24	F	None	08Ma02Hi	CHROTWELL, John	26	M	Laborer	08Ma02Hi
MCCARROLL, Rose	30	F	None	08Ma02Hi	FIRTH, Thos.	28	M	Laborer	08Ma02Hi
LARKIN, James	25	M	Laborer	08Ma02Hi	BAKER, James	25	M	Laborer	08Ma02Hi
MCDERMOTT, Patt.	24	M	Laborer	08Ma02Hi	SMITH, John	34	M	Laborer	08Ma02Hi
Jane	20	F	None	08Ma02Hi	POLLARD, James	30	M	Laborer	08Ma02Hi
CURRAN, John	28	M	Laborer	08Ma02Hi	ROGERS, Thos.	39	M	Laborer	08Ma02Hi
WATERSON, James	30	M	Laborer	08Ma02Hi	MALONE, Peter	26	M	Laborer	08Ma02Hi
RUSSELL, Wm.	22	M	Laborer	08Ma02Hi	DOOLEY, John	20	M	Laborer	08Ma02Hi
Peggy	19	F	None	08Ma02Hi	RUST, Michl.	25	M	Laborer	08Ma02Hi
CHADWICK, Alfred	30	M	Laborer	08Ma02Hi	MURRY, Ellen	14	F	Laborer	08Ma02Hi
FLYNN, Danl.	30	M	Laborer	08Ma02Hi	MOORE, Michl.	20	M	Laborer	08Ma02Hi
Margt.	28	F	None	08Ma02Hi	SULLIVAN, John	28	M	Laborer	08Ma02Hi
Pat	12	M	Laborer	08Ma02Hi	NEVITT, Saml.	28	M	Laborer	08Ma02Hi
Bridget	08	F	Child	08Ma02Hi	SAMPSON, Wm.	29	M	Laborer	08Ma02Hi
James	03	M	Child	08Ma02Hi	HALL, Thos.	23	M	Laborer	08Ma02Hi

NAMES OF PASSENGERS	AGE	SEX	OCCUPATIONS	DATE PORT SHIP
CORCORON, Thos.	24	M	Laborer	08Ma02Hi
GRANGER, Benjn.	30	M	Laborer	08Ma02Hi
U (W)	30	F	None	08Ma02Hi
Henrietta	05	F	Child	08Ma02Hi
Saml.	03	M	Child	08Ma02Hi
Joseph	.00	M	Infant	08Ma02Hi
LEVIN, George	33	M	Laborer	08Ma02Hi
MUNSEY, Thos.	20	M	Laborer	08Ma02Hi
Margt.	24	F	None	08Ma02Hi
Mary	16	F	None	08Ma02Hi
ELVIN, John	39	M	Laborer	08Ma02Hi
ARKIN, Michl.	21	M	Laborer	08Ma02Hi
Eliza	24	F	None	08Ma02Hi
Eliza	.00	F	Infant	08Ma02Hi
BARMET, Andrew	34	M	Laborer	08Ma02Hi
MURPHY, Bernd.	20	M	Laborer	08Ma02Hi
Margt.	20	F	None	08Ma02Hi
GARVEY, Bridget	20	F	None	08Ma02Hi
REILLY, Terrence	34	M	Laborer	08Ma02Hi
Mary	60	F	None	08Ma02Hi
MAHER, Thos.	27	M	Laborer	08Ma02Hi
Pat	22	M	Laborer	08Ma02Hi
PHEALIN, Martin	22	M	Laborer	08Ma02Hi
Michl.	27	M	Laborer	08Ma02Hi
CONNER, Danl.	28	M	Laborer	08Ma02Hi
BROPHY, Michl.	36	M	Laborer	08Ma02Hi
U (W)	32	F	None	08Ma02Hi
Betsey	01	F	Child	08Ma02Hi
DOHERTY, John	25	M	Laborer	08Ma02Hi
FITZGERALD, Tim	24	M	Laborer	08Ma02Hi
WALKER, Eliza	26	F	None	08Ma02Hi
CHOLHANE, Rachel	26	F	None	08Ma02Hi
USHER, James	21	M	Laborer	08Ma02Hi
LISTER, Geo.	21	M	Laborer	08Ma02Hi
OLWELL, John	40	M	Laborer	08Ma02Hi
GIBBS, George	19	M	Laborer	08Ma02Hi
FARRELL, Pat	18	M	Laborer	08Ma02Hi
Nicholas	17	M	Laborer	08Ma02Hi
Mary	14	F	None	08Ma02Hi
HARMAN, Margt.	24	F	None	08Ma02Hi

CONSTITUTION 08 MAY 1848

From Belfast

NAMES OF PASSENGERS	AGE	SEX	OCCUPATIONS	DATE PORT SHIP
BLAKE, John	55	M	Farmer	08Ma07Hi
Cath.	22	F	Farmer	08Ma07Hi
Geo.	20	M	Farmer	08Ma07Hi
Jane	18	F	Farmer	08Ma07Hi
James	16	M	Farmer	08Ma07Hi
William	11	M	Farmer	08Ma07Hi
John	05	M	Child	08Ma07Hi
Henry	.00	M	Infant	08Ma07Hi
Thomas	14	M	Farmer	08Ma07Hi
MCBRIDE, William	47	M	Farmer	08Ma07Hi
Ann	47	F	Farmer	08Ma07Hi
Thomas	22	M	Farmer	08Ma07Hi
Mary	18	F	Farmer	08Ma07Hi
Jane	16	F	Farmer	08Ma07Hi
Ann	13	F	Farmer	08Ma07Hi
William	11	M	Farmer	08Ma07Hi
John	09	M	Child	08Ma07Hi
George	06	M	Child	08Ma07Hi
Joseph	.00	M	Infant	08Ma07Hi
SMITH, Eliza	29	F	Farmer	08Ma07Hi
CROZIER, Isabella	28	F	Farmer	08Ma07Hi
TROMEY, Sara	14	F	Farmer	08Ma07Hi
Arabella	12	F	Farmer	08Ma07Hi
Maud	10	F	Farmer	08Ma07Hi
TROMEY, Jane	08	F	Child	08Ma07Hi
Emma	06	F	Child	08Ma07Hi
William	28	M	Farmer	08Ma07Hi
FERGUSON, Arabella	07	F	Child	08Ma07Hi
Mary	06	F	Child	08Ma07Hi
Hugh	03	M	Child	08Ma07Hi
George	.00	M	Infant	08Ma07Hi
Jessie	28	M	Farmer	08Ma07Hi
JOHNSTON, Anne	50	F	Farmer	08Ma07Hi
RICHARDSON, Eliza	20	F	Farmer	08Ma07Hi
JOHNSTON, James	27	M	Farmer	08Ma07Hi
SIMPSON, John	33	M	Farmer	08Ma07Hi
Rose	29	F	Farmer	08Ma07Hi
Mary	30	F	Farmer	08Ma07Hi
Terence	28	M	Farmer	08Ma07Hi
Hanna	02	F	Child	08Ma07Hi
Rose	.00	F	Infant	08Ma07Hi
DOLAUGHAN, Andrew	48	M	Farmer	08Ma07Hi
Mary	48	F	Farmer	08Ma07Hi
Jane	23	F	Farmer	08Ma07Hi
Mary	17	F	Farmer	08Ma07Hi
Nancy	13	F	Farmer	08Ma07Hi
CAMPBELL, William	22	M	Farmer	08Ma07Hi
ROBINSON, James	22	M	Farmer	08Ma07Hi
Eliza	20	F	Farmer	08Ma07Hi
MULLEN, John	40	M	Farmer	08Ma07Hi
Mary	60	F	Farmer	08Ma07Hi
LOVE, Eliza	20	F	Farmer	08Ma07Hi
Jane	18	F	Farmer	08Ma07Hi
DONALDSON, James	20	M	Farmer	08Ma07Hi
REED, Alex	29	M	Farmer	08Ma07Hi
Eliza	21	F	Farmer	08Ma07Hi
William	.00	M	Infant	08Ma07Hi
David	24	M	Farmer	08Ma07Hi
Samuel	18	M	Farmer	08Ma07Hi
Fanny	20	F	Farmer	08Ma07Hi
TODD, Jane	20	F	Farmer	08Ma07Hi
Eliza	18	F	Farmer	08Ma07Hi
TOLEN, Robert	40	M	Farmer	08Ma07Hi
Nancy	38	F	Farmer	08Ma07Hi
Betty	18	F	Farmer	08Ma07Hi
Alexander	11	M	Farmer	08Ma07Hi
HOUSTON, David	21	M	Farmer	08Ma07Hi
BOYD, Thomas	22	M	Farmer	08Ma07Hi
Jane	21	F	Farmer	08Ma07Hi
Peggy	21	F	Farmer	08Ma07Hi
Rose	22	F	Farmer	08Ma07Hi
John	22	M	Farmer	08Ma07Hi
YOUNG, William	22	M	Farmer	08Ma07Hi
DICKEY, William	21	M	Farmer	08Ma07Hi
LAMB, James	29	M	Farmer	08Ma07Hi
ROONEY, John	25	M	Farmer	08Ma07Hi
Eliza	21	F	Farmer	08Ma07Hi
Patt.	.00	M	Infant	08Ma07Hi
WARNOCK, John	30	M	Farmer	08Ma07Hi
Mary	30	F	Farmer	08Ma07Hi
Sarah	08	F	Child	08Ma07Hi
Samuel	07	M	Child	08Ma07Hi
Mary	.00	F	Infant	08Ma07Hi
DENVIR, Thomas	29	M	Farmer	08Ma07Hi
Mary	26	F	Farmer	08Ma07Hi
Cath.	04	F	Child	08Ma07Hi
Died-At-Sea				
Richard	.00	M	Infant	08Ma07Hi
MAGEE, Patrick	26	M	Farmer	08Ma07Hi
Eliza	30	F	Farmer	08Ma07Hi
Catherin	28	F	Farmer	08Ma07Hi
Rose	20	F	Farmer	08Ma07Hi
Susan	10	F	Farmer	08Ma07Hi
DENVIR, William	24	M	Farmer	08Ma07Hi
John	50	M	Farmer	08Ma07Hi
John	19	M	Farmer	08Ma07Hi
Mary	17	F	Farmer	08Ma07Hi
Cath.	15	F	Farmer	08Ma07Hi
Cath.	10	F	Farmer	08Ma07Hi

NAMES OF PASSENGERS	AGE	SEX	OCCUPATIONS	DATE PORT SHIP
PARKER, William	28	M	Farmer	08Ma07Hi
GRACY, Mary	20	F	Farmer	08Ma07Hi
WEATHERHAM, Samuel	22	M	Farmer	08Ma07Hi
HYNDMAN, Isabella	29	F	Farmer	08Ma07Hi
SCOTT, Robert	27	M	Farmer	08Ma07Hi
MCPHERSON, David	21	M	Farmer	08Ma07Hi
WATERS, James	21	M	Farmer	08Ma07Hi
Debora	20	F	Farmer	08Ma07Hi
HAGGARTY, John	18	M	Farmer	08Ma07Hi
Henry	20	M	Farmer	08Ma07Hi
KANE, Grindle	22	M	Farmer	08Ma07Hi
FERRIS, Catherine	25	F	Farmer	08Ma07Hi
Robert	24	M	Farmer	08Ma07Hi
SLOAN, Matilda	14	F	Farmer	08Ma07Hi
Margt.	28	F	Farmer	08Ma07Hi
James	24	M	Farmer	08Ma07Hi
Robert	19	M	Farmer	08Ma07Hi
HERRIOTT, Eliza	17	F	Farmer	08Ma07Hi
HIGGINS, Ann	22	F	Farmer	08Ma07Hi
Ann	18	F	Farmer	08Ma07Hi
MAGEE, Ann	21	F	Farmer	08Ma07Hi
MCKEE, Nathl.	20	M	Farmer	08Ma07Hi
Mathew	21	M	Farmer	08Ma07Hi
BRADLEY, Robert	30	M	Farmer	08Ma07Hi
DICKEY, William	24	M	Farmer	08Ma07Hi
CALDERWOOD, Samuel	24	M	Farmer	08Ma07Hi
WADES, Mary	25	F	Farmer	08Ma07Hi
LENDRUM, Francis	48	M	Farmer	08Ma07Hi
James	30	M	Farmer	08Ma07Hi
Polly	24	F	Farmer	08Ma07Hi
BLYTHE, Wm.	24	M	Farmer	08Ma07Hi
STURSON, Wm.	21	M	Farmer	08Ma07Hi
GILLES, James	21	M	Farmer	08Ma07Hi
MCDOWELL, Robert	20	M	Farmer	08Ma07Hi
Esther	20	F	Farmer	08Ma07Hi
Jane	26	F	Farmer	08Ma07Hi
Mary	24	F	Farmer	08Ma07Hi
MCKENNA, Maria	22	F	Farmer	08Ma07Hi
KENNA, John	18	M	Farmer	08Ma07Hi
KNOX, Wm.	29	M	Farmer	08Ma07Hi
MARTIN, James	34	M	Farmer	08Ma07Hi
Jane	30	F	Farmer	08Ma07Hi
Richard	.00	M	Infant	08Ma07Hi
RICHIE, Ellen	28	F	Farmer	08Ma07Hi
CLARK, James	25	M	Farmer	08Ma07Hi
Margt.	21	F	Farmer	08Ma07Hi
BRYSON, John	50	M	Farmer	08Ma07Hi
Agnes	48	F	Farmer	08Ma07Hi
Agnes	18	F	Farmer	08Ma07Hi
Mary	14	F	Farmer	08Ma07Hi
Sarah	11	F	Farmer	08Ma07Hi
MCCOLLUMN, David	24	M	Farmer	08Ma07Hi
KYLES, Thomas	20	M	Farmer	08Ma07Hi
LOYD, Alexander	29	M	Farmer	08Ma07Hi
LOUGHLIN, Esther	40	F	Farmer	08Ma07Hi
DARIGAN, William	25	M	Farmer	08Ma07Hi
DELARGY, John	27	M	Farmer	08Ma07Hi
RUDDY, Jane	30	F	Farmer	08Ma07Hi
Ellen	28	F	Farmer	08Ma07Hi
William	11	M	Farmer	08Ma07Hi
Margt.	09	F	Child	08Ma07Hi
WELSH, Mary	22	F	Farmer	08Ma07Hi
Samuel	18	M	Farmer	08Ma07Hi
MCMULLEN, John	30	M	Farmer	08Ma07Hi
KANE, John	25	M	Farmer	08Ma07Hi
GANNON, Susanna	29	F	Farmer	08Ma07Hi
Susanna	.00	F	Infant	08Ma07Hi
BALENTINE, Alexander	25	M	Farmer	08Ma07Hi
Isabella	30	F	Farmer	08Ma07Hi
CAMPBELL, John	21	M	Farmer	08Ma07Hi
BAXTER, James	21	M	Farmer	08Ma07Hi
CLEFFORTY, Bessy	18	F	Farmer	08Ma07Hi
LENNON, Daniel	40	M	Farmer	08Ma07Hi
MICHAEL, Adam	22	M	Farmer	08Ma07Hi
SOUBBEN, Rose	20	F	Farmer	08Ma07Hi
MCSHERRY, Peter	40	M	Farmer	08Ma07Hi
CUNNINGHAM, Michael	30	M	Farmer	08Ma07Hi
SCOTT, Jane	40	F	Farmer	08Ma07Hi
Sarah	12	F	Farmer	08Ma07Hi
SIMPSON, Alex	20	M	Farmer	08Ma07Hi
JOHNSTON, Jane	29	F	Farmer	08Ma07Hi
COOPER, Mary	21	F	Farmer	08Ma07Hi
DAVISON, Mary	29	F	Farmer	08Ma07Hi
Mary	.00	F	Infant	08Ma07Hi
MCCRACKEN, Thomas	30	M	Farmer	08Ma07Hi
Nancy	28	F	Farmer	08Ma07Hi
ROBERTS, John	19	M	Farmer	08Ma07Hi
RICHIE, Alexander	23	M	Farmer	08Ma07Hi
David	19	M	Farmer	08Ma07Hi
SMITH, Thomas	28	M	Farmer	08Ma07Hi
GANNEN, Hugh	21	M	Farmer	08Ma07Hi
STEELE, William	22	M	Farmer	08Ma07Hi
Ann	21	F	Farmer	08Ma07Hi
DONALDSON, Emily	20	F	Farmer	08Ma07Hi
BANNON, Rose	28	F	Farmer	08Ma07Hi
Fanny	18	F	Farmer	08Ma07Hi
STEEL, Robert	04	M	Child	08Ma07Hi
Letitia	.00	F	Infant	08Ma07Hi
DAVISON, William	21	M	Farmer	08Ma07Hi
FURY, Samuel	21	M	Farmer	08Ma07Hi
KENRAGHAN, Eliza	22	F	Farmer	08Ma07Hi
MURRAY, Jas.	52	M	Farmer	08Ma07Hi
KENRAHAN, Robert	18	M	Farmer	08Ma07Hi
Wm.	17	M	Farmer	08Ma07Hi
GUENDFIELD, Robt.	21	M	Farmer	08Ma07Hi

LEAR 08 MAY 1848

From Oporto

NAMES OF PASSENGERS	AGE	SEX	OCCUPATIONS	DATE PORT SHIP
DOUGLASS, Joseph	29	M	Servant	08Ma96Cc

COUNTESS OF DURHAM 09 MAY 1848

From Liverpool

NAMES OF PASSENGERS	AGE	SEX	OCCUPATIONS	DATE PORT SHIP
WALSH, Edmund	26	M	Baker	09Ma02Tj
Joha.	28	F	Spinster	09Ma02Tj
MAHER, Wm.	24	M	Mason	09Ma02Tj
FOLEY, Thos.	23	M	Laborer	09Ma02Tj
James	20	M	Laborer	09Ma02Tj
Ellen	17	F	Spinster	09Ma02Tj
PYNE, Michael	30	M	Laborer	09Ma02Tj
BURKE, John-D.	38	M	Unknown	09Ma02Tj
HEFFEREN, Edmund	38	M	Laborer	09Ma02Tj
Mary	35	F	Spinster	09Ma02Tj
DOYLE, Ellen	16	F	Spinster	09Ma02Tj
Bridgt.	18	F	Spinster	09Ma02Tj
HEFFEREN, Margt.	10	F	Spinster	09Ma02Tj
Mary	08	F	Child	09Ma02Tj
John	06	M	Child	09Ma02Tj
Judy	03	F	Child	09Ma02Tj
GERON, James	48	M	Smith	09Ma02Tj
FURLONG, Michl.	23	M	Laborer	09Ma02Tj
KIDNEY, John	20	M	Cooper	09Ma02Tj
HEARN, Michl.	24	M	Laborer	09Ma02Tj
Cathe.	20	F	Spinster	09Ma02Tj
FITZGERALD, James	36	M	Laborer	09Ma02Tj

AMES OF PASSENGERS	AGE	SEX	OCCUPATIONS	DATE PORT SHIP
ITZGERALD, Patrick	32	M	Laborer	09Ma02Tj
IELDS, Margt.	27	F	Spinster	09Ma02Tj
Eliza	23	F	Spinster	09Ma02Tj
OWER, Thos.	24	M	Laborer	09Ma02Tj
Mary	27	F	Spinster	09Ma02Tj
ATON, Wm.	38	M	Laborer	09Ma02Tj
OREY, Patk.	30	M	Laborer	09Ma02Tj
Joha.	27	F	Spinster	09Ma02Tj
Patk.Jnr.	02	M	Child	09Ma02Tj
UNNINGHAM, John	18	M	Laborer	09Ma02Tj
Cathe.	22	F	Spinster	09Ma02Tj
HEA, Michl.	40	M	Laborer	09Ma02Tj
Patrick	18	M	Laborer	09Ma02Tj
Edmund	15	M	Laborer	09Ma02Tj
Judy	12	F	Spinster	09Ma02Tj
URRAN, Nora	32	F	Spinster	09Ma02Tj
Mary	28	F	Spinster	09Ma02Tj
Margt.	23	F	Spinster	09Ma02Tj
ORRISSY, James	25	M	Laborer	09Ma02Tj
IERNEY, Mary	25	F	Spinster	09Ma02Tj
RIEN, Ellen	22	F	Spinster	09Ma02Tj
URLEY, Patk.	35	M	Laborer	09Ma02Tj
Brigt.	30	F	Spinster	09Ma02Tj
OWER, James	48	M	Laborer	09Ma02Tj
Bryan	24	M	Laborer	09Ma02Tj
Wm.	22	M	Laborer	09Ma02Tj
LINN, John	19	M	Laborer	09Ma02Tj
Ann	45	F	Spinster	09Ma02Tj
LANAGAN, Ann	30	F	Spinster	09Ma02Tj
OWER, Joha.	27	F	Spinster	09Ma02Tj
Thos.	32	M	None	09Ma02Tj
Bgt.	05	F	Child	09Ma02Tj
Edmund	03	M	Child	09Ma02Tj
OLLY, Patk.	01	M	Child	09Ma02Tj
ROCKET, Thos.	36	M	Laborer	09Ma02Tj
ROGER, Wm.	27	M	Laborer	09Ma02Tj
Margt.	40	F	Spinster	09Ma02Tj
WALSH, John	37	M	Laborer	09Ma02Tj
DONOHUE, John	28	M	Laborer	09Ma02Tj
MULCAHY, Ally	27	F	Spinster	09Ma02Tj
MORRISSY, Michael	22	M	Laborer	09Ma02Tj
MERNER, Martin	50	M	Laborer	09Ma02Tj
CROWLY, John	31	M	Laborer	09Ma02Tj
BRAWDERS, John	29	M	Laborer	09Ma02Tj
BYRNE, Cathe.	25	F	Spinster	09Ma02Tj
MURPHY, Wm.	29	M	Laborer	09Ma02Tj
REHOE, John	33	M	Laborer	09Ma02Tj
Ellen	27	F	Spinster	09Ma02Tj
CONNOLLY, John	21	M	Laborer	09Ma02Tj
HEARN, Patk.	41	M	Laborer	09Ma02Tj
Nora	35	F	Spinster	09Ma02Tj
Ellen	04	F	Child	09Ma02Tj
Mary	02	F	Child	09Ma02Tj
Michl.	39	M	Laborer	09Ma02Tj
Allice	34	F	Spinster	09Ma02Tj
Maure.	19	U	None	09Ma02Tj
Kate	15	F	None	09Ma02Tj
Mary	16	F	None	09Ma02Tj
Michl.	12	M	None	09Ma02Tj
Bath.	08	M	Child	09Ma02Tj
Nelly	05	F	Child	09Ma02Tj
Allice	01	F	Child	09Ma02Tj
KEARNEY, Patk.	25	M	Laborer	09Ma02Tj
POWER, Wm.	31	M	Laborer	09Ma02Tj
FOLEY, Richd.	28	M	Laborer	09Ma02Tj
BROWN, John	30	M	Baker	09Ma02Tj
CORCORAN, John	25	M	Baker	09Ma02Tj
GAMBON, Maure.	22	M	Laborer	09Ma02Tj
ROCHE, Luke	20	M	Laborer	09Ma02Tj
SMYTH, Thos.	23	M	Laborer	09Ma02Tj
POWER, Bridgt.	39	F	Spinster	09Ma02Tj
DUNPHY, Michl.	35	M	Laborer	09Ma02Tj
DOLLARD, John	17	M	Laborer	09Ma02Tj
Cathe.	11	F	None	09Ma02Tj
CARTY, Wm.	19	M	Tailor	09Ma02Tj

NAMES OF PASSENGERS	AGE	SEX	OCCUPATIONS	DATE PORT SHIP
HONEN, Cathe.	35	F	Spinster	09Ma02Tj
DEE, John	65	M	Laborer	09Ma02Tj
POWER, Wm.	37	M	Laborer	09Ma02Tj
RYAN, John	24	M	Laborer	09Ma02Tj
BALDWAN, Cathe.	26	F	Spinster	09Ma02Tj
KEARNING, Mary	23	F	Spinster	09Ma02Tj
FLEMING, Mary	21	F	Spinster	09Ma02Tj
QUINN, Brigt.	25	F	Spinster	09Ma02Tj
CASEY, Wm.	35	M	Laborer	09Ma02Tj
WALSH, Michl.	39	M	Laborer	09Ma02Tj
DAVIN, John	20	M	Laborer	09Ma02Tj
CREED, Wm.	48	M	Musician	09Ma02Tj
Wm.Jnr.	21	M	Musician	09Ma02Tj
Thos.	19	M	Musician	09Ma02Tj
DROHAN, Cathe.	26	F	Spinster	09Ma02Tj
POWER, Nann	21	F	Spinster	09Ma02Tj
SULLIVAN, Robt.	30	M	Shoemaker	09Ma02Tj
TEARNEY, Thos.	34	M	Laborer	09Ma02Tj
TOBIN, Wm.	30	M	Laborer	09Ma02Tj
James	25	M	Laborer	09Ma02Tj
Cathe.	32	F	Spinster	09Ma02Tj
Thos.	03	M	Child	09Ma02Tj
SULLIVAN, Paul	17	M	Hatter	09Ma02Tj
KEHOE, Wm.	33	M	Laborer	09Ma02Tj
BRAWDERS, Dennis	36	M	Laborer	09Ma02Tj
MEHAN, Thos.	27	M	Laborer	09Ma02Tj
BRISCOE, Wm.	28	M	Farmer	09Ma02Tj
Cathe.	27	F	Spinster	09Ma02Tj
DANIEL, Mary	21	F	Spinster	09Ma02Tj
BRISCOE, Mary	08	F	Child	09Ma02Tj
Cathe.	05	F	Child	09Ma02Tj
Wm.Jnr.	01	M	Child	09Ma02Tj
BROPHY, John	19	M	Laborer	09Ma02Tj
GRUDER, Honor	22	F	Spinster	09Ma02Tj
FITZGERALD, John	60	M	Laborer	09Ma02Tj
KEANE, Bott.	65	M	Laborer	09Ma02Tj

CHILDE-HAROLD 09 MAY 1848

From Havana

NAMES OF PASSENGERS	AGE	SEX	OCCUPATIONS	DATE PORT SHIP
FERGUSON, S.R.	35	M	Ay-Off	09Ma06Cv
REEVE, M.	35	M	Ay-Off	09Ma06Cv

WOLFSVILLE 09 MAY 1848

From Belfast

NAMES OF PASSENGERS	AGE	SEX	OCCUPATIONS	DATE PORT SHIP
DUNCAN, John	50	M	Laborer	09Ma07Cd
Ann	40	F	Laborer	09Ma07Cd
Agnes	28	F	Laborer	09Ma07Cd
John	24	M	Laborer	09Ma07Cd
Sarah	22	F	Laborer	09Ma07Cd
Mary	20	F	Laborer	09Ma07Cd
Fergus	19	M	Laborer	09Ma07Cd
NEWELL, Mary	20	F	Laborer	09Ma07Cd
MCKEE, Mary	20	F	Laborer	09Ma07Cd
SAVAGE, Thomas	22	M	Laborer	09Ma07Cd
SKINDRED, Eliza	20	F	Laborer	09Ma07Cd
RICHIE, William	60	M	Laborer	09Ma07Cd
Margt.	30	F	Laborer	09Ma07Cd
MCNEILL, James	30	M	Laborer	09Ma07Cd
VANCE, Robt.	25	M	Laborer	09Ma07Cd

NAMES OF PASSENGERS		AGE	SEX	OCCUPATIONS	DATE PORT SHIP
KERNAGHAN, James		32	M	Laborer	09Ma07Cd
HOGG, John		23	M	Laborer	09Ma07Cd
LONG, Esther		20	F	Laborer	09Ma07Cd
OHARA, John		21	M	Laborer	09Ma07Cd
BOYD, Eliza		25	F	Laborer	09Ma07Cd
KANE, Sarah		27	F	Laborer	09Ma07Cd
SHAW, Susanna		21	F	Laborer	09Ma07Cd
STEWART, Thomas		20	M	Laborer	09Ma07Cd
WATSON, Sarah		20	F	Laborer	09Ma07Cd
Arabella		20	F	Laborer	09Ma07Cd
HAYES, Saml.		30	M	Laborer	09Ma07Cd
Margt.		30	F	Laborer	09Ma07Cd
Robert		05	M	Child	09Ma07Cd
Saml.		02	M	Child	09Ma07Cd
Charlotte		.00	F	Infant	09Ma07Cd
GOURLEY, Wm.		20	M	Laborer	09Ma07Cd
HAYES, Sarah		50	F	Laborer	09Ma07Cd
Margt.		18	F	Laborer	09Ma07Cd
PINKERTON, Saml.		22	M	Laborer	09Ma07Cd
William		20	M	Laborer	09Ma07Cd
MCALISTER, Saml.		18	M	Laborer	09Ma07Cd
PINKERTON, Mary		22	F	Laborer	09Ma07Cd
Robert		01	M	Child	09Ma07Cd
Eliza		04	F	Child	09Ma07Cd
John		02	M	Child	09Ma07Cd
CAMPBELL, Mary		04	F	Child	09Ma07Cd
LOUGHRY, Mary		22	F	Spinster	09Ma07Cd
KELLY, Alexr.		27	M	Weaver	09Ma07Cd
Eliza	(W)	21	F	Wife	09Ma07Cd
DENISON, James		30	M	Laborer	09Ma07Cd
HAY, James		29	M	Laborer	09Ma07Cd
MEHERRY, Saml.		35	M	Laborer	09Ma07Cd
Sarah	(W)	30	F	Wife	09Ma07Cd
Saml.	(S)	03	M	Child	09Ma07Cd
James	(S)	.00	M	Infant	09Ma07Cd
LOUREY, Saml.		21	M	Laborer	09Ma07Cd
MCLOUGHLIN, Ann		23	F	Spinster	09Ma07Cd
HUGENTS, William		17	M	Laborer	09Ma07Cd
SHARKEY, Margt.Mrs.		17	F	Wife	09Ma07Cd
Cathe.		20	F	Unknown	09Ma07Cd
GAVIN, Margt.		04	F	Child	09Ma07Cd
FIELD, Henry		20	M	Laborer	09Ma07Cd
CUNNINGHAM, Margt.Mrs.		31	F	Wife	09Ma07Cd
ORR, Robert		22	M	Laborer	09Ma07Cd
Margt.		21	F	Spinster	09Ma07Cd
Eliza		25	F	Spinster	09Ma07Cd
Andrew.		.00	M	Infant	09Ma07Cd
MCCULLOUGH, Mary		23	F	Spinster	09Ma07Cd
MCKENNON, Ann		23	F	Spinster	09Ma07Cd
YOUNG, Jane		25	F	Spinster	09Ma07Cd
Ann		21	F	Spinster	09Ma07Cd
REYNOLDS, Sarah		25	F	Spinster	09Ma07Cd
John		04	M	Child	09Ma07Cd
Eliza		02	F	Child	09Ma07Cd
ADAM, Mary		12	F	Unknown	09Ma07Cd
WARNOCK, Saml.		25	M	Laborer	09Ma07Cd
Susanna	(W)	23	F	Wife	09Ma07Cd
Eliza	(D)	.00	F	Infant	09Ma07Cd
MOORE, Joseph		57	M	Laborer	09Ma07Cd
Jane	(W)	49	F	Wife	09Ma07Cd
Alexr.	(S)	16	M	Laborer	09Ma07Cd
Martha	(D)	14	F	Unknown	09Ma07Cd
Robt.	(S)	12	M	Unknown	09Ma07Cd
Jane	(D)	10	F	Unknown	09Ma07Cd
Nancy	(D)	08	F	Child	09Ma07Cd
Sarah	(D)	06	F	Child	09Ma07Cd
ALLEN, Robt.		21	M	Weaver	09Ma07Cd
SIMPSON, Robt.		21	M	Weaver	09Ma07Cd
ROE, Jonathan		29	M	Weaver	09Ma07Cd
CAULFIELD, Pat.		22	M	Weaver	09Ma07Cd
GRAHAM, Eliza		19	F	Weaver	09Ma07Cd
WILSON, James		31	M	Weaver	09Ma07Cd
Ann		22	F	Weaver	09Ma07Cd
Jane		02	F	Child	09Ma07Cd
Mary		.00	F	Infant	09Ma07Cd
MCMARRY, Chas.		29	M	Laborer	09Ma07Cd
MCCAUGHER, Robt.		25	M	Laborer	09Ma07Cd
HENRY, Wm.		20	M	Laborer	09Ma07Cd
MILCRIEST, Eliza-Mrs.		25	F	Wife	09Ma07Cd
MCCULLOUGH, Biddy		20	F	Unknown	09Ma07Cd
THOMPSON, James		20	M	Weaver	09Ma07Cd
NUGENT, Susan-Mrs.		45	F	Wife	09Ma07Cd
HANEY, Hanor-Mrs.		21	F	Wife	09Ma07Cd
KELLY, Sarah-Mrs.		26	F	Wife	09Ma07Cd
SMITH, Margt.Mrs.		21	F	Wife	09Ma07Cd
RODGERS, John		21	M	Laborer	09Ma07Cd
STEPHENSON, Edwd.		29	M	Laborer	09Ma07Cd
GRAHAM, Robt.		21	M	Laborer	09Ma07Cd
HALL, Achison		25	M	Laborer	09Ma07Cd
Sarah	(W)	21	F	Wife	09Ma07Cd
Thomas	(S)	07	M	Child	09Ma07Cd
John	(S)	05	M	Child	09Ma07Cd
Albert	(S)	03	M	Child	09Ma07Cd
Emily	(D)	.00	F	Infant	09Ma07Cd
GRAHAM, Grace		29	F	Unknown	09Ma07Cd
KEENAN, John		21	M	Laborer	09Ma07Cd
William		13	M	Unknown	09Ma07Cd
MAGUIRE, John		34	M	Unknown	09Ma07Cd
Mary	(W)	21	F	Wife	09Ma07Cd
BIRNEY, Thos.		18	M	Laborer	09Ma07Cd
BOGAN, Felix		18	M	Laborer	09Ma07Cd
COOPER, Wm.		30	M	Laborer	09Ma07Cd
WILLOUGHBY, Henry		29	M	Laborer	09Ma07Cd
MCGREERY, Mary		29	F	Spinster	09Ma07Cd
WOODBURN, Richd.		40	M	Laborer	09Ma07Cd
Jane	(W)	40	F	Wife	09Ma07Cd
Richd.	(S)	11	M	Unknown	09Ma07Cd
Eliza	(D)	05	F	Child	09Ma07Cd
CREIGHTON, Mary		55	F	Unknown	09Ma07Cd
HORSYTHE, Jane		30	F	Unknown	09Ma07Cd
Eliza		26	F	Unknown	09Ma07Cd
HODGE, Robt.		30	M	Laborer	09Ma07Cd
Margt.		30	F	Laborer	09Ma07Cd
Martha		.00	F	Infant	09Ma07Cd
FINLAY, Mary		30	F	Wife	09Ma07Cd
MCCONNELL, Eliza		18	F	Unknown	09Ma07Cd
CARLSON, Ellen		18	F	Unknown	09Ma07Cd
CONNOR, Dennis		23	M	Weaver	09Ma07Cd
Susan		20	F	Weaver	09Ma07Cd
Edwd.		21	M	Weaver	09Ma07Cd
MCLONINAN, Robt.		23	M	Weaver	09Ma07Cd
Sarah		22	F	Weaver	09Ma07Cd
James		03	M	Child	09Ma07Cd
Eliza		02	F	Child	09Ma07Cd
HUTCHINSON, Margt.		20	F	Spinster	09Ma07Cd
LENNOX, John		25	M	Weaver	09Ma07Cd
Margt.	(W)	20	F	Wife	09Ma07Cd
GILLON, Neil		21	M	Laborer	09Ma07Cd
MCCUSKER, John		32	M	Laborer	09Ma07Cd
Cathe.	(W)	26	F	Wife	09Ma07Cd
Mary	(D)	06	F	Child	09Ma07Cd
Rosey	(D)	04	F	Child	09Ma07Cd
Charles	(S)	02	M	Child	09Ma07Cd
Jane	(D)	.00	F	Infant	09Ma07Cd
TIERNEY, Ann		25	F	Unknown	09Ma07Cd
DONNELLY, Mary		19	F	Unknown	09Ma07Cd
Bernd.		17	M	Laborer	09Ma07Cd
Edward		14	M	Laborer	09Ma07Cd
DUGAN, James-Or-Jane		16	U	Laborer	09Ma07Cd
FARRELL, Betty		19	F	Spinster	09Ma07Cd
MCPEAK, Mary		16	F	Unknown	09Ma07Cd
FULLIN, John		23	M	Weaver	09Ma07Cd
Mary	(W)	23	F	Wife	09Ma07Cd
COSTELLO, Henry		20	M	Laborer	09Ma07Cd
KEATING, Thomas		21	M	Laborer	09Ma07Cd
TURLEY, Wm.		20	M	Laborer	09Ma07Cd
DRAMOND, Henry		17	M	Laborer	09Ma07Cd
CRAIG, Robert		20	M	Laborer	09Ma07Cd
HUGHES, Mary		21	F	Spinster	09Ma07Cd
MCGLOUGHLIN, James		21	M	Laborer	09Ma07Cd

NAMES OF PASSENGERS		AGE	SEX	OCCUPATIONS	DATE PORT SHIP
MCGLOUGHLIN, Eliza (W)		20	F	Wife	09Ma07Cd

ISABELLA-STEWART 09 MAY 1848

From Dublin

NAMES OF PASSENGERS		AGE	SEX	OCCUPATIONS	DATE PORT SHIP
CAREY, Henry		45	M	Farmer	09Ma20Cf
POWER, Thomas		25	M	Farmer	09Ma20Cf
CARNEY, James		35	M	Farmer	09Ma20Cf
Anne		22	F	Farmer	09Ma20Cf
John		13	M	Farmer	09Ma20Cf
BYRNE, Wm.		22	M	Farmer	09Ma20Cf
REILLEY, John		33	M	Farmer	09Ma20Cf
Eliza		26	F	Farmer	09Ma20Cf
ROWE, Pat		24	M	Farmer	09Ma20Cf
COSTELLO, James		40	M	Farmer	09Ma20Cf
Thomas		30	M	Farmer	09Ma20Cf
Cathe.		05	F	Child	09Ma20Cf
Mary-Ann		.00	F	Infant	09Ma20Cf
FARRELL, Simon		24	M	Farmer	09Ma20Cf
MCGUINISS, Michael		20	M	Farmer	09Ma20Cf
BARRY, James		32	M	Farmer	09Ma20Cf
CAFFE, Michael		32	M	Farmer	09Ma20Cf
LYNCH, Edward		22	M	Farmer	09Ma20Cf
QUINN, John		28	M	Farmer	09Ma20Cf
Margt.		26	F	Farmer	09Ma20Cf
Ann		09	F	Child	09Ma20Cf
Mary		.00	F	Infant	09Ma20Cf
FITZSIMONS, Ann		20	F	Farmer	09Ma20Cf
COATS, Jacob		27	M	Farmer	09Ma20Cf
Eliza		26	F	Farmer	09Ma20Cf
James		.00	M	Infant	09Ma20Cf
William		06	M	Child	09Ma20Cf
KEHOE, Peter		21	M	Farmer	09Ma20Cf
DOYLE, Margt.		20	F	Farmer	09Ma20Cf
CANAVAN, Eliza		35	F	Farmer	09Ma20Cf
RODGERS, John		30	M	Farmer	09Ma20Cf
Mary		27	F	Farmer	09Ma20Cf
MINKS, U-Mrs.		32	F	Farmer	09Ma20Cf
Michael		20	M	Farmer	09Ma20Cf
Mary-Ann		05	F	Child	09Ma20Cf
Agnes		.00	F	Infant	09Ma20Cf
James		10	M	Farmer	09Ma20Cf
KANE, Eliza		17	F	Farmer	09Ma20Cf
CONNOLLY, Eliza		66	F	Farmer	09Ma20Cf
DOYLE, Eliza		20	F	Farmer	09Ma20Cf
MAXEY, Michael		30	M	Farmer	09Ma20Cf
THOSALL, Michael		20	M	Farmer	09Ma20Cf
MERCER, James		30	M	Farmer	09Ma20Cf
WOODS, Francis		40	M	Farmer	09Ma20Cf
Pat		23	M	Farmer	09Ma20Cf
Peggy		30	F	Farmer	09Ma20Cf
KELLY, Pat		26	M	Farmer	09Ma20Cf
FLOOD, Cath.		20	F	Farmer	09Ma20Cf
HACKETT, U-Mrs.		20	F	Farmer	09Ma20Cf
HICKEY, John		24	M	Farmer	09Ma20Cf
U	(W)	22	F	Wife	09Ma20Cf
JACOB, Ebenezer		20	M	Farmer	09Ma20Cf
U	(W)	20	F	Wife	09Ma20Cf
LALOR, Francis		20	M	Farmer	09Ma20Cf
THORPE, Gabriel		50	M	Farmer	09Ma20Cf
U	(W)	45	F	Wife	09Ma20Cf
U-Mrs.		22	F	Wife	09Ma20Cf
John		16	M	Farmer	09Ma20Cf
Cath.		24	F	Farmer	09Ma20Cf
Margt.		20	F	Farmer	09Ma20Cf
Judith		18	F	Farmer	09Ma20Cf
KILBY, Mary		40	F	Farmer	09Ma20Cf
John		11	M	Farmer	09Ma20Cf
KILBY, Patrick		13	M	Farmer	09Ma20Cf
SWORDS, Denis		27	M	Farmer	09Ma20Cf
KILMENEY, Patrick		24	M	Farmer	09Ma20Cf
CONNOR, Mary		20	F	Farmer	09Ma20Cf
SWORDS, Mary		20	F	Farmer	09Ma20Cf
SCULLY, Mary		24	F	Farmer	09Ma20Cf
STERLY, Honora		23	F	Farmer	09Ma20Cf
DELANEY, Daniel		20	M	Farmer	09Ma20Cf
MCDONAGH, Pat		22	M	Farmer	09Ma20Cf
MURPHY, Richard		20	M	Farmer	09Ma20Cf
John		17	M	Farmer	09Ma20Cf
FLEMING, Catherine		20	F	Farmer	09Ma20Cf
Mary		18	F	Farmer	09Ma20Cf
KINOWN, James		20	M	Farmer	09Ma20Cf
TYRREELL, Wm.		20	M	Farmer	09Ma20Cf
QUINN, Pat		20	M	Farmer	09Ma20Cf
LYONS, Edward		22	M	Farmer	09Ma20Cf
CASEY, John		21	M	Farmer	09Ma20Cf
U	(W)	20	F	Wife	09Ma20Cf
FROLAN, Phillip		24	M	Farmer	09Ma20Cf
RABBETT, Wm.		50	M	Farmer	09Ma20Cf
U	(W)	50	F	Farmer	09Ma20Cf
Pat		18	M	Farmer	09Ma20Cf
Cath.		13	F	Farmer	09Ma20Cf
Mary-Ann		12	F	Farmer	09Ma20Cf
James		11	M	Farmer	09Ma20Cf
Wm.		08	M	Child	09Ma20Cf
Thomas		07	M	Child	09Ma20Cf
Eliza		.00	F	Infant	09Ma20Cf
MCDONAGH, Hugh		30	M	Farmer	09Ma20Cf
FOX, Charles		24	M	Farmer	09Ma20Cf
CAVANAGH, John		20	M	Farmer	09Ma20Cf
Luke		21	M	Farmer	09Ma20Cf
Margt.		17	F	Farmer	09Ma20Cf
SHEA, James		21	M	Farmer	09Ma20Cf
REGAN, Susan		26	F	Farmer	09Ma20Cf
Sarah		23	F	Farmer	09Ma20Cf
MULREADY, Pat		21	F	Farmer	09Ma20Cf
Bidelia		17	F	Farmer	09Ma20Cf
MCCABE, Brdgt.		24	F	Farmer	09Ma20Cf
KIERNAN, Wm.		24	M	Farmer	09Ma20Cf
Edward		26	M	Farmer	09Ma20Cf
BYRNE, Pat		28	M	Farmer	09Ma20Cf
Julia		23	F	Farmer	09Ma20Cf
Ann		.00	F	Infant	09Ma20Cf
GAGAN, Thomas		22	M	Farmer	09Ma20Cf
U	(W)	22	F	Wife	09Ma20Cf
KINGSWELL, Robert		26	M	Farmer	09Ma20Cf
HANRAHAN, Thomas		40	M	Farmer	09Ma20Cf
OBRINE, Mich.		22	M	Farmer	09Ma20Cf
FOY, Anthony		26	M	Farmer	09Ma20Cf
NULTY, Mick		40	M	Farmer	09Ma20Cf
BRYAN, Phillip		24	M	Farmer	09Ma20Cf
Timothy		20	M	Farmer	09Ma20Cf
MURRAY, Richard		20	M	Farmer	09Ma20Cf
BRENNAN, Edward		27	M	Farmer	09Ma20Cf
MURPHY, Mary		21	F	Farmer	09Ma20Cf
DINVEY, Robert		26	M	Farmer	09Ma20Cf
KENNEDY, Chr.		24	M	Farmer	09Ma20Cf
U	(W)	20	F	Farmer	09Ma20Cf
KEENAN, Thomas		27	M	Farmer	09Ma20Cf
PHELAN, Pat		28	M	Farmer	09Ma20Cf
COSTELLO, John		20	M	Farmer	09Ma20Cf
James		20	M	Farmer	09Ma20Cf
Margt.		12	F	Farmer	09Ma20Cf
MAGIN, Pat		20	M	Farmer	09Ma20Cf
WALL, Thomas		20	M	Farmer	09Ma20Cf
BROTHERS, Pat		30	M	Farmer	09Ma20Cf
U	(W)	28	F	Wife	09Ma20Cf
CAUGHAN, Ann		20	F	Farmer	09Ma20Cf
Pat		27	M	Farmer	09Ma20Cf
Bryan		24	M	Farmer	09Ma20Cf
Ann		22	F	Farmer	09Ma20Cf
Mary		20	F	Farmer	09Ma20Cf
KELLY, Pat		50	M	Farmer	09Ma20Cf

NAMES OF PASSENGERS		AGE	SEX	OCCUPATIONS	DATE PORT SHIP
KELLY, Ann		45	F	Farmer	09Ma20Cf
Mary		16	F	Farmer	09Ma20Cf
Ann		12	F	Farmer	09Ma20Cf
Thomas		10	M	Farmer	09Ma20Cf
CUFFE, Cath.		16	F	Farmer	09Ma20Cf
KELLY, Cath.		08	F	Child	09Ma20Cf
MOORE, Charles		30	M	Farmer	09Ma20Cf
U	(W)	30	F	Wife	09Ma20Cf
Susan		05	F	Child	09Ma20Cf
Margt.		.00	F	Infant	09Ma20Cf
CONAUGH, James		24	M	Farmer	09Ma20Cf
U		20	F	Farmer	09Ma20Cf
BALY, John		30	M	Farmer	09Ma20Cf
Margt.		30	F	Farmer	09Ma20Cf
ROBINSON, Peter		09	M	Child	09Ma20Cf
BREEN, John		21	M	Farmer	09Ma20Cf
Peter		22	M	Farmer	09Ma20Cf
CARAGH, Edward		20	M	Farmer	09Ma20Cf
MURPHY, Pat		22	M	Farmer	09Ma20Cf
U	(W)	20	F	Farmer	09Ma20Cf
BYRNE, Catherine		24	F	Farmer	09Ma20Cf
MCNEAVE, James		20	M	Farmer	09Ma20Cf
U	(W)	20	F	Farmer	09Ma20Cf
KELLEY, Lawrence		24	M	Farmer	09Ma20Cf
Denis		22	M	Farmer	09Ma20Cf
KELLY, U-Mrs.		30	F	Farmer	09Ma20Cf
Mary		05	F	Child	09Ma20Cf
James		04	M	Child	09Ma20Cf
Ann		.00	F	Infant	09Ma20Cf
SHANNON, John		22	M	Farmer	09Ma20Cf
LONERGAN, John		20	M	Farmer	09Ma20Cf
CALLY, James		20	M	Farmer	09Ma20Cf
FRANCIS, John		20	M	Farmer	09Ma20Cf
HAVERLY, Pat		24	M	Farmer	09Ma20Cf
ACTS, Wm.		24	M	Farmer	09Ma20Cf
DUIGINAN, U		27	M	Farmer	09Ma20Cf
KEILE, Joseph		27	M	Farmer	09Ma20Cf
COGHLAN, Barth.		20	M	Farmer	09Ma20Cf
DOWLING, Pat		20	M	Farmer	09Ma20Cf
GARGHRAN, Mich.		20	M	Farmer	09Ma20Cf
LENNON, Chr.		20	M	Farmer	09Ma20Cf
MAHON, Mary		28	F	Farmer	09Ma20Cf
Mary		10	F	Farmer	09Ma20Cf
Wm.		.00	M	Infant	09Ma20Cf
CONNELL, Pat		30	M	Farmer	09Ma20Cf
Mary		30	F	Farmer	09Ma20Cf
Margt.		11	F	Farmer	09Ma20Cf
Ann		.00	F	Infant	09Ma20Cf
GLENNON, Edward		40	M	Farmer	09Ma20Cf
Agnes		40	F	Farmer	09Ma20Cf
Julia		20	F	Farmer	09Ma20Cf
John		16	M	Farmer	09Ma20Cf
Sarah		05	F	Child	09Ma20Cf
Mich.		.00	F	Infant	09Ma20Cf
KERR, David		20	M	Farmer	09Ma20Cf
MALONE, Biddy		20	F	Farmer	09Ma20Cf
DAVIS, John		21	M	Farmer	09Ma20Cf
U	(W)	21	F	Wife	09Ma20Cf
RYAN, U		20	M	Unknown	09Ma20Cf
FANGHE, Ellen		30	F	Unknown	09Ma20Cf
Francis		22	M	Unknown	09Ma20Cf
Henry		16	M	Unknown	09Ma20Cf
WELSH, Mary		25	F	Unknown	09Ma20Cf
Margt.		22	F	Unknown	09Ma20Cf

ED.AUGUSTA 09 MAY 1848

From Havre

NAMES OF PASSENGERS		AGE	SEX	OCCUPATIONS	DATE PORT SHIP
ARMSTRONG, William		48	M	Farmer	09Ma05Ch
GAHARAN, John		30	M	Farmer	09Ma05Ch
Barry		24	M	Farmer	09Ma05Ch
DELANEY, Michel		30	M	Farmer	09Ma05Ch
Mary		26	F	Farmer	09Ma05Ch
Mary		.03	F	Infant	09Ma05Ch
HOGEN, James		37	M	Farmer	09Ma05Ch
QUAYLE, John		29	M	Farmer	09Ma05Ch
MORGAN, John		35	M	Farmer	09Ma05Ch
Wilson		15	M	Farmer	09Ma05Ch
Mary		34	F	Farmer	09Ma05Ch
QUAYLE, Emma		30	F	Farmer	09Ma05Ch

NAPANNA 10 MAY 1848

From Dublin

NAMES OF PASSENGERS		AGE	SEX	OCCUPATIONS	DATE PORT SHIP
HALLGAN, James		27	M	Farmer	10Ma20Ci
CHAPMAN, U-Mrs.		40	F	Farmer	10Ma20Ci
FITZPATRICK, James		35	M	Farmer	10Ma20Ci
U	(W)	32	F	Wife	10Ma20Ci
Eliza	(D)	13	F	Farmer	10Ma20Ci
Denice	(S)	10	M	Farmer	10Ma20Ci
Catherine	(D)	08	F	Child	10Ma20Ci
Thomas	(S)	04	M	Child	10Ma20Ci
Margret	(D)	.00	F	Infant	10Ma20Ci
Mary	(D)	.00	F	Infant	10Ma20Ci
HALLIGAN, Rose		20	F	Farmer	10Ma20Ci
MARTIN, U		20	F	Farmer	10Ma20Ci
MANSON, Samuel		16	M	Farmer	10Ma20Ci
LAFFAN, William		17	M	Farmer	10Ma20Ci
U-Mrs.		27	F	Farmer	10Ma20Ci
HOOLAHAN, Pat		29	M	Laborer	10Ma20Ci
MULLHALL, Mary		12	F	Laborer	10Ma20Ci
DUNNE, John		20	M	Laborer	10Ma20Ci
KENNORY, Laronce		20	M	Laborer	10Ma20Ci
MCCUNNISS, Edward		21	M	Laborer	10Ma20Ci
CLARY, Alexander		20	M	Laborer	10Ma20Ci
BYRNE, U-Mrs.		30	F	Laborer	10Ma20Ci
Catherin		08	F	Child	10Ma20Ci
FARRALL, Eliza		30	F	Unknown	10Ma20Ci
Kate		12	F	Unknown	10Ma20Ci
Patt		06	M	Child	10Ma20Ci
Mary-Jane		.00	F	Infant	10Ma20Ci
KELLY, John		40	M	Farmer	10Ma20Ci
U	(W)	40	F	Wife	10Ma20Ci
Catherin	(D)	13	F	Farmer	10Ma20Ci
Eliza	(D)	11	F	Farmer	10Ma20Ci
John	(S)	09	M	Child	10Ma20Ci
Mary-Ann	(D)	07	F	Child	10Ma20Ci
Margaret	(D)	05	F	Child	10Ma20Ci
James	(S)	03	M	Child	10Ma20Ci
Robert	(S)	.00	M	Infant	10Ma20Ci
COURTNAY, John		26	M	Farmer	10Ma20Ci
YOUNG, Willm.		21	M	Farmer	10Ma20Ci
LYONS, Edward		20	M	Farmer	10Ma20Ci
Mary-A.		24	F	Farmer	10Ma20Ci
Honora		16	F	Farmer	10Ma20Ci
TYRALL, M.		40	M	Farmer	10Ma20Ci

NAMES OF PASSENGERS		AGE	SEX	OCCUPATIONS	DATE PORT SHIP
GRIFFIN, M.		50	M	Farmer	10Ma20Ci
MOURTOGH, J.		20	M	Laborer	10Ma20Ci
THOMSON, J.		24	M	Unknown	10Ma20Ci
Mary		22	F	None	10Ma20Ci
James		.00	M	Infant	10Ma20Ci
KELLY, J.		28	M	Unknown	10Ma20Ci
Anne		28	F	Unknown	10Ma20Ci
Mary		.00	F	Infant	10Ma20Ci
HAND, Peter		20	M	Unknown	10Ma20Ci
Judeth		27	F	None	10Ma20Ci
Philip		28	M	Unknown	10Ma20Ci
Margt.		24	F	None	10Ma20Ci
Larrance		20	M	None	10Ma20Ci
U, Thoms.		18	M	None	10Ma20Ci
James		17	M	None	10Ma20Ci
GRACE, Eliza		38	F	None	10Ma20Ci
John		18	M	None	10Ma20Ci
Pat		16	M	None	10Ma20Ci
William		14	M	None	10Ma20Ci
James		12	M	None	10Ma20Ci
Edward		10	M	None	10Ma20Ci
FARRELL, Margt.		30	F	None	10Ma20Ci
Mary		25	F	None	10Ma20Ci
LEROLESS, Margt.		38	F	None	10Ma20Ci
Richard		19	M	None	10Ma20Ci
Michal		17	M	None	10Ma20Ci
James		16	M	None	10Ma20Ci
John		14	M	None	10Ma20Ci
Robt.		12	M	None	10Ma20Ci
Mary		21	F	None	10Ma20Ci
DAVIS, Mat.		33	M	Unknown	10Ma20Ci
U	(W)	26	F	Wife	10Ma20Ci
Joseph	(S)	.00	M	Infant	10Ma20Ci
Andrew		20	M	Unknown	10Ma20Ci
BEARY, J.		30	M	Unknown	10Ma20Ci
Rose		26	F	None	10Ma20Ci
NULTY, Pat		36	M	Unknown	10Ma20Ci
Thoms.		24	M	Unknown	10Ma20Ci
KEENE, Pat		28	M	Unknown	10Ma20Ci
MARTIN, J.M.		21	M	Unknown	10Ma20Ci
MONOGHAN, J.		17	M	Unknown	10Ma20Ci
Cathrn.		20	F	None	10Ma20Ci
John		38	M	Laborer	10Ma20Ci
LEE, Thos.		36	M	Unknown	10Ma20Ci
Biddy		15	F	None	10Ma20Ci
Cathn.		14	F	None	10Ma20Ci
Andrew		13	M	Unknown	10Ma20Ci
Anne		09	F	Child	10Ma20Ci
Pat		07	M	Child	10Ma20Ci
John		04	M	Child	10Ma20Ci
Wm.		12	M	Unknown	10Ma20Ci
Thoms.		.00	M	Infant	10Ma20Ci
FAGAN, G.		45	M	Unknown	10Ma20Ci
Mary		40	F	None	10Ma20Ci
Ann		21	F	None	10Ma20Ci
Mary		18	F	None	10Ma20Ci
Bridget		16	F	None	10Ma20Ci
Patt		14	M	Unknown	10Ma20Ci
Judeth		10	F	None	10Ma20Ci
Cathn.		08	F	Child	10Ma20Ci
Margt.		12	F	None	10Ma20Ci
BYRNE, John		36	M	Unknown	10Ma20Ci
Cathn.		32	F	None	10Ma20Ci
Eliza		08	F	Child	10Ma20Ci
Wm.		06	M	Child	10Ma20Ci
John		02	M	Child	10Ma20Ci
Cathn.		.00	F	Infant	10Ma20Ci
KENNEDY, John		28	M	Unknown	10Ma20Ci
BRADY, Andrew		50	M	Unknown	10Ma20Ci
Bridget		40	F	None	10Ma20Ci
John		14	M	Unknown	10Ma20Ci
Pat		10	M	Unknown	10Ma20Ci
James		07	M	Child	10Ma20Ci
DALLY, Wm.		21	M	Unknown	10Ma20Ci
Ann		17	F	None	10Ma20Ci
GOUNOR, M.		25	M	Unknown	10Ma20Ci
J.		20	M	Unknown	10Ma20Ci
NORTH, Edward		13	M	Unknown	10Ma20Ci
HANLY, May		23	F	None	10Ma20Ci
Biddy		23	F	None	10Ma20Ci
Ellen		.00	F	Infant	10Ma20Ci

NELSON-VILLAGE 10 MAY 1848

From Belfast

NAMES OF PASSENGERS		AGE	SEX	OCCUPATIONS	DATE PORT SHIP
MCEVEY, John		30	M	Carpenter	10Ma07CJ
John		11	M	Unknown	10Ma07CJ
Marianne		05	F	Child	10Ma07CJ
MARTIN, Margaret		30	F	Servant	10Ma07CJ
PERRY, Hugh		23	M	Farmer	10Ma07CJ
Jane		21	F	None	10Ma07CJ
William-J.		01	M	Child	10Ma07CJ
FORRESTER, Edward		60	M	None	10Ma07CJ
Edward-Jnr.		12	M	Farmer	10Ma07CJ
Betsey-A.		20	F	None	10Ma07CJ
Jane		18	F	None	10Ma07CJ
BOWES, John		25	M	Wheelwright	10Ma07CJ
Robert		23	M	Wheelwright	10Ma07CJ
MCKEVER, James		27	M	Carpenter	10Ma07CJ
Sally-A.		24	F	None	10Ma07CJ
FROSH, Maryann		25	F	Servant	10Ma07CJ
MCCALL, James		28	M	Farmer	10Ma07CJ
Ann		23	F	None	10Ma07CJ
Bridget		19	F	None	10Ma07CJ
MCCARTNEY, Wm.J.		18	M	Farmer	10Ma07CJ
Jane		17	F	None	10Ma07CJ
HOLMES, David		24	M	Laborer	10Ma07CJ
ROSS, John		30	M	Laborer	10Ma07CJ
HOLMES, Mary		28	F	None	10Ma07CJ
GRAHAM, Ann		22	F	None	10Ma07CJ
Margaret		65	F	None	10Ma07CJ
MCCRUM, Robert		17	M	Farmer	10Ma07CJ
Henry		15	M	Farmer	10Ma07CJ
KENNEDY, James		17	M	Farmer	10Ma07CJ
John		15	M	Farmer	10Ma07CJ
BLAIR, Alexander		21	M	Farmer	10Ma07CJ
NIXON, Joseph		20	M	Farmer	10Ma07CJ
BARTON, A.A.		35	M	None	10Ma07CJ
Frances		17	M	None	10Ma07CJ
Isabella		15	F	None	10Ma07CJ
ARMOUR, Wm.		27	M	None	10Ma07CJ
GRAHAM, Josiah		17	M	Carpenter	10Ma07CJ
HOLMES, Mary		06	F	Child	10Ma07CJ
WRIGHT, Richard		22	M	Farmer	10Ma07CJ
ARCHER, John		20	M	Farmer	10Ma07CJ
GRAHAM, John		33	M	Farmer	10Ma07CJ
STEVENSON, Samuel		26	M	Farmer	10Ma07CJ
Nancy		24	F	None	10Ma07CJ
MARSHALL, James		32	M	Farmer	10Ma07CJ
Matilda		18	F	None	10Ma07CJ
GIBSON, Ellen		20	F	None	10Ma07CJ
ABERNETHY, E.A.		18	F	None	10Ma07CJ
Sarah		10	F	None	10Ma07CJ
Richard		03	M	Child	10Ma07CJ
WILSON, James		26	M	Laborer	10Ma07CJ
Eleanor-J.	(W)	24	F	Wife	10Ma07CJ
James	(S)	03	M	Child	10Ma07CJ
Caroline	(D)	.00	F	Infant	10Ma07CJ
WATSON, Jane		20	F	Spinster	10Ma07CJ
CASSIDY, James		28	M	Laborer	10Ma07CJ
Sally		27	F	None	10Ma07CJ
Mary		04	F	Child	10Ma07CJ
John		02	M	Child	10Ma07CJ

NAMES OF PASSENGERS	AGE	SEX	OCCUPATIONS	DATE PORT SHIP
BUCKLEY, John	20	M	Laborer	10Ma07CJ
Samuel	19	M	Laborer	10Ma07CJ
DUGAN, Patrick	25	M	Laborer	10Ma07CJ
CULLIN, James	25	M	Laborer	10Ma07CJ
MCDONALL, Reben	23	M	Laborer	10Ma07CJ
WRIGHT, Alexander	14	M	Laborer	10Ma07CJ
CARMICHAEL, Ann	21	F	None	10Ma07CJ
Biddy	22	F	None	10Ma07CJ
DUFFY, Ellen	25	F	None	10Ma07CJ
DUGAN, Sarah	18	F	None	10Ma07CJ
MCGIMERY, Patrick	29	M	Laborer	10Ma07CJ
Wm.	18	M	Laborer	10Ma07CJ
SCULLAN, Robert	18	M	Laborer	10Ma07CJ
Patrick	28	M	Laborer	10Ma07CJ
CARNEY, Rosey	20	F	None	10Ma07CJ
SCULLIN, Jane	30	F	None	10Ma07CJ
Sarah	00	F	None	10Ma07CJ
Nancy	28	F	None	10Ma07CJ
DILLON, Ann	45	F	None	10Ma07CJ
Nancy	18	F	None	10Ma07CJ
Henry	13	M	None	10Ma07CJ
HENY, Patrick	18	M	Laborer	10Ma07CJ
ONEILE, Charles	23	M	Laborer	10Ma07CJ
GIBNEY, John	40	M	Laborer	10Ma07CJ
David	06	M	Child	10Ma07CJ
Mary	03	F	Child	10Ma07CJ
OWENS, James	25	M	None	10Ma07CJ
MATHIS, David	35	M	None	10Ma07CJ
Betty	35	F	None	10Ma07CJ
JAMES, Robert	11	M	None	10Ma07CJ
Charlott	07	F	Child	10Ma07CJ
Sarah-J.	00	F	None	10Ma07CJ
John	04	M	Child	10Ma07CJ
SAVAGE, Patrick	22	M	Laborer	10Ma07CJ
AUSTIN, Margaret	55	F	Dressmaker	10Ma07CJ
ROBINSON, Margaret	26	F	None	10Ma07CJ
Elizabeth	05	F	Child	10Ma07CJ
LUSK, James	26	M	Laborer	10Ma07CJ
Jane	20	F	None	10Ma07CJ
MCGIVERN, Margaret	16	F	None	10Ma07CJ
Thomas	18	M	Laborer	10Ma07CJ
MCANALLY, Wm.	24	M	Laborer	10Ma07CJ
WALSH, Sarah	30	F	None	10Ma07CJ
CAMPBELL, Joseph	22	M	None	10Ma07CJ
MCCARTNEY, James	22	M	None	10Ma07CJ
IRVIN, James	21	M	None	10Ma07CJ
Margaret	20	F	None	10Ma07CJ
Mary-J.	22	F	None	10Ma07CJ
RAINEY, Thomas	23	M	Laborer	10Ma07CJ
Margreta	24	F	Laborer	10Ma07CJ
Peggy-A.	04	F	Child	10Ma07CJ
Kitty-I.	02	F	Child	10Ma07CJ
Wm.C.	.00	M	Infant	10Ma07CJ
FARREL, James	24	M	Mechanic	10Ma07CJ
GILCHRIST, Fanny	24	F	None	10Ma07CJ
LEITCH, Samuel	22	M	None	10Ma07CJ
HOUSTON, Wm.	20	M	Laborer	10Ma07CJ
SMITH, Wm.	21	M	Laborer	10Ma07CJ
HOUSTON, Wm.	45	M	Millwright	10Ma07CJ
Eliza	15	F	None	10Ma07CJ
Sally	14	F	None	10Ma07CJ
Samuel	07	M	Child	10Ma07CJ
Margaret	03	F	Child	10Ma07CJ
CALVERT, James	34	M	Carpenter	10Ma07CJ
Martha	32	F	None	10Ma07CJ
James	12	M	None	10Ma07CJ
John	10	M	None	10Ma07CJ
James	04	M	Child	10Ma07CJ
CHAMBERS, John	32	M	Weaver	10Ma07CJ
Martha-S.	30	F	None	10Ma07CJ
John	02	M	Child	10Ma07CJ
Denis	.00	M	Infant	10Ma07CJ
GILL, Eliza	36	F	Draper	10Ma07CJ
HARVEY, James	21	M	Laborer	10Ma07CJ
MCDONALD, John	19	M	Laborer	10Ma07CJ
MCCOMB, John	04	M	Child	10Ma07CJ
Jane	30	F	None	10Ma07CJ
Margaret	11	F	None	10Ma07CJ
Jane	03	F	Child	10Ma07CJ
Joseph	.00	M	Infant	10Ma07CJ
MCDONALL, Margaret	22	F	None	10Ma07CJ
CRANE, Margaret	23	F	None	10Ma07CJ
MOORE, Hugh	35	M	Laborer	10Ma07CJ
Margaret	35	F	None	10Ma07CJ
Mary	00	F	None	10Ma07CJ
MCMULLININ, John	36	M	Laborer	10Ma07CJ
WHITE, Sally	36	F	None	10Ma07CJ
PATTERSON, M.J.	19	F	None	10Ma07CJ
Wm.J.	.00	M	None	10Ma07CJ
WRIGHT, Wm.	27	M	Smith	10Ma07CJ
U	25	M	None	10Ma07CJ
Eliza	03	F	Child	10Ma07CJ
John	.00	M	Infant	10Ma07CJ
DRENNAN, Margaret	16	F	None	10Ma07CJ
MCKENNA, Margaret	20	F	None	10Ma07CJ
GUIGEN, Sarah	20	F	None	10Ma07CJ
NELSON, Ann	.00	F	Infant	10Ma07CJ

ENGLAND 10 MAY 1848

From Liverpool

NAMES OF PASSENGERS	AGE	SEX	OCCUPATIONS	DATE PORT SHIP
DUKE, Rebecca	11	F	Spinster	10Ma02Qe
BURNS, Cathe.	11	F	Spinster	10Ma02Qe
WOODS, Michl.	25	M	Laborer	10Ma02Qe
Chas.	20	M	Laborer	10Ma02Qe
Bridgt.	21	F	Spinster	10Ma02Qe
OHAGAN, Ellen	21	F	Spinster	10Ma02Qe
GIBBON, John	25	M	Carpenter	10Ma02Qe
DORAN, Mary	21	F	Matron	10Ma02Qe
Jane	20	F	Matron	10Ma02Qe
MORGAN, Jane	20	F	Matron	10Ma02Qe
Patrick	40	M	Laborer	10Ma02Qe
MANNERY, Brigt.	20	F	Spinster	10Ma02Qe
Margt.	18	F	Spinster	10Ma02Qe
MCRICKARD, Cathr.	22	F	Spinster	10Ma02Qe
MURPHY, Jane	17	F	Spinster	10Ma02Qe
MCGRADY, Mary	18	F	Spinster	10Ma02Qe
MCAVORY, Lawrence	26	M	Farmer	10Ma02Qe
CARTER, Luke	26	M	Farmer	10Ma02Qe
ROSS, Jas.	21	M	Farmer	10Ma02Qe
Ann	17	F	Spinster	10Ma02Qe
Bessey	.00	F	Infant	10Ma02Qe
HAGAN, Thos.	26	M	Laborer	10Ma02Qe
Ellen	25	F	Spinster	10Ma02Qe
John	.00	M	Infant	10Ma02Qe
RAFFERTY, Mary	22	F	Spinster	10Ma02Qe
MORGAN, Ann	22	F	Spinster	10Ma02Qe
BOYLAN, Michl.	30	M	Laborer	10Ma02Qe
Bridgt.	24	F	Spinster	10Ma02Qe
Bessey	16	F	Spinster	10Ma02Qe
Ellen	09	F	Child	10Ma02Qe
Thos.	30	M	Carpenter	10Ma02Qe
MCGUIRE, John	19	M	Carpenter	10Ma02Qe
Margh.	21	F	Spinster	10Ma02Qe
HEALY, Wm.	20	M	Laborer	10Ma02Qe
KENWORTHY, Pat.	30	M	Laborer	10Ma02Qe
MCCARTEN, Cathr.	23	F	Spinster	10Ma02Qe
Mary	.00	F	Infant	10Ma02Qe
BAUFLE, Mary	29	F	Unknown	10Ma02Qe
MCGIVERN, Mary	26	F	Unknown	10Ma02Qe
KELLY, Cath.	13	F	Unknown	10Ma02Qe
ROBERTS, Mary	20	F	Spinster	10Ma02Qe
CAMPBELL, Rose	21	F	Spinster	10Ma02Qe

NAMES OF PASSENGERS	AGE	SEX	OCCUPATIONS	DATE PORT SHIP
LACEY, Mary	28	F	Spinster	10Ma02Qe
CAMPBELL, Mary	22	F	Spinster	10Ma02Qe
BLESSING, Bernard	55	M	Laborer	10Ma02Qe
REILLY, Barney	30	M	Laborer	10Ma02Qe
BLESSING, Sarah	14	F	Spinster	10Ma02Qe
SHERIDAN, Jas.	25	M	Laborer	10Ma02Qe
Eliza	25	F	Matron	10Ma02Qe
COLBERT, Margt.	15	F	Matron	10Ma02Qe
SMYTH, Thos.	32	M	Laborer	10Ma02Qe
BLOONEN, John	25	M	Laborer	10Ma02Qe
MATHEWS, Jas.	24	M	Laborer	10Ma02Qe
REILLY, William	40	M	Laborer	10Ma02Qe
Eliza	40	F	Matron	10Ma02Qe
Jas.	11	M	Unknown	10Ma02Qe
John	14	M	Unknown	10Ma02Qe
Mary	20	F	Unknown	10Ma02Qe
John	02	M	Child	10Ma02Qe
SEXTON, Patk.	20	M	Laborer	10Ma02Qe
STOKES, Jas.	30	M	Laborer	10Ma02Qe
Mary	22	F	Matron	10Ma02Qe
Charlotte	.00	F	Infant	10Ma02Qe
QUINN, Mary	25	F	Matron	10Ma02Qe
LAWLOR, Peter	25	M	Carpenter	10Ma02Qe
WALSH, Christopher	25	M	Unknown	10Ma02Qe
FLYNN, Michl.	20	M	Laborer	10Ma02Qe
FOX, Nicholas	40	M	Laborer	10Ma02Qe
Mary	49	F	Spinster	10Ma02Qe
Wm.	14	M	None	10Ma02Qe
Patrick	10	M	None	10Ma02Qe
Mary	08	F	Child	10Ma02Qe
Jas.	04	M	Child	10Ma02Qe
MURRAY, Jas.	60	M	Laborer	10Ma02Qe
John	30	M	Laborer	10Ma02Qe
Jas.	03	M	Child	10Ma02Qe
CONNELL, Mathew	25	M	Laborer	10Ma02Qe
HAWKINS, Thos.	20	M	Laborer	10Ma02Qe
LEWIS, Wm.	28	M	Laborer	10Ma02Qe
Sarah	29	F	Spinster	10Ma02Qe
Wm.	03	M	Child	10Ma02Qe
Sarah	.00	F	Infant	10Ma02Qe
John	27	M	Carpenter	10Ma02Qe
JONES, Jas.	32	M	Carpenter	10Ma02Qe
SLATER, Bridgt.	68	F	Spinster	10Ma02Qe
HUSHBUGH, Solom	27	M	Carpenter	10Ma02Qe
DICKINSON, Wm.	22	M	Carpenter	10Ma02Qe
Eliza	24	F	Spinster	10Ma02Qe
Emma	02	F	Child	10Ma02Qe
HILYARD, Robt.	24	M	Laborer	10Ma02Qe
REILLY, Patt.	24	M	Laborer	10Ma02Qe
Ellen	24	F	Unknown	10Ma02Qe
Margt.	17	F	Unknown	10Ma02Qe
HILYARD, Margt.	17	F	Unknown	10Ma02Qe
LAMBERT, Cor.	32	F	Unknown	10Ma02Qe
HERRON, Bernd.	25	M	Laborer	10Ma02Qe
Ellen	25	F	Spinster	10Ma02Qe
Jas.	04	M	Child	10Ma02Qe
Ellen	02	F	Child	10Ma02Qe
Ann	.00	F	Infant	10Ma02Qe
MCLAUGHLIN, Pat	25	M	Laborer	10Ma02Qe
Margt.	25	F	Matron	10Ma02Qe
Jas.	25	M	Laborer	10Ma02Qe
Cathn.	25	F	Spinster	10Ma02Qe
Bernad.	20	M	Laborer	10Ma02Qe
Mary	20	F	Spinster	10Ma02Qe
Thos.	20	M	Laborer	10Ma02Qe
CONNOR, Jas.	34	M	Laborer	10Ma02Qe
ROCHE, Patt.	20	M	Laborer	10Ma02Qe
CONNOR, Eliza	30	F	Spinster	10Ma02Qe
LENEHAN, Patt.	30	M	Laborer	10Ma02Qe
Margt.	30	F	Spinster	10Ma02Qe
DUANE, Thos.	19	M	Laborer	10Ma02Qe
FRAZER, Mary	20	F	Spinster	10Ma02Qe
COLLINS, Mary	25	F	Spinster	10Ma02Qe
OCONNELL, Wm.	20	M	Laborer	10Ma02Qe
GALLAGHER, John	27	M	Laborer	10Ma02Qe

NAMES OF PASSENGERS	AGE	SEX	OCCUPATIONS	DATE PORT SHIP
SCHOLFIELD, Sylvester	40	M	Laborer	10Ma02Qe
Ann	36	F	Spinster	10Ma02Qe
TAYLOR, Henry	24	M	Laborer	10Ma02Qe
SCHOLFIELD, Mathew	16	M	Laborer	10Ma02Qe
Hugh	13	M	Laborer	10Ma02Qe
Sarah	06	F	Child	10Ma02Qe
William	04	M	Child	10Ma02Qe
Edwd.	.00	M	Infant	10Ma02Qe
GREENWOOD, Jas.	30	M	Laborer	10Ma02Qe
Sarah	30	F	Spinster	10Ma02Qe
Isaac	20	M	Laborer	10Ma02Qe
Hannah	17	F	Spinster	10Ma02Qe
Eliza	12	F	None	10Ma02Qe
Mariah	09	F	Child	10Ma02Qe
Selina	05	F	Child	10Ma02Qe
TULLY, Patt.	24	M	Carpenter	10Ma02Qe
WHELAN, Darby	40	M	Carpenter	10Ma02Qe
John	15	M	Carpenter	10Ma02Qe
Cathe.	40	F	Spinster	10Ma02Qe
Patt	11	M	None	10Ma02Qe
Dennis	09	M	Child	10Ma02Qe
Michl.	07	M	Child	10Ma02Qe
Jas.	05	M	Child	10Ma02Qe
Thos.	03	M	Child	10Ma02Qe
GORMAN, Bernad.	30	M	Carpenter	10Ma02Qe
Sarah	36	F	Spinster	10Ma02Qe
Ann	04	F	Child	10Ma02Qe
SWEENEY, Edwd.	40	M	Laborer	10Ma02Qe
Ann	33	F	Spinster	10Ma02Qe
Ann	.00	F	Infant	10Ma02Qe
Jas.	08	M	Child	10Ma02Qe
BRADY, Arthur	34	M	Laborer	10Ma02Qe
HEFFERNAN, Michl.	28	M	Laborer	10Ma02Qe
ANDERSON, Mary	23	F	Matron	10Ma02Qe
DOYLE, Michl.	29	M	Laborer	10Ma02Qe
ATKINSON, Thos.	33	M	Laborer	10Ma02Qe
Elizabeth	22	F	Spinster	10Ma02Qe
Ann	02	F	Child	10Ma02Qe
Dorah	.00	F	Infant	10Ma02Qe
WALKER, Saml.	23	M	Laborer	10Ma02Qe
Eliza	22	F	Spinster	10Ma02Qe
Wm.	21	M	Laborer	10Ma02Qe
WALTERS, Wm.	29	M	Laborer	10Ma02Qe
Elizabeth	29	F	Matron	10Ma02Qe
HOURIGAN, Patt.	40	M	Laborer	10Ma02Qe
Bridget	38	F	Spinster	10Ma02Qe
Ellen	39	F	Spinster	10Ma02Qe
Edwd.	16	M	Laborer	10Ma02Qe
Stephen	12	M	Laborer	10Ma02Qe
Mary	.00	F	Infant	10Ma02Qe
BATH, Abraham	27	M	Carpenter	10Ma02Qe
TEADLEBURY, Jas.	40	M	Laborer	10Ma02Qe
JONES, Richd.	42	M	Laborer	10Ma02Qe
SHELCOCK, Jas.	26	M	Laborer	10Ma02Qe
COKELY, Jenny	40	F	Spinster	10Ma02Qe
RIGBY, Michl.	22	M	Laborer	10Ma02Qe
BIRMINGHAM, Cathr.	20	F	Spinster	10Ma02Qe
Margt.	18	F	Spinster	10Ma02Qe
GLASS, Saml.	27	M	Laborer	10Ma02Qe
U (W)	25	F	Matron	10Ma02Qe
Ab. (D)	.00	F	Infant	10Ma02Qe
JOHNSON, Joseph	20	M	Carpenter	10Ma02Qe
SHAW, Richd.	30	M	Carpenter	10Ma02Qe
FIELDEN, Henry	36	M	Carpenter	10Ma02Qe
Sarah-Ann	32	F	Spinster	10Ma02Qe
GALLIVAN, Hannah	20	F	Spinster	10Ma02Qe
JOHNSON, John	23	M	Laborer	10Ma02Qe
ROGAN, Wm.	27	M	Laborer	10Ma02Qe
MCCARTNAY, Wm.	26	M	Laborer	10Ma02Qe
MCGEE, Ellen	20	F	Spinster	10Ma02Qe
ROGAN, Susan	24	F	Spinster	10Ma02Qe
WHELAN, Bridget	17	F	Spinster	10Ma02Qe
MALONAY, John	20	M	Laborer	10Ma02Qe
Cathe.	26	F	Spinster	10Ma02Qe
GARDINER, Margt.	10	F	Spinster	10Ma02Qe

NAMES OF PASSENGERS	AGE	SEX	OCCUPATIONS	DATE PORT SHIP
COLGAN, Mary	20	F	Spinster	10Ma02Qe
HANLEY, Ann	09	F	Child	10Ma02Qe
MCGUIRE, Margt.	03	F	Child	10Ma02Qe
COLGAN, Jas.	50	M	Laborer	10Ma02Qe
Thos., U	20	M	Laborer	10Ma02Qe
Ellen	18	F	None	10Ma02Qe
Margt.	10	F	None	10Ma02Qe
Cath.	09	F	Child	10Ma02Qe
MALLY, Peter	20	M	Laborer	10Ma02Qe
Luke	20	M	Laborer	10Ma02Qe
REILLY, Mary	20	F	Spinster	10Ma02Qe
HORAN, Cathe.	20	F	Spinster	10Ma02Qe
COLGAN, Rose	48	F	Spinster	10Ma02Qe
Margt.	20	F	Spinster	10Ma02Qe
DEVITT, Sally	20	F	Spinster	10Ma02Qe
DUNSHOT, William	25	M	Laborer	10Ma02Qe
CRONAN, Cathr.	28	F	Spinster	10Ma02Qe
MAHONY, Mary	16	F	Spinster	10Ma02Qe
GORMAN, Eliza	21	F	Spinster	10Ma02Qe
HANNOGAN, Bridgt.	14	F	Spinster	10Ma02Qe
WALSH, John	25	M	Laborer	10Ma02Qe
LYDDON, Mary	21	F	Spinster	10Ma02Qe
FALLON, Michl.	22	M	Laborer	10Ma02Qe
FITZGERALD, Bernad.	20	M	Laborer	10Ma02Qe
BARNETT, Thos.	20	M	Laborer	10Ma02Qe
John	30	M	Laborer	10Ma02Qe
Ann	28	F	Spinster	10Ma02Qe
Adam	15	M	None	10Ma02Qe
Robert	13	M	None	10Ma02Qe
John	04	M	Child	10Ma02Qe
Matilda	02	F	Child	10Ma02Qe
Francis	.00	F	Infant	10Ma02Qe
Francis	12	F	None	10Ma02Qe
DEVITT, Sally	18	F	Spinster	10Ma02Qe
MURPHY, Mary	20	F	None	10Ma02Qe
MORGAN, Cathn.	18	F	None	10Ma02Qe
GERVIS, William	.00	M	Infant	10Ma02Qe
Died-At-Sea				
BRADY, Bridget	24	F	None	10Ma02Qe
Died-At-Sea				
STOKES, Charlotte	.00	F	Infant	10Ma02Qe
Died-At-Sea				
CAMPBELL, Cathn.	22	F	None	10Ma02Qe
CLARKE, Edwd.P.	26	M	None	10Ma02Qe
WALTER, John	50	M	None	10Ma02Qe
Francis	50	M	None	10Ma02Qe
WALKER, Eliza	20	F	None	10Ma02Qe
Margt.	18	F	None	10Ma02Qe
SHERIDAN, Eliza	.00	F	Infant	10Ma02Qe
Born-At-Sea				
BRADY, Bridget	.00	F	Infant	10Ma02Qe
Born-At-Sea				

MARCHIONESS-OF-CLYDESDAL 10 MAY 1848

From Londonderry

NAMES OF PASSENGERS	AGE	SEX	OCCUPATIONS	DATE PORT SHIP
MCCORMICK, William	30	M	Laborer	10Ma01Cl
Margaret	25	F	Spinster	10Ma01Cl
LETER, Mary	30	F	Spinster	10Ma01Cl
THOMPSON, Mary	30	F	Spinster	10Ma01Cl
MCCONEGHY, Charles	21	M	Laborer	10Ma01Cl
JOHNSTONE, James	20	M	Laborer	10Ma01Cl
BELL, James	20	M	Laborer	10Ma01Cl
GIN, John	21	M	Laborer	10Ma01Cl
Fonogon	19	F	Spinster	10Ma01Cl
John	20	M	Laborer	10Ma01Cl
KELLY, Ann	28	F	Spinster	10Ma01Cl
BALLENTINE, Ann	50	F	Spinster	10Ma01Cl
BALLENTINE, James	26	M	Laborer	10Ma01Cl
Isabella	24	F	Spinster	10Ma01Cl
Samuel	22	M	Laborer	10Ma01Cl
Margt.	20	F	Spinster	10Ma01Cl
Matilda	16	F	Spinster	10Ma01Cl
William	15	M	Laborer	10Ma01Cl
Eliza	13	F	Spinster	10Ma01Cl
John	11	M	Laborer	10Ma01Cl
MCCONNELL, Robert	21	M	Laborer	10Ma01Cl
Mary-Jane	19	F	Spinster	10Ma01Cl
KIELY, James	13	M	Laborer	10Ma01Cl
RIELY, Hannah	40	F	Spinster	10Ma01Cl
KEAN, Hugh	28	M	Laborer	10Ma01Cl
PORTER, Darcas	30	F	Spinster	10Ma01Cl
MCCOOL, Rose	50	F	Spinster	10Ma01Cl
DOUGHERTY, Nancy	21	F	Spinster	10Ma01Cl
MCGAUGHEY, Eliza	40	F	Spinster	10Ma01Cl
KYD, Robert	18	M	Laborer	10Ma01Cl
MCCUE, Magdolen	30	F	Spinster	10Ma01Cl
OROURKE, Tedy	35	M	Laborer	10Ma01Cl
CARLIN, Nancy	40	F	Spinster	10Ma01Cl
Biddy	18	F	Spinster	10Ma01Cl
Sicily	16	F	Spinster	10Ma01Cl
Gracey	08	F	Child	10Ma01Cl
CASSIDY, John	28	M	Laborer	10Ma01Cl
Mary	13	F	Spinster	10Ma01Cl
MOORE, John-Js.	20	M	Laborer	10Ma01Cl
MCCUTCHAN, Js.	23	M	Laborer	10Ma01Cl
WARDLAW, Robert	23	M	Laborer	10Ma01Cl
OBRIEN, Henery	36	M	Laborer	10Ma01Cl
Mary	20	F	Spinster	10Ma01Cl
MCGEADY, Mary	12	F	Spinster	10Ma01Cl
Catharine	10	F	Spinster	10Ma01Cl
Harry	08	M	Child	10Ma01Cl
MCKOWEN, John	20	M	Laborer	10Ma01Cl
Martha	25	F	Spinster	10Ma01Cl
BREEN, William	20	M	Laborer	10Ma01Cl
James	18	M	Laborer	10Ma01Cl
DIVEN, James	22	M	Laborer	10Ma01Cl
John	60	M	Laborer	10Ma01Cl
Hugh	40	M	Laborer	10Ma01Cl
Ellen	60	F	Spinster	10Ma01Cl
MARSHALL, Samuel	50	M	Laborer	10Ma01Cl
Martha	45	F	Spinster	10Ma01Cl
Moses	20	M	Laborer	10Ma01Cl
Mary-A.	17	F	Spinster	10Ma01Cl
William	14	M	Laborer	10Ma01Cl
Samuel	10	M	Laborer	10Ma01Cl
HUNTER, William	36	M	Laborer	10Ma01Cl
ELDER, Alex	20	M	Laborer	10Ma01Cl
MERRICK, Richard	27	M	Laborer	10Ma01Cl
Rebecca	28	F	Spinster	10Ma01Cl
Rebecca	11	F	Spinster	10Ma01Cl
Martha	08	F	Child	10Ma01Cl
Hannah	06	F	Child	10Ma01Cl
Jane	.00	F	Infant	10Ma01Cl
FISHER, John	47	M	Laborer	10Ma01Cl
Margt.	32	F	Spinster	10Ma01Cl
Hannah	32	F	Spinster	10Ma01Cl
Bernard	07	M	Child	10Ma01Cl
William	04	M	Child	10Ma01Cl
GILMOUR, James	22	M	Laborer	10Ma01Cl
ROBINSON, Mary	28	F	Spinster	10Ma01Cl
HENERY, Samuel	20	M	Laborer	10Ma01Cl
MURRAY, William	31	M	Laborer	10Ma01Cl
Samuel	64	M	Laborer	10Ma01Cl
BREEN, Isabella	16	F	Spinster	10Ma01Cl
DERMOT, Martha	20	F	Spinster	10Ma01Cl
LINDSEY, William	24	M	Laborer	10Ma01Cl
FORLES, John	20	M	Laborer	10Ma01Cl
MCLAUGHLIN, Betty	45	F	Spinster	10Ma01Cl
MULLIN, John	20	M	Laborer	10Ma01Cl
Biddy	18	F	Spinster	10Ma01Cl
MCGOLDRICK, Biddy	24	F	Spinster	10Ma01Cl
Sarah	20	F	Spinster	10Ma01Cl

NAMES OF PASSENGERS		AGE	SEX	OCCUPATIONS	DATE PORT SHIP
COLLINS, Edwd.		25	M	Laborer	10Ma01Cl
MCELHOLM, Thos.		23	M	Laborer	10Ma01Cl
Bridget		50	F	Spinster	10Ma01Cl
Catharine		27	F	Spinster	10Ma01Cl
Bridget		.00	F	Infant	10Ma01Cl

SIR-HENRY-SMITH 10 MAY 1848

From Liverpool

NAMES OF PASSENGERS		AGE	SEX	OCCUPATIONS	DATE PORT SHIP
MCGUIRE, Pat		20	M	Laborer	10Ma02Cu
TOOLE, Barney		35	M	Laborer	10Ma02Cu
MCALVIN, Hugh		23	M	Laborer	10Ma02Cu
MCBRIDE, Coleman		24	M	Laborer	10Ma02Cu
CULL, Danl.		21	M	Laborer	10Ma02Cu
Theagin		20	M	Laborer	10Ma02Cu
MCBRIDE, Danl.		20	M	Laborer	10Ma02Cu
KELLY, John		22	M	Laborer	10Ma02Cu
COLBERT, Wm.		25	M	Laborer	10Ma02Cu
LONG, Robert		21	M	Laborer	10Ma02Cu
SHOUTREN, Cathr.Mrs.		20	F	Wife	10Ma02Cu
NEWMAN, Gabriel		22	M	Laborer	10Ma02Cu
LAVELLE, Hyman		20	M	Unknown	10Ma02Cu
GREEN, James		28	M	Unknown	10Ma02Cu
MARKS, Rich.		28	M	Unknown	10Ma02Cu
SHERANS, Ellen-Mrs.		35	F	Wife	10Ma02Cu
Mary	(D)	.00	F	Infant	10Ma02Cu
CARROLL, John		23	M	Laborer	10Ma02Cu
Thomas		20	M	Laborer	10Ma02Cu
FADDEN, Roger		30	M	Laborer	10Ma02Cu
GRAHAM, Wm.		36	M	Laborer	10Ma02Cu
Ann	(W)	34	F	Wife	10Ma02Cu
Betty	(D)	06	F	Child	10Ma02Cu
Jane	(D)	04	F	Child	10Ma02Cu
Ann	(D)	.00	F	Infant	10Ma02Cu
ODONNELL, Pat		18	M	Laborer	10Ma02Cu
MOLSY, Michl.		22	M	Laborer	10Ma02Cu
JOYCE, Thos.		25	M	Laborer	10Ma02Cu
CONLEY, John		28	M	Laborer	10Ma02Cu
U	(W)	24	F	Wife	10Ma02Cu
Margt.		50	F	Unknown	10Ma02Cu
Terence		15	M	Laborer	10Ma02Cu
Pat	(S)	.00	M	Infant	10Ma02Cu
MCKENNY, Ann-Mrs.		20	F	Wife	10Ma02Cu
MCGUIRE, Mary-Mrs.		20	F	Wife	10Ma02Cu
Philip		12	M	Unknown	10Ma02Cu
DUFFY, Pat		22	M	Unknown	10Ma02Cu
DOUGHERTY, James		26	M	Laborer	10Ma02Cu
FEENY, Cathr.Mrs.		16	F	Wife	10Ma02Cu
LEE, James		23	M	Laborer	10Ma02Cu
COTRELL, Josh.		26	M	Unknown	10Ma02Cu
Margt.	(W)	24	F	Wife	10Ma02Cu
Joseph	(S)	.00	M	Infant	10Ma02Cu
Mary	(D)	.00	F	Infant	10Ma02Cu
CROWLEY, Mary-Ann		18	F	Spinster	10Ma02Cu
KERWIN, Ann		17	F	Unknown	10Ma02Cu
YORK, Pat		25	M	Laborer	10Ma02Cu
BRYAN, Martin		40	M	Unknown	10Ma02Cu
CAMPBELL, Biddy		13	F	Spinster	10Ma02Cu
MCLEON, John		20	M	Laborer	10Ma02Cu
Rose		40	F	Spinster	10Ma02Cu
COHAN, Wm.		25	M	Laborer	10Ma02Cu
KNOWLAN, Geo.		20	M	Unknown	10Ma02Cu
ROBERTS, James		25	M	Unknown	10Ma02Cu
Lucy	(W)	20	F	Wife	10Ma02Cu
BRENNAN, Pat		50	M	Laborer	10Ma02Cu
Pat		16	M	Unknown	10Ma02Cu
Honor		11	F	Unknown	10Ma02Cu
Mary		08	F	Child	10Ma02Cu

NAMES OF PASSENGERS		AGE	SEX	OCCUPATIONS	DATE PORT SHIP
BRENNAN, William		06	M	Child	10Ma02Cu
FALLON, Andw.		40	M	Laborer	10Ma02Cu
MONAGHAN, Michl.		25	M	Unknown	10Ma02Cu
MCKEOWN, John		30	M	Unknown	10Ma02Cu
Bridgt.		30	F	Spinster	10Ma02Cu
Peter		05	M	Child	10Ma02Cu
Mary		.00	F	Infant	10Ma02Cu
WILSON, Saml.		21	M	Laborer	10Ma02Cu
MORRISON, Andw.		24	M	Laborer	10Ma02Cu
HOLLINGSWORTH, Bill		25	M	Laborer	10Ma02Cu
MCKINSEY, John		30	M	Laborer	10Ma02Cu
CARNEY, Bridgt.Mrs.		24	F	Wife	10Ma02Cu
HIGGINS, James		35	M	Laborer	10Ma02Cu
U	(W)	28	F	Wife	10Ma02Cu
Mary-Ann	(D)	04	F	Child	10Ma02Cu
Robert	(S)	02	M	Child	10Ma02Cu
DUNN, Chas.		32	M	Laborer	10Ma02Cu
LYNCH, Thos.		40	M	Laborer	10Ma02Cu
U	(W)	40	F	Wife	10Ma02Cu
Thomas		26	M	Laborer	10Ma02Cu
Patk.		24	M	Laborer	10Ma02Cu
Ellen		20	F	Laborer	10Ma02Cu
Mary		12	F	Laborer	10Ma02Cu
Judy		18	F	Laborer	10Ma02Cu
James		13	M	Laborer	10Ma02Cu
GREEN, Geor.		26	M	Laborer	10Ma02Cu
NOWLAN, James		30	M	Unknown	10Ma02Cu
Anthony		26	M	Unknown	10Ma02Cu
Mary		.00	F	Infant	10Ma02Cu
SHEA, Lawr.		36	M	Farmer	10Ma02Cu
PARDON, Anty.		30	M	Unknown	10Ma02Cu
Cathr.		18	F	Spinster	10Ma02Cu
BOYD, Thomas		40	M	Laborer	10Ma02Cu
Mary	(W)	30	F	Wife	10Ma02Cu
GALLAGHER, Ellen		20	F	Unknown	10Ma02Cu
BOYD, Wm.		09	M	Child	10Ma02Cu
Mary-Ann		05	F	Child	10Ma02Cu
KEILER, Thomas		40	M	Laborer	10Ma02Cu
Biddy	(W)	40	F	Wife	10Ma02Cu
Danl.	(S)	05	M	Child	10Ma02Cu
Martin	(S)	02	M	Child	10Ma02Cu
MCGARVIN, U-Mrs.		49	F	Wife	10Ma02Cu
DOWNS, James		25	M	Laborer	10Ma02Cu
David		20	M	Laborer	10Ma02Cu
Agnes		02	F	Child	10Ma02Cu
MCKENNY, Wm.		18	M	Laborer	10Ma02Cu
WATSON, Eliza		24	F	Laborer	10Ma02Cu
SHAW, Joseph		40	M	Laborer	10Ma02Cu
FLYNN, Biddy		18	F	Spinster	10Ma02Cu
CURMISKEY, Simon		20	M	Laborer	10Ma02Cu
MULVEHILL, John		19	M	Laborer	10Ma02Cu
KING, John		20	M	Laborer	10Ma02Cu
CLARKE, Mary		19	F	Laborer	10Ma02Cu
BROGAN, Michl.		20	M	Laborer	10Ma02Cu
Nelly	(W)	27	F	Wife	10Ma02Cu
HUNTER, Thos.		50	M	Unknown	10Ma02Cu
GEOGHEGAN, Pat		20	M	Laborer	10Ma02Cu
SHARRYTELL, John		40	M	Unknown	10Ma02Cu
Pegg	(W)	40	F	Wife	10Ma02Cu
Mary	(D)	.00	F	Infant	10Ma02Cu
DUFFY, Rose-Mrs.		25	F	Wife	10Ma02Cu
Francis	(S)	.00	M	Infant	10Ma02Cu
Lenans-Or-LEONARD, Owe		25	M	Unknown	10Ma02Cu
MCCUE, John		21	M	Laborer	10Ma02Cu
MURPHY, Peter		25	M	Laborer	10Ma02Cu
Edw.		20	M	Laborer	10Ma02Cu
COOPER, Wm.		50	M	Laborer	10Ma02Cu
John		22	M	Laborer	10Ma02Cu
Margt.		25	F	Spinster	10Ma02Cu
Margt.		12	F	Spinster	10Ma02Cu
Geor.		10	M	Spinner	10Ma02Cu
Mary-Ann		24	F	Spinster	10Ma02Cu
Sarah		02	F	Child	10Ma02Cu
CARROLL, Wm.		20	M	Laborer	10Ma02Cu
BRENNAN, Pat.		35	M	Laborer	10Ma02Cu

NAMES OF PASSENGERS		AGE	SEX	OCCUPATIONS	DATE PORT SHIP
SINCLAIR, Neil		24	M	Laborer	10Ma02Cu
BELL, John		44	M	Gentleman	10Ma02Cu
Mary		44	F	Unknown	10Ma02Cu
Hannah		16	F	Unknown	10Ma02Cu
Mary-J.		12	F	Unknown	10Ma02Cu
Wm.		10	M	Unknown	10Ma02Cu
Saml.		03	M	Child	10Ma02Cu

BARBARA 11 MAY 1848

From Galway

NAMES OF PASSENGERS		AGE	SEX	OCCUPATIONS	DATE PORT SHIP
NIELAND, John		25	M	Laborer	11Ma11Cp
GREADY, Thomas		26	M	Laborer	11Ma11Cp
CONNOLLY, William		20	M	Laborer	11Ma11Cp
Patt		27	M	Smith	11Ma11Cp
JOYCE, John		28	M	Laborer	11Ma11Cp
WALSH, Mary		30	F	Spinster	11Ma11Cp
BERMINGHAM, John		30	M	Laborer	11Ma11Cp
Mary		28	F	Spinster	11Ma11Cp
Daniel		21	M	Laborer	11Ma11Cp
CLOONANE, Judy		24	F	Spinster	11Ma11Cp
Margaret		21	F	Spinster	11Ma11Cp
WALSH, John		24	M	Laborer	11Ma11Cp
Ann	(W)	20	F	Wife	11Ma11Cp
KILKENNY, Michael		22	M	Laborer	11Ma11Cp
Honor	(W)	20	F	Wife	11Ma11Cp
FLEMING, John		22	M	Laborer	11Ma11Cp
Michael		20	M	Laborer	11Ma11Cp
MADDEN, Larry		26	M	Laborer	11Ma11Cp
FORNAGHAN, Mary		19	F	Spinster	11Ma11Cp
CONNORS, Sarah		25	F	Wi	11Ma11Cp
NEASON, James		35	M	Laborer	11Ma11Cp
QUIN, Michal		22	M	Unknown	11Ma11Cp
QUINN, Mary		24	F	Spinster	11Ma11Cp
DOOLEY, Michael		28	M	Laborer	11Ma11Cp
GREELY, Mortoy		20	M	Laborer	11Ma11Cp
CONNANE, Patrick		23	M	Sawer	11Ma11Cp
DERMODY, Patrick		19	M	Laborer	11Ma11Cp
Mary		24	F	Spinster	11Ma11Cp
DOLAN, Catherine		24	F	Spinster	11Ma11Cp
QUINN, Sarah		20	F	Spinster	11Ma11Cp
REDINGTON, Mary		18	F	Spinster	11Ma11Cp
HOSER, James		30	M	Laborer	11Ma11Cp
CONNOLLY, Patt		34	M	Laborer	11Ma11Cp
KENNEDY, Thomas		16	M	Laborer	11Ma11Cp
LAWLES, John		20	M	Laborer	11Ma11Cp
FITZGERALD, Martin		26	M	Laborer	11Ma11Cp
BRODERICK, Thos.		27	M	Laborer	11Ma11Cp
GILLIGAN, Hugh		18	M	Clerk	11Ma11Cp
Mary	(T)	16	F	None	11Ma11Cp
NEAL, Henry		25	M	Laborer	11Ma11Cp
HOLLERAN, Thomas		34	M	Laborer	11Ma11Cp
FLANNERY, Michael		25	M	Laborer	11Ma11Cp
MORISON, Michael		25	M	Laborer	11Ma11Cp
DOORKAL, James		28	M	Laborer	11Ma11Cp
TIERNY, Bridget-Mrs.		25	F	Wife	11Ma11Cp
ODEA, Darby		24	M	Laborer	11Ma11Cp
FITZPATRICK, Timothy		34	M	Laborer	11Ma11Cp
CARR, Thos.		24	M	Laborer	11Ma11Cp
Mary	(W)	22	F	Wife	11Ma11Cp
GRIFFIN, Thos.		24	M	Laborer	11Ma11Cp
NAGLE, Thos.		34	M	Laborer	11Ma11Cp
MURPHY, Thos.		20	M	Laborer	11Ma11Cp
GILLIGAN, Homer		21	M	Spinner	11Ma11Cp
CONNORTON, John		21	M	Laborer	11Ma11Cp
DOOLY, Michl.		30	M	Laborer	11Ma11Cp
DEMPSY, Thos.		22	M	Bootmaker	11Ma11Cp
HORAN, Michl.		22	M	Laborer	11Ma11Cp
LARDNER, William		25	M	Mason	11Ma11Cp
RIELLY, Catharine		20	F	Spinster	11Ma11Cp
KEANE, Thos.		25	M	Laborer	11Ma11Cp
ROONEY, Honor-Mrs.		23	F	Wife	11Ma11Cp
BURKE, Wm.		26	M	Laborer	11Ma11Cp
Henry		24	M	Laborer	11Ma11Cp
CARR, Patrick		30	M	Laborer	11Ma11Cp
Mary	(W)	25	F	Wife	11Ma11Cp
NOLAN, Ellen		18	F	Spinster	11Ma11Cp
RYAN, Joseph		24	M	Laborer	11Ma11Cp
CONNOLLY, John		20	M	Laborer	11Ma11Cp
FORD, Pat.		24	M	Laborer	11Ma11Cp
CONNOLLY, Fanny		20	F	Spinster	11Ma11Cp
MCINTYRE, Pat		24	M	Laborer	11Ma11Cp
Bridget	(W)	35	F	Wife	11Ma11Cp
Thos.	(S)	13	M	Unknown	11Ma11Cp
Pat	(S)	03	M	Child	11Ma11Cp
HANNASY, Mary		17	F	Spinster	11Ma11Cp
FLANNARY, Judy		20	F	Spinster	11Ma11Cp
NEALE, Thos.		18	M	Laborer	11Ma11Cp
FURY, Martin		26	M	Laborer	11Ma11Cp
FLEMING, James		27	M	Laborer	11Ma11Cp
RAFTERRY, John		26	M	Laborer	11Ma11Cp
NEALE, Mary		16	F	Spinster	11Ma11Cp
BOHANE, Eliza		35	F	Matron	11Ma11Cp
MORAN, Ellen		20	F	Spinster	11Ma11Cp
Michl.		27	M	Clerk	11Ma11Cp
BOHANE, Eliza		21	F	Spinster	11Ma11Cp
BRANNWICK, Pat		33	M	Laborer	11Ma11Cp
BURKE, Livy		18	F	Spinster	11Ma11Cp
KENNEKEN, James		20	M	Laborer	11Ma11Cp
Margt.		23	F	Spinster	11Ma11Cp
SWEENEY, Edmond		35	M	Laborer	11Ma11Cp
GRADY, John		35	M	Laborer	11Ma11Cp
HUGHES, Martin		34	M	Laborer	11Ma11Cp
MORAINE, Martin		26	M	Laborer	11Ma11Cp
SHEA, Margt.		26	F	Spinster	11Ma11Cp
SULLIVAN, Catharine		25	F	Spinster	11Ma11Cp
SWEENEY, Michael		23	M	Laborer	11Ma11Cp
ODEA, Anne-Mrs.		30	F	Wife	11Ma11Cp
HEALY, Martin		25	M	Laborer	11Ma11Cp
Michal.		25	M	Laborer	11Ma11Cp
HENRY, Catharine		24	F	Spinster	11Ma11Cp
FINNEGAN, Honor		24	F	Spinster	11Ma11Cp
GARVY, Roger		32	M	Laborer	11Ma11Cp
KELLY, John		20	M	Laborer	11Ma11Cp
KANE, John		30	M	Laborer	11Ma11Cp
Mary	(W)	25	F	Wife	11Ma11Cp
HINDS, Bridget		20	F	Spinster	11Ma11Cp
LARPENT, Mary		30	F	Spinster	11Ma11Cp
LALLY, Mary-Anne		18	F	Spinster	11Ma11Cp
RAFFERTY, Margt.		23	F	Spinster	11Ma11Cp
DOOLY, Mary		18	F	Spinster	11Ma11Cp
KENNEDY, Margt.		21	F	Spinster	11Ma11Cp
GREEDY, Mary		35	F	Unknown	11Ma11Cp
Thos.		15	M	Unknown	11Ma11Cp
Maria		13	F	Unknown	11Ma11Cp
CONNOLLY, Honor		19	F	Spinster	11Ma11Cp
John		18	M	Unknown	11Ma11Cp
Eliza		20	F	Spinster	11Ma11Cp
FLINN, Pat		35	M	Laborer	11Ma11Cp
Nelly	(W)	30	F	Wife	11Ma11Cp
CURRIE, Paddy		35	M	Laborer	11Ma11Cp
MORIARTY, Michael		30	M	Laborer	11Ma11Cp
CULLAHAN, Mathew		20	M	Laborer	11Ma11Cp
BURKE, George		31	M	Laborer	11Ma11Cp
DORMODY, Pat.		30	M	Laborer	11Ma11Cp
NIKANE, Pat.		22	M	Laborer	11Ma11Cp
MURRAY, Pat.		30	M	Laborer	11Ma11Cp
FAY, Mary		34	F	Lad	11Ma11Cp
Mary		18	F	Spinster	11Ma11Cp
KELLY, Ellen		25	F	Spinster	11Ma11Cp
TURNGAN, Pat		30	M	Laborer	11Ma11Cp
KELLY, Darby		30	M	Laborer	11Ma11Cp
HOLANE, Catharine		17	F	Spinster	11Ma11Cp

NAMES OF PASSENGERS		A G E	S E X	OCCUPATIONS	DATE PORT SHIP
KELLY, Ellen		25	F	Spinster	11Ma11Cp
TURNGAN, Pat		30	M	Laborer	11Ma11Cp
KELLY, Darby		30	M	Laborer	11Ma11Cp
HOLANE, Catharine		17	F	Spinster	11Ma11Cp
SHERIDAN, Martin		30	M	Laborer	11Ma11Cp
MOONEY, Pat		20	M	Laborer	11Ma11Cp
SWEENEY, Michael		25	M	Laborer	11Ma11Cp
LALLY, Francis		16	M	Unknown	11Ma11Cp
TARPEY, Wm.		45	M	Laborer	11Ma11Cp
OGORMAN, Ed.		18	M	Unknown	11Ma11Cp
FAY, Michael		20	M	Laborer	11Ma11Cp
CAHALANE, Margt.		20	F	Spinster	11Ma11Cp
Ellen		16	F	Spinster	11Ma11Cp
KANE, Michael		24	M	Laborer	11Ma11Cp
SMITH, Mary		19	F	Spinster	11Ma11Cp
MULLAN, Pat		20	M	Laborer	11Ma11Cp
GREADY, Catharine		35	F	Lad	11Ma11Cp
HYNES, Michael		36	M	Laborer	11Ma11Cp
KELLY, Dermot		23	M	Laborer	11Ma11Cp
TROY, John-M.		21	M	Clerk	11Ma11Cp
Mochar	(W)	20	F	Wife	11Ma11Cp
HUGHES, Patrick		21	M	Miller	11Ma11Cp
MCNAUGHTON, Arch.		20	M	Grocer	11Ma11Cp
BRISBAN, Henry		33	M	Merchant	11Ma11Cp
LAWLES, Ellen		18	F	Spinster	11Ma11Cp
BRISBANE, William		04	M	Child	11Ma11Cp

ANN-HARLEY 11 MAY 1848

From Glasgow

NAMES OF PASSENGERS		A G E	S E X	OCCUPATIONS	DATE PORT SHIP
REILLY, John		23	M	Laborer	11Ma04Db
DEVLIN, Dennis		27	M	Laborer	11Ma04Db
MURPHY, Margaret		50	F	Wi	11Ma04Db
Margaret-Mrs.		28	F	Wife	11Ma04Db
Monoras	(S)	.10	M	Infant	11Ma04Db
MCREELY, Rose		22	F	Spinster	11Ma04Db
LOVERTY, Robert		16	M	Laborer	11Ma04Db
MELHERN, Dennis		23	M	Unknown	11Ma04Db
Elizabeth		16	F	Unknown	11Ma04Db
Margaret		14	F	Unknown	11Ma04Db

ELIZA-CAROLINE 11 MAY 1848

From Liverpool

NAMES OF PASSENGERS		A G E	S E X	OCCUPATIONS	DATE PORT SHIP
NORTH, William		20	M	Laborer	11Ma02Kn
Frances		19	F	Servant	11Ma02Kn
HOWE, Elizabeth		20	F	Servant	11Ma02Kn
DOLAN, John		20	M	Laborer	11Ma02Kn
WELSH, Patrick		40	M	Laborer	11Ma02Kn
Anne		35	F	Laborer	11Ma02Kn
Thomas		13	M	None	11Ma02Kn
Michael		12	M	None	11Ma02Kn
Mary		10	F	None	11Ma02Kn
Peter		08	M	Child	11Ma02Kn
Bridget		04	F	Child	11Ma02Kn
John		.00	M	Infant	11Ma02Kn
Michael		48	M	Farmer	11Ma02Kn
Ellen		35	F	None	11Ma02Kn
John		13	M	None	11Ma02Kn
Mark		12	M	None	11Ma02Kn
Mary		09	F	Child	11Ma02Kn
WELSH, Bridget		08	F	Child	11Ma02Kn
Michael		.00	M	Infant	11Ma02Kn
U		40	M	None	11Ma02Kn
HALLAHAN, Owen		23	M	Laborer	11Ma02Kn
John		25	M	Laborer	11Ma02Kn
TOBIN, Michael		21	M	Laborer	11Ma02Kn
HANOHAN, Patk.		20	M	Laborer	11Ma02Kn
CONNOR, Martin		20	M	Laborer	11Ma02Kn
FITZSIMMONS, Thos.		60	M	Laborer	11Ma02Kn
Mary		50	F	Servant	11Ma02Kn
Patrick		16	M	Laborer	11Ma02Kn
MAHON, Patrick		12	M	Laborer	11Ma02Kn
Betty		30	F	Servant	11Ma02Kn
Owen		20	M	Laborer	11Ma02Kn
HUGHES, Robert		30	M	Laborer	11Ma02Kn
CONLON, Patrick		24	M	Laborer	11Ma02Kn
LADELY, Thomas		20	M	Laborer	11Ma02Kn
OBRIEN, John		25	M	Laborer	11Ma02Kn
KEARNEY, Edward		22	M	Laborer	11Ma02Kn
Caroline		13	F	Servant	11Ma02Kn
GALLAGHER, Bryon		15	M	Laborer	11Ma02Kn
MURRAY, Daniel		38	M	Laborer	11Ma02Kn
Thomas		36	M	Laborer	11Ma02Kn
KELAHAN, Michl.		45	M	Laborer	11Ma02Kn
U	(W)	40	F	Servant	11Ma02Kn
DONOHOE, Jane		30	F	Servant	11Ma02Kn
John		24	M	Laborer	11Ma02Kn
MCCORMACK, Thomas		50	M	Laborer	11Ma02Kn
Patk.		20	M	Laborer	11Ma02Kn
John		18	M	Laborer	11Ma02Kn
Michl.		16	M	Laborer	11Ma02Kn
Thomas		15	M	Laborer	11Ma02Kn
Susan		15	F	Servant	11Ma02Kn
Clia.		11	F	Servant	11Ma02Kn
Denis		06	M	Child	11Ma02Kn
Hugh		20	M	Laborer	11Ma02Kn
Bridgt.		40	F	Servant	11Ma02Kn
MOORE, Mary		40	F	Servant	11Ma02Kn
COLES, Ann		20	F	Servant	11Ma02Kn
MURRAY, Patrick		13	M	Laborer	11Ma02Kn
CONNOR, John		60	M	Laborer	11Ma02Kn
Patk.		25	M	Laborer	11Ma02Kn
Bridget		13	F	Servant	11Ma02Kn
Marght.		11	F	None	11Ma02Kn
MCGUIRE, Patt.		20	M	Laborer	11Ma02Kn
TACKENEY, Jas.		28	M	Farmer	11Ma02Kn
U	(W)	28	F	Wife	11Ma02Kn
Patk.N.	(S)	.00	M	Infant	11Ma02Kn
MCDERMOTT, John		40	M	Laborer	11Ma02Kn
CULEEN, Michl.		20	M	Laborer	11Ma02Kn
Mathew		12	M	Laborer	11Ma02Kn
Thomas		10	M	Laborer	11Ma02Kn
Cathn.		12	F	None	11Ma02Kn
HAUSTON, Andrew		20	M	Laborer	11Ma02Kn
John		21	M	Laborer	11Ma02Kn
GLENSON, Mary		20	F	Servant	11Ma02Kn
MCAVOY, Anne		10	F	None	11Ma02Kn
Margh.		08	F	Child	11Ma02Kn
BLACKBURN, John		23	M	Laborer	11Ma02Kn
WHITE, James		25	M	Laborer	11Ma02Kn
KANE, John		20	M	Laborer	11Ma02Kn
MCAVOY, Mary		20	F	None	11Ma02Kn
BRADY, James		28	M	None	11Ma02Kn
Alice		17	F	None	11Ma02Kn
FINNEGAN, Thomas		17	M	None	11Ma02Kn
DUNE, Paul		50	M	None	11Ma02Kn
KELLY, Thomas		18	M	None	11Ma02Kn
Martin		25	M	None	11Ma02Kn
CONLAN, Cathr.		17	F	Servant	11Ma02Kn
KELLY, James		18	M	Laborer	11Ma02Kn
BLACKBURN, James		21	M	Laborer	11Ma02Kn
LARKIN, Michl.		21	M	Laborer	11Ma02Kn
GILCERST, Patk.		20	M	Laborer	11Ma02Kn
RERAIN, John		20	M	Laborer	11Ma02Kn
REYNOLDS, Mary		20	F	Servant	11Ma02Kn

NAMES OF PASSENGERS		AGE	SEX	OCCUPATIONS	DATE PORT SHIP
SHERIDAN, James		25	M	Laborer	11Ma02Kn
MCMANERS, Michl.		35	M	Laborer	11Ma02Kn
FRANCE, James		25	M	Laborer	11Ma02Kn
MCGRORY, Michl.		13	M	Laborer	11Ma02Kn
MCCULLOUGH, Ann		22	F	Servant	11Ma02Kn
MCGRORY, Mary		24	F	Servant	11Ma02Kn
DANDORS, John		21	M	Laborer	11Ma02Kn
BEST, John		30	M	Laborer	11Ma02Kn
Ann		20	F	Servant	11Ma02Kn
Joe		.00	M	Infant	11Ma02Kn
JONES, Edward		30	M	Laborer	11Ma02Kn
Thomas		10	M	Laborer	11Ma02Kn
MCGANNAN, Thomas		20	M	Laborer	11Ma02Kn
KIERNAN, Daniel		24	M	Laborer	11Ma02Kn
MCMANERSS, Lirnan		17	F	Servant	11Ma02Kn
MCEVOY, James		47	M	Laborer	11Ma02Kn
LAGHLAIN, Michl.		48	M	Laborer	11Ma02Kn
LEONARD, Mary-Ann		22	F	Servant	11Ma02Kn
MERCAN, John		13	M	Laborer	11Ma02Kn
OBAGLEY, Wm.		20	M	Laborer	11Ma02Kn
MCKERNEY, Mary		20	F	Servant	11Ma02Kn
DUNN, James		13	M	Laborer	11Ma02Kn
MOONEY, Peter		22	M	Laborer	11Ma02Kn
DENISON, Charles		36	M	Laborer	11Ma02Kn
MCANDREW, James		30	M	Laborer	11Ma02Kn
MARIMACK, John		28	M	Laborer	11Ma02Kn
CORCORAN, An.		20	M	Laborer	11Ma02Kn
GREENHORN, Patk.		40	M	Laborer	11Ma02Kn
Mary		30	F	Servant	11Ma02Kn
FARRELL, Patk.		20	M	Laborer	11Ma02Kn
DUNNE, Michl.		32	M	Laborer	11Ma02Kn
James		11	M	Laborer	11Ma02Kn
Philip		10	M	Laborer	11Ma02Kn
Magt.		07	F	Child	11Ma02Kn
Ann		05	F	Child	11Ma02Kn
Biddy		03	F	Child	11Ma02Kn
Mary		.00	F	Infant	11Ma02Kn
HUGHES, William		30	M	Laborer	11Ma02Kn
U	(W)	30	F	Wife	11Ma02Kn
COLLINS, U		30	M	Laborer	11Ma02Kn
U	(W)	30	F	Wife	11Ma02Kn
CONNOLLY, Michl.		26	M	Laborer	11Ma02Kn
James		04	M	Child	11Ma02Kn
GRAHAM, Thomas		24	M	Laborer	11Ma02Kn
CONNOLLY, Ann		25	F	Servant	11Ma02Kn
HAROLDS, Elizth.		26	F	Servant	11Ma02Kn
MCANULTY, Ellen		28	F	Servant	11Ma02Kn
MCKANE, Bridgt.		18	F	Servant	11Ma02Kn
FILE, Michl.		.00	M	Infant	11Ma02Kn
MCKEE, Andy		20	M	Servant	11Ma02Kn
Hugh		21	M	Servant	11Ma02Kn
Patk.		08	M	Child	11Ma02Kn
HANNAHAN, Peter		16	M	Laborer	11Ma02Kn
BRADY, Thom.		34	M	Laborer	11Ma02Kn
Judy		22	F	Servant	11Ma02Kn
CARLIN, Thomas		22	M	Laborer	11Ma02Kn
COFFEE, Patrick		40	M	Laborer	11Ma02Kn
Elizabeth		35	F	Servant	11Ma02Kn
John		19	M	Laborer	11Ma02Kn
Mick		03	M	Child	11Ma02Kn
Bernard		.00	M	Infant	11Ma02Kn
CLARK, Patrick		22	M	Laborer	11Ma02Kn
BOWES, William		24	M	Laborer	11Ma02Kn
John		24	M	Laborer	11Ma02Kn
TRAVERS, Bridget		42	F	Servant	11Ma02Kn
John		15	M	Laborer	11Ma02Kn
Brigt.		13	F	Laborer	11Ma02Kn
William		08	M	Child	11Ma02Kn
VAUGHAN, U		27	M	Laborer	11Ma02Kn
HICKING, John		20	M	Laborer	11Ma02Kn
SCANLIN, Pat		20	M	Laborer	11Ma02Kn
U-Mrs.		30	F	Servant	11Ma02Kn
Wm.		.00	M	Infant	11Ma02Kn
DREW, Bridget		30	F	Servant	11Ma02Kn
John		11	M	Laborer	11Ma02Kn
DREW, Hugh		13	M	Laborer	11Ma02Kn
Patt.		09	M	Child	11Ma02Kn
Nichs.		.00	M	Infant	11Ma02Kn
PASH, Curln.		20	M	Laborer	11Ma02Kn
SHERIDAN, Ann		26	F	Servant	11Ma02Kn
MCLAUGHLIN, Ann		26	F	Servant	11Ma02Kn
Michl.		.00	M	Infant	11Ma02Kn
Bridget		50	F	None	11Ma02Kn
Michl.		04	M	Child	11Ma02Kn
Cathe.		22	F	Servant	11Ma02Kn
Margt.		21	F	Servant	11Ma02Kn
RYAN, John		19	M	Laborer	11Ma02Kn
BARY, Mary		19	F	Servant	11Ma02Kn
JAMES, James		20	M	Laborer	11Ma02Kn
Bridget		20	F	Laborer	11Ma02Kn
COFFEE, Edward		40	M	Laborer	11Ma02Kn
Sally		40	F	Laborer	11Ma02Kn
James		26	M	Laborer	11Ma02Kn
CASTESD, Thomas		21	M	Laborer	11Ma02Kn
Margt.		20	F	Servant	11Ma02Kn
DELMIARTY, Peggt.		22	F	Servant	11Ma02Kn
JONES, Mary		20	F	Servant	11Ma02Kn
MARYMAN, Margt.		20	F	Servant	11Ma02Kn
MCELROY, Jane		10	F	Servant	11Ma02Kn
CAVANAGH, Patk.		19	F	Farmer	11Ma02Kn
RYAN, James		45	M	Farmer	11Ma02Kn
Thomas		40	M	Farmer	11Ma02Kn
Christy		09	M	Child	11Ma02Kn
Patk.		07	M	Child	11Ma02Kn
James		04	M	Child	11Ma02Kn
Eliza		.00	F	Infant	11Ma02Kn
KELLY, James		40	M	Laborer	11Ma02Kn
U	(W)	40	F	Wife	11Ma02Kn
Ann	(D)	13	F	None	11Ma02Kn
Jaine	(D)	13	F	None	11Ma02Kn
Susan	(D)	12	F	None	11Ma02Kn
Marta	(D)	10	F	None	11Ma02Kn
John	(S)	08	M	Child	11Ma02Kn
TUCKER, Ann		20	F	Servant	11Ma02Kn
Jno.		40	M	Servant	11Ma02Kn
Jane		.00	F	Infant	11Ma02Kn
MCELROY, Thomas		20	M	Laborer	11Ma02Kn
DOHERTY, Bridget		18	F	Servant	11Ma02Kn
KEHOE, Ann		18	F	Servant	11Ma02Kn
BRENNAN, Bessey		18	F	Servant	11Ma02Kn
FAGAN, Mary		20	F	Servant	11Ma02Kn
MADDEN, Magt.		20	F	Servant	11Ma02Kn
RILEY, John		30	M	Servant	11Ma02Kn
Walter		09	M	Child	11Ma02Kn
John		07	M	Child	11Ma02Kn
SCALLY, Ellen		20	F	Servant	11Ma02Kn
MADDEN, Thomas		30	M	Laborer	11Ma02Kn
GILL, Patk.		25	M	Laborer	11Ma02Kn
MCGRATH, Cathe.		20	F	Servant	11Ma02Kn
CULLEN, Mary		20	F	Servant	11Ma02Kn
LYNCH, John		24	M	Servant	11Ma02Kn
EUSTACE, Mary		17	F	Servant	11Ma02Kn
WHELAN, Fanny		20	F	Servant	11Ma02Kn
BENNETT, Peter		40	M	Laborer	11Ma02Kn
CARTY, Mary		09	F	Child	11Ma02Kn
FERSON, Mary		20	F	Servant	11Ma02Kn
Margt.		20	F	Servant	11Ma02Kn
COLLINS, Owen		26	M	Laborer	11Ma02Kn
SHERIDAN, Ellen		26	F	Servant	11Ma02Kn
MURPHY, Ellen		21	F	Servant	11Ma02Kn
PRICE, William		26	M	Laborer	11Ma02Kn
GORMAN, Thomas		30	M	Laborer	11Ma02Kn
Ann		30	F	Servant	11Ma02Kn
Thomas		.00	M	Infant	11Ma02Kn
RILEY, Philip		40	M	Laborer	11Ma02Kn
Mary		12	F	Servant	11Ma02Kn
DELUCE, Ann		21	F	Servant	11Ma02Kn
Mary		10	F	Servant	11Ma02Kn
GIBSON, Mary-Ann		12	F	Servant	11Ma02Kn
CALLAGHAN, Cathn.		24	F	Servant	11Ma02Kn

NAMES OF PASSENGERS	AGE	SEX	OCCUPATIONS	DATE PORT SHIP
JONES, Joseph	50	M	Laborer	11Ma02Kn
Bridget	25	F	Servant	11Ma02Kn
SHIRPTON, Mary	20	F	Servant	11Ma02Kn
GILHAM, Mary	06	F	Child	11Ma02Kn
Patrick	04	M	Child	11Ma02Kn
Neil	.00	M	Infant	11Ma02Kn
MARTIN, James	40	M	Laborer	11Ma02Kn
Ellen	12	F	Servant	11Ma02Kn
TRACY, Michl.	36	M	Laborer	11Ma02Kn
Ned	20	M	Laborer	11Ma02Kn
Dan	20	M	Laborer	11Ma02Kn
Cathe.	13	F	Servant	11Ma02Kn
CONNOR, John	40	M	Laborer	11Ma02Kn
U (W)	40	F	Wife	11Ma02Kn
FINCH, James	28	M	Laborer	11Ma02Kn
DULLEN, James	24	M	Laborer	11Ma02Kn
BRIEN, Patk.	25	M	Laborer	11Ma02Kn

IVANHOE 12 MAY 1848

From Liverpool

NAMES OF PASSENGERS	AGE	SEX	OCCUPATIONS	DATE PORT SHIP
MAHON, James	32	M	Merchant	12Ma02Bp
Sarah (W)	19	F	Lady	12Ma02Bp
TROTTER, Acheson	22	M	Merchant	12Ma02Bp
LABOUCHER, James	24	M	Gentleman	12Ma02Bp
MULLENS, Thos.	20	M	Laborer	12Ma02Bp
FERGUSON, Edward	21	M	Laborer	12Ma02Bp
RILEY, Mary	15	F	Servant	12Ma02Bp
FRINER, Catherine	26	F	Servant	12Ma02Bp
Susan	26	F	Servant	12Ma02Bp
MULGREW, Cicely	19	F	Servant	12Ma02Bp
CORRIGAN, Anthony	29	M	Farmer	12Ma02Bp
Catherine	22	F	None	12Ma02Bp
DOHENLLY, Catherine	48	F	None	12Ma02Bp
Margaret	15	F	None	12Ma02Bp
Catherine	11	F	None	12Ma02Bp
Mary	08	F	Child	12Ma02Bp
Bridget	06	F	Child	12Ma02Bp
Michael	04	M	Child	12Ma02Bp
Judy	02	F	Child	12Ma02Bp
DINNER, Thos.	20	M	Engineer	12Ma02Bp
MACCORMICK, Patk.	22	M	Blacksmith	12Ma02Bp
Margaret	18	F	Blacksmith	12Ma02Bp
CURLEY, Bridget	18	F	Blacksmith	12Ma02Bp
MCDERMOTT, Edwd.	25	M	Laborer	12Ma02Bp
KENNEY, Willm.	25	M	Smith	12Ma02Bp
HUESTON, Simon	21	M	Shopkeeper	12Ma02Bp
CROWE, Margaret	21	F	Unknown	12Ma02Bp
ARMSTRONG, James	19	M	Gentleman	12Ma02Bp
MACCAWLEY, Thos.	18	M	Servant	12Ma02Bp
ROURKE, Mary	20	F	Servant	12Ma02Bp
BEATTIE, William	23	M	Grocer	12Ma02Bp
LUNNEY, John	21	M	Worm Cutter	12Ma02Bp
Mary	20	F	Servant	12Ma02Bp
SMITH, Andrew	27	M	Laborer	12Ma02Bp
Pat	25	M	Laborer	12Ma02Bp
RILEY, James	30	M	Laborer	12Ma02Bp
DOYLE, John	26	M	Laborer	12Ma02Bp
BRADY, Bridget	20	F	None	12Ma02Bp
Bridget	19	F	None	12Ma02Bp
Catherine	18	F	None	12Ma02Bp
ORILEY, Ellen	20	F	None	12Ma02Bp
DINNANRY, Anne	14	F	None	12Ma02Bp
DONNELY, Owen	20	M	Laborer	12Ma02Bp
TIERNEY, John	20	M	Blacksmith	12Ma02Bp
MCCABE, Thos.	15	M	Laborer	12Ma02Bp
FLYNN, Saml.	28	M	Laborer	12Ma02Bp
Mary	26	F	None	12Ma02Bp
HALLISEY, Mary	48	F	None	12Ma02Bp
MURRAY, Patt.	36	M	Laborer	12Ma02Bp
Mary	26	F	None	12Ma02Bp
WARD, James	23	M	Laborer	12Ma02Bp
TULLY, Mark	30	M	Laborer	12Ma02Bp
Eliza	24	F	None	12Ma02Bp
SWEENEY, Hugh	25	M	Laborer	12Ma02Bp
Mary	14	F	None	12Ma02Bp
TULLY, Peter	32	M	Laborer	12Ma02Bp
Jane	20	F	Servant	12Ma02Bp
James	26	M	Laborer	12Ma02Bp
BRADY, Anne	20	F	Servant	12Ma02Bp
DONAGHUE, Mary	18	F	Servant	12Ma02Bp
BRISCOE, Edwd.	25	M	Cver	12Ma02Bp
BRYAN, Bridget	18	F	Servant	12Ma02Bp
HENEY, John	20	M	Laborer	12Ma02Bp
MEAGAHURN, Owen	40	M	Laborer	12Ma02Bp
RILEY, Eliza	21	F	Servant	12Ma02Bp
CALLAGHAN, Catherine	22	F	Storekeeper	12Ma02Bp
DOLAN, John	25	M	Laborer	12Ma02Bp
Bridget	60	F	None	12Ma02Bp
TAYLER, Peter	30	M	Laborer	12Ma02Bp
DOLAN, Patt.	28	M	Laborer	12Ma02Bp
RYAN, Margt.	32	F	Servant	12Ma02Bp
Mary	30	F	Servant	12Ma02Bp
MAHON, Eliza	30	F	Servant	12Ma02Bp
COLLINS, Mary	28	F	Servant	12Ma02Bp
RILEY, Ellen	30	F	Unknown	12Ma02Bp
James	28	M	Shoemaker	12Ma02Bp
Bridget	28	F	Servant	12Ma02Bp
DOYLE, Peter	21	M	Laborer	12Ma02Bp
KEOUGH, John	20	M	Laborer	12Ma02Bp
JOHNSON, James	24	M	Laborer	12Ma02Bp
Patt.	27	M	Laborer	12Ma02Bp
HORAHAN, Mich.	21	M	Laborer	12Ma02Bp
ANDERSON, Willm.	21	M	Laborer	12Ma02Bp
AUGHENEY, Joseph	19	M	Laborer	12Ma02Bp
ROACHE, Eliza	20	F	Servant	12Ma02Bp
JOHNSON, Mary	20	F	Servant	12Ma02Bp
MULLENS, Margt.	22	F	Servant	12Ma02Bp
DULLAHAN, Rose	26	F	Lad	12Ma02Bp
SHEA, Luke	24	M	Farmer	12Ma02Bp
Julia	21	F	None	12Ma02Bp
Thos.	19	M	None	12Ma02Bp
WALLIS, John	30	M	Joiner	12Ma02Bp
Matilda	30	F	None	12Ma02Bp
Adam	40	M	Laborer	12Ma02Bp
Letetia	38	F	None	12Ma02Bp
James	07	M	Child	12Ma02Bp
Bess	04	F	Child	12Ma02Bp
Matty	01	F	Child	12Ma02Bp
WILSON, John	60	M	Doctor	12Ma02Bp
Jane	50	F	None	12Ma02Bp
Adam	14	M	None	12Ma02Bp
Matty	12	F	None	12Ma02Bp
Thos.	10	M	None	12Ma02Bp
Catherin	08	F	Child	12Ma02Bp
ROBINSON, Willm.	18	M	Farmer	12Ma02Bp
MCELLIGHAN, James	36	M	Farmer	12Ma02Bp
Elizabeth	22	F	Unknown	12Ma02Bp
Martha	20	F	None	12Ma02Bp
Nancy	22	F	None	12Ma02Bp
ORR, Henry	24	M	None	12Ma02Bp
Abigail	20	F	None	12Ma02Bp
ROBINSON, John	20	M	Farmer	12Ma02Bp
MCLOUGHLIN, John	20	M	Cook	12Ma02Bp
CORCORAN, Mich.	20	M	Laborer	12Ma02Bp
HART, Patt.	29	M	Laborer	12Ma02Bp
Margaret	20	F	None	12Ma02Bp
Mary	18	F	None	12Ma02Bp
FLEMING, Jeremiah	21	M	Laborer	12Ma02Bp
TRAYNOR, Thos.	25	M	Bricklayer	12Ma02Bp
FAGAN, Luke	20	M	Laborer	12Ma02Bp
DONOHUE, James	20	M	Farmer	12Ma02Bp
Margaret	18	F	Servant	12Ma02Bp

NAMES OF PASSENGERS	AGE	SEX	OCCUPATIONS	DATE PORT SHIP
FLOOD, John	21	M	Farmer	12Ma02Bp
GAFFNEY, Rose	18	F	Farmer	12Ma02Bp
MCGARSHAN, Anne	03	F	Child	12Ma02Bp
CAFFREY, John	20	M	Laborer	12Ma02Bp
Philip	06	M	Child	12Ma02Bp
ENWRIGHT, Thos.	22	M	Laborer	12Ma02Bp
SANDS, John	18	M	Laborer	12Ma02Bp
DONELLY, Sally	18	F	Servant	12Ma02Bp
GOODFELLOW, Peter	06	M	Child	12Ma02Bp
MURRAY, Ellen	20	F	Servant	12Ma02Bp
POWEL, Jane	20	F	Servant	12Ma02Bp
FLANAGAN, John	14	M	Laborer	12Ma02Bp
Anne	24	F	Unknown	12Ma02Bp
WALKER, George	19	M	Laborer	12Ma02Bp
WIGGANS, William	26	M	Laborer	12Ma02Bp
BLAKELEY, James	20	M	Laborer	12Ma02Bp
Ellen	46	F	None	12Ma02Bp
MCNEICE, Matt.	15	M	None	12Ma02Bp
Eliza	16	F	None	12Ma02Bp
COGHLAN, Mary-Anne	18	F	None	12Ma02Bp
MURRAY, Mary	18	F	None	12Ma02Bp
DOWDELL, John	22	M	Laborer	12Ma02Bp
HUNT, Honora	26	F	None	12Ma02Bp
John	06	M	Child	12Ma02Bp
MILES, Catherine	20	F	Servant	12Ma02Bp
MURPHY, James	20	M	Farmer	12Ma02Bp
Marcilla	19	F	Servant	12Ma02Bp
DORAN, Catherine	22	F	Servant	12Ma02Bp
CLANDENNING, David	21	M	Bookmaker	12Ma02Bp
MURPHY, Charles	20	M	Shopman	12Ma02Bp
CAMPBELL, Barnard	20	M	Farmer	12Ma02Bp
GRAY, Patt.	21	M	Farmer	12Ma02Bp
WALL, John	22	M	Farmer	12Ma02Bp
CAMPBELL, Nicholas	21	M	Farmer	12Ma02Bp
COLMAN, Thos.	29	M	Laborer	12Ma02Bp
HAND, Peter	26	M	Laborer	12Ma02Bp
MACEVOY, James	22	M	Plasterer	12Ma02Bp
CASEY, Anne	22	F	None	12Ma02Bp
Eliza	04	F	Child	12Ma02Bp
George	02	M	Child	12Ma02Bp
DOYNE, Bridget	25	F	None	12Ma02Bp
STEACOM, Francis	18	M	Laborer	12Ma02Bp
COSTELLO, Eliza	21	F	None	12Ma02Bp
Ellen	20	F	None	12Ma02Bp
RILEY, Felix	22	M	Laborer	12Ma02Bp
LEONARD, Catherine	18	F	Servant	12Ma02Bp
MAGNIN, Charles	20	M	Laborer	12Ma02Bp
Bridget	19	F	None	12Ma02Bp
TUCKER, James	15	M	Laborer	12Ma02Bp
Jno.	17	M	Laborer	12Ma02Bp
Horner	16	F	Servant	12Ma02Bp
Cathe.	14	F	Servant	12Ma02Bp

JUDAH-FUORO 12 MAY 1848

From Liverpool

NAMES OF PASSENGERS	AGE	SEX	OCCUPATIONS	DATE PORT SHIP
BURKE, Nicholes	20	M	Farmer	12Ma02Cx
ORIAN, William	26	M	Farmer	12Ma02Cx
KOLEGH, Mathew	20	M	Farmer	12Ma02Cx
GARSIDE, Abram.	24	M	Farmer	12Ma02Cx
MCGANDIS, Michl.	20	M	Farmer	12Ma02Cx
HANNISSY, James	24	M	Farmer	12Ma02Cx
Ann	21	F	Farmer	12Ma02Cx
BUTLER, Joseph	50	M	Farmer	12Ma02Cx
Michl.	24	M	Farmer	12Ma02Cx
GALLEGAN, Bridget	20	F	Servant	12Ma02Cx
SULLIVEN, Bridget	28	F	Servant	12Ma02Cx
Mary	03	F	Child	12Ma02Cx
FORD, James	28	M	Shpc	12Ma02Cx
MULRAHULE, Michl.	22	M	Shpc	12Ma02Cx
LYNCH, Bernard	13	M	Laborer	12Ma02Cx
Michal	11	M	Laborer	12Ma02Cx
COSTELLO, Mary	40	F	Hatter	12Ma02Cx
DUFFY, Bernard	24	M	Shoemaker	12Ma02Cx
MORRIS, Edward	17	M	Shoemaker	12Ma02Cx
DWIER, Pat.	34	M	Joiner	12Ma02Cx
Eliza	24	F	Joiner	12Ma02Cx
LYONS, Heny.	20	M	Farmer	12Ma02Cx
Frances	18	F	Farmer	12Ma02Cx
Mary	20	F	Farmer	12Ma02Cx
CALLEY, James	20	M	Laborer	12Ma02Cx
MCGOOGEN, Pat	30	M	Farmer	12Ma02Cx
Ellen	22	F	Farmer	12Ma02Cx
CONNELL, Pat	31	M	Farmer	12Ma02Cx
ROURKE, Pat	30	M	Tailor	12Ma02Cx
BRADY, John	20	M	Tailor	12Ma02Cx
CULLIN, John	30	M	Tailor	12Ma02Cx
GALVIN, Pater	21	M	Stone Mason	12Ma02Cx
CASSIDY, Mary	14	F	Servant	12Ma02Cx
MCGRATH, Bridget	18	F	Servant	12Ma02Cx
MADDEN, Margret	40	F	Farmer	12Ma02Cx
Mary	09	F	Child	12Ma02Cx
Michl.	07	M	Child	12Ma02Cx
Thomas	04	M	Child	12Ma02Cx
John	02	M	Child	12Ma02Cx
MULRONEY, John	40	M	Farmer	12Ma02Cx
Mary	35	F	Farmer	12Ma02Cx
Margret	12	F	Farmer	12Ma02Cx
NOON, Bridget	50	F	Farmer	12Ma02Cx
Ann	16	F	Farmer	12Ma02Cx
Ellen	13	F	Farmer	12Ma02Cx
KILDUFF, Ellen	28	F	Servant	12Ma02Cx
NUGENT, Pat	18	M	Laborer	12Ma02Cx
Susan	16	F	Laborer	12Ma02Cx
MCCULLOUGH, Catherine	25	F	Hatter	12Ma02Cx
Mary	02	F	Child	12Ma02Cx
Mary	20	F	Hatter	12Ma02Cx
MULLIN, Patt	20	M	Lgwvr	12Ma02Cx
Mary	18	F	Lgwvr	12Ma02Cx
MARRONY, Rose	44	F	Milliner	12Ma02Cx
Rose	11	F	Milliner	12Ma02Cx
Margret	07	F	Child	12Ma02Cx
Sarah	04	F	Child	12Ma02Cx
NEGHLE, Pat	22	M	Tnm-Brz	12Ma02Cx
DAILY, Bernerd	18	M	Cooper	12Ma02Cx
RYON, Eliza	26	F	Stkw	12Ma02Cx
Mary	06	F	Child	12Ma02Cx
William	.00	M	Infant	12Ma02Cx
ONEAL, Alice	52	F	Servant	12Ma02Cx
BURK, Edw.	25	M	Brf	12Ma02Cx
CUFF, Catherine	25	F	Farmer	12Ma02Cx
Barnerd	.00	M	Infant	12Ma02Cx
Ann	04	F	Child	12Ma02Cx
John	02	M	Child	12Ma02Cx
TUNNY, Margret	20	F	Stay Maker	12Ma02Cx
NOON, Catherine	20	F	Stay Maker	12Ma02Cx
DOYLE, John	21	M	Cutler	12Ma02Cx
William	26	M	Cutler	12Ma02Cx
DEROY, Michal	09	M	Child	12Ma02Cx
WILSON, Ann	36	F	Dressmaker	12Ma02Cx
MADDEN, John	20	M	Saddler	12Ma02Cx
KILLEN, Hugh	36	M	Farmer	12Ma02Cx
Mary	36	F	Farmer	12Ma02Cx
Mary	.00	F	Infant	12Ma02Cx
William	13	M	Farmer	12Ma02Cx
Catherine	11	F	Farmer	12Ma02Cx
Hannah	09	F	Child	12Ma02Cx
Ellin	07	F	Child	12Ma02Cx
Danl.	04	M	Child	12Ma02Cx
KEOUGH, Bridget	22	F	Swhtr	12Ma02Cx
GOODWIN, Margret	16	F	Unknown	12Ma02Cx
SULLIVAN, Mary	36	F	Servant	12Ma02Cx
Ellin	.00	F	Infant	12Ma02Cx

NAMES OF PASSENGERS		AGE	SEX	OCCUPATIONS	DATE PORT SHIP
SULLIVAN, Murice		02	M	Child	12Ma02Cx
LINSKEY, John		20	M	Bootmaker	12Ma02Cx
TOLAN, Thomas		26	M	Bootmaker	12Ma02Cx
MAXWELL, Margret		36	F	Farmer	12Ma02Cx
James		21	M	Farmer	12Ma02Cx
Francis		19	M	Farmer	12Ma02Cx
John		14	M	Farmer	12Ma02Cx
CARROLL, Michl.		21	M	Engineer	12Ma02Cx
James		20	M	Engineer	12Ma02Cx
GAGHEN, Michl.		20	M	Slt-Plstr	12Ma02Cx
MAHON, Rose		21	F	Stay Maker	12Ma02Cx
TARPEY, Ann		20	F	Unknown	12Ma02Cx
Catherine		.00	F	Infant	12Ma02Cx
SMITH, Mary		20	F	Servant	12Ma02Cx
ASHWORTH, John		26	M	Farmer	12Ma02Cx
CORBET, John		22	M	Laborer	12Ma02Cx
RILEY, John-Thos.		21	M	Laborer	12Ma02Cx
REGAN, Ted		19	M	Laborer	12Ma02Cx
RILEY, Garret		25	M	Laborer	12Ma02Cx
CRAWFORD, Thomas		29	M	Cooper	12Ma02Cx
CANAN, Hannah		20	F	Servant	12Ma02Cx
MARTIN, Thomas		27	M	Joiner	12Ma02Cx
HAMMILTON, William-H.		25	M	Joiner	12Ma02Cx
U		20	F	Cnf	12Ma02Cx
CORE, Pat		20	M	Laborer	12Ma02Cx
GRADY, Mick.		28	M	Laborer	12Ma02Cx
FLEMMING, Thomas		30	M	Laborer	12Ma02Cx
Ann		29	F	Servant	12Ma02Cx
GEHAN, Joseph		34	M	Laborer	12Ma02Cx
Mary		30	F	Laborer	12Ma02Cx
Mary		.00	F	Infant	12Ma02Cx
BARNETT, Thomas		35	M	Jeweller	12Ma02Cx
HUNT, George		30	M	Farmer	12Ma02Cx
U	(W)	28	F	Wife	12Ma02Cx
U		.00	M	Infant	12Ma02Cx
Saml.		20	M	Farmer	12Ma02Cx
Thomas		02	M	Child	12Ma02Cx
Michl.		40	M	Farmer	12Ma02Cx
U	(W)	40	F	Wife	12Ma02Cx
Ann	(D)	14	F	Farmer	12Ma02Cx
Mary	(D)	12	F	Farmer	12Ma02Cx
Thomas	(S)	10	M	Farmer	12Ma02Cx
Alice	(D)	08	F	Child	12Ma02Cx
Martha	(D)	06	F	Child	12Ma02Cx
Joseph	(S)	04	M	Child	12Ma02Cx
George	(S)	03	M	Child	12Ma02Cx
Marth.	(D)	.00	F	Infant	12Ma02Cx
DEMPSIE, James		20	M	Rope Maker	12Ma02Cx
DAVIES, John		24	M	Miner	12Ma02Cx
DOWE, Thomas		40	M	Miner	12Ma02Cx
U	(W)	36	F	Wife	12Ma02Cx
Thomas	(S)	16	M	Miner	12Ma02Cx
Ann	(D)	14	F	Miner	12Ma02Cx
Mary	(D)	10	F	Miner	12Ma02Cx
Margret	(D)	06	F	Child	12Ma02Cx
John	(S)	03	M	Child	12Ma02Cx
HELEY, Peter		20	M	Farmer	12Ma02Cx
GEHAN, Mary		20	F	Servant	12Ma02Cx
KERNEN, Mary		20	F	Servant	12Ma02Cx
DEMPSY, Arther		21	M	Joiner	12Ma02Cx
DWIRE, James		22	M	Joiner	12Ma02Cx
BRYAN, Pat.		25	M	Laborer	12Ma02Cx
Henry		22	M	Laborer	12Ma02Cx
DOYLE, Hugh		22	M	Laborer	12Ma02Cx
SIMLEIN, Thomas		17	M	Laborer	12Ma02Cx
BRIAN, Terence		20	M	Laborer	12Ma02Cx
Margret		18	F	Servant	12Ma02Cx
ERIE, Margret		21	F	Servant	12Ma02Cx
CASTLEIN, John		40	M	Cchbldr	12Ma02Cx
John		12	M	Cchbldr	12Ma02Cx
John		14	M	Cchbldr	12Ma02Cx
Mary		26	F	Dressmaker	12Ma02Cx
BERIGHON, Mathew		24	M	Weaver	12Ma02Cx
OBERN, U-Mrs.		18	F	Dressmaker	12Ma02Cx
Pat.		16	M	Servant	12Ma02Cx
OBERN, Margret		15	F	Servant	12Ma02Cx
Michl.		05	M	Child	12Ma02Cx
OBRIAN, Isabella		14	F	Tailor	12Ma02Cx
Lurraine		12	F	Tailor	12Ma02Cx
AULKLIN, James		32	M	Farmer	12Ma02Cx
Rody		03	M	Child	12Ma02Cx
INREIRE, Thomas		34	M	Farmer	12Ma02Cx
OCONNELL, David		30	M	Farmer	12Ma02Cx
U	(W)	30	F	Farmer	12Ma02Cx
Julie	(D)	09	F	Child	12Ma02Cx
Michl.	(S)	07	M	Child	12Ma02Cx
James	(S)	05	M	Child	12Ma02Cx
David	(S)	03	M	Child	12Ma02Cx
Catherine	(D)	.00	F	Infant	12Ma02Cx
Eliza		20	F	Farmer	12Ma02Cx
CUMMINGS, Mary		25	F	Hatter	12Ma02Cx
GOODWIN, Ann		20	F	Hatter	12Ma02Cx
GALLAGHAR, Thomas		26	M	Servant	12Ma02Cx
KICHLOND, Ellin		21	F	Servant	12Ma02Cx
KILLIN, Grant		24	M	Butcher	12Ma02Cx
ROWEN, Mary		24	F	Servant	12Ma02Cx
ARMSTRONG, James		20	M	Farmer	12Ma02Cx
FLANAGAN, Nicholes		20	M	Farmer	12Ma02Cx
Michl.		21	M	Farmer	12Ma02Cx
WHITE, John		30	M	Farmer	12Ma02Cx
U	(W)	30	F	Farmer	12Ma02Cx
U		24	F	Farmer	12Ma02Cx
FLOOD, Patk.		26	M	Servant	12Ma02Cx
Michl.		24	M	Servant	12Ma02Cx
WARE, Pat		30	M	Shchnd	12Ma02Cx
U	(W)	28	F	Shchnd	12Ma02Cx
SIMMUNDS, Pat		21	M	Blacksmith	12Ma02Cx
BOUGHT, Francis		40	M	Blacksmith	12Ma02Cx
MEALEY, Margret		20	F	Servant	12Ma02Cx
Michl.		21	M	Servant	12Ma02Cx
BOYLE, Pat		30	M	Innkeeper	12Ma02Cx
Mary		28	F	Innkeeper	12Ma02Cx
HENEY, Bridget		35	F	Servant	12Ma02Cx
KELLY, Ewd.		40	M	Grocer	12Ma02Cx
Mary		40	F	Grocer	12Ma02Cx
DURLEY, Margret		22	F	Servant	12Ma02Cx
SHANLEY, Ann		18	F	Dressmaker	12Ma02Cx
MARTIN, Pat.		45	M	Farmer	12Ma02Cx
U	(W)	45	F	Farmer	12Ma02Cx
Pat.		20	M	Farmer	12Ma02Cx
John		21	M	Farmer	12Ma02Cx
Died-At-Sea					
Michl.		19	M	Farmer	12Ma02Cx
William		17	M	Farmer	12Ma02Cx
Mary		12	F	Farmer	12Ma02Cx
Ann		08	F	Child	12Ma02Cx
DWYER, Wallen		24	M	Farmer	12Ma02Cx
MCGRAGH, Jerry		20	M	Farmer	12Ma02Cx
FLYNN, Pat		20	F	Servant	12Ma02Cx
MANNUCK, Barney		20	M	Farmer	12Ma02Cx
WHEELEN, Catherine		20	F	Farmer	12Ma02Cx
MARTIN, Mary		20	F	Farmer	12Ma02Cx
POWELL, Frances		21	M	Farmer	12Ma02Cx
MANGEN, Jno.		25	M	Farmer	12Ma02Cx
CONLEY, Martin		23	M	Farmer	12Ma02Cx

FORFARSHIRE 12 MAY 1848

From Liverpool

NAMES OF PASSENGERS		AGE	SEX	OCCUPATIONS	DATE PORT SHIP
GARVEY, William		25	M	Mmsn	12Ma02Cy
KIRK, John		26	M	Carpenter	12Ma02Cy
Elsa		26	F	Carpenter	12Ma02Cy
SLATTERY, Denis		30	M	Bootmaker	12Ma02Cy

NAMES OF PASSENGERS		AGE	SEX	OCCUPATIONS	DATE PORT SHIP
ORILEY, Theodus		30	M	Teacher	12Ma02Cy
Thomas		28	M	Husbandman	12Ma02Cy
Eliza		27	F	Unknown	12Ma02Cy
MOLAN, Thomas		45	M	Whip Maker	12Ma02Cy
Mary-Ann		10	F	Unknown	12Ma02Cy
GALLIGAN, Jas.		20	M	Laborer	12Ma02Cy
JOHNSTON, Juilius		20	M	Laborer	12Ma02Cy
MCINTYRE, Wm.		30	M	Farmer	12Ma02Cy
Martha		38	F	Unknown	12Ma02Cy
Margaret		06	F	Child	12Ma02Cy
William		04	M	Child	12Ma02Cy
Nancy		02	F	Child	12Ma02Cy
MCGINITY, Jas.		19	M	Farmer	12Ma02Cy
GREEN, Jas.		30	M	Carpenter	12Ma02Cy
BROWN, John		20	M	Farmer	12Ma02Cy
MARSHALL, John		20	M	Farmer	12Ma02Cy
OBRIEN, Michael		22	M	Farmer	12Ma02Cy
LAINEY, John		20	M	Farmer	12Ma02Cy
LATTA, Collin		25	M	Miner	12Ma02Cy
BROPHY, Mary		26	F	Shopkeeper	12Ma02Cy
NUGENT, Paul		25	M	Farmer	12Ma02Cy
Bridget	(W)	25	F	Wife	12Ma02Cy
MURRY, Patt.		40	M	Farmer	12Ma02Cy
Lucy	(W)	40	F	Wife	12Ma02Cy
Jane	(D)	07	F	Child	12Ma02Cy
Joseph	(S)	02	M	Child	12Ma02Cy
Mary	(D)	04	F	Child	12Ma02Cy
Catherine	(D)	.00	F	Infant	12Ma02Cy
NUGENT, Pat		30	M	Farmer	12Ma02Cy
Eliza	(W)	30	F	Wife	12Ma02Cy
Wm.	(S)	02	M	Child	12Ma02Cy
MULLEN, Eliza		20	F	Housekeeper	12Ma02Cy
Margt.		09	F	Child	12Ma02Cy
BROPHY, Michl.		28	M	Shopkeeper	12Ma02Cy
Wm.		21	M	Land Agent	12Ma02Cy
John		20	M	Grocer	12Ma02Cy
FLANEDY, Patt.		35	M	Farmer	12Ma02Cy
Edmund		45	M	Farmer	12Ma02Cy
KELLREDGE, Pat		35	M	Farmer	12Ma02Cy
Mary	(W)	30	F	Wife	12Ma02Cy
SULLIVAN, John		35	M	Farmer	12Ma02Cy
RUSSELL, Bridget		22	F	Housekeeper	12Ma02Cy
HENLEY, Mathew		40	M	Farmer	12Ma02Cy
HANLEY, Mary		11	F	Unknown	12Ma02Cy
CULLINAN, Wm.		35	M	Farmer	12Ma02Cy
Mary	(W)	33	F	Wife	12Ma02Cy
John		25	M	Farmer	12Ma02Cy
CONLY, Jas.		35	M	Farmer	12Ma02Cy
MCCLOSKEY, John		40	M	Farmer	12Ma02Cy
Jas.		12	M	Farmer	12Ma02Cy
Mary-Jane		20	F	Housekeeper	12Ma02Cy
Henry		20	M	Farmer	12Ma02Cy
Patrick		20	M	Farmer	12Ma02Cy
MULRY, Mary		33	F	Housekeeper	12Ma02Cy
Thos.		14	M	Laborer	12Ma02Cy
John		12	M	Laborer	12Ma02Cy
RUDDY, Ann		20	M	Housekeeper	12Ma02Cy
STOKES, Pat		35	M	Farmer	12Ma02Cy
Mary	(W)	28	F	Wife	12Ma02Cy
Mary	(D)	08	F	Child	12Ma02Cy
Catherine	(D)	03	F	Child	12Ma02Cy
FRAWLEY, John		19	M	Farmer	12Ma02Cy
MCGREEHAN, Jerry		24	M	Laborer	12Ma02Cy
MCCARTHY, Dennis		30	M	Laborer	12Ma02Cy
BOLLARD, Michael		26	M	Stone Mason	12Ma02Cy
Ann	(W)	21	F	Wife	12Ma02Cy
Margt.	(D)	03	F	Child	12Ma02Cy
HOWARD, Catherine		22	F	Housekeeper	12Ma02Cy
John		03	M	Child	12Ma02Cy
Sarah		02	F	Child	12Ma02Cy
MCCAUN, Jas.		19	M	Baker	12Ma02Cy
HOWARD, John		35	M	Carpenter	12Ma02Cy
BRYAN, John		26	M	Farmer	12Ma02Cy
WALSH, Daniel		25	M	Farmer	12Ma02Cy
RICE, Mary		24	F	Housekeeper	12Ma02Cy
RICE, Bridget		03	F	Child	12Ma02Cy
GOLDING, Margaret		22	F	Housekeeper	12Ma02Cy
RYAN, Philip		30	M	Farmer	12Ma02Cy
Mary	(W)	36	F	Wife	12Ma02Cy
Mary	(D)	08	F	Child	12Ma02Cy
Philip	(S)	06	M	Child	12Ma02Cy
James	(S)	04	M	Child	12Ma02Cy
JOYCE, David		24	M	Farmer	12Ma02Cy
DALTON, John		20	M	Farmer	12Ma02Cy
SHEA, Thos.		22	M	Farmer	12Ma02Cy
BRIAN, Mary		29	F	Housekeeper	12Ma02Cy
QUIN, Margt.		30	F	Housekeeper	12Ma02Cy
Bridget		07	F	Child	12Ma02Cy
Alice		.00	F	Infant	12Ma02Cy
KASH, Karon		25	M	Laborer	12Ma02Cy
Mary		25	F	Housekeeper	12Ma02Cy
CARROLL, John		14	M	Baker	12Ma02Cy
Patt.		12	M	Tailor	12Ma02Cy
GAFFNEY, Thomas		32	M	Tailor	12Ma02Cy
Ann		31	F	Housekeeper	12Ma02Cy
John		.00	M	Infant	12Ma02Cy
KENESEY, Mary		25	F	Housekeeper	12Ma02Cy
CROKE, Alice		25	F	Housekeeper	12Ma02Cy
FANNEN, Ellen		25	F	Housekeeper	12Ma02Cy
HENNESY, James		.00	M	Infant	12Ma02Cy
CONNER, Patt.		20	M	Farmer	12Ma02Cy
Ellen	(W)	20	F	Wife	12Ma02Cy
Mary	(D)	.00	F	Infant	12Ma02Cy
WARDE, Catherine		28	F	Housekeeper	12Ma02Cy
Susan		05	F	Child	12Ma02Cy
Bridget		07	F	Child	12Ma02Cy
OWENS, Thos.		30	M	Laborer	12Ma02Cy
ROCHE, Michael		25	M	Coach Maker	12Ma02Cy
BRYANS, Jonathan		19	M	Laborer	12Ma02Cy
MCNAMEE, Jas.		17	M	Weaver	12Ma02Cy
Nancy		62	F	Housekeeper	12Ma02Cy
WAKEFIELD, Jas.		40	M	Farmer	12Ma02Cy
Isabella	(W)	35	F	Wife	12Ma02Cy
Wm.	(S)	05	M	Child	12Ma02Cy
Jas.	(S)	02	M	Child	12Ma02Cy
DONOVAN, Patrick		40	M	Sawer	12Ma02Cy
Bridget		35	F	Stwvr	12Ma02Cy
RYAN, John		24	M	Miller	12Ma02Cy
DOHERTY, Pat		30	M	Miller	12Ma02Cy
Jane		25	F	Housekeeper	12Ma02Cy
HOGAN, Bridget		25	F	Housekeeper	12Ma02Cy
FITZGERALD, Jas.		25	M	Shoemaker	12Ma02Cy
Bridget		20	F	Binder	12Ma02Cy
BURNS, Jas.		21	M	Tailor	12Ma02Cy
SHEA, John		21	M	Laborer	12Ma02Cy
MORRISY, Wm.		20	M	Laborer	12Ma02Cy
BURKE, Jas.		14	M	Laborer	12Ma02Cy
KERWICK, Michael		26	M	Mason	12Ma02Cy
FITZGERALD, Mary		25	F	Housekeeper	12Ma02Cy
SMITH, John-G.		35	M	Farmer	12Ma02Cy
TEARNEY, Wm.		26	M	Laborer	12Ma02Cy
LOOBY, Edmund		24	M	Laborer	12Ma02Cy
SHEA, Jas.		26	M	Laborer	12Ma02Cy
COONEY, Jas.		25	M	Laborer	12Ma02Cy
HEANY, Jas.		24	M	Laborer	12Ma02Cy
CASHEN, Wm.		29	M	Laborer	12Ma02Cy
HEANY, Jas.		20	M	Laborer	12Ma02Cy
MAHER, Johanna		21	F	Housekeeper	12Ma02Cy
HARNEY, Margaret		20	F	Housekeeper	12Ma02Cy
Catherine		22	F	Housekeeper	12Ma02Cy
SHEA, Mary		23	F	Housekeeper	12Ma02Cy
BUTLER, Mary		20	F	Housekeeper	12Ma02Cy
DWYER, Richd.		28	M	Nailer	12Ma02Cy
KENEDY, Thos.		40	M	Farmer	12Ma02Cy
Mory	(W)	40	F	Wife	12Ma02Cy
Mary	(D)	14	F	Unknown	12Ma02Cy
William	(S)	12	M	Unknown	12Ma02Cy
Margaret	(D)	18	F	Unknown	12Ma02Cy
Nory	(D)	06	F	Child	12Ma02Cy
Catherine	(D)	10	F	Unknown	12Ma02Cy

NAMES OF PASSENGERS	AGE	SEX	OCCUPATIONS	DATE PORT SHIP
BLAKE, John	24	M	Laborer	12Ma02Cy
POWER, John	22	M	Laborer	12Ma02Cy
HEALY, Ann	23	F	Housekeeper	12Ma02Cy
BEGGY, Mary	20	F	Housekeeper	12Ma02Cy
KEARY, Ellen	19	F	Housekeeper	12Ma02Cy
ROGERS, Patt.	26	M	Farmer	12Ma02Cy
Richd.	22	M	Farmer	12Ma02Cy
Denis	20	M	Farmer	12Ma02Cy
Betty	20	F	Housekeeper	12Ma02Cy
Betty	50	F	Housekeeper	12Ma02Cy
QUIN, Bridget	20	F	Housekeeper	12Ma02Cy
EMMET, Margaret	18	F	Housekeeper	12Ma02Cy
DILLON, Wm.	20	M	Laborer	12Ma02Cy
HEATH, Thos.	34	M	Laborer	12Ma02Cy
Bridget	16	F	Laborer	12Ma02Cy
Ann	14	F	Laborer	12Ma02Cy
KEARNS, Patt.	20	M	Laborer	12Ma02Cy
CONROY, Dominic	30	M	Laborer	12Ma02Cy
BURKE, Ann	18	F	Housekeeper	12Ma02Cy
NOLAN, Ann	20	F	Housekeeper	12Ma02Cy
LAVELLE, Winefred	21	F	Housekeeper	12Ma02Cy
HANRAHEN, John	18	M	Farmer	12Ma02Cy
BIRMINGHAM, Eliza	55	F	Housekeeper	12Ma02Cy
COSTELLO, Margaret	30	F	Housekeeper	12Ma02Cy
DOHENY, Michael	35	M	Farmer	12Ma02Cy
CAMPION, Richd.	20	M	Laborer	12Ma02Cy
NEWGENT, Henry	40	M	Farmer	12Ma02Cy
Mary	40	F	Housekeeper	12Ma02Cy
Joseph	12	M	Unknown	12Ma02Cy
Thos.	10	M	Unknown	12Ma02Cy
John	08	M	Child	12Ma02Cy
Lawrence	06	M	Child	12Ma02Cy
Elizabeth	04	F	Child	12Ma02Cy
Henry	.00	M	Infant	12Ma02Cy
MEEHAN, Mary	28	F	Servant	12Ma02Cy
POWER, Pat	36	M	Farmer	12Ma02Cy
Bridget	30	F	Housekeeper	12Ma02Cy
MOONEY, John	24	M	Surveyor	12Ma02Cy
KEALY, Thos.	28	M	Laborer	12Ma02Cy
Margt.	20	F	Housekeeper	12Ma02Cy
Denis	19	M	Laborer	12Ma02Cy
Matthew	12	M	Laborer	12Ma02Cy
Jas.	11	M	Laborer	12Ma02Cy
Mary	50	F	Housekeeper	12Ma02Cy
MCKENNAR, Jas.	39	M	Brick Maker	12Ma02Cy
MCCOY, Thos.	40	M	Ptdsgr	12Ma02Cy
BURNS, Samuel	26	M	Farmer	12Ma02Cy
Mary	26	F	Housekeeper	12Ma02Cy
CLANCY, Martin	32	M	Farmer	12Ma02Cy
SWENEY, Edmund	28	M	Farmer	12Ma02Cy
Thos.	30	M	Farmer	12Ma02Cy
CLIFFORD, Daniel	28	M	Farmer	12Ma02Cy
Catherine	20	F	Housekeeper	12Ma02Cy
MCGILLYENDDY, Edmund	28	M	Laborer	12Ma02Cy
HICKEY, Martin	27	M	Laborer	12Ma02Cy
HONLALEN, John	20	M	Laborer	12Ma02Cy
GARTLAM, Michael	34	M	Farmer	12Ma02Cy
SHAUGHESSY, Catherine	25	F	Housekeeper	12Ma02Cy
WOOD, Catherine	20	F	Housekeeper	12Ma02Cy
MOORE, Patrick-Thos.	20	M	Baker	12Ma02Cy
MCCOVAN, James	24	M	Laborer	12Ma02Cy
LOUGHREY, Bernard	25	M	Baker	12Ma02Cy
Ellen	25	F	Housekeeper	12Ma02Cy
Patrick	21	M	Farmer	12Ma02Cy
MCCABE, Catherine	24	F	Housekeeper	12Ma02Cy
James	20	M	Laborer	12Ma02Cy
BACON, Margaret	18	F	Housekeeper	12Ma02Cy
MILLIGAN, Margaret	20	F	Housekeeper	12Ma02Cy
EMMET, Edward	18	M	Laborer	12Ma02Cy
LEARY, Edward	20	M	Laborer	12Ma02Cy
CARROLL, John	19	M	Shoemaker	12Ma02Cy
BURNS, Francis	19	M	Laborer	12Ma02Cy
FINN, Hugh	20	M	Laborer	12Ma02Cy
MCFILLAN, Joseph	23	M	Laborer	12Ma02Cy

PHEASANT 13 MAY 1848

From St.JOHNS,N.B.

NAMES OF PASSENGERS	AGE	SEX	OCCUPATIONS	DATE PORT SHIP
GALLAGHER, Dennis	50	M	Farmer	13Ma79Cz
Margaret	45	F	Unknown	13Ma79Cz
Margaret	12	F	Unknown	13Ma79Cz
Dennis	14	M	Unknown	13Ma79Cz
James	05	M	Child	13Ma79Cz

SARAH-MILLEDGE 13 MAY 1848

From Galway

NAMES OF PASSENGERS	AGE	SEX	OCCUPATIONS	DATE PORT SHIP
WHELAN, James	28	M	Laborer	13Ma11Dc
Ann	19	F	Spinster	13Ma11Dc
WALSH, Joseph	25	M	Laborer	13Ma11Dc
LEE, Cunen	21	F	Laborer	13Ma11Dc
COWYE, Mary	22	F	Spinster	13Ma11Dc
HUBARTON, Maria	20	F	Spinster	13Ma11Dc
SHEA, Kitty	22	F	Spinster	13Ma11Dc
HAWKINS, Kitty	22	F	Spinster	13Ma11Dc
Biddy	22	F	Spinster	13Ma11Dc
JOYCE, Martin	19	M	Mechanic	13Ma11Dc
Dumerk	20	M	Laborer	13Ma11Dc
Margret	18	F	Spinster	13Ma11Dc
SWIFT, John	22	M	Laborer	13Ma11Dc
MURRAY, Ellen	30	F	Laborer	13Ma11Dc
Thomas	03	M	Child	13Ma11Dc
Mary	25	F	Laborer	13Ma11Dc
GARDNER, James	40	M	Laborer	13Ma11Dc
Ellen	40	F	Spinster	13Ma11Dc
Catarine	20	F	Spinster	13Ma11Dc
Bridget	18	F	Spinster	13Ma11Dc
Margret	16	F	Spinster	13Ma11Dc
John	13	M	Spinner	13Ma11Dc
James	11	M	Spinner	13Ma11Dc
Ellen	06	F	Child	13Ma11Dc
Mich.	04	M	Child	13Ma11Dc
CCURCANNANE, Martin	24	M	Laborer	13Ma11Dc
CONNELLY, Pate	26	M	Laborer	13Ma11Dc
HEALY, Pate	20	M	Laborer	13Ma11Dc
NEIL, Pate	30	M	Laborer	13Ma11Dc
COFFEE, Catharine	25	F	Spinster	13Ma11Dc
SHEIL, Honor-Mrs.	32	F	Wife	13Ma11Dc
ODONNELL, Stephen	36	M	Laborer	13Ma11Dc
DONNELLY, Bridget-Mrs.	22	F	Wife	13Ma11Dc
MCGRATH, James	20	M	Laborer	13Ma11Dc
FINNAGHTY, Mich.	20	M	Laborer	13Ma11Dc
SHAUGHNESSY, Mary	24	F	Spinster	13Ma11Dc
ODONNELL, Mich.	34	M	Laborer	13Ma11Dc
EGAN, Mich.	23	M	Laborer	13Ma11Dc
John	25	M	Laborer	13Ma11Dc
Jeromiah	20	M	Laborer	13Ma11Dc
James	18	M	Laborer	13Ma11Dc
Honoria-Mrs.	19	F	Wife	13Ma11Dc
Patrick	29	M	Laborer	13Ma11Dc
DOHUHY, Ellen	19	F	Spinster	13Ma11Dc
CARROLL, Pat	27	M	Laborer	13Ma11Dc
CONNOLLY, John	23	M	Laborer	13Ma11Dc
CAULKINS, Pat	32	M	Laborer	13Ma11Dc
CULKEEN, Bridget-Mrs.	20	F	Wife	13Ma11Dc
GERAGHTY, James	26	M	Laborer	13Ma11Dc

NAMES OF PASSENGERS		AGE	SEX	OCCUPATIONS	DATE PORT SHIP
GERAGHTY, Judy	(W)	26	F	Wife	13Ma11Dc
Pate	(S)	04	M	Child	13Ma11Dc
Bridget	(D)	02	F	Child	13Ma11Dc
SKAHILL, James		35	M	Laborer	13Ma11Dc
CUNNANE, John		25	M	Laborer	13Ma11Dc
Nappy	(W)	25	F	Wife	13Ma11Dc
MCMAHEN, Martin		22	M	Laborer	13Ma11Dc
Mich.		26	M	Laborer	13Ma11Dc
CONNELLY, Thomas		18	M	Laborer	13Ma11Dc
WHELAN, Mich.		24	M	Laborer	13Ma11Dc
COSTELLO, Darby		30	M	Laborer	13Ma11Dc
CONNELLY, John		30	M	Mechanic	13Ma11Dc
Catherine	(W)	24	F	Wife	13Ma11Dc
MULKINE, Peter		40	M	Laborer	13Ma11Dc
HAWLEN, Patt.		40	M	Laborer	13Ma11Dc
HYNES, Mary		20	F	Spinster	13Ma11Dc
DEALY, Honor		30	F	Spinster	13Ma11Dc
JYNAGH, John		19	M	Laborer	13Ma11Dc
MULKINN, Mary		25	F	Spinster	13Ma11Dc
KELLY, Patt.		20	M	Laborer	13Ma11Dc
MCLOUGHLIN, Thaddy		18	M	Laborer	13Ma11Dc
MULLIN, Tim		30	M	Laborer	13Ma11Dc
BURKE, Mary		23	F	Spinster	13Ma11Dc
Margret		19	F	Spinster	13Ma11Dc
MCGRATH, James		35	M	Laborer	13Ma11Dc
Mary	(W)	34	F	Wife	13Ma11Dc
Mary	(D)	08	F	Child	13Ma11Dc
MACKIN, Thomas		21	M	Laborer	13Ma11Dc
WARD, Martin		21	M	Laborer	13Ma11Dc
WALSH, John		14	M	Laborer	13Ma11Dc
NEILAN, Mich.		28	M	Laborer	13Ma11Dc
REDINGTON, Peter		20	M	Laborer	13Ma11Dc
NOLAN, John		28	M	Laborer	13Ma11Dc
MCDONNELL, Lawrence		35	M	Mechanic	13Ma11Dc
Bridget	(W)	35	F	Wife	13Ma11Dc
Wm.M.	(S)	03	M	Child	13Ma11Dc
CONNOLLY, John		10	M	Laborer	13Ma11Dc
ROWDEN, Gerelda		17	M	Laborer	13Ma11Dc
TANSY, Mary		20	F	Spinster	13Ma11Dc
Catharine		19	F	Spinster	13Ma11Dc
SWINEY, Bridget		25	F	Spinster	13Ma11Dc
RENAWE, Winy		27	F	Spinster	13Ma11Dc
Patt.		07	M	Child	13Ma11Dc
RENINS, Catharine		35	F	Lad	13Ma11Dc
Mary		11	F	Unknown	13Ma11Dc
Thomas		06	M	Child	13Ma11Dc
Narry		03	F	Child	13Ma11Dc
BURKE, Thomas		26	M	Laborer	13Ma11Dc
HOHOLAN, Thomas		26	M	Laborer	13Ma11Dc
Pat		24	M	Laborer	13Ma11Dc
HEALY, Mary		40	F	Spinster	13Ma11Dc
Jane		12	F	Unknown	13Ma11Dc
Julia		12	F	Unknown	13Ma11Dc
Daria		03	F	Child	13Ma11Dc
CAVENAGH, Bridget		20	F	Spinster	13Ma11Dc
BLAKE, Maria		12	F	Unknown	13Ma11Dc
GREALY, Mich.		07	M	Child	13Ma11Dc
Bridget		12	F	Child	13Ma11Dc
TIMICANE, Connor		24	M	Spinster	13Ma11Dc
MAHON, Patt.		25	M	Laborer	13Ma11Dc
FAHY, Edward		21	M	Laborer	13Ma11Dc
GLYN, Michael		35	M	Laborer	13Ma11Dc
HICKEY, Mich.		35	M	Laborer	13Ma11Dc
FAHERTY, Daniel		19	M	Laborer	13Ma11Dc
HYNE, John		26	M	Laborer	13Ma11Dc
CLUNDANE, Bridget		21	F	Spinster	13Ma11Dc
Ann		19	F	Spinster	13Ma11Dc
FLYNN, Bridget		30	F	Spinster	13Ma11Dc
OBRIEN, Mich.		21	M	Laborer	13Ma11Dc
TUHIDY, Thomas		21	M	Laborer	13Ma11Dc
MULRONY, Patt.		26	M	Laborer	13Ma11Dc
DILLON, Martin		16	M	Laborer	13Ma11Dc
WHITE, John		18	M	Laborer	13Ma11Dc
KELLY, D.		19	F	Spinster	13Ma11Dc
HAVENAGE, T.		40	M	Laborer	13Ma11Dc
HAVENAGE, Andy		08	M	Child	13Ma11Dc
MULLINS, Patt.		24	M	Laborer	13Ma11Dc
ELWARD, Patt.		25	M	Laborer	13Ma11Dc
MORAN, John		19	M	Laborer	13Ma11Dc
Thomas		18	M	Laborer	13Ma11Dc
Myles		17	M	Laborer	13Ma11Dc
HAWKINS, Ann		17	F	Spinster	13Ma11Dc
MOONEY, Dennis		30	M	Laborer	13Ma11Dc
JOYCE, John		25	M	Laborer	13Ma11Dc
Mich.		23	M	Laborer	13Ma11Dc
MULVEY, Andrew		22	M	Laborer	13Ma11Dc
FOSTER, John		18	M	Laborer	13Ma11Dc
GOHEGAN, Patt.		20	M	Laborer	13Ma11Dc
CUNNRE, Patt.		24	M	Laborer	13Ma11Dc
HOGAN, Thomas		25	6	Laborer	13Ma11Dc
GEARY, Patt.		30	M	Mechanic	13Ma11Dc
BURNS, Joseph		24	M	Laborer	13Ma11Dc
CONNOR, James		28	M	Laborer	13Ma11Dc
CONNER, Patt.		32	M	Laborer	13Ma11Dc
BARETE, John		40	M	Laborer	13Ma11Dc
ROANE, M.		40	M	Laborer	13Ma11Dc
BURKE, Bridget		18	F	Spinster	13Ma11Dc
HELLILIA, Julia		40	F	Spinster	13Ma11Dc
Mary		17	F	Spinster	13Ma11Dc
John		16	M	Spinster	13Ma11Dc
Martin		11	M	Unknown	13Ma11Dc
WHITE, John		18	M	Laborer	13Ma11Dc
LINN, James		24	M	Laborer	13Ma11Dc
MCMAHON, James		45	M	Laborer	13Ma11Dc
Eliza		18	F	Spinster	13Ma11Dc
John		16	M	Laborer	13Ma11Dc
Stephen		13	M	Unknown	13Ma11Dc
Mary		11	F	Unknown	13Ma11Dc
Kitty		42	F	Spinster	13Ma11Dc
MCHUGH, Patt.		25	M	Laborer	13Ma11Dc
Judeth	(W)	22	F	Wife	13Ma11Dc
HUBLINS, Margret		40	F	Spinster	13Ma11Dc
Bridget		15	F	Spinster	13Ma11Dc
John		10	M	Unknown	13Ma11Dc
MULLIN, Patt		24	M	Laborer	13Ma11Dc
EDWARD, Patt.		24	M	Laborer	13Ma11Dc
HUBLINS, Mary		20	F	Spinster	13Ma11Dc
Mary		08	F	Child	13Ma11Dc
COSTELLO, U		00	M	Clerk	13Ma11Dc

CAMBRIA 14 MAY 1848

From Liverpool-And-Halifax

NAMES OF PASSENGERS	AGE	SEX	OCCUPATIONS	DATE PORT SHIP
BROWN, Martin	46	M	Merchant	14Ma97Es
RHOADS, J.G.	28	M	Merchant	14Ma97Es
LEREZ, Chs.E.	40	M	Merchant	14Ma97Es
Jemima	24	F	None	14Ma97Es
BOXER, U	22	F	None	14Ma97Es
BUCHANAN, Mary-Ann	25	F	Servant	14Ma97Es

HOPE 15 MAY 1848

From Savanilla

NAMES OF PASSENGERS	AGE	SEX	OCCUPATIONS	DATE PORT SHIP
JOY, R.A.	30	M	Merchant	15Ma62De

WARRIOR 15 MAY 1848

From Drogheda

NAMES OF PASSENGERS	AGE	SEX	OCCUPATIONS	DATE PORT SHIP
CONAGHY, Nicholas	45	M	Farmer	15Ma32Dh
MULLAN, Mary	22	F	Farmer	15Ma32Dh
LINANEY, John	40	M	Farmer	15Ma32Dh
Cathirin	35	F	Farmer	15Ma32Dh
Margret	14	F	Farmer	15Ma32Dh
Michael	04	M	Child	15Ma32Dh
MACABARY, John	25	M	Farmer	15Ma32Dh
FARMER, Joseph	28	M	Farmer	15Ma32Dh
COOK, Henry	27	M	Farmer	15Ma32Dh
DILLAN, Mary	22	F	Farmer	15Ma32Dh
CANALAN, Pat	25	M	Tailor	15Ma32Dh
FARRELL, Ann	23	F	Tailor	15Ma32Dh
CAMEN, John	27	M	Tailor	15Ma32Dh
Mary	19	F	Laborer	15Ma32Dh
HUNELL, Thomas	24	M	Laborer	15Ma32Dh
HARLEY, Michal	24	M	Laborer	15Ma32Dh
HUGHES, Ann	20	F	Laborer	15Ma32Dh
James	23	M	Laborer	15Ma32Dh
GILLINS, Bridget	22	F	Laborer	15Ma32Dh
KELLY, Michal	24	M	Laborer	15Ma32Dh
COUGHLAN, Thomas	25	M	Laborer	15Ma32Dh
Margret	20	F	Laborer	15Ma32Dh
BROWN, William	24	M	Laborer	15Ma32Dh
Ann	22	F	Laborer	15Ma32Dh
John	19	M	Laborer	15Ma32Dh
CASSIDY, Margret	21	F	Laborer	15Ma32Dh
Bridget	25	F	Laborer	15Ma32Dh
Anne	22	F	Laborer	15Ma32Dh
Bern.	.00	M	Infant	15Ma32Dh
Rose	02	F	Child	15Ma32Dh
William	05	M	Child	15Ma32Dh
MCGEE, Thomas	45	M	Laborer	15Ma32Dh
GARGAN, Thomas	28	M	Laborer	15Ma32Dh
GAILLIN, Ellen	23	F	Laborer	15Ma32Dh
Bessy	19	F	Laborer	15Ma32Dh
Jan.	17	F	Laborer	15Ma32Dh
CALLUM, Thomas	24	M	Laborer	15Ma32Dh
GARDY, Cormick	27	M	Laborer	15Ma32Dh
Ellen	23	F	Laborer	15Ma32Dh
Eliza	20	F	Laborer	15Ma32Dh
DYLN, John	26	M	Laborer	15Ma32Dh
Mary	24	F	Laborer	15Ma32Dh
Ann	23	F	Laborer	15Ma32Dh
DUNN, Richard	25	M	Laborer	15Ma32Dh
Mary	20	F	Laborer	15Ma32Dh
Ann	17	F	Laborer	15Ma32Dh
MCGORUGH, Mary	23	F	Laborer	15Ma32Dh
Ann	00	F	Laborer	15Ma32Dh
DUFFY, Jim	21	M	Laborer	15Ma32Dh
JOHNSON, Wm.	26	M	Laborer	15Ma32Dh
YOSORPSON, Jane	28	F	Laborer	15Ma32Dh
Cath.	26	F	Laborer	15Ma32Dh
Anthony	04	M	Child	15Ma32Dh
JOHNSON, William	.00	M	Infant	15Ma32Dh
Mary	40	F	Farmer	15Ma32Dh
Pat	38	M	Farmer	15Ma32Dh
Peter	12	M	Farmer	15Ma32Dh
Peter	10	M	Farmer	15Ma32Dh
Ann	08	F	Child	15Ma32Dh
Jane	.00	F	Infant	15Ma32Dh
Bernard	07	M	Child	15Ma32Dh
Catherin	06	F	Child	15Ma32Dh
James	05	M	Child	15Ma32Dh
Peter	04	M	Child	15Ma32Dh
Wm.	03	M	Child	15Ma32Dh
JOHNSON, Catherin	02	F	Child	15Ma32Dh
KELLY, Peter	01	M	Child	15Ma32Dh
Ann	21	F	Tailor	15Ma32Dh
CAULEY, Joseph	22	M	Tailor	15Ma32Dh
Eliza	25	F	Tailor	15Ma32Dh
Ann	.00	F	Infant	15Ma32Dh
Ch.	20	M	Laborer	15Ma32Dh
GUINN, Thomas-M.	07	M	Child	15Ma32Dh
ANDREWS, James-M.	25	M	Laborer	15Ma32Dh
Bridget	22	F	Laborer	15Ma32Dh
CASIDY, Thomas	10	M	Laborer	15Ma32Dh
GORGAN, Catherine	19	F	Laborer	15Ma32Dh
MCGARLY, Thomas	22	M	Laborer	15Ma32Dh
Mary	.00	F	Infant	15Ma32Dh
HANNON, Ann	19	F	Laborer	15Ma32Dh
LAMB, Own	22	M	Laborer	15Ma32Dh
ROCKE, Rosy	20	F	Laborer	15Ma32Dh
GRANNY, Bridget	25	F	Laborer	15Ma32Dh
Catherine	22	F	Laborer	15Ma32Dh
FITZPATRICK, Mathew	19	M	Laborer	15Ma32Dh
GLENN, James-M.	10	M	Laborer	15Ma32Dh
CALLEY, James-M.	25	M	Laborer	15Ma32Dh
MASLON, Catherine	10	F	Laborer	15Ma32Dh
CANNON, Phillip	17	M	Laborer	15Ma32Dh
NOLAN, Josephine	19	F	Laborer	15Ma32Dh
MCDELANCE, Pat	20	M	Laborer	15Ma32Dh

CHAOS 16 MAY 1848

From Liverpool

NAMES OF PASSENGERS	AGE	SEX	OCCUPATIONS	DATE PORT SHIP
DOUGHERTY, Patt.	25	M	Laborer	16Ma02Gg
Margaret	20	F	None	16Ma02Gg
FLYNN, Martin	25	M	Laborer	16Ma02Gg
Mary	22	F	None	16Ma02Gg
BRIEN, William	24	M	Servant	16Ma02Gg
Sarah	25	F	None	16Ma02Gg
Sarah	05	F	Child	16Ma02Gg
FINNALLY, Sarah	30	F	Servant	16Ma02Gg
MCANNALLY, Peter	30	M	Laborer	16Ma02Gg
Patt.	34	M	Weaver	16Ma02Gg
FLANEGAN, Catherine	21	F	Servant	16Ma02Gg
Rose	18	F	Servant	16Ma02Gg
DUFFY, John	40	M	Laborer	16Ma02Gg
John	19	M	Laborer	16Ma02Gg
FINIGAN, Peter	21	M	Laborer	16Ma02Gg
MCGOVERN, James	22	M	Laborer	16Ma02Gg
MURPHY, Michael	24	M	Laborer	16Ma02Gg
MCGUIRE, Bibby	22	F	Servant	16Ma02Gg
LARMER, Mary	25	F	Servant	16Ma02Gg
SHANKLAN, William	21	M	Joiner	16Ma02Gg
LANHON, Wm.J.	20	M	Carpenter	16Ma02Gg
WALINGLEY, Alexn.	25	M	Plasterer	16Ma02Gg
DAVIS, John	28	M	Miller	16Ma02Gg
John	24	M	Rist	16Ma02Gg
EVANS, Thomas	30	M	Rist	16Ma02Gg
ROBERTS, Joseph	30	M	Shingler	16Ma02Gg
James	30	M	Shingler	16Ma02Gg
John	19	M	Unknown	16Ma02Gg
David	12	M	Unknown	16Ma02Gg
Elizabeth	08	F	Child	16Ma02Gg
DELANEY, James	40	M	Japanner	16Ma02Gg
HALLY, John	20	M	Engineer	16Ma02Gg
NAYLOR, John	23	M	Smith	16Ma02Gg
GASKELLY, James	20	M	Engineer	16Ma02Gg
CAROLIN, Bernard	26	M	Gdnr	16Ma02Gg
BURNLEY, William	22	M	Gdnr	16Ma02Gg
PURTON, John	57	M	Farmer	16Ma02Gg
Rebecca	40	F	None	16Ma02Gg

NAMES OF PASSENGERS	AGE	SEX	OCCUPATIONS	DATE PORT SHIP
PURTON, Henry	14	M	None	16Ma02Gg
Samuel	12	M	None	16Ma02Gg
James-B.	10	M	None	16Ma02Gg
John	08	M	Child	16Ma02Gg
Catherin	06	F	Child	16Ma02Gg
Robert	02	M	Child	16Ma02Gg
MAYFIELD, Samuel	30	M	Farmer	16Ma02Gg
Sarah	28	F	None	16Ma02Gg
Elizabeth	06	F	Child	16Ma02Gg
Sarah	04	F	Child	16Ma02Gg
Henry	02	M	Child	16Ma02Gg
William	.06	M	Infant	16Ma02Gg
Died-At-Sea				
THORNTON, Benjm.	23	M	Mason	16Ma02Gg
BOOTH, Ambrose	29	M	Carpenter	16Ma02Gg
Sarah	29	F	None	16Ma02Gg
Henry	.09	M	Infant	16Ma02Gg
WILLIS, Charles	30	M	Weaver	16Ma02Gg
LEWIS, Lewis	20	M	Farmer	16Ma02Gg
George	25	M	Tailor	16Ma02Gg
BRANSTON, Thom.	27	M	Mnftr	16Ma02Gg
Hannah	24	F	None	16Ma02Gg
Emily-Mary	03	F	Child	16Ma02Gg
George	.09	M	Infant	16Ma02Gg
SCULTHORP, Joseph	37	M	Mnftr	16Ma02Gg
COKELY, Samuel	28	M	Farmer	16Ma02Gg
HACKETT, James	35	M	Excavator	16Ma02Gg
Hugh	23	M	Excavator	16Ma02Gg
MCGEE, Michael	30	M	Excavator	16Ma02Gg
MCKEW, John	30	M	Excavator	16Ma02Gg
James	25	M	Excavator	16Ma02Gg
MEATHER, John	30	M	Skinner	16Ma02Gg
Ann	25	F	None	16Ma02Gg
DEGHALE, Alexn.	25	M	Baker	16Ma02Gg
GIBBS, James	28	M	Carpenter	16Ma02Gg
SHARP, Robert	30	M	Weaver	16Ma02Gg
Jarrett	30	F	None	16Ma02Gg
FORBES, James	30	M	Weaver	16Ma02Gg
Lilla	26	F	None	16Ma02Gg
James	02	M	Child	16Ma02Gg
SMITH, William	36	M	Smith	16Ma02Gg
William	12	M	None	16Ma02Gg
Thomas	05	M	Child	16Ma02Gg
MEALY, Roger	30	M	Farmer	16Ma02Gg
Catherine	27	F	None	16Ma02Gg
Patt.	30	M	Farmer	16Ma02Gg
Bridget	26	F	None	16Ma02Gg
Mary	03	F	Child	16Ma02Gg
Catherine	01	F	Child	16Ma02Gg
BARRETT, Patrick	28	M	Butcher	16Ma02Gg
Catherine	22	F	None	16Ma02Gg
Martin	03	M	Child	16Ma02Gg
ONEIL, Edward	13	M	None	16Ma02Gg
John	28	M	Shoemaker	16Ma02Gg
James	21	M	Bootmaker	16Ma02Gg
FITZGERALD, Stephen	20	M	Millwright	16Ma02Gg
KEELAHER, John	30	M	Farmer	16Ma02Gg
BROADRICK, William	36	M	Laborer	16Ma02Gg
KEELAHER, Martin	30	M	Farmer	16Ma02Gg
Mary	32	F	None	16Ma02Gg
LEAHY, Catherine	20	F	None	16Ma02Gg
Mary	21	F	None	16Ma02Gg
Mary	20	F	None	16Ma02Gg
HIGGINS, Williaml	20	M	Porter	16Ma02Gg
MURRAY, John	25	M	Mason	16Ma02Gg
SCOTT, Robert	22	M	Laborer	16Ma02Gg
KEARNEY, James	32	M	Mason	16Ma02Gg
GREALEY, Thomas	24	M	Mason	16Ma02Gg
POWER, Ally	22	F	Servant	16Ma02Gg
JONES, William	29	M	Farmer	16Ma02Gg
DONALLY, Ebenezer	30	M	Tailor	16Ma02Gg
ACTON, Frederick	30	M	Weaver	16Ma02Gg
LEWIS, Wm.Henry	22	M	Weaver	16Ma02Gg
EDWARDS, Henry	23	M	Weaver	16Ma02Gg
WEBB, William	30	M	Currier	16Ma02Gg
WEBB, Betsey	22	F	None	16Ma02Gg
Joseph	.10	M	Infant	16Ma02Gg
CULLEN, John	22	M	Laborer	16Ma02Gg
HENRY, John	45	M	Farmer	16Ma02Gg
Frances	45	F	None	16Ma02Gg
John	21	M	None	16Ma02Gg
Ann	18	F	None	16Ma02Gg
James	15	M	None	16Ma02Gg
Ralph	13	M	None	16Ma02Gg
James	11	M	None	16Ma02Gg
Sophia	09	F	Child	16Ma02Gg
Matilda	07	F	Child	16Ma02Gg
FITZSIMMONS, Philip	30	M	Laborer	16Ma02Gg
REILY, Bernard	34	M	Laborer	16Ma02Gg
WALSH, Ann	50	F	None	16Ma02Gg
BYRNE, Dennis	23	M	Cooper	16Ma02Gg
Catherine	25	F	None	16Ma02Gg
WHELAN, Peter	48	M	Farmer	16Ma02Gg
Bridget	45	F	None	16Ma02Gg
John	18	M	Laborer	16Ma02Gg
Anatonia	16	F	None	16Ma02Gg
Edward	14	M	None	16Ma02Gg
James	10	M	None	16Ma02Gg
Patrick	06	M	Child	16Ma02Gg
William	02	M	Child	16Ma02Gg
BLAKE, Richard	29	M	Smith	16Ma02Gg
Mary	35	F	None	16Ma02Gg
Bridgt.	06	F	Child	16Ma02Gg
John	18	M	Smith	16Ma02Gg
Margaret	25	F	Servant	16Ma02Gg
James	21	M	Servant	16Ma02Gg
QUINN, James	21	M	Servant	16Ma02Gg
Alice	18	F	Servant	16Ma02Gg
Catherine	16	F	Servant	16Ma02Gg
Bridget	14	F	Servant	16Ma02Gg
POWER, Michael	32	M	Laborer	16Ma02Gg
MCKAY, James	21	M	Laborer	16Ma02Gg
Bridget	22	F	Servant	16Ma02Gg
ROWE, Dennis	36	M	Laborer	16Ma02Gg
WALSH, Michael	46	M	Laborer	16Ma02Gg
HEWITT, Richard	32	M	Tinner	16Ma02Gg
CORCKRAN, Toby	27	M	Laborer	16Ma02Gg
DOWLING, Edward	37	M	Laborer	16Ma02Gg
WALLACE, Peter	22	M	Clerk	16Ma02Gg
LAIRD, James	27	M	Carpenter	16Ma02Gg
HUNCHLIFFE, Joseph	42	M	Carpenter	16Ma02Gg
GLEASON, Peter	19	M	Engineer	16Ma02Gg
DONOVAN, Johanna	22	F	Servant	16Ma02Gg
CHANDLER, Elizabeth	30	F	Servant	16Ma02Gg
CROTHMAN, William	32	M	Farmer	16Ma02Gg
James	24	M	Laborer	16Ma02Gg
BYRNES, James	24	M	Farmer	16Ma02Gg
RILLAY, Daniel	32	M	Baker	16Ma02Gg
THOMSON, Thomas	28	M	Clothier	16Ma02Gg
MORRIS, William	38	M	Cloth Maker	16Ma02Gg
YEATAN, Benjamin	48	M	Gunsmith	16Ma02Gg
PARKER, William	34	M	Spinner	16Ma02Gg
AMEAR, John	22	M	Miner	16Ma02Gg
SPEAR, Williaml	23	M	Miner	16Ma02Gg
WATERS, John	38	M	Miner	16Ma02Gg
MORRIS, William	25	M	Chandler	16Ma02Gg
KELLY, Edward	21	M	Mason	16Ma02Gg
BENNETT, Ann	36	F	None	16Ma02Gg
Lucy	24	F	Dressmaker	16Ma02Gg
HANNON, Benjamin	24	M	Miner	16Ma02Gg
LEASENDER, Thomas	32	M	Farmer	16Ma02Gg
William	19	M	Farmer	16Ma02Gg
RILEY, Michael	25	M	Dealer	16Ma02Gg
Elizabeth	25	F	None	16Ma02Gg
Stephen	02	M	Child	16Ma02Gg
Maria	.06	F	Infant	16Ma02Gg
STRINGER, John	30	M	Farmer	16Ma02Gg
GUMESTON, Richard	32	M	Laborer	16Ma02Gg
MEDCALF, John	24	M	Mason	16Ma02Gg
Mary	22	F	None	16Ma02Gg

NAMES OF PASSENGERS	AGE	SEX	OCCUPATIONS	DATE PORT SHIP
ABRAHAM, Matthew	30	M	Smith	16Ma02Gg
MALEY, Fanny	18	F	Servant	16Ma02Gg
CONRON, Michael	26	M	Porter	16Ma02Gg
HIFFERMAN, Catherine	30	F	Servant	16Ma02Gg
DONAGHRY, James	40	M	Laborer	16Ma02Gg
MURPHY, Bryan	50	M	Laborer	16Ma02Gg
EAGAN, Peter	30	M	Laborer	16Ma02Gg
MCNEAL, James	23	M	Shopman	16Ma02Gg
FARRALL, Peter	20	M	Laborer	16Ma02Gg
Elizabeth	18	F	Servant	16Ma02Gg
MURRAY, Patt.	03	M	Child	16Ma02Gg
DALY, Patrick	55	M	Laborer	16Ma02Gg
Philip	24	M	Laborer	16Ma02Gg
Patrick	22	M	Laborer	16Ma02Gg
Hugh	19	M	Laborer	16Ma02Gg
Hannah	17	F	Laborer	16Ma02Gg
MULLEN, Patt.	26	M	Laborer	16Ma02Gg
Nancy	20	F	Servant	16Ma02Gg
HENRY, Andrew-M.	24	M	Laborer	16Ma02Gg
MCKEIGH, Agnes	21	F	Servant	16Ma02Gg
Alley	18	F	Servant	16Ma02Gg
SULLLIVAN, Philip	31	M	Laborer	16Ma02Gg
CLANCEY, Edward	26	M	Laborer	16Ma02Gg
MEHAN, Ellen	24	F	Servant	16Ma02Gg
Ellen	02	F	Child	16Ma02Gg
John	.09	M	Infant	16Ma02Gg
MCGOWAN, Connar	22	M	Farmer	16Ma02Gg
Honora	20	F	Servant	16Ma02Gg
MCCORMICK, Margaret	18	F	Dressmaker	16Ma02Gg
BURKE, Daniel	40	M	Farmer	16Ma02Gg
BRACKEN, John	23	M	Laborer	16Ma02Gg
MCTIERNEY, Bridget	20	F	Servant	16Ma02Gg
KEARNEY, John	25	M	Laborer	16Ma02Gg
FLYNN, Mary	22	F	Servant	16Ma02Gg
DEVIN, John	30	M	Laborer	16Ma02Gg
Mary	28	F	None	16Ma02Gg
CONNOR, Patt	06	M	Child	16Ma02Gg
DARCY, John	20	M	Laborer	16Ma02Gg
HINCH, Charles	22	M	Laborer	16Ma02Gg
Henry	24	M	Laborer	16Ma02Gg
BLACK, Thomas	21	M	Laborer	16Ma02Gg
OBRIEN, James	30	M	Laborer	16Ma02Gg
MAHER, Thomas	50	M	Laborer	16Ma02Gg
GRAY, Thomas	21	M	Mason	16Ma02Gg
Hannah	20	F	None	16Ma02Gg
JOHNSTON, Robert	27	M	Carpenter	16Ma02Gg
Isabella	22	F	None	16Ma02Gg
James	01	M	Child	16Ma02Gg
KEARNEY, John	25	M	Farmer	16Ma02Gg
MARTIN, Ann	24	F	None	16Ma02Gg
MCCALL, John	22	M	Servant	16Ma02Gg
KEARNEY, Catherine	30	F	Servant	16Ma02Gg
Mary	22	F	Servant	16Ma02Gg
MCGINNIS, Terence	22	M	Shopkeeper	16Ma02Gg
Mary	20	F	Servant	16Ma02Gg
BURLEY, Thomas	24	M	Miner	16Ma02Gg
GREGORY, Joseph	27	M	Miner	16Ma02Gg
BROWN, James	24	M	Miner	16Ma02Gg
HAWKINS, Benjn.	27	M	Miner	16Ma02Gg
DAW, William	24	M	Miner	16Ma02Gg
WALTERS, Richard	24	M	Miner	16Ma02Gg
HAWKINS, Bartholomew	25	M	Miner	16Ma02Gg
BARRETT, John	23	M	Miner	16Ma02Gg
GRANEY, William	33	M	Miner	16Ma02Gg
ROBERTS, Thomas	16	M	Miner	16Ma02Gg
Jane	20	F	Servant	16Ma02Gg
MCLEAN, Edward	50	M	Laborer	16Ma02Gg
Daniel	50	M	Laborer	16Ma02Gg
Peter	18	M	Laborer	16Ma02Gg
Thomas	20	M	Laborer	16Ma02Gg
Bridget	21	F	Servant	16Ma02Gg
Mary	13	F	Servant	16Ma02Gg
Hugh	36	M	Farmer	16Ma02Gg
Mary	30	F	None	16Ma02Gg
Bronach	24	F	None	16Ma02Gg
MCLEAN, Matthew	08	M	Child	16Ma02Gg
Elizabeth	06	F	Child	16Ma02Gg
William	03	M	Child	16Ma02Gg
Mary	01	F	Child	16Ma02Gg
ROONEY, Mary	23	F	Servant	16Ma02Gg
GORHAM, Betty	22	F	Servant	16Ma02Gg
HUNTER, Elizabeth	26	F	Servant	16Ma02Gg
Secily	28	F	Servant	16Ma02Gg
MCLEAN, Thomas	40	M	Farmer	16Ma02Gg
Margaret	40	F	None	16Ma02Gg
Mary	08	F	Child	16Ma02Gg
Catherine	05	F	Child	16Ma02Gg
Jane	02	F	Child	16Ma02Gg
RICE, Betty	40	F	None	16Ma02Gg
CUMMINS, Samuel	20	M	Farmer	16Ma02Gg
Mary	30	F	Farmer	16Ma02Gg
HENRAN, Michael	30	M	Farmer	16Ma02Gg
MCLEAN, Thomas	40	M	Farmer	16Ma02Gg
HOLLING, Samuel	35	M	Farmer	16Ma02Gg
DAVID, Edward	27	M	Bootmaker	16Ma02Gg
DONNELLY, Patt.	30	M	Baker	16Ma02Gg
Bridget	12	F	None	16Ma02Gg
John	05	M	Child	16Ma02Gg
MCELROY, Thomas	26	M	Carpenter	16Ma02Gg
ONEIL, Mary	27	F	Servant	16Ma02Gg
MCELROY, Bridget	02	F	Child	16Ma02Gg
ZOOTILL, Richard	27	M	Bleacher	16Ma02Gg
STOTT, William	25	M	Bleacher	16Ma02Gg
JOYCE, Mary	20	F	Servant	16Ma02Gg
MCCORMICK, Catherine	20	F	Servant	16Ma02Gg
MATTHEWS, Thomas	23	M	Shoemaker	16Ma02Gg
Mary	23	M	Hatter	16Ma02Gg
Elizabeth-Jane	.06	F	Infant	16Ma02Gg
RAYESTON, James	28	M	Laborer	16Ma02Gg
LARCEY, James	26	M	Laborer	16Ma02Gg
FITZGERALD, Patrick	24	M	Carpenter	16Ma02Gg

TITCOMB 16 MAY 1848

From Londonderry

NAMES OF PASSENGERS	AGE	SEX	OCCUPATIONS	DATE PORT SHIP
MAHON, William	60	M	Shoemaker	16Ma01Dk
Mary	50	F	Unknown	16Ma01Dk
Eliza	17	F	Shoemaker	16Ma01Dk
John	11	M	Unknown	16Ma01Dk
GILIHAND, Bridget	50	F	Farmer	16Ma01Dk
William	20	M	Farmer	16Ma01Dk
Jane	17	F	Farmer	16Ma01Dk
Robert	14	M	Farmer	16Ma01Dk
Elizabeth	11	F	Farmer	16Ma01Dk
Susan	09	F	Child	16Ma01Dk
MCNEIL, Jane	11	F	Farmer	16Ma01Dk
MCCONNELL, Alexn.	20	M	Laborer	16Ma01Dk
LOVE, Elizabeth	18	F	Milliner	16Ma01Dk
IRVINE, Richard	32	M	Farmer	16Ma01Dk
Richd.John	03	M	Child	16Ma01Dk
Jane	30	F	Unknown	16Ma01Dk
Eliza-Jane	01	F	Child	16Ma01Dk
DUFFY, Peeoba	35	F	Servant	16Ma01Dk
MITCHELL, Robert	36	M	Farmer	16Ma01Dk
Jane	33	F	Unknown	16Ma01Dk
Margaret	03	F	Child	16Ma01Dk
William-John	.03	M	Infant	16Ma01Dk
ALEXANDER, Mary	20	F	Servant	16Ma01Dk
MITCHELL, John	40	M	Farmer	16Ma01Dk
Margret	60	F	Farmer	16Ma01Dk
CALHOUN, Margret-Anne	15	F	Farmer	16Ma01Dk
FERGUSON, Andrew	25	M	Laborer	16Ma01Dk
BANKS, James	19	M	Irnmldr	16Ma01Dk

NAMES OF PASSENGERS	AGE	SEX	OCCUPATIONS	DATE PORT SHIP
CANNON, Patrick	20	M	Miller	16Ma01Dk
DONAGHEY, Robert	22	M	Millwright	16Ma01Dk
Denis	16	M	Laborer	16Ma01Dk
MCGRANAGHAN, Rose	14	F	Servant	16Ma01Dk
MCCLOSKER, Matilda	22	F	Servant	16Ma01Dk
ROARTY, Grace	27	F	Servant	16Ma01Dk
MCNAMEE, Catharine	20	F	Milliner	16Ma01Dk
BROOKLOW, Sarah-Jane	19	F	Milliner	16Ma01Dk
HOOD, Mary	19	F	Milliner	16Ma01Dk
CARLIN, Alice	26	F	Cook	16Ma01Dk
TRAVERS, Henry	19	M	Laborer	16Ma01Dk
DOHERTY, John	19	M	Laborer	16Ma01Dk
BOGAN, Thomas	19	M	Student	16Ma01Dk
CRAIG, David	23	M	Laborer	16Ma01Dk
CARLIN, John	55	M	Laborer	16Ma01Dk
Bridget	54	F	Laborer	16Ma01Dk
James	14	M	Laborer	16Ma01Dk
William	09	M	Child	16Ma01Dk
STEPHENSON, Mary	78	F	Farmer	16Ma01Dk
James	36	M	Farmer	16Ma01Dk
Anne	24	F	Farmer	16Ma01Dk
James	03	M	Child	16Ma01Dk
BURKE, James	18	M	Laborer	16Ma01Dk
ADAMS, William	24	M	Laborer	16Ma01Dk
MCLUCAS, John	20	M	Laborer	16Ma01Dk
GAMBELL, John	18	M	Laborer	16Ma01Dk
YOUNG, Samuel	40	M	Laborer	16Ma01Dk
Mary	40	F	Laborer	16Ma01Dk
Samuel-Jnr.	07	M	Child	16Ma01Dk
ANDREWS, Anne	54	F	Laborer	16Ma01Dk
David	17	M	Laborer	16Ma01Dk
KYLE, Joseph	60	M	Farmer	16Ma01Dk
Mary	50	F	Farmer	16Ma01Dk
Joseph	17	M	Farmer	16Ma01Dk
William	17	M	Farmer	16Ma01Dk
Isabella	15	F	Farmer	16Ma01Dk
Thomas	12	M	Farmer	16Ma01Dk
William	12	M	Farmer	16Ma01Dk
Samuel	08	M	Child	16Ma01Dk
James	06	M	Child	16Ma01Dk
HOEY, Mary-Jane	21	F	Servant	16Ma01Dk
ALLISON, Rebecca	20	F	Servant	16Ma01Dk
Margret	18	F	Servant	16Ma01Dk
HOOD, Elizabeth	22	F	Servant	16Ma01Dk
CRESWELL, Rebecca	10	F	Servant	16Ma01Dk
Sarah	05	F	Child	16Ma01Dk
LUNNEY, Elizabeth	23	F	Laborer	16Ma01Dk
Thomas	.09	M	Infant	16Ma01Dk
GALLAHER, Winefred	20	F	Laborer	16Ma01Dk
CASSIDY, Mary	22	F	Laborer	16Ma01Dk
MCGENISS, Eliza	21	F	Laborer	16Ma01Dk
MOORE, Violet	50	F	Laborer	16Ma01Dk
Violet-Jnr.	20	F	Laborer	16Ma01Dk
Anne	16	F	Laborer	16Ma01Dk
Jane	15	F	Laborer	16Ma01Dk
Anne-Jnr.	01	F	Child	16Ma01Dk
ALLEN, Margret	57	F	Laborer	16Ma01Dk
Isabella	19	F	Laborer	16Ma01Dk
FINSTON, Jane	18	F	Laborer	16Ma01Dk
Dorothy	12	F	Laborer	16Ma01Dk
STEPHENSON, David	18	M	Laborer	16Ma01Dk
FINSTON, Hugh	22	M	Laborer	16Ma01Dk
COOPER, John	25	M	Land Agent	16Ma01Dk
ALLEN, Thomas	20	M	Laborer	16Ma01Dk
ORR, Charles	26	M	Laborer	16Ma01Dk
SMYTH, John	30	M	Laborer	16Ma01Dk
MCKANE, John	30	M	Laborer	16Ma01Dk
JAMES, Robert	23	M	Laborer	16Ma01Dk
LINDSAY, Joseph	67	M	Laborer	16Ma01Dk
Mary	64	F	Laborer	16Ma01Dk
Arthur	21	M	Laborer	16Ma01Dk
DIVER, John	24	M	Laborer	16Ma01Dk
DOHERTY, John	23	M	Laborer	16Ma01Dk
MCLAUGHLIN, James	28	M	Blacksmith	16Ma01Dk
FULLERTON, Charles	24	M	Laborer	16Ma01Dk
MARTIN, John	26	M	Laborer	16Ma01Dk
MCMONNIGLE, John	17	M	Laborer	16Ma01Dk
GILLESPIE, James	22	M	Laborer	16Ma01Dk
KENNEDY, James	35	M	Laborer	16Ma01Dk
BRAWLEY, Scott	17	M	Laborer	16Ma01Dk
FOY, Hugh	20	M	Baker	16Ma01Dk
CALAGHAN, Michael	20	M	Laborer	16Ma01Dk
BRADLEY, Paul	23	M	Laborer	16Ma01Dk
DIVINE, Michael	19	M	Laborer	16Ma01Dk
FORRENS, Matty	16	F	Laborer	16Ma01Dk
MORGAN, Mary	17	F	Laborer	16Ma01Dk
PURDY, Susan	03	F	Child	16Ma01Dk
DORAN, Edward	28	M	Laborer	16Ma01Dk
ALEXANDER, Thomas	23	M	Laborer	16Ma01Dk
FYE, James	20	M	Laborer	16Ma01Dk
MCCAUL, John	21	M	Laborer	16Ma01Dk
BRYSON, William	23	M	Joiner	16Ma01Dk
Christiana	25	F	Laborer	16Ma01Dk
HOUSTON, Esther	22	F	Laborer	16Ma01Dk
CALAGHAN, James	06	M	Child	16Ma01Dk
GALLAGHER, John	40	M	Laborer	16Ma01Dk
Margret	34	F	Laborer	16Ma01Dk
MCCARRON, Hugh	23	M	Laborer	16Ma01Dk
Edward	40	M	Laborer	16Ma01Dk
MCFADDEN, Fergal	20	M	Laborer	16Ma01Dk
CARNWORTH, James	26	M	Laborer	16Ma01Dk
STEWART, Thomas	13	M	Laborer	16Ma01Dk
CARNWORTH, Anne	38	F	Laborer	16Ma01Dk
Mary	28	F	Laborer	16Ma01Dk
STEWART, James	10	M	Laborer	16Ma01Dk
MCNALLY, Eliza	18	F	Laborer	16Ma01Dk
MCDADE, Margret	22	F	Laborer	16Ma01Dk
HEANEY, Margret	18	F	Laborer	16Ma01Dk
ALLEN, John	55	M	Blacksmith	16Ma01Dk
Margret	30	F	Laborer	16Ma01Dk
William	12	M	Laborer	16Ma01Dk
Anne	10	F	Laborer	16Ma01Dk
Catherine	08	F	Child	16Ma01Dk
Hugh	05	M	Child	16Ma01Dk
HARPER, Samuel	17	M	Laborer	16Ma01Dk
MCCONNELL, Isabella	63	F	Laborer	16Ma01Dk
CURRAN, Catharine	18	F	Laborer	16Ma01Dk
KEANE, Hugh	24	M	Laborer	16Ma01Dk
Denis	18	M	Shoemaker	16Ma01Dk
Catharine	23	F	Laborer	16Ma01Dk
QUIGLEY, William	25	M	Laborer	16Ma01Dk
MARGEY, Henry	22	M	Laborer	16Ma01Dk
MCLAUGHLIN, Bernard	21	M	Laborer	16Ma01Dk
MCILHENNY, Patrick	28	M	Laborer	16Ma01Dk
CANNEY, Hugh	21	M	Laborer	16Ma01Dk
Denis	21	M	Laborer	16Ma01Dk
Charles	23	M	Laborer	16Ma01Dk
CATHERWOOD, Michael	20	M	Laborer	16Ma01Dk
GILL, Ellen	22	F	Laborer	16Ma01Dk
CATHERWOOD, Rose	16	F	Laborer	16Ma01Dk
WALLS, Matilda	17	F	Laborer	16Ma01Dk
CARBEREY, Peter	22	M	Laborer	16Ma01Dk
Susan	20	F	Laborer	16Ma01Dk
MCCAULEY, Denis	25	M	Laborer	16Ma01Dk
Susan	25	F	Laborer	16Ma01Dk
LACKARD, Mary	23	F	Milliner	16Ma01Dk
DIVER, Anne-Jane	20	F	Servant	16Ma01Dk
MCRORY, Bridget	26	M	Laborer	16Ma01Dk
KEANE, Mary	24	M	Laborer	16Ma01Dk
BOYLE, Rosanna	30	F	Milliner	16Ma01Dk
DOHERTY, Betty	20	F	Laborer	16Ma01Dk
MCCONNELOGE, Henry	48	M	Cooper	16Ma01Dk
Catharine	60	F	Laborer	16Ma01Dk
WARDLAW, Victor	44	M	Farmer	16Ma01Dk
Isabella	38	F	Farmer	16Ma01Dk
Joseph	16	M	Farmer	16Ma01Dk
Diana	13	F	Farmer	16Ma01Dk
Anne	09	F	Child	16Ma01Dk
Robert	07	M	Child	16Ma01Dk
Jane	03	F	Child	16Ma01Dk

NAMES OF PASSENGERS	AGE	SEX	OCCUPATIONS	DATE PORT SHIP
GREGORY, George	33	M	Laborer	16Ma01Dk
MARTIN, William	20	M	Laborer	16Ma01Dk
LINDSAY, Thomas	22	M	Laborer	16Ma01Dk
RAMSEY, John	20	M	Laborer	16Ma01Dk
GALLAHER, Patrick	16	M	Miller	16Ma01Dk
KING, Elizabeth	22	F	Laborer	16Ma01Dk
GREGORY, Rebecca	60	F	Laborer	16Ma01Dk
MATTHEWS, Andrew-J.	23	M	Farmer	16Ma01Dk
Matilda	23	F	Farmer	16Ma01Dk
Sarah-Anne	.02	F	Infant	16Ma01Dk
GILLISPIE, Honor	25	F	Laborer	16Ma01Dk
Bridget	15	F	Laborer	16Ma01Dk
Patrick	.08	M	Infant	16Ma01Dk
MCKEVLIN, Denis	24	M	Unknown	16Ma01Dk
Patrick	16	M	Unknown	16Ma01Dk
Mary	20	F	Unknown	16Ma01Dk
Sydney	14	M	Unknown	16Ma01Dk
TURBITT, F.Revd.	00	M	Minister	16Ma01Dk

A.Z. 16 MAY 1848

From Liverpool

NAMES OF PASSENGERS	AGE	SEX	OCCUPATIONS	DATE PORT SHIP
BELL, Thomas	60	M	Publican	16Ma02Ei
Mulon-, Pat	30	M	Laborer	16Ma02Ei
U, U	00	M	Engineer	16Ma02Ei
U	00	M	Joiner	16Ma02Ei
GALLAGHER, U	20	F	Dressmaker	16Ma02Ei
ODONELL, Pat	20	M	Laborer	16Ma02Ei
WARD, Thomas	30	M	Laborer	16Ma02Ei
LAW, Wm.	25	M	Laborer	16Ma02Ei
MCQUADE, Rose	20	F	Dressmaker	16Ma02Ei
HAYDEN, James	30	M	Butcher	16Ma02Ei
DANIEL, Alice	40	F	Seamstress	16Ma02Ei
James	27	M	Laborer	16Ma02Ei
John	25	M	Laborer	16Ma02Ei
Magt.	20	F	Seamstress	16Ma02Ei
DONNELLY, James	26	M	Storekeeper	16Ma02Ei
ODONNELL, Simon	30	M	Laborer	16Ma02Ei
PAYTON, Pat	21	M	Farmer	16Ma02Ei
MURRAY, John	27	M	Laborer	16Ma02Ei
JONES, Wm.	22	M	Joiner	16Ma02Ei
Eliza	13	F	Seamstress	16Ma02Ei
DUNN, Richard	27	M	Bricklayer	16Ma02Ei
Magt.	21	F	Seamstress	16Ma02Ei
Catherine	17	F	Seamstress	16Ma02Ei
MAHER, Ansty.	25	F	Servant	16Ma02Ei
TIEREY, Pat	20	M	Laborer	16Ma02Ei
MAHER, Mary	20	F	Seamstress	16Ma02Ei
HARKNESS, John	25	M	Stdr	16Ma02Ei
Mary	20	F	Seamstress	16Ma02Ei
RYAL, Conner	29	M	Laborer	16Ma02Ei
Phillip	27	M	Laborer	16Ma02Ei
MCCABE, Terence	38	M	Laborer	16Ma02Ei
Rachael	36	F	Seamstress	16Ma02Ei
John	12	M	Seamstress	16Ma02Ei
Mary	05	F	Child	16Ma02Ei
Biddy	02	F	Child	16Ma02Ei
Ann	.00	F	Infant	16Ma02Ei
CAVAUGH, Rose	35	F	Servant	16Ma02Ei
Ellen	18	F	Servant	16Ma02Ei
REGAN, Pat	22	M	Laborer	16Ma02Ei
DOOLY, Pat	25	M	Laborer	16Ma02Ei
KELLEY, Bridget	30	F	Lad	16Ma02Ei
Pat	09	M	Child	16Ma02Ei
John	07	M	Child	16Ma02Ei
Michael	06	M	Child	16Ma02Ei
SMITH, Henry	16	M	Laborer	16Ma02Ei
MCMAHON, Mary	19	F	Servant	16Ma02Ei
FAGAN, Christo.	28	M	Farmer	16Ma02Ei
WHELAN, John	28	M	Farmer	16Ma02Ei
CLINTON, James	55	M	Farmer	16Ma02Ei
Mary	50	F	Unknown	16Ma02Ei
Edward	12	M	Unknown	16Ma02Ei
Patk.	13	M	Unknown	16Ma02Ei
James	08	M	Child	16Ma02Ei
Michael	06	M	Child	16Ma02Ei
John	14	M	Unknown	16Ma02Ei
MAGUINESS, Pat.	42	M	Farmer	16Ma02Ei
Elizabeth	43	F	Seamstress	16Ma02Ei
Elizabeth	17	F	Seamstress	16Ma02Ei
James	15	M	Farmer	16Ma02Ei
Mary	13	F	Seamstress	16Ma02Ei
COONEY, Margt.	18	F	Servant	16Ma02Ei
MAGUINESS, Pat.	11	M	Unknown	16Ma02Ei
Richd.	09	M	Child	16Ma02Ei
Rose	06	F	Child	16Ma02Ei
GALLAGHER, Jane	20	F	Servant	16Ma02Ei
MAGUINESS, Mary	20	F	Servant	16Ma02Ei
LEDDES, Letitia	20	F	Servant	16Ma02Ei
HIGGIN, John	30	M	Fnwk	16Ma02Ei
FRANCE, Cassandra	27	F	Dressmaker	16Ma02Ei
Thomas	05	M	Child	16Ma02Ei
Mary	.00	F	Infant	16Ma02Ei
SMALL, Anne	20	F	Servant	16Ma02Ei
WELSH, Catn.	24	F	Servant	16Ma02Ei
WITCHAM, James	30	M	Joiner	16Ma02Ei
JACKMAN, Jno.	35	M	Farmer	16Ma02Ei
Mgt.	30	F	Seamstress	16Ma02Ei
Martin	18	M	Farmer	16Ma02Ei
Cathn.	16	F	Dressmaker	16Ma02Ei
Mgt.	09	F	Child	16Ma02Ei
Marcia	07	F	Child	16Ma02Ei
Eliza	04	F	Child	16Ma02Ei
Bridget	02	F	Child	16Ma02Ei
RUDD, Jno.	28	M	Farmer	16Ma02Ei
Jane	30	F	Dressmaker	16Ma02Ei
MACKLIN, James	26	M	Laborer	16Ma02Ei
Michael	22	M	Laborer	16Ma02Ei
Wm.	22	M	Laborer	16Ma02Ei
Margt.	24	F	Servant	16Ma02Ei
SHEA, Pat.	40	M	Farmer	16Ma02Ei
U (W)	28	F	Dressmaker	16Ma02Ei
MOYLAN, Rhody	40	M	Blacksmith	16Ma02Ei
Anne	11	F	Unknown	16Ma02Ei
Joseph	09	M	Child	16Ma02Ei
PONSOBY, Pat	30	M	Cooper	16Ma02Ei
Mary	22	F	Seamstress	16Ma02Ei
Margt.	20	F	Seamstress	16Ma02Ei
LAWLER, Bartle	22	M	Laborer	16Ma02Ei
MULLALY, Jno.	20	M	Stctr	16Ma02Ei
BUTLER, Pat.	22	M	Surveyor	16Ma02Ei
COLLISON, Michl.	25	M	Laborer	16Ma02Ei
MCCARROL, Chas.	19	M	Laborer	16Ma02Ei
MOONEY, Francis	20	M	Farmer	16Ma02Ei
HARRISON, James	20	M	Bookkeeper	16Ma02Ei
GRAY, Mary	19	F	Servant	16Ma02Ei
STRAFFORD, Wm.	40	M	Surveyor	16Ma02Ei
Jane	21	F	Dressmaker	16Ma02Ei
Wm.	20	M	Brick Maker	16Ma02Ei
MORAN, Jno.	23	M	Farmer	16Ma02Ei
TOOMY, Jeremiah	23	M	Gdnr	16Ma02Ei
SCANLON, Honora	23	F	Dairymaid	16Ma02Ei
Ellen	21	F	Dairymaid	16Ma02Ei
SCULLY, Anne	20	F	Servant	16Ma02Ei
Mary	21	F	Servant	16Ma02Ei
SKELLY, Jno.	26	M	Farmer	16Ma02Ei
Cathn.	36	M	Seamstress	16Ma02Ei
Mary	07	F	Child	16Ma02Ei
Cathn.	05	F	Child	16Ma02Ei
Thomas	03	M	Child	16Ma02Ei
Michl.	.00	M	Infant	16Ma02Ei
DUFFY, Mary	20	F	Servant	16Ma02Ei
MURRAY, Cathn.	18	F	Dressmaker	16Ma02Ei

NAMES OF PASSENGERS	AGE	SEX	OCCUPATIONS	DATE PORT SHIP
MANION, Ellen	20	F	Servant	16Ma02Ei
FAHEY, Danl.	40	M	Farmer	16Ma02Ei
Danl.	23	M	Engineer	16Ma02Ei
KELLY, John	50	M	Farmer	16Ma02Ei
Pat.	25	M	Farmer	16Ma02Ei
Mary	15	F	Seamstress	16Ma02Ei
MORRISON, Mary	25	F	Servant	16Ma02Ei
BUTCHER, Wm.	28	M	Farmer	16Ma02Ei
ENWRIGHT, Danl.	20	M	Farmer	16Ma02Ei
HERON, David	25	M	Farmer	16Ma02Ei
Anne	25	F	Seamstress	16Ma02Ei
GOOKIN, Chas.	20	M	Farmer	16Ma02Ei

MARGARET 17 MAY 1848

From Grennock

NAMES OF PASSENGERS	AGE	SEX	OCCUPATIONS	DATE PORT SHIP
SAVAGE, Michael	22	M	Laborer	17Ma68Fe
MCDOUGALL, John	29	M	Miner	17Ma68Fe
Janet	24	F	Miner	17Ma68Fe
Elizabeth	04	F	Child	17Ma68Fe
Mary	02	F	Child	17Ma68Fe
Alexander	.06	M	Infant	17Ma68Fe
Alexander	27	M	Miner	17Ma68Fe
DUFFY, James	20	M	Shoemaker	17Ma68Fe
Giles	22	F	Dressmaker	17Ma68Fe
FLANAGON, Anthony	20	M	Laborer	17Ma68Fe
DIXON, Michael	20	M	Laborer	17Ma68Fe
WARD, Alexn.	21	M	Laborer	17Ma68Fe
HAMILTON, James	30	M	Laborer	17Ma68Fe
Margaret	.06	F	Infant	17Ma68Fe
FORD, Timothy	40	M	Laborer	17Ma68Fe
Nancy	34	F	Unknown	17Ma68Fe
Susan	13	F	Unknown	17Ma68Fe
John	07	M	Child	17Ma68Fe
Timothy	04	M	Child	17Ma68Fe
Andrew	01	M	Child	17Ma68Fe
Ann	.03	F	Infant	17Ma68Fe
HAMILTON, Jane	30	F	Unknown	17Ma68Fe
ALLISON, John	27	M	Laborer	17Ma68Fe
MCKIRDY, John	59	M	Laborer	17Ma68Fe
Rose	60	F	Unknown	17Ma68Fe
Isabella	25	F	Domestic	17Ma68Fe
Hannah	30	F	Domestic	17Ma68Fe
Catherine	25	F	Domestic	17Ma68Fe
Dennis	20	M	Laborer	17Ma68Fe
Mary	.06	F	Infant	17Ma68Fe
ROBERTSON, Nancy	19	F	Servant	17Ma68Fe
MAGEE, John	25	M	Laborer	17Ma68Fe
Margaret	17	F	Servant	17Ma68Fe
ARROL, John	30	M	Laborer	17Ma68Fe
Barbara	30	F	Unknown	17Ma68Fe
Jane	05	F	Child	17Ma68Fe
Janet	01	F	Child	17Ma68Fe
MCINNES, Jessie	12	F	Unknown	17Ma68Fe
MCKIRDY, Jean	35	F	Servant	17Ma68Fe
Ann-Jean	13	F	Unknown	17Ma68Fe
DUFFY, William	18	M	Shoemaker	17Ma68Fe
BATTRAY, Betsy	25	F	Servant	17Ma68Fe
LAMBIE, Robert	19	M	Weaver	17Ma68Fe
JACOB, William	44	M	Dyer	17Ma68Fe
Elizabeth	18	F	Servant	17Ma68Fe
MCKETTRICK, Cadh.	19	F	Servant	17Ma68Fe
LAIRD, Robert	38	M	Laborer	17Ma68Fe
Ann	35	F	Unknown	17Ma68Fe
Janet	04	F	Child	17Ma68Fe
Margaret	02	F	Child	17Ma68Fe
Alexander	01	M	Child	17Ma68Fe
BLAIR, Robert	24	M	Laborer	17Ma68Fe

NAMES OF PASSENGERS	AGE	SEX	OCCUPATIONS	DATE PORT SHIP
LOGAN, John	30	M	Laborer	17Ma68Fe
ODONNELL, Hugh	39	M	Servant	17Ma68Fe
John	37	M	Laborer	17Ma68Fe
Ann	24	F	Servant	17Ma68Fe
Catherine	18	F	Servant	17Ma68Fe
Marion	29	F	Servant	17Ma68Fe
FOSTER, John	35	M	Laborer	17Ma68Fe
Janet	26	F	Unknown	17Ma68Fe
Jane	05	F	Child	17Ma68Fe
Mary	03	F	Child	17Ma68Fe
Janet	01	F	Child	17Ma68Fe
DEAN, James	30	M	Wool Comber	17Ma68Fe
MCKEAN, Thomas	33	M	Irdr	17Ma68Fe
Mary	36	F	Unknown	17Ma68Fe
Margaret	09	F	Child	17Ma68Fe
William	05	M	Child	17Ma68Fe
MCALPHINNEY, Charles	28	M	Potter	17Ma68Fe
POLLOCK, Saml.	34	M	Potter	17Ma68Fe
CAVENEY, Thomas	28	M	Mpol	17Ma68Fe
Catherine	26	F	Unknown	17Ma68Fe
Michael	05	M	Child	17Ma68Fe
Thomas	01	M	Child	17Ma68Fe
HAGGERTY, Michael	54	M	Laborer	17Ma68Fe
Catherine	53	F	Unknown	17Ma68Fe
Michael	22	M	Laborer	17Ma68Fe
David	09	M	Child	17Ma68Fe
MURSAY, John	22	M	Laborer	17Ma68Fe
MCINTOSH, Robert	24	M	Weaver	17Ma68Fe
ANDERSON, Robert	24	M	Weaver	17Ma68Fe
WILSON, Andrew	23	M	Weaver	17Ma68Fe
DULLON, Patrick	23	M	Miner	17Ma68Fe
Agnes	23	F	Unknown	17Ma68Fe
KERR, William	22	M	Bricklayer	17Ma68Fe
JAMISON, John	24	M	Spdlr	17Ma68Fe
HOGG, Robert	25	M	Joiner	17Ma68Fe
ALLEN, William	24	M	Unknown	17Ma68Fe
YOUNG, Mary	12	F	Milliner	17Ma68Fe
BRAMNER, George	44	M	Potter	17Ma68Fe
MCCALLNAN, Charles	21	M	Turner	17Ma68Fe
BURNS, Alexr.	25	M	Cooper	17Ma68Fe
JAMESON, Hugh	19	M	Victualler	17Ma68Fe
BRIDGE, James	27	M	Blacksmith	17Ma68Fe
Elizabeth	28	F	Dressmaker	17Ma68Fe
James	06	M	Child	17Ma68Fe
Hamilton	03	M	Child	17Ma68Fe
Margaret	01	F	Child	17Ma68Fe
Robert	01	M	Child	17Ma68Fe
ROBERTSON, Robert	24	M	Weaver	17Ma68Fe
LOGAN, William	21	M	Miner	17Ma68Fe
GILES, Robert	24	M	Spdlr	17Ma68Fe
MURRAY, Robert	28	M	Shoemaker	17Ma68Fe
Mary	21	F	Unknown	17Ma68Fe
BROADFOOT, John	35	M	Shoemaker	17Ma68Fe
David	30	M	Shoemaker	17Ma68Fe
Christian	65	F	Unknown	17Ma68Fe
MARSHALL, William	25	M	Shoemaker	17Ma68Fe
CLARK, William	29	M	Mason	17Ma68Fe
Charles	22	M	Mason	17Ma68Fe
DAMPSTER, Daniel	26	M	Weaver	17Ma68Fe
Margaret	35	F	Dressmaker	17Ma68Fe
Catharine	03	F	Child	17Ma68Fe
BLACK, David	25	M	Blacksmith	17Ma68Fe
MCLAUGHLAN, Margaret	35	F	Spinster	17Ma68Fe
Catherine	13	F	Unknown	17Ma68Fe
John	12	M	Unknown	17Ma68Fe
Archibald	11	M	Unknown	17Ma68Fe
Janet	08	F	Child	17Ma68Fe
Daniel	05	M	Child	17Ma68Fe
Jean	03	F	Child	17Ma68Fe
Margaret	01	F	Child	17Ma68Fe
WOODBURN, Andrew	20	M	Laborer	17Ma68Fe
CLIPHAM, Thos.	30	M	Gdnr	17Ma68Fe
SMITH, William	20	M	Irnmldr	17Ma68Fe
ROBERTSON, Martin	21	M	Irnmldr	17Ma68Fe
LOCKEAD, David	30	M	Farmer	17Ma68Fe

NAMES OF PASSENGERS	AGE	SEX	OCCUPATIONS	DATE PORT SHIP
HURT, John	30	M	Farmer	17Ma68Fe
SPENDING, R.A.	30	M	Farmer	17Ma68Fe
ATKINSON, John	13	M	Laborer	17Ma68Fe
MCINTOSH, Christiana	26	F	Servant	17Ma68Fe
GRAY, John	11	M	Unknown	17Ma68Fe
MURRAY, William	33	M	Mason	17Ma68Fe
KIRK, Thomas	30	M	Joiner	17Ma68Fe
CASH, John	33	M	Miner	17Ma68Fe
MCMILLAN, James	24	M	Laborer	17Ma68Fe
LAVERTY, Robert	21	M	Laborer	17Ma68Fe
ARCHIBALD, Jas.	23	M	Mason	17Ma68Fe
MALCOMB, John	27	M	Joiner	17Ma68Fe
CRUM, Peter	25	M	Joiner	17Ma68Fe
JOHNSTON, Marion	50	F	Dressmaker	17Ma68Fe
BROWN, John	27	M	Joiner	17Ma68Fe
ROBERTSON, Robert	23	M	Joiner	17Ma68Fe
BRADLEY, Fredk.	29	M	Painter	17Ma68Fe
GLEN, Humphrey	40	M	Currier	17Ma68Fe
Agnes	33	F	Milliner	17Ma68Fe
MCADAM, John	24	M	Carpenter	17Ma68Fe
HODGES, William	25	M	Carpenter	17Ma68Fe
ALLEN, Robert	29	M	Carpenter	17Ma68Fe
HODGES, David	24	M	Carpenter	17Ma68Fe
BONNER, John	25	M	Laborer	17Ma68Fe
MCCASKEY, John	53	M	Laborer	17Ma68Fe
Elizabeth	17	F	Servant	17Ma68Fe
Robert	16	M	Unknown	17Ma68Fe
Margaret	13	F	Unknown	17Ma68Fe
Matthew	11	M	Unknown	17Ma68Fe
NETHERCOTT, Margt.	55	F	Unknown	17Ma68Fe
Susan	20	F	Servant	17Ma68Fe
CURTAN, Mary	45	F	Servant	17Ma68Fe
Francis	12	M	Unknown	17Ma68Fe
Jean	08	F	Child	17Ma68Fe
Biddy	06	F	Child	17Ma68Fe
Maria	04	F	Child	17Ma68Fe
MULLAN, Anne	19	F	Servant	17Ma68Fe
Robert	20	M	Laborer	17Ma68Fe
CURTAN, Joseph	28	M	Laborer	17Ma68Fe
MULLEN, Joseph	03	M	Child	17Ma68Fe
MCCALLINAN, Hugh	60	M	Laborer	17Ma68Fe
Eleanor	23	F	Servant	17Ma68Fe
SHIRLIN, Patrick	30	M	Laborer	17Ma68Fe
Catharine	26	F	Unknown	17Ma68Fe
Biddy	02	F	Child	17Ma68Fe
PHYFE, Giles	30	M	Laborer	17Ma68Fe
SHERIDAN, Catharine	21	F	Servant	17Ma68Fe
Sarah	18	F	Servant	17Ma68Fe
MCGRENN, Mary	25	F	Servant	17Ma68Fe
Anne	23	F	Servant	17Ma68Fe
Catherine	21	F	Servant	17Ma68Fe
MCNEIGH, William	24	M	Laborer	17Ma68Fe
Margaret	29	F	Unknown	17Ma68Fe
MCGOLERICK, Alexr.	50	M	Laborer	17Ma68Fe
RUSSEL, Edwin	22	M	Laborer	17Ma68Fe
Ann	50	F	Unknown	17Ma68Fe
MCGOLERICK, Mary	50	F	Unknown	17Ma68Fe
Arthur	20	M	Laborer	17Ma68Fe
Michael	10	M	Unknown	17Ma68Fe
Ann	16	F	Servant	17Ma68Fe
Mary	16	F	Servant	17Ma68Fe
DOHAN, Eleanor	23	F	Servant	17Ma68Fe
DONNELL, Magr.	30	F	Servant	17Ma68Fe
Daniel	06	M	Child	17Ma68Fe
Peter	05	M	Child	17Ma68Fe
COYLE, Bernard	27	M	Laborer	17Ma68Fe
NETHERCOTT, John	22	M	Laborer	17Ma68Fe
BOYLE, Peter	29	M	Laborer	17Ma68Fe
DIXON, Sophia	20	F	Servant	17Ma68Fe
GALLAGHER, Mary	20	F	Servant	17Ma68Fe
HAGERTY, John	20	M	Laborer	17Ma68Fe
MCCASKEY, Eleanor	07	F	Child	17Ma68Fe
Mary	09	F	Child	17Ma68Fe
MAGEE, Patrick	25	M	Laborer	17Ma68Fe
Ellen	22	F	Unknown	17Ma68Fe
MAGEE, Richard	02	M	Child	17Ma68Fe
JOHNSTON, John	30	M	Laborer	17Ma68Fe
SHARP, William	22	M	Laborer	17Ma68Fe
Jane	25	F	Unknown	17Ma68Fe
BLACK, Eliza	18	F	Servant	17Ma68Fe
LINN, Ann	47	F	Servant	17Ma68Fe
Mary-Ann	11	F	Unknown	17Ma68Fe
Patrick	07	M	Child	17Ma68Fe
John	05	M	Child	17Ma68Fe
FLOOD, William	17	M	Laborer	17Ma68Fe
Isabella	15	F	Servant	17Ma68Fe
David	11	M	Unknown	17Ma68Fe
Margaret-Ann	09	F	Child	17Ma68Fe
John	16	F	Servant	17Ma68Fe
Luke	50	M	Laborer	17Ma68Fe
STEWART, Margaret	25	F	Servant	17Ma68Fe
MURDOCK, Hugh	16	M	Farmer	17Ma68Fe
ANDREW, John	16	M	Farmer	17Ma68Fe
MAXWELL, Peggy-A.	21	F	Servant	17Ma68Fe
MCALLISTER, Margarit	28	F	Servant	17Ma68Fe
John	09	M	Child	17Ma68Fe
Peggy	05	F	Child	17Ma68Fe
Nancy	03	F	Child	17Ma68Fe
James	01	M	Child	17Ma68Fe
BIRNIE, William	35	M	Unknown	17Ma68Fe

GARRICK 19 MAY 1848

From Liverpool

NAMES OF PASSENGERS		AGE	SEX	OCCUPATIONS	DATE PORT SHIP
ROSS, Wm.		30	M	Naturalist	19Ma02Aa
HEARTY, Robert		27	M	Farmer	19Ma02Aa
PRINGLE, Robert		26	M	Farmer	19Ma02Aa
FORSYTH, Walter		27	M	Farmer	19Ma02Aa
LITTLE, William		28	M	Farmer	19Ma02Aa
MOORE, U-Mrs.		46	F	Unknown	19Ma02Aa
Sarah	(D)	20	F	Milliner	19Ma02Aa
Patrick	(S)	18	M	Unknown	19Ma02Aa
Jane	(D)	16	F	Milliner	19Ma02Aa
John	(S)	14	M	Unknown	19Ma02Aa
Mary	(D)	14	F	Unknown	19Ma02Aa
Margaret	(D)	12	F	Unknown	19Ma02Aa
WHELAN, Peter		30	M	Coach Maker	19Ma02Aa
U	(W)	18	F	Wife	19Ma02Aa
MITCHEL, U		21	F	Unknown	19Ma02Aa
MCLELLAN, U		00	F	Unknown	19Ma02Aa
DIVINE, Cornelius		58	M	Mason	19Ma02Aa
WHITTLE, John		15	M	Unknown	19Ma02Aa
William		13	M	Unknown	19Ma02Aa
MITCHEL, Thomas		18	M	Tailor	19Ma02Aa
ELLIOT, Thomas		00	M	Unknown	19Ma02Aa
FITZGERALD, John		34	M	Laborer	19Ma02Aa
U	(W)	21	F	Wife	19Ma02Aa
MCCARTY, Thomas		18	M	Weaver	19Ma02Aa
WOGAN, John		22	M	Laborer	19Ma02Aa
Bridget		23	F	Unknown	19Ma02Aa
ORGIN, Catharine		23	F	Unknown	19Ma02Aa
RYAN, John		04	M	Child	19Ma02Aa
FLYNN, Helen		22	F	Unknown	19Ma02Aa
Mary		40	F	Unknown	19Ma02Aa
SHERIVAN, Rose		22	F	Unknown	19Ma02Aa
BULKLEY, Patrick		50	M	Herd	19Ma02Aa
Patrick-Jr.		17	M	Unknown	19Ma02Aa
John		14	M	Unknown	19Ma02Aa
Thomas		08	M	Child	19Ma02Aa
Mary		20	F	Unknown	19Ma02Aa
GILSENAN, Lawrence		28	M	Carpenter	19Ma02Aa
Ellen		25	F	Unknown	19Ma02Aa
FINNEGAN, James		24	M	Laborer	19Ma02Aa

NAMES OF PASSENGERS	AGE	SEX	OCCUPATIONS	DATE PORT SHIP
KEGAN, John	20	M	Laborer	19Ma02Aa
FLYNN, John	29	M	Laborer	19Ma02Aa
SHERWAN, John	28	M	Laborer	19Ma02Aa
Patrick	25	M	Laborer	19Ma02Aa
Richard	14	M	Unknown	19Ma02Aa
Ann	15	F	Unknown	19Ma02Aa
Alice	09	F	Child	19Ma02Aa
Anna	12	F	Unknown	19Ma02Aa
Peter	08	M	Child	19Ma02Aa
RILEY, Bridget	20	F	Unknown	19Ma02Aa
DOBSON, Margaret	19	F	Unknown	19Ma02Aa
WHELAN, Thomas	30	M	Unknown	19Ma02Aa
LUNDIGAN, James	24	M	Laborer	19Ma02Aa
John	22	M	Laborer	19Ma02Aa
William	19	M	Laborer	19Ma02Aa
RYAN, John	24	M	Laborer	19Ma02Aa
LUNDIGAN, Ellen	40	F	Unknown	19Ma02Aa
BUTLER, Thomas	45	M	Laborer	19Ma02Aa
TOBIN, Thomas	20	M	Baker	19Ma02Aa
QUINLAN, John	24	M	Carpenter	19Ma02Aa
Catharine	23	F	Unknown	19Ma02Aa
IRWIN, Samuel-M.	21	M	Unknown	19Ma02Aa
SHANNON, Dunlap	21	M	Unknown	19Ma02Aa
WILLIAMSON, Joseph	21	M	Unknown	19Ma02Aa
CARGILL, Kitty	34	F	Unknown	19Ma02Aa
Ann	12	F	Unknown	19Ma02Aa
John	02	M	Child	19Ma02Aa
Margaret	05	F	Child	19Ma02Aa
Thomas	04	M	Child	19Ma02Aa
DOUGLASS, Arthur	22	M	Grocer	19Ma02Aa
NICOLL, Arthur	23	M	Clerk	19Ma02Aa
WILDERS, William	67	M	Minister	19Ma02Aa
Thomas	36	M	Glove Maker	19Ma02Aa
William	33	M	Glove Maker	19Ma02Aa
Henry	30	M	Glove Maker	19Ma02Aa
Israel	25	M	Glove Maker	19Ma02Aa
Samuel	22	M	Glove Maker	19Ma02Aa
TONGUE, Samuel	24	M	Tailor	19Ma02Aa
WILDERS, Frederick	07	M	Child	19Ma02Aa
Milicent	36	F	Unknown	19Ma02Aa
Elizabeth	35	F	Unknown	19Ma02Aa
Elizabeth	28	F	Unknown	19Ma02Aa
Ann	25	F	Unknown	19Ma02Aa
Sophhia	21	F	Unknown	19Ma02Aa
Sarah	04	F	Child	19Ma02Aa
THISTLE, U-Mrs.	31	F	Unknown	19Ma02Aa
Sarah	08	F	Child	19Ma02Aa
Hugh	06	M	Child	19Ma02Aa
RAFFERTY, James	19	M	Farmer	19Ma02Aa
INGHAM, James	22	M	Unknown	19Ma02Aa
WAINOCK, Mary	21	F	Unknown	19Ma02Aa
GILLIGHAN, James	20	M	Unknown	19Ma02Aa
LARDNER, Martin	34	M	Mason	19Ma02Aa
Betsey	30	F	Unknown	19Ma02Aa
William	10	M	Unknown	19Ma02Aa
Eliza	01	F	Child	19Ma02Aa
HEARTY, Thomas	30	M	Carpenter	19Ma02Aa
Biddy	22	F	Unknown	19Ma02Aa
Nancy	65	F	Unknown	19Ma02Aa
MCGOVERIN, Patrick	28	M	Laborer	19Ma02Aa
Jane	22	F	Unknown	19Ma02Aa
DUNNIGAN, Jamie	24	M	Laborer	19Ma02Aa
John	22	M	Laborer	19Ma02Aa
COFFEE, James	24	M	Laborer	19Ma02Aa
MCCONAN, Mary	15	F	Unknown	19Ma02Aa
Patrick	22	M	Laborer	19Ma02Aa
CARAHER, Rose	24	F	Unknown	19Ma02Aa
MCGUIRK, Bridget	12	F	Unknown	19Ma02Aa
SHIELDS, Dennis	27	M	Unknown	19Ma02Aa
Catharine	24	F	Unknown	19Ma02Aa
BYRNE, Judith	27	F	Unknown	19Ma02Aa
MCLACY, Bridget	21	F	Unknown	19Ma02Aa
MILES, Michel	21	M	Unknown	19Ma02Aa
RUTLIDGE, Andrew	22	M	Unknown	19Ma02Aa
WHITE, John	20	M	Unknown	19Ma02Aa
WHITE, Mary	24	F	Unknown	19Ma02Aa
FARRELL, Timothy	30	M	Baker	19Ma02Aa
Mary	57	F	Unknown	19Ma02Aa
Eliza	20	F	Unknown	19Ma02Aa
MAHAR, John	34	M	Unknown	19Ma02Aa
HYLAND, Peter	33	M	Unknown	19Ma02Aa
BRADY, Michael	38	M	Unknown	19Ma02Aa
COATES, Christopher	35	M	Unknown	19Ma02Aa
HUSTACE, James	45	M	Laborer	19Ma02Aa
John	12	M	Laborer	19Ma02Aa
James-Jr.	18	M	Laborer	19Ma02Aa
NALLY, Martin	22	M	Laborer	19Ma02Aa
DONNELL, Patrick	26	M	Laborer	19Ma02Aa
James	24	M	Laborer	19Ma02Aa
BLAKE, Thomas	16	M	Laborer	19Ma02Aa
LADIN, Daniel	55	M	Laborer	19Ma02Aa
Died-At-Sea				
John	40	M	Laborer	19Ma02Aa
Sally	35	F	Unknown	19Ma02Aa
MCWILLIAMS, George	24	M	Laborer	19Ma02Aa
Thomas	17	M	Laborer	19Ma02Aa
Ann	55	F	Unknown	19Ma02Aa
HANDLIN, Michael	18	M	Cooper	19Ma02Aa
GARLAND, Francis	24	M	Laborer	19Ma02Aa
JOHNSTON, John	24	M	Unknown	19Ma02Aa
HUGHES, Bridget	18	F	Unknown	19Ma02Aa
MCMAN, Mary	20	F	Unknown	19Ma02Aa
LINNET, Bridget	18	F	Unknown	19Ma02Aa
MCLACHLAN, Nancy	30	F	Unknown	19Ma02Aa
Owen	17	M	Unknown	19Ma02Aa
MCKUON, Peter	18	M	Unknown	19Ma02Aa
Thomas	19	M	Unknown	19Ma02Aa
RYAN, Martin	28	M	Unknown	19Ma02Aa
Mary	26	F	Unknown	19Ma02Aa
Michael	18	M	Unknown	19Ma02Aa
Margaret	19	F	Unknown	19Ma02Aa
John	04	M	Child	19Ma02Aa
Thomas	.11	M	Infant	19Ma02Aa
MURPHY, John	25	M	Trade Man	19Ma02Aa
Daniel	40	M	Unknown	19Ma02Aa
BROWN, Mary	57	F	Unknown	19Ma02Aa
Jane	20	F	Unknown	19Ma02Aa
William	22	M	Unknown	19Ma02Aa
Isabella	12	F	Unknown	19Ma02Aa
Oliver	12	M	Unknown	19Ma02Aa
WHITE, Mary	18	F	Unknown	19Ma02Aa
MCJIMSEY, Joseph	49	M	Cobbler	19Ma02Aa
Margaret	51	F	Unknown	19Ma02Aa
Eliza	17	F	Unknown	19Ma02Aa
MILLS, Catharine	17	F	Unknown	19Ma02Aa
Elicia	18	F	Unknown	19Ma02Aa
MCLACHLAN, Michael	20	M	Unknown	19Ma02Aa
MCJIMSEY, William	14	M	Unknown	19Ma02Aa
Nancy	11	F	Unknown	19Ma02Aa
Hugh	09	M	Child	19Ma02Aa
GREAVES, Thomas	22	M	Laborer	19Ma02Aa
Margaret	15	F	Unknown	19Ma02Aa
Letitia	14	F	Unknown	19Ma02Aa
DOGHERTY, Ann	17	F	Unknown	19Ma02Aa
ARMSTRONG, Sarah	19	F	Unknown	19Ma02Aa
JOHNSON, Mary-A.	19	F	Unknown	19Ma02Aa
MCGUIRE, Andrew	18	M	Laborer	19Ma02Aa
HEARY, Richard	28	M	Unknown	19Ma02Aa
MOONEY, Thomas	27	M	Unknown	19Ma02Aa
FARRELL, James	26	M	Unknown	19Ma02Aa
LOWTHE, Mary	21	F	Unknown	19Ma02Aa
LEVANS, Biddy	30	F	Unknown	19Ma02Aa
CORBLES, Peggy	21	F	Unknown	19Ma02Aa
WHELAN, John	22	M	Unknown	19Ma02Aa
MACK, Margaret	18	F	Unknown	19Ma02Aa
Bridget	16	F	Unknown	19Ma02Aa
BERGEN, James	28	M	Laborer	19Ma02Aa
Mary	27	F	Laborer	19Ma02Aa
Margaret	02	F	Child	19Ma02Aa
MCCULLOCH, Patrick	30	M	Laborer	19Ma02Aa

NAMES OF PASSENGERS	AGE	SEX	OCCUPATIONS	DATE PORT SHIP
MCCULLOCH, Mary	16	F	Unknown	19Ma02Aa
John	19	M	Laborer	19Ma02Aa
KANE, John	16	M	Unknown	19Ma02Aa
Patrick	19	M	Unknown	19Ma02Aa
TOOLE, Patrick	22	M	Laborer	19Ma02Aa
KANE, John	25	M	Laborer	19Ma02Aa
Margaret	21	F	Unknown	19Ma02Aa
DOWNEY, Eliza	20	F	Unknown	19Ma02Aa
DOOLEY, Mary	21	F	Unknown	19Ma02Aa
RHODES, Margaret	20	F	Unknown	19Ma02Aa
QUILTY, Catharine	50	F	Unknown	19Ma02Aa
Catharine	19	F	Unknown	19Ma02Aa
GARRY, William	24	M	Laborer	19Ma02Aa
CLAGHRY, John	21	M	Laborer	19Ma02Aa
CONNELL, Nora	18	F	Unknown	19Ma02Aa
John	17	M	Unknown	19Ma02Aa
CRONAN, Johannah	18	F	Unknown	19Ma02Aa
WHITTY, Dennis	25	M	Laborer	19Ma02Aa
Thomas	30	M	Laborer	19Ma02Aa
NAGH, John	30	M	Laborer	19Ma02Aa
SHANNON, James	31	M	Laborer	19Ma02Aa
AGAN, Patrick	28	M	Laborer	19Ma02Aa
KELLY, Edward	30	M	Laborer	19Ma02Aa
MCGUIGAN, Thomas	21	M	Laborer	19Ma02Aa
GORMAN, Edward	26	M	Laborer	19Ma02Aa
MCCULLEN, Neil	26	M	Laborer	19Ma02Aa
MCMAN, Francis	21	M	Laborer	19Ma02Aa
DUFFY, Mary	41	F	Unknown	19Ma02Aa
BRADY, Bridget	22	F	Unknown	19Ma02Aa
DUFFY, Catharine	21	F	Unknown	19Ma02Aa
CURRAN, John	25	M	Mason	19Ma02Aa
MAHONY, Patrick	30	M	Unknown	19Ma02Aa
COLMAN, James	30	M	Unknown	19Ma02Aa
MCREADY, Ann	21	F	Unknown	19Ma02Aa
MCCULLEN, Mary	24	F	Unknown	19Ma02Aa
Ann	22	F	Unknown	19Ma02Aa
JONES, Thomas	19	M	Unknown	19Ma02Aa

METOKA 19 MAY 1848

From Liverpool

NAMES OF PASSENGERS	AGE	SEX	OCCUPATIONS	DATE PORT SHIP
DEAN, Daniel	26	M	Farmer	19Ma02Ff
Mary	25	F	Farmer	19Ma02Ff
Thomas	32	M	Farmer	19Ma02Ff
DOOHURST, Jos.	28	M	Farmer	19Ma02Ff
Sarah	24	F	Farmer	19Ma02Ff
Mary	.00	F	Infant	19Ma02Ff
Died-At-Sea				
SUCKIN, John	40	M	Farmer	19Ma02Ff
John	20	M	Farmer	19Ma02Ff
PLATH, James	20	M	Farmer	19Ma02Ff
EGLIN, Thomas	49	M	Farmer	19Ma02Ff
Margaret	16	F	Farmer	19Ma02Ff
Ann	15	F	Farmer	19Ma02Ff
John	11	M	Unknown	19Ma02Ff
BAYNES, Wm.	25	M	Unknown	19Ma02Ff
COUN, Wm.	60	M	Unknown	19Ma02Ff
John	23	M	Unknown	19Ma02Ff
Gilbert	21	M	Unknown	19Ma02Ff
William	19	M	Unknown	19Ma02Ff
Margaret	15	F	Unknown	19Ma02Ff
Ellen	12	F	Unknown	19Ma02Ff
John	09	M	Child	19Ma02Ff
SPURLOCK, James	40	M	Unknown	19Ma02Ff
Jane	38	F	Unknown	19Ma02Ff
FRY, James	27	M	Unknown	19Ma02Ff
Herbert	03	M	Child	19Ma02Ff
PINDAR, Alexn.	24	M	Unknown	19Ma02Ff
PINDAR, Henry	20	M	Unknown	19Ma02Ff
Robert	18	M	Unknown	19Ma02Ff
James	16	M	Unknown	19Ma02Ff
Eliza	19	F	Unknown	19Ma02Ff
Margareet	18	F	Unknown	19Ma02Ff
LLOYD, Goodwin	26	M	Unknown	19Ma02Ff
Jane	24	F	Unknown	19Ma02Ff
Wm.James	.00	M	Infant	19Ma02Ff
SLATER, Wm.	30	M	Unknown	19Ma02Ff
Ellen	26	F	Unknown	19Ma02Ff
Wm.	11	M	Unknown	19Ma02Ff
Thos.	06	M	Child	19Ma02Ff
ANDREW, Samuel	30	M	Unknown	19Ma02Ff
Barbara	28	F	Unknown	19Ma02Ff
Richard	.00	M	Infant	19Ma02Ff
SLATER, James	42	M	Unknown	19Ma02Ff
LLOYD, Owen	30	M	Unknown	19Ma02Ff
SUTTON, Wm.	28	M	Unknown	19Ma02Ff
WILSON, Thomas	26	M	Unknown	19Ma02Ff
NEWGENT, Richard	24	M	Unknown	19Ma02Ff
John	20	M	Unknown	19Ma02Ff
OCONNELL, Betty	20	F	Unknown	19Ma02Ff
LYNCH, Pat	40	M	Unknown	19Ma02Ff
CALLIGAN, Pat	20	M	Unknown	19Ma02Ff
KEEFE, Richard	20	M	Unknown	19Ma02Ff
HARVEY, Pat	27	M	Unknown	19Ma02Ff
HIFFERNAN, James	27	M	Unknown	19Ma02Ff
DULTON, Margaret	20	F	Unknown	19Ma02Ff
Pat	25	M	Unknown	19Ma02Ff
GARVEY, Michael	20	M	Unknown	19Ma02Ff
KENIFICK, Peggy	20	F	Unknown	19Ma02Ff
DARLY, John	20	M	Unknown	19Ma02Ff
MALONEY, Mary	20	F	Unknown	19Ma02Ff
WESTMORLAND, Wm.	52	M	Unknown	19Ma02Ff
Margt.	40	F	Unknown	19Ma02Ff
LITTLE, John	46	M	Unknown	19Ma02Ff
JACKSON, Danl.	25	M	Unknown	19Ma02Ff
GRAHAM, John	26	M	Unknown	19Ma02Ff
KELLY, Michael	40	M	Unknown	19Ma02Ff
MCDONNELL, Catharine	30	F	Unknown	19Ma02Ff
TURNER, John	26	M	Unknown	19Ma02Ff
HANDFUTH, Thos.	24	M	Unknown	19Ma02Ff
BAMFORD, Richard	27	M	Unknown	19Ma02Ff
CAREY, Mary	40	F	Unknown	19Ma02Ff
Pat	16	M	Unknown	19Ma02Ff
JONES, John	27	M	Unknown	19Ma02Ff
U (W)	24	F	Wife	19Ma02Ff
EVANS, Edward	35	M	Unknown	19Ma02Ff
LEADFRETON, James	15	M	Unknown	19Ma02Ff
JONES, Evans	40	M	Unknown	19Ma02Ff
Ellen	30	F	Unknown	19Ma02Ff
Ann	05	F	Child	19Ma02Ff
Bridget	02	F	Child	19Ma02Ff
John	.00	M	Infant	19Ma02Ff
VALENTINE, Isaac	35	M	Unknown	19Ma02Ff
U (W)	32	F	Unknown	19Ma02Ff
Isaac (S)	.00	M	Infant	19Ma02Ff
BROOKES, Joseph	20	M	Unknown	19Ma02Ff
BAILEY, Wm.	43	M	Unknown	19Ma02Ff
BELCHER, Jos.	26	M	Unknown	19Ma02Ff
ROBINSON, Saml.	26	M	Unknown	19Ma02Ff
BELCHER, John	47	M	Unknown	19Ma02Ff
SMALLEY, Jos.	17	M	Unknown	19Ma02Ff
MILLIS, Thomas	16	M	Unknown	19Ma02Ff
BELCHER, Ann	59	F	Unknown	19Ma02Ff
GRIFFIN, Jos.	26	M	Unknown	19Ma02Ff
WEST, John	38	M	Unknown	19Ma02Ff
STINSON, Thos.	22	M	Unknown	19Ma02Ff
NATLIN, Thos.	27	M	Unknown	19Ma02Ff
LOON, John	23	M	Unknown	19Ma02Ff
TOMLINSON, Samuel	19	M	Unknown	19Ma02Ff
MORGAN, John	17	M	Unknown	19Ma02Ff
BURGESS, Joseph	36	M	Unknown	19Ma02Ff
BRIGGS, John	49	M	Unknown	19Ma02Ff
ORPHAN, George	23	M	Unknown	19Ma02Ff

NAMES OF PASSENGERS		AGE	SEX	OCCUPATIONS	DATE PORT SHIP
TIGHE, Mary		20	F	Unknown	19Ma02Ff
DILLON, John		30	M	Unknown	19Ma02Ff
Margt.		21	F	Unknown	19Ma02Ff
Edward		14	M	Unknown	19Ma02Ff
GLENAN, Maria		30	F	Unknown	19Ma02Ff
HUGHES, Pat		30	M	Unknown	19Ma02Ff
Easton		26	M	Unknown	19Ma02Ff
STOWS, Thomas		21	M	Unknown	19Ma02Ff
Mary		20	F	Unknown	19Ma02Ff
BURDON, Thomas		21	M	Unknown	19Ma02Ff
MCDANIEL, Alexn.		30	M	Unknown	19Ma02Ff
MALNAN, Mary		40	F	Unknown	19Ma02Ff
Tim		12	M	Unknown	19Ma02Ff
GLEASON, John		21	M	Unknown	19Ma02Ff
DWIER, John		21	M	Unknown	19Ma02Ff
Hannah		18	F	Unknown	19Ma02Ff
OBRIEN, Ann		25	F	Unknown	19Ma02Ff
ROBERTSON, Alexr.		30	M	Unknown	19Ma02Ff
BURGESS, Edward		24	M	Unknown	19Ma02Ff
RYAN, Jeremiah		24	M	Unknown	19Ma02Ff
PURSIL, Phil.		24	M	Unknown	19Ma02Ff
SHEA, Pat		24	M	Unknown	19Ma02Ff
BOOLAN, Danl.		22	M	Unknown	19Ma02Ff
DRENAN, Michl.		19	M	Unknown	19Ma02Ff
MCGRATH, Philip		18	M	Unknown	19Ma02Ff
PURSILL, Mary		20	F	Unknown	19Ma02Ff
SHEA, Mary		20	F	Unknown	19Ma02Ff
RYAN, Judy		20	F	Unknown	19Ma02Ff
CULLIN, Wm.		26	M	Unknown	19Ma02Ff
Philp		25	M	Unknown	19Ma02Ff
Pat		21	M	Unknown	19Ma02Ff
Bryan		15	M	Unknown	19Ma02Ff
Catharine		18	F	Unknown	19Ma02Ff
Ann		04	F	Unknown	19Ma02Ff
SMITH, Philip		27	M	Unknown	19Ma02Ff
HAND, Eliza		24	F	Unknown	19Ma02Ff
Matthew		22	M	Unknown	19Ma02Ff
NORTH, Thomas		45	M	Unknown	19Ma02Ff
Charles		24	M	Unknown	19Ma02Ff
U-Mrs.		22	F	Unknown	19Ma02Ff
Sarah		.00	F	Infant	19Ma02Ff
MORAN, Fanny		20	F	Unknown	19Ma02Ff
ODILL, John		30	M	Unknown	19Ma02Ff
U	(W)	30	F	Wife	19Ma02Ff
John	(S)	11	M	Unknown	19Ma02Ff
James		25	M	Unknown	19Ma02Ff
Jessy	(D)	10	F	Unknown	19Ma02Ff
Jane		25	F	Unknown	19Ma02Ff
SWANTON, Wm.		24	M	Unknown	19Ma02Ff
MULDANY, Selia		20	F	Unknown	19Ma02Ff
JACKSON, John		34	M	Unknown	19Ma02Ff
Mary		36	F	Unknown	19Ma02Ff
Sarah-Ann		.00	F	Infant	19Ma02Ff
Died-At-Sea					
Emma		09	F	Child	19Ma02Ff
SUTTON, John		33	M	Unknown	19Ma02Ff
MCLAUGHLIN, John		28	M	Unknown	19Ma02Ff
FARREL, Wm.		14	M	Unknown	19Ma02Ff
COLLORAN, Martin		32	M	Unknown	19Ma02Ff
MORSON, John		25	M	Unknown	19Ma02Ff
Mary-A.		22	F	Unknown	19Ma02Ff
Patrick		18	M	Unknown	19Ma02Ff
GODFREY, Margaret		25	F	Unknown	19Ma02Ff
Mary-A.		11	F	Unknown	19Ma02Ff
Bridget		09	F	Child	19Ma02Ff
FARMER, Margaret		26	F	Unknown	19Ma02Ff
WELSH, John		03	M	Child	19Ma02Ff
DADY, Cornelius		45	M	Unknown	19Ma02Ff
Ellen		46	F	Unknown	19Ma02Ff
Mary		09	F	Child	19Ma02Ff
SHIVE, Eliza		60	F	Unknown	19Ma02Ff
CONWAY, Charles		26	M	Unknown	19Ma02Ff
CONNOR, Thomas		18	M	Unknown	19Ma02Ff
Michael		17	M	Unknown	19Ma02Ff
Margaret		15	F	Unknown	19Ma02Ff
SULLIVAN, Honora		26	F	Unknown	19Ma02Ff
KANE, Michael		36	M	Unknown	19Ma02Ff
James		36	M	Unknown	19Ma02Ff
Christiana		24	F	Unknown	19Ma02Ff
BUCKLEY, Cornelius		26	M	Unknown	19Ma02Ff
CURRY, Bridget		26	F	Unknown	19Ma02Ff
GARAGAN, Laurence		23	M	Unknown	19Ma02Ff
CARTY, Bridget		17	F	Unknown	19Ma02Ff
CAHILL, John		22	M	Unknown	19Ma02Ff
CLINTON, Jane		22	M	Unknown	19Ma02Ff
DALY, Bridget		25	F	Unknown	19Ma02Ff
RILEY, Bessy		19	F	Unknown	19Ma02Ff
MCGUIRE, Hugh		53	M	Unknown	19Ma02Ff
Hugh		25	M	Unknown	19Ma02Ff
Anne		52	F	Unknown	19Ma02Ff
Bridget		11	F	Unknown	19Ma02Ff
LOVE, Sarah		18	F	Unknown	19Ma02Ff
FOLEY, Thomas		25	M	Unknown	19Ma02Ff
James		22	M	Unknown	19Ma02Ff
MURPHY, Mary		18	F	Unknown	19Ma02Ff
DONNELLY, Mary		46	F	Unknown	19Ma02Ff
James		21	M	Unknown	19Ma02Ff
Mary		18	F	Unknown	19Ma02Ff
NORTON, Pat		26	M	Unknown	19Ma02Ff
BIRMINGHAM, John		33	M	Unknown	19Ma02Ff
Margaret		36	F	Unknown	19Ma02Ff
U-Mrs.		60	F	Wi	19Ma02Ff
Mary		08	F	Child	19Ma02Ff
Anne		06	F	Child	19Ma02Ff
John		04	M	Child	19Ma02Ff
Pat		.00	M	Infant	19Ma02Ff
MALLOY, John		12	M	Unknown	19Ma02Ff
MCDONALD, George		28	M	Unknown	19Ma02Ff
CLARK, Mary-A.		26	F	Unknown	19Ma02Ff
HAST, Connor		22	M	Unknown	19Ma02Ff
Maria		18	F	Unknown	19Ma02Ff
Charles		26	M	Unknown	19Ma02Ff
ONEAL, Daniel		36	M	Unknown	19Ma02Ff
KEIRAN, Mary		18	F	Unknown	19Ma02Ff
Bridget		15	F	Unknown	19Ma02Ff
Margaret		12	F	Unknown	19Ma02Ff
MCNEIL, Ann		12	F	Unknown	19Ma02Ff
MCGRATH, Bridget		36	F	Unknown	19Ma02Ff
HART, Thomas		26	M	Unknown	19Ma02Ff
GAROLY, John		26	M	Unknown	19Ma02Ff
Bridget		17	F	Unknown	19Ma02Ff
ACHERSON, Joseph		18	M	Unknown	19Ma02Ff
Sarah		21	F	Unknown	19Ma02Ff
HOGAN, Thomas		26	M	Unknown	19Ma02Ff
BENNETT, Maria		26	F	Unknown	19Ma02Ff
ANDROS, Margaret		23	F	Unknown	19Ma02Ff
Cath.		04	F	Child	19Ma02Ff
BOYLAND, Michael		21	M	Unknown	19Ma02Ff
LAWLESS, John		26	M	Unknown	19Ma02Ff
HASLAM, Henry		22	M	Unknown	19Ma02Ff
Anne		24	F	Unknown	19Ma02Ff
MCCORMICK, Keran		18	M	Unknown	19Ma02Ff
RILEY, Bridget		16	F	Unknown	19Ma02Ff
BRODIGAN, John		24	M	Unknown	19Ma02Ff
Mary		26	F	Unknown	19Ma02Ff
Bridget		07	F	Child	19Ma02Ff
FITZGERALD, Thomas		26	M	Unknown	19Ma02Ff
CARNEY, Bridget		26	F	Unknown	19Ma02Ff
GILLON, Dennis		26	M	Unknown	19Ma02Ff
MCKEOWN, John		17	M	Unknown	19Ma02Ff
REID, James		22	M	Unknown	19Ma02Ff
KELLY, Maria		26	F	Unknown	19Ma02Ff
WALKER, Alfred		15	M	Unknown	19Ma02Ff
REDYARD, Wm.		26	M	Unknown	19Ma02Ff
George		24	M	Unknown	19Ma02Ff
SADDER, Wm.		26	M	Unknown	19Ma02Ff
EASTON, James		21	M	Unknown	19Ma02Ff
TELFER, Thomas		20	M	Unknown	19Ma02Ff
CAVENS, Walter		22	M	Unknown	19Ma02Ff
BARNEY, Richard		37	M	Unknown	19Ma02Ff

NAMES OF PASSENGERS		AGE	SEX	OCCUPATIONS	DATE PORT SHIP
SHENAN, Thomas		27	M	Unknown	19Ma02Ff
FARRELL, Peter		27	M	Unknown	19Ma02Ff
PITT, Thomas		23	M	Unknown	19Ma02Ff
TOWNSLEY, David		30	M	Unknown	19Ma02Ff
HOYLE, Joseph		27	M	Unknown	19Ma02Ff
HALL, John		30	M	Unknown	19Ma02Ff
U	(W)	28	F	Wife	19Ma02Ff
Edward	(S)	10	M	Unknown	19Ma02Ff
Mary	(D)	06	F	Child	19Ma02Ff
Thomas	(S)	04	M	Child	19Ma02Ff
MAJOR, James		30	M	Unknown	19Ma02Ff
POOLE, Sarah-N.		38	F	Unknown	19Ma02Ff
DOBSON, Thomas		25	M	Unknown	19Ma02Ff
MORGAN, Jacob		35	M	Unknown	19Ma02Ff
THOMAS, John		27	M	Unknown	19Ma02Ff
SMITH, John		20	M	Unknown	19Ma02Ff
Margaret		26	F	Unknown	19Ma02Ff
Margret		.00	F	Infant	19Ma02Ff
MARSH, Mary		18	F	Unknown	19Ma02Ff
LYDDEN, Charles		24	M	Unknown	19Ma02Ff
SHERIDAN, James		20	M	Unknown	19Ma02Ff
GALLIGAN, Catherine		20	F	Unknown	19Ma02Ff
COSGAN, Ann		20	F	Unknown	19Ma02Ff
FINNEGAN, Margaret		16	F	Unknown	19Ma02Ff
WHALAN, John		35	M	Unknown	19Ma02Ff
QUADE, Biddy		17	F	Unknown	19Ma02Ff

ROSA-LINDA 20 MAY 1848

From Belfast

NAMES OF PASSENGERS		AGE	SEX	OCCUPATIONS	DATE PORT SHIP
GREER, John		33	M	Farmer	20Ma07Fi
Samuel		12	M	None	20Ma07Fi
MCCREA, Margaret		22	F	Servant	20Ma07Fi
John		23	M	Farmer	20Ma07Fi
IRWIN, Wm.		27	M	Farmer	20Ma07Fi
MCALICE, Alexander		35	M	Farmer	20Ma07Fi
FULTON, Mary		37	F	Seamstress	20Ma07Fi
Marianne		18	F	Seamstress	20Ma07Fi
MCALICE, Ann		30	F	Seamstress	20Ma07Fi
FULTON, Sarah		08	F	Child	20Ma07Fi
KINLY, Ellen		26	F	Servant	20Ma07Fi
MCKEOWN, James		22	M	Weaver	20Ma07Fi
MCQUOID, Wm.		18	M	Weaver	20Ma07Fi
ORR, Ann		18	F	Servant	20Ma07Fi
MCCRANE, Wm.		40	M	Wheelwright	20Ma07Fi
Nancy	(W)	40	F	Wife	20Ma07Fi
Mary	(D)	13	F	Unknown	20Ma07Fi
Jane	(D)	12	F	Unknown	20Ma07Fi
Wm.	(S)	10	M	Unknown	20Ma07Fi
Margaret	(D)	08	F	Child	20Ma07Fi
Alexander	(S)	07	M	Child	20Ma07Fi
John	(S)	.09	M	Infant	20Ma07Fi
CANUGHIN, John		30	M	Farmer	20Ma07Fi
Mary		33	F	None	20Ma07Fi
Hugh		10	M	None	20Ma07Fi
George		08	M	Child	20Ma07Fi
Martha		06	F	Child	20Ma07Fi
Mary		04	F	Child	20Ma07Fi
U		.05	M	Infant	20Ma07Fi
HERALD, Samuel		27	M	Farmer	20Ma07Fi
Rose		50	F	Seamstress	20Ma07Fi
Rose		22	F	None	20Ma07Fi
Ann		19	F	None	20Ma07Fi
Patrick		16	M	None	20Ma07Fi
Elizabeth		12	F	None	20Ma07Fi
Bridget	(D)	19	F	None	20Ma07Fi
BAIELE, William		60	M	Carpenter	20Ma07Fi
Cathr.	(W)	18	F	Wife	20Ma07Fi
KELLY, Joseph		19	M	Mason	20Ma07Fi
Susannah	(W)	19	F	Wife	20Ma07Fi
SCOTT, Robert		35	M	Laborer	20Ma07Fi
Jane	(W)	35	F	Wife	20Ma07Fi
Eliza-Jane	(D)	04	F	Child	20Ma07Fi
Robert	(S)	02	M	Child	20Ma07Fi
Mary	(D)	01	F	Child	20Ma07Fi
MCWILLIAM, Charles		35	M	Shoemaker	20Ma07Fi
Margret	(W)	29	F	Wife	20Ma07Fi
Mariana	(D)	08	F	Child	20Ma07Fi
Sarah	(D)	06	F	Child	20Ma07Fi
James	(S)	04	M	Child	20Ma07Fi
Catherin	(D)	01	F	Child	20Ma07Fi
MCKEE, John		21	M	Painter	20Ma07Fi
Jane	(W)	20	F	Wife	20Ma07Fi
MURPHY, Mary		30	F	Spinster	20Ma07Fi
Mary		27	F	Spinster	20Ma07Fi
PATTERSON, Samuel		40	M	Farmer	20Ma07Fi
Martha	(W)	35	F	Wife	20Ma07Fi
Thos.	(S)	20	M	None	20Ma07Fi
William	(S)	18	M	None	20Ma07Fi
Harriet	(D)	13	F	None	20Ma07Fi
Margret	(D)	10	F	None	20Ma07Fi
Wellington	(S)	07	M	Child	20Ma07Fi
Emily	(D)	05	F	Child	20Ma07Fi
U, U		23	F	Servant	20Ma07Fi
SYNAS, James		19	M	Clerk	20Ma07Fi
ANDERSON, Saml.		46	M	Laborer	20Ma07Fi
Sarah	(W)	46	F	Wife	20Ma07Fi
Eliza	(D)	22	F	Spinster	20Ma07Fi
Mary	(D)	18	F	Spinster	20Ma07Fi
William	(S)	16	M	Laborer	20Ma07Fi
Samuel	(S)	13	M	Unknown	20Ma07Fi
Sarah-Jane	(D)	12	F	Unknown	20Ma07Fi
Bella	(D)	10	F	Unknown	20Ma07Fi
James	(S)	08	M	Child	20Ma07Fi
Francis	(S)	05	M	Child	20Ma07Fi
LAVERTY, Henry		24	M	Farmer	20Ma07Fi
SHANNON, Phillip		46	M	Farmer	20Ma07Fi
Elizabeth		10	F	Unknown	20Ma07Fi
Isabella		13	F	Unknown	20Ma07Fi
WILSON, Hugh		33	M	Laborer	20Ma07Fi
MURRAY, Mary		22	F	Spinster	20Ma07Fi
MASLING, William		17	M	Laborer	20Ma07Fi
BEATHEY, Wm.		26	M	Laborer	20Ma07Fi
Matilda	(W)	24	F	Wife	20Ma07Fi
MAIRS, John		19	M	Laborer	20Ma07Fi
HARKNESS, John		25	M	Laborer	20Ma07Fi
COLLINS, Patrick		15	M	Laborer	20Ma07Fi
CAMPBELL, John		19	M	Laborer	20Ma07Fi
QUAIL, Jane		55	F	None	20Ma07Fi
Magt.		17	F	Unknown	20Ma07Fi
MAGURY, Grace		24	F	Spinster	20Ma07Fi
MASS, Susanna		25	F	Spinster	20Ma07Fi
SIMPSON, Mary		13	F	Spinster	20Ma07Fi
Robert		20	M	Draper	20Ma07Fi
BELL, Wm.		28	M	Painter	20Ma07Fi
Phobe	(W)	25	F	Wife	20Ma07Fi
Thos.	(S)	.00	M	Infant	20Ma07Fi
BRADY, Margrt.		18	M	Laborer	20Ma07Fi
DOHERTY, John		30	M	Laborer	20Ma07Fi
BRADLEY, James		30	M	Laborer	20Ma07Fi
Letita	(W)	27	F	Wife	20Ma07Fi
Elizabeth	(D)	07	F	Child	20Ma07Fi
Robert	(S)	04	M	Child	20Ma07Fi
Magrt.	(D)	03	F	Child	20Ma07Fi
Agnes		02	F	Child	20Ma07Fi
MULLAN, Richd.		28	M	Carpenter	20Ma07Fi
Elizabeth	(W)	30	F	Wife	20Ma07Fi
Robert	(S)	03	M	Child	20Ma07Fi
GALLOGHER, Thos.		38	M	Mechanic	20Ma07Fi
MCCANN, Daniel		37	M	Laborer	20Ma07Fi
Elizabeth	(W)	45	F	Wife	20Ma07Fi
Nancy	(D)	13	F	Unknown	20Ma07Fi
KELLY, Jane		19	F	Spinster	20Ma07Fi

NAMES OF PASSENGERS		AGE	SEX	OCCUPATIONS	DATE PORT SHIP
KELLY, Nancy		16	F	Spinster	20Ma07Fi
Mary		13	F	Spinster	20Ma07Fi
DOUGLAS, Jas.		21	M	Laborer	20Ma07Fi
LAMISON, Hamilton		24	M	Laborer	20Ma07Fi
JAMISON, Jas.		20	M	Laborer	20Ma07Fi
MCCLURE, Jas.		24	M	Laborer	20Ma07Fi
Agnes	(W)	24	F	Wife	20Ma07Fi
Elizabeth	(D)	.00	F	Infant	20Ma07Fi
KELLY, William		20	M	Farmer	20Ma07Fi
CASE, Saml.		27	M	Farmer	20Ma07Fi
Henry		23	M	Farmer	20Ma07Fi
JOHNSTON, Saml.		30	M	Spinner	20Ma07Fi
WOODS, Henry		21	M	Laborer	20Ma07Fi
Ann	(W)	18	F	Wife	20Ma07Fi
MONTGOMERY, Jane		29	F	Spinster	20Ma07Fi
LEDGERT, Mary-Ann		25	F	Spinster	20Ma07Fi
DORAN, Patrick		60	M	Farmer	20Ma07Fi
Edwd.		20	M	Farmer	20Ma07Fi
Nicholas		18	M	Farmer	20Ma07Fi
Alice		16	F	Spinster	20Ma07Fi
CRAWFORD, Jas.		25	M	Laborer	20Ma07Fi
HULL, William		60	M	Laborer	20Ma07Fi
NIELL, Wm.		27	M	Laborer	20Ma07Fi
Mary-Ann	(W)	26	F	Wife	20Ma07Fi
Mary	(D)	04	F	Child	20Ma07Fi
Margrt.	(D)	02	F	Child	20Ma07Fi
MCROBERTS, Wm.		37	M	Laborer	20Ma07Fi
Jane	(W)	25	F	Wife	20Ma07Fi
William-John	(S)	06	M	Child	20Ma07Fi
James	(S)	04	M	Child	20Ma07Fi
Thomas	(S)	02	M	Child	20Ma07Fi
HOLMES, John		65	M	Laborer	20Ma07Fi
James		40	M	Laborer	20Ma07Fi
Martha	(W)	38	F	Wife	20Ma07Fi
WHITE, Matilda		14	F	Spinster	20Ma07Fi
Mary-Jane		12	F	Spinster	20Ma07Fi
John		10	M	Laborer	20Ma07Fi
HOLMES, Letty-Jane		03	F	Child	20Ma07Fi
Elizabeth		.00	F	Infant	20Ma07Fi
ONIEL, Jas.		19	M	Laborer	20Ma07Fi
NEILSON, John		20	M	Laborer	20Ma07Fi
MCGREEVY, Nielle		41	M	Farmer	20Ma07Fi
Mary	(W)	25	F	Wife	20Ma07Fi
Cathr.	(D)	04	F	Child	20Ma07Fi
Rose	(D)	02	F	Child	20Ma07Fi
Mary	(D)	.00	F	Infant	20Ma07Fi
FARRELL, Charles		21	M	Laborer	20Ma07Fi
HUGHES, Mary		24	F	None	20Ma07Fi
Patrick		01	M	Child	20Ma07Fi
HOGAN, Sally		17	F	Spinster	20Ma07Fi
WALSH, Betty		14	F	Spinster	20Ma07Fi
CUNNINGHAM, Susan		17	F	Spinster	20Ma07Fi
HUGHES, Cathr.		35	F	None	20Ma07Fi
James		13	M	Unknown	20Ma07Fi
Sally		11	F	Unknown	20Ma07Fi
Mary		09	F	Child	20Ma07Fi
Cathr.		07	F	Child	20Ma07Fi
DONALD, Alex		48	M	Laborer	20Ma07Fi
Jane	(W)	46	F	Wife	20Ma07Fi
Sarah		28	F	Spinster	20Ma07Fi
Ann-Jane		26	F	Spinster	20Ma07Fi
David		25	M	Laborer	20Ma07Fi
Mary		23	F	Spinster	20Ma07Fi
Robert		21	M	Laborer	20Ma07Fi
Matilda		13	F	Spinster	20Ma07Fi
Susan		09	F	Child	20Ma07Fi
BURNS, Patrick		25	M	Tailor	20Ma07Fi
ROONEY, Patrick		21	M	Laborer	20Ma07Fi
BRADLY, Margt.		23	F	Spinster	20Ma07Fi
SAVAGE, Henry		30	M	Laborer	20Ma07Fi
MCMURRAY, Robert		18	M	Laborer	20Ma07Fi
Mitchell		15	M	Laborer	20Ma07Fi
TODD, John		26	M	Farmer	20Ma07Fi
KELLY, John		20	M	Farmer	20Ma07Fi
GALLAGHER, Charles		21	M	Laborer	20Ma07Fi

NAMES OF PASSENGERS		AGE	SEX	OCCUPATIONS	DATE PORT SHIP
HARNER, John		18	M	Laborer	20Ma07Fi
BELL, William		24	M	Laborer	20Ma07Fi
MCMAHON, John		18	M	Laborer	20Ma07Fi
Jane	(W)	24	F	Wife	20Ma07Fi
HOUSTON, William		17	M	Laborer	20Ma07Fi
Jane		20	F	Spinster	20Ma07Fi
TYSDALE, Robert		17	M	Laborer	20Ma07Fi
Margret		23	F	Spinster	20Ma07Fi
JONES, William		28	M	Laborer	20Ma07Fi
CLARKE, Edward		27	M	Laborer	20Ma07Fi
MURPHY, Isabella		25	F	Spinster	20Ma07Fi
MEGRA, Bernard		26	M	Laborer	20Ma07Fi
KELLY, Joseph		17	M	Carpenter	20Ma07Fi
KIRK, Wm.		19	M	Carpenter	20Ma07Fi
GILMORE, Eliza		23	F	Spinster	20Ma07Fi
TOMEY, James		22	M	Farmer	20Ma07Fi
RODGERS, Wm.		22	M	Farmer	20Ma07Fi
MCMURRAY, Patrick		34	M	Farmer	20Ma07Fi
MCVIEGH, Pat		18	M	Farmer	20Ma07Fi
MCMURRY, Betty-Mrs.		25	F	Wife	20Ma07Fi
WHITE, Alex		30	M	Laborer	20Ma07Fi
Mary-Jane	(W)	23	F	Wife	20Ma07Fi
Mary	(D)	02	F	Child	20Ma07Fi
BRADY, Ellen		20	F	Servant	20Ma07Fi
HAMILTON, Wm.		26	M	Laborer	20Ma07Fi
WILSON, Andrew		35	M	Farmer	20Ma07Fi
Agnes	(W)	31	F	Wife	20Ma07Fi
Martha	(D)	15	F	Relative	20Ma07Fi
Ellen	(D)	13	F	Relative	20Ma07Fi
Joseph	(S)	11	M	Relative	20Ma07Fi
Jane	(D)	09	F	Child	20Ma07Fi
Agnes	(D)	07	F	Child	20Ma07Fi
Anne	(D)	05	F	Child	20Ma07Fi
Sarah	(D)	02	F	Child	20Ma07Fi
MAHON, Robert		35	M	Farmer	20Ma07Fi
Jane	(W)	30	F	Wife	20Ma07Fi
Mary-Jane	(D)	11	F	Unknown	20Ma07Fi
Anne	(D)	09	F	Child	20Ma07Fi
James	(S)	07	M	Child	20Ma07Fi
Robert	(S)	05	M	Child	20Ma07Fi
Hugh	(S)	02	M	Child	20Ma07Fi
MCKIBBEN, Jas.		22	M	Weaver	20Ma07Fi
Susanah	(W)	21	F	Wife	20Ma07Fi
MCCOLLOUGH, Edwd.		30	M	Wheelwright	20Ma07Fi
BURNS, David		25	M	Miller	20Ma07Fi
Mary	(W)	21	F	Wife	20Ma07Fi
MCMULLAN, George		25	M	Farmer	20Ma07Fi
Jane	(W)	26	F	Wife	20Ma07Fi
Jane	(D)	03	F	Child	20Ma07Fi
Cathr.	(D)	.00	F	Infant	20Ma07Fi
GIBSON, Robert		25	M	Laborer	20Ma07Fi
Sarah	(W)	23	F	Wife	20Ma07Fi
Samuel	(S)	01	M	Child	20Ma07Fi
WALLACE, Robert		21	M	Printer	20Ma07Fi
BLACKBURY, Joseph		26	M	Printer	20Ma07Fi
CRAWFORD, Thos.		20	M	Farmer	20Ma07Fi
William		30	M	Farmer	20Ma07Fi
PATTERSON, Mariane		22	F	Seamstress	20Ma07Fi
CRAIG, Wm.		26	M	Miller	20Ma07Fi
Anne	(W)	20	F	Wife	20Ma07Fi
Agnes	(T)	16	F	Relative	20Ma07Fi
WELSH, Jas.		30	M	Farmer	20Ma07Fi
HERPEY, Benj.		30	M	Laborer	20Ma07Fi
Sarah	(W)	30	F	Wife	20Ma07Fi
CANE, John		19	M	Carpenter	20Ma07Fi
PATTERSON, Jas.		22	M	Carpenter	20Ma07Fi
MURPHY, Mary		24	F	Servant	20Ma07Fi
AGNEW, Robt.		24	M	Engineer	20Ma07Fi
MCINTOSH, John		23	M	Engineer	20Ma07Fi
HAMILTON, Eliza		27	F	Seamstress	20Ma07Fi
FLEMING, William		36	M	Farmer	20Ma07Fi
Roddy	(T)	34	F	Relative	20Ma07Fi
Alex.	(B)	24	M	Relative	20Ma07Fi
Eliza	(T)	22	F	Relative	20Ma07Fi
Anne	(T)	22	F	Relative	20Ma07Fi

NAMES OF PASSENGERS	AGE	SEX	OCCUPATIONS	DATE PORT SHIP
MCKELVEY, Ann	15	F	Seamstress	20Ma07Fi
Eliza	12	F	Unknown	20Ma07Fi
DOWNEY, John	19	M	Laborer	20Ma07Fi
MURRAY, Jane	18	F	Spinster	20Ma07Fi
DOWNEY, Biddy	14	F	Spinster	20Ma07Fi

GEORGIA 20 MAY 1848

From Liverpool

NAMES OF PASSENGERS	AGE	SEX	OCCUPATIONS	DATE PORT SHIP
CALLAGHAN, Cornilius	23	M	Stone Mason	20Ma02Fs
Ellen-Senr.	28	F	None	20Ma02Fs
Ellen-Junr.	04	F	Child	20Ma02Fs
James	.10	M	Infant	20Ma02Fs
WYMP, Richard	30	M	Clerk	20Ma02Fs
KING, John	18	M	Painter	20Ma02Fs
DUNN, Bernard	21	M	Grocer	20Ma02Fs
DOYLE, Catherin	13	F	None	20Ma02Fs
Elizabeth	11	F	None	20Ma02Fs
Elizabeth	13	F	None	20Ma02Fs
James	12	M	None	20Ma02Fs
Margaret	09	F	Child	20Ma02Fs
James	08	M	Child	20Ma02Fs
Patrick	06	M	Child	20Ma02Fs
CUMING, William	30	M	Unknown	20Ma02Fs
POWELL, Denis	18	M	Unknown	20Ma02Fs
MEE, Michael	28	M	Shoemaker	20Ma02Fs
GALLIVAN, Patrick	21	M	Laborer	20Ma02Fs
LYNOSS, Joseph	30	M	Stone Mason	20Ma02Fs
Rebecca	27	F	Stone Mason	20Ma02Fs
Charlotte	03	F	Child	20Ma02Fs
DOWNEY, Michael	23	M	Joiner	20Ma02Fs
KELLY, Francis	24	M	Farmer	20Ma02Fs
MURPHY, Timothy	27	M	None	20Ma02Fs
TODD, William	17	M	Cooper	20Ma02Fs
HILL, Daniel	18	M	Farmer	20Ma02Fs
CAVANAGH, Thomas	33	M	Farmer	20Ma02Fs
GASS, Mary	18	F	Seamstress	20Ma02Fs
STEWART, Ann-Jane	18	F	Seamstress	20Ma02Fs
MOONEY, Charles	19	M	Baker	20Ma02Fs
COWAN, Thomas	20	M	Chandler	20Ma02Fs
KELLY, Rose-Ann	27	F	None	20Ma02Fs
Catherin	25	F	None	20Ma02Fs
KENNEDY, Esther	40	F	None	20Ma02Fs
Grace	16	F	None	20Ma02Fs
DUNKLY, John	43	M	Farmer	20Ma02Fs
HENRIGAN, Mary	25	F	None	20Ma02Fs
CRAWFORD, Margaret	18	F	None	20Ma02Fs
REILLY, Chas.	38	M	Farmer	20Ma02Fs
Judy	30	F	None	20Ma02Fs
RORKE, Hugh	20	M	Laborer	20Ma02Fs
Margaret	10	F	None	20Ma02Fs
BOOTH, James	27	M	Laborer	20Ma02Fs
Ann	25	F	None	20Ma02Fs
KENNEDY, John	30	M	Farmer	20Ma02Fs
Bridget-Senr.	26	F	None	20Ma02Fs
Bridget-Jnr.	05	F	Child	20Ma02Fs
Michael	.06	M	Infant	20Ma02Fs
RYNOLDS, Mary	24	F	None	20Ma02Fs
DOONAN, Thomas	32	M	Farmer	20Ma02Fs
Ann	25	F	None	20Ma02Fs
Thomas	.09	M	Infant	20Ma02Fs
MACKLIN, Daniel	26	M	Grocer	20Ma02Fs
Elizabeth	17	F	None	20Ma02Fs
John	.10	M	Infant	20Ma02Fs
COWAN, Francis	28	M	Baker	20Ma02Fs
Elizabeth	24	F	None	20Ma02Fs
Ellen	05	F	Child	20Ma02Fs
Bridget	03	F	Child	20Ma02Fs
RORK, Peter	26	M	Grocer	20Ma02Fs
WOODS, Patrick	14	M	None	20Ma02Fs
KEEGAN, William	26	M	Bookkeeper	20Ma02Fs
Matilda	25	F	None	20Ma02Fs
Elizabeth	01	F	Child	20Ma02Fs
DOYLE, Edward	40	M	Dealer	20Ma02Fs
Margaret	40	F	None	20Ma02Fs
Mary	15	F	None	20Ma02Fs
Mary	13	F	None	20Ma02Fs
WILLIAM, Thomas	33	M	Farmer	20Ma02Fs
DEVEREY, Peter	27	M	Farmer	20Ma02Fs
DUFFY, Bernard	20	M	Farmer	20Ma02Fs
KILLEN, Ellen	16	F	Farmer	20Ma02Fs
Patrick	09	M	Child	20Ma02Fs
Maria	08	F	Child	20Ma02Fs
KELLY, John	21	M	Farmer	20Ma02Fs
Ann	19	F	Farmer	20Ma02Fs
Christopher	18	M	Farmer	20Ma02Fs
MCDONAGH, Henry	31	M	Farmer	20Ma02Fs
DONAGHAN, Thomas	35	M	Farmer	20Ma02Fs
MOONEY, Andrew	30	M	Farmer	20Ma02Fs
CARROLL, Joseph	21	M	Farmer	20Ma02Fs
DOLAN, Thomas	25	M	Farmer	20Ma02Fs
BUTLER, Anastasia	63	F	None	20Ma02Fs
MURPHY, Ann	20	F	None	20Ma02Fs
DOLAN, Ann	25	F	None	20Ma02Fs
CARROLL, Maria	22	F	None	20Ma02Fs
CLAFFEY, Thomas	22	F	None	20Ma02Fs
Rosey	17	F	None	20Ma02Fs
BUTLER, Patrick	24	M	None	20Ma02Fs
MURPHY, Bernard	21	M	None	20Ma02Fs
MAXWELL, Stephen	28	M	None	20Ma02Fs
Caldwell	22	M	None	20Ma02Fs
MAGRATH, Michael	23	M	None	20Ma02Fs
Mary	50	F	None	20Ma02Fs
DOLAN, Catherine	42	F	None	20Ma02Fs
Mary	22	F	None	20Ma02Fs
MURRAY, Mary	15	F	None	20Ma02Fs
DOLAN, Michael	20	M	None	20Ma02Fs
BURNS, Ellen	21	F	None	20Ma02Fs
CAMPBELL, Catherine	20	F	None	20Ma02Fs
KERR, Michael	40	M	Farmer	20Ma02Fs
MCGINLEY, Neil	19	M	None	20Ma02Fs
CUNNINGHAM, John	20	M	None	20Ma02Fs
MCGINLEY, Ann	20	F	None	20Ma02Fs
Ellen	19	F	None	20Ma02Fs
Bridget	18	F	None	20Ma02Fs
Owen	27	M	None	20Ma02Fs
BRICE, Maurice	24	M	None	20Ma02Fs
MALONEY, Hugh	25	M	None	20Ma02Fs
BURNS, John	18	M	None	20Ma02Fs
LEAVEY, Mary	28	F	None	20Ma02Fs
LYNCH, Johanna	16	F	None	20Ma02Fs
LEAVEY, Bridget	16	F	None	20Ma02Fs
MCCAULEY, Connell	65	M	None	20Ma02Fs
Catherine	55	F	None	20Ma02Fs
Connell	19	M	None	20Ma02Fs
CROWLEY, Mary	16	F	None	20Ma02Fs
CAVANAGH, Judy	17	F	None	20Ma02Fs
CASHMERE, Patrick	23	M	None	20Ma02Fs
James	18	M	None	20Ma02Fs
CASEY, Thomas	30	M	Farmer	20Ma02Fs
BRENAN, John	18	M	Unknown	20Ma02Fs
DOUGHERTY, Charles	22	M	Unknown	20Ma02Fs
John	19	M	Unknown	20Ma02Fs
MCCABE, John	14	M	Unknown	20Ma02Fs
LONG, Patrick	22	M	Unknown	20Ma02Fs
GARLAND, Mary	14	F	Unknown	20Ma02Fs
MOONEY, Catherine	29	F	Unknown	20Ma02Fs
MCCARDLE, Catherine	29	F	Unknown	20Ma02Fs
CONLIN, Edward	40	M	Unknown	20Ma02Fs
HINNEASEY, Martin	25	M	Unknown	20Ma02Fs
WELCH, Michael	23	M	Unknown	20Ma02Fs
SMYTH, Jane	15	F	Unknown	20Ma02Fs
KEENAN, Rosey	17	F	Unknown	20Ma02Fs

NAMES OF PASSENGERS		AGE	SEX	OCCUPATIONS	DATE PORT SHIP
HENNESSY, Bridget		14	F	Unknown	20Ma02Fs
WELCH, David		27	M	Unknown	20Ma02Fs
ANGLEA, James		25	M	Unknown	20Ma02Fs
HOY, George		20	M	Unknown	20Ma02Fs
Francis		19	M	Unknown	20Ma02Fs
WOODS, William		20	M	Unknown	20Ma02Fs
REAY, Thomas		31	M	Unknown	20Ma02Fs
MCKEARNEY, John		30	M	Unknown	20Ma02Fs
MCARDLE, Edward		30	M	Unknown	20Ma02Fs
Mary		20	F	Unknown	20Ma02Fs
Rose		18	F	Unknown	20Ma02Fs
Peter		22	M	Unknown	20Ma02Fs
HORSFALL, John		27	M	Unknown	20Ma02Fs

JOHN-S.DEWOLF 20 MAY 1848

From Dublin

NAMES OF PASSENGERS		AGE	SEX	OCCUPATIONS	DATE PORT SHIP
GILFOYLE, James		24	M	Shoemaker	20Ma20Fp
Maria		21	F	Spinster	20Ma20Fp
RICHARDSON, U		30	M	Farmer	20Ma20Fp
U	(W)	30	F	None	20Ma20Fp
Mary		13	F	None	20Ma20Fp
John		12	M	None	20Ma20Fp
Francis		09	M	Child	20Ma20Fp
STEPHENSON, U-Mrs.		40	F	Dressmaker	20Ma20Fp
U-Mrs.Junr.		24	F	Dressmaker	20Ma20Fp
U		24	M	Hatter	20Ma20Fp
Janie		03	F	Child	20Ma20Fp
Eliza		02	F	Child	20Ma20Fp
DAVIS, U		40	M	Farmer	20Ma20Fp
U	(W)	40	F	Wife	20Ma20Fp
Maria		11	F	None	20Ma20Fp
HUNT, U		24	M	Optician	20Ma20Fp
U	(W)	20	F	None	20Ma20Fp
FEGAN, Michl.		19	M	Farmer	20Ma20Fp
Michl.		20	M	Farmer	20Ma20Fp
Catherine		40	F	Spinster	20Ma20Fp
Cathe.		20	F	Spinster	20Ma20Fp
Cathe.		07	F	Child	20Ma20Fp
Peter		14	M	Farmer	20Ma20Fp
Briget		16	F	Spinster	20Ma20Fp
REILLY, Ann		20	F	Spinster	20Ma20Fp
CAFFREYS, Cath.		20	F	Dressmaker	20Ma20Fp
WHITELY, Thos.		21	M	Carpenter	20Ma20Fp
DOYLE, Michl.		22	M	Merchant	20Ma20Fp
KEARNENN, John		22	M	Blacksmith	20Ma20Fp
Mick		20	M	Blacksmith	20Ma20Fp
PENDER, John		20	M	Painter	20Ma20Fp
CALEMAN, John		16	M	Farmer	20Ma20Fp
CARROLL, Michl.		24	M	Farmer	20Ma20Fp
U	(W)	35	F	None	20Ma20Fp
HEALY, Pat		19	M	Farmer	20Ma20Fp
Mary		18	F	Spinster	20Ma20Fp
Andy		13	M	Laborer	20Ma20Fp
Michl.		12	M	Laborer	20Ma20Fp
CARROLL, Briget		06	F	Child	20Ma20Fp
Ellen		03	F	Child	20Ma20Fp
Thomas		21	M	Laborer	20Ma20Fp
HEALY, William		21	M	Farmer	20Ma20Fp
CONNOR, Charles		40	M	Farmer	20Ma20Fp
John		14	M	Farmer	20Ma20Fp
Martin		12	M	Farmer	20Ma20Fp
SHANAHAN, William		20	M	Mason	20Ma20Fp
THOMPSON, Jane		20	F	Spinster	20Ma20Fp
MADDEN, Ellen		22	F	Spinster	20Ma20Fp
Anne		25	F	Spinster	20Ma20Fp
HOGG, William		24	M	Gdnr	20Ma20Fp
U	(W)	21	F	Spinster	20Ma20Fp
HOGG, Mary		.03	F	Infant	20Ma20Fp
JOYCE, John		20	M	Blacksmith	20Ma20Fp
HEERSOFF, Esther		20	F	Spinster	20Ma20Fp
MONTGOMERY, James		20	M	Printer	20Ma20Fp
WHELAN, Timothy		45	M	Farmer	20Ma20Fp
Bridget		40	F	Spinster	20Ma20Fp
Martin		22	M	Farmer	20Ma20Fp
Michl.		20	M	Farmer	20Ma20Fp
Pat		18	M	Farmer	20Ma20Fp
Eliza		14	F	Spinster	20Ma20Fp
Mary		12	F	Spinster	20Ma20Fp
THOMPSON, Samuel		24	M	Laborer	20Ma20Fp
DWYER, James		22	M	Farmer	20Ma20Fp
HALL, Jeremiah		26	M	Farmer	20Ma20Fp
U	(W)	20	F	Spinster	20Ma20Fp
DANIEL, Thomas		21	M	Laborer	20Ma20Fp
PLUMER, George		30	M	Painter	20Ma20Fp
FITZPATRICK, Peter		28	M	Printer	20Ma20Fp
BOID, Pat		28	M	Smith	20Ma20Fp
CROLY, Michl.		38	M	Farmer	20Ma20Fp
U	(W)	35	F	Spinster	20Ma20Fp
Mary		11	F	Spinster	20Ma20Fp
Bridget		09	F	Child	20Ma20Fp
DAY, Pat		20	M	Smith	20Ma20Fp
MALALBY, Robert		27	M	Laborer	20Ma20Fp
WALSH, Anne		20	F	Spinster	20Ma20Fp
Thos.		24	M	Laborer	20Ma20Fp
U	(W)	20	F	Spinster	20Ma20Fp
CAMPION, Edwd.		27	M	Farmer	20Ma20Fp
FOGARTY, Michl.		24	M	Farmer	20Ma20Fp
RYAN, John		21	M	Farmer	20Ma20Fp
ROWE, Jeremiah		20	M	Farmer	20Ma20Fp
HOOLOHAN, Mat.		21	M	Farmer	20Ma20Fp
CASHIN, Martin		30	M	Farmer	20Ma20Fp
BRODERICK, Thos.		25	M	Farmer	20Ma20Fp
DELANEY, Bridget		26	F	Spinster	20Ma20Fp
HEAD, Cathe.		20	F	Spinster	20Ma20Fp
CASHIN, U-Mrs.		24	F	Spinster	20Ma20Fp
Honor		22	F	Spinster	20Ma20Fp
SHEA, Mary		20	F	Spinster	20Ma20Fp
MAGUIRE, U		29	M	Servant	20Ma20Fp
FLANELLY, U-Mrs.		30	F	Spinster	20Ma20Fp
U		30	M	Farmer	20Ma20Fp
Owen		09	M	Child	20Ma20Fp
Hugh		08	M	Child	20Ma20Fp
OHALLOREN, James		48	M	Blacksmith	20Ma20Fp
John		25	M	Blacksmith	20Ma20Fp
CULLEN, Pat		24	M	Farmer	20Ma20Fp
REILLY, John		24	M	Hatter	20Ma20Fp
U	(W)	20	F	Spinster	20Ma20Fp
JUDGE, John		45	M	Farmer	20Ma20Fp
Mary		40	F	Spinster	20Ma20Fp
Bryan		25	M	Farmer	20Ma20Fp
Anne		17	F	Spinster	20Ma20Fp
John		14	M	Farmer	20Ma20Fp
Philip		07	M	Child	20Ma20Fp
Andrew		05	M	Child	20Ma20Fp
Mary		09	F	Child	20Ma20Fp
MOROME, Pat		60	M	Farmer	20Ma20Fp
Margaret		50	F	Spinster	20Ma20Fp
Margaret		16	F	Spinster	20Ma20Fp
Pat		14	M	Farmer	20Ma20Fp
Mary		12	F	Spinster	20Ma20Fp
Ellen		08	F	Child	20Ma20Fp
Ned		05	M	Child	20Ma20Fp
James		03	M	Child	20Ma20Fp
Anne		04	F	Child	20Ma20Fp
ENNIS, Richard		50	M	Farmer	20Ma20Fp
Michel.		28	M	Farmer	20Ma20Fp
John		26	M	Farmer	20Ma20Fp
Andrew		24	M	Farmer	20Ma20Fp
Mary		22	F	Spinster	20Ma20Fp
Pat		20	M	Farmer	20Ma20Fp
RYAN, William		20	M	Farmer	20Ma20Fp
CALWELL, John		20	M	Mason	20Ma20Fp

NAMES OF PASSENGERS		AGE	SEX	OCCUPATIONS	DATE PORT SHIP
BRENNAN, Pat		40	M	Farmer	20Ma20Fp
Bridget		40	F	Spinster	20Ma20Fp
Rose		15	F	Spinster	20Ma20Fp
Maria		13	F	Spinster	20Ma20Fp
Edward		11	M	Farmer	20Ma20Fp
Peter		09	M	Child	20Ma20Fp
James		07	M	Child	20Ma20Fp
Catherine		06	F	Child	20Ma20Fp
KELLY, Bridget		15	F	Spinster	20Ma20Fp
ANONAGHAM, Pat		24	M	Farmer	20Ma20Fp
U	(W)	20	F	Spinster	20Ma20Fp
BRAY, John		40	M	Farmer	20Ma20Fp
U	(W)	35	F	Spinster	20Ma20Fp
POTTS, James		24	M	Gunsmith	20Ma20Fp
CAREY, Laurence		24	M	Laborer	20Ma20Fp
FLOOD, James		22	M	Farmer	20Ma20Fp
Michl.		20	M	Farmer	20Ma20Fp
CARDIFF, John		35	M	Farmer	20Ma20Fp
U	(W)	30	F	Spinster	20Ma20Fp
James	(S)	12	M	Farmer	20Ma20Fp
Pat	(S)	10	M	Farmer	20Ma20Fp
John	(S)	08	M	Child	20Ma20Fp
Maria	(D)	02	F	Child	20Ma20Fp
WHELAN, Pat		27	M	Farmer	20Ma20Fp
BYRNE, John		27	M	Farmer	20Ma20Fp
U	(W)	25	F	Milliner	20Ma20Fp
Luke	(S)	05	M	Child	20Ma20Fp
Denis	(S)	03	M	Child	20Ma20Fp
John	(S)	.01	M	Infant	20Ma20Fp
CARTY, Pat		28	M	Farmer	20Ma20Fp
U	(W)	25	F	Spinster	20Ma20Fp
Edward	(S)	05	M	Child	20Ma20Fp
Denis	(S)	03	M	Child	20Ma20Fp
John	(S)	.01	M	Infant	20Ma20Fp
WHELAN, Michl.		20	M	Farmer	20Ma20Fp
MORIARTY, Pat		20	M	Farmer	20Ma20Fp
U	(W)	20	F	Spinster	20Ma20Fp
GIFFEN, George		25	M	Farmer	20Ma20Fp
BYRNE, Thomas		24	M	Farmer	20Ma20Fp
LYNCH, James		24	M	Laborer	20Ma20Fp
COOPER, Thos.		21	M	Mason	20Ma20Fp
Eliza		20	F	Spinster	20Ma20Fp
John		.01	M	Infant	20Ma20Fp
FLEMING, John		20	M	Laborer	20Ma20Fp
MEHAN, Pat		20	M	Farmer	20Ma20Fp
U	(W)	20	F	Spinster	20Ma20Fp
Margaret	(D)	04	F	Child	20Ma20Fp
James	(S)	.01	M	Infant	20Ma20Fp
GUNNER, Mary		20	F	Spinster	20Ma20Fp
CRAWFORD, Michl.		20	M	Farmer	20Ma20Fp
PRENTORY, Jane		28	F	Spinster	20Ma20Fp
U	(W)	26	F	Spinster	20Ma20Fp
NOWLAN, Teresa		20	F	Spinster	20Ma20Fp
FARRELL, Michl.		24	M	Farmer	20Ma20Fp
SMITH, Eliza		20	F	Spinster	20Ma20Fp
Ellen		19	F	Spinster	20Ma20Fp
BRYAN, Mary		32	F	Spinster	20Ma20Fp
FARRELLY, Robert		30	M	Farmer	20Ma20Fp
TOOHEY, Michl.		21	M	Mason	20Ma20Fp
MULVEHILL, Michl.		21	M	Farmer	20Ma20Fp
TOOHEY, Dennis		20	M	Stctr	20Ma20Fp
Hugh		24	M	Stctr	20Ma20Fp
DOWLING, James		24	M	Stctr	20Ma20Fp
U	(W)	20	F	Spinster	20Ma20Fp
Richd.	(S)	03	M	Child	20Ma20Fp
James	(S)	.01	M	Infant	20Ma20Fp
DARCY, Ellen		20	F	Spinster	20Ma20Fp
EGAN, Wm.		24	M	Laborer	20Ma20Fp
Anna		20	F	Spinster	20Ma20Fp
DEMPHRY, Maria		20	F	Spinster	20Ma20Fp
GRADY, Pat		23	M	Laborer	20Ma20Fp
DELANY, Eliza		24	F	Spinster	20Ma20Fp
FARRELL, John		28	M	Farmer	20Ma20Fp
KELLY, Maria		10	F	Spinster	20Ma20Fp
FEGAN, Joe		21	M	Farmer	20Ma20Fp
CASSIDY, Cathe.		20	F	Spinster	20Ma20Fp
PRENTICE, J.		24	M	Merchant	20Ma20Fp
U	(W)	20	F	Milliner	20Ma20Fp
Eliza	(D)	.01	F	Infant	20Ma20Fp
DOYLE, James		30	M	Merchant	20Ma20Fp
CROSBY, Mary		20	F	Spinster	20Ma20Fp
BYRNE, Laurence		30	M	Farmer	20Ma20Fp
LEACH, Ellen		30	F	Spinster	20Ma20Fp
FITZGERALD, Andrew		24	M	Farmer	20Ma20Fp
BOOTH, Anne		20	F	Spinster	20Ma20Fp
YOUNG, Eliza		20	F	Spinster	20Ma20Fp
DOYLE, Betty		26	F	Spinster	20Ma20Fp
Anne		22	F	Spinster	20Ma20Fp
James		20	M	Farmer	20Ma20Fp
William		12	M	Farmer	20Ma20Fp
Mary		10	F	Spinster	20Ma20Fp
John		06	M	Child	20Ma20Fp

LONDON 20 MAY 1848

From London

NAMES OF PASSENGERS		AGE	SEX	OCCUPATIONS	DATE PORT SHIP
TURNER, Edward		37	M	None	20Ma21Fq
Martha		35	F	None	20Ma21Fq
Harriett		30	F	None	20Ma21Fq
Edward		07	M	Child	20Ma21Fq
Stephen		04	M	Child	20Ma21Fq
Samson		03	M	Child	20Ma21Fq
Soloman		.00	M	Infant	20Ma21Fq
DICKER, James		26	M	None	20Ma21Fq
Mary		21	F	None	20Ma21Fq
LEADLEY, Thomas		50	M	Bookseller	20Ma21Fq
Lavinia		50	F	None	20Ma21Fq
Lavinia		14	F	None	20Ma21Fq
WARWICK, Thomas		54	M	None	20Ma21Fq
Sarah		54	F	None	20Ma21Fq
Elizabeth		21	F	None	20Ma21Fq
Sarah		20	F	None	20Ma21Fq
DAVIS, George		21	M	None	20Ma21Fq
MCCARTY, Dennis		27	M	None	20Ma21Fq
MEYER, Rorches		20	M	None	20Ma21Fq
OWEN, John		25	M	None	20Ma21Fq
Rachael		19	F	None	20Ma21Fq
Julia		.00	F	Infant	20Ma21Fq
CANNONS, George		21	M	None	20Ma21Fq
Mary-Ann		23	F	None	20Ma21Fq
PITHER, Charles		24	M	None	20Ma21Fq
WICKS, William		18	M	None	20Ma21Fq
George		20	M	None	20Ma21Fq
WESSEN, William		18	M	None	20Ma21Fq
WICKENS, George		22	M	None	20Ma21Fq
OWEN, George		11	M	None	20Ma21Fq
HOOPER, Emma		22	F	None	20Ma21Fq
STRADLEY, Samuel		48	M	None	20Ma21Fq
Eleonar		50	F	None	20Ma21Fq
Mary-Ann		20	F	None	20Ma21Fq
Sarah		17	F	None	20Ma21Fq
Samuel		14	M	None	20Ma21Fq
Eleonor		10	F	None	20Ma21Fq
DONCASTER, James		09	M	Child	20Ma21Fq
COHEN, Israel		21	M	Clsm	20Ma21Fq
RICHARDSON, Henry		32	M	Carpenter	20Ma21Fq
PRATT, Stephen		38	M	None	20Ma21Fq
Jane		35	F	None	20Ma21Fq
Jane		09	F	Child	20Ma21Fq
Stephen		07	M	Child	20Ma21Fq
John		05	M	Child	20Ma21Fq
William		04	M	Child	20Ma21Fq
U		.00	U	Infant	20Ma21Fq

NAMES OF PASSENGERS	AGE	SEX	OCCUPATIONS	DATE PORT SHIP
PRATT, U	.00	U	Infant	20Ma21Fq
FINKS, George	17	M	None	20Ma21Fq
CROUCHER, Robert	53	M	Cbtmkr	20Ma21Fq
TURNER, Robert	13	M	None	20Ma21Fq
WEEKS, William	70	M	None	20Ma21Fq
Charlotte	38	F	None	20Ma21Fq
Catherine	36	F	None	20Ma21Fq
DOWNEY, Mary	24	F	None	20Ma21Fq
DAVEY, John	29	M	Draper	20Ma21Fq
DORMAN, William	22	M	Tailor	20Ma21Fq
TURNER, Christopher	31	M	Tailor	20Ma21Fq
Esther	31	F	Tailor	20Ma21Fq
CARTLEDGE, William-H.	21	M	Engineer	20Ma21Fq
COCKRAN, Christopher	20	M	Clerk	20Ma21Fq
GOSLING, Edward	26	M	None	20Ma21Fq
Mary	24	F	None	20Ma21Fq
PADDINGTON, Thomas	00	M	None	20Ma21Fq
BARBER, Thomas	00	M	None	20Ma21Fq
WELLS, John	55	M	Tailor	20Ma21Fq
SEBROOK, Selina	20	F	Unknown	20Ma21Fq
COBIN, Mary	28	F	Unknown	20Ma21Fq
FIELD, Henry	27	M	Unknown	20Ma21Fq
Sarah	27	F	Unknown	20Ma21Fq
ROBINSON, John	40	M	Unknown	20Ma21Fq
DAVIE, George	31	M	Unknown	20Ma21Fq
BEDWIN, Jacob	51	M	Unknown	20Ma21Fq
Martha	48	F	Unknown	20Ma21Fq
Robert	21	M	Unknown	20Ma21Fq
Catherine	11	F	Unknown	20Ma21Fq
Israel	09	M	Child	20Ma21Fq
John	06	M	Child	20Ma21Fq
Albert	03	M	Child	20Ma21Fq
GOEPEL, John	28	M	Clerk	20Ma21Fq
ABRAHAM, Isaac	65	M	Unknown	20Ma21Fq
Ann	64	F	Unknown	20Ma21Fq
SKEET, Mary	41	F	Unknown	20Ma21Fq
SOLOMANS, Emanuel	37	M	Sugar Maker	20Ma21Fq
BARNETT, Joseph	36	M	Salesman	20Ma21Fq
Herman	26	M	Salesman	20Ma21Fq
RICHARDSON, George	30	M	Unknown	20Ma21Fq
Margaret	20	F	Unknown	20Ma21Fq
PASKET, Alice	48	F	Unknown	20Ma21Fq
CHAMBERS, Mary-Ann	30	F	Unknown	20Ma21Fq
James	18	M	Unknown	20Ma21Fq
SHEEN, Jeremiah	39	M	Laborer	20Ma21Fq
CRAY, Thomas	30	M	Laborer	20Ma21Fq
Mary	33	F	Laborer	20Ma21Fq
SHEEN, Thomas	34	F	Laborer	20Ma21Fq
WHITEHEAD, Henry	33	M	Plumber	20Ma21Fq
CROUCH, William	40	M	Unknown	20Ma21Fq
Edmond	30	M	Unknown	20Ma21Fq
HOWELL, Benjamin	37	M	Unknown	20Ma21Fq
MERTON, William	42	M	Unknown	20Ma21Fq
Elizabeth	32	F	Unknown	20Ma21Fq
TEPTON, Thomas	20	M	Farmer	20Ma21Fq
MARSHALL, William	19	M	Farmer	20Ma21Fq
HICKMOT, Edward	18	M	Farmer	20Ma21Fq
DUNN, Catherin	28	F	Farmer	20Ma21Fq
HUGHES, Barry	20	M	Farmer	20Ma21Fq
FITZGERALD, James	32	M	Farmer	20Ma21Fq
GRANGER, Georg-J.	23	M	Farmer	20Ma21Fq
BATH, John	42	M	Farmer	20Ma21Fq
CROFTS, Thomas	36	M	Farmer	20Ma21Fq
GOEPEL, John	28	M	Clerk	20Ma21Fq
RICHARDS, Thomas-W.	19	M	Unknown	20Ma21Fq
John	18	M	Unknown	20Ma21Fq
HALL, John	25	M	Laborer	20Ma21Fq
Ann	23	F	Laborer	20Ma21Fq
COLLIN, Ephraim	22	M	Laborer	20Ma21Fq
Matilda	20	F	Laborer	20Ma21Fq
HAYSON, Henry	43	M	Laborer	20Ma21Fq
Charlotte	40	M	Laborer	20Ma21Fq
REDMAYNE, Matthew	30	M	Laborer	20Ma21Fq
LORD, Charles	22	M	Laborer	20Ma21Fq
Martha	18	F	Laborer	20Ma21Fq
SAYER, Joseph	22	M	Laborer	20Ma21Fq
WHITEING, Robert	26	M	Laborer	20Ma21Fq
SCOTT, William	51	M	Laborer	20Ma21Fq
Ellen	34	F	Laborer	20Ma21Fq
George	11	M	Laborer	20Ma21Fq
Ellen	11	F	Laborer	20Ma21Fq
Walter	04	M	Child	20Ma21Fq
ISRAEL, Aaron	28	M	None	20Ma21Fq
BARRETT, John	39	M	None	20Ma21Fq
TRAVISS, Elizabeth	22	F	None	20Ma21Fq
SEYMORE, Thomas	47	M	None	20Ma21Fq
Esther	44	F	None	20Ma21Fq
Elizabeth	19	F	None	20Ma21Fq
George	12	M	None	20Ma21Fq
William	11	M	None	20Ma21Fq
Henry	09	M	Child	20Ma21Fq
Thomas	08	M	Child	20Ma21Fq
John	03	M	Child	20Ma21Fq
Mary-Ann	.00	F	Infant	20Ma21Fq
FOSSETT, Frederick	18	M	None	20Ma21Fq
PALMER, James	68	M	None	20Ma21Fq
CARTER, James	22	M	None	20Ma21Fq
BUTT, Job	28	M	None	20Ma21Fq
Maria	50	F	None	20Ma21Fq
HOLLAND, Samuel	21	M	None	20Ma21Fq
AULWICK, James	22	M	None	20Ma21Fq
Ruth	10	F	None	20Ma21Fq
BUTT, William	25	M	None	20Ma21Fq
BARKER, William	25	M	None	20Ma21Fq
BALDWIN, Aons	28	M	None	20Ma21Fq
DEARDS, John	43	M	Carpenter	20Ma21Fq
Edward	16	M	None	20Ma21Fq
Walter	13	M	None	20Ma21Fq
PFENGER, William	22	M	None	20Ma21Fq
BENZ, Fredk.	21	M	None	20Ma21Fq
ASSOLD, Frederick	22	M	None	20Ma21Fq
AMBROSE, Catherine	60	F	None	20Ma21Fq
REEVES, George	22	M	Draper	20Ma21Fq
MIDDLETON, Henry	29	M	None	20Ma21Fq
SHARP, Alfred	34	M	None	20Ma21Fq
PATCHING, James	36	M	None	20Ma21Fq
Maria	37	F	None	20Ma21Fq
BOX, George	15	M	None	20Ma21Fq
PATCHING, Edward	13	M	None	20Ma21Fq
John	11	M	None	20Ma21Fq
Lucy	09	F	Child	20Ma21Fq
Charlotte	08	F	Child	20Ma21Fq
Sarah	06	F	Child	20Ma21Fq
Alfred	04	M	Child	20Ma21Fq
George	.00	M	Infant	20Ma21Fq
Henry	.00	M	Infant	20Ma21Fq
CARTER, Edward	52	M	None	20Ma21Fq
Jane	46	F	None	20Ma21Fq
Arthur	11	M	None	20Ma21Fq
Eliza	09	F	Child	20Ma21Fq
TAYLOR, George	42	M	None	20Ma21Fq
Eliza	32	F	None	20Ma21Fq
Eliza	06	F	Child	20Ma21Fq
Henry	04	M	Child	20Ma21Fq
Albert	.00	M	Infant	20Ma21Fq
KENSIT, George	50	M	None	20Ma21Fq
Mary	45	F	None	20Ma21Fq
WINT, George	22	M	None	20Ma21Fq
PRIOR, William	18	M	None	20Ma21Fq
GODING, Isaac	38	M	None	20Ma21Fq
BRAGNE, Edward	20	M	None	20Ma21Fq
TAGDFRICH, Marie	25	F	None	20Ma21Fq
FLORENCE, Wm.	52	M	None	20Ma21Fq
Mary	49	F	None	20Ma21Fq
Geo.	15	M	None	20Ma21Fq
Died-At-Sea				
Belamy	12	U	None	20Ma21Fq
Edward	10	M	None	20Ma21Fq
Sarah	09	F	Child	20Ma21Fq
Fanny	05	F	Child	20Ma21Fq

NAMES OF PASSENGERS		AGE	SEX	OCCUPATIONS	DATE PORT SHIP
ELSON, Jos.		38	M	Unknown	20Ma21Fq
RAMSEY, Anna-Maria		35	F	Unknown	20Ma21Fq
Robt.		07	M	Child	20Ma21Fq
Allen		04	M	Child	20Ma21Fq
HANCOCK, John		30	M	Unknown	20Ma21Fq
Eliza		18	F	Unknown	20Ma21Fq
BOUCHIER, Laura		36	F	Unknown	20Ma21Fq
Georgina		11	F	Unknown	20Ma21Fq
Fanny		11	F	Unknown	20Ma21Fq
Ellen		09	F	Child	20Ma21Fq
Henry		06	M	Child	20Ma21Fq
SIKES, Christy		19	M	Unknown	20Ma21Fq
HOBBS, Frances-M.		25	F	Unknown	20Ma21Fq
DELATORRE, Anthony		40	M	Merchant	20Ma21Fq
BUTT, Chas.		20	M	None	20Ma21Fq
MEEGHAN, O.M.		28	M	Merchant	20Ma21Fq
BURTON, Chas.		42	M	None	20Ma21Fq
Ellen		25	F	Unknown	20Ma21Fq
Clara		13	F	Unknown	20Ma21Fq
WALKER, Hannah		44	F	None	20Ma21Fq
BENJAMIN, Wm.		32	M	Merchant	20Ma21Fq
Caroline		26	F	None	20Ma21Fq
Michael		03	M	Child	20Ma21Fq
Sarah		01	F	Child	20Ma21Fq
CASTLE, Goodman		21	M	None	20Ma21Fq
BARRY, Margaret		23	F	Servant	20Ma21Fq
LAWRENCE, Luke		30	M	Farmer	20Ma21Fq
Eliza		26	F	Unknown	20Ma21Fq
BOWMAN, Robt.		48	M	Tailor	20Ma21Fq
Sarah		28	F	Unknown	20Ma21Fq
BAKEWELL, Josiah		30	M	Saw Maker	20Ma21Fq
VERNON, Wm.		23	M	None	20Ma21Fq
HODGE, J.		36	M	Baker	20Ma21Fq
PRESTON, Henry		22	M	None	20Ma21Fq

MARGARET 21 MAY 1848

From Waterford

NAMES OF PASSENGERS		AGE	SEX	OCCUPATIONS	DATE PORT SHIP
BOLGER, Mary		50	F	Wi	21Ma16Fe
Patt.		19	M	Farmer	21Ma16Fe
Cath.		16	F	Spinster	21Ma16Fe
John		13	M	Farmer	21Ma16Fe
Mary		14	F	Spinster	21Ma16Fe
James		12	M	Unknown	21Ma16Fe
Johanna		10	F	Unknown	21Ma16Fe
Edward		08	M	Child	21Ma16Fe
CARTY, Bridget		25	F	Spinster	21Ma16Fe
PHELAN, Patk.		49	M	Farmer	21Ma16Fe
Cathr.	(W)	45	F	Wife	21Ma16Fe
Patrick		28	M	Farmer	21Ma16Fe
Edward		13	M	Unknown	21Ma16Fe
Simon		12	M	Unknown	21Ma16Fe
Silvester		10	M	Unknown	21Ma16Fe
Michl.		06	M	Child	21Ma16Fe
Cathe.		04	F	Child	21Ma16Fe
Mary		02	F	Child	21Ma16Fe
BEAMEY, Lawrence		32	M	Farmer	21Ma16Fe
DAVIES, Anne		25	F	Spinster	21Ma16Fe
GAUL, James		28	M	Laborer	21Ma16Fe
BRENAN, Michl.		28	M	Farmer	21Ma16Fe
NOWLAN, Edward		24	M	Laborer	21Ma16Fe
WALSHE, Patk.		30	M	Farmer	21Ma16Fe
FORTUNE, Patk.		38	M	Farmer	21Ma16Fe
Bridget	(W)	36	F	Wife	21Ma16Fe
LABOR, Judith		28	F	Spinster	21Ma16Fe
STANNERS, Garret		24	M	Spinster	21Ma16Fe
ROCHE, John		30	M	Spinster	21Ma16Fe
POWER, Martin		25	M	Spinster	21Ma16Fe
WALSHE, John		27	M	Spinster	21Ma16Fe
QUINN, James		28	M	Spinster	21Ma16Fe
RICHFORD, Patck.		30	M	Farmer	21Ma16Fe
John		26	M	Farmer	21Ma16Fe
HOWLAN, James		26	M	Laborer	21Ma16Fe
PHELAN, John		35	M	Farmer	21Ma16Fe
Johanna	(W)	37	F	Wife	21Ma16Fe
Hannah	(D)	05	F	Child	21Ma16Fe
Andy	(S)	03	M	Child	21Ma16Fe
Michl.	(S)	.11	M	Infant	21Ma16Fe
BRYAN, Richd.		27	M	Laborer	21Ma16Fe
MURPHY, John		30	M	Farmer	21Ma16Fe
Ellen	(W)	21	F	Wife	21Ma16Fe
Died-At-Sea					
Lawrence		27	M	Laborer	21Ma16Fe
HOBAN, James		50	M	Farmer	21Ma16Fe
Mary	(W)	30	F	Wife	21Ma16Fe
Mich.		26	M	Laborer	21Ma16Fe
Patt.		.00	M	Infant	21Ma16Fe
Johanna		05	F	Child	21Ma16Fe
Catherine		03	F	Child	21Ma16Fe
DOYLE, John		23	M	Laborer	21Ma16Fe
BYRNE, John		30	M	Laborer	21Ma16Fe
MURPHY, Edwd.		20	M	Farmer	21Ma16Fe
Cathe.	(W)	22	F	Wife	21Ma16Fe
Thos.		30	M	Laborer	21Ma16Fe
RYAN, Ellen		22	F	Spinster	21Ma16Fe
Margt.		20	F	Spinster	21Ma16Fe
COADY, Elize		20	F	Spinster	21Ma16Fe
GRENANN, Patk.		23	M	Farmer	21Ma16Fe
MILES, John		22	M	Farmer	21Ma16Fe
Wm.		40	M	Farmer	21Ma16Fe
Ellen	(W)	23	F	Wife	21Ma16Fe
HORLAHER, Richd.		27	M	Farmer	21Ma16Fe
DAWSON, Cath.		30	F	Spinster	21Ma16Fe
MALLREY, Wm.		18	M	Laborer	21Ma16Fe
COADY, Thos.		48	M	Laborer	21Ma16Fe
Garret		20	M	Laborer	21Ma16Fe
MURPHY, Mary		21	F	Spinster	21Ma16Fe
Dennis		24	M	Chandler	21Ma16Fe
QUIRCK, Mary		20	F	Spinster	21Ma16Fe
MCNAMARA, Pierce		40	M	Unknown	21Ma16Fe
Edwd.		12	M	Farmer	21Ma16Fe
Margt.	(W)	18	F	Wife	21Ma16Fe
BRENAN, John		47	M	Farmer	21Ma16Fe
Cathrine	(W)	18	F	Wife	21Ma16Fe
KEEFE, Wm.		25	M	Laborer	21Ma16Fe
KAVENAUGH, John		28	M	Laborer	21Ma16Fe
OFARRELL, Bernard		19	M	Laborer	21Ma16Fe
COADY, James		25	M	Laborer	21Ma16Fe
DEALIN, Eliza		21	F	Spinster	21Ma16Fe
CUDOGAN, Bridget		23	F	Spinster	21Ma16Fe
LANNAGAN, Thos.		38	M	Farmer	21Ma16Fe
Edmond		33	M	Farmer	21Ma16Fe
Honor	(W)	22	F	Wife	21Ma16Fe
KENT, Ellen		20	F	Spinster	21Ma16Fe
Anty.		24	F	Spinster	21Ma16Fe
BYRNE, Bridget		25	F	Spinster	21Ma16Fe
LYNNOT, Margt.		20	F	Spinster	21Ma16Fe
DUNNE, Margt.		18	F	Spinster	21Ma16Fe
DALTON, Andrew		36	M	Laborer	21Ma16Fe
PIBBY, Thos.		22	M	Laborer	21Ma16Fe
Michl.		20	M	Laborer	21Ma16Fe
PURCELL, Mary		20	F	Spinster	21Ma16Fe
PIBBY, Margt.		21	F	Wife	21Ma16Fe
LOFTUS, Thos.		30	M	Laborer	21Ma16Fe
Mary	(W)	20	F	Wife	21Ma16Fe
BARNIVAL, Michl.		38	M	Laborer	21Ma16Fe
Cathn.	(W)	13	F	Wife	21Ma16Fe
WALSHE, Judith		21	F	Spinster	21Ma16Fe
NOWLAN, John		25	M	Laborer	21Ma16Fe
BRYAN, John		28	M	Laborer	21Ma16Fe
Michl.		30	M	Laborer	21Ma16Fe
Michl.		42	M	Laborer	21Ma16Fe
LOUGHLIN, Judith		25	F	Spinster	21Ma16Fe

NAMES OF PASSENGERS		AGE	SEX	OCCUPATIONS	DATE PORT SHIP
GAUL, David		24	M	Laborer	21Ma16Fe
BYRNE, Edward		26	M	Laborer	21Ma16Fe
FITZGERALD, Edwd.		40	M	Laborer	21Ma16Fe
MARTIN, Bryan		38	M	Farmer	21Ma16Fe
Michl.		28	M	Farmer	21Ma16Fe
KAVANAGH, James		24	M	Laborer	21Ma16Fe
HARTLEY, James		45	M	Laborer	21Ma16Fe
KAVANAGH, Joseph		24	M	Laborer	21Ma16Fe
BOLGER, Patt.		28	M	Laborer	21Ma16Fe
DOWLING, Patk.		26	M	Laborer	21Ma16Fe
WALLACE, Danl.		36	M	Farmer	21Ma16Fe
INGHRME, Danl.		32	M	Farmer	21Ma16Fe
Cathn.	(W)	25	F	Wife	21Ma16Fe
Mary	(D)	08	F	Child	21Ma16Fe
Cathe.	(D)	04	F	Child	21Ma16Fe
BUTLER, Pat		23	M	Laborer	21Ma16Fe
HOGAN, Wm.		25	M	Laborer	21Ma16Fe
HOLLAND, Danl.		20	M	Laborer	21Ma16Fe
MURPHY, Pat		26	M	Laborer	21Ma16Fe
FEEHAN, Thos.		18	M	Laborer	21Ma16Fe
MURPHY, Michl.		27	M	Laborer	21Ma16Fe
WHELAN, John		62	M	Farmer	21Ma16Fe
Ellen	(W)	52	F	Wife	21Ma16Fe
Pierce	(S)	17	M	Farmer	21Ma16Fe
BRENAN, Garret		18	M	Farmer	21Ma16Fe
GONRAM, Richd.		16	M	Cooper	21Ma16Fe
BOLGER, Michael		27	M	Farmer	21Ma16Fe
MARSHALL, Thos.		23	M	Laborer	21Ma16Fe
BYRNE, Thos.		28	M	Laborer	21Ma16Fe
MORAN, Michael		24	M	Carpenter	21Ma16Fe
CLARKE, Wm.H.		18	M	Farmer	21Ma16Fe
Eliza		16	F	Spinster	21Ma16Fe
LYNCH, Richd.		21	M	Laborer	21Ma16Fe
MAHONY, Mary		25	F	Spinster	21Ma16Fe
BEAMY, Bridget		24	F	Spinster	21Ma16Fe
MCDONALD, James		27	M	Laborer	21Ma16Fe
MURPHY, Cath.		25	F	Spinster	21Ma16Fe
PHELAN, James		27	M	Farmer	21Ma16Fe
Philip		33	M	Farmer	21Ma16Fe
Mary	(W)	20	F	Spinster	21Ma16Fe
MORAN, Ellen		20	F	Wife	21Ma16Fe
Michl.	(S)	.03	M	Infant	21Ma16Fe
HOWLIN, Mary		25	F	Spinster	21Ma16Fe
Bridget		32	F	Laborer	21Ma16Fe
MAGINSSE, Ellen		06	F	Child	21Ma16Fe
Burke		38	M	Laborer	21Ma16Fe
GRANMEL, Mary		05	F	Child	21Ma16Fe
MCGUIRE, Judy		30	F	Unknown	21Ma16Fe
WHITE, Francis		24	M	Laborer	21Ma16Fe

STANDARD 22 MAY 1848

From Belfast

NAMES OF PASSENGERS	AGE	SEX	OCCUPATIONS	DATE PORT SHIP
WILLIAMSON, Gabriel	24	M	Laborer	22Ma07Ft
William	22	M	Laborer	22Ma07Ft
John	20	M	Laborer	22Ma07Ft
Eliza-Jane	18	F	Laborer	22Ma07Ft
ROBINSON, Arthur	21	M	Laborer	22Ma07Ft
John	19	M	Laborer	22Ma07Ft
Joseph	28	M	Laborer	22Ma07Ft
Eliza	23	F	Laborer	22Ma07Ft
Mary-Jane	05	F	Child	22Ma07Ft
Eliza	02	F	Child	22Ma07Ft
GRIFFAN, William-J.	27	M	Laborer	22Ma07Ft
KELLY, John	21	M	Laborer	22Ma07Ft
STEWARD, Jane	20	F	Laborer	22Ma07Ft
KILCHURCH, Jane	16	F	Laborer	22Ma07Ft
CANNOR, Mary	35	F	Laborer	22Ma07Ft
WILLIAMS, Joseph	19	M	Laborer	22Ma07Ft
CLARKE, William	21	M	Laborer	22Ma07Ft
FLETCHER, William	19	M	Laborer	22Ma07Ft
MCMARE, Michal	48	M	Laborer	22Ma07Ft
FITZSIMMONS, Harry	50	M	Laborer	22Ma07Ft
Mary	36	F	Laborer	22Ma07Ft
Mary	08	F	Child	22Ma07Ft
Eliza	06	F	Child	22Ma07Ft
MCKENNA, John	60	M	Farmer	22Ma07Ft
Henery	14	M	Farmer	22Ma07Ft
Sarah	19	F	Farmer	22Ma07Ft
Anne	22	F	Farmer	22Ma07Ft
WALKER, Thomas	12	M	Farmer	22Ma07Ft
DRUFFAN, John	20	M	Farmer	22Ma07Ft
SECOCK, Andrew	40	M	Farmer	22Ma07Ft
Mary-Ann	38	F	Farmer	22Ma07Ft
Anne	17	F	Farmer	22Ma07Ft
Margret	13	F	Farmer	22Ma07Ft
Samuel	13	M	Laborer	22Ma07Ft
Mary	11	F	Laborer	22Ma07Ft
Thomas	48	M	Laborer	22Ma07Ft
Eliza	46	F	Laborer	22Ma07Ft
Martha	26	F	Laborer	22Ma07Ft
Mary-Anne	18	F	Laborer	22Ma07Ft
William	15	M	Laborer	22Ma07Ft
Eliza	12	F	Laborer	22Ma07Ft
Caroline	09	F	Child	22Ma07Ft
SHEAN, Robert	19	M	Laborer	22Ma07Ft
Mary-Ann	18	F	Laborer	22Ma07Ft
KELLY, Daniel	23	M	Laborer	22Ma07Ft
Eliza	20	F	Laborer	22Ma07Ft
John	18	M	Laborer	22Ma07Ft
Sarah	21	F	Laborer	22Ma07Ft
Mary-Jane	17	F	Laborer	22Ma07Ft
MCCANN, Bridget	50	F	Laborer	22Ma07Ft
KINDY, Frances	21	F	Laborer	22Ma07Ft
MCGUIRK, Edward	24	M	Laborer	22Ma07Ft
Mary	21	F	Laborer	22Ma07Ft
Isabella	22	F	Laborer	22Ma07Ft
LOWRY, John	22	M	Laborer	22Ma07Ft
Jane	18	F	Laborer	22Ma07Ft
I----NNY, Matthew	58	M	Laborer	22Ma07Ft
Nancy	24	F	Laborer	22Ma07Ft
William	04	M	Child	22Ma07Ft
Ellen	02	F	Child	22Ma07Ft
Samuel	07	M	Child	22Ma07Ft
MULLEN, Mary-Ann	20	F	Laborer	22Ma07Ft
BELL, Harriot	25	F	Laborer	22Ma07Ft
JOHNSTON, Henry	24	M	Laborer	22Ma07Ft
HUTTAN, Hugh	24	M	Laborer	22Ma07Ft
Jane	19	F	Laborer	22Ma07Ft
ALLEN, Alexander	23	M	Laborer	22Ma07Ft
John	25	M	Laborer	22Ma07Ft
MORGAN, Katy	24	F	Laborer	22Ma07Ft
MCMURRAY, Gardon	48	M	Laborer	22Ma07Ft
Mary	40	F	Laborer	22Ma07Ft
James	19	M	Laborer	22Ma07Ft
Gordon	16	M	Laborer	22Ma07Ft
Robbert	12	M	Laborer	22Ma07Ft
Betty-Ann	10	F	Laborer	22Ma07Ft
Margret-Jane	08	F	Child	22Ma07Ft
Catherine	04	F	Child	22Ma07Ft
CORN, Debby	24	F	Farmer	22Ma07Ft
Anne-Jane	22	F	Farmer	22Ma07Ft
JACKSON, John	50	M	Farmer	22Ma07Ft
BAILIE, William	50	M	Farmer	22Ma07Ft
Joseph	18	M	Farmer	22Ma07Ft
Eliza	15	F	Farmer	22Ma07Ft
MCMURRAY, Eliza-Jane	20	F	Farmer	22Ma07Ft
HOPPER, Herchel	35	M	Farmer	22Ma07Ft
Robert	16	M	Farmer	22Ma07Ft
FORBS, P.	20	M	Farmer	22Ma07Ft
ROBBERTS, Eliza	20	F	Laborer	22Ma07Ft
MONSON, Robbert	18	M	Laborer	22Ma07Ft
Samuel	20	M	Laborer	22Ma07Ft

NAMES OF PASSENGERS	AGE	SEX	OCCUPATIONS	DATE PORT SHIP
WILLIAMS, James	40	M	Laborer	22Ma07Ft
BLAVENS, James	24	M	Laborer	22Ma07Ft
HOARSON, William	20	M	Laborer	22Ma07Ft
MCLEAN, Jane	20	F	Laborer	22Ma07Ft
CARY, Henry	25	M	Laborer	22Ma07Ft
William	13	M	Laborer	22Ma07Ft
Margret	09	F	Child	22Ma07Ft
Jane	08	F	Child	22Ma07Ft
Hanna	04	F	Child	22Ma07Ft
George	01	M	Child	22Ma07Ft
FEE, John	25	M	Laborer	22Ma07Ft
BRAEN, James	25	M	Laborer	22Ma07Ft
BAIRD, Hugh	25	M	Laborer	22Ma07Ft
WILLIAMSON, Thomas	30	M	Laborer	22Ma07Ft
RICHE, John	30	M	Laborer	22Ma07Ft
AICKIN, John	35	M	Laborer	22Ma07Ft
John	17	M	Laborer	22Ma07Ft
HUGHSE, James	22	M	Laborer	22Ma07Ft
Barbara	20	F	Laborer	22Ma07Ft
STOTT, John	38	M	Laborer	22Ma07Ft
Eliza-Ann	30	F	Laborer	22Ma07Ft
John	06	M	Child	22Ma07Ft
James	04	M	Child	22Ma07Ft
Jane	01	F	Child	22Ma07Ft
MACEY, Philip-M.	30	M	Laborer	22Ma07Ft
REMSHA, William	18	M	Laborer	22Ma07Ft
HUGHS, Robbet	37	M	Laborer	22Ma07Ft
Artha	20	M	Laborer	22Ma07Ft
KIRPATRICK, Margret	18	F	Laborer	22Ma07Ft
ROBERTS, Robetase	20	M	Laborer	22Ma07Ft
RUDDES, Hunabott	20	F	Laborer	22Ma07Ft
KIRNY, Paterick	35	M	Laborer	22Ma07Ft
Ann	30	F	Laborer	22Ma07Ft
James	07	M	Child	22Ma07Ft
CUNNINGHAM, James	28	M	Laborer	22Ma07Ft
Sarah	25	F	Farmer	22Ma07Ft
John	06	M	Child	22Ma07Ft
Susan	04	F	Child	22Ma07Ft
U	.00	U	Infant	22Ma07Ft
George	02	M	Child	22Ma07Ft
MAGAN, Edward	20	M	Farmer	22Ma07Ft
MONT, Mary	21	F	Farmer	22Ma07Ft
Ellen	19	F	Farmer	22Ma07Ft
KAINE, John	21	M	Farmer	22Ma07Ft
BURNELL, James	26	M	Farmer	22Ma07Ft
BELL, William	24	M	Farmer	22Ma07Ft
MCFADDEN, Eliza	27	F	Farmer	22Ma07Ft
PATTERSON, Thomas	34	M	Farmer	22Ma07Ft
OSWALD, John	23	M	Farmer	22Ma07Ft
GARRET, James	22	M	Farmer	22Ma07Ft
DANNAN, Frances	22	M	Farmer	22Ma07Ft
NEWBURNY, Robert	25	M	Farmer	22Ma07Ft
LOUGHAN, James	26	M	Farmer	22Ma07Ft
Margret	42	F	Farmer	22Ma07Ft
Michal	.00	M	Infant	22Ma07Ft
MCLARGAN, Henry	41	M	Laborer	22Ma07Ft
Nancy	14	F	Laborer	22Ma07Ft
Mary	12	F	Laborer	22Ma07Ft
Anne	10	F	Laborer	22Ma07Ft
Eliza	09	F	Child	22Ma07Ft
Sarah	08	F	Child	22Ma07Ft
Jane	08	F	Child	22Ma07Ft
Margret	06	F	Child	22Ma07Ft
Henry	04	M	Child	22Ma07Ft
Catherine	.00	F	Infant	22Ma07Ft
SMITH, Samuel	45	M	Laborer	22Ma07Ft
Eliza	44	F	Laborer	22Ma07Ft
Samuel	31	M	Laborer	22Ma07Ft
William	.00	M	Infant	22Ma07Ft
James	48	M	Laborer	22Ma07Ft
Eliza	46	F	Laborer	22Ma07Ft
William	22	M	Laborer	22Ma07Ft
Margret	20	F	Laborer	22Ma07Ft
James	12	M	Laborer	22Ma07Ft
Nancy	10	F	Laborer	22Ma07Ft
SMITH, Sarah	08	F	Child	22Ma07Ft
Eliza	06	F	Child	22Ma07Ft
ANDERSON, John	28	M	Laborer	22Ma07Ft
THOMSON, William	24	M	Laborer	22Ma07Ft
BELL, Sarah-Jane	24	F	Laborer	22Ma07Ft
GOODWIN, Margret	20	F	Laborer	22Ma07Ft
CONLIN, James	19	M	Laborer	22Ma07Ft
ANNCHONY, John	52	M	Laborer	22Ma07Ft
Rosey-A.	47	F	Laborer	22Ma07Ft
Edward	20	M	Laborer	22Ma07Ft
William	18	M	Laborer	22Ma07Ft
Ellen	16	F	Laborer	22Ma07Ft
Essy	14	F	Laborer	22Ma07Ft
James	13	M	Laborer	22Ma07Ft
Alexander	12	M	Laborer	22Ma07Ft
Matilda	11	F	Laborer	22Ma07Ft
Rose-Ann	09	F	Child	22Ma07Ft
George	07	M	Child	22Ma07Ft
John	05	M	Child	22Ma07Ft
BURK, Alexander	35	M	Laborer	22Ma07Ft
Anne	21	F	Laborer	22Ma07Ft
William	28	M	Laborer	22Ma07Ft
LANE, Eliza	20	F	Laborer	22Ma07Ft
KLENARD, Mathew	19	M	Laborer	22Ma07Ft
John	30	M	Laborer	22Ma07Ft
FAMPEL, Hew	25	M	Laborer	22Ma07Ft
James	27	M	Laborer	22Ma07Ft
Isabella	10	F	Laborer	22Ma07Ft
Hugh	22	M	Laborer	22Ma07Ft
MCSHEAN, Mary	24	F	Laborer	22Ma07Ft
James	20	M	Laborer	22Ma07Ft
SHINKE, Henry	25	M	Laborer	22Ma07Ft

ARLINGTON 22 MAY 1848

From Liverpool

NAMES OF PASSENGERS		AGE	SEX	OCCUPATIONS	DATE PORT SHIP
BRINAK, Richard		24	M	Saddler	22Ma02Fu
RANIHAN, Patrick		22	M	Carpenter	22Ma02Fu
HARGREAVES, James		23	M	Laborer	22Ma02Fu
DUCKWORTH, James		22	M	Laborer	22Ma02Fu
HAWKES, Thomas		24	M	Miller	22Ma02Fu
COOKSON, William		21	M	Miller	22Ma02Fu
FIRTH, William		35	M	Mechanic	22Ma02Fu
GREGSON, George		25	M	Ctnsp	22Ma02Fu
LANCASTER, Henry		40	M	Ctnsp	22Ma02Fu
BROWN, William		36	M	Surveyor	22Ma02Fu
FRYAN, Charles		18	M	Blacksmith	22Ma02Fu
DOUGHERTY, Michael		27	M	Laborer	22Ma02Fu
MCMENNENNY, Patrick		22	M	Laborer	22Ma02Fu
KEENEY, Francis		30	M	Shoemaker	22Ma02Fu
HEFFERNAN, Thomas		18	M	Farmer	22Ma02Fu
John		45	M	Farmer	22Ma02Fu
LANDERKIN, Michael		24	M	Laborer	22Ma02Fu
CUFF, William		65	M	Farmer	22Ma02Fu
BRANNAN, James		18	M	Farmer	22Ma02Fu
KELLY, Daniel		20	M	Farmer	22Ma02Fu
OCONNELL, Daniel		30	M	Farmer	22Ma02Fu
Mary		20	F	Farmer	22Ma02Fu
Margaret		18	F	Farmer	22Ma02Fu
SHERRY, William		27	M	Laborer	22Ma02Fu
MERRICK, John		32	M	Coachman	22Ma02Fu
Ellen	(W)	28	F	Coachman	22Ma02Fu
James	(S)	06	M	Child	22Ma02Fu
Mary	(D)	04	F	Child	22Ma02Fu
Thomas	(S)	.00	M	Infant	22Ma02Fu
HART, Thomas		30	M	Laborer	22Ma02Fu
Mary		32	F	Laborer	22Ma02Fu
GARRETTY, Dominic		40	M	Laborer	22Ma02Fu

NAMES OF PASSENGERS	AGE	SEX	OCCUPATIONS	DATE PORT SHIP
FORIN, Robert	15	M	Laborer	22Ma02Fu
GUINEN, Michael	35	M	Boatman	22Ma02Fu
DONOHOE, Patrick	20	M	Laborer	22Ma02Fu
Ann	18	F	Laborer	22Ma02Fu
Margaret	16	F	Laborer	22Ma02Fu
MCKENNA, Ann	40	F	Laborer	22Ma02Fu
Frank	11	M	Laborer	22Ma02Fu
Betty	09	F	Child	22Ma02Fu
Susan	06	F	Child	22Ma02Fu
Rose	04	F	Child	22Ma02Fu
Mary	.00	F	Infant	22Ma02Fu
MALLOY, Maurice	19	M	Laborer	22Ma02Fu
James	25	M	Laborer	22Ma02Fu
DALY, William	25	M	Laborer	22Ma02Fu
Mary	28	F	Laborer	22Ma02Fu
FOREST, Patrick	20	M	Laborer	22Ma02Fu
GARY, Honora	15	F	Laborer	22Ma02Fu
BROWN, James	25	M	Wheelwright	22Ma02Fu
EAGAN, Bridget	20	F	Servant	22Ma02Fu
MURRAY, Margaret	16	F	Servant	22Ma02Fu
ROONEY, Patrick	27	M	Laborer	22Ma02Fu
QUINN, William	20	M	Mason	22Ma02Fu
HAGAN, Joseph	18	M	Weaver	22Ma02Fu
MORRIS, Andrew	30	M	Laborer	22Ma02Fu
SHIEL, Bernard	20	M	Laborer	22Ma02Fu
COFFEE, Michael	22	M	Laborer	22Ma02Fu
NALLY, Michael	25	M	Laborer	22Ma02Fu
Patrick	08	M	Child	22Ma02Fu
MCBRYAN, Margaret	17	F	Laborer	22Ma02Fu
Patrick	15	M	Laborer	22Ma02Fu
BRODERICK, Maria	18	F	Laborer	22Ma02Fu
PICKENS, Ralph	19	M	Laborer	22Ma02Fu
Ellen	14	F	Laborer	22Ma02Fu
CLARY, Ellen	14	F	Laborer	22Ma02Fu
GELSHAUNNA, John	19	M	Laborer	22Ma02Fu
ODONNELL, James	18	M	Laborer	22Ma02Fu
Dominic	14	M	Laborer	22Ma02Fu
Patrick	13	M	Laborer	22Ma02Fu
John	08	M	Child	22Ma02Fu
MEGARVEY, John	25	M	Laborer	22Ma02Fu
Matthew	22	M	Laborer	22Ma02Fu
Catharine	45	F	Laborer	22Ma02Fu
MARTIN, John	20	M	Laborer	22Ma02Fu
Mary	16	F	Laborer	22Ma02Fu
BEARD, David	30	M	Laborer	22Ma02Fu
MURPHY, William	20	M	Laborer	22Ma02Fu
DAWSON, Alicia	25	F	Butcher	22Ma02Fu
Mary	.00	F	Infant	22Ma02Fu
FAGAN, James	30	M	Laborer	22Ma02Fu
NOWLAN, Garrett	30	M	Laborer	22Ma02Fu

CHESTER 22 MAY 1848

From Liverpool

NAMES OF PASSENGERS	AGE	SEX	OCCUPATIONS	DATE PORT SHIP
QUINN, Bernard	55	M	Farmer	22Ma02Hr
Bernard	13	M	Farmer	22Ma02Hr
Sarah	11	F	Seamstress	22Ma02Hr
MCMAHON, Biddy	16	F	Servant	22Ma02Hr
MURPHY, James	25	M	Servant	22Ma02Hr
John	21	M	Farmer	22Ma02Hr
CORRY, Thos.	20	M	Farmer	22Ma02Hr
Ellen	19	F	Spinster	22Ma02Hr
EAGAN, Patrick	18	M	Farmer	22Ma02Hr
CIRTON, James	30	M	Farmer	22Ma02Hr
WELCH, Mathew	25	M	Farmer	22Ma02Hr
LEAHY, David	25	M	Farmer	22Ma02Hr
MARROW, Thomas	20	M	Farmer	22Ma02Hr
MURRAY, George	20	M	Clerk	22Ma02Hr
GAITLAND, James	20	M	Clerk	22Ma02Hr
FREEMAN, Owen	20	M	Clerk	22Ma02Hr
MURRAY, Thomas	20	M	Clerk	22Ma02Hr
CONNELL, Hy.	20	M	Clerk	22Ma02Hr
MCCLARKIN, Danl.	22	M	Clerk	22Ma02Hr
WELDON, Anne	20	F	Servant	22Ma02Hr
NICKELSON, John	39	M	Farmer	22Ma02Hr
TAILOR, Geor.	50	M	Farmer	22Ma02Hr
U (W)	50	F	Dressmaker	22Ma02Hr
Mary	22	F	Dressmaker	22Ma02Hr
ADAMS, Eliza	16	F	Dressmaker	22Ma02Hr
BOYDE, John	36	M	Farmer	22Ma02Hr
MURPHY, Thos.	22	M	Farmer	22Ma02Hr
OWENS, Margaret	31	F	Servant	22Ma02Hr
KEEF, Danl.	17	M	Clerk	22Ma02Hr
DOYLE, Edward	44	M	Laborer	22Ma02Hr
CROOK, Patrick	30	M	Laborer	22Ma02Hr
CAHY, Michael	28	M	Laborer	22Ma02Hr
RYAN, Michael	28	M	Laborer	22Ma02Hr
MCCARTY, Margaret	27	F	Servant	22Ma02Hr
MCDERMOTT, Francis	40	M	Servant	22Ma02Hr
James	20	M	Servant	22Ma02Hr
Mary	20	F	Servant	22Ma02Hr
MURPHY, Anne	20	F	Servant	22Ma02Hr
MCDONNELL, James	30	M	Clerk	22Ma02Hr
BEARD, William	25	M	Clerk	22Ma02Hr
U (W)	25	F	Milliner	22Ma02Hr
PHILLIPS, James	18	M	Servant	22Ma02Hr
Mary	18	F	Servant	22Ma02Hr
BOYDE, Samuel	25	M	Servant	22Ma02Hr
Margret	65	F	Servant	22Ma02Hr
Andrew	19	M	Servant	22Ma02Hr
John	06	M	Child	22Ma02Hr
KEELEN, Sarah	50	F	Servant	22Ma02Hr
Hugh	20	M	Farmer	22Ma02Hr
COOGAN, William	46	M	Farmer	22Ma02Hr
Catherine	16	F	None	22Ma02Hr
CARPENTER, John	22	M	Farmer	22Ma02Hr
BARNET, Thos.	20	M	Farmer	22Ma02Hr
MURRAY, Thos.	26	M	Farmer	22Ma02Hr
BRADY, Mich.	22	M	Farmer	22Ma02Hr
KEHOE, John	20	M	Farmer	22Ma02Hr
MCMANUS, Jas.	30	M	Farmer	22Ma02Hr
HARDY, Hugh	35	M	Farmer	22Ma02Hr
FITZEN, James	20	M	Farmer	22Ma02Hr
Phillip	.00	M	Infant	22Ma02Hr
KENNEDY, Lawrence	25	M	Farmer	22Ma02Hr
MEALONE, Michael	25	M	Farmer	22Ma02Hr
CONNEAGHAN, Mich.	25	M	Farmer	22Ma02Hr
Margt.	25	F	Servant	22Ma02Hr
COMFORT, Catherine	18	F	Servant	22Ma02Hr
HEAGLE, Honora	23	F	Servant	22Ma02Hr
BURKE, Jas.	25	M	Clerk	22Ma02Hr
DUFFY, Hugh	19	M	Clerk	22Ma02Hr
WHITE, Mich.	40	M	Clerk	22Ma02Hr
DUFFY, Mary	22	F	Servant	22Ma02Hr
HAND, Mary	22	F	Servant	22Ma02Hr
OROURK, F.	22	M	Servant	22Ma02Hr
OHARA, Mich.	46	M	Servant	22Ma02Hr
FITZEN, William	32	M	Servant	22Ma02Hr
ROGAN, Charles	25	M	Servant	22Ma02Hr
FINNIGAN, Mich.	30	M	Servant	22Ma02Hr
MCGIVEN, Patk.	30	M	Farmer	22Ma02Hr
U (W)	27	F	None	22Ma02Hr
Bd.	03	M	Child	22Ma02Hr
Anne	.00	F	Infant	22Ma02Hr
ABRAHAM, Patrick	28	M	Farmer	22Ma02Hr
SMITH, Mich.	26	M	Farmer	22Ma02Hr
U (W)	23	F	None	22Ma02Hr
BANNEN, Mary	21	F	Servant	22Ma02Hr
MAXWELL, Ellen	24	F	Servant	22Ma02Hr
RUTHERFORD, Jane	28	F	Servant	22Ma02Hr
John	38	M	Servant	22Ma02Hr
BETTYS, William	25	M	Servant	22Ma02Hr
FETLOCK, Thos.	24	M	Servant	22Ma02Hr

NAMES OF PASSENGERS	AGE	SEX	OCCUPATIONS	DATE PORT SHIP
FETLOCK, Jane	22	F	Dressmaker	22Ma02Hr
LOUGHAN, Anne	26	F	Dressmaker	22Ma02Hr
John	03	M	Child	22Ma02Hr
OVERTON, John	28	M	Clerk	22Ma02Hr
DAVIS, Humphry	50	M	Clerk	22Ma02Hr
Mary	40	F	Housekeeper	22Ma02Hr
James	18	M	Clerk	22Ma02Hr
Maria	17	F	Dressmaker	22Ma02Hr
Ellen	16	F	Dressmaker	22Ma02Hr
ONEIL, Henry	27	M	Farmer	22Ma02Hr
CARLAN, Patrick	21	M	Farmer	22Ma02Hr
Margt.	20	F	Servant	22Ma02Hr
JACOBS, Joseph	22	M	Mechanic	22Ma02Hr
ORANGE, Samuel	47	M	Mechanic	22Ma02Hr
PURCELL, John	40	M	Clerk	22Ma02Hr
CONNELL, Peter	25	M	Clerk	22Ma02Hr
FERRELL, Daniel	24	M	Clerk	22Ma02Hr
Mary	15	F	Dressmaker	22Ma02Hr
BRENNAN, Patrick	36	M	Laborer	22Ma02Hr
Thomas	17	M	Clerk	22Ma02Hr
Mary	15	F	Dressmaker	22Ma02Hr
QUIRK, Catherine	20	F	Dressmaker	22Ma02Hr
MCDERMOTT, Peter	30	M	Printer	22Ma02Hr
MILES, George	30	M	Printer	22Ma02Hr
CONLON, Mich.	27	M	Mechanic	22Ma02Hr
KELLY, Catherine	16	F	Servant	22Ma02Hr
CARROLL, Winifrid	18	F	Servant	22Ma02Hr
HANDGROVES, Wm.	40	M	Servant	22Ma02Hr
JENNINGS, Wm.	40	M	Laborer	22Ma02Hr
RODESON, Thos.	38	M	Laborer	22Ma02Hr
ROBSON, Samuel	39	M	Coachman	22Ma02Hr
SIMPSON, Joseph	24	M	Farmer	22Ma02Hr
COWAN, John	25	M	Farmer	22Ma02Hr
SIMPSON, Christ.	46	M	Farmer	22Ma02Hr
Christ.	24	M	Farmer	22Ma02Hr
PARTINGTON, Thos.	34	M	Farmer	22Ma02Hr
Jane	26	F	Servant	22Ma02Hr
MURPHY, Daniel	30	M	Farmer	22Ma02Hr
Timothy	13	M	None	22Ma02Hr
Daniel	07	M	Child	22Ma02Hr
Michael	03	M	Child	22Ma02Hr
Johanna	20	F	Spinster	22Ma02Hr
MAHONNY, Jerry	54	M	Mechanic	22Ma02Hr
Jerry	10	M	Mechanic	22Ma02Hr
Andrew	05	M	Child	22Ma02Hr
Michael	.00	M	Infant	22Ma02Hr
BERRY, Catherine	20	F	Spinster	22Ma02Hr
SWEENEY, William	12	M	None	22Ma02Hr
Jeremiah	13	M	None	22Ma02Hr
GALLAGHAN, Bartly	25	F	Spinster	22Ma02Hr
Patrick	16	M	Clerk	22Ma02Hr
KANE, Edward	30	M	Clerk	22Ma02Hr
RYAN, Dennis	21	M	Clerk	22Ma02Hr
SHANNAGAN, Patrick	22	M	Clerk	22Ma02Hr
Thomas	20	M	Clerk	22Ma02Hr
Mary	13	F	Servant	22Ma02Hr
PRICE, Margaret	28	F	Servant	22Ma02Hr
FARRELL, Bessey	29	F	Servant	22Ma02Hr
BRENNAN, Patrick	24	M	Farmer	22Ma02Hr
KENIGAN, Hugh	22	M	Farmer	22Ma02Hr
HEARAN, James	25	M	Farmer	22Ma02Hr
ALLEN, Wm.	22	M	Farmer	22Ma02Hr
BOYLE, Terence	24	M	Farmer	22Ma02Hr
D--EGAN, Bernard	22	M	Farmer	22Ma02Hr
DOUGHERTY, James	25	M	Farmer	22Ma02Hr
MCCANN, Bernard	35	M	Farmer	22Ma02Hr
MCGERAGLE, Cath.	18	F	Dressmaker	22Ma02Hr
LOVE, William	30	M	Clerk	22Ma02Hr
Eliza	28	F	Spinster	22Ma02Hr
William	03	M	Child	22Ma02Hr
John	02	M	Child	22Ma02Hr
Thomas	.00	M	Infant	22Ma02Hr
ROWE, Samuel	29	M	Clerk	22Ma02Hr
Margaret	18	F	Milliner	22Ma02Hr
FORD, John	20	M	Mechanic	22Ma02Hr
MAHONY, James	30	M	Mechanic	22Ma02Hr
Margaret	28	F	Servant	22Ma02Hr
CLYDE, Thomas	24	M	Servant	22Ma02Hr

DEFENCE 23 MAY 1848

From Liverpool

NAMES OF PASSENGERS	AGE	SEX	OCCUPATIONS	DATE PORT SHIP
MURPHY, Ann	22	F	Servant	23Ma02Hs
Catherine	23	F	Servant	23Ma02Hs
HOBEN, Jane	20	F	Servant	23Ma02Hs
REILLY, Berryan	40	M	Laborer	23Ma02Hs
Rose	18	F	Servant	23Ma02Hs
Mary	16	F	Servant	23Ma02Hs
KERNAN, Ann	18	F	Servant	23Ma02Hs
FLOOD, Owen	34	M	Laborer	23Ma02Hs
JAMES, Patrick	22	M	Laborer	23Ma02Hs
BOADY, Peter	18	M	Laborer	23Ma02Hs
REED, Mathew	24	M	Laborer	23Ma02Hs
MCDERMOTT, Eliza	20	F	Laborer	23Ma02Hs
FOX, William	20	M	Laborer	23Ma02Hs
KANE, Mary	20	F	Servant	23Ma02Hs
Julia	18	F	Servant	23Ma02Hs
THOMPSON, Elizabeth	27	F	Servant	23Ma02Hs
GALLAHAN, Mary	30	F	Servant	23Ma02Hs
Hannah	12	F	Servant	23Ma02Hs
Patrick	10	M	Laborer	23Ma02Hs
John	08	M	Child	23Ma02Hs
HICKY, Bridget	27	F	Servant	23Ma02Hs
DUFFY, Biddy	21	F	Servant	23Ma02Hs
KENWORTHY, John	40	M	Laborer	23Ma02Hs
Jane	40	F	Servant	23Ma02Hs
Mary-Ann	12	F	Servant	23Ma02Hs
Ann	10	F	Servant	23Ma02Hs
William	08	M	Child	23Ma02Hs
Emma	06	F	Child	23Ma02Hs
EASTWOOD, Thomas	36	M	Laborer	23Ma02Hs
HALLAWOOD, Mathew	25	M	Laborer	23Ma02Hs
BARREN, Mich.	25	M	Laborer	23Ma02Hs
HORNEY, Mary	28	F	Servant	23Ma02Hs
KIDNEY, James	40	M	Laborer	23Ma02Hs
GERAHTY, Patk.	28	M	Laborer	23Ma02Hs
Bridget	22	F	Servant	23Ma02Hs
COX, Ellen	16	F	Servant	23Ma02Hs
HARLEN, Pat	40	M	Laborer	23Ma02Hs
U (W)	30	F	Servant	23Ma02Hs
James	20	M	Laborer	23Ma02Hs
James	09	M	Child	23Ma02Hs
Mary	06	F	Child	23Ma02Hs
John	04	M	Child	23Ma02Hs
MCGRATH, Alex	24	M	Laborer	23Ma02Hs
REED, Ann	16	F	Servant	23Ma02Hs
HERIS, Mary	40	F	Servant	23Ma02Hs
Biddy	16	F	Servant	23Ma02Hs
HYNES, John	24	M	Laborer	23Ma02Hs
WALSH, Andrew	24	M	Laborer	23Ma02Hs
MASLEN, Mick	23	M	Laborer	23Ma02Hs
ODEE, Thos.	25	M	Laborer	23Ma02Hs
CONNORS, James	30	M	Laborer	23Ma02Hs
Moses	27	M	Laborer	23Ma02Hs
John	23	M	Laborer	23Ma02Hs
OWENS, John	55	M	Laborer	23Ma02Hs
U (W)	45	F	Servant	23Ma02Hs
Jane	20	F	Servant	23Ma02Hs
Elizabeth	18	F	Servant	23Ma02Hs
ELLES, Thomas	25	M	Laborer	23Ma02Hs
WILLIAMS, Israel	20	M	Laborer	23Ma02Hs
BAVEN, Job	24	M	Laborer	23Ma02Hs
DAVIS, John	21	M	Laborer	23Ma02Hs

NAMES OF PASSENGERS		AGE	SEX	OCCUPATIONS	DATE PORT SHIP
CAREY, Thomas		55	M	Laborer	23Ma02Hs
U	(W)	28	F	Servant	23Ma02Hs
Daniel	(S)	09	M	Child	23Ma02Hs
SCANLAN, Patrick		20	M	Laborer	23Ma02Hs
GALAGHER, Jaque		20	M	Laborer	23Ma02Hs
ODONNELL, Cath.		17	F	Servant	23Ma02Hs
MANLENS, Mary		15	F	Servant	23Ma02Hs
MCELERACE, John		15	M	Laborer	23Ma02Hs
Patrick		17	M	Laborer	23Ma02Hs
MAGOOVAN, John		30	M	Laborer	23Ma02Hs
U	(W)	30	F	Servant	23Ma02Hs
John	(S)	09	M	Child	23Ma02Hs
Saml.		07	M	Child	23Ma02Hs
Mary		06	F	Child	23Ma02Hs
MULRANY, John		26	M	Laborer	23Ma02Hs
HURSLEY, John		27	M	Laborer	23Ma02Hs
PHILLIPS, Rich.		34	M	Laborer	23Ma02Hs
MORGAN, Ebenezer		38	M	Laborer	23Ma02Hs
JONES, William		40	M	Laborer	23Ma02Hs
CORNELL, Mich.		24	M	Laborer	23Ma02Hs
LYNCH, Owen		14	M	Laborer	23Ma02Hs
Michl.		24	M	Laborer	23Ma02Hs
BARRETT, James		27	M	Laborer	23Ma02Hs
John		22	M	Laborer	23Ma02Hs
MCQUINLAN, Alex		25	M	Laborer	23Ma02Hs
DUFFE, Elizabeth		40	F	Servant	23Ma02Hs
Martin		11	M	Laborer	23Ma02Hs
Biddy		07	F	Child	23Ma02Hs
MCGUIRE, Cath.		10	F	Servant	23Ma02Hs
LYNCH, Pat		30	M	Laborer	23Ma02Hs
Mary		20	F	Servant	23Ma02Hs
HYNE, Pat		27	M	Laborer	23Ma02Hs
BOLAN, James		19	M	Laborer	23Ma02Hs
Bernard		15	M	Laborer	23Ma02Hs
Wm.		20	M	Laborer	23Ma02Hs
MCGUIRE, Bernard		21	M	Laborer	23Ma02Hs
RYAN, Mary		20	F	Servant	23Ma02Hs
BURKE, Mary		30	F	Servant	23Ma02Hs
FLEMMING, Sally		18	F	Servant	23Ma02Hs
John		14	M	Laborer	23Ma02Hs
NAUGHTON, Thomas		50	M	Laborer	23Ma02Hs
Sarah		30	F	Servant	23Ma02Hs
Thomas		08	M	Child	23Ma02Hs
MINTON, John		13	M	Laborer	23Ma02Hs
NAUGHTON, Dennis		50	M	Laborer	23Ma02Hs
Sarah		30	F	Laborer	23Ma02Hs
Thomas		08	M	Child	23Ma02Hs
MINTON, John		13	M	Laborer	23Ma02Hs
NAUGHTON, Dennis		20	M	Laborer	23Ma02Hs
CORNWAY, Edward		22	M	Laborer	23Ma02Hs
Mary		15	F	Servant	23Ma02Hs
HOLEHAN, John		23	M	Laborer	23Ma02Hs
ROURKE, Mary		21	F	Servant	23Ma02Hs
Mary		17	F	Servant	23Ma02Hs
KEARNEY, Harry		18	M	Laborer	23Ma02Hs
HANNIGAN, Thos.		22	M	Laborer	23Ma02Hs
MCCORMICK, Dennis		19	M	Laborer	23Ma02Hs
QUINN, John		08	M	Child	23Ma02Hs
SMITH, Peter		18	M	Laborer	23Ma02Hs
CONNISKY, Patk.		24	M	Laborer	23Ma02Hs
QUILLAN, Patk.		24	M	Laborer	23Ma02Hs
MURPHY, Hugh		18	M	Laborer	23Ma02Hs
Betty		18	F	Servant	23Ma02Hs
BYRNES, Mary		22	F	Servant	23Ma02Hs
LANEY, Rose		18	F	Servant	23Ma02Hs
FITZGERALD, John		24	M	Laborer	23Ma02Hs
CRENIN, John		30	M	Laborer	23Ma02Hs
Johanna		30	F	Servant	23Ma02Hs
Mary		22	F	Servant	23Ma02Hs
HARTNELL, Mick		22	M	Laborer	23Ma02Hs
FITZPATRICK, Nancy		24	F	Servant	23Ma02Hs
Margt.		22	F	Servant	23Ma02Hs
BIRTHINGHAM, John		27	M	Laborer	23Ma02Hs
HAYES, Honna		25	F	Servant	23Ma02Hs
Joshua		22	M	Laborer	23Ma02Hs

NAMES OF PASSENGERS		AGE	SEX	OCCUPATIONS	DATE PORT SHIP
HAYES, Ellen		26	F	Servant	23Ma02Hs
RONANS, John		24	M	Laborer	23Ma02Hs
LERVEY, Henry		27	M	Laborer	23Ma02Hs
Sarah		31	F	Servant	23Ma02Hs
HYNES, Danl		18	M	Laborer	23Ma02Hs
SIMPSON, Eliza		00	F	Servant	23Ma02Hs
NEVILLE, Richd.		28	M	Laborer	23Ma02Hs
DEWYER, Simy		22	M	Laborer	23Ma02Hs
HEAP, Betty		45	F	Servant	23Ma02Hs
John		20	M	Laborer	23Ma02Hs
James		18	M	Laborer	23Ma02Hs
Mary		16	F	Servant	23Ma02Hs
Hannah		13	F	Servant	23Ma02Hs
George		07	M	Child	23Ma02Hs
Bryann		03	M	Child	23Ma02Hs
LYONS, Daniel		30	M	Laborer	23Ma02Hs
Stephen		25	M	Laborer	23Ma02Hs
Margt.		28	F	Servant	23Ma02Hs
Ellen		60	F	Servant	23Ma02Hs
OHRIN, Owen		18	M	Servant	23Ma02Hs
Daniel		18	M	Laborer	23Ma02Hs
Thomas		28	M	Laborer	23Ma02Hs
QUINLAN, Wm.		40	M	Laborer	23Ma02Hs
Johanna		40	F	Servant	23Ma02Hs
Julia		14	F	Servant	23Ma02Hs
Wm.		09	M	Child	23Ma02Hs
FITZGERALD, Sally		22	F	Servant	23Ma02Hs
HARRINGTON, Thomas		30	M	Laborer	23Ma02Hs
DALY, Dennis		25	M	Laborer	23Ma02Hs
KELLY, Mich.		13	M	Laborer	23Ma02Hs
KENNEDY, John		22	M	Laborer	23Ma02Hs
GRANFELL, Mary		50	F	Servant	23Ma02Hs
Mary		19	F	Servant	23Ma02Hs
Thomas		17	M	Laborer	23Ma02Hs
Catherine		05	F	Child	23Ma02Hs
KENNEDY, Ellen		57	F	Servant	23Ma02Hs
SULLIVAN, Patk.		23	M	Laborer	23Ma02Hs
MURPHY, Ellen		20	F	Servant	23Ma02Hs
BOLAN, Mary		09	F	Child	23Ma02Hs
DUANY, Margt.		20	F	Servant	23Ma02Hs
REYNOLDS, Mary		19	F	Servant	23Ma02Hs
LOUGHLIN, John		20	M	Laborer	23Ma02Hs
FRAINE, Michl.		18	M	Laborer	23Ma02Hs
MCGUIRE, Mary		23	F	Laborer	23Ma02Hs
MURPHY, Michl.		31	M	Laborer	23Ma02Hs
ONEILL, James		20	M	Laborer	23Ma02Hs
DAGNAN, Cath.		30	F	Servant	23Ma02Hs
MURRAY, Patk.		25	M	Laborer	23Ma02Hs
Wm.		18	M	Laborer	23Ma02Hs
CLOONAN, Patk.		20	M	Laborer	23Ma02Hs
CUFF, Mick		20	M	Laborer	23Ma02Hs
U	(W)	30	F	Servant	23Ma02Hs
DOOLAN, Rose		36	F	Servant	23Ma02Hs
Jane		27	F	Servant	23Ma02Hs
REILY, John		20	M	Laborer	23Ma02Hs
Jane		30	F	Servant	23Ma02Hs
JONES, Wm.		17	M	Laborer	23Ma02Hs
Emma		18	F	Servant	23Ma02Hs
MORRIS, Phillip		28	M	Laborer	23Ma02Hs
U	(W)	27	F	Servant	23Ma02Hs
Jane		22	F	Servant	23Ma02Hs
Emma		09	F	Child	23Ma02Hs
SMITH, John		26	M	Laborer	23Ma02Hs
Emma		19	F	Servant	23Ma02Hs
Rose		04	F	Child	23Ma02Hs
WILLIAMSON, Saml.		09	M	Laborer	23Ma02Hs
JONES, Phebe		19	F	Servant	23Ma02Hs

JENNY-LIND 24 MAY 1848

From Liverpool

NAMES OF PASSENGERS	AGE	SEX	OCCUPATIONS	DATE PORT SHIP
GREEN, Michael	60	M	Laborer	24Ma02Ak
Michael	20	M	Laborer	24Ma02Ak
Patrick	25	M	Laborer	24Ma02Ak
Neil	20	M	Laborer	24Ma02Ak
Mary	13	F	Laborer	24Ma02Ak
FISHER, Mary	20	F	Laborer	24Ma02Ak
WILLOUGHBY, Isaac	20	M	Laborer	24Ma02Ak
CUNNINGHAM, Richd.	20	M	Laborer	24Ma02Ak
CALDWELL, Wm.	35	M	Laborer	24Ma02Ak
Cathr.	04	F	Child	24Ma02Ak
BLACKWELL, Sarah	40	F	Laborer	24Ma02Ak
Richd.Jno.	14	M	Laborer	24Ma02Ak
Sarah	11	F	Laborer	24Ma02Ak
CLOONE, Daniel	19	M	Laborer	24Ma02Ak
----OR, U	16	U	Laborer	24Ma02Ak
U, Mary	00	F	Laborer	24Ma02Ak
LANNAGAN, Nano	23	F	Laborer	24Ma02Ak
James	04	M	Child	24Ma02Ak
Cath.	.00	F	Infant	24Ma02Ak
GOGAN, William	30	M	Laborer	24Ma02Ak
Cathr.	20	F	Laborer	24Ma02Ak
David	.00	M	Infant	24Ma02Ak
Margt.	06	F	Child	24Ma02Ak
L---TT, Willm.	20	M	Laborer	24Ma02Ak
GRADY, Michl.	16	M	Laborer	24Ma02Ak
GRAHAM, Margt.	18	F	Laborer	24Ma02Ak
Ellen	16	F	Laborer	24Ma02Ak
HENNESSEY, Patk.	60	M	Laborer	24Ma02Ak
U (W)	50	F	Laborer	24Ma02Ak
Martin (S)	13	M	Laborer	24Ma02Ak
Ellen (D)	16	F	Laborer	24Ma02Ak
Cathr. (D)	04	F	Child	24Ma02Ak
Brian (S)	08	M	Child	24Ma02Ak
Mary (D)	06	F	Child	24Ma02Ak
SMITH, Mary	16	F	Laborer	24Ma02Ak
HAYES, Ivory	25	F	Laborer	24Ma02Ak
Mary	20	F	Laborer	24Ma02Ak
HIGGINS, Ellen	04	F	Child	24Ma02Ak
KENNAR, James	20	M	Laborer	24Ma02Ak
MCCARTY, Wm.	24	M	Laborer	24Ma02Ak
CONNOR, Johana	20	F	Laborer	24Ma02Ak
CLEARY, John	20	M	Laborer	24Ma02Ak
Dennis	20	M	Laborer	24Ma02Ak
OBRIEN, Mary	16	F	Laborer	24Ma02Ak
FISHER, Ellen	30	F	Laborer	24Ma02Ak
Ha-----N, Julia	20	F	Laborer	24Ma02Ak
MCGIVENS, Edwd.	25	M	Laborer	24Ma02Ak
SCOTT, Maria	20	F	Laborer	24Ma02Ak
BROWN, Catherine	16	F	Laborer	24Ma02Ak
BOHAN, Margt.	28	F	Unknown	24Ma02Ak
MCDONALD, U-Mrs.	30	F	Unknown	24Ma02Ak
SWEANEY, Mary	20	F	Unknown	24Ma02Ak
MANION, Ellen	20	F	Unknown	24Ma02Ak
DUNN, Henry	16	M	Unknown	24Ma02Ak
HEARY, Bridgt.	05	F	Child	24Ma02Ak
Mary	17	F	Laborer	24Ma02Ak
HEFFERN, James	20	M	Laborer	24Ma02Ak
BRADY, Bridget	20	F	Laborer	24Ma02Ak
MARTIN, Eliza	18	F	Laborer	24Ma02Ak
THOMPSON, Robt.	20	M	Laborer	24Ma02Ak
DAILEY, Rose	20	F	Laborer	24Ma02Ak
RABBIT, Mary	05	F	Child	24Ma02Ak
DOWED, Mary	20	F	Unknown	24Ma02Ak
EGAN, James	20	M	Unknown	24Ma02Ak
MCGUIRE, Mary	24	F	Unknown	24Ma02Ak

NAMES OF PASSENGERS	AGE	SEX	OCCUPATIONS	DATE PORT SHIP
CARVEY, Edwd.	16	M	Unknown	24Ma02Ak
Mary	15	F	Unknown	24Ma02Ak
Ann	11	F	Unknown	24Ma02Ak
OROUKE, Hugh	20	M	Unknown	24Ma02Ak
Phillip	18	M	Unknown	24Ma02Ak
GELLORCK, Cath.	20	F	Unknown	24Ma02Ak
DAVIES, Michl.	20	M	Unknown	24Ma02Ak
RATHEAN, John	20	M	Unknown	24Ma02Ak
SULLIVAN, John	30	M	Unknown	24Ma02Ak
LONDON, John	22	M	Unknown	24Ma02Ak
CONWAY, Margt.	20	F	Unknown	24Ma02Ak
Mary	04	F	Child	24Ma02Ak
HILL, Arthur	18	M	Unknown	24Ma02Ak
ELLIOTT, Andr.	15	M	Unknown	24Ma02Ak
DALEY, John	18	M	Unknown	24Ma02Ak
Thos.	13	M	Unknown	24Ma02Ak
REID, Matha	20	F	Unknown	24Ma02Ak
KELLY, Catherine	20	F	Unknown	24Ma02Ak
BRADLY, Phillip	24	M	Unknown	24Ma02Ak
MCGEE, Alice	50	F	Unknown	24Ma02Ak
ROBINSON, Mich.	12	M	Unknown	24Ma02Ak
Ellen	10	F	Unknown	24Ma02Ak
Mary	09	F	Child	24Ma02Ak
Bridget	05	F	Child	24Ma02Ak
Margt.	.00	F	Infant	24Ma02Ak
BARKLEY, Dennis	12	M	Unknown	24Ma02Ak
BOHANEY, John	50	M	Unknown	24Ma02Ak
Mary	50	F	Unknown	24Ma02Ak
James	16	M	Unknown	24Ma02Ak
Patk.	11	M	Unknown	24Ma02Ak
FITZGERALD, Wm.	24	M	Unknown	24Ma02Ak
ODONNELL, James	23	M	Unknown	24Ma02Ak
BRADY, Andrew	22	M	Unknown	24Ma02Ak
GALIGAN, Thos.	18	M	Unknown	24Ma02Ak
GILMOUR, Ellen	22	F	Unknown	24Ma02Ak
HALEY, Peter	07	M	Child	24Ma02Ak
MCMANUS, Magt.	20	F	Unknown	24Ma02Ak
Ann	20	F	Unknown	24Ma02Ak
LOOBY, Mary	25	F	Unknown	24Ma02Ak
Bridgt.	17	F	Unknown	24Ma02Ak
KELLEY, Peter-S.	20	M	Unknown	24Ma02Ak
KERRY, Thos.	07	M	Child	24Ma02Ak
Esther	08	F	Child	24Ma02Ak
MCHUGH, Owen	20	M	Unknown	24Ma02Ak
BUICHAN, Hugh	12	M	Unknown	24Ma02Ak
BOYLE, Bridgh.	20	F	Unknown	24Ma02Ak
DUGAN, John	03	M	Child	24Ma02Ak
KILDAY, Patk.	30	M	Unknown	24Ma02Ak
Mary	20	F	Unknown	24Ma02Ak
Margt.	12	F	Unknown	24Ma02Ak
MCKEOWN, Michl.	20	M	Unknown	24Ma02Ak
HORLEY, Mary	16	F	Unknown	24Ma02Ak
CROLLEY, Michl.	12	M	Unknown	24Ma02Ak
CORCORAN, Ellin	18	F	Unknown	24Ma02Ak
SULLIVAN, Patk.	20	M	Unknown	24Ma02Ak
Dennis	20	M	Unknown	24Ma02Ak
FALLIN, Margt.	18	F	Unknown	24Ma02Ak
MOORE, John	20	M	Unknown	24Ma02Ak
WHILLER, Ellen	20	F	Unknown	24Ma02Ak
HOGAN, Bryan	20	M	Unknown	24Ma02Ak
KILLEN, Teady	62	M	Unknown	24Ma02Ak
Ellen	50	F	Unknown	24Ma02Ak
Thos.	15	M	Unknown	24Ma02Ak
John	11	M	Unknown	24Ma02Ak
Mary	05	F	Child	24Ma02Ak
QUINGLEY, Cath.	16	F	Unknown	24Ma02Ak
Mary	14	F	Unknown	24Ma02Ak
CLEARY, Julia	16	F	Unknown	24Ma02Ak
JOHNSTON, Saml.	20	M	Unknown	24Ma02Ak
DUFFEY, Cathr.	18	F	Unknown	24Ma02Ak
HEARNY, Patk.	20	M	Unknown	24Ma02Ak
John	22	M	Unknown	24Ma02Ak
Cath.	18	F	Unknown	24Ma02Ak
CASSIDY, Margt.	20	F	Unknown	24Ma02Ak
CONNOR, Peter	22	M	Unknown	24Ma02Ak

NAMES OF PASSENGERS	AGE	SEX	OCCUPATIONS	DATE PORT SHIP
CARROLE, Bessey	20	F	Unknown	24Ma02Ak
COUGHLIN, Patk.	20	M	Unknown	24Ma02Ak
U, U	20	F	Unknown	24Ma02Ak
Cathr.	04	F	Child	24Ma02Ak
KEENAN, Judy	26	F	Unknown	24Ma02Ak
Cathr.	02	F	Child	24Ma02Ak
HAYS, James	20	M	Unknown	24Ma02Ak
MCMANNOS, Thos.	35	M	Unknown	24Ma02Ak
HILL, Willm.	20	M	Unknown	24Ma02Ak
BEARD, Joseph	20	M	Unknown	24Ma02Ak
DUDDY, Ellin	20	F	Unknown	24Ma02Ak
HALKIN, Michl.	40	M	Unknown	24Ma02Ak
DRISKILL, Patk.	25	M	Unknown	24Ma02Ak
CREEIN, Jno.	20	M	Unknown	24Ma02Ak
FOOLEY, James	20	M	Unknown	24Ma02Ak
COLLINS, Bridget	18	F	Unknown	24Ma02Ak
NOON, John	20	M	Unknown	24Ma02Ak
CAWRBEN, Mary	20	F	Unknown	24Ma02Ak
SMYTH, Cathr.	25	F	Unknown	24Ma02Ak
John	03	M	Child	24Ma02Ak
HARRINGTON, Richd.	28	M	Unknown	24Ma02Ak
Eliza	20	F	Unknown	24Ma02Ak
Ann	21	F	Unknown	24Ma02Ak
Joseph	16	M	Unknown	24Ma02Ak
Sarah	13	F	Unknown	24Ma02Ak
SCOTT, Lancastor	36	M	Unknown	24Ma02Ak
CORCORN, Mary	18	F	Unknown	24Ma02Ak
SULLIVAN, Mary	20	F	Unknown	24Ma02Ak
DALEY, Michl.	40	M	Unknown	24Ma02Ak
MCLAUGHKIN, Edward	23	M	Unknown	24Ma02Ak
Bessey	24	F	Unknown	24Ma02Ak
Edwd.	07	M	Child	24Ma02Ak
Mary	.00	F	Infant	24Ma02Ak
Lawrn.	20	M	Unknown	24Ma02Ak
LOWENTS, Margt.	20	F	Unknown	24Ma02Ak
Cathr.	15	F	Unknown	24Ma02Ak
CORNELL, Cathr.	18	F	Unknown	24Ma02Ak
RILEY, Mary	18	F	Unknown	24Ma02Ak
DONALLY, John	20	M	Unknown	24Ma02Ak
Mary	20	F	Unknown	24Ma02Ak
CLAIR, Ann	25	F	Unknown	24Ma02Ak
FERGUSON, Margt.	30	F	Unknown	24Ma02Ak
KENNY, Michl.	50	M	Unknown	24Ma02Ak
Mary	50	F	Unknown	24Ma02Ak
James	20	M	Unknown	24Ma02Ak

MESSENGER 24 MAY 1848

From Galway

NAMES OF PASSENGERS	AGE	SEX	OCCUPATIONS	DATE PORT SHIP
MOLLAN, Thos.	30	M	Unknown	24Ma11Ht
Peter	20	M	Unknown	24Ma11Ht
BELL, Jos.	28	M	Unknown	24Ma11Ht
DALLY, Patt	20	M	Unknown	24Ma11Ht
MURPHY, Patt	30	M	Unknown	24Ma11Ht
Ellen	26	F	Unknown	24Ma11Ht
Thos.	.00	M	Infant	24Ma11Ht
LYNCH, Jas.	30	M	Unknown	24Ma11Ht
MCCORMICK, Dennis	20	M	Unknown	24Ma11Ht
LYNCH, Michl.	30	M	Unknown	24Ma11Ht
KELLY, Thos.	29	M	Unknown	24Ma11Ht
KYNE, James	24	M	Unknown	24Ma11Ht
MAUGH, Edmund	30	M	Unknown	24Ma11Ht
Nancy	26	F	Unknown	24Ma11Ht
HAIR, Bridget	23	F	Unknown	24Ma11Ht
KENNY, Wm.	20	M	Unknown	24Ma11Ht
Chas.	16	M	Unknown	24Ma11Ht
NAUGHTON, Patt	24	M	Unknown	24Ma11Ht
HIGGINS, Jas.	30	M	Unknown	24Ma11Ht
NEWELL, Patt	32	M	Unknown	24Ma11Ht
SHEARS, George	16	M	Unknown	24Ma11Ht
MOLLOY, Biddy	23	F	Unknown	24Ma11Ht
HEFIN, Thos.	50	M	Unknown	24Ma11Ht
Died-At-Sea				
Eleanor	35	F	Unknown	24Ma11Ht
Mary	18	F	Unknown	24Ma11Ht
Ally	16	F	Unknown	24Ma11Ht
Died-At-Sea				
Cath.	13	F	Unknown	24Ma11Ht
Thos.	12	M	Unknown	24Ma11Ht
CONNOR, Patt	20	M	Unknown	24Ma11Ht
GERAGHTY, Timothy	27	M	Unknown	24Ma11Ht
Mary	22	F	Unknown	24Ma11Ht
Martin	32	M	Unknown	24Ma11Ht
HYNES, Patt	20	M	Unknown	24Ma11Ht
JOYCE, Peter	30	M	Unknown	24Ma11Ht
Biddy	25	F	Unknown	24Ma11Ht
HALLORAN, Ellen	20	F	Unknown	24Ma11Ht
LALLY, Michl.	22	M	Unknown	24Ma11Ht
Mary	20	F	Unknown	24Ma11Ht
HART, Edmond	25	M	Unknown	24Ma11Ht
Biddy	24	F	Unknown	24Ma11Ht
DOOLY, John	28	M	Unknown	24Ma11Ht
Mary	21	F	Unknown	24Ma11Ht
CAHILL, John	25	M	Unknown	24Ma11Ht
Mary	23	F	Unknown	24Ma11Ht
RUANE, Bridget	21	F	Unknown	24Ma11Ht
HIGGINS, Danl.	22	M	Unknown	24Ma11Ht
MAHON, Thos.	40	M	Unknown	24Ma11Ht
Biddy	35	F	Unknown	24Ma11Ht
BANE, John	40	M	Unknown	24Ma11Ht
Patt	21	M	Unknown	24Ma11Ht
BURKE, Martin	45	M	Unknown	24Ma11Ht
Biddy	45	F	Unknown	24Ma11Ht
Mary	22	F	Unknown	24Ma11Ht
Margt.	13	F	Unknown	24Ma11Ht
Honoria	09	F	Child	24Ma11Ht
Peter	13	M	Unknown	24Ma11Ht
MANION, Peter	18	M	Unknown	24Ma11Ht
HANNON, Patt	25	M	Unknown	24Ma11Ht
KING, Timothy	23	M	Unknown	24Ma11Ht
CAHILL, John	23	M	Unknown	24Ma11Ht
Mary	21	F	Unknown	24Ma11Ht
KEARNEY, Mary	45	F	Unknown	24Ma11Ht
GALVIN, Michl.	28	M	Unknown	24Ma11Ht
Ann	23	F	Unknown	24Ma11Ht
Biddy	.00	F	Infant	24Ma11Ht
QUINN, Martin	26	M	Unknown	24Ma11Ht
Bridget	32	F	Unknown	24Ma11Ht
COLEMAN, Cornelius	29	M	Unknown	24Ma11Ht
CROW, Ann	07	F	Child	24Ma11Ht
SULLIVAN, Jas.	12	M	Unknown	24Ma11Ht
MCDERMOTT, John	30	M	Unknown	24Ma11Ht
Bridget	25	F	Unknown	24Ma11Ht
Terrence	.00	M	Infant	24Ma11Ht
BURKE, Patt.	20	M	Unknown	24Ma11Ht
DUGAN, Patt.	18	M	Unknown	24Ma11Ht
DUFFY, Mary	18	F	Unknown	24Ma11Ht
COSGROVE, Michl.	18	M	Unknown	24Ma11Ht
COMMINS, Eleanor	24	F	Unknown	24Ma11Ht
BURKE, Ann	17	F	Unknown	24Ma11Ht
LYNCH, Biddy	30	F	Unknown	24Ma11Ht
Bartley	.00	M	Infant	24Ma11Ht
Mary	.00	F	Infant	24Ma11Ht
KELLY, Biddy	28	F	Unknown	24Ma11Ht
John	10	M	Unknown	24Ma11Ht
Thos.	07	M	Child	24Ma11Ht
Wm.	.00	M	Infant	24Ma11Ht
Francis	.00	M	Infant	24Ma11Ht
COSGROVE, Ellen	13	F	Unknown	24Ma11Ht
MARTIN, Patt	24	M	Unknown	24Ma11Ht
WILLIAMS, Elizabeth	10	F	Unknown	24Ma11Ht
KELLY, Edmond	34	M	Unknown	24Ma11Ht
Margt.	55	F	Unknown	24Ma11Ht

NAMES OF PASSENGERS	AGE	SEX	OCCUPATIONS	DATE PORT SHIP
MCTIGHE, Patt	22	M	Unknown	24Ma11Ht
SUMMERLY, John	28	M	Unknown	24Ma11Ht
Biddy	25	F	Unknown	24Ma11Ht
LYBOUGH, Patt	25	M	Unknown	24Ma11Ht
COLEMAN, Mary	20	F	Unknown	24Ma11Ht
RUANE, Bryan	38	M	Unknown	24Ma11Ht
GERAGHTY, Mary	22	F	Unknown	24Ma11Ht
LAFFY, Patt	27	M	Unknown	24Ma11Ht
ODONNELL, Christopher	30	M	Unknown	24Ma11Ht
Eliza	28	F	Unknown	24Ma11Ht
Martin	05	M	Child	24Ma11Ht
Bridget	.00	F	Infant	24Ma11Ht
Roderick	.00	M	Infant	24Ma11Ht
Edmond	27	M	Unknown	24Ma11Ht
Mary	24	F	Unknown	24Ma11Ht
CONNOR, Sabina	22	F	Unknown	24Ma11Ht
KYNE, Martin	25	M	Unknown	24Ma11Ht
CUNNIFF, John	22	M	Unknown	24Ma11Ht
MCDERMOT, Michl.	29	M	Unknown	24Ma11Ht
ABBINTON, Robt.	19	M	Unknown	24Ma11Ht
WILLIAMS, John	40	M	Unknown	24Ma11Ht
Wm.	35	M	Unknown	24Ma11Ht
Cath.	21	F	Unknown	24Ma11Ht
Mary	13	F	Unknown	24Ma11Ht
Wm.	19	M	Unknown	24Ma11Ht
MCNALLY, Eliza	24	F	Unknown	24Ma11Ht
JOYCE, Wm.	24	M	Unknown	24Ma11Ht
MURPHY, Michl.	25	M	Unknown	24Ma11Ht
TAFFE, Thos.	25	M	Unknown	24Ma11Ht
CANCANNON, Thos.	22	M	Unknown	24Ma11Ht
MURPHY, Patt.	30	M	Unknown	24Ma11Ht
MCDERMOTT, Thos.	.00	M	Infant	24Ma11Ht
CARROLL, Ann	40	F	Unknown	24Ma11Ht
Bridget	18	F	Unknown	24Ma11Ht
Mary	16	F	Unknown	24Ma11Ht
NOWLAN, Matthew	20	M	Unknown	24Ma11Ht
MCDONOUGH, Phillip	26	M	Unknown	24Ma11Ht
CONELLY, Timothy	30	M	Unknown	24Ma11Ht
FINIGAN, Edmond	21	M	Unknown	24Ma11Ht
GANNON, Ann	35	F	Unknown	24Ma11Ht
Patt	13	M	Unknown	24Ma11Ht
GRIFFY, Michl.	27	M	Unknown	24Ma11Ht
Biddy	24	F	Unknown	24Ma11Ht
WALLACE, Mary	31	F	Unknown	24Ma11Ht
GERAGHTY, Richd.	40	M	Unknown	24Ma11Ht
BODKIN, Mary	17	F	Unknown	24Ma11Ht
Michl.	20	M	Unknown	24Ma11Ht
KING, Biddy	16	F	Unknown	24Ma11Ht
CAREY, Michl.	24	M	Unknown	24Ma11Ht

COMMERCE 24 MAY 1848

From Liverpool

NAMES OF PASSENGERS	AGE	SEX	OCCUPATIONS	DATE PORT SHIP
ROUSE, Stephen	30	M	Laborer	24Ma02Ic
Mary	24	F	Laborer	24Ma02Ic
LEES, Robt.	50	M	Laborer	24Ma02Ic
Betty	44	F	Laborer	24Ma02Ic
LOWE, Joseph	18	M	Laborer	24Ma02Ic
Mary	13	F	Laborer	24Ma02Ic
Robert	11	M	Laborer	24Ma02Ic
TOMPSON, John	20	M	Laborer	24Ma02Ic
HEANEY, Pat	28	M	Laborer	24Ma02Ic
Rose	25	F	Laborer	24Ma02Ic
James	03	M	Child	24Ma02Ic
Francis	.00	M	Infant	24Ma02Ic
MCGURE, Andw.	40	M	Laborer	24Ma02Ic
FARRELLY, Thos.	21	M	Laborer	24Ma02Ic
Ann	40	F	Laborer	24Ma02Ic
FARRELLY, Mattw.	10	M	Laborer	24Ma02Ic
KEITHLEY, Mattw.	45	M	Laborer	24Ma02Ic
Mary	43	F	Laborer	24Ma02Ic
FEATHERTON, John	32	M	Laborer	24Ma02Ic
Sarah	26	F	Laborer	24Ma02Ic
Wm.	07	M	Child	24Ma02Ic
John	05	M	Child	24Ma02Ic
ALLEN, Wm.	24	M	Laborer	24Ma02Ic
TETLEY, James	40	M	Laborer	24Ma02Ic
Mary	40	F	Laborer	24Ma02Ic
JONES, John	32	M	Laborer	24Ma02Ic
Jane	40	F	Laborer	24Ma02Ic
John	24	M	Laborer	24Ma02Ic
SMITH, James	25	M	Laborer	24Ma02Ic
FERGUSON, Thos.	21	M	Laborer	24Ma02Ic
ODONNELL, Hugh	22	M	Laborer	24Ma02Ic
Mary	21	F	Laborer	24Ma02Ic
SCOTT, John	20	M	Laborer	24Ma02Ic
MCCOWN, Wm.	21	M	Laborer	24Ma02Ic
FLEMMING, James	22	M	Laborer	24Ma02Ic
SHERBURN, Wm.	36	M	Laborer	24Ma02Ic
GOODWARD, Edwd.	34	M	Laborer	24Ma02Ic
Joseph	25	M	Laborer	24Ma02Ic
WALSH, James	26	M	Laborer	24Ma02Ic
Michl.	22	M	Laborer	24Ma02Ic
FADDEN, John	25	M	Laborer	24Ma02Ic
DEMPSEY, Michl.	50	M	Laborer	24Ma02Ic
John	26	M	Laborer	24Ma02Ic
Ann	45	F	Laborer	24Ma02Ic
Rose	24	F	Laborer	24Ma02Ic
Margt.	20	F	Laborer	24Ma02Ic
MURPHY, Ann	06	F	Child	24Ma02Ic
HARRISON, Benj.	24	M	Laborer	24Ma02Ic
Esther	23	F	Laborer	24Ma02Ic
John	22	M	Laborer	24Ma02Ic
Catherine	16	F	Laborer	24Ma02Ic
Bridgt.	15	F	Laborer	24Ma02Ic
Mary	19	F	Laborer	24Ma02Ic
FARRELL, Judy	16	F	Laborer	24Ma02Ic
DEMPSEY, Cathr.	30	F	Laborer	24Ma02Ic
DONOHER, Edw.	30	M	Laborer	24Ma02Ic
WELDON, Christ.	30	M	Laborer	24Ma02Ic
Michl.	26	M	Laborer	24Ma02Ic
DULLAHAN, John	34	M	Laborer	24Ma02Ic
Mary	30	F	Laborer	24Ma02Ic
MADDEN, Mary	10	F	Laborer	24Ma02Ic
DUFF, Mattw.	26	M	Laborer	24Ma02Ic
DUNN, Michl.	26	M	Laborer	24Ma02Ic
GANENAN, John	25	M	Laborer	24Ma02Ic
KENT, John	20	M	Laborer	24Ma02Ic
MILROY, Bryan	36	M	Laborer	24Ma02Ic
John	13	M	Laborer	24Ma02Ic
Cathr.	36	F	Laborer	24Ma02Ic
BROWN, Martin	25	M	Laborer	24Ma02Ic
GAHAN, Martin	24	M	Laborer	24Ma02Ic
TOSH, Sarah	40	F	Laborer	24Ma02Ic
Mary	16	F	Laborer	24Ma02Ic
BROWN, John	43	M	Laborer	24Ma02Ic
Celia	16	F	Laborer	24Ma02Ic
Ann	19	F	Laborer	24Ma02Ic
Sarah	17	F	Laborer	24Ma02Ic
Mary-Ann	17	F	Laborer	24Ma02Ic
Julia	15	F	Laborer	24Ma02Ic
DELANEY, Wm.	30	M	Laborer	24Ma02Ic
KINSELLA, Wm.	26	M	Laborer	24Ma02Ic
JONES, John	30	M	Laborer	24Ma02Ic
BUCKLEY, John	18	M	Laborer	24Ma02Ic
Wm.	08	M	Child	24Ma02Ic
CARSON, John	21	M	Laborer	24Ma02Ic
MCGAUGHEY, Saml.	21	M	Laborer	24Ma02Ic
FLEMMING, Andw.	25	M	Laborer	24Ma02Ic
U (W)	23	F	Laborer	24Ma02Ic
DONOVAN, John	30	M	Laborer	24Ma02Ic
Judith	28	F	Laborer	24Ma02Ic
Mary	05	F	Child	24Ma02Ic

NAMES OF PASSENGERS	AGE	SEX	OCCUPATIONS	DATE PORT SHIP
DONOVAN, Kate	04	F	Child	24Ma02lc
Michl.	.00	M	Infant	24Ma02lc
SHEA, Edmond	30	M	Laborer	24Ma02lc
RYAN, Charles	23	M	Laborer	24Ma02lc
Thomas	40	M	Laborer	24Ma02lc
MULALY, Pat.	30	M	Laborer	24Ma02!c
BURKE, Michl.	35	M	Laborer	24Ma02lc
Mary	30	F	Laborer	24Ma02lc
Thomas	.00	M	Infant	24Ma02lc
DANIEL, James	35	M	Laborer	24Ma02lc
FLYNN, Michl.	35	M	Laborer	24Ma02lc
RYAN, John	18	M	Laborer	24Ma02lc
HYLAND, James	40	M	Laborer	24Ma02lc
NEILL, Ann	26	F	Laborer	24Ma02lc
REILLY, Thos.	20	M	Laborer	24Ma02lc
MCEVOY, Peter	22	M	Laborer	24Ma02lc
MCCORMICK, Ann	30	F	Laborer	24Ma02lc
HOWARD, Hannah	35	F	Laborer	24Ma02lc
DUFFEY, Martin	24	M	Laborer	24Ma02lc
FISHER, Joseph	45	M	Laborer	24Ma02lc
Joseph	15	M	Laborer	24Ma02lc
MCCLEAN, Michl.	24	M	Laborer	24Ma02lc
U (W)	22	F	Laborer	24Ma02lc
BARRETT, Pat.	50	M	Laborer	24Ma02lc
MCHUGH, Phillip	33	M	Laborer	24Ma02lc
GURL, John	30	M	Laborer	24Ma02lc
TELBOYS, Thos.	25	M	Laborer	24Ma02lc
ROSS, Richd.	30	M	Laborer	24Ma02lc
CUTLES, John	30	M	Laborer	24Ma02lc
COWLEY, Mary	17	F	Laborer	24Ma02lc
CONNOR, John	46	M	Laborer	24Ma02lc
Ann	17	F	Laborer	24Ma02lc
Cathr.	15	F	Laborer	24Ma02!c
Thomas	13	M	Laborer	24Ma02lc
Bridgt.	46	F	Laborer	24Ma02lc
Maria	11	F	Laborer	24Ma02lc
Peter	10	M	Laborer	24Ma02lc
John	08	M	Child	24Ma02lc
Matty	07	F	Child	24Ma02lc
James	05	M	Child	24Ma02lc
CATHCART, Jane	20	F	Laborer	24Ma02lc
DICKENSON, James	20	M	Laborer	24Ma02lc
Eliz.	22	F	Laborer	24Ma02lc
COTTON, John	25	M	Laborer	24Ma02lc
BUSHY, Ellen	30	F	Laborer	24Ma02lc
Mary	06	F	Child	24Ma02lc
Lawrence	03	M	Child	24Ma02lc
Peggy	.00	F	Infant	24Ma02lc
Died-At-Sea				
MULHOLAN, John	25	F	Laborer	24Ma02lc
BUCHANAN, Margt.	20	F	Laborer	24Ma02lc
DOUGHERTY, James	46	M	Laborer	24Ma02lc
William	11	M	Laborer	24Ma02lc
James	09	M	Child	24Ma02lc
DOWDALL, Andw.	24	M	Laborer	24Ma02lc
CAIN, Edwd.	32	M	Laborer	24Ma02lc
ESSINGTON, Thos.	26	M	Laborer	24Ma02lc
U (W)	24	F	Laborer	24Ma02lc
BRYAN, Bernd.	26	M	Laborer	24Ma02lc
Edward	24	M	Laborer	24Ma02lc
MCCLOUD, Roger	25	M	Laborer	24Ma02lc
BRODERICK, Bridgt.	25	F	Laborer	24Ma02lc
Alley	13	F	Laborer	24Ma02lc
SMITH, Joseph	35	M	Laborer	24Ma02lc
Jane	13	F	Laborer	24Ma02lc
Ann	11	F	Laborer	24Ma02lc
FLOOD, Danl.	26	M	Laborer	24Ma02lc
Cathrn.	40	F	Laborer	24Ma02lc
Mary	13	F	Laborer	24Ma02lc
Bernard	12	M	Laborer	24Ma02lc
MONTAGUE, David	25	M	Laborer	24Ma02lc
WALSH, John	24	M	Laborer	24Ma02lc
Johana	22	F	Spinster	24Ma02lc
NULTY, Jeremiah	20	M	Laborer	24Ma02lc
MUSBRIL, David	24	M	Laborer	24Ma02lc

NAMES OF PASSENGERS	AGE	SEX	OCCUPATIONS	DATE PORT SHIP
MURRY, Mary	26	F	Laborer	24Ma02lc
KEARNS, Simon	26	M	Laborer	24Ma02lc
Lucy	22	F	Laborer	24Ma02lc
CRAWFORD, Simon	19	M	Laborer	24Ma02lc
KENEDY, Michl.	20	M	Laborer	24Ma02lc
REYNOLDS, Pat	34	M	Laborer	24Ma02lc
Cathr.	30	F	Laborer	24Ma02lc
Charles	05	M	Child	24Ma02lc
John	.00	M	Infant	24Ma02lc
SHERIDAN, Pat	25	M	Laborer	24Ma02lc
HOTSON, Thomas	36	M	Laborer	24Ma02lc
John	28	M	Laborer	24Ma02lc
Wm.	25	M	Laborer	24Ma02lc
James	16	M	Laborer	24Ma02lc
Betty	26	F	Laborer	24Ma02lc
James	03	M	Child	24Ma02lc
Michl.	.00	M	Infant	24Ma02lc
FOX, Arthur	31	M	Laborer	24Ma02lc
Sarah	24	F	Laborer	24Ma02lc
Robert	.00	M	Infant	24Ma02lc
BRETT, James	21	M	Laborer	24Ma02lc
Mary-Ann	40	F	Laborer	24Ma02lc
Mary-Ann	19	F	Laborer	24Ma02lc
Catharine	12	F	Laborer	24Ma02lc
CARR, Henry	32	M	Laborer	24Ma02lc
BERROW, James	33	M	Laborer	24Ma02lc
Mary	26	F	Laborer	24Ma02lc
KELLY, Andw.	24	M	Laborer	24Ma02lc
GILL, Michl.	18	M	Laborer	24Ma02lc
CARRAGHER, Philip	40	M	Laborer	24Ma02lc
CASH, John	17	M	Laborer	24Ma02lc
BASSIKIN, Joseph	17	M	Laborer	24Ma02lc
REILLY, Pat	29	M	Laborer	24Ma02lc
MCGOVERN, Thomas	30	M	Laborer	24Ma02lc
Cathr.	30	F	Laborer	24Ma02lc
OSHAUGHNESSEY, Michl.	21	M	Laborer	24Ma02lc
MURTHA, Edwd.	25	M	Laborer	24Ma02lc
HERREN, Cathr.	32	F	Laborer	24Ma02lc
William	03	M	Child	24Ma02lc
WALSH, Jane	16	F	Laborer	24Ma02lc
Peirce	26	M	Laborer	24Ma02lc
John	26	M	Laborer	24Ma02lc
Margt.	30	F	Laborer	24Ma02lc
Ellen	27	F	Laborer	24Ma02lc
BARRY, John	40	M	Laborer	24Ma02lc
Mary	40	F	Laborer	24Ma02lc
Ellen	60	F	Laborer	24Ma02lc
Thomas	35	M	Laborer	24Ma02lc
HUGHES, Robt.	25	M	Laborer	24Ma02lc
DUNN, Timy.	54	M	Laborer	24Ma02lc
Thos.	17	M	Laborer	24Ma02lc
Mary	50	F	Laborer	24Ma02lc
THOMPSON, Robert	20	M	Laborer	24Ma02lc
WALKER, Fredk.	29	M	Laborer	24Ma02lc
FORSETH, William	25	M	Laborer	24Ma02lc
CONNELL, Michl.	25	M	Laborer	24Ma02lc
DOWLEN, Barney	28	M	Laborer	24Ma02lc

BLAKE 24 MAY 1848

From Liverpool

NAMES OF PASSENGERS	AGE	SEX	OCCUPATIONS	DATE PORT SHIP
QUIN, John	50	M	Laborer	24Ma02ld
Alley	50	F	Laborer	24Ma02ld
Margt.	18	F	Laborer	24Ma02ld
Barnard	13	M	Laborer	24Ma02ld
John	11	M	Laborer	24Ma02ld
Alice	02	F	Child	24Ma02ld
LONOGAON, James	27	M	Laborer	24Ma02ld

NAMES OF PASSENGERS		AGE	SEX	OCCUPATIONS	DATE PORT SHIP
CLANCY, John		27	M	Laborer	24Ma02Id
ROURKE, Patt.		32	M	Laborer	24Ma02Id
Bart.		24	M	Laborer	24Ma02Id
MANSWELL, Thomas		26	M	Laborer	24Ma02Id
REGAN, John		24	M	Laborer	24Ma02Id
ROURK, Margt.		20	F	Laborer	24Ma02Id
SHANE, Mary		20	F	Laborer	24Ma02Id
CARROLL, David		28	M	Laborer	24Ma02Id
LOUGHLEN, John		20	M	Laborer	24Ma02Id
James		18	M	Laborer	24Ma02Id
SAUCE, Richard		30	M	Laborer	24Ma02Id
LACKEY, James		30	M	Laborer	24Ma02Id
U	(W)	27	F	Wife	24Ma02Id
Phil	(S)	04	M	Child	24Ma02Id
Mary-Ann	(D)	03	F	Child	24Ma02Id
CORMELL, Bridgt.		17	F	Laborer	24Ma02Id
FARLEY, Ann		17	F	Laborer	24Ma02Id
HEOG, Thomas		30	M	Laborer	24Ma02Id
James		21	M	Laborer	24Ma02Id
MCNALLY, Thomas		36	M	Laborer	24Ma02Id
Mary		34	F	Laborer	24Ma02Id
Christ.		.00	U	Infant	24Ma02Id
KELLY, John		35	M	Laborer	24Ma02Id
MCGRAGAM, Patt		24	M	Laborer	24Ma02Id
Cathr.		22	F	Laborer	24Ma02Id
Mary		20	F	Laborer	24Ma02Id
HALL, Betty		40	F	Laborer	24Ma02Id
Charles		20	M	Laborer	24Ma02Id
John		17	M	Laborer	24Ma02Id
Samuel		12	M	Laborer	24Ma02Id
HOTSON, Sarah		10	F	Unknown	24Ma02Id
BOYLAN, Patt		30	M	Unknown	24Ma02Id
PHAHAM, Mary		21	F	Unknown	24Ma02Id
JALEN, Thady		25	M	Unknown	24Ma02Id
Mary		23	F	Unknown	24Ma02Id
GORMLY, Michael		26	M	Laborer	24Ma02Id
Mary		20	F	Laborer	24Ma02Id
May		22	F	Laborer	24Ma02Id
CARROLL, James		18	M	Laborer	24Ma02Id
Daniel		13	M	Laborer	24Ma02Id
EVRY, John		33	M	Laborer	24Ma02Id
U	(W)	33	F	Laborer	24Ma02Id
Richard	(S)	09	M	Child	24Ma02Id
Eliza	(D)	04	F	Child	24Ma02Id
John	(S)	02	M	Child	24Ma02Id
JOLO, Rd.		64	M	Laborer	24Ma02Id
Mary		.00	F	Infant	24Ma02Id
BLANCH, Edward		30	M	Laborer	24Ma02Id
NALLY, Cathr.		20	F	Laborer	24Ma02Id
HARTLEY, Patt.		27	M	Laborer	24Ma02Id
SHERAN, Bridget		40	F	Laborer	24Ma02Id
SULLIVAN, Jinny		22	F	Laborer	24Ma02Id
SMITH, Andw.		25	M	Laborer	24Ma02Id
U	(W)	25	F	Laborer	24Ma02Id
John	(S)	.00	M	Infant	24Ma02Id
SHERIDAN, Matilda		19	F	Laborer	24Ma02Id
Alley		17	F	Spinster	24Ma02Id
BRADY, Mary		18	F	Spinster	24Ma02Id
Cathr.		16	F	Spinster	24Ma02Id
FINNIGAN, Ann		18	F	Spinster	24Ma02Id
WESSIN, Gedl.		40	U	Spinster	24Ma02Id
CLARK, James		20	M	Laborer	24Ma02Id
Rose		18	F	Laborer	24Ma02Id
Magt.		18	F	Laborer	24Ma02Id
MEADEN, Rd.		24	M	Laborer	24Ma02Id
MANNICK, Thomas		36	M	Laborer	24Ma02Id
COTT, Gedl.		27	U	Laborer	24Ma02Id
BURREY, Francis		25	M	Laborer	24Ma02Id
SHILES, Thomas		20	M	Laborer	24Ma02Id
RIELLY, Hugh		21	M	Laborer	24Ma02Id
MEEHAN, Margt.		23	F	Laborer	24Ma02Id
HYDEN, Wm.		28	M	Laborer	24Ma02Id
U	(W)	24	F	Spinster	24Ma02Id
Joseph	(S)	07	M	Child	24Ma02Id
Ann	(D)	04	F	Child	24Ma02Id
HYDEN, Jane	(D)	02	F	Child	24Ma02Id
BUCKLEY, John		24	M	Spinner	24Ma02Id
MCGREE, Wm.		24	M	Spinner	24Ma02Id
BURRIT, Mary		18	F	Spinster	24Ma02Id
MURPHY, Biddy		18	F	Spinster	24Ma02Id
LUCAS, James		25	M	Unknown	24Ma02Id
U	(W)	25	F	Unknown	24Ma02Id
Jesseness		.00	U	Infant	24Ma02Id
Elann		.00	F	Infant	24Ma02Id
BANNON, Daniel		35	M	Laborer	24Ma02Id
U	(W)	31	F	Wife	24Ma02Id
Jane	(D)	.00	F	Infant	24Ma02Id
COORLAN, Andw.		20	M	Laborer	24Ma02Id
Terence		20	M	Laborer	24Ma02Id
HARRISON, Wm.		25	M	Laborer	24Ma02Id
Jervis		25	M	Laborer	24Ma02Id
Robert		25	M	Laborer	24Ma02Id
Wm.		07	M	Child	24Ma02Id
CLARK, Philip		55	M	Laborer	24Ma02Id
U	(W)	53	F	Laborer	24Ma02Id
Mary	(D)	20	F	Laborer	24Ma02Id
Owen	(S)	18	M	Laborer	24Ma02Id
Thomas	(S)	16	M	Laborer	24Ma02Id
Ann	(D)	13	F	Laborer	24Ma02Id
James	(S)	11	M	Laborer	24Ma02Id
Rose	(D)	09	F	Child	24Ma02Id
REILLY, Alice		20	F	Laborer	24Ma02Id
SMITH, Cathr.		17	F	Laborer	24Ma02Id
CLARKE, Cathr.		56	F	Wife	24Ma02Id
MICHAN, James		15	M	Laborer	24Ma02Id
BURKE, James		60	M	Laborer	24Ma02Id
HENRY, Michael		25	M	Laborer	24Ma02Id
NEAVIN, James		25	M	Laborer	24Ma02Id
FINNEY, Thomas		25	M	Laborer	24Ma02Id
HONON, Martin		25	M	Laborer	24Ma02Id
RICHARDSON, Wm.W.		26	M	Laborer	24Ma02Id
U	(W)	26	F	Laborer	24Ma02Id
LOUGHLIN, Cathr.		35	F	Laborer	24Ma02Id
Michael		21	M	Laborer	24Ma02Id
Johana		12	F	Laborer	24Ma02Id
Thomas		08	M	Child	24Ma02Id
HEALY, John		45	M	Laborer	24Ma02Id
Jerh.		12	M	Laborer	24Ma02Id
REILLY, Peter		20	M	Laborer	24Ma02Id
DUFFERINN, John		46	M	Laborer	24Ma02Id
U	(W)	40	F	Laborer	24Ma02Id
PARKER, James		18	M	Laborer	24Ma02Id
FENEY, Pat		25	M	Laborer	24Ma02Id
U	(W)	24	F	Laborer	24Ma02Id
MCCORMICK, John		35	M	Laborer	24Ma02Id
Mary	(W)	30	F	Wife	24Ma02Id
John	(S)	09	M	Child	24Ma02Id
Robert	(S)	04	M	Child	24Ma02Id
Isabella	(D)	04	F	Child	24Ma02Id
Mary-Ann	(D)	.00	F	Infant	24Ma02Id
MARTIN, Mary		50	F	Wife	24Ma02Id
BERRY, Charles		21	M	Unknown	24Ma02Id
BOSWELL, Josiah		24	M	Unknown	24Ma02Id
ROBERTS, Thomas		30	M	Laborer	24Ma02Id
BUELL, Richard		32	M	Unknown	24Ma02Id
KNOX, Ann		25	F	Wife	24Ma02Id
HAIGH, Thomas		34	M	Laborer	24Ma02Id
KEENA, John		20	M	Unknown	24Ma02Id
BRANNAN, Michael		22	M	Unknown	24Ma02Id
MORRIS, Thomas		18	M	Unknown	24Ma02Id
LAWLER, Pat		21	M	Unknown	24Ma02Id
GRADY, Pat		25	M	Unknown	24Ma02Id
FELAN, Sarah		20	F	Spinster	24Ma02Id
DRENNAN, Margt.		24	F	Unknown	24Ma02Id
Ellen		20	F	Unknown	24Ma02Id
DEGAN, John		20	M	Laborer	24Ma02Id
Cathr.		18	F	Unknown	24Ma02Id
MCGUIRE, Bernd.		18	M	Unknown	24Ma02Id
STEWART, Matthew		11	M	Unknown	24Ma02Id
SULLIVAN, Peter		30	M	Unknown	24Ma02Id

NAMES OF PASSENGERS		AGE	SEX	OCCUPATIONS	DATE PORT SHIP
SULLIVAN, Mary		24	F	Unknown	24Ma02ld
Thomas		.00	M	Infant	24Ma02ld
Thomas		26	M	Laborer	24Ma02ld
KEEGAN, John		40	M	Laborer	24Ma02ld
HOFFMAN, John		31	M	Laborer	24Ma02ld
HAYES, Mary		30	F	Spinster	24Ma02ld
HOFFMAN, Sarah		24	F	Spinster	24Ma02ld
LYNCH, Ann		30	F	Spinster	24Ma02ld
Laurence		.00	M	Infant	24Ma02ld
STOCKMAN, Thomas		22	M	Spinner	24Ma02ld
Rachal		47	F	Spinster	24Ma02ld
PLATT, Robert		34	M	Laborer	24Ma02ld
HOGAN, Michael		34	M	Laborer	24Ma02ld
MULVEY, Willm.		21	M	Laborer	24Ma02ld
KELLY, Thomas		21	M	Laborer	24Ma02ld
SWORDS, Cathrin		20	F	Laborer	24Ma02ld
HAYS, Elizth.		21	F	Laborer	24Ma02ld
DUNN, Barnard		18	M	Laborer	24Ma02ld
KILONNORY, Thomas		20	M	Laborer	24Ma02ld
TAYLOR, James		24	M	Laborer	24Ma02ld
GULLEN, James		26	M	Laborer	24Ma02ld
MINTON, Thomas		24	M	Laborer	24Ma02ld
Robert		22	M	Laborer	24Ma02ld
ANDERSON, James		22	M	Laborer	24Ma02ld
HANNON, Moris		22	M	Laborer	24Ma02ld
GRADY, Judy		23	F	Laborer	24Ma02ld
ROWAN, Hugh		30	M	Laborer	24Ma02ld
John		21	M	Laborer	24Ma02ld
HOOD, Janette		30	F	Laborer	24Ma02ld
George		12	M	Laborer	24Ma02ld
Janette		07	F	Child	24Ma02ld
Mary		.00	F	Infant	24Ma02ld
EDMONDS, Benjn.		40	M	Laborer	24Ma02ld
Maria	(W)	40	F	Wife	24Ma02ld
CHEVERS, Sidney		20	M	Laborer	24Ma02ld
Isabella		20	F	Laborer	24Ma02ld
CALLAN, Christfr.		23	M	Laborer	24Ma02ld
MOODY, James		25	M	Laborer	24Ma02ld
MCGRATH, Jane		18	F	Laborer	24Ma02ld
MOONEY, Rose		18	F	Laborer	24Ma02ld
CALLAN, Hugh		50	M	Laborer	24Ma02ld
Elizth.		40	F	Laborer	24Ma02ld
John		30	M	Laborer	24Ma02ld
Margt.		14	F	Laborer	24Ma02ld
Betty		12	F	Laborer	24Ma02ld
NEAL, John		40	M	Laborer	24Ma02ld
CARROLL, Patr.		21	M	Laborer	24Ma02ld
JOHNSON, Jas.		35	M	Laborer	24Ma02ld
Cathr.		18	F	Laborer	24Ma02ld
Pat		14	M	Laborer	24Ma02ld
Margt.		09	F	Child	24Ma02ld
Jane		06	F	Child	24Ma02ld
Sarah		04	F	Child	24Ma02ld
HURLEY, James		40	M	Laborer	24Ma02ld
Margt.		35	F	Laborer	24Ma02ld
Henry		05	M	Child	24Ma02ld
Michl.		02	M	Child	24Ma02ld
Mary		.00	F	Infant	24Ma02ld
OBRIEN, Henry		24	M	Laborer	24Ma02ld
Ann		20	F	Laborer	24Ma02ld
HAND, James		35	M	Laborer	24Ma02ld
Margt.		25	F	Laborer	24Ma02ld
James		12	M	Laborer	24Ma02ld
Ann		10	F	Laborer	24Ma02ld
CONNELL, Pat		23	M	Laborer	24Ma02ld
MCATEE, Ann		25	F	Laborer	24Ma02ld
Mary		23	F	Laborer	24Ma02ld
SMITH, Cathr.		23	F	Laborer	24Ma02ld
MALONEY, Wm.		30	M	Laborer	24Ma02ld
Ellen		30	F	Spinster	24Ma02ld
Dennis		40	M	Spinner	24Ma02ld
BERNIS, Mary		28	F	Spinster	24Ma02ld
ERWIN, James		24	M	Spinner	24Ma02ld
Bridgt.		21	F	Spinster	24Ma02ld
KIRK, Thomas		24	M	Laborer	24Ma02ld
BRISTOW, Enoch		24	M	Laborer	24Ma02ld
ELLIOTT, Ann		36	F	Laborer	24Ma02ld
SIMSON, Mary-A.		30	F	Wife	24Ma02ld
James	(S)	01	M	Child	24Ma02ld
PENDERGAST, Mary		23	F	Unknown	24Ma02ld
FOGARTY, Mary		30	F	Unknown	24Ma02ld
ERWIN, Mattw.		20	M	Laborer	24Ma02ld
CUNNINGHAM, Chas.		16	M	Laborer	24Ma02ld
Mary		22	F	Laborer	24Ma02ld
James		20	M	Laborer	24Ma02ld
MCCUE, Julia		19	F	Laborer	24Ma02ld
BRADY, James		17	M	Laborer	24Ma02ld
WALSH, Mathew		12	M	Laborer	24Ma02ld
MCKEVINAN, Bernd.		25	M	Laborer	24Ma02ld
DOYLE, James		25	M	Laborer	24Ma02ld
Ellen	(W)	21	F	Wife	24Ma02ld
FLEARY, Wm.		36	M	Laborer	24Ma02ld
Julia		24	F	Laborer	24Ma02ld
Mary		07	F	Child	24Ma02ld
MEDLEY, Betty		23	F	Laborer	24Ma02ld
RYAN, Eliza		20	F	Laborer	24Ma02ld
MURPHY, Peter		20	M	Laborer	24Ma02ld
FOX, Cathr.		.00	F	Infant	24Ma02ld
DAVIES, Geo.		24	M	Laborer	24Ma02ld
FINLEY, Wm.		25	M	Laborer	24Ma02ld
Margt.		16	F	Spinster	24Ma02ld
MCMAHON, Mary		16	F	Spinster	24Ma02ld
CARTER, Betty		15	F	Spinster	24Ma02ld
OBRIAN, Thomas		11	M	Unknown	24Ma02ld
NOLAND, Pat		25	M	Unknown	24Ma02ld
HAYES, John		35	M	Unknown	24Ma02ld
HURLEY, Patk.		07	M	Child	24Ma02ld

INTRINSIC 24 MAY 1848

From Liverpool

NAMES OF PASSENGERS	AGE	SEX	OCCUPATIONS	DATE PORT SHIP
FARRA, John	27	M	Laborer	24Ma02lh
PINDAR, Elijah	30	M	Laborer	24Ma02lh
MCORMAC, Jno.	19	M	Laborer	24Ma02lh
PINDAR, Susan	25	F	Seamstress	24Ma02lh
BAXTER, Saml.	14	M	Laborer	24Ma02lh
MARTIN, John	21	M	Laborer	24Ma02lh
CONNELLY, James	21	M	Laborer	24Ma02lh
OWENS, Peter	19	M	Laborer	24Ma02lh
QUINN, James	20	M	Laborer	24Ma02lh
ONEILL, Martin	17	M	Laborer	24Ma02lh
MCGARTNLY, Barny	18	M	Laborer	24Ma02lh
Ha-----, James	00	M	Laborer	24Ma02lh
WHALLING, Pat.	26	M	Laborer	24Ma02lh
WHEELING, John	28	M	Laborer	24Ma02lh
FOLLY, Edwd.	24	M	Laborer	24Ma02lh
KENNEDY, James	27	M	Laborer	24Ma02lh
DOWD, James	21	M	Laborer	24Ma02lh
MARTIN, James	21	M	Laborer	24Ma02lh
BAXTER, Thomas	09	M	Child	24Ma02lh
Sarah	04	F	Child	24Ma02lh
William	11	M	Unknown	24Ma02lh
Florilla	34	F	Seamstress	24Ma02lh
MAGILL, John	21	M	Laborer	24Ma02lh
James	24	M	Laborer	24Ma02lh
Robt.	26	M	Laborer	24Ma02lh
Elisha	13	F	Unknown	24Ma02lh
James	55	M	Laborer	24Ma02lh
MCKAY, Mary	03	F	Child	24Ma02lh
MAGILL, Janet	22	F	Seamstress	24Ma02lh
SMITH, Andw.	24	M	Laborer	24Ma02lh
Mary	20	F	None	24Ma02lh
James	02	M	Child	24Ma02lh

NAMES OF PASSENGERS		AGE	SEX	OCCUPATIONS	DATE PORT SHIP
SMITH, Eliza		02	F	Child	24Ma02lh
Grace		.00	F	Infant	24Ma02lh
GAVIN, James		20	M	Laborer	24Ma02lh
CONOLLY, Peter		18	M	Laborer	24Ma02lh
DOHEN, Mary		27	F	Seamstress	24Ma02lh
SMYLIE, Jane		40	F	Seamstress	24Ma02lh
Margt.		21	F	Seamstress	24Ma02lh
Mary-Jane		17	F	Seamstress	24Ma02lh
John		12	M	Unknown	24Ma02lh
ONEILL, Owen		12	M	Unknown	24Ma02lh
BOYLE, Pat.		20	M	Laborer	24Ma02lh
LEWIS, Jenkin		37	M	Laborer	24Ma02lh
CAROLL, Marjery		37	F	Seamstress	24Ma02lh
FERRIE, Anne		25	F	Seamstress	24Ma02lh
INGLES, Michl.		24	M	Laborer	24Ma02lh
MCCALLUM, Wm.		25	M	Laborer	24Ma02lh
Cathrn.		24	F	Seamstress	24Ma02lh
Mary-Ann		12	F	Unknown	24Ma02lh
Lane		07	F	Child	24Ma02lh
Fany		05	F	Child	24Ma02lh
Gamble		03	M	Child	24Ma02lh
U		.00	U	Infant	24Ma02lh
RYAN, Patk.		25	M	Laborer	24Ma02lh
NETTAN, Moses		30	M	Laborer	24Ma02lh
KEEGAN, John		20	M	Laborer	24Ma02lh
MCEWEN, Collin		40	M	Laborer	24Ma02lh
MACKAN, Saml.		21	M	Laborer	24Ma02lh
CASY, John		21	M	Laborer	24Ma02lh
BROPHY, Michl.		18	M	Laborer	24Ma02lh
CLEARY, Roger		18	M	Laborer	24Ma02lh
BRADY, John		20	M	Laborer	24Ma02lh
MCGAVIN, Barny		40	M	Laborer	24Ma02lh
HANLAN, Michl.		17	M	Laborer	24Ma02lh
BRADY, John		18	M	Laborer	24Ma02lh
DOLLAN, Luke		40	M	Laborer	24Ma02lh
Michl.		30	M	Laborer	24Ma02lh
POWELL, Michl.		19	M	Laborer	24Ma02lh
COLLIGAN, Edwd.		30	M	Laborer	24Ma02lh
BRADY, Phil.		22	M	Laborer	24Ma02lh
MCWILLIAM, Jno.		22	M	Laborer	24Ma02lh
CAIN, Michl.		24	M	Laborer	24Ma02lh
MORAN, Pat.		25	M	Laborer	24Ma02lh
KENNEDY, Mgt.		21	F	Seamstress	24Ma02lh
FLYNN, Jno.		27	M	Laborer	24Ma02lh
DONAHAN, James		24	M	Laborer	24Ma02lh
DUNN, Jno.		20	M	Laborer	24Ma02lh
DILLAN, Michl.		20	M	Laborer	24Ma02lh
BRADY, James		40	M	Laborer	24Ma02lh
Pat.		16	M	Laborer	24Ma02lh
Margt.		04	F	Child	24Ma02lh
John		08	M	Child	24Ma02lh
Susan		11	F	Unknown	24Ma02lh
KENNEDY, Bridget		27	F	Seamstress	24Ma02lh
Susan		22	F	Seamstress	24Ma02lh
ONEILL, Mary		45	F	Seamstress	24Ma02lh
LETHAR, Bridgt.		25	F	Seamstress	24Ma02lh
MCCABE, Owen		21	M	Laborer	24Ma02lh
BROWN, Margt.		16	F	Seamstress	24Ma02lh
SCANLON, Thos.		26	M	Laborer	24Ma02lh
NEILL, Mary		23	F	Seamstress	24Ma02lh
William		26	M	Laborer	24Ma02lh
Helen		23	F	Seamstress	24Ma02lh
MAGNER, Mary		22	F	Seamstress	24Ma02lh
Cathrn.		17	F	Seamstress	24Ma02lh
HOGAN, John		19	M	Laborer	24Ma02lh
Margt.		21	F	Seamstress	24Ma02lh
OFARRA, Helen		24	F	Seamstress	24Ma02lh
BROADFOOT, James		40	M	Laborer	24Ma02lh
Thomas		03	M	Child	24Ma02lh
U		40	F	Seamstress	24Ma02lh
Margt.		14	F	Seamstress	24Ma02lh
LOAN, Hannah		25	F	Seamstress	24Ma02lh
SLANE, Ellen		24	F	Seamstress	24Ma02lh
CARSON, George		28	M	Laborer	24Ma02lh
BROADFOOT, Isabella		08	F	Child	24Ma02lh
SLANE, Joshua		25	M	Laborer	24Ma02lh
LAUREL, John		40	M	Laborer	24Ma02lh
U	(W)	30	F	Seamstress	24Ma02lh
Anne	(D)	.00	F	Infant	24Ma02lh
BROCK, Owen		50	M	Laborer	24Ma02lh
RYAN, Mary		21	F	Seamstress	24Ma02lh
DOLLAHIDE, Thos.		19	M	Laborer	24Ma02lh
LAMAN, Margt.		07	F	Child	24Ma02lh
BRYAN, Michl.		28	M	Laborer	24Ma02lh
MCGAVIN, Barry		.00	M	Infant	24Ma02lh
U-Mrs.		40	F	Seamstress	24Ma02lh
Margt.		18	F	Seamstress	24Ma02lh
COILL, Owen		16	M	Laborer	24Ma02lh
MCARROLL, Mary		22	F	Seamstress	24Ma02lh
FOLLIN, Mary-Anne		19	F	Seamstress	24Ma02lh
MCAROLL, Pat.		19	M	Laborer	24Ma02lh
DUNN, Michael		25	M	Laborer	24Ma02lh
MURRAY, Patk.		26	M	Laborer	24Ma02lh
MCGOLDRICK, Mary		27	F	Seamstress	24Ma02lh
FMURRAY, Anne		21	F	Seamstress	24Ma02lh
COFFIN, Thos.		35	M	Laborer	24Ma02lh
U	(W)	35	F	Seamstress	24Ma02lh
Mgt.	(D)	.00	F	Infant	24Ma02lh
Mary	(D)	11	F	Unknown	24Ma02lh
Rosy	(D)	09	F	Child	24Ma02lh
Thomas	(S)	07	M	Child	24Ma02lh
MORSY, Anne		25	F	Seamstress	24Ma02lh
COLMAN, Helen		26	F	Seamstress	24Ma02lh
TOLL, Mary-Ann		25	F	Seamstress	24Ma02lh
MCQUAY, Mary-Ann		.00	F	Infant	24Ma02lh
MCGAVIN, Ann		20	F	Seamstress	24Ma02lh
MORAN, Maria		18	F	Seamstress	24Ma02lh
MOSY, Betty		40	F	Seamstress	24Ma02lh
LOVEIN, Ann		20	F	Seamstress	24Ma02lh
RONY, James		20	M	Laborer	24Ma02lh
MORAN, Ellen		30	F	Seamstress	24Ma02lh
Pat		19	M	Laborer	24Ma02lh
RIGBY, John		24	M	Laborer	24Ma02lh
MCGLONE, Thos.		27	M	Laborer	24Ma02lh
REGAN, Pat.		21	M	Laborer	24Ma02lh
RIND, Rosy		20	F	Seamstress	24Ma02lh
HOLDEN, Anne		28	F	Seamstress	24Ma02lh
CROFTON, Mary		20	F	Seamstress	24Ma02lh
LYNCH, Thomas		22	M	Laborer	24Ma02lh
DOLLAHIDE, Pat		25	M	Laborer	24Ma02lh
BUCHAN, Pat.		20	M	Laborer	24Ma02lh
FITZPATRICK, Michl.		18	M	Laborer	24Ma02lh
CRAIG, Mary		20	F	Seamstress	24Ma02lh
KILKENNY, Cathrn.		28	F	Seamstress	24Ma02lh
GORMAN, Ellen		25	F	Seamstress	24Ma02lh
MCARTY, Lorn		18	M	Laborer	24Ma02lh
MCDERMOT, Jno.		34	M	Laborer	24Ma02lh
MORASSY, Wm.		23	M	Laborer	24Ma02lh
COLMAN, Cain		29	M	Laborer	24Ma02lh
REGAN, John		24	M	Laborer	24Ma02lh
MCQUADE, James		22	M	Laborer	24Ma02lh
KILLELY, Mic		28	M	Laborer	24Ma02lh
STINSON, John		18	M	Laborer	24Ma02lh
MURPHY, Michl.		25	M	Laborer	24Ma02lh
SCARMAN, Joseph		29	M	Laborer	24Ma02lh
SMITH, Mary		20	F	Seamstress	24Ma02lh
FLANAGAN, Pat.		30	M	Laborer	24Ma02lh
DONNELLY, Jack		26	M	Laborer	24Ma02lh
MCHUGH, U-Mrs.		40	F	Seamstress	24Ma02lh
Barny		40	M	Laborer	24Ma02lh
FARRELL, Ann		20	F	Seamstress	24Ma02lh
CUNNINGHAM, Rebecca		20	F	Seamstress	24Ma02lh
MILES, Wm.		30	M	Laborer	24Ma02lh
MOULD, John		35	M	Laborer	24Ma02lh
WELSH, Thomas		23	M	Laborer	24Ma02lh
MORRIS, Larry		26	M	Laborer	24Ma02lh
DALY, Chas.		19	M	Laborer	24Ma02lh
FOGARTY, Anne		22	F	Seamstress	24Ma02lh
LAVIN, Ellen		27	F	Seamstress	24Ma02lh
DOLLIN, Mary		23	F	Seamstress	24Ma02lh

NAMES OF PASSENGERS		AGE	SEX	OCCUPATIONS	DATE PORT SHIP
MCCAUL, Alex.		20	M	Laborer	24Ma02lh
DANIEL, Jno.		40	M	Laborer	24Ma02lh
Thomas		.00	M	Infant	24Ma02lh
Anne		04	F	Child	24Ma02lh
Martha		09	F	Child	24Ma02lh
GILLIGAN, Peter		35	M	Laborer	24Ma02lh
FLANAGAN, Thomas		30	M	Laborer	24Ma02lh
MCQUADE, Helen		20	F	Seamstress	24Ma02lh
Margt.		.00	F	Infant	24Ma02lh
KELLY, Pat		30	M	Laborer	24Ma02lh
CONNOLLY, Joseph		18	M	Laborer	24Ma02lh
FOX, Nat.		20	M	Laborer	24Ma02lh
QUIN, Dan.		24	M	Laborer	24Ma02lh
CHAMBERS, Mary		28	F	Spinster	24Ma02lh
BYRNE, Frank		23	M	Laborer	24Ma02lh
MCDERMOT, Michl.		30	M	Laborer	24Ma02lh
DANIEL, U-Mrs.		36	F	Seamstress	24Ma02lh
Chr.	(S)	07	M	Child	24Ma02lh
BRADY, U-Mrs.		40	F	Seamstress	24Ma02lh
U		.00	U	Infant	24Ma02lh
MCCARTY, U-Mrs.		30	F	Seamstress	24Ma02lh
U	(D)	03	F	Child	24Ma02lh
BRENNAN, Anne		16	F	Seamstress	24Ma02lh
Anne		60	F	Seamstress	24Ma02lh
Alice		17	F	Seamstress	24Ma02lh
MCFLAHERTY, Michl.		22	M	Laborer	24Ma02lh
Died-At-Sea					
KEARNY, Thomas		00	M	Laborer	24Ma02lh
Died-At-Sea					
DONNELLY, Helen		60	F	Seamstress	24Ma02lh
Died-At-Sea					
DOYLE, John		30	M	Laborer	24Ma02lh
Died-At-Sea					
COFFIN, Michl.		03	M	Child	24Ma02lh
Died-At-Sea					
BROADFOOT, Jane		18	F	Seamstress	24Ma02lh
Died-At-Sea					
CONNOR, Frank		19	M	Laborer	24Ma02lh
Died-At-Sea					
MCHUGH, Barny		40	M	Laborer	24Ma02lh
Died-At-Sea					
COFFIN, Cathn.		06	F	Child	24Ma02lh
Died-At-Sea					
FARRA, Sarah		.00	F	Infant	24Ma02lh
Died-At-Sea					
BRADFORD, Ellen		11	F	Unknown	24Ma02lh
Died-At-Sea					
DAVIES, George		20	M	Laborer	24Ma02lh

WAKEFIELD 24 MAY 1848

From Cork

NAMES OF PASSENGERS	AGE	SEX	OCCUPATIONS	DATE PORT SHIP
CAULFIELD, Phillip	38	M	Servant	24Ma14ll
Elzb.	36	F	Servant	24Ma14ll
Wm.	16	M	Unknown	24Ma14ll
Esther	13	F	Unknown	24Ma14ll
Mary	10	F	Unknown	24Ma14ll
John	05	M	Child	24Ma14ll
Margt.	03	F	Child	24Ma14ll
Elzb.	.00	F	Infant	24Ma14ll
SWANTON, Robt.W.	22	M	Painter	24Ma14ll
HALEY, John	28	M	Painter	24Ma14ll
Wm.	25	M	Tailor	24Ma14ll
WHITE, Mary	22	F	Servant	24Ma14ll
Honora	20	F	Servant	24Ma14ll
David	21	M	Weaver	24Ma14ll
WALSH, Michl.	21	M	Laborer	24Ma14ll
DUNN, Mary	20	F	Servant	24Ma14ll
DUNN, Mary	11	F	Unknown	24Ma14ll
MCCARTHY, Cath.	21	F	Servant	24Ma14ll
FURLONG, Ellen	60	F	Unknown	24Ma14ll
Thos.	16	M	Unknown	24Ma14ll
DALY, Joseph	12	M	Unknown	24Ma14ll
HOMBROST, John	19	M	Laborer	24Ma14ll
Rich.	17	M	Unknown	24Ma14ll
DONOVAN, Dal.	25	M	Weaver	24Ma14ll
Ellen	23	F	Unknown	24Ma14ll
Honora	21	F	Unknown	24Ma14ll
Cath.	14	F	Unknown	24Ma14ll
Julia	18	F	Unknown	24Ma14ll
WRIGHT, Thos.	21	M	Laborer	24Ma14ll
DONOHUE, Michl.	21	M	Laborer	24Ma14ll
HUDSON, Mary-A.	25	F	Servant	24Ma14ll
WELFOLY, John	26	M	Lawyer	24Ma14ll
Cath.	26	F	Unknown	24Ma14ll
Ellen	.00	F	Infant	24Ma14ll
FEHAN, Timy	28	M	Shoemaker	24Ma14ll
REGAN, Jerh.	26	M	Blacksmith	24Ma14ll
SULLIVAN, Margt.	24	F	Unknown	24Ma14ll
MCCARTHY, Mary	21	F	Unknown	24Ma14ll
Thos.	20	M	Weaver	24Ma14ll
CRONIN, Margt.	37	F	Weaver	24Ma14ll
Nancy	17	F	Unknown	24Ma14ll
Ellen	11	F	Unknown	24Ma14ll
Pat	03	M	Child	24Ma14ll
MANNING, Andr.	25	M	Tailor	24Ma14ll
Thos.	23	M	Jeweller	24Ma14ll
Johanna	18	F	Unknown	24Ma14ll
NAUGHTON, Pat	21	M	Unknown	24Ma14ll
FLYNN, Michl.	21	M	Unknown	24Ma14ll
Nancy	19	F	Unknown	24Ma14ll
BRYAN, Margt.	02	F	Child	24Ma14ll
HANLAN, John	26	M	Drover	24Ma14ll
Rich.	52	M	Drover	24Ma14ll
Michl.	27	M	Drover	24Ma14ll
John	23	M	Drover	24Ma14ll
Lawrence	21	M	Drover	24Ma14ll
Rich.	18	M	Unknown	24Ma14ll
Ellen	45	F	Unknown	24Ma14ll
BUCKLEY, Mary	18	F	Unknown	24Ma14ll
NAGLE, Edw.	32	M	Farmer	24Ma14ll
Brget.	24	F	Unknown	24Ma14ll
Rich.	.00	M	Infant	24Ma14ll
DOWD, Jerh.	44	M	Farmer	24Ma14ll
Wm.	13	M	Farmer	24Ma14ll
MCCARTHY, Mary	28	F	Servant	24Ma14ll
BROWN, John	27	M	Farmer	24Ma14ll
MCDONNELL, Thos.	23	M	Farmer	24Ma14ll
MOORE, Cath.	24	F	Unknown	24Ma14ll
SHEEHAN, John	30	M	Laborer	24Ma14ll
CALLAGHAN, Jimy	30	M	Laborer	24Ma14ll
DUNN, John	40	M	Laborer	24Ma14ll
HALLORAN, Maurice	10	M	Unknown	24Ma14ll
Norry	20	F	Unknown	24Ma14ll
Ellen	21	F	Unknown	24Ma14ll
DENNAHY, Bridget	20	F	Unknown	24Ma14ll
Bridget	20	F	Unknown	24Ma14ll
HURLEY, Ann	12	F	Unknown	24Ma14ll
RYAN, Honora	16	F	Unknown	24Ma14ll
YOUNG, Phillis	26	F	Servant	24Ma14ll
Ann	24	F	Servant	24Ma14ll
BARY, Richd.	25	M	Coachman	24Ma14ll
MAHONY, Jas.	28	M	Coachman	24Ma14ll
CALLAGHAN, Maurice	18	M	Unknown	24Ma14ll
MORRISON, Michl.	46	M	Coachman	24Ma14ll
MURPHY, Wm.	46	M	Coachman	24Ma14ll
MORRISY, Margt.	30	F	Servant	24Ma14ll
MURPHY, Mary	40	F	Servant	24Ma14ll
Ellen	.00	F	Infant	24Ma14ll
DESMOND, Andrew	60	M	Ploughman	24Ma14ll
Andrew-Jr.	19	M	Ploughman	24Ma14ll
Andrew	08	M	Child	24Ma14ll
Johanna	24	F	Unknown	24Ma14ll

NAMES OF PASSENGERS		AGE	SEX	OCCUPATIONS	DATE PORT SHIP
DESMOND, Ellen		22	F	Unknown	24Ma14II
Honora		20	F	Unknown	24Ma14II
CARROLL, Margt.		20	F	Unknown	24Ma14II
COONEY, Elza		20	F	Unknown	24Ma14II
HYNES, Mary		20	F	Unknown	24Ma14II
PLACE, John-S.		22	M	Farmer	24Ma14II
MCINTOSH, Johnson		22	M	Unknown	24Ma14II
MOON, Eliza		21	F	Lady	24Ma14II
WALSH, Robt.		26	M	Smith	24Ma14II
ALTRIDGE, Wm.		18	M	Watchmaker	24Ma14II
LINNAGHAN, Cath.		25	F	Unknown	24Ma14II
Dennis		22	M	Unknown	24Ma14II
Jas.		09	M	Child	24Ma14II
Cath.		13	F	Child	24Ma14II
CONNER, Jas.		12	M	Child	24Ma14II
KILMARTIN, Mary		20	F	Servant	24Ma14II
CRONIN, Ellen		22	F	Servant	24Ma14II
BARRY, John		25	M	Unknown	24Ma14II
HAGARTY, John		29	M	Smith	24Ma14II
GREEN, Michl.		23	M	Brick Maker	24Ma14II
WALSH, Redmond		19	M	Brick Maker	24Ma14II
MULCAHY, Chas.		28	M	Brick Maker	24Ma14II
FLEMING, Cath.		18	F	Servant	24Ma14II
HELLER, Thos.		20	M	Unknown	24Ma14II
AHERN, Michl.		11	M	Servant	24Ma14II
MULVAHILL, John		25	M	Servant	24Ma14II
HANLY, Cath.		30	F	Servant	24Ma14II
Thos.		25	M	Servant	24Ma14II
WHEELER, Fras.		25	M	Servant	24Ma14II
STACK, Ruth		26	F	Unknown	24Ma14II
Cath.		26	F	Servant	24Ma14II
HORAN, Julia		50	F	Unknown	24Ma14II
SHAHAM, Ellen		27	F	Unknown	24Ma14II
JONES, Elizb.		16	F	Unknown	24Ma14II
STACK, Ellen		02	F	Child	24Ma14II
GIVER, Edmond		24	M	Farmer	24Ma14II
SULLIVAN, John		26	M	Servant	24Ma14II
Honora		28	F	Servant	24Ma14II
Julia		03	F	Child	24Ma14II
Jas.		.00	M	Infant	24Ma14II
KELLY, Mary		22	F	Servant	24Ma14II
GUARD, Honora		27	F	Unknown	24Ma14II
MANNING, Dennis		48	M	Farmer	24Ma14II
BOWDRAPER, Pat		30	M	Farmer	24Ma14II
SCALLARD, Pat		24	M	Farmer	24Ma14II
LEARY, David		22	M	Farmer	24Ma14II
Thos.		18	M	Unknown	24Ma14II
MANNING, Margt.		12	F	Unknown	24Ma14II
POMORY, Pat		19	M	Unknown	24Ma14II
LEARY, Margt.		18	F	Servant	24Ma14II
SCALLARD, Julia		18	F	Servant	24Ma14II
MAHONY, Thos.		28	M	Shoemaker	24Ma14II
Mary		20	F	Shoemaker	24Ma14II
SULLIVAN, John		24	M	Shoemaker	24Ma14II
DONOHOE, David		27	M	Shoemaker	24Ma14II
FLYNN, Michl.		30	M	Weaver	24Ma14II
BRIAN, Timy		30	M	Chswp	24Ma14II
KELLY, Mary		17	F	Oywmn	24Ma14II
Julia		17	F	Oywmn	24Ma14II
TYNE, Hannah		20	F	Oywmn	24Ma14II
KELLY, Timy		19	M	Unknown	24Ma14II
OSULLIVAN, Pat		20	M	Butcher	24Ma14II
OCONNELL, Jimy		20	M	Butcher	24Ma14II
Cra--, Johannah		20	F	Unknown	24Ma14II
KENNY, David		20	M	Schm	24Ma14II
SULLIVAN, Ellen		18	F	Unknown	24Ma14II
Mary		20	F	Unknown	24Ma14II
DOWLING, Hannah		16	F	Unknown	24Ma14II
BIRD, Fanny		16	F	Spinster	24Ma14II
MOYNAHN, Robt.		22	M	Weaver	24Ma14II
Timy		20	M	Smith	24Ma14II
FITZPATRICK, Chas.		17	M	Smith	24Ma14II
MURPHY, Timy		20	M	Smith	24Ma14II
NAUGHTON, Michl.		23	M	Smith	24Ma14II
MURPHY, Mary		27	F	Servant	24Ma14II
FEHELY, Pat		28	M	Drover	24Ma14II
Frank		14	M	Unknown	24Ma14II
RYAN, Danl.		30	M	Unknown	24Ma14II
DILLON, David		22	M	Unknown	24Ma14II
HOGAN, Joshua		20	M	Cooper	24Ma14II
MULLAM, John		30	M	Unknown	24Ma14II
FEEHY, Wm.		30	M	Unknown	24Ma14II
CRAWLY, Barbara		25	F	Servant	24Ma14II
COFFY, Ellen		16	F	Unknown	24Ma14II
CARBERRY, Ellen		20	F	Unknown	24Ma14II
LUCAS, Geo.		22	M	Unknown	24Ma14II
MOYNAHAN, John		40	M	Farmer	24Ma14II
Mary	(W)	38	F	Wife	24Ma14II
BEGLEY, John		65	M	Unknown	24Ma14II
SULLIVAN, Michl.		45	M	Farmer	24Ma14II
CALLAGHAN, Dennis		21	M	Farmer	24Ma14II
WALSH, Garret		60	U	Farmer	24Ma14II
Wm.	(S)	22	M	None	24Ma14II
Julia	(D)	17	F	None	24Ma14II
Cath.	(D)	13	F	None	24Ma14II
Ellen	(D)	10	F	None	24Ma14II
Mary	(D)	21	F	None	24Ma14II
MCCARTHY, Conell		22	M	Cabdriver	24Ma14II
Julia		21	F	Unknown	24Ma14II
CONNELL, Julia		21	F	Unknown	24Ma14II
BARRY, David		30	M	Unknown	24Ma14II
Julia	(W)	30	F	Wife	24Ma14II
Mary	(D)	04	F	Child	24Ma14II
Pat		26	M	Unknown	24Ma14II
POWER, John		50	M	Miner	24Ma14II
Mary-Ann		45	F	Unknown	24Ma14II
Mary-Ann		20	F	Unknown	24Ma14II
Ellen		18	F	Unknown	24Ma14II
COTTER, Maurice		29	M	Saddler	24Ma14II
KENNY, Edmond		22	M	Saddler	24Ma14II
CONDON, John		28	M	Saddler	24Ma14II
Mary	(W)	36	F	Wife	24Ma14II
Eliza	(D)	07	F	Child	24Ma14II
TURNER, Mary		25	F	Unknown	24Ma14II
MCCARTHY, Dennis		25	M	Broom Maker	24Ma14II
CARRY, John		25	M	Soap Maker	24Ma14II
RIORDAN, Michl.		25	M	Butcher	24Ma14II
HURLEY, John		24	M	Butcher	24Ma14II
Mary		22	F	Butcher	24Ma14II
Mary		50	F	Butcher	24Ma14II
SANDS, Mary		20	F	Servant	24Ma14II
CONNELL, Michl.		26	M	Farmer	24Ma14II
Jane		20	F	Unknown	24Ma14II
MINTON, Mary		50	F	Unknown	24Ma14II
ROCKFORD, Thos.		05	M	Child	24Ma14II
KENT, Redmond		45	M	Unknown	24Ma14II
Edmund		25	M	Unknown	24Ma14II
Ellen		44	F	Unknown	24Ma14II
Nancy		18	F	Unknown	24Ma14II
Wm.		16	M	Unknown	24Ma14II
John		15	M	Unknown	24Ma14II
Cath.		11	F	Unknown	24Ma14II
Michl.		09	M	Child	24Ma14II
Redmond		07	M	Child	24Ma14II
FLYNN, Wm.		32	M	Unknown	24Ma14II
QUIRK, Jas.		24	M	Unknown	24Ma14II
NAGLE, Garret		40	M	Farmer	24Ma14II
BROWN, Peggy		40	F	Unknown	24Ma14II
MAHER, Mary		20	F	Servant	24Ma14II
MCGRATH, Cath.		21	F	Servant	24Ma14II
Elizb.		20	F	Servant	24Ma14II
COLEMAN, Bridget		20	F	Servant	24Ma14II
MAHONY, Barbara		30	F	Servant	24Ma14II
CROWLEY, Jerh.		46	M	Unknown	24Ma14II
DESMOND, Mary		25	F	Unknown	24Ma14II
BARRY, Phillip		18	M	Servant	24Ma14II
CASSEN, Pat		21	M	Unknown	24Ma14II
SAVAGE, Mary		20	F	Unknown	24Ma14II
SCULLY, John		30	M	Unknown	24Ma14II
Cath.		28	F	Unknown	24Ma14II

NAMES OF PASSENGERS	AGE	SEX	OCCUPATIONS	DATE PORT SHIP
BIBLE, Bridget	21	F	Unknown	24Ma14II
BARRY, Jas.	17	M	Unknown	24Ma14II
KEATING, Wm.	40	M	Unknown	24Ma14II
WHEELER, U	25	M	Unknown	24Ma14II
LYNCH, U	23	M	Unknown	24Ma14II
U	21	M	Unknown	24Ma14II

ELIZABETH 24 MAY 1848

From Bristol

NAMES OF PASSENGERS	AGE	SEX	OCCUPATIONS	DATE PORT SHIP
PALMER, John	17	M	Farmer	24Ma18IJ
STARR, Wm.	22	M	Farmer	24Ma18IJ
FISHER, Thos.	17	M	Farmer	24Ma18IJ
EVANS, Ruben	17	M	Farmer	24Ma18IJ
POPE, John	34	M	Farmer	24Ma18IJ
Sarah	33	F	Farmer	24Ma18IJ
James	02	M	Child	24Ma18IJ
Jno.	.00	M	Infant	24Ma18IJ
COLLIFRIESH, Geo.	25	M	Farmer	24Ma18IJ
GIBBS, Richd.	23	M	Farmer	24Ma18IJ
WELLS, Wm.	55	M	Shoemaker	24Ma18IJ
RADFORD, Eliza	16	F	None	24Ma18IJ
WELLS, Jane	50	F	None	24Ma18IJ
RADFORD, Ann	24	F	None	24Ma18IJ
Caroline	22	F	None	24Ma18IJ
Sarah-Ann	04	F	Child	24Ma18IJ
WELLS, Wm.	18	M	Shoemaker	24Ma18IJ
Edwin	07	M	Child	24Ma18IJ
BOYCE, Edwd.	26	M	Farmer	24Ma18IJ
Mary	21	F	None	24Ma18IJ
CRANDON, Joseph	26	M	Farmer	24Ma18IJ
Mary	25	F	Unknown	24Ma18IJ
U	.00	U	Infant	24Ma18IJ
CHURCHIS, Edwin	28	M	Farmer	24Ma18IJ
Hester	23	F	Farmer	24Ma18IJ
James	.00	M	Infant	24Ma18IJ
Sarah-A.	.00	F	Infant	24Ma18IJ
BURGE, Joseph	21	M	Farmer	24Ma18IJ
Abr.	19	M	Farmer	24Ma18IJ
POOK, Geo.	17	M	Farmer	24Ma18IJ
PARSONS, Jno.	23	M	Farmer	24Ma18IJ
NORTON, Robert	26	M	Farmer	24Ma18IJ
GALLOP, Jonathan	50	M	Farmer	24Ma18IJ
Martha	23	F	None	24Ma18IJ
HOOPER, Saml.	28	M	Carpenter	24Ma18IJ
Clara	30	F	None	24Ma18IJ
U	.00	U	Infant	24Ma18IJ
QUICK, James	28	M	Farmer	24Ma18IJ
Ann	28	F	None	24Ma18IJ
DAY, James	30	M	Farmer	24Ma18IJ
Ellen-G.	29	F	None	24Ma18IJ
HUNTABLE, Emily	22	F	None	24Ma18IJ
BROOKS, Thos.	24	M	Farmer	24Ma18IJ
Wm.	21	M	Farmer	24Ma18IJ
BINNING, Geo.	20	M	Farmer	24Ma18IJ
OTTEN, Ellen	22	F	None	24Ma18IJ
HILLIN, Mary	19	F	None	24Ma18IJ
JAMES, Jno.	45	M	Mechanic	24Ma18IJ
Elizabeth	40	F	Mechanic	24Ma18IJ
Charles	39	M	Mechanic	24Ma18IJ
John-F.	.00	M	Infant	24Ma18IJ
COOK, Wm.	37	M	Mechanic	24Ma18IJ
Ann	23	F	None	24Ma18IJ
KETHRO, Henry	30	M	Mechanic	24Ma18IJ
Hester	30	F	None	24Ma18IJ
U	.00	U	Infant	24Ma18IJ
Mary	06	F	Child	24Ma18IJ
Henry	04	M	Child	24Ma18IJ
BOND, John	39	M	Laborer	24Ma18IJ
Jemima	38	F	None	24Ma18IJ
U	.00	U	Infant	24Ma18IJ
Jno.	12	M	None	24Ma18IJ
Ann	10	F	None	24Ma18IJ
Sarah	08	F	Child	24Ma18IJ
Jas.	06	M	Child	24Ma18IJ
Amelia	04	F	Child	24Ma18IJ
BROWN, James	23	M	Carpenter	24Ma18IJ
CHRISTOPER, Jno.	23	M	Shoemaker	24Ma18IJ
BRYNE, Chas.	21	M	Farmer	24Ma18IJ
BREWER, Fredr.	18	M	Farmer	24Ma18IJ
AVERY, Edwin	22	M	Farmer	24Ma18IJ
BURNS, Jno.	20	M	Laborer	24Ma18IJ
LISTER, Richd.	22	M	Laborer	24Ma18IJ
Ann	23	F	None	24Ma18IJ
U	.00	U	Infant	24Ma18IJ
TILLEY, John	44	M	Farmer	24Ma18IJ
Mary	40	F	None	24Ma18IJ
LUKINS, Jane	06	F	Child	24Ma18IJ
TILLEY, Jno.	08	M	Child	24Ma18IJ
POPE, Thos.	18	M	Farmer	24Ma18IJ
DAY, Jane	25	F	None	24Ma18IJ
CLEMENTS, Clara	30	F	None	24Ma18IJ
Jane	07	F	Child	24Ma18IJ
Sarah	.00	F	Infant	24Ma18IJ
URCH, Eliza	22	F	None	24Ma18IJ
GAY, Francis	33	M	Farmer	24Ma18IJ
Sarah	30	F	Farmer	24Ma18IJ
MOSS, Joseph	20	M	Farmer	24Ma18IJ
PINNEY, Henry	17	M	Farmer	24Ma18IJ
DAY, Henry	17	M	Farmer	24Ma18IJ
MASLIN, Henry	35	M	Blacksmith	24Ma18IJ
Eliz.	29	F	None	24Ma18IJ
U	.00	U	Infant	24Ma18IJ
Robt.	11	M	None	24Ma18IJ
Wm.	08	M	None	24Ma18IJ
John	06	M	None	24Ma18IJ
Saml.	04	M	None	24Ma18IJ
BOWLEY, Richd.	20	M	Farmer	24Ma18IJ
CHAPPLE, Geo.	16	M	Farmer	24Ma18IJ
WALL, Mary	22	F	None	24Ma18IJ
U	.00	F	Infant	24Ma18IJ
THOMAS, Jno.	24	M	Laborer	24Ma18IJ
LANG, Benj.	29	M	Laborer	24Ma18IJ
WHINDLE, James	29	M	Laborer	24Ma18IJ
HUGGINS, Zacariah	38	M	Mason	24Ma18IJ
SKYNNER, James	20	M	Gdnr	24Ma18IJ
PRICE, Francis	25	M	Groom	24Ma18IJ
NIPPEMS, Wm.	20	M	Farmer	24Ma18IJ
Eliza	28	F	None	24Ma18IJ
Thos.	03	M	Child	24Ma18IJ
Jas.	.00	M	Infant	24Ma18IJ
DAVIS, Wm.	34	M	Tailor	24Ma18IJ
Ann	38	F	None	24Ma18IJ
Eliza	11	F	None	24Ma18IJ
Edwd.	09	M	Child	24Ma18IJ
Mary-Ann	03	F	Child	24Ma18IJ
Thos.	.00	M	Infant	24Ma18IJ
GALLOP, Jas.	25	M	Farmer	24Ma18IJ
HOWELL, Geo.	22	M	Farmer	24Ma18IJ
POPHAM, Wm.	19	M	Farmer	24Ma18IJ
JEFFERIS, Isaac	35	M	Farmer	24Ma18IJ
Sarah	36	F	None	24Ma18IJ
U	.00	U	Infant	24Ma18IJ
Jacob	05	M	Child	24Ma18IJ
Gabriel	03	M	Child	24Ma18IJ
BOWLEY, Henry	18	M	Farmer	24Ma18IJ
SHICKLAND, Geo.	20	M	Farmer	24Ma18IJ
COOMBS, George	11	M	Farmer	24Ma18IJ
SYMMONDS, Henry	45	M	Farmer	24Ma18IJ
BROWNING, Robt.	55	M	Blacksmith	24Ma18IJ
Mary	25	F	None	24Ma18IJ
William	19	M	None	24Ma18IJ
Benj.	15	M	None	24Ma18IJ

NAMES OF PASSENGERS	AGE	SEX	OCCUPATIONS	DATE PORT SHIP
BROWNING, Elizabeth	11	F	None	24Ma18lj
DAVIES, Mary-A.	00	F	None	24Ma18lj
Robt.	06	M	Child	24Ma18lj
Mary-A.	04	F	Child	24Ma18lj
Ann	.00	F	Infant	24Ma18lj
STOCK, Edwin	32	M	Butcher	24Ma18lj
Ann	32	F	None	24Ma18lj
Betsey	08	F	Child	24Ma18lj
James	06	M	Child	24Ma18lj
Fred.	.00	M	Infant	24Ma18lj
Caleb	19	M	Farmer	24Ma18lj
PERLMAN, Wm.	25	M	Farmer	24Ma18lj
EMERY, James	22	M	Farmer	24Ma18lj
GIBBS, Benj.	19	M	Farmer	24Ma18lj
EMERY, Ann	21	F	None	24Ma18lj
GIER, Peter	31	M	Miller	24Ma18lj
Sarah	31	F	None	24Ma18lj
U	.00	U	Infant	24Ma18lj
Mary	06	F	Child	24Ma18lj
James	03	M	Child	24Ma18lj
HEATH, Jno.	27	M	Laborer	24Ma18lj
BARBER, Wm.	24	M	Carpenter	24Ma18lj
FOLLETT, James	28	M	Bricklayer	24Ma18lj
ROW, Jno.	25	M	Miller	24Ma18lj
NIPPER, Francis	28	M	Farmer	24Ma18lj
Eliza	29	F	None	24Ma18lj
U	.00	U	Infant	24Ma18lj
HAISE, Henry	22	M	Laborer	24Ma18lj
BINNING, Robt.	27	M	Farmer	24Ma18lj
TAYLOR, Napohalian	19	M	Farmer	24Ma18lj
ATWOOD, Henry	18	M	Farmer	24Ma18lj
NEWTON, Jno.	24	M	Mechanic	24Ma18lj
LANDDOWN, Thos.	22	M	Mechanic	24Ma18lj
DUNN, Phillip	24	M	Mechanic	24Ma18lj
NEWCOMBE, Edw.	24	M	Mechanic	24Ma18lj
BARROW, Jno.	26	M	Carpenter	24Ma18lj
Eliza	30	F	None	24Ma18lj
MASKIN, Susan	24	F	None	24Ma18lj
U	.00	U	Infant	24Ma18lj
THORNE, Thos.	26	M	Bootmaker	24Ma18lj
Mary-A.	25	F	None	24Ma18lj
WATKINS, Henry	27	M	Farmer	24Ma18lj
James	18	M	Cooper	24Ma18lj
HARDING, Thos.	26	M	Accountant	24Ma18lj
JAMES, Wm.	29	M	Farmer	24Ma18lj
Spaaxny	25	M	None	24Ma18lj
Chas.	03	M	Child	24Ma18lj
THOMAS, Henry	21	M	Farmer	24Ma18lj
LAVELL, George	50	M	Farmer	24Ma18lj
Mary	42	F	None	24Ma18lj
SCHROOD, Jno.	30	M	Farmer	24Ma18lj
SELWOOD, Sarah	40	F	Farmer	24Ma18lj
John	19	M	Farmer	24Ma18lj
MILLARD, Ben	60	M	Farmer	24Ma18lj
Ann	55	F	Farmer	24Ma18lj
Harry	22	M	Farmer	24Ma18lj
Ann	20	F	Farmer	24Ma18lj
Ellen	17	F	Farmer	24Ma18lj
Robt.	15	M	Farmer	24Ma18lj
RAINS, John	27	M	Laborer	24Ma18lj
Elenor	29	F	None	24Ma18lj
Harry	04	M	Child	24Ma18lj
James	.00	M	Infant	24Ma18lj
CAPMAN, Jno.	29	M	Unknown	24Ma18lj
CHAPMAN, Harriet	34	F	Unknown	24Ma18lj
Harriet	05	F	Child	24Ma18lj
LEE, Harriet	30	F	Unknown	24Ma18lj
Geo.	09	M	Child	24Ma18lj
Emma	07	F	Child	24Ma18lj
Ann	04	F	Child	24Ma18lj
WILCOX, John	19	M	Unknown	24Ma18lj
TALBOT, Wm.	24	M	Unknown	24Ma18lj
HILL, Robt.	31	M	Unknown	24Ma18lj

ST.JOHN 24 MAY 1848

From Liverpool

NAMES OF PASSENGERS	AGE	SEX	OCCUPATIONS	DATE PORT SHIP
BEALE, William Died-At-Sea	70	M	Farmer	24Ma02lk
Thomas	45	M	Farmer	24Ma02lk
Mary	40	F	Farmer	24Ma02lk
Elizabeth	19	F	Farmer	24Ma02lk
John	16	M	Farmer	24Ma02lk
George	09	M	Child	24Ma02lk
GEARY, Ellen	20	F	None	24Ma02lk
GORMAN, Dennis	39	M	Unknown	24Ma02lk
Alice	35	F	Unknown	24Ma02lk
MARTIN, James	40	M	Unknown	24Ma02lk
WILSON, George	37	M	Unknown	24Ma02lk
Thomas	33	M	Unknown	24Ma02lk
HICKSON, Henry	27	M	Unknown	24Ma02lk
MILLER, Susanna	16	F	Unknown	24Ma02lk
WILSON, William	.04	M	Infant	24Ma02lk
FRIZZELL, Sarah	17	F	Unknown	24Ma02lk
HICKSON, Eliza	.10	F	Infant	24Ma02lk
MCNAMARA, James	26	M	Unknown	24Ma02lk
HARVEY, Henry	26	M	Unknown	24Ma02lk
Mary-Jane	24	F	Unknown	24Ma02lk
William	.06	M	Infant	24Ma02lk
FITZSIMMONS, Walter	26	M	Unknown	24Ma02lk
Ann	24	F	Unknown	24Ma02lk
Patt.	23	M	Unknown	24Ma02lk
Hugh	20	M	Unknown	24Ma02lk
Terrence	17	M	Unknown	24Ma02lk
Mary	15	F	Unknown	24Ma02lk
William	.06	M	Infant	24Ma02lk
BURKE, William	40	M	Unknown	24Ma02lk
NORTON, Charles	35	M	Unknown	24Ma02lk
MANNON, Thomas	20	M	Unknown	24Ma02lk
HUGHES, Winney	18	M	Unknown	24Ma02lk
CALLON, Patt	30	M	Unknown	24Ma02lk
HYANT, Marty Died-At-Sea	25	M	Unknown	24Ma02lk
Martin	24	M	Unknown	24Ma02lk
REILEY, Patt	27	M	Unknown	24Ma02lk
BURKE, Mary	20	F	Unknown	24Ma02lk
BROWN, Charles	37	M	Unknown	24Ma02lk
Ellen	07	F	Child	24Ma02lk
Owen	19	M	Unknown	24Ma02lk
MARA, William	64	M	Unknown	24Ma02lk
William	25	M	Unknown	24Ma02lk
Catherine	20	F	Unknown	24Ma02lk
Julia	19	F	Unknown	24Ma02lk
Judy	20	F	Unknown	24Ma02lk
MURAGH, Julia	20	F	Unknown	24Ma02lk
MCGUINESS, Mary	21	F	Unknown	24Ma02lk
MCGREELY, Patt	45	M	Unknown	24Ma02lk
ONEIL, Tim	20	M	Unknown	24Ma02lk
MARNON, Patt	18	M	Unknown	24Ma02lk
Jno.	25	M	Unknown	24Ma02lk
BORAN, Jno.	30	M	Unknown	24Ma02lk
MATCHETT, Richd.G.	20	M	Unknown	24Ma02lk
JOHNSTON, Jno.	35	M	Unknown	24Ma02lk
U (W)	38	F	Unknown	24Ma02lk
Mary-Ann	12	F	Unknown	24Ma02lk
Maria	08	F	Child	24Ma02lk
Harriet	06	F	Child	24Ma02lk
John	05	M	Child	24Ma02lk
Eliza	.08	F	Infant	24Ma02lk
ALLEN, Sarah	26	F	Unknown	24Ma02lk
Caroline	08	F	Child	24Ma02lk
Agnes	05	F	Child	24Ma02lk

NAMES OF PASSENGERS		AGE	SEX	OCCUPATIONS	DATE PORT SHIP
ALLEN, Virtine		03	U	Child	24Ma02Ik
BISHOP, Benjamin		34	M	Unknown	24Ma02Ik
U	(W)	29	F	Unknown	24Ma02Ik
Eliza		11	F	Unknown	24Ma02Ik
James		08	M	Child	24Ma02Ik
Robert		05	M	Child	24Ma02Ik
JOHNSTON, Wm.		18	M	Unknown	24Ma02Ik
BISHOP, Wm.		28	M	Unknown	24Ma02Ik
JOHNSTON, Edward		20	M	Unknown	24Ma02Ik
Matt.		15	M	Unknown	24Ma02Ik
BISHOP, George		38	M	Unknown	24Ma02Ik
FORE, Robert		24	M	Unknown	24Ma02Ik
U	(W)	23	F	Unknown	24Ma02Ik
Edward	(S)	.08	M	Infant	24Ma02Ik
JOHNSTON, Edward		38	M	Unknown	24Ma02Ik
U	(W)	25	F	Unknown	24Ma02Ik
Eliza		05	F	Child	24Ma02Ik
Ted		03	M	Child	24Ma02Ik
Harvey		.07	M	Infant	24Ma02Ik
BAKER, James		20	M	Unknown	24Ma02Ik
FLINT, Isaac		30	M	Unknown	24Ma02Ik
Ann		30	F	Unknown	24Ma02Ik
William		04	M	Child	24Ma02Ik
Sarah		02	F	Child	24Ma02Ik
George		.06	M	Infant	24Ma02Ik
REDHEAD, Richard		24	M	Unknown	24Ma02Ik
U	(W)	24	F	Unknown	24Ma02Ik
MCPARTLAND, Thomas		23	M	Unknown	24Ma02Ik
BURNEY, James		50	M	Unknown	24Ma02Ik
REYNOLDS, Charles		40	M	Unknown	24Ma02Ik
Jno.		18	M	Unknown	24Ma02Ik
Francis		16	M	Unknown	24Ma02Ik
Mary		11	F	Unknown	24Ma02Ik
SURDATT, Daniel		40	M	Unknown	24Ma02Ik
WARRICH, Jno.		30	M	Unknown	24Ma02Ik
MCWHENEY, Eliza		22	F	Unknown	24Ma02Ik
WILKINSON, George		30	M	Unknown	24Ma02Ik
CLARK, James		21	M	Unknown	24Ma02Ik
BROWN, Wm.		20	M	Unknown	24Ma02Ik
JOHNSTON, Richard		26	M	Unknown	24Ma02Ik
Seddy	(W)	26	F	Unknown	24Ma02Ik
Wm.		24	M	Unknown	24Ma02Ik
Ashley		.09	M	Infant	24Ma02Ik
Richard		.09	M	Infant	24Ma02Ik
ROONEY, Bessy		21	F	Unknown	24Ma02Ik
Mary		20	F	Unknown	24Ma02Ik
GORE, Thomas		23	M	Unknown	24Ma02Ik
HARDEN, Simach		22	M	Unknown	24Ma02Ik
TAYLOR, Charles		22	M	Unknown	24Ma02Ik
MCGRATH, Henry		26	M	Unknown	24Ma02Ik
U	(W)	24	F	Unknown	24Ma02Ik
Henry		.10	M	Infant	24Ma02Ik
JACKMAN, James		30	M	Unknown	24Ma02Ik
Ann		28	F	Unknown	24Ma02Ik
William		04	M	Child	24Ma02Ik
Thomas		.10	M	Infant	24Ma02Ik
William		24	M	Unknown	24Ma02Ik
POLLETLAND, George		40	M	Unknown	24Ma02Ik
Mary		20	F	Unknown	24Ma02Ik
HERRING, Wm.		32	M	Unknown	24Ma02Ik
STYLE, Richard		50	M	Unknown	24Ma02Ik
Elizth.		27	F	Unknown	24Ma02Ik
Dinah		25	F	Unknown	24Ma02Ik
Wm.		08	M	Child	24Ma02Ik
Emily-Jane		01	F	Child	24Ma02Ik
HARRISON, Aaron		25	M	Unknown	24Ma02Ik
CLANCY, Ann		55	F	Unknown	24Ma02Ik
William		30	M	Unknown	24Ma02Ik
Catherine		25	F	Unknown	24Ma02Ik
Alice		23	F	Unknown	24Ma02Ik
DANIELS, Samuel		30	M	Unknown	24Ma02Ik
Mary		30	F	Unknown	24Ma02Ik
Ellen		04	F	Child	24Ma02Ik
Thomas		03	F	Child	24Ma02Ik
Patrick		02	F	Child	24Ma02Ik
PENDERGRAST, Edwd.		40	M	Unknown	24Ma02Ik
Bridget		30	F	Unknown	24Ma02Ik
Johanna		10	F	Unknown	24Ma02Ik
James		03	M	Child	24Ma02Ik
Thomas		02	M	Child	24Ma02Ik
KING, Thomas		24	M	Unknown	24Ma02Ik
BYRNE, Jno.		35	M	Unknown	24Ma02Ik
GRIMES, Ann		20	F	Unknown	24Ma02Ik
TRACY, Bernard		20	M	Unknown	24Ma02Ik
Mary		21	F	Unknown	24Ma02Ik
Brady		20	M	Unknown	24Ma02Ik
KENNY, Martin		13	M	Unknown	24Ma02Ik
FEELY, Martin		20	M	Unknown	24Ma02Ik
MATHEWS, George		20	M	Unknown	24Ma02Ik
DONNAGAR, Lawrence		25	M	Unknown	24Ma02Ik
LANTREY, Patt		22	M	Unknown	24Ma02Ik
DONNAGAN, Mary		17	F	Unknown	24Ma02Ik
GORMAN, Mary		33	F	Unknown	24Ma02Ik
Thomas		09	M	Child	24Ma02Ik
Mary		07	F	Child	24Ma02Ik
EAGAN, Mary		20	F	Unknown	24Ma02Ik
KELLY, John		55	M	Unknown	24Ma02Ik
Ellin		55	F	Unknown	24Ma02Ik
Patt		24	M	Unknown	24Ma02Ik
Danil.		21	M	Unknown	24Ma02Ik
Eliza		15	F	Unknown	24Ma02Ik
Jane		19	F	Unknown	24Ma02Ik
ANDREWS, Michael		29	M	Unknown	24Ma02Ik
Mary		18	F	Unknown	24Ma02Ik
WHITE, William		25	M	Unknown	24Ma02Ik
Mary		18	F	Unknown	24Ma02Ik
MARTESSON, Cathe.		24	F	Unknown	24Ma02Ik
PLUNKETT, Thomas		40	M	Unknown	24Ma02Ik
Catherine		30	F	Unknown	24Ma02Ik
Catherine		12	F	Unknown	24Ma02Ik
Richard		10	M	Unknown	24Ma02Ik
William		08	M	Child	24Ma02Ik
William		40	M	Unknown	24Ma02Ik
REYNOLDS, Richard		50	M	Unknown	24Ma02Ik
John		28	M	Unknown	24Ma02Ik
Patt		20	M	Unknown	24Ma02Ik
Ann		50	F	Unknown	24Ma02Ik
Mary		20	F	Unknown	24Ma02Ik
Ann		18	F	Unknown	24Ma02Ik
RYAN, Hannah		24	F	Unknown	24Ma02Ik
BROWN, Catherine		24	F	Unknown	24Ma02Ik
HAYS, Thomas		24	M	Unknown	24Ma02Ik
SHEEHAN, John		24	M	Unknown	24Ma02Ik
KEEGAN, Eliza		24	F	Unknown	24Ma02Ik
EAGAN, Thomas		21	M	Unknown	24Ma02Ik
MCDONAGH, Mary		50	F	Unknown	24Ma02Ik
Barny		18	M	Unknown	24Ma02Ik
Catherine		24	F	Unknown	24Ma02Ik
James		13	M	Unknown	24Ma02Ik
Dennis		12	M	Unknown	24Ma02Ik
REILY, Michael		43	M	Unknown	24Ma02Ik
MCARNEY, Mary		20	F	Unknown	24Ma02Ik
LYNCH, Phil		19	M	Unknown	24Ma02Ik
HOLDEN, Sally		36	F	Unknown	24Ma02Ik
Michael		11	M	Unknown	24Ma02Ik
Thomas		04	M	Child	24Ma02Ik
GARVIN, Mary		20	F	Unknown	24Ma02Ik
INGOLDSBY, Mary		18	F	Unknown	24Ma02Ik
KELLY, Henry		17	M	Unknown	24Ma02Ik
ONEIL, Catherine		20	F	Unknown	24Ma02Ik
MCWHENNEY, Maria		20	F	Unknown	24Ma02Ik
WALSH, James		21	M	Unknown	24Ma02Ik
MCCABE, Thomas		20	M	Unknown	24Ma02Ik
CAVANAGH, Thos.		16	M	Unknown	24Ma02Ik
TANSAY, Mary		50	F	Unknown	24Ma02Ik
Margerit		20	F	Unknown	24Ma02Ik
Mary		25	F	Unknown	24Ma02Ik
John		28	M	Unknown	24Ma02Ik
FEGAN, Mary		34	F	Unknown	24Ma02Ik
James		05	M	Child	24Ma02Ik

NAMES OF PASSENGERS	A G E	S E X	OCCUPATIONS	DATE PORT SHIP
MONAGHAN, Malachi	24	M	Unknown	24Ma02lk
GEARY, Ann	30	F	Unknown	24Ma02lk
Catherine	10	F	Unknown	24Ma02lk
Mary-Ann	.10	F	Infant	24Ma02lk
FARRELL, James	18	M	Unknown	24Ma02lk
SHERIDAN, Joseph	45	M	Unknown	24Ma02lk
BURNE, James	20	M	Unknown	24Ma02lk
WILSON, James	22	M	Unknown	24Ma02lk
Betsey	18	F	Unknown	24Ma02lk
Fanny	17	F	Unknown	24Ma02lk
HICKSON, Bessy	19	F	Unknown	24Ma02lk
U, U	00	U	Unknown	24Ma02lk
Died-At-Sea				
U	.00	U	Infant	24Ma02lk
Died-At-Sea				
U	.00	U	Infant	24Ma02lk
Died-At-Sea				
U	.00	U	Infant	24Ma02lk
Died-At-Sea				

ANDREW-FOSTER 25 MAY 1848

From Liverpool

NAMES OF PASSENGERS	A G E	S E X	OCCUPATIONS	DATE PORT SHIP
WHITTAKER, Francis	37	M	Gentleman	25Ma02ll
Anne	34	F	Unknown	25Ma02ll
Bessie	07	F	Child	25Ma02ll
John	05	M	Child	25Ma02ll
Rebekah	03	F	Child	25Ma02ll
James	02	M	Child	25Ma02ll
Catharine	.06	F	Infant	25Ma02ll
BAXTER, Ann	37	F	Servant	25Ma02ll
FLANAGAN, James	15	M	Servant	25Ma02ll
MAYNARD, Johnathan	21	M	Farmer	25Ma02ll
William	19	M	Farmer	25Ma02ll
BRICE, Charles-S.	22	M	Clerk	25Ma02ll
Catherine	21	F	None	25Ma02ll
REILLY, F.G.	27	M	Laborer	25Ma02ll
COOK, Patrick	14	M	Laborer	25Ma02ll
HASKER, James	29	M	Farmer	25Ma02ll
BURNISH, Henry	44	M	Bricklayer	25Ma02ll
Mary	33	F	None	25Ma02ll
John	07	M	Child	25Ma02ll
Elizabeth	10	F	None	25Ma02ll
James	.08	M	Infant	25Ma02ll
CRANS, Elizabeth	18	F	None	25Ma02ll
DANDON, Isaac	30	M	Miner	25Ma02ll
ROBERTS, Thomas	33	M	Miner	25Ma02ll
JAMES, John	33	M	Farmer	25Ma02ll
MORAN, Thomasine-Mrs.	26	F	None	25Ma02ll
HARRISBANS, Charles	30	M	Farmer	25Ma02ll
Sarah	30	F	None	25Ma02ll
OGDEN, Margaret	22	F	None	25Ma02ll
DAVIES, Absalom	20	M	Miller	25Ma02ll
Henry	18	M	Grocer	25Ma02ll
PROSSER, John	27	M	Laborer	25Ma02ll
Margaret	05	F	Child	25Ma02ll
John	02	M	Child	25Ma02ll
SMITH, Edward	28	M	Laborer	25Ma02ll
BROWN, James	24	M	Farmer	25Ma02ll
BOYSON, George	39	M	Shoemaker	25Ma02ll
Catharine	39	F	None	25Ma02ll
BRADFORD, Charles	21	M	Shoemaker	25Ma02ll
PEARCE, John	33	M	Shoemaker	25Ma02ll
LAWSON, William	26	M	Shoemaker	25Ma02ll
Dinah	23	F	None	25Ma02ll
Georgiania	.10	F	Infant	25Ma02ll
HORNE, Thomas	52	M	Shoemaker	25Ma02ll
Leah	47	F	None	25Ma02ll
PROSSER, Margaret	27	F	None	25Ma02ll
OCONNOR, Thomas	20	M	Laborer	25Ma02ll
BRANNIGAN, Mary	28	F	None	25Ma02ll
James	12	M	None	25Ma02ll
Mary	07	F	Child	25Ma02ll
Patrick	03	M	Child	25Ma02ll
JONES, John	50	M	Laborer	25Ma02ll
Hannah	45	F	Laborer	25Ma02ll
John	21	M	Laborer	25Ma02ll
Samuel	23	M	Laborer	25Ma02ll
SAMMONDS, John	46	M	Laborer	25Ma02ll
Mary	46	F	None	25Ma02ll
John	42	F	None	25Ma02ll
Ann	18	F	None	25Ma02ll
James	12	M	None	25Ma02ll
Elizabeth	07	F	Child	25Ma02ll
POWELL, John	04	M	Child	25Ma02ll
Thomas	.03	M	Infant	25Ma02ll
PEDGATE, Henry	20	M	Laborer	25Ma02ll
Harriet	16	F	None	25Ma02ll
QUIGLEY, Margaret	17	F	None	25Ma02ll
MOONEY, Benjamin	21	M	Laborer	25Ma02ll
WALSH, James	24	M	Carpenter	25Ma02ll
LEARY, John	15	M	None	25Ma02ll
Margaret	14	F	None	25Ma02ll
DONNELLY, John	21	M	Laborer	25Ma02ll
James	18	M	Laborer	25Ma02ll
BROGAN, Mary	20	F	None	25Ma02ll
CROSSINS, Fanny	20	F	None	25Ma02ll
CARR, Mary	28	F	None	25Ma02ll
HENRY, Micheal	32	M	None	25Ma02ll
MAHEN, Micheal	18	M	None	25Ma02ll
NOLAN, Ann	16	F	None	25Ma02ll
Bridget	18	F	None	25Ma02ll
REYNOLDS, U	50	F	Wi	25Ma02ll
Rosa	20	F	None	25Ma02ll
Patrick	18	M	None	25Ma02ll
Mary	10	F	None	25Ma02ll
Catharine	08	F	Child	25Ma02ll
Margaret	.00	F	Infant	25Ma02ll
MULLIGAN, Daniel	15	M	None	25Ma02ll
MCKENNERD, Benjamin	50	M	Laborer	25Ma02ll
Sally	18	F	Unknown	25Ma02ll
SULLY, Andrew	18	M	Unknown	25Ma02ll
SULLIVAN, Mary	21	F	None	25Ma02ll
MALLONY, Mary	21	F	None	25Ma02ll
MULLONY, James	23	M	Laborer	25Ma02ll
HATTON, Catharine	28	F	None	25Ma02ll
LIMBY, James	15	M	None	25Ma02ll
LARKIN, James	20	M	Laborer	25Ma02ll
KAVENAH, Alice	40	F	None	25Ma02ll
MCWHALLEY, James	19	M	Farmer	25Ma02ll
OREILLY, Francis	24	M	Farmer	25Ma02ll
KITT John	20	M	None	25Ma02ll
SMITH, John	46	F	Unknown	25Ma02ll
BRADY, Francis	18	M	Laborer	25Ma02ll
MCCARTY, John	18	M	Laborer	25Ma02ll
John	04	M	Child	25Ma02ll
CAVANAH, Catharine	17	F	None	25Ma02ll
MCMAHON, John	22	M	Laborer	25Ma02ll
CORLIES, Thos.	24	M	Laborer	25Ma02ll
RAYNEY, William	20	M	Laborer	25Ma02ll
SULLIVAN, Margaret	20	F	None	25Ma02ll
DONNELLY, Mary	20	F	Laborer	25Ma02ll
Betsy	11	F	Laborer	25Ma02ll
Bernard	12	M	Laborer	25Ma02ll
BRADLEY, Philip	20	M	Laborer	25Ma02ll
WATTLES, John-Neil	20	M	Laborer	25Ma02ll
KIRKLAND, Ann	15	F	Laborer	25Ma02ll
AREMISH, James	18	M	Laborer	25Ma02ll
SMITH, Rose	18	F	Laborer	25Ma02ll
BOW, Andrew	25	M	Laborer	25Ma02ll
CURTAM, Biddy	22	F	None	25Ma02ll
MANN, Mary	20	F	None	25Ma02ll
FOX, Peter	22	M	Laborer	25Ma02ll

NAMES OF PASSENGERS	AGE	SEX	OCCUPATIONS	DATE PORT SHIP
BOWEN, Micheal	27	M	Farmer	25Ma0211
HEALY, John	30	M	Farmer	25Ma0211
SHORT, Mary	23	F	None	25Ma0211
FARRIS, James	27	M	Laborer	25Ma0211
Samuel	24	M	Laborer	25Ma0211
LENNARD, James	40	M	Laborer	25Ma0211
Margaret	16	F	Laborer	25Ma0211
Catharine	18	F	Laborer	25Ma0211
AMSDON, Mary	11	F	Laborer	25Ma0211
NELLY, Saul	22	M	Laborer	25Ma0211
RYAN, Susy	18	F	Laborer	25Ma0211
MCHENRY, Thomas	26	F	Laborer	25Ma0211
Patrick	16	M	Laborer	25Ma0211
Francis	14	M	Laborer	25Ma0211
FOGARTY, Micheal	25	M	Laborer	25Ma0211
KEENAN, Alexander	23	M	Laborer	25Ma0211
Eliza	20	F	Laborer	25Ma0211
Thomas	19	M	Laborer	25Ma0211
BRADY, John	20	M	Laborer	25Ma0211
Betsy	22	F	Laborer	25Ma0211
REILLY, Micheal	30	M	Laborer	25Ma0211
Ann	25	F	Unknown	25Ma0211
Mary	07	F	Child	25Ma0211
Catharine	.00	F	Infant	25Ma0211
Thomas	06	M	Child	25Ma0211
LATTIN, Joseph	18	M	Laborer	25Ma0211
COSTELLO, John	40	M	Laborer	25Ma0211
MCDARDLE, James	28	M	Laborer	25Ma0211
Micheal	24	M	Laborer	25Ma0211
COLLEN, Anthony	18	M	Laborer	25Ma0211
Patrick	12	M	Laborer	25Ma0211
MCGREGOR, Wm.	21	M	Laborer	25Ma0211
JUGGLES, Margaret	21	M	Laborer	25Ma0211
James	19	M	Laborer	25Ma0211
FAULKNER, John	50	M	Laborer	25Ma0211
KENNEY, John	20	M	Laborer	25Ma0211
POWERS, Enoch	50	M	Laborer	25Ma0211
Evan	24	M	Laborer	25Ma0211
Micheal	22	M	Laborer	25Ma0211
Margaret	19	F	Laborer	25Ma0211
James	17	M	Laborer	25Ma0211
HOWELL, John	38	M	Laborer	25Ma0211
Mary	32	F	Laborer	25Ma0211
Hannah	06	F	Child	25Ma0211
Thomas	03	M	Child	25Ma0211
OWEN, Evan	29	M	Laborer	25Ma0211
AHERN, Abraham	27	M	Laborer	25Ma0211
John	23	M	Laborer	25Ma0211
Thomas	18	M	Laborer	25Ma0211
MCSIMON, Patrick	30	M	Laborer	25Ma0211
Margaret	19	F	Unknown	25Ma0211
John	.00	M	Infant	25Ma0211
JOHNSON, John	12	M	Unknown	25Ma0211
FLYNN, Cornelius	12	M	Laborer	25Ma0211
CREW, Edward	48	M	Laborer	25Ma0211
CRAVEN, Francis	24	M	Laborer	25Ma0211
Catharine	24	F	Laborer	25Ma0211
MCCHUSON, Peter	26	M	Laborer	25Ma0211
SHEAFE, Susan	22	F	Laborer	25Ma0211
KENORS, Maria	16	F	Laborer	25Ma0211
BRADY, Eliza	18	F	Laborer	25Ma0211
SCAFES, George	.00	M	Infant	25Ma0211
DOBSON, Peter	30	M	Laborer	25Ma0211
James	24	M	Laborer	25Ma0211
Hubert	18	M	Laborer	25Ma0211
Ellen	21	F	Laborer	25Ma0211
Margaret	28	F	Laborer	25Ma0211
Bridget	.00	F	Infant	25Ma0211
Margaret	12	F	Laborer	25Ma0211
BOOTLES, Arthur	04	M	Child	25Ma0211
DONNELLY, Patrick	20	M	Laborer	25Ma0211
QUINN, Patrick	22	M	Laborer	25Ma0211
DEMPSEY, James	27	M	Laborer	25Ma0211
GALL, Mary	20	F	Laborer	25Ma0211
FITZSIMMONS, John	21	M	Laborer	25Ma0211

NAMES OF PASSENGERS	AGE	SEX	OCCUPATIONS	DATE PORT SHIP
REILLEY, Micheal	22	M	Laborer	25Ma0211
DINDHAM, Benjamin	20	M	Laborer	25Ma0211
Ann	18	F	Laborer	25Ma0211
HART, John	16	M	Laborer	25Ma0211
CLARK, Philip	27	M	Laborer	25Ma0211
RYAN, Patrick	23	M	Laborer	25Ma0211
CLARK, Mary	47	F	Laborer	25Ma0211
Susan	22	F	Laborer	25Ma0211
PHILIPS, Conrad	39	M	Laborer	25Ma0211
Sophia	29	F	Laborer	25Ma0211
Elizabeth	18	F	Laborer	25Ma0211
Mary-Ann	12	F	Laborer	25Ma0211
KESLER, Jacob	27	M	Laborer	25Ma0211
Jane	27	F	Laborer	25Ma0211
WINS, John	18	M	Laborer	25Ma0211
KEELER, Peter	46	M	Laborer	25Ma0211
Margaret	18	F	Laborer	25Ma0211
Andrew	11	M	Laborer	25Ma0211
FITZGERALD, Wm.	24	M	Laborer	25Ma0211
BURKE, Wm.	24	M	Laborer	25Ma0211
BENAKY, Thomas	20	M	Laborer	25Ma0211
GIBSON, John	36	M	Laborer	25Ma0211
LELLAN, John	30	M	Laborer	25Ma0211
KEY, Adam	24	M	Laborer	25Ma0211
George	22	M	Laborer	25Ma0211
Jane	21	F	Laborer	25Ma0211
GALLAGER, Philip	19	M	Laborer	25Ma0211
KEYS, John	53	M	Laborer	25Ma0211
PIERCE, Robert	26	M	Gdnr	25Ma0211
SIPPS, Canard	48	M	Laborer	25Ma0211
Elizabeth	18	F	Laborer	25Ma0211
Casper	11	M	Laborer	25Ma0211
LEE, Patrick	28	M	Laborer	25Ma0211
TILFORD, Thos.	26	M	Laborer	25Ma0211
Mary	26	F	Laborer	25Ma0211
Margaret	02	F	Child	25Ma0211
Agnes	01	F	Infant	25Ma0211
CAREY, John	18	M	Laborer	25Ma0211
DELANE, Owen	25	M	Laborer	25Ma0211
MURPHY, Pat	18	M	Laborer	25Ma0211
MCCARNE, Patrick	17	M	Laborer	25Ma0211
WHITE, James	20	M	Gunsmith	25Ma0211
MCPEAK, John	18	M	Laborer	25Ma0211
Catharine	17	F	Laborer	25Ma0211
DUFFE, John	35	M	Laborer	25Ma0211
KERNAN, Bernard	31	M	Laborer	25Ma0211
MCMAHON, Francis	21	M	Laborer	25Ma0211
MACKEY, Andrew	21	M	Laborer	25Ma0211
MCGORRISH, Patrick	28	M	Farmer	25Ma0211
Mary	23	F	Farmer	25Ma0211
Andrew-Foster	.00	M	Infant	25Ma0211
Born-At-Sea				
CARROLL, Catharine	20	F	Farmer	25Ma0211
MCGORISH, Mary	05	F	Child	25Ma0211
Margaret	03	F	Child	25Ma0211
Anthony	02	M	Child	25Ma0211
BENNY, Wm.	50	M	Laborer	25Ma0211
Sarah	40	F	Laborer	25Ma0211
William	11	M	Laborer	25Ma0211
Elizabeth	09	F	Child	25Ma0211
Mary	07	F	Child	25Ma0211
BARNANS, Micheal	26	M	Laborer	25Ma0211
Mary	21	F	Laborer	25Ma0211
MCCAHON, Al	20	F	Laborer	25Ma0211
MCKENNY, Pat	45	F	Laborer	25Ma0211
Catharine	40	F	Laborer	25Ma0211
Mary	21	F	Laborer	25Ma0211
Patrick	18	M	Laborer	25Ma0211
Micheal	13	M	Laborer	25Ma0211
James	11	M	Laborer	25Ma0211
Catharine	09	F	Child	25Ma0211
David	08	F	Child	25Ma0211
BENNY, Thomas	20	M	Laborer	25Ma0211
SULLIVAN, Robert	20	M	Laborer	25Ma0211
FULHAM, Kitty	21	F	Laborer	25Ma0211

NAMES OF PASSENGERS		AGE	SEX	OCCUPATIONS	DATE PORT SHIP
FLYNN, Patrick		24	M	Laborer	25Ma02Il
MCHEAS, John		25	M	Laborer	25Ma02Il
MCELLHILL, Edward		27	M	Laborer	25Ma02Il
John		03	M	Child	25Ma02Il
Catharine		05	F	Child	25Ma02Il
HENRY, John		16	M	Laborer	25Ma02Il
MORAN, Mary		28	F	Laborer	25Ma02Il
SNYDERS, Thos.		00	M	Laborer	25Ma02Il
TAYLOR, Wm.		32	M	Laborer	25Ma02Il
Ann		30	F	Laborer	25Ma02Il
SUSAN, Fredrick		30	F	Laborer	25Ma02Il
Mary		28	F	Laborer	25Ma02Il
Charles		27	M	Laborer	25Ma02Il
DOOLY, John		30	M	Laborer	25Ma02Il
Mary		25	F	Laborer	25Ma02Il
HORVICKS, Daniel		23	M	Laborer	25Ma02Il
MCGILLEN, Margaret		21	F	None	25Ma02Il
COONEY, Nancy		40	F	None	25Ma02Il
MASTER, Patrick		24	M	Laborer	25Ma02Il
CARSON, Patrick		30	M	Laborer	25Ma02Il
Ellen		21	F	Laborer	25Ma02Il
HOLLAND, Bernard		40	M	Laborer	25Ma02Il
MORAN, Andrew		18	M	Laborer	25Ma02Il
Died-At-Sea					
MCSEVEGAN, John		23	M	Laborer	25Ma02Il
DANDAS, Carrol		23	U	Laborer	25Ma02Il
Mary-Ann		.00	F	Infant	25Ma02Il
George		02	M	Child	25Ma02Il
BOYLAN, Betty		20	F	Laborer	25Ma02Il
MCCALL, Mary		20	F	Laborer	25Ma02Il
NOON, John		30	M	Laborer	25Ma02Il
Caroline		25	F	Laborer	25Ma02Il
Charles		16	M	Laborer	25Ma02Il
Alfred		02	M	Child	25Ma02Il
Edith		.00	F	Infant	25Ma02Il
Eliza		20	F	Laborer	25Ma02Il
CASLEY, Henry		25	M	Laborer	25Ma02Il
GRETON, John		25	M	Laborer	25Ma02Il
THOMPSON, Alex		09	M	Child	25Ma02Il
RYANS, Martha		59	F	Laborer	25Ma02Il
THOMPSON, John		06	M	Child	25Ma02Il
GRETON, Mary-Ann		23	F	Laborer	25Ma02Il
THOMPSON, Mary		20	F	Laborer	25Ma02Il
KENNY, James		13	M	Laborer	25Ma02Il
DANDINS, Edward		26	M	Laborer	25Ma02Il
DERKEN, Peter		25	M	Laborer	25Ma02Il

JULINDER 26 MAY 1848

From Liverpool

NAMES OF PASSENGERS		AGE	SEX	OCCUPATIONS	DATE PORT SHIP
GREENWOOD, Henry		20	M	Laborer	26Ma02Je
JOHNSTON, Geo.		20	M	Laborer	26Ma02Je
U	(W)	30	F	Wife	26Ma02Je
KIRKLAND, Thos.		20	M	Laborer	26Ma02Je
U	(W)	20	F	Wife	26Ma02Je
ROEBUCK, Geo.		36	M	Farmer	26Ma02Je
U	(W)	36	F	Wife	26Ma02Je
Henry	(S)	09	M	Child	26Ma02Je
Rachael	(D)	03	F	Child	26Ma02Je
Mary	(D)	.00	F	Infant	26Ma02Je
DUNN, John		29	M	Laborer	26Ma02Je
HOOSON, Isarael		26	M	Laborer	26Ma02Je
U	(W)	26	F	Laborer	26Ma02Je
BRADLEY, Wm.		40	M	Laborer	26Ma02Je
Sarah		40	F	Laborer	26Ma02Je
Nancy		12	F	Unknown	26Ma02Je
Arthur		09	M	Child	26Ma02Je
William		05	M	Child	26Ma02Je

NAMES OF PASSENGERS		AGE	SEX	OCCUPATIONS	DATE PORT SHIP
BRADLEY, Alfred		.00	M	Infant	26Ma02Je
WOLFENDEN, Alfred		25	M	Farmer	26Ma02Je
WILSON, James		26	M	Unknown	26Ma02Je
BUTTERSIDE, John		30	M	Unknown	26Ma02Je
DYSON, Bright.		34	F	Spinster	26Ma02Je
HARRISON, John		23	M	Laborer	26Ma02Je
ELAM, Chas.		36	M	Laborer	26Ma02Je
ROBINSON, Chas.		25	M	Laborer	26Ma02Je
DAVIES, Bernard		25	M	Laborer	26Ma02Je
FARRELL, Jas.		25	M	Laborer	26Ma02Je
MACLIN, Jas.		24	M	Laborer	26Ma02Je
MCCOLLINN, Pat		26	M	Laborer	26Ma02Je
U	(W)	24	F	Laborer	26Ma02Je
Margt.		08	F	Child	26Ma02Je
MCFEDDING, Chas.		22	M	Farmer	26Ma02Je
GALLAGHER, Darby		21	M	Farmer	26Ma02Je
MCGAINEY, Giles		16	M	Farmer	26Ma02Je
MCFADDEN, Chas.		21	M	Farmer	26Ma02Je
DWYER, Fanny		23	F	Spinster	26Ma02Je
GALLAGHER, Thos.		20	M	Spinner	26Ma02Je
OBRIEN, Mary		23	F	Spinster	26Ma02Je
ELLIOTT, Jane		25	F	Spinster	26Ma02Je
MCILHERE, Mary		18	F	Spinster	26Ma02Je
MCGINLEY, Nelly		24	F	Spinster	26Ma02Je
Ann		05	F	Child	26Ma02Je
CONNAN, Wm.		20	M	Spinner	26Ma02Je
HARNIN, Barney		21	M	Laborer	26Ma02Je
MCFADDEN, John		11	M	Unknown	26Ma02Je
MOFFATT, Patt		57	M	Unknown	26Ma02Je
Margt.	(W)	58	F	Wife	26Ma02Je
James		20	M	Laborer	26Ma02Je
Ann	(W)	18	F	Wife	26Ma02Je
Thomas		17	M	Laborer	26Ma02Je
MUNDY, John		40	M	Laborer	26Ma02Je
Wm.		40	M	Laborer	26Ma02Je
Mary		15	F	Laborer	26Ma02Je
Mathew		07	M	Child	26Ma02Je
Ann		05	F	Child	26Ma02Je
CULLEN, Cathr.		30	F	Laborer	26Ma02Je
NEAL, John		27	M	Laborer	26Ma02Je
MCCRUEN, James		24	M	Laborer	26Ma02Je
Francis		22	M	Laborer	26Ma02Je
GALLAGHER, James		40	M	Laborer	26Ma02Je
John		11	M	Unknown	26Ma02Je
Constantine		20	M	Laborer	26Ma02Je
CONNOR, Cathr.		35	F	Wife	26Ma02Je
Mary	(D)	11	F	Unknown	26Ma02Je
John	(S)	07	M	Unknown	26Ma02Je
Cathr.	(D)	05	F	Unknown	26Ma02Je
Isarel	(S)	03	M	Unknown	26Ma02Je
James	(S)	.00	M	Infant	26Ma02Je
HIGGINS, Eliza		30	F	Wife	26Ma02Je
Chas.	(S)	06	M	Child	26Ma02Je
KNIGHT, Maria		18	F	Spinster	26Ma02Je
ROBINSON, G.R.		26	M	Farmer	26Ma02Je
CARVER, J.G.		27	U	Unknown	26Ma02Je
DEAN, Danl.		45	M	Unknown	26Ma02Je
U	(W)	43	F	Wife	26Ma02Je
HAGERDOWN, Thos.		23	M	Laborer	26Ma02Je
Cathr.		14	F	Spinster	26Ma02Je
Jane		09	F	Child	26Ma02Je
Robt.		05	M	Child	26Ma02Je
BRYANT, Beng.		24	M	Laborer	26Ma02Je
HATTOCK, Josiah		35	M	Laborer	26Ma02Je
DIXON, Wm.		24	M	Laborer	26Ma02Je
HASLANN, James		46	M	Laborer	26Ma02Je
Ann	(W)	46	F	Wife	26Ma02Je
James		19	M	Laborer	26Ma02Je
Moses		17	M	Unknown	26Ma02Je
FLINAGAN, Dennis		24	M	Unknown	26Ma02Je
Ann	(W)	22	F	Wife	26Ma02Je
Mary		20	F	Unknown	26Ma02Je
PRINSON, John		28	M	Laborer	26Ma02Je
WEBB, Thomas		26	M	Unknown	26Ma02Je
EMERY, U-Mrs.		26	F	Wife	26Ma02Je

NAMES OF PASSENGERS		A G E	S E X	OCCUPATIONS	DATE PORT SHIP
EMERY, U	(D)	15	F	Unknown	26Ma02Je
U	(D)	14	F	Unknown	26Ma02Je
U	(D)	02	F	Child	26Ma02Je
U	(D)	.00	F	Infant	26Ma02Je
LOONEY, Thomas		26	M	Laborer	26Ma02Je
BRIEN, Thos.D.		18	M	Laborer	26Ma02Je
MARTIN, Jane		30	F	Laborer	26Ma02Je
QUINLAN, Jerh.		24	M	Laborer	26Ma02Je
GARRETT, Edwd.		22	M	Laborer	26Ma02Je
DWYER, Wm.		24	M	Laborer	26Ma02Je
RYAN, Thos.		24	M	Laborer	26Ma02Je
CARTHEY, Michl. Died-At-Sea		22	M	Laborer	26Ma02Je
BARRY, John		20	M	Laborer	26Ma02Je
WALLACE, Mary		20	F	Laborer	26Ma02Je
DWYER, Mary		14	F	Spinster	26Ma02Je
CARTY, Indy		20	U	Unknown	26Ma02Je
KEAL, Wm.		18	M	Laborer	26Ma02Je
GORDON, Lawn.		22	M	Unknown	26Ma02Je
Alice		17	F	Spinster	26Ma02Je
GIBNEY, Margt.		22	F	Unknown	26Ma02Je
FEGAN, Ann		12	F	Unknown	26Ma02Je
Pat		10	M	Unknown	26Ma02Je
ACHESON, Wm.		21	M	Laborer	26Ma02Je
MOONEY, John		22	M	Unknown	26Ma02Je
DONAHY, Andw.		25	M	Laborer	26Ma02Je
MURRAY, Margery		21	F	Spinster	26Ma02Je
Jane		20	F	Wife	26Ma02Je
Mary		.00	F	Infant	26Ma02Je
JOHNSTON, James		35	M	Laborer	26Ma02Je
Cathr.		18	F	Spinster	26Ma02Je
Pat.		14	M	Unknown	26Ma02Je
Margt.		09	F	Child	26Ma02Je
Jane		06	F	Child	26Ma02Je
Sarah		04	F	Child	26Ma02Je
HURLEY, James		40	M	Laborer	26Ma02Je
Margt.	(W)	35	F	Wife	26Ma02Je
Patk.	(S)	07	M	Child	26Ma02Je
Henry	(S)	05	M	Child	26Ma02Je
Michl.		23	M	Unknown	26Ma02Je
Mary	(D)	.00	F	Infant	26Ma02Je
OBRIEN, Heny.		24	M	Unknown	26Ma02Je
Ann	(W)	20	F	Wife	26Ma02Je
HAND, James		35	M	Laborer	26Ma02Je
Margt.		25	F	Unknown	26Ma02Je
CONNELL, Pat		23	M	Unknown	26Ma02Je
MCATEER, Ann		25	F	Wife	26Ma02Je
Mary		23	F	Unknown	26Ma02Je
SMITH, Cathr.		22	F	Unknown	26Ma02Je
CALLEN, Hugh		50	M	Laborer	26Ma02Je
Elizth.	(W)	48	F	Wife	26Ma02Je
John		30	M	Laborer	26Ma02Je
Margt.		14	F	Unknown	26Ma02Je
Betty		12	F	Unknown	26Ma02Je
Jane		10	F	Unknown	26Ma02Je
Mary		08	F	Child	26Ma02Je
James		06	M	Child	26Ma02Je
Pat		04	M	Child	26Ma02Je
John		02	M	Child	26Ma02Je
Elizth.		.00	F	Infant	26Ma02Je
MAHONEY, Wm.		30	M	Laborer	26Ma02Je
Ellen		30	F	Laborer	26Ma02Je
Dennis		40	M	Laborer	26Ma02Je
DENNIS, Mary		28	F	Laborer	26Ma02Je
ERWIN, James		24	M	Laborer	26Ma02Je
Bridgt.		21	F	Laborer	26Ma02Je
John		06	M	Child	26Ma02Je
Margt.		15	F	Unknown	26Ma02Je
Mary		02	F	Child	26Ma02Je
Jane		02	F	Child	26Ma02Je
BRADY, James		30	M	Laborer	26Ma02Je
Mary	(W)	28	F	Wife	26Ma02Je
Jane	(D)	12	F	Unknown	26Ma02Je
Ann	(D)	06	F	Child	26Ma02Je
WALSH, Mathew		04	M	Child	26Ma02Je
WALSH, Mary		02	F	Child	26Ma02Je
ERWIN, James		14	M	Laborer	26Ma02Je
John		06	M	Child	26Ma02Je
HOOSON, U		.00	U	Infant	26Ma02Je
NEILL, Thos.		00	M	Unknown	26Ma02Je
SHEPHERD, Dan		00	M	Unknown	26Ma02Je
RILLER, E.		00	M	Unknown	26Ma02Je
GARSHIRE, E.		00	M	Unknown	26Ma02Je
TRINLAN, U		00	M	Unknown	26Ma02Je
U	(W)	00	F	Unknown	26Ma02Je

LORD-ASHBURTON 26 MAY 1848

From Dublin

NAMES OF PASSENGERS		A G E	S E X	OCCUPATIONS	DATE PORT SHIP
FITZGERALD, John		20	M	Farmer	26Ma20Jf
STEPHENS, Edward		35	M	Farmer	26Ma20Jf
Lenard		30	M	Farmer	26Ma20Jf
NERTON, Martin		24	M	Farmer	26Ma20Jf
BRYAN, Morgan		24	M	Farmer	26Ma20Jf
MOREHOUSE, Ruth		30	F	Servant	26Ma20Jf
CARROLL, John		57	M	Bootmaker	26Ma20Jf
Mary		20	F	Bootmaker	26Ma20Jf
Biddy		30	F	Bootmaker	26Ma20Jf
Pat		19	M	Bootmaker	26Ma20Jf
Dennis		17	M	Bootmaker	26Ma20Jf
Anne		12	F	Bootmaker	26Ma20Jf
Ellen		10	F	Bootmaker	26Ma20Jf
John		07	M	Child	26Ma20Jf
Margt.		05	F	Child	26Ma20Jf
Eliza		.00	F	Infant	26Ma20Jf
GOGARTY, Pat		19	M	Bootmaker	26Ma20Jf
Mary		25	F	Bootmaker	26Ma20Jf
Cath.		04	F	Child	26Ma20Jf
Thomas		.00	M	Infant	26Ma20Jf
BROUKE, Pat		24	M	Farmer	26Ma20Jf
MAHON, Mary		15	F	Farmer	26Ma20Jf
NUGENT, Peter		07	M	Child	26Ma20Jf
BRANNIGAN, Ellen		26	F	Cabdriver	26Ma20Jf
NESBITT, William		25	M	Cabdriver	26Ma20Jf
Eliza		25	F	Cabdriver	26Ma20Jf
Susan		.00	F	Infant	26Ma20Jf
MILLAR, Thos.		35	M	Butcher	26Ma20Jf
Kitty		34	F	Butcher	26Ma20Jf
John		04	M	Child	26Ma20Jf
Bessy		02	F	Child	26Ma20Jf
Maria		11	F	Servant	26Ma20Jf
SCANLAN, William		32	M	Servant	26Ma20Jf
WOOD, Luke		40	M	Baker	26Ma20Jf
Mary		30	F	Unknown	26Ma20Jf
Thomas		11	M	Unknown	26Ma20Jf
Anne		04	F	Child	26Ma20Jf
Anne		.00	F	Infant	26Ma20Jf
CONNOLLY, Peter		25	M	Servant	26Ma20Jf
MCCABE, William		21	M	Servant	26Ma20Jf
GROSS, Jas.		26	M	Servant	26Ma20Jf
Biddy		20	F	Servant	26Ma20Jf
Wanford		17	F	Unknown	26Ma20Jf
John		15	M	Butcher	26Ma20Jf
Margt.		28	F	Butcher	26Ma20Jf
Margt.		19	F	Butcher	26Ma20Jf
Elizabeth		28	F	Butcher	26Ma20Jf
KELLY, Michl.		30	M	Farmer	26Ma20Jf
Mary		30	F	Farmer	26Ma20Jf
DOWD, Ann		20	F	Farmer	26Ma20Jf
KELLY, James		24	M	Farmer	26Ma20Jf
LYONS, Ann		22	F	Unknown	26Ma20Jf
John		50	M	Brick Maker	26Ma20Jf
Mary		50	F	Unknown	26Ma20Jf

NAMES OF PASSENGERS	AGE	SEX	OCCUPATIONS	DATE PORT SHIP
LYONS, William	24	M	Unknown	26Ma20Jf
Thomas	18	M	Unknown	26Ma20Jf
Ellen	16	F	Spinster	26Ma20Jf
BEHAN, Pat	27	M	Farmer	26Ma20Jf
Jane	29	F	Farmer	26Ma20Jf
James	.00	M	Infant	26Ma20Jf
CONNOR, William	28	M	Farmer	26Ma20Jf
Cath.	24	F	Farmer	26Ma20Jf
WILSON, Henry	25	M	Farmer	26Ma20Jf
MCGURTE, John	30	M	Farmer	26Ma20Jf
RUSH, Mike	40	M	Farmer	26Ma20Jf
Biddy	35	F	Farmer	26Ma20Jf
MEARA, John	36	M	Bootmaker	26Ma20Jf
WELDON, William	16	M	Bootmaker	26Ma20Jf
KAVANAGH, Jas.	20	M	Bootmaker	26Ma20Jf
CULLEN, Eliza	21	F	Bootmaker	26Ma20Jf
John	.00	M	Infant	26Ma20Jf
Anne	19	F	Bootmaker	26Ma20Jf
Pat	34	M	Farmer	26Ma20Jf
Biddy	24	F	Farmer	26Ma20Jf
Jane	10	F	Farmer	26Ma20Jf
Biddy	08	F	Child	26Ma20Jf
Mary	07	F	Child	26Ma20Jf
Cathr.	05	F	Child	26Ma20Jf
Sarah	03	F	Child	26Ma20Jf
Anne	.00	F	Infant	26Ma20Jf
Roseanna	00	F	Unknown	26Ma20Jf
MOLLOY, Mick	27	M	Servant	26Ma20Jf
BARRETT, Pat	30	M	Servant	26Ma20Jf
Biddy	34	F	Servant	26Ma20Jf
Ann	20	F	Servant	26Ma20Jf
John	18	M	Cabdriver	26Ma20Jf
KEOGH, Pat	19	M	Cabdriver	26Ma20Jf
Cath.	30	F	Cabdriver	26Ma20Jf
Hannah	.00	F	Infant	26Ma20Jf
BYRNE, Julia	17	F	Cabdriver	26Ma20Jf
Mary	40	F	Cabdriver	26Ma20Jf
LYONS, Denis	11	M	Gdnr	26Ma20Jf
John	09	M	Child	26Ma20Jf
Joseph	07	M	Child	26Ma20Jf
KEVANAGH, Dan	40	M	Gdnr	26Ma20Jf
Biddy	35	F	Gdnr	26Ma20Jf
Ann	10	F	Spinster	26Ma20Jf
Michl.	05	M	Child	26Ma20Jf
John	03	M	Child	26Ma20Jf
LYONS, Pat	45	M	Weaver	26Ma20Jf
Betty	19	F	Weaver	26Ma20Jf
Pat	17	M	Weaver	26Ma20Jf
Harriet	14	F	Weaver	26Ma20Jf
Mary-Anne	12	F	Weaver	26Ma20Jf
James	11	M	Weaver	26Ma20Jf
John	09	M	Child	26Ma20Jf
William	06	M	Child	26Ma20Jf
SMITH, Eliza	19	F	Cobbler	26Ma20Jf
NOWLAN, Andrew	30	M	Cobbler	26Ma20Jf
LENNON, Anne	19	F	Cobbler	26Ma20Jf
BYRNE, Geo.	50	M	Mason	26Ma20Jf
Mary	48	F	Mason	26Ma20Jf
Margt.	33	F	Mason	26Ma20Jf
Judy	20	F	Mason	26Ma20Jf
Peter	18	M	Mason	26Ma20Jf
Anne	13	F	Spinster	26Ma20Jf
Patk.	03	M	Child	26Ma20Jf
RYAN, James	25	M	Spinner	26Ma20Jf
CULLEN, Pat	25	M	Spinner	26Ma20Jf
LOUGHLIN, Jas.	22	M	Spinner	26Ma20Jf
Eliza	26	F	Baker	26Ma20Jf
Margt.	17	F	Baker	26Ma20Jf
CARROLL, Simon	26	M	Baker	26Ma20Jf
NOLAN, Mick	23	M	Baker	26Ma20Jf
BEHAN, John	40	M	Baker	26Ma20Jf
BYRNE, Eliza	16	F	Baker	26Ma20Jf
Peter	13	M	Baker	26Ma20Jf
MURPHY, John	30	M	Baker	26Ma20Jf
Cath.	27	F	Spinster	26Ma20Jf

NAMES OF PASSENGERS	AGE	SEX	OCCUPATIONS	DATE PORT SHIP
MURPHY, Mary	03	F	Child	26Ma20Jf
Cath.	.00	F	Infant	26Ma20Jf
READ, Mary-A.	25	F	Spinster	26Ma20Jf
KELLY, Pat	40	M	Butcher	26Ma20Jf
CORRIGAN, Pat	26	M	Butcher	26Ma20Jf
LOUGHLIN, Danl.	26	M	Butcher	26Ma20Jf
Dennis	22	M	Butcher	26Ma20Jf
Mary	18	F	Butcher	26Ma20Jf
WHELAN, Cath.	19	F	Servant	26Ma20Jf
NOWLAN, Eliza	17	F	Servant	26Ma20Jf
BYRNE, Martin	30	M	Servant	26Ma20Jf
Cath.	27	F	Servant	26Ma20Jf
Pat	11	M	Servant	26Ma20Jf
FARRELL, Pat	22	M	Unknown	26Ma20Jf
CRAIG, Geo.	34	M	Unknown	26Ma20Jf
Sarah	32	F	Baker	26Ma20Jf
John	05	M	Child	26Ma20Jf
Eliza	03	F	Child	26Ma20Jf
ALFRED, Geo.	.00	M	Infant	26Ma20Jf
BYRNE, Hugh	16	M	Baker	26Ma20Jf
CARTY, James	17	M	Baker	26Ma20Jf
CARROLL, Eliza	50	F	Servant	26Ma20Jf
Margt.	25	F	Servant	26Ma20Jf
Mary	21	F	Servant	26Ma20Jf
MAXWELL, Eliza	.00	F	Infant	26Ma20Jf
NOWLAN, Eliza	24	F	Servant	26Ma20Jf
WILSON, William	25	M	Servant	26Ma20Jf
Biddy	20	F	Waiter	26Ma20Jf
James	.00	M	Infant	26Ma20Jf
DOYLE, Anthony	36	M	Waiter	26Ma20Jf
Pat	16	M	Waiter	26Ma20Jf
William	13	M	Waiter	26Ma20Jf
DENNIS, John	30	M	Waiter	26Ma20Jf
Mary	34	F	Waiter	26Ma20Jf
Catherine	06	F	Child	26Ma20Jf
Thomas	04	M	Child	26Ma20Jf
Anne	.00	F	Infant	26Ma20Jf
STANLEY, James	24	M	Servant	26Ma20Jf
Marcella	28	F	Servant	26Ma20Jf
HALPIN, Ellen	24	F	Servant	26Ma20Jf
Mary	14	F	Servant	26Ma20Jf
Pat	.00	M	Infant	26Ma20Jf
FAY, Thos.	17	M	Tinker	26Ma20Jf
PASLEY, James	20	M	Tinker	26Ma20Jf
Eliza	40	F	Spinster	26Ma20Jf
Jane	18	F	Spinster	26Ma20Jf
Charles	11	M	Spinster	26Ma20Jf
DELANY, Jno.	20	M	Spinster	26Ma20Jf
Mary	18	F	Spinster	26Ma20Jf
KEANE, Peter	22	M	Spinster	26Ma20Jf
Biddy	20	F	Mason	26Ma20Jf
Henry	.00	M	Infant	26Ma20Jf
RYAN, Martin	30	M	Shoemaker	26Ma20Jf
Cath.	36	F	Shoemaker	26Ma20Jf
Jenny	19	F	Shoemaker	26Ma20Jf
Catherine	17	F	Shoemaker	26Ma20Jf
John	15	M	Shoemaker	26Ma20Jf
Margt.	13	F	Shoemaker	26Ma20Jf
Pat	09	M	Child	26Ma20Jf
Mary	11	F	Shoemaker	26Ma20Jf
Julia	07	F	Shoemaker	26Ma20Jf
TAAFE, Anne	27	F	Shoemaker	26Ma20Jf
Michl.	02	M	Child	26Ma20Jf
Peter	.00	M	Infant	26Ma20Jf
ATKINSON, Anne	25	F	Baker	26Ma20Jf
Henry	04	M	Child	26Ma20Jf
Thomas	02	M	Child	26Ma20Jf
BARTON, Thos.	21	M	Baker	26Ma20Jf
Robt.	20	M	Baker	26Ma20Jf
Eliza	16	F	Baker	26Ma20Jf
Mary	42	F	Baker	26Ma20Jf
CORLING, Margt.	12	F	Spinster	26Ma20Jf
REILLY, Lance.	22	M	Tanner	26Ma20Jf
WALSH, Owen	23	M	Tanner	26Ma20Jf
WELDON, Christopher	25	M	Tanner	26Ma20Jf

NAMES OF PASSENGERS	AGE	SEX	OCCUPATIONS	DATE PORT SHIP
RILLEY, Matt.	20	M	Tanner	26Ma20Jf
REILLY, Mary	22	F	Spinster	26Ma20Jf
WELDON, Mary	27	F	Spinster	26Ma20Jf
MULLIGAN, Anne	25	F	Spinster	26Ma20Jf
DALTON, Thomas	34	M	Blacksmith	26Ma20Jf
CULLEN, James	41	F	Blacksmith	26Ma20Jf
Eliza	31	F	Blacksmith	26Ma20Jf
Anne	02	F	Child	26Ma20Jf
CONNOR, Pat	24	M	Blacksmith	26Ma20Jf
HICKEY, Mick	29	M	Blacksmith	26Ma20Jf
Cath.	29	F	Blacksmith	26Ma20Jf
Jane	08	F	Child	26Ma20Jf
THORTON, Jane	15	F	Unknown	26Ma20Jf
CLANCY, Thos.	24	M	Farmer	26Ma20Jf
Anne	19	F	Farmer	26Ma20Jf
Eliza	12	F	Farmer	26Ma20Jf
MERRIGAN, Pat	35	M	Farmer	26Ma20Jf
Mary	38	F	Farmer	26Ma20Jf
Mary	.00	F	Infant	26Ma20Jf
FARRELL, Frank	27	M	Baker	26Ma20Jf
GOLDING, Mary	19	F	Baker	26Ma20Jf
WHITTAKER, William	21	M	Baker	26Ma20Jf
NAUGHTON, Anne	22	F	Baker	26Ma20Jf
Maria	20	F	Baker	26Ma20Jf
HOGAN, Denis	24	M	Hod Carrier	26Ma20Jf
RYAN, Eliza	50	F	Hod Carrier	26Ma20Jf
William	21	M	Hod Carrier	26Ma20Jf
Kate	11	F	Hod Carrier	26Ma20Jf
GILMORE, Owen	25	M	Hod Carrier	26Ma20Jf
JACKSON, Stephen	26	M	Paper Maker	26Ma20Jf
DOLAN, Richd.	26	M	Paper Maker	26Ma20Jf
HUTCHESON, Edwd.	26	M	Paper Maker	26Ma20Jf
KEDETT, Henry	30	M	Paper Maker	26Ma20Jf
Susan	26	F	Paper Maker	26Ma20Jf
STEPHENS, Eliza	19	F	Paper Maker	26Ma20Jf
OBRIEN, Jno.	60	M	Bookmaker	26Ma20Jf
Anne	13	F	Bookmaker	26Ma20Jf
NOLAN, Henry	21	M	Bookmaker	26Ma20Jf
CULLEN, Morris	26	M	Bookmaker	26Ma20Jf
MCCANN, Mich.	21	M	Bookmaker	26Ma20Jf
MCDOWELL, Anne	21	F	Spinster	26Ma20Jf
OBRIEN, Cath	11	F	Spinster	26Ma20Jf
Pat	09	M	Child	26Ma20Jf
James	07	M	Child	26Ma20Jf
HAUGHTON, Jno.	27	M	Spinner	26Ma20Jf
Mary	22	F	Spinster	26Ma20Jf
William	15	M	Spinner	26Ma20Jf
CARROLL, Cath.	40	F	Spinster	26Ma20Jf
Pat	20	M	Servant	26Ma20Jf
CUTHBERT, Mary	19	F	Servant	26Ma20Jf
MCGUIRE, Robt.	30	M	Servant	26Ma20Jf
DURVIN, James	24	M	Servant	26Ma20Jf
Margt.	40	F	Servant	26Ma20Jf
Anne	25	U	Servant	26Ma20Jf
Biddy	16	F	Gdnr	26Ma20Jf
Judy	15	F	Gdnr	26Ma20Jf
Pat	.00	M	Infant	26Ma20Jf
DEMPSEY, Edward	30	M	Gdnr	26Ma20Jf
Mary	23	F	Gdnr	26Ma20Jf
Kate	.00	F	Infant	26Ma20Jf
ANDERSON, Jno.	24	M	Unknown	26Ma20Jf
James	35	M	Unknown	26Ma20Jf
Jane	19	F	Farmer	26Ma20Jf
Mary	18	F	Farmer	26Ma20Jf
Thomas	25	M	Farmer	26Ma20Jf
WILSON, Anne	25	F	Farmer	26Ma20Jf
BRANEGAN, James	24	M	Tinker	26Ma20Jf
Betty	14	F	Unknown	26Ma20Jf
Catherin	40	F	Unknown	26Ma20Jf
WISEMAN, Jas.	14	M	Unknown	26Ma20Jf
CRANN, Cornelius	18	M	Bootmaker	26Ma20Jf
THORPE, Geo.	25	M	Bootmaker	26Ma20Jf
SINNOTT, Frans.	25	M	Bootmaker	26Ma20Jf
CANDLE, William	20	M	Bootmaker	26Ma20Jf
MURPHY, Roseanna	19	F	Bootmaker	26Ma20Jf
MURPHY, Biddy	19	F	Bootmaker	26Ma20Jf
Hugh	16	M	Bootmaker	26Ma20Jf
CADY, Jno.	30	M	Bootmaker	26Ma20Jf
Cath.	28	F	Bootmaker	26Ma20Jf
John	.00	M	Infant	26Ma20Jf
BRADY, Frans.	20	M	Unknown	26Ma20Jf
Cath.	23	F	Unknown	26Ma20Jf
HANDEN, Richd.	30	M	Unknown	26Ma20Jf
ROURKE, Cath.	40	F	Unknown	26Ma20Jf
Mary-Anne	20	F	Unknown	26Ma20Jf
NEVILLE, Henry	18	M	Unknown	26Ma20Jf
Charlotte	20	F	Brick Maker	26Ma20Jf
MADDEN, Cath.	26	F	Unknown	26Ma20Jf
NEVILLE, Emily	18	F	Unknown	26Ma20Jf
COLLINS, Frans.	28	F	Unknown	26Ma20Jf
MCGRAM, Michl.	30	M	Fina	26Ma20Jf
CONSTANTINE, Mary	24	F	Fina	26Ma20Jf
KERFORD, William	22	M	Fina	26Ma20Jf
CONNELL, Cath.	20	F	Fina	26Ma20Jf
Do---, Pat	18	M	Fina	26Ma20Jf
BYRNE, Hugh	18	M	Vet	26Ma20Jf
CULLEN, Pat	24	M	Baker	26Ma20Jf
John	30	M	Butcher	26Ma20Jf
Anne	17	F	Spinster	26Ma20Jf
Margt.	16	F	None	26Ma20Jf
TURNER, David	23	M	Spinner	26Ma20Jf
COLLINS, Mary	14	F	Spinster	26Ma20Jf
MCKENNA, Mary	20	F	Spinster	26Ma20Jf
TRACY, Eliza	22	F	Servant	26Ma20Jf
SMITH, Mary	22	F	Servant	26Ma20Jf
TRACY, Eliza	23	F	Servant	26Ma20Jf
BIRD, Thomas	26	M	Farmer	26Ma20Jf
BAXTER, Thomas	24	M	Farmer	26Ma20Jf
NUGENT, Peter	30	M	Farmer	26Ma20Jf
BEYLEY, John	26	M	Unknown	26Ma20Jf
WHELAN, Henry	23	M	Unknown	26Ma20Jf
DELAWARE, Thos.	30	M	Unknown	26Ma20Jf

OXFORD 27 MAY 1848

From Liverpool

NAMES OF PASSENGERS	AGE	SEX	OCCUPATIONS	DATE PORT SHIP
HUTTON, George	32	M	Gentleman	27Ma02Aj
Fanny	26	F	Unknown	27Ma02Aj
Ann-Josephine	06	F	Child	27Ma02Aj
George	04	M	Child	27Ma02Aj
Elizabeth-B.	02	F	Child	27Ma02Aj
OBEIRNE, Patrick	26	M	Gentleman	27Ma02Aj
DEWY, Rowland-W.	27	M	Physician	27Ma02Aj
Sarah	28	F	Physician	27Ma02Aj
SHAW, Samuel-M.	23	M	Mechanic	27Ma02Aj
Elizabeth	22	F	Mechanic	27Ma02Aj
Ann-Maria	03	F	Child	27Ma02Aj
Alfred Died-At-Sea	.00	M	Infant	27Ma02Aj
SOUL, Samuel	36	M	Clothier	27Ma02Aj
Emma	29	F	Clothier	27Ma02Aj
Emma	04	F	Child	27Ma02Aj
James	02	M	Child	27Ma02Aj
Elizas	.00	F	Infant	27Ma02Aj
WRIGHT, John	25	M	Merchant	27Ma02Aj
Anna	21	F	Merchant	27Ma02Aj
TOWNSAND, Matilda	18	F	None	27Ma02Aj
WARD, Jane	18	F	None	27Ma02Aj
BROWN, Thomas	22	M	Mechanic	27Ma02Aj
COOPER, James	27	M	Mechanic	27Ma02Aj
PARKER, Charles	20	M	Mechanic	27Ma02Aj
STEVENSON, John	28	M	Mechanic	27Ma02Aj
Mary	40	F	Mechanic	27Ma02Aj

NAMES OF PASSENGERS	AGE	SEX	OCCUPATIONS	DATE PORT SHIP	NAMES OF PASSENGERS	AGE	SEX	OCCUPATIONS	DATE PORT SHIP
HANNAH, William	42	M	Mechanic	27Ma02Aj	CRANE, James	02	M	Child	27Ma02Aj
Mary	42	F	Mechanic	27Ma02Aj	Ann	.00	F	Infant	27Ma02Aj
CRAIG, Margret	25	F	None	27Ma02Aj	MCNAMARA, Stephen	22	M	Laborer	27Ma02Aj
MAIN, Eliza	25	F	None	27Ma02Aj	James	22	M	Laborer	27Ma02Aj
ELLISON, Henry	26	M	Weaver	27Ma02Aj	PARK, Charles	24	M	Miner	27Ma02Aj
Nancy	22	F	Weaver	27Ma02Aj	WILLIAMS, John	24	M	Carpenter	27Ma02Aj
Robert	07	M	Child	27Ma02Aj	ANDERSON, Patrick	24	M	Laborer	27Ma02Aj
Mary	26	F	Weaver	27Ma02Aj	BLUNT, Matthew	18	M	Laborer	27Ma02Aj
GOOBRICK, Ann	18	F	Servant	27Ma02Aj	CARLIN, Ann	18	F	Laborer	27Ma02Aj
PATRICKSON, Jane	18	F	Servant	27Ma02Aj	DAVIDSON, Jeson	24	M	Butcher	27Ma02Aj
CARROL, Margret	20	F	Laborer	27Ma02Aj	BYRNES, Patrick	32	M	Farmer	27Ma02Aj
VERDINE, James	70	M	Laborer	27Ma02Aj	Margret	25	F	Farmer	27Ma02Aj
William	30	M	Laborer	27Ma02Aj	Ann	06	F	Child	27Ma02Aj
Mary	70	F	Laborer	27Ma02Aj	Patrick	04	M	Child	27Ma02Aj
SHERRY, Catherine	25	F	Servant	27Ma02Aj	Mary	.00	F	Infant	27Ma02Aj
VERDINE, Catherine	30	F	Servant	27Ma02Aj	MCQUIRK, Thomas	20	M	Laborer	27Ma02Aj
COLLINS, Patrick	35	M	Laborer	27Ma02Aj	BRANCH, James	24	M	Laborer	27Ma02Aj
GRIFFIN, John	54	M	Baker	27Ma02Aj	BURNS, Rose	20	F	Laborer	27Ma02Aj
Johannas	54	M	Baker	27Ma02Aj	CAHILL, Patrick	21	M	Farmer	27Ma02Aj
Ann	10	F	Baker	27Ma02Aj	DREYAN, Thomas	30	M	Farmer	27Ma02Aj
William	14	M	Baker	27Ma02Aj	MEILLINEAUX, Susan	18	F	Farmer	27Ma02Aj
Margret	10	F	Baker	27Ma02Aj	MCALLINEY, Patrick	20	M	Farmer	27Ma02Aj
DEVINE, Michael	24	M	Laborer	27Ma02Aj	Mary	22	F	Farmer	27Ma02Aj
HALLORAN, Patrick-O.	40	M	Farmer	27Ma02Aj	COLEMAN, Thomas	35	M	Laborer	27Ma02Aj
CREMIN, Mary	23	F	None	27Ma02Aj	CASEY, William	25	M	Farmer	27Ma02Aj
URVING, Alexander	23	M	Farmer	27Ma02Aj	MARRIGAN, David	21	M	Laborer	27Ma02Aj
Mary-Ann	30	F	Farmer	27Ma02Aj	STARKY, Ann	24	F	Laborer	27Ma02Aj
John	21	M	Farmer	27Ma02Aj	CORMIN, Thomas	19	M	Laborer	27Ma02Aj
John	.00	M	Infant	27Ma02Aj	TEYNE, Ann	20	F	Laborer	27Ma02Aj
Michael	28	M	Farmer	27Ma02Aj	MULLANE, Thomas	20	M	Laborer	27Ma02Aj
Edward	28	M	Farmer	27Ma02Aj	MCDONALD, Owen	23	M	Laborer	27Ma02Aj
MCLAUGHLIN, William	19	M	Laborer	27Ma02Aj	Charles	19	M	Laborer	27Ma02Aj
Sarah	26	F	Laborer	27Ma02Aj	Bridget	30	F	Laborer	27Ma02Aj
MARTIN, Bernard	25	M	Laborer	27Ma02Aj	ONEILL, Charles	20	M	Laborer	27Ma02Aj
Michael	27	M	Laborer	27Ma02Aj	CUMMINS, Jane	13	F	Laborer	27Ma02Aj
Andrew	18	M	Laborer	27Ma02Aj	MCCLAFFERTY, Margret	25	F	Laborer	27Ma02Aj
Mary	25	F	Laborer	27Ma02Aj	HELLIN, John	12	M	Laborer	27Ma02Aj
Mary	.00	F	Infant	27Ma02Aj	GALLAGHER, Mary	50	F	Laborer	27Ma02Aj
OSBORNE, Marshal	22	M	Laborer	27Ma02Aj	NAUGHTON, Mary	36	F	Laborer	27Ma02Aj
ROBINSON, Abel	22	M	Laborer	27Ma02Aj	Patrick	09	M	Child	27Ma02Aj
MOLLYONE, John	20	M	Laborer	27Ma02Aj	Michael	11	M	Child	27Ma02Aj
HOPKINS, Mary	28	F	Servant	27Ma02Aj	GRIFFIN, Richard	38	M	Laborer	27Ma02Aj
Thomas	.00	M	Infant	27Ma02Aj	HILBURNE, Catherine	20	F	Laborer	27Ma02Aj
BYRNE, Richard	40	M	Farmer	27Ma02Aj	PLUNKET, Mary	25	F	Laborer	27Ma02Aj
Lucy	32	F	Farmer	27Ma02Aj	Thomas	18	M	Laborer	27Ma02Aj
Margret	.00	F	Infant	27Ma02Aj	MCARDLE, Patrick	15	M	Laborer	27Ma02Aj
BENNETT, George	36	M	Farmer	27Ma02Aj	HARVEY, Rose	35	F	Laborer	27Ma02Aj
MCMAHON, Ann	16	F	Servant	27Ma02Aj	OBRIAN, Susan	16	F	Laborer	27Ma02Aj
MORGAN, Margret	13	F	Servant	27Ma02Aj	DUANE, Mairy	20	F	Laborer	27Ma02Aj
GEEHAN, Charles	11	M	Servant	27Ma02Aj	Margret	20	F	Laborer	27Ma02Aj
KENDRIE, Mackie	25	M	Laborer	27Ma02Aj	MCCABE, Mary	20	F	Laborer	27Ma02Aj
BIGLEY, John	23	M	Laborer	27Ma02Aj	CUNA, William	40	M	Laborer	27Ma02Aj
FLANNAGAN, John	24	M	Laborer	27Ma02Aj	HOLLINGWOOD, Mary	50	F	Laborer	27Ma02Aj
ODONALD, Edmund	22	M	Laborer	27Ma02Aj	HADFIELD, Edward	50	M	Laborer	27Ma02Aj
BRONAHAN, John	21	M	Laborer	27Ma02Aj	Betty	50	F	Laborer	27Ma02Aj
ENRIGHT, Catherine	24	F	Laborer	27Ma02Aj	Alfred	20	M	Laborer	27Ma02Aj
ODONALD, Mary	22	F	Laborer	27Ma02Aj	Bettey	18	F	Laborer	27Ma02Aj
FITZGERALD, Ellen	25	F	Laborer	27Ma02Aj	Frederick	14	M	Laborer	27Ma02Aj
SKELLEY, John	27	M	Laborer	27Ma02Aj	Christopher	12	M	Laborer	27Ma02Aj
Hester	28	F	Laborer	27Ma02Aj	Sarah	16	F	Laborer	27Ma02Aj
FORSYTH, John	22	M	Laborer	27Ma02Aj	BALISTEY, James	21	M	Laborer	27Ma02Aj
CRAIG, Hugh	22	M	Laborer	27Ma02Aj	John	14	M	Laborer	27Ma02Aj
BYRNE, Dennis-C.	21	M	Laborer	27Ma02Aj	Mary	15	F	Laborer	27Ma02Aj
WOODSIDE, Robert	30	M	Laborer	27Ma02Aj	FREIL, James	18	M	Laborer	27Ma02Aj
MENG, William	20	M	Laborer	27Ma02Aj	Mary	20	F	Laborer	27Ma02Aj
JUDGE, Sarah	17	F	Laborer	27Ma02Aj	BRADLEY, Frances	50	F	Laborer	27Ma02Aj
LYNCH, Ann	23	F	Laborer	27Ma02Aj	Giles	20	M	Laborer	27Ma02Aj
EVOY, Michael	15	M	Laborer	27Ma02Aj	MCDONNELL, James	20	M	Laborer	27Ma02Aj
HOWE, Thomas	35	M	Farmer	27Ma02Aj	BEIRNE, John	20	M	Laborer	27Ma02Aj
Marcella	31	F	Farmer	27Ma02Aj	CONNOLLY, Bridget	19	F	Laborer	27Ma02Aj
Catherine	03	F	Child	27Ma02Aj	SIMONS, James	25	M	Laborer	27Ma02Aj
John	02	M	Child	27Ma02Aj	DOYLE, Catherine	25	F	Laborer	27Ma02Aj
MULDOON, Patrick	35	M	Laborer	27Ma02Aj	MCGOUVAN, Margret	12	F	Laborer	27Ma02Aj
CRANE, James-Dolly	30	M	Laborer	27Ma02Aj	MCCORMACK, Edward	21	M	Laborer	27Ma02Aj
Catherine	26	F	Laborer	27Ma02Aj	SHRILL, Edward	27	M	Laborer	27Ma02Aj

NAMES OF PASSENGERS	AGE	SEX	OCCUPATIONS	DATE PORT SHIP
MURRY, Edward	14	M	Laborer	27Ma02Aj
CURR, James	20	M	Laborer	27Ma02Aj
KIRMAN, Rose	18	F	Laborer	27Ma02Aj
Ann	18	F	Laborer	27Ma02Aj
LILLY, Thomas-H.	25	M	Laborer	27Ma02Aj
SHANNON, Julia	30	F	Laborer	27Ma02Aj
MCMAHON, Julia	10	F	Laborer	27Ma02Aj
Mary	07	F	Child	27Ma02Aj
MATTHEWS, Stephen	25	M	Laborer	27Ma02Aj
MCMANNEY, James	30	M	Laborer	27Ma02Aj
PARTONE, Daniel	40	M	Laborer	27Ma02Aj
Nancy	30	F	Laborer	27Ma02Aj
Nancy	14	F	Laborer	27Ma02Aj
David	12	M	Laborer	27Ma02Aj
Catherine	10	F	Laborer	27Ma02Aj
Daniel	06	M	Child	27Ma02Aj
Robert	04	M	Child	27Ma02Aj
Mary-Jane	02	F	Child	27Ma02Aj
Catherine	.00	F	Infant	27Ma02Aj
HEALY, Catherine	22	F	Laborer	27Ma02Aj
LYNCH, Peter	20	M	Laborer	27Ma02Aj
MADDEN, Francis	19	M	Laborer	27Ma02Aj
JUDGE, Michael	30	M	Laborer	27Ma02Aj
HASSETT, John	40	M	Laborer	27Ma02Aj
MCDONALD, Margret	20	F	Laborer	27Ma02Aj
LYNCH, Farrell	19	M	Laborer	27Ma02Aj
DUFFY, John	19	M	Laborer	27Ma02Aj
Rose	23	F	Laborer	27Ma02Aj
MCKENNIE, Ann	30	F	Laborer	27Ma02Aj
HORRIGAN, Michael	16	M	Laborer	27Ma02Aj
MCKENNIE, Catherine	15	F	Laborer	27Ma02Aj
Mary	09	F	Child	27Ma02Aj
RIELLY, Andrew	10	M	Laborer	27Ma02Aj
DOWLING, James	12	M	Laborer	27Ma02Aj
HARPER, George	42	M	Farmer	27Ma02Aj
Elizabeth	38	F	Farmer	27Ma02Aj
Thomas	12	M	Farmer	27Ma02Aj
Ann	10	F	Farmer	27Ma02Aj
Emma	08	F	Child	27Ma02Aj
Alfred	06	M	Child	27Ma02Aj
Agnes	04	F	Child	27Ma02Aj
Jane	02	F	Child	27Ma02Aj
DUNN, John	29	M	Joiner	27Ma02Aj
MALONEY, James	33	M	Laborer	27Ma02Aj
MCNAMA, Ann	20	F	Laborer	27Ma02Aj
MAY, Bridget	20	F	Laborer	27Ma02Aj
HENDON, John	26	M	Laborer	27Ma02Aj
TIMMINS, Patrick	20	M	Laborer	27Ma02Aj
Sarah	20	F	Laborer	27Ma02Aj
CURTIS, Patrick	20	M	Shoemaker	27Ma02Aj
CRANE, Owen	18	M	None	27Ma02Aj
HEALEY, Margret	20	F	None	27Ma02Aj
FULLAN, Michael	15	M	None	27Ma02Aj
CONNOLLY, Catherine	18	F	None	27Ma02Aj
CRANE, James	26	M	Saddler	27Ma02Aj
LARKINS, Mary	20	F	None	27Ma02Aj
MCDONALD, Julia	20	F	None	27Ma02Aj
SHANDY, Michael	20	M	Surveyor	27Ma02Aj
CROWLEY, Catherine	20	F	Weaver	27Ma02Aj
WILLIAMS, David-M.	24	M	Laborer	27Ma02Aj
TANNON, Bernard	34	M	Laborer	27Ma02Aj
Bridget	26	F	Unknown	27Ma02Aj
GALLAGHER, Catherine	20	F	Unknown	27Ma02Aj
Sarah	11	F	Unknown	27Ma02Aj
REILLY, Mary	25	F	Unknown	27Ma02Aj
FITZGERALD, Patrick	24	M	Unknown	27Ma02Aj
MORRON, Roger	34	M	Unknown	27Ma02Aj

CALEB-GRIMSHAW 27 MAY 1848

From Liverpool

NAMES OF PASSENGERS	AGE	SEX	OCCUPATIONS	DATE PORT SHIP
HENSHAW, Mary	36	F	Unknown	27Ma02Jk
John	16	M	Unknown	27Ma02Jk
Mary-J.	11	F	Unknown	27Ma02Jk
Jackson	09	M	Child	27Ma02Jk
Elizabeth	07	F	Child	27Ma02Jk
Charles	04	M	Child	27Ma02Jk
Eleanor	01	F	Child	27Ma02Jk
EGAN, Micheal	20	M	Farmer	27Ma02Jk
Mary	22	F	Farmer	27Ma02Jk
HANSON, Jane	24	F	Unknown	27Ma02Jk
ASKEREN, Francis	27	M	Farmer	27Ma02Jk
DAWBARN, Joseph	39	M	Farmer	27Ma02Jk
Rebbecca	08	F	Child	27Ma02Jk
George	06	M	Child	27Ma02Jk
Anne	05	F	Child	27Ma02Jk
Mary	04	F	Child	27Ma02Jk
Maria	02	F	Child	27Ma02Jk
HUNT, Edward	29	M	Farmer	27Ma02Jk
BROWN, Hester	47	F	Farmer	27Ma02Jk
Thomas	47	M	Laborer	27Ma02Jk
Jane	18	F	Laborer	27Ma02Jk
Mary	22	F	Laborer	27Ma02Jk
Thomas	15	M	Laborer	27Ma02Jk
Emily	11	F	Laborer	27Ma02Jk
John	04	M	Child	27Ma02Jk
CAVVANHA, Abraham	20	M	Laborer	27Ma02Jk
JONES, Mary-Ann	17	F	Spinster	27Ma02Jk
DURCK, John	30	M	Farmer	27Ma02Jk
Charlotte	29	F	Farmer	27Ma02Jk
Thomas	05	M	Child	27Ma02Jk
George	02	M	Child	27Ma02Jk
DAUBNER, John	35	M	Laborer	27Ma02Jk
KIRK, Abraham	55	M	Laborer	27Ma02Jk
BOOTH, Henry	29	M	Laborer	27Ma02Jk
Theodesia	28	F	Laborer	27Ma02Jk
CARY, Lydia	26	F	Spinster	27Ma02Jk
SULLIVAN, Micheal	26	M	Unknown	27Ma02Jk
MCDERMOTT, Catherine	17	F	Spinster	27Ma02Jk
SULLIVAN, Catherine	20	F	Unknown	27Ma02Jk
Abraham	05	M	Child	27Ma02Jk
CONNER, Daniel	18	M	Laborer	27Ma02Jk
Honorah	16	F	Spinster	27Ma02Jk
MURPHY, Jeramiah	19	M	Laborer	27Ma02Jk
CAHEL, Micheal	60	M	Laborer	27Ma02Jk
Patt.	19	M	Laborer	27Ma02Jk
Margeret	17	F	Laborer	27Ma02Jk
Bridget	15	F	Laborer	27Ma02Jk
Jane	13	F	Laborer	27Ma02Jk
Eliza	12	F	Laborer	27Ma02Jk
CASEY, Micheal	30	M	Laborer	27Ma02Jk
Margeret	20	F	Laborer	27Ma02Jk
Walter	04	M	Child	27Ma02Jk
MITCHELL, James	59	M	Laborer	27Ma02Jk
Mary	50	F	Laborer	27Ma02Jk
SPENCE, Andrew	33	M	Laborer	27Ma02Jk
Elizabeth	36	F	Laborer	27Ma02Jk
Margaret	07	F	Child	27Ma02Jk
James	05	M	Child	27Ma02Jk
Willm.	03	M	Child	27Ma02Jk
Thomas	01	M	Child	27Ma02Jk
BURNS, Saml.	10	M	Laborer	27Ma02Jk
BATES, Sarah	20	F	Laborer	27Ma02Jk
MCKENNAY, Margerit	21	F	Laborer	27Ma02Jk
HUGHES, John	24	M	Laborer	27Ma02Jk
FLOOD, Ann	20	F	Laborer	27Ma02Jk

NAMES OF PASSENGERS	AGE	SEX	OCCUPATIONS	DATE PORT SHIP
HUGHES, Owen	47	M	Laborer	27Ma02Jk
Ann	45	F	Laborer	27Ma02Jk
Arthur	.00	M	Infant	27Ma02Jk
Bridget	20	F	Laborer	27Ma02Jk
Mary	17	F	Laborer	27Ma02Jk
Margeret	14	F	Laborer	27Ma02Jk
MCGRATH, Patt	20	M	Laborer	27Ma02Jk
LYON, Micheal	34	M	Unknown	27Ma02Jk
Betsy	25	F	Unknown	27Ma02Jk
GARRAGHAN, Edward	19	M	Unknown	27Ma02Jk
GARRAHTY, Matthew	28	M	Unknown	27Ma02Jk
Betsy	22	F	Unknown	27Ma02Jk
QUIN, Patt	36	M	Unknown	27Ma02Jk
GARRAHTY, Matthew	21	M	Unknown	27Ma02Jk
POTTS, Alexander	34	M	Unknown	27Ma02Jk
Jane	54	F	Unknown	27Ma02Jk
John	34	M	Unknown	27Ma02Jk
George	14	M	Unknown	27Ma02Jk
C.K.	12	M	Unknown	27Ma02Jk
LUCAS, Margerit	25	F	Unknown	27Ma02Jk
Elizabeth	23	F	Unknown	27Ma02Jk
MCKENNA, Charles	23	M	Unknown	27Ma02Jk
James	14	M	Unknown	27Ma02Jk
GASKILL, Samuel	24	M	Unknown	27Ma02Jk
BURGON, Jane	40	F	Unknown	27Ma02Jk
BELL, John-G.	48	M	Unknown	27Ma02Jk
Elizabeth	50	F	Unknown	27Ma02Jk
Eliza	15	F	Unknown	27Ma02Jk
SAMUELS, Daniel	16	M	Unknown	27Ma02Jk
MCGUIRE, John	24	M	Unknown	27Ma02Jk
SHORT, Willm.	21	M	Unknown	27Ma02Jk
LEWIS, Richard	32	M	Unknown	27Ma02Jk
RUSSELL, William	25	M	Unknown	27Ma02Jk
THOMAS, William	24	M	Unknown	27Ma02Jk
RUSSELL, Robert	22	M	Unknown	27Ma02Jk
STODDARD, Joseph	22	M	Unknown	27Ma02Jk
EMONDS, James	21	M	Unknown	27Ma02Jk
HAWES, George	22	M	Unknown	27Ma02Jk
LANCASTER, Thomas	24	M	Unknown	27Ma02Jk
SWEENY, Edward	20	M	Unknown	27Ma02Jk
MULHERNE, Patt	23	M	Unknown	27Ma02Jk
DONELLY, Dan	21	M	Unknown	27Ma02Jk
ROBERT, Isaiah	31	M	Unknown	27Ma02Jk
Sarah	31	F	Unknown	27Ma02Jk
Willm.	15	M	Unknown	27Ma02Jk
Mary	07	F	Child	27Ma02Jk
Eliza	05	F	Child	27Ma02Jk
Moses	03	M	Child	27Ma02Jk
John	.00	M	Infant	27Ma02Jk
HOUGHTON, Henry	30	M	Laborer	27Ma02Jk
MCGLUCKEY, Ealoner	19	F	Laborer	27Ma02Jk
Margerit	15	F	Laborer	27Ma02Jk
ODONNELLY, Honorah	30	F	Laborer	27Ma02Jk
John	06	M	Child	27Ma02Jk
Ellen	.03	F	Infant	27Ma02Jk
HACKETT, Patt	24	M	Laborer	27Ma02Jk
FITZGIBBON, Bridgett	17	F	Laborer	27Ma02Jk
FARRAR, Mary	16	F	Laborer	27Ma02Jk
FITZGIBBON, Daniel	30	M	Laborer	27Ma02Jk
FARRAR, Mary	19	F	Laborer	27Ma02Jk
FITZGIBBON, Daniel	25	M	Laborer	27Ma02Jk
DOUGHTY, Margeret	35	F	Laborer	27Ma02Jk
REDMOND, James	25	M	Laborer	27Ma02Jk
Catherine	25	F	Laborer	27Ma02Jk
John	07	M	Child	27Ma02Jk
Mary	.02	F	Infant	27Ma02Jk
DUNN, Catherine	40	F	Laborer	27Ma02Jk
BURN, Catherine	25	F	Laborer	27Ma02Jk
CRAYMAN, Ann	20	F	Laborer	27Ma02Jk
MCDERMOT, Eliza	.03	F	Infant	27Ma02Jk
MCGINLEY, Elizabeth	32	F	Laborer	27Ma02Jk
Matty	12	F	Laborer	27Ma02Jk
Francis	10	M	Laborer	27Ma02Jk
Margeret	08	F	Child	27Ma02Jk
Patt	06	M	Child	27Ma02Jk
MCGINLEY, Ellen	04	F	Child	27Ma02Jk
William	.00	M	Infant	27Ma02Jk
LORD, John	28	M	Laborer	27Ma02Jk
SHANNON, Winney	24	M	Laborer	27Ma02Jk
WILLIAMS, Ellis	23	M	Laborer	27Ma02Jk
ROWLANDS, Willm.	25	M	Laborer	27Ma02Jk
WILLIAMS, Richard	20	M	Laborer	27Ma02Jk
GRIFFITHS, Evan	25	M	Laborer	27Ma02Jk
SHAW, Catherine	46	F	Laborer	27Ma02Jk
Isabella	22	F	Laborer	27Ma02Jk
Millington	20	M	Laborer	27Ma02Jk
George	15	M	Laborer	27Ma02Jk
Jane	09	F	Child	27Ma02Jk
Agnes	06	F	Child	27Ma02Jk
Mary	04	F	Child	27Ma02Jk
WHALEN, Ellen	14	F	None	27Ma02Jk
WILLIAMS, Jane	14	F	None	27Ma02Jk
Mary	12	F	None	27Ma02Jk
Saml.	10	M	Laborer	27Ma02Jk
LANAGHAN, Bartley	55	M	Laborer	27Ma02Jk
Micheal	13	M	Laborer	27Ma02Jk
Bartly	10	M	Laborer	27Ma02Jk
Margerit	08	F	Child	27Ma02Jk
WHALEN, Thomas	17	M	Laborer	27Ma02Jk
PURCELL, John	19	M	Laborer	27Ma02Jk
CAMPBELL, Adam	20	M	Laborer	27Ma02Jk
Edward	18	M	Laborer	27Ma02Jk
MCGOVERN, Hannell	18	U	Laborer	27Ma02Jk
FLOOD, Bridgett	12	F	Laborer	27Ma02Jk
Catherine	09	F	Child	27Ma02Jk
Peter	08	M	Child	27Ma02Jk
MCDONNELL, Patt	40	M	Laborer	27Ma02Jk
LINCOLN, Willm.	35	M	Laborer	27Ma02Jk
Mary	30	F	Laborer	27Ma02Jk
Charles	07	M	Child	27Ma02Jk
FOUNTAIN, Thomas	47	M	Laborer	27Ma02Jk
Thomas	21	M	Laborer	27Ma02Jk
John	19	M	Laborer	27Ma02Jk
AHBRIDGE, George	24	M	Laborer	27Ma02Jk
Mary	28	F	Laborer	27Ma02Jk
SWARBRICK, Abraham	30	M	Laborer	27Ma02Jk
FRANKFIELD, John	20	M	Laborer	27Ma02Jk
Susan	18	F	Laborer	27Ma02Jk
OBRIEN, Dennis	21	M	Laborer	27Ma02Jk
HARGATE, John	35	M	Laborer	27Ma02Jk
MAHONEY, Daniel	50	M	Laborer	27Ma02Jk
James	20	M	Laborer	27Ma02Jk
KENNEDY, Hugh	21	M	Laborer	27Ma02Jk
James	20	M	Laborer	27Ma02Jk
BAILY, Steward	22	M	Laborer	27Ma02Jk
LAWTON, Thomas	18	M	Laborer	27Ma02Jk
BYRNE, Daniel	40	M	Laborer	27Ma02Jk
Rose	40	F	Laborer	27Ma02Jk
MAHONE, Bridget	25	F	Laborer	27Ma02Jk
Eliza	20	F	Laborer	27Ma02Jk
GURK, Delia	13	F	Laborer	27Ma02Jk
HARRIS, Eliza	20	F	Laborer	27Ma02Jk
GLASSEY, Eliza-J.	03	F	Child	27Ma02Jk
SHUDDY, Dennis	30	M	Laborer	27Ma02Jk
Ellen	28	F	Laborer	27Ma02Jk
Eleanor	03	F	Child	27Ma02Jk
Mary	.00	F	Infant	27Ma02Jk
CUNNINGHAM, Mary	18	F	Laborer	27Ma02Jk
DUGGERIN, Ellen	20	F	Laborer	27Ma02Jk
MCCONNELL, U	50	F	Wi	27Ma02Jk
Francis	18	M	Laborer	27Ma02Jk
Catherine	16	F	Laborer	27Ma02Jk
MCMANOR, Mary	10	F	Laborer	27Ma02Jk
EDAMES, Smart	28	M	Laborer	27Ma02Jk
Racheal	28	F	Laborer	27Ma02Jk
Roberts	08	M	Child	27Ma02Jk
W.J.	06	M	Child	27Ma02Jk
Mary	03	F	Child	27Ma02Jk
James	.00	M	Infant	27Ma02Jk
MCCORMICK, Patt	14	M	Laborer	27Ma02Jk

NAMES OF PASSENGERS	AGE	SEX	OCCUPATIONS	DATE PORT SHIP	NAMES OF PASSENGERS	AGE	SEX	OCCUPATIONS	DATE PORT SHIP
ODONOGHUE, Dan	19	M	Laborer	27Ma02Jk	WESTON, John	.10	M	Infant	27Ma02Jk
Mary	23	F	Laborer	27Ma02Jk	MASSEY, Joseph	33	M	Laborer	27Ma02Jk
KENNEDY, Margerit	27	F	Laborer	27Ma02Jk	KILLEN, Ellen	20	F	Laborer	27Ma02Jk
Andrew	17	M	Laborer	27Ma02Jk	JONES, John	40	M	Laborer	27Ma02Jk
PONSOBY, Mary	17	F	Laborer	27Ma02Jk	Mary	38	F	Laborer	27Ma02Jk
MCGIN, Elizabeth	15	F	Laborer	27Ma02Jk	Jane	10	F	Laborer	27Ma02Jk
Mary	11	F	Laborer	27Ma02Jk	Sarah	.00	F	Infant	27Ma02Jk
GRANT, Patt	16	M	Laborer	27Ma02Jk	BURNE, George	22	M	Unknown	27Ma02Jk
Susan	18	F	Laborer	27Ma02Jk	KELLY, James	25	M	Unknown	27Ma02Jk
STANFIELD, Thomas	50	M	Laborer	27Ma02Jk	MCBRIDE, James	26	M	Unknown	27Ma02Jk
John	19	M	Laborer	27Ma02Jk	COLGAN, Charles	25	M	Unknown	27Ma02Jk
BEIRNE, Hester	25	F	Laborer	27Ma02Jk	Mary	25	F	Unknown	27Ma02Jk
Elizabeth	.00	F	Infant	27Ma02Jk	MCCORRIE, John	30	M	Unknown	27Ma02Jk
DONELLY, James	50	M	Laborer	27Ma02Jk	Ann	25	F	Unknown	27Ma02Jk
Margerit	45	F	Laborer	27Ma02Jk	Phill.	20	M	Unknown	27Ma02Jk
Jane	15	F	Laborer	27Ma02Jk	HUMPHRIES, Humphrey	41	M	Unknown	27Ma02Jk
John	14	M	Laborer	27Ma02Jk	Phebe	39	F	Unknown	27Ma02Jk
CUNNINGHAM, Mary	40	F	Laborer	27Ma02Jk	Phebe	15	F	Unknown	27Ma02Jk
COLLINS, Bernard	34	M	Laborer	27Ma02Jk	Catherine	13	F	Unknown	27Ma02Jk
Ellen	31	F	Laborer	27Ma02Jk	Wllm.	.00	M	Infant	27Ma02Jk
HANLEY, John	45	M	Laborer	27Ma02Jk	DAVIS, John	21	M	Unknown	27Ma02Jk
Biddy	18	M	Laborer	27Ma02Jk	WILLIAMS, Margerit	52	F	Unknown	27Ma02Jk
John	15	M	Laborer	27Ma02Jk	WOODS, Wllm.	20	M	Unknown	27Ma02Jk
Peter	13	M	Laborer	27Ma02Jk	GAULT, Ellen	24	F	Unknown	27Ma02Jk
HUMPHRIES, Francis	24	M	Laborer	27Ma02Jk	Abraham	19	M	Unknown	27Ma02Jk
MAHONE, John	25	M	Laborer	27Ma02Jk	HAMILL, Connell	30	M	Unknown	27Ma02Jk
JOHNSTONE, Thomas	21	M	Laborer	27Ma02Jk	HILLMAN, Bernard	24	M	Unknown	27Ma02Jk
CARNEY, Timothy	25	M	Laborer	27Ma02Jk	ELRATH, Micheal	25	M	Unknown	27Ma02Jk
WHALEN, Patt	25	M	Laborer	27Ma02Jk	WEDGE, John	38	M	Unknown	27Ma02Jk
JONES, Mary-Ann	27	F	Laborer	27Ma02Jk	WELSH, Judith	30	M	Unknown	27Ma02Jk
Margerit	03	F	Child	27Ma02Jk	John	.02	M	Infant	27Ma02Jk
Richard	01	M	Child	27Ma02Jk	HART, Margerit	17	F	Unknown	27Ma02Jk
GREAVES, James	21	M	Laborer	27Ma02Jk	SHEA, James	25	M	Unknown	27Ma02Jk
HUNTER, William	30	M	Laborer	27Ma02Jk	FLEMING, John	35	M	Unknown	27Ma02Jk
Mary	25	F	Laborer	27Ma02Jk	QUIRK, Thomas	23	M	Unknown	27Ma02Jk
BAKER, Joseph	25	M	Laborer	27Ma02Jk	KINSHELLA, Patt.	22	M	Unknown	27Ma02Jk
CUNNINGHAM, William	30	M	Laborer	27Ma02Jk	LAWLER, Peter	17	M	Unknown	27Ma02Jk
Mary	30	F	Laborer	27Ma02Jk	DUMPLY, Patt.	21	M	Unknown	27Ma02Jk
John	04	M	Child	27Ma02Jk	QUIRK, Mary	23	F	Unknown	27Ma02Jk
LILLY, Micheal	60	M	Laborer	27Ma02Jk	BOYD, Ellen	50	F	Unknown	27Ma02Jk
Biddy	17	F	Laborer	27Ma02Jk	Jane	11	F	Unknown	27Ma02Jk
James	14	M	Laborer	27Ma02Jk	WARREN, Abraham	28	M	Unknown	27Ma02Jk
Ann	12	F	Laborer	27Ma02Jk	Maria	28	F	Unknown	27Ma02Jk
COOGAN, Micheal	16	M	Laborer	27Ma02Jk	Abraham	05	M	Child	27Ma02Jk
JASKER, Mary	38	F	Unknown	27Ma02Jk	George	.00	M	Infant	27Ma02Jk
RILEY, Bridgett	14	F	Unknown	27Ma02Jk	Thomas	23	M	Unknown	27Ma02Jk
REYNOLDS, Bessy	19	F	Unknown	27Ma02Jk	BROWN, Andrew	25	M	Unknown	27Ma02Jk
FLOOD, Honora	19	F	Unknown	27Ma02Jk	Rose	25	F	Unknown	27Ma02Jk
DOOLEY, Winnefred	24	F	Unknown	27Ma02Jk	KELLY, Catherine	16	F	Unknown	27Ma02Jk
DALTON, Eward	00	M	Unknown	27Ma02Jk	GOLDING, James	23	M	Unknown	27Ma02Jk
HOUGHTON, James	38	M	Unknown	27Ma02Jk	Margeret	34	F	Unknown	27Ma02Jk
GRIFFITHS, Edward	00	M	Unknown	27Ma02Jk	Susan	07	F	Child	27Ma02Jk
Hannah	28	F	Unknown	27Ma02Jk	Mary	05	F	Child	27Ma02Jk
Hannah	10	F	Unknown	27Ma02Jk	Abraham	03	M	Child	27Ma02Jk
Wllm.	08	M	Child	27Ma02Jk	Hannah	.00	F	Infant	27Ma02Jk
Thos.W.	04	M	Child	27Ma02Jk	GEEHON, Francis	19	M	Unknown	27Ma02Jk
Eleanor	.00	F	Infant	27Ma02Jk	COPE, Abraham	38	M	Unknown	27Ma02Jk
JAMES, Benjamin	24	M	Unknown	27Ma02Jk	SHANLEY, Patt.	25	M	Unknown	27Ma02Jk
Margeret	21	F	Unknown	27Ma02Jk	SHEVLIN, Peter	24	M	Unknown	27Ma02Jk
ASHERN, Margerit	26	F	Unknown	27Ma02Jk	MURRAY, John	24	M	Unknown	27Ma02Jk
CUSHION, Mary	09	F	Child	27Ma02Jk	DUCKWORTH, Thomas	35	M	Unknown	27Ma02Jk
Ann	07	F	Child	27Ma02Jk	BROOMHALL, John	33	M	Unknown	27Ma02Jk
John	05	M	Child	27Ma02Jk	FOX, Abraham	26	M	Unknown	27Ma02Jk
SMITH, Peter	20	M	Unknown	27Ma02Jk	Sarah	24	F	Unknown	27Ma02Jk
KELLY, Mary	18	F	Laborer	27Ma02Jk	Abraham	56	M	Unknown	27Ma02Jk
MCGIN, Sally-A.	18	F	Laborer	27Ma02Jk	ROWLANDS, Abraham	48	M	Unknown	27Ma02Jk
Willm.	13	M	Laborer	27Ma02Jk	PARRY, Thomas	26	M	Unknown	27Ma02Jk
LANNDERS, Ellen	23	F	Laborer	27Ma02Jk	MORGAN, Lewis	31	M	Unknown	27Ma02Jk
WARBIS, Thomas	20	M	Laborer	27Ma02Jk	EDWARDS, Lewis	22	M	Unknown	27Ma02Jk
WESTON, Willm.	45	M	Laborer	27Ma02Jk	MORGAN, Abraham	21	M	Unknown	27Ma02Jk
Mary	44	F	Laborer	27Ma02Jk	WALLOWS, Abraham	35	M	Unknown	27Ma02Jk
ALDRIDGE, Mary	70	F	Laborer	27Ma02Jk	MILLS, Hewey	25	M	Unknown	27Ma02Jk
WESTON, W.H.	19	M	Laborer	27Ma02Jk	CALLAGHAN, Thomas	27	M	Unknown	27Ma02Jk
Thos.	15	M	Laborer	27Ma02Jk	MANSWORTH, Abraham	29	M	Unknown	27Ma02Jk
Catherine	13	F	Laborer	27Ma02Jk	Catherine	21	F	Spinster	27Ma02Jk

NAMES OF PASSENGERS	AGE	SEX	OCCUPATIONS	DATE PORT SHIP
MULLAL, Mary	18	F	Spinster	27Ma02Jk
CALLAGHAN, Ellen	21	F	Spinster	27Ma02Jk
LEWIS, James	34	M	Laborer	27Ma02Jk
THOMAS, David	23	M	Laborer	27Ma02Jk
Abraham	18	M	Laborer	27Ma02Jk
ARTHUR, James	50	M	Laborer	27Ma02Jk
Grace	50	F	Laborer	27Ma02Jk
Elizabeth	20	F	Laborer	27Ma02Jk
James	14	M	Laborer	27Ma02Jk
DALE, Abraham	20	M	Laborer	27Ma02Jk
BIDDLE, Wm.J.	36	M	Laborer	27Ma02Jk
PATTISON, John	20	M	Laborer	27Ma02Jk
SMITH, James	20	M	Laborer	27Ma02Jk
WORKMAN, Mary-Ann	17	F	Laborer	27Ma02Jk
HARRIS, Evan	44	M	Laborer	27Ma02Jk
Hannah	50	F	Laborer	27Ma02Jk
Henry	21	M	Laborer	27Ma02Jk
Sarah	19	F	Laborer	27Ma02Jk
Ann	17	F	Laborer	27Ma02Jk
Mary	15	F	Laborer	27Ma02Jk
Hannah	11	F	Laborer	27Ma02Jk
Elvira	.08	F	Infant	27Ma02Jk
INGHRAM, Henry-W.	25	M	Laborer	27Ma02Jk
LUCAS, William	36	M	Laborer	27Ma02Jk
Mary	30	F	Laborer	27Ma02Jk
John-J.	27	M	Laborer	27Ma02Jk
Ann	46	F	Laborer	27Ma02Jk
Andrew	.07	M	Infant	27Ma02Jk
POWERS, Evan	30	M	Laborer	27Ma02Jk
JONES, John	50	M	Laborer	27Ma02Jk
GRIFFITH, Edward	33	M	Laborer	27Ma02Jk
Ann	28	F	Laborer	27Ma02Jk
JENKINS, Sarah	21	F	Laborer	27Ma02Jk
HAMILL, Owen	27	M	Laborer	27Ma02Jk
ROBERTS, Thomas	27	M	Laborer	27Ma02Jk
Mary	25	F	Laborer	27Ma02Jk
Thomas	06	M	Child	27Ma02Jk
Julia	03	F	Child	27Ma02Jk
Willm.	.00	M	Infant	27Ma02Jk
WOODCOCK, R.A.	20	M	Laborer	27Ma02Jk
CAULEY, Saml.	20	M	Laborer	27Ma02Jk
LEWIS, Arthur	18	M	Laborer	27Ma02Jk
DODDS, Ann	30	F	Laborer	27Ma02Jk
REECE, John	45	M	Laborer	27Ma02Jk

EUXINE 27 MAY 1848

From Liverpool

NAMES OF PASSENGERS	AGE	SEX	OCCUPATIONS	DATE PORT SHIP
HALPIN, James	26	M	Laborer	27Ma02Jl
REAGANS, Mary	25	F	Laborer	27Ma02Jl
Bridget	24	F	Laborer	27Ma02Jl
HOLLINGSWORTH, Robt.	30	M	Laborer	27Ma02Jl
Nancy	30	F	Laborer	27Ma02Jl
CRONAN, Tim	20	M	Laborer	27Ma02Jl
RYLIE, Bridget	20	F	Dressmaker	27Ma02Jl
BLASSING, Hugh	20	M	Laborer	27Ma02Jl
GROGAN, Eleanor	45	F	Unknown	27Ma02Jl
Charles	20	M	Unknown	27Ma02Jl
Cath.	05	F	Child	27Ma02Jl
COHEN, Cath.	20	F	Dressmaker	27Ma02Jl
ROONEY, Felix	20	M	Laborer	27Ma02Jl
FINNIGAN, Thomas	20	M	Laborer	27Ma02Jl
ROCHFORD, Ann	20	F	Dressmaker	27Ma02Jl
BRIAN, Margt.	20	F	Dressmaker	27Ma02Jl
HIGGINS, Bridget	20	F	Dressmaker	27Ma02Jl
IRVINE, James	50	M	Laborer	27Ma02Jl
Jane (W)	60	F	Wife	27Ma02Jl
James (S)	17	M	Baker	27Ma02Jl
IRVINE, Saml. (S)	22	M	Shoemaker	27Ma02Jl
FORAN, Bridget	20	F	Laborer	27Ma02Jl
Ann	19	F	Laborer	27Ma02Jl
GREEN, Willm.	22	M	Stctr	27Ma02Jl
GRADY, Maria	13	F	Dressmaker	27Ma02Jl
MAXWELL, Ann	30	F	Dressmaker	27Ma02Jl
Ann	14	F	Dressmaker	27Ma02Jl
MURPHY, Martin	26	M	Laborer	27Ma02Jl
Mary	25	F	Laborer	27Ma02Jl
BULGER, Judy	22	F	Laborer	27Ma02Jl
KEIGAN, Alley	20	F	Laborer	27Ma02Jl
LENAGHAN, John	30	M	Laborer	27Ma02Jl
Mary	25	F	Laborer	27Ma02Jl
CORRIGAN, Pat	20	M	Jailer	27Ma02Jl
HAYS, Ellen	30	F	Laborer	27Ma02Jl
Mary	06	F	Child	27Ma02Jl
MCCUE, Cath.	40	F	Dressmaker	27Ma02Jl
Cath.	25	F	Dressmaker	27Ma02Jl
John	07	M	Child	27Ma02Jl
Ann	04	F	Child	27Ma02Jl
WELSH, Mich.	20	M	Laborer	27Ma02Jl
Thomas	19	M	Laborer	27Ma02Jl
MCNAMARA, Mich.	20	M	Laborer	27Ma02Jl
OBRIAN, Danl.	20	M	Laborer	27Ma02Jl
ARMSTRONG, Eliza	24	F	Laborer	27Ma02Jl
Margt.	20	F	Laborer	27Ma02Jl
MCLARNEY, Thomas	16	M	Laborer	27Ma02Jl
DONNELL, Wm.	16	M	Laborer	27Ma02Jl
Francis	24	M	Laborer	27Ma02Jl
ROACHE, Joseph	20	M	Laborer	27Ma02Jl
NUGENT, Eliza	20	F	Laborer	27Ma02Jl
CALLIGAN, Judy	20	F	Laborer	27Ma02Jl
HALLIGAN, Hugh	22	M	Mason	27Ma02Jl
Pat	24	M	Mason	27Ma02Jl
WELSH, Pat	23	M	Laborer	27Ma02Jl
DUFFEY, Mark	07	M	Child	27Ma02Jl
MATHEWS, Ellen	20	F	Laborer	27Ma02Jl
MCGARRY, Thomas	18	M	Laborer	27Ma02Jl
MCANLIFF, Mich.	30	M	Laborer	27Ma02Jl
MURPHY, Mich.	50	M	Laborer	27Ma02Jl
Con	22	M	Laborer	27Ma02Jl
Wm.	18	M	Laborer	27Ma02Jl
LARY, Margt.	20	F	Laborer	27Ma02Jl
BARDSLEY, Joseph	20	M	Ctnsp	27Ma02Jl
HALIDAY, Ann	30	F	Dressmaker	27Ma02Jl
Francis	05	M	Child	27Ma02Jl
Fanny	04	F	Child	27Ma02Jl
William	02	M	Child	27Ma02Jl
MURPHY, Mich.	31	M	Laborer	27Ma02Jl
DONOVAN, Denis	20	M	Laborer	27Ma02Jl
DUFFY, James	18	M	Spinner	27Ma02Jl
GIBNEY, Betty	20	F	Dressmaker	27Ma02Jl
Thom.	07	M	Child	27Ma02Jl
MOFFAT, Margt.	16	F	Dressmaker	27Ma02Jl
SCULLEY, Thom.	20	M	Laborer	27Ma02Jl
COX, Math.	20	M	Laborer	27Ma02Jl
HOY, James	21	M	Laborer	27Ma02Jl
WELSH, Mich.	25	M	Laborer	27Ma02Jl
FLIN, Bart.	20	M	Laborer	27Ma02Jl
DOUGLAS, Cath.	51	F	Dressmaker	27Ma02Jl
MCNAMARA, John	50	M	Laborer	27Ma02Jl
Bridget	50	F	Laborer	27Ma02Jl
Nancy	12	F	Laborer	27Ma02Jl
James	07	M	Child	27Ma02Jl
HEAPHY, Helen	20	F	Dressmaker	27Ma02Jl
MCARTY, John	30	M	Laborer	27Ma02Jl
Mich.	20	M	Laborer	27Ma02Jl
Pat	20	M	Laborer	27Ma02Jl
Cornelius	22	M	Laborer	27Ma02Jl
Johana	18	F	Laborer	27Ma02Jl
Honora	22	F	Laborer	27Ma02Jl
Cath.	20	F	Laborer	27Ma02Jl
Johana	16	F	Laborer	27Ma02Jl
Cornelius	05	M	Child	27Ma02Jl
Mich.	02	M	Child	27Ma02Jl

NAMES OF PASSENGERS		AGE	SEX	OCCUPATIONS	DATE PORT SHIP
CARREY, Thom.		27	M	Laborer	27Ma02Jl
KENNEDY, Cath./		20	F	Laborer	27Ma02Jl
DELANY, Thom.		20	M	Laborer	27Ma02Jl
MARTIN, Walter		27	M	Laborer	27Ma02Jl
KERWICK, Mich.		20	M	Laborer	27Ma02Jl
KILDUFF, John		20	M	Laborer	27Ma02Jl
NEWMAN, Bridget		27	F	Laborer	27Ma02Jl
Thom.		03	M	Child	27Ma02Jl
Ann		20	F	Laborer	27Ma02Jl
LINEN, Pat		20	M	Laborer	27Ma02Jl
COFFEE, John		30	M	Farmer	27Ma02Jl
U	(W)	30	F	Farmer	27Ma02Jl
Peter	(S)	07	M	Child	27Ma02Jl
Maria	(D)	04	F	Child	27Ma02Jl
GAVAN, Mich.		25	M	Laborer	27Ma02Jl
Ellen		20	F	Dressmaker	27Ma02Jl
TRACEY, Mary		20	F	Dressmaker	27Ma02Jl
SMALL, Ellen		20	F	Dressmaker	27Ma02Jl
KELLY, Mary		20	F	Dressmaker	27Ma02Jl
IRVINE, Jane		20	F	Dressmaker	27Ma02Jl
Mary		23	F	Dressmaker	27Ma02Jl
Andw.		.00	M	Infant	27Ma02Jl
LEGGET, Benjamin		24	M	Clerk	27Ma02Jl
QUICK, James		20	M	Laborer	27Ma02Jl
HARAN, John		28	M	Laborer	27Ma02Jl
John		22	M	Laborer	27Ma02Jl
Denis		22	M	Laborer	27Ma02Jl
MURA, Thom.		20	F	Laborer	27Ma02Jl
SHANNON, Pat		20	F	Laborer	27Ma02Jl
DALLEY, John		20	F	Laborer	27Ma02Jl
FLEMING, James		40	M	Laborer	27Ma02Jl
Pat		15	M	Laborer	27Ma02Jl
Mich.		11	M	Laborer	27Ma02Jl
CRAIG, Hugh		24	M	Laborer	27Ma02Jl
CURREY, John		20	M	Laborer	27Ma02Jl
Pat		26	M	Laborer	27Ma02Jl
ARMSTRONG, Pheaby		30	F	Laborer	27Ma02Jl
COYLE, John		27	F	Laborer	27Ma02Jl
MCLUSKY, Mich.		20	F	Laborer	27Ma02Jl
U		.00	U	Infant	27Ma02Jl
PAYNE, David		20	M	Draper	27Ma02Jl
MCWILLIAM, Robt.		21	M	Draper	27Ma02Jl
CLARK, Peter		20	M	Laborer	27Ma02Jl
SAXTON, Stephen		20	M	Laborer	27Ma02Jl
GOLDEN, Philip		05	M	Child	27Ma02Jl
Pat		02	M	Child	27Ma02Jl
Bridget		07	F	Child	27Ma02Jl
BURK, Mich.		18	M	Laborer	27Ma02Jl
MCGLAGHLAN, Francis		19	M	Laborer	27Ma02Jl
Biddy		20	F	Laborer	27Ma02Jl
Eliza		24	F	Laborer	27Ma02Jl
HOURD, John		30	M	Laborer	27Ma02Jl
CLARK, Pat		24	M	Laborer	27Ma02Jl
Nancy		24	F	Laborer	27Ma02Jl
FAY, Pat		22	M	Laborer	27Ma02Jl
HOURIGAN, Cath.		19	F	Dressmaker	27Ma02Jl
MARTIN, Owen		19	M	Shoemaker	27Ma02Jl
GALLAGHER, Mary		20	F	Dressmaker	27Ma02Jl
LEWIS, Thom.		20	M	Dressmaker	27Ma02Jl
MULRONY, Mary		20	F	Dressmaker	27Ma02Jl
POWER, Laurence		18	M	Dressmaker	27Ma02Jl
Fanny		11	F	Dressmaker	27Ma02Jl
MORGAN, Cath.		33	F	Servant	27Ma02Jl
GOLDEN, Mich.		32	M	Laborer	27Ma02Jl
Philip		22	M	Laborer	27Ma02Jl
Bridget		40	F	Wi	27Ma02Jl
Mary		37	F	Laborer	27Ma02Jl
NAYLEN, John		30	M	Laborer	27Ma02Jl
LENON, Sarah		20	F	Dressmaker	27Ma02Jl
DOURNIN, Cath.		22	F	Dressmaker	27Ma02Jl
MARTIN, Nancy		30	F	Laborer	27Ma02Jl
Bridget		14	F	Laborer	27Ma02Jl
Cath.		12	F	Laborer	27Ma02Jl
Ann		10	F	Laborer	27Ma02Jl
Margt.		08	F	Child	27Ma02Jl

NAMES OF PASSENGERS		AGE	SEX	OCCUPATIONS	DATE PORT SHIP
MARTIN, Hanah		04	F	Child	27Ma02Jl
John		03	M	Child	27Ma02Jl
Mary		02	F	Child	27Ma02Jl
NOWLANS, Margt.		15	F	Dressmaker	27Ma02Jl
GENTLEMAN, Jane		09	F	Child	27Ma02Jl
Pat		08	M	Child	27Ma02Jl
MCDONALD, John		25	M	Laborer	27Ma02Jl
DOWD, Laurence		25	M	Laborer	27Ma02Jl
Cath.		20	F	Laborer	27Ma02Jl
MCLAUGHLAN, Martin		10	M	Laborer	27Ma02Jl
SMITH, Henry		24	M	Engineer	27Ma02Jl
MCGARRY, Mary		20	F	Servant	27Ma02Jl
OBRIAN, Pat.		25	M	Farmer	27Ma02Jl
KERSHAN, Mich.		40	M	Farmer	27Ma02Jl
U	(W)	40	F	Farmer	27Ma02Jl
U		12	U	Farmer	27Ma02Jl
U		11	U	Farmer	27Ma02Jl
U		09	U	Child	27Ma02Jl
U		08	U	Child	27Ma02Jl
U		07	U	Child	27Ma02Jl
U		06	U	Child	27Ma02Jl
U		.00	U	Infant	27Ma02Jl
DUNN, Wm.		20	M	Wool Comber	27Ma02Jl

ELLEN-FORRESTAL 27 MAY 1848

From Limerick

NAMES OF PASSENGERS	AGE	SEX	OCCUPATIONS	DATE PORT SHIP
KEOUGH, Martin	12	M	Farmer	27Ma33Jm
ODONNELL, John	27	M	Farmer	27Ma33Jm
Michael	25	M	Farmer	27Ma33Jm
WALSH, Wm.	26	M	Farmer	27Ma33Jm
FITZGIBBON, James	24	M	Farmer	27Ma33Jm
Mary	20	F	Farmer	27Ma33Jm
GLEESON, Mary	23	F	Farmer	27Ma33Jm
NEIL, Ellen	40	F	Farmer	27Ma33Jm
DWYER, Pat	12	M	Farmer	27Ma33Jm
NEAL, James	07	M	Child	27Ma33Jm
Bridget	04	F	Child	27Ma33Jm
ONEILL, Jas.	35	M	Farmer	27Ma33Jm
CONWAY, John	22	M	Farmer	27Ma33Jm
James	25	M	Farmer	27Ma33Jm
Ann	18	F	Farmer	27Ma33Jm
Johanna	30	F	Farmer	27Ma33Jm
NESTOR, Michael	27	M	Farmer	27Ma33Jm
CARROLL, James	20	M	Farmer	27Ma33Jm
HAYES, John	28	M	Farmer	27Ma33Jm
MCENERNY, Dennis	46	M	Farmer	27Ma33Jm
Mary	35	F	Farmer	27Ma33Jm
James	17	M	Farmer	27Ma33Jm
Hannah	15	F	Farmer	27Ma33Jm
Margt.	10	F	Farmer	27Ma33Jm
Patt	07	M	Child	27Ma33Jm
Mary	.00	F	Infant	27Ma33Jm
MURPHY, John	24	M	Farmer	27Ma33Jm
MCGRATH, Margt.	18	M	Farmer	27Ma33Jm
GARVEY, Lawrence	30	M	Farmer	27Ma33Jm
CONLAN, James	24	M	Farmer	27Ma33Jm
Bridget	20	F	Farmer	27Ma33Jm
Margt.	18	F	Farmer	27Ma33Jm
LOUGHNANE, Michael	24	M	Farmer	27Ma33Jm
Catherine	22	F	Farmer	27Ma33Jm
CHAMBERS, Patt	23	M	Farmer	27Ma33Jm
FLYNN, James	23	M	Farmer	27Ma33Jm
Cath.	23	F	Farmer	27Ma33Jm
WALSH, Patt	23	M	Farmer	27Ma33Jm
KERIN, Brdgt.	26	F	Farmer	27Ma33Jm
NEAGLE, John	21	M	Farmer	27Ma33Jm
MENGORAN, Thomas	26	M	Farmer	27Ma33Jm

NAMES OF PASSENGERS	AGE	SEX	OCCUPATIONS	DATE PORT SHIP
CLANCY, Michael	28	M	Farmer	27Ma33Jm
KERIN, James	24	M	Farmer	27Ma33Jm
Cath.	24	F	Farmer	27Ma33Jm
MORAN, Michael	19	F	Farmer	27Ma33Jm
LYONS, Charles	18	F	Farmer	27Ma33Jm
SPELLISSY, George	20	M	Farmer	27Ma33Jm
Ellen	18	F	Farmer	27Ma33Jm
CAREY, Stephen	21	M	Farmer	27Ma33Jm
Mary	20	F	Farmer	27Ma33Jm
LYNCH, Thomas	18	M	Farmer	27Ma33Jm
John	24	M	Farmer	27Ma33Jm
LYDEN, Charles	20	M	Farmer	27Ma33Jm
Honor	17	F	Farmer	27Ma33Jm
HART, Michael	24	M	Farmer	27Ma33Jm
SHANNON, Cath.	26	F	Farmer	27Ma33Jm
Cath.	06	F	Child	27Ma33Jm
Jane	.00	F	Infant	27Ma33Jm
MINHERNY, Thomas	22	M	Farmer	27Ma33Jm
GALVIN, Ellen	16	F	Farmer	27Ma33Jm
MAEDWARD, Rodger	20	M	Farmer	27Ma33Jm
ROUGHAN, Miney	20	F	Farmer	27Ma33Jm
DALEY, Michael	50	M	Farmer	27Ma33Jm
MORAN, Peter	20	M	Farmer	27Ma33Jm
LILLIS, Richard	23	M	Farmer	27Ma33Jm
TROUSDALE, Wm.J.	27	M	Farmer	27Ma33Jm
Saunders	23	M	Farmer	27Ma33Jm
MCMAHON, James	26	M	Farmer	27Ma33Jm
HYNS, John	22	M	Farmer	27Ma33Jm
KEANE, Michael	18	M	Farmer	27Ma33Jm
LYONS, Bridget	17	F	Farmer	27Ma33Jm
CORRY, Patt	21	M	Farmer	27Ma33Jm
MCDONAGH, Honor	43	F	Farmer	27Ma33Jm
Nancy	21	F	Farmer	27Ma33Jm
CAHILL, John	20	M	Farmer	27Ma33Jm
RYAN, Honora	18	F	Unknown	27Ma33Jm

PLENTY 28 MAY 1848

From London

NAMES OF PASSENGERS	AGE	SEX	OCCUPATIONS	DATE PORT SHIP
HUTTON, Ann	42	F	Mwdr	28Ma21Jp
Henry	13	M	Servant	28Ma21Jp
BUSNACH, Mich.	31	M	Cigar Maker	28Ma21Jp
Maria	33	F	Cigar Maker	28Ma21Jp
Fanny	06	F	Child	28Ma21Jp
Solomon	05	M	Child	28Ma21Jp
Rachael	02	F	Child	28Ma21Jp
Henry	.00	M	Infant	28Ma21Jp
BIRD, John	27	M	Unknown	28Ma21Jp
COLLINS, John	40	M	Unknown	28Ma21Jp
Ellen	32	F	Unknown	28Ma21Jp
Mary	50	F	Unknown	28Ma21Jp
Honora	11	F	Unknown	28Ma21Jp
Margaret	05	F	Child	28Ma21Jp
Cathar.	.00	F	Infant	28Ma21Jp
KELLY, John	38	M	Unknown	28Ma21Jp
CONNOR, Mary-Ann	27	F	Unknown	28Ma21Jp
Johanna	23	F	Unknown	28Ma21Jp
DALEY, Jas.	24	M	Unknown	28Ma21Jp
SINART, John	49	M	Unknown	28Ma21Jp
KELLY, Mary	40	F	Unknown	28Ma21Jp
John	11	M	Unknown	28Ma21Jp
Ellen	03	F	Child	28Ma21Jp
Anne	.00	F	Infant	28Ma21Jp
BATTER, David	22	M	Unknown	28Ma21Jp
BOHN, Henrietta	33	F	Unknown	28Ma21Jp
QUILLENT, Q.	21	U	Unknown	28Ma21Jp
BARRITT, Mary	27	F	Unknown	28Ma21Jp
BRISTMAN, Bernard	21	M	Unknown	28Ma21Jp

NAMES OF PASSENGERS	AGE	SEX	OCCUPATIONS	DATE PORT SHIP
SULLIVAN, Helen	25	F	Unknown	28Ma21Jp
JEFFREY, Sep.	70	M	Unknown	28Ma21Jp
WALKER, George	30	M	Unknown	28Ma21Jp
KISKY, Jessey	28	M	Unknown	28Ma21Jp
LANNI, Mary	38	F	Unknown	28Ma21Jp
CANNING, Jas.	35	M	Unknown	28Ma21Jp
ISAACS, Abraham	20	M	Cigar Maker	28Ma21Jp
FLETCHER, Edmund	22	M	Printer	28Ma21Jp
SMITH, George	21	M	Cbtmkr	28Ma21Jp
Jane	32	F	Unknown	28Ma21Jp
Wm.	11	M	Unknown	28Ma21Jp
Mary-Ann	09	F	Child	28Ma21Jp
Henry	.00	M	Infant	28Ma21Jp
BARNES, Harris	34	M	Unknown	28Ma21Jp
Ann	30	F	Unknown	28Ma21Jp
HUSKE, Maria	09	F	Child	28Ma21Jp
Adoplhi	07	M	Child	28Ma21Jp
Sigersmond	04	M	Child	28Ma21Jp
Ann	36	F	Unknown	28Ma21Jp
TOWNSEND, Saml.	45	M	Unknown	28Ma21Jp
Sarah	44	F	Unknown	28Ma21Jp
MOORE, Michael	20	M	Unknown	28Ma21Jp
CURSIMUS, Wm.	49	M	Unknown	28Ma21Jp
Cathe.	49	F	Unknown	28Ma21Jp
ELLEN, Henry	12	M	Unknown	28Ma21Jp
John	11	M	Unknown	28Ma21Jp
BASS, Robert	50	M	Unknown	28Ma21Jp
Thos.	18	M	Unknown	28Ma21Jp
EDWARDS, Johann	24	M	Unknown	28Ma21Jp
DAHANS, Helen	19	F	Unknown	28Ma21Jp
LEONARD, Johann	21	M	Unknown	28Ma21Jp
VOT, Wm.	26	M	Unknown	28Ma21Jp
AST, Robt.	29	M	Unknown	28Ma21Jp
Rebecca	24	F	Unknown	28Ma21Jp
John	02	M	Child	28Ma21Jp
Amillia	.00	F	Infant	28Ma21Jp
WALKER, Edwd.	02	M	Child	28Ma21Jp
Edwd.	29	M	Unknown	28Ma21Jp
BLACK, John	30	M	Unknown	28Ma21Jp
Robt.	.00	M	Infant	28Ma21Jp
MAHONEY, Danl.	36	M	Unknown	28Ma21Jp
BANN, Thos.	48	M	Unknown	28Ma21Jp
MANN, Thos.	22	M	Unknown	28Ma21Jp
WELSH, Margaret	18	F	Unknown	28Ma21Jp
LEE, David	19	M	Laborer	28Ma21Jp
BARRITT, Mary	23	F	Servant	28Ma21Jp
BANNISTER, John	21	M	Painter	28Ma21Jp
FRY, Wm.	31	M	Bookmaker	28Ma21Jp
DAY, Wm.	17	M	Bookmaker	28Ma21Jp
Henry	13	M	Bookmaker	28Ma21Jp
FRY, Elizabeth	05	F	Child	28Ma21Jp
Mary-Ann	38	F	Unknown	28Ma21Jp
BIRD, Elizth.	21	F	Unknown	28Ma21Jp
MURPHY, Michael	42	M	Laborer	28Ma21Jp
Jas.	10	M	Laborer	28Ma21Jp
FERGUSON, Jas.	24	M	Laborer	28Ma21Jp
KILLIGAN, Thos.	45	M	Laborer	28Ma21Jp
Ellen	31	F	Unknown	28Ma21Jp
Edwd.	13	M	Unknown	28Ma21Jp
Ann	03	F	Child	28Ma21Jp
Danl.	.00	M	Infant	28Ma21Jp
HARPER, John	29	M	Unknown	28Ma21Jp
Mary	29	F	Unknown	28Ma21Jp
Ellizth.	07	F	Child	28Ma21Jp
Augustus	05	M	Child	28Ma21Jp
John	03	M	Child	28Ma21Jp
Mary-Ann	.00	F	Infant	28Ma21Jp
RYAN, Michael	25	M	Unknown	28Ma21Jp
HARGRASS, Wm.	21	M	Unknown	28Ma21Jp
ARTHUR, Wm.	56	M	Unknown	28Ma21Jp
Mary	50	F	Unknown	28Ma21Jp
John	26	M	Unknown	28Ma21Jp
Elizth.	25	F	Unknown	28Ma21Jp
Ann	22	F	Unknown	28Ma21Jp
Mary	10	F	Unknown	28Ma21Jp

NAMES OF PASSENGERS	AGE	SEX	OCCUPATIONS	DATE PORT SHIP
BLACK, Sarah	26	F	Unknown	28Ma21Jp
Mary-Ann	02	F	Child	28Ma21Jp
GODSON, Wm.	28	M	Unknown	28Ma21Jp
Ann	28	F	Unknown	28Ma21Jp
Caroline	13	F	Unknown	28Ma21Jp
Elen	11	F	Unknown	28Ma21Jp
John	09	M	Child	28Ma21Jp
Robt.	02	M	Child	28Ma21Jp

SUPERIOR 29 MAY 1848

From Liverpool

NAMES OF PASSENGERS	AGE	SEX	OCCUPATIONS	DATE PORT SHIP
BOYLE, William	35	M	Farmer	29Ma02Fb
U (W)	30	F	Unknown	29Ma02Fb
Mary-Ann (D)	05	F	Child	29Ma02Fb
Lydia	03	3	Child	29Ma02Fb
William	02	M	Child	29Ma02Fb
U	.09	M	Infant	29Ma02Fb
CARRAN, Mary	24	F	Servant	29Ma02Fb
KEELAN, William	30	M	Servant	29Ma02Fb
HEARNE, Micheal	50	M	Farmer	29Ma02Fb
Judith	48	F	Unknown	29Ma02Fb
Ellen	17	F	Unknown	29Ma02Fb
Nancy	16	F	Unknown	29Ma02Fb
Thomas	07	M	Child	29Ma02Fb
DAWLEY, Thomas	20	M	Laborer	29Ma02Fb
DONELLY, Patrick	20	M	Laborer	29Ma02Fb
LEARY, John	50	M	Farmer	29Ma02Fb
Mary	48	F	Unknown	29Ma02Fb
Thomas	27	M	Unknown	29Ma02Fb
Susan	25	F	Spinster	29Ma02Fb
Prudence	23	F	Spinster	29Ma02Fb
John	19	M	Blacksmith	29Ma02Fb
MCCORMICK, Micl.	28	M	Laborer	29Ma02Fb
Bridget	22	F	Unknown	29Ma02Fb
John	02	M	Child	29Ma02Fb
Mary	.09	F	Infant	29Ma02Fb
SLATTERY, John	24	M	Mason	29Ma02Fb
Joseph	14	M	Unknown	29Ma02Fb
CRAWLEY, John	31	M	Laborer	29Ma02Fb
MOORE, Thomas	24	M	Tailor	29Ma02Fb
Ann	21	F	Unknown	29Ma02Fb
Elizath.	.10	F	Infant	29Ma02Fb
GREADY, Thomas	30	M	Tailor	29Ma02Fb
Ellen	25	F	Unknown	29Ma02Fb
Mary	06	F	Child	29Ma02Fb
Micheal	04	M	Child	29Ma02Fb
Bridget	.00	F	Infant	29Ma02Fb

DEBORAH 29 MAY 1848

From Liverpool

NAMES OF PASSENGERS	AGE	SEX	OCCUPATIONS	DATE PORT SHIP
DOHERTY, Pat	22	M	Laborer	29Ma02Js
MCGORICK, Pat	15	M	Laborer	29Ma02Js
WRIGHT, Thomas	26	M	Laborer	29Ma02Js
Eliza	26	F	Laborer	29Ma02Js
Sarah-Ann	.00	F	Infant	29Ma02Js
GREEN, Mary	20	F	Spinster	29Ma02Js
HOPKINS, Ellen	20	F	Spinster	29Ma02Js
CLARK, Mary	19	F	Spinster	29Ma02Js
Jno.	21	M	Laborer	29Ma02Js
BLAIR, Hugh	18	M	Laborer	29Ma02Js
MCCABE, Pat	16	M	Laborer	29Ma02Js
KELLY, Jno.	70	M	Laborer	29Ma02Js
HUSSEY, Pat	16	M	Laborer	29Ma02Js
KELLY, Jno.	17	M	Laborer	29Ma02Js
TIERNAN, Ann	05	F	Child	29Ma02Js
MARLOW, Jno.	18	M	Unknown	29Ma02Js
Mary	10	F	Unknown	29Ma02Js
DONOHUE, Mary	12	F	Unknown	29Ma02Js
HALL, Martin	17	M	Unknown	29Ma02Js
Ruth	11	F	Unknown	29Ma02Js
MARDOCK, Ann	16	F	Unknown	29Ma02Js
GLEEN, Mary	20	F	Unknown	29Ma02Js
FITZGERALD, Cathe.	40	F	Wife	29Ma02Js
Edward	40	M	Laborer	29Ma02Js
James	20	M	Laborer	29Ma02Js
DUNLIGG, Thomas	20	M	Laborer	29Ma02Js
COWEN, Marcella	20	F	Laborer	29Ma02Js
MCDERMOTT, Cathe.	07	F	Child	29Ma02Js
Wm.	05	M	Child	29Ma02Js
NOLAN, Mary	20	F	Laborer	29Ma02Js
LARKIN, Mary	18	F	Laborer	29Ma02Js
GRAY, Ellen	20	F	Laborer	29Ma02Js
HEFFRON, Jas.	30	M	Laborer	29Ma02Js
Ellen	50	F	Laborer	29Ma02Js
Ellen	17	F	Laborer	29Ma02Js
TAGGART, Margaret	17	F	Laborer	29Ma02Js
CORRIGAN, Jno.	21	M	Laborer	29Ma02Js
GLANCY, James	23	M	Laborer	29Ma02Js
DOWNEY, Jno.	18	M	Laborer	29Ma02Js
HAYDEN, Mary	20	F	Laborer	29Ma02Js
CANTON, Edward	19	M	Laborer	29Ma02Js
CALDWELL, Pat	40	M	Laborer	29Ma02Js
SMYTH, James	34	M	Laborer	29Ma02Js
Mary	20	F	Laborer	29Ma02Js
MCCANN, Cathe.	18	F	Spinster	29Ma02Js
Pat	17	M	Laborer	29Ma02Js
Ellen	18	F	Laborer	29Ma02Js
MCCABE, Ann	18	F	Laborer	29Ma02Js
Susan	40	F	Laborer	29Ma02Js
Margt.	08	F	Child	29Ma02Js
Jno.	06	M	Child	29Ma02Js
Thos.	04	M	Child	29Ma02Js
Pat	.00	M	Infant	29Ma02Js
DONOHUE, Jno.	20	M	Laborer	29Ma02Js
KILBURN, Jos.	20	M	Laborer	29Ma02Js
LYNCH, Cathe.	21	F	Laborer	29Ma02Js
Mary	10	F	Laborer	29Ma02Js
DONNELLY, Margaret	20	F	Laborer	29Ma02Js
KELLY, Maria	18	F	Laborer	29Ma02Js
TIGHE, Maria	20	F	Laborer	29Ma02Js
Pat	18	M	Laborer	29Ma02Js
MCGOWAN, Ann	18	F	Laborer	29Ma02Js
GIBBS, Pat	26	M	Laborer	29Ma02Js
DOOLAN, Jane	20	F	Laborer	29Ma02Js
MARA, Pat	20	M	Laborer	29Ma02Js
HYLAND, Hugh	20	M	Laborer	29Ma02Js
SHERIDAN, Kern	20	M	Laborer	29Ma02Js
BRANNAN, Luke	20	M	Laborer	29Ma02Js
Sarah	10	F	Laborer	29Ma02Js
Wm.	07	M	Child	29Ma02Js
Margt.	03	F	Child	29Ma02Js
DEMPSEY, Bridget	20	F	Laborer	29Ma02Js
MCCERREN, Saml.	20	M	Laborer	29Ma02Js
COBB, Wm.Jno.	30	M	Laborer	29Ma02Js
GILLIGAN, Ann	20	F	Laborer	29Ma02Js
COUGHLAN, Cathe.	30	F	Laborer	29Ma02Js
WALKER, Jno.	23	M	Laborer	29Ma02Js
WHITE, Jno.	29	M	Laborer	29Ma02Js
Mary	24	F	Laborer	29Ma02Js
Mary	.00	F	Infant	29Ma02Js
EGAN, Pat	20	M	Laborer	29Ma02Js
Jno.	20	M	Laborer	29Ma02Js
KELLY, Margt.	20	F	Laborer	29Ma02Js
DALEY, Pat	20	M	Laborer	29Ma02Js

NAMES OF PASSENGERS	AGE	SEX	OCCUPATIONS	DATE PORT SHIP
BROPHY, James	21	M	Laborer	29Ma02Js
DOHERTY, Pat	20	M	Laborer	29Ma02Js
WHITEHEAD, Danl.	20	M	Laborer	29Ma02Js
HOPKINS, Owen	20	M	Laborer	29Ma02Js
DONNELLY, Jas.	20	M	Laborer	29Ma02Js
Pat	18	M	Laborer	29Ma02Js
ODONNELL, Cathe.	20	F	Laborer	29Ma02Js
Eliza	20	F	Spinster	29Ma02Js
Jno.	04	M	Child	29Ma02Js
CARMOODY, Thos.	20	M	Spinner	29Ma02Js
OBRIEN, Johanna	20	F	Spinner	29Ma02Js
NOLAN, Biddy	40	F	Spinner	29Ma02Js
Owen	20	M	Spinner	29Ma02Js
Mich.	06	M	Child	29Ma02Js
Bridght.	04	F	Child	29Ma02Js
MCCROSSEL, Pat	23	M	Spinner	29Ma02Js
STAFF, Hannah	18	F	Spinster	29Ma02Js
LAVAN, Ann	19	F	Spinster	29Ma02Js
DEVANEY, Cathe.	20	F	Spinster	29Ma02Js
MCDONALD, Sarah	50	F	Spinster	29Ma02Js
JORDAN, Cathe.	12	F	Spinster	29Ma02Js
DONOHUE, Margt.	30	F	Spinster	29Ma02Js
Jno.Wm.	09	M	Child	29Ma02Js
Henry	07	M	Child	29Ma02Js
Edward	03	M	Child	29Ma02Js
Eliza	02	F	Child	29Ma02Js
JEFFARDS, Sarah	25	F	Spinster	29Ma02Js
Sarah	.00	F	Infant	29Ma02Js
CAVANAGH, Chas.	30	M	Spinner	29Ma02Js
Andrew	08	M	Child	29Ma02Js
CUNNINGHAM, Matthew	20	M	Spinner	29Ma02Js
Mary	18	F	Spinner	29Ma02Js
Jane	20	F	Spinner	29Ma02Js
MCLAUGHLIN, Michl.	25	M	Spinner	29Ma02Js
KEENAN, Mary	20	F	Spinster	29Ma02Js
Bryan	25	M	Spinner	29Ma02Js
FARREL, Pat	20	M	Spinner	29Ma02Js
DONNELLY, Bridget	20	F	Spinner	29Ma02Js
Michl.	20	M	Spinner	29Ma02Js
HARVEY, Cathe.	18	F	Spinner	29Ma02Js
MCSHEHAN, Henry	20	M	Spinner	29Ma02Js
COUGHLAN, Ann	18	F	Spinster	29Ma02Js
KELLS, Philliss	20	F	Spinster	29Ma02Js
MCGURL, Thos.	20	M	Spinner	29Ma02Js
DORAN, Margt.	20	F	Spinster	29Ma02Js
FOWLER. Peter	20	M	Spinner	29Ma02Js
HURSH, James	45	M	Spinner	29Ma02Js
Mary	25	F	Spinster	29Ma02Js
Ellen	22	F	Spinster	29Ma02Js
Grace	16	F	Spinster	29Ma02Js
Wm.	04	M	Child	29Ma02Js
JONSON, Susan	30	F	Spinster	29Ma02Js
Edwd.	11	M	Spinner	29Ma02Js
Mark	08	M	Child	29Ma02Js
Rebecca	05	F	Child	29Ma02Js
HALLY, Jeremiah	40	M	Laborer	29Ma02Js
U (W)	40	F	Laborer	29Ma02Js
Mary-Ann	17	F	Laborer	29Ma02Js
Hannah	23	F	Laborer	29Ma02Js
Geo.	19	M	Laborer	29Ma02Js
KEESHAN, Tim	20	M	Laborer	29Ma02Js
TIERNEY, Pat	18	M`	Laborer	29Ma02Js
KEESHAN, Jno.	20	M	Laborer	29Ma02Js
SLATER, James	31	M	Laborer	29Ma02Js
CLAFFERY, Keenan	20	M	Laborer	29Ma02Js
BURK, Jno.	26	M	Laborer	29Ma02Js
KENNEDY, Anty.	28	M	Laborer	29Ma02Js
FITZPATRICK, Jno.	25	M	Laborer	29Ma02Js
FOHEY, Cathe.	20	F	Laborer	29Ma02Js
Eliz.	20	F	Laborer	29Ma02Js
HENNING, Jno.	24	M	Laborer	29Ma02Js
Mu--URN, Ellen	21	F	Laborer	29Ma02Js
KILLIAN, Bridget	18	F	Laborer	29Ma02Js
FLANNERY, Thos.	20	M	Laborer	29Ma02Js
MCGOVERN, Jane	18	F	Laborer	29Ma02Js

NAMES OF PASSENGERS	AGE	SEX	OCCUPATIONS	DATE PORT SHIP
KELLFINE, Danl.	40	M	Laborer	29Ma02Js
BRENAN, Hannah	20	F	Laborer	29Ma02Js
MOYAN, Jno.	51	M	Laborer	29Ma02Js
HARKINS, Jno.	30	M	Laborer	29Ma02Js
CROLY, Cornelius	35	M	Laborer	29Ma02Js
GALLOWAY, Cons.	28	M	Laborer	29Ma02Js
KELLY, James	20	M	Laborer	29Ma02Js
BELL, Geo.	35	M	Laborer	29Ma02Js
ROE, Pat	20	M	Laborer	29Ma02Js
PRINNE, Edwd.	24	M	Laborer	29Ma02Js
Martin	20	M	Laborer	29Ma02Js
Margt.	40	F	Laborer	29Ma02Js
Mary	20	F	Laborer	29Ma02Js
MCCANN, Wm.	20	M	Laborer	29Ma02Js
HEANEY, Richd.	30	M	Laborer	29Ma02Js
SKYES, Geo.	34	M	Laborer	29Ma02Js
Ann	32	F	Laborer	29Ma02Js
Sarah	14	F	Laborer	29Ma02Js
Bridget	12	F	Laborer	29Ma02Js
Martha	10	F	Laborer	29Ma02Js
Geo.	06	M	Child	29Ma02Js
Edward	04	M	Child	29Ma02Js
Henry	.00	M	Infant	29Ma02Js
IRELAND, Geo.	40	M	Unknown	29Ma02Js
LAVAN, James	14	M	Unknown	29Ma02Js
FAIRTH, Timothy	24	M	Unknown	29Ma02Js
HURDALE, Blake	24	M	Unknown	29Ma02Js
HAGAN, Margt.	21	F	Unknown	29Ma02Js
Mary	21	F	Unknown	29Ma02Js
RIN, Thos.	21	M	Unknown	29Ma02Js
Bridget	16	F	Unknown	29Ma02Js

THOMAS-BENNETT 29 MAY 1848

From Liverpool

NAMES OF PASSENGERS	AGE	SEX	OCCUPATIONS	DATE PORT SHIP
RIELLY, John	00	M	Farmer	29Ma02Jr
Walter	.09	M	Infant	29Ma02Jr
John	.07	M	Infant	29Ma02Jr
NOBLE, James	30	M	Laborer	29Ma02Jr
GILLON, Mary	17	F	Laborer	29Ma02Jr
Ann	15	F	Laborer	29Ma02Jr
Neill	01	M	Child	29Ma02Jr
CEARNS, Richard	20	M	Farmer	29Ma02Jr
John	17	M	Farmer	29Ma02Jr
Mary	25	F	Unknown	29Ma02Jr
Sarah	17	F	Unknown	29Ma02Jr
MULCAHY, Michael	25	M	Laborer	29Ma02Jr
NEVILLE, John	25	M	Laborer	29Ma02Jr
RING, Ally	23	F	Spinster	29Ma02Jr
DUNN, Margaret	17	F	Spinster	29Ma02Jr
Ann	16	F	Spinster	29Ma02Jr
Biddy	14	F	Spinster	29Ma02Jr
Mary	27	F	Spinster	29Ma02Jr
HIGGINS, U	19	M	Laborer	29Ma02Jr
PARKER, Alexander	26	M	Laborer	29Ma02Jr
MYERS, Patt	26	M	Laborer	29Ma02Jr
FINNEGAN, Mary	24	F	Spinster	29Ma02Jr
NASH, James	40	M	Laborer	29Ma02Jr
RICHARDS, Simon	23	M	Laborer	29Ma02Jr
Jasper	29	M	Laborer	29Ma02Jr
BANNISTER, Stephen	25	M	Laborer	29Ma02Jr
GIBBONS, William	20	M	Laborer	29Ma02Jr
Michael	18	M	Laborer	29Ma02Jr
DORAN, John	41	M	Laborer	29Ma02Jr
MULLANEY, John	50	M	Laborer	29Ma02Jr
Michael	18	M	Laborer	29Ma02Jr
ONEILL, Margaret	36	F	Spinster	29Ma02Jr
Patt	11	M	Laborer	29Ma02Jr

NAMES OF PASSENGERS	AGE	SEX	OCCUPATIONS	DATE PORT SHIP
ONEILL, Mary	09	F	Spinster	29Ma02Jr
Thomas	05	M	Child	29Ma02Jr
Hugh	01	M	Child	29Ma02Jr
HIGGINS, Bryan	30	M	Laborer	29Ma02Jr
HARRIS, Elizabeth	60	F	Spinster	29Ma02Jr
Andrew	27	M	Unknown	29Ma02Jr
Ann	01	F	Child	29Ma02Jr
MALLAN, Patt	27	M	Laborer	29Ma02Jr
GAFFNEY, Ann	.00	F	Infant	29Ma02Jr
HAWTHORN, Albert	17	M	Laborer	29Ma02Jr
KANE, Mary	18	F	Spinster	29Ma02Jr
MURRAY, Sarah	15	F	Spinster	29Ma02Jr
GIBBONS, Daniel	25	M	Farmer	29Ma02Jr
Susan	28	F	Spinster	29Ma02Jr
Duncan	17	M	None	29Ma02Jr
PARKE, Curtis	24	M	None	29Ma02Jr
GUNSTAN, Thomas	20	M	None	29Ma02Jr
WHITFIELD, Susanna	20	F	Spinster	29Ma02Jr
JONES, John	50	M	Laborer	29Ma02Jr
Sarah	40	F	Spinster	29Ma02Jr
Mary	13	F	Spinster	29Ma02Jr
Susan	11	F	Spinster	29Ma02Jr
Maria	02	F	Child	29Ma02Jr
Mary	.00	F	Infant	29Ma02Jr
REID, Frank	25	M	Laborer	29Ma02Jr
SILVERWOOD, Wm.	40	M	Laborer	29Ma02Jr
U (W)	30	F	Spinster	29Ma02Jr
MOORE, Henry	27	M	Laborer	29Ma02Jr
John	29	M	Laborer	29Ma02Jr
Margaret	21	F	Spinster	29Ma02Jr
QUATTER, John	40	M	Laborer	29Ma02Jr
Michael	19	M	Laborer	29Ma02Jr
MULLAY, Mary	16	F	Spinster	29Ma02Jr
SHAKELL, Michael	27	M	Farmer	29Ma02Jr
Margaret	15	F	Spinster	29Ma02Jr
Mary	01	F	Child	29Ma02Jr
Mary	.00	F	Infant	29Ma02Jr
GILLOGHY, Bridget	40	F	Spinster	29Ma02Jr
Margaret	.00	F	Infant	29Ma02Jr
ODONOHOE, M.	26	M	Laborer	29Ma02Jr
James	28	M	Laborer	29Ma02Jr
Mary	20	F	Spinster	29Ma02Jr
WELSH, Miles	25	M	Farmer	29Ma02Jr
BELL, Geo.	50	M	Farmer	29Ma02Jr
Esther	50	F	Farmer	29Ma02Jr
STEAGER, Joseph	30	M	Farmer	29Ma02Jr
COONAN, Margaret	20	F	Spinster	29Ma02Jr
CARTER, Stephen	23	M	Laborer	29Ma02Jr
MCCARTEN, Ann	17	F	Spinster	29Ma02Jr
CLEW, John	04	M	Child	29Ma02Jr
RUSSELL, Thomas	31	M	Laborer	29Ma02Jr
MCNAMARA, Ann	20	F	Spinster	29Ma02Jr
HANLEY, Mary	20	F	Spinster	29Ma02Jr
John	16	M	Laborer	29Ma02Jr
NORTON, Henry	11	M	Laborer	29Ma02Jr
CARTHY, Thomas	26	M	Laborer	29Ma02Jr
MCCORMICK, Ellen	30	F	Spinster	29Ma02Jr
Catherine	08	F	Child	29Ma02Jr
James	07	M	Child	29Ma02Jr
Francis	06	M	Child	29Ma02Jr
Sarah	02	F	Child	29Ma02Jr
LOVE, John	30	M	Farmer	29Ma02Jr
SHEPPERD, Mary	30	F	Spinster	29Ma02Jr
DUNN, Michael	32	M	Farmer	29Ma02Jr
James	11	M	Farmer	29Ma02Jr
Phillip	10	M	Farmer	29Ma02Jr
BAXTER, Ann	17	F	Spinster	29Ma02Jr
BRENNAN, James	30	M	Laborer	29Ma02Jr
WELSH, Michael	20	M	Laborer	29Ma02Jr
MORAN, Rosey	58	F	Spinster	29Ma02Jr
Rosey	26	F	Unknown	29Ma02Jr
GILLEGHAN, Owen	50	M	Laborer	29Ma02Jr
Mary	50	F	Spinster	29Ma02Jr
ROLLERS, James	20	M	Farmer	29Ma02Jr
Mary-Ann	21	F	None	29Ma02Jr
KIERNAN, Peter	16	M	Laborer	29Ma02Jr
Edward	12	M	Laborer	29Ma02Jr
LEDWICK, Michael	30	M	Laborer	29Ma02Jr
Rose	28	F	Spinster	29Ma02Jr
Owen	03	M	Child	29Ma02Jr
John	03	M	Child	29Ma02Jr
TRESSY, Michael	19	M	Laborer	29Ma02Jr
NEALON, Margaret	14	F	Spinster	29Ma02Jr
MCCORMICK, Mary	19	F	Spinster	29Ma02Jr
Michael	30	M	Farmer	29Ma02Jr
SHESGREEN, John	25	M	Farmer	29Ma02Jr
CARLIN, Catharine	10	F	Spinster	29Ma02Jr
THOMPSON, Ralph	45	M	Farmer	29Ma02Jr
GORDON, Robert	48	M	Farmer	29Ma02Jr
MCGRATH, Catharine	27	F	Spinster	29Ma02Jr
Nara	25	M	Laborer	29Ma02Jr
CARENDAN, Labara	32	F	Spinster	29Ma02Jr
MCNALLY, Mary	21	F	Spinster	29Ma02Jr
RIELLY, Catharine	20	F	Spinster	29Ma02Jr
Michael	05	M	Child	29Ma02Jr
LYNCH, John	20	M	Laborer	29Ma02Jr
BROWN, John	30	M	Laborer	29Ma02Jr
BRADY, Bridget	13	F	Spinster	29Ma02Jr
BING, Hanh	39	F	Spinster	29Ma02Jr
MULLEN, Mary	18	F	Spinster	29Ma02Jr
CARROLL, John	50	M	Farmer	29Ma02Jr
Sarah	43	F	Spinster	29Ma02Jr
John	21	M	Farmer	29Ma02Jr
John	12	M	Farmer	29Ma02Jr
Robert	10	M	Farmer	29Ma02Jr
William	07	M	Child	29Ma02Jr
Margaret	03	F	Child	29Ma02Jr
JOHNSTONE, Jane	30	F	Spinster	29Ma02Jr
LYON, Mary	25	F	Spinster	29Ma02Jr
Sophia	17	F	Spinster	29Ma02Jr
MULLEN, Michael	21	M	Laborer	29Ma02Jr
SHERLIN, Mary	24	F	Spinster	29Ma02Jr
FLOOD, Rosey	20	F	Spinster	29Ma02Jr
DEALIN, Patt	24	M	Laborer	29Ma02Jr
OHEARY, Timothy	19	M	Laborer	29Ma02Jr
RUSSELL, Catharine	20	F	Spinster	29Ma02Jr
HENNY, Patt	24	M	Laborer	29Ma02Jr
JOHNSTONE, Nelly	19	F	None	29Ma02Jr
RUSSELL, Thomas	22	M	Farmer	29Ma02Jr
LEAHY, Ellen	19	F	Spinster	29Ma02Jr
Johanna	17	F	Spinster	29Ma02Jr
MCGOVREN, Mary	29	F	Spinster	29Ma02Jr
Margaret	09	F	Child	29Ma02Jr
John	07	M	Child	29Ma02Jr
Thomas	07	M	Child	29Ma02Jr
John	03	M	Child	29Ma02Jr
Susan	.00	F	Infant	29Ma02Jr
MCDONALD, Johana	24	F	Farmer	29Ma02Jr
HAIGH, Michael	25	M	Farmer	29Ma02Jr
STRINGER, Johana	19	F	Farmer	29Ma02Jr
MCDONOUGH, Thos.	09	M	Child	29Ma02Jr
MAHERTY, Margaret	16	F	Child	29Ma02Jr
CONERY, Eliza	37	F	Spinster	29Ma02Jr
Ann	15	F	None	29Ma02Jr
Mary	09	F	Child	29Ma02Jr
STEELE, John	22	M	Laborer	29Ma02Jr
HENRY, John	25	M	Laborer	29Ma02Jr
Susan	39	F	Spinster	29Ma02Jr
Maria	17	F	Spinster	29Ma02Jr
Martha	15	F	Spinster	29Ma02Jr
John	15	M	Unknown	29Ma02Jr
Susan	11	F	None	29Ma02Jr
MORAN, John	19	M	Laborer	29Ma02Jr
Joseph	32	M	Laborer	29Ma02Jr
Jane	15	F	Laborer	29Ma02Jr
Jerry	35	M	Laborer	29Ma02Jr
HOARTEN, Thomas	36	M	Laborer	29Ma02Jr
John	12	M	Laborer	29Ma02Jr
Thomas	07	M	Child	29Ma02Jr
Jerry	05	M	Child	29Ma02Jr

NAMES OF PASSENGERS	AGE	SEX	OCCUPATIONS	DATE PORT SHIP
FEENY, Mary	22	F	Spinster	29Ma02Jr
John	19	M	Farmer	29Ma02Jr
Catharine	07	F	Child	29Ma02Jr
John	11	M	Child	29Ma02Jr
ROSS, George	22	M	Child	29Ma02Jr
Mary	20	F	Spinster	29Ma02Jr
Sarah	15	F	Spinster	29Ma02Jr
Matilda	11	F	Spinster	29Ma02Jr
OWENS, John	50	M	Farmer	29Ma02Jr
GOODWIN, Eliz.	19	F	Unknown	29Ma02Jr
SHERMAN, Laura	32	F	Unknown	29Ma02Jr
Martha	07	F	Child	29Ma02Jr

DOWNES 29 MAY 1848

From Waterford

NAMES OF PASSENGERS	AGE	SEX	OCCUPATIONS	DATE PORT SHIP
LYNAGH, John	35	M	Laborer	29Ma16Pn
Peter	28	M	Laborer	29Ma16Pn
FAGAN, Christopher	40	M	Laborer	29Ma16Pn
STAFFORD, John	26	M	Laborer	29Ma16Pn
HEANE, Richard	28	M	Laborer	29Ma16Pn
BYRNE, Richard	30	M	Laborer	29Ma16Pn
NEILL, Richard	35	M	Laborer	29Ma16Pn
MOORE, Margaret	33	F	None	29Ma16Pn
POWER, Bridget	27	F	None	29Ma16Pn
HOLDEN, Catherine	26	F	None	29Ma16Pn
WHITTG, James	24	M	Laborer	29Ma16Pn
MOLLOY, Thomas	23	M	Laborer	29Ma16Pn
FITZGERALD, Thomas	19	M	Laborer	29Ma16Pn
PHELAN, Michael	18	M	Laborer	29Ma16Pn
FAGAN, Catherine	39	F	None	29Ma16Pn
KENT, Michael	29	M	Laborer	29Ma16Pn
COONEY, Thomas	23	M	Laborer	29Ma16Pn
James	31	M	Laborer	29Ma16Pn
Ellen	29	F	None	29Ma16Pn
BRIEN, Bridget	28	F	None	29Ma16Pn
MAHONEY, Rody	35	M	Laborer	29Ma16Pn
Ellen	30	F	None	29Ma16Pn
U	.06	U	Infant	29Ma16Pn
COGHLAN, Julia	35	F	None	29Ma16Pn
SHEA, Walter	19	M	Laborer	29Ma16Pn
RELLY, Walter	18	M	Laborer	29Ma16Pn
MURPHY, Thomas	33	M	Laborer	29Ma16Pn
RELLY, Catherine	21	F	None	29Ma16Pn
Catherine	25	F	None	29Ma16Pn
HOGAN, Patrick	24	M	Laborer	29Ma16Pn
QUINN, Thomas	23	M	Laborer	29Ma16Pn
LARKIN, Thomas	29	M	Laborer	29Ma16Pn
CARROLL, Mary	32	F	None	29Ma16Pn
RYAN, John	28	M	Laborer	29Ma16Pn
MAHONEY, John	25	M	Laborer	29Ma16Pn
BUTLER, Ellen	24	F	None	29Ma16Pn
KING, Thomas	19	M	Laborer	29Ma16Pn
VEREREN, Wm.	21	M	Laborer	29Ma16Pn
KING, James	22	M	Laborer	29Ma16Pn
DOWER, Thomas	25	M	Laborer	29Ma16Pn
WALSH, Patrick	28	M	Laborer	29Ma16Pn
JOHNSON, Ally	26	F	None	29Ma16Pn
CURTIS, Patrick	33	M	Laborer	29Ma16Pn
MURPHY, Jasper	19	M	Laborer	29Ma16Pn
CANTWELL, Michael	16	M	Laborer	29Ma16Pn
Bridget	21	F	None	29Ma16Pn
GUINEAN, Joshua	24	M	Laborer	29Ma16Pn
BROWNE, Margaret	29	F	None	29Ma16Pn
LAGAN, Bridget	32	F	None	29Ma16Pn
AYBOARD, Joshua	31	M	Laborer	29Ma16Pn
CUMMINS, Michael	17	M	Laborer	29Ma16Pn
HENNESY, Patrick	19	M	Laborer	29Ma16Pn
HENNESSY, Michael	33	M	Laborer	29Ma16Pn
MAHONEY, Andrew	35	M	Laborer	29Ma16Pn
MCGRATH, Michael	39	M	Laborer	29Ma16Pn
TOOPEY, Patrick	28	M	Laborer	29Ma16Pn
Mary	26	F	None	29Ma16Pn
PHELAN, Thomas	25	M	Laborer	29Ma16Pn
Ellen	23	F	None	29Ma16Pn
DROHAN, Joshua	20	M	Laborer	29Ma16Pn
BUTLER, Mary	39	F	None	29Ma16Pn
COUMING, Catherine	35	F	None	29Ma16Pn
SULLIVAN, John	33	M	Laborer	29Ma16Pn
CARROLL, John	27	M	Laborer	29Ma16Pn
MERGAN, Robert	30	M	Laborer	29Ma16Pn
WALSH, John	22	M	Laborer	29Ma16Pn
LARLIN, Margaret	24	F	None	29Ma16Pn
MURPHY, Ally	25	F	None	29Ma16Pn
FITZGERALD, James	25	M	Laborer	29Ma16Pn
MAHONEY, Margt.	26	F	None	29Ma16Pn
Francis	19	M	None	29Ma16Pn
MURPHY, James	17	M	None	29Ma16Pn
WALSH, Thos.	15	M	None	29Ma16Pn
Patrick	21	M	None	29Ma16Pn
ONEIL, Con	26	M	None	29Ma16Pn
MURPHY, Edward	28	M	None	29Ma16Pn
CONNORS, Michael	30	M	None	29Ma16Pn
KELLY, Patrick	33	M	None	29Ma16Pn
CONNELL, Joshua	35	M	None	29Ma16Pn
COMERFORD, Patrick	37	M	None	29Ma16Pn
EGAN, Patrick	28	M	None	29Ma16Pn
John	19	M	None	29Ma16Pn
Edward-F.	18	M	None	29Ma16Pn
Michael	16	M	None	29Ma16Pn
BRIEN, Thomas	11	M	None	29Ma16Pn

CHARLES 29 MAY 1848

From Belfast

NAMES OF PASSENGERS		AGE	SEX	OCCUPATIONS	DATE PORT SHIP
MCBRIDE, John		20	M	Farmer	29Ma07Kb
LINTON, Peter		45	M	Farmer	29Ma07Kb
MCBRIDE, Betty		24	F	Spinster	29Ma07Kb
ROBINSON, Margaret		22	F	Spinster	29Ma07Kb
MACRAW, William		60	M	Farmer	29Ma07Kb
Mary	(W)	43	F	Wife	29Ma07Kb
William	(S)	29	M	Unknown	29Ma07Kb
John	(S)	18	M	Unknown	29Ma07Kb
Nathaniel	(S)	15	M	Unknown	29Ma07Kb
David	(S)	13	M	Unknown	29Ma07Kb
Mary	(D)	11	F	Unknown	29Ma07Kb
Edward	(S)	08	M	Child	29Ma07Kb
Charlotte	(D)	06	F	Child	29Ma07Kb
Robert	(S)	03	M	Child	29Ma07Kb
Mickliffe	(S)	.00	M	Infant	29Ma07Kb
SHUTTER, Margaret		18	F	Spinster	29Ma07Kb
MCCURDY, Samuel		22	M	Weaver	29Ma07Kb
Nancy		18	F	Spinster	29Ma07Kb
MCCAMBRIDGE, Ellen		40	F	Wi	29Ma07Kb
MITCHELL, Thomas		20	M	Weaver	29Ma07Kb
MURPHY, Ann		18	F	Spinster	29Ma07Kb
FULTON, Jonathan		33	M	Farmer	29Ma07Kb
Mary	(W)	30	F	Wife	29Ma07Kb
Ellen	(D)	10	F	Unknown	29Ma07Kb
Andrew	(S)	08	M	Child	29Ma07Kb
Jane	(D)	06	F	Child	29Ma07Kb
Mathew	(S)	04	M	Child	29Ma07Kb
MOORE, Samuel		30	M	Farmer	29Ma07Kb
Margaret	(W)	28	F	Wife	29Ma07Kb
Mary	(D)	.00	F	Infant	29Ma07Kb
WALKER, William		17	M	Weaver	29Ma07Kb

NAMES OF PASSENGERS		AGE	SEX	OCCUPATIONS	DATE PORT SHIP
WALKER, Samuel		30	M	Farmer	29Ma07Kb
Catharine	(W)	28	F	Wife	29Ma07Kb
Ellen	(D)	05	F	Child	29Ma07Kb
Matilda	(D)	03	F	Child	29Ma07Kb
MCMAHON, William		27	M	Weaver	29Ma07Kb
MCCONNELL, William		17	M	Weaver	29Ma07Kb
SAMPLE, John		18	M	Weaver	29Ma07Kb
WILLIS, Joseph		21	M	Weaver	29Ma07Kb
BURRY, David		26	M	Weaver	29Ma07Kb
Eliza		18	F	Spinster	29Ma07Kb
HACKETT, Francis		21	M	Weaver	29Ma07Kb
VICTOR, Hugh		18	M	Weaver	29Ma07Kb
WARWICK, William		50	M	Farmer	29Ma07Kb
Jane	(W)	50	F	Wife	29Ma07Kb
Margaret	(D)	22	F	Unknown	29Ma07Kb
Susannah	(D)	20	F	Unknown	29Ma07Kb
Letitia	(D)	18	F	Unknown	29Ma07Kb
Sarah	(D)	16	F	Unknown	29Ma07Kb
Mary	(D)	13	F	Unknown	29Ma07Kb
Hannah	(D)	11	F	Unknown	29Ma07Kb
Eliza	(D)	09	F	Child	29Ma07Kb
BURRY, Richard		29	M	Weaver	29Ma07Kb
WILSON, John		22	M	Weaver	29Ma07Kb
ONEIL, Thomas		22	M	Weaver	29Ma07Kb
Charles		21	M	Weaver	29Ma07Kb
SCOTT, John		25	M	Weaver	29Ma07Kb
MCCLOY, Allen		18	M	Weaver	29Ma07Kb
MCLANE, Hugh		40	M	Weaver	29Ma07Kb
NEVIN, Martha		40	F	Wi	29Ma07Kb
DAVIDSON, Eliza		21	F	Spinster	29Ma07Kb
PHILLIPS, John		18	M	Weaver	29Ma07Kb
RODGERS, John		21	M	Weaver	29Ma07Kb
YOUNG, James		15	M	Weaver	29Ma07Kb
Mary		17	F	Spinster	29Ma07Kb
GONDEY, James		17	M	Weaver	29Ma07Kb
MCCLURE, William		40	M	Farmer	29Ma07Kb
Robert		25	M	Farmer	29Ma07Kb
Betty		20	F	Spinster	29Ma07Kb
Elizabeth		05	F	Child	29Ma07Kb
MELLON, Sarah		22	F	Spinster	29Ma07Kb
CRAWFORD, Thomas		30	M	Farmer	29Ma07Kb
Mary	(W)	28	F	Wife	29Ma07Kb
MILLER, Francis		21	M	Weaver	29Ma07Kb
CONNERY, David		22	M	Weaver	29Ma07Kb
ELLISON, John		21	M	Weaver	29Ma07Kb
THOMPSON, John		22	M	Weaver	29Ma07Kb
MAGUIRE, Anne		20	F	Spinster	29Ma07Kb
GAVIN, Agnes		20	F	Spinster	29Ma07Kb
MILLER, James		65	M	Farmer	29Ma07Kb
Rose	(W)	45	F	Wife	29Ma07Kb
Andrew	(S)	25	M	Unknown	29Ma07Kb
John	(S)	23	M	Unknown	29Ma07Kb
William	(S)	20	M	Unknown	29Ma07Kb
James	(S)	18	M	Unknown	29Ma07Kb
Mary	(D)	15	F	Unknown	29Ma07Kb
Kath.		13	F	Spinster	29Ma07Kb
JOHNSTON, James		20	M	Farmer	29Ma07Kb
LYSH, Andrew		30	M	Farmer	29Ma07Kb
Elizabeth	(W)	30	F	Wife	29Ma07Kb
Sarah	(D)	02	F	Child	29Ma07Kb
Margaret	(D)	.00	F	Infant	29Ma07Kb
HARE, John		18	M	Weaver	29Ma07Kb
CAIN, Robert		20	M	Weaver	29Ma07Kb
JOHNSTON, Jane		18	F	Spinster	29Ma07Kb
CROSKILL, Matilda		22	F	Spinster	29Ma07Kb
Margaret		25	F	Spinster	29Ma07Kb
ATCHESON, John		29	M	Weaver	29Ma07Kb
BIGGER, John		45	M	Farmer	29Ma07Kb
Susannah	(W)	45	F	Wife	29Ma07Kb
Margaret	(D)	20	F	Unknown	29Ma07Kb
Anne	(D)	15	F	Unknown	29Ma07Kb
Mary	(D)	13	F	Unknown	29Ma07Kb
John	(S)	10	M	Unknown	29Ma07Kb
Jane	(D)	08	F	Child	29Ma07Kb
William	(S)	06	M	Child	29Ma07Kb

NAMES OF PASSENGERS		AGE	SEX	OCCUPATIONS	DATE PORT SHIP
BIGGER, Isabella	(D)	04	F	Child	29Ma07Kb
MCMANEY, Bernard		21	M	Mason	29Ma07Kb
TUMLETTY, Margaret		20	F	Mason	29Ma07Kb
Mary		21	F	Mason	29Ma07Kb
DAVISON, Thomas		21	M	Weaver	29Ma07Kb
George		23	M	Weaver	29Ma07Kb
SMITH, Thomas		21	M	Weaver	29Ma07Kb
DAVISON, Eliza		19	F	Spinster	29Ma07Kb
DOBSON, Arthur		21	M	Weaver	29Ma07Kb
MOORE, James		21	M	Unknown	29Ma07Kb
FLEMING, Hadesse		19	F	Spinster	29Ma07Kb
CONWAY, Paul		21	M	Weaver	29Ma07Kb
DONALDSON, William		21	M	Weaver	29Ma07Kb
ONEILL, Charles		20	M	Weaver	29Ma07Kb
JOHNSTON, Samuel		21	M	Weaver	29Ma07Kb
GAGEGAN, John		30	M	Weaver	29Ma07Kb
MCMULLEN, Patt		22	M	Weaver	29Ma07Kb
PHILLIPS, Edward		40	M	Laborer	29Ma07Kb
Margaret		34	F	None	29Ma07Kb
ONEILL, John		20	M	Weaver	29Ma07Kb
Bridget	(W)	22	F	Wife	29Ma07Kb
MCCAULEY, Sarah		29	F	Spinster	29Ma07Kb
MORGAN, Margaret		29	F	Spinster	29Ma07Kb
MILLER, John		30	M	Weaver	29Ma07Kb
LOW, Robert		25	M	Weaver	29Ma07Kb
MILLER, Matilda		25	F	Spinster	29Ma07Kb
MAGEE, Ellen		19	F	Spinster	29Ma07Kb
MCMULLEN, John		23	M	Weaver	29Ma07Kb
HOOD, Mary		21	F	Spinster	29Ma07Kb
WATT, Thomas		25	M	Laborer	29Ma07Kb
MCMANEY, John		29	M	Laborer	29Ma07Kb
MCKEEVER, James		29	M	Weaver	29Ma07Kb
MOORE, Anne		18	F	Spinster	29Ma07Kb
TAIT, Hugh		21	M	Farmer	29Ma07Kb
CLARK, Robert		24	M	Farmer	29Ma07Kb
SMITH, James		16	M	Farmer	29Ma07Kb
CASSIDY, Michael		18	M	Laborer	29Ma07Kb
MOONEY, Anne		30	F	Unknown	29Ma07Kb
LAFFERTY, Luke		20	M	Weaver	29Ma07Kb
BRADFORD, John		22	M	Spinner	29Ma07Kb
Sarah		20	F	Unknown	29Ma07Kb
DALY, James		27	M	Farmer	29Ma07Kb
JOHNSTON, James		27	M	Farmer	29Ma07Kb
Alfred		23	M	Farmer	29Ma07Kb
MCCAMBRIDGE, Ellen		20	F	Spinster	29Ma07Kb
MCMARRENY, William		21	M	Weaver	29Ma07Kb

ARABIAN 29 MAY 1848

From Liverpool

NAMES OF PASSENGERS		AGE	SEX	OCCUPATIONS	DATE PORT SHIP
LAVERY, John		20	M	Laborer	29Ma02Kc
CANFIELD, Thomas		20	M	Laborer	29Ma02Kc
Alice		20	F	Matron	29Ma02Kc
HOWLEY, James		25	M	Laborer	29Ma02Kc
Mary		25	F	Matron	29Ma02Kc
U		.00	U	Infant	29Ma02Kc
MCANN, Thomas		20	M	Laborer	29Ma02Kc
JUDGE, Peter		20	M	Laborer	29Ma02Kc
Michael		18	M	Laborer	29Ma02Kc
Margaret		19	F	Spinster	29Ma02Kc
JORDAN, Anthony		20	M	Laborer	29Ma02Kc
PEARSON, Winney		16	F	Spinster	29Ma02Kc
MCANN, Sebley		16	F	Spinster	29Ma02Kc
MESHAM, Hugh		20	M	Laborer	29Ma02Kc
Patrick		20	M	Laborer	29Ma02Kc
CONNELL, James		20	M	Laborer	29Ma02Kc
SHERLOCK, Biddy		20	F	Spinster	29Ma02Kc
MCONNELL, Rose		20	F	Spinster	29Ma02Kc

NAMES OF PASSENGERS		AGE	SEX	OCCUPATIONS	DATE PORT SHIP
WATTERS, Mathew		25	M	Laborer	29Ma02Kc
FLANNERY, Biddy		30	F	Matron	29Ma02Kc
Nancy		11	F	Unknown	29Ma02Kc
Thomas		13	M	Unknown	29Ma02Kc
James		08	M	Child	29Ma02Kc
Patrick		03	M	Child	29Ma02Kc
Mary		03	F	Child	29Ma02Kc
U		.00	U	Infant	29Ma02Kc
HENRY, Patrick		25	M	Laborer	29Ma02Kc
MCCAMERON, John		36	M	Laborer	29Ma02Kc
HANAHAN, Catherine		22	F	Spinster	29Ma02Kc
SMITH, Thomas		34	M	Laborer	29Ma02Kc
HILL, George		49	M	Laborer	29Ma02Kc
Mary		49	F	Matron	29Ma02Kc
Mary		48	F	Matron	29Ma02Kc
John		07	M	Child	29Ma02Kc
Lewis		05	M	Child	29Ma02Kc
WINTERS, William		61	M	Laborer	29Ma02Kc
BROWNAN, John		27	M	Laborer	29Ma02Kc
ROONEY, Mary		40	F	Matron	29Ma02Kc
Mary		13	F	Unknown	29Ma02Kc
Nancy		01	F	Child	29Ma02Kc
Bridget		11	F	Unknown	29Ma02Kc
Patrick		07	M	Child	29Ma02Kc
Thomas		04	M	Child	29Ma02Kc
Joel		03	M	Child	29Ma02Kc
GRAY, Mary		30	F	Spinster	29Ma02Kc
SHERIDAN, J.		22	M	Laborer	29Ma02Kc
Judith		18	F	Matron	29Ma02Kc
FOY, William		30	M	Laborer	29Ma02Kc
Catherine		26	F	Matron	29Ma02Kc
MULHORAN, Thomas		42	M	Laborer	29Ma02Kc
Mary		40	F	Matron	29Ma02Kc
Mary		10	F	Unknown	29Ma02Kc
Thomas		07	M	Child	29Ma02Kc
HEADEN, John		56	M	Laborer	29Ma02Kc
Mary		46	F	Matron	29Ma02Kc
Mary		17	F	Spinster	29Ma02Kc
Anne		13	F	Unknown	29Ma02Kc
Margaret		11	F	Unknown	29Ma02Kc
Judith		11	F	Unknown	29Ma02Kc
James		09	M	Child	29Ma02Kc
Kate		07	F	Child	29Ma02Kc
U		.00	U	Infant	29Ma02Kc
BLAKE, John		23	M	Laborer	29Ma02Kc
HOOLAN, Michael		40	M	Laborer	29Ma02Kc
James		10	M	Unknown	29Ma02Kc
MILLAR, Henry		34	M	Laborer	29Ma02Kc
BRADLEY, Patrick		22	M	Laborer	29Ma02Kc
John		20	M	Laborer	29Ma02Kc
MCELREADY, David		14	M	Laborer	29Ma02Kc
Sally		13	F	Unknown	29Ma02Kc
Rachel		11	F	Unknown	29Ma02Kc
Gabriel		09	M	Child	29Ma02Kc
QUINLAN, Edward		23	M	Laborer	29Ma02Kc
Michael		16	M	Laborer	29Ma02Kc
LOGAN, John		24	M	Laborer	29Ma02Kc
MCGIVERN, Robert		37	M	Laborer	29Ma02Kc
Mary		37	F	Matron	29Ma02Kc
Mary		12	F	Matron	29Ma02Kc
Jane		07	F	Child	29Ma02Kc
Robert		04	M	Child	29Ma02Kc
Elizabeth		03	F	Child	29Ma02Kc
Eliza		.00	F	Infant	29Ma02Kc
WRIGHT, Peter		53	M	Laborer	29Ma02Kc
Benjamin		20	M	Laborer	29Ma02Kc
James		10	M	Unknown	29Ma02Kc
BULLOCK, John		33	M	Laborer	29Ma02Kc
FOX, James		29	M	Laborer	29Ma02Kc
William		03	M	Child	29Ma02Kc
CONROY, Mathew		26	M	Laborer	29Ma02Kc
FOX, Jane		.00	F	Infant	29Ma02Kc
BRADLEY, John		24	M	Laborer	29Ma02Kc
U	(W)	20	F	Matron	29Ma02Kc
Michael	(S)	.00	M	Infant	29Ma02Kc

NAMES OF PASSENGERS		AGE	SEX	OCCUPATIONS	DATE PORT SHIP
DELANEY, Mary		26	F	Spinster	29Ma02Kc
Mary		05	F	Child	29Ma02Kc
Jane		03	F	Child	29Ma02Kc
Maria		.00	F	Infant	29Ma02Kc
MCGARRY, James		30	M	Laborer	29Ma02Kc
MCELRAE, James		28	M	Laborer	29Ma02Kc
RUNCOM, John		35	M	Laborer	29Ma02Kc
James		25	M	Laborer	29Ma02Kc
HORTWELL, Edward		41	M	Laborer	29Ma02Kc
DOUGAN, Michael		19	M	Laborer	29Ma02Kc
SERLES, Joseph		22	M	Laborer	29Ma02Kc
PAINTER, Robert		30	M	Laborer	29Ma02Kc
BROWN, Charlotte		28	F	Matron	29Ma02Kc
GILLAN, James		25	M	Laborer	29Ma02Kc
Peter		30	M	Laborer	29Ma02Kc
WALTERS, Joseph		24	M	Laborer	29Ma02Kc
FLOYD, Ann		24	F	Matron	29Ma02Kc
Jacolin		10	F	Unknown	29Ma02Kc
Sampson		01	M	Child	29Ma02Kc
WATERS, John		24	M	Laborer	29Ma02Kc
BOYD, Joseph		19	M	Laborer	29Ma02Kc
BEAGLEY, William		40	M	Laborer	29Ma02Kc
DULLEN, Edward		21	M	Laborer	29Ma02Kc
MAHER, Denis		20	M	Laborer	29Ma02Kc
CALLEN, Julia		18	F	Spinster	29Ma02Kc
COLLINS, John		30	M	Laborer	29Ma02Kc
Catherine		24	F	Matron	29Ma02Kc
SIMPSON, John		28	M	Laborer	29Ma02Kc
WEBB, Thomas		26	M	Laborer	29Ma02Kc
Emery		35	F	Matron	29Ma02Kc
William		22	M	Laborer	29Ma02Kc
Louisa		19	F	Matron	29Ma02Kc
Ann		09	F	Child	29Ma02Kc
Eliza		07	F	Child	29Ma02Kc
COSGROVE, Bridget		21	F	Spinster	29Ma02Kc
COMPTON, James		58	M	Laborer	29Ma02Kc
PRICE, Jane		22	F	Spinster	29Ma02Kc
MIDDLETON, Hannah		23	F	Spinster	29Ma02Kc
DAVIS, Mary		24	F	Spinster	29Ma02Kc
JOHNSTON, Michael		20	M	Laborer	29Ma02Kc
MCKEON, Michael		20	M	Laborer	29Ma02Kc
Michael		20	M	Laborer	29Ma02Kc
HUGHES, John		36	M	Laborer	29Ma02Kc
David		32	M	Laborer	29Ma02Kc
Margaret		27	F	Matron	29Ma02Kc
Margaret		11	F	Child	29Ma02Kc
Eleanor		04	F	Child	29Ma02Kc
Mary-Ann		.00	F	Infant	29Ma02Kc
U, U		.00	U	Infant	29Ma02Kc
Born-At-Sea					
WATKINS, Evan		49	M	Laborer	29Ma02Kc
LEWIS, Job.		32	M	Laborer	29Ma02Kc
U	(W)	32	F	Matron	29Ma02Kc
Hannah	(D)	08	F	Child	29Ma02Kc
SMITH, Thomas		28	M	Laborer	29Ma02Kc
Mary		26	F	Matron	29Ma02Kc
Robert		09	M	Child	29Ma02Kc
Charles		07	M	Child	29Ma02Kc
Walter		05	M	Child	29Ma02Kc
Eaken		03	M	Child	29Ma02Kc
Edwin		.00	M	Infant	29Ma02Kc
FLYNNE, Catherine		18	F	Spinster	29Ma02Kc
CONDRA, Catherine		18	F	Spinster	29Ma02Kc
TRACEY, Ann		18	F	Spinster	29Ma02Kc
FLYNN, Patrick		22	M	Laborer	29Ma02Kc
BRANNAGAN, John		26	M	Laborer	29Ma02Kc
CARROL, Thomas		30	M	Laborer	29Ma02Kc
Ann		26	F	Matron	29Ma02Kc
John		05	M	Child	29Ma02Kc
Thomas		03	M	Child	29Ma02Kc
Catherine		02	F	Child	29Ma02Kc
U, U		.00	U	Infant	29Ma02Kc
Born-At-Sea					
HAYDEN, John		20	M	Laborer	29Ma02Kc
Hannah		22	F	Matron	29Ma02Kc

NAMES OF PASSENGERS	AGE	SEX	OCCUPATIONS	DATE PORT SHIP
HAYDEN, Ellen	18	F	Spinster	29Ma02Kc
ROARKE, Thomas	25	M	Laborer	29Ma02Kc
Bridget	50	F	Matron	29Ma02Kc
Elizabeth	20	F	Spinster	29Ma02Kc
HACKET, Ann	20	F	Spinster	29Ma02Kc
RIDING, Mary	32	F	Matron	29Ma02Kc
John	18	M	Laborer	29Ma02Kc
Henry	16	M	Laborer	29Ma02Kc
James	13	M	Laborer	29Ma02Kc
Thomas	09	M	Child	29Ma02Kc
Elizabeth	06	F	Child	29Ma02Kc
Dorothea	04	F	Child	29Ma02Kc
John	.00	M	Infant	29Ma02Kc
FEE, Mary-A.	18	F	Matron	29Ma02Kc
John	16	M	Laborer	29Ma02Kc
JUDGE, William	30	M	Laborer	29Ma02Kc
HEADAN, Thomas	25	M	Laborer	29Ma02Kc
FLYNN, James	20	M	Laborer	29Ma02Kc
RICHARDSON, Edward	26	M	Laborer	29Ma02Kc
Ann	26	F	Matron	29Ma02Kc
Mary	01	F	Child	29Ma02Kc
John	18	M	Laborer	29Ma02Kc
COLE, Joseph	24	M	Laborer	29Ma02Kc
ALLEN, James	21	M	Laborer	29Ma02Kc
Catherine	20	F	Matron	29Ma02Kc
BROWN, Mary	40	F	Matron	29Ma02Kc
John	20	M	Laborer	29Ma02Kc
Mary	18	F	Spinster	29Ma02Kc
Jane	13	F	Spinster	29Ma02Kc
Bridget	12	F	Spinster	29Ma02Kc
Mary	06	F	Child	29Ma02Kc
Jacob	04	M	Child	29Ma02Kc
HUGHES, James	36	M	Laborer	29Ma02Kc
Bridget	30	F	Matron	29Ma02Kc
Mary	12	F	Unknown	29Ma02Kc
John	10	F	Unknown	29Ma02Kc
MORAN, Michael	20	M	Laborer	29Ma02Kc
Jane	18	F	Spinster	29Ma02Kc
Margaret	02	F	Child	29Ma02Kc
John	.00	M	Infant	29Ma02Kc
BRENNA, Patrick	06	M	Child	29Ma02Kc
Mary	04	F	Child	29Ma02Kc
James	02	M	Child	29Ma02Kc
Bridget	01	F	Child	29Ma02Kc

MARTHA 29 MAY 1848

From Cork

NAMES OF PASSENGERS	AGE	SEX	OCCUPATIONS	DATE PORT SHIP
KENT, Nancy	25	F	Farmer	29Ma14Qt
LOVETT, Julia	20	F	Farmer	29Ma14Qt
LOUGHLAN, Patrick	34	M	Farmer	29Ma14Qt
HYDE, John	32	M	Farmer	29Ma14Qt
DONOVAN, Wm.	20	M	Farmer	29Ma14Qt
ABBOTT, John	18	M	Farmer	29Ma14Qt
LINES, Ellen	07	F	Child	29Ma14Qt
KENT, John	40	M	Farmer	29Ma14Qt
Mary	35	F	Farmer	29Ma14Qt
Cath.	07	F	Child	29Ma14Qt
Bess	02	F	Child	29Ma14Qt
Mick	.00	M	Infant	29Ma14Qt
Mary	04	F	Child	29Ma14Qt
JOYCE, Patrick	40	M	Farmer	29Ma14Qt
PARKER, Cath.	25	F	Farmer	29Ma14Qt
CONNELLY, Jerry	20	M	Farmer	29Ma14Qt
Timothy	18	M	Farmer	29Ma14Qt
KENNEDY, John	22	M	Farmer	29Ma14Qt
ORR, John	50	M	Farmer	29Ma14Qt
Jane	18	F	Farmer	29Ma14Qt
ORR, Crawford	16	M	Farmer	29Ma14Qt
Jessie	15	F	Farmer	29Ma14Qt
James	12	M	Farmer	29Ma14Qt
William	10	M	Farmer	29Ma14Qt
John	08	M	Child	29Ma14Qt
Cath.	06	F	Child	29Ma14Qt
Margt.	04	F	Child	29Ma14Qt
Marion	.00	F	Infant	29Ma14Qt
IVES, William	50	M	Farmer	29Ma14Qt
Ellen	55	F	Farmer	29Ma14Qt
John	25	M	Farmer	29Ma14Qt
Mary	23	F	Farmer	29Ma14Qt
Ellen	17	F	Farmer	29Ma14Qt
Norry	19	M	Farmer	29Ma14Qt
Wm.	11	M	Farmer	29Ma14Qt
COLLINGHAM, Bath.	35	M	Farmer	29Ma14Qt
SULLIVAN, Humphry	20	M	Farmer	29Ma14Qt
Johanna	20	F	Farmer	29Ma14Qt
ROACH, Bridget	22	F	Farmer	29Ma14Qt
COLLINS, James	30	M	Farmer	29Ma14Qt
Bess	35	F	Farmer	29Ma14Qt
Danl.	05	M	Child	29Ma14Qt
Wm.	03	M	Child	29Ma14Qt
Mary	.00	F	Infant	29Ma14Qt
FITZGERALD, Daniel	20	M	Farmer	29Ma14Qt
Jerry	25	M	Farmer	29Ma14Qt
Hannah	18	F	Farmer	29Ma14Qt
Gar--, Thomas	25	M	Farmer	29Ma14Qt
HOWRAN, Mary	24	F	Farmer	29Ma14Qt
HIGGINS, Danl.	24	M	Farmer	29Ma14Qt
Mary	22	F	Farmer	29Ma14Qt
LEARY, Johanna	20	F	Farmer	29Ma14Qt
Danl.	18	M	Farmer	29Ma14Qt
HIGGINS, Cath.	.00	F	Infant	29Ma14Qt
MAHONEY, Danl.	38	M	Farmer	29Ma14Qt
Danl.	18	M	Farmer	29Ma14Qt
John	20	M	Farmer	29Ma14Qt
SULLIVAN, John	20	M	Farmer	29Ma14Qt
GALLAVAN, Mary	23	F	Farmer	29Ma14Qt
MCSWEENEY, John	21	M	Farmer	29Ma14Qt
Ellen	21	F	Farmer	29Ma14Qt
KEEFE, John	25	M	Farmer	29Ma14Qt
MARSHALL, Darby	20	M	Farmer	29Ma14Qt
REGAN, Jim	28	M	Farmer	29Ma14Qt
Danl.	16	M	Farmer	29Ma14Qt
LYNCH, Daniel	20	M	Farmer	29Ma14Qt
Michael	20	M	Farmer	29Ma14Qt
Kate	18	F	Farmer	29Ma14Qt
KELLEHER, Loby	40	M	Farmer	29Ma14Qt
Cath.	40	F	Farmer	29Ma14Qt
AHEARN, Mary	20	F	Farmer	29Ma14Qt
KELLEHER, Darby	13	M	Farmer	29Ma14Qt
Thomas	11	M	Farmer	29Ma14Qt
Darby	20	M	Farmer	29Ma14Qt
Mary	18	F	Farmer	29Ma14Qt
AHEARN, Mary	22	F	Farmer	29Ma14Qt
FOX, Mary	22	F	Farmer	29Ma14Qt
NOWLAN, Mary	18	F	Farmer	29Ma14Qt
MCFEELY, Susan	20	F	Farmer	29Ma14Qt
CONNELL, Mary	23	F	Farmer	29Ma14Qt
NEIL, Andy	25	M	Farmer	29Ma14Qt
COURTNEY, James	22	M	Farmer	29Ma14Qt
DALY, --Ophny	22	U	Farmer	29Ma14Qt
DONAVAN, John	22	M	Farmer	29Ma14Qt
BURRY, Fanny	23	F	Farmer	29Ma14Qt
KINERED, Michael	30	M	Farmer	29Ma14Qt
Biddy	30	F	Farmer	29Ma14Qt
DONOVAN, Pat	35	M	Farmer	29Ma14Qt
Biddy	30	F	Farmer	29Ma14Qt
Mary	12	F	Farmer	29Ma14Qt
John	10	M	Farmer	29Ma14Qt
Honora	07	F	Child	29Ma14Qt
DUKES, Robert	20	M	Farmer	29Ma14Qt
MCCARTHY, Jerry	20	M	Farmer	29Ma14Qt
BONHAM, Michael	22	M	Farmer	29Ma14Qt

NAMES OF PASSENGERS	AGE	SEX	OCCUPATIONS	DATE PORT SHIP
CALAHAM, Margt.	21	F	Farmer	29Ma14Qt
DONOVAN, Margt.	20	F	Farmer	29Ma14Qt
John	20	M	Farmer	29Ma14Qt
MCCARTHY, Charles	40	M	Farmer	29Ma14Qt
HAYES, U	13	F	Farmer	29Ma14Qt
DONOVAN, Mary	21	F	Farmer	29Ma14Qt

MOUNTAINEER 29 MAY 1848

From Penzance

NAMES OF PASSENGERS	AGE	SEX	OCCUPATIONS	DATE PORT SHIP
PAULL, Moses	24	M	Smith	29Ma88Kd
Elizabeth-Jane	24	F	Smith	29Ma88Kd
CHUCKWINE, John	24	M	Miner	29Ma88Kd
WILLIAMS, Zachariah	34	M	Miner	29Ma88Kd
HALL, Richard	32	M	Miner	29Ma88Kd
Thomas	25	M	Miner	29Ma88Kd
HARVEY, William	27	M	Miner	29Ma88Kd
MATHEWS, John	28	M	Miner	29Ma88Kd
TAYLOR, Henry	25	M	Miner	29Ma88Kd
HALL, Susan	27	F	Miner	29Ma88Kd
RODDA, Benjamin	40	M	Miner	29Ma88Kd
Christopher	36	M	Miner	29Ma88Kd
BENNETTS, Richard	33	M	Miner	29Ma88Kd
EDDY, William	23	M	Miner	29Ma88Kd
FREZILL, Henry	44	M	Miner	29Ma88Kd
WOOLCOCK, John	29	M	Miner	29Ma88Kd
Samson	22	M	Miner	29Ma88Kd
ELLIS, John	21	M	Miner	29Ma88Kd
CHELLEN, James	22	M	Miner	29Ma88Kd
GEORGE, James	40	M	Miner	29Ma88Kd
Henry	24	M	Miner	29Ma88Kd
HOLLOW, John	26	M	Miner	29Ma88Kd
SARA, John	27	M	Smith	29Ma88Kd
BAILY, Josephis	32	M	Wool Comber	29Ma88Kd
ADAMS, William	35	M	Wool Comber	29Ma88Kd
CURTIS, Saml.	34	M	Wool Comber	29Ma88Kd
Wm.	20	M	Wool Comber	29Ma88Kd
Mary	32	F	Wool Comber	29Ma88Kd
Wm.Sr.	47	M	Wool Comber	29Ma88Kd
PERRY, Richard	22	M	Wool Comber	29Ma88Kd
MATHEWS, Peter	28	M	Wool Comber	29Ma88Kd
WOOLCOCK, Elizabeth	22	F	Wool Comber	29Ma88Kd
KING, Wm.	32	M	Fitter	29Ma88Kd
THOMAS, Wm.	24	M	Miner	29Ma88Kd
EDDY, John	36	M	Miner	29Ma88Kd
STEVENS, John	46	M	Miner	29Ma88Kd
Margaret	41	F	Miner	29Ma88Kd
James	18	M	Miner	29Ma88Kd
Thomas	15	M	Miner	29Ma88Kd
Elizabeth	10	F	Miner	29Ma88Kd
Ann	13	F	Miner	29Ma88Kd
Mary	04	F	Child	29Ma88Kd
Wm.	07	M	Child	29Ma88Kd
Ann	03	F	Child	29Ma88Kd
JOEY, John	44	M	Miner	29Ma88Kd
Matilda	35	F	Miner	29Ma88Kd
Henry	12	M	Miner	29Ma88Kd
Thomas	13	M	Miner	29Ma88Kd
Mary	07	F	Child	29Ma88Kd
William	08	M	Child	29Ma88Kd
Anne	23	F	Miner	29Ma88Kd
CLERY, Wm.	48	M	Miner	29Ma88Kd
JOEY, John	16	M	Miner	29Ma88Kd
HUGS, Stephen	20	M	Printer	29Ma88Kd
ANDREWS, James	30	M	Unknown	29Ma88Kd
Francis	27	M	Mason	29Ma88Kd
DONISHOME, John	44	M	Mason	29Ma88Kd
Anne	39	F	Mason	29Ma88Kd
DONISHOME, Anne	08	F	Child	29Ma88Kd
John	13	M	Mason	29Ma88Kd
Elizabeth	10	F	Mason	29Ma88Kd
Wm.	07	M	Child	29Ma88Kd
Richard	05	M	Child	29Ma88Kd
Emily	02	F	Child	29Ma88Kd
U	.00	U	Infant	29Ma88Kd
Mary-Ann-Emma	10	F	Unknown	29Ma88Kd
THOMAS, James	52	M	Miner	29Ma88Kd
Ann	47	F	Miner	29Ma88Kd
Mary-Ann	16	F	Miner	29Ma88Kd
Jane	13	F	Miner	29Ma88Kd
James	10	M	Miner	29Ma88Kd
Joseph	05	M	Child	29Ma88Kd
English	.11	M	Infant	29Ma88Kd
KING, Chas.	25	M	Carpenter	29Ma88Kd
NOBLE, Edw.	32	M	Carpenter	29Ma88Kd
Mary	31	F	Carpenter	29Ma88Kd
Edw.	08	M	Child	29Ma88Kd
Dorothy	07	F	Child	29Ma88Kd
Mary-Ann	05	F	Child	29Ma88Kd
Geo.	04	M	Child	29Ma88Kd
Joseph	02	M	Child	29Ma88Kd
MITCHELL, Jane	31	F	Carpenter	29Ma88Kd
FOX, James	23	M	Carpenter	29Ma88Kd
Mary	22	F	Carpenter	29Ma88Kd
Jno.	03	M	Child	29Ma88Kd
U	.10	U	Infant	29Ma88Kd
CARTER, Robert	49	M	Blacksmith	29Ma88Kd
Mary	47	F	Blacksmith	29Ma88Kd
Thomas	20	M	Blacksmith	29Ma88Kd
Susan	18	F	Blacksmith	29Ma88Kd
Richard	17	M	Blacksmith	29Ma88Kd
Jno.	14	M	Blacksmith	29Ma88Kd
Catherine	12	F	Blacksmith	29Ma88Kd
Wm.	06	M	Child	29Ma88Kd
Helen	03	F	Child	29Ma88Kd
Ros---, Catherine	49	F	Miner	29Ma88Kd
SIMMONS, Rond.	44	M	Miner	29Ma88Kd
Susan	40	F	Miner	29Ma88Kd
PENBERTHY, Thomasin	19	M	Miner	29Ma88Kd
HENDREN, Thomas	31	M	Miner	29Ma88Kd
Frey---, Edw.	47	M	Miner	29Ma88Kd
ROW, Jno.	21	M	Miner	29Ma88Kd
RICHARD, Jno.	50	M	Miner	29Ma88Kd
OATES, Chas.	45	M	Miner	29Ma88Kd
PATEZ, Saml.	47	M	Miner	29Ma88Kd
INGREM, Edw.	23	M	Unknown	29Ma88Kd
WILLS, Jas.	24	M	Unknown	29Ma88Kd
WILLIAMS, John	28	M	Unknown	29Ma88Kd
DAVEY, Wm.	34	M	Unknown	29Ma88Kd
LANYON, Urial	30	M	Unknown	29Ma88Kd
Elizabeth	33	F	Unknown	29Ma88Kd
Robert	06	M	Child	29Ma88Kd
Elizabeth	04	F	Child	29Ma88Kd
THOMAS, Benjamin	36	M	Unknown	29Ma88Kd
PASCOR, Thomas	29	M	Unknown	29Ma88Kd
Martha	30	F	Unknown	29Ma88Kd
U	01	U	Child	29Ma88Kd
Wm.	20	M	Unknown	29Ma88Kd
SHUGG, Wm.	38	M	Carpenter	29Ma88Kd
Emily	37	F	Carpenter	29Ma88Kd
William	06	M	Child	29Ma88Kd
Thomas	04	M	Child	29Ma88Kd
Mary-Ann	02	F	Child	29Ma88Kd
Anna-Martha	.10	F	Infant	29Ma88Kd
POLGLASS, Jas.	25	M	Miner	29Ma88Kd
WILLIAMS, Thos.	23	M	Miner	29Ma88Kd
Ann	22	F	Miner	29Ma88Kd
Thomas	.01	M	Infant	29Ma88Kd
Eliza	.06	F	Infant	29Ma88Kd
NICHOLLS, Stephen	32	M	Miner	29Ma88Kd
Grace	22	F	Miner	29Ma88Kd
Stephen	.04	M	Infant	29Ma88Kd
WILLIAMS, Jno.	26	M	Miner	29Ma88Kd

NAMES OF PASSENGERS	AGE	SEX	OCCUPATIONS	DATE PORT SHIP
WILLIAMS, Susan	23	F	Miner	29Ma88Kd
COCK, Thomas	21	M	Miner	29Ma88Kd
HONEYCHURCH, Oliver	37	M	Miner	29Ma88Kd
WOOLCOCK, Henry	32	M	Miner	29Ma88Kd
Cordelia	37	F	Miner	29Ma88Kd
Mary	09	F	Child	29Ma88Kd
Ellen	21	F	Miner	29Ma88Kd
U	.00	U	Infant	29Ma88Kd
Jas.	38	M	Miner	29Ma88Kd
Elizabeth	36	F	Miner	29Ma88Kd
Jas.	10	M	Miner	29Ma88Kd
Jno.	04	M	Child	29Ma88Kd
Henry	02	M	Child	29Ma88Kd
U	.00	U	Infant	29Ma88Kd
ARGALE, Jas.	34	M	Miner	29Ma88Kd
Mary-Ann	25	F	Miner	29Ma88Kd
Ann	11	F	Miner	29Ma88Kd
Jas.	09	M	Child	29Ma88Kd
Elizabeth	02	F	Child	29Ma88Kd
U	.03	U	Infant	29Ma88Kd
RANDALL, Jos.	31	M	Miner	29Ma88Kd
Elizabeth	26	F	Miner	29Ma88Kd
Wm.	03	M	Child	29Ma88Kd
U	.10	U	Infant	29Ma88Kd
ELLERY, Jno.	24	M	Miner	29Ma88Kd
TRELOAR, Henry	40	M	Miner	29Ma88Kd
Loveday	40	F	Miner	29Ma88Kd
Henry	19	M	Miner	29Ma88Kd
Bennett	17	M	Miner	29Ma88Kd
Jos.	13	M	Miner	29Ma88Kd
Elizabeth	10	F	Miner	29Ma88Kd
Loveday	08	F	Child	29Ma88Kd
Wm.	06	M	Child	29Ma88Kd
Jno.	04	M	Child	29Ma88Kd
Thomas	.06	M	Infant	29Ma88Kd
COCK, Thomas	52	M	Miner	29Ma88Kd
Elizabeth	13	F	Miner	29Ma88Kd
PRINCE, Thomasine	62	M	Miner	29Ma88Kd
Wm.	27	M	Miner	29Ma88Kd
Stephen	22	M	Miner	29Ma88Kd
PIERCE, Wm.	33	M	Miner	29Ma88Kd
Mary-Ann	37	F	Miner	29Ma88Kd
Wm.	12	M	Miner	29Ma88Kd
John	07	M	Child	29Ma88Kd
CURNON, Jno.	28	M	Miner	29Ma88Kd
MITCHELL, Henry	15	M	Miner	29Ma88Kd
TREVELEN, Wm.	27	M	Miner	29Ma88Kd
CROWGRY, Jno.	25	M	Miner	29Ma88Kd
HENRY, John	22	M	Miner	29Ma88Kd
LEROY, Daniel	25	M	Miner	29Ma88Kd
TERRY, Elishe	24	F	Miner	29Ma88Kd
JEFFERY, Edmund	21	M	Miner	29Ma88Kd
URRE, William	54	M	Miner	29Ma88Kd
Wm.Jr.	13	M	Miner	29Ma88Kd
PENROSE, Richard	24	M	Miner	29Ma88Kd
MARTIN, Mary	42	F	Miner	29Ma88Kd
John	16	M	Miner	29Ma88Kd
Saml.	18	M	Miner	29Ma88Kd
Elizabeth	12	F	Miner	29Ma88Kd
PENROSE, Jno.	34	M	Miner	29Ma88Kd
RICHARDS, Jno.	24	M	Miner	29Ma88Kd
TAYLOR, Henry	48	M	Miner	29Ma88Kd
TRENBATH, Jas.	25	M	Miner	29Ma88Kd
CHAMPION, Jno.	28	M	Miner	29Ma88Kd

BRIDGET 29 MAY 1848

From Cork

NAMES OF PASSENGERS	AGE	SEX	OCCUPATIONS	DATE PORT SHIP
CODDE, Mark	33	M	Farmer	29Ma14Kf
Patrick	30	M	Farmer	29Ma14Kf
James	26	M	Farmer	29Ma14Kf
Mary	28	F	Farmer	29Ma14Kf
FURLONG, James	26	M	Farmer	29Ma14Kf
CLOONEY, James	30	M	Farmer	29Ma14Kf
FAHEY, Maurice	45	M	Farmer	29Ma14Kf
Cathe.	43	F	Farmer	29Ma14Kf
Margt.	07	F	Child	29Ma14Kf
Wm.	05	M	Child	29Ma14Kf
Elizt.	04	F	Child	29Ma14Kf
Michl.	02	M	Child	29Ma14Kf
BREYOM, Lanc.	11	M	Farmer	29Ma14Kf
MAKESY, John	46	M	Farmer	29Ma14Kf
KINIALLY, Cathe.	23	F	Spinster	29Ma14Kf
Elizbt.	21	F	Spinster	29Ma14Kf
KIELY, Wm.	34	M	Laborer	29Ma14Kf
De---, Edmond	26	M	Unknown	29Ma14Kf
FLYNN, David	24	M	Laborer	29Ma14Kf
Ellen	21	F	Laborer	29Ma14Kf
Johana	18	F	Laborer	29Ma14Kf
Patrick	12	M	Laborer	29Ma14Kf
Thos.	10	M	Laborer	29Ma14Kf
QUANN, Ellen	26	F	Laborer	29Ma14Kf
Ellen	03	F	Child	29Ma14Kf
SHEA, Thos.	22	M	Laborer	29Ma14Kf
MORAN, Thos.	28	M	Laborer	29Ma14Kf
KENNELLY, Johana	30	F	Laborer	29Ma14Kf
CORCORAN, Ellen	28	F	Laborer	29Ma14Kf
LAHY, Henry	18	M	Laborer	29Ma14Kf
DWYER, Judith	45	F	Laborer	29Ma14Kf
Margt.	25	F	Laborer	29Ma14Kf
POWER, Thos.	24	M	Laborer	29Ma14Kf
WALSH, James	20	M	Laborer	29Ma14Kf
CONNOLLY, Cornelius	30	M	Laborer	29Ma14Kf
WILLIAMS, Lawrence	28	M	Laborer	29Ma14Kf
COLLINS, Margt.	34	F	Spinster	29Ma14Kf
SULLIVAN, Michl.	16	M	Farmer	29Ma14Kf
LONEGAN, Edmond	45	M	Farmer	29Ma14Kf
Mary	44	F	Farmer	29Ma14Kf
Cathe.	22	F	Farmer	29Ma14Kf
Anastatia	20	F	Farmer	29Ma14Kf
Mary	17	F	Farmer	29Ma14Kf
Patrick	15	M	Farmer	29Ma14Kf
Margt.	13	F	Farmer	29Ma14Kf
Richd.	10	M	Farmer	29Ma14Kf
David	08	M	Child	29Ma14Kf
Johana	06	F	Child	29Ma14Kf
John	03	M	Child	29Ma14Kf
MCGRATH, Michl.	24	M	Farmer	29Ma14Kf
BROWNE, Patrick	25	M	Farmer	29Ma14Kf
FLYNN, Johana	23	F	Dressmaker	29Ma14Kf
HANDLON, Johana	23	F	Dressmaker	29Ma14Kf
FARREL, Ellen	23	F	Dressmaker	29Ma14Kf
LAHY, Elize	20	F	Dressmaker	29Ma14Kf
MULLOWNEY, Edmond	27	M	Farmer	29Ma14Kf
Mchl.	20	M	Farmer	29Ma14Kf
MCGRATH, Maurice	28	M	Farmer	29Ma14Kf
DALTON, Joseph	28	M	Farmer	29Ma14Kf
HAYS, James	25	M	Farmer	29Ma14Kf
MCCARTHY, Lawn.	22	M	Farmer	29Ma14Kf
HENNESSY, Michl.	28	M	Farmer	29Ma14Kf
MORRISON, John	22	M	Cabdriver	29Ma14Kf
Ellen	25	F	Spinster	29Ma14Kf
MCCARTHY, Anastatia	18	F	Dressmaker	29Ma14Kf

NAMES OF PASSENGERS	A G E	S E X	OCCUPATIONS	DATE PORT SHIP
BATEMAN, John	20	M	Laborer	29Ma14Kf
LONERGAN, John	16	M	Laborer	29Ma14Kf
Alice	18	F	Laborer	29Ma14Kf
WILLS, Thomas	26	M	Boatman	29Ma14Kf
MEAGHER, Thomas	18	M	Laborer	29Ma14Kf
MCLAUGHLIN, John	36	M	Tailor	29Ma14Kf
Cathe.	35	F	Tailor	29Ma14Kf
ONEILL, Thomas	27	M	Ctldlr	29Ma14Kf
MAHER, William	16	M	Ctldlr	29Ma14Kf
Anne	14	F	Dressmaker	29Ma14Kf
MCLAUGHLIN, Anne	06	F	Child	29Ma14Kf
Cathe.	04	F	Child	29Ma14Kf
BRITT, Thomas	18	M	Tailor	29Ma14Kf
CONNELLY, Cath.	45	F	Farmer	29Ma14Kf
Michl.	24	M	Farmer	29Ma14Kf
Patrick	20	M	Farmer	29Ma14Kf
John	16	M	Farmer	29Ma14Kf
Bridget	12	F	Farmer	29Ma14Kf
Ellen	10	F	Farmer	29Ma14Kf
Judith	08	F	Child	29Ma14Kf
Margt.	06	F	Child	29Ma14Kf
FLYNN, James	48	M	Farmer	29Ma14Kf
LEARY, John	22	M	Farmer	29Ma14Kf
FLYNN, Maurice	28	M	Farmer	29Ma14Kf
SIMPSON, James-Hent.	26	M	Farmer	29Ma14Kf
MOORE, David	77	M	Farmer	29Ma14Kf
LOOBY, Mary	28	F	Farmer	29Ma14Kf
Ledious	01	U	Child	29Ma14Kf
DWYER, Michl.	.00	M	Infant	29Ma14Kf
MCLAUGHLIN, Thos.	.00	M	Infant	29Ma14Kf
CUTHBERT, Eliza	18	F	Dressmaker	29Ma14Kf
Ellicia	16	F	Dressmaker	29Ma14Kf

HARMONIA 29 MAY 1848

From Glasgow

NAMES OF PASSENGERS	A G E	S E X	OCCUPATIONS	DATE PORT SHIP
CASSIDY, Hugh	27	M	Laborer	29Ma04Sm
KILLY, Jeremiah	30	M	Tailor	29Ma04Sm
U (W)	30	F	Tailor	29Ma04Sm
Mary-Ann	06	F	Child	29Ma04Sm
James	.00	M	Infant	29Ma04Sm
BRADLEY, Mary	28	F	Tailor	29Ma04Sm
MCKINNA, Peter	48	M	Laborer	29Ma04Sm
Helen	48	F	Laborer	29Ma04Sm
Patrick	12	M	Laborer	29Ma04Sm
MCCLYNCHY, Sarah	28	F	Unknown	29Ma04Sm
Margaret	26	F	Unknown	29Ma04Sm
QUAIL, Robert	33	M	Laborer	29Ma04Sm
U (W)	30	F	Laborer	29Ma04Sm
James	.00	M	Infant	29Ma04Sm
ORYAN, James	28	M	Laborer	29Ma04Sm
DOCHARTY, Peter	30	M	Laborer	29Ma04Sm
Mary	20	F	Laborer	29Ma04Sm
MCQUADE, Margaret	23	F	Joiner	29Ma04Sm
SWEENIE, Ann	20	F	Joiner	29Ma04Sm
ODONNELL, Edward	31	M	Shoemaker	29Ma04Sm
MERNE, John	34	M	Weaver	29Ma04Sm
Jane	40	F	Weaver	29Ma04Sm
Elizabeth	08	F	Child	29Ma04Sm
TIERNEY, John	35	M	Miner	29Ma04Sm
MCEWAN, Margaret	19	F	Servant	29Ma04Sm
SLAREN, Edward	30	M	Tailor	29Ma04Sm
MCINTYRE, Martin	26	M	Laborer	29Ma04Sm
LOFTUS, James	32	M	Blacksmith	29Ma04Sm
Margt.	35	F	Blacksmith	29Ma04Sm
HOPKINS, James	35	M	Blacksmith	29Ma04Sm
HARLEY, Thomas	30	M	Painter	29Ma04Sm
ODONNELL, John	17	M	Carter	29Ma04Sm
HARLEY, Ann	20	F	Servant	29Ma04Sm
GALLAHER, Sarah	27	F	Servant	29Ma04Sm
COMPSTON, Mary	25	F	Unknown	29Ma04Sm
COLLINS, Thomas	23	M	Joiner	29Ma04Sm
Mary	48	F	Joiner	29Ma04Sm
John	19	M	Joiner	29Ma04Sm
William	16	M	Joiner	29Ma04Sm
Elizabeth	16	F	Joiner	29Ma04Sm
Helen	22	F	Pwlwvr	29Ma04Sm
HORN, Thomas	19	M	Ctnsp	29Ma04Sm
GRIERSON, Mary	30	F	Merchant	29Ma04Sm
Samuel	09	M	Child	29Ma04Sm
John	06	M	Child	29Ma04Sm
Anna	03	F	Child	29Ma04Sm
OULTON, U-Mrs.	26	F	Grocer	29Ma04Sm
U	02	F	Child	29Ma04Sm

HEATHER-BELL 30 MAY 1848

From Limerick

NAMES OF PASSENGERS	A G E	S E X	OCCUPATIONS	DATE PORT SHIP
PARKER, Thomas	20	M	Laborer	30Ma33Kh
MCCARTHY, Mary	18	F	Spinster	30Ma33Kh
RYAN, Mary	21	F	Spinster	30Ma33Kh
MASON, Jane	35	F	Spinster	30Ma33Kh
GORE, Elizabeth	27	F	Spinster	30Ma33Kh
DONAHOE, Michl.	30	M	Laborer	30Ma33Kh
RYAN, Wm.	25	M	Laborer	30Ma33Kh
DOWLEY, Hanah	25	F	Spinster	30Ma33Kh
HICKEY, Eliza	20	F	Unknown	30Ma33Kh
DOWLING, Patt	20	M	Laborer	30Ma33Kh
HOGAN, Bridget	16	F	Matron	30Ma33Kh
HERBETT, Mary	22	F	Mason	30Ma33Kh
WOODS, Mary	22	F	Spinster	30Ma33Kh
ONEILL, William	23	M	Farmer	30Ma33Kh
CROHER, Teddy	21	M	Farmer	30Ma33Kh
KING, Mary	30	F	Spinster	30Ma33Kh
CONNELL, Ellen	23	F	Spinster	30Ma33Kh
Margt.	21	F	Spinster	30Ma33Kh
OBRIEN, Timothy	21	M	Laborer	30Ma33Kh
HANNA, Mary	22	F	Spinster	30Ma33Kh
WHELAN, Ellen	35	F	Spinster	30Ma33Kh
HICKEY, Micheal	21	M	Laborer	30Ma33Kh
MCADDIGAN, Micheal	28	M	Laborer	30Ma33Kh
MCMAHON, Micheal	28	M	Laborer	30Ma33Kh
RYAN, James	17	M	Laborer	30Ma33Kh
LENY, Thos.	32	M	Laborer	30Ma33Kh
Cath. (W)	30	F	Matron	30Ma33Kh
John (S)	.00	M	Infant	30Ma33Kh
Thos. (S)	.00	M	Infant	30Ma33Kh
RUSSEL, Patt	24	M	Farmer	30Ma33Kh
BLAKE, Patt	30	M	Farmer	30Ma33Kh
Margt. (W)	30	F	Wife	30Ma33Kh
STONE, Micheal	25	M	Laborer	30Ma33Kh
Johannah (W)	20	F	Wife	30Ma33Kh
LEHTRIGHT, John	21	M	Farmer	30Ma33Kh
QUANE, Michl.	20	M	Farmer	30Ma33Kh
HAYES, Patt	20	M	Farmer	30Ma33Kh
Bridget (W)	20	F	Wife	30Ma33Kh
MAHONY, Mary	19	F	Spinster	30Ma33Kh
Margt.	16	F	Spinster	30Ma33Kh
MCMAHON, Ellen	20	F	Spinster	30Ma33Kh
LEO, James	20	M	Laborer	30Ma33Kh
RAWLEY, John	23	M	Laborer	30Ma33Kh
HENSER, Henry	20	M	Laborer	30Ma33Kh
MCINENEY, Bridgt.	30	F	Spinster	30Ma33Kh
SHINE, Ann	21	F	Spinster	30Ma33Kh
OBRIEN, Molly	30	F	Spinster	30Ma33Kh
GREENE, John	19	M	Laborer	30Ma33Kh

NAMES OF PASSENGERS		AGE	SEX	OCCUPATIONS	DATE PORT SHIP
GREENE, Eliza		15	F	Spinster	30Ma33Kh
CONNELL, Michl.		24	M	Laborer	30Ma33Kh
ROCHE, Mgt.		20	F	Spinster	30Ma33Kh
MCNAMARA, James		28	M	Laborer	30Ma33Kh
QUINN, Patt		20	M	Laborer	30Ma33Kh
ONEILL, James		18	M	Laborer	30Ma33Kh
NEWMAN, Timothy		27	M	Laborer	30Ma33Kh
HALEY, Michl.		27	M	Laborer	30Ma33Kh
MURPHY. Margt.		25	F	Spinster	30Ma33Kh
MCMAHON, Michl.		28	M	Farmer	30Ma33Kh
CONNELLY, Mary		19	F	Spinster	30Ma33Kh
Cath.		14	F	Spinster	30Ma33Kh
Bridget		16	F	Spinster	30Ma33Kh
Mgt.		10	F	Spinster	30Ma33Kh
POWER, James		26	M	Laborer	30Ma33Kh
Mgt.		24	F	Spinster	30Ma33Kh
Ellen		22	F	Spinster	30Ma33Kh
Cath.		20	F	Spinster	30Ma33Kh
BANKS, James		27	M	Farmer	30Ma33Kh
RYAN, Michl.		27	M	Laborer	30Ma33Kh
MCCARTY, Owen		20	M	Carpenter	30Ma33Kh
MORRISY, Edward		30	M	Carpenter	30Ma33Kh
MCMAHON, Judy		20	F	Spinster	30Ma33Kh
MCCORMICK, Cornelius		30	M	Farmer	30Ma33Kh
CROHEN, Hannah		40	F	Matron	30Ma33Kh
David	(S)	24	M	Unknown	30Ma33Kh
Micl.	(S)	23	M	Unknown	30Ma33Kh
John	(S)	20	M	Unknown	30Ma33Kh
Thos.	(S)	18	M	Unknown	30Ma33Kh
CROWE, Peter		30	M	Laborer	30Ma33Kh
Mary	(W)	27	F	Wife	30Ma33Kh
Thos.	(S)	.00	M	Infant	30Ma33Kh
GLEASSON, Michl.		30	M	Laborer	30Ma33Kh
FRANLEY, Cath.		20	F	Spinster	30Ma33Kh
POWER, Thos.		40	M	Farmer	30Ma33Kh
CURRY, Thos.		25	M	Laborer	30Ma33Kh
MACK, Bridget		25	F	Spinster	30Ma33Kh
JEWETT, Mary		20	F	Spinster	30Ma33Kh
MURPHY, Thos.		26	M	Farmer	30Ma33Kh
Michl.		24	M	Farmer	30Ma33Kh
FITZGERALD, James		30	M	Farmer	30Ma33Kh
POWER, Mary		18	F	Dressmaker	30Ma33Kh
HASSEL, Patk.		22	M	Laborer	30Ma33Kh
SHINE, John		34	M	Laborer	30Ma33Kh
Bridget	(W)	34	F	Unknown	30Ma33Kh
Ann	(D)	20	F	Unknown	30Ma33Kh
Ellen	(D)	20	F	Unknown	30Ma33Kh
Honora	(D)	21	F	Unknown	30Ma33Kh
Mary-Ann	(D)	09	F	Child	30Ma33Kh
Cath.	(D)	06	F	Child	30Ma33Kh
James	(S)	.00	M	Infant	30Ma33Kh
GORE, Honorah		24	F	Dressmaker	30Ma33Kh
MACK, Bridget		25	F	Dressmaker	30Ma33Kh
HEUSTIS, Nancy		28	F	Dressmaker	30Ma33Kh
KATO, James		30	M	Laborer	30Ma33Kh
HALLORAN, Thos.		25	M	Laborer	30Ma33Kh
GARNEY, Chas.		26	M	Unknown	30Ma33Kh
FITZGERALD, James		22	M	Unknown	30Ma33Kh
FARREL, William		25	M	Unknown	30Ma33Kh
MADDIGAN, Dennis		27	M	Unknown	30Ma33Kh

LOUISA 30 MAY 1848

From LIVERPOOL, Cork

NAMES OF PASSENGERS	AGE	SEX	OCCUPATIONS	DATE PORT SHIP
COLLINS, Wm.	30	M	Laborer	30Ma99Ev
KEEFE, Mary	20	F	None	30Ma99Ev
FOLEY, Francis	50	M	Farmer	30Ma99Ev
Mary	20	F	None	30Ma99Ev
FOLEY, Cathe.	13	F	Mason	30Ma99Ev
Wm.	11	M	Mason	30Ma99Ev
Elizth.	10	F	Mason	30Ma99Ev
NELIGON, Dennis	26	M	Mason	30Ma99Ev
John	30	M	Farmer	30Ma99Ev
PIGOTT, David	32	M	Farmer	30Ma99Ev
KEOHANE, Timothy	28	M	Laborer	30Ma99Ev
Mary	25	F	Dressmaker	30Ma99Ev
MCCARTHY, Cathe.	20	F	None	30Ma99Ev
HARTNETT, Mary	09	F	Child	30Ma99Ev
LANE, James	16	M	Smith	30Ma99Ev
BRIEN, Jerry	25	M	Laborer	30Ma99Ev
MURPHY, Edwd.	38	M	Laborer	30Ma99Ev
FOLEY, Mary	60	F	None	30Ma99Ev
MCSWEENEY, Cathe.	19	F	None	30Ma99Ev
FITZGERALD, Ellen	25	F	None	30Ma99Ev
MCSWINEY, Wm.	24	M	Carpenter	30Ma99Ev
Mary	60	F	None	30Ma99Ev
HOWARD, James	60	M	Hatter	30Ma99Ev
Ellen	16	F	None	30Ma99Ev
Ellanor	19	F	None	30Ma99Ev
FLYNN, John	17	M	Laborer	30Ma99Ev
David	15	M	Laborer	30Ma99Ev
NAGLE, Cathe.	24	F	None	30Ma99Ev
HENNESSY, James	40	M	Laborer	30Ma99Ev
Cathe.	26	F	None	30Ma99Ev
Jane	02	F	Child	30Ma99Ev
SULLIVAN, William	40	M	Farmer	30Ma99Ev
Jane	30	F	None	30Ma99Ev
Patrk.	09	M	Child	30Ma99Ev
HILL, Thos.	30	M	Carpenter	30Ma99Ev
Mary-Ann	07	F	Child	30Ma99Ev
HALL, Susan	05	F	Child	30Ma99Ev
Grace	03	F	Child	30Ma99Ev
Wm.	02	M	Child	30Ma99Ev
HALE, Cathe.	13	F	None	30Ma99Ev
GUIDER, Jane	28	F	None	30Ma99Ev
Richard	03	M	Child	30Ma99Ev
THOMPSON, Joseph	22	M	Carpenter	30Ma99Ev
RUSSELL, Wm.	20	M	Carpenter	30Ma99Ev
MURPHY, Johanna	54	F	None	30Ma99Ev
Patrick	24	M	Farmer	30Ma99Ev
Cathe.	18	F	None	30Ma99Ev
Michl.	15	M	None	30Ma99Ev
Daniel	13	M	None	30Ma99Ev
David	08	M	Child	30Ma99Ev
Margt.	05	F	Child	30Ma99Ev
KEEFE, Jno.	27	M	Tailor	30Ma99Ev
SULLIVAN, John	48	M	Tailor	30Ma99Ev
Mary	48	F	None	30Ma99Ev
HYDE, Humphry	20	M	Mason	30Ma99Ev
SULLIVAN, Cathe.	12	F	None	30Ma99Ev
Eliza	10	F	None	30Ma99Ev
Jno.	07	M	Child	30Ma99Ev
COURTNEY, George	22	M	Rope Maker	30Ma99Ev
MCCARTHY, Margt.	38	F	None	30Ma99Ev
Jno.	20	M	Weaver	30Ma99Ev
Margt.	13	F	None	30Ma99Ev
Bridgt.	11	F	None	30Ma99Ev
Julia	09	F	Child	30Ma99Ev
Mary	06	F	Child	30Ma99Ev
WALSH, Margt.	40	F	None	30Ma99Ev
Johanna	16	F	None	30Ma99Ev
Bridgt.	13	F	None	30Ma99Ev
CUNNINGHAM, Eliza	22	F	None	30Ma99Ev
DONOVAN, Dennis	35	M	Tailor	30Ma99Ev
CROWLEY, Cathe.	27	F	None	30Ma99Ev
Richd.	35	M	Cord Cutter	30Ma99Ev
CAHALAND, Mary	23	F	Nurse	30Ma99Ev
SHEEHAN, Michl.	25	M	Hatter	30Ma99Ev
MADAGAN, Patrk.	40	M	Hatter	30Ma99Ev
MOORE, Patrk.	20	M	Bootmaker	30Ma99Ev
NORMAL, Jno.	18	M	Bootmaker	30Ma99Ev
CARMAUL, Margt.	25	F	None	30Ma99Ev
HOURAGAN, Patrk.	40	M	Bricklayer	30Ma99Ev

NAMES OF PASSENGERS	AGE	SEX	OCCUPATIONS	DATE PORT SHIP	NAMES OF PASSENGERS	AGE	SEX	OCCUPATIONS	DATE PORT SHIP
HOURAGAN, Ellen	30	F	Tailor	30Ma99Ev	OLEARY, Ann	02	F	Child	30Ma99Ev
Thomas	25	M	Watchmaker	30Ma99Ev	BATEMAN, Saml.	24	M	Laborer	30Ma99Ev
Mary	26	F	None	30Ma99Ev	MURPHY, Jerem.	23	M	Laborer	30Ma99Ev
MCGRATH, Mary	20	F	None	30Ma99Ev	HENNESSEY, Michl.	35	M	Laborer	30Ma99Ev
HOURAGAN, Jno.	15	M	None	30Ma99Ev	Margt.	35	F	None	30Ma99Ev
Mary	13	F	None	30Ma99Ev	MONK, Jno.	24	M	Cooper	30Ma99Ev
Cathe.	11	F	None	30Ma99Ev	HENNESSY, Jas.	04	M	Child	30Ma99Ev
James	09	M	Child	30Ma99Ev	Patrk.	01	M	Child	30Ma99Ev
Patrick	07	M	Child	30Ma99Ev	BRIEN, Thos.	25	M	None	30Ma99Ev
William	05	M	Child	30Ma99Ev	PATTERSON, Jno.	32	M	Farmer	30Ma99Ev
Sarah	03	F	Child	30Ma99Ev	DONOVAN, Jeremiah	26	M	Farmer	30Ma99Ev
HOLLAND, William	13	M	None	30Ma99Ev	FLYNN, Jno.	25	M	Farmer	30Ma99Ev
Mary	40	F	None	30Ma99Ev	RYAN, Jas.	28	M	Farmer	30Ma99Ev
Ann	18	F	None	30Ma99Ev	SULLIVAN, Cathe.	19	F	None	30Ma99Ev
SULLIVAN, Connor	20	M	Shoemaker	30Ma99Ev	BARRETT, Honora	21	F	None	30Ma99Ev
HEWSTON, Sarah	28	F	Nurse	30Ma99Ev	REARDEN, Mary	24	F	None	30Ma99Ev
Elizh.	22	F	Nurse	30Ma99Ev	HOUGH, Jno.	24	M	Cooper	30Ma99Ev
Susan	20	F	None	30Ma99Ev	SULLIVAN, Jno.	33	M	Cooper	30Ma99Ev
LAYERS, Margt.	40	F	None	30Ma99Ev	Ellen	28	F	None	30Ma99Ev
Henry	12	M	None	30Ma99Ev	Dennis	08	M	Child	30Ma99Ev
FARRELL, Michl.	20	M	None	30Ma99Ev	John	03	M	Child	30Ma99Ev
Ellen	22	F	None	30Ma99Ev	Margt.	.00	F	Infant	30Ma99Ev
BUTLMAN, John	20	M	Tailor	30Ma99Ev	ALLMAN, Jno.	24	M	Laborer	30Ma99Ev
MURPHY, John	33	M	Laborer	30Ma99Ev	Timothy	20	M	Laborer	30Ma99Ev
ROCHE, Edmond	20	M	Laborer	30Ma99Ev	Margt.	16	F	None	30Ma99Ev
HYDE, Wm.	25	M	Laborer	30Ma99Ev	Cathe.	13	F	None	30Ma99Ev
Dennis	23	M	Laborer	30Ma99Ev	OBRIEN, Michl.	30	M	Shoemaker	30Ma99Ev
Johanna	50	F	None	30Ma99Ev	Mary	25	F	None	30Ma99Ev
Daniel	30	M	Laborer	30Ma99Ev	Eliza	.00	F	Infant	30Ma99Ev
Mary	20	F	None	30Ma99Ev	SCANLON, Margt.	19	F	None	30Ma99Ev
KELLY, Mary	20	F	None	30Ma99Ev	REARDEN, Mary	23	F	None	30Ma99Ev
BIRMINGHAM, Eliza	18	F	None	30Ma99Ev	BUTLER, Michl.	31	M	Bricklayer	30Ma99Ev
BRIEN, Patrk.	24	M	Farmer	30Ma99Ev	Eliza	20	F	None	30Ma99Ev
NOONAN, David	50	M	Farmer	30Ma99Ev	CONNOR, Jeremiah	40	M	Laborer	30Ma99Ev
JONES, David	25	M	Farmer	30Ma99Ev	CAHILL, Mary	20	F	None	30Ma99Ev
DAVIES, Morgan	40	M	Farmer	30Ma99Ev	MAGNIN, Cathe.	18	F	None	30Ma99Ev
ROCHE, Walter	20	M	Farmer	30Ma99Ev	CONNOR, Danl.	11	M	None	30Ma99Ev
BARRY, Honora	25	F	Tailor	30Ma99Ev	Johanna	07	F	Child	30Ma99Ev
OLEARY, Cathe.	21	F	Tailor	30Ma99Ev	David	05	M	Child	30Ma99Ev
Jno.	17	M	None	30Ma99Ev	Cornelius	03	M	Child	30Ma99Ev
WILLIAMS, Lawrence	28	M	Laborer	30Ma99Ev	Margt.	30	F	None	30Ma99Ev
Mary	20	F	None	30Ma99Ev	NAGLE, Ellen	36	F	None	30Ma99Ev
FITZGERALD, Jno.	23	M	Bricklayer	30Ma99Ev	Ellen	18	F	None	30Ma99Ev
HANRAHAN, Michl.	20	M	Bricklayer	30Ma99Ev	Eliza	16	F	None	30Ma99Ev
FLEMMING, Johanna	17	F	None	30Ma99Ev	Kate	10	F	None	30Ma99Ev
HEGARTY, Margt.	20	F	None	30Ma99Ev	Jno.	06	M	Child	30Ma99Ev
CROWLEY, Mary	22	F	None	30Ma99Ev	Mary	04	F	Child	30Ma99Ev
MCCARTHY, Jno.	30	M	Mason	30Ma99Ev	BRIEN, Ellen	17	F	None	30Ma99Ev
Ellen	20	F	None	30Ma99Ev	SULLIVAN, Michl.	24	M	Shoemaker	30Ma99Ev
James	13	M	None	30Ma99Ev	RAHILLY, James	36	M	Mason	30Ma99Ev
KENNEDY, Garrett	40	M	Watchmaker	30Ma99Ev	Mary	30	F	None	30Ma99Ev
Johanna	40	F	None	30Ma99Ev	TWOHY, Jno.	26	M	Laborer	30Ma99Ev
Cathe.	02	F	Child	30Ma99Ev	RAHILLY, Cathe.	13	F	None	30Ma99Ev
Jeremiah	.00	M	Infant	30Ma99Ev	Margt.	11	F	None	30Ma99Ev
CONLAN, Ellen	20	F	None	30Ma99Ev	Mary	09	F	Child	30Ma99Ev
BENNETT, Abrhm.	24	M	None	30Ma99Ev	Ellen	07	F	Child	30Ma99Ev
DALY, Henry	30	M	Rope Maker	30Ma99Ev	Bridgt.	06	F	Child	30Ma99Ev
Thos.	26	M	Laborer	30Ma99Ev	Thos.	02	M	Child	30Ma99Ev
HANAN, Mark	24	M	Laborer	30Ma99Ev	KING, Jno.	40	M	Weaver	30Ma99Ev
Jane	24	F	None	30Ma99Ev	Jeremiah	22	M	Cooper	30Ma99Ev
John-H.	02	M	Child	30Ma99Ev	RYAN, Wm.	50	M	Cooper	30Ma99Ev
Blessing	.00	F	Infant	30Ma99Ev	FOLEY, Jno.	19	M	Cooper	30Ma99Ev
Elizh.	30	F	None	30Ma99Ev	MCSWINEY, Patrk.	24	M	Farmer	30Ma99Ev
SLYNE, Danl.	28	M	Farmer	30Ma99Ev	Hugh	23	M	Farmer	30Ma99Ev
COLLINS, Bartholmew	40	M	Farmer	30Ma99Ev	Mary	20	F	None	30Ma99Ev
Eliza	30	F	None	30Ma99Ev	NOONAN, Honora	20	F	None	30Ma99Ev
Johanna	15	F	None	30Ma99Ev	HIGGINS, Jas.	46	M	Hatter	30Ma99Ev
Norry	13	F	None	30Ma99Ev	BABINGTON, Mary	21	F	None	30Ma99Ev
Mary	08	F	Child	30Ma99Ev	MAHONY, Thos.	25	M	Farmer	30Ma99Ev
Cathe.	06	F	Child	30Ma99Ev	MULCAHY, Hugh	25	M	Farmer	30Ma99Ev
Michl.	03	M	Child	30Ma99Ev	MAHONES, Johanna	30	F	None	30Ma99Ev
FITZGERALD, Jno.	22	M	Tailor	30Ma99Ev	MULCAHY, Anstey.	20	F	None	30Ma99Ev
OLEARY, Mary	40	F	Tailor	30Ma99Ev	RYAN, Cathe.	23	F	None	30Ma99Ev
Anne	18	F	Tailor	30Ma99Ev	TWOMEY, Edmond	18	M	None	30Ma99Ev
Mary	03	F	Child	30Ma99Ev	KISSANE, Mary	20	F	None	30Ma99Ev

NAMES OF PASSENGERS	AGE	SEX	OCCUPATIONS	DATE PORT SHIP
SHEEHAN, Wm.	24	M	Cooper	30Ma99Ev
IRELAND, Geo.	25	M	Cooper	30Ma99Ev
Ann	28	F	None	30Ma99Ev
OBRIEN, Michl.	24	M	Tailor	30Ma99Ev
Eliza	32	F	None	30Ma99Ev
NORRIS, Thos.	30	M	Clerk	30Ma99Ev
Johanna	28	F	None	30Ma99Ev
DUHANE, Danl.	22	M	None	30Ma99Ev
COGHLAN, Honora	09	F	Child	30Ma99Ev
NORRIS, John	07	M	Child	30Ma99Ev
Margt.	02	F	Child	30Ma99Ev
CASEY, Jno.	22	M	Farmer	30Ma99Ev
GRIFFIN, Thos.	24	M	Farmer	30Ma99Ev
SULLIVAN, Danl.	23	M	Farmer	30Ma99Ev
GRIFFIN, Danl.	18	M	Farmer	30Ma99Ev
GRADY, Thos.	30	M	Farmer	30Ma99Ev
TURNER, Mary	22	F	None	30Ma99Ev
CONNELL, Jno.	24	M	Laborer	30Ma99Ev
HENNESSY, Michl.	26	M	Laborer	30Ma99Ev
RYAN, Lawrence	21	M	Laborer	30Ma99Ev
CANTILLOW, Richd.	26	M	Laborer	30Ma99Ev
Julia	22	F	None	30Ma99Ev
Johanna	20	F	None	30Ma99Ev
LAWTON, Edmond	30	M	Bricklayer	30Ma99Ev
Johana	25	F	None	30Ma99Ev
BROWN, Bridget	18	F	Tailor	30Ma99Ev
CONNOR, Jno.	20	M	None	30Ma99Ev
HAYES, John	24	M	Mason	30Ma99Ev
FITZGERALD, Edmond	08	M	Child	30Ma99Ev
COTTER, Wm.	36	M	Shoemaker	30Ma99Ev
HERLIHY, Pat	33	M	Shoemaker	30Ma99Ev
MURRAY, Jas.	40	M	Shoemaker	30Ma99Ev
Cathe.	35	F	None	30Ma99Ev
Jno.	18	M	None	30Ma99Ev
SHANAHAN, Julia	20	F	Dressmaker	30Ma99Ev
MURRAY, Johanna	13	F	None	30Ma99Ev
Mary	09	F	Child	30Ma99Ev
Tade	11	M	Child	30Ma99Ev
Margt.	02	F	Child	30Ma99Ev
Michl.	06	M	Child	30Ma99Ev
DONOVAN, Mary	22	F	None	30Ma99Ev
WALSH, Margt.	20	F	None	30Ma99Ev
MALONEY, David	40	M	Farmer	30Ma99Ev
David	16	M	None	30Ma99Ev
Mary	12	F	None	30Ma99Ev
Jane	10	F	None	30Ma99Ev
Patrk.	08	M	Child	30Ma99Ev
Cathe.	05	F	Child	30Ma99Ev
Julia	35	F	None	30Ma99Ev
CALLAGHAN, Jas.	28	M	Laborer	30Ma99Ev
WEBB, Christopher	28	M	Laborer	30Ma99Ev
Ellen	22	F	None	30Ma99Ev
MALONY, Owen	28	M	Farmer	30Ma99Ev
Solomon	30	M	Shoemaker	30Ma99Ev
HICKEY, Michl.	22	M	Cooper	30Ma99Ev
Bridget	23	F	None	30Ma99Ev
ODONNELL, Margt.	22	F	None	30Ma99Ev
GEARY, Owen	22	M	Weaver	30Ma99Ev
KELLY, Jeremiah	35	M	Weaver	30Ma99Ev
DONOVAN, Mary	30	F	None	30Ma99Ev
BARRY, Bridgt.	30	F	None	30Ma99Ev
DONOVAN, Cathe.	17	F	None	30Ma99Ev
Patrk.	14	M	None	30Ma99Ev
Mary	07	F	Child	30Ma99Ev
Margt.	03	F	Child	30Ma99Ev
BISHOP, Thos.	30	M	Laborer	30Ma99Ev
RODERAN, Thos.	35	M	Watchmaker	30Ma99Ev
Mary	27	F	None	30Ma99Ev
Mary	27	F	None	30Ma99Ev
Ellen	23	F	None	30Ma99Ev
Cathe.	21	F	None	30Ma99Ev
OROURKE, Mago	33	F	None	30Ma99Ev
Julia	30	F	None	30Ma99Ev
Johanna	00	F	None	30Ma99Ev
SHANAHAN, Danl.	25	M	Farmer	30Ma99Ev
SHANAHAN, Edmond	24	M	Laborer	30Ma99Ev
SHEEHY, Bat	21	F	None	30Ma99Ev
BROWNE, Edmond	21	M	Laborer	30Ma99Ev
STACK, Cathe.	16	F	None	30Ma99Ev
SHEEHY, Margt.	16	F	None	30Ma99Ev
Patrk.	12	M	None	30Ma99Ev
WALSH, Garrett	24	M	Farmer	30Ma99Ev
Ellen	25	F	None	30Ma99Ev
MCSHEEHAN, Jeremiah	27	M	Bricklayer	30Ma99Ev
AUBREY, Mary	20	F	None	30Ma99Ev
HENNESSY, Brigt.	06	F	Child	30Ma99Ev
MCGRATH, Michl.	35	M	Mason	30Ma99Ev
Ann	30	F	None	30Ma99Ev
Jno.	13	M	None	30Ma99Ev
Michl.	11	M	None	30Ma99Ev
Roger	05	M	Child	30Ma99Ev
Timothy	02	M	Child	30Ma99Ev
BARRY, Edmond	40	M	Farmer	30Ma99Ev
FEANEY, Pat	30	M	Farmer	30Ma99Ev
GALVIN, Maurice	20	M	Farmer	30Ma99Ev
SULLIVAN, Jno.	35	M	Farmer	30Ma99Ev
TOBIN, Michl.	25	M	Laborer	30Ma99Ev
Jno.	22	M	Weaver	30Ma99Ev
LINEHAN, Jno.	26	M	Weaver	30Ma99Ev
BIRMINGHAM, Johanna	00	F	None	30Ma99Ev
KANE, Dennis	20	M	None	30Ma99Ev
Mary	24	F	Cooper	30Ma99Ev
MCCARTHY, J.	24	M	Laborer	30Ma99Ev
YOUNG, Mary	24	F	None	30Ma99Ev
HUMPHREY, Mary	30	F	None	30Ma99Ev
HARTLAND, Mary	30	F	None	30Ma99Ev
CARPENTER, U-Mrs.	30	F	None	30Ma99Ev
William (S)	04	M	Child	30Ma99Ev
Elizabeth (D)	08	F	Child	30Ma99Ev
Susan (D)	04	F	Child	30Ma99Ev
Thomas (S)	01	M	Child	30Ma99Ev
LAWRENCE, Isabella	24	F	Farmer	30Ma99Ev
HEILLARD, David	28	M	Farmer	30Ma99Ev
CHAMBERS, U	21	M	None	30Ma99Ev

DEBORAH 31 MAY 1848

From Liverpool

NAMES OF PASSENGERS	AGE	SEX	OCCUPATIONS	DATE PORT SHIP
LOUGHLIN, Mary	20	F	Servant	31Ma02Js
CAREY, Pat	44	M	Baker	31Ma02Js
U (W)	44	F	Baker	31Ma02Js
John (S)	21	M	Baker	31Ma02Js
Margaret (D)	13	F	Baker	31Ma02Js
Mary (D)	12	F	Servant	31Ma02Js
Pat (S)	10	M	None	31Ma02Js
Catherine (D)	06	F	Child	31Ma02Js
CONLEY, John	26	M	Laborer	31Ma02Js
Ellen	19	F	Servant	31Ma02Js
MALLAM, Sarah	20	F	Servant	31Ma02Js
HUGHSTON, Wm.	16	M	Laborer	31Ma02Js
ANDERSON, Ann	30	F	Servant	31Ma02Js
MANN, Jane	20	F	Servant	31Ma02Js
CLARK, Jane	20	F	Servant	31Ma02Js
OLIVERS, Margt.	35	F	Servant	31Ma02Js
Mary	09	F	Child	31Ma02Js
George	.04	M	Infant	31Ma02Js
HOMES, Daniel	32	M	Laborer	31Ma02Js
U (W)	28	F	None	31Ma02Js
Mary (D)	07	F	Child	31Ma02Js
Margt. (D)	.04	F	Infant	31Ma02Js
FERGUSON, Ann	50	F	Servant	31Ma02Js
James	17	M	Laborer	31Ma02Js
Willm.	.04	M	Infant	31Ma02Js

NAMES OF PASSENGERS		AGE	SEX	OCCUPATIONS	DATE PORT SHIP
PERCY, James		21	M	Laborer	31Ma02Js
Saml.		19	M	Laborer	31Ma02Js
PETERS, John		30	M	Laborer	31Ma02Js
Joseph		20	M	Laborer	31Ma02Js
John		18	M	Laborer	31Ma02Js
STEPHENSON, David		28	M	Laborer	31Ma02Js
MCGILAM, James		26	M	Laborer	31Ma02Js
CUMMINS, James		27	M	Laborer	31Ma02Js
Thomas		40	M	Laborer	31Ma02Js
DUFF, Wm.		27	M	Laborer	31Ma02Js
BRANNON, Mary		30	F	Servant	31Ma02Js
Mary		18	F	Servant	31Ma02Js
Thomas		09	M	Child	31Ma02Js
Josiah		.04	M	Infant	31Ma02Js
SMITH, Bridget		19	F	Servant	31Ma02Js
KEGNEY, Owen		35	M	Laborer	31Ma02Js
CAULEY, Daniel		24	M	Accountant	31Ma02Js
KEANEY, John		30	M	Laborer	31Ma02Js
SHEA, Nancy		20	F	Servant	31Ma02Js
MCALENY, Sarah		18	F	Servant	31Ma02Js
Margaret		16	F	Servant	31Ma02Js
CAMPBELL, Susan		20	F	Servant	31Ma02Js
MCGUIRE, John		20	M	Laborer	31Ma02Js
LYNCH, Phil		50	M	Laborer	31Ma02Js
ROACH, James		26	M	Laborer	31Ma02Js
LYNCH, Nicholas		20	M	Laborer	31Ma02Js
MCDONALD, James		20	M	Laborer	31Ma02Js
DONNAN, Malone		55	M	Laborer	31Ma02Js
Robert		20	M	Laborer	31Ma02Js
Andrew		16	M	Laborer	31Ma02Js
James		14	M	Laborer	31Ma02Js
FERGUSON, Andrew		27	M	Laborer	31Ma02Js
HANNAH, John		20	M	Laborer	31Ma02Js
LENOID, Ned		45	M	Laborer	31Ma02Js
U	(W)	40	F	None	31Ma02Js
Bridget	(D)	04	F	Child	31Ma02Js
Mary	(D)	02	F	Child	31Ma02Js
MALAWNEY, Pat		14	M	Laborer	31Ma02Js
MCCANN, Frank		24	M	Laborer	31Ma02Js
U	(W)	24	F	None	31Ma02Js
GAUGHAN, Anthony		20	M	Laborer	31Ma02Js
Nancy		18	F	Servant	31Ma02Js
Harrison		16	M	Laborer	31Ma02Js
RUDDY, John		25	M	Laborer	31Ma02Js
MCANDREW, Michael		25	M	Laborer	31Ma02Js
CAFFERTY, Michael		60	M	Laborer	31Ma02Js
U	(W)	60	F	None	31Ma02Js
Michael		20	M	Laborer	31Ma02Js
Bridget		18	F	Servant	31Ma02Js
Mary		14	F	Servant	31Ma02Js
CONWAY, Mary		18	F	Servant	31Ma02Js
GOUDAN, John		20	M	Laborer	31Ma02Js
DONNELLY, Pat		30	M	Laborer	31Ma02Js
CAFFERTY, Jacob		30	M	Laborer	31Ma02Js
Anthony		06	M	Child	31Ma02Js
Michael		13	M	None	31Ma02Js
RILEY, Barney		20	M	Laborer	31Ma02Js
GAAGHAN, Pat		40	M	Laborer	31Ma02Js
MORAN, Thomas		22	M	Laborer	31Ma02Js
Catherine		21	F	None	31Ma02Js
James		.06	M	Infant	31Ma02Js
CARTY, Pat.		30	M	Laborer	31Ma02Js
WALSH, Michael		25	M	Laborer	31Ma02Js
Patrick		22	M	Laborer	31Ma02Js
REELY, John		20	M	Laborer	31Ma02Js
MULROONEY, Thomas		38	M	Laborer	31Ma02Js
HEFEN, Denis		26	M	Laborer	31Ma02Js
MURPHY, Pat.		24	M	Laborer	31Ma02Js
James		38	M	Laborer	31Ma02Js
BRENNAN, John		26	M	Laborer	31Ma02Js
HUGHES, Thomas		40	M	Laborer	31Ma02Js
Bridget		10	F	Laborer	31Ma02Js
WALSH, Martin		22	M	Laborer	31Ma02Js
CORHAM, James		15	M	Laborer	31Ma02Js
FEHAN, James		24	M	Laborer	31Ma02Js

NAMES OF PASSENGERS	AGE	SEX	OCCUPATIONS	DATE PORT SHIP
FERGUSON, William	28	M	Hjnr	31Ma02Js
Elizabeth	28	F	None	31Ma02Js
GIVEN, James	24	M	Laborer	31Ma02Js
Jane	28	F	Servant	31Ma02Js
ALLEN, James	51	M	Laborer	31Ma02Js
Daniel	17	M	Laborer	31Ma02Js
SHERIDAN, Catherine	30	F	Servant	31Ma02Js
Mary	06	F	Child	31Ma02Js
GRATTAN, James	24	M	Laborer	31Ma02Js
SHAW, Thomas	26	M	Laborer	31Ma02Js
DOLAN, Willm.	26	M	Laborer	31Ma02Js
Thomas	30	M	Laborer	31Ma02Js
Pat	17	M	Laborer	31Ma02Js
Anne	30	F	Laborer	31Ma02Js
Judy	24	F	Laborer	31Ma02Js
Michael	02	M	Child	31Ma02Js
Peter	.06	M	Infant	31Ma02Js
RYAN, Michael	24	M	Laborer	31Ma02Js
James	18	M	Laborer	31Ma02Js
Bridget	20	F	Servant	31Ma02Js
SYKES, Michl.	23	M	Laborer	31Ma02Js
SULLIVAN, Ellen	06	F	Child	31Ma02Js
NEIL, P.	17	M	Laborer	31Ma02Js
MELLAY, Thomas	24	M	Laborer	31Ma02Js
PURCELL, Margt.	25	F	Servant	31Ma02Js
Antony	20	M	Laborer	31Ma02Js
BURKE, John	28	M	Laborer	31Ma02Js
MCCORMICK, Patrick	20	M	Laborer	31Ma02Js
Mary	24	F	Servant	31Ma02Js
GILBRIDE, Owen	39	M	Laborer	31Ma02Js
Bernard	15	M	Laborer	31Ma02Js
John	11	M	Laborer	31Ma02Js
COWEN, David	22	M	Laborer	31Ma02Js
GAHAN, Thomas	30	M	Laborer	31Ma02Js
MCQUILLAN, Arthur	29	M	Laborer	31Ma02Js
CAIN, Darby	18	M	Laborer	31Ma02Js
Mary	15	F	Servant	31Ma02Js
MULLIGAN, Anne	40	F	Servant	31Ma02Js
CARROLL, Daniel	28	M	Laborer	31Ma02Js
FITZPATRICK, Julia	27	F	Servant	31Ma02Js
HANNEGAN, Thomas	28	M	Laborer	31Ma02Js
BURTH, Sally	20	F	Servant	31Ma02Js
LEESON, Cathe.	31	F	Servant	31Ma02Js
CURRY, Michl.	26	M	Laborer	31Ma02Js
Sylvester	24	M	Laborer	31Ma02Js
MCCURKE, James	40	M	Laborer	31Ma02Js
Jane	30	F	Servant	31Ma02Js
GAFNEY, Betsey	30	F	Servant	31Ma02Js
CLARY, Michael	12	M	Laborer	31Ma02Js
Patrick	10	M	Laborer	31Ma02Js
LARKIN, Thomas	50	M	Laborer	31Ma02Js
Margaret	50	F	None	31Ma02Js
Mary	.06	F	Infant	31Ma02Js
LYNCH, Pat	20	M	Laborer	31Ma02Js
HANNEGAN, Owen	28	M	Laborer	31Ma02Js
WRIGHT, Darby	21	M	Laborer	31Ma02Js
Thomas	21	M	Laborer	31Ma02Js
Ellen	24	F	Servant	31Ma02Js
CARROLL, Naffy	26	M	Laborer	31Ma02Js
WHITE, Thomas	26	M	Laborer	31Ma02Js
Michael	18	M	Laborer	31Ma02Js
CARTY, Michael	30	M	Laborer	31Ma02Js
MCCARTY, Jane	28	F	Servant	31Ma02Js
Michl.	.06	M	Infant	31Ma02Js

ELIZABETH-DENTLEY 31 MAY 1848

From Liverpool

NAMES OF PASSENGERS	AGE	SEX	OCCUPATIONS	DATE PORT SHIP
QUIN, Ann	40	F	Unknown	31Ma02Wg
Ann	10	F	Unknown	31Ma02Wg
DORNON, Thos.	35	M	Farmer	31Ma02Wg
Catharine	30	F	Unknown	31Ma02Wg
Morgon	04	M	Child	31Ma02Wg
Patrick	02	M	Child	31Ma02Wg
Mary	.09	F	Infant	31Ma02Wg
COLLINGS, Patt	33	M	Farmer	31Ma02Wg
James	12	M	Farmer	31Ma02Wg
John	06	M	Child	31Ma02Wg
Mary	06	F	Child	31Ma02Wg
BURKE, Patrick	50	M	Farmer	31Ma02Wg
Mary	40	F	Unknown	31Ma02Wg
Pat.	19	M	Farmer	31Ma02Wg
John	17	M	Farmer	31Ma02Wg
James	12	M	Unknown	31Ma02Wg
Catharine	13	F	Unknown	31Ma02Wg
Pearce	11	M	Unknown	31Ma02Wg
Ann	.09	F	Infant	31Ma02Wg
Nelley	06	F	Child	31Ma02Wg
James	03	M	Child	31Ma02Wg
Judith	.00	F	Infant	31Ma02Wg
WALSH, Andrew	36	M	Farmer	31Ma02Wg
Winford	35	U	Unknown	31Ma02Wg
Andrew	06	M	Child	31Ma02Wg
Walter	03	M	Child	31Ma02Wg
NOONAN, Pat	32	M	Farmer	31Ma02Wg
Margaret	29	F	Unknown	31Ma02Wg
Ellen	09	F	Child	31Ma02Wg
Thos.	06	M	Child	31Ma02Wg
Patrick	04	M	Child	31Ma02Wg
TARNEY, James	55	M	Farmer	31Ma02Wg
Dorothy	21	F	Farmer	31Ma02Wg
Pat	16	M	Farmer	31Ma02Wg
Catharine	11	F	Farmer	31Ma02Wg
Mary	22	F	Farmer	31Ma02Wg
Wm.	30	M	Farmer	31Ma02Wg
David	22	M	Tailor	31Ma02Wg
FITZGERALD, Mary	26	F	Unknown	31Ma02Wg
Ann	08	F	Child	31Ma02Wg
Pat	06	M	Child	31Ma02Wg
ALLEN, Mary	26	F	Unknown	31Ma02Wg
SAMMON, Pat	26	M	Farmer	31Ma02Wg
DOCKERTY, Mikel	26	M	Farmer	31Ma02Wg
MCAVOY, Richard	27	M	Farmer	31Ma02Wg
RARIDON, John	26	M	Farmer	31Ma02Wg
GILLLIGAN, Richard	18	M	Farmer	31Ma02Wg
BIRD, Byand	30	M	Farmer	31Ma02Wg
RAFFERTY, Mary	20	F	Unknown	31Ma02Wg
RILEY, Thos.	19	M	Farmer	31Ma02Wg
BUCKLEY, James	30	M	Mason	31Ma02Wg
CONWAY, Salley	17	F	Unknown	31Ma02Wg
Mikel	13	M	Unknown	31Ma02Wg
Connor	11	M	Unknown	31Ma02Wg
Catharine	09	F	Child	31Ma02Wg
Hugh	07	M	Child	31Ma02Wg
CALLIHAN, Hannah	03	M	Child	31Ma02Wg
Bridget	03	M	Child	31Ma02Wg
MCANDERSON, Thos.	30	M	Farmer	31Ma02Wg
LANGDON, Pat	20	M	Blacksmith	31Ma02Wg
MCGINLEY, Robert	70	M	Farmer	31Ma02Wg
Ann	60	F	Unknown	31Ma02Wg
Robert-Jnr.	22	M	Farmer	31Ma02Wg
Rebecca	16	F	Unknown	31Ma02Wg
Mary-Ann	10	F	Unknown	31Ma02Wg
DUNN, Pat	50	M	Farmer	31Ma02Wg
SANDERS, Mikel	26	M	Tailor	31Ma02Wg
LAPSLEY, Thos.	50	M	Farmer	31Ma02Wg
Bridget	50	F	Unknown	31Ma02Wg
Mikel-Jr.	26	M	Tailor	31Ma02Wg
Thos.	.00	M	Infant	31Ma02Wg
Bridget-Jr.	02	F	Child	31Ma02Wg
Larry	.04	M	Infant	31Ma02Wg
Patrick	30	M	Farmer	31Ma02Wg
MURPHY, Mikel	20	M	Farmer	31Ma02Wg
FAHY, Cornelius	25	M	Farmer	31Ma02Wg
MURPHY, Jerry	25	M	Farmer	31Ma02Wg
FORD, Ellen	18	F	Unknown	31Ma02Wg
NEEL, John	21	M	Farmer	31Ma02Wg
THOMAS, Sollomon	20	M	Farmer	31Ma02Wg
WARD, Catharine	26	F	Unknown	31Ma02Wg
SHEAN, Pat	20	M	Laborer	31Ma02Wg
Owan	20	M	Laborer	31Ma02Wg
HAFFEY, John	18	M	Laborer	31Ma02Wg
CRONAN, John	14	M	Laborer	31Ma02Wg
MURPHY, Jerry	29	M	Farmer	31Ma02Wg
Mary	20	F	Unknown	31Ma02Wg
REID, John	29	M	Cabdriver	31Ma02Wg
NULTY, James	26	M	Farmer	31Ma02Wg
SULLIVAN, Patrick	21	M	Farmer	31Ma02Wg
Margaret	26	F	Farmer	31Ma02Wg
CLARY, John	27	M	Farmer	31Ma02Wg
BURKE, Richard	26	M	Farmer	31Ma02Wg
MCGUIRE, Elizabeth	50	F	Unknown	31Ma02Wg
James	30	M	Farmer	31Ma02Wg
Thos.	25	M	Farmer	31Ma02Wg
Elizabeth-Jr.	18	F	Unknown	31Ma02Wg
Catharine	17	F	Unknown	31Ma02Wg
Margaret	14	F	Unknown	31Ma02Wg
Mary	12	F	Unknown	31Ma02Wg
Susan	11	F	Unknown	31Ma02Wg
Phillip	10	M	Unknown	31Ma02Wg
MURPHY, Mary	25	F	Unknown	31Ma02Wg
ROATCH, Catharine	20	F	Unknown	31Ma02Wg
Ann	20	F	Unknown	31Ma02Wg
HANNEGAN, Margaret	25	F	Unknown	31Ma02Wg
MCANDREWS, Patrick	20	M	Tailor	31Ma02Wg
GORMAN, John	48	M	Farmer	31Ma02Wg
John-Jr.	13	M	Unknown	31Ma02Wg
Mikel	11	M	Unknown	31Ma02Wg
Catharine	21	F	Unknown	31Ma02Wg
Judith	19	F	Unknown	31Ma02Wg
Mary	13	F	Unknown	31Ma02Wg
DELANY, Bridget	30	F	Unknown	31Ma02Wg
HANDALEN, Mary	22	F	Unknown	31Ma02Wg
GAGAN, Dennis	25	M	Farmer	31Ma02Wg
MCGUIRE, Susan	20	F	Unknown	31Ma02Wg
MANING, Rose	20	F	Unknown	31Ma02Wg
WALSH, Saml.	40	M	Farmer	31Ma02Wg
BULGER, Edward	40	M	Farmer	31Ma02Wg
BARRICK, Edward	20	M	Farmer	31Ma02Wg
BRATHY, Catharine	20	F	Unknown	31Ma02Wg
CRADY, Margaret	20	F	Unknown	31Ma02Wg
DELLANY, Margaret	13	F	Unknown	31Ma02Wg
Mary	11	F	Unknown	31Ma02Wg
OBRIAN, Pat	24	M	Farmer	31Ma02Wg
Mary	22	F	Unknown	31Ma02Wg
MCLIN, Pat	40	M	Farmer	31Ma02Wg
Mary	30	F	Unknown	31Ma02Wg
Ann	06	F	Child	31Ma02Wg
Wm.	09	M	Child	31Ma02Wg
Patrick	.00	M	Infant	31Ma02Wg
Thos.	30	M	Farmer	31Ma02Wg
Ann	30	F	Farmer	31Ma02Wg
RIGAN, Richard	20	M	Laborer	31Ma02Wg
MADDEN, Pat	25	M	Waterman	31Ma02Wg
Edward	20	M	Waterman	31Ma02Wg
Jane	22	F	Unknown	31Ma02Wg
Bridget	18	F	Unknown	31Ma02Wg
MOLLONEY, Peter	30	M	Farmer	31Ma02Wg

NAMES OF PASSENGERS	AGE	SEX	OCCUPATIONS	DATE PORT SHIP
STADLER, John	26	M	Farmer	31Ma02Wg
SWEENY, Pat	26	M	Farmer	31Ma02Wg
Valentine	20	M	Farmer	31Ma02Wg
ASPINALE, Ellen	20	F	Unknown	31Ma02Wg
HOGGARD, Thos.	25	M	Farmer	31Ma02Wg
Mary	27	F	Farmer	31Ma02Wg
Martha	08	F	Child	31Ma02Wg
CANADA, David	30	M	Shepherd	31Ma02Wg
KINLEY, Wm.	40	M	Pawn Broker	31Ma02Wg
Bridget	30	F	Unknown	31Ma02Wg
Mary	06	F	Child	31Ma02Wg
GRAHAM, Phillip	20	M	Farmer	31Ma02Wg
John	21	M	Farmer	31Ma02Wg
QUICKLEY, Patrick	20	M	Farmer	31Ma02Wg
Catharine	25	F	Unknown	31Ma02Wg
CASTON, James	40	M	Farmer	31Ma02Wg
SNELE, James	29	M	Farmer	31Ma02Wg
CALORY, Mikel	21	M	Farmer	31Ma02Wg
CROW, Francess	31	M	Farmer	31Ma02Wg
Wm.	08	M	Child	31Ma02Wg
Francess	18	F	Farmer	31Ma02Wg
Wm.	27	M	Farmer	31Ma02Wg
FORSTER, Thos.	25	M	Farmer	31Ma02Wg
Wm.	25	M	Farmer	31Ma02Wg
Thos.Jr.	04	M	Child	31Ma02Wg
CONEY, Andrew	25	M	Farmer	31Ma02Wg
MCREADY, John	22	M	Blacksmith	31Ma02Wg
CONDY, Mikel	24	M	Farmer	31Ma02Wg
Owen	24	M	Farmer	31Ma02Wg
DOYLE, Peter	30	M	Farmer	31Ma02Wg
Patrick	30	M	Farmer	31Ma02Wg
John	26	M	Farmer	31Ma02Wg
Ann	50	F	Unknown	31Ma02Wg
James	13	M	Unknown	31Ma02Wg
Mary	25	F	Unknown	31Ma02Wg
Margaret	11	F	Unknown	31Ma02Wg
Patrick	05	M	Child	31Ma02Wg
KIRK, James	25	M	Farmer	31Ma02Wg
Margret	26	F	Unknown	31Ma02Wg
BURKE, Mikel	26	M	Farmer	31Ma02Wg
Thos.	20	M	Farmer	31Ma02Wg
SHELLEY, Mary	30	F	Unknown	31Ma02Wg
HOGGINS, Wm.	30	M	Farmer	31Ma02Wg
CREED, Alexander	21	M	Laborer	31Ma02Wg
MILEGAN, Mikel	30	M	Farmer	31Ma02Wg
Margaret	25	F	Unknown	31Ma02Wg
MORISH, Samuel	18	M	Laborer	31Ma02Wg
PHELAN, Pat	20	M	Laborer	31Ma02Wg
BYRNE, Mikel	50	M	Farmer	31Ma02Wg
Mary	06	F	Child	31Ma02Wg
Hannah	16	F	Unknown	31Ma02Wg
John	19	M	Laborer	31Ma02Wg
Thos.	12	M	Unknown	31Ma02Wg
Catharine	09	F	Child	31Ma02Wg
Margaret	06	F	Child	31Ma02Wg
Pat	05	M	Child	31Ma02Wg
COLLINGS, Margaret	23	F	Unknown	31Ma02Wg
BURKE, Ann	20	F	Unknown	31Ma02Wg
Any	21	F	Unknown	31Ma02Wg
Eliza	20	F	Unknown	31Ma02Wg
James	30	M	Farmer	31Ma02Wg
Ellen	30	F	Unknown	31Ma02Wg
Catharine	07	F	Child	31Ma02Wg
Mary	05	F	Child	31Ma02Wg
Ellen	03	F	Child	31Ma02Wg
Patrick	.00	M	Infant	31Ma02Wg
HUGGON, John	27	M	Farmer	31Ma02Wg
MARTIN, Mikel	24	M	Farmer	31Ma02Wg
RICK, Betty	20	F	Unknown	31Ma02Wg
CONLEY, Mary	26	F	Unknown	31Ma02Wg
Rufas	02	M	Child	31Ma02Wg
MCNULTY, Betty	18	F	Unknown	31Ma02Wg
CONLEY, Margaret	13	F	Unknown	31Ma02Wg
CALLIAN, John	29	M	Jockey	31Ma02Wg
Mary	27	F	Farmer	31Ma02Wg
FITZPATRICK, Edward	18	M	Farmer	31Ma02Wg
Thos.	16	M	Unknown	31Ma02Wg
Margaret	13	F	Unknown	31Ma02Wg
Mary	11	F	Unknown	31Ma02Wg
James	09	M	Child	31Ma02Wg
Margaret	10	F	Unknown	31Ma02Wg
Margaret	40	F	Unknown	31Ma02Wg
RALLEY, John	32	M	Shoemaker	31Ma02Wg
RICE, John	25	M	Farmer	31Ma02Wg
James	20	M	Farmer	31Ma02Wg
SHERIDAN, Mary	16	F	Unknown	31Ma02Wg
KERNAN, James	48	M	Farmer	31Ma02Wg
CLARK, Thos.	26	M	Farmer	31Ma02Wg
John	20	M	Farmer	31Ma02Wg
Mary	20	F	Unknown	31Ma02Wg
CONNOR, Catharine	26	F	Unknown	31Ma02Wg
MURPHY, John	20	M	Farmer	31Ma02Wg
Ann	20	F	Unknown	31Ma02Wg
Thos.	03	M	Child	31Ma02Wg
CUSSAK, Pat	20	M	Farmer	31Ma02Wg
HALLAHAN, Mary	26	F	Unknown	31Ma02Wg
CAVINO, John	29	M	Unknown	31Ma02Wg
CONNOR, Biddy	29	F	Unknown	31Ma02Wg
CALLIHAN, Mikel	20	M	Tailor	31Ma02Wg
MORGON, Winford	29	U	Unknown	31Ma02Wg
SMITH, Ebray	19	U	Unknown	31Ma02Wg
LANGDON, Ann	02	F	Child	31Ma02Wg
MAGLAN, Mary	04	F	Child	31Ma02Wg
MARKEY, Pat	24	M	Farmer	31Ma02Wg
Mary	27	F	Unknown	31Ma02Wg
MULLAN, Richard	23	M	Farmer	31Ma02Wg
GILE, Hugh	20	M	Farmer	31Ma02Wg
KICKAM, John	31	M	Farmer	31Ma02Wg
DOWLING, Mikel	25	M	Farmer	31Ma02Wg
Mary	28	F	Unknown	31Ma02Wg
Ellen	06	F	Child	31Ma02Wg
James	05	M	Child	31Ma02Wg
Mary	03	F	Child	31Ma02Wg
Walter	03	M	Child	31Ma02Wg
MCHAFFEY, Wm.	39	M	Farmer	31Ma02Wg
Margaret	29	F	Unknown	31Ma02Wg
Mary	12	F	Unknown	31Ma02Wg
MCCLAIN, Wm.	08	M	Child	31Ma02Wg
Samuel	08	M	Child	31Ma02Wg
Nancy	05	F	Child	31Ma02Wg
Mary	40	F	Unknown	31Ma02Wg
Samuel	12	M	Unknown	31Ma02Wg
James	10	M	Unknown	31Ma02Wg
John	08	M	Child	31Ma02Wg
RADFORD, Wm.	27	M	Clerk	31Ma02Wg
RYAN, John	16	M	Farmer	31Ma02Wg
James	20	M	Farmer	31Ma02Wg
ALLAN, Thos.	20	M	Farmer	31Ma02Wg
HANNIHAN, Petre	16	M	Farmer	31Ma02Wg
WALSH, Pat	56	M	Farmer	31Ma02Wg
Ann	35	F	Unknown	31Ma02Wg
Thos.	16	M	Farmer	31Ma02Wg
Mikel	14	M	Farmer	31Ma02Wg
Mary	10	F	Unknown	31Ma02Wg
Pat	08	M	Child	31Ma02Wg
Bridget	06	F	Child	31Ma02Wg
John	03	M	Child	31Ma02Wg
Morgon	60	M	Farmer	31Ma02Wg
Mikel	45	M	Farmer	31Ma02Wg
Ellen	40	F	Unknown	31Ma02Wg
John	14	M	Unknown	31Ma02Wg
Mark	12	M	Unknown	31Ma02Wg
Mary	10	F	Unknown	31Ma02Wg
Biddy	09	F	Child	31Ma02Wg
Mikel	03	M	Child	31Ma02Wg
HALAHAN, Owen	23	M	Farmer	31Ma02Wg
John	25	M	Farmer	31Ma02Wg
HANAHAN, Pat	20	M	Farmer	31Ma02Wg
GIBBIN, Bridget	23	F	Unknown	31Ma02Wg
FILBEN, Mikel	21	M	Farmer	31Ma02Wg

NAMES OF PASSENGERS	AGE	SEX	OCCUPATIONS	DATE PORT SHIP
COMMUS, John	30	M	Stone Mason	31Ma02Wg
WOOD, Mikel	28	M	Stone Mason	31Ma02Wg
HUTCHINSON, Wm.	25	M	Laborer	31Ma02Wg
LOGAN, Daniel	30	M	Farmer	31Ma02Wg
WALSH, Wm.	40	M	Farmer	31Ma02Wg
Peggy	30	F	Unknown	31Ma02Wg
Mary	18	F	Unknown	31Ma02Wg
Nancy	08	F	Child	31Ma02Wg
James	06	M	Child	31Ma02Wg
MCCABE, James	33	M	Farmer	31Ma02Wg
RICE, James	30	M	Farmer	31Ma02Wg
NEWELE, Mikel	26	M	Gameskeeper	31Ma02Wg
COMOCLE, Thos.	26	M	Farmer	31Ma02Wg
MCKINLEY, John	30	M	Farmer	31Ma02Wg
WARD, Owen	70	M	Farmer	31Ma02Wg
Mary	55	F	Unknown	31Ma02Wg
John	21	M	Farmer	31Ma02Wg
Bridget	19	F	Unknown	31Ma02Wg
Patrick	16	M	Unknown	31Ma02Wg
James	13	M	Unknown	31Ma02Wg
John	09	M	Child	31Ma02Wg
JONES, David	25	M	Miner	31Ma02Wg
RILEY, John	18	M	Laborer	31Ma02Wg
BUCKLY, Edwd.	22	M	Laborer	31Ma02Wg

UNITED-STATES 31 MAY 1848

From Liverpool

NAMES OF PASSENGERS	AGE	SEX	OCCUPATIONS	DATE PORT SHIP
OCONNOR, J.	26	U	Unknown	31Ma02Wd
BUTLER, Wm.	24	M	Unknown	31Ma02Wd
BARNARD, G.	29	U	Unknown	31Ma02Wd
DARCY, Jno.	30	U	Unknown	31Ma02Wd
DYER, Thomas	25	M	Mechanic	31Ma02Wd

MARY-MORRIS 31 MAY 1848

From Glasgow

NAMES OF PASSENGERS	AGE	SEX	OCCUPATIONS	DATE PORT SHIP
QUIGLY, Sarah	28	F	Servant	31Ma0401
CLERK, Sam	28	M	Miner	31Ma0401
Mary	25	F	None	31Ma0401
GREY, Pat	35	M	Weaver	31Ma0401
KILGOUR, Wm.	25	M	Bleacher	31Ma0401
OLIPHANT, Geo.	42	M	Bleacher	31Ma0401
BUCHANAN, And.	30	M	Plumber	31Ma0401
SHANE, Alex	39	M	Machinist	31Ma0401
BIGGER, Wm.	50	M	Farmer	31Ma0401
Martha	21	F	Unknown	31Ma0401
Martha	60	F	Unknown	31Ma0401
DONNACHY, Jane	22	F	Weaver	31Ma0401
Mary	18	F	Weaver	31Ma0401
WILSON, James	43	M	Weaver	31Ma0401
THOMPSON, Rob.	24	M	Weaver	31Ma0401
SCOTT, Chas.	25	M	Stctr	31Ma0401
GILCHRIST, Jas.	25	M	Joiner	31Ma0401
CURRE, John	20	M	Joiner	31Ma0401
Miln--, Geo.	28	M	Mason	31Ma0401
LANDIS, John	22	M	Machinist	31Ma0401
Gr----, Alex.	23	M	Laborer	31Ma0401
WILSON, William	26	M	Blacksmith	31Ma0401
DOCHERTY, John	24	M	Dyer	31Ma0401
CONLIN, Owen	21	M	Laborer	31Ma0401
WALKER, James	24	M	Fefndr	31Ma0401
FRAZER, David	22	M	Machinist	31Ma0401
DUNCAN, Wm.	32	M	Stctr	31Ma0401
Geo.	28	M	Laborer	31Ma0401
MCGIE, Geo.	23	M	Laborer	31Ma0401
MCKNIGHT, Jas.	28	M	Machinist	31Ma0401
KENNEDY, Rob.	32	M	Laborer	31Ma0401
Mary	30	F	Unknown	31Ma0401
John	28	M	Unknown	31Ma0401
Mary-Ann	26	F	Unknown	31Ma0401
Martha	04	F	Child	31Ma0401
MCQUAKER, Wm.	33	M	Weaver	31Ma0401
KENNIDY, Wm.	34	M	Laborer	31Ma0401
MILLER, Monk	30	M	Blacksmith	31Ma0401
KENNEDY, Thos.	30	M	Carpenter	31Ma0401
GRIERE, Wm.	21	M	Litgr	31Ma0401
SMITH, Alice	18	F	Servant	31Ma0401
Peter	21	M	Laborer	31Ma0401
RODIN, Philip	19	M	Laborer	31Ma0401
MCDONNELL, Wm.	26	M	Gdnr	31Ma0401
SINCLAIR, Alex	24	M	Clcp	31Ma0401
BROGAN, Felix	35	M	Ctnsp	31Ma0401
CRAWFORD, Agnes	26	F	Unknown	31Ma0401
BLAIR, Cath.	74	F	Unknown	31Ma0401
GILLESPIE, Jas.	28	M	Mason	31Ma0401
CUNNINGHAM, Jas.	22	M	Coachman	31Ma0401
SCOTT, Rob.D.	42	M	Farmer	31Ma0401
MCKIE, Ann	26	F	Unknown	31Ma0401
QUAGE, John	21	M	Carpenter	31Ma0401
ARTHUR, Janet	24	F	Unknown	31Ma0401
Elizabeth	50	F	Unknown	31Ma0401
MCCONNOCHY, Sarah	19	F	Unknown	31Ma0401
ROBERTSON, Rob.	26	M	Painter	31Ma0401
Jane	21	F	Unknown	31Ma0401
James	02	M	Child	31Ma0401
William	.09	M	Infant	31Ma0401
SORLEY, Jane	35	F	Unknown	31Ma0401
John	14	M	Unknown	31Ma0401
William	12	M	Unknown	31Ma0401
DOBSON, Wm.	33	M	Wdmcht	31Ma0401
CALLAHAN, Chas.	28	M	Laborer	31Ma0401
Eliza	28	F	Unknown	31Ma0401
Charles	07	M	Child	31Ma0401
James	04	M	Child	31Ma0401
Eliza	01	F	Child	31Ma0401
Mary	.01	F	Infant	31Ma0401
BLAIR, Cath.	25	F	Swhtr	31Ma0401
TURNER, Ed.	21	M	Laborer	31Ma0401
KEITH, Wm.	24	M	Clerk	31Ma0401
FRATER, Wm.	26	M	Weaver	31Ma0401
SHANGAN, Wm.	18	M	Weaver	31Ma0401
SHIELDS, And.	23	M	Dyer	31Ma0401
LEITCH, Jas.	21	M	Turner	31Ma0401
EUMAN, John	23	M	Weaver	31Ma0401
ANDREWS, Geo.	30	M	Warper	31Ma0401
THOMPSON, Arch.	26	M	Baker	31Ma0401
Christine	20	F	Unknown	31Ma0401
FERGUSON, Wm.	25	M	Fefndr	31Ma0401
Janet	25	F	Unknown	31Ma0401
David	.10	M	Infant	31Ma0401
COOPER, Jas.	18	M	Carpenter	31Ma0401
YORK, Rich.	22	M	Mason	31Ma0401
WHITE, John	27	M	Tailor	31Ma0401
Janet	29	F	Unknown	31Ma0401
George	09	M	Child	31Ma0401
Henry	07	M	Child	31Ma0401
Lucy-Ann	03	F	Child	31Ma0401
John	05	M	Child	31Ma0401
REICH, Arkam	37	M	Clcp	31Ma0401
MCMILLAN, Thos.	30	M	Farmer	31Ma0401
BRUCE, Elis.	18	F	Milliner	31Ma0401
KERR, Mary	24	F	Servant	31Ma0401
STEWARD, H.C.	29	M	Baker	31Ma0401
Mary	27	F	Unknown	31Ma0401
James	05	M	Child	31Ma0401

NAMES OF PASSENGERS	AGE	SEX	OCCUPATIONS	DATE PORT SHIP
PROUDFOOT, Wm.	33	M	Farmer	31Ma0401
PRINGLE, Wm.	25	M	Farmer	31Ma0401
RUTHERFORD, Joan	24	F	Unknown	31Ma0401
CAMBELL, Mike	22	M	Blacksmith	31Ma0401
OHARA, John	25	M	Laborer	31Ma0401
MCILROY, James	30	M	Laborer	31Ma0401
Mary	20	F	Unknown	31Ma0401
MCINTYRE, Susan	30	F	Unknown	31Ma0401
Niel	28	M	Laborer	31Ma0401
MCFARLANE, Geo.	34	M	Glsctr	31Ma0401
Mary	34	F	Unknown	31Ma0401
Janet	06	F	Child	31Ma0401
George	05	M	Child	31Ma0401
Mary	01	F	Child	31Ma0401
CORDTER, Joseph	21	M	Irnmldr	31Ma0401
MCDONALD, Hugh	38	M	Butcher	31Ma0401
MCINTYRE, John	35	M	Carpenter	31Ma0401
FRAZER, Donald	23	M	Laborer	31Ma0401
DUNNING, Susan	23	F	Sspnr	31Ma0401
MCNEIL, Neil	20	M	Bookseller	31Ma0401
STEWARD, John	16	M	Mill Worker	31Ma0401
ANDERSON, John	20	M	Engt	31Ma0401
HUGES, Hugh	29	M	Weaver	31Ma0401
COLVILLE, Rob.	30	M	Ptmkr	31Ma0401
HOUSTON, Diana	16	F	Unknown	31Ma0401
GREY, Mary	18	F	Nurse	31Ma0401
MCINTYRE, Wm.	04	M	Child	31Ma0401
John	01	M	Child	31Ma0401
HARK, Walter	25	M	Tailor	31Ma0401
Elisabeth	24	F	Unknown	31Ma0401
WATSON, Arch.	20	M	Weaver	31Ma0401
Mary	21	F	Unknown	31Ma0401
TURNAN, Mary	23	F	Servant	31Ma0401
Mathew	13	M	Unknown	31Ma0401
SPIERS, George	25	M	Stone Mason	31Ma0401
MCKIE, W.B.	15	M	Stone Mason	31Ma0401
THOMPSON, Thos.	20	M	Potter	31Ma0401
MCKENZIE, Geo.	26	M	Blacksmith	31Ma0401
REID, Alex	34	M	Weaver	31Ma0401
COLLINS, Joseph	00	M	Blr	31Ma0401
MOVILL, Henry	00	M	Seaman	31Ma0401
WHITE, John	35	M	Merchant	31Ma0401
Ellis	35	F	Merchant	31Ma0401
HUNTER, James	18	M	Merchant	31Ma0401
BOWER, Wm.	24	M	Merchant	31Ma0401

KENT 31 MAY 1848

From Liverpool

NAMES OF PASSENGERS	AGE	SEX	OCCUPATIONS	DATE PORT SHIP
MCNIGHT, Richard	60	M	Laborer	31Ma02We
Ann	50	F	Spinster	31Ma02We
Sarah	10	F	Unknown	31Ma02We
RYAN, Patt	20	M	Laborer	31Ma02We
ONEILL, Rose	30	F	Spinster	31Ma02We
GRAHAM, Patt	25	M	Carpenter	31Ma02We
Proctor	25	F	Spinster	31Ma02We
HOGAN, Richard	25	M	Laborer	31Ma02We
HALPIN, Thos.	20	M	Laborer	31Ma02We
HOGAN, Loughlin	25	M	Laborer	31Ma02We
MONKS, Richard	25	M	Laborer	31Ma02We
CARTHEY, Edwd.	25	M	Laborer	31Ma02We
KINNAY, Nicholas	21	M	Laborer	31Ma02We
Mary	21	F	Spinster	31Ma02We
DUNN, Peter	25	M	Laborer	31Ma02We
KELLEY, Peter	20	M	Laborer	31Ma02We
NOLAN, Michael	25	M	Carpenter	31Ma02We
CROW, Jas.	25	M	Carpenter	31Ma02We
DUNN, Thos.	25	M	Carpenter	31Ma02We

NAMES OF PASSENGERS	AGE	SEX	OCCUPATIONS	DATE PORT SHIP
TOOLE, Patt	25	M	Carpenter	31Ma02We
KAIN, Patt	46	M	Carpenter	31Ma02We
ISDELL, Cathe.	28	F	Spinster	31Ma02We
MULLIGAN, John	30	M	Laborer	31Ma02We
CURTIS, Andrew	32	M	Laborer	31Ma02We
ANDERSON, Jas.	35	M	Laborer	31Ma02We
Margt.	20	F	Carpenter	31Ma02We
CARLTON, James	19	M	Carpenter	31Ma02We
Wm.	19	M	Carpenter	31Ma02We
FARR, John	21	M	Carpenter	31Ma02We
Eliza	18	F	Spinster	31Ma02We
HALPIN, Francis	40	M	Laborer	31Ma02We
Mary	50	F	Matron	31Ma02We
Jane	18	F	Matron	31Ma02We
BYRNES, Agnes	20	F	Matron	31Ma02We
RUSSELL, Elizabeth	20	F	Matron	31Ma02We
MCGOREY, Edwd.	22	M	Laborer	31Ma02We
GINNS, Bridget	17	F	Spinster	31Ma02We
DOWNNY, John	25	M	Carpenter	31Ma02We
CARROLL, Jas.	26	F	Spinster	31Ma02We
DOWNEY, Jane	24	F	Spinster	31Ma02We
RIGNEY, Kearne	20	M	Laborer	31Ma02We
Cathe.	18	F	Spinster	31Ma02We
MCLOUGHLIN, Wm.	30	M	Carpenter	31Ma02We
SHAIN, Ann	20	F	Spinster	31Ma02We
Wm.	22	M	Brick Maker	31Ma02We
MCKENNA, Patt	29	M	Brick Maker	31Ma02We
COMERFORD, Michl.	21	M	Brick Maker	31Ma02We
U (W)	22	F	Spinster	31Ma02We
TUITT, Edwd.	27	M	Mmsn	31Ma02We
Patt	23	M	Mmsn	31Ma02We
WARD, Patt	24	M	Mmsn	31Ma02We
Lawrence	18	M	Mmsn	31Ma02We
MCGUINESS, Mary	18	F	Spinster	31Ma02We
CARR, Thos.	25	M	Laborer	31Ma02We
Ann	28	F	Spinster	31Ma02We
FANRATT, Bridget	18	F	Spinster	31Ma02We
BRANNAN, Patrick	25	M	Carpenter	31Ma02We
NOWLAN, John	26	M	Carpenter	31Ma02We
Mary	04	F	Child	31Ma02We
MILEY, Thomas	26	M	Carpenter	31Ma02We
LYONS, Mary	35	F	Spinster	31Ma02We
John	12	M	Unknown	31Ma02We
Margt.	08	F	Child	31Ma02We
Timothy	08	M	Child	31Ma02We
Mary	03	F	Child	31Ma02We
Judy	03	F	Child	31Ma02We
RICHARD, Thomas	40	M	Spinner	31Ma02We
Thos.	11	M	Unknown	31Ma02We
Rose	09	F	Child	31Ma02We
George	07	M	Child	31Ma02We
Ann	16	F	Spinster	31Ma02We
EVANS, Edw.	42	M	Carpenter	31Ma02We
Mary	37	F	Spinster	31Ma02We
Jane	13	F	Unknown	31Ma02We
Edwd.	09	M	Child	31Ma02We
Elizabeth	03	F	Child	31Ma02We
John	02	M	Child	31Ma02We
GRIFFITH, John	44	M	Carpenter	31Ma02We
LYNCH, James	20	M	Carpenter	31Ma02We
PORTER, Joseph	20	M	Carpenter	31Ma02We
MARNACK, John	28	M	Carpenter	31Ma02We
Betsey	28	F	Spinster	31Ma02We
John-Thos.	02	M	Child	31Ma02We
WEAVER, George	25	M	Laborer	31Ma02We
Ann	24	F	Spinster	31Ma02We
BANNING, George	26	M	Laborer	31Ma02We
WILLIAMS, Richard	24	M	Laborer	31Ma02We
COLLINS, John	26	M	Laborer	31Ma02We
Mary	22	F	Spinster	31Ma02We
RUTHERFORD, David	23	M	Laborer	31Ma02We
WALTER, John	38	M	Laborer	31Ma02We
FAHILY, Mary	23	F	Matron	31Ma02We
CORAGHTY, Roxana	12	F	Matron	31Ma02We
RALF, John	25	M	Laborer	31Ma02We

NAMES OF PASSENGERS	AGE	SEX	OCCUPATIONS	DATE PORT SHIP
MCCABE, Danl.	45	M	Laborer	31Ma02We
BOURKE, Jeny	27	M	Laborer	31Ma02We
RYAN, Paddy	25	M	Laborer	31Ma02We
HART, Bridgt.	25	F	Spinster	31Ma02We
BURKE, Nancy	22	F	Spinster	31Ma02We
Bridgt.	30	F	Spinster	31Ma02We
HARTY, Margt.	.00	F	Infant	31Ma02We
DEMPSEY, Cathe.	20	F	Spinster	31Ma02We
BYRNE, Patt	20	M	Carpenter	31Ma02We
DOYLE, Patt	20	M	Carpenter	31Ma02We
NOWLAN, Michl.	27	M	Carpenter	31Ma02We
WALL, Michl.	27	M	Carpenter	31Ma02We
Patt	25	M	Carpenter	31Ma02We
RIENAN, John	20	M	Carpenter	31Ma02We
DOYLE, John	20	M	Carpenter	31Ma02We
REILLY, Joseph	21	M	Carpenter	31Ma02We
Rose	19	F	Spinster	31Ma02We
Fanny	17	F	Spinster	31Ma02We
Cathe.	45	F	Spinster	31Ma02We
Cathe.	12	F	Spinster	31Ma02We
Owen	10	M	Unknown	31Ma02We
MCGUIRE, Ann	34	M	Carpenter	31Ma02We
Mary	15	F	Spinster	31Ma02We
Bridget	13	F	Spinster	31Ma02We
Cathn.	11	F	Spinster	31Ma02We
Ann	06	F	Child	31Ma02We
HARLIN, Patt	28	M	Laborer	31Ma02We
William	29	M	Laborer	31Ma02We
CRILLY, Mary	25	F	Spinster	31Ma02We
WILSON, John	16	M	Carpenter	31Ma02We
Elizabeth	20	F	Spinster	31Ma02We
FINNEGAN, Nancy	15	F	Spinster	31Ma02We
CANAGHER, Alice	20	F	Spinster	31Ma02We
FEE, Bridget	19	F	Spinster	31Ma02We
FINNEGAN, Mary	19	F	Spinster	31Ma02We
WARD, Mary	15	F	Spinster	31Ma02We
BREEN, Mathew	37	M	Laborer	31Ma02We
CONDON, Edwd.	20	M	Laborer	31Ma02We
HARRIS, Mary	24	F	Spinster	31Ma02We
BYRNES, Michl.	24	M	Laborer	31Ma02We
ORR, Ellen	30	F	Spinster	31Ma02We
CONNELLY, Bridget	36	F	Spinster	31Ma02We
KEARNY, Cathn.	18	F	Spinster	31Ma02We
CONNELLY, Thos.	.00	M	Infant	31Ma02We
CARNEY, Thos.	18	M	Laborer	31Ma02We
LATHROM, Barney	20	M	Laborer	31Ma02We
FOLEY, James	25	M	Laborer	31Ma02We
CROW, Donate	21	M	Laborer	31Ma02We
DOGGAN, Mary	24	F	Laborer	31Ma02We
REILLY, Patrick	55	M	Laborer	31Ma02We
CAMPBELL, Patrick	30	M	Laborer	31Ma02We
Cathe.	30	F	Spinster	31Ma02We
HENRY, Michl.	21	M	Carpenter	31Ma02We
Ann	18	F	Spinster	31Ma02We
James	28	M	Laborer	31Ma02We
CLENDUNERY, Mary-Ann	25	F	Spinster	31Ma02We
WILSON, John	34	M	Laborer	31Ma02We
Jane	30	F	Spinster	31Ma02We
Richd.	11	M	Spinner	31Ma02We
LANEGAN, Danl.	22	M	Spinner	31Ma02We
BASH, William	30	M	Carpenter	31Ma02We
Ann	24	F	Spinster	31Ma02We
YARDLY, Mary	29	F	Spinster	31Ma02We
PEPPER, William	30	M	Carpenter	31Ma02We
KIERNAN, John	26	M	Carpenter	31Ma02We
Rose-Ann	22	F	Spinster	31Ma02We
Jas.	03	M	Child	31Ma02We
Teresa	.00	F	Infant	31Ma02We
MANDLY, Edwd.	30	M	Laborer	31Ma02We
CLAFFAY, Danl.	25	M	Laborer	31Ma02We
MAGEE, John	28	M	Laborer	31Ma02We
FARRELL, Bernard	23	M	Laborer	31Ma02We
ATCHON, John	25	M	Laborer	31Ma02We
ANDERSON, John	21	M	Laborer	31Ma02We
REID, James	25	M	Laborer	31Ma02We
CAVNAUGH, Jas.	20	M	Laborer	31Ma02We
NOONAN, Fredk.	27	M	Laborer	31Ma02We
NEILE, John	20	M	Laborer	31Ma02We
HAMMOND, Wm.	29	M	Laborer	31Ma02We
CARTIN, Thos.	24	M	Laborer	31Ma02We
GATESWORTH, John	23	M	Laborer	31Ma02We
MCDONNALL, Ann	20	F	Spinster	31Ma02We
MCENRUE, U	25	F	Laborer	31Ma02We
MCCARTNAY, John	20	M	Laborer	31Ma02We
Mary-Ann	20	F	Spinster	31Ma02We
LYNCH, James	20	M	Laborer	31Ma02We
MCCABE, Danl.	45	M	Laborer	31Ma02We
MCCARTNEY, Mary	20	F	Spinster	31Ma02We

CHIEFTAIN 31 MAY 1848

From Belfast

NAMES OF PASSENGERS	AGE	SEX	OCCUPATIONS	DATE PORT SHIP
CAMPBELL, Thomas	19	M	Laborer	31Ma07Wf
MCKEOWN, Thomas	24	M	Laborer	31Ma07Wf
MCSHAVERTY, Barney	24	M	Laborer	31Ma07Wf
LAWSON, Betty	20	F	Laborer	31Ma07Wf
DEVINE, Catherine	40	F	Laborer	31Ma07Wf
William	15	M	Laborer	31Ma07Wf
Mary	13	F	Laborer	31Ma07Wf
Catherine	11	F	Laborer	31Ma07Wf
MCKEWON, Hugh	18	M	Laborer	31Ma07Wf
CONLIN, James	45	M	Laborer	31Ma07Wf
Mary	40	F	Laborer	31Ma07Wf
Jane	07	F	Child	31Ma07Wf
Catherine	05	F	Child	31Ma07Wf
Patrick	.00	M	Infant	31Ma07Wf
John	22	M	Laborer	31Ma07Wf
FOSTER, Michal	40	M	Laborer	31Ma07Wf
John	21	M	Laborer	31Ma07Wf
STEELE, David	18	M	Laborer	31Ma07Wf
HUGHS, Philex	23	M	Laborer	31Ma07Wf
GILLESPIE, James	19	M	Laborer	31Ma07Wf
QUINN, Marget	18	F	Laborer	31Ma07Wf
JINNINGS, Mary	13	F	Laborer	31Ma07Wf
John	17	M	Laborer	31Ma07Wf
MCCORT, Catherine	23	F	Laborer	31Ma07Wf
BEST, Richard	21	M	Laborer	31Ma07Wf
Jane	18	F	Laborer	31Ma07Wf
William	27	M	Laborer	31Ma07Wf
FOX, George	22	M	Laborer	31Ma07Wf
EDWARD, Thomas	18	M	Laborer	31Ma07Wf
SHIELDS, Ann	19	F	Laborer	31Ma07Wf
BERN, William	51	M	Laborer	31Ma07Wf
MCNAGHLAN, Mary	27	F	Laborer	31Ma07Wf
CANDLE, Margret	.00	F	Infant	31Ma07Wf
MCNAGHLAN, Eliza	00	F	Laborer	31Ma07Wf
MCGREGOR, Eliza	10	F	Laborer	31Ma07Wf
BLACK, Danial	17	M	Laborer	31Ma07Wf
Margret	19	F	Laborer	31Ma07Wf
BROWN, Matilda	19	F	Laborer	31Ma07Wf
FOX, Eliza	35	F	Laborer	31Ma07Wf
Mary-Jane	01	F	Child	31Ma07Wf
BEST, Jane	50	F	Laborer	31Ma07Wf
BEAR, James	32	M	Laborer	31Ma07Wf
Eliza	30	F	Laborer	31Ma07Wf
Mary-Anne	08	F	Child	31Ma07Wf
Thomas	06	M	Child	31Ma07Wf
Eliza-Jane	04	F	Child	31Ma07Wf
Mathar	02	F	Child	31Ma07Wf
Margret	.00	F	Infant	31Ma07Wf
WILSON, Nancy	15	F	Laborer	31Ma07Wf
DONAGHY, Ann	35	F	Laborer	31Ma07Wf
Ann	11	F	Laborer	31Ma07Wf

NAMES OF PASSENGERS	A G E	S E X	OCCUPATIONS	DATE PORT SHIP
DONAGHY, Alice	07	F	Child	31Ma07Wf
YORKINGHOUSE, John	24	M	Laborer	31Ma07Wf
LINSEY, Mather	35	M	Laborer	31Ma07Wf
CLARK, William	40	M	Laborer	31Ma07Wf
STEPHENS, John	23	M	Laborer	31Ma07Wf
CLOVER, James	26	M	Laborer	31Ma07Wf
Mary-Ann	27	F	Laborer	31Ma07Wf
John	04	M	Child	31Ma07Wf
Nancy	02	F	Child	31Ma07Wf
MOONEY, William	21	M	Laborer	31Ma07Wf
SCOTT, Alexander	20	M	Laborer	31Ma07Wf
FOULER, Edward	22	M	Laborer	31Ma07Wf
KENNY, William	13	M	Laborer	31Ma07Wf
LEVANY, Stephen-M.	16	M	Laborer	31Ma07Wf
SWANSEY, James	57	M	Laborer	31Ma07Wf
Margrit	45	F	Laborer	31Ma07Wf
Eliza	17	F	Laborer	31Ma07Wf
Catherine	13	F	Laborer	31Ma07Wf
Mary	10	F	Laborer	31Ma07Wf
James	09	M	Child	31Ma07Wf
Margret	07	F	Child	31Ma07Wf
John	03	M	Child	31Ma07Wf
GIBSON, Eliza	20	F	Laborer	31Ma07Wf
STEPHANSON, Rebecca	18	F	Laborer	31Ma07Wf
PHILLIPS, Eliza	20	F	Laborer	31Ma07Wf
HURRY, Mary-Ann	20	F	Laborer	31Ma07Wf
MCDOUGAL, Nancey	18	F	Laborer	31Ma07Wf
John	22	M	Laborer	31Ma07Wf
KING, John	26	M	Laborer	31Ma07Wf
HAMILL, Margret	30	F	Laborer	31Ma07Wf
CORR, John	19	M	Laborer	31Ma07Wf
FITZIMONS, Hugh	45	M	Laborer	31Ma07Wf
NICKLUSON, John	36	M	Laborer	31Ma07Wf
Mary-Ann	25	F	Laborer	31Ma07Wf
Lucinda	20	F	Laborer	31Ma07Wf
Mal---Da	18	U	Laborer	31Ma07Wf
FISHER, James	30	M	Laborer	31Ma07Wf
RANKIN, Joseph	28	M	Laborer	31Ma07Wf
SHIELDS, James	25	M	Laborer	31Ma07Wf
MCGUCKIN, William	45	M	Laborer	31Ma07Wf
BURNS, John	30	M	Laborer	31Ma07Wf
MICHELL, Thomas-C.	29	M	Laborer	31Ma07Wf
CANN, Eliza	38	F	Laborer	31Ma07Wf
Eliza	16	F	Laborer	31Ma07Wf
John	13	M	Laborer	31Ma07Wf
Edmond	11	M	Laborer	31Ma07Wf
James	10	M	Laborer	31Ma07Wf
Jane	04	F	Child	31Ma07Wf
QUINN, Thomas	44	M	Laborer	31Ma07Wf
Sarah	24	F	Laborer	31Ma07Wf
James	19	M	Laborer	31Ma07Wf
Eliza	13	F	Laborer	31Ma07Wf
William	11	M	Laborer	31Ma07Wf
Mary	09	F	Child	31Ma07Wf
Ellen	07	F	Child	31Ma07Wf
John	04	M	Child	31Ma07Wf
Joseph	02	M	Child	31Ma07Wf
MCLEARY, John	20	M	Laborer	31Ma07Wf
FLEMING, Mary	22	F	Laborer	31Ma07Wf
WALLACE, Robert	20	M	Laborer	31Ma07Wf
MCCAUGHEY, Samuel	20	M	Laborer	31Ma07Wf
Ann	20	F	Laborer	31Ma07Wf
HANANN, Joseph	22	M	Laborer	31Ma07Wf
CALLEY, Mary	26	F	Laborer	31Ma07Wf
Rose	03	F	Child	31Ma07Wf
MCGRA, John	30	M	Laborer	31Ma07Wf
Mary	20	F	Laborer	31Ma07Wf
Molly	65	F	Laborer	31Ma07Wf
SCOTT, Thomas	47	M	Laborer	31Ma07Wf
Agnes	47	F	Laborer	31Ma07Wf
William-George	20	M	Laborer	31Ma07Wf
John	18	M	Laborer	31Ma07Wf
Alexander	14	M	Laborer	31Ma07Wf
Thomas	16	M	Laborer	31Ma07Wf
GRACY, James	23	M	Laborer	31Ma07Wf
GRACY, Flosee	47	F	Laborer	31Ma07Wf
Nancy	18	F	Laborer	31Ma07Wf
LOVE, Samuel	47	M	Laborer	31Ma07Wf
ONEAL, Yavey	24	M	Laborer	31Ma07Wf
Margret	50	F	Laborer	31Ma07Wf

ROSETTA 31 MAY 1848

From Belfast

NAMES OF PASSENGERS		A G E	S E X	OCCUPATIONS	DATE PORT SHIP
RENSHAW, James		21	M	Laborer	31Ma07Wl
Jane	(W)	21	F	Wife	31Ma07Wl
LOWRY, John		25	M	Laborer	31Ma07Wl
Magt.	(W)	23	F	Wife	31Ma07Wl
MCCLERY, Cathe.		19	F	Spinster	31Ma07Wl
BLACK, Mary		30	F	Spinster	31Ma07Wl
MOONY, Ally		28	F	None	31Ma07Wl
MCMULLEN, Thos.		55	M	None	31Ma07Wl
Eliza		56	F	None	31Ma07Wl
Eliza		20	F	None	31Ma07Wl
Robt.		17	M	Laborer	31Ma07Wl
Nancy		15	F	Spinster	31Ma07Wl
MCAREVY, Bernard		60	M	Spinner	31Ma07Wl
MCMICHL, M.		45	M	Spinner	31Ma07Wl
Robt.		20	M	Spinner	31Ma07Wl
MCKEE, Hugh		19	M	Spinner	31Ma07Wl
WILSON, Saml.		25	M	Spinner	31Ma07Wl
Eliza		24	F	Spinner	31Ma07Wl
MORRISON, Jane		21	F	Spinner	31Ma07Wl
JOHNSTON, James		50	M	Laborer	31Ma07Wl
Richd.		18	M	Laborer	31Ma07Wl
Eliza		15	F	None	31Ma07Wl
John		23	M	None	31Ma07Wl
KENNEDY, Thomas		55	M	None	31Ma07Wl
Mary		56	F	Spinster	31Ma07Wl
Elizth.		16	F	Spinster	31Ma07Wl
LAWRENCE, Ann		20	F	Spinster	31Ma07Wl
DIXON, James		60	M	Spinster	31Ma07Wl
Johanna		48	F	Spinster	31Ma07Wl
Jane		22	F	Spinster	31Ma07Wl
Eliza		13	F	Spinster	31Ma07Wl
James		05	M	Child	31Ma07Wl
DODSON, James		28	M	Laborer	31Ma07Wl
Jane		26	F	Laborer	31Ma07Wl
REID, Michl.		40	M	Laborer	31Ma07Wl
MCNALLY, John		19	M	Laborer	31Ma07Wl
MCNAMEE, Sarah		22	F	Laborer	31Ma07Wl
TAGGART, Betty-O.		16	F	Laborer	31Ma07Wl
MCKIBBIN, James		40	M	Laborer	31Ma07Wl
Joseph		21	M	Laborer	31Ma07Wl
Simpson		24	M	Laborer	31Ma07Wl
Elizth.		40	F	Laborer	31Ma07Wl
Martha		18	F	Laborer	31Ma07Wl
BRANNAN, Biddy		40	F	Laborer	31Ma07Wl
BECK, James		20	M	Laborer	31Ma07Wl
MCGIVEN, Mary		25	F	Laborer	31Ma07Wl
HANLON, Mary		18	F	Laborer	31Ma07Wl
MCEON, Elias		18	M	Laborer	31Ma07Wl
OHARA, Bridge		30	F	Laborer	31Ma07Wl
DUFF, Ann		22	F	Laborer	31Ma07Wl
MCKEYE, Robt.		17	M	Laborer	31Ma07Wl
MCHERRAN, Patk.		67	M	Laborer	31Ma07Wl
Patk.		30	M	Laborer	31Ma07Wl
Elizth.		30	F	Spinster	31Ma07Wl
HUGHES, Ann		34	F	Spinster	31Ma07Wl
TAGGART, James		25	M	Spinster	31Ma07Wl
BALLINTIN, Eliza		29	F	Spinster	31Ma07Wl
MCCORD, James		28	M	Spinner	31Ma07Wl
FITZSIMMONS, Patk.		21	M	Spinner	31Ma07Wl

NAMES OF PASSENGERS	AGE	SEX	OCCUPATIONS	DATE PORT SHIP
FITZSIMMONS, Mary	21	F	Spinster	31Ma07WI
MCELINN, Rosy	17	F	Spinster	31Ma07WI
MCGLUCK, Patk.	38	M	Spinster	31Ma07WI
Mary	38	F	Spinster	31Ma07WI
Mary	.00	F	Infant	31Ma07WI
HAGAN, Chas.	24	M	Laborer	31Ma07WI
DEVELIN, James	20	M	Laborer	31Ma07WI
ONEILL, Danl.	23	M	Laborer	31Ma07WI
DONALDSON, Thomas	20	M	Laborer	31Ma07WI
MCCORMICK, Michl.	30	M	Laborer	31Ma07WI
WHITE, Thomas	26	M	Laborer	31Ma07WI
James	24	M	Laborer	31Ma07WI
Ann	28	F	Spinster	31Ma07WI
Cathn.	50	F	Spinster	31Ma07WI
Marcy	19	F	Spinster	31Ma07WI
MCCORMICK, John	20	M	Laborer	31Ma07WI
Henry	20	M	Laborer	31Ma07WI
MCBLAIN, Eliza	21	F	Spinster	31Ma07WI
ONEVIE, Eliza	20	F	Spinster	31Ma07WI
MCCLELLAND, Jane	50	F	Spinster	31Ma07WI
Elanor	12	F	Spinster	31Ma07WI
James	09	M	Child	31Ma07WI
WOODS, Wm.	32	M	Spinner	31Ma07WI
STEWART, Jane	21	F	Spinner	31Ma07WI
WHITE, James	17	M	Spinner	31Ma07WI
James	18	M	Spinner	31Ma07WI
Danl.	46	M	Spinner	31Ma07WI
Patk.	09	M	Child	31Ma07WI
CRAG, James	30	M	Spinner	31Ma07WI
John	16	M	Spinner	31Ma07WI
LOUGHRAN, John	34	M	Spinner	31Ma07WI
MCQUEN, John	10	M	Spinner	31Ma07WI
Magt.	04	F	Child	31Ma07WI
Cath.M.	02	F	Child	31Ma07WI
Patk.	.00	M	Infant	31Ma07WI
TENAN, Michl.	60	M	Laborer	31Ma07WI
Michl.	24	M	Laborer	31Ma07WI
Mary	60	F	Laborer	31Ma07WI
Susan	20	F	Laborer	31Ma07WI
Mary	02	F	Child	31Ma07WI
CUNNINGHAM, Rose	30	F	Laborer	31Ma07WI
MCKAYE, John	27	M	Laborer	31Ma07WI
GRIFFIN, John	13	M	Laborer	31Ma07WI
Anthony	15	M	Laborer	31Ma07WI
Fitzpatk., Mary	30	F	Laborer	31Ma07WI
HANNAH, Wm.	32	M	Laborer	31Ma07WI
Jane	30	F	Laborer	31Ma07WI
Ann	60	F	Spinster	31Ma07WI
THOMPSON, Robt.	24	M	Spinner	31Ma07WI
HANNAH, Ann	09	F	Child	31Ma07WI
Annabella	07	F	Child	31Ma07WI
Mary	02	F	Child	31Ma07WI
Magt.	.00	F	Infant	31Ma07WI
GRIFFIN, James	28	M	Spinner	31Ma07WI
Peter	60	M	Spinner	31Ma07WI
Sarah	56	F	Spinner	31Ma07WI
Patk.	24	M	Spinner	31Ma07WI
Wm.	22	M	Spinner	31Ma07WI
Henry	18	M	Spinner	31Ma07WI
John	20	M	Spinner	31Ma07WI
MCMULLEN, Heyl.	23	M	Spinner	31Ma07WI
SIMPSON, James	07	M	Child	31Ma07WI
Mary	19	F	Spinster	31Ma07WI
MULLHOLLAND, Jas.	26	M	Spinner	31Ma07WI
MCELENAN, Mar.	25	F	Spinster	31Ma07WI
ARNOLD, Clarence	02	M	Child	31Ma07WI
John	.00	M	Infant	31Ma07WI
Eliza	50	F	Laborer	31Ma07WI
M.	05	M	Child	31Ma07WI
Alfee	03	M	Child	31Ma07WI
HUGHS, Peter	30	M	Laborer	31Ma07WI

ANN-MCLESTER 31 MAY 1848

From Londonderry

NAMES OF PASSENGERS	AGE	SEX	OCCUPATIONS	DATE PORT SHIP
KING, Joseph	35	M	Laborer	31Ma01Wh
MCBRIDE, James	21	M	Laborer	31Ma01Wh
HIGGINS, Mary	22	F	Spinster	31Ma01Wh
MCCAFFREY, James	24	M	Spinner	31Ma01Wh
JAMISON, John	26	M	Spinner	31Ma01Wh
GUINNESS, William	23	M	Spinner	31Ma01Wh
BRADLEY, Mary	25	F	Wife	31Ma01Wh
Michl.	18	M	Laborer	31Ma01Wh
MCGURK, Mattw.	20	M	Laborer	31Ma01Wh
MCCULLOUGH, Thomas	22	M	Laborer	31Ma01Wh
KELLY, James	23	M	Laborer	31Ma01Wh
KERR, John	21	M	Laborer	31Ma01Wh
ALLESON, Saml.	24	M	Laborer	31Ma01Wh
Jane (W)	24	F	Wife	31Ma01Wh
GRAHAM, Mary-J.	21	F	Unknown	31Ma01Wh
Alexr.	14	M	Unknown	31Ma01Wh
Matilda	13	F	Unknown	31Ma01Wh
BOWER, John	22	M	Unknown	31Ma01Wh
MCFADDEN, Geo.	12	M	Unknown	31Ma01Wh
BONNER, Wm.	11	M	Unknown	31Ma01Wh
MCFADDEN, John	40	M	Laborer	31Ma01Wh
BONER, James	20	M	Laborer	31Ma01Wh
MITCHELL, John	22	M	Laborer	31Ma01Wh
PERRY, John	25	M	Laborer	31Ma01Wh
STEVENSON, Margt.	24	F	Wife	31Ma01Wh
Elizth.B.	.00	F	Infant	31Ma01Wh
Born-At-Sea				
BLAKELY, Elizth.	23	F	Spinster	31Ma01Wh
LYNCH, Neal	38	M	Laborer	31Ma01Wh
Sally	37	F	Unknown	31Ma01Wh
Mary	14	F	Unknown	31Ma01Wh
Ellen	12	F	Unknown	31Ma01Wh
John	10	M	Unknown	31Ma01Wh
Andw.	05	M	Child	31Ma01Wh
Teresa	.00	F	Infant	31Ma01Wh
SWEENY, Wm.	29	M	Laborer	31Ma01Wh
CORRIGAN, Mary	24	F	Unknown	31Ma01Wh
Michl.	27	M	Unknown	31Ma01Wh
Judy	06	F	Child	31Ma01Wh
COX, Domnick	20	M	Laborer	31Ma01Wh
BLACK, James	22	M	Unknown	31Ma01Wh
CAWFIELD, Mary	18	F	Unknown	31Ma01Wh
BOWEN, Sarah	20	F	Wife	31Ma01Wh
CANNING, James	21	M	Laborer	31Ma01Wh
MCCRACKEN, Susan	21	F	Laborer	31Ma01Wh
THOMPSON, James	24	M	Laborer	31Ma01Wh
KENNEDY, Peggy	32	F	Wife	31Ma01Wh
Leteticia	12	F	Unknown	31Ma01Wh
Isabella	10	F	Unknown	31Ma01Wh
RODGERS, Ellen	50	F	Unknown	31Ma01Wh
GALLAGHER, Wm.	22	M	Laborer	31Ma01Wh
CONNOLLY, Mary	18	F	Spinster	31Ma01Wh
ROONEY, Mary	22	F	Unknown	31Ma01Wh
DUNLEAVEY, John	18	M	Laborer	31Ma01Wh
MCATAGGERT, Hugh	34	M	Laborer	31Ma01Wh
BRADY, Hugh	38	M	Laborer	31Ma01Wh
James	19	M	Laborer	31Ma01Wh
KELLIM, Mary	18	F	Laborer	31Ma01Wh
REILLY, Bernd.	16	M	Laborer	31Ma01Wh
CONAGHAN, John	30	M	Laborer	31Ma01Wh
Sally (W)	28	F	Wife	31Ma01Wh
MARTIN, Wm.B.	03	M	Child	31Ma01Wh
BINGHAM, Robt.	43	M	Laborer	31Ma01Wh
Rachael	40	F	Spinster	31Ma01Wh
Johnson	30	M	Spinner	31Ma01Wh

NAMES OF PASSENGERS	AGE	SEX	OCCUPATIONS	DATE PORT SHIP
BINGHAM, Margt.	21	F	Spinster	31Ma01Wh
MILEY, Moses	07	M	Child	31Ma01Wh
ODONNELL, Margery	20	F	Spinster	31Ma01Wh
BASSIN, Eliza	25	F	Unknown	31Ma01Wh
MILLS, Thomas	20	M	Laborer	31Ma01Wh
John	14	M	Laborer	31Ma01Wh
MITCHELL, Francis	21	M	Laborer	31Ma01Wh
SMITH, John	22	M	Laborer	31Ma01Wh
Ann	20	F	Laborer	31Ma01Wh
MCLOUGHLIN, John	35	M	Laborer	31Ma01Wh
DEVINE, Michl.	22	M	Laborer	31Ma01Wh
BURKE, John	20	M	Laborer	31Ma01Wh
HEFFERN, Wm.	18	M	Laborer	31Ma01Wh
BULLION, Nancy	28	F	Wife	31Ma01Wh
HENRY, Henry	29	M	Laborer	31Ma01Wh
Nancy	27	F	Laborer	31Ma01Wh
MCILWAINE, Ann	23	F	Laborer	31Ma01Wh
MOORE, Saml.	24	M	Laborer	31Ma01Wh
Susan	21	F	Laborer	31Ma01Wh
William	18	M	Laborer	31Ma01Wh
Margt.	16	F	Spinster	31Ma01Wh
Margt.	17	F	Spinster	31Ma01Wh
HILLIARD, William	24	M	Laborer	31Ma01Wh
HARKIN, Michl.	23	M	Laborer	31Ma01Wh
MCCUE, Denis	19	M	Laborer	31Ma01Wh
GALLAGHER, Brian	24	M	Laborer	31Ma01Wh
BOYLE, Mary	19	F	Spinster	31Ma01Wh
MCGURN, Susan	20	F	Unknown	31Ma01Wh
CONAGHAN, Pat	22	M	Laborer	31Ma01Wh
GEATON, John	18	M	Laborer	31Ma01Wh
HANLIN, Philip	27	M	Laborer	31Ma01Wh
MCGINLEY, Pat	19	M	Laborer	31Ma01Wh
GALLAGHER, Pat	22	M	Laborer	31Ma01Wh
ODONNELL, Rose	19	F	Spinster	31Ma01Wh
Denis	22	M	Laborer	31Ma01Wh
Mary (W)	20	F	Wife	31Ma01Wh
MCCLOSKEY, Mary	20	F	Unknown	31Ma01Wh
MCFADDEN, John	21	M	Laborer	31Ma01Wh
MILLER, John	18	M	Laborer	31Ma01Wh
MCGINLEY, Unity	19	M	Laborer	31Ma01Wh
FORBIS, Saml.	29	M	Laborer	31Ma01Wh
HENRY, Chas.	21	M	Laborer	31Ma01Wh
Cathe.	20	F	Spinster	31Ma01Wh
MCFADDEN, Michl.	22	M	Laborer	31Ma01Wh
MCCLOSKEY, Ann	23	F	Laborer	31Ma01Wh
MULLEN, Maria	20	F	Spinster	31Ma01Wh
Arthur	19	M	Laborer	31Ma01Wh
DOHERTY, John	18	M	Laborer	31Ma01Wh
LYNCH, Danl.	24	M	Laborer	31Ma01Wh
WOODS, John	28	M	Laborer	31Ma01Wh
FRANE, Wm.	21	M	Laborer	31Ma01Wh
IRWIN, Jane	20	F	Wife	31Ma01Wh
KANE, Susana	19	F	Unknown	31Ma01Wh
MCLOUGHLIN, Edwd.	24	M	Laborer	31Ma01Wh
MILLAN, Eliza-Jane	20	F	Laborer	31Ma01Wh
ODONNELL, John	19	M	Laborer	31Ma01Wh
STEWART, Joseph	23	M	Laborer	31Ma01Wh
MCLOUGHLIN, Mary	19	F	Spinster	31Ma01Wh
Biddy	14	F	Unknown	31Ma01Wh
SWEENY, Hugh	24	M	Laborer	31Ma01Wh
KENNEDY, Murdoch	19	M	Laborer	31Ma01Wh
ARMSTRONG, John	20	M	Laborer	31Ma01Wh
DOAK, Wm.	25	M	Laborer	31Ma01Wh
PATTON, Cathr.	19	F	Spinster	31Ma01Wh
James	15	M	Spinner	31Ma01Wh
MCLOUGHLIN, John	22	M	Spinner	31Ma01Wh
PERRY, Saml.	40	M	Spinner	31Ma01Wh
Rebecca	39	F	Spinner	31Ma01Wh
ALEXANDER, James	20	M	Spinner	31Ma01Wh
PERRY, John	10	M	Spinner	31Ma01Wh
MAGILL, Chas.	29	M	Laborer	31Ma01Wh
MANEYERS, Wm.	19	M	Laborer	31Ma01Wh
Thomas	23	M	Laborer	31Ma01Wh
David	26	M	Laborer	31Ma01Wh
MORRIS, Charles	20	M	Laborer	31Ma01Wh
BOYLE, Conl.	18	M	Laborer	31Ma01Wh
MOORE, Jane	20	F	Spinster	31Ma01Wh
GILLRAITH, Wm.	23	M	Farmer	31Ma01Wh
HARLEY, James	19	M	Farmer	31Ma01Wh
MCGRANNELL, John	22	M	Farmer	31Ma01Wh
WARD, Mary	19	F	Wife	31Ma01Wh
CARR, James	20	M	Laborer	31Ma01Wh
Sally	18	F	Spinster	31Ma01Wh
BINGHAM, Robert	02	M	Child	31Ma01Wh
WARD, John	19	M	Laborer	31Ma01Wh
MCGURKE, Ann	23	F	Wife	31Ma01Wh

ALPINE 31 MAY 1848

From Belfast

NAMES OF PASSENGERS	AGE	SEX	OCCUPATIONS	DATE PORT SHIP
RITCHIE, William	20	M	Laborer	31Ma07Wi
KENNEY, Michl.	50	M	Laborer	31Ma07Wi
Ellen	50	F	None	31Ma07Wi
Patrick	20	M	Laborer	31Ma07Wi
Isabella	18	F	None	31Ma07Wi
Michl.	13	M	None	31Ma07Wi
James	11	M	None	31Ma07Wi
THOMPSON, Wm.	32	M	Laborer	31Ma07Wi
MCGRAW, James	25	M	Laborer	31Ma07Wi
Sarah	20	F	None	31Ma07Wi
HUGHES, Joseph	21	M	None	31Ma07Wi
MCCORD, Wm.	35	M	Farmer	31Ma07Wi
Eliza	35	F	None	31Ma07Wi
Wm.John	02	M	Child	31Ma07Wi
MCAVOY, Thomas	21	M	Laborer	31Ma07Wi
DOUGAL, John	20	M	Laborer	31Ma07Wi
ANDERSON, Wm.	31	M	Laborer	31Ma07Wi
HILL, Mary	20	F	None	31Ma07Wi
Edwd. Died-At-Sea	.00	M	Infant	31Ma07Wi
LIVINGSTON, Robt.	24	M	Laborer	31Ma07Wi
Elizth.	20	F	Spinster	31Ma07Wi
BEASSY, Ann	19	F	Spinster	31Ma07Wi
TOWNSEND, Robert	24	M	Laborer	31Ma07Wi
Mary (W)	20	F	Wife	31Ma07Wi
MARTIN, Wm.	25	M	Laborer	31Ma07Wi
M.A.	20	F	Spinster	31Ma07Wi
Elizth.	17	F	Spinster	31Ma07Wi
DUNLOP, Ann	48	F	Wi	31Ma07Wi
John	13	M	Unknown	31Ma07Wi
Wm.	10	M	Unknown	31Ma07Wi
Charles	07	M	Child	31Ma07Wi
REID, Robert	20	M	Unknown	31Ma07Wi
ATKINSON, Joseph	23	M	Laborer	31Ma07Wi
Eliza	21	F	Laborer	31Ma07Wi
BURNS, Mary	18	F	Wife	31Ma07Wi
MCNICOL, Daniel	18	M	Laborer	31Ma07Wi
DOUGLAS, James	20	M	Laborer	31Ma07Wi
BURBAGH, Peter	24	M	Laborer	31Ma07Wi
MCGOUGH, Patk.	46	M	Laborer	31Ma07Wi
Mary	46	F	Laborer	31Ma07Wi
John	23	M	Laborer	31Ma07Wi
Morgon	12	M	Laborer	31Ma07Wi
Margt.	06	F	Child	31Ma07Wi
NUGENT, Mary	23	F	Child	31Ma07Wi
BROWN, James	35	M	Spinster	31Ma07Wi
KENNEDY, Samuel	22	M	Laborer	31Ma07Wi
WOODS, Rose	35	F	Wi	31Ma07Wi
Stewart	13	M	None	31Ma07Wi
ACHESON, John	20	M	Laborer	31Ma07Wi
LITTLE, Geo.	30	M	Laborer	31Ma07Wi
Robt.	30	M	Laborer	31Ma07Wi
Joseph	28	M	Laborer	31Ma07Wi

NAMES OF PASSENGERS		AGE	SEX	OCCUPATIONS	DATE PORT SHIP
GLASS, Elizth.		21	F	None	31Ma07Wi
REDFERS, Elizth.		20	F	None	31Ma07Wi
SINCLAIR, Saml.		17	M	Laborer	31Ma07Wi
MORROWS, Ellen		40	F	Wi	31Ma07Wi
Sarah		18	F	Spinster	31Ma07Wi
James		04	M	Child	31Ma07Wi
MCALIFFE, John		28	M	Laborer	31Ma07Wi
REDFORM, Geo.		26	M	Laborer	31Ma07Wi
Mary	(W)	18	F	Wife	31Ma07Wi
GIBSON, Wm.John		09	M	Child	31Ma07Wi
DENNISON, Joseph		50	M	Farmer	31Ma07Wi
Margt.	(W)	47	F	Wife	31Ma07Wi
Isabella	(D)	08	F	Child	31Ma07Wi
Margt.	(D)	02	F	Child	31Ma07Wi
MATCHER, Thomas		22	M	Laborer	31Ma07Wi
Samuel		28	M	Laborer	31Ma07Wi
MILLER, James Died-At-Sea		45	M	Farmer	31Ma07Wi
Jane	(W)	40	F	Wife	31Ma07Wi
Saml.		20	M	Laborer	31Ma07Wi
Sarah-Ann		18	F	Spinster	31Ma07Wi
Robt.		10	M	Laborer	31Ma07Wi
CLARK, Joseph		45	M	Farmer	31Ma07Wi
Ann	(W)	40	F	Wife	31Ma07Wi
Robert		20	M	Laborer	31Ma07Wi
Thomas		17	M	Laborer	31Ma07Wi
Sarah		17	F	Spinster	31Ma07Wi
Ann		13	F	Spinster	31Ma07Wi
CONNA, Ellen		18	F	Spinster	31Ma07Wi
BOOTH, Geo.		16	M	Laborer	31Ma07Wi
Mi.		17	F	Servant	31Ma07Wi
LILLY, A.		20	F	Servant	31Ma07Wi
MCCLEANN, James		18	M	Laborer	31Ma07Wi
MURRAY, Hugh		40	M	Laborer	31Ma07Wi
Eliza	(W)	42	F	Wife	31Ma07Wi
Hugh		18	M	Laborer	31Ma07Wi
BRISON, Robert		30	M	Laborer	31Ma07Wi
WEIR, Wm.		28	M	Laborer	31Ma07Wi
MCANNICK, Oliver		55	M	Laborer	31Ma07Wi
Jane	(W)	54	F	Wife	31Ma07Wi
Letty		27	F	None	31Ma07Wi
Wm.		25	M	Laborer	31Ma07Wi
Arthur		22	M	Laborer	31Ma07Wi
James		20	M	Laborer	31Ma07Wi
ORR, James		10	M	Laborer	31Ma07Wi
SHAW, James		29	M	Laborer	31Ma07Wi
GILMORE, Robt.		23	M	Laborer	31Ma07Wi
MCCAUSEY, Robt.		35	M	Laborer	31Ma07Wi
FATE, Wm.		35	M	Laborer	31Ma07Wi
HOLMES, Vance		21	M	Laborer	31Ma07Wi
MURPHY, Patk.		25	M	Laborer	31Ma07Wi
Henry		22	M	Laborer	31Ma07Wi
KERR, James		25	M	Laborer	31Ma07Wi
STEWART, Francis		25	M	Laborer	31Ma07Wi
GRAHAM, Saml.		17	M	Laborer	31Ma07Wi
WALLACE, James		16	M	Laborer	31Ma07Wi
POLL, Mary		22	F	Spinster	31Ma07Wi
COTTIER, Wm.		20	M	Laborer	31Ma07Wi
MORRISON, Ann		18	F	Spinster	31Ma07Wi
MCARONA, Alex		27	M	Laborer	31Ma07Wi
CORD, Wm.		20	M	Laborer	31Ma07Wi
James		18	M	Laborer	31Ma07Wi
Kirkpatk., James		20	M	Laborer	31Ma07Wi
MULHOLLAND, James		28	M	Laborer	31Ma07Wi
John		40	M	Laborer	31Ma07Wi
SMITH, Thomas		28	M	Laborer	31Ma07Wi
Mary	(W)	26	F	Wife	31Ma07Wi
DEVIN, Isabella		17	F	None	31Ma07Wi
Wm.		15	M	Laborer	31Ma07Wi
MURRAY, John		15	M	Laborer	31Ma07Wi
Patk.		05	M	Child	31Ma07Wi
Daniel		06	M	Child	31Ma07Wi
James		02	M	Child	31Ma07Wi
SLOAN, Moses		20	M	Laborer	31Ma07Wi
YATES, Thomas		20	M	Laborer	31Ma07Wi
COATES, John		25	M	Laborer	31Ma07Wi
DIXON, Henry		30	M	Laborer	31Ma07Wi
Martha	(W)	30	F	Wife	31Ma07Wi
RITCHIE, Geo.		40	M	Farmer	31Ma07Wi
Mary	(W)	38	F	Wife	31Ma07Wi
Mary	(D)	13	F	Unknown	31Ma07Wi
Geo.	(S)	13	M	Unknown	31Ma07Wi
Mary-Ann	(D)	09	F	Child	31Ma07Wi
Nancy	(D)	05	F	Child	31Ma07Wi
James	(S)	04	M	Child	31Ma07Wi
Jane	(D)	02	F	Child	31Ma07Wi
BEATTY, Eliza		30	F	Wi	31Ma07Wi
Robt.		02	M	Child	31Ma07Wi
TAGGART, Margt.		28	F	Spinster	31Ma07Wi
SENDER, Mary-Ann		40	F	Wi	31Ma07Wi
David		20	M	Laborer	31Ma07Wi
Alice		18	F	Spinster	31Ma07Wi
Jane		15	F	Spinster	31Ma07Wi
Edmund		11	M	Unknown	31Ma07Wi
Joseph		09	M	Child	31Ma07Wi
Robt.		03	M	Child	31Ma07Wi
Nancy		05	F	Child	31Ma07Wi
MCGEE, James		21	M	Laborer	31Ma07Wi

DEVON 31 MAY 1848

From Liverpool

NAMES OF PASSENGERS		AGE	SEX	OCCUPATIONS	DATE PORT SHIP
DOWNEY, Mary-Ann		25	F	Laborer	31Ma02Wj
George		22	M	Laborer	31Ma02Wj
John		22	M	Laborer	31Ma02Wj
CEANE, Ceasar		33	M	Laborer	31Ma02Wj
Ann	(W)	21	F	Wife	31Ma02Wj
COWAN, Margt.		21	F	Unknown	31Ma02Wj
Jane		19	F	Unknown	31Ma02Wj
BOBS, Francis		20	M	Laborer	31Ma02Wj
DOCKEY, Thos.		17	M	Laborer	31Ma02Wj
SAVAGE, Pat		18	M	Laborer	31Ma02Wj
FAHAY, Martin		19	M	Laborer	31Ma02Wj
MANN, Margt.		18	F	Spinster	31Ma02Wj
BRENNAN, Sarah		20	F	Spinster	31Ma02Wj
Bridgt.		22	F	Unknown	31Ma02Wj
ROBY, James		22	M	Laborer	31Ma02Wj
Margt.		25	F	Spinster	31Ma02Wj
Margt.		.00	F	Infant	31Ma02Wj
LINDSEY, Mary		25	F	Unknown	31Ma02Wj
CANLEY, Farrell		26	M	Laborer	31Ma02Wj
U	(W)	22	F	Spinster	31Ma02Wj
Mary	(D)	03	F	Child	31Ma02Wj
Ann	(D)	02	F	Child	31Ma02Wj
Margt.	(D)	.00	F	Infant	31Ma02Wj
HAYES, James		30	M	Laborer	31Ma02Wj
Ellen	(W)	30	F	Wife	31Ma02Wj
Bridgt.		22	F	Unknown	31Ma02Wj
Nicholas		.00	M	Infant	31Ma02Wj
DEVINE, Martin		35	M	Laborer	31Ma02Wj
Margt.	(W)	35	F	Wife	31Ma02Wj
Luke	(S)	11	M	Unknown	31Ma02Wj
Michael	(S)	10	M	Unknown	31Ma02Wj
Maria	(D)	08	F	Child	31Ma02Wj
Pat	(S)	06	M	Child	31Ma02Wj
Elizth.	(D)	.00	F	Infant	31Ma02Wj
NEILL, Pat		25	M	Unknown	31Ma02Wj
Eliza		25	F	Unknown	31Ma02Wj
Pat		06	M	Child	31Ma02Wj
DEVINE, John		04	M	Child	31Ma02Wj
Ellen		.00	F	Infant	31Ma02Wj
FINNEGAN, Charles		28	M	Laborer	31Ma02Wj
James		40	M	Unknown	31Ma02Wj

NAMES OF PASSENGERS		AGE	SEX	OCCUPATIONS	DATE PORT SHIP
FINNEGAN, U	(W)	30	F	Wife	31Ma02Wj
Ann	(D)	10	F	Unknown	31Ma02Wj
Cathe.	(D)	08	F	Child	31Ma02Wj
Biddy	(D)	06	F	Child	31Ma02Wj
Hugh	(S)	04	M	Child	31Ma02Wj
Margt.		.00	F	Infant	31Ma02Wj
BYRNE, Pat		12	M	Unknown	31Ma02Wj
HILL, Owen		30	M	Farmer	31Ma02Wj
DUNIGAN, John		32	M	Farmer	31Ma02Wj
BYRNE, Bridgt.		25	F	Farmer	31Ma02Wj
HENNESSY, Michl.		18	M	Farmer	31Ma02Wj
U	(W)	17	F	Wife	31Ma02Wj
Owen	(S)	13	M	Unknown	31Ma02Wj
Pat	(S)	12	M	Unknown	31Ma02Wj
HARRISON, John		37	M	Laborer	31Ma02Wj
BLAKE, Thos.		40	M	Laborer	31Ma02Wj
FLYNN, Wm.		11	M	Laborer	31Ma02Wj
CARROLL, Mary		35	F	Laborer	31Ma02Wj
ROGERS, Mary		20	F	Laborer	31Ma02Wj
LOUCKLIN, Andw.		20	M	Unknown	31Ma02Wj
Ellen	(W)	21	F	Wife	31Ma02Wj
HINCHCLIFFE, Josh.		21	M	Laborer	31Ma02Wj
MCIROINE, Pat		28	M	Laborer	31Ma02Wj
CORCRAN, John		24	M	Laborer	31Ma02Wj
DONOLANS, Thos.		50	M	Laborer	31Ma02Wj
BYRNE, Pat		20	M	Laborer	31Ma02Wj
WALLACE, Malry		20	F	Laborer	31Ma02Wj
DICKS, Thomas		30	M	Unknown	31Ma02Wj
Susan		30	F	Unknown	31Ma02Wj
Ellen		.00	F	Infant	31Ma02Wj
ONEILL, Neal		22	M	Laborer	31Ma02Wj
Mary		21	F	Laborer	31Ma02Wj
Cathr.		20	F	Laborer	31Ma02Wj
MCBRIDE, Bridgt.		28	F	Laborer	31Ma02Wj
Nancy		20	F	Laborer	31Ma02Wj
MCINTIRE, Cathr.		15	F	Laborer	31Ma02Wj
Patt		12	M	Unknown	31Ma02Wj
RYAN, John		40	M	Laborer	31Ma02Wj
Margt.		11	F	Unknown	31Ma02Wj
DUFFY, Andw.		20	M	Farmer	31Ma02Wj
NEWMAN, Bryan		20	M	Farmer	31Ma02Wj
RYAN, U-Mrs.		35	F	Farmer	31Ma02Wj
James		.00	M	Infant	31Ma02Wj
BURKE, Law.		24	M	Laborer	31Ma02Wj
Thomas		24	M	Laborer	31Ma02Wj
WOODLOCK, Danl.		24	M	Laborer	31Ma02Wj
MCCAWE, Francis		24	M	Laborer	31Ma02Wj
DENING, John		26	M	Laborer	31Ma02Wj
DUFFEY, Stephen		30	M	Laborer	31Ma02Wj
BOYD, Pat		23	M	Laborer	31Ma02Wj
MOONEY, Chas.		20	M	Laborer	31Ma02Wj
John		21	M	Laborer	31Ma02Wj
YOUNG, Henry		23	M	Laborer	31Ma02Wj
Martha	(W)	26	F	Wife	31Ma02Wj
MAYNOY, Patt		20	M	Farmer	31Ma02Wj
GROVER, Geol.		40	M	Farmer	31Ma02Wj
Ann		40	F	Farmer	31Ma02Wj
SMITH, Andw.		40	M	Farmer	31Ma02Wj
WHITE, Mary		16	F	Farmer	31Ma02Wj
Pat		13	M	Farmer	31Ma02Wj
SHALL, Michl.		26	M	Farmer	31Ma02Wj
RICE, Jane		21	F	Farmer	31Ma02Wj
LLOYD, John		26	M	Farmer	31Ma02Wj
Mary	(W)	26	F	Wife	31Ma02Wj
CADDEN, Pat		21	M	Laborer	31Ma02Wj
Susan	(W)	21	F	Wife	31Ma02Wj
JONES, Richd.		24	M	Laborer	31Ma02Wj
FOX, John		24	M	Laborer	31Ma02Wj
MUCHARKY, Margt.		26	F	Laborer	31Ma02Wj
LOOBY, John		27	M	Laborer	31Ma02Wj
KEEFFE, John		27	M	Laborer	31Ma02Wj
LOOBY, John		50	M	Laborer	31Ma02Wj
Ellen		23	F	Laborer	31Ma02Wj
Bridgt.		19	F	Laborer	31Ma02Wj
LUCAS, Morris		28	M	Laborer	31Ma02Wj
MEEHAN, Morris		27	M	Laborer	31Ma02Wj
U	(W)	25	F	Wife	31Ma02Wj
HUGGAN, Thos.		25	M	Laborer	31Ma02Wj
Mary		23	F	Laborer	31Ma02Wj
Matitias		08	M	Child	31Ma02Wj
LOOBY, Michl.		30	M	Laborer	31Ma02Wj
Mary		30	F	Laborer	31Ma02Wj
John		.00	M	Infant	31Ma02Wj
ROACH, David		26	M	Laborer	31Ma02Wj
ANDREWS, Pat		26	M	Laborer	31Ma02Wj
Danl.		12	M	Unknown	31Ma02Wj
Johans		20	F	Spinster	31Ma02Wj
MULHOLLAND, Pat		50	M	Farmer	31Ma02Wj
U	(W)	40	F	Farmer	31Ma02Wj
Hugh		20	M	Farmer	31Ma02Wj
Cath.		17	F	Spinster	31Ma02Wj
Anabella		13	F	Spinster	31Ma02Wj
Margt.		11	F	Spinster	31Ma02Wj
John		09	M	Child	31Ma02Wj
HAMMILL, Hugh		18	M	Laborer	31Ma02Wj
MCGILL, Rose		28	F	Laborer	31Ma02Wj
HANNAH, Wm.		25	M	Laborer	31Ma02Wj
HANNAHAN, Peter		16	M	Laborer	31Ma02Wj
MORAN, Richd.		13	M	Laborer	31Ma02Wj
SPLANE, Julia		40	F	Laborer	31Ma02Wj
REILLY, Edwd.		21	M	Laborer	31Ma02Wj
Charles		20	M	Laborer	31Ma02Wj
Phil		19	M	Laborer	31Ma02Wj
NULTY, Mary		18	F	Spinster	31Ma02Wj
Eliza		24	F	None	31Ma02Wj
JACKSON, Christe.		50	M	Farmer	31Ma02Wj
MORGAN, Mary		28	F	Farmer	31Ma02Wj
Alice		25	F	Farmer	31Ma02Wj
DEVON, Judy		13	F	Farmer	31Ma02Wj
John		18	M	Farmer	31Ma02Wj
Mary		16	F	Farmer	31Ma02Wj
Jane		30	F	Farmer	31Ma02Wj
SHERAN, Mary		20	F	Farmer	31Ma02Wj
LANGAN, Mary		21	F	Farmer	31Ma02Wj
CARROLL, Geol.		30	F	Farmer	31Ma02Wj
MCGRADY, Mary		00	F	Unknown	31Ma02Wj
Arthur		21	M	Laborer	31Ma02Wj
FINEGAN, Thos.		00	M	Unknown	31Ma02Wj
HODSON, William		.00	M	Infant	31Ma02Wj
MCCANN, Sarah		30	F	Wife	31Ma02Wj
SMITH, Owen		24	M	Farmer	31Ma02Wj
ODONNELL, D.		35	M	Farmer	31Ma02Wj
WILLIAMS, Michl.		35	M	Farmer	31Ma02Wj
DUFFEY, Geol.		18	M	Farmer	31Ma02Wj
POWELL, John		20	M	Farmer	31Ma02Wj
CAVANAGH, Dennis		13	M	Farmer	31Ma02Wj
GINNOTT, Danl.		20	M	Farmer	31Ma02Wj
Mary	(W)	21	F	Wife	31Ma02Wj
Andy		20	M	Laborer	31Ma02Wj
CLARKE, John		21	M	Laborer	31Ma02Wj
CUNNINGHAM, Peter		20	M	Laborer	31Ma02Wj
Ann		13	F	Laborer	31Ma02Wj
LYNCH, Michl.		26	M	Laborer	31Ma02Wj
KENNAY, Edwd.		18	M	Laborer	31Ma02Wj
GOLDEN, Pat		40	M	Laborer	31Ma02Wj
Ann		35	F	Laborer	31Ma02Wj
Judith		14	F	Laborer	31Ma02Wj
CONNELL, Wm.		20	M	Laborer	31Ma02Wj
James		20	M	Laborer	31Ma02Wj
U-Mrs.		20	F	Laborer	31Ma02Wj
Wm.		06	M	Child	31Ma02Wj
Christ.		04	M	Child	31Ma02Wj
RATECLIFFE, John		24	M	Laborer	31Ma02Wj
CONNELL, John		20	M	Laborer	31Ma02Wj
NEILL, William		20	M	Laborer	31Ma02Wj
QUNE, Francis		20	M	Laborer	31Ma02Wj
DERMODDY, Thomas		20	M	Laborer	31Ma02Wj
U	(W)	20	F	Wife	31Ma02Wj
John	(S)	.00	M	Infant	31Ma02Wj
CHRISTIAN, John		20	M	Laborer	31Ma02Wj

NAMES OF PASSENGERS	AGE	SEX	OCCUPATIONS	DATE PORT SHIP
LEGG, Thos.	21	M	Laborer	31Ma02Wj
John	19	M	Laborer	31Ma02Wj
DOWNEY, Robt.	27	M	Laborer	31Ma02Wj
HODSON, Ann	27	F	Wife	31Ma02Wj
U, U	.00	U	Infant	31Ma02Wj
Born-At-Sea				
U	.00	U	Infant	31Ma02Wj
Born-At-Sea				
U	.00	U	Infant	31Ma02Wj
Born-At-Sea				
U	.00	U	Infant	31Ma02Wj
Born-At-Sea				
NEILL, U	26	M	Unknown	31Ma02Wj
HUGH, U	26	M	Unknown	31Ma02Wj
CAMPBELL, U	26	M	Unknown	31Ma02Wj
TAYLOR, U	26	M	Unknown	31Ma02Wj

AGNES 31 MAY 1848

From Dublin

NAMES OF PASSENGERS		AGE	SEX	OCCUPATIONS	DATE PORT SHIP
BENTON, George		20	M	Farmer	31Ma20Lx
MURPHY, John		22	M	Farmer	31Ma20Lx
U	(W)	20	F	Farmer	31Ma20Lx
MOREWOOD, Samuel		26	M	Farmer	31Ma20Lx
FANNIN, Charles		26	M	Farmer	31Ma20Lx
DOYLE, Pat		20	M	Farmer	31Ma20Lx
RYAN, Mary		20	F	Farmer	31Ma20Lx
WARD, G.		24	M	Farmer	31Ma20Lx
U	(W)	20	F	Farmer	31Ma20Lx
Harriet	(D)	.00	F	Infant	31Ma20Lx
DUNGAN, P.		27	M	Farmer	31Ma20Lx
U	(W)	24	F	Farmer	31Ma20Lx
MOONEY, Michael		24	M	Farmer	31Ma20Lx
CLAN, James		27	M	Farmer	31Ma20Lx
TUTLY, Wm.		27	M	Farmer	31Ma20Lx
James		11	M	Farmer	31Ma20Lx
CURRY, James		24	M	Farmer	31Ma20Lx
MAHON, Denis		24	M	Farmer	31Ma20Lx
DUNN, Mary		19	F	Farmer	31Ma20Lx
BARRON, James		50	M	Farmer	31Ma20Lx
U	(W)	48	F	Farmer	31Ma20Lx
Mary	(D)	27	F	Farmer	31Ma20Lx
Ann	(D)	25	F	Farmer	31Ma20Lx
Sarah	(D)	23	F	Farmer	31Ma20Lx
James	(S)	19	M	Farmer	31Ma20Lx
Robt.	(S)	18	M	Farmer	31Ma20Lx
MORRISON, Hannah		11	F	Farmer	31Ma20Lx
KINLY, John		25	M	Farmer	31Ma20Lx
GARDINER, Anty.		20	F	Farmer	31Ma20Lx
RIPPERAN, James		23	M	Farmer	31Ma20Lx
SHAUGHNESSY, Lawrence		21	M	Farmer	31Ma20Lx
WEIR, John		22	M	Farmer	31Ma20Lx
LODEN, Mary-J.		20	F	Farmer	31Ma20Lx
MANGAN, Thomas		20	M	Farmer	31Ma20Lx
RENNETT, Thomas		20	M	Farmer	31Ma20Lx
GILLICK, Pat		20	M	Farmer	31Ma20Lx
Bridgt.		14	F	Farmer	31Ma20Lx
NEIL, Edward		12	M	Farmer	31Ma20Lx
Ann		34	F	Farmer	31Ma20Lx
Edward		28	M	Farmer	31Ma20Lx
Bridgit		.00	F	Infant	31Ma20Lx
LEONARD, Paul		24	M	Farmer	31Ma20Lx
Eliza		22	F	Farmer	31Ma20Lx
Ann		.00	F	Infant	31Ma20Lx
MULLIGAN, John		21	M	Farmer	31Ma20Lx
CORLEY, Michael		20	M	Farmer	31Ma20Lx
POWELL, Wm.		25	M	Farmer	31Ma20Lx
U	(W)	20	F	Farmer	31Ma20Lx
EAGAN, Wm.		24	M	Farmer	31Ma20Lx
DORAN, Richard		24	M	Farmer	31Ma20Lx
Maria		20	F	Farmer	31Ma20Lx
MATHEWS, Richd.		22	M	Farmer	31Ma20Lx
HORAN, U		25	M	Farmer	31Ma20Lx
ROONEY, John		22	M	Farmer	31Ma20Lx
OBRIEN, John		22	M	Farmer	31Ma20Lx
SMITH, Rose		20	F	Farmer	31Ma20Lx
Betty		30	F	Farmer	31Ma20Lx
MAHON, James		40	M	Farmer	31Ma20Lx
Margt.		12	F	Farmer	31Ma20Lx
Dora		11	F	Farmer	31Ma20Lx
Eliza		09	F	Child	31Ma20Lx
Mary		07	F	Child	31Ma20Lx
Margt.		05	F	Child	31Ma20Lx
Teresa		02	F	Child	31Ma20Lx
Thomas		.00	M	Infant	31Ma20Lx
MORAN, Edward		30	M	Farmer	31Ma20Lx
Pat		06	M	Child	31Ma20Lx
Cath.		04	F	Child	31Ma20Lx
FLYNN, Tim		50	M	Farmer	31Ma20Lx
Mary		45	F	Farmer	31Ma20Lx
Thomas		16	M	Farmer	31Ma20Lx
Tim		12	M	Farmer	31Ma20Lx
Cath.		07	F	Child	31Ma20Lx
May		.00	F	Infant	31Ma20Lx
RYAN, Danl.		32	M	Farmer	31Ma20Lx
Ellen		31	F	Farmer	31Ma20Lx
Mary		09	F	Child	31Ma20Lx
Lawrence		07	M	Child	31Ma20Lx
KEARNS, Cath.		21	F	Farmer	31Ma20Lx
MAHONY, John		40	M	Farmer	31Ma20Lx
Thomas		20	M	Farmer	31Ma20Lx
Mary		19	F	Farmer	31Ma20Lx
Ellen		18	F	Farmer	31Ma20Lx
Cath.		15	F	Farmer	31Ma20Lx
Margt.		13	F	Farmer	31Ma20Lx
Johanna		.00	F	Infant	31Ma20Lx
BOTTS, David		25	M	Farmer	31Ma20Lx
Margt.		21	F	Farmer	31Ma20Lx
Andrew		06	M	Child	31Ma20Lx
DONNELLY, John		25	M	Farmer	31Ma20Lx
CONNELLY, Wm.		20	M	Farmer	31Ma20Lx
BAVENS, Thomas		20	M	Farmer	31Ma20Lx
DOWD, Richard		20	M	Farmer	31Ma20Lx
HOOLAHANN, Pat		24	M	Farmer	31Ma20Lx
FITZGERALD, Bridget.		20	F	Farmer	31Ma20Lx
DELANY, Margt.		57	F	Farmer	31Ma20Lx
CARTHCAT, Michael		53	M	Farmer	31Ma20Lx
Ellen		32	F	Farmer	31Ma20Lx
Mary		04	F	Child	31Ma20Lx
Joseph		03	M	Child	31Ma20Lx
Ann		02	F	Child	31Ma20Lx
Ellen		.00	F	Infant	31Ma20Lx
WHITE, Mary-A.		20	F	Farmer	31Ma20Lx
CARTHCAT, Hamilton		57	M	Farmer	31Ma20Lx
Wm.		20	M	Farmer	31Ma20Lx
DUNNE, Robt.		20	M	Farmer	31Ma20Lx
BRADY, James		20	M	Farmer	31Ma20Lx
KENNY, Mary		20	F	Farmer	31Ma20Lx
FRANEER, Mary		20	F	Farmer	31Ma20Lx
CLYNE, Frank		27	M	Farmer	31Ma20Lx
Micl.		25	M	Farmer	31Ma20Lx
Mary-Ann		23	M	Farmer	31Ma20Lx
Eliza		20	F	Farmer	31Ma20Lx
MORAN, Cath.		20	F	Farmer	31Ma20Lx
DUNN, Pat		35	M	Farmer	31Ma20Lx
U	(W)	30	F	Farmer	31Ma20Lx
James	(S)	05	M	Child	31Ma20Lx
Biddy	(D)	03	F	Child	31Ma20Lx
Phelix	(S)	.00	M	Infant	31Ma20Lx
CAROLL, Matty		20	M	Farmer	31Ma20Lx
BROWN, Henry		25	M	Farmer	31Ma20Lx
U	(W)	20	F	Farmer	31Ma20Lx
CRONIN, Ann		20	F	Farmer	31Ma20Lx

NAMES OF PASSENGERS		AGE	SEX	OCCUPATIONS	DATE PORT SHIP
CAROLL, Matty		20	M	Farmer	31Ma20Lx
BROWN, Henry		25	M	Farmer	31Ma20Lx
U	(W)	20	F	Farmer	31Ma20Lx
CRONIN, Ann		20	F	Farmer	31Ma20Lx
BURNETT, U		45	M	Farmer	31Ma20Lx
WALSH, Thomas		10	M	Farmer	31Ma20Lx
Walter		08	M	Child	31Ma20Lx
Mary		.00	F	Infant	31Ma20Lx
KING, Mathew		30	M	Farmer	31Ma20Lx
Pat		28	M	Farmer	31Ma20Lx
Mary		55	F	Farmer	31Ma20Lx
Mary		09	F	Child	31Ma20Lx
SULLIVAN, U		30	F	Farmer	31Ma20Lx
RYAN, James		30	M	Farmer	31Ma20Lx
SMITH, Thomas		36	M	Farmer	31Ma20Lx
Ann		36	F	Farmer	31Ma20Lx
James		18	M	Farmer	31Ma20Lx
William		16	M	Farmer	31Ma20Lx
Patrick		14	M	Farmer	31Ma20Lx
Bridget		12	F	Farmer	31Ma20Lx
Ann		10	F	Farmer	31Ma20Lx
Thomas		03	M	Child	31Ma20Lx
MULREADY, Kate		40	F	Farmer	31Ma20Lx
PURCELL, James		24	M	Farmer	31Ma20Lx
FERGAN, Wm.		24	M	Farmer	31Ma20Lx
BENRARD, Thomas		50	M	Farmer	31Ma20Lx
U	(W)	17	F	Farmer	31Ma20Lx
Nora		09	F	Child	31Ma20Lx
Cath.		04	F	Child	31Ma20Lx
Michal		.00	M	Infant	31Ma20Lx
ARCHER, Wm.		24	M	Farmer	31Ma20Lx
BONARD, John		30	M	Farmer	31Ma20Lx
Eliza		26	F	Farmer	31Ma20Lx
BURELL, Ann		21	F	Farmer	31Ma20Lx
Mary		20	F	Farmer	31Ma20Lx
FITZGILL, David		30	M	Farmer	31Ma20Lx
Mary		30	F	Farmer	31Ma20Lx
Danl.		06	M	Child	31Ma20Lx
Mary		03	F	Child	31Ma20Lx
FLINN, Thomas		30	M	Farmer	31Ma20Lx
Ann		30	F	Farmer	31Ma20Lx
Mary		20	F	Farmer	31Ma20Lx
David		12	M	Farmer	31Ma20Lx
Mary		10	F	Farmer	31Ma20Lx
Thomas		08	M	Child	31Ma20Lx
Michal		06	M	Child	31Ma20Lx
BYRNE, Honor		35	F	Farmer	31Ma20Lx
John		05	M	Child	31Ma20Lx
CASSIDY, William		28	M	Farmer	31Ma20Lx
MOLLOY, Thomas		28	M	Farmer	31Ma20Lx
Brdget.		26	F	Farmer	31Ma20Lx
Jane		24	F	Farmer	31Ma20Lx
Mary		13	F	Farmer	31Ma20Lx
DOGHNAN, Ann		20	F	Farmer	31Ma20Lx
MCMANUS, Thoms.		30	M	Farmer	31Ma20Lx
U	(W)	30	F	Farmer	31Ma20Lx
Thomas	(S)	.00	M	Infant	31Ma20Lx
BULICK, William		22	M	Farmer	31Ma20Lx
BUKER, Richd.		34	M	Farmer	31Ma20Lx
MCCARTY, Honor		21	F	Farmer	31Ma20Lx
FITZGERALD, Henry		22	M	Farmer	31Ma20Lx
James		21	M	Farmer	31Ma20Lx
RYAN, Thomas		25	M	Farmer	31Ma20Lx
Patt		22	M	Farmer	31Ma20Lx
GALLAGHER, John		20	M	Farmer	31Ma20Lx
GLECIVIN, Maria		19	F	Farmer	31Ma20Lx
Bridgt.		18	F	Farmer	31Ma20Lx
COURTNY, Cath.		20	F	Farmer	31Ma20Lx
REILEY, G.		28	M	Farmer	31Ma20Lx
NOLAN, Patt		40	M	Farmer	31Ma20Lx
FLYNNS, John		40	M	Farmer	31Ma20Lx
Margt.		30	F	Farmer	31Ma20Lx
MCMANN, James		21	M	Farmer	31Ma20Lx
KINLY, Michal		18	M	Farmer	31Ma20Lx
Patt		18	M	Farmer	31Ma20Lx

NAMES OF PASSENGERS	AGE	SEX	OCCUPATIONS	DATE PORT SHIP
KINLY, Ellen	20	F	Farmer	31Ma20Lx
MURPHY, Marty	25	M	Farmer	31Ma20Lx
Mary	22	F	Farmer	31Ma20Lx
Cath.	24	F	Farmer	31Ma20Lx
HICKEY, Ann	24	F	Farmer	31Ma20Lx
KEANY, Patt	25	M	Farmer	31Ma20Lx
Eliza	18	F	Farmer	31Ma20Lx
JOYCE, John	30	M	Farmer	31Ma20Lx
Bridgt.	30	F	Farmer	31Ma20Lx
Cath.	08	F	Child	31Ma20Lx
Luke	04	M	Child	31Ma20Lx
Ellen	.00	F	Infant	31Ma20Lx
GERAGHTY, E.	26	M	Farmer	31Ma20Lx
Mary	40	F	Farmer	31Ma20Lx
DALTON, Mary	20	F	Farmer	31Ma20Lx
Pat	20	M	Farmer	31Ma20Lx
Thomas	24	M	Farmer	31Ma20Lx
John	26	M	Farmer	31Ma20Lx
George	21	M	Farmer	31Ma20Lx
Francis	22	M	Farmer	31Ma20Lx
Simon	22	M	Farmer	31Ma20Lx
Mary	00	F	Farmer	31Ma20Lx

MARIA 31 MAY 1848

From Dublin

NAMES OF PASSENGERS	AGE	SEX	OCCUPATIONS	DATE PORT SHIP
GILBISH, Susan	26	F	Laborer	31Ma20Wk
DALTON, Robt.	30	M	Unknown	31Ma20Wk
DUNNE, Mary	31	F	Unknown	31Ma20Wk
Ann	19	F	Unknown	31Ma20Wk
Margt.	15	F	Unknown	31Ma20Wk
Pat	27	M	Unknown	31Ma20Wk
MCNAMARA, Brid.	22	F	Servant	31Ma20Wk
MOORE, Brid.	24	F	Unknown	31Ma20Wk
RIELLY, Maria	19	F	Unknown	31Ma20Wk
Mary-Ann	13	F	Unknown	31Ma20Wk
COTTER, Cornl.	39	M	Unknown	31Ma20Wk
WHELAN, Eliza	17	F	Unknown	31Ma20Wk
DUNNE, Peter	17	M	Farmer	31Ma20Wk
DALY, Bryan	16	M	Farmer	31Ma20Wk
Ann	36	F	Servant	31Ma20Wk
Ann	20	F	Unknown	31Ma20Wk
Margt.	18	F	Unknown	31Ma20Wk
Cath.	13	F	Unknown	31Ma20Wk
Brid.	11	F	Unknown	31Ma20Wk
Died-At-Sea				
Mary	09	F	Child	31Ma20Wk
CONNELL, Thos.	30	M	Laborer	31Ma20Wk
DALY, Mich.	07	M	Child	31Ma20Wk
Jane	05	F	Child	31Ma20Wk
Danl.	.00	M	Infant	31Ma20Wk
Died-At-Sea				
MAGAIN, Philim	60	M	Unknown	31Ma20Wk
John	24	M	Unknown	31Ma20Wk
Abby	20	F	Servant	31Ma20Wk
DONOHER, Jas.	61	M	Unknown	31Ma20Wk
Cathr.	40	F	Unknown	31Ma20Wk
HANLY, Michl.	20	M	Unknown	31Ma20Wk
CASHRY, Brid.	46	F	Unknown	31Ma20Wk
Mary	10	F	Unknown	31Ma20Wk
BERN, James	30	M	Unknown	31Ma20Wk
John	20	M	Unknown	31Ma20Wk
Ann	16	F	Unknown	31Ma20Wk
Thos.	13	M	Unknown	31Ma20Wk
Bryan	06	M	Child	31Ma20Wk
THOMPSON, Wm.	40	M	Farmer	31Ma20Wk
Mary	40	F	Unknown	31Ma20Wk
Pat	14	M	Unknown	31Ma20Wk

NAMES OF PASSENGERS		AGE	SEX	OCCUPATIONS	DATE PORT SHIP
THOMPSON, Ann		12	F	Unknown	31Ma20Wk
Mary		10	F	Unknown	31Ma20Wk
Cath.		07	F	Child	31Ma20Wk
FOLEY, Mich.		60	M	Farmer	31Ma20Wk
Cathr.		50	F	Unknown	31Ma20Wk
Mary		25	F	Unknown	31Ma20Wk
Thomas		20	M	Cooper	31Ma20Wk
Pat		18	M	Unknown	31Ma20Wk
Bernd.		12	M	Unknown	31Ma20Wk
Biddy		10	F	Unknown	31Ma20Wk
Eleanor		16	F	Unknown	31Ma20Wk
Eliza		12	F	Unknown	31Ma20Wk
KIMICAN, Mary		24	F	Unknown	31Ma20Wk
CARROLL, Pat		21	M	Unknown	31Ma20Wk
KRMARDY, John		20	M	Farmer	31Ma20Wk
MCCANN, Susan		18	F	Unknown	31Ma20Wk
SEBOLD, Stephen		22	M	Unknown	31Ma20Wk
BOLGER, Dennis		30	M	Unknown	31Ma20Wk
ROACH, Brid.		56	F	Unknown	31Ma20Wk
Died-At-Sea					
BOLGER, Eliza		26	F	Servant	31Ma20Wk
Died-At-Sea					
Dennis		08	M	Child	31Ma20Wk
Cath.		06	F	Child	31Ma20Wk
Ellen		03	F	Child	31Ma20Wk
Sarah		.00	F	Infant	31Ma20Wk
Died-At-Sea					
WADE, Mary		26	F	Unknown	31Ma20Wk
Died-At-Sea					
Thomas		12	M	Unknown	31Ma20Wk
Died-At-Sea					
Mary-Ann		07	F	Child	31Ma20Wk
Died-At-Sea					
Robert		03	M	Child	31Ma20Wk
Died-At-Sea					
DRIGAN, Thomas		48	M	Servant	31Ma20Wk
Died-At-Sea					
KELLEY, Bernd.		25	M	Servant	31Ma20Wk
VANLED, Ann		23	F	Servant	31Ma20Wk
DUGGAN, Biddy		18	F	Servant	31Ma20Wk
LEONARD, Margt.		12	F	Servant	31Ma20Wk
GANNON, Wm.		18	M	Unknown	31Ma20Wk
DONEGAN, Cath.		19	F	Unknown	31Ma20Wk
Ann		16	F	Unknown	31Ma20Wk

QUEEN 01 JUNE 1848

From Liverpool

NAMES OF PASSENGERS		AGE	SEX	OCCUPATIONS	DATE PORT SHIP
SELBY, William-J.		38	M	Carpenter	01Ju02Qx
Segler-T.	(W)	26	F	Wife	01Ju02Qx
Anna		07	F	Child	01Ju02Qx
John		02	M	Child	01Ju02Qx
Robert		.00	M	Infant	01Ju02Qx
MEATH, Ruth		18	F	Spinster	01Ju02Qx
REDMOND, Frances		32	M	Glazier	01Ju02Qx
Eliza-Jane	(W)	28	F	Wife	01Ju02Qx
FORTUNEL, Ann-Jane		52	F	Milliner	01Ju02Qx
Jane-Jane		24	F	Milliner	01Ju02Qx
Sarah		19	F	Milliner	01Ju02Qx
Theresa		16	F	Milliner	01Ju02Qx
LANNAN, Elizabeth		52	F	Servant	01Ju02Qx
BARNUS, Hannah		26	F	Milliner	01Ju02Qx
WHEELHOUSE, Thomas		35	M	Cld	01Ju02Qx
Charlotte	(W)	34	F	Wife	01Ju02Qx
William		12	M	Child	01Ju02Qx
Henry		10	M	Child	01Ju02Qx
Robert		08	M	Child	01Ju02Qx
Mary-A.		05	F	Child	01Ju02Qx
WHEELHOUSE, Emma		.00	F	Infant	01Ju02Qx
DIXON, William		45	M	Schm	01Ju02Qx
Mary	(W)	44	F	Wife	01Ju02Qx
Margaret		11	F	Child	01Ju02Qx
Ann		26	F	None	01Ju02Qx
GILLIGAN, John		30	M	Porter	01Ju02Qx
BUCKLEY, William		30	M	Machmkr	01Ju02Qx
Sarah-W.	(W)	30	F	Dressmaker	01Ju02Qx
HALLOWELL, James		31	M	Spinner	01Ju02Qx
GROVES, Charles		28	M	Butcher	01Ju02Qx
Thomas		20	M	Butcher	01Ju02Qx
MOLEY, William		17	M	Butcher	01Ju02Qx
GROVES, Mary		30	F	Dressmaker	01Ju02Qx
MOLEY, Harriet		17	F	Dressmaker	01Ju02Qx
HENDERSON, John		22	M	Laborer	01Ju02Qx
Ann	(W)	22	F	Dressmaker	01Ju02Qx
GILDON, Maria		38	F	Laborer	01Ju02Qx
Mary-Ann		16	F	Laborer	01Ju02Qx
Matilda		15	F	Child	01Ju02Qx
Maria		13	F	Child	01Ju02Qx
Joseph		11	M	Child	01Ju02Qx
John		09	M	Child	01Ju02Qx
Emma		07	F	Child	01Ju02Qx
Anna		06	F	Child	01Ju02Qx
Hannah		.00	F	Infant	01Ju02Qx
TUNGATE, Samuel		45	M	Laborer	01Ju02Qx
Sarah	(W)	45	F	Wife	01Ju02Qx
Mary-Ann		18	F	None	01Ju02Qx
William		13	M	Child	01Ju02Qx
John		11	M	Child	01Ju02Qx
Edward		07	M	Child	01Ju02Qx
MILEM, Robert		40	M	Brick Maker	01Ju02Qx
WALSH, Richard		35	M	Laborer	01Ju02Qx
Mary	(W)	35	F	Wife	01Ju02Qx
James		09	M	Child	01Ju02Qx
Pat		11	M	Child	01Ju02Qx
SUTCLIFF, James		24	M	Farmer	01Ju02Qx
Martha	(W)	24	F	Wife	01Ju02Qx
FOLEY, Pat		23	M	Laborer	01Ju02Qx
Ellen	(W)	21	F	Wife	01Ju02Qx
DUFF, Robert		37	M	Farmer	01Ju02Qx
Isabella	(W)	37	F	Wife	01Ju02Qx
William		.00	M	Infant	01Ju02Qx
GERROND, William		21	M	Farmer	01Ju02Qx
James		19	M	Farmer	01Ju02Qx
Margaret		18	F	Spinster	01Ju02Qx
ARTHUR, William		21	M	Miner	01Ju02Qx
John		19	M	Miner	01Ju02Qx
Martha		23	F	Milliner	01Ju02Qx
PIERCE, Elizabeth		55	F	Wi	01Ju02Qx
Mary		24	F	Servant	01Ju02Qx
Elizabeth		18	F	Servant	01Ju02Qx
Ann		13	F	Servant	01Ju02Qx
SAUNDERS, Jane		22	F	Spinster	01Ju02Qx
Harriet		.00	F	Infant	01Ju02Qx
CARSON, William		19	M	Farmer	01Ju02Qx
Elizabeth		20	F	Dressmaker	01Ju02Qx
Mary		12	F	Dressmaker	01Ju02Qx
LIVINGSTON, Robert		23	M	Farmer	01Ju02Qx
John		21	M	Farmer	01Ju02Qx
RIDDLE, Samuel		23	M	Farmer	01Ju02Qx
BALLEY, John		19	M	Farmer	01Ju02Qx
DUGAN, Andrew		19	M	Farmer	01Ju02Qx
HINERY, Jane		24	F	Spinster	01Ju02Qx
FORREST, Thomas		26	M	Smith	01Ju02Qx
HARRISON, John		28	M	Smith	01Ju02Qx
STORM, William		24	M	Joiner	01Ju02Qx
WILSON, John		20	M	Farmer	01Ju02Qx
WEUR, Nathan		18	M	Farmer	01Ju02Qx
FLESHER, Thomas		30	M	Machmkr	01Ju02Qx
GLASCO, John		30	M	Machmkr	01Ju02Qx
HOGART, Mat.		28	M	Farmer	01Ju02Qx
Bridget	(W)	25	F	Wife	01Ju02Qx
Mary		02	F	Child	01Ju02Qx
EDWARDS, Ball		20	M	Shoemaker	01Ju02Qx

NAMES OF PASSENGERS		AGE	SEX	OCCUPATIONS	DATE PORT SHIP
EDWARDS, Eliza		18	F	Spinster	01Ju02Qx
RILEY, Eliza		18	F	Dressmaker	01Ju02Qx
DOOLEY, Pat		24	M	Farmer	01Ju02Qx
Sarah		19	F	Dressmaker	01Ju02Qx
MULLONER, Owen		24	M	Laborer	01Ju02Qx
MULLOWN, James		26	M	Groom	01Ju02Qx
Fanny		20	F	Servant	01Ju02Qx
PIERCE, Richard		24	M	Miner	01Ju02Qx
ROARK, Matthew		28	M	Laborer	01Ju02Qx
RILEY, Michael		50	M	Laborer	01Ju02Qx
Mary		19	F	Servant	01Ju02Qx
HAGUE, Samuel		74	M	Farmer	01Ju02Qx
Elizabeth		40	F	Spinster	01Ju02Qx
Grace		28	F	Spinster	01Ju02Qx
MULLIN, Stephen		43	M	Laborer	01Ju02Qx
Sarah	(W)	42	F	Wife	01Ju02Qx
Pat		10	M	Child	01Ju02Qx
DONNELLY, Mary		44	F	Servant	01Ju02Qx
MCCARN, Rose		04	F	Child	01Ju02Qx
MCCARDAL, Pat		25	M	Mill Worker	01Ju02Qx
Mary	(W)	23	F	Wife	01Ju02Qx
MCKALL, James		24	M	Joiner	01Ju02Qx
MOONEY, Pat		28	M	Laborer	01Ju02Qx
WALSH, Edward		20	M	Laborer	01Ju02Qx
CARLETON, Joseph		23	M	Laborer	01Ju02Qx
NOBLE, Robert		24	M	Laborer	01Ju02Qx
KEGS, Thomas		16	M	Laborer	01Ju02Qx
MOLEY, Peter		24	M	Laborer	01Ju02Qx
Mary		22	F	Servant	01Ju02Qx
MCQUEEN, Andrew		24	M	Laborer	01Ju02Qx
MOLEY, Bridget		.00	F	Infant	01Ju02Qx
WIHM, Bridget		18	F	Servant	01Ju02Qx
MCLAUCHLAN, Thomas		22	M	Laborer	01Ju02Qx
James		13	M	Laborer	01Ju02Qx
Catherine		06	F	Servant	01Ju02Qx
SWEENEY, Maria		18	F	Servant	01Ju02Qx
PRYOR, Dalia		18	F	Servant	01Ju02Qx
MOLDOM, John		18	M	Weaver	01Ju02Qx
HAND, Mick		28	M	Laborer	01Ju02Qx
John		22	M	Laborer	01Ju02Qx
Mary		21	F	Servant	01Ju02Qx
HACKETTS, William		22	M	Joiner	01Ju02Qx
Ann	(W)	22	F	Wife	01Ju02Qx
WILKINSON, William		30	M	Weaver	01Ju02Qx
MANU, Ann		20	F	Servant	01Ju02Qx
QUIGLA, Michel		22	M	Laborer	01Ju02Qx
Margaret		24	F	Servant	01Ju02Qx
CARINE, Peter		30	M	Laborer	01Ju02Qx
CONLEY, Michael		36	M	Laborer	01Ju02Qx
MCGINNIS, Thomas		29	M	Farmer	01Ju02Qx
JACKSON, Frederick		25	M	Farmer	01Ju02Qx
DUNN, Francis		20	M	Clerk	01Ju02Qx
COCHRAN, Daniel		24	M	Joiner	01Ju02Qx
CASEY, Edward		20	M	Joiner	01Ju02Qx
FITZWILLIAMS, Pat		35	M	Laborer	01Ju02Qx
HART, William		39	M	Shoemaker	01Ju02Qx
HOWLAND, William		27	M	Tailor	01Ju02Qx
QUIXLEY, Thomas		27	M	Laborer	01Ju02Qx
MCSHANE, Terrance		40	M	Farmer	01Ju02Qx
Owen		16	M	Farmer	01Ju02Qx
Peter		13	M	Farmer	01Ju02Qx
Mary		11	F	Servant	01Ju02Qx
MCBRIDE, Pat		16	M	Tailor	01Ju02Qx
LANNON, Pat		16	M	Laborer	01Ju02Qx
Dennis		15	M	Laborer	01Ju02Qx
VEATCH, John		43	M	Farmer	01Ju02Qx
Jane		13	F	Child	01Ju02Qx
Margaret		11	F	Child	01Ju02Qx
John		07	M	Child	01Ju02Qx
SULLIVAN, Ann		26	F	Dressmaker	01Ju02Qx
Letitia		19	F	Dressmaker	01Ju02Qx
ENNIS, Andrew		25	M	Farmer	01Ju02Qx
HIGHLAND, John		30	M	Farmer	01Ju02Qx
Catherine	(W)	30	F	Wife	01Ju02Qx
Thomas		06	M	Child	01Ju02Qx

NAMES OF PASSENGERS		AGE	SEX	OCCUPATIONS	DATE PORT SHIP
ELDERS, James		25	M	Carpenter	01Ju02Qx
Ann	(W)	25	F	Wife	01Ju02Qx
MCEWEN, Mary		14	F	Servant	01Ju02Qx
CREVY, William		14	M	Joiner	01Ju02Qx
FOOT, Pat		35	M	Nailer	01Ju02Qx
FRINGLESS, Jane		25	F	Servant	01Ju02Qx
AGEW, Maria		22	F	Servant	01Ju02Qx
DIXON, James		25	M	Farmer	01Ju02Qx
Sarah	(W)	21	F	Wife	01Ju02Qx
James		02	M	Child	01Ju02Qx
Walter		.00	M	Infant	01Ju02Qx
EDGAR, Walter		40	M	Farmer	01Ju02Qx
Jannet	(W)	40	F	Wife	01Ju02Qx
William		18	M	Joiner	01Ju02Qx
Walter		13	M	Child	01Ju02Qx
James		10	M	Child	01Ju02Qx
Thomas		08	M	Child	01Ju02Qx
Robert		03	M	Child	01Ju02Qx
MURRY, Samuel		23	M	Farmer	01Ju02Qx
Margaret	(W)	22	F	Wife	01Ju02Qx
William		.00	M	Infant	01Ju02Qx
LITTLE, John		45	M	Tailor	01Ju02Qx
KIRK, James		25	M	Groom	01Ju02Qx
Maria	(W)	26	F	Wife	01Ju02Qx
BALL, Martin		20	M	Mechanic	01Ju02Qx
LITTLE, John		13	M	Tailor	01Ju02Qx
BUCK, Matthew		26	M	Joiner	01Ju02Qx
POACH, Jane		25	F	Spinster	01Ju02Qx
William		11	M	Child	01Ju02Qx
Eliza		09	F	Child	01Ju02Qx
MITCHELL, Cudy		18	F	Servant	01Ju02Qx
MASRAFIELD, John		30	M	Farmer	01Ju02Qx
EVANS, John		31	M	Farmer	01Ju02Qx
Jane	(W)	33	F	Wife	01Ju02Qx
John-T.		02	M	Child	01Ju02Qx
BAXTER, Sarah		20	F	Milliner	01Ju02Qx
HOLMES, William		36	M	Farmer	01Ju02Qx
COTTON, Thomas		19	M	Iron Roller	01Ju02Qx
HOOTH, William		43	M	Weaver	01Ju02Qx
Julia	(W)	43	F	Wife	01Ju02Qx
Ellen		10	F	Child	01Ju02Qx
William		07	M	Child	01Ju02Qx
Hugh		05	M	Child	01Ju02Qx
Susanna		03	F	Child	01Ju02Qx
Sarah-A.		.00	F	Infant	01Ju02Qx
KILROY, Mary		45	F	Pms	01Ju02Qx
Elizabeth		20	F	Spinster	01Ju02Qx
Margaret		18	F	Spinster	01Ju02Qx
Edwin		17	M	Agent	01Ju02Qx
Frances		15	F	Spinster	01Ju02Qx
Winifred		14	F	Spinster	01Ju02Qx
DART, Jessey		23	M	Puddler	01Ju02Qx
PIERCE, Samuel		21	M	Puddler	01Ju02Qx
Benjamin		24	M	Puddler	01Ju02Qx
COX, Charles		45	M	Laborer	01Ju02Qx
BUSH, Giles		45	M	Smith	01Ju02Qx
GREENOW, Thomas		25	M	Shoemaker	01Ju02Qx
AUSTIN, Laurence		39	M	Laborer	01Ju02Qx
Jane	(W)	25	F	Wife	01Ju02Qx
SMART, John		48	M	Laborer	01Ju02Qx
Rebecca	(W)	54	F	Wife	01Ju02Qx
Laurence		16	M	Child	01Ju02Qx
BARNETT, William		24	M	Lace Maker	01Ju02Qx
Ellen	(W)	24	F	Wife	01Ju02Qx
POISEY, John		21	M	Laborer	01Ju02Qx
SMART, Newton		21	M	Laborer	01Ju02Qx
HALL, William		20	M	Laborer	01Ju02Qx
KILSALA, Thomas		24	M	Laborer	01Ju02Qx
MURPHY, Morris		21	M	Bootmaker	01Ju02Qx
KALLAHAN, Daniel		28	M	Laborer	01Ju02Qx
NAILEN, James		27	M	Bootmaker	01Ju02Qx
MCCANE, John		25	M	Gdnr	01Ju02Qx
Mary	(M)	50	F	Mother	01Ju02Qx
Daniel		02	M	Child	01Ju02Qx
QUINLAN, Thomas		25	M	Farmer	01Ju02Qx

NAMES OF PASSENGERS		AGE	SEX	OCCUPATIONS	DATE PORT SHIP
QUINLAN, Mary	(W)	30	F	Wife	01Ju02Qx
WILSON, Robert		28	M	Farmer	01Ju02Qx
WOOD, Thomas		32	M	Unknown	01Ju02Qx
MCGACHIE, Charles		23	M	Laborer	01Ju02Qx
Sarah	(W)	23	F	Servant	01Ju02Qx
BLAKE, Ann		29	F	Servant	01Ju02Qx
CONROY, Julia		42	F	Cook	01Ju02Qx
MATCHELL, William		19	M	Tmkr	01Ju02Qx
FORSYTH, George		20	M	Tmkr	01Ju02Qx
Robert		25	M	Tmkr	01Ju02Qx
CURREY, John		30	M	Tmkr	01Ju02Qx
NOX, John		45	M	Farmer	01Ju02Qx
Martha	(W)	45	F	Farmer	01Ju02Qx
Thomas		18	M	Farmer	01Ju02Qx
Elizabeth		16	F	Farmer	01Ju02Qx
DAVIS, John		35	M	Farmer	01Ju02Qx
BOWNE, Samuel		22	M	Farmer	01Ju02Qx
Ann	(W)	22	F	Wife	01Ju02Qx
Mary		15	F	Child	01Ju02Qx
RANSON, William		35	M	Farmer	01Ju02Qx
COCHRANE, Edward		28	M	Tailor	01Ju02Qx
DEAN, John		38	M	Butcher	01Ju02Qx
Sarah	(W)	30	F	Wife	01Ju02Qx
Mary		06	F	Child	01Ju02Qx
Joseph		04	M	Child	01Ju02Qx
Jane		02	F	Child	01Ju02Qx
BLOWER, William		30	M	Farmer	01Ju02Qx
Eliza	(W)	26	F	Wife	01Ju02Qx
DUGGAN, Thomas		19	M	Servant	01Ju02Qx
GILLIGHAN, Pat		24	M	Laborer	01Ju02Qx
MILLS, Samuel		24	M	Farmer	01Ju02Qx
Susan	(W)	25	F	Wife	01Ju02Qx
MURRY, John		18	M	Farmer	01Ju02Qx
BYARM, Ann		18	F	Servant	01Ju02Qx
MASON, Joseph		53	M	Miner	01Ju02Qx
Susanna	(W)	46	F	Wife	01Ju02Qx
Joseph		28	M	Miner	01Ju02Qx
Susan		27	F	Wife	01Ju02Qx
John		25	M	Miner	01Ju02Qx
PARRY, David		25	M	Miner	01Ju02Qx
Mary	(W)	23	F	Wife	01Ju02Qx
MASON, Ann		20	F	Spinster	01Ju02Qx
Samuel		17	M	Miner	01Ju02Qx
Elizabeth		14	F	Spinster	01Ju02Qx
Susanna		12	F	Spinster	01Ju02Qx
William		07	M	Miner	01Ju02Qx
Rosanna		03	F	Child	01Ju02Qx
RILEY, Pat		12	M	Servant	01Ju02Qx
HANEY, Richard		24	M	Servant	01Ju02Qx
Elizabeth		18	F	Servant	01Ju02Qx
CAGAN, Catherine		19	F	Servant	01Ju02Qx
KIARNAN, James		22	M	Laborer	01Ju02Qx
Bridget	(W)	22	F	Wife	01Ju02Qx
RILEY, Pat		21	M	Laborer	01Ju02Qx
WALSH, David		35	M	Glsctr	01Ju02Qx
FORREL, George		22	M	Weaver	01Ju02Qx
KELLEY, Pat		30	M	Miller	01Ju02Qx
DAFFY, John		25	M	Laborer	01Ju02Qx
AKEN, Andrew		36	M	Mlov	01Ju02Qx
Christina	(W)	37	F	Wife	01Ju02Qx
CUNNINGHAM, Edward		28	M	Laborer	01Ju02Qx
HANOVAN, Pat		22	M	Laborer	01Ju02Qx
Elizabeth		15	F	Servant	01Ju02Qx
BENT, Abram		24	M	Weaver	01Ju02Qx
DEPLATCH, William		21	M	Spinner	01Ju02Qx
QUNLISK, Dennis		30	M	Groom	01Ju02Qx
Ellen	(W)	27	F	Wife	01Ju02Qx
WEIR, Thomas		21	M	Farmer	01Ju02Qx
TIFFINY, Mary		29	F	Farmer	01Ju02Qx
Anna		09	F	Child	01Ju02Qx
John		07	M	Child	01Ju02Qx
EVANS, William		30	M	Miner	01Ju02Qx
ROBINSON, Samuel		38	M	Slpl	01Ju02Qx
Lucy	(W)	40	F	Wife	01Ju02Qx
Walter		11	M	Child	01Ju02Qx
RENWICK, Alice		48	F	Grocer	01Ju02Qx
FOXLOW, Margaret		23	F	Grocer	01Ju02Qx
RENWICK, Jiles		13	M	Child	01Ju02Qx
John		11	M	Child	01Ju02Qx
Bryan		09	M	Child	01Ju02Qx
MCCULLOCH, John		35	M	Farmer	01Ju02Qx
FLAHERTY, John		21	M	Clerk	01Ju02Qx
Margaret		17	F	Spinster	01Ju02Qx
Sophia		16	F	Miner	01Ju02Qx
WHITE, Smith		32	M	Traveller	01Ju02Qx
FOSTER, Peter		30	M	Miner	01Ju02Qx
BEADLY, George		25	M	Gunsmith	01Ju02Qx
MULLOVY, Allicia		19	F	Spinster	01Ju02Qx
REDMOND, Francis		.00	F	Infant	01Ju02Qx
Died-At-Sea					

INFANTA 01 JUNE 1848

From Dublin

NAMES OF PASSENGERS		AGE	SEX	OCCUPATIONS	DATE PORT SHIP
MEPETT, James		28	M	Laborer	01Ju20FJ
BRADY, Eliza		20	F	None	01Ju20FJ
GALLAGHER, Michael		40	M	Laborer	01Ju20FJ
Michael		20	M	Laborer	01Ju20FJ
HARDEN, U		45	F	None	01Ju20FJ
Henry		17	M	Laborer	01Ju20FJ
Robert		20	M	Laborer	01Ju20FJ
GUINESS, Pat		45	M	Laborer	01Ju20FJ
Michael		22	M	Laborer	01Ju20FJ
James		11	M	Laborer	01Ju20FJ
Pat		09	M	Child	01Ju20FJ
Catherine		10	F	Child	01Ju20FJ
Everard		24	M	Laborer	01Ju20FJ
SWEENEY, Eliza		20	F	Servant	01Ju20FJ
POWDERLY, Hugh		40	M	Laborer	01Ju20FJ
Ellen	(W)	38	F	Wife	01Ju20FJ
Pat		12	M	Child	01Ju20FJ
James		10	M	Child	01Ju20FJ
Margaret		07	F	Child	01Ju20FJ
James		01	M	Child	01Ju20FJ
SMITH, Simon		55	M	Laborer	01Ju20FJ
Mary		19	F	None	01Ju20FJ
Dolly		09	F	Child	01Ju20FJ
Edward		07	M	Child	01Ju20FJ
Simon		05	M	Child	01Ju20FJ
MARTIN, Bridget		20	F	Servant	01Ju20FJ
DALY, John		28	M	Laborer	01Ju20FJ
Pat		20	M	Tailor	01Ju20FJ
Ellen		20	F	Tailor	01Ju20FJ
FEGAN, Mary		30	F	Servant	01Ju20FJ
KEEFE, John		47	M	Laborer	01Ju20FJ
Deborah	(W)	47	F	Wife	01Ju20FJ
Austy		19	F	None	01Ju20FJ
Mary		17	F	None	01Ju20FJ
Catherine		15	F	Child	01Ju20FJ
Margaret		13	F	Child	01Ju20FJ
Joseph		11	M	Laborer	01Ju20FJ
Michael		09	M	Laborer	01Ju20FJ
John		06	M	Laborer	01Ju20FJ
RYAN, William		50	M	Schm	01Ju20FJ
William		28	M	Laborer	01Ju20FJ
Catherine		24	F	None	01Ju20FJ
Alley		16	F	None	01Ju20FJ
Sally		13	F	Child	01Ju20FJ
MAHER, Pat		22	M	Laborer	01Ju20FJ
John		25	M	Laborer	01Ju20FJ
MURPHY, Dennis		20	M	Laborer	01Ju20FJ
URITELY, George-B.		29	M	Butcher	01Ju20FJ
LORD, William		24	M	Miner	01Ju20FJ

NAMES OF PASSENGERS		AGE	SEX	OCCUPATIONS	DATE PORT SHIP
TINGER, James		21	M	Miner	01Ju20Fj
IRWIN, Stephen		28	M	Miner	01Ju20Fj
KEARNS, William		26	M	Miner	01Ju20Fj
KNIGHT, Susan		22	F	Servant	01Ju20Fj
TINGER, Amelia		26	F	Servant	01Ju20Fj
Eliza		24	F	Servant	01Ju20Fj
Anne		65	F	Servant	01Ju20Fj
ARKEN, Susan		24	F	Servant	01Ju20Fj
LORD, Ann		18	F	Servant	01Ju20Fj
ROSRITA, George		50	M	Cooper	01Ju20Fj
U	(W)	45	F	Wife	01Ju20Fj
John		23	M	Cooper	01Ju20Fj
Thomas		20	M	Cooper	01Ju20Fj
George		18	M	Cooper	01Ju20Fj
Pat		12	M	Cooper	01Ju20Fj
Ellen		13	F	Child	01Ju20Fj
Mick		24	M	Cooper	01Ju20Fj
GEACON, John		21	M	Farmer	01Ju20Fj
NICHOLAS, Thomas		42	M	Laborer	01Ju20Fj
Maria	(W)	40	F	Wife	01Ju20Fj
Maria		10	F	Child	01Ju20Fj
Thomas		07	M	Child	01Ju20Fj
MILNE, Bridget		45	F	Dressmaker	01Ju20Fj
Catherine		17	F	Dressmaker	01Ju20Fj
Margaret		15	F	Dressmaker	01Ju20Fj
MILLER, James		24	M	Irnmldr	01Ju20Fj
Teresa		21	F	None	01Ju20Fj
Nannette		42	F	None	01Ju20Fj
PAINTING, William		20	M	Carpenter	01Ju20Fj
CLIFFORD, James		30	M	Servant	01Ju20Fj
Catherine	(W)	28	F	Servant	01Ju20Fj
CARTER, William		30	M	Shoemaker	01Ju20Fj
BOYLE, Michael		50	M	Fireman	01Ju20Fj
Catherine		20	F	Fireman	01Ju20Fj
CORCORAN, Patrick		27	M	Laborer	01Ju20Fj
MILLER, Jane		01	F	Child	01Ju20Fj
Nanette		02	F	Child	01Ju20Fj
DOOLAN, Michael		40	M	Laborer	01Ju20Fj
James		10	M	Laborer	01Ju20Fj
HOUGH, Martin		22	M	Laborer	01Ju20Fj
FINNEL, Mary		20	F	Servant	01Ju20Fj
HONOR, Catharina		20	F	Servant	01Ju20Fj
BLAKE, John		25	M	Laborer	01Ju20Fj
BRADLY, Pat		22	M	Laborer	01Ju20Fj
John		20	M	Laborer	01Ju20Fj
HARRIETT, Anty		30	M	Laborer	01Ju20Fj
Margaret	(W)	28	F	None	01Ju20Fj
Thomas		24	M	Laborer	01Ju20Fj
Patrick		05	M	Child	01Ju20Fj
Mary		03	F	Child	01Ju20Fj
Kate		02	F	Child	01Ju20Fj
Martin		.09	M	Infant	01Ju20Fj
HUTTON, Henry		24	M	Servant	01Ju20Fj
Margaret	(W)	22	F	Servant	01Ju20Fj
John		04	M	Child	01Ju20Fj
BUMWELL, Margarette		20	F	Servant	01Ju20Fj
HUTTON, John		22	M	Carpenter	01Ju20Fj
James		20	M	Servant	01Ju20Fj
MCCABE, James		50	M	Tailor	01Ju20Fj
Henry		21	M	Tailor	01Ju20Fj
Letechia		16	F	Tailor	01Ju20Fj
Edmund		15	M	Tailor	01Ju20Fj
Ann	(W)	41	F	Tailor	01Ju20Fj
COYLE, William-J.		25	M	Farmer	01Ju20Fj
Ann		23	F	None	01Ju20Fj
James		19	M	Servant	01Ju20Fj
BLUETT, Mary		51	F	Servant	01Ju20Fj
Jane		25	F	Servant	01Ju20Fj
Emily		23	F	Servant	01Ju20Fj
Thomas		27	M	Farmer	01Ju20Fj
William		21	M	Farmer	01Ju20Fj
John		20	M	Tailor	01Ju20Fj
Margarette		18	F	Tailor	01Ju20Fj
Emily		02	F	Child	01Ju20Fj
William		04	M	Child	01Ju20Fj

NAMES OF PASSENGERS		AGE	SEX	OCCUPATIONS	DATE PORT SHIP
MACDONNELL, Edward		45	M	Farmer	01Ju20Fj
Isabella	(W)	26	F	Wife	01Ju20Fj
Sarah		07	F	Child	01Ju20Fj
George		05	M	Child	01Ju20Fj
Valinda		03	F	Child	01Ju20Fj
Elizabeth		.03	F	Infant	01Ju20Fj
BOYLE, Thomas		25	M	Bilen	01Ju20Fj
MURPHY, Pat		21	M	Laborer	01Ju20Fj
Ann		16	F	None	01Ju20Fj
MCMANUS, Margaret		20	F	Servant	01Ju20Fj
CONJUGHAM, Charles		21	M	Laborer	01Ju20Fj
RENEDY, Jonas		21	M	Laborer	01Ju20Fj
MCQUADE, Thomas		24	M	Whitesmith	01Ju20Fj
Harrette	(W)	30	F	Whitesmith	01Ju20Fj
CONDON, Ann		40	F	None	01Ju20Fj
SMITH, Ann		13	F	Child	01Ju20Fj
MCQUADE, Hannah-Ann		08	F	Child	01Ju20Fj
William		06	M	Child	01Ju20Fj
Thomas		04	M	Child	01Ju20Fj
John		.03	M	Infant	01Ju20Fj
MCCORMICK, Ally		50	M	Whitesmith	01Ju20Fj
Pat		22	M	Laborer	01Ju20Fj
Thomas		20	M	Laborer	01Ju20Fj
Mary		09	F	Child	01Ju20Fj
MALENE, Laurence		25	M	Laborer	01Ju20Fj
WHITE, John		25	M	Laborer	01Ju20Fj
Eliza		.04	F	Infant	01Ju20Fj
REGNEY, John		23	M	Laborer	01Ju20Fj
EGAN, Maria		22	F	None	01Ju20Fj
FOX, Alexander		13	M	Servant	01Ju20Fj
Joseph		11	M	Servant	01Ju20Fj
COSTELLO, Martin		22	M	Laborer	01Ju20Fj
KENEDY, John		23	M	Laborer	01Ju20Fj
KEIRNAN, Charles		26	M	Laborer	01Ju20Fj
CORMICK, Mary		18	F	None	01Ju20Fj
KENIGAN, Mary		18	F	None	01Ju20Fj
QUINLAN, Edward		23	M	Laborer	01Ju20Fj
Michael		16	M	Laborer	01Ju20Fj
BYRNE, Thomas		25	M	Laborer	01Ju20Fj
GAHAN, Daniel		25	M	Laborer	01Ju20Fj

FIDELIA 01 JUNE 1848

From Liverpool

NAMES OF PASSENGERS		AGE	SEX	OCCUPATIONS	DATE PORT SHIP
FITZGERALD, James		24	M	Laborer	01Ju02Ax
Mary		20	F	Servant	01Ju02Ax
EGAN, Micheal		19	M	Laborer	01Ju02Ax
BRYAN, Timothy		20	M	Laborer	01Ju02Ax
MCGLINE, Catherine		18	F	Servant	01Ju02Ax
QUIRK, Bridget		20	F	Servant	01Ju02Ax
FORY, Timothy		20	M	Laborer	01Ju02Ax
RIGBY, John		24	M	Carpenter	01Ju02Ax
DOYLE, James		29	M	Joiner	01Ju02Ax
MILLS, Micheal		26	M	Joiner	01Ju02Ax
DOYLE, Elizabeth		19	F	Servant	01Ju02Ax
WILLIS, Anne		20	F	Servant	01Ju02Ax
SULLIVAN, Jeremiah		20	M	Carpenter	01Ju02Ax
Micheal		40	M	Carpenter	01Ju02Ax
Julia		28	F	Servant	01Ju02Ax
KANAGHER, Catherine		18	F	Servant	01Ju02Ax
QUIN, Allice		30	F	Servant	01Ju02Ax
John		40	M	Laborer	01Ju02Ax
FALLAR, Jane		14	F	Servant	01Ju02Ax
POWELL, Thomas		35	M	Laborer	01Ju02Ax
William		20	M	Laborer	01Ju02Ax
Sarah		15	F	Servant	01Ju02Ax
DUFFY, Bridget		30	F	Servant	01Ju02Ax
CLANCY, John		30	M	Laborer	01Ju02Ax

NAMES OF PASSENGERS	AGE	SEX	OCCUPATIONS	DATE PORT SHIP
HICKEY, Bridgette	20	F	Servant	01Ju02Ax
ROACH, Patrick	22	M	Laborer	01Ju02Ax
CLANCY, Thomas	21	M	Laborer	01Ju02Ax
Mary	20	F	Servant	01Ju02Ax
Catherine	21	F	Servant	01Ju02Ax
Honora	18	F	Servant	01Ju02Ax
RYAN, Ellen	20	F	Servant	01Ju02Ax
CONNOR, Edmund	35	M	Laborer	01Ju02Ax
DARCY, Maurice	26	M	Shoemaker	01Ju02Ax
HALPIN, Patrick	24	M	Laborer	01Ju02Ax
DONEGAN, Anne	18	F	Servant	01Ju02Ax
GLENCHAN, Margaret	18	F	Servant	01Ju02Ax
TANDIE, Mary	22	F	Servant	01Ju02Ax
CONNOR, Thomas	22	M	Laborer	01Ju02Ax
WEST, Edward	14	M	Laborer	01Ju02Ax
HOPKINS, William	25	M	Bleacher	01Ju02Ax
MCLOUGHLIN, James	20	M	Laborer	01Ju02Ax
MEARNS, Samuel	40	M	Laborer	01Ju02Ax
ANDERSON, James	21	M	Laborer	01Ju02Ax
ODONNELL, Thade	25	M	Laborer	01Ju02Ax
SULLIVAN, Jeremiah	26	M	Laborer	01Ju02Ax
CONNELL, Margaret	24	F	Servant	01Ju02Ax
Mary	27	F	Servant	01Ju02Ax
WILSON, Josiah	25	M	Laborer	01Ju02Ax
Anne	25	F	Servant	01Ju02Ax
Eliza	01	F	Child	01Ju02Ax
Eliza-Jane	01	F	Child	01Ju02Ax
MOHAN, Patrick	50	M	Laborer	01Ju02Ax
Anne	50	F	Servant	01Ju02Ax
Thomas	25	M	Laborer	01Ju02Ax
James	22	M	Laborer	01Ju02Ax
Patrick-Jr.	18	M	Laborer	01Ju02Ax
Catherine	20	F	Servant	01Ju02Ax
GUARGIAN, Anne	16	F	Servant	01Ju02Ax
MCGARRY, James	25	M	Laborer	01Ju02Ax
Catherine	27	F	Servant	01Ju02Ax
Mary	18	F	Servant	01Ju02Ax
MACKEY, Judith	19	F	Servant	01Ju02Ax
Mary	.00	F	Infant	01Ju02Ax
QUIN, Ellen	18	F	Servant	01Ju02Ax
MOURICE, John	22	M	Laborer	01Ju02Ax
CLEESON, Micheal	28	M	Wool Comber	01Ju02Ax
MEINY, Thomas	22	M	Laborer	01Ju02Ax
John	18	M	Laborer	01Ju02Ax
IRVIN, David	35	M	Laborer	01Ju02Ax
BREW, Thade	55	M	Laborer	01Ju02Ax
Thade-Jr.	18	M	Laborer	01Ju02Ax
CASEY, Charles	26	M	Bricklayer	01Ju02Ax
OCONNOR, Alice	20	F	Servant	01Ju02Ax
MCDERMOTT, Isabella	19	F	Milliner	01Ju02Ax
BOLAND, Mary	24	F	Servant	01Ju02Ax
OBRIAN, Mary	22	F	Milliner	01Ju02Ax
MACKIN, Marian	22	F	Milliner	01Ju02Ax
BURKE, John	19	M	Tailor	01Ju02Ax
MILBY, Charles	24	M	Servant	01Ju02Ax
DIVERS, Lawrence	22	M	Servant	01Ju02Ax
PURSELL, Elizabeth	20	F	Servant	01Ju02Ax
GRADY, Patrick	27	M	Farmer	01Ju02Ax
MCREON, Phil	35	M	Cooper	01Ju02Ax
Ann	30	F	None	01Ju02Ax
Ann	06	F	Child	01Ju02Ax
BRADY, Ann	20	F	Servant	01Ju02Ax
Phil	30	M	Laborer	01Ju02Ax
DAVIS, Allice	50	F	Milliner	01Ju02Ax
Andrew	17	M	None	01Ju02Ax
RYAN, William	17	M	None	01Ju02Ax
MORRIS, Micheal	17	M	Laborer	01Ju02Ax
COLMAN, John	26	M	Laborer	01Ju02Ax
FITZPATRICK, Judy	19	F	None	01Ju02Ax
BRADY, Mary	20	F	None	01Ju02Ax
BURNS, Margaret	19	F	None	01Ju02Ax
BRADY, Patrick	16	M	None	01Ju02Ax
SHINE, Johanna	30	F	None	01Ju02Ax
John	.00	M	Infant	01Ju02Ax
KEEFE, Catherine	21	F	None	01Ju02Ax
COLLINS, Sylvester	17	M	None	01Ju02Ax
LAWLER, Julia	26	F	None	01Ju02Ax
GAVIN, Brian	20	M	None	01Ju02Ax
COWRY, Martin	21	M	None	01Ju02Ax
WARD, Margt.	22	F	None	01Ju02Ax
CANE, Bridget	20	F	None	01Ju02Ax
BROWN, James	28	M	Mason	01Ju02Ax
Charlotte	32	F	None	01Ju02Ax
Sarah	05	F	Child	01Ju02Ax
Margaret	03	F	Child	01Ju02Ax
Robert	.01	M	Infant	01Ju02Ax
Thomas	32	M	None	01Ju02Ax
Letitia	18	F	None	01Ju02Ax
COLLINS, Mary	40	F	None	01Ju02Ax
Anne	15	F	None	01Ju02Ax
John	17	M	None	01Ju02Ax
HARKWELL, Elizabeth	21	F	None	01Ju02Ax
Hannah	15	F	None	01Ju02Ax
RONAN, Mary	25	F	None	01Ju02Ax
REARDON, Julia	18	F	None	01Ju02Ax
FRUNTY, Ellen	17	F	None	01Ju02Ax
SHEERAN, Bridgette	16	F	None	01Ju02Ax
CANE, James	22	M	Seaman	01Ju02Ax
Mary	18	F	None	01Ju02Ax
WILSON, Hannah	23	F	None	01Ju02Ax
Eliza	13	F	None	01Ju02Ax
MCHUGH, Thos.	27	M	Laborer	01Ju02Ax
MCGURRAN, Arthur	30	M	Laborer	01Ju02Ax
DURSEN, Patrick	30	M	Laborer	01Ju02Ax
RONAN, John	26	M	Laborer	01Ju02Ax
OBRIAN, Micheal	26	M	Laborer	01Ju02Ax
COSTELLO, William	30	M	Laborer	01Ju02Ax
WILLIAMS, Patrick	56	M	Laborer	01Ju02Ax
Bridgett	56	F	None	01Ju02Ax
Timothy	24	M	None	01Ju02Ax
Catherine	18	F	None	01Ju02Ax
FARRELL, Catherine	50	F	Servant	01Ju02Ax
MCHUGH, Bridgett	20	F	Servant	01Ju02Ax
HYNES, Anne	05	F	Child	01Ju02Ax
Maria	07	F	Child	01Ju02Ax
Patrick	11	M	Child	01Ju02Ax
GERAGHTY, Patrick	20	M	Laborer	01Ju02Ax
Elizabeth	20	F	None	01Ju02Ax
KIERNAN, Patrick	20	M	Laborer	01Ju02Ax
WATSON, John	35	M	Coach Maker	01Ju02Ax
Patrick	42	M	Dairyman	01Ju02Ax
KELLY, Ellen	20	F	None	01Ju02Ax
Bridgett	22	F	None	01Ju02Ax
DEVIN, John	28	M	Draper	01Ju02Ax
CROOKE, U	42	M	Physician	01Ju02Ax
CAMPBELL, James	25	M	Laborer	01Ju02Ax
Catherine	23	F	None	01Ju02Ax
Mary	20	F	None	01Ju02Ax
Mary	16	F	None	01Ju02Ax
BRIAN, Ellen	20	F	None	01Ju02Ax
HACKETT, Peter	30	M	None	01Ju02Ax
COX, Charles	18	M	None	01Ju02Ax
DOWD, Micheal	25	M	None	01Ju02Ax
TINNERTON, Sarah	20	F	None	01Ju02Ax
LEARY, James	20	M	Laborer	01Ju02Ax
John	25	M	Shoemaker	01Ju02Ax
WAIT, John	20	M	Shoemaker	01Ju02Ax
MURPHY, Mary	23	F	None	01Ju02Ax
MOONEY, Thomas	.00	M	Infant	01Ju02Ax
WILLIAMS, Catherine	26	F	Servant	01Ju02Ax
RONAN, Johanna	20	F	Servant	01Ju02Ax
RIBERAN, James	30	M	Laborer	01Ju02Ax
Mary	27	F	Laborer	01Ju02Ax
Thomas	01	M	Child	01Ju02Ax
DAVIS, James	20	M	Laborer	01Ju02Ax
RIBERAN, Micheal	20	M	Laborer	01Ju02Ax
GORRIGAN, Catherine	20	F	Servant	01Ju02Ax
LYONS, Mary	20	F	Servant	01Ju02Ax
MCGOWN, Ann	25	F	Servant	01Ju02Ax
Daniel	23	M	Laborer	01Ju02Ax

NAMES OF PASSENGERS	AGE	SEX	OCCUPATIONS	DATE PORT SHIP
MCGORRY, Bridget	20	F	Servant	01Ju02Ax
John	.09	M	Infant	01Ju02Ax
CAVANAGH, Alice	11	F	None	01Ju02Ax
Edwd.	10	M	None	01Ju02Ax
MOONEY, Mary	32	F	Servant	01Ju02Ax
MCMAKIN, Jeremiah	33	M	Wheelwright	01Ju02Ax
BUTLER, Micheal	26	M	Laborer	01Ju02Ax
FLOOD, Mary	30	F	Servant	01Ju02Ax
SMITH, Eliza	08	F	Child	01Ju02Ax
CAVANAGH, Laurence	30	M	Laborer	01Ju02Ax
MOORE, John	23	M	Laborer	01Ju02Ax
CONOLLY, Jane	28	F	Dressmaker	01Ju02Ax
Bridget	07	F	Child	01Ju02Ax
Catherine	03	F	Child	01Ju02Ax
Sarah	01	F	Child	01Ju02Ax
James	.00	M	Infant	01Ju02Ax
MCGRATH, Bridget	22	F	None	01Ju02Ax
NARY, Bridget	21	F	None	01Ju02Ax
CARBERRY, Margaret	18	F	None	01Ju02Ax
KILLIDY, James	12	M	None	01Ju02Ax
CARBERRY, Patrick	23	M	None	01Ju02Ax
MURRAY, John	23	M	None	01Ju02Ax
GAPHREEN, Hugh	24	M	None	01Ju02Ax
Charles	22	M	Baker	01Ju02Ax
Honor	52	F	None	01Ju02Ax
Margaret	18	F	None	01Ju02Ax
FOLEY, Anne	18	F	None	01Ju02Ax
LUNDY, Thomas	21	M	None	01Ju02Ax
John	20	M	None	01Ju02Ax
CONNOR, Mary	26	F	None	01Ju02Ax
MCGEEHAN, John	33	M	None	01Ju02Ax
John	10	M	None	01Ju02Ax
Hugh	06	M	Child	01Ju02Ax
James	04	M	Child	01Ju02Ax
Edward	01	M	Child	01Ju02Ax
Alice	30	F	None	01Ju02Ax
MCCORT, John	21	M	None	01Ju02Ax
Catherine	19	F	None	01Ju02Ax
WARD, Samuel	25	M	None	01Ju02Ax
Jane	23	F	None	01Ju02Ax
Margaret	.00	F	Infant	01Ju02Ax
REILLY, Micheal	30	M	None	01Ju02Ax
CAFFREY, Hugh	18	M	None	01Ju02Ax
ROGERS, Dawson	19	M	Clerk	01Ju02Ax
ARMSTRONG, Robert	22	M	Draper	01Ju02Ax
Edwd.	30	M	Cmmr	01Ju02Ax
TOLEY, Bridget	24	F	Servant	01Ju02Ax
LEERY, James	.00	M	Infant	01Ju02Ax
BRADY, Ann	15	F	Servant	01Ju02Ax
CONNATT, John	10	M	None	01Ju02Ax
Patrick	07	M	Child	01Ju02Ax
KEEFE, David	20	M	Laborer	01Ju02Ax
HOLMAN, Judith	50	F	None	01Ju02Ax
ODONNELL, Mary	18	F	None	01Ju02Ax
COLMAN, Julia	50	F	None	01Ju02Ax
DILLON, Edmund	26	M	Laborer	01Ju02Ax

GARLAND-GROVE 02 JUNE 1848

From London

NAMES OF PASSENGERS	AGE	SEX	OCCUPATIONS	DATE PORT SHIP
MARKS, William	22	M	Engineer	02Ju21Ky
WILLIAMS, James	47	M	Unknown	02Ju21Ky
Fredrick	18	M	Unknown	02Ju21Ky
George	14	M	Unknown	02Ju21Ky
BOWER, John	26	M	Unknown	02Ju21Ky
MEKEN, Fredk.	21	M	Unknown	02Ju21Ky
JOWER, John	25	M	Unknown	02Ju21Ky
GERDS, John	22	M	Sugar Baker	02Ju21Ky
BROWNS, Colin	23	M	Unknown	02Ju21Ky
MENDERS, Harman	26	M	Unknown	02Ju21Ky
WOLHLS, John	18	M	Unknown	02Ju21Ky
KELDERS, Fredk.	24	M	Unknown	02Ju21Ky
HINCHIN, Fredk.	20	M	Unknown	02Ju21Ky
HESMAN, Fredk.	22	M	Unknown	02Ju21Ky
WEBB, Charles	23	M	Chwkr	02Ju21Ky
Robert	22	M	Chwkr	02Ju21Ky
STEVEN, John	21	M	Farmer	02Ju21Ky
Ann	23	F	Unknown	02Ju21Ky
OGADDY, Patrick	30	M	Unknown	02Ju21Ky
Annora	30	F	Unknown	02Ju21Ky
KIMBAL, Fredk.	21	M	Laborer	02Ju21Ky
CONNER, Bartholomew	19	M	Unknown	02Ju21Ky
ROPER, Causon	26	M	Unknown	02Ju21Ky
BYERS, James	27	M	Unknown	02Ju21Ky
MOORE, Thomas	20	M	Unknown	02Ju21Ky
JONES, John	33	M	Haberdasher	02Ju21Ky
HURLEY, John	18	M	Haberdasher	02Ju21Ky
TYLOR, Ann	40	F	Haberdasher	02Ju21Ky
HURLEY, Timothy	08	M	Child	02Ju21Ky
DWYER, Richard	47	M	Unknown	02Ju21Ky
Bridget	47	F	Unknown	02Ju21Ky
Ann	18	F	Clerk	02Ju21Ky
James	02	M	Child	02Ju21Ky
GALWAY, David	40	M	Unknown	02Ju21Ky
Mary	42	F	Unknown	02Ju21Ky
Mary	12	F	Unknown	02Ju21Ky
John	10	M	Unknown	02Ju21Ky
Thomas	05	M	Child	02Ju21Ky
MILLER, Stephen	38	M	Laborer	02Ju21Ky
ABRAM, Harry	27	M	Laborer	02Ju21Ky
ROAKE, Catharine	30	F	Laborer	02Ju21Ky
SHANE, Mary	30	F	Laborer	02Ju21Ky
LEARY, Mary	30	F	Laborer	02Ju21Ky
LANE, Dennis	25	M	Laborer	02Ju21Ky
SMITH, Richard	53	M	Laborer	02Ju21Ky
Sophia	44	F	Laborer	02Ju21Ky
John	10	M	Laborer	02Ju21Ky
Benjamin	08	M	Child	02Ju21Ky
Henry	06	M	Child	02Ju21Ky
Mary-Ann	02	F	Child	02Ju21Ky
PARSONS, John	21	M	Laborer	02Ju21Ky
MARSDEN, John	28	M	Laborer	02Ju21Ky
TOMKINS, William	30	M	Laborer	02Ju21Ky
HARVEY, Charles	25	M	Laborer	02Ju21Ky
Eliza	27	F	Laborer	02Ju21Ky
Eliza	05	F	Child	02Ju21Ky
OBRIEN, James	54	M	Laborer	02Ju21Ky
John	24	M	Laborer	02Ju21Ky
Flora	54	F	Unknown	02Ju21Ky
James	26	M	Gentleman	02Ju21Ky
David	22	M	Unknown	02Ju21Ky
Jeremiah	19	M	Unknown	02Ju21Ky
CAMPBELL, Charles	28	M	Unknown	02Ju21Ky
BENFIELD, Charles	27	M	Unknown	02Ju21Ky
Elizabeth	25	F	Unknown	02Ju21Ky
Sarah	03	F	Child	02Ju21Ky
BORLECK, Henry	21	M	Unknown	02Ju21Ky
CLARK, Samuel	21	M	Unknown	02Ju21Ky
KATES, Elijah	28	M	Unknown	02Ju21Ky
CHADWICK, John	60	M	Unknown	02Ju21Ky
BIRD, George	19	M	Unknown	02Ju21Ky
SAUNDERS, William	40	M	Unknown	02Ju21Ky
Mary-Ann	30	F	Unknown	02Ju21Ky
William	03	M	Child	02Ju21Ky
Emily	01	F	Child	02Ju21Ky
Mary-Ann	.00	F	Infant	02Ju21Ky
KENBEN, Fredk.	27	M	Unknown	02Ju21Ky
PIERCE, Thomas	34	M	Unknown	02Ju21Ky
JENKINS, Welham	32	M	Unknown	02Ju21Ky
RUTHERFORD, James	32	M	Unknown	02Ju21Ky
BROWN, William	50	M	Unknown	02Ju21Ky
Mary	50	F	Unknown	02Ju21Ky
Mary	21	F	Unknown	02Ju21Ky

NAMES OF PASSENGERS	AGE	SEX	OCCUPATIONS	DATE PORT SHIP
BROWN, Elizabeth	06	F	Child	02Ju21Ky
BARNARD, Thomas-H.	40	M	Unknown	02Ju21Ky
MALIE, John	42	M	Unknown	02Ju21Ky
WIGSTON, William	30	M	Unknown	02Ju21Ky
Jane	34	F	Unknown	02Ju21Ky
Francis	06	M	Child	02Ju21Ky
SAMPSON, Charles	18	M	Unknown	02Ju21Ky
FEANS, Phillip	27	M	Unknown	02Ju21Ky
Catharine	29	F	Unknown	02Ju21Ky
NACHO, Frank	23	M	Unknown	02Ju21Ky
Caroline	24	F	Unknown	02Ju21Ky
Lendane	20	U	Unknown	02Ju21Ky
HALLINTING, Jacob	22	M	Unknown	02Ju21Ky
HELEN, John	35	M	Unknown	02Ju21Ky
Eliza	27	F	Unknown	02Ju21Ky
LEHORAR, Phillip	18	M	Unknown	02Ju21Ky
KING, Charles	21	M	Unknown	02Ju21Ky
GORTNER, Daniel	28	M	Unknown	02Ju21Ky
Eliza	22	F	Unknown	02Ju21Ky
William	.00	M	Infant	02Ju21Ky
SCHWARTZ, William	29	M	Unknown	02Ju21Ky
DERBE, John	26	M	Unknown	02Ju21Ky
Peter	18	M	Unknown	02Ju21Ky
LERMON, Valentine	19	M	Unknown	02Ju21Ky
GARDNER, Peter	25	M	Unknown	02Ju21Ky
Catharine	22	F	Unknown	02Ju21Ky
Peter	.00	M	Infant	02Ju21Ky
HARTMANN, George	24	M	Unknown	02Ju21Ky
CHRISTIAN, Ricker	22	M	Unknown	02Ju21Ky
WERTBOCK, Charles	29	M	Unknown	02Ju21Ky
PIFAFF, George	19	M	Unknown	02Ju21Ky
LEHR, Mary	28	F	Unknown	02Ju21Ky
CHEMERS, Henry	22	M	Unknown	02Ju21Ky
WERGEL, Peter	32	M	Unknown	02Ju21Ky
Maria	35	F	Unknown	02Ju21Ky
Peter	06	M	Child	02Ju21Ky
Henry	04	M	Child	02Ju21Ky
Jacob	.00	M	Infant	02Ju21Ky
HELWIG, William	27	M	Unknown	02Ju21Ky
STILZ, Jacob	27	M	Unknown	02Ju21Ky
Charlotte	30	F	Unknown	02Ju21Ky
Eliza	24	F	Unknown	02Ju21Ky
FENA, William	31	M	Unknown	02Ju21Ky
Catharine	31	F	Unknown	02Ju21Ky
George	05	M	Child	02Ju21Ky
John	.00	M	Infant	02Ju21Ky
BROWN, George	57	M	Unknown	02Ju21Ky
Francisco	27	M	Unknown	02Ju21Ky
SCHNEIDER, Jacob	20	M	Unknown	02Ju21Ky
BLAS, Jacob	23	M	Unknown	02Ju21Ky
VOYCT, Fredrick	25	M	Unknown	02Ju21Ky
FEIGHT, Charles	25	M	Unknown	02Ju21Ky
Gustavus	15	M	Unknown	02Ju21Ky
LEOPOLD, Henry	20	M	Unknown	02Ju21Ky
RONEY, Charles	27	M	Unknown	02Ju21Ky
WERLAND, Jacob	23	M	Unknown	02Ju21Ky
SCHILLING, Fredk.	25	M	Unknown	02Ju21Ky
INGRAM, Anton	28	M	Unknown	02Ju21Ky
GERD, John	28	M	Unknown	02Ju21Ky
James	27	M	Unknown	02Ju21Ky
NETH, Phillip	45	M	Unknown	02Ju21Ky
Madeline	43	F	Unknown	02Ju21Ky
Jacob	18	M	Unknown	02Ju21Ky
WALL, Johan	40	M	Unknown	02Ju21Ky
Louisa	38	F	Unknown	02Ju21Ky
Wilhelm	20	M	Unknown	02Ju21Ky
Valentine	18	M	Unknown	02Ju21Ky
Wilhelm	30	M	Unknown	02Ju21Ky
Elizabeth	30	F	Unknown	02Ju21Ky
SCHLIFFE, Wilhelm	40	M	Unknown	02Ju21Ky
Margaretia	40	F	Unknown	02Ju21Ky
Johan	20	M	Unknown	02Ju21Ky
Maria	16	F	Unknown	02Ju21Ky
Catharine	10	F	Unknown	02Ju21Ky
VOYT, Sebastian	25	M	Unknown	02Ju21Ky
SCHLAFF, Peter	30	M	Unknown	02Ju21Ky
HOBRENAGN, Henry	25	M	Unknown	02Ju21Ky
GRADY, Margaret	25	F	Unknown	02Ju21Ky

OREGON 02 JUNE 1848

From Liverpool

NAMES OF PASSENGERS		AGE	SEX	OCCUPATIONS	DATE PORT SHIP
LAWSON, Alexander		20	M	Farmer	02Ju02Ux
BUCKLEY, Ann		22	F	Farmer	02Ju02Ux
Ellen		20	F	Farmer	02Ju02Ux
Michael		21	M	Farmer	02Ju02Ux
David		18	M	Farmer	02Ju02Ux
MURPHY, Catherine		18	F	Farmer	02Ju02Ux
FRANEY, Thomas		20	M	Poulterer	02Ju02Ux
Margaret	(W)	21	F	Poulterer	02Ju02Ux
FLOOD, Maria		22	F	Poulterer	02Ju02Ux
Margaret		21	F	Poulterer	02Ju02Ux
MORGAN, Patrick		21	M	Clerk	02Ju02Ux
MURRAY, Catherine		30	F	Servant	02Ju02Ux
HART, John		20	M	Farmer	02Ju02Ux
DEVENEY, Patrick		24	M	Farmer	02Ju02Ux
Catherine		26	F	Farmer	02Ju02Ux
SCANLAN, Bridget		22	F	Farmer	02Ju02Ux
JUDGE, Cathrine		16	F	Farmer	02Ju02Ux
BOYLE, Margaret		17	F	Farmer	02Ju02Ux
EAGAN, Jane		15	F	Farmer	02Ju02Ux
GAUGHRAN, Peter		22	M	Draper	02Ju02Ux
Patrick		20	M	Grocer	02Ju02Ux
LERRISEY, Thomas		20	M	Laborer	02Ju02Ux
MCDONALD, Mary		21	F	Seamstress	02Ju02Ux
TOBIN, Martin		45	M	Laborer	02Ju02Ux
DUNN, Patrick		22	M	Laborer	02Ju02Ux
HEALY, Martin		25	M	None	02Ju02Ux
FOX, Ann		18	F	Servant	02Ju02Ux
TRAINOR, Thomas		22	M	Laborer	02Ju02Ux
John		24	M	Laborer	02Ju02Ux
HUNT, Mathew		20	M	None	02Ju02Ux
CONNOR, Ann		30	F	Dressmaker	02Ju02Ux
John		02	M	Child	02Ju02Ux
Maria		.00	F	Infant	02Ju02Ux
DOYLE, Kat.		20	F	Servant	02Ju02Ux
WARREN, Thomas		22	M	Engineer	02Ju02Ux
SHANNON, Michael		19	M	Car Man	02Ju02Ux
LEECHY, James		20	M	Laborer	02Ju02Ux
Thom		10	M	Laborer	02Ju02Ux
Mary		07	F	Laborer	02Ju02Ux
LARYTON, Patrick		30	M	Laborer	02Ju02Ux
MCCULLOCH, James		25	M	Laborer	02Ju02Ux
MCKEON, Hugh		27	M	Weaver	02Ju02Ux
Eliza	(W)	25	F	Weaver	02Ju02Ux
KENNEDY, Susan		25	F	Seamstress	02Ju02Ux
DAVEY, John		25	M	Laborer	02Ju02Ux
BOYLE, Charles		20	M	Laborer	02Ju02Ux
James		17	M	Laborer	02Ju02Ux
HENNESEY, Michael		30	M	Laborer	02Ju02Ux
CONDON, Bridget		22	F	Wife	02Ju02Ux
Mary		04	F	Child	02Ju02Ux
FITZPATRICK, Mary		30	F	Wife	02Ju02Ux
MCNULTY, Peter		28	M	Laborer	02Ju02Ux
KENNEDY, Ellen		10	F	Child	02Ju02Ux
MULLEN, Thomas		22	M	Laborer	02Ju02Ux
CLEAREY, Julia		31	F	Laborer	02Ju02Ux
Jeremiah	(S)	05	M	Servant	02Ju02Ux
LEADER, Bridget		27	F	Servant	02Ju02Ux
FLANIGAN, Thomas		19	M	Laborer	02Ju02Ux
COOK, John		17	M	Laborer	02Ju02Ux
BONATON, Jane		20	F	Servant	02Ju02Ux
BROWN, Mary		30	F	Servant	02Ju02Ux

NAMES OF PASSENGERS	AGE	SEX	OCCUPATIONS	DATE PORT SHIP
BROWN, Ellen	09	F	Servant	02Ju02Ux
Daniel	06	M	Servant	02Ju02Ux
Alexander	04	M	Servant	02Ju02Ux
HEMPBELL, John	14	M	Laborer	02Ju02Ux
MCCURREY, W.J.	20	M	Hairdresser	02Ju02Ux
Charlotte	19	F	Hairdresser	02Ju02Ux
BRUNSAN, Ellen	30	F	Hairdresser	02Ju02Ux
Peter	35	M	Hairdresser	02Ju02Ux
Margaret	30	F	Hairdresser	02Ju02Ux
CONNOR, Arthur	27	M	Laborer	02Ju02Ux
COLLIN, Kevan	26	M	Boot Closer	02Ju02Ux
Ellen (W)	26	F	Wife	02Ju02Ux
James	04	M	Child	02Ju02Ux
William	03	M	Child	02Ju02Ux
John	.00	M	Infant	02Ju02Ux
DUNN, Mary	26	F	Servant	02Ju02Ux
William	24	M	Servant	02Ju02Ux
John	20	M	Servant	02Ju02Ux
BOYLEN, James	19	M	Laborer	02Ju02Ux
KNOWLES, Philip	37	M	Shoemaker	02Ju02Ux
Ann	13	F	Shoemaker	02Ju02Ux
Mary	11	F	Shoemaker	02Ju02Ux
John	10	M	Shoemaker	02Ju02Ux
Phillip	05	M	Shoemaker	02Ju02Ux
KELLY, Thomas	20	M	Farmer	02Ju02Ux
BURKE, Catherine	30	F	Farmer	02Ju02Ux
Catherine	30	F	Farmer	02Ju02Ux
MURRAY, Michael	12	M	Farmer	02Ju02Ux
FLINN, James	24	M	Laborer	02Ju02Ux
Mary (W)	22	F	Laborer	02Ju02Ux
MORAN, Michael	25	M	Laborer	02Ju02Ux
NALLY, Patrick	20	M	Laborer	02Ju02Ux
GILLIGAN, Patrick	14	M	Laborer	02Ju02Ux
Mary	09	F	Child	02Ju02Ux
DOHERTY, Elizabeth	19	F	Seamstress	02Ju02Ux
Hugh	15	M	Seamstress	02Ju02Ux
MCCARTHY, Daniel	20	M	Laborer	02Ju02Ux
DUMPHEY, Richard	20	M	Laborer	02Ju02Ux
OHAGAN, Patrick	19	M	Shoemaker	02Ju02Ux
DUNN, John	24	M	Shoemaker	02Ju02Ux
SMITH, Ann	16	F	Servant	02Ju02Ux
KILDUFF, Peter	30	M	None	02Ju02Ux
HARLAN, Jno.	21	M	None	02Ju02Ux
SCANLAN, Thomas	22	M	None	02Ju02Ux
GALLIGHER, William	36	M	None	02Ju02Ux
Mary	10	F	Child	02Ju02Ux
TAYLOR, James	12	M	Child	02Ju02Ux
SMITH, Ann	14	F	Child	02Ju02Ux
REAL, Pat	10	M	Child	02Ju02Ux
MURPHY, Owen	20	M	Laborer	02Ju02Ux
Bridget	20	F	Servant	02Ju02Ux
Patrick	15	M	Servant	02Ju02Ux
LOFTUS, Mary	22	F	Seamstress	02Ju02Ux
PHILLIPS, James	40	M	Ploughman	02Ju02Ux
MCMANUS, John	28	M	Worm Cutter	02Ju02Ux
Ellen	40	F	Worm Cutter	02Ju02Ux
MCKEE, Patrick	13	M	Worm Cutter	02Ju02Ux
CONAGHTON, John	32	M	Laborer	02Ju02Ux
Margaret (W)	30	F	Wife	02Ju02Ux
FLAHERTY, Mary	20	F	Servant	02Ju02Ux
MONAHAN, Patrick	42	M	Laborer	02Ju02Ux
Nancy (W)	28	F	Laborer	02Ju02Ux
Catherine	09	F	Child	02Ju02Ux
Michael	10	M	Child	02Ju02Ux
Ann	06	F	Child	02Ju02Ux
Patrick	.00	M	Infant	02Ju02Ux
MEIGHIN, Edward	40	M	Farmer	02Ju02Ux
Elizabeth (W)	38	F	Farmer	02Ju02Ux
James	21	M	Farmer	02Ju02Ux
Patrick	18	M	Farmer	02Ju02Ux
Rose	16	F	Farmer	02Ju02Ux
CAPLIN, Margaret	45	F	Farmer	02Ju02Ux
Jane	18	F	Farmer	02Ju02Ux
DUFF, Catherine	22	F	Farmer	02Ju02Ux
Mary	.00	F	Infant	02Ju02Ux
MURTHA, Ann	18	F	Farmer	02Ju02Ux
DONOLLY, Bridget	22	F	Seamstress	02Ju02Ux
MCCOLLOUGH, Robert	25	M	Laborer	02Ju02Ux
SHEANE, Patrick	27	M	Laborer	02Ju02Ux
DORAN, William	23	M	Laborer	02Ju02Ux
SHUMMUCK, Richard	27	M	Servant	02Ju02Ux
CONWAY, Patrick	25	M	Sawer	02Ju02Ux
Bridget (W)	20	F	Seamstress	02Ju02Ux
RICHY, Mary	22	F	Seamstress	02Ju02Ux
SOMERS, Hugh	22	M	Blacksmith	02Ju02Ux
Michael	21	M	Blacksmith	02Ju02Ux
Ann	20	F	Blacksmith	02Ju02Ux
Eliza	.00	F	Infant	02Ju02Ux
LYONS, John	29	M	Stone Mason	02Ju02Ux
Bridget	21	F	Stone Mason	02Ju02Ux
Michael	20	M	Stone Mason	02Ju02Ux
Rose-Wrinkle	20	F	Stone Mason	02Ju02Ux
CRILEY, James	28	M	Laborer	02Ju02Ux
Patrick	27	M	Laborer	02Ju02Ux
FAGAN, John	25	M	Laborer	02Ju02Ux
Ellen (W)	22	F	Laborer	02Ju02Ux
WILSON, James	35	M	Laborer	02Ju02Ux
ENGLISH, Margaret	19	F	Laborer	02Ju02Ux
MCGUIRE, Ann	18	F	Laborer	02Ju02Ux
RYAN, Michael	20	M	Laborer	02Ju02Ux
Thomas	26	M	Laborer	02Ju02Ux
CONNOR, Mary	30	F	Dressmaker	02Ju02Ux
ROGERS, Mary	26	F	Servant	02Ju02Ux
SLACK, John	38	M	Laborer	02Ju02Ux
Ellen	24	F	Laborer	02Ju02Ux
Thomas	24	M	Laborer	02Ju02Ux
James	.00	M	Infant	02Ju02Ux
CROAKE, Michael	26	M	Carpenter	02Ju02Ux
OWENS, Rose	20	F	Dressmaker	02Ju02Ux
RILEY, Ellen	20	F	Dressmaker	02Ju02Ux
DUNNIGAN, Daniel	22	M	Laborer	02Ju02Ux
ROUGHAN, Mary	22	F	Servant	02Ju02Ux
LAEHY, Ellen	23	F	Servant	02Ju02Ux
DEVLIN, Charles	20	M	Tpf	02Ju02Ux
CULLEN, Bessy	20	F	Servant	02Ju02Ux
FORD, Catherine	14	F	Servant	02Ju02Ux
KELLY, John	25	M	Coach Maker	02Ju02Ux
Bridget (W)	31	F	Coach Maker	02Ju02Ux
CULLEN, Peter	06	M	Child	02Ju02Ux
KELLY, Margaret-A.	02	F	Child	02Ju02Ux
Mary-Ann (T)	.00	F	Infant	02Ju02Ux
HATFIELD, Thomas	21	M	Farmer	02Ju02Ux
Margaret (W)	20	F	Farmer	02Ju02Ux
GARRY, Ellen	23	F	Farmer	02Ju02Ux
Mary	22	F	Farmer	02Ju02Ux
RILEY, Philip	24	M	Laborer	02Ju02Ux
RUBY, Margaret	24	F	Laborer	02Ju02Ux
SHEHAN, William	32	M	Farmer	02Ju02Ux
KEEP, Oween	19	M	Servant	02Ju02Ux
CURRY, Catherine	16	F	Servant	02Ju02Ux
QUADE, Catherine	14	F	Farmer	02Ju02Ux
BRADY, Bryan	40	M	Laborer	02Ju02Ux
SHANNON, John	20	M	Laborer	02Ju02Ux
KELLY, James	30	M	Laborer	02Ju02Ux
MURTAGH, James	22	M	Laborer	02Ju02Ux
Owen	20	M	Laborer	02Ju02Ux
SHIPPARD, James	24	M	Groom	02Ju02Ux
NIXON, Michael	42	M	Mason	02Ju02Ux
Febe (W)	45	F	Mason	02Ju02Ux
Hannah	14	F	Mason	02Ju02Ux
Matilda	12	F	Child	02Ju02Ux
Robert	10	M	Child	02Ju02Ux
Eliza	08	F	Child	02Ju02Ux
Phebe	06	F	Child	02Ju02Ux
John	04	M	Child	02Ju02Ux
DUFFEY, Mary	40	F	Mason	02Ju02Ux
MCNALLY, Thomas	20	M	Backer	02Ju02Ux
Catherine (W)	20	F	Backer	02Ju02Ux
ELLIS, Robert	30	M	Clerk	02Ju02Ux
DOHERTY, Margaret	40	F	Servant	02Ju02Ux

NAMES OF PASSENGERS		AGE	SEX	OCCUPATIONS	DATE PORT SHIP
TRAVERS, Philip		21	M	Laborer	02Ju02Ux
CROWN, John		20	M	Laborer	02Ju02Ux
GLINN, Susan		20	F	None	02Ju02Ux
Ann		21	F	Seamstress	02Ju02Ux
BENTLEY, Catherine		35	F	Seamstress	02Ju02Ux
Emma		.00	F	Infant	02Ju02Ux
Died-At-Sea					
Sarah		11	F	Child	02Ju02Ux
Eliza		06	F	Child	02Ju02Ux
Caroline		04	F	Child	02Ju02Ux
Robert		12	M	Child	02Ju02Ux
RINKLE, Edward		30	M	Laborer	02Ju02Ux
THOMPSON, Jeremiah		22	M	Laborer	02Ju02Ux
FOX, Catherine		20	F	Seamstress	02Ju02Ux
Eliza		20	F	Seamstress	02Ju02Ux
SMITH, John		20	M	Saddler	02Ju02Ux
Henry		20	M	Saddler	02Ju02Ux
FITZGIBBON, Honora		19	F	Seamstress	02Ju02Ux
SHANLEY, Francis		26	M	Farmer	02Ju02Ux
Bridget		27	F	Farmer	02Ju02Ux
NOALE, Patrick		22	M	Blacksmith	02Ju02Ux
LANGAN, Patrick		30	M	Laborer	02Ju02Ux
Bridget		24	F	Laborer	02Ju02Ux
SWIFT, Nancy		16	F	Servant	02Ju02Ux
COLLINS, Michael		20	M	Laborer	02Ju02Ux
Andrew		16	M	Laborer	02Ju02Ux
Ellen		21	F	Laborer	02Ju02Ux
CONOLLY, Patrick		45	M	Farmer	02Ju02Ux
Julia	(W)	35	F	Farmer	02Ju02Ux
John		12	M	Farmer	02Ju02Ux
Julia		11	F	Farmer	02Ju02Ux
Ann		09	F	Farmer	02Ju02Ux
Bridget		.00	F	Infant	02Ju02Ux
Died-At-Sea					
ODONNELL, John		25	M	Farmer	02Ju02Ux
DEVENEY, Peter		24	M	Laborer	02Ju02Ux
HEAVY, John		24	M	Laborer	02Ju02Ux
COUGHLAN, John		11	M	Child	02Ju02Ux
DEVERRY, Mary		18	F	Seamstress	02Ju02Ux
Biddy		18	F	Seamstress	02Ju02Ux
DERMODY, James		20	M	Laborer	02Ju02Ux
BYRNE, Daniel		35	M	Farmer	02Ju02Ux
FLOOD, Mary		16	F	Fysvnt	02Ju02Ux
SMITH, Catherine		20	F	Fysvnt	02Ju02Ux
REAL, Thomas		35	M	Farmer	02Ju02Ux
Mary	(W)	35	F	Farmer	02Ju02Ux
Mary		14	F	Farmer	02Ju02Ux
Margaret		12	F	Farmer	02Ju02Ux
Nicholas		05	M	Child	02Ju02Ux
Betsey		.00	F	Infant	02Ju02Ux

INDUSTRY 05 JUNE 1848

From Dublin

NAMES OF PASSENGERS		AGE	SEX	OCCUPATIONS	DATE PORT SHIP
KARVE, Martin		30	M	Farmer	05Ju20Hn
MATHEWS, Judy		24	F	Farmer	05Ju20Hn
CONNOLLY, John		24	M	Farmer	05Ju20Hn
U	(W)	20	F	Farmer	05Ju20Hn
BARNET, Samuel		30	M	Farmer	05Ju20Hn
Ann		28	F	Farmer	05Ju20Hn
HUTCHINSON, U		17	F	Farmer	05Ju20Hn
HANCHISSY, James		24	M	Farmer	05Ju20Hn
U	(W)	22	F	Farmer	05Ju20Hn
MCEVOY, William		50	M	Farmer	05Ju20Hn
U	(W)	50	F	Farmer	05Ju20Hn
James		26	M	Farmer	05Ju20Hn
Margret		24	F	Farmer	05Ju20Hn
Mary-Ann		22	F	Farmer	05Ju20Hn
MCEVOY, Francis		21	M	Farmer	05Ju20Hn
Eliza.		19	F	Farmer	05Ju20Hn
William		17	M	Farmer	05Ju20Hn
John		14	M	Farmer	05Ju20Hn
KEARNS, Pat		25	M	Farmer	05Ju20Hn
MCEVOY, Eliza		11	F	Farmer	05Ju20Hn
Stephen		08	M	Child	05Ju20Hn
Charles		05	M	Child	05Ju20Hn
MARTIN, Stephen		24	M	Farmer	05Ju20Hn
U	(W)	20	F	Farmer	05Ju20Hn
DONNAN, Richard		30	M	Farmer	05Ju20Hn
Julia		24	F	Farmer	05Ju20Hn
Michal		.00	M	Infant	05Ju20Hn
NORTON, Pat		26	M	Farmer	05Ju20Hn
BYRNE, Richard		28	M	Farmer	05Ju20Hn
QUINN, Edward		17	M	Farmer	05Ju20Hn
DUNN, Michal		30	M	Farmer	05Ju20Hn
John		18	M	Farmer	05Ju20Hn
Ann		50	F	Farmer	05Ju20Hn
James		15	M	Farmer	05Ju20Hn
COATIS, Pat		20	M	Farmer	05Ju20Hn
WHELAN, Jer.		50	M	Farmer	05Ju20Hn
U	(W)	40	F	Farmer	05Ju20Hn
Danial		18	M	Farmer	05Ju20Hn
Pate		16	M	Farmer	05Ju20Hn
CULLEN, Patt		26	M	Farmer	05Ju20Hn
U	(W)	20	F	Farmer	05Ju20Hn
James		.00	M	Infant	05Ju20Hn
MAHONEY, Patt		24	M	Unknown	05Ju20Hn
U	(W)	20	F	Unknown	05Ju20Hn
HACHY, Michal		34	M	Unknown	05Ju20Hn
U	(W)	28	F	Unknown	05Ju20Hn
David		07	M	Child	05Ju20Hn
Catharine		05	F	Child	05Ju20Hn
Ann		03	F	Child	05Ju20Hn
Bridget		.00	F	Infant	05Ju20Hn
KEANN, John		30	M	Farmer	05Ju20Hn
U	(W)	26	F	Farmer	05Ju20Hn
Moses		02	M	Child	05Ju20Hn
Edward		.00	M	Infant	05Ju20Hn
Timothy		.00	M	Infant	05Ju20Hn
HUGGAN, Daily		34	M	Farmer	05Ju20Hn
U	(W)	26	F	Farmer	05Ju20Hn
Darby		08	M	Child	05Ju20Hn
John		06	M	Child	05Ju20Hn
Edward		.00	M	Infant	05Ju20Hn
HALPIN, Willm.		20	M	Farmer	05Ju20Hn
HIGGINS, Edward		20	M	Farmer	05Ju20Hn
HAURPEY, Catharine		20	F	Farmer	05Ju20Hn
KENEDY, Martin		17	M	Farmer	05Ju20Hn
SCHOLLAND, John		26	M	Farmer	05Ju20Hn
Edward		20	M	Farmer	05Ju20Hn
William		18	M	Farmer	05Ju20Hn
Eliza		21	F	Farmer	05Ju20Hn
HAIT, John		20	M	Farmer	05Ju20Hn
BROWN, U		40	M	Farmer	05Ju20Hn
Anne		40	F	Farmer	05Ju20Hn
William		18	M	Farmer	05Ju20Hn
James		13	M	Farmer	05Ju20Hn
Mary-A.		11	F	Farmer	05Ju20Hn
Richard		07	M	Child	05Ju20Hn
John		04	M	Child	05Ju20Hn
Bridget		.00	F	Infant	05Ju20Hn
MCGANN, Edward		20	M	Farmer	05Ju20Hn
MURRAY, Edward		20	M	Farmer	05Ju20Hn
SHERIDAN, Pat		26	M	Farmer	05Ju20Hn
DUNPURY, Ann		20	F	Farmer	05Ju20Hn
WILSON, Mary		20	F	Farmer	05Ju20Hn
PHELAN, James		24	M	Farmer	05Ju20Hn
Alley		21	F	Farmer	05Ju20Hn
MCCLAINE, Eliza		24	F	Farmer	05Ju20Hn
BYRNE, Murtagh		55	M	Farmer	05Ju20Hn
Ann		20	F	Farmer	05Ju20Hn
Andy		22	M	Farmer	05Ju20Hn
AIKIN, Murrie		42	M	Farmer	05Ju20Hn

NAMES OF PASSENGERS		AGE	SEX	OCCUPATIONS	DATE PORT SHIP
AIKIN, James		40	M	Farmer	05Ju20Hn
Alexander		22	M	Farmer	05Ju20Hn
Samuel		20	M	Farmer	05Ju20Hn
James		18	M	Farmer	05Ju20Hn
John		16	M	Farmer	05Ju20Hn
Mary-Ann		14	F	Farmer	05Ju20Hn
REILLY, Anne		24	F	Farmer	05Ju20Hn
MCLAUGHLIN, U-Mrs.		24	F	Farmer	05Ju20Hn
KELLY, Peter		27	M	Farmer	05Ju20Hn
George		26	M	Farmer	05Ju20Hn
BRAGG, Francis		24	M	Farmer	05Ju20Hn
SCOTT, James		21	M	Farmer	05Ju20Hn
MURRAY, Mary		24	F	Farmer	05Ju20Hn
ENTYART, M.-Miss		22	F	Farmer	05Ju20Hn
BRENNAN, Cath.		48	F	Farmer	05Ju20Hn
U	(W)	35	F	Farmer	05Ju20Hn
Matt		18	M	Farmer	05Ju20Hn
Bridget		16	F	Farmer	05Ju20Hn
Rose		13	F	Farmer	05Ju20Hn
Charles		09	M	Child	05Ju20Hn
B.		07	M	Child	05Ju20Hn
Michael		05	M	Child	05Ju20Hn
Pat		03	M	Child	05Ju20Hn
Chr.		.00	M	Infant	05Ju20Hn
KING, Esther		24	F	Farmer	05Ju20Hn
CLEARY, Denis		28	M	Farmer	05Ju20Hn
DUFFEY, James		21	M	Farmer	05Ju20Hn
CANVEL, Anne		20	F	Farmer	05Ju20Hn
Pat		16	M	Farmer	05Ju20Hn
Owen		19	M	Farmer	05Ju20Hn
HAMMOND, Eliza		19	F	Farmer	05Ju20Hn
FERRNS, Cr.		20	M	Farmer	05Ju20Hn
HUNT, Sally		24	F	Farmer	05Ju20Hn
BYRNE, Eliza		24	F	Farmer	05Ju20Hn
CARROLL, James		24	M	Farmer	05Ju20Hn
U	(W)	20	F	Farmer	05Ju20Hn
CONNOLLY, Bridget		25	F	Farmer	05Ju20Hn
FITZPATRICK, Barth.		18	M	Farmer	05Ju20Hn
BAILEY, James		24	M	Farmer	05Ju20Hn
Mary		30	F	Farmer	05Ju20Hn
Mary		21	F	Farmer	05Ju20Hn
TOOLE, John		20	M	Farmer	05Ju20Hn
CARROLL, Edward		21	M	Farmer	05Ju20Hn
Margt.		00	F	Farmer	05Ju20Hn
FITZGERALD, Simon		20	M	Farmer	05Ju20Hn
CORR, Ann		24	F	Farmer	05Ju20Hn
Bridget		26	F	Farmer	05Ju20Hn
Jane		27	F	Farmer	05Ju20Hn
Emilia		08	F	Child	05Ju20Hn
Thomas		.00	M	Infant	05Ju20Hn
BRENNAN, John		.00	M	Infant	05Ju20Hn
KELLY, Ann		27	F	Farmer	05Ju20Hn
HILLIARD, Walter		20	M	Farmer	05Ju20Hn
BYERS, U		24	F	Farmer	05Ju20Hn
MCMAHON, Mary		24	F	Farmer	05Ju20Hn
Pat		10	M	Farmer	05Ju20Hn
HEENEY, John		48	M	Farmer	05Ju20Hn
U	(W)	44	F	Farmer	05Ju20Hn
James		20	M	Farmer	05Ju20Hn
John		14	M	Farmer	05Ju20Hn
Eliza		17	F	Farmer	05Ju20Hn
Ellen		12	F	Farmer	05Ju20Hn
Ann		07	F	Child	05Ju20Hn
SHEAL, John		21	M	Farmer	05Ju20Hn
MOONEY, Henry		28	M	Farmer	05Ju20Hn
U	(W)	20	F	Farmer	05Ju20Hn
MCGINNISS, U-Mrs.		20	F	Farmer	05Ju20Hn
BROPHY, Martin		20	M	Farmer	05Ju20Hn
U-Mrs.		50	F	Farmer	05Ju20Hn
Edward		19	M	Farmer	05Ju20Hn
Mark		18	M	Farmer	05Ju20Hn
Richard		16	M	Farmer	05Ju20Hn
John		13	M	Farmer	05Ju20Hn
William		12	M	Farmer	05Ju20Hn
BEYEN, Lawrence		21	M	Farmer	05Ju20Hn
BEYEN, Ann		16	F	Farmer	05Ju20Hn
HYNES, John		30	M	Farmer	05Ju20Hn
Mary		30	F	Farmer	05Ju20Hn
Dan		25	M	Farmer	05Ju20Hn
Ellen		50	F	Farmer	05Ju20Hn
Michael		.00	M	Infant	05Ju20Hn
CORCORAN, John		24	M	Farmer	05Ju20Hn
TOOMEY, Denis		30	M	Farmer	05Ju20Hn
DORARY, Pat		27	M	Farmer	05Ju20Hn
LESLY, James		40	M	Farmer	05Ju20Hn
U	(W)	38	F	Farmer	05Ju20Hn
Thomas		13	M	Farmer	05Ju20Hn
MURRAY, Ann		24	F	Farmer	05Ju20Hn
Thomas		.00	M	Infant	05Ju20Hn
Biddy		04	F	Child	05Ju20Hn
LAWLESS, Peter		24	M	Farmer	05Ju20Hn
Cath.		22	F	Farmer	05Ju20Hn
ODONNELL, Pat		27	M	Farmer	05Ju20Hn
GALLAGHIR, Pat		28	M	Farmer	05Ju20Hn
SLEOWIN, George		24	M	Farmer	05Ju20Hn
LESLEY, Ann		16	F	Farmer	05Ju20Hn
BUTLER, Mgt.		18	F	Farmer	05Ju20Hn

NANCY 06 JUNE 1848

From Waterford

NAMES OF PASSENGERS		AGE	SEX	OCCUPATIONS	DATE PORT SHIP
QUOR, Patrick		24	M	Laborer	06Ju16Kz
HAYES, Pat		23	M	Laborer	06Ju16Kz
POWER, Michl.		18	M	Laborer	06Ju16Kz
Martin		19	M	Laborer	06Ju16Kz
NOONAN, Margt.		20	F	Wife	06Ju16Kz
DOYLE, Ellen		21	F	Spinster	06Ju16Kz
James		24	M	Laborer	06Ju16Kz
Thos.		27	M	Unknown	06Ju16Kz
LIDDIN, Mary		18	F	Spinster	06Ju16Kz
FLAHERTY, James		21	M	Unknown	06Ju16Kz
Mary		22	F	Unknown	06Ju16Kz
Mary		.00	F	Infant	06Ju16Kz
Born-At-Sea					
Wm.		09	M	Child	06Ju16Kz
Susan		05	F	Child	06Ju16Kz
Mary		03	F	Child	06Ju16Kz
ROACH, Cathr.		19	F	Unknown	06Ju16Kz
BOYDE, John		21	M	Laborer	06Ju16Kz
Mary	(W)	24	F	Wife	06Ju16Kz
Thos.		.00	M	Infant	06Ju16Kz
Born-At-Sea					
FLYNN, Danl.		24	M	Laborer	06Ju16Kz
FLAHERTY, Jno.		24	M	Laborer	06Ju16Kz
LONERGAN, Pat.		22	M	Laborer	06Ju16Kz
BRASSILL, Thos.		30	M	Laborer	06Ju16Kz
HICKEY, Ellen		21	F	Laborer	06Ju16Kz
CLEARY, Julia		24	F	Laborer	06Ju16Kz
DALTON, Andw.		36	M	Laborer	06Ju16Kz
BRENNAN, Pat		52	M	Laborer	06Ju16Kz
WALSH, Adam		22	M	Laborer	06Ju16Kz
BYRNE, Ann		23	F	Laborer	06Ju16Kz
WALSH, Lawn.		28	M	Laborer	06Ju16Kz
FLYNN, John		23	M	Laborer	06Ju16Kz
WALSH, John		30	M	Laborer	06Ju16Kz
POWER, John		26	M	Laborer	06Ju16Kz
FLYNN, Mary		22	F	Laborer	06Ju16Kz
HYMAN, Pat		26	M	Laborer	06Ju16Kz
BARRY, Wm.		24	M	Laborer	06Ju16Kz
John		21	M	Laborer	06Ju16Kz
KAVANAGH, TGIS,		29	M	Laborer	06Ju16Kz
GLEESON, John		22	M	Laborer	06Ju16Kz
FLYNN, Mary		25	F	Laborer	06Ju16Kz

NAMES OF PASSENGERS		AGE	SEX	OCCUPATIONS	DATE PORT SHIP
OCALLAGHAN, Thos.		21	M	Laborer	06Ju16Kz
HYDE, Robt.		31	M	Laborer	06Ju16Kz
LARRMIE, John		20	M	Laborer	06Ju16Kz
WILLIAMS, John		20	M	Laborer	06Ju16Kz
CATSHIRE, Lawn.		20	M	Laborer	06Ju16Kz
SHANAHAN, James		22	M	Laborer	06Ju16Kz
WHELAN, James		30	M	Laborer	06Ju16Kz
WALSH, Wm.		24	M	Laborer	06Ju16Kz
MURPHY, Cathr.		23	F	Wife	06Ju16Kz
POWER, James		43	M	Laborer	06Ju16Kz
Bridgt.		40	F	Unknown	06Ju16Kz
Ellen		16	F	Spinster	06Ju16Kz
Edw.		14	M	Laborer	06Ju16Kz
Michl.		10	M	Laborer	06Ju16Kz
Cathr.		07	F	Child	06Ju16Kz
James		03	M	Child	06Ju16Kz
CAREWY, Johana		23	F	Laborer	06Ju16Kz
MCGRATH, Johana		29	F	Wife	06Ju16Kz
KEHOE, Peter		19	M	Unknown	06Ju16Kz
LOOBY, Patk.		26	M	Laborer	06Ju16Kz
Mary		20	F	Laborer	06Ju16Kz
SHEA, Ellen		22	F	Laborer	06Ju16Kz
CONWAY, Michl.		50	M	Laborer	06Ju16Kz
James		14	M	Laborer	06Ju16Kz
Michl.Jnr.		10	M	Laborer	06Ju16Kz
John		30	M	Laborer	06Ju16Kz
Ellen	(W)	43	F	Wife	06Ju16Kz
Ann		12	F	Unknown	06Ju16Kz
Cath.		24	F	Unknown	06Ju16Kz
Judith		20	F	Unknown	06Ju16Kz
Cathr.		03	F	Child	06Ju16Kz
DORAN, John		23	M	Farmer	06Ju16Kz
KELLY, Pat		22	M	Farmer	06Ju16Kz
James		20	M	Farmer	06Ju16Kz
DALEY, Ichl.		34	M	Farmer	06Ju16Kz
Margt.		30	F	Spinster	06Ju16Kz
Galle-Or-GILLE, Ann		28	F	Spinster	06Ju16Kz
Mary-Ann		05	F	Child	06Ju16Kz
Margt.		04	F	Child	06Ju16Kz
FLYNN, Ellen Born-At-Sea		.00	F	Infant	06Ju16Kz
GALE, William Born-At-Sea		.00	M	Infant	06Ju16Kz

ENTERPRISE 06 JUNE 1848

From Dublin

NAMES OF PASSENGERS		AGE	SEX	OCCUPATIONS	DATE PORT SHIP
MURRAY, Mary		24	F	Laborer	06Ju20Hh
MCCUTAGAT, Mary		24	F	Laborer	06Ju20Hh
HILLARD, Walter		24	M	Laborer	06Ju20Hh
DUGANN, John		40	M	Laborer	06Ju20Hh
Michal		18	M	Laborer	06Ju20Hh
James		16	M	Laborer	06Ju20Hh
Ann		13	F	Laborer	06Ju20Hh
John		11	M	Laborer	06Ju20Hh
Thomas		09	M	Child	06Ju20Hh
Patt		07	M	Child	06Ju20Hh
LEARY, Pat		30	M	Laborer	06Ju20Hh
Bridget		20	F	Laborer	06Ju20Hh
WAELSH, Susan		20	F	Laborer	06Ju20Hh
KIERNAN, Thomas-S.		19	M	Laborer	06Ju20Hh
NOWLAN, Eliza		21	F	Laborer	06Ju20Hh
SMITH, Peter		24	M	Laborer	06Ju20Hh
U	(W)	20	F	Laborer	06Ju20Hh
MCENTON, Margret		20	F	Laborer	06Ju20Hh
Ann		20	F	Laborer	06Ju20Hh
MARTIN, Mary		20	F	Laborer	06Ju20Hh
FARREL, Owen		24	M	Laborer	06Ju20Hh
KENAN, Philip		27	M	Laborer	06Ju20Hh
BARRETT, Thomas		24	M	Laborer	06Ju20Hh
MCEVOY, U-Mrs.		45	F	Laborer	06Ju20Hh
Patt		24	M	Laborer	06Ju20Hh
Bridget		15	F	Laborer	06Ju20Hh
CHESTAL, Eliza		26	F	Laborer	06Ju20Hh
Eliza		21	F	Laborer	06Ju20Hh
Thomas		.00	M	Infant	06Ju20Hh
ANSTER, Samuel		27	M	Laborer	06Ju20Hh
GILLIGAN, John		28	M	Laborer	06Ju20Hh
KENNY, Mary		20	F	Laborer	06Ju20Hh
GRADY, Joseph		28	M	Laborer	06Ju20Hh
KELLON, John		26	M	Laborer	06Ju20Hh
FALLAN, John		30	M	Laborer	06Ju20Hh
U	(W)	24	F	Laborer	06Ju20Hh
Mary		.00	F	Infant	06Ju20Hh
DEECAN, Jane		20	F	Laborer	06Ju20Hh
LYNCH, James		24	M	Laborer	06Ju20Hh
MCKEOWN, Thomas		30	M	Laborer	06Ju20Hh
Bridget		20	F	Laborer	06Ju20Hh
DONNOLY, Eliza		20	F	Laborer	06Ju20Hh
SMITH, Bartle		25	M	Laborer	06Ju20Hh
HALPIN, Pat		26	M	Laborer	06Ju20Hh
Bridget		21	F	Laborer	06Ju20Hh
BEHAN, Catharine		30	F	Laborer	06Ju20Hh
Mary-A.		20	F	Laborer	06Ju20Hh
MKEON, Catharine		26	F	Laborer	06Ju20Hh
Susana		20	F	Laborer	06Ju20Hh
GREHAN, William		15	M	Laborer	06Ju20Hh
John		25	M	Laborer	06Ju20Hh
Ellen		34	F	Laborer	06Ju20Hh
Samuel		15	M	Laborer	06Ju20Hh
WHEALAHAN, Pat		26	M	Laborer	06Ju20Hh
RONAN, Heb.		20	M	Laborer	06Ju20Hh
SMITH, Pat		27	M	Laborer	06Ju20Hh
COLON, John		13	M	Laborer	06Ju20Hh
MCGUINASS, John		26	M	Laborer	06Ju20Hh
Margret		20	F	Laborer	06Ju20Hh
KARY, Mary		20	F	Laborer	06Ju20Hh
Judy		19	F	Laborer	06Ju20Hh
Michal		21	M	Laborer	06Ju20Hh
DOLAN, Peggy		20	F	Laborer	06Ju20Hh
DOLANY, John		26	M	Laborer	06Ju20Hh
Anne		21	F	Laborer	06Ju20Hh
Anne		03	F	Child	06Ju20Hh
MULLAN, Jane		20	F	Laborer	06Ju20Hh
BUTELL, John		19	M	Laborer	06Ju20Hh
LYAL, James		27	M	Laborer	06Ju20Hh
RILLEY, Patt		27	M	Laborer	06Ju20Hh
U	(W)	22	F	Laborer	06Ju20Hh
Thomas		03	M	Child	06Ju20Hh
KELLY, Margret		24	F	Laborer	06Ju20Hh
MCENGAT, Catharine		20	F	Laborer	06Ju20Hh
QUINN, Michal		30	M	Laborer	06Ju20Hh
MAHAN, Hew		21	M	Laborer	06Ju20Hh
ALHANE, Mary		25	F	Laborer	06Ju20Hh
Wm.		.00	M	Infant	06Ju20Hh
KEHAN, Patrick		24	M	Laborer	06Ju20Hh
MARTAN, U-Mrs.		24	F	Laborer	06Ju20Hh
MALL, Joseph		20	M	Laborer	06Ju20Hh
CALL, Anna		18	F	Laborer	06Ju20Hh
John		09	M	Child	06Ju20Hh
KEHOW, Wm.		24	M	Laborer	06Ju20Hh
MAHON, Owen		30	M	Laborer	06Ju20Hh
HICKY, Samuel		21	M	Laborer	06Ju20Hh
WHELAN, Anne		20	F	Laborer	06Ju20Hh
THRYANE, Mary		20	F	Laborer	06Ju20Hh
Pat.		17	M	Laborer	06Ju20Hh
RILLEY, Patt		30	M	Laborer	06Ju20Hh
U	(W)	28	F	Laborer	06Ju20Hh
Thomas		04	M	Child	06Ju20Hh
Mary-A.		.00	F	Infant	06Ju20Hh
Patt		.00	M	Infant	06Ju20Hh
RICHFORD, Mary		20	F	Laborer	06Ju20Hh
Margret		16	F	Laborer	06Ju20Hh

NAMES OF PASSENGERS		AGE	SEX	OCCUPATIONS	DATE PORT SHIP
RYAN, Edward		40	M	Laborer	06Ju20Hh
Mary		30	F	Laborer	06Ju20Hh
Ann		07	F	Child	06Ju20Hh
Bridget		06	F	Child	06Ju20Hh
Michal		04	M	Child	06Ju20Hh
Maria		02	F	Child	06Ju20Hh
Charles		.00	M	Infant	06Ju20Hh
PITKEGHE, Bridget		50	F	Laborer	06Ju20Hh
MCNALLY, Silvesta		21	M	Laborer	06Ju20Hh
REAAN, Pat		21	M	Laborer	06Ju20Hh
WHILLY, Martin		15	M	Laborer	06Ju20Hh
FAY, Charles		35	M	Laborer	06Ju20Hh
U	(W)	30	F	Laborer	06Ju20Hh
Patrick		.00	M	Infant	06Ju20Hh
Patrick		06	M	Child	06Ju20Hh
Jane		04	F	Child	06Ju20Hh
Mary-A.		02	F	Child	06Ju20Hh
Bridget		22	F	Laborer	06Ju20Hh
RUSSEL, George		27	M	Laborer	06Ju20Hh
KENNY, Luke		27	M	Laborer	06Ju20Hh
Cath.		05	F	Child	06Ju20Hh
MUNOWAN, Jane		50	F	Laborer	06Ju20Hh
Mary		50	F	Laborer	06Ju20Hh
KENNY, Margret		30	F	Laborer	06Ju20Hh
BAXTEN, Ellen		20	F	Laborer	06Ju20Hh
DOLE, Frances		28	F	Laborer	06Ju20Hh
OHARE, Peter		21	M	Laborer	06Ju20Hh
MCLAUGHAN, Mary		20	F	Laborer	06Ju20Hh
PURCELL, Bridget		50	F	Laborer	06Ju20Hh
Mary		26	F	Laborer	06Ju20Hh
Margret		25	F	Laborer	06Ju20Hh
Ann		23	F	Laborer	06Ju20Hh
John		22	M	Laborer	06Ju20Hh
Ellen		19	F	Laborer	06Ju20Hh
Patt		17	M	Laborer	06Ju20Hh
Thomas		15	M	Laborer	06Ju20Hh
Bridget		10	F	Laborer	06Ju20Hh
Eliza		06	F	Child	06Ju20Hh
CONNOR, Pat		25	M	Laborer	06Ju20Hh
U	(W)	25	F	Unknown	06Ju20Hh
Matt		04	M	Child	06Ju20Hh
Susan		02	F	Child	06Ju20Hh
Anne		.00	F	Infant	06Ju20Hh
Anne		30	F	Laborer	06Ju20Hh
HEARY, John		25	M	Laborer	06Ju20Hh
U	(W)	25	F	Laborer	06Ju20Hh
Bith-, Peggy		20	F	Laborer	06Ju20Hh
SWINNY, Mary		20	F	Laborer	06Ju20Hh
FLANAGAN, Catharine		20	F	Laborer	06Ju20Hh
DONNOY, Rose		20	F	Laborer	06Ju20Hh
Briddy		20	F	Laborer	06Ju20Hh
MURTAGH, Wm.		21	M	Laborer	06Ju20Hh
Mary		20	F	Laborer	06Ju20Hh
HEANEY, Ellen		20	F	Laborer	06Ju20Hh
MCCORMICK, Catharine		20	F	Laborer	06Ju20Hh
HALL, U		50	M	Laborer	06Ju20Hh
MCQUADE, Joseph		28	M	Laborer	06Ju20Hh
U	(W)	26	F	Laborer	06Ju20Hh
HANY, Rey.		21	M	Laborer	06Ju20Hh
COOK, U-Mrs.		50	F	Laborer	06Ju20Hh
Mary		18	F	Laborer	06Ju20Hh
HALL, U		20	F	Laborer	06Ju20Hh
CARBOY, Michl.		32	M	Laborer	06Ju20Hh
Ellen		30	F	Laborer	06Ju20Hh
Eliza		12	F	Laborer	06Ju20Hh
John		08	M	Child	06Ju20Hh
Elias		.00	M	Infant	06Ju20Hh
ROCHFORD, Mary		20	F	Laborer	06Ju20Hh
Margt.		16	F	Laborer	06Ju20Hh
CLORRY, Judy		20	F	Laborer	06Ju20Hh
THURSON, Mary		20	F	Laborer	06Ju20Hh

PROGRESS 07 JUNE 1848

From Liverpool

NAMES OF PASSENGERS		AGE	SEX	OCCUPATIONS	DATE PORT SHIP
HASSET, Anthony		30	M	Farmer	07Ju02Uy
Margt.		28	F	Farmer	07Ju02Uy
Thomas		.00	M	Infant	07Ju02Uy
Patk.		05	M	Child	07Ju02Uy
Mary		03	F	Child	07Ju02Uy
Cathr.		.00	F	Infant	07Ju02Uy
Martin		.00	M	Infant	07Ju02Uy
NIX, Anthony		25	M	Laborer	07Ju02Uy
Margt.	(W)	22	F	Wife	07Ju02Uy
Johana		06	F	Child	07Ju02Uy
Anthony		04	M	Child	07Ju02Uy
Michl.		02	M	Child	07Ju02Uy
Ellen		.00	F	Infant	07Ju02Uy
OFLAGHERTY, Eliza		18	F	Unknown	07Ju02Uy
STAFF, James		20	M	Laborer	07Ju02Uy
OFLAGHERTY, Mary		20	F	Laborer	07Ju02Uy
STAFF, John		18	M	Laborer	07Ju02Uy
Thomas		17	M	Laborer	07Ju02Uy
Mary		40	F	Wife	07Ju02Uy
Bridget		24	F	Unknown	07Ju02Uy
Cathr.		16	F	Spinster	07Ju02Uy
Mary		14	F	Spinster	07Ju02Uy
Honora		21	F	Spinster	07Ju02Uy
BRADY, Patk.		22	M	Farmer	07Ju02Uy
John		20	M	Farmer	07Ju02Uy
HOUGH, Martin		22	M	Farmer	07Ju02Uy
FINNELL, Mary		20	F	Wife	07Ju02Uy
HANAHAN, Cathr.		20	F	Unknown	07Ju02Uy
MCKENNY, Isabella		35	F	Unknown	07Ju02Uy
Mary		09	F	Child	07Ju02Uy
Christ.		16	F	Unknown	07Ju02Uy
James		05	M	Child	07Ju02Uy
Patk.		03	M	Child	07Ju02Uy
Ellen		.00	F	Infant	07Ju02Uy
DARCY, Michl.		38	M	Laborer	07Ju02Uy
U	(W)	38	F	Wife	07Ju02Uy
Edward		09	M	Child	07Ju02Uy
FRISBY, Wm.		24	M	Farmer	07Ju02Uy
BURNS, Pat		18	M	Farmer	07Ju02Uy
Eliza		19	F	Spinster	07Ju02Uy
CAMPBELL, John		24	M	Laborer	07Ju02Uy
Pat		26	M	Laborer	07Ju02Uy
Susan		45	F	Laborer	07Ju02Uy
MOORE, John		27	M	Laborer	07Ju02Uy
Margt.		21	F	Laborer	07Ju02Uy
FUBISHER, Robt.		24	M	Laborer	07Ju02Uy
TAYLOR, John		22	M	Laborer	07Ju02Uy
ROBERTSON, Isabel		20	F	Laborer	07Ju02Uy
TAYLOR, Mary		25	F	Laborer	07Ju02Uy
Isabel		.00	F	Infant	07Ju02Uy
BRADY, B.		50	U	Unknown	07Ju02Uy
Mary		40	F	Unknown	07Ju02Uy
Bridgt.		16	F	Unknown	07Ju02Uy
Ellen		12	F	Unknown	07Ju02Uy
Mary		11	F	Unknown	07Ju02Uy
Pat		09	M	Child	07Ju02Uy
BOYLAN, Mattw.		24	M	Laborer	07Ju02Uy
Mary		12	F	Laborer	07Ju02Uy
WITHERS, Dafney		20	F	Unknown	07Ju02Uy
MCMAHON, Peter		20	M	Unknown	07Ju02Uy
TYSON, Geo.		52	M	Farmer	07Ju02Uy
U	(W)	50	F	Wife	07Ju02Uy
Jane		27	F	Unknown	07Ju02Uy
Sarah		21	F	Unknown	07Ju02Uy
Mary		17	F	Spinster	07Ju02Uy

NAMES OF PASSENGERS		AGE	SEX	OCCUPATIONS	DATE PORT SHIP
TYSON, Eliza		15	F	Unknown	07Ju02Uy
John		13	M	Unknown	07Ju02Uy
Charlotte		11	F	Unknown	07Ju02Uy
Wm.		25	M	Laborer	07Ju02Uy
U	(W)	24	F	Wife	07Ju02Uy
George		.00	M	Infant	07Ju02Uy
HORNER, Joseph		22	M	Laborer	07Ju02Uy
WILLIAMS, Isaac		20	M	Laborer	07Ju02Uy
CAVENEY, Luke		46	M	Laborer	07Ju02Uy
Mary		46	F	Laborer	07Ju02Uy
Patk.		17	M	Laborer	07Ju02Uy
Thomas		15	M	Laborer	07Ju02Uy
Edward		12	M	Unknown	07Ju02Uy
Luke		10	M	Unknown	07Ju02Uy
Mary		19	F	Unknown	07Ju02Uy
Ann		07	F	Child	07Ju02Uy
KELLY, Pat		40	M	Laborer	07Ju02Uy
Eliza		26	F	Unknown	07Ju02Uy
Thomas		12	M	Unknown	07Ju02Uy
Wm.		08	M	Child	07Ju02Uy
Maria		14	F	Unknown	07Ju02Uy
Ann		10	F	Unknown	07Ju02Uy
CONNOR, James		45	M	Laborer	07Ju02Uy
Honora		44	F	Laborer	07Ju02Uy
Martin		22	M	Laborer	07Ju02Uy
BIRMINGHAM, E.		45	M	Laborer	07Ju02Uy
Mary	(W)	30	F	Wife	07Ju02Uy
Michl.		08	M	Child	07Ju02Uy
Mary		06	F	Child	07Ju02Uy
Essey		04	F	Child	07Ju02Uy
Wm.		.00	M	Infant	07Ju02Uy
REILLY, John		28	M	Laborer	07Ju02Uy
Ann		17	F	Laborer	07Ju02Uy
DEVINE, Mary		25	F	Laborer	07Ju02Uy
HANLEY, Bridgt.		24	F	Laborer	07Ju02Uy
Honora		27	F	Laborer	07Ju02Uy
NEARY, Margt.		28	F	Laborer	07Ju02Uy
KAY, Danl.		30	M	Laborer	07Ju02Uy
WHALEN, Margt.		20	F	Laborer	07Ju02Uy
CONIGAN, James		42	M	Laborer	07Ju02Uy
U	(W)	38	F	Spinster	07Ju02Uy
Ann		05	F	Child	07Ju02Uy
James		03	M	Child	07Ju02Uy
GAFFRY, Biddy		17	F	Unknown	07Ju02Uy
LEWIS, Isaac		36	M	Unknown	07Ju02Uy
U	(W)	30	F	Unknown	07Ju02Uy
FORD, Danl.		27	M	Laborer	07Ju02Uy
Jerh.		22	M	Laborer	07Ju02Uy
COMERFORD, W.		27	M	Laborer	07Ju02Uy
REILLY, Patk.		43	M	Laborer	07Ju02Uy
Andw.		09	M	Child	07Ju02Uy
HEALY, Honora		25	F	Child	07Ju02Uy
MCDONALD, James		20	M	Child	07Ju02Uy
Michl.		17	M	Child	07Ju02Uy
MULOY, Felix		25	M	Child	07Ju02Uy
U	(W)	25	F	Wife	07Ju02Uy
Honora		20	F	Unknown	07Ju02Uy
FARREL, Peter		16	M	Laborer	07Ju02Uy
GARIFT, James		25	M	Laborer	07Ju02Uy
ROLLEY, Andw.		25	M	Laborer	07Ju02Uy
U	(W)	25	F	Laborer	07Ju02Uy
SHANLY, Bidddy		27	F	Laborer	07Ju02Uy
KEWAN, Michl.		26	M	Laborer	07Ju02Uy
DONOVAN, Wm.		26	M	Laborer	07Ju02Uy
GERETY, Cathr.		40	F	Laborer	07Ju02Uy
GARRETY, Edward		23	M	Laborer	07Ju02Uy
Cathr.	(W)	20	F	Wife	07Ju02Uy
Ann		18	F	Unknown	07Ju02Uy
Margt.		11	F	Unknown	07Ju02Uy
MONTGOMERY, Margt.		26	F	Unknown	07Ju02Uy
MILES, James		26	M	Laborer	07Ju02Uy
Sarah	(W)	20	F	Wife	07Ju02Uy
Lydia		21	F	Unknown	07Ju02Uy
MILLIGAN, Robt.		30	M	Laborer	07Ju02Uy
FINEGAN, Mattw.		35	M	Laborer	07Ju02Uy

NAMES OF PASSENGERS		AGE	SEX	OCCUPATIONS	DATE PORT SHIP
HITHERHEAD, Jose.		25	M	Laborer	07Ju02Uy
Ann-E.		.00	F	Infant	07Ju02Uy
CURRAN, Arthur		35	M	Unknown	07Ju02Uy
U	(W)	35	F	Wife	07Ju02Uy
John		.00	M	Infant	07Ju02Uy
MCCABE, Ann		26	F	Unknown	07Ju02Uy
Thos.		.00	M	Infant	07Ju02Uy
FOX, U-Mrs.		34	F	Unknown	07Ju02Uy
Geo.		34	M	Unknown	07Ju02Uy
Jos.		08	M	Child	07Ju02Uy
Robert		06	M	Child	07Ju02Uy
Elizth.		05	F	Child	07Ju02Uy
Amelia		03	F	Child	07Ju02Uy
Chas.		.00	M	Infant	07Ju02Uy
KINDALE, U-Mrs.		35	F	Wife	07Ju02Uy
Elizth.		05	F	Child	07Ju02Uy
CONON, Wm.		25	M	Farmer	07Ju02Uy
Johana		25	F	Farmer	07Ju02Uy
Mary		20	F	Spinster	07Ju02Uy
WHITECHURCH, James		40	M	Unknown	07Ju02Uy
HAGEN, E.		40	M	Laborer	07Ju02Uy
Pat		22	M	Laborer	07Ju02Uy
Biddy		26	F	Laborer	07Ju02Uy
Rose		24	F	Laborer	07Ju02Uy
LARKIN, Ellen		56	F	Laborer	07Ju02Uy
Owen		20	M	Laborer	07Ju02Uy
Peter		20	M	Laborer	07Ju02Uy
John		19	M	Laborer	07Ju02Uy
Pat		12	M	Laborer	07Ju02Uy
OHANLON, Philip		20	M	Laborer	07Ju02Uy
WHITE, Richd.		20	M	Laborer	07Ju02Uy
Ellen		20	F	Spinster	07Ju02Uy
THORNTON, Alice		34	F	Spinster	07Ju02Uy
Geo.		12	M	Unknown	07Ju02Uy
Francis		09	M	Child	07Ju02Uy
Cathr.		07	F	Child	07Ju02Uy
Owen		04	M	Child	07Ju02Uy
Mary-Ann		.00	F	Infant	07Ju02Uy
Patrick		40	M	Spinner	07Ju02Uy
U-Mrs.		40	F	Wife	07Ju02Uy
Mary		08	F	Child	07Ju02Uy
Ann		06	F	Child	07Ju02Uy
Biddy		04	F	Child	07Ju02Uy
Peter		39	M	Laborer	07Ju02Uy
Peter		.00	M	Infant	07Ju02Uy
QUIN, John		12	M	Unknown	07Ju02Uy
CARTER, Robt.		39	M	Unknown	07Ju02Uy
U	(W)	39	F	Wife	07Ju02Uy
REILLY, Peter		20	M	Unknown	07Ju02Uy
BRISCOE, Pat		25	M	Laborer	07Ju02Uy
BRIDGART, Wm.		50	M	Laborer	07Ju02Uy
Elizth.	(W)	50	F	Wife	07Ju02Uy
Saml.		16	M	Laborer	07Ju02Uy
Elizth.		13	F	Laborer	07Ju02Uy
Ann		07	F	Child	07Ju02Uy
WHEATLY, Hiram		38	M	Laborer	07Ju02Uy
SHORT, Walter		38	M	Laborer	07Ju02Uy
WARNER, Geo.		23	M	Laborer	07Ju02Uy
FARRELLY, Bryan		40	M	Laborer	07Ju02Uy
Pat		12	M	Laborer	07Ju02Uy
Edw.		09	M	Child	07Ju02Uy
Ellen		07	F	Child	07Ju02Uy
Ann		05	F	Child	07Ju02Uy
HUGHES, Thomas		20	M	Laborer	07Ju02Uy
MCNEALS, Rose		20	F	Unknown	07Ju02Uy
Cathr.		18	F	Spinster	07Ju02Uy
COYLE, Michl.		40	M	Unknown	07Ju02Uy
Pat		24	M	Laborer	07Ju02Uy
Ellen		22	F	Unknown	07Ju02Uy
Alice		14	F	Spinster	07Ju02Uy
MCKENNA, Mary		24	F	Spinster	07Ju02Uy
DEWLAN, Margt.		20	F	Spinster	07Ju02Uy
Pat		20	M	Spinner	07Ju02Uy
WILKINS, John		55	M	Laborer	07Ju02Uy
BOLAN, John		21	M	Laborer	07Ju02Uy

NAMES OF PASSENGERS		AGE	SEX	OCCUPATIONS	DATE PORT SHIP
KELLY, Mary		20	F	Laborer	07Ju02Uy
BARNES, James		40	M	Laborer	07Ju02Uy
ROOME, Geo.		16	M	Laborer	07Ju02Uy
LEARY, Michl.		30	M	Laborer	07Ju02Uy
Ann		25	F	Laborer	07Ju02Uy
MCDONALD, Andw.		25	M	Laborer	07Ju02Uy
GIBBONS, Mark		20	M	Laborer	07Ju02Uy
ROGER, John		30	M	Laborer	07Ju02Uy
MCCOUGHLIN, John		24	M	Laborer	07Ju02Uy
MALONE, Joseph		24	M	Laborer	07Ju02Uy
FORTUNE, James		30	M	Laborer	07Ju02Uy
CULLEN, Wm.		24	M	Laborer	07Ju02Uy
TIPPING, Martha		24	F	Laborer	07Ju02Uy
Simon		.00	M	Infant	07Ju02Uy
BERGAN, Margt.		21	F	Spinster	07Ju02Uy
LOUGHLIN, Eliza		20	F	Spinster	07Ju02Uy
CARTY, Ann		24	F	Spinster	07Ju02Uy
DOWNEY, Eliza		26	F	Spinster	07Ju02Uy
BOURKE, Edward		20	M	Laborer	07Ju02Uy
FOGERTY, Michl.		27	M	Unknown	07Ju02Uy
Ellen	(W)	24	F	Wife	07Ju02Uy
John		05	M	Child	07Ju02Uy
Mary		03	F	Child	07Ju02Uy
WRIGHT, Wm.		30	M	Unknown	07Ju02Uy
MATHEWS, Jno.		35	M	Unknown	07Ju02Uy
MALONE, Judith		22	F	Wife	07Ju02Uy
KEENE, Ann		22	F	Unknown	07Ju02Uy
JONES, Margt.		24	F	Unknown	07Ju02Uy
DOWDELL, Patk.		21	M	Laborer	07Ju02Uy
Bridgt.		17	F	Laborer	07Ju02Uy
SPIER, Geo.		41	M	Laborer	07Ju02Uy
Franky		40	M	Laborer	07Ju02Uy
John		17	M	Laborer	07Ju02Uy
Harriett		16	F	Spinster	07Ju02Uy
Geo.		14	M	Unknown	07Ju02Uy
Honora		09	F	Child	07Ju02Uy
Sarah		07	F	Child	07Ju02Uy
Wm.		04	M	Child	07Ju02Uy
Edward		.00	M	Infant	07Ju02Uy
BURTON, Henry		32	M	Farmer	07Ju02Uy
Harriet	(W)	31	F	Wife	07Ju02Uy
James		07	M	Child	07Ju02Uy
Elizth.		05	F	Child	07Ju02Uy
Joseph		.00	M	Infant	07Ju02Uy
HOWES, James		48	M	Laborer	07Ju02Uy
Hannah	(W)	45	F	Wife	07Ju02Uy
Eliza		20	F	Unknown	07Ju02Uy
Edmond		16	M	Laborer	07Ju02Uy
Matilda		14	F	Wife	07Ju02Uy
Isaac		12	M	Unknown	07Ju02Uy
Sarah		06	F	Child	07Ju02Uy
Charles		02	M	Child	07Ju02Uy
ANTTY, Emma		20	F	Unknown	07Ju02Uy
Richd.		02	M	Child	07Ju02Uy
BURTON, Stephen		17	M	Laborer	07Ju02Uy
Jonas		20	M	Laborer	07Ju02Uy
Saml.		15	M	Laborer	07Ju02Uy
WATTS, Henry		34	M	Laborer	07Ju02Uy
Wm.		09	M	Child	07Ju02Uy
Rich.		07	M	Child	07Ju02Uy
ARCHIBALD, Pat		28	M	Laborer	07Ju02Uy
CAMPBELL, Bridgt.		20	F	Laborer	07Ju02Uy
SMITH, James		25	M	Laborer	07Ju02Uy
KELLY, Cormick		23	M	Laborer	07Ju02Uy
TULLY, Catharine		24	F	Wife	07Ju02Uy
Honor		25	F	Unknown	07Ju02Uy
MCMANUS, Ellen		30	F	Unknown	07Ju02Uy
Michl.		06	M	Child	07Ju02Uy
John		04	M	Child	07Ju02Uy
Pat		.00	M	Infant	07Ju02Uy
MCNEALY, Elizth.		30	F	Wife	07Ju02Uy
BERGEN, Ann		26	F	Unknown	07Ju02Uy
PHILLIPS, Stephen		20	M	Laborer	07Ju02Uy
LANGAN, Jas.		45	M	Unknown	07Ju02Uy
WILSON, Ellen		26	F	Wife	07Ju02Uy

NAMES OF PASSENGERS	AGE	SEX	OCCUPATIONS	DATE PORT SHIP
WILSON, Hannah	18	F	Unknown	07Ju02Uy
Margt.	.00	F	Infant	07Ju02Uy
RUDDEN, Cathr.	32	F	Unknown	07Ju02Uy
MAGUIRE, James	24	M	Laborer	07Ju02Uy
SULLIVAN, Jerry	35	M	Laborer	07Ju02Uy
CROWE, John	23	M	Laborer	07Ju02Uy
MARTIN, Margt.	21	F	Spinster	07Ju02Uy
FOX, Michl.	40	M	Spinner	07Ju02Uy
Pat	34	M	Spinner	07Ju02Uy
Margt.	27	F	Spinster	07Ju02Uy
Mary	19	F	Spinster	07Ju02Uy
James	13	M	Unknown	07Ju02Uy
Cathr.	07	F	Child	07Ju02Uy
John	06	M	Child	07Ju02Uy
Michl.	04	M	Child	07Ju02Uy
Margt.	.00	F	Infant	07Ju02Uy
CROWLEY, Peter	13	M	Unknown	07Ju02Uy
Mary	89	F	Unknown	07Ju02Uy
Cathr.	19	F	Spinster	07Ju02Uy
CAREY, Jas.	45	M	Laborer	07Ju02Uy
John	20	M	Laborer	07Ju02Uy
Mathew	18	M	Laborer	07Ju02Uy
Mary	13	F	Spinster	07Ju02Uy
Ellen	20	F	Unknown	07Ju02Uy
COFFEY, Michl.	20	M	Laborer	07Ju02Uy
KING, Honora	25	F	Unknown	07Ju02Uy
CLEARY, Ann	21	F	Spinster	07Ju02Uy
DUFFEY, Michl.	13	M	Laborer	07Ju02Uy
CARBEY, David	27	M	Unknown	07Ju02Uy
Bridgt.	25	F	Spinster	07Ju02Uy
Thomas	02	M	Child	07Ju02Uy
Martha	.00	F	Infant	07Ju02Uy
QUINLAN, Michl.	40	M	Laborer	07Ju02Uy
WITHERHEAD, U-Mrs.	25	F	Wife	07Ju02Uy
FARELLY, Mary	40	F	Unknown	07Ju02Uy
BRIDGART, Charlotte	30	F	Unknown	07Ju02Uy
Sarah	24	F	Wife	07Ju02Uy
U, U Died-At-Sea	.00	U	Infant	07Ju02Uy
U Died-At-Sea	.00	U	Infant	07Ju02Uy
MCCANN, Hugh	38	M	Unknown	07Ju02Uy
COX, John	35	M	Unknown	07Ju02Uy
GRIFFIN, John	20	M	Unknown	07Ju02Uy
HAMILTON, Chas.	21	M	Unknown	07Ju02Uy
BARR, Mary-Ann	23	F	Unknown	07Ju02Uy
WARD, John	22	M	Unknown	07Ju02Uy
ARCHER, Benj.	22	M	Unknown	07Ju02Uy

MARY-T.RUNDLETT 09 JUNE 1848

From Cork

NAMES OF PASSENGERS	AGE	SEX	OCCUPATIONS	DATE PORT SHIP
EVANS, Thos.	52	M	Merchant	09Ju14Lc
Esther	50	F	Merchant	09Ju14Lc
DUNNE, Anne	52	F	Merchant	09Ju14Lc
EVENS, Elizabeth	19	F	Merchant	09Ju14Lc
Thos.	17	M	Merchant	09Ju14Lc
Wm.B.	14	M	None	09Ju14Lc
HORTETT, John	20	M	Unknown	09Ju14Lc
Ellen	24	F	Draper	09Ju14Lc
BARNETT, Wm.	22	M	Draper	09Ju14Lc
Mary	20	F	Draper	09Ju14Lc
BURKE, Miles	25	M	Draper	09Ju14Lc
ROTCHE, John	30	M	Draper	09Ju14Lc
Margret	28	F	Draper	09Ju14Lc
-----, -----	00	M	Unknown	09Ju14Lc
MCCARTEY, Pat	20	M	Laborer	09Ju14Lc
Dennis	20	M	Laborer	09Ju14Lc

NAMES OF PASSENGERS	AGE	SEX	OCCUPATIONS	DATE PORT SHIP
DARLY, Eliza	22	F	Laborer	09Ju14Lc
BRIMAR, John	26	M	Laborer	09Ju14Lc
BYRN, Fanny	22	F	Laborer	09Ju14Lc
SHEEHAN, Eliza	34	F	Laborer	09Ju14Lc
HANIGAN, Catharine	20	F	Unknown	09Ju14Lc
MURPHY, John	23	M	Unknown	09Ju14Lc
HEAPHY, Daniel	26	M	Unknown	09Ju14Lc
CEAHILL, John	20	M	Unknown	09Ju14Lc
SHEEHAN, Michael	20	M	Unknown	09Ju14Lc
MCCARTY, Andrew	25	M	Unknown	09Ju14Lc
COLLINS, Mary	20	F	Unknown	09Ju14Lc
HAGAN, Jerry	21	M	Unknown	09Ju14Lc
DRISCOLL, Nelley	20	F	Unknown	09Ju14Lc
FROLEY, Mary-Ann	25	F	Unknown	09Ju14Lc
Richard	21	M	Unknown	09Ju14Lc
SHEEHIN, Daniel	20	M	Laborer	09Ju14Lc
ROCHE, Bridget	22	F	None	09Ju14Lc
REEFFE, James	18	M	None	09Ju14Lc
NAGLE, Maria	18	F	Servant	09Ju14Lc
HARTNETT, Mary	20	F	Servant	09Ju14Lc
CONOVAN, Patt	30	M	Laborer	09Ju14Lc
CRONIN, Honora	20	F	None	09Ju14Lc
BLUTE, James	26	M	Weaver	09Ju14Lc
MCCARTHY, Eliza	18	F	Servant	09Ju14Lc
BURKLEY, Jerimiah	40	M	Farmer	09Ju14Lc
Catharine	38	F	None	09Ju14Lc
Tim	13	M	None	09Ju14Lc
Mary	12	F	None	09Ju14Lc
CUBB, John	33	M	Servant	09Ju14Lc
MCCARTHEY, Pat	30	M	None	09Ju14Lc
Margret	28	F	Farmer	09Ju14Lc
HARLEY, Margret	20	F	Farmer	09Ju14Lc
MCCARTEY, Michal	12	M	Servant	09Ju14Lc
Catharine	10	F	Servant	09Ju14Lc
James	04	M	Child	09Ju14Lc
BRIAN, Daniel	30	M	Laborer	09Ju14Lc
CAVANA, Thomas	28	M	Laborer	09Ju14Lc
BRENNAN, Daniel	20	M	Laborer	09Ju14Lc
MCCARTEY, Daniel	28	M	Laborer	09Ju14Lc
MORIARTY, Pat	20	M	Farmer	09Ju14Lc
CONDON, Edmond	24	M	Farmer	09Ju14Lc
BRENNAN, Mary	20	F	Servant	09Ju14Lc
WILLIAMS, Mary	18	F	Servant	09Ju14Lc
SWEENEY, Jery	30	M	Servant	09Ju14Lc
STRATTLES, George	25	M	Servant	09Ju14Lc
Catharine	50	F	Servant	09Ju14Lc
MURPHY, Tim	19	M	None	09Ju14Lc
RASIDON, Mary	25	F	Servant	09Ju14Lc
WALSH, Michael	40	M	Laborer	09Ju14Lc
Ellen	28	F	Servant	09Ju14Lc
Michael	18	M	None	09Ju14Lc
LYONS, Michael	25	M	Servant	09Ju14Lc
MURPHY, Joseph	30	M	Farmer	09Ju14Lc
LAVETT, John	30	M	Farmer	09Ju14Lc
Ellen	30	F	Farmer	09Ju14Lc
SMITH, Catharine	45	F	Farmer	09Ju14Lc
SULLIVAN, Jeremiah	26	M	Farmer	09Ju14Lc
CONNELL, Bessey	26	F	Farmer	09Ju14Lc
HICKEY, Michal	30	M	Farmer	09Ju14Lc
Edmond	30	M	Farmer	09Ju14Lc
WALSH, John	23	M	Farmer	09Ju14Lc
HICKEY, Catharine	28	F	Farmer	09Ju14Lc
Bridget	20	F	Farmer	09Ju14Lc
MOORE, Catharine	14	F	None	09Ju14Lc
HICKEY, Catharine	06	F	Child	09Ju14Lc
James	04	M	Child	09Ju14Lc
James	01	M	Child	09Ju14Lc
MCCARTEY, Pat	60	M	Laborer	09Ju14Lc
Cornellas	20	M	None	09Ju14Lc
Ellen	18	F	None	09Ju14Lc
CALLAGHAN, Catharine	21	F	None	09Ju14Lc
DONAGHUE, John	27	M	Farmer	09Ju14Lc
DUGGAN, Mary	20	F	None	09Ju14Lc
RESIDON, John	30	M	Weaver	09Ju14Lc
Margret	28	F	Weaver	09Ju14Lc
RESIDON, Catharine	02	F	Child	09Ju14Lc
Andrew	01	M	Child	09Ju14Lc
PINDAGAS, Patrick	40	M	Laborer	09Ju14Lc
Catharine	38	F	None	09Ju14Lc
RARIDON, Dennis	25	M	Weaver	09Ju14Lc
COLLINS, Thos.	20	M	Weaver	09Ju14Lc
HAYES, Margret	22	F	None	09Ju14Lc
Hannah	20	F	None	09Ju14Lc
RUSHELL, Patt	00	M	Servant	09Ju14Lc
OCONNELL, Joseph	30	M	Servant	09Ju14Lc
SULLIVAN, Silvestor	24	M	Servant	09Ju14Lc
DOYLE, Margret	32	F	Servant	09Ju14Lc
CRENING, Timothy	25	M	Servant	09Ju14Lc
LIHAN, James	25	M	Laborer	09Ju14Lc
CALLAGHAN, Julia	40	F	None	09Ju14Lc
Hannah	09	F	Child	09Ju14Lc
FLYNN, John	26	M	Servant	09Ju14Lc
BARRETT, Richard	24	M	Farmer	09Ju14Lc
WISE, John	25	M	Farmer	09Ju14Lc
Sally	13	F	Farmer	09Ju14Lc
BURNS, James	19	M	None	09Ju14Lc
PIYANE, Paddy	18	M	Servant	09Ju14Lc
BLACKHEM, Thos.	23	M	Laborer	09Ju14Lc
Wm.	25	M	Laborer	09Ju14Lc

SIR-JAMES-MCDONALD 09 JUNE 1848

From Dublin

NAMES OF PASSENGERS	AGE	SEX	OCCUPATIONS	DATE PORT SHIP
JOHNSTON, Richard	39	M	Farmer	09Ju20Ty
Catherine (W)	32	F	Wife	09Ju20Ty
Ann	32	F	Relative	09Ju20Ty
John	10	M	Relative	09Ju20Ty
Josh	12	M	Relative	09Ju20Ty
Mary	08	F	Child	09Ju20Ty
Margaret	05	F	Child	09Ju20Ty
Theresa	.00	F	Infant	09Ju20Ty
Samuel	.00	M	Infant	09Ju20Ty
COLEMAN, John	23	M	Laborer	09Ju20Ty
SHERLOCK, Jane	18	F	Servant	09Ju20Ty
BRADY, James	18	M	Laborer	09Ju20Ty
Ann	44	F	Relative	09Ju20Ty
Ann	22	F	Relative	09Ju20Ty
Maria	17	F	Relative	09Ju20Ty
Pat	13	M	Relative	09Ju20Ty
John	12	M	Relative	09Ju20Ty
Edwd.	11	M	Relative	09Ju20Ty
Kate	08	F	Child	09Ju20Ty
Eliza	06	F	Child	09Ju20Ty
MCCORMICK, Mary	20	F	Servant	09Ju20Ty
LYNCH, James	21	M	Laborer	09Ju20Ty
MCDONALD, Mary	30	F	Spinster	09Ju20Ty
Pat	13	M	Relative	09Ju20Ty
Mary	10	F	Relative	09Ju20Ty
DELAHUNT, Mary	32	F	Spinster	09Ju20Ty
MCGLADE, Henry	62	M	Farmer	09Ju20Ty
Ellen (W)	29	F	Wife	09Ju20Ty
Mary	03	F	Child	09Ju20Ty
Peter	.00	M	Infant	09Ju20Ty
FARRELL, Catherine	26	F	Servant	09Ju20Ty
FLYNN, Mary	24	F	Servant	09Ju20Ty
EGAN, Wm.	30	M	Laborer	09Ju20Ty
HEMINGWAY, John	22	M	Laborer	09Ju20Ty
DUNNE, Eliza	17	F	Servant	09Ju20Ty
RYAN, Catherine	23	F	Servant	09Ju20Ty
GLEESON, Pat	50	M	Farmer	09Ju20Ty
MORAN, Maria	12	F	Unknown	09Ju20Ty
Ann	09	F	Child	09Ju20Ty
RYAN, Wm.	35	M	Laborer	09Ju20Ty

NAMES OF PASSENGERS	AGE	SEX	OCCUPATIONS	DATE PORT SHIP
RYAN, Pat	05	M	Child	09Ju20Ty
Martha	.00	F	Infant	09Ju20Ty
GREGORY, James	24	M	Laborer	09Ju20Ty
Mary (W)	21	F	Wife	09Ju20Ty
Ellen	.00	F	Infant	09Ju20Ty
CRAWFORD, Thomas	18	M	Laborer	09Ju20Ty
MULLALY, Ann	24	F	Servant	09Ju20Ty
KELLY, James	23	M	Laborer	09Ju20Ty
DEVERIL, Martha	22	F	Servant	09Ju20Ty
WADE, Susan	21	F	Servant	09Ju20Ty
JEGGINS, John	24	M	Laborer	09Ju20Ty
HIGGINS, Mary	35	F	Spinster	09Ju20Ty
Mary-Ann	22	F	Relative	09Ju20Ty
Michael	37	M	Relative	09Ju20Ty
Teresa	10	F	Relative	09Ju20Ty
PIKE, Chas.	28	M	Laborer	09Ju20Ty
EGAN, Jos.	21	M	Servant	09Ju20Ty
PIKE, Josh.	42	M	Farmer	09Ju20Ty
PURDUE, Jane	26	F	Servant	09Ju20Ty
MCGARRY, Pat	13	M	Servant	09Ju20Ty
MCARDLE, Jas.	30	M	Farmer	09Ju20Ty
Harriet (W)	25	F	Wife	09Ju20Ty
WALSH, William	28	M	Laborer	09Ju20Ty
Biddy (W)	18	F	Wife	09Ju20Ty
WILLIAMS, Josh.	20	M	Laborer	09Ju20Ty
John	18	M	Laborer	09Ju20Ty
HORAN, Pat	24	M	Laborer	09Ju20Ty
RENTRY, Alice	15	F	Servant	09Ju20Ty
DOYLE, Ann	28	F	Spinster	09Ju20Ty
KINSELLY, Jas.	34	M	Farmer	09Ju20Ty
LYNCH, Mary	20	F	Servant	09Ju20Ty
Jane	16	F	Servant	09Ju20Ty
FALLARD, Bessy	34	F	Spinster	09Ju20Ty
CULLEN, Biddy	24	F	Servant	09Ju20Ty
REID, Daniel	40	M	Laborer	09Ju20Ty
Pat	15	M	Servant	09Ju20Ty
Josh.	11	M	Servant	09Ju20Ty
John	42	M	Laborer	09Ju20Ty
James	18	M	Laborer	09Ju20Ty
Alice	20	F	Servant	09Ju20Ty
CHRISTY, William	17	M	Laborer	09Ju20Ty
MULLEN, Pat	18	M	Laborer	09Ju20Ty
MILLER, Jas.	24	M	Laborer	09Ju20Ty
Marcella	26	F	Servant	09Ju20Ty
HOWES, Mick	25	M	Laborer	09Ju20Ty
SALTER, Thomas	19	M	Laborer	09Ju20Ty
KELLY, James	20	M	Laborer	09Ju20Ty
NUGENT, Richd.	30	M	Laborer	09Ju20Ty
BERGEN, Martin	30	M	Laborer	09Ju20Ty
DELANY, James	25	M	Laborer	09Ju20Ty
WELSH, U	25	M	Laborer	09Ju20Ty
BENNETT, Peter	22	M	Clerk	09Ju20Ty

WELLINGTON 10 JUNE 1848

From London

NAMES OF PASSENGERS	AGE	SEX	OCCUPATIONS	DATE PORT SHIP
CANSEL, Edward	18	M	Cutler	10Ju21Bl
DOUGHERTY, George	35	M	Reporter	10Ju21Bl
REED, Richard	25	M	Silversmith	10Ju21Bl
Elizabeth	28	F	Unknown	10Ju21Bl
LEPROVEST, Nicholas	53	M	Farmer	10Ju21Bl
Elizabeth	53	F	Unknown	10Ju21Bl
Louisa	18	F	Unknown	10Ju21Bl
HAKET, Mary	35	F	Unknown	10Ju21Bl
NICHOLAS, Peter	27	M	Painter	10Ju21Bl
MEDOLA, Frederick	20	M	Farmer	10Ju21Bl
LETIFSIER, Thomas	14	M	Farmer	10Ju21Bl
ROBILLARD, Peter	16	M	Unknown	10Ju21Bl
ARMSTRONG, John	24	M	Cbtmkr	10Ju21Bl
LEPEDLY, Adolphus	16	M	Unknown	10Ju21Bl
HONEYCOMB, John	27	M	Carpenter	10Ju21Bl
Elizabeth	27	F	Unknown	10Ju21Bl
Annickoln	18	F	Unknown	10Ju21Bl
Charles	30	M	Carpenter	10Ju21Bl
Margaret	30	F	Unknown	10Ju21Bl
JOHN, Wm-John	05	M	Child	10Ju21Bl
Charlotte	12	F	Unknown	10Ju21Bl
Elizabeth-Ann	.00	F	Infant	10Ju21Bl
MARTIN, William	30	M	Miner	10Ju21Bl
Elizabeth	25	F	Unknown	10Ju21Bl
HOPKINSON, George	19	M	Miner	10Ju21Bl
WHEELER, George	29	M	Miner	10Ju21Bl
ADAMS, Caleb	24	M	Miner	10Ju21Bl
WESTRON, Frederick	20	M	Miner	10Ju21Bl
PLIVAR, Henry	25	M	Miner	10Ju21Bl

GREAT-WESTERN 10 JUNE 1848

From Bermuda

NAMES OF PASSENGERS	AGE	SEX	OCCUPATIONS	DATE PORT SHIP
SHERIFF, S.	38	M	Lawyer	10Ju75Uj
ZUILKE, U-Mrs.	21	F	Wi	10Ju75Uj
J.	01	M	Child	10Ju75Uj
BUTLER, M.	44	M	Surgeon	10Ju75Uj
MORRISON, J.	65	M	Banker	10Ju75Uj
CORREA, M.A.	28	M	Merchant	10Ju75Uj
MARTIN, J.	30	M	Merchant	10Ju75Uj

ACADIA 10 JUNE 1848

From Liverpool

NAMES OF PASSENGERS	AGE	SEX	OCCUPATIONS	DATE PORT SHIP
OGROMAN, U	18	M	Gentleman	10Ju02Tu
BURSTALL, Edwd.	34	M	Merchant	10Ju02Tu
GORMEN, A.	32	F	None	10Ju02Tu
MAGUIRE, A.	19	F	None	10Ju02Tu
HERMAN, A.	19	F	None	10Ju02Tu
HEARN, A.	18	F	None	10Ju02Tu
LOMBARD, A.	23	F	None	10Ju02Tu

CHARTER-OAK 12 JUNE 1848

From Belfast

NAMES OF PASSENGERS	AGE	SEX	OCCUPATIONS	DATE PORT SHIP
NIEHAN, Patrick	24	M	Laborer	12Ju07Tw
Eliz.	20	F	None	12Ju07Tw
Mary-Jane	02	F	Child	12Ju07Tw
MALHOLLAND, Biddy	28	F	Spinster	12Ju07Tw
REY, James	26	M	Laborer	12Ju07Tw
Jane	22	F	Spinster	12Ju07Tw
KILPATRICK, Alex.	18	M	Laborer	12Ju07Tw
LAWRENCE, Sarah	20	F	Spinster	12Ju07Tw
MASON, Martha	16	F	Spinster	12Ju07Tw
NETTLETON, Fanney	40	F	Wi	12Ju07Tw
HANNA, Ellen	26	F	Spinster	12Ju07Tw

NAMES OF PASSENGERS	AGE	SEX	OCCUPATIONS	DATE PORT SHIP
BOYLE, Jane	06	F	Child	12Ju07Tw
SCOTT, Edwd.	30	M	Laborer	12Ju07Tw
GORMAN, Hugh	23	M	Laborer	12Ju07Tw
HILL, James	34	M	Laborer	12Ju07Tw
OTOOLE, Biddy	20	F	Spinster	12Ju07Tw
WILSON, Wm.	18	M	Laborer	12Ju07Tw
Margret	16	F	Spinster	12Ju07Tw
ADAMS, Jas.	18	M	Laborer	12Ju07Tw
CORD. Hugh	60	M	Farmer	12Ju07Tw
Jane	50	F	Wife	12Ju07Tw
HASLEY, Ann	16	F	Spinster	12Ju07Tw
MCGUINPSEY, Robt.	19	M	Laborer	12Ju07Tw
CORD, Isaac	35	M	Farmer	12Ju07Tw
Mary	30	F	Wife	12Ju07Tw
Isaac	07	M	Child	12Ju07Tw
Jane	04	F	Child	12Ju07Tw
James	02	M	Child	12Ju07Tw
QUINN, James	24	M	Laborer	12Ju07Tw
CLARK, Hugh	24	M	Laborer	12Ju07Tw
HUNT, George	21	M	Laborer	12Ju07Tw
WILSON, Margret	24	F	Spinster	12Ju07Tw
MAYLON, Wm.	20	M	Laborer	12Ju07Tw
OLIVER, Adam	50	M	Farmer	12Ju07Tw
KETTEY, John	30	M	Farmer	12Ju07Tw
FARLEY, Robert	18	M	Farmer	12Ju07Tw
LACKEY, Clark	19	M	Farmer	12Ju07Tw
Hannah	21	F	Spinster	12Ju07Tw
FOX, Mary	30	F	Wi	12Ju07Tw
DONNELLY, Mary	17	F	Spinster	12Ju07Tw
Margret	15	F	Spinster	12Ju07Tw
Catherine	13	F	Spinster	12Ju07Tw
Anna	11	F	Spinster	12Ju07Tw
MCODERY, Alex.	20	M	Laborer	12Ju07Tw
CHAWBER, James	21	M	Laborer	12Ju07Tw
Margret	20	F	Spinster	12Ju07Tw
MCAUNETHY, Edwd.	34	M	Laborer	12Ju07Tw
MCBRIDE, Thos.	40	M	Farmer	12Ju07Tw
Eliz.	25	F	Spinster	12Ju07Tw
RICE, Henry	30	M	Farmer	12Ju07Tw
HARVEY, Patrick	40	M	Farmer	12Ju07Tw
Eliz.	40	F	Wife	12Ju07Tw
MCAUATHEY, Jane	26	F	Spinster	12Ju07Tw
Sarah	16	F	Spinster	12Ju07Tw
SMYTHE, John	19	M	Laborer	12Ju07Tw
CONNOR, John	20	M	Laborer	12Ju07Tw
SMYTHE, Mary	20	F	Spinster	12Ju07Tw
John	14	M	Laborer	12Ju07Tw
Sally	12	F	Unknown	12Ju07Tw
MCMULLEN, Jas.	60	M	Farmer	12Ju07Tw
Mahel	60	F	Wife	12Ju07Tw
Patrick	25	M	Laborer	12Ju07Tw
KELLY, Jas.	20	M	Laborer	12Ju07Tw
Mary	20	F	Spinster	12Ju07Tw
MCMULLEN, Jas.	20	M	Laborer	12Ju07Tw
KILLAN, Patrick	26	M	Laborer	12Ju07Tw
Jane	30	F	Wife	12Ju07Tw
BEATHY, Hatz-Ann	30	F	Spinster	12Ju07Tw
FURGERSON, Mary	40	F	Wi	12Ju07Tw
Ellen-Jane	18	F	Spinster	12Ju07Tw
Rachel	16	F	Spinster	12Ju07Tw
James	14	M	Laborer	12Ju07Tw
George	12	M	Unknown	12Ju07Tw
Joseph	10	M	Unknown	12Ju07Tw
FERGERSON, Robert	08	M	Child	12Ju07Tw
Mary-Ann	04	F	Child	12Ju07Tw
Sarah	02	F	Child	12Ju07Tw
JUNK, Jas.	40	M	Laborer	12Ju07Tw
Daniel	13	M	Unknown	12Ju07Tw
MEARUSLEY, Eliza	17	F	Spinster	12Ju07Tw
Sarah	15	F	Spinster	12Ju07Tw
EDGAR, Mary	25	F	Spinster	12Ju07Tw
TEUPTELLOW, John	20	M	Clerk	12Ju07Tw
THOMPSON, Wm.	30	M	Laborer	12Ju07Tw
DICKEY, Elenor	40	F	Wi	12Ju07Tw
MCGENTLY, Letha	40	F	Wi	12Ju07Tw
MCGENTLY, Robert	14	M	Laborer	12Ju07Tw
Eleanor	14	F	Spinster	12Ju07Tw
David	10	M	Unknown	12Ju07Tw
Ruth	07	F	Child	12Ju07Tw
Eliza	03	F	Child	12Ju07Tw
MARSHALL, Jane	26	F	Spinster	12Ju07Tw
MCCANDREY, Daniel	26	M	Laborer	12Ju07Tw
Alberth	22	F	Spinster	12Ju07Tw
COLENCOURT, Wm.	19	M	Laborer	12Ju07Tw
----, ----	19	U	Laborer	12Ju07Tw
BRESLIN, Robert	23	M	Laborer	12Ju07Tw
MILLER, Robert	17	M	Laborer	12Ju07Tw
MURPHY, U	45	F	Lady	12Ju07Tw
Eliza	18	F	Lady	12Ju07Tw
Rebecca	21	F	Lady	12Ju07Tw

CORNELIA 12 JUNE 1848

From Liverpool

NAMES OF PASSENGERS	AGE	SEX	OCCUPATIONS	DATE PORT SHIP
ARMSTEAD, Wm.	26	M	Gentleman	12Ju02Am
U	22	F	None	12Ju02Am
Anna-Sophia	01	F	Child	12Ju02Am
BLACKBURN, Mary	29	F	None	12Ju02Am
WOODHALL, Wm.	23	M	Gentleman	12Ju02Am
NEILE, Thos.R.	28	M	Gentleman	12Ju02Am
WOODCOCK, R.A.	20	M	Gentleman	12Ju02Am
COWLEY, Saml.	20	M	Gentleman	12Ju02Am
LEWIS, Arthur	18	M	Gentleman	12Ju02Am
Mary	28	F	Unknown	12Ju02Am
Mary-Ann	01	F	Child	12Ju02Am
BURN, Thos.	20	M	Laborer	12Ju02Am
REILLY, John	40	M	Lawyer	12Ju02Am
MCKEOWN, Dennis	41	M	Laborer	12Ju02Am
Pat	35	M	Jockey	12Ju02Am
Mary-Ann	08	F	Child	12Ju02Am
Miles	06	M	Child	12Ju02Am
Alick	04	M	Child	12Ju02Am
MAGUIRE, Ann	20	F	Unknown	12Ju02Am
MURRAY, Wm.	59	M	Weaver	12Ju02Am
DIXONE, Thos.	25	M	Weaver	12Ju02Am
Rachael	24	F	Unknown	12Ju02Am
Jane	02	F	Child	12Ju02Am
Mary-Ann	01	F	Child	12Ju02Am
LITTLE, John	22	M	Clerk	12Ju02Am
RODGERS, Pat	20	M	Laborer	12Ju02Am
MAHON, Thos.	17	M	Laborer	12Ju02Am
RUSSIAAN, Thos.	06	M	Child	12Ju02Am
Ann	05	F	Child	12Ju02Am
DOLAN, Margt.	19	F	Unknown	12Ju02Am
HARDEN, Wm.	30	M	Laborer	12Ju02Am
SILIEU, Thomas	24	M	Laborer	12Ju02Am
SWEENEY, Hugh	30	M	Laborer	12Ju02Am
GALLAGHAN, Mary	30	F	Unknown	12Ju02Am
Hannah	13	F	Unknown	12Ju02Am
Biddy	12	F	Unknown	12Ju02Am
Sarah	10	F	Unknown	12Ju02Am
James	.10	M	Infant	12Ju02Am
Daniel	08	M	Child	12Ju02Am
Sophia	07	F	Child	12Ju02Am
Madge	04	F	Child	12Ju02Am
COYLE, John	20	M	Laborer	12Ju02Am
CROSBY, Isabella	35	F	Unknown	12Ju02Am
Mary	37	F	Unknown	12Ju02Am
JAMISON, Ann	26	F	Unknown	12Ju02Am
CARDELL, Sarah	22	F	Servant	12Ju02Am
COFFIN, Jane	11	F	Unknown	12Ju02Am
John	09	M	Child	12Ju02Am
James	07	M	Child	12Ju02Am

NAMES OF PASSENGERS	AGE	SEX	OCCUPATIONS	DATE PORT SHIP
CULLERAN, John	20	M	Laborer	12Ju02Am
Pat	12	M	Laborer	12Ju02Am
MCCULLOCK, John	40	M	Gdnr	12Ju02Am
Mary	39	F	Unknown	12Ju02Am
Mary	13	F	Unknown	12Ju02Am
John	09	M	Child	12Ju02Am
POLLACK, Isabella	23	F	Unknown	12Ju02Am
BENSON, Robt.	21	M	Gdnr	12Ju02Am
MCKENNA, Nancy	50	F	Unknown	12Ju02Am
Henry	12	M	Unknown	12Ju02Am
BALFE, Cathn.	28	F	Unknown	12Ju02Am
MCSHANE, Wm.	32	M	Tailor	12Ju02Am
WARD, Bridget	30	F	Unknown	12Ju02Am
James	11	M	Unknown	12Ju02Am
Ellen	07	F	Child	12Ju02Am
PEWETETON, James	20	M	Clerk	12Ju02Am
DEVINE, Margt.	20	F	Unknown	12Ju02Am
LYONS, Eliza	18	F	Unknown	12Ju02Am
DONNELLY, Bernard	30	M	Smith	12Ju02Am
SMITH, Bridget	20	F	Unknown	12Ju02Am
FLEMING, Michl.	21	M	Laborer	12Ju02Am
CONNOLEY, Cath.	20	F	Unknown	12Ju02Am
SCHOLES, George	26	M	Dyer	12Ju02Am
KEHOR, Cath.	23	F	Unknown	12Ju02Am
Peter	22	M	Laborer	12Ju02Am
Michl.	20	M	Laborer	12Ju02Am
OLARKEY, James	23	M	Laborer	12Ju02Am
NOALAN, Henry	41	M	Grocer	12Ju02Am
DUGAN, Mary	41	F	Unknown	12Ju02Am
John	08	M	Child	12Ju02Am
Mary	06	F	Child	12Ju02Am
Sarah	01	F	Child	12Ju02Am
HEALY, Kyle	20	M	Laborer	12Ju02Am
MOORE, Samuel	21	M	Laborer	12Ju02Am
CAMPBELL, Edward	18	M	Clerk	12Ju02Am
MORROW, Ann	16	F	Unknown	12Ju02Am
AICKEE, Martha	16	F	Unknown	12Ju02Am
QUINN, Mary	18	F	Unknown	12Ju02Am
HEARSON, Margt.	18	F	Unknown	12Ju02Am
RYAN, Elizth.	17	F	Unknown	12Ju02Am
Sarah	19	F	Unknown	12Ju02Am
HURSON, Wm.	21	M	Laborer	12Ju02Am
EDWARDS, Wm.	24	M	Quarryman	12Ju02Am
PRITCHARD, Wm.	24	M	Miner	12Ju02Am
RICHARDS, Thomas	30	M	Miner	12Ju02Am
THOMAS, Russel	21	M	Engineer	12Ju02Am
WILLIAMS, Elizabeth	32	F	Unknown	12Ju02Am
Cath.	25	F	Unknown	12Ju02Am
Ann	02	F	Child	12Ju02Am
GALE, John	28	M	Servant	12Ju02Am
WHATELY, Martin	20	M	Servant	12Ju02Am
John	18	M	Servant	12Ju02Am
Wm.	20	M	Servant	12Ju02Am
MAHER, Richard	31	M	Baker	12Ju02Am
DEWHURST, Margt.	21	F	Unknown	12Ju02Am
Jane	61	F	Unknown	12Ju02Am
MARTIN, Mary	50	F	Unknown	12Ju02Am
Thos.	18	M	Laborer	12Ju02Am
BRADY, Ann	16	F	Unknown	12Ju02Am
Michael	12	M	Unknown	12Ju02Am
DUNN, Ann	24	F	Servant	12Ju02Am
Sarah	22	F	Unknown	12Ju02Am
CAMPBELL, Jno.	27	M	Tailor	12Ju02Am
U	25	F	Unknown	12Ju02Am
Geo.	01	M	Child	12Ju02Am
COCKAIGN, Geo.	21	M	Irnmldr	12Ju02Am
CURRAN, Cath.	25	F	Unknown	12Ju02Am
THOMAS, Thomas	25	M	Laborer	12Ju02Am
WOODHALE, Wm.	24	M	Laborer	12Ju02Am
MCKENNA, Cath.	21	F	Unknown	12Ju02Am
KING, Sarah	28	F	Unknown	12Ju02Am
John	23	M	Laborer	12Ju02Am
MARTIN, Cathn.	28	F	None	12Ju02Am
Rosey	16	F	None	12Ju02Am
Patrick	03	M	Child	12Ju02Am

NAMES OF PASSENGERS	AGE	SEX	OCCUPATIONS	DATE PORT SHIP
MARTIN, Thomas	01	M	Child	12Ju02Am
MOUTEGH, Michael	21	M	Laborer	12Ju02Am
MCDONALD, Pat	22	M	Clerk	12Ju02Am
MCKERWIN, Hugh	22	M	Clerk	12Ju02Am
REILLY, Biddy	25	F	Unknown	12Ju02Am
Mary	23	F	Unknown	12Ju02Am
BENSON, Pat	30	M	Laborer	12Ju02Am
PROWLEY, Jno.	50	M	Laborer	12Ju02Am
Bridget	20	F	Unknown	12Ju02Am
MALLON, Mary	26	F	Unknown	12Ju02Am
HEALLY, Mary	20	F	Unknown	12Ju02Am
Thomas	10	M	Unknown	12Ju02Am
MCEVAY, Thomas	18	M	Clerk	12Ju02Am
ROACH, Ed.	18	M	Clerk	12Ju02Am
COYLE, Daniel	15	M	Unknown	12Ju02Am
Margaret	08	F	Child	12Ju02Am
MCMAHAN, John	28	M	Laborer	12Ju02Am
DALTON, John	24	M	Laborer	12Ju02Am
Teresa	24	F	Unknown	12Ju02Am
DUNGAN, Pat	35	M	Laborer	12Ju02Am
MCDANIEL, Nicholas	30	M	Laborer	12Ju02Am
GIBBONS, Owen	20	M	Laborer	12Ju02Am
WELSH, Peter	30	M	Laborer	12Ju02Am
EATON, Phillip	23	M	Miner	12Ju02Am
THOMPSON, Wm.	30	M	Dyer	12Ju02Am
Jane	30	F	Unknown	12Ju02Am
Mary-Ann	04	F	Child	12Ju02Am
GARDNER, John	30	M	Laborer	12Ju02Am
HURT, Geo.	39	M	Laborer	12Ju02Am
LEWIS, Edward	28	M	Laborer	12Ju02Am
MCMAHON, Rose	29	F	Miner	12Ju02Am
Tery	20	M	Unknown	12Ju02Am
Ann	28	F	Unknown	12Ju02Am
Mary	03	F	Child	12Ju02Am
KELLY, Wm.	45	M	Laborer	12Ju02Am
MCMANUS, Phillip	36	M	Laborer	12Ju02Am
Caroline	30	F	Unknown	12Ju02Am
Owen	07	M	Child	12Ju02Am
Phillip	03	M	Child	12Ju02Am
Mary	05	F	Child	12Ju02Am
James	.10	M	Infant	12Ju02Am
BONES, Henry	32	M	Laborer	12Ju02Am
BRAUCKER, Frances	45	M	Laborer	12Ju02Am
Eliza	20	F	Unknown	12Ju02Am
Elleanore	17	F	Unknown	12Ju02Am
PARKE, Henry	30	M	Clerk	12Ju02Am
EDWARDS, Elias	23	M	Hatter	12Ju02Am
FLANNAGAN, Felix	27	M	Unknown	12Ju02Am
Eleanor	25	F	Unknown	12Ju02Am
MULLER, Christoph.	27	M	Laborer	12Ju02Am
HUGHES, Alice	22	F	Unknown	12Ju02Am
FLANNAGAN, Mary	05	F	Child	12Ju02Am
James	01	M	Child	12Ju02Am
FITZPATRICK, Andw.	20	M	Laborer	12Ju02Am
Ellen	19	F	Unknown	12Ju02Am
DONNELLY, Margt.	27	F	Unknown	12Ju02Am
James	04	M	Child	12Ju02Am
Charles	03	M	Child	12Ju02Am
Bernard	01	M	Child	12Ju02Am
BUCKHANON, Wm.	18	M	Clerk	12Ju02Am
QUINN, Bernard	27	M	Laborer	12Ju02Am
TRAUPLESURE, Elizth.	30	F	Farmer	12Ju02Am
Mary-Ann	25	F	Farmer	12Ju02Am
Thomas	18	M	Farmer	12Ju02Am
BURGERS, John	19	M	Farmer	12Ju02Am
BOOTH, Alfred	19	M	Farmer	12Ju02Am
Sydney	20	M	Farmer	12Ju02Am
BRIERLY, Edwd.	31	M	Farmer	12Ju02Am
TUCKER, Wm.	23	M	Farmer	12Ju02Am
ALBIRE, Henry	30	M	Farmer	12Ju02Am
U	30	F	None	12Ju02Am
Wm.	01	M	Child	12Ju02Am
HEARTLAND, U	21	F	Unknown	12Ju02Am
BONN, Wm.	22	M	Farmer	12Ju02Am
ATCHERTY, Wm.	31	M	Farmer	12Ju02Am

NAMES OF PASSENGERS	A G E	S E X	OCCUPATIONS	DATE PORT SHIP
ATCHERTY, U	30	F	None	12Ju02Am
Annie	10	F	None	12Ju02Am
Sarah	07	F	Child	12Ju02Am
Jane	06	F	Child	12Ju02Am
Elizabeth	05	F	Child	12Ju02Am
NAPTON, Fredk.	29	M	Farmer	12Ju02Am
U	31	F	Farmer	12Ju02Am
Jno.	05	M	Child	12Ju02Am
Edward	02	M	Child	12Ju02Am
BIRNE, Wm.	42	M	Unknown	12Ju02Am
U	42	F	Unknown	12Ju02Am
Wm.	10	M	Unknown	12Ju02Am
James	08	M	Child	12Ju02Am
John	06	M	Child	12Ju02Am
Mary	04	F	Child	12Ju02Am
Elizth.	03	F	Child	12Ju02Am
KITSON, Sarah	26	F	Unknown	12Ju02Am
THOMLY, H.D.	20	M	Unknown	12Ju02Am
CARLISLE, Wm.	29	M	Whitesmith	12Ju02Am
PARKINSON, Geo.	23	M	Spinner	12Ju02Am
Alice	32	F	Unknown	12Ju02Am
Mary	21	F	Unknown	12Ju02Am
STAFFORD, Wm.	40	M	Laborer	12Ju02Am
Bridgt.	40	F	Unknown	12Ju02Am
Wm.	15	M	Unknown	12Ju02Am
Richd.	10	M	Unknown	12Ju02Am
Joseph	06	M	Unknown	12Ju02Am
Mary-Ann	04	F	Unknown	12Ju02Am
MURPHY, John	30	M	Laborer	12Ju02Am
FAULKNER, Geo.	20	M	Laborer	12Ju02Am
RUTLEDGE, Ann	11	F	Unknown	12Ju02Am
REILLY, Bernard	20	M	Laborer	12Ju02Am
MCMANUS, Barney	25	M	Laborer	12Ju02Am
Ann	22	F	Unknown	12Ju02Am
Sally	20	F	Unknown	12Ju02Am
HORTON, Thos.	28	M	Mason	12Ju02Am
DEVLIN, Ann	20	M	Shoemaker	12Ju02Am
DUGGAN, Saml.	15	M	Laborer	12Ju02Am
MCCABE, Michl.	25	M	Laborer	12Ju02Am
POWELL, Martin	22	M	Laborer	12Ju02Am
Thos.	22	M	Laborer	12Ju02Am
MCGREGAN, Michl.	60	M	Retired	12Ju02Am
Susan	55	F	Retired	12Ju02Am
Ann	20	F	None	12Ju02Am
MULLEN, Rose	20	F	None	12Ju02Am
GORDON, Abraham	28	M	Farmer	12Ju02Am
Mary	28	F	Unknown	12Ju02Am
Jno.	.10	M	Infant	12Ju02Am
MIDDLETON, Saml.	40	M	Laborer	12Ju02Am
MANNON, Michl.	25	M	Laborer	12Ju02Am
HENNESEY, Chas.	14	M	Laborer	12Ju02Am
Mary	15	F	Unknown	12Ju02Am
CAMPBELL, Mary	30	F	Unknown	12Ju02Am
FITZGERALD, Edwd.	28	M	Laborer	12Ju02Am
DOUGHERTY, Pat	28	M	Laborer	12Ju02Am
QUGLEY, Jno.	23	M	Laborer	12Ju02Am
CANNON, Wm.	35	M	Unknown	12Ju02Am
DOFF, Ann	22	F	Unknown	12Ju02Am
DAILEY, David	40	M	Laborer	12Ju02Am
MAGUIRE, Bridget	18	F	Unknown	12Ju02Am
KERNON, Saml.	20	M	Clerk	12Ju02Am
RAFFERTY, Patt	20	M	Laborer	12Ju02Am
FARQUHAN, Wm.	18	M	Spinner	12Ju02Am
GALLAGHER, Rose	30	F	Unknown	12Ju02Am
HORKEN, Jane	20	F	Unknown	12Ju02Am
FRANCIS, Pat	20	M	Laborer	12Ju02Am
GEORGE, Henry	23	M	Baker	12Ju02Am
MAHEN, Bridget	24	F	Unknown	12Ju02Am
OBRIAN, Elicia	20	F	Unknown	12Ju02Am
SMITH, John	34	M	Laborer	12Ju02Am
HEATON, Wm.	24	M	Mason	12Ju02Am
JONES, John	23	M	Laborer	12Ju02Am
BRIAN, Dennis	55	M	Laborer	12Ju02Am
WATKINS, Peter	30	M	Laborer	12Ju02Am
JAMES, Vannel	20	M	Laborer	12Ju02Am
DAVIS, David	20	M	Laborer	12Ju02Am
MURRAY, Pat	27	M	Laborer	12Ju02Am
CAVANAGH, Pat	38	M	Laborer	12Ju02Am
KENNY, Mary	18	F	Unknown	12Ju02Am
RATTEY, Thos.	35	F	Miner	12Ju02Am
Thomas	12	M	Unknown	12Ju02Am
John	10	M	Unknown	12Ju02Am
BRYAN, Pat	25	M	Thatcher	12Ju02Am
MAHON, Thomas	23	M	Mason	12Ju02Am
WHALEN, Michael	23	M	Laborer	12Ju02Am
Peggy	22	F	Unknown	12Ju02Am
BROOKS, Thomas	35	M	Laborer	12Ju02Am
COUGHLAN, Christoph	22	M	Laborer	12Ju02Am
GALAGHER, Mary	10	F	Unknown	12Ju02Am
Ann	08	F	Child	12Ju02Am
Rosey	05	F	Child	12Ju02Am
Bridget	01	F	Child	12Ju02Am
DENNISON, Edwd.	24	M	Clerk	12Ju02Am
REYNOLDS, Thos.	25	M	Unknown	12Ju02Am
Elizth.	24	F	Unknown	12Ju02Am
HUGHES, Mary	40	F	Unknown	12Ju02Am
SMITH, Pat	32	M	Laborer	12Ju02Am
Ann	26	F	Unknown	12Ju02Am
James	01	M	Child	12Ju02Am
EUSTACE, James	22	M	Laborer	12Ju02Am
BROWN, Pat	22	M	Laborer	12Ju02Am
MCCANCE, Nancy	11	F	Laborer	12Ju02Am
DAUSON, Wm.	23	M	Laborer	12Ju02Am
BEACH, Henry	31	M	Laborer	12Ju02Am
DEATON, Christoph	29	M	Laborer	12Ju02Am
MCLOUHGLIN, Pat	20	M	Unknown	12Ju02Am
Dennis	28	M	Unknown	12Ju02Am
CAMPBELL, Hugh	34	M	Farmer	12Ju02Am
MACKLE, James	36	M	Farmer	12Ju02Am
CAMPBELL, Henry	28	M	Farmer	12Ju02Am

GONDAR 12 JUNE 1848

From Liverpool

NAMES OF PASSENGERS	A G E	S E X	OCCUPATIONS	DATE PORT SHIP
CAIN, Ann	24	F	Servant	12Ju02Ub
LAHERZ, Michal	22	M	Laborer	12Ju02Ub
DONOTZ, Neil	32	M	Weaver	12Ju02Ub
Mary	50	F	Housekeeper	12Ju02Ub
Ellen	25	F	Servant	12Ju02Ub
KELLY, Thomas	24	M	Weaver	12Ju02Ub
FOLARD, Roger	24	M	Laborer	12Ju02Ub
Bridget	21	F	Housekeeper	12Ju02Ub
GRALEY, Sicley	20	F	Servant	12Ju02Ub
BYRNE, John	26	M	Joiner	12Ju02Ub
Eliza	24	F	Housekeeper	12Ju02Ub
Mary	.00	F	Infant	12Ju02Ub
FENLON, Cathran	23	F	None	12Ju02Ub
HAGADEN, John	44	M	Baker	12Ju02Ub
John	18	M	Clerk	12Ju02Ub
Catheran	12	F	Child	12Ju02Ub
Timothy	16	M	Baker	12Ju02Ub
WARD, Peter	35	M	Laborer	12Ju02Ub
BRADLEY, Thomas	20	M	Laborer	12Ju02Ub
MITCHELL, Patt.	20	M	Laborer	12Ju02Ub
HENERZ, Eliza	30	F	Dressmaker	12Ju02Ub
DAGIN, James	30	M	Laborer	12Ju02Ub
CLOSE, James	22	M	Laborer	12Ju02Ub
U	21	F	Housekeeper	12Ju02Ub
GROGAN, Mary	30	F	Housekeeper	12Ju02Ub
Ann	.00	F	Infant	12Ju02Ub
CROWLEY, Samuel	25	M	Laborer	12Ju02Ub
Mary	24	F	Housekeeper	12Ju02Ub
Mary	05	F	Child	12Ju02Ub

NAMES OF PASSENGERS	AGE	SEX	OCCUPATIONS	DATE PORT SHIP
CROWLEY, William	03	M	Child	12Ju02Ub
CORMACK, Thomas	32	M	Laborer	12Ju02Ub
CAIN, Mary	18	F	Servant	12Ju02Ub
DONGAN, A.	35	M	Laborer	12Ju02Ub
Died-At-Sea				
John	14	M	Laborer	12Ju02Ub
Elizabeth	60	F	Housekeeper	12Ju02Ub
George	12	M	Child	12Ju02Ub
William	10	M	Child	12Ju02Ub
ROOK, Betsey	18	F	Servant	12Ju02Ub
MALAN, Hugh	20	M	Ctldlr	12Ju02Ub
MCGOVERN, Hugh	40	M	Laborer	12Ju02Ub
KENEDY, Rody	27	M	Farmer	12Ju02Ub
RIGHT, John	40	M	Laborer	12Ju02Ub
Thomas	13	M	Child	12Ju02Ub
Mary	11	F	Child	12Ju02Ub
Jane	.00	F	Infant	12Ju02Ub
OGGANS, Michal	21	M	Laborer	12Ju02Ub
TRACY, John	24	M	Laborer	12Ju02Ub
FITZPATRICK, Patt	50	M	Laborer	12Ju02Ub
Elen	30	F	Servant	12Ju02Ub
Ann	28	F	Housekeeper	12Ju02Ub
Frances	26	F	Housekeeper	12Ju02Ub
RYAN, John	25	M	Laborer	12Ju02Ub
Patrick	22	M	Laborer	12Ju02Ub
DELANEY, Eliza.	33	F	Servant	12Ju02Ub
Banard	16	M	Laborer	12Ju02Ub
Mary	13	F	Servant	12Ju02Ub
John	.00	M	Infant	12Ju02Ub
MURPHY, Fredrick	35	M	Laborer	12Ju02Ub
Dennis	20	M	Laborer	12Ju02Ub
John	13	M	Laborer	12Ju02Ub
Patrick	12	M	Laborer	12Ju02Ub
William	11	M	Laborer	12Ju02Ub
RILEY, Margrett	18	F	Servant	12Ju02Ub
GREEN, Elen	16	F	Servant	12Ju02Ub
EVEY, Cathran	16	F	Servant	12Ju02Ub
MCGOVERN, Ann	47	F	Housekeeper	12Ju02Ub
KINLESS, Richard	24	M	Laborer	12Ju02Ub
RUDDER, James	20	M	Laborer	12Ju02Ub
Cathran	18	F	Servant	12Ju02Ub
GOVERN, Lary	20	M	Shoemaker	12Ju02Ub
Margrett	19	F	Servant	12Ju02Ub
RYAN, Patt	50	M	Laborer	12Ju02Ub
Oner	20	F	Servant	12Ju02Ub
FARRALL, William	21	M	Laborer	12Ju02Ub
GARAGUN, Mary	20	F	Servant	12Ju02Ub
CONOTTON, Biddy	17	F	Servant	12Ju02Ub
KENEDY, John	35	M	Smith	12Ju02Ub
Jula	27	F	Housekeeper	12Ju02Ub
Marria	07	F	Child	12Ju02Ub
Honory	04	F	Child	12Ju02Ub
Edward	03	M	Child	12Ju02Ub
Martin	.00	M	Infant	12Ju02Ub
QUINLINN, Ann	20	F	Servant	12Ju02Ub
BRANAGAN, John	40	M	Laborer	12Ju02Ub
Betty	40	F	Housekeeper	12Ju02Ub
Harthur	10	M	Child	12Ju02Ub
Patrick	08	M	Child	12Ju02Ub
MCANLEY, Cathran	30	F	Housekeeper	12Ju02Ub
Biddy	10	F	Child	12Ju02Ub
Cathran	08	F	Child	12Ju02Ub
John	.00	M	Infant	12Ju02Ub
PLUNKETT, James	19	M	Miller	12Ju02Ub
MONAGAN, Richard	30	M	Carpenter	12Ju02Ub
U	30	F	Housekeeper	12Ju02Ub
Mary	.00	F	Infant	12Ju02Ub
GRIFFIN, Charles	30	M	Laborer	12Ju02Ub
MONAGAN, Bridgett	19	F	Servant	12Ju02Ub
HALIGAN, Mary	20	F	Servant	12Ju02Ub
RILEY, Margrett	22	F	Servant	12Ju02Ub
MONAGAN, Biddy	18	F	Servant	12Ju02Ub
Mary	16	F	Servant	12Ju02Ub
GRIFFIN, Andrew	26	M	Laborer	12Ju02Ub
Jane	21	F	Housekeeper	12Ju02Ub
GRIFFIN, Martin	02	M	Child	12Ju02Ub
CARROLL, John	19	M	Laborer	12Ju02Ub
RATIGAN, James	25	M	Stone Mason	12Ju02Ub
RILEY, Phillip	40	M	Laborer	12Ju02Ub
U	40	F	Housekeeper	12Ju02Ub
Michal	20	M	Laborer	12Ju02Ub
Mary	18	F	Servant	12Ju02Ub
Patt	13	M	Laborer	12Ju02Ub
Thomas	11	M	Child	12Ju02Ub
Hugh	04	M	Child	12Ju02Ub
Cathran	.00	F	Infant	12Ju02Ub
DUFFEY, Peter	25	M	Smith	12Ju02Ub
EAGAN, John	25	M	Weaver	12Ju02Ub
Charles	18	M	Weaver	12Ju02Ub
DONNELY, Barney	35	M	Laborer	12Ju02Ub
U	25	F	Housekeeper	12Ju02Ub
MCGUIRE, Gerrad	30	M	Farmer	12Ju02Ub
DONNELY, William	.00	M	Infant	12Ju02Ub
MCGUIRE, U	28	F	Housekeeper	12Ju02Ub
James	07	M	Child	12Ju02Ub
Betsey	05	F	Child	12Ju02Ub
Anne	03	F	Child	12Ju02Ub
Mary	02	F	Child	12Ju02Ub
Biddy	.00	F	Infant	12Ju02Ub
CARR, Andrew	25	M	Laborer	12Ju02Ub
MCMANNA, Ann	20	F	Servant	12Ju02Ub
MCDONNALD, Mary	30	F	Servant	12Ju02Ub
MCGRUE, Patt	40	M	Servant	12Ju02Ub
U	30	F	Housekeeper	12Ju02Ub
Biddy	20	F	Servant	12Ju02Ub
Anne	19	F	Servant	12Ju02Ub
WYNNE, Patt	20	M	Servant	12Ju02Ub
U	20	F	Housekeeper	12Ju02Ub
LEONARD, Honora	20	F	Servant	12Ju02Ub
Maryann	.00	F	Infant	12Ju02Ub
FITZPATRICK, John	31	M	Laborer	12Ju02Ub
U	28	F	Housekeeper	12Ju02Ub
SMITH, Hugh	30	M	Laborer	12Ju02Ub
HENRICK, William	30	M	Laborer	12Ju02Ub
Mary	30	F	Servant	12Ju02Ub
KENEDY, Bridgett	18	F	Servant	12Ju02Ub
COMMINS, Jonnah	46	F	Housekeeper	12Ju02Ub
Ellen	26	F	Dressmaker	12Ju02Ub
Cathran	24	F	Dressmaker	12Ju02Ub
Pattrick	22	M	Painter	12Ju02Ub
SHEELEY, Cathran	18	F	Servant	12Ju02Ub
DUFFEY, John	21	M	Tailor	12Ju02Ub
CALLAGAN, Tullus	21	M	Laborer	12Ju02Ub
Mary	50	F	Housekeeper	12Ju02Ub
Nancy	19	F	Servant	12Ju02Ub
Peter	14	M	Child	12Ju02Ub
Margrett	11	F	Child	12Ju02Ub
DUFFEY, Peter	19	M	Baker	12Ju02Ub
SHAW, Mary	19	F	Servant	12Ju02Ub
MCMADDEN, Peter	19	M	Laborer	12Ju02Ub
CALLAGAN, Bridgett	20	F	Servant	12Ju02Ub
Nancy	18	F	Servant	12Ju02Ub
Betty	12	F	Servant	12Ju02Ub
KEENAN, Barnard	19	M	Laborer	12Ju02Ub
DONHOE, John	30	M	Laborer	12Ju02Ub
KALLAN, Cathran	50	F	Housekeeper	12Ju02Ub
DONHOE, Ellen	22	F	Servant	12Ju02Ub
Dennis	16	M	Laborer	12Ju02Ub
Betty	13	F	Servant	12Ju02Ub
SULAVAN, Carley	20	M	Laborer	12Ju02Ub
ORMEROD, Henery	27	M	Paver	12Ju02Ub
LAWLER, Thomas	22	M	Laborer	12Ju02Ub
TAYLOR, Ann	19	F	Servant	12Ju02Ub
LANE, John	25	M	Carpenter	12Ju02Ub
U	25	F	Housekeeper	12Ju02Ub
NAUGHTON, James	25	M	Laborer	12Ju02Ub
WHATTON, Michael	20	M	Laborer	12Ju02Ub
LANDRAGAN, Patt	20	M	Laborer	12Ju02Ub
DOUGAN, Mary	20	F	Servant	12Ju02Ub
BAXTER, John	40	M	Laborer	12Ju02Ub

NAMES OF PASSENGERS	AGE	SEX	OCCUPATIONS	DATE PORT SHIP
BAXTER, U	40	F	Housekeeper	12Ju02Ub
RILEY, Mary-Ann	18	F	Servant	12Ju02Ub
FOGATY, Martin	24	M	Laborer	12Ju02Ub
KEENAN, Margrett	20	F	Servant	12Ju02Ub
CONWAY, Patt	25	M	Laborer	12Ju02Ub
MANHALL, Winfred	19	F	Dressmaker	12Ju02Ub
LAMBERT, Susan	29	F	Servant	12Ju02Ub
SWEENEY, Robert	26	M	Laborer	12Ju02Ub
DOWD, John	21	M	Laborer	12Ju02Ub
James	16	M	Laborer	12Ju02Ub
Cathran	23	F	Servant	12Ju02Ub
Jane	18	F	Servant	12Ju02Ub
KENEDY, Mary	18	F	Housekeeper	12Ju02Ub
Anne	16	F	Servant	12Ju02Ub
GARRAGAN, John	21	M	Laborer	12Ju02Ub
MORAN, Christy	19	M	Laborer	12Ju02Ub
SPRINNIGAN, James	30	M	Musician	12Ju02Ub
MULDOON, Patt	10	M	Child	12Ju02Ub
MCKENNA, Phillip	20	M	Laborer	12Ju02Ub
MCBUDS, Patt	16	M	Cooper	12Ju02Ub
RENCH, William	30	M	Carpenter	12Ju02Ub
BELTON, Mary	20	F	Dressmaker	12Ju02Ub
CUNNINGHAM, Hugh	20	M	Tailor	12Ju02Ub
COOGAN, Ellen	20	F	Servant	12Ju02Ub
DAY, James	18	M	Laborer	12Ju02Ub
CAGAN, James	35	M	Laborer	12Ju02Ub
FARRALL, Mary	44	F	Housekeeper	12Ju02Ub

FANCHION 12 JUNE 1848

From Liverpool

NAMES OF PASSENGERS	AGE	SEX	OCCUPATIONS	DATE PORT SHIP
OHAGAN, Pat	22	M	Laborer	12Ju02Tm
CALDWELL, Thomas	18	M	Laborer	12Ju02Tm
Margaret	19	F	Servant	12Ju02Tm
MCDONALD, Ann	33	F	Unknown	12Ju02Tm
Ann	03	F	Child	12Ju02Tm
Mary	02	F	Child	12Ju02Tm
Hugh	.00	M	Infant	12Ju02Tm
Barnard	20	M	Butcher	12Ju02Tm
OBRIEN, U	50	F	Wi	12Ju02Tm
Pat	21	M	Laborer	12Ju02Tm
Ann	14	F	Servant	12Ju02Tm
HAWKINS, John	25	M	Laborer	12Ju02Tm
GANNON, Bernard	14	M	Laborer	12Ju02Tm
William	10	M	Child	12Ju02Tm
NOON, Martin	46	M	Laborer	12Ju02Tm
DALY, John	26	M	Laborer	12Ju02Tm
Ellen	18	F	Servant	12Ju02Tm
GALLAGHAN, Michael	20	M	Laborer	12Ju02Tm
MORAN, Bridget	10	F	Child	12Ju02Tm
GOLDING, Biddy	25	F	Servant	12Ju02Tm
GORDON, Pat	21	M	Laborer	12Ju02Tm
GAUGHAN, Harry	20	M	Laborer	12Ju02Tm
CAVANAUGH, Michael	19	M	Laborer	12Ju02Tm
MYNE, Catherine	13	F	Servant	12Ju02Tm
MULDOWN, John	22	M	Mason	12Ju02Tm
COYLE, John	23	M	Laborer	12Ju02Tm
Mary	26	F	Servant	12Ju02Tm
CARTY, William	25	M	Laborer	12Ju02Tm
OBRIEN, John	28	M	Laborer	12Ju02Tm
COONEY, Pat	40	M	Laborer	12Ju02Tm
Bridget	30	F	Unknown	12Ju02Tm
Bryan	18	M	None	12Ju02Tm
Richard	16	M	None	12Ju02Tm
Catherine	11	F	Child	12Ju02Tm
Pat	09	M	Child	12Ju02Tm
Mary	07	F	Child	12Ju02Tm
OBRIAN, James	40	M	Laborer	12Ju02Tm

NAMES OF PASSENGERS	AGE	SEX	OCCUPATIONS	DATE PORT SHIP
JOHNSTONE, William	31	M	Farmer	12Ju02Tm
James	22	M	Farmer	12Ju02Tm
James	50	M	Farmer	12Ju02Tm
MULLAGEN, Isabella	40	F	Servant	12Ju02Tm
ADAMS, Arthur	63	M	Weaver	12Ju02Tm
Archibald	21	M	None	12Ju02Tm
Arthur	17	M	None	12Ju02Tm
Eleanor	14	F	None	12Ju02Tm
WATERS, John	37	M	Weaver	12Ju02Tm
Mary-Jane	37	F	Unknown	12Ju02Tm
Robert	12	M	Child	12Ju02Tm
Andrew	10	M	Child	12Ju02Tm
Rebecca	08	F	Child	12Ju02Tm
John	06	M	Child	12Ju02Tm
Eleanora	02	F	Child	12Ju02Tm
SIMMINS, James	40	M	Cooper	12Ju02Tm
John	20	M	Laborer	12Ju02Tm
HALFPENNY, Ann	17	F	Servant	12Ju02Tm
John	16	M	Laborer	12Ju02Tm
IVORY, Thomas	30	M	Carpenter	12Ju02Tm
Biddy	20	F	Unknown	12Ju02Tm
FARRELL, John	26	M	Laborer	12Ju02Tm
HOGG, Samuel	35	M	Joiner	12Ju02Tm
KELLY, Pat	30	M	Laborer	12Ju02Tm
HANNETON, Michael	30	M	Laborer	12Ju02Tm
MONAGHAN, Dennis	22	M	Laborer	12Ju02Tm
TUCKER, James	13	M	Child	12Ju02Tm
HANLEY, Ellen	55	F	Wi	12Ju02Tm
DOOLAN, Peter	14	M	Unknown	12Ju02Tm
Betty	18	F	Servant	12Ju02Tm
Catherine	16	F	Servant	12Ju02Tm
Mary	13	F	Servant	12Ju02Tm
DOWLING, John	21	M	Laborer	12Ju02Tm
FANTIMAN, Francis	20	M	Laborer	12Ju02Tm
DOWD, Michael	20	M	Laborer	12Ju02Tm
HOLMES, John	60	M	Shoemaker	12Ju02Tm
Benjamin	30	M	Cbtmkr	12Ju02Tm
Ann	30	F	None	12Ju02Tm
Henry	24	M	Joiner	12Ju02Tm
Margaret	08	F	Child	12Ju02Tm
Kate	06	F	Child	12Ju02Tm
Benjamin	01	M	Child	12Ju02Tm
LENDRAN, William	30	M	Shoemaker	12Ju02Tm
Ellen	26	F	Unknown	12Ju02Tm
Mary-A.	.08	F	Infant	12Ju02Tm
ANDERSON, John	24	M	Hairdresser	12Ju02Tm
THACKER, William	35	M	Weaver	12Ju02Tm
Esther	30	F	Unknown	12Ju02Tm
BURN, Peter-J.	20	M	Laborer	12Ju02Tm
SMITH, Matilda	20	F	Servant	12Ju02Tm
HEARN, Pat	20	M	Laborer	12Ju02Tm
BYRNE, Michael	45	M	Laborer	12Ju02Tm
CROAKEN, Margaret	60	F	None	12Ju02Tm
Margaret	34	F	Servant	12Ju02Tm
Ann	22	F	Servant	12Ju02Tm
Pat	19	M	Laborer	12Ju02Tm
KELLY, Alice	25	F	Servant	12Ju02Tm
MCCANDLES, John	50	M	Farmer	12Ju02Tm
Martha	30	F	Unknown	12Ju02Tm
Samuel-James	12	M	Child	12Ju02Tm
William-H.	10	M	Child	12Ju02Tm
Matilda	08	F	Child	12Ju02Tm
John	05	M	Child	12Ju02Tm
Mary	03	F	Child	12Ju02Tm
David-George	.05	M	Infant	12Ju02Tm
David	18	M	Saddler	12Ju02Tm
BOYD, Eliza	17	F	Servant	12Ju02Tm
MCCANDLES, Martha Died-At-Sea	75	F	Mother	12Ju02Tm
SHAW, William	35	M	Smith	12Ju02Tm
DONLAN, Rose	50	F	Laborer	12Ju02Tm
Ann	20	F	Servant	12Ju02Tm
Rosey	18	F	Servant	12Ju02Tm
Bessey	16	F	Servant	12Ju02Tm
Peter	11	M	Child	12Ju02Tm

NAMES OF PASSENGERS	AGE	SEX	OCCUPATIONS	DATE PORT SHIP
DONLAN, John	09	M	Child	12Ju02Tm
Margaret	07	F	Child	12Ju02Tm
BRAY, Rosey	19	F	Servant	12Ju02Tm
DORIES, Ann	20	F	Servant	12Ju02Tm
TRADINICK, John	23	M	Miner	12Ju02Tm
FARRELL, George	30	M	Miner	12Ju02Tm
SHERLOCK, Pat	46	M	Farmer	12Ju02Tm
Bridget	36	F	Unknown	12Ju02Tm
John	17	M	Farmer	12Ju02Tm
Anna	13	F	Child	12Ju02Tm
Patt	11	M	Child	12Ju02Tm
Stephen	08	M	Child	12Ju02Tm
Theobald	03	M	Child	12Ju02Tm
Edmund	.10	M	Infant	12Ju02Tm
BROOME, Robert	37	M	Miner	12Ju02Tm
Mary	43	F	Unknown	12Ju02Tm
Eli	14	M	Child	12Ju02Tm
Samuel	11	M	Child	12Ju02Tm
Caroline	09	F	Child	12Ju02Tm
Charles	07	M	Child	12Ju02Tm
CARROLL, Tim	20	M	Laborer	12Ju02Tm
HOCKER, Ann	40	F	Laborer	12Ju02Tm
Pat	26	M	Laborer	12Ju02Tm
Mary	20	F	Unknown	12Ju02Tm
Ann	13	F	Child	12Ju02Tm
Edward	10	M	Child	12Ju02Tm
MURRY, Bridget	18	F	Servant	12Ju02Tm
MALLON, Patt	20	M	Laborer	12Ju02Tm
LINAGHAN, Peter	21	M	Laborer	12Ju02Tm
Catherine	20	F	Unknown	12Ju02Tm
CONDRICK, Thomas	19	M	Laborer	12Ju02Tm
FARLEY, Bessy	25	F	Servant	12Ju02Tm
Ellen	.11	F	Infant	12Ju02Tm
MACNAMARA, Judy	08	F	Child	12Ju02Tm
Daniel (F)	30	M	Laborer	12Ju02Tm
Bridget (M)	28	F	Unknown	12Ju02Tm
Mary	06	F	Child	12Ju02Tm
Patt	04	M	Child	12Ju02Tm
Michael	.11	M	Infant	12Ju02Tm
DONOHOE, Patt	22	M	Laborer	12Ju02Tm
Ellen	25	F	Unknown	12Ju02Tm
HANLON, Mathew	45	M	Laborer	12Ju02Tm
MCGUIRE, Lawrence	26	M	Laborer	12Ju02Tm
Mary	20	F	Servant	12Ju02Tm
Rose	17	F	Servant	12Ju02Tm
MARTIN, Lawrence	33	F	Farmer	12Ju02Tm
Mary	09	F	Child	12Ju02Tm
Eliza	07	F	Child	12Ju02Tm
Ann	06	F	Child	12Ju02Tm
KENNEDY, George	30	M	Farmer	12Ju02Tm
CARROLL, John	24	M	Pardner	12Ju02Tm
Ann	23	F	Unknown	12Ju02Tm
DIGNAN, James	30	M	Laborer	12Ju02Tm
HIGGINS, Owen	29	M	Shoemaker	12Ju02Tm
MARTIN, Francis	21	M	Farmer	12Ju02Tm
Catherine	22	F	Servant	12Ju02Tm
FULHAM, Mary	25	F	Servant	12Ju02Tm
MARTIN, Bessy	26	F	Servant	12Ju02Tm
CAFFREY, John	36	M	Laborer	12Ju02Tm
Mary	32	F	Unknown	12Ju02Tm
WALSH, Micael	24	M	Farmer	12Ju02Tm
NEAL, William	24	M	Farmer	12Ju02Tm
MINNICK, John	40	M	Farmer	12Ju02Tm
Ellen	40	F	Unknown	12Ju02Tm
Abby	20	F	Servant	12Ju02Tm
Peggy	11	F	Child	12Ju02Tm
MONIN, James	22	M	Blacksmith	12Ju02Tm
COULTER, John	21	M	Farmer	12Ju02Tm
FARRELL, Handy	24	M	Laborer	12Ju02Tm
TRACEY, Ann	22	F	Servant	12Ju02Tm
Mary	17	F	Servant	12Ju02Tm
MCLAUGHLIN, Owen	19	M	Laborer	12Ju02Tm
FIFE, Catherine	17	F	Servant	12Ju02Tm
KELLY, Alice	15	F	Servant	12Ju02Tm
James	08	M	Child	12Ju02Tm
MCCULLOCH, Jane	18	F	Servant	12Ju02Tm
Rosey	17	F	Servant	12Ju02Tm
GLAVIN, Ann	21	F	Servant	12Ju02Tm
Ann	10	F	Child	12Ju02Tm
CROATH, Anty	11	F	Child	12Ju02Tm
FIERNAN, Pat	30	M	Laborer	12Ju02Tm
SHERIDAN, Daniel	30	M	Laborer	12Ju02Tm
MOONEY, Thomas	22	M	Laborer	12Ju02Tm
BLANCHFORD, Richard	20	M	Shoemaker	12Ju02Tm

MONTREAL 12 JUNE 1848

From Liverpool

NAMES OF PASSENGERS	AGE	SEX	OCCUPATIONS	DATE PORT SHIP
CONWAY, Richard	26	M	Laborer	12Ju02Lz
GATELY, Peter	22	M	Laborer	12Ju02Lz
Jane	22	F	Unknown	12Ju02Lz
CRUMNIN, Thomas	25	M	Laborer	12Ju02Lz
WINOHAM, Edward	36	M	Laborer	12Ju02Lz
Catharine	35	F	Laborer	12Ju02Lz
Patrick	.10	M	Infant	12Ju02Lz
Margaret	02	F	Child	12Ju02Lz
HALL, Thomas	24	M	Mechanic	12Ju02Lz
MCCABE, John	24	M	Mechanic	12Ju02Lz
MCEVERY, John	24	M	Mechanic	12Ju02Lz
SHEIVLING, Mary	20	F	Laborer	12Ju02Lz
ROGERS, Catherine	20	F	Laborer	12Ju02Lz
DUFFY, William	50	M	Farmer	12Ju02Lz
HOY, Daniel	54	M	Farmer	12Ju02Lz
NOWLIN, Matin	25	M	Farmer	12Ju02Lz
DOLTAN, James	30	M	Farmer	12Ju02Lz
HECHY, Thomas	16	M	Farmer	12Ju02Lz
QUINN, Thomas	25	M	Mechanic	12Ju02Lz
MAHON, Peter	23	M	Mechanic	12Ju02Lz
CONNORS, Thomas	22	M	Mechanic	12Ju02Lz
JOY, Catherine	19	F	None	12Ju02Lz
HACHEETT, Ellen	19	F	None	12Ju02Lz
RYAND, Maria	19	F	None	12Ju02Lz
LAYHEE, Mary	20	F	None	12Ju02Lz
COX, James-Mrs	21	F	None	12Ju02Lz
Ellen	.09	F	Infant	12Ju02Lz
Marcellas	07	M	Child	12Ju02Lz
James	03	M	Child	12Ju02Lz
HANNGAN, Anthony	40	M	Mechanic	12Ju02Lz
Honoria	40	F	Unknown	12Ju02Lz
Catherine	18	F	None	12Ju02Lz
HANLY, Mary	16	F	None	12Ju02Lz
Jane	15	F	None	12Ju02Lz
POOL, Francis	27	M	Mechanic	12Ju02Lz
U	26	F	Unknown	12Ju02Lz
John	.07	M	Infant	12Ju02Lz
BRADY, Patrick	24	M	Mechanic	12Ju02Lz
Mary	05	F	Child	12Ju02Lz
BARING, James	35	M	Farmer	12Ju02Lz
Michael	21	M	Farmer	12Ju02Lz
William	19	M	Farmer	12Ju02Lz
Susan	17	F	None	12Ju02Lz
KEELY, Bridget	20	F	None	12Ju02Lz
LERMON, William	40	M	Farmer	12Ju02Lz
John	30	M	Farmer	12Ju02Lz
Patrick	18	M	Farmer	12Ju02Lz
Winferd	20	M	Farmer	12Ju02Lz
HANAGAN, Thomas	28	M	Farmer	12Ju02Lz
CASEY, Patrick	49	M	Farmer	12Ju02Lz
KILLEN, Juline	40	F	None	12Ju02Lz
Michael	20	M	Farmer	12Ju02Lz
Brian	16	M	Farmer	12Ju02Lz
SWEENY, Mary	22	F	Farmer	12Ju02Lz
CLOTHEN, James-Mrs.	23	F	Unknown	12Ju02Lz

NAMES OF PASSENGERS	AGE	SEX	OCCUPATIONS	DATE PORT SHIP
CLOTHEN, Ann-Jane	.03	F	Infant	12Ju02Lz
Mary	19	F	None	12Ju02Lz
MCCLELLAND, John	27	M	Farmer	12Ju02Lz
MCMAHON, Mary	20	F	None	12Ju02Lz
MCCLELLAND, Isabella	34	F	None	12Ju02Lz
FAYEN, Ellen	18	F	None	12Ju02Lz
ELMORE, Peter	46	M	Farmer	12Ju02Lz
HILL, Henry	22	M	Farmer	12Ju02Lz
REGENY, Hugh	26	M	Farmer	12Ju02Lz
COGRAGE, John	24	M	Farmer	12Ju02Lz
LARKIN, Pegg	19	F	None	12Ju02Lz
FLYAN, Ann	24	F	None	12Ju02Lz
LARKIN, Bridget	38	F	None	12Ju02Lz
TULLY, Patrick	30	M	Farmer	12Ju02Lz
STEANE, William	30	M	Farmer	12Ju02Lz
CANNOLY, Rose	23	F	Farmer	12Ju02Lz
Mary	08	F	Child	12Ju02Lz
WHEELAHN, Biddy	22	F	None	12Ju02Lz
FARREL, James	26	M	Mechanic	12Ju02Lz
U	24	F	Unknown	12Ju02Lz
James	03	M	None	12Ju02Lz
Reenan	07	M	None	12Ju02Lz
FEELY, Patrick	27	M	Mechanic	12Ju02Lz
U	26	F	Unknown	12Ju02Lz
William	.09	M	Infant	12Ju02Lz
Owen	09	M	Child	12Ju02Lz
James	07	M	Child	12Ju02Lz
Patrick	05	M	Child	12Ju02Lz
MORAN, Julia	27	F	None	12Ju02Lz
HOG, Ann	24	F	None	12Ju02Lz
U	.00	F	Infant	12Ju02Lz
BELL, George	21	M	Mechanic	12Ju02Lz
COX, James	27	M	Mechanic	12Ju02Lz
SCANNEL, Honoria	07	M	Child	12Ju02Lz
MAHONY, Catherine	28	F	None	12Ju02Lz
Margarett	18	F	None	12Ju02Lz
MCHONDOY, Catherine	11	F	Child	12Ju02Lz
COLLINS, Mary-A.	10	F	Child	12Ju02Lz
MCDONNALD, James	30	M	Farmer	12Ju02Lz
MALLAGAN, Brigett	17	F	None	12Ju02Lz
ELMORE, Michel	50	M	Farmer	12Ju02Lz
William	15	M	Farmer	12Ju02Lz
Elizabeth	50	F	Unknown	12Ju02Lz
MCKEE, Ann	42	F	Farmer	12Ju02Lz
Mary	20	F	None	12Ju02Lz
Lydia-Ann	17	F	None	12Ju02Lz
Joseph	11	M	Child	12Ju02Lz
William	08	M	Child	12Ju02Lz
Alfred	05	M	Child	12Ju02Lz
KENNEDY, Catherine	21	F	None	12Ju02Lz
MACKMAHON, Thomas	26	M	Mechanic	12Ju02Lz
HADFIELD, John	21	M	Mechanic	12Ju02Lz
William	20	M	Mechanic	12Ju02Lz
HALLORAN, Thomas	30	M	Mechanic	12Ju02Lz
TAYHEE, John	25	M	Mechanic	12Ju02Lz
ROACH, Michel	36	M	Mechanic	12Ju02Lz
U	27	M	Mechanic	12Ju02Lz
Francis	05	M	Child	12Ju02Lz
John	03	M	Child	12Ju02Lz
WOOLLEY, Joseph	30	M	Mechanic	12Ju02Lz
THORMLY, Mhel	24	M	Farmer	12Ju02Lz
CONNOLY, Thomas	24	M	Farmer	12Ju02Lz
GARLAND, James	20	M	Farmer	12Ju02Lz
SCANLAND, Margaret	20	F	Farmer	12Ju02Lz
CROSBY, John	20	M	Farmer	12Ju02Lz
POTTERS, John	28	M	Farmer	12Ju02Lz
KENNEDY, John	25	M	Farmer	12Ju02Lz
HOLLOKIN, Mickel	30	M	Farmer	12Ju02Lz
MCMONIE, Steven	25	M	Farmer	12Ju02Lz
HOY, Peter	30	M	Farmer	12Ju02Lz
Margaret	25	F	None	12Ju02Lz
Catharine	27	F	None	12Ju02Lz
Patrick	40	M	Farmer	12Ju02Lz
John	28	M	Farmer	12Ju02Lz
MAHONY, John	24	M	Mechanic	12Ju02Lz
BARRY, Ann	16	F	None	12Ju02Lz
MAHONY, Eliza	18	F	None	12Ju02Lz
Margaret	20	F	None	12Ju02Lz
DALY, Biddy	50	F	None	12Ju02Lz
EVERT, Abby-Duca	22	F	None	12Ju02Lz
DURCIN, Anthony	30	M	None	12Ju02Lz
GOSHAM, Edward-Gr.	40	M	Farmer	12Ju02Lz
DARCY, John	25	M	Farmer	12Ju02Lz
WARD, Honora	40	M	Laborer	12Ju02Lz
Sarah	06	F	Child	12Ju02Lz
CONWAY, U-Mrs.	20	F	Laborer	12Ju02Lz
WALLACE, Bridgett	10	F	Laborer	12Ju02Lz
SCANNEL, Bridgett	17	F	Laborer	12Ju02Lz
Mary	09	F	Child	12Ju02Lz

MERCY 12 JUNE 1848

From Bristol

NAMES OF PASSENGERS	AGE	SEX	OCCUPATIONS	DATE PORT SHIP
CREED, William	32	M	Farmer	12Ju18Tn
Harriet	30	F	Farmer	12Ju18Tn
Sarah	07	F	Farmer	12Ju18Tn
John	06	M	Farmer	12Ju18Tn
Elizabeth	04	F	Farmer	12Ju18Tn
Thomas	02	M	Farmer	12Ju18Tn
Mary-Jane	.00	F	Infant	12Ju18Tn
SOLWAY, Cornelius	40	M	Mechanic	12Ju18Tn
Louisa	34	M	Mechanic	12Ju18Tn
HOBBS, Ann	55	F	Wi	12Ju18Tn
SIMS, Mary	20	F	Dressmaker	12Ju18Tn
HOOK, William	25	M	Farmer	12Ju18Tn
COOMBS, William	24	M	Farmer	12Ju18Tn
Elizabeth	20	F	Farmer	12Ju18Tn
WATTS, Joseph	12	M	Farmer	12Ju18Tn
Ellen	11	F	Dressmaker	12Ju18Tn
WHITE, George	30	M	Farmer	12Ju18Tn
JENKINSON, John	34	M	Mechanic	12Ju18Tn
Ann	26	F	Unknown	12Ju18Tn
Thomas	03	M	Unknown	12Ju18Tn
Elizabeth	02	F	Unknown	12Ju18Tn
Ann	.00	F	Infant	12Ju18Tn
STONEMAN, Philip	24	M	Mechanic	12Ju18Tn
CLEMENTS, Mary	20	F	Dressmaker	12Ju18Tn
WHITELOCK, Fanny	19	F	Farmer	12Ju18Tn
LLOYD, James	33	M	Farmer	12Ju18Tn
Elizabeth	27	F	Farmer	12Ju18Tn
Henry-James	.00	M	Infant	12Ju18Tn
BABER, Joseph	26	M	Laborer	12Ju18Tn
HUDSON, William	27	M	Shpc	12Ju18Tn
POTTER, Frederick	30	M	Blacksmith	12Ju18Tn
GREGORY, Charlotte	18	F	Servant	12Ju18Tn
TAYLOR, Ann	18	F	Servant	12Ju18Tn
Luke	17	M	Mechanic	12Ju18Tn
William	21	M	Mechanic	12Ju18Tn
LAMB, Hiram	16	M	Hrsm	12Ju18Tn
SUMMERFIELD, William	46	M	Mechanic	12Ju18Tn
William	22	M	Mechanic	12Ju18Tn
RAVENHILL, James	23	M	Mechanic	12Ju18Tn
VEALE, Sarah	36	F	Nurse	12Ju18Tn
Robert	04	M	Child	12Ju18Tn
COGSWILL, John	22	M	Sailor	12Ju18Tn
HARDINAN, Dionicia	40	M	Cst	12Ju18Tn
Sarah	18	F	Cst	12Ju18Tn
Charles	17	M	Cst	12Ju18Tn
Joesph	14	M	Cst	12Ju18Tn
Samuel	12	M	Cst	12Ju18Tn
John	21	M	Cst	12Ju18Tn
George	09	M	Cst	12Ju18Tn
Thomas	17	M	Cst	12Ju18Tn

NAMES OF PASSENGERS	AGE	SEX	OCCUPATIONS	DATE PORT SHIP
GOODFELLOW, Maria	30	F	Cst	12Ju18Tn
STRONG, William	24	M	Farmer	12Ju18Tn
Jane	23	F	Unknown	12Ju18Tn
John	.00	M	Infant	12Ju18Tn
REED, Thomas	26	M	Laborer	12Ju18Tn
Fanny	27	F	Unknown	12Ju18Tn
George	05	M	Child	12Ju18Tn
Thomas	03	M	Child	12Ju18Tn
Henry	02	M	Child	12Ju18Tn
Mercy	.00	F	Infant	12Ju18Tn
FORREST, William	34	M	Engineer	12Ju18Tn
Jane	32	F	Unknown	12Ju18Tn
Jean	08	F	Child	12Ju18Tn
Jeannest	07	F	Child	12Ju18Tn
William	05	M	Child	12Ju18Tn
Elizabeth	03	F	Child	12Ju18Tn
SMITH, William	26	M	Blacksmith	12Ju18Tn
ROWLAND, John	27	M	Mechanic	12Ju18Tn
BENNETT, John	28	M	Laborer	12Ju18Tn
DEANE, Daniel	22	M	Rope Maker	12Ju18Tn
RICHARDS, Benjamin	47	M	None	12Ju18Tn
Mary	27	F	None	12Ju18Tn
Elizabeth	24	F	None	12Ju18Tn
John	04	M	Child	12Ju18Tn
Benjamin	26	M	Unknown	12Ju18Tn
Salina	22	F	Unknown	12Ju18Tn
BENJAMIN, Abraham	17	M	Mechanic	12Ju18Tn
VIVIAN, Francis	22	M	Mechanic	12Ju18Tn
Simon	21	M	Mechanic	12Ju18Tn
SUGG, William	22	M	Mechanic	12Ju18Tn
BANNETTS, James	23	M	Mechanic	12Ju18Tn
MULLINS, William	27	M	Mechanic	12Ju18Tn
HOWELL, George	26	M	Laborer	12Ju18Tn
BROWNING, John	44	M	Laborer	12Ju18Tn
Jane	45	F	Laborer	12Ju18Tn
John	20	M	Laborer	12Ju18Tn
Sarah	16	F	Laborer	12Ju18Tn
Emma	15	F	Laborer	12Ju18Tn
Samuel	14	M	Laborer	12Ju18Tn
William	12	M	Laborer	12Ju18Tn
JAMES, George	24	M	Mill Worker	12Ju18Tn
MILLS, George	25	M	Mill Worker	12Ju18Tn
MCHALE, Austen	22	M	Laborer	12Ju18Tn
ODONNELL, Bernard	21	M	Laborer	12Ju18Tn
ONSELY, Isaac	36	M	Mechanic	12Ju18Tn
FRY, Henry	17	M	Laborer	12Ju18Tn
Morley	26	M	Shoemaker	12Ju18Tn
MORLEY, John	30	M	Shoemaker	12Ju18Tn
Nathan	.00	M	Infant	12Ju18Tn
Mary	28	F	Unknown	12Ju18Tn
Jesse	06	M	Child	12Ju18Tn
Clara	05	F	Child	12Ju18Tn
David	03	M	Child	12Ju18Tn
Eliza	17	F	None	12Ju18Tn
HEALE, George	55	M	Paper Maker	12Ju18Tn
Sarah	53	F	Unknown	12Ju18Tn
SHILDON, James	30	M	Laborer	12Ju18Tn
Emma	29	F	Unknown	12Ju18Tn
Mary-Ann	05	F	Child	12Ju18Tn
Emily	03	F	Child	12Ju18Tn
Sarah-Jane	.00	F	Infant	12Ju18Tn
SIMMONDS, Ester	34	F	Diet Maker	12Ju18Tn
George	14	M	Child	12Ju18Tn
Jonathan	12	M	Child	12Ju18Tn
Ellen	09	F	Child	12Ju18Tn
Martha	07	F	Child	12Ju18Tn
Mary	05	F	Child	12Ju18Tn
SIMS, Etan	40	M	Stctr	12Ju18Tn
Zebra	38	F	Stctr	12Ju18Tn
James	13	M	Stctr	12Ju18Tn
Louisa	11	F	Stctr	12Ju18Tn
Isabella	07	F	Stctr	12Ju18Tn
Mary-Ann	05	F	Stctr	12Ju18Tn
John	.00	M	Infant	12Ju18Tn
ROGERS, James	27	M	Bootmaker	12Ju18Tn
ROGERS, Jane	28	F	Unknown	12Ju18Tn
William	03	M	Child	12Ju18Tn
Sarah	.00	F	Infant	12Ju18Tn
EVANS, Edward	30	M	Laborer	12Ju18Tn
Sarah	28	F	Laborer	12Ju18Tn
James	03	M	Child	12Ju18Tn
HILL, Hannah	18	F	None	12Ju18Tn
RINES, George	40	M	Laborer	12Ju18Tn
Charlotte	28	F	Laborer	12Ju18Tn
Ann	17	F	Laborer	12Ju18Tn
Charlotte	13	F	Laborer	12Ju18Tn
Henry	12	M	Laborer	12Ju18Tn
Caroline	20	F	Laborer	12Ju18Tn
Eliza	04	F	Child	12Ju18Tn
George	.00	M	Infant	12Ju18Tn
COOPER, William	37	M	Laborer	12Ju18Tn
Elizabeth	24	F	Unknown	12Ju18Tn
Henry	.00	M	Infant	12Ju18Tn
DAVEY, Lydia-J.	27	F	Dressmaker	12Ju18Tn
Elizabeth	03	F	Child	12Ju18Tn
William	.00	M	Infant	12Ju18Tn
ENGLAND, William	34	M	Shoemaker	12Ju18Tn
Hannah	34	F	Unknown	12Ju18Tn
Oliver	15	M	None	12Ju18Tn
William	14	M	None	12Ju18Tn
Morris	12	M	None	12Ju18Tn
Mary	09	F	Child	12Ju18Tn
Ann	04	F	Child	12Ju18Tn
Charles	.00	M	Infant	12Ju18Tn
WINTER, William-Thomas	18	M	None	12Ju18Tn

SAMOSET 12 JUNE 1848

From Liverpool

NAMES OF PASSENGERS	AGE	SEX	OCCUPATIONS	DATE PORT SHIP
MCGORVY, Cath	20	F	House Maid	12Ju02Tt
BOYLE, Nancey	20	F	House Maid	12Ju02Tt
KINNEY, Jane	15	F	House Maid	12Ju02Tt
DUGAN, Mans	20	M	Laborer	12Ju02Tt
GILLESPIE, Mary	18	F	House Maid	12Ju02Tt
Cath	20	F	House Maid	12Ju02Tt
DIRER, Allice	18	F	House Maid	12Ju02Tt
MCABE, Henry	57	M	Laborer	12Ju02Tt
COYLE, Michael	30	M	Laborer	12Ju02Tt
LEE, Michael	20	M	Laborer	12Ju02Tt
CUMMINGS, Pat	18	M	Laborer	12Ju02Tt
BRIEN, Judy	20	F	House Maid	12Ju02Tt
DAILEY, Pat	20	M	Laborer	12Ju02Tt
Thomas	21	M	Laborer	12Ju02Tt
THORNTON, Ellen	30	F	Night Nurse	12Ju02Tt
KELCHN, Ellen	22	F	House Maid	12Ju02Tt
BRADLEY, Jane	20	F	House Maid	12Ju02Tt
TAGNE, Isabella	20	F	House Maid	12Ju02Tt
VAUGHN, James	20	M	Shoemaker	12Ju02Tt
LEDREN, John	20	M	Laborer	12Ju02Tt
DENHAM, Robert	40	M	Nearer	12Ju02Tt
Agnes	40	M	Nearer	12Ju02Tt
Eliza	20	F	Nearer	12Ju02Tt
Thomas	13	M	Nearer	12Ju02Tt
MCARTY, Eliza	12	F	Servant	12Ju02Tt
QUINN, Ellen	15	F	Servant	12Ju02Tt
MCINCHU, Bridget	40	F	Servant	12Ju02Tt
SMYTHE, Bridget	40	F	House Maid	12Ju02Tt
Peter	08	M	Child	12Ju02Tt
Ann	10	F	Child	12Ju02Tt
Mary	05	F	Child	12Ju02Tt
HATTAN, Ann	20	F	House Maid	12Ju02Tt
Mary	16	F	House Maid	12Ju02Tt
Bridget	15	F	House Maid	12Ju02Tt

NAMES OF PASSENGERS	AGE	SEX	OCCUPATIONS	DATE PORT SHIP
OBRIEN, Mary	23	F	House Maid	12Ju02Tt
William	04	M	Child	12Ju02Tt
John	.00	M	Infant	12Ju02Tt
Died-At-Sea				
SHERIDAN, Bridget	17	F	House Maid	12Ju02Tt
Julia	18	F	House Maid	12Ju02Tt
JOHNSTON, James	50	M	Laborer	12Ju02Tt
GALLAGHAN, Francis	20	M	Baker	12Ju02Tt
GOLDING, Bridget	17	F	House Maid	12Ju02Tt
LAGGINS, Ann	18	F	House Maid	12Ju02Tt
FLYN, Maria	14	F	House Maid	12Ju02Tt
Ellen	11	F	House Maid	12Ju02Tt
MULBERG, Charles	21	M	Laborer	12Ju02Tt
DOLPHIN, Mina	40	F	Night Nurse	12Ju02Tt
Cath	25	F	Servant	12Ju02Tt
BRYM, Eliza	45	F	House Maid	12Ju02Tt
Margaret	19	F	House Maid	12Ju02Tt
BROWN, Mary-Jane	19	F	House Maid	12Ju02Tt
BROTHELL, Pat	12	M	Unknown	12Ju02Tt
MOONEY, James	32	M	Laborer	12Ju02Tt
CRUMNEY, Bridget	20	F	House Maid	12Ju02Tt
DEMPSEY, Mary	20	F	House Maid	12Ju02Tt
MURPHY, Cath	20	F	House Maid	12Ju02Tt
MCGEE, Mary	20	F	House Maid	12Ju02Tt
MCALANELEY, Allay	18	M	House Maid	12Ju02Tt
SULLIVAN, James	17	M	Laborer	12Ju02Tt
SHOULDER, Kildy	20	F	House Maid	12Ju02Tt
MCINTIGN, Cath	20	F	House Maid	12Ju02Tt
HOSTIH, Charles	63	M	Nearer	12Ju02Tt
Sarah	60	F	Wife	12Ju02Tt
Sarah	15	F	Child	12Ju02Tt
JURNE, James	10	M	Child	12Ju02Tt
KERNAHIN, William	24	M	Clerk	12Ju02Tt
DARLEY, Cath.	20	F	House Maid	12Ju02Tt
CRAIG, John	20	M	Carpenter	12Ju02Tt
Ann	21	F	Carpenter	12Ju02Tt
NERIM, Margaret	20	F	House Maid	12Ju02Tt
BURNS, James	13	M	Child	12Ju02Tt
MCNITYRE, Mathew	30	M	Laborer	12Ju02Tt
CONLAN, Ann	20	F	House Maid	12Ju02Tt
U, U	20	U	Laborer	12Ju02Tt
U	18	F	House Maid	12Ju02Tt
U	20	M	Carpenter	12Ju02Tt
U	20	M	Carpenter	12Ju02Tt
U	20	M	Shoemaker	12Ju02Tt
U	21	M	Farmer	12Ju02Tt
U	00	M	Farmer	12Ju02Tt
U	00	M	Farmer	12Ju02Tt
U	18	M	Farmer	12Ju02Tt
U	21	M	Laborer	12Ju02Tt
U	21	M	Laborer	12Ju02Tt
U	20	F	House Maid	12Ju02Tt
U	20	F	House Maid	12Ju02Tt
U	20	F	Nurse	12Ju02Tt
U	20	M	Laborer	12Ju02Tt
U	20	M	Carpenter	12Ju02Tt
U	20	M	Carpenter	12Ju02Tt
U	20	M	Carpenter	12Ju02Tt
U	26	M	Brewer	12Ju02Tt
U	23	U	Clerk	12Ju02Tt
U	30	U	Farmer	12Ju02Tt
U	20	U	Farmer	12Ju02Tt
U	20	U	Farmer	12Ju02Tt
U	21	U	Farmer	12Ju02Tt
U	22	U	Farmer	12Ju02Tt
U	20	U	Laborer	12Ju02Tt
U	26	U	Spinner	12Ju02Tt
U	19	U	Spinner	12Ju02Tt
U	18	F	Servant	12Ju02Tt
U	14	F	Servant	12Ju02Tt
U	12	F	Servant	12Ju02Tt
U	18	U	Laborer	12Ju02Tt
U	17	F	Servant	12Ju02Tt
U	40	U	Laborer	12Ju02Tt

LORD-BYRON 12 JUNE 1848

From Glasgow

NAMES OF PASSENGERS	AGE	SEX	OCCUPATIONS	DATE PORT SHIP
MAHAFFEY, Leatheam	16	M	None	12Ju04Tq
PATTERSON, James	21	M	Farmer	12Ju04Tq
SCOTT, Jane	17	F	None	12Ju04Tq
Joseph	20	M	Farmer	12Ju04Tq
Jane	64	M	None	12Ju04Tq
QUIGLEY, Margaret	20	F	None	12Ju04Tq
SMITH, Thomas	14	M	None	12Ju04Tq
TIMONEY, Rose	20	F	None	12Ju04Tq
RODGERS, Fanny	32	F	None	12Ju04Tq
James	05	M	None	12Ju04Tq
DOCHERTY, Edward	28	M	Laborer	12Ju04Tq
MCDEAD, Patrick	58	M	Laborer	12Ju04Tq
John	23	M	Laborer	12Ju04Tq
Catherine	15	F	Servant	12Ju04Tq
GILLESPY, Peter	23	M	Laborer	12Ju04Tq
FANNAN, Dennis	20	M	Laborer	12Ju04Tq
Elin	18	F	Seamstress	12Ju04Tq
William	18	M	Butcher	12Ju04Tq
KAIN, Catherine	14	F	None	12Ju04Tq
DOCHERTY, John	19	M	Laborer	12Ju04Tq
MCGLAUGHLAN, Daniel	46	M	Farmer	12Ju04Tq
Patrick	11	M	None	12Ju04Tq
MCGROREY, Mary	17	F	Servant	12Ju04Tq
COIL, Cathrine	16	F	Servant	12Ju04Tq
BROWN, Joseph	18	M	Laborer	12Ju04Tq
Sarah	19	F	Seamstress	12Ju04Tq
LOWEL, Ann	18	F	Servant	12Ju04Tq
ANNOVER, Joseph	19	M	Servant	12Ju04Tq
GIBBONS, John	24	M	Laborer	12Ju04Tq
PORTER, James	20	M	Coachman	12Ju04Tq
REID, Eliza	14	F	None	12Ju04Tq
Eliza	40	F	None	12Ju04Tq
MCLAUGHLAN, Elwen	26	M	Farmer	12Ju04Tq
DENNY, James	25	M	Farmer	12Ju04Tq
LENNYSTON, James	19	M	Farmer	12Ju04Tq
Margaret	15	F	None	12Ju04Tq
MCHUGH, John	26	M	Stctr	12Ju04Tq
Eleanore	24	F	None	12Ju04Tq
Catherine	26	F	Servant	12Ju04Tq
LAFERTY, John	21	M	Farmer	12Ju04Tq
WOCSKEY, Micheal	20	M	Miller	12Ju04Tq
NIXON, Thomas	21	M	Coppersmith	12Ju04Tq
HEAGERTY, Patrick	25	M	Laborer	12Ju04Tq
MCLAUGHLIN, Biddy	18	F	Servant	12Ju04Tq
MCCRADEN, Micheal	22	M	Laborer	12Ju04Tq
BOYERS, Robert	27	M	Farmer	12Ju04Tq
DOCHARTY, Bernard	60	M	Farmer	12Ju04Tq
Bernard	12	M	None	12Ju04Tq
Margaret	15	F	None	12Ju04Tq
BANKS, Margaret	20	F	Seamstress	12Ju04Tq
MCKENNY, William	25	M	Farmer	12Ju04Tq
MCDERMONT, Fanny	27	F	None	12Ju04Tq
James	02	M	None	12Ju04Tq
NIXON, Mary	30	F	None	12Ju04Tq
MCLAUGHLAN, John	16	M	Tailor	12Ju04Tq
LESLIE, Joseph	27	M	Farmer	12Ju04Tq
Margaret	24	F	Wife	12Ju04Tq
Jane	04	F	None	12Ju04Tq
David	07	M	None	12Ju04Tq
PENDERGRASS, Eliza	20	F	Servant	12Ju04Tq
CAMPBELL, Jane	22	F	Dressmaker	12Ju04Tq
LOGAN, Cathrine	60	F	None	12Ju04Tq
Samuel	21	M	Farmer	12Ju04Tq
Betsey	30	F	House Cook	12Ju04Tq
Isabela	18	F	Seamstress	12Ju04Tq

NAMES OF PASSENGERS	AGE	SEX	OCCUPATIONS	DATE PORT SHIP
LOGAN, Jeremiah	15	M	None	12Ju04Tq
Thomas	11	M	None	12Ju04Tq
Jane	06	F	Child	12Ju04Tq
Rebeca	06	F	Child	12Ju04Tq
Isabela	01	F	Child	12Ju04Tq
Robert	26	M	Laborer	12Ju04Tq
MCGILL, William	23	M	Laborer	12Ju04Tq
LINTON, Jane	63	F	None	12Ju04Tq
MCNAMARA, Charles	23	M	Carpenter	12Ju04Tq
FLETCHER, Eliza	20	F	Servant	12Ju04Tq
Mary	18	F	Servant	12Ju04Tq
CAMPBELL, Thomas	20	M	Farmer	12Ju04Tq
CONWAY, Susan	20	F	Servant	12Ju04Tq
CAMPBELL, Ann	55	F	None	12Ju04Tq
MCLAUGHLAN, Biddy	22	F	Servant	12Ju04Tq
CONNOR, Nancy	20	F	Servant	12Ju04Tq
MCLAUGHLAN, Charles	20	M	Laborer	12Ju04Tq
HARSHAW, Samuel	20	M	Farmer	12Ju04Tq
BUCHANAN, Andrew	17	M	Farmer	12Ju04Tq
SEMPLE, Mary	24	F	Seamstress	12Ju04Tq
MCINTYRE, Martha	19	F	Seamstress	12Ju04Tq
MCLOSKEY, John	16	M	None	12Ju04Tq
Margaret	15	F	Servant	12Ju04Tq
CAITON, Margaret	19	F	Servant	12Ju04Tq
MCRONNEY, Thomas	21	M	Saddler	12Ju04Tq
Ellen	18	F	Servant	12Ju04Tq
MCGETTINGHAM, John	17	M	Laborer	12Ju04Tq
MCGUGAN, Biddy	18	F	Servant	12Ju04Tq
CUNNINGHAM, Jane	30	F	Servant	12Ju04Tq
WOODS, William	19	M	Farmer	12Ju04Tq
PARKER, Eliza	18	F	Servant	12Ju04Tq
STURREY, Andrew	22	M	Farmer	12Ju04Tq
GOURLEY, Margaret	20	F	Servant	12Ju04Tq
KILPATRICK, U-Mrs.	24	F	None	12Ju04Tq
BOND, Martha	19	F	Seamstress	12Ju04Tq
CRAWFORD, Thomas	27	M	Farmer	12Ju04Tq
ROAFESTOR, James	21	M	Farmer	12Ju04Tq
TRONE, Cathrine	18	F	Seamstress	12Ju04Tq
CRAWFORD, Eliza	20	F	Servant	12Ju04Tq
Ann	17	F	Servant	12Ju04Tq
ALEXANDER, Nancy	17	F	Seamstress	12Ju04Tq
MAHAFFEY, U-Mrs.	60	F	None	12Ju04Tq
John	20	M	Farmer	12Ju04Tq
Moses	17	M	Farmer	12Ju04Tq
Robert	18	M	Farmer	12Ju04Tq
Samuel	14	M	Farmer	12Ju04Tq
Thomas	12	M	None	12Ju04Tq
William	10	M	None	12Ju04Tq
DOCHERTY, William	20	M	Laborer	12Ju04Tq
COLHOUN, Galbreath	18	M	Laborer	12Ju04Tq
ROSS, John	27	M	Farmer	12Ju04Tq
James	21	M	Farmer	12Ju04Tq
Sarah	20	F	Servant	12Ju04Tq
Jane-Ann	25	F	Keeper	12Ju04Tq
COLHOUN, Ann	25	F	Seamstress	12Ju04Tq
KEARNEY, William	24	M	Laborer	12Ju04Tq
Hamilton	22	M	Laborer	12Ju04Tq
Margaret	30	F	Servant	12Ju04Tq
MCMANNAN, Mary	15	F	None	12Ju04Tq
ALEXANDER, William	36	M	Weaver	12Ju04Tq
Mary	35	F	Wife	12Ju04Tq
Eliza	03	F	None	12Ju04Tq
Isabela	.04	F	Infant	12Ju04Tq
KANE, Patrick	31	M	Laborer	12Ju04Tq
Ann	12	F	None	12Ju04Tq
Eliza	15	F	None	12Ju04Tq
Jane	13	F	None	12Ju04Tq
MCGLAUGHLAN, Daniel	16	M	Tailor	12Ju04Tq
HAGAN, Rossana	16	F	Servant	12Ju04Tq
MCGINTEY, James	16	M	Laborer	12Ju04Tq
CAMPBELL, Eliza	18	F	Seamstress	12Ju04Tq
MCGONIGEL, Niell	28	M	Farmer	12Ju04Tq
COULTER, James	28	M	Farmer	12Ju04Tq
STEINPHILL, John	19	M	Laborer	12Ju04Tq
COULTER, Margaret	28	F	None	12Ju04Tq
COULTER, James	10	M	None	12Ju04Tq
Robert	04	M	Child	12Ju04Tq
Lucy	02	F	Child	12Ju04Tq
FOY, Rebaca	20	F	Servant	12Ju04Tq
LOGAN, William	20	M	Farmer	12Ju04Tq
MCGUIRE, Charles	25	M	Farmer	12Ju04Tq
MCCULLOUGH, James	24	M	Blacksmith	12Ju04Tq
WATSON, John	18	M	None	12Ju04Tq
U, U	.00	U	Infant	12Ju04Tq

CHENAGO 12 JUNE 1848

From London

NAMES OF PASSENGERS	AGE	SEX	OCCUPATIONS	DATE PORT SHIP
SHELLY, Richard	29	M	Hatter	12Ju21Tr
FARRELL, John	28	M	Tailor	12Ju21Tr
Ellen	26	F	Tailor	12Ju21Tr
SANDS, Michael	29	M	Laborer	12Ju21Tr
Jane	23	F	Laborer	12Ju21Tr
CODDER, John	32	M	Carpenter	12Ju21Tr
Catherine	31	F	Carpenter	12Ju21Tr
Michael	.11	M	Infant	12Ju21Tr
CURLEY, John	33	M	Laborer	12Ju21Tr
Ellen	30	M	Laborer	12Ju21Tr
Mary	03	M	Laborer	12Ju21Tr
CAUGHLIN, Jeremiah	27	M	Laborer	12Ju21Tr
Catherine	31	F	Laborer	12Ju21Tr

HELENA 13 JUNE 1848

From Galway

NAMES OF PASSENGERS	AGE	SEX	OCCUPATIONS	DATE PORT SHIP
RAFTERY, Bridget	18	F	Spinster	13Ju11Jd
FAHEY, Margret	14	F	Spinster	13Ju11Jd
CONNELL, Bridget	00	F	Spinster	13Ju11Jd
BERGAN, John	20	M	Laborer	13Ju11Jd
Mary	20	F	Spinster	13Ju11Jd
BEEGAN, Kitty	19	F	Spinster	13Ju11Jd
HEALEY, Thomas	27	M	Laborer	13Ju11Jd
John	13	M	Child	13Ju11Jd
HEALY, May	48	F	Matron	13Ju11Jd
CONNOR, Michael	21	M	Laborer	13Ju11Jd
FITZGERALD, Thomas	21	M	Laborer	13Ju11Jd
Margret	20	F	Spinster	13Ju11Jd
KERSE, Patt	22	M	None	13Ju11Jd
Mary	18	F	Spinster	13Ju11Jd
Bridget	16	F	Spinster	13Ju11Jd
KEARNEY, Pat	26	M	Laborer	13Ju11Jd
OLAUGHLAN, Coleman	18	M	Laborer	13Ju11Jd
WALSH, Mathias	30	M	Laborer	13Ju11Jd
Margaret	30	F	Wife	13Ju11Jd
VERNON, Mary	20	F	Spinster	13Ju11Jd
BURNS, Michel	25	M	Laborer	13Ju11Jd
LEONARD, Thomas	20	M	Laborer	13Ju11Jd
KEARNY, May	24	F	Spinster	13Ju11Jd
CREAN, James	25	M	None	13Ju11Jd
Margaret	24	F	None	13Ju11Jd
BUTLER, John	21	M	Laborer	13Ju11Jd
HAVERTY, Michel	18	M	Laborer	13Ju11Jd
REGAN, Catharin	20	F	Spinster	13Ju11Jd
Bridget	16	F	Spinster	13Ju11Jd
SHANAHAN, Margaret	18	F	Spinster	13Ju11Jd
COVELS, Pat	21	M	None	13Ju11Jd

NAMES OF PASSENGERS	AGE	SEX	OCCUPATIONS	DATE PORT SHIP
ROYONA, Mary	23	F	Spinster	13Ju11Jd
DOGERTY, Catharine	20	F	Spinster	13Ju11Jd
MCTIGNE, May	20	F	Spinster	13Ju11Jd
FINEGAN, Thomas	21	M	Laborer	13Ju11Jd
GAWSON, Thomas	15	M	Laborer	13Ju11Jd
ARMSTRONG, Fanny	22	F	Spinster	13Ju11Jd
MCCARRTY, Elenor	20	F	Spinster	13Ju11Jd
WILLIAMS, Jane	13	F	None	13Ju11Jd
BURNS, Michel	35	M	Laborer	13Ju11Jd
MALONEY, Margaret	16	F	Spinster	13Ju11Jd
DUGGAN, Mathew	23	M	Saddler	13Ju11Jd
TRACY, Michel	22	M	Saddler	13Ju11Jd
NOON, William	24	M	Laborer	13Ju11Jd
Honor (W)	24	F	Wife	13Ju11Jd
FINEGAN, Daniel	18	M	Laborer	13Ju11Jd
MCDERMOTT, Michel	24	M	Laborer	13Ju11Jd
JENINGS, Patck.	30	M	Servant	13Ju11Jd
Patt	30	M	Laborer	13Ju11Jd
Celia (W)	28	F	Wife	13Ju11Jd
NOON, John	35	M	Laborer	13Ju11Jd
Honor (W)	28	F	Wife	13Ju11Jd
HORERE, John	26	M	Laborer	13Ju11Jd
HAVERTY, Thomas	25	M	Laborer	13Ju11Jd
HIGINS, Daniel	25	M	Laborer	13Ju11Jd
Michel	23	M	Laborer	13Ju11Jd
READY, Margaret	25	F	Spinster	13Ju11Jd
HOGAN, Mary	28	F	Spinster	13Ju11Jd
HOPKINS, John	28	M	Laborer	13Ju11Jd
WALSH, Michel	20	M	Laborer	13Ju11Jd
Michel	30	M	Laborer	13Ju11Jd
MOVOREY, Mathew	25	M	Laborer	13Ju11Jd
MULLINS, Michel	22	M	Clerk	13Ju11Jd
MOVONEY, Symon	22	M	Laborer	13Ju11Jd
DONAHOE, Martin	35	M	Laborer	13Ju11Jd
MONESSY, Jane	40	F	Wi	13Ju11Jd
JOURDAN, Thomas	30	M	Laborer	13Ju11Jd
GILL, Margaret	30	F	Matron	13Ju11Jd
QUICK, Honor	16	F	Spinster	13Ju11Jd
LYONS, Catharine	14	F	Spinster	13Ju11Jd
DOOLY, John	20	M	Shoemaker	13Ju11Jd
FRAINY, Roderick	40	M	Laborer	13Ju11Jd
QUINN, John	40	M	Laborer	13Ju11Jd
KOONAN, Peter	35	M	Laborer	13Ju11Jd
COLOHAN, Frank	25	M	Laborer	13Ju11Jd
MORAN, Edward	22	M	Laborer	13Ju11Jd
TOOLE, Mary	26	F	Spinster	13Ju11Jd
KELLY, Patt	40	M	Laborer	13Ju11Jd
FLYNN, William	35	M	Laborer	13Ju11Jd
BOONEY, Mary	20	F	Dressmaker	13Ju11Jd
CURRAN, Catharine	24	F	Spinster	13Ju11Jd
HAVERTY, Mary	19	F	Spinster	13Ju11Jd
SHEENAN, Thimothy	21	M	Laborer	13Ju11Jd
BURNS, Michel	22	M	Laborer	13Ju11Jd
Mary	19	F	Spinster	13Ju11Jd
MANNION, Martin	23	M	Laborer	13Ju11Jd
CARTHY, Bernard	18	M	Tailor	13Ju11Jd
MCGRATH, Peter	17	M	Servant	13Ju11Jd
DONOHUE, Mary	28	F	Spinster	13Ju11Jd
Patt	04	M	Child	13Ju11Jd
Thomas	02	M	Child	13Ju11Jd
KEATING, Michel	30	M	Laborer	13Ju11Jd
Fardy	30	M	Laborer	13Ju11Jd
Died-At-Sea				
Bridget	27	F	Spinster	13Ju11Jd
BROWN, Mary	35	F	Spinster	13Ju11Jd
DOOLEY, Michel	30	M	Laborer	13Ju11Jd
Mary	22	F	Spinster	13Ju11Jd
CASSEDY, James	23	M	Laborer	13Ju11Jd
LALLY, May	19	F	Spinster	13Ju11Jd
Catharine	21	F	Spinster	13Ju11Jd
OLAUGLIN, Margaret	20	F	Spinster	13Ju11Jd
WARD, John	27	M	Laborer	13Ju11Jd
Malachi	18	M	Laborer	13Ju11Jd
Peggy	50	F	None	13Ju11Jd
Judy	32	F	Spinster	13Ju11Jd

NAMES OF PASSENGERS	AGE	SEX	OCCUPATIONS	DATE PORT SHIP
CAHALIN, William	20	M	Laborer	13Ju11Jd
Michel	30	M	Laborer	13Ju11Jd
DUFFY, Hugh	30	M	Laborer	13Ju11Jd
GLENAN, Martin	24	M	Laborer	13Ju11Jd
BURKE, Thomas	21	M	Shoemaker	13Ju11Jd
STAUNTON, William	22	M	Laborer	13Ju11Jd
Ann (W)	20	F	Wife	13Ju11Jd
MCALAIN, Patt	28	M	Laborer	13Ju11Jd
Mary	18	F	Spinster	13Ju11Jd
COOKE, Michel	20	M	Tailor	13Ju11Jd
KENNEDY, Catharine	23	F	Matron	13Ju11Jd
BURKE, Catharine	22	F	Spinster	13Ju11Jd
Maria	20	F	Spinster	13Ju11Jd
HANLON, Jeremiah	20	M	Laborer	13Ju11Jd
COVANEY, Dennis	20	M	Laborer	13Ju11Jd
KING, Honor	26	F	Spinster	13Ju11Jd
HANLIN, Thomas	24	M	Laborer	13Ju11Jd
Bridget (W)	16	F	Wife	13Ju11Jd
COLEMAN, Bedelia	14	F	Spinster	13Ju11Jd
Mary (T)	16	F	Spinster	13Ju11Jd
HOLORAN, Patt	35	M	Laborer	13Ju11Jd
FORD, Patt	26	M	Laborer	13Ju11Jd
Ellen (W)	27	F	Wife	13Ju11Jd
MCDONNELL, Ann	33	F	Matron	13Ju11Jd
SHEEHAN, Margaret	28	F	Spinster	13Ju11Jd

HOTTINGUER 13 JUNE 1848

From Liverpool

NAMES OF PASSENGERS	AGE	SEX	OCCUPATIONS	DATE PORT SHIP
OBRIEN, William-Smith	30	M	Cver	13Ju02Bc
Eliza	28	F	None	13Ju02Bc
Jean	27	F	None	13Ju02Bc
BYRNE, James	23	F	Clerk	13Ju02Bc
Margaret	30	F	None	13Ju02Bc
MCHUGH, Isabella	26	F	None	13Ju02Bc
CASSIDY, Mary	16	F	None	13Ju02Bc
MCHUGH, Margaret	01	F	Child	13Ju02Bc

EMERALD 13 JUNE 1848

From Londonderry

NAMES OF PASSENGERS	AGE	SEX	OCCUPATIONS	DATE PORT SHIP
MCGEE, Michael	00	M	Laborer	13Ju01Cs
BOYCE, John	00	M	Laborer	13Ju01Cs
MCGINLEY, John	00	M	Laborer	13Ju01Cs
MCFADDEN, Sally	00	F	Spinster	13Ju01Cs
KEENAN, James	30	M	Gdnr	13Ju01Cs
Jane	25	F	Milliner	13Ju01Cs
James	01	M	Child	13Ju01Cs
MCLAUGHLIN, Biddy	16	F	Spinster	13Ju01Cs
DOUGHERTY, Nancy	14	F	Spinster	13Ju01Cs
Matty	16	F	Spinster	13Ju01Cs
Mcnult---, Mary	22	F	Spinster	13Ju01Cs
MCGREW, Eliza	34	F	Spinster	13Ju01Cs
John	06	M	Child	13Ju01Cs
Mary-Ann	04	F	Child	13Ju01Cs
HERRAN, Daniel	40	M	Laborer	13Ju01Cs
John	18	M	Laborer	13Ju01Cs
Allice	16	F	None	13Ju01Cs
Bridget	14	F	None	13Ju01Cs
Peter	12	M	Laborer	13Ju01Cs
STUART, Joseph	21	M	Laborer	13Ju01Cs

NAMES OF PASSENGERS		AGE	SEX	OCCUPATIONS	DATE PORT SHIP
BRADLEY, Patrick		26	M	Laborer	13Ju01Cs
LADEN, Mary		18	F	Spinster	13Ju01Cs
JACOB, Ann		18	F	Spinster	13Ju01Cs
DOOGAN, Mary		25	F	Spinster	13Ju01Cs
MCBRIDE, Micky		20	M	Laborer	13Ju01Cs
HENRY, John		32	M	Laborer	13Ju01Cs
Robert		14	M	Laborer	13Ju01Cs
ROCK, Thomas		52	M	Miller	13Ju01Cs
MCGINNIS, Denis		29	M	Laborer	13Ju01Cs
John		21	M	Laborer	13Ju01Cs
MCGEE, Ann		25	F	Spinster	13Ju01Cs
ELLISON, Robert		17	M	Laborer	13Ju01Cs
LAGAN, John		32	M	Laborer	13Ju01Cs
Biddy		32	F	Spinster	13Ju01Cs
Mary		20	F	Spinster	13Ju01Cs
MCGLABL, Susan		20	F	None	13Ju01Cs
MCCREADY, Charles		24	M	Laborer	13Ju01Cs
SHANNON, John		18	M	Butler	13Ju01Cs
HASLITT, Allexander		21	M	Laborer	13Ju01Cs
SHIELDS, Patrick		22	M	Laborer	13Ju01Cs
Michael		28	M	Laborer	13Ju01Cs
KARR, Darby		30	M	Laborer	13Ju01Cs
KERR, Owen		40	M	Laborer	13Ju01Cs
MCCOUGHEY, Giles		24	F	Spinster	13Ju01Cs
YOUNG, John		27	M	Joiner	13Ju01Cs
Eliza		21	F	Joiner	13Ju01Cs
Eliza		17	F	None	13Ju01Cs
WILSON, Mary-J.		16	F	Dressmaker	13Ju01Cs
LYNCH, Margaret		17	F	Dressmaker	13Ju01Cs
SMALL, James		23	M	Laborer	13Ju01Cs
TUMBLIN, John		33	M	Laborer	13Ju01Cs
Ann	(W)	30	F	Seamstress	13Ju01Cs
Eliza	(D)	09	F	Child	13Ju01Cs
Jane	(D)	08	F	Child	13Ju01Cs
George	(S)	05	M	Child	13Ju01Cs
Daniel	(S)	04	M	Child	13Ju01Cs
Mary	(D)	02	F	Child	13Ju01Cs
Susan	(D)	.03	F	Infant	13Ju01Cs
MCCONNELL, Thomas		21	M	Laborer	13Ju01Cs
WASON, John		17	M	Laborer	13Ju01Cs
MCGLOUGHLEN, Elliot		48	M	Stone Mason	13Ju01Cs
QUIGLEY, Denis		18	M	Laborer	13Ju01Cs
DONNELLY, Margaret		28	F	Seamstress	13Ju01Cs
MCLAUGHLIN, Mary		29	F	Spinster	13Ju01Cs
MCGREW, Sarah		09	F	Spinster	13Ju01Cs
LOGAN, Lititia		30	F	Dressmaker	13Ju01Cs
MCCEW, Ellen		22	F	Seamstress	13Ju01Cs
MURREY, Mary-A.		21	F	Seamstress	13Ju01Cs
LOGUE, Magy		17	F	Seamstress	13Ju01Cs

MILAN 13 JUNE 1848

From Liverpool

NAMES OF PASSENGERS		AGE	SEX	OCCUPATIONS	DATE PORT SHIP
GRIFFIN, John		35	M	Laborer	13Ju02Uq
William		24	M	Laborer	13Ju02Uq
WILLIAMS, Ryland		23	M	Laborer	13Ju02Uq
Rowland		53	M	Laborer	13Ju02Uq
Elizabeth	(W)	44	F	Laborer	13Ju02Uq
Edward	(S)	18	M	Laborer	13Ju02Uq
Margaret	(D)	16	F	Laborer	13Ju02Uq
Rowland	(S)	06	M	Child	13Ju02Uq
Robert	(S)	04	M	Child	13Ju02Uq
Ellen	(D)	.00	F	Infant	13Ju02Uq
BROWN, William		45	M	Laborer	13Ju02Uq
Mary		26	F	Laborer	13Ju02Uq
DIXON, Charlott		63	F	Laborer	13Ju02Uq
George		58	M	Laborer	13Ju02Uq
WAKELY, Robert		23	M	Laborer	13Ju02Uq
BIXLIN, William		31	M	Laborer	13Ju02Uq
Elizabeth	(W)	35	F	Wife	13Ju02Uq
Henry	(S)	13	M	None	13Ju02Uq
Charles	(S)	11	M	Child	13Ju02Uq
Jane	(D)	09	F	Child	13Ju02Uq
Mary-Ann	(D)	06	F	Child	13Ju02Uq
Caroline	(D)	04	F	Child	13Ju02Uq
William	(S)	.00	M	Infant	13Ju02Uq
BROWN, James		26	M	Laborer	13Ju02Uq
LAMMY, Solomon		40	M	Laborer	13Ju02Uq
Jane	(W)	30	F	Wife	13Ju02Uq
John	(S)	11	M	Child	13Ju02Uq
William	(S)	08	M	Child	13Ju02Uq
Mary	(D)	06	F	Child	13Ju02Uq
Christie	(D)	04	F	Child	13Ju02Uq
Sarah-Jane	(D)	.00	F	Infant	13Ju02Uq
COULTON, John		25	M	Laborer	13Ju02Uq
MCCANNY, Michael		26	M	Laborer	13Ju02Uq
MCGOLDRICH, Michael		25	M	Laborer	13Ju02Uq
APPLEBY, J.M.		40	M	Laborer	13Ju02Uq
Mary	(W)	40	F	Laborer	13Ju02Uq
John	(S)	23	M	Laborer	13Ju02Uq
Mary	(D)	23	F	Laborer	13Ju02Uq
CALLAGHAN, Margaret		25	F	Laborer	13Ju02Uq
Ann		20	F	Laborer	13Ju02Uq
Elizabeth		10	F	Laborer	13Ju02Uq
MANGINSON, Marth.		30	F	Laborer	13Ju02Uq
Helen	(D)	03	F	Child	13Ju02Uq
John-Henry	(S)	.00	M	Infant	13Ju02Uq
CULNTON, Nichols		28	M	Laborer	13Ju02Uq
DOYLE, Phil		27	M	Laborer	13Ju02Uq
Elizabeth		23	F	Laborer	13Ju02Uq
DEVANY, Pat.		18	M	Laborer	13Ju02Uq
CASSADY, Hugh		44	M	Laborer	13Ju02Uq
Catherine	(D)	16	F	Laborer	13Ju02Uq
Julia	(D)	14	F	Laborer	13Ju02Uq
MASINTY, Mary		20	F	Laborer	13Ju02Uq
MCDERMODY, Mary		20	F	Laborer	13Ju02Uq
OBAY, Pat.		19	M	Laborer	13Ju02Uq
MCKIRMAN, Thomas		18	M	Laborer	13Ju02Uq
MURPHY, Elizabeth		18	F	Laborer	13Ju02Uq
LYNCH, Daniel		24	M	Laborer	13Ju02Uq
CLOSE, Samuel		25	M	Laborer	13Ju02Uq
BOOTHE, James		25	M	Laborer	13Ju02Uq
CARNRY, Mary		22	F	Laborer	13Ju02Uq
DOLAN, Mary		48	F	Laborer	13Ju02Uq
Lawrence	(S)	18	M	Laborer	13Ju02Uq
Andrew	(S)	17	M	Laborer	13Ju02Uq
Bridget	(D)	13	F	Laborer	13Ju02Uq
FORRELL, Michael		15	M	Laborer	13Ju02Uq
Peter		14	M	Laborer	13Ju02Uq
CORSLEY, Thomas		18	M	Laborer	13Ju02Uq
ROURHE, Mary		22	F	Laborer	13Ju02Uq
Laehny		51	M	Laborer	13Ju02Uq
MORRIN, Bridget		36	F	Laborer	13Ju02Uq
MILLS, George		25	M	Laborer	13Ju02Uq
Ann	(W)	25	F	Wife	13Ju02Uq
Ann	(D)	.00	F	Infant	13Ju02Uq
MORRIN, Daniel		36	M	Laborer	13Ju02Uq
MCINTYRE, Rose		35	F	Laborer	13Ju02Uq
COUSINS, John		30	M	Laborer	13Ju02Uq
Ann	(W)	25	F	Wife	13Ju02Uq
Elizabeth	(D)	.00	F	Infant	13Ju02Uq
WALKER, Robert		40	M	Laborer	13Ju02Uq
Mary	(W)	40	F	Wife	13Ju02Uq
Mary-Jane	(D)	02	F	Child	13Ju02Uq
Lewis	(S)	03	M	Child	13Ju02Uq
Elizabeth	(D)	07	F	Child	13Ju02Uq
Benjamin		30	M	Laborer	13Ju02Uq
DIXON, Mary-Ann		11	F	None	13Ju02Uq
DENNY, Pat.		28	M	Laborer	13Ju02Uq
LYNCH, John		08	M	Child	13Ju02Uq
Mathew		07	M	Child	13Ju02Uq
BAYLAN, Pat.		19	M	Laborer	13Ju02Uq
SMITH, Pat.		22	M	Laborer	13Ju02Uq

NAMES OF PASSENGERS		AGE	SEX	OCCUPATIONS	DATE PORT SHIP
HODSON, Mary-Ann		44	F	Laborer	13Ju02Uq
Ann	(D)	20	F	Laborer	13Ju02Uq
Lustim	(D)	13	F	Child	13Ju02Uq
Mary	(D)	14	F	Child	13Ju02Uq
Kenedy	(S)	08	M	Child	13Ju02Uq
John	(S)	06	M	Child	13Ju02Uq
Thomas	(S)	03	M	Child	13Ju02Uq
William	(S)	.00	M	Infant	13Ju02Uq
GRUNNETH, George		60	M	Laborer	13Ju02Uq
William		40	M	Laborer	13Ju02Uq
PLATT, Robert		28	M	Laborer	13Ju02Uq
WHITMIN, John		26	M	Laborer	13Ju02Uq
GRAY, John		27	M	Laborer	13Ju02Uq
LEMESTN, William		27	M	Laborer	13Ju02Uq
SHARPE, Thomas		22	M	Laborer	13Ju02Uq
Mary	(W)	24	F	Laborer	13Ju02Uq
Mary-Ester	(D)	.00	F	Infant	13Ju02Uq
MCGOVERN, Cath.		17	F	Laborer	13Ju02Uq
SMITH, Ellen		20	F	Laborer	13Ju02Uq
BYRNE, Mary		18	F	Laborer	13Ju02Uq
DOOLY, Anastatia		21	F	Laborer	13Ju02Uq
LANLIN, Margaret		08	F	Child	13Ju02Uq
Julia		06	F	Child	13Ju02Uq
BRADLEY, Nancy		24	F	Laborer	13Ju02Uq
MILLS, James		24	M	Laborer	13Ju02Uq
Jane		22	F	Laborer	13Ju02Uq
REYNOLDS, Cath.		25	F	Laborer	13Ju02Uq
FLANAGEN, Mary		34	F	Laborer	13Ju02Uq
William	(S)	12	M	Child	13Ju02Uq
Betty	(D)	10	F	Child	13Ju02Uq
GIBLIN, Betty		40	F	Laborer	13Ju02Uq
William	(S)	20	M	Laborer	13Ju02Uq
Pat.	(S)	05	M	Child	13Ju02Uq
Ellen	(D)	.00	F	Infant	13Ju02Uq
COYLE, Mary		40	F	Laborer	13Ju02Uq
Cath.	(D)	19	F	Laborer	13Ju02Uq
Edward	(S)	17	M	Laborer	13Ju02Uq
Eleanor	(D)	14	F	Laborer	13Ju02Uq
Rose	(D)	11	F	None	13Ju02Uq
Ann	(D)	.00	F	Infant	13Ju02Uq
Mary	(D)	05	F	Child	13Ju02Uq
MCKINNY, Mary-Ann		40	F	Laborer	13Ju02Uq
Robert	(S)	20	M	Laborer	13Ju02Uq
Nancy	(D)	18	F	Laborer	13Ju02Uq
Alex	(S)	15	M	Laborer	13Ju02Uq
Margaret	(D)	14	F	Laborer	13Ju02Uq
Mary-Ann	(D)	09	F	Child	13Ju02Uq
Jane	(D)	07	F	Child	13Ju02Uq
William	(S)	.00	M	Infant	13Ju02Uq
HALPIN, Mary		27	F	Laborer	13Ju02Uq
KILLAGHIN, Ellen		08	F	Child	13Ju02Uq
MCGRATH, Edward		24	M	Laborer	13Ju02Uq
DUNN, John		24	M	Laborer	13Ju02Uq
KELLY, Cath.		21	F	Laborer	13Ju02Uq
MARSH, John		37	M	Laborer	13Ju02Uq
Francis		35	M	Laborer	13Ju02Uq
Francis	(S)	.00	M	Infant	13Ju02Uq
SMITH, William		40	M	Laborer	13Ju02Uq
CLARK, John		17	M	Laborer	13Ju02Uq
SMITH, Alen		30	U	Laborer	13Ju02Uq
JONES, Evan		34	M	Laborer	13Ju02Uq
Elizabeth		38	F	Laborer	13Ju02Uq
DAVIS, Elizabeth		25	F	Laborer	13Ju02Uq
EDWARDS, Margaret		20	F	Laborer	13Ju02Uq
GRIFFITH, Edward		39	M	Laborer	13Ju02Uq
Benjamin	(S)	18	M	Laborer	13Ju02Uq
Jonathan	(S)	11	M	Laborer	13Ju02Uq
ROBERTS, John		30	M	Laborer	13Ju02Uq
MASON, Enoch		23	M	Laborer	13Ju02Uq
CNID, Charles		20	M	Laborer	13Ju02Uq
HAYES, George		19	M	Laborer	13Ju02Uq
MIZIN, James		23	M	Laborer	13Ju02Uq
Mary-Ann		23	F	Laborer	13Ju02Uq
Samuel		22	M	Laborer	13Ju02Uq
WAGGITT, William		26	M	Laborer	13Ju02Uq
KUMAN, Edward		30	M	Laborer	13Ju02Uq
MCGUIRE, Mary		15	F	Laborer	13Ju02Uq
Ann		14	F	Laborer	13Ju02Uq
Margaret		11	F	Laborer	13Ju02Uq
Pat.		09	M	Laborer	13Ju02Uq
Bridget		06	F	Laborer	13Ju02Uq
DAVEY, Lawrence		28	M	Laborer	13Ju02Uq
MCCABE, Mary		13	F	Laborer	13Ju02Uq
GOOLIN, Martha		35	F	Laborer	13Ju02Uq
STANLEY, Pat.		12	M	Laborer	13Ju02Uq
John		09	M	Laborer	13Ju02Uq
James		08	M	Laborer	13Ju02Uq
William-L.		.00	M	Infant	13Ju02Uq
JOHNS, George		28	M	Laborer	13Ju02Uq
STEWART, Mary		25	F	Laborer	13Ju02Uq
Isabella	(D)	.00	F	Infant	13Ju02Uq
HINES, Pat.		22	M	Laborer	13Ju02Uq
Margaret		55	F	Laborer	13Ju02Uq
KELLY, Michael		18	M	Laborer	13Ju02Uq
MOLLOY, Mary		16	F	Laborer	13Ju02Uq
WOODHAN, Sam		30	M	Laborer	13Ju02Uq
BAKER, Isaiah		35	M	Laborer	13Ju02Uq
GRIMSHAW, Bing		45	M	Laborer	13Ju02Uq
William		45	M	Laborer	13Ju02Uq
BRISLOE, Henry		20	M	Laborer	13Ju02Uq
JONES, John		25	M	Laborer	13Ju02Uq
Joshua		28	M	Laborer	13Ju02Uq
Edward		11	M	Laborer	13Ju02Uq
DAVIS, James		48	M	Laborer	13Ju02Uq
RICHARDS, John		55	M	Laborer	13Ju02Uq
DAVIS, Evan		27	M	Laborer	13Ju02Uq
SMITH, Pat.		24	M	Laborer	13Ju02Uq
Larry		18	M	Laborer	13Ju02Uq
CHAPMAN, Thomas		26	M	Laborer	13Ju02Uq
Elizabeth		20	F	Laborer	13Ju02Uq
MULLINGTON, Margaret		22	F	Laborer	13Ju02Uq
Ann		19	F	Laborer	13Ju02Uq
APPLEBY, Alfred		04	M	Child	13Ju02Uq
Betsey		02	F	Child	13Ju02Uq
John		.00	M	Infant	13Ju02Uq
FARRELL, James		31	M	Laborer	13Ju02Uq
GLENNERITE, Thomas		30	M	Laborer	13Ju02Uq
Hannah	(W)	25	F	Laborer	13Ju02Uq
Sarah-Ann	(D)	.00	F	Infant	13Ju02Uq
DONOGHUE, Michael		24	M	Laborer	13Ju02Uq
Bernard		36	M	Laborer	13Ju02Uq
SMITH, Pat.		25	M	Laborer	13Ju02Uq
IBBOTSON, Edward		23	M	Laborer	13Ju02Uq
HENDERSON, Alex		36	M	Laborer	13Ju02Uq
PALEME, Sarah-Jane		20	F	Laborer	13Ju02Uq
DONNELLY, James		23	M	Laborer	13Ju02Uq
Sarah		22	F	Laborer	13Ju02Uq
MCAULY, Henry		50	M	Laborer	13Ju02Uq
Ann	(W)	50	F	Laborer	13Ju02Uq
Ann-Maria		06	F	Laborer	13Ju02Uq
HULL, Richard		25	M	Laborer	13Ju02Uq
Cath.	(W)	25	F	Laborer	13Ju02Uq
DENGEN, Ann		20	F	Laborer	13Ju02Uq
HALL, Dobbin		18	M	Laborer	13Ju02Uq
Leurnda		21	M	Laborer	13Ju02Uq
MOIN, Terance		34	M	Laborer	13Ju02Uq
Mary	(W)	28	F	Laborer	13Ju02Uq
Cath.	(D)	.00	F	Infant	13Ju02Uq
OCONNIN, James		30	M	Laborer	13Ju02Uq
DORYLAND, James		30	M	Laborer	13Ju02Uq
Thos.	(S)	08	M	Laborer	13Ju02Uq
WHALIN, Pat.		30	M	Laborer	13Ju02Uq
Mary	(W)	30	F	Laborer	13Ju02Uq
FARRELL, Margaret		18	F	Laborer	13Ju02Uq
HAGAN, Ally		30	F	Laborer	13Ju02Uq
SPALIN, Mary		30	F	Laborer	13Ju02Uq
KARNEY, Bridget		19	F	Laborer	13Ju02Uq
MURPHY, Mary		21	F	Laborer	13Ju02Uq
WHITEHEAD, Henry-A.		25	M	Laborer	13Ju02Uq
NAYLOR, John		24	M	Laborer	13Ju02Uq

NAMES OF PASSENGERS		AGE	SEX	OCCUPATIONS	DATE PORT SHIP
HANOP, John		23	M	Laborer	13Ju02Uq
CRADICK, Ann		27	F	Laborer	13Ju02Uq
Thos.	(S)	.00	M	Infant	13Ju02Uq
WALL, Thos.		26	M	Laborer	13Ju02Uq
LEONARD, Ann		35	F	Laborer	13Ju02Uq
John	(S)	15	M	Laborer	13Ju02Uq
Thos.	(S)	13	M	Laborer	13Ju02Uq
Richard	(S)	10	M	Laborer	13Ju02Uq
Ann	(D)	07	F	Child	13Ju02Uq
Cath.	(D)	05	F	Child	13Ju02Uq
Andrew	(S)	02	M	Child	13Ju02Uq
MADDIN, Isabella		24	F	Laborer	13Ju02Uq
MCSHEA, Cath.		20	F	Laborer	13Ju02Uq
MANSON, Joseph		38	M	Laborer	13Ju02Uq
BATES, George		30	M	Laborer	13Ju02Uq
SMITH, John		95	M	Laborer	13Ju02Uq
JONES, John		03	M	Child	13Ju02Uq

COURIER 14 JUNE 1848

From Liverpool

NAMES OF PASSENGERS	AGE	SEX	OCCUPATIONS	DATE PORT SHIP
SMITH, Matthew	25	M	Laborer	14Ju02Qd
Susan	25	F	Spinster	14Ju02Qd
John	03	M	Child	14Ju02Qd
Anne	.00	F	Infant	14Ju02Qd
GAFFNEY, Cath.	40	F	Spinster	14Ju02Qd
MCCABE, Ann	26	F	Spinster	14Ju02Qd
Mary	.00	F	Infant	14Ju02Qd
KELLY, John	26	M	Laborer	14Ju02Qd
Margaret	24	F	Spinster	14Ju02Qd
Mary-Anne	21	F	Spinster	14Ju02Qd
Maria	10	F	Child	14Ju02Qd
Margaret	09	F	Child	14Ju02Qd
Peter	07	M	Child	14Ju02Qd
Wm.	.00	M	Infant	14Ju02Qd
BRENNAN, Michael	25	M	Laborer	14Ju02Qd
James	17	M	Laborer	14Ju02Qd
Mary	21	F	Spinster	14Ju02Qd
Anne	15	F	Spinster	14Ju02Qd
Magy	10	M	Child	14Ju02Qd
FOLEY, James	18	M	Laborer	14Ju02Qd
Edward	20	M	Laborer	14Ju02Qd
KELLY, Michael	21	M	Laborer	14Ju02Qd
STEWART, Ellen	16	F	Spinster	14Ju02Qd
CREANEY, Isabella	52	F	Spinster	14Ju02Qd
Bernard	23	M	Laborer	14Ju02Qd
Bessy	19	F	Spinster	14Ju02Qd
Ellen	17	F	Spinster	14Ju02Qd
Isabella	13	F	Spinster	14Ju02Qd
John	10	M	Child	14Ju02Qd
Teresa	07	F	Child	14Ju02Qd
STAPLETON, Thomas	45	M	Laborer	14Ju02Qd
Peter	17	M	Laborer	14Ju02Qd
TURNEY, Michael	30	M	Laborer	14Ju02Qd
GORMAN, William	24	M	Laborer	14Ju02Qd
Mary	17	F	Spinster	14Ju02Qd
RYAN, Pat	25	M	Laborer	14Ju02Qd
LITTLE, Joseph	40	M	Laborer	14Ju02Qd
Esther	40	F	Spinster	14Ju02Qd
Margaret	20	F	Spinster	14Ju02Qd
Betty	19	F	Spinster	14Ju02Qd
John	13	M	Child	14Ju02Qd
Joseph	12	M	Child	14Ju02Qd
Esther	10	F	Child	14Ju02Qd
Matilda	06	F	Child	14Ju02Qd
HARRIS, John	24	M	Laborer	14Ju02Qd
MCGANNEY, Dom.	28	M	Laborer	14Ju02Qd
PENTROY, Edward	30	M	Laborer	14Ju02Qd
PENTROY, Margaret	30	F	Spinster	14Ju02Qd
Martha	13	F	Child	14Ju02Qd
KELLY, Margaret	20	F	Spinster	14Ju02Qd
ARTHURS, Dolly	40	F	Spinster	14Ju02Qd
Elizabeth	20	F	Spinster	14Ju02Qd
Thomas	17	M	Laborer	14Ju02Qd
John	11	M	Child	14Ju02Qd
FITZGERALD, Jim	30	M	Laborer	14Ju02Qd
CLOAKY, Michael	30	M	Laborer	14Ju02Qd
CORRIGAN, Pat.	22	M	Laborer	14Ju02Qd
Mary	25	F	Spinster	14Ju02Qd
William	.00	M	Infant	14Ju02Qd
CLONES, John	35	M	Laborer	14Ju02Qd
Betty	30	F	Spinster	14Ju02Qd
Thomas	03	M	Child	14Ju02Qd
James	.00	M	Infant	14Ju02Qd
KENNY, Pat.	20	M	Laborer	14Ju02Qd
BELL, John	40	M	Laborer	14Ju02Qd
ORR, James	20	M	Laborer	14Ju02Qd
HARRISON, William	30	M	Laborer	14Ju02Qd
ORR, Alex	40	M	Laborer	14Ju02Qd
Sarah	14	F	Spinster	14Ju02Qd
KEEMAN, Margaret	30	F	Spinster	14Ju02Qd
REILY, Mary	20	F	Spinster	14Ju02Qd
WILLIAMS, Anne	20	F	Spinster	14Ju02Qd
BUCKLY, William	30	M	Laborer	14Ju02Qd
MCKEOWN, Pat.	20	M	Laborer	14Ju02Qd
DOBBIN, Sarah	19	F	Spinster	14Ju02Qd
KENNEDY, Thomas	30	M	Laborer	14Ju02Qd
John	28	M	Laborer	14Ju02Qd
Jane	20	F	Spinster	14Ju02Qd
KEENAN, Bridget	35	F	Spinster	14Ju02Qd
KANE, John	45	M	Laborer	14Ju02Qd
Peter	22	M	Laborer	14Ju02Qd
James	09	M	Child	14Ju02Qd
John	07	M	Child	14Ju02Qd
Mary	10	F	Child	14Ju02Qd
MCKEENAN, Mary	20	F	Spinster	14Ju02Qd
Lucy	17	F	Spinster	14Ju02Qd
LINN, James	18	M	Laborer	14Ju02Qd
SCULLEN, Rose	20	F	Spinster	14Ju02Qd
BRENNAN, Peter	22	M	Laborer	14Ju02Qd
CROSBY, James	24	M	Laborer	14Ju02Qd
MURRAY, Peter	23	M	Laborer	14Ju02Qd
Michael	30	M	Laborer	14Ju02Qd
BARRY, Thomas	23	M	Laborer	14Ju02Qd
KENNY, Peter	26	M	Laborer	14Ju02Qd
CONNOLLY, Owen	24	M	Laborer	14Ju02Qd
SCOTT, John	25	M	Laborer	14Ju02Qd
CONWAY, Mary	18	F	Spinster	14Ju02Qd
GOLDEN, Ellen	18	F	Spinster	14Ju02Qd
MAHON, Andrew	28	M	Laborer	14Ju02Qd
MACNAMARA, Pat.	25	M	Laborer	14Ju02Qd
Judy	20	F	Spinster	14Ju02Qd
MONAHAN, Martin	26	M	Laborer	14Ju02Qd
Honora	20	F	Spinster	14Ju02Qd
Pat.	06	M	Laborer	14Ju02Qd
Bridget	06	F	Spinster	14Ju02Qd
James	.00	M	Infant	14Ju02Qd
MCGINTY, Martin	18	M	Laborer	14Ju02Qd
MONAHAN, Bryan	24	M	Laborer	14Ju02Qd
MORRAN, Thomas	28	M	Laborer	14Ju02Qd
SWEENY, F.	20	M	Laborer	14Ju02Qd
DONOHUE, Martin	27	M	Laborer	14Ju02Qd
COYLE, Michael	27	M	Laborer	14Ju02Qd
REDMOND, Ellen	20	F	Spinster	14Ju02Qd
MITTON, John	40	M	Laborer	14Ju02Qd
Philip	13	M	Child	14Ju02Qd
Mary	35	F	Spinster	14Ju02Qd
Michael	04	M	Child	14Ju02Qd
Mary	07	F	Child	14Ju02Qd
George	04	M	Child	14Ju02Qd
Honora	02	F	Child	14Ju02Qd
WELSH, William	34	M	Laborer	14Ju02Qd
WYNN, Thomas	22	M	Laborer	14Ju02Qd

NAMES OF PASSENGERS	AGE	SEX	OCCUPATIONS	DATE PORT SHIP
KENNEDY, Sally	16	F	Spinster	14Ju02Qd
ANNDLEY, Ellen	20	F	Spinster	14Ju02Qd
KILROY, Mary	20	F	Spinster	14Ju02Qd
Ned	30	M	Laborer	14Ju02Qd
MOFFAT, Richard	20	M	Laborer	14Ju02Qd
Pat.	20	M	Laborer	14Ju02Qd
BURKE, Edward	20	M	Laborer	14Ju02Qd
TUNNEN, George	24	M	Laborer	14Ju02Qd
LARKEN, Margaret	21	F	Spinster	14Ju02Qd
CONNOR, Catherine	29	F	Spinster	14Ju02Qd
Margaret	07	F	Child	14Ju02Qd
FINLAY, Joseph	02	M	Child	14Ju02Qd
DILLON, Mary	40	F	Spinster	14Ju02Qd
Biddy	10	F	Child	14Ju02Qd
Anne	09	F	Child	14Ju02Qd
Thomas	07	M	Child	14Ju02Qd
Jane	04	F	Child	14Ju02Qd
MORAN, Catherine	20	F	Spinster	14Ju02Qd
Isaac	13	M	Child	14Ju02Qd
Mary	10	F	Child	14Ju02Qd
Henry	04	M	Child	14Ju02Qd
Dinah	05	F	Child	14Ju02Qd
Alice	07	F	Child	14Ju02Qd
James	.00	M	Infant	14Ju02Qd
Hy.	35	M	Laborer	14Ju02Qd
HANIGAN, Owen	30	M	Laborer	14Ju02Qd
COGANS, M.	18	M	Laborer	14Ju02Qd
DOWN, Michael	25	M	Laborer	14Ju02Qd
LARKIN, Michael	30	M	Laborer	14Ju02Qd
CONLIN, Martin	30	M	Laborer	14Ju02Qd
BOLAND, Michael	21	M	Laborer	14Ju02Qd
WALSH, U	22	F	Spinster	14Ju02Qd
DUTTON, James	23	M	Laborer	14Ju02Qd
WELSH, Joseph	26	M	Laborer	14Ju02Qd
Julia	26	F	Spinster	14Ju02Qd
WILLIAMS, Samuel	34	M	Laborer	14Ju02Qd
Anne	34	F	Spinster	14Ju02Qd
Mary	12	F	Child	14Ju02Qd
Samuel	10	M	Child	14Ju02Qd
Sarah-Anne	08	F	Child	14Ju02Qd
Lucia	04	F	Child	14Ju02Qd
Grace	04	F	Child	14Ju02Qd
James	.00	M	Infant	14Ju02Qd
MIDDELTON, Maria	26	F	Spinster	14Ju02Qd
John	09	M	Child	14Ju02Qd
BRENNAN, Chr.	28	M	Laborer	14Ju02Qd
MURRAY, John	30	M	Laborer	14Ju02Qd
GARRY, William	28	M	Laborer	14Ju02Qd
MITCHELL, William	24	M	Laborer	14Ju02Qd
HOYLE, Pat.	20	M	Laborer	14Ju02Qd
CANNING, William	21	M	Laborer	14Ju02Qd
Owen	18	M	Laborer	14Ju02Qd
COYLE, Rose	16	F	Spinster	14Ju02Qd
MAGEE, Honor	16	F	Spinster	14Ju02Qd
DIFFEN, Mary	16	F	Spinster	14Ju02Qd
CANNING, Joseph	10	M	Child	14Ju02Qd
MAGEE, Michael	10	M	Child	14Ju02Qd
MCFINLAY, Grace	10	F	Child	14Ju02Qd
LOWDEN, Andrew	22	M	Laborer	14Ju02Qd
BURNS, Mary-Anne	16	F	Spinster	14Ju02Qd
FOLY, William	20	M	Laborer	14Ju02Qd
MULEEY, Thomas	22	M	Laborer	14Ju02Qd
SEALEY, John	20	M	Laborer	14Ju02Qd
DOWSIE, Biddy	20	F	Spinster	14Ju02Qd
SCULLION, Jane	30	F	Spinster	14Ju02Qd
Hanna	30	F	Spinster	14Ju02Qd
Anne	.00	F	Infant	14Ju02Qd
DUGAN, Sally	40	F	Spinster	14Ju02Qd
Michael	24	M	Laborer	14Ju02Qd
James	20	M	Laborer	14Ju02Qd
Biddy	14	F	Spinster	14Ju02Qd
Mary	20	F	Spinster	14Ju02Qd
Mary	09	F	Spinster	14Ju02Qd
MCCLONE, Mary	25	F	Spinster	14Ju02Qd
DOHERTY, Mary-Ann	25	F	Spinster	14Ju02Qd
LOGAN, James	49	M	Laborer	14Ju02Qd
RYAN, Jno.	27	M	Laborer	14Ju02Qd
Edward	23	M	Laborer	14Ju02Qd
SOUTHEY, Richard	21	M	Laborer	14Ju02Qd
KELLY, Pat.	25	M	Laborer	14Ju02Qd
FOLEY, Pat.	30	M	Laborer	14Ju02Qd
PICKETT, John	25	M	Laborer	14Ju02Qd
Garratt	13	M	Laborer	14Ju02Qd
PARKER, Margaret	13	F	Child	14Ju02Qd
DOLTER, John	25	M	Laborer	14Ju02Qd
HUNTER, Jno.	25	M	Laborer	14Ju02Qd
CRILLY, Pat.	22	M	Laborer	14Ju02Qd
NEILY, Joseph	21	M	Laborer	14Ju02Qd
CRILLY, Eliza	18	F	Spinster	14Ju02Qd
Peggy	17	F	Spinster	14Ju02Qd
Betsy	19	F	Spinster	14Ju02Qd
NEILLY, Ellen	27	F	Spinster	14Ju02Qd
MORAN, Allen	36	M	Laborer	14Ju02Qd
BROWN, Joseph	50	M	Laborer	14Ju02Qd
Catherine	17	F	Spinster	14Ju02Qd
WALLS, Henry	23	M	Laborer	14Ju02Qd
William	25	M	Laborer	14Ju02Qd
NEIL, John	50	M	Laborer	14Ju02Qd
Owen	18	M	Laborer	14Ju02Qd
Bryan	14	M	Laborer	14Ju02Qd
HENRY, James	24	M	Laborer	14Ju02Qd
MCCLEARY, M.	21	F	Spinster	14Ju02Qd
Eliza	17	F	Spinster	14Ju02Qd
PATERSON, James	22	M	Laborer	14Ju02Qd
Owen	19	M	Laborer	14Ju02Qd
RILY, Biddy	19	F	Spinster	14Ju02Qd
KANE, Julia	22	F	Spinster	14Ju02Qd
MUSSO, Bridget	23	F	Spinster	14Ju02Qd
CUNNINGHAM, Rose	20	F	Spinster	14Ju02Qd
CULLEN, James	34	M	Laborer	14Ju02Qd
OWENS, Owen	30	M	Laborer	14Ju02Qd
Anne	30	M	Spinster	14Ju02Qd
Mary-Ann (M)	55	M	Spinster	14Ju02Qd
Mary	03	M	Child	14Ju02Qd
Robert	.00	M	Infant	14Ju02Qd
NUGENT, Alice	30	F	Spinster	14Ju02Qd
Mary-A.	07	F	Child	14Ju02Qd
Allen	05	M	Child	14Ju02Qd
James	03	M	Child	14Ju02Qd
Charles	.00	M	Infant	14Ju02Qd
GRANT, Michael	26	M	Laborer	14Ju02Qd
HUGHES, Richard	24	M	Laborer	14Ju02Qd
LARKIN, Eliza	24	F	Spinster	14Ju02Qd
Richard	26	M	Laborer	14Ju02Qd
Charles	19	M	Laborer	14Ju02Qd
Rose-Ann	02	F	Child	14Ju02Qd
Mary	.00	F	Infant	14Ju02Qd
Died-At-Sea				
HIGGINSON, Mary	30	F	Spinster	14Ju02Qd
James	03	M	Child	14Ju02Qd
Laura	17	F	Spinster	14Ju02Qd
NOLAN, Ellen	26	F	Spinster	14Ju02Qd
BOW, Pat.	25	M	Laborer	14Ju02Qd
Died-At-Sea				
DOWEY, Ned.	24	M	Laborer	14Ju02Qd
BRENNAN, Nancy	20	F	Spinster	14Ju02Qd
HAND, Jane	26	F	Spinster	14Ju02Qd
Catherine	24	F	Spinster	14Ju02Qd
TIERNAN, Pat.	26	M	Laborer	14Ju02Qd
BRENNAN, M.	17	M	Laborer	14Ju02Qd
CASSIDY, Thomas	35	M	Laborer	14Ju02Qd
REGAN, Pat.	35	M	Laborer	14Ju02Qd
Mary	30	F	Spinster	14Ju02Qd
CONWAY, Hy	30	M	Laborer	14Ju02Qd
FEENEY, My.A.	25	F	Spinster	14Ju02Qd
SHANNON, Bessy	25	F	Spinster	14Ju02Qd
COWREY, Margaret	06	F	Child	14Ju02Qd
FEELY, Anne	20	F	Spinster	14Ju02Qd
KELLY, John	30	M	Laborer	14Ju02Qd
LOUGHRAN, M.	35	M	Laborer	14Ju02Qd

NAMES OF PASSENGERS		AGE	SEX	OCCUPATIONS	DATE PORT SHIP
ROURK, Pat.		25	M	Laborer	14Ju02Qd
KELLY, Hugh		22	M	Laborer	14Ju02Qd
NOLAN, Mary		23	F	Spinster	14Ju02Qd
DOGHERTY, Michael		25	M	Laborer	14Ju02Qd
MCBRIDE, Charles		24	M	Laborer	14Ju02Qd
JORDAN, Joseph		21	M	Laborer	14Ju02Qd
Chr.		20	M	Laborer	14Ju02Qd
KELLY, Sally		30	F	Spinster	14Ju02Qd
GREENAN, Richard		20	M	Laborer	14Ju02Qd
Eliza		20	F	Spinster	14Ju02Qd
Thomas		20	M	Laborer	14Ju02Qd
Elias		20	M	Laborer	14Ju02Qd
WARDEN, George		20	M	Laborer	14Ju02Qd
Sarah		20	F	Spinster	14Ju02Qd
HARRISON, David		20	M	Laborer	14Ju02Qd
WARDEN, William		09	M	Child	14Ju02Qd
FRANCIS, James		25	M	Laborer	14Ju02Qd
Joseph		22	M	Laborer	14Ju02Qd
DEVANY, Catherine		20	F	Spinster	14Ju02Qd
THORPE, John		25	M	Laborer	14Ju02Qd
INGHAM, William		33	M	Laborer	14Ju02Qd
Mary		32	F	Spinster	14Ju02Qd
BROWN, Ed.		20	M	Laborer	14Ju02Qd
Thomas		21	M	Laborer	14Ju02Qd
POWER, William		50	M	Laborer	14Ju02Qd
Margaret	(W)	50	F	Spinster	14Ju02Qd
William	(S)	21	M	Laborer	14Ju02Qd
Michael	(S)	19	M	Laborer	14Ju02Qd
Onasten	(S)	19	M	Laborer	14Ju02Qd
John	(S)	13	M	Child	14Ju02Qd
Mary	(D)	11	F	Child	14Ju02Qd
Pat.	(S)	08	M	Child	14Ju02Qd
Tom	(S)	06	M	Child	14Ju02Qd
James	(S)	04	M	Child	14Ju02Qd
Michael	(S)	02	M	Child	14Ju02Qd
BOYLE, Mick		50	M	Laborer	14Ju02Qd
POWER, Thomas		28	M	Laborer	14Ju02Qd
Biddy		28	F	Spinster	14Ju02Qd
PACKWOOD, William		48	M	Laborer	14Ju02Qd
Mary	(W)	47	F	Spinster	14Ju02Qd
Ebenezer	(S)	15	M	Laborer	14Ju02Qd
PRATT, Joseph		36	M	Laborer	14Ju02Qd
Bethra		22	F	Spinster	14Ju02Qd
LEMON, Mike		24	M	Laborer	14Ju02Qd
Eliza	(W)	20	F	Spinster	14Ju02Qd
James	(S)	03	M	Child	14Ju02Qd
Catherine	(D)	.00	F	Infant	14Ju02Qd
HORNER, William		30	M	Laborer	14Ju02Qd
U	(W)	29	F	Spinster	14Ju02Qd
Mary		19	F	Spinster	14Ju02Qd
Susan		05	F	Child	14Ju02Qd
Kidman		03	M	Child	14Ju02Qd
James		.00	M	Infant	14Ju02Qd
SKULE, John		43	M	Laborer	14Ju02Qd
STAFFORD, Joseph		25	M	Laborer	14Ju02Qd
Jesse		19	F	Spinster	14Ju02Qd
BOSS, William		21	M	Laborer	14Ju02Qd
UFFINDALE, John		50	M	Laborer	14Ju02Qd
Sarah	(D)	12	F	Child	14Ju02Qd
CONNOLLY, Pat.		19	M	Laborer	14Ju02Qd
Mary		19	F	Spinster	14Ju02Qd
CLARK, James		35	M	Laborer	14Ju02Qd
Rosy		18	F	Spinster	14Ju02Qd
KELLY, Anne		20	F	Spinster	14Ju02Qd
MADDEN, James		35	M	Laborer	14Ju02Qd
HYLAND, Mary		30	F	Spinster	14Ju02Qd
ROCHFORD, Mary		25	F	Spinster	14Ju02Qd
DEE, Timothy		25	M	Laborer	14Ju02Qd
Jeremiah		23	M	Laborer	14Ju02Qd
Richard		12	M	Child	14Ju02Qd
GORMAN, U-Mrs.		32	F	Spinster	14Ju02Qd
CARTER, Thomas		40	M	Laborer	14Ju02Qd
COLLINS, Stephen		21	M	Laborer	14Ju02Qd
FARRELL, Michael		25	M	Laborer	14Ju02Qd
MILLOTT, Thomas		23	M	Laborer	14Ju02Qd
PEASLAND, William		27	M	Laborer	14Ju02Qd
Elijah		20	M	Laborer	14Ju02Qd
Job		09	M	Child	14Ju02Qd
KEENAN, Catherine		22	F	Spinster	14Ju02Qd
LOOBY, John		25	M	Laborer	14Ju02Qd
MCAFEE, Samuel		39	M	Unknown	14Ju02Qd
Rose		30	F	Unknown	14Ju02Qd
Margaret-Jane		17	F	Unknown	14Ju02Qd
Ann		12	F	Unknown	14Ju02Qd
John		07	M	Unknown	14Ju02Qd
Julia		06	F	Unknown	14Ju02Qd
Charles		03	M	Unknown	14Ju02Qd
Ann		02	F	Unknown	14Ju02Qd
William		37	M	Unknown	14Ju02Qd
Rachael		37	F	Unknown	14Ju02Qd
Margaret-Jane		07	F	Unknown	14Ju02Qd
Cathn.		06	F	Unknown	14Ju02Qd
Mary-Ann		04	F	Unknown	14Ju02Qd
William		.00	M	Infant	14Ju02Qd

CALIFORNIA 14 JUNE 1848

From Liverpool

NAMES OF PASSENGERS		AGE	SEX	OCCUPATIONS	DATE PORT SHIP
HEELAN, Daniel		23	M	Laborer	14Ju02Qh
MUSGRAVE, Bell		20	F	Servant	14Ju02Qh
FULVA, Julia		20	F	Servant	14Ju02Qh
MULDOON, Mary		20	F	Spinster	14Ju02Qh
BAXTER, Charles		16	M	Laborer	14Ju02Qh
HUGHES, Robert		61	M	Laborer	14Ju02Qh
Margaret	(W)	59	F	Wife	14Ju02Qh
Hannah	(D)	14	F	Servant	14Ju02Qh
FLYNN, Michael		24	M	Laborer	14Ju02Qh
KELLY, Bridget		40	F	Servant	14Ju02Qh
Jane	(D)	04	F	Child	14Ju02Qh
William	(S)	03	M	Child	14Ju02Qh
MUHAN, Charles		08	M	Child	14Ju02Qh
ONEILL, U		48	F	Servant	14Ju02Qh
Michael	(S)	20	M	Laborer	14Ju02Qh
GANNON, Ann		20	F	Spinster	14Ju02Qh
OBRYAN, Patt		16	M	Laborer	14Ju02Qh
KIRWIN, William		12	M	Child	14Ju02Qh
Patt		12	M	Child	14Ju02Qh
BRYAN, Mary		16	F	Spinster	14Ju02Qh
SHANGHNESSY, Catherine		20	F	Servant	14Ju02Qh
HIGGINS, Bridget		40	F	Mother	14Ju02Qh
James	(S)	16	M	Laborer	14Ju02Qh
Sarah	(D)	14	F	Servant	14Ju02Qh
Bridget	(D)	13	F	Child	14Ju02Qh
MURRAY, Catherine		50	F	Mother	14Ju02Qh
Edward	(S)	14	M	Laborer	14Ju02Qh
Edward	(S)	05	M	Child	14Ju02Qh
MORRISON, Bridget		16	F	Spinster	14Ju02Qh
KELLY, James		25	M	Laborer	14Ju02Qh
MURPHY, Simeon		26	M	Laborer	14Ju02Qh
Mary	(W)	20	F	Wife	14Ju02Qh
SMITH, Agnes		16	F	Servant	14Ju02Qh
Thomas	(B)	11	M	Child	14Ju02Qh
MCGEE, Isabella		26	F	Servant	14Ju02Qh
Margaret	(D)	11	F	Child	14Ju02Qh
Patt	(S)	09	M	Child	14Ju02Qh
HOGAN, Michael		16	M	Laborer	14Ju02Qh
Ann	(T)	09	F	Child	14Ju02Qh
RUSH, Patt		26	M	Laborer	14Ju02Qh
GAFFNEY, Catherine		22	F	Spinster	14Ju02Qh
FAGAN, Bessy		20	F	Spinster	14Ju02Qh
RIGGS, Bessy		24	F	Spinster	14Ju02Qh
BARRY, Margaret		16	F	Spinster	14Ju02Qh
MCKENNA, Bridget		08	F	Child	14Ju02Qh

NAMES OF PASSENGERS		AGE	SEX	OCCUPATIONS	DATE PORT SHIP
SMITH, Patt		15	M	Laborer	14Ju02Qh
MCINTYRE, John		40	M	Laborer	14Ju02Qh
MORRISON, Joseph		21	M	Laborer	14Ju02Qh
Andrew		36	M	Laborer	14Ju02Qh
OSULLIVAN, Mary		40	F	Servant	14Ju02Qh
Michael	(S)	06	M	Child	14Ju02Qh
KENNAHAN, Francis		20	M	Laborer	14Ju02Qh
TIPPING, Catherine		19	F	Servant	14Ju02Qh
LAUGHLAN, James		25	M	Laborer	14Ju02Qh
KEOUGH, Mary		18	F	Spinster	14Ju02Qh
TIPPING, John		25	M	Laborer	14Ju02Qh
George	(B)	22	M	Laborer	14Ju02Qh
TRYHE, Mary		20	F	Servant	14Ju02Qh
MADDEN, Johanna-S.		60	F	Servant	14Ju02Qh
COUGHLIN, Catherine		30	F	Servant	14Ju02Qh
NIXON, Ann		35	F	Servant	14Ju02Qh
LOVELL, William		30	M	Laborer	14Ju02Qh
MCGINNESS, Ephraim		20	M	Laborer	14Ju02Qh
MARTIN, Mary-Jane		19	F	Servant	14Ju02Qh
MCCORMICK, Francis		21	M	Laborer	14Ju02Qh
Patt		28	M	Laborer	14Ju02Qh
BRYANS, William		11	M	Child	14Ju02Qh
Ellen		09	F	Child	14Ju02Qh
HARGADEN, Catherine		20	F	Servant	14Ju02Qh
DOYLE, Maria		19	F	Servant	14Ju02Qh
MCCABE, Patt		20	M	Laborer	14Ju02Qh
CONLAN, John		30	M	Laborer	14Ju02Qh
Mary		19	F	Servant	14Ju02Qh
RYAN, Roger		25	M	Laborer	14Ju02Qh
Peggy		22	F	Servant	14Ju02Qh
DIGMAN, John		18	M	Laborer	14Ju02Qh
HAGNEY, Ann		20	F	Servant	14Ju02Qh
WELSH, Henry		25	M	Laborer	14Ju02Qh
KULAN, Michael		17	M	Laborer	14Ju02Qh
DENNAN, Patt		40	M	Laborer	14Ju02Qh
Mary	(W)	35	F	Wife	14Ju02Qh
Mary	(D)	11	F	Child	14Ju02Qh
John	(S)	09	M	Child	14Ju02Qh
Ann	(D)	07	F	Child	14Ju02Qh
Michael	(S)	04	M	Child	14Ju02Qh
Rose	(D)	03	F	Child	14Ju02Qh
MCENTYRE, Susan		22	F	Spinster	14Ju02Qh
MATTHEWS, Margaret		30	F	Mother	14Ju02Qh
Frances	(D)	03	F	Child	14Ju02Qh
Thomas	(S)	.00	M	Infant	14Ju02Qh
TUMILTY, Ellen		50	F	Servant	14Ju02Qh
Patt	(S)	20	M	Laborer	14Ju02Qh
MCFADDEN, Catherine		28	F	Spinster	14Ju02Qh
GOGHERTY, Alice		48	F	Servant	14Ju02Qh
MCLAUGHLIN, Patt		24	M	Laborer	14Ju02Qh
CONNELLY, Catherine		26	F	Servant	14Ju02Qh
MCCARTIN, Bernard		20	M	Laborer	14Ju02Qh
MURPHY, Eliza		24	F	Servant	14Ju02Qh
DOYLE, Daniel		28	M	Laborer	14Ju02Qh
DOCKNEY, Mary		17	F	Servant	14Ju02Qh
Patt		04	M	Child	14Ju02Qh
HANLEY, Luke		42	M	Laborer	14Ju02Qh
FANNIN, Winifred		06	F	Child	14Ju02Qh
REILLY, Rose		25	F	Servant	14Ju02Qh
Anthony	(S)	08	M	Child	14Ju02Qh
KAIN, Ellen		16	F	Servant	14Ju02Qh
GILROY, Michael		23	M	Laborer	14Ju02Qh
FINLAY, Owen		18	M	Laborer	14Ju02Qh
Ann	(T)	16	F	Servant	14Ju02Qh
ROONEY, Ann		40	F	Mother	14Ju02Qh
Betty	(D)	10	F	Child	14Ju02Qh
Michael	(S)	08	M	Child	14Ju02Qh
Ann	(D)	05	F	Child	14Ju02Qh
FURGUSON, Judy		20	F	Servant	14Ju02Qh
MARTIN, Robert		20	M	Laborer	14Ju02Qh
Martha		14	F	Servant	14Ju02Qh
HUNSON, Ellen		25	F	Servant	14Ju02Qh
Bryan	(S)	04	M	Child	14Ju02Qh
Michael	(S)	02	M	Child	14Ju02Qh
TURLEY, James		14	M	Child	14Ju02Qh
TURLEY, Catherine		15	F	Child	14Ju02Qh
Honor		11	F	Child	14Ju02Qh
LEONARD, Patt		25	M	Laborer	14Ju02Qh
LONG, William		20	M	Laborer	14Ju02Qh
READON, Pat		48	M	Laborer	14Ju02Qh
FEELY, Mary		20	F	Servant	14Ju02Qh
ROON, Timothy		30	M	Laborer	14Ju02Qh
WALLIS, Morris		22	M	Laborer	14Ju02Qh
REILLY, Mary		21	F	Servant	14Ju02Qh
NOCKER, Bernard		27	M	Laborer	14Ju02Qh
DONNELLY, Patt		36	M	Laborer	14Ju02Qh
MCKENNA, Daniel		26	M	Laborer	14Ju02Qh
MOILER, Pat		40	M	Laborer	14Ju02Qh
John		24	M	Laborer	14Ju02Qh
SIMPSON, William		26	M	Laborer	14Ju02Qh
Thomas		19	M	Laborer	14Ju02Qh
MCKEEVER, Mary		19	F	Servant	14Ju02Qh
CRANNAEY, Jane		16	F	Servant	14Ju02Qh
Sarah	(D)	11	F	Child	14Ju02Qh
LEARY, Honora		26	F	None	14Ju02Qh
Bridget	(D)	04	F	Child	14Ju02Qh
REILLY, Owen		18	M	Laborer	14Ju02Qh
Bart		17	M	Laborer	14Ju02Qh
MULLIGAN, Mary		20	F	Spinster	14Ju02Qh
MCKENNA, Michael		20	M	Laborer	14Ju02Qh
MCCRORY, Terence		40	F	Servant	14Ju02Qh
HAGAN, Margaret		40	F	Servant	14Ju02Qh
PATTEN, John		18	M	Laborer	14Ju02Qh
James	(B)	15	M	Laborer	14Ju02Qh
Pat	(B)	10	M	Child	14Ju02Qh
DONNELLY, James		26	M	Laborer	14Ju02Qh
REARDON, Johanna		45	F	Servant	14Ju02Qh
Honnor		30	F	Servant	14Ju02Qh
CALLAGAN, Tim		25	M	Laborer	14Ju02Qh
READON, Tim		10	M	Child	14Ju02Qh
Owen		07	M	Child	14Ju02Qh
Mary		05	F	Child	14Ju02Qh
Johanna	(D)	.00	F	Infant	14Ju02Qh
DEE, Honor		40	F	Mother	14Ju02Qh
Morris	(S)	14	M	Child	14Ju02Qh
Pat	(S)	10	M	Child	14Ju02Qh
Mary	(D)	08	F	Child	14Ju02Qh
Ellen	(D)	04	F	Child	14Ju02Qh
Johanna	(D)	02	F	Child	14Ju02Qh
MCGARRITY, James		55	M	Laborer	14Ju02Qh
JENNETT, Archibald		12	M	Child	14Ju02Qh
MCCARTY, Dennis		24	M	Laborer	14Ju02Qh
Michael	(S)	14	M	Child	14Ju02Qh
Thomas	(S)	09	M	Child	14Ju02Qh
John	(S)	04	M	Child	14Ju02Qh
JONES, Thomas		42	M	Laborer	14Ju02Qh
MCGINN, Ellen		40	F	Servant	14Ju02Qh
OCONNOR, Thomas		30	M	Laborer	14Ju02Qh
WALSH, Fanny		34	F	Mother	14Ju02Qh
Catherine	(D)	12	F	Child	14Ju02Qh
John	(S)	07	M	Child	14Ju02Qh
Mary	(D)	03	F	Child	14Ju02Qh
GLADDEN, John		26	M	Laborer	14Ju02Qh
SHEEHAN, Mary		20	F	Servant	14Ju02Qh
KELLY, Sally		50	F	Servant	14Ju02Qh
LEDDY, John		40	M	Laborer	14Ju02Qh
Margaret	(W)	40	F	Wife	14Ju02Qh
Ellen	(D)	17	F	Servant	14Ju02Qh
Mary	(D)	17	F	Servant	14Ju02Qh
Pat	(S)	12	M	Child	14Ju02Qh
James	(S)	19	M	Laborer	14Ju02Qh
DANARY, John		04	M	Child	14Ju02Qh
Margaret	(D)	03	F	Child	14Ju02Qh
MOINER, Patt		24	M	Laborer	14Ju02Qh
MCKENNA, Bernard		28	M	Laborer	14Ju02Qh
GOOWIN, Mary		18	F	Servant	14Ju02Qh
FAILS, Margaret		20	F	Servant	14Ju02Qh
HACKETT, Ann		50	F	Servant	14Ju02Qh
William		12	M	Child	14Ju02Qh
WRIGHT, Elizabeth		30	F	Servant	14Ju02Qh

NAMES OF PASSENGERS		AGE	SEX	OCCUPATIONS	DATE PORT SHIP
WRIGHT, Joseph		11	M	Child	14Ju02Qh
HAMILTON, John		10	M	Child	14Ju02Qh
FLYNN, Ann		20	F	Servant	14Ju02Qh
TACKETT, Susan		20	F	Servant	14Ju02Qh
FREEMAN, Catherine		20	F	Servant	14Ju02Qh
MCCABE, Ann		20	F	Servant	14Ju02Qh
Catherine	(T)	16	F	Servant	14Ju02Qh
DONOHOE, John		20	M	Laborer	14Ju02Qh
COLLINS, Margaret		18	F	Servant	14Ju02Qh
HAGNAY, Daniel		20	M	Laborer	14Ju02Qh
REILLY, Mary		30	F	Servant	14Ju02Qh
GEOGHAN, Margaret		20	F	Servant	14Ju02Qh
MARRON, Margaret		15	F	Servant	14Ju02Qh
AINLEY, Hannah		30	F	Servant	14Ju02Qh
Charlotte		28	F	Servant	14Ju02Qh
WEBB, Mary		28	F	Servant	14Ju02Qh
WHITEHEAD, Edward		22	M	Servant	14Ju02Qh
CRAWFORD, William		21	M	Laborer	14Ju02Qh
KEENAN, James		24	M	Laborer	14Ju02Qh
HANLIN, Daniel-John		35	M	Laborer	14Ju02Qh
GIBSON, James		48	M	Laborer	14Ju02Qh
CRANAGE, James		33	M	Laborer	14Ju02Qh
BROWN, Samuel		22	M	Laborer	14Ju02Qh
KIMBLELANE, Thomas		23	M	Laborer	14Ju02Qh
Mary	(W)	24	F	Wife	14Ju02Qh
CAIN, Mary		20	F	Spinster	14Ju02Qh
RIELLY, Phillip		50	M	Laborer	14Ju02Qh
Rosey		20	F	Servant	14Ju02Qh
DUNN, Dennis		20	M	Laborer	14Ju02Qh
DOUGHERTY, Biddy		35	F	Servant	14Ju02Qh
TURLY, Margaret		38	F	Servant	14Ju02Qh
Died-At-Sea					
ROONEY, Alley		02	M	Child	14Ju02Qh
Died-At-Sea					

CALEDONIA 16 JUNE 1848

From Londonderry

NAMES OF PASSENGERS		AGE	SEX	OCCUPATIONS	DATE PORT SHIP
MILLER, Samuel		54	M	Unknown	16Ju01lo
Hannah		39	F	Spinster	16Ju01lo
Samuel		18	M	Unknown	16Ju01lo
Martha		13	F	Child	16Ju01lo
Ann		10	F	Child	16Ju01lo
ROBERTS, William		10	M	Child	16Ju01lo
Hannah		07	F	Child	16Ju01lo
MATHEWS, Mathew		20	M	Laborer	16Ju01lo
PORTER, Sarah		17	F	Unknown	16Ju01lo
KENNEDY, Sarah		14	F	Spinster	16Ju01lo
Caroline		04	F	Child	16Ju01lo
BOGAN, William		25	M	Laborer	16Ju01lo
James		27	M	Laborer	16Ju01lo
Jane		33	F	Laborer	16Ju01lo
Margt.		16	F	Laborer	16Ju01lo
Nancy		16	F	None	16Ju01lo
KILFEATHER, Mary-Ann		18	F	Spinster	16Ju01lo
Jane		16	F	Spinster	16Ju01lo
ARLEY, John		18	M	Laborer	16Ju01lo
NEELY, Matthew		60	M	Laborer	16Ju01lo
Samuel		18	M	Laborer	16Ju01lo
Jane		50	F	Laborer	16Ju01lo
Gabriel		16	M	Laborer	16Ju01lo
TEMPLE, Sarah-Ann		23	F	Laborer	16Ju01lo
BARY, May		21	F	Laborer	16Ju01lo
FULLERTON, David		17	M	Laborer	16Ju01lo
CONWAY, Bride		19	F	Spinster	16Ju01lo
LOGAN, Nathaniel		25	M	Laborer	16Ju01lo
Samuel		22	M	Laborer	16Ju01lo
Robert-H.		17	M	Laborer	16Ju01lo
TAYLOR, Sarah-Jane		20	F	Laborer	16Ju01lo
BOYD, Samuel		19	M	Laborer	16Ju01lo
Eliza		21	F	Laborer	16Ju01lo
Charlotte		15	F	Laborer	16Ju01lo
MCGOWAN, Ann		24	F	Laborer	16Ju01lo
CONNELL, John		22	M	Laborer	16Ju01lo
Sarah	(W)	21	F	Wife	16Ju01lo
KING, William		17	M	Laborer	16Ju01lo
JOHNSTONE, Janette		48	F	Laborer	16Ju01lo
Geoe.	(S)	12	M	Child	16Ju01lo
Isabella	(D)	06	F	Child	16Ju01lo
Wm.John	(S)	.00	M	Infant	16Ju01lo
ALCORM, Robert		24	M	Laborer	16Ju01lo
Ann		60	F	Laborer	16Ju01lo
Elizabeth		22	F	Laborer	16Ju01lo
Rose-Ann		20	F	Laborer	16Ju01lo
CAMPBELL, Ann		18	F	Laborer	16Ju01lo
MCKELVEY, Robert		21	M	Laborer	16Ju01lo
CAMPBELL, Eliza		16	F	Laborer	16Ju01lo
BELL, Thomas		32	M	Laborer	16Ju01lo
Ann		45	F	Laborer	16Ju01lo
James		06	M	Laborer	16Ju01lo
Jane		04	F	Laborer	16Ju01lo
Mary		.00	F	Infant	16Ju01lo
GIBSON, Martha		19	F	Spinster	16Ju01lo
BLAKE, Samuel		19	M	Unknown	16Ju01lo
MCCAFFREY, James		25	M	Laborer	16Ju01lo
Pat		23	M	Laborer	16Ju01lo
Philip		20	M	Laborer	16Ju01lo
MCDONALD, Daniel		24	M	Laborer	16Ju01lo
ONEILL, John		23	M	Laborer	16Ju01lo
KNOX, William		20	M	Laborer	16Ju01lo
DONAGHEY, Robert		20	M	Laborer	16Ju01lo
William		20	M	Laborer	16Ju01lo
GALLAGHER, Michael		24	M	Laborer	16Ju01lo
MOORE, Eliza		18	F	Spinster	16Ju01lo
KERRIGAN, Hugh		22	M	Laborer	16Ju01lo
KNOX, Eliza		20	F	Spinster	16Ju01lo
PERRY, Isabella		35	F	Spinster	16Ju01lo
REYNOLDS, Elizabeth		23	F	Spinster	16Ju01lo
WILEY, Robert		26	M	Spinster	16Ju01lo
MCCLEARY, Wm.		15	M	Spinster	16Ju01lo
Ann		51	F	Spinster	16Ju01lo
Mary-Ann		20	F	Spinster	16Ju01lo
James		19	M	Spinster	16Ju01lo
Cathr.		17	F	Spinster	16Ju01lo
Rebecca		10	F	Spinster	16Ju01lo
GILLILAND, Mary		20	F	Spinster	16Ju01lo
BREDON, John		21	M	Laborer	16Ju01lo
MARTIN, John		20	M	Laborer	16Ju01lo
SHERRAND, Elizabeth		22	F	Spinster	16Ju01lo
MCCANNY, Margt.		23	F	Spinster	16Ju01lo
TORMLEY, Ann		14	F	Spinster	16Ju01lo
John		10	M	Child	16Ju01lo
EAKIN, John		70	M	Unknown	16Ju01lo
Bridgt.	(W)	40	F	Wife	16Ju01lo
John		15	M	Laborer	16Ju01lo
BOYLE, Owen		29	M	Laborer	16Ju01lo
EAKIN, Mary		14	F	Laborer	16Ju01lo
Isabella		12	F	Laborer	16Ju01lo
PORTER, James		23	M	Laborer	16Ju01lo
PLATT, George		22	M	Laborer	16Ju01lo
ONEILL, Charles		20	M	Laborer	16Ju01lo
Joseph		20	M	Laborer	16Ju01lo
DALLAS, Thomas		20	M	Laborer	16Ju01lo
MOORE, John		22	M	Laborer	16Ju01lo
BROLLY, William		56	M	Laborer	16Ju01lo
James		14	M	Laborer	16Ju01lo
MCHUGH, Margt.		20	F	Spinster	16Ju01lo
MCLENAHAM, John		30	M	Laborer	16Ju01lo
NEILANS, Robert		20	M	Laborer	16Ju01lo
MCCURDY, Robert		13	M	Laborer	16Ju01lo
Isabella		15	F	Spinster	16Ju01lo
CALDWELL, James		24	M	Laborer	16Ju01lo
Eleanor	(W)	23	F	Wife	16Ju01lo

NAMES OF PASSENGERS		AGE	SEX	OCCUPATIONS	DATE PORT SHIP
CALDWELL, Jane		18	F	None	16Ju01lo
SMITH, Wm.		23	M	Laborer	16Ju01lo
Jane	(W)	30	F	Wife	16Ju01lo
Wm.	(S)	08	M	Child	16Ju01lo
Peggy	(D)	03	F	Child	16Ju01lo
James	(S)	.00	M	Infant	16Ju01lo
Jane	(D)	.00	F	Infant	16Ju01lo
HAGERTY, William		19	M	Laborer	16Ju01lo
CULLEN, James		23	M	Laborer	16Ju01lo
LYNCH, James		19	M	Laborer	16Ju01lo
HUGHES, Sarah		20	F	Laborer	16Ju01lo
GONNY, James		25	M	Laborer	16Ju01lo
Elizabeth		23	F	Laborer	16Ju01lo
James		21	M	Laborer	16Ju01lo
MCLAUGHLIN, Cathr.		20	F	Laborer	16Ju01lo
MILLER, James		37	M	Laborer	16Ju01lo
Mary	(W)	36	F	Wife	16Ju01lo
Mary	(D)	18	F	None	16Ju01lo
Jane	(D)	16	F	None	16Ju01lo
Ruth	(D)	14	F	Child	16Ju01lo
Margt.	(D)	12	F	Child	16Ju01lo
Hannah	(D)	10	F	Child	16Ju01lo
HOPKINS, James		30	M	Laborer	16Ju01lo
LYNCH, Mary		22	F	Laborer	16Ju01lo
OLLINAN, Margt.		21	F	Laborer	16Ju01lo
MURGG, Com.		20	M	Laborer	16Ju01lo
HULL, Margaret		41	F	Laborer	16Ju01lo
Isabella	(D)	15	F	Laborer	16Ju01lo
MCKYE, William		31	M	Laborer	16Ju01lo
MCKEE, James		18	M	Laborer	16Ju01lo
CARLIN, John		23	M	Laborer	16Ju01lo
SAWYERS, Josh.		23	M	Laborer	16Ju01lo
LYNCH, Richard		21	M	Laborer	16Ju01lo
BAILEY, Robert		56	M	Laborer	16Ju01lo
Margt.	(D)	18	F	Spinster	16Ju01lo
John	(S)	15	M	None	16Ju01lo
DALLAS, Thomas		20	M	Laborer	16Ju01lo
MOORE, John		22	M	Laborer	16Ju01lo
BROLLY, William		56	M	Laborer	16Ju01lo
MCGINTY, Hugh		26	M	Laborer	16Ju01lo
CULLEN, John		20	M	Laborer	16Ju01lo
Anthony		18	M	Laborer	16Ju01lo
Ellen		17	F	Spinster	16Ju01lo
Dominick		18	M	Laborer	16Ju01lo
KEIGHTLY, Jane		21	F	Laborer	16Ju01lo
MCGITTIGAN, Danl.		26	M	Laborer	16Ju01lo
Pat		14	M	Laborer	16Ju01lo
Pat		20	M	Laborer	16Ju01lo
Danl.		10	M	Laborer	16Ju01lo
Rose		28	F	Laborer	16Ju01lo
Ann		12	F	Child	16Ju01lo
Margery		17	F	Laborer	16Ju01lo
Philip		40	M	Laborer	16Ju01lo
JOHNSON, Joseph		20	M	Laborer	16Ju01lo
RICHEY, Mary		20	F	Laborer	16Ju01lo
MORRIS, Cath.		25	F	Laborer	16Ju01lo
Jane		28	F	Laborer	16Ju01lo
MCQUADE, Cath.		18	F	Laborer	16Ju01lo
CRINNLISH, Elisha		18	M	Laborer	16Ju01lo
MCKEOWN, James		23	M	Laborer	16Ju01lo
DOUGHERTY, Jonas		22	M	Laborer	16Ju01lo
FARRAN, John		20	M	Laborer	16Ju01lo
MCGINLEY, Charles		20	M	Laborer	16Ju01lo
KANE, Jane		20	F	Spinster	16Ju01lo
OLPHURT, John		19	M	Laborer	16Ju01lo
STEVENSON, Robert		19	M	Laborer	16Ju01lo
MCPHERSON, William		19	M	Laborer	16Ju01lo
HILL, Robert		22	M	Laborer	16Ju01lo
SMITH, Alex.		26	M	Laborer	16Ju01lo
BRACKEN, Geoe.		38	M	Laborer	16Ju01lo
WALLACE, Cath.		20	F	Spinster	16Ju01lo
Mary		23	F	Spinster	16Ju01lo
ARMSTRONG, Thompson		18	M	Laborer	16Ju01lo
FERGUSON, Geoe.		20	M	Laborer	16Ju01lo
CONNOR, Cath.		20	F	Laborer	16Ju01lo

NAMES OF PASSENGERS		AGE	SEX	OCCUPATIONS	DATE PORT SHIP
GORDON, John		25	M	Laborer	16Ju01lo
HARGON, James		20	M	Laborer	16Ju01lo
Margt.		17	F	Laborer	16Ju01lo
RUTLEDGE, Edward		23	M	Laborer	16Ju01lo
Hugh		18	M	Laborer	16Ju01lo
PHILLIPS, Geoe.		22	M	Laborer	16Ju01lo
MCLAUGHLIN, John		20	M	Laborer	16Ju01lo
KELLY, James		17	M	Laborer	16Ju01lo
MCCAFFREY, Edward		26	M	Laborer	16Ju01lo
BARNETT, Jas.		20	M	Laborer	16Ju01lo
HUGHES, Sarah		20	F	Spinster	16Ju01lo
BOYD, Nancy		17	F	Spinster	16Ju01lo
GANLY, Wm.		22	M	Laborer	16Ju01lo
GODFREY, Robert		59	M	Laborer	16Ju01lo
FARRELL, James		24	M	Laborer	16Ju01lo
GALLAGHER, Dennis		18	M	Laborer	16Ju01lo
Ellen		22	F	Spinster	16Ju01lo
TOLLON, Biddy		49	F	Spinster	16Ju01lo
Sally		18	F	Spinster	16Ju01lo
Biddy		17	F	Spinster	16Ju01lo
Pat		17	M	Laborer	16Ju01lo
James		17	M	Laborer	16Ju01lo
MCGRENON, Biddy		17	F	Laborer	16Ju01lo
SCOTT, William		28	M	Laborer	16Ju01lo
BRISTOE, Mary		20	F	Laborer	16Ju01lo
HENRY, David		40	M	Laborer	16Ju01lo
Jessie		37	M	Laborer	16Ju01lo
KEE, Oliver		21	M	Laborer	16Ju01lo
AUSSON, John		27	M	Laborer	16Ju01lo
WARD, Hannah		15	F	Spinster	16Ju01lo
ANSSON, John		27	M	Laborer	16Ju01lo
JOHNSON, William		19	M	Laborer	16Ju01lo
ALGOE, Robert		19	M	Laborer	16Ju01lo
MCQUADE, Hugh		18	M	Laborer	16Ju01lo
Esther		17	F	Laborer	16Ju01lo
Margt		14	F	Spinster	16Ju01lo
James		30	M	Laborer	16Ju01lo
MCGONGHEY, John		20	M	Laborer	16Ju01lo
GALLAGHER, Susan		34	F	Laborer	16Ju01lo
Michael	(S)	11	M	Laborer	16Ju01lo
Henry	(S)	09	M	Laborer	16Ju01lo
Dennis	(S)	07	M	Laborer	16Ju01lo
MULLIN, John		18	M	Laborer	16Ju01lo
GALLAGHER, William		18	M	Laborer	16Ju01lo
GORDON, James		24	M	Laborer	16Ju01lo
MITCHELL, Mary		32	F	Laborer	16Ju01lo
Eliza	(D)	04	F	Child	16Ju01lo
Pat	(S)	.00	M	Infant	16Ju01lo
MEEHAN, Jane		25	F	Spinster	16Ju01lo
FORD, Matthew		26	M	Laborer	16Ju01lo
Bophit		20	M	Laborer	16Ju01lo
Ellen		60	F	Wife	16Ju01lo
MAYCE, Ann		25	F	None	16Ju01lo
MCLOUGHLIN, George		30	M	Laborer	16Ju01lo
Mary	(W)	25	F	Wife	16Ju01lo
MCFEELY, Ellen		36	F	None	16Ju01lo
RYAN, Michael		36	M	Laborer	16Ju01lo
DONAGHEY, Voniks		23	M	Laborer	16Ju01lo
CARLIN, Pat		20	M	Laborer	16Ju01lo
BREWSTER, James		20	M	Laborer	16Ju01lo
HASLETT, Samuel		26	M	Laborer	16Ju01lo
Samuel		70	M	Laborer	16Ju01lo
Martha		67	F	Spinster	16Ju01lo
Margt.Ann		23	F	None	16Ju01lo
Jane		28	F	None	16Ju01lo
MCCONNELL, Hannah		18	F	None	16Ju01lo
REANY, John		04	M	Child	16Ju01lo
John		.00	M	Infant	16Ju01lo
QUEARNS, Samuel		23	M	Laborer	16Ju01lo
Mary-Jane		22	F	Laborer	16Ju01lo
FINLEY, James		60	M	Laborer	16Ju01lo
FINLAY, Matty		60	M	Laborer	16Ju01lo
John		20	M	Laborer	16Ju01lo
John		20	M	Laborer	16Ju01lo
Mary		20	F	Spinster	16Ju01lo

NAMES OF PASSENGERS		AGE	SEX	OCCUPATIONS	DATE PORT SHIP
FINLAY, Martha		22	F	Spinster	16Ju01lo
Margt.		.00	F	Infant	16Ju01lo
HUNTER, Paul		19	M	Laborer	16Ju01lo
KERR, Samuel		20	M	Laborer	16Ju01lo
MCGAUGHRY, James		22	M	Laborer	16Ju01lo
KELVEY, Alexander-P.		24	M	Laborer	16Ju01lo
QUIGLEY, Thomas		28	M	Laborer	16Ju01lo
WATSON, Martha		18	F	Spinster	16Ju01lo
WILLS, Chas.		25	M	Drafe	16Ju01lo
COPELAND, Nicholina		48	F	Drafe	16Ju01lo
James		30	M	Drafe	16Ju01lo
Eliza		25	F	None	16Ju01lo
William		27	M	Drafe	16Ju01lo
Hugh		23	M	Drafe	16Ju01lo
Henry		21	M	Drafe	16Ju01lo
Jane		17	F	None	16Ju01lo
Mary		16	F	None	16Ju01lo
John		14	M	None	16Ju01lo
Geoe.		12	M	None	16Ju01lo
Robert		10	M	None	16Ju01lo

CLUTHA 16 JUNE 1848

From Glasgow

NAMES OF PASSENGERS		AGE	SEX	OCCUPATIONS	DATE PORT SHIP
LAW, John		36	M	Farmer	16Ju04Kv
BEVERIDGE, Matthew		40	M	Farmer	16Ju04Kv
PATE, Isabella		42	F	Servant	16Ju04Kv
LUMSDEN, John		19	M	Farmer	16Ju04Kv
BAIRD, Robert		32	M	Weaver	16Ju04Kv
U	(W)	40	F	Wife	16Ju04Kv
James		28	M	Weaver	16Ju04Kv
JOHNSTONE, James		11	M	Unknown	16Ju04Kv
BAIRD, Margaret		04	F	Child	16Ju04Kv
Christiana		.04	F	Infant	16Ju04Kv
PATERSON, Wanchope		29	M	Tailor	16Ju04Kv
U	(W)	29	F	Wife	16Ju04Kv
CLEGHORN, Andrew		45	M	Ctnsp	16Ju04Kv
U	(W)	45	F	Ctnsp	16Ju04Kv
Mary	(D)	22	F	Ctnsp	16Ju04Kv
Margaret	(D)	21	F	Ctnsp	16Ju04Kv
Janet	(D)	16	F	Ctnsp	16Ju04Kv
Andrew	(S)	13	M	Unknown	16Ju04Kv
William	(S)	12	M	Unknown	16Ju04Kv
George	(S)	12	M	Unknown	16Ju04Kv
Anne	(D)	08	F	Child	16Ju04Kv
Mary	(D)	06	F	Child	16Ju04Kv
Robert	(S)	.11	M	Infant	16Ju04Kv
John	(S)	25	M	Ctnsp	16Ju04Kv
MUIR, John		50	M	Weaver	16Ju04Kv
U	(W)	48	F	Wife	16Ju04Kv
Agnes	(D)	11	F	Unknown	16Ju04Kv
DAVIS, John		10	M	Child	16Ju04Kv
SLOAN, Mary		24	F	Servant	16Ju04Kv
MURDOCK, David		20	M	Tailor	16Ju04Kv
ADAM, James		15	M	Calenderer	16Ju04Kv
GALLAWAY, Isabella		43	F	Wi	16Ju04Kv
Neralja	(D)	18	F	Servant	16Ju04Kv
Catherine	(D)	16	F	Servant	16Ju04Kv
MILNE, James		36	M	Farmer	16Ju04Kv
BEVERIDGE, Mary		20	F	Servant	16Ju04Kv
ONEIL, Arthur		30	M	Sawer	16Ju04Kv
U	(W)	25	F	Wife	16Ju04Kv
Elizabeth	(D)	.11	F	Infant	16Ju04Kv
Anne	(D)	02	F	Child	16Ju04Kv
PATERSON, James		29	M	Shoemaker	16Ju04Kv
Isabella	(W)	21	F	Wife	16Ju04Kv
THOMSON, James		26	M	Ctnsp	16Ju04Kv
STEWART, William		20	M	Bookbinder	16Ju04Kv
MALCOLM, Henry		40	M	Miner	16Ju04Kv
U	(W)	45	F	Wife	16Ju04Kv
Andrew	(S)	11	M	Unknown	16Ju04Kv
Isabella	(D)	08	F	Child	16Ju04Kv
Henry	(S)	04	M	Child	16Ju04Kv
MCQUEEN, Robert		25	M	Engineer	16Ju04Kv
U	(W)	25	F	Wife	16Ju04Kv
James	(S)	02	M	Child	16Ju04Kv
Robert	(S)	.11	M	Infant	16Ju04Kv
Adam		20	M	Miner	16Ju04Kv
Margaret		18	F	Servant	16Ju04Kv
MCLEAN, Allan		25	M	Fnkp	16Ju04Kv
U	(W)	22	F	Wife	16Ju04Kv
MILLEN, William		26	M	Shpc	16Ju04Kv
HANNAY, William		23	M	Tailor	16Ju04Kv
MCGEE, Alex		30	M	Laborer	16Ju04Kv
U	(W)	30	W	Laborer	16Ju04Kv
Edward	(S)	04	M	Child	16Ju04Kv
SMITH, U		25	F	Wife	16Ju04Kv
Henry		28	M	Laborer	16Ju04Kv
ROSS, Hamilton		24	M	Engineer	16Ju04Kv
U	(W)	24	F	Wife	16Ju04Kv
Alexander	(S)	03	M	Child	16Ju04Kv
BROWN, U		24	F	Wife	16Ju04Kv
CONNELL, Mary		28	F	Servant	16Ju04Kv
MILLAR, Euphemia		22	F	Servant	16Ju04Kv
MEHAN, Thomas		45	M	Farmer	16Ju04Kv
U	(W)	45	F	Wife	16Ju04Kv
James		47	M	Farmer	16Ju04Kv
Margaret		18	F	Servant	16Ju04Kv
SMITH, Robert		25	M	Bricklayer	16Ju04Kv
THORBURN, Robert		19	M	Blacksmith	16Ju04Kv
John		19	M	Mason	16Ju04Kv
MCMURRAY, Thomas		31	M	Shoemaker	16Ju04Kv
ADAM, James-Sr.		84	M	Farmer	16Ju04Kv
U	(W)	60	F	Wife	16Ju04Kv
James	(S)	35	M	Shoemaker	16Ju04Kv
U	(W)	35	F	Wife	16Ju04Kv
James	(S)	13	M	Unknown	16Ju04Kv
Elizabeth	(D)	10	F	Unknown	16Ju04Kv
Janet	(D)	08	F	Child	16Ju04Kv
Catherine	(D)	03	F	Child	16Ju04Kv
MCMILLAN, William		12	M	Unknown	16Ju04Kv
Alex		13	M	Unknown	16Ju04Kv
SMITH, Francis		40	M	Printer	16Ju04Kv
U	(W)	35	F	Wife	16Ju04Kv
Catherine	(D)	11	F	Unknown	16Ju04Kv
David	(S)	09	M	Child	16Ju04Kv
James	(S)	07	M	Child	16Ju04Kv
Agnes	(D)	02	F	Child	16Ju04Kv
CAMPBELL, Alex		12	M	Unknown	16Ju04Kv
JAMIESON, Samuel		24	M	Husband	16Ju04Kv
Jane	(W)	25	F	Wife	16Ju04Kv
Sarah	(T)	16	F	Sister	16Ju04Kv
Margaret		.06	F	Infant	16Ju04Kv
DIVINE, Margaret		19	F	Servant	16Ju04Kv
MEKAL, David		38	M	Laborer	16Ju04Kv
BOYLE, James		34	M	Plasterer	16Ju04Kv
John		24	M	Slater	16Ju04Kv
BROWNLIE, Alex		19	M	Clerk	16Ju04Kv
WHITEHEAD, U		24	F	Wife	16Ju04Kv
Sarah	(D)	03	F	Child	16Ju04Kv
MOIR, Andrew		23	M	Gdnr	16Ju04Kv
Alexander		20	M	Gdnr	16Ju04Kv
WALLACE, James		32	M	Carpenter	16Ju04Kv
PATRICK, William		30	M	Baker	16Ju04Kv
CAMPBELL, James		24	M	Baker	16Ju04Kv
U	(W)	20	F	Wife	16Ju04Kv
STEWART, John		30	M	Smith	16Ju04Kv
MUIR, William		29	M	Carter	16Ju04Kv
RICE, Samuel		50	M	Weaver	16Ju04Kv
U	(W)	50	F	Wife	16Ju04Kv
James	(S)	16	M	Weaver	16Ju04Kv
Margaret	(D)	13	F	Unknown	16Ju04Kv
John	(S)	06	M	Child	16Ju04Kv

NAMES OF PASSENGERS		AGE	SEX	OCCUPATIONS	DATE PORT SHIP
RICE, Samuel	(S)	23	M	Weaver	16Ju04Kv
U	(W)	23	F	Wife	16Ju04Kv
Samuel	(S)	.02	M	Infant	16Ju04Kv
THOMSON, William		29	M	Porter	16Ju04Kv
WILKIN, U		34	F	Wife	16Ju04Kv
JONES, Henry		28	M	Fefndr	16Ju04Kv
WALKER, James		20	M	Mason	16Ju04Kv
MCDONALD, John		23	M	Joiner	16Ju04Kv
GRAHAM, James		17	M	Farmer	16Ju04Kv
WARDLAW, R.		24	M	Porter	16Ju04Kv
SHEARER, Mary		30	F	Servant	16Ju04Kv
Rose-Anne		28	F	Servant	16Ju04Kv
HARRISON, Robert		28	M	Porter	16Ju04Kv
MCGORLICK, James		45	M	Laborer	16Ju04Kv
U	(W)	45	F	Wife	16Ju04Kv
James	(S)	16	M	Laborer	16Ju04Kv
MORTON, James		23	M	Cooper	16Ju04Kv
William		26	M	Cooper	16Ju04Kv
Robert		20	M	Carter	16Ju04Kv
DONALDSON, John		30	M	Blr	16Ju04Kv
U	(W)	30	F	Wife	16Ju04Kv
Catherine	(D)	03	F	Child	16Ju04Kv
Cecilia	(D)	.03	F	Infant	16Ju04Kv
James		23	M	Blr	16Ju04Kv
ALLAN, Alex		35	M	Farmer	16Ju04Kv
U	(W)	26	F	Wife	16Ju04Kv
MUIR, Martha		24	F	Servant	16Ju04Kv
ALLAN, Jean		04	F	Child	16Ju04Kv
Alex		.06	M	Infant	16Ju04Kv
ANDERSON, Thomas		25	M	Joiner	16Ju04Kv
RAMSAY, Alex		24	M	Joiner	16Ju04Kv
INGRAM, Alex		32	M	Printer	16Ju04Kv
RIDDELL, Robert		28	M	Mason	16Ju04Kv
MCNAB, Agnes		26	F	Servant	16Ju04Kv
MCLAREN, John		34	M	Ctnsp	16Ju04Kv
PARK, David		46	M	Mason	16Ju04Kv
U	(W)	48	F	Wife	16Ju04Kv
David	(S)	13	M	Unknown	16Ju04Kv
Margaret	(D)	10	F	Child	16Ju04Kv
KELLY, James		20	M	Tailor	16Ju04Kv
MCLARTY, William		26	M	Dyer	16Ju04Kv
CARLIN, James		30	M	Laborer	16Ju04Kv
U	(W)	25	F	Wife	16Ju04Kv
Agnes		18	F	Servant	16Ju04Kv
Catherine		13	F	Child	16Ju04Kv
Rosanna		20	F	Servant	16Ju04Kv
Rosanna	(D)	08	F	Child	16Ju04Kv
John	(S)	.06	M	Infant	16Ju04Kv
MEHAN, Daniel		45	M	Laborer	16Ju04Kv
Alley	(W)	35	F	Wife	16Ju04Kv
GALLAGHER, Daniel		30	M	Laborer	16Ju04Kv
SIMPSON, James		25	M	Joiner	16Ju04Kv
MURPHY, Bartley		19	M	Laborer	16Ju04Kv
TORRENCE, David		25	M	Shoemaker	16Ju04Kv
STEWART, James		30	M	Draper	16Ju04Kv
MCKETCHIE, A.		27	M	Gentleman	16Ju04Kv
MCWADE, W.		18	F	Servant	16Ju04Kv
BLECKENRIDGE, Walter		38	M	Weaver	16Ju04Kv
CARMICHAEL, Helen		48	F	Servant	16Ju04Kv
TORRENCE, U		24	F	Wife	16Ju04Kv
MCKAY, John		20	M	Laborer	16Ju04Kv
MOIR, U		20	F	Wife	16Ju04Kv
WALLACE, Thomas		20	M	Carpenter	16Ju04Kv
CAMPBELL, Angus		23	M	Farmer	16Ju04Kv

ADONIS 17 JUNE 1848

From Liverpool

NAMES OF PASSENGERS		AGE	SEX	OCCUPATIONS	DATE PORT SHIP
JOHNSON, Owen		20	M	Laborer	17Ju02Kw
TOBIN, Bridget		20	F	Spinster	17Ju02Kw
REILLY, Mary		20	F	Spinster	17Ju02Kw
Cath.		18	F	Spinster	17Ju02Kw
TREMAN, John		30	M	Laborer	17Ju02Kw
JUDGE, Nancy		26	F	Spinster	17Ju02Kw
BROADBENT, Mary		16	F	Spinster	17Ju02Kw
KEANE, Michael		35	M	Laborer	17Ju02Kw
KELLY, E.		37	M	Laborer	17Ju02Kw
U	(W)	28	F	Spinster	17Ju02Kw
U		.00	U	Infant	17Ju02Kw
Martin		05	M	Child	17Ju02Kw
Patrick		03	M	Child	17Ju02Kw
Mathew		28	M	Laborer	17Ju02Kw
CULLEN, Mathew		30	M	Laborer	17Ju02Kw
U	(W)	20	F	Spinster	17Ju02Kw
Ellen		26	F	Spinster	17Ju02Kw
Margaret		15	F	Spinster	17Ju02Kw
RYAN, Mich.		20	M	Laborer	17Ju02Kw
PELON, James		40	M	Laborer	17Ju02Kw
Margret		26	F	Spinster	17Ju02Kw
HART, Andrew		28	M	Laborer	17Ju02Kw
Mary		25	F	Spinster	17Ju02Kw
Patrick		03	M	Child	17Ju02Kw
John		01	M	Child	17Ju02Kw
FARRELL, Patrick		50	M	Laborer	17Ju02Kw
Mary		50	F	Spinster	17Ju02Kw
ROCHE, Thomas		25	M	Laborer	17Ju02Kw
NEILE, Jane		20	F	Spinster	17Ju02Kw
MCKEE, Margt.		21	F	Spinster	17Ju02Kw
MCCLUE, Wm.		22	M	Laborer	17Ju02Kw
KING, Wm.		27	M	Laborer	17Ju02Kw
BIGGENS, David		21	M	Laborer	17Ju02Kw
MCILVENE, John		25	M	Laborer	17Ju02Kw
COALES, E.		22	M	Laborer	17Ju02Kw
JACKSON, Moses		23	M	Laborer	17Ju02Kw
COALES, Martha		21	F	Spinster	17Ju02Kw
FORD, Thomas		19	M	Laborer	17Ju02Kw
MCDERMOTT, Mich.		30	M	Laborer	17Ju02Kw
Patrick		20	M	Laborer	17Ju02Kw
DOLPHIN, Mich.		22	M	Laborer	17Ju02Kw
MUNNELL, Martin		22	M	Laborer	17Ju02Kw
TOOHEY, Thomas		22	M	Laborer	17Ju02Kw
MULVENE, Pat		22	M	Laborer	17Ju02Kw
FAHEY, Cath.		20	F	Spinster	17Ju02Kw
Bridget		18	F	Spinster	17Ju02Kw
MURIAL, Happy		16	F	Spinster	17Ju02Kw
MADDIN, Mary		16	F	Spinster	17Ju02Kw
MCDERMOTT, Ann		06	F	Child	17Ju02Kw
Mary		04	F	Child	17Ju02Kw
Bridget		07	F	Child	17Ju02Kw
FAHEY, Thomas		07	M	Child	17Ju02Kw
WALSH, John		22	M	Laborer	17Ju02Kw
Pat.		26	M	Laborer	17Ju02Kw
MARTIN, John		22	M	Laborer	17Ju02Kw
TRUMBLE, Wm.		22	M	Laborer	17Ju02Kw
MCVAIL, Wm.		22	M	Laborer	17Ju02Kw
John		24	M	Laborer	17Ju02Kw
FLANNERTY, Martin		22	M	Laborer	17Ju02Kw
CONWAY, Honor		14	F	Spinster	17Ju02Kw
KELLY, John		23	M	Laborer	17Ju02Kw
Edmund		32	M	Laborer	17Ju02Kw
TRAINER, Patrick		25	M	Laborer	17Ju02Kw
James		22	M	Laborer	17Ju02Kw
William		07	M	Child	17Ju02Kw

NAMES OF PASSENGERS		AGE	SEX	OCCUPATIONS	DATE PORT SHIP
TRAINER, Margaret		35	F	Spinster	17Ju02Kw
Sarah		30	F	Spinster	17Ju02Kw
Arthur		34	M	Laborer	17Ju02Kw
FORRESTER, John		33	M	Laborer	17Ju02Kw
U		.00	U	Infant	17Ju02Kw
Cath.		28	F	Spinster	17Ju02Kw
Robert		08	M	Laborer	17Ju02Kw
Mary		03	F	Child	17Ju02Kw
ARCHIBOLD, Alex		33	M	Laborer	17Ju02Kw
Cath.		26	F	Spinster	17Ju02Kw
James		04	M	Child	17Ju02Kw
Alex		02	M	Child	17Ju02Kw
SMITH, Wm.		19	M	Laborer	17Ju02Kw
MCCRADY, John		28	M	Laborer	17Ju02Kw
DUNN, James		22	M	Laborer	17Ju02Kw
NAIL, Bridget		22	F	Spinster	17Ju02Kw
Mary		09	F	Spinster	17Ju02Kw
KIEMAN, Cath.		18	F	Spinster	17Ju02Kw
FLYNN, Bridget		18	F	Spinster	17Ju02Kw
ASHTON, John		23	M	Laborer	17Ju02Kw
CONWAY, Ellen		35	F	Spinster	17Ju02Kw
James		10	M	Laborer	17Ju02Kw
LLOYD, Ellen		17	F	Spinster	17Ju02Kw
LYMAN, John		16	M	Laborer	17Ju02Kw
SWELL, John		38	M	Laborer	17Ju02Kw
Betty		37	F	Spinster	17Ju02Kw
Honora		17	F	Spinster	17Ju02Kw
George		15	M	Laborer	17Ju02Kw
Samuel		13	M	Laborer	17Ju02Kw
John		11	M	Laborer	17Ju02Kw
Sarah		10	F	Spinster	17Ju02Kw
Harriet		08	F	Spinster	17Ju02Kw
Betty		06	F	Child	17Ju02Kw
Jane		02	F	Child	17Ju02Kw
MERGAN, Mary		30	F	Spinster	17Ju02Kw
MCGREAL, Mick		28	M	Laborer	17Ju02Kw
Owen		40	M	Laborer	17Ju02Kw
James		10	M	Laborer	17Ju02Kw
Bridget		08	F	Spinster	17Ju02Kw
Maxwell		06	M	Child	17Ju02Kw
Ann		04	F	Child	17Ju02Kw
TOBIN, Francis		24	M	Laborer	17Ju02Kw
CAMPBELL, John		21	M	Laborer	17Ju02Kw
MURPHY, Mich.		19	M	Laborer	17Ju02Kw
KEERGAN, John		23	M	Laborer	17Ju02Kw
VERDON, Rich		30	M	Laborer	17Ju02Kw
STEWART, Anastasia		42	F	Laborer	17Ju02Kw
BRADY, Mary		22	F	Laborer	17Ju02Kw
DUFFY, Thomas		19	M	Laborer	17Ju02Kw
Mich.		15	M	Laborer	17Ju02Kw
MCMALAN, Marg.		40	F	Spinster	17Ju02Kw
Mich.		18	M	Laborer	17Ju02Kw
Jane		16	F	Spinster	17Ju02Kw
TEAGAN, M.		09	M	Laborer	17Ju02Kw
DEAVY, Mary		17	F	Spinster	17Ju02Kw
CARMAN, Hugh		21	M	Laborer	17Ju02Kw
CAFNEY, Peter		22	M	Laborer	17Ju02Kw
FOGAN, Thomas		24	M	Laborer	17Ju02Kw
John		21	M	Laborer	17Ju02Kw
GAFFNEY, Hugh		20	M	Laborer	17Ju02Kw
MCKEE, Thomas		20	M	Laborer	17Ju02Kw
GALLAGAN, Thomas		20	M	Laborer	17Ju02Kw
LYNCH, Peter		18	M	Laborer	17Ju02Kw
REILLY, Mary		18	F	Spinster	17Ju02Kw
Ann		20	F	Spinster	17Ju02Kw
CARROL, Mary		20	F	Spinster	17Ju02Kw
KEEMAN, Pat.		18	M	Laborer	17Ju02Kw
BROWN, Mark		24	M	Laborer	17Ju02Kw
Henry		20	M	Laborer	17Ju02Kw
GRANT, Jeremiah		27	M	Laborer	17Ju02Kw
U	(W)	25	F	Spinster	17Ju02Kw
Martha		02	F	Child	17Ju02Kw
HUGHES, Edward		24	M	Laborer	17Ju02Kw
MCKENNA, Dennis		12	M	Laborer	17Ju02Kw
Mary		14	F	Spinster	17Ju02Kw

NAMES OF PASSENGERS		AGE	SEX	OCCUPATIONS	DATE PORT SHIP
MARTIN, Wm.		28	M	Laborer	17Ju02Kw
DOYLE, Ann		24	F	Spinster	17Ju02Kw
BYRNES, James		28	M	Laborer	17Ju02Kw
Cath.		20	F	Spinster	17Ju02Kw
Thomas		21	M	Laborer	17Ju02Kw
Patrick		19	M	Laborer	17Ju02Kw
BRICK, Mich.		18	M	Laborer	17Ju02Kw
COLEMAN, John		19	M	Laborer	17Ju02Kw
QUINLAN, John		30	M	Laborer	17Ju02Kw
CARTY, Daniel		23	M	Laborer	17Ju02Kw
MOORE, James		12	M	Laborer	17Ju02Kw
BYRNES, Edmund		01	M	Child	17Ju02Kw
ONEILE, Daniel		26	M	Laborer	17Ju02Kw
SULLIVAN, Margaret		30	F	Spinster	17Ju02Kw
WESH, Bridget		20	F	Spinster	17Ju02Kw
WINES, Martin		20	M	Laborer	17Ju02Kw
CLARY, Elizabeth		20	F	Spinster	17Ju02Kw
CLEARY, Patrick		04	M	Child	17Ju02Kw
TUM, Rich		22	M	Laborer	17Ju02Kw
SULLIVAN, Johanna		30	F	Spinster	17Ju02Kw
RYAN, Edward		30	M	Laborer	17Ju02Kw
Elizabeth		30	F	Spinster	17Ju02Kw
Mich.		04	M	Child	17Ju02Kw
FLANGON, Mich.		38	M	Laborer	17Ju02Kw
MALEY, Mich.		38	M	Laborer	17Ju02Kw
MCKENNA, Marg.		40	F	Spinster	17Ju02Kw
Sarah-A.		05	F	Child	17Ju02Kw
REILLY, Cath.		26	F	Spinster	17Ju02Kw
Mary		02	F	Child	17Ju02Kw
MURPHY, Patrick		26	M	Laborer	17Ju02Kw
MONTON, Rose		30	F	Spinster	17Ju02Kw
Cath.		08	F	Child	17Ju02Kw
Patrick		06	M	Child	17Ju02Kw
CLARK, T.P.		21	M	Laborer	17Ju02Kw
BOYLAN, Mich.		23	M	Laborer	17Ju02Kw
FARRELL, James		30	M	Laborer	17Ju02Kw
Mary		00	F	Spinster	17Ju02Kw
U		.00	U	Infant	17Ju02Kw
Cath.		04	F	Child	17Ju02Kw
FARELLY, James		30	M	Laborer	17Ju02Kw
U	(W)	00	F	Spinster	17Ju02Kw
U		.00	U	Infant	17Ju02Kw
Cath		08	F	Child	17Ju02Kw
George		06	M	Child	17Ju02Kw
Patrick		03	M	Child	17Ju02Kw
SMITH, Hugh		25	M	Laborer	17Ju02Kw
DUDY, Thomas		22	M	Laborer	17Ju02Kw
CUNNINGHAM, Pat		28	M	Laborer	17Ju02Kw
MUNLAGH, Cath.		24	F	Spinster	17Ju02Kw
DONNELLY, Thomas		24	M	Laborer	17Ju02Kw
RYAN, John		40	M	Laborer	17Ju02Kw
GRADY, Math.		27	M	Laborer	17Ju02Kw
Cath		25	F	Spinster	17Ju02Kw
U		.00	U	Infant	17Ju02Kw
Ann	(D)	02	F	Child	17Ju02Kw
FORAN, Maurice		27	M	Laborer	17Ju02Kw
KELLY, Edward		30	M	Laborer	17Ju02Kw
EARLY, Mary		28	F	Spinster	17Ju02Kw
Pat		00	M	Laborer	17Ju02Kw
GORMON, Thomas		20	M	Laborer	17Ju02Kw
BARLOW, James		24	M	Laborer	17Ju02Kw
U	(W)	24	F	Spinster	17Ju02Kw
REILLY, Bridget		16	F	Spinster	17Ju02Kw
MCCREY, U		28	M	Laborer	17Ju02Kw
GASKAYNE, Pat		27	M	Laborer	17Ju02Kw
James		03	M	Child	17Ju02Kw
Dominick		01	M	Child	17Ju02Kw
Mary-Ann		28	F	Spinster	17Ju02Kw
Ann		46	F	Spinster	17Ju02Kw
MCDONNELL, Wm.		46	M	Laborer	17Ju02Kw
REILLY, James		27	M	Laborer	17Ju02Kw
HOLLAND, George		22	M	Laborer	17Ju02Kw
ROSEMAN, John		22	M	Laborer	17Ju02Kw
Betty		26	F	Spinster	17Ju02Kw
NUGENT, Pat		36	M	Laborer	17Ju02Kw

NAMES OF PASSENGERS		AGE	SEX	OCCUPATIONS	DATE PORT SHIP
KELLY, Cath.		20	F	Spinster	17Ju02Kw
HYLAN, John		28	M	Laborer	17Ju02Kw
MCGEE, John		24	M	Laborer	17Ju02Kw
MCINTIRE, William		27	M	Laborer	17Ju02Kw
Daniel		20	M	Laborer	17Ju02Kw
Sarah		11	F	Spinster	17Ju02Kw
MCQUADE, Mich.		20	M	Laborer	17Ju02Kw
SUMMERS, Wm.		30	M	Laborer	17Ju02Kw
ARTHUR, Joseph		20	M	Laborer	17Ju02Kw
CLOHENY, P.		36	M	Laborer	17Ju02Kw
DUFFY, Cath.		28	F	Spinster	17Ju02Kw
GERANY, Cath.		22	F	Spinster	17Ju02Kw
ROONEY, Cath.		22	F	Spinster	17Ju02Kw
BURK, Mich.		18	M	Laborer	17Ju02Kw
FAY, Margaret		20	F	Spinster	17Ju02Kw
RILEY, Christiana		16	F	Spinster	17Ju02Kw
CLANCY, Sarah		20	F	Spinster	17Ju02Kw
BERMAN, John		58	M	Laborer	17Ju02Kw
Jane	(W)	48	F	Spinster	17Ju02Kw
Elizabeth	(D)	27	F	Spinster	17Ju02Kw
Mary-A.		26	F	Spinster	17Ju02Kw
Peter		22	M	Laborer	17Ju02Kw
BANKS, Iabas		22	M	Laborer	17Ju02Kw
Jane		19	F	Spinster	17Ju02Kw
BUCKLY, Johanna		50	F	Spinster	17Ju02Kw
Margaret		04	F	Child	17Ju02Kw
KENALY, Margaret		16	F	None	17Ju02Kw
CONLY, Mary		23	F	Spinster	17Ju02Kw
MCCARTY, C.		25	F	Spinster	17Ju02Kw
U-Mrs.		20	F	Spinster	17Ju02Kw
MULLIGAN, Bridget		50	F	Spinster	17Ju02Kw
Mary		08	F	Child	17Ju02Kw
HARRIS, Joseph		41	M	Laborer	17Ju02Kw
KENT, Mary		40	F	Spinster	17Ju02Kw
RYAN, John		17	M	Laborer	17Ju02Kw
Bridget		18	F	Spinster	17Ju02Kw
GONDAR, Thomas		30	M	Laborer	17Ju02Kw
EVERETT, Mary		20	F	Spinster	17Ju02Kw
KENNEDY, Johanna		26	F	Spinster	17Ju02Kw
MAHER, Johanna		25	F	Spinster	17Ju02Kw
KENAN, Mary		20	F	Spinster	17Ju02Kw
FITZPATRICK, R.		21	M	Laborer	17Ju02Kw
HONLY, Ellen		17	F	Spinster	17Ju02Kw
BARRY, Mary		20	F	Spinster	17Ju02Kw
LEARY, Margaret		18	F	Spinster	17Ju02Kw
ELLIS, M.A.		30	M	Laborer	17Ju02Kw
Mary		06	F	Child	17Ju02Kw
Isabella		04	F	Child	17Ju02Kw
PENDAR, Winny		15	F	Spinster	17Ju02Kw
Owen		15	M	Laborer	17Ju02Kw
BAAM, Mich.		20	M	Laborer	17Ju02Kw
MCMANUS, Rose		20	F	Spinster	17Ju02Kw
PEARRY, Margaret		24	F	Spinster	17Ju02Kw
BROOKS, John		36	M	Laborer	17Ju02Kw
Mary		30	F	Spinster	17Ju02Kw
HARRINGTON, Bridget		20	F	Spinster	17Ju02Kw
Ann		20	F	Spinster	17Ju02Kw
Mary		18	F	Spinster	17Ju02Kw
LEARY, James		07	M	Child	17Ju02Kw
Mary		05	F	Child	17Ju02Kw
Ellen		03	F	Child	17Ju02Kw
CASSIDY, Pat		30	M	Laborer	17Ju02Kw
HILL, Mich.		25	M	Laborer	17Ju02Kw
WILSON, James		40	M	Laborer	17Ju02Kw
U	(W)	30	F	Spinster	17Ju02Kw
Emma		09	F	Child	17Ju02Kw
John		07	M	Child	17Ju02Kw
MOORE, Phillip		30	M	Laborer	17Ju02Kw
William		09	M	Child	17Ju02Kw
Mary		30	F	Spinster	17Ju02Kw

ARGYLE 17 JUNE 1848

From Cork

NAMES OF PASSENGERS	AGE	SEX	OCCUPATIONS	DATE PORT SHIP
KELCHER, Edward	49	M	Farmer	17Ju14Kx
Ellen	40	F	Spinster	17Ju14Kx
Margaret	17	F	Spinster	17Ju14Kx
James	08	M	None	17Ju14Kx
SULLIVAN, Alexander	50	M	Farmer	17Ju14Kx
LAMASNEY, Thomas	24	M	Farmer	17Ju14Kx
MORRISSY, Michael	18	M	Farmer	17Ju14Kx
Margaret	28	F	Spinster	17Ju14Kx
Ellen	19	F	Spinster	17Ju14Kx
KEIFFE, Cornelius	30	M	Farmer	17Ju14Kx
Daniel	26	M	Farmer	17Ju14Kx
Hannah	30	F	Spinster	17Ju14Kx
BEALYS, Francis	34	M	Laborer	17Ju14Kx
MORGAN, Ellen	22	F	Spinster	17Ju14Kx
DUGGAN, Daniel	26	M	Farmer	17Ju14Kx
Johannah	24	F	Spinster	17Ju14Kx
Charles	18	M	Laborer	17Ju14Kx
DONEGHEN, Johannah	20	F	Spinster	17Ju14Kx
ARCHDEACON, Johannah	22	F	Spinster	17Ju14Kx
RAY, Mathew	35	M	Farmer	17Ju14Kx
SULLIVAN, Ellen	30	F	Spinster	17Ju14Kx
Catherine	04	F	Child	17Ju14Kx
HELEN, Robert	55	M	Farmer	17Ju14Kx
Elizabeth	50	F	Spinster	17Ju14Kx
Roger	18	M	Farmer	17Ju14Kx
Robert	13	M	Farmer	17Ju14Kx
Isabella	10	F	Spinster	17Ju14Kx
Joseph	07	M	None	17Ju14Kx
TOOMEY, Michael	21	M	Laborer	17Ju14Kx
SULLIVAN, Daniel	12	M	Laborer	17Ju14Kx
DWYER, Mathew	13	M	Laborer	17Ju14Kx
Ellen	20	F	Spinster	17Ju14Kx
Mathew	50	M	Farmer	17Ju14Kx
Bridget	22	F	Spinster	17Ju14Kx
BAITEN, Thomas	30	M	Farmer	17Ju14Kx
KEANE, Michael	22	M	Farmer	17Ju14Kx
BAITEN, Mary	30	F	Spinster	17Ju14Kx
Mary	.08	F	Infant	17Ju14Kx
MORIATY, Ellen	22	F	Spinster	17Ju14Kx
DRISCOLL, Jeremiah	23	M	Laborer	17Ju14Kx
GAHEGAN, James	26	M	Laborer	17Ju14Kx
BATEMAN, Jeremiah	28	M	Laborer	17Ju14Kx
GANNAN, Jeremiah	30	M	Laborer	17Ju14Kx
GEAR, Richard	38	M	Laborer	17Ju14Kx
Margaret	36	F	Spinster	17Ju14Kx
Richard	09	M	None	17Ju14Kx
Morris	05	M	None	17Ju14Kx
Catherine	04	F	None	17Ju14Kx
Johannah	02	F	None	17Ju14Kx
BOUCK, Mary	26	F	Spinster	17Ju14Kx
CONNELL, William	20	M	Farmer	17Ju14Kx
REGAN, Honorah	30	F	Spinster	17Ju14Kx
FERNILLS, William	40	M	Laborer	17Ju14Kx
MCCARTHY, Jeremiah	25	M	Laborer	17Ju14Kx
Edmond	25	M	Laborer	17Ju14Kx
HICKEY, David	25	M	Laborer	17Ju14Kx
BUCKLEY, John	30	M	Farmer	17Ju14Kx
DEMPSEY, Michael	27	M	Farmer	17Ju14Kx
Margaret	23	F	Spinster	17Ju14Kx
KEITY, Daniel	46	M	Laborer	17Ju14Kx
Catherine	45	F	Spinster	17Ju14Kx
Ellen	08	F	Child	17Ju14Kx
Nancy	16	F	Spinster	17Ju14Kx
Catherine	11	F	None	17Ju14Kx
Margaret	05	F	None	17Ju14Kx

NAMES OF PASSENGERS	AGE	SEX	OCCUPATIONS	DATE PORT SHIP
KEITY, Daniel	03	M	None	17Ju14Kx
ENGLISH, Lawrence	20	M	Farmer	17Ju14Kx
Thomas	18	M	Farmer	17Ju14Kx
OBRIEN, Michael	35	M	Farmer	17Ju14Kx
RURDEN, John	20	M	Farmer	17Ju14Kx
LEAHY, Thomas	35	M	Farmer	17Ju14Kx
SPELECY, Andrew	26	M	Farmer	17Ju14Kx
MOONY, John	30	M	Laborer	17Ju14Kx
DELLIN, James	30	M	Laborer	17Ju14Kx
Catherine	28	F	Spinster	17Ju14Kx
Hannah	07	F	Child	17Ju14Kx
Thomas	05	M	None	17Ju14Kx
Mary	03	F	None	17Ju14Kx
HEGARTY, Annie	60	F	Spinster	17Ju14Kx
MURPHY, William	20	M	Laborer	17Ju14Kx
Ellen	22	F	Spinster	17Ju14Kx
LEAHY, Thomas	20	M	Farmer	17Ju14Kx
Michael	18	M	Farmer	17Ju14Kx
Fanny	16	F	Spinster	17Ju14Kx
Johannah	15	F	Spinster	17Ju14Kx
Mathew	05	M	None	17Ju14Kx
John	16	M	Farmer	17Ju14Kx
COTTRELL, James	20	M	Farmer	17Ju14Kx
Anne	18	F	Spinster	17Ju14Kx
SARSFIELD, Jeremiah	24	M	Laborer	17Ju14Kx
CASEY, Michael	22	M	Laborer	17Ju14Kx
Abby	20	F	Spinster	17Ju14Kx
MACKEY, William	17	M	Farmer	17Ju14Kx
COLLINS, Catherine	20	F	Spinster	17Ju14Kx
MCCARTHY, Charles	27	M	Farmer	17Ju14Kx
Margaret	27	F	Spinster	17Ju14Kx
SULLIVAN, David	48	M	Farmer	17Ju14Kx
Catherine	38	F	Spinster	17Ju14Kx
Ellen	08	F	None	17Ju14Kx
Eliza	11	F	None	17Ju14Kx
Thomas	04	M	None	17Ju14Kx
David	60	M	Farmer	17Ju14Kx
SPILLANE, Michael	23	M	Laborer	17Ju14Kx
GARVON, Michael	25	M	Laborer	17Ju14Kx
HENNELSY, Richard	26	M	Laborer	17Ju14Kx
DUGGAN, Daniel	27	M	Laborer	17Ju14Kx
CORMELL, David	25	M	Laborer	17Ju14Kx
DUGGAN, Ellen	24	F	Spinster	17Ju14Kx
TOOMEY, Mary	36	F	Spinster	17Ju14Kx
DUGGAN, John	.04	M	Infant	17Ju14Kx
HURLEY, Ellen	13	F	Spinster	17Ju14Kx
WINTER, John	20	M	Laborer	17Ju14Kx
PARKER, James	30	M	Laborer	17Ju14Kx
MALONE, Morris	20	M	Laborer	17Ju14Kx
WALSH, Margaret	20	F	Spinster	17Ju14Kx
BARRETT, James	18	M	Farmer	17Ju14Kx
CORMERS, Cornelius	27	M	Farmer	17Ju14Kx
Ellen	19	F	Spinster	17Ju14Kx
SEXTON, Mary	19	F	Spinster	17Ju14Kx
SCULLY, Dennis	20	M	Laborer	17Ju14Kx
MORRISSON, Joseph	22	M	Laborer	17Ju14Kx
GEARY, John	35	M	Laborer	17Ju14Kx
WHOLOHEN, Michael	20	M	Laborer	17Ju14Kx
Ellen	10	F	Spinster	17Ju14Kx
KENNEDY, Catherine	40	F	Spinster	17Ju14Kx
Peggy	05	F	Child	17Ju14Kx
CONNORS, Bridget	20	F	Spinster	17Ju14Kx
CASHEN, Patrick	35	M	Laborer	17Ju14Kx
Margaret	30	F	Spinster	17Ju14Kx
Hannah	06	F	Child	17Ju14Kx
Edmond	05	M	None	17Ju14Kx
Patrick	03	M	None	17Ju14Kx
Garret	01	M	None	17Ju14Kx
MAHONY, Patrick	40	M	Farmer	17Ju14Kx
SHEA, James	20	M	Farmer	17Ju14Kx
Mary	25	F	Spinster	17Ju14Kx
BARRETT, Margaret	24	F	Spinster	17Ju14Kx
OBRIEN, Michael	21	M	Laborer	17Ju14Kx
CREWLY, Catherine	25	F	Spinster	17Ju14Kx
JOHNSON, William	24	M	Laborer	17Ju14Kx
DOWLING, Patrick	28	M	Laborer	17Ju14Kx
Catherine	20	F	Spinster	17Ju14Kx
GILLEY, Michael	40	M	Farmer	17Ju14Kx
BARRY, Patrick	40	M	Farmer	17Ju14Kx
FLYNN, Timothy	50	M	Laborer	17Ju14Kx
Daniel	24	M	Laborer	17Ju14Kx
Mary	55	F	Spinster	17Ju14Kx
Catherine	16	F	Spinster	17Ju14Kx
Mary	12	F	Spinster	17Ju14Kx
Ellen	24	F	Spinster	17Ju14Kx
WALSH, Honora	23	F	Spinster	17Ju14Kx
HENRIGHT, Augustus	22	M	Farmer	17Ju14Kx
BARRY, Patrick	23	M	Farmer	17Ju14Kx
RYAN, William	40	M	Laborer	17Ju14Kx
John	10	M	Laborer	17Ju14Kx
William	07	M	Child	17Ju14Kx
KEHEY, Patrick	19	M	Laborer	17Ju14Kx
HAYES, Edmond	18	M	Laborer	17Ju14Kx
KEHEY, Mary	20	F	Spinster	17Ju14Kx
WALSH, Bridget	20	F	Spinster	17Ju14Kx
SHEEHAN, Ellen	20	F	Spinster	17Ju14Kx
MURPHY, Catharine	20	F	Spinster	17Ju14Kx
HEDGER, Bartholomew	30	M	Farmer	17Ju14Kx
PENDERGAST, John	45	M	Farmer	17Ju14Kx
DUANE, Ellen	45	F	Spinster	17Ju14Kx
PENDERGAST, Catherine	12	F	Spinster	17Ju14Kx
James	10	M	None	17Ju14Kx
Ellen	08	F	None	17Ju14Kx
Mary	07	F	None	17Ju14Kx
John	04	M	None	17Ju14Kx
WALLIS, Anzty	24	F	Spinster	17Ju14Kx
ROCHE, James	25	M	Farmer	17Ju14Kx
WALLIS, Betty	26	F	Spinster	17Ju14Kx
Mary	25	F	Spinster	17Ju14Kx
U	.00	U	Infant	17Ju14Kx
BOULER, Michael	35	M	Farmer	17Ju14Kx
John	30	M	Farmer	17Ju14Kx
Johanna	28	F	Spinster	17Ju14Kx
Ellen	22	F	Spinster	17Ju14Kx
Ellen	21	F	Spinster	17Ju14Kx
MURPHY, John	25	M	Laborer	17Ju14Kx
SHIEL, Catherine	19	F	Spinster	17Ju14Kx
LEE, Simon	35	M	Farmer	17Ju14Kx
Mary	28	F	Spinster	17Ju14Kx
POWER, John	24	M	Farmer	17Ju14Kx
Anthony	20	M	Farmer	17Ju14Kx
Margaret	22	F	Spinster	17Ju14Kx
TRENDAWAY, Honora	20	F	Spinster	17Ju14Kx
CONSHEY, Terry	16	M	Laborer	17Ju14Kx
RYAN, Julia	23	F	Spinster	17Ju14Kx
Dennis	18	M	Farmer	17Ju14Kx
Mary	50	F	Spinster	17Ju14Kx
Sally	18	F	Spinster	17Ju14Kx
HEROLD, Margaret	25	F	Spinster	17Ju14Kx
CARNEY, John	26	M	Laborer	17Ju14Kx
BOLAND, James	20	M	Laborer	17Ju14Kx
HALY, John	28	M	Laborer	17Ju14Kx
MOORONEY, John	25	M	Laborer	17Ju14Kx
Daniel	04	M	None	17Ju14Kx
Mary	12	F	None	17Ju14Kx
Thomas	.00	M	Infant	17Ju14Kx
DOREGAN, Batholomew	20	M	Farmer	17Ju14Kx
FLAHERTY, Mary	27	F	Spinster	17Ju14Kx
DALY, John	25	M	Laborer	17Ju14Kx
CROWLY, Mary	20	F	Spinster	17Ju14Kx
BARRETT, Margaret	23	F	Spinster	17Ju14Kx
Matt	04	M	None	17Ju14Kx
Leonard	05	M	None	17Ju14Kx
GLORA, James	29	M	Farmer	17Ju14Kx
HALY, Margaret	25	F	Spinster	17Ju14Kx
HENEBRY, William	23	M	Farmer	17Ju14Kx
Henry	20	M	Farmer	17Ju14Kx
Bess	18	F	Spinster	17Ju14Kx
David	50	M	Farmer	17Ju14Kx
Francis	21	M	Farmer	17Ju14Kx

NAMES OF PASSENGERS	AGE	SEX	OCCUPATIONS	DATE PORT SHIP
HENEBRY, Thomas	19	M	Farmer	17Ju14Kx
David	12	M	Farmer	17Ju14Kx
James	12	M	Farmer	17Ju14Kx
Bess	10	F	Spinster	17Ju14Kx
Michael	09	M	None	17Ju14Kx
Patt	08	M	None	17Ju14Kx
Bridget	06	F	None	17Ju14Kx
Garrett	04	M	None	17Ju14Kx
Jane	44	F	Spinster	17Ju14Kx
John	06	M	None	17Ju14Kx
William	23	M	Farmer	17Ju14Kx
John	20	M	Farmer	17Ju14Kx
James	30	M	Farmer	17Ju14Kx
Ellen	25	F	Spinster	17Ju14Kx
Michael	.00	M	Infant	17Ju14Kx
Thomas	02	M	None	17Ju14Kx
Bridget	04	F	None	17Ju14Kx
KENNEY, John	22	M	Laborer	17Ju14Kx
BYRON, Michael	30	M	Laborer	17Ju14Kx
Bridget	30	F	Spinster	17Ju14Kx
James	04	M	None	17Ju14Kx
Thomas	06	M	None	17Ju14Kx
Mary	08	F	None	17Ju14Kx
DONAPHAE, Joh.	28	M	Laborer	17Ju14Kx
BARRETS, John	35	M	Farmer	17Ju14Kx
Ellen (D)	06	F	Farmer	17Ju14Kx
BROPHY, John	28	M	Laborer	17Ju14Kx
KEIFFE, Elizabeth Died-At-Sea	.00	F	Infant	17Ju14Kx
WALSH, Margaret Died-At-Sea	03	F	None	17Ju14Kx

WIDGEON 19 JUNE 1848

From Nassau

NAMES OF PASSENGERS	AGE	SEX	OCCUPATIONS	DATE PORT SHIP
WARD, Rebecca	21	F	Milliner	19Ju93Lf

CHIEFTAIN 20 JUNE 1848

From Cork

NAMES OF PASSENGERS	AGE	SEX	OCCUPATIONS	DATE PORT SHIP
GARRETT, Francis	23	M	Farmer	20Ju14Wf
ORR, Richard	18	M	Farmer	20Ju14Wf
REIDY, Pat	30	M	Farmer	20Ju14Wf
KANE, Simon	30	M	Farmer	20Ju14Wf
FLYNN, Thomas	26	M	Farmer	20Ju14Wf
WHITE, Wm.	23	M	Farmer	20Ju14Wf
SHANAHAN, Hannah	48	F	Spinster	20Ju14Wf
BENNETT, Wm.	19	M	Farmer	20Ju14Wf
CONWAY, Johanna	20	F	Unknown	20Ju14Wf
FITZGERALD, Johanna	20	F	Unknown	20Ju14Wf
MAHONY, Margaret	20	F	Spinster	20Ju14Wf
CONNOR, Jerry	22	M	Laborer	20Ju14Wf
MURPHY, Tim	26	M	Laborer	20Ju14Wf
LEARY, John	09	M	Child	20Ju14Wf
CONNOR, Morte	12	M	Unknown	20Ju14Wf
Morte	60	M	Unknown	20Ju14Wf
MOLONY, Wm.	23	M	Laborer	20Ju14Wf
Maria	21	F	Laborer	20Ju14Wf
MURPHY, Margt.	20	F	Laborer	20Ju14Wf
HEGARTY, Denis	20	M	Laborer	20Ju14Wf
WALSH, Cath.	22	F	Laborer	20Ju14Wf
FLANAGAN, John	40	M	Laborer	20Ju14Wf
Cath.	36	F	Laborer	20Ju14Wf
Ellen	18	F	Laborer	20Ju14Wf
Pat	16	M	Laborer	20Ju14Wf
Catherine	13	F	Laborer	20Ju14Wf
Michael	03	M	Child	20Ju14Wf
John	.00	M	Infant	20Ju14Wf
HOCK, Edmond	24	M	Laborer	20Ju14Wf
CONNORS, Edmond	28	M	Laborer	20Ju14Wf
CONNON, Richard	28	M	Laborer	20Ju14Wf
MCENERY, Cath.	26	F	Laborer	20Ju14Wf
RIORDAN, Pat	30	M	Laborer	20Ju14Wf
BUTTINER, Andrew	40	M	Laborer	20Ju14Wf
John	20	M	Laborer	20Ju14Wf
Mary	30	F	Laborer	20Ju14Wf
Ellen	19	F	Laborer	20Ju14Wf
CHAMBERS, Richard	20	M	Laborer	20Ju14Wf
MAHONEY, John	40	M	Laborer	20Ju14Wf
CULLANANE, Julia	50	F	Laborer	20Ju14Wf
MARKS, Honor	25	F	Laborer	20Ju14Wf
DONNELL, Cath.	19	F	Laborer	20Ju14Wf
BURK, Michael	23	M	Laborer	20Ju14Wf
Thomas	19	M	Laborer	20Ju14Wf
DELANY, James	19	M	Laborer	20Ju14Wf
BUCKLY, Denis	24	M	Laborer	20Ju14Wf
KENNY, Jeremiah	40	M	Laborer	20Ju14Wf
KANE, Maurice	30	M	Laborer	20Ju14Wf
FLYNN, Thomas	40	M	Laborer	20Ju14Wf
QUILLAN, Bridget	40	F	Laborer	20Ju14Wf
KIELLY, Edmond	35	M	Laborer	20Ju14Wf
Thomas	30	M	Laborer	20Ju14Wf
GIFFIN, John	16	M	Laborer	20Ju14Wf
KEILY, John	13	M	Laborer	20Ju14Wf
SHEEDY, Mary	24	F	Farmer	20Ju14Wf
KENNY, Danial	20	M	Unknown	20Ju14Wf
HERBETT, Mainice	20	U	Unknown	20Ju14Wf
FITTON, Thomas	36	M	Unknown	20Ju14Wf
John	20	M	Unknown	20Ju14Wf
Biddy	21	F	Unknown	20Ju14Wf
Hannah	04	F	Child	20Ju14Wf
Ally	02	U	Child	20Ju14Wf
Bridget	.00	F	Infant	20Ju14Wf
ONEILL, John	40	M	Unknown	20Ju14Wf
SHARMON, Mathias	21	M	Unknown	20Ju14Wf
WALSH, Mannie	27	U	Unknown	20Ju14Wf
David	21	M	Unknown	20Ju14Wf
RYAN, William	18	M	Unknown	20Ju14Wf
TUOMEY, Con.	12	M	Unknown	20Ju14Wf
COGHLAN, Matthew	35	M	Unknown	20Ju14Wf
COLLINS, John	30	M	Unknown	20Ju14Wf
MAHONY, Patt	28	M	Unknown	20Ju14Wf
Mary	25	F	Unknown	20Ju14Wf
CORKERAN, James	21	M	Unknown	20Ju14Wf
FANELL, John	30	M	Unknown	20Ju14Wf
Cath.	28	F	Unknown	20Ju14Wf
COAKLEY, Mary	24	F	Unknown	20Ju14Wf
CLEARY, Martin	40	M	Unknown	20Ju14Wf
RYAN, Patt	30	M	Unknown	20Ju14Wf
FANELE, Maurice	21	M	Unknown	20Ju14Wf
OBRIEN, John	47	M	Unknown	20Ju14Wf
REA, Thomas	30	M	Unknown	20Ju14Wf
WALSH, Julia	20	F	Unknown	20Ju14Wf
Mary	18	F	Unknown	20Ju14Wf
HEAFFY, Frank	20	M	Unknown	20Ju14Wf
Cath.	18	F	Unknown	20Ju14Wf
MURPHY, Mary	25	F	Unknown	20Ju14Wf
WALE, Frank	20	M	Unknown	20Ju14Wf
WILLETT, Mary	18	F	Unknown	20Ju14Wf
OBRIEN, Thomas	40	M	Unknown	20Ju14Wf
BEGLEY, James	20	M	Unknown	20Ju14Wf
Ellen	20	F	Unknown	20Ju14Wf
HENNESSEY, Maurice	21	M	Unknown	20Ju14Wf
HUMPHREYS, Jane	27	F	Unknown	20Ju14Wf
MAHONY, John	25	M	Unknown	20Ju14Wf
MADIGAN, Edward	18	M	Unknown	20Ju14Wf

NAMES OF PASSENGERS	AGE	SEX	OCCUPATIONS	DATE PORT SHIP
COLLINS, Martha	30	F	Unknown	20Ju14Wf
MAHONY, Johanna	27	F	Unknown	20Ju14Wf
ATKINS, Alice	24	F	Unknown	20Ju14Wf
KEAN, Catherine	24	F	Unknown	20Ju14Wf
VALE, Cath.	40	F	Unknown	20Ju14Wf
KEAN, Margaret	02	F	Child	20Ju14Wf
John	.00	M	Infant	20Ju14Wf
Mary	25	F	Farmer	20Ju14Wf
GROVES, Margt.	19	F	Farmer	20Ju14Wf
TOBIN, Mary	20	F	Farmer	20Ju14Wf
MURRAY, Ellen	20	F	Farmer	20Ju14Wf
ODONOVAN, Jerry	26	M	Farmer	20Ju14Wf
Mary	20	F	Farmer	20Ju14Wf
BUCKLEY, Lawrence	32	M	Farmer	20Ju14Wf
Ellen	25	F	Farmer	20Ju14Wf
SULLIVAN, Mary	21	F	Farmer	20Ju14Wf
RIORDON, Johanna	22	F	Farmer	20Ju14Wf
BURCHILL, George	35	M	Farmer	20Ju14Wf
Marty	30	M	Farmer	20Ju14Wf
Math.	16	M	Farmer	20Ju14Wf
Leah	45	F	Farmer	20Ju14Wf
Mary	35	F	Farmer	20Ju14Wf
KNIGHT, Thomas	30	M	Farmer	20Ju14Wf
Ellen	25	F	Farmer	20Ju14Wf
Mary	21	F	Farmer	20Ju14Wf
BURN, Ann	25	F	Farmer	20Ju14Wf
MALONY, Pat	20	M	Farmer	20Ju14Wf
MURPHY, Jerry	26	M	Farmer	20Ju14Wf
RYAN, Thomas	24	M	Farmer	20Ju14Wf
SMITH, Bridget	26	F	Farmer	20Ju14Wf
Ellen	24	F	Farmer	20Ju14Wf
MAHONY, Margt.	24	F	Farmer	20Ju14Wf
KELCHER, Con.	24	M	Farmer	20Ju14Wf
BARRY, Wm.	30	M	Farmer	20Ju14Wf
KELCHER, Eleanor	60	F	Farmer	20Ju14Wf
DOWNEY, Abby	20	F	Farmer	20Ju14Wf
MANNIN, Mary	24	F	Farmer	20Ju14Wf
FLYNN, Ann	18	F	Farmer	20Ju14Wf
John	13	M	Farmer	20Ju14Wf
BEAMISH, Sarah	22	F	Farmer	20Ju14Wf
OKEEFE, Con.	21	M	Farmer	20Ju14Wf
BARRY, John	26	M	Farmer	20Ju14Wf
WALSH, Ellen	20	F	Farmer	20Ju14Wf
DONGAN, John	25	M	Farmer	20Ju14Wf
COLLINS, Elisa	20	F	Farmer	20Ju14Wf
FLENNING, Sarah	30	F	Farmer	20Ju14Wf
Elisa	24	F	Farmer	20Ju14Wf
ALSPIN, Michael	20	M	Farmer	20Ju14Wf
NESH, Ellen	20	F	Farmer	20Ju14Wf
TWOHIG, John	22	M	Farmer	20Ju14Wf
BUCKLEY, Mary	20	F	Farmer	20Ju14Wf
MCNAMARA, David	24	M	Farmer	20Ju14Wf
Cath.	21	F	Farmer	20Ju14Wf
GALLAGHER, Cath.	26	F	Farmer	20Ju14Wf
SHORT, John	26	M	Farmer	20Ju14Wf
GALLAGHER, Daniel	30	M	Farmer	20Ju14Wf
MCGRATH, Thos.	18	M	Farmer	20Ju14Wf
EGAN, Patt	30	M	Farmer	20Ju14Wf
MANNING, John	30	M	Farmer	20Ju14Wf
BARRY, Honora	18	F	Farmer	20Ju14Wf
Ellen	05	F	Child	20Ju14Wf
Ellen	50	F	Unknown	20Ju14Wf
BARREY, Margt.	12	F	Unknown	20Ju14Wf
Ellen	11	F	Unknown	20Ju14Wf
FLANNERY, Francis	45	M	Unknown	20Ju14Wf
LOVETT, Richd.	25	M	Unknown	20Ju14Wf
Thos.	26	M	Unknown	20Ju14Wf
Patk.	07	M	Child	20Ju14Wf
DALEY, Michael	19	M	Unknown	20Ju14Wf
WALSH, John	19	M	Unknown	20Ju14Wf
DALLY, Ann	16	F	Unknown	20Ju14Wf
OSULLIVAN, John	25	M	Unknown	20Ju14Wf
KINCAID, Thos.	24	M	Unknown	20Ju14Wf
RIELEY, Mannie	30	M	Unknown	20Ju14Wf
Edmund	28	M	Unknown	20Ju14Wf
RIELEY, Matthew	29	M	Unknown	20Ju14Wf
AHEM, Wm.	30	M	Unknown	20Ju14Wf
MYLES, Wm.	10	M	Unknown	20Ju14Wf
Bridget	09	F	Child	20Ju14Wf
Michl.	08	M	Child	20Ju14Wf
KEAYS, Jerry	56	M	Unknown	20Ju14Wf
Margt.	16	F	Unknown	20Ju14Wf
Cath.	20	F	Unknown	20Ju14Wf
Jerry	12	M	Unknown	20Ju14Wf
BUCKLEY, James	26	M	Unknown	20Ju14Wf
WALSH, Honora	15	F	Unknown	20Ju14Wf
ISEHEY, Edwd.	30	M	Unknown	20Ju14Wf
Ellen	30	F	Unknown	20Ju14Wf
FORE, Margt.	35	F	Unknown	20Ju14Wf
Nancy	25	F	Unknown	20Ju14Wf
ISEHEY, John	07	M	Child	20Ju14Wf
Edwd.	05	M	Child	20Ju14Wf
Mary	04	F	Child	20Ju14Wf
RYAN, John	30	M	Unknown	20Ju14Wf
Honorah	25	F	Unknown	20Ju14Wf
Matthew	.00	M	Infant	20Ju14Wf
MCENERREY, James	25	M	Unknown	20Ju14Wf
Hannah	30	F	Unknown	20Ju14Wf
Mary	.00	F	Infant	20Ju14Wf
OBRIEN, Daniel	23	M	Unknown	20Ju14Wf
Margt.	21	F	Unknown	20Ju14Wf
CALLAGHAN, Jas.	30	M	Unknown	20Ju14Wf
HALY, John	25	M	Unknown	20Ju14Wf
LYNCH, Timothy	27	M	Unknown	20Ju14Wf
Mary	60	F	Unknown	20Ju14Wf
BROSNAHAN, Hugh	20	M	Unknown	20Ju14Wf
BRUME, Bridgit	35	F	Unknown	20Ju14Wf
FOHRAN, Bridgit	12	F	Unknown	20Ju14Wf
Kate	06	F	Child	20Ju14Wf
Mary	04	F	Child	20Ju14Wf
Bridget	.00	F	Infant	20Ju14Wf
CORBETT, Alex.	23	M	Unknown	20Ju14Wf
MOONEY, John	21	M	Unknown	20Ju14Wf
CONNELL, Mary	30	F	Unknown	20Ju14Wf
Cath.	17	F	Unknown	20Ju14Wf
REDWICK, John	25	M	Unknown	20Ju14Wf
Ann	23	F	Unknown	20Ju14Wf
Jane	23	F	Unknown	20Ju14Wf
Julia	.00	F	Infant	20Ju14Wf
KEEFE, James	26	M	Unknown	20Ju14Wf
MCCARTHY, Dennis	24	M	Unknown	20Ju14Wf
Thos.	20	M	Unknown	20Ju14Wf
Johanna	23	F	Unknown	20Ju14Wf
OKEEFE, Jeremiah	30	M	Unknown	20Ju14Wf
MAHONY, Ellen	32	F	Unknown	20Ju14Wf
BUCKLEY, Dan	26	M	Unknown	20Ju14Wf
Timothy	18	M	Unknown	20Ju14Wf
DORE, Jas.	30	M	Unknown	20Ju14Wf
Laurence	26	M	Unknown	20Ju14Wf
CORBETT, Patt	30	M	Unknown	20Ju14Wf
LYONS, Mary	40	F	Unknown	20Ju14Wf
Johanna	06	F	Child	20Ju14Wf
HALLANAN, Mary	23	F	Unknown	20Ju14Wf
Julia	20	F	Unknown	20Ju14Wf
COTTER, Cath.	30	F	Unknown	20Ju14Wf
DOYLE, Edmund	25	M	Unknown	20Ju14Wf
HARRIS, Thos.	21	M	Unknown	20Ju14Wf
CONNELL, Richd.	24	M	Unknown	20Ju14Wf
DALY, Pat	30	M	Unknown	20Ju14Wf
Norry	22	F	Unknown	20Ju14Wf
GALLANAN, James	22	M	Unknown	20Ju14Wf
MULEHILL, Pat	30	M	Unknown	20Ju14Wf
COLTHURST, Ann	19	F	Unknown	20Ju14Wf
RYAN, James	25	M	Unknown	20Ju14Wf
Honorah	25	F	Unknown	20Ju14Wf
SULLIVAN, Dennis	25	M	Unknown	20Ju14Wf
Ellen	23	F	Unknown	20Ju14Wf
CURTIN, Patt	28	M	Unknown	20Ju14Wf
Ellen	28	F	Unknown	20Ju14Wf
MULLANE, John	30	M	Unknown	20Ju14Wf

NAMES OF PASSENGERS	AGE	SEX	OCCUPATIONS	DATE PORT SHIP
BLEWITT, John	24	M	Unknown	20Ju14Wf
Margt.	02	F	Child	20Ju14Wf
FLEMING, Honora	20	F	Unknown	20Ju14Wf
LYNCH, Thomas	30	M	Unknown	20Ju14Wf
JOHNSON, Patt	19	M	Unknown	20Ju14Wf
DILWORTH, Michl.	45	M	Unknown	20Ju14Wf
REILY, Fanny	40	F	Unknown	20Ju14Wf
SULLIVAN, Mannie	32	M	Unknown	20Ju14Wf

REPUBLIC 20 JUNE 1848

From Liverpool

NAMES OF PASSENGERS	AGE	SEX	OCCUPATIONS	DATE PORT SHIP
MANNS, Hugh	12	M	Laborer	20Ju02Nv
Elizabeth	10	F	None	20Ju02Nv
Mary	04	F	None	20Ju02Nv
Anna	.00	F	Infant	20Ju02Nv
GRAHAM, Felix	19	M	Laborer	20Ju02Nv
DUFFY, Catherine	20	F	None	20Ju02Nv
MAHN, Bridget	28	F	None	20Ju02Nv
BURKE, Catherine	19	F	None	20Ju02Nv
DOWLING, Saville	28	M	Mechanic	20Ju02Nv
Mary	36	F	None	20Ju02Nv
FLETCHER, Mary	21	F	None	20Ju02Nv
LITTLE, U	16	F	None	20Ju02Nv
CAFFREY, Mary	14	F	None	20Ju02Nv
John	12	M	None	20Ju02Nv
MCCABE, Ann	10	F	None	20Ju02Nv
LONGHRAN, Mary	20	F	None	20Ju02Nv
HASPEY, Daniel	18	M	Laborer	20Ju02Nv
HANANS, Bridget	19	F	None	20Ju02Nv
SHEPHARD, William	19	M	Mechanic	20Ju02Nv
FEEHAN, Eliza	26	F	None	20Ju02Nv
GRIMLEY, John	26	M	Laborer	20Ju02Nv
Mary	21	F	None	20Ju02Nv
MAHONEY, James	23	M	Laborer	20Ju02Nv
Jane	18	F	None	20Ju02Nv
GRIMLEY, Peter	21	M	Laborer	20Ju02Nv
ENNIS, John	20	M	Laborer	20Ju02Nv
MCGANN, Catherine	20	F	None	20Ju02Nv
WALSH, James	37	M	Laborer	20Ju02Nv
Jane	30	F	Unknown	20Ju02Nv
Mary	13	F	None	20Ju02Nv
Michael	10	M	None	20Ju02Nv
Thomas	08	M	None	20Ju02Nv
William	06	M	None	20Ju02Nv
CAMPION, James	32	M	Laborer	20Ju02Nv
MARTIN, John	19	M	Laborer	20Ju02Nv
Mary	17	F	None	20Ju02Nv
LARKIN, John	23	M	Mechanic	20Ju02Nv
MURPHY, Maria	19	F	None	20Ju02Nv
LEE, Anastatia	19	F	None	20Ju02Nv
LITTLE, Alexander	18	M	Mechanic	20Ju02Nv
SMITH, William	39	M	Mechanic	20Ju02Nv
MORRIS, John	20	M	Laborer	20Ju02Nv
SHEA, John	27	M	Laborer	20Ju02Nv
Ellen	22	F	None	20Ju02Nv
HEALY, Mary	21	F	None	20Ju02Nv
NOWLAN, John	28	M	None	20Ju02Nv
HODSON, U	20	F	None	20Ju02Nv
PLUNKETT, U	20	F	None	20Ju02Nv
CONNOLLY, Catherine	18	F	None	20Ju02Nv
GOGARTHY, Ann	20	F	None	20Ju02Nv
HOGAN, Michael	18	M	None	20Ju02Nv
MCEVANS, Morris	22	M	None	20Ju02Nv
ROACH, Thomas	21	M	Mechanic	20Ju02Nv
CAMPBELL, Jane	20	F	None	20Ju02Nv
CLARKE, Thomas	36	M	Mechanic	20Ju02Nv
MOORE, William	37	M	Mechanic	20Ju02Nv
SMITH, Honora	30	F	None	20Ju02Nv
Thomas	11	M	None	20Ju02Nv
Patrick	09	M	None	20Ju02Nv
MCGEE, James	40	M	Laborer	20Ju02Nv
Jane	30	F	None	20Ju02Nv
NEAL, Patrick	40	M	Laborer	20Ju02Nv
Eleanor	19	F	None	20Ju02Nv
Rose	16	F	None	20Ju02Nv
HORNDEL, James	26	M	Mechanic	20Ju02Nv
Phoeby	12	F	None	20Ju02Nv
KEIRMAN, Agnes	25	F	None	20Ju02Nv
MCMANNS, U	48	F	None	20Ju02Nv
BURTON, U	32	F	None	20Ju02Nv
DELANY, Thomas	19	M	Mechanic	20Ju02Nv
DARRIGAN, Michael	23	M	Mechanic	20Ju02Nv
LILLY, Margaret	30	F	None	20Ju02Nv
FINLAN, Mary	16	F	None	20Ju02Nv
Patrick	07	M	None	20Ju02Nv
Matthew	05	M	None	20Ju02Nv
MCCABE, Philip	25	M	Laborer	20Ju02Nv
CARROL, Thomas	18	M	Laborer	20Ju02Nv
DONOHUE, Edward	25	M	Laborer	20Ju02Nv
BRADY, Daniel	20	M	Laborer	20Ju02Nv
MCMANNS, Catherine	20	F	None	20Ju02Nv
Bridget	26	F	None	20Ju02Nv
MCGOWAN, Catherine	50	F	None	20Ju02Nv
Betty	21	F	None	20Ju02Nv
Honora	19	F	None	20Ju02Nv
William	25	M	None	20Ju02Nv
MCCABE, Peter	25	M	Laborer	20Ju02Nv
Margaret	21	F	None	20Ju02Nv
OBRIEN, Mary	18	F	None	20Ju02Nv
Francis	15	M	None	20Ju02Nv
DENNISTON, Fanny	20	F	None	20Ju02Nv
KELROY, Daniel	20	M	Laborer	20Ju02Nv
DONOHOE, Rose	50	F	None	20Ju02Nv
MASTERSON, Mary	16	F	None	20Ju02Nv
MCGUIRE, Mary	24	F	None	20Ju02Nv
HAVERTY, Mary	30	F	None	20Ju02Nv
Catherine	06	F	None	20Ju02Nv
Mary	32	F	None	20Ju02Nv
Patrick	21	M	None	20Ju02Nv
Mary	45	F	None	20Ju02Nv
CURREN, Bridget	47	F	None	20Ju02Nv
MCCORMACK, Mary	26	F	None	20Ju02Nv
HEFFRON, Juliet	21	F	None	20Ju02Nv
DARGAN, Julia	04	F	None	20Ju02Nv
WALKER, Robert	26	M	Mechanic	20Ju02Nv
Eliza	24	F	Unknown	20Ju02Nv
John	02	M	None	20Ju02Nv
MCGUIRE, Ellen	25	F	None	20Ju02Nv
WOODS, Alice	19	F	None	20Ju02Nv
Eliza	14	F	None	20Ju02Nv
HACKETT, Bridget	20	F	None	20Ju02Nv
FAGAN, Patrick	22	M	Mechanic	20Ju02Nv
BURDEN, Henry	46	M	Mechanic	20Ju02Nv
Rosanna	23	F	None	20Ju02Nv
DOWLING, William	32	M	Mechanic	20Ju02Nv
KELLY, William	32	M	Mechanic	20Ju02Nv
Catherine	28	F	None	20Ju02Nv
Catherine (D)	.00	F	Infant	20Ju02Nv
HOWARD, George	17	M	None	20Ju02Nv
FITZGERALD, James	20	M	Laborer	20Ju02Nv
Ellen	20	F	None	20Ju02Nv
MCCAFFERTY, Dominick	18	M	Laborer	20Ju02Nv
GRUBB, Frederick	25	M	Laborer	20Ju02Nv
U (W)	20	F	Unknown	20Ju02Nv
John	.00	M	Infant	20Ju02Nv
JOHNSTON, Thomas	30	M	Mechanic	20Ju02Nv
TAAFFE, John	40	M	Mechanic	20Ju02Nv
BUCKLEY, Thomas	22	M	Mechanic	20Ju02Nv
KIRKPATRICK, John	22	M	Mechanic	20Ju02Nv
MCGREAL, Ann	24	F	None	20Ju02Nv
ROURKE, Catherine	20	F	None	20Ju02Nv
MCGOWAN, Pat.	25	M	Mechanic	20Ju02Nv

NAMES OF PASSENGERS		AGE	SEX	OCCUPATIONS	DATE PORT SHIP
RYAN, Timothy		30	M	Mechanic	20Ju02Nv
Ellen		20	F	None	20Ju02Nv
KENNEDY, Judy		18	F	None	20Ju02Nv
MCGUIRE, William		50	M	Laborer	20Ju02Nv
Mary	(W)	46	F	Unknown	20Ju02Nv
Edward		30	M	Laborer	20Ju02Nv
Catherine	(D)	20	F	None	20Ju02Nv
Ellen		18	F	None	20Ju02Nv
Margaret		16	F	None	20Ju02Nv
Mary		20	F	None	20Ju02Nv
Eliza		12	F	None	20Ju02Nv
HICKLEY, Daniel		11	M	None	20Ju02Nv
CUMMINGS, Michael		25	M	Laborer	20Ju02Nv
LONGHRAN, Mary		48	F	None	20Ju02Nv
Thomas		21	M	Laborer	20Ju02Nv
James		16	M	None	20Ju02Nv
Edward		13	M	None	20Ju02Nv
ROUNDTREE, James		58	M	Mechanic	20Ju02Nv
John		07	M	None	20Ju02Nv
LONGHRAN, Stephen		19	M	Mechanic	20Ju02Nv
COTTON, James		32	M	Mechanic	20Ju02Nv
Catherine		25	F	None	20Ju02Nv
MCSHAW, Mary		50	F	None	20Ju02Nv
Biddy		36	F	None	20Ju02Nv
Betty		15	F	None	20Ju02Nv
Mary		13	F	None	20Ju02Nv
Patrick		11	M	None	20Ju02Nv
Ann		09	F	None	20Ju02Nv
Teresa		07	F	None	20Ju02Nv
GARVEN, Patrick		40	M	Laborer	20Ju02Nv
EVAN, Alice		42	F	None	20Ju02Nv
TWISS, John		40	M	Laborer	20Ju02Nv
Mary		30	F	Unknown	20Ju02Nv
Francis		16	M	None	20Ju02Nv
Richard		12	M	None	20Ju02Nv
Patrick		12	M	None	20Ju02Nv
Hannah		10	F	None	20Ju02Nv
MAHONEY, James		16	M	Laborer	20Ju02Nv
THOMPSON, Ann		50	F	None	20Ju02Nv
Jonathan		57	M	Mechanic	20Ju02Nv
Ann		30	F	None	20Ju02Nv
John		20	M	Mechanic	20Ju02Nv
Thomas		13	M	None	20Ju02Nv
DREW, Joseph		19	M	Mechanic	20Ju02Nv
KERLING, Thomas		24	M	Mechanic	20Ju02Nv
FARRELL, Bridget		35	F	None	20Ju02Nv
Eliza		18	F	None	20Ju02Nv
Ambrose		10	M	None	20Ju02Nv
LAWLIE, Peter		23	M	Laborer	20Ju02Nv
GORMAN, Patrick		25	M	Laborer	20Ju02Nv
CORCORAN, Charles		24	M	Laborer	20Ju02Nv
KELLY, Michael		50	M	Laborer	20Ju02Nv
Patrick		23	M	Laborer	20Ju02Nv
Mary		20	F	None	20Ju02Nv
Biddy		26	F	None	20Ju02Nv
ROURKE, James		18	M	Laborer	20Ju02Nv
MCGOWAN, Mary		22	F	None	20Ju02Nv
FARRELL, Edward		22	M	Laborer	20Ju02Nv
Daniel		25	M	Laborer	20Ju02Nv
Catherine		21	F	None	20Ju02Nv
ROLPH, Frederick		24	M	Laborer	20Ju02Nv
Ann		21	F	None	20Ju02Nv
FARRELL, Catherine		35	F	None	20Ju02Nv
OBRYAN, Peter		25	M	Laborer	20Ju02Nv
Mary		25	F	Unknown	20Ju02Nv
CARBERRY, Patrick		28	M	Laborer	20Ju02Nv
BOYLE, William		25	M	None	20Ju02Nv
CLUTTERHEAD, R.S.		23	M	Mechanic	20Ju02Nv
BOYLAN, John		26	M	Mechanic	20Ju02Nv
Catherine		22	F	Unknown	20Ju02Nv
Honora		.00	F	Infant	20Ju02Nv
MORAN, William		43	M	Mechanic	20Ju02Nv
Mary		25	F	None	20Ju02Nv
NORTH, Eliza		25	F	None	20Ju02Nv
DONOHUE, Mary		40	F	None	20Ju02Nv
JONES, Ann		12	F	None	20Ju02Nv
WILSON, George		25	M	Mechanic	20Ju02Nv
Alice		28	F	None	20Ju02Nv
COSGREVE, Mary		25	F	None	20Ju02Nv
Margaret		19	F	None	20Ju02Nv
James		17	M	Mechanic	20Ju02Nv
DARMONDY, James		30	M	Mechanic	20Ju02Nv
KELLY, Patrick		24	M	Laborer	20Ju02Nv
FAHEY, Martin		25	M	Mechanic	20Ju02Nv
KILROY, John		28	M	Mechanic	20Ju02Nv

ARETHUSA 20 JUNE 1848

From Newry

NAMES OF PASSENGERS		AGE	SEX	OCCUPATIONS	DATE PORT SHIP
CUNNINGHAM, Maria		26	F	Spinster	20Ju19Ib
HEMING, Nancy		30	F	Spinster	20Ju19Ib
LIVISON, Samuel		23	M	Farmer	20Ju19Ib
Maria	(W)	25	F	Wife	20Ju19Ib
MCKEOWN, James		58	M	Farmer	20Ju19Ib
Ketty	(W)	35	F	Wife	20Ju19Ib
Mary		23	F	Relative	20Ju19Ib
Peggy-Anne		20	F	Relative	20Ju19Ib
Hugh		05	M	Child	20Ju19Ib
BARNS, Mary		22	F	Unknown	20Ju19Ib
MCKAIN, Hugh		25	M	Laborer	20Ju19Ib
GRAHAM, John		25	M	Laborer	20Ju19Ib
Gussey	(W)	24	F	Wife	20Ju19Ib
MCWORTHY, Margaret		19	F	Spinster	20Ju19Ib
CLEMENTS, Sarah		21	F	Spinster	20Ju19Ib
THOMPSON, William		20	M	Laborer	20Ju19Ib
John		19	M	Laborer	20Ju19Ib
LAWSEN, David		23	M	Farmer	20Ju19Ib
Easter	(W)	20	F	Wife	20Ju19Ib
James		22	M	Laborer	20Ju19Ib
SMITH, James		24	M	Laborer	20Ju19Ib
Mary		22	F	Relative	20Ju19Ib
Fanny		20	F	Relative	20Ju19Ib
Elizabeth		18	F	Relative	20Ju19Ib
Catharine		12	F	Relative	20Ju19Ib
Thomas		16	M	Relative	20Ju19Ib
Richard		13	M	Relative	20Ju19Ib
DAVIDSON, Agnes		20	F	Spinster	20Ju19Ib
ROWEN, Mary		60	F	Farmer	20Ju19Ib
Eliza		20	F	Relative	20Ju19Ib
William		25	M	Relative	20Ju19Ib
MORGAN, James		27	M	Laborer	20Ju19Ib
Catharine	(W)	20	F	Wife	20Ju19Ib
MURPHY, Arthur		15	M	Laborer	20Ju19Ib
STEWART, William		22	M	Farmer	20Ju19Ib
John		15	M	Relative	20Ju19Ib
Easter		18	F	Relative	20Ju19Ib
Eliza-Margaret		14	F	Relative	20Ju19Ib
MCCLENIGAN, John		20	M	Laborer	20Ju19Ib
JAMISON, Samuel		35	M	Rope Maker	20Ju19Ib
Mary	(W)	32	F	Wife	20Ju19Ib
John		16	M	Relative	20Ju19Ib
Margaret		14	F	Relative	20Ju19Ib
Robert		12	M	Relative	20Ju19Ib
Mary		10	F	Relative	20Ju19Ib
Samuel		08	M	Child	20Ju19Ib
Margaret		38	F	Relative	20Ju19Ib
Elizabeth		.02	F	Infant	20Ju19Ib
CUMINGHAM, Patrick		20	M	Laborer	20Ju19Ib
FLOOD, Arthur		22	M	Laborer	20Ju19Ib
MCAVOY, Sarah		24	F	Spinster	20Ju19Ib
Margaret		12	F	Spinster	20Ju19Ib
Hugh		11	M	Laborer	20Ju19Ib
CUNNINGHAM, James		20	M	Laborer	20Ju19Ib

NAMES OF PASSENGERS		AGE	SEX	OCCUPATIONS	DATE PORT SHIP
MARTIN, Colon		20	M	Farmer	20Ju19lb
Harriet	(W)	19	F	Wife	20Ju19lb
ROWEN, James		18	M	Laborer	20Ju19lb
Jane		20	F	Spinster	20Ju19lb
MACKIN, Patrick		21	M	Laborer	20Ju19lb
MCBRIDE, James		20	M	Laborer	20Ju19lb
WATSON, Samuel		21	M	Laborer	20Ju19lb
William		18	M	Laborer	20Ju19lb
ADAMS, Samuel		35	M	Farmer	20Ju19lb
Eliza	(W)	30	F	Wife	20Ju19lb
David		08	M	Child	20Ju19lb
John		07	M	Child	20Ju19lb
Joseph		05	M	Child	20Ju19lb
Robert		03	M	Child	20Ju19lb
Martha		.00	F	Infant	20Ju19lb
KEOWN, Hamilton		40	M	Farmer	20Ju19lb
Elizabeth	(W)	40	F	Wife	20Ju19lb
Betty-Anne		26	F	Relative	20Ju19lb
Penelope		18	F	Relative	20Ju19lb
Mary		14	F	Relative	20Ju19lb
Margaret		11	F	Relative	20Ju19lb
Hamilton		08	M	Child	20Ju19lb
Nancy		06	F	Child	20Ju19lb
Sarah		04	F	Child	20Ju19lb
Charlotte		01	F	Child	20Ju19lb
CLUGISH, Charlotte		19	F	Spinster	20Ju19lb
WATERSON, Nancy		17	F	Spinster	20Ju19lb
ONEIL, Charles		27	M	Laborer	20Ju19lb
MCKULVENY, James		23	M	Laborer	20Ju19lb
Eliza	(W)	20	F	Wife	20Ju19lb
SHANNON, Elizabeth		20	F	Spinster	20Ju19lb
TALL, Robert		22	M	Laborer	20Ju19lb
Agnes	(W)	20	F	Wife	20Ju19lb
HANNAH, David		23	M	Laborer	20Ju19lb
PEEL, William		26	M	Laborer	20Ju19lb
Isabella	(W)	25	F	Wife	20Ju19lb
Prudence		28	F	Spinster	20Ju19lb
MCCUSKEE, Margaret		20	F	Spinster	20Ju19lb
DELLANEY, Sarah		20	F	Spinster	20Ju19lb
BROWN, Margaret		20	F	Spinster	20Ju19lb
MARKS, Hugh		42	M	Laborer	20Ju19lb
Thomas		17	M	Laborer	20Ju19lb
William		13	M	Laborer	20Ju19lb
ROWNY, Peter		25	M	Laborer	20Ju19lb
Ally		20	F	Spinster	20Ju19lb
Biddy		22	F	Spinster	20Ju19lb
Patrick		20	M	Laborer	20Ju19lb
GIBSON, Cornelius		25	M	Farmer	20Ju19lb
Sarah	(W)	22	F	Wife	20Ju19lb
Patt		.00	M	Infant	20Ju19lb
HUTCHESON, William		30	M	Farmer	20Ju19lb
Mary-Anne	(W)	25	F	Wife	20Ju19lb
WILSON, Mary		18	F	Spinster	20Ju19lb
MCKIN, Redmond		20	M	Laborer	20Ju19lb
PARKER, Isaac		17	M	Laborer	20Ju19lb
MCKANE, Thomas		28	M	Farmer	20Ju19lb
Jane	(W)	20	F	Wife	20Ju19lb
David		07	M	Child	20Ju19lb
Jane		02	F	Child	20Ju19lb
Mary-Anne		.06	F	Infant	20Ju19lb
DISMORE, Margaret		20	F	Spinster	20Ju19lb
WATSON, Joseph		40	M	Laborer	20Ju19lb
LARKIN, Mary		50	F	Farmer	20Ju19lb
Michael		29	M	Relative	20Ju19lb
Mary		26	F	Relative	20Ju19lb
Peter		21	M	Relative	20Ju19lb
Margaret		19	F	Relative	20Ju19lb
Biddy		15	F	Relative	20Ju19lb

MARGARET-EVANS 20 JUNE 1848

From London

NAMES OF PASSENGERS	AGE	SEX	OCCUPATIONS	DATE PORT SHIP
EAVES, Sarah	36	F	Unknown	20Ju21lp
Sarah	08	F	Child	20Ju21lp
Mary	06	F	Child	20Ju21lp
TYRRELL, Thos.	50	M	Farmer	20Ju21lp
MCCULLOCH, Rebecca	25	F	Unknown	20Ju21lp
KING, George	24	M	Unknown	20Ju21lp
Michl.	60	M	Printer	20Ju21lp
Mary	60	F	Unknown	20Ju21lp
Naomi	25	F	Unknown	20Ju21lp
PAIN, Mary	40	F	Unknown	20Ju21lp
Mary-H.	15	F	Unknown	20Ju21lp
Fanny	13	F	Unknown	20Ju21lp
John	10	M	Unknown	20Ju21lp
Charlotte	08	F	Child	20Ju21lp
David	05	M	Child	20Ju21lp
LAZARUS, Rose	20	F	Unknown	20Ju21lp
HENESSY, David	45	M	Laborer	20Ju21lp
CONNELL, Michl.	27	M	Laborer	20Ju21lp
DOWNING, John-G.	30	M	Jeweller	20Ju21lp
Eliza-H.	26	F	Unknown	20Ju21lp
MACKAY, Jas.	35	M	Laborer	20Ju21lp
STONE, George	20	M	Laborer	20Ju21lp
LYNCH, John	21	M	Bootmaker	20Ju21lp
RAPHAEL, Ellis	24	M	Cigar Maker	20Ju21lp
Rosetta	22	F	Unknown	20Ju21lp
Anne	.00	F	Infant	20Ju21lp
ELDRIDGE, Benja.	26	M	Whitesmith	20Ju21lp
Josiah	18	M	Blacksmith	20Ju21lp
BARNETT, Barnett	24	M	Cigar Maker	20Ju21lp
Henrietta	23	F	Unknown	20Ju21lp
Elizt.	.00	F	Infant	20Ju21lp
SIMMONDS, Benj.	20	M	Cigar Maker	20Ju21lp
BENJAMIN, John	22	M	Cigar Maker	20Ju21lp
ROGERS, Wm.	41	M	Shoemaker	20Ju21lp
Cath.	41	F	Unknown	20Ju21lp
Jemina	17	F	Unknown	20Ju21lp
Maria	13	F	Unknown	20Ju21lp
Mellicent	09	F	Child	20Ju21lp
Elizt.	05	F	Child	20Ju21lp
Emily	02	F	Child	20Ju21lp
COSE, Wm.	17	M	Tailor	20Ju21lp
BARRETT, Cole	42	M	Shoemaker	20Ju21lp
Esther	27	F	Unknown	20Ju21lp
Rebecca	08	F	Child	20Ju21lp
Esther	06	F	Child	20Ju21lp
Louisa	.00	F	Infant	20Ju21lp
QUIN, John	27	M	Tailor	20Ju21lp
LEMESURRIERS, Chas.	22	M	Carpenter	20Ju21lp
HUSSEY, Young	38	F	Unknown	20Ju21lp
Sarah	.00	F	Infant	20Ju21lp
MASSEY, Wm.	22	M	Shoemaker	20Ju21lp
HAGGARTY, John	26	M	Laborer	20Ju21lp
STEPHEN, Philip	21	M	Mason	20Ju21lp
PARRY, Thos.	17	M	Laborer	20Ju21lp
HUNT, John	41	M	Piano Maker	20Ju21lp
DINGLEY, Robt.	43	M	Cbtmkr	20Ju21lp
OSMOND, Geo.	23	M	Baker	20Ju21lp
Mary-Ann	22	F	Unknown	20Ju21lp
ADAMS, Richd.	29	M	Carpenter	20Ju21lp
Sophia	26	F	Unknown	20Ju21lp
Richd.	03	M	Child	20Ju21lp
Geo.	.00	M	Infant	20Ju21lp
CLARKE, Sarah	24	F	Unknown	20Ju21lp
Wm.	.00	M	Infant	20Ju21lp
CUGGAN, Alfred	27	M	Yeoman	20Ju21lp

NAMES OF PASSENGERS		AGE	SEX	OCCUPATIONS	DATE PORT SHIP
SANTELL, John		26	M	Yeoman	20Ju21Ip
JONES, John		16	M	None	20Ju21Ip
MIDMEN, Willm.		27	M	Laborer	20Ju21Ip
JONES, Thos.		18	M	Smith	20Ju21Ip
MATTHEWS, Hannah		25	F	Unknown	20Ju21Ip
Henry		06	M	Child	20Ju21Ip
Gideon		03	M	Child	20Ju21Ip
John		.00	M	Infant	20Ju21Ip
RUSSELL, Robt.		30	M	Laborer	20Ju21Ip
Jas.		22	M	Laborer	20Ju21Ip
CHAFFEY, Geo.		21	M	Farmer	20Ju21Ip
RUSSELL, Harriet		26	F	Unknown	20Ju21Ip
REEVE, Wm.		23	M	Blacksmith	20Ju21Ip
George		26	M	Wheelwright	20Ju21Ip
BOONMANN, Friend.		44	M	Gcr-Bkr	20Ju21Ip
Mary		45	F	Unknown	20Ju21Ip
Ellen		20	F	Unknown	20Ju21Ip
Susan		18	F	Unknown	20Ju21Ip
Friend.		14	M	Unknown	20Ju21Ip
Brinchley		12	M	Unknown	20Ju21Ip
John		10	M	Unknown	20Ju21Ip
Betsey		05	F	Child	20Ju21Ip
BRISBY, John		55	M	Bootmaker	20Ju21Ip
HARPER, Thos.		48	M	Baker	20Ju21Ip
Sarah		26	F	Unknown	20Ju21Ip
Thos.		10	M	Unknown	20Ju21Ip
John		08	M	Child	20Ju21Ip
Mary		05	F	Child	20Ju21Ip
Alexr.		03	M	Child	20Ju21Ip
Matthew		.00	M	Infant	20Ju21Ip
LEACH, Geo.		20	M	Farmer	20Ju21Ip

ISAAC-WRIGHT 22 JUNE 1848

From Liverpool

NAMES OF PASSENGERS		AGE	SEX	OCCUPATIONS	DATE PORT SHIP
MOONEY, Patrick		25	M	Laborer	22Ju02Qk
CARROLL, Francis		20	M	Laborer	22Ju02Qk
DUFFEY, Bridget		25	F	None	22Ju02Qk
CLARK, John		30	M	Carpenter	22Ju02Qk
Ann	(D)	03	F	Child	22Ju02Qk
WHEATON, Elizabeth		35	F	Weaver	22Ju02Qk
George	(S)	16	M	Weaver	22Ju02Qk
Eliza	(D)	13	F	Weaver	22Ju02Qk
BUMBY, William		30	M	Tanner	22Ju02Qk
U	(W)	28	F	None	22Ju02Qk
CARROLL, Pat.		24	M	Laborer	22Ju02Qk
ORNSTON, Joseph		30	M	Laborer	22Ju02Qk
Margret		50	F	None	22Ju02Qk
MAHER, Cornelis		40	M	Laborer	22Ju02Qk
DWIRE, James		20	M	Laborer	22Ju02Qk
TRACEY, Mary		20	F	Weaver	22Ju02Qk
DWINN, William		20	M	Weaver	22Ju02Qk
ONEIL, Bridget		26	F	Weaver	22Ju02Qk
BIGLEY, William		45	M	Tinker	22Ju02Qk
HAIGH, James		31	M	Tinker	22Ju02Qk
Sarah		26	F	None	22Ju02Qk
Job		28	M	Tinker	22Ju02Qk
Lydia		30	F	None	22Ju02Qk
James		03	M	Child	22Ju02Qk
HANLEY, James		30	M	Laborer	22Ju02Qk
CRONING, Jno.		20	M	Laborer	22Ju02Qk
Michael		21	M	Laborer	22Ju02Qk
Patrick		18	M	Laborer	22Ju02Qk
GAINEY, Tim		26	M	Baker	22Ju02Qk
MCDONNELL, Eustace		50	M	Farmer	22Ju02Qk
Patrick		30	M	Farmer	22Ju02Qk
Michael		36	M	Farmer	22Ju02Qk
James		26	M	Farmer	22Ju02Qk

NAMES OF PASSENGERS		AGE	SEX	OCCUPATIONS	DATE PORT SHIP
MCKENNA, Margaret		20	F	None	22Ju02Qk
BYRON, Pat.		20	M	Farmer	22Ju02Qk
JOHNSON, George		49	M	Farmer	22Ju02Qk
Harriet	(W)	39	F	None	22Ju02Qk
Antony	(S)	20	M	Farmer	22Ju02Qk
Jane	(D)	15	F	None	22Ju02Qk
Eliza	(D)	09	F	Child	22Ju02Qk
George	(S)	04	M	Child	22Ju02Qk
Harriett	(D)	15	F	None	22Ju02Qk
CONROY, Margaret		20	F	Servant	22Ju02Qk
MANNON, John		30	M	Laborer	22Ju02Qk
MCCORD, James		24	M	Farmer	22Ju02Qk
HUMLEY, Patrick		22	M	Weaver	22Ju02Qk
DOCKRAY, Louisa		23	F	Weaver	22Ju02Qk
U		.00	U	Infant	22Ju02Qk
KETHSLEY, Grace		26	U	Infant	22Ju02Qk
MURPHEY, Edward		25	M	Laborer	22Ju02Qk
REGAN, Mathew		28	M	Laborer	22Ju02Qk
Maurice		24	M	Laborer	22Ju02Qk
FOX, James		26	M	Laborer	22Ju02Qk
DOYLE, Mary		20	F	Dressmaker	22Ju02Qk
SUMOT, Michel		24	M	Saddler	22Ju02Qk
Charles		18	M	Saddler	22Ju02Qk
BRADLEY, Abraham		29	M	Saddler	22Ju02Qk
U	(W)	26	F	None	22Ju02Qk
Eliza		22	F	None	22Ju02Qk
Mary		07	F	Child	22Ju02Qk
Ellen		06	F	Child	22Ju02Qk
William		.00	M	Infant	22Ju02Qk
GAY, Thomas		20	M	Laborer	22Ju02Qk
FITZPATRIC, Mary		15	F	None	22Ju02Qk
DERMOODY, William		18	M	Laborer	22Ju02Qk
MCCABE, Norah		26	F	Servant	22Ju02Qk
ROBINSON, James		30	M	Joiner	22Ju02Qk
U	(W)	28	F	None	22Ju02Qk
Betty	(D)	03	F	Child	22Ju02Qk
HASKETH, Thomas		38	M	Carpenter	22Ju02Qk
LEND, Andrew		24	M	Blacksmith	22Ju02Qk
NEBBY, Dennis		20	M	Wheelwright	22Ju02Qk
Catherine		20	F	None	22Ju02Qk
PARKINSON, U		26	M	Clerk	22Ju02Qk
U	(W)	24	F	None	22Ju02Qk
HORAGHAN, Martha		30	F	Weaver	22Ju02Qk
DOONEY, Mary		35	F	Weaver	22Ju02Qk
DOOLEY, James		20	M	Weaver	22Ju02Qk
MCCUSKER, Edward		18	M	Priest	22Ju02Qk
GIBLAN, Patrick		22	M	Laborer	22Ju02Qk
BARSLEY, James		37	M	Laborer	22Ju02Qk
U	(W)	30	F	None	22Ju02Qk
DENHAM, Patrick		22	M	Laborer	22Ju02Qk
FEY, Bernerd		28	M	Laborer	22Ju02Qk
HALTON, John		26	M	Laborer	22Ju02Qk
HERD, U		26	F	Servant	22Ju02Qk
KYE, Benjamin		26	M	Servant	22Ju02Qk
Elizabeth		22	F	Servant	22Ju02Qk
DEEGAN, John		26	M	Laborer	22Ju02Qk
Biddy	(W)	20	F	None	22Ju02Qk
NOLTON, Catherine		20	F	None	22Ju02Qk
QUIGGINS, Robert		20	M	Tailor	22Ju02Qk
Mannian		20	M	Tailor	22Ju02Qk
GEHERTY, Miles		21	M	None	22Ju02Qk
KING, Dennis		20	M	None	22Ju02Qk
TABLEY, Edward		20	M	Farmer	22Ju02Qk
John		20	M	Farmer	22Ju02Qk
MOORE, Thomas		20	M	Laborer	22Ju02Qk
CART, Thomas		40	M	Laborer	22Ju02Qk
William		30	M	Laborer	22Ju02Qk
GOODEN, Mary		40	F	Weaver	22Ju02Qk
DALEY, James		20	M	Laborer	22Ju02Qk
DOWD, Jane		20	F	None	22Ju02Qk
MCNULTY, Bridget		20	F	Servant	22Ju02Qk
REYNOLDS, Rose		19	F	Servant	22Ju02Qk
CONROY, Eliza		21	F	Servant	22Ju02Qk
SILVER, Bridget		20	F	Servant	22Ju02Qk
Catharine		25	F	Servant	22Ju02Qk

NAMES OF PASSENGERS		AGE	SEX	OCCUPATIONS	DATE PORT SHIP
SINE, Mary		20	F	Servant	22Ju02Qk
RYCROFT, Mary		19	F	Servant	22Ju02Qk
Sarah		18	F	Servant	22Ju02Qk
KEIF, Mary		17	F	Servant	22Ju02Qk
PURCELL, James		17	M	Laborer	22Ju02Qk
HOGAN, Eliza		20	F	Servant	22Ju02Qk
RYAN, Elenna		17	F	Servant	22Ju02Qk
Bridget		10	F	Child	22Ju02Qk
Honora		08	F	Child	22Ju02Qk
BRENNAN, Thomas		24	M	Laborer	22Ju02Qk
Edward		20	M	Laborer	22Ju02Qk
MASTERSON, Patrick		25	M	Laborer	22Ju02Qk
DORSEY, John		19	M	Laborer	22Ju02Qk
Kate		17	F	Servant	22Ju02Qk
Elizabeth		25	F	Servant	22Ju02Qk
COLLINS, Bridget		23	F	Servant	22Ju02Qk
Arthur		23	M	Laborer	22Ju02Qk
CONWAY, Ann		12	F	Child	22Ju02Qk
Ellen		15	F	Servant	22Ju02Qk
MAGUIRE, Rosa		18	F	Servant	22Ju02Qk
MULICK, Bernard		23	M	Tailor	22Ju02Qk
GILL, Patrick		25	M	Baker	22Ju02Qk
DOYLE, Edward		09	M	Child	22Ju02Qk
BOYLE, Bernard		27	M	Painter	22Ju02Qk
Mary		27	F	Weaver	22Ju02Qk
GLENNAN, Julia		30	F	Farmer	22Ju02Qk
Catharine	(D)	02	F	Child	22Ju02Qk
Bridget	(D)	04	F	Child	22Ju02Qk
Ellen	(D)	08	F	Child	22Ju02Qk
Anne	(D)	06	F	Child	22Ju02Qk
Patrick	(S)	10	M	Child	22Ju02Qk
CASSIDY, Bridget		20	F	Servant	22Ju02Qk
MCGARRY, John		21	M	Laborer	22Ju02Qk
CAMPHAN, Patrick		25	M	Laborer	22Ju02Qk
HICKY, Louise		22	F	Servant	22Ju02Qk
PURSALL, John		18	M	Laborer	22Ju02Qk
HUNTER, Samuel		25	M	Laborer	22Ju02Qk
HENDERSON, Jane		25	F	Dressmaker	22Ju02Qk
KEENAN, Catharine		21	F	Dressmaker	22Ju02Qk
Bridget		20	F	Dressmaker	22Ju02Qk
BOILESTY, James		40	M	Wheelwright	22Ju02Qk
Mary	(W)	40	F	None	22Ju02Qk
Patrick	(S)	16	M	None	22Ju02Qk
Mary	(D)	17	F	None	22Ju02Qk
FLAHERTY, Patrick		15	M	Brick Maker	22Ju02Qk
Edward		09	M	Child	22Ju02Qk
MCGUCKIAM, Hugh		50	M	Builder	22Ju02Qk
Terese	(D)	16	F	None	22Ju02Qk
SLAIN, Eliza		16	F	Servant	22Ju02Qk
DOWD, Mary-Ann		18	F	Servant	22Ju02Qk
HOWGATE, Michael		24	M	Laborer	22Ju02Qk
ANDERSON, Eliza		26	F	Dressmaker	22Ju02Qk
DONAHOE, U		50	F	Dressmaker	22Ju02Qk
Kathrine		13	F	Dressmaker	22Ju02Qk
Mary		03	F	Child	22Ju02Qk
MURPHY, John		42	M	Farmer	22Ju02Qk
Catharine	(W)	40	F	None	22Ju02Qk
John	(S)	14	M	None	22Ju02Qk
Michael	(S)	11	M	Child	22Ju02Qk
Bridget	(D)	08	F	Child	22Ju02Qk
Widow		50	F	None	22Ju02Qk
KEEFE, Bridget		23	F	Weaver	22Ju02Qk
CONROY, Bernard		18	M	Laborer	22Ju02Qk
MCCORMICK, John		16	M	Peddler	22Ju02Qk
Edward		15	M	Peddler	22Ju02Qk
CONROY, Mary		50	F	Servant	22Ju02Qk
LUIGE, Catherine		40	F	Servant	22Ju02Qk
SLEVIN, Mary		50	F	Servant	22Ju02Qk
CRONAN, Catherine		26	F	Servant	22Ju02Qk
HAMILTON, John		24	M	Laborer	22Ju02Qk
Michael		11	M	Child	22Ju02Qk
MURPHEY, Sarah		20	F	Servant	22Ju02Qk
HAND, John		22	M	Farmer	22Ju02Qk
TIERNEY, Maria		17	F	Servant	22Ju02Qk
OWENS, William		20	M	Farmer	22Ju02Qk
MURRY, Thomas		20	M	Farmer	22Ju02Qk
DOHERTY, George		20	M	Farmer	22Ju02Qk
LYNCH, William		30	M	Tailor	22Ju02Qk
HENRY, Peter		20	M	Shoemaker	22Ju02Qk
MALONE, Peter		50	M	Shoemaker	22Ju02Qk
OFARRELL, Francis		20	M	Shoemaker	22Ju02Qk
DOBSON, Catherine		20	F	Servant	22Ju02Qk
Peter		13	M	Servant	22Ju02Qk
Elizabeth		15	F	Servant	22Ju02Qk
FEE, Patrick		20	M	Mason	22Ju02Qk
James		20	M	Mason	22Ju02Qk
HARA, Sarah		40	F	Weaver	22Ju02Qk
MCMELLONY, Anne		13	F	Weaver	22Ju02Qk
Ellen		14	F	Weaver	22Ju02Qk
Patrick		17	M	Laborer	22Ju02Qk
MCCALL, Henry		26	M	Laborer	22Ju02Qk
MCCORD, John		35	M	Laborer	22Ju02Qk
GORMLY, Mary-A.		21	F	Servant	22Ju02Qk
MCLEAN, Mary		20	F	Servant	22Ju02Qk
MCCANN, James		20	M	Farmer	22Ju02Qk
FITZPATRIC, John		45	M	Wheelwright	22Ju02Qk
U, Biddy		20	M	Weaver	22Ju02Qk
GARRY, James		20	M	Laborer	22Ju02Qk
Antony		21	M	Laborer	22Ju02Qk
BYRNE, Mary		25	F	Weaver	22Ju02Qk
HILLARD, John		20	M	Farmer	22Ju02Qk
CLINTON, Margaret		20	F	Dressmaker	22Ju02Qk
HARKEY, Mary		21	F	Dressmaker	22Ju02Qk
RILEY, Mary		18	F	Dressmaker	22Ju02Qk
ROBINSON, Shepherd		55	M	Artisan	22Ju02Qk
Mary	(W)	34	F	None	22Ju02Qk
MCNULTY, Andrew		21	M	Laborer	22Ju02Qk
HEGARTY, James		20	M	Laborer	22Ju02Qk
Catherine		18	F	Servant	22Ju02Qk
MCHUGH, Thomas		15	M	Laborer	22Ju02Qk
GOUGH, Bridget		25	F	Servant	22Ju02Qk
DONNELLY, Michel		19	M	Laborer	22Ju02Qk
RILEY, Mathew		20	M	Laborer	22Ju02Qk
KEAMES, Michel		20	M	Laborer	22Ju02Qk
READMOND, Peter		20	M	Laborer	22Ju02Qk
FITZPATRIC, Nancy		40	F	None	22Ju02Qk
CASSON, Ann		26	F	Servant	22Ju02Qk
BRADLEY, Anne		40	F	Weaver	22Ju02Qk
CORCORAN, Mary		20	F	Dressmaker	22Ju02Qk
REYNOLDS, Rose		20	F	Dressmaker	22Ju02Qk
MCDONNALL, Alexander		28	M	Baker	22Ju02Qk
Anne	(W)	20	F	None	22Ju02Qk
MAHONE, Margaret		20	F	Servant	22Ju02Qk
CASSY, Catherine		22	F	Servant	22Ju02Qk
MEEHAN, Catherine		19	F	Dressmaker	22Ju02Qk
SWEENEY, Mary		20	F	Dressmaker	22Ju02Qk
DOWN, U-Mrs.		30	F	Lad	22Ju02Qk
Anne	(D)	13	F	None	22Ju02Qk
Alfred	(S)	12	M	Child	22Ju02Qk
James	(S)	10	M	Child	22Ju02Qk
Jennette	(D)	08	F	Child	22Ju02Qk
Francis	(S)	06	M	Child	22Ju02Qk
Edward	(S)	04	M	Child	22Ju02Qk
HUNTER, Mark		20	M	Laborer	22Ju02Qk
STINSON, William		50	M	Shoemaker	22Ju02Qk
MCGOVIM, James		25	M	Laborer	22Ju02Qk
FLANAGAN, Catherine		18	F	Servant	22Ju02Qk
PLUNKET, Bridget		20	F	Servant	22Ju02Qk
HIGGINS, Montague		49	M	Farmer	22Ju02Qk
DALY, U-Mrs.		20	F	None	22Ju02Qk
BRENARD, Sally		20	F	Servant	22Ju02Qk
BROWN, U		27	M	Gentleman	22Ju02Qk

CHUSAN 22 JUNE 1848

From Belfast

NAMES OF PASSENGERS	AGE	SEX	OCCUPATIONS	DATE PORT SHIP
MCSHANE, Cath.	20	F	Spinster	22Ju07Ts
KERR, Cath.	20	F	Spinster	22Ju07Ts
WHITE, James	28	M	Laborer	22Ju07Ts
WOLFENDEN, John	24	M	Laborer	22Ju07Ts
WILSON, Wm.	24	M	Laborer	22Ju07Ts
Eliz.	20	F	Matron	22Ju07Ts
Eliz.	03	F	Child	22Ju07Ts
MCCULLIN, Bridget	21	F	Spinster	22Ju07Ts
MCGEE, Susanna	18	F	Spinster	22Ju07Ts
CONKEY, Alexr.N.	20	M	Laborer	22Ju07Ts
FLETCHER, Sarah-Jane	20	F	Spinster	22Ju07Ts
MULLAN, Miles	56	M	Farmer	22Ju07Ts
Susanna	50	F	Matron	22Ju07Ts
Cath.	15	F	Spinster	22Ju07Ts
Ann	12	F	None	22Ju07Ts
Cath.	06	F	Child	22Ju07Ts
YOUNG, Eliza	25	F	Spinster	22Ju07Ts
MATHERS, Ann	21	F	Spinster	22Ju07Ts
Mary	19	F	Spinster	22Ju07Ts
Mich.	14	M	Laborer	22Ju07Ts
Hannah	12	F	None	22Ju07Ts
Ellen	10	F	None	22Ju07Ts
MCCULLIN, Pat	22	M	Laborer	22Ju07Ts
CONYAN, Margt.	16	F	Spinster	22Ju07Ts
SMYTH, Thos.	20	M	Laborer	22Ju07Ts
James	18	M	Laborer	22Ju07Ts
HIGGINS, John	40	M	Laborer	22Ju07Ts
Ann	30	F	Matron	22Ju07Ts
Barry	25	M	Laborer	22Ju07Ts
Sarah	08	F	Child	22Ju07Ts
Mary	04	F	Child	22Ju07Ts
HUGHES, James	29	M	Farmer	22Ju07Ts
Patrick	25	M	Farmer	22Ju07Ts
John	30	M	Farmer	22Ju07Ts
Sarah	23	F	Spinster	22Ju07Ts
FINNEGAN, Arthur	24	M	Farmer	22Ju07Ts
CANEN, John-M.	40	M	Farmer	22Ju07Ts
MCGUCKIAN, Robt.	22	M	Farmer	22Ju07Ts
Sarah	22	F	Spinster	22Ju07Ts
Marianne	35	F	Spinster	22Ju07Ts
Mary-Jane	.00	F	Infant	22Ju07Ts
MCDONNELL, M.J.	32	M	Farmer	22Ju07Ts
MURPHY, Jane	20	F	Spinster	22Ju07Ts
Bernard	20	M	Laborer	22Ju07Ts
KEEN, Chas.	21	M	Laborer	22Ju07Ts
FORSYTH, Eliz.	19	F	Spinster	22Ju07Ts
COCHRAN, Mary	50	F	Matron	22Ju07Ts
James	17	M	Laborer	22Ju07Ts
SCOTT, John	15	M	Laborer	22Ju07Ts
FARRELL, Mary	22	F	Spinster	22Ju07Ts
WRIGHT, Thos.	22	M	Laborer	22Ju07Ts
MCDONNELL, Rose	20	F	Spinster	22Ju07Ts
MCLOUGHLIN, Richd.	21	M	Laborer	22Ju07Ts
Eliza	22	F	Matron	22Ju07Ts
WALKER, Mary	20	F	Matron	22Ju07Ts
MCGRATH, Mary	25	F	Spinster	22Ju07Ts
CANON, Mary	30	F	Spinster	22Ju07Ts
CURRAN, Michael	21	M	Laborer	22Ju07Ts
MCKEON, Hugh	24	M	Laborer	22Ju07Ts
Isabella	26	F	Spinster	22Ju07Ts
MCKAY, Archibald	30	M	Weaver	22Ju07Ts
BODELE, Agnes	50	F	Wi	22Ju07Ts
Hugh	25	M	Laborer	22Ju07Ts
Died-At-Sea				
SMITH, John	21	M	Laborer	22Ju07Ts
DANAGH, Robt.	29	M	Laborer	22Ju07Ts
DORNAN, Robt.	40	M	Laborer	22Ju07Ts
John	10	M	None	22Ju07Ts
BOSLAND, Eliza	20	F	Spinster	22Ju07Ts
HUTCHINSON, Wm.	50	M	Farmer	22Ju07Ts
Margt. (W)	18	F	Wife	22Ju07Ts
Samuel	11	M	None	22Ju07Ts
Carlile	09	M	Child	22Ju07Ts
NEILLY, Thos.	26	M	Laborer	22Ju07Ts
WILSON, Wm.	20	M	Laborer	22Ju07Ts
MCCURRY, John	20	M	Laborer	22Ju07Ts
DIOLIN, Jas.	21	M	Weaver	22Ju07Ts
Peter	20	M	Weaver	22Ju07Ts
William	22	M	Weaver	22Ju07Ts
QUIN, Isabella	21	F	Wife	22Ju07Ts
Sarah	02	F	Child	22Ju07Ts
Cath.	.00	F	Infant	22Ju07Ts
MCKEWER, John	16	M	Laborer	22Ju07Ts
Died-At-Sea				
GRANT, John	28	M	Laborer	22Ju07Ts
Eliz.	28	F	Matron	22Ju07Ts
Charles	02	M	Child	22Ju07Ts
FARRELL, Bridget	36	F	Matron	22Ju07Ts
Aly	08	M	Child	22Ju07Ts
Bridget	06	F	Child	22Ju07Ts
Mary	04	F	Child	22Ju07Ts
Theresa	.00	F	Infant	22Ju07Ts
WHITTLE, Hugh	24	M	Laborer	22Ju07Ts
CORROE, Danl.	27	M	Laborer	22Ju07Ts
MAGORY, Ann	19	F	Spinster	22Ju07Ts
Mary	26	F	Spinster	22Ju07Ts
BERRY, Danl.	50	M	Farmer	22Ju07Ts
John	16	M	Laborer	22Ju07Ts
Mary	12	F	None	22Ju07Ts
Sarah	10	F	None	22Ju07Ts
MAIARTUEY, Eliz.	40	F	Matron	22Ju07Ts
Died-At-Sea				
MCDONELL, Phillip	24	M	Laborer	22Ju07Ts
DANLEAVEY, Mary	20	F	Spinster	22Ju07Ts
HANLON, Margt.	23	F	Spinster	22Ju07Ts
PATRICK, Jas.	30	M	Laborer	22Ju07Ts
MCMANUS, W.	27	M	Laborer	22Ju07Ts
JONES, John	30	M	Weaver	22Ju07Ts
Died-At-Sea				
Margt.	28	F	Matron	22Ju07Ts
Margt.	.00	F	Infant	22Ju07Ts
Died-At-Sea				
NICHOLE, Andrew	22	M	Smith	22Ju07Ts
HAFFEY, John	20	M	Smith	22Ju07Ts
WALKER, Alexr.	20	M	Smith	22Ju07Ts
NELSON, Jane	21	F	Spinster	22Ju07Ts
MOORE, Thos.	40	M	Farmer	22Ju07Ts
Jane	16	F	None	22Ju07Ts
William	13	M	None	22Ju07Ts
KELLY, Jas.	20	M	Laborer	22Ju07Ts
SHUNK, Jas.	20	M	Laborer	22Ju07Ts
MCKEE, Jane	30	F	Spinster	22Ju07Ts
WARD, Mary	13	F	Spinster	22Ju07Ts
CURRANS, Agnes	20	F	Spinster	22Ju07Ts
HAYES, Robt.	26	M	Weaver	22Ju07Ts
George	24	M	Weaver	22Ju07Ts
ANDERSON, David	11	M	Weaver	22Ju07Ts
MCATAMANY, W.	40	F	Wi	22Ju07Ts
Rosey	20	F	Spinster	22Ju07Ts
Jane	13	F	None	22Ju07Ts
Anna	10	F	None	22Ju07Ts
DIAMOND, John	30	M	Weaver	22Ju07Ts
Died-At-Sea				
Patk.	28	M	Weaver	22Ju07Ts
Mary	26	F	Spinster	22Ju07Ts
SKILLING, Bernard	21	M	Weaver	22Ju07Ts
MCGILL, Biddy	20	F	Spinster	22Ju07Ts
RIGES, Mary	21	F	Spinster	22Ju07Ts
TOGHILE, Biddy	19	F	Spinster	22Ju07Ts
Mary	20	F	Spinster	22Ju07Ts

NAMES OF PASSENGERS	AGE	SEX	OCCUPATIONS	DATE PORT SHIP
DUFFY, Cath.	23	F	Spinster	22Ju07Ts
SCOTT, John	26	M	Weaver	22Ju07Ts
COCHRAN, Jas.	21	M	Weaver	22Ju07Ts
FLANAGHAN, Hugh	20	M	Weaver	22Ju07Ts
DEVOIR, Jas.	20	M	Weaver	22Ju07Ts
MOORE, Eliza	25	F	Spinster	22Ju07Ts
TRAVIRS, Ann	25	F	Spinster	22Ju07Ts
CLENDENNING, Eliza	24	F	Spinster	22Ju07Ts
HAYES, Sarah	20	F	Spinster	22Ju07Ts
BURNS, John	25	M	Laborer	22Ju07Ts
MURRAY, Jas.	25	M	Farmer	22Ju07Ts
Eliza (W)	24	F	Wife	22Ju07Ts
Mary	07	F	Child	22Ju07Ts
Jane	05	F	Child	22Ju07Ts
Hugh	03	M	Child	22Ju07Ts
Eliza	.00	F	Infant	22Ju07Ts
SENGTH, Simon	21	M	Laborer	22Ju07Ts
BOYD, Wm.	29	M	Laborer	22Ju07Ts

GERTRUDE 23 JUNE 1848

From Liverpool

NAMES OF PASSENGERS	AGE	SEX	OCCUPATIONS	DATE PORT SHIP
KIRKPATRICK, Margt.	20	F	Servant	23Ju02Eq
DOWZANE, William	25	M	Policeman	23Ju02Eq
Bridgt.	22	F	Unknown	23Ju02Eq
OMSBY, Francis	22	M	Laborer	23Ju02Eq
BICKLEY, George	25	M	Laborer	23Ju02Eq
Mary	25	F	Unknown	23Ju02Eq
HAYES, Nicholas	35	M	Laborer	23Ju02Eq
John	25	M	Unknown	23Ju02Eq
BYRNES, George	26	M	Baker	23Ju02Eq
ABBOTT, Mary	27	F	Servant	23Ju02Eq
KENNER, William	24	M	Farmer	23Ju02Eq
Mary	28	F	Servant	23Ju02Eq
WALLACE, Michael	20	M	Farmer	23Ju02Eq
BRENNAN, William	50	M	Weaver	23Ju02Eq
Martha	50	F	Unknown	23Ju02Eq
COGHLN, Michl.	24	M	Farmer	23Ju02Eq
FITZGERALD, Cathn.	25	F	Unknown	23Ju02Eq
Edwin	04	M	Child	23Ju02Eq
FITZHARRIS, James	28	M	Farmer	23Ju02Eq
Thomas	31	M	Unknown	23Ju02Eq
MOLOY, James	27	M	Farmer	23Ju02Eq
REYNOLDS, Bernard	28	M	Unknown	23Ju02Eq
HOPKINS, Terrence	50	M	Farmer	23Ju02Eq
Mary	20	F	Unknown	23Ju02Eq
John	13	M	Unknown	23Ju02Eq
SCANTON, Mary	18	F	Servant	23Ju02Eq
MCKEEN, Belle	18	F	Unknown	23Ju02Eq
FOY, Ellen	40	F	Servant	23Ju02Eq
WALSH, Frederick	26	M	Coachman	23Ju02Eq
FITZGERALD, Honora	16	F	Servant	23Ju02Eq
WALSH, Patrick	04	M	Child	23Ju02Eq
Cath.	12	F	Unknown	23Ju02Eq
U	.04	U	Infant	23Ju02Eq
Thomas	34	M	Farmer	23Ju02Eq
Joseph	30	M	Unknown	23Ju02Eq
James	22	M	Unknown	23Ju02Eq
Mary	18	F	Unknown	23Ju02Eq
COHAN, Thomas	30	M	Farmer	23Ju02Eq
BOWING, William	30	M	Unknown	23Ju02Eq
Amelia	30	F	Unknown	23Ju02Eq
CONNER, Ellen	26	F	Unknown	23Ju02Eq
U	.00	U	Infant	23Ju02Eq
MOSS, Michael	23	M	Gasfitter	23Ju02Eq
JACOBS, John	45	M	Tailor	23Ju02Eq
MOUSLEY, Joseph	20	M	Tailor	23Ju02Eq
JACOBS, Jacob	30	M	Unknown	23Ju02Eq

NAMES OF PASSENGERS	AGE	SEX	OCCUPATIONS	DATE PORT SHIP
BROOKS, John-H.	30	M	Ivt	23Ju02Eq
KELLY, Patt	26	M	Laborer	23Ju02Eq
QUINN, Dennis	26	M	Laborer	23Ju02Eq
Patt	25	M	Unknown	23Ju02Eq
FOGARTY, Cath.	18	F	Servant	23Ju02Eq
LAHY, Mary	18	F	Servant	23Ju02Eq
LEVY, William	50	M	Gdnr	23Ju02Eq
Mary	50	F	Unknown	23Ju02Eq
Edward	18	M	Unknown	23Ju02Eq
Mary	16	F	Unknown	23Ju02Eq
Cathn.	13	F	Unknown	23Ju02Eq
RYAN, Mary	60	F	Servant	23Ju02Eq
Betty	20	F	Servant	23Ju02Eq
GOCENT, Alex.	41	M	Farmer	23Ju02Eq
Died-At-Sea				
MILLARD, William	31	M	Clerk	23Ju02Eq
HARRINGTON, Anne	19	F	Servant	23Ju02Eq
LEGGALT, William	25	M	Laborer	23Ju02Eq
DEEN, Patk.	19	M	Shoemaker	23Ju02Eq
Thomas	13	M	Laborer	23Ju02Eq
MCGARRY, James	14	M	Laborer	23Ju02Eq
ONEILL, Bernd.	30	M	Laborer	23Ju02Eq
Bernd.	32	M	Farmer	23Ju02Eq
LOGAN, William	08	M	Child	23Ju02Eq
ONEILL, Matilde	13	F	Unknown	23Ju02Eq
John	11	M	Unknown	23Ju02Eq
CLOGHANY, Mary	55	F	Servant	23Ju02Eq
QUINTAN, David	05	M	Child	23Ju02Eq
ANDERLY, Edwd.	26	M	Farmer	23Ju02Eq
CONER, Michl.	26	M	Whitesmith	23Ju02Eq
DONNELLY, Patt	21	M	Servant	23Ju02Eq
KENTWILL, Ellen	21	F	Unknown	23Ju02Eq
Elizabeth	27	F	Unknown	23Ju02Eq
BYRNE, Patt	34	M	Farmer	23Ju02Eq
CAHOY, Edward	40	M	Farmer	23Ju02Eq
MCELROY, Patt	20	M	Farmer	23Ju02Eq
MCGUIRK, Patt	40	M	Laborer	23Ju02Eq
Michl.	11	M	Unknown	23Ju02Eq
MAHER, Roger	75	M	Farmer	23Ju02Eq
Maria	35	F	Servant	23Ju02Eq
NEVIN, James	33	M	Farmer	23Ju02Eq
Bridgt.	27	F	Farmer	23Ju02Eq
MCFESUN, Alex.	21	M	Calender	23Ju02Eq
COCELTES, Andrew	26	M	Flaxdr	23Ju02Eq
REYNOLDS, William	25	M	Coach Maker	23Ju02Eq
LEWIS, George	21	M	Clerk	23Ju02Eq
DOGHERY, Jno.	18	M	Laborer	23Ju02Eq
RINGLE, Jno.	26	M	Laborer	23Ju02Eq
MAHEN, Patt	32	M	Laborer	23Ju02Eq
LANGY, Jno.	18	M	Laborer	23Ju02Eq
Mary	26	F	Unknown	23Ju02Eq
BROOKS, Edwd.	20	M	Saddler	23Ju02Eq
ANDERSON, David	27	M	Carpenter	23Ju02Eq
Nancy	30	F	Unknown	23Ju02Eq
HOGAN, Naha	30	F	Laborer	23Ju02Eq
MCKENZIE, David	30	M	Stone Mason	23Ju02Eq
James	25	M	Stone Mason	23Ju02Eq
NUGNET, James	30	M	Laborer	23Ju02Eq
QUINN, Terence	23	M	Laborer	23Ju02Eq
FLANAGAN, Jno.	25	M	Shoemaker	23Ju02Eq
KELLY, Tho.	21	M	Laborer	23Ju02Eq
KEILLY, Patt	21	M	Carpenter	23Ju02Eq
DIGNAN, Edwd.	21	M	Molder	23Ju02Eq
BRADY, James	54	M	Laborer	23Ju02Eq
Patt	26	M	Laborer	23Ju02Eq
James	03	M	Child	23Ju02Eq
Mary	04	F	Child	23Ju02Eq
Cathn.	.08	F	Infant	23Ju02Eq
Mary	23	F	Wife	23Ju02Eq
CONN, John	25	M	Tailor	23Ju02Eq
MCCLERLEY, James	50	M	Farmer	23Ju02Eq
LEVY, Bernd.	40	M	Plasterer	23Ju02Eq
OTTERSON, John	35	M	Farmer	23Ju02Eq
BERN, Patt	24	M	Farmer	23Ju02Eq
MOLLOY, Michl.	28	M	Miner	23Ju02Eq

NAMES OF PASSENGERS		AGE	SEX	OCCUPATIONS	DATE PORT SHIP
HOGAN, John		31	M	None	23Ju02Eq
STANGE, Robert		40	M	None	23Ju02Eq
U	(W)	32	F	Unknown	23Ju02Eq
U		.00	U	Infant	23Ju02Eq
BLACK, John		27	M	Unknown	23Ju02Eq
WHITE, Richd.		26	M	Unknown	23Ju02Eq
RUE, Wm.		24	M	Unknown	23Ju02Eq
Sarah		29	F	Unknown	23Ju02Eq
DONNELL, J.		31	M	Unknown	23Ju02Eq
U		10	F	Unknown	23Ju02Eq
U		07	F	Unknown	23Ju02Eq

AGNES 24 JUNE 1848

From Liverpool

NAMES OF PASSENGERS		AGE	SEX	OCCUPATIONS	DATE PORT SHIP
THRING, Frederick		20	M	Laborer	24Ju02Lx
Jane		20	F	Spinster	24Ju02Lx
BELLEW, Michael		20	M	Laborer	24Ju02Lx
Mary		21	F	Spinster	24Ju02Lx
NUGENT, Thomas		28	M	Laborer	24Ju02Lx
Pat.		25	M	Laborer	24Ju02Lx
MADAGAN, Thomas		25	M	Laborer	24Ju02Lx
CROSSETT, Jane		20	F	Spinster	24Ju02Lx
KENNEDY, Robert		26	M	Laborer	24Ju02Lx
RICHARDSON, Thomas		20	M	Laborer	24Ju02Lx
CAULFIELD, Thomas		24	M	Laborer	24Ju02Lx
Margaret		19	F	Spinster	24Ju02Lx
CREAGH, Hanna		28	F	Spinster	24Ju02Lx
Frances		02	F	Child	24Ju02Lx
Hanna		.00	F	Infant	24Ju02Lx
SULLIVAN, Daniel		40	M	Laborer	24Ju02Lx
NEHER, Samuel		25	M	Laborer	24Ju02Lx
William		20	M	Laborer	24Ju02Lx
James		03	M	Child	24Ju02Lx
Lucy		02	F	Child	24Ju02Lx
Alfred		.00	F	Infant	24Ju02Lx
READ, James		24	F	Laborer	24Ju02Lx
LYNCH, Pat		40	F	Laborer	24Ju02Lx
COLEMAN, Ellen		20	F	Spinster	24Ju02Lx
Michael		20	M	Laborer	24Ju02Lx
BRIEN, Bridget		22	F	Spinster	24Ju02Lx
MAGUIRE, Thomas		25	M	Laborer	24Ju02Lx
MCINTYRE, Kennedy		25	M	Laborer	24Ju02Lx
FANNEY, Pat.		26	M	Laborer	24Ju02Lx
KEARNEY, William		30	M	Laborer	24Ju02Lx
MULLIGAN, Jno.		29	M	Laborer	24Ju02Lx
MCKAY, Joseph		22	M	Laborer	24Ju02Lx
GAVAN, William		22	M	Laborer	24Ju02Lx
HUGHES, Jno.		35	M	Laborer	24Ju02Lx
Patrick		20	M	Laborer	24Ju02Lx
Thomas		18	M	Laborer	24Ju02Lx
Michael		11	M	None	24Ju02Lx
DINNIN, Michael		21	M	Laborer	24Ju02Lx
GAVAN, Jno.		20	M	Laborer	24Ju02Lx
CARLY, Brian		20	M	Laborer	24Ju02Lx
HUGHES, Charles		28	M	Laborer	24Ju02Lx
CAVANAGH, George		36	M	Laborer	24Ju02Lx
RILY, Edwin		26	M	Laborer	24Ju02Lx
GORDON, Jno.		40	M	Laborer	24Ju02Lx
Nancy		40	F	Spinster	24Ju02Lx
Martha		40	F	Spinster	24Ju02Lx
QUIN, Pat.		40	M	Laborer	24Ju02Lx
STEVENS, Henry		50	M	Laborer	24Ju02Lx
Richard		30	M	Laborer	24Ju02Lx
ALLEN, William		27	M	Laborer	24Ju02Lx
STEVENS, Jno.		17	M	Laborer	24Ju02Lx
RILY, Phil.		20	M	Laborer	24Ju02Lx
FOX, Edwd.		24	M	Laborer	24Ju02Lx
MCKENNA, Catherine		20	F	Spinster	24Ju02Lx
BUTLER, Ellen		26	F	Spinster	24Ju02Lx
Rachel		25	F	Spinster	24Ju02Lx
WHITE, Nancy		26	F	Spinster	24Ju02Lx
POWER, Jeffry		24	M	Laborer	24Ju02Lx
Bridget		20	F	Spinster	24Ju02Lx
ROBINSON, Solomon		24	M	Laborer	24Ju02Lx
Jissy		09	F	Child	24Ju02Lx
Hanna		40	F	Spinster	24Ju02Lx
WORK, Esther		30	F	Spinster	24Ju02Lx
David		02	M	Child	24Ju02Lx
Mary		.00	F	Infant	24Ju02Lx
MCCARTY, Charles		30	M	Laborer	24Ju02Lx
WATERS, Michael		30	M	Laborer	24Ju02Lx
BUTLER, Daniel		26	M	Laborer	24Ju02Lx
William		25	M	Laborer	24Ju02Lx
Ellen		21	F	Spinster	24Ju02Lx
Elvira		16	F	Spinster	24Ju02Lx
Michael		16	M	Laborer	24Ju02Lx
Ellen		22	F	Spinster	24Ju02Lx
GARDNER, M.		31	M	Laborer	24Ju02Lx
MILLS, Margaret		08	F	Child	24Ju02Lx
Isabella		06	F	Child	24Ju02Lx
Michael		04	M	Child	24Ju02Lx
Alexander		.00	M	Infant	24Ju02Lx
MALONE, Denis		20	M	Laborer	24Ju02Lx
MONSEY, James		25	M	Laborer	24Ju02Lx
HYUM, Nancy		30	F	Spinster	24Ju02Lx
MCNALLY, Mary		16	F	Spinster	24Ju02Lx
Rose		20	F	Spinster	24Ju02Lx
FOGARTY, Bridget		21	F	Spinster	24Ju02Lx
JOHNSON, Edward		20	M	Laborer	24Ju02Lx
SHINGFELLEN, M.		18	M	Laborer	24Ju02Lx
BANAN, Isaac		21	M	Laborer	24Ju02Lx
FENEY, Robert		28	M	Laborer	24Ju02Lx
CONNOR, Henry		30	M	Laborer	24Ju02Lx
WILLIAMS, Jno.		20	M	Laborer	24Ju02Lx
HENDERSON, James		20	M	Laborer	24Ju02Lx
BURKE, William		32	M	Laborer	24Ju02Lx
Jno.		50	M	Laborer	24Ju02Lx
Mary		50	F	Spinster	24Ju02Lx
Martin		18	M	Laborer	24Ju02Lx
Margaret		23	F	Spinster	24Ju02Lx
Margaret		.00	F	Infant	24Ju02Lx
CURRIE, Pat.		25	M	Laborer	24Ju02Lx
GULEN, Hanna		25	F	Spinster	24Ju02Lx
MCGLADDERY, Pat.		28	M	Laborer	24Ju02Lx
FANSEY, William		30	M	Farmer	24Ju02Lx
FAMDFORT, Walter		30	M	Farmer	24Ju02Lx
HAIGH, Charles		40	M	Laborer	24Ju02Lx
Jane		25	F	Seamstress	24Ju02Lx
U		13	M	None	24Ju02Lx
Isabella		09	F	Child	24Ju02Lx
Ellen		07	F	Child	24Ju02Lx
WINSON, Thomas		32	M	Laborer	24Ju02Lx
Mary	(W)	28	F	Seamstress	24Ju02Lx
Denis		03	M	Child	24Ju02Lx
Henry		.00	M	Infant	24Ju02Lx
HARRIS, William		26	M	Laborer	24Ju02Lx
Mary		25	F	Seamstress	24Ju02Lx
Mary-Anne		.00	F	Infant	24Ju02Lx
FOLEY, Thomas		40	M	Laborer	24Ju02Lx
FLYNN, Pat.		22	M	Laborer	24Ju02Lx
DWYER, Thomas		27	M	Laborer	24Ju02Lx
WALSH, Jno.		17	M	Laborer	24Ju02Lx
KING, Ellen		30	F	Seamstress	24Ju02Lx
WILLIAMS, Timothy		40	M	Laborer	24Ju02Lx
Dolly		40	F	Seamstress	24Ju02Lx
Nancy		16	F	Seamstress	24Ju02Lx
Margaret		13	F	Seamstress	24Ju02Lx
William		09	M	Child	24Ju02Lx
Martha		06	F	Child	24Ju02Lx
Nancy		03	F	Child	24Ju02Lx
Judy		.00	F	Infant	24Ju02Lx
CAVANAGH, Edward		16	M	Laborer	24Ju02Lx

NAMES OF PASSENGERS	AGE	SEX	OCCUPATIONS	DATE PORT SHIP
NUGENT, Thomas	28	M	Laborer	24Ju02Lx
CAMPBELL, Robert	27	M	Laborer	24Ju02Lx
Elvira	26	F	Seamstress	24Ju02Lx
Neal	20	M	Laborer	24Ju02Lx
HENRY, Anna	19	F	Seamstress	24Ju02Lx
Nancy	.00	F	Infant	24Ju02Lx
Neal	.00	M	Infant	24Ju02Lx
CONLAN, Pat.	25	M	Laborer	24Ju02Lx
Anne	21	F	Seamstress	24Ju02Lx
MCINTAGGART, Michael	21	M	Laborer	24Ju02Lx
SCHIND, Lewis	21	M	Laborer	24Ju02Lx
MCGOVERN, Pat.	60	M	Laborer	24Ju02Lx
Nancy	50	F	Seamstress	24Ju02Lx
Jno.	16	M	Laborer	24Ju02Lx
James	18	M	Laborer	24Ju02Lx
Bridget	13	F	Seamstress	24Ju02Lx
Mary	10	F	None	24Ju02Lx
Betty	02	F	Child	24Ju02Lx
Mary	08	F	Child	24Ju02Lx
KENNEDY, Mary	20	F	Seamstress	24Ju02Lx
BRENNAN, Mary	20	F	Seamstress	24Ju02Lx
HULL, Hugh	35	M	Laborer	24Ju02Lx
MILTON, William	30	M	Laborer	24Ju02Lx
MCSERRON, Catherine	.00	F	Infant	24Ju02Lx
Ellen	40	F	Seamstress	24Ju02Lx
Agnes	18	F	Seamstress	24Ju02Lx
Sarah-Jane	14	F	Seamstress	24Ju02Lx
Edward	12	M	Laborer	24Ju02Lx
James	10	M	None	24Ju02Lx
Ellen	08	F	Child	24Ju02Lx
Elvira	07	F	Child	24Ju02Lx
Mary	07	F	Child	24Ju02Lx
CURLSHAW, Morris	18	M	Laborer	24Ju02Lx
BOYLUN, Catherine	20	F	Seamstress	24Ju02Lx

ELIZA 24 JUNE 1848

From Waterford

NAMES OF PASSENGERS	AGE	SEX	OCCUPATIONS	DATE PORT SHIP
DOYLE, James	45	M	Farmer	24Ju16Lk
Margaret	38	F	Seamstress	24Ju16Lk
Mary	19	F	Seamstress	24Ju16Lk
Ellen	12	F	Seamstress	24Ju16Lk
John	09	M	Child	24Ju16Lk
William	05	M	Child	24Ju16Lk
Thomas	05	M	Child	24Ju16Lk
Catharine	.00	F	Infant	24Ju16Lk
HAYDEN, Mary	24	F	Seamstress	24Ju16Lk
IVY, Catharine	21	F	Seamstress	24Ju16Lk
RYAN, Bridget	30	F	Seamstress	24Ju16Lk
MCDONALD, Sylvester	30	M	Laborer	24Ju16Lk
Mary	34	F	Seamstress	24Ju16Lk
WALSH, James	50	M	Laborer	24Ju16Lk
BRYAN, John	21	M	Laborer	24Ju16Lk
RYAN, Mary	20	F	Seamstress	24Ju16Lk
NEIL, Bridget	20	F	Seamstress	24Ju16Lk
ROE, Thomas	20	M	Laborer	24Ju16Lk
OSULLIVAN, Margaret	30	F	Seamstress	24Ju16Lk
ROE, John	27	M	Farmer	24Ju16Lk
Pat.	30	M	Farmer	24Ju16Lk
Catharine	40	F	Seamstress	24Ju16Lk
Catharine	28	F	Seamstress	24Ju16Lk
Ellen	12	F	Seamstress	24Ju16Lk
WALLACE, James	40	M	Laborer	24Ju16Lk
Margaret	12	F	None	24Ju16Lk
Robt.	10	M	None	24Ju16Lk
HOLDING, Jno.	20	M	Laborer	24Ju16Lk
James	20	M	Laborer	24Ju16Lk
MAHER, Pat.	29	M	Laborer	24Ju16Lk
WHELAN, Jno.	35	M	Laborer	24Ju16Lk
CARROLL, Martin	25	M	Laborer	24Ju16Lk
MOORE, Mary	25	F	Seamstress	24Ju16Lk
PHELAN, Alice	21	F	Seamstress	24Ju16Lk
Bridget	20	F	Seamstress	24Ju16Lk
MAHONEY, Thomas	25	M	Laborer	24Ju16Lk
FLYNN, Pat.	25	M	Laborer	24Ju16Lk
SHEA, David	30	M	Laborer	24Ju16Lk
Bridget	24	F	Seamstress	24Ju16Lk
Philip	04	M	Child	24Ju16Lk
Ellen	.00	F	Infant	24Ju16Lk
DANIEL, John	38	M	Laborer	24Ju16Lk
Mary	34	F	Seamstress	24Ju16Lk
DOBBIN, Martin	24	M	Laborer	24Ju16Lk
POWER, Thomas	20	M	Laborer	24Ju16Lk
CARROLL, Margaret	26	F	Seamstress	24Ju16Lk
MANSFIELD, James	24	M	Laborer	24Ju16Lk
COADY, Jno.	23	M	Laborer	24Ju16Lk
Bridget	.00	F	Infant	24Ju16Lk
TALBOT, Michael	47	M	Laborer	24Ju16Lk
Jno.	19	M	Laborer	24Ju16Lk
Anty	16	F	Seamstress	24Ju16Lk
COADY, Margaret	36	F	Seamstress	24Ju16Lk
BRENAN, Thomas	25	M	Laborer	24Ju16Lk
BRITON, Thomas	25	M	Laborer	24Ju16Lk
DOHERTY, James	21	M	Laborer	24Ju16Lk
COMERFORD, Richard	19	M	Laborer	24Ju16Lk
ODONNELL, Catharine	21	F	Seamstress	24Ju16Lk
POWER, Johanna	17	F	Seamstress	24Ju16Lk
Anne	25	F	Seamstress	24Ju16Lk
GALLAVAN, John	21	M	Shoemaker	24Ju16Lk
DRUIN, Stephan	45	M	Shoemaker	24Ju16Lk
PHELAN, James	19	M	Laborer	24Ju16Lk
BAKER, Benjamin	24	M	Laborer	24Ju16Lk
POWER, Pat.	19	M	Laborer	24Ju16Lk
OCONNOR, Michael	30	M	Gentleman	24Ju16Lk
HENESSY, Pat.	30	M	Gentleman	24Ju16Lk

KING PHILIP 26 JUNE 1848

From Santiago De Cuba

NAMES OF PASSENGERS	AGE	SEX	OCCUPATIONS	DATE PORT SHIP
BOYLAN, Philip	21	M	Merchant	26Jua1Vp

ASHBURTON 26 JUNE 1848

From Liverpool

NAMES OF PASSENGERS	AGE	SEX	OCCUPATIONS	DATE PORT SHIP
BRADY, Brian	35	M	Laborer	26Ju02Bd
WILEY, Jno.	25	M	Laborer	26Ju02Bd
MCQUE, John	27	M	Laborer	26Ju02Bd
CULINGAN, Michael	24	M	Laborer	26Ju02Bd
JESSEIS, Edward	20	M	Laborer	26Ju02Bd
HURLEY, Thos.	28	M	Laborer	26Ju02Bd
RYAN, Wm.	45	M	Laborer	26Ju02Bd
CHOVLIN, Owen	20	M	Laborer	26Ju02Bd
ODONNELL, Edward	40	M	Brick Maker	26Ju02Bd
DEVIT, Patrick	30	M	Laborer	26Ju02Bd
HUGHES, Patrick	36	M	Weaver	26Ju02Bd
CROCKHAN, Thos.	45	M	Farmer	26Ju02Bd
KOE, Dominick	60	M	Laborer	26Ju02Bd
Mary	45	F	Laborer	26Ju02Bd
Margaret	23	F	Laborer	26Ju02Bd

NAMES OF PASSENGERS	AGE	SEX	OCCUPATIONS	DATE PORT SHIP
KOE, Edward	25	M	Laborer	26Ju02Bd
Lally	22	M	Laborer	26Ju02Bd
Ann	18	F	Laborer	26Ju02Bd
Henry	15	M	Laborer	26Ju02Bd
Robert	13	M	Laborer	26Ju02Bd
CAVONEY, Martin	32	M	Laborer	26Ju02Bd
Annora	30	F	Laborer	26Ju02Bd
Wm.	13	M	Laborer	26Ju02Bd
Mary	09	F	Child	26Ju02Bd
Eliza	05	F	Child	26Ju02Bd
Martin	02	M	Child	26Ju02Bd
CONNOR, James	35	M	Carpenter	26Ju02Bd
CIVEN, Peter	21	M	Laborer	26Ju02Bd
DORTON, Catherine	18	F	Laborer	26Ju02Bd
CEVEY, Bridget	25	F	Laborer	26Ju02Bd
Patrick	30	M	Laborer	26Ju02Bd
Michael	.00	M	Infant	26Ju02Bd
SULLIVAN, Jerry	50	U	Laborer	26Ju02Bd
JOSEY, Mary	30	F	Laborer	26Ju02Bd
BOYLE, Mary	43	F	Laborer	26Ju02Bd
Bridget	20	F	Laborer	26Ju02Bd
John	12	M	Laborer	26Ju02Bd
Rose	10	F	Laborer	26Ju02Bd
Peter	07	M	Child	26Ju02Bd
Pat.	03	M	Child	26Ju02Bd
KOE, Eliza	11	F	Laborer	26Ju02Bd
James	08	M	Child	26Ju02Bd
Wm.	02	M	Child	26Ju02Bd
DUNNAVAN, Jno.	45	M	Laborer	26Ju02Bd
Margaret	17	F	Laborer	26Ju02Bd
MCLAUGHLIN, Mary	24	F	Laborer	26Ju02Bd
Catherine	22	F	Laborer	26Ju02Bd
GREEN, Math.	22	M	Laborer	26Ju02Bd
MCMAHAN, Thos.	22	M	Laborer	26Ju02Bd
DENNAN, John	31	M	Laborer	26Ju02Bd
Margaret	26	F	Laborer	26Ju02Bd
Catherine	03	F	Child	26Ju02Bd
Margaret	.00	F	Infant	26Ju02Bd
SMITH, Catherine	23	F	Laborer	26Ju02Bd
MCMANUS, Catherine	21	F	Laborer	26Ju02Bd
TOWERS, Betsy	23	F	Laborer	26Ju02Bd
DONNIGAN, Christy	30	M	Mason	26Ju02Bd
Ellen	25	F	Unknown	26Ju02Bd
Christy	.00	M	Infant	26Ju02Bd
GATITY, Mary	40	F	Servant	26Ju02Bd
May	11	F	Unknown	26Ju02Bd
Thos.	10	M	Unknown	26Ju02Bd
MUIR, Geo.	30	M	Teacher	26Ju02Bd
Geo.Jr.	13	M	Child	26Ju02Bd
Robt.	30	M	Farmer	26Ju02Bd
LITTLE, Jno.	25	M	Laborer	26Ju02Bd
DAVIES, Patrick	21	M	Laborer	26Ju02Bd
SMITH, Jno.	36	M	Rope Maker	26Ju02Bd
MCGUFFOCK, Jno.	38	M	Farmer	26Ju02Bd
Ellen	35	F	Unknown	26Ju02Bd
James	14	M	Unknown	26Ju02Bd
Jno.	12	M	Unknown	26Ju02Bd
Elizabeth	10	F	Unknown	26Ju02Bd
Wm.	08	M	Child	26Ju02Bd
Marion	06	F	Child	26Ju02Bd
Jane	04	F	Child	26Ju02Bd
Mathew	02	M	Child	26Ju02Bd
DINNEDY, Michele	26	M	Laborer	26Ju02Bd
Catherine	26	F	Unknown	26Ju02Bd
Ann	.00	F	Infant	26Ju02Bd
MILLOG, Geo.	20	M	Laborer	26Ju02Bd
COTTON, Martha	26	F	Lace Maker	26Ju02Bd
Wm.	04	M	Child	26Ju02Bd
AKEN, Jno.	19	M	Laborer	26Ju02Bd
Ann	15	F	Unknown	26Ju02Bd
CROSS, James	23	M	Blr	26Ju02Bd
BUNDELL, Evan	30	M	Mechanic	26Ju02Bd
SHAW, Jno.	19	M	Wls	26Ju02Bd
Emelin	17	M	Unknown	26Ju02Bd
KERY, Wm.	23	M	Clcp	26Ju02Bd
MECHINSON, John	24	M	Molder	26Ju02Bd
CELLIGAN, Eugine	18	M	Hatter	26Ju02Bd
REGAN, Johanna	40	F	Laborer	26Ju02Bd
Johanna	19	F	Laborer	26Ju02Bd
RAGAIN, Wm.	16	M	Laborer	26Ju02Bd
David	13	M	Laborer	26Ju02Bd
Thos.	11	M	Laborer	26Ju02Bd
Mary	09	F	Child	26Ju02Bd
Ellen	07	F	Child	26Ju02Bd
RICHARDS, John	32	M	Laborer	26Ju02Bd
Bridget	32	F	Unknown	26Ju02Bd
M.J.	13	U	Unknown	26Ju02Bd
Margaret	09	F	Child	26Ju02Bd
Edward	06	M	Child	26Ju02Bd
James	06	M	Child	26Ju02Bd
LEJUL, Benjamin	34	M	Spinner	26Ju02Bd
BOYLE, John	40	M	Carpenter	26Ju02Bd
Biddy	40	F	Unknown	26Ju02Bd
Michele	18	M	Unknown	26Ju02Bd
Andrew	13	M	Unknown	26Ju02Bd
John	11	M	Child	26Ju02Bd
Phillip	08	M	Child	26Ju02Bd
Pat.	03	M	Child	26Ju02Bd
LINCH, Rosey	16	F	Laborer	26Ju02Bd
MAHAR, Bridget	18	F	Laborer	26Ju02Bd
HAZELL, Wm.	23	M	Blr	26Ju02Bd
HEARTHAN, Peter	30	M	Blr	26Ju02Bd
DOYLE, Jos.	20	M	Laborer	26Ju02Bd
WOOD, Mary	22	F	Dressmaker	26Ju02Bd
QUEEN, Bridget	66	F	Laborer	26Ju02Bd
MCGOVERN, Bissey	19	F	Laborer	26Ju02Bd
MARTIN, Mary	15	F	Laborer	26Ju02Bd
FARRAE, Catherine	25	F	Laborer	26Ju02Bd
CROCKHAN, Elizabeth	45	F	Laborer	26Ju02Bd
May	17	F	Unknown	26Ju02Bd
James	15	M	Unknown	26Ju02Bd
Simon	13	M	Unknown	26Ju02Bd
Bartel	11	M	Child	26Ju02Bd
Wm.	09	M	Child	26Ju02Bd
Pat.	08	M	Child	26Ju02Bd
Thos.	06	M	Child	26Ju02Bd
Ann	05	F	Child	26Ju02Bd
John	.00	M	Infant	26Ju02Bd
MCCORMOCK, Ann	20	F	Servant	26Ju02Bd
BRADY, Hugh	20	M	Laborer	26Ju02Bd
BUCKLY, Daniel	50	M	Farmer	26Ju02Bd
Kate	16	F	Unknown	26Ju02Bd
LINNEN, Thos.	20	M	Laborer	26Ju02Bd
CONNER, Jerry	28	M	Laborer	26Ju02Bd
MERIGHER, Luke	28	M	Laborer	26Ju02Bd
HICKEY, Margaret	23	F	Laborer	26Ju02Bd
Ellen	24	F	Laborer	26Ju02Bd
FAGAN, Peter	21	M	Laborer	26Ju02Bd
KENNON, Ellen	17	F	Laborer	26Ju02Bd
BURKE, Jos.	20	M	Laborer	26Ju02Bd
RILEY, Hugh	45	M	Laborer	26Ju02Bd
Catherine	40	F	Unknown	26Ju02Bd
Thos.	15	M	Unknown	26Ju02Bd
Bessey	13	F	Unknown	26Ju02Bd
May	12	F	Unknown	26Ju02Bd
Ann	10	F	Unknown	26Ju02Bd
Catherine	09	F	Child	26Ju02Bd
Margaret	07	F	Child	26Ju02Bd
Lucy	05	F	Child	26Ju02Bd
Alley	03	F	Child	26Ju02Bd
Owen	01	M	Child	26Ju02Bd
CORMCK, Bessy	09	F	Child	26Ju02Bd
KELLY, Juda-S.	16	F	Laborer	26Ju02Bd
CRONNON, Pat.	18	M	Laborer	26Ju02Bd
MCGURROK, Arthur	22	M	Laborer	26Ju02Bd
CLEARY, Nat.	32	M	Laborer	26Ju02Bd
LEVEY, Wm.	22	M	Laborer	26Ju02Bd
Bridget	22	F	Laborer	26Ju02Bd
DONNAHOE, John	32	M	Laborer	26Ju02Bd
BULKLEY, Brian	23	M	Tailor	26Ju02Bd

NAMES OF PASSENGERS	AGE	SEX	OCCUPATIONS	DATE PORT SHIP
SHANE, Jonna	17	M	Laborer	26Ju02Bd
MCQUAN, Sarah	17	F	Laborer	26Ju02Bd
Ellen	20	F	Unknown	26Ju02Bd
MAID, Jane	29	F	Unknown	26Ju02Bd
Barnard	15	M	Unknown	26Ju02Bd
Jane	11	F	Unknown	26Ju02Bd
Jno.	03	M	Child	26Ju02Bd
FOLBY, Daniel	19	M	Joiner	26Ju02Bd
BRADY, Catherine	20	F	Unknown	26Ju02Bd
JACKSON, Samuel	43	M	Unknown	26Ju02Bd
CONNOR, Hannah	44	F	Unknown	26Ju02Bd
Edward	24	M	Unknown	26Ju02Bd
Ann	22	F	Unknown	26Ju02Bd
James	00	M	Unknown	26Ju02Bd
Fanny	20	F	Unknown	26Ju02Bd
Hannah	13	M	Unknown	26Ju02Bd
Agnes	12	F	Unknown	26Ju02Bd
Eliza	08	F	Unknown	26Ju02Bd
FLYN, May	21	F	Unknown	26Ju02Bd
GALLATHER, Elizabeth	18	F	Unknown	26Ju02Bd
FLATHERTY, Mary	17	F	Unknown	26Ju02Bd
BARBER, Hugh	53	M	Farmer	26Ju02Bd
Sarah	43	F	Unknown	26Ju02Bd
Ellzebeth	20	F	Unknown	26Ju02Bd
Jane	16	F	Unknown	26Ju02Bd
John	14	M	Unknown	26Ju02Bd
Emma	12	F	Unknown	26Ju02Bd
Anna	10	F	Unknown	26Ju02Bd
Thos.	08	M	Child	26Ju02Bd
Henry	06	M	Child	26Ju02Bd
Geo.	04	M	Child	26Ju02Bd
Sarah	02	F	Child	26Ju02Bd
BROADHURST, Elizebeth	63	F	Laborer	26Ju02Bd
UNNIS, Catherine	16	F	Laborer	26Ju02Bd
LARREN, Wm.	30	M	Laborer	26Ju02Bd
DOHERTY, Mary	20	F	Laborer	26Ju02Bd
KUTE, Daniel	24	M	Laborer	26Ju02Bd
DUFFIE, John	20	M	Laborer	26Ju02Bd
SUTE, Edward	31	M	Laborer	26Ju02Bd
FEGAN, Pat.	27	M	Laborer	26Ju02Bd
LUN, Lanthy	20	M	Blacksmith	26Ju02Bd
CURE, Domerick	24	M	Laborer	26Ju02Bd
Mary	50	F	Laborer	26Ju02Bd
BARRETT, Brion	35	M	Laborer	26Ju02Bd
Mary	30	F	Unknown	26Ju02Bd
Martin	04	M	Child	26Ju02Bd
John	02	M	Child	26Ju02Bd
POWERS, Michael	32	M	Laborer	26Ju02Bd
John	40	M	Laborer	26Ju02Bd
James	38	M	Laborer	26Ju02Bd
HUSKIN, Pat.	27	M	Laborer	26Ju02Bd
CALLAGAN, Nancy	21	F	Laborer	26Ju02Bd
RUSH, Wm.	27	M	Shoemaker	26Ju02Bd
HALE, Mary	25	F	Laborer	26Ju02Bd
Mary-Ann	04	F	Child	26Ju02Bd
MCKENZIE, Ellen	24	F	Unknown	26Ju02Bd
MCGREE, Susan	28	F	Unknown	26Ju02Bd
CARBERRY, John	30	M	Unknown	26Ju02Bd
DEVANY, Thos.	48	M	Unknown	26Ju02Bd
MCSAGERT, Ann	22	F	Unknown	26Ju02Bd
BURS, Hugh	26	M	Unknown	26Ju02Bd
BURR, Ann	36	F	Unknown	26Ju02Bd
Eliza	16	F	Unknown	26Ju02Bd
KELLY, May	30	F	Unknown	26Ju02Bd
MCDONNAL, Jane	19	F	Dressmaker	26Ju02Bd
DURFEE, Catherine	20	F	Laborer	26Ju02Bd
MESOTON, Bridget	24	F	Laborer	26Ju02Bd
HURLEY, Daniel	30	M	Tailor	26Ju02Bd
Mary	20	F	Unknown	26Ju02Bd
ROE, John	21	M	Laborer	26Ju02Bd
FOX, James	20	M	Laborer	26Ju02Bd
QUEEN, Edward	25	M	Laborer	26Ju02Bd
MELEY, Bridget	20	F	Laborer	26Ju02Bd
RAYNOLD, B.	20	U	Laborer	26Ju02Bd
BOHAN, Michael	15	M	Laborer	26Ju02Bd

NAMES OF PASSENGERS	AGE	SEX	OCCUPATIONS	DATE PORT SHIP
BRUMAN, Michael	16	M	Laborer	26Ju02Bd
EVERETT, Larana	24	U	Laborer	26Ju02Bd
May	28	F	Laborer	26Ju02Bd
MCDONNAL, John	17	M	Laborer	26Ju02Bd
MCKILLERN, Thos.	26	M	Laborer	26Ju02Bd
CARNEY, John	23	M	Laborer	26Ju02Bd
FAMLINSON, Robt.	24	M	Laborer	26Ju02Bd
BIRON, Michael	30	M	Farmer	26Ju02Bd
Ellen	24	F	Unknown	26Ju02Bd
Margaret	02	F	Child	26Ju02Bd
HASTINGS, Peter	30	M	Unknown	26Ju02Bd
Eliza	20	F	Unknown	26Ju02Bd
Phillip	04	M	Child	26Ju02Bd
Eliza	02	F	Child	26Ju02Bd
BURKE, Mary	20	F	Servant	26Ju02Bd
WILLS, Bedella	17	F	Servant	26Ju02Bd
ROONEY, Nora	15	F	Servant	26Ju02Bd
LEFIA, Harriet	20	F	Servant	26Ju02Bd
SMITH, Mary-A.	24	F	Servant	26Ju02Bd
Lewis	03	M	Child	26Ju02Bd
GARRET, G.	20	M	Servant	26Ju02Bd
FARRAL, Richard	26	M	Carpenter	26Ju02Bd
MCGUIRE, May	20	F	Servant	26Ju02Bd

ADAM-CARR 26 JUNE 1848

From Glasgow

NAMES OF PASSENGERS	AGE	SEX	OCCUPATIONS	DATE PORT SHIP
OBRIAN, Patrick	40	M	Laborer	26Ju04Aw
Mary (W)	35	F	Wife	26Ju04Aw
MCNINEMA, Edward-M.	28	M	Laborer	26Ju04Aw
MCGUIRE, Bernard	50	M	Laborer	26Ju04Aw
Edward	19	M	Laborer	26Ju04Aw
Hellen	48	F	Laborer	26Ju04Aw
CURRIE, John	24	M	Miner	26Ju04Aw
HIGGINS, Mary-Bella	28	F	Spinster	26Ju04Aw
WARD, William	38	M	Laborer	26Ju04Aw
Nancy	30	F	None	26Ju04Aw
Michael	06	M	None	26Ju04Aw
Daniel	04	M	None	26Ju04Aw
Bridget	02	F	None	26Ju04Aw
John	.06	M	Infant	26Ju04Aw
CONNOLLY, Elizabeth	18	F	Spinster	26Ju04Aw
GREEN, Elizabeth	20	F	Spinster	26Ju04Aw
LAURIE, William	25	M	Shoemaker	26Ju04Aw
MCGREGOR, Francis	24	M	Shoemaker	26Ju04Aw
CAMPBELL, Thomas	26	M	Printer	26Ju04Aw
BALLENTINE, William	25	M	Engineer	26Ju04Aw
FORSON, Robert	25	M	Engineer	26Ju04Aw

BRITTANIA-OF-GLASGOW 26 JUNE 1848

From Liverpool

NAMES OF PASSENGERS	AGE	SEX	OCCUPATIONS	DATE PORT SHIP
DRUMMOND, William	51	M	Clergyman	26Ju02Va
MURRAY, Peter	36	M	Merchant	26Ju02Va
MILLAN, J.	32	M	Merchant	26Ju02Va
MITCHELL, William	19	M	Servant	26Ju02Va

NAMES OF PASSENGERS		AGE	SEX	OCCUPATIONS	DATE PORT SHIP

GRAMPION 26 JUNE 1848

From Belfast

NAMES OF PASSENGERS		AGE	SEX	OCCUPATIONS	DATE PORT SHIP
MCKANE, Wm.		28	M	Laborer	26Ju07Up
WHISKER, James		23	M	Laborer	26Ju07Up
Mary	(W)	24	F	Wife	26Ju07Up
James	(S)	06	M	Child	26Ju07Up
Robt.	(S)	04	M	Child	26Ju07Up
Wm.	(S)	02	M	Child	26Ju07Up
John	(S)	.00	M	Infant	26Ju07Up
MOLES, James		20	M	Laborer	26Ju07Up
MCVEY, Robt.		20	M	Laborer	26Ju07Up
BURN, John		67	M	Laborer	26Ju07Up
Margt.	(W)	63	F	Wife	26Ju07Up
Saml.	(S)	24	M	Farmer	26Ju07Up
Margt.	(W)	22	F	Wife	26Ju07Up
Robt.		18	M	Laborer	26Ju07Up
GROGAN, Eliza		22	F	Spinster	26Ju07Up
HESLIP, Agnes		26	F	Spinster	26Ju07Up
Joseph	(S)	04	M	Child	26Ju07Up
Eliza	(D)	.00	F	Infant	26Ju07Up
MCGERM, Andw.		37	M	Laborer	26Ju07Up
GRAHAM, Geo.		28	M	Laborer	26Ju07Up
ONEILL, James		22	M	Laborer	26Ju07Up
Bern.		18	M	Laborer	26Ju07Up
SMALL, Robt.		26	M	Laborer	26Ju07Up
Cath.	(W)	21	F	Wife	26Ju07Up
MCCAGHENY, Rosey		24	F	Wife	26Ju07Up
GRAHAM, John		30	M	Laborer	26Ju07Up
CLOSE, John		17	M	Laborer	26Ju07Up
RUSSELL, Hugh		50	M	Laborer	26Ju07Up
Francis		22	M	Laborer	26Ju07Up
Saml.		18	M	Laborer	26Ju07Up
Agnes		16	F	Spinster	26Ju07Up
Jane		15	F	Spinster	26Ju07Up
MCGRADY, Bern.		35	M	Laborer	26Ju07Up
TAGGERTS, James		15	M	Laborer	26Ju07Up
JOHNSTONE, Robt.		53	M	Laborer	26Ju07Up
NEILL, Mary		20	F	Spinster	26Ju07Up
Eliza		16	F	Spinster	26Ju07Up
SLOAN, David		25	M	Laborer	26Ju07Up
Eliza		25	F	Spinster	26Ju07Up
Margt.		26	F	Spinster	26Ju07Up
Mary		20	F	Spinster	26Ju07Up
GIBSON, Robt.		52	M	Laborer	26Ju07Up
Isabella	(W)	41	F	Laborer	26Ju07Up
Robt.	(S)	18	M	Laborer	26Ju07Up
Isabella	(D)	17	F	Laborer	26Ju07Up
Eliza	(D)	15	F	Laborer	26Ju07Up
Margt.	(D)	14	F	Laborer	26Ju07Up
Sarah	(D)	12	F	Laborer	26Ju07Up
Ann	(D)	08	F	Laborer	26Ju07Up
John	(S)	06	M	Child	26Ju07Up
Mary	(D)	04	F	Child	26Ju07Up
James	(S)	.00	M	Infant	26Ju07Up
MCCORMELL, Eliza		25	F	Spinster	26Ju07Up
MCKELVEY, Alex.		20	M	Laborer	26Ju07Up
GILMORE, Margt.		50	F	Spinster	26Ju07Up
RUSSELL, Joseph		13	M	Child	26Ju07Up
Wm.		11	M	Child	26Ju07Up
Jane		09	F	Child	26Ju07Up
Martha		05	F	Child	26Ju07Up
MCALLISTER, Nancy		22	F	Spinster	26Ju07Up
MCCULLY, Wm.		36	M	Laborer	26Ju07Up
Mary		34	F	Spinster	26Ju07Up
Ann		09	F	Spinster	26Ju07Up
Jane		07	F	Spinster	26Ju07Up
John		04	M	Child	26Ju07Up
ROGERS, Eliza		60	F	Spinster	26Ju07Up
Margt.		50	F	Spinster	26Ju07Up
MCMEEHAM, James		22	M	Laborer	26Ju07Up
John		20	M	Laborer	26Ju07Up
COBEEN, James		60	M	Laborer	26Ju07Up
HENRY, Wm.		22	M	Laborer	26Ju07Up
MCCORMICK, Mich.		20	M	Laborer	26Ju07Up
KIRK, James		20	M	Laborer	26Ju07Up
Andrew		18	M	Laborer	26Ju07Up
Alex.		16	M	Laborer	26Ju07Up
GREEMAN, Mary		26	F	Spinster	26Ju07Up
PATTISON, Mary		20	F	Spinster	26Ju07Up
MCFARLAND, Mary		20	F	Spinster	26Ju07Up
Nancy		18	F	Spinster	26Ju07Up
MOONEY, Cath.		20	F	Spinster	26Ju07Up
BOYD, Mary		29	F	Spinster	26Ju07Up
GRAHAM, James		24	M	Laborer	26Ju07Up
Mary		24	F	Laborer	26Ju07Up
SPENCE, Robt.		21	M	Laborer	26Ju07Up
LINDSAY, Thos.		26	M	Laborer	26Ju07Up
Eliza	(W)	22	F	Laborer	26Ju07Up
Isaac	(S)	.00	M	Infant	26Ju07Up
WARD, Hugh		18	M	Laborer	26Ju07Up
Arthur		13	M	Laborer	26Ju07Up
MCCAY, Wm.		20	M	Laborer	26Ju07Up
KEENAN, Peter		25	M	Laborer	26Ju07Up
MCLOUGHLIN, Hugh		26	M	Laborer	26Ju07Up
CAULFIELD, Pat.		24	M	Laborer	26Ju07Up
HUSTON, Alex.		25	M	Laborer	26Ju07Up
Ann		26	F	Laborer	26Ju07Up
KELLY, John		19	F	Laborer	26Ju07Up
GORDON, Dan.		25	F	Laborer	26Ju07Up
COLYE, Jane		40	F	Wife	26Ju07Up
Alex.	(S)	13	M	Child	26Ju07Up
Mary	(D)	17	F	Child	26Ju07Up
Eliza	(D)	09	F	Child	26Ju07Up
Isabella	(D)	07	F	Child	26Ju07Up
WILEY, Eliz.		60	F	Spinster	26Ju07Up
TURNER, Henry		25	M	Laborer	26Ju07Up
WILLIAMS, Jane		20	F	Spinster	26Ju07Up
MCKELVEY, Sarah		35	F	Spinster	26Ju07Up
MCCLUSKEY, Henry		25	M	Laborer	26Ju07Up
Margt.		44	F	Spinster	26Ju07Up
MCAULEY, Mary		22	F	Spinster	26Ju07Up
DORMAN, John		25	M	Laborer	26Ju07Up
THOMPSON, John		23	M	Laborer	26Ju07Up
JACKSON, Robt.		35	M	Laborer	26Ju07Up
Eliz.		30	F	Unknown	26Ju07Up
John		13	M	Laborer	26Ju07Up
Isabella		11	F	Unknown	26Ju07Up
James		08	M	Unknown	26Ju07Up
Eliz.		.00	F	Infant	26Ju07Up
Margt.		15	F	Spinster	26Ju07Up
Robt.		26	M	None	26Ju07Up
John		20	M	None	26Ju07Up
Andrew		18	M	None	26Ju07Up
VANCE, Robt.		20	M	Laborer	26Ju07Up
ELLISON, Jas.		25	M	Laborer	26Ju07Up
CRAY, George		22	M	Laborer	26Ju07Up
BANNEN, Francis		25	M	Laborer	26Ju07Up
VANCE, Martha		22	F	Laborer	26Ju07Up
Margt.		18	F	Laborer	26Ju07Up
MARSHALL, Wm.		21	M	Laborer	26Ju07Up
Jane		23	F	Laborer	26Ju07Up
Mary		19	F	Laborer	26Ju07Up
Susanna		17	F	Laborer	26Ju07Up
Margt.		15	F	Laborer	26Ju07Up
Bishop		12	M	Laborer	26Ju07Up
Eliza		10	F	Laborer	26Ju07Up
DODDS, Francis		21	M	Laborer	26Ju07Up
BENNETT, Robt.		21	M	Laborer	26Ju07Up
RUSSELL, Wm.		46	M	Laborer	26Ju07Up
Sarah		36	F	Laborer	26Ju07Up
John		15	M	Laborer	26Ju07Up
SHANNON, Mathew		35	M	Laborer	26Ju07Up

NAMES OF PASSENGERS	AGE	SEX	OCCUPATIONS	DATE PORT SHIP
MCGLADE, Eliza	18	F	Spinster	26Ju07Up
CULBERT, Margt.	22	F	Spinster	26Ju07Up
GILLON, Robt.	25	M	Laborer	26Ju07Up
MCMURRAY, Robt.	27	M	Laborer	26Ju07Up
Hannah	36	F	Spinster	26Ju07Up
Margt.	04	F	Child	26Ju07Up
Ellen	.00	F	Infant	26Ju07Up
SONLLIN, Nancy	36	F	Unknown	26Ju07Up
Mary	20	F	Unknown	26Ju07Up
Jane	13	F	Unknown	26Ju07Up
ONIELL, Mary	18	F	Unknown	26Ju07Up
Teresa	19	F	Unknown	26Ju07Up
MCROBERTS, Wm.	45	M	Laborer	26Ju07Up
Jane	48	F	Laborer	26Ju07Up
Andrew	16	M	Laborer	26Ju07Up
John	13	M	Laborer	26Ju07Up
Mary	12	F	Child	26Ju07Up
Nancy	10	F	Child	26Ju07Up
Jane	08	F	Child	26Ju07Up
Simon	06	M	Child	26Ju07Up
GRAHAM, Margt.	21	F	Unknown	26Ju07Up
Pat.	04	M	Child	26Ju07Up
James	.00	M	Infant	26Ju07Up
RANEY, Wm.	30	M	Laborer	26Ju07Up
BAILEY, Wm.	21	M	Laborer	26Ju07Up
FINLAY, Eliz.	20	F	Spinster	26Ju07Up
HANNAGH, Ann	18	F	Spinster	26Ju07Up
WRIGHTMAN, Mathew	21	M	Laborer	26Ju07Up
STREHAM, Andrew	20	M	Laborer	26Ju07Up
DAVISON, Wm.	20	M	Laborer	26Ju07Up
PAUL, Saml.	23	M	Laborer	26Ju07Up
MCCULLOUGH, Nath.	22	M	Laborer	26Ju07Up
SCOTT, James	22	M	Laborer	26Ju07Up
SEYMONS, Jane	20	F	Laborer	26Ju07Up
MCCEAFNEY, Jane	17	F	Laborer	26Ju07Up
SPENCE, James	17	M	Laborer	26Ju07Up
Sarah	22	F	Laborer	26Ju07Up
WARNOCK, Ann	40	F	Laborer	26Ju07Up
Saml.	19	M	Laborer	26Ju07Up
Susanna	18	F	Laborer	26Ju07Up
Mary	16	F	Laborer	26Ju07Up
CREIGHTON, John	18	M	Laborer	26Ju07Up
SCOTT, John	19	M	Laborer	26Ju07Up
WOODS, Margt.	17	F	Laborer	26Ju07Up
ANDERSON, Sarah	25	F	Laborer	26Ju07Up
WOODBURN, Robt.	26	M	Laborer	26Ju07Up
CRILLY, Mich.	25	M	Laborer	26Ju07Up
Anny	23	F	Laborer	26Ju07Up
GRIBBIN, Mary	17	F	Laborer	26Ju07Up
Matty	15	F	Laborer	26Ju07Up
MILLER, Jane	27	F	Wife	26Ju07Up
Jane	27	F	None	26Ju07Up
SCOLLION, Mich.	26	M	Laborer	26Ju07Up
CRILLY, Mary	18	F	Laborer	26Ju07Up
BLARKLEY, Jos.	23	M	Laborer	26Ju07Up
NIXON, James	23	M	Laborer	26Ju07Up
Hugh	21	M	Laborer	26Ju07Up
Saml.	18	M	Laborer	26Ju07Up
John	33	M	Laborer	26Ju07Up
MOARELAND, James	17	M	Laborer	26Ju07Up
MICKLE, Ellen	20	F	Laborer	26Ju07Up
BURNS, Henry	20	M	Laborer	26Ju07Up
DENALER, Hugh	46	M	Laborer	26Ju07Up
MCCARTNEY, Eliz.	60	F	Wife	26Ju07Up
MCQUILLAN, Cath.	24	F	Wife	26Ju07Up
BRADLEY, Andrew	18	M	Laborer	26Ju07Up
MCCOY, Molly	20	F	Spinster	26Ju07Up
Nancy	18	F	Spinster	26Ju07Up
BLANEY, Hugh	20	M	Unknown	26Ju07Up
BARREN, Agnes	20	F	Unknown	26Ju07Up
WILSON, Stewart	20	M	Laborer	26Ju07Up
BAILEY, Wm.	18	M	Laborer	26Ju07Up
Francis	30	M	Laborer	26Ju07Up
ALEXANDER, John	30	M	Laborer	26Ju07Up
Ellen	23	F	Wife	26Ju07Up
BOGAN, Cath.	31	F	Wife	26Ju07Up
BURNS, Mary	25	F	Wife	26Ju07Up
MCKENNA, Anny	40	F	Wife	26Ju07Up
BROWN, Mark	21	M	Laborer	26Ju07Up
MCAULA, Saml.	30	M	Laborer	26Ju07Up
John	28	M	Laborer	26Ju07Up
PATTERSON, Sarah	23	F	Wife	26Ju07Up
Margt.	24	F	Wife	26Ju07Up
MCGLADE, Wm.	27	M	Unknown	26Ju07Up
SHANNON, James	35	M	Unknown	26Ju07Up
ELLIOTT, Thos.	22	M	Laborer	26Ju07Up
GARRATT, Saml.	26	M	Laborer	26Ju07Up
Alex.	21	M	Laborer	26Ju07Up
Eliza (W)	25	F	Wife	26Ju07Up
Robt. (S)	.00	M	Infant	26Ju07Up
KIRK, Jane	16	F	Spinster	26Ju07Up
MCMAHON, Eliza	46	F	Spinster	26Ju07Up
Eliza	22	F	Spinster	26Ju07Up
READ, Jane	18	F	Spinster	26Ju07Up
HACKETT, Pat.	28	M	Laborer	26Ju07Up
Felix	21	M	Laborer	26Ju07Up
Cath.	18	F	Spinster	26Ju07Up
MURRAY, Anne	50	F	Spinster	26Ju07Up
CROW, Jane	40	F	Spinster	26Ju07Up
Margt.	18	F	Spinster	26Ju07Up
Peter	45	M	Farmer	26Ju07Up
MCAFFEE, Rose	27	F	Wife	26Ju07Up
CREELIN, Hugh	25	M	Laborer	26Ju07Up
ENGLISH, James	30	M	Laborer	26Ju07Up
Margt.	25	F	Wife	26Ju07Up
MCGARMOND, James	18	M	Laborer	26Ju07Up
BATTEY, Jane	26	F	Wife	26Ju07Up
AROND, John-Simon	24	M	Laborer	26Ju07Up
BELL, James	18	M	Laborer	26Ju07Up
KIRKLEY, Esther	16	F	Spinster	26Ju07Up
COATES, Isabela	19	F	Spinster	26Ju07Up
CARGO, Robt.	32	M	Spinster	26Ju07Up
ALLISON, Mary	25	F	Wife	26Ju07Up
James	19	M	Laborer	26Ju07Up
TAYLOR, Mary-Ann	20	F	Spinster	26Ju07Up
MCDUNTON, Martha	53	F	Spinster	26Ju07Up
Cath.	14	F	Spinster	26Ju07Up
Brice	19	M	Laborer	26Ju07Up
MCGINN, Chas.	25	M	Laborer	26Ju07Up
HAMILL, Bernard	26	M	Laborer	26Ju07Up
CHAPMAN, Grace	30	F	Spinster	26Ju07Up
RUSSEL, Robt.	22	M	Laborer	26Ju07Up
MARCHALL, James	23	M	Laborer	26Ju07Up
KEENAN, John	26	M	Laborer	26Ju07Up
THANEY, Hugh	23	M	Laborer	26Ju07Up
MCQUILLAN, George	20	M	Laborer	26Ju07Up
LYONS, Eliza	18	F	Spinster	26Ju07Up
MCCUDLISH, Matty	24	F	Spinster	26Ju07Up
WALSH, Margt.	20	F	Spinster	26Ju07Up
ONEILL, Teresa	24	F	Spinster	26Ju07Up
DODD, Robt.	21	M	Laborer	26Ju07Up
CLEHAN, John	20	M	Laborer	26Ju07Up
LARK, Thos.	25	M	Laborer	26Ju07Up
ELLIOTT, Henry	30	M	Laborer	26Ju07Up

MEMNON 27 JUNE 1848

From Liverpool

NAMES OF PASSENGERS	AGE	SEX	OCCUPATIONS	DATE PORT SHIP
CAGLIN, Paterick	16	M	Laborer	27Ju02Gd
Frances	18	F	Unknown	27Ju02Gd
Bridget	28	F	Unknown	27Ju02Gd
MANEY, Pat.	22	M	Unknown	27Ju02Gd
Morris	22	M	Unknown	27Ju02Gd

NAMES OF PASSENGERS	AGE	SEX	OCCUPATIONS	DATE PORT SHIP
FOLEYE, Margaret	21	F	Unknown	27Ju02Gd
KEEF, Catherine	25	F	Unknown	27Ju02Gd
Margaret	22	F	Unknown	27Ju02Gd
3RADEY, Thomas	30	M	Carpenter	27Ju02Gd
Mary	28	F	Unknown	27Ju02Gd
Philip	02	M	Child	27Ju02Gd
CONALL, Jane	28	F	Unknown	27Ju02Gd
Catherine	24	F	Unknown	27Ju02Gd
Esther	12	F	Unknown	27Ju02Gd
Jane	10	F	Unknown	27Ju02Gd
SMITH, Rosa	20	F	Unknown	27Ju02Gd
BROWN, Ann	30	F	Unknown	27Ju02Gd
Philip	04	M	Child	27Ju02Gd
Pat	05	M	Child	27Ju02Gd
SHEILS, Charles	30	M	Unknown	27Ju02Gd
FRIEL, Brien	25	M	Unknown	27Ju02Gd
Hannah	20	F	Unknown	27Ju02Gd
EGAN, Bridget	40	F	Unknown	27Ju02Gd
Thomas	25	M	Unknown	27Ju02Gd
John	20	M	Unknown	27Ju02Gd
Bridget	16	F	Unknown	27Ju02Gd
Ann	14	F	Unknown	27Ju02Gd
Eliza	25	F	Unknown	27Ju02Gd
CURAN, James	40	M	Farmer	27Ju02Gd
CONELL, Pat	28	M	Farmer	27Ju02Gd
MALONE, Michael	40	M	Farmer	27Ju02Gd
CONDON, Bridget	50	F	Unknown	27Ju02Gd
DELMER, William	40	M	Tailor	27Ju02Gd
CONDON, Catherine	30	F	Unknown	27Ju02Gd
Margaret	24	F	Unknown	27Ju02Gd
Ann	22	F	Unknown	27Ju02Gd
Eliza	20	F	Unknown	27Ju02Gd
Ellen	18	F	Unknown	27Ju02Gd
Keean	16	M	Unknown	27Ju02Gd
Margaret	09	F	Child	27Ju02Gd
Michael	13	M	Unknown	27Ju02Gd
Fanny	08	F	Child	27Ju02Gd
William	.10	M	Infant	27Ju02Gd
HALL, Stephen	22	M	Unknown	27Ju02Gd
HORAN, Mary	21	F	Unknown	27Ju02Gd
LONG, Ellen	24	F	Unknown	27Ju02Gd
Catherine	18	F	Unknown	27Ju02Gd
LINCH, Margaret	22	F	Unknown	27Ju02Gd
FELTON, Jonama	30	F	Unknown	27Ju02Gd
FITZGERALD, Edmond	50	M	Farmer	27Ju02Gd
Margaret	40	F	Unknown	27Ju02Gd
Margaret	16	F	Unknown	27Ju02Gd
MIRLEY, Timothy	25	M	Unknown	27Ju02Gd
SULLIVAN, Ellen	20	F	Unknown	27Ju02Gd
FORHANT, Denis	22	M	Unknown	27Ju02Gd
BRYAN, James	23	M	Unknown	27Ju02Gd
Honora	21	F	Unknown	27Ju02Gd
MAHONEY, Denis	25	M	Unknown	27Ju02Gd
BRADEY, Philip	28	M	Farmer	27Ju02Gd
Eliza	28	F	Unknown	27Ju02Gd
NOONAN, Michael	50	M	Unknown	27Ju02Gd
John	16	M	Unknown	27Ju02Gd
Edmond	11	M	Child	27Ju02Gd
LEARY, Honora	20	F	Unknown	27Ju02Gd
Jeremiah	30	M	Farmer	27Ju02Gd
MCDOWELL, Thomas	40	M	Mason	27Ju02Gd
Mary	35	F	Unknown	27Ju02Gd
Thomas	04	M	Child	27Ju02Gd
John	02	M	Child	27Ju02Gd
Pat.	.01	M	Infant	27Ju02Gd
DALEY, Timothy	20	M	Farmer	27Ju02Gd
Catherin	18	F	Unknown	27Ju02Gd
Lucy	14	F	Unknown	27Ju02Gd
Mary	12	F	Unknown	27Ju02Gd
WILSON, John	25	M	Farmer	27Ju02Gd
Elizabeth	24	F	Unknown	27Ju02Gd
Ann	20	F	Unknown	27Ju02Gd
Sara	17	F	Unknown	27Ju02Gd
HALL, Robert	18	M	Unknown	27Ju02Gd
FLEMMING, William	20	M	Unknown	27Ju02Gd
MULLEN, James	22	M	Unknown	27Ju02Gd
DOGHERTY, John	22	M	Unknown	27Ju02Gd
FRAYNOR, Frances	55	M	Unknown	27Ju02Gd
Ellen	16	F	Unknown	27Ju02Gd
Felix	13	M	Unknown	27Ju02Gd
QUIN, Mary	21	F	Unknown	27Ju02Gd
CALLAHAN, Pat.	28	M	Unknown	27Ju02Gd
MCCARTY, Pat.	25	M	Shoemaker	27Ju02Gd
LEARY, Jermiah	25	M	Farmer	27Ju02Gd
HARINGTON, Pat.	21	M	Farmer	27Ju02Gd
GREEN, Richard	30	M	Farmer	27Ju02Gd
George	24	M	Farmer	27Ju02Gd
ROACH, Michael	18	M	Unknown	27Ju02Gd
KEOGH, John	33	M	Unknown	27Ju02Gd
BAKER, John	30	M	Unknown	27Ju02Gd
MORE, Thomas	30	M	Unknown	27Ju02Gd
GARVEY, John	30	M	Unknown	27Ju02Gd
Johana	08	F	Child	27Ju02Gd
KEANE, Moses	30	M	Unknown	27Ju02Gd
Bridget	36	F	Unknown	27Ju02Gd
Pat.	13	M	Unknown	27Ju02Gd
BUTTERMAN, John	30	M	Shoemaker	27Ju02Gd
RYAN, Matthew	18	M	Grocer	27Ju02Gd
NOOLAN, Malachia	40	M	Unknown	27Ju02Gd
NEAL, William	19	M	Unknown	27Ju02Gd
POWER, Thomas	30	M	Farmer	27Ju02Gd
LYONS, Michael	27	M	Farmer	27Ju02Gd
John	20	M	Farmer	27Ju02Gd
Daniel	26	M	Farmer	27Ju02Gd
SULLIVAN, Daniel	24	M	Farmer	27Ju02Gd
BEAGAN, John	26	M	Farmer	27Ju02Gd
Catherine	20	F	Unknown	27Ju02Gd
SIMPSON, James	30	M	Unknown	27Ju02Gd
KEALEY, Mary	17	F	Unknown	27Ju02Gd
EVANS, Richard	30	M	Farmer	27Ju02Gd
Mary-Ann	25	F	Unknown	27Ju02Gd
Richard	04	M	Child	27Ju02Gd
John	18	M	Unknown	27Ju02Gd
Hannah	18	F	Unknown	27Ju02Gd
MAGRATH, George	24	M	Hairdresser	27Ju02Gd
SULLIVAN, John	21	M	Cmcl	27Ju02Gd
MCCOY, Thomas	24	M	Coachman	27Ju02Gd
DUN, Michael	30	M	Grocer	27Ju02Gd
Mary	32	F	Unknown	27Ju02Gd
Catherine	31	F	Unknown	27Ju02Gd
Margaret	08	F	Child	27Ju02Gd
Mary	06	F	Child	27Ju02Gd
COLEMAN, Mathias	27	M	Gdnr	27Ju02Gd
Bridget	28	F	Unknown	27Ju02Gd
CONDON, Mary	24	F	Dressmaker	27Ju02Gd
SHORT, Paterick	30	M	Painter	27Ju02Gd
Mary-Ann	28	F	Unknown	27Ju02Gd
Paterick	10	M	Child	27Ju02Gd
John	08	M	Child	27Ju02Gd
Francis	03	M	Child	27Ju02Gd
Michael	01	M	Child	27Ju02Gd
SHEAN, William	28	M	Dyer	27Ju02Gd
Simon	22	M	Cbtmkr	27Ju02Gd
DOGHERLY, Robert	20	M	Cbtmkr	27Ju02Gd
MCDARRAH, Joshua	50	M	Brush Maker	27Ju02Gd
JONES, Thomas	40	M	Unknown	27Ju02Gd
Mary	40	F	Unknown	27Ju02Gd
WILKINS, John	20	M	Farmer	27Ju02Gd
STEWART, Hamilton	20	M	Farmer	27Ju02Gd
KIRWIN, John	24	M	Farmer	27Ju02Gd
GRANT, Ellen	24	F	Unknown	27Ju02Gd
GANNON, Thomas	45	M	Unknown	27Ju02Gd
MCCARRAHER, Catherine	24	F	Unknown	27Ju02Gd
POTTS, James	38	M	Farmer	27Ju02Gd
Jane	36	F	Unknown	27Ju02Gd
William	08	M	Child	27Ju02Gd
COLLIN, Mary	19	F	Unknown	27Ju02Gd
MCCANN, Catherine	24	F	Unknown	27Ju02Gd
CRINION, Mary	24	F	Unknown	27Ju02Gd
MARCAN, Catherine	20	F	Unknown	27Ju02Gd

NAMES OF PASSENGERS	AGE	SEX	OCCUPATIONS	DATE PORT SHIP
DALEY, Edward	36	M	Farmer	27Ju02Gd
Betsy	36	F	Unknown	27Ju02Gd
GALL, Michael	28	M	Unknown	27Ju02Gd
MCGRAN, Thomas	24	M	Farmer	27Ju02Gd
Christopher	26	M	Baker	27Ju02Gd
MORE, John	24	M	Smith	27Ju02Gd
CALLAHAN, Pat	30	M	Unknown	27Ju02Gd
KILPATRICK, William	24	M	Mill Worker	27Ju02Gd
COGLEY, William	25	M	Joiner	27Ju02Gd
Anastasia	24	F	Unknown	27Ju02Gd
DOYLE, John	28	M	Joiner	27Ju02Gd
MORGAN, Paterick	25	M	Unknown	27Ju02Gd
FLYNN, Brien	22	M	Unknown	27Ju02Gd
Margaret	20	F	Unknown	27Ju02Gd
CAROLL, Margaret	22	F	Unknown	27Ju02Gd
SIMMONS, John	25	M	Gdnr	27Ju02Gd
HAND, Frances	40	F	None	27Ju02Gd
DANAH, Thomas	40	M	Carpenter	27Ju02Gd
MCMURRAH, Thomas	30	M	Carpenter	27Ju02Gd
MCDOWELL, Frances	23	F	Unknown	27Ju02Gd
Margaret	20	F	Unknown	27Ju02Gd
MONK, Jane	45	F	Unknown	27Ju02Gd
Julia	20	F	Dressmaker	27Ju02Gd
Jane	17	F	Bookbinder	27Ju02Gd
PURFIELD, Annah	40	F	Unknown	27Ju02Gd
Mary	19	F	Unknown	27Ju02Gd
BRAIDY, Ellen	17	F	Unknown	27Ju02Gd
WALL, Paterick	30	M	Unknown	27Ju02Gd
SMITH, Bartley	30	M	Farmer	27Ju02Gd
MALADY, Thomas	22	M	Farmer	27Ju02Gd
DONOHUE, Edward	21	M	Farmer	27Ju02Gd
RILEY, Pat.	20	M	Farmer	27Ju02Gd
CLINTON, Michael	28	M	Farmer	27Ju02Gd
Mary	25	F	Unknown	27Ju02Gd
Martha	03	F	Child	27Ju02Gd
Mary	01	F	Child	27Ju02Gd
HARLAN, John	34	M	Farmer	27Ju02Gd
CONES, James	20	M	Farmer	27Ju02Gd
HODGE, Robert	21	M	Farmer	27Ju02Gd
GARDNER, Catherine	16	F	Unknown	27Ju02Gd
DICKSON, James	26	M	Weaver	27Ju02Gd
BRENNAN, Anna	24	F	None	27Ju02Gd
MCEROY, Mary	22	F	None	27Ju02Gd
MCNAMEE, William	50	M	Baker	27Ju02Gd
KEOUGH, Bridget	22	F	Shirt Maker	27Ju02Gd
LOOBY, Margaret	20	F	Unknown	27Ju02Gd
LYNCH, Bridget	18	F	Unknown	27Ju02Gd
CLARK, Catherine	17	F	Unknown	27Ju02Gd
CRUMMY, James	35	M	Farmer	27Ju02Gd
Samuel	30	M	Farmer	27Ju02Gd
KEAN, Anna	18	F	Unknown	27Ju02Gd
CRUMMY, Anna	08	F	Child	27Ju02Gd
William	06	M	Child	27Ju02Gd
CUNNINGHAM, Cristopher	30	M	Farmer	27Ju02Gd
Mary	20	F	Unknown	27Ju02Gd
Martin	30	M	Unknown	27Ju02Gd
GORMAN, Thomas	21	M	Unknown	27Ju02Gd
Catherine	20	F	Unknown	27Ju02Gd
FALEN, Michael	24	M	Farmer	27Ju02Gd
DALANEY, James	22	M	Farmer	27Ju02Gd
Mary	20	F	Unknown	27Ju02Gd
BRENNAN, Fanny	21	F	Unknown	27Ju02Gd
JUDGE, Charles	28	M	Baker	27Ju02Gd
DOOLY, Cornelius	30	M	Unknown	27Ju02Gd
CAROLL, Mary	28	F	Unknown	27Ju02Gd
CARIS, Daniel	28	M	Unknown	27Ju02Gd
MADDOCK, Louis	22	M	Farmer	27Ju02Gd
BOLAND, John	21	M	Unknown	27Ju02Gd
SHERMOND, Pat.	21	M	Unknown	27Ju02Gd
PENDEGRAST, John	24	M	Unknown	27Ju02Gd
COMERFORD, Mary	22	F	Unknown	27Ju02Gd
FITZPATRICK, Ann	23	F	Unknown	27Ju02Gd
KAVANAH, Edward	30	M	Unknown	27Ju02Gd
DOYLE, Michael	20	M	Unknown	27Ju02Gd
FITZPATRICK, Matthew	23	M	Shoemaker	27Ju02Gd

NAMES OF PASSENGERS	AGE	SEX	OCCUPATIONS	DATE PORT SHIP
ERWIN, Henry	15	M	Unknown	27Ju02Gd
ROARK, Pat.	30	M	Farmer	27Ju02Gd
CARSON, John	20	M	Unknown	27Ju02Gd
MCKINN, James	20	M	Unknown	27Ju02Gd
Andrew	12	M	Unknown	27Ju02Gd
John	06	M	Child	27Ju02Gd
Sara-Jane	14	F	None	27Ju02Gd
Martha	08	F	Child	27Ju02Gd
Isabella	02	F	Child	27Ju02Gd
Jane	50	F	None	27Ju02Gd
COLVIN, Samuel	26	M	Gdnr	27Ju02Gd
RYAN, Edward	24	M	Farmer	27Ju02Gd
SHEA, Michael	20	M	Carpenter	27Ju02Gd
TOD, John	22	M	Saddler	27Ju02Gd
LEE, Ruben	25	M	Shoemaker	27Ju02Gd
DENIS, John	21	M	Unknown	27Ju02Gd
MANEN, Owen	40	M	Farmer	27Ju02Gd
Bridget	40	F	Unknown	27Ju02Gd
Ann	.11	F	Infant	27Ju02Gd
RAFFERTY, John	25	M	Unknown	27Ju02Gd
Catherine	60	F	Unknown	27Ju02Gd
EBBITT, George	40	M	Weaver	27Ju02Gd
Jane	35	F	Unknown	27Ju02Gd
George	08	M	Child	27Ju02Gd
Robert	05	M	Child	27Ju02Gd
CHERRY, James	30	M	Jeweller	27Ju02Gd
Jane	30	F	Unknown	27Ju02Gd
Margaret	10	F	Child	27Ju02Gd
Samuel	08	M	Child	27Ju02Gd
Sara-Ann	05	F	Child	27Ju02Gd
Mary	02	F	Child	27Ju02Gd
HODGSON, Sara	40	F	None	27Ju02Gd
CARRY, James	26	M	Hdwmr	27Ju02Gd
BRUTON, John	45	M	Unknown	27Ju02Gd
DOYLE, John	25	M	Unknown	27Ju02Gd
RYAN, John	21	M	Unknown	27Ju02Gd
KELLEY, Richardson	45	M	Carpenter	27Ju02Gd

E.Z. 27 JUNE 1848

From Liverpool

NAMES OF PASSENGERS	AGE	SEX	OCCUPATIONS	DATE PORT SHIP
JONES, John	40	M	Farmer	27Ju02Vt
Eliz.	02	F	Farmer	27Ju02Vt
June	11	F	Farmer	27Ju02Vt
Edw.	25	M	Farmer	27Ju02Vt
Ann	13	F	Farmer	27Ju02Vt
June	11	F	Farmer	27Ju02Vt
Charles	26	M	Farmer	27Ju02Vt
Eliz.	43	F	Farmer	27Ju02Vt
John	09	M	Farmer	27Ju02Vt
Michl.	07	M	Farmer	27Ju02Vt
William	28	M	Farmer	27Ju02Vt
Edw.	05	M	Farmer	27Ju02Vt
Evan	30	M	Farmer	27Ju02Vt
POWELL, Margaret	46	F	Farmer	27Ju02Vt
June	.00	F	Infant	27Ju02Vt
CABOTT, Mary	25	F	Farmer	27Ju02Vt
Ann	03	F	Farmer	27Ju02Vt
Michael	.00	M	Infant	27Ju02Vt
KILLEP, Margaret-W.	19	F	Farmer	27Ju02Vt
DAVIS, Thos.	42	M	Farmer	27Ju02Vt
GREGORY, Jane	30	F	Farmer	27Ju02Vt
MURPHY, Patt	12	M	Child	27Ju02Vt
Dennis	08	M	Child	27Ju02Vt
Winfried	10	F	Child	27Ju02Vt
REYNOLDS, Ann	30	F	Farmer	27Ju02Vt
Lucy	02	F	Child	27Ju02Vt
BOLF, Margaret	21	F	Farmer	27Ju02Vt

NAMES OF PASSENGERS		AGE	SEX	OCCUPATIONS	DATE PORT SHIP
POWELL, John		17	M	Farmer	27Ju02Vt
John		48	M	Farmer	27Ju02Vt
Thos.		17	M	Farmer	27Ju02Vt
Robt.		03	M	Farmer	27Ju02Vt
Ann		12	F	Farmer	27Ju02Vt
Betsy		03	F	Child	27Ju02Vt
Edw.		09	M	Child	27Ju02Vt
Mary		14	F	Farmer	27Ju02Vt
WILLIAM, Ann		22	F	Farmer	27Ju02Vt
David		25	M	Farmer	27Ju02Vt
WILLIAMS, William		16	M	Farmer	27Ju02Vt
DONNAHU, Margt.		16	F	Farmer	27Ju02Vt
LARD, Michael		48	M	Farmer	27Ju02Vt
LOHER, Law.		49	M	Farmer	27Ju02Vt
NEAL, James		30	M	Farmer	27Ju02Vt
LOGAN, William		22	M	Farmer	27Ju02Vt
CHAPMAN, Edw.		20	M	Farmer	27Ju02Vt
BLACKBURN, Robt.		35	M	Farmer	27Ju02Vt
Robt.		08	M	Child	27Ju02Vt
John		06	M	Child	27Ju02Vt
Eliz.		09	F	Child	27Ju02Vt
Margt.		25	F	Farmer	27Ju02Vt

SOPHIA 27 JUNE 1848

From Waterford

NAMES OF PASSENGERS		AGE	SEX	OCCUPATIONS	DATE PORT SHIP
WHELAN, Pat.		25	M	Farmer	27Ju16Vs
BYRMAME, Edw.		26	M	Unknown	27Ju16Vs
POWER, Mary		19	F	Spinster	27Ju16Vs
CARROLL, Pat.		27	M	Laborer	27Ju16Vs
Mary		30	F	Wife	27Ju16Vs
WALSH, John		41	M	Laborer	27Ju16Vs
FLYNN, Edw.		36	M	Laborer	27Ju16Vs
DALEY, James		30	M	Laborer	27Ju16Vs
Mary		30	F	Spinster	27Ju16Vs
MAYLOR, Frances		27	F	Spinster	27Ju16Vs
MURPHY, Mich.		14	M	Child	27Ju16Vs
JORDAN, Pat.		35	M	Farmer	27Ju16Vs
KEEFFE, Pat.		30	M	Farmer	27Ju16Vs
Mary		30	F	Spinster	27Ju16Vs
John		.00	M	Infant	27Ju16Vs
MURPHY, Ann		16	F	Unknown	27Ju16Vs
SEXTON, Thos.		25	M	Laborer	27Ju16Vs
SLAHERY, Edmond		40	M	Laborer	27Ju16Vs
RYAN, Pat.		35	M	Laborer	27Ju16Vs
MURPHY, Thos.		20	M	Laborer	27Ju16Vs
FARRELL, Jno.		28	M	Laborer	27Ju16Vs
SULLIVAN, Jno.		22	M	Laborer	27Ju16Vs
GRADY, Mich.		23	M	Laborer	27Ju16Vs
POWER, Cath.		20	F	Spinster	27Ju16Vs
FARRELL, Pat.		23	M	Laborer	27Ju16Vs
BULGER, Mich.		18	M	Laborer	27Ju16Vs
KENNEDY, Pat.		23	M	Laborer	27Ju16Vs
BURKE, James		23	M	Laborer	27Ju16Vs
CORCORAN, James		32	M	Laborer	27Ju16Vs
CASEY, Ellen		54	F	Wife	27Ju16Vs
Philip		20	M	Laborer	27Ju16Vs
Pat.		17	M	Laborer	27Ju16Vs
SHEA, James		32	M	Laborer	27Ju16Vs
MCGRATH, Bridget		25	F	Wife	27Ju16Vs
TOBIN, Thos.		21	M	Laborer	27Ju16Vs
KENNDEY, Robt.		23	M	Laborer	27Ju16Vs
MURRAY, Mich.		23	M	Laborer	27Ju16Vs
HARDY, Man.		58	M	Laborer	27Ju16Vs
Cath.		40	F	Spinster	27Ju16Vs
Mich.	(S)	11	M	Child	27Ju16Vs
Rich.	(S)	23	M	Laborer	27Ju16Vs
Mary	(D)	18	F	Wife	27Ju16Vs
HARDY, Mich.	(S)	32	M	Laborer	27Ju16Vs
Manrich	(S)	07	M	Child	27Ju16Vs
Wm.	(S)	09	M	Child	27Ju16Vs
Cath.	(D)	.00	F	Infant	27Ju16Vs
John	(S)	17	M	Laborer	27Ju16Vs
DOYLE, Davis		27	M	Laborer	27Ju16Vs
John		16	M	Laborer	27Ju16Vs
SHEA, Thos.		32	M	Laborer	27Ju16Vs
GORMAN, Law.		32	M	Laborer	27Ju16Vs
BRODRICK, M.		21	M	Laborer	27Ju16Vs
WALSH, Jas.		30	M	Laborer	27Ju16Vs
KINSETTA, Philip		30	M	Laborer	27Ju16Vs
Brdgt.		28	F	Wife	27Ju16Vs
Mich.		28	M	Laborer	27Ju16Vs
Pat.		.00	M	Infant	27Ju16Vs
Alice		06	F	Child	27Ju16Vs
DELAHUNTY, Thos.		24	M	Laborer	27Ju16Vs
HALLY, John		20	M	Unknown	27Ju16Vs
SHIEL, Wm.		54	M	Unknown	27Ju16Vs
Mary	(W)	62	F	Wife	27Ju16Vs
Bridget	(D)	18	F	Spinster	27Ju16Vs
Margt.	(D)	17	F	Spinster	27Ju16Vs
Wm.	(S)	13	M	Child	27Ju16Vs
James	(S)	.00	M	Infant	27Ju16Vs
FURLONG, Pat.		17	M	Laborer	27Ju16Vs
CLEARY, Wm.		35	M	Laborer	27Ju16Vs
FOGARTY, Mich.		25	M	Laborer	27Ju16Vs
CLEARY, Mary		25	F	Wife	27Ju16Vs
PENDERGRAST, John		19	M	Laborer	27Ju16Vs
TYRELL, Pat.		18	M	Laborer	27Ju16Vs
BYRNE, Edw.		25	M	Laborer	27Ju16Vs
SHIEL, Ann		40	F	Wife	27Ju16Vs
MCMAHON, Wm.		22	M	Gentleman	27Ju16Vs

GOV.HINCKLEY 28 JUNE 1848

From Cork

NAMES OF PASSENGERS		AGE	SEX	OCCUPATIONS	DATE PORT SHIP
JONES, Patrick		27	M	Flabr	28Ju14Ui
Margaret		01	F	Child	28Ju14Ui
CORCORRAN, Patrick		26	M	Currier	28Ju14Ui
MURPHY, John		30	M	Flabr	28Ju14Ui
MACKEY, Mary		20	F	Fsvnt	28Ju14Ui
FLANIGAN, Kitty		25	F	Unknown	28Ju14Ui
WORTHINGTON, James		20	M	Carpenter	28Ju14Ui
MYLES, Michael		20	M	Butcher	28Ju14Ui
FITZGERALD, Ellen		20	F	Unknown	28Ju14Ui
LEARYS, Kitty		19	F	Unknown	28Ju14Ui
MAHONY, Ellen		22	F	Unknown	28Ju14Ui
MORRISSON, John		40	M	Flabr	28Ju14Ui
Eliza		38	F	Unknown	28Ju14Ui
HAYES, Ellen		30	F	Unknown	28Ju14Ui
MORRISSON, John		10	M	Unknown	28Ju14Ui
Catherine		08	F	Child	28Ju14Ui
Richard		07	M	Child	28Ju14Ui
Peter		04	M	Child	28Ju14Ui
William		01	M	Child	28Ju14Ui
GREANY, Ellen		38	F	Unknown	28Ju14Ui
ROCHE, Dominick		40	M	Blacksmith	28Ju14Ui
Dominick		13	M	Unknown	28Ju14Ui
John		25	M	Blacksmith	28Ju14Ui
William		20	M	Blacksmith	28Ju14Ui
Ellen		20	F	Unknown	28Ju14Ui
David		12	M	Unknown	28Ju14Ui
Margaret		40	F	Unknown	28Ju14Ui
DONEGAN, Patrick		21	M	Painter	28Ju14Ui
FOLEY, William		30	M	Flabr	28Ju14Ui
James		20	M	Flabr	28Ju14Ui
Bridget		23	F	Unknown	28Ju14Ui

NAMES OF PASSENGERS	AGE	SEX	OCCUPATIONS	DATE PORT SHIP
MCAULIFFE, Norry	23	F	Unknown	28Ju14UI
CALLAGHAN, Eliza	20	F	Unknown	28Ju14UI
Hannah	20	F	Unknown	28Ju14UI
LANE, Henry	28	M	Flabr	28Ju14UI
Kate	26	F	Unknown	28Ju14UI
Edward	04	M	Child	28Ju14UI
Alice	02	F	Child	28Ju14UI
BAILY, Robert	22	M	Carpenter	28Ju14UI
RYAN, James	21	M	Flabr	28Ju14UI
CUNNINGHAM, Patrick	30	M	Laborer	28Ju14UI
Honorah	26	F	Unknown	28Ju14UI
Hannah	06	F	Child	28Ju14UI
Margaret	05	F	Child	28Ju14UI
SULLIVAN, Bridget	45	F	Unknown	28Ju14UI
RYAN, Andrew	60	M	Laborer	28Ju14UI
BEARY, Thomas	25	M	Flabr	28Ju14UI
Honorah	27	F	Unknown	28Ju14UI
FITZPATRICK, Sandy	32	M	Flabr	28Ju14UI
John	18	M	Flabr	28Ju14UI
KENNEDY, John	31	M	Flabr	28Ju14UI
COSGREVE, Ellen	30	F	Unknown	28Ju14UI
CONNELL, Mary	20	F	Unknown	28Ju14UI
SCANNELLY, Ellen	20	F	House Maid	28Ju14UI
William	20	M	Flabr	28Ju14UI
FITZGERALD, John	30	M	Flabr	28Ju14UI
KEEFFE, Edward	26	M	Flabr	28Ju14UI
MCCARTHY, Honorah	22	F	Unknown	28Ju14UI
FOLEY, Catherine	36	F	Unknown	28Ju14UI
SULLIVAN, William	30	M	Flabr	28Ju14UI
COWHIG, Margt.	23	F	Unknown	28Ju14UI
COUGHLAN, Mary	24	F	Unknown	28Ju14UI
MCCARTHY, Eliza	20	F	Unknown	28Ju14UI
MANNIX, Catharine	24	F	Unknown	28Ju14UI
LEAHY, Michael	28	M	Flabr	28Ju14UI
OBRIEN, Margt.	26	F	Unknown	28Ju14UI
AHERN, William	20	M	Stone Mason	28Ju14UI
FITZGERALD, Mary	30	F	Unknown	28Ju14UI
CADDIGAN, Ellen	23	F	Unknown	28Ju14UI
BARRETT, Johannah	20	F	Unknown	28Ju14UI
CONWAY, Denis	25	M	Flabr	28Ju14UI
WALSH, John	18	M	Ploughman	28Ju14UI
CONWAY, Ellen	19	F	Unknown	28Ju14UI
ROCHE, Thomas	20	M	Accountant	28Ju14UI
Mary	21	F	Unknown	28Ju14UI
MURPHY, James	23	M	Butcher	28Ju14UI
MAHONY, Mary	24	F	Unknown	28Ju14UI
HENESSY, Richd.	20	M	Tailor	28Ju14UI
Norry	28	F	Unknown	28Ju14UI
Bess	21	F	Unknown	28Ju14UI
GEARY, Maurice	21	M	Carpenter	28Ju14UI
BANOTE, William	30	M	Laborer	28Ju14UI
BRUNOCK, Patrick	20	M	Groom	28Ju14UI
CALLAGHAN, John	25	M	Lawyer	28Ju14UI
DESMOND, John	13	M	Unknown	28Ju14UI
FITZGERALD, Catharine	35	F	Unknown	28Ju14UI
MCCARTHY, Patrick	25	M	Flabr	28Ju14UI
Timothy	20	M	Carpenter	28Ju14UI
RYAN, Patrick	23	M	Flabr	28Ju14UI
MURPHY, Denis	17	M	Accountant	28Ju14UI
Anne	24	F	Dairymaid	28Ju14UI
Dan	36	M	Gdnr	28Ju14UI
SPILLANE, Micchl.	40	M	Carpenter	28Ju14UI
Bridget	60	F	Unknown	28Ju14UI
John	21	M	Carpenter	28Ju14UI
Margt.	19	F	Dressmaker	28Ju14UI
HARTIGAN, Mary	20	F	Unknown	28Ju14UI
THOMAS, Henry	22	M	Carpenter	28Ju14UI
Alice	20	F	Milliner	28Ju14UI
Richard	30	M	Carpenter	28Ju14UI
GARDES, Henry-Davis	02	M	Child	28Ju14UI
OBRIEN, Maria	21	F	Dressmaker	28Ju14UI
PURCELL, Ellen	20	F	Unknown	28Ju14UI
GIBBON, John	50	M	Farmer	28Ju14UI
Matthew	20	M	Farmer	28Ju14UI
WARNER, Margt.	20	F	Dressmaker	28Ju14UI
LUCY, Timothy	20	M	Tailor	28Ju14UI
OCONNELE, Charles	24	M	Accountant	28Ju14UI
Ellen	26	F	Unknown	28Ju14UI
Margt.	26	F	Unknown	28Ju14UI
BENNETTE, Thomas	28	M	Watchmaker	28Ju14UI
FLYNN, Ellen	20	F	Unknown	28Ju14UI
SULLIVAN, John	30	M	Farmer	28Ju14UI
JULIAN, Henry	30	M	Coach Maker	28Ju14UI
QUIGLEY, John	30	M	Stone Mason	28Ju14UI
Margt.	30	F	Unknown	28Ju14UI
MANLY, Robert	30	M	Coach Maker	28Ju14UI
Mary-Ann	07	F	Child	28Ju14UI
U	05	F	Child	28Ju14UI
SHEA, John	30	M	Laborer	28Ju14UI
DANIS, Joseph	44	M	Unknown	28Ju14UI
Jane	42	F	Unknown	28Ju14UI
Henry-J.	20	M	Unknown	28Ju14UI
Josh-H.	19	M	Unknown	28Ju14UI
Bridget-W.	17	F	Unknown	28Ju14UI
Jane	16	F	Unknown	28Ju14UI
William	13	M	Unknown	28Ju14UI
Maria	11	F	Unknown	28Ju14UI
Henry	10	M	Unknown	28Ju14UI
John	08	M	Child	28Ju14UI
Rebecca	04	F	Child	28Ju14UI
Lucinda	01	F	Child	28Ju14UI
REARDEN, William	27	M	Flabr	28Ju14UI
Owen	30	M	Flabr	28Ju14UI
Andrew	26	M	Flabr	28Ju14UI
Ellen	27	F	Unknown	28Ju14UI
Owen	03	M	Child	28Ju14UI
Margaret	01	F	Child	28Ju14UI
TONKIN, James	30	M	Miner	28Ju14UI
Anne	30	F	Unknown	28Ju14UI
Mary	15	F	Unknown	28Ju14UI
Jane	13	F	Unknown	28Ju14UI
Susan	11	F	Unknown	28Ju14UI
Sarah	09	F	Child	28Ju14UI
Lydia	05	F	Child	28Ju14UI
Elizabeth	03	F	Child	28Ju14UI
Lavinia	01	F	Child	28Ju14UI
PEAL, James	36	M	Flabr	28Ju14UI
Ellen	30	F	Unknown	28Ju14UI
Philip	10	M	Unknown	28Ju14UI
James	08	M	Child	28Ju14UI
Ellen	04	F	Child	28Ju14UI
Catharine	02	F	Child	28Ju14UI
LINIHAN, James	22	M	Gdnr	28Ju14UI
DELEA, James	30	M	Flabr	28Ju14UI
Julia	26	F	Unknown	28Ju14UI
John	05	M	Child	28Ju14UI
CORCORRAN, Denis	22	M	Currier	28Ju14UI
FLYNN, John	21	M	Baker	28Ju14UI
OSULLIVAN, Mortimer	22	M	Unknown	28Ju14UI
MARROW, John	17	M	Unknown	28Ju14UI
GORT, Richard	41	M	Unknown	28Ju14UI
HARTLOW, Hester	22	F	Unknown	28Ju14UI
Christine	25	F	Unknown	28Ju14UI

LEONIDAS 28 JUNE 1848

From Liverpool

NAMES OF PASSENGERS	AGE	SEX	OCCUPATIONS	DATE PORT SHIP
HARGARAUS, Wm.	40	M	Unknown	28Ju02VJ
BERTWITTLE, Henry	24	M	Unknown	28Ju02VJ
Mary	20	F	Unknown	28Ju02VJ
Ellen	17	F	Unknown	28Ju02VJ
Wm.	14	M	Unknown	28Ju02VJ
James	10	M	Unknown	28Ju02VJ

NAMES OF PASSENGERS		AGE	SEX	OCCUPATIONS	DATE PORT SHIP
BERTWITTLE, Alice		06	F	Unknown	28Ju02VJ
Richard		05	M	Unknown	28Ju02VJ
BURN, Brid.		20	F	Unknown	28Ju02VJ
BUNION, Mary		20	F	Unknown	28Ju02VJ
MASTERSON, John		21	M	Unknown	28Ju02VJ
BRYAN, Mary		30	F	Unknown	28Ju02VJ
CORMICK, John		30	M	Unknown	28Ju02VJ
Thomas		25	M	Unknown	28Ju02VJ
KELLY, John		24	M	Unknown	28Ju02VJ
Thomas		21	M	Unknown	28Ju02VJ
Henry		20	M	Unknown	28Ju02VJ
BRADLY, Brid.		20	F	Unknown	28Ju02VJ
JHONSTONE, John		20	M	Unknown	28Ju02VJ
Mary		19	F	Unknown	28Ju02VJ
CROSLEY, Wm.		24	M	Unknown	28Ju02VJ
MITCHELL, Eliza		20	F	Unknown	28Ju02VJ
CASEY, Peter		26	M	Unknown	28Ju02VJ
BRYAN, Thos.		20	M	Unknown	28Ju02VJ
HICKEY, Pat.		20	M	Unknown	28Ju02VJ
DIVAN, Alex.		21	M	Unknown	28Ju02VJ
HANLEY, Bridget		16	F	Unknown	28Ju02VJ
JONES, Oliver		26	M	Unknown	28Ju02VJ
Michael		24	M	Unknown	28Ju02VJ
John		.00	M	Infant	28Ju02VJ
LEWIS, John		21	M	Unknown	28Ju02VJ
REYNOLDS, Thos.		27	M	Unknown	28Ju02VJ
TRACEY, Tim		24	M	Unknown	28Ju02VJ
CENDY, James		20	M	Unknown	28Ju02VJ
NUGENT, Michael		21	M	Unknown	28Ju02VJ
FARREL, Mary		18	F	Unknown	28Ju02VJ
HAMMOND, J.L.		40	M	Unknown	28Ju02VJ
Janet	(W)	40	F	Unknown	28Ju02VJ
Francis		17	M	Unknown	28Ju02VJ
Janet		15	F	Unknown	28Ju02VJ
Susanah		13	F	Unknown	28Ju02VJ
Thos.		09	M	Unknown	28Ju02VJ
James		07	M	Unknown	28Ju02VJ
Alex.		06	M	Unknown	28Ju02VJ
Chas.		05	M	Unknown	28Ju02VJ
Wm.		.00	M	Infant	28Ju02VJ
John		02	M	Unknown	28Ju02VJ
KINSLEY, Jos.		24	M	Unknown	28Ju02VJ
ROE, James		37	M	Unknown	28Ju02VJ
U	(W)	35	F	Unknown	28Ju02VJ
Charles		07	M	Unknown	28Ju02VJ
Mary		04	F	Unknown	28Ju02VJ
Barbara		03	F	Unknown	28Ju02VJ
Thos.	(S)	.00	M	Infant	28Ju02VJ
CLARK, Richard		30	M	Unknown	28Ju02VJ
Johnathan		21	M	Unknown	28Ju02VJ
James		25	M	Unknown	28Ju02VJ
OUSLEY, John		30	M	Unknown	28Ju02VJ
Mary		29	F	Unknown	28Ju02VJ
Able		12	M	Unknown	28Ju02VJ
HYDE, Samuel		30	M	Unknown	28Ju02VJ
REY, Wm.		40	M	Unknown	28Ju02VJ
KELLEY, Agnes		19	F	Unknown	28Ju02VJ
POOLE, Abraham		29	M	Unknown	28Ju02VJ
Ann		26	F	Unknown	28Ju02VJ
CANDELS, Thos.H.		30	M	Unknown	28Ju02VJ
U	(W)	25	F	Unknown	28Ju02VJ
DWIRE, Cen		24	M	Unknown	28Ju02VJ
Tead		21	M	Unknown	28Ju02VJ
Judy		20	F	Unknown	28Ju02VJ
LIND, Wm.		18	M	Unknown	28Ju02VJ
BRYAN, Ellen		30	F	Unknown	28Ju02VJ
DRASFIELD, Richard		35	M	Unknown	28Ju02VJ
U	(W)	32	F	Unknown	28Ju02VJ
Lucy		05	F	Unknown	28Ju02VJ
GOLDWELL, Mathew		20	M	Unknown	28Ju02VJ
HAYTIN, John		22	M	Unknown	28Ju02VJ
Eliza		20	F	Unknown	28Ju02VJ
HUGHES, Thos.		26	M	Unknown	28Ju02VJ
U	(W)	24	F	Unknown	28Ju02VJ
ROLLINS, Hugh		30	M	Unknown	28Ju02VJ
ROLLINS, U	(W)	26	F	Unknown	28Ju02VJ
ELLIOT, Ann		56	F	Unknown	28Ju02VJ
COLLINS, Mary		06	F	Unknown	28Ju02VJ
Eliza		.00	F	Infant	28Ju02VJ
BLACK, Robert		20	M	Unknown	28Ju02VJ
NOWLAN, Thos.		20	M	Unknown	28Ju02VJ
NEILUS, Daniel-W.		24	M	Unknown	28Ju02VJ
Philip		30	M	Unknown	28Ju02VJ
SWEENEY, Johann-W.		20	M	Unknown	28Ju02VJ
GORMLEY, Mary		20	F	Unknown	28Ju02VJ
SEHAHAL, Pat.		30	M	Unknown	28Ju02VJ
RILEY, Margaret		20	F	Unknown	28Ju02VJ
FOWLER, Sarah		20	F	Unknown	28Ju02VJ
GRIMES, Ann		18	F	Unknown	28Ju02VJ
MALRONEY, Mary		20	F	Unknown	28Ju02VJ
PURREL, Bridget		20	F	Unknown	28Ju02VJ
Ann		21	F	Unknown	28Ju02VJ
BRIAN, Lawrence		22	M	Unknown	28Ju02VJ
MURPHY, Alice		18	F	Unknown	28Ju02VJ
RINK, Mary		16	F	Unknown	28Ju02VJ
CONNOLLY, James		20	M	Unknown	28Ju02VJ
STRAINE, Rose		17	F	Unknown	28Ju02VJ
DRISCOL, John		30	M	Unknown	28Ju02VJ
BLACK, Mary		21	F	Unknown	28Ju02VJ
PERCEVAL, Mary		03	F	Unknown	28Ju02VJ
BOWLER, James		16	M	Unknown	28Ju02VJ
Richard		11	M	Unknown	28Ju02VJ
MOONEY, John		17	M	Unknown	28Ju02VJ
BELL, Margaret		30	F	Unknown	28Ju02VJ
JOHNSTONE, Wm.		30	M	Unknown	28Ju02VJ
BELL, David		04	M	Unknown	28Ju02VJ
FOX, Luke		50	M	Unknown	28Ju02VJ
Ann		50	F	Unknown	28Ju02VJ
ROWANTREE, Peter		26	M	Unknown	28Ju02VJ
RILEY, James		20	M	Unknown	28Ju02VJ
MORTON, Geo.		10	M	Unknown	28Ju02VJ
Jane		18	F	Unknown	28Ju02VJ
ROBINSON, Jane		18	F	Unknown	28Ju02VJ
SMYTH, John		30	M	Unknown	28Ju02VJ
NOONAN, Catherine		17	F	Unknown	28Ju02VJ
HEAVEY, Margaret		28	F	Unknown	28Ju02VJ
Ann		07	F	Unknown	28Ju02VJ
James		06	M	Unknown	28Ju02VJ
CARROL, Andrew		21	M	Unknown	28Ju02VJ
John		08	M	Unknown	28Ju02VJ
THORN, Martha		30	F	Unknown	28Ju02VJ
John		11	M	Unknown	28Ju02VJ
Emma		08	F	Unknown	28Ju02VJ
Wm.		05	M	Unknown	28Ju02VJ
Mary		03	F	Unknown	28Ju02VJ
Alex.		.00	M	Infant	28Ju02VJ
WELSH, John		25	M	Unknown	28Ju02VJ
FINARAN, Rose		18	F	Unknown	28Ju02VJ
CONOLLY, Rose		28	F	Unknown	28Ju02VJ
CURREN, Thos.		21	M	Unknown	28Ju02VJ
DOWD, Thos.		30	M	Unknown	28Ju02VJ
Bridget		50	F	Unknown	28Ju02VJ
REARDEN, Thos.		08	M	Unknown	28Ju02VJ
Mary		06	F	Unknown	28Ju02VJ
John		04	M	Unknown	28Ju02VJ
ROBINSON, Ellen		24	F	Unknown	28Ju02VJ
TIGHE, Mary		20	F	Unknown	28Ju02VJ
PHILLIPS, Pat.W.		20	M	Unknown	28Ju02VJ
Bridget		24	F	Unknown	28Ju02VJ
SMITH, Hellen		20	F	Unknown	28Ju02VJ
DOWLING, Geo.		20	M	Unknown	28Ju02VJ
GREEN, Mary		25	F	Unknown	28Ju02VJ
RERNEY, John		.00	M	Infant	28Ju02VJ
KERR, Robert		18	M	Unknown	28Ju02VJ
John		20	M	Unknown	28Ju02VJ
SMYTH, James		15	M	Unknown	28Ju02VJ
Eleanr		15	M	Unknown	28Ju02VJ
FITZGERALD, Sarah		20	F	Unknown	28Ju02VJ
TODD, Thos.		35	M	Unknown	28Ju02VJ
Ruth		35	F	Unknown	28Ju02VJ

NAMES OF PASSENGERS		AGE	SEX	OCCUPATIONS	DATE PORT SHIP
TODD, Wm.		06	M	Unknown	28Ju02Vj
Jos.		13	M	Unknown	28Ju02Vj
John		10	M	Unknown	28Ju02Vj
CLARK, Mary		54	F	Unknown	28Ju02Vj
Thos.		15	M	Unknown	28Ju02Vj
Alexander		12	M	Unknown	28Ju02Vj
Hugh		09	M	Unknown	28Ju02Vj
Isabella		08	F	Unknown	28Ju02Vj
Wm.		07	M	Unknown	28Ju02Vj
John		05	M	Unknown	28Ju02Vj
COWLAN, James		28	M	Unknown	28Ju02Vj
HENWOOD, John		28	M	Unknown	28Ju02Vj
MCCABREY, Alex		21	M	Unknown	28Ju02Vj
MILLER, Alex.		18	M	Unknown	28Ju02Vj
MILLMORE, Margaret		30	F	Unknown	28Ju02Vj
James		04	M	Unknown	28Ju02Vj
Margaret		.00	F	Infant	28Ju02Vj
THOMPSON, Rose		20	F	Unknown	28Ju02Vj
READY, Catharine		20	F	Unknown	28Ju02Vj
AVERY, Eliza-W.		20	F	Unknown	28Ju02Vj
RYAN, John		20	M	Unknown	28Ju02Vj
BREEN, Pat.		20	M	Unknown	28Ju02Vj
DUNN, Agnes		20	F	Unknown	28Ju02Vj
FAY, Bridget		18	F	Unknown	28Ju02Vj
REES, Morris		55	M	Unknown	28Ju02Vj
Martha		52	F	Unknown	28Ju02Vj
Wm.		22	M	Unknown	28Ju02Vj
Richard		22	M	Unknown	28Ju02Vj
SULLY, Mary		15	F	Unknown	28Ju02Vj
MARA, Catharine		40	F	Unknown	28Ju02Vj
DIXION, Francis		22	M	Unknown	28Ju02Vj
Margaret		30	F	Unknown	28Ju02Vj
EAGAN, Wm.		06	M	Unknown	28Ju02Vj
Bridget		08	F	Unknown	28Ju02Vj
Maria		04	F	Unknown	28Ju02Vj
FLYNN, Maria		03	F	Unknown	28Ju02Vj
SMYTH, James		17	M	Unknown	28Ju02Vj
FARLEY, Julia		18	F	Unknown	28Ju02Vj
CHRISTAL, Ann		20	F	Unknown	28Ju02Vj
WILLS, Thos.		40	M	Unknown	28Ju02Vj
ARLEY, Peter-W.		20	M	Unknown	28Ju02Vj
CORTELLO, Pat.		20	M	Unknown	28Ju02Vj
HANLY, Abby		25	F	Unknown	28Ju02Vj
BUTLER, Julia		22	F	Unknown	28Ju02Vj
CREGIN, Dennis		26	M	Unknown	28Ju02Vj
MURRY, Catherine		20	F	Unknown	28Ju02Vj
Margaret		16	F	Unknown	28Ju02Vj
CARROL, Catherine		50	F	Unknown	28Ju02Vj
BURBEN, James		18	M	Unknown	28Ju02Vj
BLACK, Rebecca		37	F	Unknown	28Ju02Vj
MEIGHAN, Rebeca		50	F	Unknown	28Ju02Vj
Pat.		20	M	Unknown	28Ju02Vj
Catherine		15	F	Unknown	28Ju02Vj
SCANLAN, Bill		40	M	Unknown	28Ju02Vj
GALLAGHER, Leady		50	M	Unknown	28Ju02Vj
Rose		45	F	Unknown	28Ju02Vj
Bridget		18	F	Unknown	28Ju02Vj
Frances		11	F	Unknown	28Ju02Vj
Thos.		09	M	Unknown	28Ju02Vj
RIGDON, Jos.		26	M	Unknown	28Ju02Vj
POWER, Wm.		30	M	Unknown	28Ju02Vj
SHARP, Gibbert		24	M	Unknown	28Ju02Vj
GILL, James		24	M	Unknown	28Ju02Vj
DENBY, Richard		26	M	Unknown	28Ju02Vj
MADDEN, John		20	M	Unknown	28Ju02Vj
RATEN, Mary		25	F	Unknown	28Ju02Vj
BROOMFIELD, Murphy		20	M	Unknown	28Ju02Vj
NAMARA, Mathew-W.		26	M	Unknown	28Ju02Vj
Catherine	(W)	20	F	Unknown	28Ju02Vj
MARRISEY, Michael		24	M	Unknown	28Ju02Vj
SIMPSON, John		35	M	Unknown	28Ju02Vj
FLYNN, Sarah		30	F	Unknown	28Ju02Vj
FOOLEY, Margarett		20	F	Unknown	28Ju02Vj
BURNE, Wm.		27	M	Unknown	28Ju02Vj
Alice		25	F	Unknown	28Ju02Vj
DENIS, Robert		30	M	Unknown	28Ju02Vj
U, Jos.		45	M	Unknown	28Ju02Vj
NELSON, Jos.		20	M	Unknown	28Ju02Vj
SMALL, John		36	M	Unknown	28Ju02Vj
HARRIDEN, Jos.		30	M	Unknown	28Ju02Vj
SMALL, Ann		38	F	Unknown	28Ju02Vj
Charles		10	M	Unknown	28Ju02Vj
Sarah		05	F	Unknown	28Ju02Vj
Mary-Ann		.00	F	Infant	28Ju02Vj
MULRINAN, Henry		20	M	Unknown	28Ju02Vj
MADIGIN, Thos.		20	M	Unknown	28Ju02Vj
SHIELD, Senior		20	M	Unknown	28Ju02Vj
Mary		45	F	Unknown	28Ju02Vj
MANEY, Ellen		12	F	Unknown	28Ju02Vj
SPOON, Samuel		30	M	Unknown	28Ju02Vj
Mary		28	F	Unknown	28Ju02Vj
WIGAN, John		20	M	Unknown	28Ju02Vj
U	(W)	20	F	Unknown	28Ju02Vj
CASSEN, John		40	M	Unknown	28Ju02Vj
RING, Ann		15	F	Unknown	28Ju02Vj
RYLEY, Mary		50	F	Unknown	28Ju02Vj
SMITH, Julia		18	F	Unknown	28Ju02Vj
MCLAUGHLIN, Mary		20	F	Unknown	28Ju02Vj
MITCHEAL, Pat.		20	M	Unknown	28Ju02Vj
MCGEE, James		18	M	Unknown	28Ju02Vj
Daniel		14	M	Unknown	28Ju02Vj
MAYHAN, James		20	M	Unknown	28Ju02Vj
FINLEY, Peter		17	M	Unknown	28Ju02Vj
DUFFEY, Mary		17	F	Unknown	28Ju02Vj

SARAH-SANDS 28 JUNE 1848

From Liverpool

NAMES OF PASSENGERS		AGE	SEX	OCCUPATIONS	DATE PORT SHIP
FRANKLIN, Joseph		40	M	Merchant	28Ju02Kp
Sophia	(W)	35	F	Wife	28Ju02Kp
Joshua	(S)	15	M	Unknown	28Ju02Kp
Mary	(D)	13	F	Unknown	28Ju02Kp
George	(S)	11	M	Unknown	28Ju02Kp
Henry	(S)	09	M	Child	28Ju02Kp
James	(S)	07	M	Child	28Ju02Kp
A.		05	U	Child	28Ju02Kp
MCMULLON, Thos.		42	M	Merchant	28Ju02Kp
Ann	(W)	36	F	Wife	28Ju02Kp
Selina	(D)	16	F	Unknown	28Ju02Kp
Arabella	(D)	14	F	Unknown	28Ju02Kp
Mary	(D)	13	F	Unknown	28Ju02Kp
Thos.Alex	(S)	11	M	Unknown	28Ju02Kp
Rebecca	(D)	09	F	Child	28Ju02Kp
Anne-Georgina	(D)	07	F	Child	28Ju02Kp
Emma	(D)	03	F	Child	28Ju02Kp
MARCHBACK, Mary		18	F	Lady	28Ju02Kp
EVANS, Henry		27	M	Servant	28Ju02Kp
COMBERFORD, Fanny		25	F	Servant	28Ju02Kp
BLATELY, Sophia		24	F	Servant	28Ju02Kp
FEENEY, Michael		17	M	Merchant	28Ju02Kp
HESON, John		16	M	Merchant	28Ju02Kp
TORBITT, Jas.Jnr.		25	M	Lnmftr	28Ju02Kp
CALLIGAN, James		24	M	Merchant	28Ju02Kp
HASSETT, Cathr.		20	F	Merchant	28Ju02Kp
CORBETT, S.H.		20	M	Merchant	28Ju02Kp
THOMPSON, Sarah		10	F	Merchant	28Ju02Kp
Eliza		05	F	Child	28Ju02Kp
Lydia		02	F	Child	28Ju02Kp
SHEA, Ellen		20	F	None	28Ju02Kp
MEYERS, Wm.		23	M	Salesman	28Ju02Kp
JOHNSTON, Sarah		22	F	Unknown	28Ju02Kp
PUSSY, Ellen		23	F	None	28Ju02Kp
KIDD, Stephen		24	M	Engineer	28Ju02Kp

NAMES OF PASSENGERS		AGE	SEX	OCCUPATIONS	DATE PORT SHIP
ROSE, Joseph		26	M	Laborer	28Ju02Kp
MCGRATH, Richd.		30	M	Laborer	28Ju02Kp
Anne	(W)	30	F	Wife	28Ju02Kp
BROWN, John		28	M	Merchant	28Ju02Kp
CASSWELL, Clarke		37	M	Farmer	28Ju02Kp
HILL, Wm.		40	M	Unknown	28Ju02Kp
THORNTON, James		26	M	Joiner	28Ju02Kp
Dorothea	(W)	20	F	Wife	28Ju02Kp
SPRUCE, Ann		50	F	Unknown	28Ju02Kp
James		10	M	Ruler	28Ju02Kp
DOUGLAS, Margt.		21	F	Ruler	28Ju02Kp
SLOAN, Margt.		22	F	Ruler	28Ju02Kp
TURNER, James		23	M	Laborer	28Ju02Kp
HOLSID, Thomas		25	M	Spinner	28Ju02Kp
RITCHIE, Robt.		24	M	Joiner	28Ju02Kp
BRYAN, James		30	M	Tailor	28Ju02Kp
Mary	(W)	28	F	Wife	28Ju02Kp
DEVAN, Mary		29	F	Wife	28Ju02Kp
MCCANN, Mary		55	F	Wife	28Ju02Kp
MONTGOMERY, Alice		20	F	Wife	28Ju02Kp
MOORE, John		35	M	Weaver	28Ju02Kp
Winifred		35	F	Weaver	28Ju02Kp
Anna		09	F	Child	28Ju02Kp
DEACON, John		20	M	Joiner	28Ju02Kp
SMITH, Rose		45	F	Joiner	28Ju02Kp
MCCORMICK, Margt.		18	F	Joiner	28Ju02Kp
SMITH, John		25	M	Laborer	28Ju02Kp
KELLY, James		25	M	Mason	28Ju02Kp
MCCRACKEN, Alex		20	M	Joiner	28Ju02Kp
COLLINS, George		34	M	Joiner	28Ju02Kp
BEWS, John		27	M	Farmer	28Ju02Kp
HUNTER, James		25	M	Farmer	28Ju02Kp
Jane		23	F	Farmer	28Ju02Kp
James		01	M	Child	28Ju02Kp
NEWELL, Adam		30	M	Farmer	28Ju02Kp
NEWELLY, Patrick		26	M	Laborer	28Ju02Kp
Frances		24	F	None	28Ju02Kp
Michael		04	M	Child	28Ju02Kp
Mary		.06	F	Infant	28Ju02Kp
DILLON, Mary-Ann		20	F	Unknown	28Ju02Kp
COLLINS, John		26	M	Weaver	28Ju02Kp
SKIDMORE, Thos.		49	M	Farmer	28Ju02Kp
BALL, Wm.		27	M	Mechanic	28Ju02Kp
DEEHAN, John		30	M	Blacksmith	28Ju02Kp
MULLON, John		40	M	Blacksmith	28Ju02Kp
BROWN, Abraham		27	M	Clerk	28Ju02Kp

TRITON 29 JUNE 1848

From Dublin

NAMES OF PASSENGERS		AGE	SEX	OCCUPATIONS	DATE PORT SHIP
MCMAHAN, Barney		33	M	Laborer	29Ju20Vc
Anne	(W)	28	F	Laborer	29Ju20Vc
Annie		13	F	Laborer	29Ju20Vc
Owen	(S)	06	M	Laborer	29Ju20Vc
Mary-Ann		03	F	Laborer	29Ju20Vc
GALLAGHER, Patrick		42	M	Laborer	29Ju20Vc
Margaret		32	F	Laborer	29Ju20Vc
Michael		15	M	Laborer	29Ju20Vc
Patrick		13	M	Laborer	29Ju20Vc
Anne		10	F	Laborer	29Ju20Vc
Maria		06	F	Laborer	29Ju20Vc
Catherine		03	F	Laborer	29Ju20Vc
Margaret		.00	F	Infant	29Ju20Vc
REYNOLDS, Patrick		25	M	Laborer	29Ju20Vc
James		24	M	Laborer	29Ju20Vc
Mary		20	F	Laborer	29Ju20Vc
MCCABE, Edward		28	M	Laborer	29Ju20Vc
Mary		25	F	Laborer	29Ju20Vc
MCCABE, Hanna		20	F	Laborer	29Ju20Vc
Rose		.00	F	Infant	29Ju20Vc
SHEA, Matthew		22	M	Laborer	29Ju20Vc
TULLY, Thos.		20	M	Laborer	29Ju20Vc
FANELL, M.		20	M	Laborer	29Ju20Vc
DEENGAN, Mary		20	F	Laborer	29Ju20Vc
WILSON, Patrick		30	M	Laborer	29Ju20Vc
MURRAY, John		24	M	Laborer	29Ju20Vc
MASTERSEN, Michael		22	M	Laborer	29Ju20Vc
Julia		22	F	Laborer	29Ju20Vc
HEALY, Francis		22	M	Laborer	29Ju20Vc
Michael		20	M	Laborer	29Ju20Vc
WALSH, Patrick		21	M	Laborer	29Ju20Vc
LAWLER, Patrick		21	M	Laborer	29Ju20Vc
LEE, Mary		27	F	Laborer	29Ju20Vc
CASTLE, Catherine		20	F	Laborer	29Ju20Vc
BYRNE, Anthrin		24	M	Laborer	29Ju20Vc
U	(W)	20	F	Laborer	29Ju20Vc
CAVANAGH, Edward		20	M	Laborer	29Ju20Vc
TOWMAY, Mary		29	F	Laborer	29Ju20Vc
HIGGINS, Patrick		20	M	Laborer	29Ju20Vc
Ann		28	F	Laborer	29Ju20Vc
DARCA, Martha		20	F	Laborer	29Ju20Vc
CLARKE, Margaret		17	F	Laborer	29Ju20Vc
Died-At-Sea					
Ann		13	F	Laborer	29Ju20Vc
Patrick		12	M	Laborer	29Ju20Vc
Edward		10	M	Laborer	29Ju20Vc
Julia		07	F	Laborer	29Ju20Vc
DOWLING, Julia		18	F	Laborer	29Ju20Vc
BYRNE, Michael		35	M	Laborer	29Ju20Vc
Margaret		31	F	Laborer	29Ju20Vc
Elisa		10	F	Laborer	29Ju20Vc
Peter		08	M	Laborer	29Ju20Vc
Edward		06	M	Laborer	29Ju20Vc
Maria		04	F	Farmer	29Ju20Vc
Patrick		02	M	Farmer	29Ju20Vc
MAHER, James		21	M	Farmer	29Ju20Vc
MCDONALD, Martha		28	F	Farmer	29Ju20Vc
KERWAN, Wm.		28	M	Farmer	29Ju20Vc
LAWLER, Michael		20	M	Farmer	29Ju20Vc
DOECY, John		22	M	Farmer	29Ju20Vc
LAMB, Bridget		21	F	Farmer	29Ju20Vc
BREUN, Christina		19	F	Farmer	29Ju20Vc
CLARKE, Anne		21	F	Farmer	29Ju20Vc
FLYNN, Patrick		26	M	Farmer	29Ju20Vc
Michael		24	M	Farmer	29Ju20Vc
DOWNIE, James		21	M	Farmer	29Ju20Vc
LIGNAM, John		24	M	Farmer	29Ju20Vc
LANG, Henry		26	M	Farmer	29Ju20Vc
Eliza		25	F	Farmer	29Ju20Vc
Mary		06	F	Farmer	29Ju20Vc
Alex.		04	M	Farmer	29Ju20Vc
WINGFIELD, Cuerly		30	M	Farmer	29Ju20Vc
Ann		28	F	Farmer	29Ju20Vc
REDDY, John		20	M	Farmer	29Ju20Vc
U	(W)	20	F	Farmer	29Ju20Vc
RICE, Richard		40	M	Farmer	29Ju20Vc
U	(W)	20	F	Farmer	29Ju20Vc
FEGAN, John		40	M	Farmer	29Ju20Vc
MANNING, Matthew		30	M	Farmer	29Ju20Vc
KEARNEY, Bridget		30	F	Farmer	29Ju20Vc
Mary		20	F	Farmer	29Ju20Vc
Bridget		20	F	Farmer	29Ju20Vc
Margaret		13	F	Farmer	29Ju20Vc
Jane		12	F	Farmer	29Ju20Vc
Daniel		10	M	Farmer	29Ju20Vc
BREMAN, Rachel		20	F	Farmer	29Ju20Vc
FEGAN, Mary		45	F	Farmer	29Ju20Vc
Lawrence		18	M	Farmer	29Ju20Vc
Terrence		16	M	Farmer	29Ju20Vc
Maria		14	F	Farmer	29Ju20Vc
Patrick		10	M	Farmer	29Ju20Vc
John		08	M	Farmer	29Ju20Vc
Thos.		13	M	Farmer	29Ju20Vc

NAMES OF PASSENGERS		AGE	SEX	OCCUPATIONS	DATE PORT SHIP
FEGAN, Margaret		06	F	Child	29Ju20Vc
Catherine		05	F	Child	29Ju20Vc
Phillip		04	M	Child	29Ju20Vc
OCALLAGHAN, Cornelius		30	M	Farmer	29Ju20Vc
MCEVEY, Catherine		40	F	Farmer	29Ju20Vc
Michael		29	M	Farmer	29Ju20Vc
Patrick		15	M	Farmer	29Ju20Vc
John		17	M	Farmer	29Ju20Vc
Luke		13	M	Farmer	29Ju20Vc
DIGNAN, Ann		40	F	Farmer	29Ju20Vc
TWOURLEY, Margaret		34	F	Farmer	29Ju20Vc
CODY, Mary		24	F	Farmer	29Ju20Vc
MENIA, Edward		26	M	Laborer	29Ju20Vc
LAWLER, James		28	M	Laborer	29Ju20Vc
DUFFY, William		24	M	Laborer	29Ju20Vc
TAGGERTY, Mary		40	F	Laborer	29Ju20Vc
John		18	M	Laborer	29Ju20Vc
James		14	M	Laborer	29Ju20Vc
COMAN, Margaret		45	F	Laborer	29Ju20Vc
Dennis		18	M	Laborer	29Ju20Vc
John		10	M	Laborer	29Ju20Vc
Margaret		15	F	Laborer	29Ju20Vc
KELLY, Thos.		24	M	Laborer	29Ju20Vc
MCDERMITT, May		21	F	Laborer	29Ju20Vc
LAWLEY, Martin		36	M	Laborer	29Ju20Vc
LAWLES, Bridget		20	F	Laborer	29Ju20Vc
HUGHES, Bridget		20	F	Laborer	29Ju20Vc
OHARA, Jane		28	F	Laborer	29Ju20Vc
DUNN, Thos.		34	M	Laborer	29Ju20Vc
U	(W)	34	F	Laborer	29Ju20Vc
John		18	M	Laborer	29Ju20Vc
Matthew		16	M	Laborer	29Ju20Vc
Anne		14	F	Laborer	29Ju20Vc
ROCHEFORT, John		30	M	Laborer	29Ju20Vc
Elisa	(W)	30	F	Laborer	29Ju20Vc
Wm.		07	M	Laborer	29Ju20Vc
Catherine		05	F	Child	29Ju20Vc
Mary		.00	F	Infant	29Ju20Vc
STEEL, Catherine		60	F	Laborer	29Ju20Vc
ROCHEFORT, Wm.		15	M	Laborer	29Ju20Vc
FEGAN, John		21	M	Laborer	29Ju20Vc
Margaret		19	F	Laborer	29Ju20Vc
CARRIGAN, Patrick		60	M	Laborer	29Ju20Vc
BRUTEN, John		21	M	Laborer	29Ju20Vc
BOSHILL, John		28	M	Laborer	29Ju20Vc
CORRIGAN, U		23	F	Laborer	29Ju20Vc
Anne		06	F	Laborer	29Ju20Vc
John		02	M	Laborer	29Ju20Vc
DOYLE, Elisa		20	F	Laborer	29Ju20Vc
MILEY, John		14	M	Laborer	29Ju20Vc
DUNN, Wm.		20	M	Laborer	29Ju20Vc
SMITH, Patrick		21	M	Laborer	29Ju20Vc
DOYLE, John		20	M	Laborer	29Ju20Vc
GORMLEY, Mary		20	F	Laborer	29Ju20Vc
DEVLIN, Anne		20	F	Laborer	29Ju20Vc
HENDERSON, Peter		22	M	Laborer	29Ju20Vc
Mary		20	F	Laborer	29Ju20Vc
John		.00	M	Infant	29Ju20Vc
COCKBURN, Margaret		22	F	Laborer	29Ju20Vc
John		14	M	Laborer	29Ju20Vc
Elisa		11	F	Laborer	29Ju20Vc
Julia		09	F	Laborer	29Ju20Vc
LARKIN, Peter		21	M	Laborer	29Ju20Vc
DIVINE, Peter		20	M	Laborer	29Ju20Vc
FLUDDY, Patrick		23	M	Laborer	29Ju20Vc
MCCORMICK, Patrick		18	M	Laborer	29Ju20Vc
FLUDDY, Catherine		19	F	Laborer	29Ju20Vc
CURRAN, Anne		20	F	Farmer	29Ju20Vc
LEPAGHT, Elisabeth		20	F	Farmer	29Ju20Vc
MCKENNA, Julia		20	F	Farmer	29Ju20Vc
GERAGHTY, John		21	M	Farmer	29Ju20Vc
COONEY, Thos.		30	M	Farmer	29Ju20Vc
DOUGLAS, James		24	M	Farmer	29Ju20Vc
U	(W)	20	F	Farmer	29Ju20Vc
QUINN, U		40	F	Farmer	29Ju20Vc
QUINN, Mary		18	F	Farmer	29Ju20Vc
Bridget		06	F	Child	29Ju20Vc
Patrick		13	M	Farmer	29Ju20Vc
Peter		07	M	Farmer	29Ju20Vc
DICKSON, Thos.		45	M	Farmer	29Ju20Vc
John		12	M	Farmer	29Ju20Vc
Thos.		06	M	Farmer	29Ju20Vc
Catherine		14	F	Farmer	29Ju20Vc
KELLY, Patrick		30	M	Farmer	29Ju20Vc
DUNN, Patrick		25	M	Farmer	29Ju20Vc
RYAN, Wm.		24	M	Farmer	29Ju20Vc
HEARY, Mary		40	F	Farmer	29Ju20Vc
John		13	M	Farmer	29Ju20Vc
Michael		11	M	Farmer	29Ju20Vc
Anne		09	F	Farmer	29Ju20Vc
Margaret		05	F	Child	29Ju20Vc
BURNS, Charles		25	M	Farmer	29Ju20Vc
U	(W)	22	F	Farmer	29Ju20Vc
Michael		.00	M	Infant	29Ju20Vc
KENNEDY, Dennis		21	M	Farmer	29Ju20Vc
U	(W)	20	F	Farmer	29Ju20Vc
MOWATT, James		28	M	Farmer	29Ju20Vc
U	(W)	40	F	Farmer	29Ju20Vc
HEYA, Patrick		24	M	Farmer	29Ju20Vc
U	(W)	22	F	Farmer	29Ju20Vc
QUINN, James		22	M	Farmer	29Ju20Vc
Stephen		20	M	Farmer	29Ju20Vc
MCDONALD, Ann		20	F	Farmer	29Ju20Vc
HOARE, John		21	M	Farmer	29Ju20Vc
REILLY, Rose		18	F	Farmer	29Ju20Vc
RUPEL, Ellen		18	F	Farmer	29Ju20Vc
CREIGHTON, John		22	M	Farmer	29Ju20Vc
CAFFRAY, Anne		20	F	Farmer	29Ju20Vc
CAVANAGH, Arthur		25	M	Farmer	29Ju20Vc
BRIEN, William		26	M	Farmer	29Ju20Vc
QUINN, Catherine		21	F	Farmer	29Ju20Vc
May		20	F	Farmer	29Ju20Vc
ARNOLA, Mary		21	F	Farmer	29Ju20Vc
MOONEY, M.		25	M	Farmer	29Ju20Vc
FITZPATRICK, Thos.		11	M	Farmer	29Ju20Vc
Catherine		27	F	Farmer	29Ju20Vc
FEEGAN, Lawrence		18	M	Farmer	29Ju20Vc
MCEVEY, James		20	M	Farmer	29Ju20Vc
DWYER, Edward		22	M	Farmer	29Ju20Vc
Margaret		25	F	Farmer	29Ju20Vc
TALLON, James		23	M	Farmer	29Ju20Vc
FITZPATRICK, Margaret		20	F	Farmer	29Ju20Vc
TRACEY, Sarah		20	F	Farmer	29Ju20Vc
KERWAN, Richard		24	M	Farmer	29Ju20Vc
CULLEN, John		22	M	Farmer	29Ju20Vc
RAFFERTY, Paul		20	M	Farmer	29Ju20Vc
Margaret		20	F	Farmer	29Ju20Vc
MCLAUGHLIN, James		24	M	Farmer	29Ju20Vc
CLARKE, John		24	M	Farmer	29Ju20Vc
ANDREWS, Mary		22	F	Farmer	29Ju20Vc
Alice		30	F	Farmer	29Ju20Vc
MAULEY, John		24	M	Farmer	29Ju20Vc
Richard		20	M	Farmer	29Ju20Vc
STEELE, T.		21	M	Farmer	29Ju20Vc
DEMPSEY, U		34	F	Farmer	29Ju20Vc
Jane		14	F	Farmer	29Ju20Vc
Patrick		02	M	Child	29Ju20Vc
Anne		16	F	Farmer	29Ju20Vc
BYRNE, Marcella		22	F	Farmer	29Ju20Vc
OBRIEN, Edward		26	M	Farmer	29Ju20Vc
DUNN, James		26	M	Farmer	29Ju20Vc
OBRIEN, Ann		03	F	Child	29Ju20Vc
GERRAGHTY, Michael		24	M	Farmer	29Ju20Vc
U	(W)	22	F	Farmer	29Ju20Vc
MORSE, Edward		21	M	Farmer	29Ju20Vc
GALLAGHER, Michael		21	M	Farmer	29Ju20Vc
CUNNINGHAN, Thos.		21	M	Farmer	29Ju20Vc
REILLY, Wm.		21	M	Farmer	29Ju20Vc
U	(W)	20	F	Farmer	29Ju20Vc
Edward		05	M	Farmer	29Ju20Vc

NAMES OF PASSENGERS		AGE	SEX	OCCUPATIONS	DATE PORT SHIP
FEGAN, Margaret		50	F	Farmer	29Ju20Vc
John		20	M	Farmer	29Ju20Vc
CARNEY, Michael		30	M	Farmer	29Ju20Vc
Sarah	(W)	25	F	Farmer	29Ju20Vc
HILLYER, Margaret		18	F	Farmer	29Ju20Vc
FRASER, John		30	M	Farmer	29Ju20Vc
U	(W)	32	F	Farmer	29Ju20Vc
Sarah		04	F	Child	29Ju20Vc
KEATING, Redmond		23	M	Farmer	29Ju20Vc
ALPINE, Patrick		24	M	Farmer	29Ju20Vc
Fanny	(W)	21	F	Farmer	29Ju20Vc
Kate		.00	F	Infant	29Ju20Vc
MORAN, Kate		15	F	Farmer	29Ju20Vc
MASON, U		25	M	Farmer	29Ju20Vc
U	(W)	20	F	Farmer	29Ju20Vc
Robert		18	M	Farmer	29Ju20Vc
Joseph		04	M	Child	29Ju20Vc
Traven		03	M	Child	29Ju20Vc
Edward		02	M	Child	29Ju20Vc
Elisabeth		.00	F	Infant	29Ju20Vc
DUNN, Bridget		20	F	Farmer	29Ju20Vc
CONWAY, Elisa		18	F	Farmer	29Ju20Vc
KENNEDY, D.		21	M	Farmer	29Ju20Vc
HIGGINS, J.		21	M	Farmer	29Ju20Vc

SULTAN 29 JUNE 1848

From Dublin

NAMES OF PASSENGERS		AGE	SEX	OCCUPATIONS	DATE PORT SHIP
MOUNTJOY, Sarah		55	F	Wi	29Ju20Vq
Margaret		20	F	None	29Ju20Vq
BARTON, John-B.		25	M	Clerk	29Ju20Vq
DALE, Isabella		18	F	Spinster	29Ju20Vq
CARROL, Chas.		25	M	Mason	29Ju20Vq
FRASIER, Mary		20	F	Seamstress	29Ju20Vq
POWELL, John		20	M	Clerk	29Ju20Vq
RAFERTY, Thomas		21	M	Clerk	29Ju20Vq
LOYDEN, William		21	M	Laborer	29Ju20Vq
Ann		20	F	Laborer	29Ju20Vq
FLOOD, Peter		32	M	Carpenter	29Ju20Vq
DORAN, Dennis		24	M	Engineer	29Ju20Vq
Cate		10	F	None	29Ju20Vq
John		50	M	Traveller	29Ju20Vq
Eleaner		40	F	Traveller	29Ju20Vq
FLANNERY, Mary		21	F	Spinster	29Ju20Vq
BEHAN, William		20	M	Bookbinder	29Ju20Vq
DONAHOO, Bridget		22	F	Seamstress	29Ju20Vq
Anne		20	F	Spinster	29Ju20Vq
KANNEY, Ewd.		24	M	Servant	29Ju20Vq
ROCHFORD, Thos.		24	M	Clerk	29Ju20Vq
Catherine		20	F	Clerk	29Ju20Vq
BEATTY, Jas.		25	M	Flaxdr	29Ju20Vq
OREELEY, Byan		21	M	Clerk	29Ju20Vq
CONLAN, Daniel		21	M	Clerk	29Ju20Vq
CONROY, Patrick		21	M	Farmer	29Ju20Vq
ODLAM, P.		24	M	Carpenter	29Ju20Vq
HARE, Ewd.		18	M	Carpenter	29Ju20Vq
HIGGINS, Mary		22	F	Spinster	29Ju20Vq
DAILEY, Peter		54	M	Farmer	29Ju20Vq
Bridget		20	F	Farmer	29Ju20Vq
Mark		18	M	Farmer	29Ju20Vq
Dan		16	M	Farmer	29Ju20Vq
Catherine		15	F	Farmer	29Ju20Vq
Mary		13	F	Farmer	29Ju20Vq
OBRINE, J.J.		22	M	Carpenter	29Ju20Vq
PENTONY, Thos.		21	M	Carpenter	29Ju20Vq
CASTEY, Benard		27	M	Carpenter	29Ju20Vq
REILEY, Ewd.		27	M	Shoemaker	29Ju20Vq
KELLY, Catharin		25	F	Shoemaker	29Ju20Vq

NAMES OF PASSENGERS		AGE	SEX	OCCUPATIONS	DATE PORT SHIP
CULLEN, Elisa		20	F	Dressmaker	29Ju20Vq
Mary		19	F	Dressmaker	29Ju20Vq
COLMAY, Andrew		24	M	Servant	29Ju20Vq
William		20	M	Laborer	29Ju20Vq
COLGAN, Jas.		37	M	Farmer	29Ju20Vq
Bess		24	F	Farmer	29Ju20Vq
Ann		01	F	Farmer	29Ju20Vq
BURGAN, William		48	M	Laborer	29Ju20Vq
Ann		40	F	Laborer	29Ju20Vq
Honor		22	F	Laborer	29Ju20Vq
Pat		20	M	Laborer	29Ju20Vq
Julia		15	F	Laborer	29Ju20Vq
John		13	M	Laborer	29Ju20Vq
Biddy		11	F	Laborer	29Ju20Vq
Fanton		07	M	Child	29Ju20Vq
CANOL, John		45	M	Butcher	29Ju20Vq
Mary		30	F	Butcher	29Ju20Vq
Mary		11	F	Butcher	29Ju20Vq
John		07	M	Child	29Ju20Vq
CARROL, Pat		03	M	Child	29Ju20Vq
COWLAY, Frank		36	M	Laborer	29Ju20Vq
Mary		31	F	Laborer	29Ju20Vq
Mary		05	F	Child	29Ju20Vq
Pat		02	M	Laborer	29Ju20Vq
WHITAKER, Arthur		50	M	Farmer	29Ju20Vq
Sarah		42	F	Farmer	29Ju20Vq
Arthur		22	M	Farmer	29Ju20Vq
Amelia		20	F	Farmer	29Ju20Vq
FLOOD, Julia		30	F	Farmer	29Ju20Vq
Maria		10	F	Farmer	29Ju20Vq
Cate		09	F	Child	29Ju20Vq
Teresa		07	F	Child	29Ju20Vq
MAYTAN, Thomas		42	M	Distiller	29Ju20Vq
Mary		38	F	Distiller	29Ju20Vq
Thos.		10	M	Distiller	29Ju20Vq
Sally		11	F	Distiller	29Ju20Vq
Celelue		12	F	Distiller	29Ju20Vq
Thos.		10	M	Distiller	29Ju20Vq
REILEY, Michael		20	M	Saddler	29Ju20Vq
COLDWELL, Thomas		50	M	Saddler	29Ju20Vq
Mary		43	F	Saddler	29Ju20Vq
CONNER, Pat		45	M	Laborer	29Ju20Vq
Robt.		21	M	Laborer	29Ju20Vq
Anne		16	F	Spinster	29Ju20Vq
LAWLESS, Thos.		30	M	Laborer	29Ju20Vq
Jane		28	F	Laborer	29Ju20Vq
Elisa		07	F	Child	29Ju20Vq
Gregory		05	M	Child	29Ju20Vq
Fany		03	F	Child	29Ju20Vq
Annie		01	F	Child	29Ju20Vq
COOGAN, John		40	M	Laborer	29Ju20Vq
Mary		35	F	None	29Ju20Vq
MAURRY, Patrick		25	M	Servant	29Ju20Vq
DOWALL, Richard		30	M	Blacksmith	29Ju20Vq
Bridget		22	F	Blacksmith	29Ju20Vq
MCMELLY, Elisa		26	F	Spinster	29Ju20Vq
DOWALL, Ewd.		05	M	Child	29Ju20Vq
Mary		03	F	Child	29Ju20Vq
Catherine		01	F	Child	29Ju20Vq
RECLERY, Robt.		25	M	Cooper	29Ju20Vq
GORMAN, Pat.C.		30	M	Cooper	29Ju20Vq
Martin-C.		07	M	Child	29Ju20Vq
MENTON, Michael		15	M	Cooper	29Ju20Vq
QUAYLE, Ewd.		27	M	Laborer	29Ju20Vq
Ann		24	F	Laborer	29Ju20Vq
LEE, William		24	M	Gilder	29Ju20Vq
MURPHY, Ewd.		40	M	Druggist	29Ju20Vq
ROBINSON, Fredrick		21	M	Accountant	29Ju20Vq
HALPIN, George		24	M	Shepherd	29Ju20Vq
Thos.		13	M	Shepherd	29Ju20Vq
OBRINE, Thos.		18	M	Cooper	29Ju20Vq
QUINLAN, Ewd.		21	M	Cooper	29Ju20Vq
Michael		22	M	Laborer	29Ju20Vq
DAY, Richard		27	M	Farmer	29Ju20Vq
Peggy		24	F	Farmer	29Ju20Vq

NAMES OF PASSENGERS		AGE	SEX	OCCUPATIONS	DATE PORT SHIP
BURK, Thos.		24	M	Laborer	29Ju20Vq
CUSHIN, Michael		22	M	Farmer	29Ju20Vq
John		20	M	Laborer	29Ju20Vq
Mary		19	F	Spinster	29Ju20Vq
CULLEN, Pat.		21	M	Gdnr	29Ju20Vq
WHITAKER, Samuel		18	M	Gdnr	29Ju20Vq
Sarah		16	F	Gdnr	29Ju20Vq
Susan		25	F	Gdnr	29Ju20Vq
MATTHEWS, James		25	M	Farmer	29Ju20Vq
SHERMAN, Chas.		50	M	Clerk	29Ju20Vq
KEITH, Pat		38	M	Servant	29Ju20Vq
KEHOE, Michael		24	M	Laborer	29Ju20Vq
QUIGLEY, Bridget		16	F	Spinster	29Ju20Vq
Kitty		15	F	Spinster	29Ju20Vq
DUGAN, Andy		30	M	Laborer	29Ju20Vq
MCAVOY, Judy		20	F	Spinster	29Ju20Vq
HENNISSY, John		24	M	Farmer	29Ju20Vq
MCGOWN, Dennis		39	M	Sawer	29Ju20Vq

W.M.VAIL 29 JUNE 1848

From Liverpool

NAMES OF PASSENGERS		AGE	SEX	OCCUPATIONS	DATE PORT SHIP
DALRYMPLE, Anne	(W)	39	F	Wife	29Ju02Vr
Jane		20	F	Spinster	29Ju02Vr
Cloluith		18	M	Laborer	29Ju02Vr
James		12	M	Child	29Ju02Vr
Anne		10	F	Child	29Ju02Vr
Helen		06	F	Child	29Ju02Vr
Martha		04	F	Child	29Ju02Vr
Eliza		02	F	Child	29Ju02Vr
KELLY, John		28	M	Weaver	29Ju02Vr
Anne	(W)	28	F	Wife	29Ju02Vr
James		01	M	Child	29Ju02Vr
Mary		.00	F	Infant	29Ju02Vr
MCKILVEY, Mary		22	F	Spinster	29Ju02Vr
QUINLEY, Catherine		26	F	Mother	29Ju02Vr
James		09	M	Child	29Ju02Vr
Daniel		07	M	Child	29Ju02Vr
Mary-Ann		03	F	Child	29Ju02Vr
SWEENEY, John		23	M	Laborer	29Ju02Vr
RYAN, Patrick		50	M	Laborer	29Ju02Vr
MURPHY, Thomas		26	M	Laborer	29Ju02Vr
Mary	(W)	25	F	Wife	29Ju02Vr
RYAN, Judith		14	F	Spinster	29Ju02Vr
Nancy		22	F	Spinster	29Ju02Vr
Edward		12	M	Child	29Ju02Vr
MURPHY, Patrick		.00	M	Infant	29Ju02Vr
HARAN, Sarah		25	F	Mother	29Ju02Vr
Maria		04	F	Child	29Ju02Vr
DURNIN, Hugh		25	M	Laborer	29Ju02Vr
Patrick		22	M	Laborer	29Ju02Vr
CURRIN, James		21	M	Laborer	29Ju02Vr
LAFFERTY, James		27	M	Laborer	29Ju02Vr
MCLOUGHLIN, Mary		18	F	Spinster	29Ju02Vr
GALLAGHER, Michael		30	M	Laborer	29Ju02Vr
MCNALLY, James		20	M	Laborer	29Ju02Vr
Rose		18	F	Spinster	29Ju02Vr
BRIER, John		28	M	Laborer	29Ju02Vr
FISHER, John		27	M	Laborer	29Ju02Vr
Mary	(W)	26	F	Wife	29Ju02Vr
Samuel		04	M	Child	29Ju02Vr
William		06	M	Child	29Ju02Vr
John		.00	M	Infant	29Ju02Vr
HAMILTON, Stewart		50	M	Grocer	29Ju02Vr
Ann	(W)	50	F	Wife	29Ju02Vr
Stewart		20	M	Laborer	29Ju02Vr
Eliza		18	F	Spinster	29Ju02Vr
Rebecca		15	F	Spinster	29Ju02Vr

NAMES OF PASSENGERS		AGE	SEX	OCCUPATIONS	DATE PORT SHIP
MCCULLOH, Jane		17	F	Spinster	29Ju02Vr
MCCANLY, Sarah		20	F	Spinster	29Ju02Vr
MCCARTHY, Philip		40	M	Laborer	29Ju02Vr
Sarah		30	F	Wife	29Ju02Vr
SLAVEN, Ellen		22	F	Spinster	29Ju02Vr
ROSBOROUGH, William		25	M	Shoemaker	29Ju02Vr
Margaret	(W)	25	F	Wife	29Ju02Vr
Charlotte		20	F	Spinster	29Ju02Vr
William		02	M	Child	29Ju02Vr
KELLY, Mary		30	F	Wife	29Ju02Vr
GERALY, Michael		30	M	Laborer	29Ju02Vr
MCQUAID, James		25	M	Laborer	29Ju02Vr
MURPHY, James		22	M	Laborer	29Ju02Vr
KEARNEY, Patrick		30	M	Laborer	29Ju02Vr
Bridget	(W)	24	F	Wife	29Ju02Vr
Mary		23	F	Spinster	29Ju02Vr
KEWON, Lizz		22	F	Spinster	29Ju02Vr
ARTHURS, John		37	M	Ctnsp	29Ju02Vr
Mary	(W)	36	F	Wife	29Ju02Vr
William		13	M	Child	29Ju02Vr
Mary		11	F	Child	29Ju02Vr
Alexander		09	M	Child	29Ju02Vr
Helen		07	F	Child	29Ju02Vr
Eliza		04	F	Child	29Ju02Vr
Maria		.00	F	Infant	29Ju02Vr
BALEY, Maria		30	F	Spinster	29Ju02Vr
LINDSAY, James		18	M	Laborer	29Ju02Vr
MAHON, Daniel		25	M	Laborer	29Ju02Vr
U	(W)	23	F	Wife	29Ju02Vr
Honora		.00	F	Infant	29Ju02Vr
HEALY, John		20	M	Laborer	29Ju02Vr
HAGARTY, Hugh		19	M	Laborer	29Ju02Vr
BOYLE, Margaret		18	F	Spinster	29Ju02Vr
GRULL, James		21	M	Laborer	29Ju02Vr
Patrick		19	M	Laborer	29Ju02Vr
HOMES, John		26	M	Laborer	29Ju02Vr
Mary		20	F	Spinster	29Ju02Vr
HAGARTY, Philip		22	M	Laborer	29Ju02Vr
HANNAHAN, Michael		25	M	Laborer	29Ju02Vr
MCMANNINGS, Ellen		14	F	Spinster	29Ju02Vr
DEVENEY, Margaret		18	F	Spinster	29Ju02Vr
GOULY, Andrew		20	M	Laborer	29Ju02Vr
MCMULLEN, Mark		20	M	Shoemaker	29Ju02Vr
LINDLEY, Thomas		21	M	Carpenter	29Ju02Vr
BEA, Mary-Ann		22	F	Spinster	29Ju02Vr
TAYLOR, James		23	M	Laborer	29Ju02Vr
MECHAN, John		21	M	Farmer	29Ju02Vr
SULLIVAN, George		48	M	Laborer	29Ju02Vr
Patrick		24	M	Shoemaker	29Ju02Vr
Henry		18	M	Laborer	29Ju02Vr
Bernard		15	M	Laborer	29Ju02Vr
Margaret		22	F	Spinster	29Ju02Vr
Peter		10	M	Child	29Ju02Vr
MCARDLE, Mary		30	F	Spinster	29Ju02Vr
GOUR, Margaret		18	F	Spinster	29Ju02Vr
WALLS, Bridget		18	F	Spinster	29Ju02Vr
MUILLIGAN, John		24	M	Laborer	29Ju02Vr
Anne		14	F	Spinster	29Ju02Vr
BRODLY, Philip		22	M	Laborer	29Ju02Vr
MCTEGE, Peter		25	M	Laborer	29Ju02Vr
RONAN, Patrick		14	M	Laborer	29Ju02Vr
Mary		16	F	Spinster	29Ju02Vr
ELWELL, Rose		22	F	Wife	29Ju02Vr
MURRAY, Bess		16	F	Spinster	29Ju02Vr
JOICE, William		28	M	Laborer	29Ju02Vr
CABE, Michael		24	M	Laborer	29Ju02Vr
TOOHY, Martin		35	M	Laborer	29Ju02Vr
CAROLIN, Mary		13	F	None	29Ju02Vr
SHANNON, Thomas		35	M	Farmer	29Ju02Vr
Margaret	(W)	32	F	Wife	29Ju02Vr
Bridget		08	F	Child	29Ju02Vr
Peter		06	M	Child	29Ju02Vr
LINCH, Catherine		24	F	Spinster	29Ju02Vr
DWYER, Bridget		19	F	Spinster	29Ju02Vr
LINCH, Catherine		13	F	None	29Ju02Vr

NAMES OF PASSENGERS		AGE	SEX	OCCUPATIONS	DATE PORT SHIP
LINCH, James		10	M	Child	29Ju02Vr
GARAJAN, Michael		35	M	Laborer	29Ju02Vr
CONNELLY, William		34	M	Laborer	29Ju02Vr
MURDAH, James		41	M	Quarryman	29Ju02Vr
NEWSON, Henry		32	M	Laborer	29Ju02Vr
U	(W)	27	F	Wife	29Ju02Vr
CAHILL, Thomas		36	M	Laborer	29Ju02Vr
RYAN, John		21	M	Laborer	29Ju02Vr
GENNINS, James		20	M	Laborer	29Ju02Vr
MURPHY, Patrick		35	M	Laborer	29Ju02Vr
U	(W)	26	F	Wife	29Ju02Vr
Ann		02	F	Child	29Ju02Vr
Michael		.00	M	Infant	29Ju02Vr
CONNELLY, John		46	M	Laborer	29Ju02Vr
REED, Peter		26	M	Laborer	29Ju02Vr
CONLON, Anne		18	F	Spinster	29Ju02Vr
BOYDE, Edward		25	M	Mason	29Ju02Vr
MATHEWS, Lawrence		24	M	Clerk	29Ju02Vr
CARROLL, Peter		39	M	Laborer	29Ju02Vr
U	(W)	30	F	Wife	29Ju02Vr
Mary		05	F	Child	29Ju02Vr
Bridget		03	F	Child	29Ju02Vr
Anne		.00	F	Infant	29Ju02Vr
MURRAY, James		35	M	Butcher	29Ju02Vr
Elizabeth	(W)	20	F	Wife	29Ju02Vr
TEENEY, John		22	M	Laborer	29Ju02Vr
Nancy		49	F	Wife	29Ju02Vr
Mary		16	F	Spinster	29Ju02Vr
Bridget		13	F	None	29Ju02Vr
Susan		12	F	Child	29Ju02Vr
Patrick		10	M	Child	29Ju02Vr
Nancy		08	F	Child	29Ju02Vr
SMITH, John		16	M	Laborer	29Ju02Vr
FREEMAN, James		20	M	Laborer	29Ju02Vr
Ann		18	F	Spinster	29Ju02Vr
CLANNINGS, David		22	M	Fitter	29Ju02Vr
DOGHERTY, Catherine		21	F	Wife	29Ju02Vr
MOONEY, Patrick		24	M	Laborer	29Ju02Vr
Sabina	(W)	22	F	Wife	29Ju02Vr
REGAN, Bridget		35	F	Wife	29Ju02Vr
Michael		11	M	Child	29Ju02Vr
Mary-Ann		.00	F	Infant	29Ju02Vr
MCDERMOTT, John		45	M	Laborer	29Ju02Vr
Margaret	(W)	40	F	Wife	29Ju02Vr
Hugh		20	M	Laborer	29Ju02Vr
Thomas		24	M	Laborer	29Ju02Vr
Patrick		18	M	Laborer	29Ju02Vr
James		16	M	Laborer	29Ju02Vr
IVERS, Michael		50	M	Laborer	29Ju02Vr
Michael		25	M	Laborer	29Ju02Vr
Mary	(W)	24	F	Wife	29Ju02Vr
Sarah		01	F	Child	29Ju02Vr
Patrick		.00	M	Infant	29Ju02Vr
CURLEY, Mary		24	F	Spinster	29Ju02Vr
GREGORY, Richard		34	M	Clerk	29Ju02Vr
Mary-Ann	(W)	30	F	Wife	29Ju02Vr
Jane		03	F	Child	29Ju02Vr
SNELL, Bridget		21	F	Spinster	29Ju02Vr
CALCRAFT, Alfred		33	M	Baker	29Ju02Vr
LAVEY, Ann		45	F	Wife	29Ju02Vr
Mary-Ann		11	F	Child	29Ju02Vr
Margaret		08	F	Child	29Ju02Vr
KENNEDY, Patrick		22	M	Laborer	29Ju02Vr
GIBSON, Thomas		25	M	Clock Maker	29Ju02Vr
U	(W)	22	F	Wife	29Ju02Vr
Fenton		07	M	Child	29Ju02Vr
Walter		05	M	Child	29Ju02Vr
William		03	M	Child	29Ju02Vr
Catherine		.00	F	Infant	29Ju02Vr
HYNES, Patrick		22	M	Laborer	29Ju02Vr
CONNER, John		22	M	Laborer	29Ju02Vr
MONTGOMERY, John		20	M	Laborer	29Ju02Vr
DEVINE, Mary		18	F	Spinster	29Ju02Vr
HEERY, Mary		40	F	Spinster	29Ju02Vr
Bridget		16	F	Spinster	29Ju02Vr
HEERY, Rose		11	F	Child	29Ju02Vr
CASEY, Patrick		30	M	Laborer	29Ju02Vr
MCCALLAN, Bernard		30	M	Laborer	29Ju02Vr
JOHNSON, James		23	M	Laborer	29Ju02Vr
FLOOD, John		22	M	Laborer	29Ju02Vr
HEANEY, Bridget		20	F	Spinster	29Ju02Vr
REGAN, Terence		20	M	Laborer	29Ju02Vr
RIDWAY, Jane		20	F	Spinster	29Ju02Vr
MCEVOY, John		18	M	Laborer	29Ju02Vr
Richard		30	M	Laborer	29Ju02Vr
Sally		12	F	Child	29Ju02Vr
WILLIAMS, Edward		18	M	Laborer	29Ju02Vr
Jane		17	F	Spinster	29Ju02Vr
William		20	M	Laborer	29Ju02Vr
MCDONALD, Fanny		16	F	Spinster	29Ju02Vr
MU, Jane		19	F	Spinster	29Ju02Vr
MCAUNLTY, Hugh		20	M	Laborer	29Ju02Vr
CARR, Bessy		29	F	Spinster	29Ju02Vr
REILLY, Mary		29	F	Spinster	29Ju02Vr
MORGAN, Davis		30	M	Laborer	29Ju02Vr
MCNALLY, William		20	M	Clerk	29Ju02Vr
MORAN, John		33	M	Laborer	29Ju02Vr
Michael		07	M	Child	29Ju02Vr
CONNOR, Martin		37	M	Laborer	29Ju02Vr
HICKEY, Patrick		30	M	Brick Maker	29Ju02Vr
KELLY, Patrick		24	M	Laborer	29Ju02Vr

JANE 29 JUNE 1848

From Liverpool

NAMES OF PASSENGERS		AGE	SEX	OCCUPATIONS	DATE PORT SHIP
MCDONNELL, Thomas		25	M	Laborer	29Ju02Dv
Mary		20	F	Servant	29Ju02Dv
HUMPHREYS, Mathw.		40	M	Laborer	29Ju02Dv
Catherine		30	F	Servant	29Ju02Dv
Mary-Anne		04	F	Child	29Ju02Dv
Margaret		01	F	Child	29Ju02Dv
Died-At-Sea					
MCDERMOTT, Pat		19	M	Laborer	29Ju02Dv
FOSTER, Jane		30	F	Seamstress	29Ju02Dv
John		12	M	Seamstress	29Ju02Dv
Elizabeth		10	F	Seamstress	29Ju02Dv
SHORT, John		19	M	Laborer	29Ju02Dv
COBB, Anne		23	F	Spinster	29Ju02Dv
BRYAN, Denis		50	M	Laborer	29Ju02Dv
FENNESSY, John		23	M	Laborer	29Ju02Dv
BRYAN, Danl.		18	M	Laborer	29Ju02Dv
Margt.		04	F	Child	29Ju02Dv
Mary		06	F	Child	29Ju02Dv
WHITE, Judy		40	F	Servant	29Ju02Dv
BASMON, Martin		23	M	Laborer	29Ju02Dv
Mary		23	F	Seamstress	29Ju02Dv
MORRISSY, Margt.		22	F	Servant	29Ju02Dv
BRYAN, Cathn.		15	F	Servant	29Ju02Dv
HERSON, Michl.		20	M	Laborer	29Ju02Dv
JARNAN, Bernard		23	M	Laborer	29Ju02Dv
U, Laurence		17	M	Laborer	29Ju02Dv
Anne		50	F	Seamstress	29Ju02Dv
Anne		16	F	Seamstress	29Ju02Dv
DUFFY, Jane		40	F	Seamstress	29Ju02Dv
Ellen		22	F	Seamstress	29Ju02Dv
MAHONY, Pat		27	M	Laborer	29Ju02Dv
BUCKLY, John		22	M	Laborer	29Ju02Dv
CONNELL, Tim		22	M	Laborer	29Ju02Dv
Died-At-Sea					
MAHONY, Pat-Jnr.		23	M	Laborer	29Ju02Dv
DONOLOY, Mary		24	F	Servant	29Ju02Dv
BUCKLY, Honor		22	F	Servant	29Ju02Dv
HANKINSON, Wm.		40	M	Carpenter	29Ju02Dv

NAMES OF PASSENGERS	AGE	SEX	OCCUPATIONS	DATE PORT SHIP
HANKINSON, Eliza	18	F	Servant	29Ju02Dv
Jane	13	F	Servant	29Ju02Dv
Wm.Jnr.	11	M	Servant	29Ju02Dv
U, Mary	19	F	Servant	29Ju02Dv
Eliza	17	F	Servant	29Ju02Dv
Wm.	26	M	Laborer	29Ju02Dv
John	37	M	Baker	29Ju02Dv
By---, Cathe.	15	F	Servant	29Ju02Dv
BYRNE, James	21	M	Laborer	29Ju02Dv
MORAN, Margt.	50	F	Seamstress	29Ju02Dv
MURPHY, Maria	19	F	Servant	29Ju02Dv
KENNY, John	35	M	Laborer	29Ju02Dv
Mary	30	F	Seamstress	29Ju02Dv
Rose	09	F	Child	29Ju02Dv
Mary-Jnr.	.02	F	Infant	29Ju02Dv
COLGAN, Arthur	26	M	Joiner	29Ju02Dv
Eliza	21	F	Seamstress	29Ju02Dv
Bridgt.	.10	F	Infant	29Ju02Dv
MCGRAH, Danl.	36	M	Plasterer	29Ju02Dv
Eliza	33	F	Seamstress	29Ju02Dv
CLARKE, Charlotte	08	F	Child	29Ju02Dv
MCGRAH, Ellen	01	F	Child	29Ju02Dv
DAVIS, John	50	M	Farmer	29Ju02Dv
Geo.	22	M	Laborer	29Ju02Dv
KERR, Thomas	23	M	Laborer	29Ju02Dv
CAMORGHAM, Mary	25	F	Seamstress	29Ju02Dv
FARRELL, Mary	22	F	Seamstress	29Ju02Dv
DONNELLY, Ellen	17	F	Seamstress	29Ju02Dv
BRADY, Edwd.	18	M	Laborer	29Ju02Dv
ONEAL, Peter	22	M	Laborer	29Ju02Dv
CONNELL, Catherine	25	F	Servant	29Ju02Dv
Rose	20	F	Servant	29Ju02Dv
RIELLY, Susan	18	F	Servant	29Ju02Dv
MCDONNOTT, Michl.	22	M	Laborer	29Ju02Dv
COOK, Edward	20	M	Laborer	29Ju02Dv
CAFFREY, James	22	M	Laborer	29Ju02Dv
RIELLY, Jane	40	F	Servant	29Ju02Dv
Bessy	10	F	Servant	29Ju02Dv
Martha	06	F	Child	29Ju02Dv
FARLEY, Thomas	40	M	Laborer	29Ju02Dv
MCENROE, John	30	M	Laborer	29Ju02Dv
FARLEY, Christina	40	F	Seamstress	29Ju02Dv
Cathrine	13	F	Servant	29Ju02Dv
Mary	12	F	Servant	29Ju02Dv
Rose	07	F	Child	29Ju02Dv
MCGOVERN, Cathn.	20	F	Servant	29Ju02Dv
MCCABE, Pat	55	M	Laborer	29Ju02Dv
MARSHALL, Sam	18	M	Laborer	29Ju02Dv
MCCABE, Michl.	37	M	Laborer	29Ju02Dv
Mary	30	F	Spinster	29Ju02Dv
MURPHY, Mary	20	F	Servant	29Ju02Dv
JOY, Bess	20	F	Servant	29Ju02Dv
MULLOWNY, Honora	20	F	Servant	29Ju02Dv
MCCLEAN, Bridgt.	20	F	Servant	29Ju02Dv
Anne	16	F	Servant	29Ju02Dv
DOYLE, Anne	11	F	Servant	29Ju02Dv
MULLEN, Pat	34	M	Laborer	29Ju02Dv
Biddy	34	F	Seamstress	29Ju02Dv
Cathrine	.09	F	Infant	29Ju02Dv
Margt.	06	F	Child	29Ju02Dv
Biddy	21	F	Seamstress	29Ju02Dv
COOGAN, Ellen	18	F	Seamstress	29Ju02Dv
CASSEDY, Edwd.	21	M	Laborer	29Ju02Dv
MCCUE, Margt.	21	F	Servant	29Ju02Dv
Rose	21	F	Servant	29Ju02Dv
Ellen	20	F	Servant	29Ju02Dv
Bridgt.	18	F	Seamstress	29Ju02Dv
MCQUADE, Mathw.	23	M	Laborer	29Ju02Dv
FITZPATRICK, Mathw.	15	M	Laborer	29Ju02Dv
DALTAN, John	25	M	Laborer	29Ju02Dv
Bridgt.	25	F	Seamstress	29Ju02Dv
SCOTT, Cathn.	18	F	Spinster	29Ju02Dv
BROTHERS, Martin	27	M	Laborer	29Ju02Dv
Judith	25	F	Seamstress	29Ju02Dv

NAMES OF PASSENGERS	AGE	SEX	OCCUPATIONS	DATE PORT SHIP
Jane	.00	F	Infant	29Ju02Dv
Born-At-Sea				
DOYLE, Dan	40	M	Laborer	29Ju02Dv
CARNEY, Edwd.	22	M	Laborer	29Ju02Dv
WIGGANS, Thomas	22	M	Laborer	29Ju02Dv
SMITH, Cathrine	78	F	Spinster	29Ju02Dv
QUINLAN, Cathrine	28	F	Seamstress	29Ju02Dv
Johanna	18	F	Seamstress	29Ju02Dv
MAHONY, Jane	18	F	Seamstress	29Ju02Dv
CAMPBELL, Wm.	30	M	Watchmaker	29Ju02Dv
WOODRUFF, Wm.	21	M	Laborer	29Ju02Dv
DOOLAN, Martin	25	M	Laborer	29Ju02Dv
GILLIGAN, Charles	30	M	Laborer	29Ju02Dv
Mary	25	F	Servant	29Ju02Dv
James	07	M	Child	29Ju02Dv
Pat	06	M	Child	29Ju02Dv
FARRELL, Terry	20	M	Laborer	29Ju02Dv
MCENERNY, John	21	M	Laborer	29Ju02Dv
FARRELL, Bryan	20	M	Laborer	29Ju02Dv
MURTAGH, John	30	M	Laborer	29Ju02Dv
Cathn.	07	F	Child	29Ju02Dv
Mary	04	F	Child	29Ju02Dv
MAHER, John	35	M	Laborer	29Ju02Dv
MCEVOY, Jab.	31	M	Laborer	29Ju02Dv
CHAMBERLAIN, Wm.	36	M	Laborer	29Ju02Dv
NOON, Charles	22	M	Laborer	29Ju02Dv
Ellen	22	F	Servant	29Ju02Dv
Cathn.	20	F	Servant	29Ju02Dv
THORNTON, John	22	M	Laborer	29Ju02Dv
KILROY, Michl.	28	M	Laborer	29Ju02Dv
GIBBONS, Bridgt.	20	F	Seamstress	29Ju02Dv
WALSH, Tom	45	M	Laborer	29Ju02Dv
Bridgt.	40	F	Seamstress	29Ju02Dv
Michl.	13	M	Seamstress	29Ju02Dv
Margt.	09	F	Child	29Ju02Dv
Anne	07	F	Child	29Ju02Dv
GUINESS, Edwd.	28	M	Laborer	29Ju02Dv
MCGRAH, Michl.	28	M	Laborer	29Ju02Dv
Pat	19	M	Laborer	29Ju02Dv
MAHER, James	30	M	Laborer	29Ju02Dv
Anne	30	F	Seamstress	29Ju02Dv
Margt.	.11	F	Infant	29Ju02Dv
MCCORMICK, Michl.	20	M	Laborer	29Ju02Dv
KAVANAH, Martin	18	M	Laborer	29Ju02Dv
CARROLL, James	17	M	Laborer	29Ju02Dv
GIBBINS, Mary	45	F	Servant	29Ju02Dv
CUMMINS, Cathrine	18	F	Servant	29Ju02Dv
CONWAY, Anne	19	F	Servant	29Ju02Dv
MORRIS, Cathrine	16	F	Servant	29Ju02Dv
SHEA, Pat	24	M	Baker	29Ju02Dv
KEENAN, Owen	30	M	Laborer	29Ju02Dv
DOOLAN, Pat	35	M	Laborer	29Ju02Dv
MCGANN, Rose	50	F	Servant	29Ju02Dv
BOW, Mary	20	F	Hatter	29Ju02Dv
LAWLER, Mary	22	F	Dressmaker	29Ju02Dv
Richd.	.01	M	Infant	29Ju02Dv
Died-At-Sea				
MCCUE, Frank	24	M	Laborer	29Ju02Dv
Rose	25	F	Servant	29Ju02Dv
SHEVLAN, Jane	22	F	Seamstress	29Ju02Dv
FALLON, Michl.	23	M	Laborer	29Ju02Dv
Anne	30	F	Servant	29Ju02Dv
HANLON, Rose	20	F	Servant	29Ju02Dv
CARROLL, Sally	20	F	Servant	29Ju02Dv
DOWDALL, Pat	20	M	Laborer	29Ju02Dv
DOYLE, Thomas	35	M	Laborer	29Ju02Dv
DOWDALL, Cathn.	25	F	Servant	29Ju02Dv
DOYLE, Mary	07	F	Child	29Ju02Dv
MCGOVERN, Wm.	18	M	Laborer	29Ju02Dv
Margt.	20	F	Servant	29Ju02Dv
Owen	.09	M	Infant	29Ju02Dv
WHELAN, Edward	60	M	Farmer	29Ju02Dv
Pat	23	M	Laborer	29Ju02Dv
Judy	21	F	Servant	29Ju02Dv
Eliza	19	F	Servant	29Ju02Dv

NAMES OF PASSENGERS		AGE	SEX	OCCUPATIONS	DATE PORT SHIP
WHELAN, Mary		16	F	Servant	29Ju02Dv
Bridgt.		13	F	Servant	29Ju02Dv
James		12	M	Servant	29Ju02Dv
Anne		09	F	Child	29Ju02Dv
Edwd.Jnr.		07	M	Child	29Ju02Dv
Michl.		03	M	Child	29Ju02Dv
Cathn.		04	F	Child	29Ju02Dv
HYNNE, Michl.		30	M	Laborer	29Ju02Dv
MCDONALD, John		25	M	Laborer	29Ju02Dv
BARRY, Kevin		20	M	Laborer	29Ju02Dv
CLEARY, Pat		21	M	Laborer	29Ju02Dv
HELAN, John		26	M	Laborer	29Ju02Dv
KIERNAN, Thomas		28	M	Laborer	29Ju02Dv
HYNNE, Jane		20	F	Servant	29Ju02Dv
BARRY, Anne		18	F	Servant	29Ju02Dv
FARRELL, John		23	M	Laborer	29Ju02Dv
OXLEY, Jas.		25	M	Laborer	29Ju02Dv
NEVILLE, Michl.		18	M	Laborer	29Ju02Dv
THOMPSON, Peter		25	M	Servant	29Ju02Dv
CUMMINS, Jane		18	F	Servant	29Ju02Dv
NEVILLE, Bridgt.		18	F	Servant	29Ju02Dv
DUGLEY, Mary		19	F	Servant	29Ju02Dv
GREY, Pat		30	M	Dealer	29Ju02Dv
KEASY, Thomas		22	M	Laborer	29Ju02Dv
MORRIS, Robt.		21	M	Laborer	29Ju02Dv
CORRIGAN, Jane		16	F	Servant	29Ju02Dv
ODONNELL, Jane		26	F	Servant	29Ju02Dv
LEAHY, Cathn.		23	F	Servant	29Ju02Dv
FARRELL, Michl.		30	M	Carpenter	29Ju02Dv
DALTAN, Robt.		40	M	Shoemaker	29Ju02Dv
Wm.		14	M	Shoemaker	29Ju02Dv
LARKIN, Mathw.		56	M	Steward	29Ju02Dv
KENNY, John		36	M	Laborer	29Ju02Dv
FOLEY, Frank		16	M	Laborer	29Ju02Dv
BUTLER, John		30	M	Clerk	29Ju02Dv
HAYS, Edwd.		52	M	Laborer	29Ju02Dv
Thomas		20	M	Laborer	29Ju02Dv
BUTLER, Bridgt.		23	F	Servant	29Ju02Dv
HAYS, Jane		18	F	Servant	29Ju02Dv
BUTLER, Margt.		20	F	Servant	29Ju02Dv
QUILLAN, Martin		01	M	Child	29Ju02Dv

BRITISH-QUEEN 29 JUNE 1848

From Sligo

NAMES OF PASSENGERS		AGE	SEX	OCCUPATIONS	DATE PORT SHIP
COLLEARY, Pat.		23	M	Laborer	29Ju28Vw
Andrew		20	M	Laborer	29Ju28Vw
JOHNSTON, Ellen		19	F	Spinster	29Ju28Vw
Thomas		20	M	Laborer	29Ju28Vw
SWEENEY, Biddy		24	F	Spinster	29Ju28Vw
Mary		03	F	Child	29Ju28Vw
John		04	M	Child	29Ju28Vw
DALEY, Pat.		17	M	Laborer	29Ju28Vw
Mary		14	F	Spinster	29Ju28Vw
ROONEY, James		20	M	Laborer	29Ju28Vw
Anne		28	F	Spinster	29Ju28Vw
SHUMMS, Mary		24	F	Spinster	29Ju28Vw
Anne		18	F	Spinster	29Ju28Vw
MCFADDEN, John		50	M	Laborer	29Ju28Vw
FETANAGUN, Mich.		50	M	Laborer	29Ju28Vw
CULLEN, Charles		22	M	Farmer	29Ju28Vw
James		22	M	Laborer	29Ju28Vw
KELLORAN, Mich.		19	M	Laborer	29Ju28Vw
DAVY, Thomas		30	M	Laborer	29Ju28Vw
FLYNN, Mich.		22	M	Laborer	29Ju28Vw
SCANLON, James		25	M	Laborer	29Ju28Vw
BRENNAN, James		45	M	Shopkeeper	29Ju28Vw
Bridget	(W)	45	F	Wife	29Ju28Vw

NAMES OF PASSENGERS		AGE	SEX	OCCUPATIONS	DATE PORT SHIP
FITZPATRICK, Bess		30	F	Spinster	29Ju28Vw
BRENNAN, Bess		16	F	Spinster	29Ju28Vw
Mary		14	F	Spinster	29Ju28Vw
James		10	M	Child	29Ju28Vw
Honor		03	F	Child	29Ju28Vw
MAGLOIN, Mary		15	F	Spinster	29Ju28Vw
DEVANY, Mary		.06	F	Infant	29Ju28Vw
MAGOWEN, Biddy		22	F	Spinster	29Ju28Vw
FOLEY, Mary		20	F	Spinster	29Ju28Vw
BERNE, Mich.		24	M	Laborer	29Ju28Vw
James		25	M	Laborer	29Ju28Vw
Cath.		25	F	Spinster	29Ju28Vw
Judy		59	F	Spinster	29Ju28Vw
COLLEARY, Anne		20	F	Spinster	29Ju28Vw
KILHY, Biddy		24	F	Spinster	29Ju28Vw
KERRIGAN, John		20	M	Laborer	29Ju28Vw
Biddy		24	F	Spinster	29Ju28Vw
BURKE, Cath.		18	F	Spinster	29Ju28Vw
HANNAN, Bessey		21	F	Spinster	29Ju28Vw
MCDERMOTT, Mich.		19	M	Laborer	29Ju28Vw
MELL, Dan.		35	M	Laborer	29Ju28Vw
Jane		24	F	Spinster	29Ju28Vw
DOWDIOAN, Hannah		19	F	Spinster	29Ju28Vw
SCANLON, Mich		19	M	Laborer	29Ju28Vw
SILY, John		15	M	Laborer	29Ju28Vw
HART, Anne		30	F	Spinster	29Ju28Vw
AVENT, Joseph		20	M	None	29Ju28Vw
James		20	M	None	29Ju28Vw
GALLAGHER, John		21	M	Laborer	29Ju28Vw
Cath.		10	F	Child	29Ju28Vw
ROONY, James		21	M	Laborer	29Ju28Vw
REED, Margt.		20	F	Spinster	29Ju28Vw
MURPHEY, Pat.		21	M	Laborer	29Ju28Vw
Cath.		15	F	Spinster	29Ju28Vw
Judy		17	F	Spinster	29Ju28Vw
SPENCE, Mary		18	F	Spinster	29Ju28Vw
FARRELL, Bridget		20	F	Spinster	29Ju28Vw
Alice		12	F	Spinster	29Ju28Vw
Mary		40	F	Spinster	29Ju28Vw
WALSH, Sarah		20	F	Spinster	29Ju28Vw
Sabrina		22	F	Spinster	29Ju28Vw
KAVERNY, Cath.		22	F	Spinster	29Ju28Vw
MAGUIRE, Mich.		28	M	Laborer	29Ju28Vw
WEIR, Peggy		24	F	Spinster	29Ju28Vw
MCDONNELL, Alice		24	F	Spinster	29Ju28Vw
MCGOWAN, James		26	M	Laborer	29Ju28Vw
Biddy	(W)	24	F	Wife	29Ju28Vw
Pat.	(S)	03	M	Child	29Ju28Vw
CARROLL, Mary		14	F	Spinster	29Ju28Vw
FARRY, Mich		22	M	Laborer	29Ju28Vw
James		20	M	Laborer	29Ju28Vw
BRENNAN, Anne		24	F	Spinster	29Ju28Vw
MAGOWAN, James		26	M	Laborer	29Ju28Vw
WATERS, Biddy		26	F	Spinster	29Ju28Vw
BRAL, Anne		24	F	Spinster	29Ju28Vw
QUINN, John		17	M	Laborer	29Ju28Vw
FOLEY, James		26	M	Laborer	29Ju28Vw
Mary		21	F	Spinster	29Ju28Vw
DYER, Bessy		20	F	Spinster	29Ju28Vw
MCANDREW, Pat.		12	M	Child	29Ju28Vw
KERR, Robt.		24	M	Farmer	29Ju28Vw
MATTIMORE, Mick		28	M	Sawer	29Ju28Vw
LAEKEN, Mick		23	M	Laborer	29Ju28Vw
Ellen		30	F	Spinster	29Ju28Vw
TANREY, John		30	M	Laborer	29Ju28Vw
TERNPANY, John		20	M	Laborer	29Ju28Vw
EGAN, Pat.		25	M	Laborer	29Ju28Vw
MCNULTAY, Pat.		24	M	Laborer	29Ju28Vw
DOOGAN, Pat.		20	M	Laborer	29Ju28Vw
Mary		18	F	Spinster	29Ju28Vw
Anne		16	F	Spinster	29Ju28Vw
MCSWEENEY, Terence		14	M	Laborer	29Ju28Vw
MORISON, Martin		30	M	Laborer	29Ju28Vw
Rose		25	F	Spinster	29Ju28Vw
CONLAN, Mary		20	F	Spinster	29Ju28Vw

NAMES OF PASSENGERS	AGE	SEX	OCCUPATIONS	DATE PORT SHIP
DONOHUE, Owen	50	M	Laborer	29Ju28Vw
Rose	48	F	Matron	29Ju28Vw
Mary	18	F	Spinster	29Ju28Vw
Biddy	16	F	Spinster	29Ju28Vw
James	12	M	Child	29Ju28Vw
Nancy	06	F	Child	29Ju28Vw
OHARA, Ellen	18	F	Spinster	29Ju28Vw
SMITH, Mary	21	F	Spinster	29Ju28Vw
DOONEY, Mary	20	F	Spinster	29Ju28Vw
FILBIN, Anthony	24	M	Laborer	29Ju28Vw
Andrew	24	M	Laborer	29Ju28Vw
KILCAULY, Martin	22	M	Laborer	29Ju28Vw
Anne	20	F	Spinster	29Ju28Vw
SHANNON, Pat.	17	M	Laborer	29Ju28Vw
BERGEN, John	26	M	Laborer	29Ju28Vw
COURTEREY, Margt.	20	F	Spinster	29Ju28Vw
KILLIHA, John	14	M	Laborer	29Ju28Vw
James	16	M	Laborer	29Ju28Vw
HUNT, Cath	40	F	Spinster	29Ju28Vw
Bessy	40	F	Spinster	29Ju28Vw
Eliza-Anne	14	F	Spinster	29Ju28Vw
Emily	10	F	Spinster	29Ju28Vw
DALTON, Margt.	30	F	Spinster	29Ju28Vw
BRENNAN, Margt.	22	F	Spinster	29Ju28Vw
Anne	20	F	Spinster	29Ju28Vw
MCHUGH, John	25	M	Laborer	29Ju28Vw
DIXON, James	23	M	Laborer	29Ju28Vw
Ellen	20	F	Spinster	29Ju28Vw
MCQUINN, Mich.	47	M	Laborer	29Ju28Vw
MCGRATH, Jane	46	F	Matron	29Ju28Vw
Mary	48	F	Spinster	29Ju28Vw
Margt.	16	F	Spinster	29Ju28Vw
Bridget	14	F	Spinster	29Ju28Vw
James	12	M	Child	29Ju28Vw
Cath	09	F	Child	29Ju28Vw
Anne	07	F	Child	29Ju28Vw
KEMS, Pat.	30	M	Laborer	29Ju28Vw
CONAGHLIN, Mary	24	F	Spinster	29Ju28Vw
GRAHEM, James	25	M	Laborer	29Ju28Vw
KILBRIDE, Owen	25	M	Laborer	29Ju28Vw
Cath	24	F	Wife	29Ju28Vw
HANELLY, Mary	40	F	Spinster	29Ju28Vw
Pat.	20	M	Laborer	29Ju28Vw
Cath.	17	F	Spinster	29Ju28Vw
Thos.	10	M	Child	29Ju28Vw
James	09	M	Child	29Ju28Vw
MCCANN, Pat.	26	M	Laborer	29Ju28Vw
SMITH, Mark	25	M	Laborer	29Ju28Vw
Margt.	20	F	Spinster	29Ju28Vw
Roger	40	M	Laborer	29Ju28Vw
ROGAR, Owen	26	M	Laborer	29Ju28Vw
CAVANAGH, Biddy	16	F	Spinster	29Ju28Vw
HURT, Thomas	26	M	Laborer	29Ju28Vw
ROONY, Thomas	18	M	Laborer	29Ju28Vw
MCARDLE, Maria	14	F	Spinster	29Ju28Vw
Bessey	14	F	Spinster	29Ju28Vw
GRILGEN, Ellen	24	F	Spinster	29Ju28Vw
MCCLOUD, Mich.	30	M	Laborer	29Ju28Vw
BOLAND, Susan	24	F	Spinster	29Ju28Vw
MOFFIT, Margt.	50	F	Spinster	29Ju28Vw
OHARA, Bryan	30	M	Laborer	29Ju28Vw
ROONEY, Sarah	18	F	Spinster	29Ju28Vw
HONAN, James	20	M	Laborer	29Ju28Vw
DYER, Pat.	21	M	Laborer	29Ju28Vw
GARNEY, Anne	20	F	Spinster	29Ju28Vw
MCGOWAN, Anne	24	F	Spinster	29Ju28Vw
BOLUNSE, Pat.	50	M	Laborer	29Ju28Vw
MCHUGH, Biddy	20	F	Spinster	29Ju28Vw
KERN, Henry	35	M	Printer	29Ju28Vw
KERR, Ann	30	F	Wife	29Ju28Vw
Mortyre (S)	.06	M	Infant	29Ju28Vw
SMITH, Sarah	22	F	Spinster	29Ju28Vw
OMALLEY, Mary	17	F	Spinster	29Ju28Vw
SHEA, Pat.	40	M	Laborer	29Ju28Vw
HENRY, Margt.	25	F	Spinster	29Ju28Vw
ELLIOTT, John	20	M	Farmer	29Ju28Vw
Ellen	45	F	Spinster	29Ju28Vw
Adam	50	M	Farmer	29Ju28Vw
DOWD, Ellen	19	F	Spinster	29Ju28Vw
MCFEMAN, Hugh	40	M	Laborer	29Ju28Vw
WATER, Mary	20	F	Spinster	29Ju28Vw
CREGG, Mary-Ann	21	F	Spinster	29Ju28Vw
HIGGINS, Mich.	23	M	Laborer	29Ju28Vw
DAVERY, John	30	M	Laborer	29Ju28Vw
Peggy	40	F	Spinster	29Ju28Vw
OHARA, James	30	M	Laborer	29Ju28Vw
OCONNOR, Luke	27	M	Laborer	29Ju28Vw
Mart.	17	F	Spinster	29Ju28Vw
OHARA, Sarah	26	F	Spinster	29Ju28Vw
MULLEN, Mary	22	F	Spinster	29Ju28Vw
FRIZELL, Wm.	25	M	Laborer	29Ju28Vw
FALLOW, Cath	20	F	Spinster	29Ju28Vw
GORDON, Mary	26	F	Spinster	29Ju28Vw
MCHUGH, Margt.	24	F	Spinster	29Ju28Vw
MCMONIN, James	45	M	Laborer	29Ju28Vw
MCCORMICK, Biddy	20	F	Spinster	29Ju28Vw
CAMPBELL, Ellen	22	F	Spinster	29Ju28Vw
DONOHUE, Pat.	24	M	Laborer	29Ju28Vw
FARRELL, John	22	M	Laborer	29Ju28Vw
BEGLEY, Thomas	27	M	Laborer	29Ju28Vw
Mich.	26	M	Laborer	29Ju28Vw
James	25	M	Laborer	29Ju28Vw
Catharine	24	F	Spinster	29Ju28Vw
KERR, William	30	M	Farmer	29Ju28Vw
Jane (W)	35	F	Wife	29Ju28Vw
Nancy (D)	12	F	Child	29Ju28Vw
Fanny (D)	08	F	Child	29Ju28Vw
Eliza-Jane (D)	04	F	Child	29Ju28Vw
Isabella (D)	02	F	Child	29Ju28Vw
Wm.Rockfort (S)	01	M	Child	29Ju28Vw
FAVRY, Bessy	21	F	None	29Ju28Vw
HART, Pat.	19	M	None	29Ju28Vw
CREGG, Antery	20	M	Laborer	29Ju28Vw

VANDALIA 29 JUNE 1848

From Liverpool

NAMES OF PASSENGERS	AGE	SEX	OCCUPATIONS	DATE PORT SHIP
MCLAUGHLIN, Thomas	28	M	Laborer	29Ju02Vk
ELLENSWORTH, Charles	26	M	Laborer	29Ju02Vk
GRACIOUS, William	24	M	Laborer	29Ju02Vk
HEARTY, Michael	30	M	Laborer	29Ju02Vk
MCQUADE, John	56	M	Laborer	29Ju02Vk
Mary	14	F	Laborer	29Ju02Vk
FOX, Francis	28	M	Laborer	29Ju02Vk
TUCKWOOD, Thomas	32	M	Laborer	29Ju02Vk
Crodins (W)	31	F	Laborer	29Ju02Vk
Elisabeth	07	F	Laborer	29Ju02Vk
John	06	M	Laborer	29Ju02Vk
Thomas	04	M	Laborer	29Ju02Vk
George	02	M	Laborer	29Ju02Vk
William	.03	M	Infant	29Ju02Vk
MCCULLOUGH, Bridget	20	F	Spinster	29Ju02Vk
HORAN, Patt	24	M	Laborer	29Ju02Vk
ARMSTRONG, John	16	M	Laborer	29Ju02Vk
Thomas	16	M	Laborer	29Ju02Vk
ORR, Mary	18	F	Spinster	29Ju02Vk
KENNEDY, Nancy	14	F	Spinster	29Ju02Vk
DYER, John	40	M	Laborer	29Ju02Vk
PEAKE, Edward	50	M	Laborer	29Ju02Vk
GLASS, Benjamin	47	M	Laborer	29Ju02Vk
B.	47	F	Laborer	29Ju02Vk
George	19	M	Laborer	29Ju02Vk
KANE, Ellen	17	F	Spinster	29Ju02Vk

NAMES OF PASSENGERS		AGE	SEX	OCCUPATIONS	DATE PORT SHIP
MORAN, Michael		30	M	Laborer	29Ju02Vk
HURLEY, James		35	M	Laborer	29Ju02Vk
RING, Daniel		18	M	Laborer	29Ju02Vk
CROWLEY, Mary		24	F	Spinster	29Ju02Vk
SULLIVAN, Ellen		21	F	Spinster	29Ju02Vk
GALLAGHER, Mary		31	F	Spinster	29Ju02Vk
Patt		.00	M	Infant	29Ju02Vk
DILLON, Thomas		30	M	Laborer	29Ju02Vk
SHEAN, Patt		10	M	Laborer	29Ju02Vk
Johamm		07	M	Laborer	29Ju02Vk
BULKLY, Dennis		35	M	Laborer	29Ju02Vk
Betty		35	F	Laborer	29Ju02Vk
David		16	M	Laborer	29Ju02Vk
Patt		14	M	Laborer	29Ju02Vk
Daniel	(S)	12	M	Laborer	29Ju02Vk
Ellen	(D)	07	F	Laborer	29Ju02Vk
Mary	(D)	04	F	Laborer	29Ju02Vk
Margaret	(D)	02	F	Laborer	29Ju02Vk
LEAKY, John		27	M	Laborer	29Ju02Vk
Mary		26	F	Laborer	29Ju02Vk
SHEAN, John		20	M	Laborer	29Ju02Vk
DAHILL, Patt		24	M	Laborer	29Ju02Vk
DUGGAN, Michael		20	M	Laborer	29Ju02Vk
John		22	M	Laborer	29Ju02Vk
MURPHY, John		25	M	Laborer	29Ju02Vk
FIZGERALD, John		30	M	Laborer	29Ju02Vk
Johanna		20	F	Laborer	29Ju02Vk
Margaret		18	F	Laborer	29Ju02Vk
MOVILLE, Ellen		14	F	Laborer	29Ju02Vk
HANLEY, Michael		17	M	Laborer	29Ju02Vk
Honor		15	F	Laborer	29Ju02Vk
SHEENAN, Timothy		19	M	Laborer	29Ju02Vk
DELANEY, Hetty		19	F	Spinster	29Ju02Vk
FLYN, Catharine		24	F	Spinster	29Ju02Vk
KELLY, Margaret		25	F	Spinster	29Ju02Vk
MORAN, Mary		27	F	Spinster	29Ju02Vk
Ellen		27	F	Spinster	29Ju02Vk
Ann		04	F	Spinster	29Ju02Vk
James		.00	M	Infant	29Ju02Vk
MCCORMICK, James		20	M	Laborer	29Ju02Vk
Ann		18	F	Laborer	29Ju02Vk
HAYES, Patt		21	M	Laborer	29Ju02Vk
RAYNOR, Thomas		20	M	Laborer	29Ju02Vk
GAVIN, Ann		11	F	Spinster	29Ju02Vk
RIELLY, William		19	M	Laborer	29Ju02Vk
DONAGHUE, Patt		48	M	Laborer	29Ju02Vk
SLAVIN, Margaret		26	F	Spinster	29Ju02Vk
WHEELER, Margaret		26	F	Spinster	29Ju02Vk
WELSH, James		31	M	Laborer	29Ju02Vk
ROURKE, Ann		20	F	Spinster	29Ju02Vk
BANNAN, Ann		19	F	Spinster	29Ju02Vk
CARNEY, John		20	M	Laborer	29Ju02Vk
Ann		10	F	Spinster	29Ju02Vk
CAMPBELL, Ann		30	F	Spinster	29Ju02Vk
MURPHY, James		30	M	Laborer	29Ju02Vk
JOHNSON, John		30	M	Laborer	29Ju02Vk
OBREIN, John		14	M	Laborer	29Ju02Vk
Margaret		21	F	Spinster	29Ju02Vk
JONES, Thomas		29	M	Laborer	29Ju02Vk
John		29	M	Laborer	29Ju02Vk
Ann		29	F	Spinster	29Ju02Vk
Thomas		05	M	Child	29Ju02Vk
Ann	(D)	03	F	Child	29Ju02Vk
John		.00	M	Infant	29Ju02Vk
KEENAN, Honor		18	F	Spinster	29Ju02Vk
KANE, James		58	M	Laborer	29Ju02Vk
Elisabeth		55	F	Laborer	29Ju02Vk
CLOVER, Ann		20	F	Spinster	29Ju02Vk
MULHALL, Margaret		18	F	Spinster	29Ju02Vk
AUGUST, Catherine		20	F	Spinster	29Ju02Vk
MAGUINNESS, John		22	M	Laborer	29Ju02Vk
FALLEN, Patt		21	M	Laborer	29Ju02Vk
RIELLY, John		12	M	Laborer	29Ju02Vk
RINSLY, Ann		21	F	Seamstress	29Ju02Vk
FIGUBY, Bridget		18	F	Seamstress	29Ju02Vk
MCPHILIPS, Mary		40	F	Nurse	29Ju02Vk
Thomas		12	M	Laborer	29Ju02Vk
Sally	(D)	09	F	Spinster	29Ju02Vk
WARD, Patt		20	M	Laborer	29Ju02Vk
Mary		26	F	Laborer	29Ju02Vk
MCGAVIN, Ann		34	F	Nurse	29Ju02Vk
MULLOLY, Jerry		25	M	Laborer	29Ju02Vk
Phill		27	M	Laborer	29Ju02Vk
MCGRATH, Johanna		21	F	Spinster	29Ju02Vk
MCCLEAN, Patt		35	M	Laborer	29Ju02Vk
Elisabeth		30	F	Laborer	29Ju02Vk
Sarah		04	F	Laborer	29Ju02Vk
Rose		03	F	Laborer	29Ju02Vk
William		02	M	Laborer	29Ju02Vk
Mary		.03	F	Infant	29Ju02Vk
SMITH, Nicholas		30	M	Laborer	29Ju02Vk
CLARKE, Patt		30	M	Laborer	29Ju02Vk
HANNAN, Maria		19	F	Spinster	29Ju02Vk
KIERNAN, Michael		17	M	Laborer	29Ju02Vk
Patt		14	M	Laborer	29Ju02Vk
ONEILL, John		23	M	Laborer	29Ju02Vk
CORRELL, Edward		23	M	Laborer	29Ju02Vk
MORRELL, Edward		45	M	Laborer	29Ju02Vk
E.		45	F	Laborer	29Ju02Vk
Edward		15	M	Laborer	29Ju02Vk
Charles		13	M	Laborer	29Ju02Vk
James		10	M	Laborer	29Ju02Vk
Bernard		09	M	Laborer	29Ju02Vk
Thomas		30	M	Laborer	29Ju02Vk
Mary		24	F	Spinster	29Ju02Vk
PUGH, David		20	M	Laborer	29Ju02Vk
EWENS, Thomas		50	M	Laborer	29Ju02Vk
THOMAS, Henry		25	M	Laborer	29Ju02Vk
MCFADDEN, James		30	M	Laborer	29Ju02Vk
SMITH, Patt		24	M	Laborer	29Ju02Vk
Biddy		20	F	Laborer	29Ju02Vk
MCLAUGHLIN, Edward		24	M	Laborer	29Ju02Vk
FARILY, Phill		40	M	Laborer	29Ju02Vk
Catharine		30	F	Laborer	29Ju02Vk
Mary		02	F	Laborer	29Ju02Vk
John		.00	M	Infant	29Ju02Vk
CUSICK, Marry		16	F	Spinster	29Ju02Vk
MCGUINESS, Arthur		20	M	Laborer	29Ju02Vk
Daniel-Long		35	M	Laborer	29Ju02Vk
Mathew-Fettes		27	M	Laborer	29Ju02Vk

KATE-HOWE 30 JUNE 1848

From Liverpool

NAMES OF PASSENGERS	AGE	SEX	OCCUPATIONS	DATE PORT SHIP
PHELEN, Edward	34	M	Farmer	30Ju02Vl
Michael	28	M	Farmer	30Ju02Vl
LACY, Pat	34	M	Coachman	30Ju02Vl
Mary	37	F	Coachman	30Ju02Vl
Mary	03	F	None	30Ju02Vl
GARRITY, Joseph	22	M	Blacksmith	30Ju02Vl
HARWOOD, John	33	M	Ctnsp	30Ju02Vl
LEVERY, Robert	35	M	Ctnsp	30Ju02Vl
POWDERLY, Eliza	21	F	Servant	30Ju02Vl
MCGAGHAM, Mary	13	F	Servant	30Ju02Vl
DAVIS, Bridget	16	F	Servant	30Ju02Vl
MAHONEY, Denis	36	M	Iron Worker	30Ju02Vl
CONOLLY, Michael	20	M	Laborer	30Ju02Vl
Daniel	16	M	Laborer	30Ju02Vl
QUINN, Thomas	30	M	Laborer	30Ju02Vl
OHILL, Moses	26	M	Laborer	30Ju02Vl
CARBERY, Ann	24	F	Servant	30Ju02Vl
Julia	40	F	Wi	30Ju02Vl
SMYTH, Eleano	36	F	Wi	30Ju02Vl

NAMES OF PASSENGERS	AGE	SEX	OCCUPATIONS	DATE PORT SHIP
HACKETT, Johana	26	F	Dressmaker	30Ju02VI
SMYTH, Cath.	08	F	None	30Ju02VI
Thomas	04	M	None	30Ju02VI
RAID, John	36	M	Sawer	30Ju02VI
Cath.	40	F	None	30Ju02VI
Margaret	16	F	None	30Ju02VI
Sarah	13	F	None	30Ju02VI
Ellen	11	F	None	30Ju02VI
Eliza	09	F	None	30Ju02VI
Cath	06	F	None	30Ju02VI
Mary	.01	F	Infant	30Ju02VI
KIRVING, John	17	M	Gvts	30Ju02VI
GARRITY, Michael	22	M	Ploughman	30Ju02VI
James	28	M	Laborer	30Ju02VI
CARROLL, Pat.	23	M	Shopkeeper	30Ju02VI
Michael	22	M	Farmer	30Ju02VI
FALLON, John	20	M	Saddler	30Ju02VI
LALY, James	30	M	Laborer	30Ju02VI
MALONEY, Tim	36	M	Blacksmith	30Ju02VI
LOWE, William	15	M	Piecer	30Ju02VI
James	40	M	Ctnsp	30Ju02VI
Mary	40	F	None	30Ju02VI
James	10	M	Piecer	30Ju02VI
Eliza	06	F	Child	30Ju02VI
Alice	02	F	Child	30Ju02VI
KINNEY, Hen	23	M	Carpenter	30Ju02VI
Mary	22	F	None	30Ju02VI
FARRELL, Bridget	08	F	None	30Ju02VI
KELLY, Hugh	42	M	Stone Mason	30Ju02VI
JOHNSTON, James	20	M	Servant	30Ju02VI
CANNON, Michl	22	M	Bartender	30Ju02VI
Ann	20	F	Servant	30Ju02VI
MCKINNEY, Pat	30	M	Farmer	30Ju02VI
DAVY, Arthur	25	M	Farmer	30Ju02VI
LAVERY, Robert	24	M	Farmer	30Ju02VI
LENON, Susan	30	F	Housekeeper	30Ju02VI
Mary-Ann	13	F	None	30Ju02VI
Isabella	11	F	None	30Ju02VI
Susan	09	F	None	30Ju02VI
DONEGAN, Fanny	21	F	Servant	30Ju02VI
DALTON, Eliza	23	F	Servant	30Ju02VI
HAYES, Bridget	25	F	Servant	30Ju02VI
HEFFERTY, Annistatia	24	F	Servant	30Ju02VI
LASKIN, Christopher	19	M	Bookkeeper	30Ju02VI
BROWN, Cath.	16	F	Servant	30Ju02VI
REILY, Ann	30	F	Housekeeper	30Ju02VI
Philip	12	M	None	30Ju02VI
MCDERMIT, Henry	24	M	Farmer	30Ju02VI
BARNEY, John	18	M	Servant	30Ju02VI
BOYL, William	08	M	Servant	30Ju02VI
Mu--PR, Ann	20	F	Servant	30Ju02VI
DERKEN, Maria	25	F	Servant	30Ju02VI
KEENAN, Mary	17	F	Servant	30Ju02VI
CLARKE, Andrew	27	M	Carter	30Ju02VI
Isabella	26	F	None	30Ju02VI
Cath.	04	F	None	30Ju02VI
Timothy	40	M	Laborer	30Ju02VI
Margt.	24	F	None	30Ju02VI
Tim.	.02	M	Infant	30Ju02VI
Mary	60	F	None	30Ju02VI
FITZPATRICK, John	47	M	Weaver	30Ju02VI
Edward	45	M	Weaver	30Ju02VI
MENTONE, Tim.	24	M	Carpenter	30Ju02VI
FITZPATRICK, Ann	43	F	None	30Ju02VI
DELANEY, Cath.	37	F	WI	30Ju02VI
Judah	13	F	Servant	30Ju02VI
MCGOVERN, Pat	31	M	Laborer	30Ju02VI
MCGUIRE, Pat	13	M	None	30Ju02VI
Hanna	22	F	Servant	30Ju02VI
BUTLER, William	25	M	Laborer	30Ju02VI
KERSE, Daniel	26	M	Laborer	30Ju02VI
Marg.	26	F	None	30Ju02VI
Mary	01	F	None	30Ju02VI
DALY, Cath	26	F	Housekeeper	30Ju02VI
DONOLY, Hugh	24	M	Laborer	30Ju02VI

NAMES OF PASSENGERS	AGE	SEX	OCCUPATIONS	DATE PORT SHIP
AGOE, Mary	13	F	Servant	30Ju02VI
BURNS, Julia	12	F	Servant	30Ju02VI
Ellen	14	F	None	30Ju02VI
KINNEY, Margaret	24	F	Housekeeper	30Ju02VI
CUMINGS, Thomas	06	M	None	30Ju02VI
MCGLINE, Sarah	23	F	Housekeeper	30Ju02VI
COLLAGHAN, Bridget	20	F	Servant	30Ju02VI
TOAL, Bridget	20	F	Servant	30Ju02VI
GORMAN, Pat.	20	M	Tailor	30Ju02VI
REYNOLDS, Mathew	17	M	Tailor	30Ju02VI
HAGAN, William	17	M	Laborer	30Ju02VI
SULLIVAN, Pat.	24	M	Laborer	30Ju02VI
Mary	18	F	None	30Ju02VI
DEMPSEY, Julia	14	F	None	30Ju02VI
MCCURDY, Laughlin	27	M	Laborer	30Ju02VI
Isabella	27	F	None	30Ju02VI
BROWN, William	20	M	Molder	30Ju02VI
MCDONAUGH, Michl	48	M	Clerk	30Ju02VI
MAHONEY, Daniel	21	M	Dealer	30Ju02VI
OCALAGHAN, Eugene	23	M	Inspector	30Ju02VI
GREEN, Maurice	23	M	Farmer	30Ju02VI
OCALAGHAN, Marg.	24	F	Dressmaker	30Ju02VI
DELANEY, James	22	M	Laborer	30Ju02VI
Sally	21	F	None	30Ju02VI
FLYNN, Cath	15	F	Servant	30Ju02VI
Eliza	38	F	Housekeeper	30Ju02VI
Mary	11	F	None	30Ju02VI
Sarah	13	F	None	30Ju02VI
Judith	07	F	None	30Ju02VI
Eliza	04	F	None	30Ju02VI
CULLERTON, Mary	18	F	Servant	30Ju02VI
CARROLL, Thomas	45	M	Tailor	30Ju02VI
William	15	M	Tailor	30Ju02VI
DEADY, David	26	M	Tailor	30Ju02VI
KINNEY, John	01	M	None	30Ju02VI
BRENNAN, Michl.	24	M	Laborer	30Ju02VI
GARRETT, Michl.	56	M	Tailor	30Ju02VI
Anne	58	F	None	30Ju02VI
Jane	26	F	Servant	30Ju02VI
Ellen	24	F	Servant	30Ju02VI
CORLET, Mary	22	F	Servant	30Ju02VI
GARRET, James	16	M	Laborer	30Ju02VI
Henry	16	M	Laborer	30Ju02VI
COLLISTER, John-James	17	M	Laborer	30Ju02VI
KISOG, Elizabeth	.03	F	Infant	30Ju02VI
SMYTH, James	44	M	Farmer	30Ju02VI
Mary	41	F	None	30Ju02VI
Bridg.	19	F	Servant	30Ju02VI
Mich.	09	M	None	30Ju02VI
Pat.	03	M	None	30Ju02VI
Honora	01	F	None	30Ju02VI
COYL, Judith	07	F	None	30Ju02VI
Mathew	18	M	Laborer	30Ju02VI
GUINAN, John	25	M	Laborer	30Ju02VI
Cath	23	F	None	30Ju02VI
SMYTH, Thomas	11	M	Dealer	30Ju02VI
Franc.	37	U	None	30Ju02VI
Mary	33	F	None	30Ju02VI
John	09	M	None	30Ju02VI
William	07	M	None	30Ju02VI
Francis	05	M	None	30Ju02VI
Mary	01	F	None	30Ju02VI
MADDEN, Thomas	41	M	Stevedore	30Ju02VI
Ellen	30	F	None	30Ju02VI
Mary	06	F	None	30Ju02VI
John	03	M	None	30Ju02VI
Ellen	05	F	None	30Ju02VI
Bridg.	01	F	None	30Ju02VI
DAVIS, John	27	M	Dealer	30Ju02VI
HEGGARTY, John	20	M	Laborer	30Ju02VI
MAHER, William	20	M	Ndm	30Ju02VI
MORAN, Alice	22	F	Servant	30Ju02VI
Eliza	20	F	Dressmaker	30Ju02VI
PAULEY, Cath.	20	F	Servant	30Ju02VI
HAGGARTY, Ann	22	F	Servant	30Ju02VI

NAMES OF PASSENGERS		A G E	S E X	OCCUPATIONS	DATE PORT SHIP	NAMES OF PASSENGERS	A G E	S E X	OCCUPATIONS	DATE PORT SHIP
CORCORAN, John		35	M	Laborer	30Ju02VI					
Ellen		28	F	Laborer	30Ju02VI					
SULLIVAN, Eliza		20	F	Servant	30Ju02VI					
MAHER, Robt.		11	M	None	30Ju02VI					
RYAN, Daniel		24	M	Servant	30Ju02VI					
Mary		22	F	None	30Ju02VI					
HACKET, James		17	M	None	30Ju02VI					
MCCABE, Hen		17	M	None	30Ju02VI					
BRESNON, John		30	M	None	30Ju02VI					
Mary	(W)	25	F	None	30Ju02VI					
WELSH, Johanna		18	F	Servant	30Ju02VI					
SHEEHAN, Mich.		24	M	None	30Ju02VI					
GRAUNY, Mich.		25	M	None	30Ju02VI					
WALSH, Pat.		25	M	None	30Ju02VI					
HAYDEN, Winfred		20	M	None	30Ju02VI					
Mary		23	F	None	30Ju02VI					
LYNCH, Eliza		24	F	None	30Ju02VI					
KEENAN, Mary		18	F	None	30Ju02VI					
MARTIN, Andrew		25	M	Farmer	30Ju02VI					
CUNNINGHAM, Pat		22	M	None	30Ju02VI					
KEENAN, Thomas		19	M	None	30Ju02VI					
MCCLEAN, William		57	M	None	30Ju02VI					
Anne		18	F	None	30Ju02VI					
Maria		16	F	Servant	30Ju02VI					
SARAHAN, Bernard		20	M	None	30Ju02VI					
Lawrence		25	M	None	30Ju02VI					
FITSIMMINS, Cath.		20	F	None	30Ju02VI					
CRONAN, Pat		48	M	Laborer	30Ju02VI					
Mary		40	F	None	30Ju02VI					
Margt.		13	F	None	30Ju02VI					
Mary		02	F	Child	30Ju02VI					
LARKIN, Mary		18	F	None	30Ju02VI					
MURPHY, Mary		12	F	None	30Ju02VI					
Bridg.		50	F	Housekeeper	30Ju02VI					
Eliza		15	F	None	30Ju02VI					
BOYL, John		08	M	None	30Ju02VI					
LAVERY, John		27	M	Farmer	30Ju02VI					
MCKINNY, Peter		24	M	None	30Ju02VI					
MCCORMACH, Hugh		26	M	None	30Ju02VI					
FARREL, Pat.		30	M	Farmer	30Ju02VI					
Bridget		22	F	None	30Ju02VI					
John		07	M	None	30Ju02VI					
Mary		03	F	None	30Ju02VI					

Index